THE OXFORD HANDBOOK OF
THE EUROPEAN IRON AGE

THE OXFORD HANDBOOK OF

THE EUROPEAN IRON AGE

Edited by

COLIN HASELGROVE,

KATHARINA REBAY-SALISBURY,

and

PETER S. WELLS

Great Clarendon Street, Oxford, OX2 6DP,
United Kingdom

Oxford University Press is a department of the University of Oxford. It furthers the University's objective of excellence in research, scholarship, and education by publishing worldwide. Oxford is a registered trade mark of Oxford University Press in the UK and in certain other countries

First Edition published in 2023

Published in the United States of America by Oxford University Press
198 Madison Avenue, New York, NY 10016, United States of America

British Library Cataloguing in Publication Data
Data available

Library of Congress Control Number: 2023937474

ISBN 978–0–19–969682–6

DOI: 10.1093/oxfordhb/9780199696826.001.0001

Printed in the UK by
Bell & Bain Ltd., Glasgow

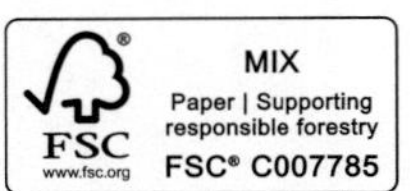

Preface

The Iron Age was a critical era in European development. Starting before 1000 BC in the lands bordering the eastern Mediterranean, this final period of prehistory is understood as having continued into the later first millennium AD in the many regions that never became part of the Roman Empire. During this period, new technologies, agricultural innovation, and demographic growth saw much of the landscape opened up to near modern limits. We also see growing social and economic complexity and the emergence of much larger settlements, but this was by no means universal. Centuries after city states emerged in Greece and Italy, much of Europe was inhabited by agrarian communities with few overt signs of status distinction or centralized institutions.

Why a Handbook on the European Iron Age? Bordering as it does on written history, study of Iron Age Europe has been strongly influenced by its relationship to the classical world, with archaeological evidence often more or less subordinated to the partial accounts of Greek and Roman writers. No recent works have attempted to survey the European Iron Age as a whole, and many accounts terminate with the Roman conquest and privilege above all the 'Celtic' regions with their iconic fortified sites, lavish burials, and distinctive art, relegating much of Europe to the margins of Iron Age studies. Preoccupation with cultural and economic connections with the classical Mediterranean has also led to the relative neglect of terrestrial and maritime networks within Europe, and links to other continents. In the past thirty years, however, our knowledge of Iron Age societies and how they varied in time and space has increased almost exponentially, due above all to large-scale excavations ahead of modern development and international collaborations enabled by political changes in the former eastern bloc. At the same time, the application of many techniques of modern science has opened up significant new avenues of research, while theoretical reappraisals have both cast doubt on old assumptions and provoked alternative interpretations of Iron Age monuments and societies.

Drawing on these advances, this Handbook offers the first archaeologically led account of the European Iron Age in its geographical and chronological entirety, written by specialists from many countries. Part I sets the scene and explains the basics of the period. Part II provides an overview of the period across Europe, eschewing traditional national narratives as far as possible by presenting the material in terms of fourteen broad regions. The focus of Part III is thematic, covering a wide range of topics including lifeways, economy, complexity, identity, ritual, and expression. Some areas and subjects feature more than others, whether because of the nature of the material, or the importance they are accorded by current researchers. Recognizing both the plurality of intellectual traditions and variability of the archaeological record across Europe, we encouraged authors to interpret their original brief according to their preferred theoretical standpoints, believing this approach to enrich the overall perspective. It is our hope that this Handbook will provide a valuable and stimulating synthesis for anyone interested in this fascinating period.

Our thanks are due to the many staff at Oxford University Press who have supported us in the production of this Handbook over the years, particularly Hilary O'Shea, who commissioned the volume, and her successor Charlotte Loveridge, along with Laura Heston, Alexander Johnston, Clare Kennedy, Jenny King, Celine Louasli, Will Richards, Brad Rosenkrantz, Cathryn Steele, and Emma Varley. OUP arranged for the translation of chapters into English, where needed. We are indebted to Pamela Lowther for her help with copy-editing the chapters, and preparing and standardizing many of the authors' original figures and tables. Roderick Salisbury kindly created the maps that accompany many of the regional chapters. Many different sources have been used to provide illustrations. We are grateful to all who provided permission to reproduce copyright material; should there have been any inadvertent omissions or errors in our acknowledgements, we would be pleased to set this right in any subsequent edition (and the online version).

Thanks are due to student assistants Michaela Fritzl, Hanna Skerjanz, and Domnika Verdianu at the Austrian Archaeological Institute for checking the bibliographies, and for their help in creating an online bibliographic resource for the Handbook, which can be accessed via Oxford Handbooks Online. The idea for the Handbook coalesced in the course of the research programme *Tracing Networks: Craft Traditions in the Ancient Mediterranean and Beyond* funded by the Leverhulme Trust (PI: Lin Foxhall), based at the University of Leicester. We wish to acknowledge the generous support of the Trust for work undertaken in the preparation of the Handbook. The School of Archaeology and Ancient History, University of Leicester kindly funded some of the editorial work.

For various reasons, not least the 2020 pandemic, this Handbook has been long in gestation; we would like to thank all our contributors for their forbearance. This print book collects chapters published online between 2018 and 2022.

Colin Haselgrove, Katharina Rebay-Salisbury, and Peter S. Wells

Contents

List of Figures xi
List of Tables xxiii
List of Contributors xxv

PART I INTRODUCTION

1. Introduction: The Iron Age in Europe 3
COLIN HASELGROVE, KATHARINA REBAY-SALISBURY, AND PETER S. WELLS

2. Europe in the Iron Age: Landscapes, Regions, Climate, and People 19
COLIN HASELGROVE, KATHARINA REBAY-SALISBURY, AND PETER S. WELLS

3. Chronology in Iron Age Europe: Current Approaches and Challenges 37
COLIN HASELGROVE, KATHARINA REBAY-SALISBURY, AND PETER S. WELLS

PART II REGIONAL SYNTHESES

4. North-West Europe 67
COLIN HASELGROVE AND SOPHIE KRAUSZ

5. Scandinavia and Northern Germany 145
FRANDS HERSCHEND

6. The Eastern Baltic 173
VALTER LANG

7. Eastern Central Europe: Between the Elbe and the Dnieper 193
WOJCIECH NOWAKOWSKI

8. Central Europe 217
CAROLA METZNER-NEBELSICK

9. Southern France 275
DOMINIQUE GARCIA

10. The Iberian Peninsula 305
XOSÉ-LOIS ARMADA AND IGNACIO GRAU MIRA

11. The Northern Adriatic 345
RAFFAELE DE MARINIS AND BIBA TERŽAN

12. The Central Mediterranean and the Aegean 407
LIN FOXHALL

13. Northern Greece and the Central Balkans 449
STEFANOS GIMATZIDIS

14. The Carpathian and Danubian Area 477
AUREL RUSTOIU

15. The Northern Black Sea and North Caucasus 525
SABINE REINHOLD AND VALENTINA I. MORDVINTSEVA

16. Europe to Asia 575
LUDMILA KORYAKOVA

17. Edges and Interactions beyond Europe 619
NAOÍSE MAC SWEENEY AND PETER S. WELLS

PART III: THEMES IN IRON AGE ARCHAEOLOGY

LIFEWAYS

18. Food, Foodways, and Subsistence 659
HANSJÖRG KÜSTER

19. Animals and Animal Husbandry 675
MAAIKE GROOT

20. Households and Communities 693
LEO WEBLEY

21. Urbanization and *Oppida* 717
STEPHAN FICHTL

22. Monuments — 741
HOLGER WENDLING AND MANFRED K. H. EGGERT

ECONOMY

23. Iron and Iron Technology — 773
TIMOTHY CHAMPION

24. Raw Materials, Technology, and Innovation — 797
RUPERT GEBHARD

25. Material Worlds — 819
FRASER HUNTER

26. Textiles and Perishable Materials — 843
JOHANNA BANCK-BURGESS

27. Trade and Exchange — 871
CHRIS GOSDEN

28. Coinage and Coin Use — 887
COLIN HASELGROVE

COMPLEXITY

29. Politics and Power — 927
JOHN COLLIS AND RAIMUND KARL

30. Warriors, War, and Weapons; or Arms, the Armed, and Armed Violence — 947
SIMON JAMES

31. Wealth, Status, and Occupation Groups — 971
TOM MOORE

32. Horses, Wagons, and Chariots — 999
KATHARINA REBAY-SALISBURY

IDENTITY

33. Demographic Aspects of Iron Age Societies — 1025
STEFAN BURMEISTER AND MICHAEL GEBÜHR†

34. Gender and Society 1049
RACHEL POPE

35. Regions, Groups, and Identity: An Intellectual History 1079
T. L. THURSTON

36. Writing, Writers, and Iron Age Europe 1103
DAPHNE NASH BRIGGS

37. Migration 1137
ANDREW P. FITZPATRICK

38. Indigenous Communities under Rome 1187
ADAM ROGERS

RITUAL AND EXPRESSION

39. Feasting and Commensal Rituals 1213
JODY JOY

40. Funerary Practices 1237
PATRICE BRUN

41. Ritual Sites, Offerings, and Sacrifice 1261
IAN ARMIT

42. Formal Religion 1283
MIRANDA ALDHOUSE-GREEN

43. Art on the Northern Edge of the Mediterranean World 1305
MARTIN GUGGISBERG

Index 1337

Figures

2.1 Map showing the regional framework adopted for Chapters 4 to 17. 20

3.1 Time spans covered by the regional chapters in this Handbook. 40

3.2 Chronological periodizations for the pre-Roman and Roman Iron Age in north-west and central Europe. 42

3.3 Brooch types typifying the La Tène D1 and D2 periods in Germany. 45

3.4 Competing regional chronologies for non-Mediterranean France and adjacent areas. 46

3.5 Tree-ring fixed dates from western and central Europe. 50

3.6 Model estimates for the major occupation phases, cemetery, and late houses at Broxmouth, Scotland. 51

3.7 Spans of radiocarbon-dated activity at later prehistoric sites around Traprain Law, Scotland. 53

3.8 Probability distributions for the use of figure-of-eight palisade enclosures at the Rath of the Synods Tara, Navan, and Dún Ailinne, Ireland. 54

4.1 Map of principal Iron Age sites in north-west Europe. 68

4.2 Mont Lassois-Vix, Côte d'Or: general plan and the large building. 74

4.3 The Gaulish aristocratic settlement at Paule, Côtes d'Armor, in the third century BC. 77

4.4 Mierlo-Hout, Noord-Brabant, plan of urnfield graves and Haps-type byre houses. 80

4.5 Early Iron Age timber roundhouse at Pimperne, Dorset. 84

4.6 The Period 2 defences and longhouses at Crickley Hill, Gloucestershire. 85

4.7 Building PC15 under excavation at Mont Beuvray, Burgundy. 92

4.8 Sheet-bronze carnyces and a bird-helmet deposited in the sanctuary at Tintignac, Corrèze. 97

4.9 The later Iron Age hillfort at Burrough Hill, Leicestershire, showing settlement area outside east entrance. 102

4.10 Navan, Co. Armagh: '40m structure' and overlying mound. 107

4.11 Gold hoard from Blair Drummond, Stirling, third or second century BC. 110

4.12 Broch and 'village' at Gurness, Orkney. 115

5.1 The human landscape in Iron Age Scandinavia, showing the location of sites mentioned in the text. 146
5.2 Southern Scandinavian house and central Scandinavian house. 151
5.3 Roman and Byzantine base metal coins from Scandinavia. 157
5.4 The distribution of Scandinavian lev/leben-names. 161
6.1 Early tarand graves of the pre-Roman Iron Age and stone-cist grave of the late Bronze Age at Tõugu, Estonia. 176
6.2 Main cultural regions in the pre-Roman Iron Age in the eastern Baltic. 177
6.3 Main grave types in the eastern Baltic region in the Roman Iron Age. 181
6.4 Classical tarand grave at Pada, Estonia. 182
6.5 Reconstructed barrows at Karmazinai, Lithuania. 185
6.6 Miniature hillfort at Lavariškės, Lithuania. 186
7.1 Early pre-Roman Iron Age cultural groupings in east central Europe. 195
7.2 Early pre-Roman Iron Age pottery of the Pomeranian culture and the West Balt barrow culture in Poland. 196
7.3 Late pre-Roman Iron Age cultural groupings in east central Europe. 200
7.4 Late pre-Roman Iron Age cremation grave of the Przeworsk culture at Dobrzankowo (Poland). 202
7.5 Early Roman Iron Age cultural groupings in east central Europe. 205
7.6 Late Roman Iron Age cultural groupings in east central Europe. 207
7.7 Late Roman Iron Age finds from the Wielbark culture cemetery at Elbląg (Poland). 208
7.8 Early Roman Iron Age dress accessories from a female inhumation grave from the Sambian peninsula (Kovrovo, Russian Federation). 209
7.9 Migration period brooches from a cemetery of the Olsztyn group (Tumiany, Poland). 212
8.1 Map of principal Iron Age sites in central Europe. 218
8.2 Italian imported bronze bowl from Frankfurt-Stadtwald, tumulus 1, Grave 12. 220
8.3 Bowl of embossed sheet gold from tumulus 8, Wehringen-Hexenbergle, near Augsburg. 224
8.4 Hallstatt period wagon burial of a woman in the barrow cemetery of Niedererlbach, Lower Bavaria. 226
8.5 Banqueting equipment comprising different types of bronze vessels from the central grave of tumulus 3, Kappel am Rhein. 228
8.6 Spouted bronze jugs from the princely tombs of Reinheim and Waldalgesheim. 241

8.7 Sandstone sculpture of the prince from Glauberg barrow 1, grave 1. 243
9.1 Map of Mediterranean France showing sites mentioned in the text. 277
9.2 Stela from La Ramasse (Clermont l'Hérault), with representation of a warrior panoply. 279
9.3 The back of the warrior (lancer?) from Lattes, sixth century BC. 280
9.4 Reconstruction of a monumental portico featuring the seated warrior from Glanon. 281
9.5 Aerial view of Saint-Blaise. 285
9.6 Aerial view of the site of Tamaris. 286
9.7 The Hellenistic ramparts at Saint-Blaise. 293
9.8 Model showing part of the first fortified settlement at L'Ile de Martigues. 293
9.9 Destruction level in a house of the first settlement at L'Ile de Martigues. 294
9.10 Set of ceramic vessels of the later Iron Age from Provence. 296
9.11 Plan of the *oppidum* of Entremont (Aix-en-Provence). 298
10.1 Map of the Iberian Peninsula showing geographical and linguistic areas. 308
10.2 Aerial views of Iron Age sites: 1 Chao Samartín (Asturias); 2 Numancia (Soria); 3 Cancho Roano (Badajoz); 4 Puente Tablas (Jaén); 5 Monte Molião (Algarve); 6 Els Vilars d'Arbeca (Lleida). 309
10.3 Zoomorphic stone sculptures (*verracos*) from Guisando (Ávila). 313
10.4 Iron Age iconography: 1 bronze object with a scene of sacrifice (north-west Iberian Peninsula); 2 decorated diadem-belt from Moñes (Asturias); 3 ceramic jug from Numancia (Soria); 4 symbolic ceramic iconography from Ilici (Elche). 332
10.5 Stone sculpture: 1 fight scene from Cerrillo Blanco de Porcuna (Jaén); 2 Dama de Baza (Granada); 3 warrior from Castro Lezenho (Vila Real). 334
10.6 Late Iron Age decorated silver tableware (páteras) from Castellet de Banyoles (Tarragona). 335
10.7 Samples of writing and monetization. 337
11.1 Map of northern Italy showing principal sites mentioned in the text. 346
11.2 Chiavari cemetery, Genoa: urn and orientalizing gold ear-rings. Seventh century BC. 353
11.3 Grave assemblage from Moncucco, Como, *c.*800 BC. Golasecca phase IA2. 355
11.4 Orientalizing basin and ribbed cist found in a grave at Motto Fontanile, Castelletto Ticino. Golasecca phase IC. 357
11.5 Pottery from a grave at Castelletto Ticino. Golasecca phase IIB. 358
11.6 Bronze figurines of a horseman and of horses from votive deposit found at Sanzeno, Trentino. Fourth to third century BC. 363

11.7 Mounted warriors engraved on ice-polished rock at Naquane, Camonica valley. 365

11.8 Bronze disc depicting a priestess or *kleidoukos* (bearer of keys), from Montebelluna, Treviso. Fourth–third century BC. 370

11.9 Map of the north-east Adriatic, western Balkans, south-east Alpine, and Pannonian regions showing sites mentioned in the text. 371

11.10 Santa Lucia/Most na Soči: grave with prestige goods and bow fibulae of Santa Lucia type with pendants. 373

11.11 Nesactium/Nezakcij: stone statue of ithyphallic horseman and birth-giving woman breast-feeding a child. 375

11.12 Examples of Iapodic jewellery. 376

11.13 Liburnian silver jewellery. 378

11.14 Stična, tumulus 48. 381

11.15 Prestige armour of the Dolenjska and Styrian-Pannonian warrior elites and schematic representation of warrior ranks in the Dolenjska group. 382

11.16 Kleinklein, Kröllkogel: reconstruction and plan of the grave chamber. 386

11.17 The Strettweg cult-wagon. 388

12.1 Map showing principal sites in the central Mediterranean and Aegean Sea area. 408

12.2 Nichoria, Greece: house IV-1. 412

12.3 Lefkandi, Euboea: *Heroon* and Toumba cemetery. 413

12.4 Broglio di Trebesacce, southern Italy: area of forge and *pithos* store. 422

12.5 Torre di Satriano, southern Italy: later sixth-century BC rectangular house. 425

12.6 View from Broglio di Trebesacce, looking towards Timpone della Motta. 427

12.7 The acropolis at Francavilla Marittima, Timpone della Motta, southern Italy. 427

12.8 The ancient city of Morgantina, Sicily. 432

12.9 Cuciurpula, Corsica, Structure 1. 440

13.1 Map of principal sites in northern Greece and the central Balkans. 450

13.2 Complex tell-settlement with toumba and table at Pentalofos, Thessaloniki. 452

13.3 Hilltop settlement at Chorygi, Kilkis, Greece. 454

13.4 The tumulus of Kamenicë in the basin of Korçë, Albania. 460

13.5 Dolmen at Lalapaşa, Edirne, Turkey. 467

13.6 Niches at the rocky cliffs of Gluhite Kamani, Bulgaria. 469

14.1 The geography of the Carpathian and Danubian area. 478
14.2 The earliest iron artefacts, thirteenth to eleventh and tenth to eighth centuries BC. 481
14.3 Archaeological cultures of the early Iron Age. 483
14.4 The fortified settlement at Teleac, Transylvania. 485
14.5 Archaeological cultures of the seventh to third centuries BC. 492
14.6 The Celtic horizon in the Carpathian basin (fourth to third centuries BC) and the aristocratic horizon in the northern Balkans (fifth to third centuries BC). 494
14.7 1 Panoply of weapons from a grave at Remetea Mare, Banat; 2 helmet from Ciumeşti, Romania; 3 helmet found in Transylvania. 495
14.8 The Dacian kingdom. 504
14.9 Late La Tène weapons and harness fittings from Bulbuc, Transylvania, late second century to first half of the first century BC. 505
14.10 Late La Tène artefacts from a tumulus cremation grave near the Dacian fortress at Cugir, Transylvania, late second century to first half of the first century BC. 506
14.11 The Dacian fortress at Piatra Craivii, Transylvania, showing its constituent functional zones. 507
14.12 Temples in the sacred area at Sarmizegetusa (Romania). 510
15.1 Late Bronze–early Iron Age cultures of the first half of the first millennium BC. 526
15.2 Late Chernogovka burials. 533
15.3 (A) Kizil Koba aligned stone cists at Urkusta; (B) Proto-Maeotian burials at Fars/Klady. 536
15.4 The necropolis at Serzhen' Yurt, Chechenia; 1 plan; 2 pre-Scythian grave; 3 Scythian period grave. 538
15.5 Houses and domestic pottery of the Cozia-Sacharna culture. 540
15.6 Early Scythian burial mounds, seventh century BC. 541
15.7 Early Scythian burials. 542
15.8 (A) The late Scythian settlement at Lyubimovka; (B) typical finds from late Scythian settlements of the lower Dnieper region, first century BC to first century AD. 547
15.9 (A) Single burials from kurgan mounds of the lower Dnieper area, second to first century BC. (B) Solontsy, probably votive hoard, second to first century BC. 548
15.10 The Kachalinskaya votive hoard, north Pontic region, second century BC. 549

15.11 The settlement of Neapolis Scythica, Crimea. 552
15.12 Crypt grave at Bitak necropolis, Crimea. 553
15.13 Niche grave from the eastern necropolis at Neapolis Scythica, Crimea. Late second century AD. 554
15.14 Flat burials from the cemetery of the settlement of Starokorsunskaya-3, Kuban region. Late first to second century AD. 558
15.15 Kurgan 3, burial from Proletarskiy cemetery, Kuban region, second century BC. 559
15.16 Burials in kurgan mounds at Verkhnee Pogromnoe, lower Volga region, second to first century BC. 561
15.17 Burials in the flat cemetery of Kobyakovo, lower Don region. 564
16.1 Cultural map of easternmost Europe, seventh to third centuries BC. 578
16.2 Cultural map of easternmost Europe, third century BC to third century AD. 579
16.3 Kichigino cemetery, barrow 1, burial 1. 584
16.4 Kichigino cemetery, barrow 3, burial 5. 587
16.5 Objects from the Filippovka burial ground. 588
16.6 Burials and objects of the early Sarmatian (Prokhorovo) culture. 590
16.7 Decorative objects of the middle and late Sarmatian culture in the lower Don area. 593
16.8 Burials and objects of the middle and late Sarmatian culture. 595
16.9 The Dyakovo culture: hillfort, houses, and artefacts. 599
16.10 Dyakovo culture mortuary house. 600
16.11 (A)–(B) Burials from the Akkozinsky burial ground; (C) artefacts from Ananyino cemeteries. 604
16.12 Burials and objects from the Tarasovo burial ground. 607
16.13 Female ornaments of the Pyanobor style. 608
16.14 Copper cult figurines from the Glyadenovo bone-producing site. 610
17.1 The Near East in the Iron Age, with principal sites mentioned in the text. 622
17.2 North Africa in the Iron Age, with principal sites mentioned in the text. 627
17.3 Principal sites in temperate Europe mentioned in the text. 634
17.4 Bronze *situla* from Straubing, Bavaria, Germany. 635
17.5 Ivory and amber pommel on an iron sword from Hallstatt, Austria. 636
19.1 Species proportions for the main domestic livestock on Iron Age sites. 677
19.2 Greek vase showing sacrificial animal being led to the altar. 680

19.3 Three ritual deposits of a sheep's head and feet, Alorda Park, Catalonia, fifth to fourth century BC. 685

19.4 A byre-house excavated at Ezinge, Netherlands, showing the cattle stalls. 686

20.1 Iron Age houses from Mediterranean Europe. 695

20.2 Iron Age houses from temperate Europe. 697

20.3 Burnt houses showing floor artefact distributions. 701

20.4 Multi-household settlements from Mediterranean Europe. 705

20.5 Multi-household settlements from temperate Europe. 707

21.1 Aerial view of the *oppidum* of Besançon (Vesontio), France. 721

21.2 The *oppidum* of Bracquemont on the chalk cliffs of Seine-Maritime, France. 722

21.3 Reconstruction of rampart with vertical post construction at the *oppidum* of the Donnersberg, Germany. 723

21.4 Reconstruction of the *murus gallicus* at the Porte du Rebout entrance to the *oppidum* of Bibracte, Burgundy. 724

21.5 Stone facing of the *murus gallicus* at the *oppidum* of Hérisson, France. 726

21.6 Model of the plots or *îlots* in the centre of Manching, Bavaria. 728

21.7 The public centre at the *oppidum* of Corent in the Auvergne. 732

22.1 Late La Tène fortified farmstead (*Viereckschanze*) and Hallstatt barrows around the giant Hohmichele tumulus near the Heuneburg (south-west Germany). 744

22.2 Natural springs and reservoirs incorporated by annexe walls at the early Iron Age hillforts of Glauberg, Altkönig, and Ipf, Germany. 746

22.3 Hallstatt C and D burial monuments at the Schirndorf cemetery, south-east Germany. 747

22.4 Lines of barrows at Grundsheim, south-west Germany. 748

22.5 Large building in the centre of a *Viereckschanze* farmstead near Manching, Bavaria, with comparative plans of buildings at Westenhausen and Manching. 753

22.6 Linear ditches and earthworks around the Glauberg hillfort. 755

22.7 Natural features incorporated into the defensive system of the Heidengraben *oppidum*, south-west Germany. 756

22.8 Middle La Tène gold-foil covered representation of an ivy-leaved branch or small tree from Manching. 759

22.9 LiDAR topographical model of the fortification at Manching; reconstruction of the building sequence; and remains of the *murus gallicus* phase. 761

23.1 The stone-walled hilltop enclosure at Bryn y Castell, north Wales, indicating the location of ironworking in the late Iron Age and early Roman periods. 777

23.2 Iron firedog from Capel Garmon, north Wales. 787

24.1 Tools and equipment of the third to first centuries BC from the *oppidum* of Manching, Bavaria. 799

24.2 Pottery of the second to first centuries BC from Manching. 803

24.3 Ceramic vessels with hammer-scale and iron remnants from a forge at Manching. 809

24.4 Coin dies made of iron with corresponding coins from Kleinsorheim, Bavaria, first century BC. 810

25.1 Datable finds of rotary querns from the European Iron Age. 821

25.2 Reconstruction of the chariot from Newbridge, Edinburgh. 822

25.3 Hybrid torc from Blair Drummond (Stirling, Scotland). 824

25.4 Bone and antler combs for textile processing and a bone hide-rubber from Midhowe and Gurness (Orkney, Scotland). 826

25.5 Comparison of the proportions of different material types found in settlement and cemetery contexts from East Yorkshire, England, and the Traisen valley, Austria. 829

25.6 Bone and antler objects with varying styles of decoration from Broxmouth (East Lothian, Scotland). 833

26.1 Tablet-woven fabric from the late Hallstatt burial at Hochdorf, south-west Germany. 851

26.2 Tablet-woven textiles from Hochdorf. 852

26.3 Reconstruction of the burial chamber at Hochdorf. 857

28.1 Map of the earliest Iron Age coinages in Celtic Europe, showing Greek prototypes and location of key sites mentioned in the text. 889

28.2 Composite images of Iron Age coins struck from a single die: (A) Gallo-Belgic C gold; (B) British J gold; (C) South-Western silver stater. 894

28.3 Iron Age gold coin hoards containing Rainbow cup staters and other coin types, showing the extent of die-linking between hoards. 898

28.4 Cut-marked 'sitting person' silver coins from the Martberg, Germany. 907

28.5 *Denarius* hoard and circular building from Birnie, Scotland. 910

30.1. Skull fragment from Danebury hillfort, southern England, exhibiting blunt-force trauma and a graphic perimortem injury. 951

30.2. Iron Age swords from Spain and Switzerland. 955

30.3 Top left and centre: Steppe equestrian combat with bow and lance: engraved figures from the Kosika cup, *c.*50 BC–AD 50. Top right: reconstruction of Roman saddle design, probably of Steppe origin. Bottom left: head of a Roman *draco* from Niederbieber, Germany. Bottom right: Sarmatian troops with windsock standards, Arch of Galerius, Thessaloniki, Greece. 956

30.4 Reconstruction of a Gallic war trumpet (*carnyx*) found at Tintignac, France. 959

31.1 The traditional Celtic model of society. 973

31.2 The varied expression of wealth and status through metalwork: the distribution of gold torcs in Europe. 976

31.3 Graph showing change in deposition of metalwork in the latest Bronze Age/earliest Iron Age of central France. 977

31.4 Gold torc and bracelets from Waldalgesheim, Rheinland-Pfalz, Germany. 981

31.5 The elaborate earthworks of Maiden Castle hillfort, southern England. 984

31.6 Grave of possible ironworker from Rudston, East Yorkshire, England. 988

32.1 Two breeds of horses on the belt plate from Vače, Slovenia, fifth century BC. 1001

32.2 Riders with saddles and spurs depicted on the Gundestrup cauldron, Denmark, second to first century BC. 1004

32.3 Four-wheeled ceremonial wagon used in the funerary display at Mitterkirchen, Austria, eighth/seventh century BC. 1007

32.4 The distribution of wagon graves and depictions of wagons in the early Iron Age. 1009

32.5 Burial of eight men and their horses at Gondole, France, first century BC. 1013

32.6 The Uffington Horse (Oxfordshire) from the air. 1015

33.1 Mortality curve and life pyramid of the Iron Age population in Schleswig-Holstein, north Germany. For comparison, the modern population of Schleswig-Holstein. 1031

33.2 Gender- and age-specific high-status burials in late Hallstatt south-west Germany. 1034

33.3 Mortality in the Roman Empire according to epitaphs on gravestones, first to sixth centuries AD. 1036

33.4 Opposing mortality curves and life pyramids of the Viking Age population from the cemeteries and settlement of Haithabu, Denmark. 1038

33.5 Simulated mortality curve and life pyramid of a population experiencing a long-lasting emigration vs a population experiencing immigration, compared to the Migration period/early Anglo-Saxon populations from Issendorf, Lower Saxony, Germany, and Spong Hill, East Anglia, England. 1043

34.1 Map of sites mentioned in the text. 1051

34.2 Hallstatt Grave 505: gold, amber, and bronze items. 1054

34.3 Gendered cemetery populations. 1056

34.4 Burmeister's seriation methodology: North Württemberg, Germany, Hallstatt D1. 1057

34.5 Selection of Hallstatt D dagger handles, revealing anthropomorphism and cattle symbolism. 1058

34.6 Links between German and French 'dynasties', potentially denoting kinship. 1064

36.1 'Duenos' inscription on the shoulders of three conjoint vases, Rome, *c.* sixth century BC. 1105

36.2 Tartessian and Celtiberian symbols. 1106

36.3 Alphabets mentioned in the text, arranged to show morphological connections. 1107

36.4 Schematic map showing spread of early writing systems based on Iberian, Etruscan, Greek, and Latin scripts. 1109

36.5 1 Espanca stone (Portugal), *c.* seventh to fifth century BC. 2 Silver *denarius*, *c.*150–100 BC, Vascones (Spain), with Iberic inscription. 3 Silver *denarius*, *c.*120–30 BC, Segobriges (Spain), with Celtiberian inscription. 4 Bronze *as*, *c.* first century BC, people of Narbo (France). 1111

36.6 1 Briona stone (Italy), *c.* third century BC. 2 Silver drachm, *c.* second to first century BC, Insubres (Italy), with Lepontic inscription. 3 Celtic inscription on Negau Helmet A (Slovenia). 4 Germanic inscription on Negau Helmet B. 5 Inscription ARATIEPOS, from silver tetradrachms in the Ribnjačka hoard, third/early second century BC. 6 Old runic futhark, Kylver stone (Sweden), *c.*AD 400. 1113

36.7 1 Stone from Vaison-la-Romaine (France). 2 Silver unit inscribed KALETEDOU, Lingones (Gaul), *c.*120–50 BC. 3 Bronze coin of Kavaros, Tylis (Thrace), *c.*225–218 BC. 4 Gold ring from Erezovo (Bulgaria), fifth century BC. 5 Silver *denarius* inscribed RAVIS, Eravisci (Pannonia), *c.* first century BC. 6 Silver unit inscribed [AN]TEĐ, *c.*AD 20–43. 1116

36.8 Ogam script, basic system. 1118

36.9 British kings named by Augustus, on gold staters. 1132

37.1 Map of selected sites mentioned in the text. 1141

37.2 The discovery of the Celtic migration to Italy: Marzabotto and Marne. 1142

37.3 Celtic migration embodied: the 'Dying Gaul'. 1147

37.4 The leitmotif of the 'dragon pair' on sword scabbards. 1153

37.5 The distribution of early La Tène burials in the Carpathian basin and the possible directions of Celtic migration. 1158
37.6 Heavily worn neck-rings (*Scheibenhalsringe*) in relation to all neck-rings. 1159
37.7 Detail from a relief from the acropolis of Athena Nikephoros at Pergamon with a photograph of a Celtic helmet from Batina, Croatia, superimposed. 1164
38.1 Period 2 Alphen-Ekeren-type timber buildings at Kielenstraat, Tongeren, Belgium, probably dating to the beginning of the first century AD. 1194
38.2 Birdlip Quarry, Gloucestershire, England: plan of roundhouse and nearby features. 1195
38.3 The cemetery of Wadern-Oberlöstern, Saarland, Germany. 1199
38.4 The location of the Moor House excavations in relation to Roman London and the upper Walbrook valley. 1200
39.1 Layout of the cauldrons in the pit at Chiseldon, Wiltshire, England. 1219
39.2 Decorated cauldron from Chiseldon, detail. 1220
39.3 One of a pair of copper-alloy flagons, Basse-Yutz, Lorraine, France. 1223
39.4 Basse-Yutz flagon: close-up of the duck swimming on a 'river' of wine. 1223
39.5 Copper-alloy stave bindings and handle of a tankard found near Brackley, Northamptonshire, England. 1224
40.1 Model of the ideological messages conveyed by funerary practices. 1239
40.2 The Vix-Mont Lassois complex, Burgundy. 1243
40.3 Burial with cart and Mediterranean imports at La Gorge-Meillet, France. 1248
40.4 The sequence of graves at the cemetery of Lamadeleine near the *oppidum* of the Titelberg, Luxembourg. 1250
40.5 Mortuary practices in Britain. 1252
41.1 Details of wagon and chariot from the upper frieze of the *situla* from Vače, Slovenia, from digital 3D model. 1263
41.2 One of the warrior statues from Entremont, southern France. 1274
42.1 Stone carving of a woodman, bearing the inscription 'Esus'. 1286
42.2 Copper-alloy sceptre head from a high-status cremation grave in a cemetery at Numantia, Spain, second century BC. 1290
42.3 Armorican Iron Age gold coin depicting a naked horsewoman with shield and sword, accompanied by wheel and lyre symbols, first century BC. 1291
42.4 Inner plate from a gilded silver cauldron, depicting an antlered human figure accompanied by a stag, a ram-horned snake, and other creatures, second to first century BC. From a bog at Gundestrup, Denmark. 1293

42.5 Ceramic *turibulum* (incense-burner) from an underground sanctuary at Chartres (Autricum), France. 1296

43.1 Stepped plate (*Stufenteller*) of Alb-Hegau ware from Gomadingen-Sternberg, south-west Germany, seventh century BC. 1308

43.2 The lion figures from the Hochdorf cauldron, south-west Germany. 1310

43.3 Handle attachment of the beaked flagon (*Schnabelkanne*) and *stamnos* from Kleinaspergle, south-west Germany. 1312

43.4 Gold openwork mount from Schwarzenbach, Saarland, Germany, probably from a drinking horn. 1313

43.5 The torc from Waldalgesheim, Rheinland-Pfalz, Germany: detail of terminal decorated with a palmette and tendrils. 1314

43.6 Bronze knob in Plastic style. 1315

43.7 Scabbard from Cernon-sur-Coole, Marne, France. 1317

43.8 Wooden figure from Fellbach-Schmiden, south-west Germany. 1318

43.9 Vessel with deer figure from Puy de la Poix, Clermont-Ferrand, Auvergne, France. 1319

43.10 Scabbard from Kelermes, north Caucasus, Russia, with procession of griffins: detail of lion griffin. 1322

43.11 Wooden bridle attachment in the shape of a mouflon from *kurgan* 3, Pazyryk, Siberia, Russia. 1323

43.12 Breastplate from the Seven Brothers *kurgan*, Taman peninsula, Russia. 1325

43.13 Silver beaker from Agighiol, Romania. 1327

43.14 Griffin sculpture from Cerrillo Blanco de Porcuna, Andalusia, Spain. 1328

Tables

5.1 Chronological overview of the Scandinavian Iron Age. 148

11.1 Chronological table for northern Italy. 350

12.1 Chronologies employed in the central Mediterranean and the Aegean. 409

15.1 Correlation of Scythian and Sarmatian chronologies in the Circumpontic area. 529

15.2 Correlation of cultures and chronological phases in the Circumpontic area, thirteenth to seventh centuries BC. 531

16.1 Chronological chart for the steppe and forest zones in easternmost Europe. 580

20.1 Typical roofed area of domestic units in selected areas of Iron Age Europe. 699

25.1 Ratio of decorated to undecorated material culture in Pomerania (Germany/Poland). 832

28.1 Principal coinages in different regions of Iron Age Europe. 890

34.1 Gendered grave assemblages and status groups for the Ramsauer graves at Hallstatt, Austria. 1053

34.2 Examples of disproportionate deposition in graves in late Hallstatt and early La Tène Europe. 1066

39.1 Sources of evidence for feasting. 1214

Contributors

Miranda Aldhouse-Green, Cardiff University

Xosé-Lois Armada, Spanish National Research Council (CSIC), Santiago de Compostela

Ian Armit, University of York

Johanna Banck-Burgess, Landesamt für Denkmalpflege, Esslingen am Neckar

Daphne Nash Briggs, University of Oxford

Patrice Brun, Institut Universitaire de France, Paris

Stefan Burmeister, Museum und Park Kalkriese

Timothy Champion, University of Southampton

John Collis, University of Sheffield

Raffaele de Marinis, University of Milan

Manfred K. H. Eggert, University of Tübingen

Stephan Fichtl, University of Strasbourg

Andrew P. Fitzpatrick, University of Leicester

Lin Foxhall, University of Liverpool

Dominique Garcia, University of Aix-Marseille 1

Rupert Gebhard, Museum für Vor- und Frühgeschichte, Munich

Michael Gebühr†, University of Hamburg

Stefanos Gimatzidis, Austrian Academy of Sciences, Vienna

Chris Gosden, University of Oxford

Ignacio Grau Mira, University of Alicante

Maaike Groot, Berlin Free University

Martin Guggisberg, University of Basel

Colin Haselgrove, University of Leicester

Frands Herschend, University of Uppsala

Fraser Hunter, National Museums Scotland, Edinburgh

Simon James, University of Leicester

Jody Joy, University of Cambridge

Raimund Karl, University of Vienna

Ludmila Koryakova, Russian Academy of Sciences, Moscow

Sophie Krausz, University of Paris 1 Panthéon-Sorbonne

Hansjörg Küster, Leibniz University, Hannover

Valter Lang, University of Tartu

Naoíse Mac Sweeney, University of Vienna

Carola Metzner-Nebelsick, Ludwig-Maximilians University, Munich

Tom Moore, Durham University

Valentina I. Mordvintseva, National Academy of Sciences of Ukraine, Kiev

Wojciech Nowakowski, University of Warsaw

Rachel Pope, University of Liverpool

Katharina Rebay-Salisbury, University of Vienna

Sabine Reinhold, German Archaeological Institute, Berlin

Adam Rogers, University of Leicester

Aurel Rustoiu, Romanian Academy of Sciences, Kluj-Napoca

Biba Teržan, University of Ljubljana

T. L. Thurston, University at Buffalo, The State University of New York

Leo Webley, Oxford Archaeology

Peter S. Wells, University of Minnesota

Holger Wendling, Salzburg Museum/Keltenmuseum Hallein

PART I

INTRODUCTION

CHAPTER 1

INTRODUCTION

The Iron Age in Europe

COLIN HASELGROVE,
KATHARINA REBAY-SALISBURY,
AND PETER S. WELLS

The Concept of the Iron Age

Early in the nineteenth century, researchers in Europe began applying Christian Jürgensen Thomsen's Three Age System of Stone Age, Bronze Age, and Iron Age to the arranging of objects in museum collections. New museums—local, regional, and national—were being established all over Europe during that century and receiving a steady stream of objects, some recovered by farmers, others through early purposeful excavations. Several sites that were to be of immense importance were discovered and investigated in the middle decades of the century, notably at Hallstatt in Austria (Kern et al. 2009) and La Tène in Switzerland (Betschart 2007). In the second half of the nineteenth century, following these and other discoveries, a series of international congresses were held to organize study of the rapidly growing collections of Iron Age materials. Archaeologists including Hans Hildebrand, Otto Tischler, Oscar Montelius, Paul Reinecke, and Joseph Déchelette worked out detailed chronological frameworks for the Iron Age, based on changes in artefact typology. The assembled researchers decided to call the earlier part of the Iron Age the Hallstatt period, after the excavation of hundreds of well outfitted graves at that site, and the second part the La Tène period, after the recovery of large numbers of iron weapons and other implements from that lakeshore deposit (Kühn 1976: 51–83, 171–97).

As it is understood today, the term 'Iron Age' refers in Europe to the period between the time when iron first came into general use—around 800 BC for central regions of the continent, earlier in Mediterranean lands, and later in the north and north-west—and the Roman conquests in Europe. These began in the early third century BC in northern

Italy and continued up to the early second century AD in the Carpathians, with much of central and north-west Europe coming under Roman dominion in a comparatively short period beginning with Caesar's conquest of Gaul in the 50s BC. The term 'Roman Iron Age' is often applied to indigenous societies in lands north and east of the Roman imperial frontier during the Roman period, from the time of the conquests until the mid-fifth century AD. In some northern regions, this era is usually regarded as part of a longer late Iron Age, encompassing the so-called Migration period up to the start of the Viking age (*c.*AD 400–800). Even at its maximum extent, the Roman Empire covered less than half of the area considered in this volume.

The Iron Age was the final period of 'prehistory' in temperate Europe, between the Bronze Age, for which we have no textual (written, historical) sources of information outside the eastern Mediterranean, and the Roman period, which is considered 'historic' in the sense that we have abundant written documents. In many parts of Europe, the Iron Age is therefore regarded as a 'protohistoric' period. It is during the Iron Age that we have the first Greek and Roman texts that refer to temperate Europe, from Hecataeus and Herodotus in the sixth and fifth centuries BC to Caesar, Strabo, Livy, and Pliny just before and after the Roman conquests (Champion 1985). For northern Europe, texts written in southern regions from the Roman period onward, by authors such as Pliny and Tacitus, provide information that complements the evidence of archaeology. This situation offers special opportunities and challenges to investigators, since for the first time in European archaeology they have access to written sources—from outside temperate Europe and by writers whose comprehension of the peoples they described was not comparable to modern anthropologists' understandings. Through these written sources, we have the earliest references to named 'peoples' who came to play important roles in historical and literary contexts, such as Celts, Gauls, Cimmerians, Scythians, Sarmatians, Germans, and Dacians (Szabó 2006).

Prominent among the changes that distinguish the Iron Age from earlier times were the development and expansion of iron-working technology, leading to changes in and intensification of farming techniques; the formation of larger communities, some of which have been called 'towns' and even 'cities'; much more intensive and extensive interactions with other communities, both within and beyond Europe; the introduction and development of coinage and eventually of a money economy; the emergence of more formalized religious practices; and the beginnings of writing, adopted from Greek and Roman societies.

As serious interest in the ancient past of Europe began to intensify during the eighteenth century, field monuments that we now know to be of Iron Age date and collections of Iron Age objects started to attract scholarly attention. The systematic excavations of the great cemetery at Hallstatt, begun in the middle of the nineteenth century, marked a watershed in the development of Iron Age archaeology. The scale of the excavations and the wealth of finds created an international sensation, and large numbers of prominent people visited the excavations and spread the word about their importance. Around the same time, rich deposits of Iron Age weapons, tools, and coins were recovered at lakeside sites in Switzerland, especially at La Tène on the shore of Lake Neuchâtel. Many of the early discoveries—and the Iron Age peoples with whom they were supposedly associated—were quickly invoked in the refashioning of national identities that was taking place across Europe at this era, and have continued to occupy an important place in national and popular culture to the present day (e.g. Dietler 1994; Wells 2001: 19–21, 131–132).[1]

Following the results from Hallstatt, early archaeologists undertook excavations of burial mounds in many parts of Europe, quickly uncovering vast quantities of objects and information about the Iron Age. Hilltop sites with enclosing walls, such as Stradonice in Bohemia and Bibracte in France, were investigated (Rybová and Drda 1994; Guichard and Paris 2013). Low-lying wetland settlements, such as Glastonbury and Meare in south-west England, yielded organic materials in unusually good states of preservation (Coles and Minnit 1995). Large deposits of metal and wooden weapons were recovered in bog environments, such as those at Nydam and Vimose in Denmark (Jørgensen et al. 2003). Thanks to the richness of the evidence, and the evolution of new investigative and analytical techniques, many of these sites continue to attract high-quality, innovative research.

During the twentieth century, as the field of archaeology expanded with the establishment of increasing numbers of museums, universities, and government posts, research on Iron Age sites was carried out at an intensive pace throughout much of Europe, interrupted only by the two World Wars. Recent developments in Iron Age studies include greater attention to interactions between humans and the environments in which they lived, subsistence practices, landscape analyses, social systems, ritual activities, and the expression of individual and group identities.

From the beginning, the objects of the Iron Age have always been a major focus of research. Studies of 'Celtic art' loom large in this regard (Farley and Hunter 2015) and specialist studies of pottery, iron tools, glass ornaments, and other categories of material culture play important roles in our understanding of the period. In the past few decades, increased attention has been paid to exploring religion and ritual, representation and symbolism, and issues associated with gender and identity.

This volume presents the Iron Age of Europe in the widest sense, from the Atlantic in the west to the Ural Mountains in the east, from Scandinavia in the north to the Mediterranean in the south. The coverage is comprehensive, with equal treatment given to those regions not as familiar to most readers of English scholarship as the core parts of temperate Europe, and including the pre-classical periods in the Mediterranean societies of Greece and Italy. As the reader will note, much of the archaeology of the Mediterranean world is not fundamentally different from that of the rest of Europe, though the divide often appears to be greater than it is because of the different research traditions that focus on parts of the continent that are illuminated by classical literary texts and those that are not. The chronological range is from the earliest Iron Age around 1000 BC in the Mediterranean region to the greatest extent of Iron Age societies in northern Scandinavia and beyond around AD 1000. There have of course been many excellent previous studies of the Iron Age, which the reader will find referred to throughout this volume (e.g. Collis 1984; Kristiansen 1998; Metzner-Nebelsick et al. 2009; Vandkilde

2007; Buchsenschutz 2015). All of these, however, are in some ways subject to tighter geographical and chronological limits.

The Nature of the Archaeological Evidence

Iron Age material culture is found in a variety of contexts, including principally cemeteries and settlements, as well as deliberate deposits of different kinds, and representations. The character and frequency of the surviving remains vary considerably from region to region, often in quite localized ways.

Cemeteries

Much early research on Iron Age sites involved the excavation of graves (Chapter 40). Especially during the early Iron Age, many burials were in mounds and thus were easy for antiquarians to find and to explore. Flat grave cemeteries were often discovered as the result of digging into the ground for agricultural purposes. Some of the early cemetery excavations, such as those at Hallstatt, were relatively well documented by their excavators, others were not. The majority of Iron Age objects that we see in museums and illustrated in books about the Iron Age come from graves.

Iron Age cemeteries can be large, with hundreds and even thousands of graves, as at Hallstatt, and they can be small, consisting of just a few graves. Burials can be in mounds or tumuli, as at Hradenín in the Czech Republic and at Magdalenska gora in Slovenia (Filip 1966; Tecco Hvala 2012), or flat, as in the cemeteries of the middle La Tène period such as Münsingen-Rain in Switzerland and Jenišův Újezd in the Czech Republic (Hodson 1968; Waldhauser 1978). Tumuli can contain just one burial, or over a hundred, as at Stična in Slovenia and the Magdalenenberg in south-west Germany (Gabrovec 1999; Spindler 1999). Graves can be pits in the ground, whether simple or more complex, or they can include elaborate wooden chambers such as those at Hochdorf in south-west Germany and Vix in eastern France (Biel 1985; Rolley 2003). Burial can be by inhumation, usually with the body laid out flat on its back in an extended position, or by cremation, sometimes with an urn buried in the ground, sometimes not. Burial practices were closely linked to the beliefs and traditions of the different communities and varied greatly over time and with geography, with some parts of Europe lacking archaeologically visible methods for disposal of the dead for some or all of the period.

Throughout the Iron Age, the quantity of objects placed in graves varied greatly. Some graves contain no objects (at least none that survived to be recognized by the excavators). Some contain quantities of objects, some everyday and some of special significance. In many early Iron Age rich graves, personal ornaments of bronze and gold adorn the deceased, sets of drinking vessels of pottery and of bronze accompany the dead, and wheeled vehicles were included in the chamber. Weapons and sometimes tools were also placed in many graves (Chapter 30). The body of the deceased can be positioned in a variety of different ways, and each detail of arrangement has meaning.

In earlier traditions of scholarship, grave wealth was often equated with the wealth, status, and power of the buried individuals during their lifetimes (Chapter 31). Today, archaeologists tend to interpret grave inventories as results of a reflective discourse that includes both the community's desires and expressions, and the individual's personal identity. The objects and their disposition are also understood as active statements about the social group and of the aspirations of the individuals who conducted the funerary ritual. The bodies of the buried persons themselves can reveal detailed information on diet, disease, and stress that can be contextualized with the grave inventories (Chapters 3, 34).

With all of the multifarious data that can be extracted from graves, cemeteries continue to be very rich sources of information concerning Iron Age communities and societies. Cemeteries generally offer the best evidence upon which to base population estimates for communities, and well-preserved bones allow for major studies of demographic composition. Thanks to scientific advances, ancient DNA and isotope analyses provide rich new possibilities for understanding biological sex, family relationships within and beyond cemeteries, as well as patterns of mobility and migration of individuals from place to place (Chapters 3, 37).

Settlements

In most parts of Europe, settlements have generally received less attention than burials, but the situation is fast changing, partly with the application of more effective technologies for locating settlement sites, including air photography, magnetometry, ground-penetrating radar, and LIDAR, and above all as a result of the dramatic increase since the 1990s in archaeological interventions legally required in advance of building works in most European countries. In some parts of Europe, settlements are well documented, in others less so. Iron Age settlements range from individual farmsteads, to villages, to towns, to the fortified *oppida*, which many investigators consider to have been cities (Chapter 21).

The vast majority of Iron Age settlements were small, consisting of a few farmsteads and with populations usually fewer than 100 persons (Chapter 20). Most people were primary producers of food through agriculture and the raising of livestock. Plant and animal remains inform us about diet and subsistence as well as their economic implications (Chapters 18, 19). But even in the smallest settlements, some people participated in making things—pottery, iron tools, ornaments of various materials. In larger settlements, such as the so-called *Fürstensitze* of the early Iron Age, as at Mont Lassois and the Heuneburg, specialized crafts are evident (Chaume et al. 2011; Krausse et al. 2016), and at the large unenclosed agglomerations and *oppida* that developed at the end of the Iron Age, specialists worked in many different materials (Chapters 21, 24).

Different from typical agricultural settlements were enclosed hilltop sites, both small and large, known as hillforts. Some hilltop settlements were permanently occupied, others seem to have seen intermittent use, perhaps only in times of danger. The late Iron Age *oppida* were often, but by no means always, situated on hilltops.

Some larger settlements specialized in the production of particular materials and products destined specifically for trade. The salt-mining sites of Hallstatt and the Dürrnberg at Hallein (Stöllner 1999) are examples of communities situated at particular natural resources, whose members specialized in the production of that one material. Kelheim in Bavaria, Germany, the site of an *oppidum* at the end of the Iron Age, was a production centre of iron (Schäfer 2002) as was Mšec in the Czech Republic (Pleiner and Princ 1984). The community at Lovosice, also in the Czech Republic, was specialized in the quarrying and exporting of quernstones (Wefers 2012). At the opposite end of the spectrum, we find a multitude of small, specialized sites engaged in producing materials like salt, jet and shale, particularly in coastal and wetland areas, and at altitude; these were often seasonally occupied.

As archaeological research on settlements has progressed all over Europe, some important changes have taken place in our understanding of them. At the Heuneburg, for example, what was once seen as a special central place of high status but modest size in the sixth and early fifth centuries BC is now believed to have been part of a vast urban complex, with relatively densely inhabited suburbs extending around the hilltop fortress. Its population is now estimated at around 5,000 persons, much larger than had previously been thought likely for any early Iron Age settlement (Krausse et al. 2016). At one time, it was assumed that the *oppida* were 'cities', often compared to urban centres of the Mediterranean world. But excavations within the enclosing walls have indicated that many of them were not densely settled and may have served mainly as places of refuge in times of danger. Some researchers interpret even the major *oppida*, such as Manching, as more like assemblages of village communities than as urban centres (Moore 2017). For several decades, the rectangular enclosures of temperate Europe—*Viereckschanzen*—were believed to have been primarily places of ritual activity (Chapter 41), with deep shafts into which objects were ceremonially deposited. More recent research suggests that they were instead enclosed settlements in which ritual activity took place, but only as part of the multifarious activities of daily life in late Iron Age farmsteads (von Nicolai 2009).

In eastern regions of Europe, in the lands associated with the Scythians, many communities were nomadic or semi-nomadic (Chapters 15–16). Although these groups are often represented by their great burial mounds known as kurgans, with a few exceptions, their settlements are still poorly understood. Most of the Continent, however, was densely and permanently settled with movement restricted to periodic rebuilding of dwelling sites in a landscape that was also increasingly divided up into discrete territorial units during the Iron Age. Throughout the period, we see a gradual rise in the number of rural settlements, albeit subject to various regional peaks and fluctuations. In the harsher northern regions, settlement densities were lower, and focused on areas best suited to agriculture, hunting and fishing.

Deposits

A third major category of Iron Age 'site' is the deposit. Objects, especially those made of metal, were deposited in pits in the ground (in which case they are often called 'hoards') and in bodies of water. Land deposits include those at unusual natural features, such as the stone arch at Egesheim in south-west Germany (Dehn and Klug 1993) or at the site of fourteen pits at Snettisham in Norfolk in Britain (Joy 2015). Some deposits include mostly metal jewellery, others iron weapons or tools, and others coins.

Water deposits are found at springs, as in the case of Duchcov (Dux) in the Czech Republic (Kruta 1971), at the sources of streams, as at the Douix in France (Buvot 1998), in rivers such as the Thames and the Witham in Britain (Bradley 1998), and in lakes and ponds, as at La Tène in Switzerland. The purpose of deposits in both land and water has been much debated over the years, whether they contain objects regarded as treasure, or hidden assets, or as votive offerings to supernatural beings. Today most investigators seem to hold with the final interpretation.

Deposits at architecturally constructed 'sanctuary' sites such as Gournay and Ribemont in northern France appear to be linked to ritualized warfare (Brunaux 2004). Places for ritual activities such as rectangular enclosures were built at the edges of larger settlements, for instance at Roseldorf in Austria (Holzer 2014). Several sanctuaries with large numbers of votive deposits are known from around the city of Este in Italy. Especially in the Alpine regions of Europe, deposits of metal objects in context with large heaps of cremated animal bones and evidence of fire, known as *Brandopferplätze* (Steiner 2010), constitute another kind of ritual site linked to the specific Alpine landscape.

Representations

Representations of humans and animals provide important information about the ways that the Iron Age people of Europe perceived the world in which they lived. The Strettweg cult wagon from an early Iron Age grave in Austria (Egg 1996) can be understood to inform us about ideas concerning relations between humans and animals, including both wild animals (the stags) and domestic animals (the horses), as well as about gender, with the female, male, and sexless representations of people on the vehicle. The sword scabbard from Hallstatt Grave 994, dating to the early fourth century BC, bears a scene of soldiers, some marching on foot, some mounted on horseback, providing information about military organization and its practices, costume, and weaponry (Egg and Schönfelder 2009). Stone statues such as those from Hirschlanden and from the Glauberg in Germany, from Vix on the river Seine in France, and others in

Mediterranean France and Iberia, represent persons outfitted with garments, weapons, and insignia representative of high status (Frey 2002). Many interpretations have been proposed for the Gundestrup cauldron from late Iron Age Denmark (Nielsen et al. 2005), none of them as yet convincing the majority of investigators. The imagery is complex and varied and seems to represent interactions between humans, supernatural beings, and animals. Finally, the Situla art of 600–300 BC in central southern Europe provides what appear to be much more realistic representations of humans engaged in a variety of ritual practices (Turk 2005). Two main schools of thought propose that the scenes represent the lives and activities of deities on the one hand, and those of Iron Age elites on the other, intersecting in the idea of heroization in which members of the elite became deified.

Greek and Roman Written Sources

In the later phases of the Iron Age, a few written sources from the Mediterranean world provide information about the prehistoric peoples to their north. But none of the sources can be understood in terms of our understanding of modern social anthropological studies (although some regard Tacitus' *Germania* as an ethnographic account). The earliest substantial accounts are by Greeks, notably Herodotus, who describes in some depth the Scythians and other nomadic peoples inhabiting the lands north of the Black Sea, in the fifth century BC (Chapter 36). Later, Julius Caesar tells much about the Gauls against whom he was fighting in the years 58–51 BC, and he makes a few statements about the peoples he calls Germans. At the end of the first century AD, Tacitus provides information about the peoples he calls Germans living beyond the frontiers of the Empire. Whereas at one time these sources were accepted as historical statements about the peoples whom the Greeks and Romans were encountering, more recent interpretations are much more nuanced, seeking to understand what the classical commentators were writing (and why) in the context of their own experiences as individuals and as elite members of society. Thus they can be useful sources, and in some cases appear to be remarkably accurate, but they must always be used with critical care, in conjunction with the archaeological evidence.

Themes in Iron Age Archaeology

Part I continues with a discussion of the physical geography of Europe and of the climate, environment, and people in the Iron Age (Chapter 2), followed by an overview of the chronology and dating methods currently in use for the period (Chapter 3). Part II presents overviews of the Iron Age archaeology of all the major regions of Europe, from the Atlantic coast and the Mediterranean to the Urals (Chapters 4–17). In Part III, a primarily thematic approach is adopted (Chapters 18–43). For convenience, the thematic chapters are grouped under five main headings—lifeways, economy, complexity, identity, and ritual and expression—but in practice there is considerable overlap in subject matter, and many of the themes are also taken up in the regional chapters. Some topics—particularly mortuary archaeology—have been a feature of Iron Age studies virtually from the outset, whereas others have come to the fore relatively recently as knowledge of the period has advanced and in response to wider changes in perspective in the discipline of archaeology as a whole.

The lifeways and economies of prehistoric societies have long been a focus in European archaeology. The Iron Age is no exception, with excellent data now available from excavated sites across the continent. As regards lifeways, the bulk of the population throughout the period under consideration practised a subsistence economy and in the main lived in small domestic units and settlements of rural character (Chapters 18–20), although as noted earlier there was a marked tendency to aggregation and urbanization at certain times and places, which remains one of the enduring research themes of the period (Chapter 21). Significant differences can however be observed across the continent in terms of the plants and animals consumed, both domestic and wild, and the technologies to manage and exploit the environment, while the character of these essentially local communities, whether dispersed or nucleated, also varied. The sheer scale of human intervention in the landscape during the Iron Age has only become clear in recent decades (Chapter 22).

The exploitation of raw materials, and the technology and organization of manufacturing to process those materials into products for consumption and trade, developed apace in the course of the Iron Age (Chapters 23–24). Forms of trade, whether exchange or commerce, provided communities with raw materials and finished goods that were unavailable in the local environment, bringing communities into contact with one another, both regionally and interregionally on a scale that penetrated society more widely than before (Chapter 27). In the final phase of the late Iron Age, coinage (Chapter 28) became an important medium of trade, as well as of political expression.

The study of material culture—objects—remains a fundamental part of Iron Age research. Already in the nineteenth century, close attention was being paid to establishing typologies of fibulae, pottery, and other objects in order to work out local chronologies and to identify connections between different regions of Europe (Kühn 1976). Recently the study of objects has included analysis of the roles that they played as agents—as active things in the social lives of individuals and communities (Chapter 25). Among the categories of material culture that have received considerable attention recently are textiles (Chapter 26), often well preserved in wet and slightly acidic environments, and wheeled vehicles (Chapter 32).

The social organization and complexity of Iron Age communities, particularly as reflected in mortuary evidence, have been much discussed. Burial evidence can now provide rich data for our understanding of demography and health of Iron Age populations (Chapter 33). Graves are understood to embody complex meanings, such as those linked to issues of identity (Chapter 35), gender (Chapter 34), and specialist roles (Chapter 31). Gender studies are yielding information about kinship, for example regarding marriage patterns and how elite individuals were interconnected. No longer is grave wealth interpreted as directly correlated with status and wealth in life (Chapter 40). There has been a tendency to treat all Iron Age societies as more or less hierarchical, but archaeologists are increasingly beginning to think in terms of other models of social organization as perhaps more appropriate to many Iron Age communities.

Political systems of Iron Age Europe have also been long debated, with much discussion about the most appropriate models to apply to the archaeological evidence (Chapter 29). Were Iron Age societies comparable to the chiefdoms studied by cultural anthropologists, or were they more like the principalities or small kingdoms of medieval Europe? Or were they organized in ways completely different from any historically or ethnohistorically documented societies? Political organization certainly varied widely, from the beginning of the early Iron Age to the much larger scale societies encountered and described by Julius Caesar in the middle of the final century BC. And political systems varied by region as well as by time.

Warfare has been much studied, mostly from the point of view of weapons, which are abundant in graves, in deposits, and on battlefields, and of defensive structures, notably hillforts. After a period of neglect, its agency in Iron Age societies is deservedly receiving renewed attention (Chapters 5, 30). A persistent debate is about the prevalence of armed violence during the Iron Age. Does the presence of weapons necessarily indicate a time of much warfare? Or do weapons often protect the peace and serve largely symbolic functions? There is much direct evidence for the conduct of war in Iron Age Europe, but how typical was it of any given time and place?

Ritual, religion, and their expression in the archaeological record of Iron Age Europe can be approached from many different perspectives. The classical authors give us their views of the religion of peoples they called 'Celts', 'Germans', and 'Scythians' during the later centuries of the Iron Age (Chapter 42). The archaeological evidence provides rather different information about the practices of the period, such as making offerings of valued objects in bodies of water or pits in the ground (Chapter 41). Feasting (Chapter 39) has become a major theme in Iron Age studies, as it has in many different archaeological contexts worldwide. Feasting is a complex practice that has social, political, and economic overtones as well as those linking it to the practice of religion. The art of the Iron Age—a field that has seen a range of interpretative approaches over the years, as has the field of art history as a whole—is a fruitful source of insights into the ideologies and connectivities of Iron Age societies (Chapter 43).

Interaction between the inhabitants of Iron Age Europe, and contacts between them and communities elsewhere, has been a topic of interest since the beginning, one interwoven with the theme of trade and exchange. From the early twentieth century, the 'amber route' has been invoked to account for the large quantities of apparently Baltic amber found in graves all over Europe (Chapter 7), notably in the cemetery at Hallstatt. Invasions of groups from the east, such as those named by the classical authors 'Cimmerians' and 'Scythians', and from the north, called 'Cimbri' and 'Teutones', have long been subjects of concern to archaeologists. Interactions between temperate Europe and the Mediterranean coasts were recognized already in the nineteenth century through imports manufactured in the Greek, Etruscan, and Roman worlds found in graves to the north; for many years, these were also the mainstay of our chronologies (Chapter 3). Recently, evidence for connections with the Near East has become more abundant, with increasing suggestions of contacts with places yet further afield to the east, south, and west (Chapter 17).

Migrations have always played an important part in thinking about the dynamics of Iron Age societies. Greek written sources attest to migrations from central regions of temperate Europe into Greece and on into Anatolia. Roman sources, notably Livy, describe migrations of Gauls across the Alps into Italy, but the archaeological dimension of these movements of people and the character and scale of such displacements remain a matter of vigorous debate. Some archaeologists think that significant cultural changes observed in the archaeological material can be best explained through migration, others feel that migration is overused as an explanation, and that local indigenous developments deserve greater prominence. Isotope analyses, in particular using strontium and oxygen, are contributing to our understanding of how and at what age individuals changed residence (Chapter 37). Studies of the genetic composition of Iron Age communities demonstrate influx and admixture patterns that arise from migrations.

Already around the middle of the pre-Roman Iron Age, a few objects from temperate Europe bear writing in Greek letters. By the final centuries of prehistory, legends in Greek and in Latin letters on Iron Age coins, letters scratched onto sherds of pottery, and other occasional inscriptions show that some Iron Age individuals were adopting the practice of writing from their Mediterranean neighbours to the south (Chapter 36). Such borrowing attests to the impact of interactions between persons in temperate Europe and people in the Mediterranean world, perhaps merchants and diplomats.

During the final two centuries BC, evidence from much of Europe, especially in the form of imported wine amphorae, indicates growing connectivities with the expanding world of Rome. Following the Roman conquests between the middle of the final century BC and the middle of the first century AD, we observe aspects of local indigenous cultures that altered radically with the newly imposed political system, and others that preserved existing traditions (Chapter 38). The complex and varied patterns of change raise the fascinating question—how much impact did Rome actually have on the communities of Iron Age Europe?

Periods of Transformation

During the fifth century BC a number of profound changes took place throughout much of Europe. Most of the early Iron Age centres were abandoned, and a new style of decoration and representation developed, known as the La Tène style. Whereas the main decorative style of the early Iron Age was based on geometric patterns of straight lines, rectangles, circles, and triangles, and more-or-less naturalistic representations of humans and animals, the new style was based on floral ornament and on highly stylized representations of humans and animals. The new style accompanied changes in settlement location and in some aspects of burial practice, with two-wheeled chariots replacing four-wheeled wagons in the more richly outfitted graves. The sources of the La Tène style have long been sought in the arts of Greece and Etruria, but new evidence suggests that we need to take a much broader view of design and motif in this dynamic period, as we recognize striking similarities in design and representation across much of Eurasia.

A couple of generations after the creation of the new style, fundamental changes occurred in burial practice. During the early Iron Age and the first part of the late Iron Age, burial was frequently in mounds of varying sizes. But after 400 BC, mounds were largely abandoned as the media for burial, and the practice of inhuming the dead in flat graves became dominant. With the disappearance of burial mounds, exceptionally richly outfitted burials became much less common than they had been. A great many flat grave cemeteries are known from all over temperate Europe, often containing hundreds of graves each. Women were often outfitted with such jewellery as neck-rings, bracelets, and chain belts, and men sometimes with sets of weapons, including swords and spears, and less often shields and helmets. Long viewed as a replacement of the population by incoming Celts, these changes in burial practice are now quite often interpreted as signs of a revolution of some kind against the elites of the preceding period, but the evidence suggests much greater complexity to the transformations that were taking place.

During this time, Greek sources document the service of what are called 'Celtic' mercenaries in armies fighting in the lands of the eastern Mediterranean. Attempts to link such mercenaries with archaeological materials in temperate Europe have not been fully successful to date, but the mention of such mercenary service contributes to our picture of intensifying relations between the Iron Age peoples of temperate Europe and those of the Mediterranean south, connectivities which were also undoubtedly a factor in the rapid spread of coinage at this time. The changes of the fourth and third centuries BC reached far beyond the La Tène world. Major cultural discontinuities are apparent over much of the north European plain, while north of the Black Sea, the Scythians gave way to the Sarmatians (Chapter 15). Areas as far apart as western Iberia, Mediterranean France and southern Britain witnessed a nucleation of population into fortified sites.

During the final centuries BC, before the conquests by Roman armies, the landscape of the central regions of temperate Europe was increasingly dominated by settlement sites much larger than any known from earlier periods. These sites had populations in the thousands, and they were centres for the production of a wide range of goods, many—such as pottery and iron tools—produced in a system of mass production. We can now see that the growth of these larger aggregations was part of a wider process of agricultural intensification, settlement expansion, increased specialization of production, and population growth, driven or enabled by a mature iron technology, with its roots in the fourth and third centuries BC. Against this background, some scholars are starting to argue that the proliferation of fortified *oppida* was a response to a crisis affecting much of temperate Europe, comparing the eruption of rampart building in the late second century BC with the *incastellamento* of feudal Europe at the end of the first millennium AD (e.g. Guichard 2017). The interplay of population movement, the rising threat of Rome, and indigenous or natural phenomena, have yet to be disentangled as possible contributory factors. What is clear, however, is that Roman imperialism was a major driver in many of the highly visible social and economic changes that we see from this point onward in Iron Age societies across Europe from the Mediterranean to the North Atlantic and the Baltic.

Traditions of Research

Until very recently, and to some extent today as well, different traditions of research have been practised in different countries. Archaeologists working in different parts of Europe ask different questions of the evidence, and they interpret it according to different frameworks. In parts of Europe, and for some researchers, terms such as 'Celts' and 'Scythians' are automatically used to refer to the peoples under study. Other investigators prefer not to use names deriving from the writings of Greek and Roman authors. Over much of the continent, culture history remains the dominant paradigm, and population replacement is still the preferred explanation for culture change for some. A hierarchical model of Iron Age society based on Caesar's writings is still deeply entrenched, whereas anthropological models and post-processual ideas remain largely the preserve of Anglophone archaeologists. Until the fall of the Iron Curtain, an essentially Marxist model of social organization prevailed in eastern Europe, but in recent decades scholars from these regions have been energetically developing new ideas of wide applicability that deserve attention. In the chapters that follow, the editors have chosen to allow authors to use the terminologies that they employ in their own research. In this sense, the book provides an overview of the practice of archaeological thinking in Europe today, as well as of the material evidence of the Iron Age.

Note

1. For discussion of various appropriations of Iron Age archaeology to support national territorial claims, including those of the unjust regimes of the twentieth century, see e.g. Kohl 1998, Arnold 2006, and papers in Diaz-Andreu and Champion 1996 and Popa and Stoddart 2014.

References

Arnold, B. 2006. '"Arierdämmerung": Race and archaeology in Nazi Germany'. *World Archaeology* 38, 1: 8–31.

Betschart, M. (ed.) 2007. *La Tène: Die Untersuchung, die Fragen, die Antworten*. Biel: Museum Schwab.

Biel, J. 1985. *Der Keltenfürst von Hochdorf.* Stuttgart: Theiss.

Bradley, R. 1998. *The Passage of Arms: An Archaeological Analysis of Prehistoric Hoards and Votive Deposits*, 2nd edition. Oxford: Oxbow.

Brunaux, J.-L. 2004. *Guerre et religion en Gaule: Essai d'anthropologie celtique.* Paris: Errance.

Buchsenschutz, O. (ed.) 2015. *L'Europe celtique à l'âge du Fer.* Paris: Presses Universitaires de France.

Buvot, P. 1998. 'Découverte d'un lieu de culte antique. La source de la Douix à Châtillon-sur-Seine'. *Archéologia* 344: 26–33.

Champion, T. C. 1985. 'Written sources and the study of the European Iron Age', in T. C. Champion and J. V. S. Megaw (eds) *Settlement and Society: Aspects of West European Prehistory in the 1st Millennium BC*: 9–22. Leicester: Leicester University Press.

Chaume, B., C. Mordant, and C. Allag. 2011. *Le complexe aristocratique de Vix: Nouvelles recherches sur l'habitat et le système de fortification et l'environnement du Mont Lassois.* Dijon: Editions Universitaires de Dijon.

Coles, J., and J. Minnit. 1995. *Industrious and Fairly Civilised: The Glastonbury Lake Village.* Taunton: Somerset Levels Project and Somerset County Council Museums Service.

Collis, J. 1984. *The European Iron Age.* London: Batsford.

Dehn, R., and J. Klug. 1993. 'Fortführung der Grabungen am "Heidentor" bei Egesheim, Kreis Tuttlingen'. *Archäologische Ausgrabungen in Baden-Württemberg* 1992: 99–103.

Diaz-Andreu, M., and T. C. Champion (eds). 1996. *Nationalism and Archaeology in Europe.* London: UCL Press.

Dietler, M. 1994. '"Our Ancestors the Gauls": Archaeology, ethnic nationalism, and the manipulation of Celtic identity in modern Europe'. *American Anthropologist* 96: 584–605.

Egg, M. 1996. *Das Hallstattzeitliche Fürstengrab von Strettweg bei Judenburg in der Obersteiermark.* RGZM Monographien 37. Mainz: Römisch-Germanisches Zentralmuseum.

Egg, M., and M. Schönfelder. 2009. 'Zur Interpretation der Schwertscheide aus Grab 994 von Hallstatt', in C. Bockisch-Bräuer and B. Mühldorfer (eds) *Beiträge zur Hallstatt- und Latènezeit in Nordostbayern und Thüringen: Tagung vom 26.–28. Oktober 2007 in Nürnberg.* Beiträge zur Vorgeschichte Nordostbayerns 7: 27–44. Nürnberg: Fürth.

Farley, J., and F. Hunter (eds). 2015. *In Search of the Celts.* London: The British Museum.

Filip, J. 1966. 'Hradenín', in J. Filip (ed.) *Enzyklopädisches Handbuch zur Ur- und Frühgeschichte Europas*: 507. Stuttgart: Kohlhammer.

Frey, O.-H. 2002. 'Menschen oder Heroen? Die Statuen vom Glauberg und die frühe Keltische Großplastik', in H. Baitinger and B. Pinsker (eds) *Glaube—Mythos—Wirklichkeit: Das Rätsel der Kelten vom Glauberg*: 208–218. Stuttgart: Theiss.

Gabrovec, S. 1999. 'Die Ausgrabungen in Stična und ihre Bedeutung für die Geschichte der Eisenzeit in the Südostalpen'. *Mitteilungen der Anthropologischen Gesellschaft in Wien* 123–124: 73–88.

Guichard, V. 2017. 'Les *oppida*, une parenthèse dans l'histoire de l'Europe tempérée?' *Pallas* 105: 159–171.

Guichard, V., and P. Paris. 2013. 'Chronique des recherches sur le Mont Beuvray 2009–2012'. *Revue Archeologique de l'Est* 62: 113–155.

Hodson, F. R. 1968. *The La Tène Cemetery at Münsingen-Rain: Catalogue and Relative Chronology.* Acta Bernensia 5. Bern: Stämpfli.

Holzer, V. 2014. 'Roseldorf: An enclosed central settlement of the Early and Middle La Tène period in Lower Austria (Roseldorf/Němêice Centre)', in M. Fernández-Götz, H. Wendling, and K. Winger (eds) *Paths to Complexity: Centralisation and Urbanisation in Iron Age Europe*: 122–131. Oxford: Oxbow Books.

Jørgensen, L., B. Storgaard, and L. Gebauer (eds). 2003. *The Spoils of Victory: The North in the Shadow of the Roman Empire*. Copenhagen: Nationalmuseet.

Joy, J. 2015. 'Snettisham: Shining new light on an old treasure'. *British Archaeology* September/October 2015: 18–26.

Kern, A., K. Kowarik, A. W. Rausch, and H. Reschreiter (eds). 2009. *Kingdom of Salt: 7000 years of Hallstatt*. Veröffentlichungen der Prähistorischen Abteilung 3. Vienna: Natural History Museum.

Kohl, P. L. 1998. 'Nationalism and archaeology: On the constructions of nations and the reconstructions of the remote past'. *Annual Review of Anthropology* 27: 223–246.

Krausse, D., M. Fernández-Götz, L. Hansen, and I. Kretschmer. 2016. *The Heuneburg and the Early Iron Age Princely Seats: First Towns North of the Alps*. Budapest: Archaeolingua.

Kristiansen, K. 1998. *Europe Before History*. Cambridge: Cambridge University Press.

Kruta, V. 1971. *Le trésor de Duchcov dans les collections tchécoslovaques*. Ustí nad Labem: Severoceske Nakladatelství.

Kühn, H. 1976. *Geschichte der Vorgeschichtsforschung*. Berlin: Walter de Gruyter.

Metzner-Nebelsick, C., R. Müller, and S. Sievers. 2009. 'Die Eisenzeit—800 v. Chr.–Christi Geburt', in S. Schnurbein (ed.) *Atlas der Vorgeschichte*: 150–225. Stuttgart: Theiss.

Moore, T. 2017. 'Beyond Iron Age "Towns": Examining *oppida* as examples of low-density urbanism'. *Oxford Journal of Archaeology* 36, 3: 287–305.

Nielsen, S., J. H. Andersen, J. A. Baker, C. Christensen, J. Glastrup, P. M. Grootes, et al. 2005. 'The Gundestrup Cauldron: New scientific and technical investigations'. *Acta Archaeologica* 76, 2: 1–58.

Pleiner, R., and M. Princ. 1984. 'Die latènezeitliche Eisenverhüttung und die Untersuchung einer Rennschmelze in Mšec, Böhmen'. *Památky Archeologické* 75: 133–180.

Popa, C. N., and S. Stoddart (eds). 2014. *Fingerprinting the Iron Age: Approaches to Identity in the European Iron Age: Integrating South-Eastern Europe into the Debate*. Oxford: Oxbow.

Rolley, C. (ed.) 2003. *La tombe princière de Vix*. Paris: Picard/Société des amis du Musée du Châtillonnais.

Rybová, A., and P. Drda. 1994. *Hradiště by Stradonice: Rebirth of a Celtic Oppidum*. Prague: Institute of Archaeology.

Schäfer, A. 2002. 'Manching—Kelheim—Berching-Pollanten', in C. Dobiat, S. Sievers, and T. Stöllner (eds) *Dürrnberg und Manching: Wirtschaftsarchäologie im ostkeltischen Raum: Akten des internationalen Kolloquiums in Hallein/Bad Dürrnberg vom 7. bis 11. Oktober 1998*. Kolloquien zur Vor- und Frühgeschichte 7: 219–241. Bonn: Habelt.

Spindler, K. 1999. *Der Magdalenenberg bei Villingen: Ein Fürstengrabhügel des 7. vorchristlichen Jahrhunderts*, 2nd edition. Führer zu archäologischen Denkmälern in Baden-Württemberg 5. Stuttgart: Theiss.

Steiner, H. 2010. *Alpine Brandopferplätze: Archäologische und naturwissenschaftliche Untersuchungen/Roghi votivi alpini. Archeologiae scienze naturali*. Forschungen zur Denkmalpflege in Südtirol/Beni culturali in Alto Adige: studi e ricerche 5. Trento: Editrice Temi.

Stöllner, T. 1999. *Der prähistorische Salzbergbau am Dürrnberg bei Hallein I: Forschungsgeschichte—Forschungsstand—Forschungsanliegen*. Dürrnberg-Forschungen 1. Rahden: Leidorf.

Szabó, M. (ed.) 2006. *Celtes et Gaulois: L'archéologie face à l'histoire: Les Civilisés et les Barbares du Ve au IIe siècle avant J.-C.: Actes de la table ronde de Budapest, 17–18 juin 2005*. Collection Bibracte 12/3. Glux-en-Glenne: Centre archéologique européen du Mont Beuvray.

Tecco Hvala, S. 2012. *Magdalenska gora: družbena struktura in grobni rituali železnodobne skupnosti [Social Structure and Burial Rites of the Iron Age Community]*. Opera Instituti Archaeologici Sloveniae 26. Ljubljana: Inštitut za arheologijo ZRC SAZU, Založba ZRC.

Turk, P. 2005. *Images of Life and Myth: Exhibition Catalogue*. Ljubljana: Narodni muzej Slovenije.

Vandkilde, H. 2007. *Culture and Change in Central European Prehistory, 6th to 1st Millennium BC*. Aarhus: Aarhus University Press.

Von Nicolai, C. 2009. 'La question des "Viereckschanzen" d'Allemagne du Sud revisitée', in I. Bertrand, A. Duval, J. Gomez De Soto, and P. Maguer (eds) *Les Gaulois entre Loire et Dordogne: Actes du XXXI colloque international de l'AFEAF*. Mémoire 34: 245–280. Chauvigny: Association des publications chauvinoises.

Waldhauser, J. 1978. *Das keltische Gräberfeld bei Jenišův Újezd in Böhmen*. Teplice: Kranjské Muzeum.

Wefers, S. 2012. *Latènezeitliche Mühlen aus dem Gebiet zwischen den Steinbruchrevieren Mayen und Lovosice. Vulkanpark-Forschungen 9*. RGZM Monographien 95. Mainz: Verlag des Römisch-Germanischen Zentralmuseums.

Wells, P. S. 2001. *Beyond Celts, Germans and Scythians: Archaeology and Identity in Iron Age Europe*. London: Duckworth.

CHAPTER 2

EUROPE IN THE IRON AGE

Landscapes, Regions, Climate, and People

COLIN HASELGROVE,
KATHARINA REBAY-SALISBURY,
AND PETER S. WELLS

Physical Geography

This Handbook aims to provide a continent-wide coverage of Iron Age archaeology, including making accessible regions that have often been overlooked in Iron Age research. Traditionally, the continental core, with its Hallstatt and La Tène cultures, has dominated discussion, in part in opposition to the scholarly dominance of the Graeco-Roman world. Since fascination with the past began with interest in the standing monuments of the Mediterranean, such as the Athenian Acropolis or the Roman Forum, it is no surprise that the subtler remains of the continental Iron Age took longer to discover. Moreover, the foundations for their systematic study were first laid during the late nineteenth and early twentieth centuries, at a time when national borders were being redrawn and new nation states emerging, so that subsequent research was often trapped within these boundaries. In parts of Europe, Iron Age archaeology was even instrumentalized to justify the boundaries of modern geopolitical units (Diaz-Andreu and Champion 1996; Kohl 1998). Following World War II, the second half of the twentieth century saw a convergence of Europe in geopolitical, administrative, and social terms, through increased personal mobility and not least through the growth of the European Union (Kristiansen 2015). Nevertheless, linking research across modern national borders remains a major challenge.

Recognizing the artificial divisions inhibiting Iron Age research, and overcoming them, are two quite different issues. In an effort to define meaningful geographical and topographical entities that transcend these historically rooted national research boundaries, while taking on board what we know about Iron Age ethnicity, we have divided the coverage of this Handbook into fourteen zones (Figure 2.1). While each of these broader entities encompasses smaller regions suitable for different, complementary subsistence strategies, all are linked by high levels of internal interaction and exchange. Providing a balanced overview is nevertheless a challenge, since the archaeological evidence—the one primary source available for the whole area and period—is not only unevenly researched, but also unequally distributed across Europe. Thus, while the most extreme latitudes were inhabited by dispersed or mobile groups and much of northern Europe was dominated until a relatively late stage by agrarian communities with little evidence of centralized political institutions or status distinctions, population levels were much higher in the middle latitudes closer to the complex city state-based societies that emerged in Greece and the Italian peninsula, creating greater densities of material remains.

In a break from traditional subject boundaries, we have included parts of Mediterranean Europe that are more often regarded as the domain of classical archaeology in our geographical coverage, as well as the Near East and North Africa. The former present many features in common with the rest of Europe in the early Iron Age, while links with more distant places had a significant influence on European

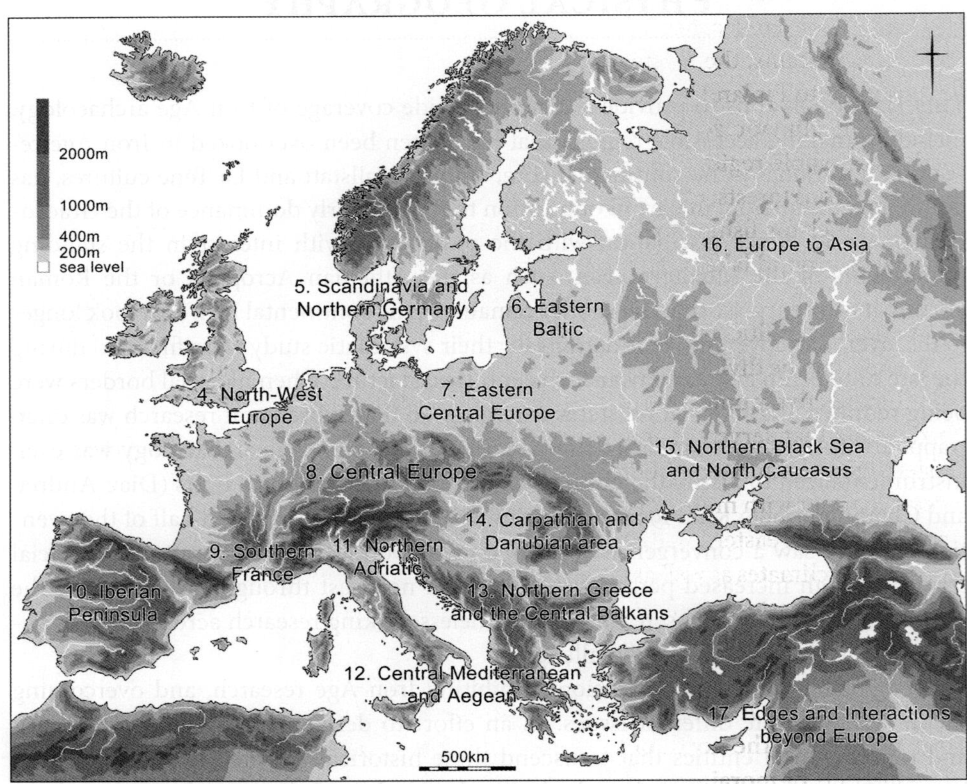

FIGURE 2.1 Map showing the regional framework adopted for Chapters 4 to 17.

developments throughout the period. Additionally, we have opted for a long view of the Iron Age in the two-thirds of the continent that never became subject to direct Roman rule and so effectively preserved an Iron Age lifestyle until the advent of literacy and Christianity.

Regional Framework

The order of the regional chapters follows roughly west to east and north to south, starting with 'north-west Europe' (Chapter 4), covering Britain, Ireland, northern France, and the Low Countries. Rather than forming a divide, the English Channel and the southern North Sea have together acted as maritime connectors between Britain and the near continent since at least the Bronze Age. Within this broader region, a wetter Atlantic zone can be differentiated from a drier, inland and continental zone. The landscape is predominantly flat, with no major mountain ranges, but there are significant wetlands and bogs.

Moving north-east, 'Scandinavia and northern Germany' (Chapter 5) covers modern Norway, Sweden, and Denmark, as well as those parts of Germany bordering Denmark and the Baltic Sea. With its long coastline, the sea is again a dominant feature of this region. Major landscapes include the mountainous western seaboard, the north-central mountains, the foothills of the Scandinavian mountains, and the eastern plain extending into Finland and the Baltic states. A maritime influence is noticeable in the west, while climatic zones range from arctic and subarctic to temperate/continental across the whole region. The variable landscape is covered with tundra, boreal forest, and coniferous forests; temperate mixed forests continue towards the south. With ample opportunities for fishing and hunting, farming is limited to areas near the coasts, on the plains, around lakes, and in the low-lying areas of modern Denmark and southern Sweden.

The 'eastern Baltic' region (Chapter 6), comprising modern-day Estonia, Latvia, and Lithuania, can be divided into three: a coastal zone, which has a mild, maritime climate and thin, relatively unfertile soils; a central zone with moraine heights and thicker, more fertile soils that served as the main agricultural area in the Roman Iron Age; and an eastern zone dominated by bogs, lakes, and small hills—an area of forests with plenty of access to water with more opportunities for fishing and hunting than for farming. In climatic terms, the eastern Baltic region represents a transitional zone between marine and continental climates as well as between subarctic and temperate/continental climates.

Chapter 7, 'eastern central Europe', continues the survey towards the south-west. Delineated by the river Elbe in the west and the river Dnieper in the east, this region corresponds to the eastern parts of modern Germany, Poland, Belarus, and Ukraine. The Baltic shores are important as rich sources of amber, which was widely traded in later prehistory. The north of the region forms part of the flat North European Plain; hilly districts of moraines and glacially formed lakes are characteristic for some areas. The Oder and Vistula river basins dominate the central area. Towards the south, a more mountainous area includes the Sudetes and the Carpathian mountains. The climate is temperate throughout: the north is influenced by the sea, but towards the south and east, the climate becomes warmer and drier. The wood cover includes mixed forests and conifer forest in the mountains.

'Central Europe' (Chapter 8) provides an overview of the heartland of Iron Age research, including the seminal sites of Hallstatt in Austria and La Tène in Switzerland. The region extends from the North European Plain to the Alps and includes eastern France, central and southern Germany, Austria, Switzerland, and the Czech Republic, as well as parts of Hungary, France, Poland, and Slovenia. The landscape is varied and includes lowlands well suited to farming, especially along the major rivers and their tributaries, as well as uplands and high mountains. Although landlocked, the region is connected by west–east (Danube) and north–south (Rhine) river systems. The climate is temperate and largely dependent on elevation above sea level; the change of four seasons provides a natural rhythm for the agricultural year. Temperate broadleaf and mixed forests prevail, changing to coniferous forests at higher elevations.

'Southern France' bordering the Mediterranean (Chapter 9) was another key region in the development of Iron Age Europe. Thanks to the river Rhône and the corridor it provides between the main Alpine massif and the uplands of the Massif Central, Mediterranean goods and ideas were able to travel northwards, into the western Hallstatt and La Tène core areas of central Europe. It is the ritual landscape of southern France that is most striking; the sanctuaries around summits and springs provide rich insights into the idiosyncratic religious practices of Iron Age people. This region is characterized by a Mediterranean climate with hot, dry summers and mild winters, while the location enables seafaring connections along the coastline and beyond.

The 'Iberian Peninsula', encompassing modern Spain and Portugal, forms a discrete geographical entity, linked to, but separated from, the rest of the continent by the Pyrenees mountain range (Chapter 10). The Atlantic and Mediterranean coastlines are both defining geographic features, and at the point where they meet, at the Straits of Gibraltar, Europe and Africa are separated by less than 15 km. The coastal regions are relatively narrow, and in the interior of the peninsula is a large elevated plateau, known as the Central Meseta, which is bordered by mountain systems and connected to the oceans by five major rivers—of which only the Ebro flows into the Mediterranean, the others into the Atlantic. In terms of climate, a wetter Atlantic zone can be differentiated from a warmer and drier Mediterranean zone.

During the Iron Age, the 'northern Adriatic' (Chapter 11), today's northern Italy, southern Austria and Hungary, Slovenia, Croatia, and Bosnia, was another important connector between the Mediterranean and central Europe. The region encompasses a diverse and fragmented landscape, with a share of the high, mountainous terrain of the main Alpine massif and the Dinaric Alps, cut by numerous rivers, as well as lakes and river plains. The river Po and its basin are the most prominent landscape feature in northern Italy, while in the eastern part of the region the rivers Sava and Drava are both tributaries of the Danube. Behind the Adriatic coastline with its many peninsulas and islands, limestone plateaus provide good conditions for settlement. Over short distances, the climate changes from Alpine to Mediterranean.

Chapter 12, the 'central Mediterranean and the Aegean', continues our survey southward, examining the early Iron Age in southern Greece and southern Italy, along with the major islands of Crete, Corsica, Sicily, and Sardinia, all tied together by the Mediterranean. As the birthplace of classical Greece and Rome, this region is normally discussed in the framework of the scholarly tradition of classics, rather than on equal terms with other parts of Europe. Developments in the Aegean are the centre of traditional core–periphery models for the Iron Age; in this chapter, the interconnections around the Mediterranean and beyond take centre stage. The survey is complemented by Chapter 13, 'northern Greece and the central Balkans', covering the modern political entities of northern Greece, the Republic of North Macedonia, Serbia, Kosovo, and Bulgaria. Dominant landscape features include the Balkan and the Rhodope mountains, the Struma and Nestos/Mesta river systems, and the Danube and Thracian plains leading to the Black Sea.

The 'Carpathian and Danubian' region (Chapter 14) brings together eastern Hungary, south-eastern Slovakia, northern Serbia, northern Bulgaria, Moldova, and parts of western and south-western Ukraine. The Carpathian mountains frame the Great Hungarian Plain, a steppe with marshlands along the Tisza river, and the Transylvanian plateau, a higher plain with steppe vegetation framed by forests. The area is rich with sources of salt, copper, and gold. The Danube is the dominant feature of its lower basin, emptying into the Black Sea. Temperate, continental climate prevails. Chapter 15, the 'northern Black Sea and north Caucasus', covers the neighbouring region ranging from the hilly landscapes of the rivers Dniester and Prut in Moldavia, to the inland steppe belt of Ukraine, stretching to the Caucasus mountains in Russia. The most important river is the Dnieper, separated from the river Don by the Donec hills; the steppe continues into the Kuma-Manych basin. The long coastline of the Black Sea, the Crimean peninsula, and the Azov Sea are important landscape features.

Finally, Chapter 16, 'Europe to Asia', surveys the Iron Age archaeology of the Russian plain, the European part of the Russian Federation, to the border with Asia, the Ural mountains and Ural river. The plain comprises several upland areas and the basins of the Dnieper, Oka, Don, and Volga rivers. Given the vast north–south extent of this region, climate and vegetation vary greatly according to latitude, from arctic tundra via coniferous and mixed forests to temperate steppes, with mild and arid continental climate predominant. Our geographical survey concludes with 'edges and interactions beyond Europe' (Chapter 17), which, by looking beyond the continent, seeks to highlight archaeological evidence for connections between its inhabitants and those of Asia, Africa, and even the North Atlantic, thereby seeking to improve our understanding of Europe's position in the globalized world of the long Iron Age.

Clearly, both landscape and climate have undergone significant changes since the Iron Age—and indeed during the period, as we discuss later in the chapter. Across the continent, Iron Age populations will have encountered challenges, constraints, and possibilities that were very different from today. Nevertheless, the relative differences between the constituent parts of Iron Age Europe are likely to have been broadly similar to those we find today, a view supported by the archaeobotanical and palynological evidence from the period (Chapter 18).

Topography and Soils

Europe, effectively a peninsula surrounded by oceans at the western end of the vast continent of Eurasia (Cunliffe 2008), is a landscape that affords many different and suitable forms of settling and living. It may seem obvious, but it is worth pointing out that landscape and climate affect not only subsistence and settlement practices, but also the way in which regions were able to connect with each other.

Europe has long coastlines abundant in harbours, with the Baltic and North Sea in the north, the Atlantic and the English Channel in the west, the Mediterranean in the south, and the Black and Caspian Seas in the east; all these seas played important roles in shaping cultural connectivities during later prehistory. Many of Europe's rivers are long, relatively flat, and navigable for trade, but the major rivers do not meet. Indeed, it took until 1992 to connect the Rhine, a major south–north route, to the Danube, the main west–east artery (Marshall 2015: 91). Standing back from the detail, Kristiansen (1998: 27–28) sees the principal river systems as defining four persistent interaction zones: a western corridor, connecting south-west and north-west Europe via the Rhône, Rhine, and Weser, and on to Britain and Scandinavia; a second connecting Denmark and the western Baltic, via the Elbe and Oder, with Bohemia, the Carpathians, and beyond; a third linking Scandinavia and the central Baltic with eastern Europe and the Black Sea, via the Vistula, Dnieper, and Dniester river systems; the Danube articulates the fourth zone, not only connecting eastern and western Europe, but also via its tributaries reaching northwards and southwards, including into the Balkans.

The vast North European Plain extending from north-west France to the Urals forms a contrast to the upland and mountainous landscapes of the south. The Pyrenees, the Alps, and the Carpathians are significant high mountain chains; such terrain is difficult to cross and partly explains the great degree of diversity in cultures and communities found in areas such as the Balkans. The temperate grasslands of the Eurasian steppe, extending from the Carpathian basin eastwards, have connected Europe to the Middle East and Central Asia since the Palaeolithic. Europe became, and continues to be, populated via the steppes and the east Mediterranean coastline, and numerous studies of ancient DNA (Reich 2018) support the idea of continuous gene flow into Europe. In general, Europe is blessed with good farmland and the right types of soils, even if the coastal plains in the south, the hinterland of the Mediterranean Sea, are not extensive.

Since soil is the medium in which food, natural fibre, and wood grow, its composition and quality was vital for the survival and economic success of Iron Age societies. It is also a crucial material for potting and architecture, especially in temperate Europe. Soil types, the bedrock on which they form, and inherent characteristics such as permeability, acidity/alkalinity, and grain size, are important factors for a range of archaeological applications, including palaeoenvironmental reconstructions, soil chemistry and activity areas research, archaeobotany, zooarchaeology, and strontium isotope studies. An overview of the many different soil types of Europe and their distributions over the continent can be found in compilations by the European Soil Bureau Network and European Commission (Jones et al. 2005). To assist comparability, these soil descriptions follow internationally agreed standards and therefore differ from the terms commonly used in different countries and regions across Europe. At the same time, however, because they aim to be globally relevant, these standard terms hide a great deal of variability that was captured in older, national soil taxonomies. Local variability in soil qualities can be very relevant for small-scale preindustrial agriculture.

Cambisols prevail in western and central Europe, whereas chernozems are widely distributed in eastern Europe from the southern Urals to Ukraine. Both these types of soil form on fine-grained material such as alluvium and loess, and are very fertile, although chernozems in particular can be heavy and difficult to till. Fluvisols are highly fertile soils, which are present along rivers everywhere in Europe. Sandy podzols occur primarily in northern Europe, in the plains as well as in the mountains. Forming in boreal forests and heathlands, podzols have a low organic content and tend to be poor for agriculture. Gleysols occur near wetlands and in other areas where the water table is close to the surface, for example in Ireland and the Baltic states. They can be suitable for grazing, but unless artificially drained, their agricultural potential is limited. Regosols are weakly developed mineral soils found in particular along coasts and in arid mountain areas, for example in the western Iberian Peninsula and in Sicily. Prone to erosion, they are best suited to low volume grazing; cultivation usually requires intensive irrigation and fertilization. Luvisols are mineral soils, generally with a high nutrient content and good drainage; they include the red Mediterranean soils that form primarily on limestone in Spain, southern France, Italy, the Balkan countries, Bulgaria, Turkey, and Greece and they play a role as a secondary soil in most of Europe except for cold regions. The last class is the lithosols, which comprise any soils of 10 cm or less in depth over hard bedrock; in Europe they are mainly associated with moderate and high mountain ranges such as the Urals, the Alps, the Pyrenees, the Caucasus, and the Balkans, including areas permanently covered by snow and ice (Jones et al. 2005).

Metals such as gold, silver, copper, tin, and good-quality iron ores are unevenly distributed across the continent. The same is true of other minerals and natural resources that were in demand during the Iron Age, whether for ornamental or utilitarian purposes, from amber, coral, and lignite to rocks with good milling properties such as lava and puddingstone, and also clay. Salt was extensively produced from sea water in coastal areas through evaporation, as well as from inland brine springs and rock salt deposits such as those at Hallstatt and the Dürrnberg. Differential access to raw materials and technologies had a major impact both on the nature of Iron Age economies and on connectivity between different regions (Chapters 23–25).

Climate

Europe is positioned between several very different and very strong climatic agents that generate its four climate zones: the subarctic to the north, Mediterranean to the south, Eurasian continental to the east, and Atlantic oceanic to the west. Although each part of Europe lies in a given zone, most of the continent, and central Europe in particular, is influenced by the combined effects of two or more of these zones. Thus the climate of north-west Europe is significantly influenced by the North Atlantic Gulf Stream and by winds originating in the Rocky mountains, which results in a warmer and milder winter climate than would otherwise be expected for the latitude. From north to south, the climate gradually becomes warmer, as it shifts from subarctic to temperate and then Mediterranean. The average temperature difference between north and south varies by season, but may be as much as 20°C. The maritime influence is particularly noticeable in the west; from west to east, there is a shift from Oceanic to Continental influences. Apart from latitude and longitude, altitude is the third decisive factor for climatic patterns across Europe. For the most part, the continent has the right amount of rainfall for successful agriculture; precipitation is high along the Atlantic seaboard and in the Alps, but somewhat less in central Europe and the east. Central and eastern Iberia, the Mediterranean, and the steppe regions north of the Black and Caspian Seas present especially arid conditions.

Four distinct seasons can be differentiated in most of Europe, providing a rhythm for agriculture and a recurrent way to structure community life and ritual. The climate is mild enough for outdoor work generally to be possible all year round, even at the height of the summer; winter work takes place mostly indoors. It is likely that cold winters play a role in killing germs (Marshall 2015: 90) and preventing the spread of diseases. The climate in Mediterranean Europe includes distinct wet and dry seasons—hot, arid summers and mild, wet winters.

Given the predominantly temperate climate of much of the continent, Europe by and large lacks the extremes of aridity and cold that have led to the spectacular survival of archaeological sites in other parts of the world. Where Iron Age organic materials do survive well, they are usually in wetland environments—as with lake settlements and the Danish and Irish bog bodies—or at other sites in features such as wells, where ground conditions have created localized waterlogging or anaerobic conditions. Due to its preservative properties, the deep salt mines at Hallstatt are a notable exception; others include the accidentally burnt-down ninth-century BC settlement at Must Farm, Cambridgeshire (Knight et al. 2016) and the early Iron Age midden site of Potterne, also in southern England (Lawson 2000), where the particular manner in which deposits gradually built up, coupled with a chemical reaction leading to rapid mineralization, resulted in a level of preservation exceptional outside a wetland environment. In general, organic survival is determined by the surrounding matrix: alkaline soils such as occur on chalk generally preserve human and animal bone, whereas acidic soils tend to destroy bone and wood in only a short period (e.g. Kibblewhite et al. 2015), leaving many upland and heathland parts of Europe devoid of even basic evidence of Iron Age animal husbandry and human remains.

The European Iron Age spans the transition of two distinct climatic periods within the Holocene: the Subboreal (*c.*3710–450 BC; both dates vary) and the Subatlantic (*c.*450 BC to present). The former encompasses a long, stable climate optimum that may have contributed to the rise of civilizations from the European Bronze Age to the Middle East, India, and China (Brooke 2014), while a slight decline in average temperatures and changes in humidity and precipitation after the mid-second millennium BC has long been linked to social changes at the end of the Bronze Age.

Reconstruction of the Iron Age climate and the investigation of climate change as a driver of social change have both become important foci of research in the first decades of the twenty-first century. The repertoire of proxies used to infer climatic changes and associated environmental changes during the Holocene include, but are by no means limited to, oxygen isotope ratios from lacustrine and ice cores, speleothems, and corals; microfossils such as diatoms, cladocera, pollen, and chironomids; macrofossil data from molluscs, insects, and macrobotanicals; sedimentary data in marine and lake cores, palaeosols, and cave sediments; and dendroclimatic records (Bell and Walker 2005; Roberts 2014; Tinner et al. 2003: 1455). Some proxies, such as tree-rings, lake varves, and mollusc shells, provide evidence at the scale of single years or even seasons. Many of these can also be used to infer changes in anthropogenic land use and resource extraction, and as chronological markers, thereby providing high-resolution chronometric, environmental, and behavioural data.

The Greenland ice cores, along with bog and lake deposits, have traditionally provided a coarse framework for climatic reconstructions. As more data from micro-regions become available, it transpires that large-scale trends do not always fit a particular case study, and climate change affects different regions and landscapes in different ways. Problems of dating and synchronizing various climate proxies make linking climate change to the archaeological record and to historical events challenging. Stable, favourable climatic conditions may lead to population expansion and the use of marginal landscapes (Berglund 2003) such as high-altitude Alpine regions. Extreme weather events may be at the root of floods and landslides causing the destruction of settlement and farming areas. Cold and wet winters may lead to crop failure and the death of farm animals; humid conditions during the growing season provide ideal conditions for some crop parasites. The resulting food shortages may cause famine and high susceptibility to disease, leading to death and depopulation.

Gradual, long-term change is more easily adjusted to than rapidly changing, unstable conditions. A large-scale overview of mid- to late Holocene climate (Wanner et al. 2008) thus focuses on identifying periods of significant rapid climate change, one of which falls between 3500 and 2500 BP (*c.*1550–550 BC). Archaeological evidence for Iron Age cultural resilience and human actions to mitigate changing environmental conditions may be found in changes in settlement locations or subsistence strategies, and bioarchaeological and material evidence for migration, as well as signs of conflict between groups. Understanding the impact of climate change on societies, however, requires detailed climatic reconstruction and a precise chronological synchronization of the archaeological evidence with climate events.

One obvious candidate to link to climate change is the collapse of the late Bronze Age civilizations around 1200 BC and the transition to the Iron Age in the eastern Mediterranean. Between the thirteenth and tenth centuries BC, arid and cooler, unstable conditions seem to have prevailed in the region (Finné et al. 2011). Extreme droughts in Anatolia and the Levant (also referred to as the 3.2 kyr cal BP event) may be connected to large-scale population movements and destructions in the Aegean—the Sea Peoples on the move (Kaniewski and Van Campo 2017). Many sites were destroyed or abandoned during this time, and societies transformed. As Knapp and Manning argue, the climatic conditions were 'the context for change but not necessarily its only or specific cause' (Knapp and Manning 2016: 137).

The end of the Bronze Age in north-west Europe and the subsequent Bronze to Iron Age transition coincided with a rapid climatic downturn from relatively warm and dry to colder, wetter conditions, beginning around 800–750 BC and lasting until *c.*300 BC (also known as the Iron Age Cold Epoch). This change unfolded in different ways in different regions. In Ireland, research shows that the decline in farming and population density as well as cultural changes began at around 1050–900 BC, shortly after the late Bronze Age peak and thus before the start of the climate trend; climate change alone can thus not explain the changes (Armit et al. 2014). In north-east Scotland, in contrast, pollen data suggest that people shifted agricultural activities from the uplands to intensify them in the lowlands in response to the climate deterioration at the end of the Bronze Age, but did not abandon settlements on account of climate change (Tipping et al. 2008). In the Netherlands, the same climatic trend caused a significant rise in the groundwater table, which led to the extension of fens and bogs and triggered the abandonment of low-lying areas; instead, coastal salt marshlands became inhabitable (Van Geel et al. 1996).

The end of Bronze Age Alpine lake-shore settlements in Switzerland and France at around 850 BC may be explained by rising lake water levels linked to the onset of cooler, wetter and less stable conditions between 800 and 400 BC (Magny 2004; Magny et al. 2009). Tinner and colleagues combined Alpine dendroclimatic and Greenland oxygen isotope records with pollen data from sediments of two Swiss lakes north of the Alps and two lakes south of the Alps to reconstruct phases of land use (Tinner et al. 2003). They demonstrated that forest clearance and intensified land use coincided with phases of warm and dry climate at around 1450–1250 BC, 650–450 BC, and 50 BC–100 AD. A decrease in cereal pollen and increase in tree pollen, suggesting the abandonment of previously arable land and reforestation, was noted between 800–650 BC and 400–100 BC, in response to a shift towards colder and wetter climate. Comparable data from southern Germany and northern Italy confirm the broad trends (e.g. Giraudi et al. 2011; Zolitschka et al. 2003).

In eastern Europe, the archaeologically and historically documented incursions of Asian nomads may correlate with climatic shifts towards wetter conditions in the steppes (Bokovenko 2005). In southern Siberia, an increase in precipitation around 850 BC changed deserts into attractive steppe landscapes, triggering an expansion in the Scythian population and subsequent migrations westward. The extent to which Celtic migrations in the fourth to third centuries BC (Chapter 37) may be linked to a short-lived climatic downturn remains a question for further research, but by *c.*250 BC the tables had in any case turned and the Roman Warm Period began, lasting until the final decades of the fourth century AD. The rise of Rome thus coincided with a period of favourable, stable climate. Written records, archaeological evidence, and climate proxies now illuminate the connections between climate events and food production on the one hand and political crises as well as military actions at the boundaries of the Roman Empire on the other (Manning 2013; McCormick et al. 2012).

Biogeography: Flora and Fauna

During the early and middle Holocene, vegetation dynamics were influenced almost exclusively by climate, topography, and other natural factors, but by the late Holocene humans are recognized as a primary agent of environmental change and biodiversity (Crees et al. 2016; Davis et al. 2015). In some areas like Fennoscandia and the Alps, factors such as latitude and topography have continued to play a major role, and in these areas vegetation has remained fairly constant throughout the Holocene. While there is ample evidence from most parts of Europe for small-scale land clearance and vegetation changes during the Neolithic, these developments were for the most part localized, and many were reversed when people moved away (e.g. Bogucki et al. 2012; Salisbury et al. 2013).

This trend changed during the Bronze Age, when we have evidence for rapid increase of deforestation and changing biomes. By *c.*4000 years ago, most of Europe had vegetation broadly similar to today, although the rates of processes of environmental change varied in northern, central, and southern Europe (Davis et al. 2015). The Iron Age saw further extensive deforestation and settlement expansion in many areas of the continent, both lowland and upland. The exploitation of the Iron Age environment for agricultural and other requirements such as wood for fuel and building materials, and the extent of anthropogenic changes on the landscape and in the configuration of proto-urban spaces are discussed further in Part III, 'Lifeways'.

Biogeography of Iron Age People

The focus of investigation into the skeletons and cremated remains of Iron Age people has shifted away from metrics and morphology with the aim of classifying ethnic groups, to a concern with individuals' nutrition, health, and life histories including migrations and genetic heritage. Members of the wealthy and well-connected elite, such as the 'Dame de Vix' in France (Knüsel 2002; Ginolhac et al. 2003), have attracted much attention, as for a while her sex was under dispute (Arnold 2012). A comparison between high-status individuals from graves in south-west Germany such as Eberdingen-Hochdorf, Grafenbühl-Asperg, and the central chamber of the Magdalenenberg near Villingen (Wahl et al. 2010) revealed that men of the elite were on average 177 cm tall, 6 cm taller than men from non-elite burial contexts. This result compares well with a study of the 144 individuals from the burial mound of Magdalenenberg (Gallay 1977: 107), which found an average height of 168 cm for men and 164 cm for women.

There are, however, considerable site-specific and regional differences in average body height, physical stress, and involvement in physical labour (Rebay-Salisbury 2016: 54–58). The study of musculoskeletal markers reveals gender- and age-specific patterns of strain, allowing researchers to show that the population buried at the cemetery with rich grave goods at Hallstatt, Austria was the same as the one working in the salt mines (Pany et al. 2003). The individuals revealed degenerative signs and alterations of their skeletons from a young age, pointing to the involvement of children in the mining operation; men had musculoskeletal markers consistent with striking movements employed in salt mining; women showed different patterns consistent with lifting, carrying, and pulling heavy loads. Young adults from the Dürrnberg population, in contrast, showed fewer signs of hard physical labour (Wiltschke-Schrotta 2014).

Isotopic analyses of human bones and teeth are bringing valuable insights into people's diet and mobility. The proportion of animal protein intake apparent through the carbon and nitrogen isotopic system reveals important information on access to milk and meat. The men and women buried in the Magdalenenberg near Villingen had equal access to animal proteins, but some men consumed a diet dominated by animal protein that also included some millet (Oelze et al. 2012: 413). A similar dietary signal was found for La Tène period individuals associated with warrior equipment in graves at Kutná Hora-Karlov and Radovesice, Czech Republic (Le Huray and Schutkowski 2005). High levels of animal protein, but a curious absence of any indication of eating marine resources such as fish—given their availability along the coastlines—was noted in individuals from Iron Age Britain (Jay and Richards 2006, 2007).

Mobility is primarily inferred from differences in strontium isotope levels in the enamel of teeth formed at different ages and by comparison to the geological background; oxygen isotopes supplement the data with information on climatic conditions. The success of these methods depends on the variability of the geological environment and the age at which persons moved; studies of individual sites are thus not directly comparable or easily reconcilable into broader patterns. The dead of the Magdalenenberg revealed very heterogeneous isotopic patterns (Oelze et al. 2012). Around one-third of the individuals could well have grown up at the local hillfort of Kapf, but others had different regions of origin such as the Black Forest, the Lake Constance area, and perhaps even south of the Alps. Men and women were evidently highly mobile in the early Iron Age, a finding which is also supported by the many 'foreign' objects in graves. Interestingly, however, burials with foreign isotopic signals and foreign objects hardly overlap (Koch 2017).

Isotope signatures of early and middle Iron Age individuals buried at Cliffs End Farm in Kent, Britain (McKinley et al. 2014) display evidence of long-distance maritime mobility, pointing to origins to the south of Britain as well as in Scandinavia. Isotopic investigation of cemeteries believed to be connected to the Celtic migrations of the fourth and third centuries BC, namely Nebringen in Germany, Monte Bibele in Italy, and Radovesice and Kutná Hora in Bohemia (Scheeres et al. 2013, 2014), found no evidence for the movement of large groups of people; instead, patterns of mobility and migration were more complex and less unidirectional than expected. The individuals from the fourth- to second-century BC Sajópetri cemetery in Hungary (Alt and Schönfelder 2017) appear to represent a local community that adopted La Tène culture, rather than newcomers; the high mitochondrial DNA (mtDNA) variability moreover suggests a community with diverse ancestry. Interesting insights into typical age and gender mobility come from isotopic analysis of individuals from Basel-Gasfabrik, Switzerland (Knipper et al. 2018). People buried in graves and settlement features at this site were frequently born elsewhere or had spent parts of their childhood away, perhaps in the context of an Iron Age fostering network; differences in mobility between gender groups point to patrilocal residential rules.

In comparison to isotope studies, DNA studies of Iron Age individuals are still relatively uncommon (cf. Reich 2018). A few studies focus on the reconstruction of biological kinship in cemetery populations: paternal relationships have been established at Mitterkirchen, Austria (Kiesslich et al. 2005) and at Nebringen, Germany (Scholz et al. 1999), where closely related individuals were buried near one another. In Switzerland, the Münsingen-Rain cemetery included two kinship groups and shows genetic continuity over many generations from the late fifth to the early second century BC (Alt et al. 2005).

Studies of population history are not (yet) fine-grained enough to differentiate Iron Age groups of divergent genetic signatures, but rapidly evolving technical advancements are bringing new insights into the way populations mixed at an astonishing rate. Samples are taken from ancient skeletons and modern populations; increasingly, mitrochondrial and Y-chromosome data—which represent the maternal and paternal genetic lines respectively—are supplemented with full genome data, bringing insights into patterns of genetic admixture. Despite Herodotus' claim of a Near Eastern origin for the Etruscans and the presence of Near Eastern mtDNA haplogroups in central Italy (Achilli et al. 2007; Vernesi et al. 2004), DNA analysis of ancient Etruscan and medieval skeletal remains in conjunction with modern individuals in fact points to a local origin for Etruscan culture (Ghirotto et al. 2013).

Attempts to understand the genetic contribution of 'Celts' in Britain and Ireland (McEvoy and Bradley 2010; Oppenheimer 2010; Røyrvik 2010) suggest little genetic change since the post-glacial expansion—certainly not enough movement of genetically distinct groups to leave a lasting imprint on the modern gene pool. The presence of Vikings in Britain, however, has been ascertained by combined analysis of patrilineal surnames and Y-chromosomal haplotypes (Bowden et al. 2008). As more fine-grained methods of analysing genetic difference are developed, the analysis of their geographic distribution is revealing ever finer patterns. The proximity of Irish and Scottish samples, for example, reflects ancient maritime connections, and the Viking contribution to the Irish gene pool is greater than previously thought (Byrne et al. 2018). A study of the mtDNA, Y-chromosomes, and genome-wide SNP profiles of speakers of Balto-Slavic languages in the European context (Kushniarevich et al. 2015) found that the populations are both genetically close to one another and to their neighbours. Geography was revealed as one of the most important factors in gene distribution; East and West Slavs are closer to their Baltic and Estonian-speaking neighbours than to the South Slavs. These examples, more than anything else, demonstrate the difficulty of aligning the results of genetic studies with archaeological cultures or language groups. That archaeological and linguistic concepts of 'ethnicity' do not map easily onto genetic heritage underlines that descent is only one small element of group affiliation.

Genetic analysis also helps in tracing the history of diseases. Disabilities and diseases with a genetic cause may be traced directly in the human genome. For example, the F508del mutation responsible for cystic fibrosis was present in three Iron Age individuals, two from Franzhausen and one from Pöttsching, Austria (Farrell et al. 2007). Pathogen DNA, such as the DNA of *Yersinia pestis* responsible for the plague, has been found in several Bronze Age and Iron Age burial contexts, including the early Iron Age cemetery of Kapan-Shahumyan, Armenia (Rasmussen et al. 2015). An analysis of proteins in sherds of vessels from a burial mound near the Heuneburg, Germany claims to have found evidence of a haemorrhagic fever virus (Wiktorowicz et al. 2017). If true, this is not only evidence of an unusual disease and possible cause of death in this geographic region, but also for mortuary practices such as evisceration and the deposition of body parts in ceramic vessels.

Whereas isotopic analyses of human bones and teeth may now be considered tried and tested, although doubtless there will be further methodological advances, the study of biomarkers and ancient DNA is still evolving, but with several large-scale projects now under way (e.g. Armit 2023; Fischer et al. 2022; Patterson et al. 2022), we may confidently look forward to the exciting insights they will bring for Iron Age studies in the future.

References

Achilli, A., A. Olivieri, M. Pala, E. Metspalu, S. Fornarino, V. Battaglia, et al. 2007. 'Mitochondrial DNA variation of modern Tuscans supports the Near Eastern origin of Etruscans'. *American Journal of Human Genetics* 80, 4: 759–768.

Alt, K. W., P. Jud, F. Müller, N. Nicklisch, A. Uerpmann, and W. Vach. 2005. 'Biologische Verwandtschaft und soziale Struktur im latènezeitlichen Gräberfeld von Münsingen-Rain'. *Jahrbuch des Römisch-Germanischen Zentralmuseums* 52, 1: 157–210.

Alt, K. W., and M. Schönfelder. 2017. 'Keltenwanderungen und Ausbreitung der Latènekultur—Fakt oder Fiktion? Historische und naturwissenschaftliche Konzepte auf dem Prüfstand', in H. Meller, F. Daim, J. Krause, and R. Risch (eds) *Migration und Integration von der*

Urgeschichte bis zum Mittelalter. Tagungen des Landesmuseums für Vorgeschichte Halle 17: 169–183. Halle: Landesamt für Denkmalpflege und Archäologie Sachsen-Anhalt.

Armit, I. 2023. 'The COMMIOS project', in M. Fernández-Götz, C. Nimura, P. Stockhammer, and R. Cartwright (eds) *Rethinking Mobility in Late Prehistoric Eurasia. Proceedings of the British Academy* 254: 280–291. London: The British Academy.

Armit, I., G. T. Swindles, K. Becker, G. Plunkett, and M. Blaauw. 2014. 'Rapid climate change did not cause population collapse at the end of the European Bronze Age'. *Proceedings of the National Academy of Sciences* 111, 48: 17045–17049.

Arnold, B. 2012. 'The Vix Princess Redux: A retrospective on European Iron Age gender and mortuary studies', in L. Prados Torreira (ed.) *La Arqueología funeraria desde una perspectiva de género*: 215–232. Madrid: UA Ediciones.

Bell, M. G., and M. J. C. Walker. 2005. *Late Quaternary Environmental Change: Physical and Human Perspectives*, 2nd edition. Harlow: Pearson/Prentice Hall.

Berglund, B. E. 2003. 'Human impact and climate changes—synchronous events and a causal link?' *Quaternary International* 105, 1: 7–12.

Bogucki, P., D. Nalepka, R. Grygiel, and B. Nowaczyk. 2012. 'Multiproxy environmental archaeology of Neolithic settlements at Osłonki, Poland, 5500–4000 BC'. *Environmental Archaeology* 17, 1: 45–65.

Bokovenko, N. A. 2005. 'Migrations of early nomads of the Eurasian Steppe in a context of climatic changes', in E. Marian Scott, A. Y. Alekseev, and G. Zaitseva (eds) *Impact of the Environment on Human Migration in Eurasia*: 21–33. Dordrecht: Springer.

Bowden, G. R., P. Balaresque, T. E. King, Z. Hansen, A. C. Lee, G. Pergl-Wilson, et al. 2008. 'Excavating past population structures by surname-based sampling: The genetic legacy of the Vikings in northwest England'. *Molecular Biology and Evolution* 25, 2: 301–309.

Brooke, J. L. 2014. 'Optimum and crisis in early civilizations, 3000–500 BC', in J. L. Brooke (ed.) *Climate Change and the Course of Global History: A Rough Journey*. Studies in Environment and History: 288–316. Cambridge: Cambridge University Press.

Brunaux, J.-L. 2004. *Guerre et religion en Gaule: Essai d'anthropologie celtique*. Paris: Errance.

Byrne, R. P., R. Martiniano, L. M. Cassidy, M. Carrigan, G. Hellenthal, O. Hardiman, D. G. Bradley, and R. L. McLaughlin. 2018. 'Insular Celtic population structure and genomic footprints of migration'. *PLOS Genetics* 14, 1: e1007152.

Crees, J. J., C. Carbone, R. S. Sommer, N. Benecke, and S. T. Turvey. 2016. 'Millennial-scale faunal record reveals differential resilience of European large mammals to human impacts across the Holocene'. *Proceedings of the Royal Society B: Biological Sciences* 283: 1827.

Cunliffe, B. 2008. *Europe Between the Oceans*. New Haven: Yale University Press.

Davis, B. A. S., P. M. Collins, and J. O. Kaplan. 2015. 'The age and post-glacial development of the modern European vegetation: A plant functional approach based on pollen data'. *Vegetation History and Archaeobotany* 24, 2: 303–317.

Diaz-Andreu, M., and T. C. Champion (eds). 1996. *Nationalism and Archaeology in Europe*. London: UCL Press.

Farrell, P., C. Le Marechal, C. Ferec, M. Siker, and M. Teschler-Nicola. 2007. 'Discovery of the principal cystic fibrosis mutation (F508del) in ancient DNA from Iron Age Europeans'. *Nature Proceedings* hdl:10101/npre.2007.1276.1.

Finné, M., K. Holmgren, H. S. Sundqvist, E. Weiberg, and M. Lindblom. 2011. 'Climate in the eastern Mediterranean, and adjacent regions, during the past 6000 years—a review'. *Journal of Archaeological Science* 38, 12: 3153–3173.

Fischer, C.-E., M.-H. Pemonge, I. Ducossau, A. Arzelier, M. Rivollat, F. Santos, et al. 2022. 'Origin and mobility of Iron Age Gaulish groups in present-day France revealed through archaeogenomics'. *iScience* 25: 104094. https://doi.org/10.1016/

Gallay, G. 1977. 'Die Körpergräber aus dem Magdalenenberg bei Villingen', in K. Spindler (ed.) *Magdalenenberg: Der hallstattzeitliche Fürstenhügel bei Villingen im Schwarzwald V*: 69–78. Villingen: Neckar Verlag.

Ghirotto, S., F. Tassi, E. Fumagalli, V. Colonna, A. Sandionigi, M. Lari, et al. 2013. 'Origins and evolution of the Etruscans' mtDNA'. *PLOS ONE* 8, 2: e55519.

Ginolhac, A., L. Orlando, A. Thenot, and C. Hänni. 2003. 'Détermination du sexe de la "Dame de Vix"', in C. Rolley (ed.) *La tombe princière de Vix*: 47–57. Paris: Picard/Société des amis du Musée du Châtillonnais.

Giraudi, C., M. Magny, G. Zanchetta, and R. N. Drysdale. 2011. 'The Holocene climatic evolution of Mediterranean Italy: A review of the continental geological data'. *The Holocene* 21, 1: 105–115.

Jay, M., and M. P. Richards. 2006. 'Diet in the Iron Age cemetery population at Wetwang Slack, East Yorkshire, UK: Carbon and nitrogen stable isotope evidence'. *Journal of Archaeological Science* 33, 5: 653–662.

Jay, M., and M. P. Richards. 2007. 'British Iron Age diet: Stable isotopes and other evidence'. *Proceedings of the Prehistoric Society* 73: 169–190.

Jones, A., L. Montanarella, and R. Jones (eds). 2005. *Soil Atlas of Europe*. Luxembourg: European Soil Bureau Network and European Commission.

Kaniewski, D., and E. van Campo. 2017. 'The climatic context of the 3.2 kyr cal BP event', in P. M. Fischer and T. Bürge (eds) *'Sea Peoples' Up-to-Date: New Research on Transformations in the Eastern Mediterranean in the 13th–11th Centuries BCE*: 85–94. Vienna: Austrian Academy of Sciences.

Kibblewhite, M., G. Tóth, and T. Hermann. 2015. 'Predicting the preservation of cultural artefacts and buried materials in soil'. *Science of the Total Environment* 529: 249–263.

Kiesslich, J., F. Neuhuber, H. J. Meyer, M. P. Baur, and J. Leskovar. 2005. 'DNA analysis on biological remains from archaeological findings—sex identification and kinship analysis on skeletons from Mitterkirchen, Upper Austria', in R. Karl and J. Leskovar (eds) *Interpretierte Eisenzeiten 1*: 147–154. Linz: Oberösterreichisches Landesmuseum.

Knapp, A. B., and S. W. Manning. 2016. 'Crisis in context: The end of the late Bronze Age in the eastern Mediterranean'. *American Journal of Archaeology* 120: 99–149.

Knight, M., S. Harris, and G. Appleby. 2016. 'Must Farm: An extraordinary tale of the everyday'. *Current Archaeology* 319: 12–18.

Knipper, C., S. L. Pichler, D. Brönnimann, H. Rissanen, M. Rosner, N. Spichtig, et al. 2018. 'A knot in a network: Residential mobility at the late Iron Age proto-urban centre of Basel-Gasfabrik (Switzerland) revealed by isotope analyses'. *Journal of Archaeological Science: Reports* 17: 735–753.

Knüsel, C. 2002. 'More Circe than Cassandra: The princess of Vix in ritualised social context'. *European Journal of Archaeology* 5, 3: 275–308.

Koch, J. K. 2017. 'Between the Black Forest and the Mediterranean Sea. Individual mobility in the early Iron Age', in S. Scharl and B. Gehlen (eds) *Mobility in Prehistoric Sedentary Societies*. Kölner Studien zur Prähistorischen Archäologie 8: 215–228. Rahden: Marie Leidorf.

Kohl, P. L. 1998. 'Nationalism and archaeology: On the constructions of nations and the reconstructions of the remote past'. *Annual Review of Anthropology* 27: 223–246.

Kristiansen, K. 1998. *Europe before History*. Cambridge: Cambridge University Press.

Kristiansen, K. 2015. 'National archaeology in the age of European integration'. *Antiquity* 64, 245: 825–828.

Kushniarevich, A., O. Utevska, M. Chuhryaeva, A. Agdzhoyan, K. Dibirova, I. Uktveryte, et al. 2015. 'Genetic heritage of the Balto-Slavic speaking populations: A synthesis of autosomal, mitochondrial and Y-chromosomal data'. *PLOS ONE* 10, 9: e0135820.

Lawson, A. J. 2000. *Potterne 1982–5: Animal Husbandry in Later Prehistoric Wiltshire*. Wessex Archaeology Report 17. Salisbury: Wessex Archaeology.

Le Huray, J. D., and H. Schutkowski. 2005. 'Diet and social status during the La Tène period in Bohemia: Carbon and nitrogen stable isotope analysis of bone collagen from Kutná Hora-Karlov and Radovesice'. *Journal of Anthropological Archaeology* 24, 2: 135–147.

McCormick, M., U. Büntgen, M. A. Cane, E. R. Cook, K. Harper, P. Huybers, et al. 2012. 'Climate change during and after the Roman Empire: Reconstructing the past from scientific and historical evidence'. *Journal of Interdisciplinary History* 43: 169–220.

McEvoy, B. P., and D. G. Bradley. 2010. 'Irish genetics and Celts', in B. Cunliffe and J. T. Koch (eds) *Celtic from the West: Alternative Perspectives from Archaeology, Genetics, Language and Literature*: 107–120. Oxford: Oxbow.

McKinley, J. I., M. Leivers, J. Schuster, P. Marshall, A. J. Barclay, and N. Stoodley. 2014. *Cliffs End Farm, Isle of Thanet, Kent: A Mortuary and Ritual Site of the Bronze Age, Iron Age and Anglo-Saxon Period with Evidence for Long-Distance Maritime Mobility*. Wessex Archaeology Report 31. Salisbury: Wessex Archaeology.

Magny, M. 2004. 'Holocene climate variability as reflected by mid-European lake-level fluctuations and its probable impact on prehistoric human settlements'. *Quaternary International* 113, 1: 65–79.

Magny, M., O. Peyron, E. Gauthier, Y. Rouèche, A. Bordon, Y. Billaud, et al. 2009. 'Quantitative reconstruction of climatic variations during the Bronze and early Iron ages based on pollen and lake-level data in the NW Alps, France'. *Quaternary International* 200, 1: 102–110.

Manning, S. W. 2013. 'The Roman world and climate: Context, relevance of climate change, and some issues', in W. V. Harris (ed.) *The Ancient Mediterranean Environment between Science and History*: 103–170. Leiden: Brill.

Marshall, T. 2015. *Prisoners of Geography: Ten Maps That Tell You Everything You Need to Know About Global Politics*. London: Elliott & Thompson.

Oelze, V. M., J. K. Koch, K. Kupke, O. Nehlich, S. Zäuner, J. Wahl, et al. 2012. 'Multi-isotopic analysis reveals individual mobility and diet at the early Iron Age monumental tumulus of Magdalenenberg, Germany'. *American Journal of Physical Anthropology* 148, 3: 406–421.

Oppenheimer, S. 2010. 'A reanalysis of multiple prehistoric immigrations to Britain and Ireland aimed at identifying the Celtic contributions', in B. Cunliffe and J. T. Koch (eds) *Celtic from the West: Alternative Perspectives from Archaeology, Genetics, Language and Literature*: 121–150. Oxford: Oxbow.

Pany, D., M. Teschler-Nicola, and H. Wilfing. 2003. 'Miners or mine owners—do the Hallstatt skeletons reflect occupation and social structure?' *American Journal of Physical Anthropology* Supplement 36: 164.

Patterson, N., M. Isakov, T. Booth, L. Büster, C.-E. Fischer, I. Olalde, et al. 2022. 'Large-scale migration into Britain during the Middle to Late Bronze Age'. *Nature* 601: 588–594.

Rasmussen, S., M. E. Allentoft, K. Nielsen, L. Orlando, M. Sikora, K.-G. Sjögren, et al. 2015. 'Early divergent strains of *Yersinia pestis* in Eurasia 5,000 years ago'. *Cell* 163, 3: 571–582.

Rebay-Salisbury, K. 2016. *The Human Body in Early Iron Age Central Europe: Burial Practices and Images of the Hallstatt World*. London: Routledge.

Reich, D. 2018. *Who We Are and How We Got Here: Ancient DNA and the New Science of the Human Past*. Oxford: Oxford University Press.

Roberts, N. 2014. *The Holocene: An Environmental History*, 3rd edition. Oxford: Blackwell.

Røyrvik, E. C. 2010. 'Western Celts? A genetic impression of Britain in Atlantic Europe', in B. Cunliffe and J. T. Koch (eds) *Celtic from the West: Alternative Perspectives from Archaeology, Genetics, Language and Literature*: 83–106. Oxford: Oxbow.

Salisbury, R. B., G. Bácsmegi, and P. Sümegi. 2013. 'Preliminary environmental historical results to reconstruct prehistoric human–environmental interactions in eastern Hungary'. *Central European Journal of Geosciences* 5, 3: 331–343.

Scheeres, M., C. Knipper, M. Hauschild, M. Schönfelder, W. Siebel, C. Pare, and K. W. Alt. 2014. '"Celtic migrations": Fact or fiction? Strontium and oxygen isotope analysis of the Czech cemeteries of Radovesice and Kutná Hora in Bohemia'. *American Journal of Physical Anthropology* 155: 496–512.

Scheeres, M., C. Knipper, M. Hauschild, M. Schönfelder, W. Siebel, D. Vitali, C. Pare, and K. W. Alt. 2013. 'Evidence for "Celtic migrations"? Strontium isotope analysis at the early La Tène (LT B) cemeteries of Nebringen (Germany) and Monte Bibele (Italy)'. *Journal of Archaeological Science* 40: 3614–3625.

Scholz, M., J. Hald, P. Dicke, S. Hengst, and C. M. Pusch. 1999. 'Das frühlatènezeitliche Gräberfeld von Gäufelden-Nebringen. Neue Erkenntnisse zur inneren Gliederung unter Anwendung archäobiologischer Analyseverfahren'. *Archäologisches Korrespondenzblatt* 29, 2: 223–235.

Tinner, W., A. F. Lotter, B. Ammann, M. Conedera, P. Hubschmid, J. F. N. van Leeuwen, and M. Wehrli. 2003. 'Climatic change and contemporaneous land-use phases north and south of the Alps 2300 BC to 800 AD'. *Quaternary Science Reviews* 22, 14: 1447–1460.

Tipping, R., A. Davies, R. McCulloch, and E. Tisdall. 2008. 'Response to late Bronze Age climate change of farming communities in north east Scotland'. *Journal of Archaeological Science* 35, 8: 2379–2386.

Van Geel, B., J. Buurman, and H. T. Waterbolk. 1996. 'Archaeological and palaeoecological indications of an abrupt climate change in The Netherlands, and evidence for climatological teleconnections around 2650 BP'. *Journal of Quaternary Science* 11, 6: 451–460.

Vernesi, C., D. Caramelli, I. Dupanloup, G. Bertorelle, M. Lari, E. Cappellini, et al. 2004. 'The Etruscans: A population-genetic study'. *American Journal of Human Genetics* 74, 4: 694–704.

Wahl, J., O. Nehlich, T. D. Price, and C. M. Pusch. 2010. 'Fürsten, Fakten, Forschungslücken. Anthropologische Schlaglichter zur Urnenfelder- und Hallstattzeit in Südwestdeutschland', in J. Bofinger and D. Krausse (eds) *Aktuelle Forschungen zu den Kelten in Europa*. Archäologische Informationen aus Baden-Württemberg 59: 45–51. Esslingen: Regierungspräsidium Stuttgart, Landesamt für Denkmalpflege.

Wanner, H., J. Beer, J. Bütikofer, T. J. Crowley, U. Cubasch, J. Flückiger, et al. 2008. 'Mid- to late Holocene climate change: An overview'. *Quaternary Science Reviews* 27, 19: 1791–1828.

Wiktorowicz, C. J., B. Arnold, J. E. Wiktorowicz, M. L. Murray, and A. Kurosky. 2017. 'Hemorrhagic fever virus, human blood, and tissues in Iron Age mortuary vessels'. *Journal of Archaeological Science* 78: 29–39.

Wiltschke-Schrotta, K. 2014. 'Anthropologische Auswertung der Gräbegruppe Dürrnberg/Hexenwandfeld', in G. Tiefengraber and K. Wiltschke-Schrotta (eds) *Der Dürrnberg bei Hallein: Die Gräbergruppe Hexenwandfeld*. Dürrnberg-Forschungen 7: 208–235. Rahden: Leidorf.

Zolitschka, B., K.-E. Behre, and J. Schneider. 2003. 'Human and climatic impact on the environment as derived from colluvial, fluvial and lacustrine archives—examples from the Bronze Age to the Migration period, Germany'. *Quaternary Science Reviews* 22, 1: 81–100.

CHAPTER 3

CHRONOLOGY IN IRON AGE EUROPE

Current Approaches and Challenges

COLIN HASELGROVE,
KATHARINA REBAY-SALISBURY,
AND PETER S. WELLS

Introduction

This chapter examines the chronological frameworks used to study Iron Age Europe and the dating methods that underpin them. Understandings of the definition and duration of this last period of prehistory vary across the continent, with the result that multiple chronological systems are employed in parallel, sometimes within quite small regions. Here, we look at how perceptions differ, and the ways in which this has shaped the terminologies used in different regions. We will also examine the relative and absolute dating methods used to construct Iron Age chronologies, from historical cross-dating to modern scientific techniques, and review their strengths and weaknesses.

As we shall see, many chapters in this Handbook employ periodizations that originated with the founding figures of European prehistoric archaeology. Despite refinements by later generations, the labelling and broad dating of the phases would still be familiar to their authors. We conclude by exploring how scientific dating is not only opening up fresh avenues for studying Iron Age settlement and social dynamics, but also creating a new kind of 'big data' able to provide insights into wider demographic and environmental trends during the first millennia BC and AD.

Defining the Iron Age

The starting date and duration of the Iron Age in Europe are as much a matter of academic convention as of archaeological realities. In some regions, the term 'Iron Age' covers just a few centuries, whereas in the two-thirds of the continent never under direct Roman rule, it is generally applied to over a millennium of archaeology. Iron itself was known and worked long before the period that takes its name, if only on a small scale. Conceived as a technological epoch, the Iron Age may be said to have commenced once iron became the prime working metal, but in practice the point when this somewhat subjective threshold was reached is rarely easy to determine from the archaeological record. Despite widespread availability of quality ores, iron industries did not emerge at the same time everywhere, or grow at the same rate. Early in the Iron Age, the metal was often used to make weapons and other prestigious accoutrements for the social elite, such as wagon fittings (Berranger 2014), and its economic and technological impact was limited. Only more gradually did iron come into generalized use, as new types of tools were developed for agriculture and crafts including carpentry and metalworking. With a few exceptions, it is not until the later Iron Age that we see many indications of large-scale iron production, or find iron artefacts in any quantity (Chapter 23).

Dating the transition to iron use in different parts of Europe faces numerous obstacles. These include an unknown extent of iron recycling; poor survival of the metal in many environments; and local variations in the archaeological record (especially whether mortuary/depositional practices favoured, or inhibited, discard of iron objects), compounded by uneven research. These factors have understandably deterred quantitative comparisons between regions, for which we must go back to the classic study by Snodgrass (1980a) of early iron metallurgy in Greece and other Mediterranean lands. This revealed that over four-fifths of weapons, knives, and tools, and some three-quarters of pins and brooches included in Athenian burials dating between *c.*1050–900 BC were made of iron, not bronze. At Vergina (Greece), which had a similar start date, iron weapons were absolutely dominant, although here burials continued later, and all but a few pins and brooches were bronze. Morris (1987) has since argued convincingly that at this era burial in Athens and elsewhere was reserved for a small elite, but this does not negate Snodgrass' conclusion that, by the later eleventh century BC, Greece and Cyprus had entered 'a full Iron Age' as he termed it (Snodgrass 1980a: 341).

A survey of the Near Eastern evidence shows a notable expansion in ironworking after *c.*1200 BC, albeit with regional variations (Erb-Satullo 2019). This followed over a millennium when iron objects occurred sporadically, often in a decorative context or with associations implying that iron was initially a prestige material.[1] Anatolia was probably the first region to develop extractive iron metallurgy early in the second millennium BC, but lagged behind Cyprus and the Levant (and perhaps parts of Greece) in becoming predominantly iron-using. Maritime networks in which the Phoenicians had a leading role have long been seen as instrumental in the spread of iron technologies to other Mediterranean lands early in the first millennium BC (Erb-Satullo 2019: 567), although this might underestimate the significance of contacts with Cyprus for some regions (Chapter 12), while in others largely independent development is not to be excluded.

In non-Mediterranean Europe the sequence is broadly similar, although the timing varies. Apart from in the far north, iron objects occur occasionally from the second millennium BC, and more frequently in the final stages of the Bronze Age, mostly as ornaments or small tools (Chapter 23; Kristiansen 1998; Berranger 2014). As noted earlier, it is difficult to be certain when metalworkers in different regions began to replicate in iron weapons and tools previously made from bronze, and on what scale. Current indications are that in parts of the Circum-Pontic zone, the shift began around the start of the first millennium BC, but in northern Europe not until mid-millennium, with temperate Europe between the two. The picture could yet change, however. For example in Ireland, where iron objects are vanishingly rare until the last centuries BC, radiocarbon dates from hearths used for smelting or smithing suggest iron production by the eighth or seventh century BC (Gartski 2019). Slags may ultimately prove a better indicator of early ironworking than the objects themselves.

For much of temperate Europe, a date around 800 BC can be inferred for the onset of iron metallurgy on a significant scale, supported by the early Hallstatt C wagon burial with an iron sword at Wehringen in southern Germany that is tree-ring dated to within five years of 778 BC (Friedrich and Hennig 1996). In central Europe, the start of Hallstatt C is also marked by changes in elite burial ritual and material culture (Chapter 8; Pare 1991, 1998; Torbrügge 1991, 1992), although not everywhere. In north-west Europe, bronze hoarding declined sharply after 800 BC, while in Britain the divide also saw changes in pottery and domestic architecture and—along with Ireland—in the character of the bronze industry (Chapter 4; Needham 2007). While the extent to which these developments were intertwined remains a matter of debate, together they form a distinct horizon covering much of central and western Europe, which provides a convenient proxy for the start of the Iron Age both in areas where iron artefacts soon became more common—generally because they were placed in burials—and in those where they remained rare until later in the first millennium BC.

When the Iron Age is deemed to end is highly variable, but easier to put a date on. From a technological perspective, the repertoire of iron tools used by farmers in the late first millennium BC would have been immediately recognizable to nineteenth-century rural populations in many parts of Europe (Zvelebil 1985). In practice, the end of the Iron Age is determined by the subsequent histories of different regions and the disciplinary divides to which these have given rise. In Greece and most of Italy, the emergence of classical civilizations acts as the boundary. Elsewhere in the Mediterranean zone and in much of temperate Europe, the Iron Age is concluded by incorporation into the Roman Empire, which occurred variably across three centuries. Beyond the Roman frontiers in northern and eastern Europe, however, the 'prehistoric' Iron Age is perceived as continuing until the start of the Middle Ages, itself defined variously in different academic traditions by horizons such as the Great Migration, the adoption of Christianity, or the Viking diaspora.

Figure 3.1 shows the chronological spans of the Iron Age employed by the authors of the regional surveys that follow. At the top are the early adopters of iron in south-east Europe—this includes the Danubian Black Sea coast—and the eastern Mediterranean (Chapters 12, 13, 14, 17). Their trajectories diverge thereafter: the Iron Age in the Carpathian-Danubian region and the Mediterranean coastlands of Asia and Africa is seen as continuing to the Roman period, but in Greece and Italy to cease with the rise of Greek and Etruscan city states. In this zone, the period after *c.*750 BC is considered the preserve of classical archaeologists and ancient historians, whose approach is generally quite different to that of pre- and protohistorians.[2] This is unfortunate, since Archaic Greece and Italy, and the equivalent Iron Age beyond the Alps, have many archaeological features in common. This academic divide has hindered fruitful comparison and analysis, as younger scholars on both sides are increasingly recognizing (e.g. Stoddart 2017; Zamboni et al. 2020).

At the opposite end of the chart are the eastern Baltic and Scandinavia, which on current evidence were relatively late adopters of iron technology. In this zone, both the start and the end of the Iron Age are set later than elsewhere (Chapters 5 and 6). The rest of Europe is essentially divided between regions where the Iron Age began in the early first millennium BC and was ended by the Roman conquest (Chapters 8, 9, 10, 11), and those where the Iron Age continued well into the first millennium AD (Chapters 7, 15, 16); north-west Europe, never fully conquered by Rome, straddles both (Chapter 4). The arbitrary nature of this division should however be underlined; in many areas, the Roman conquest does not represent a clear horizon in the archaeological record. Outside obviously 'Roman' foci such as forts and towns, major changes are often not apparent in rural areas for some decades. For many people, their lives continued largely as before, hence our inclusion of a chapter on this theme (Chapter 38). Conversely, areas beyond the frontier were not immune to contact and manipulation, with concomitant social and economic changes compared to earlier periods; indeed, similar processes began before the Roman conquest in many areas that were incorporated into the Empire.

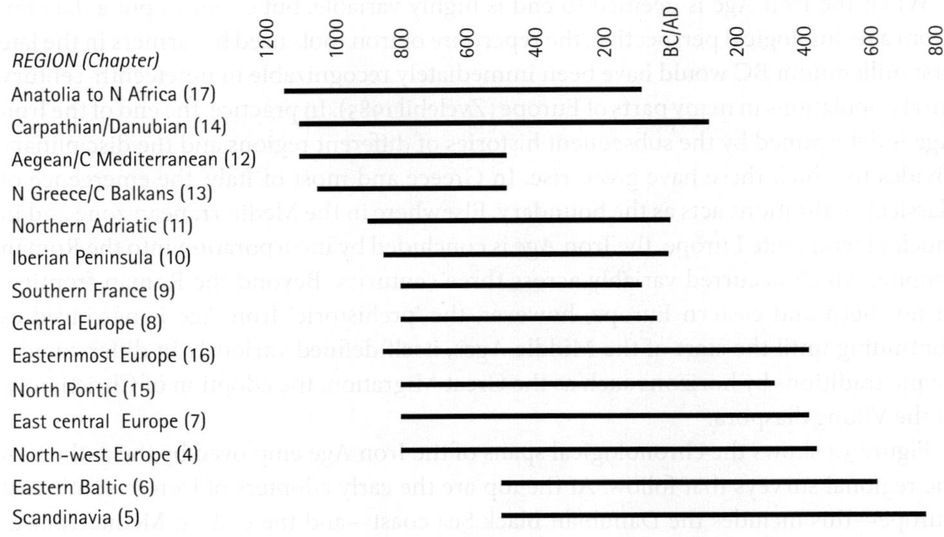

FIGURE 3.1 Time spans covered by the regional chapters in this Handbook (Chapter 17 also covers the long Iron Age in the North Atlantic).

The combination of different intellectual constructs and time spans of the Iron Age, and the regional variability of the archaeological record, has led to the development of a plethora of chronological schemes and terminologies across Europe. These are often not methodologically compatible (Hedeager 1992: 13) and in some cases very localized. This makes it difficult to impose a single, overarching framework on the period. It is not unusual to find different systems within one country: for example, southern Germany uses the Hallstatt–La Tène periodization (see later), whereas in northern Germany beyond the Roman frontier another scheme holds sway (see Chapters 7 and 8). In some regions, several chronologies operate at the same time (Figure 3.2). In north-west Europe, there are at least five schemas, which can easily lead to confusion! For instance, in both the Netherlands and southern Britain, archaeologists divide the pre-Roman Iron Age into Early, Middle, and Late (Chapter 4), but the boundaries do not coincide.[3] The concept of a 'long Iron Age' on the Scandinavian model (Chapter 5; Price 2020: 66) has gained traction among many Scottish archaeologists, so that in northern Britain, 'Earlier Iron Age' and 'Later Iron Age' mean quite different things than in the south, where the period is deemed to end with the Roman conquest (Haselgrove and Pope 2007; Harding 2017). Bearing such complications in mind, the basis of the current chronological frameworks can be discussed.

Cultural Frameworks and Relative Dating

Across Europe, many of the dating schemes used by Iron Age archaeologists are simply more elaborate versions of typo-chronologies first developed in the late nineteenth and early twentieth centuries in the wake of Thomsen's Three Age system (e.g. Moore and Armada 2011: 13–21). The Nordic area, for example, still uses the basic periods devised by Montelius (1895–7, 1986) for the Bronze and Iron Ages (Hedeager 1992: 6–14; Kristiansen 1998: 31–35). In eastern Europe, temporal (and geographical) boundaries are typically framed in terms of successive cultural and/or ethnic constructs such as Scythians and Sarmatians (Chapters 6, 7, 14, 15, 16). Around the Mediterranean, a variety of systems are used, some based on cultural entities (e.g. Este, Golasecca, Villanovan in northern Italy), others on Greek pottery styles (Chapter 9, 11, 12, 13; Morris 1987). Iberia is divided into two zones on linguistic criteria, one 'Iberian', the other 'Celtic', each with its own chronological subdivisions (Chapter 10). In large parts of north-west and northern Europe, where cultural material is often sparse and radiocarbon dating is by default the primary means of building chronologies (see later), the tendency is increasingly towards simple generic divisions (Chapters 4, 5; Figure 3.2).

Perhaps the most widely applied periodization—at least as measured by the number of countries where it is employed, if not necessarily by the geographical extent of the zone where it is used—and the best known, is the Hallstatt–La Tène framework for

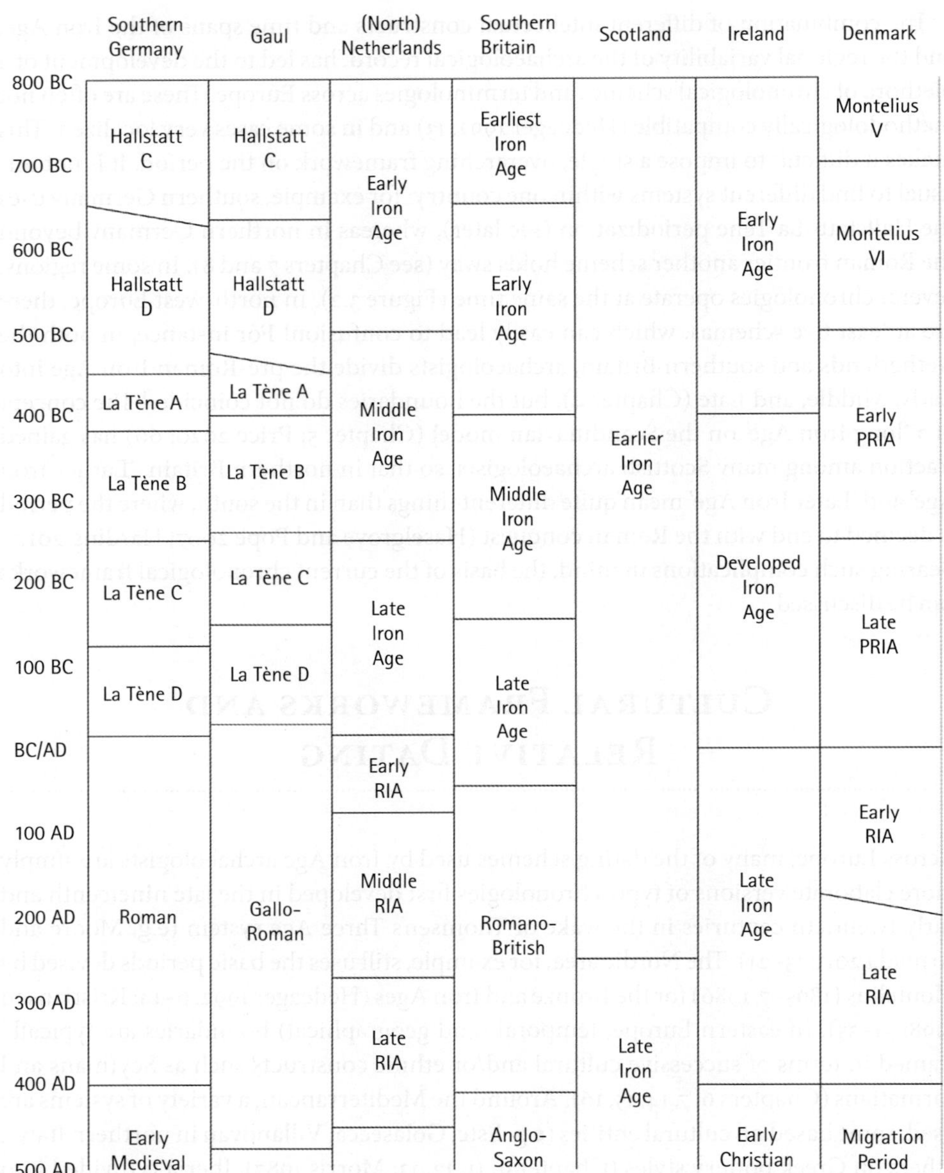

FIGURE 3.2 Chronological periodizations for the pre-Roman and Roman Iron Age in different regions of north-west and central Europe.

'Celtic' western and central Europe (Chapters 4, 7, 8, 11, 14; cf. Kaenel 2008: ill. 1); this terminology is also often invoked as a convenient way of equating different regional typo-chronologies.[4] Following two key congresses in the 1870s at Bologna and Stockholm, prehistorians espoused the idea of dividing the European Iron Age into two principal parts, the first characterized by finds from the Hallstatt cemetery in Austria, the second named after the Swiss lakeside site of La Tène and seen as an archaeological expression of the Celts (de Mortillet 1876; Hildebrand 1876). La Tène finds from burials in Italy and the Marne region (France), and from the battlefield at Alesia—where in 52 BC, Caesar's legions definitively defeated the Gauls led by Vercingetorix—also played a substantial part in these formulations (Olivier 2019; Chapter 37). Soon afterwards, Tischler proposed splitting the Hallstatt Iron Age into earlier and later phases, and—following the discovery of a votive deposit at Duchcov (Czech Republic)—subdivided the La Tène period into early, middle, and late phases, or I–III (Tischler 1881, 1885). This formative work was consolidated by Déchelette, Montelius, Reinecke, Viollier, and others, drawing on newly and increasingly well-excavated settlements and cemeteries such as Mont Beuvray (France) and Münsingen (Switzerland). Its culmination was Déchelette's Europe-wide syntheses of the Hallstatt and La Tène Iron Ages published in his *Manuel d'Archéologie* (Déchelette 1913, 1914).

The periodization formulated by Reinecke (reprinted 1965) differed from those of his near contemporaries in two significant respects. Acknowledging the continuities between the earlier Iron Age and the preceding late Bronze Age urnfields, Reinecke included them both within the Hallstatt period.[5] He also adopted a discrete early La Tène phase (christened La Tène A). These modifications produced fourfold divisions for both periods, with Hallstatt C–D and La Tène A–D representing the Iron Age. Reinecke's scheme has continued to evolve as new finds have prompted reconsideration. All the main phases have been further subdivided, sometimes sparking lengthy debates over their interregional equivalence and/or the methods used to define them (e.g. Kossack 1959; Demoule 1999; Trachsel 2004).[6] The dating of individual phases has also been subject to revision over the years, with the pendulum swinging between shorter and longer time spans (e.g. Miron 1986, 1991; Pare 1991, 1998).

In its developed form, the Reinecke system is the most widely accepted in Iron Age studies. A common nomenclature has its advantages, but can mask the fact that similarly labelled phases in different regions are not always defined by the same archaeological criteria, and may not be chronologically equivalent. This is a particular problem for the later La Tène period west and east of the Rhine, where the use of identical terminology for successive subphases (La Tène C2-D1a-D1b-D2a-D2b) hides significant contradictions in their dating and definition (Rieckhoff 1995; Kaenel 2008; Danielisová 2020; Kysela 2020). There are also lingering tensions from the use of Hallstatt and La Tène as both cultural and chronological constructs (e.g. Moore and Armada 2011), while the Hallstatt–La Tène distinction essentially encapsulates the adoption of a new decorative style of art and craft products across a large part of Europe, rather than a fundamental cultural or social divide (Wells 2012: 1–4; Rebay-Salisbury 2016: 35–49). The well-known Vix burial (France) is usually assigned to Hallstatt D3 based on the brooches, whereas Trachsel (2004) attributes it to La Tène A on account of the decoration on the torc. It is important to be transparent about the criteria used to distinguish each period, as in reality few if any period boundaries will be clear-cut, since the artefact types that collectively characterize a phase will not have had identical life cycles.

The periodizations employed in Europe today rest on 150 years of analysis using the basic tools of typology, stratigraphy, seriation, and artefact associations in closed contexts to determine the relative order of different classes of Iron Age objects and sites, and their contemporaneity (or not). Tischler's (1885) tripartite division of the La Tène period hinged on distinctive brooch and sword types, while it is primarily to Déchelette and Reinecke that we owe the characterization of successive stages of the Iron Age in terms of the association of diagnostic types of artefact in contemporary burials, hoards, and settlements (Collis 2008; Kaenel 2008; Sørensen and Rebay-Salisbury 2008). Since then, typologies have been devised for almost every kind of (non-perishable) object known to Iron Age societies, with ubiquitous items like brooches—that are both plentiful in archaeological contexts and subject to frequent changes of fashion—among the most useful for dating purposes (Figure 3.3). Periodizations based on artefact typology are most easily constructed for regions and phases with furnished burials, since diagnostic metalwork is often rare on settlements. Periods of transition (see e.g. Chapter 5) are a recurrent weak point with all these schemes, as changes in burial rites or depositional behaviour may give a false impression of discontinuity in other spheres, as arguably at the start of the Iron Age in central Europe (Kristiansen 1998: 33–34).

Settlement and burial chronologies are often difficult to relate, as they frequently depend on mutually exclusive categories of objects. Although pottery occurs in both domains, funerary and domestic wares may be quite different in character. As the most abundant material recovered from settlements, pottery forms the basis of most regional chronologies in use today, some honed to a degree of precision that theoretically allows us to follow changes on a timescale of little more than a generation (Figure 3.4). These, however, are the exception. Pottery is not unproblematic as a means of dating sites: in many areas and periods, domestic wares are conservative and exhibit minimal change over time, while a lack of stratification on most Iron Age settlements makes it difficult to refine ceramic typologies beyond a certain point.

Due to poor survival of occupation deposits and floor levels, vertical stratigraphy has played a lesser role in building Iron Age site chronologies than in many branches of archaeology, although some fortified sites and agglomerations do possess good stratification that has yet to be exploited to the full (Collis 2008). Horizontal stratigraphy can provide a valuable check on the validity of artefact typo-chronologies, as with the gradual spatial expansion of occupation at the agglomeration at Manching in Germany (Stöckli 1974; Chapter 8), or the displacements from one short-lived centre to another nearby, each with a distinct archaeological facies, seen in many parts of Europe in the last centuries BC; the Aisne valley (France) provides several examples (Haselgrove and Guichard 2013; Chapter 4). The horizontal stratigraphy of the Münsingen cemetery, which expanded along a ridge, was employed by Hodson (1968) to evaluate his seriation of La Tène B–C grave assemblages using quantitative methods.[7] Although multivariate analysis has been little used in building Iron Age chronologies, it has proved effective at isolating social groupings, as at the Hallstatt

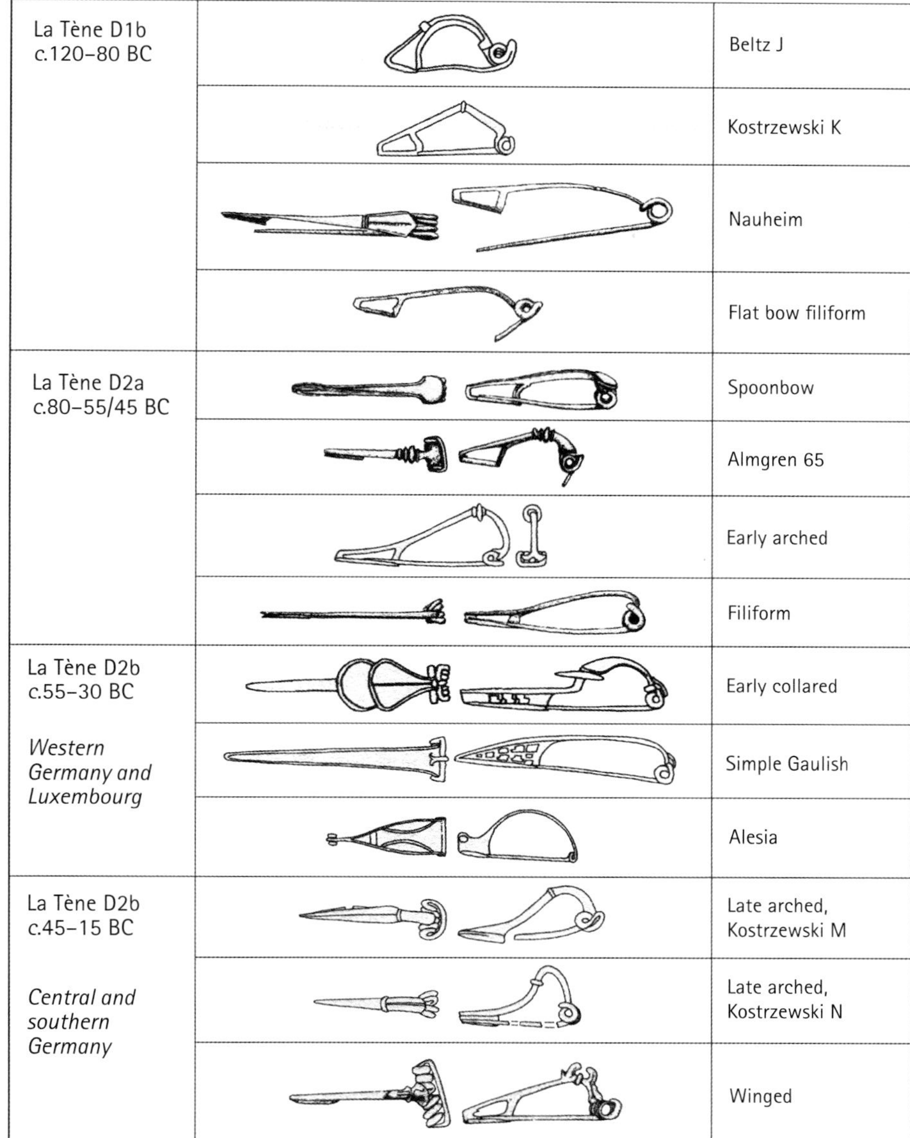

FIGURE 3.3 Brooch types typifying the La Tène D1 and D2 periods in Germany.

Source: adapted from Rieckhoff (2012: fig. 3)

cemetery, where intercutting graves provide a modicum of vertical stratigraphy (Hodson 1990).

In parts of northern Europe where acidic soils are common, pottery often survives poorly or was never common, so that before the advent of scientific dating it was necessary to rely on site typologies to provide crude frameworks for both relative and absolute

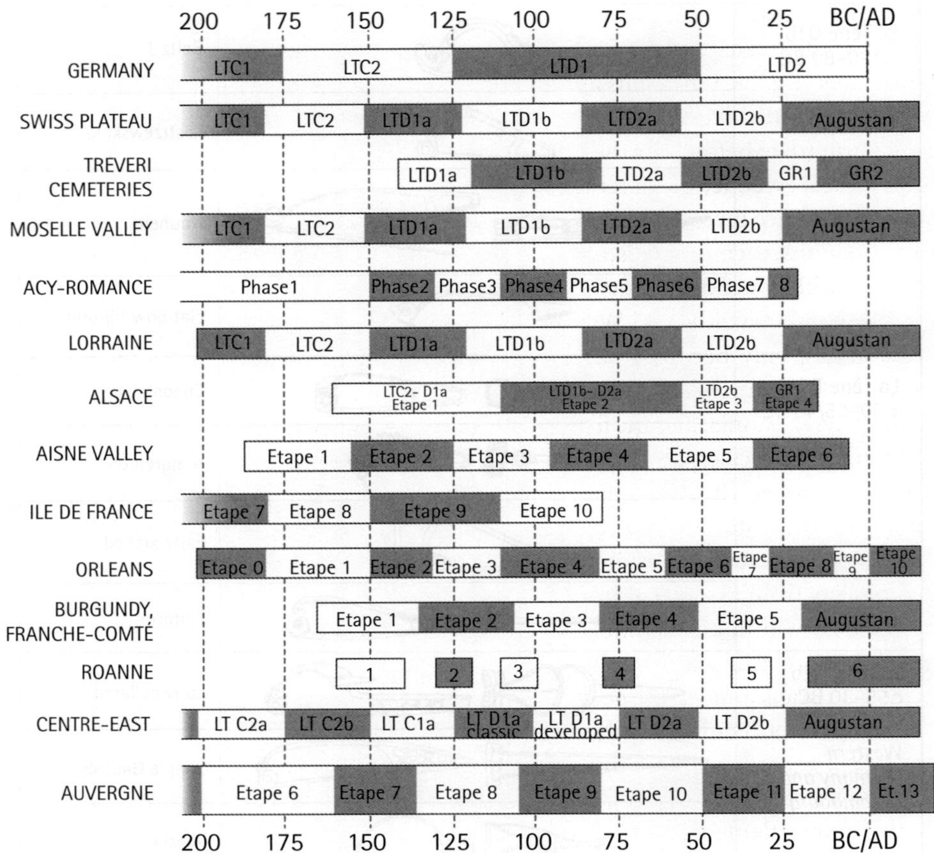

FIGURE 3.4 Competing chronological schemes identified for selected sites and areas in non-Mediterranean France from 200 BC to the start of the Roman period.

Source: adapted from Ralston (2019: fig. 3.2)

dating. More recent research has, however, often cast doubt on such models: the so-called 'Hownam sequence' for fortified sites in northern Britain is a case in point (Armit and McKenzie 2013).

Absolute Dating in the European Iron Age

Until the late twentieth century, the absolute dating of the Iron Age depended very largely on cross-dating with the historical chronologies of the classical world and—at the start of the period—with those of Egypt and the Levant. The main sources of cross-correlation are the presence of Mediterranean imports in Iron Age contexts (e.g. Greek or Etruscan goods in Hallstatt burials), and of Iron Age material at historically dated sites (e.g. La Tène coins and weapons at Alesia), or preferably both (Collis 1984). The first provides a *terminus post quem* (date after) for the context, the latter a *terminus ante quem* (date before) for the finds. Cross-dating is most dependable where (a) there is reciprocal evidence of contemporaneity, and (b) similar associations recur at different sites. It becomes increasingly insecure where it is reliant on a chain of connections between regions, each more distant than the last from the source of calendar dates. In the Greek world, dependable synchronisms are rare before the eighth century BC (Morris 1987: 11–14; Gimatzidis and Weniger 2020), and in most of Transalpine Europe direct cross-dating only becomes possible with Roman expansion from 200 BC onwards. In the early centuries AD, Roman imports and coins reached as far afield as northern Scandinavia, Estonia, and the forest zone of Russia (Chapters 5, 6, 7, 15, 16).

Although the calendar dates for successive periods of the Iron Age first proposed over a century ago by Montelius, Déchelette, and Reinecke via cross-dating rested on a fraction of the material now available, they have broadly stood the test of time. It remains challenging, however, to establish reliable absolute dates for individual sites, contexts, and objects from associated imports and/or on historical grounds. Some imports can be dated to within a generation or less (e.g. Attic Black and Red Figure wares, Greek and Roman coins, wine amphorae with consular inscriptions, samian pottery), but many are datable only to the nearest century, if that (most amphorae and metal vessels).[8] Moreover, imports may have had long use-lives before finding their way into the archaeological record, without this being apparent from wear or repair. Many Roman silver coins remained in circulation long after issue, and single finds of coins or other items from settlements may easily be residual, even if stratified. Significant quantities of imports are needed to establish robust dating frameworks for sites, and even then, certainty is not guaranteed. Despite the presence of Roman coins and other imports in many graves at Ornavasso (Italy), a range of chronologies have been proposed for the two late La Tène cemeteries there (Chapter 11; Graue 1974).[9]

The chronology of Hallstatt and La Tène graves containing southern imports has attracted much critical discussion over the years, partly on account of their significance for the dating of subphases and development of art styles (Dehn and Frey 1979; Parzinger 1988; Trachsel 2004; Guggisberg 2007; Garrow and Gosden 2012; Rebay-Salisbury 2016). Imports provide only a *terminus post quem* for the grave in which they occur; other associated grave goods could be older or younger. Some items were manufactured specifically for deposition with the deceased person, as at Hochdorf (Germany; Chapter 8), but others—especially those connected to identity, such as jewellery, dress elements, or weapons—would have been acquired over a person's lifetime. Women often received objects at adolescence, which might then be decades old when put in the grave; burials can also contain repaired and/or curated objects, perhaps heirlooms handed down over generations (Rebay-Salisbury 2016: 47). Swords of antique style occur in several elite graves of the south-eastern Hallstatt area, as at Stična (Slovenia) and Strettweg (Austria; Chapter 11), and a fragment of a decorated *situla* made early in the fifth century BC was placed in a high-status third-century BC grave at Dürrnberg (Austria; Moser 2010: 108–113). Consequently, it is essential to try and unpick the entangled relationships between the dated import(s), associated objects, and their place of deposition.

Historically dated sites are of mixed value for anchoring chronologies. From what we know now, the foundation dates claimed for many Greek colonies in the Black Sea and the Mediterranean are mythical, although for others such as Olbia (Ukraine), Massalia (France), and Pithekoussai and Cumae (Italy) they accord well enough with the archaeology (Morris 1996; Osborne 1996: 119–129).[10] Roman forts, such as those linked to the Celtiberian wars in Iberia (153–133 BC) or the German campaigns of Augustus (12 BC–AD 16), are of most use for dating Roman goods like amphorae and pottery which were exported to other regions—although some identifications of forts with particular campaigns can be questioned (Morillo and Sala-Sellés 2019). Altogether more problematic is the recurrent desire to link Iron Age sites and deposits with recorded events, for example in Mediterranean France, where the destruction or abandonment of fortified sites such as Buffe-Arnaud and Entremont (Chapter 9) is often tied to the Roman conquest (125–123 BC). Episodes like the incursions of the Cimbri and Teutones (113–101 BC; Chapter 37) and the Gallic War (58–51 BC) have acted as magnets for dating coin hoards and the minting of Iron Age coinages, giving rise to misleading and overprecise numismatic chronologies bunched around 'known' historical events, and drawing our eyes away from alternative interpretations (Haselgrove 2019; Chapter 28). Iron Age coins are of limited value for dating. Many are uninscribed, and few of the individuals named are known from independent sources. Caesar's Gaulish opponent Vercingetorix is a notable exception. Indeed, most Iron Age coins should be treated like any other item of material culture, to be dated from their find contexts, rather than vice versa.

Using copies of imports as a second-hand source of absolute dating is subject to all the pitfalls already mentioned, with an additional layer of uncertainty over time lapse, as with Iron Age coins copied at various removes from Greek originals, or locally manufactured spouted flagons modelled on Etruscan prototypes placed in early La Tène graves. In the past, art styles have been used as a means of dating objects, but this is to be avoided. Complex iconographies cannot just be reduced to a simple ladder-like sequence. Styles overlapped, 'early' and 'late' motifs could be combined together on later pieces, and—as noted earlier—individual objects often had long and complicated biographies (Macdonald 2007; Garrow et al. 2009; Nimura et al. 2020).

Scientific Dating Methods

In the last thirty years, absolute dating for the Iron Age has been increasingly revolutionized by the application of independent scientific methods first introduced in the mid-twentieth century, releasing archaeologists from their dependence on Mediterranean historical chronologies. The most widely used methods are dendrochronology and radiocarbon dating. Luminescence and archaeomagnetic dating have also proved valuable in specific situations.

In areas where suitable wood samples are preserved and reference curves have been established, dendrochronology (tree-ring dating) is capable of great precision. The method is not without potential problems, the most significant being whether the final growth rings of the tree survive or the felling date has to be estimated, and the degree of confidence with which a specimen can be matched to the correct part of the reference curve. As with any category of archaeological material, the exact relationship of the specimen to the event to be dated (if not an *in situ* structure)[11] needs to be evaluated. An error in the German oak chronology that was not rectified until the 1980s (Lambert 2008) meant that many early tree-ring dates prior to 500 BC—including those for the Hallstatt D1 burial mound at the Magdalenenberg (Germany; Chapter 8)—were wrong. The resultant conflict with the received archaeological dating for Hallstatt D prompted some distrust of dendrochronology for a while.[12] Many regions now have continuous master curves.

Dendrochronology is ideal for dating wetland sites with well-preserved timber structures, from Biskupin in Poland (Chapter 7) to the many crannogs of Ireland and southern Scotland (Chapter 4). At Biskupin, much of the wood used for the first settlement was felled between 739 and 736 BC; three other stockaded lake sites of 'Biskupin type' were built during the later eighth century BC (Ważny 1994; Harding and Rączkowski 2010). The Cults Loch 3 and Black Loch crannogs in south-west Scotland were both constructed in the later fifth century BC (Cavers and Crone 2018, 2019; see later). Tree-ring dating of the Swiss lake villages is a mainstay of later Bronze Age chronology in the Circum-Alpine zone (Pare 1996: 102–103). Wood can also survive in dry environments, not least in the Alpine salt mines (e.g. Stöllner 2003), or when charred, as in timber-laced ramparts.

A significant contribution of dendrochronology has been to vindicate the essential accuracy of the Hallstatt–La Tène typo-chronology, with some minor modifications. There are now enough dates to provide a comprehensive framework for the period (Figure 3.5), including from key sites such as the Wehringen burial, the long-lived fortified site at the Heuneburg, and the salt mining centres at Dürrnberg and Hallstatt itself (Friedrich and Hennig 1996; Krausse 2006; Billamboz 2008). New fixed points are being added all the time, a case in point being the well-furnished female burial attributed to Hallstatt D1 at Bettelbühl—just across the river Danube from the Heuneburg—where the chamber is dated to 583 BC (Krausse et al. 2017). Dendrochronology was a key driver in the lengthening of the La Tène D period in the 1990s (Kaenel 1990). Occasionally, individual dates throw up challenges: grave 352 at Dürrnberg belongs to Hallstatt D3 in typo-chronological terms, but has a tree-ring date of 464 BC (Sormaz and Stöllner 2005). Some would regard this date as being right at the limit of the period, although in all probability, all this does is expose the inadvisability of trying to draw a sharp division between periods.

Radiocarbon dating was long neglected for the Iron Age, largely on account of the infamous 800–400 BC plateau and other 'wiggles' in the calibration curve, which resulted in dates seen as too broad to be useful compared to those given by artefact typo-chronologies. Thanks to continuous gains in measurement precision and increasingly

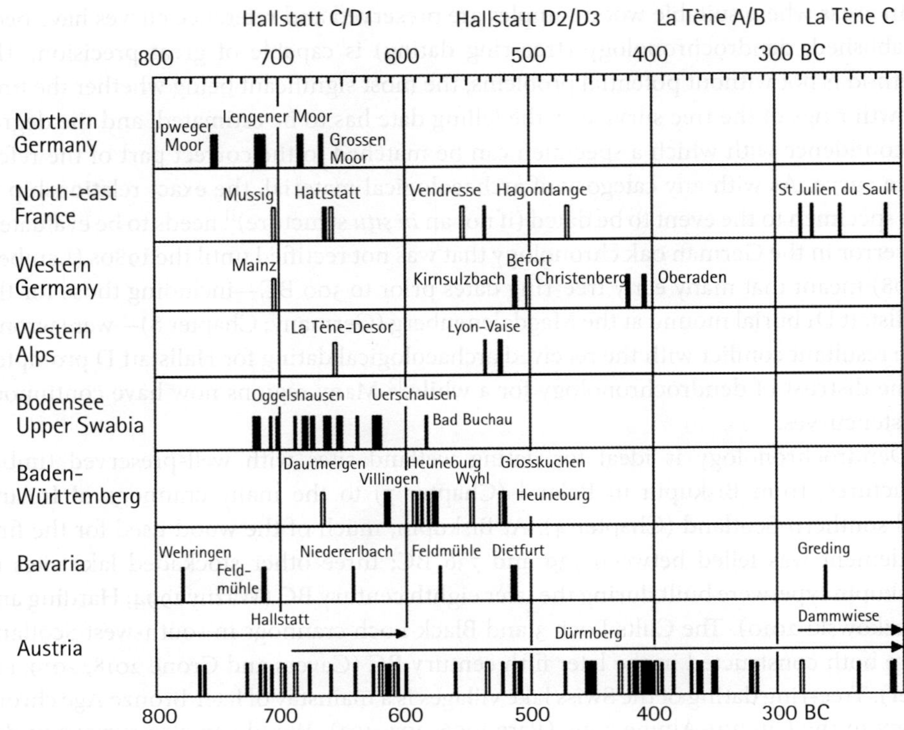

FIGURE 3.5 Tree-ring fixed dates from western and central Europe.

Source: adapted from Billamboz (2008: Abb. 11)

sophisticated methods of analysis—above all the introduction of Bayesian modelling—radiocarbon dating has transformed our ability to build robust Iron Age chronologies that are independent of existing archaeological models (Hamilton et al. 2015). Unlike dendrochronology, radiocarbon dating is possible almost everywhere, as viable dates require only tiny amounts of organic material, although the taphonomy of samples and contemporaneity to the event being dated is again crucial. Short-lived, single-entity samples (e.g. cereals, bone, coppiced wood) from primary deposits (e.g. human burials, animal sacrifices, stored grain) are the most secure. Artefacts with organic components can also be dated. Single determinations are of limited value: to date entire sites or phases with any accuracy or precision, multiple samples are necessary, ideally from stratified sequences or deposits that can be reliably ordered by another means. These stratigraphic controls are then built into chronological model(s) following a Bayesian approach, generating estimates for the timing and duration of site episodes often accurate to less than a century, sometimes to just a few decades (Bayliss 2009).

By and large, those parts of Europe where metalwork is scarce and pottery (if used) rarely closely dateable were the first to adopt radiocarbon dating as routine. In these areas its impact was immediate, often resulting in a substantial lengthening of existing chronologies for various classes of monuments. In Britain, hillforts were long considered an exclusively Iron Age phenomenon, but it soon became apparent from radiocarbon dating that here, as on the continent, many hilltop enclosures originated in the later Bronze Age. Closer to the classical world, the view until quite recently was that traditional periodizations and ceramic dating provided greater precision for the Iron Age than radiocarbon chronologies (Collis 1984: 23), but attitudes have shifted; over much of Europe, radiocarbon dating and Bayesian modelling are now perceived as indispensable for building Iron Age chronologies, from the Danube to Iberia (e.g. Holzer 2008; Prieto Martínez et al. 2017) and from Scandinavia to the Adriatic (e.g. Teržan and Črešna 2014; Herschend 2016; Rose 2020), or acknowledged as a lacuna to be remedied (Danielisová 2020). Hesitancy over radiocarbon dating persists in some quarters, for example where dates clash with long-established historically based chronologies (see Gimatzidis and Weninger 2020), but such views are increasingly infrequent.

In Britain, phases of settlement and midden accumulation on the 'Hallstatt plateau' have been closely dated using Bayesian approaches (Figure 3.6; Armit and McKenzie 2013; Waddington et al. 2019), as have many later sites (Hamilton et al. 2015). These include unfurnished inhumation cemeteries that would otherwise have been assigned to another period, as could prove true in other parts of Europe. The level of resolution obtained from Bayesian models is often comfortably superior to that achievable by conventional means. Many critics overlook the point that error margins for radiocarbon estimates are transparent, which is not the case for typo-chronological dating.

Radiocarbon dating has been successfully used to investigate artefact typo-chronologies (e.g. Hamilton et al. 2022). In some cases, both methods give similar results, as at Glastonbury Lake Village, where brooches and radiocarbon dates suggest comparable time spans for the occupation (Marshall et al. 2020). In others, Bayesian models imply that the artefact dating was conservative (Fitzpatrick et al. 2017). Another programme of radiocarbon dating has shown that the earliest style of La Tène art reached

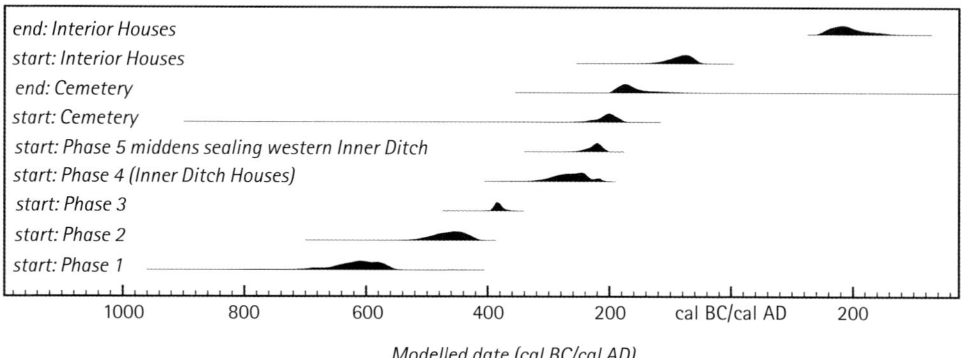

FIGURE 3.6 Model estimates for the major occupation phases, cemetery, and late houses at Broxmouth, Scotland.

Source: Armit and McKenzie (2013: fig. 9:12)

Britain soon after its inception, and later styles were not strictly successive (Garrow et al. 2009; see earlier). A lesson from all these studies is that new artefact styles spread rapidly between regions without the time lags often assumed by cross-dating. Finally, Bayesian modelling combining radiocarbon dates from stratified graves at Dietfurt (Germany) and tree-ring dates from other sites now suggest that the Hallstatt C–D transition in Bavaria occurred before 650 BC, several decades earlier than the accepted date of this transition (Rose et al. 2022).[13]

Other scientific methods have been successfully applied to more niche contexts, from archaeomagnetic dating of hearths (Clark 1991) to optical stimulated luminescence (OSL) dating of sediments (Reece-Jones and Tite 2003). OSL dating is useful for linear earthworks, which may be far from any habitation and thus lacking in other datable material. Although these other methods give wide date ranges, Bayesian models can integrate dates generated by different techniques, which can be used to narrow them down (Millard 2013; Rose et al. 2022). Archaeomagnetic and luminescence dating have been applied to vitrified ramparts of Iron Age fortifications in several parts of Europe, but without conspicuous success to date (Ralston 2006: 143–163).[14]

Pottery has been dated using luminescence (Barnett 2000), but radiocarbon dating of carbonized residues on ceramic vessels has potential for greater precision. Already, site-based radiocarbon models are suggesting issues with the Iron Age ceramic chronology for southern England (Waddington et al. 2019; Haselgrove et al. forthcoming). A study of settlements in the Danebury area exposed various conflicts between ceramic and radiocarbon dating: some sites proved to have shorter occupation spans, others to be earlier than thought. At one site, activity of some kind continued when the pottery implied a break. The ramifications are potentially significant, since even in regions with solid artefact typo-chronologies, pottery sequences are generally the mainstay of settlement dating, but are not always as well linked to metalwork typologies as archaeologists might wish.

Future Perspectives

In the next twenty-five years, we can expect a wholesale shift to absolute chronologies for Iron Age Europe, based on high-precision radiocarbon dating, supported by dendrochronological fixed points, and tailored to individual regions and classes of monument or material. Indeed, in parts of Europe where radiocarbon dating is already routine, this is happening fast (Figure 3.7). This does not mean the end of artefact typo-chronologies, which will continue to play a key role in interrogating social patterns and processes. However, while the traditional dating frameworks have stood the test of time remarkably well, the confusion stemming from the mixing of ethnocultural and chronological constructs renders them open to criticism (Moore and Armada 2011). The use of parallel terminologies may also have the effect of masking periods of transition common to large areas.[15] As Collis and others have argued, we need to build new chronological

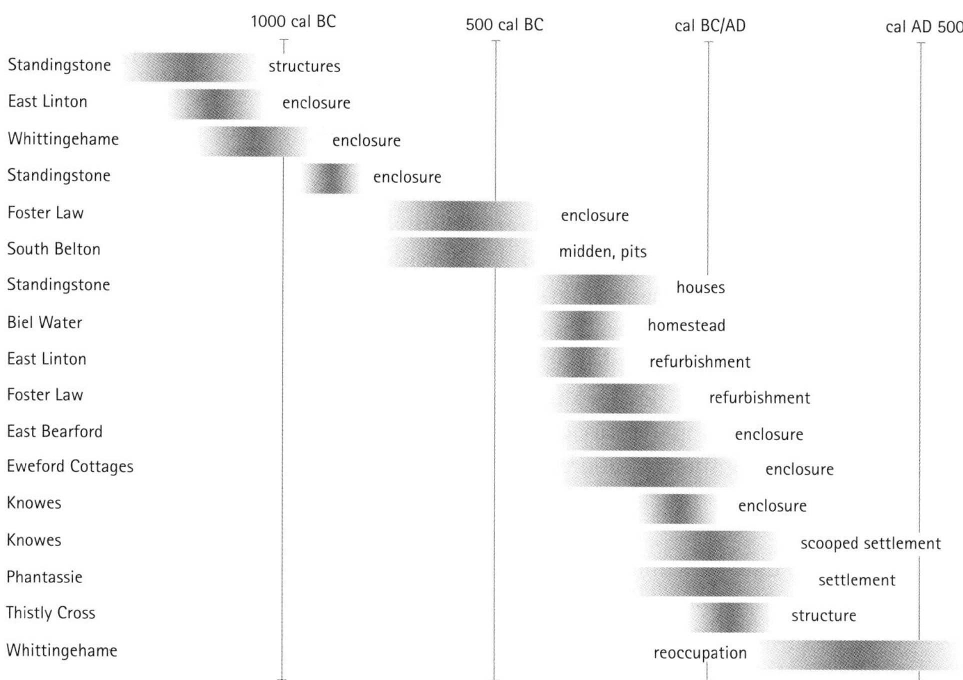

FIGURE 3.7 Chronological spans of radiocarbon-dated activity at later prehistoric sites around Traprain Law, Scotland. Some sites were excavated ahead of a new road (Lelong and McGregor 2007), the rest during a research project (Haselgrove 2009).

Source: adapted from Haselgrove (2009: fig. 11.1)

models and regional typo-chronologies that are suited to the tasks for which they are required (Collis 2008, 2019).

While the ability to date individual sites robustly is important, ultimately the greatest impact of Bayesian chronologies will be in enabling archaeologists to compare the timing and duration of events, and hence tempos of change, across Iron Age Europe, irrespective of prevailing models and terminologies. Already, scientific dating is indicating that some changes visible in the archaeological record were the outcome of long-drawn-out processes, whereas others represent short-lived episodes. For example, the main spate of hillfort construction in Britain was between *c.*450–350 BC, and the custom of chariot burial in East Yorkshire had a *floruit* of a few decades around 200 BC—in both cases, shorter time spans than previously allowed (Jay et al. 2012; Hamilton and Haselgrove 2019).

In the Circum-Alpine region, a flurry of timber road and bridge building in the later seventh century BC coincided with the intensification of Transalpine exchange networks (Nebelsick and Metzner-Nebelsick 2020: 48). If episodic phenomena were indeed frequent, the idea of framing typo-chronologies around 'horizons' (rather than phases) may have much to commend it (Collis 2008: 95–99). Robust site chronologies also open up the possibility of measuring the tempo of events at a scale of decades rather than centuries, for example how often buildings were replaced, enclosures refurbished, or farms relocated (Hamilton et al. 2015; Hamilton and Haselgrove 2019).

The resource created by scientific dating is dynamic, and will continue to grow in quality as well as quantity. New techniques and calibrations will enhance the precision of our frameworks, and existing dates can be remodelled to the latest standards.[16] Sites excavated in the past can be dated retrospectively, where suitable organic material survives in the archives (Needham and Ambers 1994) or can be obtained by targeted excavations, as at Glastonbury (Marshall et al. 2020). Where adequate stratigraphic controls exist, Bayesian approaches can be used to build tighter chronologies even for sites dated using bulk samples, as for some British hillforts (Hamilton et al. 2022) and the Irish 'Royal sites' (Bayliss and Grogan 2013). While the level of resolution may not be as good as for single-entity dates, the resultant site biographies are sufficiently detailed to reveal significant differences: the figure-of-eight enclosures at Navan, for example, proved to be much older than their counterparts at Tara and Dún Ailinne (Figure 3.8).

Being able to date sites and events to within the span of human lifetimes has major implications for the practice of Iron Age archaeology. It could help bridge the academic divide between the 'historical' Iron Age societies of the classical Mediterranean and their counterparts in the rest of Europe (see earlier), by allowing pre- and protohistorians to explore short-term episodes and patterns in behaviour in the way that historical archaeologists can, rather than having to focus on longer-term trends due to poor chronological resolution (Foxhall 2000).[17] Together, Bayesian chronologies and tree-ring dating will permit different forms of archaeological and environmental evidence (e.g. from pollen cores) to be properly integrated and deployed in wider historical debates (Bayliss 2009). As an example, timbers from successive builds of the rampart defending the *oppidum* at Metz yielded felling dates between 114–110 BC and then of 55 BC, highly suggestive of a link to the Gallic War, and before that to the marauding

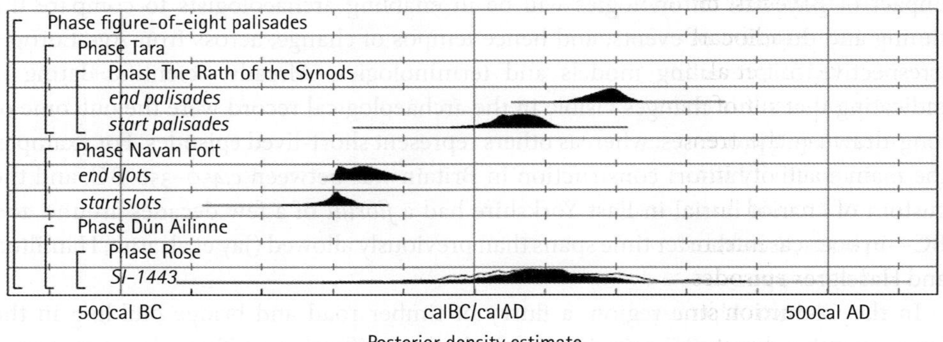

FIGURE 3.8 Probability distributions for the use of figure-of-eight palisade enclosures at the Rath of the Synods Tara, Navan, and Dún Ailinne, Ireland.

Source: Bayliss and Grogan (2013: fig. 22)

of the Cimbri and Teutones (Ralston 2019). Sometimes, we may even perceive the motivations of Iron Age people. The votive causeway built in 456 BC over the river Witham at Fiskerton (Britain) was reconstructed several times in the next 150 years at dates coinciding with midwinter lunar eclipses, suggesting a cosmological significance to the rebuilds (Field and Parker Pearson 2003).

Precise dating can also provide glimpses of the short timescales of 'lived life' and ordinary patterns of the everyday (Foxhall 2000: 484). At Black Loch of Myrton crannog, tree-ring dates established that oaks used for building one of the roundhouses were felled in winter/spring 437–436 BC and spring/summer of 435 BC (Crone et al. 2018). Alder and ash wood from the structure were also felled over a two-year period, suggesting that preparations for the work began twelve to eighteen months beforehand. Radiocarbon dates from successive hearths and floor layers, and deposits over the house indicate that it was only occupied for about a generation. The next-door house was also built in 435 BC.

As well as reconstructing additional individual site biographies, tree-ring data from crannogs in south-west Scotland will in time enable us to determine whether the foundation of these lake dwellings was part of a recurrent regional pattern or a short-lived episode, as well as how they fit in with settlement dynamics on dry land (Cavers and Crone 2018, 2019). The Cults Loch 3 crannog was constructed at much the same time as Black Loch. Multiple tree-ring data can also provide insights into the histories of larger, more complex sites. Over a hundred sequences from different areas of the *oppidum* on Mont Beuvray show that the peak period of building in timber on the hilltop occurred in the decades around 100 BC (Guichard et al. 2018: 201–205). At Hallstatt, dating of 763 wood samples from the mines by a combination of dendrochronology and radiocarbon 'wiggle-matching' has allowed the history of salt extraction to be elucidated, showing which galleries belonged to the same operational phase, and when they fell out of use (Grabner et al. 2021).

Ever more widespread use of scientific dating methods is also generating 'big data' that open the door to properly large-scale analysis of demographic and environmental trends during the first millennia BC and AD. In Ireland, where occupied sites are rare, a data set of 1,554 radiocarbon determinations was used as a proxy for analysing Iron Age settlement (Armit et al. 2013). This study revealed a low level of activity in the earlier Iron Age (the result of a decline starting in the late Bronze Age), a recovery after 400 BC—mirroring the trend across north-west Europe—and a second (unanticipated) reduction in activity in the Roman Iron Age (see Chapter 4). Radiocarbon dates from Britain and Ireland have been incorporated in an analysis spanning the Holocene, which examined inferred population levels in a long-term perspective, identifying these and other episodes of decline and recovery, which were then compared to changing food-production strategies and climatic factors (Bevan et al. 2017). Tree-ring data of course offer a direct means of reconstructing variations in rainfall and temperature over time (e.g. Büntgen et al. 2011), which can be combined with independently dated archaeological evidence for agricultural productivity, conflict, settlement densities, and anthropogenic impacts on the environment.

Overall, the prospects for dating different facets of life in Iron Age Europe look brighter than at any time in the past. There is every hope that we may look forward to an era when chronologies simply become a means to an end, as they are supposed to be, rather than an obstacle to overcome before we can make coherent sense of the Iron Age past.

Notes

1. Modern analytical studies suggest that most early objects were made from meteoric iron, but small amounts of iron were apparently smelted from the early second millennium BC in Anatolia (Erb-Satullo 2019: 563–566). Large-scale smelting does not seem to have taken off until the end of the second millennium BC.
2. Notable exceptions to such a sweeping generalization include the work of Anthony Snodgrass (1980b) and Ian Morris (1987), to cite just two of many.
3. In southern Britain, the first two centuries of the pre-Roman Iron Age are often referred to as the 'earliest' Iron Age, or the Bronze Age/Iron Age transition, adding to the complexities.
4. 'Hallstatt' and/or 'La Tène' (usually both) occur in nine of the fourteen regional chapters in this Handbook; Celtic is used as a synonym for La Tène in two further chapters.
5. Reinecke saw the Hallstatt period as a phase of transition between the Bronze and Iron Ages, during which iron gradually gained ascendancy over bronze, whereas Montelius and Déchelette adhered to the period divisions of the Three Age System. For background, see Sørensen and Rebay-Salisbury (2008).
6. In the mid-twentieth century, Hallstatt D3 in south-west Germany was thought to overlap with La Tène A elsewhere. This led many archaeologists to label this phase Hallstatt D3/La Tène A (e.g. Spindler 1983: 31), a usage still sometimes found today.
7. The chronology of the middle La Tène period rests primarily on the seriation of grave goods (e.g. Kysela 2020).
8. In some cases, there is a danger of circular argument, as finds from Iron Age settlements and cemeteries in temperate Europe have become the means of dating the imports, rather than vice versa—e.g. some types of Roman Republican wine serving equipment (Sueur 2018).
9. The difficulties of dating the cemeteries are partly due to a break in the arrival of new Roman coinage between the 80s BC and the Augustan period (cf. Kysela 2020: 51).
10. As Morris (1996) notes, the colonial evidence contributes nothing before 750 BC.
11. There are of course instances where good-quality building timber has been reused.
12. Spindler's (1983) chronology for Hallstatt D and La Tène A—starting the former at 550 BC—was predicated on tree-ring dates for Villingen that were seventy-one years too late.
13. Trachsel (2004) did in fact suggest a mid-seventh century BC date for the transition, but this found little favour.
14. See Ralston (2006: 213–215) for further references.
15. The extent to which the fourth and third centuries BC can be considered a pan-European turning point was the subject of a session at the 2018 meeting of the European Association of Archaeologists.
16. The current standard calibration curve is IntCal20, launched in 2020.
17. In Britain, archaeologists have been quick to adapt Bayesian approaches for the early Anglo-Saxon period, which is in effect an equivalent to the Long Iron Age in Scandinavia (e.g. Scull and Bayliss 1999; Hines 2021).

References

Armit, I., and J. McKenzie. 2013. *An Inherited Place: Broxmouth Hillfort and the South-East Scottish Iron Age*. Edinburgh: Society of Antiquaries of Scotland.

Armit, I., G. T. Swindles, and K. Becker. 2013. 'From dates to demography in later prehistoric Ireland? Experimental approaches to the meta-analysis of large 14C data-sets'. *Journal of Archaeological Science* 40, 1: 433–438.

Barnett, S. M. 2000. 'Luminescence dating of pottery from later prehistoric Britain'. *Archaeometry* 42, 2: 431–457.

Bayliss, A. 2009. 'Rolling out revolution: Using radiocarbon dating in archaeology'. *Radiocarbon* 51, 1: 123–147.

Bayliss, A., and E. Grogan. 2013. 'Chronologies for Tara and comparable royal sites of the Irish Iron Age', in M. O'Sullivan, C. Scarre, and M. Doyle (eds) *Tara: From the Past to the Future*: 105–144. Dublin: Wordwell.

Berranger, M. 2014. *Le Fer, entre matière première et moyen d'échange, en France, du VIIe au Ier siècle avant J.-C : Approches interdisciplinaires*. Dijon: Éditions Universitaires de Dijon.

Bevan, A., S. Colledge, D. Fuller, R. Fyfe, S. Shennan, and C. Stevens. 2017. 'Holocene fluctuations in human population demonstrate repeated links to food production and climate'. *Proceedings of the National Academy of Sciences* 114, 49: E10524–E10531. Available at www.pnas.org/cgi/doi/10.1073/pnas.1709190114 [accessed 15 August 2022].

Billamboz, A. 2008. 'Stand der Dendrochronologie der Eisenzeit nördlich der Alpen mit neuen Daten aus der Heuneburg-Vorburg', in D. Krausse (ed.) *Frühe Zentralisierungs- und Urbanisierungsprozesse: Zur Genese und Entwicklung frühkeltischer Fürstensitze und ihres territorialen Umlandes: Kolloquium des DFG-Schwerpunktprogramms 1171 in Blaubeuren, 9.–11. Oktober 2006: Festschrift Jörg Biel*. Forschungen und Berichte zur Vor- und Frühgeschichte in Baden-Württemberg 101: 229–248. Stuttgart: Theiss.

Büntgen, U., W. Tegel, K. Nicolussi, M. McCormick, D. Frank, V. Trouet, et al. 2011. '2500 years of European climate variability and human susceptibility'. *Science* 331, 6017: 578–582.

Cavers, G., and A. Crone. 2018. *A Lake Dwelling in its Landscape: Iron Age Settlement at Cults Loch, Castle Kennedy, Dumfries & Galloway*. Oxford: Oxbow Books.

Cavers, G., and A. Crone. 2019. 'The chronology of wetland settlement and its impact on Iron Age settlement dynamics in southwest Scotland', in D. C. Cowley, M. Fernández-Götz, T. Romankiewicz, and H. Wendling (eds) *Rural Settlement: Relating Buildings, Landscape, and People in the European Iron Age*: 115–124. Leiden: Sidestone Press.

Clark, A. 1991. 'Archaeomagnetic dating', in N. Sharples, *Maiden Castle: Excavations and Field Survey 1985–6*. English Heritage Archaeological Report 19: 105. London: English Heritage.

Collis, J. 1984. *The European Iron Age*. London: Batsford.

Collis, J. 2008. 'Constructing chronologies: Lessons from the Iron Age', in A. Lehoërff (ed.) *Construire le Temps: Histoire et méthodes des chronologies et calendriers des derniers millénaires avant notre ère en Europe occidentale: Actes du 30e colloque international de Halma-Ipel, UMR 8164 (CNRS, Lille 3, MCC) 7–9 décembre 2006, Lille*. Collection Bibracte 16: 85–104. Glux-en-Glenne: Centre archéologique européen.

Collis, J. 2019. 'Oram's Arbour, Winchester: A new interpretation', in T. Romankiewicz, M. Fernández-Götz, G. Lock, and O. Buchsenschutz (eds) *Enclosing Space, Opening New Ground: Iron Age Studies from Scotland to Mainland Europe*: 65–85. Oxford: Oxbow Books.

Crone, A., G. Cavers, E. Allison, K. Davies, W. D. Hamilton, A. Henderson, et al. 2018. 'Nasty, brutish and short? The life cycle of an Iron Age roundhouse at Black Loch of Myrton, SW Scotland'. *Journal of Wetland Archaeology* 18, 2: 138–162.

Danielisová, A. 2020. 'Bohemia at the end of the La Tène period: Objects, materials, chronology, and main development trends—a review'. *Památky Archeologické* 111: 113–157.

Déchelette, J. 1913. *Manuel d'Archéologie Préhistorique, Celtique et Gallo-Romaine. II-2: Premier âge du Fer ou époque de Hallstatt*. Paris: Picard.

Déchelette, J. 1914. *Manuel d'Archéologie Préhistorique, Celtique et Gallo-Romaine. II-3: Deuxième âge du Fer ou époque de La Tène*. Paris: Picard.

Dehn, W., and O. H. Frey. 1979. 'Southern imports and the Hallstatt and early La Tène chronology of central Europe', in D. Ridgeway and F. Ridgeway (eds) *Italy Before the Romans: The Iron Age, Orientalizing and Etruscan Periods*: 489–511. London: Academic Press.

Demoule, J.-P. 1999. *Chronologie et société dans les nécropoles celtiques de la culture Aisne-Marne du Vie au IIIe siècle avant notre ère*. Revue Archéologique de Picardie Numéro spécial 15. Amiens: Revue Archéologique de Picardie.

Erb-Satullo, N. L. 2019. 'The Innovation and Adoption of Iron in the Ancient Near East'. *Journal of Archaeological Research* 27, 4: 557–607.

Field, N., and M. Parker Pearson. 2003. *Fiskerton: An Iron Age Timber Causeway with Iron Age and Roman Votive Offerings*. Oxford: Oxbow Books.

Fitzpatrick, A. P., W. D. Hamilton, and C. Haselgrove. 2017. 'Radiocarbon dating and modelling of a late Iron Age cremation cemetery at Westhampnett, West Sussex, UK'. *Archäologisches Korrespondenzblatt* 47, 3: 359–381.

Foxhall, L. 2000. 'The running sands of time: Archaeology and the short-term'. *World Archaeology* 31, 3: 484–498.

Friedrich, M., and H. Hennig. 1996. 'A dendrodate for the Wehringen Iron Age wagon grave (778 ± 5 BC) in relation to other recently obtained absolute dates for the Hallstatt period in southern Germany'. *Journal of European Archaeology* 4, 1: 281–303.

Garrow, D., and C. Gosden. 2012. *Technologies of Enchantment? Exploring Celtic Art 400 BC–100 AD*. Oxford: Oxford University Press.

Garrow, D., C. Gosden, J. D. Hill, and C. Bronk Ramsey. 2009. 'Dating Celtic art: A major radiocarbon dating programme of Iron Age and early Roman metalwork'. *Archaeological Journal* 166, 1: 79–123.

Gartski, K. 2019. 'The social production of iron in first millennium BC Ireland'. *Oxford Journal of Archaeology* 38, 4: 443–463.

Gimatzidis, S., and B. Weninger. 2020. 'Radiocarbon dating the Greek Protogeometric and Geometric periods: The evidence of Sindos'. *PLoS ONE* 15, 5: e0232906. Available at https://doi.org/10.1371/journal.pone.0232906 [accessed 15 August 2022].

Grabner, M., E. Wächter, K. Nicolussi, M. Bolka, T. Sormaz, P. Steier, et al. 2021. 'Prehistoric salt mining in Hallstatt, Austria. New chronologies out of small wooden fragments'. *Dendrochronologia* 66, 2: 125814. Available at https://doi.org/10.1016/j.dendro.2021.125814 [accessed 15 August 2022].

Graue, J. 1974. *Die Gräberfelder von Ornavasso: Eine Studie zur Chronologie der späten Latène- und frühen Kaiserzeit*. Hamburger Beiträge zur Archäologie Beiheft 1. Hamburg: Helmut Buske Verlag.

Guggisberg, M. A. 2007. 'Zur absoluten Chronologie der späten Hallstatt- und frühen Latènezeit: der Beitrag der Klassischen Archäologie'. Available at http://hdl.handle.net/10900/44022 [accessed 15 August 2022].

Guichard, V., A. Meunier, and P. Paris. 2018. 'Chronique des recherches sur le Mont Beuvray 2013–2016'. *Revue Archéologique de l'Est* 67: 151–211.

Hamilton, W. D., J. A. Horn, S. Adams, K. McCaskill, and S. McDonald. 2022. 'More detailed approaches to dating the Iron Age hillforts of Britain', in G. Lock and I. Ralston (eds) *Atlas of the Hillforts of Britain and Ireland*: 342–368. Edinburgh: Edinburgh University Press.

Hamilton, W. D., and C. Haselgrove. 2019. 'Exploring settlement dynamics through radiocarbon dating', in T. Romankiewicz, M. Fernández-Götz, G. Lock, and O. Buchsenschutz (eds) *Enclosing Space, Opening New Ground: Iron Age Studies from Scotland to Mainland Europe*: 111–119. Oxford: Oxbow Books.

Hamilton, W. D., C. Haselgrove, and C. Gosden. 2015. 'The impact of Bayesian chronologies on the British Iron Age'. *World Archaeology* 47, 642–660.

Harding, A., and W. Raczkowski. 2010. 'Living on the lake in the Iron Age: New results from aerial photographs, geophysical survey and dendrochronology on sites of Biskupin type'. *Antiquity* 84, 324: 386–404.

Harding, D. W. 2017. *The Iron Age in Northern Britain: Britons and Romans, Natives and Settlers*. London: Routledge.

Haselgrove, C. 2009. *The Traprain Law Environs Project: Excavations and Fieldwork 2000–2004*. Edinburgh: Society of Antiquaries of Scotland.

Haselgrove, C. 2019. 'The Gallic War in the chronology of Iron Age coinage', in A. P. Fitzpatrick, and C. Haselgrove (eds) Julius *Caesar's Battle for Gaul: New Archaeological Perspectives*: 241–266. Oxford: Oxbow Books.

Haselgrove, C., and R. Pope. 2007. 'Characterising the earlier Iron Age', in C. Haselgrove and R. Pope (eds) *The Earlier Iron Age in Britain and the Near Continent*: 1–23. Oxford: Oxbow Books.

Haselgrove, C., and V. Guichard. 2013. 'Les gaulois sont-ils dans la plaine? Reflections on settlement patterns in Gaul in the 1st century BC', in S. Krausz, A. Colin, K. Gruel, I. Ralston, and T. Dechezleprêtre (eds) *L'âge du Fer en Europe: Mélanges offerts à Olivier Buchsenschutz*: 317–328. Bordeaux: Ausonius.

Haselgrove, C., W. D. Hamilton, C. Gosden, L. Davenport, and C. Poole. forthcoming. *Iron Age Settlement and Society in Central Southern Britain: A New Chronological Perspective*. Oxford: Oxford University School of Archaeology Monographs.

Hedeager, L. 1992. *Iron Age Societies: From Tribe to State in Northern Europe, 500 BC–AD 700*. Oxford: Blackwell.

Herschend, F. 2016. 'Towards a standardized discussion of priors in Bayesian analyses of 14C dated archaeological periods: A study based on the dates from Gjøsund'. *Journal of Archaeology and Ancient History* 19: 1–28.

Hildebrand, H. 1876. *Sur les commencements de l'âge du Fer en Europe: Congrès Internationale d'Anthropologie et d'Archéologie Préhistorique*. Stockholm: P. A. Norstedt.

Hines, J. 2021. 'The chronological framework of early Anglo-Saxon graves and grave goods. New radiocarbon data from RAF Lakenheath, Eriswell, Suffolk, and a new calibration curve (IntCal20)'. *Antiquaries Journal* 101: 106–142.

Hodson, F. R. 1968. *The La Tène Cemetery at Münsingen-Rain: Catalogue and Relative Chronology*. Acta Bernensia 5. Bern: Stämpfli.

Hodson, F. R. 1990. *Hallstatt: The Ramsauer Graves: Quantification and Analysis*. RGZM Monographien 16. Mainz: Römisch-Germanisches Zentralmuseum.

Holzer, V. 2008. 'Ein latènezeitlicher Getreidespeicher aus der keltischen Grosssieldlung am Sandberg in Roseldorf (Niederösterreich)'. *Germania* 86, 1: 135–179.

Jay, M., C. Haselgrove, W. D. Hamilton, J. D. Hill, and J. Dent. 2012. 'Chariots and context: New radiocarbon dates from Wetwang and the chronology of Iron Age burials and brooches in East Yorkshire'. *Oxford Journal of Archaeology* 31, 2: 161–189.

Kaenel, G. 1990. 'La dendrochronologie appliquée aux IIe et Ier siècles avant J.C.', in A. Duval, J.-P. Morel, and Y. Roman (eds) *Gaule interne et Gaule Méditerranéenne aux IIe et Ier siècles avant J.C.: Confrontations chronologiques*. Revue Archéologique de Narbonnaise, supplément 21: 321–326. Paris: Éditions CNRS.

Kaenel, G. 2008. 'Entre histoire et typologies: les chronologies de la période de La Tène', in A. Lehoërff (ed.) *Construire le Temps: Histoire et méthodes des chronologies et calendriers des derniers millénaires avant notre ère en Europe occidentale: Actes du 30e colloque international de Halma-Ipel, UMR 8164 (CNRS, Lille 3, MCC) 7–9 décembre 2006, Lille*. Collection Bibracte 16: 321–326. Glux-en-Glenne: Centre archéologique européen.

Kossack, G. 1959. *Südbayern während der Hallstattzeit*. Römisch-Germanische Forschungen 25. Berlin: De Gruyter.

Krausse, D. 2006. *Eisenzeitlicher Kulturwandel und Romanisierung im Mosel-Eifel Raum*. Römisch-Germanische Forschungen 63. Mainz: Philipp von Zabern.

Krausse, D., N. Ebinger-Rist, S. Million, A. Billamboz, J. Wahl, and E. Stephan. 2017. 'The "Keltenblock" project: Discovery and excavation of a rich Hallstatt grave at the Heuneburg, Germany'. *Antiquity* 91, 355: 108–123.

Kristiansen, K. 1998. *Europe before History*. Cambridge: Cambridge University Press.

Kysela, J. 2020. *Things and Thoughts: Central Europe and the Mediterranean in the 4th–1st centuries BC*. Studia Hercynia monographs 1. Prague: Charles University.

Lambert, G. 2008. 'A century for dendrochronology and archaeology quiet activities', in A. Lehoërff (ed.) *Construire le Temps: Histoire et méthodes des chronologies et calendriers des derniers millénaires avant notre ère en Europe occidentale: Actes du 30e colloque international de Halma-Ipel, UMR 8164 (CNRS, Lille 3, MCC) 7–9 décembre 2006, Lille*. Collection Bibracte 16: 113–122. Glux-en-Glenne: Centre archéologique européen.

Lelong, O., and G. MacGregor (eds). 2007. *The Lands of Ancient Lothian: Interpreting the Archaeology of the A1*. Edinburgh: Society of Antiquaries of Scotland.

Macdonald, P. 2007. 'Perspectives on insular La Tène art', in C. Haselgrove and T. Moore (eds) *The Later Iron Age in Britain and Beyond*: 329–338. Oxford: Oxbow Books.

Marshall, P., R. Brunning, S. Minnitt, C. Bronk Ramsey, E. Dunbar, and P. J. Reimer. 2020. 'The chronology of Glastonbury Lake Village'. *Antiquity* 94, 378: 1464–1481.

Millard, A. 2013. 'Appendix 7. Integrated dating analysis', in J. Zant and C. Howard-Davis, *Scots Dyke to Turnpike: The Archaeology of the A66, Greta Bridge to Scotch Corner*. Lancaster Imprints 18: 203–207. Lancaster: Oxford Archaeology North.

Miron, A. 1986. 'Das Gräberfeld von Horath: Untersuchungen zur Mittel- und Spätlatènezeit im Saar-Mosel-Raum'. *Trierer Zeitschrift* 49: 7–198.

Miron, A. 1991. 'Die späte Eisenzeit im Hunsrück-Nahe-Raum: mittel- und spätlatènezeitliche Gräberfelder', in A. Haffner and A. Miron (eds) Studien zur Eisenzeit im Hunsrück-Nahe-Raum. Trierer Zeitschrift Beiheft 13: 151–169. Trier: Rheinisches Landesmuseum Trier.

Montelius, O. 1895–7. 'Den nordiska Jernålderns kronologi 1–3'. *Svenska Fornminnesföreningens Tidskrift* 9, 2: 155–214.

Montelius, O. 1986 [1885]. *Dating in the Bronze Age with special reference to Scandinavia*. Kungliga Vitterhets Historie och Antikvitets Akademien Handlingar 30. Stockholm: Kungliga Vitterhets Historie och Antikvitets Akademien.

Moore, T., and X.-L. Armada. 2011. 'Crossing the divide: Opening a dialogue on approaches to western European first millennium BC studies', in T. Moore and X.-L. Armada (eds) *Atlantic Europe in the First Millennium BC: Crossing the Divide*: 3–77. Oxford: Oxford University Press.

Morillo, Á., and F. Sala-Sellés. 2019. 'The Sertorian wars in the conquest of Hispania: From data to archaeological assessment', in A. P. Fitzpatrick and C. Haselgrove (eds) Julius *Caesar's Battle for Gaul: New Archaeological Perspectives*: 49–72. Oxford: Oxbow Books.

Morris, I. 1987. *Burial and Ancient Society: The Rise of the Greek City-State.* Cambridge: Cambridge University Press.

Morris, I. 1996. 'The absolute chronology of the Greek colonies in Sicily'. *Acta Archaeologica* 67: 51–59.

Mortillet, G. de. 1876. *Tableau archéologique de la Gaule.* Paris: Ernest Leroux.

Moser, S. 2010. *Die Kelten am Dürrnberg: Eisenzeit am Nordrand der Alpen.* Schriften aus dem Keltenmuseum Hallein 1. Hallein: Keltenmuseum Hallein.

Nebelsick, L., and C. Metzner-Nebelsick. 2020. 'From Genoa to Günzburg. New trajectories of urbanisation and acculturation between the Mediterranean and south-central Europe', in L. Zamboni, M. Fernández-Götz, and C. Metzner-Nebelsick (eds) *Crossing the Alps: Early Urbanism Between Northern Italy and Central Europe (900–400 BC)*: 43–69. Leiden: Sidestone Press.

Needham, S. 2007. '800 BC, the Great Divide', in C. Haselgrove and R. Pope (eds) *The Earlier Iron Age in Britain and the Near Continent*: 39–63. Oxford: Oxbow Books.

Needham, S., and J. Ambers. 1994. 'Redating Rams Hill and reconsidering Bronze Age enclosure'. *Proceedings of the Prehistoric Society* 60, 1: 225–243.

Nimura, C., H. Chittock, P. Hommel, and C. Gosden (eds). 2020. *Art in the Eurasian Iron Age: Context, Connections and Scale.* Oxford: Oxbow Books.

Olivier, L. 2019. 'The second battle of Alesia: The 19th-century investigations at Alise-Sainte-Reine and international recognition of the Gallic period of the late Iron Age', in A. P. Fitzpatrick and C. Haselgrove (eds) Julius *Caesar's Battle for Gaul: New Archaeological Perspectives*: 285–309. Oxford: Oxbow Books.

Osborne, R. 1996. *Greece in the Making 1200–479 BC.* London: Routledge.

Pare, C. F. E. 1991. *Swords, Wagon-Graves, and the Beginning of the Early Iron Age in Central Europe: Kleine Schriften aus dem Vorgeschichtlichen Seminar Marburg.* Marburg: Universität Marburg.

Pare, C. F. E. 1996. 'Chronology in Central Europe at the end of the Bronze Age'. *Acta Archaeologica* 67: 99–120.

Pare, C. F. E. 1998. 'Beiträge zum Übergang von der Bronze- zur Eisenzeit in Mitteleuropa. Teil I. Grundzüge der Chronologie im östlichen Mitteleuropa (11.–8. Jahrhundert v. Chr.)'. *Jahrbuch des Römisch-Germanischen Zentralmuseums Mainz* 45, 1: 293–433.

Parzinger, H. 1988. *Chronologie der Späthallstatt- und Frühlatènezeit: Studien zu Fundgruppen zwischen Mosel und Save: Acta Humaniora.* Quellen und Forschungen zur prähistorischen und provinzialrömischen Archäologie 4. Weinheim: VCH.

Price, N. 2020. *The Children of Ash and Elm: A History of the Vikings.* London: Allen Lane.

Prieto Martínez, M. P., Y. Alvarez González, M. Fernández-Götz, M. V. García Quintela, A. C. González García, and L. F. López González. 2017. 'The contribution of Bayesian analysis to the chronology of Iron Age north-western Iberia: New data from San Cibrán de Las (Galicia, Spain)'. *Journal of Archaeological Science: Reports* 16: 397–408.

Ralston, I. 2006. *Celtic Fortifications*. Stroud: Tempus.

Ralston, I. 2019. 'The Gauls on the eve of the Roman conquest', in A. P. Fitzpatrick and C. Haselgrove (eds) *Julius Caesar's Battle for Gaul: New Archaeological Perspectives*: 19–47. Oxford: Oxbow Books.

Rebay-Salisbury, K. 2016. *The Human Body in Early Iron Age Central Europe: Burial Practices and Images of the Hallstatt World*. London: Routledge.

Reece-Jones, J., and M. Tite. 2003. 'Appendix 1: Optically stimulated luminescence (OSL) dating results from the White Horse and linear ditch', in D. Miles, S. Palmer, G. Lock, C. Gosden, and A. M. Cromarty, *Uffington White Horse and its Landscape: Investigations at White Horse Hill Uffington, 1989–95 and Tower Hill Ashbury, 1993–4*. Thames Valley Landscapes Monograph 18: 269–271. Oxford: Oxford Archaeology.

Reinecke, P. 1965. *Mainzer Aufsätze zur Chronologie der Bronze- und Eisenzeit. Nachdrucke aus Altertümer unserer heidnischen Vorzeit und Festschrift RGZM 1901*. Bonn: Habelt.

Rieckhoff, S. 1995. *Süddeutschland im Spannungsfeld von Kelten, Germanen und Römern: Studien zur Chronologie der Spätlatènezeit im südlichen Mitteleuropa*. Trierer Zeitschrift Beiheft 19. Trier: Rheinisches Landesmuseum.

Rieckhoff, S. 2012. 'L'histoire de la chronologie de La Tène finale en Europe centrale et le paradigme de continuité', in P. Barral and S. Fichtl (eds) *Regards sur la chronologie de la fin de l'âge du Fer (IIIe–Ier siècle avant notre ère) en Gaule non-méditerannéenne: Actes de la table ronde tenue à Bibracte du 15 au 17 octobre 2007*. Collection Bibracte 22: 25–38. Glux-en-Glenne: Centre archéologique européen.

Rose, H. A. 2020. 'Bayesian chronological modelling of the Early Iron Age in southern Jutland, Denmark'. PhD thesis, Kiel University.

Rose, H. A., N. Müller-Scheessel, J. Meadows, and C. Hamann. 2022. 'Radiocarbon dating and Hallstatt chronology: A Bayesian chronological model for the burial sequence at Dietfurt an der Altmühl "Tennisplatz", Bavaria, Germany'. *Archaeological and Anthropological Sciences* 14: 72. Available at https://doi.org/10.1007/s12520-022-01542-1 [accessed 15 August 2022].

Scull, C., and Bayliss, A. 1999. 'Radiocarbon dating and Anglo-Saxon graves', in U. von Freeden, U. Koch, and A. Wieczorek (eds) *Völker an Nord- und Ostsee und die Franken: Aken des 48. Sachsensymposiums in Mannheim vom 7. bis 11. September 1997*: 39–50. Bonn: Habelt.

Snodgrass, A. M. 1980a. 'Iron and early metallurgy in the Mediterranean', in T. A. Wertime and J. D. Muhly (eds) *The Coming of the Age of Iron*: 335–374. New Haven, CT: Yale University Press.

Snodgrass, A. M. 1980b. *Archaic Greece: The Age of Experiment*. London: Dent.

Sørensen, M. L. S., and K. Rebay-Salisbury. 2008. 'The impact of 19th century ideas on the construction of "Urnfield" as chronological and cultural concept', in A. Lehoërff (ed.) *Construire le Temps: Histoire et méthodes des chronologies et calendriers des derniers millénaires avant notre ère en Europe occidentale: Actes du 30e colloque international de Halma-Ipel, UMR 8164 (CNRS, Lille 3, MCC) 7–9 décembre 2006, Lille*. Collection Bibracte 16: 57–67. Glux-en-Glenne: Centre archéologique européen.

Sormaz, T., and T. Stöllner. 2005. 'Zwei hallstattzeitliche Grabkammern vom Dürrnberg bei Hallein—Neue dendrochronologische Ergebnisse zum Übergang von der Hallstatt- zur Frühlatènezeit'. *Archäologisches Korrepondenzblatt* 35, 3: 361–376.

Spindler, K. 1983. *Die frühen Kelten*. Stuttgart: Reclam.

Stoddart, S. (ed.) 2017. *Delicate Urbanism in Context: Settlement Nucleation in Pre-Roman Germany*. Cambridge: McDonald Institute for Archaeological Research.

Stöllner, T. 2003. 'The economy of Dürrnberg-bei-Hallein: An Iron Age salt-mining centre in the Austrian Alps'. *Antiquaries Journal* 83: 123–194.

Sueur, Q. 2018. *La vaisselle métallique en Gaule septentrionale à la veille de la Conquête: Typologie, fonction et diffusion*. Monographie instrumentum 55. Drémil Lafage: Éditions Mergoil.

Teržan, B., and M. Črešna. 2014. *Absolute Dating of the Bronze and Iron Ages in Slovenia*. Katalogi in Monografije 40. Ljubljana: Narodni musej Slovenije.

Tischler, O. 1881. 'Gliederung der vorrömischen Metallzeit'. *Korrespondenzblatt der Deutschen Gesellschaft für Anthropologie, Ethnologie und Urgeschichte* 12: 121–127.

Tischler, O. 1885. 'Über die Gliederung der La Tène Periode und über die Dekorierung der Eisenwaffen in dieser Zeit'. *Korrespondenzblatt der Deutschen Gesellschaft für Anthropologie, Ethnologie und Urgeschichte* 14: 157–161.

Torbrügge, W. 1991. 'Die frühe Hallstattzeit (HA C) in chronologischen Ansätzen und notwendige Randbemerkungen I. Bayern und der "westliche Hallstattkreis"'. *Jahrbuch des Römisch-Germanischen Zentralmuseums Mainz* 38, 2: 223–463.

Torbrügge, W. 1992. 'Die frühe Hallstattzeit (HA C) in chronologischen Ansätzen und notwendige Randbemerkungen II. Der sogenannte östliche Hallstattkreis'. *Jahrbuch des Römisch-Germanischen Zentralmuseums Mainz* 39, 2: 425–615.

Trachsel, M. 2004. *Untersuchungen zur relativen und absoluten Chronologie der Hallstattzeit*. Universitätsforschungen zur Prähistorischen Archäologie 104. Bonn: Habelt.

Waddington, K., A. Bayliss, T. Higham, R. Madgwick, and N. Sharples. 2019. 'Histories of deposition: Creating chronologies for the late Bronze Age–early Iron Age transition in southern Britain'. *Archaeological Journal* 176, 1: 84–133.

Ważny, T. 1994. 'Dendrochronology of Biskupin—absolute chronology of the Iron Age settlement'. *Bulletin of the Polish Academy of Sciences, Biological Sciences* 43, 3: 283–289.

Wells, P. S. 2012. *How Ancient Europeans saw the World: Vision, Patterns and the Shaping of the Mind in Prehistoric Times*. Princeton: Princeton University Press.

Zamboni, L., M. Fernández-Götz, and C. Metzner-Nebelsick (eds). 2020. *Crossing the Alps: Early Urbanism Between Northern Italy and Central Europe (900–400 BC)*. Leiden: Sidestone Press.

Zvelebil, M. 1985. 'Iron Age transformations in northern Russia and the northeast Baltic', in G. Barker and C. Gamble (eds) *Beyond Domestication in Prehistoric Europe*: 147–180. London: Academic Press.

PART II

REGIONAL SYNTHESES

CHAPTER 4

NORTH-WEST EUROPE

COLIN HASELGROVE AND SOPHIE KRAUSZ

Introduction

This chapter focuses on the pre-Roman Iron Age in non-Mediterranean France, the Low Countries, Britain, and Ireland, following through into the early centuries AD in areas not incorporated into the Roman Empire. In recent decades, our understanding of Iron Age societies in north-west Europe has benefited greatly from development-led excavations on an unprecedented scale, often in areas that previously received little attention (Bradley et al. 2016; Guilane and Garcia 2018). Among other things, this has greatly expanded our knowledge of rural settlement, especially unenclosed sites, complementing earlier research concentrated on upstanding fortified sites and burial mounds.

Significant regional diversity is apparent across north-west Europe, but also many common trends. Rather than acting as a barrier, the sea was a unifying factor. The short crossings to Britain and Ireland were comfortably within the capabilities and range of Iron Age sailing vessels, ensuring good connectivity between mainland Europe and the offshore islands. The Irish Sea was also a crucial element in a long-lived maritime corridor extending some 2,000 km from the Shetland Islands to Iberia (Cunliffe 2015). Inland routes by water and land were increasingly well developed during the period too, with travel further speeded up in the late Iron Age by the building of timber bridges across significant rivers.

While the nature and intensity of interaction varied in time and space, insular Iron Age developments broadly echo changes in mainland Europe. Many implement types appearing for the first time take identical forms on both sides of the Channel (Webley 2015). Not all influence was from south to north. Insular swords played a key role in the evolution of Hallstatt C sword types (Milcent 2017) and, in the later Iron Age, rotary querns may have been introduced from Britain to northern France.[1] The much-cited contrast between insular circular architecture and continental rectangular houses has been blurred by the discovery of several circular structures in northern France and

FIGURE 4.1 Map of principal Iron Age sites in north-west Europe.
France: 1 Acy-Romance, 2 Batilly-en-Gâtinais, 3 Bobigny, 4 Bourges, 5 Bragny-sur-Saône, 6 Châteaumeillant, 7 Chavéria, 8 Condé-sur-Suippe, 9 Corent, 10 Aulnat-Gandaillat, 11 Crévéchamps, 12 Fléré-la-Rivière, 13 Gournay-sur-Aronde, 14 Grotte des Perrats, Agris, 15 Isle-Saint-Georges, 16 Ifs, 17 Lacoste, 18 Lavau, 19 Levroux, 20 Luant, 21 Lyon-Vaise, 22 Marsal, 23 Mez-Notariou, Ouessant, 24 Mont Beuvray, 25 Moulay, 26 Orléans, 27 Paule-Saint-Symphorien, 28 Le Plessis-Gassot, 29 Le Puy d'Issolud, Vayrac, 30 Reims, 31 Ribemont-sur-Ancre, 32 Thézy-Glimont, 33 Tintignac, 34 Trégueux, 35 Urville-Nacqueville, 36 Villejoubert, Saint-Denis-des-Murs, 37 Villeneuve-Saint-Germain, 38 Vix-Le Mont Lassois. *Belgium*: 39 Beringen, 40 Kemmelberg, 41 Kontich-Alfberg. *Luxembourg*: 42 Goeblange-Nospelt, 43 Titelberg. *Netherlands*: 44 Assendelver Polders, 45 Bernisse, 46 Den Haag, 47 Empel, 48 Ezinge, 49 Geldermalsen,

rectangular buildings in Britain (Haselgrove 2001). The same applies to burials. The low visibility of mortuary practices in Britain and Ireland for much of the Iron Age is replicated in parts of mainland Europe, where burials are similarly restricted to certain regions, phases, and sections of society.

Most regions discussed here are relatively low-lying, some including extensive wetlands and coastal areas prone to inundation in times of rising sea level. The Massif Central and the Jura-Vosges mountains are the only really high ground; other upland expanses include the Belgian Ardennes, and much of western Britain and Ireland. The constraints on land use posed by latitude and topography were exacerbated by cooler, wetter conditions at the start of the Iron Age, and briefly in the mid-first millennium BC (Brun and Ruby 2008: 55). Mixed farming was nevertheless the norm in most areas, albeit with more emphasis on animal husbandry in uplands and the wetter Atlantic regions, as well as on poorer lowland soils such as the cover sands at the western end of the North European Plain in the Low Countries. In upland areas, our understanding is hindered by poor artefact and bone preservation due to soil acidity, albeit offset to some extent by better earthwork survival in areas that have escaped intensive agriculture and by the widespread use of drystone construction in the Atlantic zone (including Brittany), where some Iron Age buildings and enclosure walls still stand metres high (Henderson 2007).

Landscape and connectivity helped shape cultural links and divides within north-west Europe (Figure 4.1). Throughout later prehistory, coastal communities in the west participated in maritime networks extending along the Atlantic seaboard (Milcent 2012; Cunliffe 2015), whereas eastern Britain looked across the North Sea towards the heart of Europe, a difference in outlook accentuated by the Pennine uplands down the spine of

---

50 Hannut, 51 Haps, 52 Heunen, 53 Koningsbosch, 54 Mierlo-Hout, 55 Oss, 56 Someren, 57 Tiel-Passewaaij, 58 Weert, 59 Zeijen, 60 Zeist. *England*: 61 Bagendon, 62 Bredon Hill, 63 Bryher, Scilly, 64 Burrough Hill, 65 Colchester, 66 Crick, 67 Crickley Hill, 68 Danebury, 69 Deal, 70 Fin Cop, 71 Fiskerton, 72 Fison Way, Thetford, 73 Garton-Wetwang Slack, 74 Glastonbury, 75 Hallaton, 76 Ham Hill, 77 Hengistbury Head, 78 Hunsbury, 79 Leicester, 80 Little Woodbury, 81 Maiden Castle, 82 Mucking, 83 Must Farm, 84 Newcastle Great Park, 85 Pimperne, 86 Pocklington, 87 Silchester, 88 Snettisham, 89 St Albans, 90 Stanwick, 91 Sutton Common, 92 Trevelgue Head, 93 Westhampnett, 94 Winchester, 95 Winterbourne Kingston, 96 Wittenham Clumps, 97 Yarnton. *Ireland (RoI and NI)*: 98 Barrees, 99 Baysrath, 100 Broighter, 101 Carrickmines Great, 102 Clonycavan, 103 Cloongownagh, 104 Corlea, 105 Drumanagh, 106 Dún Aonghasa, 107 Killalane, 108 Killoran, 109 Knockaulin, 110 Knockcommane, 111 Lough Gara, 112 Navan, 113 Newgrange, 114 Old Croghan, 115 Rathcroghan, 116 Rathgall, 117 Rosepark, 118 Tara. *Scotland*: 119 Birnie, 120 Blair Drummond, 121 Broxmouth, 122 Caterthuns, 123 Clachtoll, 124 Cnip, Lewis, 125 Cults Loch, 126 Dunnicaer, 127 Gurness, Orkney, 128 Howe, Orkney, 129 Milla Skerra, Shetland, 130 Old Scatness, Shetland, 131 Over Rig, 132 Tap O'Noth, 133 Traprain Law. *Wales*: 134 Breiddin, 135 Castell Henllys, 136 Llanmaes, 137 Llyn Cerrig Bach, Anglesey, 138 Meillonydd.

Drawing: R. Salisbury for authors

central Britain. On the mainland, the barrier of the Mittelgebirge—with the Ardennes at their tip—added to the separation of the North European Plain from the core of Hallstatt and La Tène Europe, while the Massif Central delimited this zone from Mediterranean France, as well as channelling contacts with the Graeco-Roman world towards the Rhône valley and the Garonne basin.

Agriculture

As agriculture underpinned all other aspects of Iron Age societies, a brief overview is useful before examining cultural developments. Communities across the region typically practised some form of mixed farming, employing agro-pastoral strategies adapted to climatic and environmental conditions. Wheat (emmer, spelt, or bread wheat) and barley (naked or hulled) were the principal cereals, with millet, oats, and rye grown in some areas, sometimes possibly for fodder (see Chapter 18). Peas, beans, lentils, bitter vetch, and flax were also widely cultivated. In the earlier Iron Age in northern France, other species were grown alongside the main crop, but later in the period monoculture became the rule. Extensive and intensive cultivation regimes were followed, involving crop rotation and periods of fallow (Zech-Matterne and Brun 2016). Cattle and sheep were the principal livestock, their relative significance varying with the local environment. Pigs usually played a subsidiary role; small horses, dogs, and domestic fowl were also kept.

Wild species were rarely consumed, although hunting had an important symbolic role. In Britain, fish were largely avoided, apart from shellfish on coastal sites. Salt making on the coast and at inland brine springs became more intensive during the period, occurring as far north as southern Scotland (Bradley et al. 2016: 236–237). As with wetland and upland grazing, salt making was often seasonal, but facilities also occur at permanent settlements. Salt was important for preserving meat and dairy produce, and was transported to sites many hundreds of kilometres from the source. Similar types of storage structure found on both sides of the Channel include souterrains (underground chambers) in Brittany, Cornwall, and Scotland;[2] grain silos, a recurrent feature of chalk and limestone areas in Britain and France; and small four- and six-post structures for above-ground storage, which are even more widespread.

In the earlier Iron Age, smaller farming settlements were most numerous in river valleys and on lighter soils, but from the third century BC onwards, there was a marked rise in site numbers (and by implication in total population) on heavier soils, from the loess-covered plateau tops of northern France to the boulder clays of central Britain. The availability of mature iron technology for plough sheaths, axes, and other tools was a major factor in opening up these heavier but fertile soils to cultivation, although convincing evidence for the use of mould-board ploughs to turn the soil before the Roman period is so far confined to the Netherlands (van Heeringen 1989: 235). Remains of fields and paddocks are well represented in some areas, but over much of north-west Europe field boundaries were fluid, especially in the earlier Iron Age (Bradley 2019: 281–286). Spade cultivation was practised in some upland areas (Topping et al. 1989).

Initially, iron was principally used for making elite items such as weapons and wagon fittings and for replicating implements made in bronze, but from the fifth century BC onwards, the number of objects found in settlements and cemeteries expanded and several centres of intensive iron production emerged. By the late Iron Age, iron was used to make a wide range of tools for agriculture, carpentry, metalworking, and other crafts (see Chapter 23). Bipyramidal ingots, semi-products ('currency bars'), and billets provided a means of distributing iron in standard units; distinct regional ingot types have distributions extending over several hundred kilometres (Berranger and Fluzin 2012; Berranger 2014). While smelting was a more specialist craft, smithing is common on farms throughout north-west Europe, showing that the skills required to make and repair simple iron objects were widespread.

Chronology

As in central Europe, most French archaeologists now use a version of Reinecke's typo-chronology (Hallstatt C–D; La Tène A–D) for the Iron Age (see Chapters 3, 8). This scheme is underpinned by a growing number of tree-ring dates on the one hand and well-defined local chronologies on the other (Ralston 2019). In Britain, Ireland, and the Low Countries, where diagnostic pottery or metalwork are often scarce, there is more reliance on radiocarbon dating, leading to broader periodizations only loosely linked to the Hallstatt–La Tène scheme or to one another. For the earlier Iron Age, dating is impeded by the 'Hallstatt plateau' in the radiocarbon calibration curve (800–400 BC), although use of Bayesian modelling to construct site and artefact chronologies is fast improving matters (see Chapter 3).

Given these issues, we opted to present the material in three chronological blocks, subdivided as necessary. The first covers the period up to *c.*400 BC, when changes are apparent across the region. The second concludes with the conquest of Gaul by Julius Caesar and his armies in the 50s BC and the integration of its three parts (*Aquitania*, *Belgica*, and *Celtica*) into the Roman Empire.[3] Within these first two chronological blocks, the continent is presented first, followed by Britain and Ireland. The Netherlands and Flanders are considered separately on account of the distinctive character of Iron Age settlement and society in the North European Plain.

The third block examines Roman impact on societies outside the Empire following the conquest of Gaul up until AD 400. The Claudian invasion in AD 43 brought southern Britain under Roman control, but not Scotland or Ireland. Across the North Sea, the peoples north of the Rhine also remained beyond the frontier, if heavily influenced by its proximity. Although the rise of Rome after 200 BC, and particularly her late second-century BC annexation of Mediterranean Gaul, opened up much of Gaul to Roman trade, leading to the import of vast quantities of wine and other goods (Poux 2004; Loughton 2009; Olmer et al. 2013; Olmer 2018), most Roman imports in the far north of Gaul and in Britain and Ireland post-date Caesar.

Roman expansion also generated the first accounts of north-west Europe by Graeco-Roman authors including Caesar, Strabo, and Tacitus. Used critically, these provide tantalizing (if one-sided and highly selective) glimpses of Iron Age communities and their political and social geography in the first centuries BC and AD to set alongside the increasingly comprehensive perspective provided by the archaeological record.

The Earlier Iron Age in Mainland North-West Europe (c.800–400 BC)

In France and adjoining parts of Belgium and Luxembourg, settlements and their architecture at the start of Hallstatt C (800–625 BC) differed little from the preceding Late Bronze Age, with small upland fortifications and hamlets scattered across the countryside. In many respects, the picture is one of stability, but some changes are nevertheless apparent. Around 800 BC the long-lived lake margin settlements were abandoned in eastern France, and the deposition of bronze object hoards that had characterized the Atlantic complex largely ceased, replaced by grave goods and funerary offerings. The eighth century BC marked the beginning of ironworking and the appearance of the first long iron swords of Hallstatt type (Milcent 2017). This period is primarily known from cemeteries, for example in Belgium (De Mulder and Bourgeois 2011; Warmenbol 2017), in the Haguenau forest of Alsace, and in various parts of central France—Auvergne, Berry, Limousin, and the Sologne (Milcent 2004). Cremation burial under a barrow in the late Bronze Age tradition was the most frequent mortuary rite.

At Chavéria near Lons-le-Saunier in the Jura, the funerary rites of a particular family can be followed over several generations during the eighth century BC (Vuaillat 1977). The cemetery includes two groups of eight barrows, each with a larger mound over 20 m in diameter. Each barrow contained a single individual, either inhumed or cremated, and some were surrounded by a ring of stone. The burials were of wealthy warriors, accompanied by swords and sheaths, razors and horse gear. One of the latest included a bronze vessel, probably of Etruscan origin. This cemetery displays the continuation of local Bronze Age traditions, but also shows the first indications of the Hallstatt Iron Age.

In south-west France, cremation, either under a barrow or in a pit, was the dominant rite in Hallstatt C (Colin et al. 2013). Cemeteries were generally dispersed, apart from an exceptional concentration that developed during the early Iron Age in Gascony in the valley of the river Leyre (Mohen 1980). Settlements included single farmsteads, fortified enclosures, and villages such as Isle-Saint-Georges (Gironde) and favoured the alluvial plains of the major rivers, a pattern repeated in many other regions. The site at Crévéchamps in Lorraine is a good example. Here, some fifteen domestic units of Hallstatt C–D1 date—each comprising a dwelling and ancillary structures—were identified on the bank of the river Moselle; they are thought to represent a series of farms moving cyclically from one gravel dome to another within an area of *c.*30 ha, constrained by palaeochannels (Koenig 2016). The region is also notable for the important salt production complex that developed at this date at brine springs in the upper Seille valley near Marsal: large accumulations of ceramic waste, containers, supports, and ovens attest the production of salt from brine by evaporation from the seventh to the first century BC (Jusseret et al. 2013).

Hallstatt D and La Tène A

Our understanding of the sixth and fifth centuries BC was long dominated by isolated burials and cemeteries (see e.g. Baray 2003), but since the 1990s many settlements on the river terraces and plains have been excavated ahead of mineral extraction or infrastructure projects; there has also been important research on fortified sites of aristocratic type (Augier et al. 2012; Chaume and Mordant 2011; Brun and Chaume 2013). Throughout non-Mediterranean France, settlement numbers rose steadily at this period, peaking around 500 BC (Malrain et al. 2013).

Although most rural sites of this date were unenclosed, palisaded enclosures—often with prominent above-ground storage structures—are also now being identified in increasing numbers (Maitay et al. 2022). Some might be high-status farms, whereas others appear to be linked to systems of agro-pastoral exploitation in the river valleys. The majority of structures at rural sites were relatively insubstantial and probably used for agricultural and other everyday purposes, but larger timber buildings—generally rectangular, occasionally circular—occur more often than at the start of the Iron Age (Riquier et al. 2018). Most of these larger structures were presumably dwellings, but some could have had another role. There is nothing to indicate a division of building interiors between people and animals in the manner of the north European longhouse tradition (see later).

There have been major advances in our knowledge of princely seats and their settings, in particular at Vix in Burgundy and Bourges in central France. These wealthy sites emerged during Hallstatt D (*c.*625–475 BC) in a zone around the northern fringes of the Alps and along the upper Rhine and Danube valleys, from Zàvist (Bohemia) to Bourges, over 1,000 km to the west (see Chapters 8 and 21). At Vix, the settlement, which covered around 45 ha, was focused on Mont Lassois, overlooking the river Seine, and was protected by multiple fortifications (Figure 4.2). Excavations on the summit revealed several enormous timber buildings, one nearly 35 m long, with a plan presently unparalleled in temperate Europe: the key feature is an apsidal end with arcs of major posts interpreted as an external gallery (Chaume and Mordant 2011; Filgis 2011). This building is exceptional both in its monumental scale and architectural style, just as the Heuneburg in southern Germany had mud-brick fortifications of Mediterranean inspiration (Krausse et al. 2016).

The excavators interpret the apsidal structure at Mont Lassois as a palace, rather than as a building with a public function. Dating to the late sixth or early fifth century BC, it may even have been the residence of the so-called 'Princess of Vix', whose grave lay

FIGURE 4.2 Mont Lassois-Vix, Côte d'Or: (a) general plan of complex; (b) view of the large building.

Illustrations Bruno Chaume

in the plain below the hill. Excavated in 1953, her burial contained a dismantled four-wheel wagon and a rich array of other prestige goods, many of them imports from the Mediterranean world, including a huge bronze *krater*, which was probably a diplomatic gift (Joffroy 1962). Nearby were several more barrows and a small cult enclosure, in the ditch of which were the remains of limestone figures of a seated woman and a male warrior, with their heads broken off (Chaume and Reinhardt 2013). Numerous fragments of Greek pottery and wine amphorae from Massalia (Marseille) have also been found on Mont Lassois.

The palace lay within a settlement some 5 ha in extent (Chaume et al. 2011). Geophysical prospection has shown that the plateau was divided into two roughly equal parts by a road running north–south. To the east of the road, a series of rectangular plots defined by ditches contained post-built structures; the palace lay in the biggest plot, close to the centre. Subsequent survey has identified further traces of settlement below the hill on both banks of the Seine, perhaps also fortified, and possibly a port area (Chaume et al. 2020). The subdivisions, road network, and hierarchy of building types on Mont Lassois, and the 'suburb' all find parallels in an urban milieu at other times and places, and it is tempting to envisage a precocious town here. However, it remains to be established how wide a range of activities was undertaken or how varied the population was in socio-economic terms—two key attributes of urban societies—or indeed whether the complex belongs to a single phase. That said, the grid layout on the summit strongly suggests a planned foundation rather than the juxtaposition of smaller settlement units over time.

Bourges presents a different picture. Here, several series of rich barrow burials dating from the late sixth to the late fifth century BC have been identified in the hinterland of a 39 ha promontory on which the modern town stands (Augier and Krausz 2021; Krausz 2021a). The long-term inhabitation of the promontory makes detecting underlying Iron Age occupation difficult, but a range of finds, from Greek Attic pottery to painted wall plaster, from several locations, suggests that it was the core of another princely complex (Augier et al. 2007). Unlike Mont Lassois, however, craft areas are known in the immediate environs of the promontory, notably at Port Sec, where there is extensive evidence of bronzeworking and ironworking, including hundreds of drum brooches abandoned in the course of manufacture, as well as pottery kilns and debris from making lignite bracelets and bone-working (Augier et al. 2009, 2012).

This craftworking started with the emergence of the elite centre and intensified considerably in the fifth century BC. Domestic debris and traces of buildings indicate that the artisans lived in the craft zone; these 'suburbs' around the promontory covered some 470 ha and included funerary areas. Further areas of craft activity and burial beyond this inner zone suggest the complex extended to over 1.5 km^2 (Augier and Krausz 2012). A similar arrangement existed at the Heuneburg, where dwellings and workshops coexisted over several dozen hectares around the fortified core (Krausse et al. 2016).

It thus appears that these princely sites formed the core of extended urban territories, with an 'acropolis', 'suburbs', and a wider periphery containing farms, hamlets, and further craft sectors. Across temperate Europe, these centres collapsed as suddenly as they appeared, around 475 BC (the start of La Tène A). Although they did not all implode at this time (Bourges continued for another fifty years), the collapse was geographically widespread. And it was not simply the sites that succumbed, but the economic and political systems that lay behind them. This disintegration disrupted contacts with the Mediterranean world and destabilized the elite dynasties that had controlled these princely centres (Fernández-Götz and Ralston 2017; Krausz 2020; Krausz 2021a). Rural site numbers also declined rapidly at this period from their earlier peak across non-Mediterranean France.

The princely centres are far from representative of the diversity of settlement types now recognized in the sixth and fifth centuries BC. While some sites share elements with them, they also include different components. Bragny-sur-Saône, located near the confluence of the rivers Saône, Doubs, and Dheune in eastern France, is a good example (Collet and Flouest 1997). Some 3 ha in area, this site is much smaller than those just considered. Its occupation extends to late La Tène, but its main use is attributable to Hallstatt D and La Tène A. This agglomeration was not enclosed or fortified, a major contrast with the princely centres. Evidence for timber buildings indicates settlement associated with workshops where both iron and bronze were worked. The craftworkers at Bragny-sur-Saône had access to products from the south—from the Golasecca area in northern Italy, and amphorae from Massalia—showing that although not itself a major centre, this smaller agglomeration also participated in long-distance networks. It seems that it was either the satellite of a yet-unidentified princely seat, or developed independently on account of its favourable location.

Lyon-Vaise presents another variant (Carrara et al. 2021). The archaeological remains cover about 300 ha with a denser area of 70 ha in the southern part of the plain, beside the river Saône, close to its confluence with the Rhône. Its location on this major communication corridor explains the quantities of Mediterranean imports, akin to those from the princely seats. To date, no trace of a Hallstatt-period acropolis has been identified at Lyon. Thus Bragny-sur-Saône and Lyon-Vaise, while contemporary with the princely seats and sharing their extensive craft activities and access to Greek and Etruscan imports, lack any clear evidence for a locally resident elite or of rich burials in their vicinity. It is likely that these agglomerations had particular roles relative to the network of princely seats, but how this relationship functioned is as yet unclear.

Aristocratic settlements of a rather different type occur from the sixth century BC onwards in Brittany. These sites are characterized by rectilinear or curvilinear ditched enclosures, and include evidence for domestic settlement, storage (souterrains, cellars, cisterns), and cemeteries—in the form of dug graves and barrows. The most fully examined is at Paule-Saint-Symphorien (Menez 2012; 2016; 2021). From the outset, this settlement, although small, was wealthier and more monumental than most Armorican sites, and in the third century BC it was rebuilt on an even grander scale (Figure 4.3). The residential enclosure with its substantial buildings and souterrains was now enclosed by a stone rampart with four gate towers and a ditch, while ancillary structures and workshops were housed in an adjacent compound. Subsequent reconfigurations of this stronghold culminated in an even larger fortified agglomeration, or *oppidum*, 10 ha in extent, encompassing the original settlement core. The sequence from aristocratic rural settlement to *oppidum* remains without ready parallel.[4]

In northern France, equivalent elite settlements have not been identified for these centuries, but with some 15,000 excavated graves, society can be approached through its funerary archaeology. The Aisne-Marne culture of the sixth to fourth centuries BC has the largest concentration of chariot graves in Europe, with more than 200 examples known from cemeteries such as Chouilly (Jogasses), Manre, and Pernant (Demoule 1999; Diepeveen-Jansen 2001).[5] Most contained males, although some twenty vehicles accompanied women. The men's graves included weapons, notably swords and throwing-spears, and sometimes a shield laid over the body; body armour and helmets were rare. Torcs were the most frequent items of jewellery in rich female graves. Greek or Etruscan imports were rare. The rich tumulus burial near the Seine at Lavau was accompanied by a dozen imported metal vessels (Dubuis et al. 2015), but this early fifth-century BC grave is essentially transitional both in space and time, lying at the interface of Champagne and the zone of princely centres to the south, and marking the end of the earlier Iron Age tradition of rich burials (see Chapters 34, 40).

While numerous settlements are known in the Aisne-Marne region, none apart from Chassemy are associated with burial grounds.[6] Most occupation sites were short-lived

FIGURE 4.3 Reconstruction of the Gaulish aristocratic settlement at Paule, Côtes d'Armor, in the first half of the third century BC.

Artwork Laurence Stéphanon, Arts graphiques et patrimoine/Yves Menez, ministère de la culture

and housed only a few domestic units, and cemeteries may have provided the principal territorial foci, as on the North European Plain (see later). The general picture presented by the Aisne-Marne culture is one of small communities, with little or no indication of centralization. Grave numbers increased rapidly during the fifth century BC, but then declined steadily over the next two centuries; many established cemeteries were abandoned altogether, suggesting a significant depopulation (Demoule 1999). It is tempting to link this to the Celtic migrations of the fourth and third centuries BC (see later); the warrior societies of the Aisne-Marne region could have participated significantly in this exodus.

North-east of the Aisne-Marne region, in the uplands of the Ardennes and the Hunsrück-Eifel, many smaller hilltop sites were occupied in Hallstatt D or La Tène A.[7] Recent research has shown that a group of large sites in this region that went on to become *oppida* in the late Iron Age, such as Wallendorf (Germany) and the Titelberg (Luxembourg), were first fortified in La Tène A (Fernández-Götz 2014; Metzler et al. 2016). There is no sign, however, of elite centres comparable to the princely seats further south, but both hillforts and some lowland settlements have yielded high-status finds including a single sherd of imported Attic pottery from the Kemmelberg (Belgium; De Mulder and Bourgeois 2011; Warmenbol 2017), less than 40 km from the Channel coast. A cluster of cemeteries with chariot burials in the Belgian Ardennes provide a link with the Aisne-Marne region; again, most of the chariot graves are of La Tène A date, and few of the cemeteries continue into La Tène B (Cahen-Delhaye 1999).

The North European Plain 800–400 BC

In northern Belgium and the Netherlands, the patterns established in the later Bronze Age on the sandy landscapes south and north of the river Rhine, and on the clays and peats of the Rhine-Meuse delta and along the North Sea coast, largely continued into the earlier Iron Age. Settlement was dominated by dispersed farms, which regularly shifted their location. Over much of this region, dwellings were typically occupied for no more than a generation or so, before being replaced by new farms not far away (Gerritsen 2003). On the other hand, the characteristic Urnfield cemeteries of the period were often long-lived, providing focal points for communities distributed across the local landscape. The area around Weert, where several late Bronze Age and/or early Iron Age settlements have been uncovered within 1 km of a large cemetery, offers a good example (Roymans et al. 1998). More rarely, both occupation sites and burial grounds periodically shifted location, as at Nijmegen-Waalsprung (Van den Broeke and Ball 2012).

Throughout the Iron Age, occupation of the coastal zone was shaped by periodic marine transgressions. As inland, many earlier Iron Age settlements near the coast, such as Assendelver Polders in the western Netherlands (Therkorn et al. 1984), were short-lived or only seasonally occupied. The northern coastal marshes were mainly used for summer pasture until the sixth century BC, when the area began to be colonized for settlement (Nieuwhof and Schepers 2016). With the onset of renewed wet conditions, the inhabitants of some sites responded by raising their dwellings on artificial mounds (terps) made of marsh turfs, creating permanent settlements. Many of these mounded settlements never passed beyond their primary stage, but others were occupied continuously until the early medieval period; founded around 500 BC and still inhabited today, the terp at Ezinge near Groningen can lay claim to be among the oldest surviving Iron Age settlements in Europe (Nieuwhof 2020). Due to their wetland setting, many coastal sites are exceptionally well preserved, with posts and internal partitions of timber buildings, and features such as hearths, still surviving, along with normally perishable artefacts (see Chapter 19; Figure 4.4).

The normal Iron Age dwelling form throughout the Netherlands, extending into north-west Germany and south Scandinavia, was the three-aisled longhouse. Allowing for regional variations in construction, their basic tripartite layout was remarkably consistent, comprising a living area at the western end, and stalling for animals at the eastern end, divided by a hall with opposed entrances, as at Oss and Someren (Gerritsen 2003). This tradition originated in the middle Bronze Age, but buildings of this period were much larger. After 1000 BC, houses became smaller (10–20 m long), interpreted by Fokkens (1997) as signifying a shift from extended to nuclear families as the primary domestic unit. The byre areas were primarily for cattle, economically the most important domestic animal in this region, but horses and goats were also kept in them. Many earlier Iron Age houses lie within complexes of 'Celtic' fields, within which they moved periodically, but with limited dating evidence, debate continues over whether these fields were laid out in the Bronze Age, or were contemporary with the dwellings (Arnoldussen and de Vries 2014; 2017; Løvschal 2014). Farmyards commonly contained outbuildings and ancillary structures such as four-post granaries, storage pits, ovens, and wells.

The Urnfield burial tradition of the later Bronze Age also continued into the Iron Age, with cremations (both urned and unurned) interred in elongated or circular mounds, or in flat graves, generally with few goods. Some cemeteries comprised hundreds of burial monuments (e.g. Someren), but most are smaller (e.g. Beeglen), and many have a close spatial relationship with contemporary settlements. Some variations in practice are apparent between the northern and southern Netherlands, and in coastal areas formal burials are essentially absent throughout the Iron Age (Hessing and Kooi 2005). In the Dutch Rivers area, many cemeteries contain inhumations alongside cremations (Van den Broeke and Ball 2012), but this is not repeated elsewhere. In general, urnfields emphasize the local community rather than the individual as the most important unit of identity in society (Roymans and Kortland 1999). In the first half of the earlier Iron Age, many new cemeteries were founded, with numbers doubling in the southern Netherlands; coupled with rising settlement numbers, this points to significant demographic increase. During the fifth century BC, however, most urnfields fell out of use, amidst other changes in mortuary practice, including the adoption of square-ditched monuments, as at Mierlo-Hout (Figure 4.4; Roymans 1991).

Against the background of seemingly limited social differentiation in both domestic and mortuary spheres—reality may have differed (Fokkens 1997)—a dozen early Hallstatt elite graves in the southern Netherlands containing combinations of long

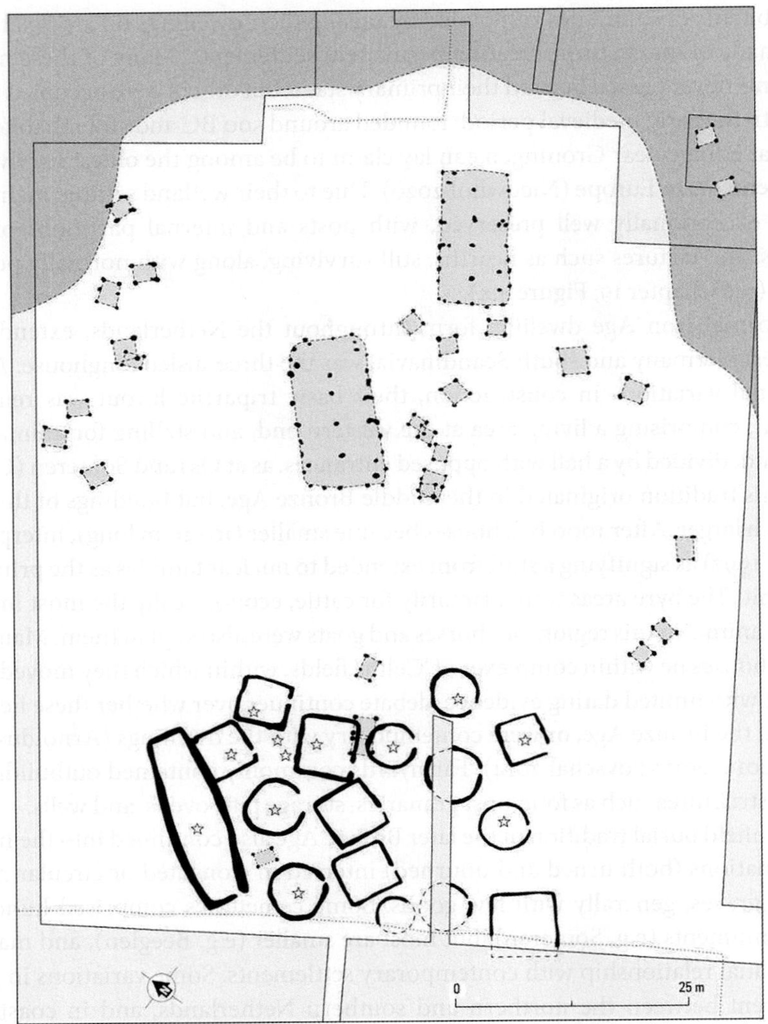

FIGURE 4.4 Mierlo-Hout, Noord-Brabant, plan of Urnfield graves and Haps-type byre houses. Illustration courtesy Nico Roymans

swords, horse gear, and bronze vessels stand out. They include the well-known 'chieftain's burial' from Oss (Fontijn and Fokkens 2007; Bourgeois and Van der Vaart-Verschoof 2017). Nearly all are cremations, but inhumations also occur (Uden-Slabroek). While these Dutch burials display some affinities with rich Hallstatt C graves in central Europe (Chapter 8), their association with Urnfield cemeteries implies a parallel tradition rather than any direct connection. After a seeming hiatus in Hallstatt D, there are hints of a new cycle of social ranking, manifested by a scatter of La Tène A burials with bronze vessels and other elite gear, mostly in the south of the region (Gerritsen 2003). Two fifth-century BC chariot burials from the Nijmegen area resemble examples in the middle

Rhine-Moselle and Aisne-Marne regions (see earlier), with which other contemporary links have been inferred (Roymans 1991).[8]

Some of the changes that mark the inception of the Iron Age in France have echoes further north. Bronze hoarding—never prolific in the Netherlands—and other forms of metalwork deposition on dry land and in wet places declined sharply, only partly balanced by an increase in weaponry and dress accessories in graves (Fontijn 2002). As the Iron Age progressed, domestic sites increasingly became a focus for ritualized deposition, albeit mostly of pottery and other everyday objects rather than metalwork, as well as animal and human remains. Detailed case studies suggest that many placed deposits on occupation sites derive from rituals performed when farms were founded or abandoned, or enacted at other key points in the inhabitants' life cycles (van den Broeke 2002; Gerritsen 2003).

Overall, the funerary and settlement records suggest that in this part of the North European Plain, the period up to 500 BC saw gradual infilling of the landscape, consistent with a rising population. Apart from the scatter of Hallstatt C rich burials, there is little, however, to point to marked social hierarchization. In the fifth century BC, there are hints of new connections between the southern Netherlands and lands further south, while new burial practices and the disuse of many older urnfields provide a prelude to other changes that were to follow during the later Iron Age.

The Earlier Iron Age in Britain and Ireland

As on the continent, the inception of the Iron Age in Britain and Ireland is marked less by the appearance of iron than by a sharp decline in bronze hoards, which after 800 BC were largely confined to south-west Britain and the south of Ireland, and often contained non-functional axes (Needham 2007; O'Connor 2007). In eastern Britain and Ireland, long swords continued to be placed in wet places, but unlike their Hallstatt C equivalents across the Channel, were nearly all bronze. Both traditions petered out in the sixth century BC. Despite evidence of ironworking in the tenth century BC in southern Britain (Collard et al. 2006) and by the eighth or seventh centuries BC in Ireland (Gartski 2019), iron objects are extremely rare. A scatter of iron socketed axes from Britain (Boughton 2015), and the iron sword, spearhead, and sickle in the Llyn Fawr votive hoard from South Wales remain exceptions to the rule.

In the sixth and fifth centuries BC, material culture in southern and eastern England remained in step with continental styles. Short iron swords supplanted longer types in Hallstatt D, only to lengthen again after 400 BC, and La Tène bow brooches replaced pins, although the insular products also have distinguishing features (Stead 2006). A few Mediterranean exotica such as the Attic cup from the Thames at Reading made their way to south-east England (Haselgrove 2001). Elsewhere in Britain and Ireland, little metalwork entered the record, while a lack of pottery (Ireland was aceramic after 800 BC) makes earlier Iron Age sites difficult to date with precision.[9] The destruction in a catastrophic fire of a pile dwelling built in the ninth century BC over a freshwater channel at Must Farm in East Anglia is a valuable reminder of how little of everyday life survives even on 'prolific' sites. As well as the burnt buildings and their contents, nine log boats used to navigate the Fenland waterways were found near the settlement (Knight et al. 2019).

In Wessex, the onset of the Iron Age was marked by new types of highly decorated pottery (Cunliffe 2005), often slipped with red iron ore (haematite) and polished to imitate bronze vessels. This ceramic repertoire may be linked to new arenas of social competition replacing the lavish ritual sacrifices of metal through which power and prestige were previously maintained, now rendered redundant by the primacy of iron over bronze. Another case of colour manipulation referencing the changing roles of these metals is offered by the large Langton Matravers hoard of socketed axes, dating to the seventh century BC; they were made in high-tin alloy, rendering them too brittle to use, but making them look like iron (Roberts et al. 2015).

The changes in the ceramic repertoire were associated with a new category of midden site, of which around thirty have now been identified across southern Britain. The middens appeared around the time that iron began to be worked, and were at their most active from the eighth to fifth centuries BC (Waddington et al. 2019). Some built up into substantial mounds, but unlike the Dutch terps they have little structural evidence and consisted largely of manure, with huge amounts of fine pottery and animal bone, and often debris from craft production (Bradley 2019). They occupy a range of settings, often liminal, including islands in the river Thames (Runnymede, Wallingford) and coastal locations (Mount Batten, Thanet, Worth Matravers), and several developed at earlier occupation sites or hilltop enclosures (Balksbury, East Chisenbury, Llanmaes, Potterne, Wittenham Clumps).

Opinion is divided over the roles of the midden sites, but they were probably places of assemblies and fairs, where goods were exchanged and other business transacted, accompanied by feasting and rituals. At Llanmaes (South Wales), finds included fragments of cauldrons and large amounts of pork were consumed; most of the bones were from right forequarters and the pigs were reared in several different areas (Gwilt et al. 2016). Some Wessex middens might have been base camps for grazing higher ground (Valdez-Tullett 2017). While usually seen as an insular phenomenon, there are parallels in France, notably the long-lived midden near the early Iron Age settlement at Mez-Notariou on Ouessant (Le Bihan and Villard 2001). Here, too, bones from the right forequarter predominated (for all animal species) and the deposition of miniature axe-heads is also paralleled at insular middens (Bradley et al. 2016).

The insular middens coexisted with a range of other sites. Hilltop occupation is attested in the late Bronze Age in many parts of Britain, but was more sporadic in the early centuries of the Iron Age. Some large hilltop enclosures in Wessex and the Welsh Marches may be of this period (Cunliffe 2005: 378–382; Payne et al. 2006), although where closely dated, their relatively slight defences were either built in the late Bronze

Age—but not maintained after the eighth century BC (Balksbury, Breiddin)—or in the mid-first millennium BC (Winklebury). These sites were lightly occupied and probably only used periodically. They may have complemented the middens, although Balksbury has midden deposits in the interior, which probably continued accumulating after the defences ceased to be maintained. Some ridge-end forts may also be early (Cunliffe 2005: 382–383), but the most securely dated early Iron Age settlements in Wessex are a group of curvilinear ditched enclosures like Houghton Down, Old Down Farm, or Overton Down, and a cluster of open sites on the Isle of Purbeck with houses and middens (Sharples 2010; Ladle 2018).

Enclosed and unenclosed settlements occur widely in other parts of Britain. Timber palisades were a common form of enclosure in the earlier Iron Age in both upland and lowland settings, palisaded settlements ranging in size from a single household unit to small communities. Palisades were often also the earliest form of boundary at hillforts or settlements later surrounded with banks and ditches (Harding 2017).[10] Large post-ring roundhouses with imposing porches of the type first recognized in the 1930s at Little Woodbury in Wessex and subsequently on many other sites (Figure 4.5) were another feature of the period, suggesting a greater role for domestic architecture in signalling social distinctions and/or a shift to endogamous marriage patterns linked with the growing importance of land ownership (Sharples 2010). Sharing living space with livestock might also have contributed to the increased size of houses, particularly in northern Britain, where new land use strategies after 800 BC linked to the worsening climate led to many upland sites shifting to lower locations (Haselgrove and Pope 2007; Pope 2015); many early Iron Age houses in Scotland have internal ring ditches, as at Ravelrig and Broxmouth (Rennie 2013; Armit and McKenzie 2013).

The earlier Iron Age also saw a shift away from the single-generation farms typical in the Bronze Age to longer-lived and often more aggregated sites (Davies 2018). Open settlements characterized by four-post settings, pit clusters, and circular buildings became common in lowland river valleys across Britain. Thanks to large-scale excavations at sites like Cotswold Community and Mucking on the Thames (Powell et al. 2010; Evans et al. 2016); Trumpington in East Anglia (Evans et al. 2018); and Newcastle Great Park in the Tyne valley (Hodgson et al. 2012), their dynamics are much better understood. Typically, settlements comprised between three and five domestic units, as at Clifton Quarry on the Severn (Mann and Jackson 2018) and Yarnton or Gravelly Guy on the Thames (Lambrick and Allen 2004; Hey et al. 2011), and many houses stood for up to a century before being rebuilt on the same or adjacent stances. As in the Netherlands, domestic sites were increasingly a focus for structured deposits of artefacts, and animal and human remains (Hill 1995). Much of the material from the large roundhouses at Longbridge Deverill Cow Down and other sites derived from closure rituals after they went out of use; some houses were deliberately burnt down (Webley 2007).

Early in the first millennium BC, field systems in the chalklands of Wessex and East Yorkshire were supplanted by territories defined by linear boundaries (Bradley 2019). As the Iron Age progressed, landscapes in other parts of Britain were divided up by earthworks or pit alignments—another hint of growing interest in land. Each land unit

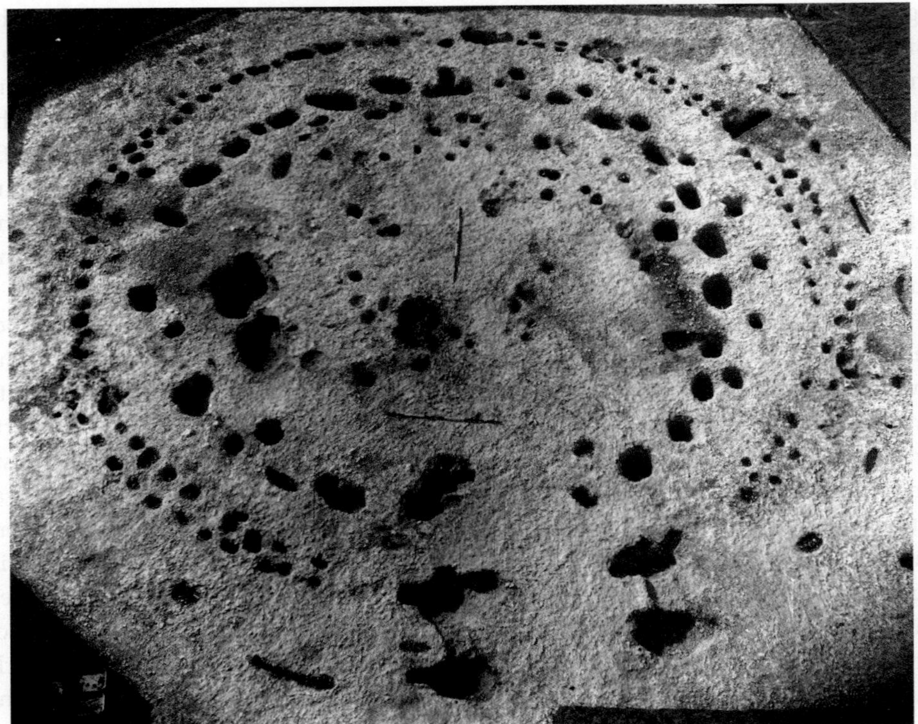

FIGURE 4.5 Early Iron Age timber roundhouse at Pimperne, Dorset.

Photo: © I. M. Blake and D. W. Harding.

was farmed from one or more sites—open or enclosed, as in the Vale of Pickering—situated either at the edge or more centrally. Several early Iron Age farms occupy old fields, as at Flint Farm and Rowbury Farm, established soon after 600 BC just 350 m apart in the same system, close to the later hillfort at Danebury (Cunliffe 2009). In general, there were fewer boundaries within land holdings than in the later Bronze Age, perhaps indicating a system of temporary divisions that were constantly changed (Bradley 2019), although over time territories were subdivided and some hillforts were built where several linear earthworks converged, perhaps replacing earlier meeting places at these nodes.

In the sixth to fifth centuries BC, settlement numbers rose across Britain and new types emerged, including a rash of highly visible hilltop enclosures collectively known as hillforts, fortified with imposing timber-framed or stone-revetted ramparts, and found principally in southern England and the Welsh Marches.[11] Some hillforts were well occupied and/or had substantial storage capacities, but many were lightly used, or never finished. This class of monument clearly had a range of sociopolitical and symbolic roles, with visual impact and/or status projection perhaps as important as defence. Although some ramparts were deliberately fired, this is not proof of attack. Among the earliest hillforts was Crickley Hill on the Cotswold scarp. In its first phase, long rectangular buildings—unusual for Britain—lined the track leading from the gate (Figure 4.6). After the primary timber-laced rampart was burnt, it was replaced by a stone-revetted version (itself later enlarged, and eventually burnt), while the interior was filled with roundhouses (Dixon 1994, 2019). Other scarp-edge hillforts such as Liddington and Uffington along the Berkshire Ridgeway may also be relatively early (Lambrick and Robinson 2009; Davies 2018).

Radiocarbon dating suggests that hillfort building in southern Britain peaked in the decades around 400 BC, later than once thought. At Danebury, one of the most extensively investigated hillforts in Europe, intensive activity began late in the fifth century BC (Hamilton and Haselgrove 2019). Another iconic Wessex hillfort at Maiden Castle is

FIGURE 4.6 Reconstruction of the Period 2 defences and longhouses lining the internal roadway at Crickley Hill, Gloucestershire.

Drawing: Philip Dixon

no earlier (Sharples 1991). On this redating, hillforts barely overlapped the large midden sites (see earlier) and may have assumed their role as gathering places, with highly visible acts of boundary construction supplanting feasting as a means of communal integration and/or elite competition (Waddington et al. 2019). Intriguingly, dumps of curated pottery typical of the midden sites occur in several hillfort ramparts (Davies 2018), providing a tangible link between the two types of focus. In its early phase, the northern half of Danebury contained rows of four-post settings with some circular structures in its southern part and around the circumference (Cunliffe 1995), but there is still debate over just how intensively or permanently the hillfort was occupied.

Increased ostentation and monumentality is also apparent in northern Britain. At the coastal site at Broxmouth, a palisade was replaced in the fifth century BC by a ditch and rampart (Armit and McKenzie 2013). Broxmouth is deemed a fairly typical 'hillfort' for southern Scotland, but its initial internal area was less than a twelfth that of Danebury (5 ha). While Broxmouth was later enlarged to over 1 ha by a new rampart, and both sites display a long-term attachment to place on the part of a single community, in other respects they represent different phenomena. A handful of larger hilltop enclosures emerged in the north at this period, including the Brown and White Caterthuns on adjacent hills in eastern Scotland; these seem more likely to be places of assembly than occupation foci on account of their multiple entrances and segmented earthworks (Dunwell and Strachan 2007).

In Atlantic Scotland, a new tradition of thick-walled drystone roundhouses emerged in the Northern Isles. By the mid-first millennium BC, this had given rise to larger and more complex dwellings like those excavated at Bu and Howe on Orkney (Hedges 1987; Ballin Smith 1994), which seem to be ancestral to the tower-like brochs (see later). Another innovation, likely to have been driven primarily by display, was the building of detached drystone 'blockhouses' at the entrances to Clickhimin and other promontory forts on Shetland, which must have looked formidable but had no real defensive value. At the other end of the socio-economic spectrum, Milla Skerra (Shetland) is probably typical of many mid-first-millennium BC dwelling sites in northern Scotland; throughout its life, this seaside settlement consisted of stone buildings, yards, and middens constructed over one another and preserved beneath the blown sand that caused its abandonment in the second century AD (Lelong 2019).

In central and south-western Scotland, crannogs and lake dwellings were a significant component of the early Iron Age settlement pattern (Cavers 2006). The well-preserved sites at Black Loch of Myrton and Cults Loch in Galloway were both occupied in the fifth century BC, Cults Loch being just one part of a complex of sites that included a palisaded enclosure and a promontory fort (Cavers and Crone 2018). There were also changes further south in Atlantic Britain. At Meillionydd in Wales, an open settlement spanning the earlier Iron Age was converted into a double ringwork in the fifth century BC, around the same time as the cliff castle at Trevelgue Head in south-west England was first fortified (Nowakowski and Quinnell 2011; Waddington 2013; Higgins 2016).

Despite a vast increase in development-led fieldwork, few earlier Iron Age sites are known in Ireland (Becker et al. 2008). Buildings are rare and habitation traces consist mostly of pits, hearths, or postholes. Late Bronze Age forts such as Rathgall, Haughey's

Fort, and Dún Aonghasa show little sign of continued activity, nor do crannogs like those at Lough Gara and Ballinderry (Raftery 1994; Fredengren 2002; Cavers 2006). The central enclosure at Rathgall might date to the earlier Iron Age, as may the enclosure and pit circle heading the Navan sequence, but if so, they are exceptions; the Navan enclosure was, in any case, followed by a hiatus (Bayliss and Grogan 2013). Overall, radiocarbon dates from Ireland suggest low levels of activity between 800 and 400 BC, but on balance the lack of sites is more likely to be the result of altered subsistence strategies and/or increased mobility than a sharp fall in population (Becker 2012; Armit et al. 2013; Gartski 2019).

Evidence for the dead is minimal on both sides of the Irish Sea. In Ireland, cremations associated with small ring ditches and barrows appear to span the first millennium BC, but few are attributable to the earlier Iron Age (McGarry 2009). In Britain, cremation petered out and normative burial practices are hard to recognize. A handful of small inhumation cemeteries have been excavated near settlements, as at Melton near the Humber, and Little Woodbury (Fenton-Thomas 2011; Powell 2015). Isolated graves of fifth century BC date include a burial under a barrow at Bromfield, Shropshire, and a chariot burial at Newbridge in Scotland (Hughes 1994; Carter et al. 2010). The chariot was buried intact, unusually for Britain, but typical of continental practice (see earlier). Some of the dead were deposited in water from causeways like the one built in 456 BC (and reconstructed several times in the next 150 years) over the river Witham at Fiskerton in eastern England, which is associated with metalwork offerings and human remains, or those on the Thames at Eton (Field and Parker Pearson 2003; Lambrick and Robinson 2009: 232). More generally, the sixth and fifth centuries BC saw a sharp rise in human remains—from single bones to whole bodies—and other forms of structured deposits in pits or ditches at sites in Wessex, the Thames Valley, and elsewhere, which intensified after 400 BC (Davies 2018).

Discussion of social and political structure in earlier Iron Age Britain and Ireland is hindered by the paucity of burials. Many archaeologists lean towards non-hierarchical or heterarchical models of social organization, but hierarchical readings of the material are also possible (Cunliffe 2005; Sharples 2010; Hill 2011). The breakdown of the large-scale metalwork style zones characteristic of the later Bronze Age and the emergence in Britain of regional pottery traditions was often taken to indicate that long-distance interaction declined in the earlier Iron Age and that the two islands were less integrated with the continent than before or after, but this is undoubtedly overstated (Webley 2015; Bradley et al. 2016).

The Later Iron Age in Mainland North-West Europe (c.400–50 BC)

After the collapse of the princely seats and their aristocratic societies in the later fifth century BC, the following two centuries in mainland north-west Europe were marked by instability and political and social restructuring (La Tène B–C1, *c*.400–200 BC). The exchange networks that had brought Greek and Etruscan goods northwards diminished. The visible changes in the archaeological record are often related to classical texts which record Celtic migrations southward in the fourth and third centuries BC. The steady decline in grave numbers in the Aisne-Marne region during this period was noted earlier; interestingly, although male burials were still in the majority, the proportion of female burials, especially of rich females, rose markedly in cemeteries such as Bucy-le-Long (Desenne et al. 2009). Might this reflect the rising political importance of women in societies where many men had gone abroad?

Settlements of the fourth to third centuries BC remain poorly documented; although some established sites such as Paule in Brittany prospered (see earlier), site numbers were low in most areas throughout the period (Malrain et al. 2013). New types of site appeared, specializing in agricultural storage, marked especially by dense clusters of storage pits. Several examples have been excavated in northern France, where they began in early La Tène (Gransar 2002). The pit clusters could be interpreted as a retreat to a more rural world, but could equally signal rising surpluses and real prosperity. These installations are more than just storage sites, as some are juxtaposed with settlements or cemeteries. Built on agricultural wealth amassed in the absence of urban forms of settlement, they point to the emergence of communities organized differently from those led by the earlier aristocratic dynasties. Nor did these groups practise ostentatious mortuary rites of the kind seen earlier, with a few exceptions such as the earlier third-century BC cemetery at Plessis-Gassot in Ile-de-France. Among the eighteen inhumation graves was a chariot burial in a wood-lined tomb; it held an elite warrior accompanied by high-quality weapons, decorated fabrics, and two pottery cups from Hellenistic Etruria (Ginoux 2009).

Also an exception for the period is the large third-century BC cemetery at Bobigny (Ile-de-France), immediately pre-dating a craftworking agglomeration (see later). With over 500 graves (499 inhumations, 20 cremations), the cemetery provides temperate Europe's largest skeletal assemblage for this period (Marion et al. 2006–2007). The burials included all age groups except perinatal infants, who are rarely recovered. Accompanying them were personal items such as brooches, bracelets, and belt components; weapons were recovered from a few male graves. Overall, goods were relatively uncommon and there were no very wealthy graves. The Bobigny burials indicate a population of varying status, but clearly dominated by the middle ranks. There are limited traces of contemporary settlement in the excavated areas, so it remains unclear whether there was already a nucleated settlement here, or whether the cemetery served a larger territory.

The most spectacular sites of this period were religious sanctuaries such as Gournay-sur-Aronde and Ribemont-sur-Ancre in Picardy, and Fesques in Normandy (Brunaux 2004). These sanctuaries originated in the fourth century BC and evoke two dominant themes—religion and war. Gournay-sur-Aronde was the first to be excavated: it comprised a quadrangular enclosure delimited by two deep ditches containing successive post-built structures (Brunaux et al. 1985), compared by Brunaux to an ancient Greek *propylaion*, serving to separate the worlds of the divine and the profane. The internal ditch produced fragmentary remains of some sixty people, as well as of sacrificed animals—cattle, lambs, piglets, and sheep; there were also over 200 swords, 250 scabbards, and about the same numbers of shield bosses and suspension chains. Many of these items were well used and had undergone repairs. Brunaux suggests that most or all of them were war booty, inferring from this that warfare was particularly frequent between *c*.280–200 BC, and diminishing thereafter.

The sanctuary at Ribemont-sur-Ancre is rather different in character. The remains are focused on an area of *c*.3 ha, set at a high point which Brunaux (2004) believes had been the site of a battle, where two monuments were built to mark the victory. One was a quadrangular enclosure, interpreted as a trophy containing the spoils of victory. The other enclosure, polygonal in plan, functioned as a shrine to the fallen heroes, akin to a Greek *heroon*. The material recovered from the monuments consists almost exclusively of human bones and iron weapons (Brunaux et al. 1999). The human remains may represent over 1,000 individuals, all young or middle-aged men. There were several thousand weapons, some 75% of which date to the first half of the third century BC. They are a quite different selection to Gournay. At Ribemont, spearheads were by far the commonest type of weapon. In contrast, swords were not especially frequent, and are less well represented than shield bosses or suspension chains. The impression is one of abandoned weaponry gathered up from a battlefield. Ribemont thus appears to commemorate an important battle, with the human and material remains of the two sides treated very differently, although this interpretation is subject to some debate (Fercoq du Leslay et al. 2019).

The Picardy sanctuaries are thought to have served as symbolic and political foci, cementing together the populations of several territories. Although weapon-rich sanctuaries are particularly characteristic of Belgic Gaul, similar sites have been investigated in other parts of France, for example, at Mirebeau-sur-Bèze in Burgundy (Joly and Barral 2007). Other types of cult site range from open-air foci to natural caves. Some of the human remains found in caves alongside Iron Age objects bear signs of dismembering, but it does not necessarily follow that this occurred in the course of cult rather than funerary practices. The best-known is the Grotte des Perrats near Agris (Charente), which was in use from the fourth century BC to Roman times (Gomez de Soto and Lejars 2009). Finds included a spectacular copper alloy and iron helmet, covered in gold and decorated with coral studs. During the second century BC, deposits at sanctuaries became more diverse, with other categories of material such as brooches, jewellery, tools, miniature objects, and coins all represented (Demierre et al. 2019).

A novelty of the third century BC was the minting of gold coins copied from Greek originals, which soon gave rise to distinctive regional coinages across France. These were followed in the second century BC by the widespread adoption of silver types alongside or instead of gold, and cast bronze (potin) coins, superseded in the mid-first century BC by struck bronze issues (see Chapter 28). The expanding use of coinage was tightly bound up with the emergence of proto-urban communities, living in lowland agglomerations and, increasingly from *c*.120–110 BC, in fortified *oppida*. Many of these sites have been important centres ever since (e.g. Besançon, Geneva, Metz, Orléans, Reims, Toulouse) or preceded major Gallo-Roman towns in the vicinity (e.g. Mont Beuvray/Autun, Titelberg/Trier).

The Rise of Proto-Urban Communities

The first lowland agglomerations in France appeared in La Tène C1, multiplying rapidly during the second century BC (Fichtl and Barral 2019). Such sites extended over tens of hectares and are marked by intensive craft production (e.g. metallurgy, pottery-making), as at Bobigny (Marion et al. 2006–2007), Châteaumeillant (Centre; Krausz 2009; Bouchet 2017), Kergoven (Brittany; Le Goff 2019), Lacoste (Aquitaine; Sireix 2013), Levroux (Centre; Buchsenschutz et al. 2000) and Verdun-sur-le-Doubs (Burgundy; Barral and Lallemand 2014).[12] They were often near major routes and functioned as markets for the exchange of goods imported from Italy (e.g. wine amphorae, Campanian pottery) or other parts of La Tène Europe (e.g. pottery, glass bracelets). Some agglomerations seem to have had distinct religious sectors, as at Acy-Romance beside the river Aisne (see later), while others may have possessed mints (e.g. Saumeray, Centre).

These agglomerations are western examples of a series extending to Manching (Bavaria) and Němčice Nad Hanou (Moravia); all display evidence for the economic surge under way during La Tène C across temperate Europe. In the decades after 100 BC some sites were abandoned, but their inhabitants and functions moved to a nearby hill, which became an *oppidum*. Levroux and Basel (Switzerland) are classic examples of such shifts, but instances occur across France. This model suggests the deliberate creation of some *oppida* as a kind of planned 'new town' to which populations moved, while remaining within their established territory.[13]

In other cases, there was no displacement: the *oppidum* developed at the same place as the La Tène C2 craft agglomeration. This happened at Châteaumeillant, where an agglomeration developed early in the second century BC on a promontory between two streams (Krausz 2009). Around 100 BC, the community erected a fortification around the settlement, which developed rapidly through the first half of the first century BC. Other lowland agglomerations did not become *oppida*, but fell into decline (Acy-Romance, Lacoste). Their populations drifted away to *oppida* or more economically propitious settings elsewhere. In Auvergne, the inhabitants abandoned the previously flourishing lowland agglomeration at Aulnat-Gandaillat (Deberge et al. 2007a) and moved to the hilltop *oppidum* of Corent around 100 BC—where a cult site had been established a few decades earlier (Poux and Demierre 2015)—and probably to other settlements.[14]

There are no essential differences in terms of the activities undertaken at the craft agglomerations and the *oppida*, but there were changes in morphology and layout. The principal novelty was the building of a substantial enclosing earthwork, a key attribute of the *oppidum*. These earthworks were variants on the traditional temperate European construction of earth, timber, and stone—the *murus gallicus* described by Caesar at Bourges-*Avaricum* in 52 BC (*de Bello Gallico* VII, 23). While not particularly effective militarily in the face of new styles of warfare, earthworks of this kind were widely distributed at this period west of the Rhine (Krausz 2018; 2021b). *Muri gallici* were built at major *oppida*—the likely regional centres—as well as around smaller sites, the equivalents perhaps of modest towns, and even wealthy aristocratic farms as at Luant (Centre; Buchsenschutz et al. 2010). *Muri gallici* were often interrupted by complex entrances, whether inturned defensive gateways of *Zangentor* type, or truly monumental edifices with a paved road leading through them, as at Mont Beuvray (Burgundy) or Hérisson (Auvergne; Lallemand 2009).

Across Celtic and Belgic Gaul, the appearance of *oppida* enclosed by *muri gallici* seems to have been near-synchronous, occurring around the turn of the second and first centuries BC (Krausz 2021b). Where the topography allowed, most examples were elevated (e.g. Titelberg; Châteaumeillant; Villejoubert, Limousin); some were on conspicuous hills (e.g. Mont Beuvray). But fortified *oppida* also occur in lowland settings, as at Condé-sur-Suippe and Villeneuve-Saint-Germain on the Aisne in Picardy. The same is true of other sites beside major rivers, such as Orléans-*Cenabum* on the Loire and Besançon-*Vesontio* in a bend of the Doubs. The enclosed areas vary considerably from about 10 ha to several hundred hectares for the largest sites (Fichtl 2005; Chapter 21).

A slightly later type of fortification, known as the Fécamp type after the *oppidum* in upper Normandy, consisted of high dump ramparts, characteristically preceded by a wide, flat-bottomed ditch. There are two main concentrations—one along and north-east of the Seine in Belgic Gaul (Wheeler and Richardson 1957), the other in central France (Ralston 1992; Krausz 2014). At Châteaumeillant, the rampart was originally 14–15 m high (without the parapet) and was fronted by a 45 m-broad ditch. Built in the mid-first century BC, it replaced an earlier wall in *murus gallicus* style (Krausz 2019; 2021c). Many other earlier timber-laced ramparts were similarly re-engineered at this period (Ralston 2019), making it highly likely that this new form of massive earthwork defence was specifically designed as a response to Roman artillery and siege warfare.

As much past excavation at *oppida* has been directed at the defences and many of the sites have been occupied continuously to the present day, knowledge of the interiors is often based on fairly limited interventions. That said, evidence is emerging for organized layouts at many sites. Zones given over to particular activities have been identified at, for example, Corent, Mont-Beuvray, Moulay,[15] the Titelberg, and Villeneuve-Saint-Germain, containing housing and workshops, sanctuaries, public buildings, and open spaces used as assembly and marketplaces, subdivided by roads and internal boundaries (e.g. Poux 2012; Le Goff 2016).

Such arrangements, already developing in lowland agglomerations,[16] suggest an urban style of planning. At Mont Beuvray, a two-aisled timber courtyard structure was built just before the mid-first century BC on an artificial terrace revetted on the north and east by a wall of *murus gallicus* style (Figure 4.7; Barral et al. 2019). While presumably a public building, its function has yet to be established. Courtyard buildings of similar form and size have been excavated at Trégueux, a lowland agglomeration

FIGURE 4.7 Drone view of building PC15 under excavation at Mont Beuvray, Burgundy.
Photo: © Bibracte, Antoine Maillier

in Brittany, and Thézy-Glimont, a cult site in Picardy. Large buildings with economic functions include a long building with a cellar for the storage of wine at Corent, interpreted as a warehouse (Poux 2012). An area next to the main road traversing the Titelberg is thought to have been a Roman traders' quarter established there just before the Gallic War (Metzler et al. 2016), similar to the one at Orléans-*Cenabum*, where according to Caesar the resident Roman traders were massacred (*de Bello Gallico* VII, 3).

Contemporary activity outside the walled circuits has been identified at a number of *oppida* (e.g. the Titelberg). At Gondole (Auvergne), the extramural craft quarter was larger than the area inside the rampart, which could be secondary, as at Châteaumeillant (Deberge et al. 2009). With better dating evidence, other lowland agglomerations may prove to have continued to function, if at a reduced level, after they were 'replaced' by a nearby *oppidum* in a more defensible location (Champigny-lès-Langres/Langres?). In the later stages at Mont Beuvray, a new agglomeration of similar extent to the *oppidum* developed around the nearby source of the river Yonne (Moore et al. 2013), while for Auvergne, it has been argued that the neighbouring *oppida* of Corent-Gergovie-Gondole effectively formed a single extended complex, with different functions dispersed between the three fortified foci (Poux 2014).[17] And while many *oppida* had sizeable populations and well-developed infrastructure, some were only ever lightly occupied (e.g. Mont Vully, Switzerland; Puy d'Issolud, Aquitaine), suggesting they were intended as refuges, or were places where people came together periodically, with few permanent inhabitants.

Over most of France, the *oppida* were fairly regularly distributed across the landscape. This mirrors the political and territorial pattern of *civitates* described by Caesar as more or less independent territories (Fichtl 2004). Each *civitas* had a leading *oppidum* as its capital—e.g. *Avaricum* (Bourges) for the *Bituriges*; *Bibracte* (Mont Beuvray) for the *Aedui*; and *Durocortorum* (Reims) for the *Remi*. Such a territorial structure organized around a single central place implies a strong administrative organization, and by extension the existence of early state entities controlling the *oppida* and defining their functions (Krausz 2016). The *oppida* acted as key nodes in the political system, from which control was exercised over the rest of the region. Their foundation thus provided a political solution to the challenge of controlling social groups in the increasingly diverse societies that are evident from La Tène C1 onwards, as in the Bobigny cemetery with its male and female graves representing different social groups (see earlier). Against a background of societies that were becoming wealthier and more complex, the political *raison d'être* of the *oppida* concerned the control and organization of territory.

After a century or more of unprecedented economic and demographic growth, what changes brought about the proliferation of fortified *oppida* at the end of the second century BC, not only in France but all over La Tène Europe? This remains a subject of lively debate. Given their diversity, a single, straightforward explanation is unlikely. While many *oppida* succeeded existing craft agglomerations and absorbed their inhabitants, others began as, or succeeded, sanctuaries (Corent, Gournay-sur-Aronde, Moulay), and at least one developed from an elite residence (Paule; Menez 2021). Some *oppida* were certainly *de novo* foundations, as in the Aisne valley, and these must have acquired their substantial populations in other ways.

Some archaeologists have suggested that elite competition and interests played a key role in the emergence of *oppida* (e.g. Buchsenschutz 2004: 109; Buchsenschutz and Ralston 2012). The aristocrats who controlled the economic output of the lowland agglomerations reorganized their territories, maintaining some established production centres but at the same time creating new foci (*oppida*), whose populations grew over time. Under this impetus, the settlement pattern became more hierarchical, with *oppida*, whose functions and activities varied, surrounded by lesser hamlets and farms which furnished the primary agricultural production.

Others, however, argue that the proliferation of fortified sites was too sudden and affected too large an area (from the Atlantic to the middle Danube) for this hypothesis to be viable (Fichtl and Guichard 2016; Guichard 2017). Given the simultaneous decline in agglomerations and also rural sites (see later), they see *oppida* as a response to a wider crisis affecting the La Tène world. Even if they were built partly to impress and their very construction helped to reinforce collective identity, ramparts had a military dimension. Also, attention has focused on the larger *oppida*, but many smaller sites were fortified or refortified at this period: an eruption of rampart building that might even be compared with the *incastellamento* of feudal Europe. Events that might have engendered such chronic instability were the passage of the Cimbri and their allies through middle Europe and Gaul between 113 and 101 BC (Luginbühl 2014; Krausz 2021b) and further population movements set off by this and Roman military expansion into Mediterranean Gaul (see Chapter 37).

Rural Settlement

Our knowledge of the organization of the rural landscapes and communities, and the agricultural systems that underpinned the *oppida*, is also now much better understood. In areas that have seen the greatest level of large-scale excavation, it is possible to follow the development of settlement over several centuries in considerable detail. At Ifs on the Caen plain in Normandy, for example, a sequence of farms has been traced from the Bronze Age onwards (Le Goff 2009). The first enclosed settlements appeared late in Hallstatt D within an agricultural landscape already subdivided by systems of routeways. From early La Tène onwards, more substantial farms appeared, which developed in essentially the same locations through to the early Roman period. The Ifs group consists of a series of farms set within a regular field system subdivided by a network of tracks, some of which have been traced for over 800 m. The farms were accompanied by small cemeteries for family-sized groups.

Across northern and western France, later Iron Age farmsteads were often surrounded by ostentatious ditches (Fichtl 2021; Menez 2021); rather than being fortifications, the enclosures symbolized the importance of the aristocratic owners of the largest agricultural units (Maguer and Lusson 2009; Menez 2021). One of the most imposing of these establishments is Batilly-en-Gâtinais, near Orléans. This La Tène D1–D2a trapezoidal enclosure was almost 700 m long, with a separate quadrangular compound inside its narrower end, delimited by a massive ditch and entered through a tower gateway (Fichtl 2013; 2021). The interior of the compound contained several complex buildings and was subdivided by palisades that were plastered with daub and painted. Buildings were ranged along the long sides of the bigger enclosure.

Many smaller farming settlements occur, some enclosed, others open. Based on evidence from the Oise valley in Picardy, Malrain et al. (2002: 137–158) propose a social hierarchy of four levels of site. Settlement in the loess belt in Belgium was dominated by enclosed sites similar to those in northern France (Bourgeois et al. 2003). While mixed farming was the paramount activity at all these rural sites, other pursuits ranged from the processing of secondary products (weaving textiles, working leather or bone, basketry) to more specialized undertakings such as salt making at the coast (e.g. Pont-Rémy near the Somme estuary; Prilaux 2000), and metallurgy (e.g. Ronchères; Malrain et al. 2010). In Normandy, bracelet roughouts made out of Kimmeridge shale from southern England have been found at the coastal site of Urville-Nacqueville on the Cotentin peninsula, together with roundhouses and a mixed cemetery, which includes inhumations buried in a manner more typical of late Iron Age Dorset (Lefort et al. 2015). At the very least, this indicates the strength of cross-Channel contact at this period across the short sea crossing, and probably the presence of people from southern Britain (Ralston 2019).

Ancient DNA analysis of the Urville burials has revealed two maternally differentiated subgroups, one with genetic affinities with Channel/Atlantic coast groups, the other with individuals from the Paris basin (Fischer et al. 2019).

In eastern France, the countryside shows little sign of wider organization prior to the La Tène C2–D1 transition (*c.*150 BC), when the landscape was structured and large rectilinear enclosed farmsteads appear (Nouvel et al. 2009). On the Limagne plain in Auvergne, exploitation of the countryside became more intensive in the third century BC. Farms were now enclosed and spaced *c.*1 km apart (compared to *c.*2 km in the fifth century BC); each probably exploited land of 100–200 ha (Deberge et al. 2007b). Le Pâtural was one of many farms that sprang up in the environs of the Aulnat-Gandaillat agglomeration, illustrating the interrelationship between different components of the second-century BC settlement pattern; the rural sites provided foodstuffs and secondary agricultural products, receiving in return goods manufactured in the agglomeration, together with some of the Roman imports now increasingly penetrating the region in exchange for slaves and other commodities (Loughton 2014; Mata 2019).

In Auvergne, most lowland farms, as well as the larger agglomerations, were abandoned around 100 BC for two generations before being reoccupied after the Gallic War (Haselgrove and Guichard 2013). The pattern is repeated across the northern half of France, with rural site numbers rising to a peak in the late second century BC, after which they fell back and did not recover until the Roman period (Malrain et al. 2013). The detail differs from area to area, and the downturn was less pronounced in plateau areas, many of them only colonized in the later Iron Age. This suggests a variety of factors were responsible for the desertion of farms and the aggregation of their inhabitants into defended *oppida*, ranging from internal coercion or crises (disease, declining yields) to external threats (e.g. population movements; slaving), later compounded by the devastation wrought by Caesar's armies.

Mortuary and Ritual Practices at the End of the Iron Age

In the final centuries BC, cremation supplanted inhumation as the principal burial rite in northern and eastern France, whereas west and south of the Seine, inhumation largely continued, mixed to some extent with cremation (Bradley et al. 2016: 316–323). Mont Beuvray and the Titelberg are among the few *oppida* with known burial grounds; the Lamadeleine cemetery outside the Titelberg was used by a handful of family groups (Metzler-Zens et al. 1999), whereas its eastern cemetery had several hundred graves (Metzler et al. 2016: 411). Some rural areas were marked by the revival of earlier elite practices, including occasional chariot burials. Groups of aristocratic burials of La Tène D and early Roman date are known from south-west France (e.g. Boé, near Agen), in the middle Aisne valley (Hannogne; Vieux-lès-Asfeld), and in Luxembourg (Clémency; Goeblange-Nospelt).

The Fléré group from Berry comprises a series of wealthy male graves (e.g. Châtillon-sur-Indre, Dun-sur-Auron, Fléré-la-Rivière), accompanied by weapons that imply that they were cavalrymen (Ferdière and Villard 1993). The graves also contained banqueting equipment, including joints of meat, iron utensils, imported Italian bronze vessels, ceramic cooking pots and tablewares, and amphorae of wine. These burials show that despite the centralization of political decision-making in *oppida*, the elite maintained close links with the rural estates on which their power and wealth were founded (Ralston 2019). Apart from Châtillon, the burials are post-Caesarian in date, suggesting that the deceased were aristocrats who had taken the Roman side (and probably served as auxiliaries).[18] Nevertheless, in death they chose to assert their indigenous origins and ancient privileges through conspicuous burial rites in the La Tène tradition on their ancestral lands.

Until relatively recently, archaeological knowledge of religious and ritual practices in this period was limited, but excavations have now produced evidence from sites of all types. A key structuring element of the agglomeration of Acy-Romance was a large open space which may have been used for commercial activities, public gatherings, and religious ceremonies, the last involving animal sacrifice (Méniel 1998) and the execution of young men (Lambot 2006; Bocquillon et al. 2012). Along its north-west margin were monumental structures interpreted as temples; north of these were the graves of nineteen young men, spanning the duration of the site, and buried in an unusual, seated position. Although cause of death could not always be established, it was linked to a particularly violent ritual; one man had been killed by an axe-blow to the forehead.

At Corent, the sanctuary initially took the form of a palisaded enclosure, but this was demolished and replaced by a monumental covered gallery early in the first century BC. Nearby, across an open space, a semi-circular timber arena is thought to have been an assembly or meeting place (Poux 2012; Poux and Demierre 2015). In the Roman period, the sanctuary was rebuilt, first in timber then in stone, and a theatre was erected on the site of the assembly building. At the Titelberg, the eastern side of the *oppidum* was divided from the rest of the interior by a ditch, creating a large area interpreted as a 'public space' from its succession of unusual corridor-like structures and monumental buildings, associated with religious, political, and perhaps economic activities (Metzler et al. 2016). Later on, a Roman *fanum* was built here. Other *oppida* such as Boviolles and Mont Beuvray replicate this sequence of earlier cult areas replaced by a Gallo-Roman sanctuary.

Some light on the religious and political ceremonies performed at these places is shed by the remains of banquets or feasts lubricated by Italian wine (Poux 2004); such residues have been identified at Corent and other centres such as Lyons or Arnac-La-Poste (Limousin) as well as on some rural sites (e.g. Braine; Auxiette et al. 2017). A wide variety of ritualized practices are also attested in domestic settings on sites of all types, from major centres to small farmsteads, involving the deposition of material culture and/or animal and human remains, in recurrent ways and combinations (Gransar et al. 2007). Objects were often rendered unfit for further use before deposition (like weapons at sanctuaries), and whole or partial animal and human bodies are regularly found. Many such deposits were placed in pits and ditches; others occur in domestic structures. Away from settlements and formal cult sites, rivers, bogs, and springs were frequently

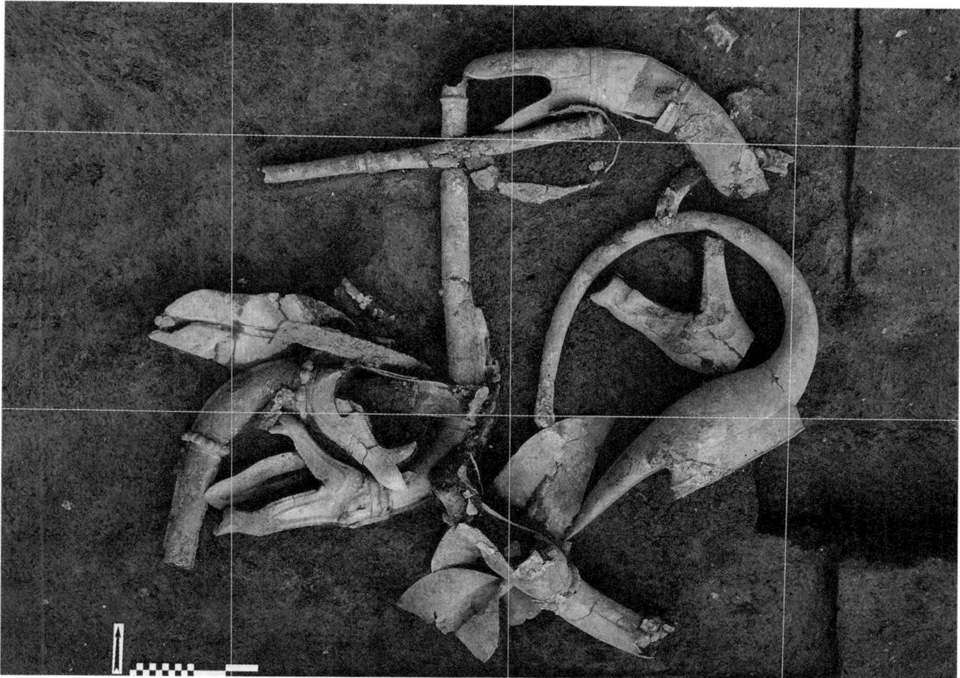

FIGURE 4.8 Sheet-bronze *carnyces* and a bird-helmet deposited at the base of a pit in the sanctuary at Tintignac, Corrèze. The pit contained around sixty objects, including a range of weapons, helmets, and a cauldron.

Photo: © Patrick Ernaux, INRAP

the scene of deposition of prestige objects and metalwork (weaponry, coins, torcs). In sum, the archaeological evidence indicates a hugely elaborate suite of ritual practices.

Gallo-Roman religious complexes were built over many Iron Age rural sanctuaries, from Ribemont-sur-Ancre in the north to Tintignac in the Limousin. There, an Iron Age cult place was established in the early first century BC. Later in that century, a spectacular group of sacrificed weapons (swords, spearheads, helmets, and shields) and several war trumpets or *carnyces* were buried together in a pit (Figure 4.8; Maniquet 2008; Maniquet et al. 2011). Tintignac is over 50 km from the supposed capital of the *Lemovices*, the *oppidum* of Villejoubert near Limoges, but this rural sanctuary could have been a ceremonial centre for one of the groups that formed part of the *Lemovices*.

The North European Plain 400–50 BC

In Flanders and the Netherlands many aspects of society continued into the later Iron Age, but changes can also be seen, particularly in the funerary sphere. Cremation remained the dominant rite, but after 400 BC burial grounds were fewer and smaller, and flat graves were the norm. Many burials now consisted mostly of pyre debris, and were unaccompanied or contained a pot or ornament at most; other objects were burnt on the pyre. Meat portions placed on the pyre were commonly of pork or sheep/goat (see Chapter 19), contrasting with the emphasis on cattle at settlements. Just a few burials stand out for their richer contents, e.g. the set of 'female' ornaments (belt hook, ankle rings, and La Tène C brooch) from Koningsbosch, Limburg (Roymans 2007). As previously, cemeteries were often near contemporary farms. Late in the period, larger communal burial grounds reappear, often continuing into the Roman era, some of flat graves, others with small square burial enclosures (Gerritsen 2003).

Later Iron Age farms appear similar to their predecessors, but settlement location became more stable, with buildings now displaced over shorter distances, or even rebuilt on the same plot, shown by overlapping house plans (Gerritsen 2003). North of the Rhine, three-aisled houses remained the norm, as at Bernisse on an island in the estuary, where successive floor levels survived, and deposits of dung in the byre area confirmed that cattle were kept indoors for part of the year (Gerritsen 2008: 147–148). Further south, extending into the loess belt fringing the Ardennes, byre-houses now became two-aisled (Bourgeois et al. 2003; Gerritsen 2003; Hiddink and Roymans 2015), although this seems merely to be a change in plan form, not of function. The Haps type[19] with its hipped roof, was the earliest (see earlier, Figure 4.4), giving way in the second century BC to longer structures (Oss-Ussen type 5), and eventually at the turn of era to sturdier forms (Alphen-Ekeren type), all named after the settlements where they were first defined. Four-aisled buildings, first attested in the earlier Iron Age, also occur at this period, albeit infrequently. As Roymans (1995) has indicated, the sheer longevity of the byre-house tradition implies a deep-rooted importance for these buildings beyond the purely functional, connected to the ideology and value systems of the overwhelmingly pastoral societies inhabiting the North European Plain, for whom animals had a special importance.

Greater clustering of contemporary farms is apparent, as for example at Haps, and some were enclosed within ditched plots, although this was much less common than in the loess belt of southern Belgium (see earlier). At Oss-Schalkskamp, Oss-Almstein, and Zeist-Kroostweg Noord, late Iron Age settlements were surrounded by rectilinear enclosures (Gerritsen 2003; Waldus and Verelst 2005; Arnoldussen and Jansen 2010), while three longhouses constructed around 50 BC at Tiel-Passewaaij were ranged along a palaeochannel, each associated with ditched plots (Roymans et al. 2007). More equivocal is a large double-ditched enclosure at Weert-Laarderweg, where there are few signs of contemporary activity, but after the ditches silted up in the late first century BC, the site was occupied by a cluster of farms (Roymans et al. 1998). In the north Netherlands, excavations at Noordbarge, Peelo, and Zeijen demonstrate that by the first centuries BC and AD, settlements with two to three farms had developed, which remained fixed in the landscape for significant periods. Some of these were surrounded by 'defensive' enclosures, defined by earthworks and palisades (e.g. Zeijen I and II; Vries; Waterbolk 1995; Arnoldussen and Jansen 2010).

Nucleated settlements were uncommon in inland areas of the region before the Roman period, but in the coastal marshes terp sites expanded in size. At Ezinge, the later Iron Age settlement consisted of a dozen farms grouped radially around an open space. In the dune areas of the west coast, grid-like ditched field or paddock systems laid out in the late Iron Age (e.g. Den Haag, Monsterseweg, and World Forum sites) might be linked to the adoption of the true plough, probably in the third century BC, shown by the presence of furrows from mould-board ploughing at the World Forum site. Seasonal or temporary occupation remained common in areas too wet for permanent settlement (Bradley et al. 2016).

Towards the end of the Iron Age, ritual practices were increasingly segregated, both in domestic sites and dedicated cult places. At Geldermalsen-Hondsgamet, an area by a ditch at the edge of the farm was a focus for ritual deposition; finds included an animal burial, a horse skull, charred grain, brooches, a pot, and a Neolithic axe. What seem to be cult enclosures are also found in settlements (Oss R49; Tiel-Passewaaij) and out in the landscape (Lomm, Oss R26; Sittard-Hoogveld, Zundert), some with a funerary association. Isolated cult enclosures are also known in Belgium (Hannut; Kontich-Alfberg, which overlay an earlier settlement; Bourgeois et al. 2003). Lastly, Empel provides a rare regional example of the sequence familiar in Gaul (see earlier) of a Roman temple that succeeded a late Iron Age open-air cult site, attested by the deposition of pottery, animal bone, metal objects, and coins (Roymans and Aarts 2005).

As elsewhere in north-west Europe, dress accessories and objects associated with personal status are more frequent as settlement finds in the closing phases of the Iron Age. La Tène influence also became more apparent, notably in the wearing of glass bracelets closely resembling central European models. These were made in the Lower Rhine-Meuse region from the second century BC, although direct evidence for workshops is so far lacking (Roymans and Verniers 2010). Gold coins appear around the same time, including a hoard of coins and torcs buried in the second century BC within a settlement at Beringen, Limburg (Van Impe et al. 2002), but coinage was not minted locally until La Tène D2, and only west of the Rhine. Mediterranean imports are rare until after Caesar, although the glass and colourants used for making bracelets and beads came ultimately from eastern Mediterranean sources (Huisman et al. 2017).

The settlement expansion seen earlier continued in most areas during the later Iron Age. An exception is the Meuse-Demer-Scheldt region, where many farms and field systems were abandoned, probably due to over-exploitation of the sandy soils (Roymans and Gerritsen 2002), although some sites continued (e.g. Oss-Ussen). In the mid-first century BC, a major break in the settlement record occurred west of the Rhine, with sites abandoned and not reoccupied until the Augustan period, when new sites were also founded (Roymans 2019). Whatever caused the similar ruptures in northern France, the timing makes it likely that the episode here was linked to the Roman invasion and ensuing resettlement of Germanic groups from over the Rhine. Roymans has argued persuasively that the mass of La Tène D weaponry and human remains recovered from Kessel-Lith at the Rhine-Meuse confluence was linked to the defeat and massacre of the Usipetes and Tencteri by Caesar in 55 BC, although the river here was a focus of offerings from the Bronze Age through to the early medieval period, so votive deposition cannot be excluded.

The Later Iron Age in Britain and Ireland

The rise in settlement numbers that began in the earlier Iron Age continued unabated after 400 BC across Britain. As well as infilling around existing farms, this involved colonization of hitherto thinly inhabited landscapes, often with heavier, damper clay soils, made easier to clear and work by mature iron technology. Woodland clearance points to agricultural expansion into upland areas; other changes included manuring and crop rotation to maintain soil fertility and a surge in salt making sites. These suggest a rising population. Increased specialization is evident in the emergence of centres of iron production in areas like the Midlands, the Vale of York, and North Wales, and a growth of craft activities in marginal environments, whose inhabitants exploited local resources for exchange to offset their other disadvantages. By the late Iron Age, many craft industries were large-scale enterprises, distributing their products—iron bars and billets, salt-cakes, decorated pottery, rotary querns—over long distances.

La Tène-style decoration was adopted in Britain—if not yet Ireland—before 400 BC, earlier than once thought but consistent with the evidence in western France (Milcent 2006; Garrow et al. 2009). Hillfort occupancy in lowland Britain peaked in the fourth century BC and the quality of pottery declined, signifying a period of stress and social change. After 300 BC, houses became smaller and new regional ceramic traditions emerged across southern Britain, which endured for the rest of the later Iron Age (Cunliffe 2005; Sharples 2010). These changes imply an increased emphasis on group identity and a decline in the role of the house as an arena for social interaction.

Developed Hillforts

In parallel with these developments, many hillforts were abandoned, some after violence, as at Fin Cop in the Peak District (Waddington 2012). This left fewer hillforts dominating larger territories. Typically these were aggrandized with glacis earthworks (where the faces of dump ramparts formed a continuous profile with deep V-ditches) and elongated entrances, often augmented by outworks. At Danebury one entrance was blocked, a partial outer circuit added, and the interior reorganized. Much of its southern half was given over to regimented rows of four- and six-post structures along the internal roads, while circular buildings were now mostly in the north, and more tightly packed (Cunliffe 1995; Davis 2013). The enclosed area at Maiden Castle was more than doubled and eventually surrounded by three ramparts, with complex outworks at the entrances (Sharples 1991). The incidence of special deposits increased at both sites, while rich finds assemblages attest to far-flung contacts and a range of agricultural and manufacturing activities. These 'developed hillforts'—as they are often termed—are concentrated in Wessex, the Cotswolds, and the Welsh Marches. Other excavated examples include Cadbury Castle and Ham Hill in Somerset, and the Breiddin and Croft Ambrey in the Marches (Cunliffe 2005).

Various models have been proposed for the rise of developed hillforts. The Wessex examples are thought to have achieved dominance by overcoming weaker neighbours and then more distant rivals (Sharples 1991; Cunliffe 2005). At Maiden Castle, Sharples suggests that vanquished neighbours were absorbed into the hillfort, while groups further away were demilitarized and obliged to furnish labour (Sharples 2010: 74). The victors used this labour to maintain and enlarge the earthworks surrounding their own hillfort, which came to symbolize the success and prestige of the community. Many sites around Danebury were deserted around the time it was remodelled (Cunliffe 2009), supporting the view that aggregation of population was a factor in the growth of these dominant communities.

While some archaeologists have argued that developed hillforts were lightly occupied, Danebury and Maiden Castle had sizeable populations, swelled by seasonal visitors for assemblies and festivals (Davis 2013). Older models of these sites as elite residences or central places where a rural population came to exchange its produce for other goods are difficult to sustain, given the sparsely populated environs. If it is going too far to call them hilltop towns, developed hillforts nevertheless had much in common with many Greek *poleis*, most of whose population lived in the city but farmed the surrounding countryside, or medieval hilltop towns whose inhabitants went out daily to cultivate the fields. In size and density of occupation, the largest developed hillforts are comparable with *oppida* (see earlier): indeed, Ham Hill (88 ha) is larger than all but a few Gaulish *oppida* and shares many of their other attributes (Sharples 2014; Stewart and Russell 2017).

From the later second century BC onwards, the occupants of many developed hillforts dispersed to smaller sites in the environs. There is little to indicate what occasioned this exodus—at Danebury, the east gate was destroyed by fire, but not necessarily in an attack—and some activity often continued. One entrance at Maiden Castle was used for burial, while a farm was later installed inside Danebury. At about the same time, a handful of large fortified sites were established in river valleys in southern England, as at Oram's Arbour, Winchester, perhaps the successor to a nearby hillfort on St Catherine's Hill. While there have been few modern excavations, these low-lying enclosures—like the developed hillforts—were intensively occupied and may have performed similar roles.

Not all later hillforts in southern Britain conform to the Wessex template. On Bredon Hill, Worcestershire, a small hillfort (Conderton Camp) and a promontory fort (Bredon

Camp, known for the mass of human bone from the entranceway) coexisted for much of the period and overlapped an extensive settlement at Beckford in the valley beneath (Thomas 2005). In the East Midlands, Burrough Hill was the same size as Danebury, but had a settlement outside (Figure 4.9; Taylor et al. 2012). Hunsbury hillfort was packed with pits, which yielded over 100 querns from sources as far afield as Bristol, Kent, and the Pennines—reflecting the importance of the Jurassic geology for iron production (Cunliffe 2005: 396, 509). In the Thames Valley, a later Iron Age open settlement has been excavated below Wittenham Clumps hillfort, notable for its human remains and the site of a late Bronze Age enclosure and early Iron Age midden (Lambrick and Robinson 2009; see earlier).

Other later Iron Age hillforts were unoccupied, possibly hosting periodic gatherings or used as refuges. Sutton Common in the Humber wetlands, built about 350 BC, is an interesting example. Initially, the interior was packed with rows of four-post storage structures recalling Danebury, but no houses were found. Later, the site was used for cremation (Van de Noort et al. 2007). Several East Anglian ringworks like Arbury Camp seem to be devoid of occupation, while later hillforts in Kent and Sussex are often low-lying, implying a different role to the earlier hillforts high up on the Downs. Some Wealden sites incorporate striking rock formations and might have been special places before the earthworks were constructed (Hamilton and Manley 2001).

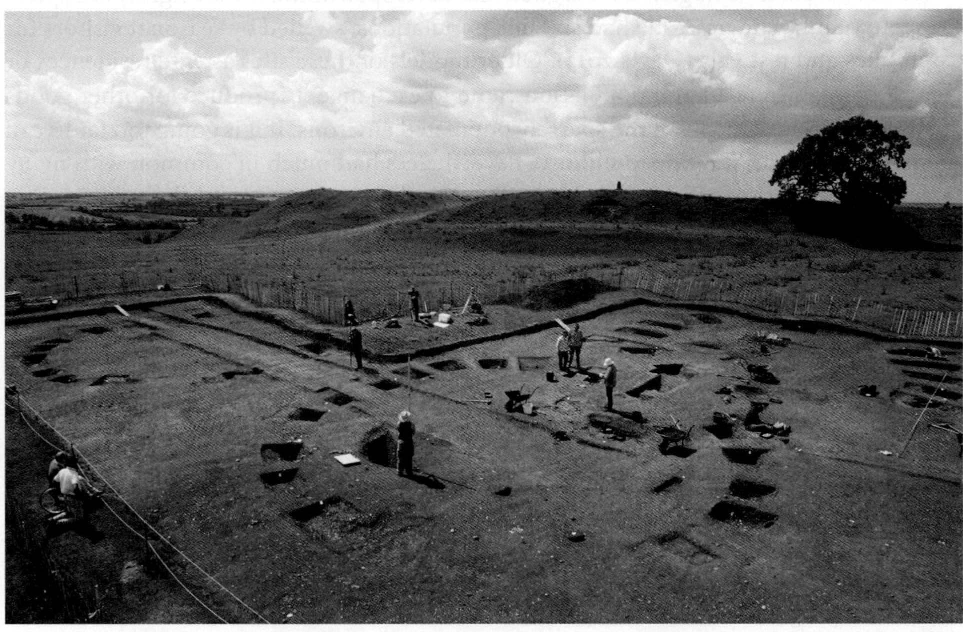

FIGURE 4.9 The later Iron Age hillfort at Burrough Hill, Leicestershire, showing contemporary roundhouses in the settlement area outside the east entrance.

Photo: University of Leicester Archaeological Services

Atlantic Britain

Large parts of western and northern Britain were dominated by small fortified sites, often with room for little more than two or three households. From Trevelgue Head—where there was an important iron smelting operation—to Broxmouth, sites were regularly embellished or acquired extra defences (Nowakowski and Quinnell 2011; Armit and McKenzie 2013). Often the earthworks were out of all proportion to the scale of the settlement, suggesting social display was the primary motive, not defence (e.g. Frodsham et al. 2007; Driver 2013). At the inland promontory site of Castell Henllys in Wales, a palisade built a little before 400 BC was refortified within a generation, with a dump rampart and elaborate entrance (later modified three times) fronted by stone *chevaux de frise*—familiar throughout Atlantic Europe, but more common in western Ireland or Scotland than southern Britain (Mytum 2013).

The overall distribution of forts masks significant regional variation (Lock and Ralston 2017). Multiple-enclosure forts with widely spaced ramparts were common in south-west England and parts of Wales (e.g. Clovelly Dykes, Devon; Collfryn, Powys; Killibury, Cornwall), reflecting the importance of pastoral farming and the need to protect valuable livestock. In North Wales, large stone-walled forts such as Conwy Mountain, Garn Boduan, and Tre'r Ceiri may be of this period, but are unlikely to have been used all year round given the altitude, and many of the visible hut circles are probably Roman Iron Age (Waddington 2013: 108). In east-central Scotland, a group of small oblong forts stands out, distinguished by massive timber-laced stone walls, often vitrified, and lacking entrances. They span the period 400–100 BC (O'Driscoll and Noble 2020; Noble 2020). Some were built inside earlier hillforts (White Caterthun, Turin Hill), while Tap O'Noth was later the focus of a Roman Iron Age hillfort (see later). They show little sign of occupation—Tap O'Noth is the second highest hillfort in Scotland—or defensive *raison d'être*. Given the deliberate firing of many sites, a ceremonial function seems likely (Harding 2017: 113–119).

In Atlantic Scotland, small promontory forts occur, but thick-walled drystone structures of varying degrees of complexity, some freestanding, others with outworks, dominated the settlement pattern. Known collectively as 'Atlantic roundhouses', they range from substantial roundhouses such as Dun Glashan and Rathoy in Argyll to the striking tower-like brochs of Caithness and the Northern and Western Isles, originally two or more storeys in height, with intramural staircases and galleries (Armit 2003; Henderson 2007; Harding 2017). Their wall faces were functionally independent, the inner wall taking the roof weight, the outer wall bearing the brunt of the weather (Romankiewicz 2011). Internally, brochs had a central living space surrounded by cells for sleeping and storage. Long viewed as defensive structures, they appear to be the ultimate in extravagant dwellings. Like contemporary forts, they were frequently embellished and located to be highly visible (from land and/or sea), while in easy reach of better-quality land and other resources.

From excavations at Old Scatness on Shetland and elsewhere, brochs probably emerged not long after 400 BC, albeit not reaching their full extent and development until later (Dockrill et al. 2015). Many northern brochs, including Old Scatness, Howe, and Gurness, occupied small enclosures, packed with conjoining buildings clustered around the central structure. Analysis of the layout of these 'broch villages' implies a gulf in rank between the broch dwellers and the rest of the community (Foster 1989). In the Western Isles, brochs tend to be isolated, albeit possibly because open sites are difficult to recognize, rather than indicating a fundamentally different social structure (Harding 2017: 171–172). But even if there were significant social differences, both the northern and the western brochs were clearly occupied by locally prominent households who could command the requisite resources for building them.

While brochs were at their peak, a new type of structure—the wheelhouse—appeared in Shetland and the Western Isles, so-called because of the way they were divided up by piers radiating from a central space, creating a series of bays with corbelled roofs around the circumference. Most wheelhouses were isolated, but others were built in the shells of older roundhouses, brochs, and 'broch villages'. To what extent this reflects status, chronology, or changing attitudes to monumentality is yet to be unpicked. Wheelhouses are far less visually prominent in the landscape than brochs—indeed, many like Cnip on Lewis were semi-subterranean—but they required similar architectural skills, were internally impressive, and arguably mimicked broch interiors (Armit 2003: 41–45). Another innovation at this period was the souterrain, with early versions on Skye, at several unenclosed sites in north-east Scotland, and in south-west England at Carn Euny (Henderson 2007: 142–147; Harding 2017: 126–127, 184).[20]

Farms and Agglomerations in Lowland Britain

In the course of the later Iron Age, farmsteads in many lowland areas of central and southern Britain were enclosed with banks and ditches, with open or palisaded settlements becoming progressively less common. The scale of earthworks around some farms was large enough for them to be classed as hillforts had their banks not been flattened by later agriculture. Whether their inhabitants were able to call on subordinate labour, or groups of farms cooperated, social competition was probably a driving factor behind specific episodes of accelerated enclosure like that seen around 200 BC in east-central Britain (Hamilton and Haselgrove 2019). Many later Iron Age farms were rectilinear in form, contrasting with the irregular, curvilinear enclosures hitherto prevalent over much of this zone, and one particular group in southern Scotland probably relates to infilling of the already well-occupied coastal plain as the population rose (Armit 2003; Haselgrove 2009).

Along the terraces of the Thames, from Mucking at the estuary to Cotswold Community near its source, the earlier unenclosed settlement clusters gave way to a landscape of enclosed farms, fields, and tracks, including seasonally occupied sites on the floodplain (Lambrick and Robinson 2009; Davies 2018). Shifts from open to enclosed sites are seen in other river valleys such as the Trent, as well as in areas in between (Knight 2007; Moore 2020). Many farms display features such as antenna ditches linked to stock raising, notably the distinctive 'banjo' enclosures, common from the South Coast to Wales (Cunliffe 2005). Their elongated entrances were useful for rounding up livestock, often now moved over long distances (Hamilton et al. 2019). Some banjo enclosures were occupied, perhaps seasonally. One at Nettlebank Copse in the Danebury environs had only a short lifespan, whereas two at Bagendon were used for much longer and were complementary, one associated with pig rearing, the other with sheep; animal remains from the sites might be debris from feasting at gatherings for livestock management (Moore 2020: 127–133). The hillfort at Bury Hill, near Danebury, was refortified and reoccupied for around a generation in the second century BC, perhaps for breeding horses (Cunliffe 2009).

Against this background of some regions dominated by large hillforts and others by smaller fortified sites or enclosed homesteads, eastern England stands out. Here, many earlier Iron Age open sites developed into larger agglomerations. Several have been explored, including Beaumont Leys and Glenfield near Leicester, and Dragonby (May 1996; Thomas 2011, 2018). Sometimes their limits were defined by earthworks of modest scale, while the inhabited areas consisted of clusters of houses and compounds following no clear pattern, often separated by open spaces. The agglomeration at Crick was focused around a low-lying area used as summer pasture (Hughes and Woodward 2015; Masefield 2015). Several long-distance routes met here and some structures were not permanently occupied, implying that the population was swelled by seasonal visitors coming here for exchange. While there is limited evidence of craft activity at these agglomerations, they could have played a role similar to the developed hillforts in other parts of southern Britain (Thomas 2011; Bradley 2019). Burrough Hill, combining hillfort and open settlement, may be the exception that proves the rule. Moreover, the abandonment of developed hillforts in other parts of southern Britain seems to coincide with the development of large new unenclosed settlements in these areas, from the newly discovered site at Winterbourne Kingston in Dorset, which covered some 20 ha (Russell 2016), to Beckford at the foot of Bredon Hill. Glastonbury Lake Village was founded in the earlier second century BC and grew rapidly, reaching around fourteen households, before increasingly wet conditions forced its desertion around 50 BC. Craft activity was more prominent at Glastonbury than at the East Midlands sites, while the nearby sites at Meare seem to have been seasonally occupied craft and trading centres—glass beads made at Meare have been found as far afield as Cornwall and Scotland (Coles and Minnitt 1995; Marshall et al. 2020). All three Lake Villages provide a good example of groups inhabiting environments poorly suited for cultivation, developing specialist skills (see earlier).

Ireland

In Ireland, the pattern of ephemeral unenclosed sites with few buildings or artefacts continued (Becker 2012). While occupation sites remain elusive, this seems to reflect continuing mobility rather than lack of people, shown by the increase in radiocarbon dates after 400 BC, mirroring trends across north-west Europe (Armit et al. 2013). Another proxy for settlement is the network of timber tracks in the Irish midlands, notably the 2 km long Corlea trackway (Co Longford; McDermott et al. 2009). This was built in a single year (148 BC), implicating a significant number of people (Raftery 1994: 103–104). Many sites were used on a short-term or intermittent basis, often for activities such as ironworking. Smelting furnaces are not uncommon, but rarely associated with structures. A furnace near a roundhouse at Carrickmines Great (Co Dublin) and one in a circular structure at Knockcommane (Co Limerick) are exceptions (Ó Drisceoil 2007; Dolan 2016; Gartski 2019). Two crannogs at Lough Gara returned later Iron Age radiocarbon dates, the first Irish examples to do so, but this could be from seasonal use, not permanent occupation (Fredengren 2002).

Metalwork—now in La Tène style—reappeared in the archaeological record, and rotary querns—some decorated—replaced saddle types, indicating changes in the agricultural sphere (Raftery 1994). The metalwork consisted mostly of high-status objects, particularly bronze horse-gear, martial items, and gold torcs. Despite the widespread evidence of smelting, few iron objects were deposited. Almost all the metalwork comes from natural places, but weaponry is restricted to wet contexts, particularly rivers, gold to dryland and bogs, and there are fewer bronze hoards on dryland than gold (Becker 2011). Metalwork finds thin out in the southern half of Ireland, and rotary querns are wholly absent (Becker 2012), perhaps indicating that such objects did not hold the same meaning in processes of social reproduction here as they did further north (Bradley 2019). The period also saw the emergence of formal ceremonial foci or places of regional assembly. One of the earliest, constructed in three phases around 400 BC, was the circular palisaded site at Lismullin (near Tara), where a post avenue astronomically aligned with the Pleiades led from an east-facing entrance to a smaller inner enclosure (O'Connell 2013).

Larger, and some centuries later, than Lismullin are the monumental centres at Navan, Knockaulin, Rathcroghan, and Tara (Raftery 1994; Newman 1997; Lynn 2003; Johnston and Wailes 2007). All four feature in later Irish sources as the former residences of kings, and so are known, albeit anachronistically, as royal sites. While not a uniform group, the similarities outweigh the differences (Becker 2019). They lie in landscapes full of earlier monuments and occupied prominent hilltops or ridges—Rathacrogan was focused on a vast mound—surrounded by large curvilinear ditched enclosures with external banks. Linear earthworks were also part of all the complexes except Knockaulin. In the interiors (sometimes outside) were mounds, ring ditches, and successive timber palisades, including distinctive conjoined double-skinned 'figure-of-eight' structures, often with funnel entrances, and in many cases built before the enclosing earthworks. Many of the internal structures were probably unroofed and they became increasingly monumental with time.

The most extensively explored and best dated is the complex at Navan (Lynn 2003; Bayliss and Grogan 2013; O'Driscoll et al. 2020), which lies near Haughey's Fort (see earlier), and two lakes with late Bronze Age offerings. Around 200 BC, after a hiatus of some centuries, timber figure-of-eight structures began to be constructed on Navan hill. In the 90s BC, the hill was enclosed; a construction 40 m across was erected, quickly filled with stones, destroyed by fire, and covered beneath a mound (Figure 4.10); and the Dorsey earthwork was created, subdividing the landscape south of Navan. Similar sequences at Knockaulin and Tara probably unfolded broadly in parallel (Becker 2019).[21]

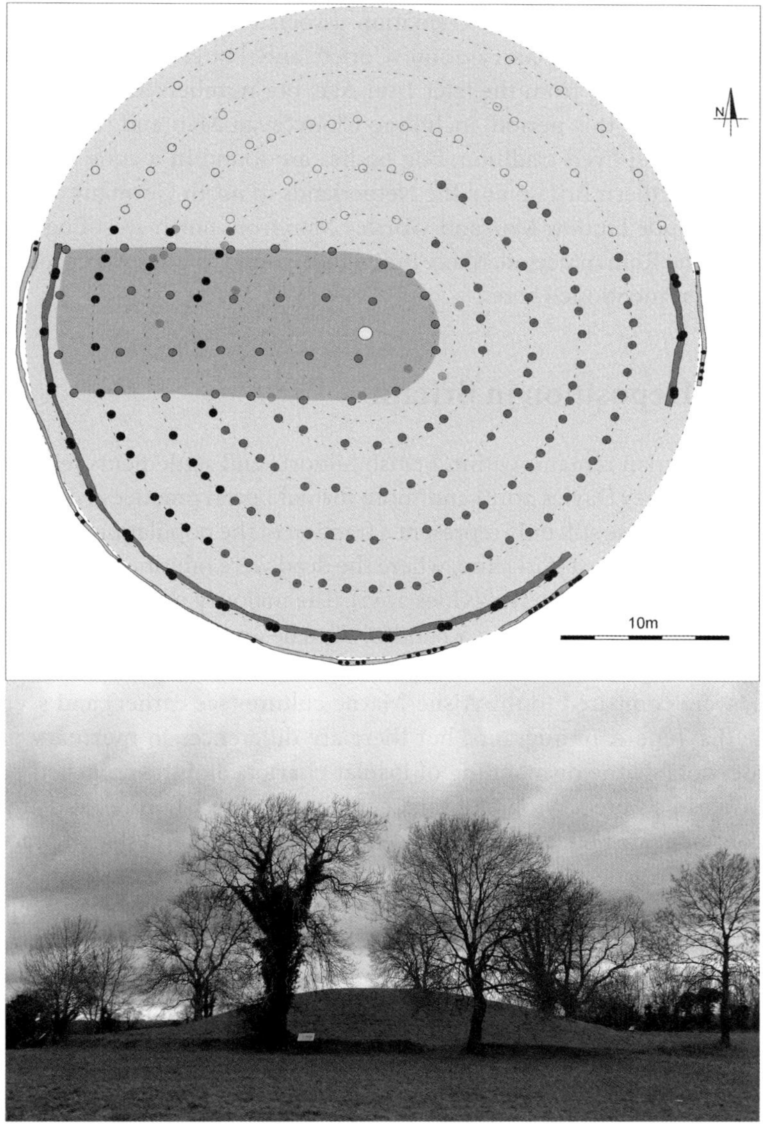

FIGURE 4.10 Navan, Co. Armagh: (a) reconstructed plan of '40 m structure'; (b) photo of the overlying mound.

Illustrations Tanja Romankiewicz

Activities at these complexes included burial, feasting on pork, and metalworking, while isotope analysis shows that people and their animals came to Navan from afar (Madgwick et al. 2019). Contacts over longer distances are attested by the remains of a North African macaque from a feature pre-dating the 40 m structure. What led to the burst of monumentalization at Navan at the turn of the second and first centuries BC is unclear, but the coincidence with the peak of *oppidum* building on the continent is intriguing (Bradley et al. 2016).

The Irish tradition of unurned cremation associated with ring ditches and older monuments continued (McGarry 2009; Corlett and Potterton 2012). More cremation deposits are known from the later Iron Age, but numbers are still small. Several bog bodies belong to this period, including Clonycavan Man and Old Croghan Man (Giles 2020). A long-lived tradition, bog bodies are found in a zone extending from Ireland across northern Britain and the Netherlands to north Germany and Denmark. British finds include Lindow Man and Worsley Man from north-west England, both of whom died in the Roman period. Many individuals found in bogs were violently killed, including all four mentioned here.

Burial and Deposition in Britain

Deposition of human remains within British hillforts and settlements reached its peak in the later Iron Age (Davies 2018) and more formal burial practices emerged in some regions, although these still only represent a fraction of the population. The most prominent tradition was in East Yorkshire, where the dead were inhumed in square barrows, often grouped in large cemeteries (Giles 2012). The majority of graves date to the third or second centuries BC, including a handful of male and female chariot graves, some containing swords or mirrors (Garton-Wetwang Slack). In the past, the Yorkshire chariot graves were compared to the Aisne-Marne culture (see earlier) and seen as a rite brought by La Tène A immigrants, but there are differences in mortuary practice as well as date, notably the dismantling of insular chariots and the crouched position of the dead. Chariots were a symbol of rank across north-west Europe, and any parallels with the continent are better explained by elite-level contacts and shared practices than mass migration. In 2017–18, two unusual chariot burials were excavated at Pocklington in separate cemeteries: both included pairs of ponies, and one a shield (Stephens and Ware 2020).

Localized cist grave traditions developed in Cornwall (Harlyn Bay, Trethellan Farm) and eastern Scotland (Broxmouth, Dryburn Bridge), while radiocarbon dating has identified several unfurnished inhumation cemeteries in southern England, as at Suddern Farm, Yarnton, and Fison Way (Gregory 1992; Sharples 2010; Hey et al. 2011). A few inhumations with weapons may be founder burials. At Mill Hill, Deal, a male buried with sword, shield, and bronze headdress around 200 BC was the earliest grave at a long-lived dispersed cemetery (Parfitt 1995); near Winchester, the first-century BC Owslebury 'warrior' was associated with a small cemetery; a cist grave with sword and mirror at Bryher, Isles of Scilly, may be another example (Johns 2002–3). In East Yorkshire, a group of extended inhumations with weapons (mostly at Rudston) seems to be a late development within that regional tradition, parallel with the rise in weapon burials in southern Britain. A man with a Gaulish helmet and sword buried at North Bersted (Sussex) could be a Gallic War refugee (Taylor 2020).

Late in the second century BC, a new cremation rite with links to Belgic Gaul began to be practised in south-east England. Typically, burials were in urns, sometimes accompanied by one or two pots, brooches, or other personal items. A handful of graves with buckets, hearth furniture, or bronze vessels anticipate the wealthy Welwyn graves found in the area from after 50 BC (see later). Most cemeteries were small, and clusters of burials hint at kin groups, as at Aylesford in Kent. The early and unusually large cemetery at Westhampnett, near Chichester, in use until the mid-first century BC, differed in several regards from those nearer the Thames. Its 161 graves were close to pyre sites and shrines, the cremations were unurned, many objects were burnt on the pyre, and animal sacrifice was common (Fitzpatrick 2007). Some of the pottery has affinities with Normandy, suggesting that the users of this cemetery and the builders of the Gaulish-style timber shrine erected in the first century BC on nearby Hayling Island were linked into different cross-Channel networks from groups in south-east England.

Hoarding of metalwork resumed in the later Iron Age, above all in southern Britain. Iron features in many more deposits than in Ireland. Study of iron hoards and semi-products ('currency bars') reveals two broad zones linked to differing practices (Haselgrove and Hingley 2006). The majority of iron bars occur in Wessex and the Severn-Cotswolds, often near the boundaries or entrances of hillforts and enclosed settlements. Outside this zone, ironwork deposits are rarer, and mainly from natural places; at some wet foci such as Fiskerton and Llyn Cerrig Bach on Anglesey, the offerings spanned centuries. As well as iron bars and billets, weapons, domestic and personal items, agricultural implements, and metalworking tools all feature in deposits, reflecting the role the metal had acquired in everyday life and ideology.

While some dryland hoards from southern England might have been intended for recovery, the choice of symbolically charged boundary locations, the referencing of agriculture and metalworking, and the inclusion of broken objects imply that these deposits—like their counterparts in rivers or bogs—were sacrificed for the well-being of the community. Two big cauldron hoards from Chiseldon in Wessex and Glenfield near Leicester provide a tantalizing glimpse of the lavish banquets that were another important feature of the period. The eighteen iron-rimmed bronze cauldrons from Chiseldon would have held stew for 600 people, while faunal deposits that may be actual remnants of communal feasts occur at Aylesbury and High Post (Baldwin and Joy 2017; Thomas 2018; Bradley 2019: 292).

As in Ireland, gold reappeared in Britain, initially as torcs and bracelets like those in the Leekfrith (Staffordshire) and Blair Drummond (Stirling) hoards (Figure 4.11), followed by gold coins imported from Belgic Gaul into the regions around the Thames estuary (Farley and Hunter 2015). In the second century BC, the inhabitants of East Kent began casting potin coins similar to those in use in Gaul, while by the time of Julius

FIGURE 4.11 Gold hoard from Blair Drummond, Stirling, third or second century BC. The torcs show widespread connections: the two twisted ribbon torcs are a local style; the fragmentary torc is modelled on French examples, while the elaborate torc at the front mixes Iron Age form and Mediterranean technique (Farley and Hunter 2015: 93–94). Excavation revealed that the hoard was buried inside a circular timber building in an isolated wet location.

Photo: National Museums Scotland, Edinburgh

Caesar's invasions in 55–54 BC most British peoples as far as the Severn-Humber line were minting gold coins. Together with over 200 precious metal torcs, bracelets, and rings, gold and potin coins were among the contents of fourteen hoards buried in the late second or early first century BC at an open-air sanctuary on a low hill at Snettisham, East Anglia (Joy 2015).

Around the same date, the fast potter's wheel was adopted in parts of southern Britain (although its use only became widespread after 50 BC) and Italian wine amphorae began to be imported. These reached the South Coast via the cross-Channel networks linking coastal trading places such as Hengistbury Head (Cunliffe 1987) and Urville-Nacqueville (see earlier), rather than through direct exchange with the Roman world. A handful of pre-Caesarian imports from burials and settlements near the Thames estuary, notably Dressel 1A amphorae from Baldock and Stansted, and a bronze wine service from Aylesford, were probably passed on from Belgic Gaul by means of the alliances that previously introduced gold coinage. The imports were a portent of the rapid changes to come in Britain between Caesar's conquest of Gaul and the Claudian invasion a century later.

The Roman Iron Age (50 BC–AD 400)

The Gallic War effectively brought the south and east of Britain into the Roman orbit, although not yet the Atlantic zone or Ireland. In south-east England, the treaties put in place by Caesar and his successors altered the political arena, opening the way to the formation of new polities headed by rulers friendly to Rome, who styled themselves kings and minted inscribed coinages, borrowing Roman imagery (Creighton 2000; Hill 2007). Other markers of increased political centralization and social hierarchy after 50 BC include the emergence of new seats of royal power, associated with imposing linear dykes, such as Colchester or St Albans, and the richly furnished Welwyn burials north of the Thames. The latter resemble contemporary aristocratic Gaulish graves and, like them, are mainly rural and mix indigenous status items (buckets, hearth furniture) and luxury imports, with an emphasis on feasting and drinking (Champion 2016). Weapons are missing from the British graves, however, apart from chain mail in a few unusually elaborate graves like the Lexden tumulus, Colchester, and Folly Lane, St Albans. These graves are also exceptional in being associated with dyke complexes, and might be of client rulers.

Although often compared to *oppida*, the British linear dyke complexes are a distinct class of site (Haselgrove 2016; Garland 2020; Moore 2020). They emerged late in the first century BC, after the reorganization of Gaul into Roman provinces. Their locations suggest an intention to unite different groups and some are named on coins,[22] confirming their links with lineages friendly to Rome. Like *oppida*, some developed from ritual foci and they show signs of functional zoning (habitation, funerary, workshops), but spread over large areas within the dykes, separated by fields or open space, giving them a polyfocal character. There is little indication of planned layouts, however, or sizeable resident populations—although the King Harry Lane cemetery at St Albans is larger than most known burial grounds at *oppida*.

The site most resembling Gaulish *oppida* is Silchester (Hampshire), where a street grid was laid out early in the first century AD, flanked by rectilinear buildings, still more familiar across the Channel at this date, but attested at some other British dyke complexes. Among the buildings was a timber hall over 40 m long, one of three built on the same spot in little over a generation (Fulford et al. 2018). Silchester displays other ties with Belgic Gaul, including a high level of pork consumption, perhaps indicating the presence of migrants or traders, whose familiarity with the new Roman towns of Gaul could have contributed to these developments. All the British dyke complexes have yielded abundant imports, often now Gaulish or Spanish rather than Italian. At Stanwick in northern England, initial contacts with the Roman world were largely indirect, but intensified between AD 40–70 when the complex achieved new significance as the centre of a client kingdom on the northern flanks of the fledgling Roman province (Haselgrove 2016; Fell 2020). Unlike Silchester, circular buildings remained the norm at Stanwick throughout the life of the core settlement. They included a large unroofed timber structure erected around the change of era, soon replaced by another short-lived building of similar dimensions, this time roofed.[23] This frequent rebuilding of imposing structures at both British sites recalls the pattern seen at Irish ceremonial complexes like Navan.

Alongside the dyke complexes, new forms of agglomerated settlements emerged, particularly in eastern England. Many lay at river crossings, but as most became Roman towns, evidence for their origins is patchy. The port at Heybridge on the Blackwater estuary was centred on a shrine (Atkinson and Preston 2015), and a strong ritual focus is also apparently at Baldock and Canterbury, whereas exchange and craft activity are prominent at Braughing-Puckeridge and Old Sleaford. Only a few sites were fortified (e.g. Abingdon). Leicester may have begun as a meeting place for agglomerations in the environs, which were progressively deserted as the focus beside the river Soar grew. Like the dyke complexes, the agglomerations often broke with traditional architecture, mixing rectangular and circular structures.

Imported Gallo-Roman tablewares, brooches, and toilet implements were extensively imitated in southern and eastern England, as a wider section of society espoused new ways of preparing, serving, and consuming food and drink, and of bodily adornment. Literacy was another innovation, if only for a few, evidenced by finds of styli, graffiti on pots, and coin legends. Silver coinages minted from Roman *denarii* and bullion entering Britain as gifts or subsidies (Farley 2012: 73–84) displaced gold as the principal medium, although bronze was confined to the regions near the Thames. The relative significance of Roman diplomacy and hostage taking, Gaulish immigrants or refugees from failed uprisings in Belgic Gaul, traders, and existing elite networks in driving these changes is a matter of debate, but it is fair to say that south-east Britain was as much Gallicized as Romanized at this period, with the inhabitants of Roman Gaul key intermediaries in the process (Gosden 2004: 109).

Mortuary and ritual practices were increasingly segregated from the domestic sphere in cemeteries and cult sites. A rectilinear space lined by funerary structures at Mucking recalls Acy-Romance (see earlier) and was presumably a place for the community to gather (Evans et al. 2016). Aylesford-type cemeteries multiplied in south-east England, and crouched inhumation cemeteries appeared in Dorset. Simply furnished burials remained the norm, but more graves now contained swords or mirrors (Hunter 2005; Joy 2010). Built sanctuaries range from square and circular shrines set within ditches or palisades (Heathrow; Welwick Farm) to more elaborate complexes such as Fison Way or Springhead (Gregory 1992; Andrews et al. 2011). As in Gaul, many Roman temples superseded earlier sacred sites with scant structural remains, inferred principally from feasting debris and coins or brooch offerings (Harlow, Uley, Wanborough). The Hayling Island temple is unusual in its structural continuity, but also stands out for its Gaulish affinities (see earlier).

Ironwork deposits in Wessex declined with the demise of the hillforts, but deposits of other metals increased significantly. Distinct regional traditions can be discerned, favouring horse and chariot equipment, personal adornment, or coins (Hunter 1997; Garrow and Gosden 2012). Certain finds graphically chart the evolving relationship with Rome, from the gold jewellery including a pair of necklace-torcs made in a Mediterranean workshop deposited in the first century BC on a low hilltop near Winchester (Hill et al. 2004), to the multiple hoards of Iron Age and Roman coins to Claudius, silver ingots, and Roman cavalry helmet excavated at an open-air sanctuary at Hallaton. Possibly captured after AD 43, the helmet could also have been an elite-level gift—as the necklace-torcs surely were—or acquired through auxiliary service (Score 2011). Large quantities of young pig were consumed at Hallaton, recalling the feasting at midden sites like Llanmaes, although this time the right forelimbs are missing.

While the most striking changes before the Roman invasion occurred in the 'Gallicized' zone nearest the continent, similar trends can be detected further west and north. Across southern Britain, settlement numbers climb rapidly after 50 BC (Smith et al. 2016). In northern England and southern Scotland, enclosed farms and hillforts gave way to open settlements, their houses spilling out over former boundaries. A similar development occurred in the Cotswolds (Moore 2020). Wales and south-west England, on the other hand, saw a refocusing of occupation away from fortified hilltops to enclosed farms such as the Welsh raths and Cornish rounds, which emerged a little earlier and now multiplied. Coaxial field systems were laid out over tracts of central England and East Anglia. Various forms of 'grouped' farms appeared, often comprising conjoined enclosures with clearly differentiated internal spaces, including the distinctive 'ladder' and 'washing line' settlements of Yorkshire (Melton, Newbridge, Wattle Syke).[24] In Cornwall, courtyard house clusters developed, and the souterrain at Carn Euny was altered to give access from one of the houses (Henderson 2007: 144). Across Scotland, there was a surge in souterrain construction, notably in the lowlands north of the Tay (Harding 2017: 247–250).

Beyond south-east Britain, overt signs of social hierarchy are fairly limited, notwithstanding the recent Pembrokeshire find of a chariot burial dating to the first century AD, the first from Wales. The failure of groups west and north of the Severn-Humber line to adopt coinage implies different value systems, and perhaps non-hierarchical social structures (Hill 2011). However, the impression of difference is reinforced by the rarity of Roman imports in Atlantic regions prior to the conquest, and by higher levels of conspicuous consumption in south-east Britain. Finds like the Welsh chariot burial, the Llyn Cerrig Bach objects (Macdonald 2007), and a few peri-conquest hoards show that individuals in Atlantic Britain had access to metalwork of the same quality as the leading sections of society in south-east Britain, but usually chose not to deposit them in the same manner (Haselgrove 2004). Distinctions of rank might in any case have been expressed in other ways, from architecture to ownership of movables like cattle. The coalescence of kingdoms under Roman influence in the south and east is also distorting the picture. Coin distributions and historical sources reveal the underlying complexity and fluidity of these polities, which were to a greater or lesser extent Roman creations, fossilized in the *civitates* of Roman *Britannia*.

Beyond the Frontiers

The creation of permanently garrisoned frontiers left the north Netherlands, Scotland, and Ireland outside the Roman Empire, albeit all were affected to a greater or lesser extent by its proximity. There is little sign of military activity north of the Rhine after the first century AD and no record of official Roman interventions in Ireland (Cahill Wilson 2014),[25] whereas Scotland suffered repeated aggression (Hunter 2007, 2016). As in southern Britain before AD 43, Rome manipulated groups beyond the frontiers, even imposing rulers,[26] and the later Roman army relied on recruitment outside the Empire. Trade was another driver of cross-border interaction, with the export of Roman goods in return for raw materials, slaves, and other commodities. In Free Germany, low-value items such as pottery were concentrated near the frontiers, with luxury exports and weaponry travelling further afield (Hedeager 1978; Cunliffe 1988), although depositional practices may have exaggerated the distinction.

In the North Sea coastal region of the north Netherlands and as far east as the river Weser,[27] the early centuries AD saw many tendencies evident in the later Iron Age continuing. Nucleated settlements, some enclosed, multiplied on both sides of the Rhine (Waterbolk 1995; Hiddink and Roymans 2015). Many of them began as groups of one to three farms, as at Wijster (Drenthe), where the earlier houses were replaced in the third century AD by an ordered layout of buildings, enclosures, and trackways, and at Flögeln (Lower Saxony). These villages and hamlets coexisted with single farms like Fochteloo (Friesland). Variants of three-aisled byre-houses remained the norm, complemented in the late Roman period by sunken-featured ancillary structures associated with the immigration of new Germanic groups (Roymans et al. 2020).[28] Renewed settlement expansion in the coastal marshes is attested by new terp sites,[29] including the extensively excavated site at Feddersen Wierde on the Weser estuary, occupied from the late Iron Age to the fifth century AD, when it was deserted due to rising sea levels. Initially comprising two houses, it grew quickly, developing a typical radial plan; at its peak in the third century AD, there were over twenty-five farms (Haarnagel 1979).

At Feddersen Wierde, a large house with its own palisade and a concentration of Roman imports is seen as the residence of the leading household, but there is little sign of a pronounced social hierarchy—a view seemingly shared by Tacitus.[30] Simple cremation burials (urned or unurned) continued as the dominant rite, and several bog bodies of the period are known in the north Netherlands,[31] but there are no counterparts to the Lübsow burials with their imported feasting equipment and other wealthy Roman Iron Age burials beyond the Elbe (Todd 1987; Grane 2013; see Chapter 5). Many of the *denarius* hoards and Roman gold coins found north of the Rhine may have arrived as subsidies, or to recruit troops (Blackwell et al. 2017; Roymans et al. 2020),[32] but most imports to the region—like samian pottery and brooches—were introduced through seaborne trade, as they are concentrated on coastal sites like Feddersen Wierde (Erdrich 2001). There is little sign of agricultural intensification to supply the Roman market for cattle and horses such as we see within the province, with cattle remaining small beyond the frontier (Roymans 1996: 60, 82–83), although increased craftworking (e.g. textiles) in the later part of the period has been inferred at some settlements.

The Roman arrival in northern Britain in the later first century AD and short-lived occupation of southern Scotland initially had little tangible impact on settlement (Harding 2017). In lowland areas, open sites predominated. Interspersed with these were a few brochs (mostly built on extant settlements) but no larger foci, apart from Traprain Law on the East Lothian coastal plain, where there is an exceptional amount of Roman material (Hunter 2007). South of the Forth-Clyde isthmus, settlements and dwellings were often scooped, while in the Southern Uplands small enclosures were common. The picture is more fragmented in Atlantic regions, with broch 'villages' still occupied in Caithness and the Northern Isles (Figure 4.12), and wheelhouses gaining ground at the

FIGURE 4.12 Broch and 'village' at Gurness, Orkney.

Photo: Tanja Romankiewicz

expense of brochs in Shetland and the Western Isles, but steadfastly absent in the Inner Hebrides and Argyll (where other forms of Atlantic roundhouses continued in use) as well as Orkney. At Clachtoll, excavation of a broch that burnt down around AD 50 is providing a detailed picture of the possessions and daily lives of its occupants (Cavers and Sleight 2018).

Votive practices continued largely unaltered, albeit often now incorporating Roman objects alongside native ones—as in a group of ironwork hoards from southern Scotland—or replacing them (Hunter 1997). Apart from an unusual valley bottom enclosure at Over Rig near the earlier hillfort of Castle O'er in south-west Scotland (Mercer 2019), built sanctuaries are unknown, and cult activity remained focused on long-established special places such as older monuments (Dairsie) and the Covesea Caves on the Moray coast, which were used for excarnation in the Roman Iron Age (Armit and Büster 2020). The complexity of the rites accorded by communities to the dead can also be glimpsed at settlements such as Phantassie, close to Traprain Law, where token amounts of cremated bone were brought back to the site after ceremonies elsewhere (Lelong and MacGregor 2007). A scatter of sword burials around the Firth of Forth recalls those in southern Britain (Hunter 2005; Roy 2015).

The picture changes radically in the later Roman Iron Age. In eastern Scotland, a new tradition emerged of inhumation burial (often in cists) under square- or round-ditched barrows grouped in small cemeteries like Lunan Bay, where they were accompanied by unenclosed inhumations (Alexander 2005). Most souterrains were infilled before the fourth century AD, some when settlements remained occupied (Harding 2017). In the Atlantic zone, brochs and wheelhouses gave way to smaller cellular structures, while across the Central Lowlands there was a drop-off in settlement (e.g. Cook et al. 2019). Much of the farming population around Traprain Law moved onto the hilltop, to which a stone wall was added in the fifth century AD (Haselgrove 2009). Other hillforts were reoccupied and/or refortified, from Castle O'er in the south-west to Tap O'Noth in the north-east, where a sizeable Roman Iron Age settlement grew up around the earlier oblong fort (Noble 2020).[33] If the stone plaques with simple Pictish symbols found at Dunnicaer promontory fort, near Aberdeen, were indeed integral to its rampart, this implies that their iconic tradition of stone carving and symbols had emerged by the late third century AD, when Roman sources first mention the Picts (Noble et al. 2018, 2019). The enclosed ceremonial site at Rhynie, in existence in the late fourth century AD (and overlooked from Tap O'Noth) also had a number of early Pictish symbol stones.

Roman impact north of Hadrian's Wall was far greater in some areas than others. Unsurprisingly, Roman material is commonest in the areas that were garrisoned, but goods filtered north by a variety of mechanisms. East Lothian had a negligible military presence, which along with the rich array of imports at Traprain Law implies that its inhabitants had client status for much of the period (Hunter 2016). In general, Roman imports are concentrated at settlements that are also 'richer' in other ways, such as the lowland brochs, which perhaps implies a hierarchical society where control over Roman goods may have enabled leading groups to increase their social distance from the rest (Hunter 2007). In the admittedly more sparsely inhabited Atlantic regions, there are fewer imports and these are mostly at coastal sites, pointing to arrival through seaborne contacts. The spread of Roman goods implies more even access in this zone, although in some areas such as Orkney and Caithness focal sites again have more finds (albeit still in single figures). Across Scotland, samian occurs at the most sites, followed by brooches, coarsewares, glassware, metal vessels, beads, and coins.

A series of later second- and early third-century AD *denarius* hoards from central and north-east Scotland, including two from an extensive open settlement at Birnie in Moray, may reflect a Roman policy of subsidies or pay-offs to troublesome groups after the failed Antonine reoccupation of southern Scotland (Hunter 2007). After *c.*AD 230, the policy ceased. South-east Scotland saw continued access to Roman goods—although focused on fewer sites—but in the Pictish homeland in the north-east, imports ceased (Hunter 2016). Roman interference is widely accepted as a factor in the ethnogenesis of the Picts, but opinion is divided over whether this came about because the Roman threat caused smaller groups to coalesce, or because the loss of subsidies led to the collapse of an elite that had grown dependent on them, from which an antagonistic new social order emerged. North-east Scotland had already developed a clear regional identity in the early Roman Iron Age, which points to changes in social and political organization (Hunter 2007).

A handful of hoards containing late Roman 'hacksilver' from sites in eastern Scotland including Traprain Law show that contacts with Rome ran on beyond the formal end of Roman Britain. Long thought to be loot, the fifth-century Traprain 'treasure' was either a diplomatic gift to long-standing allies, or pay brought home by warriors returning from service in the late Roman army; military equipment has also been found there (Blackwell et al. 2017; see also Chapter 28). Imported silver was increasingly recycled into local types of personal objects such as pins, and used to manufacture massive silver chains that combined the old custom of wearing neck-rings to symbolize high status with the new metal of power to which elites had become habituated in their dealings with the Roman Empire. Silver chains cluster in south-east Scotland, where they were presumably made; a scatter along the north-east coast may reflect elite contacts between the two areas. Two hoards from north of the Forth mixing hacksilver and early medieval objects were both buried at older monuments—a stone circle (Gaulcross) and a burial mound (Norrie's Law)—indicating not only that earlier practices carried on into the late fifth or sixth centuries AD, but also that Roman silver was still highly prized (Blackwell et al. 2017).

While never subjected to military adventures, Ireland was clearly of interest to the Romans. Ptolemy listed its peoples, places, coastal features, and offshore islands in some detail (Mattingly 2006). The limited number of Roman finds from Irish sites suggests that interactions focused on coastal areas. Three main clusters of imports in the north, east, and south-east of Ireland correspond to the main sea crossings. The majority belong to the late first or second century AD, or the later Roman period (Raftery 1994; Cahill Wilson 2014). Coins and personal items like brooches are most frequent, some perhaps arriving with their owners or via established networks across the Irish Sea and along the Atlantic seaways, rather than in commercial exchange.[34]

Two coastal sites near Dublin are relevant in this regard. The promontory fort at Drumanagh has yielded Roman coins and brooches of later first to mid-second century AD date along with unfinished Irish horse-bits and some forty bun-shaped copper, bronze, and brass ingots, one stamped with Roman numerals. By implication, Drumanagh was a metalworking centre using metal from Britain as well as obtained locally. Other Roman finds include a seal box and possible writing styli (Cahill Wilson 2014).[35] Some items, such as a British mirror and bronze vessels, imply an exchange network active before the Roman period, and Drumanagh can be compared with Hengistbury Head, where metalworking continued into the Roman period. The wider distribution of Roman imports in Ireland broadly echoes that of metal sources, probably a reason for the interest in Ireland. Another possible port was Lambay Island, intervisible with Drumanagh. First-century AD metalwork recovered in the early twentieth century from an inhumation cemetery points to a community with links to south-west England (Rynne 1976; Cahill Wilson et al. 2014). One grave may have contained a sword, shield, and mirror, recalling the Bryher burial, and the harbour-edge location of the Lambay burials echoes Urville-Nacqueville across the Channel from Hengistbury Head (see earlier).

Samian ware occurs quite widely on Irish sites (including Drumanagh), but more decorated forms and larger sherds are found in the north (Cahill Wilson 2014), suggesting that the military zone of northern Britain was the source of supply for this area.[36] Three second-century AD *denarius* hoards, two from Antrim and one from Dublin (Burnett 2020), suggest that the Roman policy of subsidies may have extended to Irish groups who were well placed to aid troublesome peoples in Scotland. Two hacksilver hoards from Ballinrees (Co Derry) and Balline (Co Limerick) were probably pay for Irish warriors recruited for the late Roman army, rather than booty from Irish raiding in Britain, since they included stamped ingots from an officially controlled source (Mattingly 2006).

As well as occurring on occupation sites, Roman imports were integrated into local ritual practice. The Broighter hoard, which included two gold necklaces of Mediterranean origin reminiscent of the Winchester find (see earlier), as well as the celebrated model boat and a buffer torc, was buried in wetland (Raftery 1994), as were the hacksilver hoards. Many long-standing ceremonial foci like the Newgrange and Knowth passage graves on the River Boyne, and the Rath of the Synods at Tara, have multiple imports. At Newgrange, Roman gold jewellery was buried near the entrance; other deposits included gold coins and a torc terminal inscribed with Roman letters (Raftery 1994). Large amounts of samian and glass drinking vessels, perhaps feasting debris, are present at Knowth and Tara, along with more unusual items such as a cosmetic spoon, a stylus, and a lead seal.[37] In the funerary sphere, cremation continued, but some crouched (or flexed) inhumations occur in the Meath-Dublin area (e.g. Lambay Island, Knowth), albeit not beyond the early third century AD. A few graves with Roman goods—a cremation at Stoneyford (Co Kilkenny) and cist burials at Bray Head (Co Wicklow)—might belong to immigrants. During the fourth century AD, extended supine inhumation began to take hold across Ireland, undoubtedly influenced by changes in the Roman world across the water (Cahill Wilson 2014).

While radiocarbon dates seem to imply a decline in settlement activity in the early centuries AD (Armit et al. 2013), this may simply be the product of a growing attachment to place. Unenclosed sites remained the norm, but some now had several dwellings, which might denote multiple households (Dowling 2014). Most houses were small, but a few larger structures stand out, as at Killoran (Co Tipperary), and the stone 'enclosure' at Barrees (Co Cork), although this was probably unroofed (O'Brien 2009). A growing number of long-lived open settlements have been found to precede early medieval enclosures, as at Cloongownagh (Co Roscommon), while at Lagore (Co Meath) Iron Age activity spanning several centuries provides a context for the Roman imports found when the early medieval crannog was excavated (Dowling 2014).[38]

Apart from a palisaded settlement at Baysrath (Co Kilkenny) and a large irregular stone-walled compound at Barrees, enclosed sites were exceptional before the third century AD. The small double-ditched 'ring fort' excavated at Killalane (Co Tipperary) closely resembles the 50,000 known Irish raths and cashels conventionally assigned an early medieval date, amongst which future research will surely reveal more small enclosures of Iron Age origin (Henderson 2007: 173–198). Other ditched enclosures range from the multivallate Rath of the Synods at Tara—constructed around AD 200, and possibly residential, but at a place of great symbolic significance (Grogan 2008; Bayliss and Grogan 2013)—to large compounds with agricultural or craft functions, such as Lismullin, overlooking the earlier ceremonial focus, or Rosepark (Co Dublin) with drying kilns and ironworking (Dowling 2014). Tara apart, there is little sign of building activity at the leading Irish politico-religious centres in the early centuries AD.[39]

The many cereal-drying kilns of second to fourth century AD date in eastern Ireland—where there are also most enclosures—imply that the reconfiguration of settlement after AD 200 was accompanied, in this area at least, by an intensification of arable farming. An indication that the changes extended to the social and political sphere was the adoption—at the latest by the fourth century AD—of the Irish ogham script; derived from the Latin alphabet and preserved as short inscriptions on standing stones and objects, this soon spread to Atlantic Britain.[40] Like the Pictish symbol system, which emerged at same period, the genesis of this epigraphical system may have been bound up with ethnic self-definition in reaction to Roman influence (see Chapter 36). Ogham inscriptions are especially common in southern Ireland, the area with strongest evidence of continuing contact with the Mediterranean world after the Roman withdrawal from Britain.

Conclusion

Over the eight centuries of the pre-Roman Iron Age, population densities across north-west Europe reached unprecedented levels, underpinned by an increasingly reliable agricultural base, and settlement became progressively more stable (Bradley et al. 2016). Various new types of central foci emerged, some with important economic functions, although ritual and reinforcement of collective identity were often the primary factors bringing people together.[41] Despite their disparate forms, such centres were key to the management of social power and status, and became increasingly monumental in character as larger polities coalesced. Not all developments, however, fit a narrative of growing social complexity. Episodes of instability occurred at the start of the Iron Age, in the mid-first millennium BC and after 125 BC. Roman intervention has been given too much primacy in the rise of *oppida*, but after the Gallic War it impacted forcefully on many societies on the fringes of the Empire, promoting ethnogenesis and other changes that would ultimately contribute to its demise.

Regional variations in settlement architecture and depositional practices (compounded by variable preservation) have obscured an underlying cultural unity at the level of shared Hallstatt and La Tène artefact types and art styles.[42] From the striking brochs of northern Britain to the more functional longhouses of the North European Plain, and from the state-like polities of central Gaul to the barely visible peoples of Ireland, societies were highly interconnected, while maintaining their individual characters. Perhaps the most fundamental divide was between peoples who embraced coinage and those who did not—with implications for social structures and ideologies.

To what extent Iron Age groups were hierarchical and dominated by elites remains a matter of debate, but a simple overarching model is unlikely. For Gaul, interpretation is still swayed by the stratified model of society presented by Caesar, but its wider applicability is doubtful given the variations in the archaeological record across time and space. Rich burials were restricted to certain periods and areas; generally, overt signs of social differentiation in death were muted or absent, although it does not follow that such societies were more egalitarian. Status differences might have been articulated in other ways. In many cases, heterarchy may be a more useful model than hierarchy (Hill 2011; Currás and Sastre 2020). Given the rate at which data continue to accumulate, we may expect to come closer to resolving these questions in the years to come, while archaeogenetic and isotopic analyses will revolutionize our understanding of population make-up and movement.

Notes

1. Rotary querns appeared in southern Britain by the end of the fifth century BC, but only reached northern France in the later third or second century BC and the Low Countries even later (Wefers 2011).
2. Irish souterrains are thought to date after the mid-first millennium AD, although some simpler forms may have Iron Age origins (Henderson 2007: 145).
3. According to Caesar's commentaries (*de Bello Gallico*), Belgic Gaul extended from the Seine to the Rhine, Aquitania was south-west of the Garonne, and Celtic Gaul lay between the other two, bounded by the Rhône.

4. Paule is famous for four small anthropomorphic stone figures, one holding a lyre and wearing a torc, buried in two late Iron Age ditches and a souterrain (Menez et al. 2009). Thought to depict gods or ancestors, some thirty statues of this type are known from France. In 2019, four were found at Trémuson, another aristocratic settlement in Brittany, three of them in a well (Bourne 2020). All four statues were burnt, as were three from Paule.
5. Unlike the four-wheeled wagons from Hallstatt D burials such as Vix, vehicles in the Aisne-Marne cemeteries are two-wheeled, apart from in the late Hallstatt cemetery at Chouilly.
6. A three-aisled building of early La Tène date with stake-walls fortuitously preserved in woodland at Chassemy is probably typical of many earlier Iron Age dwellings. Had the building been ploughed, little trace would have survived (Haselgrove 2007: 406).
7. Mata (2019) links the construction of fortified hilltop sites at this period to a rise in slaver activity, driven by growing demand in the Mediterranean world, foreshadowing the more visible Roman slave trade of the final centuries BC.
8. One of these chariot burials was found in 2020 at Heumen, near the river Meuse (N. Roymans pers. comm.).
9. An issue even in pottery-using areas owing to the longevity of earlier Iron Age ceramic traditions in Britain, which display little typological change between the eighth and fifth centuries BC.
10. Earlier Iron Age palisaded settlements include Broxmouth, Dryburn Bridge, Hayhope Knowe, Huckoe, Little Woodbury, Moel-y-Gaer, Ravelrig, Staple Howe, West Brandon, and West Harling (see Cunliffe 2005; Harding 2017). Some features that appear in plan to be 'palisades' may have been timber revetments for banks, particularly where accompanied by ditches.
11. The term hillfort is applied to a wide variety of sites, merging at the lower end of the size range with smaller enclosures of the kind that proliferated in the later Iron Age. The term is best reserved to larger, visually dominant fortified sites (see Sharples 2010: 57–61 for discussion).
12. Verdun-sur-le-Doubs lies on the opposite side of the confluence to the earlier craftworking centre at Bragny-sur-Saône.
13. Isotope analysis suggests that part of the population at Basel-Gasfabrik was born or spent some of their childhood elsewhere, a few of whom may be from well outside the region (Knipper et al. 2018).
14. At 70 ha, Corent seems too small to have housed the entire population of Aulnat-Gandaillat, even allowing for the 'suburb' at the foot of the *oppidum* (Guichard 2017: 162).
15. At Moulay (Pays-de-la-Loire), excavations examined a 1 km long transect through a 135 ha *oppidum* at the confluence of the Aron and the Mayenne, revealing residential and craft quarters, a public space, and an earlier sanctuary. Only a smaller fortified enclosure at the apex of the promontory was previously known (Le Goff 2016).
16. Grids of dwelling units interspaced with open spaces and streets at Aulnat-Gandaillat imply that parts of some lowland agglomerations were deliberately laid out (Deberge et al. 2007a).
17. A grave of nine men and nine horses at Gondole may relate to the clearance of a Gallic War battle site. Siegeworks from Caesar's attempt in 52 BC to capture Gergovia have been traced between the *oppida* (Deberge et al. 2014). Alésia and Puy d'Issolud (Uxellodunum) also have archaeological evidence of Gallic War sieges, while lead sling bullets from the rampart at Thuin (Belgium) suggest this was the *oppidum* of the Aduatuci stormed by Caesar in 57 BC (Roymans 2019).

18. Some Fléré graves contain Roman weapons or fittings (e.g. Berry-Bouy); see Pernet (2019).
19. Also known as Oss-Ussen type 4.
20. North-east Scotland was among the few parts of Britain where unenclosed settlements remained the norm during the later Iron Age, often continuing without a break into the Roman Iron Age (Harding 2017: 124–129, 136–142). Some of these settlements were engaged in iron-smelting and other industrial activity on a significant scale. The metalwork assemblage from Culduthel, near Inverness, is the largest from any Scottish site after Traprain Law and Fairy Knowe (Murray 2007).
21. The externally banked enclosure at Tara (the Fort of the Kings) is contemporary to Navan, but their counterpart at Knockaulin is not closely dated (Bayliss and Grogan 2013). Radiocarbon dates place the monumental internal structures at Knockaulin in the early centuries AD, but there are doubts over the reliability of these dates, and a La Tène C sword from the final palisaded structure would have to be curated. Given the similarities between the sequences, the question remains open (Becker 2019: 297). The figure-of-eight enclosures preceding the Rath of the Synods at Tara are later than similar structures at Navan, but are external and secondary to the main enclosure.
22. Colchester (*Camulodunum*), St Albans (*Verlamion*), and Silchester (*Calleva*). Other examples include Chichester and Bagendon.
23. Not far away from these buildings at Stanwick is an unexcavated quadrangular enclosure, with an uncanny resemblance to the Belgic sanctuary at Gournay-sur-Aronde. The two enclosures were of similar size and sited on slopes looking out over marshy valleys, with their entrances aligned on the midsummer solstice. The Gournay sanctuary was later incorporated in the annexe of a La Tène D2 oppidum, just as the enclosure at Stanwick lay within an extensive dyke complex (Haselgrove 2016).
24. Exactly when some of these settlement forms emerged is a matter of debate; they were at their most numerous in the Roman period, but some might pre-date the first century BC.
25. Tacitus (*Agricola*: 24) states that Julius Agricola, who conquered northern Britain in the late first century AD, contemplated invading Ireland, and that an expelled Irish ruler took refuge with him.
26. Tacitus (*Annals* XI: 16) recounts how in AD 47 the Cherusci asked Rome for a king. Claudius chose Italicus—the last of the Cheruscan royal line and nephew of the German leader Arminius, but raised in Rome and a Roman citizen—and gave him money and an escort. The Cherusci later ejected Italicus, but he was restored with the backing of the Langobardi.
27. According to Roman authors, the North Sea coastal region was inhabited by the Frisii; to their east were the Chauci (Tacitus, *Germania*: 34–35). For overviews of the Roman Iron Age in this region, see Todd (1987); Cunliffe (1988); Wells (1999).
28. The difficulty of keeping sunken-featured buildings dry accounts for their near-absence in the coastal marshes (Hamerow 2004: 31–32). The north Netherlands seems to have escaped the fall in settlement numbers in the later third to early fourth century AD that affected the west and south Netherlands, and is seen as paving the way for Germanic migration into those areas (Roymans et al. 2020).
29. The elevated mounds and artificial platforms that caught the eye of Pliny the Elder during his visit to the north between AD 40 and 50 were undoubtedly terp settlements (Todd 1987: 79).

30. According to Tacitus, a move by the Frisii in AD 58 to settle on land reserved for Roman troops was 'led by Verritus and Malorix—their kings (in so far as Germans have any)' (*Annals* XIII: 54).
31. Although bog burials have a long currency in the Netherlands, the majority date to the centuries around the beginning of our era (Hessing and Kooi 2005). Late Iron Age or early Roman bog bodies from the area include the Weerdinge couple, Exloërmond man, Yde girl, and Zweeloo woman. While resonating with Tacitus' remark that those convicted of certain crimes among the Germans were put to death by being staked down in bogs (*Germania*: 12), individuals found in bogs died in a range of circumstances, not always violent (Giles 2020).
32. Only one late Roman hacksilver hoard is recorded from the North Sea coastal region, unlike Jutland and Scotland, where there are several (Blackwell et al. 2017). It was found at Winsum, Friesland, between known Iron Age terp settlements (information F. Hunter).
33. Previously it was assumed that most of the hut circles here were pre-Roman. It remains to be seen whether Tap O'Noth provides a model for other large hillforts in Scotland such as Eildon Hills, or in North Wales (see earlier) where the Roman use is thought to be secondary. Several promontory forts in Wales and south-west England also show renewed activity in the Roman period.
34. Tacitus' comment (*Agricola*: 24) that Irish harbours had become better known from merchants is sometimes read as indicating that the traders were Romans, but this is unwarranted.
35. Geophysical survey has revealed occupation at and near Drumanagh, but only excavation can establish how much of this relates to the Roman imports and metalworking, or indeed whether the defences of the promontory fort belong to the same period.
36. Samian ware might have been passed on by groups in south-west Scotland who had access to Roman goods, rather than coming directly from the military.
37. Cahill Wilson (2014: 31–32) speculates on a relationship between Tara and Drumanagh similar to that between the Roman Iron Age politico-religious focus at Gudme on Funen in Denmark, and its port and metalworking adjunct at Lundeborg. Haselgrove (2016: 486–487) has similarly compared the Stanwick-Scotch Corner complex in northern England to Gudme-Lundeborg. The Irish sites are, however, much further apart (40 km) than the others.
38. The radiocarbon dates suggest occupation spanning the fourth century BC to sixth century AD.
39. But see note 21. The figure-of-eight palisaded enclosures and other structures preceding the Rath of the Synods at Tara date to the first and second centuries AD.
40. An ogham-inscribed knife handle dated to cal. AD 340–540 was found at the broch of Gurness (Orkney) in the same phase as small unelaborated symbol-stones (Noble et al. 2018).
41. This seems to be as true of the developed hillforts of southern Britain as of the contemporary Belgic warrior sanctuaries.
42. Variations in depositional behaviour have also led archaeologists into erroneous judgements about 'poverty' or 'wealth'. The Aisne-Marne culture seems 'rich' most of all because of the number of furnished graves, but there is no reason to suppose that peoples who disposed of their dead without this element of display were fundamentally different, or had inferior possessions.

References

Alexander, D. 2005. 'Redcastle, Lunan Bay, Angus: The excavation of an Iron Age timber-lined souterrain and a Pictish barrow cemetery'. *Proceedings of the Society of Antiquaries of Scotland* 135: 41–118.

Andrews, P., E. Biddulph, A. Hardy, and R. Brown. 2011. *Settling the Ebbsfleet Valley: High Speed 1 Excavations at Springhead and Northfleet. Vol. 1: The Sites*. Oxford and Salisbury: Oxford Wessex Archaeology.

Armit, I. 2003. *Celtic Scotland*. London: Batsford & Historic Scotland.

Armit, I., and L. Büster. 2020. *Darkness Visible: The Sculptor's Cave, Covesea, from the Bronze Age to the Picts*. Edinburgh: Society of Antiquaries of Scotland.

Armit, I., and J. McKenzie. 2013. *An Inherited Place: Broxmouth Hillfort and the South-East Scottish Iron Age*. Edinburgh: Society of Antiquaries of Scotland.

Armit, I., G. T. Swindles, and K. Becker. 2013. 'From dates to demography in later prehistoric Ireland? Experimental approaches to the meta-analysis of large 14C data-sets'. *Journal of Archaeological Science* 40, 1: 433–438.

Arnoldussen, S., and K. M. de Vries. 2014. 'Of farms and fields: The Bronze Age and Iron Age settlement and Celtic field at Hijken-Hijkerveld'. *Palaeohistoria* 55, 56: 85–104.

Arnoldussen, S., and K. M. de Vries. 2017. 'A plan in place? Celtic field habitation at Westeinde (prov. Drenthe, The Netherlands)'. *Lunula: Archaeologia protohistorica* 25: 79–89.

Arnoldussen, S., and R. Jansen. 2010. 'Iron Age habitation patterns on the southern and northern Dutch Pleistocene covers and soils: The process of settlement nucleation', in M. Meyer (ed.) *Haus—Gehöft—Weiler—Dorf, Siedlungen der vorrömischen Eisenzeit im nördlichen Mitteleuropa*. Berliner Archäologische Forschungen 8: 379–397. Rahden: Verlag Marie Leidorf.

Atkinson, M., and S. Preston. 2015. *Heybridge, a Late Iron Age and Roman Settlement: Excavations at Elms Farm 1993–5. Vol. 1: East Anglian Archaeology 154*. Chelmsford: E ssex County Council.

Augier, L., A. Baron, A. Filippini, P. Y. Milcent, B. Pescher, and M. Salin. 2009. 'Les activités artisanales de la fin du VIe et du Ve S. av. J.-C. attestées sur le site de Bourges (Cher)', in M. B. Chardenoux, S. Krausz, O. Buchsenschutz, and M. Vaginay (eds) *L'âge du Fer dans la boucle de la Loire: Les Gaulois sont dans la ville: Actes du XXXIIe colloque de l'AFEAF (Bourges, 2008)*. Revue Archéologique du Centre de la France supplément 35: 39–66. Paris/Tours: FERACF.

Augier, L., O. Buchsenschutz, and I. Ralston. 2007. *Un complexe Princier de l'âge du Fer: L'habitat du promontoire de Bourges (Cher), VIe–IVe s. av. J.-C.* Revue Archéologique du Centre de la France supplément 32. Bourges: Bourges Plus, Service d'archéologie préventive, Bituriga.

Augier, L., O. Buchsenschutz, R. Durand, A. Filipini, D. Germinet, M. Levéry, et al. 2012. *Un complexe princier à l'âge du Fer: le quartier artisanal de Port Sec sud à Bourges (Cher), Vols 1–2*. Revue Archéologique du Centre de la France supplément 41. Bourges/Tours: Bourges Plus.

Augier, L., and S. Krausz. 2012. 'Du complexe princier a l'oppidum: les modèles du Berry', in S. Sievers and M. Schönfelder (eds) *Die Frage der Protourbanisation in der Eisenzeit: La question de la protourbanisation à l'âge du Fer.* Akten des 34. internationalen Kolloquiums der AFEAF (Aschaffenburg, 2010), Kolloquien zur Vor- und Frühgeschichte 16: 167–192. Bonn: Habelt.

Augier, L., and S. Krausz. 2021. 'Le complexe princier de Bourges: nouvelles perspectives sur la chronologie et le territoire', in P. Brun, B. Chaume, and F. Sacchetti (eds) *Vix et le phénomène princier: Actes du colloque de Châtillon, 2016*: 77–94. Pessac: Ausonius Éditions. Available at https://una-editions.fr/vix-et-le-phenomene-princier [accessed 15 August 2022].

Auxiette, G., S. Desenne, S. Bauvais, S. Gaudefroy, F. Gransar, B. Gratuze, et al. 2017. 'Une trajectoire singulière. Les enclos de Braine "la Grange des Moines" (Aisne) à La Tène finale'. *Revue archéologique de Picardie*, 3, 4: 7–340.

Baldwin, A., and J. Joy. 2017. A Celtic Feast: The Iron Age Cauldrons from Chiseldon, Wiltshire. Research Publication 203. London: British Museum Press.

Ballin Smith, B. (ed.) 1994. *Howe: Four Millennia of Orkney Prehistory: Excavations 1978–1982*. Society of Antiquaries of Scotland Monograph 9. Edinburgh: Society of Antiquaries of Scotland.

Baray, L. 2003. *Pratiques funéraires et sociétés de l'âge du fer dans le bassin parisien: Fin du VIIe s.–troisième quart du IIe s. avant J.-C.* Gallia supplément 56. Paris: CNRS.

Barral, P., J. Hantrais, M. Joly, P. Nouvel, and M. Thivet. 2019. 'Un nouveau type d'architecture publique? Le complexe monumentale de PC15 à Bibracte et es bâtiments sur cour de la fin de l'âge du Fer en Gaule interne', in A. Villard-Le Tiec (ed.) *Architectures de l'âge du fer en Europe Occidentale et centrale: Actes du 40e Colloque international de l'AFEAF (Rennes, 2016)*: 489–508. Rennes: Presses Universitaires de Rennes.

Barral, P., and D. Lallemand. 2014. 'Les agglomérations ouvertes du IIe siècle av. J.-C. à spécialisation artisanale et commerciale: deux exemplaires du centre-est de la France, Varennes-sur-Allier (Allier) et Verdun-sur-le-Doubs (Sâone-et-Loire)', in S. Hornung (ed.) *Produktion–Distribution–Ökonomie, Siedlungs- und Wirtschaftsmuster der Latènezeit*. Akten des internationalen Kolloquiums in Otzenhausen, Institut für Vor- und Frühgeschichte der Universität Mainz 258: 205–230. Bonn: Habelt.

Bayliss, A., and E. Grogan. 2013. 'Chronologies for Tara and comparable royal sites of the Irish Iron Age', in M. O'Sullivan, C. Scarre, and M. Doyle (eds) *Tara: From the Past to the Future*: 105–144. Dublin: Wordwell.

Becker, K. 2011. 'Iron Age Ireland. Continuity, change and identity', in T. Moore and X. L. Armada (eds) *Atlantic Europe in the First Millennium BC: Crossing the Divide*: 449–467. Oxford: Oxford University Press.

Becker, K. 2012. 'Redefining the Irish Iron Age', in C. Corlett and M. Potterton (eds) *Life and Death in Iron Age Ireland*: 1–14. Dublin: Wordwell.

Becker, K. 2019. 'Irish Iron Age settlement and society: Reframing royal sites'. *Proceedings of the Prehistoric Society* 85: 273–306.

Becker, K., J. Ó Néill, and L. O'Flynn. 2008. *Iron Age Ireland: Finding an Invisible People*. Final Report to the Heritage Council Project 16365. Dublin: University College Dublin.

Berranger, M. 2014. *Le fer, entre matière première et moyen d'échange, en France du VIIe au Ier siècle avant J.-C: Approches interdisciplinaires*. Dijon: Éditions Universitaires de Dijon.

Berranger, M., and P. Fluzin. 2012. 'From raw iron to semi-product: Quality and circulation of materials during the Iron Age in France'. *Archaeometry* 54, 4: 664–684.

Blackwell, A., M. Goldberg, and F. Hunter. 2017. *Scotland's Early Silver: Transforming Roman Pay-Off to Pictish Treasures*. Edinburgh: National Museums Scotland.

Bocquillon, H., B. Lambot, P. Méniel, and M. Saurel. 2012. *Le site protohistorique d'Acy-Romance (Ardennes)*, IV: *Les constructions du village*. Société Archéologique Champenoise Mémoire 20. Reims: Société Archéologique Champenoise.

Bouchet, M. 2017. *La céramique de la fin de l'âge du fer dans le Berry: Approches chronologique, culturelle et territoriale de la société des Bituriges (IIe–Ier siècle av. J.-C.)*. Revue Archéologique du Centre de la France supplément 67. Tours: FERAC.

Boughton, D. 2015. 'The early Iron Age socketed axes in Britain'. Unpublished PhD thesis, University of Central Lancashire.

Bourgeois, I., B. Cherretté, and J. Bourgeois. 2003. 'Bronze Age and Iron Age settlements in Belgium: An overview', in J. Bourgeois, I. Bourgeois, and B. Cherretté (eds) *Bronze and Iron Age Communities in North-Western Europe*: 175–297. Brussels: Koninklijke Vlaamse Academie van Belgie voor Wetenschappen en Kunsten.

Bourgeois, Q., and S. Van der Vaart-Verschoof. 2017. 'A practice perspective. Understanding early Iron Age elite burials in the southern Netherlands through events-based analysis', in R. Schumann and S. van der Vaart-Verschoof (eds) *Connecting Elites and Regions: Perspectives on Contacts, Relations and Differentiation During the Early Iron Age Hallstatt C Period in Northwest and Central Europe*: 305–318. Leiden: Sidestone Press.

Bourne, S. 2020. 'Découverte récente d'un établissement aristocratique de La Tène finale à Trémuson (Côtes-d'Armor)'. *Bulletin de l'AFEAF* 38: 61–64.

Bradley, R. 2019. *The Prehistory of Britain and Ireland*, 2nd edition. Cambridge: Cambridge University Press.

Bradley, R., C. Haselgrove, L. Webley, and M. Vander Linden. 2016. *The Later Prehistory of North-West Europe: The Evidence of Development-Led Fieldwork*. Oxford: Oxford University Press.

Brun, P., and P. Ruby. 2008. *L'âge du fer en France: Premières villes, premiers états celtiques*. Paris: La Découverte.

Brun, P., and B. Chaume. 2013. 'Une éphémère tentative d'urbanisation en Europe centre-occidentale durant les VIe et Ve siècles av. J.-C.?' *Bulletin de la Société préhistorique française* 110, 2: 319–349.

Brunaux, J. L., M. Amandry, V. Brouquier-Reddé, L.-P. Delestrée, H. Duday, G. Fercoq Du Leslay, et al. 1999. 'Ribemont-sur-Ancre, Somme: bilan préliminaire et nouvelles hypothèses'. *Gallia* 56, 1: 177–283.

Brunaux, J. L. 2004. *Guerre et religion en gaule: Essai d'anthropologie celtique*. Paris: Errance.

Brunaux, J.-L., P. Méniel, and P. Poplin. 1985. *Gournay I: Les fouilles sur le sanctuaire et l'oppidum*. Revue Archéologique de Picardie Numéro Spécial. Amiens: Revue Archéologique de Picardie.

Buchsenschutz, O. 2004. *Les Celtes de L'âge du Fer dans la moitié nord de la France*. Paris: Maison des Roches.

Buchsenschutz, O., A. Colin, G. Firmin, B. Fischer, J.-P. Guillaumet, S. Krausz, et al. 2000. *Le village celtique des Arènes à Levroux: Synthèses. Levroux 5*. Revue Archéologique du Centre de la France supplément 19. Levroux: ADEL/Tours: FERAC.

Buchsenschutz, O., S. Krausz, and I. Ralston. 2010. 'Architecture et chronologie des remparts celtiques du Berry et du Limousin', in S. Fichtl (ed.) *Murus celticus: Architecture et fonctions des remparts de l'âge du Fer: Actes de la table ronde à Glux-en-Glenne les 11 et 12 octobre*. Collection Bibracte 19: 297–313. Glux-en-Glenne: Centre archéologique européen du Mont Beuvray.

Buchsenschutz, O., and I. Ralston. 2012. 'Urbanisation et aristocratie Celtique', in S. Sievers and M. Schönfelder (eds) *Die Frage der Protourbanisation in der Eisenzeit: La question de la protourbanisation à l'âge du Fer: Akten des 34. internationalen Kolloquiums der AFEAF (Aschaffenburg, 2010)*. Kolloquien zur Vor- und Frühgeschichte 16: 347–364. Bonn: Habelt.

Burnett, A. M. 2020. 'New light on three Roman hoards from Scotland and Ireland'. *British Numismatic Journal* 90: 193–197.

Cahen-Delhaye, A. 1999. 'Tombes à char du Ve siècle en Ardenne belge', in A. Villes and A. Bataille-Melkon (eds) *Fastes des Celtes entre Champagne et Bourgogne au VIIe–IIIe siècles avant notre ère*. Société Archéologique Champenoise Mémoire 15: 391–410. Reims: Société Archéologique Champenoise.

Cahill Wilson, J. 2014. 'Romans and Roman material in Ireland: A wider social perspective', in J. Cahill Wilson, G. Dowling, M. A. Bevivino, and P. Barry (eds) *Late Iron Age and 'Roman' Ireland*. Discovery Programme Reports 8: 11–58. Dublin: Wordwell.

Cahill Wilson, J., G. Cooney, G. Dowling, and I. Elliott. 2014. 'Investigations on Lambay, Co. Dublin', in J. Cahill Wilson, G. Dowling, M. A. Bevivino, and P. Barry (eds) *Late Iron Age and 'Roman' Ireland*. Discovery Programme Reports 8: 91–112. Dublin: Wordwell.

Carrara, S., E. Bertrand, C. Mège, and G. Maza. 2021. 'Le site de Lyon et ses céramiques importées à la fin du VIe s. et au Ve s. a. C.: marqueurs de circuits commerciaux, indices de mixité ethnique et de mutations socio-culturelles', in P. Brun, B. Chaume, and F. Sacchetti (eds) *Vix et le phénomène princier: Actes du colloque de Châtillon, 2016*: 95–132. Pessac: Ausonius. Available at https://una-editions.fr/vix-et-le-phenomene-princier [accessed 15 August 2022].

Carter, S., F. Hunter, and A. Smith. 2010. 'A 5th century BC Iron Age chariot burial from Newbridge, Edinburgh'. *Proceedings of the Prehistoric Society* 76: 31–74.

Cavers, G. 2006. 'Late Bronze and Iron Age lake settlement in Scotland and Ireland: The development of the 'crannog' in the north and west'. *Oxford Journal of Archaeology* 25, 4: 389–412.

Cavers, G., and A. Crone. 2018. *A Lake Dwelling in its Landscape: Iron Age Settlement at Cults Loch, Castle Kennedy, Dumfries & Galloway*. Oxford: Oxbow Books.

Cavers, G., and G. Sleight. 2018. 'Clachtoll: Saving an Iron Age broch'. *British Archaeology* 159: 16–21.

Champion, T. 2016. 'Britain before the Romans', in M. Millett, L. Revell, and A. Moore (eds) *The Oxford Handbook of Roman Britain*: 150–178. Oxford: Oxford University Press.

Chaume, B., and C. Mordant. 2011. *Le complexe aristocratique de Vix: Nouvelles recherches sur l'habitat, le système de fortification et l'environnement du Mont Lassois*. Dijon: Editions universitaires de Dijon.

Chaume, B., and W. Reinhardt. 2013. 'Les statues du sanctuaire de Vix/Les Herbues dans le contexte de la statuaire anthropomorphe hallstattienne', in P. Gruat and D. Garcia (eds) *Stèles et statues du début de l'âge du Fer dans le Midi de la France (VIIIe–IVe s. av. J.-C.): chronologies, fonctions et comparaisons*. Documents d'Archéologie Méridionale 34: 293–310.

Chaume, B., P. Cheetmam, R. Komp, R. Lüth, T. Pertlweiser, W. Reinhardt, et al. 2020. 'Vix (Côte-d'Or) et l'émergence des principautés celtiques: l'hypothèse portuaire et le concept de port of trade'. *Gallia* 77, 1: 435–452.

Chaume, B., N. Nieszery, and W. Reinhardt. 2011. 'Le bâtiment palatial du mont Saint-Marcel: The house of the rising sun', in B. Chaume and C. Mordant (eds) *Le complexe aristocratique de Vix: nouvelles recherches sur l'habitat, le système de fortification et l'environnement du mont Lassois*: 795–838. Dijon: Editions universitaires de Dijon.

Coles, J. M., and S. Minnitt. 1995. *Industrious and Fairly Civilized: The Glastonbury Lake Village*. Taunton: Somerset Levels Project.

Colin, A., F. Verdin, and A. Dumas. 2013. 'Dynamique du peuplement dans le nord de l'Aquitaine: quelques pistes de réflexion', in A. Colin and F. Verdin (eds) *L'âge du Fer en Aquitaine et sur ses marges: Mobilité des hommes, diffusion des idées, circulation des biens dans l'espace européen à l'âge du Fer: Actes du 35e Colloque international de l'AFEAF (Bordeaux, 2011)*. Aquitania supplément 30: 23–45. Bordeaux: Aquitania.

Collard, M., T. Darvill, and M. Watts. 2006. 'Iron working in the Bronze Age? Evidence from a 10th century BC settlement at Hartshill Copse, Upper Bucklebury, West Berkshire'. *Proceedings of the Prehistoric Society* 72: 367–421.

Collet, S., and J. L. Flouest. 1997. 'Activités métallurgiques et commerce avec le monde Méditerranéen au Ve siècle av. J.-C. à Bragny-sur-Saône (Saône-et-Loire)', in P. Brun and B. Chaume (eds) *Vix et les éphémères principautés celtiques: Les VIe–Ve siècles avant J.-C. en Europe centre-occidentale: Actes du colloque de Châtillon-sur-Seine*: 165–172. Paris: Errance.

Cook, M., T. McCormick, J. McAlpine, R. Greenshields, G. Cook, and A. McLean. 2019. 'A new look at the late prehistoric settlement patterns of the Forth Valley', in T. Romankiewicz, M. Fernández-Götz, G. Lock, and O. Buchsenschutz (eds) *Enclosing Space, Opening New Ground: Iron Age Studies from Scotland to Mainland Europe*: 87–100. Oxford: Oxbow Books.

Corlett, C., and M. Potterton (eds) 2012. *Life and Death in Iron Age Ireland*. Dublin: Wordwell.

Creighton, J. 2000. *Coins and Power in Late Iron Age Britain*. Cambridge: Cambridge University Press.

Cunliffe, B. 1987. *Hengistbury Head, Dorset, Vol. 1: Prehistoric and Roman settlement, 3500 BC–AD 500*. OUCA Monograph 13. Oxford: Oxford University Committee for Archaeology.

Cunliffe, B. 1988. *Greeks, Romans and Barbarians: Spheres of Interaction*. London: Batsford.

Cunliffe, B. 1995. *Danebury, an Iron Age Hillfort in Hampshire: A Hillfort Community in Perspective. Vol. 6*. CBA Research Report 102. London: Council for British Archaeology.

Cunliffe, B. 2005. *Iron Age Communities in Britain*, 4th edition. London: Routledge.

Cunliffe, B. 2009. 'Continuity and change in a Wessex landscape'. *Proceedings of the British Academy* 162: 161–210.

Cunliffe, B. 2015. 'Facing the northern Ocean: The British late Bronze and Iron Ages in their continental perspective', in F. Hunter and I. Ralston (eds) *The Later Bronze and Iron Ages of Scotland in their European Setting*: 5–17. Edinburgh: Society of Antiquaries of Scotland.

Currás, B. X., and I. Sastre (eds). 2020. *Alternative Iron Ages: Social Theory from Archaeological Analysis*. New York: Routledge.

Davies, A. 2018. *Creating Society and Constructing the Past: Social Change in the Thames Valley from the Late Bronze Age to the Middle Iron Age*. British Archaeological Reports, British Series 637. Oxford: BAR Publishing.

Davis, O. P. 2013. 'Re-interpreting the Danebury Assemblage: Houses, Households and Community'. *Proceedings of the Prehistoric Society* 79: 353–375.

De Mulder, G., and J. Bourgeois. 2011. 'Shifting centres of power and changing elite symbolism in the Scheldt Fluvial Basin during the late Bronze Age and the Iron Age', in T. Moore and X. L. Armada (eds) *Atlantic Europe in the First Millennium BC: Crossing the Divide*: 302–318. Oxford: Oxford University Press.

Deberge, Y., F. Baucheron, U. Cabezuelo, P. Caillat, E. Gatto, C. Landry, et al. 2014. 'Témoignages de la Guerre des Gaules dans le bassin clermontois, nouveaux apports'. *Revue archéologique du Centre de la France* 53: 1–47.

Deberge, Y., U. Cabezuelo, M. Cabanis, S. Foucras, M. Garcia, K. Gruel, et al. 2009. 'L'oppidum arverne de Gondole (Le Cendre, Puy-de-Dôme). Topographie de l'occupation protohistorique (La Tène D2) et fouille du quartier artisanal: un premier bilan'. *Revue archéologique du Centre de la France* 48: 33–130.

Deberge, Y., C. Vermeulen, and J. Collis. 2007a. 'Le complexe de Gandaillat/La Grande Borne: un état de la question', in C. Mennessier-Jouannet and Y. Deberge (eds) *L'archéologie de l'âge du fer en Auvergne: Actes du XXVIIe colloque international de l'AFEAF (Clermont-Ferrand, 2003)*: 267–290. Lattes: Monographies d'archéologie Méditerranéenne.

Deberge, Y., J. Collis, and J. Dunkley (eds). 2007b. *Le Pâtural, Clermont-Ferrand, Puy-de-Dôme: un établissement agricole gaulois en Limagne d'Auvergne. Documents d'Archéologie en Rhône-Alpes 30*. Lyon: Association de liaison pour le Patrimoine et de l'Archéologie en Rhône-Alpes et en Auvergne.

Demierre, M., G. Bataille, and R. Perruche. 2019. 'Faciès mobiliers et espaces rituels. Les ensembles des sanctuaires laténiens du IVe au Ier siècle av. J.-C', in P. Barral and M. Thivet (eds) *Sanctuaires de l'âge du Fer: Actes du 41e colloque international de l'AFEAF (Dole, 2017), Collection AFEAF 1*: 331–342. Paris: AFEAF.

Demoule, J. P. 1999. *Chronologie et société des nécropoles celtiques de la culture Aisne-Marne, du VIème au IIIème siècle avant notre ère. Revue Archéologique de Picardie Numéro Spéciale 15*. Amiens: RAP.

Desenne, S., C. Pommepuy, and J. P. Demoule. 2009. *Bucy-le-Long (Aisne): Une nécropole de la Tène ancienne (Ve–IVe siècle avant notre ère)*. Revue Archéologique de Picardie Numéro Spéciale 26. Amiens: RAP.

Diepeveen-Jansen, M. 2001. *People, Goods and Ideas: New Perspectives on 'Celtic Barbarians' in Western and Central Europe (500–250 BC)*. Amsterdam Archaeological Studies 7. Amsterdam: Amsterdam University Press.

Dixon, P. 1994. *Crickley Hill. Vol. 1. The Hillfort Defences*. Nottingham: Crickley Hill Trust and Department of Archaeology, University of Nottingham.

Dixon, P. 2019. *Crickley Hill. Vol. 2. The Hillfort Settlements*. Nottingham: Crickley Hill Trust.

Dockrill, S. J., J. M. Bond, V. E. Turner, L. D. Brown, D. J. Bashford, J. E. Cussans, et al. 2015. *Excavations at Old Scatness, Shetland: The Broch and Iron Age Village. Vol. 2*. Lerwick: Shetland Heritage Publications.

Dolan, B. 2016. 'Making iron in the Irish midlands: The social and symbolic role of Iron Age ironworkers'. *Journal of Irish Archaeology* 25: 31–48.

Dowling, G. 2014. 'Landscape and settlement in late Iron Age Ireland: Some emerging trends', in J. Cahill Wilson, G. Dowling, M. A. Bevivino, and P. Barry (eds) *Late Iron Age and 'Roman' Ireland*. Discovery Programme Reports 8: 151–174. Dublin: Wordwell.

Driver, T. 2013. *Architecture, Regional Identity and Power in the Iron Age Landscapes of Mid Wales: The Hillforts of North Ceredigion*. British Archaeological Reports, British Series 583. Oxford: BAR Publishing.

Dubuis, B., D. Josset, E. Millet, and C. Villenave. 2015. 'La tombe princière du Ve siècle avant notre ère de Lavau "ZAC du Moutot" (Aube)'. *Bulletin de la société préhistorique française* 112, 2: 371–374.

Dunwell, A., and R. Strachan. 2007. Excavations at Brown Caterthun and White Caterthun, Angus, 1995–1997. Tayside and Fife Archaeological Committee Monograph 5. Perth: TAFAC.

Erdrich, M. 2001. *Rom und die Barbaren: Das Verhältnis zwischen dem Imperium Romanum und den germanischen Stämmen vor seiner Nordwestgrenze seit der späten römischen Republik bis zum Gallischen Sonderreich*. Römisch-Germanische Forschungen 58. Mainz: von Zabern.

Evans, C., G. Appleby, and S. Lucy. 2016. *Lives in Land: Mucking Excavations by Margaret and Tom Jones, 1965–78: Prehistory, Context and Summary*. Oxford: Oxbow Books.

Evans, C., S. Lucy, and R. Patten. 2018. *Riversides: Neolithic Barrows, a Beaker Grave, Iron Age and Anglo-Saxon Settlement at Trumpington, Cambridge*. Cambridge: McDonald Institute for Archaeological Research.

Farley, J., and F. Hunter (eds). 2015. *Celts, Art and Identity. London: British Museum Press.*

Farley, J. M. 2012. 'At the edge of empire: Iron Age and early Roman metalwork in the East Midlands'. Unpublished PhD thesis, University of Leicester.

Fell, D. W. 2020. *Contact, Concord and Conquest: Britons and Romans at Scotch Corner*. Northern Archaeological Associates Monograph 5. Barnard Castle: Northern Archaeological Associates.

Fenton-Thomas, C. 2011. *Where Sky and Yorkshire and Water Meet: The Story of the Melton Landscape from Prehistory to the Present*. OSA Monograph 2. York: On-Site Archaeology.

Fercoq du Leslay, G., G. Bataille, and C. Chaidron. 2019. 'Évolution du pratiques rituelles laténiennes et de leurs contextes: le cas du sanctuaire de Ribemont-sur-Ancre (Somme)', in P. Barral and M. Thivet (eds) *Sanctuaires de l'âge du fer: Actes du 41e Colloque international de l'AFEAF (Dole, 2017)*. Collection AFEAF 1: 291–312. Paris: AFEAF.

Ferdière, A., and A. Villard. 1993. *La tombe augustéenne de Fléré-la-Rivière (Indre) et les sépultures aristocratiques de la cité des Bituriges—En Berry au début de l'époque gallo-romaine: le fer, le vin, le pouvoir et la mort*. Revue Archéologique du Centre de la France supplément 7. Saint-Marcel: Musée d'Argentomagus.

Fernández-Götz, M. 2014. *Identity and Power: The Transformation of Iron Age Societies in Northeast Gaul*. Amsterdam Archaeological Studies 21. Amsterdam: Amsterdam University Press.

Fernández-Götz, M., and I. Ralston. 2017. 'The complexity and fragility of early Iron Age urbanism in west-central temperate Europe'. *Journal of World Prehistory* 30, 3: 259–279.

Fichtl, S. 2004. *Les peuples Gaulois: IIIe-Ie siècles av. J.-C.* Paris: Errance.

Fichtl, S. 2005. *La ville celtique: Les oppida de 150 av. J.-C. à 15 apr. J.-C*, 2nd edition. Paris: Errance.

Fichtl, S. 2013. 'À propos des résidences aristocratiques de la fin de l'âge du Fer: l'exemple de quelques sites du Loiret', in S. Krausz, A. Colin, K. Gruel, I. Ralston, and T. Dechezleprêtre (eds) *L'âge du Fer en Europe. Mélanges offerts à Olivier Buchsenschutz*: 329–343. Bordeaux: Ausonius.

Fichtl, S. 2021. 'Des remparts dans les établissement ruraux?', in F. Delrieu, C. Féliu, P. Gruat, M.-C. Kurzaj, and E. Nectoux (eds) *Les espaces fortifiés à l'âge du Fer en Europe: Actes du 43e colloque international de l'AFEAF (Le Puy-en-Velay, 2019)*. Collection AFEAF 3: 97–136. Paris: AFEAF.

Fichtl, S., and P. Barral. 2019. 'Quelques réflexions sur les agglomérations celtiques de La Tène moyenne et finale', in S. Fichtl, P. Barral, G. Pierrevelcin, and M. Schönfelder (eds) *Les agglomérations ouvertes de l'Europe celtique IIIe–Ier s. av. J.-C. Table ronde internationale Glux-en-Glenne, 28–30 October 2015*. Mémoires d'Archéologie du Grand Est 4: 439–450. Strasbourg: AVAGE.

Fichtl, S., and V. Guichard. 2016. 'Ne faut-il pas repenser les oppida?'. *L'Archéologue* 139: 56–59.

Field, N., and M. Parker Pearson. 2003. *Fiskerton: An Iron Age Timber Causeway with Iron Age and Roman Votive Offerings*. Oxford: Oxbow Books.

Filgis, M. N. 2011. 'La maison à abside du mont Saint-Marcel: conception et restitution architecturale', in B. Chaume and C. Mordant (eds) *Le complexe aristocratique de Vix: nouvelles recherches sur l'habitat, le système de fortification et l'environnement du mont Lassois*: 739–751. Dijon: Editions universitaires de Dijon.

Fischer, C.-E., M.-H. Pemonge, F. Santos, H. Houzelot, C. Couture-Veschambre, A. Lefort, et al. 2019. 'Multi-scale archaeogenetic study of two French Iron Age communities: From internal social- to broad-scale population dynamics'. *Journal of Archaeological Science: Reports* 27: 101942.

Fitzpatrick, A. 2007. 'The fire, the feast and the funeral. Late Iron Age burial rites in southern England', in V. Kruta and G. Leman-Delerive (eds) *Feux des morts, foyers des vivants: Les rites et symbols du feu dans les tombes de l'Âge du Fer et de l'époque romaine*. Revue de Nord Hors série Art et Archéologie 11: 123–142. Lille: Revue de Nord.

Fokkens, H. 1997. 'The genesis of Urnfields: Economic crisis or ideological change?' *Antiquity* 71, 272: 360–373.

Fontijn, D. 2002. *Sacrificial Landscapes: Cultural Biographies of Persons, Objects, and 'Natural' Places in the Bronze Age of the Southern Netherlands, 2300–600 BC*. Analecta Praehistorica Leidensia 33/34. Leiden: University of Leiden.

Fontijn, D., and H. Fokkens. 2007. 'The emergence of early Iron Age 'chieftains' graves' in the southern Netherlands: Reconsidering transformations in burial and depositional practices', in C. Haselgrove and R. Pope (eds) *The Earlier Iron Age in Britain and the Near Continent*: 354–373: Oxford: Oxbow Books.

Foster, S. 1989. 'Analysis of spatial patterns in buildings (access analysis) as an insight into social structure. Examples from the Scottish Atlantic Iron Age'. *Antiquity* 63, 238: 43–50.

Fredengren, C. 2002. *Crannogs: A Study of People's Interaction with Lakes, with Special Reference to Loch Gara, in the North-West of Ireland*. Bray: Wordwell.

Frodsham, P., I. Hedley, and R. Young. 2007. 'Putting the neighbours in their place? Displays of position and possession in northern Cheviot 'hillfort' design', in C. Haselgrove and T. Moore (eds) *The Later Iron Age in Britain and Beyond*: 250–265. Oxford: Oxbow Books.

Fulford, M., A. Clarke, E. Durham, and N. Pankhurst. 2018. *Late Iron Age Calleva: The Pre-Conquest Occupation at Silchester Insula IX, 77–91*. Britannia Monograph 32. London: Society for the Promotion of Roman Studies.

Garland, N. 2020. 'The origins of British oppida: Understanding transformation in Iron Age practice and society'. *Oxford Journal of Archaeology* 39, 1: 107–125.

Garrow, D., and C. Gosden. 2012. *Technologies of Enchantment?: Exploring Celtic Art 400 BC–100 AD*. Oxford: Oxford University Press.

Garrow, D., C. Gosden, J. D. Hill, and C. Bronk Ramsey. 2009. 'Dating Celtic art: A major radiocarbon dating programme of Iron Age and early Roman metalwork in Britain'. *Archaeological Journal* 166, 1: 79–123.

Gartski, K. 2019. 'The social production of iron in first millennium BC Ireland'. *Oxford Journal of Archaeology* 38, 4: 443–463.

Gerritsen, F. 2003. *Local Identities: Landscape and Community in the Late Prehistoric Meuse-Demer-Scheldt Region*. Amsterdam Archaeological Studies 9. Amsterdam: Amsterdam University Press.

Gerritsen, F. 2008. 'Domestic times: Houses and temporalities in late prehistoric Europe', in A. Jones (ed.) *Prehistoric Europe: Theory and Practice*: 143–161. Oxford: Blackwell.

Giles, M. 2012. *A Forged Glamour: Landscape, Identity and Material Culture in the Iron Age*. Oxford: Windgather Press.

Giles, M. 2020. *Bog Bodies: Face to Face with the Past*. Manchester: Manchester University Press.

Ginoux, N. 2009. *Élites guerrières au nord de la Seine au début du IIIe siècle av. J.-C.: la nécropole celtique du Plessis-Gassot (Val-d'Oise)*. Revue du Nord Hors série Art et Archéologie 15. Lille: Université Charles de Gaule-Lille III.

Gomez de Soto, J., and T. Lejars. 2009. 'Les lieux de culte des âge du Fer en Centre-Ouest', in I. Bertrand, A. Duval, J. Gomez de Soto, and P. Maguer (eds) *Les Gaulois entre Loire et Dordogne: Actes du XXXIe colloque international de l'AFEAF (Chauvigny, 2007), Vol. 1*. Association des Publications Chauvinoises Mémoire 34: 227–244. Chauvigny: Association des Publications Chauvinoises.

Gosden, C. 2004. *Archaeology and Colonialism: Cultural Contact from 5000 BC to the Present.* Cambridge: Cambridge University Press.

Grane, T. 2013. 'Roman imports in Scandinavia: Their purpose and meaning?', in P. Wells (ed.) *Roman Beyond its Frontiers: Imports, Attitudes and Practices.* Journal of Roman Archaeology Supplementary Series 94: 29–44. Portsmouth: Journal of Roman Archaeology.

Gransar, F. 2002. 'La batterie de silos de Soupir "Le Champ Grand Jacques" (Aisne): contribution à l'identification d'une centralisation du stockage à La Tène B dans le nord de la France', in P. Méniel and B. Lambot (eds) *Découvertes récentes de l'âge du Fer dans le massif des Ardennes et ses marges: Repas des vivants et nourritures pour les morts en Gaule: Actes du XXV Colloque international de l'AFEAF (Charleville-Mézières, 2001)*: Société Archéologique Champenoise Mémoire 16: 67–80. Reims: Société Archéologique Champenoise.

Gransar, F., G. Auxiette, S. Desenne, B. Henon, F. Malrain, V. Matterne, and E. Pinard. 2007. 'Expressions symboliques, manifestations rituels et culturels en contexte domestique au Ier millénaire avant notre ère dans le nord de la France', in P. Barral, A. Daubigney, C. Dunning, G. Kaenel, and M. J. Roulière-Lambert (eds) *L'âge du Fer dans l'arc jurassien et ses marges. Dépôts, lieux sacrés et territorialité à l'âge du Fer: Actes du XXIXe colloque international de l'AFEAF (Bienne, 2005)*: 549–564. Besançon: Presses universitaires de Franche-Comté.

Gregory, T. 1992. *Excavations in Thetford, 1980–1982, Fison Way.* East Anglian Archaeology 53. Dereham: Norfolk Museums Service.

Grogan, E. 2008. *The Rath of the Synods, Tara, Co. Meath: Excavations by Seán P. Ó Ríordáin.* Bray: Wordwell.

Guichard, V. 2017. 'Les *oppida*, une parenthèse dans l'histoire de l'Europe tempérée?' *Pallas* 105: 159–171.

Guilaine J., and D. Garcia (eds). 2018. *La protohistoire de la France.* Paris, Hermann.

Gwilt, A., M. Lodwick, J. Deacon, N. Wells, R. Madgwick, and T. Young. 2016. 'Ephemeral abundance at Llanmaes: Exploring the residues and resonances of an earliest Iron Age midden and its associated archaeological context in the Vale of Glamorgan', in J. T. Koch and B. Cunliffe (eds) *Celtic from the West 3: Atlantic Europe in the Metal Ages: Questions of Shared Language*: 294–329. Oxford: Oxbow Books.

Haarnagel, W. 1979. *Die Grabung Feddersen Wierde, 2: Methode, Hausbau, Siedlungs- und Wirtschaftformen sowie Sozialstruktur.* Wiesbaden: Steiner.

Hamerow, H. 2004. *Early Medieval Settlements: The Archaeology of Rural Communities in Northwest Europe 400–900.* Oxford: Oxford University Press.

Hamilton, D., and C. Haselgrove. 2019. 'Exploring settlement dynamics through radiocarbon dating', in T. Romankiewicz, M. Fernández-Götz, G. Lock, and O. Buchsenschutz (eds) *Enclosing Space, Opening New Ground: Iron Age Studies from Scotland to Mainland Europe*: 111–119. Oxford: Oxbow Books.

Hamilton, D., K. L. Sayle, M. Boyd, C. Haselgrove, and G. Cook. 2019. '"Celtic cowboys" reborn: Application of multi-isotopic analysis (δ13C, δ15N, and δS) to examine mobility and movement of animals within an Iron Age British society'. *Journal of Archaeological Science* 101: 189–198.

Hamilton, S., and J. Manley. 2001. 'Hillforts, monumentality and place: A chronological and topographic review of first millennium BC hillforts of south-east England'. *European Journal of Archaeology* 4, 1: 7–42.

Harding, D. W. 2017. *The Iron Age in Northern Britain: Britons and Romans, Natives and Settlers,* 2nd edition. London: Routledge.

Haselgrove, C. 2001. 'Iron Age Britain and its European setting', in J. R. Collis (ed.) *Society and Settlement in Iron Age Europe: Actes du XVIIIe Colloque de l'AFEAF (Winchester, 1994)*. Sheffield Archaeological Monograph 11: 37–72. Sheffield: J. R. Collis Publications.

Haselgrove, C. 2004. 'Society and polity in late Iron Age Britain', in M. Todd (ed.) *The Blackwell Companion to Roman Britain*: 12–29. Oxford: Blackwell.

Haselgrove, C. 2007. 'Rethinking earlier Iron Age settlement in the eastern Paris Basin', in C. Haselgrove and R. Pope (eds) *The Earlier Iron Age in Britain and the Near Continent*: 400–428. Oxford: Oxbow Books.

Haselgrove, C. 2009. *The Traprain Law Environs Project: Excavations and Fieldwork 2000–2004*. Edinburgh: Society of Antiquaries of Scotland.

Haselgrove, C. 2016. Cartimandua's Capital? The late Iron Age royal site at Stanwick, North Yorkshire, fieldwork and analysis 1981–2011. CBA Research Report 175. York: Council for British Archaeology.

Haselgrove, C., and V. Guichard. 2013. 'Les gaulois sont-ils dans la plaine? Reflections on settlement patterns in Gaul in the 1st century BC', in S. Krausz, A. Colin, K. Gruel, I. Ralston, and T. Dechezleprêtre (eds) *L'âge du Fer en Europe: Mélanges offerts à Olivier Buchsenschutz*: 317–328. Bordeaux: Ausonius.

Haselgrove, C., and R. Hingley. 2006. 'Iron deposition and its significance in pre-Roman Britain', in G. Bataille and J. P. Guillaumet (eds), *Les dépôts d'objets métalliques aux âges du fer*. Collection Bibracte 11: 147–163. Glux-en-Glenne: Centre archéologique européen du Mont Beuvray.

Haselgrove, C., and R. Pope. 2007. 'Characterising the earlier Iron Age', in C. Haselgrove and R. Pope (eds) *The Earlier Iron Age in Britain and the Near Continent*: 1–23. Oxford: Oxbow Books.

Hedeager, L. 1978. 'A quantitative analysis of Roman imports in Europe north of the Limes (0–400 AD), and the question of Roman-Germanic exchange', in K. Kristiansen and C. Paludan-Müller (eds) *New Directions in Scandinavian Archaeology*. Studies in Scandinavian Prehistory and Early History 1: 191–216. Copenhagen: National Museum of Denmark.

Hedges, J. 1987. *Bu, Gurness and the Brochs of Orkney*. British Archaeological Reports, British Series 163–164. Oxford: British Archaeological Reports.

Henderson, J. 2007. *The Atlantic Iron Age: Settlement and Identity in the First Millennium BC*. London: Routledge.

Hessing, W., and Kooi, P. 2005. 'Urnfields and cinerary barrows. Funerary and burial ritual in the Late Bronze and Iron Ages', in L. P. Louwe Kooijmans, P. W. van den Broeke, H. Fokkens, and A. L. van Gijn (eds) *The Prehistory of the Netherlands, Vol. 2*: 631–654. Amsterdam: Amsterdam University Press.

Hey, G., P. Booth, and J. Timby. 2011. Yarnton Iron Age and Romano-British Settlement and Landscape. Thames Valley Landscapes Monograph 35. Oxford: Oxford Archaeology.

Hiddink, H., and N. Roymans. 2015. 'Exploring the rural landscape of a peripheral region', in N. Roymans, T. Derks, and H. Hiddink (eds) *The Roman Villa of Hoogeloon and the Archaeology of the Periphery*. Amsterdam Archaeological Studies 22: 45–86. Amsterdam: Amsterdam University Press.

Higgins, M. 2016. 'Meillionydd. The life and death of an Iron Age community in Wales'. *Current Archaeology* 321: 28–33.

Hill, J. D. 1995. *Ritual and Rubbish in the Iron Age of Wessex: A Study on the Formation of a Specific Archaeological Record*. British Archaeological Reports, British Series 242. Oxford: Tempus Reparatum.

Hill, J. D. 2007. 'The dynamics of social change in later Iron Age eastern and south-eastern England *c.*300 BC–AD 43', in C. Haselgrove and T. Moore (eds) *The Later Iron Age in Britain and Beyond*: 16–40. Oxford: Oxbow.

Hill, J. D. 2011. 'How did British middle and late pre-Roman Iron Age societies work (if they did)?', in T. Moore and X. L. Armada (eds) *Atlantic Europe in the First Millennium BC: Crossing the Divide*: 242–263. Oxford: Oxford University Press.

Hill, J. D., A. J. Spence, S. La Niece, and S. Worrell. 2004. 'The Winchester hoard. A find of unique Iron Age gold jewellery from southern England'. *Antiquaries Journal* 84: 1–22.

Hodgson, N., J. McKelvey, and W. Muncaster. 2012. *The Iron Age on the Northumberland Coastal Plain: Excavations in Advance of Development 2002–2010*. Tyne and Wear Archives and Museums Archaeological Monograph 3. Newcastle-upon-Tyne: Arbeia Society.

Hughes, E. G. 1994. 'An Iron Age barrow, burial at Bromfield, Shropshire'. *Proceedings of the Prehistoric Society* 60, 1: 395–402.

Hughes, G., and A. Woodward. 2015. *The Iron Age and Romano-British Settlement at Crick Covert Farm, Northamptonshire: Excavations 1997–1998 (DIRFT Vol. I)*. Oxford: Archaeopress.

Huisman, D. J., J. van der Laan, G. R. Davies, B. J. H. van Os, N. Roymans, B. Fermin, et al. 2017. 'Purple haze: Combined geochemical and Pb-Sr isotope constraints on colourants in Celtic glass'. *Journal of Archaeological Science* 81: 59–78.

Hunter, F. 1997. 'Iron Age hoarding in Scotland and northern England', in A. Gwilt and C. Haselgrove (eds) *Reconstructing Iron Age Societies*. Oxbow Monograph 71: 108–133. Oxford: Oxbow.

Hunter, F. 2005. 'The image of the warrior in the British Iron Age—coin iconography in context', in C. Haselgrove and D. Wigg-Wolf (eds) *Iron Age Coinage and Ritual Practices*. Studien zu Fundmünzen der Antike 20: 43–68. Mainz: Philipp von Zabern.

Hunter, F. 2007. *Beyond the Edge of Empire—Caledonians, Picts and Romans*. Rosemarkie: Groam House Museum.

Hunter, F. 2016. 'Beyond Hadrian's Wall', in M. Millett, L. Revell, and A. Moore (eds) *The Oxford Handbook of Roman Britain*: 179–202. Oxford: Oxford University Press.

Joffroy, R. 1962. *Le Trésor de Vix: Histoire et portée d'une grande découverte*. Paris: Fayard.

Johns, C. 2002–3. 'An Iron Age sword and mirror cist burial from Bryher, Isles of Scilly'. *Cornish Archaeology* 41–42: 1–70.

Johnston, S. A., and B. Wailes. 2007. *Dún Ailinne: Excavations at an Irish Royal Site, 1968–1975*. Philadelphia: University of Pennsylvania Museum.

Joly, M., and P. Barral. 2007. 'Le sanctuaire de Mirebeau-sur-Bèze (Côte-d'Or): bilan des recherches récentes', in P. Barral, A. Daubigney, C. Dunning, G. Kaenel, M.-J. Roulière-Lambert (eds) *L'âge du Fer dans l'arc jurassien et ses marges: dépôts, lieux sacrés et territorialité à l'âge du Fer: Actes du XXIXe colloque international de l'AFEAF (Bienne, 2005)*: 5–72. Besançon: Presses universitaires de Franche-Comté.

Joy, J. 2010. *Iron Age Mirrors: A Biographical Approach*. British Archaeological Reports, British Series 518. Oxford: Archaeopress.

Joy, J. 2015. 'Snettisham: Shining new light on an old treasure'. *British Archaeology* 144: 18–25.

Jusseret, S., L. Olivier, N. G. Riddiford, N. P. Branch, and M. Watteaux. 2013. 'Le Briquetage de la Seille (Moselle): géoarchéologie et archéogéographie d'un complexe d'exploitation intensive du sel à l'âge du Fer', in F. Olmer and R. Roure (eds) *Les Gaulois au fil de l'eau: Actes du 37e colloque international de l'AFEAF (Montpellier, 2013), Vol. 1*: 515–537. Bordeaux: Ausonius.

Knight, D. 2007. 'From open to enclosed. Iron Age landscapes of the Trent Valley', in C. Haselgrove and T. Moore (eds) *The Later Iron Age in Britain and Beyond*: 190–218. Oxford: Oxbow Books.

Knight, M., R. Ballantyne, I. Robinson Zeki, and D. Gibson. 2019. 'The Must Farm pile-dwelling settlement'. *Antiquity* 93, 369: 645–663.

Knipper, C., S. L. Pichler, D. Brönnimann, H. Rissanen, M. Rosner, N. Spichtig, et al. 2018. 'A knot in a network: Residential mobility at the Late Iron Age proto-urban centre of Basel-Gasfabrik (Switzerland) revealed by isotope analyses'. *Journal of Archaeological Science: Reports* 17: 735–753.

Koenig, M. P. (ed.) 2016. *Le gisement de Crévéchamps (Lorraine): Du néolithique à l'époque romaine dans la vallée de la Moselle*. Documents d'archéologie française 110. Paris: Maison des sciences de l'homme.

Krausse, D., M. Fernández-Götz, L. Hansen, and I. Kretschmer. 2016. *The Heuneburg and the Early Iron Age Princely Seats: First Towns North of the Alps*. Budapest: Archaeolingua.

Krausz, S. 2009. 'L'oppidum de Châteaumeillant-Mediolanum (Cher)', in O. Buchsenschutz, M. B. Chardenoux, S. Krausz, and M. Vaginay (eds) *L'âge du Fer dans la boucle de la Loire. Les Gaulois sont dans la ville. Actes du XXXIIe colloque de l'AFEAF (Bourges, 2008)*. Revue Archéologique du Centre de la France supplément 35: 67–73. Bourges: FERAC.

Krausz, S. 2014. 'Stratégie et défense des oppida celtiques: les remparts de guerre des Bituriges Cubi', in O. Buchsenschutz, O. Dutour, and C. Mordant (eds) *Archéologie de la violence et de la guerre dans les sociétés pré et protohistoriques: Congrès National du CTHS, Perpignan mai 2011*: 193–207. Paris: Editions du CTHS.

Krausz, S. 2016. *Des premières communautés paysannes à la naissance de l'état dans le Centre de la France 5000–50 a.C.* Scripta Antiqua 86. Bordeaux: Ausonius.

Krausz, S. 2018. 'L'art de la fortification celtique: Architecture et ingénierie des systèmes défensifs', in A. Villard-Le Tiec (ed.) *Architectures de l'âge du Fer en Europe occidentale et centrale: Actes du 40e colloque de l'AFEAF (Rennes, 2016)*: 243–259. Rennes: Presses Universitaires de Rennes.

Krausz, S. 2019. 'Gauls under siege: Defending against Rome', in A. P. Fitzpatrick and C. Haselgrove (eds) *Julius Caesar's Battle for Gaul: New Archaeological Perspectives*: 159–178. Oxford: Oxbow Books.

Krausz, S. 2020. 'Le modèle politique des Bituriges', in J. Kysela and G. Pierrevelcin (eds) *Unité et diversité du monde celtique: Actes du 42e Colloque international de l'AFEAF (Prague, 2018)*. Collection AFEAF 2: 285–300. Paris: AFEAF.

Krausz, S. 2021a. 'Les Gaulois contre l'État'. *Études Celtiques* 46: 7–26.

Krausz, S. 2021b. 'Les remparts de l'âge du Fer ont-ils été construits pour la guerre ou pour la paix?', in F. Delrieu, C. Féliu, P. Gruat, M.-C. Kurzaj, and E. Nectoux (eds) *Les espaces fortifiés à l'âge du Fer en Europe: Actes du 43e colloque international de l'AFEAF (Le Puy-en-Velay, 2019)*. Collection AFEAF 3: 123–136. Paris: AFEAF.

Krausz, S. 2021c. 'Le dernier rempart des Bituriges. La poliorcétique à la fin de l'âge du Fer à Châteaumeillant (Cher)', in F. Delrieu, C. Féliu, P. Gruat, M.-C. Kurzaj, and E. Nectoux (eds) *Les espaces fortifiés à l'âge du Fer en Europe: Actes du 43e colloque international de l'AFEAF (Le Puy-en-Velay, 2019)*. Collection AFEAF 3: 63–76. Paris: AFEAF.

Ladle, L. 2018. *Multi-Period Occupation at Football Field, Worth Matravers, Dorset: Excavations 2006–2011*. Oxford. BAR Publishing.

Lallemand, D. 2009. 'Hérisson, oppidum de Cordes Chateloi (Allier): fouille de la Porte de Babylone', in O. Buchsenschutz, M. B. Chardenoux, S. Krausz, and M. Vaginay (eds) *L'âge du Fer dans la boucle de la Loire: Les Gaulois sont dans la ville: Actes du XXXII colloque international de l'AFEAF (Bourges, 2008)*. Revue Archéologique du Centre de la France supplément 35: 75–87. Bourges: FERAC.

Lambot, B. 2006. 'Religion et habitat, les fouilles d'Acy-Romance', in C. Goudineau (ed.) *Religion et société en Gaule*: 177–188. Paris: Errance.

Lambrick, G., and T. Allen. 2004. Gravelly Guy, Stanton Harcourt, Oxfordshire: The development of a prehistoric and Romano-British community. Thames Valley Landscapes Monograph 21. Oxford: Oxford Archaeology.

Lambrick, G., and M. Robinson. 2009. *The Archaeology of the Terraces of the Upper and Middle Thames: The Thames Valley in Late Prehistory, 1500 BC–AD 50*. Thames Valley Landscapes Monograph 29. Oxford: Oxford Archaeology.

Le Bihan, J. P., and J. F. Villard. 2001. *Archéologie d'une île à la pointe de l'Europe: Ouessant. 1: Le site archéologique de Mez-Notariou et le village du premier âge du fer*. Quimper: Centre de recherche archéologique du Finistère.

Le Goff, E. 2009. 'Habitats, terroir et paysage rural: aménagement et structuration du territoire et de la campagne gauloise: Ifs, ZAC "Object'Ifs Sud" (Calvados)', in I. Bertrand, A. Duval, J. Gomez de Soto, and P. Maguer (eds) *Habitats et paysages ruraux en Gaule et regards sur d'autres régions du monde celtique: Actes du XXXI colloque international de l'AFEAF (Chauvigny, 2007), Vol. 2*. Association des Publications Chauvinoises Mémoire 35: 93–107. Chauvigny: Association des Publications Chauvinoises.

Le Goff, E. 2016. 'L'oppidum de Moulay, capitale gauloise des Aulerques Diablintes', in S. Fichtl, E. Le Goff, A. Mathiaut-Legros, and Y. Menez (eds) *Les premières villes de l'ouest: Agglomérations gauloises de Bretagne et Pays de la Loire*: 123–138. Jublains: Deco 72.

Le Goff, E. 2019. 'Une agglomération artisanale et commerciale de l'ouest de la Gaule; le site de Kergolvez à Quimper (Finistère)', in S. Fichtl, P. Barral, G. Pierrevelcin, and M. Schönfelder (eds) *Les agglomérations ouvertes de l'Europe celtique IIIe–Ier s. av. J.-C: Table ronde internationale Glux-en-Glenne, 28–30 October 2015*. Mémoires d'Archéologie du Grand Est 4: 119–134. Strasbourg: AVAGE.

Lefort, A., A. Baron, F. Blondel, M. Méniel, and S. Rottier. 2015. 'Artisanat, commerce et nécropole. Un port de La Tène D1 à Urville-Nacqueville', in F. Olmer and R. Roure (eds) *Les gaulois au fil de l'eau: Actes du 37e colloque international de l'AFEAF (Montpellier, 2013)*: 441–474. Montpellier: Ausonius.

Lelong, O. (ed.) 2019. *Excavations at Milla Skerra, Sandwick, Unst: Rhythms of Life in Iron Age Shetland*. Oxford: Oxbow Books.

Lelong, O., and G. MacGregor (eds). 2007. *The Lands of Ancient Lothian: Interpreting the Archaeology of the A1*. Edinburgh: Society of Antiquaries of Scotland.

Lock, G., and I. Ralston. 2017. *Atlas of Hillforts of Britain and Ireland*. Edinburgh: Edinburgh University Press. Available at https://hillforts.arch.ox.ac.uk/ accessed 15 August 2022.

Loughton, M. 2009. 'Getting smashed: The deposition of amphorae and the drinking of wine in Gaul during the late Iron Age'. *Oxford Journal of Archaeology* 28, 1: 77–110.

Loughton, M. 2014. *The Arverni and Roman Wine: Roman Amphorae from Late Iron Age Sites in the Auvergne (Central France): Chronology, Fabrics, and Stamps*. Archaeopress Roman Archaeology 2. Oxford: Archaeopress.

Løvschal, M. 2014. 'Emerging boundaries. Social embedment of landscape and settlement divisions in north-western Europe during the first millennium BC'. *Current Anthropology* 55, 6: 727–750.

Luginbühl, T. 2014. 'La "migration des Cimbres et des Teutons". Une histoire sans archéologie?', in C. Gaeng (ed.) *Hommage à Jeannot Metzler*. Archaeologia Mosellana 9: 343–360.

Lynn, C. 2003. *Navan Fort: Archaeology and Myth*. Bray: Wordwell.

Macdonald, P. 2007. *Llyn Cerrig Bach: A Study of the Copper Alloy Artefacts from the Insular La Tène Assemblage*. Cardiff: University of Wales Press.

Madgwick, R., V. Grimes, A. L. Lamb, A. J. Nederbragt, J. A. Evans, and F. McCormick. 2019. 'Feasting and mobility in Iron Age Ireland: Multi-isotope analysis reveals the vast catchment of Navan Fort, Ulster'. *Science Reports* 9, 1: 19792.

Maguer, P., and D. Lusson. 2009. 'Fermes, hameaux et résidences aristocratiques entre Loire et Dordogne', in I. Bertrand, A. Duval, J. Gomez de Soto, and P. Maguer (eds) *Les Gaulois entre Loire et Dordogne: Actes du XXXI colloque international de l'AFEAF (Chauvigny, 2007), Vol. 1*. Association des Publications Chauvinoises Mémoire 34: 423–457. Chauvigny: Association des Publications Chauvinoises.

Maitay, C., C. Marcigny, and V. Riquier. 2022. *L'habitat rural du premier âge du Fer: Enclos palissadés de l'Atlantique à la Moselle*. Collection Recherches archéologiques 21. Paris: CNRS/Inrap.

Malrain, F., S. Bauvais, M. Boulen, B. Hénon, V. Legros, M. Saurel, et al. 2010. 'Le site artisanal de La Tène finale et du Gallo-Romain de Ronchères (Aisne) "Le Bois de la Forge"'. *Revue archéologique de Picardie*, 1, 2: 41–165.

Malrain, F., G. Blancquaert, and T. Lorho (eds). 2013. *L'habitat rural du second âge du Fer: Rythmes de création et d'abandon au nord de la Loire*. Collection Recherches archéologiques 7. Paris: CNRS/Inrap.

Malrain, F., V. Matterne, and P. Méniel. 2002. *Les paysans Gaulois (IIIe siècle–52 av. J.-C.)*. Paris: Errance/Inrap.

Maniquet, C. 2008. 'Le dépôt cultuelle du sanctuaire Gaulois de Tintignac à Naves (Corrèze)'. *Gallia* 65, 1: 273–326.

Maniquet, C., T. Lejars, B. Armbruster, M. Pernot, M. Drieux-Daguerre, P. Mora, et al. 2011. 'Le carnyx et le casque oiseau celtique de Tintignac (Naves-Corrèze). Description et étude technologique'. *Aquitania* 27: 63–150.

Mann, A., and R. Jackson. 2018. *Clifton Quarry, Worcestershire: Pits, Posts and Cereals: Archaeological Investigations 2006–2009*. Oxford: Oxbow Books.

Marion, S., Y. Le Bechennec, and C. Le Forestier. 2006–2007. 'Nécropole et bourgade d'artisans: l'évolution des sites de Bobigny, entre La Tène B et La Tène D'. *Revue archéologique du Centre de la France* 45–46: 6–50.

Marshall, P., R. Brunning, S. Minnitt, C. Bronk Ramsey, E. Dunbar, and P. J. Reimer. 2020. 'The chronology of Glastonbury Lake Village'. *Antiquity* 94, 378: 1464–1481.

Masefield, R. (ed.) 2015. *Origins, Development and Abandonment of an Iron Age Village (DIRFT Vol. II)*. Oxford: Archaeopress.

Mata, K. 2019. *Iron Age Slaving and Enslavement in Northwest Europe*. Oxford: Archaeopress.

Mattingly, D. J. 2006. *An Imperial Possession: Britain in the Roman Empire, 54 BC–AD 409*. London: Allen Lane.

May, J. 1996. *Dragonby: Report on Excavations at an Iron Age and Romano-British Settlement in North Lincolnshire*. Oxbow Monograph 61. Oxford: Oxbow Books.

McDermott, C., C. Moore, C. Murray, G. Plunkett, and M. Stanley. 2009. 'A colossus of roads: The Iron Age archaeology of Ireland's peatlands', in G. Cooney, K. Becker, J. Coles, M. Ryan, and S. Sievers (eds) *Relics of Old Decency: Archaeological Studies of Later Prehistory*: 49–64. Dublin: Wordwell.

McGarry, T. 2009. 'Irish late prehistoric burial ring-ditches', in G. Cooney, K. Becker, J. Coles, M. Ryan, and S. Sievers (eds) *Relics of Old Decency: Archaeological Studies of Later Prehistory*: 413–423. Dublin: Wordwell.

Menez, Y. 2012. 'Die Entstehung städlischer Siedlungen: Das Beispiel von Paule (Côtes d'Armor)', in S. Sievers and M. Schönfelder (eds) *Die Frage der Protourbanisation in der Eisenzeit: Akten des 34. internationalen Kolloquiums der AFEAF (Aschaffenburg 2010)*. Kolloquien zur Vor- und Frühgeschichte 16: 289–301. Bonn: Habelt.

Menez, Y. 2016. 'De la résidence rurale à l'agglomération', in S. Fichtl, E. Le Goff, A. Mathiaut-Legros, and Y. Menez (eds) *Les premières villes de l'ouest: Agglomérations gauloises de Bretagne et Pays de la Loire*: 139–146. Jublains: Deco 72.

Menez, Y. (ed.) 2021. *Une résidence de la noblesse gauloise: Le camp de Saint-Symphorien à Paule (Côtes-d'Armor)*. Documents d'Archéologie Française 112. Paris: Éditions de la Maison des sciences de l'homme.

Menez, Y., P. R. Giot, F. Laubenheimer, E. Le Goff, and C. Vendries. 2009. 'Les sculptures Gauloises de Paule (Côtes-d'Amor)'. *Gallia* 56: 357–414.

Méniel, P. 1998. *Le site protohistorique d'Acy-Romance (Ardennes), III: Les animaux et l'histoire d'un village gaulois*. Reims: Société Archéologique Champenoise Mémoire 14.

Mercer, R. 2019. *Native and Roman on the Northern Frontier: Excavations and Survey in a Later Prehistoric Landscape in Upper Eskdale, Dumfriesshire*. Edinburgh: Society of Antiquaries of Scotland.

Metzler, J., C. Gaeng, and P. Méniel. 2016. *L'espace public du Titelberg*. Dossiers d'Archéologie XVII. Luxembourg: Centre National de Recherche Archéologique.

Metzler-Zens, N., J. Metzler-Zens, and P. Méniel. 1999. *Lamadelaine: Une nécropole de l'oppidum du Titelberg*. Dossiers d'Archéologie VI. Luxembourg: Musée Nationale d'Histoire et d'Art.

Milcent, P. Y. 2004. *Le premier âge du Fer en France centrale*. SPF Mémoire 34. Paris: Société Préhistorique Française.

Milcent, P. Y. 2006. 'Premier âge du Fer médio-atlantique et genèse multipolaire des cultures matérielles laténiennes', in D. Vitali (ed.) *Celtes et Gaulois, l'Archéologie face à l'Histoire, 2: la Préhistoire des Celtes: Actes de la table ronde de Bologne-Monterenzio, 28–29 Mai 2005*. Collection Bibracte 12/2: 81–105. Glux-en-Glenne: Centre archéologique européen du Mont Beuvray.

Milcent, P. Y. 2012. *Le temps des élites en Gaule Atlantique: Chronologie des mobiliers et rythmes de constitution des dépôts métalliques dans le contexte Européen (XIIIe–VIIe s. av. J.-C.)*. Rennes: Presses Universitaires de Rennes.

Milcent, P. Y. 2017. 'Hallstatt C sword graves in Continental Gaul. Rise of an elite or new system of representation of self in a context of crisis?', in R. Schumann and S. van der Vaart-Verschoof (eds) *Connecting Elites and Regions: Perspectives on Contacts, Relations and Differentiation During the Early Iron Age Hallstatt C Period in Northwest and Central Europe*: 85–107. Leiden: Sidestone Press.

Mohen, J. P. 1980. *L'âge du Fer en Aquitaine*. SPF Mémoire 14. Paris: Société Préhistorique Française.

Moore, T. 2020. *A Biography of Power: Research and Excavations at the Iron Age Oppidum of Bagendon, Gloucestershire (1979–2017)*. Oxford: Archaeopress.

Moore, T., A. Braun, J. Creighton, L. Cripps, P. Haupt, I. Klenner, et al. 2013. '*Oppida*, agglomerations and suburbia: The Bibracte environs and new perspectives on late Iron Age urbanism in central-eastern France'. *European Journal of Archaeology* 16, 3: 491–517.

Murray, R. 2007. *Culduthel Mains Farm, Inverness. Phase 5: Excavation of a Later Prehistoric Settlement: Assessment Report. Report 1769*. Edinburgh: Headland Archaeology.

Mytum, H. 2013. *Monumentality in Later Prehistory: Building and Rebuilding Castell Henllys Hillfort*. New York: Springer.

Needham, S. 2007. '800 BC, the Great Divide', in C. Haselgrove and R. Pope (eds) *The Earlier Iron Age in Britain and the Near Continent*: 39–63. Oxford: Oxbow Books.

Newman, C. 1997. *Tara: An Archaeological Survey*. Discovery Programme Monographs 2. Dublin: Royal Irish Academy.

Nieuwhof, A. 2020. *Ezinge Revisited: The Ancient Roots of a Terp Settlement: Excavation, Environment and Economy: Catalogue of Plans and Finds. Vol. 1*. Groningen Archaeological Studies 37. Groningen: Groningen Institute of Archaeology and Barkhuis Publishing.

Nieuwhof, A., and M. Schepers. 2016. 'Living on the edge: Synanthropic salt marshes in the coastal area of the northern Netherlands from around 600 BC'. *Archaeological Review from Cambridge* 31, 2: 48–74.

Noble, G. 2020. 'The problem of the Picts. Searching for a lost people in northern Scotland'. *Current Archaeology* 364: 28–35.

Noble, G., N. Evans, D. Hamilton, C. MacIver, E. Masson-Maclean, and J. O'Driscoll. 2019. 'Dunnicaer, Aberdeenshire, Scotland: A Roman Iron Age promontory fort beyond the frontier'. *Archaeological Journal* 177, 2: 256–338.

Noble, G., M. Goldberg, and D. Hamilton. 2018. 'The development of the Pictish symbol system: Inscribing identity beyond the edges of Empire'. *Antiquity* 92, 365: 1329–1348.

Nouvel, P., P. Barral, S. Deffressigne, V. Riquier, J.-M. Séguier, N. Tikonoff, et al. 2009. 'Rhythmes de création, fonctionnement et abandon des établissements ruraux de la fin de l'âge du Fer dans l'Est de la France', in I. Bertrand, A. Duval, J. Gomez De Soto, and P. Maguer (eds) *Habitats et paysages ruraux en Gaule et regards sur d'autres régions du monde celtique: Actes du XXXIe colloque de l'AFEAF (Chauvigny, 2007), Vol. 2*. Association des Publications Chauvinoises Mémoire 35: 109–151. Chauvigny: Association des Publications Chauvinoises.

Nowakowski, J. A., and H. Quinnell. 2011. *Trevelgue Head, Cornwall: The Importance of C. K. Croft Andrew's 1939 Excavations for Prehistoric and Roman Cornwall*. Truro: Cornwall County Council.

Ó Drisceoil, C. 2007. 'Life and death in the Iron Age at Carrickmines Great, County Dublin'. *Journal of the Royal Society of Antiquaries of Ireland* 137: 5–28.

O'Brien, W. 2009. *Local Worlds: Early Settlement Landscapes and Upland Farming in South-West Ireland*. Cork: Collins Press.

O'Connell, A. 2013. *Harvesting the Stars: A Pagan Temple at Lismullin, Co. Meath*. Dublin: National Roads Authority.

O'Connor, B. 2007. 'Llyn Fawr metalwork in Britain: A review', in C. Haselgrove and R. Pope (eds) *The Earlier Iron Age in Britain and the Near Continent*: 64–79. Oxford: Oxbow Books.

O'Driscoll, J., P. Gleeson, and G. Noble. 2020. 'Re-imagining Navan fort: New light on the evolution of a major Ceremonial Centre in northern Europe'. *Oxford Journal of Archaeology* 39: 247–273.

O'Driscoll, J., and G. Noble. 2020. 'Survey and excavation at an Iron Age enclosure complex on Turin Hill and environs'. *Proceedings of the Society of Antiquaries of Scotland* 149: 83–114.

Olmer, F. 2018. 'Le commerce et les importations en Gaule au Second Âge du Fer', in J. Guilaine and D. Garcia (eds) *La Protohistoire Française*: 453–469. Paris: Hermann.

Olmer, F., B. Girard, G. Verrier, and H. Bohbot. 2013. 'Voies, acteurs et modalités du grand commerce en Europe occidentale', in A. Colin and F. Verdin (eds) *L'Âge du Fer en Aquitaine et sur ses marges: Mobilité des hommes, diffusion des idées, circulation des biens dans l'espace européen à l'Âge du Fer: Actes du 35e colloque international de l'AFEAF (Bordeaux, 2011)*. Aquitania supplément 30: 665–691. Bordeaux: Aquitania.

Parfitt, K. 1995. *Iron Age Burials from Mill Hill, Deal*. London: British Museum Press.

Payne, A., M. Corney, and B. Cunliffe. 2006. *The Wessex Hillforts Project: Extensive Survey of Hillfort Interiors in Central Southern England*. London: English Heritage.

Pernet, L. 2019. 'Fighting for Caesar: The archaeology and history of Gallic auxiliaries in the 2nd–1st centuries BC', in A. P. Fitzpatrick and C. Haselgrove (eds) *Julius Caesar's Battle for Gaul: New Archaeological Perspectives*: 179–199. Oxford: Oxbow Books.

Pope, R. 2015. 'Bronze Age architectural traditions: Dates and landscapes', in F. Hunter and I. Ralston (eds) *The Later Bronze and Iron Ages of Scotland in their European Setting*: 159–184. Edinburgh: Society of Antiquaries of Scotland.

Poux, M. 2004. *L'Âge du vin: rites de boisson, festins et libations en Gaule indépendante*. Collection Protohistoire européenne 8. Montagnac: Monique Mergoil.

Poux, M. (ed.) 2012. *Corent, voyage au cœur d'une ville gauloise*. Paris: Errance.

Poux, M. 2014. 'Enlarging oppida: Multi-polar town patterns in late Iron Age Gaul', in M. Fernández-Götz, H. Wendling, and K. Winger (eds) *Paths to Complexity: Centralisation and Urbanisation in Iron Age Europe*: 156–166. Oxford: Oxbow Books.

Poux, M., and M. Demierre. 2015. *Le sanctuaire de Corent (Puy-de-Dôme, Auvergne): vestiges et rituel*. Gallia supplément 62. Paris: CNRS.

Powell, A. B. 2015. 'Bronze Age and early Iron Age burial grounds and later landscape development outside Little Woodbury, Salisbury, Wiltshire'. *Wiltshire Archaeological and Natural History Magazine* 108: 44–78.

Powell, K., A. Smith, and G. Laws. 2010. *Evolution of a Farming Community in the Upper Thames Valley: Excavation of a Prehistoric, Roman and Post-Roman Landscape at Cotswold Community, Gloucestershire and Wiltshire*. Thames Valley Landscapes Monograph 31. Oxford: Oxford Archaeology.

Prilaux, G. 2000. 'Une ferme gauloise spécialisée dans le travail du sel à Pont-Rémy "La Queute" et "Le Fond de Baraquin" (Somme). Évolution et particularités de l'espace enclos'. *Revue archéologique de Picardie*, 1–2: 233–254.

Raftery, B. 1994. *Pagan Celtic Ireland: The Enigma of the Irish Iron Age*. London: Thames and Hudson.

Ralston, I. 1992. *Les enceintes fortifiées du Limousin: les habitats protohistoriques de la Luxembourg non méditerranéenne*. Documents d'archéologie française 36. Paris: Maison des sciences de l'homme.

Ralston, I. 2019. 'The Gauls on the eve of the Roman conquest', in A. P. Fitzpatrick and C. Haselgrove (eds) *Julius Caesar's Battle for Gaul: New Archaeological Perspectives*: 19–47. Oxford: Oxbow Books.

Rennie, C. 2013. 'A room with a view: Excavations at Ravelrig quarry'. *Proceedings of the Society of Antiquaries of Scotland* 143: 137–156.

Riquier, V., C. Maitay, E. Leroy-Langelin, and P. Maguer. 2018. 'Maisons et dépendences à l'âge du fer dans le nord et l'ouest de la France: du premier âge du fer au début de La Tène', in A. Villard-Le Tiec (ed.) *Architectures de l'âge du fer en Europe Occidentale et centrale: Actes du 40e Colloque international de l'AFEAF (Rennes, 2016)*: 273–347. Rennes: Presses Universitaires de Rennes.

Roberts, B. W., D. Boughton, M. Dinwiddy, N. Doshi, A. P. Fitzpatrick, D. Hook, et al. 2015. 'Collapsing commodities or lavish offerings? Understanding massive metalwork deposition at Langton Matravers, Dorset during the Bronze Age–Iron Age transition'. *Oxford Journal of Archaeology* 34, 4: 365–395.

Romankiewicz, T. 2011. *The Complex Roundhouses of the Scottish Iron Age*. British Archaeological Reports, British Series 550. Oxford: Archaeopress.

Roy, M. 2015. 'An Iron Age burial with weapons, on a site with evidence of medieval and post-medieval occupation from Dunbar, East Lothian'. *Proceedings of the Society of Antiquaries of Scotland* 145: 177–212.

Roymans, N. 1991. 'Late Urnfield societies in the Northwest European Plain and the expanding networks of Central European Hallstatt groups', in N. Roymans and F. Theuws (eds) *Images of the Past: Studies on Ancient Societies in Northwestern Europe*. Studies in Prae-en Protohistoire 7: 9–89. Amsterdam: University of Amsterdam.

Roymans, N. 1995. 'Romanization, cultural identity and the ethnic discussion. The integration of lower Rhine populations into the Roman empire', in J. Metzler, M. Millett, N. Roymans, and J. Sloftstra (eds) *Integration in the Early Roman West: The Role of Culture and Ideology*. Dossiers d'Archéologie du Musée National d'Histoire et d'Art IV: 47–64. Luxembourg: Musée National d'Histoire et d'Art.

Roymans, N. 1996. 'The sword or the plough. Regional dynamics in the Romanisation of Belgic Gaul and the Rhineland area', in N. Roymans (ed.) *From the Sword to the Plough: Three Studies on the Earliest Romanization of Northern Gaul*. Amsterdam Archaeological Studies 1: 9–126. Amsterdam: Amsterdam University Press.

Roymans, N. 2007. 'On the latènisation of Late Iron Age material culture in the lower Rhine/Meuse area', in S. Möllers, W. Schlüter, and S. Sievers (eds) *Keltische Einflüsse im nördlichen Mitteleuropa während der mittleren und jüngeren vorrömischen Eisenzeit*: 311–325. Frankfurt am Main: Römisch-Germanische Komission.

Roymans, N. 2019. 'Caesar's conquest and the archaeology of mass violence in the Germanic frontier zone', in A. P. Fitzpatrick and C. Haselgrove (eds) *Julius Caesar's Battle for Gaul: New Archaeological Perspectives*: 113–133. Oxford: Oxbow Books.

Roymans, N., and J. Aarts. 2005. 'Coins, soldiers and the Batavian Hercules cult. Coin deposition at the sanctuary of Empel in the Lower Rhine region', in C. Haselgrove and D. Wigg-Wolf (eds) *Iron Age Coinage and Ritual Practices*. Studien zu Fundmünzen der Antike 20: 337–359. Mainz: Philipp von Zabern.

Roymans, N., T. Derks, and S. Heeren. 2007. *Een Bataafse gemeenschap in de wereld van het Romeinse rijk: Opgravingen te Tiel-Passawaaij*. Utrecht: Matrijs.

Roymans, N., T. Derks, and S. Heeren. 2020. 'Roman imperialism and the transformation of rural society in a frontier province: Diversifying the narrative'. *Britannia* 51: 265–294.

Roymans, N., and F. Gerritsen. 2002. 'Landscape, ecology and mentalités: A long-term perspective on developments in the Meuse-Demer-Scheldt region'. *Proceedings of the Prehistoric Society* 68: 257–287.

Roymans, N., and F. Kortland. 1999. 'Urnfield symbolism, ancestors and the land in the lower Rhine region', in N. Roymans and F. Theews (eds) *Land and Ancestors: Cultural Dynamics in the Urnfield Period and the Middle Ages in the Southern Netherlands*. Amsterdam Archaeological Studies 4: 33–61. Amsterdam: Amsterdam University Press.

Roymans, N., A. Tol, and H. Hiddink. 1998. *Opgravingen in Kampershoek en de Molenakker te Weert: Campagne 1996–1998*. Zuidnederlandse Archeologische Rapporten 5. Amsterdam: ACVU.

Roymans, N., and L. Verniers. 2010. 'Glass La Tène Bracelets in the Lower Rhine Region: Typology, chronology and social interpretation'. *Germania* 88, 1/2: 195–219.

Russell, M. 2016. 'Finding Duropolis. A new kind of Iron Age settlement'. *Current Archaeology* 313: 12–18.

Rynne, E. 1976. 'The La Tène and Roman finds from Lambay, County Dublin: A reassessment'. *Proceedings of the Royal Irish Academy* 76: 231–244.

Score, V. 2011. *Hoards, Hounds and Helmets: A Conquest-Period Ritual Site at Hallaton, Leicestershire*. Leicester Archaeology Monograph 21. Leicester: University of Leicester.

Sharples, N. 2014. 'Are the developed hillforts of southern England urban?', in M. Fernández-Götz, H. Wendling, and K. Winger (eds) *Paths to Complexity: Centralisation and Urbanisation in Iron Age Europe*: 224–232. Oxford: Oxbow Books.

Sharples, N. M. 1991. *Maiden Castle: Excavations and Field Survey 1985–6*. English Heritage Archaeological Report 19. London: HBMC(E).

Sharples, N. M. 2010. *Social Relations in Later Prehistory: Wessex in the First Millennium BC*. Oxford: Oxford University Press.

Sireix, C. 2013. 'L'agglomération artisanale de Lacoste à Mouliets-et-Villemartin (Gironde)', in A. Colin and F. Verdin (eds) *L'âge du Fer en Aquitaine et sur ses marges: Mobilité des hommes, diffusion des idées, circulation des biens dans l'espace européen à l'âge du Fer: Actes du 35e Colloque international de l'AFEAF (Bordeaux, 2011)*. Aquitania supplément 30: 79–122. Bordeaux: Aquitania.

Smith, A., M. Allen, T. Brindle, and M. Fulford. 2016. *The Rural Settlement of Roman Britain*. Britannia Monograph 29. London: Society for the Promotion of Roman Studies.

Stead, I. M. 2006. *British Iron Age Swords and Scabbards*. London: British Museum Press.

Stephens, M., and P. Ware. 2020. 'The Iron Age cemetery at Pocklington and other excavations by MAP', in P. Halkon (ed.) *The Arras Culture of Eastern Yorkshire: Celebrating the Iron Age*: 17–31. Oxford: Oxbow Books.

Stewart, D., and M. Russell. 2017. *Hillforts and the Durotriges: A Geophysical Survey of Iron Age Dorset*. Oxford: Archaeopress.

Taylor, A. 2020. 'Farewell to arms. The North Bersted warrior burial'. *British Archaeology* 158: 16–23.

Taylor, J., J. Thomas, and C. Haselgrove. 2012. 'Burrough Hill, Leicestershire: Excavations at the hillfort in 1960, 1967 and 1970–1'. *Transactions of the Leicestershire Archaeological and Historical Society* 86: 49–102.

Therkorn, L. L., R. W. Brandt, J. P. Pals, and M. Taylor. 1984. 'An early Iron Age farmstead: Site Q of the Assendelver Polders project'. *Proceedings of the Prehistoric Society* 50: 351–373.

Thomas, J. 2011. *Two Iron Age 'Aggregated' Settlements in the Environs of Leicester: Excavations at Beaumont Leys and Humberstone*. Leicester Archaeology Monograph 19. Leicester: University of Leicester.

Thomas, J. 2018. 'Glenfield Park: Living with cauldrons'. *British Archaeology* 158: 14–21.

Thomas, N. 2005. *Conderton Camp, Worcestershire: A Small Middle Iron Age Hillfort on Bredon Hill*. York: Council for British Archaeology Research Report 143.

Todd, M. 1987. *The Northern Barbarians*, 2nd edition. Oxford: Blackwell.

Topping, P., S. Halliday, and A. Welfare. 1989. 'Early cultivation in Northumberland and the Borders'. *Proceedings of the Prehistoric Society* 55: 161–179.

Valdez-Tullett, A. 2017. 'Sheep in wealth's clothing: Social reproduction across the Bronze Age to Iron Age transition in Wiltshire, southern England'. *European Journal of Archaeology* 20, 4: 663–681.

Van de Noort, R., H. P. Chapman, and J. R. Collis. 2007. *Sutton Common: The Excavation of an Iron Age 'Marsh Fort'*. Council for British Archaeology Research Report 154. York: Council for British Archaeology.

Van den Broeke, P. W. 2002. 'Een vurig afscheid? Aanwijzingen voor verlatingsrituelen in ijzertijdnederzettingen', in H. Fokkens and R. Jansen (eds) *2000 Jaar Bewoningsdynamiek: Brons- en Ijzertijdbewoning in het Maas-Demer-Scheldegebied*: 45–61. Leiden: Leiden University.

Van den Broeke, P. W., and E. A. G. Ball. 2012. 'Unveiling Bronze Age, Iron Age and native Roman communities in lower Nijmegen (the Netherlands)—twelve years of excavations in a fluvial area', in J. Bofinger and D. Krausse (eds) *Large-Scale Excavations in Europe: Fieldwork Strategies and Scientific Outcome*: 65–83. Brussels: Europae Archaeologia Consilium.

Van Heeringen, R. M. 1989. 'The Iron Age in the western Netherlands V: Synthesis'. *Berichten van de Rijksdienst voor het Oudheidkundig Bodemonderzoek* 39: 157–268.

Van Impe, L., G. Creemers, R. Vanm Laere, S. Scheers, H. Wouters, and B. Ziegaus. 2002. 'De Keltische goudschat van Beringen (prov. Limburg)'. *Archaeology in Vlaanderen* VI, 1997/1998: 9–132.

Vuaillat, D. 1977. *La Nécropole tumulaire de Chavéria (Jura)*. Annales littéraires de l'Université de Besançon 28. Paris: Les Belles Lettres.

Waddington, C. 2012. 'Excavations at Fin Cop, Derbyshire: An Iron Age hillfort in conflict?' *Archaeological Journal* 169, 1: 159–236.

Waddington, K. 2013. *The Settlements of Northwest Wales, from the Late Bronze Age to the Early Medieval Period*. Cardiff: University of Wales Press.

Waddington, K., A. Bayliss, T. Higham, R. Madgwick, and N. Sharples. 2019. 'Histories of deposition: Creating chronologies for the late Bronze Age–Iron Age transition in Southern Britain'. *Archaeological Journal* 176, 1: 84–133.

Waldus, W., and K. Verelst. 2005. *Zeist Kroostweg-Noord, proefsleuvenonderzoek en DO fase 1*. ADC ArcheoProjecten Rapport 382. Amersfoort: ADC ArcheoProjecten.

Warmenbol, E. 2017. 'The early Iron Age in Belgium. Earth and fire, and also water', in R. Schumann and S. van der Vaart-Verschoof (eds) *Connecting Elites and Regions: Perspectives on Contacts, Relations and Differentiation During the Early Iron Age Hallstatt C period in Northwest and Central Europe*: 201–219. Leiden: Sidestone Press.

Waterbolk, H. T. 1995. 'Patterns of the peasant landscape'. *Proceedings of the Prehistoric Society* 61: 1–36.

Webley, L. 2007. 'Using and abandoning roundhouses: A reinterpretation of the evidence from late Bronze Age–early Iron Age southern England'. *Oxford Journal of Archaeology* 26, 2: 127–144.

Webley, L. 2015. 'Rethinking Iron Age connections across the Channel and North Sea', in H. Anderson-Whymark, D. Garrow, and F. Sturt (eds) *Continental Connections: Cross-Channel Relationships from the Lower Palaeolithic to the Iron Age*: 122–144. Oxford: Oxbow Books.

Wefers, S. 2011. 'Still using your saddle quern? A compilation of the oldest known rotary querns in western Europe', in D. Williams and D. Peacock (eds) *Bread for the People: The Archaeology of Mills and Milling: Proceedings of a Colloquium held in the British School at Rome 4th–7th November 2009*. British Archaeological Reports International Series 2274: 67–76. Oxford: Archaeopress.

Wells, P. S. 1999. *The Barbarians Speak: How the Conquered Peoples Shaped Roman Europe*. Princeton: Princeton University Press.

Wheeler, R. E. M., and K. M. Richardson. 1957. *Hill-Forts of Northern France*. Reports of the Research Committee of the Society of Antiquaries of London 19. Oxford: Oxford University Press.

Zech-Matterne, V., and C. Brun. 2016. 'Vers une agriculture extensive? Étude diachronique des productions végétales et des flores associés, au cours de la période Laténienne, en France sepentrionale', in G. Blancquaert and F. Malrain (eds) *Évolution des sociétés gauloises du Second âge du Fer, entre mutations internes et influences externes: Actes du 38e colloque international de l'AFEAF (Amiens, 2014)*. Revue Archéologique de Picardie Numéro Spécial 30: 623–638. Amiens: Revue Archéologique de Picardie.

CHAPTER 5

SCANDINAVIA AND NORTHERN GERMANY

FRANDS HERSCHEND

Introduction

This chapter covers modern Norway, Sweden, and Denmark, collectively known as Scandinavia, together with the parts of Germany bordering Denmark and the Baltic (Figure 5.1). Thanks to its enormously long coastline, the sea has played a crucial role in the economy, culture and communications of this vast region. While southern and eastern Scandinavia are closely linked to the main European continental mass across the Baltic, the northern part of the peninsula looks more towards the circumpolar zone. The best agricultural land is to be found in the south (Denmark, the islands, southern Sweden), which like northern Germany is relatively low-lying. In central Sweden and southern Norway, land suitable for arable farming exists near the coast, on the plains, and around the Swedish lakes. In the north and in the mountainous interior, possibilities for agriculture are limited and the focus is on fishing and hunting.

Archaeological Background

Checked by legislation, modern society pushes forward Scandinavian and with less restriction north-west German archaeology. Regional authorities decide where, when, and how most archaeology is carried out (cf. Kristiansen 2009). In inland central and northern Scandinavia, Iron Age heritage management is considered relatively simple: monuments are few, and sites threatened by forestry are not yet sufficiently acknowledged. In eastern Scandinavia, owing to shoreline displacement, the Iron Age landscape is little affected by the limited development of these presently declining areas. Excavations are thus few. In western Norway there has been little shore displacement and Iron Age settlement landscapes are limited. These locations have, moreover,

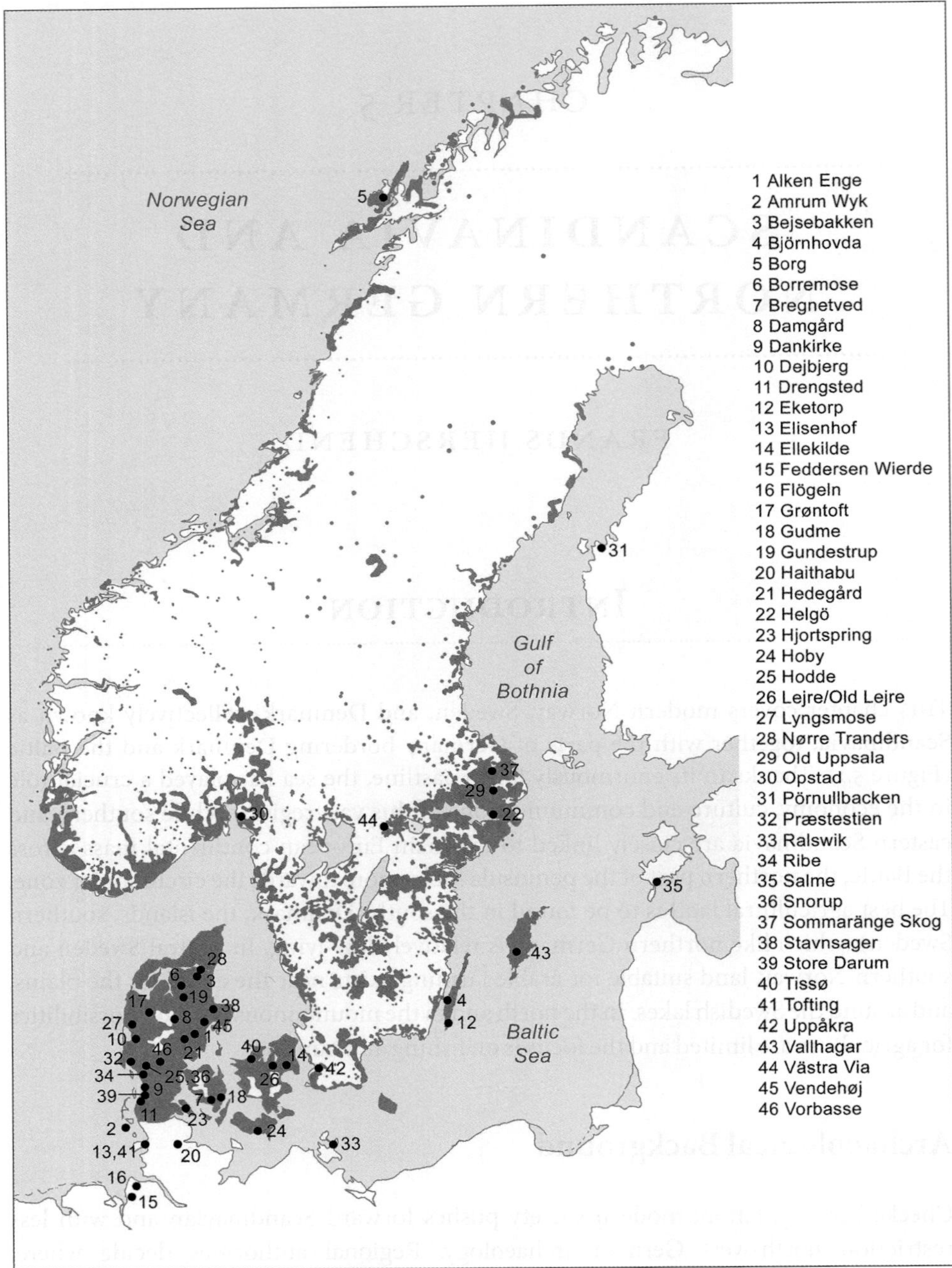

FIGURE 5.1 The human landscape in Iron Age Scandinavia, showing the location of sites mentioned in the text. For Sweden and Norway, quarrying the national FMIS and Askeladden databases and mapping areas with Iron Age cemeteries (as a proxy for the markers by which one navigated the human landscape) provide a good way of representing areas of permanent settlement (shaded grey). In densely occupied Denmark, cemeteries and settlements recorded in Fund og Fortidsminder result in a similar map. The number of burial markers grows during the Iron Age except in Denmark, where cemeteries become fewer from the fifth century AD onwards. Cemeteries designate permanently settled areas, but not a specific mode of subsistence. Agriculture, husbandry, and inland hunting formed the backbone of the Iron Age economy.

been exploited ever since the Iron Age. The destruction of graves in the late nineteenth century is emblematic (cf. Solberg 1986). After World War II, excavations were limited, but more recently large investments in Norwegian infrastructure have given new opportunities for development-led archaeology. Due to their size and generally southern Scandinavian and coastal distribution, the capital cities and large towns have impacted on areas that were important to Iron Age societies, but until recently Iron Age archaeology was unknown in urban areas because development was considered so essential. In greater Stockholm, Copenhagen, and Århus, Iron Age farms were not recognized until the 1990s (e.g. Klasro in Sollentuna, Sweden: Herschend et al. 1993: 79–99; or Høje Tåstrup and Vendehøj).[1]

Despite decentralization, heritage management is still centrally controlled, aiming at preserving visible monuments. The focus of Iron Age archaeology, on the other hand, has shifted from visible to concealed monuments, from graves to farms, from small-scale to large sites, and from individual sites to landscapes. Tensions between administrative traditions, society, and reformed archaeology have resulted in a situation in which Iron Age archaeology developed neither in the urban centres nor in peripheral regions, but instead in more dynamic provincial areas. The best archaeological data therefore come from Jutland (Bejsebakken), Rogaland (Forsandmoen), Scania (Fosie, Järrestad), and parts of the Mälar valley. More recently, urban fringes have come into focus, turning points being the excavations for Gardemoen airport (Oslo), Høje Tåstrup (Copenhagen), and Nordortsleden (Stockholm). Historically speaking, archaeology in Germany has lacked the legislative support that characterizes Scandinavian archaeology, and suffered from long periods of war and undemocratic rule (Kunow 2002).

In north-west Germany, large areas of marshland disappeared in the marine transgression of 400–150 BC. Despite a series of lesser trans- and regressions, this created the high water levels that resulted in the still surviving terp settlements (Behre 2008). Rescue excavations on these sites are uncommon, although there have been several model research excavations (e.g. Feddersen Wierde, Flögeln, Elisenhof). Danish projects have favoured provincial Jutland (Grøntoft, Hodde, Vorbasse) and, later, the islands (Gudme, Tissø, Hoby). In Sweden (with the exception of Helgö) large post-war projects were also situated at peripheral locations, such as Vallhagar in Gotland, and Eketorp in Öland. In Norway, Borg in the Lofoten archipelago and Romerike (Skre 1998) were purely research projects, as were those at Gene in Ångermanland (Sweden) and projects in Ostrobothnia (Baudou et al. 1991). For a time, rescue archaeology brought large research excavations almost to a halt, but in the twenty-first century they have started up again.

Chronological Overview

The framework used in this chapter is based on transformations in the archaeological data, a general view of the eras and epochs of European pre- and early history, and geographical characteristics. Taking Scandinavia and north-west Germany as one region (which is relatively common when discussing the early Iron Age), the links to a wider European past become obvious. Nevertheless, studies combining region and chronology are common, and today there are four main source materials that structure the period: artefacts, graves, farms, and infrastructure—including offering lakes and defence works. The evidence they provide is not synchronous; on the contrary, some periods of stability or transformation are evident more readily in one material than another. Nevertheless, we can point to major periods of transformation in the first century BC, in the mid-first millennium AD, and in the eighth century AD. The start and end of the Iron Age are difficult to determine—the beginning because it is diffuse and hard to date, the end because it is strongly influenced by biased historical sources (cf. Myhre 1993).

For this overview, we define the early Iron Age as the period from 500 BC to AD 400 and the late Iron Age as AD 400 to 750. Some iron objects already occur in the final phase of the late Bronze Age in the south of Scandinavia (Montelius Period VI, corresponding roughly to Hallstatt C–D; e.g. Kristiansen 1998: 213, fig. 106), but this period is conventionally treated as part of the Bronze Age (e.g. Thrane 2013) and is not discussed here. The transition to the Iron Age proper was evidently long-drawn-out; while the presence of new objects indicating connections with the Hallstatt communities of central Europe marks something of a break with earlier centuries, many elements of daily life continue uninterrupted (Thrane 2013: 749).

The early Iron Age essentially consists of a pre-Roman Iron Age, up to the start of the first millennium AD, and a Roman Iron Age, lasting until *c.*AD 400. The late Iron Age spans the period from then until *c.*AD 750. The last hundred years or so of the first millennium BC constitute a period of transition and so do roughly the first hundred years of the late Iron Age. Disregarding the very end of the Iron Age, there are three periods of predictable 'order' during the 'long' Iron Age and two periods of 'transformation' (Table 5.1).

Up to the first period of transformation, the pre-Roman Iron Age is characterized by a relatively simple material culture. While this may in fact have been the case, we suspect that our source material is biased because it cannot show the full complexity of a material culture largely characterized by artefacts made of organic materials. The period,

Table 5.1 Chronological overview of the Scandinavian Iron Age

late Bronze Age	Montelius Period VI	c.750–500 BC
early Iron Age	pre-Roman Iron Age	c.500–1 BC
	Roman Iron Age	c.AD 1–400
late Iron Age		c.AD 400–750
first period of transformation		c.100–1 BC
second period of transformation		c.AD 400–500

moreover, is marked by an unwillingness to deposit metal objects, Hjortspring being an exception. Since the dead were cremated in plain dress with few grave goods, and their bodily remains were reduced to anonymity (although the tradition on Gotland is slightly different), burials also provide disappointingly little information. In the south-western part of our region, La Tène influences become visible in the second century BC. The reason we may talk of a first period of transformation in the middle of the Scandinavian early Iron Age is based on the introduction of a more varied material culture, the appearance of larger households and villages, and changes in burial customs. The range of finds signifies a growing material wealth, and in the wake of this transition, regional variation becomes apparent.

In the Roman Iron Age, the links between southern Denmark/north-west Germany (as well as further north) and the Roman world stand out, and a border zone fringing the European continent becomes apparent around a line from Schleimünde in the east to Eiderstedt in the west. As throughout the Iron Age, economic geography establishes coastal and inland Scandinavia as distinct kinds of human landscapes. The resources of the interior are exploited partly on a seasonal basis and the sedentary coastal population grows. Coastal–inland relations enhance connectivity, and the period is characterized by different forms of warfare, acquisition, and trade. Farms become larger and more varied, indicating growing social stratification. Although the social pyramid is still relatively flat, complex burials become a significant social marker. Eventually there are signs of demographic stress in areas where deforestation started early, such as north-west Germany, Jutland, Rogaland, parts of Scania, Öland, and Gotland. Some areas are depopulated, but are still used for herding.

Rudimentary verbal and numeric literacy was introduced in the Roman Iron Age, and verse lines suggest that oral poetry and epics gained ground during a period of increasing social stratification. Warfare becomes endemic in southernmost Scandinavia. The second period of transformation is complex and much disputed (cf. Löwenborg 2012). It seems to grow out of a subsistence crisis with its roots in the fourth and fifth centuries AD, beginning in the south. Successful Scandinavian mercenaries become a fact and instability grows, ultimately because of the declining Roman Empire (Fischer et al. 2011). Starting in north-west Germany, demographic and political aspects of the transformation become apparent from the fifth century onwards; a political shift in the upper echelons of society (cf. Näsman 2006) and a change of ideology are apparent (cf. Hedeager 2011), while social stratification and dependency continued to grow.

The late Iron Age is characterized by continued migration and a declining or stagnating population, until the eighth century AD. At this point, a new upper class emerges, sharing a series of ideological notions and material expressions in a network constructed by means of nodes based on manorial hall farms that are no longer distributed solely with an eye to subsistence. East Scandinavian influences in southern Scandinavia are an important part of a scene defining a Scandinavia prepared to renew contacts with a 'Romanized' Europe now represented by Carolingian France, Friesland, and Anglo-Saxon England. The first autonomous urban communities, bordering on resettled north-west Germany, belong to this end phase of the Iron Age.

The Iron Age Economy

In the pre-Roman Iron Age, subsistence was characterized by sedentary and non-sedentary family-based households. Although there may have been some entirely self-sufficient hunter-gatherers, it appears that non-sedentary families were linked in with sedentary economies able to produce a surplus, which facilitated interaction with people engaged, for example, in communal reindeer drives in mountain areas and on glaciers (Nesje et al. 2012). Mixed economies combining and balancing two or more of the variables hunting, fishing, husbandry, and agriculture characterize large parts of Scandinavia. The inhabitants were sedentary, grew in importance, and tended to form communities. Self-sufficient communities, relying on agriculture and husbandry, covered north-west Germany and southern Scandinavia, and expanded north along the Scandinavian coastlands.

The Iron Age house was adapted to this arrangement inasmuch as the building that generally constituted the farm housed humans and animals under the same roof, keeping dairy economy close to daily indoor life. Barley was the main source of bread and was continuously processed through the year, threshing and cleaning the crops being a recurring indoor activity. Agriculture was practised on small fertilized fields, and in densely populated areas systems of small, regular plots—so-called 'Celtic fields'—developed (cf. Viklund 1998; Behre 2008; Odgaard and Rømer 2009). Overwintering animals, mainly sheep kept primarily for meat production, played an important role. Weaving was an ongoing indoor activity. Indoor–outdoor was an essential complementary pair, and farmyards, the 'in-between', were uncommon. Judging from the size of the pre-Roman Iron Age house, subsistence, especially in the south, was based on a nuclear family living in a small one-house, one-generation farm for about thirty years (Chapter 20). Houses were never rebuilt and the size of the byre was always matched by that of the dwelling. The household's production of dung was thus fixed, allowing a family to graze the same number of cows and to spread the same amount of manure on the same field area. The house effectively defined the size of the family and its share of the common wealth. Some south Scandinavian households were so small, with dwelling quarters less than 10 m^2, that they could hardly reproduce themselves. Together with the few large farms, this indicates dependency and social stratification (Herschend 2009: 44–47, 156–171).

Further north, as at Opstad in Östfold (Løken 1977), some large, self-sufficient family structures, reminiscent of the Bronze Age, may have persisted. Pre-Roman Iron Age settlements did not form villages until late in the period, and never in central and northern Scandinavia, with Rogaland and the Mälar valley presently being the limit of distribution of the Iron Age village. While there were 'Celtic fields' in southern Scandinavia, in central Scandinavia there were areas with clearance cairns and stone-fenced fields, starting in the Bronze Age, for example in Rogaland (Juhl 2002). Most farm sites that were continuously settled in the Roman Iron Age had temporary pre-Roman Iron Age forerunners.

The first period of transformation marks the end of one-generation farms and eventually of the 'balanced' house/byre. Starting in the south-west, byres grew in size and outhouses became the norm. Separate field systems disappeared, probably because they were inefficient, and single farms (in central Scandinavia) or villages (in south Scandinavia) became permanent. The creation of the central Scandinavian house is significant because it marks the origin of a new way of living (Figure 5.2). These developed southern and central Scandinavian houses indicate that farms and households were becoming more complex, fewer in number, larger, and more stable. The first tendencies to fence individual farms belong to the end of the first period of transformation, around the sturn of era. Change was primarily one of family structure and the right to form a farming household, but the essence of the developments apparent during the Roman Iron Age is consistent with a new economic situation. With larger households, greater division of labour and intensification of work became possible. In this transitory phase of great social change, conditions for the unfree seem to have worsened, with some people living in byres in southern Scandinavia. We know of their existence because in some burnt-down houses people found in the compartments furthest away from the doors had been killed in the fire, while animals in the outer stalls were saved and animals in between suffocated (e.g. Norre Tranders in northern Jutland, Nielsen 2002a). Given the situation in the pre-Roman Iron Age with the stratification of households, it stands to reason that the households of the new, fewer and larger farms consisted of farm

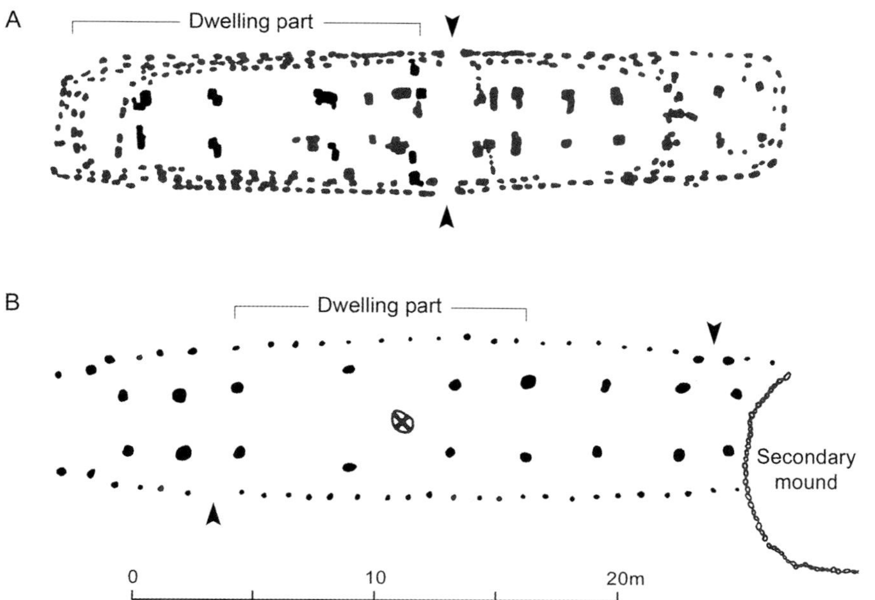

FIGURE 5.2 (A) Southern Scandinavian house with central entrance and dwelling area in the left, or western, side of the house. (B) Central Scandinavian house with diagonally placed entrances and central dwelling room. This house had no specific orientation.

owners (landowners) and their farmhands, i.e. landless and thus dependent members of the household. Most farms still comprised one household.

In the Roman Iron Age, apart from the introduction of rye, the use of the *plaggen* system for manuring (see Chapter 18), and probably larger cattle in north-west Germany and south-west Jutland, subsistence continued on the same basis as in the first period of transformation (Herschend 2009: 224). The economy was enhanced by means of the new households, more farmhands, and a better spatial relationship between fields, manure, and farms. The social change of the first period of transformation was at the root of this.

A number of weeds grew in the fields, and fat hen (*Chenopodium album*) is common in samples of plant remains (Viklund 1998). When harvesting the fields, the sheaves were cut at ground level and immediately taken home to dry. Threshing divided the crop into food and fodder. The basis of farming continued to be crop cultivation and animal husbandry, and the expansion of the latter led to a more open landscape. Deforestation had clearly been going on since the Bronze Age in several parts of southern Scandinavia, such as Jutland (Odgaard and Rømer 2009) and Rogaland (Bakkevik et al. 2002), as well as in northern Germany (Behre 2008). Öland and Gotland are the most obvious Roman Iron Age additions. The German coastland lacked forests, but they were close at hand on the heathlands (*Geest*) bordering the marsh, and found across the north German plain.

Settlement expansion into the central Scandinavian coastlands reflects the enhanced opportunities for single family-based households to sustain themselves. The settlements at Pörnullbacken in Ostrobothnia (Viklund and Gullberg 2002), Gene in Ångermanland, and Vestvågøy in Lofoten (Johansen 1979) are good examples. To some degree this expansion is the result of colonization, but local populations too may have become farmers. Hunting continued to be the norm in central and northern Scandinavia, but reindeer herding, based on the annual cycle of the wild reindeer, did not become important until the late Iron Age (Sommerseth 2011). In the late Iron Age, the amount of roofed dwelling space in square metres indicates that the population had grown, and in the large main houses of the farms in the Mälar valley there were sometimes primary as well as secondary households (Herschend 2009: 236–250), and in Østfold (Brådseth 2007: 130). This indicates not only population growth, but also social stratification, and suggests a crisis similar to the one observed during the pre-Roman Iron Age in southern Scandinavia.

The second period of transformation represents a twofold crisis. In part it was the start of a subsistence crisis, forcing some farms to be abandoned, and in part was due to escalating social stratification. Perhaps the bad summers of AD 536–550 killed people and closed down farms for good, but other systemic factors must be considered, since a number of farms and villages had already been deserted in the late fourth century AD and were never resettled. In some cases they were perhaps replaced by new settlements, and some central settlements seem just to have shrunk, but the majority were deserted. This means that between the late fourth and the mid-sixth century AD a large number of settlements disappeared. The exceptions are the new late Iron Age manors, such as Gausel, Lejre, and Old Uppsala. In some areas where buildings and fences were built partly in stone, such as Öland and Gotland, the settlement structure was completely reconfigured. It would seem therefore that one way of overcoming this crisis was the restructuring of the settlement landscape. In southern Scandinavia we may speak of a concentration of farms to form the villages that still exist today.

Extensive radiocarbon dating of settlement remains has recently shown that farm sites have a specific Iron Age history. Most places would have been frequented at intervals perhaps as far back as the late Neolithic, but sometimes, starting in the first period of transformation in south Scandinavia, the farm site was permanently and more intensively settled for two or three hundred years before it disappeared. It seems that over-intensive usage of the farmland brought subsistence problems for the farmers, creating an imbalance between the size of the population and the capacity of the agricultural system. In some semi-marginal areas, additional signs of the crisis are apparent: small households in pit houses resettled formerly abandoned sites, apparently without engaging in agriculture, as at Västra Via and Sommaränge Skog (Sundkvist 2010: 134; Forsman and Victor 2007: 31, 286). Iron production, as well as hunting and animal husbandry, is a feature of these households. The subsistence crisis may also be apparent in summer hunting on the glaciers and the use of summer pasture shielings in mountain areas (cf. Prescott 1998). These settlements worked, not because they were primarily self-sufficient, but because they cooperated with other types of settlement. Despite farms being closed down, there was not enough cultivable land to go round.

These solutions are typical of central Scandinavia. In the south, solutions are more difficult to come by, the permanently inhabited Ölandic ring forts being the exception to the rule. The fifth-century AD population density on Öland was about eight per km^2 and the overall population about 10,000. In Eketorp some twenty-five households were engaged in husbandry, cooperating for their other subsistence needs with surrounding farms in a completely deforested environment. It stands to reason that the inhabitants of Eketorp would have preferred a farm of their own but the system could not provide one; they were thus victims of a subsistence crisis. It is not surprising that Ölandic mercenaries emigrated temporarily to Italy in AD 460 (Fischer et al. 2011).

In the late Iron Age few radical changes in subsistence took place. Farms continued to become larger and fewer in number. Perhaps haymaking improved and cattle may have become bigger. We might expect larger fields, with more ploughed land, but that is difficult to prove. The landscape became more forested, signalling a decreasing human impact on the land, perhaps in part because of a diminishing population. This view might be correct, but a rise in agricultural production and a decline in husbandry would have the same effect. The catastrophic scenario is still disputed, but the bad weather of *c.* AD 536–550 and a decline in the north European population are undeniable. It is noteworthy that in remote and late colonizations, such as Borg in Lofoten or Pörnullbacken, Ostrobothnia, subsistence does not seem to have been a problem. The eventual solution to the late Iron Age problem was to be larger fields, crop rotation, better farming methods, better meadows, and larger animals, but these changes were not to occur until later.

Social stratification becomes apparent in several ways, as indicated by the following fourfold hierarchy. (1) Very large manors came into being, as well as manors sited in the landscape in such a way that their economic base could hardly have been their immediate surroundings only; they must instead have been sustained by dues from a larger area. (2) Farms in village communities; these may well have been dependant on the owners of the manors, but were probably free estates. In the Ribe area around AD 500 there are two villages (Præstestien and Store Darum) with modular farms, implying that each equated to a certain proportion of the village's production and thus was subject to some form of taxation. This system seems to have disappeared after a generation or two and was not revived until the Viking Age. (3) One-generation farms on the outskirts of villages (e.g. Rasmussen and Nielsen 2009); these indicate that although people were allowed to build a farm, it was not passed on by inheritance. (4) Pit house dwellings, whether forming homogenous settlements or ancillary buildings at farms (e.g. Bejsebakken; Nielsen 2002b), could function as dwellings as well as workshops. During the late Iron Age they spread from northern Germany and Jutland into the rest of Scandinavia. As dwellings, they were second-rate and low-cost, and some of them were evidently intended for a dependant population engaged in handicrafts—mainly textile production and ironworking. They disappeared with the onset of urbanization.

Throughout the Iron Age, then, we may speak of social dependency and growing social stratification based on owning or not owning land. At first, land ownership seems to have been a matter of having rights as a member of a community settled in its own subsistence area, but gradually land became linked to farm ownership and the site of the farmstead, before eventually becoming formalized, which allowed the owner not to live on his land. Since all the activities taking place in pit houses were also performed in more capacious buildings, we may interpret pit house dwellers as a segment of the population attached to farms as farmhands. It goes without saying that there could be no urbanization until this social segment had been created and had come to understand that, while not ideal, towns were better for them than the countryside.

The issue of resource exploitation comes to the fore in deforestation and local overgrazing. They are symptomatic of grave structural problems in an economy unable to cope with its own success and population growth, on the fringes of the world economic system of the Roman Empire. Otherwise, the exploitation of natural resources was an unproblematic way to fulfil the needs of the household, enhance exchange, and develop material culture as well as life quality. Even hunter-gatherers could produce surplus commodities, such as hides and wool, just as in a more complex economy, but the main by-product of a subsistence economy was free time and eventually a population surplus. It is typical of the Iron Age that production, primarily intended to fulfil the requirements of the household, was also designed or enhanced in such a way as to create a surplus.

Iron production is a case in point (Rasmussen et al. 2006). In the early Iron Age, production was farm- or village-based. Any farm could produce iron, bog ore being abundant, but in some farms or villages (e.g. Drengsted, Snorup) production was greater than local needs. In south Scandinavia and northern Germany, such small-scale production eventually came to an end in the seventh century AD. At the same time production in central Scandinavia moved into the forests on a seasonal basis. Similarly, during the Roman Iron Age only some farms in forested areas produced wood tar in excess of their own needs, but in the late Iron Age, as with iron, production moved into the woods (Hennius et al. 2005). Seal and whale blubber was used to produce marine mammal oil in the Baltic, especially around the Bay of Bothnia (Bottenviken), and on the Atlantic coast of Norway north of the area with sedentary coastal farms. Non-sedentary north Scandinavians probably produced this commodity in growing amounts, particularly in the late Iron Age (Heron et al. 2010). In technologically similar processes, all three raw materials are heated in ovens in order for iron to run out of the ore, tar out of the wood, and oil out of the blubber, the end products being collected below the ovens. Iron, tar, and blubber are only needed in small quantities in a subsistence economy, but in central and northern Scandinavia, people produced for market as well.

Animal husbandry too could produce surplus by-products in the form of hides and wool. A mid-first millennium AD farm (Vallhagar) on Gotland, where sheep were abundant, had several looms, suggesting more than household production. That weaving was so common in pit houses suggests the same, in a similar manner to the farms producing iron and tar. Thus we cannot rule out the possibility that calves and lambs were sometimes produced primarily for their wool and hides. This kind of exploitation was also the origin of craftworking and a more complex and stratified society; the differences between pre- and post-Roman Iron Age societies are thus significant, partly on account of the growing importance of specialization.

In the pre-Roman Iron Age, acquisition of wealth was related to small-scale internal rather than external factors, in a system of dependency that controlled people's time. Over the course of the Iron Age, the gradually shrinking number of landowners, and the consequent division between people with and without land rights, indirectly testifies to the growing importance of internal acquisition. Social stratification and dependency reflect the general long-term change mirrored in the material structure of society. In this system, surplus tended to accumulate, with free landowners demonstrating their position, for example by means of halls. Dependency eventually existed at all status levels without making slaves the backbone of the economy (cf. Brink 2012). In the Roman Iron Age, before status display took the form of halls and large manors, the archaeological material suggests that burial contexts were ostentatiously used to mirror status, and signal material wealth and exterior contacts. It has been noticed that while farms grew in the Roman Iron Age, male burials became less ostentatious and female ones more materially outstanding, while males became more and females less physically fit (Balslev Jørgensen et al. 1984; Ethelberg et al. 2000; Jensen 2003: 498).

Contact with the Roman World

Prior to contacts with the Roman world, external acquisition was of little importance, but the world system character of the Imperial economy made it easy to tap into with commodities, slaves, and mercenaries. The material benefits ensuing from this interaction were obvious in terms of access to exotic goods, materiality, and prestige. Long-distance contacts are apparent in Jutland before Roman expansion north of the Rhine, through finds such as the Gundestrup cauldron, the Dejbjerg wagon, and the Hedegård grave (Madsen 1997), but the political context of the first century AD created an openness to Roman culture in south Scandinavia, i.e. north of the regions where the Roman advance into Germany met with fierce resistance (Hedeager and Tvarnø 1991). This positive attitude is reflected in the use of Roman imports as grave goods, as a public exhibition of the cultural affinities of the individual, and became a long-lasting trend (Hedeager 1992; Grane 2013). Trade was to become the backbone of these interactions, but as early as the first century AD, political and military overtones were apparent.

Mapping Roman imports across the region displays a clear pattern in which the parts of Scandinavia and north-west Germany with better connections to the Roman Empire are the ones richest in coins and other objects. Intra-regional variation is best explained by a tendency now and again to show off the success of a family, family member, or farm. South Scandinavia seems to have been a hub in interaction with the Roman world (cf. Lund Hansen 1987; Grane 2013: 35). Roman and Byzantine base metal coins are commonest in south Scandinavia, indicating relatively intensive contacts with the Roman economy, but there are also notable clusters in central and northern Scandinavia (Figure 5.3).

In terms of general composition, the coins from south Scandinavia appear similar to the rest, but a closer look reveals that coin types that are common in the south are rare in the north, where conversely there are coins that are unknown or scarce in the south (Horsnæs 2010). If we compare the coast and the interior in central and north Scandinavia, a similar filtering effect seems to be in action. Since hunters and trappers penetrated the Scandinavian interior in Sweden, Norway, and Finland, they would benefit from having some kind of currency or economic token, which they could exchange at intervals for supplies. Selling one's furs just once a year in exchange for foodstuffs and other commodities is obviously irrational. Using the odd Roman coin as a token in a limited economy, on the other hand, is rational, but could not work where Roman coins were abundant.

The distribution pattern thus suggests the following: southern Scandinavia had good access to Roman base metal coinage; some of these coins were then used in interactions with central, northern, and eastern Scandinavia, where certain coastal regions characterized by agriculture functioned as hubs in the exchange system, allowing a few uncommon coins eventually to filter into circulation. The coins used range from the third century BC to the seventh century AD. The lack of coins in Norway may be explained partly by archaeological non-recovery, or because direct contacts with the continent undermined this kind of system. In the Viking Age, silver was introduced into the north Scandinavian economy, but inland hoards continued to attract base metal coins until Ottoman times (Zachrisson 2010).

The ostentatious burials of the dominant Iron Age landholding families are emblematic of their capability to acquire, store, and eventually send on commodities via a network of hubs interacting with the Roman economy as a means of procuring

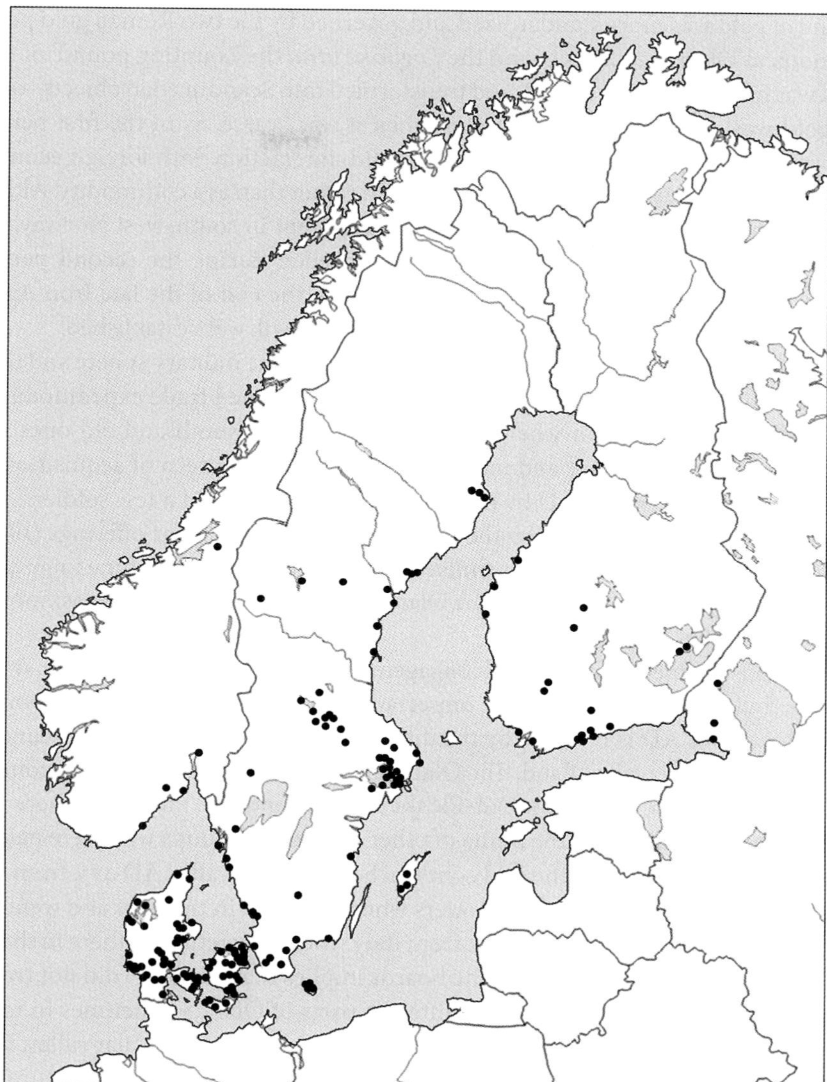

FIGURE 5.3 Roman and Byzantine base metal coins from Scandinavia, stray finds, and hoards. In the coastal belt and inland central Scandinavia, distribution is significant, as well as marking routes between the coast and the interior. The Baltic countries are not mapped.

prestige goods. It seems that the whole of Scandinavia was involved in such a network, even if some people did not venture to exhibit foreign prestige goods in their graves, as offerings, or in their settlements until the late Iron Age. Commodities such as weapons, quernstones, scrap metal, glass beads, drinking services, and tableware were part of the trade in prestige goods, gold, and silver. An essential part of contact with the Empire is attested by the use of Roman weight systems. While length measures vary regionally, the weighing of gold was more standardized and governed by the two Roman gold pounds, the Canonical Libra of *c.*327.45 g, and the *Logarikē litra*, the 'counting pound' of *c.*322.8 g. Gold was melted down, weighed, and transformed into Scandinavian objects—simple when gold was abundant, more complex when it was scarce, as in the first period of transformation. Except for payment rings of gold, interaction with foreign economies revolved around the artefact as an individual item rather than as a commodity. Although contacts with continental Europe were already apparent in south-west Norway, in the Limfjord area of Denmark, and in south-west Sweden during the second period of transformation (Segschneider 2002), it was not until the end of the late Iron Age that *emporia* such as Amrum Wyk, Ribe, Haithabu, and Ralswik were established.

An essential part of external acquisition was related to the military sphere and the service of Scandinavian mercenaries in the Roman army. Armed trade expeditions might well have been a mechanism whereby fresh soldiers went south and old ones north, but there is a definite military and individual aspect to the pattern of acquisition. This is shown in the first century AD by the Hoby drinking cups and a few soldiers' graves (Hørløkke); in the third century by the presence of weapons in war offerings (Illerup); in the fourth by Roman awards (*dona militaria*) and military belts (Böhme 1999: 49–73); and in the fifth by the construction of the Öland ring forts and by the composition of *solidus* hoards (Fischer et al. 2011).

Acquisition by means of martial engagement is not possible without systemic structures, but individuals played an important role, too. The pattern of importation in the fifth century AD is revealed by the distribution of *solidi* in the Baltic islands, the Mälar valley, and especially Öland. The Ölandic *solidi* to a large extent reflect coins paid to troops in Italy in the mid-460s. Outside the Empire, finds are numerous there and in northern France, presumably the home of other mercenary groups who were paid with *solidi* in Italy. On Öland, only the odd coin reached the island after AD 473, from which we may perhaps conclude that the Ölanders who succeeded in the 460s and went home to hoard their coins, did not come back from Italy when they returned there in the 470s. The distribution and composition of the hoards implies that Ölanders did not travel en bloc, but in groups originating in four different parts of Öland, sometimes in tandem with Gotlanders, who in turn were associated with people from the Mälar valley. It takes a system with recurrent (and sometimes failed) expeditions to reveal the nature of the imported materials, which in cases of success would have been circulated and melted down. Earlier Ölandic hoards suggest that the imports were being transformed within twenty to thirty years of their arrival. Gotlandic contacts with Merovingian France in the sixth century AD mark the end of the period of *solidus* import (Fischer et al. 2011).

Warfare

The archaeological material and contexts at our disposal for the study of this theme comprise human bodies or body parts, sacrificed war gear, military pay, defence structures, battlegrounds, and place names relating to military organization. Weapon graves are best seen as projecting an image of martiality rather than necessarily being the burials of actual warriors or reflecting the incidence of warfare, but image, fear, and trauma were all part and parcel of the Iron Age martial universe (see Chapter 30). Most often our sources relate to non-specific conflicts between unknown antagonists involving ambiguous concepts such as 'defence', 'strife', or 'battle'. Now and again, however, the character of the conflict is less vague.

Jutland is a case to which a number of more disparate contexts link in. In the pre-Roman Iron Age strategies relating to landscape and community explain a number of phenomena such as forts, fortified villages, lines of *lilia* (concealed pits) and dykes. These phenomena disappear, albeit slowly, in the Roman Iron Age. Spread over much of the peninsula, their purpose was defensive or passive. Borremose fort is difficult to access, being erected in a bog, and as a settlement its location seems quite irrational from the subsistence point of view. Defended settlements range from earth-walled and palisaded villages and farms (Lyngsmose, Grøntoft, Damgård) to fenced settlements (Hodde), and eventually in the first period of transformation individual farms were enclosed by fences that had no defensive purpose. In the second period of transformation the fence became symbolic, with the formal quality of delimiting and defining the plot (as at Præstestien).

The dykes typically face in a variety of directions, implying roaming war bands and local defence. The belts of *lilia* are strategically placed as traps in particular situations, such as points of approach. We know of only a small number of these features, partly owing to the rarity of large excavations, and partly because many have been destroyed, as the *lilia* were placed in shallow pits. Although such defence systems will help against any enemy, their distribution, like that of hillforts and ring forts in Scandinavia, must primarily be understood in a local context. They reflect common-sense strategies and recurrent occasional needs, rather than long-term regional investment in defence. It seems relevant that when these fortifications lost their significance, weapon graves started to become popular for a while in the early Iron Age. In the process the division of Jutland into sub-regions becomes more apparent. It stands to reason therefore that after a socially turbulent period, leading up to the change of era, relative peace was accompanied by the display of martiality in burials (Jensen 2003: 171–176).

If these traits are indicative of internal warfare and power struggles, an increasing number of Roman Iron Age finds point to external warfare. This evidence is not specifically Jutish, but more generally south Scandinavian, and predominantly coastal. There are three kinds of finds: sacrificed war gear, dismembered bodies, and coastal and river barrages. The war gear consisted of spoils taken from the battlefield and partly destroyed in or after battle, prior to their deposition in lakes that were already traditional votive sites. The find from Hjortspring is the oldest and is unique, but just before the start of the first millennium AD, offerings started to become more common, growing in frequency up until the second period of transformation (Nydam). There is only one obvious find of dismembered bodies marked by battle, buried in Lake Mossø at Alken Enge, and belonging early in the first period of transformation.

There were two kinds of barrages: those preventing attacks on the countryside, and those preventing a coastal bay from becoming a naval base. Their distribution and analysis of the weapons indicate that Jutland and the southernmost part of Scandinavia were attacked from the sea. The general landscape of conflict in southern Jutland was orientated towards the east, whereas interactions along the North Sea coast seem to have been peaceful until the late Iron Age. Calculations based on the number of weapons sacrificed at one time suggest that the armies involved in late Roman Iron Age warfare could comprise as many as 1,000 soldiers and officers in an organization seemingly inspired by the Roman army (Jensen 2003: 525–528). The armament as well as the distribution of finds suggests external warfare. Warfare between regions, as related in the Old English poem Widsith (referring to different regionally based peoples), was thus already firmly established in the archaeological record in the late Roman Iron Age.

Until the late Iron Age the landscape of warfare was related to internal and eventually external struggles concerning strategy and ritual traditions, but not to political landscapes. The small kingdom around Gudme, on Fyn, is a case in point. The peripheries of Fyn display signs of warfare but the political centre, Gudme, is devoid of defences, although one might expect the centre to be the prime military goal. That centres *were* targeted is indicated by the relatively abrupt downfall of Gudme and possible destruction of its largest hall. In the late Iron Age, combat technique changed (Ystgaard 2014: 245–270) and warfare started to incorporate a political dimension inasmuch as centres such as Dejbjerg, Uppåkra, Helgö, and Borg in Lofoten were targeted. As mentioned, old centres, such as Gudme, and perhaps Dankirke and Björnhovda, were abandoned, while new ones, e.g. Lejre, Tissø, Stavnsager (Fiedel et al. 2011), Old Uppsala (Ljungkvist et al. 2011), and Högom were implanted in the landscape. The construction of the Dannevirke border in southern Jutland must also be seen as a military way of building a political landscape.

Given the military experience provided by the Roman army—attested by the *solidi*—and the skills learnt—attested by the portcullis gate at Eketorp ring fort (Herschend 1985)—professionalization of armies and warriors should not come as a surprise. In north-west Germany, military belts tell the same story. The most obvious political scenes of warfare are the many destroyed halls accompanied by weapons lost on the battlefield or by retainers settled in the manors. These contexts are new to the late Iron Age and they fit the geography of the so-called lev-names. Lev-names combine a personal male name with a gift of land, a village left by or to someone. Early runic inscriptions show naming to be relatively varied, and comparison with lev-names shows the latter to be strongly related to warrior names. Lev-villages exist in Scandinavia and eastern Germany (as 'leben' village names)—and some personal names in Germany are Scandinavian. Their distribution clusters, for example, at Magdeburg, where they are surrounded by German names; the incidence of Scandinavian names falls off with distance from Magdeburg (Figure 5.4). The implication is that late Iron Age south Scandinavian warriors settled as a group among German warriors near a power centre. They were in all probability granted land for military services. If we take this political notion of settling warriors on farms next to power centres back to Scandinavia, lev-villages tend to cluster near

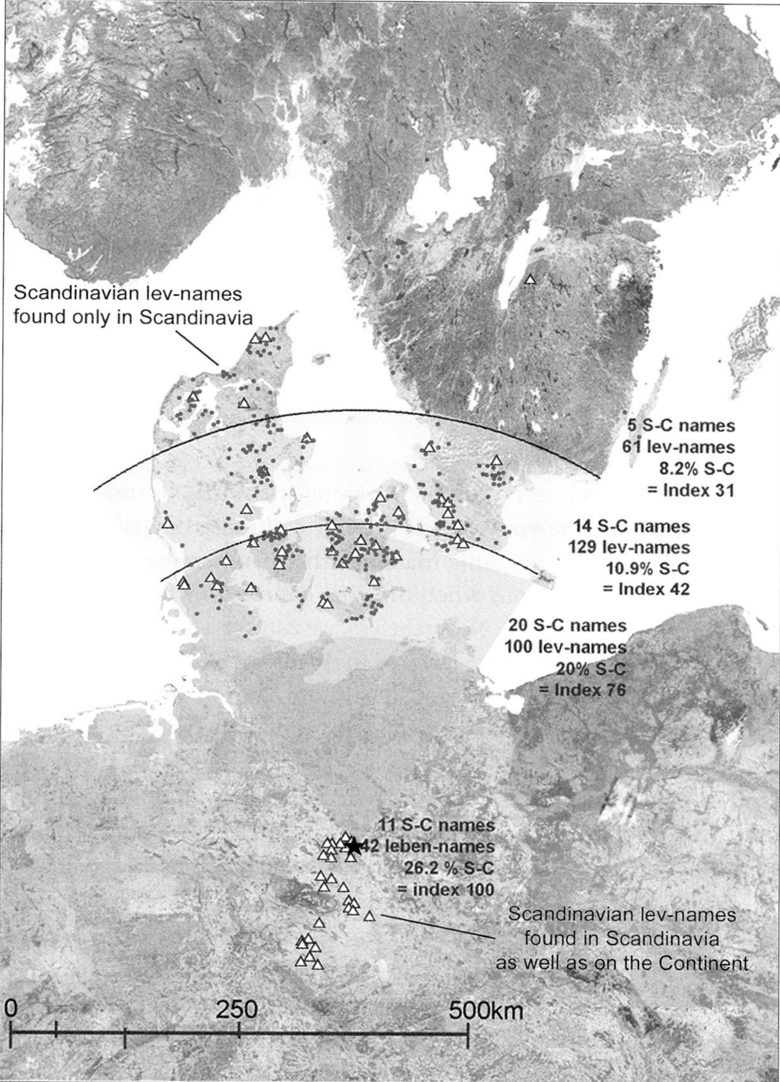

FIGURE 5.4 The distribution of Scandinavian lev-/leben-names. These names are common in the Magdeburg area, but become less frequent with distance from Magdeburg (star). Together with the empty space between Magdeburg and the Baltic, this suggests that people with Scandinavian names colonized the Magdeburg area.

the new late Iron Age power centres. Unsurprisingly, lev-villages are more common in coastal areas than inland—coastal situations, generally speaking, being more strategic from a south Scandinavian defensive viewpoint.

During the Iron Age, warfare acquired additional characteristics—local defence and field battle—and, in the Roman Iron Age, a maritime and super-regional dimension.

Eventually, no doubt inspired by the Roman military, warriors became professional. Power in the late Iron Age was organized partly with an eye to settling warrior families on farms in the vicinity of power centres. Scandinavian warriors being granted land abroad sounds Viking Age, but seems to have deeper roots, and it is thus unsurprising that the warriors buried in their early eighth-century AD sailing ship at Salme on the island of Saaremaa off Estonia were equipped as Scandinavians (Konsa et al. 2009). The way that warfare developed into a supra-regional phenomenon suggests that we should be prepared to understand the late Iron Age in relation to social strata and class, not just in terms of community and the *longue durée*.

Artefacts and Material Culture

Wooden artefacts from the terp settlements along the north German coast, and to a certain extent finds from the votive lakes, provide a glimpse of a rich material culture expressed in wood and other organic materials that is otherwise almost unknown to us. We must therefore be cautious when drawing conclusions from the general run of surviving archaeological material. Nevertheless, we can see a growth in the number and variety of metal and glass artefacts, as well as in the use of antler. Ceramics, which vary in popularity in prehistoric times, became less important in the course of the Iron Age, implying that metal cauldrons and wooden table- and kitchenware grew in importance in daily life.

Thanks to Roman contacts, an element of narrative decoration entered this material world, not least depictions of humans and animals. To begin with, the difference between domestic and foreign objects was striking, inasmuch as indigenous craftwork was reluctant to combine figurative elements with functional and abstract elements. In the late Roman Iron Age, the use of domestic figurative elements nevertheless grew continuously, and a desire to decorate whole surfaces became fashionable for expensive objects. This development echoes Roman culture. In the second period of transformation, figurative and narrative decoration in the form of zoomorphic decoration became distinctively Scandinavian and non-Roman (cf. Kristoffersen 2000). In the late Iron Age, the new decorative elements started to be reproduced on inexpensive artefacts such as brooches. Gold objects led the change in figurative decoration, but this metal became scarce before the decorative revolution of the zoomorphic narrative styles occurred. Some of the decoration on high-status objects can be understood as narrative illustration, and Eddic myth is apparent in several scenes (Axboe 2007). It has been convincingly argued that the change in the picture repertoire, which took place during the second period of transformation, was connected to a change in ontology. Odinic qualities of Ostrogothic and Hunnic origin lay behind this prominent ideological change and its manifestation in material culture (Hedeager 2011).

Because burial practices vary, we have little knowledge of the spread of different classes of artefact into the lower social strata. The wearing of glass beads, nevertheless, was a trend that spread socially starting in the second period of transformation, as did the use of decorated combs, simple bronze brooches, and dress pins. From the contents of cremation graves in the Mälar valley dating to the end of the Roman Iron Age and the start of the late Iron Age, it would seem that the willingness to supply the deceased with metal, glass, and bone objects fell away in the fourth to fifth centuries AD, only to escalate again markedly from the start of the sixth century AD. The increase in grave goods at the beginning of the sixth century was followed by an even more significant rise—typical of central Scandinavia—in the second half of the eighth century (Fischer and Victor 2011).

Rich burials follow more or less the same ups and downs. During the Roman Iron Age, up to the fourth century AD, they grew in number; rather than enhancing graves with many different objects, the tendency was to add more of the same to the grave goods. After the dip in the fourth to fifth centuries—a period to which relatively few (mostly Norwegian and central Scandinavian) graves belong—a new lavishness and narrative character is apparent in high-status graves. These introduce a narrative scene with complex symbolic connotations. To begin with, chamber graves typify this trend, but soon boat burial was revived and developed to accommodate complex burials (Müller-Wille 1971; Norr 2008). It would seem that the need for professional craftsmanship paralleled the professionalization and individuation of warriors.

Architecture—in the sense of the design of buildings and the organization of indoor living space—was an essential aspect of Iron Age material culture. As a rule, houses reflect the building materials available in their local environments. Traditional techniques nevertheless overruled a number of rational solutions dependent on the environment. Already in the pre-Roman Iron Age in inland northern Germany two-aisled buildings with relatively stout walls and few internal posts, resembling Dutch houses, are found (Fries 2010). Their construction technique relied on the load-bearing properties of the walls—a solution befitting a forested landscape with a good supply of timber. Elsewhere, the three-aisled house predominated, and in less heavily forested landscapes, the insulating and load-bearing walls were distinct. In the first period of transformation the two types were merged, in a more skilled type of construction, where the space between the evenly spaced load-bearing elements was filled with insulation, in the form of wattle and daub, sometimes whitewashed. This technique dominated even in densely forested eastern Denmark and Scandinavia, where one might have expected stouter walls. Access to heavy timber is demonstrated by the dimensions of the roof-bearing posts; during the Roman Iron Age in the Mälar valley, the local supply of wood sometimes forced the builders to use two slender timbers instead of one stout trunk to craft the interior posts.

In the late Roman Iron Age and the second period of transformation in western Norway, inner plank walls, set on a sill-beam and with no load-bearing function, were accompanied by outer supporting walls of stone and earth, creating an insulating air gap between the two (e.g. Borg in Lofoten). This mirrors a building tradition in a landscape where postholes may be difficult to dig because of the bedrock. Here too insulation, skilled craftsmanship, and in some places the ability to import timber (see Chapter 18) were advantages. In even more barren landscapes, such as Öland, the insulating wall was made of wattle and daub.

Reflecting the relative scarcity of wood, coastal north-west German houses were three-aisled, often with radially wedged pieces of timber as supporting elements, and insulating daub made from dung mixed with straw (e.g. Tofting).

The traditional importance of the internal roof-supporting 'trestles' anchored in the ground is apparent in the Ölandic ring forts. The limestone walls of the buildings inside these forts could easily have carried a wall-plate that would have held the weight of the roof, but the builders insisted on interior posts. Although perfectly able to copy a portcullis gate and a Roman building technique using quarried limestone blocks to build double-faced walls *c.*70 cm wide without mortar, the builders were not prepared to allow the walls to carry any load. In fact, Iron Age Scandinavian and northern German traditions stubbornly resisted the roof truss, preferring to develop their own ideas of roof support.

The idea that vertical timbers must be anchored in the ground was only reluctantly given up, although the technique of jointing timbers was known from at least the late Iron Age. The walls were the first to lose their ground anchoring. With the notable exception of the plank walls of west Norway, this happened in the late Roman Iron Age, starting in the north-east, with a change in the width of the central aisle. This led to the roof becoming underbalanced, meaning that nearly all its weight was taken by the interior trestles. In underbalanced roofs, the top of the walls and the trestles must be tied together; thus the roof and walls become an outer shell attached to the trestles, like the hull to the frame of a boat. The technical problems of the underbalanced roof can be solved with skill and better timber. The change was not as radical in the south-west as in the forested north-east, where in the late Iron Age the central aisle shrank to 25–30% of the overall width of the building, compared to 55–60% in the pre-Roman Iron Age.

In the first period of transformation, builders began to construct larger houses: to begin with, buildings were longer with fewer trestles, later taller, and eventually broader, and the rest of the Iron Age is characterized by changing building techniques. Every development demanded better timber and more professional craftsmanship. Access to timber led developments: conservative solutions were typical of the south-west, radical ones typical of the north-east. By and large the sequence of development strongly suggests north-eastern influence reaching the Danish islands in the late Iron Age and Jutland in the Viking Age. The curved walls and outer wall-support posts, so emblematic of the reconstructed Viking Age hall, belong to the eastern tradition.

The original Iron Age dwelling was the one-room dwelling of a nuclear family, organized around a central hearth between four posts. The size of dwelling eventually grew, introducing partition walls and rooms with different functions. The cardinal change came in the Roman Iron Age, when a basic pattern of four rooms in a row introduced a new household structure that became the norm. This development followed the growth of farms as economic units, but in the second period of transformation and in the late Iron Age, when the byres of a number of farms became much smaller than during the Roman Iron Age, the structure and size of the dwelling quarters remained unchanged. This means that the organization of the dwelling was itself a measure of social status in a period of economic downturn.

The change in the social norms of the farming household which began in the late Roman Iron Age links in with the introduction of free-standing halls, inasmuch as they were small houses that became enormous buildings despite economic crisis, demographic loss, and political turmoil. Architecturally, halls are interesting because they led the way to large, lavish open rooms, which are difficult to build, while at the same time conforming to the early Iron Age ideal of the open dwelling room where everyone—farm owner and guests—gathered around the hearth to eat and drink. Nobody needs a hall purely for the purposes of subsistence, and this makes the mixture of modern lavishness and traditional values all the more significant. It suggests an architectural expression marked by aesthetics as well as ideology—a conscious way of expressing upper-class values in much the same way as the ideological value of a farmer's four-room dwelling.

The growing number of pit houses, albeit starting in the second period of transformation, parallels the rise of the hall. The first ones were built in the south-west, the last in the north-east. They are part of a wider trend, with still earlier continental Roman Iron Age examples. The function of these houses in Scandinavia is debated according to a false dichotomy: either they were workshops or they were multifunctional, including dwelling quarters. Basically, pit houses are a way of constructing a small and cheap building without roof trestles, of a type that may suit a number of different purposes. Although there are pit house communities or households (e.g. Västra Via; Strömberg 1978) where people lived, most pit houses occur in conjunction with farms, but more often than not lay outside the farmyard in groups of their own (as at Præstestien). Pit houses are short-lived, and although they can be repaired, generally they were not. Instead people preferred to sink a new house into the subsoil; in comparison to traditional buildings, pit houses therefore now appear more common than they actually were. They were often used for crafts—textiles and metalworking being the most frequent uses. There is no doubt, however, that anything produced in pit houses was also produced in ordinary buildings. Since large and capacious rooms as well as large households were the preferred social environments, it would seem less attractive to spend one's days, even rainy ones, in a pit house. However, if we imagine a landless and/or peripatetic workforce, such as the late Iron Age squatters who lived in the ruins of the deserted Eketorp ring fort, it makes sense to attach one or more pit houses to a farm to accommodate these workers. Just like farmhouses and halls, pit houses reflected their users, and we may infer that in the late Iron Age social status—whether high, middle, or low—could be attached to houses.

Narrative, Belief, and Ritual

Narrative is taken for granted in any society, but the lack of Iron Age written narrative in the historical sense is manifest, although the region was not totally illiterate. From the late Roman Iron Age, runic inscriptions on wood, stone, and other materials were used for magical purposes, messages, and charms, but no extended texts in this form are known (Hedeager 2011: 21–32). Ideologically tinted myth relating to the later Iron Age societies of the region is, however, preserved in poems written down at a later date such as Widsith, Hildebrandslied, the Finnsburg Fragment, Beowulf, Hêliand, and late Eddic poetry. Royalty, warriors, and retinues are central to these. There are also hints of specific narratives in Tacitus (Herschend 2009: 160–171). But, importantly, there are archaeological contexts that have narrative and metaphoric qualities. To find a narrative that orders events in a meaningful, not too formal, time series, we must look for intent, time dimension, and metaphor in the material record.

Votive lakes go back to the Stone Age, some continuing in use until organized Christianity (Backe et al. 1993; Stjernquist 1997). In this respect, they constitute the time dimension of a place—a quality rather than a narrative. In the pre-Roman Iron Age, some lakes became war-offering sites. This tradition linked large communities to traumatic, albeit victorious events, primarily in the earlier first millennium AD. Some lake offerings continued beyond the late Iron Age, indicating a more general notion behind the depositions. The narrative point is the repetition of offerings in particular lakes, and variation in their composition over time. It would seem that a lake landscape such as Illerup/Alken Enge constitutes a context supporting the memory of a series of regional wars (Jensen 2003: 511). Initially, deposition centred on objects damaged by warfare; during the Roman Iron Age, the range widened to include belts, coins, and blowing horns, i.e. not just items related to conflict. Later, weapons are again favoured. In the second period of transformation and in the late Iron Age, horse-gear continued to be worth offering. When war offerings became more frequent, the significance of the objects changed according to a time-specific understanding, played out against a general backdrop of warfare. It takes historical reasoning—a narrative—to agree on what should and should not be offered.

Over time, graves and cemeteries become more and more likely to exhibit the deceased as an individual. This development, expressed by inhumation graves, starts to come to the fore in the first period of transformation in the south. It moves slowly north, but without replacing cremation. Although cremation is often anonymous, permitting us to infer little about the status of the deceased, the late Iron Age pyre was sometimes an elaborate and extravagant display of material wealth, individualizing the deceased. There are indications that lavish funerals were prolonged rituals, especially in the case of boat graves. Chamber graves were visited and partly emptied years after they were sealed. The habit of burying a person on top of someone previously interred indicates that graves continued to be an active part of ritual and myth for some time (Ørsnes 1955; Price 2010). Given that Saxo Grammaticus and Snorre Sturluson were keen to inform us about who was buried where, the archaeological evidence can be said to link in with later mythic narratives.

Pre-Roman Iron Age cemeteries give the impression of representing the community, although in fact by no means all the population were buried in a way that can be recovered archaeologically. Amidst this commonality, some graves nevertheless stand out as the roots of their cemetery. The idea of a cemetery built up around a founder's grave is supported by the small but lavishly equipped two- or three-generation cemeteries connected with the leading farms of new Roman Iron Age villages, such as Hoby, Vendehøj, or Vorbasse (cf. Hedeager 1992). Supported by the cemeteries, narratives about origin are thus to be expected. Western Norway in the second period of transformation is a good model (Myhre 1987). Owing to the characteristics of the landscape—and in contrast to southern Scandinavia, where late Iron Age centres were often new—many west Norwegian centres such as Avaldsnes revived Roman Iron Age foci. The third-century Ellekilde cemetery has exceptional narrative qualities. Around thirty graves built up over three or four generations around a central mound containing a horn-blower's grave. This unarmed man had been shot and cut down from his horse from behind in battle (Iversen 2011). It stands to reason that the memory of the horn-blower formed the roots of a narrative related to this individual's qualities or virtues.

Halls and hall rooms created by the well-off were an interface for interacting with their peers and clients. Echoing the Roman *aula*, they were social arenas and a sign of wealth rather than class, and in the late Iron Age social stratification favoured impressive halls. Since they continued to be important, they are central to many Saxon, Anglo-Saxon, and Norse texts. In these sources, hall life focuses on the individual, and the hall was a paragon of ordered as well as conflicting society, where rituals, moral and entertaining tales, and juridical and political deliberations all took place. It is not surprising, then, that in the early ninth-century Hêliand, Jesus was born in King David's hall in Bethlehem. His parents belonged to David's lineage and consequently, when in Bethlehem, lived in his hall. Starting in the first century AD in north Germany and on Jutland, halls were added to the main dwelling quarters. In south Scandinavia, the small, free-standing hall became popular in the late Roman Iron Age. In Norway it continued to be incorporated as a room in the main house (Løken 2001). In the late Iron Age, some halls became the dwelling quarters of the owner. This is also the period in which halls were targeted for attack and the sites preserved as ruined monuments of a lost cause. In this capacity they too illustrate a historical narrative.

Beliefs are difficult to grasp by means of archaeological sources, but the intertwined balance and symmetry hinted at by Tacitus seems to fit the binary structure of the early Iron Age house (e.g. in Jutland), in which the equally sized dwelling and byre balance one another irrespective of the size of the building. These ideas were superseded by the asymmetry of Roman and later Iron Age settlements with an obvious 'head', in the form of a dominant farm, and adjacent dependent farms. This shift goes hand in hand with the individual rich graves that appeared at the start of the first millennium AD. Later, the hall attests to the rise of the individual and individual leadership. Lordship developed as indicated by the chronological series *froh–hlaford–herro*, terms indicating a change from caretaking, via bread-giving, to formal leadership (Green 1965: 19–29).

Today we consider gods to be old, distant, and rather inactive, but the indications are that Odin (Oðinn) was seen as present and active in the late Iron Age, when his prominence grew, and the new ontology of parallel worlds and travels in between them became significant (Hedeager 2011). According to myth, Odin took out an eye in order to gain more knowledge. There are several representations of this one-eyed Odin, but others depict a god with one of his two eyes removed. A third-century Roman equestrian mask found in a sixth-century context on Gotland was originally provided with eyeballs, but one was later removed and buried in the floor beneath the post where the mask presumably hung. This suggests that the mask was turned into an idol representing a god who took out an eye just like Odin, part of actively building up his image in the second period of transformation. We may thus suppose that the story about Odin's adventure was believed to be true (Price and Mortimer 2014).

In many respects the late Iron Age stands out as a period when divine or semi-divine leaders interacted with an otherworldly pantheon whose gods took part in human life. Compared to the early Iron Age, this seems to represent new kinds of belief, in a society also marked by new royal centres such as Old Uppsala and Old Lejre. When the early sixth century is described as a period of transformation in Beowulf, when the Hêliand author chose to make Jesus a hall-born prince with a retinue, and when Eddic poets refer to gods in halls, it seems that their understanding of the late Iron Age is correct. Their tales qualify as myth, but then again people probably actually believed that Odin took out an eye in around AD 500. Venantius Fortunatus, King Sigbert's court poet, for one, considered Brunhild's marriage bed in Metz in AD 565 an 'earthly' one, because her mother was the goddess Venus, whose bed was not.

Archaeologically speaking, rituals come to the fore in burials and offerings. There are several types of burials, and offerings occur in different contexts. The divide between them is not always clear. The early Iron Age habit of submerging people in lakes can be viewed as either offering or burial; how should graves full of weapons in cemeteries be interpreted (as at Bregentved)? Some offerings mark a beginning, such as unburnt foundation deposits in houses; others signify an end, like the burnt offerings associated with the demolition of early Iron Age houses. Anything submerged into water was seemingly once and for all dispatched to a netherworld, whereas destroying something by fire sent it into the air and an elevated world.

Both dry land and water offerings existed from the start of the early Iron Age, but in the second period of transformation, those on dry land expanded (cf. Fabech 1991) to include the deposition of war offerings and battle spoils next to halls, as at Uppåkra. Nevertheless, giving something to the upper world and the netherworld, from where it cannot easily be retrieved, as opposed to placing something in a grave where it is still in principle accessible—that is to say still in some respect present in our world—seems to relate to three different kinds of ritual behaviour. We may imagine that all three offering 'locales'—air, water, and land—were essential, for example in connection with houses—a foundation offering for the building, a food offering in the lake for its ability to provide, and a fire offering and burial to end its life (cf. Herschend 2009: 143–156).

To judge from the growing popularity of offerings on land, it seems that the middle world, the 'Midgard', grew in prominence during the Iron Age. The willingness to destroy, but not to burn down, halls points to their sacred qualities as the houses of deities and their representatives on earth. This fits with the idea that, with more kings and queens descended from gods, more divine objects found a place in the human world, at the expense of water and fire offerings. After 1,250 years of the Iron Age, the upper classes had set themselves up as everyone's interface with divinity in a social, ritual, religious, and narrative sense. Christianity built on that.

Note

1. Archaeological site names are given without a reference if they are readily found in *Reallexikon der germanischen Altertumskunde* (Beck et al. 1968–2007), *Danmarks Oldtid* (Jensen 2003), *Norsk arkeologisk leksikon* (Østmo and Hedeager 2005), or *The Early Iron Age in South Scandinavia* (Herschend 2009), all of which are recommended for further reading. Most twenty-first-century excavation reports can be found in print or online.

References

Axboe, M. 2007. *Brakteatstudier*. Copenhagen: Det Kongelige Nordiske Oldskriftselskab.

Backe, M., B. Edgren, and F. Herschend. 1993. 'Bones thrown into a water hole', in G. Arwidsson (ed.) *Sources and Resources: Studies in Honor of Birgit Arrhenius*. PACT 38: 327–342. Belgium: PACT.

Bakkevik, S., K. Griffin, L. Prøsch-Danielsen, P. Utigard-Sandvik, A. Simonsen, E.-C. Soltvedt, et al. 2002. 'Archaeobotany in Norway', in K. Viklund (ed.) *Nordic Archaeobotany*: 23–48. Umeå: Umeå University.

Balslev Jørgensen, J., U. Lund Hansen, and B. Jansen Sellevold (eds). 1984. *Iron Age Man in Denmark*. Nordiske fortidsminder Serie B 8. Copenhagen: Det Kongelige Nordiske Oldskriftselskab.

Baudou, E., R. Engelmark, L. Liedgren, U. Segerström, and J.-E. Wallin. 1991. *Järnåldersbygd i Österbotten: en ekologisk-arkeologisk studie av bosättningskontinuitet och resursutnyttjande*. Vasa: Scriptum.

Beck, H., D. Geuenich, H. Steuer, and R. Müller. (eds). 1968–2007. *Reallexikon der germanischen Altertumskunde*. Berlin: Walter de Gruyter.

Behre, K.-E. 2008. *Landschaftsgeschichte Norddeutschlands*. Neumünster: Wachholtz.

Böhme, H. W. 1999. 'Sächsiche Söldner im römischen Reich', in F. Both and H. Aouni (eds) *Über allen Fronten*: 46–73. Oldenburg: Isensee.

Brådseth, G. A. (ed.) 2007. *Hus og gård langs E6 i Råde kommune*. Varia 65. Oslo: Kulturhistorisk Museum.

Brink, S. 2012. *Vikingarnes slavar*. Stockholm: Atlantis.

Ethelberg, P., U. L. Hansen, and B. Storgaard. 2000. *Skovgårde: Eine Bestattungsplatz mit reichen Frauengräbern des 3. Jahrhunderts n. Chr. auf Seeland*. Nordiske fortidsminder Serie B 19. Copenhagen: Det Kongelige Nordiske Oldskriftselskab.

Fabech, C. 1991. 'Booty sacrifices in Southern Scandinavia: A reassessment', in P. Garwood, D. Jennings, R. Skeates, and J. Toms (eds) *Sacred and Profane: Proceedings of a Conference on Archaeology, Ritual and Religion, Oxford, 1989*. OUCA Monograph 32: 88–99. Oxford: Oxford University Committee for Archaeology.

Fiedel, R., K. Høilund Nielsen, and C. Loveluck. 2011. 'From hamlet, to central place, to manor. Social transformation of the settlement at Stavnsager, eastern Jutland, and its networks,

AD 400–1100', in T. Panhuysen (ed.) *Transformation in North-Western Europe (AD 300–1000)*: 161–176. Stuttgart: Theiss.

Fischer, S., F. López Sánchez, and H. Victor. 2011. 'A result from the LEO-Project: The 5th century hoard of Theodosian solidi from Stora Brunneby, Öland, Sweden'. *Fornvännen* 106: 189–204.

Fischer, S., and H. Victor. 2011. 'New horizons for Helgö', in B. Arrhenius and U. O'Meadhra (eds) *Excavations at Helgö 18*: 79–92. Stockholm: KVHAA.

Forsman, C., and H. Victor. 2007. *Sommaränge Skog*. SAU Skrifter 18. Uppsala: Societas Archaeologica Upsaliensis.

Fries, J. E. 2010. 'Mehr als gedacht—Häuser und Gehöfte der Vorrömischen Eisenzeit zwischen Weser und Vechte', in M. Meyer (ed.) *Haus—Gehöft—Weiler—Dorf: Siedlungen der Vorrömischen Eisenzeit im nördlichen Mitteleuropa*: 343–355. Rahden: Marie Leidorf.

Grane, T. 2013. 'Roman imports in Scandinavia: Their purpose and meaning?', in P. S. Wells (ed.) *Rome beyond its Frontiers: Imports, Attitudes and Practices*. Journal of Roman Archaeology Supplementary Series 94: 29–44. Portsmouth, RI: Journal of Roman Archaeology.

Green, D. 1965. *The Carolingian Lord*. Cambridge: Cambridge University Press..

Hedeager, L. 1992. *Iron Age Societies: From Tribe to State in Northern Europe 500 BC to AD 700*. Oxford: Blackwell.

Hedeager, L. 2011. *Iron Age Myth and Materiality: An Archaeology of Scandinavia, AD 400–1000*. London: Routledge.

Hedeager, L., and H. Tvarnø. 1991. *Romerne og germanerne: Det europeiske hus*, vol. 2. Copenhagen: Gyldendal.

Hennius, A., J. Svensson, A. Ölund, and H. Göthberg. 2005. *Kol och tjära—Arkeologi i norra Upplands skogsmarker*. Rapport 2005.02. Uppsala: Upplandsmuseet.

Heron, C., G. Nilsen, B. Stern, O. Craig, and C. Nordby. 2010. 'Application of lipid biomarker analysis to evaluate the function of "slab-lined pits" in Arctic Norway'. *Journal of Archaeological Science* 37, 9: 2188–2197.

Herschend, F. 1985. 'Fallgallerporten i Eketorp-II, Öland'. *Tor* 20: 165–216.

Herschend, F. 2009. *The Early Iron Age of South Scandinavia: Social Order in Settlement and Landscape*. Uppsala: Uppsala University.

Herschend, F., S. Norr, and S. Reisborg. 1993. 'Klasro i Sollentuna'. *Tor* 25: 79–99.

Horsnæs, H. W. 2010. *Crossing Boundaries: An Analysis of Roman Coins in Danish Contexts*, vol. 1. Copenhagen: University Press of Southern Denmark.

Iversen, R. 2011. 'Ellekilde—en gravplads fra romersk jernalder med fyrstegrav og cirkusbægre'. *Aarbøger for nordisk oldkyndighed og historie* 2009: 69–120.

Jensen, J. 2003. *Danmarks oldtid, Vol. 3–4: Ældre jernalder. Yngre jernalder og vikingetid*. Copenhagen: Gyldendal.

Johansen, O. S. 1979. 'Early farming north of the Arctic Circle'. *Norwegian Archaeological Review* 12, 1: 22–35.

Juhl, K. 2002. 'Theoretical and methodological aspects of investigating stone built structures of ancient farms and field systems', in K. Viklund (ed.) *Nordic Archaeobotany*. Archaeology and Environment 15, 111–132. Umeå: Umeå University.

Konsa, M., R. Allmäe, L. Maldre, and J. Vasilyev. 2009. 'Rescue excavations of a Vendel era boat-grave in Salme, Saaremaa'. *Archaeological Fieldwork in Estonia 2008*, 53–64.

Kristiansen, K. 1998. *Europe before History*. Cambridge: Cambridge University Press.

Kristiansen, K. 2009. 'Contract archaeology in Europe: An experiment in diversity'. *World Archaeology* 41, 4: 641–648.

Kristoffersen, S. 2000. 'Expressive objects', in D. Olausson and H. Vandkilde (eds) *Form, Function and Context*: 265–274. Lund: Almqvist & Wiksell International.

Kunow, J. 2002. 'Die Entwicklung von archäologischen Organisationen und Institutionen in Deutschland im 19. und 20. Jahrhundert und das "öffentliche Interesse"—Bedeutungsgewinne und Bedeutungsverluste und deren Folgen', in P. F. Biehl, A. Gramsch, and A. Marciniak (eds) *Archäologien Europas: Geschichte, Methoden und Theorien*. Tübinger Archäologische Taschenbücher 3: 147–184. Münster: Waxmann.

Ljungkvist, J., P. Frölund, H. Göthberg, and D. Löwenborg. 2011. 'Gamla Uppsala: Structural development of a centre in middle Sweden'. *Archäologisches Korrespondenzblatt* 41: 571–585.

Løken, T. 1977. 'Nye funn fra gammelt gravfelt. Kan gård og gravplass gå tilbake til eldre bronsealder?' *Viking* 41: 133–165.

Løken, T. 2001. 'Oppkomsten av den germanska hallen: Hal og sal i eldre jernalder i Rogaland'. *Viking* 64: 49–86.

Löwenborg, D. 2012. 'An Iron Age shock doctrine: Did the AD 536–7 event trigger large-scale social changes in the Mälaren valley area?' *Journal of Archaeology and Ancient History* 4: 1–29.

Lund Hansen, U. 1987. *Römischer Import im Norden*. Nordiske fortidsminder 10. Copenhagen: Det kongelige oldskriftsselskab.

Madsen, O. 1997. 'Hedegård—a rich village and cemetery complex of the Early Iron Age on the Skjern river'. *Journal of Danish Archaeology* 13, 1: 57–93.

Müller-Wille, M. 1971. 'Pferdegrab und Pferdeopfer im frühen Mittelalter'. *Berichten van de Rijksdienst voor het Oudheidkundig Bodemonderzoek* 1970/71: 119–248.

Myhre, B. 1987. 'Chieftain's graves and chiefdom territories in southern Norway in the Migration period'. *Studien zur Sachsenforschung* 6: 169–187.

Myhre, B. 1993. 'The beginning of the Viking age: Some current archaeological problems', in A. Faulkes and R. Perkins (eds) *Viking Revaluations*: 182–197. London: Viking Society for Northern Research.

Näsman, U. 2006. 'Danerne og deras danske kongerigers opkomst'. *Kuml* 2006: 205–241.

Nesje, A., L. H. Pilø, E. Finstad, B. Solli, V. Wangen, R. S. Ødegård, et al. 2012. 'The climatic significance of artefacts related to prehistoric reindeer hunting exposed at melting ice patches in southern Norway'. *The Holocene* 22, 4: 485–496.

Nielsen, J. N. 2002a. 'Flammernes bytte'. *Skalk* 2002, 6: 5–10.

Nielsen, J. N. 2002b. 'Bejsebakken, a central site near Aalborg in Northern Jutland', in B. Hårdh and L. Larsson (eds) *Central Places in the Migration and Merovingian Periods*: 197–213. Stockholm: Almqvist & Wiksell International.

Norr, S. (ed.) 2008. *Valsgärde Studies: The Place and its People Past and Present*. OPIA 42. Uppsala: Uppsala University Press.

Odgaard, B., and J. R. Rømer. 2009. *Danske landbrugslandskaber gennem 2000 år*. Århus: Aarhus Universitetsforlag.

Ørsnes, M. 1955. 'Kyndby. Ein Seeländischer Grabplatz aus dem 7.–8. Jahrhundert nach Christus'. *Acta Archaeologica* 26: 69–162.

Østmo, E., and L. Hedeager (eds). 2005. *Norsk arkeologisk leksikon*. Oslo: Pax.

Prescott, C. 1998. 'Long-term patterns of non-agrarian exploitation in southern Norwegian highlands', in C. Fabech and J. Ringtved (eds) *Settlement and Landscape*: 213–223. Århus: Aarhus University Press.

Price, N. 2010. 'Passing into poetry: Viking-Age mortuary drama and the origin of Norse mythology'. *Medieval Archaeology* 54: 123–156.

Price, N., and P. Mortimer. 2014. 'An eye for Odin: Divine role-playing in the age of Sutton Hoo'. *European Journal of Archaeology* 17, 3: 517–538.

Rasmussen, K. L., U. Rahbek, and O. Voss. 2006. 'Radiocarbon dating of the iron production slag-pit furnaces in Jutland'. *Journal of Danish Archaeology* 14: 127–138.

Rasmussen, T., and J. Nielsen. 2009. *To gårdstomter fra yngre germansk jernalder/vikingetid ved Himmelev Boldbaner*. Bygherrerapport. J. nr. ROM 2503. Roskilde: Roskilde Museum.

Segschneider, M. 2002. 'Trade and centrality between the Rhine and the Limfjord around 500 AD. The beachmarket on the Northfrisian island Amrum and its context', in B. Hårdh and L. Larsson (eds) *Central Places in the Migration and Merovingian Periods*: 247–256. Stockholm: Almqvist & Wiksell International.

Skre, D. 1998. *Herredømmet: Bosetning og besittelse på Romerike 200–1350 e.Kr.* Oslo: Universitetsforlaget.

Solberg, B. 1986. 'Førhistorisk tid i Sogndal', in P. Sandal (ed.) *Sogndal bygdebok 1. Allmenn bygdesøge, tida før 1800*: 119–235. Sogndal: Sogndal Sogelag.

Sommerseth, I. 2011. 'Archaeology and the debate on the transition from reindeer hunting to pastoralism'. *Rangifer* 31, 1: 111–127.

Stjernquist, B. 1997. *The Roekillorna Spring: Spring-Cult in Scandinavian Prehistory.* Stockholm: Almqvist & Wiksell International.

Strömberg, M. 1978. *En kustby I Ystad—före stadens tillkomst.* Ystadiana 23. Ystad: Ystads Allehanda.

Sundkvist, A. 2010. 'Vendeltida järnframställning i Västra Via', in E. Pettersson (ed.) *Västra via vid vägen.* SAU reports 2010, 2: 134–145. Uppsala: Societas Archaeologica Upsaliensis.

Thrane, H. 2013. 'Scandinavia', in H. Fokkens and A. Harding (eds) *The Oxford Handbook of the European Bronze Age*: 746–766. Oxford: Oxford University Press.

Viklund, K. 1998. *Cereals, Weeds and Crops: Processing in Iron Age Sweden.* Umeå: Umeå University.

Viklund, K., and K. Gullberg. 2002. *Från romartid till vikingatid.* Vasa: Scriptum.

Ystgaard, I. 2014. *Krigens praksis: Organisert voldsbruk og maretiell kultur i Mitt-Norge ca. 100–900 e.Kr.* Trondheim: Norges teknisk-naturvitenskaplige universitet.

Zachrisson, I. 2010. 'Vittnesbörd om pälshandel?' *Fornvännen* 105: 187–202.

CHAPTER 6

THE EASTERN BALTIC

VALTER LANG

Introduction

The eastern Baltic region is today divided between the states of Estonia, Latvia, and Lithuania, covering altogether about 175,000 km^2. People in the northern part of this region spoke Finnic languages (Estonian and Livonian), whereas the southernmost part was inhabited by Baltic-speaking (Latvian and Lithuanian) populations. This language division goes back at least to the late Bronze Age (Lang 2015a).

In geographical terms, the eastern Baltic can be divided into three main sub-regions:

(1) The coastal zone, which rose from the sea during the Holocene, with thin and unfertile (in the modern sense) agricultural soils and a mild, maritime climate. The coastal zone is widest in the north-west, i.e. low-lying west Estonia (together with its numerous islands), becoming significantly narrower further south where isostatic uplift of the earth's surface after the retreat of the ice sheet was modest. Many areas in the coastal zone, particularly in west and north Estonia, had favourable conditions for early (i.e. Neolithic to Bronze Age) agriculture and stock-breeding, although in the long run they were overtaken by the central zone.

(2) The central zone, characterized by thick and rather fertile soils formed on the base of moraine landscapes. Moraine heights such as Žemaitija, Vidzeme, Sakala, Otepää, Haanja, and Pandivere became the principal agricultural areas of the region from the Roman Iron Age.

(3) In the eastern zone, few and small agricultural lands are divided between numerous bogs, lakes, and small hills; the region is rich in bodies of water and forests that are very suitable for hunting and fishing.

There are also remarkable differences in climate, both from north to south and from west to east. In the northern part of the east Baltic region, it is colder, summer is shorter, and winter longer than in the southern part; the frost-free period in Estonia is three months shorter than in Lithuania, whereas the growing period (above 5°C) in central Estonia is three weeks shorter than in central Lithuania. As a transitional zone between a marine and a continental climate, there are also big differences in rainfall and temperature when one moves from west to east across the eastern Baltic region.

The Iron Age of the east Baltic region covers the timespan from *c.*500 cal. BC to *c.*AD 1200 and is divided into several sub-periods. Allowing for minor differences between the chronologies used in the three countries, the period can be subdivided as follows:

- Pre-Roman Iron Age: 500 BC–AD 50 (divided into early and late, with the border in the third century BC).
- Roman Iron Age: AD 50–400/450 (divided into early and late, with the border around AD 200).
- Middle Iron Age: AD 450–800 (consisting of the Migration period: AD 450–550/600 and the pre-Viking Age: AD 550/600–800).
- Late Iron Age: 800–1200/1250 (divided into the Viking Age: AD 800–1050 and final Iron Age: AD 1050–1200/1250).

This chapter will examine the earlier part of the Iron Age up to the end of the Migration period (*c.*500 BC–AD 550/600). The reasons for stopping in the middle of the Iron Age can be found in the major ethnocultural change that took place at around that time. The use of artefacts characteristic of the Roman Iron Age ended during the late Migration period and new forms of material culture were introduced after that (e.g. Tvauri 2012: 327–329). The third quarter of the first millennium AD has also been considered a period of disintegration of (eastern) Proto-Baltic into northern (Latvian) and southern (Lithuanian) language branches (Dini 2014: 259–260); Proto-Finnic, too, is supposed to have lasted until the second half of the first millennium, when it too split into different languages (e.g. Kallio 2006). People living on the south-eastern shores of the Baltic Sea have been called the Aestii (*Aestiorum gentes*) following Tacitus' *Germania* (AD 98); some researchers have thought that this name also held good for all the tribes living in the east Baltic region.

From Bronze to Iron

The start of the Iron Age at 500 BC is conventional. The very first items of iron occur in the final Bronze Age (800–500 BC), for example the small iron awls found at the fortified settlements at Iru and Asva in coastal Estonia (Lang 2007: 121). Iron artefacts of the final Bronze Age and early pre-Roman Iron Age from Estonia and Latvia were either imported or made locally; in some cases the iron for locally produced artefacts (axes) was imported from what is now Poland (Anteins 1976: 9–10). Judging from artefact typology, the other direction of import was from Scandinavia. The earliest direct evidence for local iron production—in the form of both smelting furnaces and iron objects—comes from western Lithuania (at Lazdininkai and Banduziai) and dates from about 300 BC (A. Merkevičius pers. comm.; Grigalavičienė 1979: 37). There is little doubt that iron was also produced at this time in the northern part of the east Baltic region, as evidenced by many local forms of iron ornaments and tools. Iron-producing sites became common in all Baltic countries from the turn of our era (Peets 2003: 51–82). In this way, the early pre-Roman Iron Age is something of a transitional period, when iron was already being locally produced, between the late Bronze Age and the Iron Age proper.

When speaking about the Bronze Age to Iron Age transition in a wider cultural and economic sense, the entire pre-Roman Iron Age should be taken into account. First, in the (early) pre-Roman Iron Age, there were remarkable changes in burial customs: traditions characteristic of the Bronze Age were gradually replaced by new customs, which then remained in use for many centuries. These developments mostly affected the coastal zone, which had already seen monumental grave building in the Bronze Age, but the changes were different in nature in different places. Second, there were notable changes in material culture: many new forms of ornaments, tools, and pottery were introduced *after* the earlier pre-Roman Iron Age. In terms of material culture, this period formed something of a continuation of the late Bronze Age. Third, during the later pre-Roman Iron Age, one can trace the start of a settlement shift and/or expansion of burial with grave goods across the central zone of the east Baltic region. The eastern zone did not face all these changes during the pre-Roman Iron Age, the cultural and economic systems of the Bronze Age remaining little changed until the Roman Iron Age.

Sites of the Pre-Roman Iron Age

The main archaeological sources for the pre-Roman Iron Age are cemeteries in the coastal regions; settlements and hillforts are less well known and less studied. Other types of site—such as fossil field systems or iron-producing sites—are few in number. The burial evidence from coastal Estonia and coastal Lithuania is particularly rich.

Late Stone Cist Graves and Cairn Graves

Stone cist graves were the first above-ground stone burial structures to appear in northern coastal Estonia at around 1200 BC. As convincingly proved by AMS radiocarbon dates on a number of skeletons, the building of graves of this type continued well into the pre-Roman Iron Age, until at least 400 BC; in addition, they often contain burials of later periods (see e.g. Laneman and Lang 2013; Laneman et al. 2015). Stone cist graves are above-ground structures of around 10–15 m in diameter and up to 1.5 m in height; they contain a stone cist (or several cists) in the middle, with one or more circular stone walls around it (or them), all covered with a mound of stones and turf (see Lang

2007: 147–153). Although these structures were seemingly built for individual burials, the actual number of burials can vary from two or three to twenty or more, but they are usually spread over a long time period. Inhumation is the most common form of burial, but cremations also occur, particularly outside the cists. Grave goods are rare, consisting mostly of ornaments and small tools or everyday items. Although they are smaller in size and later in date, in terms of their structure and burial practices the Estonian stone cist graves very much resemble stone barrows in central Sweden and on Gotland in the earlier part of the Bronze Age. In the east Baltic region, stone cist graves occur in northern and western Estonia (but seldom in interior areas) and in northern Latvia.

Cairn graves resemble stone cist graves in their general shape and size, but lack either a cist or a surrounding wall or both. They are known so far in the same area as stone cist graves and can be regarded as a later development. The excavated cairn grave mounds belong to the pre-Roman Iron Age.

Early *Tarand* Graves

Tarand graves can be divided into two large groups, the so-called typical (dated to the Roman Iron Age) and early *tarand* graves. The latter emerged in the last centuries of the Bronze Age and continued through the pre-Roman Iron Age (*c.*800 BC–AD 100). *Tarands* are quadrangular stone enclosures for burials, built on the ground (Figure 6.1). The number of *tarands* in one grave can vary from one to a few dozen (see e.g. Lang 2007: 170–180). The earliest *tarands* were usually built for only a few inhumations; *tarands* of the later pre-Roman Iron Age mostly contain numerous cremations. On the basis of their construction and general layout, several sub-groups can be distinguished

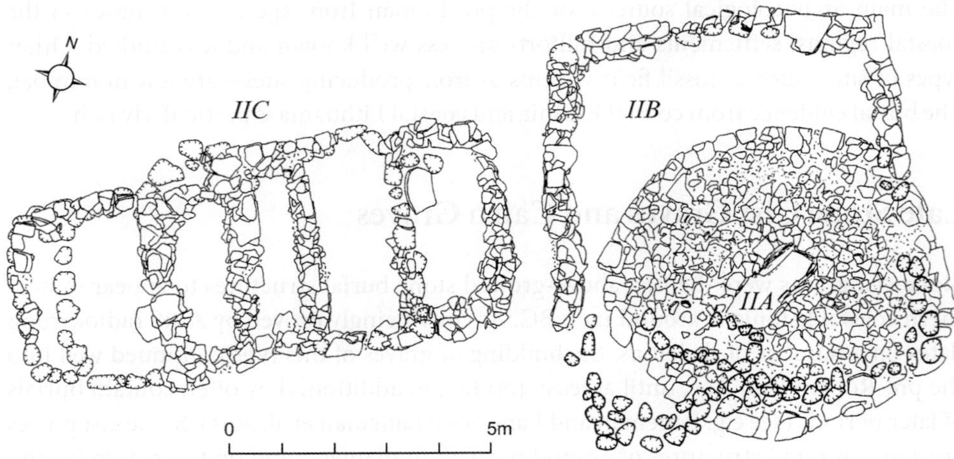

FIGURE 6.1 Early *tarand* graves IIB and IIC of the pre-Roman Iron Age and stone cist grave IIA of the late Bronze Age at Tõugu, Estonia.

among the early *tarand* graves, but the whole group shares common chronological developments in burial customs and grave goods. The main distribution of early *tarand* graves covers coastal Estonia, south-west Finland, and east central Sweden, but a few are also found in what are today Courland (Latvia) and Ingermanland (north-west Russia; Figure 6.2).

AMS dates on skeletons indicate that burials in the first *tarands* (*c*.800–500 BC) were unfurnished. The use of grave goods began in the early pre-Roman Iron Age;

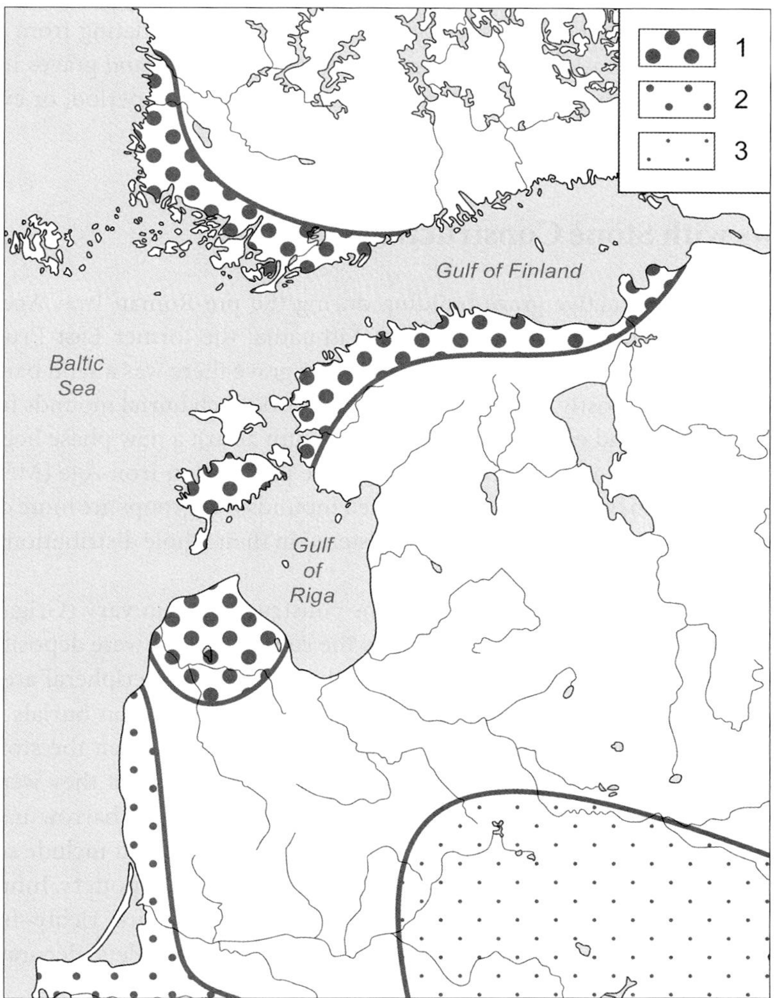

FIGURE 6.2 Main cultural regions in the pre-Roman Iron Age: 1 early *tarand* graves in the coastal regions of Estonia, Finland, and Courland (Latvia); 2 barrows with stone constructions in coastal Latvia, Lithuania, and former East Prussia (Kaliningrad district); 3 late striated pottery and fortified settlements in eastern Lithuania, south-eastern Latvia, and north-western Byelorussia.

they consisted of bronze neck-rings, bronze and (massive) iron bracelets, decorative pins, some imported single items, and so-called Ilmandu-style ceramics (e.g. graves at Ilmandu, Tõugu). The *tarand* graves of the late pre-Roman Iron Age are richer in grave goods, at least in quantitative terms: shepherd's crook pins, thin bronze and iron bracelets, the spiral and other bronze decorative items worn on the head known as 'temple ornaments' (Lang 2007: 112–113), knives, cord- and comb-impressed pottery, and a number of imported items (e.g. graves at Kõmsi, Poanse, Kurevere, and Uusküla). Weapons and larger tools are very rare in Estonian *tarand* graves. No early Roman Iron Age fibulae have so far been found in such graves. Early *tarand* graves in north-west Latvia (e.g. Strazde and Lazdiņi) are somewhat later in origin, dating from the third to first centuries BC (Vasks 2006). It is not unusual for early *tarand* graves in Estonia and Latvia to contain later burials (Roman Iron Age, Migration period, or even later) and finds.

Barrows with Stone Constructions

Another region with active grave-building during the pre-Roman Iron Age covered coastal areas of south-west Latvia, western Lithuania, the former East Prussia, and north-west Poland (Figure 6.2). The leading type of grave there was a sand barrow with stone constructions, mostly concentric circles and cists. Such burial mounds first occur in the late Neolithic and early Bronze Age (Hoffmann 2001); a new phase began at the end of the Bronze Age and continued through the pre-Roman Iron Age (Merkevičius 2016). The barrows may occur as single, isolated mounds, but groups are more common. There are 470 groups, with 1,450 barrows registered in their whole distribution area; 423 barrows (28%) have been investigated to date.

Burial customs in sand barrows with stone constructions can vary (Grigalavičienė 1979, 1995; Hoffmann 2001). Most commonly the earliest burials were deposited in the central part, within the innermost circle, with later burials in peripheral areas of the mounds (e.g. Ėgliškiai, Padvariai, Głamsławki, Bauska). Cremation burials predominate. Cremated bones were put either in compact clusters between the stones or in urns; sometimes small cists were built. Inhumations also occur, but they were mostly deposited higher in the mounds and belong to the final stage of barrow use (*c.*200/150 BC–AD 100). Cremations are poor in terms of grave goods, but include some iron bracelets, iron fibulae of La Tène type, bronze decorative pins, and pottery. Inhumations of the late pre-Roman Iron Age were more often–and more richly–furnished, containing spiral temple ornaments, pendants, neck-rings, bracelets, decorative pins, and finger-rings.

At the very end of the pre-Roman Iron Age, new stone constructions were built alongside earlier barrows (e.g. Kurmaičiai). These vary in size and shape (being round, oval, rectangular, and irregular), while their walls may sometimes reach 0.5–0.7 m in height. Usually only one (in some cases more) cremation burial was deposited in each construction, either in small pits or scattered over the entire area within the structure. This tradition of grave-building developed further during the Roman Iron Age.

Other Grave Types

As palaeodemographic calculations demonstrate, only a minority of members of society were buried in monumental above-ground graves of the kinds described above (Lang 2011). Evidence of other burial customs is, however, very limited. Some cemeteries with both inhumations and cremations in pit graves are known in the interior of Latvia and Lithuania. For instance, 110 pit graves have been excavated at Raganukalns in central Latvia, but they were totally lacking in grave goods. Eighty-one burials in an area of 3,600 m^2 were studied at Lankiškės in Byelorussia, close to the Lithuanian border; pottery with striated surfaces, some stone axes, and flint flakes permit the dating of the cemetery to the pre-Roman Iron Age (Grigalavičienė 1995: 93). In 2015, two inhumations were discovered at Alu, north Estonia (but far from the sea); the burials had been dug into moraine deposits close to some larger boulders, but no special constructions were observed. The burials had no grave goods, but were AMS dated to *c.*400–100 BC (Laneman et al. 2016).

Settlement Sites and Hillforts

The main types of sites were open settlements, which are so small and have such thin occupation layers that they can hardly be interpreted as other than traces of single (semi-) permanent farmsteads. Such sites have been recorded in all the Baltic countries, but to date have been very poorly investigated.

Enclosed settlements have been of much greater interest to archaeologists. The major group are the so-called fortified settlement sites that spread from the late Bronze Age everywhere across the east Baltic region, and further to the east and south-east. Their main distribution is in the valley of the river Daugava and what is today north-east Lithuania and north-west Byelorussia (Figure 6.2); in Estonia they were few in number and were all abandoned at the end of the Bronze Age. In the Daugava basin, however, most fortified settlements stayed in use until the early Roman Iron Age, although the pre-Roman Iron Age layers at such sites are usually barely distinguishable, and the period is represented mostly by ceramics and a few metal artefacts. What is clear is that fortifications, which in the Bronze Age consisted mostly of ditches and wooden palisades, became more complicated in the later part of the pre-Roman Iron Age, with wooden chambers, built in corner-jointed technique, keeping the rampart sand together (Ķivutkalns, Latvia; Jägala, Estonia).

A few centuries after the abandonment of Bronze Age fortified settlements in Estonia, a new wave of fortifications appeared across the northern east Baltic region. At least a dozen excavated hilltop sites have yielded either archaeological material or radiocarbon dates of the middle and late pre-Roman Iron Age. At some places there were remarkable fortifications for the time; at others, nothing but a few potsherds or traces of (possibly defensive) buildings were found.

Another group of enclosed sites is found in western Estonia—the so-called early ring forts on flat ground. Such sites are usually round or oval in plan, *c*.50–80 m in diameter, and surrounded by a low circular rampart of stones and earth. Traces of occupation are either sparse or altogether absent. These sites—examples are also reported from western Lithuania—are comparable to sites in Gotland and Öland, dated from the pre-Roman Iron Age to the later Iron Age (see Chapter 5). The Estonian sites date to the late pre-Roman Iron Age and/or early Roman Iron Age (Lang 2007: 78–81).

Roman Iron Age and Migration Period Sites

The main archaeological sources for the Roman Iron Age and Migration period are burial sites. These now occur in far greater numbers and cover much larger areas than in previous centuries (Figure 6.3). Settlement sites and enclosed/fortified sites are still noticeably fewer in number than cemeteries. Yet from this period there are many interesting sites that have been more or less thoroughly examined. Several iron-smelting sites are well studied, some fossil field systems are known, and—particularly towards the end of this period—the number of hoards increased remarkably.

Classical *Tarand* Graves

So-called classical or typical *tarand* graves are monumental (up to 100 m in length, 20–30 m wide, and 1–1.5 m in height) above-ground burial mounds built of stone, as at Pada, Nurmsi, or Virunuka (Figure 6.4). They presumably developed out of one group of early *tarand* graves (Poanse) characterized by *tarands* that were joined to one another in a single straight row. Individual *tarands* usually have a north–south orientation, and a row often consists of more than a dozen enclosures arranged on an east–west axis. During the early Roman Iron Age, the *tarands*, which were previously quite small, became larger and were designed for collective burials. During the early Roman Iron Age cremation gradually replaced the inhumation tradition throughout the distribution area of classical *tarand* graves (continental Estonia, north and north-west Latvia, south-west Finland, and Ingermanland); during the late Roman Iron Age cremation strongly prevailed (although inhumation did not disappear entirely), while in the Migration period both customs can again be found side by side. The building of new *tarands* ended during the fourth century AD; the latest *tarand* grave was erected in the late fourth to early fifth century AD at Viimsi, north Estonia. However, burial in such graves often

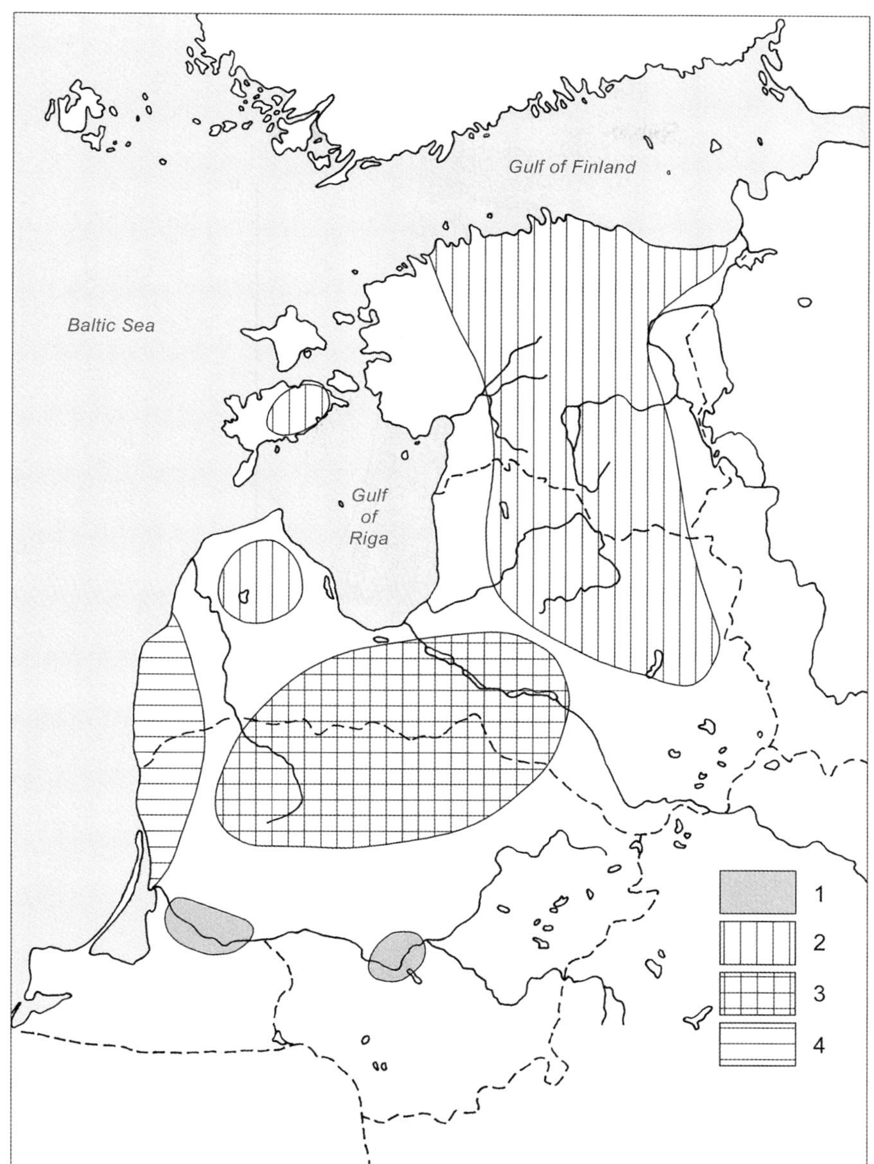

FIGURE 6.3 Main grave types in the eastern Baltic region in the Roman Iron Age: 1 pit graves; 2 *tarand* graves; 3 sand barrows with stone circles; 4 cemeteries with stone constructions.

continued until the sixth century, and it is not unusual to find burials or grave goods up to the twelfth to thirteenth centuries AD.

The majority of (but not all) classical *tarand* graves were richly furnished. Grave goods were more numerous and diverse than in the pre-Roman Iron Age, but were mainly

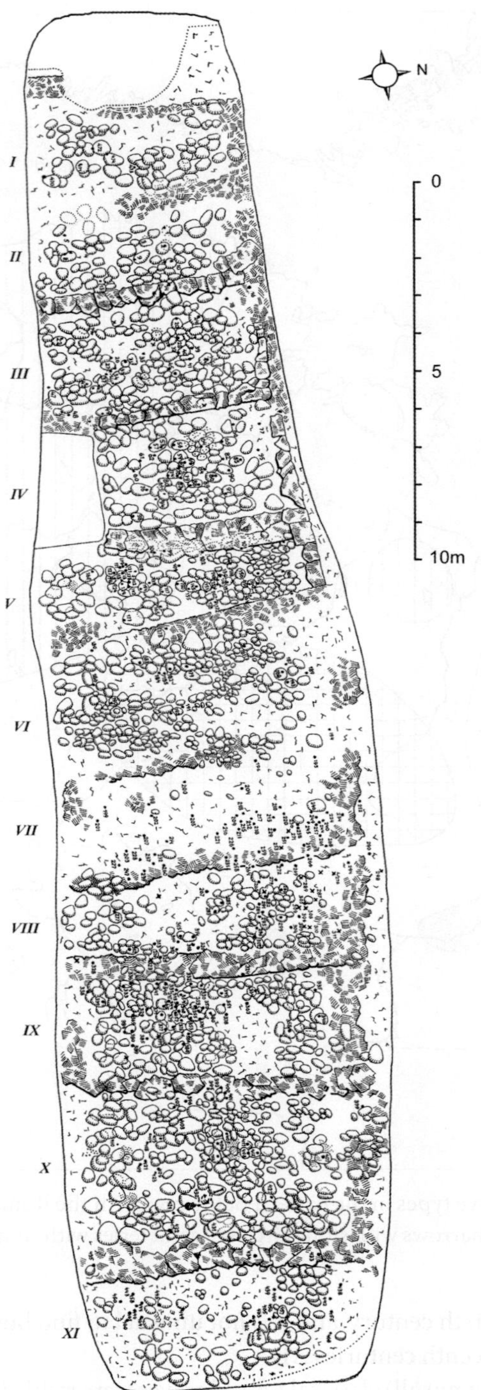

FIGURE 6.4 Classical *tarand* grave at Pada, Estonia.

Drawing: Marta Schmiedehelm

restricted to ornaments, small tools, and everyday items. Bigger tools and weapons are almost entirely absent from Estonian graves during the Roman Iron Age, although they occur in a number of north Latvian, Finnish, and Russian graves. In the Migration period, weapons and larger tools also occurred in Estonian stone graves, but these were already of a new type characterized by the absence of internal constructions. These so-called stone grave-fields became typical burial places of Finnic populations in the east Baltic region and Finland for the entire later Iron Age.

Sand Barrows with Stone Circles

For large parts of central, southern, and eastern Latvia and northern Lithuania it became widespread from the early Roman Iron Age to bury the dead in sand barrows surrounded by stone circles (e.g. Šnore 1993; Michelbertas 2004, 2011). Such barrows are usually located in groups of twenty to thirty, situated in forested areas close to bodies of water. In this sense they differ from *tarand* graves, which are usually found on or near the agricultural fields. The barrows vary in diameter from 7–20 m and in height from 0.5–1.1 m (e.g. Sāviena, Pajuostis). The site would first be cleared by burning all vegetation. The first inhumation was placed in the centre, at the level of the original ground surface; the next burials were located in the peripheral areas of the circle, and were often also at a higher level. While the central burial is generally oriented with the head to the west or north-west, peripheral burials lie concentric to the stone circle. Stones and sometimes even hearths can be found within a barrow.

The burials are usually quite rich in grave goods. Unlike those in *tarand* graves, burials in sand barrows were often furnished with weapons (spearheads, battle knives, axes), tools (sickles, axes, hoes), and sometimes even spurs and swords. Ornaments of bronze are represented by neck-rings, bracelets, decorative pins, chains, and pendants. Fibulae and finger-rings are quite rare in the Latvian part of the barrow area, but are more frequent in north Lithuania. Artefact typologies indicate that most sand barrows with stone circles were built during the second to fifth centuries AD, but they often yield burials of the sixth to eighth centuries too. The barrow tradition was later replaced by burial in pit graves, but this happened in different places at different times: in eastern Latvia during the seventh to eighth centuries AD, in central Latvia and northern central Lithuania during the Migration period, and in north-western Lithuania (Žemaitija) as early as the late fourth century AD.

Cemeteries with Stone Constructions

Cemeteries with various stone constructions or enclosures (round, oval, and rectangular) are spread over what are today western Lithuania and south-western Latvia in roughly the same coastal region as the barrows with stone constructions of the previous period (Tautavičius 1968; Banytė-Rowell 2016). Initially, the dead were buried in pits 0.2–0.3 m deep, and each burial was marked with a stone circle. Neighbouring circles touched one another. In the early Roman Iron Age the circles measured 4–6 m in diameter; later they became smaller and their shape started to change (becoming oval or rectangular). Grave goods are rich: males usually had two spearheads, an axe, a scythe, knives, a miniature clay vessel, sometimes even a horse; females were furnished with numerous ornaments (e.g. Tūbausiai, Kurmaičiai, Žviliai). Particularly from AD 175–250, Roman coins were often put in graves (Lazdininkai). Such cemeteries were established in the late pre-Roman Iron Age and remained in use until *c.*AD 600.

Pit Graves

In the Roman Iron Age, pit grave cemeteries occasionally occur in different micro-regions (e.g. in central Lithuania and on the lower reaches of the river Nemunas; e.g. Bertašius 2016), but they are so far not well investigated. From the fifth to sixth centuries AD, however, inhumations in pit graves gradually spread, both to the areas where barrows with stone circles occurred in the Roman Iron Age and to areas with no known earlier burial traditions. Some cemeteries are extraordinarily rich in grave goods, as at Plinkaigalis in central Lithuania, where 379 inhumations, eight cremations, and four horse burials of the fifth to sixth centuries AD have been investigated (Kazakevičius 1993). From the fifth century AD in southern Lithuania, and the fifth to sixth centuries in central Lithuania, cremations in pit graves also started to spread.

Round Barrows in East and South-East Lithuania

At variance with the rest of the southern east Baltic region, where barrow burial ended during the Migration period, in eastern Lithuania and western Byelorussia the custom started to spread more widely from that time (Tautavičius 1996: 46–57; Kurila 2016; Bliujienė 2016). Sand barrows 6–10 m in diameter and 0.6–1 m in height are sited in groups, ranging from dozens to several hundred. They were built and used for burial between the fifth or sixth and twelfth centuries AD (e.g. Taurapilis, Karmazinai; Figure 6.5). Early barrows were surrounded by stone circles, but during the fifth to seventh centuries, the circles became irregular in shape and 'disappeared' into the barrow, so they became invisible from outside. Later, stone circles became rare.

The earlier inhumation custom was gradually replaced by cremation during the fifth (to sixth) century AD. The number of burials per barrow increased in the course of time: in the fifth century there were usually only one or two burials, but in the seventh to eighth centuries there could be from four to seven burials in one barrow. Pieces of burnt bone were either put in small pits or scattered over larger areas; with a few exceptions, urns were not used. Grave goods are usually not numerous but weapons (spearheads, parts of shields, axes, knives) and horse harness (and horses) seem to dominate among the male attributes, while spindle-whorls are quite common in female burials, whose ornaments are modest. Some Migration period barrow groups were exceptionally rich in grave goods, but quite a number of barrows were completely empty of both burials and finds.

FIGURE 6.5 Reconstructed barrows at Karmazinai, Lithuania.

Photo: Valter Lang

Long Barrows in East Estonia and East Latvia

From the fifth to sixth centuries AD, sand barrows also started to spread in what are today eastern Estonia, eastern Latvia, and neighbouring areas of north-west Russia. Because of their characteristic shape they are called 'long barrows': their length can reach 100 m, although it is more usually around 20–30 m; oval and round formations also occur next to long ones (e.g. Rõsna-Saare, Mikitamäe). Barrows are located in groups of up to two dozen, most commonly on sandy soils close to rivers. The number of cremations in one barrow is always more than one; the bones were either put in urns or pits, or were scattered over larger areas. Stones occur in some barrows, particularly in the areas close to stone graves; traces of log buildings ('houses of the dead') have been found in several barrows. Grave goods were minimal: single ornaments, knives, buckles, strike-a-lights, clay pots, and horse bones.

Settlement Sites and Hillforts

In comparison to the many graves and cemeteries, known settlement sites are very few in number. Sites are mostly small, and occupation layers thin and poor in finds; most were probably just single farmsteads. There is some evidence for bigger village-like units, particularly at the foot of hillforts (e.g. Aukštadvaris in Lithuania), and several of the settlements investigated in Latvia (Kerkūzi, Spietiņi, Jaunlīve, and Kivti) were hamlets or villages rather than single farms. In Estonia, the majority of known settlement sites were single farms located close to stone graves (e.g. Ilumäe), but there is also some evidence of villages close to hillforts (Alt-Laari). Houses were mostly rectangular (4–6 x 4–6 m), sometimes oval, with floors dug into the ground. In the southern part of the east Baltic region, the houses were post-built, whereas in the northern part they were mostly log houses, built using the corner-jointed technique. The latter spread southwards at the end of the Roman Iron Age and during the Migration period.

The best evidence for Roman Iron Age hillforts comes from Lithuania (Vengalis 2016). In the early Roman Iron Age many fortified settlements typical of the Bronze Age and pre-Roman Iron Age were still in use, but they were abandoned after that. Particularly from the third to fourth centuries AD, a new type of fortification became widespread: the small, well-fortified hilltop, with an open settlement at its foot. Sometimes the forts are so small (100–120 m^2) that there may have been no dwellings behind the ramparts (Figure 6.6), but more often there were houses situated around the perimeter of the fort. The fortifications consisted of ramparts (which became higher over time, and contained stone, timber, and clay for strengthening) and ditches. During the late Roman Iron Age and Migration period, settlement units comprising a fort and an open settlement at its foot spread widely throughout the east Baltic region.

Other Types of Site

Iron-smelting furnaces became more numerous from the start of the first millennium AD. They can be divided into two main types (Peets 2003: 51–71). The furnaces of the

FIGURE 6.6 Miniature hillfort at Lavariškės, Lithuania.

Photo: Valter Lang

first type were log chambers (*c*.1.5 x 2.5 m) dug into the ground, in the centre of which there were shafts (diameter *c*.0.3–0.4 m), with an air channel in one corner (Tindimurru and Metsküla in Estonia). Furnaces of the other type were built above the ground; they had clay shafts, usually with a large stone on the bottom. The latter type were distributed all over the eastern Baltic region and beyond (e.g. Spietiņi in Latvia, Aukštadvaris and Bakšiai in Lithuania).

No hoards are reported from the pre-Roman Iron Age, but they do occur in the (late) Roman Iron Age. One type of hoard consists mostly of Roman coins: they have been found in all three countries, but the density of finds decreases from the south-eastern shores of the Baltic to the north. The quantity of Roman coins in the region of the western Balts is explained through the amber trade. West Lithuanian cemeteries often contain Roman coins dating from between AD 175–250 (mostly bronze *sestertii*, very rarely also silver *denarii*), whereas coins from hoards can be of later date. Roman coin hoards in Estonia are dated back to the early third century (Kiudsoo 2013); the largest was discovered in 2015 at Varudi-Vanaküla and yielded fifty-one coins (*sestertii* and local emissions).

Some other late Roman Iron Age hoards consist only of bronze ornaments. The number of hoards increased noticeably in the fifth and sixth centuries AD (Oras 2015); at this time silver hoards also occur, some of them quite remarkable (e.g. Kardla in Estonia, Rijnieki in Latvia, Baubliai in Lithuania). Another group of late Roman Iron Age and Migration period deposits consist only (or mostly) of iron weapons and tools, deposited in wetlands over many centuries. The most remarkable are Kokmuiža in Latvia (600 spearheads, several swords, and other items, weighing 120 kg altogether) and a recent find at Kohtla in Estonia (more than 200 sickles, 100 spearheads, and other items; Oras and Kriiska 2014).

Culture, Economy, and Society

In the pre-Roman Iron Age, three sub-regions are clearly distinguishable—though without exact borders—in the east Baltic region, each with its own cultural traditions (see Figure 6.2). One was coastal Estonia with its early *tarand* graves, pottery styles (Ilmandu, cord- and comb-impressed wares), and ornaments. The second covered what are today coastal Lithuania, former east Prussia, north-west Poland, and south-west Latvia, with different burial customs and material culture. The third (so-called Late Striated Pottery culture) covered inland parts of north-east Lithuania, south-east Latvia (the Daugava valley) and north-west Byelorussia with fortified settlements, striated pottery, distinctive material culture, and almost unknown burial customs (apart from a few pit graves). Large interior areas between these three culturally distinct regions were sparsely populated, mostly indicated by isolated finds and sites.

The Roman Iron Age saw a remarkable unification of material culture: almost everywhere in the east Baltic region and even beyond (south-west Finland, north-west

Russia) communities made use of ornaments, tools, weapons, and everyday items of types developed on the south-eastern shores of the Baltic Sea. In terms of their material culture, dress, and outlook people in the whole east Baltic region were quite similar to one another. Ceramic styles, however, were different in different geographical areas, as were burial customs, the main border of which runs between the stone graves and sand barrow traditions in northern Latvia. Many researchers believe that the latter boundary probably marked the border of Finnic- and Baltic-speaking populations. The unity of material culture continued until the Migration period, after which regional differences started to become increasingly marked.

From the Bronze Age onwards, the principal mode of subsistence was based on agriculture and stock rearing. However, in different regions the economy was oriented differently. In coastal Estonia field cultivation was already quite well developed in the late Bronze Age, as one can conclude from the occurrence of extensive field systems of (pre-) Celtic type (e.g. Saha-Loo and Loo). Numerous relict field complexes are known from the pre-Roman Iron Age, such as Proosa and Rebala (Lang 2015b). At the start of our era there was a change in farming systems, with earlier field complexes being abandoned; evidence for field cultivation in the Roman Iron Age and Migration period is scant. It is likely that at that time the heavier and more fertile soils of the central zone were taken into use; as these soils have been cultivated until the present day, earlier traces are not preserved.

The inhabitants of Bronze Age and pre-Roman Iron Age fortified settlements further inland practised stock rearing, some agriculture, hunting, and fishing. Evidence for genuine field cultivation in this region is debatable. Around 80% of the animal bones recovered belong to domesticated species, indicating that herds consisted of cattle, sheep/goats, pigs, and horses.

In the Roman Iron Age, the central zone became the principal agricultural area in the east Baltic region. Although direct evidence in the form of fossil field systems is very rare, the general pattern of settlement development and distribution speaks in favour of agricultural use of moraine soils. The most important crop plants were wheat and barley, but oats, peas, and rye also occurred (the latter first as a weed, but after the Migration period also as a cultivated plant).

Society was organized in small communities, each headed by a dominant farm or family. Such a social structure has been suggested for Estonia in the pre-Roman and Roman Iron Age but is also plausible for other parts of the east Baltic region with open settlements and monumental graves. Palaeodemographic calculations indicate that not more than around 20% of the people living at a given time were buried in archaeologically recognizable graves; these graves should thus be interpreted as the burial places of one element of society, an elite. At the same time, the excavated cemeteries display variation in terms of grave assemblages: there are richer and poorer groups of graves or cemeteries, while really lavish 'princely' burials are absent until the end of the Roman Iron Age and Migration period (Lang 2011; Banytė-Rowell et al. 2012; Jovaiša 2016). In the landscape, a richer grave was usually accompanied by some poorer ones in the same micro-region, allowing one to infer some social difference between adjacent landowning farms. In the area of fortified settlements, however, the social structure was probably different: groups inhabiting the fortified sites probably dominated the surrounding open settlements, evidence of which is scanty.

Social stratification increased in the Migration period. In Taurapilis, east Lithuania, the excavations yielded a princely burial with extremely rich grave goods in a central barrow and burials of warriors (with weapons and horses) in surrounding barrows (Tautavičius 1981). This is a new social occurrence—a 'prince' and his military retinue or entourage—which in one way or another was followed for many cemeteries after the Migration period. The erection of fortifications on hills and the spread of forts-and-settlements everywhere in the east Baltic region also fit well with this picture. Although it is impossible to study individual burials in the northern east Baltic area due to their being mixed cremations in stone graves, even there one can still follow the foundation of cemeteries with extraordinarily rich grave goods, indicating foreign contacts and military concerns (e.g. Proosa).

The End of the Early Iron Age

In AD 536 a climatic catastrophe took place in the northern hemisphere, caused probably by an immense volcanic eruption. As a result of this, sunlight was reduced and the air temperature became cooler, followed by crop failures, serious famine, and mass fatalities. It is not yet clear how serious the consequences of this event were for the populations living in the east Baltic region, but a notable decrease in the number of archaeological sites and changes in material culture are apparent in many areas during the sixth century AD (Tvauri 2014 and references therein). The suggested crisis in population numbers and cultural development is an appropriate point at which to end the thousand-year-long prehistoric period of the east Baltic region.

References

Anteins, A. 1976. *Melnais metals Latvijâ*. Riga: Zinātne.

Banytė-Rowell, R. 2016. 'West Lithuanian cemeteries', in G. Zabiela, Z. Baubonis, and E. Marcinkevičiūtė (eds) *A Hundred Years of Archaeological Discoveries in Lithuania*: 256–267. Vilnius: Lietuvos Archeologijos Draugija.

Banytė-Rowell, R., A. Bitner-Wróblewska, and C. Reich. 2012. 'Did they exist? The question of elites in western Lithuania in the Roman and early Migration periods, and their interregional contacts'. *Archaeologia Baltica* 18: 192–220.

Bertašius, M. 2016. 'Central Lithuanian cemeteries', in G. Zabiela, Z. Baubonis, and E. Marcinkevičiūtė (eds) *A Hundred Years of Archaeological Discoveries in Lithuania*: 226–235. Vilnius: Lietuvos Archeologijos Draugija.

Bliujienė, A. 2016. 'South Lithuanian barrows', in G. Zabiela, Z. Baubonis, and E. Marcinkevičiūtė (eds) *A Hundred Years of Archaeological Discoveries in Lithuania*: 208–225. Vilnius: Lietuvos Archeologijos Draugija.

Dini, P. U. 2014. *Foundations of Baltic Languages* (trans. M. B. Richardson and R. E. Richardson). Vilnius: Eugrimas.

Grigalavičienė, E. 1979. 'Egliškių pilkapiai'. *Lietuvos Archeologija* 1: 5–43.

Grigalavičienė, E. 1995. *Žalvario ir ankstyvasis geležies amžius Lietuvoje*. Vilnius: Mokslo ir Enciklopedijų Leidykla.

Hoffmann, M. J. 2001. 'Früheisenzeitliche Hügelgräber in der westbaltischen Zone—das Problem ihrer Genese und Differenzierung'. *Archaeologia Lituana* 2: 5–21.

Jovaiša, E. 2016. 'Military aristocracy in Lower Nemunas', in G. Zabiela, Z. Baubonis, and E. Marcinkevičiūtė (eds) *A Hundred Years of Archaeological Discoveries in Lithuania*: 236–247. Vilnius: Lietuvos Archeologijos Draugija.

Kallio, P. 2006. 'On the earliest Slavic loanwords in Finnic', in J. Nuorluoto (ed.) *The Slavicization of the Russian North: Mechanisms and Chronology*. Slavica Helsingiensia 27: 154–166. Helsinki: Department of Slavonic and Baltic Languages and Literatures.

Kazakevičius, V. 1993. *Plinkaigalio kapinynas*. Lietuvos Archeologija 10. Vilnius: Mokslo ir Enciklopedijų Leidykla.

Kiudsoo, M. 2013. 'New Roman coin find in Estonia'. *Archaeological Fieldwork in Estonia* 2012: 289–296.

Kurila, L. 2016. 'East Lithuanian barrows—burial in the cradle of Lithuanian tribes', in G. Zabiela, Z. Baubonis, and E. Marcinkevičiūtė (eds) *A Hundred Years of Archaeological Discoveries in Lithuania*: 192–207. Vilnius: Lietuvos Archeologijos Draugija.

Laneman, M., and V. Lang. 2013. 'New radiocarbon dates for two stone-cist graves at Muuksi, northern Estonia'. *Estonian Journal of Archaeology* 17, 2: 89–122.

Laneman, M., V. Lang, M. Malve, and E. Rannamäe. 2015. 'New data on Jaani stone graves at Väo, northern Estonia'. *Estonian Journal of Archaeology* 19, 2: 110–137.

Laneman, M., V. Lang, and R. Saage. 2016. 'Burial site hidden in a clearance cairn at Alu, Raplamaa'. *Archaeological Fieldwork in Estonia* 2015: 35–46.

Lang, V. 2007. *The Bronze and Early Iron Ages in Estonia*. Estonian Archaeology 3. Tartu: Tartu University Press.

Lang, V. 2011. 'Traceless death. Missing burials in Bronze Age and Iron Age Estonia'. *Estonian Journal of Archaeology* 15, 2: 109–129.

Lang, V. 2015a. 'Formation of Proto-Finnic—an archaeological scenario from the Bronze Age/Early Iron Age', in H. Mantila, K. Leinonen, S. Brunni, S. Palviainen, and J. Sivonen (eds) *Congressus Duodecimus Internationalis Fenno-Ugristarum*: 63–84. Oulu: University of Oulu.

Lang, V. 2015b. 'Stability and changes in the agricultural use of limestone soils in northern Estonia', in F. Retamero, I. Schjellerup, and A. Davies (eds) *Agricultural and Pastoral Landscapes in Pre-Industrial Society: Choices, Stability and Change*: 125–142. Oxford: Oxbow.

Merkevičius, A. 2016. 'West Lithuania during the Early Metal Age', in G. Zabiela, Z. Baubonis, and E. Marcinkevičiūtė (eds) *A Hundred Years of Archaeological Discoveries in Lithuania*: 130–147. Vilnius: Lietuvos Archeologijos Draugija.

Michelbertas, M. 2004. *Pajuosčio pilkapynas*. Vilnius: Vilniaus universiteto leidykla.

Michelbertas, M. 2011. *Paalksnių archeologijos paminklai*. Vilnius: Vilniaus universiteto leidykla.

Oras, E. 2015. *Practices of Wealth Depositing in the 1st–9th Century AD Eastern Baltic*. Leiden: Sidestone Press.

Oras, E., and A. Kriiska. 2014. 'The Kohtla weapon deposit: preliminary results'. *Archaeological Fieldwork in Estonia* 2013: 55–66.

Peets, J. 2003. *The Power of Iron: Iron Production and Blacksmithy in Estonia and Neighbouring Areas in Prehistoric Period and the Middle Ages*. Muinasaja teadus 12. Tallinn: Institute of History.

Šnore, E. 1993. *Agrā dzelzs laikmeta uzkalniņi Latvijas austrumu daļā*. Riga: Zinātne.

Tautavičius, A. (ed.) 1968. *Lietuvos pajûrio I–VII a. kapinynai: Lietuvos archeologiniai paminklai*. Vilnius: Mintis.

Tautavičius, A. 1981. 'Taurapilio "Kunigaikščio" kapas', in R. Volkaitė-Kulikauskienė (ed.) *Pirmykštės bendruomenės irimas*. Lietuvos Archeologija 2: 18–43. Vilnius: Mokslas.

Tautavičius, A. 1996. *Vidurinis geležies amžius Lietuvoje (V–IX a.)*. Vilnius: Pilių tyyimų centras 'Lietuvos Pilys'.

Tvauri, A. 2012. *The Migration Period, Pre-Viking Age, and Viking Age in Estonia*. Estonian Archaeology 4. Tartu: Tartu University Press.

Tvauri, A. 2014. 'The impact of the climate catastrophe of 536–537 AD in Estonia and neighbouring areas'. *Estonian Journal of Archaeology* 18, 1: 30–56.

Vasks, A. 2006. 'Stone grave cemeteries in western Latvia', in H. Valk (ed.) *Ethnicity and Culture: Studies in Honour of Silvia Laul*. Muinasaja teadus 18: 99–111. Tartu/Tallinn: Tartu Ülikool arheoloogia õppetool/TLÜ Ajaloo Instituut.

Vengalis, R. 2016. 'Old and Middle Iron Age settlements and hillforts', in G. Zabiela, Z. Baubonis, and E. Marcinkevičiūtė (eds) *A Hundred Years of Archaeological Discoveries in Lithuania*: 160–181. Vilnius: Lietuvos Archeologijos Draugija.

CHAPTER 7

EASTERN CENTRAL EUROPE

Between the Elbe and the Dnieper

WOJCIECH NOWAKOWSKI

Introduction

Eastern central Europe (*Ostmitteleuropa*) can be defined primarily on historical and cultural grounds. The area is not delimited by any clear physiographic boundaries, but both in prehistory and in the historic period—as well as in more recent times—it functioned as a distinct transitional zone, albeit with much stronger ties to the Rhine and the upper and middle Danube basins than to the Don and Volga regions. The centre of this area lay in the Oder and Vistula river basins, its western border being the eastern edge of the Elbe basin, while to the east at certain periods this zone extended as far as the Dnieper basin, and introduced a cultural model typical of central European *Barbaricum* into the territory of modern-day Belarus (the Zarubincy culture). Most of the area covered by this chapter is now Poland.

The Beginnings: The Early Pre-Roman Iron Age (800–200 BC)

The early Iron Age, characterized by a clear departure from the cultural structures of the Bronze Age, is marked by the formation of the so-called Hallstatt culture on the northern fringes of the Alps and in the upper and middle Danube region, a development related to influences from the Mediterranean world reaching central Europe at this time. A decisive role in these contacts was played by the Etruscans, who at that time occupied most of central and northern Italy and whose settlements reached as far as the foothills of the Alps. Even though the Etruscans adopted numerous elements of Greek culture, they maintained relations with peoples outside the Mediterranean world, in particular with the Hallstatt area. Testimonies of these extensive contacts are the Greek and Etruscan luxury items found in the tombs of local rulers (see Chapter 8).

Late Lusatian Culture and the Hallstatt Zone

One reason for the intensive contact between the Etruscans and their Hallstatt partners was the trade in amber, which was in high demand in the Mediterranean world (Gediga et al. 2016: 147–195). This raw material did not occur in the Danube region, and had to be imported from amber-rich coastal zones. Initially the main supply came from the North Sea, but from the mid-first millennium BC the Baltic coast took the lead. Evidence of this trade is provided by amber used on objects produced in the Hallstatt area, mainly brooches, but also by Italian goods that reached the territory of the Lusatian culture through the Hallstatt zone, the most impressive of these being bronze buckets (Kaczanowski and Kozłowski 1998: 165–176; cf. Gediga et al. 2016: 16–20).

Hallstatt influences included the adoption of cultural models. In Silesia, a region close to the Hallstatt zone, we find barrows that resemble tombs of the Danube basin as well as painted vessels imitating Hallstatt pottery. Given the scale of these influences, one cannot completely exclude the possibility that Hallstatt groups migrated, creating a remote outpost of the amber trade north of the Sudeten mountains (Gedl 1991). Another significant development was the appearance of a group of fortified settlements, including the celebrated lake site of Biskupin with its ordered street grid lined with near identical log buildings, surrounded by a wooden stockade (e.g. Niesiołowska-Wędzka 1991). Tree-ring dates indicate that wood used in the construction of the first settlement was felled between 750 and 708 BC, contemporary with other fortified wetland sites in the region, such as Sobiejuchy (Harding et al. 2004; Harding and Rączkowski 2010). Many of the later Bronze Age Urnfield cemeteries typical of the earlier Lusatian culture continued in use in the Hallstatt period, among them the vast cemetery at Kietrz in Silesia (Gedl 1980); it was seemingly used without a break from the middle Bronze Age right through into the La Tène period (see later in the chapter).

The development of the Lusatian culture was halted by Scythian raids. Towards the end of the first half of the sixth century BC, Scythians occupied the steppe of the Carpathian basin (Parducz 1974) and proceeded to attack lands north of the Carpathian mountains. Evidence of these raids is to be found in the form of burnt-down settlements of the Lusatian culture, such as Wicina, yielding tri-lobed arrowheads typical of Scythian military equipment (Bukowski 1977).

Pomeranian Culture

A new phenomenon in the Hallstatt period was the formation of the Pomeranian culture in the lower Vistula region (Figure 7.1), out of a local group of the late Lusatian culture. This was associated with a pronounced change in social structure, marked by the replacement of large late Bronze Age Urnfield cemeteries composed of individual cremation burials with smaller burial grounds featuring stone-set graves containing up to twenty urns. One may suspect that in this period the earlier large groups disintegrated into small, scattered communities living in open settlements with close internal ties manifesting themselves in the construction of communal tombs (Kaczanowski and Kozłowski 1998: 183–187).

A distinctive trait of the Pomeranian culture was the occurrence of urns with a bulbous body and a tall, conical neck with a schematic representation of a human face, an attached nose, and incised eyes (Figure 7.2, A; Kneisel 2012). Bronze ear-rings with glass beads often adorned small ears attached to the sides, while lids were shaped like hats. The appearance of these face-urns was for a long time interpreted as the result of contacts with Etruscan traders who reached the Baltic coast and brought with them the custom of making anthropomorphic vases—canopic urns to contain the ashes of the dead. But it seems more justified to view the face-urns as an effect of specific local transformations occurring over the entire Baltic coastal region from Jutland to the mouth of the river Vistula.

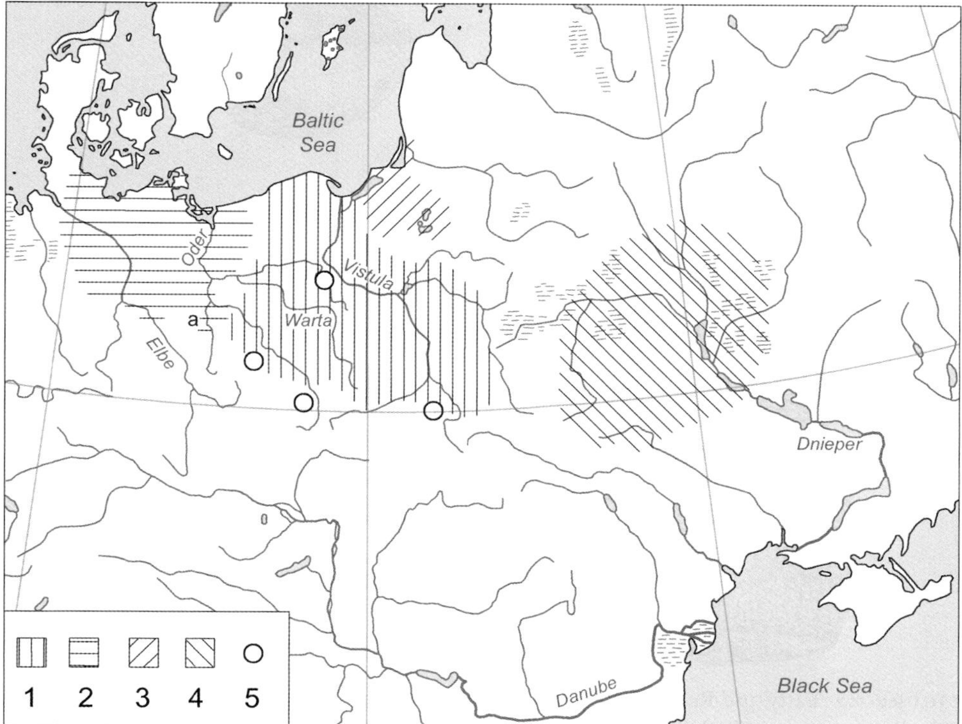

FIGURE 7.1 Early pre-Roman Iron Age cultural groupings in east central Europe: 1 Pomeranian culture, 2 Jastorf culture (a = Gubin group), 3 West Balt barrow culture, 4 Milogrady culture, 5 Celtic enclaves north of the Sudeten and Carpathian mountains.

In the later Hallstatt period, the Pomeranian culture expanded territorially to include not only Pomerania, but also the entire Vistula, Warta, and Oder basins, although the archaeological evidence does not permit us to determine whether this was due to migration of population, conquest, or solely cultural expansion consisting of the adoption of new burial customs (cf. Dzięgielewski 2010). It must be pointed out, however, that cemeteries of the Pomeranian culture featured yet another distinctive type of burial: so-called cloche-graves, in which the urn, sometimes together with additional vessels, was covered by a large (up to 1 m high) inverted globular vessel or 'cloche' (Figure 7.2, C–D). Such graves are particularly numerous in the eastern part of the area occupied by the Pomeranian culture, which compels some archaeologists to distinguish a separate Cloche-grave culture. The differences between the two, however, are limited to the burial rite, while pottery and elements of dress, weapons, and tools are identical (Czopek 1992).

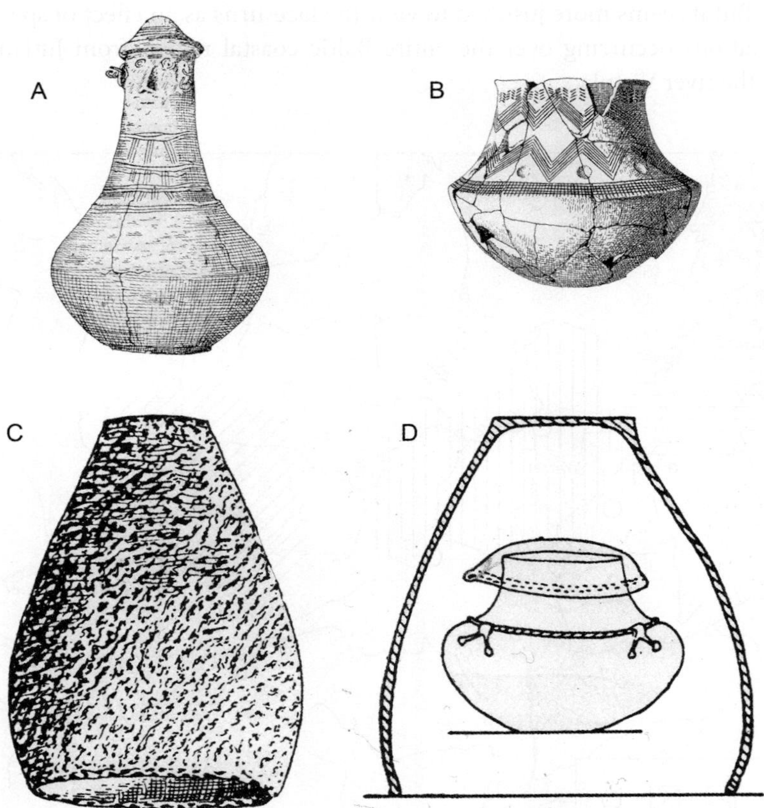

FIGURE 7.2 Early pre-Roman Iron Age pottery: (A) Face-urn of the Pomeranian culture (Rzadkowo, county Chodzież, Poland); (B) Urn of the West Balt barrow culture with rounded base (Piórkowo, county Braniewo, Poland); (C) Cloche of the Pomeranian culture (Szymborze, county Inowrocław, Poland); (D) Section of cloche-grave (Brachnówko, county Toruń, Poland).

Sources: A–C after Kostrzewski et al. 1965; D after Engel 1935

The West Balt Barrow Culture

Another group in indirect contact with the Hallstatt zone via the Pomeranian culture was the West Balt barrow culture (Okulicz 1967), located on the Sambian peninsula and in the Masurian lake region (Figure 7.1). Finds from archaeological sites attributed to this culture, especially bronze ornaments, as well as tools and weapons (some of which were already made of iron), closely resemble Pomeranian types. The West Balt barrows with stone settings, containing up to thirty urns, also recall sepulchral features of the Pomeranian culture and point to the existence of similar social structures. Vessels with bulbous bodies and long, cylindrical necks found in the barrows are morphologically similar to face-urns—the only clear difference lies in their rounded bases, which constitute a distinctive trait of West Balt pottery (Figure 7.2, B). Small fortified settlements on hilltops or built in shallow lacustrine bays, on platforms made of tree trunks, are another characteristic trait of the West Balt barrow culture.

The vessels with rounded bottoms became the basis for formulating a hypothesis concerning the origin of the West Balt barrow culture. Similar pottery found in the middle Dnieper region is attributed to the Milograd culture (Shadyra and Vyargey 1999: 29–112). Other shared features are barrows, albeit without stone settings, and a settlement model based on small hillforts. These common features have led to the West Balt barrow culture being considered an effect of the migration of Milograd population groups to the Baltic Sea region. The West Balt barrow culture population is also classified as a western faction of the Balts, which was the first to break away from the community of Balt-Slavs in the middle of the first millennium BC (Okulicz 1969). This hypothesis is nowadays treated with some caution: the evident Lusatian cultural traditions and very strong Pomeranian influences indicate beyond doubt that the West Balt barrow culture was in effect a synthesis of various cultural threads, the Milograd culture constituting just one of many elements. One can thus hardly consider the creators of the West Balt barrow culture as homogeneous West Balts—rather, this population appears to have been multi-ethnic, and its possible 'Baltization' may have occurred no earlier than in the late pre-Roman Iron Age.

La Tène Influences (500–100 BC)

Sites of both the Pomeranian and the West Balt barrow cultures feature imports from the Celtic or La Tène world to the south, mainly decorated, most commonly brooches and bracelets, but also iron tools: scythes and axe-heads with distinctive rectangular sockets. The interest of these groups in the territories north of the Sudeten and Carpathian mountains was probably driven by the same motives as the earlier Hallstatt culture: the 'gold of the north' (amber), available on the shores of the Baltic Sea.

Archaeological finds indicate beyond doubt that Celtic settlements progressed northward, beyond the Sudeten mountains (Figure 7.1). In Silesia there are typical La Tène cemeteries with inhumation burials rich in weapons, ornaments, and vessels made using a potter's wheel, a technique unknown to northern peoples at this date. Further north, there are traces of Celtic settlement in the Kujawy region, and Celtic groups also crossed the Carpathian mountains, reaching the upper Vistula and San rivers (Woźniak 1970; see also Chapter 37). The technical skill of the people who migrated to the Vistula, Warta, and Oder basins manifested itself in their ability to produce wheel-thrown pottery, as well as in their sophisticated technology of iron smelting (cf. Orzechowski 2012) and production of excellent quality weapons and tools. The wealth of finds from the settlement at Nowa Cerekwia in Silesia (Rudnicki 2014) leaves little doubt that this was a major regional centre with international connections, on a par with other large middle La Tène aggregations of a kind that developed throughout Celtic Europe at this time, such as Němčice in Moravia and Roseldorf in Austria.

The greatest difference between the Celtic incomers and the indigenous population seems, however, to have lain in their social system. This is often classified as a 'military democracy' (see Chapter 30), in the belief that the main political power in each community lay in the assembly of all free male warriors. War, which brought glory and spoils if it resulted in victory, was at the same time the only career path that permitted the gaining of wealth and authority in a community. Archaeologically detectable traces of this system are burials furnished with complete sets of weaponry resembling examples from the La Tène world: a long, double-edged sword, a spear, a shield with iron fittings, as well as spurs, which hint at a growing significance of cavalry. An additional element of identity was the torc, a neck ornament made of a thin bar of metal bent into a circle—usually bronze, but occasionally silver or even gold—worn by both men and women.

Social and cultural differences created a clear divide between the Celts and the indigenous inhabitants of the Vistula, Warta, and Oder basins. As mentioned, La Tène ornaments and iron tools also reached the Pomeranian culture and West Balt barrow culture populations, but no attempts were made to launch local production imitating these imports. One possible explanation for this failure may reside in the very different social system of the Celts. With its emphasis on individual military success, this will have been completely alien to the small communities of the two indigenous cultures, which emphasized their strong internal ties by building communal tombs. They were only compelled to depart from this traditional model by events that changed the face of central Europe in the third century BC.

Germanic Tribes in East Central Europe (250 BC–AD 50)

The issue of the presence of Germanic tribes in central Europe, especially its eastern part, used to provoke heated debate among archaeologists. Nowadays it is generally accepted that the first archaeological unit whose population can be considered Germanic with a high degree of certainty is the Jastorf culture, which formed on the lower Elbe and in Mecklenburg at the start of the early Iron Age (Figure 7.1; Müller 2000; Woźniak et al. 2013; Brandt and Rauchfuss 2014). Its characteristic feature was flat cremation cemeteries—often very large—the graves without stone settings, and containing urns with bulbous bodies, cylindrical necks, and flared rims, often decorated with semicircular lugs applied to the body. Relatively rare finds in the graves were elements of dress, usually bronze or iron pins with distinctively curved shafts, or iron hook clasps, sometimes found with iron rings, forming sets used to fasten belts.

In a late phase of the early pre-Roman Iron Age, the Jastorf culture found itself in the zone of Celtic influence (Brandt and Rauchfuss 2014)—brooches modelled on La Tène types appear in grave assemblages in place of traditional pins. A remarkable phenomenon was the appearance of so-called crown neck-rings, constituting a development of the Celtic torc.

Expansion and Influences of the Jastorf Culture in Central and South-Eastern Europe

In the third century BC, for obscure reasons, the population of the Jastorf culture began to expand towards the south and east. The main axis was the Elbe, which naturally oriented the migration in a southerly direction (Figure 7.3). However, this path was blocked by the Celts occupying territories north of the Danube. Thus, the migrant Germanic population of the Jastorf culture only reached the north-western edge of the Czech basin, where it formed the Podmokly-Kobily group (Mähling 1944). This was a local variant of the Jastorf culture, which over time adopted elements of La Tène culture, above all wheel-thrown pottery. Another trace of expansion of the Jastorf culture to the south and east is the Gubin group on the Nysa and middle Oder rivers (Domański 1975), indicating the movement of compact population groups from the middle Elbe region to the east.

Besides peripheral groups of the Jastorf culture, abundant testimonies of the migration of this population are found in the Warta and middle Vistula river basins (Machajewski 2004). They are almost exclusively relics of small, short-lived settlements, possibly rest stops of small population groups moving relatively quickly in a south-easterly direction. Similar scattered finds occur in the upper Dniester region, while further south, in the middle Dniester region, they form a distinct cluster of settlements and cemeteries distinguished as the Poieneşti-Lukaševka culture (Figure 7.3; Babeş 1992). Its clear parallels to the Jastorf culture, such as the presence of vessel forms similar to specimens from the western Baltic area, or characteristic objects such as the crown neck-rings just mentioned, leave no doubt that these relics represent a Germanic population.

The formation of the Poieneşti-Lukaševka culture in the late third to early second century BC was contemporary with the arrival of 'new' barbarians in the Black Sea region; the Scirii and Bastarnae were both identified by Roman historians as Germanic tribes. In the second and first centuries BC, the historical sources mention numerous raids by

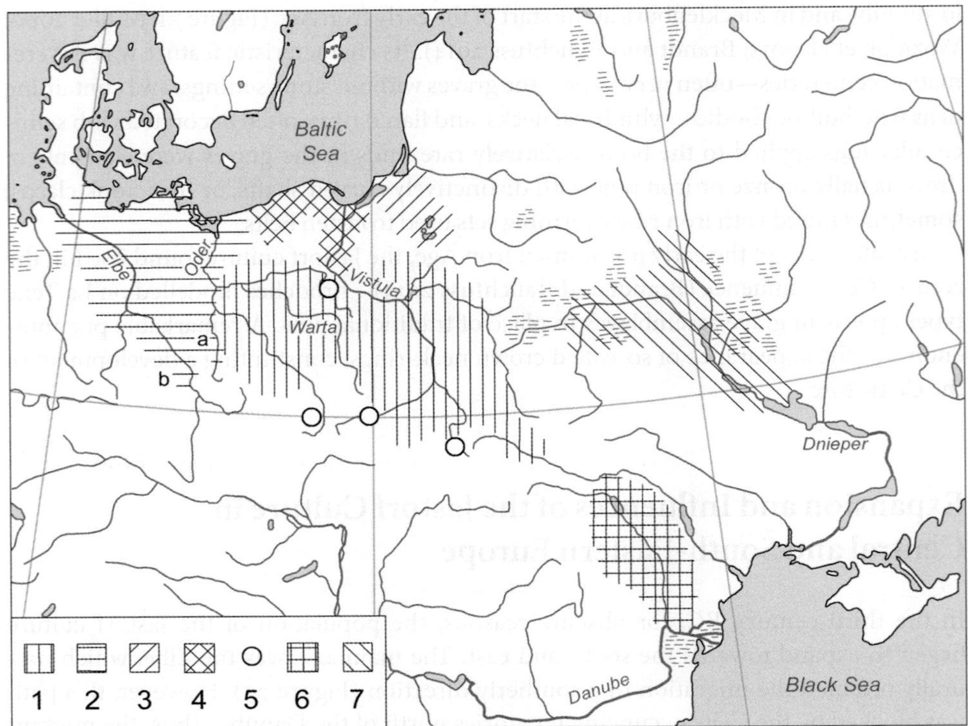

FIGURE 7.3 Late pre-Roman Iron Age cultural groupings in east central Europe: 1 Przeworsk culture, 2 Jastorf culture (a = Gubin group; b = Podmokly-Kobily group), 3 West Balt barrow culture, 4 Oksywie culture, 5 Celtic enclaves, 6 Poieneşti-Lukaševka culture, 7 Zarubincy culture.

the Bastarnae into the Balkans, from the Dniester region almost to the Adriatic coast—these are reflected in the archaeological record of the Poieneşti-Lukaševka culture by the presence of Thracian and Celtic objects from that area. By the mid-first century BC, in turn, Dacian raids led to depopulation of the territory of the Poieneşti-Lukaševka culture.

A significantly weaker and much more indirect echo of the Jastorf culture was the Zarubincy culture in the middle reaches of the Dnieper (Figure 7.3; Shadyra and Vyargey 1999: 232–289). It was more or less contemporary with the Poieneşti-Lukaševka culture, and the evident parallels between their material records seem to be the result of mutual contacts, as well as a shared tradition traceable to the Jastorf culture. For example, vessels of the Zarubincy culture are decorated with applied semi-circular lugs, similar to those of the Jastorf culture. In addition, carefully made and smoothed pottery and abundant metal objects (pins, brooches, belt buckles, spearheads) distinguish the Zarubincy culture from other cultures of the north-east European forest zone. Cemeteries of the Zarubincy culture feature cremation burials containing numerous vessels, metal ornaments, elements of dress, and weapons. They resemble the burial grounds in the Vistula, Oder, and Elbe basins, but are exceptional in this part of eastern Europe, whose inhabitants otherwise cultivated funerary practices that left no traces in the archaeological record. These differences constitute a sound basis for associating the emergence of the Zarubincy culture with an influence or even a migration of a part of the population from the west, namely from the lower Elbe and the western shores of the Baltic Sea.

Przeworsk Culture

The passage of 'foreigners' through the territory of the Pomeranian culture led to a crisis of the established social and cultural order, and compelled the local population to seek new solutions, or to adopt the ways of Celtic peoples. This brought technological progress, especially learning the highly sophisticated methods of smelting and forging iron, but above all the introduction of a new social structure in which warriors played a leading role. An effect of this process was the formation in the late pre-Roman Iron Age of the Przeworsk culture (Dąbrowska 1988a), whose territory encompassed Silesia, Greater Poland with Kujawy, and Mazovia (Figure 7.3). In various forms, the Przeworsk culture was to last until the end of the Roman Iron Age (for a summary of the archaeology, see Andrzejowski 2010).

Vast cemeteries in which almost all men were buried with weapons indicate that the population embraced so-called military democracy. Weaponry, especially long double-edged swords, matched La Tène models. Brooches too imitated La Tène examples, but with few exceptions they were made of iron, which makes these objects distinctive markers of the Przeworsk culture. Other distinguishing elements are vessels with faceted rims. The funerary customs of the Przeworsk culture are also notable: graves in the vast newly founded cemeteries, such as Dobrzankowo in Masovia, took the form of large rectangular pits filled with cremated human bones and charcoal from the funeral pyre (Figure 7.4). Many of the grave goods, which included elements of dress, weaponry (in male burials), and numerous (up to twenty) hand-made vessels, bear traces of burning and intentional damage.

During the earlier first century BC, the territory of the Przeworsk culture was significantly reduced. The entire western frontier on the middle Oder and lower Warta rivers also became depopulated at this period (Godłowski 1978). Meanwhile, sites far to the west, in the middle Elbe region and on the river Main, feature pottery with faceted rims typical of the Przeworsk culture (Dąbrowska 1988b: 156–167). It is therefore possible that there were migrant groups from the Przeworsk culture among the peoples living close to the Gaulish border.

Oksywie Culture

The late pre-Roman Iron Age also saw changes in the lower Vistula region. As in the territory of the Przeworsk culture, one can see the emergence of large flat-grave cremation cemeteries with pyre remains in pits and grave goods in the form of elements of

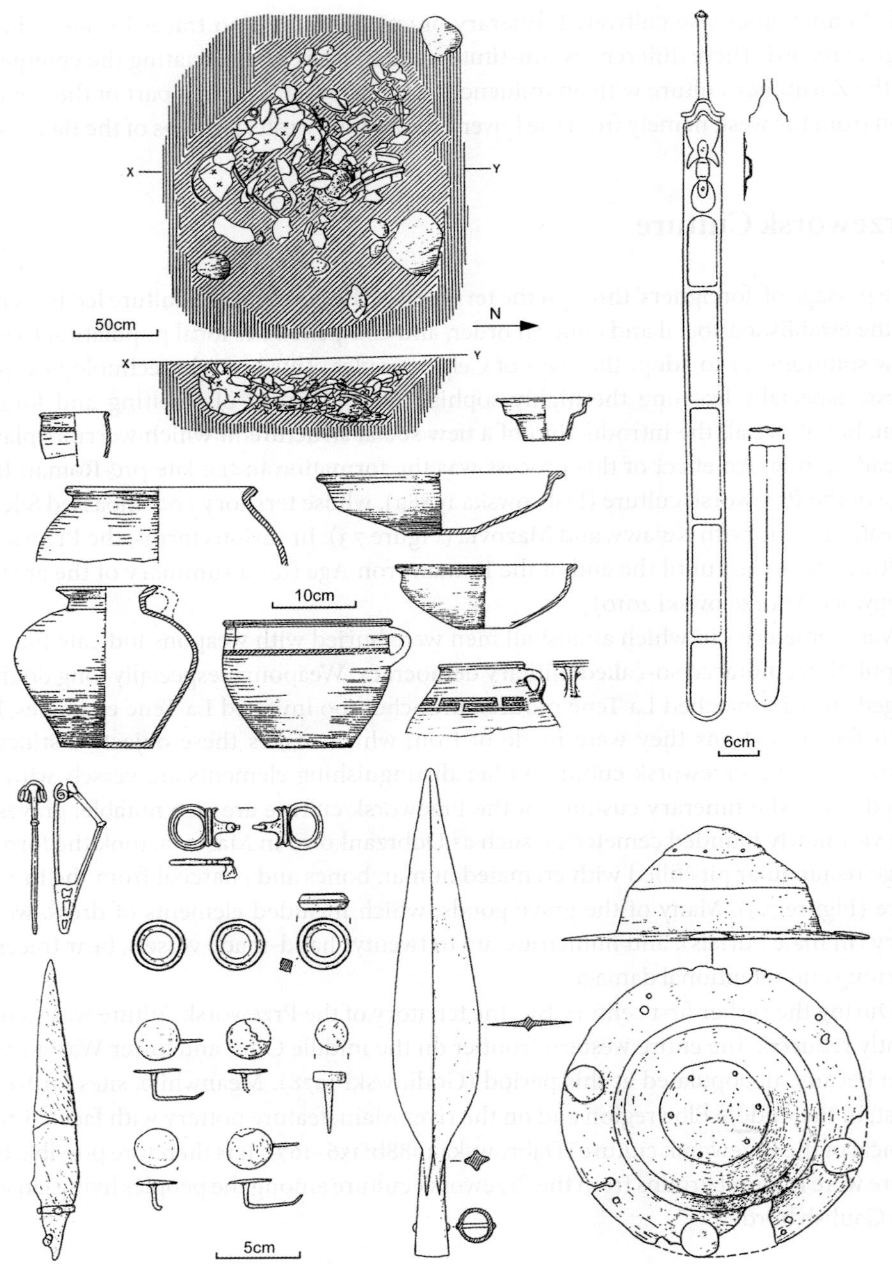

FIGURE 7.4 Late pre-Roman Iron Age cremation grave of the Przeworsk culture at Dobrzankowo (county Przasnysz, Poland).

Source: Okulicz 1971

dress and weaponry imitating La Tène models. There are also vessels with faceted rims, which resemble the pottery of the Przeworsk culture. All these markers point to significant influence from the Przeworsk culture, then occupying Greater Poland and Kujawy to the south. At the same time one can see a major impact of the Jastorf culture, which is apparent, for instance, in the widespread use of hook-clasps. Another peculiarity is the frequent occurrence of one-edged swords and javelin heads, which are otherwise exceptional in central Europe at this date. These characteristics have permitted the definition of the Oksywie culture (Dąbrowska 2003) in the lower Vistula region and the stretch of Baltic coast to the west (Figure 7.3). It probably formed somewhat later than the Przeworsk culture, in the developed late pre-Roman Iron Age (*c.*100 BC).

Towards the end of the late pre-Roman Iron Age, around the mid-first century BC, metal elements of women's belts are found in the Vistula delta region, for which parallels can only be found on Gotland. The belts are so distinctive that these finds should not be treated as imitations or imports, but as evidence for natives of that island reaching the lower Vistula region. On this basis, the Oksywie culture population can be considered a multi-ethnic community in which immigrants from Scandinavia played an increasingly important role (Bierbrauer 1994: 75–87).

The Oksywie culture played a singular role in the history of studies on the ethnogenesis of Germanic peoples. In the nineteenth and early twentieth centuries, it was believed to be the earliest material trace of the Burgundians. At that time the original location of this tribe was thought to have been Bornholm, on the grounds of its medieval name *Burgundarholmr*. As a result of the similarity of finds from Bornholm and the lower Vistula region, the formation of the Oksywie culture was believed to have been the effect of migration of the inhabitants of Bornholm to the lower Vistula—a conviction that subsequently found expression in the designation 'Burgundian culture' (cf. Bohnsack 1938). The current state of research offers no support for this hypothesis, however, as the similarities in archaeological material between Bornholm and sites of the Oksywie culture appear to reflect parallel cultural processes taking place throughout the entire Baltic Sea region in the late pre-Roman Iron Age.

The Roman Iron Age (50 BC–AD 400)

Towards the end of the first century BC, Rome engulfed territories along the upper and middle Danube, but the conquest did not sever all earlier ties: for example, brooches made in traditional La Tène style but using Roman methods of craftsmanship are found in the region, indicating beyond doubt that the native inhabitants of territories on the south bank of the Danube, at this point formally Romans, still ventured to the 'amber coast'.

Archaeologists' suppositions that Romans did indeed directly reach the Baltic shore find confirmation in classical texts. Pliny the Elder mentions an expedition organized in the last years of the Emperor Nero, *c.*AD 65, sent north in search of amber (*Natural*

History 37.11.3; cf. Kolendo 1981). The destination of this expedition lay at a distance of 600 Roman miles from the Imperial border on the middle Danube; it was *litora et commercia*, a coast that featured 'ports of trade', or centres for obtaining and further distributing amber. The expedition delivered an enormous amount of amber to Rome, which enabled the emperor to hold particularly spectacular gladiatorial games.

Of much greater importance for archaeologists and historians than the description of Nero's propagandistic success is the context in which the account of the 'amber expedition' was placed. It is clear that Pliny considered it relevant only because it was a state initiative that most likely generated a detailed written report describing the route and documenting the distance between the amber-rich coast and the Roman frontier. In turn, Pliny treated the very fact that Romans travelled to the 'Northern Ocean' as a fairly commonplace affair.

Lugiorum Nomen—The Guards of the Amber Route

A more important source is the detailed description of central European *Barbaricum* in Tacitus' *Germania*. According to this historian, to the north of the Marcomanni, who inhabited the Czech basin and with whom the Romans were familiar, was the 'Lugian league' (*Lugiorum nomen*)—most likely a political construct created to protect the amber route (*Germania* 43). The league united many tribes, but Tacitus names only the five 'mightiest' ones and includes very brief descriptions of just two. We thus learn that in the territory of the Nahanarvali there was a sacred grove that was also the federation's main cult centre, while the Harii carried black shields and were trained in nocturnal combat. It seems, however, that Tacitus has misinterpreted his sources, classifying different vocational groups as tribes: the Nahanarvali were most likely priests, and the Harii were warriors in charge of safety and order on the amber route.

The location of the 'Lugian league' given by Tacitus matches the territory of the Przeworsk culture in the early Roman Iron Age (Figure 7.5), permitting us to establish that its population was, at least in part, identifiable with the Lugians (Kokowski and Leiber 2003: 39–48, 77–183). This identification is corroborated to a degree by the archaeological evidence: the Przeworsk culture features some graves that take the form of a chamber with walls of stone or logs and that contain inhumation burials. These are a clear violation of the 'normal' funerary rite followed by the Przeworsk culture, in which cremation burials without stone settings were the rule, which points to an exceptional social status of the buried individuals. Their position is confirmed by very rich grave goods, which included abundant Roman imports, mainly metal and glass vessels, but not weapons, which were otherwise very common in Przeworsk culture burials. These traits permit us to interpret these funerary structures as tombs of an elite, most likely local chieftains and their families, as for example the four inhumations at Łęg Piekarski, in Greater Poland (Nowakowski 2001). The geographical focus of these so-called 'princely burials' is along a corridor connecting the Moravian Gate and the lower Vistula, pointing to the existence of a hierarchical social structure associated with the existence of a political organization guarding the 'amber road'. In general terms these high-status burials are part of a wider phenomenon of rich Roman Iron Age burials, extending across northern Germany and Denmark, which have come to be known as the Lübsow/Lubieszewo group after the burials in western Pomerania (Eggers 1950; Chapter 5).

Roman goods are also found on settlements of the Przeworsk culture. At Jakuszowice in southern Poland (occupied from the second century BC to the fifth century AD), Roman imports included fibulae, gold and silver ornamented jewellery, glass finger-rings and gaming pieces, bronze mirrors, samian vessels (*terra sigillata*), and silver coins (Godłowski 1986, 1991). Gold, silver, and bronze were all worked at the settlement, together with amber, as demonstrated by carving debris. Iron, lead, and tin were also processed there. The finds suggest that an elite family resided at Jakuszowice, and that the settlement may have been involved in shipping iron and amber west to the Roman provinces in exchange for luxury goods (Wells 1999: 246–247). Jakuszowice lies near the Holy Cross mountains (Góry Swietokrzyskie), where mining of high-grade iron ores was carried out throughout the late pre-Roman and Roman Iron Ages (Bielenin 1992; Hošek et al. 2011: 31–54). Hundreds of shaft furnaces for iron production have been discovered in the region, often set out in rows (e.g. Jeleniów, Stara Słupia); each

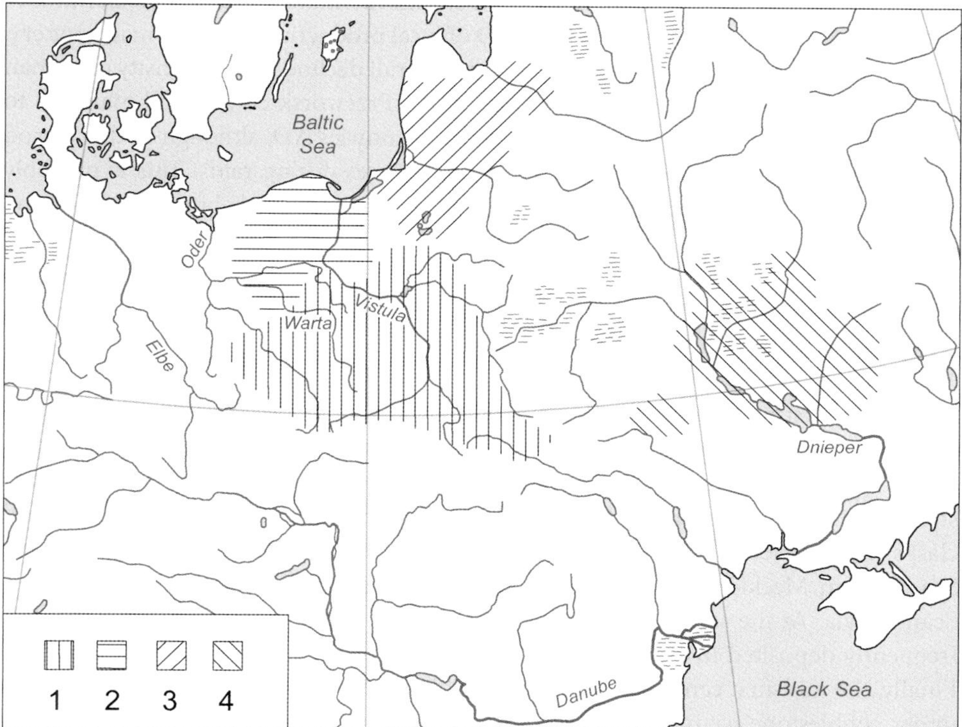

FIGURE 7.5 Early Roman Iron Age cultural groupings in east central Europe: 1 Przeworsk culture, 2 Wielbark culture, 3 West Balt circle, 4 Post-Zarubincy culture.

furnace was probably only used once, but production was clearly on an industrial scale (Todd 1975: 131–133). The important La Tène settlement at Nowa Cerekwia (see 'La Tène influences (500–100 BC)' earlier) was reoccupied at this period, after a break, but most Przeworsk culture settlements seem to have been small, unenclosed hamlets made up of a few houses, often semi-sunken.

A series of events changed the face of central Europe beyond the Imperial frontier and disrupted the operation of the 'amber road': the wars against the Marcomanni in AD 166–180, when nearly all barbarian tribes rebelled against Rome. Around the same time, probably as a result of the pressure on the Roman Empire, settlements of the Przeworsk culture population extended further south, crossing the Carpathians and reaching the upper Tisza, in the immediate vicinity of the Roman border. This coincides chronologically with the appearance in the textual record of the Germanic Hasdingi, a faction of the Vandals, in the Carpathian basin (Godłowski 1984). This may indicate that the disruption of the 'amber road' caused by the Marcomannic wars led to the disintegration of the Lugian league and the formation of a new tribal construct under a new name.

One may suppose that the Marcomannic wars also played an important role in the economic development of the Przeworsk culture. Large numbers of captives from the Danubian provinces of the Roman Empire were taken to the territory north of the Carpathians, bringing new technological skills with them: the most spectacular innovation was the launch in the third century AD of local production of wheel-made pottery. Despite the collapse of the 'amber road' and the overall decline in the intensity of Roman activity beyond the frontier, the population of the Przeworsk culture still managed to acquire Roman products in the third and fourth centuries AD, although in this period they were mostly spoils looted from Roman provinces during raids. This is probably how silver and glass vessels and Roman coins found in the princely burials of Wrocław-Zakrzów reached Silesia.

The Goths and the Wielbark Culture

In the early first century AD, a cultural change occurs in the region of the lower Vistula and the Baltic coast east of the river mouth. Cemeteries of the Oksywie culture grow richer in ornaments and dress accessories: bronze and silver brooches, bracelets with stylized snake heads, and necklaces of glass and amber beads fastened with S-shaped clasps. These objects imitate products that occur in the coastal zone around the Baltic Sea, both in Mecklenburg and on the Danish archipelago, as well as in continental Scandinavia. At the same time, weapons and iron objects in general are less and less frequently deposited in graves, and inhumations appear alongside cremation burials. Finally, the mid-first century AD saw the establishment of new cemeteries with graves under cobblestone paving and barrows within stone circles. These changes provide a basis for distinguishing a new archaeological unit, the Wielbark culture (Figure 7.5). Its formation in the area previously dominated by the Oksywie culture is largely attributable

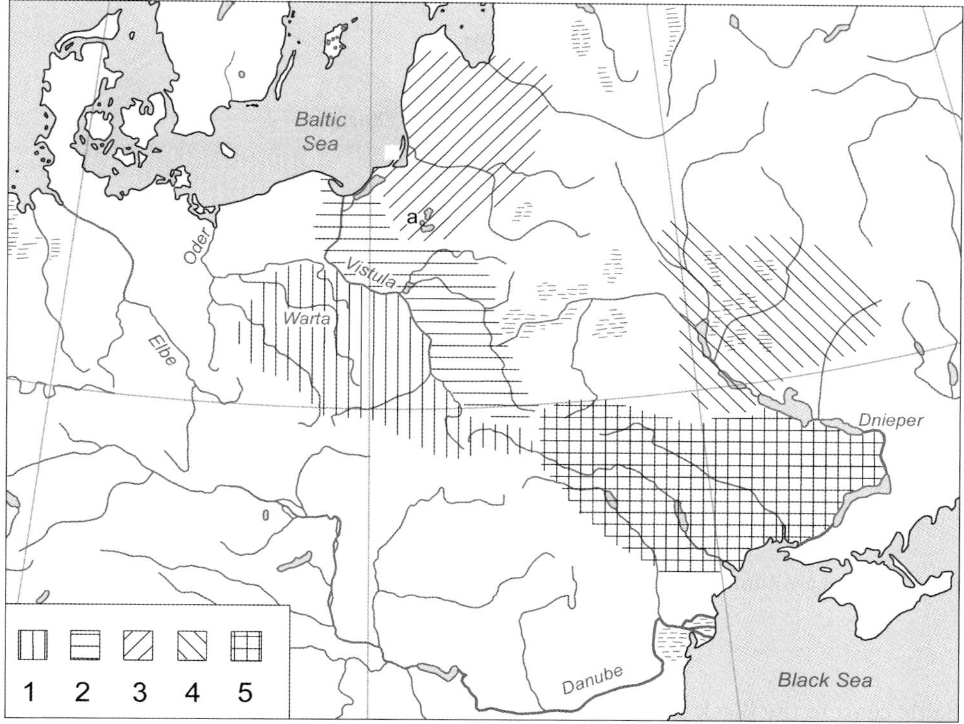

FIGURE 7.6 Late Roman Iron Age cultural groupings in east central Europe: 1 Przeworsk culture, 2 Wielbark culture, 3 West Balt circle (a = Olsztyn group in the Great Migration period), 4 Kiev culture, 5 Chernyakhov culture.

to Scandinavian influences, perhaps associated with the arrival of Scandinavian newcomers to the southern shore of the Baltic (Kokowski and Leiber 2003: 325–339).

Towards the end of the second and in the early third century AD, the territorial focus of the Wielbark culture changed decisively (Figure 7.6). Many cemeteries in Pomerania were abandoned, although a few carried on in the area nearest the Vistula, such as Elbląg (Figure 7.7); instead, burial grounds typical of the Wielbark culture now appeared east of the middle Vistula, in Mazovia and the Lublin upland, and even further south-east, in Volhynia. The same period saw the formation in southern Ukraine of the Chernyakhov culture (Figure 7.6), which displays close links to the Wielbark culture. These developments imply that a major group of the Wielbark culture may have abandoned its homeland and headed south, creating a vast settlement zone ranging from the Baltic to the Black Sea (Kokowski and Leiber 2003: 340–354).

This migration seems to find an echo in the ancient texts. Tacitus (*Germania* 44) and Ptolemy (*Geography* 3.5.20) are nearly unanimous in their reports, both locating the original late first-century AD homeland of the Goths on the south coast of the Baltic, specifically on the lower Vistula, in the territory of the Wielbark culture. The late antique historian Jordanes (*Getica* 26–29) mentions the passage of this group from its seat on the

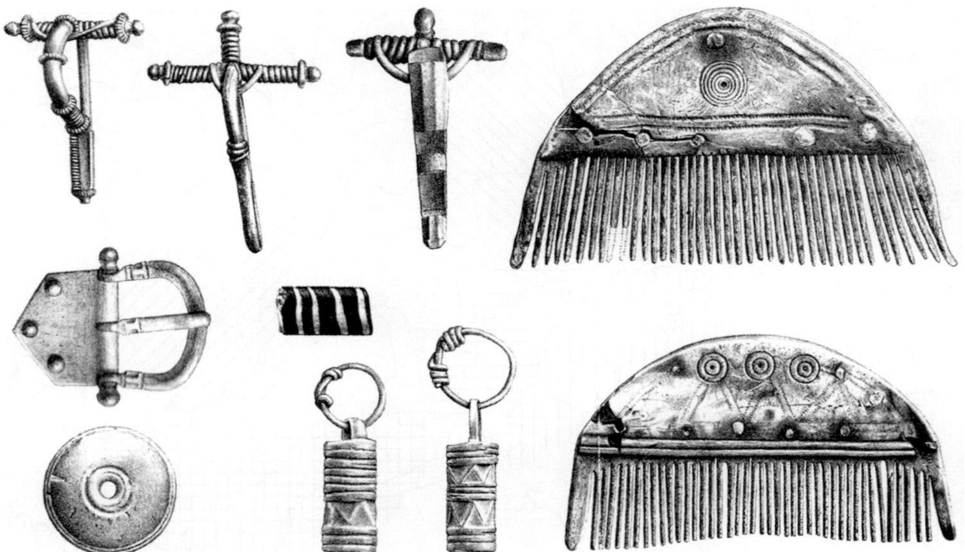

FIGURE 7.7 Late Roman Iron Age finds from the Wielbark culture cemetery at Elbląg (Poland).
Source: after Anger 1880

Baltic coast to the Black Sea, where they sacked Greek cities at the mouths of the Don, Dnieper, and Boh rivers. This remarkable convergence of texts and archaeology permits us to identify with some certainty the population of the Wielbark and Chernyakhov cultures as Goths (Bierbrauer 1994).

The Balts: Tribes at the End of the World

The eastern neighbour of the Goths in the territory of the Wielbark culture on the lower Vistula was a people Tacitus calls *Aestiorum gentes* (*Germania* 45), which suggests that the name was a general designation of several groups. The Aestii were reportedly the only people to collect amber on the Baltic beaches, which implies they were located on the Sambian peninsula, in the region where amber deposits were richest. According to Tacitus, although the homelands of the Aestii were located in the farthest reaches of *Barbaricum*, they did not differ in dress from other Germanic peoples. This is confirmed by the remarkable similarity of finds from the Sambian peninsula to material attributed to the neighbouring Wielbark culture. Sambian cemeteries contain inhumation burials under stone paving which are very similar to those of the Wielbark culture. A notable difference is the presence of weapons in the graves of the Aestii, while the Gothic rite excluded them from funerary assemblages. The Aestii also differed from the Goths and other Germanic tribes in language, permitting us to identify this population as Balts (Kokowski and Leiber 2003: 359–375).

The description of the Aestii in Tacitus' work indicates that despite the distance from the borders of the Empire, this people was well known to the Romans, most likely through their activity collecting and selling amber to Roman merchants. In the early Roman Iron Age, women from the Sambian peninsula began to wear belts with abundant fittings (e.g. Kovrovo; Figure 7.8), modelled on an element of dress attested for female inhabitants of the Danubian provinces of the Empire, no doubt as a result of these contacts.

The Alexandrian geographer Ptolemy also refers to regions near the Baltic coast. He does not mention the Aestii, but lists the Galindai (*Γαλινδαί*) and Sudinoi (*Σουδινοί*) as the south-eastern neighbours of the Goths (*Geography* 3.5.21). The correspondence of both ethnonyms with the names of Prussian tribes (Galindite and Sudowite; Peter von Dusburg *Chronicon terrae Prussiae* 3.3) vanquished by the Teutonic Knights permits us to locate both population groups in the Masurian lake region and identify them as Balts, perhaps two distinct branches of the multi-ethnic *Aestiorum gentes*. On the other hand, there are clear archaeological arguments in favour of distinguishing the inhabitants of the Masurian lake region from the Aestii: inhumation burials are lacking, and instead of influences of the Wielbark culture one can see the powerful impact of the Przeworsk culture, from which this population adopted its weaponry and the attire of male warriors (Kokowski and Leiber 2003: 359–375).

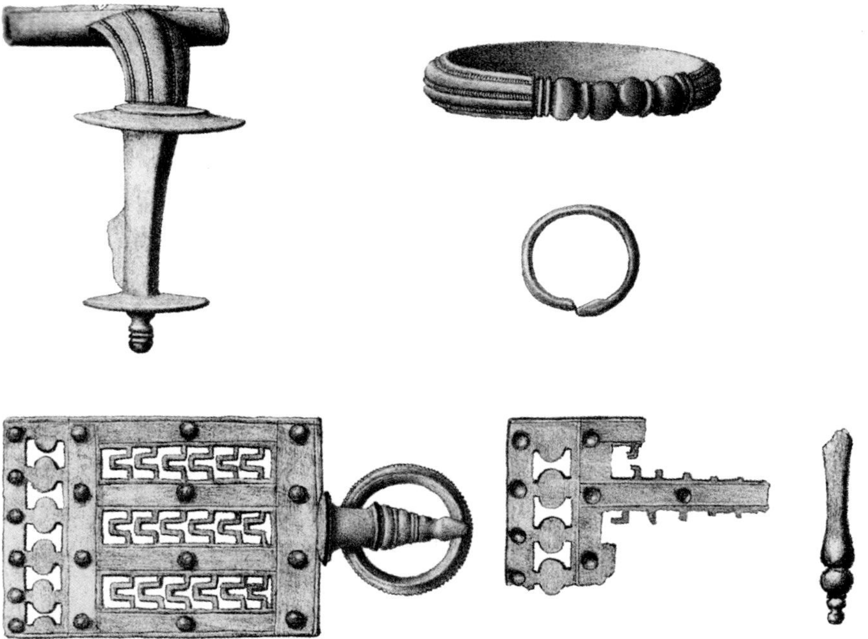

FIGURE 7.8 Early Roman Iron Age dress accessories from a female inhumation grave from the Sambian peninsula (Kovrovo, Kaliningrad district, Russian Federation).

Source: after Tischler and Kemke 1902

The Time of the Storm: The Great Migration Period (AD 400–600)

At the end of the fourth century AD, the inhabitants of the Vistula and Oder basins began to feel the effects of events taking place far to the south. The invasion of the Black Sea steppe zone by the Huns, and their vanquishing of the hitherto dominant Ostrogothic state caused more wars and large-scale migrations, including, in the early fifth century, the westward shift of the Vandals. In turn, the death of Attila and the fall of his empire were followed by another phase of Germanic population movement south into the Carpathian basin.

Migration to the West and the End of Germanic Settlement in the Oder and Vistula Areas

Towards the end of the fourth century, evidence of settlement becomes increasingly sparse in the northern part of the territory occupied by the Przeworsk culture, although major economic and political centres in the southern part of the region still flourished. One such example was the substantial settlement at Jakuszowice in southern Poland (see '*Lugiorum nomen*—the guards of the amber route' earlier), which had numerous workshops producing wheel-thrown pottery and metal objects at this period (Godłowski 1986). Next to this settlement was a princely burial containing, among other things, a bow with gold fittings, a symbol of authority among the Huns. This was presumably still a local seat of power in the late Roman Iron Age, which nonetheless recognized the supremacy of the powerful Hun state in the Carpathian basin.

At the same time, a change occurred in the burial rite in part of the territory of the Przeworsk culture, in the form of cemeteries where cremated remains of the dead were scattered on the surface. Cemeteries with inhumation burials also appear, perhaps evidence for the brief appearance of new population groups in the territory vacated by the Przeworsk culture. By the turn of the fifth and sixth centuries AD there is no longer any trace of settlement that can be associated with the Przeworsk culture (Kokowski and Leiber 2003: 185–201).

The fate of the Wielbark culture in the Vistula and Oder basins was slightly different. Here there is evidence for a marked depopulation and contraction of its territory, which by the mid-fifth century AD was reduced to the lower Vistula region. A hoard of some 10 kg of bronze ornaments and elements of dress from Łubiana in north-west Poland illustrates this process of depopulation, as these objects were undoubtedly looted from graves in abandoned cemeteries of the vacated territories of the Przeworsk and Wielbark cultures (Mączyńska 2009). Inhabitants of the lower Vistula region maintained contacts with the Mediterranean world, leading to their appearance in the written record as the

Vidivarii, who were evidently a conglomerate consisting of relics of various Germanic peoples (Jordanes *Getica* 36). Around the mid-sixth century AD, settlement drawing on Roman Iron Age traditions disappeared also from this area (Godłowski 1980).

The Arrival of Slavonic Peoples

The abandonment of the Oder and Vistula basins in the late fifth and early sixth centuries AD opened this region to Slavonic expansion from the middle Dnieper region. The territory in which the Zarubincy culture developed in the late pre-Roman Iron Age came under Sarmatian raids in the later first century BC, becoming severely depopulated. Small, scattered population groups cultivating the tradition of the Zarubincy culture survived there through the early Roman Iron Age (the so-called post-Zarubincy culture), but the third century AD saw the formation of a new archaeological unit, the Kiev culture (see Figures 7.5 and 7.6), which presented a completely new set of characteristics (Shadyra and Vyargey 1999: 290–298). Its typical dwelling was a small, quadrangular, semi-subterranean blockhouse with an oven in one corner. Its pottery was typical kitchenware—somewhat carelessly made S-profiled pots, as well as occasional wheel-made vases and bowls imported from the Chernyakhov culture. One may suppose that tableware was made of wood, as is typical in the forest zone of eastern Europe. Fewer than twenty cremation burials are known from the territory of the Kiev culture, indicating that after cremation the remains of the deceased were either scattered or placed in organic containers on the ground surface, leaving no traces in the archaeological record. The characteristics of the Kiev culture are almost entirely consistent with the cultural model of tribes referred to as Slavs in textual sources of the fifth and sixth centuries AD (Godłowski 2005).

The link between the Kiev culture and the Slavs is confirmed by late antique sources, according to which the Ostrogoths on the Black Sea subjugated their northern neighbours, the Antes, in the fourth century AD (Jordanes *Getica* 119, 247). This fits in well with the clear cultural influence exerted on the Kiev culture by the Gothic Chernyakhov culture. In the mid-sixth century AD the Antes were unambiguously classified as Slavs by Byzantine authors (Jordanes *Getica* 34–35), although most likely at that time this population also included groups of Iranian nomads (cf. Curta 2010: 53–82).

The destruction of the Ostrogothic state by the Huns was followed in the first half of the fifth century AD by destabilization of the political situation on the middle and lower Danube. Together with the turmoil that ensued after the collapse of Attila's state, it caused westward and southward movements of local Germanic populations, paving the way for Slavonic expansion. Most likely, the Slavs already occupied territories stretching as far as the eastern and northern slopes of the Carpathian mountains in the late fifth century AD, filled the Vistula and Oder river basins during the sixth century, and subsequently marched on to the Elbe, carrying with them the cultural model derived from the Kiev culture. The Slavonic expansion brought about a complete change in the face of central Europe, heralding the formation of new cultural communities and political structures in the early Middle Ages.

The 'Quiet Corner': The Balts and the Olsztyn Group (AD 450–650)

Despite its location on the fringe of the territory affected by the great migrations, the Masurian lake region and the Sambian peninsula to the north, appear to have experienced no major population changes in the fifth and sixth centuries AD. Apart from minor disturbances, cultural continuity is observable in this region from the Roman to the Migration period. Stability of settlement is also indicated by the uninterrupted use of cemeteries established in the late Roman Iron Age.

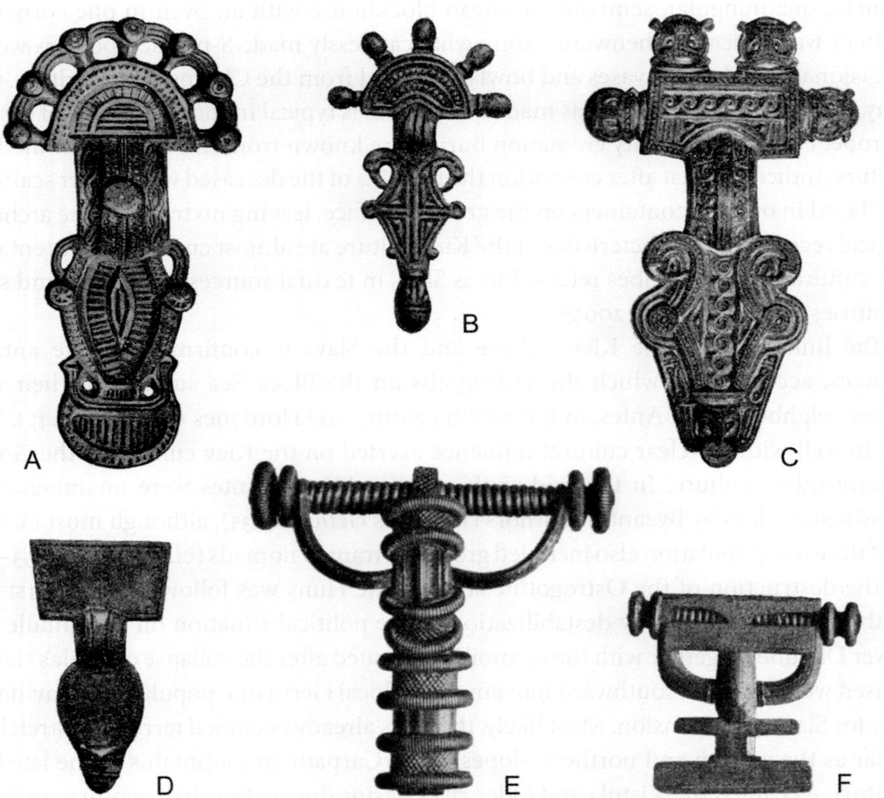

FIGURE 7.9 Migration period brooches from a cemetery of the Olsztyn group (Tumiany, county Olsztyn, Poland).

Source: after Engel 1935

This stability seems to have led to the emergence of the Olsztyn group in the Masurian lake region in the sixth century AD (cf. Curta 2010: 31–52). This small area most likely played an important role as a 'quiet corner', serving as a potential foothold in trans-European contacts. Such a role is implied by imports reaching this area from virtually every part of Europe: products of Merovingian states on the Rhine and upper Danube dominate, but there is no lack of objects from the Black Sea region, the lower Danube, and Scandinavia. The most distinctive finds attributed to the Olsztyn group are bow fibulae (e.g. from Tumiany; Figure 7.9, A–D), first imported and later produced locally in simplified form.

In the course of the following century, the stabilization of Slavonic settlement in the Vistula basin deprived the Olsztyn group of its unique position. At the same time the proximity of the Slavs, who dominated central Europe at the time, resulted in the gradual adoption of Slavonic cultural traits by the Balts from the Masurian lake region. These influences are observable in pottery, but above all in the funerary customs, as no later than the start of the eighth century AD the cemeteries of the Olsztyn group fell into disuse, with the local population instead adopting the Slavonic custom of disposing of the cremated remains of the deceased in a manner that left no traces in the archaeological record. This period, which saw the formation of the tribal structure of medieval Prussia, definitively closes a cultural development cycle with roots going back to the early Iron Age.

References

Andrzejowski, J. 2010. 'The Przeworsk culture: A brief story (for the foreigners)', in U. Lund Hansen and A. Bitner-Wróblewska (eds) *Worlds Apart? Contacts Across the Baltic Sea in the Iron Age*: 1–52. Copenhagen/Warsaw: Det Kongelige Nordiske Odlskriftselskab/Państwowe Muzeum Archeologiczne.

Anger, S. 1880. 'Das gemischte Gräberfeld auf dem Neustädter Felde bei Elbing'. *Zeitschrift für Ethnologie* 12: 106–125.

Babeş, M. 1992. *Die Poieneşti-Lukaševka-Kultur: Ein Beitrag zur Kulturgeschichte im Raum östlich der Karpaten in den letztem Jahrhunderten vor Christi Geburt*. Saarbrücker Beiträge zur Altertumskunde 30. Bonn: Habelt.

Bielenin, K. 1992. *Starożytne górnictwo i hutnictwo żelaza w Górach Świętokrzyskich [Ancient Mining and Iron Smelting in the Holy Cross Mountains]*. Kielce: Kieleckie Towarzystwo Naukowe.

Bierbrauer, V. 1994. 'Archäologie und Geschichte der Goten vom 1.–7. Jahrhundert'. *Frühmittelalterliche Studien* 23: 51–171.

Bohnsack, D. 1938. *Die Burgunden in Ostdeutschland und Polen während des letzten Jahrhunderts v. Chr.* Quellenschriften zur ostdeutschen Vor- und Frühgeschichte 4. Leipzig: Kabitzsch.

Brandt, J., and B. Rauchfuss (eds). 2014. *Das Jastorf-Konzept und die vorrömische Eisenzeit im nördlichen Mitteleuropa*. Hamburg: Archäologisches Museum.

Bukowski, Z. 1977. *The Scythian Influences in the Area of Lusatian Culture*. Wrocław/Warsaw/Kraków/Gdańsk: Zakład Narodowy im. Ossolińskich.

Curta, F. (ed.) 2010. *Neglected Barbarians*. Studies in the Early Middle Ages 32. Turnhout: Brepols.

Czopek, S. 1992. *Południowo-wschodnia strefa kultury pomorskiej*. Rzeszów: Muzeum Okręgowe.

Dąbrowska, T. 1988a. 'Bemerkungen zur Entstehung der Przeworsk-Kultur'. *Praehistorische Zeitschrift* 63, 1: 53–80.

Dąbrowska, T. 1988b. *Wczesne fazy kultury przeworskiej: Chronologia—zasięg—powiązania*. Warsaw: Państowe Wydawnictwo Naukowe.

Dąbrowska, T. 2003. 'Oksywie-Kultur', in *Reallexikon der Germanischen Altertumskunde* 22: 45–54. Berlin/New York: Walter de Gruyter.

Domański, G. 1975. *Studia z dziejów środkowego Nadodrza*. Wrocław: Zakład Narodowy im. Ossolińskich.

Dzięgielewski, K. 2010. 'Expansion of the Pomeranian culture in Poland during the early Iron Age: Remarks on the mechanism and possible causes', in K. Dzięgielewski, M. S. Przybyła, and A. Gawlik (eds) *Migration in Bronze and Early Iron Age Europe*. Prace Archeologiczne 63: 173–196. Kraków: Księgarnia Akademicka.

Eggers, H.-J. 1950. 'Lübsow, ein germanischer Fürstensitz der älteren Kaiserzeit'. *Prähistorische Zeitschrift* 34–35: 58–111.

Engel, C. 1935. *Aus ostpreußischer Vorzeit*. Königsberg in Preußen: Gräfe und Unzer.

Gediga, B., A. Grossman, and W. Piotrowski (eds). 2016. *Europa w okresie od VIII wieku przed narodzeniem Chrystusa do I wieku naszej ery*. Biskupin-Wrocław: Muzeum Archeologiczne w Biskupinie.

Gedl, M. 1980. 'Studia nad periodyzacją kultury łużyckiej w południowej części Śląska'. *Archaeologia Polski* 25, 1: 79–129.

Gedl, M. 1991. *Die Hallstatteinflüsse auf den polnischen Gebieten in der Früheisenzeit*. Prace Archeologiczne 48. Kraków: Uniwersytet Jagielloński.

Godłowski, K. 1978. 'Zu Besiedlungsveränderungen in Schlesien und den Nachbarräumen während der jüngeren vorrömischen Eisenzeit', in M. Gedl (ed.) *Beiträge zum Randbereich der Latènekultur*: 110–125. Warsaw/Kraków: Państwowe Wydawnictwo Naukowe.

Godłowski, K. 1980. 'Zur Frage der völkerwanderungszeitlichen Besiedlung in Pommern'. *Studien zur Sachsenforschung* 2: 63–106.

Godłowski, K. 1984. '"Superiores barbari" und die Markomannenkriege im Lichte archäologischer Quellen'. *Slovenska Archeologia* 32, 2: 327–350.

Godłowski, K. 1986. 'Jakuszowice, eine Siedlung der Bandkeramik, älteren Bronzezeit, jüngeren vorrömischen Eisenzeit, römischen Kaiserzeit und der frühen Völkerwanderungszeit in Südpolen'. *Die Kunde* 37: 109–132.

Godłowski, K. 1991. 'Jakuszowice: A multi-period settlement in southern Poland'. *Antiquity* 65: 662–675.

Godłowski, K. 2005. *Frühe Slawen in Mitteleuropa: Schriften von Kazimierz Godłowski (herausgegeben von Jan Bemmann und Michał Parczewski)*. Studien zur Siedlungsgeschichte und Archäologie der Ostseegebiete 6. Neumünster: Wachholtz Verlag.

Harding, A., J. Ostoja-Zagórski, J. Rackham, and C. Palmer. 2004. *Sobiejuchy: A fortified site of the early Iron Age in Poland*. Warsaw: Institute of Archaeology and Ethnology Polish Academy of Sciences.

Harding, A., and W. Rączkowski. 2010. 'Living on the lake in the Iron Age: New results from aerial photographs, geophysical survey and dendrochronology on sites of Biskupin type'. *Antiquity* 84: 386–404.

Hošek, J., H. Cleere, and Ľ. Mihok. (eds). 2011. *The Archaeometallurgy of Iron: Recent Developments in Archaeological and Scientific Research Dedicated to Professor Radomír Pleiner*. Prague: Insititute of Archaeology of the ASCR.

Kaczanowski, P., and J. K. Kozłowski. 1998. *Najdawniejsze dzieje ziem polskich*. Kraków: Fogra.

Kneisel, J. 2012. *Anthropomorphe Gefäße in Nord- und Mitteleuropa während der Bronze- und Eisenzeit: Studien zu den Gesichtsurnen—Kontaktzonen, Chronologie und sozialer Kontext*. Studien zur Archäologie in Ostmitteleuropa 7, 1–2. Bonn: Habelt.

Kokowski, A., and C. Leiber (eds). 2003. *Die Vandalen: Die Könige, die Eliten, die Krieger, die Handwerker*. Nordstemmen: Trigena.

Kolendo, J. 1981. *A la recherche de l'ambre baltique: L'expédition d'un chevalier romain sous Néron*. Studia Antiqua 1. Warsaw: Wydawnictwa Uniwersytetu Warszawskiego.

Kostrzewski, J., W. Chmielewski, and K. Jażdżewski. 1965. *Pradzieje Polski*. Wrocław/Warsaw/Kraków: Zakład Narodowy im. Ossolińskich.

Machajewski, H. 2004. *Kultura jastorfska na Nizinie Wielkopolsko-Kujawskiej*. Poznań: Stowarzyszenie Naukowe Archeologów Polskich.

Mączyńska, M. 2009. 'Der frühvölkerwanderungszeitliche Hortfund aus Łubiana, Kreis Kościerzyna (Pommern)'. *Bericht der Römisch-Germanischen Kommission* 90: 7–481.

Mähling, W. 1944. *Die Bodenbacher Gruppe: Zur Frage der latènezeitlichen elbgermanischen Landnahme in Nordböhmen*. Abhandlungen der Deutschen Akademie der Wissenschaften in Prag, Philosophisch-Historische Klasse 15. Prague: Verlag der Deutschen Akademie der Wissenschaften Prag.

Müller, R. 2000. 'Jastorf-Kultur', in *Reallexikon der Germanischen Altertumskunde 16*: 43–55. Berlin/New York: De Gruyter.

Niesiołowska-Wędzka, A. 1991. 'Procesy urbanizacyjne w kulturze łużckiej', in J. Jaskanis (ed.) *Prehistoryczny gród w Biskupinie: Problematyka osiedli obronnych na początku opoki żelaza*: 57–80. Warsaw: State Archaeological Museum.

Nowakowski, W. 2001. 'Łęg Piekarski', in *Reallexikon der Germanischen Altertumskunde 19*: 75–77. Berlin/New York: De Gruyter.

Okulicz, J. 1971. 'Cmentarzysko z okresu późnolateńskiego i rzymskiego w miejscowości Dobrzankowo, pow. Przasnysz'. *Materiały Starożytne i Wczesnośredniowieczne* 1, 127–170.

Okulicz, Ł. 1967. 'Studies on the culture of West Balts tumuli in the early Iron Age'. *Archaeologia Polona* 11: 35–57.

Okulicz, Ł. 1969. 'Uwagi o etnogenezie zachodniego odłamu Bałtów'. *Archeologia Polski* 14, 2: 391–416.

Orzechowski, S. 2012. 'The role of Celts in popularising iron smelting in the Polish territories'. *Notize Archologiche Bergomensi* 20: 107–116.

Parducz, M. 1974. 'Die charakteristischen skythischen Funde aus dem Karpatenbecken und die damit verbundenen ethnischen Fragen', in B. Chropovský (ed.) *Symposium zu Problemen der jüngeren Hallstattzeit in Mitteleuropa*: 311–336. Bratislava: Vydavateľstvo Slovenskej Akadémie Vied Veda.

Rudnicki, M. 2014. 'Nowa Cerekwia—the middle La Tène centre of power north of the Carpathians', in J. Čižmářová, N. Venclová, and G. Březinová (eds) *Moravské Křižovatky: Střední Podunají mezi pravěkem a historií*: 421–436. Brno: Moravské Zemské Muzeum.

Shadyra, V. I., and V. S. Vyargey (eds). 1999. *Arkhealogiya Belarusi, Vol. 2: Zhalezny vek i rannyae syarednyavechcha*. Minsk: Belaruskaya Navuka.

Tischler, O., and H. Kemke. 1902. *Ostpreußiche Alterthümer aus der Zeit der großen Gräberfelder nach Christi Geburt*. Königsberg: Wilh. Koch.

Todd, M. 1975. *The Northern Barbarians 100 BC–AD 300*. Oxford: Blackwell.

Wells, P. S. 1999. *The Barbarians Speak: How the Conquered Peoples Shaped Roman Europe*. Princeton: Princeton University Press.

Woźniak, Z. 1970. *Osadnictwo celtyckie w Polsce*. Wrocław/Warsaw/Kraków: Zakład Narodowy im Ossolińskich.

Woźniak, Z., M. Grygiel, H. Machajewski, and A. Michałowski. 2013. *The Jastorf Culture in Poland*. British Archaeological Reports International Series 2579. Oxford: Archaeopress.

CHAPTER 8

CENTRAL EUROPE

CAROLA METZNER-NEBELSICK

INTRODUCTION

CENTRAL Europe is traditionally regarded as the home of Iron Age research, principally on account of the mid-nineteenth-century discovery of the extraordinary sites at Hallstatt in Austria and La Tène in Switzerland. This chapter focuses on the zone extending from eastern France to western Hungary, and from the Alps to the North European Plain (Figure 8.1). This effectively equates to the core of the Hallstatt cultural sphere, and in terms of modern geography corresponds to central and southern Germany, Austria, Switzerland, and the Czech Republic, as well as parts of Hungary, France, Poland, and Slovenia.

The early/Hallstatt Iron Age (*c.*800–450 BC) and later/La Tène Iron Age (*c.*450–50 BC) mark the first periods in Europe when ethnic labels are habitually applied to specific groups. These names were used by classical writers, but we do not know what peoples living in the region called themselves, and the attribution of ethnic terms to areas or cultures with no literary sources of their own remains highly controversial (Collis 2003). The Hallstatt inhabitants of Switzerland, south-west Germany, and eastern France are commonly regarded as early Celts. The argument is based partly on Herodotus, who wrote that the river Istros (Danube) rose among the Celts (*Histories* 2.33). Since the source of the Danube is in south-west Germany, the Hallstatt culture in this area has been associated with the historic Celts.

Regional diversity is a prominent feature of central Europe's Iron Age cultural landscape, not least because of its varied topography and terrain, ranging from prime agricultural lowlands in major river valleys, such as those of the Danube, the Rhine, and their tributaries, via upland valleys and lakes, to inhospitable mountains. For the first time in European history, a significant difference developed between the literate city states of the Mediterranean and the largely tribally organized societies of central Europe. While iron ore occurs virtually everywhere and could be exploited without the need for long-distance networks like those of the Bronze Age, exchange was nevertheless a key part of

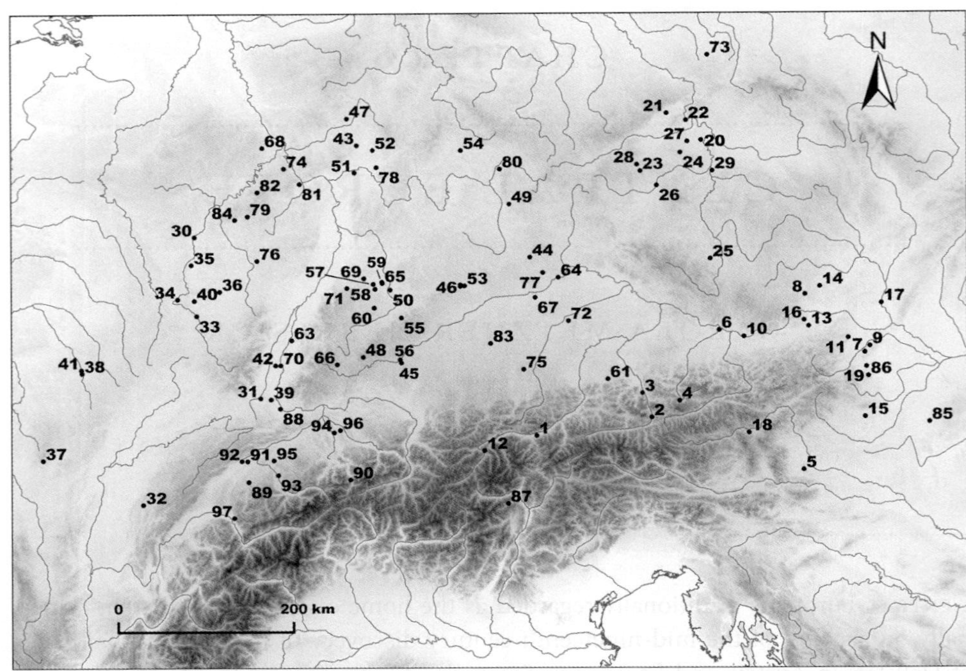

FIGURE 8.1 Map of principal Iron Age sites in central Europe. *Austria*: 1 Ampass-Demlfeld, 2 Bischofshofen-Pestfriedhof, 3 Dürrnberg, 4 Hallstatt, 5 Kleinklein, 6 Linz-St Peter, 7 Loretto, 8 Maiersch, 9 Mannersdorf, 10 Mitterkirchen, 11 Mödling, 12 Piller Sattel, 13 Pottenbrunn, 14 Roseldorf, 15 Schandorf, 16 Statzendorf, 17 Stillfried, 18 Strettweg, 19 Zagersdorf. *Czech Republic*: 20 Chřín, 21 Duchcov, 22 Lovosice, 23 Manětín-Hrádek, 24 Mšecké Žehrovice, 25 Němčice, 26 Nynice, 27 Stradonice, 28 Vladař, 29 Závist. *France*: 30 Basse Yutz, 31 Britzgyberg, 32 Chavéria, 33 Crévéchamps, 34 Gondreville, 35 Marly, 36 Marsal La Digue, 37 Mont Beuvray, 38 Sainte-Colombe, 39 Sierentz, 40 Tomblaine Le Pré Chenu, 41 Vix, 42 Wolfgantzen. *Germany*: 43 Bad Nauheim, 44 Berching-Pollanten, 45 Bettelbühl, 46 Bopfingen, 47 Dünsberg, 48 Egesheim, 49 Ehrenbürg, 50 Fellbach-Schmiden, 51 Frankfurt-Stadtwald, 52 Glauberg, 53 Goldberg, 54 Großeibstadt, 55 Heidengraben, 56 Heuneburg, 57 Hirschlanden, 58 Hochdorf, 59 Hohenasperg, 60 Holzgerlingen, 61 Holzhausen, 62 Ipf, 63 Kappel, 64 Kelheim-Alkimoennis, 65 Kleinaspergle, 66 Magdalenenberg, 67 Manching, 68 Mayen, 69 Mühlacker, 70 Münsterberg, 71 Neuenbürg, 72 Niedererlbach, 73 Niederkaina, 74 Pfalzfeld, 75 Pöcking, 76 Reinheim, 77 Riedenburg-Untereggersberg, 78 Rodenbach, 79 Schwarzenbach, 80 Staffelberg, 81 Waldalgesheim, 82 Wederath-Belginum, 83 Wehringen-Hexenbergle, 84 Weiskirchen. *Hungary*: 85 Somlóvásárhely, 86 Sopron-Burgstall. *Italy*: 87 St Walburg-Ulten. *Switzerland*: 88 Basel-Gasfabrik, 89 Châtillon-sur-Glâne, 90 Erstfeld, 91 Ins, 92 La Tène, 93 Münsingen-Rain, 94 Unterlunkhofen-Bärhau, 95 Urtenen, 96 Ütliberg, 97 Villeneuve.

Drawing: R. Salisbury for author

elite social practices throughout the Iron Age. Much of the region came under Roman domination in the century following Julius Caesar's conquest of Gaul, but north of the Danube, the Iron Age continued uninterrupted through the early centuries AD, albeit subject to extensive exchange across the Roman frontiers (Todd 1987; Wells 1999, 2013).

The Early Iron Age (800–450 BC): Terminology, Chronology, Spheres

The term 'Hallstatt' is applied in multiple ways: as a chronological period and synonym for the early Iron Age in central Europe, and as a cultural concept or type site. Although lending its name to the period, as we know today, the Hallstatt cemetery is an exceptionally rich burial site associated with proto-industrial salt mining, and cannot be regarded as typical of society at large. The community that buried its dead there often included abundant metal grave goods, reflecting both regional identity and wide-ranging connections with other parts of Europe, such as northern Italy, Bohemia, Slovenia, and the Pannonian basin (Kern et al. 2008; Dörrer 2002).

Today a distinction is made between a west and an east Hallstatt culture. The western zone is characterized by wagon graves, sword graves, inhumation burials, geometric pottery designs and, later, by princely graves, fortified hilltop sites, and gold ornaments. Features of the eastern zone include plastic ornament on pottery, figurative art, cremation burials, battleaxes, and defensive armour (Müller-Scheeßel 2000: maps 1–2). These traits are widely regarded as the material manifestation of shared norms for the representation of status and prestige as well as regional identity. For a long time, Hallstatt archaeology focused on burials, with research on settlements concentrated on fortified sites, and regional differences were diagnosed largely from grave goods, while in the Czech Republic there has always been more emphasis on settlement archaeology (Chytráček and Metlička 2004). Nowadays development-led excavations are fast expanding our knowledge of large and small settlements across the whole region.

A century ago, Paul Reinecke (reprinted 1965) created the first widely recognized framework for the Bronze and Iron Ages in central Europe. His scheme, which divided both Hallstatt and La Tène each into four stages labelled A–D, is still widely used. The former spans the later Bronze Age and the early Iron Age, with Hallstatt C and D belonging to the Iron Age. These were later subdivided by Kossack into Hallstatt C1–C2 and D1–D2 based on his work in Bavaria (Kossack 1959) and by Zürn for south-west Germany into three subphases D1–D3 employing brooch typo-chronology (Zürn 1942; Mansfeld 1973; Trachsel 2004). Initially, the absolute dating rested on links with the Graeco-Etruscan world, but radiocarbon dating (although still of restricted utility for the period 800–400 BC due to the so-called Hallstatt plateau) and dendrochronology have made important contributions, notably in establishing the existence of an early phase of Hallstatt C in the early eighth century BC (Pare 1991, 1998, 1999; Friedrich and Hennig 1995, Hennig 2001).

The Western and Eastern Hallstatt Spheres

Barrow cemeteries are the most characteristic burial feature of the entire Hallstatt area. Kossack (1959) remains the best account of mortuary practices in southern Bavaria, but even in this benchmark region our understanding is far from adequate, as much of the data comes from old excavations. North of the Danube, the Altmühl valley is well researched (Nikulka 1998; Schumann 2015: 45–109; Augstein 2015), along with cemeteries in Franconia and western Bavaria (Torbrügge 1979; Hoppe 1986, 2005; Ettel 1996; Hughes 1999, 2001). Thuringia (Simon 1972) and Hesse (Schumacher 1972–1974) form the northern border of the Hallstatt zone. At the Frankfurt-Stadtwald cemetery in Hesse (Fischer 1979), the ostentatious tumulus 1 grave 12, a burial of a sword-bearer and wagon driver with horse harness and a set of bronze drinking vessels, includes one of the earliest (Hallstatt C1) southern imports north of the Alps—an Italian bronze drinking bowl (*phiale*; Figure 8.2).

In the central eastern Alps, the cemeteries of the salt mining sites at Hallstatt and Dürrnberg have been extensively studied (e.g. Kromer 1959; Hodson 1990; Moosleitner et al. 1974; Wendling and Wiltschke-Schrotta 2015). Many questions remain concerning the integrity of the grave groups excavated at Hallstatt in the nineteenth century, but ongoing excavations have revealed more than eighty new graves, adding fascinating details

FIGURE 8.2 Italian imported bronze bowl from Frankfurt-Stadtwald, tumulus 1, Grave 12
Photo: Archäologisches Museum Frankfurt

of ceramic grave goods and stone-lined chambers (Kern et al. 2008). The Dürrnberg offers a rather different picture to the crowded Hallstatt cemetery. Several tumulus groups have been defined (Wendling and Wiltschke-Schrotta 2015: 9) around the fortified settlement of the Ramsaukopf (Irlinger 1995). Most of the Dürrnberg burials date to the late Hallstatt and early La Tène period, in contrast to Hallstatt, which declined as a salt mining site after Hallstatt D1. Other cemeteries in the central eastern Alps offer a picture of different cultural traditions (Lippert and Stadler 2009; Moosleitner 1992; Stöllner 1996, 2002). Knowledge of sites in the Inn valley and along the Danube into Upper Austria is still limited (Lang 1998), but the tumulus cemetery of Mitterkirchen (Schumann 2015: 137–143) and larger flat grave cemeteries, such as Linz-St Peter (Adler 1965), show affinities to regions further down the Danube. Along its tributary, the Enns, close to Linz, an imaginary border can be drawn between the western and eastern Hallstatt zones.

The Hallstatt culture in Switzerland is also still largely an archaeology of graves (Kurz 1997; Müller-Scheeßel 2013), and includes several cemeteries excavated under modern conditions (Lüscher 1993; Müller and Lüscher 2004). In the upper Rhine valley, some richly equipped barrows have been investigated in Alsace (Plouin 2012). Alsace-Lorraine is one of the few regions where open settlements have been excavated on a large scale, including the site at Crévéchamps in the Moselle valley (Koenig 2016). To the north, the Hunsrück-Eifel forms the north-western limit of the Hallstatt world. Rich in iron ore, this hilly region with its many small valleys has a high density of small hillforts and barrow cemeteries with distinctive local pottery forms and female dress accessories, which continued in use well into the middle La Tène period (Haffner 1976; Nakoinz 2005; Hornung 2008; Schneider 2012).

Bohemia was a core part of the western Hallstatt zone. This prominence carried on into the La Tène period, when Bohemia was one of the major centres for early Celtic art and later the home of the Boii, hence its modern name (Karwowski et al. 2015). In the earlier Iron Age, it was divided into several subregions. During Hallstatt C–D1, most of Bohemia belonged to the Bylany group and the Tumulus group of the western Hallstatt culture (Michálek and Chytráček 2013),[1] whereas the Silesian-Platěnice group in the north-east and the Billendorf/Białowice group north of the Ore mountains in Brandenburg, Saxony-Anhalt, and western Poland formed parts of the Lusatian culture (Vokolek 1999; Koutecký and Vokolek 2013; Venclová 2013: 13–18). Cemeteries of the Billendorf group contained many hundreds of cremation burials; their large size is a result of an unusually long-lived attachment to place. They probably served only one or a few villages. Analysis of the large cemetery at Niederkaina in Saxony has provided numerous insights into the religious beliefs and rituals that underpinned the cremation rite (Nebelsick 2001, 2016: 41–72; Puttkammer 2003).

As noted, the river Enns effectively divides the western and eastern Hallstatt zones. The Alpine piedmont between Lower Austria, northern Burgenland, south-west Slovakia, and north-west Hungary was home to the flat grave cemeteries and tumuli of the distinctive Kalenderberg group (Nebelsick 1996, 1997). In Burgenland, huge barrow cemeteries such as Schandorf offer a glimpse into a landscape of funerary monuments that extends into western Hungary (Czajlik et al. 2012). In Styria and Carinthia, large tumulus cemeteries are again the norm, with clusters around hillforts (Dobiat 1980; Teržan 1990; Egg 1996; Egg and Kramer 2005; Tomedi 2002). Moravia, western Slovakia, western Hungary (Patek 1993), eastern and central Croatia (Metzner-Nebelsick 2002, 2017a), and northern Bosnia also formed part of the eastern Hallstatt zone, although sometimes displaying stronger connections with the Balkans or Transylvania.

Mortuary Practices in the Hallstatt World

The most prominent Hallstatt monument type is the burial mound or tumulus. Mounds can be seen as forms of status representation of the people entitled to such burial, and as an expression of an ancestor cult. In the preceding Urnfield period (1300–780 BC) flat cremation cemeteries were the norm. This pattern changed in the eighth to seventh centuries BC, when many burial grounds were newly founded or in some cases continued in use, but now with barrows instead of flat graves.

South-Central Germany

The steppe-based lifestyle of semi-nomadic groups inhabiting the eastern Carpathian basin from the ninth century BC onwards had a noticeable impact on the formation of the Hallstatt culture in Bavaria and other areas (Kossack 1954; Metzner-Nebelsick 2002). The typical bridled horse equipment for wagons was modelled on east European prototypes. The disruptions that affected the Carpathian basin in the ninth and eighth centuries BC (see Chapter 14) were probably caused by multiple factors, setting in motion a chain reaction that extended into central Europe. A cooler, wetter climate (Maise 1998), over-exploitation of resources such as wood, and groups of migrating steppe nomads may all have undermined economic systems and political structures, causing the late Bronze Age elites to lose power. New ways of perceiving the role of rulers may have helped new families to ascend to power.

The most distinctive features of Hallstatt tumuli are large rectangular burial chambers, roughly 3 x 3 or 4 x 5 m in size, sometimes with their timber walls preserved (Biel 1985; Hennig 2001; Müller-Scheeßel 2013). Underground chambers are common in some areas (Kossack 1970); elsewhere, they were at ground level (Ettel 1996). Where stone was available, chambers were protected by a stone covering. Cremation and inhumation are both attested. The cremated bones were mostly scattered in heaps inside the chamber. Again, regional differences are apparent. In Bavaria the ratio of cremations to inhumations was roughly even at first (Kossack 1959: 119; Hennig 2001), but inhumation became most common in Hallstatt D.

The two Hallstatt C cemeteries at Großeibstadt in Franconia are renowned for their wagon burials beneath mounds (Kossack 1970: 44–61; Wamser 1981; Pare 1992). The Großeibstadt I tumulus cemetery has no fewer than seven graves with below-ground rectangular burial chambers containing four-wheeled wagons or at least a double set of horse-gear, the latter either purely symbolic or the only remains of a wagon without any metal fittings. In barrow I, the deceased was laid on the wagon with his sword next to him. Horse gear for two horses and a yoke were also deposited; horses themselves were rarely buried in graves (Kmeťová 2013). A set of thirty-three ceramic vessels was packed into the southern part of the grave to provide the dead warrior with an everlasting feast in the afterlife with symbolically present guests. The importance of the dead warrior was further emphasized by a set of two plate-like sheet-bronze bowls and a conical necked amphora, probably containing drink (Kossack 1970: pls 40–41). Animal bones represent the remains of a meat offering. Such drinking and eating sets are a ubiquitous feature of Hallstatt C burials. Kossack stressed the similarity with graves of the Bylany group in Bohemia and suggested that a caste of warriors with wide-ranging contacts was the driving social force at the start of the period. Male dominance may be suspected given the lack of rich female graves in Hallstatt C1 and a wider difficulty of discerning female dress accessories at this date north of the Alps.[2] The latest wagon burial at Großeibstadt I dates to Hallstatt D1, indicating a use-life of around 150 years for the cemetery, and confirming its interpretation as an elite burial ground.

If burials beneath mounds were long seen as the dominant grave type in south-central Europe, the 1980–1982 excavations in the larger Großeibstadt II cemetery have revealed a more complex picture. The forty-three burials included not only rectangular graves of the elite, but also cremation graves between the eight barrows, and inhumation graves without mounds. The coexistence of different grave types implies that individuals of different status, who were not entitled to the same mortuary rites, were buried alongside the elite (Fries 2005). Another important new feature of Großeibstadt II is the presence of elite female graves. Cremation burials with modest grave goods, apart from urns, were also found between the barrows at Riedenburg-Untereggersberg in the Altmühl valley (Nikulka 1998).

How large the Hallstatt tumulus cemeteries were originally is hard to say, as many barrows have been destroyed. Groups of ten to twenty-five are the most common, but in areas with less intensive agriculture, cemeteries can contain from seventy to a hundred barrows, as at Pöcking, south of Munich.[3] Around Lake Starnberg, some 720 barrows are recorded from fifty-two cemeteries (Uenze and Lang 2013: 127); the mounds vary from 5 to over 20 m in diameter. Hennig (2001) has emphasized the standardized way in which wooden burial chambers were constructed in Bavarian Swabia. The inhumations were placed in the centre or in the western part of the chamber, whereas the four-wheeled wagon was always placed in the western half, with sword and horse-gear to the south-west. Normally there were two groups of pottery, the first of large vessels with conical necks in which drink for the hereafter or an afterlife banquet was stored, together with drinking bowls. These were usually placed in the eastern part of the chamber opposite the wagon, whereas large plates or platters were located along the north or northwestern wall.

Tumulus 8 at Wehringen in Swabia is dated by dendrochronology to the early eighth century BC. The small wagon is of late Urnfield type with bronze-sheathed wheels, but the tomb and the associated equipment, such as the bronze Gündlingen sword, are of Hallstatt type (Pare 1987: 191–192, 1992). The grave contained pottery drinking and dining sets for four people, each with a large storage vessel covered by a lid with a drinking bowl inside, two larger bowls, and a plate, apart from one set which had another large bowl instead of a large plate (Hennig 2001: pls 107–110). The set associated with the dead individual comprised only a serving bowl, and instead of a ceramic bowl, the large vessel contained a rare sheet-gold bowl (Figure 8.3). Fewer than ten drinking bowls of gold or silver are known from the central European Iron Age. This bowl, however, may never have been used, since the embossed gold sheet would have been very fragile, emphasizing the special status of the Wehringen burial.

The dominant status item of Hallstatt C was the iron-clad wagon with four large wheels. In male graves, the wagons were combined with swords as the other main status symbol; in Hallstatt D, the sword was replaced by a short sword or dagger.[4] Variations in wagon construction indicate regional traditions, especially in Hallstatt D (Pare 1992). Knowledge of iron-clad wagons probably spread from the Near East to Italy and thence across the Alps (Kossack 1971). Hallstatt C wagon graves are concentrated in Bavaria

FIGURE 8.3 Bowl of embossed sheet gold from tumulus 8, Wehringen-Hexenbergle near Augsburg. The Wehringen bowl was found inside a large pottery vessel. It is the only metal vessel among a pottery banqueting set and is the oldest gold vessel from a Hallstatt culture grave. The burial chamber is dendro-dated to 778 ±5 BC.

Photo: M. Eberlein, Archäologische Staatssammlung München

and Franconia (up to the river Main) as well as in Bohemia; in Hallstatt D the custom spread west to Baden-Württemberg, eastern France, western Switzerland, and the middle Rhine and Moselle regions (Pare 1987: fig. 1), but almost disappeared in Bavaria.

The first graves of high-status women occur in central Austria in Hallstatt C, and slightly later in Bavaria, as at Niedererlbach (Figure 8.4) and Großeibstadt II. In Hallstatt D, more female wagon graves are found in the west, including a large group in eastern France, attesting to the changing role of women in a more stratified society (Metzner-Nebelsick 2009; Chapter 34).

South-West Germany

The numerous rich graves between the upper Rhine and the Swabian Alb are the best-known feature of Hallstatt D2–D3. The number of burials in south-west Germany is vast. Some cemeteries started in the Bronze Age and continued until the end of the Hallstatt period (Reim 1988; Bräuning et al. 2012), but the majority began in late Hallstatt C or Hallstatt D1, with the introduction, around 600 BC, of new concepts for the representation of status in the form of wagon burials and large sets of metal vessels. Many burial mounds in south-west Germany were constructed differently from those in Bavaria, which may reflect a more lineage-based social organization. Indeed, some large mounds were cemeteries in their own right. In the centre of the mound was a rectangular wooden chamber *c.*5 m across; smaller secondary burials with less elaborate inventories were grouped concentrically around it. The dominant Hallstatt D burial rite was inhumation.

The largest 'kin group' burial mound (*Familiengrabhügel*) is the Magdalenenberg near Villingen (Spindler 1971–1980, 1999; Teržan 1990; Oelze et al. 2012). Grouped around the 8 x 6.5 m wooden chamber were 126 inhumations of both sexes, all dating to Hallstatt D1. The concept of an enlarged family—that is, a lineage or patronage relationship between the person in the central grave and those in the secondary burials—is convincing. The central chamber was built in *c.*616 BC and was robbed in *c.*500 BC, when the mound was no longer used for burial. The number of graves at the Magdalenenberg is matched only by the huge family mounds found in the Slovenian landscape of Dolenjsko (Gabrovec 1966: Beilage 1; Gabrovec and Teržan 2010; Križ 2000; Tecco Hvala 2012), although unlike in south-west Germany, the south-east Alpine family barrows were integrated into cemeteries of varying sizes.

Other single barrows or small barrow cemeteries in the Hallstatt west contain central graves, but usually had few or no secondary burials. The function of barrows as places of ancestral cults is best documented by the Hirschlanden tumulus, where a life-size stone statue of a warrior was found at the foot of the barrow (Zürn 1970: fig. 23). This statue is one of the few known images of a late Hallstatt warrior (Frey 2002a). The man is depicted in heroic nakedness—as reported by Roman authors regarding the Celts in battle—adorned only with symbols of his status, including a dagger tucked into a belt, a torc around his neck, and a conical hat. The last was probably made of birch bark, like

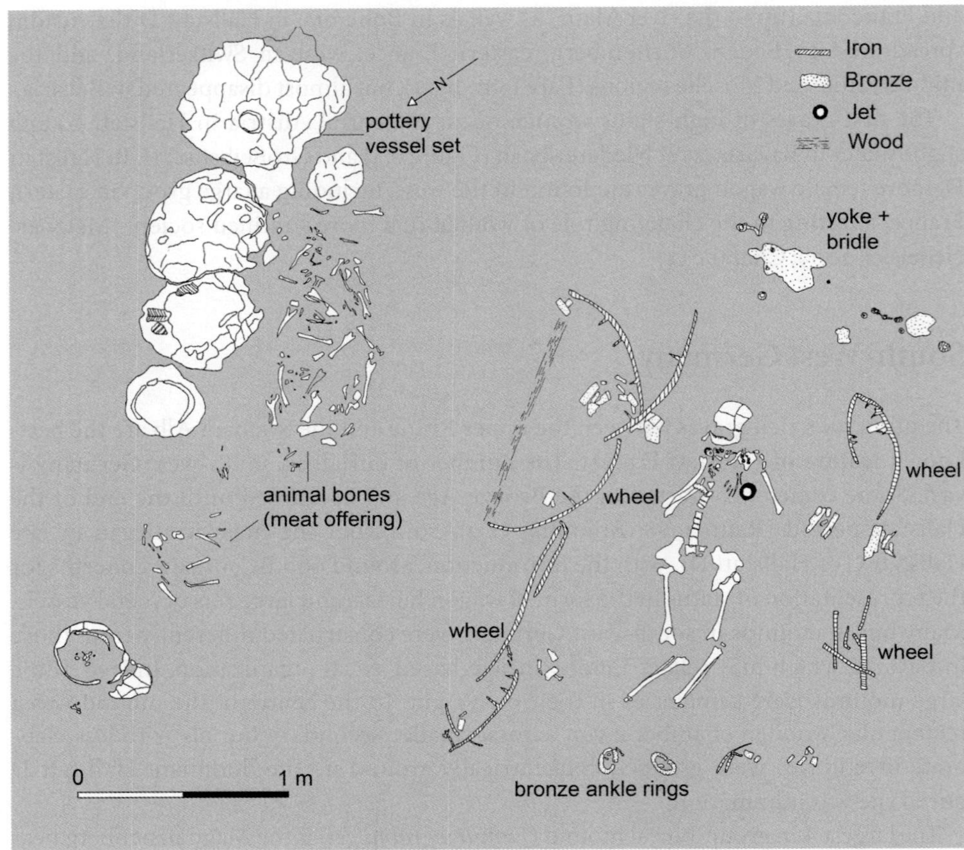

FIGURE 8.4 Hallstatt period wagon burial of a woman in the barrow cemetery of Niedererlbach near Landshut, Lower Bavaria, grave 1998/11.

Drawing: S. Peisker, after Engelhardt and Häck 1999: 46, fig. 32

the example from Hochdorf (Biel 1985: pl. 15). The face of the warrior is strangely abstract, because a mask covers his facial features.

Central graves were also occupied by women in the late Hallstatt period, as at Mühlacker in Württemberg, pointing to their role as heads of lineages in a matrilineal sense (Pauli 1971). Rich female burials occur in greater number around the Heuneburg (Riek 1962; Zürn 1987; Kurz and Schiek 2002). The Bettelbühl grave, dated by dendrochronology to 583 BC, contained a woman adorned with precious, partly Etruscan, gold and amber jewellery (Krausse et al. 2017). Horse gear portrays her as a rider. A second woman without regal attire was buried with her. The burial in a nearby barrow of an infant girl wearing gold ear-rings of Etruscan type reinforces the idea that power and status were hereditary and that women played important roles in Hallstatt societies (Krausse 1999, 2006, 2010; Krausse et al. 2017). The importance of elite women can also be deduced from the presence in female graves of status indicators for activities in public spaces, such as wagons and metal drinking sets (Metzner-Nebelsick 2009).

The contrast to Hallstatt D1 burials of the late seventh and early sixth centuries BC is illustrated by Kappel near the Rhine in Baden, which marks a turning point in funerary status display (Dehn et al. 2005). The central grave in tumulus 3, which was nearly 40 m in diameter and surrounded by a palisade, is a wagon burial of early Hallstatt D1 date with an extraordinary set of bronze vessels (Figure 8.5). The deceased wore a bronze neck-ring and dragon-type and bow fibulae—both originally Italian types. A dagger and two iron spears denote him as a warrior. Bronze neck-rings of Iron Age date are found mainly in south-west Germany, in the middle Rhine-Moselle region, and in east central France (Dehn et al. 2005: fig. 21). The drinking set is not only the largest of the period, but was deposited in a special way. A Kurd-type *situla* 1.09 m high was placed in a large bronze handled cauldron. Inside the *situla* were nine small ribbed bronze buckets (*ciste a cordoni*), a small Kurd-type *situla*, two bronze jugs, two bronze footed bowls, and a large drinking horn, of which only the elaborate metal mouthpiece and handle survived. The complexity of the ceremony in which this set was to be used may be deduced from the pottery vessels that augmented the bronze set. Two large knives to cut meat indicate an aspect of symbolic duplication, but also the presence of meat offerings or symbolic feasting in the grave.

Thus, by the last quarter of the seventh century BC, the west Hallstatt elites were developing intensive contacts with regions south of the Alps, particularly northern Italy. They adopted a southern style of dressing by wearing Italian fibulae as fasteners, and incorporated elaborate Italic drinking and eating customs into their burial rites and probably their lifestyles. The prestigious character of the mostly imported vessels is evident and reflects the ability of the deceased person to entertain a large party of guests, family, or people of comparable rank. Status representation had gained a new and more public facet.

This pattern finds its most iconic expression in the Hochdorf burial, near Stuttgart, erected around 530 BC, and situated not far from the Hohenasperg, a prominent plateau and probably an important Iron Age hilltop settlement, now largely destroyed by later buildings (Balzer 2010). Excavated between 1978 and 1982, the Hochdorf burial is one of the richest in Europe, with numerous gold dress accessories and a unique selection of bronze artefacts and imports; detailed studies of the grave and its contents have transformed our knowledge of the late Hallstatt period (Biel 1985; Krausse 1996; Bieg 2002; Koch 2006; Hansen 2010). The mound is nearly 60 m in diameter, with a stone *krepis* (revetment) and a wooden chamber underneath a massive stone mantle.

In contrast to the earlier grave at Kappel, at Hochdorf the deceased man was adorned with gold objects, including a belt plaque, coverings for his pointed shoes of Etruscan fashion, serpentine fibulae, and a torc. His iron dagger in a bronze sheath was covered by a second, richly ornamented gold sheath. The body was clad in luxurious textiles dyed with *Kermes vermilio* imported from the Mediterranean (Banck-Burgess 1999; Chapter 26). His body was laid on a bronze couch with a figuratively ornamented back, supported by eight female figures on wheels, placed along the western wall of

FIGURE 8.5 Banqueting equipment comprising different types of bronze vessels from the central grave of tumulus 3, Kappel am Rhein. An additional drinking horn, possibly signifying the owner of the grave, as well as two large knives for cutting meat are not on the picture.

Photo: Manuela Schreiner, Archäologisches Landesmuseum Baden-Württemberg

the chamber. The mobile couch was probably locally made, but with the expertise of craftworkers from northern Italy, possibly Lombardy (Hoppe 2012). Unlike the gold dress accessories, which were specially produced in a workshop at the burial site, the couch had been in use for some time. At its foot was a large cauldron of Mediterranean type with three bronze lions on the rim, each of a different design, one of local production. A gold bowl and a bright blue cloth with an embroidered edge had been placed on the rim.

Opposite the dead man, along the eastern wall of the chamber, stood a four-wheeled wagon on top of which a variety of objects were piled, including bronze dishes, a quiver of arrows, an iron axe, a butcher's knife, and an antler pick. These objects depicted the deceased as host, hunter, and a person entitled to perform blood sacrifice (Pauli 1988–1989; Krausse 1999). All the objects were hidden from the eyes of spectators and attendants by various kinds of textiles wrapped round them. Hooks found close to the walls indicate that they too were covered in cloth. Eight drinking horns with gold and bronze mounts were hung on the southern wall, together with a ninth made of iron and adorned with gold mounts, imitating a bull's horn, which belonged to the deceased. This huge horn weighed more than 2.7 kg. According to one interpretation, the prince and his eight companions are represented by the nine horns. This number corresponds to the number of buckets in the Kappel grave, and to the vessels in the princely grave of the Kröllkogel at Kleinklein in Austrian Styria (see 'The eastern Hallstatt sphere and situla art'). Religious symbolism may thus be implicit in the composition of Hallstatt grave assemblages.

Debate over the status of the deceased Hochdorf man is ongoing (Schier 2010), but ancient DNA analysis suggests that he was related to other high-ranking individuals in the area via the maternal bloodline (Hummel et al. 2005). Krausse's argument for hereditary status among privileged families (see earlier) is supported by the recurrent combination of symbols of power such as weapons, gold rings, and wagons associated with ritual activities or duties of the deceased. Political power and ritual competence are signs of status, which, in accord with the classical sources, we can liken to that of a prince rather than a mere chieftain. The gold attire of the Hochdorf ruler and other wearers of gold neck-rings of Hallstatt D2–D3 and La Tène A date (Schönfelder 2002) arguably represents a new symbol of power absent from Hallstatt D1 graves such as Kappel. We may assume that the status of individuals of the highest social standing had changed and that they could now dispose of symbolic artefact types hitherto reserved for sacrifice to the gods in hoards. After their death, members of the princely elite became or mutated into heroic ancestors, entombed beneath giant monuments for eternity, and commemorated in an almost god-like manner (Metzner-Nebelsick 2017b).

Eastern France and Switzerland

The predominant burial monuments in eastern France are tumuli. In Hallstatt C, the most noteworthy attributes of the male elite were swords placed next to the warrior as well as parts of wagons and horse harness. In Alsace, tumuli of differing dimensions are often grouped in large cemeteries (Plouin 1996). Extended inhumation dominated, although in Burgundy and central France, cremation and inhumation are attested in some tumuli (Piningre 1996; Milcent 2004). In Hallstatt C, inhumation burials were comparatively modestly equipped, with swords the supreme status marker of a male sword-fighting elite. This may indicate a more regionally organized society with village chiefs at the top of the hierarchy, as in the late Bronze Age. Social continuity is indicated by uninterrupted use of barrow cemeteries such as Chavéria in Jura from the ninth to the seventh century BC (Vuaillat 1977; Milcent 2004: 118–134).

A more complex social organization is evident in Hallstatt D, with the appearance in eastern France of wagon graves in barrows containing inhumations of men and women (Mohen et al. 1987; Piningre 1996; Brun and Chaume 1997). These culminated in the remarkable cluster of female burials lavishly equipped with gold dress accessories, including torcs, and imported Greek and Etruscan pottery and bronze vessels around Mont Lassois, most notably at Sainte-Colombe and Vix (Joffroy 1958; Chaume 2001; Rolley 2003). As at the Magdalenenberg (see earlier, 'South-west Germany'), many late Hallstatt tumuli in eastern France—irrespective of whether the primary burial was male or female—contain numerous secondary burials of men, women, and children, sometimes protected by stone cists and arranged concentrically in the mound. This arrangement of burials with a balanced sex ratio indicating a family- or lineage-based structure is also found in the Slovenian Dolenjsko, where the custom started in Hallstatt C. The significant role of high-status women in these 'family' barrows and especially in monumental graves like Vix can be seen as manifestations of the inherited status of elite families in which women played a significant part in the power structure (Metzner-Nebelsick 2009). Some tumuli in Burgundy continued in use into La Tène A (Chaume 2001).

Hallstatt Switzerland is characterized by regional diversity. Many of the principal settlements and cemeteries were in the Swiss central plateau between the Jura, Lake Geneva, and Lake Constance (Drack 1958–1959, 1964). A high percentage of wagon burials of men and women are attested here. Other foci of settlement are apparent in the Valais, Tessin, and Engadin regions to the south-east. The Alps did not form a barrier, the passes connecting northern Italy with eastern France and south-west Germany (Schmid-Sikimić 2001). Rich resources of copper and iron (Müller and Lüscher 2004: 36, fig. 38) provided ample trading goods.

Unterlunkhofen-Bärhau is the largest Hallstatt cemetery in Switzerland, with sixty-three barrows (Lüscher 1993). Most contained cremations in urns, but a few were inhumations. The standard equipment in elite burials comprised a wagon and a bronze *situla*, as well as weapons and rich ornaments. Imports of Italian gold jewellery occur in graves at Ins and Urtenen in Kanton Bern (Drack 1958; Schmid-Sikimić 1984). The female costumes in graves on the Swiss plateau resemble those from south-west Germany, with richly ornamented sheet-bronze armlets, bracelets, and ankle-rings made of bronze or sapropelite (Schmid-Sikimić 1996), and bronze belt plates as well as various types of fibulae. Bronze headdress pins were sometimes covered with sheet gold.

From the Central Eastern Alps to Bohemia

The eponymous cemetery of Hallstatt contained both inhumation and cremation burials. With over 1,500 recorded graves (Kern et al. 2008: 130), the cemetery is large for prehistoric Europe, but still may not represent the entire mining community, since the social mechanisms of access to burial in a grave do not leave archaeological evidence. A model of a society divided into an upper class benefiting from the economic gains of salt mining, and various unrepresented lower ranks, dependent workers, or slaves, may not match reality either. Anthropological analyses reveal that even people in burials furnished with prestige items such as bronze vessels, who might be regarded as members of a privileged elite, worked hard during their lives. Status items such as wagons and sets of horse-gear are absent, although single items of horse-gear were worn as amulets by some women and girls and seem to be symbols of their special status (Metzner-Nebelsick and Nebelsick 1999).

The second salt mining site in the Austrian Alps is the Dürrnberg near Hallein in the Salzach valley. Despite their proximity, there are significant chronological differences between Hallstatt (late Bronze Age to Hallstatt D) and the Dürrnberg (Hallstatt D to La Tène C), where the topography also allowed a wider dispersal of settlements and burials. Burial started at the Eislfeld (Penninger 1972; Moosleitner et al. 1974) near the Ramsaukopf settlement (Irlinger 1995), with burial grounds later spreading to other areas. The onset of activity coincided quite closely with the time when mining at Hallstatt was temporarily halted by a massive landslide, but it is unlikely that the founders were refugees from Hallstatt, since the mining techniques were different (Stöllner 1999, 2002).

More than 400 graves are known at the Dürrnberg, with inhumations alongside cremations. Burials were placed in stone-lined chambers, some with preserved wooden constructions. In some cases, secondary and multiple burials in one chamber and reuse of chambers over a long period can be observed (i.e. Moser et al. 2012: tabs 1–2). This hints at family traditions and the right of certain members of the social unit to be buried in a prestigious grave. Anthropological analyses reveal a balanced sex and age ratio, which hints also at long-term stability of family structures. The chambers were covered by earth mounds, now eroded, while at the Hallersbichl cemetery, two graves were covered by mining debris and preserved. A dendrochronological date of 464 BC was obtained for Hallstatt D3 costume accessories (Sormaz and Stöllner 2005); other finds included carved wood and a birch bark hat like the one from Hochdorf.

Salt was the foundation of the wealth of both communities. In addition to institutionalized gift giving among the elites, we find evidence for organized trade as early as the late middle Bronze Age at Hallstatt (Kern et al. 2008), while at the Dürrnberg, where several mines were in use at the same time, Thomas Stöllner (1999, 2002) argues in favour of a complex economic centre with various specialized crafts accompanying the mining activity. The nearby cremation cemetery at Bischofshofen-Pestfriedhof on the terraces of the ore-rich Salzach valley adheres to local traditions of grave construction, with modestly sized pits and often stone settings or cists, while the grave goods show strong affinities to assemblages from Bavaria and the south-east Alps. This cemetery was founded in the tenth century BC and used until the fifth century BC (Lippert and Stadler 2009).

The Bylany group of Hallstatt C barrow burials of north-western and central Bohemia have long attracted attention on account of their four-wheeled wagons, horse harnesses, and lavishly ornamented wooden yokes with geometric decoration composed of thousands of bronze nails and rivets (Filip 1936–1937; Dvořák 1938; Chvojka and Michálek 2011). These wooden burial chambers housed members of a sword-bearing warrior elite with wide-ranging contacts. The cemeteries contained inhumations and cremations, sometimes in the same chamber; large pit graves are also attested. The chambers can reach up to 25 m^2, whereas the pit graves tend to be from 1.5 to 10 m^2 in size (Koutecký 1968, 2013; Půlpan and Reszczyńska 2013). As in southern Germany, graves between the barrows attest to a more complex social stratification than the old model of an elite caste of wagon-driving warriors (see earlier). The similarity of the bronze ornamented yokes in western Bohemia, Bavaria, Hesse, and Lower Austria shows that mobile craftworkers, including wainwrights and saddlers as well as smiths, were active across central Europe (Gebhard et al. 2016).

In central Bohemia, cremation predominated, while inhumed individuals were placed north–south with their heads to the north, along the western wall of the grave pit or burial chamber.

Graves range from small burial chambers with cremations in Nynice (Šaldová 1968) and stone constructions, to larger square or rectangular chambers. The burnt bones were either placed in urns in the southern or south-western part of the grave, or scattered on a layer of ash in the case of Nynice (Michálek and Chytráček 2013: 86–90). As in Franconia, southern Bavaria, and Württemberg, the dead were buried in an extended position on their backs, this time with the head to the south. There are, however, other regional variations, with east–west orientations in some parts of Bohemia (Koutecký 2013: 67). Some of the larger cemeteries like Nynice remained in use for several centuries, starting in the late Urnfield period and continuing until the La Tène period.

The Eastern Hallstatt Sphere and Situla Art

Wagons do not belong to the standard status set in the eastern Hallstatt area. The only real wagon east of Vienna is from the warrior grave in tumulus I of Somlóvásárhely in western Hungary, which dates to Hallstatt C2 (Patek 1993: figs 54–64), although re-excavation of the grave at Strettweg (Austria) from which the famous cult wagon (see later in this section) was recovered, shows that this chamber also originally contained a life-size wagon (Tiefengraber and Tiefengraber 2013: 47).

Instead, sets of horse-gear or single wagon parts symbolize the presence of a wagon. Bridles for two horses are sometimes found alongside the riding equipment for a single horse, emphasizing the social role of the rider. Contact with communities with a steppe lifestyle and subsistence strategy in the eastern Carpathian basin and beyond is apparent in the introduction of new types of horse-gear, in the role of the rider as a form of funeral representation, and in the presence of Caucasian iron weapon types and luxury pottery of Basarabi style in elite graves (Tomedi 1994; Nebelsick 1997: fig. 25). Basarabi pottery, with its complex incisions and encrustations, was produced in the Iron Gates and Banat region in northern Serbia and south-west Romania (Vulpe 1986; Metzner-Nebelsick 1992; Gumă 1993; Chapter 14).

The Kalenderberg group, named after the hillfort at Mödling near Vienna, is the largest on the north-east Alpine fringe (Nebelsick 1997). Metal objects as status and prestige markers are rare, especially in Hallstatt C, when cremation was the exclusive burial rite in the east Hallstatt sphere (Nebelsick 1997; Rebay 2006). Both tumuli and flat grave cemeteries occur, such as Statzendorf, Loretto, and Maiersch (Berg 1962; Nebelsick 1997; Rebay 2006). In these cemeteries, elite burials with swords or metal vessel drinking sets are absent. In Hallstatt D, inhumation burials became a more prominent feature in the flat grave cemeteries. In contrast to the flat graves, the tumulus graves with central rectangular wooden burial chambers displayed a lavish set of drinking vessels composed of colourful red-and-black-painted lustrous ware, sometimes adorned with animal protomes (Preinfalk 2003; Siegfried-Weiss 1979). The staged arrangements of drinking sets in the burial chambers may directly reflect rituals performed during the funeral ceremony (Nebelsick 1997, 2016: 11–40).

The status of women in Kalenderberg graves is noteworthy. Their social role as lady of the house is represented by spindle whorls and sometimes loom weights signifying textile production, echoing the symbolism of Etruscan and north-east Italian graves (Gleba 2011). The social role of elite women entailed the ability and right to invite guests to a drinking feast, or at least to play that part in the context of death and burial. The first evidence of domesticated grapes north of the Alps comes from an ostentatious female burial at Zagersdorf, near Eisenstadt (Rebay 2002). Ritual competences of women in domestic cults and prophecy are displayed by ritual hearths and clay prisms in graves (Teržan 1996).

Many large late Bronze Age hillforts in the eastern Alps have tumulus cemeteries outside their entrances (Nebelsick 1997). This arrangement helped to emphasize the importance of the political groups in command of these sites and might imitate the model of the extramural Etruscan necropolis. Examples include Stillfried in north-east Austria (Hellerschmid 2006), Sopron-Burgstall in western Hungary (Patek 1982), and Strettweg and Kleinklein in Styria, both located near major iron ore deposits (Dobiat 1980; Jerem and Urban 2000; Czajlik et al. 2012). At Kleinklein, several clusters of tumuli of various sizes are known. Each mound contained a cremation burial at the centre. The finds span the ninth to early sixth centuries BC. There may originally have been as many as 2,000 barrows.[5] Presumably several lineages or village populations (or certain segments of the society) were burying their dead close to the hillfort, which functioned as the central place of power for the region.

The tumuli include a number of discrete groups of very large mounds with diameters of over 40 m. The Kröllkogel, one of a group of four barrows first excavated in 1860, has been the subject of a major new study (Egg and Kramer 2013). The burial dates to 600–580 BC (Hallstatt D1). In the large drystone-walled chamber and long *dromos* (passage), four cremated individuals were buried. The leading occupant was represented as a warrior with a bronze cuirass and helmet. He wore a sword and carried an axe and probably three spears. The bronze sword, which was burned on the pyre, is anachronistic, since elsewhere daggers were the fashion of the time (Sievers 1982). Four spears and two socketed axes presumably belonged to two brothers-in-arms who followed the chieftain into the grave. Cremated horse bones deposited in the *dromos* suggest that horses were sacrificed during the burial ceremony, but no wagon fittings were recovered—unlike princely graves in the west, wagons were not a regular feature of high-status burials in the east Hallstatt region (Pare 1992; Metzner-Nebelsick 2009)—and all three men were portrayed as riders. Spindle whorls, a necklace, and bronze hair-rings indicate the possible sacrificing of a woman who was burnt and buried together with the chieftain.

The most remarkable feature of the Kröllkogel is a sheet-bronze mask depicting a human face, and two left hands, both made from embossed bronze sheet (Egg and Kramer 2013: pls 19–20), reminiscent of the Etruscan custom of imaging the deceased and of canopic urns. Iron spits and a lavish set of bronze and ceramic drinking and eating vessels also point to Italian connections. Ritual feasting at the grave may be inferred from the large number of smashed pots (*c.*80), some of them burnt on the pyre, as well as bones of sheep/goat, cattle, and pig. The bronze vessel set is one of the largest north of the Alps. Richly and partly figuratively ornamented, it consists of five *situlae*, a large hanging bowl, three biconical vessels, a ladle, a strainer, and seven buckets with lids but no bottoms.[6] Given the three other large tumuli nearby—the oldest of which contains one of the earliest bell-shaped cuirasses of the Hallstatt period (Egg and Kramer 2016)—Markus Egg argues convincingly for inherited status within a lineage, linking the Kleinklein graves with high-ranking chieftains or minor kings in the sense of the Greek *basileus* of the Homeric Age (Metzner-Nebelsick 2017b).

Italic influence on the eastern Hallstatt culture is most apparent in the realm of art. In contrast to the almost aniconic west, figural art was one of the principal characteristics of the Hallstatt east (Nebelsick 1992). The human body is depicted in a stylized manner, mostly in combination with animals, composed in scenic arrangements in the form of painted or incised decoration on clay vessels, as little clay figurines on pots, or as bronze statuettes. The most prominent composition of this kind is the Strettweg cult wagon (Egg 1996: fig. 17). A nude female deity is depicted in a complex sacrificial scene; she stands on a four-wheeled wagon, balancing a flat bowl or plate on her head. Two identical groups of figurines are placed at her feet. A deer is led by two naked people and followed by a naked female figure and an axe-wielding man, indicating that the deer is about to be sacrificed. The group is flanked by two mounted warriors with helmets and shields. The figurines are arranged so that the vehicle could be moved back and forth, stressing the performative aspect of a ritual in which it was probably used (Rebay-Salisbury 2016).

Around 600 BC, situla art was introduced in northern Italy, and slightly later in the east Hallstatt sphere and the central Alpine Fritzens-Sanzeno culture (Chapter 11). This unique figurative art dates from between the sixth and fourth centuries BC (Frey 1969; Eibner 2001; Turk 2005; Chapter 43). It is the first complex narrative art north of the Alps, with detailed depictions of people, clothes, artefacts, and animals realistically executed in embossed half-relief on bronze buckets (*situlae*), lids, belt plates, and sometimes other forms of vessels. Its emergence was clearly influenced by Etruscan communities settling north of the Apennines. Three major production areas can be distinguished, transcending regional cultural borders: north-east upper Italy, the south-east Alps (where the Dolenjsko group was the most prominent micro-centre), and South Tyrol. A relative lack of situla art in Styria may be chronological, as high-status burials are unknown there after the early sixth century BC, whereas in Carinthia activity in some tumulus cemeteries continued well into the La Tène period (Gleirscher 2009).

While the symbolic character of the scenes must be emphasized, situla art provides a good source for reconstructing various aspects of Hallstatt life, including social differentiation, costume, and activities in public spaces, as well as ritual activities in contexts such as funerals and fertility rituals, and mythological scenes. The themes are manifold: processions; preparations for feasts, including animal sacrifice and drinking rituals; banquets; musical performances or competitions; and boxing and wrestling contests. Chariot races, battles, hunting, dancing, and sex scenes also occur.

After Hallstatt D1 a power shift can be observed in the south-east Alpine fringe zone. In the Slovenian Dolenjsko, tumulus cemeteries and hillforts continued in use—although some burials show Scythian influence in terms of armour and rite—but in Styria, the use of long-lived hilltop sites such as Kleinklein and Strettweg and their surrounding cemeteries ceased (Egg and Kramer 2013), with settlement activity now focused in lowland locations. At around the time these Styrian centres lost their significance, those in south-west Germany started to flourish. Intensive contacts between the two regions can be inferred from similarities in dress accessories (Stöllner 2002), and the appearance in south-west Germany of 'lineage' burial mounds such as the Magdalenenberg, recalling the 'family' graves of the Slovenian Dolenjsko. Whether or not this was connected with the migration of people, a growing connectivity between aristocratic families around 600 BC is evident.

Earlier Iron Age Settlement

Over much of central Europe, settlement archaeology remains a relatively recent focus of research, although in the last three decades investigations linked to road, rail, and pipeline construction, as well as ever increasing building activity, have vastly increased our knowledge of Iron Age settlement types, particularly rural sites and lowland habitations. Recognition of Hallstatt C–D sites is hindered by a broad similarity of house types, construction details, and domestic wares to the preceding Urnfield period, but a wide variety of open settlements, single farmsteads, and house types are now known to have existed, often characterized by specific local manifestations. The majority of small-scale settlements appear quite short-lived, but rather than pointing to a high level of instability of society, this may simply reflect the fact that before the advent of artificial fertilizers and more sophisticated forms of crop rotation, rural settlements and farms may have frequently been relocated within a specific area.

House forms in Hallstatt C open settlements generally resemble those of the late Bronze Age (Schefzik 2001), although their dimensions are often larger. Two-storey buildings are likely, to judge from the large and deep postholes. Buildings with special functions are recorded, as on the Goldberg in southern Germany (Parzinger 1998). In southern Bavaria and elsewhere, village-size settlements of late Hallstatt and early La Tène date have been excavated, containing both post-built houses and smaller sunken dwellings (Schefzik 2001; Bagley et al. 2010). Large open settlements occur widely in the river valleys of eastern France, as at Sierentz-ZAC Hoell and Wolfgantzen in Alsace (Roth-Zehner 2013), and Crévéchamps, Gondreville, and Marly in Lorraine (Deffressigne and Tikonoff 2013; Koenig 2016), although here the dwellings and other structures seem to be entirely post-built. How many dwellings were contemporary is often unclear, but many sites undoubtedly consisted of multiple domestic units.

Enclosed farmsteads with no connection to these larger 'villages' are also common and widely seen as the residences of a rural elite. A specific type found mainly in Bavaria and western Bohemia is the rectangular farmstead with multiple ditches and a single entrance, sometimes called a *Herrenhof* (elite farmstead). The earliest examples date to the late Urnfield period (Wells 1983), but most are of Hallstatt D or early La Tène date (Kas and Schussmann 1998; Berg-Hobohm 2002–2003). Some show traces of craft production, as at Niedererlbach in lower Bavaria (Müller-Depreux 2005).

There is a significant divide between the early and late Hallstatt periods in the use of hillforts, which also display different rhythms of occupation in the eastern and western zones. Many fortified hilltop sites in the east reveal continuity between the late Urnfield period, when they were founded, and Hallstatt C–D1—Sopron-Burgstall in western Hungary, the Burgstallkogel at Kleinklein in Styria, and Stillfried in north-east Austria being prominent examples (Dobiat 1990; Jerem and Urban 2000; Hellerschmid 2006; Metzner-Nebelsick 2012a). In the west, however, particularly in Bohemia and southern Germany, late Urnfield hillforts were generally abandoned in Hallstatt C (Jockenhövel 1974; Michálek and Chytráček 2013: 73), to be followed in Hallstatt D by a new phase of fortified sites, often grouped together as *Fürstensitze* (princely sites), and variously interpreted as aristocratic residences, central places of power, or proto-urban centres. They occur across a zone stretching from south-west Germany to eastern France, including parts of Switzerland (Krausse 2010; Chaume 2001; Chaume and Mordant 2011).

The multi-period Heuneburg, strategically located on a plateau above the river Danube, has long served as the archetype of these early Iron Age princely seats (Kimmig 1983). New excavations have revealed that the plateau, fortified around 600 BC with a unique mud-brick wall, bastions, and gates, was just the defended 'acropolis' of a settlement complex with a gated lower town and a vast suburb of enclosed farmsteads, some with prestigious larger buildings, divided by a planned road grid. There are good arguments for calling this phase of the Heuneburg 'urban', and it might be the city of Pyrene, associated by Herodotus with the Celts and the source of the Danube as Dirk Krausse and Manuel Fernández-Götz have proposed (Krausse et al. 2016: 84–87). Around 540 BC, the settlement on the plateau was burnt down and the mud-brick wall destroyed, but the fortifications were rebuilt in traditional earth, timber, and stone construction and occupation carried on until the mid-fifth century BC, when the site was definitively abandoned following another catastrophic fire. In the later phase, the lower town was noticeably more densely occupied, whereas the citadel housed a smaller number of prestigious larger structures than before, while a group of rich burial mounds were constructed over the remains of the now deserted outer settlement (Krausse et al. 2016: 91–110).

The mud-brick fortifications of the Heuneburg and a monumental stone gateway built in ashlar technique discovered in 2005 were clearly of Mediterranean inspiration, and attest to knowledge of Mediterranean technology if not the presence of foreign craftworkers. Together with an array of Greek and Etruscan imports, mostly from the later phases, these underline the significance of transalpine contacts for these late Hallstatt centres north of the Alps (Krausse 2008, 2010). A similar picture is apparent for Mont Lassois, where investigations on the fortified plateau above the river Seine have revealed an enclosure containing four or five huge apsidal buildings, which are unprecedented north of the Alps, as well as several immense storage buildings—possibly granaries—in a second enclosure, and a third compound containing possible residential buildings (Chaume and Mordant 2011; Mötsch 2011; Fougère 2016). This complex can surely be regarded as the residential seat of the family of the Vix 'princess'. The strategic importance of this location on the Seine is stressed by the fact that the river is navigable from here. Mont Lassois could have controlled a trade route stretching from the Mediterranean all the way to the Channel, which increased in importance following the Greek foundation of Massalia in 600 BC. Imports such as the enormous bronze crater from Vix and other rich burials in the area as well as from Mont Lassois itself can be explained in such a context. Other potential *Fürstensitze* include Châtillon-sur-Glâne and the Ütliberg in Switzerland, the Münsterberg near Breisach and Britzgyberg on the upper Rhine and, less certainly, the Hohenasperg in Baden-Württemberg. This group of sites does not seem significantly to outlast the Hallstatt period, although in other areas fortified sites continued into the early La Tène period, or were resettled in the late La Tène period.

Mediterranean imports are also found in lowland occupation sites such as large farmsteads. At Hochdorf-Reps, a settlement of several farmsteads with large timber houses, the presence of red-figure Greek pottery imports, slightly later in date than the famous Hallstatt D2 princely tomb (see earlier), indicates that at the end of the Hallstatt and in the early La Tène periods, rural elites apparently also participated in long-distance exchange networks (Biel 2015). At the Ipf near Bopfingen in south-west Germany, Greek amphorae and finewares were found in the hillfort as well as in two adjacent contemporary rectangular settlement enclosures at the foot of the hill (Krause et al. 2010; Krause 2014).

Although the late Hallstatt period was marked by intensive contacts with the Mediterranean world, some areas such as southern Bavaria seem to have been outside these interregional trade networks (Kossack 1959; Schefzik 2001). Here, the only prominent fortified site with Mediterranean imports is the Ehrenbürg in Upper Franconia, which also has early La Tène occupation (Abels 2010). This contrasts with Bohemia, where Greek black-figure and red-figure pottery and Etruscan metal vessel imports occur regularly in elite burials and at late Hallstatt and early La Tène lowland settlements (Chytráček 2008). So intensive was this interaction between the Bohemian elites and the Mediterranean that it led to a unique case of local imitation of Attic red-figure painted pottery at the late Hallstatt to early La Tène settlement of Chřín. Závist, near Prague, is the best documented example in this region of an acropolis with complex buildings, partly in stone, and different functional units, among them buildings with a religious connotation (Drda and Rybová 2008). The large fortified site at Vladař in western Bohemia, occupied intensively in the mid-first millennium BC, belongs to the same class of site (Chytráček and Metlička 2004). After a period of abandonment in the fourth and third centuries BC, Závist was reoccupied and became one of the most important *oppida* in central Europe.

The Later Iron Age (*c*.450–50 BC)

When the first iron artefacts came to light in 1857 at La Tène on Lake Neuchâtel, it could hardly have been imagined that this ensemble would become the 'type site' and give its name to the younger Iron Age in Europe. Pile structures uncovered in an old channel of the river Thièle initially suggested that a new Alpine lake dwelling had been discovered. Excavations in the 1870s and early 1900s by Emile Vouga and his son Paul revealed many iron weapons, including swords with their scabbards, spearheads, along with horse-gear and wagon equipment (rings, bits, a wooden yoke, and a wheel), tools (a wooden plough, scissors, scythes), and human remains, including crania. The non-Roman character of the weapons supported the interpretation of the site as a fortified camp of the Helvetii, whose exodus from their homeland in the first century BC eventually led to the conquest of Gaul by Julius Caesar.

In all, more than 2,500 objects and human remains were recovered (E. Vouga 1885; P. Vouga 1923). Their meaning has been much debated ever since: Klaus Raddatz (1952) was the first to view La Tène as a sacrificial place (*Opferplatz*), followed by Réné Wyss (1955). Hanni Schwab (1989) reverted to a settlement interpretation, despite the lack of artefacts with female associations. However, several features point in a different direction, and today La Tène is regarded as a bridge from which sacrifices were made, perhaps during a military conflict, functioning as a kind of *tropaion* or victory monument (Müller 2002; Honegger et al. 2009). Some weapons had been destroyed; others were wrapped in textiles, while in among them were the human skulls, and bones of horses and cattle. Most of the finds date to the second century BC, long before Caesar's interventions north of the Alps.

Chronology

Like Hallstatt, the eponymous site for the younger pre-Roman Iron Age is unique. The unprecedented quantity of high-quality metal finds of specific character led Swedish antiquarian Hans Hildebrand (1874) to call the second part of the Iron Age 'La Tène'. Otto Tischler introduced the first basic chronology for central Europe, defining early, middle, and late La Tène periods based on fibula and sword types (Tischler 1885; Collis 2003). Paul Reinecke later subdivided this into four phases, La Tène A–D, following the system he established for the Hallstatt period (Reinecke 1902, 1965). There have been further refinements, based mainly on German finds, especially for the late La Tène period (Krämer 1962, 1985; Polenz 1971; Gebhard 1989, 1991; Rieckhoff 1995: 145 tab. 18).

In France, Joseph Déchelette, inspired by Josef Píč's excavations at the Bohemian *oppidum* of Stradonice between 1897 and 1907, excavated at Mont Beuvray—Bibracte, the capital of the Aedui, where Caesar installed his winter camp in 52 BC, and wrote his famous commentaries on the Gallic War. Déchelette recognized the similarity of materials from Stradonice and Mont Beuvray, and coined the phrase 'civilisation des *oppida*'. His *Manuel d'Archéologie* defined the *Second Âge du Fer ou époque de La Tène* (Déchelette 1914) and the term gained widespread acceptance. Unlike Reinecke, Déchelette divided the La Tène period into three phases: I—early, II—middle, and III—late La Tène. The period has subsequently been subdivided by other scholars, with slight differences in the absolute dating of the subphases, depending on the author and region.

The end of the La Tène period was always defined by the arrival of the Romans—under Caesar in the mid-first century BC in France, while Augustus' campaign across the Alps in 15 BC marked the end of La Tène D2 in southern Germany. The start, on the other hand, was more controversial. Martin Trachsel (2004) proposed a very early date of 520–500 BC, but dendrochronological dates in the mid-fifth century BC from the Dürrnberg for a grave with late Hallstatt material (Sormaz and Stöllner 2005) suggest a start around 460/450 BC. The end of the early La Tène period is placed around 270/250 BC and connected with the Celtic migrations, although their destruction of Delphi in 279 BC was only one of several such episodes during the period (Chapter 37). The beginning of the late La Tène period (La Tène D1), associated with the *oppida*, is dated to 150/130 BC.

La Tène Mortuary Evidence

Although La Tène A material culture differs markedly from the late Hallstatt period in its dress accessories, the reintroduction of the long sword, and the appearance of the so-called Early style of figurative art, with its human bodies and body parts, human–animal hybrids, and Celtic adaptations of Greek ornamental motifs (Jacobsthal 1944; Megaw 1970; Megaw and Megaw 1989; Chapter 43), its mortuary practices and settlement structures show greater continuity. The custom of princely burials under large mounds survived until La Tène B1, although—apart from the Dürrnberg—the most sumptuous La Tène A burials now occurred in areas further north, where they were previously rare or absent: in the Rhine-Eifel-Moselle area, in Hesse, and in Bohemia (Krausse 2010). Their disappearance from south-west Germany possibly indicates a shift of political power away from the former centres at the Hohenasperg and the Heuneburg. In Bavaria, early La Tène burials are rare, partly because they were often secondary burials in older barrows and thus easily lost with the destruction of the mounds by agricultural activities over time.

One exceptional early La Tène A burial in south-west Germany is the Kleinaspergle, near Ludwigsburg, a huge barrow 60 m in diameter (Kimmig 1988). Its central chamber had been robbed, but a second wooden chamber contained an elaborate drinking set, composed of an Italian bronze *stamnos*, ribbed bucket (*cista con cordone*), and spouted jug with a handle attachment in the form of a Celtic adaptation of a satyr; two Greek red-figure drinking bowls (*kylikes*) dating to 450 BC, adorned with gold foil appliqués with typical Early style floral motifs; and finally, two drinking horns with sheet gold ends.

The most remarkable item among the personal attire of the deceased was a decorative openwork plaque in an early La Tène style floral design, crafted in bronze and iron, and covered with gold foil and inlays. Similar pieces of jewellery occur in princely tombs from the Rhine-Moselle region to Bohemia (Chytráček 1999: 375, fig. 17), attesting to the connectivity of early La Tène elites and artisans.

At the Dürrnberg, stone-lined burial chambers containing inhumations and cremations stand for continuity in burial rites, although a significant impact of western artefact types and modes of elite representation is evident. In barrow 44, grave 2 of the Eislfeld group, a sword-bearer was entombed lying on a chariot with a Berru-type helmet (both common at the time in the Marne culture in northern France), and equipped with several bronze vessels (Moosleitner et al. 1974; Zeller 2001). The Sonneben barrow group has yielded several more warrior graves with Berru helmets in bronze and iron (Moser et al. 2012).

The early La Tène shift of regional centres is most obvious in the middle Rhine-Main and Hunsrück-Eifel-Moselle regions (Haffner 1976). In the Hunsrück-Eifel, numerous sumptuous burials, many with prestigious artefacts in the Early style, occur in a relatively restricted geographical area (Joachim 1968). A stratified society with an emerging nobility is identified not only by Etruscan imports, chariot burials, and outstanding artefacts like the gold-rich furnishings in graves such as Weiskirchen, Rodenbach, and Schwarzenbach (Verger 1995), but also by the establishment of aristocratic cemeteries, isolated small groups of barrows with rich finds. Another indicator of a hierarchically organized society can be seen in the larger percentage of elite female burials. Some of the richest early La Tène burials are those of women, such as Reinheim in the Saarland (Keller 1965; Echt 1999), or the later grave at Waldalgesheim, after which the second La Tène art style is named (Joachim 1995).

These women were entitled to wear gold jewellery, like male members of the ruling elite of the time. Gold jewellery was a manifest symbol of power, particularly torcs, otherwise the attribute of gods and thus also found in votive deposits. The Reinheim 'princess' was adorned with a gold torc with a complex iconography and terminals in the form of a helmeted female deity. One of the two accompanying bracelets carries a similarly intriguing three-dimensional depiction of a female being. The burial also contained a bronze mirror, one of very few from continental Europe, and other ritually charged objects. The woman is often seen as a priestess or person whose high status was mainly based on her religious competence (Schickler 2001). This is, however, only one aspect of her social standing, as comparison with other rich female graves indicates. The exquisite quality of early La Tène craftsmanship is displayed not only by the jewellery, but also by outstanding sheet-bronze metalwork, exemplified by the spouted bronze jug (*Röhrenkanne*) from Reinheim (Figure 8.6), with incised geometric ornament executed using a pair of compasses. The same type of jug, with similar decoration, was found in the Waldalgesheim grave, dating to around 330 BC, and one of the very latest princely graves (Joachim 1995). The dead woman wore a torc with Waldalgesheim-style floral design; as well as other gold and bronze items of personal attire, her grave goods included the *Röhrenkanne*, an Italian-type bronze bucket, and, most importantly, a chariot, symbolizing her power.

FIGURE 8.6 Spouted bronze jugs from the princely tombs of Reinheim (left, height 504 mm) and Waldalgesheim (right, height 350 mm).

Source: Kimmig 1988: 98–99, figs 27–28

As these examples show, the triad of status representation comprising a vehicle, gold paraphernalia, and metal drinking equipment survived into the early La Tène period, albeit with variations. Instead of the multiple vessel sets found in late Hallstatt princely burials, La Tène A drinking equipment was often reduced to two vessels, such as the pairs of drinking horns (and two red-figure *kylikes*) at Kleinaspergle and Reinheim. In other graves such as Rodenbach in Rheinland-Pfalz, one of the few La Tène A princely graves with an iron weapon set, a personalized endowment of four different types of Etruscan bronze vessels and one Greek pottery drinking vessel was chosen to equip the deceased.

One of the most important discoveries for the early La Tène period is the Glauberg in Hesse, dating to the later fifth century BC (Baitinger and Pinsker 2002; Baitinger 2010). Two tumuli with three princely burials, two inhumations, and one cremation, were discovered at the foot of a fortified hilltop settlement (Schwitalla 2008). The barrows were embedded into a complex system of ditches and banks with a 350 m long processional way leading up to barrow 1 (see Chapter 22). The most remarkable is burial 1 in barrow 1, in which a man was inhumed carrying his sheathed, elaborately ornamented sword, a shield, spearheads, and bow and arrow. Regalia and symbols of power included a gold torc, bracelet, and finger-ring, and a headdress or leaf crown. A bronze spouted jug of Celtic manufacture, originally wrapped in textile, displays a complex iconography, with a seated man in a short tunic flanked by beasts. Judging from the close correspondence between the finds in burial 1 and a monumental, slightly larger than life-size, sandstone statue found in the ditch surrounding barrow 1, an idealized image of the dead prince survived, showing him as a warrior in a short leather cuirass holding a shield and wearing a sword (Figure 8.7).[7] His torc, with three baluster shaped ornaments, resembles the one in the grave. The statue also wears a leaf crown which, according to the finds from the burial, was constructed of iron wire with an organic covering, most likely made of padded leather.

Pieces of several other deliberately destroyed stone sculptures with similar features were found nearby. The combination of monumental architectural features, anthropomorphic stone sculptures and, most importantly, the positioning of a number of posts in the vicinity of barrow 1 have led to the assumption that the Glauberg complex was a cosmological observatory or calendar, as well as the postmortem veneration monument for a powerful ruler and his successor. This discovery, as well as large-scale investigations at the hillfort, have led to a better understanding of early La Tène society. Analysis of the bones of the man from barrow 1, grave 1 reveals a prestigious diet dominated by animal protein, contrasting sharply with the people interred—or rather thrown—into storage pits nearby (Knipper et al. 2014). Pollen preserved in the mead found in the spouted jug implies that the man's dominion may have included land 200 km away.

Regionally different burial practices are seen in Bohemia (Collis 2003: 185–188). Barrow and flat grave cemeteries with cremations were typical in La Tène A in south and west Bohemia. The late Hallstatt flat grave cemetery of Manětín-Hrádek near Plzeň continued in use, its La Tène phase represented by modestly equipped burials with handmade and wheel-thrown pottery, and personal ornaments (Soudská 1994). A mask fibula of a human figure with amber inlays and pointed, beak-shaped shoes, was found in a female cremation (Soudská 1991). Bronze fibulae with zoomorphic, anthropomorphic, or hybrid figures are typical of the early La Tène world (Binding 1993), often occurring in women's graves. In other parts of Bohemia, sumptuous graves with wagons and harness, and bronze vessels such as beaked flagons embody the traditional pattern of princely behaviour (Drda 1995).

In northern Bohemia (Filip 1960) and Bavaria (Krämer 1985), a noticeable change in burial practice in La Tène B2 (330/320 to 270/260 BC) may express fundamental social changes on the eve of the great Celtic migration. Instead of the traditional elaborate barrow burials for a select few, larger parts of society were now buried in flat grave inhumation cemeteries with consistent sets of personal equipment. Women and men were adorned with Duchcov and Münsingen fibulae and their variants. Women wore bracelets, ankle- and neck-rings and—from La Tène C1 onwards—glass arm-rings, whereas men were equipped with iron swords, sometimes combined with iron sword chains or shields. The high percentage of weapon burials may indicate that the flat grave period of La Tène B2–C1 (*Flachgräber Latène*) still represents the social elite, but the whole warrior class and their families, not just princes.

FIGURE 8.7 Sandstone sculpture of the prince from Glauberg barrow 1, grave 1, found at the bottom of the barrow.

Photo: Pavel Obody, Keltenwelt am Glauberg

Probably the most iconic La Tène flat grave cemetery is Münsingen-Rain near Bern in Switzerland (Müller 1998). Almost completely excavated in 1904, it contained 230 graves, spanning some 300 years between La Tène A and La Tène C2 (Hodson 1968; Stöckli 1975). This equates to around fifteen to twenty people per generation, a figure that can only represent the upper part of a much larger population (Jud 1998), and the Münsingen burial ground is now believed to be that of a single extended family (Müller et al. 2008). The graves contained gender- and age-based dress accessories for women and children (Martin-Kilcher 1973). Meat offerings were only found in male burials. Other status items were weapons, the sword being the most conspicuous marker of male social distinction—there were eighteen sword graves in all. The number of sword graves was highest in La Tène B1, shortly before the onset of migration towards eastern Europe. Other indicators of social distinction are finger-rings of gold or silver. In the Hunsrück-Eifel culture, the right to wear them first appears in La Tène A2, in Bohemia in La Tène B1, and at Münsingen in La Tène B2, where 66% of the ring-wearers were women (Waldhauser 1998).

In eastern Austria, as in parts of Bohemia, the transition to the La Tène period was at first a continuous one. Some Hallstatt cemeteries continued in use until La Tène A (Neugebauer 1992), indicating that the local population adopted the new La Tène style. The founding in La Tène B of several new cemeteries in Lower Austria, such as Mannersdorf and Pottenbrunn, might reflect incoming groups or families from the west and north-west (Ramsl 2002, 2011).[8] Distinctive dress accessories like Münsingen-style combinations (at Pottenbrunn) or types of female attire common in north Bavaria and Bohemia-Moravia enable us to identify their possible places of origin.

After La Tène C1, a fundamental change in burial practice can be observed throughout the La Tène zone. The flat grave cemeteries were no longer used, possibly reflecting inter alia migration and an accompanying change in social and religious behaviour. Generally, archaeological traces of burial practice are scarce after La Tène C1; presumably different rites were practised, which are not easily detected, such as the deposition of cremated remains in rivers or lakes. At the very end of the La Tène period, small cremation burials—Kronwinkl-type burials—occur in Bavaria (Krämer 1959), but would account for only a very small part of society. A variety of multiphased burial practices is also attested. At the *oppidum* of Manching in Bavaria (Sievers 2003) and the settlement of Basel-Gasfabrik in Switzerland (Jud 2008; Hecht and Niederhäuser 2011), parts of human skeletons were placed in pits. At Basel, the repeated combination with imported amphorae attests complex death rituals in the late La Tène period.

The middle and late La Tène periods in the Moselle-Hunsrück region were characterized by a continuing practice of burial in graves. The cemetery of Wederath-Belginum was established during the early La Tène period, with seven mounds containing cremation and inhumation burials; around 500 flat graves were dug between the mid-third century BC and the Roman conquest (Haffner and Abegg 1989). Other cemeteries of late La Tène date occur in the area (Gleser 2005).

Settlement in the Later Iron Age

As with mortuary practices, La Tène A is characterized by continuity of settlement patterns. Defended hilltop settlements continued as centres of power and residences of the ruling elites, but now mainly occur between the middle Rhine and Bohemia (Pare 2009), mirroring the northward shift of princely burials (Kimmig 1983). One of these defended settlements is the Glauberg, on the hill above the princely tombs (Baitinger 2010). Like others of its kind, the Glauberg was already occupied in the Hallstatt period (Hansen and Pare 2016), but its main use was in the early La Tène period.

Comparable sites are the Ehrenbürg (Abels 2010) and the Staffelberg in Upper Franconia (Schussmann 2010), and the acropolis of Závist, near Prague in Bohemia (Drda and Rybová 2008). All have a late Hallstatt phase and continued into early La Tène. The picture is, however, regionally very variable. Whereas hilltop sites were already abandoned in La Tène A in Middle Franconia, in the Upper Palatinate, Hesse, and Bohemia, occupation continued (Schussmann 2010: 165). Some information is available about the interior layouts of these hilltop sites of Glauberg type (Baitinger et al. 2012). At the Ehrenbürg, hundreds of closely set earth cellars have been detected by magnetometer survey and trial excavation, leading to the assumption that the above-ground buildings were erected using log or *Blockbau* technique. A fragment of a glass flask (*aryballos*) is a Mediterranean import, while clay imitations of spouted jugs at the Ehrenbürg show that imports remained precious items that were probably not available everywhere. At Závist—despite the complex and impressive stone-built structures on the acropolis—Mediterranean imports are absent (Drda and Rybová 2008).

Settlement evidence is scarce after the end of La Tène A, possibly because parts of the population participated in the great Celtic migration. Sudden climatic deterioration has been posited as a trigger (Maise 1998: 220, 224), but population growth and an agricultural economy unable to adjust to the needs of a growing population, or to exploit the environment in a sustainable manner, could also have contributed in some areas (Chapter 37). In contrast to the large defended settlements of Glauberg and Ehrenbürg type, which functioned as supra-regional centres, in the Hunsrück-Eifel a dense scatter of small hillforts was the norm in the early La Tène period (Nortmann 1999, 2009, 2015), along with smaller hamlets.

Starting in later La Tène B, but mainly during La Tène C, a new type of settlement emerged, known as 'production and distribution centres of Němčice-Roseldorf type' (Salač 2005: 11, 2012, 2014), also called open agglomerations (Haselgrove and Guichard 2013). Němčice in Bohemia (Salač 2005), Roseldorf in Lower Austria (Holzer 2009, 2014), and Berching-Pollanten in Bavaria (Schäfer 2010) have all been extensively excavated. They were complex and diversely organized settlements with residential areas, storage facilities for agricultural products (Roseldorf), and artisan quarters with large-scale production of goods and semi-products, including glass, bronze objects (Němčice), and iron (Berching-Pollanten). At Bad Nauheim in Hesse, salt was produced on an industrial scale (Hansen 2016).

A shared aspect of these agglomerations is an emphasis on religious practice. At Roseldorf, three distinct cult areas with several sanctuaries suggest a district-like organization of the settlement (Holzer 2009, 2014). A site of urban character with around fifty buildings dating to La Tène D1, with areas for commercial and ritual activities, and residential and artisanal quarters, has been excavated at Tomblaine Le Pré Chenu in Lorraine (Deffressigne-Tikonoff and Tikonoff 2005; Deffressigne et al. 2012). The regular presence of coinage, a typical attribute of urban sites, adds to the close similarities between the settlements of Němčice-Roseldorf type and some *oppida*, long seen as the first towns north of the Alps (Collis 1984, 1993). None of the agglomerations, however, were substantially fortified, and they thus do not meet the definition of an *oppidum*, which needs a wall. A fortification as a marker of 'inside' and 'outside' is one criterion for a town in antiquity as well as in later periods. This apparent contradiction has led to an intensive discussion of the phenomenon of centralization and urbanization in the late Iron Age (e.g. Guichard et al. 2000; Sievers and Schönfelder 2012).

The open agglomerations with their production, religious, and residential quarters often come closer to a modern understanding of a town than the *oppida*. In contrast to many hilltop *oppida* with a prominent defensive character, the centres of Němčice-Roseldorf type were sited in fertile lowlands; they also occupied favourable locations along road systems and communication routes, or lay near resources such as iron deposits, as at Berching-Pollanten and Manching, which started life as an open agglomeration. Consequently, Vladimir Salač and others regard them as towns and envisage a more dynamic picture of La Tène settlement patterns with episodes of urbanization and de-urbanization (Salač 2012). The hilltop *oppida* represent a more traditional concept, showing closer similarities to late Bronze Age or early Iron Age fortified settlements with a stronger emphasis on hierarchy and defensibility.

Since John Collis' important work on the *oppida*, this most prominent type of late La Tène settlement has been extensively discussed (e.g. Fichtl 2000; see Chapter 21). Except for the lowland site of Manching, our knowledge of the internal organization of central European *oppida* is still relatively limited. The function of the vast areas enclosed by ramparts of post-and-groove type (*Pfostenschlitzmauer*),[9] with intermittent gates of complex construction, remains largely unknown. This is true of the largest *oppidum* in southern Germany, the Heidengraben near Grabenstetten in the Swabian Alb, which covers 1,660 ha (Knopf 2006). At Kelheim-Alkimoennis above the Danube gorge, several iron quarries were enclosed within its more than 600 ha (Burger 1984; Leicht 2000). This site represents an interesting crossover between urban sites of Němčice-Roseldorf type and well-fortified mountain *oppida*. For long, little was known about the hinterlands of the *oppida* (e.g. Wells 1993), but new data from southern Bavaria indicate a high density of large single farmsteads, in the form of small settlements, surrounded by a strictly rectangular ditch and palisade, generally known as *Viereckschanzen*.

The *Viereckschanzen* were at first interpreted as fortifications, next as large farms or estates, and then as cult enclosures, a view seemingly strengthened by excavations at Holzhausen near Munich, which uncovered an isolated square building, deep shafts with chemically proven traces of blood, and a setting for a wooden pole (Schwarz and Wieland 2005). However, more recent excavations at a number of *Viereckschanzen* in southern Germany have revealed buildings of various types and functions inside these enclosures: residential houses, storage buildings or granaries, sunken huts (*Grubenhäuser*), and even traces of craft production, as at Bopfingen, in Baden-Württemberg (Wieland 1999). Today, *Viereckschanzen* are seen as the residential seats of a rural aristocratic elite, who at times may also have resided in the *oppida*. Interestingly, a few south Bavarian enclosed farms outlasted the *oppida* and continued in use into La Tène D2 (Wieland 2004), clearly representing a process of de-urbanization.

Production and Material Culture in the Later Iron Age

La Tène Europe was subject to a series of major technological innovations, which had a tremendous impact not just on crafts and craftsmanship, but on the organization of society as a whole (see Chapter 24). For the first time, large-scale workshop production—in some cases at an almost industrial level—can be traced in the archaeological record. Surprisingly, the potter's wheel, invented in the fourth millennium BC in the Near East, was only adopted in central Europe around 500 BC. The technology was probably transmitted along the Rhône valley from the Greek colony of Massalia, then via Burgundy to south-west Germany and its princely seats (Balzer 2009: 148). The *poterie grise* from southern France is a likely role model. In the Carpathian lands east of the Danube, wheel-turned pottery was introduced slightly earlier, in the sixth century BC (Romsauer 1991), thanks to exchange networks across the Carpathians and along the Dniester valley—one of the main transit routes to the Greek colonies on the western Black Sea coast such as Histria.

At the Heuneburg (Lang 1974) and the Münsterberg near Breisach (Balzer 2009), the fast potter's wheel led to a complete change in the repertoire of forms and the production of a new type of dark greyish, unornamented but grooved pottery. As shown by Ines Balzer for the Münsterberg and by Claudia Tappert (2006) for lowland open settlements in eastern Bavaria, wheel-thrown pottery existed alongside handmade wares for a long time. Only in the middle La Tène period did wheel-made ceramics become dominant (Zeiler 2010). A shift to professional craft production, a characteristic of the La Tène period, is best shown by the replacement of formerly household-based pottery manufacture in the Hallstatt period (supposedly performed by women and thus part of gender-specific regional communication networks), to workshop-based production on a larger scale. New kiln types with several fire-channels permitted higher firing temperatures (Zeiler 2009). Harder pots could also be transported more easily over longer distances. Incised stamps on early La Tène pottery (Schwappach 1977; Jerem et al. 2009) have enabled the identification of particular workshops and interregional trade networks. In the late La Tène period, painted pottery, mainly with a white coating and red coloured stripes, became the hallmark of prestigious ceramic dishes. Graphite-clay pottery, with a high percentage of graphite mixed into the clay matrix and with distinctive combed incisions (*Kammstrichkeramik*; Trebsche 2011), made the pots tolerant of higher cooking temperatures and allowed a change in cooking styles and food production.

As a result of increased craft specialization and productivity, as well as the development of trade networks and long-distance contacts (Lang and Salač 2002), full-time craftworkers may well have become a social rank in their own right. Other goods and commodities such as iron objects (especially swords), glass bangles, and bracelets made of sapropelite (a fossilized sediment of organic origin) were also produced on a large scale at sites of Němčice-Roseldorf type and *oppida* like Manching (Later 2014).

Large-scale rock salt production is known at Hallstatt from the Bronze Age to the early Iron Age (Hallstatt D1), and at the Dürrnberg from the late Hallstatt period (Stöllner 2002). The Dürrnberg mines continued into the La Tène period, as also indicated by the large number of La Tène burials there. A different production technique was used at Bad Nauheim, where salt springs were exploited on an industrial scale by boiling brine, using briquetage—a coarse ceramic container placed on pedestals in furnaces to evaporate the brine. After the evaporation process was concluded, the containers were smashed to release salt cakes or ingots, which could easily be exported. Excavations at Bad Nauheim have revealed a vast production complex, with cobbled working areas enclosed by wickerwork and fences, and a complex system of channels for directing the brine to the furnaces. Due to the saline conditions, wooden troughs and tubs have been preserved. The lifespan of production is attested by dendrochronological dates spanning the second to the earlier first century BC, and a sequence of several furnaces stratified above one another (Kull and Becker 2003; Hansen 2016). At Marsal La Digue, in the Seille valley in Lorraine, rows of furnaces produced tens of thousands of tonnes of salt over a long period of time (Olivier 2010; Harding 2013: 75–76).

Evidence for Hallstatt ironworking is still limited, although some regional centres of iron smelting are known, in the Slovenian Dolensjko (Dular and Tecco Hvala 2007: 217) and in the Black Forest near Neuenbürg (Gassmann et al. 2006). This changed dramatically in the La Tène period. Large-scale production sites have been identified at various places, including Berching-Pollanten (Schäfer 2010), Kelheim, and Manching. More than fifty smelting furnaces have been excavated at Neuenbürg, a site used continuously throughout the early La Tène period. The supra-regional supply of iron is also attested by the dense cluster of large iron ingots (*Doppelspitzenbarren*) and already-forged sword ingots (Metzner-Nebelsick et al. 2009: 155, fig. 165).

An advanced iron technology helped to improve agricultural techniques and food production. Iron ploughshares, scythes, scissors, flat tongs, and various other types of tools were used, or at least are found, for the first time in La Tène Europe (Jacobi 1974; Nothdurfter 1979; Chapter 24). The repertoire resembles that of the Middle Ages, and attests to the high standard of Celtic craftsmanship. More advanced tools enabled the carpenters, cartwrights, and blacksmiths to create the basic equipment and wherewithal to supply growing urban populations with agricultural produce and items such as houses, workshops, vehicles, weapons, and storage facilities—as well as luxury items (e.g. glass)—to sustain the more complex lifeways of later Iron Age society. Surplus production, with agricultural products and food as a potential source of wealth, is difficult to prove, but has been argued for the Glauberg area in the early La Tène period (Kreuz and Friedrich 2014). More advanced implements undoubtedly helped to raise agricultural yields. The wide distribution of rotary querns of volcanic rock from Mayen in the Eifel and Lovosice in Bohemia indicates that agricultural production was both improved and pursued on a supra-household level (Wefers 2011).

As a side effect of extended trade and more centralized distribution networks (as well as the Celtic migrations), certain types of objects and tastes or aesthetic norms became more unified and widespread. This has led to the comparatively easy recognizability of objects in almost all parts of the expanding La Tène sphere. Typical male/warrior items are long swords and sheaths,[10] long oval wooden shields with iron frames and spindle-shaped shield bosses, and iron spearheads. More rarely, bronze and iron helmets (Schaaff 1988) functioned as markers of special distinction. For both sexes, personal ornaments consisted of a variety of fibula types and neck-rings or torcs. Female dress accessories were complemented by armlets and ankle-rings of bronze, sapropelite, and from La Tène C1 by glass bracelets (Gebhard 1989). These functioned as a medium for expressing social standing as well as affiliation to different age groups. In La Tène A–B1, fibulae of zoomorphic and other forms occur mainly in women's graves (Binding 1993; Metzner-Nebelsick 2007). In female graves of La Tène B1–B2 and C1, sets of several fibulae indicate multi-layered costumes, as at Münsingen, Mannersdorf, and Pottenbrunn (Hodson 1968; Ramsl 2002, 2011). Jewellery and local copies of prestigious bronze vessels such as spouted jugs, like those from Reinheim or Waldalgesheim (Figure 8.6), or the pair from Basse Yutz in Lorraine, reveal the expertise of the goldsmiths and bronzesmiths. They were not only skilled craftworkers, but must also have been well educated in mythology and religious beliefs to be able to express the vivid figurative depictions of Early style art (Jacobsthal 1944; Megaw and Megaw 1989; Bagley 2014). The craftworkers must also have been experienced in geometry. The use of metal compasses enabled the designers to create the intriguing patterns of early La Tène art (e.g. Frey 2002b). Majolie Lenerz-de Wilde (1977) calculated that 25% of early La Tène metal artworks were ornamented with patterns composed with compasses and a ruler (*Zirkelornamentik*); she proposes that this 'stimulus diffusion' of the rules of geometry came about via the Greeks in southern France. But instead of just copying Greek models, this transfer of knowledge resulted in the creation of a genuinely new art style, its curvilinear and floral patterns marking a stark contrast to the former square and rectangular Hallstatt patterns. Knowledge of the 'golden section' and the multiple segmentation of the circle probably also reflects the intention of the Celtic fine smiths to visualize concepts of eternity in their work.

La Tène period imports from south of the Alps now focused on Italian bronze vessels like the spouted jug, or exotic materials such as coral, used as inlays for weapons and jewellery (Harding 2007: 41). From La Tène D1, imports of wine in amphorae of Dressel 1A type to *oppida* such as the Heidengraben (Stegmaier 2014) and Manching, and other settlements (Jud 2008) confirm the famous wine consumption of the Celts remarked on by classical authors. Imported foodstuffs such as prunes, coriander, figs, and grapes are attested by the early La Tène period (Kreuz and Friedrich 2014).

Later Iron Age Religion and Ritual

Ritual practices in the later Iron Age were complex and diverse; they also changed over time. As for all prehistoric cultures, it is difficult if not impossible to reconstruct religious ideas and beliefs solely from ritual practices or mortuary practices, but two factors help us to gain insights into Iron Age religious concepts. One is classical sources that mention the names of Celtic gods and the beliefs of the Celts (Hofeneder 2005, 2008, 2011; see Chapter 42). The second is figurative art showing human beings, animals, and hybrid creatures, often interpreted as expressions of religious meaning. One must, however, be aware that not only do the written sources report on an alien culture from an etic perspective, but also that we are hardly ever able to evaluate how far back into the past these reports can be projected.

Intentional deposition of material items (mostly metal) on dry land, at special places such as peat bogs, on mountain tops, or in rivers, has a long tradition in European prehistory. Such deposits are most commonly interpreted as the material relics of ritual acts of devotion, offering personal or group belongings to supernatural entities, to ensure their benevolence or to plead for favours according to the principle of '*do—ut—des*' (I give in order to be given; Bradley 1990; Fontijn 2002; Hansen et al. 2012; Metzner-Nebelsick 2012b). After a sharp decline in votive hoards and river deposits in Hallstatt C, the custom of offering metal objects rose again in the early La Tène period, exemplified by the hoard from Erstfeld in Switzerland, at the foot of the Saint Gotthard pass, one of the most important transit routes through the western Alps (Wyss 1975; Guggisberg 2000). The objects offered here comprised four gold torcs and three bracelets. The complex iconography recalls the Reinheim finds, combining human and animal aspects, and floral symbols with anthropomorphic hybrids of divine character.

River deposits, predominantly of swords, are well attested along the Rhine and the Bavarian Danube (Torbrügge 1971; Kurz 1995). Another variant of ritual deposition is offerings at springs, most famously at Duchcov (Dux) in Bohemia (Karasová 2012). This enormous La Tène jewellery deposit was offered to an unknown goddess, the emanation of the thermal spring *Obří pramen* (the Giant spring). More than 1,600 bronze items—among them 850 fibulae (including several variants of the eponymous Duchcov or Dux-type fibula), bracelets, and rings—were found in and around a bronze cauldron of late Hallstatt type.

Cultural continuity between the late Hallstatt and La Tène periods extended to ritual practices. Striking natural places were frequent foci for material sacrifices and devotions (Müller 2002). More than sixty Hallstatt D1 to La Tène B2 fibulae were found by metal detecting at the Heidentor ('pagan's gate'), a rock formation at Egesheim in south-west Germany. Judging from the glass beads also found there, and from contemporary offerings at the source of the Douix in Burgundy, the dedicants were mostly female. In contrast, the deposits of late La Tène weaponry and horse-gear at the Dünsberg *oppidum* in Hesse—long seen as relics of a battle—are more convincingly interpreted as ritual deposits of a male clientele (Schulze-Forster 2015), their composition similar to the offerings at La Tène.

Sanctuaries and/or built space for acts of religious devotion and worship become more frequent from the middle La Tène period onwards. At Roseldorf, a remarkable group of finds was discovered in the large sanctuary (Holzer 2009: 53–73), where an offering pit contained iron weapons including swords and chain mail, as well as vehicle parts. So far unique is a headdress made of iron bands, sometimes called a Druidic crown. Large stag antlers are tentatively seen by the excavator Veronika Holzer as a symbol of the Gallic god *Cernunnos*, who may have been venerated there. Traces of animal offerings and libations of wine suggest cult practices involving blood and material sacrifice and the presence of religious personnel. Similar structures are known at Manching. Built sacred space—in the form of sanctuaries as the homes of gods or places of intensive religious activities—may be a response to the temples encountered by the Celts through their contacts with the Mediterranean world. Images of deities are also well attested. A dismantled cult image of oak, originally painted yellow, was found in a well in a *Viereckschanze* at Fellbach-Schmiden in south-west Germany. It was intentionally deposited after the destruction of the enclosure by fire; the well was then poisoned with manure and infilled. Two male goats, each with a human hand embracing their body, are the remains of a 'Master or Mistress of the Animals' sculpture (see Chapter 43). A stag 80 cm high with its forelegs pulled up formed part of the same cult image. It was manufactured in *c*.127 BC (Müller 2009: 238–241).

One of the most famous La Tène sculptures is the life-size stone head of a bearded man wearing a torc from Mšecké Žehrovice in Bohemia (Müller 2009: 232–233). It was found just outside a large rectangular ditched enclosure, one part of which housed a settlement with buildings, the other an empty space that may have been a *temenos* or sacred space. The head sculpture could represent a hero—as at the Glauberg, where there is a close connection between princely burial and hero cult (as well as observatory)—or may be the image of a god. Early La Tène stone sculptures which fall more clearly into this latter category are the monumental pillar from Pfalzfeld, and the 2.3 m high 'Janus' of Holzgerlingen near Stuttgart, a double-faced anthropomorphic sandstone statue with a leaf crown (Frey 2002b).

Religious activities are more easily determined in the late Iron Age. Cult images attest the veneration of gods of anthropomorphic shape, while votive offerings show that powerful natural places such as springs were seen as the emanation of deities. From the middle La Tène period, cult buildings became more frequent and were sometimes clustered in ritual complexes within *oppida* or open agglomerations. They show traces of ritual deposition of various artefact types, often weapons, as well as evidence for blood sacrifice and feasting. The connection between the princely elites and the divine sphere was close, especially in the early La Tène period. This is also apparent from the role of gold jewellery as both a status symbol and a projection of religious competence. As well as in burials, gold jewellery occurs as votive offerings (Erstfeld) and ornamenting wooden statues of deities, such as those from Villeneuve in Geneva harbour, which were adorned with golden torcs (Birkhan 1997).

A different form of religious practice existed in the burnt offering sites or *Brandopferplätze* of the Alpine Fritzens-Sanzeno culture, associated with the historical Raeti (Chapter 11). These places of sacrifice were part of a long-lived tradition reaching back to the Bronze Age. Many were located on mountain tops or promontories overlooking valleys, but in the Iron Age *Brandopferplätze* also occurred in inner Alpine valleys and on the fringes of the central Alps (Steiner 2010: 493, fig. 228). They vary in character, changing form and showing various types of construction and deposition over time (Steiner 2010: 219–662). Blood sacrifice was the central feature: that is, the offering of animals to the gods by burning their carcasses on a stone altar, very like Olympic sacrifice, and sometimes involving an identical choice of body parts (Völling 2002). Parts of the sacrificed animals were consumed in acts of communal ritual feasting, and large quantities of Fritzens-Sanzeno bowls, used for drink or libations, were intentionally smashed and deposited. The *Brandopferplätze* thus come close to a religious practice known in contemporary Mediterranean cultures.

The burnt offering sites had remarkably long lifespans (Steiner 2010: 652–653), sometimes continuing into the late Roman period, as at the Piller Sattel near Fließ in North Tyrol. The repeated sacrifice of animals resulted in a stratigraphy more than 2 m deep, with alternating layers of burnt and crushed animal bones and ashes (Tschurtschenthaler and Wein 2002). Offering activities did, however, change in character over time. In the late Iron Age, the Piller Sattel was characterized by deposition of La Tène swords, helmet parts, and iron tools, pointing to male dedicants. Elsewhere, as at Demlfeld near Ampass in North Tyrol, fibulae and other dress accessories hint at female worshippers (Tomedi et al. 2006). Fragments of bronze vessels and dedications in the Raetic alphabet are also frequent finds at burnt offering sites. *Potnia theron* ('Mistress of the Animals') bronze pendants of a female figure flanked by horse heads are commonly identified with the goddess Raetia (Egg 1986). Artefact offerings of Iron Age date were often intentionally deformed or cut into pieces, and thus represent acts of ritual violence mirroring the destructive nature of the burning. Sometimes sanctuaries, built structures, or houses in which dedicated objects may have been stored are associated with these sites. At Saint Walburg-Ulten in South Tyrol, several *Brandopferplätze* consisting of clay floors and stone-framed altars have been excavated (Steiner 2010: 121–217).

Conclusion

Since the nineteenth century, the finds-rich sites of Hallstatt and La Tène have provided the basis for the chrono-typological divisions still used throughout much of Europe. However, looked at from a different perspective, the material changes used to define the transitions from the late Bronze Age to the early Iron Age and from the Hallstatt to the La Tène periods seem less obvious. In terms of both burial rituals and settlement patterns, the links between the late Urnfield and early Hallstatt periods are in some ways stronger than those between Hallstatt C and D. Similarly, the affinities between Hallstatt D2–D3 and La Tène A are often closer than those between the early and middle La Tène periods—a reminder that historical processes cannot be understood on the basis of material culture alone.

Regional divergences at the start of the Iron Age would lead to the emergence of distinct eastern and western Hallstatt cultural spheres. Cremation remained predominant in the east, whereas in the west a new memorial culture was expressed by the barrow burials of a sword-bearing male elite of wagon drivers. Influences from the steppes and northern Italy are evident in the east, but burial continued Urnfield traditions of elite behaviour and there is greater settlement continuity than in the west. Around 600 BC, significant changes can be observed both in the eastern Hallstatt sphere, where long occupied hillforts were abandoned and burial ceased in some tumulus cemeteries, hinting at contingent sociopolitical changes, and in the west, where unprecedented social stratification and centralization become apparent in the emergence of town-like princely seats and associated princely tombs of both men and women with strong Mediterranean contacts.

Although iron quickly became the favoured material for weapons and wagon-building, bronze remained in use for jewellery and prestige vessels throughout the first millennium BC. Apart from the supra-regional salt production sites, the Hallstatt economy was based primarily on the large household (*oikos*). A division between consumer and producer sites developed in the late Hallstatt period, when new techniques such as the potter's wheel, better furnace types, and advances in iron smelting technology created the preconditions for the shift in the middle La Tène period to an economy based on proto-urban centres with specialized craft workshops and large-scale production of goods, and, from the third century BC, the adoption from the classical world of coinage as an equivalent for material value.

Mediterranean contacts, particularly during the Celtic migrations, thus not only led to economic changes, but also affected social organization, seen in the rise of more distinct social groups. A larger warrior elite, alongside well-dressed elite women, dominate the burial record, complemented by specialized craftsmen, and perhaps craftswomen, and ritual and religious specialists. A large part of the population, particularly those of low or non-free status, is difficult to trace in either the Hallstatt or La Tène burial record, while from La Tène C2, burial of any kind is generally rare, possibly reflecting changing beliefs. The renunciation of princely burial accords well with new, centralized forms of living in town-like agglomerations and fortified *oppida*, regarded as the first towns north of the Alps, which functioned over generations as foci of group identity until the Roman conquest.

The expression of religious beliefs shows both continuity and discontinuity over the eight centuries of the Iron Age. A significant novelty was the overcoming of the Bronze Age taboo on depicting the human body or divine entities of anthropomorphic shape. Initially a preserve of the eastern sphere, figurative and scenic art became fairly common in La Tène Europe. The interruption during Hallstatt C of votive metalwork hoarding is another important departure from the Bronze Age, although the practice of making offerings soon resumed. A new concept of veneration and more institutionalized religious activity is apparent from the middle La Tène period, with the appearance of built structures or temples in settlements.

Notes

1. The Bylany group is considered a 'culture' in Czech archaeology (Koutecký 2013).
2. For north-east Bavaria, Sabine Pabst-Dörrer (2000) has suggested a Hallstatt C date for rich female dress accessories with spectacle fibulae.

3. Despite these very substantial numbers, both here and elsewhere in Hallstatt central Europe, archaeologically recoverable graves were clearly the preserve of a small minority.
4. Pare (1992: 204) recorded just over 200 sword graves from southern Germany, emphasizing the exclusive character of the weapon type. In Hallstatt D, only around sixty dagger graves are known, implying a diminished role for warfare in the symbolic context of burial (Kull 1997).
5. In 1883, 1,124 barrows were recorded; today around 700 barrows are still visible around Kleinklein, of which fewer than 10% have been excavated (Egg and Kramer 2005: 4).
6. Whether the cists covered wooden vessels, or were non-functional and just for display at the funeral is unclear.
7. The statue is 1.86 m high, but missing the feet. The man in the (non-central) burial 1 was 1.69 m tall and 28–30 years old (Schwitalla 2008).
8. At Pottenbrunn, an existing cemetery was replaced at the end of La Tène A by another burial ground with a new kind of grave architecture of ditched enclosures marking the burials.
9. In contrast to the *murus gallicus* type of rampart—with a stone front and timber frame construction fixed together with iron nails, and filled with a stone packing—which predominates west of the Rhine.
10. The long sword now appears again in graves after a break in deposition in Hallstatt D.

References

Abels, B.-U. 2010. 'Die Ehrenbürg bei Forchheim. Die frühlatènezeitliche Zentralsiedlung Nordostbayerns', in D. Krausse (ed.) *'Fürstensitze' und Zentralorte der frühen Kelten: Abschlusskolloquium des DFG-Schwerpunktprogramms 1171 in Stuttgart, 12.–15. Oktober 2009*. Forschungen und Berichte zur Vor- und Frühgeschichte in Baden-Württemberg 120–121: 101–128. Stuttgart: Theiss.

Adler, H. 1965. *Das urgeschichtliche Gräberfeld Linz-St. Peter*. Linzer archäologische Forschungen 2. Linz: Stadtmuseum Linz-Nordico.

Augstein, M. 2015. *Das Gräberfeld der Hallstatt- und Frühlatènezeit von Dietfurt an der Altmühl (›Tankstelle‹): Ein Beitrag zur Analyse einer Mikroregion*. Universitätsforschungen zur Prähistorischen Archäologie 262. Bonn: Habelt.

Bagley, J. M. 2014. *Zwischen Kommunikation und Distinktion: Ansätze zur Rekonstruktion frühlatènezeitliche Bildpraxis*. Vorgeschichtliche Forschungen 25. Rahden: Marie Leidorf.

Bagley, J. M., C. Eggl, D. Neumann, and R. Schumann. 2010. 'Die späthallstatt-/frühlatènezeitliche Siedlung an der Haffstraße in München-Trudering'. *Bericht der Bayerischen Bodendenkmalpflege* 51: 67–125.

Baitinger, H. 2010. *Der Glauberg—ein Fürstensitz der Späthallstatt-/Frühlatènezeit in Hessen*. Materialien zur Vor- und Frühgeschichte in Hessen. Wiesbaden: Landesamt für Denkmalpflege Hessen.

Baitinger, H., L. Hansen, and C. F. E. Pare. 2012. 'Ein Zentrum an der Peripherie? Der Fürstensitz auf dem Glauberg', in R. Röber, M. Jansen, S. Rau, C. von Nicolai, and I. Frech (eds) *Die Welt der Kelten: Zentren der Macht—Kostbarkeiten der Kunst. Ausstellungskatalog Stuttgart*: 157–164. Ostfildern: Thorbecke.

Baitinger, H., and B. Pinsker (eds). 2002. *Das Rätsel der Kelten vom Glauberg: Glaube—Mythos—Wirklichkeit*. Darmstadt: Wissenschaftliche Buchgesellschaft.

Balzer, I. 2009. *Chronologisch-chorologische Untersuchung des späthallstatt- und frühlatènezeitlichen 'Fürstensitzes' auf dem Münsterberg von Breisach (Grabungen 1980–1986)*. Materialhefte zur Archäologie in Baden-Württemberg 84. Stuttgart: Theiss.

Balzer, I. 2010. 'Neue Forschungen zu alten Fragen. Der früheisenzeitliche "Fürstensitz" Hohenasperg (Kr. Ludwigsburg) und sein Umland', in D. Krausse (ed.) *'Fürstensitze' und Zentralorte der frühen Kelten: Abschlusskolloquium des DFG-Schwerpunktprogramms 1171 in Stuttgart, 12.–15. Oktober 2009*. Forschungen und Berichte zur Vor- und Frühgeschichte in Baden-Württemberg 120–121: 209–238. Stuttgart: Theiss.

Banck-Burgess, J. 1999. *Hochdorf IV: Die Textilfunde aus dem späthallstattzeitlichen Fürstengrab von Eberdingen-Hochdorf (Kreis Ludwigburg) und weitere Grabtextilien aus hallstatt- und latènezeitlichen Kulturgruppen*. Forschungen und Berichte zur Vor- und Frühgeschichte in Baden-Württemberg 70. Stuttgart: Theiss.

Berg, F. 1962. *Das Flachgräberfeld der Hallstattkultur von Maiersch*. Veröffentlichungen der Österreichischen Arbeitsgemeinschaft für Ur- und Frühgeschichte 4. Vienna: Institut für Ur- und Frühgeschichte der Universität Wien.

Berg-Hobohm, S. 2002–2003. 'Umfriedete Höfe der Hallstattzeit in Bayern. Aktueller Forschungsstand zu den Herrenhöfen und den zeitgleichen rechteckigen Grabenwerken'. *Bericht der Bayerischen Bodendenkmalpflege* 43–44: 161–189.

Bieg, G. 2002. *Hochdorf V: Der Bronzekessel aus dem späthallstattzeitlichen Fürstengrab von Eberdingen-Hochdorf (Kr. Ludwigsburg)*. Forschungen und Berichte zur Vor- und Frühgeschichte in Baden-Württemberg 83. Stuttgart: Theiss.

Biel, J. 1985. *Der Keltenfürst von Hochdorf*. Stuttgart: Theiss.

Biel, J. 2015. *Hochdorf IX: Die eisenzeitliche Siedlung in der Flur Reps und andere vorgeschichtliche Fundstellen von Eberdingen-Hochdorf (Kreis Ludwigsburg)*. Forschungen und Berichte zur Vor- und Frühgeschichte in Baden-Württemberg 111. Stuttgart: Theiss.

Binding, U. 1993. *Studien zu den figürlichen Fibeln der Frühlatènezeit*. Universitätsforschungen zur Prähistorischen Archäologie 16. Bonn: Habelt.

Birkhan, H. 1997. *Kelten—Versuch einer Gesamtdarstellung ihrer Kultur*. Vienna: Verlag der Österreichischen Akademie der Wissenschaften.

Bradley, R. 1990. *The Passage of Arms: An Archaeological Analysis of Prehistoric Hoards and Votive Deposits*. Cambridge: Cambridge University Press.

Bräuning, A., W. Löhlein, and S. Plouin. 2012. *Die frühe Eisenzeit zwischen Schwarzwald und Vogesen/Le Premier âge du Fer entre la Forêt-Noire et les Vosges*. Stuttgart: Landesamt für Denkmalpflege.

Brun, P., and B. Chaume (eds) 1997. *Vix et les éphemères principautés celtiques. Les VIe–Ve siècles avant J.-C. en Europe centro-occidentale*. Paris: Éditions Errance.

Burger, I. 1984. *Das Oppidum Alkimoennis*. Abendsberg: Verlag der Weltenburger Akademie.

Chaume, B. 2001. *Vix et son territoire à l'Age du Fer. Fouilles du mont Lassois et environnement du site princier*. Protohistoire Européene 6. Montagnac: Monique Mergoil.

Chaume, B., and C. Mordant (eds). 2011. *Le complexe aristocratique de Vix: Nouvelles recherches sur l'habitat, le système de fortification et l'environnement du mont Lassois*. Dijon: Éditions Universitaires de Dijon.

Chvojka, O., and J. Michálek. 2011. *Výzkumy Josefa Ladislava Píče na mohylových pohřebištích doby bronzové a halštatské v jižních Čechách/Ausgrabungen von Josef Ladislav Píč aus den Hügelgräberfeldern aus der Bronze- und Hallstattzeit in Südböhmen*. Prague: Národní Muzeum.

Chytráček, M. 1999. 'Élite burials in Bohemia from the 6th–5th century BC and the beginnings of a new art-style', in A. Villes and A. Bataille-Melkon (eds) *Fastes des Celtes entre Champagne et Bourgogne aux VIIe–IIIe siècles avant notre ère: Actes du colloque de l'AFEAF tenu à Troyes en 1995*. Mémoire de la Société Archéologique Champenoise 15: 359–377. Reims: Société Archéologique Champenoise.

Chytráček, M. 2008. 'Die Nachahmung einer rotfigurigen Trinkschale aus der frühlatènezeitlichen Flachlandsiedlung von Chržín (Mittelböhmen) und das überregionale Verkehrsnetz der Hallstatt- und Frühlatènezeit in Böhmen'. *Germania* 86: 47–101.

Chytráček, M., and M. Metlička. 2004. *Die Höhensiedlungen der Hallstatt- und Latenezeit in Westböhmen*. Památky archeologické Supplementum 16. Prague: Institute of Archaeology, Academy of Sciences of the Czech Republic.

Collis, J. R. 1984. *Oppida: Earliest Towns North of the Alps*. Sheffield: University of Sheffield.

Collis, J. R. 1993. 'Die Oppidazivilisation', in H. Dannheimer and R. Gebhard (eds) *Das keltische Jahrtausends*: 102–106. Mainz: Philipp von Zabern.

Collis, J. R. 2003. *The Celts: Origins, Myths and Inventions*. Stroud: Tempus.

Czajlik, Z., G. Király, A. Czövek, S. Puszta, B. Holl, and G. Brolly. 2012. 'The application of remote sensing technology and geophysical methods in the topographic survey of early Iron Age burial tumuli in Transdanubia', in S. Berecki (ed.) *Iron Age Rites and Rituals in the Carpathian Basin: Proceedings of the International Colloquium from Târgu Mureş 7–9 October 2011*: 65–76. Târgu Mureş: Editura Mega.

Déchelette, J. 1914. *Manuel d'Archéologie Préhistorique, Celtique et Gallo-Romaine. II-3: Deuxième âge du Fer ou époque de La Tène*. Paris: Picard.

Deffressigne, S., and N. Tikonoff. 2013. 'La Lorraine', in F. Malrain, G. Blancquaert, and T. Lorho (eds) *L'habitat rural du second âge du Fer: Rhythmes de création et d'abandon au nord de la Loire*: 45–66. Paris: CNRS Éditions/Inrap.

Deffressigne, S., N. Tikonoff, and M. Georges-Leroy. 2012. 'La proto-urbanisation dans le bassin de Nancy (Lorraine) de la fin du VIe au Ier siècle av. J.-C.', in S. Sievers and M. Schönfelder (eds) *Die Frage der Protourbanisation in der Eisenzeit/ La question de la protourbanisation à l'âge du Fer: Akten des 34. internationalen Kolloquiums der AFEAF vom 13.–16. Mai 2010 in Aschaffenburg*. Kolloquien zur Vor- und Frühgeschichte 16: 127–137. Bonn: Habelt.

Deffressigne-Tikonoff, S., and N. Tikonoff. 2005. 'L'habitat à la fin du deuxième âge du Fer en Meurthe-et-Moselle: présentation des données récentes', in S. Fichtl (ed.) *Hiérarchie de l'habitat rural dans le nord-est de la Gaule à la La Tène Moyenne et Finale*. Archaeologia Mosellana 6: 103–150.

Dehn, R., M. Egg, and R. Lehnert. 2005. *Das hallstattzeitliche Fürstengrab im Hügel 3 von Kappel am Rhein in Baden*. RGZM Monographien 63. Mainz: Römisch-Germanisches Zentralmuseum.

Dobiat, C. 1980. *Das hallstattzeitliche Gräberfeld von Kleinklein und seine Keramik. Schild von Steier Beiheft 1*. Graz: Landesmuseum Joanneum.

Dobiat, C. 1990. *Der Burgstallkogel bei Kleinklein I: Die Ausgrabungen der Jahre 1982 und 1984*. Marburger Studien zur Vor- und Frühgeschichte 13. Marburg: Hitzeroth.

Dörrer, O. 2002. 'Das Grab eines nordostalpinen Kriegers in Hallstatt. Zur Rolle von Fremdpersonen in der alpinen Salzmetropole'. *Archaeologia Austriaca* 86: 55–82.

Drack, W. 1958. 'Wagengräber und Wagenbestandteile aus Hallstattgrabhügeln der Schweiz'. *Zeitschrift für Schweizer Archäologie und Kunstgeschichte* 18: 1–67.

Drack, W. 1958–1959. *Ältere Eisenzeit der Schweiz: Kanton Bern 1–2*. Materialhefte zur Ur- und Frühgeschichte der Schweiz 1–2. Basel: Birkhäuser.

Drack, W. 1964. *Ältere Eisenzeit der Schweiz: Die Westschweiz: Kantone Freiburg, Genf, Neuenburg, Waadt und Wallis*. Materialhefte zur Ur- und Frühgeschichte der Schweiz 4. Basel: Birkhäuser.

Drda, P. 1995. *Les Celtes de Bohême*. Paris: Errance.

Drda, P., and A. Rybová. 2008. *Akropole na hradišti Závist v 6.–4. stol. př. Kr. (Akropolis von Závist im 6.–4. Jh. v. Chr.)*. Památky archeologické Supplementum 19. Prague: Institute of Archaeology, Academy of Sciences of the Czech Republic.

Dular, J., and S. Tecco Hvala. 2007. *South-Eastern Slovenia in the Early Iron Age: Settlement—Economy—Society*. Opera Instituti Archaeologici Sloveniae 12. Ljubljana: Založba ZRC.

Dvořák, F. 1938. *Knížecí pohřby na vozech ze starší doby Železné/Wagengräber der älteren Eisnezeit in Böhmen*. Prague: Prehistorický ústav Karlowy university.

Echt, R. 1999. *Das Fürstinnengrab von Reinheim: Studien zur Kulturgeschichte der Früh-Latènezeit*. BLESA 2/Saarbrücker Beiträge zur Altertumskunde 69. Bonn: Habelt.

Egg, M. 1986. 'Die Herrin der Pferde im Ostalpengebiet'. *Archäologisches Korrespondenzblatt* 16: 69–78.

Egg, M. 1996. *Das Hallstattzeitliche Fürstengrab von Strettweg bei Judenburg in der Obersteiermark*. RGZM Monographien 37. Mainz: Römisch-Germanisches Zentralmuseum.

Egg, M., and D. Kramer. 2005. *Krieger—Feste—Totenopfer: Der letzte Hallstattfürst von Kleinklein in der Steiermark*. Mosaiksteine. Forschungen am Römisch-Germanischen Zentralmuseum 1. Mainz: Römisch-Germanisches Zentralmuseum.

Egg, M., and D. Kramer (eds). 2013. *Die Hallstattzeitlichen Fürstengräber von Kleinklein in der Steiermark: Der Kröllkogel*. RGZM Monographien 110. Mainz: Römisch-Germanisches Zentralmuseum.

Egg, M., and D. Kramer. 2016. *Die hallstattzeitlichen Fürstengräber von Kleinklein in der Steiermark: die beiden Harnermichelkogel und der Pommerkogel*. RGZM Monographien 125. Mainz: Römisch-Germanisches Zentralmuseum.

Eibner, A. 2001. 'Die Stellung der Frau in der Hallstattkultur anhand der bildlichen Zeugnisse'. *Mitteilungen der Anthropologischen Gesellschaft in Wien* 130/131: 107–136.

Engelhardt, B., and B. Häck. 1999. 'Neue Ausgrabungen im späthallstattzeitlichen Grabhügelfeld von Niedererlbach Gemeindes Buch a. Erlbach, Landkreis Landshut, Niederbayern'. *Das archäologische Jahr in Bayern* 1998: 45–47.

Ettel, P. 1996. *Gräberfelder der Hallstattzeit aus Oberfranken*. Materialhefte zur Bayerischen Vorgeschichte 72. Kallmünz: Lassleben.

Fichtl, S. 2000. *La ville celtique: Les oppida de 150 av. J.-C. à 15 ap. J.-C.* Paris: Errance.

Filip, J. 1936–1937. *Popelnicová pole a počátky dobyželezné v Čechách/Die Urnenfelder und die Anfänge der Eisenzeit in Böhmen*. Prague: Vytiskla Státní Tiskárna.

Filip, J. 1960. *Keltská Civilizace a jeji Dedictvi*. Prague: Akademia.

Fischer, U. 1979. *Ein Grabhügel der Bronze- und Eisenzeit im Frankfurter Stadtwald*. Frankfurt: Kramer.

Fontijn, D. 2002. *Sacrificial Landscapes: Cultural Biographies of Persons, Objects and 'Natural' Places in the Bronze Age of the Southern Netherlands, c.2300–600 BC*. Analecta Praehistorica Leidensia 33/34. Leiden: University of Leiden.

Fougère, F. 2016. *La tombe de Vix: Un trésor Celte entre histoire et légende*. Lyon: Editions Fage.

Frey, O.-H. 1969. *Die Entstehung der Situlenkunst: Studien zur figürlich verzierten Toreutik von Este*. Römisch-Germanische Forschungen 31. Berlin: De Gruyter.

Frey, O.-H. 2002a. 'Menschen oder Heroen? Die Statuen vom Glauberg und die frühe Keltische Großplastik', in H. Baitinger and B. Pinsker (eds) *Glaube—Mythos—Wirklichkeit: Das Rätsel der Kelten vom Glauberg*: 208–218. Stuttgart: Theiss.

Frey, O.-H. 2002b. 'Frühe keltische Kunst—Dämonen und Götter', in H. Baitinger and B. Pinsker (eds) *Glaube—Mythos—Wirklichkeit: Das Rätsel der Kelten vom Glauberg*: 186–205. Stuttgart: Theiss.

Friedrich, M., and H. Hennig. 1995. 'Dendrochronologische Untersuchung der Hölzer des hallstattzeitlichen Wagengrabes 8 aus Wehringen, Lkr. Augsburg und andere Absolutdaten zur Hallstattzeit'. *Bayerische Vorgeschichtsblätter* 60: 289–300.

Fries, J. E. 2005. *Die Hallstattzeit im Nördlinger Ries*. Materialhefte zur bayerischen Vorgeschichte 88. Kallmünz: Lassleben.

Gabrovec, S. 1966. 'Zur Hallstattzeit in Slowenien'. *Germania* 44: 1–48.

Gabrovec, S., and B. Teržan. 2010. *Gomile starjše železne dobe. Razprave: Grabhügel aus der älteren Eisenzeit*. Katalogi in monografije 38. Ljubljana: Narodni muzej Slovenije.

Gassmann, G., M. Rösch, and G. Wieland. 2006. 'Das Neuenbürger Erzrevier im Nordschwarzwald als Wirtschaftsraum während der Späthallstatt- und Frühlatènezeit'. *Germania* 84, 2: 273–306.

Gebhard, R. 1989. *Der Glasschmuck aus dem Oppidum von Manching*. Die Ausgrabungen in Manching 11. Stuttgart: Steiner.

Gebhard, R. 1991. *Die Fibeln aus dem Oppidum von Manching*. Die Ausgrabungen in Manching 14. Stuttgart: Steiner.

Gebhard, R., C. Metzner-Nebelsick, and R. Schumann. 2016. 'Excavating an extraordinary burial of the early Hallstatt period from Otzing, eastern Bavaria, in the museum laboratories'. *Past: Newsletter of the Prehistoric Society* 82: 1–3.

Gleba, M. 2011. 'The "distaff side" of early Iron Age aristocratic identity in Italy', in M. Gleba and H. Horsnaes (eds) *Communicating Identity in Italic Iron Age Communities*: 26–32. Oxford: Oxbow.

Gleirscher, P. 2009. 'Ente, Entenmann und Heros in der Situalenkunst. Zur mythologischen Deutung eines Deckelfrieses mit Tierbildern aus Waisenberg (Kärtnen)'. *Germania* 87: 411–436.

Gleser, R. 2005. *Studien zu sozialen Strukturen der historischen Kelten in Mitteleuropa aufgrund der Gräberanalyse: die keltisch-römische Nekropole von Hoppstädten-Weiersbach im Kontext latènezeitlicher Fundgruppen und römischer Okkupation*. Bonn: Habelt.

Guggisberg, M. A. 2000. *Der Goldschtz von Erstfeld: Ein keltischer Bilderzyklus zwischen Mitteleuropa und der Mittelmeerwelt*. Antiqua 24. Basel: Verlag der Schweizerischen Gesellschaft für Ur- und Frühgeschichte.

Guichard, V., S. Sievers, and O. Urban. 2000. *Les processus d'urbanisation à l'âge du Fer*. Collection Bibracte 4. Glux en Glenne: Centre Archéologique Européen du Mont Beuvray.

Gumă, M. 1993. *Civilizația primei epoci a fierului în sud-vestul României*. Bucharest: București Institutul Român de Tracologie.

Haffner, A. 1976. *Die westliche Hunsrück-Eifel-Kultur*. Römisch-Germanische Forschungen 36. Berlin: De Gruyter.

Haffner, A., and A. Abegg. 1989. *Gräber—Spiegel des Lebens: zum Totenbrauchtum der Kelten und Römer am Beispiel der Treverer-Gräberfeldes Wederath-Belginum*. Mainz: Philipp von Zabern.

Hansen, L. 2010. *Hochdorf VIII: Die Goldfunde und Trachtbeigaben des späthallstattzeitlichen Fürstengrabes von Eberdingen-Hochdorf (Kr. Ludwigsburg)*. Forschungen und Berichte zur Vor- und Frühgeschichte in Baden-Württemberg 118. Stuttgart: Theiss.

Hansen, L. 2016. *Die Latènezeitliche Saline von Bad Nauheim: Die Befunde der Grabungen der Jahre 2001–2004 in der Kurstraße 2*. Fundberichte aus Hessen Beiheft 8/Glauberg Forschungen 2. Bonn: Habelt.

Hansen, L., and C. F. E. Pare. 2016. *Untersuchungen im Umland des Glaubergs Zur Genese und Entwicklung eines frühlatènezeitlichen Fürstensitzes in der östlichen Wetterau*. Materialien zur Vor- und Frühgeschichte von Hessen/Glauberg Studien 2. Wiesbaden: Landesamt für Denkmalpflege Hessen.

Hansen, S., D. Neumann, and T. Vachta (eds). 2012. *Hort und Raum: Aktuelle Forschungen zu bronzezeitlichen Deponierungen in Mitteleuropa*. Berlin/Boston: De Gruyter.

Harding, A. 2013. *Salt in Prehistoric Europe*. Leiden: Sidestone Press.

Harding, D. W. 2007. *The Archaeology of Celtic Art*. London/New York: Routledge.

Haselgrove, C., and V. Guichard. 2013. 'Les gaulois sont-ils dans la plaine? Reflections on settlement patterns in Gaul in the 1st century BC', in S. Krausz, A. Colin, K. Gruel, I. Ralston, and T. Dechezleprêtre (eds) *L'âge du Fer en Europe: Mélanges offerts à Olivier Buchsenschutz*: 317–328. Bordeaux: Ausonius.

Hecht, J., and A. Niederhäuser. 2011. *Alltagskultur und Totenrituale der Kelten/The Everyday Culture and Funerary Rituals of the Celts*. Basel: Merian.

Hellerschmid, I. 2006. *Die urnenfelder-/hallstattzeitliche Wallanlage von Stillfried an der March: Ergebnisse der Ausgrabungen 1969–1989 unter besonderer Berücksichtigung des Kulturwandels an der Epochengrenze Urnenfelder/Hallstattkultur*. Mitteilungen der Prähistorischen Kommission 63. Vienna: Verlag der Österreichischen Akademie der Wissenschaften.

Hennig, H. 2001. *Die Gräber der Hallstattzeit in Bayerisch-Schwaben*. Monographien der Archäologischen Staatssammlung München. Stuttgart: Theiss.

Hildebrand, H. 1874. 'Sur les commencements de l'âge du Fer en Europe', in *Congrès Internationale d'Anthropologie et d'Archéologie Préhistorique*: 592–601. Stockholm: P. A. Norstedt.

Hodson, F. R. 1968. *The La Tène Cemetery at Münsingen-Rain: Catalogue and Relative Chronology*. Acta Bernensia 5. Bern: Stämpfli.

Hodson, F. R. 1990. *Hallstatt: The Ramsauer Graves: Quantification and Analysis*. RGZM Monographien 16. Mainz: Römisch-Germanisches Zentralmuseum.

Hofeneder, A. 2005. *Die Religion der Kelten in den antiken literarischen Zeugnissen: Sammlung, Übersetzung und Kommentierung 1: Von den Anfängen bis Caesar*. Vienna: Verlag der Österreichischen Akademie der Wissenschaften.

Hofeneder, A. 2008. *Die Religion der Kelten in den antiken literarischen Zeugnissen: Sammlung, Übersetzung und Kommentierung 2: Von Cicero bis Florus*. Vienna: Verlag der Österreichischen Akademie der Wissenschaften.

Hofeneder, A. 2011. *Die Religion der Kelten in den antiken literarischen Zeugnissen: Sammlung, Übersetzung und Kommentierung 3: Von Arrianos bis zum Ausklang der Antike*. Vienna: Verlag der Österreichischen Akademie der Wissenschaften.

Holzer, V. (ed.) 2009. *Roseldorf: Interdisziplinäre Forschungen zur größten keltischen Zentralsiedlung Österreichs; KG. Roseldorf, MG. Sitzendorf an der Schmieda*. Schriftenreihe der Forschung im Verbund 102. Vienna: Österreichische Elektrizitätswirtschafts-Aktiengesellschaft.

Holzer, V. 2014. 'Roseldorf: An enclosed central settlement of the early and middle La Tène period in Lower Austria (Roseldorf/Němčice Centre)', in M. Fernández-Götz, H. Wendling, and K. Winger (eds) *Paths to Complexity: Centralisation and Urbanisation in Iron Age Europe*: 122–131. Oxford: Oxbow Books.

Honegger, M., D. Ramseyer, G. Kaenel, B. Arnold, and M.-A. Kaeser (eds). 2009. *Le site de La Tène: bilan des connaissances—état de la question: Actes de la Table ronde internationale de Neuchâtel, 1–3 novembre 2007*. Archéologie neuchâteloise 43. Neuchâtel: Office et musée cantonal d'archéologie.

Hoppe, M. 1986. *Die Grabfunde der Hallstattzeit in Mittelfranken*. Materialhefte zur bayerischen Vorgeschichte A55. Kallmünz: Lassleben.

Hoppe, M. 2005. *Das hallstattzeitliche Gräberfeld von Beilngries 'Im Ried-Ost', Lkr. Eichstätt, Oberbayern: kommentierter Katalog der Funde und Befunde der Untersuchungen von 1988–1992*. Rahden: Marie Leidorf.

Hoppe, T. 2012. 'Die "Kline" von Hochdorf', in R. Röber, M. Jansen, S. Rau, C. von Nicolai, and I. Frech (eds) *Die Welt der Kelten: Zentren der Macht—Kostbarkeiten der Kunst: Ausstellungskatalog Stuttgart 2012*: 222–225. Ostfildern: Thorbecke.

Hornung, S. 2008. *Die südöstliche Hunsrück-Eifel-Kultur: Studien zu Späthallstatt- und Frühlatènezeit in der deutschen Mittelgebirgsregion*. Universitätsforschungen zur Prähistorischen Archäologie 153. Bonn: Habelt.

Hughes, R. 1999. *Das hallstattzeitliche Gräberfeld von Schirndorf, Ldkr. Regensburg V*. Materialhefte zur Bayerischen Vorgeschichte A 78. Kallmünz: Lassleben.

Hughes, R. 2001. *Das hallstattzeitliche Gräberfeld von Schirndorf, Ldkr. Regensburg VI*. Materialhefte zur Bayerischen Vorgeschichte A 79. Kallmünz: Lassleben.

Hummel, S., D. Schmidt, and B. Hermann. 2005. 'Molekulargenetische Analysen zur Verwandtschaftfeststellung an Skelettproben aus Gräbern frühkeltischer Fürstensitze', in J. Biel and D. Krausse (eds) *Frühkeltische Fürstensitze: Älteste Städte und Herrschaftszentren nördlich der Alpen? Internationaler Workshop zur keltischen Archäologie in Eberdingen-Hochdorf 2003*. Archäologische Informationen aus Baden-Württemberg 51: 67–70. Stuttgart: Landsamt für Denkmalpflege.

Irlinger, W. 1995. *Der Dürrnberg bei Hallein V: Die Siedlung auf dem Ramsaukopf*. Munich: Beck.

Jacobi, G. 1974. *Werkzeug und Gerät aus dem Oppidum von Manching*. Die Ausgrabungen von Manching 5. Wiesbaden: Steiner.

Jacobsthal, P. 1944 (reprinted 1969). *Early Celtic Art*. Oxford: Clarendon Press.

Jerem, E., and O. H. Urban. 2000. 'Höhensiedlungen—Befestigungen—Zentralsiedlungen: Prozesse der Urbanisierung im Donau-Karpaten-Raum', in V. Guichard, S. Sievers, and O. H. Urban (eds) *Les processus d'urbanisation à l'âge du Fer/Eisenzeitliche Urbanisierungsprozesse*. Collection Bibracte 4: 157–164. Glux-en-Glenne: Centre archéologique européen du Mont Beuvray.

Jerem, E., M. Zeiler, P. Ramsl, and J. V. S. Megaw. 2009. 'Stempelgleiche Frühlatènekeramik zwischen Traisental und Neusiedlersee', in G. Cooney, K. Becker, J. Coles, M. Ryan, and S. Sievers (eds) *Relics of Old Decency: Archaeological Studies in Later Prehistory: Festschrift for Barry Raftery*: 259–276. Dublin: Wordwell.

Joachim, H.-E. 1968. *Die Hunsrück-Eifel-Kultur am Mittelrhein*. Beihefte der Bonner Jahrbücher 29. Cologne: Böhlau Verlag.

Joachim, H.-E. 1995. *Waldalgesheim: Das Grab einer keltischen Fürstin*. Kataloge des Rheinischen Landesmuseums Bonn 3. Cologne/Puhlheim: Rheinland-Verlag.

Jockenhövel, A. 1974. 'Zur Benennung urnenfelderzeitlicher Stufen im östlichen Mitteleuropa'. *Jahresbericht des Instituts für Vorgeschichte der Universität Frankfurt a. M.* 1974: 57–69.

Joffroy, R. 1958. *Les sépultures à char du premier âge du fer en France*. Paris: Picard.

Jud. P. 1998. 'Untersuchungen zur Struktur des Gräberfeldesvon Münsingen-Rain', in F. Müller (ed.) *Münsingen-Rain: Ein Markstein der keltischen Archäologie: Funde, Befunde und Methoden im Vergleich. Akten des Internationalen Kolloquiums 'Das keltische Gräberfeld von*

Münsingen-Rain 1906–1996' in Münsingen bei Bern vom 9. bis 12. Oktober 1996. Schriften des Bernischen Historischen Museums 2: 123–144. Bern: Bernisches Museum.

Jud, P. 2008. *Die Töpferin und der Schmied: Basel-Gasfabrik, Grabung 1989/5*. Basel: Archäologische Bodenforschung des Kantons Basel-Stadt.

Karasová, Z. 2012. 'Dux—Duchcov', in S. Sievers, O. Urban, and P. Ramsl (eds) *Lexikon der keltischen Archäologie*: 455–457. Vienna: Verlag der Österreichischen Akademie der Wissenschaften.

Karwowski, M., V. Salač, and S. Sievers (eds). 2015. *Boier zwischen Realität und Fiktion: Akten des internationalen Kolloquiums in Český Krumlov vom 14.–16.11.2013. Römisch-Germanische Kommission des Deutschen Archäologischen Instituts*. Kolloquien zur Vor- und Frühgeschichte 21. Bonn: Habelt.

Kas, S., and M. Schussmann. 1998. 'Einige Überlegungen zu den hallstattzeitlichen Herrenhöfen', in B. Berthold, E. Kahler, S. Kas, D. Neubauer, S. Schmidt, and M. Schußmann (eds) *Zeitenblicke: Ehrengabe W. Janssen*: 93–123. Rahden: Marie Leidorf.

Keller, J. 1965. *Das keltische Fürstengrab von Reinheim I: Ausgrabungsbericht und Katalog der Funde*. Mainz/Bonn: Habelt.

Kern, A., K. Kowarik, A. W. Rausch, and H. Reschreiter (eds). 2008. *Salz—Reich: 7000 Jahre Hallstatt*. Veröffentlichungen der Prähistorischen Abteilung 2. Vienna: Naturhistorisches Museum Wien.

Kimmig, W. 1983. 'Die griechische Kolonisation im westlichen Mittelmeergebiet und ihre Wirkung auf die Landschaften des westlichen Mitteleuropa'. *Jahrbuch des Römisch-Germanischen Zentralmuseums Mainz* 30: 5–78.

Kimmig, W. 1988. *Das Kleinaspergle: Studien zu einem Fürstengrabhügel der frühen Latènezeit bei Stuttgart*. Forschungen und Berichte zur Vor- und Frühgeschichte in Baden-Württemberg 30. Stuttgart: Theiss.

Kmeťová, P. 2013. 'The spectacle of the horse: on early Iron Age burial customs in the Eastern-Alpine Hallstatt region'. *Archaeological Review from Cambridge* 28, 2: 67–81.

Knipper, C., C. Mayer, F. Jacobi, et al. 2014. 'Social differentiation and land use at an early Iron Age "princely seat": bioarchaeological investigations at the Glauberg (Germany)'. *Journal of Archaeological Science* 41: 818–835.

Knopf, T. 2006. *Der Heidengraben bei Grabenstetten: archäologische Untersuchungen zur Besiedlungsgeschichte*. Universitätsforschungen zur Prähistorischen Archäologie 141. Bonn: Habelt.

Koch, J. 2006. *Hochdorf VI: Der Wagen und das Pferdegeschirr aus dem späthallstattzeitlichen Fürstengrab von Eberdingen-Hochdorf (Kr. Ludwigsburg)*. Forschungen und Berichte zur Vor- und Frühgeschichte in Baden-Württemberg 89. Stuttgart: Theiss.

Koenig, M.-P. 2016. *Le gisement de Crévéchamps (Lorraine): Du néolithique à l'époque romaine dans la vallée de la Moselle*. Documents d'archéologie française 110. Paris: Éditions de la Maison des sciences de l'homme.

Kossack, G. 1954. *Studien zum Symbolgut der Urnenfelder- und Hallstattzeit Mitteleuropas*. Römisch-Germanische Forschungen 20. Berlin: De Gruyter.

Kossack, G. 1959. *Südbayern während der Hallstattzeit*. Römisch-Germanische Forschungen 25. Berlin: De Gruyter.

Kossack, G. 1970. *Gräberfelder der Hallstattzeit an Main und Fränkischer Saale*. Materialhefte zur bayerischen Vorgeschichte 24. Kallmünz: Lassleben.

Kossack, G. 1971. 'The construction of the felloe in Iron Age spoked wheels', in J. Boardman, M. A. Brown, and T. G. E. Powell (eds) *The European Community in Prehistory: Studies in Honour of C. F. C. Hawkes*: 141–163. London: Routledge and Kegan Paul.

Koutecký, D. 1968. 'Velké hroby, jeich konstrukce, pohřebí ritus a sociální struktura obyvatelstva bylanské kultury/Grossgräber, ihre Konstruktion, Grabritus und soziale Struktur der Bevölkerung der Bylaner Kultur'. *Památky archeologické* 59: 400–487.

Koutecký, D. 2013. 'Hallstatt period, Ha C to Ha D1: culturally specific characteristics', in N. Venclová (ed.) *The Early Iron Age—The Hallstatt Period*. The Prehistory of Bohemia 5: 51–73. Prague: Archeologický ústav AV ČR.

Koutecký, D., and V. Vokolek. 2013. 'The Billendorf culture', in N. Venclová (ed.) *The Early Iron Age—The Hallstatt Period*. The Prehistory of Bohemia 5: 106–107. Prague: Archeologický ústav AV ČR.

Krämer, W. 1959. 'Endlatènezeitliche Brandgräber aus Kronwinkl in Niederbayern'. *Germania* 37: 140–149.

Krämer, W. 1962. 'Manching II. Zu den Ausgrabungen in den Jahren 1957 bis 1961'. *Germania* 40: 293–317.

Krämer, W. 1985. *Die Grabfunde in Manching und die latènezeitlichen Grabfunde in Südbayern*. Die Ausgrabungen in Manching 9. Stuttgart: Steiner.

Krause, R., A. Stobbe, D. Euler, and K. Fuhrmann. 2010. 'Zur Genese und Entwicklung des frühkeltischen Fürstensitzes auf dem Ipf bei Bopfingen (Ostalbkreis, Baden-Württemberg) und seines Umlandes im Nördlinger Ries', in D. Krausse and D. Beilharz (eds) *"Fürstensitze" und Zentralorte der frühen Kelten. Abschlusskolloquium des DFG-Schwerpunktprogramms 1171 in Stuttgart, 12.–15. Oktober 2009*. Forschungen und Berichte zur Vor- und Frühgeschichte in Baden-Württemberg 120–121: 169–207. Stuttgart: Konrad Theiss.

Krause, R. 2014. *Neue Forschungen zum frühkeltischen Fürstensitz auf dem Ipf*. Bonn: Habelt.

Krausse, D. 1996. *Hochdorf III: Das Trink- und Speiseservice aus dem späthallstattzeitlichen Fürstengrab von Eberdingen-Hochdorf (Kr. Ludwigsburg)*. Forschungen und Berichte zur Vor- und Frühgeschichte in Baden-Württemberg 64. Stuttgart: Theiss.

Krausse, D. 1999. 'Der "Keltenfürst" von Hochdorf: Dorfälterster oder Sakralkönig? Anspruch und Wirklichkeit der sog. kulturanthropologischen Hallstatt-Archäologie'. *Archäologisches Korrespondenzblatt* 29: 339–358.

Krausse, D. 2006. 'Prunkgräber der nordwestalpinen Späthallstattkultur. Neue Fragestellungen und Untersuchungen zu ihrer sozialhistorischen Deutung', in C. von Carnap-Bornheim, D. Krausse, and A. Wesse (eds) *Herrschaft—Tod—Bestattung: Zu den vor- und frühgeschichtlichen Prunkgräbern als archäologisch-historische Quelle*. Universitätsforschungen zur prähistorischen Archäologie 139: 61–80. Bonn: Habelt.

Krausse, D. (ed.) 2008. *Frühe Zentralisierungs- und Urbanisierungsprozesse: Zur Genese und Entwicklung frühkeltischer Fürstensitze und ihres territorialen Umlandes: Kolloquium des DFG-Schwerpunktprogramms 1171 in Blaubeuren, 9.–11. Oktober 2006. Festschrift Jörg Biel*. Forschungen und Berichte zur Vor- und Frühgeschichte in Baden-Württemberg 101. Stuttgart: Theiss.

Krausse, D. (ed.) 2010. *'Fürstensitze' und Zentralorte der frühen Kelten: Abschlusskolloquium des DFG-Schwerpunktprogramms 1171 in Stuttgart, 12.–15. Oktober 2009*. Forschungen und Berichte zur Vor- und Frühgeschichte in Baden-Württemberg 120–121. Stuttgart: Theiss.

Krausse, D., N. Ebinger-Rist, S. Million, A. Billamboz, J. Wahl, and E. Stephan. 2017. 'The "Keltenblock" project: discovery and excavation of a rich Hallstatt grave at the Heuneburg, Germany'. *Antiquity* 91: 108–123.

Krausse, D., M. Fernández-Götz, L. Hansen, and I. Kretschmer. 2016. *The Heuneburg and the Early Iron Age Princely Seats: First Towns North of the Alps*. Budapest: Archaeolingua.

Kreuz, A., and K. Friedrich. 2014. 'Iron Age agriculture a potential source of wealth?', in S. Hornung (ed.) *Produktion—Distribution—Ökonomie: Siedlungs- und Wirtschaftsmuster der Latènezeit. Akten des internationalen Kolloquiums in Otzenhausen 28.–30. Oktober 2011.* Universitätsforschungen zur Prähistorischen Archäologie 258: 307–317. Bonn: Habelt.

Križ, B. 2000. *Novo Mesto V: Kapiteljska njiva: Gomila IV in gomila V.* Carniola archaeologica 5. Novo Mesto: Dolenjski Muzej.

Kromer, K. 1959. *Das Gräberfeld von Hallstatt.* Florence: Sansoni.

Kull, B. 1997. 'Tod und Apotheose. Zur Ikonographie in Grab und Kunst der jüngeren Eisenzeit an der unteren Donau und ihre Bedeutung für die Interpretation von "Prunkgräbern"'. *Bericht der Römisch-Germanischen Kommission* 78: 197–466.

Kull, B., and A. Becker. 2003. *Sole und Salz schreiben Geschichte: 50 Jahre Landesarchäologie, 150 Jahre Archäologische Forschung in Bad Nauheim.* Mainz: Philipp von Zabern.

Kurz, G. 1995. *Keltische Hort- und Gewässerfunde in Mitteleuropa: Deponierungen der Latènezeit.* Materialhefte zur Archäologie in Baden-Württemberg 33. Stuttgart: Theiss.

Kurz, S. 1997. *Bestattungsbrauch in der westlichen Hallstattkultur.* Tübinger Schriften zur Ur- und Frühgeschichtlichen Archäologie 2. Münster: Waxmann.

Kurz, S., and S. Schiek. 2002. *Bestattungsplätze im Umfeld der Heuneburg.* Forschungen und Berichte zur Vor- und Frühgeschichte in Baden-Württemberg 87. Stuttgart: Theiss.

Lang, A. 1974. *Die geriefte Drehscheibenkeramik der Heuneburg 1950–1970 und verwandte Gruppen.* Heuneburgstudien III/Römisch-Germanische Forschungen 34. Mainz: Philipp von Zabern.

Lang, A. 1998. *Das Gräberfeld von Kundl im Tiroler Inntal: Studien zur vorrömischen Eisenzeit in den zentralen Alpen.* Frühgeschichtliche und Provinzialrömische Archäologie 2. Rahden: Marie Leidorf.

Lang, A., and V. Salač (eds). 2002. *Fernkontakte in der Eisenzeit: Konferenz Liblice 2000.* Prague: Archäologisches Institut der Akademie der Wissenschaften der Tschechischen Republik.

Later, C. E. 2014. *Die Sapropelitefunde aus dem Oppidum von Manching.* Die Ausgrabungen in Manching 19. Wiesbaden: Reichert Verlag.

Leicht, M. 2000. *Die Wallanlagen des Oppidums Alkimoennis, Kelheim: zur Baugeschichte und Typisierung spätkeltischer Befestigungen.* Rahden: Marie Leidorf.

Lenerz-de Wilde, M. 1977. *Zirkelornament in der Kunst der Latènezeit.* Münchner Beiträge zur Vor- und Frühgeschichte 17. Munich: Beck.

Lippert, A., and P. Stadler. 2009. *Das spätbronze- und früheisenzeitliche Gräberfeld von Bischofshofen-Pestfriedhof.* Universitätsforschungen zur prähistorischen Archäologie 168. Bonn: Habelt.

Lüscher, G. 1993. *Unterlunkhofen und die hallstattzeitliche Grabkeramik in der Schweiz.* Antiqua 24. Basel: Schweizerische Gesellschaft für Ur- und Frühgeschichte.

Maise, C. 1998. 'Archäoklimatologie—vom Einfluss nacheiszeitlicher Klimavariabilität in der Ur- und Frühgeschichte'. *Jahrbuch der Schweizerischen Gesellschaft für Ur- und Frühgeschichte* 81: 197–235.

Mansfeld, G. 1973. *Die Fibeln der Heuneburg 1950–1970: Ein Beitrag zur Geschichte der Späthallstattfibel.* Römisch-Germanische Forschungen 33. Berlin: Walter de Gruyter.

Martin-Kilcher, S. 1973. 'Zur Tracht- und Beigabensitte im keltischen Gräberfeld von Münsingen-Rain (Kt. Bern)'. *Schweizerische Zeitschrift für Archäologie und Kunstgeschichte* 30: 26–39.

Megaw, J. V. S. 1970. *Art of the European Iron Age: A Study of the Elusive Image*. Bath: Adams and Dart.

Megaw, J. V. S., and R. Megaw. 1989. *Celtic Art from its Beginnings to the Book of Kells*. London: Thames and Hudson.

Metzner-Nebelsick, C. 1992. 'Gefäße mit basaraboider Ornamentik aus Frög', in A. Lippert and K. Spindler (eds) *Festschrift zum 50jährigen Bestehen des Institutes für Ur- und Frühgeschichte der Leopold-Franzens-Universität Innsbruck*. Universitätsforschungen zur Prähistorischen Archäologie 8: 349–383. Bonn: Habelt.

Metzner-Nebelsick, C. 2002. *Der 'thrako-kimmerische' Formenkreis aus der Sicht der Urnenfelder- und Hallstattzeit im südöstlichen Pannonien*. Vorgeschichtliche Forschungen 23. Rahden: Marie Leidorf.

Metzner-Nebelsick, C. 2007. 'Pferdchenfibeln—Zur Deutung einer frauenspezifischen Schmuckform der Hallstatt- und Frühlatènezeit', in M. Blečić, M. Črešnar, B. Hänsel, A. Hellmuth, E. Kaiser, and C. Metzner-Nebelsick (eds) *Scripta praehistorica in honorem Biba Teržan*. Situla 44: 707–735. Ljubljana: Narodni muzej Slovenije.

Metzner-Nebelsick, C. 2009. 'Wagen- und Prunkbestattungen von Frauen der Hallstatt- und frühen Latènezeit in Europa. Ein Beitrag zur Diskussion der sozialen Stellung der Frau in der älteren Eisenzeit', in J. M. Bagley, C. Eggl, D. Neumann, and M. Schefzik (eds) *Alpen, Kult und Eisenzeit: Festschrift für Amei Lang zum 65. Geburtstag*. Internationale Archäologie, Studia honoraria 30: 237–270. Rahden: Marie Leidorf.

Metzner-Nebelsick, C. 2012a. 'Social transition and spatial organisation: the problem of the early Iron Age occupation of the strongholds in northeast Hungary', in P. Anreiter, E. Bánffy, L. Bartosiewicz, W. Meid, and C. Metzner-Nebelsick (eds) *Archaeological, Cultural, Linguistic Heritage: Festschrift for Erzsébet Jerem in Honour of her 70th Birthday*. Archaeolingua Main Series 25: 425–447. Budapest: Archaeolingua.

Metzner-Nebelsick, C. 2012b. 'Das Opfer Betrachtungen aus archäologischer Sicht', in A. Lang and P. Marinković (eds) *Bios—Cultus—(Im)mortalitas: Internationale Archäologie—Arbeitsgemeinschaft, Symposium, Tagung, Kongress 16*: 157–179. Rahden: Marie Leidorf.

Metzner-Nebelsick, C. 2017a. 'At the crossroads of the Hallstatt East', in R. Schumann and S. von der Vaart-Verschoof (eds) *Connecting Elites and Regions: Perspectives on Contacts, Relations and Differentiations during the Early Iron Age Hallstatt C Period in Northwest and Central Europe*: 349–379. Leiden: Sidestone Press.

Metzner-Nebelsick, C. 2017b. 'Königtum in prähistorischen Kulturen? Annäherungen an den archäologischen Befund am Beispiel der Kelten und Skythen', in S. Rebenich (ed.) *Monarchische Herrschaft im Altertum*. Schriften des Historischen Kollegs 94: 364–400. Berlin: Walter de Gruyter.

Metzner-Nebelsick, C., R. Müller, and S. Sievers. 2009. 'Die Eisenzeit, 800 v. Chr.–Christi Geburt', in S. von Schnurbein (ed.) *Atlas der Vorgeschichte*: 150–225. Stuttgart: Theiss.

Metzner-Nebelsick, C., and L. D. Nebelsick. 1999. 'Frau und Pferd. Ein Topos am Übergang von der Bronze- zur Eisenzeit Europas'. *Mitteilungen der Anthropologischen Gesellschaft in Wien* 129: 69–106.

Michálek, J., and Chytráček, M. 2013. 'The Hallstatt Tumulus culture', in N. Venclová (ed.) *The Early Iron Age—The Hallstatt Period*. The Prehistory of Bohemia 5: 73–91. Prague: Archeologický ústav AV ČR.

Milcent, P.-Y. 2004. *Le premier âge du Fer en France centrale*. Mémoire XXXIV de la Société Préhistorique Française. Paris: Société Préhistorique Française.

Mohen, J.-P., A. Duval, and C. Eluère. 1987. 'Trésors des princes celtes', in J.-P. Mohen, A. Duval, and C. Eluère (eds) *Trésors des princes celtes*. Paris: Éditions de la Réunion des Musées Nationaux.

Moosleitner, F. 1992. *Das hallstattzeitliche Gräberfeld von Uttendorf im Pinzgau: archäologische Forschungen in der Nationalparkregion Hohe Tauern*. Beiheft zur Sonderausstellung Zell am See 1992 und im Salzburger Museum Carolino Augusteum 1993. Salzburg: Amt der Salzburger Landesregierung.

Moosleitner, F., L. Pauli, and E. Penninger. 1974. *Der Dürrnberg bei Hallein II: Katalog der Grabfunde aus der Hallstatt- und Latènezeit*. Münchner Beiträge zur Vor- und Frühgeschichte 17. Munich: Beck.

Moser, S., G. Tiefengraber, and K. Wiltschke-Schrotta. 2012. *Der Dürrnberg bei Hallein: Die Gräbergruppen Kammelhöhe und Sonneben*. Dürrnberg Forschungen 5. Rahden: Marie Leidorf.

Mötsch, A. 2011. *Der späthallstattzeitliche 'Fürstensitz' auf dem Mont Lassois: Ausgrabungen des Kieler Instituts für Ur- und Frühgeschichte 2002–2006*. Universitätsforschungen zur Prähistorischen Archäologie 202. Bonn: Habelt.

Müller, F. 1998. *Münsingen-Rain, ein Markstein der keltischen Archäologie: Funde, Befunde und Methoden im Vergleich: Akten des Internationalen Kolloquiums 'Das keltische Gräberfeld von Münsingen-Rain 1906–1996' in Münsingen bei Bern vom 9. bis 12. Oktober 1996*. Schriften des Bernischen Historischen Museums 2. Bern: Bernisches Museum.

Müller, F. 2002. *Götter, Gaben, Rituale: Religion in der Frühgeschichte Europas*. Mainz: Philipp von Zabern.

Müller, F. (ed.) 2009. *Kunst der Kelten. 700 v.Chr.–700 n.Chr.* Stuttgart: Belser Verlag.

Müller, F., P. Jud, and K. W. Alt. 2008. 'Artefacts, skulls and written sources: the social ranking of a Celtic family buried at Münsingen-Rain'. *Antiquity* 82: 462–469.

Müller, F., and G. Lüscher. 2004. *Die Kelten in der Schweiz*. Stuttgart: Theiss.

Müller-Depreux, A. 2005. *Die Hallstatt- und frühlatènezeitliche Siedlung 'Erdwerk I' von Niedererlbach, Landkreis Landshut*. Materialien zur bayerischen Vorgeschichte A 87. Kallmünz: Lassleben.

Müller-Scheeßel, N. 2000. *Die Hallstattkultur und ihre räumliche Differenzierung: Der West- und Osthallstattkreis aus forschungsgeschichtlich-methodologischer Sicht*. Tübinger Texte 3. Rahden: Marie Leidorf.

Müller-Scheeßel, N. 2013. *Untersuchungen zum Wandel hallstattzeitlicher Bestattungssitten in Süd- und Südwestdeutschland*. Universitätsforschungen zur prähistorischen Archäologie 245. Bonn: Habelt.

Nakoinz, O. 2005. *Studien zur räumlichen Abgrenzung und Strukturierung der älteren Hunsrück-Eifel-Kultur*. Universitätsforschungen zur Prähistorischen Archäologie 118. Bonn: Habelt.

Nebelsick, L. D. 1992. 'Figürliche Kunst der Hallstattzeit am Nordostalpenrand im Spannungsfeld zwischen alteuropäischer Tradition und italischem Lebensstil', in A. Lippert and K. Spindler (eds) *Festschrift zum 50jährigen Bestehen des Institutes für Ur- und Frühgeschichte der Leopold-Franzens-Universität Innsbruck*. Universitätsforschungen zur prähistorischen Archäologie 8: 401–432. Bonn: Habelt.

Nebelsick, L. D. 1996. 'Herd im Grab? Zur Deutung der kalenderbergverzierten Ware am Nordostalpenrand', in E. Jerem and A. Lippert (eds) *Die Osthallstattkultur: Akten des Internationalen Symposiums, Sopron, 10.–14. Mai 1994*. Archaeolingua Main Series 7: 327–364. Budapest: Archaeolingua.

Nebelsick, L. D. 1997. 'Die Kalenderberggruppe der Hallstattzeit am Nordostalpenrand', in L. D. Nebelsick, A. Eibner, E. Lauermann, and J.-W. Neugebauer (eds) *Hallstattkultur im Osten Österreichs*: 9–128. St Pölten/Vienna: Niederösterreichisches Pressehaus.

Nebelsick, L. D. 2001. *Das prähistorische Gräberfeld von Niederkaina bei Bautzen* 5. Veröffentlichungen des Landesamtes für Archäologie mit Landesmuseum für Vorgeschichte 31. Dresden: Landesamt für Archäologie.

Nebelsick, L. D. 2016. *Drinking against Death: Studies on the Materiality and Iconography of Ritual, Sacrifice and Transcendence in Later Prehistoric Europe*. Warsaw: Naukowe UKSW.

Neugebauer, J.-W. 1992. *Die Kelten im Osten Österreichs*. St Pölten: Verlag Niederösterreichisches Pressehaus.

Nikulka, F. 1998. *Das hallstatt- und frühlatènezeitliche Gräberfeld von Riedenburg-Untereggersberg, Lkr. Kelheim, Niederbayern*. Archäologie am Main-Donau Kanal 13. Rahden: Marie Leidorf.

Nortmann, H. 1999. 'Burgen der Hunsrück-Eifel-Kultur', in A. Jockenhövel (ed.) *Ältereisenzeitliches Befestigungswesen zwischen Maas/Mosel und Elbe: Internationales Kolloquium am 8. November 1997 in Münster anläßlich des hundertjährigen Bestehens der Altertumskommission für Westfalen*. Veröffentlichungen der Altertumskommission für Westfalen 11: 69–80. Münster: Aschendorf.

Nortmann, H. 2009. 'Befestigungen der Eisenzeit im Hunsrück-Nahe-Raum. Forschungsstand, Fragen und Hypothesen'. *Trierer Zeitschrift* 71/72: 15–25.

Nortmann, H. 2015. 'Wie viel Gefolge hat der "Fürst"? Keltische Gesellschaft und Demographie in der Region Trier', in M. Koch (ed.) *Archäologie in der Großregion: Beiträge des internationalen Symposiums zur Archäologie in der Großregion in der Europäischen Akademie Otzenhausen vom 7.–9. März 2014*: 91–108. Nonnweiler: Europäische Akademie Otzenhausen.

Nothdurfter, J. 1979. *Die Eisenfunde von Sanzeno im Nonsberg*. Römisch-Germanische Forschungen 38. Mainz: Philipp von Zabern.

Oelze, V. M., J. K. Koch, K. Kupke, O. Nehlich, S. Zäuner, J. Wald, et al. 2012. 'Multi-isotopic analysis reveals individual mobility and diet at the early Iron Age monumental tumulus of Magdalenenberg, Germany'. *American Journal of Physical Anthropology* 148, 3: 406–421.

Olivier, L. 2010. 'Nouvelles recherches sur le site de sauniers du premier âge du Fer de Marsal "La Digue" (Moselle)'. *Antiquités nationales* 41: 127–160.

Pabst-Dörrer, S. 2000. *Untersuchungen zu hallstattzeiltichen Frauentrachten mit Spiralbrillenfibeln zwischen Alpen, Karpaten und Ostsee*. Internationale Archäologie 51. Rahden: Marie Leidorf.

Pare, C. F. E. 1987. 'Der Zeremonialwagen der Hallstattzeit—Untersuchungen zu Konstruktion, Typologie und Kulturbeziehungen', in F. E. Barth (ed.) *Vierrädrige Wagen der Hallstattzeit: Untersuchungen zu Geschichte und Technik*. RGZM Monographien 12: 189–248. Mainz: Römisch-Germanisches Zentralmuseum.

Pare, C. F. E. 1991. *Swords, Wagon-Graves, and the Beginning of the Early Iron Age in Central Europe*. Kleine Schriften aus dem Vorgeschichtlichen Seminar Marburg. Marburg: Universität Marburg.

Pare, C. F. E. 1992. *Wagons and Wagon-Graves of the Early Iron Age in Central Europe*. OUCA Monograph 35. Oxford: Oxford University Committee for Archaeology.

Pare, C. F. E. 1998. 'Beiträge zum Übergang von der Bronze- zur Eisenzeit in Mitteleuropa. Teil I. Grundzüge der Chronologie im östlichen Mitteleuropa (11.–8. Jahrhundert v. Chr.)'. *Jahrbuch des Römisch-Germanischen Zentralmuseums Mainz* 45, 1: 293–433.

Pare, C. F. E. 1999. 'Beiträge zum Übergang von der Bronze- zur Eisenzeit in Mitteleuropa. Teil II. Grundzüge der Chronologie im westlichen Mitteleuropa (11.–8. Jahrhundert v. Chr.)'. *Jahrbuch des Römisch-Germanischen Zentralmuseums Mainz* 46, 1: 175–315.

Pare, C. F. E. 2009. 'Zu den Großbefestigungen des 5. Jahrhunderts v. Chr. zwischen Mittelrhein-Mosel und Böhmen', in C. Bockisch-Bräuer (ed.) *Beiträge zur Hallstatt- und Latènezeit in Nordostbayern und Thüringen: Tagung vom 26.–28. Oktober 2007 in Nürnberg*. Beiträge zur Vorgeschichte Nordostbayerns 7: 67–85. Nürnberg: Naturhistorische Gesellschaft.

Parzinger, H. 1998. *Der Goldberg, die metallzeitliche Besiedlung*. Römisch-Germanische Forschungen 57. Mainz: Philipp von Zabern.

Patek, E. 1982. 'Neue Untersuchungen auf dem Burgstall bei Sopron'. *Berichte der Römisch-Germanischen Kommission* 63: 105–177.

Patek, E. 1993. *Westungarn in der Hallstattzeit*. Acta Humaniora: Quellen und Forschungen zur prähistorischen und provinzialrömischen Archäologie 7. Weinheim: VCH.

Pauli, L. 1971. *Studien zur Golasecca Kultur: ein Beitrag zur Geschichte des Handels über die Alpen*, Vol. I/1. Hamburger Beiträge zur Archäologie. Hamburg: Buske.

Pauli, L. 1988–1989. 'Zu Gast bei einem keltischen Fürsten'. *Mitteilungen der Anthropologischen Gesellschaft in Wien* 118/119: 291–303.

Penninger, E. 1972. *Der Dürrnberg bei Hallein I: Katalog der Grabfunde aus der Hallstatt- und Latènezeit*. Münchner Beiträge zur Vor- und Frühgeschichte 16. Munich: Beck.

Piningre, J.-F. (ed.) 1996. *Nécropoles et société au premier âge du Fer: la tumulus de Courtsoult (Haute-Saône)*. Documents d'archéologie Française 54. Paris: Éditions de la Maison des Sciences de l'Homme.

Plouin, S. (ed.) 1996. *Trésors Celtes et Gaulois: Le Rhin supérieur entre 800 et 50 avant J.-C. Exposition présentée au musée d'Unterlinden du 16 mars au 2 juin 1996*. Colmar: Musée d'Unterlinden.

Plouin, S. 2012. 'Nécropoles et rites funéraire en Alsace à l'époque hallstattiene', in A. Bräuning and W. Löhlein (eds) *Die frühe Eisenzeit zwischen Schwarzwald und Vogesen*. Archäologische Informationen aus Baden-Württemberg 66: 218–261, 283. Freiburg: Regierungspräsidium Stuttgart Landesamt für Denkmalpflege.

Polenz, H. 1971. 'Mittel- und spätlatènezeitliche Brandgräber von Dietzenbach, Kr. Offenbach a. Main'. *Studien und Forschungen N.F.* 4: 3–115.

Preinfalk, F. 2003. *Die hallstattzeitlichen Hügelgräber von Langenlebarn, Niederösterreich*. Fundberichte aus Österreich, Materialheft A 12. Horn: Berger.

Půlpan, M., and A. Reszczyńska. 2013. 'Chamber graves of the Bylany culture (Ha C–Ha D1) in north-western Bohemia'. *Analecta Archaeologica Ressoviensia* 8: 173–235.

Puttkammer, T. 2003. *Das prähistorische Gräberfeld von Niederkaina bei Bautzen 8*. Dresden: Landesamt für Archäologie.

Raddatz, K. 1952. 'Zur Deutung der Funde von La Tène'. *OFFA* 11: 24–27.

Ramsl, P. 2002. *Das eisenzeitliche Gräberfeld von Pottenbrunn*. Fundberichte aus Österreich, Materialhefte A 11. Vienna: Bundesdenkmalamt.

Ramsl, P. 2011. *Das latènezeitliche Gräberfeld von Mannersdorf am Leithagebirge, Flur Reinthal Süd, Niederösterreich: Studien zu Phänomenen der latènezeitlichen Kulturausprägungen*. Vienna: Verlag der Österreichischen Akademie der Wissenschaften.

Rebay, K. C. 2002. *Die hallstattzeitliche Grabhügelgruppe von Zagersdorf im Burgenland*. Wissenschaftliche Arbeiten aus dem Burgenland 107. Eisenstadt: Amt der Burgenländischen Landesregierung.

Rebay, K. C. 2006. *Das hallstattzeitliche Gräberfeld von Statzendorf, Niederösterreich*. Universitätsforschungen zur Prähistorischen Archäologie 135. Bonn: Habelt.

Rebay-Salisbury, K. 2016. *The Human Body in Early Iron Age Central Europe: Burial Practices and Images of the Hallstatt World*. London: Routledge.

Reim, H. 1988. *Das keltische Gräberfeld bei Rottenburg am Neckar: Grabungen 1984–1987: Begleitheft zur Ausstellung Archäologie in Rottenburg, das keltische Gräberfeld im 'Lindele'*. Archäologische Informationen aus Baden-Württemberg 3. Stuttgart: Gesellschaft für Vor- und Frühgeschichte in Württemberg und Hohenzollern.

Reinecke, P. 1902. 'Zur Kenntnis der La Tène-Denkmäler der Zone nordwärts der Alpen', in L. Lindenschmidt, L. Beck, K. Schumacher, W. Reeb, and P. Reinecke (eds) *Festschrift des Römisch-Germanischen Zentralmuseums Mainz*: 53–109. Mainz: Römisch-Germanisches Zentralmuseum.

Reinecke, P. 1965. *Mainzer Aufsätze zur Chronologie der Bronze- und Eisenzeit: Nachdrucke aus Altertümer unserer heidnischen Vorzeit und Festschrift RGZM 1901*. Bonn: Habelt.

Rieckhoff, S. 1995. *Süddeutschland im Spannungsfeld von Kelten, Germanen und Römern: Studien zur Chronologie der Spätlatènezeit im südlichen Mitteleuropa*. Trierer Zeitschrift Beiheft 19. Trier: Rheinisches Landesmuseum.

Riek, G. 1962. *Der Hohmichele: Ein Fürstengrabhügel der späten Hallstattzeit bei der Heuneburg*. Heuneburgstudien I/Römisch-Germanische Forschungen 25. Berlin: De Gruyter.

Rolley, C. (ed.) 2003. *La tombe princière de Vix*. Paris: Picard/Société des amis du Musée du Châtillonnais.

Romsauer, P. 1991. 'The earliest wheel-turned pottery in the Carpathian Basin'. *Antiquity* 65: 358–367.

Roth-Zehner, M. 2013. 'L'Alsace', in F. Malrain, G. Blancquaert, and T. Lorho (eds) *L'habitat rural du second âge du Fer: Rhythmes de création et d'abandon au nord de la Loire*: 25–43. Paris: CNRS Editions/Inrap.

Salač, V. 2005. 'Vom Oppidum zum Einzelgehöft und zurück—zur Geschichte und dem heutigen Stand der Latèneforschung in Böhmen und Mitteleuropa'. *Alt-Thüringen* 38: 279–300.

Salač, V. 2012. 'Les oppida et les processus d'urbanisation en Europe centrale', in S. Sievers and M. Schönfelder (eds) *Die Frage der Protourbanisation in der Eisenzeit: La question de la protourbanisation à l'âge du Fer: Akten des 34. internationalen Kolloquiums der AFEAF vom 13.–16. Mai 2010 in Aschaffenburg*. Kolloquien zur Vor- und Frühgeschichte 16: 319–345. Bonn: Habelt.

Salač, V. 2014. 'Oppida and urbanisation process in central Europe', in M. Fernández-Götz, H. Wendling, and K. Winger (eds) *Paths to Complexity: Centralisation and Urbanisation in Iron Age Europe*: 64–75. Oxford: Oxbow Books.

Šaldová, V. 1968. 'Halštatská mohylová kultura v zá padních Čechách—pohřebiště Nynice. Die hallstattzeitliche Hügelgräberkultur in Westböhmen. Das Gräberfeld von Nynice'. *Památky archeologické* 59: 297–399.

Schaaff, U. 1988. 'Keltische Helme', in *Antike Helme: Sammlung Lipperheide und andere Bestände des Antikenmuseums Berlin*. RGZM Monographien 14: 293–326. Mainz: Verlag des Römisch-Germanischen Zentralmuseums.

Schäfer, A. 2010. *Berching-Pollanten II: Die Kleinfunde der jüngerlatènezeitlichen Siedlung Berching-Pollanten, Lkr. Neumarkt i.d. Oberpfalz*. Rahden: Marie Leidorf.

Schefzik, M. 2001. *Die bronze- und eisenzeitliche Besiedlungsgeschichte der Münchner Ebene: eine Untersuchung zu Gebäude- und Siedlungsformen im süddeutschen Raum*. Internationale Archäologie 68. Rahden: Marie Leidorf.

Schickler, H. 2001. *Heilige Ordnungen: Zu keltischen Funden im Württembergischen Landesmuseum*. Stuttgart: Württembergisches Landesmuseum.

Schier, W. 2010. 'Soziale und politische Strukturen der Hallstattzeit. Ein Diskussionsbeitrag', in D. Krausse (ed.) 2010. *'Fürstensitze' und Zentralorte der frühen Kelten: Abschlusskolloquium des DFG-Schwerpunktprogramms 1171 in Stuttgart, 12.–15. Oktober 2009*. Forschungen und Berichte zur Vor- und Frühgeschichte in Baden-Württemberg 120–121: 375–405. Stuttgart: Theiss.

Schmid-Sikimić, B. 1984. 'Das Wagengrab von Gunzwil-Adiswil: ein Frauengrab'. *Helvetia Archaeologica* 15: 103–118.

Schmid-Sikimić, B. 1996. *Der Arm- und Beinschmuck der Hallstattzeit in der Schweiz*. Prähistorische Bronzefunde X, 5. Stuttgart: Steiner.

Schmid-Sikimić, B. 2001. 'Wasserwege, Passrouten und der Handel über die Alpen', in Schweizerisches Landesmuseum (ed.) *Die Lepontier: Grabschätze eines mythischen Alpenvolkes: Exhibition Catalogue*. Collectio Archaeologica I-1: 59–74. Zürich: Chronos-Verlag.

Schneider, F. N. 2012. *Neue Studien zur Hunsrück-Eifel-Kultur*. Münchner Archäologische Forschungen 2. Rahden: Marie Leidorf.

Schönfelder, M. 2002. *Das spätkeltische Wagengrab von Boé (Dép. Lot-et-Garonne): Studien zu Wagen und Wagengräbern der jüngeren Latènezeit*. RGZM Monographien 54. Mainz: Römisch-Germanisches Zentralmuseum.

Schulze-Forster, J. 2015. *Die latènezeitlichen Funde vom Dünsberg*. Berichte der Kommission für Archäologische Landesforschung in Hessen 13. Rahden: Marie Leidorf.

Schumacher, A. 1972–1974. *Die Hallstattzeit im südlichen Hessen*. Bonner Hefte zur Vorgeschichte 5–6. Bonn: Institut für Vor- und Frühgeschichte.

Schumann, R. 2015. *Status und Prestige in der Hallstattkultur*. Münchner Archäologische Forschungen 3. Rahden: Marie Leidorf.

Schussmann, M. 2010. 'Siedlungshierarchien und Zentralisierungsprozesse in der Südlichen Frankenalb zwischen dem 9. und 4. Jh. v.Chr.', in D. Krausse (ed.) *'Fürstensitze' und Zentralorte der frühen Kelten: Abschlusskolloquium des DFG-Schwerpunktprogramms 1171 in Stuttgart, 12.–15. Oktober 2009*. Forschungen und Berichte zur Vor- und Frühgeschichte in Baden-Württemberg 120–121: 129–167. Stuttgart: Theiss.

Schwab, H. 1989. *Archéologie de la 2e correction des eaux du Jura, Vol. 1: Les Celtes sur la Broye et la Thielle*. Archéologie fribourgoise 5. Fribourg: Editions Universitaires Fribourg Suisse.

Schwappach, F. 1977. 'Die stempelverzierte Latène-Keramik aus den Gräbern von Braubach'. *Bonner Jahrbücher des Rheinischen Landesmuseums Bonn und des Rheinischen Amtes für Bodendenkmalpfelge im Landschaftsverband Rheinland und des Vereins von Altertumsfreunden im Rheinlande* 177: 119–183.

Schwarz, K., and G. Wieland. 2005. *Die Ausgrabungen in der Viereckschanze 2 von Holzhausen. Grabungsgerichte von K. Schwarz. Zusammengestellt und kommentiert von G. Wieland*. Frühgeschichtliche und provinzial-römische Archäologie 7. Rahden: Marie Leidorf.

Schwitalla, G. (ed.) 2008. *Der Glauberg in keltischer Zeit: Zum neuesten Stand der Forschungen: Öffentliches Symposium 14.–16. September 2006, Darmstadt*. Fundberichte aus Hessen Beiheft 6. Bonn: Habelt.

Siegfried-Weiss, A. 1979. *Der Ostalpenraum in der Hallstattzeit und seine Beziehungen zum Mittelmeergebiet*. Hamburger Beiträge zur Archäologie 6. Hamburg: Buske.

Sievers, S. 1982. *Die mitteleuropäischen Hallstattdolche*. Prähistorische Bronzefunde VI, 6. Munich: Beck.

Sievers, S. 2003. *Manching—Die Keltenstadt*. Führer zu archäologischen Denkmälern in Bayern, Oberbayern 3. Stuttgart: Theiss.

Sievers, S., and M. Schönfelder (eds). 2012. *Die Frage der Protourbanisation in der Eisenzeit: La question de la protourbanisation à l'âge du Fer: Akten des 34. internationalen Kolloquiums der AFEAF vom 13.–16. Mai 2010 in Aschaffenburg*. Kolloquien zur Vor- und Frühgeschichte 16. Bonn: Habelt.

Simon, K. 1972. *Die Hallstattzeit in Ostthüringen*. Forschungen zur Vor- und Frühgeschichte 8. Berlin: Deutscher Verlag des Wissenschaft.

Sormaz, T., and T. Stöllner. 2005. 'Zwei hallstattzeitliche Grabkammern vom Dürrnberg bei Hallein—Neue dendrochronologische Ergebnisse zum Übergang von der Hallstatt- zur Frühlatènezeit'. *Archäologisches Korrespondenzblatt* 35: 361–376.

Soudská, E. 1991. 'Manětín-Hrádek', in S. Moscati (ed.) *The Celts*: 182–183. London: Thames and Hudson.

Soudská, E. 1994. *Die Anfänge der keltischen Zivilisation in Böhmen: Das Gräberfeld Manětín-Hrádek*. Prague: Krystal OP.

Spindler, K. 1971–1980. *Magdalenenberg: Der hallstattzeitliche Fürstenhügel bei Villingen im Schwarzwald I–VI*. Villingen: Neckar Verlag.

Spindler, K. 1999. *Der Magdalenenberg bei Villingen: Ein Fürstengrabhügel des 7. vorchristlichen Jahrhunderts*, 2nd edition. Führer zu archäologischen Denkmälern in Baden-Württemberg 5. Stuttgart: Theiss.

Stegmaier, G. 2014. '"Die Stadt im Kornfeld". Untersuchungen zur Wirtschafts- und Besiedlungsstruktur des Oppidums Heidengraben', in S. Hornung (ed.) *Produktion—Distribution—Ökonomie Siedlungs- und Wirtschaftsmuster der Latènezeit: Akten des internationalen Kolloquiums in Otzenhausen 28.–30. Oktober 2011*. Universitätsforschungen zur Prähistorischen Archäologie 258: 271–292. Bonn: Habelt.

Steiner, H. 2010. *Alpine Brandopferplätze: Archäologische und naturwissenschaftliche Untersuchungen. Roghi Votivi Alpini. Archeologia e scienze naturali*. Forschungen zur Denkmalpflege in Südtirol 5. Trento: Editrice Temi.

Stöckli, W. E. 1975. *Chronologie der jüngeren Eisenzeit im Tessin*. Antiqua 2. Basel: Verlag der Schweizerischen Gesellschaft für Ur- und Frühgeschichte.

Stöllner, T. 1996–2002. *Die Hallstattzeit und der Beginn der Latènezeit im Inn-Salzach-Raum*. Archäologie in Salzburg 3, 1–2. Salzburg: Amt der Salzburger Landesregierung.

Stöllner, T. 1999. *Der prähistorische Salzbergbau am Dürrnberg bei Hallein I: Forschungsgeschichte—Forschungsstand—Forschungsanliegen*. Dürrnberg Forschungen 1. Rahden: Marie Leidorf.

Stöllner, T. 2002. *Der prähistorische Salzbergbau am Dürrnberg bei Hallein II: Die Funde und Befunde der Bergwerksausgrabungen zwischen 1990 und 2000*. Dürrnberg Forschungen 3. Rahden: Marie Leidorf.

Tappert, C. 2006. *Die Gefäßkeramik der latènezeitlichen Siedlung von Straubing-Bajuwarenstrasse*. Kallmünz: Lassleben.

Tecco-Hvala, S. 2012. *Magdalenska Gora: Social Structure and Burial Rites of the Iron Age Community*. Opera Instituti Archaeologici Sloveniae 26. Ljubljana: Založba ZRC.

Teržan, B. 1990. *Starejša železna doba na Slovenskem Štajerskem/The Early Iron Age in Slovenian Styria*. Katalogi in monografije 25. Ljubljana: Narodni muzej Slovenije.

Teržan, B. 1996. 'Weben und Zeitmessen im südostalpinen und westpannonischen Gebiet', in E. Jerem and A. Lippert (eds) *Die Osthallstattkultur: Akten des Internationalen Symposiums, Sopron, 10.–14. Mai 1994*. Archaeolingua Main Series 7: 507–536. Budapest: Archaeolingua.

Tiefengraber, G., and S. Tiefengraber. 2013. *Reiterkrieger? Priesterin? Das Rätsel des Kultwagengrabes von Strettweg bei Judenburg*. Judenburg: Arbeitskreis Falkenberg.

Tischler, O. 1885. 'Über die Gliederung der La-Tène-Periode und die Dekorierung der Eisenwaffen in dieser Zeit'. *Correspondenz-Blatt der deutschen Gesellschaft für Anthropologie, Ethnologie und Urgeschichte Berlin* 14: 157–161.

Todd, M. 1987. *The Northern Barbarians 100 BC–AD 300*, second edition. Oxford: Blackwell.

Tomedi, G. 1994. 'Der Übergang von der Bronze- zur Eisenzeit am Beispiel von Frög, Tumulus "K"', in P. Schauer (ed.) *Archäologische Untersuchungen zum Übergang von der Bronze- zur Eisenzeit zwischen Nordsee und Kaukasus. Ergebnisse eines Kolloquiums in Regensburg 28.–30. Oktober 1992*. Regensburger Beiträge zur prähistorischen Archäologie 1: 365–382. Bonn: Habelt.

Tomedi, G. 2002. *Das hallstattzeitliche Gräberfeld von Frög: Die Altgrabungen von 1883 bis 1892*. Archaeolingua Main Series 14. Budapest: Archaeolingua.

Tomedi, G., S. Hye, R. Lachberger, and S. Nicolussi Castellan. 2006. 'Denkmalschutzgrabungen am Heiligtum vom Demlfeld in Ampass 2006', in *ArchaeoTirol Kleine Schriften* 5: 116–122. Wattens: Verein ArchaeoTirol.

Torbrügge, W. 1971. 'Vor- und frühgeschichtliche Flußfunde. Zur Ordnung und Bestimmung einer Denkmälergruppe'. *Bericht der Römisch-Germanischen Kommission* 51/52: 1–146.

Torbrügge, W. 1979. *Die Hallstattzeit in der Oberpfalz*. Materialhefte zur Bayerischen Vorgeschichte 39. Kallmünz: Lassleben.

Trachsel, M. 2004. *Untersuchungen zur relativen und absoluten Chronologie der Hallstattzeit*. Universitätsforschungen zur Prähistorischen Archäologie 104. Bonn: Habelt.

Trebsche, P. 2011. 'Eisenzeitliche Graphittonkeramik im mittleren Donaugebiet', in *Vorträge des 29. Niederbayerischen Archäologentages*: 449–481. Rahden: Marie Leidorf.

Tschurtschenthaler, M., and Wein, U. 2002. 'Das Heiligtum auf der Pillerhöhe', in L. Zemmer-Plank (ed.) *Kult der Vorzeit in den Alpen: Opfergaben, Opferplätze, Opferbrauchtum/Culti nella Preistoria delle Alpi: Le offerte, i santuari, i riti*: 635–674. Bozen-Bolzano: Athesia.

Turk, P. 2005. *Images of Life and Myth: Exhibition Catalogue*. Ljubljana: Narodni muzej Slovenije.

Uenze, H. P., and A. Lang. 2013. 'Auf den Spuren der Kelten', in M. Fesg-Martin, A. Lang, and M. Peters (eds) *Der Starnberger See: Natur- und Vorgeschichte einer bayerischen Landschaft*: 121–132. Munich: Verlag Dr Friedrich Pfeil.

Venclová, N. (ed.) 2013. *The Early Iron Age – The Hallstatt Period*. The Prehistory of Bohemia 5. Prague: Czech Academy of Sciences.

Verger, S. 1995. 'De Vix à Weiskirchen. La transformation des rites funéraires aristocratiques en Gaule du Nord et de l'Est au Ve siècle avant J.-C.'. *Mélanges de l'École Française de Rome* 107, 2: 335–458.

Vokolek, V. 1999. *Východočeská halštatská pohřebiště/The Hallstatt Period Cemeteries in East Bohemia*. Pardubice: Východočké muzeum Pardubice.

Völling, T. 2002. 'Weihungen in griechischen Heiligtümern am Beispiel des Artemisheiligtums von Kombotheka und des Zeusheiligtums von Olympia', in L. Zemmer-Plank (ed.) *Kult der Vorzeit in den Alpen: Opfergaben, Opferplätze, Opferbrauchtum/Culti nella Preistoria delle Alpi: Le offerte, i santuari, i riti*: 83–112. Bozen-Bolzano: Athesia.

Vouga, E. A. 1885. *Les Helvètes à La Tène: Notice historique*. Neuchâtel: Attinger.

Vouga, P. 1923. *La Tène: Monographie de la station*. Leipzig: Hiersemann.

Vuaillat, D. 1977. *La necropole tumulaire de Chavéria (Jura)*. Paris: Les Belles Lettres.

Vulpe, A. 1986. 'Zur Entstehung der geto-dakischen Zivilisation. Die Basarabikultur'. *Dacia N.S.* 30: 49–90.

Waldhauser, J. 1998. 'Die Goldfingerringe aus Münsingen-Rain', in F. Müller (ed.) *Münsingen-Rain: Ein Markstein der keltischen Archäologie: Funde, Befunde und Methoden im Vergleich. Akten des Internationalen Kolloquiums 'Das keltische Gräberfeld von Münsingen-Rain 1906–1996' in Münsingen bei Bern vom 9. bis 12. Oktober 1996*. Schriften des Bernischen Historischen Museums 2: 85–121. Bern: Bernisches Museum.

Wamser, L. 1981. 'Wagengräber der Hallstattzeit in Franken'. *Frankenland: Zeitschrift für Fränkische Landeskunde und Kulturpflege N.F.* 33: 225–261.

Wefers, S. 2011. 'Still using your saddle quern? A compilation of the oldest known rotary querns in western Europe', in D. Williams and D. Peacock (eds) *Bread for the People: The Archaeology of Mills and Milling: Proceedings of a colloquium held in the British School at Rome 4th–7th November 2009*. British Archaeological Reports International Series 2274: 67–76. Oxford: Archaeopress.

Wells, P. S. 1983. *Rural Economy in the Early Iron Age: Excavations at Hascherkeller 1978–1981*. American School of Prehistoric Research Bulletin 36. Cambridge, MA: Peabody Museum, Harvard University.

Wells, P. S. 1993. *Settlement, Economy, and Cultural Change at the End of the European Iron Age: Excavations at Kelheim in Bavaria, 1987–1991*. Archaeological Series 6. Ann Arbor: International Monographs in Prehistory.

Wells, P. S. 1999. *The Barbarians Speak: How the Conquered Peoples Shaped Roman Europe*. Princeton: Princeton University Press.

Wells, P. S. (ed.) 2013. *Rome Beyond its Frontiers: Imports, Attitudes and Practices*. Journal of Roman Archaeology Supplementary Series 94. Portsmouth, RI: Journal of Roman Archaeology.

Wendling, H., and K. Wiltschke-Schrotta. 2015. *Der Dürrnberg bei Hallein: Die Gräbergruppe am Römersteig*. Dürrnberg Forschungen 9. Rahden: Marie Leidorf.

Wieland, G. 1999. *Keltische Viereckschanzen: Kultplätze oder Gehöftsiedlungen?* Stuttgart: Theiss.

Wieland, G. 2004. 'Zur Frage der Kontinuität von der Spätlatènezeit in die frühe römische Kaiserzeit an der oberen Donau', in C.-M. Hüssen, W. Irlinger, and W. Zanier (eds) *Spätlatènezeit und frühe römische Kaiserzeit zwischen Alpenrand und Donau: Akten des Kolloquiums in Ingolstadt am ll. und 12. Oktober 2001*: 113–122. Bonn: Habelt.

Wyss, R. 1955. 'Funde aus der alten Zihl und ihre Deutung'. *Germania* 33: 349–354.

Wyss, R. 1975. *Der Schatzfund von Erstfeld: frühkeltischer Goldschmuck aus den Zentralalpen*. Zürich: Gesellschaft für das Schweizer Landesmuseum.

Zeiler, M. 2009. 'Rekonstruktion von Töpfereien der jüngeren vorrömischen Eisenzeit (Ha D–Lt D)', in P. Trebsche, I. Balzer, C. Eggl, J. Fries-Knoblach, J. K. Koch, and J. Wiethold (eds) *Architektur: Interpretation und Rekonstruktion: Beiträge zur Sitzung der AG Eisenzeit während des 6. Deutschen Archäologie-Kongresses in Mannheim 2008*. Beiträge zur Ur- und Frühgeschichte Mitteleuropas 55: 263–280. Langenweissbach: Verlag Dr Faustus.

Zeiler, M. 2010. *Untersuchungen zur jüngerlatènezeitlichen Keramikchronologie im östlichen Mitteleuropa*. Rahden: Marie Leidorf.

Zeller, K. W. 2001. *Der Dürrnberg bei Hallein: Ein Zentrum keltischer Kultur am Nordrand der Alpen*. Hallein: Keltenmuseum.

Zürn, H. 1942. 'Zur Chronologie der späten Hallstattzeit'. *Germania* 26: 116–124.

Zürn, H. 1970. *Hallstattforschungen in Nord-Württemberg: Die Grabhügel von Asperg (Kr. Ludwigsburg), Hirschlanden (Kr. Leonberg) und Mühlacker (Kr. Vaihingen)*. Veröffentlichungen des Staatlichen Amtes für Denkmalpflege Stuttgart A16. Stuttgart: Müller und Gräff.

Zürn, H. 1987. *Hallstattzeitliche Grabfunde in Württemberg und Hohenzollern*. Forschungen und Berichte zur Vor- und Frühgeschichte in Baden-Württemberg 25. Stuttgart: Theiss.

CHAPTER 9

SOUTHERN FRANCE

DOMINIQUE GARCIA

Introduction

Marseille, the Greek Massalia, can be considered the oldest city in Gaul. Its creation as an *emporion* dates back to the 600s BC, even if the urban and economic development that would turn it into one of the most prominent Greek colonies in the west is only perceptible from the 530s BC. Its foundation triggered the development of a network of indigenous settlements, trading posts, and production sites. This was profoundly to modify the nature of local Iron Age societies over the following four centuries, until Roman rule was progressively imposed over southern France from the 120s BC onwards.

This 'civilization of the *oppida*' in the south of France has been the subject of much research since the 1950s, documenting its uniqueness within the urban or proto-urban phenomenon which characterizes the early Iron Age in the western Mediterranean (Garcia 2004, Garcia 2005, Py 1993). Research on the cultural sphere, economy, and the environment of sites complements the detailed stratigraphic and architectural analyses presented in site monographs. Beyond the coast and lower valleys, the influence of the Mediterranean merchants eventually extended to the hinterland and to the Gaulish interior: to Toulouse and Bordeaux, via the Carcassonne Gap, to the Massif Central via the Hérault valley (Garcia 1993, 1995), and to the western Alps and Burgundy via the Rhône and its tributaries.

It is this phenomenon, with its significant social and economic implications, which during the sixth century BC was to put its stamp on the lifestyles of pre-Roman communities from Catalonia to Liguria, which is addressed in this chapter, after initially touching upon the earliest part of the Iron Age.

Pre-Urban Societies from the Late Bronze Age to the Early Iron Age

In the south of France, the late Bronze Age (Bronze final III) seems to correspond to a relatively uniform society. A fairly homogeneous cultural community extended from the Alps to the Pyrenees, counterbalanced by an apparent diversity in the forms of settlements: isolated establishments, villages on plateaus or plains, and caves. Our knowledge of settlement at the Bronze Age/Iron Age transition is limited by a lack of large-scale excavation, but the evidence suggests that some non-sedentary populations remained in the region. Construction techniques using perishable materials, mostly cob or daub on load-bearing posts, the absence of stone fortifications, and the limited number of storage structures all suggest lifeways incompatible (in most cases) with permanent settlement and the development of urbanism. In eastern Languedoc, these semi-sedentary lifestyles are associated with the practice of inverse transhumance, whereas in Provence, territorial mobility can be linked to soil depletion caused by the practice of slash-and-burn agriculture, a system which supposedly marks a stage of agrarian development prior to the widespread adoption of the plough and soil improvement by manuring. Similar observations can be made for other southern micro-regions, but detailed evidence is still lacking, meaning that we are unable to describe the socio-economic organization of these populations in any detail.

The Cult Domain

It is to the early part of the Iron Age (725–550 BC) that most of the anepigraphic and often aniconic stelae commonly encountered on southern French sites—mainly in Provence, the lower Rhône valley, the south of the Massif Central, and central and eastern Languedoc—should be dated. In these regions, a votive tradition involving the erection of monolithic monuments had existed from the late Neolithic. Close to 500 examples are now known, from more than forty sites. These monuments were usually made from soft sandstones and shelly limestones, which were rarely available in the immediate locality. The natural outcrops that could have provided the stone are generally situated around 15–20 km from their place of discovery. Analysis of the methods of quarrying and surface dressing indicate fairly basic techniques and the absence of any kind of mass production. The stelae would have been set directly in the ground or in stone bases, probably on rudimentary plinths, as shown by rare *in situ* discoveries. Some of these monuments must have been protected by porticos, as demonstrated by the discovery of fragments of lintels and pillars on sites such as Le Marduel (Saint-Bonnet du Gard), Les Caisses de Saint-Jean (Mouriès, Bouches-du-Rhône), and Les Touriès (Aveyron) in the southern Massif Central (Figure 9.1; Roure and Pernet 2011).

These monuments mark the presence of sanctuaries devoted to natural cults, located at special places in the landscape, often on summits overlooking the settlements and their countryside (e.g. Saint-Blaise, Le Marduel), or close to a river mouth (Lattes), or near a spring (Glanon). Due to their heterogeneous character, geologically as much as technically and typologically, the stelae can be interpreted as *ex votos* made outside specialized workshops and placed in sanctuaries by individuals or families from the surrounding countryside. For the eighth to sixth centuries BC, it has been suggested that the populations were organized into acephalous societies: local egalitarian societies without rulers, whose structure was not favourable to collective undertakings and for which religion was a rare cohesive element, or at least certain ritual activities.

Prior to the development of social hierarchy and the rise of urbanization, these stelae would have acted as veritable 'geosymbols', marking, inhabiting, and structuring the landscape at a time before long-term appropriation of territory occurred. Most of these places were inhabited from the sixth century BC, because during the period of synœcism that characterizes the end of the early Iron Age, people recognized them as

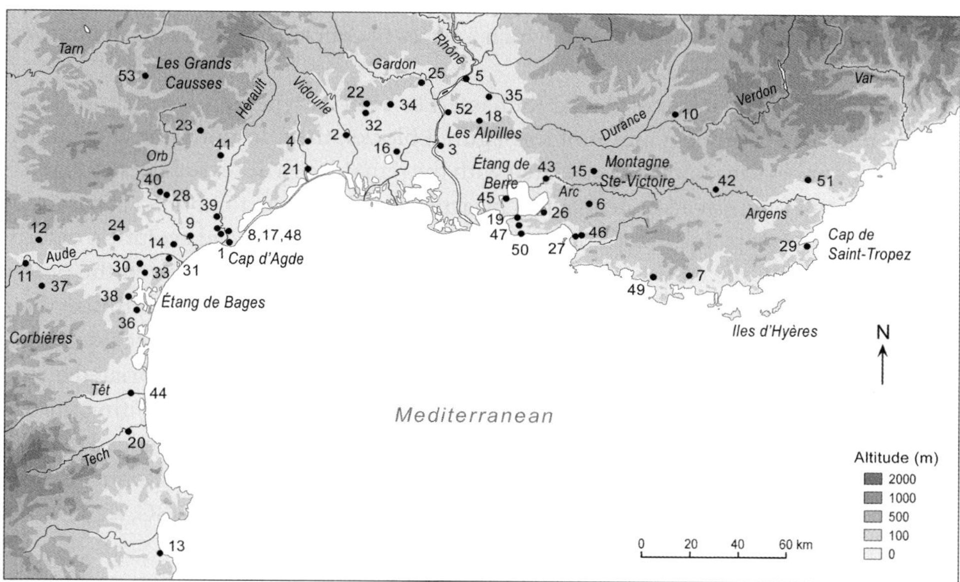

FIGURE 9.1 Map of Mediterranean France showing sites mentioned in the text. 1 Agde, 2 Ambrussum, 3 Arles, 4 Assas, 5 Avignon, 6 Le Baou-Roux, 7 Baudouvin-la-Bigoye, 8 Bessan, 9 Béziers, 10 Buffe-Arnaud, 11 Carcassonne, 12 Le Cros, 13 Emporion (Ampurias), 14 Ensérune, 15 Entremont, 16 Espeyran, 17 Florensac, 18 Glanon, 19 L'Ile de Martigues, 20 Illeberis (Elne), 21 Lattes, 22 La Liquière, 23 Lodève, 24 Mailhac, 25 Le Marduel, 26 Marignane, 27 Marseille, 28 Montfau, 29 Montjean, 30 Montlaurès, 31 La Moulinasse, 32 Nages, 33 Narbonne, 34 Nîmes, 35 Noves, 36 Pech-Maho, 37 Le Peyra, 38 Peyriac-de-Mer, 39 Pézenas, 40 Pradines, 41 La Ramasse, 42 Robernier-Monfort, 43 Roquepertuse, 44 Ruscino (Perpignan), 45 Saint-Blaise, 46 Saint-Marcel, Les Baou, 47 Saint-Pierre, 48 Saint-Thibéry, 49 Sanary, 50 Tamaris, 51 Taradeau, 52 Tarascon, 53 Les Touriès.

federative spaces and symbols of their identity. Stelae, pillars, and lintels were frequently built into the foundations and faces of ramparts: we may assume that they retained a cult value and were deliberately incorporated in the mass of the perimeter which marked out the new agglomeration, thereby ensuring its defence and affirming the cohesion of the social group. In addition to a political and military role, the enclosure would have assumed a symbolic character like that of the *pomœrium* in the Etrusco-Roman world.

Various monuments reference the symbolism of the heroic warrior, in particular the remarkable collection from Les Touriès, which are among the oldest decorated stelae or statues (Gruat and Garcia 2016). The unusual stela from the *oppidum* of Castelnau-le-Lez, in the hinterland of Lattes, displays the attributes of a warrior (shield, lance, and sword). Other finds come from La Ramasse (Clermont-l'Hérault) in the middle Hérault valley (Figure 9.2) and the *oppidum* at Le Pègue (Drôme) in the middle Rhône valley; incorporated in later defensive circuits, both display a pattern of concentric circles similar to the representation of the shield from Castelnau-le-Lez. Another find, this time an old discovery without context, from Robernier-Monfort (Var), in eastern Provence, bears at least three representations of this motif, together with zoomorphic and geometric engravings. This small group has been augmented by a recent find from Assas in the garrigue north of Montpellier on which a series of concentric circles (*kardiophylax*) and a belt can be discerned.

Anthropomorphic stelae of the La Ramasse/Les Touriès type do not mark the location of a tomb. As faceless and limbless figured blocks, they do not represent known individuals or personal objects associated with the remains of a deceased person to illustrate his status, but instead endeavour to incarnate or give shape to mythical characters or heroized ancestors. Indeed, the early Iron Age saw a phase of social evolution of local communities with the emergence of 'Big Men' (Sahlins 1976), who asserted the power of a small group or a lineage over a particular territory, and needed to legitimize their nascent supremacy. The panoply displayed was not so much that of a deceased warrior as the mystical image of an armed power dominating the space appropriated by the group: at first essentially cultic, the geosymbol now became political, exhibiting the authority of one or more lineages over the ethnic territory. It is now acknowledged that the series of well-known sitting warrior statues found at sites such as Glanon, Roquepertuse, and Lattes (Figures 9.3–9.4) began as early as the sixth or fifth centuries BC, rather than belonging to the late Iron Age, as was once thought (Garcia 2004: 111).

The earliest representations pre-date the earliest phase of urbanization and ethnic regrouping, but are contemporary with the nascent assertion of small local powers and the first contacts with exogenous Mediterranean populations. During a phase which sees shifting ethnic spaces, where populations get together and settle down within territories which were no longer just travelled through and exploited, but also politically dominated, these anthropomorphic stelae erected at formal inter-community sanctuaries such as Les Touriès testify to the emergence of local elites, the representation of proto-historic myths, and the first aristocracies of the Mediterranean region. In so doing, the social and cultural phenomena which these figural monuments symbolize can be compared to the statue-menhirs of the Chalcolithic period, reflecting political

FIGURE 9.2 Stela from La Ramasse (Clermont l'Hérault), with representation of a warrior panoply.

Photo: Dominique Garcia

restructurings, the reinforcement and assertion of lineage links, the promotion of elites, and the writing of myths.

The World of the Dead

Even if the evidence is unevenly distributed (present from the Pyrenees to Hérault and in the foothills of the Massif Central and the Alps, but absent in the lower Rhône region and in lower Provence), cemeteries of pit graves or tumuli dating to the seventh century BC, as well as isolated tombs, are relatively numerous.

FIGURE 9.3 The back of the warrior (lancer?) from Lattes, sixth century BC, found in the wall of a later residential building.

Photo: Centre Camille Jullian

Pit grave cemeteries occur in Catalonia, Roussillon, western Languedoc, the Pyrenees, and Aquitaine (Nickels et al. 1989; Gailledrat 1997; Sanmartí et al. 2006). They are linked to the Grand Bassin I facies, as defined on the basis of excavations at Mailhac (Aude). They range from several dozen to several hundred cremation graves. The funerary urn was placed in a pit, usually with food offerings and grave goods (pottery, metal objects, and various other items). The graves were probably covered with wood and/or mounds of stones or earth. They were sometimes surrounded by enclosures, as at Pradines (Causses-et-Veyran, Hérault), and organized into well-structured zones, as at Agde (Nickels et al. 1989). Most cemeteries were not associated with any known nearby settlements. Indeed, we know no contemporary settlements near the large Grand Bassin I cemeteries at Agde, Mailhac, or Pézenas.

FIGURE 9.4 Reconstruction of a monumental portico featuring the seated warrior from Glanon.

Photo: Dominique Garcia

These cemeteries were situated either at places where the rocky substrate outcropped on the surface, or in areas likely to be regularly submerged. The first applies at Agde, where the Le Peyrou cemetery was established directly on the basalt bedrock. The Causse necropolis at Labruguière and La Génibrette at Lautrec (both Tarn) share the same topographical criteria. In lower Languedoc, cemeteries like Mailhac or Le Peyra (Montlaur, Aude) are located in depressions, with recent excavations at Le Peyra revealing lacustrine or marshy conditions. At Mailhac, the Grand Bassin and Le Moulin cemeteries developed in a flat area, extending over nearly 5 ha (Taffanel et al. 1998). The soil profiles and the fills of some graves indicate that this depression was probably partially and/or temporarily submerged. The low-lying situation of these cemeteries is comparable to others in the Albi region, such as La Traytié, near the settlement of Catusse, Mondi (Algans), as well as the large burial grounds of La Gourjade and Martinet near Castres on the lower terrace of the Agout. At these last, the substrate is composed of a thick layer of silty soil, while the burials at La Gourjade are covered with silt some 0.3 m deep. In Hérault, the cemetery of Pradines also seems to have been located in a marshy environment.

For some researchers, these topographical choices appear to be governed by a wish to avoid arable land. This is possible, but seems incompatible with the presumed lack of agricultural pressure at this period. For some cemeteries (Mailhac especially), we might consider that the situation was inherited from the late Bronze Age, but in many other cases (such as Agde) this solution is not likely. For the cemeteries situated close to wet land, it may not be too simplistic to seek an answer in the ritual domain. The establishment of a cemetery next to a marsh is reminiscent of the geographical location of some Neolithic tombs or Bronze and Iron Age sanctuaries in eastern Europe.

The cultural homogeneity of the grave goods from the Grand Bassin I cemeteries in the Hérault and Aude valleys suggests that they could be related to the people known as the Elisyces, first mentioned by Hecataeus of Miletus around the end of the sixth century BC. Their mercenaries took part in the battle of Himera on the Carthaginian side in 480 BC (Herodotus *Histories* 7.195), and Narbo/Naro (Narbonne) was their capital according to the *Ora Maritima* of Festus Avienus. Study of finds from seventh-century BC graves in Roussillon implies that these cemeteries belonged to a different group.

In the Pyrenees, and from the Grands-Causses (Dedet 2001) to the southern Alps via the Montagne Sainte-Victoire, the tumuli of the eighth century BC show different funerary practices from those in force in Roussillon and western Languedoc. Analysis of the grave goods and architecture of the mounds seems to indicate, far more than in the Grand Bassin I zone, a certain hierachization of the population. But, as with the major Grand Bassin I cemeteries, there are no known contemporary settlements adjacent to these tumulus cemeteries. These 'cities of the dead' may reflect not so much single agglomerations but instead have served a dispersed population inhabiting small isolated sites and hamlets, and may perpetuate (or indeed structure) lineage or community links. This hypothesis makes social interpretation difficult. Indeed, differences in the number and types of objects (especially those of metal), in the way the grave was arranged, or the identification of different burial zones within some cemeteries may not so much translate into a strongly hierarchized society, but instead reflect groups living in different places in a territory. However, the overall size of the population should not be overestimated. The group that used the Grand Bassin I cemetery at Agde is estimated as between 220 and 280 individuals (Nickels et al. 1989: 199–200).

Analysis of the grave assemblages enables us to identify four separate regional groups: a Pyrenean cluster; the '*suspendien*' facies between the Hérault and the Rhône; an Alpine cluster north of the Durance; and finally a quite heterogeneous lower Provençal cluster, including the Alpilles and Sainte-Victoire.

After the apparent homogeneity of the Mailhac I facies, six major groups can be seen to emerge, which would last through the Iron Age: Catalonia/eastern Pyrenees, the Aude and Hérault basins, eastern Languedoc, western Provence, and the lower Alps. This next phase—if not a crisis, at least a rupture—may well have triggered the development of new ethnic groupings, which arose from the new lifestyles and social reorganization (emerging proto-chieftainships) that followed the abandonment of slash-and-burn agriculture. Paradoxically, we see both a geographical spread and regional regrouping of the population, linked to the emergence of wider networks. This process was not exclusively 'Gaulish'. Similar trends are observable elsewhere in the north-west Mediterranean zone: in Spain, the individualization of local cultural groups following the segmentation of larger groups during the late Bronze Age (Chapter 10), and in north-west Italy the emergence of distinctive local facies out of the apparent ethnic homogeneity of the middle Bronze Age (Chapter 11).

Commerce and Economy Before Massalia

If the seventh century BC was a century of disruption, it was nevertheless characterized by remarkable technical borrowings or innovations (in particular the use of iron) on the one hand, and by the first contacts with Mediterranean merchants on the other. These were almost concomitant events, but with different origins, and would have a major impact on the development of protohistoric societies. Iron made metal production less dependent on distant extraction centres for raw materials, and enabled widespread use of metal tools, especially for agriculture. For historians and agronomists, the introduction of iron to agriculture constitutes a true technical revolution.

The organization of Mediterranean commerce has been analysed extensively; here we shall simply stress that it started at a time when the local populations seemingly lacked dynamism, and where their lifestyles and modes of production were most open to change (Dedet 1995; Gras 1995). In their topographic situation and their economy, a number of sites founded or reoccupied at the end of the seventh or the beginning of the sixth century BC—such as Carsac, La Liquière, Saint-Blaise, and Sanary—exhibit one or more distinctive features which were later to become the norm: an elevated position, the presence of a fortified *enceinte* (walled enclosure), and an openness to Mediterranean commerce.

Before tackling the formation of urban centres, it is appropriate to sketch out a possible explanation for this phase of disruption between 725 and 625 BC. Natural events that might have weakened these populations should be ruled out at the outset. No notable markers have been observed in palaeoenvironmental analysis, except perhaps in the lagoon areas. The abandonment of the lagoon sites can be associated with critical riverine alluvial build-up. War-related explanations can also be rejected: there is no evidence of invasion or of major battles which might have swept away these societies. The continuity of material culture and persistence of funerary practices, often on the very same sites, do not support this idea.

The most likely explanation lies in a series of unfavourable conjunctions around the lifestyles of these early Iron Age populations. In the long run, slash-and-burn agriculture leads to a double crisis: an ecological crisis (deforestation, erosion, or even climatic deterioration) and a subsistence crisis. The crisis which may have affected the south of France from the last third of the eighth century BC was only averted by the general introduction of a system of fallow and light ploughing during the later seventh century BC, along with the adoption of iron and the first Mediterranean contacts. The social organization of these groups must also have played a part. As already mentioned, 'Big Man' societies are poorly hierarchized, and the inertia inherent in the domestic mode of production leads to a revival of social segmentation during periodic crises.

The Growth of Towns in the Sixth Century BC

A First Phase of Urbanization

The phenomenon of urbanization really began in the sixth century BC. A rapid survey, from west to east, will help delineate its chronological framework. South of the Pyrenees, no sedentary settlement is recorded in the hinterland of Emporion (Ampurias) before the arrival of the Phocaeans. In Roussillon, the site of Ruscino (near Perpignan) shows little sign of occupation before the end of the seventh or beginning of the sixth century BC, the most closely datable finds being a few sherds of Etruscan black *bucchero* and amphorae, and a fragment of Italo-Corinthian *œnochoe*. This Iron Age Phase I has long been recognized on the highest part of the hill at Ruscino, and is described as a settlement that shifted regularly. Structures were of perishable materials, and no fortifications are known at this date. The site of Illeberis (Elne, Roussillon) was also established during the sixth century BC.

The primitive bourgade of Pech-Maho (Sigean, Aude), formed of houses with a rectangular plan, was founded at around the same date as Ruscino, while Le Moulin—a rocky platform which stands some 15 m above the western bank of the Étang de Bages lagoon at Peyriac-de-Mer—was inhabited from the later sixth century BC. At Carcassonne, the plateau of Carsac was deserted before the mid-sixth century, but the spur now occupied by the medieval town was inhabited from the second half of the century. In Minervois, the enceinte of the *oppidum* of Le Cros (Caunes), which covers more than 5 ha, was also built at the end of the seventh or start of the sixth century BC.

Near Narbonne, houses with timber and daub walls of the sixth century BC are known on the lower slopes of Montlaurès before the hilltop itself was developed. At Mailhac, Le Cayla was reoccupied from the second quarter of the sixth century BC after more than a century of abandonment. The *oppidum* of La Moulinasse (Salles d'Aude), dominating the alluvial plain of the Aude on the northern edge of the La Clape massif, has yielded surface finds ranging from the late Bronze Age to the Roman period. A ditch enclosing around 0.8 ha might date to the late Bronze Age or the early Iron Age. In the last third of the sixth century BC, this settlement had houses built of mud-brick or stone; its tightly organized plan, without dividing walls, was a kind of intermediate step between a settlement with a completely organic structure and one with buildings laid out in regular blocks (*îlots* or *insulae*). The *oppidum* of Ensérune at Nissan was occupied from the second quarter of the sixth century BC. Further north, the site of Montfau (Magalas) in the Libron valley was also founded in the sixth century. The first permanent settlements of the middle Hérault valley and the Lodévois were created shortly before 500 BC, not long after those of the lower valley such as Agde, Bessan, Florensac, and Saint-Siméon (Pézenas).

At Lattes (Lattara), a date around 525 BC has been proposed for the first occupation of Saint-Sauveur, and 525–475 BC for the first phase of the town itself (Garcia 1999; Py 1995, Py 2009). Many other sites in eastern Languedoc were founded around this period, along with the trading post at Espeyran on the bank of the Petit Rhône, at the eastern end of the chain of coastal lagoons (Barruol and Py 1978). At the head of the Rhône delta, the settlement at Arles (Theline), which had existed from the beginning of the sixth century BC (Arcelin 1995), saw a sudden expansion in the 540s–530s BC.

In western Provence (Chausserie-Laprée 2000), the development of settlement was not very different from west of the Rhône. Elevated locations and expansion of built-up areas are two notable characteristics of the late Bronze Age, the site of Le Baou-Roux (Bouc-Bel-Air) being a good example. On the banks of the Étang de Berre, a hierarchy of settlement can be observed: farms, small agglomerations, and especially a large fortified site, high up on the plateau of Saint-Blaise (Figure 9.5). Occupation at both Saint-Blaise and the coastal promontory site at Tamaris (Figure 9.6) probably began in the very early sixth century BC, while the *oppidum* of Les Baou de Saint-Marcel, close to Massalia, was also founded around 575 BC. New architectural elements appeared more and more frequently in the Marseille region (but nowhere else in the south); these included enceintes, dwellings of quadrangular plan, buildings with load-bearing walls, and use of adobe, all of them designed with optimal organization and permanence in mind. In eastern Provence, hilltop settlements became widespread in the seventh to sixth centuries BC, even if slightly earlier occupation is attested at Baudouvin-la-Bigoye (Var). In the southern Alps, however, no permanent sites are known that pre-date 525 BC.

FIGURE 9.5 Aerial view of Saint-Blaise.

Photo: Centre Camille Jullian

To sum up, sites show few if any signs of significant or sustained development in the form of fortifications or settlement quarters in the seventh century BC. The first permanent settlements were founded in the first quarter of the sixth century, but the phenomenon only became widespread from the middle of the century, and particularly in its last third. While the towns thought to be the oldest were all close to Massalia (Saint-Blaise, Tamaris) or near the mouth of coastal rivers (Arles, Béziers, Bessan, Lattes, Montlaurès), the reoccupation of some late Bronze Age proto-urban centres can also be noted (Le Baoux-Roux, Mailhac).

FIGURE 9.6 Aerial view of the site of Tamaris.

Photo: City of Martigues

Topography and Architecture of the Southern Sites

The natural settings of early Iron Age settlements fall into two main categories. The first group of sites occur in low fluvial valleys, near the mouths of coastal rivers or slightly inland at the head of the deltas, or even along the lagoon shores; this is where most major pre-Roman urban centres were located. The second group is situated on the tops of hills, plateau edges, or flanks of the foothills, dominating the valleys and plains. These were 'high sites' par excellence, and include most of the known *oppida* or secondary agglomerations. Some sites do not fall completely into either topographic category, since their siting was seemingly governed by specific factors, such as the presence of a sanctuary, a crossroads, or mineral deposits.

Long underrated with respect to their agro-pastoral potential, the deltas and coastal valleys around the major pre-Roman agglomerations appear propitious environments on the basis of palaeoenvironmental analyses. The plain of the Lattes delta, for instance, is composed of two tightly interlocking natural environments with complementary resources: one aquatic (sea, lagoons, the River Lez), the other terrestrial and favouring cattle raising and agriculture. This type of diverse environment is a constant in the settlements of Mediterranean agro-pastoral communities for whom self-sufficiency was essential; this is particularly true of sites in Languedoc belonging to the first phase of permanent occupation in the early Iron Age. Most likely their lifestyles could not be changed abruptly. Landscapes selected for settlement had to meet the varied needs of a population experiencing economic change: land suitable for cattle raising, fruit picking, and agriculture, as well as fishing, water sources, and availability of building materials. The natural resources of the environs of these sites were such that they could sustain their communities through such changes and allow them to thrive.

In the interior, along the valleys and in the foothills of the Massif Central, the settlement pattern takes on a conventional character of villages practising a cultivation regime of fallow and light ploughing on the river terraces up to the plateaus and foothills. In the Hérault valley, the types of terrain encompassed in the territories of the major centres are diverse and complementary. The alluvial plains were probably dedicated to hunting and cattle raising; the middle terraces were suitable for cultivation; the lighter soils on the plateaus were propitious for cereal growing and sheep farming; these were bordered with more rugged and probably wooded areas, for fruit picking and pig grazing.

Natural routes were an important element structuring the settlement network. Ancient authors like Strabo acknowledge the role of valleys as communication routes. Whether it was the proximity of the coast, the presence of a navigable route, or the circulation of goods and commodities, all seem to have been indispensable for the development of settlements. The practice of transhumance was another factor, as were links with Mediterranean merchants. The main east–west axis, largely parallel to the coast, is that taken by the ancient long-distance land route between Iberia and Italy dedicated to commerce in specific products. It probably provided services to the Greek colonies (Massalia, Emporion) and the major indigenous coastal centres. The secondary axes generally have a north–south orientation. These followed river valleys such as the Aude, Orb, and Hérault, enabling manufactured goods (wine first and foremost) to be transported to the hinterland and bulk commodities (cereals, metals) to the coast. There must also have been a network of branching connections linking settlements in different valleys. The Rhône formed a second principal axis, joining up to routes along its main tributaries, while a third axis led through the Carcassone gap towards Aquitaine.

The Structuring Components of Urban Sites: Enclosure and Districts

The enclosure circuit constitutes a fundamental element of the highly symbolic, possibly sacred agglomeration. It delineates the occupied space, reflects a certain political autonomy, and demonstrates that the group is capable of undertaking a significant collective work. At present, no open agglomerations dating from the early Iron Age are known. The oldest ramparts date to the mid-sixth century BC, others to its last third. The enceintes often surrounded a space larger than the built-up area. They exploit natural defences to the maximum, and sometimes enclose a specific element of the landscape, such as a delta, part of a plateau, or the summit of a hill, but there was clearly a deliberate intention to incorporate a wider area. In the classical world as well as in 'barbarian' societies, the purpose of the enceinte—the very image of the urban space—was to attract rather than contain people. The 'crystallizing' nature of the enclosure, like that of the sanctuary, may help to explain the original surface areas of the newly founded cities and their remarkable demographic boom. Lattes, Arles, and Nîmes—which from the outset covered significant areas—would triple in size over a few generations. Both for these extreme examples, and for many other agglomerations, such demographic growth cannot be described as normal.

In addition to lacking areas for grazing or agriculture, the enceintes did not contain facilities for storing fodder, or even water sources, however indispensable these might seem. The enclosed space was essentially dedicated to houses, although the layout of the buildings could be quite diffuse. Further investigation is required, especially large-scale excavation, but the situation may not correspond to a simple linear progression or gentle evolution from 'loose' to 'dense' forms of urbanism. On the contrary, the evidence points to the adoption of urban schemes on a case-by-case basis, linked to demographic pressure and economic development. In less densely populated agglomerations, houses were preferentially constructed first against the rampart, then, according to the topography, spread into the interior. On larger sites, elongated *îlots* of abutting houses were often laid out perpendicular to the slope: either in simple blocks one room deep, or in double blocks formed of two aligned rows separated by an axial wall. In these cases, access routes are generally not well developed and probably not planned. Sites with a higher density of occupation probably had a more strictly regulated plan, both major sites such as Lattes and Arles, but also smaller agglomerations.

The Economic, Cultural, and Social Implications of Urbanization

Rather than being concerned with criteria that define urbanization (which are quite difficult both to establish and to recognize in the field), we should instead think in terms of the necessary preconditions for urbanization and the rising importance of urban functions (Garcia 2013). Four elements, at least, theoretically seem to need to come together:

(1) The possibility of generating a surplus capable of feeding non-producers, hence the need for more intensive exploitation of the surrounding countryside; however, the larger the agglomeration, the less easily its needs may be satisfied by its immediate hinterland, requiring wider-scope tribute and larger-scale interregional commerce.
(2) The establishment of commercial activities. Commerce is an integral part of the city and, for the largest sites, implies the presence of a class of merchants specialized in the collection and redistribution of foodstuffs, with a body of specialists dedicated to storage, transport, bookkeeping, and possibly the organization of a market.
(3) The presence of integrative elements (religious, political) for attracting and crystallizing the population.
(4) The emergence of political power—i.e. of a class of leaders capable of organizing the use of the surplus for the agriculturally non-productive. This power also enables the imposition of the stability needed for the production and circulation of foodstuffs.

Agriculture, Surplus, and Mediterranean Commerce

The criterion common to every urban phenomenon—which may even lie at its very heart—is above all economic: 'non-self-sufficiency'. It is expressed in the way the inhabitants of an agglomeration feed themselves (and more widely speaking, consume goods), not solely relying on local agro-pastoral activities but involving trade and the emergence of a class of craftworkers. Paradoxically, this transition from a 'rural' to an 'urban' economy went hand in hand with the intensification of agricultural production or, at least, of a type of production that would guarantee the food supply of the group and/or provide the means for exchange.

As we have seen, the slash-and-burn system of the late Bronze Age may have led to a double ecological and subsistence crisis only averted by a shift to fallow and light ploughing. The break between the early Iron Age and the following period is very tangible. Archaeobotanists have noted a substantial increase in the number of cultigens, especially cereals, across the north-west Mediterranean region, while pollen analysis reveals significant deforestation. At Le Marduel in Gard, increased exploitation of oak woodland and activity over a wider area around 525/450 BC was followed by a phase of deforestation. As well as these relatively limited archaeological traces for agriculture, the siting of agglomerations shows a real control over their territories. We may also note increased use of iron tools from the fifth century BC, if not yet on the scale of the late Iron Age. The archaeology of storage suggests a substantial increase in production after the end of the sixth century BC. Absent from sites prior to 500 BC, by the mid-fifth century BC *pithoi* (large vessels for storing cereals) represent 25–35% of the objects found on indigenous sites. This increase in quantity is accompanied by an increase in size. The first granaries appear at this time. If supra-family management of granaries (whether with open storage or in *pithoi*) is not certain, it was undeniably the case for the long-term cereal reserves represented by the silo fields of western Languedoc (e.g. at Aumes near Pézenas, Ensérune, Montfau) and Roussillon (Illeberis, Ruscino), where some pits could contain as much as 350 hectolitres.

This increase in the cereal storage capacities of southern French sites has been linked with Mediterranean commerce, especially around Marseille (Py 1990). Directly or indirectly, it suggests significant modifications of indigenous social structures: full sedentarization, new agrarian practices, stock management and control, and the beginnings of specialization. This intensification of agricultural production and increase in exchange marks a fundamental step in the process of urbanization, reflecting the existence of an indigenous urban network and its introduction to the commercial world of the Mediterranean: a dual urban/rural and indigenous/Greek relationship.

This commercial model, probably associated with an urban model, was undoubtedly more or less imposed upon the natives by the Greeks, but cannot have been the sole (let alone principal) cause of the social upheavals observed. The start of Massaliot wine production in the later sixth century BC, probably associated with the arrival of Phocaean immigrants and the establishment of a commercial network out of Massalia, accelerated the development of indigenous cities: in the mid-sixth century BC along the coast, shortly afterwards along the river axes, in the fifth century BC in the hinterland.

Specialization is the step that follows significant agricultural development in all societies. It is indispensable for cities to flourish, whether for para-agricultural production (particularly metalworking and ceramics) or service activities. The organization of commerce is difficult to demonstrate archaeologically, but lead sheets inscribed in Etruscan and Greek from Pech-Maho that mention indigenous go-betweens in the fifth century BC, and (slightly later) in Iberic from the Narbonne-Béziers region, contribute to our understanding of these phenomena.

The Prominence of Religion and Politics

Many known Iron Age place-names are in fact theonyms and refer to local divinities, after which the sites are named. Recent work supports the hypothesis of sanctuaries, sources, or chthonic divinities being at the origin of large urban sites like Nîmes (Nemausos, 'the village of the sacred spring') and Glanon in the Alpilles. This may also be the case for Montlaurès and the Œuillals spring (the oldest occupation on the site was in the area near this perennial Vaucluse spring) or Béziers on the Plateau des Poètes.

These sanctuaries, previously visited by a dispersed local population, may have played an important role in crystallizing human groups, which might help account for the extent of the earliest phases of urban occupation. Foundation of a city would not only take advantage of pre-existing networks, in particular the road network, but the settlement would also benefit from the protection afforded by occupying a sacred place. Such an evolution, still poorly documented in southern France, is well attested in other regions, especially in the Greek world. A similar process may be at the origin of many Celtic *oppida* (Chapter 21).

Development of the southern French agglomerations could only take place within the framework of a more hierarchical social structure than those of the late Bronze Age and early Iron Age. The nucleation of population, the development of an urban site, the building of an enclosure, the exploitation of the countryside, and the management of exchange are among the many elements that could only thrive in structured societies. The urban network of the sixth to fifth centuries BC also reflected a regional political and administrative power. A real political organization gradually replaced the earlier Iron Age ethnic and lineage links, the social process matching that of urbanization. The emergence of a class of leaders capable of imposing the stability needed for the production and circulation of foodstuffs, and organizing the use of surplus to support specialists, was a phenomenon associated with the development of cities in all periods and everywhere in the world.

Cultural practices, exchange, architecture, and to an extent funerary rites, have long enabled us to distinguish different cultural zones in western and eastern Languedoc, and western and eastern Provence. Within these areas, different networks (especially economic and religious) based on natural regions (the basins of the coastal rivers) are superimposed. The economic weight of agglomerations such as Lattes or Arles cannot be denied, nor the political role of cities like Nîmes. But within each settlement, it is difficult to describe the political system in force. The allusions of ancient texts to aristocratic systems do not suffice for an answer. A communal type of organization has often been put forward since the 1970s to explain the apparent uniformity of the housing modes of the later Iron Age, but ethnology and history provide many examples where material culture does not reflect a well-established social hierarchy. It seems logical that starting from a chieftainship system and network of chiefs mainly concerned with subsistence, the development of exchange promoted the arrival of new classes (first merchants, then craftworkers) and strengthened the religious and political power of certain individuals. The crystallizing role of the sanctuaries and the existence of an agricultural surplus were the basis of the more hierarchical society whose first manifestations of prestige (statuary, public edifices) emerged in the fourth century BC.

Urban Concentration: The Fourth to Third Centuries BC

The second part of the Iron Age (particularly the fourth and third centuries BC) represents the high point of nucleated settlement in Mediterranean France; this reflects a strong political and economic evolution. Paradoxically, *oppida* are less numerous than in the 500s BC, but their internal structure reflects a greater regularity and their occupation density is sometimes higher. Isolated farms or hamlets are extremely rare.

In eastern Provence, no lowland settlements are known from the end of the fifth century to the end of the second century BC. The number of *oppida* was also in decline: Montjean on the coastal heights above Saint-Tropez was abandoned in the mid-fourth century BC. In western lower Provence (Arcelin 1992), total or partial desertion occurs at sites such as Le Baou-Roux and Les Baou de Saint-Marcel. Le Mont-Garou at Sanary was also abandoned between the early fourth and second century BC. The *oppidum* of Saint-Blaise (Figure 9.7) probably saw a reduction of population in the fourth century BC, but this phase is still not fully understood (Isoardi 2013). Along with other sites of the Ouvèze valley, the *oppidum* of Saint-Laurent at Vaison-la-Romaine seems to have been abandoned as early as at the start of the fourth century.

Among the best-known sites, the two successive fortified settlements at L'Ile de Martigues have highly organized layouts (Figures 9.8–9.9), but over restricted areas, reflecting a high occupation density (Chausserie-Laprée 2000; Chausserie-Laprée 2005). The second village was built in the later third century BC. The occupation is characterized not only by a change in layout, but also by a marked extension of the inhabited area to the west, delimited by a new boundary wall. At the nearby hilltop *oppidum* of Saint-Pierre, the internal organization was apparently not disrupted.

Several new creations are attested in the Marseille area (Notre-Dame-de-Pitié at Marignane, Teste-Nègre in Les Pennes-Mirabeau), but these are small sites whose area is substantially less than 1 ha. Elsewhere in Provence, particularly in the Alpilles, the large fortified agglomerations of the early Iron Age on high ground appear to have been abandoned or, at least, lost importance. In this micro-region, the beginning of the later Iron Age presents a picture of territorial reconfiguration characterized by the declining importance of elevated, nucleated, and fortified settlements, even if a few survive. This development coincided with the maximum expansion of Arles. The extensive southern districts of this agglomeration, covering over 30 ha, were densely occupied and attest the economic drawing power of this centre over the surrounding regions. Avignon apparently developed at the same time (in the third century BC?). Few sites are known in the southern Alps.

The few fourth-century BC sites known in the middle Rhône valley include Vienne, Soyons, and Saint-Etienne-de-Dions. At Le Pègue, a timber-framed rampart was constructed at the start of the fourth century BC, but the site was deserted around 325–300 BC. The situation changed at the start of the third century BC, when most

FIGURE 9.7 The Hellenistic ramparts at Saint-Blaise.

Photo: Centre Camille Jullian

FIGURE 9.8 Model showing part of the first fortified settlement at L'Ile de Martigues.

Photo: Jean-Chausserie Laprée

FIGURE 9.9 Destruction level in a house of the first settlement at L'Ile de Martigues.
Photo: Jean-Chausserie Laprée

sites abandoned in the fifth century were reoccupied. Sites such as Feurs, Roanne, and Aulnat indicate the spread of extensive open settlements from the Rhône-Saône confluence towards the eastern Massif Central. On the Provence border, the *oppidum* of Barry (Bollène, Vaucluse) saw major development from the third century BC; this fortified site of 45 ha has yielded abundant ceramics and many coins.

In eastern Languedoc, the period between the end of the fifth century and the second century BC saw the large-scale abandonment of lower-lying sites, suggesting that the agricultural land was now mainly managed from the *oppida* and other nucleated settlements. In the Nîmes region, there were fewer settlements than before (albeit over a longer time period), but they are generally larger and probably represent a greater occupied area. Important sites founded in the late fourth and early third century BC include Ambrussum and Nages (Py 1978). At Nîmes, we see the creation of an enceinte, the first stone-built dwellings, and progressive desertion of the slopes in favour of the agglomeration at the foot of the hill, which expanded from 20 to 25 ha; the enceinte, incorporating the spring of La Fontaine and part of Mont Cavalier, may enclose a total area of over 40 ha.

The coastal lagoon area was also losing population in the later Iron Age, with the exception of the agglomerations of Espeyran and Lattes. The latter was about to see a remarkable expansion: on the lagoon side, the addition of an outer defensive wall which delineated a harbour terrace, a new gate linked to the presence of metallurgical workshops, and an abundance of imports from the interior (Py 2009). Economic boom and urban development seem to go hand in hand. At Lattes, we observe an expansion of the occupied area (to around 20 ha) and increased density of dwellings in the 'historic centre'. This urban growth seems to have been organized in a rational manner. Public space (mainly the rampart, streets, and lanes) was respected. The fortifications were strengthened with additional bastions and stone facing, which may have replaced mud-brick walls, and the streets were relaid and paved, making them more durable and helping improve sanitation by managing the evacuation of foul water.

In the fourth century BC, central Languedoc was affected by an important regional event (Garcia 1995): the creation *c*.400 BC of the colony of Agathé (Agde) on the site of the earlier agglomeration. The Greeks probably imposed or prompted a reorganization of the hinterland settlements and countryside. In the lower Hérault valley, sites such as Bessan and Florensac were abandoned by their native occupants and absorbed into the *chôra*. At Saint-Thibéry (Cessero), no native occupation is apparent in the fourth to third centuries, when the site was exploited for basalt by the Greeks. We can surmise that the indigenous population either retreated further inland or was subjugated by the Greeks. Aumes, the *oppidum* closest to the sites annexed by the settlers, seems to develop at this time. Situated at a suitable stopping point for heavy loads, it may have acted as a relay station. Further up the Hérault valley, the *oppidum* of La Ramasse underwent a major transformation, with the building of an irregular rampart onto which a series of single-room houses abutted, enclosing an area of 1 ha, during its Phase 3 (400/375 to 250/225 BC), shortly after Agde was founded.

In western Languedoc, sites like Montfau and Mailhac continued to develop, while Béziers had a remarkable standard of living and a large occupation area (20 ha) up to its desertion at the end of the fourth century BC. At Ensérune, Phase III saw the development of stone architecture, including two public buildings in dressed stone, which might perhaps be the source of a series of voluted capitals found in the same phase. Sites like Combo de la Semal and Le Calla de Durban in the Corbières were abandoned between 350 and 300 BC. The *oppidum* of Montlaurès near Narbonne was still occupied, but saw no appreciable development. The maritime trading post of Le Moulin at Peyriac-de-Mer was abruptly abandoned around 300–250 BC and Pech-Maho a little later. A few sites in Roussillon were still inhabited, and Ruscino and Illeberis even experienced a phase of expansion, the latter exceeding 10 ha.

In north-east Iberia, the history of Emporion in the fourth century BC is interesting. Both classical sources (e.g. Livy *History of Rome*, 34.9) and excavations, especially those at the suburban sanctuary, suggest the presence of natives on the Greek site. The assimilation of local populations seems to have started early in the fifth century BC, and to have been complete around a century later. Possibly at Emporion, the Greeks had to opt for peaceful coexistence due to their small numbers, whereas at Massalia they were more numerous and able to impose harsher terms on the indigenous population. In Iberia, the end of this phase coincided with the second Punic War (Sanmartí et al. 2006).

The fourth and third centuries BC saw the development of nucleated settlements and the expansion of an essentially agricultural economy of which Massalia was the main beneficiary. Craftworking (metallurgy, and the production of wheel- and handmade ceramics; Figure 9.10) was thriving, but did not go beyond regional commercial activity. Some coin hoards occur, but there is nothing to suggest that coinage was regularly in

FIGURE 9.10 Set of ceramic vessels of the later Iron Age from Provence.

Photo: Centre Camille Jullian

circulation in a native context. The development of statuary seems to have played a part in the reinforcement of the political powers of local elites. Funerary practices remain poorly known, with the exception of Ensérune, whose cemetery yielded abundant grave goods attesting to a wide variety of cultural influences (Iberian, Celtic, Greek, and Italic; Schwaller et al. 2001).

Monumental Development and Late Foundations (Second to First Centuries BC)

In central and eastern Provence, small *oppida* continued to be quite numerous in the first century BC. Taradeau (Var) is typical of settlements of this date. Buildings were essentially ranged in a row against the fortifications around a virtually empty central space. These features were fundamentally different from those encountered in the Languedoc plains and the lower Rhône valley, and appear to be more in keeping with a fortified space used temporarily or periodically.

Again, we cannot speak of real urbanism in the southern Alps, where settlements of the later Iron Age combined optimal use of topography with a rational organization of dwellings in elongated blocks. Nucleated and elevated settlements are the most widespread form of occupation recognized, although the second century BC saw the creation of numerous farms. Sites located at the boundary of complementary landscapes seem to be linked with the existence of communication routes marked by valleys, as at La Platrière de Lazer (third to first centuries BC), on the hill of Saint-Mers (Gap), and Le Plan des Ribiers. After a phase of abandonment between 425 and 225 BC, the small confluence site of Buffe-Arnaud (Saint-Martin-de-Brômes) was provided with an enceinte incorporating a tower-gate of a distinctive southern type, and terraced residential quarters. The destruction of the *oppidum* by fire in the later second century BC, and the presence of catapult bolts, suggests the abandonment may be linked with the Roman campaign against the Saluvii in 124 BC.

In the Marseille area, numerous sites were abandoned between 220 and 175 BC, sometimes after violent destruction (Le Verduron, Teste-Nègre). Afterwards, new settlements were created or restructured, as at L'Ile de Martigues, Pierredon, and perhaps Le Baou-Roux (Chausserie-Laprée 2000; Chausserie-Laprée 2005), occupying larger areas than before, notably at Entremont (Figure 9.11). The discovery of sculptured elements and the presence of public spaces attest to a new conception of settlement. The fall of the Saluvian confederation in 123 BC provided Massalia with a subservient domain which it could organize to suit its economic needs. Other sites experienced violent destruction, for example Saint-Blaise around 140–120 BC, or less brutal abandonment, as at Les Baou de Saint-Marcel in the last quarter of the second century BC.

In the Alpilles, the late Iron Age was marked by reoccupation of several elevated settlements (Les Caisses de Saint-Jean at Mouriès, Mont de Cordes at Fontvielle) and the creation of some new ones (Notre-Dame-du-Château at Saint-Etienne-du-Grès, Le Castellas at Maussanne). At the same time, we see an increased structuring of space, the monumentalization of some centres (Glanon, Tarascon), and the development of residential quarters on slopes or lower hillsides (Sainte-Cécile at Eyguières, Le Puech at Noves). Until then indistinguishable from other proto-historic sites, Glanon experienced a veritable 'municipal fever' after the mid-second century BC, marked by the erection of many public buildings of late Hellenistic type (Roth-Congès 1997). This can be linked to the development of cult and therapeutic practices around a sacred well entered by a stairway, which was later ransacked, like all Glanon's monuments, probably during the last Roman intervention in 90 BC.

Glanon was not the only 'new city'. At Tarascon, located at a major crossroads at the western end of the Alpilles, the second century BC saw the installation of a new settlement below the abandoned early Iron Age *oppidum*. Arles seems to have been precociously open to Italic commerce, reaching 30 ha in extent at this date. The remains of a dressed stone building under the future Augustan forum should be seen in the perspective of urban change in the second century BC, accompanied by a new politics of monumentality in public life. This new Graeco-Italian cultural ambiance largely accounts for why Arles was selected as a Roman colony 150 years later.

New sites in the middle Rhône valley include Saint-Just-d'Ardèche, at the confluence of the Ardèche and the Rhône, which was probably a place where goods were transshipped; it was active between the end of the third and the start of the first century BC. Occupation layers of around 200 BC have been recognized at Vienne, capital of

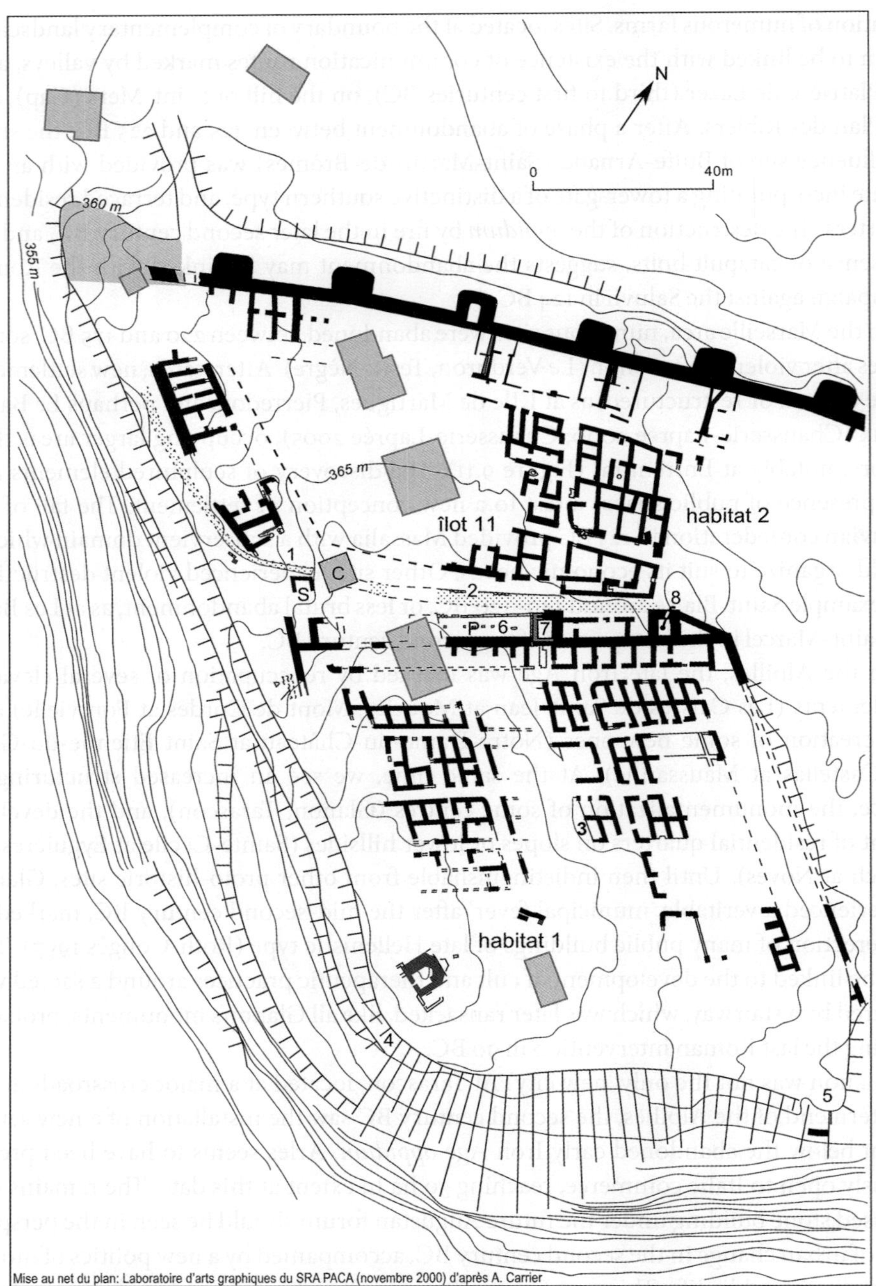

FIGURE 9.11 Plan of the oppidum of Entremont (Aix-en-Provence).

Drawing: Laboratoire d'arts graphiques du SRA PACA, after A. Carrier

the Allobroges, and at Feurs, Goincet, and Roanne on the eastern fringes of the Massif Central.

In eastern Languedoc, the second century BC marks a phase of development and growth. Around 175 BC, Nages was extended to the west and provided with a new rampart. The second-century BC boundaries of Nîmes were identical to those of the fourth and third centuries BC. From the perspective of urban development, the century was one of transition, marked by continuity of occupation of the foothills and the gradual reconquest of the slopes of Mont Cavalier, until then at least partly reserved for agriculture, at all events certainly uninhabited. In the first century BC, but before the Augustan period, the lower city extended beyond its walls to the south and south-east. Monumental building (porticos and statues) around the spring of La Fontaine should also be noted (Monteil 1999).

Lattes had by then reached an area of close to 25 ha; this period provides the most complete overview of urbanism. At this time, the city was extensively renovated, as shown by the building of Mediterranean-style courtyard houses, a harbour terrace, and a monumental public centre, indicated by finds of late Hellenistic architectural fragments (Py 2009).

In central Languedoc, we may note the abandonment of a number of sites, perhaps because of internal or external conflicts, along with the creation of lower-lying settlement areas, or even the development of new agglomerations in the plains (Garcia 1995). This period saw the final disappearance of cave sites and, above all, large numbers of new settlements on the plains. This was the first period when upland settlement did not represent the highest percentage of sites, even though the number of hilltop sites was actually increasing. As in Provence at this time, these were generally small-scale. There are undoubtedly multiple reasons for their occupation, but their topographic situation—difficult to access, and surrounded by land unsuited to agriculture—suggests that many were sites of refuge for those not inclined to blend into the new economic model. While architecturally (the presence of drystone walls or walls of undressed stone and earth) and materially (handmade ceramics) they have a clearly indigenous aspect, the abundance of fragments of Italic amphorae testify to communities open to exchange. These late sites were generally short-lived, and most were abandoned in the Augustan period.

In the Corbières, the process of site abandonment initiated in the third century BC seems to accelerate in the second century. Conversely, the development of new agglomerations can be observed in western Languedoc, among them La Lagaste (Pomas-et-Rouffiac), the origins of which lie at the end of the second century BC. The agglomeration encompasses two nuclei: a dense one on the plateau, and a much less structured occupation on the peripheral areas and slopes; all told, more than 60 ha were built up into residential and craft districts, with pottery and metallurgical workshops. Among the other sites flourishing from the second century BC was Ensérune, which saw the construction of large courtyard houses of Italic type. It was probably in the second half of the first century BC that the public buildings of Hellenistic type were destroyed. At the start of the second century BC, the *oppidum* of Montlaurès saw large-scale urban development; residential blocks terraced along the slope were erected on both sides of a wide street over the former ditch; the hill slopes were probably also now inhabited, perhaps on account of significant population growth. At Carcassonne, extramural quarters developed outside the *oppidum* of La Cité, particularly to the north-east, along the line of the Aquitaine road. After limited occupation between the sixth and third century BC, the agglomeration of Castelnaudary (Sostomagus) reached a size of some 7 ha in the second century BC; it may have been a 'relay *oppidum*' on the Aquitaine road.

Further inland on the Aude-Garonne axis, the settlement of Le Cluzel at Toulouse seems to have been abandoned, but the development of Vieille-Toulouse, which was about to become a major commercial centre within the Roman world, can be observed. The abundance of Italic amphorae discovered in the wells testify to its role as an *emporion*: a place for commerce, production, and redistribution to the Gallic world (Vaginay and Izac-Imbert 2007). The agglomeration of Lacoste in Aquitaine exemplifies the dynamism of the south-western Gaulish populations. Ceramic and iron production reflect its role as a centre for commerce (Colin et al. 2011).

Evidence from Roussillon is limited, but we may note a reduction of the occupied area at Illeberis, perhaps to the benefit of Ruscino, which gained the status of Latin colony at that time, along with the creation of numerous isolated sites.

Conclusions

At the end of the Bronze Age, the emphasis was on pastoral activities in the Pyrenees, the south of the Massif Central, and the southern Alps. A dynamism in metallurgical activity is, however, also apparent: local copper resources were exploited and the production of bronze objects attests exceptional craft skills. Further south, only limited activity is apparent in lower-lying areas around the lagoons and on the lower hills, and settlements show a lack of permanence. Contact with the Mediterranean world was intermittent, but should not be underestimated. The presence of Italic fibulae dated to the eighth century BC points to limited exchange, with Mediterranean influences becoming more tangible during the seventh century BC. Some objects (cups, *œnochoes*, amphorae) can be associated with the consumption of Greek or Etruscan wine, a prestige good which would link indigenous elites and Mediterranean merchants. Even before the foundation of Massalia in 600 BC, the first 'Mediterraneanization' of southern Gaul occurred. Around 540 BC, the beginning of wine growing and the setting up of a commercial network around Massalia, probably associated with the arrival of Phocaean immigrants (Gras 1995), triggered an explosion of merchant activity in the city with profound repercussions for indigenous societies.

A dense network of *oppida* developed from the end of the sixth century BC: the production centres of the southern hinterland were matched by redistribution centres situated close to the coast, in the lower Rhône valley and along the Aude-Garonne axis near indigenous places of commerce and trans-shipment. Such specialization in a relatively small geographical area, where agrarian production exceeded self-sufficiency, implies a degree of geopolitical stability, whence came the adoption of common rules or laws. With various twists and turns, the Massaliot market system lasted at least up to the second Punic War. Native integration into this, in two stages, is perfectly summed up by the historian Justin (*Epitome* 43.4):

> Consequently, the Gauls learned from them how to live in a more civilized way, after softening and forsaking their Barbarian ways; they learned to cultivate fields and to surround cities with ramparts. They also became accustomed to live governed by laws, sometimes compelled by arms, to cut vineyards, to plant olive trees, and men like things reflected that blinding change to the extent that one could have thought that Gaul had been transported to Greece instead of the Greeks having invaded Gaul.

This phenomenon resulted from an evolution of indigenous social organization (probably communities with aristocratic tribal systems) on the one hand, and from the integration of southern Gaul into Mediterranean commercial networks on the other. During the later Iron Age, larger ethnic configurations progressively came into being. Political organization was based on existing economic networks and led to the emergence of political capitals: Ruscino for the Sordi, Narbonne for the Elisyces, Toulouse for the Volcae Tectosages, Nîmes for the Volcae Arecomici, Saint-Blaise(?) then Entremont(?)for the Saluvii (Barruol 1969; Garcia and Verdin 2002; Collin-Bouffier and Garcia 2012).

At the Conquest, the structuring character of the indigenous territorial system (politically and economically) was clearly perceived by Rome. In the context of the Augustan organization of the *Provincia*, the coastal road system, the Gaulish isthmus, and the Rhône axis were defined (or even fixed) by Roman towns, *fora*, and colonies. But more important than these urban centres, and the status granted to them, was the manner in which the territorial organization of the pre-Roman network was modified. Whereas the indigenous territories (or Greek, in the case of the Agde region) seem to have comprised portions of river courses and occupied segments of the overall network, the frontiers of the Roman *civitates* followed these axes and so broke them up. Rome and its military, then political, power were about to get the upper hand in these regions, which were now fully integrated to Mediterranean cultural and economic networks.

References

Arcelin, P. 1992. 'Sociétés indigènes et propositions culturelles massaliotes en basse Provence occidentale', in M. Bats, G. Bertucchi, G. Congès, and H. Tréziny (eds) *Marseille grecque et la Gaule*. Études Massaliètes 3: 305–336. Lattes: ADAM Éditions.

Arcelin, P. 1995. 'Arles protohistorique, centre d'échanges économiques et culturels', in P. Arcelin, M. Bats, D. Garcia, G. Marchand, and M. Schwaller (eds) *Sur les pas des Grecs en Occident*. Études Massaliètes 4: 325–338. Lattes/Paris: ADAM-Errance.

Barruol, G. 1969. *Les peuples préromains du sud-est de la Gaule: Étude de géographie historique*. Paris: de Boccard.

Barruol, G., and M. Py. 1978. 'Recherches récentes sur la ville antique d'Espeyran à Saint-Gilles-du-Gard'. *Revue archéologique de Narbonnaise* 11: 19–100.

Chausserie-Laprée, J. (ed.) 2000. *Le temps des Gaulois en Provence*. Martigues: Musée Ziem.

Chausserie-Laprée, J. 2005. *Martigues, Terre Gauloise Entre Celtique et Méditerranée*. Paris: Éditions Errance.

Colin, A., C. Sireix, and F. Verdin. 2011. *Gaulois d'Aquitaine*. Bordeaux: Ausonius.

Collin-Bouffier, S., and D. Garcia. 2012. 'Greeks, Celts and Ligurians in south-east Gaul: ethnicity and archaeology', in A. Hermary and G. R. Tsetskhladze (eds) *From the Pillars of Hercules to the Footsteps of the Argonauts*: 21–36. Louvain: Peeters.

Dedet, B. 1995. 'Etrusques, Grecs et Indigènes dans les Garrigues du Languedoc oriental au premier âge du Fer. Habitats et sépultures', in P. Arcelin, M. Bats, D. Garcia, G. Marchand, and M. Schwaller (eds) *Sur les pas des Grecs en Occident*. Études Massaliètes 4: 277–308. Lattes/Paris: ADAM-Errance.

Dedet, B. 2001. *Tombes et pratiques funéraires protohistoriques des Grands Causses du Gévaudan*. Documents d'archéologie Française 84. Paris: Éditions de la Maison des sciences de l'homme.

Gailledrat, E. 1997. *Les Ibères de l'Ebre à l'Hérault*. Monographie d'Archéologie Méditerranéenne 1. Lattes: Association pour la recherche archéologique en Languedoc oriental.

Garcia, D. 1993. *Entre Ibères et Ligures: Moyenne vallée de l'Hérault et Lodévois protohistoriques*. Supplément à la Revue archéologique de Narbonnaise 26. Paris: CNRS éditions.

Garcia, D. 1995. 'Le territoire d'Agde grecque et l'occupation du sol en Languedoc central durant l'âge du Fer', in P. Arcelin, M. Bats, D. Garcia, G. Marchand, and M. Schwaller (eds) *Sur les pas des Grecs en Occident*. Études Massaliètes 4: 137–168. Lattes/Paris: ADAM-Errance.

Garcia, D. 1999. 'La gestion de l'espace urbain de la cité de Lattes au IVe avant notre ère', in M. Py (ed.) *Recherches sur le quatrième siècle avant notre ère à Lattes*. Lattara 12: 641–650. Lattes: Association pour la recherche archéologique en Languedoc oriental.

Garcia, D. 2004. *La Celtique méditerranéenne: Habitats et sociétés en Languedoc et en Provence du VIIIe au IIe s. av. J.-C.* Paris: Éditions Errance.

Garcia, D. 2005. 'Urbanization and spatial organization in southern France and north-eastern Spain during the Iron Age', in B. W. Cunliffe and R. Osborne (eds) *Mediterranean Urbanization 800–600 BC*. Proceedings of the British Academy 126: 169–186. Oxford: Oxford University Press.

Garcia, D. 2013. 'La ville préclassique en Gaule méridionale', in D. Garcia (ed.) *L'habitat en Europe celtique et en Méditerranée préclassique: Domaines urbaines*: 193–199. Arles: Éditions Errance.

Garcia, D., and F. Verdin (eds). 2002. *Territoires celtiques: Espaces ethniques et territoires des agglomérations protohistoriques d'Europe occidentale*. Paris: Éditions Errance.

Gras, M. 1995. 'L'arrivée d'immigrés à Marseille au milieu du VIe s. avant J.-C.', in P. Arcelin, M. Bats, D. Garcia, G. Marchand, and M. Schwaller (eds) *Sur les pas des Grecs en Occident*. Études Massaliètes 4: 263–266. Lattes/Paris: ADAM-Errance.

Gruat, P., and D. Garcia. 2016. *Guerriers Celtes du Midi: Stèles et sculptures du premier âge du Fer*. Rodez: Musée Fenaille.

Isoardi, D. 2013. 'L'habitat groupé, la démographie et le cas de Saint-Blaise. Quelques pistes sur les modèles urbains protohistoriques méridionaux', in D. Garcia (ed.) *L'habitat en Europe celtique et en Méditerranée préclassique: Domaines urbaines*: 45–95. Arles: Éditions Errance.

Monteil, M. 1999. *Nîmes antique et sa proche campagne*. Monographie d'Archéologie Méditerranéenne 3. Lattes: Association pour la recherche archéologique en Languedoc oriental.

Nickels, A., G. Marchand, and M. Schwaller (eds). 1989. *Agde: La nécropole du premier âge du Fer*. Supplément à la Revue archéologique de Narbonnaise 19. Paris: Centre national de la recherche scientifique.

Py, M. 1978. *L'oppidum des Castels à Nages (Gard), fouilles 1958–1974*. Supplément à Gallia 35. Paris: Centre national de la recherche scientifique.

Py, M. 1990. *Culture, économie et sociétés protohistoriques dans la région nimoise*. Collection de l'Ecole Française de Rome 131. Rome: École française de Rome.

Py, M. 1993. *Les Gaulois du Midi: De la fin de l'âge du Bronze à la conquête romaine*. Paris: Hachette.

Py, M. 1995. 'Les Etrusques, les Grecs et la fondation de Lattes', in P. Arcelin, M. Bats, D. Garcia, G. Marchand, and M. Schwaller (eds) *Sur les pas des Grecs en Occident*. Études Massaliètes 4: 261–276. Lattes/Paris: ADAM-Errance.

Py, M. 2009. *Lattara, Lattes, Hérault: Comptoir gaulois méditerranéen entre Etrusques, Grecs et Romains*. Paris: Éditions Errance.

Roth Congès, A. 1997. 'La fortune éphémère de Glanum. Du religieux à l'économique'. *Gallia* 54: 157–202.

Roure, R., and L. Pernet. 2011. *Des rites et des hommes*. Paris: Éditions Errance.

Sahlins, M. 1976. *Age de pierre, âge d'abondance: L'économie des sociétés primitives*. Paris: Gallimard.

Sanmartí, J., D. Asensio, M. C. Belarte, A. Martín, and J. Santacana. 2006. 'La iberització a la Catalunya costanera i central', in M. C. Belarte and J. Sanmartí (eds) *De les comunitats locals als estats arcaics: la formació de les societats complexes a la costa del Mediterrani occidental: Homenatge a Miquel Cura. Actes de la III Reunió Internacional d'Arqueologia de Calafell*. Arqueomediterrània 9: 145–164. Calafell: Rea d'arqueologia/Universitat de Barcelona/Institut Català d'arqueologia clàssica.

Schwaller, M., G. Marchand, T. Lejars, D. Orliac, A. Rapin, and E. Sanmarti. 2001. 'Echanges, influences et productions dans la nécropole du deuxième âge du Fer d'Ensérune'. *Documents d'Archéologie Méridionale* 24: 173–184.

Taffanel, O., J. Taffanel, and T. Janin. 1998. *La nécropole du Moulin à Mailhac (Aude)*. Monographie d'archéologie Méditerannéenne 2. Lattes: Association pour la recherche archéologique en Languedoc oriental.

Vaginay, M., and L. Izac-Imbert (eds). 2007. *Les âges du Fer dans le sud-ouest de la France: Actes du XXVIIIe colloque de l'AFEAF, Toulouse, 20–23 mai 2004*. Aquitania Supplément 14/1. Bordeaux: Aquitania.

CHAPTER 10

THE IBERIAN PENINSULA

XOSÉ-LOIS ARMADA AND IGNACIO GRAU MIRA

Introduction

The Iberian Peninsula is a territory of some 583,000 km^2 in the far south-west of Europe, linked to the rest of the continent by the Pyrenees mountains. This situation meant it was relatively on the margins of the important historical processes that took place on the European continent and in the Mediterranean lands during the Iron Age. However, that same geographical position also made it a nexus between the Atlantic and the Mediterranean. It shares this characteristic with France, although the Iberian Peninsula contains the only point where both seas meet, at the Strait of Gibraltar, which is also the link between Europe and north Africa.

This situation as a geographical connector, with more than 4,000 km of coastline, a mild climate, and a relative abundance of natural resources (e.g. for mining/metallurgy, agriculture, and fishing), has aroused the interest of outsiders since prehistoric times and helps to explain the colonial movements seen in the Iron Age. In the interior of the peninsula there is a large central plateau known as the Central Meseta. It has an average height of around 650 m and is bordered by large mountain systems: the Cordillera Cantábrica (the Cantabrian range) to the north, the Sistema Ibérico (the Iberian system) to the east, and the Sierra Morena to the south. The mouths of the main rivers have historically been points of trade and cultural contact, and their courses have acted as communication routes to the interior. Four of the five major rivers (the Duero, Tajo, Guadiana, and Guadalquivir) flow into the Atlantic; the Ebro, Spain's second longest river and the one carrying the largest volume of water, empties into the Mediterranean.

Research into the Iron Age as a chronological period on the Iberian Peninsula has a long history. Both the concept itself and the Three Age System appear in the bibliography of the nineteenth century and were well established by the beginning of the twentieth century.[1] Since then, and up to the present day, one of the main characteristics of research into that period has been the division of the peninsula into two large areas according to linguistic criteria, one Celtic or Indo-European and the other Iberian or non-Indo-European (Untermann 1963; Jordán Cólera 2008: 191–193). This division has strongly conditioned archaeological and historical reconstruction of the past by carrying over the influence of obsolete diffusionist models. Researchers working in the Indo-European area have tended to seek out influences and parallel situations in central and western Europe and the British Isles, while those dealing with the non-Indo-European area have done the same with the Mediterranean. In the central and western sector of the Pyrenees, in particular on their northern slopes, investigators have documented an ancient language—probably not of Indo-European origin (Gorrochategui and Lakarra 2013)—that is the predecessor of present-day Basque. There is some dispute over the dating of the earliest evidence of this language south of the Pyrenees, in the territory of the Vascones, but it is probably in the pre-Roman period (Gorrochategui 2009). In 2021, a bronze plaque in the shape of a hand, dating from the first century BC, was discovered in Irulegui (Pamplona), and is considered to be the oldest testimony of this language south of the Pyrenees. The study of the linguistic situation in the Balearic Islands before Romanization is hindered by the lack of available data, and it has not been possible to reach any reliable conclusions (Velaza 2014).

A second important characteristic in the development of research has been the interaction with linguists and historians of antiquity. There are well over 2,000 inscriptions in pre-Roman languages, and the number of pre-Roman theonyms (names of divinities) recorded in the Latin epigraphy of the north-west is among the highest in the Roman Empire. The equally high number of mentions of the Iberian Peninsula in Graeco-Roman sources led to the collaboration between the German historian of antiquity, Adolf Schulten, and the Catalan archaeologist and professor, Pere Bosch Gimpera, on the *Fontes Hispaniae Antiquae*, a project to publish the ancient sources that started in 1922 and continued until 1959, with the final volume not published until 1987. In the 1990s a new project was begun to publish an updated edition of the sources, *Testimonia Hispaniae Antiqua* (López Barja de Quiroga 1995–1996). A good example of this interdisciplinary cooperation between archaeologists, linguists, and historians is the Colloquia of Palaeohispanic Languages and Cultures that have been held in Spain and Portugal since 1974.[2]

The labels used by classical writers to designate the different ethnicities or cultural groups of antiquity—such as Iberians, Celtiberians, Vaccaei, and Vettones—have served to make smaller or larger 'boxes' around which doctoral theses, scientific congresses, and exhibitions have been structured (Lorrio 1997; Burillo 1998; Ruiz Rodríguez and Molinos 1998; Álvarez-Sanchís 1999; Romero Carnicero and Sanz Mínguez 2010). However, the use of these labels, whose meaning varied with different Graeco-Roman writers over time, runs the risk of giving an appearance of historical uniformity and continuity to what was in reality a complex and changing situation. These perspectives have led non-experts to construct an excessively simplified social image of the pre-Roman past.

On the other hand, academia itself has paid particular attention to specific historical processes, areas, and elements of material culture characterized by a greater visual attraction and proximity to the 'great cultures' of the Mediterranean. Even in recent syntheses, areas such as the north-west or north-east of the Iberian Peninsula have received much less attention (Bendala 2000; Almagro-Gorbea et al. 2001; Gracia Alonso 2008a), despite the fact that in recent years they have been the subject of major research with international impact (González Ruibal 2006; Sastre 2008, 2011; Sanmartí 2009; González García et al. 2011). It is to be hoped that this recent internationalization will contribute to remedying the sparse attention that has traditionally been paid to the Iron Age on the Iberian Peninsula in synopses produced in the Anglophone environment, with notable exceptions such as the work of Barry Cunliffe (e.g. Cunliffe 2001, 2017).

The division of the peninsular Iron Age into two large areas has led to two main types of periodization (Moore and Armada 2011b: 17–18). In the area with Indo-European roots, the division is normally into two phases (early and late Iron Age), with the exception of the eastern Meseta and nuclear Celtiberia (Lorrio 1997, 2008). The sequence for the Iberian area tends to be divided into three stages beginning around the year 550 BC, with a prior formative period designated the early Iron Age in areas such as Catalonia. The date given for the beginning of the Iron Age also varies, but we believe that the mid-ninth century (*c.*850 BC) can be taken as a valid reference point for the different areas of Spain and Portugal, as it is from then that some of the principal characteristics of the period begin to be seen: colonial processes, sedentarization and fortification in some areas, and the consolidation of inequalities. Nevertheless, it is worth clarifying that the beginning of the Iron Age by no means implies the general adoption of that metal on the peninsula (Parcero-Oubiña 2002: 19–20), where bronze working continued to be important until the Roman period.

These introductory comments serve as a starting point for our overview of the Iberian Peninsula. For this purpose, we have adopted a framework of ten geographical areas (Figure 10.1). We accept that definition of these areas has a certain component of randomness and that other divisions may be equally valid; the view we offer is not necessarily homogenous and puts different emphasis on particular questions and themes. Finally, we reflect on the principal socio-cultural processes of the Iron Age on the Iberian Peninsula and the questions raised about that period today.

Regional Developments

The North-West

Beginning at the end of the second millennium BC, a process of agricultural intensification is recorded in the north-west (Figure 10.1, 1), the best examples of which are the open villages with large silo pits found in northern Portugal and southern Galicia. The intensification of production marks the emergence of a new period, the Iron Age, the most outstanding feature of which is fortified settlement. Nevertheless, the first fortified

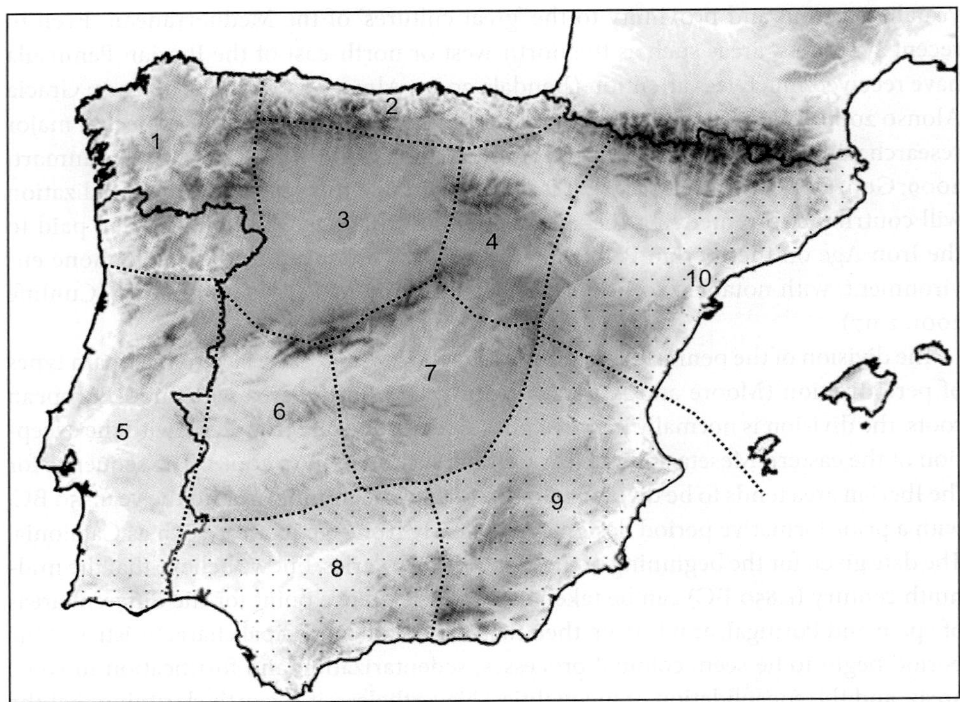

FIGURE 10.1 Map of the Iberian Peninsula showing the geographical areas used in this chapter. 1 North-west; 2 Cantabrian strip; 3 Northern Meseta; 4 Iberian range; 5 Central and southern Portugal; 6 Extremadura; 7 Southern Meseta; 8 South; 9 South-east; 10 North-east and Balearics. The Iberian linguistic area as usually defined by scholars is shown stippled.

sites (*castros*) in the north-west were, as we will see, part of a different logic to that of the late Bronze Age.

These first *castros* appeared in the north of Portugal during the tenth century BC and spread to the rest of the north-west in the following two centuries. In the early Iron Age most *castros* were small and positioned mainly on prominent elevations with good views of the surrounding area; these favourable natural defensive conditions were reinforced by ditches and artificial walls that marked the boundaries of the interior space, which was occupied by round huts built of perishable materials on a stone platform (Figure 10.2, 1).

We concur with the current view that links these settlements to a break in the trend towards inequality that began to manifest itself in the late Bronze Age (Parcero-Oubiña 2002; González Ruibal 2008: 902–905; González García et al. 2011). The collective effort and community cohesion represented by the construction of the *castros* are consistent with the absence of evidence for the accumulation of surpluses, a relative uniformity in the domestic space, and a notable decrease in the number of prestige objects characteristic of the late Bronze Age. Everything appears to indicate a retreat from the ideology

FIGURE 10.2 Aerial views of Iron Age sites: 1 Chao Samartín (Asturias), eighth century BC to second century AD; 2 Numancia (Soria), third century BC to fourth century AD; 3 Cancho Roano (Badajoz), sixth to early fourth centuries BC; 4 Puente Tablas (Jaén), seventh to fourth centuries BC; 5 Monte Molião (Algarve), late fourth to second centuries BC; 6 Els Vilars d'Arbeca (Lleida), eighth to fourth centuries BC.

Photos: 1 © A. Villa Valdés; 2 © A. Jimeno; 3 © S. Celestino; 4 © IAI, University of Jaén; 5 © R. Parreira, DGPC, Direcção Regional de Cultura do Algarve; 6 © Grup d'Investigació Prehistòrica, UdL

and practice of inequality. At that time Atlantic communities were also experiencing greater isolation, although material evidence is found in the *castros* of contact with the Mediterranean world from a very early date, in many cases indirectly via settlements further to the south (Ferrer 2019).

This situation changed in the fourth century BC. At that time *castros* began to be located in lower-lying areas, on land with better resources and greater agricultural potential; in coastal areas fish and seafood resources were intensively exploited. As a rule these *castros* were larger, with more monumentalized artificial defences and a higher intramural population density. Their layouts were more complex, with family units made up of various functional areas surrounding a courtyard; circular houses continued to be in the majority, although rectangular dwellings have been found in some zones. Some structures can be interpreted as storehouses and linked to the accumulation of surpluses. In addition, new types of building appear, probably of a public nature, such as the so-called monuments with furnaces (*pedras formosas*) that were used as ritual saunas (García Quintela and Santos 2015).

From the fifth century BC, contacts with the Mediterranean area became more common, probably as a result of foreign seafarers' interest in the mining and metallurgical resources of the north-west (Ferrer 2019). In a large percentage of *castros*, especially those in the southern zone, Punic and, to a lesser extent, Greek imports are found. Some evidence of oriental cults, such as altars and figurines, has also been discovered, on the basis of which it has been hypothesized that small Punic communities may have resided seasonally in Galician *castros* (González Ruibal 2008: 911). These southern influences are apparent in some of the locally produced pottery and in the adoption of goldworking techniques such as filigree and granulation. The same period saw an increase in prestige material culture, and gold objects became heavier and more complex.

A common feature in the north-west throughout the Iron Age is the absence of a funerary record, except for a few very tenuous indications. Burial sites have always been a basic element used for reconstructing Iron Age social structure, so their absence in the north-west deprives us of an important source of information. Despite this limitation, the diversity we see in other facets of the archaeological record leads us to believe that there was more than one form of sociopolitical organization during the late Iron Age. González Ruibal (2006, 2008: 909–910) maintains that there were three: a 'heroic society' for the northern area, in which the acquisition and maintenance of power was supported by warrior values and movable property (jewellery and cattle); 'house societies' for the south-western sector, where the household—understood in its widest sense—was the key element in competition for power; and, lastly, 'deep rural societies' for the interior of Galicia and the bordering mountainous areas, where hierarchization was averted by means of an ideology and economic practice that prevented the accumulation of surpluses, prestige objects, and imports. Nevertheless, despite the progress made in recent years, certain key issues are still subject to debate. These include determining when the large population centres known as *oppida* first appeared and when political structures superior to the settlements first existed. We will return to these questions later.

The Cantabrian Strip

The Cantabrian area shows a similar dynamic to adjacent regions, although with some particularities due to the mountainous nature of a large part of its geography (Figure

10.1, 2). The Bronze Age communities were nomadic, with temporary or seasonal habitats and an economy based mainly on livestock, and they frequented places that were later occupied during the Iron Age (Marín Suárez 2009). As happened in the north of Galicia, in the west of this zone the stable fortified settlements built at high altitude with artificial defences that characterized the early Iron Age first appeared around 800 BC, somewhat later than in adjacent areas (Marín Suárez 2009: 31–36). In the central and eastern parts of Cantabria, almost 80% of the first early Iron Age settlements were apparently already occupied in the late Bronze Age (Torres Martínez 2011: 267). Inland, to the north of the provinces of Palencia and Burgos, the first settlements show similarities to the Meseta group of El Soto de Medinilla (Peralta Labrador 2000: 47–51). As a rule, all these settlements had mixed economies, with agriculture, hunting, and a large amount of stockbreeding; the accumulation of surpluses was limited, although some silos and large storage vessels are documented.

In the western zone a period of change in the settlement pattern is detected between 600 and 400 BC, characterized by the construction of houses in stone and the appearance of ramparts of modular construction (Marín Suárez 2009: 33). In the central and eastern areas fewer changes can be detected. Around 50% of early Iron Age settlements continued to be inhabited in the following period; of these only about 10% can be classified as new foundations (Torres Martínez 2011: 267). Furthermore, they include a number of settlements that were continuously occupied from the late Bronze Age to the late Iron Age. As in adjacent areas, the second half of the first millennium BC is characterized by a demographic increase, a more intensive occupation of the territory, particularly in the areas with the most agricultural potential, and a concentration of population in larger settlements. In some cases these settlements can be classified as true *oppida*, including, for example, Monte Bernorio (Peralta Labrador 2000; Torres Martínez 2011; Torres Martínez et al. 2016).

In the late Iron Age, the Cantabrian strip, particularly its central and eastern sectors, shows a penetration of Celtiberian and Meseta influences through the Duero and Ebro valleys. These influences reached the north of the mountain chain, although they are especially noticeable in the so-called Miraveche-Monte Bernorio culture that developed to the north of the provinces of Palencia and Burgos in the fourth and third centuries BC. One of the most outstanding features is rich metalwork at the service of the elites, particularly a type of profusely decorated dagger and sheath (Quesada 1997; Peralta Labrador 2000: 55–77; Pablo Martínez 2022).

The classical sources, together with epigraphy and other elements of the archaeological record, have provided the raw material for an abundant literature on the social organization, rituals, and general way of life of the Cantabrians. The conclusions reached are not always easy to accept, but there is agreement on establishing their cultural connection with an archaic Indo-European substratum. The funerary evidence is only partially known: there was widespread use of caves for burial in the late Bronze Age and throughout the Iron Age, initially of inhumation and later also of cremation. Cremation cemeteries with pottery urns constitute the other principal funerary practice, especially to the north of the provinces of Burgos and Palencia, although examples are also known north of the mountain range (Peralta Labrador 2000: 45–77; Torres Martínez 2011: 514–541). The fact that a large part of this area was the scene of the Cantabrian wars—the final campaign in the Roman conquest of the Iberian Peninsula (29–19 BC)—has contributed to bestowing a certain legendary aura on its proto-historic communities and main archaeological sites.

The Northern Meseta

During the late Bronze Age the landscape of the northern Meseta (Figure 10.1, 3) was characterized by a low population density and a dispersed settlement pattern of small, non-permanent villages consisting of huts (Blanco González 2011). They were often situated on the plains and were unfortified; their economies were agricultural-pastoral and they used silos or large vessels to store surpluses.

The first permanent settlements appeared in the eighth century BC and took definitive shape from the beginning of the following century; they were generally newly founded, with artificial defences and huts made of stone and mud brick (Ruiz Zapatero 2011: 300). Among the outstanding archaeological features of the settlements in the so-called Soto de Medinilla group, which developed in the middle of the Duero river basin, are the round mud-brick huts. These generally have a single interior space, although some exceptions to this pattern have been found (Romero Carnicero et al. 2008: 652–654; Delibes de Castro and Romero Carnicero 2011). The permanent nature of the settlements and the centrality of the house in the social life of the community represent, for some scholars, a fundamental change with respect to the communities of huts made of perishable materials in the previous period (Blanco González 2011). One of the questions most debated by researchers is whether this and other cultural changes recorded at the time were due to the arrival of foreigners. Ruiz Zapatero (2011: 300) has recently opted for continuity in the basic population of this central part of the Meseta, combined with cultural influences arriving from the Ebro area, and climatic and environmental changes that altered farming and stockbreeding conditions, allowing more intensive exploitation of the natural surroundings.

The western Meseta shares some features with the central area, notably a self-sufficient economy and a largely non-hierarchical settlement pattern. We know almost nothing of the internal organization of the settlements (Esparza 2011). 'Orientalizing' stimuli are evident here from finds in some settlements of ritual metal objects linked to emerging elites and changes in rituality (Álvarez-Sanchís 1999: 85–91; Esparza 2011). The centres where these items are found would have played an important role in the exchange of goods and economic relations with the areas to the south. In fact, Berrocal-Rangel (2004: 34) links the stable long-distance exchange of prestige goods to the spread of fortified settlements from the sixth century BC in the middle Duero valley.

A common pattern in these early Iron Age communities on the Meseta is the scarcity of funerary evidence, if we exclude some infant inhumations inside villages (below the floors of dwellings) or the group of pits with ashes and fragments of metal objects that had been exposed to fire in Sanchorreja, for which there are no parallels and the interpretation of which is controversial (Esparza 2011: 36–37). The only exceptions are in the eastern part of the Meseta, in the upper Duero, and on the spurs of the Iberian range, where the influence of the Ebro area is clear. In this part of the Meseta cremation was practised extensively by the sixth century BC, with grave goods that included weapons providing clear signs of social hierarchization.

A reduction in the number of settlements is detected from the beginning of the late Iron Age (*c.*400 BC), due to their merging with larger fortified and more densely populated villages with orthogonally laid out rectangular houses. At the same time, this process of demographic concentration—in *oppida* that could hold up to several thousand inhabitants—led to population vacuums in some areas. The large population centres possessed extensive areas of cultivated farmland and from the end of the fourth century BC may have controlled territories of a significant size (around 500 km^2; Ruiz Zapatero 2011: 301).

The Vettonian communities of the south-western Meseta underwent a similar process, although their *oppida* show a less ordered internal layout and lower populations, rarely more than a thousand inhabitants (Álvarez-Sanchís 2011). One of the most characteristic features of that time is the appearance of large stone sculptures known as *verracos* representing bulls and pigs (Figure 10.3); they are interpreted as property boundary markers or indicators of pasture rights, particularly in periods of crisis, although a possible complementary role as ethnic identifiers cannot be ruled out (Álvarez-Sanchís 1999: 215–294, 2000: 75, figs 7–8).

Although towns appeared on the eastern Meseta somewhat later (at the end of the third century BC) and show some differences, we should also emphasize the general

FIGURE 10.3 Zoomorphic stone sculptures (*verracos*) from Guisando (Ávila).
Photo: © J. R. Álvarez-Sanchís

nature of the political integration processes or synoecisms on the northern Meseta during the late Iron Age. Later, we will set out some of our ideas on the changes that allow this process to be explained, but it is important to emphasize the role played by the emergence of an equestrian warrior aristocracy and its link to the need to protect the community. The presence of these warriors can be detected, among other manifestations in the archaeological record, in the grave goods of the cremation cemeteries that appear in the Vettonian area in the fifth century BC and spread shortly afterwards throughout the northern Meseta (Álvarez-Sanchís 1999: 169–213; Romero Carnicero et al. 2008: 686–691, 710–717). These burial sites are often very large (e.g. more than 2,200 graves at La Mesa de Miranda) and tend to be in the vicinity of *oppida*, with the tombs marked by stone stelae.

By the time of the first Roman incursions (at the beginning of the second century BC), urban settlements were widespread on the northern Meseta. This urbanization process went hand in hand with the emergence of new forms of power and institutions of a civil and military nature. Nevertheless, much work remains to be done on the identification and study of public or politically orientated spaces.

The Iberian Range

The highlands of the eastern edge of the Meseta and the left bank of the Ebro make up the cultural area of Celtiberia (Figure 10.1, 4). This group with Indo-European roots that goes back to the late Bronze Age, or even earlier, was strongly influenced by the Iberian world, exemplified in such aspects as their weapons and the adoption of the potter's wheel, writing, and town planning (Burillo 1998; Lorrio 2008). The areas situated to the north and north-east demonstrate some particularities, but they can be framed within a very similar dynamic (Armendáriz Martija 2008). At the beginning of the Iron Age there were profound changes in the population, including the appearance of small, stable settlements located on promontories and other defendable sites. These settlements (*castros*) were built with simple layouts of quadrangular dwellings adjoining the walls and in rows adapted to the terrain. With the passing of time they expanded and the fortification systems were developed. These changes can be related to a phase of population growth and expansion around the year 400 BC that involved the appropriation and delimitation of the *castro* territories, among which a certain hierarchization of settlements according to size can be recognized. The considerable extent of this region favoured the appearance of local models of settlement, such as the so-called 'Sorian *castros*', a type of small, solidly fortified enclave.

These communities developed cremation cemeteries in which a certain variability of funerary customs is evident, with the grave goods demonstrating the differences between the distinct sectors of society. Some cemeteries were organized in streets, while others are characterized by a predominance of tumuli covered with stone slabs or the appearance of stelae; differences in the burials can also be seen in the depositions of arms, adornments, and other offerings.

The economic bases of the region's groups were largely oriented towards stockbreeding, mainly sheep and goats, with cattle as a secondary species, although the literary sources and iconography show a preponderance of the latter, possibly because they constituted expressions of wealth. Stockbreeding was complemented to varying degrees by agriculture. Artisanal activities show a major development, with rich metalwork and decorated wheel-made pottery (Lorrio 1997).

The evidence of stratification at the burial sites, the fortified landscapes, and the hierarchization of the settlements all imply the emergence of a lineage-based warrior aristocracy. In their early stages, in the early Iron Age, the peasant communities were ruled by small aristocratic groups that expanded during the late Iron Age to form castes of mounted warriors commanded by leaders.

At the time of contact with Rome, around the second century BC, the urbanization and hierarchization of the settlement pattern accelerated noticeably, together with the development of civic institutions. This period saw the appearance of region-wide state institutions and the development of writing and coinage.

Central and Southern Portugal

The territory that is now Portugal was heterogeneous and experienced diverse dynamics during the Iron Age. There are also gaps in the information, which can be attributed both to the nature of the archaeological record and to the direction taken by research. During this period the north of Portugal bore similarities to Galicia and the west of Asturias and as such has already been analysed in a previous section. Here we will deal with the central and southern areas (Figure 10.1, 5).

The late Bronze Age in the central districts of Portugal saw the appearance from the twelfth century BC of settlements on high ground with good defensive attributes and territorial control. They had huts made of perishable materials with stone foundations, and there is evidence of small-scale metalworking (Vilaça 1998, 2013); the material culture also shows that they were part of the networks linking the Atlantic and the Mediterranean at that time (Celestino et al. 2008). However, the majority of these settlements did not survive into the Iron Age. Today there is a major gap in our information for much of the territory between the rivers Vouga and Tajo (Fabião 2001: 228). The sparse evidence available indicates similar dynamics to the more northerly zones, meaning that the early Iron Age would have been characterized by fortified settlements on high ground, with circular houses normally built of perishable material. Subsequently, the late Iron Age would see the population concentrated into larger sites that were able to act as central places, coexisting with smaller settlements.

In the areas further to the south, the beginning of the Iron Age was marked by an early colonial presence along the coastal strip. There is disagreement as to whether these colonists were Phoenicians (Arruda 2011) or Tartessians (Almagro-Gorbea and Torres 2009), but in any case they were peoples from the south of the Iberian Peninsula whose material repertoire included Phoenician and Orientalizing grey pottery. In the

Tajo estuary, which was characterized by its dynamic nature from the late Bronze Age (Vilaça and Arruda 2004; Aubet 2009: 296–300), we find the earliest evidence of a colonial presence (end of the ninth to beginning of the eighth century BC), barely twenty-five years after the first Phoenician colonies in the south of the peninsula (Arruda 2005: 26–28). This suggests that there was no linear colonizing process from south to north, but rather a predetermined jump to a specific zone, probably linked to an interest in the tin and gold resources of the Beira interior region (Arruda 2005: 50–51), which were already known and exploited in the late Bronze Age. From that time the colonial presence continued to be concentrated around the river mouths, first of the Tagus and the Mondego, and later the Sado. This process affected the settlements with good visibility near ports occupied from the late Bronze Age, where mixed local and foreign populations coexisted during the Iron Age. Around these main enclaves, which were responsible for the dynamic trade, small farming settlements grew up from the seventh century BC. In the late sixth century BC, sites such as Abul and Santa Olaia, for which a purely colonial origin is proposed, were abandoned, while the other settlements on the Atlantic coast remained occupied, although cut off from the socio-economic dynamics of the south of the peninsula (Arruda 2005).

On the southernmost tip of the Portuguese coast, the main archaeological sites such as Castro Marim or Tavira were already occupied in the late Bronze Age and were also affected by Phoenician colonial influence. However, this zone underwent notable development in the late Iron Age, including the emergence of new settlements and the colonization of interior zones, with cultural links to the Turdetani area in Andalusia. For this period Arruda (2005: 81) proposes an oligarchic social model in which a dominant elite would have controlled agriculture, fish and seafood processing, and trade.

Some differences can be seen in the interior zones. The Orientalizing influence came later there than on the coast, and the first archaeological sites of the period are located on high ground, generally in places that were not occupied during the late Bronze Age. At a later period, around the sixth century BC, small farming settlements grew up on low-lying ground, as well as places of worship that show certain similarities to those in the area of Extremadura (Arruda 2005: 87–104). In these interior lands of the Alentejo and the Algarve, and particularly in the area of Ourique, we find concentrations of slabs with the so-called 'writing of the southwest', together with the graffiti on Tartessian pottery, the first examples of writing on the Iberian Peninsula. Although the funerary nature of the inscriptions and their association with burial sites has been suggested, we cannot completely exclude the possibility that their presence in cemeteries is the result of reuse. In any event, the appearance of these written expressions is symptomatic of the changes occurring in the local communities (Ruiz-Gálvez 2013: 257–311).

From the mid-fifth century BC and above all from 400 BC onwards, there were major changes. The most important consequence of these was concentration of the population in fortified *castros*. Depending on their geographical location they were related culturally to the area of Extremadura known as Celtic Baeturia or to Turdetania. This phenomenon of *oppida* formation in the interior of southern Portugal is interpreted in different ways: while some scholars believe that people from other areas joined the local population (Arruda 2005), others maintain there was a robust cultural continuity based on sustained demographic growth (Fabião 2001).

Extremadura

The territory of Extremadura (Figure 10.1, 6) offers a wealth of interesting archaeological manifestations, some of which have become true Iberian Peninsula proto-historic icons.

Although late Bronze Age settlement and burial evidence is sparse, a clear preference for pasture over cultivation can be detected. This is apparent in the distribution of all the main forms of evidence for the period (deposits of bronzes, gold jewellery, and warrior stelae). Taken together, these indicate a trend towards hierarchization and a mixing of the Atlantic and Mediterranean influences characteristic of this stage of Extremaduran proto-history (Bendala 2000: 66–82; Celestino 2008: 179–193).

Analysis of the geographical distribution and iconography of the stelae has led Celestino (2008: 183) to propose a gradual demographic displacement towards the south, probably linked to the increase in mining operations in the Tartessian core area. The Extremaduran elites of the late Bronze Age and early Iron Age would have contributed agricultural resources and labour to this production focus. However, the importance of the Extremaduran mining and metallurgical resources emphasized in the past by some researchers has been questioned (Celestino 2008: 314), although in our opinion it is a subject that needs to be investigated in greater depth.

The mid- to late seventh century BC saw Tartessian interest in Extremaduran agricultural resources. The most evident example of this is the hypothetical—and insufficiently known—*oppidum* and cemetery of Medellín. Plains settlements such as El Palomar, with a chronology centred on the sixth century BC, are further examples of this new dynamic, which some scholars class as agrarian colonization. Located on flat land in the Guadiana valley, with an urban structure without walls, El Palomar demonstrates an agricultural model of exploitation designed to produce surpluses for trade (Jiménez Ávila and Ortega Blanco 2008).

These socio-economic changes in the areas surrounding the river Guadiana, which were mainly linked to agricultural exploitation, became even more evident from the middle of the sixth century BC, coinciding with the crisis of the Tartessian settlements located further to the south (Celestino 2008: 330). It was at this time that singular, quadrangular-shaped buildings, clearly linked to the sociopolitical control and organization of the territory, emerged or grew in importance. The most famous are El Turuñelo and Cancho Roano (Figure 10.2, 3), whose functional interpretation has oscillated between a shrine and a palatial residence. Without joining this debate, we can affirm that there can be no doubt about their similarities to the Phoenician shrines of the Bajo Guadalquivir and about the role of the ritual and religious activities in the Cancho Roano building, the main feature of which is an altar situated in the same position as the altars of two earlier buildings, the oldest dating to the beginning of the sixth century BC (Bendala 2000: 91–93; Celestino 2008: 331–336). In another excavated building, that of

La Mata de Campanario, this religious dimension appears to be of less importance, with its economic, commercial, and territorial control functions standing out (Rodríguez Díaz 2009: 129–185). Taken as a whole, the available data, which include small nuclei or groups of houses in the vicinity of these buildings, indicate a clientage-based model of aristocratic power whose legitimization would have had a strong ideological and ritual basis. These buildings disappeared at the end of the fifth century BC, some after a fire, giving rise to what is known as 'the crisis of 400' (Rodríguez Díaz 2009: 209–213).

To the north, in the Tajo valley, the late Bronze Age socio-economic model showed more resistance, and the archaeological record of the early Iron Age shows affinities with that of the surrounding areas of the Meseta, with certain Mediterranean influences evident, particularly in material culture. In addition to those that had survived from earlier periods, new settlements were established at the end of the sixth or during the fifth century BC. Taken as a whole they demonstrate a consolidation of sedentarization, demographic growth, and technological and commercial development throughout that century until the aforementioned crisis of 400 BC, which also appears to have affected these more northerly lands (Celestino et al. 2009).

This crisis gave rise to the emergence of fortified *oppida* or *castros* at sites with good defensive conditions dominating the surrounding area, but with less agricultural potential than in earlier periods. In the area around the river Tajo, these settlements were culturally linked to the *castros* in the Vettonian area, and its landscapes were demarcated by zoomorphic sculptures (*verracos*). Some of these Extremaduran *castros* had associated burial grounds with grave goods that also reflected links with the Meseta. According to the classical sources, a large part of this territory coincided with Celtic Baeturia, and they mention a series of ethnonyms (Lusitanians, Celts, Turduli, Vettones, etc.) that undoubtedly reflect a varied cultural mosaic. At that time the Extremadura was receiving influences from the Meseta, Portugal, and western Andalusia. Various authors have emphasized the Celtic or Indo-European cultural component of these populations, which would have been the result of a reactivation of the local substratum following a lessening of the Orientalizing influence and new cultural contacts with other interior areas of the Iberian Peninsula (Berrocal-Rangel 1992).

Although some *castros* survived the Roman conquest and continued into the first century AD, from the second century BC and above all during the first century BC tower-enclosures of Cyclopean construction linked to territorial control appeared in Extremadura. These would be an important component in the Romanization process, although some of them may have been established prior to the conquest of the territory. There are high concentrations of these tower-enclosures in some areas of the province of Badajoz, such as the county of La Serena (Mayoral and Celestino 2010).

The Southern Meseta (Submeseta Sur)

As is the case with the bordering lands of Extremadura, the extensive area of the southern part of the Meseta (Figure 10.1, 7) can be divided into two sectors corresponding to the two fluvial axes that articulate the zone: the Tajo valley to the north and the Guadiana valley to the south. We will therefore describe them separately. The beginning of the Iron Age in the Tajo valley was characterized by significant changes in cultural patterns and the organization of space. In contrast to the traditional cultural links with the north of the Meseta, relations with other regions expanded at this time, particularly with the south of the peninsula, from where feelers related to Phoenician trade were being sent out (Urbina 2000). These influences encouraged a process of complete sedentarization and an economic development based on the intensification of farming influenced by the introduction of iron.

The settlement pattern is characterized by fairly small sites with little concern for territorial control, that were more likely to be located on low hills with the idea of overlooking the surrounding farmland. Settlements were restricted to hut bases of perishable materials, with only a few more solid buildings standing out. These plains settlements controlled smaller, subordinate nuclei that grew up in their vicinity.

The fourth century BC saw the emergence of small or mid-size defensive settlements, with fortifications located on small hills and escarpments. These sites, which at first complemented the earlier settlements on the plains, acquired increasing importance in the unstable conditions of the late third century BC, eventually taking on a central role in the organization of the territory (Urbina 2000). The cemeteries associated with these settlements have smaller groupings of graves in pits and tumuli, with cremations and grave goods; they show marked regional trends, such as structures marking the tombs and the absence of arms. These patterns reveal little structuring in lineages or large groups in the social organization schemes. Everything points towards a cultural group with clear signs of the survival of earlier traditions and limited influence resulting from opening up to the Mediterranean.

The Guadiana valley was included in the processes linked to the Iberian zone in the south and east of the peninsula (Morales Hervás 2010), which were tied to the formalization of the urban clientage-based societies. The early Iron Age was characterized by the opening up of the region to the trading channels from the southern coasts with Orientalizing roots. That process favoured the reorganization of settlement towards control of the region's principal resources and circulation routes, as part of an economic intensification and opening up to new regional trade networks. Solid settlements of quadrangular stone buildings developed, generally on promontories that dominated the surrounding territory.

From the late fifth century BC a process of urbanization and hierarchization is evident from the settlement pattern. We find *oppida* of a considerable size with a notable urban aspect, solid fortifications, and control of extensive stockbreeding and agricultural and mining resources, related to which secondary *oppida* and farming villages were established. These large centres housed places of worship or concentrations of agricultural resources.

The South

The south of the Iberian Peninsula (Figure 10.1, 8) is an extensive geographical area surrounding the river Guadalquivir, the main territorial axis, which flows into the

Atlantic through a large estuary that was an important port area in antiquity. Based on this river and its tributaries, the territory was organized in the form of a mosaic of spaces with dense forms of settlement and wide-ranging possibilities for exploitation, both in agricultural and mineral resources.

The beginning of the Iron Age saw profound changes that were rapidly to transform the late Bronze Age villages into large urban centres around which production and trade were organized. This process affected the regions of lower Andalusia with its rich mineral resources, such as the areas around the Odiel and Riotinto rivers, which were the focus of the mythical region of Tartessos, and the agricultural lands along the upper reaches of the Guadalquivir. The booming economic development attracted early colonization, focused on the Phoenician town of Gadir. The proximity of the Phoenician colonies and their trade networks was soon felt in the transformation of the local towns and villages, which underwent early processes of synoecism and urban concentration (Ruiz Mata 1997). These urban nuclei, such as Onuba, Ilipla, Hasta Regia, and Carmo, controlled the trade networks and began a process of agricultural colonization by establishing farming settlements (Ferrer et al. 2007). Certain manifestations, such as the early adoption of writing, attest to the intense economic and cultural interaction within the colonial sphere.

The economic developments involving the intensification and integration of the trade networks with the Phoenician colonies were subjected to profound changes as a consequence of the transformation of the colonial system at the end of the sixth century BC (Aubet 2009). In the mining areas of Huelva, metal was replaced by the production and processing of agricultural products, while a salt industry developed in the Cádiz area. In general, the whole Guadalquivir area was boosted by the strengthening of the urban nuclei (García Fernández and Ferrer 2021) in which production was focused and trade organized (Escacena and Belén 1997).

This intensive urban consolidation, agrarian colonization, and territorial configuration had resulted in a dense urban landscape by the time the Romans arrived towards the end of the third century BC. The classical sources bear witness to this dense urban organization into networks of settlements that were dependent on the most important towns, one example being Lascuta, which was dependent on the town of Hasta. This territorial articulation suggests the development of complex urban territorial policies, although unfortunately the funerary record provides us with very little additional evidence with which to delve more deeply into social characterization. This dearth of evidence could be due to a cultural pattern that inhibited funerary manifestations, although we cannot rule out that it is the result of other factors, such as poor archaeological preservation.

The South-East

The groups of south-eastern Iberia—which corresponds roughly to upper Andalusia, Murcia, Albacete, and the south of the Valencian country—can be joined together in an area with a similar cultural environment, despite the fact that obvious local differences are attested (Figure 10.1, 9). Urbanization came early in this zone thanks to local socio-economic changes and the influence of a series of colonial settlements in nearby coastal areas. The result of these changes is that from the beginning of the Iron Age we find mid-size fortified settlements known as *oppida*, with complex, regular layouts and rectilinear streets lined with adjoining quadrangular dwellings. The towns were the organizational centres of complex economies, in which technological innovations and the development of trade configured a new social and cultural model. In upper Andalusia the entire population was concentrated in *oppida* (Ruiz Rodríguez and Molinos 2007), while in the other areas subordinate nuclei in the form of villages, hamlets, and rural establishments of varying morphology and function are documented (Bonet and Mata 2001; Grau Mira 2007).

The basis of this new society was the consolidation of lineages and dominant families who imposed their power on a base of peasant families. The leaders portrayed themselves as warrior aristocrats to whom the other families were connected through links of dependence. The main evidence supporting this social characterization comes from the graves in which the members of the ruling warrior aristocracies and their family and client groups were buried (Blánquez and Antona 1992). The elite were buried in complex monuments with funerary chambers, large tumuli, or stelae-pillars finished off with stone sculptures, sometimes of an exceptional nature, such as at Cerrillo Blanco in Porcuna (Jaén). We see a variable degree of wealth in the structures and grave goods of the subordinate groups. Also in the ritual sphere, the process of making sacred the heroic ancestor of the princes contributed to the formalization of social inequality (Olmos 2002).

The economic structure of these towns was orientated towards cereal production on the open land and fields surrounding the Guadalquivir, whereas in the eastern zone the agriculture was mixed, with importance given to the cultivation of trees, including fruit trees and vines. This was complemented by stockbreeding and especially the exploitation of the mineral resources of upper Andalusia and the Cartagena area. The complex economy of surpluses allowed the development of dense trade networks oriented towards exterior trade with the Mediterranean lands and governed by the social elite, who deployed social strategies such as ritual commensality and the redistribution of prestige goods.

Following the consolidation of the *oppida* around the fourth century BC, the domains of certain towns were expanded through colonization and the foundation of settlements dependent on the main town. These expansion projects shaped a political space based on a valley or a natural geographical unit. On occasions the political project was ratified by building places of worship or shrines on the limits of the town's domain. These structures acted as frontier markers (Ruiz Rodríguez 2008) or, in the main urban centres, as elements designed to unite the population of the territory through religious bonds. The inhabitants of the territory would periodically visit the community sanctuary located at the capital, thus reinforcing its role from a symbolic and representative point of view.

The elites who ruled these *oppida* were interrelated through ties of clientage and alliances that elevated powerful chiefs to the leadership of true federations of towns. These pacts show us how the town constituted the basic territorial unit, and above it there were aggregations that were set up and dissolved according to the changing social and political relations and historical contexts (Ruiz Rodríguez 2008; Bonet et al. 2015).

The North-East and the Balearic Islands

The origins of the Iron Age in the north-eastern Iberian Peninsula are characterized by a certain regional diversity that is the result, in part, of the prior evolution of the different areas during the late Bronze Age (Figure 10.1, 10).

In the thirteenth to twelfth centuries BC, the Ebro basin saw the emergence of a village model with a central open space, the most significant example of which is Genó (Aitona, Lleida). The houses were built of adobe on a stone base; they adjoined one another and shared a rear wall, which also served as the settlement enclosure wall. Although this new urban design can be explained by demographic growth and the insecurity brought about by greater competition for territorial resources (Sanmartí 2004), the characteristics of the settlements suggest communities of between forty and a hundred inhabitants, with a marked cooperative component and low levels of social inequality. Their economies were mainly agricultural, with stockbreeding being more important in the mountain areas. In the tenth century BC this model appears to have expanded towards lower Aragón and then up the river Ebro to Navarra and La Rioja (Burillo 2011: 281). In the areas nearest the coast and on the lower reaches of the Ebro, urbanism became generalized at a later time, although recent finds indicate that the first villages with an urban layout in areas such as the Priorat also appeared during the late Bronze Age. We cannot rule out that this precocity was linked to the exploitation of the area's mineral resources (Armada et al. 2013; Rafel and Armada 2023). Similar patterns can be seen in Castellón province, although with a lower population density. In contrast, stone-built villages did not become common on the Catalan coast until the second Iron Age.

The low levels of social inequality are also reflected in the funerary record, which does not show any marked differences between tombs (Ruiz Zapatero 2004). In the late Bronze Age the communities of the north-eastern Iberian Peninsula experienced the arrival of trans-Pyrenean elements linked to the Urnfield tradition, which they assimilated and reinterpreted in their different local contexts. The first cremation cemeteries appeared around 1100 BC and became widespread from the ninth century BC. They can be classified typologically in two major groups: urnfields and small tumuli.

The settlement model with streets or a central open space survived, with different variations, into the early Iron Age, and is documented in various parts of north-eastern Iberia. This continuity of some of the characteristic late Bronze Age features explains the lack of consensus on when the Iron Age began, although majority opinion inclines towards sometime in the eighth century BC. The increase in population and social complexity that had begun at least as early as the eleventh century BC, with the consequent pressure on certain territories, continued into the Iron Age. This trend grew with the upsurge in Phoenician trade, a phenomenon that, although it began in the previous century, increased dramatically in the seventh century BC, especially from the second half of the century. The main archaeological indicator of this is the amphorae—probably for wine—found in the majority of settlements belonging to this period and suggesting widespread wine consumption, albeit channelled through the local elites (Sanmartí 2004: 16–19).

From the mid-seventh century BC the archaeological record suggests increased levels of social inequality: larger villages with more complex layouts, different-sized houses, differences in grave goods, differentiated zones in cemeteries, and an increase in the number of storage jars linked to the accumulation of surpluses. Other indications, such as the iron weapons or defensive structures found in some settlements, reflect the growing role of conflict and an increased competition for territory. Although Phoenician commerce was not the trigger for these phenomena, it contributed decisively to accelerating dynamics that were already in train. We cannot always know what the Phoenician traders received in exchange for wine and other prestige goods, but it is known that the mining and metallurgical resources—especially lead—from areas such as the Baix Priorat played an important role, even reaching as far as the south-west of the Iberian Peninsula (Murillo-Barroso et al. 2016). At the same time, the communities of the north-east received copper from the mining area of Linares (Jaén; Rafel 2011–2012).

The Phoenician presence on the island of Ibiza began towards the end of the eighth century BC with the foundation of what is now the Sa Caleta archaeological site, where the exploitation and trade of silver-bearing galena played an important role. Its abandonment at the end of the seventh century BC coincides with the foundation of a new settlement on the bay of Ibiza, the origin of the present-day town. For many years researchers believed that the island of Ibiza acted as the almost exclusive intermediary for Phoenician trade with the north-east. However, both lead isotope analyses and the pottery record lead this hypothesis to be questioned, as they indicate much more diverse trade networks (Ramon et al. 2011).

The seventh century BC saw the emergence of segregated buildings known as tower-houses, which are interpreted as the residences of heads of lineages. This phenomenon is initially identified in lower Aragon, but recent studies have shown that it was present in other parts of the north-east, including Castellón province. Although there are still many unknown factors regarding its interpretation, it clearly appears to be related to an unstable social system that was about to enter into crisis and die out in the mid-sixth century BC. At this time settlements in areas such as the Baix Priorat were also abandoned. The chronological coincidence of these phenomena indicates a crisis related to the discontinuation of Phoenician trade and the settlement in Ampurias of the Phocaeans, who would soon begin to expand their influence beyond their immediate surroundings. In the following decades investigators detect a certain information vacuum that leads some to speak of a 'dark period' or 'crisis of the early Iberian period'.

In contrast, there are tombs with rich grave goods that appear to belong to this period (Graells 2010).

Towards the second half of the fifth century BC, we see the beginning of the middle Iberian period, a time of profound changes among the populations of this area. The general interpretation is of an increase in population, economic development based on the expansion of agricultural production and exchange, and, as a consequence of these developments, the consolidation of institutionalized forms of inequality in the shape of complex chiefdoms and archaic states (Sanmartí and Belarte 2001; Sanmartí 2016).

The main archaeological evidence for these changes comes from territorial studies that attest to the development of the population on all levels of settlement, from the growth in the size of power centres to an increase in the number of dependent rural settlements.

The increase in farming settlements, together with evidence of environmental changes—specifically a decrease in tree pollen levels (Burjachs et al. 1999)—would indicate an expansion of land for cultivation and an increase in agricultural production. The economic development went hand in hand with the increase in inequality, as in parallel to these changes we find clear evidence that production was being controlled by elites who accumulated the grain in large silo fields. We also see the development of administrative systems, such as Iberian writing on lead sheets to record production and exchange.

These economic changes and their associated political forms did not develop equally across the north-east, as once again the political forms and processes differed between coastal and inland areas. While in the former we see the clearly hierarchized structures associated with archaic states, the inland areas had power structures of a heterarchical nature (Sanmartí 2016: 462).

Four large geopolitical areas have been identified on the coastal façade. They correspond to the territories of the regions mentioned in the textual sources: Indigecia, Layetania, Cessetania, and Ilercavonia. Each of these regions would have been presided over by the largest enclaves recognized: urban-type nuclei covering approximately 10 ha with outstanding elements in their archaeological record. They are the Iberian towns of Ullastret (Girona), Burriac-Ilturo (Barcelona province), Tarracon-Kese (present-day Tarragona), and Castellet de Banyoles (Tarragona province), at least from the third century BC (Sanmartí 2016: 464).

Within these political areas there were other urban enclaves, such as Alorda Park or El Turó de Ca n'Oliver, that may have held sway over their respective localities, although under the authority of the larger towns. Finally, at the bottom of the population structure we find the rural settlements, which were either scattered or clustered together.

These political territories on the coastal strip of the north-east present differences in settlement type, especially in terms of their size, which at approximately 2200–2600 km^2 is far larger than the geopolitical areas of other Iberian territories.

An important aspect of the way they organized their economic activity is their relationship with the Punic trading network established on the island of Ibiza. Without forgetting that in the far north-east of the Iberian Peninsula the Greek colony of

Emporion strongly influenced trade and cultural relations in that area, in the other territories a special relationship with Ibiza is attested. Although the Ebusitanian colonial settlement would have begun around the end of the eighth century BC, with the establishment of Sa Caleta, the true development would have come about with the consolidation of the settlement on the bay of Ibiza and the expansion of the urban nucleus of Puig de Vila from the beginning of the sixth century BC. Sometime later, around the fifth century BC, the island was colonized agriculturally with the development of surplus agricultural production for exchange with the outside world and a commercial sphere that encompassed the Balearic Islands and the eastern coasts of the Iberian Peninsula, possibly with exclusivity and with considerable intensity during the fourth and third centuries BC.

This commercial activity also impacted on the rest of the Balearic Islands, especially the island of Mallorca, which in return provided the contingents of mercenaries that would swell the Punic armies in their altercations in the central Mediterranean lands. The El Sec, Binisafuller, and Cabrera II shipwrecks illustrate the trading relations between the coasts of Iberia and the islands of Ibiza and the Balearics (Gracia Alonso 2008b). The driving force behind these interchanges would be demand among the Iberian groups for the prestige manufactured goods with which they nourished their social networks. Commodities from the Iberian territories, particularly the agricultural surpluses and metallurgical resources of southern Catalonia, were traded for Attic vessels and processed foods from Ibiza, especially wine and salted products.

In contrast to the coastal strip, the inland territories of the north-east region do not demonstrate such hierarchized settlement patterns, and show us glimpses of less centralized forms of political control. These are the territories occupied by the Ausetani, Lacetani, Ilergetes, Suesetani, and Sedetani of the Ebro according to the classical texts. Unlike on the coast, here we do not find large towns that act as capitals; in fact the largest of the fortified settlements barely cover a single hectare. These larger places would have controlled the dependent rural settlements, about which we know very little in this region.

Although we do not find large towns, the main settlements in this area have major fortifications and singular buildings in their interior, for example Els Vilars until the fourth century BC (Figure 10.2, 6) and, very similarly, El Molí d'Espígol. These features are proof of the existence of aristocratic groups of a markedly warrior-like nature empowered with the leadership of this society, which was possibly of a heterarchical nature, to judge by the dispersion of the power centres and the meagre prevalence of capitals such as those recognized in the coastal band. The dominant groups would have controlled a society of peasant farmers established in dependent productive settlements or in small villages associated with silo fields, such as that of Missatges, near El Molí d'Espígol, or in secondary settlements with a regular urban layout and defensive stockades, such as Els Estinclells (Garcés 2005).

In exceptional circumstances—during wars for example—these inland Iberian villages of the north-east may have united in confederations under the control of a chieftain or leader who would have emerged at the cusp of the pyramid of power.

This, according to the classical sources, is the case of Indibil, the leader of the Ilergetes (Polybius *Histories* 21.11).

The funerary practices of this period are virtually unknown. We barely have any documentation on cemeteries, which once again suggests that funerary rites were restricted to a small minority of society, possibly the ruling elite. Proof of this could be that, at least in the coastal region, the only two known cemeteries are associated with the towns of Ullastret and Burriac.

This north-eastern region was particularly affected by the conflicts associated with the Second Punic War and the beginning of Roman domination, with the pacification of the population by the consul Cato. These episodes are evidenced by considerable destruction in the villages and show the drastic end to the Iberian period and its associated organizational structures. The beginning of a new era is indicated by the strong Roman influence that radiated out from the towns of Tarraco and Emporion, Rome's principal bases in the region.

A profound transformation came about in the population from the late second century BC. There began an authentic programme of founding new towns and imposing new forms of organization on the countryside, based on villa-type settlements and the Roman plantation agricultural system. This process culminated during the reign of Augustus.

The Iron Age in Iberia: Building a Synopsis

General Politics and Local Processes

One of the most important processes in the Iron Age on the Iberian Peninsula, shared with other temperate regions of Europe and the Mediterranean, was the generalization of nuclei that aggregated the population and constituted embryonic forms of urbanism. These centres were normally fortified and located in strategic positions, on hills and controlling communication routes. With the passing of time, in some parts of Iberia, particularly in the south, east, and north-east, the settlement agglomerations turned into true towns that controlled dependent settlements spread around territorial areas of a regional nature (Belarte et al. 2019). In the central and north-western regions this process took place to a lesser extent, and quite often the nucleated settlements did not expand their domains beyond their immediate hinterland.

This dynamic of aggregation into larger, protected nuclei reflects profound socio-economic and political transformations that, on the one hand, have common patterns, but on the other are a product of particular local dynamics and processes. With regard to the former, we should refer to the social dynamic itself with the consolidation of inequalities and the emergence of elites who gained followers and linked groups of dependents. With the aim of increasing production they encouraged population concentration in order to manage the workforce and control the production of related groups more effectively. To do this they deployed social control and promotion mechanisms such as ritual commensality, the circulation of prestige goods, violence, or sacred bonds with heroized ancestors (see examples of these strategies in Moore and Armada 2011a). We will return to these later.

Also beginning in the late Bronze Age, intensive contacts and trade were developed with the objective of supplying metals over long-distance networks that linked the Atlantic and Mediterranean zones (Celestino et al. 2008). The integration of local economies into regional and supra-regional frameworks necessitated their transformation into forms designed to increase production in order to satisfy the needs of trade. A consequence of the rise in production incentivized by the leaders and in part channelled through trade was a demographic increase, through which the population concentration and economic expansion processes could be sustained. On the other hand, technological improvements such as iron metallurgy and the potter's wheel, which reached the Iberian Peninsula through interaction with Mediterranean peoples, favoured the expansion of productive forces and the growing specialization of production. The expansive nature of these forms of power generated friction between groups competing for land and communication routes, which in turn became a factor of sociopolitical change and favoured fortified nucleated settlement models.

As we have indicated, the considerable variability in territorial models nevertheless suggests different trajectories in each region, in which local traditions, socio-economic models, and responses to external influences were involved. We see some territorial models that express these differences and are undoubtedly due to the forms of social organization in each territory. The nucleation process was particularly intense and early in the Mediterranean zone, where the pre-existing trade networks served as a basis for a commerce that saw strong growth as a result of the establishment of Phoenician populations on the coasts. These contacts provided the prestige goods with which to foster the leaders' social networks and growing prestige (Sanmartí 2009).

In upper Andalusia there was a complete aggregation of the population into medium-sized urban centres covering around 5–10 hectares, although the main *oppida* were larger. These were solidly fortified settlements on promontories, such as Puente Tablas (Figure 10.2, 4), in which the whole population of the area was concentrated. Ruiz Rodríguez and Molinos (2007) link the aggregation process to the formalization of a clientage model of society in which the elite were able to bind the dependent population together through networks that allowed the leaders to take control of the workforce and the collection of taxes. Neighbourhood relations in the urban settlements are an expression of the success of this model of social inequality that began to develop in the sixth century BC and appears to have been fully consolidated by the fourth century BC.

Other zones in the south and south-east of Iberia do not show an absolute urban concentration. Modestly sized fortified centres coexisted with networks of smaller subordinate settlements. In some cases there were constellations of farms and villages that depended on the fortified centres (Bonet et al. 2007; Grau Mira 2007); this model can be linked to less rigid forms of clientage in which the dependence of the peasant would not have been so strict. The need for refuge and protection would have been a key factor in the relationship between the *oppida* and their secondary settlement networks. Sometimes they were aggregated nuclei of different sizes, as in the southern Meseta area (Urbina 2000; Morales Hervás 2010), where the communities maintained a certain degree of independence, although they also formed part of regional networks.

On occasions, it seems that the forms of nucleated settlement cannot be linked to an increase in social inequality and the consolidation of chiefdoms and archaic states. As we have already observed, in the north-west the development of fortified nucleated settlements in the early Iron Age appears to have been a form of community cohesion in the face of the risk of the emergence of accentuated forms of inequality. As such, monumental fortification led to the channelling of collective material resources and the deflection of intergroup friction into rivalry between communities. In some inland areas, such as the mountainous zones of Galicia, Asturias, and the west of the province of León, this situation may have continued almost up to the Roman conquest (González Ruibal 2008: 909–910; Sastre 2011). However, in many other cases, particularly in those areas most open to external trade, this strategy of binding communities to the land established a basis for the intensification of production and the emergence of armed elites, the end result of which would be the consolidation of social inequality (González García et al. 2011). Until a few years ago, the chronology of the population nucleation processes and the emergence of *oppida* or large *castros* in the north-west were attributed by some scholars to contact with Rome, although we now have evidence to support the hypothesis that these processes began earlier than that in the most dynamic areas (González Ruibal 2006–2007: 328–401; Sande Lemos et al. 2011; Prieto Martínez et al. 2017). *Oppida* appeared even earlier on the northern Meseta and are apparent from the fourth century BC (Ruiz Zapatero 2011).

As we can see, the nucleated fortified settlement formula does not have a single cause, but rather reflects societies that, due to internal developments, confronted diverse situations. Within this framework, the constant and conspicuous presence of fortifications obliges us to reflect on their social significance and, in a wider sense, on the role of conflict in the social formations of the Iron Age in Iberia. In fact, in each region it is possible to appreciate the more or less complex development of impressive settlement fortification programmes, as well as of strategic positions from which to control the immediate territory.

The frequency of towers and walls makes us reflect on the role of fortification as a principal element in the monumentalization of settlements and virtually the only public project to which collective resources were devoted. The rich evidence of reconstruction of gates and towers, the most important parts of a fortification system, attests the importance of these elements, which were renewed periodically. Moreover, the frequent and intensive adoption of Mediterranean defensive system models shows us the importance given to and care taken with their construction.

From a functional point of view, the majority of the fortification systems in Iberia are characterized by their simplicity, with only a few and very late examples of the advanced poliorcetics (defensive technology) of contemporary Mediterranean cultures (Berrocal-Rangel and Moret 2007). Only from the third century BC onwards did the Carthaginian and Roman invasions of the Iberian Peninsula lead to the development of complex fortification systems suitable for actively defending settlements. Prior to this period generally only simple walled enclosures, frequently reinforced with towers and ditches, are attested. This type of construction may have been designed to protect the population in the face of a surprise attack, as such defences would have been hard pressed to stand up to a siege or to the war machines that reached Iberia in the centuries immediately before the turn of the era (Quesada 1997). Before that time any conflict would have been based on the protection of the population and the dispatching of warriors to confront aggressors outside the settlement.

Walls, ditches, and other defensive systems emphasize the instability of the period, although they are not the only elements associated with this bellicose context. Equally important, and a constant presence in the extensive territories of the Iberian Peninsula, was the emergence of the warrior figure as the image of the elites who dominated the social body. A large proportion of the societies on the peninsula were headed by leaders accompanied by warrior retinues, who assumed power over the running of the community. The warrior figure is particularly evident in the funerary record of the eastern and central regions of the peninsula from the end of the fifth century BC. Iberian and Celtiberian burial sites have tombs with outstanding and varied grave goods providing emphatic evidence of status and power.

Sculptural and pictorial manifestations also indicate the pre-eminence of these warrior groups, among which the figure of the knight, as the chief of the aristocratic group, stands out. Sculptures of Galician-Lusitanian warriors (Schattner 2003) or those from Cerrillo Blanco de Porcuna (Ruiz Rodríguez and Molinos 2007), as well as scenes painted on the pottery of Llíria (Aranegui 2012: 270–274) and Numancia (Wattenberg 1963), give a good account of the pre-eminence of the warrior figure.

From all this evidence we can deduce that war was important in the historical context of the time in the Iberian Peninsula, as it was in the rest of Iron Age Europe. In social terms, we would like to emphasize that this latent or real instability was conducive to the emergence of the armed leader as the protector of the community and the justification of his rise to political power. As in other geographical areas, belonging to the social caste that guaranteed the security of the group was a powerful ideological mechanism through which to consolidate social inequality and the fracturing of the social body into a dominant class and common people. Likewise, control of technological innovations, particularly iron metallurgy, was in the hands of the dominant classes, thus favouring specialization of economic activity and the rupture of the domestic mode of production.

The Forms of Social Life: Tradition and Innovation

The sociopolitical processes analysed were closely related to new forms of social life. On the Iberian Peninsula, as in the rest of Europe, the Iron Age was a period of cultural contact and widening of horizons. This meant access to new materialities, new technologies, and, in general, new knowledge that contributed to modifying ways of life and identities. The forms of social life in proto-history have often been explained in terms of ethnic identity and cultural tradition. According to this approach, Iberians, Celtiberians, and western Phoenicians would have had certain associated cults, rituals, and institutions. However, recent studies have shown the difficulty in applying such simplistic views. These cultural practices often formed part of long-standing traditions with roots buried deep in prehistoric times. Almagro-Gorbea pioneered the theory of the existence of a 'proto-Celtic' substratum of Atlantic origin, whose gestation dated back to the time of Bell Beaker pottery and to which we can attribute rock altars, *pedra formosa*-type saunas, warrior initiation rites, offerings of arms to water, and the absence of cremation tombs (Almagro-Gorbea 2011: 33). These ancient traditions probably survived until the Roman period in areas such as the west or the north of the Iberian Peninsula. Other Indo-European influences that would have been introduced across the Pyrenees in the late Bronze Age are associated with the Urnfields and would explain the Indo-European rituals and beliefs detected among the Iberian peoples of the north-east (Almagro-Gorbea 2001). While this latter phenomenon breaks with the radical disassociation of the Iberian area from other Indo-European areas, we should also point out that the whole of the territory of Iberia was subjected to common historical processes during the Iron Age.

A second relevant aspect is the reconceptualization of ethnicity in archaeological studies. In contrast to the traditional essentialist view, scholars such as Díaz-Andreu (1998) defend the fluid and polyform character of ethnicity; its relation to subjective perception; its changing nature depending on the interlocutor and the situation; the coexistence of various ethnic identities in a single individual; and the coexistence of ethnicity with other forms of identity (e.g. gender, religion, status). Similarly, postcolonial approaches, which in recent years have achieved a certain popularity in Spain (Vives-Ferrándiz 2008), emphasize hybridism as a characteristic typical of colonial situations, claiming that local communities played an active role, and proposing that local and foreign populations lived together in the same settlements at certain times during the Phoenician-Punic colonial dynamic (Arruda 2005: 105; González-Ruibal 2008: 911). Thus, the relations between forms of social life and ethnic identities are complex and multiple and are included in the fluid dynamics that combined tradition with innovation.

Taking these caveats into account, we may explore some of the main forms of social life in the proto-history of the Iberian Peninsula. First of all we will mention sacrificial and banqueting rituals as a setting for social negotiation. Of particular interest is the geographical spread and long duration of a type of combinational animal sacrifice that is attested in a large part of the western territory. Thanks to diverse sources of information (archaeological remains, epigraphy, and iconography) we know that cattle, pigs, sheep, and goats were offered in combined sacrifices to different divinities within the framework of rituals in which objects such as cauldrons—or torcs in the north-west—played a special role (Armada and García Vuelta 2006; Figure 10.4, 1). Animal sacrifices were often associated with banquets, a subject to which special attention has been paid in the last two decades (Sanz Mínguez and Romero Carnicero 2009; Aranda et al. 2011). Bronze objects (cauldrons, flesh-hooks, and spits) appeared during the late Bronze Age on the European Atlantic façade, constituting a new materiality linked to commensality (Armada 2011).

In the early Iron Age the repertory of metal objects linked to banquets expanded and these began to appear in the tombs of outstanding warriors, particularly in the north-east of the peninsula and in Vettonian burial sites, underlining the political nature of these practices and their connection to the warrior elites. In other cases, banquets had obvious religious and ritual connotations, as suggested by finds of spits and vessels—both bronze and pottery—in the shrine of Cancho Roano (Celestino 2008: 331–336). The outstanding items brought by Phoenician and Greek traders were processed food products and pottery vessels for consumption, once again highlighting the importance of commensality in social life. The presence of conspicuous consumption items in most of Iberia suggests the importance of political commensality as a form of aggregation and power negotiation. The materiality of this ritualized consumption must have channelled a large part of the surpluses and can possibly be linked to the sparse development of emphatic programmes for the expression of power that are frequently found in similar social contexts.

An important innovation with respect to the previous stage was the growing formalization and monumentalization of shrines and places of worship resulting from these social changes, and influenced by contacts with Mediterranean societies. These shrines could be buildings inside urban settlements (Almagro-Gorbea and Moneo 2000) or isolated structures that simultaneously exercised an economic and territorial control function, as is the case of Cancho Roano and other Extremaduran and Portuguese complexes. Whatever the type, in the 'Orientalizing' or Phoenician-influenced shrines it is common to find altars in the shape of a bull skin or a Cypriot ingot (Celestino 2008: 308–309; Escacena and Amores 2011: 118–121), a symbol that provides another example of traditional and cultural continuity, as it is documented over a chronological arc of several centuries. Across a large part of the northern half of the Iberian Peninsula the shrines were less formal and monumental, maintaining traditions such as altars on rocks or sanctifying natural spaces that probably dated back to the late Bronze Age. However, evidence of oriental cults is documented in the south of Galicia and the north of Portugal, including the structure with *baetyli* (sacred stones) in the *castro* of Punta do Muiño (González Ruibal 2006–2007: 267–268).

Together with the shrines, the cemetery was a key element in social life and ritual. As we have already seen, the proto-historic funerary record of the Iberian Peninsula shows wide variability, including cremation and inhumation. There are also large areas in which we know nothing of the funerary rituals and how bodies were dealt with, probably due to the existence of mortuary practices that have scant archaeological visibility. The most common type of burial rite is probably cremation with pottery urns and other grave goods beneath a tumulus. These cemeteries are an outstanding example of the expression of relationships of dependency between individuals and groups, at the same

FIGURE 10.4 Iron Age iconography: 1 Late Iron Age bronze object with a scene of sacrifice from the Instituto Valencia de Don Juan, Madrid (north-west Iberian Peninsula, unknown provenance); 2 Decorated diadem-belt from Moñes (Asturias); 3 Ceramic jug from Numancia (Soria, inv. N-11967); 4 Symbolic ceramic iconography from Ilici (Elche), second to first century BC.

Photos: 1–2 © O. García-Vuelta; 3 © Junta de Castilla y León, Museo Numantino de Soria, Alejandro Plaza; 4 © Lexicon Iberian Iconography Project

time as they evidence social stratification through differences in tombs and grave goods. For example, in parallel to the aforementioned monumentalization of the shrines, from the sixth century BC in the areas subject to Mediterranean influence we document monumental sepulchres with a tower-shape, with a hypogeum (underground chamber), or with stela-pillars. These stone structures are associated with sculptural programmes, some of which are complex and reveal the importance given to images from this time on.

Two main trends can be seen in the development of this stone sculpture (Bendala 2007). The first is linked to the 'Orientalizing' tendency resulting from the Phoenician colonization and dates back to the seventh century BC. The most outstanding example is the tower-shaped monument of Pozo Moro, which is endowed with a complex iconographic programme with clear oriental influences. Based on this first influx, a second trend developed from the late sixth century BC; this was highly influenced by Greek workshops and has its main exponent in the sculptural group of Porcuna, which was found in hundreds of pieces in a pit that can be dated to around 400 BC (Figure 10.5, 1). The adoption of this type of sculpture probably implies contact with foreign artisans who would have established themselves on the Iberian Peninsula during the colonial contact. Other important examples of Iberian sculpture can be found in the so-called 'ladies' (*damas*), especially the Lady of Elche and the seated Lady of Baza (Figure 10.5, 2), who were probably heroized women who founded lineages. They are usually dated to the fifth century BC, probably towards the end of the century, and they would have been placed in funerary chambers containing the ashes of the deceased (Bendala 2000: 154–158; Ruiz Rodríguez 2008: 802–803).

In addition to these manifestations linked to the funerary sphere, images in general took on a much greater presence and power in the Iron Age than in previous periods. A rich iconography in gold and silver jewellery, bronze objects, stone sculpture, painted pottery, and other objects developed all over the Iberian Peninsula (Figure 10.4). The human figure also increased in importance, being depicted in day-to-day actions, combat, and acts of worship. There were also images from the plant and animal worlds, as well as mythological beings and geometric shapes. However, each area and period are characterized by particular manifestations, with monumental sculpture, as we have already seen, predominating in areas more open to Mediterranean stimuli. Of particular interest, although they are less well carved, are the *verracos* or zoomorphic sculptures of the south-western part of the northern Meseta, which date to the late Iron Age and were linked to the demarcation of grazing areas (Álvarez-Sanchís 1999). Also outstanding are the late Iron Age warrior statues of the north-west, such as the find from Castro Lezenho (Figure 10.5, 3), which had a similar function to those from other areas of Celtic Europe, although in this case they are not linked to funerary tumuli (Schattner 2003). Painted pottery is typical of eastern Iberia and some zones of the Meseta. Also on the Meseta, skilled artisans produced fine bronzeware, including arms, belt buckles, pectorals, and fibulae (Lorrio 1997). Gold jewellery is typical of the north-west and some parts of the Phoenician-Tartessian area, while silver jewellery predominates on the Meseta and in the Iberian world, areas which also produced silver tableware with a rich iconography and fine technical quality (Figure 10.6).

Both the gold and silver jewellery as adornments and the bronze weapons reflect the importance acquired in this period by the body as the expression of belonging to a group, gender, or social position (González Ruibal 2006–2007: 419). Nevertheless, it should be emphasized that jewellery does not have an unambiguous significance as a personal adornment, as it must also have acted as an element of ritual accumulation of treasure and even as adornments for sacrificial animals (Escacena and Amores 2011).

The last innovations to which we will refer are the use of writing and coinage, which are crucial for explaining the emergence of state-type social formations (Figure 10.7). As we have already seen, the first examples of writing appeared in the south and south-west of the peninsula in the form of graffiti on pottery and engraved slabs, probably

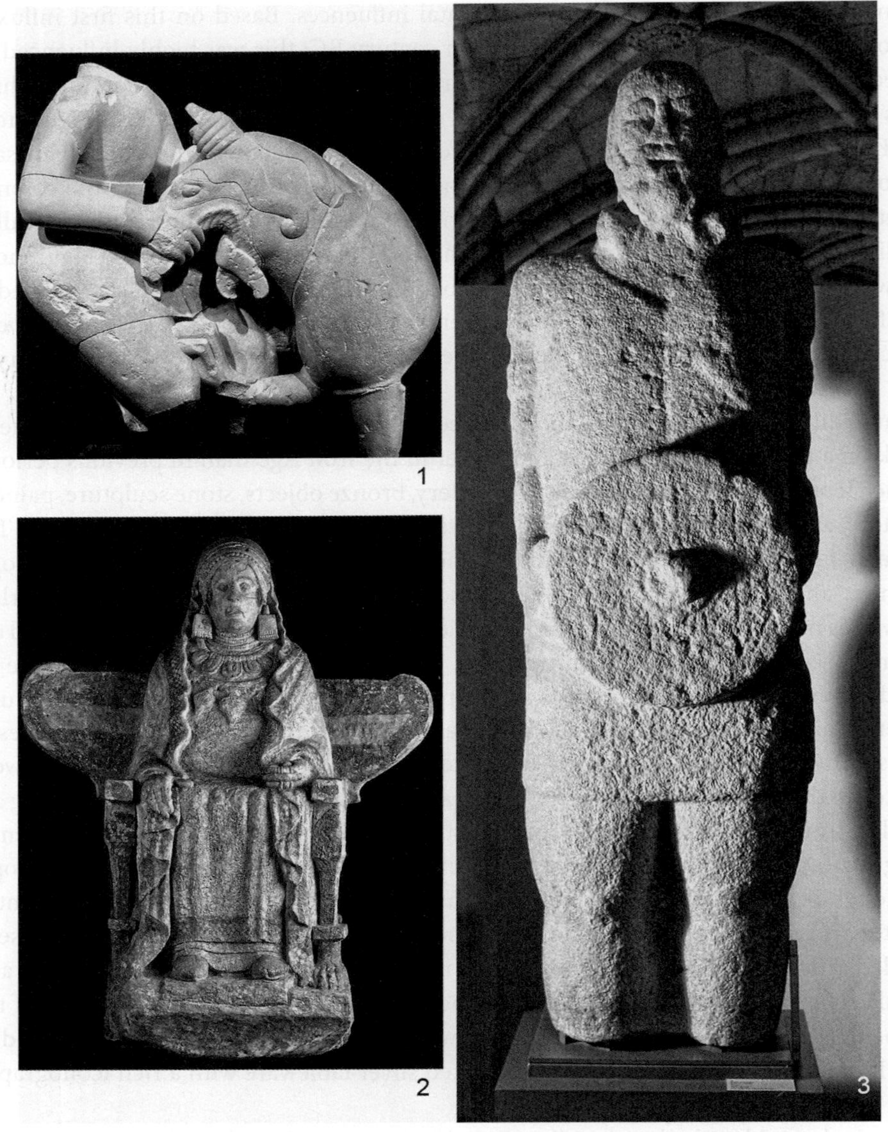

FIGURE 10.5 Stone sculpture: 1 Fight scene on a memorial monument from Cerrillo Blanco de Porcuna (Jaén), late fifth century BC; 2 Dama de Baza funerary sculpture (Granada), fourth century BC; 3 Warrior sculpture from Castro Lezenho (Vila Real), first century BC to first century AD.

Photos: 1–2 © Lexicon Iberian Iconography Project; 3 © Incipit—CSIC

tombstones. The origin and chronology of this writing are disputed. De Hoz, one of the principal experts, defended the theory that the semi-syllabic writing of the south-west is derived from the Phoenician alphabet and dates from no later than 650 BC (de Hoz 2005); others consider it to be a local adaptation of eastern Mediterranean script, although not necessarily Phoenician (Ruiz-Gálvez 2013: 304–311). Although there must have been other examples of writing on perishable material in the southern region, which are now lost, the concentration of slabs in a very specific zone of the interior of Portugal is explained in strictly social terms by the existence of budding aristocracies that used them to display their social position. This system of writing shows a notable period of survival in the southern and eastern coastal areas of the Iberian Peninsula.

A new type of writing derived from the earlier one subsequently appeared in the Iberian area and lasted until the Roman period (Untermann 1990). At least from the middle of the second century BC, but probably prior to that (Lorrio 2008: 566), the Celtiberians adopted Iberian writing for mainly practical and institutional uses (e.g. coinage, hospitality tokens or *tesserae*, institutional bronzes). In addition to this Iberian writing, in the eastern Iberian Peninsula (the areas of Valencia and Murcia), probably

FIGURE 10.6 Late Iron Age decorated silver tableware (*páteras*) from Castellet de Banyoles (Tivissa, Tarragona).

Photo: © X.-L. Armada

due to the influence of Massalia, around the fourth century BC, the Ionic alphabet was adapted to the local languages, although this innovation failed to take root (Aranegui 2012: 56–57). In large parts of the peninsula indigenous use of writing did not come about until the Roman period; we know of important inscriptions in pre-Roman languages and in the Latin alphabet in both Celtiberia and Lusitania.

The introduction of coinage to the Iberian Peninsula was also a slow and geographically varied process. Coinage was first used in the Greek colony of Emporion, although there was a long tradition of using weight systems and pre-monetary objects throughout the peninsula that dates back to at least the late Bronze Age (García-Bellido 2011). In Emporion a mint was founded around 470–460 BC, although coinage was evidently already in circulation, and its use for economic purposes spread progressively throughout the colony's area of influence. In commercially dynamic areas all over Mediterranean Iberia there were other early foci of coin minting, including Arse-Saguntum (second half of the fourth century BC) and Gadir (around 300 BC). However, the peak of monetization did not come until the turn of the third to the second century BC, as a consequence of the Second Punic War (García-Bellido 2011: 133–134; Aranegui 2012: 235–236). In the Celtiberian area the first mints appeared during the first half of the second century BC (Burillo 1998: 238).

As was the case with writing—they are closely related phenomena—large areas of the northern and western sectors of the Iberian Peninsula were not monetized until the end of the Roman conquest period, no doubt for historical and social reasons. García-Bellido (2011: 133–134) defends the interesting theory of a relationship between monetization and the necessities of war (e.g. payments to mercenaries), which would explain both the peak linked to the Second Punic War in the Iberian area and the beginning of monetization in the north-west as a consequence of the Cantabrian Wars, the final campaign in the definitive Roman conquest of the peninsula.

From the Past to the Present

The Iron Age has always been a major historical reference point for constructing the identities of modern Spain, with ideological to-ing and fro-ing resulting from the political contexts of the period. The complexity of the subject prevents an adequate treatment of it here, but we would like to point out some of its most important features. Since the beginning of modern research, the study of the Iron Age has oscillated between two cultural traditions of great weight, the Celtic and the Iberian, both of which have had a decisive influence on identity building. The Celts represented the relationship with the powerful historical reference of western Europe, whereas the Iberians formed the link to the classical Mediterranean world. Moreover, the latter group was the first autochthonous culture on the Iberian Peninsula whose name was known and brought with it a powerful corpus of images. The potency of naming an ancient people and the attractiveness of its icons turned the Mediterranean Iron Age into an important national

FIGURE 10.7 Samples of writing and monetization: 1 Iberian administrative lead inscription from La Serreta d'Alcoi (Alicante), third century BC; 2 Drachma from Arse (Sagunto), *c*.200 BC, 15 mm; 3 Bronze unit, Konterbia Karbika, mid-first century BC, 23 mm; 4 As from Ercavica, minted with the name of Augustus (27 BC–14 AD), 28 mm.

Photos: 1 © Archaeological Museum of Alcoi; 2 © Royal Coin Cabinet, Stockholm; 3 © Bibliothèque nationale de France, Paris; 4 American Numismatic Society, New York

historical reference at the beginning of the twentieth century (Aranegui 2012: 29–53). The Franco dictatorship wanted to see in the fusion of these two large groups the emergence of the Celtiberian people mentioned in the textual sources: in other words the remote origin of a much desired national unity (Ruiz Zapatero 2003; Ruiz Rodríguez et al. 2006).

With the passing of time, the simple uniform view of large Iron Age populations gave way to the regional division of studies. This view is consistent with the particularities of the archaeological record and with the ways in which the societies of the period organized themselves, but it was also in line with the political interests of the last quarter of the twentieth century. The return to democracy in Spain brought with it political and administrative decentralization. As a result, the respective governments of the regional autonomous communities have found in the Iron Age elements with which to build their own regional identities, especially in regions with nationalist traditions, such as Galicia or Catalonia. This is further contributed to by the values of independence and cultural resistance that European tradition has associated with Iron Age communities, as well as with the monumentality and evocative power of the remains of that period.

On the other hand, decentralization has meant that each region runs its own cultural and heritage management programmes. In contrast to the centralized models of other countries (such as INRAP or English Heritage), archaeological practice and scientific programmes are preferentially divided into regional areas of action, a fact that contributes to insufficiently generalizing interpretative models (Moore and Armada 2011b: 23–24, 36–37). This is a similar problem, albeit on a different scale, to that pointed out by Kristiansen (2008) for European proto-history.

Acknowledgements

We would like to thank the editors for inviting us to contribute to this volume. This chapter is part of the following research projects: 'From the workshop to the body: metals as power expressions in the Late Bronze Age and the Iron Age of NW Iberia' (10 PXIB 606 016 PR), funded by the Xunta de Galicia; 'Archaeological analysis and heritage evaluation of three landscapes of the Roman conquest of Hispania (2nd–1st cent.). East of Hispania Citerior' (HAR2015-64601-C3-2-R), funded by the MINECO, and 'Navigation and coastal heritage in Northwestern Iberia' (Network CN2011/56), funded by the Xunta de Galicia. Our thanks also go to Ana Pernas for her help with the figures, as well as to the institutions and colleagues who gave us permission to use their photographs.

Notes

1. Vilanova y Piera (1872: 438) is probably the first Spanish writer to mention an 'Iron Epoch' as the chronological period that followed a 'Bronze Epoch' (Ayarzagüena pers. comm.).
2. With a similar orientation, the journal *Palaeohispanica* has been published since 2001.

References

Almagro Gorbea, M. 2001. 'Los íberos: nuevas perspectivas sobre sus orígenes', in A. J. Lorrio (ed.) *Los íberos en la comarca de Requena-Utiel (Valencia)*: 33–47. Alicante: Universidad de Alicante.

Almagro Gorbea, M. 2011. 'La celtización de la Península Ibérica: bases para la investigación en el siglo XXI', in G. Ruiz Zapatero and J. R. Álvarez-Sanchís (eds) *Castros y verracos: Las gentes de la Edad del Hierro en el occidente de Iberia*: 19–44. Ávila: Diputación de Ávila.

Almagro Gorbea, M., O. Arteaga, M. Blech, D. Ruiz Mata, and H. Schubart. 2001. *Protohistoria de la Península Ibérica*. Barcelona: Ariel.

Almagro Gorbea, M., and T. Moneo. 2000. *Santuarios urbanos en el mundo ibérico*. Madrid: Real Academia de la Historia.

Almagro Gorbea, M., and M. Torres. 2009. 'La colonización de la costa atlántica de Portugal: ¿fenicios o tartesios?' *Palaeohispanica* 9: 113–142.

Álvarez-Sanchís, J. R. 1999. *Los Vettones*. Madrid: Real Academia de la Historia.

Álvarez-Sanchís, J. R. 2000. 'The Iron Age in western Spain (800 BC–AD 50): An overview'. *Oxford Journal of Archaeology* 19, 1: 65–89.

Álvarez-Sanchís, J. R. 2011. 'La segunda Edad del Hierro en el Oeste de la Meseta', in G. Ruiz Zapatero and J. R. Álvarez-Sanchís (eds) *Castros y verracos: Las gentes de la Edad del Hierro en el occidente de Iberia*: 101–127. Ávila: Diputación de Ávila.

Aranda, G., S. Montón-Subías, and M. Sánchez (eds). 2011. *Guess Who's Coming to Dinner: Feasting Rituals in the Prehistoric Societies of Europe and the Near East*. Oxford: Oxbow.

Aranegui, C. 2012. *Los iberos ayer y hoy: Arqueologías y culturas*. Madrid: Marcial Pons.

Armada, X.-L. 2011. 'Feasting metals and the ideology of power in the Late Bronze Age of Atlantic Iberia', in G. Aranda, S. Montón-Subías, and M. Sánchez (eds) *Guess Who's Coming to Dinner: Feasting Rituals in the Prehistoric Societies of Europe and the Near East*: 158–183. Oxford: Oxbow.

Armada, X.-L., and O. García Vuelta. 2006. 'Symbolic forms from the Iron Age in the north-west of the Iberian Peninsula: Sacrificial bronzes and their problems', in M. V. García Quintela, F. J. González García, and F. Criado Boado (eds) *Anthropology of the Indo-European World and Material Culture*: 163–178. Budapest: Archaeolingua.

Armada, X.-L., N. Rafel, R. Graells, and R. Roqué. 2013. 'Orígenes del urbanismo y dinámicas sociales en el Bronce Final de Cataluña meridional: El Avenc del Primo (Bellmunt del Priorat, Tarragona)'. *Trabajos de Prehistoria* 70, 2: 278–294.

Armendáriz Martija, J. 2008. *De aldeas a ciudades: El poblamiento durante el primer milenio a.C. en Navarra*. Pamplona: Gobierno de Navarra.

Arruda, A. M. 2005. 'O 1º milénio a.n.e. no Centro e no Sul de Portugal: leituras possíveis no início de um novo século'. *O Arqueólogo Português, série IV* 23: 9–156.

Arruda, A. M. 2011. 'Indígenas, fenicios y tartésicos en el occidente peninsular: mucha gente, poca tierra', in M. Álvarez (ed.) *Fenicios en Tartesos: nuevas perspectivas*. British Archaeological Reports International Series 2245: 151–160. Oxford: Archaeopress.

Aubet, M. E. 2009. *Tiro y las colonias fenicias de Occidente*, 3rd edition. Barcelona: Bellaterra.

Belarte, M. C., J. Noguera, R. Plana-Mallart, and J. Sanmartí (eds). 2019. *Urbanization in Iberia and Mediterranean Gaul in the First Millennium BC*. Tarragona: ICAC.

Bendala, M. 2000. *Tartesios, iberos y celtas: Pueblos, culturas y colonizadores de la Hispania antigua*. Madrid: Temas de Hoy.

Bendala, M. 2007. 'El arte ibérico en el ámbito andaluz: notas sobre la escultura', in L. Abad and J. A. Soler (eds) *Arte ibérico en la España mediterránea*: 21–38. Alicante: Diputación Provincial.

Berrocal-Rangel, L. 1992. *Los pueblos célticos del Suroeste de la Península Ibérica*. Complutum Extra 2. Madrid: Universidad Complutense.

Berrocal-Rangel, L. 2004. 'La defensa de la comunidad: sobre las funciones emblemáticas de las murallas protohistóricas en la Península Ibérica'. *Gladius* 24: 27–98.

Berrocal-Rangel, L., and P. Moret (eds). 2007. *Paisajes fortificados de la Edad del Hierro: Las murallas protohistóricas de la Meseta y la vertiente atlántica en su contexto europeo*. Madrid: Real Academia de la Historia/Casa de Velázquez.

Blanco González, A. 2011. 'From huts to "the house": The shift in perceiving home between the Bronze Age and the early Iron Age in central Iberia (Spain)'. *Oxford Journal of Archaeology* 30, 4: 393–410.

Blánquez, J., and V. Antona (eds). 1992. *Congreso de Arqueología Ibérica: Las necrópolis*. Madrid: Universidad Autónoma de Madrid.

Bonet, H., I. Grau, and J. Vives-Ferrándiz. 2015. 'Estructura social y poder entre las comunidades ibéricas de la franja central mediterránea', in M. C. Belarte, D. Garcia, and J. Sanmartí (eds) *Les estructures socials a la Gàl·lia i a Ibèria: Homenatge a Aurora Martín i Enriqueta Pons. Actes de la VII Reunió Internacional d'Arqueologia de Calafell (Calafell, 7 al 9 de marc de 2013). Arqueo mediterrània* 14: 251–272. Barcelona: Universitat de Barcelona/ICAC.

Bonet, H., and C. Mata. 2001. 'Organización del territorio y poblamiento en el País Valenciano entre los siglos VII al II a.C.', in L. Berrocal-Rangel and P. Gardes (eds) *Entre Celtas e Iberos: Las poblaciones protohistóricas de las Galias e Hispania*: 175–186. Madrid: Real Academia de la Historia/Casa de Velázquez.

Bonet, H., C. Mata, and A. Moreno. 2007. 'Paisaje y hábitat rural en el territorio edetano durante el Ibérico Pleno (siglos IV–III a.C.)', in A. Rodríguez Díaz and I. Pavón (eds) *Arqueología de la tierra: Paisajes rurales de la protohistoria peninsular*: 247–276. Cáceres: Universidad de Extremadura.

Burillo, F. 1998. *Los Celtíberos: Etnias y estados*. Barcelona: Crítica.

Burillo, F. 2011. 'Oppida y "ciudades estado" celtibéricos'. *Complutum* 22, 2: 277–295.

Burjachs, F., M. Blech, D. Marzoli, and R. Julià. 1999. 'Evolución del paisaje vegetal en relación con el uso del territorio en la Edad del Hierro en el NE de la Península Ibérica', in R. Buxó and E. Pons (eds) *Els productes alimentaris d'origen vegetal a l'edat del Ferro de l'Europa Occidental: de la producció al consum. Actes du XXIIe Colloque de l'AFEAF (Girona, 1988)*. Serie Monogràfica 18: 31–42. Gerona: Museu d'Arqueologia de Catalunya.

Celestino, S. 2008. 'Tartessos', in F. Gracia Alonso (ed.) *De Iberia a Hispania*: 93–345. Barcelona: Ariel.

Celestino, S., N. Rafel, and X.-L. Armada (eds). 2008. *Contacto cultural entre el Mediterráneo y el Atlántico (siglos XII–VIII ANE): La precolonización a debate*. Madrid: Escuela Española de Historia y Arqueología en Roma-CSIC.

Celestino, S., J. A. Salgado, and R. Cazorla. 2009. 'El siglo V a.C. en la Alta Extremadura', in P. Sanabria (ed.) *Lusitanos y vettones*: 197–211. Cáceres: Museo de Cáceres.

Cunliffe, B. W. 2001. *Facing the Ocean: The Atlantic and its Peoples 8000 BC–AD 1500*. Oxford: Oxford University Press.

Cunliffe, B. W. 2017. *On the Ocean. The Mediterranean and the Atlantic from Prehistory to AD 1500*. Oxford: Oxford University Press.

de Hoz, J. 2005. 'La recepción de la escritura en Hispania como fenómeno orientalizante', in S. Celestino and J. Jiménez (eds) *El periodo orientalizante* 1: 363–381. Mérida: CSIC.

Delibes de Castro, G., and F. Romero Carnicero. 2011. 'La plena colonización agraria del Valle Medio del Duero'. *Complutum* 22, 2: 49–94.

Díaz-Andreu, M. 1998. 'Ethnicity and Iberians: The archaeological crossroads between perception and material culture'. *European Journal of Archaeology* 1, 2: 199–218.

Escacena, J. L., and F. Amores. 2011. 'Revestidos como dios manda. El tesoro del Carambolo como ajuar de consagración'. *Spal* 20: 107–141.

Escacena, J. L., and M. Belén. 1997. 'Economía y sociedad en la Turdetania de los siglos V–IV a.C.', in J. Fernández, P. Rufete, and C. García (eds) *La Andalucía Ibero-turdetana (siglos V–IV a.C.)*. Huelva Arqueológica 14: 137–161. Huelva: Diputación de Huelva.

Esparza, A. 2011. 'Los castros del oeste de la Meseta'. *Complutum* 22, 2: 11–47.

Fabião, C. 2001. 'O povoamento do Sudoeste peninsular na segunda metade do I milénio a.C.: continuidades e rupturas', in L. Berrocal-Rangel and P. Gardes (eds) *Entre Celtas e Iberos: Las poblaciones protohistóricas de las Galias e Hispania*: 227–246. Madrid: Real Academia de la Historia/Casa de Velázquez.

Ferrer, E. (ed.) 2019. *La ruta de las Estrímnides. Navegación y conocimiento del litoral atlántico de Iberia en la Antigüedad*. Alcalá de Henares: Universidad de Alcalá-Universidad de Sevilla.

Ferrer, E., M. L. Bandera, and F. J. García. 2007. 'El poblamiento rural protohistórico en el Bajo Guadalquivir', in A. Rodríguez Díaz and I. Pavón (eds) *Arqueología de la tierra: Paisajes rurales de la protohistoria peninsular*: 195–224. Cáceres: Universidad de Extremadura.

Garcés, I. 2005. 'Ilergets i lacetans occidentals: deu anys de recerques i algunes propostes de síntesi', in O. Mercadal (ed.) *Món Ibèric als Països Catalans: XIII Col·loqui Internacional d'Arqueologia de Puigcerdà*: 411–440. Puigcerdà: Institut d'Estudis Ceretans.

García-Bellido, M. P. 2011. 'Hackgold and hacksilber in protomonetary Iberia', in M. P. García-Bellido, L. Callegarin, and A. Jiménez (eds) *Barter, Money and Coinage in the Ancient Mediterranean (10th–1st centuries BC)*: 121–135. Madrid: CSIC.

García Fernández, F. J., and E. Ferrer. 2021. Ciudad y territorio: los orígenes del urbanismo en el Bajo Guadalquivir. Jaén: Universidad de Jaén.

García Quintela, M. V., and M. Santos Estévez. 2015. 'Iron Age saunas of northern Portugal: State of the art and research perspectives'. *Oxford Journal of Archaeology* 34, 1: 67–95.

González García, F. J., C. Parcero-Oubiña, and X. Ayán Vila. 2011. 'Iron Age societies against the state: An account of the emergence of the Iron Age in north-western Iberia', in T. Moore and X.-L. Armada (eds) *Atlantic Europe in the First Millennium BC: Crossing the Divide*: 285–301. Oxford: Oxford University Press.

González Ruibal, A. 2006. 'House societies vs. kinship-based societies: An archaeological case from Iron Age Europe'. *Journal of Anthropological Archaeology* 25: 144–173.

González Ruibal, A. 2006–2007. *Galaicos: Poder y comunidad en el Noroeste de la Península Ibérica (1200 a.C.–50 d.C.)*. Brigantium 18–19. A Coruña: Museo Arqueolóxico e Histórico.

González Ruibal, A. 2008. 'Los pueblos del Noroeste', in F. Gracia Alonso (ed.) *De Iberia a Hispania*: 899–930. Barcelona: Ariel.

Gorrochategui, J. 2009. 'Vasco antiguo: algunas cuestiones de geografía e historia lingüísticas'. *Palaeohispanica* 9: 539–555.

Gorrochategui, J., and J. A. Lakarra. 2013. 'Why Basque cannot be, unfortunately, an Indo-European language'. *Journal of Indo-European Studies* 41, 1–2: 203–237.

Gracia Alonso, F. (ed.) 2008a. *De Iberia a Hispania*. Barcelona: Ariel.

Gracia Alonso, F. 2008b. 'Colonización y comercio púnico en la península Ibérica', in F. Gracia Alonso (ed.) *De Iberia a Hispania*: 845–893. Barcelona: Ariel.

Graells, R. 2010. *Las tumbas con importaciones y la recepción del Mediterráneo en el nordeste de la Península Ibérica (ss. VII–VI a.C.)*. Lleida: Universitat de Lleida.

Grau Mira, I. 2007. 'Dinámica social, paisaje y teoría de la práctica. Propuestas sobre la evolución de la sociedad ibérica en el área central del oriente peninsular'. *Trabajos de Prehistoria* 64, 2: 119–142.

Jiménez Ávila, J., and J. Ortega Blanco. 2008. 'El poblamiento en llano del Guadiana Medio durante el período post-orientalizante', in J. Jiménez (ed.) *Sidereum Ana I: El río Guadiana en época post-orientalizante*: 251–281. Mérida: CSIC.

Jordán Cólera, C. 2008. 'Las lenguas celtas de la Península Ibérica', in M. Alberro and C. Jordán Cólera (eds) *Los celtas de la Península Ibérica*: 177–330. Noia: Toxosoutos.

Kristiansen, K. 2008. 'Do we need the "archaeology of Europe"?' *Archaeological Dialogues* 15, 1: 5–25.

López Barja de Quiroga, P. 1995–1996. 'Testimonia Antiqua Hispaniae'. *Studia Historica. Historia Antigua* 13–14: 165–179.

Lorrio, A. J. 1997. *Los Celtíberos*. Complutum Extra 7. Alicante: Universidad de Alicante/ Universidad Complutense.

Lorrio, A. J. 2008. 'Los celtíberos', in F. Gracia Alonso (ed.) *De Iberia a Hispania*: 553–647. Barcelona: Ariel.

Marín Suárez, C. 2009. 'De nómadas a castreños. Los orígenes de la Edad del Hierro en Asturias', in C. Marín and J. F. Jordá (eds) *Arqueología castreña en Asturias*. Entemu 16: 21–46. Gijón: UNED.

Mayoral, V., and S. Celestino (eds). 2010. *Los paisajes rurales de la romanización: Arquitectura y explotación del territorio*. Madrid: La Ergástula.

Moore, T., and X.-L. Armada (eds). 2011a. *Atlantic Europe in the First Millennium BC: Crossing the Divide*. Oxford: Oxford University Press.

Moore, T., and X.-L. Armada. 2011b. 'Crossing the divide: Opening a dialogue on approaches to western European first millennium BC studies', in T. Moore and X.-L. Armada (eds) *Atlantic Europe in the First Millennium BC: Crossing the Divide*: 3–77. Oxford: Oxford University Press.

Morales Hervás, J. 2010. *El poblamiento de época ibérica en Ciudad Real*. Toledo: Universidad de Castilla-La Mancha.

Murillo-Barroso, M., I. Montero-Ruiz, N. Rafel, M. A. Hunt, and X.-L. Armada. 2016. 'The macro-regional scale of silver production in Iberia during the first millennium BC in the context of Mediterranean contacts'. *Oxford Journal of Archaeology* 35, 1: 75–100.

Olmos, R. 2002. 'Los grupos escultóricos del Cerrillo Blanco de Porcuna (Jaén). Un ensayo de lectura iconográfica convergente'. *Archivo Español de Arqueología* 75: 23–48.

Pablo Martínez, R. 2022. *Puñales de la Segunda Edad del Hierro en el Alto Ebro y el Duero Medio: los puñales de tipo Monte Bernorio, enmangue en espiga y filos curvos y su influencia sobre el "pugio" romano*. Madrid: Editorial CSIC.

Parcero-Oubiña, C. 2002. *La construcción del paisaje social en la Edad del Hierro del Noroeste ibérico*. Ortigueira: Fundación F. M. Ortegalia.

Peralta Labrador, E. 2000. *Los Cántabros antes de Roma*. Madrid: Real Academia de la Historia.

Prieto Martínez, M. P., Y. Álvarez González, M. Fernández-Götz, M. V. García Quintela, A. C. González García, and L. F. López González. 2017. 'The contribution of Bayesian analysis to the chronology of Iron Age north-western Iberia: New data from San Cibrán de Las (Galicia, Spain)'. *Journal of Archaeological Science: Reports* 16: 397–408.

Quesada, F. 1997. *El armamento ibérico: Estudio tipológico, geográfico, funcional, social y simbólico de las armas en la Cultura Ibérica (siglos VI–I a.C.)*. Montagnac: Monique Mergoil.

Rafel, N. 2011–2012. 'La cuenca minera del Baix Priorat (Tarragona): explotación y distribución en época colonial. Recursos locales versus recursos alóctonos', in M. E. Aubet and P. Sureda (eds) *Interacción social y comercio en la antesala del colonialismo*: 71–85. Barcelona: Universitat Pompeu Fabra.

Rafel, N., and X.-L. Armada. 2023. *La cuenca minera del Baix Priorat (Tarragona): poblamiento protohistórico y relaciones con el ámbito fenicio*. Madrid: Editorial CSIC.
Ramon, J., N. Rafel, I. Montero, M. Santos, M. Renzi, M. A. Hunt, et al. 2011. 'Comercio protohistórico: el registro del Nordeste peninsular y la circulación de mineral de plomo en Ibiza y el Bajo Priorato (Tarragona)'. *Saguntum* 43: 55–81.
Rodríguez Díaz, A. 2009. *Campesinos y 'señores del campo': Tierra y poder en la protohistoria extremeña*. Barcelona: Bellaterra.
Romero Carnicero, F., and C. Sanz Mínguez (eds). 2010. *De la región vaccea a la arqueología vaccea*. Valladolid: Centro de Estudios Vacceos Federico Wattenberg.
Romero Carnicero, F., C. Sanz Mínguez, and J. R. Álvarez-Sanchís. 2008. 'El primer milenio a.C. en las tierras del interior peninsular', in F. Gracia Alonso (ed.) *De Iberia a Hispania*: 649–731. Barcelona: Ariel.
Ruiz-Gálvez, M. 2013. *Con el fenicio en los talones. Los inicios de la Edad del Hierro en la cuenca del Mediterráneo*. Barcelona: Bellaterra.
Ruiz Mata, D. 1997. 'Fenicios, tartesios y turdetanos', in J. Fernández, P. Rufete, and C. García (eds) *La Andalucía Ibero-turdetana (siglos V–IV a.C.)*. Huelva Arqueológica 14: 325–366. Huelva: Diputación de Huelva.
Ruiz Rodríguez, A. 2008. 'Iberos', in F. Gracia Alonso (ed.) *De Iberia a Hispania*: 733–844. Barcelona: Ariel.
Ruiz Rodríguez, A., and M. Molinos. 1998. *The Archaeology of Iberians*. Cambridge: Cambridge University Press.
Ruiz Rodríguez, A., and M. Molinos. 2007. *Iberos en Jaén*. Jaén: Universidad de Jaén.
Ruiz Rodríguez, A., A. Sánchez, and J. P. Bellón. 2006. *Los archivos de la arqueología ibérica: una arqueología para dos Españas*. Jaén: Universidad de Jaén.
Ruiz Zapatero, G. 2003. 'Historiografía y "uso público" de los celtas en la España franquista', in F. Wulff and M. Álvarez (eds) *Antigüedad y franquismo (1936–1975)*: 217–240. Málaga: Centro de Ediciones de la Diputación de Málaga.
Ruiz Zapatero, G. 2004. 'Casas y tumbas. Explorando la desigualdad social en el Bronce Final y primera Edad del Hierro del NE de la Península Ibérica'. *Mainake* 26: 293–330.
Ruiz Zapatero, G. 2011. 'El caleidoscopio urbano en el mundo "céltico" de la Meseta'. *Complutum* 22, 2: 297–309.
Sande Lemos, F., G. Cruz, J. Fonte, and J. Valdez. 2011. 'Landscape in the late Iron Age of northwest Portugal', in T. Moore and X.-L. Armada (eds) *Atlantic Europe in the First Millennium BC: Crossing the Divide*: 187–204. Oxford: Oxford University Press.
Sanmartí, J. 2004. 'From local groups to early states: the development of complexity in protohistoric Catalonia'. *Pyrenae* 35, 1: 7–41.
Sanmartí, J. 2009. 'Colonial relations and social change in Iberia (seventh to third centuries BC)', in M. Dietler and C. López-Ruiz (eds) *Colonial Encounters in Ancient Iberia: Phoenicians, Greeks and Indigenous Relations*: 49–88. Chicago/London: University of Chicago Press.
Sanmartí, J. 2016. 'Long-term social change in Iron Age northern Iberia (ca. 700–200 BC)', in A. B. Knapp and P. van Dommelen (eds) *The Cambridge Prehistory of the Bronze and Iron Age Mediterranean*: 454–470. Cambridge: Cambridge University Press.
Sanmartí, J., and C. Belarte. 2001. 'Urbanización y desarrollo de estructuras estatales en la costa de Cataluña (siglos VII–III A.C.)', in L. Berrocal-Rangel and P. Gardes (eds) *Entre Celtas e Iberos: Las poblaciones protohistóricas de las Galias e Hispania*: 161–174. Madrid: Real Academia de la Historia/Casa de Velázquez.

Sanz Mínguez, C., and F. Romero Carnicero (eds). 2009. *El vino y el banquete en la Europa prerromana*. Valladolid: Centro de Estudios Vacceos Federico Wattenberg.

Sastre, I. 2008. 'Community, identity and conflict. Iron Age warfare in the Iberian northwest'. *Current Anthropology* 49, 6: 1021–1051.

Sastre, I. 2011. 'Social inequality during the Iron Age: Interpretation models', in T. Moore and X.-L. Armada (eds) *Atlantic Europe in the First Millennium BC: Crossing the Divide*: 264–284. Oxford: Oxford University Press.

Schattner, T. G. (ed.) 2003. 'Die lusitanisch-galläkischen Kriegerstatuen'. *Madrider Mitteilungen* 44: 1–307.

Torres Martínez, J. F. 2011. *El Cantábrico en la Edad del Hierro*. Madrid: Real Academia de la Historia.

Torres Martínez, J. F, M. Fernández Götz, A. Martínez-Velasco, D. Vacas-Madrid, and E. Rodríguez-Millán. 2016. 'From the Bronze Age to the Roman conquest: The oppidum of Monte Bernorio (northern Spain)'. *Proceedings of the Prehistoric Society* 82: 363–382.

Untermann, J. 1963. 'Estudio sobre las áreas lingüísticas pre-romanas de la península Ibérica'. *Archivo de Prehistoria Levantina* 10: 165–192.

Untermann, J. 1990. *Monumenta Linguarum Hispanicarum III: Die iberischen Inschriften aus Spanien*. Wiesbaden: Reichert.

Urbina, D. 2000. *La Segunda Edad del Hierro en el centro de la Península Ibérica: Un estudio de arqueología espacial en la Mesa de Ocaña (Toledo, España)*. British Archaeological Reports International Series 855. Oxford: Archaeopress.

Velaza, J. 2014. 'Antroponimia y lenguas prerromanas en las islas Baleares'. *Emerita* 82, 1: 51–67.

Vilaça, R. 1998. 'Hierarquização e conflito no Bronze Final da Beira Interior', in S. O. Jorge (ed.) *Existe uma Idade do Bronze Atlântico?*: 203–217. Lisbon: Instituto Português de Arqueologia.

Vilaça, R. 2013. 'O povoamento da Beira Interior durante o Bronze Final: evidências, interacção e simbolismos'. *Estudos Arqueológicos de Oeiras*, 20: 191–220.

Vilaça, R., and A. M. Arruda. 2004. 'Ao longo do Tejo, do Bronze ao Ferro'. *Conimbriga* 43: 11–45.

Vilanova y Piera, J. 1872. *Origen, naturaleza y antigüedad del hombre*. Madrid: Imprenta de la Compañía de Impresores y Libreros del Reino.

Vives-Ferrándiz, J. 2008. 'Negotiating colonial encounters: Hybrid practices and consumption in Eastern Iberia (8th–6th centuries BC)'. *Journal of Mediterranean Archaeology* 21, 2: 241–272.

Wattenberg, F. 1963. *Corpus Vasorum Hispanorum: Las cerámicas indígenas de Numancia*. Madrid: CSIC.

CHAPTER 11

THE NORTHERN ADRIATIC

RAFFAELE DE MARINIS AND BIBA TERŽAN

Introduction

This chapter covers an area extending from Liguria on the Mediterranean coast of north-west Italy, around the head of the Adriatic, to the western Balkans and the western Carpathian basin, taking in the southern part of the Alpine massif. Spanning high, mountainous terrain to low-lying river basins, the varied geography is mirrored in a cultural diversity expressed in both settlement patterns and ways of life. Throughout the Iron Age, this zone was a key interface between the Mediterranean world and the peoples of central Europe and beyond.

Aside from the Alps, the most striking geographical feature of northern Italy is the vast basin of the river Po, running broadly west to east towards the Adriatic, bounded to the south by the Apennines and to the north by the Alps, with some areas of low hills, as in Piedmont and the Veneto (Figure 11.1). The alluvial plain provides fertile soils, but frequent flooding and marshy conditions combined to make the lowest-lying areas difficult to inhabit until relatively recently; in some places alluviation has covered archaeological sites to a great depth. The Alpine area is marked by rivers cutting deep valleys that feed the Po, the Adriatic, and the Danube, and provide access to the rich mineral resources of the mountains and, via a handful of passes, to lands to the north. The river valleys and the large lakes found in some of them, such as Maggiore, Como, and Garda, were attractive areas for settlement from an early date.

To the east of the Adriatic, running south-east from the main Alpine massif, the Dinaric Alps dominate the western Balkans. The Adriatic coast is punctuated by numerous peninsulas and islands, while the hinterland from Slovenia to Bosnia is characterized by limestone plateaus (*poljes*), both environments being well suited to settlement. East of the Dinaric Alps, lower hills descend to the Danube basin. Several major rivers, including the Drava and the Sava, flow into the Danube, and there are again large lakes, led by Balaton and Neusiedl/Fertő.

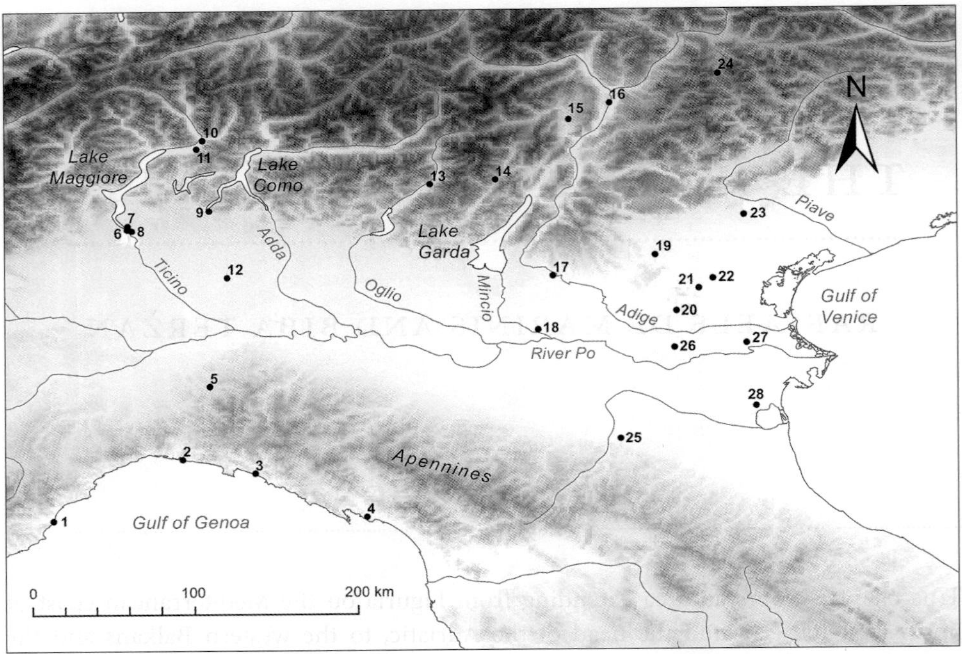

FIGURE 11.1 Map of northern Italy showing principal sites mentioned in the text. 1 Albenga, 2 Genoa, 3 Chiavari, 4 Ameglia, 5 Guardamonte, 6 Castelletto Ticino, 7 Sesto Calende, 8 Golasecca, 9 Como, 10 Arbedo, 11 Giubiasco, 12 Milan, 13 Breno (Valcamonica), 14 Roncone (Trentino), 15 Sanzeno, 16 Vadena, 17 Verona, 18 Castellazzo della Garolda, 19 Vicenza, 20 Este, 21 San Pietro-Montagnon (Abano Terme), 22 Padua, 23 Montebelluna (Treviso), 24 Altino, 25 Bologna, 26 Frattesina, 27 Adria, 28 Spina.

Drawing: R. Salisbury for author

The evolution of Iron Age groups was neither uniform nor contemporaneous throughout this area, so a regional approach is adopted here, working broadly from west to east. Iron itself came into wider use in the ninth and eighth centuries BC (Teržan and Črešnar 2014: 706–713). At the other end of the period, Roman domination was established only gradually; the process started in the third century BC, but much of our region was only absorbed into the Empire during the reign of Augustus.

The Bronze Age Background in Northern Italy

The late Bronze Age in Italy was characterized by groups inhabiting large territories, among them the Terramare culture in the Po valley. While there was a tendency over time towards aggregation, with the rise of larger sites, the settlement pattern essentially remained dispersed. Cemeteries such as Olmo di Nogara (Verona) imply a society dominated by a warrior aristocracy who exercised power in various fields: control of trade (amber, copper, tin, probably salt), territorial defence, metal hoarding, management of places of worship, and probably the distribution of land for agriculture and grazing. Olmo di Nogara provides no evidence for a more restricted elite at the very top of society: the burials of armed men (38% of adult males) do not exhibit signs of wealth differentiation, nor do the female burials containing grave goods (Salzani 2005; de Marinis 2010; Nicolis 2013).

The Bronze Age socio-economic system seemingly underwent a crisis shortly after 1200 BC. The Terramare settlements in the plains north and south of the Po were abandoned, as were the numerous pile-dwellings of Lake Garda and settlements in the Garda basin. It is doubtful that climate was the sole factor behind this crisis (Cremaschi 2009). In north-west Italy, there is continuity between the Canegrate culture and the Ascona (Protogolasecca) complex, although further east, more discontinuity in the archaeological record can be detected (de Marinis 2009).

The final Bronze Age—once considered a short period of transition, but now known to have lasted from the twelfth to tenth centuries BC—is closely linked to developments in the early Iron Age (Bietti Sestieri 2013). It was in the final Bronze Age that the regional archaeological cultures that went on to form the substrate of Italy's regional diversity first appeared. These were of more limited territorial extent than before, but displayed greater individuality—differences that would become more pronounced in the Iron Age.

The spread of the Terramare culture southwards into peninsular Italy may have played a role in the formation of Proto-Villanovan groups, but current evidence is insufficient to understand this phenomenon (Cardarelli 2009). In the northern Po plain, the abandonment of the pile-dwellings and Terramare sites was followed by a noticeable break in settlement patterns, structures, and material culture. The final Bronze Age saw large, relatively densely populated settlement areas emerge along some rivers, the best known being Frattesina on the Adria, a palaeochannel of the Po (Bietti Sestieri 1981, 1997, 2008; Scarfì 1984; Bellintani et al. 2009). Covering around 20 hectares, it contained specialized workshops for working bone, antler, bronze, Baltic amber, and notably glass, on a scale indicating that production was not solely for local consumption. Glassworking is attested by crucibles and ingot fragments; annular and barrel-shaped beads were produced, monochromatic (blue or red) or decorated with white or red threads. Frattesina displays trade links with the Proto-Villanovan Chiusi-Cetona group, the mid-Tyrrhenian area, central Europe, and the eastern Mediterranean. Ostrich eggs and elephant ivory were imported, the latter worked on site. Other imports included Late Mycenaean pottery and Proto-Geometric pottery manufactured in southern Italy. The Narde and Fondo Zanotto cemeteries have yielded more than 1,000 tombs (De Min 1982, 1986; Salzani and Colonna 2010; Nicolis 2013).

Etruscans and Romans

Developments in Etruria exercised a major influence in northern Italy during the Iron Age. Early in the final Bronze Age, southern Etruria and Latium were culturally unified, but we subsequently see a separation between the Proto-Villanovan Tolfa-Allumiere facies and the culture of *Latium Vetus*. Around 1000 BC, the Roma-Colli Albani group developed its own identity, reflected in grave goods characterized by numerous miniaturized objects. The grave goods let us infer the presence of prominent individuals with priestly and political-military functions (De Santis 2009, 2011). However, the population still lived in scattered villages, a pattern that persisted until the Iron Age (Fulminante 2014).

In Etruria, on the other hand, settlement numbers rose considerably in the final Bronze Age, with the formation of extensive 'districts' of up to twenty-five settlements, some of which, located on naturally defended plateaus, appear to have played a dominant role. At the end of the final Bronze Age, a further hierarchical process took place, the so-called Villanovan revolution: most of the hundreds of settlements of southern Etruria were abandoned and the population gathered into a few larger centres on the tuff plateaus, centres that extended over more than 100 ha, which would become the major Etruscan cities of Veii, Cerveteri, Tarquinia, Vulci, Bisenzio, and Orvieto (di Gennaro 1982, 1986; Bietti Sestieri 1997, 2008, 2013; Guidi 2000; Pacciarelli 2000; Barbaro 2010).

The Villanovan world experienced both rapid development and steady expansion, including through movements of colonization, as may be the case at Bologna (Etruscan Felsina), at the southern edge of the Po plain at the end of one of the principal routes across the Apennines to Tuscany. The Villanovans represent the most important cultural entity of protohistoric Italy, whose identification with the Etruscans can no longer be doubted; the culture is named after the cemetery 8km south-east of Bologna, which was excavated in the mid-nineteenth century. Villanovan communities were characterized by a strong political and territorial organization and a society firmly divided into classes. Analysis of eighth-century BC grave goods enables us to recognize the existence of a hegemonic social class, composed of aristocratic lineages (*gentes*), which reached its peak in the display of wealth accumulated in the tombs of the Orientalizing period that followed (Bartoloni 1989, 2003; Bietti Sestieri 2012). During the Iron Age, the urban aggregation of Bologna, with its famous surrounding cemeteries (Arnoaldi, Benacci, Certosa, San Vitale, Villanova), became one of the main centres of bronze metallurgy and trade in northern Italy.[1]

Further north, Frattesina and the other thriving centres of the lower Po plain were abandoned in the early ninth century BC, almost certainly due to unfavourable weather conditions: the increase in rainfall which marked the beginning of the Sub-Atlantic period must have caused widespread flooding and created a chaotic hydrographic situation at a time when the rivers had not yet been contained. Although the relationship between archaeological cultures and populations with a well-defined ethnic identity is complex and controversial, the extent to which the major protohistoric entities in existence at the time iron came into widespread use prefigure the main pre-Roman peoples of northern Italy is remarkable.[2] The chronological correlations between the various regional archaeological cultures are set out in Table 11.1.

The Etruscan cities reached the peak of their power and prosperity in the sixth century BC (Chapter 12), by which time the zone under Etruscan political and cultural domination extended as far as the Po delta, where the ports of Adria and Spina were established. Following the Gallic invasion of 388 BC, Padanian Etruria, as the area is known, became part of the La Tène cultural sphere in northern Italy (otherwise known as Cisalpine Gaul).[3] Roman conquests beyond the Apennines started in the early third century BC, with the seizure of the territory of the Gallic Senones, and the establishment of colonies at Sena Gallica and Rimini on the Adriatic coast. Following the battle of Telamon in 225 BC, the Po basin was subdued and Latin colonies were founded at Cremona and Piacenza, but many of the peoples north of the Po were not formally brought under Roman dominion until much later.

Liguria

The Ligurians appear for the first time from the seventh century BC. Brief mentions in Greek texts state that they were one of the peoples settled along the northern shores of the western Mediterranean between the Iberians, Celts, and Tyrrheni (Etruscans). The sources agree that the Greek colony of Massalia lay in Ligurian territory. In the Archaic period, Greek geographical knowledge was largely limited to coastal regions, and only with Roman historians and geographers (Polybius, Strabo, Livy, Pliny the Elder) do we gain any clear indication of the extent of Ligurian territory inland. As well as present-day Liguria and southern Piedmont (*regio IX Liguria* of Augustan Italy), their territory evidently included much of Provence up to the Rhône delta, the southern part of the western Alps, the Tuscan-Emilian Apennines, and Lunigiana and Garfagnana.

The Ligurians comprised several groups, whose *nomina* are recorded in the written sources (see Forni 1976), although they were variously labelled Ligurian, Celtic, and Gallic by different ancient authors.[4] The language they spoke is barely known, but almost certainly related to Celtic. The few reliable data include a Celtic name, Nemetios, on an inscription from Genoa written in the Etruscan alphabet and language (De Simone 1980). The only inscriptions from the Ligurian hinterland, at Busca and Mombasiglio, are Etruscan (Colonna 1998).[5]

The recent and final Bronze Age in Liguria saw a differentiation between the Canegrate culture north of the Po and a specifically Ligurian area south of the Po, the latter influenced by the Rhine-Switzerland-eastern France group of the Urnfield culture. Recently, the Pont-Valperga group has been defined, whose extent corresponds to the territory of the Taurini-Salassi in the Iron Age (Rubat Borel 2006). In early Iron Age Liguria, there is no trace of the proto-urban developments found elsewhere in northern Italy as early as the eighth century BC. The archaeological record is particularly patchy for the ninth and eighth centuries BC, but for the late eighth and the seventh centuries

Table 11.1 Chronological table for northern Italy

yrs BC	Hallstatt/La Tène	Golasecca	Este	Bologna	Etruria
	Hallstatt B1	Final Bronze Age 3	Final Bronze Age 3	?	Final Bronze Age 3
900					
	Hallstatt B3	Golasecca IA 1	Este I	Villanovan I	Villanovan I
800				II	IIA
	Hallstatt C1a	IA 2	II early	III A	IIB
				III B	IIC
	Hallstatt C1b	IB	II middle	III C/IV A	
700					
	Hallstatt C2	IC	II late	IV B1	Orientalizing
600		IIA	II–III	IV B2	
	Hallstatt D1				
		IIA-B	III early	IV C	
					Archaic
	Hallstatt D2	II B	III middle		
500					
	Hallstatt D3	IIIA 1		Certosa	
		IIIA 2	Este III late		
	La Tène A				
400					Classical
		IIIA 3			
	La Tène B1	La Tène B1		La Tène B1	
300					Hellenistic
	La Tène B2	La Tène B2	Este IV	La Tène B2	
					Roman conquest
	La Tène C1	La Tène C1		La Tène C1	
200					
				Roman conquest	
	La Tène C2	La Tène C2			
			Romanization		Late Republican
100	La Tène D1	La Tène D1			
	La Tène D2	La Tène D2			
			Augustan period		

Sources: Golasecca after R. C. de Marinis; Este after Frey (1969); Bologna after Carancini (1969), Dore (2005), and D. Vitali; Etruria/Villanovan after Toms (1986).

the Chiavari cemetery provides a firmer basis for reconstructing the cultural history of the region. The sixth century BC is again known only from a few scattered finds, whereas the fifth and fourth centuries find an important attestation in the cemetery and settlement of Genoa. Between the mid-fourth and early third century BC, the cemetery of Ameglia at the mouth of the river Magra is a key point of reference, although few tombs are yet published, but the rest of the third and second centuries are documented by a small number of cist graves (de Marinis 1988a: 248–259; de Marinis and Spadea 2004, 2006; Venturino Gambari and Gandolfi 2004).

Despite the gaps, ancient sources and archaeology agree that the story of the pre-Roman Ligurians shifts between two opposite poles, the mountains and the sea. The first revolves around the harsh conditions of life in an almost entirely mountainous terrain, with an inland side facing the Po valley and a maritime one sloping towards the sea with its often high and rugged coasts, a naturally tough and poor environment. Thanks to modern landscape archaeology, it has been possible to reconstruct the formation of the characteristic Ligurian landscape. The reduction of tree cover—a process that began in the Neolithic—produced depleted soils, intense colluviation, landslides, and mudslides. To counter this, slopes were terraced, creating one of the most unmistakable features of the Ligurian landscape. Terracing is attested from the Bronze Age thanks to the excavation of hillforts (*castellari*) such as Uscio (near Portofino), Camogli, Zignago, and Pignone.

The agro-silvo-pastoral system mentioned in the ancient sources was fully developed by the Bronze Age. It remained more or less intact until modern times, even if the land was probably impoverished, with a reduced carrying capacity due to excessive human pressure exerted on the fragile upland environment for thousands of years (Maggi 2004). Half a century ago, Emilio Sereni investigated this world through a careful analysis of the historical sources (Sereni 1955). In the period of the wars with Rome (the third and second centuries BC), Sereni recognized some Ligurian groups who had reached a more advanced stage of social organization and constituted stable territorial communities subject to a hegemonic *oppidum* (such as the Ingauni, Intemelii, Statielli, and Genuates), alongside others organized in confederations that lacked a main *oppidum* (the Apuani, Friniates, and Bagienni), or subdivided into small communities who lived scattered *per vicos et castella* (the tribes of the Alpine valleys). These forms of economic and social organization seem to have lasted for a long time, reflected in non-hierarchical settlement patterns, characterized by small dispersed nuclei and sparsely populated villages. This is also seen in the limited spread of writing in Iron Age Liguria, unique in northern Italy. The archaeological evidence thus to some extent supports the rural image of Liguria handed down by the written sources.[6]

The second long-term phenomenon is the maritime orientation of part of the territory and the Ligurians' relationship with the sea. For a long time, the only major site for the period between the start of the Iron Age and the end of the sixth century BC was the Chiavari cemetery (Paltineri 2010), but thanks to evidence from Genoa-Portofranco and Albenga, we can now advance a more detailed picture. The inhabitants both of the coastal region and of the hinterland were involved in Mediterranean trade and in networks linking the Mediterranean to early Iron Age central Europe. The concentration of sites around the Gulf of Genoa clearly indicates a gravitation of the Ligurian world towards the sea, and the creation of a series of ports where boats going along the coast to and from southern France could stop over. Ports such as Genoa and at the mouth of the Magra lay at the end of important inland routes. Exchange enriched the Ligurian world both materially and through a variety of cultural relations that transformed it. The influence of Greeks, Etruscans, and Phoenicians was suddenly and explosively grafted onto the existing agro-silvo-pastoral economy.

The evidence from Chiavari shows the complexity of the dynamics of interaction at these ports. Imports from north and south Etruria, and a multiplicity of objects from other cultural spheres, whether direct or mediated (Villanovan, Orientalizing, Hallstatt, Golasecca, Greek, and perhaps even Phoenician in the case of gold ear-rings), reveal the existence of a port of trade frequented primarily by the Etruscans of Pisa, but which also welcomed visitors from other directions and greater distances (Figure 11.2). From the late seventh century BC, a consistent flow of Etruscan wine amphorae and black *bucchero* vessels—notably the carinated handled cup (*kantharos*)—reached southern France, especially Languedoc. Other finds attest to Etruscan expansion into Versilia up to the mouth of the Magra. Of great importance are discoveries at Genoa-Portofranco, where Corinthian, Etruscan-Corinthian, and Ionian pottery, Etruscan amphorae, and *bucchero* from Pisa—all wares that pre-date the Etruscan foundation of Genoa—testify to the use of this natural port, an indispensable stopover for maritime traffic between Etruria and the south of France (Melli 2007). This process reached its peak in the late sixth century BC when the Etruscans established an emporium at Genoa, following an exceptional set of events that saw the foundation of Etruscan Pisa, Greek Massalia, and Adria and Spina in the Po delta.

The new emporium at Genoa took on a hegemonic role in relation to other Ligurian ports, and, from then on, constituted the principal access to the sea for the west-central Po valley. The finds from the cemetery and settlement indicate intense commercial activity both along maritime routes and overland towards the Po valley—the latter network reflected in finds from inland sites such as Guardamonte in the Apennines. The quantity of inscriptions at Genoa written in the Etruscan alphabet on vases reveals a strong Etruscan presence, but, like all great ports, in the fifth and fourth century BC it was a place where different cultures and traditions met: trade was accompanied by cultural exchange and acculturation (Colonna 2004; Melli 2004, 2007).

With the Gallic invasion of 388 BC and the collapse of Padanian Etruria, the cultural geography of northern Italy was altered. The Ligurians, like other populations, were heavily influenced by the La Tène culture introduced by the invaders, especially weaponry. Finds from settlements (particularly the *castellari*) and cemeteries such as Ameglia document the culture, economy, and territorial organization of the main Ligurian communities between the fourth and second centuries BC. Although influenced by the Gauls who settled in the Po valley, the Ligurians still maintained a strong awareness of their own identity, shown by the persistence of centuries-old cultural traditions of ornamentation and female costume. It was not by chance that these people strenuously

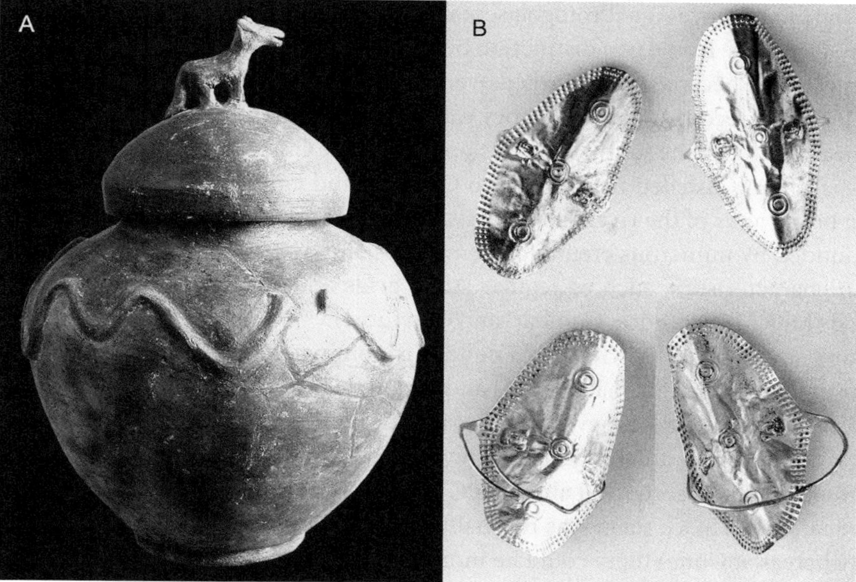

FIGURE 11.2 Chiavari cemetery, Genoa. (A) Urn with applied relief decoration and bowl over it for lid, with moulded animal, Grave 10. (B) Pair of Orientalizing gold ear-rings from Grave 61. Seventh century BC.

defended their independence from Rome in wars that lasted from 236–117 BC, but their gradual 'Romanization' is attested in the imposition of colonies, starting with Lucca and Luni in 177 BC, the construction of monumental buildings and roads, and land reorganization in lowland areas.

The Golasecca Culture

The Golasecca culture was the fundamental ethnocultural entity in eastern Piedmont, western Lombardy, Ticino, and the Mesolcina valley until the fourth century BC, when first La Tène and then Roman influence became increasingly apparent. Its territory stretched from the Alpine watershed to the river Po, and between the river Sesia to the west and the Serio to the east. The ancient sources mention the Orobii from Bergamo to Como, the Lepontii in Ticino, and the Insubres on the plains (Pliny *Natural History* 3.124, 3.134; Strabo *Geography* 4.6.8).[7] In this large area, the archaeological record enables us to follow the successive stages of what was effectively a single culture from the thirteenth century BC until the eve of the Roman period. The Golasseca culture and its chronology have been the subject of numerous studies (e.g. Pauli 1971; de Marinis 1981a, 2014; Schindler 1998; de Marinis and Biaggio 2000; de Marinis and Gambari 2005; de Marinis et al. 2009; see Table 11.1).

In the final Bronze Age (Protogolasecca), cultural aspects were relatively uniform, but at the start of the Iron Age a distinction between an eastern and a western area began to emerge, which became more marked over time. From the late ninth to mid-eighth century BC (Golasecca IA 2), the territory was organized around two proto-urban centres, one near Como, on the south-western slopes of Monte Croce, the second comprising the aggregation of Castelletto Ticino, Sesto Calende, and Golasecca (henceforth CTSCG) along both banks of the river Ticino at its exit from Lake Maggiore.[8] Both centres were surrounded by numerous cremation cemeteries and over time developed increasingly urban characteristics, such as regular street grids and drainage systems (de Marinis 1992; de Marinis et al. 2001; Gambari and Cerri 2011).

Our knowledge of the Golasecca culture is dominated by cemetery data. Funerary enclosures—circular for male burials and rectangular for female ones—were common at CTSCG in the eighth to seventh centuries BC, but absent at Como. The cemeteries at the two centres also differed in their grave goods. The *situla*-shaped urn was frequent in female graves at Como, but absent at CTSCG, where the urns of the first period were biconical. At CTSCG, there was normally a single accessory beaker, placed inside the urn, whereas at Como there could be more than one beaker, in a variety of shapes, and these were placed beside the urn. Footed rectangular bowls and cordoned-footed cups were typical of CTSCG but absent from Como, while bowls and cups with a cordoned rim, ladles made first of bronze and then of iron, and sheet-bronze dipper-cups are attested only at Como. The repertoire of impressed stamp and pattern-burnished decoration also differed between the two centres in Golasecca II.

The situation in the Alpine Ticino and the Mesolcina valley was different. After the Protogolasecca period, there follows a data vacuum spanning the whole of Golasecca I, perhaps due to the worsening climate of the early Sub-Atlantic. From the late seventh century BC (Golasecca IIA), the Alpine area was repopulated; cemeteries are known at Minusio, Gudo, Giubiasco, in the surroundings of Arbedo (Cerinasca, Molinazzo, Castione, Claro), and later also in the Leventina (Quinto, Dalpe Vidresco, Osco) and Mesolcina (Castaneda, Mesocco) valleys. At first, the funerary rite was cremation, as at Como and CTSCG, but burial soon became bi-ritual, and within a few generations inhumation was exclusively used. Along with distinctive large bronze belt plates and ear-rings with amber beads, both typical of female costume, grave goods include pottery that recalls traits of both Como and CTSCG.

The rise of the two large proto-urban centres was a consequence of structural changes in society, observable in the funerary record. Starting from the Protogolasecca period, cemetery burial was restricted to adults; burial of children and adolescents became an exception. In the final Bronze Age and at the beginning of the Iron Age (ninth to mid-eighth century BC), funerary equipment was modest and homogeneous, with only gender-based distinctions apparent: pins, serpentine fibulae, and, in some cases, weapons for men; simple arc, thickened bow, or ribbed fibulae, spindle whorls, and bobbins for women. Luxury and parade weapons did not become part of the grave inventory, although they were certainly in circulation: indeed, the three greaves from the twelfth-century BC Malpensa hoard are among the oldest and most finely decorated in Europe (de Marinis et al. 2009: 146–154, 673–680). Bronze hilted swords from Gattinara (Novara) and Prato Pagano di Bernate (Como) attest to the practice of deposition in water by hegemonic warrior elites. Compared to a relatively large number of tombs containing bronze spearheads, only three tombs with swords are known: Ca' Morta 292 (tenth century BC), Moncucco (late ninth to early eighth century BC; Figure 11.3), and Ca' Morta cava Ballerini (eighth century BC). In these tombs, the social role of the deceased as lord and chief rather than warrior is emphasized, their superiority expressed precisely through the privilege of being accompanied in the grave by a sword.

Around the mid-eighth century BC, we find the first tombs denoting the existence of individuals able to concentrate considerable economic and political power in their hands. Contacts with the Mediterranean world intensified, as demonstrated by imports, particularly from Etruria. Bologna was the centre from which this network radiated. The first signs of social stratification can be seen at Como, the tombs of Vigna di Mezzo and Ca' Morta being particularly important. Vigna di Mezzo, a male (probable) chariot burial (de Marinis 1988a, 2001), contained a sheet-bronze amphora, a knife, a pair of horse bits, and a two-pronged implement—perhaps used during sacrifices and banquets, or a sacred and power insignia, rather like the tridents found in Etruria, for instance in the Circolo del Tridente at Vetulonia, or the insignia of Etruscan magistrates in the fourth and third centuries BC. The Ca' Morta wagon burial (Bertolone 1957; Kossack 1957; Pare 1992) provides evidence of a warlord able to access prestige objects from the Etruscan world, but who retained local traditions more akin to the transalpine zone (the

FIGURE 11.3 Grave assemblage from Moncucco, Como, *c.*800 BC. The urn is decorated with false-cord impressions. The sword had been broken into six pieces and placed in the urn together with the burnt bones. Golasecca phase IA2.

composition of the drinking set, and the custom of cremation with a wagon). The inventory included a sheet-bronze amphora similar to the Veii-Gevelinghausen type, a Bologna-type bronze dipper-cup, a San Francesco-type socketed axe,[9] a knife with a serpentine blade, two ribbed sheet-bronze bowls from Vetulonia, one of them mounted on a cultic four-wheeled cauldron cart (*Kesselwagen*), a bronze hooked key, and a pair of iron horse bits derived from Thraco-Cimmerian models.

Other eighth- to early seventh-century BC finds attesting Como's connections with Bologna and Etruria include a fragment of a Villanovan belt plaque from Prestino and the boot-shaped pot from a tomb at Villa Giovio (de Marinis 1999a: figs 1–7). Later in the seventh century BC (Golasecca IC), rich funerary assemblages—characterized by a vehicle, weapons, and imports—no longer occur at Como, but are found in the CTSCG area. Among the grave goods at Castelletto Ticino was an elaborately decorated bronze basin depicting a line of winged sphinxes and lions, an Orientalizing import from Vetulonia (Figure 11.4; Brown 1960; de Marinis 1988a: figs 163–165). Other Etruscan imports include a *bucchero* ladle-cup (*kyathos*) decorated with Orientalizing animal friezes found at Sesto Calende, a *kylix* in light (*sottile*) *bucchero* at Golasecca, and a *situla* with crescent-shaped handle attachments, this last paralleled in Populonia, Marsiliana d'Albegna, and Orvieto, as well as in Hallstatt graves in Germany (Oberempt in Westphalia, Frankfurt-Stadtwald). It thus seems that the CTSCG centre played a leading role in the management of trade and relations with the Etruscan world, serving as an intermediary with central Europe.

During Golasecca IC, the first inscriptions appear on pottery and stone in the Golasecca area (but not at Como).[10] In Golasecca II, evidence of writing remains restricted to the CTSCG area, suggesting that the alphabet was introduced from Etruria via a more westerly route than Bologna, perhaps through Liguria. Pre-Roman inscriptions in the Golasecca area are conventionally referred to as Lepontic (Lejeune 1970, 1971; Gambari and Colonna 1986; de Marinis and Motta 1990–1991; Solinas 1994; Chapter 36), since the first examples were discovered in Ticino, the territory of the Lepontii. Modern scholars now see the Lepontic language as a Celtic dialect, which, thanks to this early epigraphic evidence, can be taken back at least as early as the seventh century BC.

The flourishing economy brought about by the trade with Etruria and regions beyond the Alps is reflected in the grave goods. The two later seventh-century BC warrior graves with two-wheeled chariots at Sesto Calende are emblematic. Both had rich grave goods including pairs of horse bits, horse trappings, a Kurd-type decorated bronze *situla*, a four-wheeled cauldron cart, bronze helmets, Etruscan bronze greaves, Hallstattian iron antennae daggers, iron spearheads, and abundant pottery (de Marinis 1975; de Marinis et al. 2009: 162–203). The second warrior grave is a true 'princely' tomb, exceptional for the Golasecca culture. It dates to a generation after the first, suggesting that these could be the burials of a father and son of a dynasty that exercised power in the proto-urban centre of CTSCG. Two of the chariot wheels have partly preserved metal components, their construction revealing Etruscan technologies transmitted to the west Hallstatt world via the Golasecca culture (cf. naves [hubs] of the Ins and Erkenbrechtsweiler

FIGURE 11.4 Orientalizing basin, probably imported from Vetulonia, and ribbed cist found in a grave discovered in 1884 at Motto Fontanile, Castelletto Ticino. The grave was covered by a stone mound or cairn 2.2 m high. Golasecca phase IC.

types, and wagons of types 4 and 5; Pare 1992: 72–74, 117). In contrast, the horse-gear recalls types found throughout the Hallstatt world, but known in Italy only in the CTSCG area. This diversity of influences not only illustrates the role of the Golasecca communities in trade between the Italian peninsula and central Europe, but also how local leaders took control of these exchanges, adopting the customs and ideologies of the aristocracies with whom they came into contact.

In the seventh century BC, about one third of tombs at both Como and CTSCG contained much more ceramic material than the norm. Another distinction was the use of bronze vases as funerary urns or as part of the grave goods, as well as the presence of imports from Etruria, and in some cases Este. During the sixth century BC signs of contact with the Etruscan world extended to innovations in local pottery production: the introduction of the slow potter's wheel, shiny black-surfaced pottery that seems to imitate *bucchero* (Figure 11.5; de Marinis et al. 2009: 162–203, figs 4–5; Gambari 2001: figs 19–20, pls 7–10), new forms such as stamnoid urns, and impressed stamp decorations from Bologna and northern Etruria.

The evidence for richly equipped male graves with weapons and insignia of power declines at this period, but it is not clear whether this is an accident of the archaeological record[11] or because the display of wealth, at least in funerary ritual, became a female prerogative, as occurred in the Venetic world. Here we should mention the Golasecca IIB tomb with a monumental stone cist at Sesto Calende (Mulini Bellaria). Although disturbed, it still contained rich grave goods, including a bronze *situla*, a tripod with human-shaped legs, and many amber pendants, beads, and fibulae (de Marinis et al. 2009: 431–454).

FIGURE 11.5 Pottery decorated with pattern/burnished designs, and pear-shaped urn from a grave discovered at Castelletto Ticino in 1876. Golasecca phase IIB.

After about 490 BC we see a series of changes that are largely due to the contacts with Padanian Etruria. Along with an increase in valuable imports, Etruscan cultural influence is apparent in many aspects of Golasecca IIIA, although there was continuity in ceramic production and dress accessories. In the fifth century BC, the Golasecca culture experienced an intense flourishing and vitality, demonstrated by the dense and widespread population distributed all over the territory (Primas 1970; de Marinis 1981b, 2007; de Marinis and Biaggio 2000). An exception was CTSCG, which declined suddenly, although discoveries at Sesto Calende (Mulini Bellaria-Via Marconi) indicate that the area was not totally abandoned. The settlement at Como especially benefited from this situation, undergoing a phase of expansion in the fifth century BC, seen also in Ticino, at cemeteries near Arbedo and in the Magadino plain, and in the Mesolcina valley at sites such as Mesocco, the last stopover before the San Bernardino pass, which gave access to the upper Rhine valley (Schmid-Sikimić 2002). The important settlement at Milan was also founded in Golasecca IIIA (Casini and Tizzoni 2014).

Technological advances in the fifth century BC include the introduction of the fast potter's wheel and other manufacturing techniques (selection of clay, modelling, firing). The use of thick coral-red paint was added to the traditional methods of slipping and graphite painting. New pottery types inspired by Etruscan-Padanian forms appeared, such as spouted flagons (replacing *situla*-shaped beakers), ring-footed bowls, and mortars. A remarkable quantity and variety of bronze vessels was imported from Bologna and southern Etruria via the centres of Padanian Etruria, including beaked flagons (*Schnabelkannen*), stamnoid *situlae*, basins, ladles (*kyathoi*), cordoned cists with two side handles, as well as examples of a strainer, a basket-shaped *situla* (*kalathos*), and a stool with small bronze feet. The greatest variety of types is found in the Como facies, but never the complete set of bronze vessels used for consumption of wine during banquets; stamnoid *situlae* were used as funerary urns and *Schnabelkannen* were also part of the funerary equipment (de Marinis 2008). Attic black- and red-figure pottery occurs in small quantities in graves, but more frequently in the settlement at Como.

The range of imports from Padanian and Tyrrhenian Etruria was undoubtedly more extensive than appears from just the grave goods—a good example being the Populonian coin found at Como (de Marinis 1988a: fig. 190)—but whether the associated behaviour patterns were also acquired along with the luxury goods related to the *symposium* is another matter. While this could have occurred in everyday life, it certainly did not happen in the realm of funerary ideology, which retained its own traditions.

In Golasecca IIIA, warrior tombs with swords reappeared. The Ca' Morta 'Helmet Tomb' is particularly important: along with an Etruscan stamnoid *situla* and two small bronze buckets, it contained an iron sword with a pseudo-anthropoid handle, three spearheads, and a Negau-type bronze helmet. Costume accessories, some made of silver and even gold, were of both male and female character. A woman may have been cremated on the funerary pyre along with the warrior. Other tombs with iron swords are known at Brembate Sotto, Gravellona Toce, Montecrestese, Cerinasca d'Arbedo, Castione Bergàmo, and Castaneda, perhaps a sign that power was now more widely spread than seems to have been the case at the turn of the seventh to sixth centuries BC, to judge from the two Sesto Calende warrior graves.

In sum, the archaeological evidence points to a Golasecca society with a stable territorial structure, where some aristocratic groups had gained a hegemonic social and economic position. Initially, the power of leaders appears to have been based on religious and ritual practices, such as offerings in water; later, involvement in a network of long-distance exchanges between the Etruscans and central Europe led to more pronounced social stratification and strengthened the role of the warrior aristocracy.

As in Liguria, the Gallic invasion and the ensuing collapse of Padanian Etruria and the trade of luxury goods had a major impact on the area. The ongoing process of urbanization stalled, and the direction of cultural evolution changed radically. A progressive Latènization can be detected, first in male and then in female burials (Stöckli 1975; de Marinis 1986; Rapi 2009). The extent of actual Gallic settlement remains a matter of debate, but acculturation clearly played a part, and the Golasecca area retained its own distinct identity. The region was an early adopter of coinage, an initial phase of copies of Greek coins giving way in the third century BC to silver coinages (the Padane drachm, imitating the light drachm of Massalia), issued by the Insubres of the Milan area and other peoples north of the Po from Liguria to the Veneto (e.g. Gorini 2014). From about 200 BC, a growth of Roman influence and imports (black glazed ware, bronze drinking services, coins) is apparent, for example in the cemeteries of the Ticino valley, such as Ornavasso (Piana Agostinetti 1999). But despite military incursions—notably in the wake of the Second Punic War, when the Romans defeated the Insubres at Como in 196 BC—the greater part of the old Golasecca region was not brought formally under Roman control until the first century BC.

The Central Alpine Region

In the heart of the Alpine region, the population was divided into many separate communities, whom the ancient writers called, in a broad sense, Raeti. Their territory included the Alpine sector of the Adige basin, coinciding with present-day Trentino-Alto Adige/South Tyrol. Although different periodizations exist, there is consensus that Luco, Meluno, and Fritzens-Sanzeno were stages in an uninterrupted evolution from the final Bronze Age to the Roman conquest, and the material expression of the Raetian peoples (see Lunz 1973, 1974; de Marinis 1988b; Metzger and Gleirscher 1992; Ciurletti and Marzatico 1999; Marzatico 2014). This continuity is apparent in pottery production—which, although it changed over the centuries, retained for a long time some distinctive features—and in the persistence of certain ritual traditions and a territorial organization lacking proto-urban phenomena.

For most of the Bronze Age, the Trentino belonged to a cultural sphere that had its epicentre in the Garda amphitheatre and the Po valley, exemplified by the pile-dwelling lake sites at Ledro and Fiavè. From the thirteenth century BC, a progressive separation, that lay at the root of later developments, is apparent in the Dos Gustinaci facies at Fiavè. The earliest phase of the Luco culture belongs to the final Bronze Age (Luco A, twelfth to tenth centuries BC); its most characteristic feature was a 'beaker' (actually a jug) with two lateral protuberances on the rim and a triangular spout, an elaborate form indicative of a specific identity, whose subsequent evolution defines the Luco B (ninth to eighth centuries BC) and Luco C or Meluno (seventh to early sixth centuries BC) phases. Late forms of Meluno-type beaker occur in the subsequent Fritzens-Sanzeno culture, which emerged in the mid-sixth century BC and lasted to the first century BC.

Luco A was a period of cultural uniformity over a very large territory including the lower Engadine and Alpenrheintal.[12] In Luco B, relationships were established with the Golasecca and Este cultures and especially with the Villanovans, as evidenced by types of razors, horse bits with a twisted mouthpiece, horse-shaped cheek-pieces, lozenge-shaped belt plaques and sheet-bronze *pyxides* from Vadena, and the Bambolo- and San Francesco-type axes from the Calliano hoard (de Marinis 1988b: figs 112–113; Lunz 1991; Dal Ri 1992; Gleirscher 1994). The Vadena cemetery typifies funerary practices at this period. Cremation was the exclusive rite, the ashes deposited in a pit or in a clay urn, with an upturned bowl placed over the burnt bones. Graves were covered with heaps of small stones and were arranged in family groups. Weapons and rich funerary equipment were absent; nor were there any burials with ceramic drinking sets referencing banquets. This absence of social differentiation, which persisted into subsequent periods, finds a correspondence in the lack of proto-urban centres and the existence of a territorial organization focused instead on cult places known as *Brandopferplätze*—sanctuaries where animals were sacrificed, burnt, and deposited with various objects (Gleirscher et al. 2002; Tecchiati 2002; Zemmer-Plank 2002; Steiner 2010).[13]

In Luco C—the period of the Meluno-type beaker—Raetian territory was influenced by the neighbouring Este and Santa Lucia di Tolmino cultures, and by eastern Hallstatt groups, as documented by pins with a multi-knobbed head, lunate and double-looped types of fibula, and cauldrons with cross-shaped handle attachments. The subsequent Fritzens-Sanzeno culture—named after two sites in North Tyrol and Trentino—is divided into three periods: A (mid-sixth to mid-fifth centuries BC), B (mid-fifth to mid-fourth centuries BC), and C (third to second centuries BC). Its most characteristic pottery form was the small S-profiled *omphalos* cup, whose evolution can be followed across this period, from undecorated specimens or ones with ring-and-dot ornament, through vessels with a flatter, S-shaped profile and decorated with stamped or combed vertical bands, to more recent forms with a distinct neck. Burials took the form of small pits with scattered cremated bones, and grave goods often show traces of intentional destruction, a feature shared with the *Brandopferplätze*.

The mid-sixth to fourth centuries BC represent the greatest cultural flowering of the Raetian populations. The Fritzens-Sanzeno culture showed a great capacity for expansion: its burial rites, dress accessories, and pottery styles are found over an area that also includes North and East Tyrol, the lower Engadine, and the western Veneto. Settlement spread from the valley bottoms to the narrower and lateral valleys (such as the Fiemme, Fassa, and Gardena valleys in the Dolomites). The typical house form is the *casa retica*, a two- or more storey building with several rooms, a stone foundation, and an angular entrance corridor (Castiglioni et al. 2014; Tecchiati and Rizzi 2014), and Sanzeno itself was a centre of iron artefact production for the Adige valley (de Marinis 2004: 78). Hilltop settlements controlled the central passes through the Alps (Dal Ri et al. 2010). Fibulae manufactured by central Alpine workshops (e.g. *Zweiknopffibeln* and Castellin di Fisterre types) are found in the Golasecca and Venetic areas, as well as at Santa Lucia di Tolmino and in the south-east Alps. Certosa-type VII-c fibulae, widespread from the mid-fifth to the end of the fourth century BC, probably also originated in the central Alps (Teržan 1976). Relations with Padanian Etruria must have been intense; the modest amount of Etruscan and Greek prestige objects, such as bronze *Schnabelkannen*, Attic pottery, and small coloured glass vases, found in the region is primarily a function of the burial rite, which did not provide for their deposition in graves.

The spread of writing is attested by growing use of inscriptions on tombstones or for dedications on votive bronze statuettes, *situla* handles and rims, and pottery. These were written in the so-called Sanzeno alphabet, an adaptation of the Etruscan alphabet to the needs of the local language. The Etruscan Negau helmet inspired a local production that evolved over time and spread throughout many parts of the Alpine region (Egg 1986). Use of the traditional burnt offering sites continued, alongside a new practice of depositing offerings near springs and at shrines. Votive bronze statuettes, inspired by Etruscan models, were locally produced, ranging from the warrior of Sanzeno and the so-called 'Mars von Gutenberg' (from Balzers, Liechtenstein), to simpler figures of male and female worshippers.

Large numbers of figurines have been found at Sanzeno. Typically, they were only modelled on the front, with a flat back; they depict horses, riders, 'Siamese twins', fish, scorpions, and anthropomorphs; some were inlaid with coral (Figure 11.6). Also mediated by Etruscan influence are the cut-out bronze sheets decorated with embossed points and studs (sometimes made from old belt plates or *situlae*) from the Campi Neri at Cles, Mechel, Fiè, and Sanzeno (de Marinis 1988b: 122–123, figs 116–121; Gleirscher 1994: figs 11–12). The situla art of the central Alps resembles that of contemporary examples in the south-eastern Alpine area, apart from the use of decorative motifs borrowed from Greek pottery, such as the friezes of alternating palmettes and buds linked by continuous wavy tendrils (de Marinis 1988b: 123–124; Egg 1992: figs 12–13, pls 6–7) and the absence of warrior parades.

The Gallic invasion of the Po valley did not directly affect the Alpine area, but La Tène influence nevertheless spread rapidly, seen especially on weapons and brooches. With the decline of relations with the Etruscan and Italic worlds, connections within the Alpine region—e.g. between the Adige and Ticino valleys—assumed greater importance, seen in the spread of typical Alpine artefacts, such as brooches with anthropomorphic masks (*Helmkopffibeln*), Alpine-type crested helmets, and iron axe-halberds.

The Camonica Valley

The Camonica valley, north of Brescia in eastern Lombardy, derives its name from the Camuni named in the ancient sources.[14] Between the fifth and first centuries BC, this and adjacent Alpine valleys were home to the Breno-Dos dell'Arca culture (de Marinis 1992, 1999b), named after a cemetery and hillfort (*castelliere*). Its most distinctive element was a one-handled beaker with an incurving wall on the handle side (*Henkeldellenbecher*), often decorated with stamped patterns. The funerary rite in the middle and late Iron Age was inhumation, but cremation spread after the Roman conquest in 16 BC. At Breno itself, we see continuity from a protohistoric cult site of *Brandopferplatz* type to a Roman sanctuary dedicated to Minerva (Rossi 2005).

The Breno-Dos dell'Arca culture is notable for its inscriptions on stone stelae, pottery, and especially on rocks bearing rock art of styles IV-3–5 (see later in this section). Written in an alphabet once termed 'of Sondrio', but now generally called Camunic, such inscriptions are known at Naquane, Foppe di Nadro, Paspardo, and many other places in the Camonica valley, as well as at Roncone in Trentino to the east (de Marinis 1999b; Solano 2012). Given the lack of a critical corpus of Camunic inscriptions (there are great difficulties in reading and transcription), the language is hard to classify and interpret, but is probably not Indo-European.

The Camonica and neighbouring Valtellina valleys are most famous for their rock art, which represents one of the largest groups in Europe (Anati 1975, 1979; Sansoni 1987; Fossati 1991; Sansoni and Gavaldo 1995; de Marinis and Fossati 2012). The engraved rock surfaces display a wide variety of themes, and cover a broad chronological range spanning the Mesolithic to the medieval periods, with many carvings thought to belong to the first millennium BC. The sheer abundance of engravings undoubtedly reflects the important mineral resources of the valley, which were exploited from at least the third

FIGURE 11.6 Bronze figurines of a horseman and of horses, with inscriptions in the local Rhaetic script, from the large votive deposit found at Sanzeno, Trentino. Fourth to third century BC.

millennium BC. The latest phase of exploitation at a copper mine at Campolungo, south of Bienno, at an altitude of 1,550 m, has been radiometrically dated to the eighth to fifth centuries BC (Cucini Tizzoni and Tizzoni 1999). Iron ores were also prospected and exploited in the first millennium BC, a tradition that has continued to the present day.

The petroglyphs were engraved on conglomerates and sandstones smoothed by the passage of Pleistocene glaciers; these *roches moutonnées* are frequent between 400 and 750 m above sea level on both sides of the Camonica valley around Capo di Ponte and in the Darfo Boario Terme area. Two groups can be distinguished according to technique: they are either incised (carved into the rock with a sharp tool to obtain a thin, shallow groove), or pecked (the surface hammered to obtain a continuous series of points, which form the contours of the figures and their interior patterning). There is no definition of the figurative space, nor any reference to the natural landscape and plant world. The figures appear to be randomly dispersed on the rock surface, and images often overlap, sometimes being so numerous as to form an inextricable tangle. Such palimpsests are valuable for reconstructing the succession of styles and constructing a chronology. The carvings include figurative and non-figurative representations—geometric patterns such as dotted and concentric circles, cup-marks, and five-pointed stars. The Camonica valley art is fundamentally schematic, only rarely resulting in naturalistic representations.

The transition from a symbolic to a narrative-descriptive art took place at the start of the Iron Age, in the ninth to eighth centuries BC (style IV-1), although the geometric linear style persisted. Thus, iconographic content changed before stylistic mode. The most frequent themes of style IV, to which most of the Camunian rock art belongs, are scenes of ritual duels, military parades, warriors with raised weapons, deer hunting, racing and dancing warriors, houses (sometimes isolated, sometimes linked to form villages), four-wheeled wagons, weapons, musical instruments, ploughing and agriculture, images of deities (e.g. Cernunnos), and topographical representations or 'maps'. There are also figures of symbolic meaning, such as paddles (*palette*), the so-called Camunian rose, cup-marks, and footprints. In the fifth century BC, a naturalistic figurative style (IV-3) made its appearance, different elements of human and animal figures being organically represented by fluid and continuous contour lines. This does not mean that it is a 'photographic' reproduction of reality; on the contrary, images were always stylized according to certain conventions. The later styles IV-4 and IV-5 saw a return to more schematic art, the mode of representation becoming ever more stylized.

Figures of warriors and deer played a central role in Camunian rock art (Figure 11.7; de Marinis 1988b). However, while the warrior figure is the dominant theme, scenes where armed men are engaged in actual fighting are uncommon—a warrior art that rarely depicts 'war'. Warriors equipped with heavy weapons are most often depicted with their arms raised in exultation, while in numerous duel scenes, opponents fight using light weapons, as if in a sporting competition, their armament comprising a stick or small sword and what is probably a small leather bag to protect the arm. Fighters and referees are depicted close together, the former smaller than the latter, from which we might infer that they were young individuals. Even the footprints and shoes with laces seem to belong to youths, being smaller in size than those of an adult. Such details lead us to think that Camunian rock art can be considered as votive images, incised on the occasion of initiation rites through which the youths of the local warrior aristocracy entered adult society. Another sign of social inequality is provided by petroglyphs depicting horsemen escorted by squires, as on rock 27 at Foppe di Nadro and rocks 59 and 60 at Naquane. Some scenes seem to illustrate tests to which the young were subjected: duels, races and feats of acrobatic riding, armed racing, sword dances, and deer hunting were all probably conceived as actual initiation rites.

The Roman annexation of the valley interrupted the centuries-old engraving tradition. The local aristocracy, whose traditional (ritual or not) motifs had formed the iconographic heritage of rock engraving, lost their power in the face of the economic, cultural, and religious influence exerted by the new Roman settlements, such as *Civitas*

FIGURE 11.7 Mounted warriors with shield and spear engraved on the ice-polished surface of a rock at Naquane, in the Camonica valley. Style IV-2, probably about seventh century BC.

Drawing: Andrea Arcà

Camunnorum. Ancient local traditions, including the practice of engraving on rocks, were gradually abandoned.

The Veneti

The name of the Augustan *regio X, Venetia et Histria*, recalls the people who lived in north-eastern Italy from the Alps to the Po in previous centuries. The Veneti spoke a language of their own and adopted writing probably in the late seventh century BC, using an alphabet adapted from the Etruscans, and known from numerous short inscriptions on votive tablets and stelae. Long-term allies of Rome, they were drawn increasingly into the Roman sphere following the foundation in 181 BC of the *colonia* at Aquileia at the head of the Adriatic, but continued to speak their own language even after Latin became the official language.[15] According to Strabo (*Geography* 5.1.4), citing earlier authors, they were once noted breeders of racehorses, but the ancient sources otherwise provide little useful information about the pre-Roman Veneti.[16] They, too, minted silver coinage in the Padane tradition from the third century BC (Gorini 2014).

Based on their archaeological correlate, the Este culture, the territory of the Veneti corresponded closely to the modern Veneto, but excluding the Lessini mountains and the Asiago plateau and with the addition of part of the eastern Lombardy plain. Over time, the western border shifted progressively eastwards. In the final Bronze Age, the Casalmoro settlements along the Chiese river resembled those of the Veneto, but in the early Iron Age, settlements like Castellazzo della Garolda on the river Mincio seem to mark the western limit. More territory was lost following the penetration of the Etruscans in the sixth and fifth centuries BC along the axis of the Mincio, while after the Gallic invasion of 388 BC, the area up to the Adige was occupied by the Cenomani (de Marinis 1999c). The eastern border probably lay along the Livenza river, as Strabo says that 'Aquileia is located outside the borders of the Veneti' (*Geography* 5.1.8). Archaeological data would seem to confirm this, as it is here that the Este culture gives way to the Santa Lucia di Tolmino group in Friuli and western Slovenia (see next section, 'The Santa Lucia/Sv. Lucija and Notranjska groups').

The main aspects of the Este culture were revealed in the late nineteenth-century excavations of burials at the Villa Benvenuti and other locations around Este by Alessandro Prosdocimi and the Abbot Soranzo.[17] In a still fundamental overview published in *Notizie degli Scavi* in 1882, Prosdocimi divided the Este culture into four periods on the basis of the stratigraphy (frequent floodings of the river Adige had led to the formation of deposits thicker than 5 m) and the associations of artefact types from closed grave finds. Following cremation, the burnt remains were apparently carefully collected and probably washed, since charcoal and pyre debris are never found inside the urns. The dead were cremated on the funerary pyre fully clothed, since fibulae and ornaments show clear signs of burning. Intact artefacts could have been added as offerings by relatives of the dead at the time of burial.

Although cremation was by far the dominant funerary rite at Padua, Este, and other cemeteries, inhumation burials with the dead placed in a supine position also occur, but these never exceed 20% of the cases. The lack of grave goods, with a few exceptions, leads us to attribute these inhumations to lower-status individuals, perhaps kept in servile conditions. The oldest tombs were simple pits, sometimes lined with stones or calcareous tufa slabs, where the urn and possibly other pottery vessels were placed, together with the pyre debris. Cist graves lined with volcanic trachyte slabs appeared by the eighth century BC. Surrounded by the pyre debris, they took on a more regular shape over time, with accurately worked interlocking slabs. In the sixth century BC, alongside the cist tombs spread the use of large storage vessels (*dolia*) with smooth or cordoned walls, which served as containers for the funerary urn and other vessels and grave goods.

At Este, groups of tombs were located within enclosures constructed from vertically placed limestone slabs, very likely linked to individual households or lineages; groups of enclosures were in turn bordered by low drystone walls that delimited the burial areas. Burials could be single or contain several urns relating to different depositions. Excavations at the Casa di Ricovero cemetery, Este, have shown that cist tombs were reopened to place new deposits of bone; this has allowed the development of the funerary structures to be documented (Bianchin Citton et al. 1998). Arranged in small groups, the oldest pit-graves were covered by modest mounds delimited by small blocks of trachyte. Around 600 BC, mounds delimited by standing limestone slabs making a sort of monumental entrance were built. In the fifth century BC, a large pear-shaped mound was constructed, with two cist tombs in the centre and a third one in a peripheral position. The area was encircled by trachyte pillars. The last phase includes the great third-century BC tomb of Nerka (Chieco Bianchi 1987). All members of the Este community were buried in the cemeteries, regardless of age. Individuals up to 6 years of age were widely represented, with percentages which approach those of populations predating the introduction of the smallpox vaccine. In this aspect, the Este culture is linked to the preceding Bronze Age, and resembles the Villanovan culture, but differs from Golasecca.

Although the subject of great debate over the years, Prosdocimi's sequence has to a large extent stood the test of time, although it has been subdivided in different ways by various scholars, with adjustments to the absolute dating based on correlations with other cultural sequences and the presence of Greek pottery (e.g. Müller-Karpe 1959; Fogolari and Frey 1965; Frey 1969; Ridgeway 1979). Pottery provides the main tool for chronological seriation. During Este I (ninth century BC), ceramics are nearly indistinguishable from those of the final Bronze Age. In Este II (eighth to seventh centuries BC), ceramics include biconical and *situla*-shaped urns, high-footed cups, bowls, small cups with upraised handles, and boot-shaped pots. Characteristic features were decoration with bronze studs, applied to the wet clay and arranged in geometric patterns, and engraved geometric and schematic figurative patterns, especially of horses. The surface could be shiny, graphite-black in colour, against which the golden-yellow bronze studs stood out. Este III (sixth to fourth centuries BC) pottery is typified mainly by a decoration of red and black bands separated by small horizontal plastic cordons. Stamped decoration with figurative or geometric patterns, tin strip decorations applied to the vessel surface, and pattern-burnished decoration also spread.

In the Venetic area, two large proto-urban centres, Este and Padua, emerged in the eighth century BC. The nearly rectangular settlement at Este lay on a north-west to south-east axis, around which the river Adige flowed, and covered at least 110 ha. Around it there were numerous cemeteries: those to the north-east contained at least 625 burials, with at least another 350 tombs in the burial areas to the south-west and south-east.[18] Padua too extended over approximately 110 ha, and was bordered by two possibly already fossil meanders of the river Brenta, which at that time flowed along the southern side of the settlement. A large funerary area, extending for some 550 m, lay to the north-east, with another to the south-west (Fogolari and Chieco Bianchi 1976; Ruta

Serafini 1990; De Min et al. 2005); so far, nearly 1,000 graves have been excavated.[19] The burials, grouped into low subcircular mounds up to 1m high, bordered by a wooden fence, consisted of wooden cists surrounded by pyre debris, or from the early sixth century BC were dolium burials, as at Este. A stone or wooden funerary marker was placed on the tomb, but individuals of importance received a funerary stela with figurative representations (such as a horseman with a helmet, shield, and spear) and an inscription, where the term *ekupetaris*—variously interpreted, but now understood as referring to social class and to correspond to the Latin *equites*—was frequently used (Marinetti and Prosdocimi 2005). Padua, however, differs from Este in some aspects of funerary rite and especially ceramics. The pottery is characterized by a preference for pattern-burnished decoration and plastic figurative relief decoration, and certain vessel shapes, such as the chalice, are typical of Padua. In addition, Greek imports, which occur in the settlement, are absent from graves. Other large Este settlements with their attendant cremation cemeteries are known at Vicenza and Oppeano, near Verona.

Tomb construction and grave goods attest to the economic and social development of the region, as far as this can be inferred from the funerary record. In the ninth century BC (Este I), an 'egalitarianism' prevailed, albeit with gender distinctions expressed by pins, serpentine fibulae, and weapons for men and by thickened arc fibulae, spindle whorls, and bobbins for women. In the eighth century BC, a clear differentiation became evident between high-ranked individuals, who displayed their status through the quantity and quality of their grave goods, and more modest tombs with simpler equipment. In addition, burials of couples appeared. Ricovero Tomb 236 at Este is emblematic: a double burial, in which the man's ashes were placed in a bronze urn, along with a broken sword, an axe, burnt bronze vessels, and many other objects, including carpentry tools placed in the bottom of the cist. A similar artisan identity occurs in a rich tomb from Padua (via Umberto 1, tomb 318), which dates to some decades later.

In the seventh century BC, the diversification in burial equipment increased, with three levels now apparent: rich tombs belonging to the higher social class, an intermediate group, and tombs with simple grave goods. Weapons disappeared from male burials: social dominance was no longer indicated by the warrior identity, but instead was expressed through wealth displayed in female burials, such Benvenuti tomb 122 at Este, or the slightly later tomb 126 with its famous decorated bronze *situla*. In the sixth and fifth centuries BC, grave goods conspicuous for their quantity and quality became frequent (ceramic drinking sets, bronze vases, ornaments), but overall the trend for displaying wealth in burials seems to decrease. Only a few graves at Este, mainly in the southern necropolis, contained Attic pottery.

Tombs of Este IV (mid-fourth to second century BC) are still poorly studied, and opinions diverge on the chronological boundary between late Este III and Este IV. La Tène influence is now attested, mainly by fibulae and swords. Ricovero tomb 23, attributed to Nerka Trostaia from two inscribed bronze vessels in the grave, stands out for its abundance of Volterran black-glazed pottery and other prestige objects: a Gnathia-type *skyphos*, Italic bronze vases, sheet-gold pendants, silver fibulae coated in gold leaf, miniature models of hearth furniture, and a sheet-bronze model of a couch, whose headboard depicts four horses chased by a wolf, dating to the early third century BC (Chieco Bianchi 1987). In cemeteries such as Zevio or Isola Rizza in the Gallic area on the west bank of the Adige south-east of Verona, many second- and first-century BC burials include coins, mostly Roman but including some Padanian drachms (Biondani 2014).

Along with Bologna and the central and south-eastern Alps, the Este region was at the heart of the extensive zone where situla art flourished during the early Iron Age (Lucke and Frey 1962; Frey 1969; Chapter 8; Chapter 43). Situla art—a term that encompasses all decorated sheet-bronze artefacts—rendered obsolete schematic art imbued with religious symbols, such as the so-called solar boat and waterfowl typical of the Urnfield period. In its stead, a figurative language and descriptive-narrative discourse were adopted under the impetus of eastern Mediterranean influence assimilated through the mediation of Bologna's Etruscans (Colonna 1980). Different cultural environments reacted differently to these influences, giving rise to artistic workshops each with their own characteristics. The Este workshops produced figurative, but mostly ornamental works, which rarely resulted in narrative representations; the most famous of these is the Benvenuti *situla*. Products included lids, *situlae*, dagger sheaths, belt buckles and plaques, and votive plaques that were deposited as offerings in sanctuaries. Among the earliest works are the lids ornamented with friezes of animals interspersed with vegetal motifs, which circulated widely, being found at Grandate (near Como), Sesto Calende, Scuol in Engadine, Numana in the Piceno, Santa Lucia, Stična, and Hallstatt. More recent products circulated over a smaller area, with finds of *situlae* outside the Veneto being restricted mainly to Bologna, Spina, Nesactium, and Slovenia. Etruscan influences on these objects, besides engraving and repoussé techniques, included the repertoire of ornamental and figurative elements. Palmettes, intertwined vegetal motifs, and rosettes are all elements that derive from Proto-Corinthian and Orientalizing pottery, as well as many figures of the animal repertoire, including lions, centaurs, griffins, and winged sphinxes. The local element can be recognized especially in weaponry and clothing, which retained their traditional character.

Numerous cult places are known in the Veneto (Dämmer 1986; Capuis 1993: 237–264; Ruta Serafini 2002). Around the settlement of Este lay four suburban sanctuaries: Caldevigo, Scolo di Lozzo, Morlungo, and Meggiaro, while about 2 km to the south-east was the important extra-urban sanctuary of Baratella. Other sanctuaries include Altino (Trentino), San Pietro Montagnon near Abano Terme, Vicenza, and at Lagole Calalzo and Monte Calvario di Auronzo in the Cadore valley in the Alps. All these sanctuaries have yielded figured bronze plaques (Figure 11.8)—sometimes bearing votive inscriptions, as for example at Altino and Baratella—bronze statuettes, bronze and iron artefacts, sheet-bronze miniature objects, pottery, and burnt animal bones (especially pig, ovicaprids, and cattle). There were shrines for the deposition of offerings and burnt animal sacrifices. From the inscriptions, we learn that the deity of the Baratella sanctuary was female—Pora/Reitia—to whom is attributed the epithet 'goddess of healing'. At Altino the deity was male—Altno—whose name can be recognized in that of the town.

FIGURE 11.8 Bronze disc depicting a priestess or kleidoukos (bearer of keys), from an unexplored sanctuary at Montebelluna, Treviso. Fourth to third century BC.

The Santa Lucia/Sv. Lucija and Notranjska Groups

Several cultural groups emerged along the northern Adriatic and its hinterland around the turn of the second to the first millennium BC, namely the Santa Lucia, Kras-Notranjska, Istrian, Iapodic, and Liburnian groups. Some of these exhibit recognizable ties with local Bronze Age communities, but Urnfield elements are more prominently represented. At the same time, these groups displayed contacts with the wider Mediterranean world from the Aegean to Italy. Although there are variations, the major developments occurred in more or less synchronous chronological phases (see Gabrovec and Čović 1987: 903, 905).

At the start of the Iron Age, the Posočje (Soča/Isonzo valley) and the eastern part of Friuli were inhabited by the Santa Lucia/Sv. Lucija group, while the Notranjska and Kras (Karst area) regions in western Slovenia were home to the Notranjska group (Gabrovec 1987a). Their most prominent sites are Santa Lucia/Most na Soči near Tolmin (Gabrovec and Svoljšak 1983; Teržan et al. 1984–1985; Marchesetti 1993; Svoljšak and Dular 2016), Tolmin (Svoljšak and Pogačnik 2001–2002; Teržan 2002) and Kobarid (Kruh 2014),

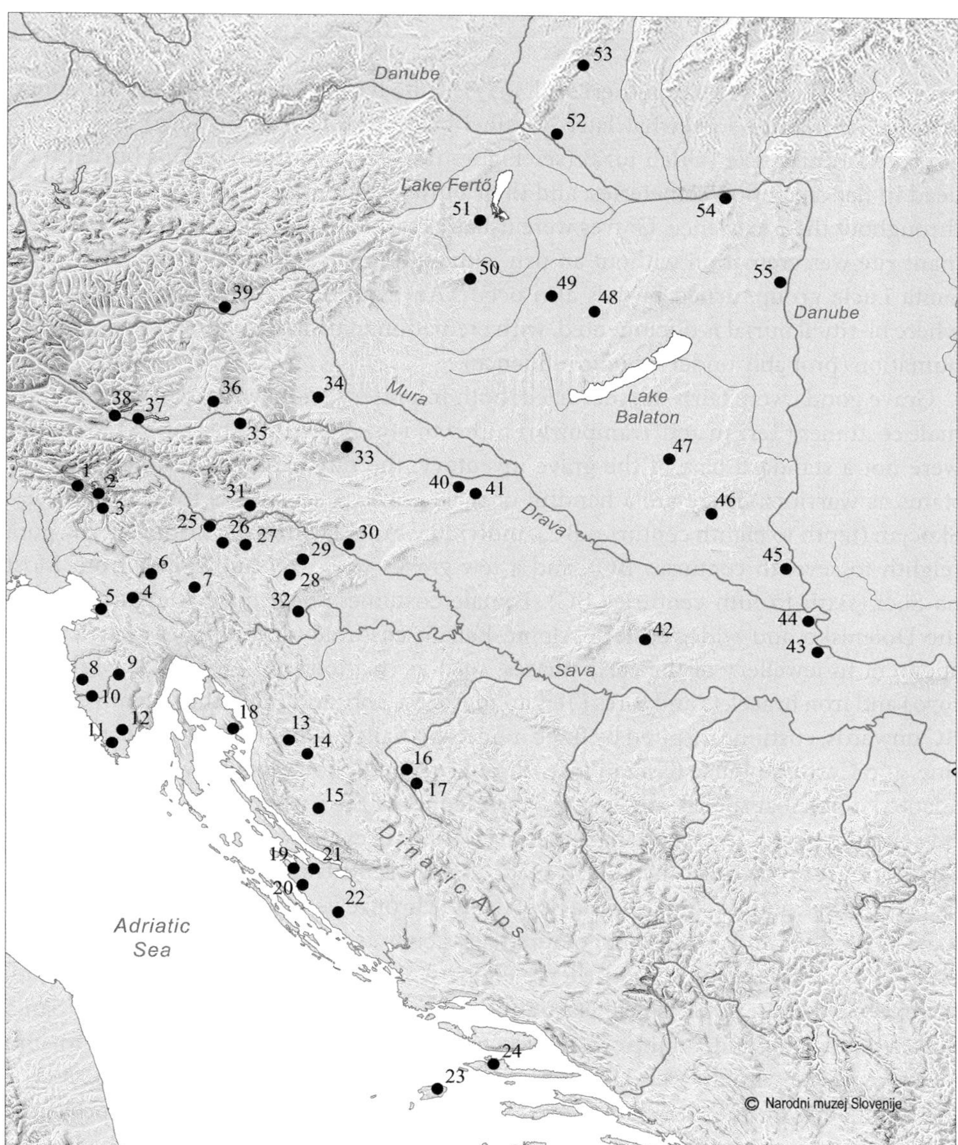

FIGURE 11.9 Map of the north-east Adriatic, western Balkans, south-east Alpine, and Pannonian regions showing sites mentioned in the text. 1 Kobarid, 2 Tolmin, 3 Most na Soči/Santa Lucia, 4 Brežec near Škocjan, 5 Santa Barbara near Muggia/Milje, 6 Šmihel, 7 Križna gora near Lož, 8 Picugi near Poreč, 9 Beram, 10 Limska gradina, 11 Pula, 12 Nesactium/Nezakcij, 13 Kompolje, 14 Prozor near Otočac, 15 Gospič-Lipe, 16 Jezerine, 17 Golubić, 18 Baška, 19 Nin, 20 Zadar, 21 Radovin, 22 Jagodnja Gornja, 23 Issa/Vis, 24 Pharos/Starigrad na Hvaru, 25 Ljubljana, 26 Magdalenska gora, 27 Stična, 28 Novo mesto, 29 Šmarjeta, 30 Libna, 31 Vače, 32 Podzemelj, 33 Poštela near Maribor, 34 Kleinklein, 35 Katharinenkogel and Tscherberg/Čergoviče near Bleiburg/Pliberk, 36 Lamprechtskogel-Waisenberg and Führholz near Mittertrixen, 37 Frög/Breg, 38 Villach/Beljak, 39 Strettweg, 40 Martijanec, 41 Jalžabet, 42 Kaptol near Slavonska Požega, 43 Vukovar, 44 Dalj, 45 Batina, 46 Pecs-Jakabhegy, 47 Nagyberki-Szalacska, 48 Somlohegy, 49 Saghegy, 50 Velem Szentvid, 51 Sopron-Varhely and Krautacker, 52 Velika Košariska, 53 Smolenice-Molpír, 54 Süttő, 55 Százhalombatta.

Drawing: Vesna Svetiličič, Narodni muzej Slovenije, for author

Brežec near Škocjan (Ruaro Loseri et al. 1977), Santa Barbara near Muggia (Montagnari Kokelj 1996), and—somewhat later—Šmihel below Nanos (Guštin 1979) and Križna gora at Cerknica lake (Urleb 1974) (see Figure 11.9, nos 1–7). Both groups buried their dead in flat cremation cemeteries, and their burial rite remained practically unaltered throughout their existence. Graves were usually marked with stone slabs. The predominant rite was cremation without an urn, although in later phases, particularly in the Santa Lucia group, urned burials also occur. An exception is Križna gora cemetery, where bi-ritual burial is documented, with cremation in urns and without urns, and inhumation (probably under Iapodic influence).

Grave goods were fairly standardized, both in pottery and jewellery of male and female costumes (Teržan and Trampuž 1973; Teržan 1992: 464–471, Abb. 9a–12). Weapons were not a standard part of the grave inventory; the rare exceptions indicate special status as warriors. There are a handful of male graves with swords from Brežec near Škocjan (tenth to eighth centuries BC), individual graves with spears from Križna gora (eighth to seventh centuries BC), and a few graves with axes and spears from Most na Soči (sixth to fifth centuries BC). Female costumes show many similarities with the Dolenjsko and wider eastern Alpine-Balkan costume type, which is particularly apparent in jewellery of the early phases, such as two-looped bow fibulae (Gabrovec 1970) and iron bracelets and torcs (Teržan 1995a: 97, Abb. 20). From the seventh century BC onwards, costume inspired by Italic models prevailed, notably types of boat, serpentine, and Certosa fibulae (Teržan 1976). These were not, however, imported, but locally adapted items that specifically marked the identity of the wearer as a member of a particular community (crescent-shaped fibulae, Santa Lucia bow fibulae, two-looped bow fibulae of Vače type, and others: Teržan 2002; Teržan and Trampuž 1973: figs 2.1, 4.1).

The prestige goods from Most na Soči include bronze vessels (buckets, *situlae, cistae*, jugs; Jereb 2016) and small multicoloured glass cups as well as imported Greek pottery (*skyphoi*) and some pieces of jewellery (Figure 11.10). These indicate, on the one hand, the existence of an upper social class and hence social stratification among the Santa Lucia community, and, on the other, lively trade links with the regions to the south and north, as well as with the west Hallstatt sphere (Frey 1971; Krause 2002: 503, Abb. 18).

Settlements of the Kras-Notranjska group were predominantly well-protected hillforts, with impressive defensive walls built in the drystone technique of the Bronze Age *castellieri* tradition. The settlements of the Santa Lucia group instead favoured naturally protected and strategically important locations: Most na Soči, for example, overlooks the canyon-like confluence of the Idrijca and the Soča. Excavations there revealed a proto-urban settlement layout, with a division between craft, trading, residential, and cult areas (Gabrovec and Svoljšak 1983: figs 1, 18, 19; Svoljšak 2001; Svoljšak and Dular 2016).

Based on the size of cemeteries and the grave goods, the Kras-Notranjska group prospered most in the eighth and seventh centuries, and again in the fourth and third centuries BC (Guštin 1979), whereas the Santa Lucia group reached its peak between the seventh and the fifth century BC—particularly Most na Soči, with over 7,000 graves found so far (Gabrovec and Svoljšak 1983; Teržan et al. 1984–1985; Marchesetti

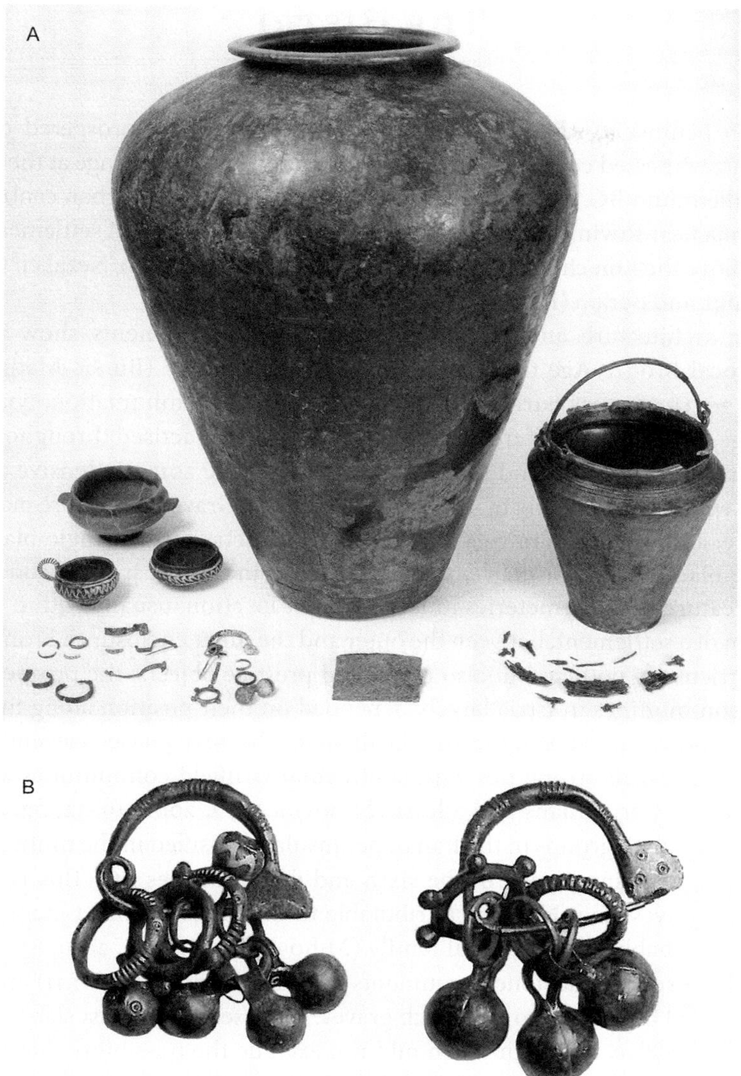

FIGURE 11.10 Santa Lucia/Most na Soči: (A) Grave with prestige goods such as a bronze urn and a bronze *situla*, an imported Greek cup, two glass cups, and dress accessories including fibulae, pendants, and a belt. (B) Bow fibulae of Santa Lucia type with pendants.

Source: Vitri 2004

1993)—after which it fell into decline. In the La Tène period, the population moved to the nearby hills, forming the Idrija group (Guštin 1991). This local population continued the Santa Lucia tradition, but also embraced influences of La Tène culture such as swords and brooches. Based on Roman sources, Jaroslav Šašel (1972) identifies them with the Ambisonti, while other authors suppose them to be the Celtic tribe of the Carni (Guštin 2011a).

The Histri

The Istrian peninsula, where the so-called Castellieri culture prospered during the Bronze Age, witnessed considerable demographic and cultural change at the end of the second millennium BC. This is visible both in abandoned proto-urban centres such as Monkodonja near Rovinj (Hänsel et al. 2007, 2015) and in the rise of settlements such as Gradina above the Lim channel (Mihovilić 1972), Pula, Nesactium/Nezakcij (Mihovilić 2001), Picugi, and Beram (Kučar 1979; Figure 11.9, nos 8–12).

In their architecture and structure, the Iron Age settlements show continuity with the local Bronze Age tradition of hillforts or *castellieri* (Buršić-Matijašić 2007; Mihovilić 2013), whereas burial ritual changed completely: inhumation, typical of the Bronze Age, was replaced by cremation, which was then practised throughout the first millennium BC (Gabrovec and Mihovilić 1987; Mihovilić 2013). Extensive cemeteries appeared, with burials usually in stone cists, with urns. Grave goods were mainly items of costume, and weapons are very rare (conical helmets, curved single-blade knives, and single-blade swords or *machairas*) and seem to indicate a special taboo (Cestnik 2009). A feature of the cemeteries in Istria is their location, usually within the defensive system of a settlement, between the outer and the inner enclosures. From the grave goods, particularly pottery, but also metal and prestige objects, the prosperity of the Iron Age communities in Istria largely depended on their position along the Adriatic sea routes and from the trading this facilitated. The first phase (eleventh to tenth centuries BC) reveals strong ties with continental Urnfield communities all the way to the northern Carpathians and Silesia (Mihovilić 1972, 2001: 49–52, fig. 43; Teržan 1996). Contacts with groups in the Italian peninsula intensified in the ninth and eighth centuries BC, reaching a peak in the sixth and fifth centuries BC. This is evidenced by very rich graves from Nezakcij attributable to the highest ranked members of the aristocracy, probably even the royal family (Mihovilić 1995, 1996, 2001: 83–105, pls 8–25, 2013). The exceptional stone monuments from Nezakcij (Figure 11.11) are probably best understood in relation to these rich graves: some seem to be cist slabs, and others to be funerary stelae, although we should not exclude the possibility that some were anthropomorphic statues based on Greek or Italic models, which adorned the sanctuary of a local female divinity or a *heroon* situated near the royal graves (Fischer 1984; Mihovilić 2001, 2013).

Material culture in Istria shows only faint La Tène influences, notably in fibulae (Guštin 1987; Mihovilić 2009). Greek and Hellenistic influences are far more prominent, probably a result of contacts with Adria and Spina in the Po delta (both ports were home to sizeable numbers of Greek traders as well as Etruscans, shown by the presence of graffiti in both languages), and with later colonies on the middle Adriatic coast such as Issa and Pharos (Mihovilić 2002). The Istrian group seemingly enjoyed a fairly high level of prosperity and existed without noticeable internal upheavals or changes, until 178/177 BC when its capital at Nesactium fell after a lengthy Roman siege. Following this,

FIGURE 11.11 Nesactium/Nezakcij: Stone statue of ithyphallic horseman and birth-giving woman breast-feeding a child.

Source: Mihovilić 2001

their last king, Epulon, committed suicide together with the members of the aristocracy, while in Rome the victory was celebrated by a triumph (Križman 1997: 220–229).

The Iapodes

Extending behind the high mountain ridge of Velebit is Lika, the core area of the Iapodes (Figure 11.9, nos 13–17). Some authors also attribute to the Iapodes the areas extending to the middle reaches of the Kolpa, on the one side, and to the upper Una, on the other; they may also have occasionally controlled parts of the Kvarner coast around Senj (Drechsler-Bižić 1987; Balen-Letunić 2006; Olujić 2007). The contribution of the pre-existing local tradition to the early phase of the Iapodic culture remains to be established, as Bronze Age settlement is poorly documented in this area. Burial practice was bi-ritual from the outset. Alongside typical urn graves (Kompolje, Gospić-Lipe, Jezerine, Golubić) and items of jewellery, particularly dress pins, which clearly reflect an Urnfield connection (Drechsler-Bižić 1961, 1987: Sl. 22; Marić 1968: Tab. 1, 19–29; Raunig 1968: Tab. 4, 29–30), were inhumations, which gradually prevailed. From the grave goods with these inhumations, particularly large bow fibulae with two discs, we infer

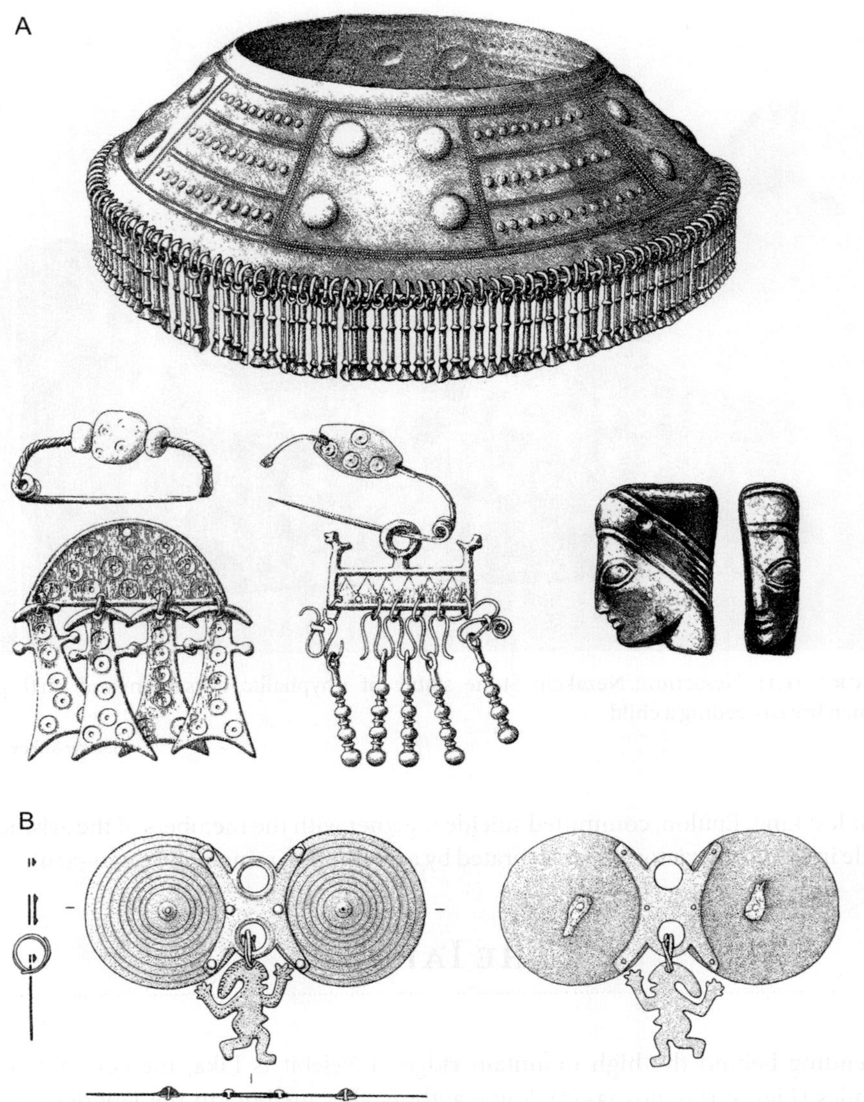

FIGURE 11.12 Examples of Iapodic jewellery: (A) Bronze female cap, fibulae with glass and amber beads on the bow and various pendants, and a female head in amber from Kompolje. (B) Spectacle fibula with a pendant in the form of a warrior figurine from Gračac.

Sources: Drechsler-Bižić 1987; Balen-Letunić 2007

an association with other Adriatic communities, primarily the Liburnian and southern Balkan groups (Teržan 1995b: Abb. 23–24, 2007: pl. 36, 2016: 233–237; Pabst 2009: Abb. 2–3, 5).

Iapodic cemeteries are generally large, with either flat or tumulus graves. They are usually close to the settlements, often at the foot of the settlement hill, as at Kompolje (Drechsler-Bižić 1961) or Prozor near Otočac (Drechsler-Bižić 1972–1973). Graves, primarily inhumations, yield relatively rich jewellery, including items made of amber (Figure 11.12) (Palavestra 1993: 68–109; Balen-Letunić 2006). This points to marked social stratification with a relatively large and rich upper class, and to trade links with distant lands, probably extending all the way to the Baltic (Todd et al. 1976: 321–322, table 2). That said, these components of the local costume, such as special parts of female bronze caps, fibulae with amber beads and various pendants, as well as special types of spectacle fibulae (Figure 11.12), were distinctive products specific to the Iapodic area (Lo Schiavo 1970: 503–513, maps 1–8; Tessmann 2001; Balen-Letunić 2006; Kukoč 2009; Teržan 2009, 2010; Pabst 2012). They also indicate a great measure of autarchy, underlined by the extremely rare imports. Despite the bi-ritual burial practice, placing weapons in graves was also taboo for the Iapodes; the very rare exceptions mostly date to the La Tène period. In general, La Tène influences are rather slight, seen primarily in items of costume such as brooches (Lo Schiavo 1970: maps 7–8; Tessmann 2001). This is rather surprising in view of Strabo's description of them as a mixed Illyrian and Celtic people (Šašel 1977; Šašel-Kos 2005: 424; Olujić 2007: 66).

Settlements fortified with stone walls predominate in the Iapodic area. Most occupy elevated locations at the edges of the karst *polje*, but a few exceptions lie in central positions on the plateau, as at Kompolje, Gradina on the hill of Veliki, and Mali Vital by Prozor. Individual settlements seem to have been located to facilitate intervisibility, which could mean that the whole territory of Lika was tied into a single communication network (Drechsler-Bižić 1975). An exceptional settlement type are the pile-dwelling sites in the Una valley. Given the relatively high altitude of the terrain, the mainstay of the economy was probably pastoral farming, primarily of ovicaprids, although the people must also have been engaged in commerce, probably bulk transport.

As in Istria, Iapodic culture persisted right up to their loss of independence in 35–33 BC, when their main centres (Monetium, Avendo, Arupium, and Metulum) fell one by one to the Roman conqueror Octavian (Šašel-Kos 2005; Olujić 2007).

The Liburni

The coastal part of northern Dalmatia, between the Zrmanja and Krka rivers, was the main territory of the Liburni, who also controlled the Adriatic islands from the Kvarner gulf to Corfu (Figure 11.9, nos 18–24; Batović 1965, 1987). Ancient sources report that they were driven off Corfu by the Greeks towards the end of the eighth century BC, and much later from the middle Dalmatian islands, probably when the Greek colonies on the islands of Vis, Hvar, and Korčula were being established in the fourth and third centuries BC, contemporary with the rise of the Illyrian kingdoms in middle and south Dalmatia.

In contrast to the Iapodic area, the formative phase of the Liburnian group shows pronounced ties with the local Bronze Age tradition. This is most clearly discernible in mortuary practice, with stone cist burials in tumuli, into which the dead were generally laid uncremated, in a crouched position (Batović 1965: Taf. 1). This practice continued throughout the entire first millennium BC.

Recently, urn graves that indicate Urnfield influence have been found in the Zadar area (tenth to eighth centuries BC), although these graves, too, are covered by tumuli following the local tradition (Kukoč 2010; Marijanović 2012). A few graves in large storage vessels (*pithoi*), primarily of children, occur in settlements (e.g. Nin)—a widespread phenomenon in the Mediterranean world. Grave goods—and some hoards (Baška, Jagodnja Gornja)—include rich sets of jewellery, which in later periods (i.e. from the fourth to first centuries BC) were made predominantly of silver (Batović 1965, 1974, 1987). These items reveal a lavish costume for Liburnian women (Figure 11.13),

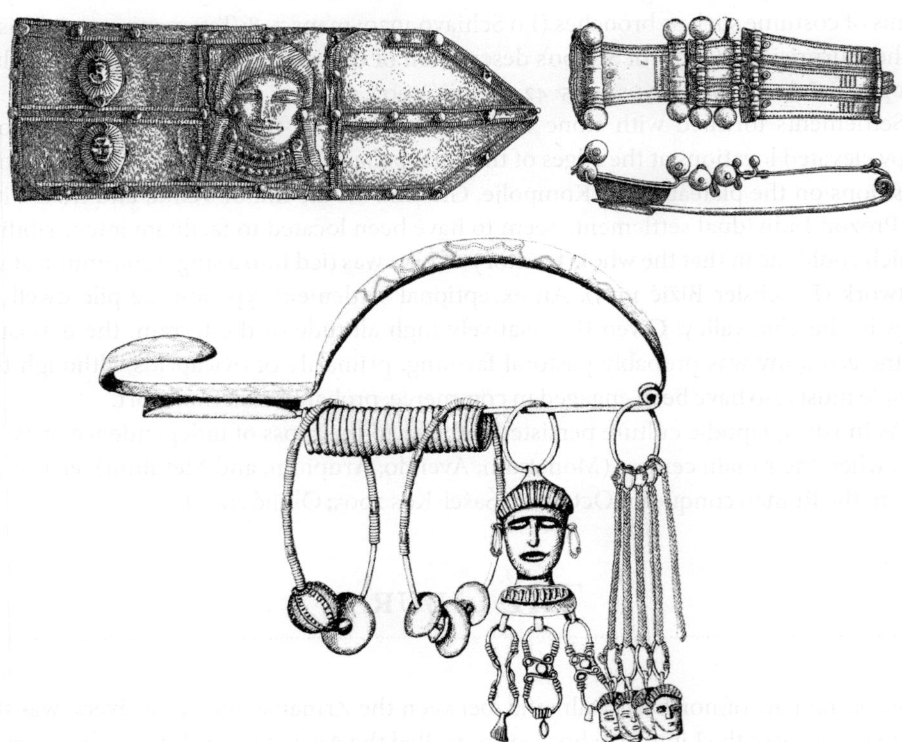

FIGURE 11.13 Liburnian silver jewellery: belt plate and plate fibula from Lisičić, Predgrađe-Asseria, and bow fibula with several pendants from Baška, island of Krk.

Source: Batović 1987

possibly tied to a special role or status in the community (Teržan 2013). The jewellery also indicates a dominant upper social class, as does the existence of a few warrior graves with weapons, primarily bronze swords (Batović 1968a, pl. 10). These warrior graves appeared over a very short time span in the ninth and the eighth centuries BC; the origins of the model can probably be sought in central or northern Italy (Picenum, Bologna, Este). However, like other north Adriatic groups, the Liburni did not generally include weapons in graves, a practice that persisted until the Roman conquest.

Impressive, well-defended hillforts that exercised visual control over the immediate and more distant surroundings were the main settlement type in Liburnia. Well-investigated examples, such as at Radovin (Batović 1968b), show a proto-urban layout with buildings of various functions in the interior, but mostly intended for storing large quantities of goods. This suggests large-scale trading, which may also be inferred from the coastal location of sites such as Nin and Zadar, both well protected and originally probably island settlements. In this context, we may also mention the relatively frequent finds of imported Apulian, south Italian, and Greek pottery on Liburnian sites; this not only supports the hypothesis of maritime trade links with other areas of the Mediterranean, but also the idea that the Liburnians acted as intermediaries for the lands in the Adriatic hinterland (Teržan 1995a: 130–134).

The Dolenjska Group

The south-east Alpine area and Transdanubia were host to various cultural groups that formed in the early part of the Iron Age. Apart from the Santa Lucia and Kras-Notranjska groups—discussed in an earlier section owing to their being more comparable with groups living along the northern Adriatic—the main groups of this region are the Dolenjska (Carniola) Hallstatt group (see Figure 11.9, nos 25–32), the east Alpine or Styrian-Pannonian (Štajerska/Steiermark-Transdanubia) group, and the Carinthian or Frög/Breg group. Their beginnings are somewhat later than those of the groups to the west, and date between the ninth and early eighth centuries BC. Their subsequent development shows numerous differences, particularly in their specific cultural characteristics.[20]

The Dolenjska group inhabited the Dolenjska and Bela krajina regions, extending to the Brežice Gate on the lower Sava valley on the one side and to the Gorjanci hills on the other (Gabrovec 1964–1965, 1966a, 1987b). This predominantly hilly terrain was densely populated, with numerous hilltop settlements that were usually well fortified either with stone walls of the Stična type or with earthen ramparts and palisades. Standing apart in size and fortifications is the best investigated Iron Age settlement in Slovenia, Cvinger above Vir near Stična, which was undoubtedly a key centre. This settlement was evidently conceived according to a plan, with its several-kilometre-long walls being constructed in a single campaign in the eighth century BC. This building feat clearly speaks of an act of colonization and marks the formative phase of the Dolenjska community (Gabrovec 1994). Several other sites were founded at the same period, in the late ninth or eighth century BC (Dular and Tecco-Hvala 2007). These settlements were inhabited practically throughout the whole time span of the Dolenjska group, to its end in the late fourth or early third century BC, when it was overthrown by Celtic incomers.

The main characteristics of the Dolenjska Hallstatt community include the specific form of their cemeteries and their burial rite. Unlike the flat cemeteries of the Dobova and Ljubljana groups of the Urnfield period—a tradition which was continued only partly and at the very beginning by the Dolenjska group—the cemeteries were now dominated by a new monument type, the tumulus (Gabrovec 1964–1965, 1966a, 1987b; Dular and Tecco-Hvala 2007: 123–130). The tumulus cemeteries were extensive and usually divided into clusters arranged around the fortified hilltop settlements, particularly along the main roads. They can consist of several dozen tumuli, sometimes over 100 (Stična, Šmarjeta, Novo mesto, Libna, Podzemelj). Each individual tumulus, generally containing numerous dead—several hundred at Stična (Gabrovec et al. 2006; Gabrovec and Teržan 2008) and Magdalenska gora (Tecco-Hvala et al. 2004)—represents the burial site of an extended family or clan. At first, some graves in the tumuli were cremations, but inhumation quickly prevailed throughout the area.

The internal structure of the tumuli was usually strictly standardized: the centre was occupied either by the founder of the family or clan, or left empty as a sort of cenotaph or memorial to a mythical ancestor. Subsequent graves were arranged concentrically and tangentially around the central part, generation after generation, often in several circles, serving to emphasize the importance and status of the first individual buried. The position and orientation of individual graves within tumuli not only followed the logic described earlier, but also depended on the celestial sphere and cardinal points. Judging from the orientation of the graves, the tumuli must originally have been divided into two halves—east and west, or north and south—around which individual graves ran clockwise or anti-clockwise. The position of a grave within a tumulus was also influenced by the sex, age, and status of the deceased. The tumuli thus reveal a community with a complex social structure, organized according to a dualistic principle. This is well illustrated by the large tumulus from Stična (Figure 11.14): buried on the east side of the tumulus, where the sun rises, are warrior-horsemen, with their retinue, as well as women of the highest rank, while the west side holds other burials, predominantly women of other categories and men of a lower social standing (Gabrovec and Teržan 2008).

The burial customs reveal the Dolenjska community as a society with a markedly military organization. Offensive weapons (swords, axes, spears, arrows) were mandatory in male burials, while the leading warrior-horsemen—i.e. the top of the military elite—were marked out by the provision of prestige armour in the form of cuirasses and helmets (Figure 11.15, A–B; Gabrovec 1962–1963; Egg 1986; Teržan 2008: figs 17–19, 31–37, 54–62) along with sacrificed horses and/or horse-gear. Typical sets of weapons suggest that the male part of the population in the late Hallstatt period (sixth to fourth century BC) had as many as six classes, five of which were ranks of warrior (Figure 11.15, C). This indicates a strictly military organization of society headed by a horseman-commander-prince-king (Teržan 1985; Gabrovec and Teržan 2008). A reflection of this organization

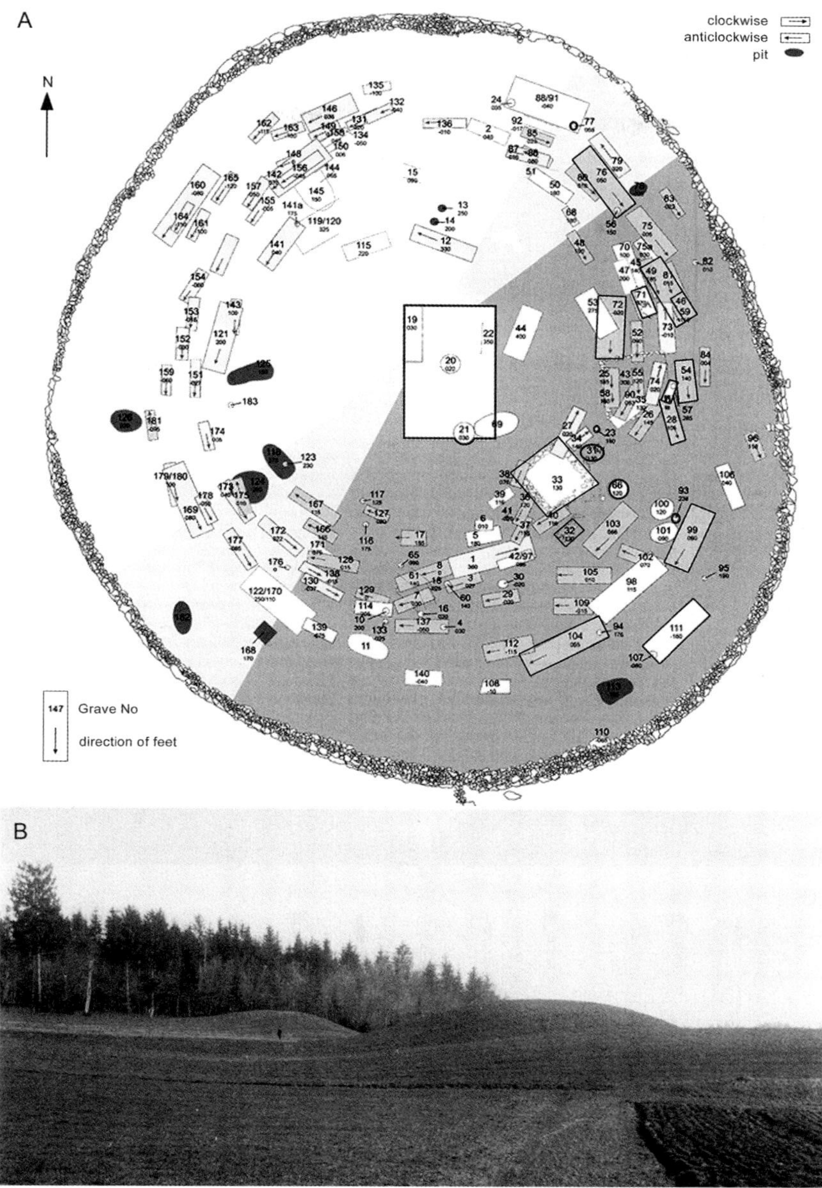

FIGURE 11.14 Stična: (A) Plan of tumulus 48, showing the orientation of the graves: clockwise in the eastern part of the tumulus and anti-clockwise in the western part. The graves outlined in black, mainly in the eastern part of the tumulus, also contained sacrificed horses, parts of horses, or just horse-gear. (B) View of the tumuli at the beginning of the twentieth century.

Sources: Gabrovec et al. 2006; Gabrovec and Teržan 2008

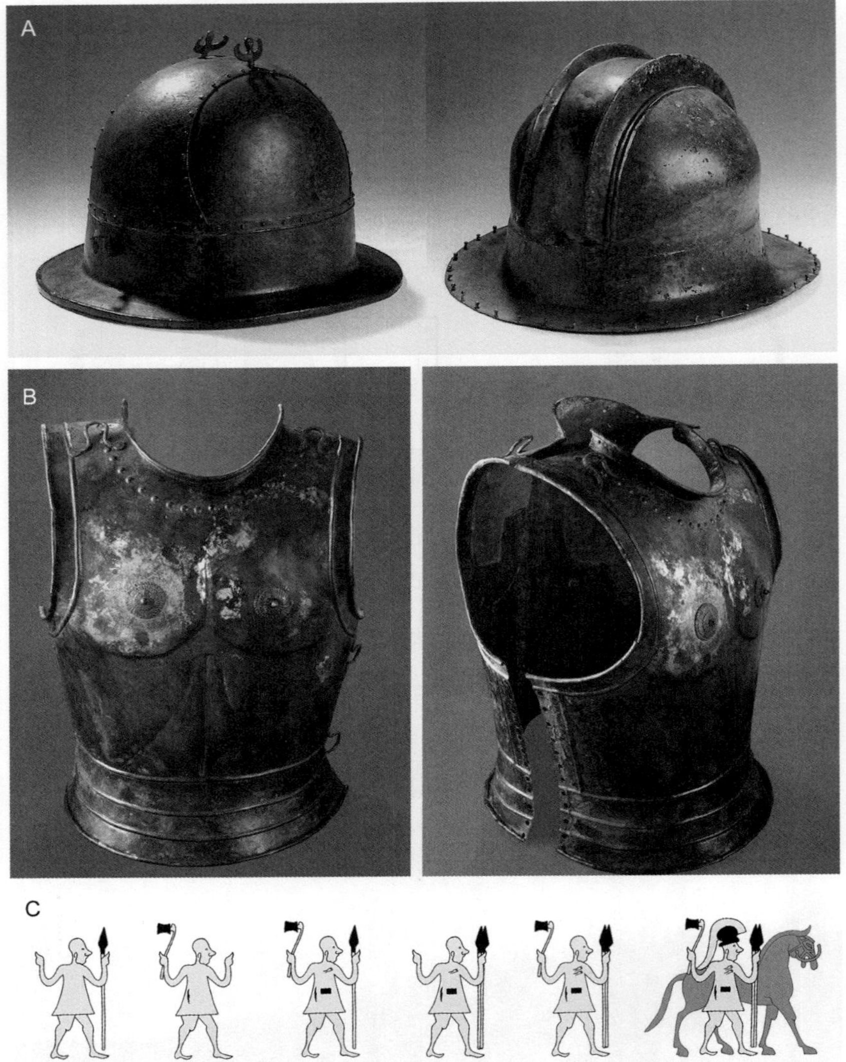

FIGURE 11.15 (A) Helmets from Vače and (B) Cuirass from Stična-Vrhpolje, representing prestige armour of the Dolenjska and Styrian-Pannonian warrior elites. (C) Schematic representation of five warrior ranks with typical sets of weapons in the Dolenjska group.

Various sources

can be observed in the iconography of situla art, which represents the most typical figural imagery as decoration on bronze items, especially ritual bronze vessels, in the region of the Dolenjska group (Lucke and Frey 1962; Teržan 1997, 2011a; Jereb 2016).

The main source of prosperity of the Dolenjska group lay in ironworking, enabled by easy access to surface sources of iron ore. Exploitation of other minerals (copper, lead, etc.) can be inferred from the extremely rich array of glass jewellery (Matthäus and Braun 1983; Dobiat et al. 1987; Kunter 1987). Animal husbandry must have been important, particularly cattle farming (Bökönyi 1994; Bartosiewicz 1996, 1999; Dular and Tecco-Hvala 2007: 204–212). The group probably also served as middlemen for (race) horses between Pannonia and northern Italy (Bökönyi 1968; Teržan 1995a, 2011a), and as traders of wine (Apulian pottery) and possibly other products of various origins.

The group died out at the end of the fourth or the start of the third century BC. Newcomers of Celtic origin appeared, occupying previously uninhabited parts of the lowlands, for example the Krško plain (Brežice, Veliko Mraševo, Dobova, and others) as well as old Hallstatt sites such as those in Novo mesto and near Mokronog. This latter site gave its name to the La Tène population in Dolenjska—the Mokronog group (Gabrovec 1966b; Guštin 1984). To date, the group is primarily known from mortuary evidence, and settlement finds are limited. The cemeteries are mostly small, with flat cremation burials, some in urns, but devoid of any grave constructions. The only exception is the flat burial ground of Novo mesto, which extends alongside the Hallstatt tumuli and has yielded over 700 La Tène graves so far (Križ 2006). Noteworthy is the relatively high number of graves with typical La Tène weapons, usually ritually destroyed by fire and bent before being laid into graves. The weapons consist primarily of swords, spears, and shields, but also iron helmets. It seems that the Celtic tribes in Dolenjska, supposed to be the Taurisci, had an enormous military potential in the middle and late La Tène periods (Guštin 2011b). The concentration of warrior graves of first-century BC date at and near Novo mesto (Verdun, Mihovo, Bela cerkev) has even fuelled the suggestion that some inhabitants of Dolenjska or newcomers like the Latobici (Petru 1971) served as auxiliaries in the Roman army and perhaps participated in the conquest of Pannonia.

The Styrian-Pannonian Group

The Styrian-Pannonian cultural group is a characteristic representative of the east Hallstatt sphere (Figure 11.9, nos 33–55); see also Chapter 8). As the name reveals,[21] the group extends across Styria (in Slovenia and Austria) from the Savinja valley in the south to the Mura basin in the north, and from the Koralpe mountains in the west to Pannonia and the river Danube (in Hungary) in the east. In Pannonia, the group borders on other communities belonging to the same cultural phenomenon (see later in this section), but who are given various names by local researchers because of different political and historical backgrounds (Teržan 1990). Alongside Strettweg (Schmid 1934; Egg 1996), one of the most important sites of the entire Styrian-Pannonian group is the famous archaeological complex of Kleinklein,[22] both investigated in the nineteenth century. Here, the hilltop settlement on the Burgstallkogel was surrounded by vast tumulus cemeteries (Dobiat 1990, 1980) extending all the way down to the eponymous village in the Sulm/Solba valley. Excavations of other large tumuli at Martijanec and Jalžabet in the Podravina region and at Kaptol near Slavonska Požega have shown this cultural phenomenon to be far wider than initially thought, reaching all the way to the Slavonija region in Croatia. Also related are sites in the Baranja and east Slavonija region, such as Batina, Dalj, and Vukovar, known under the name of the Dalj group (Metzner-Nebelsick 2002).

Transdanubia in Hungary shows a similar cultural picture. Three or four cultural areas are discernible: the south Pannonian group with centres such as Pecs-Jakabhegy and Nagyberki-Szalacska; the Raab group, north-west of Lake Balaton, with centres such as Sághegy and Somlóhegy; the north-east group in the Danube bend, with famous sites such as Süttő and Százhalombatta; and finally the western group located around Sopron, south-west of Lake Neusiedl (Patek 1982a, 1982b, 1993; Eibner-Persy 1980; Teržan 1990).[23] The same cultural complex can be traced in south Slovakia, the Danubian plain and its fringes between the Danube and the Little Carpathians, with sites such as Velika Košariská (Pichlerová 1969; Studeníková 1996) and Smolenice-Molpír (Dušek and Dušek 1984, 1995).

To the west of Styria, beyond the Koralpe mountains, was the Carinthian Hallstatt group. It is also known as the Frög/Breg group after one of its key sites (Pittioni 1954; Gabrovec 1966a; Tomedi 2002; Gleirscher 2011); others include Villach/Beljak, Lamprechtskogel-Waisenberg and Führholz near Mittertrixen, and Katharinenkogel and Tscherberg/Čergoviče near Bleiburg/Pliberk (Teržan 1990: 183–203; Gleirscher 2005). Miniature lead sculptures in the form of horsemen, other anthropomorphic and animal figurines, and various symbols, primarily of the sun, were a feature of this group. These attest not only the local nature of burial customs and religious concepts, but also the source of the group's prosperity, the exploitation of nearby lead deposits and the trading or exchange of this commodity.

With the onset of the Hallstatt Iron Age, the entire area shows a marked decrease in settlement numbers compared to the late Bronze Age, divided among numerous small and large regional groups. Most lowland settlements of the previous Urnfield culture were abandoned, while new settlements, established or renovated at the start of the Iron Age, were located predominantly on elevations of greater or lesser strategic importance, or on isolated hills. A minority were settled in previous periods, for example Sághegy and Velem Szentvid, and retained their dominant role into the early Iron Age. Other settlements such as Poštela (Teržan 1990), Burgstallkogel near Kleinklein (Dobiat 1990), and Sopron-Varhely (Patek 1982b) grew up afresh in the ninth to eighth centuries BC. Excavations show that most hilltop settlements were fortified with earthen ramparts as well as wooden palisades and ditches (Poštela, Burgstallkogel), some displaying a combination of stone and timber walls (Sopron-Varhely, Smolenice-Molpír). Most settlements are relatively large and their interiors were divided into artificial terraces that are still clearly visible, allowing us to infer relatively intense occupation. It thus seems possible to propose for the early Iron Age a model of settlement aggregation into larger centres that controlled fairly wide areas.

The second characteristic of this group is tied to their religion and concerns the burial of cremated remains of the deceased under tumuli. Cremation stands in the tradition of the Urnfield culture, but the tumulus as a tomb marker/funerary monument was an important innovation. Vast tumulus cemeteries were usually arranged in clusters in the general vicinity of the settlement hill, and often at its foot. They can comprise several hundred tumuli, which is even reflected in the name of one famous Hungarian site on the Danube—Százhalombatta, 'one hundred tumuli' (Holport 1984). In contrast to the Dolenjska type of extended family/clan tumuli with inhumation burials, the Styrian-Pannonian group was characterized by tumuli that each cover the grave of a single individual, often accompanied by a (sacrificed) retinue of one or more persons, all of them cremated—a feature found elsewhere in the east Hallstatt sphere. In the middle of the tumuli there are usually burial chambers of stone and/or wood, of a square or rectangular plan orientated according to the cardinal points; round chambers are rare. Very large tumuli are also known (Teržan 1990, 2008: figs 13–14), often with a *dromos*, or passage with lined walls and a paved floor, leading to the burial chamber (Figure 11.16; Dobiat 1985; Egg 1996: Abb.7). After the burial, the *dromos* was often walled up or otherwise blocked; sometimes there was a burial in it (Kleinklein-Kröllkogel, Sopron-Varhely, Süttő), perhaps a human sacrifice intended to act as a guard. Some cemeteries had clusters of small tumuli around larger ones, serving as visual expressions of social differentiation, although these smaller tumuli can themselves contain the remains of wooden or stone grave constructions.

Typical grave goods in the tumuli are principally rich and varied pottery and bronze vessels, from storage vessels to eating and drinking sets, usually intended for serving several people, i.e. for *symposia*. Special cult vessels and idols are not uncommon, especially in rich female graves. Metal dress accessories were usually burnt with the deceased person and thus are generally unidentifiable, but a few pieces were laid undamaged directly in the grave. Male graves often yield weapons (swords, spears, axes) and horse-gear; in some exceptional warrior graves we also find helmets, cuirasses, shields, and even sacrificed horses (Figure 11.16), which signifies that here too the social hierarchy was crowned by warrior-horsemen (Teržan 1990, 2011a, 2011b; Egg and Kramer 2005, 2013, 2016).

The mortuary rite is well illustrated by the tumulus at Süttő on the Danube, and the re-excavated Kröllkogel tumulus at Kleinklein. At Süttő (Vadász 1983), the burial chamber was constructed on the same spot that served as the funerary pyre (*ustrina*), where the deceased was burnt together with several humans and animals (horses, dogs, pigs, and smaller numbers of cattle and sheep/goats). The burial chamber was carefully laid out with bedding for the cremated remains of an elderly man and a younger woman with relatively modest goods of personal nature in one part, while the other part held a number of vessels arranged along the wall. On the roof of the chamber was the inhumation burial of a child, a dog, and horse-gear for three horses, perhaps for the yoke of a wagon (*troika*) to carry the dead to the other world. The importance and wealth of the buried man was thus measured in the number of sacrificed individuals, both human and animal, as well as in the number of vessels for food and drink.

A similar observation can be made for the Kröllkogel tumulus at Kleinklein (Egg and Kramer 2005, 2013), where at least three individuals and three horses were buried. The rich grave goods consisted of assault weapons and armour as well as other valuable

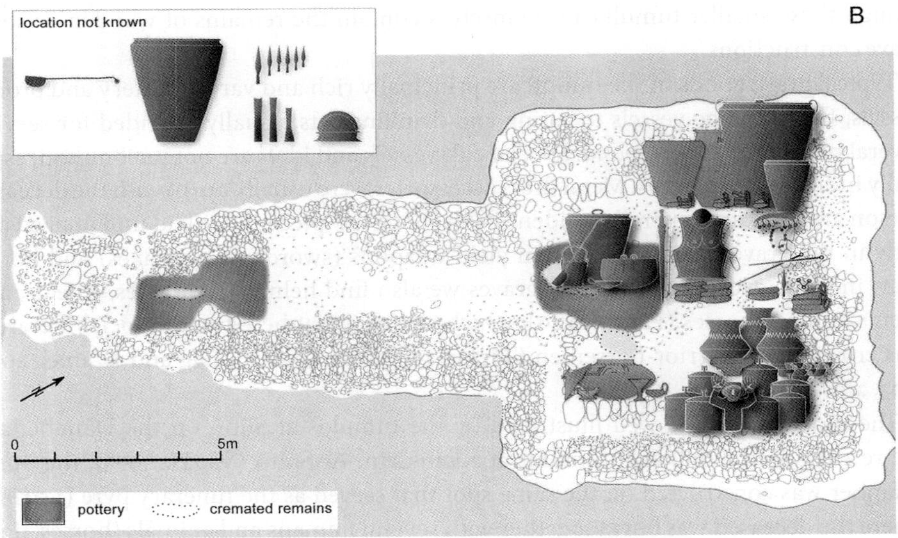

FIGURE 11.16 Kleinklein, Kröllkogel. (A) Reconstruction of the deceased and their grave goods. (B) Plan of the grave chamber, showing the position of the grave goods.

Source: after Egg and Kramer 2005: fig 28; fig 6

goods, primarily metal vessels, while there were around 100 ceramic vessels, approximately half of them with signs of burning (Egg and Kramer 2013: 305; Figure 11.16). Detailed analyses of the extensive tumulus cemeteries around Kleinklein allow us to infer a complex social stratification into several classes (Dobiat 1980; Teržan 1990: 124–145, figs 27–32; Brosseder 2004: 309–313, figs 194–195) and show beyond doubt that this cluster of rich tumuli (Hartnermichel-, Pommer- und Kröllkogel) was the resting place of the Kleinklein ruling dynasty (Gleirscher 2001; Egg and Kramer 2005, 2013, 2016). The famous Tumulus I from Strettweg (Egg 1996) also fits the pattern, particularly in the exceptional cult wagon with its figural composition as the focal point of the ideological concept of Hallstatt society (Figure 11.17; Teržan 2011b). Re-excavation of this grave showed that the chamber originally contained the remains of four people—two male and two female, one of them probably a young girl—a life-size wagon, and recovered items missed in the original investigation (Tiefengraber and Tiefengraber 2013; Tiefengraber 2015).[24]

The east Hallstatt sphere, including the Styrian-Pannonian group, witnessed a catastrophic end around 600 BC, at the transition from Hallstatt C2 to Hallstatt D1. Most settlements were either abandoned or only lasted a short while longer, while burial under tumuli ceased. This was probably connected with incursions of nomadic horse-riding peoples, primarily those of Scythian origin (Teržan 1998). Illuminating for these events are the abrupt end to the occupation revealed by excavations at the fortified settlement of Smolenice-Molpír in Slovakia, as well as detailed analysis of Scythian trilobate arrowheads (Hellmuth 2006a, 2006b, 2010). Not only was Molpír devastated, but so were other settlements in the eastern Alps all the way to Sopron-Varhely, Poštela, and Ljubljana. Following a short pause, some parts of Transdanubia were reinhabited by the newcomers. However, they did not choose the old hillforts, but instead occupied lowland sites, such as the settlement and cemetery at Sopron-Krautacker, or Szentlőrinc (Jerem 1968, 1980, 1986). In Styria, no such traces of habitation have been found thus far. The origin of the new cultural groups should be sought in the so-called Szentes-Vekerzug culture, which primarily spread across the Tisza basin and, in the sixth century BC, occupied areas beyond the Danube all the way to south-east Slovakia and the Alpine foothills (Chochorowski 1985; Kemenczei 2009; Chapter 14).

In the fifth century BC, the areas along the Danube and in northern Pannonia reveal not only the influence of La Tène A culture, but most probably also an influx of newcomers from the west (Frey 1996; Neugebauer 1992; Ramsl 2002; Hauschild 2010). These gradually spread across Lower Austria, Burgenland, and along the Danube towards the east and the south all the way to southern Pannonia (Horváth et al. 1987; Horváth and Németh 2011), Podravina and Slavonia (Guštin 1984; Dizdar 2011), but also west to Styria (Pahič 1966; Lubšina-Tušek and Kavur 2009, 2011). The earliest known grave finds in this area date to the late fourth and early third centuries BC (La Tène B2). It seems that Celtic expansion across this sparsely populated zone took place without major complications. This is also observable from the distribution of typical La Tène swords in the Carpathian basin (Szabó and Petres 1992). The tribes that settled in southern Pannonia all the way to the eastern Alps during the third century BC retained their military character, as we observed for the Mokronog group in Dolenjska. Some authors identify them as Taurisci (Dizdar 2011); others believe that the La Tène communities of southern Pannonia, Baranja, and east Slavonia belonged to the powerful Scordisci, whose core territory extended along the middle reaches of the Sava and its confluence with the Danube all the way to the mouth of the Morava or the Iron Gates. In common with many other Celtic peoples, they adopted coinage in the

FIGURE 11.17 The Strettweg cult-wagon.

Source: Egg 1996

third century BC, and their major centre was probably on the Danube at Singidunum, modern Belgrade (Todorović 1968; Guštin 1984; Jovanović 1987). From the mid-second century BC, the Scordisci came increasingly into conflict with the Romans and were eventually subjugated by Tiberius in 15 BC, while the Pannonian peoples were finally subdued in AD 6–9.

NOTES

1. Piana Agostinetti (2012) provides a useful summary of the archaeological evidence and bibliography for Bologna and other Iron Age urban centres in northern Italy.
2. The Villanovan culture and the Etruscans; the Golasecca culture and the Celts; the Luco-Meluno, then Fritzens-Sanzeno and the Raeti; the Breno-Dos dell'Arca and the Camunni; and the Este culture and the Veneti.
3. For further discussion of Gallic settlement in northern Italy, see Chapter 37; Lejars 2006; Barral et al. 2014.
4. The Taurini were Celtic according to Polybius (*Histories* 3.60.8–11), Ligurian for Strabo (*Geography* 4.6.6) and Pliny (*Natural History* 3.123), and semi-Gallic for Livy (*History of Rome* 21.38.5). Some tribes considered Ligurian (e.g. the Oxybii and Deciates) have names

of typically Celtic character. On the other hand, if the sources perceived a distinction between Celts and Ligurians, there may indeed have been actual cultural and linguistic elements underlying this judgement (cf. Strabo *Geography* 2.5.28).

5. Inscriptions are concentrated in Lunigiana, some stelae dating back to the sixth and fifth centuries BC, but too poorly preserved to read with certainty. The Busca inscription may be that of a Ligurian who had served as an Etruscan mercenary, who, after returning home, wanted a funerary stone for himself in Etruscan (Colonna 1998).
6. According to Strabo (*Geography* 4.6.2), their economy was based on transhumant herding. Diodorus Siculus (*Library of History* 5.20, 5.39) paints a picture of subsistence agriculture. The Ligurians are described as illiterate by Cato (*apud* Dionysius of Halicarnassus *Roman Antiquities* 1.10–13) and as tough peasants by Cicero (*de lege agraria* 2.35), while Virgil (*Georgics* 2.168) mentions their physical endurance.
7. According to Livy (*History of Rome* 5.33–35), the Insubres were already settled in the territory of Milan before the Gallic invasions.
8. In the CTSCG area, the Golasecca IA 1 phase (ninth century BC) is lacking.
9. Named after the huge eighth-century BC hoard of some 14,800 bronze objects and fragments found in 1887 at Bologna-San Francesco.
10. A cup from Sesto Calende, a stone inscription from the settlement of Castelletto Ticino, a bowl in the Bellini collection, and the inscription on a Hallstatt ceramic vessel from Montmorot (Jura) seemingly written by a person from the Golasecca area (Verger 2001).
11. A recently discovered warrior burial at Grandate (Como) with a rich set of grave goods, including a late Hallstatt short iron sword with Neuenegg-type bronze grip, fragments of a composite calotte helmet, and a decorated bronze lid imported from Este, is assigned to Golasecca IIA.
12. One of the most characteristic products of local metallurgy were harvesting knives, attested as early as the twelfth century BC in the Mezzocorona hoard; these were probably an Alpine invention to facilitate harvesting and the preparation of winter fodder for domestic animals.
13. *Brandopferplätze* also occur widely north of the Alps.
14. Cato (apud Pliny *Natural History* 3.133–135; Strabo *Geography* 4.206). Along with the neighbouring Trumplini, the name Camunni appears among the defeated Alpine populations recorded in the inscription on the Tropaeum Augusti at La Turbie near Nice.
15. According to Polybius (*Histories* 2.17.46), the Veneti differed from the Celts only with respect to their language, which implies that it was still commonly spoken in the mid-second century BC when he was writing. A period of bilingualism is attested by funerary stelae such as those of Marcus Gallienus and Ostiala Galliena at Padua.
16. Often referred to in the archaeological literature as palaeo-Veneti to differentiate them from the modern inhabitants of the region.
17. For a general picture of Este civilization, see Fogolari 1975; Chieco Bianchi 1988; Capuis 1993; Chieco Bianchi and Calzavara Capuis 1985; Chieco Bianchi and Capuis 2006).
18. Burial areas north-east of the settlement, at the foot of the Principe hill: Alfonsi, Benvenuti, Candeo, Casa di Ricovero, Castello, Muletti Prosdocimi, and Rebato. To the south-west: Costa Martini, Franchini, Lachini-Pelà, Nazari, Palazzina Capodaglio, Pelà, Prà d'Este, and Randi; to the south-east: Boldù Dolfin.
19. At Via S. Massimo, via Tiepolo, and vicolo Ognissanti to the north-east; and via Umberto I, via Paoli, and via Boito to the south-west.

20. For research on Hallstatt cultural groups in Slovenia see also *Arheološki vestnik* volumes 70–74 (2019–2023) under the title "Gabrovčev dan = Gabrvec day".
21. The Styrian-Pannonian group is also known in the literature under various other names: Type Wies (Pittioni 1954), Kleinklein-Martijanec-Kaptol (Vinski-Gasparini 1987), Sulmtal (Dobiat 1980), or simply east Alpine.
22. Previously called Klein-Glein (Schmid 1933).
23. The latter entity is ascribed by some researchers, primarily Austrians, to the local Kalenderberg group (Nebelsick 1997; Rebay 2002).
24. The undisturbed Strettweg Tumulus II, excavated in 2012, contained two men and a woman. Tumulus III (re-excavated in 2013) had been thoroughly robbed in antiquity, but also contained at least two people.

References

Anati, E. 1975. *Evoluzione e stile nell'arte rupestre camuna [Evolution and Style in Camunian Rock Art]*. Archivi 6. Capo di Ponte: Edizioni del Centro.

Anati, E. 1979. *I Camuni: Alle radici della civiltà europea*. Milan: Jaca Book.

Balen-Letunić, D. 2006. *Japodi: Arheološka svjedočanstva o japodskoj kulturi u posljednem pretpovijesnom tisućljeću*. Ogulin: Matica hrvatska.

Balen-Letunić, D. 2007. 'Novi prikaz japodskog ratnika iz okolice Gračaca. A new representation of a Iapodian warrior from the Gračac area', in M. Blečić, M. Črešnar, B. Hänsel, A. Hellmuth, E. Kaiser, and C. Metzner-Nebelsick (eds) *Scripta praehistorica in honorem Biba Teržan*. Situla 44: 381–390. Ljubljana: Narodni muzej Slovenije.

Barbaro, B. 2010. *Insediamenti, aree funerarie ed entità territoriali in Etruria meridionale nel Bronzo Finale*. Florence: All'insegna del Giglio.

Barral, P., J.-P. Guillaumet, M.-J. Roullière-Lambert, M. Saracino, and D. Vitali (eds). 2014. *I Celti e l'Italia del Nord: Prima e Seconda Età del ferro. Actes du XXXVIe colloque international de l'AFEAF, Vérone, 17–20 mai 2012*. Revue Archéologique de l'Est supplément 36. Dijon: Revue Archéologique de l'Est.

Bartoloni, G. 1989. *La cultura villanoviana: All'inizio della storia etrusca*. Rome: La Nuova Italia Scientifica.

Bartoloni, G. 2003. *Le società dell'Italia primitiva: Lo studio delle necropoli e la nascita delle aristocrazie*. Rome: Carocci.

Bartosiewicz, L. 1996. 'Continuity in the animal keeping of Hallstatt period communities in Slovenia', in E. Jerem and A. Lippert (eds) *Die Osthallstattkultur: Akten des Internationalen Symposiums, Sopron, 10.–14. Mai 1994*. Archaeolingua Main Series 7: 29–35. Budapest: Archaeolingua.

Bartosiewicz, L. 1999. 'Recent developments in archaeological research in Slovenia'. *Arheološki vestnik* 50: 311–322.

Batović, Š. 1965. 'Die Eisenzeit auf dem Gebiet des illyrischen Stammes der Liburnen'. *Archaeologia Iugoslavica* 6: 55–70.

Batović, Š. 1968a. 'Nin u prapovijesti. Nin in Prehistory', in M. Suić, Š. Batović, and J. Belošević (eds) *Nin: Problemi arheoloških istraživanja/Problems of archaeological excavations*: 7–33. Zadar: Arheološki muzej.

Batović, Š. 1968b. 'Istraživanje ilirskog naselja u Radovinu'. *Diadora* 4: 53–74.

Batović, Š. 1974. 'Ostava iz Jagodnje Gornje u okviru zadnje faze liburnske kulture'. *Diadora* 7: 159–245.

Batović, Š. 1987. 'Liburnska grupa', in A. Benac and S. Gabrovec (eds) *Praistorija jugoslavenskih zemalja V: Željezno doba*: 339–390. Sarajevo: Akademija nauka i umjetnosti Bosne i Hercegovine, Centar za balkanološka ispitivanja.

Bellintani, P., E. Bianchin Citton, A. M. Bietti Sestieri, C. Colonna, L. Salzani, M. Saracino, et al. 2009. *Il villaggio di Frattesina e le sue necropoli, XII–X secolo a. C.* Fratta Polesine: Museo Archeologico Nazionale di Fratta Polesine.

Bertolone, M. 1957. 'Tomba della prima età del Ferro, con carrettino, scoperta alla Ca' Morta di Como'. *Sibrium* 3: 37–40.

Bianchin Citton, E., G. Gambacurta, and A. Ruta Serafini. 1998. *'Presso l'Adige ridente'... Recenti rinvenimenti archeologici da Este e Montagnana*. Padua: ADLE edizioni.

Bietti Sestieri, A. M. 1981. 'Lo scavo dell'abitato protostorico di Frattesina di Fratta Polesine (Rovigo). I. La sequenza stratigrafica del quadrato U6'. *Bullettino Paletnologia Italiana* 1975–1980: 221–256.

Bietti Sestieri, A. M. 1997. 'Italy in Europe in the early Iron Age'. *Proceedings of the Prehistoric Society* 63: 371–402

Bietti Sestieri, A. M. 2008. 'L'età del Bronzo Finale nella penisola italiana'. *Padusa* 44: 7–54.

Bietti Sestieri, A. M. 2012. 'Il Villanoviano, un problema storico di archeologia mediterranea', in V. Bellelli (ed.) *Le origini degli Etruschi: Storia Archeologia Antropologia*: 249–277. Rome: L'Erma di Bretschneider.

Bietti Sestieri, A. M. 2013. 'Peninsular Italy', in D. Fontijn, and A. Harding (eds) *The Oxford Handbook of the European Bronze Age*: 632–652. Oxford: Oxford University Press.

Biondani, F. 2014. 'Monete celtico-padane e monete romane nelle necropoli celtiche del Veronese', in P. Barral, J.-P. Guillaumet, M.-J. Roullière-Lambert, M. Saracino, and D. Vitali (eds) *I Celti e l'Italia del Nord: Prima e Seconda Età del ferro. Actes du XXXVIe colloque international de l'AFEAF, Vérone, 17–20 mai 2012*. Revue Archéologique de l'Est supplément 36: 489–494. Dijon: Revue Archéologique de l'Est.

Bökönyi, S. 1968. *Mecklenburg Collection, Part I: Data on Iron Age Horses of Central and Eastern Europe*. American School of Prehistoric Research Bulletin 25. Cambridge, MA: Peabody Museum, Harvard University.

Bökönyi, S. 1994. 'Analiza živalskih kosti. Die Tierknochenfunde', in S. Gabrovec (ed.) *Stična I: Naselbinska izkopavanja: Siedlungsausgrabungen*. Katalogi in monografije 28: 190–213. Ljubljana: Narodni muzej Slovenije.

Brosseder, U. 2004. *Studien zur Ornamentik hallstattzeitlicher Keramik zwischen Rhonetal und Karpatenbecken*. Universitätsforschungen zur Prähistorischen Archäologie 106. Bonn: Habelt.

Brown, W. L. 1960. *The Etruscan Lion*. Oxford: Clarendon Press.

Buršić-Matijašić, K. 2007. *Gradine Istre*. Povijest Istre 6. Pula: ZN »Žakan Juri«.

Capuis, L. 1993. *I Veneti: Società e cultura di un popolo dell'Italia preromana*. Biblioteca di archeologia 19. Milan: Longanesi.

Carancini G. L. 1969. 'Osservazioni sulla cronologia del Villanoviano IV a Bologna'. *Bulletino di Paletnologia Italiana* 78: 277–288.

Cardarelli, A. 2009. 'The collapse of the Terramare culture and growth of new economic and social systems during the late Bronze Age in Italy'. *Scienze dell'Antichità* 15: 449–520.

Casini, S. and Tizzoni, M. 2014. 'Mediolanum: dati inedita dallo studio dei levelli preromani', in P. Barral, J.-P. Guillaumet, M.-J. Roullière-Lambert, M. Saracino, and D. Vitali (eds) *I Celti e l'Italia del Nord: Prima e Seconda Età del ferro. Actes du XXXVIe colloque international de l'AFEAF, Vérone, 17–20 mai 2012*. Revue Archéologique de l'Est supplément 36: 355–373. Dijon: Revue Archéologique de l'Est.

Castiglioni, E., L. Dal Ri, B. Leitner, U. Tecchiati, M. Cottini, and F. Groppi. 2014. 'Laives Reif: approccio multidisciplinare allo studio di un abitato della seconda età del Ferro in Val d'Adige', in R. Roncador and F. Nicolis (eds) *Antichi popoli delle Alpi: Sviluppi culturali durante l'età del Ferro nei territori alpini centro-orientali*: 105–125. Trento: Giunta della Provincia autonoma di Trento.

Cestnik, V. 2009. *Željeznodobna nekropola Kaštel kod Buja: Analiza pokopa željeznodobne Istre. Iron Age Necropolis Kaštel near Buje: Analysis of Burial Practice in the Iron Age Istria*. Monografije i katalozi 18. Pula: Arheološki muzej Istre.

Chieco Bianchi, A. M. 1987. 'Dati preliminari su nuove tombe di III secolo da Este', in D. Vitali (ed.) *Celti ed Etruschi nell'Italia centro-settentrionale dal V secolo a.C. alla Romanizzazione*: 191–236. Bologna: Bologna University Press.

Chieco Bianchi, A. M. 1988. 'I Veneti', in G. Pugliese Carratelli (ed.) *Italia omnium terrarum alumna*: 1–98. Milan: Scheiwiller.

Chieco Bianchi, A. M., and L. Calzavara Capuis. 1985. *Este I: Le necropoli Casa di Ricovero, Casa Muletti Prosdocimi e Casa Alfonsi*. Monumenti antichi 51. Serie monografica 2. Rome: Bretschneider.

Chieco Bianchi, A. M., and L. Capuis. 2006. *Este II: La Necropoli di Villa Benvenuti*. Monumenti Antichi 65. Serie monografica 7. Rome: Bretschneider.

Chochorowski, J. 1985. 'Die Rolle der Vekerzug-Kultur (VK) im Rahmen der skythischen Einflüsse in Mitteleuropa'. *Praehistorische Zeitschrift* 60: 204–271.

Ciurletti, G., and F. Marzatico (eds). 1999. *Die Räter/I Reti. Atti del Simposio 23–25 settembre 1993, Castello di Stenico*. Archaeoalp 5. Trento: Provincia autonoma di Trento.

Colonna, G. 1980. 'Rapporti artistici tra il mondo paleoveneto e il mondo etrusco', in Istituto di studi etruschi ed italici (ed.) *Este e la civiltà paleoveneta a cento anni dalle prime scoperte. Atti XI convegno di Studi Etruschi e Italici*: 177–190. Florence: Olschki.

Colonna, G. 1998. 'Etruschi sulla via delle Alpi occidentali', in L. Mercando and M. Venturino Gambari (eds) *Archeologia in Piemonte I: La preistoria*: 261–266. Turin: U. Allemandi.

Colonna, G. 2004. 'Scrittura e onomastica', in R. C. de Marinis and G. Spadea (eds) *I Liguri: Un antico popolo europeo tra Alpi e Mediterraneo*: 298–307. Geneva/Milan: Skira.

Cremaschi, M. 2009. 'Ambiente, clima ed uso del suolo nella crisi della cultura delle terramare'. *Scienze dell'Antichità* 15: 521–534.

Cucini Tizzoni, C., and Tizzoni, M. (eds). 1999. *La Miniera perduta: Cinque anni di ricerche archeometallurgiche nel territorio di Bienno*. Bienno: Comune di Bienno.

Dal Rì, L. 1992. 'Note sull'insediamento e sulla necropoli di Vadena', in I. R. Metzger and P. Gleirscher (eds) *Die Räter / I Reti*: 475–522. Bolzano: Athesia.

Dal Rì, L., P. Gamper, and H. Steiner (eds). 2010. *Höhensiedlungen der Bronze- und Eisenzeit Kontrolle der Verbindungswege über die Alpen/Abitati dell'Età del Bronze e del Ferro controlle delle vie di comunicazione attraverso le Alpi*. Forschungen zur Denkmalpflege in Südtirol. Beni culturali in Alto Adige VI. Trento: Temi Editrice.

Dämmer, H.-W. 1986. *San Pietro Montagnon (Montegrotto): Ein vorgeschichtliches Seeheiligtum in Venetien*. Studien zu vor- und frühgeschichtlichen Heiligtümern 1. Mainz: Philipp von Zabern.

de Marinis, R. C. 1975. 'Le tombe di guerriero di Sesto Calende e le spade e i pugnali hallstattiani scoperti nell'Italia nord-occidentale', in *Archeologica: Scritti in onore di A. Neppi Modona*: 213–269. Florence: Olschki.

de Marinis, R. C. 1981a. 'La ceramica della prima tomba di guerriero di Sesto Calende e nuove osservazioni sulla cronologia del Golasecca I'. *Rivista Archeologica dell'Antica Provincia e Diocesi di Como* 163: 5–47.

de Marinis, R. C. 1981b. 'Il periodo Golasecca III A in Lombardia'. *Studi Archeologici* 1: 41–284, tavv. 1–69, 290–303.

de Marinis, R. C. 1986. 'L'età gallica in Lombardia (IV–I secolo a.C.): risultati delle ultime ricerche e problemi aperti', in *Atti II convegno archeologico regionale, Como 1984*: 93–156. Como: Società Archeologica Comense.

de Marinis, R. C. 1988a. 'Liguri e Celto-Liguri', in G. Pugliese Carratelli (ed.) *Italia omnium terrarum alumna*: 157–259. Milan: Scheiwiller.

de Marinis, R. C. 1988b. 'Le popolazioni alpine di stirpe retica', in G. Pugliese Carratelli (ed.) *Italia omnium terrarum alumna*: 99–155. Milan: Scheiwiller.

de Marinis, R. C. 1992. 'Il territorio prealpino e alpino tra i laghi di Como e di Garda dal Bronzo recente alla fine dell'età del Ferro', in I. R. Metzger and P. Gleirscher (eds) *Die Räter / I Reti*: 145–174. Bolzano: Athesia.

de Marinis, R. C. 1999a. 'Rapporti culturali tra Reti, Etruria Padana e Celti golasecchiani', in G. Ciurletti and F. Marzatico (eds) *Die Räter/I Reti. Atti del Simposio 23–25 settembre 1993, Castello di Stenico.* Archaeoalp 5: 603–649. Trento: Provincia autonoma di Trento.

de Marinis, R. C. 1999b. 'La cultura di Breno-Dos dell'Arca e il problema degli Euganei', in R. Poggiani Keller (ed.) *Atti del II Convegno Archeologico Provinciale, Grosio 20–21 ottobre 1995*: 117–125. Sondrio: Parco Incisioni Rupestri di Grosio.

de Marinis, R. C. 1999c. 'Il confine occidentale del mondo proto-veneto/paleoveneto dal Bronzo Finale alle invasioni galliche del 388 a.C.', in *Protostoria e storia del 'Venetorum angulus'. Atti XX convegno di Studi Etruschi e Italici*: 511–564. Pisa/Rome: Istituti Editoriali e Poligrafici Internazionali.

de Marinis, R. C. 2001. 'L'età del Ferro in Lombardia: stato attuale delle conoscenze e problemi aperti', in *Atti del 3° convegno archeologico regionale 'La Protostoria in Lombardia'*: 27–76. Como: Società Archeologica Comense.

de Marinis, R. C. 2004. 'Iron metallurgy in protohistoric Italy', in W. Nicodemi (ed.) *The Civilization of Iron from Prehistory to the Third Millennium*: 63–81. Milan: Olivares.

de Marinis, R. C. 2007. 'Il periodo Golasecca III A nelle necropoli dei dintorni di Como: nuovi aggiornamenti', in *La circolazione di beni di lusso e di modelli culturali nel VI e V secolo a.C. Atti giornata di studi, Brescia, Università Cattolica, 3 marzo 2006*: 75–96. Milan: Vita e Pensiero.

de Marinis, R. C. 2008. 'Aspetti degli influssi dell'espansione etrusca in Val padana verso la civiltà di Golasecca'. *Annali Fondazione Faina* 15: 115–146.

de Marinis, R. C. 2009. 'Continuity and discontinuity in Northern Italy from the Recent to the Final Bronze Age: a view from north-western Italy'. *Scienze dell'Antichità* 15: 535–545.

de Marinis, R. C. 2010. 'L'immagine del guerriero e i segni del potere nell'età del Rame e del Bronzo dell'Italia settentrionale alla luce della documentazione funeraria', in *Les manifestations du pouvoir dans les Alpes, de la Préhistoire au Moyen-Age, XIIeme colloque international sur les Alpes dans l'Antiquité, 2–4 octobre 2009, Yenne, Savoie*. Bulletin d'Etudes Préhistoriques Alpines 21: 127–141.

de Marinis, R. C. 2014. 'Correlazioni chronologiche tra Italia nord-occidentale (area della cultura di Golasecca) e ambiti culturali transalpine e cisalpine dal Bronzo Recente alla fine del VII secolo a.C.', in P. Barral, J.-P. Guillaumet, M.-J. Roullière-Lambert, M. Saracino, and D. Vitali (eds) *I Celti e l'Italia del Nord: Prima e Seconda Età del ferro. Actes du XXXVIe colloque international de l'AFEAF, Vérone, 17–20 mai 2012*. Revue Archéologique de l'Est supplément 36: 17–35. Dijon: Revue Archéologique de l'Est.

de Marinis, R. C., and S. Biaggio (eds). 2000. *I Leponti tra mito e realtà, I–II*. Locarno: A. Didò.

de Marinis, R. C., S. Casini, and M. Rapi. 2001. 'L'abitato protostorico dei dintorni di Como', in *La Protostoria in Lombardia. Atti del 3° Convegno archeologico regionale, Como Villa Olmo 22–24 ottobre 1999*: 97–140. Como: Società Archeologica Comense.

de Marinis, R. C., and A. Fossati. 2012. 'A che punto è lo studio dell'arte rupestre della Valcamonica'. *Atti della XLII Riunione Scientifica, Istituto Italiano di Preistoria e Protostoria. Preistoria alpina* 46, 2: 17–43.

de Marinis, R. C., and F. M. Gambari. 2005. 'La cultura di Golasecca dal X agli inizi del VII secolo a.C.: cronologia relativa e correlazioni con altre aree culturali', in G. Bartoloni and F. Delpino (eds) *Oriente e Occidente: metodi e discipline a confronto: Riflessioni sulla cronologia dell'età del Ferro italiana. Atti dell'Incontro di Studio, Roma 30–31 ottobre 2003*: 197–225. Pisa/Rome: Istituti Editoriali e Poligrafici Internazionali.

de Marinis, R. C., S. Massa, and M. Pizzo (eds). 2009. *Alle origini di Varese e del suo territorio: Le collezioni del sistema archeologico provinciale*. Rome: L'Erma di Bretschneider.

de Marinis, R. C., and F. Motta. 1990–1991. 'Una nuova iscrizione lepontica su pietra da Mezzovico, Lugano'. *Sibrium* 21: 201–225.

de Marinis, R. C., and G. Spadea (eds). 2004. *I Liguri: Un antico popolo europeo tra Alpi e Mediterraneo*. Geneva/Milan: Skira.

de Marinis, R. C., and G. Spadea (eds). 2006. *Ancora su I Liguri: Un antico popolo europeo tra Alpi e Mediterraneo*. Genoa: De Ferrari.

De Min, M. 1982. 'La necropoli protovillanoviana di Frattesina di Fratta Polesine (Rovigo)'. *Padusa* 18: 3–25.

De Min, M. 1986. 'Frattesina di Fratta Polesine. La necropoli protostorica', in M. De Min and R. Peretto (eds) *L'Antico Polesine: Testimonianze archeologiche e paleoambientali. Catalogo delle esposizioni di Adria e Rovigo*: 143–169. Rovigo: Museo nazionale archeologico di Adria, Museo Civico delle Civiltà in Polesine di Rovigo.

De Min, M., M. Gamba, G. Gambacurta, and A. Ruta Serafini (eds). 2005. *La città invisibile: Padova preromana: Trent'anni di scavi e ricerche*. Ozzano dell'Emilia: Edizioni Tipoarte Industrie Grafiche.

De Santis, A. 2009. 'La definizione delle figure sociali riconoscibili in relazione alla nascita e allo sviluppo della cultura laziale'. *Scienze dell'Antichità* 15: 359–370.

De Santis, A. (ed.) 2011. *Politica e leader nel Lazio ai tempi di Enea*. Rome: Soprintendenza Beni Archeologici Roma.

De Simone, C. 1980. 'Gallisch *Nemetios—etruskisch Nemetie'. *Zeitschrift für Vergleichende Sprachforschung* 94: 198–202.

Di Gennaro, F. 1982. 'Organizzazione del territorio nell'Etruria meridionale protostorica: applicazione di un modello grafico'. *Dialoghi di Archeologia, N. S.* 4: 102–112.

Di Gennaro, F. 1986. *Forme di insediamento tra Tevere e Fiora dal Bronzo Finale al principio dell'età del Ferro*. Florence: Olschki.

Dizdar, M. 2011. 'The La Tène culture in central Croatia. The problem of eastern border of the Taurisci in the Podravina region', in M. Guštin and M. Jevtić (eds) *The Eastern Celts: The Communities between the Alps and the Black Sea*. Annales Mediterranei: 99–118. Koper: Univerza na Primorskem.

Dobiat, C. 1980. *Das hallstattzeitliche Gräberfeld von Kleinklein und seine Keramik*. Schild von Steier Beiheft 1. Graz: Landesmuseum Joanneum.

Dobiat, C. 1985. 'Der Kröll-Schmiedkogel und seine Stellung innerhalb der ostalpinen Hallstattkultur', in A. Reichenberger and C. Dobiat (eds) *Kröll-Schmiedkogel: Beiträge zu einem 'Fürstengrab' der östlichen Hallstattkultur in Kleinklein (Steiermark)*. Kleine Schriften aus dem Vorgeschichtlichen Seminar Marburg 18: 29–61. Marburg: Philipps-Universität Marburg.

Dobiat, C. 1990. *Der Burgstallkogel bei Kleinklein I: Die Ausgrabungen der Jahre 1982 und 1984*. Marburger Studien zur Vor- und Frühgeschichte 13. Marburg: Hitzeroth.

Dobiat, C., H. Matthäus, B. Raftery, and J. Henderson. 1987. *Ringaugenperlen und verwandte Perlengruppen: Glasperlen der vorrömischen Eisenzeit II. Nach Unterlagen von Thea Elisabeth Haevernick (†)*. Marburger Studien zur Vor- und Frühgeschichte 9. Marburg: Hitzenroth.

Dore, A. 2005. 'Il Villanoviano I–III di Bologna: problem di cronologia relativa e assoluta', in G. Bartolini and F. Delpino (eds) *Oriente e Occidente: metodi e discipline a confronto: Riflessioni sulla cronologia dell'età del Ferro italiana. Atti dell'Incontro di Studio, Roma 30–31 ottobre 2003*: 255–292. Pisa/Rome: Istituti Editoriali e Poligrafici Internazionali.

Drechsler-Bižić, R. 1961. 'Rezultati istraživanja japodske nekropole u Kompolju 1955–1956. godine. Ergebnisse der in den Jahren 1955/56 durchgeführten Ausgrabungen in der japodischen Nekropole von Kompolje'. *Vjesnik Arheološkog muzeja u Zagrebu* 3, 2: 67–113.

Drechsler-Bižić, R. 1972–1973. 'Nekropola prahistorijskih Japoda u Prozoru kod Otoćca. Gräberfelder vorgechichtlicher Japoden in Prozor bei Otoćac'. *Vjesnik Arheološkog muzeja u Zagrebu* 3, 6–7: 1–54.

Drechsler-Bižić, R. 1975. 'Caractéristiques des agglomérations fortifiées dans la région centrale des Japodes. Utvrđena ilirska naselja—Agglomérations fortifiées illyriennes', in A. Benac (ed.) *Međunarodni kolokvij—Colloque international, Mostar, 24.–26. oktobar 1974*. Posebna izdanja 24: 71–79. Sarajevo: Centar za balkanološka ispitivanja.

Drechsler-Bižić, R. 1987. 'Japodska grupa', in A. Benac and S. Gabrovec (eds) *Praistorija jugoslavenskih zemalja V. Željezno doba*: 391–441. Sarajevo: Akademija nauka i umjetnosti Bosne i Hercegovine, Centar za balkanološka ispitivanja.

Dular, J., and S. Tecco Hvala. 2007. *South-eastern Slovenia in the Early Iron Age: Settlement—Economy—Society*. Opera Instituti Archaeologici Sloveniae 12. Ljubljana: Založba ZRC.

Dušek, M., and S. Dušek. 1984. *Smolenice-Molpír I: Befestigter Fürstensitz der Hallstattzeit*. Materialia Archaeologica Slovaca 6. Nitra: Instituti Archaeologici Nitrensis Academiae Scientiarum Slovacae.

Dušek, M., and S. Dušek. 1995. *Smolenice-Molpír II: Befestigter Fürstensitz der Hallstattzeit*. Materialia Archaeologica Slovaca 13. Nitra: Instituti Archaeologici Nitrensis Academiae Scientiarum Slovacae.

Egg, M. 1986. *Italische Helme: Studien zu den ältereisenzeitlichen Helmen Italiens und der Alpen*. RGZM Monographien 11. Mainz: Römisch-Germanisches Zentralmuseum.

Egg, M. 1992. 'Ein eisenzeitlicher Altfund von Schloss Greifenstein bei Siebeneich in Südtirol', in A. Lippert and K. Spindler (eds) *Festschrift zum 50jährigen Bestehen des Institutes für Ur- und Frühgeschichte der Leopold-Franzens-Universität Innsbruck*: 135–172. Bonn: Habelt.

Egg, M. 1996. *Das Hallstattzeitliche Fürstengrab von Strettweg bei Judenburg in der Obersteiermark*. RGZM Monographien 37. Mainz: Römisch-Germanisches Zentralmuseum.

Egg, M., and D. Kramer. 2005. *Krieger—Feste—Totenopfer: Der letzte Hallstattfürst von Kleinklein in der Steiermark: Mosaiksteine*. Forschungen am Römisch-Germanischen Zentralmuseum 1. Mainz: Römisch-Germanisches Zentralmuseum.

Egg, M., and D. Kramer. 2013. *Die hallstattzeitlichen Fürstengräber von Kleinklein in der Steiermark: Der Kröllkogel*. RGZM Monographien 110. Mainz: Römisch-Germanisches Zentralmuseum.

Egg, M., and D. Kramer. 2016. *Die hallstattzeitlichen Fürstengräber von Kleinklein in der Steiermark: die beiden Hartnermichelkogel und der Pommerkogel*. RGZM Monographien 125. Mainz: Römisch-Germanisches Zentralmuseum.

Eibner-Persy, A. 1980. *Hallstattzeitliche Grabhügel von Sopron (Ödenburg): Die Funde der Grabungen 1890–92 in der Prähistorischen Abteilung des Naturhistorischen Museums in Wien und im Burgenländischen Landesmuseum in Eisenstadt*. Wissenschaftliche Arbeiten aus dem Burgenland 62. Eisenstadt: Amt der Burgenländischen Landesregierung.

Fischer, J. 1984. 'Die vorrömischen Skulpturen von Nesactium'. *Hamburger Beiträge zur Archäologie* 11: 9–98.

Fogolari, G. 1975. 'La protostoria delle Venezie', in *Popoli e civiltà dell'Italia antica 4*: 61–222. Rome: Biblioteca di Storia Patria.

Fogolari, G., and A. M. Chieco Bianchi (eds). 1976. *Padova Preromana*. Padua: Comune di Padova/Soprintendenza Archeologica delle Venezie.

Fogolari, G., and O.-H. Frey. 1965. 'Considerazioni tipologiche e cronologiche sul II e il III periodo atestino'. *Studi Etruschi* 33: 237–293.

Forni, G. (ed.) 1976. *Fontes Ligurum et Liguriae Antiquae, Vol. 90: Atti della Società Ligure di Storia Patria*. Genoa: Società ligure di storia patria.

Fossati, A. 1991. 'L'età del Ferro nelle incisioni rupestri della Valcamonica', in E. Arslan (ed.) *Immagini di un'aristocrazia dell'età del Ferro nell'arte rupestre camuna*: 11–71. Milan: Edizioni ET.

Frey, O.-H. 1969. *Die Entstehung der Situlenkunst: Studien zur figürlich verzierten Toreutik von Este*. Römisch-Germanische Forschungen 31. Berlin: Walter de Gruyter.

Frey, O.-H. 1971. 'Fibeln vom westhallstättischen Typus aus dem Gebiet südlich der Alpen. Zum Problem der keltischen Wanderung', in A. Dominioni (ed.) *Oblatio: Raccolta di studi di Antichità ed Arte in onore del Prof. Aristide Calderini*: 355–386. Como: Societa Archaeologica Comense.

Frey, O.-H. 1996. 'Bemerkungen zu einigen Fundstücken der Frühlatènezeit aus Niederösterreich', in E. Jerem, A. Krenn-Leeb, J.-W. Neugebauer, and O. H. Urban (eds) *Die Kelten in den Alpen und an der Donau. Akten des internationalen Symposions, St. Pölten, 14.–18. Oktober 1992*. Studien zur Eisenzeit im Ostalpenraum: 193–215. Budapest: Archaeolingua.

Fulminante, F. 2014. *The Urbanisation of Rome and Latium Vetus from the Bronze Age to the Archaic Era*. Cambridge: Cambridge University Press.

Gabrovec, S. 1962–1963. 'Halštatske čelade jugovzhodnoalpskega kroga'. *Arheološki vestnik* 13–14: 293–347.

Gabrovec, S. 1964–1965. 'Halštatska kultura v Sloveniji'. *Arheološki vestnik* 15–16: 21–63.

Gabrovec, S. 1966a. 'Zur Hallstattzeit in Slowenien'. *Germania* 44: 1–48.

Gabrovec, S. 1966b. 'Srednjelatensko obdobje v Sloveniji. Zur Mittellatènezeit in Slowenien'. *Arheološki vestnik* 17: 169–242.

Gabrovec, S. 1970. 'Dvozankaste ločne fibule. Doprinos k problematiki začetka železne dobe na Balkanu in v jugovzhodnih Alpah'. *Godišnjak. Centar za balkanološka ispitivanja* 8, 6: 5–65.

Gabrovec, S. 1987a. 'Svetolucijska grupa. Notranjska grupa', in A. Benac and S. Gabrovec (eds) *Praistorija jugoslavenskih zemalja V. Željezno doba*: 120–177. Sarajevo: Akademija nauka i umjetnosti Bosne i Hercegovine, Centar za balkanološka ispitivanja.

Gabrovec, S. 1987b. 'Dolenjska grupa', in A. Benac and S. Gabrovec (eds) *Praistorija jugoslavenskih zemalja V. Željezno doba*: 29–119. Sarajevo: Akademija nauka i umjetnosti Bosne i Hercegovine, Centar za balkanološka ispitivanja.

Gabrovec, S. 1994. *Stična I: Naselbinska izkopavanja/Siedlungsgrabungen*. Katalogi in monografije 28. Ljubljana: Narodni muzej Slovenije.

Gabrovec, S., and B. Čović. 1987. 'Zaključna razmatranja. Periodizacija i kronologija', in A. Benac and S. Gabrovec (eds) *Praistorija jugoslavenskih zemalja V. Željezno doba*: 901–928. Sarajevo: Akademija nauka i umjetnosti Bosne i Hercegovine, Centar za balkanološka ispitivanja.

Gabrovec, S., A. Kruh, I. Murgelj, and B. Teržan. 2006. *Stična II/1: Gomile starejše železne dobe/Grabhügel aus der älteren Eisenzeit*. Katalogi in monografije 37. Ljubljana: Narodni muzej Slovenije.

Gabrovec, S., and K. Mihovilić. 1987. 'Istarska grupa', in A. Benac and S. Gabrovec (eds) *Praistorija jugoslavenskih zemalja V. Željezno doba*: 293–338. Sarajevo: Akademija nauka i umjetnosti Bosne i Hercegovine, Centar za balkanološka ispitivanja.

Gabrovec, S., and D. Svoljšak. 1983. *Most na Soči (S. Lucia) I: Zgodovina raziskovanj in topografija/Storia delle ricerche e topografia*. Katalogi in monografije 22. Ljubljana: Narodni muzej Slovenije.

Gabrovec, S., and B. Teržan. 2008. *Stična II/2: Gomile starejše železne dobe/Grabhügel aus der älteren Eisenzeit*. Katalogi in monografije 37. Ljubljana: Narodni muzej Slovenije.

Gambari, F. M. (ed.) 2001. *La birra e il fiume: Pombia e le vie dell'Ovest Ticino tra VI e V secolo a. C.* Turin: Celid.

Gambari, F. M., and R. Cerri (eds). 2011. *L'alba della città: Le prime necropoli del centro proto-urbano di Castelletto Ticino*. Novara: Interlinea edizioni.

Gambari, F. M., and G. Colonna. 1986. 'Il bicchiere con iscrizione arcaica da Castelletto Ticino'. *Studi Etruschi* 54: 130–164.

Gleirscher, P. 1994. 'Zum etruskischen Fundgut zwischen Adda, Etsch und Inn'. *Helvetia Archaeologica* 93/94: 69–105.

Gleirscher, P. 2001. 'Norische Könige. Historische Quellen und archäologischer Befund'. *Praehistorische Zeitschrift* 76: 87–104.

Gleirscher, P. 2005. 'Hügelgräber und Herrschaftsbereiche im Ostalpenraum'. *Arheološki vestnik* 56: 99–112.

Gleirscher, P. 2011. *Die Hügelgräber von Frög: Ein eisenzeitliches Herrschaftszentrum in Rosegg*. Klagenfurt/Celovec–Laibach/Ljubljana–Vienna/Dunaj: Hermagoras, Mohorjeva založba.

Gleirscher, P., H. Nothdurfter, and E. Schubert. 2002. *Das Rungger Egg: Untersuchungen an einem eisenzeitlichen Brandopferplatz bei Seis am Schlern in Südtirol*. Römisch-Germanische Forschungen 61. Mainz: Philipp von Zabern.

Gorini, G. 2014. 'Nuove indagini sulle emission preromane dell'Italia settentrionale nell'Età del ferro (IV–I sec. a.C.)', in P. Barral, J.-P. Guillaumet, M.-J. Roullière-Lambert, M. Saracino, and D. Vitali (eds) *I Celti e l'Italia del Nord: Prima e Seconda Età del ferro. Actes du XXXVIe colloque international de l'AFEAF, Vérone, 17–20 mai 2012*. Revue Archéologique de l'Est supplément 36: 475–482. Dijon: Revue Archéologique de l'Est.

Guidi, A. 2000. *Preistoria della complessità sociale*. Rome/Bari: Laterza.

Guštin, M. 1979. *Notranjska: k začetkom železne dobe na severnem Jadranu/Notranjska: zu den Anfängen der Eisenzeit an der nördlichen Adria*. Katalogi in monografije 17. Ljubljana: Narodni muzej Slovenije.

Guštin, M. 1984. 'Die Kelten in Jugoslawien. Übersicht über das archäologische Fundgut'. *Jahrbuch des Römisch-Germanischen Zentralmuseums Mainz* 31: 305–363.

Guštin, M. 1987. 'La Tène fibulae from Istria'. *Archaeologia Iugoslavica* 24: 43–56.

Guštin, M. 1991. *Posočje in der jüngeren Eisenzeit/Posočje v mlajši železni dobi*. Katalogi in monografije 27. Ljubljana: Narodni muzej Slovenije.

Guštin, M. 2011a. 'Carnium (Kranj, Slovenia): insediamento dei Carni', in S. Casini (ed.) *'Il filo del tempo': Studi di preistoria e protostoria in onore di Raffaele Carlo de Marinis*. Notizie Archeologiche Bergomensi 19: 447–458. Bergamo: Civico Museo Archaeologico.

Guštin, M. 2011b. 'On the Celtic tribe of Taurisci', in M. Guštin and M. Jevtić (eds) *The Eastern Celts: The Communities between the Alps and the Black Sea*. Annales Mediterranei: 119–128. Koper: Univerza na Primorskem.

Hänsel, B., K. Mihovilić, and B. Teržan. 2015. *Monkodonja 1: Istraživanje protourbanog naselja brončanog doba Istre: Knjiga 1: Iskopavanje i nalazi građevina. Forschungen zu einer protourbanen Siedlung der Bronzezeit Istriens: Teil 1: Die Grabung und der Baubefund*. Monografije i katalozi 25. Pula: Arheološki muzej Istre.

Hänsel, B., B. Teržan, and K. Mihovilić. 2007. 'Radiokarbondaten zur älteren und mittleren Bronzezeit Istriens'. *Praehistorische Zeitschrift* 82: 23–50.

Hauschild, M. 2010. '"Celticised" or "assimilated"? In search of foreign and indigenous people at the time of the Celtic migrations. Proceedings of the International Colloquium from Târgu Mureş, October 2009', in B. Sándor (ed.) *Iron Age Communities in the Carpathian Basin*. Biblioteca Musei Marisiensis Seria Archaeologica 2: 171–180. Cluj-Napoca: Editura Mega.

Hellmuth, A. 2006a. 'Untersuchungen zu den sogenannten skythischen Pfeilspitzen aus der befestigten Höhensiedlung von Smolenice-Molpír', in A. Hellmuth and D. Yalçikli (eds) *Pfeilspitzen*. Universitätsforschungen zur Prähistorischen Archäologie 128: 10–204. Bonn: Rudolf Habelt.

Hellmuth, A. 2006b. 'Zum Untergang der hallstattzeitlichen befestigten Höhensiedlung von Smolenice-Molpír in der Südwestslowakei'. *Mitteilungen der Berliner Gesellschaft für Anthropologie, Ethnologie und Urgeschichte* 27: 41–56.

Hellmuth, A. 2010. *Bogenschützen des pontischen Raumes in der Älteren Eisenzeit: Typologische Gliederung, Verbreitung und Chronologie der skythischen Pfeilspitzen*. Universitätsforschungen zur Prähistorischen Archäologie 177. Bonn: Rudolf Habelt.

Holport, A. 1984. 'Questions in connection with recent excavations at Százhalombatta', in L. Török (ed.) *Hallstattkolloquium Veszprém 1984*. Antaeus: Mitteilungen des Archäologischen Instituts der Ungarischen Akademie der Wissenschaften, Beiheft 3: 93–98, 349–356. Budapest: Ungarische Akademie der Wissenschaften.

Horváth, L., M. Kelemen, A. Uzsoki, and É. Vadász. 1987. *Transdanubia 1: Corpus of Celtic Finds in Hungary 1*. Budapest: Akadémiai Kiadó.

Horváth, L., and P. G. Németh. 2011. 'Celtic warriors from Szabadi (Somogy County, Hungary)', in M. Guštin and M. Jevtić (eds) *The Eastern Celts: The Communities between the Alps and the Black Sea*. Annales Mediterranei: 19–30. Koper: Univerza na Primorskem.

Jereb, M. 2016. *Die Bronzegefäße in Slowenien*. Prähistorische Bronzefunde II, 19. Stuttgart: Franz Steiner.

Jerem, E. 1968. 'The late iron age cemetery of Szentlörinc'. *Acta Archaeologica Academiae Scientiarum Hungaricae* 20: 159–208.

Jerem, E. 1980. 'Zur Späthallstatt- und Frühlatènezeit in Transdanubien', in D. Straub (ed.) *Die Hallstattkultur: Frühform europäischer Einheit. Internationale Ausstellung des Landes Oberösterreich 25. April bis 26. Oktober 1980, Schloß Lamberg, Steyr*: 105–136. Linz: OÖ Landesverlag.

Jerem, E. 1986. 'Bemerkungen zur Siedlungsgeschichte der Späthallstatt- und Frühlatènezeit im Ostalpenraum', in L. Török (ed.) *Hallstattkolloquium Veszprém 1984*. Antaeus: Mitteilungen des Archäologischen Instituts der Ungarischen Akademie der Wissenschaften, Beiheft 3: 107–118. Budapest: Ungarische Akademie der Wissenschaften.

Jovanović, B. 1987. 'Keltska kultura u Jugoslaviji. Istoćna grupa', in A. Benac and S. Gabrovec (eds) *Praistorija jugoslavenskih zemalja V. Željezno doba*: 805–854. Sarajevo: Akademija nauka i umjetnosti Bosne i Hercegovine, Centar za balkanološka ispitivanja.

Kemenczei, T. 2009. *Studien zu den Denkmälern skythisch geprägter Alföld Gruppe*. Budapest: Magyar Nemzeti Múzeum.

Kossack, G. 1957. 'Zu den Metallbeigaben des Wagengrabes von Ca' Morta (Como)'. *Sibrium* 3: 41–54.

Krause, R. 2002. 'Ein frühkeltischer Fürstensitz auf dem Ipf am Nördlinger Ries'. *Antike Welt* 33, 5: 493–508.

Križ, B. 2006. *Novo Mesto VI: Kapiteljska njiva: Mlajšeželeznodobno grobišče/Late Iron Age Cemetery*. Carniola archaeologica 6. Novo Mesto: Dolenjski muzej.

Križman, M. 1997. *Antička svjedočanstva o Istri: Povijest Istre I*. Pula: ZN »Žakan Juri«.

Kruh, A. 2014. 'Kobarid', in B. Teržan and M. Črešnar (eds) *Absolutno datiranje bronaste in železne dobe na Slovenskem/Absolute Dating of the Bronze and Iron Ages in Slovenija*. Katalogi in monografije 40: 615–627. Ljubljana: Narodni muzej Slovenije.

Kučar, V. 1979. 'Prahistorijska nekropola Beram. Le necropole prehistorique de Beram'. *Histria archaeologica* 10, 1: 85–131.

Kukoč, S. 2009. *Japodi—fragmenta symbolica*. Biblioteka znanstvenih dela 164. Split: Književni krug Split.

Kukoč, S. 2010. 'Osvrt na spaljivanje pokojnika u liburnskom kulturnem kotekstu. A review of the cremation rite in the liburnian cultural context'. *Prilozi Instituta za arheologiju u Zagrebu* 27: 95–109.

Kunter, K. 1987. *Schichtaugenperlen: Glasperlen der vorrömischen Eisenzeit IV. Nach Unterlagen von Thea Elisabeth Haevernick (†)*. Marburger Studien zur Vor- und Frühgeschichte 18. Espelkamp: Marie Leidorf.

Lejars, T. 2006. 'Les Celtes d'Italie', in M. Szabó (ed.) *Celtes et gaulois: l'archéologie face à l'histoire: Les Civilisés et les Barbares du Ve au IIe siècle avant J.-C. Actes de la table ronde de Budapest, 17–18 juin 2005*. Collection Bibracte 12/3: 77–96. Glux-en-Glenne: Centre archéologique européen du Mont Beuvray.

Lejeune, M. 1970. 'Lepontica. Documents gaulois et para-gaulois de Cisalpine'. *Études Celtiques* 12, 2: 337–500.

Lejeune, M. 1971. *Lepontica*. Paris: Les Belles Lettres.

Lo Schiavo, F. 1970. *Il Gruppo Liburnico-Japodico per una definizione nell´ ambito della protostoria balcanica*. Atti della Accademia Nazionale dei Lincei 367. Memorie Ser. VIII, Vol. XIV, Fasc. 6. Rome: Accademia Nazionale dei Lincei.

Lubšina-Tušek, M., and B. Kavur. 2009. 'A sword between. The Celtic warriors grave from Srednica in North-Eastern Slovenia', in G. Tiefengraber, B. Kavur, and A. Gaspari (eds) *Keltske študije II: Studies in Celtic Archaeology. Papers in honour of Mitja Guštin*. Protohistoire Européenne 11: 125–142. Montagnac: Monique Mergoil.

Lubšina-Tušek, M., and B. Kavur. 2011. 'Srednica near Ptuj. A contribution to the beginning of the La Tène period in Eastern Slovenia', in M. Guštin and M. Jevtić (eds) *The Eastern Celts: The Communities between the Alps and the Black Sea*. Annales Mediterranei: 31–50. Koper: Univerza na Primorskem.

Lucke, W., and O.-H. Frey. 1962. *Die Situla in Providence (Rhode Island): Ein Beitrag zur Situlenkunst des Osthallstattkreises*. Römisch-Germanische Forschungen 26. Berlin: Walter de Gruyter.

Lunz, R. 1973. *Ur- und Frühgeschichte Südtirols*. Bolzano: Athesia.

Lunz, R. 1974. *Studien zur Endbronzezeit und älteren Eisenzeit im Südalpenraum*. Florence: Sansoni.

Lunz, R. 1991. 'Ur- und Frühgeschichte des Pfattener Raumes', in G. Tengler (ed.) *Pfatten: Landschaft und Geschichte*: 53–179. Bolzano: Athesia.

Maggi, R. 2004. 'L'eredità della Preistoria e la costruzione del paesaggio', in R. C. de Marinis and G. Spadea (eds) *I Liguri: Un antico popolo europeo tra Alpi e Mediterraneo*: 34–49. Geneva/Milan: Skira.

Marchesetti, C. 1993. *Scritti sulla necropoli di S. Lucia di Tolmino (Scavi 1884–1902)*. Reprinted 1993. Trieste: Comune di Trieste, Civici Musei di Storia ed Arte.

Marić, Z. 1968. 'Japodske nekropole u dolini Une'. *Glasnik Zemaljskog muzeja Bosne i Hercegovine u Sarajevu N.S.* 23: 5–79.

Marijanović, B. 2012. *Tumuli iz Krneze i Podvršja kod Zadra/Tumuli from Krneza and Podvršje near Zadar*. Zadar: Sveučilište.

Marinetti, A., and A. L. Prosdocimi. 2005. 'Lingua e scrittura', in M. De Min, M. Gamba, G. Gambacurta, and A. Ruta Serafini (eds) *La città invisibile: Padova preromana: Trent'anni di scavi e ricerche*: 32–47. Ozzano dell'Emilia: Edizioni Tipoarte Industrie Grafiche.

Marzatico, F. 2014. 'L'età del Ferro in area alpina centro-orientale', in R. Roncador and F. Nicolis (eds) *Antichi popoli delle Alpi: Sviluppi culturali durante l'età del Ferro nei territori alpini centro-orientali*: 11–28. Trento: Giunta della Provincia autonoma di Trento.

Matthäus, H., and C. Braun. 1983. *Glasperlen der vorrömischen Eisenzeit I: Nach Unterlagen von Thea Elisabeth Haevernick (†)*. Marburger Studien zur Vor- und Frühgeschichte 5. Mainz: Philipp von Zabern.

Melli, P. 2004. 'Genova dall'approdo del Portofranco all'emporio dei Liguri; Genova. La necropoli preromana', in R. C. de Marinis and G. Spadea (eds) *I Liguri: Un antico popolo europeo tra Alpi e Mediterraneo*: 285–297, 308–315. Geneva/Milan: Skira.

Melli, P. 2007. *Genova preromana*. Genoa: Frilli editori.

Metzger, I. R., and P. Gleirscher (eds). 1992. *Die Räter: I Reti*. Bolzano: Athesia.

Metzner-Nebelsick, C. 2002. *Der 'Thrako-Kimmerische' Formenkreis aus der Sicht der Urnenfelder- und Hallstattzeit im südöstlichen Pannonien*. Vorgeschichtliche Forschungen 23. Rahden: Marie Leidorf.

Mihovilić, K. 1972. *Nekropola Gradine iznad Limskog kanala/La necropoli del castelliere 'Gradina' sovrastante il Canale di Leme*. Histria archaeologica 3.2. Pula: Arheološki muzej Istre.

Mihovilić, K. 1995. 'Reichtum durch Handel in der Hallstattzeit Istriens', in B. Hänsel (ed.) *Handel, Tausch und Verkehr im bronze- und früheisenzeitlichen Südosteuropa*. Prähistorische Archaeologie in Südosteuropa 11: 283–329. Munich/Berlin: Südosteuropa-Gesellschaft und Seminar für Ur- und Frühgeschichte der Freien Universität zu Berlin.

Mihovilić, K. 1996. *Nezakcij: Nalaz grobnice 1981. Godine/Nesactium: The Discovery of a Grave Vault in 1981*. Monografije i katalozi 6. Pula: Arheološki muzej Istre.

Mihovilić, K. 2001. *Nezakcij: Prapovijesni nalazi 1900–1953/Nesactium: Prehistoric finds 1900–1953*. Monografije i katalozi 11. Pula: Arheološki muzej Istre.

Mihovilić, K. 2002. 'Grčki i helenistični nalazi u Istri i Kvarneru. Greek and Hellenistic Finds in Istria and the Kvarner bay', in N. Cambi, S. Čače, and B. Kirigin (eds) *Grčki utecaj na istočnoj obali Jadrana/Greek Influence along the east Adriatic coast. Proccedings of the International Conference held in Split from September 24th to 26th 1998*: 499–519. Split: Književni krug.

Mihovilić, K. 2009. 'New finds of La Tène fibulae from Istria', in G. Tiefengraber, B. Kavur, and A. Gaspari (eds) *Keltske študije II: Studies in Celtic Archaeology. Papers in honour of Mitja Guštin*. Protohistoire Européenne 11: 209–216. Montagnac: Monique Mergoil.

Mihovilić, K. 2013. *Histri u Istri: Željezno doba Istre/Gli Istri in Istria: L´età del ferro in Istria/The Histri in Istria: The Iron Age in Istria*. Monografije i katalozi 23. Pula: Arheološki muzej Istre.

Montagnari Kokelj, E. 1996. 'Le necropoli di S. Barbara presso castelliere di Monte Castellier degli Elleri (Muggia-Trieste)'. *Aquilea Nostra* 67: 9–46.

Müller-Karpe, H. 1959. *Beiträge zur Chronologie der Urnenfelderzeit nördlich und südlich der Alpen*. Römisch-Germanische Forschungen 22. Berlin: Walter de Gruyter.

Nebelsick, L. D. 1997. 'Die Kalenderberggruppe der Hallstattzeit am Nordostalpenrand', in L. D. Nebelsick, A. Eibner, E. Lauermann, and J.-W. Neugebauer (eds) *Hallstattkultur im Osten Österreichs*. Wissenschaftliche Schriftenreihe Niederösterreich 106–109: 9–128. St Pölten/ Vienna: Niederösterreichisches Pressehaus.

Neugebauer, J.-W. (ed.) 1992. *Die Kelten im Osten Österreichs*. Wissenschaftliche Schriftenreihe Niederösterreich 92–94. St Pölten/Vienna: Niederösterreichisches Pressehaus.

Nicolis, F. 2013. 'Northern Italy', in D. Fontijn and A. Harding (eds) *The Oxford Handbook of the European Bronze Age*: 692–705. Oxford: Oxford University Press.

Olujić, B. 2007. *Povijest Japoda*. Zagreb: Pristup.

Pabst, S. 2009. 'Bevölkerungsbewegungen auf der Balkanhalbinsel am Beginn der Früheisenzeit und die Frage der Ethnogenese der Makedonen'. *Jahrbuch des Deutschen Archäologischen Instituts* 124: 1–74.

Pabst, S. 2012. *Die Brillenfibeln: Untersuchungen zu spätbronze- und ältereisenzeitlichen Frauentrachten zwischen Ostsee und Mittelmeer*. Marburger Studien zur Vor- und Frühgeschichte 25. Rahden: Marie Leidorf.

Pacciarelli, M. 2000. *Dal villaggio alla città: La svolta protourbana del 1000 a.C. nell'area tirrenica*. Florence: All'insegna del Giglio.

Pahič, S. 1966. 'Keltske najdbe v Podravju'. *Arheološki vestnik* 17: 271–336.

Palavestra, A. 1993. *Praistorijski ćilibar na centralnom i zapadnom Balkanu/Prehistoric Amber in Central and Western Balkans*. Belgrade: Srpska akademija nauka i umjetnosti, Balkanološki institut.

Paltineri, S. 2010. *La necropoli di Chiavari: Scavi Lamboglia 1959–1969*. Bordighera: Istituto Internazionale di Studi Liguri.

Pare, C. F. E. 1992. *Wagons and Wagon-Graves of the Early Iron Age in Central Europe*. OUCA Monograph 35. Oxford: Oxford University Committee for Archaeology.

Patek, E. 1982a. 'Neue Untersuchungen auf dem Burgstall bei Sopron'. *Bericht der Römisch-Germanischen Kommission* 63: 105–177.

Patek, E. 1982b. 'Recent excavations at the Hallstatt and La Tène hill-fort of Sopron-Várhely (Burgstall) and the predecessors of the Hallstatt culture in Hungary', in D. Gabler, E. Patek, and I. Vörös (eds) *Studies in the Iron Age of Hungary*. British Archaeological Reports International Series 144: 1–56. Oxford: Archaeopress.

Patek, E. 1993. *Westungarn in der Hallstattzeit*. Acta Humaniora. Quellen und Forschungen zur prähistorischen und provinzialrömischen Archäologie 7. Weinheim: VCH.

Pauli, L. 1971. *Studien zur Golasecca-Kultur*. Mitteilungen des Deutschen Archäologischen Instituts, Römische Abteilung, Ergänzungsheft 19. Heidelberg: Kerle.

Petru, P. 1971. *Hišaste žare Latobikov*. Situla 11. Ljubljana: Narodni muzej Slovenije.

Piana Agostinetti, P. (ed.) 1999. *I sepolcreti di Ornavasso: Cento anni di studi, Vols I–IV*. Rome: Nardini.

Piana Agostinetti, P. 2012. 'Contribution à l'étude de l'émergence du phénomène urbain en Cisalpine celtique', in S. Sievers and M. Schönfelder (eds) *Die Frage der Protourbanisation in der Eisenzeit/La question de la protourbanisation à l'âge du Fer. Akten des 34. internationalen*

Kolloquiums der AFEAF vom 13.–16. Mai 2010 in Aschaffenburg. Kolloquien zur Vor- und Frühgeschichte 16: 267–287. Bonn: Habelt.

Pichlerová, M. 1969. *Nové Košariská: Kniežacie mohyly zo staršej doby železnej*. Fontes Historického ústavu Slovenského národného múzea v Bratislave 4. Bratislava: Slovenské národné múzeum.

Pittioni, R. 1954. *Urgeschichte des österreichischen Raumes*. Vienna: Deuticke.

Primas, M. 1970. *Die südschweizerischen Grabfunde der älteren Eisenzeit und ihre Chronologie*. Monographien zur Ur- und Frühgeschichte der Schweiz 16. Basel: Birkhäuser.

Ramsl, P. C. 2002. *Das eisenzeitliche Gräberfeld von Pottenbrunn*. Fundberichte aus Österreich, Materialhefte A 11. Vienna: Bundesdenkmalamt.

Rapi, M. 2009. *La seconda età del Ferro nell'area di Como e dintorni: Materiali La Tène nelle collezioni del civico museo archeologico P. Giovio*. Archeologia dell'Italia settentrionale 11. Como: Musei Civici.

Raunig, B. 1968. 'Japodska nekropola na Crkvini u Golubiću'. *Glasnik Zemaljskog muzeja Bosne i Hercegovine u Sarajevu N.S.* 23: 81–98.

Rebay, K. C. 2002. *Die hallstattzeitliche Grabhügelgruppe von Zagersdorf im Burgenland*. Wissenschaftliche Arbeiten aus dem Burgenland 107. Eisenstadt: Amt der Burgenländischen Landesregierung.

Ridgeway, F. R. 1979. 'The Este and Golasecca cultures: A chronological guide', in D. Ridgeway and F. R. Ridgeway (eds) *Italy Before the Romans: The Iron Age, Orientalizing and Etruscan Periods*: 419–487. London: Academic Press.

Rossi, F. 2005. *La dea sconosciuta e la barca solare: Una placchetta votiva del santuario protostorico di Breno in Valcamonica*. Milan: ET.

Ruaro Loseri, L., G. Steffe De Piero, S. Vitri, and G. Righi. 1977. *La necropoli di Brežec presso S. Canziano del Carso: Scavi Marchesetti 1896–1900*. Monografie di Preistoria degli Atti dei Civici Musei di Storia ed Arte. Trieste: Electa Editrice.

Rubat Borel, F. 2006. 'Il Bronzo Finale nell'estremo Nord-Ovest italiano: il gruppo Pont-Valperga'. *Rivista di Scienze Preistoriche* 56: 429–482.

Ruta Serafini, A. (ed.) 1990. *La necropoli paleoveneta di via Tiepolo a Padova*. Padua: Zielo.

Ruta Serafini, A. (ed.) 2002. *Este preromana: Una città e i suoi santuari*. Treviso: Canova.

Salzani, L. (ed.) 2005. *La necropoli dell'età del Bronzo all'Olmo di Nogara*. Verona: Memorie del Museo Civico di Storia Naturale.

Salzani, L., and C. Colonna (eds). 2010. *La fragilità dell'urna: I recenti scavi a Narde necropoli di Frattesina (XII–IX sec.a.C.)*. Rovigo: Museo dei Grandi Fiumi.

Sansoni, U. 1987. *L'arte rupestre di Sellero*. Studi Camuni 9. Capo di Ponte: Edizioni del Centro.

Sansoni, U., and S. Gavaldo. 1995. *L'arte rupestre di Pià d'Ort*. Archivi 10. Capo di Ponte: Edizioni del Centro.

Šašel, J. 1972. 'Zur Erklärung der Inschrift am Tropaeum Alpium (Plin. n.h. 3, 136–7. CIL V 7817)'. *Živa antika* 22: 135–144.

Šašel, J. 1977. 'Strabo, Ocra and archaeology', in V. Markotić (ed.) *Ancient Europe and the Mediterranean: Studies Presented in Honour of Hugh Hencken*: 157–169. Warminster: Aris & Phillips.

Šašel-Kos, M. 2005. *Appian and Illyricum*. Situla 43. Ljubljana: Narodni muzej Slovenije.

Scarfì, B. M. (ed.) 1984. *Preistoria e Protostoria nel Polesine*. Padusa 20. Rovigo: Centro Polesano di studi storici, archeologici ed etnografici.

Schindler, M. P. 1998. *Der Depotfund von Arbedo TI und die Bronzedepotfunde des Alpenraums vom 6. bis zum Beginn des 4. Jh. v. Chr.* Antiqua 10. Basel: Verlag der Schweizerische Gesellschaft für Ur- und Frühgeschichte.

Schmid, W. 1933. 'Die Fürstengräber von Klein Glein in Steiermark'. *Praehistorische Zeitschrift* 24: 219–282.

Schmid, W. 1934. *Der Kultwagen von Strettweg*. Führer zur Urgeschichte 12. Leipzig: C. Kabitzsch.

Schmid-Sikimić, B. 2002. *Mesocco Coop (GR): Eisenzeitlicher Bestattungsplatz im Brennpunkt zwischen Süd und Nord*. Universitätsforschungen zur prähistorischen Archäologie 88. Bonn: Rudolf Habelt.

Sereni, E. 1955. *Comunità rurali nell'Italia antica*. Rome: Editori Riuniti.

Solano, S. 2012. 'L'iscrizione di Roncone (Trento) nel quadro dell'epigrafia preromana in alta quota fra area retica e camuna'. *Notizie archeologiche bergomensi* 18: 155–164.

Solinas, P. 1994. 'Il Celtico in Italia'. *Studi Etruschi* 60: 11–408.

Steiner, H. 2010. *Alpine Brandopferplätze: Archäologische und naturwissenschaftliche Untersuchungen/Roghi votivi alpini: Archeologiae scienze naturali*. Forschungen zur Denkmalpflege in Südtirol. Beni culturali in Alto Adige: studi e ricerche 5. Trento: Editrice Temi.

Stöckli, W. E. 1975. *Chronologie der jüngeren Eisenzeit im Tessin*. Antiqua 2. Basel: Verlag der Schweizerischen Gesellschaft für Ur- und Frühgeschichte.

Studeníková, E. 1996. 'Neue Ausgrabungen hallstattzeitlicher Hügelgräber in der Südwestslowakei', in E. Jerem and A. Lippert (eds) *Die Osthallstattkultur. Akten des Internationalen Symposiums, Sopron, 10.–14. Mai 1994*. Archaeolingua Main Series 7: 497–506. Budapest: Archaeolingua.

Svoljšak, D. 2001. 'Zametki urbanizma v železnodobni naselbini na Mostu na Soči. Zur Entstehung der Urbanisation in der eisenzeitlichen Siedlung von Most na Soči'. *Arheološki vestnik* 52: 139–142.

Svoljšak, D., and J. Dular. 2016. *Železnodobno naselje Most na Soči: Gradbeni izvidi in najdbe/The Iron Age Settlement at Most na Soči: Settlement Structures and Small Finds*. Opera Instituti Archaeologici Sloveniae 33. Ljubljana: Založba ZRC.

Svoljšak, D., and A. Pogaćnik. 2001–2002. *Tolmin, prazgodovinsko grobišće/Tolmin, the Prehistoric Cemetery. Vols I–II*. Katalogi in monografije 34–35. Ljubljana: Narodni muzej Slovenije.

Szabó, M., and É. F. Petres. 1992. *Decorated Weapons of the La Tène Iron Age in the Carpathian Basin*. Inventaria Praehistorica Hungariae 5. Budapest: Magyar Nemzeti Múzeum.

Tecchiati, U. (ed.) 2002. *Der heilige Winkel: Der Bozner Talkessel zwischen der Späten Bronzezeit und der Romanisierung (13.–1. Jh. v. Chr.)*. Schriften des Südtiroler Archäologiemuseums 2. Bolzano/Vienna: Folio-Verlag.

Tecchiati, U. and Rizzi, G. 2014. 'La "Casa delle botti e delle ruote" di Rosslauf (Bressanone): studi archeologici e technologici su un edificio del V. sec. a.C.', in R. Roncador and F. Nicolis (eds) *Antichi popoli delle Alpi: Sviluppi culturali durante l'età del Ferro nei territori alpini centro-orientali*: 73–103. Trento: Giunta della Provincia autonoma di Trento.

Tecco Hvala, S., J. Dular, and E. Kocuvan. 2004. *Železnodobne gomile na Magdalenski Gori/Eisenzeitliche Grabhügel auf der Magdalenska Gora*. Katalogi in monografije 36. Ljubljana: Narodni muzej Slovenije.

Teržan, B. 1976. 'Certoška fibula'. *Arheološki vestnik* 27: 317–536.

Teržan, B. 1985. 'Poskus rekonstrukcije halštatske družbene strukture v dolenjskem kulturnem krogu. Ein Rekonstruktionsversuch der Gesellschaftsstruktur im Dolenjsko-Kreis der Hallstattkultur'. *Arheološki vestnik* 36: 77–105.

Teržan, B. 1990. *Starejša železna doba na Slovenskem Štajerskem/The Early Iron Age in Slovenian Styria*. Katalogi in monografije 25. Ljubljana: Narodni muzej Slovenije.

Teržan, B. 1992. 'Beobachtungen zu den ältereisenzeitlichen Bestattungssitten im mittleren und südostalpinen Raum. Osservazioni sulla modalità sepolcrali dell'antica età del Ferro nel territorio delle Alpi centrali e sud-orientali', in I. R. Metzger and P. Gleirscher (eds) *Die Räter/I Reti*: 451–475. Bozen/Bolzano: Athesia.

Teržan, B. 1995a. 'Handel und soziale Oberschichten im früheisenzeitlichen Südosteuropa', in B. Hänsel (ed.) *Handel, Tausch und Verkehr im bronze- und früheisenzeitlichen Südosteuropa*. Prähistorische Archäologie in Südosteuropa 11: 81–160. Munich/Berlin: Südosteuropa-Gesellschaft und Seminar für Ur- und Frühgeschichte der Freien Universität zu Berlin.

Teržan, B. 1995b. 'Stand und Aufgaben der Forschungen zur Urnenfelderzeit in Jugoslawien', in M. zu Erbach (ed.) *Beiträge zur Urnenfelderzeit nördlich und südlich der Alpen*. RGZM Monographien 35: 323–372. Mainz: Römisch-Germanisches Zentralmuseum.

Teržan, B. 1996. 'Urnenfelderzeitliche Halsringe zwischen der nördlichen Adria und Südpolen', in J. Chochorowski (ed.) *Problemy epoki brązu i wczesnej epoki żelaza w Europie srodkowej: Księga jubileuszowa poświęcona Markowi Gedlowi/Probleme der Bronze- und der frühen Eisenzeit in Mitteleuropa: Festschrift für Marek Gedl*: 489–501. Krakow: Uniwersytet Jagielloński, Instytut archeologii.

Teržan, B. 1997. 'Heros der Hallstattzeit', in C. Becker, M.-L. Dunkelmann, C. Metzner-Nebelsick, H. Peter-Röcher, M. Roeder, and B. Teržan (eds) *Χρόνος: Beiträge zur prähistorischen Archäologie zwischen Nord- und Südosteuropa: Festschrift für Bernhard Hänsel*. Internationale Archäologie, Studia honoraria 1: 653–669. Espelkamp: Marie Leidorf.

Teržan, B. 1998. 'Auswirkungen des skythisch geprägten Kulturkreises auf die hallstattzeitlichen Kulturgruppen Pannoniens und des Ostalpenraumes', in B. Hänsel and J. Machnik (eds) *Das Karpatenbecken und die osteuropäische Steppe*. Prähistorische Archäologie in Südosteuropa 12: 511–560. Rahden: Marie Leidorf.

Teržan, B. 2002. 'Kronološki oris. Chronological Outline', in D. Svoljšak and A. Pogaćnik (eds) *Tolmin, prazgodovinsko grobišće, II/Tolmin, The Prehistoric Cemetery, II*. Katalogi in monografije 35: 85–102. Ljubljana: Narodni muzej Slovenije.

Teržan, B. 2007. 'Cultural connections between Caput Adriae and the Aegean in the Late Bronze and Early Iron Age', in I. Galanaki, H. Tomas, Y. Galanakis, and R. Laffineur (eds) *Between the Aegean and Baltic Seas: Prehistory across Borders: Proceedings of the International Conference 'Bronze and Early Iron Age Interconnections and Contemporary Developments between the Aegean and the Regions of the Balkan Peninsula, Central and Northern Europe', University of Zagreb, 11–14 April 2005*. Aegaeum 27: 157–165. Liège: Université de Liège.

Teržan, B. 2008. 'Stiške skice. Stična-Skizzen', in S. Gabrovec and B. Teržan (eds) *Stična II/2: Gomile starejše železne dobe, Razprave/Grabhügel aus der älteren Eisenzeit, Studien*. Katalogi in monografije 38: 189–325. Ljubljana: Narodni muzej Slovenije.

Teržan, B. 2009. 'Japodska nevesta iz okolice Novega mesta. A Iapodian bride from the vicinity of Novo mesto'. *Vjesnik Arheološkog muzeja u Zagrebu* 3, 42: 213–230.

Teržan, B. 2010. 'Japodske tropentljaste fibule. Iapodian three-looped fibulae'. *Prilozi Instituta za arheologiju u Zagrebu* 27: 111–122.

Teržan, B. 2011a. 'Horses and cauldrons. Some remarks on horse and chariot races in situla art', in S. Casini (ed.) *'Il Filo del Tempo': Studi di preistoria e protostoria in onore di Raffaele Carlo de Marinis*. Notizie Archeologiche Bergomensi 19: 303–325. Bergamo: Civico Museo Archaeologico.

Teržan, B. 2011b. 'Hallstatt Europe: Some aspects of religion and social structure', in G. R. Tsetskhladze (ed.) *The Black Sea, Greece, Anatolia and Europe in the First Millennium BC*. Colloquia Antiqua 1: 233–264. Leuven: Peeters.

Teržan, B. 2013. 'Liburnske dvodelne fibule s stožčastimi spiralicami—označevalke stanu in izobilja. Liburnian two-part fibulae with conical helices—identifiers of status and affluence', in S. Gluščević (ed.) *Batovićev zbornik*. Diadora 26/27: 241–266. Zadar: Arheološki muzej.

Teržan, B. 2016. 'Fibule. Obročast nakit/Oggetti di ornamento ad anello', in B. Teržan, E. Borgna, and P. Turk (eds) *Depo iz Mušje jame pri Škocjanu na Krasu/Il ripostiglio della Grotta delle Mosche presso San Canziano del Carso*. Katalogi in monografije 42: 233–284. Ljubljana: Narodni muzej Slovenije.

Teržan, B., and M. Črešnar. 2014. 'Poskus absolutnega datiranja starejše železne dobe na Slovenskem. Attempt at an absolute dating of the Early Iron Age in Slovenia', in B. Teržan and M. Črešnar (eds) *Absolutno datiranje bronaste in železne dobe na Slovenskem/Absolute Dating of the Bronze and Iron Ages in Slovenija*. Katalogi in monografije 40: 703–725. Ljubljana: Narodni muzej Slovenije.

Teržan, B., F. Lo Schiavo, and N. Trampuž-Orel. 1984–1985. *Most na Soči (S. Lucia) II: Die Ausgrabungen von J. Szombathy*. Katalogi in monografije 23. Ljubljana: Narodni muzej Slovenije.

Teržan, B., and N. Trampuž. 1973. 'Prispevek h kronologiji svetolucijske skupine. Contributto alla cronologia del gruppo preistorico di Santa Lucia'. *Arheološki vestnik* 24: 416–460.

Tessmann, B. 2001. 'Schmuck und Trachtzubehör aus Prozor. Kroatien. Ein Beitrag zur Tracht im japodischen Gebiet'. *Acta Praehistorica et Archaeologica* 33: 28–151.

Tiefengraber, G. 2015. 'Eine ausgewählte Fundstelle: Die Falkenberg und die Fürstengräber von Strettweg', in B. Hebert (ed.) *Urgeschichte und Römerzeit in der Steiermark*. Geschichte der Steiermark 1: 541–555. Vienna/Cologne/Wiemar: Böhlau.

Tiefengraber, G., and S. Tiefengraber. 2013. *Reiterkrieger? Priesterin? Das Rätsel des Kultwagengrabes von Strettweg bei Judenburg*. Judenburg: Arbeitskreis Falkenberg.

Todd, J. M., M. H. Eichel, C. W. Beck, and A. Macchiarulo. 1976. 'Bronze and Iron Age amber artifacts in Croatia and Bosnia-Hercegovina'. *Journal of Field Archaeology* 3, 3: 313–327.

Todorović, J. 1968. *Kelti u jugoistoćnoj Evropi. The Celts in Southeastern Europe*. Dissertationes 7. Belgrade: Muzej grada Beograda.

Tomedi, G. 2002. *Das hallstattzeitliche Gräberfeld von Frög: Die Altgrabungen von 1883 bis 1892*. Archaeolingua Main Series 14. Budapest: Archaeolingua.

Toms, J. 1986. 'The relative chronology of the Villanovan cemetery of Quatro Fontanili at Veii'. *AION Archeologia e Storia Antica* 7: 41–97.

Urleb, M. 1974. *Križna gora pri Ložu. Hallstattzeitliches Gräberfeld Križna gora*. Katalogi in monografije 11. Ljubljana: Narodni muzej Slovenije.

Vadász, É. 1983. 'Előzetes jelentés egy koravaskori halomsír feltárásáról Süttőn (Vorbericht über die Erschließung eines früheisenzeitlichen Hügels von Süttő)'. *Communicationes Archaeologicae Hungariae*: 19–54.

Venturino Gambari, M., and D. Gandolfi (ed.) 2004. *Ligures celeberrimi: La Liguria interna nella seconda età del Ferro. Atti del congresso internazionale, Mondovì 26–28 aprile 2002*. Bordighera: Istituto Internazionale di Studi Liguri.

Verger, S. 2001. 'Un graffite archaique dans l'habitat hallstattien de Montmorot (Jura, France)'. *Studi Etruschi* 64: 265–316.

Vinski-Gasparini, K. 1987. 'Grupa Martijanec-Kaptol', in A. Benac and S. Gabrovec (eds) *Praistorija jugoslavenskih zemalja V. Željezno doba*: 182–231. Sarajevo: Akademija nauka i umjetnosti Bosne i Hercegovine, Centar za balkanološka ispitivanja.

Vitri, S. 2004. 'Testimonianze dell'età del ferro nel Caput Adriae', in F. Marzatico and P. Gleirscher (eds) *Guerrieri, Principi ed Eroi fra il Danubio e il Po dalla Preistoria all'Alto Medioevo*: 284–291. Trento: Castello del Bonconsiglio.

Zemmer-Plank, L. (ed.) 2002. *Kult der Vorzeit in den Alpen: Opfergaben, Opferplätze, Opferbrauchtum*. Bolzano: Athesia.

CHAPTER 12

THE CENTRAL MEDITERRANEAN AND THE AEGEAN

LIN FOXHALL

Introduction

With very few exceptions (Broodbank 2013: 506–592), the Iron Age of the Aegean and the Mediterranean has generally been studied in a fragmentary way, within distinctive national scholarly traditions, often pursued in isolation. This chapter aims to break down the imaginary walls that scholars have traditionally built to divide the Mediterranean region in this period. In some parts of the region covered (southern Greece, Crete, southern Italy, Sicily, Sardinia, and Corsica; Figure 12.1), the Iron Age was a period of enormous change, while in others there appears to be much more continuity between the latest phases of the Bronze Age and the Iron Age. In all areas, it is fair to say, localism is paramount. Particularly in the Aegean relatively few well-preserved Iron Age sites survive, so our evidence is limited in some places, and we are regularly confronted with gaps (for example, only cemeteries but not settlements). Using well-documented case studies dating between about 1100 and 500 BC, I will explore changes and continuities across the region (and how we might understand them by bringing together a range of scholarly traditions), the interconnections between different localities around the Mediterranean, and the significance of Iron Age developments, including the impact of Greek and Phoenician settlement, for the region as a whole.

In much of the region under consideration, this period lies at the interface of prehistory and classical archaeology. In some scholarly traditions this period is labelled 'protohistory', a term that is as problematic as it is useful. In particular, it is sometimes deployed to justify the application of evidence from written sources, mostly Greek and Latin, which are geographically and/or chronologically distant in origin from the material they seek to interpret, and which is in reality beyond the reach of the texts.

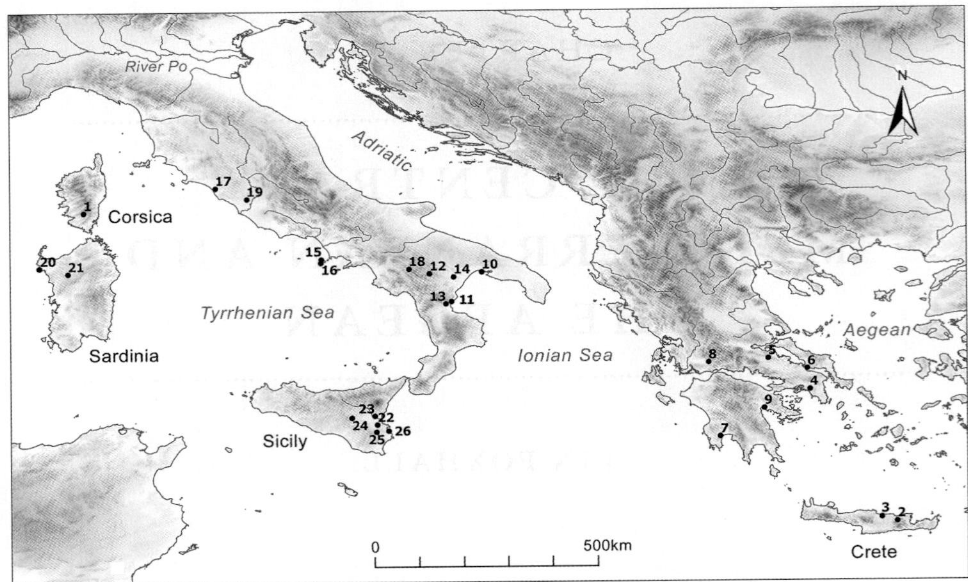

FIGURE 12.1 Map showing principal sites in the central Mediterranean and Aegean Sea area. *Corsica*: 1 Cuciurpula. *Crete*: 2 Karphi, 3 Knossos. *Greece*: 4 Athens, 5 Kalapodi, 6 Lefkandi, 7 Nichoria, 8 Thermon, 9 Tiryns. *Italy*: 10 L'Amastuola, 11 Broglio di Trebisacce, 12 Cozzo Presepe, 13 Francavilla-Marittima, Timpone della Motta, 14 Incoronata, 15 Pithekoussai, 16 Punta Chiarito, 17 Tarquinia, 18 Torre di Satriano, 19 Veii. *Sardinia*: 20 Sant'Imbenia, 21 Santu Antine. *Sicily*: 22 Lentini, 23 Lipari, 24 Morgantina Cittadella, 25 Pantalica, 26 Thapsos.

Drawing: R. Salisbury for author

However, the use of this term is an apt reminder that the divide between prehistorians and classical archaeologists, and their methodologies and intellectual frameworks, is artificial and needs to be transcended if we are to understand this fascinating and transformative phase in Mediterranean cultures, a theme to which I shall return.

Chronologies

Different chronological systems and divisions prevail across the regions covered by this chapter according to particular national scholarly traditions, and this can be very confusing. Much of the dating has been formulated on the basis of pottery styles, so that while the relative chronologies for specific localities are often (but not always) quite secure, the same cannot be said of the absolute dating, which is much debated (Nizzo 2007, 2016a, 2016b; Nijboer 2016; Núñez 2016). The chronology presented here (Table 12.1) is based on Dickinson (1994: 13, 19, 2006): 23; Leighton (1999: 147, 187); Kleibrink (2006: 30); Shelmerdine (2008: 4–5); Cascino (2012: 349); Peche-Quilicini (2012);

Table 12.1 Chronologies employed in the central Mediterranean and the Aegean

Mainland Greece	Crete	Sicily	Southern Italy	Central Italy	Sardinia	Corsica
Late Helladic IIIB 1300–1200	Late Minoan IIIB 1300–1200	Middle/late Bronze Age 1425–1200	Middle/late Bronze Age 1425–1200	Late Bronze Age 1365–1200	Middle/late Bronze Age 1500–1200	Late Bronze Age 1500–1200
Late Helladic IIIC 1200–1050	Late Minoan IIIC 1200–1050	Final Bronze Age 1200–c.1000	Final Bronze Age 1200–c.1000	Final Bronze Age 1200–1000	Final Bronze Age 1200–900	Final Bronze Age 1200–800
Sub-Mycenaean 1050–1000	Sub-Minoan 1050–950			Early Iron Age 1 1000–880		
Protogeometric 1000–900	Protogeometric 950–900 Protogeometric B 900–800					
Early Geometric 900–800		First Iron Age (Ausonian II) c.1000–700/680	First Iron Age c.1100?–c.730	Early Iron Age 2 880–750	First Iron Age c.900–538	First Iron Age 850/800–c.565
Middle Geometric 860–750	Middle Geometric 800–750					
Late Geometric 750–700	Late Geometric 750–700	Second Iron Age c.730/700–650?	Second Iron Age c.730/700–650?	Orientalizing 750–580		
Archaic 700–500	Archaic 700–500	Archaic c.650?–480	Archaic c.650?–480	Archaic 580–480	Second Iron Age 538–238	Second Iron Age c.565–238
Classical 480–323	Classical 480–323	Classical 480–323	Classical 480–323	Classical 480–350		

Peche-Quilicini et al. (2012); Sciappelli (2012: 329). Wallace (2010: 28) uses slightly earlier dates for the Minoan sequence. All dates are approximate and much debated.

Greece and the Aegean

The initial phases of the Iron Age in Greece and the Aegean are frequently represented in the scholarly literature as a 'Dark Age' of decay and decline after the materially and archaeologically rich era of the later Bronze Age palatial states. Certainly, the region saw great changes in political, economic, and social organization from around 1200–1100 BC, and the number and size of occupied sites diminishes and shifts in location to some extent, though the extent of abandonment of the palatial sites has often been exaggerated. Tiryns actually increased slightly in size; occupation continued at a reduced level and different in character at Mycenae and Knossos, and even at Pylos there are traces of low-level Iron Age occupation of the palace site. This is the region through which the invention of ironworking was introduced into Europe, probably via Cyprus (Muhly et al. 1985: 68; Dickinson 2006: 146; Chapter 23). Moreover, although the nature of the state changed radically, the idea that the highly centralized palace-led societies simply degenerated into stateless or 'tribal' societies consisting of isolated communities is probably, in its crudest form at least, incorrect.

For a start, communities were not as isolated as often depicted, and there was considerable variation across the region. Crete continued to maintain links with the Near East, and major sites such as the palatial centre at Knossos continued to be occupied, albeit rather differently than in the Bronze Age. What appear to be refuge sites, such as Karphi, also emerged (Wallace 2010), perhaps indicating a perception of danger from invaders or social and political disruption. Although the island of Euboea may have momentarily lost contact with the outside world, it rapidly regained it, and there is considerable evidence of links between Lefkandi and other sites in Greece and the Near East from not much after 1100 BC, while in Athens contact with the Near East becomes evident during the ninth century BC (Lemos 2002: 226–229, 2006: 525–526).

Nichoria and the South-Western Peloponnese

The kinds of changes that took place at the beginning of the Iron Age are best illustrated via a case study. The site of Nichoria was an important Bronze Age settlement, a second-order centre where local administrators, perhaps the leaders of an elite household inhabiting house IV-4A, were based (Foxhall 2014) under the authority of the so-called Palace of Nestor at Pylos. It is set on a flat hilltop surrounded by well-watered and fertile agricultural land. In some ways, Nichoria is a 'typical' site of the period in that it consisted of a compact village in a secure and defendable location, which exploited the good agricultural land and grazing resources in its immediate vicinity. Although dispersed settlement in the countryside was characteristic of Greek landscapes from about the sixth century BC onward, in this early period the land was farmed from nucleated settlements.

Beyond its geographical proximity and material cultural links, Linear B tablets found in the palace attest to its role in the political hierarchy. The site continued into the Iron Age, one of the few that provides archaeological evidence of a settlement in this period, though it was considerably smaller, and its regional role changed considerably. After a phase of abandonment of about 100 years, new houses were built directly on the Bronze Age foundations, starting shortly after 1000 BC. The site was abandoned for good around 700 BC and not inhabited thereafter, which no doubt partially explains why it is one of the few Iron Age settlements to survive reasonably intact. Area IV, inhabited by the local elites in the Bronze Age, was the core of the Iron Age community and remained the centre for its leading family, though of course we have no idea whether it was the same leading family as that of the Bronze Age settlement. As in other parts of Greece, Bronze Age *tholos* tombs were the object of cult activity in the Iron Age, but this may indicate a desire on the part of local elites or communities to identify themselves with the past inhabitants rather than reflecting a genuine direct connection. In Iron Age Nichoria, there is no evidence of the specialist artisans who serviced the Bronze Age palace and very little metal was in use—the only meagre metal finds came from the one elite house IV-1/IV-4. This may reflect the economic circumstances of the community more than the state of technological knowledge.

Unlike the Bronze Age inhabitants, Iron Age households, even the elites, preferred one-roomed houses. House IV-1/IV-4 was considerably larger than the rest (Figure 12.2). A one-room rectangular structure built of wattle and daub and supported by posts, it was considerably modified over its lifespan, starting in its second phase around 850–800 BC. An apse was added, which seems to have been used for storage. A large paved circle, which was part of the house from the start, was made more prominent; this may have had a ritual function, but this is uncertain. A new entrance was added on the northern side and a courtyard area—perhaps to provide additional work and social space—at the eastern end. Most of the material found in the house is modest in character and indicates a domestic assemblage (60% coarsewares, 40% fine wares; McDonald et al. 1983: 19–33). This was probably the only house on the site with permanently fixed cooking facilities. Especially in its larger second phase, the building may also have hosted communal events such as feasting (suggested by the relatively large number of animal bones) and/or religious ritual, although it is difficult to be sure of this. Evidence is less strong for the architectural history of other Iron Age houses, but there certainly seems to be an increase in house numbers and settlement density in Area IV over time, whatever the precise spatial organization.

Lefkandi

Lefkandi, on the island of Euboea, is again a somewhat unusual site. Later Archaic and Classical period settlement on the island focused on nearby Chalkis and Eretria,

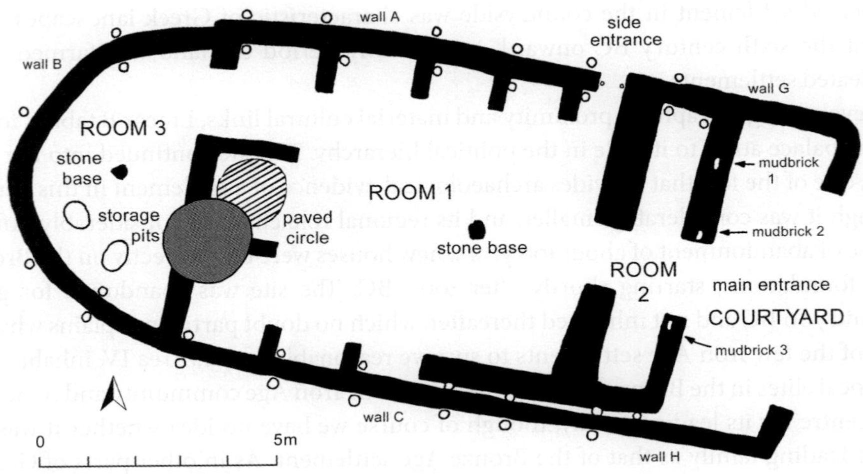

FIGURE 12.2 Nichoria, Greece: house IV-1, phase 2.

Source: courtesy of the University of Minnesota Press

whereas Lefkandi was abandoned around 700 BC and thus both settlement and cemetery areas survive. The settlement at Xeropolis in Lefkandi is not well understood in the Iron Age, though in recent years a very large tenth-century BC house has been excavated (but is not yet fully published).

The cemeteries were the first areas to be explored when the site was discovered. There were at least six, but the Toumba cemetery, adjacent to the so-called *Heroon* (Figure 12.3), has been most extensively investigated, published, and discussed (Popham 1988–1989; Dickinson 2006: 190–193; Lemos and Mitchell 2011). The *Heroon* itself is a remarkable monumental building. In form and construction, it is rather like the elite house—originally a rectangular structure with an apse added at the western end for storage—but much larger (45 x 10 m). In the centre of the building were two burial pits. The southern pit contained the inhumed body of a woman with rich grave goods including gold hair coils, embossed gold discs and bronze, gilded iron, and bone pins. Next to her, the cremated body of a man had been placed in a large bronze vessel decorated with human figures and animals; an iron sword and spear were also found. The man's remains had been wrapped in a cloth, which survived where it was in contact with the bronze. The adjacent pit contained four horses, two with iron bits. Shortly after the structure was built it was covered over with an earthen mound (*toumba* in modern Greek). The adjoining cemetery to the east of the building came into use almost immediately, around 1100 BC, and the latest burials date to about 825 BC (Popham et al. 1982). Many are very rich and include iron weapons. Unlike Nichoria, this was a wealthy site with many imported objects and a considerable amount of metal, demonstrating contacts within Greece and across the Mediterranean. Though house-like in form, it is uncertain whether the *Heroon* was built as a dwelling or always intended as a tomb. Clearly those

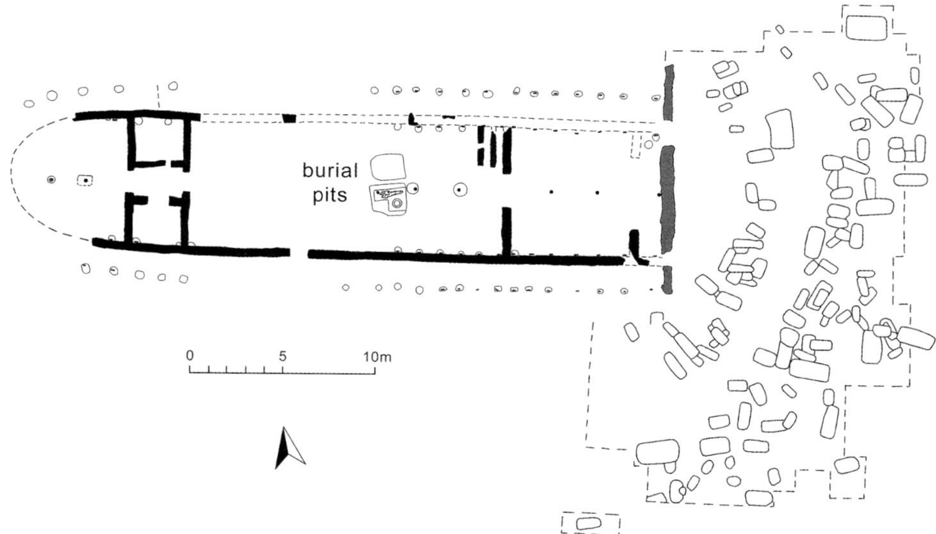

FIGURE 12.3 Lefkandi, Euboea: *Heroon* and Toumba cemetery.

Source: courtesy of the British School at Athens

buried there were elites of some kind, and the graves in the adjacent cemetery could be individuals who considered themselves part of their establishment or related to the people buried in the *Heroon*. In the cemetery there are both male and female cremations and inhumations, including children (for the most part in one section), as well as a few horse burials.

The Euboeans had settlements abroad from at least the early eighth century BC, and possibly earlier, both on the coast of the Levant (e.g. al Mina, Turkey) and in southern Italy (notably Pithekoussai, the island of Ischia; Ridgway 1992). At Lefkandi there are Levantine imports, for example an ornate bronze bowl, and clear connections with Cyprus, as documented by finds of Cypriot pottery including some marked with signs of the Cypriot syllabary. In turn, Euboean pottery appears in southern Italy and the Levant from an early date. The connection with Cyprus suggests that the Euboeans, who were some of the first Greeks to work iron, learned the technology directly from the Cypriots, and some areas of Euboean activity in southern Italy, such as the mainland adjacent to Ischia, are rich in iron ores.

Athens

Evidence for the Iron Age occupation of Athens comes largely from burials, notably those revealed by the extensive excavations in the Agora (on the slopes of the Acropolis and the Areopagus) and the Kerameikos (Morris 1987). Other evidence survives in sanctuaries around Attica. This situation exemplifies the difficulty we have with those

Iron Age sites in Greece which were the most successful: Athens had clearly been a substantial and prosperous community, but millennia of construction in the Archaic, Classical, Hellenistic, Roman, and later periods has obliterated virtually all traces of the Iron Age settlement.

Athenian graves provide a complete pottery sequence from the latest phases of the Bronze Ages (late Helladic IIIC) through to the end of the eighth century BC. The relative chronology derived from ceramics in other parts of Greece is linked to this key sequence, and there were clearly particularly close ties between Athens and Euboea. Although the quality of workmanship declines in the Sub-Mycenaean phase, skilled craftspeople remained working in Athens and Attica throughout the Protogeometric and Geometric periods. Like Lefkandi, Athens regained contact with the Near East quite early, but not until the ninth century BC, rather later than Lefkandi.

Graves were also often highly gendered. A ninth-century middle Protogeometric female grave from the slopes of the Areopagus is one of the richest found, with costlier grave goods than in most male graves of the period (ASCSA n.d.). The remains of the cremated corpse were contained in a large decorated belly amphora, the typical shape for female graves. Among other finds, the grave contained a pair of elaborate gold ear-rings employing the techniques of both granulation and filigree. Although the techniques were surely learned from Near Eastern artisans, the ear-rings were made locally. The most extraordinary find in the grave, however, was a ceramic chest with five smaller pointed pots upended on top of it, each with a hole in the top. This is normally interpreted as a granary, although there is no evidence for the use of granaries of this type at this period, and the granaries in the Xeropolis settlement at Lefkandi are quite different. A more probable interpretation might be that this item represents a row of ovens or kilns—in form they resemble closely the depictions of kilns for manufacturing pottery and metal that are depicted on the Penteskaphe plaques from seventh-century BC Corinth, and there are plenty of actual examples of such installations.

In contrast, an early Protogeometric male grave of the ninth century BC contained a spear point, dagger, and sword (wrapped around the cremation urn) and a set of ceramic vessels associated with wine drinking (*œnochoe*, cups); the cremated remains were contained in a large shoulder amphora of the type typical of male graves. Similar kinds of 'warrior graves' appear regularly but sporadically throughout Greece at this time, the one in the *Heroon* at Lefkandi being perhaps an extreme example. It seems likely that these are particularly high-status men, though what roles they played in life is unknown, and Homeric epic does not help us.

It seems plain that Athens in this period, like Lefkandi, was ruled by wealthy elite families who competed with one another, probably among other ways through lavish display in funerals and the deposition of grave goods. This practice stopped in the second half of the eighth century BC (late Geometric period) when competitive display shifted to sanctuary contexts (Osborne 2009: 86–88).

Crete

Crete had its own, very different, trajectory in the Iron Age, displaying much more apparent continuity with Bronze Age traditions, although social and political organization was plainly very different in many ways. Crete lacks the 'Dark Age' perceived elsewhere in Greece by many scholars. It kept its connections with the outside world much more firmly: as in Lefkandi, iron appears in Crete about 1100 BC, and it seems likely that the technology was acquired directly from Cyprus. There is considerable, if scattered, evidence for Iron Age settlement at Knossos (Kotsonas et al. 2012). As at Lefkandi, there are also several well-preserved cemeteries. Bronze Age Cretans buried their dead in communal (probably family-based) chamber tombs, and this habit was maintained during the Iron Age, even though the burial ritual switched for the most part from inhumation to cremation. Other kinds of tombs, small pit tombs, and shaft graves were also used. Sometimes Bronze Age chamber tombs were reused or continued in use, but many new ones were also constructed during the Iron Age. Iron tools, weapons, and jewellery appear in these graves from as early as 1100 BC, some imported from Cyprus, others made locally. Other objects in bronze, lead, ivory, and faience from the Near East and Cyprus also appear in these cemeteries, and one bronze bowl bears a Phoenician inscription. The twenty-eight Attic Protogeometric pots discovered—a larger number than were imported from any other area of Greece—suggest reasonably regular contact with Athens and Attica. Clearly a prosperous, thriving, and well-connected community lived at Knossos during this period.

However, other patterns also emerged at this time in Crete. A number of 'refuge' sites appeared, of which Karphi is one, located so as to be invisible from below on an inaccessible saddle between two steep hills (Wallace 2010). The site was abandoned around 1000 BC. The tightly nested cluster of houses is a phenomenon we see at other Cretan Iron Age sites. Like the chamber tombs, the development of these 'agglutinative' settlements, where new units are built on to existing units, seems to be based on household and kinship organization.

In east Crete, in the Kavousi area, sites moved inland and upward, and became larger and more nucleated during the later phases of the Bronze Age and the early Iron Age. Single farmhouses disappear from the archaeological record. Sites appear to be organized in clusters, which Haggis (1993) has suggested are probably family based. Within sites, houses were also tightly packed (Haggis 1993: 143–149; Wallace 2010: 63–66) and agglutinative settlements were characteristic in many places (Wallace 2010: 108–112). This process continued down to the seventh century BC.

Although these small early Iron Age sites were defensible, with many being quite inaccessible, all had good agricultural land in the vicinity (Wallace 2010: 59–60). Houses were much smaller than in the Bronze Age, suggesting smaller household units and possibly less status differentiation within the household. Buildings were much more similar in size across different settlements. In many of these communities one or more houses may be larger than the rest, suggesting that there were still significant social or status differences within the community (Wallace 2010: 114–116), but there is no indication that they had much impact on the use of space within the settlement. Communities appear to be made up of relatively autonomous households (Glowacki 2004: 134), at least in terms of taking decisions about organizing the space available to them, although we cannot be certain about what social or political obligations or relationships bound them to such elite families as there were. Agglutinative building patterns within settlements suggest that individual household reproduction and decisions were the major factor in settlement growth and construction, with the apparent absence of any large-scale centralized authority. This pattern of settlement appears elsewhere in the Aegean, most notably at Zagora on the island of Andros (Foxhall 2009, 2014).

Kalapodi and Thermon

Both these sites demonstrate somewhat divergent patterns of development from other Greek settlements in the Iron Age, suggesting that they are different kinds of communities with a rather different kind of trajectory than those that developed into city states in the later Iron Age and Archaic periods. In most places the development of monumental architecture in the form of temple buildings emerges in the later eighth century BC. This phenomenon, visible at Eretria on Euboea (Apollo Daphnephoros), Dreros on Crete (Apollo Delphinios), Samos (Hera), Argos (Hera) and Sparta (the so-called Menelaion) is characteristic of communities which later became full-fledged city states (*poleis*).

However, at Kalapodi and Thermon there is evidence of substantial cult activity, and of built temples, at a much earlier date. At Kalapodi in Phokis, central Greece, there is evidence of extensive cult activity from the twelfth century BC (late Helladic IIIC). Cult activity continued at a high level through the early Iron Age, although in the middle of the tenth century BC domesticated animals took over from deer as the most common form of sacrifice. The construction of the first monumental temple began in the middle of the ninth century, and two more buildings were added in the late eighth or early seventh century BC. At Thermon in Aetolia, west of Kalapodi, cult activity appears to have been continuous from the Bronze Age. The earliest temple building, Megaron A, was built sometime between the twelfth and tenth centuries BC. The much larger Megaron B dates to the ninth century BC.

What both communities have in common is that they never developed the urban centre characteristic of *poleis* (sing. *polis*), but instead, focused their social, religious, political, and communal activities on a sanctuary, while the members of the community lived in small, scattered settlements. This probably explains the very early emergence of monumental temple buildings on the key sanctuary sites of these communities. Such political entities are normally identified as *ethnē* (sing. *ethnos*) by modern scholars, adopting Aristotle's terminology of the fourth century BC, and indeed they certainly turned into *ethnē* in later periods. However, one could equally find parallels to these communities across the Mediterranean in Sicily, southern Italy, Sardinia, Corsica, and

Iberia, where a central place, often but not always dominated by an elite family, became a core focus for the communal activities of people living spread out over a wide area.

Conclusions

In contrast to the relative cultural and material cultural homogeneity of the Bronze Age, one of the greatest changes in the Iron Age was the strong and rapid emergence of distinctive local habits and traditions. This is not to say that regions were isolated from one another, as has sometimes been suggested, or that they did not share many fundamental elements of culture, including language (with dialectical differences). A core repertoire of pottery shapes and decorative elements, for example, is widely shared across the Greek world, although there are many local—sometimes highly localized—variations as well as eccentric shapes and decorative motifs peculiar to a specific community or region. Crete is particularly distinctive culturally, linguistically, and material culturally because of its Minoan heritage, and perhaps because of its continuing links with the Levant, but nonetheless its inhabitants shared beliefs and maintained active links with other Greeks.

As we shall see, Greeks were very much a part of the wider world in which they lived—the Mediterranean has no fences or boundaries. However, it was in this period, even before the adoption of alphabetic writing toward the end of the Iron Age in the eighth century BC, that we can see that despite their local differences, Greek communities shared beliefs, traditions, customs, and habits that underpinned a common identity.

Central Italy

When Greek incomers first arrived at Pithekoussai early in the eighth century BC, they will have encountered the Italic peoples on the mainland to the north, whom modern scholars have come to know as the Etruscans. These Iron Age communities and their later successors ranged at their furthest extent from the Po valley to northern Campania, but were concentrated mainly in what is now Tuscany and Lazio. By the time the Greeks encountered them, these were sophisticated societies, but their development from the late and final Bronze Ages down into the Iron Age is complex. Two key methodological approaches have had a considerable impact on how the Etruscans and the development of their culture have been interpreted by modern scholars. First, much past research has taken the later Greek and Roman literary tradition as a core body of evidence for this period, and some more recent work still depends heavily on these written sources (Riva 2010: 4–7). Almost inevitably, this has meant that the Etruscans have been considered as part of the evolution of Rome and its political and social structures, so it can be difficult to disentangle their specific cultural and political development in its own terms and in its own time from views about later Roman society in hindsight. Secondly, partly as a result of this first approach, much discussion of Etruscan sites and polities has focused on the issues of state-formation and urbanization (di Gennaro 1986, 1999; Peroni 1994, 2000; Pacciarelli 2000), which, as Riva (2010: 13) observes, are not the same thing, although scholars have often conflated them. Here the development of these Etruscan communities will be approached primarily through archaeological evidence. I will focus principally on two sites, Tarquinia and Veii, as case studies, although many of the same trends can be observed at other sites.

A fundamental archaeological problem is that most of the Etruscan sites that have been intensively investigated and published are cemeteries; far less work has been carried out on settlements and other types of site (Izzet 2007: 165). One reason for this is that many Etruscan settlements lie under Roman and modern towns, while their cemeteries were situated in less densely inhabited parts of the landscape. However, even in the case of the cemeteries, many were excavated, or raided for their treasures, before the twentieth century, so the archaeology of these sites is far from complete and often not intact. More recently, archaeological survey has enabled this balance to be corrected in part (e.g. Sciappelli 2012).

During the final Bronze Age, from about 1200 BC, numbers of sites increased. Small to medium-sized settlements of around 3–15 ha in size (most in the lower part of the range), located on steep-sided hilltops, proliferated in central Italy. These appear to be organized as independent, but interacting and possibly competing, communities. Although few have been comprehensively excavated, most appear to consist of groups of oval houses with groups of tombs located a short distance away, with indications of elite groups and hierarchal structure (di Gennaro 1999), as at San Giovenale (Hanell 1962) or the Isola Farnese site at Veii. However, density and character of settlement varied considerably over central Italy. In some areas rich in mineral resources, such as around the Monti della Tolfa, settlements are quite close together (Riva 2010: 14). In contrast, the intensively surveyed area around Veii revealed no other late Bronze Age sites in the immediate vicinity (Sciappelli 2012: 329–330). These late Bronze Age sites are often represented as 'pre-urban' centres, though this may owe more to the perceived evolution of Etruscan society and states than to the actual evidence of the archaeological remains, for which, in most instances, high-resolution data are lacking.

From the period of the first Iron Age (often referred to as the Villanovan period), starting around 1000 BC, most of the final Bronze Age settlements disappear, and settlement focused on fewer, but much larger sites, from about 35 ha up to 100 ha or more, on the big plateaux (Riva 2010: 18–19). Some of these, such as Tarquinia, had already been occupied on a smaller scale in the later Bronze Age, but others were completely new settlements, such as Vulci, and in some cases (as at Veii) the settlement moved from one location to another. These settlements too have generally been characterized as 'proto-urban' (Peroni 1994, 2000; Pacciarelli 2000). They were generally located in proximity to good agricultural land, and in some cases within easy reach of mineral resources, especially metal ores, or were positioned to exploit maritime resources and trade networks. This development is particularly striking in southern Etruria where several particularly large settlements—Veii, Caere, Tarquinia, and Vulci—stand out in comparison with smaller ones further inland such as Bisenzio, Chiusi, and Orvieto, or the more widely spaced settlement centres in northern Etruria at Populonia, Vetulonia, or Volterra. Although this dramatic settlement shift has often been interpreted as 'state formation', there is little solid archaeological support for idea, and size and density of settlement alone need not indicate a state organization (Riva 2010: 21–22).

From the later tenth through eighth centuries BC, there is evidence at Tarquinia for a substantial Iron Age community, covering up to 150 ha, with cemeteries located around it. Because it was largely covered by the later Etruscan cemeteries, it is hard to get a full picture of the Iron Age settlement. However, surface survey indicates clusters of habitation of varying size, with open spaces in between. Geophysical survey and test excavations over about 2 ha in the area of the sixth century BC necropolis revealed considerable portions of eleven structures and traces of at least fourteen more. Four were certainly oval and substantial in size (12–16 x 7–8 m), while another seven could be identified as rectangular, albeit variable in size and form. The few artefacts recovered suggest cooking and storage, probably indicating that these buildings were houses. Cult activity began in the final Bronze Age in a natural crevasse in the rock, and continued to be elaborated and developed down to the sixth century and beyond.

At Veii, excavations on the Piazza d'Armi, a small hilltop just off the southern edge of the main plateau, revealed circular and elliptical structures ('huts') and burials dating to the early Iron Age. Within one hut located in the settlement area was the grave of a young man, dated to the early ninth century BC. In the seventh century, the hut was replaced with a rectangular timber building, suggesting that this grave remained a focus of cult activity (Cascino 2012: 341). Survey has revealed that during the Iron Age, settlement activity was thinly scattered across virtually the whole plateau, with a greater concentration along the northern side in proximity to the main roads entering the site from the north and north-west, and at the southern tip, just north of the Piazza d'Armi, leaving an apparent gap in the central-eastern sector. Cemeteries were located off the plateau, especially but not exclusively to the north and west (Cascino 2012: 345–349; Sciappelli 2012: 334–339).

During the eighth and seventh centuries BC, occupation of the plateau intensified, as documented in survey by a much greater amount of pottery found, and the site developed into a truly urban centre. This period is usually seen as the transition from the earlier Iron Age Villanovan period to the Etruscans. At Veii, the earliest traces of grid planning dating to the mid-seventh century appear on the Piazza d'Armi (Riva 2010: 27; Cascino 2012: 347). In the more densely occupied northern sector of the city from the first half of the seventh century BC, rectangular timber structures, some of which had stone foundations and mud-brick walls, were situated next to elliptical huts. There is also evidence of major monumental buildings and ceramic workshops (Cascino 2012: 347–349). The earliest cult activity at Portonaccio, a site which later became a major sanctuary south-west of the main plateau, also appeared in the seventh century BC.

Over the eighth and seventh centuries, in the great burial grounds to the north and west outside the settlement area, tombs became much more elaborate, developing from single graves (generally cremations) with an additional pit (*loculus*) used for offerings or banqueting vessels, to square chamber tombs housing inhumations, many with more than one chamber, benches, an entry passage (*dromos*) and *loculi*. In some, the walls were painted, and many contained a wide range of prestigious grave goods, including banqueting assemblages, valuable personal ornaments and tools, and chariot and 'warrior' burials with an array of weapons and armour. Many of these graves and cemeteries emphasized status and gender; some also seem to be organized in family groups. Between 650 and 600 BC, small numbers of exceptionally rich tumulus tombs (nine or ten are known at Veii) also appeared along main roads and in cemeteries (Riva 2010: 37; Cascino 2012: 343). Most scholars interpret these funerary trends, which occur at most major Etruscan sites, as indicating the development of a wealthy aristocratic elite, whose wealth was founded on land ownership, although the latter supposition is not well supported by the archaeological evidence (Riva 2010: 8).

One of the most important features of the mid-eighth to seventh-century BC phase was the explosion of imported objects from Greece, the Near East, and elsewhere, which appears to have exerted a major influence on Etruscan craft production, to the extent that it is regularly dubbed the 'Orientalizing' period. A much wider range of shapes and new wares—including the well-known highly burnished black *bucchero* production and Italo-geometric wares—appeared, in addition to large quantities of Greek pottery and Near Eastern objects. Simultaneously, the Etruscans also adopted a version of the Euboean Greek alphabet to write their own language. This elaboration of material culture is particularly evident in funerary contexts (Riva 2010: 141–176). Traditionally scholars attributed the developments in Etruscan society and material culture at this period to outside influences, particularly the Greeks, but it is now generally agreed that Etruscan urbanization was very much an indigenous development. It is clear, however, that the Etruscans were exceptionally well networked in the Mediterranean, especially the western Mediterranean, and that this web of relationships may well have played a significant part in the dramatic social, political, and material cultural developments of the later eighth and seventh centuries BC.

Etruscan interactions with the Greeks are often stressed in the scholarly literature, and are perhaps obvious from the large amounts of Greek material that appear in Etruscan tombs. However, Etruscan material also occurs in Greek sanctuaries (Izzet 2007: 215–223). Etruscan links with Sardinia and Sicily are well documented, and contact between central Italy and Iberia and eastern Languedoc in France is evident. In the early eighth century BC, Villanovan pottery appears at Huelva in Iberia along with Euboean (Sub-Protogeomentric), Attic (middle Geometric), Cypriot (black on red), Sardinian, and Phoenician (Tyrian) ceramics (González de Canales et al. 2006). Phoenician pottery constitutes the bulk of the material, perhaps suggesting that Phoenician traders brought pottery from elsewhere along with their own. Nonetheless, this implies that even at this early date, the Villanovan/Etruscan inhabitants of central Italy were in contact with the Phoenicians, perhaps via Pithekoussai, Sicily, or Sardinia, where Phoenician settlements were well established. By the sixth century BC, at the indigenous settlement of Lattes, west of the Greek city of Massalia (Marseille), two houses can be identified as belonging to Etruscan merchants. These houses were unusual in construction for the site, 90% of the ceramics present were Etruscan, and included cooking pots (some with graffiti in Etruscan script) and tablewares as well as amphorae (Dietler 2010: 97–99). Perhaps via France, Etruscan material made its way into central Europe, and these links may explain the regular appearance of amber, presumably from the Baltic, in many elite Etruscan graves.

The impact of the Etruscans and their earlier Iron Age Villanovan predecessors on these wider Mediterranean networks is often overshadowed by the waves of Greek and Phoenician overseas activity and settlement in the period between the ninth and sixth centuries BC. On the other hand, too often the Etruscans have been viewed as the 'predecessors' of the Romans, and scholars have attempted to retroject Roman political and social institutions to interpret the Villanovan and Etruscan archaeological record. The creative internal dynamics of these central Italian societies, and their wide network, about which we still have much to learn, deserve to be interpreted and analysed on their own terms.

Southern Italy

Between the late Bronze Age, the final Bronze Age, and the Iron Age significant changes took place in southern Italic societies and polities, but these do not appear to be as dramatic as in the Aegean, or possibly even elsewhere in Italy (Attema et al. 2010: 116). Much scholarly debate has focused on 'urbanization' and 'proto-urbanization', though this may not be the most useful approach for understanding the social and political organization of this period. It is generally accepted that Iron Age societies in this region were somewhat less hierarchical, and probably smaller in scale, than in the middle and late Bronze Age. Although the Iron Age cultures of the region share many features, local areas develop quite differently. Almost everywhere, our knowledge of the Iron Age depends heavily on burial evidence, and relatively few well-excavated settlement sites are published, although this is changing. Graves are exceptionally variable, sometimes even within the same site and the same cemetery. Individual inhumations (*tombe a fossa*) are common across the entire region, but burial in large storage jars and cremation were also regularly practised. Perhaps the most widely shared feature, especially in elite graves, is the emphasis on gender demarcation.

In the late and final Bronze Age in Campania, Puglia, Basilicata, Calabria, and Sicily at sites such as Roccagloriosa, Rocavecchia, Termito, Broglio di Trebisacce, Syracuse, Morgantina, and Lentini, there is evidence of small amounts (or in the case of Rocavecchia, substantial amounts) of imported Mycenaean pottery, as well as larger numbers of imitations made locally, but using firing and manufacturing techniques (including the use of the potter's wheel) that were not employed for indigenous wares. Although it is probable that some of the Mycenaean material was brought by Cypriots and others, the distinctive manufacture of Mycenaean imitations suggests the possibility of some direct contact with Mycenaean craftworkers, although the nature and degree of that contact is much debated (van Wijngaarden 2002; Blake 2008; Iacono 2015; Russell 2017). This Mycenaean material is critical for dating. A few sites maintained direct or indirect contact with other Mediterranean cultures, as documented by finds at sites such as Torre Galli (Kleibrink 2006: 28). In some areas such as Basilicata, key centres of the late Bronze Age and final Bronze Age were abandoned, especially those closer to the coast, and only a few coastal sites, such as Termito, retained low levels of occupation. Broglio di Trebisacce has also produced some of the earliest evidence for iron production in southern Italy, with a forge dating to the final Bronze Age/early Iron Age (Figure 12.4). A sherd with a mark which could be a Cypriot ideogram has been interpreted to suggest that the knowledge of ironworking came with Cypriot contact (Vanzetti n.d.).

In some areas, for example around the fertile plain of Sybaris in northern Calabria, early Iron Age settlements sprang up on Bronze Age sites (Kleibrink 2006: 24; Attema et al. 2010: 112–117). Sites such as Torre di Mordillo and Broglio di Trebisacce supported smaller Iron Age communities, while Francavilla Marittima (Timpone della Motta) became the main Iron Age settlement in the region (Kleibrink 2006; Handberg et al. 2009). In the case of L'Amastuola in Puglia, the well-preserved Iron Age settlement dates to late eighth century BC, although there are also traces of a Bronze Age presence near the site (Burgers and Crielaard 2011: 36–38). Although not far from the coast, these sites are situated some distance inland. They are generally located on the tops of flat hills or ridges, significantly higher than the fertile plains and flatter lands they overlook, but rarely at altitudes over 300–500 m above sea level. They often have a view of the sea, but were not usually visible from the sea (cf. Pacciarelli 2016). Another focus of the vigorous and long-lasting Iron Age settlement in southern Italy was on the well-watered and fertile upland plateaux away from the coast, at sites like Torre di Satriano in Basilicata (Osanna et al. 2009; Osanna and Capozzoli 2012; Osanna 2014), or around the northern side of the Aspromonte massif at sites such as Castellace (Sica 2011), Torre d'Inferrata, and Palazzo in Calabria (Agostino and Sica 2009), and L'Amastuola in Puglia (Burgers and Crielaard 2007, 2012).

FIGURE 12.4 Broglio di Trebisacce, southern Italy, area of forge and *pithos* store.

Photo: Lin Foxhall

The arrival of Greek settlers in small numbers in Italy and Sicily is first detectable in the eighth century BC. Pithekoussai (the island of Ischia off the Bay of Naples) remains the earliest documented Greek presence, and the nature of the settlement here has been much debated (Ridgway 1992; Buchner and Ridgway 1993). Although there appears to be a strong Greek element in the material culture of the site, with elements from all over the Greek world, as well as Cypriot and Levantine material, the many indigenous elements which appear in the graves suggest that this was a complex, mixed community (Nizzo 2016b: 59–60). In particular, the fibulae in the female graves are indigenous, not Greek, in style (Coldstream 1993; Hodos 1999; Leighton 2000: 194) and virtually all the 'Greek' graves contained indigenous handmade pottery, including as a standard item one small jug, which was perhaps a key element in local funerary ritual.

Even more interesting is the rural house at Punta Chiarito, occupied from the mid-eighth to early sixth centuries BC (Gialnella 1994; de Caro and Gialnella 1998). This is a small elliptical, one-roomed house with evidence of large numbers of storage vessels. A small elliptical outbuilding in its final phase (late seventh to early sixth century) included a large tufa basin, which Brun (2004: 162–163) has identified as for grape treading; carbonized remains of both grapes and olives appeared on the site (Coubray 1994). Given the mixture of artefacts and the style of building, it is impossible to identify this establishment, especially in its earlier phases, as definitively occupied by either Greeks or indigenous people. Instead, it would seem to be a classic example of a 'hybrid' site.

Although modern scholars regularly identify Italic Iron Age people by the later 'ethnic' designations used by classical authors (Enotrian, Messapian, Lucanian, etc.), this is probably not generally appropriate until at least the later Archaic and Classical periods, when such ethnic designations may have been taken up in response to the challenges posed by the growth of Greek cities at this time. The material culture evidence, including architectural and ceramic styles as well as burial customs, demonstrates a range of local traditions on common themes, suggesting that in earlier times each settlement was relatively independent and in competition with (as well as linked to) other similar settlements, but there appears to be relatively little sense of common regional or 'ethnic' identity. However, from the eighth century BC onward, contact between indigenous Italic communities and the Greek (and later, Roman) incomers had a significant impact on all of these cultures.

Basilicata and the Metapontino

In Basilicata during the ninth to sixth centuries BC, prosperous hilltop communities, often identified as 'Lucanian', thrived in the uplands around Matera and Potenza. Climatically, the area is cooler and wetter than areas closer to the coast, is excellent for agriculture and stock rearing, and had good access to forest products. Substantial settlements with associated graves such as Difesa di San Biagio (seventh to third centuries BC) flourished, situated in an area of sandy conglomerate marine terraces, offering fertile and easily worked soils.

Torre di Satriano, on the upper reaches of the River Bradano (Osanna and Capozzoli 2012; Osanna 2014), began as a large one-roomed apsidal house constructed on a stone foundation with a wattle and daub or mud-brick superstructure, with the roof supported by a line of posts down the centre. There were a couple of adjacent graves. The house included substantial work areas and storage facilities, including partially buried large storage jars. This structure was occupied between the eighth and early sixth centuries BC, on a hilltop dominating a number of smaller sites on the broad upland plain below, and was probably inhabited by an elite family who controlled the territory in the immediate vicinity. The pottery is all local and indigenous, consisting of handmade impasto and fine matt-painted wares, many of them drinking vessels. There were also two portable braziers and a considerable number of animal bones, as well as large undecorated impasto loom weights. No metal finds occurred in the house, but some, including an iron spear, occurred in the nearby sanctuary. This is not entirely surprising since metal objects are most commonly found in graves, many of which are very rich.

However, during the sixth century a new residence consisting of a large rectangular, multiroomed building was constructed lower down the hill (Figure 12.5). This building too had graves close by (seven). It was decorated with a Greek terracotta frieze made of local clay by Lakonian workers from Taras (modern Taranto), identifiable by the distinctive Lakonian letters incised on the back before firing. In a Greek context, such a frieze would have featured only on a temple or a major public building, not a private house. The material culture of this house was overall much more varied and richer than that of the earlier apsidal house, suggesting that contact with Greek incomers on the coast had a major impact on the consumption and production habits of the inhabitants. In addition, loom weights from three looms stacked on the outside wall of the house indicate that at least thirty women were employed in textile manufacture, operating at a workshop scale. These loom weights, also made in local clay, although only about forty years later than those from the apsidal house, are completely regular, small pyramidal weights, suitable for weaving fine textiles. Evidently, there were Greek women in the house of this elite indigenous family, whether slaves, concubines, or wives. Osanna (2014) interprets these two structures as the headquarters of different families, but both conceivably belonged to different generations of the same prosperous and powerful family.

To the east, down towards the coast, there were a few Iron Age sites, smaller than those inland. Two important sites in what eventually became the territory of the Greek city of Metaponto were Incoronata and Cozzo Presepe. These sites began in the ninth century BC, along with Termito closer to the coast, where there had also been late Bronze Age occupation. In this period there was little Italic dispersed settlement in the countryside, and it seems that population concentrated in the village centres and exploited the limited amount of good agricultural land nearby. However, from the eighth century BC there were significant changes. These settlements had always had quite extensive contacts with other settlements in the region and limited external connections. Initially

Greek Geometric wares appeared sporadically, but increased substantially in the later eighth to early seventh centuries, well before the Greek urban settlement of Metaponto developed. Incoronata consisted of a substantial village with a nearby necropolis. In the late eighth century one sector of the site, Incoronata greca, acquired a Greek presence of some sort, the nature of which is much debated (Osanna 2014: 233–235). It seems probable that a few Greek settlers moved into the indigenous community, developing into a mixed community (Denti 2016; Savelli 2016). Large numbers of Greek imports appeared, especially transport amphorae, and a new local style of pottery called 'colonial' ware (inspired by a wide range of Greek types) developed alongside the traditional impasto wares. 'Colonial' ware does not appear at Cozzo Presepe. There is good evidence for the cultivation of cereals, olives, and vines, and for exploitation of domestic animals, especially sheep and pig. There is also interesting evidence of the 'scaling up' of local agricultural production: the earliest known rotary olive crusher appears here in an excavated context of the late seventh century BC. This discovery raises the possibility that it may be a western Mediterranean invention stimulated by a changing political and economic environment, rather than a Greek innovation as is generally assumed. Such developments suggest that the links to a broader network of external connections via the Greeks provided new opportunities for elite activities and competition.

FIGURE 12.5 Torre di Satriano, southern Italy: later sixth-century BC rectangular house in the foreground, with hill in the background where the earlier eighth to sixth-century BC house is located.

Photo: Lin Foxhall

The inland limit of Greek settlement in the Metapontine countryside is about 27 km from the coast, near Pomarico. Archaic and Classical Greek rural settlement displays geological clustering on the easily tilled soils of the Pleistocene marine terraces, in areas where the blue clays meet the overlying sands and gravels, so ground water was easily accessible via wells and springs. Although Folk (2011) suggests that the Greeks forced the indigenous peoples inland, the archaeological record contradicts this interpretation. In fact, the upland plateaux of the mountains, where Greeks do not appear to have settled, provide good, or even better, conditions for agriculture. Rather, it seems that powerful local indigenous communities relegated the Greek incomers to the land near the coast, which they considered less desirable because it was inclined to flood. It was only after the inhabitants of Metaponto constructed major drainage works starting in the sixth century (the so-called 'division lines') that dispersed rural settlement began to flourish here (Prieto 2006; Carter and Prieto 2011).

Francavilla Marittima and the Sybaride

Timpone della Motta, near Francavilla Marittima, is situated on a series of terraces ranging from 135–180 m above sea level, in what was later the territory of the Greek city of Sybaris. The sizeable cemetery at Macchiabate, just to the east, must belong to this settlement. The earliest Greek settlers appear to have moved into this indigenous community, named by classical authors and modern scholars as 'Oinotrians'. During the late Bronze Age the main settlement was probably at Broglio di Trebisacce (Peroni and Vanzetti 1998), and the two sites are intervisible (Figure 12.6). In the final Bronze Age and first Iron Age some settlements disappeared, but some of those which remained increased in size (Kleibrink 2006: 28). Partial remains of a basically rectangular early Iron Age house constructed of posts with wattle and daub, measuring at least 8 x 5 m, have been excavated (Kleibrink 2006: 79–110). The structure had substantial storage facilities associated with it. The site (but probably not the house itself) appears to have been inhabited from the late ninth to the end of the seventh centuries BC.

However, the most fully excavated and published buildings from Timpone della Motta are those on the acropolis (Figure 12.7). The earliest was a middle Bronze Age 'hut'. There was no late Bronze Age material, but in the first Iron Age two large apsidal houses of wattle and daub set between two rows of posts were constructed, building I at the northern end and building Vb at the southern end. Radiocarbon dates suggest that building Vb was in use in the mid-ninth century BC (Kleibrink 2006: 163). The associated assemblages, particularly well-documented for building Vb, suggest they were the headquarters of elite families. The building could have been as large as 16 x 8 m. It included a substantial fixed hearth, ceramic cooking stands, numerous animal bones, a double row of thirty large decorated loom weights against the wall indicating an active loom *in situ*, spindle-whorls, considerable storage facilities and large storage jars (*pithoi*), a wide range of beads, jewellery, and other metal objects (including an iron knife next to the loom), and a wide range of matt-painted and impasto pottery. Opinion is divided on the function of this building and whether it served as a house or a

FIGURE 12.6 View from Broglio di Trebisacce, looking towards Timpone della Motta.

Photo: Lin Foxhall

FIGURE 12.7 The acropolis at Francavilla Marittima, Timpone della Motta, southern Italy.

Photo: Lin Foxhall

sanctuary. While it is clear that ritual functions were incorporated within this building, and its successors were indeed sanctuaries, it seems most probable that this was an elite dwelling house in the ninth century BC, although its function and that of its successors changed later. From the eighth century BC, a large ash deposit incorporating artefacts and animal bones built up outside the south-west corner of the building. Around 725/700 BC a rectangular timber temple (building Vc) was constructed on the site, probably using a different building technique from that used for the Iron Age house Vb (Kleibrink 2006: 174). In the seventh and sixth centuries BC, when the Greek settlers were developing the urban sites of Sybaris and Croton on the coast, the acropolis housed a succession of temples dedicated to Athena. Substantial amounts of Greek pottery began to appear in addition to the indigenous wares, suggesting that the sanctuary was used by Greek, indigenous, and mixed communities of the area.

L'Amastuola

L'Amastuola (Burgers and Crielaard 2007, 2011, 2012, 2016) is a village of about 3.3 ha located on a flat hilltop in the Salento peninsula, 200–213 m above sea level, some 15 km inland from the later Greek city of Taras (modern Taranto). Both survey and excavation suggest that the site was first occupied by local indigenous Italic groups in the late eighth century BC as a nucleated settlement, with no scatter of occupation in the surrounding territory. Late Bronze Age occupation was located on three sites at lower elevations, not on the Amastuola hilltop. There is no evidence of any final Bronze Age activity, suggesting a considerable gap in the occupation between *c.*1200 and 725 BC (Burgers and Crielaard 2007: 95–96, 2011: 36–38). The site had a complex system of defensive walls, and traces of indigenous curvilinear houses have been excavated.

During the seventh century BC, L'Amastuola became a mixed community as Greek settlers moved in, but the indigenous presence continued throughout the century (Burgers and Crielaard 2016). Houses built from this period onward were rectilinear. The cemetery to the south-east of the site, which has graves dating from *c.*675 through to the mid-fifth century BC, is probably associated with the immigration of Greeks (Burgers and Crielaard 2007: 99, 106). The local indigenous pottery suggests strong connections with the Metapontino and Matera area, and there are many Greek imports from a wide range of different places, including Corinth, Attica, east Greece, and Corcyra, as well as Greek-style pottery from Metaponto and the Sybaride. The settlement history of l'Amastuola points to a community far more threatened by Greek incomers, and ultimately overwhelmed by them compared to the indigenous communities of Torre di Satriano and Francavilla Marittima.

Conclusions

Before the arrival of the Greeks, powerful, well-organized, and prosperous societies inhabited the southern half of the Italian peninsula. Political organization seems to have been based on the activities of competing elite families. Despite distinguishable regional material cultural traditions in the Iron Age, there is no firm evidence for the use of the 'ethnic' designations assigned by later classical authors (although by the fourth century BC these had genuinely become more real). Recent work suggests that 'ethnicity' in these mixed communities needs to be conceptualized more flexibly, not simply as 'Greek' or 'indigenous' (Burgers and Crielaard 2016). Instead, political/social authority seems to be quite local. In terms of sophistication these indigenous societies were very little different from the Greek incomers who arrived in the eighth and seventh centuries BC. In many cases the incomers appear to have been both welcomed and regulated—indigenous groups often seem to have been glad of the opportunities for wider connectivity (potentially leading to greater prestige for individuals and particular families, as in the case of Torre di Satriano). However, sometimes there was clearly considerable hostility, and this might often have been much more complex than the stories of 'Greeks vs natives' that appear in the later classical sources.

Sicily

In many Sicilian sites, the transition from the later phases of the Bronze Age to the first Iron Age are relatively smooth, despite the literary tradition (which some archaeologists perceive in the material cultural evidence) that around this time Sicily was the recipient of migrations by 'peoples' from mainland Italy (e.g. Albanese Procelli 2016: 199–200). For this reason, the first Iron Age is often called the 'Ausonian'. The type-site for this phase, from which the ceramic sequence was developed, is Pantalica, with over 1,000 rock-cut chamber tombs dating from the latest phases of the Bronze Age right through the Iron Age. It is located on a flat ridge with steep ravines on three sides about 20 km from the coast and the later Greek city of Megara Hyblaea. In the early twentieth century, Orsi excavated a multi-roomed structure thought to be an elite house of the late Bronze Age, but more recently considerable doubt has been cast on this dating; the building seems more likely to be of Byzantine construction.

Dating for the earlier phases of the period is difficult in the absence of the kinds of Aegean wares that allowed for cross-dating in the Bronze Age, and there are still few radiocarbon dates. The situation is complicated by the strong archaeological tradition of attempting to 'reconcile' the literary traditions of migration of named 'peoples' with the archaeological evidence within a chronological framework (see Chapter 37). The validity of these approaches is still widely accepted (Albanese Procelli 2016), although other scholars have cast considerable doubt on them (Leighton 2000; Hodos 2006: 92–93). Towards the end of the Iron Age, sometime during the eighth century BC, Greeks began to settle on the coasts, largely on the eastern half of the island. Phoenician/Punic settlers took up residence on the western shores probably around the same time, facing toward the parts of the western Mediterranean such as Sardinia and Iberia where they were already well established.

Leighton (1993: 106, 1999: 187–188, 2000: 15–17) has convincingly shown that the traditional chronologies for the Iron Age in Sicily were placed too early and should be downdated (cf. Hodos 2006: 94–98; Kleibrink 2006: 30). It is clear from their assemblages that many sites continued well into the eighth and in some cases the seventh century BC, after the arrival of Greek incomers. Some of the 'type-fossil' artefacts regularly used for dating, such as the serpentine fibula, continued in production much longer than had previously been assumed, and the origin and dating of other artefacts traditionally supposed to relate to the earliest Greek settlers, such as the 'Thapsos cups', are highly problematic (see following section).

It is also becoming more widely accepted that the social and political reality of the 'peoples' such as Sikels, Sikans, and Elymii named by later writers like Thucydides and Diodorus Siculus, is dubious (Leighton 2000: 19–21). It is extremely difficult to understand whether the names that appear in the literary sources have any 'ethnic', social, cultural, or any other kind of reality in the Iron Age; the likelihood is that they do not. Leighton has suggested that these groups were segmentary, 'tribal' societies, and this suggestion has been used to underpin the analyses of others (Leighton 1996, 1999: 198–9, 2000: 17–19; cf. Albanese Procelli 2003: 122–128; Hodos 2006: 93). However, as Leighton himself emphasizes, the evidence is limited and 'at present there is no label which convincingly characterizes the societies in question' (Leighton 2000: 19).

Thapsos

Such a change of population has been suggested for Thapsos, a fortified site with a good harbour situated on a peninsula on the south-east coast of Sicily, which had prospered from the middle Bronze Age and was a gateway for Mycenaean contact in the late Bronze Age, with evidence of large-scale storage areas, although the extent and impact of this Aegean contact has been challenged (Russell 2017). In the final Bronze Age and first Iron Age (in the eleventh to ninth centuries BC), evidence for interaction with the Aegean declines, although links with the western Mediterranean continue and develop. The circular houses with central hearths and the regular rectilinear buildings along what appear to be streets of the Bronze Age (Areas 1, 2A, and possibly 2B) were replaced in the first Iron Age with a poorly preserved cluster of rectilinear rooms (Area 2C). One area has been interpreted as for food storage, and there were millstones for grinding grain in the room opposite, as well as spaces with evidence of textile manufacture (represented by loom weights) and perhaps craft production (in the form of deer antlers; Albanese Procelli 2003: 38). Whether this group of rooms was a domestic house with specialist and/or commercial activities incorporated within the household is difficult to say, but that seems the most likely interpretation on present evidence.

One of the most important but problematic discoveries for the Sicilian Iron Age and its chronology has proven to be a group of fineware cups, more or less early Protocorinthian in style, which have become known as 'Thapsos cups'. These were long considered to be Corinthian imports which could be used to date finds in Sicily and southern Italy, and to demonstrate the presence of Greek incomers. These cups (and more rarely other shapes) occur at a number of Sicilian and southern Italian sites, as well as on sites in western and central Greece, including Kalapodi and Delphi, with occasional examples in the Cyclades. However, their origin has been questioned, because they often bear decorative motifs such as spirals, which never appear on actual Corinthian examples, because the range of shapes (particularly cups) is rather different from the repertoire of Corinth, and because of macroscopic analysis of the clay, which is greener than Corinthian clays (Coldstream 1977: 168–172; Bosana-Kourou 1983; Hodos 2006: 94–98; Jacobsen and Handberg 2010: 263). In the absence of recent and conclusive scientific analyses of the fabric, none of the suggestions for their place of origin (Corinth, Aegina, Megara) seem very convincing. These cups, at least in terms of the received wisdom concerning the decorative motifs used, appear to cover a long period, from the end of the late Geometric to middle Protocorinthian in style (Bosana-Kourou 1983: 267)—in theory, from about the last third of the eighth century to the end of the first quarter of the seventh century BC (Coldstream 1977: 385). However, since their place of origin is unknown, it is difficult to be certain about the chronological significance of the decorative motifs, as the chronology of stylistic sequences can vary considerably from one region to another for many reasons. Hence, it is wise to be cautious about the chronological or cultural significance often claimed for this category of pottery when it appears on Sicilian and other Iron Age sites.

Morgantina Cittadella

In addition to the coastal sites, a number of inland hilltop communities retained some continuity across the transition between the Bronze and Iron Ages, but many new communities also sprang up at this time, and some, like Morgantina, continued to be occupied after the arrival of Greek incomers. The best evidence for second Iron Age occupation at Morgantina appears on the Cittadella (Area III of the excavations), a prominent conical hill (578 m above sea level) at most about 600 m in diameter, with two flat ridges at a lower altitude on the eastern side (Figure 12.8). The hilltop appears to have been well supplied with springs, and there is good agricultural land in the valley bottom below (Leighton 1993: 127–128). The remains of the Iron Age settlement are fragmentary, with parts of a number of what are most likely to be domestic houses, and in places subsequent Archaic and Classical building has destroyed the Iron Age levels. This seems to have been a fairly substantial, though not densely packed, settlement. Occupation in this period appears over a wide area of the hill and the lower ridges, but it is impossible to ascertain whether all parts were occupied concurrently, or indeed if all the excavated houses were inhabited at the same time. There is no evidence of any 'urban' planning, nor of a street grid. It is possible that the settlement consisted of several clusters of houses, with empty space in between, though this is speculative (Leighton 1993: 138–139).

It is difficult to generalize about the houses at Morgantina Cittadella because no complete houses have been excavated. House floors were constructed to be below ground

FIGURE 12.8 The ancient city of Morgantina, Sicily, with the hill of Morgantina Cittadella in the background.

Photo: Alexander van Loon [own work, CC BY-SA 4.0, https://commons.wikimedia.org/w/index.php?curid=36402961], via Wikimedia Commons

level, and where possible, one side of the house was cut into the bedrock, a widespread building tradition in Sicily and southern Italy from the Iron Age to the Classical period. In several cases the floors were deliberately constructed on two levels, and there is at least one raised platform whose purpose is unknown. The walls consisted of a stone socle or foundation, preserved to a maximum of 0.8 m in excavated houses, with a wattle-and-daub superstructure. Several houses had benches built into the walls or cut out of the natural bedrock. The position of entrances cannot generally be determined, and the construction and materials of the roof are unknown. Several houses had substantial permanent hearths set on a bedding of potsherds, and in some there is evidence for internal divisions in the form of postholes. Insofar as it can be determined, the one house (trench 29) where the full dimensions can be guessed was at least 10 m long and 5 m wide. It is likely that the buildings were a range of different sizes, though they seem relatively large compared to Iron Age houses at Lentini and Lipari (see following sections). This could suggest that they were inhabited by relatively large extended households, but there is little direct evidence to support this hypothesis.

Most houses appear to be sub-rectangular in shape, a feature that appears at other Sicilian sites such as Lentini. Where preserved, as in the house in trench 31, there is evidence for storage (this particular building had a particularly large number of *pithoi*), living space, and areas for processing and cooking food, including an oven. However, although all the houses are slightly different there seems to be little specialization in terms of crafts or productive activities, and few obvious differences in wealth or status (Leighton 1993: 141–146). Handmade coarsewares predominate, with a range of shapes and items characteristic of domestic assemblages. These include large *pithoi* (occasionally used for intra-mural burials, probably of children), amphorae and other large storage jars, jugs, carinated cups and bowls, cooking stands, bone and stone tools, loom weights and spindle-whorls, millstones, and moulds for casting bronze. There is a smaller amount of painted finewares (plumed and geometric), but like the coarsewares these largely seem to be locally made (Leighton 1993: 146–147).

Rock-cut tombs that presumably belonged to this community were located on the slopes of the Cittadella at an altitude of about 500 m above sea level, alongside cemeteries of the Archaic period. The Iron Age necropolis (Area III, Necropolis IV) was comprised of scattered clusters of oven-shaped tombs, most of which had been disturbed. The three undisturbed tombs (4, 5, and 6) contained varying numbers of individuals and grave goods. Tomb 4 contained one adult with pottery, and items of personal adornment and jewellery in bronze, iron, and a bead of glass paste. Two adults and the skulls of two small children were found in Tomb 5, with only one small jug. Tomb 6 was the largest and most complicated of the undisturbed tombs, containing two adults, with a cow horn and a bowl standing on a large flat sherd in the most recent level, and four adults side by side at a lower level, with numerous grave goods, including pottery, jewellery, and personal ornaments in bronze and iron, and one bead of glass paste. Of these earlier skeletons, one was a man over 50 with signs of arthritis, along with a second man and two women aged between 25 and 45. This tomb also contained the only pot with painted decoration, although four of the fifteen pots found in these three tombs were wheel-made. These tombs seem to be contemporary with the latest excavated Iron Age levels on the Cittadella, suggesting that an Iron Age community later than most of the occupied dwellings on the top of the Cittadella may have lived nearby.

Unlike the chamber tombs of the Bronze Age, in which large numbers of bodies were deposited, the Iron Age tombs seem to represent much smaller social groupings, possibly household based. The intact Iron Age tombs in Morgantina seem to show quite different amounts of archaeologically visible grave goods, although this could be related to factors other than wealth and status—such as gender or age. However, with such a small sample it is impossible to generalize.

The finds at Morgantina Cittadella suggest a relatively long-lived Iron Age farming community inhabiting the site from perhaps some time before 800 BC down to the seventh century (Leighton 1993: 123–125), but not necessarily always focused in the same place. In addition to the fertile land for growing crops below the settlement, the inhabitants also exploited cattle, sheep/goats, pigs, and deer, although no bones of horses or donkeys are reported from the limited animal bone samples collected. The restricted material culture suggests no great differences in wealth, but the samples from both the settlement and cemetery sites are, of course, very small from what was probably a relatively large community. We can glean little about the political organization of the site from the excavated remains, although the diffuse arrangement of the settlement and the graves, shifting over time and with nothing that suggests any kind of long-lived 'chief's house' or major monuments, might suggest that it was relatively fluid and volatile. In the later phases, when Greek imports began to be present on the site, there is no evidence to suggest that the inhabitants were 'Hellenized'. Rather, they seem to have adapted the habits and material culture of the Greek incomers to suit themselves (Lyons 1996).

Lipari

The acropolis on Lipari remains a key 'Sicilian' site, not least because it has been published in detail (Bernabò Brea and Cavalier 1980), although the Aeolian Islands have cultural traditions of their own which are somewhat different from those of Sicily. Located on the top of a steep-sided volcanic hill, the site was inhabited from the Neolithic. The Iron Age settlement, which must have been quite extensive, appears to have been built directly on top of that of the Bronze Age, although it was oriented and organized differently. There are no springs on the island, so in all periods water must have come from cisterns; those of historic periods have considerably disturbed the underlying archaeology. Remains of the first Iron Age (Ausonian II) are most complete in what were dubbed Insulae III and IV of the Classical-Hellenistic city, an area with no major Classical buildings.

Two structures of this period have been investigated in considerable detail. Hut α I survives as only a small stretch of north–south wall, but three postholes and considerable areas of floor surfaces remain. The internal floor was cut down into the soil, so the internal space was at a lower level than the external surface. A sizeable internal hearth was rebuilt over four phases across the lifetime of the house; an additional hearth lay outside. Large quantities of carbonized material and food remains were found in and around all the hearths (but not analysed). The hut was covered by the burned layer which often covers Ausonian II levels on this site, and the top layers were mixed with Greek material (Bernabò Brea and Cavalier 1980: 24–26).

The second structure, Hut α II, was almost complete except for the south-west corner (Bernabò Brea and Cavalier 1980: 20–42). It appears to be a large, single-roomed domestic house, sub-rectangular in shape, with an internal length of 13.8 m (15.6 m external) and a width of 5.5 m at the east end, 4.75 m at the west (maximum width 5.7 m). The only entrance was at the east end; the door probably faced north-east, with a covered area in front (Bernabò Brea and Cavalier 1980: 39–40). Hut α II directly overlay traces of two other houses, α III (which actually adjoins α II) and α IV to the west and north; it was built on a stone socle (approximately five rows of stone survived up to a height of *c.*0.7 m; thickness 0.8–0.9 m) with wooden posts around 0.6 m apart. In some parts of the site traces of carbonized structural timbers were found. The two long walls had posts on the edge of the wall, but the posts on the short sides were internal. The house was built directly into a natural slope of the bedrock, and the south/south-eastern side of the floor was about 1 m lower than the north/north-west side (Bernabò Brea and Cavalier 1980: 31–33). There was a hearth outside the west end with carbonized material and food remains. A considerable amount of pottery, lithics, and weaving tools were associated with this building.

This was clearly an extensive hilltop settlement, well connected to the outside world, which appears to have existed right down to the occupation of the site by Greeks in the later eighth and seventh centuries BC. Because of later construction it is impossible to deduce much about the spatial or political organization of the Iron Age site, but Hut α II seems plausible as the base of a substantial household, and frequent modifications of the hearth used for food preparation in Hut α I suggests a dynamic household composition changing over time.

Lentini

Lentini, the site of the later Greek city of Leontinoi, remains one of the most important sites for understanding the Sicilian Iron Age and the arrival of the Greeks, despite the limited scope of its publication (primarily Rizza 1962, 1978, 1980). Both the Metapiccola and the San Mauro hills have the remains of Iron Ages houses, but the cluster of seven houses on Metapiccola (Rizza 1962), certainly part of a settlement which may have been more extensive, are the best preserved and excavated. The one-roomed rectangular houses varied in size from 3.5 x 4.1 m to 19 x 5.1 m. They were constructed by carving out the bedrock to produce a sunken floor; the floor of Hut B (capanna B) was 0.7 m deep. The walls and roofs of the houses were supported by posts along the sides, documented by postholes carved into the bedrock to a depth of 0.4–0.5 m and averaging 0.4 m in diameter. Four of the seven houses also had one or more posts in the centre of the house, presumably to support the roof. The substantial size of the timbers indicates access to areas of mature forest inland. The house walls were possibly built of wattle and daub, though other materials could have been used, and the central posts could imply a thatched roof. In Hut B, the excavators suggested that the eastern end, with a slight dip in the middle, was the entrance. There was a post immediately outside the house here, aligned with the central posts inside the house, and another that more or less lines up with the north-east corner post—perhaps for some kind of covered area at this end of the house (Rizza 1962: 3–6).

Subsequent early Greek houses of the later eighth and perhaps early seventh centuries BC on the site of San Mauro at Lentini (Rizza 1980) were also built using the technique of carving out the bedrock—in this case, right into the side of the hill. It seems that the Greeks were exploiting local building traditions and techniques (Rizza 1980: 127). Fitzjohn (2007: 221–222) has further suggested that this is an example of 'cultural translation', drawing on traditions from both cultures to produce something which has elements of both and yet is characteristic of neither in their original forms. Certainly, this appears to be an excellent example of the face-to-face exchange of ideas and techniques between the indigenous and Greek inhabitants of the site, perhaps especially among builders and craftworkers. It suggests that the literary tradition (Thucydides *History of the Peloponnesian War* 6.3; Polyainos *Stratagems* 5.5) of hostility between the

Greek and indigenous inhabitants of eighth-century Leontinoi should not be taken at face value.

Initially, much emphasis was placed on the rectangular form of the houses (Rizza 1962: 4–6) and on finding parallels for this shape of building, since many Sicilian houses are round or elliptical, although rectangular examples do occur at other sites (Panvini 1997) and in southern Italy. In part this was probably because at the time rectangular buildings may have been seen as 'more advanced', and greater importance was assigned to the shape of houses than was perhaps warranted. Also, the excavator was attempting to reconcile the later classical literary traditions of Iron Age immigration from the mainland with the archaeological remains. In fact there is no evidence for any of these underlying premises. What Rizza (1962: 8–12) correctly established, however, were the parallels with the 'Ausonian II' phase at Melegunìs Lipára (Lipari), where in fact, Hut α II is very nearly rectangular and was constructed in a very similar way. The similarities between the two sites were long viewed as 'evidence' for the migration of Iron Age peoples from the mainland to Sicily via the Aeolian Islands, and were dated too early. The connections and parallels (some more convincing than others) which Rizza points out between the material culture of Lentini Metapiccola and other parts of Sicily, Italy (e.g. Puglia), and Crete may indicate substantial interactions with other places, though the nature of such interactions is difficult to specify (Leighton 2000: 40; Albanese Procelli 2003: 101–111).

Conclusions

Although there are some common themes across Sicilian Iron Age sites, there are also many regional variations depending in part on local topographies and available materials. But a common pattern emerges of settlements, some potentially quite large, without much evidence of wide socio-economic divisions within them. Like Greeks in the Iron Age, there appears to be a preference for one-roomed houses, though we have little idea about how space was arranged and used, or what, if any, less permanent divisions might have operated. The differences between these buildings and those of the incoming Greeks have been exaggerated: Hodos' (2006: 101) statement that 'multi-roomed rectilinear houses are a feature characteristic of Greek domestic architecture' is only really true from the sixth century BC; earlier, one- or two-roomed houses of varying sizes were regularly found in many places. Albanese Procelli's (2003: 122) suggestion that these houses were the base for some kind of extended household seems highly plausible, but on the available evidence it is difficult to elaborate on this without speculation.

We still face major problems with chronology, though Leighton's down-dating of the Ausonian seems most plausible at present. There are also major issues with how we understand the later Classical literary sources. Nothing in the material culture of Morgantina, Lipari, Lentini, or elsewhere conclusively supports the later Classical accounts of migration from mainland Italy. The Morgantina Cittadella material has many features in common with the settlements of Lipari and Lentini, as well as with the

Iron Age cultures of southern Italy, but in a way that suggests that they were entangled in the same networks and cultural traditions. Perhaps this led classical writers—or maybe even indigenous peoples themselves—to present the relationship as a migration from one area to another.

Sicily was on a Mediterranean crossroads, and from the eighth century BC onward was politically and culturally extremely complex. Common cultural elements, imported material, and evidence for wider cross-cultural interactions across sites with many regional/local variations suggests complex networks, perhaps kinship-based, which we do not yet understand. We know little about the precise relationships of sites to one another and with the wider world.

Sardinia

The Iron Age of Sardinia is far less well understood and documented than the late and final Bronze Age societies of the island, characterized by their monumental settlements with stone towers known as *nuraghi* (sing. *nuraghe*), usually built on hilltops. The location of the island in the middle of the western Mediterranean made it a stopping point for traders and travellers traversing the sea, and a point of exchange. In the late and final Bronze Age and even in the earliest part of the first Iron Age this included close contacts with Cyprus and the Aegean on the one hand and the maritime indigenous Sardinian communities on the other (Lilliu 1988). Sometimes the specific dating of these contacts is hard to pin down, for example it is not clear whether the copper oxhide ingots from Cyprus, which appear in Sardinia, should all be dated to the Bronze Age or whether some of them belong to the early Iron Age. Later in the Iron Age, Phoenician/Punic peoples from Carthage, Etruscans (Tronchetti 1988), and later Greeks (Tronchetti 1985) became the main external contacts, and especially in the case of the first group, settlers.

The earliest Phoenician/Punic settlement was at Sulcis, in the mid-eighth century BC. From this point the long-established links with other parts of the Mediterranean appear to change in character. The Iron Age phases of nuraghic settlements are comparatively poorly published in comparison with the Bronze Age phases, but the Iron Age settlements were generally smaller than the previous ones and continued to occupy earlier buildings, or, as in the case of the eighth to seventh century phase at Genna Maria near Villanovaforru, were built directly on the earlier structures. Unlike Sicily and southern Italy, the societies of Iron Age Sardinia were seemingly more hierarchical than those of the Bronze Age, with the rise of a new elite (van Dommelen 2006: 144). This change may be related to the exploitation of new networks by particular individuals and families, in conjunction with the Punic presence on the island.

The settlement at Santu Antine consists of a *nuraghe* built in the fifteenth century BC and abandoned in the first Iron Age (tenth to ninth centuries BC). The surrounding village was inhabited from the final Bronze Age (twelfth century BC to fourth century AD; Colombi 2010: 14–15). Indigenous nuraghic pottery dominates the fifth to fourth century BC assemblage, and although some Phoenician/Punic ceramics appear, the strongest connections appear to be with central Italy rather than the eastern Mediterranean (Colombi 2010: 15–16).

The settlement of Sant'Imbenia offers a good example of this kind of cultural contact. Located on a peninsula on the west coast of northern Sardinia, it was occupied from the middle Bronze Age down to the sixth century BC. The settlement consisted of a cluster of round and rectilinear rooms around courtyards, which included habitation, assembly, and storage areas. The Iron Age ceramic assemblage contained Punic/Phoenician and Euboean Greek imports, including transport amphorae and drinking cups from the ninth to seventh centuries BC. At this time, local Sardinian potters also began to make transport amphorae that closely imitated the Phoenician ones. These indigenous Sardinian amphorae appear in Carthage and Spain (Huelva and Málaga), suggesting strong external links across the western Mediterranean region.

This is typical of the impact which Phoenician/Punic craftworkers and traditions had on indigenous nuraghic pottery manufacture, and is discernible in other classes of pottery, notably askoid jugs, the shapes of which change apparently under foreign influence in the Iron Age (Hayne 2010: 152). However, like other indigenous groups in Sicily and southern Italy, the nuraghic peoples seem to have been quite selective in what customs they adopted from incomers, and how (van Dommelen 2006; Roppa 2013: 134–135). In metalworking, the Sardinians appear to have adopted the lost wax process from the Phoenicians. Small bronze figurines of warriors (*bronzetti*) were made using this process from the final Bronze Age through to the sixth century, so no two are alike. They are mostly found in sanctuaries, which appear to increase in importance, within and beyond Sardinia, in mainland Italy and in the Aegean. It has been suggested that the *bronzetti* represent a distinctive Sardinian use of the technique (Hayne 2010: 152; Tronchetti 1997), deployed to express the greater role that individuality played in Iron Age societies on the island, by emphasizing distinctive details of dress, posture, and gesture.

Corsica

As in Sardinia, the Corsican Iron Age is comparatively poorly known compared to earlier periods, especially the Neolithic and earlier Bronze Age. However, recent research is closing this gap. One of the most important and well-excavated sites is Cuciurpula (Peche-Quilicini et al. 2012). Here was a settlement of about thirty-five structures over about 12 ha, mostly domestic houses, dating from the eighth to the early sixth centuries BC. Residual sherds of the final Bronze Age from the lowest levels suggest that the area had been occupied earlier. A large circular structure located on the slopes, paralleled at Nuciaresa and Riccu, perhaps served some kind of communal function. The site is located on a granite hilltop, on terraces built on a sloping ledge 1,164 m above sea level. Environmental analyses suggest a thriving mixed agricultural community, with evidence of arable agriculture, arboriculture, and stock rearing. Houses appear to have been occupied permanently and fairly continuously, and were regularly modified. The buildings are stone-built and elliptical/oval in shape, ranging in length from about 9–12 m and about 2.5 m in width.

Structure 1 has been fully excavated, consisting of a single room 11.8 m long, with a maximum width of 3.8 m (Figure 12.9). A vessel under one of the walls is probably a foundation deposit, as it appears to have been deliberately place there. The entrance was at the north end, and a line of blocks on the eastern side formed a kind of 'porch' sheltering the door. A line of postholes lengthwise along the centre of the structure was probably for supporting the roof, and there were other postholes of varying sizes within and outside the building. These were probably used for internal divisions of the space, specific installations (e.g. a loom), and externally for lean-to sheds or similar structures. Near the front of the house, a small pit with charcoal and burnt pottery is interpreted as a kiln or oven; there was also a hearth and an internal bench. Traces of metalworking (iron and copper alloys) were present in the form of ore fragments, part of a crucible, and slag. Radiocarbon determinations place the main phase of the site in the seventh to early sixth centuries, with the earliest levels dated not before 760 BC. Spatial analysis of the large amount of handmade pottery is somewhat inconclusive, not least because much material was dumped on the site shortly after it was abandoned. However, it appears that the area towards the back (south) of the house contained many of the larger storage vessels, and there was a considerable amount of material, including a millstone, near the front of the house and in the 'porch', which appear to be work areas near the hearth and kiln. Although the material demonstrates affinities with wares found elsewhere in the southern part of the island, there is nothing at this stage to indicate that the inhabitants were linked into wider western Mediterranean networks, in contrast with the later Bronze Age (Peche-Quilicini 2012: 221–222).

Although no other sites have been excavated and published in such detail as Cuciurpula, Iron Age activity is documented elsewhere on Corsica. Similar village-type settlements have been investigated at Nuciaresa (Peche-Quilichini 2013) and Cozza Torte (Milanini 2012); rock-built tombs, terracing, and enclosure/fortification walls are also documented. Many earlier sites were also occupied in the Iron Age, and de Lanfranchi and Alessandri (2012) have argued that it is possible to distinguish construction techniques of the Iron Age at Alta Rocca Caleca-Lévie, Cumpulaghja-Santa Lucia di Tallà, Pertalba-Lévie, Cucuruzzu-Lévie, and Stantari de Pacciunituli.

Corsica has Iron Age settlements that appear to have many similarities to those of Sicily and southern Italy (though they are, interestingly, less similar to Sardinia), but the history of the island and its contacts is quite different from other parts of the western Mediterranean. Contact with other areas drops off in the later Bronze Age, and the material culture of the earlier Iron Age seems to develop smoothly out of the later and final Bronze Age traditions. Only in the sixth century BC, with the arrival of Etruscan and Greek incomers, did Corsica once again become linked in to external networks.

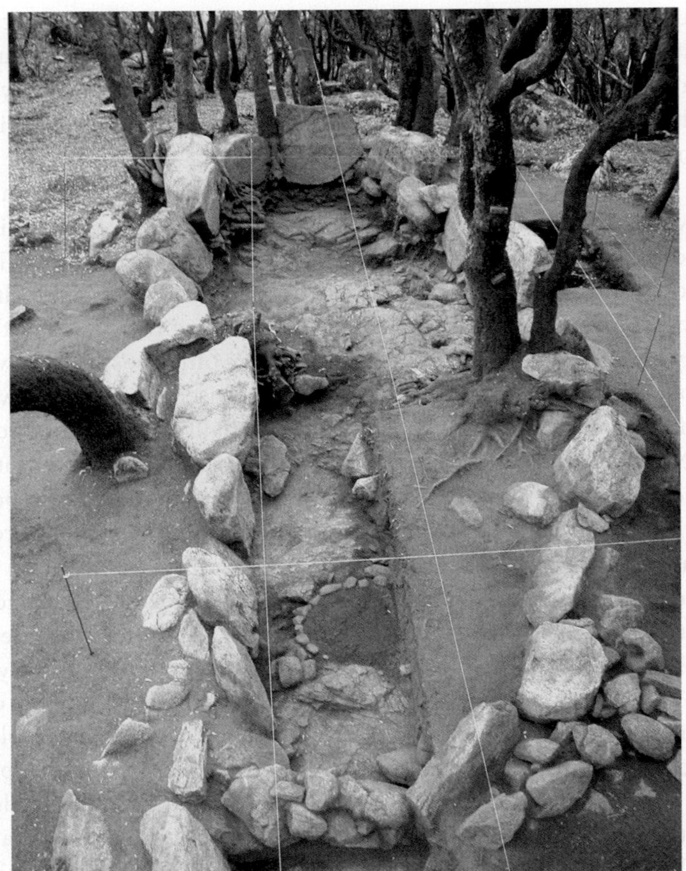

FIGURE 12.9 Cuciurpula, Corsica, Structure 1.

Photo: Caprica6 [own work, CC BY-SA 3.0 http://creativecommons.org/licenses/by-sa/3.0], via Wikimedia Commons

Conclusion

One of the major difficulties for understanding Greece, southern Italy, and the western Mediterranean is the plethora of diverse scholarly traditions, which sometimes make the Iron Age cultures of the region seem much more different than they probably were. This trend is exacerbated by an unhelpful divide between 'prehistoric' and 'Classical' archaeology, traditionally pursued by different groups of scholars using different approaches and methodologies.

An intellectual framework regularly applied by Italian and French scholars, though not generally taken as seriously in Anglophone scholarship, is the notion of 'protohistory' (Leighton 2000: 15). This is, in fact, an extremely useful perspective for understanding the range of evidence for the Iron Age societies of the wider Mediterranean region, although it needs to be precisely and analytically thought out theoretically and methodologically. Protohistory implies that writing and written sources exist which purport to provide relevant information for the period, areas, and societies in question, but that (if contemporary) these sources are either short and not very informative, or they are contextually remote from their subjects regionally, chronologically, or both, and embedded in completely different political, social, and literary contexts. Another crucial feature is that even where literacy existed in these societies, its use may have been limited to particular individuals and settings. In consequence, ideas and information rapidly and regularly move in and out of the realm of written texts, and we are lucky if we can spot it by chance in the texts. Consequently, we need a major rethink about how we might relate text, landscape, and material culture in such protohistoric periods where literacy might exist but documents, in any real historical sense, do not.

As has been stressed throughout this chapter, development through the Iron Age is highly localized, and varies considerably from place to place and site to site. However, it is possible to recognize some broadly common features across the whole region, even though there are many exceptions. Settlement is characteristically in nucleated 'villages' or settlements, consisting for the most part of one-roomed houses, with little evidence of dispersed settlement in the countryside as is characteristic of many parts of the Mediterranean in the Classical Greek, Hellenistic, and Roman periods. Houses are built in a range of shapes from round to elliptical to sub-rectangular/rectangular, often with a stone socle and wattle-and-daub or similar perishable superstructures supported by posts. Roofs were likewise supported by posts. Houses often seem to have been used for a wide range of activities carried out by stem or extended families, and perhaps their dependants.

These settlements often appear to have been internally quite homogeneous, perhaps implying relatively egalitarian societies, especially in comparison to those of the Bronze Age in the same areas. However, there are clearly differences in wealth within communities, and in some areas and periods wealthier or 'higher-status' families plainly competed with others for power and prestige; indeed some sites appear to be focused around one or more elite families, as in the case of Torre di Satriano. Sometimes the presence of elites is indicated by one or more particularly large houses in a settlement, or by a few outstandingly wealthy graves. Nonetheless, political organization seems to have been flexible and volatile, and political power comparatively short-lived, with little evidence of fixed offices or political roles until at least the seventh century BC in the Greek world and often (though not always) later among some of the indigenous cultures of the western Mediterranean. During this period the first buildings, structures, and areas with communal functions began to emerge (for example, temples in Greece), though at different times in different places.

Genuine 'urbanization' on any significant scale is generally not visible archaeologically in most places before the early sixth century BC. Communities appear to be politically and socially quite self-contained, although across a specific area local family-based groups and small communities interacted regularly with one another. While there are some material cultural similarities across specific areas, it is difficult to see any convincing evidence in this period for the kinds of clearly demarcated group and ethnic identities presented by later classical writers. Even in Greece, identities appear to be focused for the most part on the very local community except, ironically, in areas where nucleated settlements of the kind that later became the urban centres of *poleis* did not exist. Albanese Procelli's (2003: 122) notion of the 'household-based' society seems to be a good starting point: in most of these societies it appears that larger, wealthier, and more powerful families which aspired to be elites competed with one another to varying degrees for patronage, power, and prestige.

One very striking difference between areas—across the whole region—is the degree and specific details of connectivity beyond the immediate locale. It is interesting to observe how differently islands such as Euboea, Crete, Sardinia, Corsica, Sicily, and Ischia were networked, both in terms of to whom and when. Euboea, Crete, and Sardinia retained ties with Cyprus and the Levant, even in the earliest part of the Iron Age from the eleventh to tenth centuries BC. For Sardinia, these connections were probably fostered by the activities of Phoenician/Punic peoples in the western Mediterranean (including in Carthage and Iberia), which opened up wider networks for indigenous Sardinian navigators. In contrast, Phoenician activity in Sicily does not begin until the eighth century BC, about the same time as the arrival of the Greeks. Ischia appears to serve as a key node in networks including Euboeans and other Greeks, Phoenicians, and indigenous Italic peoples from the mainland. In contrast, the arrival of Greek and Etruscan incomers on Corsica does not occur until the sixth century BC. For indigenous societies located inland in southern Italy, coastal areas take on a renewed importance beginning in the eighth century BC; here as well as in Sicily sites that had been important coastal contact points with outsiders in the later Bronze Age were revitalized. In many cases, indigenous societies (or at least their elites) evidently welcomed the new links offered by contact with incomers (Leighton 2000: 28). All over the region, the renewal and strengthening of cross-cultural contacts in many forms had profound effects, both positive and negative, on all.

References

Agostino, R., and M. Sica. 2009. *Palazzo: una struttura fortificata in Aspromonte*. Soveria Mannelli: Rubbettino.

Albanese Procelli, R. M. 2003. *Sicani, Siculi, Elimi: Forme di indentità, modo di contatto e processi di trasformazione*. Milan: Longanesi.

Albanese Procelli, R. M. 2016. 'Gli indigeni della Sicilia tra la Prima e la Seconda Età del Ferri: il contest locale della "prima colonizzazione"', in L. Donnellan, V. Nizzo, and G.-J. Burgers (eds) *Contexts of Early Colonization: Papers of the Royal Netherlands Institute in Rome 64*: 199–210. Rome: Palombi.

ASCSA (American School of Classical Studies at Athens). n.d. 'The Athenian Aristocracy'. Available at http://agathe.gr/democracy/the_athenian_aristocracy.html [accessed 4 August 2017].

Attema, P., G.-J. Burgers, and P. M. van Leusen. 2010. *Regional Pathways to Complexity: Settlement and Land-use Dynamics in Early Italy from the Bronze Age to the Republican Period*. Amsterdam: Amsterdam University Press.

Bernabò Brea, L., and M. Cavalier. 1980. *Meligunìs–Lipára IV: L'acropoli di Lipari nella preistoria*. Palermo: Flaccovio.

Blake, E. 2008. 'The Mycenaeans in Italy: A minimalist position'. *Papers of the British School at Rome* 76: 1–34.

Bosana-Kourou, N. 1983. 'Some problems concerning the origin and the dating of the Thapsos class vases'. *Annuario della Scuola Archeologica di Atene* 61 (N. S. 45): 257–267.

Broodbank, C. 2013. *The Making of the Middle Sea: A History of the Mediterranean from the Beginning to the Emergence of the Classical World*. London: Thames and Hudson.

Brun, J.-P. 2004. *Archéologie du vin et de l'huile dans l'Empire romain*. Paris: Errance.

Buchner, G., and D. Ridgway. 1993. *Pithekoussi I: La necropolis: tombe 1–723 scavate dal 1952 al 1961*. Rome: Bretschneider.

Burgers, G.-J., and J. P. Crielaard. 2007. 'Greek colonists and indigenous populations at L'Amastuola, southern Italy'. *BABESCH* 82: 77–114.

Burgers, G.-J., and J. P. Crielaard. 2011. *Greci e indigeii a L'Amastuola*. Mottola: Stampasud.

Burgers, G.-J., and J. P. Crielaard. 2012. 'Greek colonists and indigenous populations at L'Amastuola, southern Italy II'. *BABESCH* 87: 59–96.

Burgers, G.-J., and J. P. Crielaard. 2016. 'The migrant's identity. "Greeks" and "natives" at l'Amastuola, southern Italy', in L. Donnellan, V. Nizzo, and G.-J. Burgers (eds) *Conceptualising Early Colonisation*: 225–238. Brussels/Rome: Belgian Historical Institute in Rome.

Carter, J. C., and A. Prieto (eds). 2011. *The Chora of Metaponto 3: Archaeological Field Survey Bradano to Basento 1*. Austin: University of Texas Press.

Cascino, R. 2012. 'Veii in the orientalizing, archaic and classical periods', in R. Cascino, H. di Giuseppe, and H. Patterson (eds) *Veii: The Historical Topography of the Ancient City*. Archaeological Monographs of the British School at Rome 19: 336–349. London: British School at Rome.

Coldstream, J. N. 1977. *Geometric Greece*. London: Methuen.

Coldstream, J. N. 1993. 'Mixed marriages at the frontiers of the early Greek world'. *Oxford Journal of Archaeology* 12: 89–107.

Colombi, R. 2010. 'Indigenous settlements and Punic presence in Roman Republican northern Sardinia. International Congress of Classical Archaeology, Rome 2008'. *Bolletino di Archeologia on line*, Volume speciale A/A7/3. Available at http://www.bollettinodiarcheologiaonline.beniculturali.it/documenti/generale/3_Colombi_paper.pdf [accessed 12 March 2018].

Coubray, S. 1994. 'Étude paléobotanique des macrorestes végétaux provenant de Ischia', in B. D'Agostino and D. Ridgway (eds) *Apoikia: I più antichi insediamenti greci in occidente: funzioni e modi dell'orgazzazione politica e sociale: Scritti in onore di Giorgio Buchner*. Annali di archeologia e storia antica N. S. 1: 205–209. Naples: Istituto Universitario Orientale.

de Caro, S., and C. Gialnella. 1998. 'Novità pitecusane. L'insediamento dio Punta Chiarito a Forio d'Ischia', in M. Bats and B. D'Agostino (eds) *Euboica: L'Eubea e la presenza euboica in Calcidi e in occidente*: 337–353. Naples: Centre Jean Bérard.

de Lanfranchi, F., and J. Alessandri. 2012. 'L'apparition d'une technique constructive protohistorique (âge du Fer) en Alta Rocca documentée par quelques fouilles anciennes', in K. Peche-Quilichini (ed.) *L'âge du Fer en Corse: acquis et perspectives*: 13–26. Serra-di-Scopamena: Associu Cuciurpula.

Denti, M. 2016. 'Gli Enotri—e I Greci—sul Basento. Nuovi dati sul Metapontino in Età proto-coloniale', in L. Donnellan, V. Nizzo, and G.-J. Burgers (eds) *Contexts of Early Colonization*. Papers of the Royal Netherlands Institute in Rome 64: 223–236. Rome: Palombi.

di Gennaro, F. 1986. *Forme de insediamento tra Trevere e Fiora dal bronzo finale al principio dell'età del ferro*. Firenze: L. S. Olschki.

di Gennaro, F. 1999. 'Indizi archeologici di élites nell'età del bronzo dell'Italia mediotirrenica', in *Eliten in der Bronzezeit: Ergebnisse Zweiter Kolloquien in Mainz und Athen. RGZM Monographien* 43: 185–196. Mainz: Römisch-Germanisches Zentralmuseum.

Dickinson, O. 1994. *The Aegean Bronze Age*. Cambridge: Cambridge University Press.

Dickinson, O. 2006. *The Aegean from Bronze Age to Iron Age: Continuity and Change between the Twelfth and Eighth Centuries BC*. London: Routledge.

Dietler, M. 2010. *Archaeologies of Colonialism: Consumption, Entanglement and Violence in Ancient Mediterranean France*. Berkeley and Los Angeles: University of California Press.

Fitzjohn, M. 2007. 'Equality in the colonies: concepts of equality in Sicily during the eighth to sixth centuries BC'. *World Archaeology* 39, 2: 215–228.

Folk, R. L. 2011. 'Geologic background of the Metapontino', in J. C. Carter and A. Prieto (eds) *The Chora of Metaponto 3: Archaeological Field Survey: Bradano to Basento*: 3–30. Austin: University of Texas Press.

Foxhall, L. 2009. 'Gender', in K. Raaflaub and H. van Wees (eds) *Blackwell Companion to Archaic Greece*: 483–507. Oxford: Blackwell.

Foxhall, L. 2014. 'Households, hierarchies, territories and landscapes in Bronze Age and Iron Age Greece', in A. B. Knapp and P. van Dommelen (eds) *The Cambridge Prehistory of the Bronze and Iron Age Mediterranean: 417–436* . Cambridge: Cambridge University Press.

Gialnella, C. 1994. 'Pithecusa: gli insediamenti di Punta Chiarito. Relazione preliminarie', in B. D'Agostino and D. Ridgway (eds) *Apoikia: I più antichi insediamenti greci in occidente: funzioni e modi dell'orgazzazione politica e sociale: Scritti in onore di Giorgio Buchner*. Annali di archeologia e storia antica N. S. 1: 168–204. Naples: Istituto Universitario Orientale.

Glowacki, K. 2004. 'Household analysis in Dark Age Crete', in L. Preston Day, M. Mook, and J. Muhly (eds) *Crete beyond the Palaces: Proceedings of the Crete 2000 Conference*: 125–136. Philadelphia: INSTAP Academic Press.

Gonzáles de Canales, F., L. Serrano, and J. Llompart. 2006. 'The pre-colonial Phoenician emporium of Huelva ca. 900–770 BC'. *BABESCH* 81: 13–29.

Haggis, D. 1993. 'Intensive survey, traditional settlement patterns, and Dark Age Crete: The case of Early Iron Age Kavousi'. *Journal of Mediterranean Archaeology* 6: 131–174.

Handberg, S., J. K. Jacobsen, and G. P. Mittica. 2009. 'Recent Dutch and Danish excavations at the sanctuary of Timpone della Motta close to Francavilla Marittima, south Italy', in T. Fischer-Hansen and B. Poulsen (eds) *From Artemis to Diana: The Goddess of Man and Beast*. Acta Hyperborea 12: 554–558. Copenhagen: Museum Tusculanum Press, University of Copenhagen.

Hanell, K. 1962. 'The excavations of the Swedish Institute in Rome in San Giovenale and its environs', in A. Boëthius (ed.) *Etruscan Culture, Land and People: Archaeological Research and Studies Conducted in San Giovenale and its Environs*: 277–288. New York/Malmö: Columbia University Press/Allhem Publishing House.

Hayne, J. 2010. 'Entangled identities on Iron Age Sardinia?', in P. van Dommelen and A. B. Knapp (eds) *Material Connections in the Ancient Mediterranean*: 147–169. London: Routledge.

Hodos, T. 1999. 'Intermarriage in the western Greek colonies'. *Oxford Journal of Archaeology* 18: 61–78.

Hodos, T. 2006. *Local Responses to Colonization in the Iron Age Mediterranean*. London: Routledge.

Iacono, F. 2015. 'Feasting at Roca: Cross-cultural encounters and society in the southern Adriatic during the Late Bronze Age'. *European Journal of Archaeology* 18, 2: 259–281.

Izzet, V. 2007. *The Archaeology of Etruscan Society*. Cambridge: Cambridge University Press.

Jacobsen, J. K., and S. Handberg. 2010. *Excavation on the Timpone della Motta, Francavilla Marittima (1992–2004), I: The Greek Pottery*. Bari: Edipuglia.

Kleibrink, M. (ed.) 2006. *Oenotrians at Lagaria near Sybaris: A Native Proto-Urban Centralised Settlement*. Accordia Specialist Studies on Italy 11. London: Accordia Research Institute, University of London.

Kotsonas, A., T. Whitelaw, A. Vasilakis, and M. Bredaki. 2012. 'Early Iron Age Knossos: An overview from the Knossos Urban Landscape Project (KULP)'. Submitted for web publication of the 11th International Cretological Congress 2011. Available at http://www.academia.edu/31012077 [accessed 4 August 2017].

Leighton, R. 1993. *Morgantina IV: The Protohistoric Settlement on the Cittadella*. Princeton: Princeton University Press.

Leighton, R. 1996. 'From chiefdom to tribe? Social organisation and change in later prehistory', in R. Leighton (ed.) *Early Societies in Sicily*: 101–116. London: Accordia Research Institute, University of London.

Leighton, R. 1999. *Sicily before History: An Archaeological Survey from the Palaeolithic to the Iron Age*. London: Duckworth.

Leighton, R. 2000. 'Indigenous society between the ninth and sixth centuries BC: Territorial, urban and social evolution', in C. J. Smith (ed.) *Sicily from Aenaes to Augustus: New Approaches in Archaeology and History*: 15–40. Edinburgh: Edinburgh University Press.

Lemos, I. 2002. *The Protogeometric Aegean*. Oxford: Oxford University Press.

Lemos, I. 2006. 'Athens and Lefkandi: A tale of two sites', in E. Lemos and S. Deger-Jalkotzy (eds) *From the Mycenaean Palaces to the Age of Homer*: 505–530. Edinburgh: Edinburgh University Press.

Lemos, I. and D. Mitchell. 2011. 'Elite burial in the Early Iron Age Aegean. Some preliminary observations concerning the spatial organisation of the Toumba cemetery at Lefkandi', in A. Mazarakis-Ainian (ed.) *Dark Ages Revisited*: 635–644. Volos: University of Thessaly.

Lilliu, C. 1988. *La civiltà dei Sardi dal Paleolitico all' età dei nuraghi*, 3rd edition. Turin: Nuova ERI.

Lyons, C. 1996. 'Sikel burials at Morgantina: Defining social and ethnic identities', in R. Leighton (ed.) *Early Societies in Sicily*: 177–188. London: Accordia Research Institute, University of London.

McDonald, W., W. Coulson, and J. Rosser. 1983. *Excavations at Nichoria in Southwest Greece, Vol. III: Dark Age and Byzantine Occupation*. Minneapolis: University of Minnesota Press.

Milanini, J.-L. 2012. 'Cozza Torta et la question du premier âge du Fer dans l'extrème sud de la Corse', in K. Peche-Quilichini (ed.) *L'âge du fer en Corse: acquis et perspectives*: 27–34. Serra-di-Scopamena: Associu Cuciurpula.

Morris, I. 1987. *Burial and Ancient Society: The Rise of the Greek City-State*. Cambridge: Cambridge University Press.
Muhly, J. D., R. Maddin, and T. Stech. 1985. 'Iron in Anatolia and the nature of the Hittite iron industry'. *Anatolian Studies* 35: 67–84.
Nijboer, A. 2016. 'Is the tangling of events in the Mediterranean around 770–60 BC in the Conventional Absolute Chronology (CAC) a reality or a construct?', in L. Donnellan, V. Nizzo, and G.-J. Burgers (eds) *Contexts of Early Colonization*. Papers of the Royal Netherlands Institute in Rome 64: 35–48. Rome: Palombi.
Nizzo, V. 2007. *Ritorno ad Ischia: Dalla stratigrafia della necropolis di Pithekoussai alla tipologia dei materiali*. Naples: Centre Jean Bérard.
Nizzo, V. 2016a. 'Tempus fugit. Datare e interpretare la "prima colonizzazione": una riflessione "retrospettiva" e "prospettiva" su cronologie, culture e contesti', in L. Donnellan, V. Nizzo, and G.-J. Burgers (eds) *Conceptualising Early Colonisation*: 105–116. Brussels/Rome: Belgian Historical Institute in Rome.
Nizzo, V. 2016b. 'Cronologia versus archeologia. L'ambiguo scorrere del tempo alle soglie della "colonizzazione". Il caso di Cuma e Pithekoussai', in L. Donnellan, V. Nizzo, and G.-J. Burgers (eds) *Contexts of Early Colonization: Papers of the Royal Netherlands Institute in Rome 64*: 49–72. Rome: Palombi.
Núñez, F. 2016. 'Considerations around a polarized Mediterranean Iron Age chronology', in L. Donnellan, V. Nizzo, and G.-J. Burgers (eds) *Contexts of Early Colonization: Papers of the Royal Netherlands Institute in Rome* 64: 73–88. Rome: Palombi.
Osanna, M. 2014. 'The Iron Age in south Italy: Settlement, mobility and culture contact', in A. B. Knapp and P. van Dommelen (eds) *The Cambridge Prehistory of the Bronze and Iron Age Mediterranean* : 230–248. Cambridge: Cambridge University Press.
Osanna, M., and V. Capozzoli (eds). 2012. *Lo spazio di potere II: Nuove ricerche nell'area del anaktoron di Torre di Satriano*. Venosa: Osanna Edizioni.
Osanna, M., L. Colangelo, and G. Carollo. 2009. *Lo spazio di potere: La residenza ad abside, l'anaktoron, l'episcopio di Torre di Satriano*. Venosa: Osanna Edizioni.
Osborne, R. 2009. *Greece in the Making 1200–479 BC*, 2nd edition. London: Routledge.
Pacciarelli, M. 2000. *Dal villagio alla città: La svolta protourbana del 1000 a.C nell'Italia tirrenica*. Florence: All'Insegna del Giglio.
Pacciarelli, M. 2016. 'Forme di insediamento del Primo Ferro in Calabria', in L. Donnellan, V. Nizzo, and G.-J. Burgers (eds) *Contexts of Early Colonization*. Papers of the Royal Netherlands Institute in Rome 64: 177–182. Rome: Palombi.
Panvini, R. 1997. 'Osservazioni sulle dinamiche formative socio-culturali a Dessuerii', in S. Tusa (ed.) *Prima Sicilia: alle origini della società siciliana*: 493–501. Palermo: Ediprint.
Peche-Quilichini, K. 2012. 'Le Bronze final et le premier âge du Fer de la Corse: chronologie, production céramique et espaces culturels'. *Acta Archeologica* 83: 203–223.
Peche-Quilichini, K. 2013. 'Villages et fortifications indigènes de l'âge du Fer en Corse'. *Archéothéma* 28, 74–79.
Peche-Quilichini, K., L. Bergerot, T. Lachenai, D. Martinetti, V. Py, and M. Regert. 2012. 'Les fouilles de Cuciurpula: la structure I', in K. Peche-Quilichini (ed.) *L'âge du Fer en Corse: acquis et perspectives*: 35–57. Serra-di-Scopamena: Associu Cuciurpula.
Peroni, R. 1994. *Introduzione all a protoistoria italiana*. Bari: Laterza.
Peroni, R. 2000. 'Formazione e sviluppi dei centri protourbani medio-tirrenici', in A. Carandini and R. Capelli (eds) *Roma: Romolo, Remo e la fondazione della città: Catalogo di mostra*: 26–30. Rome/Milan: Ministerio per i Beni e le Attività Culturali/Electa.
Peroni, R., and A. Vanzetti. 1998. *Broglio di Trebisacce 1990–1994. Elementi e problem nuovi dale recenti campagne di scavi*. Soveria Mannelli: Rubbettino.

Popham, M. R., P. G. Calligas, and L. H. Sackett. 1988–1989. 'Further excavation of the Toumba cemetery at Lefkandi, 1984 and 1986: A preliminary report'. *Archaeological Reports of the Society for the Promotion of Hellenic Studies* 35: 117–129.

Popham, M. R., E. Touloupa, and L. H. Sackett. 1982. 'The Hero of Lefkandi'. *Antiquity* 56: 169–174.

Prieto, A. 2006. 'The Metaponto Division Lines'. PhD thesis, University of Texas at Austin.

Ridgway, D. 1992. *The First Western Greeks*. Cambridge: Cambridge University Press.

Riva, C. 2010. *The Urbanisation of Etruria: Funerary Practices and Social Change, 700–600 BC*. Cambridge: Cambridge University Press.

Rizza, G. 1962. 'Siculi e Greci sui colli di Leontini'. *Cronache di Archeologia* 1: 3–27.

Rizza, G. 1978. 'Leontini nel'VIII e nel VII secolo a. C.', in G. Rizza (ed.) *Insediamento coloniali Greci in Sicilia nell VIII e nel VII secolo a. C.* Cronache di Archeologia 17: 26–37.

Rizza, G. 1980. 'Osservazioni sull'architettura e sull'impianto urbano di Leontini in età arcaica'. *Cronache di Archeologia* 19: 115–129.

Roppa, A. 2013. *Comunità urbane e rurali nella Sardegna punica di età ellenistica: Sagvntvm Extra 14*. València: Universitat de València.

Russell, A. 2017. 'Sicily without Mycenae: A cross-cultural consumption analysis of connectivity in the Bronze Age central Mediterranean'. *Journal of Mediterranean Archaeology* 30, 1: 59–83.

Savelli, S. 2016. 'Models of interaction between Greeks and indigenous populations on the Ionian coast: Contributions from the excavations at Incoronata by the University of Texas at Austin', in L. Donnellan, V. Nizzo, and G.-J. Burgers (eds) *Contexts of Early Colonization*. Papers of the Royal Netherlands Institute in Rome 64: 372–384. Rome: Palombi.

Sciappelli, A. 2012. 'Veii in the protohistoric period: A topographical and territorial analysis', in R. Cascino, H. di Giuseppe, and H. Patterson (eds) *Veii: The Historical Topography of the Ancient City*. Archaeological Monographs of the British School at Rome 19: 327–336. London: British School at Rome.

Shelmerdine, C. W. (ed.) 2008. *The Cambridge Companion to the Aegean Bronze Age*. Cambridge: Cambridge University Press.

Sica, M. 2011. 'Castellace tra Greci e indigeni', in G. De Sensi Sestito and S. Mancuso (eds) *Enotri e Brettii in Magna Grecia: Modi e forme di interazione culturale*: 95–122. Soveria Mannelli: Rubbettino.

Tronchetti, C. 1985. 'I Greci e la Sardegna'. *Dialoghi di Archeologia N. S.* 7: 17–34.

Tronchetti, C. 1988. 'La Sardegna e gli Etruschi'. *Mediterranean Archaeology* 1: 66–82.

Tronchetti, C. 1997. 'I bronzetti "nuragici": ideologia, iconografia, cronologia'. *Annali di archeologia e storia antica N. S.* 4: 9–34.

van Dommelen, P. 2006. 'The orientalising phenomenon: Hybridity and material culture in the western Mediterranean', in C. Riva and N. Vella (eds) *Debating Orientalization: Multidisciplinary Approaches to Change in the Ancient Mediterranean*: 135–152. London/Oakville: Equinox.

van Wijngaarden, J. 2002. *Use and Appreciation of Mycenaean Pottery in the Levant, Cyprus and Italy (ca. 1600–1200 BC)*. Amsterdam: Amsterdam University Press.

Vanzetti, A. n.d. 'Broglio di Trebisacce'. *Fasti Online*. Available at http://www.fastionline.org/excavation/micro_view.php?fst_cd=AIAC_3047&curcol=main_column [accessed 4 August 2017].

Wallace, S. 2010. *Ancient Crete: From Successful Collapse to Democracy's Alternatives, Twelfth to Fifth centuries BC*. Cambridge: Cambridge University Press.

CHAPTER 13

NORTHERN GREECE AND THE CENTRAL BALKANS

STEFANOS GIMATZIDIS

INTRODUCTION

NORTHERN Greece and the central Balkans are neither a culturally nor a historically uniform region in the Iron Age. In archaeological terms, this region is often perceived as a periphery of the Aegean or of central Europe, or at best as a buffer zone. Extending from the Aegean Sea to the Balkan mountains (Stara Planina), and from the Adriatic to the Black Sea, it comprises the historical landscapes of Epirus, southern Illyria, Macedonia, and Thrace (Figure 13.1). These historical place names were all constructed and established within the ancient Greek collective memory and literature; there was hardly any direct association between them and individual ethnic groups, with the probable exception of the Macedonians and the land named after them.

The ancient Greeks conceived Macedonia as the land where the Macedonians lived, together with other affiliated or subordinate nations (*ethne*). Hence, the name was a political rather than a geographical term and applied to a land with constantly changing borders following the expansion of the Macedonian kingdom. Epirus means 'continent' in Greek, and has been used since the early historical period to mean the land opposite the Ionian islands. Thrace and Illyria are among the vaguest geographical terms in ancient literature. Greeks indiscriminately conceived as Thracian all the peoples who lived between the north Aegean coast, the Balkan mountains, and the Danube, but the place name held no political significance until the Roman period (Oberhummer and Lenk 1936: 392–423). Finally, the Illyrians were just one among many groups who inhabited the western Balkans (Wilkes 1992: 92).

Within the area covered by this chapter, the Iron Age is defined in different ways and various chronological systems are used. Here, the early Iron Age is taken as the period from *c*.1050–700 BC; after this, we enter the Archaic period which saw the emergence of the Greek city states and colonies (see Chapter 12). The archaeology is presented in terms

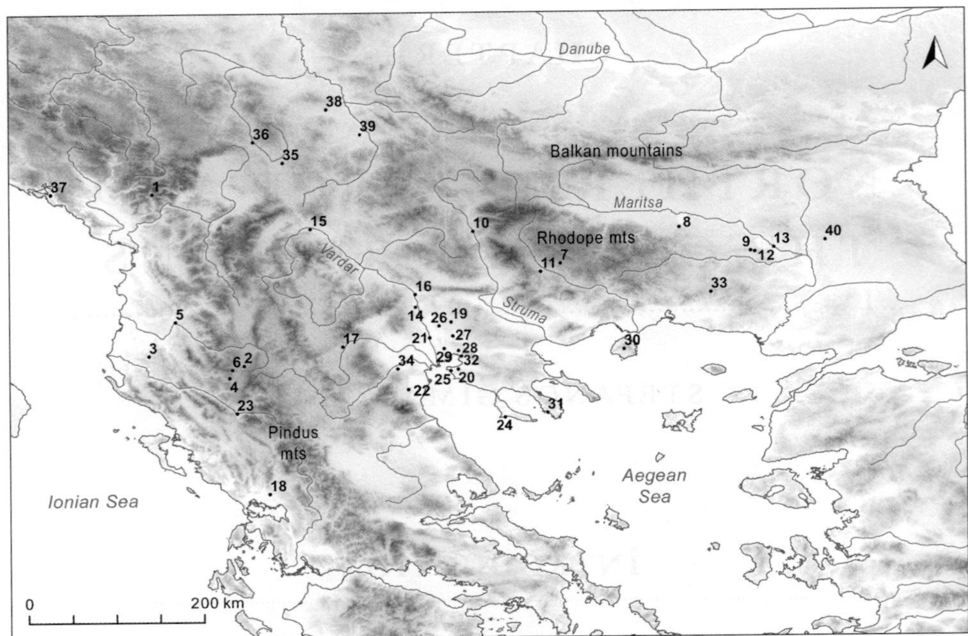

FIGURE 13.1 Map of principal sites in northern Greece and the central Balkans. *Albania*: 1 Grunas, 2 Kamenicë, 3 Lofkënd, 4 Luaras, 5 Pazhok, 6 Rehovë. *Bulgaria*: 7 Cochan-Satovcha, 8 Dragoyna, 9 Gluhite Kamani, 10 Kamenska Čuka, 11 Koprivlen, 12 Kush Kaya, 13 Svilengrad. *North Macedonia*: 14 Gevgelija, 15 Kluçka/Skopje, 16 Marvinci. *Greece*: 17 Agios Panteleimonas, 18 Ambracia/Arta, 19 Chorygi, Kilkis, 20 Karabournaki, 21 Kastanas, 22 Kastro, 23 Liatovouni, 24 Mende, 25 Nea Michaniona, 26 Palio Gynaekokastro, 27 Pentalofos (Thessaloniki), 28 Polichni, 29 Sindos, 30 Thasos, 31 Torone, 32 Toumba, 33 Sarakini, 34 Vergina. *Kosovo*: 35 Donja Brnjica, 36 Karagač. *Montenegro*: 37 Velika Gruda, 38 Gornja Stražava. *Serbia*: 39 Hisar/Leskovac. *Turkey*: 40 Lalapaşa.

Drawing: R. Salisbury for author

of its constituent natural geographical landscapes, starting from the Aegean coast. The traditional model of archaeological cultures is partly used in the region, but owing to its dependence on ill-defined pottery and artefact typologies and sequences, often from poorly documented older excavations, has tended to confuse more than to illuminate.

From Chalkidike, via Central and North Macedonia to Kosovo and South Serbia

Central Macedonia is one of the best-studied areas of the Balkans, with a history of archaeological research going back to the late nineteenth century. The landscape of the lower courses of the Axios/Vardar and Gallikos rivers and the Langadas basin has been subject to powerful silting and erosion mechanisms through the millennia, which have caused major geomorphological transformations from the Bronze Age, and especially the early Iron Age (Gimatzidis 2010: 24–58). Chalkidike is administratively considered part of modern central Macedonia, but it is distinct and more Mediterranean in geographical, ecological, and cultural terms. The upper Axios/Vardar valley (north Macedonia) with its tributaries, the Breglnica and Pčinja rivers, in the eastern part of the former Yugoslav Republic (FYR) of Macedonia, and the south Morava valley in southern Serbia are usually regarded as the natural routes from the Aegean to the Balkan hinterland. The Demir Kapija gorge, north of the Doiran basin, is the only natural barrier to this important axis of communication.

Settlement and Apoikia

A socially complex and morphologically coherent settlement system developed during the Bronze Age and early Iron Age in the valleys and plains of central Macedonia, comprising numerous small sites in the form of low tells that first appeared during the early Bronze Age (Andreou et al. 1996: 576–586). These artificial hills, known as *toumbas*, were usually erected on geologically stable areas within the alluvial valleys or on the lower surrounding hills; they gained height over time through a long-lasting, controlled depositional process involving rebuilding on the levelled debris of earlier settlement phases (Gimatzidis 2010: 59–62).

In the early first millennium BC, a demographic boom caused a significant change in the nature of the settlement system. After many years of occupation, the available surface area on the increasingly tall and conical tells was no longer sufficient for the size of the population. This was probably one of the main reasons for the appearance of a new form of settlement at the start of the early Iron Age. These new sites were located on hills with a larger, flat surface area suitable for habitation; known as 'tables' in the regional literature after their form, they were built either next to existing *toumbas* or as completely independent new settlements, during the tenth and ninth centuries BC (Figure 13.2).

A complex network of unfortified tell settlements developed around the ancient Thermaic Gulf, which at that time projected further inland into the Balkan landmass. Lagoon conditions emerged some time in the Bronze Age and spread gradually south during a long period of significant geomorphological transformation in the lower Axios valley (Gimatzidis 2010: 53–58, fig. 1). The development of the central Macedonian tell settlement system was at least partly linked with this process, which severely affected the morphology and ecology of the region. Most of these sites, which today are inland—like Sindos—lay right on the shores of the ancient Thermaic Gulf and next to rivers in the early Iron Age. Their subsistence strategies were thus at least partly determined by their watery environment, but at the same time they were subject to floods, erosion, and sedimentation of a very active fluvial system that consisted of the central Macedonian Gallikos, Axios, Loudias, and Aliakmon rivers.

FIGURE 13.2 Complex tell settlement with toumba and table at Pentalofos, Thessaloniki.

Photo: © Stefanos Gimatzidis

Late Bronze Age and early Iron Age occupation transformed the archaeological landscape once and for all in central Macedonia, where *toumbas* and tables became the most distinctive archaeological features. Assumptions about a hierarchical organization of this settlement system were based solely on the grounds of the size of settlements or sporadic evidence for agricultural production (Wardle and Wardle 2007: 461; cf. Andreou et al. 1996: 579). More significantly, not a single tell settlement among the many excavated in the last century was ever fortified. Terraces at one of the best excavated tells, Toumba Thessaloniki, which were constructed in the casemate technique (using conjoined cells) around the tell edge in order to enlarge the occupation area, were also seen as potential defensive structures. Such massive earthworks are most typical at the largest tells (Toumba Thessaloniki, Sindos), but are not documented at smaller tells such as Kastanas (Gimatzidis 2010: 82–84). Their construction required the engagement of the whole community and implies some kind of central organization within the individual settlements, but the domestic architecture, consisting of houses of similar size and form—as known from levels 8 to 5 at Kastanas (Hänsel 1989: 232–304) and Phase 2 at Assiros (Wardle and Wardle 2007: 462, 473–475, fig. 3)—points more to a non-stratified society. Overall, the pattern of small communities living in practically unfortified tells suggests the absence of any centralized inter-settlement political organization and a pre-urban network of co-dependent communities.

Significant changes took place during the eighth century BC in central Macedonia, when the tell settlements had reached their largest extent. Excavations at the complex tell settlement at Sindos, which consisted of a Bronze Age *toumba* and two early Iron Age tables, have revealed twelve successive settlement phases on the upper table, as well as a well-investigated building phase on the lower table, dating to the period of the settlement's greatest extent in the mid-eighth century BC. Statistical analysis of pottery from well-dated closed contexts has demonstrated major changes in ceramic technology at Sindos that may indicate significant social transformations. In Late Geometric Ia (760–750 BC), local wheel-thrown pottery of Aegean type outnumbered handmade wares of Balkan style for the first time. At the same time, there was a significant increase in central and south Aegean pottery imports, especially of Euboean origin (Gimatzidis 2011). These changes were not, however, due to settlement of newcomers from the south, but were actually triggered by the rapid economic and political developments of the preceding period in Macedonia. Instead of reflecting colonization, we are seeing the development of a more standardized and centrally organized system of agricultural production (reflected in material culture by amphorae and storage facilities), along with a more complex social organization, which together fuelled mobility and led to intensification of contacts with the south.

Sindos was never perceived as a colony in ancient literature. It was only a local Thracian settlement, and we will perhaps never know if even a single person from central or south Greece ever settled there during the eighth or seventh centuries BC. If there was only the pottery evidence, we might even have claimed that Sindos had a more 'colonial' profile than Mende, which according to Thucydides was a proper Eretrian colony (*apoikia*).[1] The fact that, in contrast to Sindos, a renowned Euboean colony such as Mende actually shows no break in its material culture during the so-called colonization period, may well indicate a different process of 'colonization' from that once envisaged, but modern scholarship has only very recently cut free from the colonial ideology that dominated the discipline from its beginning.

The links between Chalkidike and the central Aegean are apparent in the archaeological record for almost every period from the middle Bronze Age onwards. In contrast to central Macedonia, hilltop sites on rocky promontories or steep hills in the hinterland were the most usual form of settlements here. Inhabited sites that were easily accessible were equipped with fortifications (e.g. Lagomandra). This shows an intent to define and protect the occupied area, which could indicate a politically unstable and less centralized system with inter-settlement tensions.

Artificial mounds were no longer constructed for occupation in the middle Axios valley, in the basin of Lake Doiran, and to the north of the Kerkini/Belasica mountain range, where the sedimentation activity of regional rivers and their effect on the environment had diminished. Instead, naturally fortified hills became the dominant settlement form, alongside some flat occupation sites (Figure 13.3). Settlement density here was seemingly no less than in the lower Axios valley, but is less well-studied (Savvopoulou 2004: 307–311). However, some sites may have acted as central places—e.g. Isar-Marvinci, Vardarski Rid-Gevgelija (Mitrevski 2005), Prdejska Cuka near Grciste, and Isar-Prsten—if we lay any value upon size and location as indicators for such classifications (Ristov 2004: 46–117, plans 7, 9, 17).

Settlements on the top of usually steep hills equipped with defensive ramparts and ditches also appeared along the northern course of the Vardar and Pčinja rivers, as well as in the valley of the south Morava river in south Serbia, and the tributaries Ibar, Raška, and Sitnica of the west Morava river in Kosovo. The hillfort settlements of the south Morava valley seem to have replaced earlier lowland habitation sites during the early

FIGURE 13.3 Hilltop settlement at Chorygi, Kilkis, Greece.

Photo: © Stefanos Gimatzidis

Iron Age, but lowland settlements continued to exist along the middle course of the Axios (Kalica-Miravci, Beli Most-Petrovo, Grobista-Furka) and in the Vranje region (Kapuran 2009: 149–166; Bulatović 2007: 291–292). However, due to a lack of systematic archaeological survey or excavation in this region, any attempt to reconstruct inter-settlement organization—for example, the relationships between lowland and highland settlements—is not yet possible.

Cultural Divides and Connectivity in Mortuary Ideology from Donja Brnija to Kerameikos

The most characteristic aspect of the regional material culture in Kosovo, south Serbia, and the northern FYR Macedonia at the end of the Bronze Age is the 'Donja Brnjica-Gornja Stražava Cultural Group', or more simply the Brnijca culture, which is known principally from its cremation cemeteries. Aegean imports and metal artefact seriations suggest that the Brnjica culture began in the thirteenth century BC, and continued into the ninth century BC, but the chronological span is not beyond question (Tasić 1997: 290–293; Stojić 2000). One of the very few available stratigraphic sequences comes from the excavated settlement site of Hisar near Leskovac (Stojić 2000: 10–20; Bulatović 2007: 58–60).

This most characteristic feature of the group was its cremation burial rite (Vasić 2013: 173–179, figs 3–7): corpses were cremated outside the cemeteries and the ashes placed in urns. Very few grave goods—usually one bronze or clay artefact and some smaller pottery vessels—were laid in or next to the urn, which was finally covered with an open bowl placed upside down or a flat stone (Trbucović 1970: 107–108, pl. 2). Care was taken in the construction of the grave where the urn—often a bi-conical amphora—was deposited. Sometimes graves were revetted with stones or slabs, and could contain more than one urn (Srejović 1959–1960: 84–101, figs 3, 7, and 13; Luci 1984: plans 1–3; Mitrevski 1992–1993). At the two flat cemeteries after which the culture is named—Donja Brnjica, a village near Pristina (Srejović 1959–1960; Luci 1984; Tasić 1997), and Gornja Stražava, not far from Niš (Krstić 1991: 231–237, pls 1–2)—the cremation urns were arranged in groups. At the cemeteries of Kluçka, next to the Hippodrome of Skopje, which dates to the thirteenth to twelfth centuries BC (Mitrevski 1992–1993), and Karagač in northern Kosovo (Srejović 1973: 45–49, fig. 4), they were arranged in rows. A cist grave inhumation equipped with a bronze leaf-blade sword (*Griffzungenschwert*) that is older than the numerous cremation urns at the necropolis of Donja Brnjica, may have been treated as an 'ancestor', around whom the cremations of the descendants clustered (Srejović 1959–1960: 94–95, fig. 8).

In contrast to Kosovo and south Serbia, late Bronze Age burial rites are far less well known in northern and especially central Macedonia, where burial practices at this period are almost archaeologically invisible. However, at the transition to the Iron Age or a little earlier, some flat cemeteries with cist tombs appear in north Macedonia, as at Vodovratski Rid and Ulanci (Mitrevski 1997: 35–40, figs 5–6, pls 5–12). Cremation and inhumation in an extended position in pit or cist graves were also practised during the eleventh to ninth centuries BC in central Macedonia (Savvopoulou 2004: 311–316), both under tumuli (Palio Gynaekokastro) and in flat cemeteries (Polichni, Nea Philadelphia, Oreokastro, Torone). In some of these extensive bi-ritual cemeteries, cremations prevail (Palio Gynaekokastro, Koukos, Torone), while in others inhumations constitute the dominant burial rite (Polichni). In Chalkidike, only flat cemeteries occur.

Around the same time as these developments in central Macedonia, the first formal cemeteries with cist tombs appeared in the south of Greece, exemplified by the well-studied cemetery of Kerameikos in Athens. The early eleventh century BC saw a transition from multiple burials in chamber tombs to single inhumations in pit, cist, or *pithos* graves. Soon after, cremation began to be practised on an increasingly wide scale, eventually superseding inhumation in mainland Greece. Culture-historical archaeologists long imagined a diffusion of these new burial rites from north—where they appeared earlier—to south, introduced by migrating populations, and linked the phenomenon either with a rather abstract 'Aegean immigration' (Garašanin 1973: 635), or more concretely to the legendary Dorian invasion (Desborough 1964: 244–257). However, unlike the migration of the Sea People—an historical event attested by contemporary sources—the Dorian invasion was clearly a narrative of the classical period, and cannot be taken at face value. In spite of this, many Aegean scholars used to put historic value on this information (and in certain quarters still do), seeing the new burial practices and the gradual adoption during the twelfth and eleventh centuries BC of new types of weapons, pottery, and dress accessories (e.g. violin and arched fibulae, spiral and hair rings, and long pins), as intrusive cultural features, and thus hard evidence of migration.

Returning to central Macedonia, the small cemetery at Torone is the only fully published burial ground in the whole region (Papadopoulos 2005). In all, there were 120 graves with cremations in urns, together with thirteen pit graves and one cist tomb. On the assumption that it was the only or principal burial ground for the settlement, the excavator suggested the very act of being buried in the cemetery was an expression of status and rank (Papadopoulos 2005: 404). Other early Iron Age cemeteries, such as Polichni, have yielded hundreds of burials, which hardly show any differentiation, be it in the form of tomb, or quantity and quality of grave goods. These cemeteries were in use from around 1050 to 850/800 BC. No cemeteries are known, however, from the late ninth to late eighth centuries BC, despite the accompanying settlements continuing to be occupied; indeed, it was in the eighth century BC that most of the central Macedonian settlements reached their greatest extent, as already mentioned.

In the early Archaic period, cemeteries reappear on the coast at Mende and Polychrono in Chalkidike (Vokotopoulou 1994), and from the mid-sixth century BC in the lower Axios valley and Thessaloniki plain (e.g. Karabournaki, Polichni, Sindos, Souroti, Thermi). After many years of systematic rescue excavations—especially within the conurbation of Thessaloniki, where there were continuously inhabited Iron Age settlements at Polichni, Toumba Thessaloniki, and Karabournaki—the lack of cemeteries between the later ninth and seventh centuries BC cannot be attributed to a lack of fieldwork. A similar phenomenon is apparent in the middle Axios valley and the Doiran basin, where after a gap of a few centuries extensive flat cemeteries reappear in the seventh or sixth century BC at several sites near Gevgelija (e.g. Ristov 2002–2004), Dedeli, and Marvinci. In the Bregalnica valley, hundreds of tumuli were erected from the latest phases of the early Iron Age onwards (e.g. Sanev 1975–1978).

During these periods with no cemeteries, the dead of the central Macedonian communities must have been treated in a manner that left no archaeological traces. This does not, however, mean that they were buried in an 'improper' way, or without due ritual process. Moreover, even when organized cemeteries existed, such as Torone, they probably did not receive all the dead members of the community.

West Macedonia, Pelagonia, Polog, and Metohija

The mountainous terrain of west Macedonia, Pelagonia, and Polog, which extends from Mount Olympus to the Prespa lakes and the Šar mountains, contrasts strongly with the broad valleys of central and northern Macedonia. The middle course of the river Aliakmon, and the region to the north of it, are regarded as the heartland of Macedonia before its expansion into the plain of Pieria, allegedly in the early Archaic period (Zahrnt 1984).

The early Iron Age archaeological landscape of the Pierian plains east and north of Mount Olympus is striking for several reasons. On the one hand there is a relative uniformity in the mortuary behaviour in south Pieria, which contrasts with the variability of burial rites in central Macedonia. During the later Bronze Age, and up to and including the Sub-Mycenaean period, inhumation was practised in cist graves both in tumulus (Pigi Athinas close to Platamon and Valtos at Leptokaria) and flat cemeteries (Agios Dimitrios and Treis Elies). During the first centuries of the early Iron Age (eleventh to ninth centuries BC), tumulus cemeteries with inhumations in cist graves dominated the alluvial plain of south Pieria. Cremation, which used to be so popular in central Macedonia, was practised rarely, if at all, in Pieria. On the other hand, there is a conspicuous scarcity of settlements all over Pieria during the early Iron Age. The site of Kastro at Neokaisaria, located on the flat top of a steep hill next to the river Mavroneri, is the only well-documented habitation site in central Pieria, with a single phase dating to the later Protogeometric period (950–900 BC; Gimatzidis and Jung 2008). This discrepancy in the archaeological record may be due to the existence of semi-permanent settlements during the Bronze and early Iron Ages, which have left little trace in the archaeological record of the intensively eroded and silted Pierian plain.

There is barely any evidence for settlement in the rest of western Macedonia, Pelagonia, and Polog, where hilltops were generally preferred as habitation sites. The dominant burial rite in the mountainous region from Olympus to the Šar mountains was single (or very occasionally multiple) inhumations; more rarely, there were cremations in cists, pits, and sometimes *pithos* burials under tumuli. At the unusually large cemetery of Vergina with its more than 500 tumuli—some of them arranged in groups—the graves were usually arranged in a ring around central male and also female tombs (Andronikos 1969; Bräuning and Kilian-Dirlmeier 2013). Further west in Lynkestis, and north in Pelagonia, inhumations took place over many generations in the same large tumuli, each of them containing numerous—sometimes hundreds (Patele/Agios Panteleimonas) or many dozens (Visoi-Beranci)—of cist graves regularly arranged in a circular plan around an ancient central burial (Simoska and Sanev 1976: 24–27; Mitrevski 1997: 96–100, fig. 26). The ability to keep order in the arrangement of the individual graves within the large tumuli of west Macedonia and Pelagonia over many decades or centuries requires a form of political stability and respect for old social norms. No matter what the real social status of the deceased person in the central tomb was, the evident long-term planning in the organization of these large tumuli speaks for a highly hierarchical social system.

Burial practice—again the main surviving cultural expression—in the Metohija basin in south-west Kosovo, does not share many common features with the rest of Kosovo and central Macedonia. In the late Bronze Age and early Iron Ages the dead were inhumed (and rarely cremated), in tumulus and flat cemeteries, in contrast to neighbouring regions, where cremations of the Brnjica type were dominant (Bunguri 2006: 48–53). Burial rites in Metohija show more affinities with the Drina valley in western Serbia and Bosnia, and with Montenegro, where inhumation in tumuli—usually arranged in groups—was also the dominant practice (Della Casa 1996: 157–162, 189, fig. 174).

North-West Greece and Albania

The southern Dinaric Alps and the northern Pindus mountains, together with the coastal plains and valleys of Albania, constituted a more uniform archaeological landscape during the late Bronze and early Iron Age than those just discussed, albeit not without significant cultural differences. This region constitutes the areas known as Epirus and south Illyria—in other words, the north-west part of mainland Greece and Albania.

Subsistence Strategies in South Illyria and Epirus

Upland sites and sites located on steep rocky hills along river valleys, in coastal plains, and especially around big lakes—such as Scutari in the north, or the ancient dried-up Lake Maliq in the Korçë basin in the south—were the dominant forms of settlement during the early Iron Age, along with tells and flat lowland settlements. The building techniques and plans of the impressive 2–3 m thick fortification walls of the sites in highland Albania and Epirus have often served as typological and chronological criteria for their development, although it is almost impossible to date many of them due to the long occupation and intensive erosion they have endured. The same is true of the few remains of houses and other structures of oval, circular, and rectangular plan within and outside these impressively fortified acropolises (Korkuti 1982: 242–248, figs 8–12n; for late Bronze Age settlement in Epirus see Tartaron 2004: 24–70).

As far as we can tell, these fortified sites were more intensively occupied in the early Iron Age than previously (e.g. Tren, Gaijtan), and show signs of productive functions, whereas in the Bronze Age they may have served more as refuges or cult sites, with open settlements like Maliq still the main habitation type. The appearance of a new network of fortified nucleated settlements, surrounded by smaller agricultural establishments, in the valleys and plains of Albania from the later seventh century BC onwards, was accompanied by changes in the organization of pottery and metalwork production and by a marked increase in Greek imports (Ceka 1983). In Epirus, unfortified hilltop sites represent the commonest form of settlement at the start of the Iron Age, but most were abandoned in the eighth century BC.

The reconstruction of protohistoric social and economic organization in Albania and Epirus has changed over the decades, with several conflicting models having been proposed, the focus always on the existence, or not, of transhumance.[2] More concrete information on the issue comes from the multidisciplinary fieldwork project in the Shala valley in north Albania. The settlement system that emerged there in the late Bronze Age/early Iron Age was highly nucleated, exemplified by the site of Grunas. This was a complex fortified terrace system with huge walls, interpreted as a fort facilitating control of the valley route from the Albanian coast to the hinterland. Chemical analysis of lithic artefacts from sites in the Shala valley and the southern region of Shosh indicates interaction in the form of flint exchange, whereas chemical analysis of pottery has demonstrated domestic production with a limited exchange potential. The idea that Grunas was inhabited by a pastoral community is not contradicted by the faunal remains, while residue analysis points to a predominantly meat-based diet. Soil phosphate and archaeobotanical analyses yield further support by demonstrating that cereals were not cultivated on the terraces, but imported to the site, while the western part of the settlement housed the human population and the eastern part was reserved for animals. The assumption that Grunas was a seasonal settlement used by a mobile pastoral population as part of its transhumance strategy within a network of nucleated sites along the north Albanian river valleys is still attractive, in spite of the site's monumental architecture (Galaty et al. 2013).

Your Ancestors Are Ours: Falsification of the Past during the Early Iron Age

More information about the social organization of indigenous communities in Epirus and Albania comes from the numerous excavated tumuli, the typical form of burial ground in the region from the early Bronze Age. More than 130 tumuli have been excavated in Albania and several dozen in Epirus, presenting a more or less coherent picture. Single tumuli erected on small hills, or next to ancient roads, still dominate their localities (Lofkënd, Patos, Bajkaj, Luaras); others appear in small (Vajzë) or large (Pazhok) groups of 5–25 tumuli in the valleys of the Mat, Drin, and Vjosë rivers (Korkuti et al. 2008: 36–37, 51–52). A feature shared by tumuli in Albania, Epirus, western Macedonia, and Pelagonia is the gradual construction of the monument around a central tomb. The size of the tumuli and the number of tombs vary significantly. Tumuli can contain from a single tomb (for example, the tumuli at Kakavia and Bodrishtë; Prendi 1959: 190–211, figs 3, 7), to a few dozen or even hundreds, as at Kamenicë, the largest tumulus in Albania, with 396 tombs (Figure 13.4). Inhumation was the most common mortuary rite, while cremation *in situ* or in urns—sometimes made of perishable material—was occasionally practised (for example at Lofkënd, Papadopoulos et al. 2007: 125; and Rehovë, Aliu 2012: 274).

The largest and most complex late Bronze Age and early Iron Age tumuli were constructed around an ancient tomb, first covered by a small mound earlier in the Bronze Age. The central monument could be a simple pit (Rehovë), or a platform (Luaras) enclosed by a massive ring of stones (Rehovë, Pazhok, Piskovë, Vodhinë) and covered with a large pile of stones (Bodinaku 1999: 11–17, figs 1, 5; Korkuti et al.

FIGURE 13.4 The tumulus of Kamenicë in the basin of Korçë, Albania.
Photo: © Stefanos Gimatzidis

2008: 36–43, figs 3–5, 8–11; Aliu 2012: 37–42, figs 21–24). The area around the central monument, which stood out because of its size and elaborate construction, was levelled, often with material brought in from other sites, while a second stone ring defined the space for the burials that clustered in later periods around the Bronze Age 'ancestor'. Successive layers of settlement debris were added to enlarge mounds and create space for new burials during the Iron Age (Papadopoulos et al. 2007: 127–135; Aliu 2012: 271). The central monument was usually reserved for a single burial and rarely for multiple burials (Pazhok, Lofkënd). At some tumuli, such as Rehovë, one or more distinct tombs were constructed within the massive inner ring of the central burial mound (Aliu 2012: 54, 126, 272, figs 23, 45).

The central tomb or tombs stand out for their elaborate construction and spatial position within the larger tumuli (Amore 2010: 96–97). The question that arises at this point is whether the person buried in the central monument was recognized as a hero after death, perhaps many years or even centuries after burial, or whether she/he already stood at a high rank in the social hierarchy of their community at the time of their death. One answer may lie in the high degree of differentiation reflected in the elaborate equipment of some central tombs, such as Liatovouni (Douzougli and Papadopoulos 2010) and Pazhok (Korkuti et al. 2008: 39, figs 8–10). Even though the rich equipment of some central tombs is usually regarded as an indication of the high social status of the deceased, one cannot exclude the possibility that it also reflected the emotions or desires of the active members of the communities who furnished the tomb. Burial gifts alone are not a valid indicator of social differentiation: several central and elaborately constructed tombs that are completely devoid of grave goods testify to this fact.

Nevertheless, it is tricky—not to say methodologically problematic—to use tomb types or everyday artefacts such as pins, fibulae, and pottery vessels as indicators of social variability, a method deeply embedded in the old-fashioned cultural-historical perspective of the Balkans (see e.g. Bejko 2002).

Several significant points emerge from the social characterization of mortuary practice in Epirus and Albania. The first is that the largest tumuli developed around an ancient tomb, evoking the image of descendants who took their place around a venerable ancestor. The central tomb stands out not only because it is the most ancient monument, but also because it is usually the most richly equipped and elaborately constructed. This, however, is not enough evidence to speak of an ancestor cult, which must not be confused with burial practice (Morris 1991: 150). More robust indications of veneration may be represented by the presence of an ox skull (bucranium) in the central tomb at Pazhok, and animal remains in the central tombs of other tumuli (Bodinaku 1999: 13–15, fig. 4; Korkuti et al. 2008: 39, 53); even more conspicuous is a stone platform with clay figurines above the central tomb at Shtoj (Korkuti et al. 2008: 37, fig. 5), although all these features may be of earlier Bronze Age date.

But if there was no ancestor veneration during the late Bronze and early Iron Age, what lies behind the choice of later generations to bury their dead in or next to those tumuli? Debate over these monuments in the western Balkans was previously defined by socioeconomic determinism and often resulted in generalizations (cf. Morris 1991: 152; Hodder 1982: 140). The tumulus at Velika Gruda, on the coastal plain of Tivat close to the bay of Kotor in Montenegro, is one of few scientifically excavated and published burial sites in the western Balkans with a wide range of archaeometric analyses, which offers detailed evidence for the formation process of the burial mound (another is Lofkënd; Papadopoulos et al. 2014).

At the core of the Velika Gruda burial mound was a tumulus covering an unusually rich Copper Age tomb (*c.*2800–2700 cal BC) with valuable and exotic burial gifts, including a golden dagger from the Near East, which betray a highly differentiated social behaviour and status for the deceased person and those in charge of the burial (Primas 1996: 25–112). More than a thousand years later, the tumulus was enlarged and received new burials. After another long interval, it was reused as a burial place in the early Iron Age, and then in the medieval period (Della Casa 1996: 21–82, figs 18–27). It never stopped being regarded as a significant ritual place in the collective memory and a point of reference in the imagination of subsequent generations.

The Velika Gruda tumulus, with its fine radiocarbon chronology, shows beyond doubt that the first 'descendant' burial occurred at least a thousand years after the 'ancestor' was placed in the central tomb (Della Casa 1996: 24–27; Primas 1996: 48–52). Typo-chronological analysis of the Albanian tumuli leads to much the same conclusion, with most tombs constructed in the late Bronze Age and early Iron Age next to a central tomb or small group of tombs of the early Bronze Age. There is no doubt that these small western Balkan communities decided to bury their dead next to some very old tombs, with which they did not share any direct linear descent. Ancestors were invented in the collective memory of 'orphan' descendants, and a fictive lineage constructed by reuse of the burial space around the old tumuli, a way of legitimizing claims over territories, resources, or cultural heritage. This is a clear case of some individuals becoming after death what they never were in life (Hodder 1982: 146).

Pottery Stories

One of the most interesting aspects of early Iron Age material culture of Albania and Epirus is so-called matt-painted pottery. This fine handmade ceramic ware, decorated with sophisticated linear and geometric motives made with a dull paint (Gimatzidis 2010: 274–280, figs 86–87), forms part of a more widespread pottery tradition rooted in the Bronze Age, also found in Macedonia and Thessaly. Long treated as evidence for migrations and ethnogenesis of either Illyrians or Dorians, recent research has shown that in Albania and Epirus the greatest part of its production falls in the early Iron Age, later than in Macedonia or Thessaly (Horejs 2007: 218–286).

By the later eighth century BC, and before the earliest colonies were established on the Ionian and Adriatic coasts, local communities in the hinterlands of Epirus and Albania were already importing and consuming Greek pottery, mostly of Corinthian origin, and other non-local luxury goods (Douzougli and Papadopoulos 2010: 46–62). Also noteworthy is the presence, at a slightly later date, of large quantities of Thapsos ware at the Corinthian colony of Ambracia (modern Arta). This ware was widely distributed in Italy, so if it was partly produced in western Greece this would change our understanding of regional cultural contacts as we traditionally infer them from pottery distributions.

Pirin and East Macedonia

Two major fluvial systems, the Struma (ancient Strymon) and Nestos/Mesta rivers that rise in the mountains south of Sofia and flow into the Aegean, cut from north to south through the Kerkini (Belasica), Maleševo, Rila, Pirin, and Rhodope mountains that stand as major barriers between the Aegean and the central Balkans. The Struma valley would undoubtedly have been a more convenient route of communication than that of the Nestos, which has numerous narrow gorges in its middle and upper course.

Alluviation and erosion in the lower courses of these rivers created extremely unstable geomorphological conditions in antiquity with severe ecological consequences for the population. It is likely that these unstable conditions partly determined the settlement pattern of the late Bronze and early Iron Ages on small tells, or fort sites on the hills fringing the Struma and Nestos valleys (Grammenos 1984). Evidence for settlement is scarce in east Macedonia, whereas in the adjacent Pirin Macedonia, numerous excavations and surveys present a better picture of settlement history in the middle Struma and Nestos valleys. After a long period with very few habitation sites following on from a more or less dense settlement pattern during the late Neolithic, new sites appeared again in the late Bronze Age within a complex settlement system (Gergova 1995: 32–34, fig. 1; Grębska-Kulowa and Kulow 2007: 279–294).

A very distinctive form of settlement is the fort on a small hill that stands over passes, water resources, or fertile valleys. Kamenska Čuka, next to the river Struma in the Blagoevgrad basin, is the best-excavated and most extensively published site of this kind (Stefanovic and Bankoff 1998). Dominating this very fertile part of the Struma valley from the fourteenth to twelfth centuries BC, this site is notable for its exceptional architectural form, comprising a small rectangular fort of two storeys surrounded by a very strong and high stone wall with a single entrance. Interpretation of this structure of only 320 m^2, which was never intensively occupied, as its modest depositional history betrays, is puzzling. Apart from being a perfect place of refuge, it seems to have been a centre with special storage facilities and distributional duties, as attested by its 30 *pithoi* and numerous amphorae. More than ten forts of this type are known in the middle Struma valley, all in the Blagoevgrad basin north the Kresna gorge (Grębska-Kulowa and Kulow 2007: 291).

Another feature of the middle Struma and Nestos valleys during the late Bronze Age and the transition to the Iron Age was the flat settlement, generally located next to forts of the Kamenska Čuka type or other fortified sites (Grębska-Kulowa and Kulow 2007: 294, fig. 12). There is still little information on these flat settlements, which may however have been the main sites of permanent occupation in the region. At Koprivlen near Gotze Delchev in the middle Nestos valley, rescue excavations by Anelia Bozkova have yielded two late Bronze Age and one early Iron Age settlement phases on a terrace on the right bank of the Nestos (Bozkova et al. 2002), but apart from a very conspicuous pit complex (see later), the early Iron Age levels yielded no remains of domestic architecture.

Earlier archaeological research in east and Pirin Macedonia focused on cemeteries, many of them still only partially published. The Cochan-Satovcha necropolis, with more than 100 tumuli, is one of the largest, spanning a long period from the late Bronze Age to the Roman period (Gergova 1995: 35–37, figs 2–6). If we wish to generalize about mortuary practice, we would say that cremation was mostly practised during the initial phases of the early Iron Age, with inhumation becoming more common later.

The Rhodope Mountains and Adjacent Plains

Traditionally regarded as natural barriers hampering interaction between the Aegean and the Balkan hinterland, recent and some older finds from the Bulgarian hinterland attest—contrary to earlier views—contact over the Rhodope mountains with the Aegean long before the foundation of the first Greek colonies on the Thracian coast. As early as the fifteenth century BC, some artefacts of Aegean type were used and deposited in the Bulgarian hinterland (Bozhinova et al. 2010: 70–84, fig. 4). These contacts seem to have broken off before the end of the late Bronze Age and only become archaeologically visible again, after a long gap, from the eighth century BC onwards, with the import and consumption of a few pieces of Geometric pottery in Svilengrad in the middle Maritsa valley (Karadzhinov 2010).

From the early Archaic period (seventh century BC), artefacts of Greek type or origin appear more frequently in the Bulgarian hinterland, this time as a result of more intensive contacts following the foundation of the Greek colonies on the western shores of the Black Sea and on the Aegean shores of Thrace. During the early Iron Age the Rhodope mountains and the adjacent plain to the north do not demonstrate any archaeologically traceable contact with the Aegean, with the exception of the sparse finds from Svilengrad. This does not mean that the Rhodope mountains were a physical barrier that prevented the exchange of goods or concepts. They were instead a connective zone, as the uniformity in burial rites, settlement forms, pottery, and other artefact types both north and south of the mountains attests. The most noticeable differences in material culture are between the western and eastern Rhodope mountains. For example, while fluted wares decorated with knobs are found across the region in the early Iron Age, and continued to be produced at later periods, a distinctive new type of pottery with elaborate geometric motifs (Pšeničevo ware) was used in the eastern Rhodope mountains from the tenth century BC onwards; this is closely related to ceramics of the Basarabi and Babadag groups north of the Balkan mountains (see Chapter 14).

Domestic and Ritual Space on the Thracian Highlands

The most typical early Iron Age sites in southern Thrace are located on the peaks of the Rhodope, Sakar, and Strandzha mountains and on surrounding lower hills. These highland sites, which were usually equipped with double- or triple-walled enclosures, with walls several hundred metres long and up to 3 m thick, form the densest settlement system that the Rhodope mountains ever witnessed in prehistory (Triantafyllos 1990; Efstratiou 2002: 108). Although many of these upland sites have been excavated, interpretation is still controversial due to their complex depositional history. Most of their impressive defensive walls were probably actually built in later periods, but some megalithic 'cyclopean' defensive structures may date to the late Bronze or early Iron Age (Triantafyllos 1990: 302, figs 3–4). Apart from a scatter of pottery sherds there are usually barely any other finds or structures in the highly disturbed contexts at these Thracian highland sites that can be securely dated to these periods. Very few sites in the Bulgarian part of the Rhodope mountains have yielded any stratigraphy or well-dated structures of the early Iron Age.

Remoteness and inaccessibility, together with their megalithic architecture, provide the main arguments for interpreting these rocky sites as either fortified settlements or sanctuaries, a long-lasting debate in Bulgarian archaeology (cf. Popov 2009; Bozhinova 2018). The truth is that while a complex and multi-dimensional settlement system existed in the Rhodope mountains, it remains difficult to understand in the current state of archaeological knowledge (cf. Archibald 1998: 34–47). Small-scale ethnoarchaeological research in the Greek part of the Rhodope mountains has demonstrated the methodological weakness in invoking generalizations for interpreting archaeological phenomena of consistent form (Efstratiou 2002). The hilltop site at Tsouka, close to Sarakini, was equipped with a still visible low enclosure and a few rectangular structures built adjacent to it. Modern rural settlements in the region that share common features with Tsouka support its interpretation as an early Iron Age pastoral site with particular production, organization, and management strategies. Strongly contrasting is the nearby settlement on the barely accessible Kremastos hill (Asar-tepe), which rises 900 m above the surrounding landscape and is partly enclosed by a strong defensive wall 1.70 m thick and 700 m long. If there had been a large open settlement next to it, this could perhaps be explained as a refuge, but this is not the case (Efstratiou 2002: 105–109). These highland sites, which were strategically conceived to control passes to valuable resources or routes of communication, were occupied for a long period of time from the early Bronze Age to late Antiquity and even modern times.

Some fortified hilltop sites were much larger and could have functioned as freestanding settlements. Kush Kaya on a ridge between two rocky peaks in the north-eastern Rhodope mountains, close to the Ardas valley, extends over some 100 ha (Popov 2009, 2015). Excavation yielded a complex sequence of late Bronze Age and early Iron Age buildings. Dragoyna in the foothills of the central Rhodope mountains is another well-excavated fortified hilltop site (Bozhinova et al. 2010). Thanks to these and other recent excavations, the missing settlements of the late Bronze Age and early Iron Age are gradually coming to light, deconstructing the old narrative about the dominance of sanctuaries in Thrace.

Unfortified open settlements, and perhaps tells, were also occupied in the early Iron Age in the central plain along the Maritsa and Tundza rivers and in the south-eastern lowlands of Bulgaria (e.g. at Pšeničevo, Rogozinovo, and Ovcharitsa), but evidence for the overall settlement pattern is still limited (Shalganova and Gotzev 1995: 334; Georgieva 2001: 83–85; Gyuzelev 2008: 67–150; Popov 2015). Several sites, however, possessed extensive storage facilities in the form of pit complexes. In Bulgaria, there is still a tendency to regard the pits as places of ritual performance, and the sites as sanctuaries, due to finds of human and animal skeletons and body parts in some pits and the absence of other traces of settlement at excavated pit complexes (e.g. Koprivlen, Svilengrad, Malko Tranovo, Gledacevo), but in north and central Greece they are seen simply as rubbish pits. In central Macedonia, where domestic buildings had stone foundations and mud-brick walls instead of wattle and daub, the pit complexes clearly belong to settlements. Future research should focus on the economic implications of storage facilities on such a large scale, surely indicative of surplus agricultural production that resulted from increased specialization in cereals, as well as to secondary use of the pits for disposal of the dead and other ritual acts—similar practices are attested in many parts of Iron Age Europe (cf. Chapter 4).

Mortuary Practice in Thrace

The most intriguing aspect of the early Iron Age in the Rhodope mountains and adjacent plains is the variability of mortuary practice, where 'we face already a rich mosaic of burial and cult practices connected with the Thracian barrow-graves' (Gergova 1989: 235). Although flat cemeteries are far from rare, the chief feature of the mortuary landscape in Thrace is the tumulus, and inhumation was the dominant burial rite. Cremation in urns was also practised, often deposited under the same tumulus next to inhumations. The variety of grave forms is also remarkable, with megalithic burial monuments (dolmens) under tumuli being the most impressive. Burials also occur in cist and pit graves, stone enclosures, and on platforms—usually under tumuli—during the early Iron Age. The distinctive social status enjoyed by women in some regions becomes explicit by the central position reserved for them in the burial tumuli. On the other hand, several double female graves have been interpreted as victims of sacrifice. Primary and secondary burials, pseudo-graves without burials, cult structures, and various offerings in tumuli form part of an extremely complex and highly variable, in both time and space, mortuary habitus (Gergova 1989; Shalganova and Gotzev 1995: 336–338; Archibald 1998: 48–78; Georgieva 2001: 63–65, 86–88; Kisyov 2009).

The Megalithic Monuments

Dolmens, rings of upright stones (cromlechs or peristaliths), rock-cut tombs, menhirs, large complexes of niches, as well as various other rock-cut features including basins known as *sharapans*, steps, cup-marks, and engraved linear and figural motives constitute what is known today as the megalithic aspect of mortuary and ritual material culture in the eastern Rhodope, Sakar, and Strandzha mountains (Nekhrizov 2015). The dolmens have attracted archaeological interest since the late nineteenth century (Triantafyllos 1983: 145–154; Delev 1984: 18–20; Akman 1997: 151–153). These conspicuous megalithic tombs, constructed with large granite or gneiss slabs, form the most visible and impressive material expression of mortuary behaviour in this mountainous region (Akman 1997: 153–154, fig. 2; Özdoğan 1998). There are many different treatments of their typology, but they may be subsumed into two main groups, with one, or more commonly two, chambers (Delev 1984: 20–24, figs 1–10; Akman 1997: 155–156, fig. 4; Nekhrizov 2015: 126–130). A front slab with an oval or quadrangular opening usually separates the main chamber or chambers from the entrance corridor, which—when present—usually opens south onto a stone façade. Unfortunately, almost all dolmens were looted in the past and very few have been well excavated and documented, but we know that they were in use from the end of the late Bronze Age to the Archaic period. Excavations at the impressive monument at Lalapaşa, north-east of Edirne, have yielded in its middle chamber four individual inhumations dating to the early Iron Age (Figure 13.5). The few Hellenistic sherds in the main chamber speak either for its looting or for continuous use until that period (Akman 1997: 160–170). Each dolmen was covered by a

FIGURE 13.5 Dolmen at Lalapaşa, Edirne, Turkey.

Photo: © Stefanos Gimatzidis

single tumulus, and only rarely were two dolmens erected parallel to one another under the same mound. These tumuli usually appear singly or in small groups, but occasionally belong to more extensive cemeteries (Triantafyllos 1973).

The rock-cut tomb was a less common type of early Iron Age burial monument in the eastern Rhodope mountains, with a few examples also on the Sakar mountain and on Thasos. They can occur in groups of two or three, but are usually single, comprising a rectangular or rounded chamber that is often vaulted and accessible from a side opening—sometimes with an anteroom—and may have an opening on the roof (Delev 1984: 28–29; Nekhrizov 2015: 134–137). Another megalithic feature of the funerary or cultic landscape in Thrace was standing stones, often called menhirs. They are sometimes directly linked with dolmens, as for example at Hacilar. More usually, they appear in hundreds as independent monuments of different shapes (rectangular, cylindrical, pyramidal, and irregular) and sizes (from 0.5m to 3 m in height), erected in rows and covering large areas (Özdoğan 1998). In at least one case, more than two thousand menhirs have been recorded around Muhittin Baba mountain in the Lalapaşa region (Erdoğu 2003). Their mortuary connotations cannot be doubted because of their spatial relationship to other burial monuments, although they also occur well beyond the region where dolmens are found—for example, in the Gallipoli peninsula (Özbek 2008: 89–90). The standing stones must have had a more complex function than other funerary monuments. It is probable that they commemorated deceased members of the community in the same way as the megalithic tombs, but they could also have been erected as a post-funerary appeal to the ancestors. Another possibility is that they commemorated particular events or even marked a territory (Parker Pearson and

Ramilisonina 1998). Rows of erected stones forming circles or quadrants, usually called cromlechs or peristaliths, were also part of the extraordinary mortuary and ritual landscape of Thrace.

Menhirs and other megalithic monuments or rocks were sometimes decorated with simple linear engravings or more elaborate geometric and figurative motifs depicting human figures, animals, and abstract geometric motifs. The most characteristic feature is, however, the so-called cup-mark: small hollows carved, usually in large groups, on rocks that show no other sign of working, or even on stone monuments probably used for some kind of ritual activity (Erdoğu et al. 2002). It is preferable to see petroglyphs as an iconographic expression of variable ideologies according to their social context, which apart from mortuary beliefs may also reflect social rivalry, as the hunting scenes on the rocks of Pangaion imply (Moutsopoulos 1969).

The last and most intriguing aspect of the megalithic archaeological landscape in Thrace are large groups of niches cut into the vertical façades of mountain cliffs and rocks in eastern Rhodope (Figure 13.6). These niches are 0.5–1 m high, usually of trapezoidal form, and cluster in groups—ranging from a single one to several hundred—on high cliffs in upland locations (Nekhrizov 2015: 138–141). As Peter Delev has pointed out, the niches must have been cut over a long period of time, as they are grouped in different sizes and forms at each site (Delev 1984: 30–31, figs 13–14). Cutting these niches many metres above the ground was a difficult and dangerous undertaking, usually requiring the engagement of a person hanging by a rope from the top of the rock. The two most popular interpretations are that the niches were places for the storage of burial urns or of votive tablets, but whatever their function, their social and ideological importance can be in no doubt. This is manifest both in the effort invested in their construction and the care taken to ensure their visibility and dominance over the landscape within inhabited sites, or next to cemeteries (Nehrizov et al. 2012: 228–229; Nekhrizov 2015: 139, fig. 10.3).

The largest known group of niches is at Gluhite Kamani near Malko Gradishte, where 459 niches in eighty-one clusters on twenty-eight individual rocks are recorded (Nehrizov et al. 2012). Gluhite Kamani is one of very few sites in the eastern Rhodope mountains with a good stratified sequence of at least three Iron Age phases, and good-quality botanical and faunal remains. The occupants ate an impressive variety of cereals and exploited an unusually large number of wild animals, while open-air hearths and other features of non-permanent character are suggestive of seasonal occupation. A cult dimension to the activity is implied by numerous finds of miniature vases and anthropomorphic figurines (Nehrizov et al. 2012: 223–229).

Final Remarks

In the first millennium BC, north Greece and the central Balkans are widely perceived as a periphery or buffer zone between Greece and the rest of continental Europe. According to this modernist viewpoint, which found support in world system theory, the only

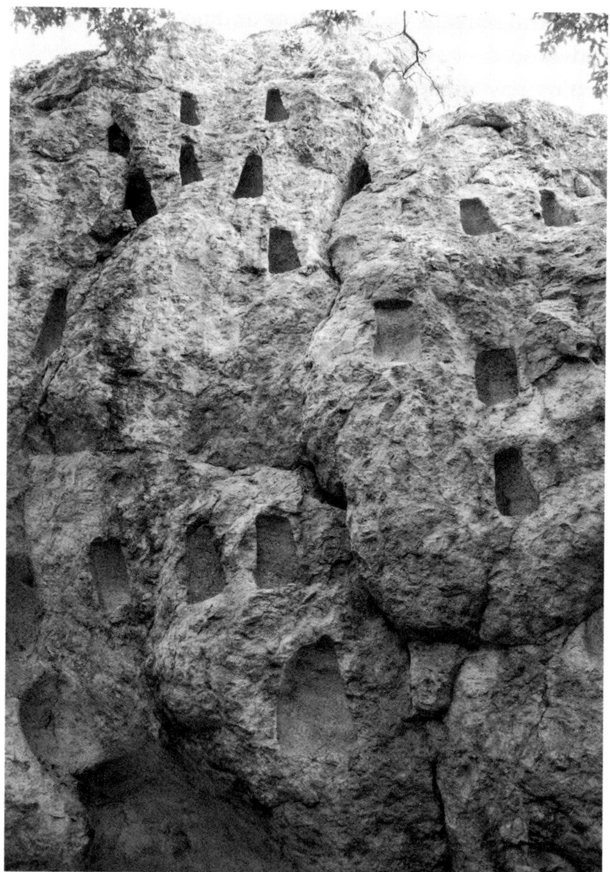

FIGURE 13.6 Niches at the rocky cliffs of Gluhite Kamani (meaning deaf stones), Bulgaria.
Photo: © Stefanos Gimatzidis

connective factor was the Greek colonists, who, after settling on the east, west, and south Balkan coasts from the eighth century BC onwards, initiated cultural homogenization through a 'Hellenization' process. The dualist point of view—Greek and non-Greek—is still common in Aegean and Balkan prehistory, as well as in classical archaeology. A similar oversimplification of origins is inherent in the labelling of cultural and historical landscapes in the Balkans with the names Illyria, Epirus, Macedonia, and Thrace, as if these were self-defined cultural or even ethnic entities with characteristics similar to modern nation states.

Contrary to these traditional views, this chapter has sought to demonstrate the archaeological complexities concealed by these oversimplifications and to argue that the Iron Age landscape of the central Balkans was not just a field between two distorting poles; it comprised, instead, a network of numerous independent and interacting social systems and agents. If we accept that there are no sterile cultural entities, we can also recognize that the central Balkans were no more and no less a buffer zone than any other archaeological landscape.

John Papadopoulos has suggested that genuine urbanization started in this 'periphery' during the fourth century BC as a response of the rising tribal societies (*ethne*) that inhabited Epirus, Macedonia, and other regions neighbouring the Greek city states, after a long period of economic and social transformations (Papadopoulos 2016). All this may have started in a period when the Greek *polis* was losing its prestige in a changing world, where powerful kingdoms were emerging out of the old tribal societies, and new large cities came into being through synoecism of numerous pre-existing small villages (*komai*). This view overturns older essentialist theories that perceived urbanization as a direct result of contacts with the Greek world through its colonies from the Archaic period onwards. We may also agree that, elusive though theoretical definitions of the term urbanization may be (see Osborne 2005 for a concise discussion), archaeologists in the Mediterranean lands have been overly reluctant to embrace a robust theoretical framework and definition of the term. If we wish to avoid swinging between vaguely defined terms of pre-, proto-, and proper urbanization, we should recognize that complex urban entities had in fact already emerged in Macedonia in a previous period.

While we still do not know a great deal about the seventh century BC in Macedonia, there are certainly changes in the archaeological record dating to the later Archaic period. In the later sixth and early fifth centuries BC, some communities expanded well beyond the limits of the old tell settlements, and the first clearly recognizable public buildings were erected. Some of these were very elaborate, such as the late Archaic monumental marble temple at Aineia at Nea Michaniona (which was not a colony), whereas others were more modest, as at Sindos. New extended cemeteries appeared next to almost every settlement with exceptional groups of rich warrior and female graves reflecting a more complex social differentiation—albeit not necessarily a hierarchy. These changes were not confined to sites along the Aegean shores that might be conceived as privileged recipients of impulses from the south, but reached the Balkan hinterland (e.g. Aiani, Trebenishte). Some of the largest, most prominent cities of the classical and Hellenistic periods in the lower and middle Axios valley, such as Chalastra, Morrylos, and Europos, were already regional centres in the Archaic period.

In sum, the process of centralization does not just begin in the northern Aegean region during the Archaic period, but patently follows on from the rapid development of more complex economic relationships evident in the early Iron Age archaeology of central Macedonia, a process that was definitely not triggered by impulses from the south.

Notes

1. Study of the archaeological material from Mende is a work in progress.
2. See, for example, Cherry (1988) and Halstead (1996) who argue that models based on modern transhumance patterns are inappropriate for reconstructing practices at this early period.

REFERENCES

Akman, M. 1997. 'Megalithforschungen in Thrakien'. *Istanbuler Mitteilungen* 47: 151–170.

Aliu, S. 2012. *Tuma e Rehovës*. Korçë: Akademia e Shkencave e Shqipërisë.

Amore, M. G. 2010. *The Complex of Tumuli 9, 10 and 11 in the Necropolis of Apollonia (Albania)*. British Archaeological Reports International Series 2059. Oxford: Archaeopress.

Andreou, S., M. Fotiadis, and K. Kotsakis. 1996. 'Review of Aegean Prehistory V: The Neolithic and Bronze Age of Northern Greece'. *American Journal of Archaeology* 100: 537–597.

Andronikos, M. 1969. *Βεργίνα I: Το νεκροταφείο των τύμβων*. Athens: Βιβλιοθήκη της εν Αθήναις Αρχαιολογικής Εταιρείας.

Archibald, Z. H. 1998. *The Odrysian Kingdom of Thrace: Orpheus Unmasked*. Oxford Monographs on Classical Archaeology. Oxford: Clarendon Press.

Bejko, L. 2002. 'Mortuary customs in the late Bronze Age of southeastern Albania', in G. Touchais and J. Renard (eds) *L'Albanie dans l'Europe Préhistorique*. Bulletin de Correspondance Hellénique Supplément 42: 171–198. Paris: De Boccard.

Bodinaku, N. 1999. 'Some tumulus burials of early Bronze Age in Albania (Problem of migrations)', in P. Cabanes (ed.) *L'Illyrie méridionale et l'Epire dans l'antiquité 3. Actes du IIIe colloque international de Chantilly (16–19 octobre 1996)*: 11–17. Paris: De Boccard.

Bozhinova, E. 2018. 'Settlements or sanctuaries? Interpretational dilemma concerning 2nd–1st millennium BC sites in Bulgaria', in S. Gimatzidis, M. Pieniążek, and S. Mangaloğlu-Votruba (eds) *Archaeology across Frontiers and Borderlands: Fragmentation and Connectivity in the North Aegean and the Balkans during the Late Bronze Age and Early Iron Age*. OREA 9: 333–358. Vienna: Austrian Academy of Sciences.

Bozhinova, E., R. Jung, and H. Mommsen. 2010. 'Dragojna: Eine spätbronzezeitliche Höhensiedlung in den bulgarischen Rhodopen mit importierter mykenischer Keramik'. *Mitteilungen des Deutschen Archäologischen Instituts, Athenische Abteilung* 125: 45–97.

Bozkova, A., P. Delev, and D. Vulcheva (eds). 2002. *Koprivlen, Vol. 1: Rescue Archaeological Investigations Along the Gotse Delchev-Drama Road: 1998–1999*. Sofia: NOUS.

Bräuning, A., and I. Kilian-Dirlmeier. 2013. *Die eisenzeitlichen Grabhügel von Vergina: Die Ausgrabungen von Photis Petsas 1960–1961*. RGZM Monographien 119. Mainz: Römisch-Germanisches Zentralmuseum.

Bulatović, A. 2007. 'South Morava basin in the transitional period from the Bronze to the Iron Age'. *Starinar* 57: 57–82.

Bunguri, A. 2006. 'Drini i Bardhë area in Prehistory', in L. Përzhita, K. Luci, G. Hoxha, A. Bunguri, F. Peja, and T. Kastrati (eds) *The Archaeological Map of Kosova I*. Prishtina/Tirana: The Museum of Kosova and The Institute of Archaeology.

Ceka, N. 1983. 'Lindja e jetës qytetare tek Ilirët e jugut (La naissance de la vie urbaine chez les Illyriens du Sud)'. *Iliria. Revistë arkeologjike* 2: 144–192.

Cherry, J. 1988. 'Pastoralism and the role of animals in the pre- and protohistoric economies of the Aegean', in C. R. Whittaker (ed.) *Pastoral Economies in Classical Antiquity*. Cambridge Philological Society Supplement 14: 6–34. Cambridge: Cambridge Philological Society.

Delev, P. 1984. 'Megalithic Thracian tombs in south-eastern Bulgaria'. *Anatolica* 11: 1–45.

Della Casa, P. 1996. *Velika Gruda II: Die bronzezeitliche Nekropole Velika Gruda (Opš. Kotor, Montenegro)*. Universitätsforschungen zur prähistorischen Archäologie 33. Bonn: Habelt.

Desborough, V. R. d'A. 1964. *The Last Mycenaeans and Their Successors: An Archaeological Survey, c.1200–c.1000 BC*. Oxford: Clarendon Press.

Douzougli, A., and J. K. Papadopoulos. 2010. 'Liatovouni: A Molossian cemetery and settlement in Epirus'. *Archäologischer Anzeiger* 125: 1–87.

Efstratiou, N. 2002. *Εθνοαρχαιολογικές αναζητήσεις στα Πομακοχώρια της Ροδόπης*. Thessaloniki: Vanias.

Erdoğu, B., R. Erdoğu, and J. Chapman. 2002. 'Kirikköy—The largest megalithic complex in Turkish Thrace'. *Antaeus* 25: 547–569.

Erdoğu, R. 2003. 'A major new megalithic complex in Europe'. *Antiquity* 77, 297. Project Gallery available at http://www.antiquity.ac.uk/projgall/erdogu297 [accessed 12 March 2018].

Galaty, M. L., O. Lafe, W. E. Lee, and Z. Tafilica. 2013. *Light and Shadow: Isolation and Interaction in the Shala Valley of Northern Albania*. Monumenta Archaeologica 28. Los Angeles: The Cotsen Institute of Archaeology Press.

Garašanin, M. V. 1973. *Praistorija na tlu SR Srbije [La préhistoire sur le territoire de la république socialiste de Serbie]*. Belgrade: Srpska književna zadruga.

Georgieva, R. 2001. 'Thracian culture of the Early Iron Age', in I. Panayotov, B. Borisov, and R. Georgieva (eds) *Maritsa-Iztok Archaeological Research* 5: 83–94. Radnevo: Archaeological Museum 'Maritsa-Iztok' and Archaeological Expedition 'Maritsa-Iztok'.

Gergova, D. 1989. 'Thracian burial rites of late Bronze and early Iron Age', in J. G. P. Best and N. M. W. de Vries (eds) *Thracians and Mycenaeans. Proceedings of the Fourth International Congress of Thracology, Rotterdam, 24–26 September 1984*: 231–240. Leiden: E. J. Brill and Terra Antiqua Balcanica.

Gergova, D. 1995. 'Culture in the late Bronze and early Iron Age in southwest Thrace'. Зборник Нова Серија, бр. *1, 1995*, археологија: 31–48.

Gimatzidis, S. 2010. *Die Stadt Sindos: Eine Siedlung von der späten Bronze- bis zur Klassischen Zeit am Thermaischen Golf in Makedonien*. Prähistorische Archäologie in Südosteuropa 26. Rahden: Marie Leidorf.

Gimatzidis, S. 2011. 'Counting sherds at Sindos: Pottery consumption and construction of identities in the Iron Age', in S. Verdan, T. Theurillat, and A. Kenzelmann Pfyffer (eds) *Early Iron Age Pottery: A Quantitative Approach. Proceedings of the International Round Table Organized by the Swiss School of Archaeology in Greece, Athens, November 28–30 2008*. British Archaeological Reports International Series 2254: 97–110. Oxford: Archaeopress.

Gimatzidis, S., and R. Jung. 2008. 'Νέα στοιχεία για την Εποχή Χαλκού και Σιδήρου από την Πιερία: Κάστρο Νεοκαισάρειας 2007'. *Archaeologiko Ergo sti Makedonia kai Thrake* 22: 211–218.

Grammenos, D. 1984. 'Prähistorische Siedlungen in Ostmazedonien', in A. Peschew, D. Popov, K. Jordanov, and I. von Bredow (eds) *Dritter internationaler thrakologischer Kongress zu Ehren W. Tomascheks, 2.–6. Juni 1980, Wien*: 75–87. Sofia: Staatlicher Verlag Swjat.

Grębska-Kulowa, M., and I. Kulow. 2007. 'Prehistoric sites in the middle Struma river valley between the end of the VIIth mill. BC and the beginning of the 1st mill. BC', in H. Todorova, M. Stefanovich, and G. Ivanov (eds) *The Struma/Strymon River Valley in Prehistory. Proceedings of the International Symposium Strymon Praehistoricus, Kjustendil–Blagoevgrad (Bulgaria), Serres–Amphipolis (Greece), 27.09–01.10.2004: In The Steps of James Harvey Gaul, Vol. 2*: 279–296. Sofia: Gerda Henkel Stiftung.

Gyuzelev, M. 2008. *The West Pontic Coast between Emine Cape and Byzantion During the First Millennium BC*. Burgas: Lotus Advertising Publishing House.

Halstead, P. 1996. 'Pastoralism or household herding? Problems of scale and specialization in early Greek animal husbandry'. *World Archaeology* 28: 20–42.

Hänsel, B. 1989. *Kastanas: Ausgrabungen in einem Siedlungshügel der Bronze- und Eisenzeit Makedoniens 1975–1979: Die Grabung und der Baubefund*. Prähistorische Archäologie in Südosteuropa 7. Berlin: Wissenschaftsverlag Volker Spiess.

Hodder, I. 1982. *The Present Past: An Introduction to Anthropology for Archaeologists*. London: Batsford.

Horejs, B. 2007. *Das Prähistorische Olynth: Ausgrabungen in der Toumba Agios Mamas 1994–1996: Die spätbronzezeitliche handgemachte Keramik der Schichten 13–1*. Prähistorische Archäologie in Südosteuropa 21. Rahden: Marie Leidorf.

Kapuran, A. 2009. *Late Bronze and Early Iron Age Architecture in the Južna Morava Basin*. Belgrade: University of Belgrade, Centre for Archaeological Research.

Karadzhinov, I. 2010. 'Early Greek painted pottery from the middle currents of Hebros and Tonzos', in R. Georgieva, T. Stoyanov, and D. Momchilov (eds) *Югоизточна България през II—I хилядолетие пр. Хр./South-Eastern Bulgaria during the 2nd–1st millennium BC*: 158–180. Varna: Zograf Press.

Kisyov, K. 2009. *Pogrebalni praktiki v Rodopite (II–I hil. pr. Hr.)/Burial Practices in the Rhodope Mountain (II–I mil. BCE)*. Plovdiv: Avtospektar.

Korkuti, M. 1982. 'Die Siedlungen der späten Bronze- und der frühen Eisenzeit in Südwest-Albanien', in B. Hänsel (ed.) *Südosteuropa zwischen 1600 und 1000 v. Chr*. Prähistorische Archäologie in Südosteuropa 1: 235–253. Berlin/Bad Bramstedt: Moreland Editions.

Korkuti, M., A. Baçe, N. Ceka, and P. Cabanes. 2008. *Carte archéologique de l'Albanie*. Tirana: Pegi.

Krstić, D. 1991. 'Preistorijske nekropole u Gornjoj Stražavi/Prehistoric Necropolii in Gornja Stražava'. *Zbornik Narodnog Muzeja. Arheologija* 14, 1: 231–243.

Luci, K. 1984. 'Nova grupa grobova na praistorijskoj nekropoli u Donjoj Brnjici/The new group of graves on a prehistoric necropolis in lower Brnjca'. *Glasnik Muzeja I Metohije/Bulletin du Musée de Kosovo et Metohie* 13–14: 25–34.

Mitrevski, D. 1992–1993. 'A Brnjica type necropolis near Skopje'. *Starinar N.S.* 43–44: 115–124.

Mitrevski, D. 1997. *Proto-Historical Communities in Macedonia through Burials and Burial Manifestations*. Cultural and Historic Heritage of Republic of Macedonia 37. Skopje: Institute for the Protection of Cultural Monuments of Macedonia.

Mitrevski, D. 2005. *Vardarski Rid I*. Skopje: Foundation Vardarski Rid.

Morris, I. 1991. 'The archaeology of ancestors: The Saxe/Goldstein hypothesis revisited'. *Cambridge Archaeological Journal* 1: 147–169.

Moutsopoulos, N. 1969. *Τα ακιδογραφήματα του Παγγαίου*. Athens.

Nehrizov, G., L. E. Roller, M. Vassileva, J. Tsvetkova, and N. Kecheva. 2012. 'The Gloukhite Kamani site: Old questions and new approaches'. *Thracia* 20: 215–233.

Nekhrizov, G. 2015. 'Dolmens and rock-cut monuments', in J. Valeva, E. Nankov, and D. Graninger (eds) *A Companion to Ancient Thrace*: 126–143. Malden: Wiley Blackwell.

Oberhummer, E., and B. Lenk (ed.) 1936. *Thrake: Real-Encyclopädie der Classischen Altertumswissenschaft VI A,1*. Stuttgart: Metzler-Verlag.

Osborne, R. 2005. 'Urban sprawl: What is urbanisation and why does it matter?', in R. Osborne and B. W. Cunliffe (eds) *Mediterranean Urbanisation 800–600 BC*. Proceedings of the British Academy 126: 1–16. Oxford: Oxford University Press.

Özbek, O. 2008. 'Menhirs in the graveyards: fact or fiction? A reconsideration of erected stone monuments of Gallipoli Peninsula', in O. Özbek (ed.) *Funeral Rites, Rituals and Ceremonies from Prehistory to Antiquity. Proceedings of the International Workshop 'Troas and its Neighbours', Çanakkale and Ören 2–6 October 2006*: 83–96. Istanbul: Institut Français d'Études Anatoliennes Georges-Dumézil.

Özdoğan, M. 1998. 'Early Iron Age in eastern Thrace and the megalithic monuments', in N. Tuna, Z. Aktüre, and M. Lynch (eds) *Thracians and Phrygians: Problems of Parallelism. Proceedings of an International Symposium on the Archaeology, History and Ancient Languages of Thrace and Phrygia, Ankara 3–4 June 1995*: 29–40. Ankara: MTEU Faculty of Architecture Press.

Papadopoulos, J. 2005. *The Early Iron Age Cemetery at Torone*. Los Angeles: Cotsen Institute of Archaeology at UCLA.

Papadopoulos, J. 2016. 'Komai, colonies and cities in Epirus and southern Albania: The failure of the polis and the rise of urbanism on the fringes of the Greek world', in B. P. C. Molloy (ed.) *Of Odysseys and Oddities: Scales and Modes of Interaction Between Prehistoric Aegean Societies and their Neighbours*. Sheffield Studies in Aegean Archaeology, 435–460. Oxford: Oxbow.

Papadopoulos, J., L. Bejko, and S. Morris. 2007. 'Excavations at the prehistoric burial tumulus of Lofkënd in Albania: A preliminary report for the 2004–2005 seasons'. *American Journal of Archaeology* 111: 105–147.

Papadopoulos, J., S. P. Morris, L. Bejko, and L. A. Schepartz. 2014. *The Excavation of the Prehistoric Burial Tumulus at Lofkënd, Albania*. Monumenta Archaeologica 34. Los Angeles: Cotsen Institute of Archaeology at UCLA.

Parker Pearson, M., and M. Ramilisonina. 1998. 'Stonehenge for the ancestors: The stones pass on the message'. *Antiquity* 72: 308–326.

Popov, H. 2009. 'Selishten Obekt Kush kaya. Harakteristiki na Obitavaneto prez Kasnata Bronzova I Rannata Zhelyazna Epoha/Occupation characteristics of the residential site Kush kaya during the late Bronze and the early Iron Age'. *Arheologiya* 1, 2: 21–39.

Popov, H. 2015. 'Settlements', in J. Valeva, E. Nankov, and D. Graninger (eds) *A Companion to Ancient Thrace*: 109–125. Malden: Wiley Blackwell.

Prendi, F. 1959. 'Tumat në fshatin Kakavi dhe Bodrishtë të rrethit të Gjirokastrës'. *Buletin i Universitetit shtetëror të Tiranës, Seria e shkencat shoqërore* 2: 190–211.

Primas, M. 1996. *Velika Gruda I: Hügelgräber des frühen 3: Jahrtausends v. Chr. im Adriagebiet—Velika Gruda, Mala Gruda und ihr Kontext*. Universitätsforschungen zur prähistorischen Archäologie 32. Bonn: Habelt.

Ristov, K. 2002–2004. 'Три нови некрополи од Гевгелиско/Three new cemeteries in Gevgelia region'. *Macedoniae Acta Archaeologica* 18: 153–174.

Ristov, K. 2004. *Утврдени пајонски населбиво долно повардарје*. Sofia: Bogdanci.

Sanev, V. 1975–1978. 'The tombs from Kunovo-Chuki near the village Orizari, Kochani. Tomb III'. *Zbornik. Recueil des Travaux (Skopje)*: 7–14.

Savvopoulou, T. 2004. 'Η περιοχή του Αξιού στην Πρώιμη Εποχή του Σιδήρου', in N. C. Stampolidis and A. Giannikouri (eds) *Το Αιγαίο στην Πρώιμη Εποχή του Σιδήρου: Πρακτικά του Διεθνούς Συμποσίου, Ρόδος, 1–4 Νοεμβρίου 2002*: 307–316. Athens: Panepistimio Kritis.

Shalganova, T., and A. Gotzev. 1995. 'Problems of research on the early Iron Age', in D. W. Bailey and I. Panayotov (eds) *Prehistoric Bulgaria*. Monographs in World Archaeology 22: 327–343. Madison, WI: Prehistory Press.

Simoska, D., and V. Sanev. 1976. *Praistorija vo centralna Pelagonija/Prehistory in Central Pelagonia*. Bitola: Naroden muzej.

Srejović, D. 1959–1960. 'Praistorijska Nekropola u Donjoj Brnjici/Nécropole préhistorique à Donja Brnjica'. *Glasnik Muzeja I Metohije/Bulletin du Musée de Kosovo et Metohie* 4–5: 83–129.

Srejović, D. 1973. 'Karagač and the problem of the ethnogenesis of the Dardanians'. *Balcanica* 4: 39–82.

Stefanovic, M., and H. A. Bankoff. 1998. 'Kamenska Čuka 1993–1995', in M. Stefanovich, H. Todorova, and H. Hauptmann (eds) *James Harvey Gaul In Memoriam: In the Steps of James Harvey Gaul, Vol. 1*: 254–338. Sofia: The James Harvey Gaul Foundation.

Stojić, M. 2000. 'The Brnjica cultural group in the south the Morava basin'. *Starinar* 50: 9–59.

Tartaron, T. F. 2004. *Bronze Age Landscape and Society in Southern Epirus, Greece*. British Archaeological Reports International Series 1290. Oxford: Archaeopress.

Tasić, N. 1997. 'Einige Fragen über die Chronologie und Genese der Brnjica-Kultur', in D. Srejović (ed.) *Antidoron: Dragoslavo Srejovic, Completis LXV annis ab amicis collegis discipulis oblatum*: 287–299. Belgrade: Centre for Archaeological Research.

Trbucović, V. 1970. *Donja Toponica: dardanska i slovenska nekropola/Dardanian and Slavic necropolis*. Belgrade/Prokuplje: Narodni muzej Toplice.

Triantafyllos, D. 1973. 'Μεγαλιθικά μνημεία (Dolmen) και βραχογραφίαι εις την δυτικήν Θράκην'. *Archaeologika Analekta ex Athenon* 6: 241–255.

Triantafyllos, D. 1983. 'Les monuments mégalithiques en Thrace occidentale', in A. Fol (ed.) *Pulpudeva: Semaines Philippopolitaines de l'histoire et de la Culture Thrace 4, Plovdiv, 3–17 Octobre 1980*: 145–163. Sofia: Académie Bulgare des Sciences.

Triantafyllos, D. 1990. 'Η Θράκη του Αιγαίου πριν από τον Ελληνικό Αποικισμό'. *Thrakike Epeterida* 7 (1987–1990): 297–322.

Vasić, R. 2013. 'Cremation burials in the Morava valley between 1300 and 750 BC', in M. Lochner and F. Ruppenstein (eds) *Brandbestattungen von der mittleren Donau bis zur Ägäis zwischen 1300 und 750 v. Chr. Akten des Internationalen Symposiums an der Österreichischen Akademie der Wissenschaften in Wien, 11.–12. Februar 2010*: 173–183. Vienna: Verlag der Österreichischen Akademie der Wissenschaften.

Vokotopoulou, J. 1994. 'Anciennes nécropoles de la Chalcidique', in J. de Genière (ed.) *Nécropoles et sociétés antiques (Grèce, Italie, Languedoc). Actes du Colloque International du Centre de Recherches Archéologique de l'Université de Lille III, Lille, 2–3 décembre 1991*. Cahiers du Centre Jean Bérard 18: 79–98. Naples: Centre Jean Bérard.

Wardle, K., and D. Wardle. 2007. 'Assiros Toumba. A brief history of the settlement', in H. Todorova, M. Stefanovich, and G. Ivanov (eds) *The Struma/Strymon River Valley in Prehistory. Proceedings of the International Symposium Strymon Praehistoricus, Kjustendil–Blagoevgrad (Bulgaria), Serres–Amphipolis (Greece), 27.09–01.10.2004: In The Steps of James Harvey Gaul, Vol. 2*: 451–479. Sofia: Gerda Henkel Stiftung.

Wilkes, J. 1992. *The Illyrians*. Oxford: Blackwell.

Zahrnt, M. 1984. 'Die Entwicklung des makedonischen Reiches bis zu den Perserkriegen'. *Chiron* 14: 325–368.

CHAPTER 14

THE CARPATHIAN AND DANUBIAN AREA

AUREL RUSTOIU

Introduction: Geography and Environment

This chapter covers the eastern Carpathian basin and the lower Danube region (Figure 14.1). These areas have quite different geographical characteristics, which have significantly influenced human settlement patterns from prehistory to modern times, as well as affecting the nature and orientation of communication and exchange with surrounding regions. In modern terms, the region encompasses Romania, along with eastern Hungary, south-eastern Slovakia, northern Serbia, northern Bulgaria, Moldova, and parts of western and south-western Ukraine.

The southern, eastern, and northern limits of the eastern Carpathian basin are delimited by the Carpathian mountains, with the Danube forming its western and part of its southern side. Within it are two major landscape units: to the west, the Great Hungarian Plain, which is crossed from north to south by the River Tisza; and to the east, the Transylvanian plateau, which connects with the Great Hungarian Plain by a series of rivers of which the Mureş and the Someş are the most important. Passes across the Carpathians facilitated communication eastward with the Pontic region, and southward with the northern Balkans. Some passes were major routes—for example, north-east into Ukraine—whereas others were of more local importance. The Danube connects the region with central Europe, while the Sava and Drava rivers link the Carpathian basin with northern Italy and the south-eastern Alpine region. The corridor formed by the Vardar and Morava rivers was an important axis of communication with Macedonia and northern Greece.

From a landscape viewpoint, the Great Hungarian Plain is a steppe (Sümegi 2011: 13–15, fig. 8). The vast marshes that once existed along the Tisza and to its west have all been

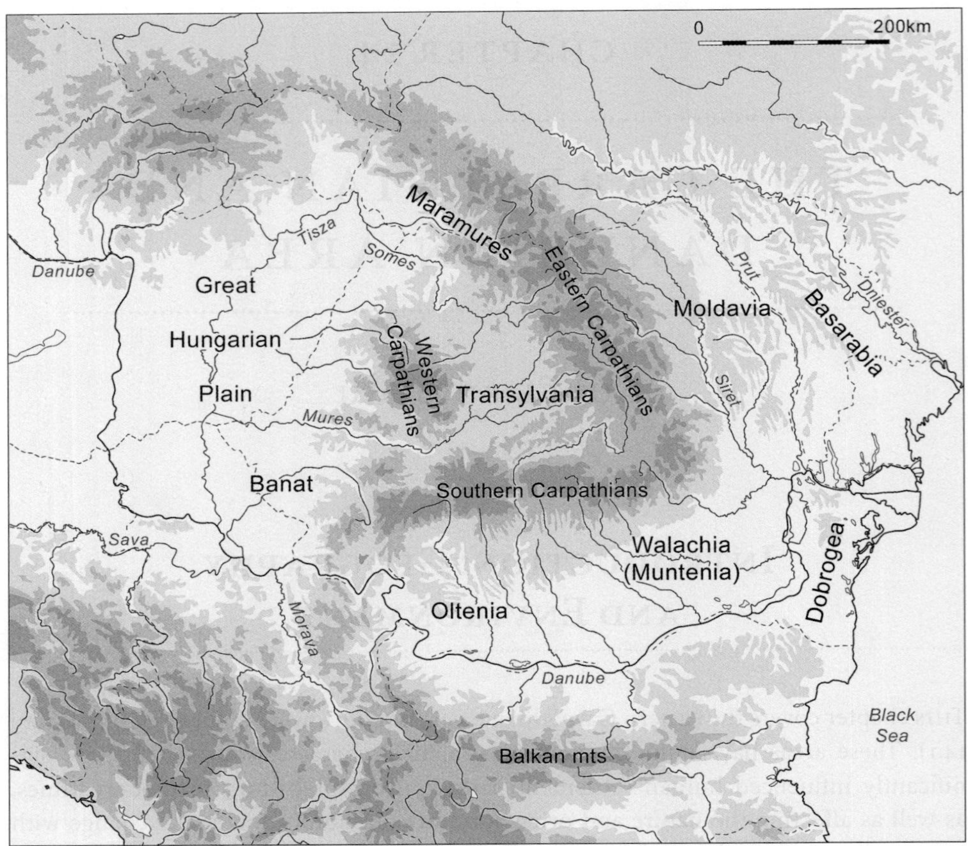

FIGURE 14.1 The geography of the Carpathian and Danubian area.

drained since the eighteenth century (see Hänsel and Medović 1991: 52, pl. 1). Prehistoric dwellings, as well as later ones, were located on the shores of these marshes, and sometimes, probably seasonally, on top of ridges across the wetlands. Transylvania has a higher plain characterized by steppe vegetation; the remaining territory is a plateau that was once mostly forested (Sümegi 2011: 13–15, fig. 8; Pop 2009: 23). The very name Transylvania recalls the vast forests that once separated this region from the Great Hungarian Plain. Massive deforestation accompanied the development of human settlement along the waterways. In broad terms, the Great Hungarian Plain represents the westernmost extreme of the Eurasian steppe, and the Transylvanian plateau marks the eastern limit of temperate Europe.

The Transylvanian plateau has important mineral resources, notably the many rock salt deposits close to the surface and around the plateau edges, and salt springs (Medeleţ 1995). Dendrochronological analyses demonstrate that some deposits were exploited in prehistory (Harding and Kavruk 2010; Harding and Szemán 2011; Ciugudean 2012: 117, fig. 13). The salt was used not only locally, but also by communities from the Great Hungarian Plain and the northern Balkans (Medeleţ 1995). Non-ferrous ores were also important. The western Carpathians contain rich deposits of complex ores (copper, silver, gold) often close to the surface, so allowing open-pit mining (Rustoiu 1996: 28–32; Iaroslavschi 1997: 11–19). At Roşia Montană in western Transylvania, gold was exploited in the pre-Roman period by open-pit mining, gallery mining only appearing after the Roman conquest (Cauuet et al. 2010). Similar complex ores were mined in the upper Tisza valley (Rusu 1972), while alluvial gold was extracted from river gravels in Transylvania.

The landscape, vegetation, and distribution of natural resources all influenced the nature of human settlement, the social structure of the local communities, and strategies for controlling and distributing these resources. Despite the differences in their geography and economy, the Great Hungarian Plain and the Transylvanian plateau were always interconnected and interdependent. In general, lowland communities were reliant on Transylvanian salt, wood, and ores, so access to them had to be permanently negotiated. These relationships can be identified in the archaeological record through material culture.

The lower Danube basin covers the lower course of the river from the Iron Gates gorge to the Black Sea; it is bordered to the north by the southern Carpathians and to the south by the Balkan mountains (the Stara Planina massif). This region widens out to include the historical regions of Moldavia and Basarabia, its eastern limits formed by the Black Sea coast and the River Dniester—an important route of communication towards central and northern Europe. From west to east, the relief descends gradually from the Carpathians through hilly areas, down to the Danube plain. Several rivers join the Danube, most of them providing north–south routes of communication. Away from the mountains, the region has a steppe or forest steppe climate and vegetation (Sümegi 2011: 13–15, fig. 8; Meshinev 2007). Mineral resources include rock salt from the southern and eastern foothills of the Carpathians, this time supplying the northern Balkans and the northern Pontic region as well as the local population (Medeleţ 1995; Ciobanu 2002; Alexianu et al. 2011). Copper and iron are found in northern Dobrogea, close to the Black Sea.

The geography and mineral resources of the lower Danube basin favoured an orientation of its communities towards the northern Pontic steppes, the northern Balkans and the Aegean/Anatolian area, although in some periods contacts were established with the eastern Carpathian basin. The latter region was sometimes significantly influenced by socio-cultural patterns from the south, as during the period of the Dacian kingdom at the very end of the Iron Age, which encompassed both regions. Prior to this point in time, the development of Iron Age communities in the eastern Carpathian basin and the lower Danube region, with their very different geographical characteristics, is best analysed in parallel.

The Beginning of Iron Use

The first iron objects from the inner Carpathian region of Romania are among the earliest from temperate Europe. This has prompted several specialists to search for evidence of the beginnings of iron use and the routes through which iron metallurgy reached the region. The earliest iron finds (Figure 14.2), dated to the thirteenth century BC (or slightly later for some researchers: Vasiliev 1983; Vasiliev et al. 1991: 126–128), come from northern Transylvania (Boroffka 1987). An iron knife in a deposit of bronze objects was discovered at Rozavlea, a socketed axe-head in a grave at Lăpuş and an unidentified object from a settlement at Viştea. Iron artefacts dating to the twelfth to eleventh centuries BC are known from the Banat area of western Romania: a sword and a long pin from unidentified sites, a bracelet from a grave at Bobda, and a dagger from Tirol (Boroffka 1987: 60).

The earliest finds from south-east Transylvania, including iron slag (from settlements at Peteni and Cernatu), metalworking tools, and half-finished objects (Cernatu) date to the tenth to eighth centuries BC. At this period both the number of iron objects (weapons and tools) and traces of metallurgical production (slag, blooms, and ingots) increased in quantity and are distributed more widely across Transylvania (Boroffka 1987). The presence of such finds in fortified settlements or in their environs (for example at Cernatu, Mediaş, Teleac, and Tilişca) is significant for the information it provides on the status of the people who controlled iron production, distribution, and consumption.

Different routes have been proposed for the spread of iron and related technologies to the Carpathian basin. The distribution of the earliest iron artefacts in Banat and northern Transylvania suggests an initial importation from the south, either from the north-west Balkans (László 1975) or from Greece, along the Vardar–Morava corridor (Pleiner 2000: 23). Another possibility is the 'Cimmerian' route from Armenia, the Caucasus, and the northern Pontic steppes (Berciu 1963). A third hypothesis suggests an earlier (twelfth century BC) spread of iron objects and technologies along the maritime route from Asia Minor and the Aegean to the western Black Sea: to Dobrogea, thence to Walachia and Transylvania (Boroffka 1987). However, these models merely suggest different phases and modalities through which iron artefacts and technologies came into the eastern Carpathian basin. Gradual diffusion is also supported by analysis of the distribution areas, contexts of discovery, and typology of the earliest iron artefacts.

The earliest iron objects occur in contexts attributable to very late phases of Bronze Age cultures with established connections with Mycenaean Greece. The grave from Lăpuş with its socketed axe-head belongs to a group deriving from the Suciu de Sus culture, and the settlement of Viştea to the Wietenberg culture (Boroffka 1987). The earliest object from central Europe, the iron handle of a dagger from Gánovce, Slovakia (Pleiner 2000: 24), which has been dated to the fifteenth century BC, was found in a context of the Otomani culture. The arrival of such artefacts in the Carpathian basin can be linked

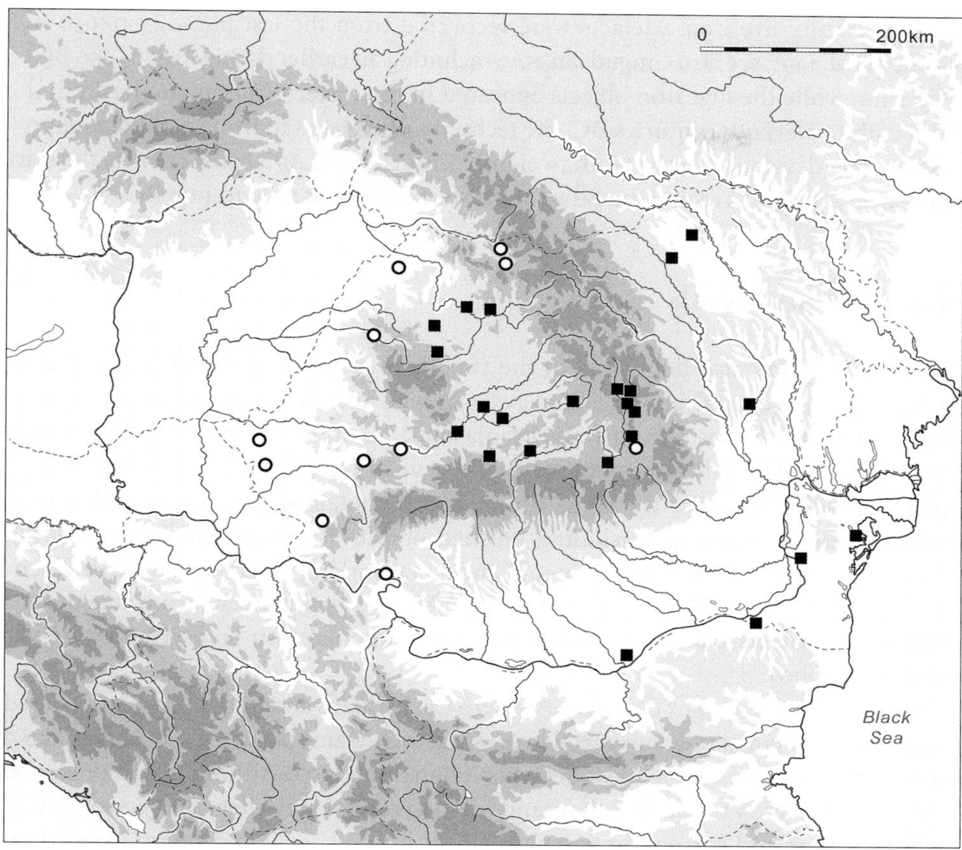

FIGURE 14.2 The earliest iron artefacts. Circles: first distribution phase (thirteenth to eleventh centuries BC); squares: second distribution phase (tenth to eighth centuries BC).

to long-distance exchange relationships with southern communities, through which prestige goods, including iron objects, might have been transmitted. Other similar items might have been brought in by mobile individuals such as craftworkers, marriage partners, warriors, or diplomats.

The second phase in the spread of iron dates to the tenth to eighth centuries BC (Figure 14.2). During this period, a series of regional power centres appeared in Transylvania, characterized archaeologically by large fortified settlements. These centres controlled various natural resources (copper, precious metals, iron, and salt) and their related 'industries', which also attracted specialized craftworkers and facilitated an accelerated transfer of technologies. The first clear traces of activity related to the extraction and manufacture of iron belong to this phase; the range of products diversified and their distribution expanded. Increasing access to iron is reflected by the finds from the fortified settlement at Teleac (Transylvania), a site that has been extensively investigated over several decades. Only four iron objects were found in the early phases of the settlement, whereas twenty-five iron artefacts were recovered from the last phase (750–650 BC; Vasiliev et al. 1991; see also Ciugudean 2012 including an earlier dating to 880–650 BC).

In sum, while the first iron objects appeared in the eastern Carpathian basin in the thirteenth to eleventh centuries BC, the technologies related to iron smelting and processing only developed in the tenth to eighth centuries BC. As a consequence, the start of the Iron Age in this region can be set at the start of the first millennium BC.

Non-ferrous Metals

Bronze metallurgy also flourished in the twelfth to eleventh centuries BC (equating to Hallstatt A in central Europe). Dozens of bronze hoards, consisting of over 23,000 objects in total, are known from Transylvania alone. A number of metalworkers' hoards from the vicinity of salt mines exemplify the scale of the phenomenon (Ocna Mureş, Şpălnaca, Ocna Sibiului). The Ocna Mureş hoard contained 5,812 items with a total weight of around 1,100 kg, including finished objects (socketed axe-heads, sickles), recycled pieces, bronze blooms, tin ingots, and metalworking tools (Rusu 1963; Petrescu-Dîmboviţa 1977, 1978). Workshops in the Great Hungarian Plain, an area where dozens of bronze hoards have been discovered, were also supplied with Transylvanian copper (Mozsolics 2000).

The presence of complex ores in the western Carpathians and Maramureş contributed to the development of precious metal processing at the same period. Gold was obtained both from open-pits and alluvial deposits. Flourishing goldworking is demonstrated by dozens of hoards containing thousands of items of gold jewellery and vessels found in Transylvania and surrounding regions (Rusu 1972). The Hinova hoard (Mehedinţi county), discovered in a cemetery dated to Hallstatt A, contains jewellery weighing 4.92 kg. Metallographic analysis confirms that the gold used for making the jewellery came from the western Carpathians (Davidescu 1981).

During the following centuries, the importance of bronze working gradually diminished. Bronze hoards of the eighth to seventh centuries BC generally contain only clothing accessories (e.g. Coldău and Vinţu de Jos, Transylvania), and sometimes harness fittings or vessels (Petrescu-Dîmboviţa 1977, 1978).

The Earlier Iron Age (*c*.1100–650 BC)

The Eastern Carpathian Basin

Archaeologically the most representative culture of the early phase of the early Iron Age in the eastern Carpathian basin is the Gáva culture (Figure 14.3), named after a cremation cemetery in north-east Hungary and first defined by Amalia Mozsolics (1957), later renamed Gáva-Holihrady (Smirnova 1974) following the recognition of similar artefacts in Ukraine. In contrast to the late Bronze Age groups from which it emerged, the Gáva culture is characterized by its widespread distribution and apparent uniformity of material culture, notably fluted ceramics with a black burnished exterior and red interior surface, although there are some regional differences in settlement structure and mortuary practices.

The development of the Gáva culture is still debated, but it seems to have first appeared in the upper Tisza basin at a date equivalent to Hallstatt A in central Europe. Its settlements and cemeteries yield pottery of types that have also been identified in north-east Hungary, north-west Romania (as the Lăpuş II-Gáva I group), and Transcarpathian Ukraine (Kemenczei 1984: 58–86). Recently an early extension of the Gáva culture into central Transylvania has been proposed (Ciugudean 2012). In the next phase, around 1000 BC, the distinctive fluted pottery became more widespread across the Great

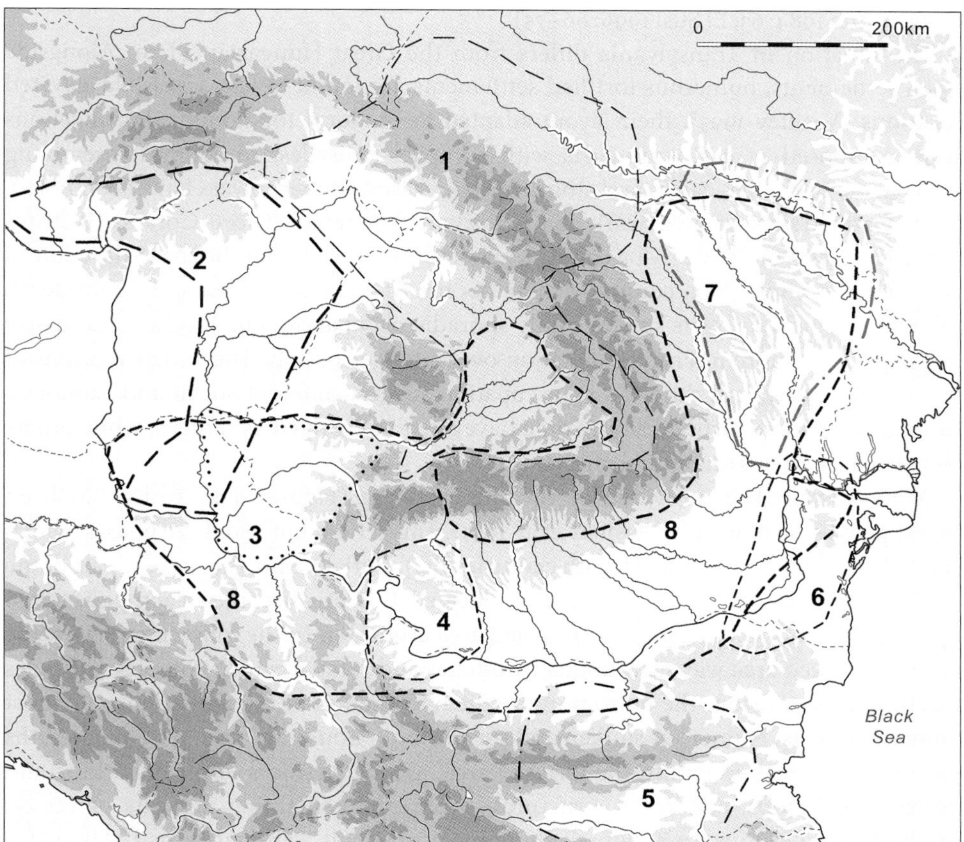

FIGURE 14.3 Archaeological cultures of the early Iron Age. 1 Gáva culture, 2 Mezőcsát group, 3 Gornea-Kalakača group, 4 Insula Banului group, 5 Pšeničevo culture, 6 Babadag culture, 7 Corlăteni-Chişinău culture, Cozia group, and Saharna-Solonceni group, 8 Basarabi culture.

Hungarian Plain, in Banat and northern Serbia, in south-east Slovakia, Transylvania, and in the Carpathians (Gumă 1993: 181–194; Vasiliev et al. 1991; László 1994). The third phase of the Gáva culture is characterized by various local manifestations: in Transylvania it continued up to Hallstatt C, whereas in Banat and the Great Hungarian Plain it ceased with the appearance of the Mezőcsát and Gornea-Kalakača cultures respectively (cf. Kemenczei 1984; Gumă 1993; Vasiliev et al. 1991).

Rural settlements located along waterways or on natural hills and ridges have been identified in the lower-lying western part of the Gáva culture area, although few have been systematically investigated. At some settlements occupation was clearly short-lived, whereas others had more than one phase (e.g. Poroszló and Nagykálló, in Hungary). Settlement features consist of sunken huts and surface-built dwellings with simple hearths or ovens, and storage and rubbish pits. Pits containing deposits of pottery are common and are considered ritual features (Patay 1976; Kemenczei 1984; Gumă 1993: 186–197; Szabó 1996, 2004). Animal remains from the settlements point to a pastoralist economy based mainly on cattle-rearing and to a lesser extent on ovicaprines (Kemenczei 1984: 63; El Susi 1996: 66–75).

The situation in Transylvania differs from the Great Hungarian Plain. Alongside open settlements, numerous fortified settlements are found in less accessible elevated locations (Vasiliev 1995), their layout adapted to the local topography. Fortifications were composed of earth ramparts with complex palisades, sometimes resembling walls made of timber, earth, and stone. In some cases, timber towers have been noted. Some fortified sites reached nearly 30 ha in extent, for example Ciceu-Corabia (Bistrița-Năsăud county) or Teleac (Alba county), but others are far smaller: Bozna (Sălaj county) is 4.2 ha and Şona (Alba county) a mere 0.4 ha. At some settlements, the thin depth of archaeological deposits suggests only sporadic occupation, but at others successive layers point to more intensive habitation over a longer period. The wide variations of the size, intensity, and duration of occupation suggest different social and economic functions for these fortified sites. Some have been interpreted as refuges, while others were tribal centres with multiple functions.

A good example is provided by the site at Teleac (Figure 14.4), which has been investigated systematically (Vasiliev et al. 1991). This settlement had three phases, which span Hallstatt B–C (tenth to seventh centuries BC). Initially only the highest part of the hill was fortified, where the settlement was located; this later became an acropolis for an open settlement occupying the unfortified area around it. In the following phases, the entire inhabited area was surrounded by ditches and ramparts with complex palisades reaching 12–13 m from the bottom of the ditch to the top of the palisade in the most vulnerable areas. Numerous sunken and surface-built houses, storage pits, and hearths have been discovered within the fortified area, as well as traces of metalworking and pottery workshops, and ritual structures—from pits containing deposits of vessels or children's skeletons, to a 'house' where magical rituals were performed. All of this suggests that Teleac was a major social, economic, military, and religious centre.

In sum, there are important differences in settlement pattern between Transylvania and the Great Hungarian Plain. The Transylvanian fortified settlements were evidently

FIGURE 14.4 The fortified settlement at Teleac.

Photo: Z. Czajlik

centres of power around which rural communities gravitated. Variations in size, intensity of habitation, and range of functions suggest a hierarchy of local communities and territorial centres. The fortified centres controlled the exploitation and distribution of natural resources (metal ores and salt), as well as local agricultural production and manufacturing. The rural communities of the Great Hungarian Plain had close connections with the Transylvanian centres, as they relied on salt supplies and mineral resources from that region. Indeed, in the tenth century BC, the northern part of the Great Hungarian Plain experienced a resurgence of bronze metallurgy based on Transylvanian copper.

Important differences also exist in the mortuary practices of the two regions. In the Great Hungarian Plain, flat cremation cemeteries with the remains placed in urns continued Bronze Age traditions (Kemenczei 1984: 63–64). At the same time, burial mounds were used in north-western Romania, as at Lăpuş (Kacsó 2011). On the other hand, in Transylvania the appearance of large fortified settlements coincided with the disappearance of traditional cemeteries of Bronze Age type. Here the deceased were treated in a manner that left no archaeological traces (for example, by scattering cremated ashes in special places such as forest groves or rivers, or the deceased might have been exposed/dismembered and left to decay naturally),[1] although some of the pits with vessel deposits found on settlements might be related to collective funerary ceremonies or rites of passage performed by mourners during funerals (Egri 2012: 509). In sum, despite the apparent uniformity of material culture in the earliest Iron Age, the differences in settlement and mortuary practices imply different models of social organization and practice in the Great Hungarian Plain and in Transylvania.

These communities experienced new cultural transformations during the middle phase of the early Iron Age. In the Great Hungarian Plain, the so-called Mezőcsát group appeared between the ninth and the start of the seventh century BC (Figure 14.3), identified through a new funerary rite. The dead were now inhumed, the skeletons usually being oriented west to east; only one or two vessels were included in the graves (a large biconical pot and a beaker or bowl), as well as a meat offering (cattle or sheep). Cemeteries were small, rarely with more than ten graves, and were located on natural heights such as sand dunes, or on abandoned tells. They are mainly found in the northern part of the Great Hungarian Plain, with some further south along the Tisza and west in south-west Slovakia (Metzner-Nebelsick 1998, 2000, 2010).

At the same time as these cemeteries appeared, some bronze hoards began to include artefacts with parallels in the northern Pontic area, mainly harness fittings. This 'Cimmerian' or 'Thracian-Cimmerian' horizon (the latter to include material of local origin associated with finds of eastern origin) was long explained by a presumed migration of groups from the northern Pontic steppes and the northern Caucasus, which brought an end to the Gáva communities (Kemenczei 1984; Romsauer 1999). Recently, however, it has been noted that Mezőcsát mortuary practices, as well as the structure of their funerary assemblages, differ from graves of the northern Caucasus and the northern Pontic region, and in fact display local features.

The transformation of beliefs and funerary practices of the Mezőcsát communities of the Great Hungarian Plain was perhaps related to changes in their lifestyle and economy, based on pastoral nomadism and transhumance, and linked to climate change and anthropogenic modifications of the environment following the massive deforestations of the late second millennium BC. Their mobile lifestyle contributed to the development of new social networks with neighbouring populations, including those to the north of the Black Sea. These contacts may explain the presence of eastern and central European artefacts (mostly horse gear and weaponry, both symbols of status). A massive immigration of peoples from the northern Pontic region can be excluded. The phenomenon was a consequence of the transformation of the local economic and social structures, while the symbols of status through which the elites chose to express the new ideology combined local and 'Cimmerian' elements (Metzner-Nebelsick 1998, 2000, 2010).

A similar phenomenon occurred in Banat, and later in Transylvania and the lower Danube basin. In Banat, settlements of the Gáva horizon were replaced at the turn of the ninth century BC by sites of the Gornea-Kalakača group (Figure 14.3),[2] characterized by distinctive ceramics decorated with grooves and incisions. The group is found over a well-delimited area including northern Serbia (mainly the Morava and Danube valleys), the region between the lower Sava and Drava, Vojvodina, and Banat. Settlements had a rural character, and were located on the middle and upper terraces of major waterways. Dwellings usually consisted of sunken houses accompanied by storage and rubbish pits; thin archaeological deposits (less than 20 cm), indicate a short-lived occupation. Settlements were often established on previously uninhabited sites, perhaps due to the climate changes of the early first millennium BC, although the transformation of economic structures must have also played a role. To date, not a single cemetery has been identified (Gumă 1993). Ceramics of Gornea-Kalakača type have also been discovered in Transylvania, both in rural (Tărtăria) and fortified (the second phase at Teleac) settlements of the Gáva horizon, which suggests a series of contacts along the Mureş valley (Vasiliev et al. 1991).

The Gornea-Kalakača group disappeared around the mid-eighth century BC, to be followed by the Basarabi culture, which was widespread between 800–650 BC in the lower Danube basin (Figure 14.3). This culture is characterized by pottery combining fluted, impressed, and incised decoration consisting of complex motifs, like triangles and rhombi with hatching, spirals, meanders, and aquatic birds, expressing a particular ideology. Its origins are thought to be in Banat, Oltenia, and the neighbouring Danubian regions, broadly the same area as the Gornea-Kalakača group. In Banat, a number of Basarabi settlements overlay predecessors belonging to the Gornea-Kalakača group (Vulpe 1986; Gumă 1993; Garašanin and Roman 1996). This culture expanded east along the Danube, down to southern Moldavia, and along the Mureş valley, occupying the southern half of Transylvania (Ursuţiu 2002). Similar finds occur further north, up to the southern part of the Great Hungarian Plain. Some vessels decorated in the Basarabi style are documented further west, and even reached the south-east Alpine region (Metzner-Nebelsick 1992; Eibner 1996).

Despite the widespread distribution and apparent uniformity of Basarabi ceramic forms and decoration, aspects of the settlements and mortuary practices differ from one region to another. For example, rural settlements from Banat were located on the terraces of major waterways and are characterized by thin archaeological layers (Gumă 1993: 217–219). In Transylvania, Basarabi ceramics have been identified on fortified settlements, for example in structures of the third phase at Teleac (Vasiliev et al. 1991; Ursuţiu 2002).

Burial mounds containing inhumation graves and others with cremation graves are known along the Danube and in Banat. Some metal objects in the inhumation graves (weapons, jewellery) suggest close connections with the north-western Balkans (Gumă 1993). In Transylvania, graves are absent altogether; this may indicate a continuity of population, the groups who used pottery of Basarabi type continuing to practice the old, archaeologically 'invisible' mortuary rites. Continuity in ritual practices is also apparent in the presence of pits with vessel deposits. A pit containing four large flagons and four drinking vessels (three beakers and an *askos*) decorated with a typical Basarabi motif, including the image of birds, has been discovered at Iernut (Vulpe 1986: 58; Ursuţiu 2002: 90, pls 155–157); although the composition of objects differs, the mode of deposition is similar to the pit offerings of the Gáva horizon.

In sum, Basarabi pottery is found across a wide geographical area from the lower Danube and Transylvania to the south-eastern Alpine region, but was used by communities with different origins, traditions, and ways of expressing identity. It can be linked to a mobile lifestyle, based on nomadic pastoralism and transhumance, similar to that of the Mezőcsát group, which may also help explain the establishment of cultural contacts between distant territories and of some new networks of social interaction at community level.

The Lower Danube Basin

The start of the early Iron Age is less clearly defined in the lower Danube basin, with one archaeological 'horizon' at the end of the second millennium BC characterized by fluted pottery and another by incised and impressed pottery at the start of the first millennium BC. The spread of fluted ceramics was long considered a result of 'influences' or 'impulses' from Banat or Transylvania, but is more likely to be a product of a period of frequent direct contacts between the Danube basin and the peoples of the inner Carpathian region. These contacts are demonstrated, for example, by the presence of bronze objects of Transylvanian origin south of the Carpathians (Petrescu-Dîmbovița 1977: 79, 120), or of jewellery made from Transylvanian gold, like items from the aforementioned Hinova hoard (Davidescu 1981).

Archaeological evidence suggests a smooth transition from the end of the Bronze Age to the start of the early Iron Age, without any major transformations of the local communities that might have been caused by significant population movements. Changes can only be noted in some aspects of material culture, for example the decorative styles of ceramics and the increased use of iron objects. The settlements have a rural character and the deposits suggest short-lived occupation (Lazăr 2007). The cemeteries are flat and consist of urned cremation burials. Some tumulus cremation burials have been identified in Muntenia, for example at Meri, in Teleorman county (Moscalu 1976).

Archaeological investigations at Ghidici provide a coherent picture of habitation and funerary customs in Oltenia at the end of the second and start of the first millennium BC (Nica 1995; Lazăr 2007). Several dwellings have been excavated, each containing ceramic vessels of the Žuto Brdo-Gârla Mare culture of the late Bronze Age. The surface buildings are oval or rectangular and cover between 30 and 50 m^2. Some simple hearths or ovens have been identified in the central part of these houses. The subsequent settlement phase consists of dwellings dated by pottery to the beginning of the Iron Age. The shape, building technique, and internal layout of the structures are similar to the previous period, which suggests a continuity of lifestyle. The dwellings were grouped in two areas separated by several tens of metres, suggesting that the community comprised two separate families or clans.

Two cremation cemeteries have been identified nearby (Nica 1995), one of late Bronze Age date, the other used by the early Iron Age inhabitants. The grave goods included a large number of vessels, placed in the grave pit according to consistent rules. Ceramic sets consisted of functionally similar vessels: large or medium-sized biconical jars, bowls, and two-handled drinking vessels. The only differences concern vessel morphology and decoration, which are characteristic of their respective periods. Thus, the settlement and cemeteries at Ghidici illustrate a gradual transition from the end of the Bronze Age to the start of the Iron Age. Over a number of generations, the community preserved a particular lifestyle and funerary practices, whereas elements of their material culture underwent changes reflecting the spread of new vessel forms and decorative techniques (perhaps with different symbolic significance) at the beginning of the Iron Age.

The fluted pottery 'horizon' is also present east of the Carpathians, in the Suceava depression in north-west Moldavia (László 1994: 48–104). Some rural settlements have been identified, usually on higher ground or the upper river terraces. Most dwellings were surface-built, although some sunken huts were used. A settlement with three precincts, fortified with earth ramparts, palisades, and ditches, has been investigated at Preuteşti. Only the tiny inner precinct (0.12 ha) was inhabited; the occupation was of low intensity and lasted only a short time. In the mortuary sphere, cremation with the remains placed in urns was favoured, using both flat graves and tumulus burials (László 1994: 57–62). Certain details of the flat grave cemetery at Cucorăni recall the Gáva culture. At Volovăţ, five groups of mounds were built at a distance of 0.5 to 1.5 km from one another, along a ridge of hills some 400 m in height. An unusual feature of Volovăţ is the way that the funerary mounds were built first and the grave pits were dug out later, each tumulus perhaps being used by a different family. The urns were placed upside down, with the base cut off, and the human remains and other pyre debris deposited inside them.

The similarities in mortuary rites and pottery might suggest that Gáva communities had migrated to the Suceava depression from the upper Tisza region or northern Transylvania, preserving some of their customs. Similar movements across the Carpathians have been noted at other periods, due to the economic importance of the rock salt and salt springs of the Suceava depression. The remainder of the hills and forest steppe between the eastern Carpathians and the Dniester basin was occupied by another group characterized by fluted pottery, the Corlăteni-Chişinău culture (László 1994: 105–141; Leviţki 1994). Its origin is poorly defined, but some ceramic forms have closer analogies in Banat and Oltenia than in Transylvania. These communities had contacts with pastoral populations from the northern Pontic steppes. Their settlements were located on river terraces and meadows, and consisted exclusively of surface-built dwellings. The pastoral economy was based on cattle rearing. The cremation cemeteries were flat, with the remains placed in lidded urns. Some of the graves contained more than one urn, each vessel containing one individual, and sometimes the urns were accompanied by bowls or drinking vessels.

Early in the first millennium BC, part of the territory of the Corlăteni-Chişinău culture in central and southern Moldavia was taken over by the Cozia group (László 1980: 185–186, 1989), one of several regional entities in the lower Danube basin characterized by the use of incised and impressed pottery (Hänsel 1976). Also part of this complex were the Insula Banului group in the Iron Gates region (Morintz and Roman 1969); the Babadag culture in Dobrogea, eastern Muntenia, southern Moldavia and north-east Bulgaria (Morintz 1987; Jugănaru 2005); the Saharna-Solonceni group in southern Basarabia and the north-west Pontic region (Kašuba 2000, 2003); and, south of the Balkan mountains expanding into northern Bulgaria, the Pšeničevo culture (Čičikova 1972: 97–98, fig. 20;

Gotzev 1994). These various entities shared a style of pottery decorated with incised and impressed motifs—usually combining lines, zigzags, and triangles with dots and circles, and in certain cases with stylized aquatic birds—sometimes associated with grooves and plastic details, one of the most typical forms being the so-called 'knobbed ware' (German *Buckelkeramik*; Todorova 1972). This decorative repertoire was used by various peoples with different settlement types and funerary traditions, hence the distinguishing of several regional entities. The style spread north and north-west from the south-eastern Balkan peninsula and north-western Anatolia, apparently appearing at broadly the same time throughout the lower Danube basin. The presence of vessels of this style in deposits of phase VIIb 2–3 at Troy suggests a date at the end of the second or start of the first millennium BC (de Boer 2007: 123–126; László 2012).

Two factors affected the ways in which this pottery circulated. During the Sub-Mycenaean and Protogeometric periods in Greece (Chapter 12), maritime contacts developed between Aegean and Anatolian centres, and the southern and western Black Sea coasts, prefiguring later Greek colonization (de Boer 2007). Significantly, one route along which iron metallurgy spread followed the Black Sea coast up to the Danube delta in Dobrogea, where iron ores were first exploited in the tenth century BC (Boroffka 1987). Fortified settlements of the Babadag culture appear there at the same time (the eponymous site is well-known archaeologically: Jugănaru 2005: 21–22). These power centres had complex functions and were involved in social and economic networks with distant contacts.

Relations established as early as the end of the Bronze Age between the peoples of the lower Danube and the Aegean/Anatolia were another important factor in the spread of incised and impressed pottery. These contacts mainly involved the elites and were sometimes expressed through gift exchange, which included prestige goods, for example the gold vessels and other objects discovered in the Vulchitran hoard near Pleven in northern Bulgaria. Its inventory illustrates connections with Asia Minor and the region north of the Danube. The gold vessels from the Rădeni hoard in eastern Romania (Vulpe and Mihăilescu-Bîrliba 1980–1982) are morphologically and technologically very similar to those from Vulchitran, dated to the early first millennium BC (Gergova 1994).

All the groups using incised and impressed pottery disappeared during the seventh century BC. In the Danube valley and southern Moldavia, they were succeeded from the mid-eighth century BC onward by the 'expansion' of the Basarabi culture. Analysis of the pottery from several recently excavated settlements of the Babadag culture shows that incised and impressed decoration gradually diminished during the seventh century BC, until it finally disappeared altogether (Ailincăi 2011); at the same time, new ceramic forms which distinguish the end of the early Iron Age appeared.

In conclusion, at the start of the early Iron Age the lower Danube basin was a contact area between central-eastern Europe, the Balkans, and the Aegean/Anatolian region. This is most clearly seen in the distribution and popularity of certain decorative elements on pottery. On the other hand, the local communities perpetuated many Bronze Age socio-cultural traditions. These features gradually evolved at the end of the early Iron Age, reflecting new cultural and historical circumstances.

The Seventh to Third Centuries BC in the Carpathian Basin

The Scythian Horizon (*c.*650–350 BC)

The final phase of the early Iron Age in the eastern Carpathian basin was marked by a cultural reorientation towards the northern Pontic region (see Chapter 15). This situation may have been brought about by the migration of some groups from the steppes, who came through the passes of the northern Carpathians in successive stages, bringing new models of culture and identity. Based on these new features, the period is often called the Scythian Age, although the archaeological record, especially mortuary practices, points to a mixture of locals and newcomers (Párducz 1973; Chochorowski 1985; Kemenczei 2009).

Flat cemeteries, where the deceased were either interred in a crouched or extended position or cremated with the remains placed in pits or urns, appeared in the northern and central parts of the Great Hungarian Plain, down to the confluence of the Mureş and the Tisza, as well as in south-west Slovakia. Sometimes horses with complete harnesses and wagons were placed in graves together with the deceased, and weaponry typical of the nomadic warriors of the northern Pontic region (arrows, daggers or short swords of *akinakes* type, swords, armour). Female graves contain hair loops, bracelets, hairpins, sometimes gold foil appliqués sewn onto clothes, rows of glass beads and kauri shells, and mirrors. A few of them also include weapons, mainly spears. Burial mounds or graves with funerary chambers made of timber and including objects decorated in the Animal style, typical of the northern Pontic elites, are less numerous. The entire archaeological phenomenon is known as the Vekerzug culture or Alföld group (Figure 14.5; Párducz 1973; Chochorowski 1985; Kemenczei 2009).

In the upper Tisza region, cremation graves predominate, with the remains placed in simple pits or in urns. From the mid-fifth century BC and in the following century, flat cremation cemeteries with the remains placed in urns were used almost exclusively; artefacts of eastern origin were very rare. At the periphery of the Vekerzug culture area, this phenomenon is known as the Sanislău-Nir group (Németi 1982).

Contemporary settlements have a rural character and are limited in size. Dwellings are mainly sunken huts of rectangular or oval shape (Scholtz 2010). Importantly, about 25% of the ceramics from these settlements are wheel-thrown; this new technique was usually used to produce local forms that were previously handmade. The potter's wheel was probably introduced by craftworkers trained in the hinterland of the Greek colonies in the northern Pontic region, who worked for the steppe elites and followed the groups migrating to the west (Romsauer 1991). Connections with these colonies are also attested by Greek bronze vessels in some graves, for example the water-carrying *hydriai* from Artand and Dobroselie (formerly Bene), made in Peloponnesian workshops (Popovich

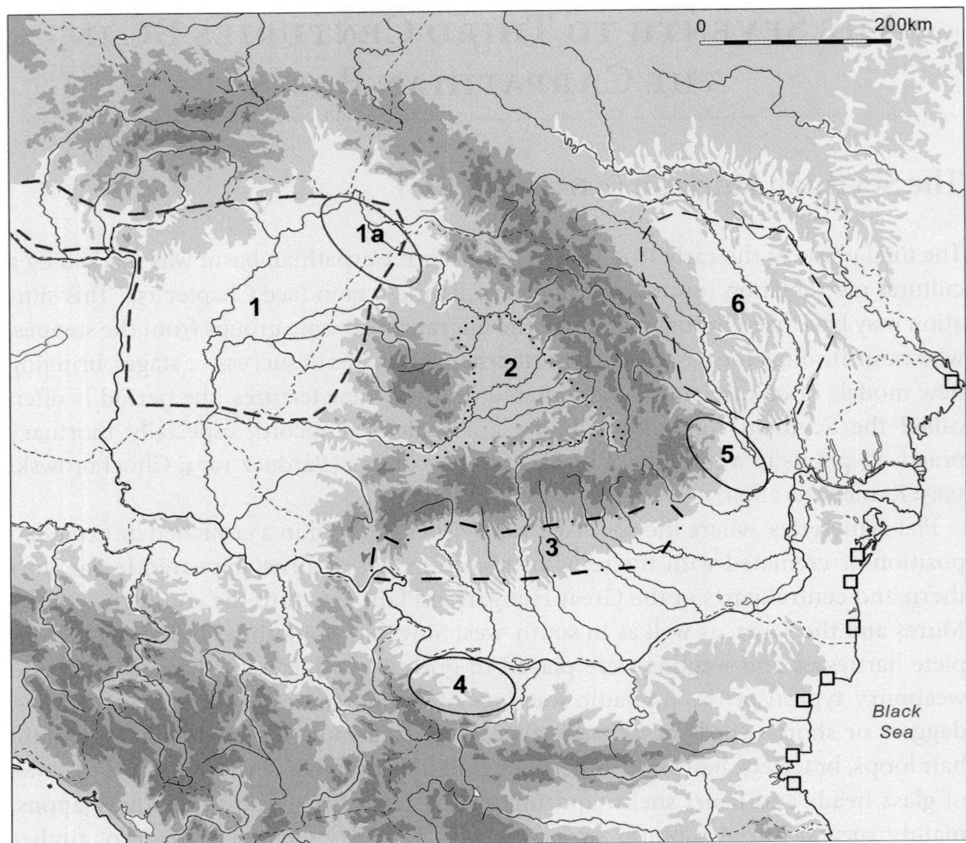

FIGURE 14.5 Archaeological cultures of the seventh to third centuries BC. 1 Vekerzug culture, 1a Sanislău-Nir group, 2 'Scythian' group in Transylvania, 3 Ferigile group, 4 Vraca group, 5 Bârseşti group, 6 Huşi-Suruceni group. Squares: Greek colonies on the western Pontic coast.

1995–1996: 86–87; Teleagă 2008: 254–257). These finds reached the Great Hungarian Plain through the northern Pontic region and not directly from Greece.

Some flat inhumation cemeteries have been discovered in Transylvania, many graves containing weaponry typical of the northern Pontic region. The earliest graves date to the beginning of the sixth century BC (Vasiliev 1980). Towards the mid-fifth century BC the rite gradually changed, and cremation with the remains placed in rectangular pits became preponderant, as at Băiţa and Uioara de Sus (Vasiliev 1976, 1999). Timber structures belonging to a kind of funerary chamber were occasionally identified in these rectangular pits. Certain prolonged funerary practices requiring the removal and cremation of inhumed corpses, followed by the reburying of remains in the same pits, were also noted (Babeş and Miriţoiu 2012). It was long presumed that Scythian migration from the northern Black Sea region brought an end to fortified settlements such as Teleac (Vasiliev et al. 1991), but it now seems more likely that their abandonment reflects the gradual disintegration of the social and cultural structures that had previously maintained control over local resources, a transformation that also facilitated the immigration of pastoral groups from north of the Black Sea.

From a cultural viewpoint, the 'Scythian Age' covers a diversity of aspects, but particularly the amalgamation of local communities with warrior groups from the northern Pontic region, starting in the later seventh century BC. The development of these mixed groups with their predominantly eastern and/or north Balkan connections was interrupted after the mid-fourth century BC by the arrival of Celtic communities from the west.

The Celtic Horizon (*c.*350–200 BC)

During the later Iron Age, the Great Hungarian Plain and Transylvania underwent a complex process of colonization by Celtic groups, mainly from Transdanubia, but also from other parts of central Europe (Rustoiu 2008, 2014). The relatively small number of early graves from different cemeteries suggests that the colonizing groups were not large, while the diversity of new communal identities implies that they probably came from different places (Figure 14.6). Continued use of cemeteries in Transdanubia and south-western Slovakia implies selective rather than mass migration to the east.

Warrior elites—one of the most mobile segments of society—played an important part in the colonization and migration process (see Chapter 37). This mobility contributed to the widespread dissemination of La Tène style material culture associated with their lifestyle and ideology, such as scabbards decorated with facing dragon pairs, or swords of Hatvan-Boldog type (Figure 14.7; Stöllner 1998: 162–170, maps 2–3). Social contacts between neighbouring and more distant communities probably also had a significant role in the creation of colonizing groups (Ramsl 2003: 104) and would have been a factor in the selection of individuals destined to leave their original community for a new one. The colonization of new territories also required the establishment of new social networks involving the existing communities.

The first groups moved east from Transdanubia into the northern Great Hungarian Plain and the upper Tisza region. From there, they went along the Carpathians to Transylvania. This advance is documented by a series of cemeteries located along the route. Some cemeteries began at the La Tène B1/B2 transition, but others were only established in La Tène B2, suggesting a slow advance, in successive phases, during the later fourth and early third century BC (Rustoiu 2008: 69, fig. 27).

The arrival of the Celts initiated a cultural reconfiguration of the regions east of the middle Danube. The newly formed communities, based on the amalgamation of different population groups, frequently chose different ways of expressing communal identity, incorporating both local and foreign elements. There was clearly a variety of interactions between the local populations and the incomers, which should be detectable through close analysis of funerary practices. In some cases, the local populations preserved their traditional practices, at least during the initial period

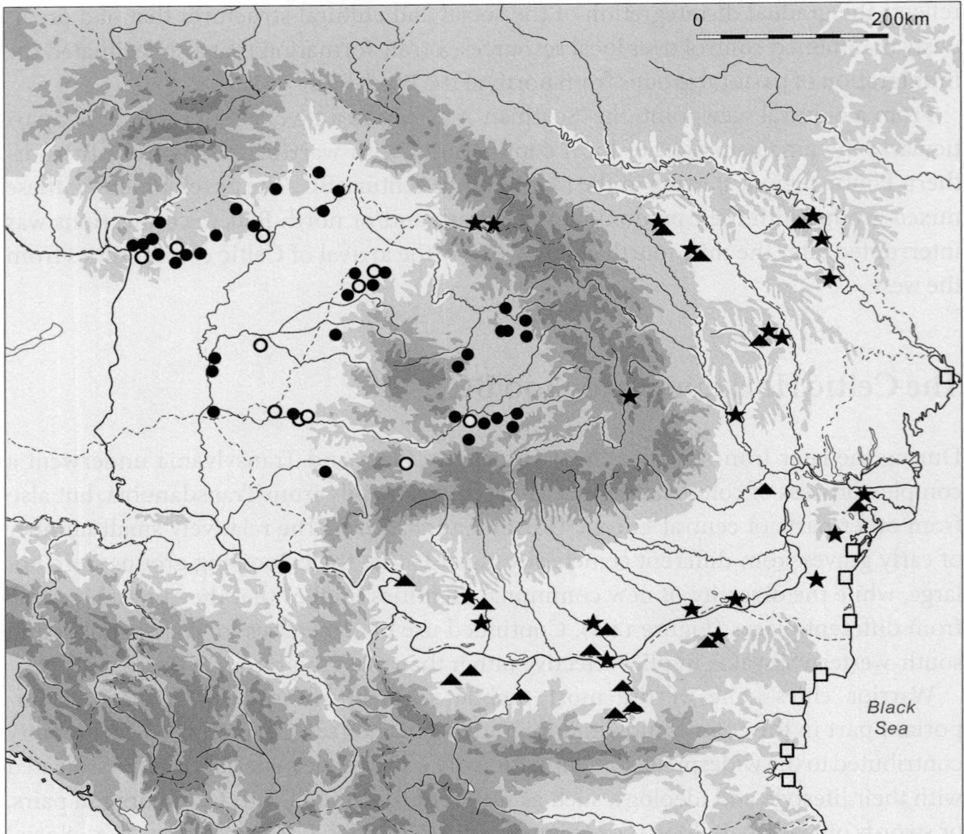

FIGURE 14.6 The Celtic horizon in the Carpathian basin (fourth to third centuries BC) and the aristocratic horizon in the northern Balkans (fifth to third centuries BC). Circles: cemeteries beginning in La Tène B1/B2; dots: cemeteries beginning in La Tène B2; stars: fortified settlements; triangles: aristocratic tumulus graves with funerary chamber and hoards of gold and silver objects; squares: Greek colonies on the Black Sea coast.

of cohabitation, for example in the cemeteries at Muhi in Hungary (Hellebrandt 1999) or Pişcolt in Romania (Németi 1988, 1989). We may infer that they deliberately maintained a specific manner of expressing their identity, while at the same time the absence of weaponry in indigenous graves suggests that they were not integrated into the warrior elite of the newcomers. In other cases, for example in Transylvania, the adoption of new funerary practices may indicate that the existing populations were quite rapidly integrated into new communal structures, although they continued to influence material culture and use local ceramics for a few generations (Rustoiu 2008: 76–78, 2014). Recent analyses of strontium isotopes focusing on different areas in central Europe seem to confirm this mixing of newcomers and local groups (Scheeres et al. 2014).

FIGURE 14.7 1 Panoply of weapons from a grave at Remetea Mare in Banat; 2 Helmet from Ciumeşti, in north-west Romania; 3 Helmet with vegetal-style ornament on the neck-guard, found in Transylvania.

Photos: 1 A. Rustoiu, 2 I. V. Ferencz, 3 M. Egri

The integration of local populations into the new communities can also be seen in settlement organization. Throughout the Celtic horizon, rural settlements were small, mostly containing only a few sunken huts. These were sometimes grouped in such a way as to suggest a social organization based on families or clans, as at the excavated sites at Moreşti in Transylvania (Berecki 2008), Ciumeşti in north-western Romania (Zirra 1980), and Polgár in north-east Hungary (Szabó et al. 2008). The presence of both local and central European pottery forms points to the adoption of mixed culinary practices.

Alongside these rural settlements, a number of large manufacturing centres appeared across the Carpathian basin, usually functioning as central places. One such settlement is Sajópetri-Hosszú-dűlő, in the northern part of the Great Hungarian Plain (Szabó 2007), which dates to the third century BC (La Tène B2–C1). This site was organized into three sectors, each corresponding to a specific craft activity: iron smelting, blacksmithing, and pottery making. This concentration of craft production in large manufacturing centres serving a rural hinterland anticipates the structural transformation that took place a few generations later, which was to lead to industrial-scale production in large fortified settlements or *oppida* (Rustoiu 2009).

Celtic groups did not penetrate the entire region. The Maramureş depression on the upper Tisza and the intra-montane depressions of eastern Transylvania continued to be inhabited by indigenous populations. In Maramureş, archaeological investigations in the last decade have identified some fortified settlements dated to the fourth to third centuries BC, for example Bila Cerkva and Solotvino, both on the right bank of the Tisza. These were fortified with earth ramparts, ditches, and complex palisades made of timber and compacted soil. Settlement elements consist of surface dwellings and storage pits. The ceramic assemblage includes handmade vessels continuing the traditional forms of the early Iron Age. More generally, the fortifications and settlement structure, as well as the range of pottery forms, have analogies in Thracian settlements east of the Carpathians (Rustoiu 2002a; Nemeth et al. 2005).

The settlements of Bila Cerkva and Solotvino illustrate the smooth transition of local communities from the early to the late Iron Age, uninfluenced by foreign immigration. Settlement organization in Maramureş indicates a social structure similar to that found east and south of the Carpathians and different from late Iron Age rural communities in Transylvania. At the same time, their location at the periphery of the so-called 'Thracian' model of social and settlement organization hampered the development of exchange relationships with the Greek Pontic area and the eastern Scythian region. In contrast, ceramic assemblages from sites to the east of the Carpathians include numerous Greek vessels, and their rulers accumulated prestige goods and material symbols of power, as seen for example in hoards of gold and silver objects recovered from settlements and graves (Rustoiu 2008: 80–86).

Recent research in the eastern Transylvanian depressions has revealed another example of local evolution, exemplified by a cremation cemetery and contemporary rural settlement dating to the fourth to third century BC excavated at Olteni (Cavruc and Buzea 2005). The burials and grave groups have analogies to the east of the Carpathians. Like the inhabitants of the Maramureş depression, the community from Olteni seems to have lacked interest in La Tène material culture. Furthermore, the archaeology suggests an undisturbed transition from the early to the late Iron Age, away from the influence of the Celtic groups in Transylvania. The patterns of local social organization resemble the model characterizing communities from the east of the Carpathians (Rustoiu 2008: 80–86).

The local communities from Maramureş and the eastern Transylvanian depressions were not influenced by foreign groups and experienced their own model of social and economic development. This is relevant for understanding the evolution of many other communities from the Great Hungarian Plain and Transylvania. Celtic colonization brought about the disintegration of old relationships and created new ones through the incorporation of indigenous populations into new social and cultural structures. One result was the development of a specific material culture, which sets the Carpathian basin apart from the Celtic communities of central and western Europe. Its most important characteristic is the combination of La Tène elements with local ones developed at the end of the early Iron Age.

These newly created communities in the Carpathian basin were also connected with the eastern Mediterranean region. These relations took a variety of forms, from the Great Expedition into Greece and the Balkans in 280–277 BC, via smaller-scale plundering and raids, to more peaceful contacts, whether commercial and diplomatic (including political agreements, gift exchanges, and matrimonial alliances between members of the elites), of a 'professional' nature, such as mercenary service, or other forms of communication through which goods and ideas circulated over long distances (Rustoiu 2006, 2008: 99–134). Contacts with the eastern Mediterranean world led to a fascination with certain elements of material culture of Hellenistic origin (and probably also ideology). Mediterranean influence in western Europe in the late Hallstatt and early La Tène period was mostly mediated through Massalia and the Etruscans. A similar phenomenon happened in the Carpathian basin in La Tène B2–C1: in this case, transfers of goods and ideas from the eastern Mediterranean Greek space were transmitted via the Balkans and the Greek colonies on the Black Sea coast. However, these influences were not automatically adopted, but were reinterpreted by local craftspeople according to the interests and ideologies of the elites who dominated the rural communities. As a result, various Hellenistic forms were transformed and invested with specific meanings in the Carpathian basin, the results being morphologically and ideologically different from the originals. For example, *kantharos* cups were copied from the Greek ceramic repertoire, but were adapted to suit local needs and manners of consumption (Rustoiu and Egri 2010, 2011).

The Seventh to Third Centuries BC in the Lower Danube Region

The final phase of the early Iron Age in the lower Danube basin coincided with the foundation of Greek colonies on the western shores of the Black Sea (Figure 14.5). These played an important role in the networks of communication between local communities and the Mediterranean world. At the same time, the northward extension of political control exerted successively by the Persians, Odrysians, and Macedonians contributed to the orientation of local elites towards southern social models, starting at the end of the sixth century BC, but especially during the fifth to third centuries BC. For the first time, some of the inhabitants of the region are mentioned in ancient historical sources.[3]

Histria (Istros), the first colony of Miletus on the western Black Sea coast, was founded around 657 BC, followed by Apollonia and others. The majority of Black Sea colonies appeared during the following century. In contrast with southern Italy and Sicily, where Greek colonization often generated military confrontations, the foundation of Histria was based on bilateral agreements with the indigenous populations, which governed land use and the exploitation of local resources. These agreements were probably confirmed by diplomatic gift exchanges and matrimonial alliances (Avram 1991; Ruscu 2002: 253–307). The rural and quasi-urban settlements founded in the agricultural hinterland of Histria during the sixth century BC were not fortified and the finds attest to cohabitation of newcomers and local people (Avram 1991). Within a few generations of their foundation, Histria and the other western Black Sea colonies developed a network of commercial exchange with the lower Danube basin, links which in turn facilitated the mobility of Greek craftworkers across the region. The adoption of the potter's wheel was one of the first important technological transfers resulting from such contacts.

In the final phase of the early Iron Age, the number of sites in the Danube plain diminished significantly and the period from the later seventh century BC to the mid-fifth century BC is largely represented by cemeteries (Vulpe 1970; Vulpe and Popescu 1972; Popescu and Vulpe 1982). The hilly region south of the Carpathians was inhabited by communities who cremated their dead, placing the remains in urns and covering them with mounds. They are known as the Ferigile group (Figure 14.5), after the eponymous cemetery where the mounds were grouped according to familial affiliations (Vulpe 1967). Pottery from the earliest graves displays a continuity of forms and decoration specific to the earlier Basarabi culture, leading the excavator to believe that these communities resulted from the migration of elements of the Basarabi culture population from the plains into the sub-Carpathian hills. Metal grave goods (jewellery, weaponry) indicate the initial orientation of these communities towards the north-western Balkans, whereas numerous eastern elements (such as short swords of *akinakes* type, battle axes, arrowheads) appeared later (Vulpe 1970: 130–138). In north-west Bulgaria, the mortuary practices of the Vraca group—tumuli with cremations and some inhumations—point to a similar development of Basarabi communities from the previous period (Vulpe 1970: 150–2). Tumulus burials in southern Moldavia too display very similar funerary practices and grave inventories to those from south of the Carpathians. Despite the close similarities (only some differences in ceramic morphology can be noted) this cultural group has been named Bârseşti, after a cemetery in this region (Vulpe 1970: 139–140).

The central parts of Moldavia and Basarabia, between the Prut and Dniester rivers, are characterized by small inhumation cemeteries of the Huşi-Suruceni group (Figure 14.5; Ignat 2004). The graves contain many metal artefacts of eastern origin, such as short swords of *akinakes* type and trilobate arrowheads; some female inventories also contain weapons. Harness fittings are absent. Many elements of the mortuary rites and grave goods are replicated in Transylvania in the area occupied by the Ciumbrud group. The graves point to small, mobile communities that practised transhumance or nomadic pastoralism and had connections with Transylvania (for example bronze propeller-shaped nailheads are almost exclusively encountered in these areas and in Dobrogea;

Măndescu 2010: 334–339) and Scythian communities from the northern Pontic region. We may therefore presume that the elites adopted symbols of martial identity specific to the nomadic populations of the northern Pontic steppes; the *akinakes* short sword or dagger in particular became an emblem of the warrior for peoples throughout the lower Danube basin and the inner Carpathian region, regardless of whether their lifestyle was sedentary or nomadic.

Communities in Dobrogea practised cremation, the remains being placed in urns. The long-lived cemeteries at Dobrina and Ravna, in north-east Bulgaria, are among the best known. From the sixth century BC onwards, grave goods included Greek vessels, illustrating the contacts between local populations and colonists, and numerous wheel-thrown vessels imitating Greek prototypes are present in the second phase of the Ravna cemetery (Vulpe 1970: 193–194; Hänsel 1974; Măndescu 2010: 263–268).

Known habitation sites are restricted to a few rural settlements with both surface and sunken dwellings. Wheel-thrown pottery was used as early as the seventh century BC in Alexandria, Bălăneşti, and Oprişor. These vessels were either imported from the Greek colonies and the southern Balkans, or are local imitations of prototypes from those regions (Măndescu 2010: 192–195).

The Northern Balkan Aristocratic Horizon of the Fifth to Third Centuries BC

The start of the late Iron Age in the lower Danube basin coincided with the appearance of a new horizon of fortified settlements across an area extending from the north-western Pontic region to the northern Balkans (Figure 14.6; Florescu 1971; Zanoci 1998; Stoyanov and Mihaylova 1996; Sîrbu and Trohani 1997; Kašuba et al. 2000). The first sites date to the end of the sixth or the start of the fifth century BC, and most were still occupied in the fourth and third centuries BC (Măndescu 2010). Dozens are known, but very few have been systematically investigated. They are set in various landscapes, on mountainous plateaus and high hills, as well as on upper river terraces, occupying sites that required minimal construction effort due to the presence of natural defences such as steep slopes or ravines. Many are also located close to rich natural resources and along the most important trade and communication routes, such as the Danube, Dniester, and Siret rivers.

Some of these fortified sites cover tens of hectares. The two precincts identified at Stânceşti in Moldavia, which has extensively investigated, together cover 45 ha (Florescu and Florescu 2005). Others are much smaller, for example Cotnari, also in Moldavia, which is around 4 ha (Florescu 1971). Most of the sites have earth ramparts with more or less complex palisades (simple or of rectangular shape) and ditches, closely following the natural topography (Florescu 1971; Sîrbu and Trohani 1997; Zanoci 1998). In certain cases, the fortifications were built using Mediterranean techniques perhaps by Greek masons; some have a polygonal plan. These 'foreign' building features are found in settlements that had social or economic connections with the Greek Pontic area or with the regions controlled by Odrysian or Macedonian rulers. At Sboryanovo (north-east Bulgaria) and Căscioarele (on the Danube) the fortifications were constructed using the *emplecton* technique, comprising two outer wall faces of dressed ashlar masonry with a compacted earth and rubble core (Stoyanov and Mihaylova 1996: 55–57; Sîrbu and Trohani 1997: 515). At Coţofenii din Dos and Bâzdâna in Oltenia, the outer walls were made of brick, similar to fortifications in the Mediterranean region (Trohani 1988; Babeş 1997).

Depending on their size, houses or sunken huts, storage pits, hearths, and other features are more or less densely packed in the interiors of the fortified settlements, along with workshops for metal and pottery, and ritual structures (some sanctuaries have stone masonry). Their agricultural hinterlands are full of rural settlements, pointing to the role of these fortified sites as regional centres with multiple economic, social, and religious functions. They developed social and economic links with distant territories. Numerous Greek amphorae, as well as kitchen and tableware from the Greek colonies or neighbouring areas, bronze vessels, and silver and gold jewellery are found at many of the fortified sites, as well as in the rural settlements in their environs (Mateevici 2007; Teleagă 2008; Măndescu 2010).

Numerous cemeteries have been identified in the lower Danube region, some containing only a few dozen burials, others with hundreds. Around 2,000 burials of the fifth to third centuries BC have been identified (Sîrbu 1993a; 41–42; 2006: 119–120; Măndescu 2010). They come from flat cremation cemeteries, with the remains placed in urns. Funerary assemblages mostly comprise pottery vessels (medium-sized jars used as urns, bowls, and sometimes beakers) and only rarely dress accessories, jewellery, or weaponry, as in the case of Zimnicea (Alexandrescu 1980). All told, fewer than 5% of the graves are inhumations. Some of these may relate to small-scale immigration from the northern Pontic region, as at Chiscani, in eastern Muntenia, where the individuals are associated with grave goods specific to Scythian populations (Sîrbu 1983). In other cases, there is a hint of parallel funerary practices within the community, a good example being the Stelnica cemetery on the Muntenia plain, where the number of inhumation and cremation burials is roughly equal (Conovici and Matei 1999).

Standing out from these more ordinary burials are a series of opulent graves, from which we may infer the existence of an aristocratic elite with a well-defined identity and ideology. These aristocratic burials occur south of the Balkan mountains in the territory of the Odrysians, as well as further north on both banks of the Danube, reaching as far as Moldavia (Figure 14.6; Kull 1997: 202–203, fig. 1; Măndescu 2010). Many of the graves are close to fortified settlements, either as isolated burials or grouped in cemeteries (Sîrbu and Florea 2000: 52; Sîrbu 2006: 121–128). They were predominantly inhumations, with the dead men and women interred in carefully constructed stone funerary chambers covered by impressive mounds. In some cases (e.g. Vraca, Sboryanovo, Agighiol), these structures also had antechambers (some containing sacrificed horses) or adjacent rooms, and ashlar masonry in the Greek technique (Tsetskhladze 1998).

These tombs were quite possibly inspired by Macedonian funerary monuments, with the royal cemetery at Vergina often cited as a parallel (Măndescu 2010: 377–418). Symbolic and decorative details of Mediterranean origin were sometimes copied and interpreted in a local manner. Relevant examples include the stone caryatids from a burial mound at Sboryanovo, and paintings showing royal investitures on the walls of some funerary chambers at the same site (Čičikova 1992; Fol et al. 1986). Not all the funerary monuments in the area display such quality of construction, however; others, mostly north of the Danube, are of simpler style, at as Peretu and Zimnicea (Moscalu 1989; Alexandrescu 1980). The differences could reflect variable access to the network of contacts between indigenous rulers and the Greek world that provided Mediterranean craftworkers and goods, or levels of hierarchy among the regional elites (Babeş 1997: 232–233; Rustoiu and Berecki 2012: 169–170, pl. 8).

The social hierarchy is illustrated by the grave goods placed with the elite burials. From a functional point of view they consist of: (a) weaponry and military equipment, (b) harness fittings, (c) jewellery and garment accessories, and (d) metal vessels in silver and bronze and ceramic tableware. These categories of object also occur in hoards[4] and at fortified settlements (Kull 1997; Sîrbu and Florea 2000; Măndescu 2010: 377–418).

The weaponry consists mainly of spears and arrowheads; swords of Mediterranean type are rare. The spear and the bow were emblematic weapons of the warrior aristocracy. Both are frequently depicted in hunting scenes in figurative art. These weapons occur with defensive military equipment, sometimes of very ostentatious character. For example, silver or even gold helmets (as at Coţofeneşti) inspired by the north Balkan variant of Chalcidian bronze helmets (Pflug 1988: 141–142; Rustoiu and Berecki 2012) have been found in burials such as Agighiol, Vraca, and Peretu, and in hoards or isolated finds at Cucuteni-Băiceni, Coţofeneşti, and in the Iron Gates region—each of them with cheek-pieces and neck-guards richly decorated with complex scenes (Sîrbu and Florea 2000). Many graves of warriors of lower rank contain bronze helmets of Chalcidian or occasionally of Attic type, like the one from Găvani in eastern Muntenia (Sîrbu and Harţuche 2000). Chalcidian helmets also occur in Banat and southern Transylvania (Rustoiu and Berecki 2012). The Agighiol and Vraca burials also contained silver greaves decorated with human heads and other features that follow the same iconographic structure as the silver helmets (Kull 1997; Sîrbu and Florea 2000).

The horse was another important symbol of aristocratic status (Chapter 32). In figurative art, warriors are shown riding in hunting or investiture scenes. Their horses were sometimes buried in the funerary antechambers, or in pits within the cemeteries, as at Zimnicea (A. D. Alexandrescu 1983). Osteological analyses indicate that in the fourth to third centuries BC, selective horse breeding was practised to obtain taller animals (Haimovici 1971). Given the significance of the horse as a status symbol, it is no coincidence that we find decorative silver harness fittings, including strap appliqués or frontals decorated in zoomorphic style, in burials such as Agighiol and Vraca, as well as in graves of lower ranked warriors, such as Găvani. They are accompanied by horse bits and strap dividers of iron or bronze. Sometimes ceremonial wagons were placed in the mortuary chamber, as at Vraca (Torbov 2005).

Bronze, silver, and gold jewellery and dress accessories include both local types (brooches of so-called Thracian type being common: Zirra 1996–1998; Măndescu 2010: 339–357) and Greek ones (ear-rings, chains, necklaces, diadems, seal rings). The latter were either imported from the Greek cities, or made locally by Greek craftworkers or individuals trained in Hellenistic workshops. Artefacts were adapted stylistically and morphologically to the preferences of local clients. The range of forms is noticeably different to those encountered in the Greek cities on the Black Sea coast (Tonkova 1994, 1998, 2000–2001) indicating that the take-up of imports was selective, and restricted to those types of jewellery and dress accessories that corresponded to the local norms of aristocratic bodily adornment.

The ceramic vessels from the burials, mostly tablewares, are also a mixture of local and Greek products. They were accompanied by Mediterranean amphorae, and bronze *situlae* and beakers (Teleagă 2008). Some of the most prized items were silver drinking vessels of Achaemenid or Greek inspiration, the repertoire including *phialae* (shallow bowls), beakers, cups, and drinking horns or *rhyta* (Măndescu 2010: 376–400). The later fourth-century BC Rogozen hoard contained 165 silver vessels of different origins, some of them over a century old (Nikolov 1988–1989; Marazov 1996). Some vessels were inscribed in the Greek alphabet with the names of their owners—Kotys, Sadokos, and Kersebleptes—presumably the Odrysian kings of the written sources, or perhaps local rulers with similar names. The Rogozen hoard also illustrates the local system of sociopolitical relationships based on the exchange of prestige gifts; the practice is also mentioned in various historical sources (see Măndescu 2010: 400–409).

The figurative art on metal artefacts (vessels, helmets, greaves, decorative plaques) and the painted scenes on the walls of the funerary chambers illustrate a coherent ideological code specific to the aristocracy of the northern Balkans. Its visual structure combines and interprets in a particular and original manner various stylistic and iconographic elements of Scythian, Achaemenid, and Greek origin (P. Alexandrescu 1983, 1984). Typical subjects include male riders in hunting scenes (the boar, bear, and lion being the preferred prey), male and female characters seated in ceremonial wagons, scenes of sacrifice, female winged deities shown as the 'mistress of the animals', hierogamies, fighting beasts, processions of real and fantastic animals, and mythical heroes such as Heracles (Kull 1997; Sîrbu and Florea 2000).

In conclusion, the funerary evidence of the fifth to third centuries BC from the lower Danube basin documents the social distance between ordinary members of society and the ruling elites. However, the latter social group was not monolithic, but had its own internal hierarchy. Its members were strongly influenced by cultural models promoted by the Odrysian or Macedonian rulers, but as their iconography and funerary practices show, the aristocracy of the northern Balkans constructed their own ideology, heroizing their rulers. At Sboryanovo, for example, the funerary chamber had moveable doors that were frequently opened and closed, presumably during commemorative rituals. Other burials from the lower Danube region (e.g. Yankovo, Fântânele, Zimnicea) contain sacrificial altars, which were used during such ceremonies (Sîrbu 2006: 24–25, 121–126).

The fortified settlements and opulent funerary monuments came to an end in or soon after the mid-third century BC. This is often attributed, on the one hand, to the Celtic invasion of the Balkans and Greece from 280–277 BC, and, on the other, to the migration of the Germanic Bastarnae into the region east of the Carpathians. However, many sites of this horizon continued for some decades after the Celtic invasion, so their disappearance cannot be directly related to those events. The La Tène jewellery and dress accessories discovered in the northern Balkans are more likely to be a result of contacts and exchanges based on individual mobility—diplomatic contacts, matrimonial alliances—between the elites of the northern Balkans and Carpathian basin (Emilov 2010; Anastassov 2011; Rustoiu 2011).

East of the Carpathians, the Poienești-Lukaševka culture, which is attributed to the arrival of the Bastarnae, began around 200 BC, a few decades after the end of the horizon of opulent burials and fortified settlements (Figure 14.8). This culture flourished until the end of the first century BC (see also Chapter 7). Several flat cremation cemeteries have been identified, with ritual features and funerary assemblages of ceramics, jewellery, and dress accessories resembling those from Germanic cemeteries in northern Europe. The settlements had a rural character, the pottery pointing to an amalgamation of the newcomers with the existing population. We can therefore suggest that this culture was the result of successive migrations from various parts of Poland, north Germany, and Denmark, which probably also drew in some La Tène groups. The heterogeneous character of the material culture from this region, which differs from that of Germanic communities in northern Europe, reflects this demographic mix (see Babeș 1993). The sudden demise of the northern Balkan aristocracy and its particular ways of expressing its identity thus seems more likely to be the product of an internal sociopolitical transformation, perhaps similar to the end of the Hallstatt period in western Europe. Not long afterwards, around 200 BC, a new warrior elite, which chose to express its identity through a specific panoply of arms, was to appear in the region in their place.

The Late Iron Age and the Rise of the Dacian Kingdom

In spite of local variations, for example in the Great Hungarian plain, the second century BC (La Tène C2–D1) was a period of relative cultural homogeneity across much of the Carpathian-Danubian area. The existing cemeteries went out of use at the end of La Tène C1, implying a profound change in mortuary beliefs (Egri 2012: 507–509), while over a zone extending from the middle Danube to the Atlantic coast, large fortified settlements known as *oppida* emerged (Chapter 21).

Although the Great Hungarian Plain had previously seen a concentration of manufacturing activities in large aggregations such as Sajópetri (as already mentioned), fortified *oppida* did not appear in this region, and the settlement pattern remained rural

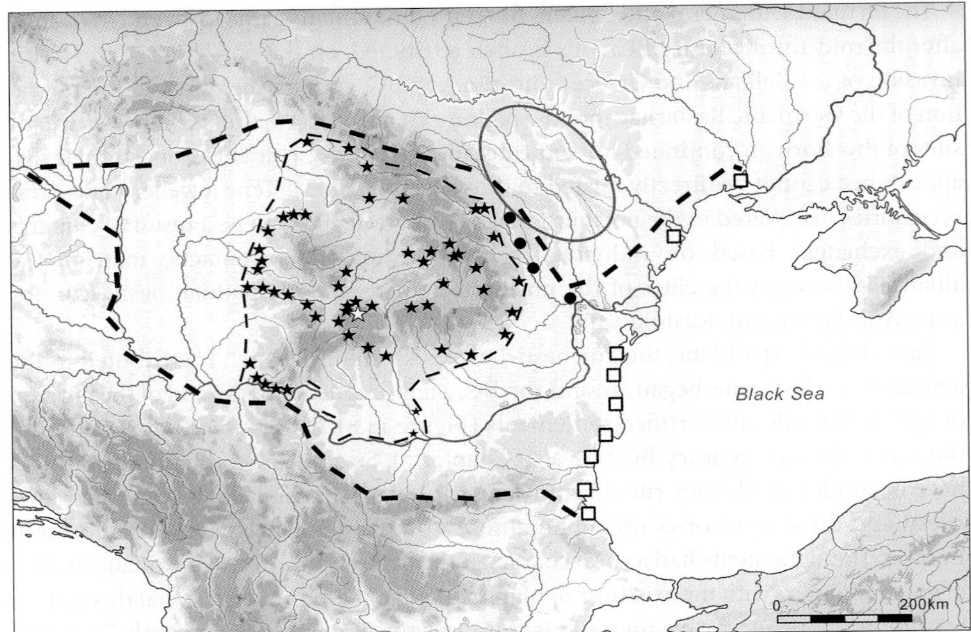

FIGURE 14.8 The Dacian kingdom. Key: thick dashed line—extent of Burebista's kingdom; thin dashed line—extent of Decebalus' kingdom; oval outline—Poieneşti-Lukaševka culture; small stars—fortresses and fortified settlements; larger white star—Sarmizegetusa Regia; dots—manufacturing and commercial centres outside the kingdom's control after Burebista's reign; squares—Greek cities.

in character. Settlements were limited in size, with only small numbers of houses, in tighter or looser clusters, surrounded by storage pits, some of which were reused as rubbish pits. The settlements at Tiszafüred-Maratvapart (La Tène C2) and Tápiószele (La Tène D1) illustrate a continuity of habitation, lifestyle, and material culture (for example, the ceramics point to the preservation of existing culinary practices) from the later third century to the first century BC (Kriveczky 1991; Hellebrandt 1999: 42–50). Moreover, various elements of La Tène material culture are still found in many settlements dating to the first decades of Roman rule, mixed with Dacian or Sarmatian elements, underlining a particular development of this region at the start of the first millennium AD (Almássy 2001).

In Transylvania the situation was different. Burials dated to La Tène C2–D1 display different funerary practices and inventories from the previous Celtic horizon. The cremated remains were buried in flat or tumulus graves (e.g. Blandiana, Tărtăria, Hunedoara, Cugir) with a distinctive panoply of arms: long swords of La Tène type, spears, curved daggers of northern Balkan origin (some with blades decorated with incised or stamped zoomorphic and/or celestial symbols), shields, and sometimes chain mails and helmets. Horse bits of Thracian type (Werner 1988, type XVI) are also

FIGURE 14.9 Late La Tène weapons and harness fittings from Bulbuc, Transylvania, specific to the Padea-Panagjurski Kolonii group, late second century to first half of the first century BC.

Photo: A. Rustoiu

known (Figures 14.9–14.10). The ceramic assemblages consisted of vessels without close parallels in the previous Celtic horizon, but derived instead from typical north Balkan forms. Among them are jar-like vessels decorated with knobs, tall, footed 'fruit bowls' (the bigger ones used in commensal/feasting practices), beakers with one handle (often handmade, sometimes used as urns), and large biconical vessels with two handles (Rustoiu 2005a, 2008: 142–163). No burials that can be attributed to women are known, but as there are still only a few osteological analyses (Rustoiu and Comşa 2004), female inventories may be identified in the future.

These burials have analogies in the northern Balkans (mainly northern Bulgaria, southern Romania, and the Iron Gates region). More than four decades ago Zenon

FIGURE 14.10 Late La Tène artefacts from a tumulus cremation grave near the Dacian fortress at Cugir, southern Transylvania, late second century to first half of the first century BC. A: Bronze *situla*; B: Military equipment: iron chain mail and helmet cheek-pieces.

Photo: A. Rustoiu

Wožniak (1974) identified this phenomenon as the Padea-Panagjurski Kolonii group. Regional variations in mortuary practice, such as the preponderance of burial mounds south of the Danube and of flat graves north of the river, suggest different population groups (Triballi, Moesi, Lesser Scordisci, Dacians), whose elites nevertheless shared a common ideology and identity, related to warrior status rather than ethnicity. This identity was probably created around the La Tène C1–C2 transition, and was principally expressed through the use of particular sets of weapons.

In north-west Bulgaria, some burials yield artefacts dated to the end of La Tène C1, whereas north of the Danube in Oltenia the earliest such burials date to La Tène C2. This chronology suggests a gradual northwards extension of the area controlled by warrior groups from the northern Balkans, who effected a substantial transformation of society and political authority in Transylvania (Rustoiu 2005a, 2008). This migration from the lower Danube region also brought about demographic changes, with some areas witnessing a significant increase in the number of rural settlements compared to before; these settlements yielded ceramics similar to those recovered from contemporary burials (Rustoiu and Rustoiu 2000). At the same time, fortified settlements and small fortresses appeared, located on dominant heights controlling important strategic places (e.g. Piatra Craivii, Cugir, and Costeşti), with specific military, economic, and sociopolitical functions (Figure 14.11). In contrast to the essentially rural pattern of settlement that characterized the Celtic horizon in Transylvania, these fortifications point to the emergence of a different kind of elite and of new mechanisms of social control and subordination of the local communities (Rustoiu 2008). These Dacian fortresses are quite different from the *oppida* of central and western Europe, both in their layouts and in their roles.

A few generations later, during the reign of King Burebista, a contemporary of Julius Caesar, these warrior elites were transformed into a coherent military and political force. Caesar is the first author to mention the Dacians, writing that the western borders of their lands extend to the middle Danube and the Hercynian Forest, in modern Slovakia (*de Bello Gallico* 6.25.2). Little is known of the biography of Burebista. Contemporary and later epigraphic and literary sources mention him as a *basileus* who defeated a coalition of the Boii and Taurisci somewhere in the middle Danube region, probably around 60 BC (*Sylloge Inscriptionum Graecarum* 762; Strabo *Geography* 7.3.11). After 55 BC he extended his authority to include Greek cities on the Black Sea coast, either by force of arms (Olbia and Histria: Alexandrescu 1994, 2007; Ruscu 2002: 297–299), or through diplomatic agreements (Dionysopolis). He also led raids into Thrace, Macedonia, and Illyricum (Florus *Epitome* 1.39.1–6; Appian *Illyrian Wars* 14), similar to those of the Padea-Panagjurski Kolonii warrior groups in the second to first centuries BC.

During the Civil Wars, Burebista was an ally of Pompey against Caesar, the agreement being negotiated in 48 BC with the diplomatic support of Akornion of Dionysopolis, an adviser to the king, who was designated *filius* (a frequently used title in the late Hellenistic kingdoms of the eastern Mediterranean) in the honorific decree issued by

FIGURE 14.11 The Dacian fortress at Piatra Craivii, Transylvania, showing its constituent functional zones: 1 fortress, 2 sanctuaries, 3 civilian area and workshops, 4 presumed 'familial' cemeteries.

Photo: Z. Czajlik

the Greek colony (*Sylloge Inscriptionum Graecarum* 762). By these various means, the Dacian king extended his political control over a territory stretching from the middle Danube to the Black Sea and from the northern Carpathians to the Balkans (Figure 14.8; Crişan 1978; Babeş 1980). After the death of Burebista (who was deposed during a revolt; Strabo *Geography* 7.3.11), an event that must have happened before Octavian's Illyrian campaign in 35–33 BC (Dobesch 1995: 15–19), his kingdom was divided first into four parts, then into five during the reign of Augustus.

The breakaway territories mentioned by Strabo cannot be easily identified. One was probably in the Siret valley. The fortifications built during the rule of Burebista at some sites in this region (Brad, Răcătău) were dismantled in the later first century BC (Ursachi 1986–1987; 1995: 99–112). Other territories formerly belonging to the Dacian kingdom may have been in Dobrogea, where three local chieftains—Rholes, Dapyx, and Zyraxes—are mentioned in the 29–28 BC (Cassius Dio *Roman History* 51.23–27), or between the Danube and the Balkans, where the Romans gradually advanced, and along the middle Danube. Some local chieftains are mentioned in ceramic graffiti from Ocniţa and Cârlomăneşti, outside the Carpathians (Russu 1977: 33–40; Babeş 2010). Thus it seems that the border regions of Burebista's former kingdom were ruled, at least temporarily, by a series of independent chieftains. On the other hand, the rulers who succeeded Burebista managed to preserve political control over Banat, Crişana, Maramureş, Transylvania, Oltenia, the sub-Carpathian area in Muntenia, and some outposts in western Moldavia, where some settlements and fortresses continued through the first centuries BC and AD (Glodariu 1983).

The territory occupied by the Padea-Panagjurski Kolonii group, as well as the expansion of Burebista's kingdom, is defined by the distribution of a series of artefacts generally ascribed to the Dacians, including typical ceramic forms such as the 'fruit bowl', the jar-shaped pot, and the truncated mug (Babeş 1980). Their presence indicates a preference for particular cooking and dining practices among the newly established communities. At the same time the appearance of fortified sites and fortresses in dominant positions, with complex economic and social functions, illustrates a specific pattern of sociopolitical organization. These centres had artisan quarters nearby and were surrounded by an agricultural hinterland comprising a network of dependant rural settlements (Florea 2011; Egri 2014a: 177).

The extent of Burebista's kingdom from the middle Danube region to the western Pontic shores allowed the establishment of close connections with the Greek Black Sea cities and with the areas under Roman control in the north-west Balkans, which influenced the culture of the Dacian kingdom until the Roman conquest. After subjugating the former Greek colonies, Burebista initiated a vast programme of civilian, military, and religious construction in the Orăştie mountains in south-west Transylvania. At Grădiştea de Munte, a truly urban centre was built on a ridge at an altitude of 1,000 m to act as the capital. Later rulers added new architectural elements (Glodariu 1983, 1995; Daicoviciu et al. 1989; Iaroslavschi 1995; Glodariu et al. 1996; Florea 2011). This ridge was almost certainly the sacred *Kogaionon* mentioned by Strabo (*Geography* 7.3.5), known later as *to basileion* (Cassius Dio

Roman History 67.10.3; 68.8.3; 68.14.3), or Sarmizegetusa *to basileion* (Ptolemy *Geography* 3.8.4).

The contribution of Greek craftworkers and stonemasons to the building of Sarmizegetusa and other fortresses in its surroundings is attested by various architectural features and techniques. The structures were erected on artificial terraces, supported by walls of cut stone brought from different limestone quarries located tens of kilometres away. They include rectangular and circular sanctuaries (Figure 14.12), a monumental paved road, cisterns, and a system of ceramic pipes for water distribution. A civilian settlement located on a large hilltop and mainly dating to the first century AD occupied dozens of artificial terraces, east and west of the sacred area, with a total length of around 3 km (Florea 2011: 132). Excavations have unearthed civilian buildings made of timber, some of two storeys. The ceramics recovered from these buildings are different from those encountered on other Dacian settlements. They include many imported Greek and Roman forms, and copies by local potters, as well as a distinctive pottery decorated with vegetal and zoomorphic elements, stylistically different from types produced in late La Tène central Europe (Florea 1998). Several workshops for metal and glass have also been discovered, some using technologies of Mediterranean origin, suggesting the presence of some Greek or Roman craftworkers (Rustoiu 1996; Iaroslavschi 1997; Florea 2011). A small fortification built in the *emplecton* technique was erected just prior to the wars with Domitian. Its final layout suggests that it was rebuilt and extended after the Roman conquest, in the reign of Trajan, by the garrison that controlled the region (Glodariu 1995).

All access routes to the capital were controlled by a system of fortresses with similar ashlar masonry (Costeşti-Cetăţuie, Costeşti-Blidaru, Piatra Roşie, Vârful lui Hulpe). Some of them had rectangular multistorey towers of stone and brick. These fortresses had a military role, but also served as power centres for the aristocracy associated with the royal court (Glodariu 1983, 1995; Daicoviciu et al. 1989; Glodariu et al. 1996; Florea 2011). Members of the court may have competed for control of local resources and of the religious centre at Sarmizegetusa, which was probably perceived as important for legitimizing royal status (Lockyear 2004; Egri 2014b: 235–237).

Fortifications and fortresses in other parts of Dacia were usually built using traditional earthen ramparts and wooden palisades, although in some peripheral areas they have rubble masonry and rectangular towers imitating the spectacular constructions of the capital, such as Bâtca Doamnei in Moldavia, Cetăţeni in Muntenia, and Divici in Banat (Gumă et al. 1999; Rustoiu 2006–2007). Workshops for ceramics, metal, and bone have been identified in many of these sites, pointing to their importance as production centres (Glodariu and Iaroslavschi 1979; Rustoiu 1996; Iaroslavschi 1997). A system of inter-community exchange has also been identified. For example, the metal workshops from the mountainous area near Sarmizegetusa supplied rural communities in the Mureş valley with iron goods (mainly agricultural tools), and the latter provided agricultural produce that could not be obtained in the mountains (Florea 2011: 162).

Some settlements developed into large commercial centres, for example those located in the Siret valley (Brad, Răcătău, Poiana: Ursachi 1995; Rustoiu 2002b; Vulpe

FIGURE 14.12 Temples in the sacred area at Sarmizegetusa (Grădiştea de Munte, Romania), seat of the Dacian kings, in the Orăştie mountains.

Photo: A. Rustoiu

and Teodor 2003), and Ocniţa in Oltenia, near a large salt mine, and Piatra Craivii in Transylvania (Rustoiu 2002b: 200). The wide variety of finds recovered points to a commercial exchange network that included distant connections with Italy and the eastern Mediterranean. However, most imports (metal, ceramics, and glass objects) have been recovered from settlements in south-west Transylvania and around Sarmizegetusa, underlining the importance of this area, where many economic resources were concentrated (Glodariu 1976; Rustoiu 2005b).

Contact with the Mediterranean world also resulted in widespread imitation of Roman Republican *denarii* in Dacia, probably in workshops established by foreign craftworkers (Glodariu et al. 1992). More than 30,000 such coins have been discovered, mostly in hoards (Glodariu 1976; Mihăilescu-Bîrliba 1980, 1990), which may indicate that the silver *denarii* had no economic role, but were seen as prestige goods. Roman bronze issues were used in the first century AD after the foundation of the province of Moesia, but only in settlements along the frontier (Rustoiu 2006–2007: 20; Egri 2014a: 177–179, n. 4).

After Burebista's demise, power was taken over by the high priest Deceneus. From this time until the reign of Decebalus, the last Dacian king, the rulers combined the function of high priest with political and military prerogatives. Royal authority became both martial and theocratic. These fundamental modifications of the nature of royal power are apparent both in the transformation of the funerary practices of the elites, and in the imposition of an 'official' state religion, evidenced by the appearance of monumental sanctuaries.

Warrior burials containing weaponry specific to the Padea-Panagjurski Kolonii group disappeared at the end of the first century BC (Babeş 1988). Tumulus burials appear in the vicinity of the settlements in the Siret valley during the first century AD, when the region ceased to belong to the Dacian kingdom in Transylvania. Elements of the burial rite point to strong connections with Sarmatian communities from the northern Pontic region. Finds from the fortresses and iconographic representations suggest that changes occurred in weapon panoplies during the first century AD, long swords of La Tène type being replaced by curved swords of the *falx* type. However, curved daggers of *sica* type continued to be used, becoming an ethnic emblem of the Dacians in Roman visual and symbolic language after the campaigns of Domitian and Trajan (Rustoiu 2007).

Other important changes can be seen in the mortuary practices of ordinary members of society. In the earlier second century BC, the flat grave cemeteries characteristic of the fifth to third centuries BC disappeared, and the deceased were treated in an archaeologically invisible manner. As at an earlier period, pits containing vessel deposits found at some settlements might perhaps be related to rituals associated with death. At the same time, human skeletons are sometimes found in or near settlements, whether isolated or in batteries of pits. In most cases the skeletons were not placed in anatomical position and were frequently incomplete; it is thought that they could be human sacrifices, with some skeletons bearing traces of violence (Babeş 1988; Sîrbu 1993a). Children's skeletons (see Rustoiu et al. 1993; Sîrbu and Dăvîncă 2016), and sometimes those of certain craftworkers (Vagalinski 2011), were buried in anatomical position in settlements or in their vicinity—in contexts interpreted as non-funerary—suggesting that some social or professional groups were treated differently upon death.

Sanctuaries appeared in the vicinity of late Iron Age fortified centres, as an expression of the 'official' state religion. The earliest sanctuaries were rectangular timber structures, albeit significantly larger than ordinary domestic buildings, with an apse oriented to the north-west (Sîrbu 2006: 33–34). New types of sanctuary appeared in Burebista's time and during the reigns of his successors. These include circular and rectangular structures like those discovered in the sacred area at Sarmizegetusa and elsewhere (Sîrbu 2006: 25–33). The circular sanctuaries consisted of a rectangular chamber with an apse oriented to the north-west, surrounded by a ring of stone or timber. The rectangular structures included wooden columns sometimes supported by limestone or andesite bases, resembling Mediterranean temples.

As well as these monumental religious buildings, other types of sacred cult places have been identified, pointing to different religious practices on the part of rural communities and/or the existence of 'unofficial' popular religious beliefs and behaviours. At Conţeşti, on the shores of a lake in southern Romania, a large area where numerous domestic animals were cremated has been found, the place perhaps a sacred grove. Most of the animal remains were limb bones, associated with ceramic vessels, reinforcing the sacrificial nature of the assemblage (Nicolăescu-Plopşor 1976; Vulpe and Popescu 1976).

Evidence of magical practices is also found at many settlements, especially outside the Carpathians, including anthropomorphic clay figurines, sometimes displaying signs of stabbing or mutilation, and a few 'witchcraft sets' (Sîrbu 1993b).

Numerous hoards of silver artefacts have also been discovered, buried outside settlements. Generally, they consist of a female costume set, including brooches, bracelets, and necklaces, as well as metal drinking vessels. Some objects were intentionally destroyed before burial (Spânu 2012). These costume sets were never replicated in bronze or iron, which might suggest that their use was restricted to individuals of particular status within the community, for whom they probably served as identity symbols. It is likely that they were ceremonial costumes exclusively worn by priestesses (Medeleţ 1993, 1994; Egri and Rustoiu 2014).

The Roman Conquest

The development of the Dacian kingdom was abruptly halted by the Roman conquest. Following a first attempt by Domitian in the late first century AD, Trajan organized two major campaigns in AD 101–102 and 105–106, at the end of which most of the Dacian territory was incorporated into a new Roman province. The Roman strategy was to conquer the capital and annihilate the religious centre at Sarmizegetusa, as this was a key place of resistance for the Dacian theocratic elites. All the sanctuaries were completely dismantled after the conquest, suffering violent destruction comparable to that of the Temple in Jerusalem (Rustoiu 2002c: 139–140; Ruscu 2003: 48–67). The definitive collapse of the entire power structure happened after the death of Decebalus. The disappearance of the theocratic and military hierarchy that had governed the kingdom is attested archaeologically by the sudden abandonment of all the Dacian fortresses, even of those located outside the new province, for example in the upper Tisza basin (Rustoiu 2002a; Babeş 2000).

In contrast to the neighbouring Danubian provinces, the Dacian elites were not integrated into the early administrative structures of the new province, nor apparently were the late Iron Age local deities incorporated into provincial religious life through syncretism or *interpretatio romana* (Ruscu 2003: 48–67). This latter might, however, have been the result of a different local manner of perceiving and acknowledging divine beings and actions, which was difficult to accommodate within Roman religion. Although Roman Dacia experienced massive immigration, with people brought from all over the Empire,[5] some local rural communities from the province and its bordering territories revived cultural practices that pre-dated the Dacian kingdom, such as the reappearance of flat cremation cemeteries with urns (Babeş 2000: 333–335). Others were gradually integrated into the provincial administrative system (Nemeti 2006; Nemeti and Bărbulescu 2010). During Trajan's and Hadrian's reigns, the Dacian auxiliary units that served in Britannia, Cappadocia, and Syria were probably recruited from these communities. Thus, the conquest of the Dacian kingdom and the subsequent organization of the Roman province ended the trajectory of local late Iron Age sociopolitical structures, and gradually introduced new social, administrative, economic, and cultural practices.

Notes

1. A similar situation occurred in the late Iron Age, when the emergence of the *oppida* coincided with the abandonment of formal burial across a large part of Europe, and the disposal of the dead became archaeologically invisible.
2. Known as Bosut IIIa in Serbian literature.
3. Herodotus (*Histories* 4.93) writes that the Getae from Dobrogea, ethnically related to the Thracians, blocked the Persian advance into the region during King Darius' Scythian campaign in 519 (or 514–512) BC. Thucydides (*History of the Peloponnesian War* 2.96.1) mentions that the Getae inhabited the territory between the Balkans and the mouth of the Danube. The region west of the Iskăr up to the confluence of the Serbian Morava and the Danube was inhabited by the Triballi. Alexander the Great campaigned against them in 335 BC, and also led an incursion against the Getae across the Danube, somewhere near the mouth of the Morava (Arrian *Anabasis* 1.3–4; Strabo *Geography* 7.3.8). For the location of this campaign see Medeleţ (1982).
4. As many of these 'hoards' are poorly recorded chance discoveries. Some of them might conceivably originally have been from graves.
5. See, for example, Husar (1999) for the epigraphic and archaeological evidence for Celtic and Germanic communities.

References

Ailincăi, S.-C. 2011. 'Ceramica din siturile culturii Babadag. Cu privire specială asupra siturilor din Dobrogea'. *Peuce* 9: 55–178.

Alexandrescu, A. D. 1980. 'La nécropole Gète de Zimnicea'. *Dacia N. S.* 24: 19–126.

Alexandrescu, A. D. 1983. 'Tombes de chevaux et pièces du harnais dans la nécropole gète de Zimnicea'. *Dacia N. S.* 27: 67–78.

Alexandrescu, P. 1983. 'Le groupe de trésors thraces du Nord des Balkans (I)'. *Dacia N. S.* 27: 45–66.

Alexandrescu, P. 1984. 'Le groupe de trésors thraces du Nord des Balkans (II)'. *Dacia N. S.* 28: 85–97.

Alexandrescu, P. 1994. 'La destruction d'Istros par les Gètes. 1. Dossier archéologique'. *Il Mar Nero* 1: 179–214.

Alexandrescu, P. 2007. 'La fin de la zone sacrée d'époque Greque d'Istros'. *Dacia N. S.* 51: 211–219.

Alexianu, M., O. Weller, and R.-G. Curcă (eds). 2011. *Archaeology and Anthropology of Salt: A Diachronic Approach*. British Archaeological Reports International Series 2198. Oxford: Archaeopress.

Almássy, K. 2001. 'New data on the Celto-Dacian relationship in the Upper Tisza region', in E. Istvánovits and V. Kulcsár (eds) *International Connections of the Barbarians of the Carpathian Basin in the 1st–5th centuries AD*: 45–55. Aszód/Nyiregyháza: Jósa András Múzeum/Osváth Gedeon Museum Foundation.

Anastassov, J. 2011. 'The Celtic presence in Thrace during the 3rd century BC in light of new archaeological data', in M. Guštin and M. Jevtić (eds) *The Eastern Celts: The Communities Between the Alps and the Black Sea*: 227–239. Koper/Belgrade: Univerza na Primorskem.

Avram, A. 1991. 'Beziehungen zwischen Griechen und Geten im archaischen Histria'. *Studii Clasice* 27: 19–30.

Babeş, M. 1980. 'L'unité et la diffusion des tribus géto-daces à la lumière des données archéologiques', in R. Vulpe (ed.) *Actes du IIe Congrès International de Thracologie (Bucarest, 4–10 septembre 1976)*: 7–23. Bucharest: Editura Academiei.

Babeş, M. 1988. 'Descoperirile funerare şi semnificaţia lor în contextul culturii geto-dacice clasice'. *Studii şi cercetări de istorie veche şi arheologie* 39: 3–32.

Babeş, M. 1993. *Die Poieneşti-Lukaševka-Kultur: Ein Beitrag zur Kulturgeschichte im Raum östlich der Karpaten in den Jahrhunderten vor Christi Geburt*. Bonn: Habelt.

Babeş, M. 1997. 'Despre fortificaţiile "Cetăţii Jidovilor" de la Coţofenii din Dos'. *Studii şi cercetări de istorie veche şi arheologie* 48: 199–236.

Babeş, M. 2000. '"Devictis Dacis". La conquête trajane vue par l'archéologie', in A. Avram and M. Babeş (eds) *Civilisation greque et cultures antiques périphériques. Hommage à P. Alexandrescu à son 70e anniversaire*: 323–338. Bucharest: Editura Enciclopedică.

Babeş, M. 2010. 'Staţiunea geto-dacă de la Cârlomăneşti: dava sau centru religios?'. *Mousaios* 15: 123–146.

Babeş, M., and N. Miriţoiu 2012. 'Verlängerte, mehrstufige birituelle Bestattungen im Donau-Karpaten-Raum', in S. Berecki (ed.) *Iron Age Rites and Rituals in the Carpathian Basin: Proceedings of the International Colloquium from Târgu Mureş, 7–9 October 2011* : 139–160. Târgu Mureş: Editura Mega.

Berciu, D. 1963. 'Este şi o cale cimmeriană în difuziunea metalurgiei fierului?' *Studii şi cercetări de istorie veche* 14: 395–402.

Berecki, S. 2008. *The La Tène Settlement from Moreşti*. Cluj-Napoca: Editura Mega.

Boroffka, N. 1987. 'Folosirea fierului în România de la începuturi până în sec. al VIII-lea î.e.n.'. *Apulum* 24: 55–77.

Cauuet, B., B. Ancel, C. Rico, and C. Tamaş. 2010. 'Ancient mining networks. The French archaeological missions 1999–2001', in P. Damian (ed.) *Alburnus Maior I*: 453–510. Cluj-Napoca: Editura Mega.

Cavruc, V., and D. Buzea. 2005. 'Vestigiile dacice timpurii de la Olteni. Raport preliminar'. *Angustia* 9: 121–153.

Chochorowski, J. 1985. *Die Vekerzug-Kultur: Charakteristik der Funde*. Kraków/Warsaw: Uniwersytet Jagielloński/Państwowe Wydawn.

Čičikova, M. 1972. 'Nouvelles données sur la culture thrace de l'époque de Hallstatt en Bulgarie du sud'. *Thracia* 1: 79–100.

Čičikova, M. 1992. 'The Thracian tomb near Sveshtari'. *Helis* 2: 143–163.

Ciobanu, D. 2002. *Exploatarea sării în perioada marilor migraţii în spaţiul carpato-dunărean*. Buzău: Biblioteca Mousaios.

Ciugudean, H. 2012. 'The chronology of the Gáva culture in Transylvania', in W. Blajer (ed.) *Peregrinationes Archaeologicae in Asia et Europa Joanni Chochorowski Dedicate*: 107–121. Kraków: Instytut Archeologii Uniwersytetu Jagiellońskiego.

Conovici, N., and G. Matei. 1999. 'Necropola getică de la Stelinca—Grădiştea Mare. Raport general pentru anii 1987–1996'. *Materiale şi cercetări arheologice S. N.* 1: 99–144.

Crişan, I. H. 1978. *Burebista and his time*. Bucharest: Editura Academiei.

Daicoviciu, H., A. Ferenczi, and I. Glodariu. 1989. *Cetăți și așezări dacice în sud-vestul Transilvaniei*. Bucharest: Editura Științifică și Enciclopedică.

Davidescu, M. 1981. 'Un tezaur de podoabe tracice descoperit la Hinova'. *Thraco-Dacica* 2: 7–22.

de Boer, J. G. 2007. 'The earliest possible date of Greek colonization along the western Pontic coast', in *Ancient Civilisations and the Sea*. Acta Musei Varnaensis 5: 123–142. Varna: Zograf.

Dobesch, G. 1995. 'Die Boier und Burebista', in J. Tejral, J. Rajtár, and K. Pieta (eds) *Kelten, Germanen, Römer im Mitteldonaugebiet vom Ausklang der Latène-Zivilisation bis zum 2. Jahrhundert*: 15–19. Brno/Nitra: Spisy Archeologického ústavu AV ČR.

Egri, M. 2012. 'A warrior never dies. The manipulation of tradition in early funerary contexts from Pannonia', in S. Berecki (ed.) *Iron Age Rites and Rituals in the Carpathian Basin: Proceedings of the International Colloquium from Târgu Mureș, 7–9 October 2011* : 503–529. Târgu Mureș: Editura Mega.

Egri, M. 2014a. 'Enemy at the gates? The interactions between Dacians and Romans in the 1st century AD', in M. A. Janković, V. D. Mihajlović, and S. Babić (eds) *The Edges of the Roman World*: 172–193. Newcastle: Cambridge Scholars Publishing.

Egri, M. 2014b. 'Desirable goods in the Late Iron Age—the craftsman's perspective', in S. Berecki (ed.) *Iron Age Crafts and Craftsmen in the Carpathian Basin: Proceedings of the International Colloquium from Târgu Mureș, 10–13 October 2013* : 233–248. Târgu Mureș: Editura Mega.

Egri, M., and A. Rustoiu. 2014. 'Sacred conviviality in the Lower Danube region. The case of the Sâncrăieni hoard', in L. Ruscu (ed.) *Banquets of Gods, Banquets of Men: Conviviality in the Ancient World*. Studia Universitatis Babeș-Bolyai. Series Historia 59, 1: 153–188. Cluj-Napoca: Argonaut.

Eibner, A. 1996. 'Die Bedeutung der Basarabi-Kultur in der Entwiklung des Osthallsattkreis', in M. Garašanin and P. Roman (eds) *Der Basarabi-Komplex in Mittel- und Südosteuropa*: 105–118. Bucharest: Vavila Edinf.

El Susi, G. 1996. *Vânători, pescari și crescători de animale în Banatul mileniilor VI î. Ch.–I d. Ch.* Timișoara: Editura Mirton.

Emilov, J. 2010. 'Ancient texts on the Galatian royal residence of Tylis and the context of La Tène finds in southern Thrace. A reappraisal', in L. F. Vagalinski (ed.) *In Search of Celtic Tylis in Thrace (III C BC): Proceedings of the Interdisciplinary Colloquium arranged by the National Archaeological Institute and Museum at Sofia and the Welsh Department, Aberystwyth University, held at the National Archaeological Institute and Museum, Sofia, 8 May 2010*: 67–87. Sofia: NOUS Publishers.

Florea, G. 1998. *Ceramica pictată: Artă, meșteșug și societate în Dacia preromană*. Cluj-Napoca: Presa universitară clujeană.

Florea, G. 2011. *Dava et Oppidum: Débuts de la genèse urbaine en Europe au deuxième âge du Fer*. Cluj-Napoca: Academia Română.

Florescu, A. C. 1971. 'Unele considerații asupra cetăților traco-getice din mileniul I î.e.n. de pe teritoriul Moldovei'. *Cercetări istorice* 2: 103–118.

Florescu, A., and M. Florescu. 2005. *Cetățile traco-getice din secolele VI–III a. Chr. de la Stâncești (jud. Botoșani)*. Târgoviște: Editura Cetatea de Scaun.

Fol, A., M. Čičikova, T. Ivanov, and T. Teofilov. 1986. *The Thracian Tomb near the Village of Sveshtari*. Sofia: Svyat Publishers.

Garašanin, M., and P. Roman (eds). 1996. *Der Basarabi-Komplex in Mittel—und Südosteuropa*. Bucharest: Vavila Edinf.

Gergova, D. 1994. 'The treasure from Vulchitran and the amber route in the Balkans', in H. Ciugudean and N. Boroffka (eds) *The Early Hallstatt Period (1200–700 BC) in South-Eastern Europe*. Bibliotheca Musei Apulensis 1: 69–80. Alba Iulia: Muzeul National al Unirii.

Glodariu, I. 1976. *Dacian Trade with the Hellenistic and Roman World*. British Archaeological Reports International Series 8. Oxford: Archaeopress.

Glodariu, I. 1983. *Arhitectura dacilor: Civilă şi militară*. Bucharest: Editura Dacia.

Glodariu, I. 1995. 'Addenda aux "Points de repère pour la chronologie des citadelles et des établissements daciques des Monts d'Orăştie"'. *Acta Musei Napocensis* 32: 119–134.

Glodariu, I., and E. Iaroslavschi. 1979. *Civilizaţia fierului la daci*. Cluj-Napoca: Editura Dacia.

Glodariu, I., E. Iaroslavschi, and A. Rusu. 1992. 'Die Münzstätte von Sarmizegetusa Regia'. *Ephemeris Napocensis* 2: 57–68.

Glodariu, I., E. Iaroslavschi, A. Rusu-Pescaru, and F. Stănescu. 1996. *Sarmizegetusa Regia: Capitala Daciei preromane*. Acta Musei Devensis. Deva: Muzeul Civilizaţiei Dacice şi Romane.

Gotzev, A. M. 1994. 'Decoration of the early Iron Age pottery from south-east Bulgaria', in H. Ciugudean and N. Boroffka (eds) *The Early Hallstatt Period (1200–700 BC) in South-Eastern Europe*. Bibliotheca Musei Apulensis 1: 97–128. Alba Iulia: Muzeul National al Unirii.

Gumă, M. 1993. *Civilizaţia primei epoci a fierului în sud-vestul României*. Bucharest: Institutul Român de Tracologie.

Gumă, M., A. Rustoiu, and C. Săcărin. 1999. 'Les fibules du site fortifié de Liubcova-Stenca et de la citadelle de Divici-Grad', in M. Vasić (ed.) *Le Djerdap/Les Portes de Fer à la deuxième moitié du premier millénaire av. J.-C. jusqu'aux guerres daciques: Kolloquium in Kladovo—Drobeta-Tr.Severin (September–October 1998)*: 65–70. Belgrade: Arheološki institut.

Haimovici, S. 1971. 'Les caractéristiques des chevaux découverts dans la nécropole Gète de Zimnicea'. *Analele Ştiinţifice ale Univ. "Al. I. Cuza" Iaşi, S. II, a. Biologie* 17, 1: 169–185.

Hänsel, B. 1974. 'Zur Chronologie des 7. bis 5. Jahrhunderts v. Chr. im Hinterland von Odessos an der westlichen Schwarzmeerküste'. *Praehistorische Zeitschrift* 49, 2: 193–217.

Hänsel, B. 1976. *Beiträge zur regionalen und chronologischen Gliederung der älteren Hallstattzeit an der unteren Donau*. Bonn: Habelt.

Hänsel, B., and P. Medović. 1991. 'Vorbericht über die jugoslawisch-deutschen Ausgrabungen in der Siedlung von Feudvar bei Mošorin von 1986–1990. Bronzezeit–vorrömische Eisenzeit'. *Berichte der Römisch-Germanischen Kommission* 72: 45–204.

Harding, A. F., and V. Kavruk. 2010. 'A prehistoric salt production site at Băile Figa, Romania'. *Eurasia Antiqua* 16: 131–167.

Harding, A. F., and A. Szemán. 2011. 'Evidence for prehistoric salt extraction rediscovered in the Hungarian central mining museum'. *The Antiquaries Journal* 91: 27–49.

Hellebrandt, M. 1999. *Celtic Finds from Northern Hungary: Corpus of Celtic Finds in Hungary III*. Budapest: Akadémiai Kiadó.

Husar, A. 1999. *Celţii şi germanii în Dacia romană*. Cluj-Napoca: Presa universitară clujeană.

Iaroslavschi, E. 1995. 'Conduits et citernes d'eau chez les daces des Monts d'Orăştie'. *Acta Musei Napocensis* 32: 135–143.

Iaroslavschi, E. 1997. *Tehnica la daci*. Cluj-Napoca: Muzeul National de Istorie a Transilvaniei.

Ignat, M. 2004. 'Un aspect particulier du Hallstatt récent à l'Est des Carpathes', in I. Niculiţă, A. Zanoci, and M. Băţ (eds) *Thracians and Circumpontic World: Proceedings of the Ninth International Congress of Thracology, Chişinău-Vadu lui Vodă, 6–11 September 2004* : 5–12. Chişinău: Cartdidact.

Jugănaru, G. 2005. *Cultura Babadag*. Constanţa: Ex Ponto.

Kacsó, K. 2011. 'Die Hügelnekropole von Lăpuş. Eine zusammenfassende Einleitung', in S. Berecki, R. E. Németh, and B. Rezi (eds) *Bronze Age Rites and Rituals in the Carpathian Basin: Proceedings of the International Colloquium from Târgu Mureş, 8–10 October 2010*: 213–244. Târgu Mureş: Editura Mega.

Kašuba, M. T. 2000. 'Rannee železo v lesostepi meždu Dnestrom i Siretom (Cul'tura Cozia-Saharna)'. *Stratum Plus* 3: 241–476.

Kašuba, M. T. 2003. 'Periferia de est a complexului hallstattian timpuriu cu ceramică incizată şi imprimată (secolele X–VIII î.e.n. în interfluviul Nistru-Siret)', in E. Sava (ed.) *Interferenţe cultural-cronologice în spaţiul nord-pontic*: 183–210. Chişinău: Institutul de Arheologie şi Etnografie.

Kašuba, M., V. Haheu, and O. Leviţki. 2000. *Vestigii traco-getice pe Nistrul mijlociu*. Bucharest: Vavila Edinf.

Kemenczei, T. 1984. *Die Spätbronzezeit Nordostungarns*. Archaeologia Hungarica N.S. 51. Budapest: Akadémiai Kiadó.

Kemenczei, T. 2009. *Studien zu den Denkmälern skythisch geprägter Alföld Gruppe*. Budapest: Magyar Nemzeti Múzeum.

Kriveczky, B. 1991. 'Régészeti ásatások Tiszafüred-Morotvaparton'. *Szolnok megyei múzeumi adattár* 32: 65–96.

Kull, B. 1997. 'Tod und Apotheose: zur Ikonographie in Grab und Kunst der jüngeren Eisenzeit an der unteren Donau und ihrer Bedeutung für die Interpretation von "Prunkgräbern"'. *Berichte der Römisch-Germanischen Kommission* 78: 197–466.

László, A. 1975. 'Începuturile metalurgiei fierului pe teritoriul României'. *Studii şi cercetări de istorie veche* 26: 17–40.

László, A. 1980. 'La région extracarpatique orientale à la fin du IIe millénaire et dans la première moitié du Ier millénaire av. n. è.', in R. Vulpe (ed.) *Actes du IIe Congrès International de Thracologie (Bucarest, 4–10 septembre 1976)*: 181–187. Bucharest: Editura Academiei.

László, A. 1989. 'Les groupes régionaux anciens du Hallstatt à l'est des Carpathes. La Moldavie aux XII–VII siècles av. n. è.', in M. Ulrix-Closset and M. Otte (eds) *La civilisation de Hallstatt—bilan d'une rencontre 1987*: 111–129. Liège: Université de Liège.

László, A. 1994. *Începuturile epocii fierului la est de Carpaţi: Culturile Gáva-Holihrady şi Corlăteni-Chişinău pe teritoriul Moldovei*. Bucureşti: S. C. Melior Trading.

László, A. 2012. 'Troy and the lower Danube region at the end of the Bronze Age', in G. Korres, N. Karadimas, and G. Flouda (eds) *Archaeology and Heinrich Schliemann—A Century after his Death: Assessments and Prospects. Myth—History—Science*: 50–60. Athens: Aegeus/Society for Aegean Prehistory.

Lazăr, S. 2007. 'Types of habitat at the end of the Bronze Age and the beginning of the Iron Age in Oltenia'. *Arhivele Olteniei* 21: 7–22.

Leviţki, O. 1994. *Cultura Hallstattului canelat la răsărit de Carpaţi*. Bucharest: Vavila Edinf.

Lockyear, K. 2004. 'The late Iron Age background to Roman Dacia', in W. S. Hanson and I. P. Haynes (eds) *Roman Dacia: The Making of a Provincial Society*: 33–74. Portsmouth, RI: Journal of Roman Archaeology.

Măndescu, D. 2010. *Cronologia perioadei timpurii a celei de a doua vârste a fierului (sec. V–III a. Chr.) între Carpaţi, Nistru şi Balcani*. Brăila: Editura Istros.

Marazov, I. 1996. *The Rogozen Treasure*. Sofia: Secor.

Mateevici, N. 2007. *Amforele greceşti din mediul barbar din nord-vestul Pontului Euxin în sec. VI–începutul sec. II a. Chr.* Biblioteca Tyragetia 14. Chişinău: Bons Offices.

Medeleț, F. 1982. 'În legătură cu expediția întreprinsă de Alexandru Macedon la Dunăre în 335 î.e.n.'. *Acta Musei Napocensis* 19: 13–22.
Medeleț, F. 1993. *Au sujet d'une grande spirale dacique en argent du Musée National de Belgrade*. Reșița: Caietele Banatica.
Medeleț, F. 1994. 'În legătură cu o mare spirală dacică de argint aflată în Muzeul Național din Belgrad'. *Analele Banatului, s.n., Arheologie-Istorie* 3: 192–230.
Medeleț, F. 1995. 'Über das Salz in Dakien'. *Archäologie Österreichs* 6, 2: 53–57.
Meshinev, T. 2007. 'Vegetation and phytogeography: a brief characteristic', in V. Fet and A. Popov (eds) *Biogeography and Ecology of Bulgaria*: 581–588. Dordrecht: Springer.
Metzner-Nebelsick, C. 1992. 'Gefäße mit basaraboider Ornamentik aus Frög', in A. Lippert and K. Spindler (eds) *Festschrift zum 50jährigen Bestehen des Institutes für Ur—und Frühgeschichte der Leopold-Franzens-Universität Innsbruck*. Universitätsforschungen zur Prähistorischen Archäologie 8: 349–383. Bonn: Habelt.
Metzner-Nebelsick, C. 1998. 'Abschied von den "Thrako-Kimmeriern"?—Neue Aspekte der Interaktion zwischen karpatenländischen Kulturgruppe der späten Bronze—und frühen Eisenzeit mit der osteuropäischen Steppenkoine', in B. Hänsel and J. Machnik (eds) *Das Karpatenbecken und die osteuropäische Steppe*. Prähistorische Archäologie in Südosteuropa 12: 361–422. Rahden: Marie Leidorf.
Metzner-Nebelsick, C. 2000. 'Early Iron Age nomadism in the Great Hungarian Plain—migration or assimilation? The Thraco-Cimmerian problem revisited', in J. Davis-Kimball, E. Murphy, L. Koryakova, and L. T. Yablonsky (eds) *Kurgans, Ritual Sites, and Settlements: Eurasian Bronze and Iron Age*. British Archaeological Reports International Series 890: 160–184. Oxford: Archaeopress.
Metzner-Nebelsick, C. 2010. 'Aspects of mobility and migration in the eastern Carpathian basin and adjacent areas in the early Iron Age (10th–7th centuries BC)', in K. Dzięgielewski, M. S. Przybyła, and A. Gawlik (eds) *Migrations in Bronze and Iron Age Europe*: 121–151. Kraków: Księgarnia Academicka.
Mihăilescu-Bîrliba, V. 1980. *La monnaie romaine chez les Daces Orientaux*. Bucharest: Editura Academiei.
Mihăilescu-Bîrliba, V. 1990. *Dacia răsăriteană îm sec. VI-I a. Chr. Economie și monedă*. Iași: Editura Junimea.
Morintz, S. 1987. 'Noi date și probleme privind perioadele hallstattiană timpurie și mijlocie în zona istro-pontică (Cercetările de la Babadag)'. *Thraco-Dacica* 8: 39–71.
Morintz, S., and P. Roman. 1969. 'Un nou grup hallstattian timpuriu în sud-vestul României—Insula Banului'. *Studii și cercetări de istorie veche* 20, 3: 393–423.
Moscalu, E. 1976. 'Die frühhallstattzeitlichen Gräber von Meri'. *Thraco-Dacica* 1: 77–86.
Moscalu, E. 1989. 'Das thrako-getische Fürstengrab von Peretu in Rumänien'. *Berichte der Römisch-Germanischen Kommission* 70: 129–190.
Mozsolics, A. 1957. 'Archäologische Beiträge zur Geschichte der Grossen Wanderung'. *Acta Archaeologica Hungaricae* 8: 119–156.
Mozsolics, A. 2000. *Bronzefunde aus Ungarn: Depotfundhorizonte Hajdúböszömény, Románd und Bükkszentlászló*. Prähistorische Archäologie in Südosteuropa 17. Kiel: Oetker-Voges.
Nemeth, E., A. Rustoiu, and H. Pop. 2005. *Limes dacicus occidentalis: Die Befestigungen im Westen Dakiens vor und nach der römischen Eroberung*. Cluj-Napoca: Editura Mega.
Németi, I. 1982. 'Das späthallstattzeitliche Gräberfeld von Sanislău.' *Dacia N. S.* 26: 115–144.
Németi, I. 1988. 'Necropola Latène de la Pișcolt, jud. Satu Mare. I'. *Thraco-Dacica* 9: 49–74.
Németi, I. 1989. 'Necropola Latène de la Pișcolt, jud. Satu Mare. II'. *Thraco-Dacica* 10: 75–114.

Nemeti, S. 2006. 'Scenarios on the Dacians: The indigenous districts'. *Studia Universitatis "Babeş-Bolyai" Series Historia* 51, 1: 86–98.

Nemeti, S., and M. Bărbulescu. 2010. 'Arcobadara'. *Latomus* 69: 446–455.

Nica, M. 1995. 'Câteva date despre necropola şi locuinţele hallstattiene timpurii de la Ghidici punctul "Balta Ţarova"'. *Cercetări arheologice în aria nord-tracă* 1: 236–246.

Nicolăescu-Plopşor, D. 1976. 'Considérations anthropologiques sur l'ensemble ritual géto-dace de Conţeşti-Argeş'. *Thraco-Dacica* 1: 227–230.

Nikolov, B. 1988–1989. 'Der Fund von Rogozen und seine Zusammensetzung', in A. Fol (ed.) *Der thrakische Silberschatz aus Rogozen Bulgarien*: 46–50. Sofia: Komitee für Kultur der Volksrepublik Bulgarien.

Párducz, M. 1973. 'Probleme der Skythenzeit im Karpatenbecken'. *Acta Archaeologica Academiae Scientiarum Hungaricae* 25: 27–63.

Patay, P. 1976. 'Vorbericht über die Ausgrabungen zu Poroszló-Aponhát'. *Folia Archaeologica* 27: 193–201.

Petrescu-Dîmboviţa, M. 1977. *Depozitele de bronzuri din România*. Bucharest: Editura Academiei Republicii Socialiste România.

Petrescu-Dîmboviţa, M. 1978. *Die Sicheln in Rumänien mit Corpus der jung- und spätbronzezeitlichen Horte Rumäniens*. Prähistorische Bronzefunde XVIII, 1. Munich: Beck.

Pflug, H. 1988. 'Chalkidische Helme', in A. Bottini (ed.) *Antike Helme: Sammlung Lipperheide und andere Bestände des Antikenmuseums Berlin*: 137–150. Mainz: Römisch-Germanisches Zentralmuseum.

Pleiner, R. 2000. *Iron in Archaeology: The European Bloomery Smelters*. Prague: Archeologický ústav AV ČR.

Pop, G. P. 2009. 'Transilvania, Banat, Crişana şi Maramureş. Caracteristici geografice', in I.-A. Pop and T. Nägler (eds) *Istoria Transilvaniei I*: 11–27. Cluj-Napoca: Institutul Cultural Român.

Popescu, E., and A. Vulpe. 1982. 'Nouvelles découvertes du typ Ferigile'. *Dacia N. S.* 26: 77–114.

Popovich, I. 1995–1996. 'Periodization and chronology of Kushtanovica type sites in the Transcarpathian region'. *A Nyíregyházi Jósa András Múzeum évkönyve* 37–38: 77–114.

Ramsl, P. 2003. 'Migrationsphänomene (?!) in der Frühlatènezeit'. *Mitteilungen der Anthropologischen Gesellschaft Wien* 133: 101–109.

Romsauer, P. 1991. 'The earliest wheel-turned pottery in the Carpathian Basin'. *Antiquity* 65: 358–367.

Romsauer, P. 1999. 'Zur Frage der Westgrenze der Mezőcsát-Gruppe', in E. Jerem and I. Poroszlai (eds) *Archaeology of the Bronze and Iron Age: Experimental Archaeology, Environmental Archaeology, Archaeological Parks*: 167–176. Budapest: Archaeolingua.

Ruscu, D. 2003. *Provincia Dacia în istoriografia antică*. Cluj-Napoca: Editura Nereamia Napocae.

Ruscu, L. 2002. *Relaţiile externe ale oraşelor greceşti de pe litoralul românesc al Mării Negre*. Cluj-Napoca: Presa universitară clujeană.

Russu, I. I. 1977. 'Die griechische und lateinische Schrift im vorrömischen Dakien', in D. M. Pippidi and E. Popescu (eds) *Epigraphica: Travaux dédié au VIIe Congrès d'épigraphie greque et latine (Constantza, 9–15 septembre 1977)*: 33–50. Bucharest: Editura Academiei.

Rustoiu, A. 1996. *Metalurgia bronzului la daci (sec. II î.Chr.–I d.Chr.). Tehnici, ateliere şi produse de bronz*. Bibliotheca Thracologica 15. Bucharest: Institutul Român de Tracologie.

Rustoiu, A. 2002a. 'Die östliche Gruppe der dakischen Schmucks. Eine Untersuchung bezüglich der interregionalen Beziehungen im vorrömischen Dakien', in A. Rustoiu and A.

Ursuțiu (eds) *Interregionale und Kulturelle Beziehungen im Karpatenraum*: 191–226. Cluj-Napoca: Nereamia Napocae.

Rustoiu, A. 2002b. 'Locuirile dacice', in V. Vasiliev, A, Rustoiu, E. Balaguri, and C. Cosma (eds) *Solotvino-Cetate (Ucraina Transcarpatică): Așezările din epoca bronzului, a doua vârstă a fierului și din evul mediu timpuriu*. Bibliotheca Thracologica 33. Cluj-Napoca: Napoca star.

Rustoiu, A. 2002c. *Războinici și artizani de prestigiu în Dacia preromană*. Cluj-Napoca: Editura Nereamia Napocae.

Rustoiu, A. 2005a. 'Dacia și Italia în sec. I a. Chr. Comerțul cu vase de bronz în perioada republicană târzie (Studiu preliminar)', in C. Cosma and A. Rustoiu (eds) *Comerț și civilizație: Transilvania în contextul schimburilor comerciale și culturale în antichitate—Trade and civilisation: Transylvania in the frame of trade and cultural exchanges in Antiquity*: 53–117. Cluj-Napoca: Editura Mega.

Rustoiu, A. 2005b. 'The Padea-Panagjurski Kolonii group in south-western Transylvania (Romania)', in H. Dobrzańska, V. Megaw, and P. Poleska (eds) *Celts on the Margin: Studies in European Cultural Interaction (7th Century BC–1st Century AD) Dedicated to Zenon Woźniak*: 109–119. Krakow: Institute of Archaeology and Ethnology of the Polish Academy of Sciences.

Rustoiu, A. 2006. 'A journey to Mediterranean. Peregrinations of a Celtic warrior from Transylvania'. *Studia Universitatis "Babeș-Bolyai" Series Historia* 51, 1: 42–85.

Rustoiu, A. 2006–2007. 'În legătură cu datarea fortificației dacice de la Divici'. *Ephemeris Napocensis* 16–17: 17–30.

Rustoiu, A. 2007. 'Thracian "sica" and Dacian "falx". The history of a "national" weapon', in S. Nemeti, F. Fodorean, E. Nemeth, et al. (eds) *Dacia felix: Studia Michaeli Bărbulescu oblata*: 67–82. Cluj-Napoca: Editura Tribuna.

Rustoiu, A. 2008. *Războinici și societate în aria celtică transilvăneană: Studii pe marginea mormântului cu coif de la Ciumești*. Cluj-Napoca: Editura Mega.

Rustoiu, A. 2009. 'Masters of metals in the Carpathian Basin (workshops, production centres and funerary manifestations in the early and middle La Tène)'. *Ephemeris Napocensis* 19: 7–21.

Rustoiu, A. 2011. 'The Celts from Transylvania and the eastern Banat and their southern neighbours. Cultural exchanges and individual mobility', in M. Guštin and M. Jevtić (eds) *The Eastern Celts: The Communities Between the Alps and the Black Sea*: 163–170. Koper/Belgrade: Annales Mediterranei.

Rustoiu, A. 2014. 'Indigenous and colonist communities in the eastern Carpathian Basin at the beginning of the Late Iron Age. The genesis of an eastern Celtic world', in C. N. Popa and S. Stoddart (eds) *Fingerprinting the Iron Age: Approaches to Identity in the European Iron Age: Integrating South-Eastern Europe into the Debate*: 142–156. Oxford: Oxbow.

Rustoiu, A., and S. Berecki. 2012. '"Thracian" warriors in Transylvania at the beginning of the late Iron Age. The grave with a Chalcidian helmet from Ocna Sibiului', in S. Berecki (ed.) *Iron Age Rites and Rituals in the Carpathian Basin: Proceedings of the International Colloquium from Târgu Mureș, 7–9 October 2011*: 161–182. Târgu Mureș: Editura Mega.

Rustoiu, A., and A. Comșa. 2004. 'The Padea-Panagjurski Kolonii group in southwestern Transylvania. Archaeological, historical and paleo-anthropological remarks', in A. Pescaru and I. V. Ferencz (eds) *Daco-Geții: 80 de ani de cercetări arheologice sistematice la cetățile dacice din Munții Orăștiei*: 267–276. Deva: Muzeul Civilizației Dacice și Romane.

Rustoiu, A., A. Comșa, and C. Lisovschi-Chelesanu. 1993. 'Practici funerare în așezarea dacică de la Sighișoara-Wietenberg (Observații preliminare)'. *Ephemeris Napocensis* 3: 81–94.

Rustoiu, A., and M. Egri. 2010. 'Danubian kantharoi—almost three decades later', in S. Berecki (ed.) *Iron Age Communities in the Carpathian Basin: Proceedings of the International Colloquium from Târgu Mureş, 9–11 October 2009* : 217–287. Cluj-Napoca: Editura Mega.

Rustoiu, A., and M. Egri. 2011. *The Celts from the Carpathian Basin between Continental Traditions and the Fascination of the Mediterranean: A Study of the Danubian Kantharoi.* Cluj-Napoca: Editura Mega.

Rustoiu, A., and G. T. Rustoiu. 2000. 'Aşezări din a doua vârstă a fierului descoperite recent pe teritoriul oraşului Alba Iulia'. *Apulum* 37, 1: 177–192.

Rusu, M. 1963. 'Die Verbreitung der Bronzehorte in Transilvanien vom Ende der Bronzezeit in die mittlere Hallstattzeit'. *Dacia N. S.* 7: 177–210.

Rusu, M. 1972. 'Consideraţii asupra metalurgiei aurului din Transilvania în Bronz D şi Hallstatt A'. *Acta Musei Napocensis* 9: 29–63.

Scheeres, M., C. Knipper, M. Hauschild, M. Schönfelder, W. Siebel, C. Pare, et al. 2014. '"Celtic migrations": fact or fiction? Strontium and oxygen isotope analysis of the Czech cemeteries of Radovesice and Kutna Hora in Bohemia'. *American Journal of Physical Anthropology* 155, 4: 496–512.

Scholtz, R. 2010. 'New data on the Skythian Age settlement history of Szabolcs County, Hungary', in S. Berecki (ed.) *Iron Age Communities in the Carpathian Basin: Proceedings of the International Colloquium from Târgu Mureş, 9–11 October 2009* : 79–98. Cluj-Napoca: Editura Mega.

Sîrbu, V. 1983. 'Câmpia Brăilei în sec. V–III î.e.n. Descoperiri arheologice şi interpretări istorice'. *Studii şi cercetări de istorie veche şi arheologie* 34, 1: 11–41.

Sîrbu, V. 1993a. *Credinţe şi practici funerare, religioase şi magice în lumea geto-dacilor.* Galaţi: Editura Porto-Franco.

Sîrbu, V. 1993b. 'Credinţe şi practici magico-vrăjitoreşti la traco-geto-daci'. *Banatica* 12: 129–175.

Sîrbu, V. 2006. *Man and Gods in the Geto-Dacian World.* Braşov: Editura C2 Design.

Sîrbu, V., and D. Dăvîncă. 2016. 'Children burials in northern Thracian settlements during the Iron Age'. *Istros* 22: 317–346.

Sîrbu, V., and G. Florea. 2000. *Les Géto-Daces: Iconographie et imaginaire.* Cluj-Napoca: Fondation Culturelle Roumaine.

Sîrbu, V., and N. Harţuche. 2000. 'Remarques sur le tumulus aristocratique de Găvani', in V. Lungu (ed.) *Pratiques funéraires dans l'Europe des XIIIe–Ier s. av. J.-C.: Actes du IIIe Colloque International d'Archéologie Funéraire, Tulcea 1997*: 139–153. Tulcea: Institutul de Cercetări Eco-Muzeale.

Sîrbu, V., and G. Trohani. 1997. 'Cités et établissements fortifiés entre les Carpathes Méridionales, le Danube et la mer Noire (Ve–IIIe s. av. J.-C.)', in P. Roman (ed.) *The Thracian World at the Crossroads of Civilisation 1*: 512–539. Bucharest: Vavila Edinf.

Smirnova, G. I. 1974. 'Complexe de tip Gáva-Holyhrady: o comunitate cultural-istorică'. *Studii şi cercetări de istorie veche şi arheologie* 25, 3: 359–380.

Spânu, D. 2012. *Tezaurele dacice: Creaţia în metale preţioase din Dacia preromană.* Bucharest: Editura Simetria.

Stöllner, T. 1998. 'Grab 102 vom Dürrnberg bei Hallein. Bemerkungen zu den Dürrnberger Kriegergräbern der Frühlatènezeit'. *Germania* 76, 1: 67–176.

Stoyanov, T., and Z. Mihaylova. 1996. 'Metal working in the Getic city in "Sboryanovo"'. *Ephemeris Napocensis* 6: 55–78.

Sümegi, P. 2011. 'A link between regions—the role of the Danube in the life of European communities', in G. Kovacs and G. Kulcsár (eds) *Ten Thousand Years along the Middle Danube.* Varia Archaeologica Hungarica 26: 9–41. Budapest: Archaeolingua.

Szabó, M. 2007. *L'habitat de l'époque de La Tène à Sajópetri Hosszú-dűlő*. Budapest: L'Harmattan.

Szabó, M., Z. Czajlik, K. Tankó, and L. Timár. 2008. 'Polgár 1: l'habitat du second Âge du Fer (IIIe siècle av. J.-Chr.)'. *Acta Archaeologica Academiae Scientiarum Hungaricae* 59: 183–223.

Szabó, V. G. 1996. 'A Csorva-csoport és a Gáva-kultúra kutatásának problémái néhány Csongrád megyei leletegyüttes allapján'. *A Móra Ferencz Múzeum Évkönyve. Studia Archaeologica* 2: 9–110.

Szabó, V. G. 2004. 'Ház, település és településszerkezet a késő bronzkori (BD, HA, HB periódus) Tisza-vidéken', in E. G. Nagy (ed.) *Momos II: Őskoros kutatók II: Összejövetelének konferenciakötete*: 137–170. Debrecen: Debreceni Déri Múzeum Kiadványai.

Teleagă, E. 2008. *Griechische Importe in den Nekropolen an der unteren Donau. 6. Jh.–Anfang des 3. Jh. v. Chr.* Marburger Studien zur Vor-und Frühgeschichte 23. Rahden: Marie Leidorf.

Todorova, H. 1972. 'Über einige Probleme der südosteuropäischen Früheisenzeit'. *Thracia* 1: 67–78.

Tonkova, M. 1994. 'Vestiges d'ateliers d'orfèvrerie thrace des Ve–IIIe s. av. J.-C. sur le territoire de la Bulgarie'. *Helis* 3: 175–200.

Tonkova, M. 1998. 'Les ateliers d'orfèvres de luxe en Thrace: mêthodes de localisation'. *Topoi* 8: 749–764.

Tonkova, M. 2000–2001. 'Classical jewellery in Thrace: Origins and development, archaeological contexts'. *Talanta* 32–33: 277–288.

Torbov, N. 2005. *Mogilanskata tumulus in Vratsa*. Vratza: Obština.

Trohani, G. 1988. 'Materiale de construcţie din lut ars descoperite în aşezările geto-dacice'. *Thraco-Dacica* 9: 161–170.

Tsetskhladze, G. 1998. 'Who built the Skythian and Thracian royal and elite tombs?' *Oxford Journal of Archaeology* 17, 1: 55–92.

Ursachi, V. 1986–1987. 'Fortificaţii dacice pe valea Siretului'. *Carpica* 18–19: 31–52.

Ursachi, V. 1995. *Zargidava: Cetatea dacică de la Brad*. Bucharest: Vavila Edinf.

Ursuţiu, A. 2002. *Etapa mijlocie a primei vârste a fierului în Transilvania*. Cluj-Napoca: Editura Nereamiae Napocae.

Vagalinski, L. 2011. 'A new late La Tène pottery kiln with a bread oven on the lower Danube (northern Bulgaria)', in M. Guštin and M. Jevtić (eds) *The Eastern Celts: The Communities Between the Alps and the Black Sea*: 219–226. Koper/Belgrade: Annales Mediterranei.

Vasiliev, V. 1976. 'Necropola de la Băiţa şi problema tracizării enclavei scitice din Transilvania'. *Marisia* 6: 49–87.

Vasiliev, V. 1980. *Sciţii agatârşi pe teritoriul României*. Cluj-Napoca: Editura Dacia.

Vasiliev, V. 1983. 'Probleme ale cronologiei Hallstattului în Transilvania'. *Acta Musei Napocensis* 20: 33–57.

Vasiliev, V. 1995. *Fortifications de refuge et établissements fortifiés du premier Âge du Fer en Transylvanie*. Bucharest: Institut Roumain de Thracologie.

Vasiliev, V. 1999. 'Date noi despre necropola de la sfârşitul primei vârste a fierului descoperită la Uioara de Sus (jud. Alba)'. *Thraco-Dacica* 20: 181–188.

Vasiliev, V., I. A. Aldea, and H. Ciugudean. 1991. *Civilizaţia dacică timpurie în aria intracarpatică a României*. Cluj-Napoca: Editura Dacia.

Vulpe, A. 1970. 'Archäologische Forschungen und historische Betrachtungen über die Periode des 7.–5. Jh. im Donaukarpatenraum'. *Memoria Antiquitatis* 2: 115–213.

Vulpe, A. 1986. 'Zur Entstehung der geto-dakischen Zivilisation. Die Basarabikultur'. *Dacia N. S.* 30: 49–90.

Vulpe, A., and V. Mihăilescu-Bîrliba. 1980–1982. 'Tezaurul de la Rădeni—Neamţ'. *Memoria Antiquitatis* 12–14: 41–63.

Vulpe, A., and E. Popescu. 1972. 'Contribution à la connaissance des débuts de la culture géto-dacique dans la zone subcarpatique Vâlcea-Argeş (La nécropole tumulaire de Tigveni)'. *Dacia N. S.* 16: 75–111.

Vulpe, A., and E. Popescu. 1970. 'Une contribution archéologique à l'étude de la religion des Géto-Daces'. *Thraco-Dacica* 1: 217–226.

Vulpe, R., and S. Teodor. 2003. *Piroboridava: Aşezarea geto-dacică de la Poiana.* Bucharest: Vavila Edinf.

Werner, W. M. 1988. *Eisenzeitliche Trensen an der unteren und mittleren Donau*. Prähistorische Bronzefunde XVI, 4. Munich: Beck.

Wožniak, Z. 1974. *Wschodnie pogranicze kultury latènskiej*. Wrocław/Warsaw/Kraków/Gdansk: Zakł. Narod. im. Ossolińskich.

Zanoci, A. 1998. *Fortificaţiile geto-dacice din spaţiul extracarpatic în secolele VI–III a. Chr.* Bucharest: Vavila Edinf.

Zirra, V. 1980. 'Locuiri din a doua vârstă a fierului în nord-vestul României (Aşezarea contemporană cimitirului La Tène de la Ciumeşti şi habitatul indigen de la Berea)'. *Satu Mare. Studii şi Comunicări* 4: 39–84.

Zirra, V. V. 1996–1998. 'Bemerkungen zu den thraco-getischen Fibeln'. *Dacia N. S.* 40–42: 29–53.

CHAPTER 15

THE NORTHERN BLACK SEA AND NORTH CAUCASUS

SABINE REINHOLD AND
VALENTINA I. MORDVINTSEVA

Introduction

For most of the last 150 years, the archaeology of the first millennium BC in the northern Black Sea region has been dominated by research on two intertwined peoples, both of whom left behind spectacular monuments and magnificent objects—the 'Scythians' and the 'north Pontic Greeks'. The latter arrived on the Black Sea shores as traders and early colonists—the foundation of the trading post at Berezan in the mid-seventh century BC is the earliest fixed point (Solov'ev 1999)—while the former had occupied the inland steppe belt north of the Black Sea for just a few decades longer.

The origin of the mounted warrior federations, labelled in ancient Greek literature as 'Scythians', lay far away in the steppes of central Asia and the Altai mountains (for an overview, see Parzinger 2004). Elite burial paraphernalia rich in gold, with similar stylistic codes found from southern Siberia to Ukraine, have been displayed at several major international exhibitions such as *Gold of the Nomads, Scythian Treasures from Ancient Ukraine* in the USA (2001), *Under the Sign of the Golden Griffin* in Germany (2007), and *Scythians, Warriors of Ancient Siberia* in the UK (2017), to name but a few. These exhibitions brought this spectacular material to a wider audience and shed light on the vast Eurasian dimension of early Iron Age eastern Europe. The splendid gold and silver jewellery, impressive scale armour, and humans and horses dressed up with precious metal that were buried in Scythian royal tombs of the fifth and fourth centuries BC have until recently eclipsed many other no less important archaeological remains of the Iron Age populations living between the Caucasus and the northern shores of the Black Sea.[1]

Geography

The Black Sea is surrounded by varied environments and habitats: dense forests on the eastern and southern shores, the Eurasian steppe to the north, and the Caucasus mountains to the east (Figure 15.1). Its cultural diversity to some degree reflects adaptations to these very different settings, from mountain dwellers to nomadic steppe inhabitants. The western shores are dominated by the plains of the Danube, Dniester, and Prut, which rise in the Carpathian mountains. They surround a well-watered hilly environment, which belongs to the steppe belt stretching from here to central Asia.

The Dnieper (Greek *Borysthenēs*) is the principal river in the centre of the northern Black Sea region. Its lower course runs through the steppe, but north-west of Dnipropetrovs'k, the river flows through hilly forest steppe. Until the nineteenth century, the famous Dnieper rapids hindered about 70 km of its course across the crystalline bedrock; they form an important geographical division. The archaeological literature often discusses the right and left banks of the Dnieper separately. To the east, the Donec hills divide the Dnieper from the Don basin. The flat steppe continues into the Kuma-Manych basin, which divides the south Russian plains from Caucasia. To the south lies the Sea of Azov.

The northern (premontane) part of the Crimean peninsula belongs to the steppe, but its southern part is mountainous, with forest vegetation. Crimea is today linked

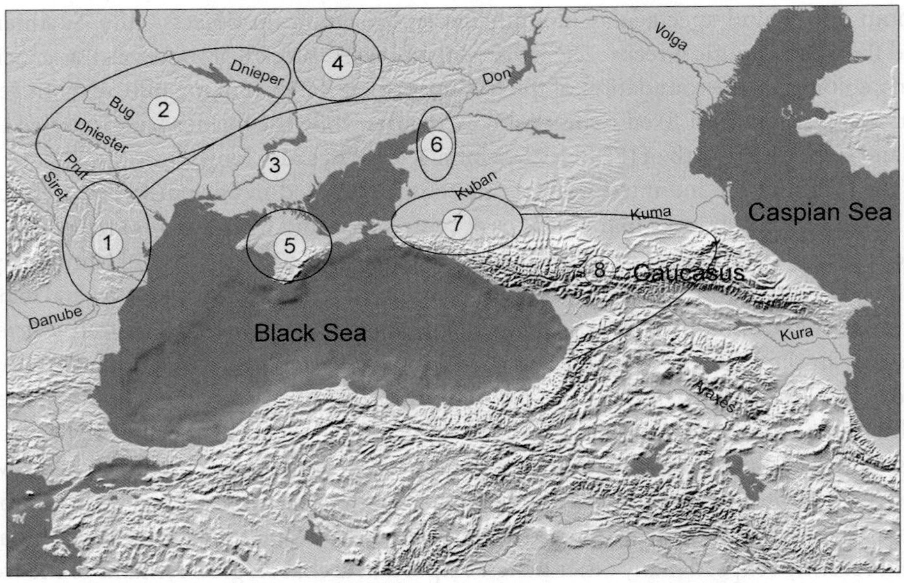

FIGURE 15.1 Late Bronze Age to early Iron Age cultures of the first half of the first millennium BC. 1 Cozia-Sacharna culture, 2 Chernoles-Zhabotin cultures, 3 Chernogorovka culture, 4 Bondarikha culture, 5 Kizil Koba culture, 6 Late Bronze Age Kobyakovo culture, 7 Proto-Maeotian culture, 8 Koban-Colchis culture.

to the mainland by a narrow isthmus of rather marshy land. The Strait of Kerch (the Cimmerian-Bosporos) divides Crimea from the Taman peninsula to the east, and gives entry to the Sea of Azov and the Don river system. Until the first century BC, a second strait (the Taman-Bosporus) existed where the Taman peninsula is now connected to the mainland (Kelterbaum et al. 2011). This allowed early Greek colonists to pass along the coast much further to the east than previously thought, and calls into question the locations of ancient Greek cities in this part of the Black Sea region (Dan and Gehrke forthcoming).

The Great Caucasus mountains east of the Black Sea form the last coherent sub-region. Their peaks rise to 4,500 m, with the volcano of Mount El'brus the highest point (5,642 m). The Caucasus is divided into separate micro-regions by rivers running south to north, but crossing the mountains in summer is not difficult. The piedmonts are characterized by fairly flat plateaus and a hilly, well-watered, and wooded environment. The largest rivers are the Kuban, disgorging into the Black Sea, and the Kuma and Terek, flowing into the Caspian Sea.

Research Paradigms, Chronologies, and Historical Overview

Herodotus (*c.*484–425 BC) is our major historical source for the non-Greek peoples in the northern Black Sea area (Ivantchik 2001, 2005). Beside the Scythians, the most important group were the Cimmerians, who according to Herodotus inhabited the area prior to the Scythians, by whom they were expelled from their homeland (*Histories* 1.15). The Cimmerians appear as 'Gimirrāia' in Assyrian texts for the year 714 BC in the reign of Sargon II, when they defeated an Urartian army under Rusa I. In the late eighth and early seventh centuries BC, 'Gimirrāia' operated in the area north of Assyria, and are mentioned in passing in Lykia, Ionia, and Phrygia (Ivantchik 2001; Metzner-Nebelsick 2000: 504–506).

The strong interdependence of archaeology and history for previous generations of Russian and Soviet scholars[2] led them to scour the archaeological record for traces of this oldest mentioned population. For a time, a Bronze Age substrate was discussed as representing Herodotus' Cimmerians, who later lost their homeland (Metzner-Nebelsick 2000). In a seminal work, A. A. Iessen (1953) shifted this event to the start of the Iron Age, and for the first time systematized early Iron Age material from the north Black Sea area, defining two pre-Scythian phases (Chernogorovka and Novocherkassk), with different sets of horse-gear and weapons, arguing that both reflected 'Cimmerians'. From then on, the archaeological material has been discussed under this label, and deemed to reflect the ethnic reality of later prehistory in the region as documented by ancient authors (e.g. Chochorowski 1993; Makhortych 1994).

In an overview of Chernogorovka and Novocherkassk sites in the northern Black Sea area, A. I. Terenozhkin (1976) related both phases to a 'Cimmerian' culture. Since the 'Gimirrāia' were first mentioned in 714 BC, a date in the eighth century BC seemed realistic for the Pontic sites. In the 1970s to 1990s, however, excavations brought to light a much larger number of characteristic horse-gear and weaponry at north Caucasian sites than in the northern Black Sea area. After an episode of searching for Cimmerians in the Caucasus (e.g. Makhortych 1994), most scholars now agree that these objects do not relate directly to Pontic cultures, but evolved in the north Caucasus (Dudarev 1991; Dubovskaya 1997; Metzner-Nebelsick 2002; Erlikh 2007; Reinhold 2007). North of the Black Sea, material of this period is still assigned to 'Cimmerians' (Skoryj 1999; Makhortych 2005), despite critiques of the purely ethnic interpretation of archaeological cultures (Dubovskaya 1997).

Defining the earliest 'Scythians' in the west is similarly dominated by discussion of which archaeological remains reflect what kind of historical ethnic group (e.g. Ivantchik 2001). Assyrian sources name the 'Ishkuzai', assumed to be the Greek 'Scythians', in connection with the 'Gimirrāia' under Sargon II (Parzinger 2004: 19–24; Ivantchik 2001). During the reign of Asarhaddon in the seventh century BC, the 'Ishkuzai' achieved political influence as confederates and were a constant threat to several Near Eastern kingdoms. At the start of the sixth century BC their role faded, and it is assumed that they moved via the Caucasus into the north Pontic steppe.

The sixth century BC was thus long considered the earliest possible date for Scythian material in the north Caucasus (Iessen 1953), but the discovery of Novocherkassk-related elements in early mounds at Kelermes in the Kuban region led to a reconsideration (Galanina 1997: 173–193). The earliest Scythian impact on north Caucasian and north Black Sea groups was shown to be reflected in specific types of horse-gear, either parallel to, or even part of, the Novocherkassk horizon in the later eighth century BC (Kossack 1987; Medvedskaja 1992). Based on the sequence at Kelermes and other burials with Near Eastern imports, a tripartite chronology has been developed, extending from the eighth century until 600 BC (early Scythian I–III; Table 15.1).

Scythian chronology of the fifth and fourth centuries BC is based on the splendid 'royal' burial mounds, with their Greek imports, from both sides of the river Dnieper. The historical sources inform us about this period and name several Scythian kings, but the political history, and especially the assignment of excavated tombs to specific kings, is problematic (Alekseev 1996). The fifth and fourth centuries BC nevertheless saw the blossoming of Scythian culture in the north Black Sea area (Chernenko et al. 1986; Ol'chovskij 1991; Mozolevskiy and Polin 2005; Alekseev 2007; Polin 2007).

The end of the Scythian culture in the north Pontic region is usually associated with the appearance of a new Iranian people—the Sarmatians (or Sauromatians). It is generally accepted that in the course of the Sarmatian invasion, the Scythians moved from the Dnieper region to Crimea and Dobrudzha (Dobrogea). 'Late Scythian culture' was the name given to the non-Greek archaeological sites of Crimea dated from the third century BC to the mid-third century AD (Koltukhov and Yurochkin 2004: 42). The same label was attributed to the settlements and flat cemeteries that appeared by the second century BC along the lower Dnieper (Bylkova 2007) and lower Dniester (Popa 2012). The burial mounds, on the contrary, were ascribed to the Sarmatians, who advanced into the north Pontic steppe from the east. A similar

Table 15.1 Correlation of Scythian and Sarmatian chronologies in the Circumpontic area

North Pontic area		North-west Caucasus	
Pre-Scythian	10th/9th century BC		
Early Scythian I / Novocherkassk	8th century BC	Proto-Maeotian	9th to mid-7th century BC
Early Scythian II	700–650 BC	Early Maeotian	Late 7th to early 4th century BC
Early Scythian III	650–600 BC	Middle Maeotian I	4th to early 3rd century BC
Royal Scythian	5th to 4th century BC	Middle Maeotian II	3rd to mid-1st century BC
Late Scythian	3rd century BC to mid-3rd century AD	Late Maeotian / Sarmatian	1st to 3rd century AD

situation can be observed in the Kuban region. The main sedentary population of this area is regarded as Maeotian, a group who, according to the ancient authors, were divided into several tribes. The archaeological sites here were accordingly united as the Maeotian culture, although the kurgan cemeteries are generally ascribed to the Sarmatians. N. V. Anfimov (1954, 1961) developed an evolutionary model for the region divided into five periods spanning the eighth century BC to the third century AD.

The appearance of the Sarmatians seems to be mentioned in a passage of Diodorus Siculus (*Library of History* 2.43.7), and might have happened at the end of the fourth or in the early third century BC (Tokhtasyev 2005: 292). Later, the whole northern Black Sea territory was called European Sarmatia (Ptolemy *Geography* 3.5). In Russian academic literature the term 'Sarmatian period' was introduced for the period from the third century BC to the fourth century AD.

There are several views on the origins of the Sarmatian archaeological culture in the northern Black Sea area. M. I. Rostovtzeff (1929) proposed long-distance migration (Mordvintseva 2013), whereby the north Pontic steppes were periodically invaded by new groups of Iranian-speaking nomads from the Far East, their presence supposedly marked by certain objects in the ostentatious burials. Rostovtzeff ascribed the first wave of migration to the Saka, who brought gold polychrome brooches and silver *phalerae* from horse harnesses, and the second wave to the Ÿue-chi with gold Animal style objects (Rostovtzeff 1929: 45, 67–68, 93–94), noting that the spread of the Sarmatian Animal style coincided with the first written mention of the Alani or Alans (Rostovtzeff 1922: 116). In the mid-twentieth century this idea was replaced by models of short-distance migration. According to this hypothesis, the homeland of the Sarmatians was the Volga-Ural steppe. The spread of Sarmatian culture was envisaged in terms of four successive stages dating between the sixth century BC and the fourth century AD (Grakov 1947).[3] From this region, the culture spread westward and eastward by diffusion. Thus, while the starting point was now the Volga-Ural area, Rostovtzeff's thesis about a continuous migration of Sarmatian hordes over the Caspian steppes to the west remained partly valid.

A different model of long-distance migration was formulated by A. Skripkin (1990, 1997), drawing on new material that had accumulated by the end of the 1980s. He regarded each stage of the Sarmatian culture as corresponding to a new nomadic wave from the east, emphasizing the cyclical character of these movements. He attributed the early Sarmatian (Prokhorovka) culture to the Aorsi, the middle Sarmatian to the Alani, and the late Sarmatian to nameless tribes of Iranian origin. Specific artefacts were correlated with each new wave, brought about by ethnic changes in the eastern steppes. All the rich burials from the Dniester to the Volga were interpreted as Alanian (Skripkin 1997: 12). The chronology of Sarmatian cultures was also formulated in accordance with ideas about when certain peoples appeared on the historical scene. This scheme is reflected in the latest periodization (Berlizov 2011). However, neither migration model can explain the absence from the lower Dnieper region of archaeological sites similar to those of the archetypical Volga-Don culture in the period of the inferred Sarmatian invasion.

The disappearance of Scythian barrows by the third century BC, followed by an almost total absence of archaeological sites, gave rise to a new research approach. According to this view, the changes in the north Pontic region were a product of an environmental catastrophe and economic factors (Polin 1992), but this theory has been criticized by both archaeologists and historians (Vinogradov 1997: 106–107; Bruyako 1999). Yet another hypothesis, drawing on literary sources, epigraphy, and archaeology, proposes that the invasion happened in the opposite direction, and was a 'Celtic' movement from the west (Ruban 1985: 43–44; Vinogradov 1997).

The problem cannot be solved by a simple choice between migration from west or east. Although great advances have been made, the archaeological data are still primarily used to illustrate paradigms rooted in the written sources. The complexity and diversity of the archaeology of the north Pontic region could have been affected by a multiplicity of factors: the arrival of Greek settlers on the northern shores of the Black Sea, the expansion of the Roman Empire, pressure of nomadic tribes from the east, an advance of Celtic-Thracian peoples from the west, changing environmental conditions, and others besides. To reveal the nature of cultural exchange and interaction between various groups on the periphery of the classical world, one must disengage from the narrative tradition and previous explanatory models, and rely on analysis of the archaeological data, the quantity and representativeness of which have meanwhile moved to a qualitatively new level.

Regional Groups in the Early Iron Age

The earliest horse-mounted nomads arrived from the central Asian steppes in the mid to late eighth century BC, first in the lower Volga and the north Caucasus, then later in

Table 15.2 Correlation of cultures and chronological phases in the Circumpontic area, thirteenth to seventh centuries BC

	North-west Pontic	North Pontic steppe	North Pontic forest steppe	Crimea	Caucasus
14th/13th–10th/ 9th century BC	Belogrudovskaya	Belozërka	Bondarikha	Belozërka Crimean variant	Late Bronze Age/Koban A
10th/9th century BC	Cozia-Sacharna	Early Chernogorovka	Chernoles	Kizil Koba	Koban-Colchis/ Koban B
early 8th century BC		Late Chernogorovka/ Novocherkassk	Zhabotin I		Koban-Colchis/ Koban C1
~ 750 BC	Soldanesti		Zhabotin II		Koban C2
7th century BC		Early Scythian II	Zhabotin III		Koban-Colchis/ Koban D

the northern Black Sea region. They changed the lifeways of the indigenous late Bronze Age population considerably, introducing a new mobile lifestyle, social structure, and very different material culture. However, this profound caesura—which affected the whole interwoven network of local cultures from the north Caucasus to the mouth of the Danube (Table 15.2) at more or less the same time but in very different ways—took place after the late Bronze Age to early Iron Age transition, and was not linked to the adoption of iron. In some cultures, the metal was a marker for these changes, but in other areas, such as the Caucasus, iron was already used in the fourteenth and thirteenth centuries BC (Khakhutaishvili 2009).

The Central Northern Black Sea Area

During the later Bronze Age, the north Pontic steppe was inhabited by various groups with a predominantly settled lifestyle, mixed economy, and medium to large cemeteries, derived from the earlier Timber-grave culture. The Belozërka culture is characterized by small settlements with stone architecture and sunken pit-houses much as in the preceding centuries (Pieniążek 2012). Burials generally occur in small, linear flat-grave cemeteries, sometimes with one or two burials in larger pits, covered by mortuary chambers and mounds (Vanchugov 1990). During its later phase, the number of settlements diminished, indicating a shift towards a more mobile lifestyle. By the twelfth or eleventh century BC, settlements had disappeared, and the number of burial sites also decreased dramatically (Makhortych and Ievlev 1992; Pieniążek 2012). A significant increase in temperature, resulting in severe desiccation of the steppe belt, is held responsible for this depopulation. Signs of desertification are found at several sites and the process is illustrated in pollen diagrams. At the end of the second millennium BC, the north Pontic area was almost completely depopulated, apart from small groups with apparently semi-nomadic lifestyles.

The early Iron Age in the north Pontic region starts in the first quarter of the tenth century BC and is divided into several cultural groups situated in specific environments (see Figure 15.1). The Chernogorovka culture in the steppe extends from the lower Dniester to the middle Don and the northern part of the Caucasian steppe. In the forest steppe the Chernoles culture emerged from the Bronze Age Belogrudovskaya culture, later spawning the Zhabotin culture of the eighth and seventh centuries BC in the central Dnieper area (Daragan 2011). The Zhabotin culture has three variants. Zhabotin pottery is frequently found in the steppe zone, where it is associated with Chernogorovka burials. For a long time Zhabotin imports were considered to be a characteristic of the Novocherkassk horizon, but M. Daragan has shown that the internal chronology was much longer; stylistically, the material is closely related to eastern European Hallstatt groups[4] such as Cozia-Sacharna, Cisinau-Korlaten, Gava, and Gornia-Kalakača.

There are two opposing models for the north Pontic steppe. Emphasizing the heterogeneity of archaeological complexes subsumed as Novocherkassk, Dubovskaya (1997) rejects this term as a cultural group or chronological stage. Burials with Novocherkassk elements in the forest steppe (such as Kvitki, Butënki, Nosachevo, and Olshana) and the steppe (e.g. Vysokaya mogila burial 2) contain similar sets of weapons—iron spears, socketed arrowheads, and horse-gear—associated with local pottery and burial customs. Pointing to the warrior character of these elite burials, Dubovskaya (1997) supposes them to be local leaders partaking in an 'international' style. She therefore restricts the Chernogorovka culture to the steppe zone and proposes a three-stage development: transitional Berëzovka/Chernogorovka (tenth to ninth centuries BC), early Chernogorovka, and late Chernogorovka (this last identical with the Novocherkassk horizon). Following this, the earliest 'Scythian' cultures developed from a mixture of local and foreign elements.

The early Chernogorovka phase is linked with crouched burials in pits, which contain a medium-sized pot or small beaker, sometimes decorated with a band of incised geometric patterns. In the north-eastern regional variant, elements of horse harness made of bone and bronze are found. Late Chernogorovka/Novocherkassk graves are characterized by extended burials in pits or catacomb-like niches (Figure 15.2). They contain similar pots and beakers, albeit now decorated with more complex patterns, like Zhabotin pottery. Iron daggers, lances and knives, whetstones, bone and socketed bronze arrowheads, and horse-gear with decorated buckles complete the grave sets. The bronze types of both Chernogorovka phases are of Caucasian origin.

A very different view of the material is presented by Makhortych (2005), who divides the steppe burials into a Chernogorovka group with crouched burials and a Novocherkassk group with extended burials, both representing 'Cimmerian' tribes and

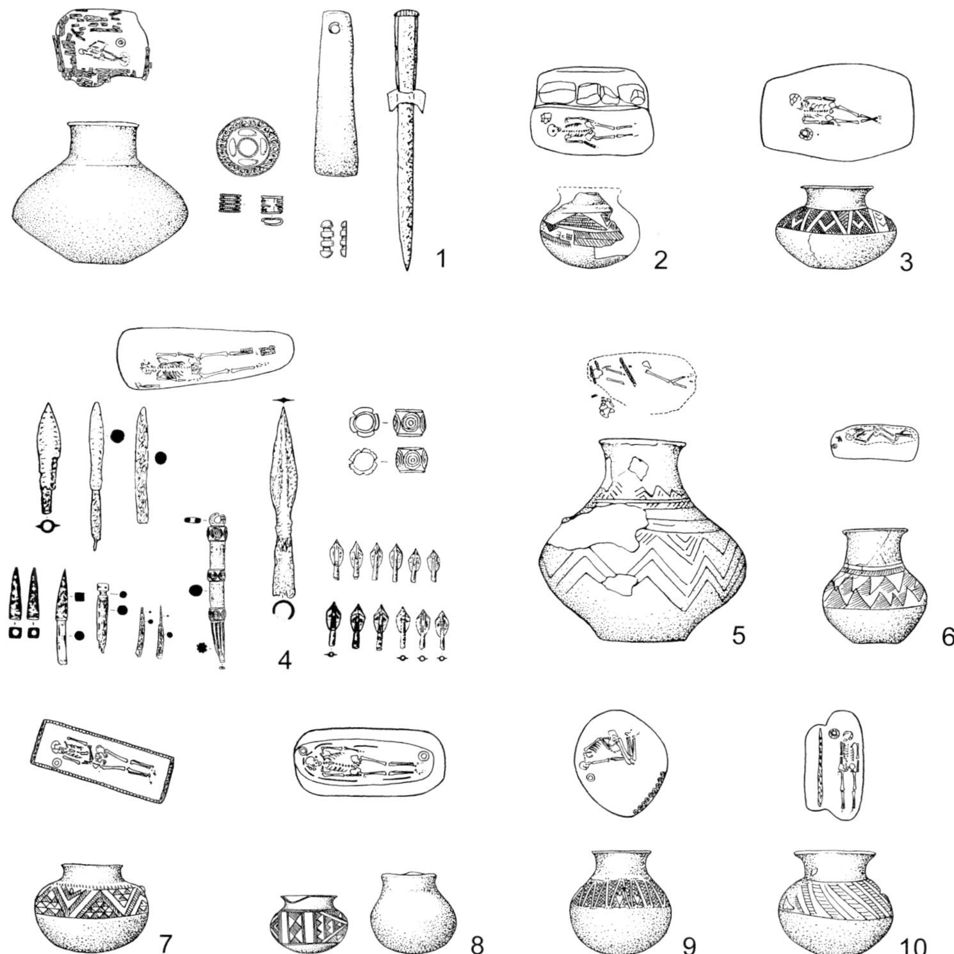

FIGURE 15.2 Late Chernogorovka burials. 1 Vysokaya mogila 2; 2 Kostychi 1/8; 3 Sofievka 40/2; 4 Baranovka I/10/11; 5 Balkovo kurgan 1/1; 6 Krasnaya Polyana 3/6; 7 Kaushany 1/2; 8 Vasil'evka 1/8; 9 Spasskoe 11/3/3; 10 Ivanovka 4/11. Various scales.

Source: after Dubovskaya 1997: figs 2–14

divided into three phases. The models cannot be reconciled, but the chronological stages are more or less comparable. Finally, Skoryj (1999) identifies thirteen burial complexes from the forest steppe with wealthy equipment and burial chambers under mounds as 'Cimmerian'. For Dubovskaya (1997), however, they would be local Chernoles chiefs using weapons of Caucasian origin to symbolize leadership.

No more than 150–160 burial complexes are known for the entire period, essentially single graves at separate sites. The low density of burials, as well as the lack of settlements point to a mobile, nomadic lifestyle (Makhortych 2005: 282–286), but Dubovskaya would see the regional groups as representing a semi-nomadic economy.

In contrast to the steppe, the Chernoles and later Zhabotin cultures of the forest steppe represent settled communities with permanent sites and mixed agriculture (Daragan 2011). During the later phase of the Chernoles culture, many small hillforts were established on lower river terraces. Burials seem to be dominated by cremations. At the end of the ninth century BC, the existing sites were abandoned. This was long supposed to be the result of 'Cimmerian' raids, but a shift in the settlement system is more likely (Daragan 2009, 2011: 49–73, 706–735). Huge (up to 100 ha), impressively fortified hillforts such as Zhabotin were now built on plateaus amidst the former Chernoles landscape. The process reflects a concentration of population into fewer, larger sites. At the moment ten such sites are known between the Dnieper and Dniester. At Zhabotin several buildings have been excavated, most of them built with wooden posts of a considerable size. Two houses had decorated hearths, which Daragan interprets as altars, and the buildings consequently as ritual or cultic places. Over the next 200 years we also see the development of more complex ornaments and new vessel forms, such as cups with high handles and carinated bowls.

Early Zhabotin cremation burials are found under small mounds without any interior constructions. During the third Zhabotin phase, the earliest 'Scythian' imports appear, e.g. in mound no. 524 near Zhabotin. At the end of the eighth and start of the seventh century BC, people started to move from Zhabotin, and by the end of Zhabotin III the site was practically abandoned.

The post-Zhabotin phase saw another fundamental change in settlement patterns and ceramic traditions. By the end of the seventh century BC, vast fortified sites of between 100 and 800 ha replaced the Zhabotin sites. The best known is the gigantic complex at Belsk, which comprises three separate fortified areas, linked by earthworks, in all covering around 4,400 ha, and is held to be a 'Scythian' agricultural site (Rolle and Murzin 1998). Another important site is Nemirovskoe (Daragan 2009). The post-Zhabotin phase corresponds to the early Scythian II–III burials and the first Greek settlements on the Black Sea shore at Olbia, Panticapaion, and Mymekrion. Greek pottery occurs on inland sites from a very early date. The first imports are painted Greek wares; from the sixth century onwards a grey, wheel-made pottery was developed under Greek influence, mostly in the north-western part of the Black Sea region (Kashuba et al. 2010).

Crimea

Apart from a few steppe-related burials, Crimea forms a rather isolated cultural entity. In the thirteenth to tenth centuries BC, a variant of the Belozërka culture developed out of the local Timber-grave culture, on its western shore and in the mountains (Kolotuchin 1996). Fifteen settlements and several cave sites are known. Some excavated sites have revealed a subterranean stone architecture of square houses with entrance corridors; others had subterranean post-framed houses. The inhabitants were clearly settled and practised mixed agriculture with a preference for sheep. Burials are crouched inhumations, some under mounds, some not. At first stone cists are found, but pit burials were more common.

At the turn of the tenth century BC, many new sites were founded in the mountains, the foothills, and on the coast. They have a changed material culture, including cups and beakers, some with incised geometric motifs. This phenomenon is related to the formation of the Kizil Koba culture, which spans the tenth to the third or second century BC. The first settlements were small hamlets along the mountain rivers. Settlement density increased, and houses were predominantly built with a post frame. The economy seems to include some kind of mobile herding, since the preference for sheep shifted towards a dominance of cattle and horses. A distinctive feature of the Kizil Koba culture was a specific form of burial in lined-up stone cists with up to fifty burials. In the earlier phase small cists were built in neat rows, surrounded by interlinked/conjoining square enclosures (Figure 15.3, A). From the sixth century BC onwards, multiple burials occurred, which resulted in larger stone cists, and more objects were found in graves.

Attempts have been made to link the Kizil Koba culture with the Taurs known from written sources as inhabitants of the Crimea in later periods, through the use of the term proto-Taurian, but Kolotuchin (1996: 71–86) warns against an overly narrow ethnic perspective, using the presence of both Chernogorovka/Novocherkassk and early 'Scythian' imports and burial sites to argue for a culturally open and integrative population.

The North Caucasus

The piedmont of the north Caucasus is an ideal landscape for mountain agriculture and a settled lifestyle. A mild climate and a well-watered but not over-steep terrain form an excellent basis for supporting a large population. However, until recently the late Bronze Age was a rather shadowy epoch, with only a handful of known sites, among them settlements of the Kobyakovo variant of the late Timber-grave culture in the Kuban area.

Recent research has revealed an unexpected new settlement landscape on a plateau at between 1,400 m and 2,400 m altitude south of the Caucasian Mineral Waters area with its abundant springs (Reinhold et al. 2007; Belinskiy et al. 2009). A complex stone architecture developed here from the seventeenth century BC onwards. Between the fourteenth/thirteenth and tenth/ninth centuries BC, when lower temperatures and increased precipitation fostered settled life in the steppe belt as well, the highlanders developed multifunctional houses incorporating stables (Reinhold et al. 2017) and a dairy economy based on summer transhumance (*Almwirtschaft*). In the neighbouring high mountain valleys of Abchazia, Svantia, and Racha a great number of copper and antimony mines date to this period (Maisuradze and Gobedishvili 2001), as do the well-known rich burials of highland Ossetia, such as Verchnyaya Rutcha and Faskau (Motzenbäcker 1996). This flourishing period ended in the tenth century BC, when most mountain sites have reduced numbers of burials or were abandoned altogether.

It was at this time that the early Iron Age cultures of the Caucasus took shape. They are traditionally divided into the Koban culture on the northern, and the Colchis culture

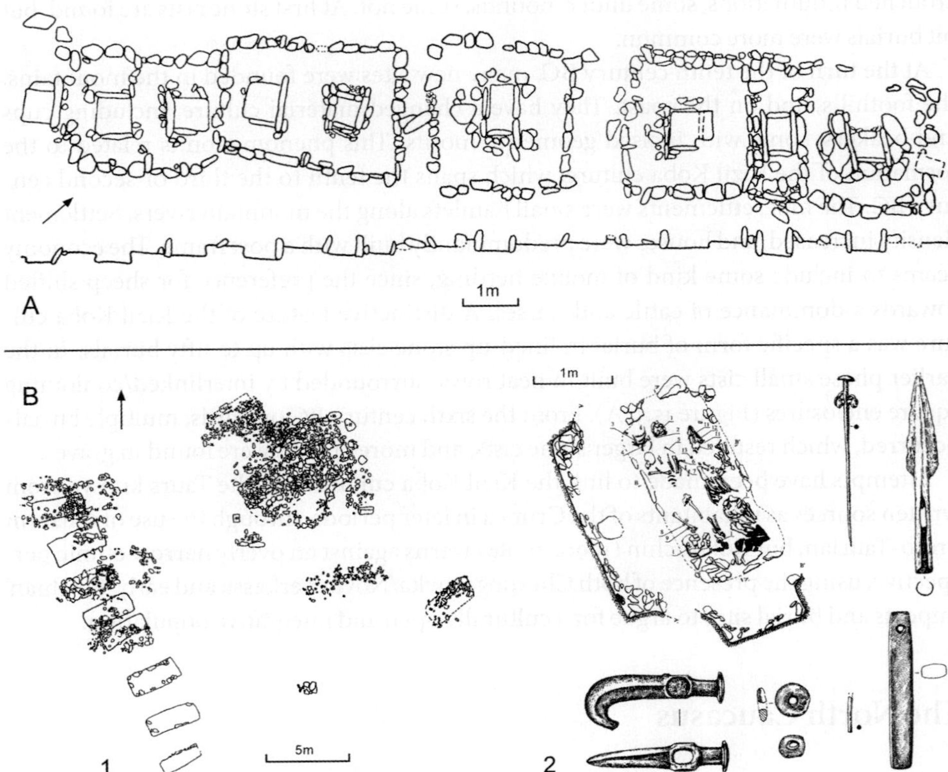

FIGURE 15.3 (A) Kizil Koba aligned stone cists at Urkusta; (B) Proto-Maeotian burials at Fars/Klady: 1 Plan of part of the necropolis, 2 grave 35.

Source: A after Kris 1981: tabs 3, 6; B after Leskov and Erlikh 1999

on the southern flanks of the Great Caucasus, as well as the Proto-Maeotian culture in the north-west (see Figure 15.1, 7–8). New analysis of the artefacts shows, however, that these cultures have been rather artificially disaggregated and the idea of a combined Koban-Colchis culture is increasingly accepted (Erlikh 2007; Reinhold 2007; Skakov 2009). The early Iron Age is characterized by a dichotomy of local traits—costumes, types of ornaments, ceramics, and weapons—and supra-regional elements. The previously mentioned horse-gear, with one- or two-looped bridles and bronze *psalia*,[5] and specific types of daggers found in elite burials of the northern Black Sea area are the most prominent interregional elements.

The regional chronology is founded on a large body of burials with rich grave goods. In the central north Caucasus stone cist graves prevail, while in the Kuban area pit burials are found. Here horse burials, either complete or partial, are frequent, as at the important site of Fars/Klady (Figure 15.3, B; Leskov and Erlikh 1999). In the Caucasian Mineral Waters area they are less frequent, but at the eastern fringe complete horses were buried beside humans in nine graves at the Serzhen'-Yurt cemetery in Chechenia (Figure 15.4; Kozenkova 1992, 2002). The large cemeteries and extensive burial complexes have made it possible to compile chronological sequences on a statistical basis (Reinhold 2007). Four late Bronze Age and early Iron Age phases can be distinguished, during which local ceramic styles and metal types changed visibly. The variety of bronze horse-gear is large, which provides another argument that the north Caucasus, especially the Kuban and the Mineral Waters area, was the origin of such types. The same can be said for the bimetallic daggers; these are mainly found in this area, although finds go as far as Stare Achmylovo on the middle Volga and Pec-Jakobhegy in Hungary (Reinhold 2007: 39–42). Iron objects, including small knives, spears, and bimetallic daggers, are present from the eleventh/tenth century BC onwards (Koban B).

Unlike the steppe burials, graves in the north Caucasus were well furnished, with clear gender distinctions. Male and female graves contain similar numbers of objects, and both genders were evidently classified according to social rank, although no real elite class can be identified. Burials such as grave 186 in the Klin Yar burial ground near Kislovodsk with its Assyrian-inspired helmet are exceptions (Belinskiy 1990). In all regions, settlements are known, allowing us to reconstruct densely inhabited landscapes. Intensive agriculture and mixed animal husbandry formed the economic basis of these communities, and many of the artificial agricultural terraces in the Kislovodsk basin were built in the early Iron Age (Korobov and Borisov 2013).

Across the northern flanks of the Caucasus, a short horizon can be singled out in Koban C that includes objects characteristic of the Novocherkassk horizon of the north Black Sea area (Reinhold 2007: 304–308). This supports Dubovskaya's idea of a short period when Caucasian materials were distributed to the steppes more frequently than before. Koban D (seventh to sixth centuries BC) shows a definite break in nearly all aspects. Cemeteries fall sharply in number or were abandoned. Ceramics are no longer decorated, vessel shapes change to small drinking cups and large S-shaped flasks, and iron is now the dominant metal. In all groups 'Scythian'-looking influence is traceable. The short iron daggers with heart-shaped handles (*akinakai*), so frequent in contemporary early Scythian burials, also occur in local contexts up in the high mountains. Iron axes on the other hand seem to originate there and were transferred into the Scythian sphere. The same is true for metal vessels, especially buckets with ear-shaped handles. Cross-links are frequent enough to correlate the two chronological sequences. Whether Scythian impact was responsible for the visible population decline in the north Caucasian piedmont remains an open question. Study of the Kislovodsk terraces has revealed evidence of an environmental catastrophe, which saw the terrace systems covered by infertile eroded soil as a result of over-exploitation and heavy rainfall. This disaster must have had a severe effect on such a large community, and while not precisely dated, would correlate well with the decrease in burials in the seventh and sixth centuries BC, when the Kuban area also saw a sharp decrease in sites (Erlikh 2007). The situation stabilized in the late sixth century BC and site numbers recovered in the following centuries (Kamenetskiy 1989).

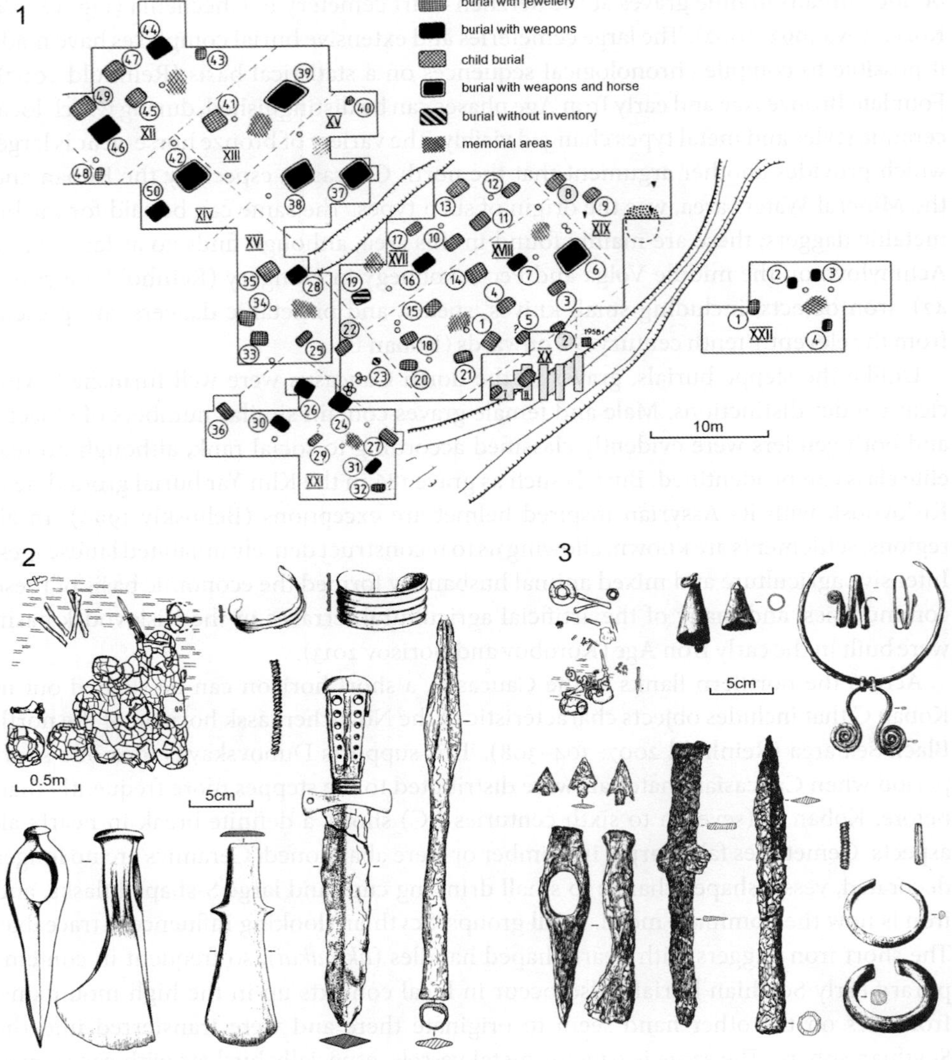

FIGURE 15.4 1 Plan of part of the necropolis at Serzhen' Yurt; 2 Pre-Scythian grave 26; 3 Scythian period grave II/2.

Source: after Kozenkova 2002: tabs 17, 71

The Lower Danube Area

On the other side of the Black Sea near the mouth of the Danube, as in the Caucasus, settled life continued during the late Bronze Age. A recent study revealed the development of the Babadag I-Tămăoani-Holercani-Balta cultural facies at the turn of the second to first millennium BC, with antecedents in the south-east European Bronze Age cultures (Nicic 2008). The tradition of stamped ceramic decoration in particular shows strong cultural links to the area south and west of the Carpathian mountains.

This link is strengthened with the formation of the Cozia-Sacharna culture in the forest steppe zone between the Dniester and the Siret from the middle of the tenth to the eighth centuries BC. Recent research, especially the excavations at Sacharna, demonstrates the strong cross-links with the Balkan-Danubian Hallstatt groups, from which Kashuba (2000: 352–360) infers considerable movement of population into the area from the lower Danube. The internal variants Cozia and Sacharna are both represented by a dense settlement network along the rivers Prut and Dniester with small sites clustered around larger hillforts of up to 12 ha. Houses were either dug into the ground or stood on the surface, and were fairly small (Figure 15.5). Pits of different uses are equally typical elements of the Cozia-Sacharna culture. The roots of the highly polished and decorated pottery lie in Danubian stamped ceramics, yet this culture developed its own particular style of geometric carved decoration and specific vessel forms. Both settlement and burial sites for the first time reveal objects made of iron, among them bow- and knot-fibulae, knives, and socketed adzes (Kashuba 2000).

The burials include flat graves in stone cists and graves below small mounds of stones, some surrounded by stone circles. The graves contain crouched inhumations, and are found in small cemeteries set apart from the settlements in elevated positions. Grave goods were limited to ceramic vessels and items of personal adornment. Together with stratigraphic sequences, the grave goods permit the subdivision of the Cozia-Sacharna culture and cross-link it with the Carpathian basin and the north Pontic steppe region (Kashuba 2000: 340–352, 2008). In the Carpathian basin, the Basarabi culture took shape from the start of the eighth century BC (see also Chapter 14). Although its influence is found deep in the north Pontic steppe, it is not a genuine Pontic culture. At this period, the Cozia-Sacharna culture transformed into a cultural complex, known as Soldanesti (Kashuba 2008).

A New Epoch: Scythians and Greeks, Seventh to Fourth Centuries BC

Early Scythians in the North Caucasus

The earliest 'Scythian' burials, such as Kelermes, Kraznoe Znamya, and Novozavedënoe in the north Caucasus, Zhabotin, mound 2 on the Dnieper, and Temir gora in the Crimea, include objects which reveal a very specific new stylistic design—the so-called Scythian Animal style. Found predominantly carved on bone *psalia* or on small bone or bronze buttons, griffins and fantastical animals illustrate a stylistic tradition that is foreign to the Caucasus and areas further west.

FIGURE 15.5 Houses from Cozia-Sacharna settlements: 1 Orlovec; 2 Soldanesti; 3 Alchedar III. 4 Domestic pottery of the Cozia-Sacharna culture. Various scales.

Sources: after Kashuba 2000; Daragan 2011: fig. IV, 55

Most sites of the seventh and sixth centuries BC are found in the north Caucasus. The most famous is the cemetery of Kelermes, where huge burial mounds were excavated as early as 1904. Excavations in the 1980s revealed more early burials, with grave goods including golden figurines in Animal style, Near Eastern imports, and weapons and horse-gear (Galanina 1997). Beside the mounds, there were flat inhumation graves, with the same Scythian-style burial goods as in the mounds. Yet the burial custom is a different, local one. On the basis of the Kelermes burials, Galanina proposed a four-stage sequence for the seventh and sixth centuries BC, which with some modifications was adopted by Kossack (1987) and Medvedskaja (1992) in their definition of the early Scythian phases II–III (see Table 15.1).

Another exceptional monument of this period is the burial mound of Kraznoe Znamya near Pyatigorsk in the piedmont steppe (Petrenko 2006). Excavated in the mid-1970s, it is one of the largest known Caucasian burial mounds, more than 90 m in diameter and standing 13 m high (Figure 15.6). There were two successive central stone chambers with a *dromos* built in several stages, a stone *krepis* (revetment), and a third burial chamber. The mound was surrounded by a ditch 20 m wide, the edges of which were retained by drystone walls. Beside the mound and inside the *krepis*, a separate building was uncovered, comprising a closed inner room with an altar with remains of burning, surrounded by another wall. The closest parallels for such a building are found among the later fire temples of ancient Iran (Petrenko 2006: 59–62).

The two central chambers were completely robbed, but in the third chamber, although also robbed, remains of the burial equipment survived. The deceased was a man aged 45–50 years. With him two horses were buried, which formed a double-harnessed team. Remains of the bronze coating of a driving collar and a pole, as well as other details, permit the reconstruction of a chariot as a burial gift. The pole coating displays the Near Eastern motif of Ishtar, found in exactly the same position on chariots on reliefs of Ashurbanipal II, allowing this last burial to be dated to the 630s BC. The central chambers were older and date to the early seventh century BC. The stone constructions at Krasnoe Znamya are exceptional in Scythian burial architecture, but can be linked to oriental building traditions with which the Scythians became familiar at this period. Both the moat and complex burial architecture were to become characteristic features of later Scythian mounds.

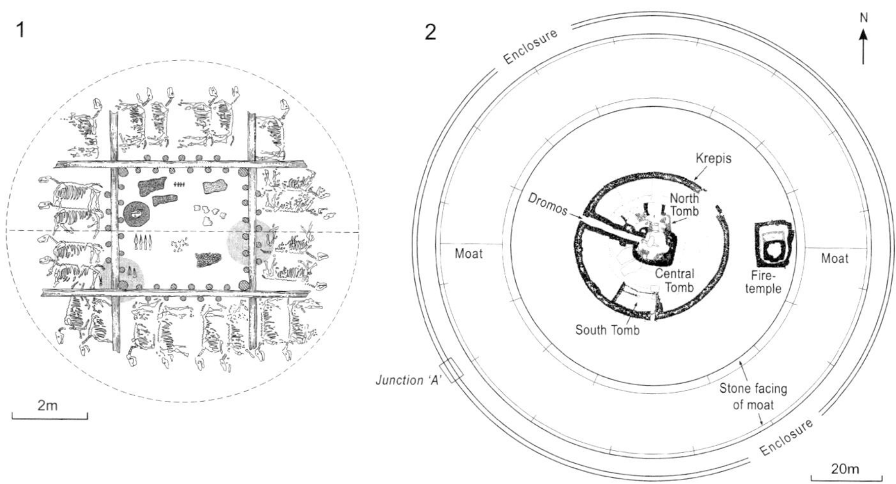

FIGURE 15.6 Early Scythian burial mounds, seventh century BC: 1 Komstromskaya; 2 Krasnoe Znamya mound 1.

Sources: after Galanina 1997: fig. 1; Petrenko 2006: tab. 2; 7

Early Scythians in the Northern Black Sea Region

In the north Black Sea area, Scythian burial mounds of the seventh and sixth centuries BC remain few in number, concentrated around the lower Don and the Sea of Azov. Dubovskaya (1997: 303–316, fig. 1) lists sixty-one burial sites, Polin (2007) no more than thirty for the steppe zone. These early graves are much less rich than those of the north Caucasus. Among the grave goods, arrowheads were common, as well as small mushroom-shaped buttons (Figure 15.7). These little objects—presumably belonging to the bow-case—are chronological markers of the seventh century BC and also occur in north Caucasian Scythian graves. The southernmost findspot of an object of this type is Nush-i-Jan in Iran (Curtis 1984: fig. 12, 372); it serves as a small but important indicator of Scythian presence in this region, otherwise known only from the written sources.

Most early Scythian burials were placed in square burial pits, with or without wooden constructions, and from the sixth century BC in catacomb shafts, under mounds

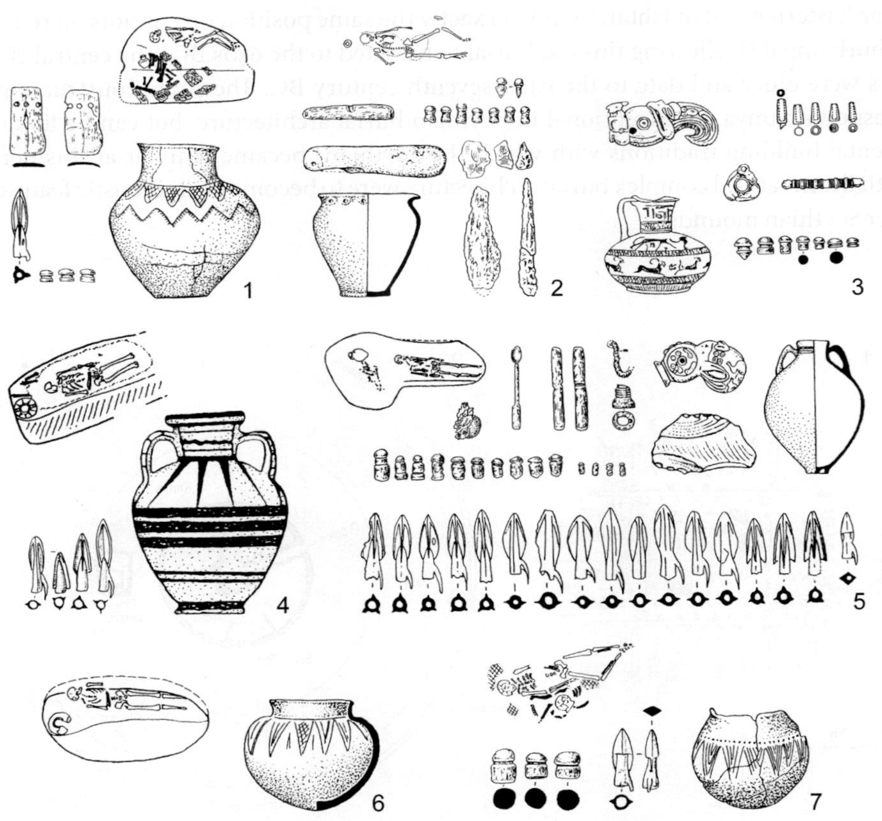

FIGURE 15.7 Early Scythian burials: 1 Novokorsunkaya 2/3; 2 Vysochino; 3 Temir-gora; 4 Bushuyka 2/10; 5 Novoalexandrovka 7/8; 6 Kamyshevakha 5/4; 7 Primorskiy I/1/3. Various scales.

Source: after Dubovskaya 1997: figs 18, 21

(Murzin 1984: 48–56). The Temir gora complex on the Kerch peninsula in Crimea is notable for its imported *œnochoe* dating to the third quarter of the seventh century BC, found alongside a wealthy Scythian grave inventory. The *œnochoe* is one of the earliest examples of Greek pottery from the Black Sea area (Kerschner and Schlotzhauer 2007). Other parts of Crimea are lacking in settlements during the seventh and sixth centuries BC. Apparently the new Scythian population was not large and led a nomadic way of life.

Greek Colonies and Local People

The first presence of Greek traders is found at the same period as early Scythian groups established themselves in the northern Black Sea area. In the mid-seventh century BC, an *emporion* (trading post) was founded at Berezan, an island in the Dnieper-Bug estuary (Solov'ev 1999; Povalahev 2008: 65–110). Finds of the same date from Taganrog at the mouth of the Don suggest a similar but as yet unlocated settlement here. More settlements were founded in quick succession from the start of the sixth century BC onwards around the Black Sea coast. Most are said to have Miletus in Asia Minor as their point of origin. Early colonies are known at Olbia on the lower Bug and on both sides of the Strait of Kerch. The newly revealed eastern passage to the Sea of Azov (Kelterbaum et al. 2011) will probably add the shores of the Kuban region to this list.

Greek impact on the local populations was initially quite limited. Painted pottery appears in some early Scythian contexts (Bruyako 2005: 229–238, map 61); the low density of sites makes the intensity of contact difficult to gauge (Povalahev 2008: 208–215), although the distribution of Greek pottery in the hinterland reveals the extent of interaction. The Greek colonies soon developed their own cultural landscapes (Ochotnikov 2006). During the sixth and fifth centuries BC, a new scene had developed around the Black Sea coast, although the extent of interaction with cultures whose territories were several hundred kilometres inland is still under discussion (Daragan 2011). The development of Greek-influenced grey wheel-made pottery in the north-western part of the Black Sea region in the sixth century BC indicates an intensive transfer of technologies (Kashuba et al. 2010).

The formation of the Bosporan kingdom in the mid-fifth century BC changed the quality of interactions considerably. This global player of its time was founded on the exploitation of the fertile soils of the northern Black Sea coast, and on trade and the production of luxury goods, many of which ended up in the so-called Scythian royal burials. Local peoples such as the Maeotians and Taurians were part of this polity, as the titles of the Bosporan rulers indicate. These groups are generally thought to belong to the pre-Scythian population of the region (Kolotuchin 1996), but the crisis of the sixth/fifth centuries BC, which led to the disappearance of nearly all the archaeological groups in the north Caucasus, renders this ancestry problematic. More research into interaction between local populations and the earliest Greek settlers is required to understand the transfer of indigenous cultural aspects into the later Greek political system.

Scythians of the Fifth and Fourth Centuries BC

Despite the information provided by Herodotus, our understanding of Scythian history is still vague (Alekseev 2007). The sources inform us about ruling dynasties and name as many as eight rulers of this period (see Ivantchik 2001), among them Ariapeites and Skyles, who both ruled in the earlier fifth century BC. From an archaeological viewpoint, Herodotus' narrative on the funerals of Scythian kings is extremely important (*Histories* 4.71–2). Practically all the details described by Herodotus are reflected in the archaeological record of the period, starting with the construction of graves using walls of wattle and wooden ceilings, the placing of the dead including funeral gifts, the killing and burial of horses and servants, and the successive building of the huge mounds (Ivantchik 2007). The royal burials of the fourth century BC were in subterranean catacombs with vertical shafts and several chambers. The offering of women and servants is perhaps authenticated by the multiple burials found at nearly all these sites. The guard of fifty dead attendants posted as watchmen around a royal burial mound (*Histories* 4.72) is similarly echoed by the human remains from the large Chertomlyk mound (Rolle and Murzin 1998: 84–93). Reinvestigation of the Alexandropol' mound revealed a radial system of side burials of males aged 20–55 years old, which the excavators read as similar proof of ritually killed and buried attendants (Polin and Daragan 2011: 193).

Fourteen or fifteen huge mounds are termed royal, five of them dating to the late fifth and fourth centuries BC. These royal burial sites, such as the Oguz, Chertomlyk, Solokha, and Alexandropol' mounds along the Dnieper and the Kul' Oba mound in Crimea, have been objects of excavation since the nineteenth century (Polin 2007). Details of grave construction from the old interventions were limited, but re-excavation, as at Chertomlyk, Alexandropol', and Oguz, has added much contextual detail to the fabulous gold and silver objects from these mounds (Rolle and Murzin 1998; Polin and Daragan 2010). The elite burials of Tolstaya/Tovsta mogila, Soboleva mogila, and other mounds in the middle Dnieper region have also been excavated (Mozolevskiy 1979; Mozolevskiy and Polin 2005). The big Ryzhanovka tumulus in western Ukraine is one of the youngest and the most western of the giant Scythian mounds (Chochorowski and Skoryj 2000).

The burial mounds rise up to 20 m and have a diameter of 100–120 m. Stone *krepis* up to 3 m high and ditches surround the mounds. As at Alexandropol', burials of attendants can be found outside the ditch. Inside the mounds, beside the central graves, were usually several catacomb graves dug over a period of one generation. Some can be very elaborate, as with the multilobed central chamber at Chertomlyk. Here, as in other mounds, several people were buried in the side-chambers, associated with exquisite equipment, including gilded weapons, jewellery, and large numbers of imported Greek amphorae. Women and men are found with equally rich furnishings. Some chambers seem to reflect more 'domestic' aspects, e.g. those with huge numbers of amphorae or cooking installations—such as the Ryzhanovka mound (Chochorowski and Skoryj 2000).

Horses are buried in side-chambers, saddled and with full harness. More horses are found outside the mounds, as at Chertomlyk. Traces of funeral rituals, which included drinking of huge quantities of wine, indicated by large numbers of amphorae, are found at several sites. At Alexandropol', where the complete area of the mound was re-excavated, large areas where such rituals could have taken place were covered with amphora sherds, animal bones, and equipment (Polin and Daragan 2011: 191–204, figs 6–9). Similar finds were made at Gaymanova mogila and Krasnokutinskiy (Polin 2007: 258–260). A martial character to the burials is displayed by weapons and often scale armour (Ochotnikov 1990; Marchenko 1999).

The mounds themselves were complex constructions. The Chertomlyk mound was made from thousands of square metres of steppe-grassland turf divots (Rolle and Murzin 1998: 34–65, pls 4–8). About 75 ha of 'eternal pasture' were piled up to secure for the deceased eternal access to good pasture for his horse. Based on mound size, several ranks of burials are suggested.

Regional Groups from the Third Century BC to the Third Century AD

From the third century BC onwards, developments in the Black Sea area took a new direction.

The Lower Dnieper Region

A range of archaeological sites dating to this period are known in the lower Dnieper area, including settlements, kurgan mounds, flat cemeteries, and deposits of objects without any human remains—the so-called votive hoards.

The settlements are more or less well studied, partly because of the attention given in the mid-twentieth century to the question of continuity between Scythian and Slavic cultures. There are two main groups of settlements (Bylkova 2007). Those in the hinterland (*chora*) of Olbia appeared at the same time as the Greek colonies; those of the so-called late Scythian culture developed in the first century BC, and may be linked with the arrival of a new population (Bylkova 2007: 29). Settlements of both groups have a regular plan. The main features are one-room and multi-roomed houses, semi-dugouts, and pits. Also present are ash-hills or middens, seemingly with a cult dimension. They consist of layers of ash and clay, and contain a range of special artefacts such as anthropomorphic statuettes, terracotta, graffiti, and small clay loaves. In the mid-third century AD most of the building constructions of Olbia and its *chora* were abandoned, and the dwellings fell into decay.

The late Scythian settlements are situated along the Dnieper and were mostly founded on previously unoccupied sites (Bylkova 2007: 110–114). One of the main economic activities was iron mining and processing. As a rule, these settlements are surrounded by several lines of fortifications, comprising either natural barriers, such as precipices or ravines, and a ditch; or stone walls and towers (Figure 15.8). Their regular layout and some of the building types are usually regarded as influenced by the classical world (Kryžytskiy 1993: 228). These sites fell into decay during the second century AD, but soon after, in the late second or third century AD, settlements of the Chernyakhov culture appeared in the western part of the lower Dnieper area (Magomedov 2001: 133–134). These are non-fortified dwelling places with regular lines of houses and dugouts.

In marked contrast to the abundant burial sites of the fourth century BC, burials of the third to the mid-first century BC are few in number, although this may be partly due to a lack of dating material. Large kurgan cemeteries and flat cemeteries did not exist at this time. The standard burial rite is a simple rectangular pit inserted into a barrow of earlier times, of which around seventy are known (Figure 15.9); there are also around thirty so-called votive hoards (Smirnov 1984; Simonenko 1993). Other types of graves (square-shaped, niche-grave, catacomb, grave with shelves) are very rare at this period and occur mainly in the cemeteries of the northern Azov area (Novo-Filippovka, Akkermen). The contents of kurgan burials differ according to local burial practices.

There is one elite grave cut into the occupation layer of the Kamenka settlement (Pogrebova 1956), but for the most part, the elite may be represented by status objects in the so-called votive hoards containing 'male' sets of objects, rather than by burial constructions. The 'male' sets comprise high-status objects with a clear military orientation, which show connections mainly with the west (Figure 15.10). These include silver *phalerae*, Montefortino-type helmets, bronze *situlae*, and silver cups of western Mediterranean provenance. A clear connection to Crimea appears in the gold mouth- and eye-pieces from the Kamenka burial. Such objects are also abundant in the elite graves of Neapolis Scythica (Pogrebova 1961) and some other cemeteries of premontane Crimea.

In the first century BC, votive hoards start to become rarer (disappearing by the mid-second century AD), while along with the settlements, several important flat and kurgan cemeteries appeared, often in close proximity. Burials from the kurgan cemeteries (Ust'-Kamenka) show similarities with graves of the Volga and Don areas (with a sheep's leg, a knife, and a clay vessel as a standard set, and weapons in male graves; Kostenko 1993). The graves in the flat cemeteries are more like the rare single kurgan burials of the former period (Vyaz'mitina 1972). These burial grounds existed until the later second century AD.

Distinctive changes occurred in the types of artefacts and composition of elite assemblages around the mid-first century BC. Ostentatious burials appear, containing Roman goods ranging in quality from highly artistic silverware to bronze vessel stands reused as amulets. The elite female graves of the highest level (Chuguno-Krepinka, Sokolova mogila) are remarkable for their high-quality jewellery of eastern Mediterranean provenance and items and materials originating from distant lands

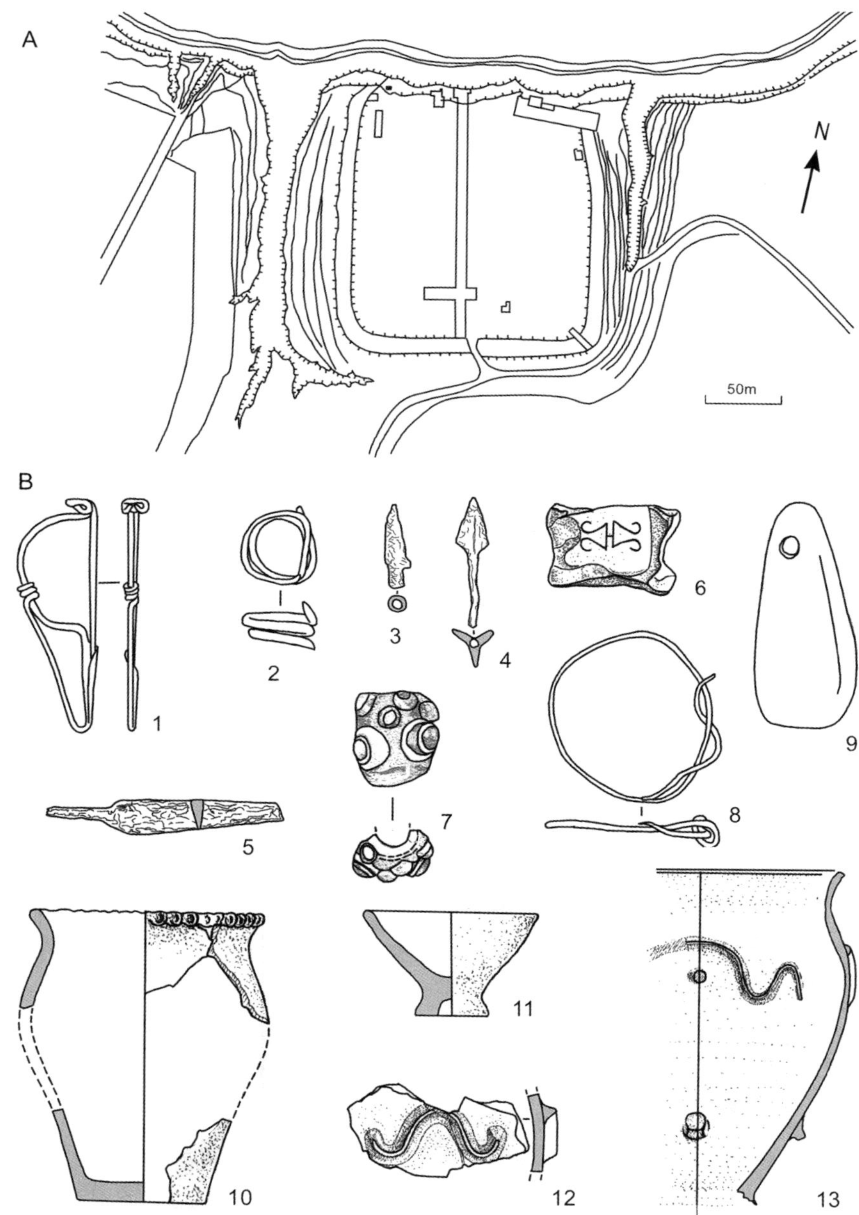

FIGURE 15.8 (A) Schematic plan of the late Scythian settlement at Lyubimovka. (B) Typical finds from late Scythian settlements of the lower Dnieper region: 1 brooch, 2 temple-pendant, 3–4 arrowheads, 5 knife, 6 astragalus with inscribed tamga-sign, 7 glass bead, 8 arm-ring, 9 weight, 10–13 handmade pots. First century BC to first century AD. Various scales.

Source: after Bylkova 2007

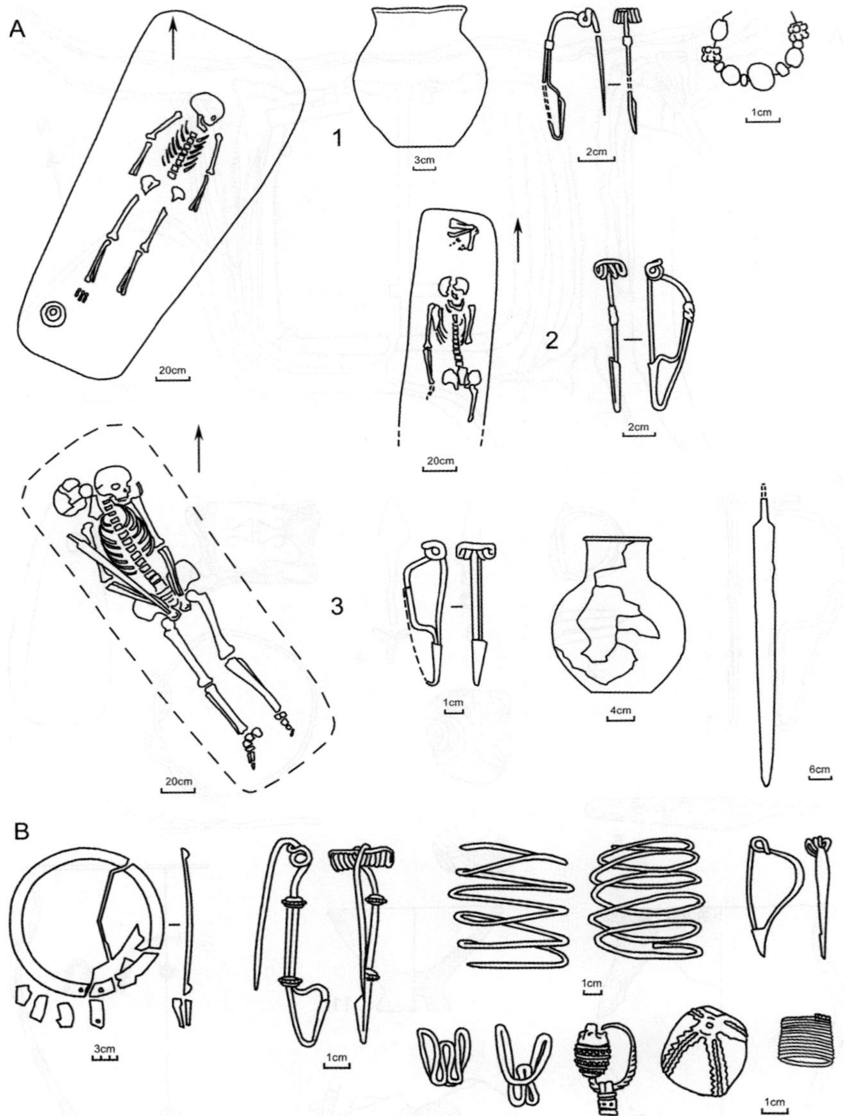

FIGURE 15.9 (A) Single burials from kurgan mounds of the lower Dnieper area: 1 Gromovka, kurgan 2, burial 2; 2 Vasil'evka, kurgan 1, burial 4; 3 Brylevka, kurgan 16, burial 1. Second to first centuries BC. (B) Solontsy, chance find, probably votive hoard, second to first century BC.

Source: after Simonenko 1993

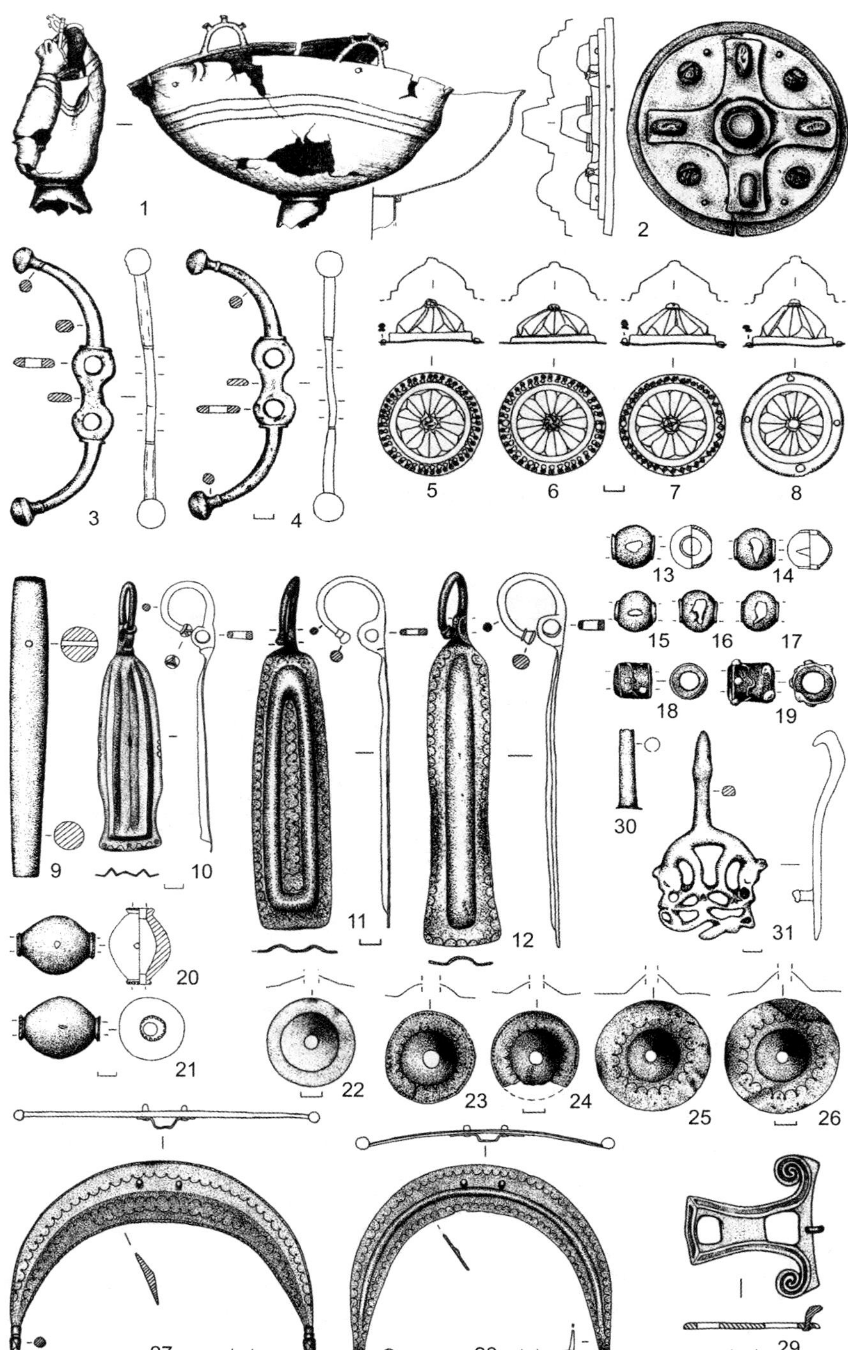

FIGURE 15.10 The Kachalinskaya votive hoard, north Pontic region, second century BC. 1 bronze cauldron; 2, 5–8 silver *phalerae* from horse harnesses; 3–4 iron horse bits; 9 whetstone; 10 silver head-piece from horse harness; 11–12 bronze head-pieces from horse harness; 13–17, 20–21 bronze beads from horse harness; 18–19 glass beads; 22 silver ornament from horse harness; 23–26 bronze ornaments from horse harness; 27–28 bronze front-pieces from horse harness; 29 silver attachment from a drinking cup; 30 bronze tube; 31 bronze hook. Various scales.

Source: after Sergatskov 2009

such as China (silks, lacquer, mirrors) and the Near East (stands for mirrors, fans, toilet vessels; Kovpanenko 1986; Simonenko et al. 2008: Cat. No. 70, tables 56–66). In the male burial of the highest rank (Tsvetna), in addition to gold jewellery, belt fittings, and Roman provincial tableware, there were gold leaves from a funeral wreath, which was customary in Greek and Roman burial rites.

Around the mid-second century AD, the number of burials in the lower Dnieper region declined. From then until the fourth century AD, they cluster mainly on the fringes of the area, in the lower Danube and northern Azov littoral (Gudkova and Fokeev 1984; Simonenko 1993: 99). Most are single burials in kurgans. Graves that could be interpreted as elite are rare and contain status objects of local, Bosporan, and Roman provincial origin. The changes of burial rite in the lower Dnieper area are traditionally interpreted as reflecting pressure from nomadic migrations from the east. However, this explanatory model has no foundation in the archaeological material (Mordvintseva 2008, 2013).

The Crimea

The non-Greek archaeological monuments of the Crimea dating from the third century BC to the mid-third century AD are regarded as late Scythian, following the idea that after the Sarmatian invasion, the Scythians advanced into the Crimea peninsula, which became the centre of a new Scythian state (Artamonov 1948: 57; Dashevskaya 1991; Popova 2011; Popa 2012). Archaeological sites include settlements, flat cemeteries, kurgan burials, and sanctuaries.

Around eighty fortified and unfortified settlements of the late Scythian culture are known in the premontane zone, from Chersonesos Taurica to Theodosia, and on the north-west coast (Vysotskaya 1972, 1979; Khrapunov 1991; Koltukhov 1999; Zaytsev 2004). Most are known only from surface remains, with fewer than ten settlements excavated. One of the largest (some 10 ha) and earliest fortified settlements, Ak-Kaya, was built on a rocky plateau in the late fourth to early third century BC in central Crimea.[6] The shallower slopes were protected by a wall, *c.*5 m wide, with towers, and on the north-west side a fore wall (*proteichisma*) and enclosed space (*peribolos*). In sight of the fortress are several groups of large burial mounds up to 10 m high, comparable with those in the vicinity of Panticapaion (Kerch). The burials from these kurgans date to the later fourth century BC (Koltukhov 2007). Inside the fortress, several buildings have been excavated, one of which, judging by the presence of an altar-fireplace, could be of religious purpose. The excavated deposits yielded evidence of several fires between the late fourth and mid-second centuries BC. The upper horizon belongs to the Augustan period. The size of the fortress, the high level of its fortifications, and the finds (a seven-line graffito in Greek, rare forms of black-glazed ware, and the quantity and quality of amphora sherds) underline the high status of this settlement.

Most of the other settlements that have been investigated started later, in the late third or second century BC (e.g. Neapolis Scythica, Kermen-Kyr, Bulganak in central Crimea,

Ust'-Al'ma in south-western Crimea, and Beliaus, Kulchuk, Kara-Tobe in north-western Crimea). In central and south-western Crimea, they tended to be founded on new sites, but some in north-western Crimea emerged on the Greek settlements (Kutaisov and Uzhentsev 1997; Shcheglov 1998). Settlements on the north-west coast disappeared between the mid-first and early second century AD; others survived until the mid-third century AD.

In the first century BC, a group of new settlements were founded in south-western and central premontane Crimea, as at Alma-Kermen, Krasnozorenskoe, and Druzhnoe (Koltukhov 1999: 20–27). The destruction of the late Scythian fortresses in the mid-third century AD is generally associated with the raids of the Goths (Vysotskaya 1972: 186–187, 1979: 204; Koltukhov 1999: 27). The settlement of Kermenchik, in the modern city of Simferopol, is identified as Strabo's Neapolis Scythica (*Geography* 7.4.7). At about 17 ha, it is the largest Iron Age fortified settlement in the Crimea (Vysotskaya 1979; Koltukhov 1999: 29–38; Zaytsev 2004), situated on a rocky plateau of triangular shape, its eastern side naturally protected by cliffs (Figure 15.11). The earliest layers date to the late fourth or early third century BC, but the fortifications seem to have been built in the second century BC. On the plateau side the settlement was defended by a stone wall with towers, with a *proteichism* and a *peribolos* in its southern part. There is limited information on the internal layout, but mud-brick and stone buildings and sunken-floor structures are attested, and there was a large undeveloped space or square. Intensive building in stone began in the later second century BC, around the time Ak-Kaya in central Crimea started to decline. Opposite the main entrance to Kermenchik, a major stone complex was built, which is known as the Southern Palace (Figure 15.11, 2). The finds from this area revealed strong Hellenistic influence. In the first century BC the defensive wall was partly destroyed, then reconstructed in the first century AD. During the later second century AD a new building complex appeared in the northern part of the settlement—the so-called Northern Palace. Around the mid-third century AD the settlement was completely destroyed.

Flat cemeteries appeared in considerable numbers in the second century BC along with new settlements (Puzdrovskiy 2007). Those in western Crimea were used up to the early first century AD (Beliaus, Kulchuk, Chaika), whereas in central and south-western Crimea most of the burial grounds lasted until the mid-third century AD. Some of these flat cemeteries contain thousands of tombs, but few are fully published (Symonovich 1983; Vysotskaya 1994). Scholars have often selectively published certain graves united by particular themes—warrior burials, female or children's burials, elite burials (e.g. Khrapunov 2007; Stoyanova 2012), but we lack an overall picture of their development.

From the mid-second to late first century BC, multiple burials (up to 100 skeletons) in earth crypts are typical (Figure 15.12). Not every burial is accompanied by burial goods. The male set includes belt fittings, brooches, and sometimes weapons (spearheads). Female burials are usually accompanied by mirrors and jewellery, mainly beads or rarely foot-rings. Crypts usually contain several ceramic vessels (handmade pots and incense burners, wheel-made jugs and plates), which do not seem to belong to any specific burial. Animal bones are extremely rare. Male and female burials of higher social

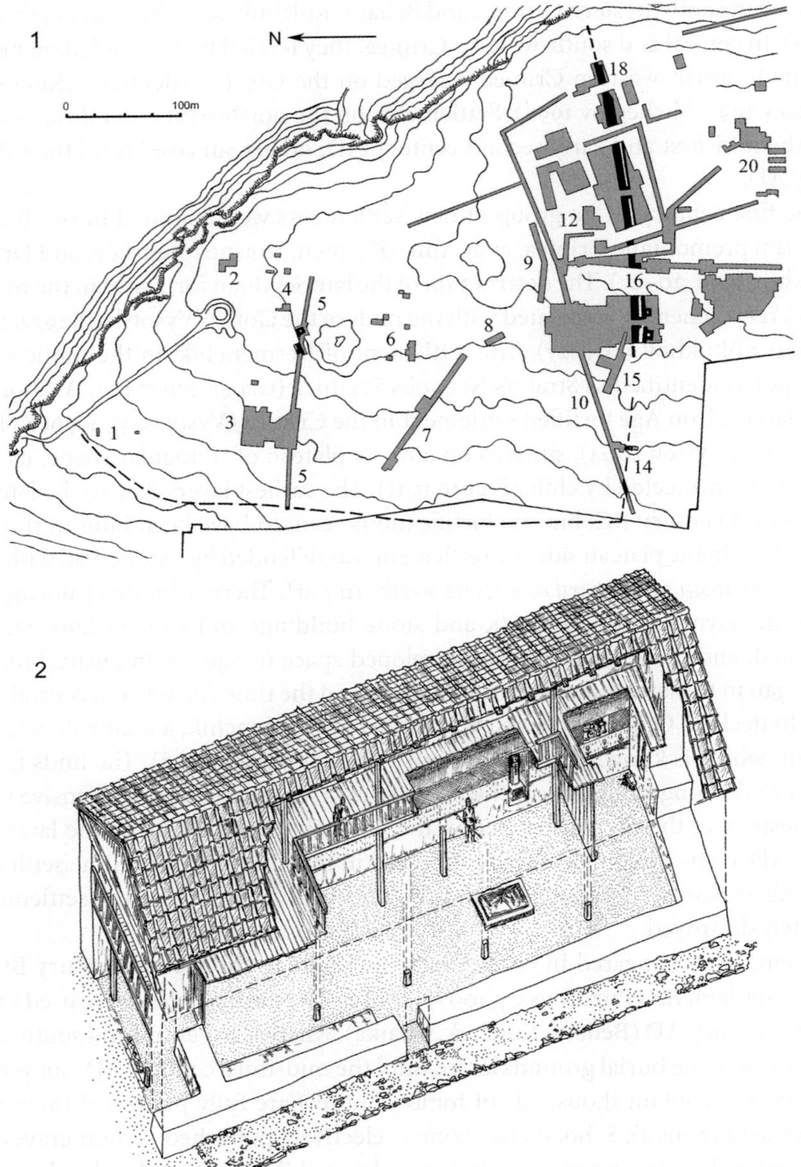

FIGURE 15.11 1 Plan of the settlement of Neapolis Scythica, Crimea, showing excavated areas. 2 Reconstruction of the megaron of the Southern Palace in the late second century BC.

Source: after Zaytsev 2004

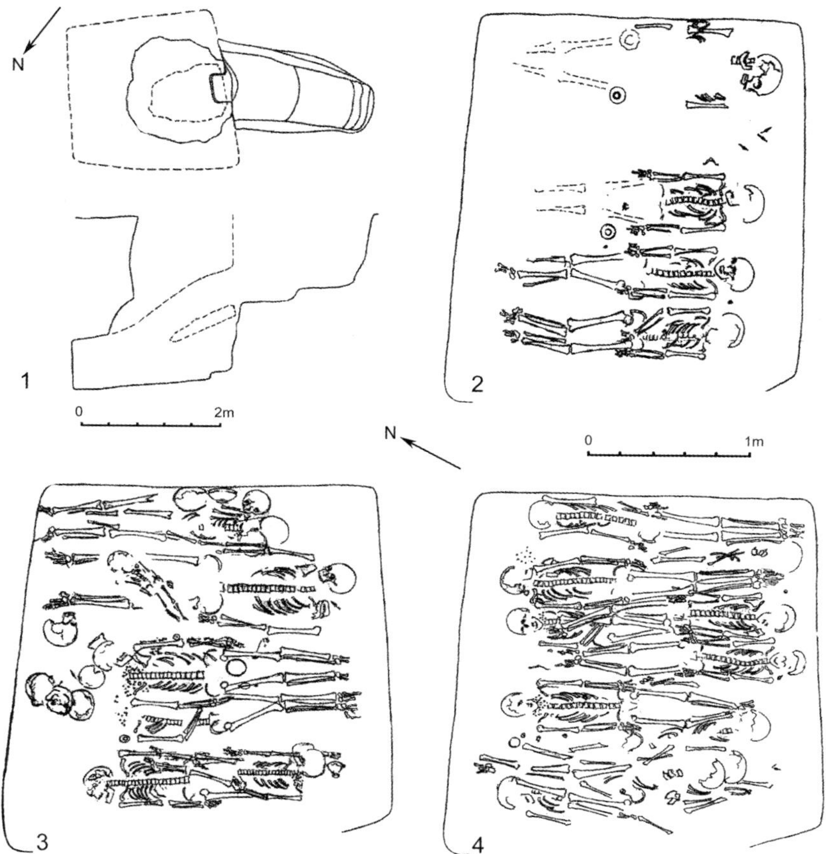

FIGURE 15.12 Crypt no. 155 at Bitak necropolis, Crimea. 1 Plan and section. 2–4 lower, middle, and upper levels of burials.

Source: after Zaytsev 2004

status are differentiated from the standard ones in the same crypts by the presence of particular types of belt plaque and weapons, and more elaborate jewellery respectively. As a rule, there are no grave goods in children's burials.

Around the start of the first millennium AD, changes in burial rite occurred. Niche graves appeared alongside the earth crypts, becoming widespread between the first and third centuries AD. Niche graves were used primarily for individual burials, but some had two niches, or several skeletons in one niche (Figure 15.13). Some children were buried in amphorae, a characteristic Greek custom. The standard set of grave goods also changed; regardless of sex, the deceased were now accompanied by a set of red-slip pottery (a jug or cup and a plate), brooches, beads, and amulets. Meat joints occur but are still quite rare. Rarely, in elite burials, horses were interred in pits at the entrance to the burial chamber. Weapons still only occur in male burials of high social status. Female and children's graves are often furnished with a rich set of amulets,

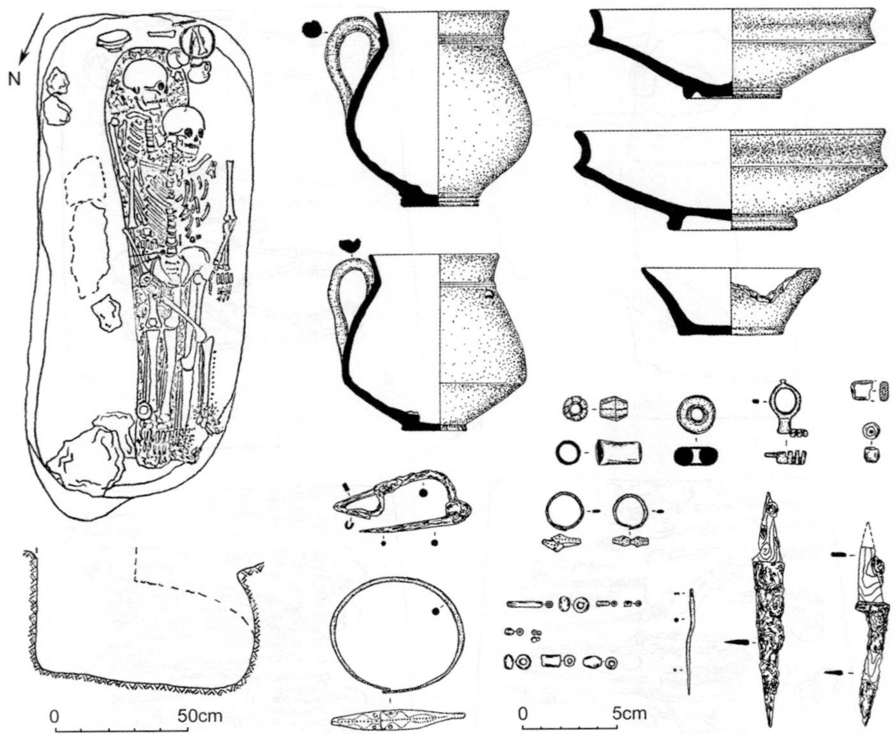

FIGURE 15.13 Niche grave no. 76/1984 from the eastern necropolis at Neapolis Scythica, Crimea. Late second century AD.

Source: after Zaytsev 2004

and women were sometimes accompanied by caskets and perfume flasks. The material remains of the burial rite, including the burial structures, are very similar to graves in the cemeteries of the Crimean Greek cities.

Between the early first and mid-second centuries AD, high-status ostentatious burials in earth crypts are found in some cemeteries, as at Ust'-Al'ma (Loboda et al. 2002; Puzdrovskiy and Zajcev 2004; Puzdrovskiy 2013). These crypts were located in one particular part of the cemetery, apparently along the road leading to the settlement of Ust'-Al'ma. The graves contained Roman imports, Chinese lacquer boxes, golden funeral wreaths, and many other high-status objects, which demonstrate the wide connections of the local elite, and its orientation toward Greek customs.

Burials in kurgan mounds take a variety of forms: stone crypts, stone cists, and earth-cut graves. Stone crypts with multiple burials repeat, in a simpler form, the constructions of Bosporan tombs in mounds with a stepped internal structure. Stone cists are made of four vertical stone slabs, following a local form of burial construction known from the Bronze Age. Both types of burial contain either skeletons lying in an extended position, accompanied by grave goods, or disarticulated human bones with some, often damaged, items. Stone crypts and cists were used from the fourth century BC to the late first century AD across premontane Crimea. Starting a little later, earth graves with the same burial rite appear in the flat cemeteries of north-western, western, and central Crimea. The main difference lies in the presence or absence of stone structures, which can be explained by the natural paucity of stone in the steppe areas.

A notable stone crypt is the mausoleum near the main gate of Neapolis Scythica (Babenchikov 1957; Shults 1957; Pogrebova 1961; Zaytsev 2004). It is regarded as a funeral place of the nobility, because of its remarkable differences to burials in the flat cemeteries near the city. The stone cist inside the mausoleum is suggested to be the burial place of king Skiluros, who is known from the written sources (Strabo), Olbian coins, and inscriptions (Frolova 1964: 44; Zaytsev 2004).

Earthen burials in kurgan mounds were rare from the third century BC to the third century AD. It seems that the kurgan burials sporadically found in earlier (Bronze Age) mounds belonged to the social elite, for example the Chisten'koe grave (Zaytsev and Koltukhov 2004). To the later group belong several elite kurgan burials in south-western Crimea (Zaytsev 2005; Puzdrovskiy 2007). Full details are yet to be published, but some of the finds from these assemblages show great similarity to the ostentatious burials from the flat necropolis of Ust'-Al'ma.

Sanctuaries in Crimea

Iron Age sanctuaries in Crimea are mainly found in the mountainous part of the peninsula (Lysenko 2009), apart from one on the western littoral (Lantsov 2003). Three types of sacred places are distinguished by their layouts and types of finds (Lysenko 2009). The first variant is represented by open sanctuaries on the tops of mountains, with dispersed offerings: animal parts, and objects of everyday life and religious purpose (Gurzuf pass, Eklizi-Burun, Autka, Aligor). The sanctuary at the Gurzuf pass seems to be the earliest (Novichenkova 2002). The objects found there range in date from the seventh century BC to the eighteenth century AD, but the stratified archaeological layers belong to two periods: (1) early Roman (Augustan to early second century AD), represented by burnt animal bones, coins, gold jewellery, rare Roman and provincial imports (military equipment, silver and glass vessels, brooches, etc.), and cult objects (silver and bronze votive statuettes and altars, amulets, etc.), and (2) later Roman (mid-second to fourth centuries AD), consisting of unburnt animal bones and some objects (brooches, mirrors, coins). The sanctuary of Eklizi-Burun is situated at the top of Chatyr-Dag (Lysenko 2009: 383–384), the highest mountain in Crimea, and visible from most parts of the peninsula. Cultural layers dated from the late first century BC to the early fourth century AD have yielded animal bones, ceramics, knives, coins, brooches, belt fittings, amulets, silver cups, and imported Roman objects. The sanctuaries of Aligor and Autka belong to the second to fourth centuries AD (Lysenko 2009). Open sanctuaries also appeared in premontane Crimea (Zaytsev et al. 2007).

To the second category belongs a sanctuary with two temples on the slopes of Taraktash ridge, which functioned from the first to the late fourth century AD (Myts and Lysenko 2001; Lysenko 2009). The first temple was rectangular in plan, constructed of stone and wood. Its entrance was oriented to sunrise at the winter solstice. Opposite the entrance was an offering place and a ledge in an earthen wall that was probably an altar. Animal bones, sherds of ceramic and glass vessels, arrowheads, brooches, and beads had been inserted into the fabric of the building. Animal bones and fragments of about 250 red-slip cups were found inside the temple. The second temple was square in plan, its entrance oriented to sunrise at the vernal equinox. In the middle of the floor there was a hollow. Finds from inside the temple included three hand-formed clay statuettes, incense burners, portable altars, and red-slip cups. Both temples were covered by a layer of stones, earth, small fragments of burnt animal bone, and fragments of glass and ceramic vessels.

The third type of sanctuary is represented by a temple near the ruins of the Roman fortress of Kharax on the cape of Ai-Todor (Rostovtzeff 1911). It spanned the early second to the mid-third century AD. The remains of a destroyed stone building were found, with fragments of two limestone altars dedicated to Jupiter Optimus Maximus, and of marble votive reliefs (Thracian horseman, Dionysus, Mithras, Hermes, and Hecate). This sanctuary was presumably used by Roman troops quartered at Kharax.

The three types of sanctuaries have been interpreted as belonging to societies with different degrees of social complexity (Lysenko 2009). All were abandoned around the fourth century AD.

The Kuban Region

Between the third century BC and the third century AD, the Kuban region is characterized by various kinds of archaeological monument: fortified and unfortified settlements, flat cemeteries, barrows, votive deposits, and sanctuaries. The settlements and flat cemeteries are generally ascribed to the Maeotians[7] (Kamenetskiy 2000: 74) and the burial mounds to the Siracae—nomadic tribes, rivals of the Aorsi mentioned in written sources (Marchenko 1996).

Although settlements are well known in the Kuban region, few have been excavated. Most of the information comes from Elizavetinskaya (Shilov 1955); a few other settlements are briefly described in publications with only very rough plans (Anfimov 1973; Kamenetskiy 2000). They all have a central 'citadel', separated from the rest of the settlement by a deep ditch. Archaeological deposits yield local grey and red wheel-made ceramics and some handmade pots. Pottery kilns have been found at the settlements of Elizavetinskaya (Shilov 1955: 235), Pashkovskaya (Anfimov 1973: 109), and Kavkazskaya.

Most of the settlements are situated along the river Kuban, mainly in its middle reaches. Their abandonment in the third century AD has been linked to the appearance of the Goths (Kamenetskiy 1989: 240). In the Kirpili valley, more than twenty settlements existed between the third century BC and early first century AD, their demise being interpreted as due to resettlement of their population in the Don delta.

Most of the flat burial grounds are found near settlements in these river valleys, particularly in the middle reaches of the Kuban. Many have been excavated, but none fully published. All are regarded as belonging to various sedentary Maeotian peoples. From the third to mid-first centuries BC, the standard form of burial is inhumation in a simple rectangular pit. As a rule, the skeleton was laid on its back, head to the east, often placed in a ceramic bowl, noted as a special Maeotian custom. The standard set of burial offerings includes wheel-made pottery (generally placed to the right of the deceased), animals or animal parts (usually sheep and pigs, more rarely cows and horses), and a knife. Male burial goods include weapons (mainly spear- and arrowheads), horse harness, and whetstones. The female set consists of jewellery, mirrors, needles, and spindle-whorls (Kamenetskiy 1989: 240–241). In the period from the mid-first century BC to the third century AD, catacombs and niche graves became more common, while the custom of putting the head of the deceased in a bowl disappeared. Animal bones are found less frequently, but other categories of grave goods remained substantially the same, albeit in line with wider changes in the material culture of the time (Figure 15.14; Kamenetskiy 1989: 246–247). However, more detailed analysis of the burial rites of the Kuban flat cemeteries is still required.

Kurgan Cemeteries

Kurgan mounds are better published than flat burial grounds (Marchenko 1996; Marchenko and Limberis 2008). Some scholars attribute them to Sarmatian tribes (Alekseeva 1976; Gushchina and Zasetskaya 1994: 38–39; Marchenko 1996: 6), others regard some of them as Maeotian (Shilov 1959: 353). There are two main territorial groups of kurgans. The first is in the middle Kuban valley and between the Kuban and Laba rivers. The second is situated in the lower Kuban steppe, between the right bank of the Kuban and the Kirpili valley.

From the third to the late first centuries BC, burials were inserted into kurgan mounds of the Bronze Age, as in Crimea. Most are on the right bank of the Kuban. Groups of kurgans have also been excavated between the Kuban and the Laba rivers (the so-called Zubov-Vozdvizhenskaya group). Burial constructions include rectangular pits, graves with side shelves, niche graves, and catacombs (Marchenko 1996: 95). Most of the burials are single, with the deceased lying on his or her back in an extended position, with the head to the west. The standard set of grave goods, regardless of sex, consists of wheel-made pottery (plate and/or jug), part of a sheep or horse, with a knife near the head or feet of the deceased, mirrors or their fragments, and beads on the chest or near the hands and feet (Figure 15.15). Some handmade pots contain pebbles and sometimes coal. Male graves are often accompanied by a sword, and spear- and arrowheads. Female burials contained jewellery. Elite grave assemblages of this period contain cups of gold, silver, and glass; gold torcs, arm- and foot-rings, sometimes with Animal style decoration; small plaques; and elaborate polychrome brooches. Ostentatious male burials can also contain silver *phalerae* and swords in golden sheaths (Mordvintseva et al. 2010: 53–64). From a comparative analysis of kurgans and flat burials of this period, I. Marchenko (1996: 96–112) concluded

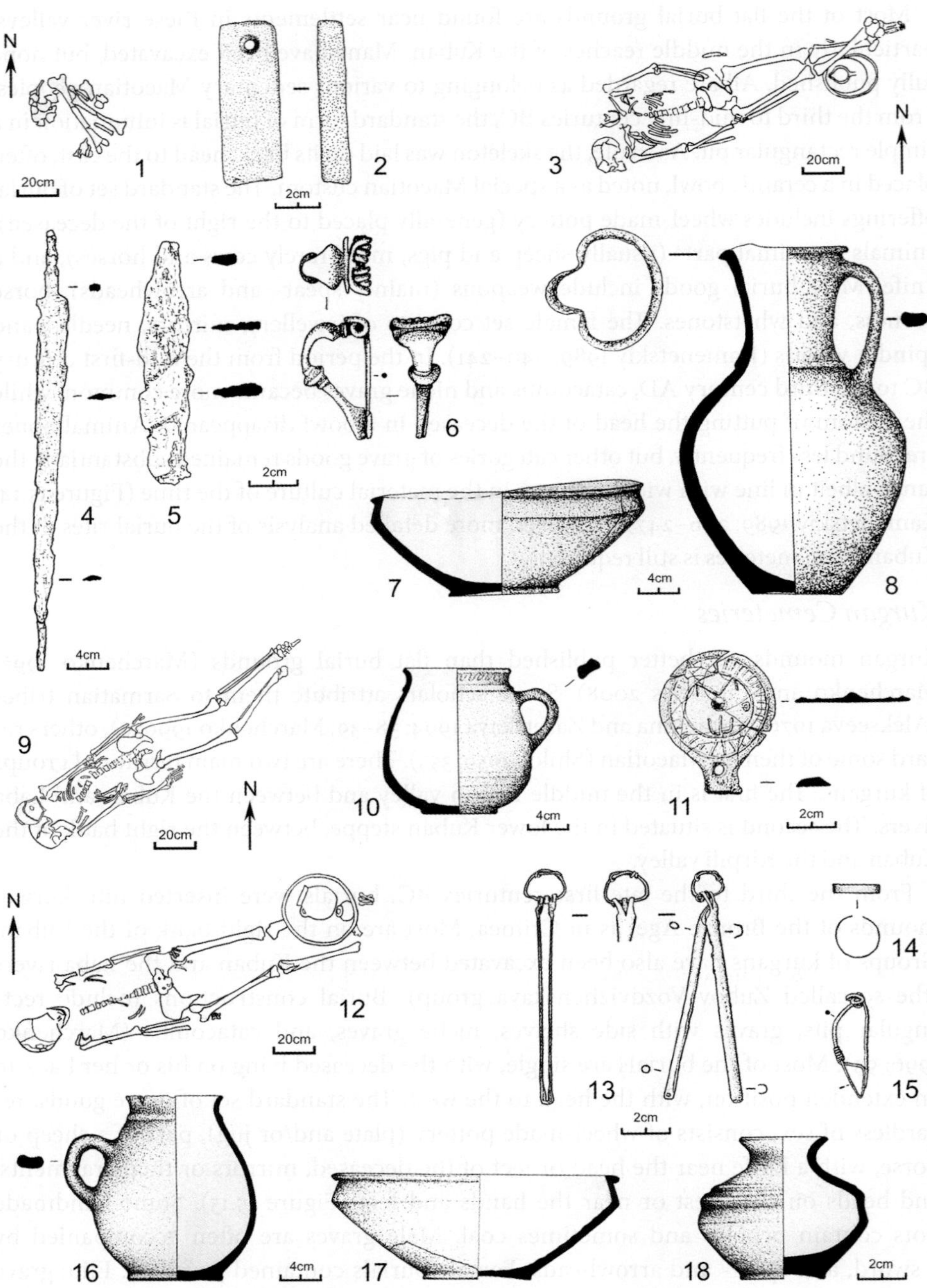

FIGURE 15.14 Flat burials from the cemetery of the settlement of Starokorsunskaya-3, Kuban region. 1–2 Burial 9/1986; 3–8 Burial 4/1986; 9–11 Burial 18/1986; 12–18 Burial 203/1988. Late first to second century AD.

Source: excavations of A.V. Kondrashov 1986, 1988; we are grateful for permission to use these materials

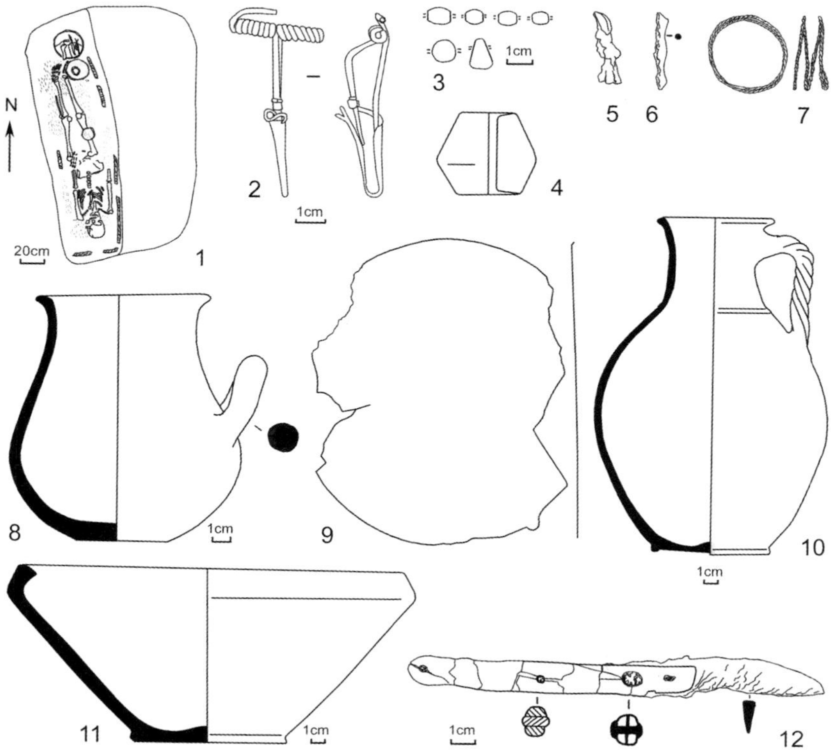

FIGURE 15.15 Kurgan 3, burial 3/1984 from Proletarskiy cemetery, Kuban region, second century BC. 1 Plan of grave, 2 bronze fibula, 3 glass beads, 4 ceramic spindle-whorl, 5 iron ornament, 6 iron needle, 7 gold temple-pendants, 8, 10–11 ceramic vessels, 9 bronze mirror, 12 iron knife with bone handle.

Source: excavations of N. F. Shevchenko 1984, 1986; we are grateful for permission to use these materials

that the kurgan burials on the right bank of the Kuban belonged to the Sarmatians (i.e. nomads).

In the late period, from the first to third centuries AD, burials are concentrated in the middle Kuban valley and between the Kuban and the Laba. The 'Golden cemetery' is a group of kurgan burial grounds along the northern part of the middle Kuban (Gushchina and Zasetskaya 1994). These kurgans are located near the settlements and flat burial grounds. The burials take the form of catacombs. As often happened in early twentieth-century excavations, some groups of artefacts, such as ceramics, were not properly recorded, leaving uncertainties over the standard burial rite. It has been suggested that these kurgans belonged to the Alani (Spitsyn 1909; Gushchina and Zasetskaya 1994: 38–39), but the abundant Roman imports, silver tableware, weapons, pieces of armour, precious belts, and jewellery suggest that these graves may instead be the elite burials of the same population as the settlements, which are ascribed to the Maeotians.

Sanctuaries and Votive Hoards

A number of hoards of high-status objects of military character (Celtic helmets, weapons, horse harness) have been found in burial mounds, as at Sergievskaya, Korenovsk, and Verkhniy. In contrast to the lower Dnieper and Volga-Don regions, such objects also occur in kurgan burials.

Several complexes with evidence for human and animal sacrifice have been excavated in the Kuban region. Offerings of status objects—weapons, golden jewellery, tools—found in the region were once regarded as the remains of ostentatious burials, but have been reinterpreted as sanctuaries following excavation of the Ul' and Ulyap kurgan mounds (Leskov 1985: 26–44; Beglova 2002, 2005). The earliest sanctuaries of this kind date to the fourth century BC; many belong to the third and second centuries BC. The best studied are the sanctuaries near the Tenginskaya settlement.

The Lower Don and Volga Region

Archaeological sites of the lower Volga and Don region from the third to mid-first century BC consist of burials in kurgan cemeteries and a few so-called votive hoards. Later, from the mid-first century BC to the mid-third century AD, there were only kurgan burials. Around the mouth of the Don settlements and flat cemeteries appeared by the mid-first century BC.

Kurgan Cemeteries

Large-scale excavations of kurgan cemeteries from the 1950s to 1990s have generated a great quantity of archaeological material. The Volga cemeteries, regarded as archetypes for the Sarmatian culture, have been extensively published (Smirnov 1960; Shilov 1959, 1975; Mamontov 2000; Sergatskov 2002), but the Don cemeteries are less well known (Maksimenko 1983), albeit with some recent publications to a high standard (Bespalyi et al. 2007). There are few burial complexes of the third century BC, and they are hard to date because of the paucity of imported grave goods (Klepikov 2002). By about the mid-second century BC, the quantity of both cemeteries and graves increased greatly, with most burial grounds remaining in use until the third century AD.

Burials of the early Sarmatian culture (third to late first century BC) are represented by simple grave pits, grave pits with shelves, niche graves, and catacombs inserted into earlier (mainly Bronze Age) burial mounds. The deceased lay, as a rule, on their back with the head to the south (Figure 15.16). A standard set of burial goods consisted of a sheep's leg bones with a knife, and handmade pottery. Weapons and a whetstone are also typical for ordinary male burials. In standard female burials one finds beads, temple-pendants, a spindle-whorl, and a mirror (often fragmentary). Some female graves, however, have weapons, and male graves have beads and spindle-whorls. At this time, there are many separate child burials (normally one-third of the total number of graves). From the third to the mid-second century BC, social stratification is reflected by a full

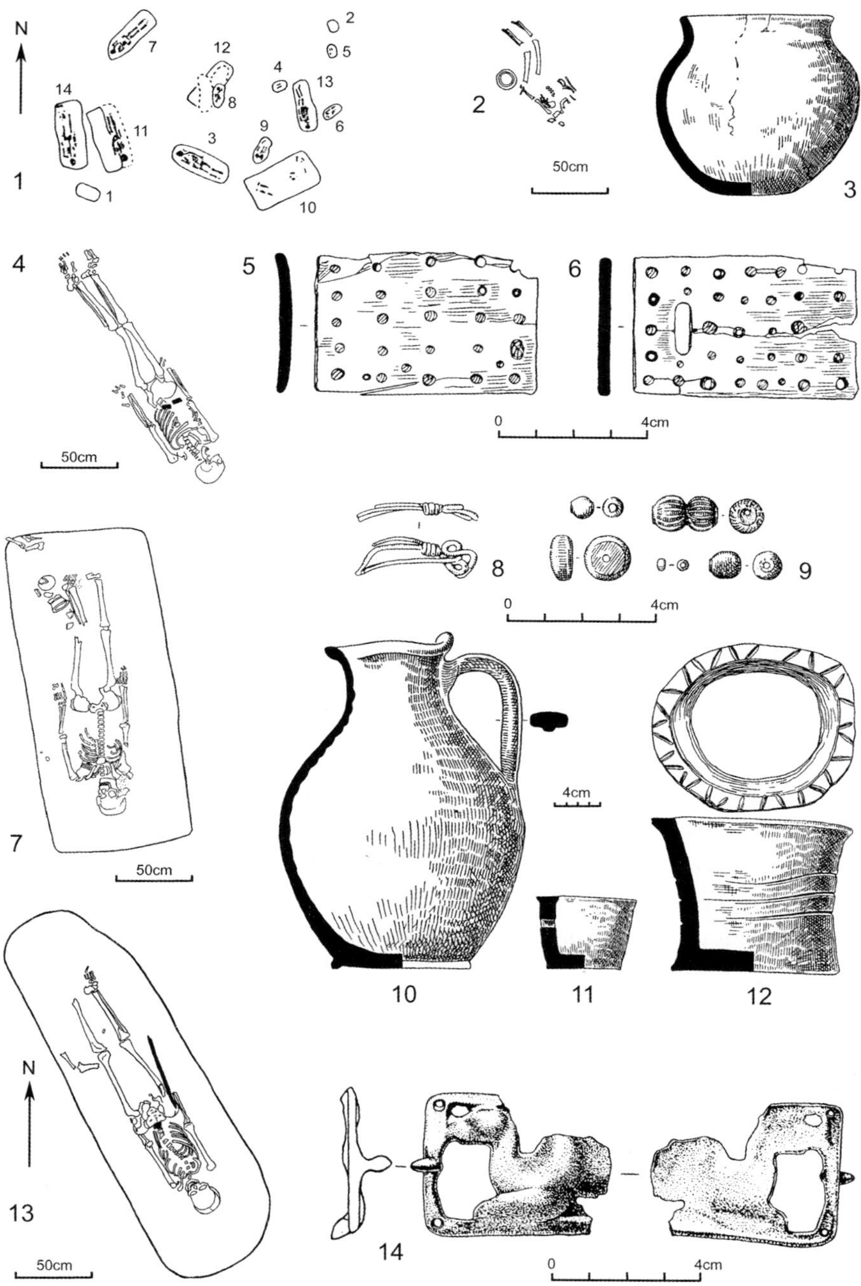

FIGURE 15.16 Burials in kurgan mounds at Verkhnee Pogromnoe, lower Volga region, second to first century BC. 1 Plan of burials in kurgan 1. 2–3 Burial 1, kurgan 1, plan and handmade vessel. 4–6 Burial 13, plan and belt plaques made of horn. 7–12 Burial 14, plan and finds. 13–14 Burial 4, kurgan 4, plan and bronze belt plaque.

Source: after Shilov 1975

set of weapons in the male graves (long sword, short sword/dagger, spear, arrowheads), and by a more diverse set of jewellery in female graves. Most items found in graves of this date seem to be of local origin. Some female jewellery (gold finger-rings, beads) could point to connections with the lower Dniester area and with the Greek colonies, probably via the city of Tanais, founded in the third century BC at the Don delta (Mordvintseva and Khabarova 2006).

The situation changed around the mid-second century BC. Although the standard burial rite and grave goods remained the same, social stratification was now more explicitly displayed in the cemeteries, manifested by connections in a variety of different directions. Male burials indicate links with nomadic groups from the Eurasian steppes (e.g. belt plaques [Figure 15.16, 5–6, 14], *phalerae*, and Animal style objects), with Hellenistic Iran (precious cups), with the Kuban region (jewellery, horse harness), and the lower Dnieper region (some of the *phalerae* from votive deposits; Mordvintseva 2011). Status objects from female graves tend to be of local or Kuban origin, but occasionally female burials contain items from Hellenistic Iran. Some elite graves of both sexes contain Greek pottery and ceramic *unguentaria*. It is worth noting that the ostentatious burials of this period occur in the same cemeteries as other graves, sometimes in the same kurgan mound and using the same burial rite.

The most ostentatious burial ever found in this region—Kosika burial 1—dates to the end of this period, in the later first century BC (Dvornichenko and Fedorov-Davydov 1993; Treister 2005). It has a non-standard burial rite and is located far away from any kurgan cemetery. The grave goods include a set of silver drinking vessels of the highest artistic quality, a golden funeral wreath, a gold pectoral with Animal style decoration, and many other imported precious objects. The funeral wreath and the drinking vessels can be considered as insignia obtained from a culture of greater social complexity.

The middle Sarmatian period (from the first to the mid-second century AD) is marked by changes in burial rite and the disappearance of votive hoards. Instead of burials inserted into ancient kurgans, graves were now under their own mounds. Square pits with the deceased person lying diagonally across the grave became widespread, and seem to have been preferred by the elite. The standard set of grave goods remained the same, but instead of handmade pots, sets of wheel-made pottery are found, represented by a plate and a jug. From then on, the geographical origin of status objects indicates a remarkable change in the connections of the social elite of the lower Volga and Don territory. Female and male graves were now furnished with Roman provincial bronze and silver vessels, while the jewellery and belt fittings, even Animal style objects, often came from the Greek workshops of the north Pontic region. The elite burials of the highest rank sometimes now appeared in separate groups of kurgans (e.g. Berdia, Oktyabr'skiy; Sergatskov 2002); in the Don delta these might be on the boundary of flat cemeteries (as at Kobyakovo; Prokhorova and Guguev 1992).

The late Sarmatian period (mid-second to fourth century AD) is characterized by further changes in burial rite. Most graves were now of the niche type. The buried person lay with their head to the north, and many show a deformation of the skull. The main set of burial goods remained, however, the same: a sheep's leg with a knife and pottery.

The number of elite burials decreased sharply, however. Most of the jewellery and status objects are types widespread in the north Pontic region; Animal style objects are no longer represented.

Changes in burial rite in the lower Volga region were long explained by nomadic migration from the east, but the fact that most kurgan cemeteries contain burials of all chronological periods suggests that the population remained largely unchanged. The changes can be explained by many causes, above all social factors (Mordvintseva 2011).

'Maeotian' Settlements and Cemeteries of the Lower Don Area

In the late first century BC a number of settlements appeared in the Don delta, but there has been little excavation. Associated with these are flat cemeteries, which display a different burial rite from the kurgan cemeteries. These sites in the lower Don area are similar to those of the Kuban region (Kamenetskiy 1989: 241, 2000: 74, 134), which has led scholars to explain their appearance in the delta in terms of a movement of Maeotian people north from the Kuban area at this date.

The flat cemeteries associated with the lower Don settlements (e.g. Kobyakovo, Nizhne-Gnilovskoe, Krepostnoe, Temernitskoe) show three basic forms of burial, although only part of the Kobyakovo burial ground is published (Kosyanenko 2008). The first type is characterized by catacombs with a chamber made in the narrow wall of the entrance. The burial chamber was cut down from the entrance pit, on the same axis, making the grave L-shaped in section (Figure 15.17, A). Many entrance pits for such catacombs contained a 'scarecrow'—the skull and leg bones of a horse or bull, or (rarely) a sheep. The deceased usually lay on their back, with the head pointing to the entrance of the chamber. The other two types of burial are niche graves and grave pits with side shelves (Figure 15.17, B). By the later second century AD, the number of niche graves increased. These graves often contained skeletons with skull deformation.

Conclusions

The material differences between regional groups noted for the period before the mid-first century BC most likely reflect different economic types and self-identifications of the respective populations. The archaeological evidence of the lower Volga region is characteristic of nomadic economies and cultures. The nature and connectivities of the regional elites also support this view. The appearance in male elite graves of status objects from the central Asian and Eurasian steppes may be linked to the well-known events at the end of the second century BC on the northern frontiers of Graeco-Bactria. These events resulted in increased mobility in the nomadic world throughout the steppe

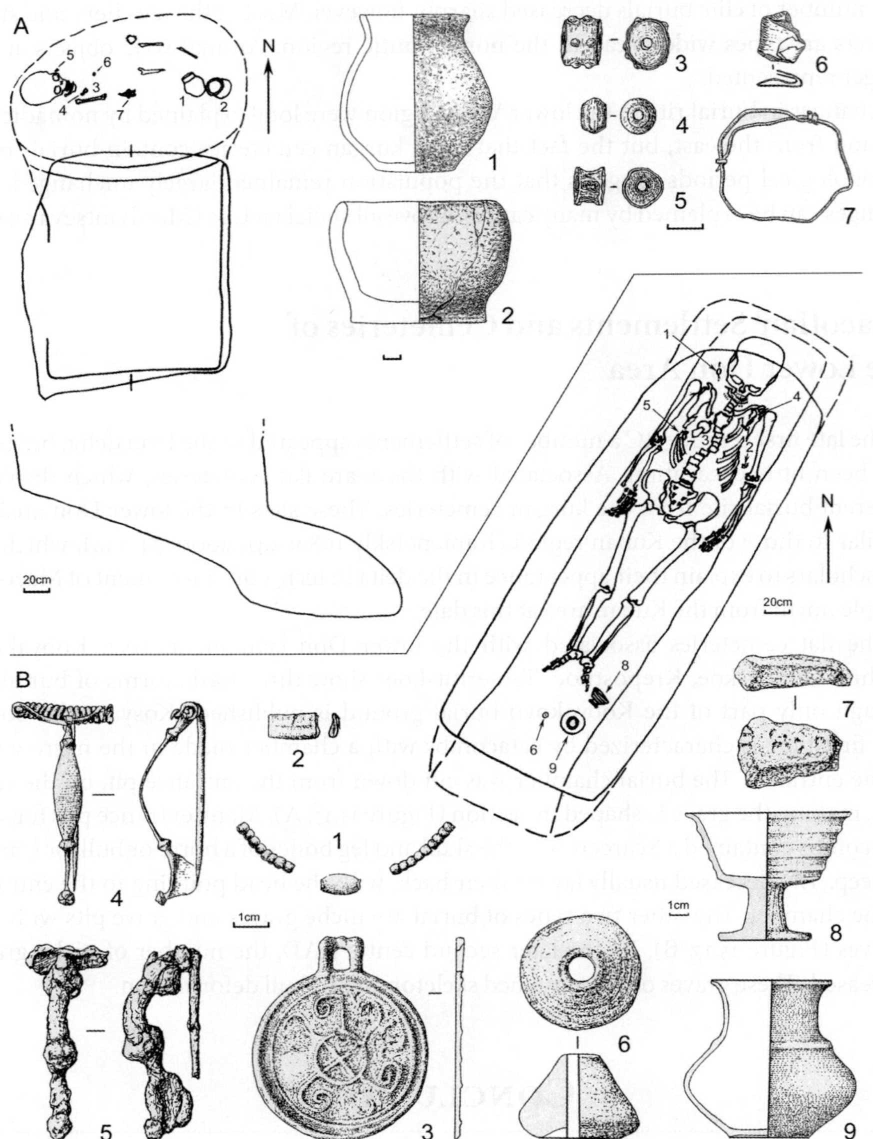

FIGURE 15.17 Burials in the flat cemetery of Kobyakovo, lower Don region. (A) Grave 27/1984: 1–2 hand-made vessels, 3–6 glass and bronze beads, 7 bronze arm-ring. (B) Grave 20/1984: 1 beads, 2 bronze tube, 3 mirror pendant, 4–5 fibulae, 6 clay spindle-whorl, 7 chalk, 8–9 ceramic vessels.

Source: excavations of V. K. Guguev 1984; we are grateful for permission to use these materials.

belt, and the intensified activity of Xiungnu people, which might have influenced the spread of certain status objects (for instance, belt plates) in the elite graves in this region.

The archaeological culture of the lower Dnieper region in the closing centuries of the first millennium BC belonged to a different type and contained no elements of material culture that can be identified with nomads. It is worth recalling the literary and epigraphic sources, which mention the presence of Celts and Bastarnae at precisely this time in the northern Black Sea region. This might explain why the lower Dnieper archaeological culture resembles that of neighbouring territories to the west. In the following period, however, this local culture changed, introducing a more nomadic-looking aspect. Crimea and the Kuban region show an even more complicated picture. There is a range of archaeological sites, which could be identified with various economic-cultural types.

By the mid-first century BC, the overall diversity of cultures in the north Pontic region was replaced by greater cultural uniformity over a broad territory from the Dniester to the Kuban and the Volga. This phenomenon is usually attributed to the process of 'Sarmatization' of the territories neighbouring the Volga-Don region, but there could be other possible explanations.

At the end of the second century BC, Rome's struggle for supremacy resulted in several wars with the king of Pontus, Mithridates VI Eupator, whose allies were barbarian peoples of the northern Caucasus and Crimea. The defeat of Mithridates radically changed the situation in the northern Black Sea region. It resulted in the subordination to Rome of the Greek *poleis* and the Bosporan kingdom, which was for a short time under the direct governance of the Empire in the reign of Nero. Later, Rome followed a policy of support for the Bosporan state, which kept some barbarian peoples subordinated, and prevented others from invading territory in the zone of interest to Rome. The general standardization of burial rites in the north Pontic region in the second and early third centuries AD can be interpreted as a certain stabilization of the political situation on the frontiers of the Bosporan kingdom, which lasted until the disastrous Gothic wars.

Notes

1. Good overviews of the Scythians and their art can be found in recent exhibition catalogues (e.g. Menghin et al. 2007; Trofimova 2007; Simpson and Pankova 2017).
2. For an overview to the methodological background of Soviet archaeology, see Klejn (1982). The importance of the historical-ethnic paradigm to Soviet and Russian archaeology alike is most influential.
3. The four stages comprised: (1) the Blumenfeld or Sauromatian, sixth to fourth century BC; (2) the Prokhorovka or Sauromatian-Sarmatian, fourth to second century BC; (3) the Susly or Sarmatian, late second century BC to second century AD; and (4) Shipovo or Alan, second to fourth century AD (see Grakov 1947).

4. From a central European perspective one might wonder about using the term Hallstatt in this context. The term has transferred to the lower Danube region as a result of the application of Reinecke's Hallstatt A–B to the Danubian Bronze Age.
5. Rods attached to the end of a horse bit, serving to attach the reins and as a stop piece.
6. Unpublished excavations by Y. Zaytsev.
7. The northern boundary of the Maeotian territory runs from Primorsko-Atkharsk on the shore of the Sea of Azov, along the Kirpili river and the right bank of the Kuban to Prochnookopskaya in the foothills of the north Caucasus. The western part of the territory borders the Bosporan kingdom at the Taman peninsula. The southern boundary is less clear.

References

Alekseev, A. Y. 1996. 'Skifskie tsari i "tsarskie kurgany" V–IV vv. do. n.e.' *Vestnik drevney istorii* 1996, 3: 99–113.

Alekseev, A. Y. 2007. 'Skythische Könige und Fürstenkurgane', in W. Menghin, H. Parzinger, A. Nagler, and M. Nawroth (eds) *Im Zeichen des goldenen Greifen: Königsgräber der Skythen*: 242–255. Berlin: Staatliche Museen zu Berlin, Preußischer Kulturbesitz.

Alekseeva, E. P. 1976. *Etnicheskie svyazi sarmatov i rannikh alan s mestnym naseleniem Severo-Zapadnogo Kavkaza*. Cherkessk: Karachaevo-Cherkesskoe Otdelenie of the Stavropol Publisher House.

Anfimov, N. V. 1954. 'Osnovnye etapy razvitiya meoto-sarmatskikh plemen Prikuban'ya (po materialam gruntovykh mogil'nikov)'. Avtoreferat dissertatsii, Institute of Archaeology, Moscow.

Anfimov, N. V. 1961. 'Protomeotskiy mogil'nik s. Nikolaevskogo'. *Sbornik materialov po arkheologii Adygei* 2: 103–130.

Anfimov, N. V. 1973. *Raskopki na pravoberezh'e r. Kubani: Arkheologicheskie otkrytiya 1972 g.* Moscow: Nauka.

Artamonov, M. I. 1948. 'Skifskoe tsarstvo v Krymu'. *Vestnik Leningradskogo Universiteta* 8: 56–78.

Babenchikov, V. P. 1957. 'Nekropol' Neapolya skifskogo', in P. N. Shults (ed.) *Istoriya i arkheologiya drevnego Krima*: 94–141. Kiev: Naukova dumka.

Beglova, E. 2002. 'Kopflos und gefesselt—Bestattungen der ganz anderen Art. Ein Ritualkomplex mit menschlichen Opfergaben aus der Grabstätte von Tenginskaja (Nordkaukasus)'. *Antike Welt* 3: 297–304.

Beglova, E. 2005. 'The first ritual complex of the Tenginskii burial-ground'. *Ancient Civilizations from Scythia to Siberia* 11: 41–84.

Belinskiy, A. B. 1990. 'K voprosu o vremeni poyavleniya shlemov assiriyskogo tipa na Severnom Kavkaze'. *Sovetskaya Archeologiya* 1990, 4: 190–195.

Belinskiy, A. B., D. S. Korobov, and S. Reinhold. 2009. 'Landshaftnaya archeologiya na Severnom Kavkaze: pervie rezul'taty issledovaniya predgornogo landshafta Kislovodska epochi pozdnego bronzovogo i rannego zheleznogo veka'. *Materialy po Izucheniyu Istoriko-kul'turnogo Naslediya Severnogo Kavkaza* 9: 177–220.

Berlizov, N. E. 2011. *Ritmy Sarmatii: Savromatsko-sarmatskie plemena Yuzhnoi Rossii v VII v. do n.e.–V v.n.e.* Krasnodar: Parabellum.

Bespalyi, E. I., N. E. Bespalaya, and B. A. Raev. 2007. *Drevnee naselenie Nizhnego Dona: Kurgannyi mogil'nik "Valovyi 1"*. Rostov-on-Don: Yuzhnyi nauchnyi tsentr Rossiyskoy Akademii nauk.

Bruyako, V. 1999. 'O sobytiyakh III v.do n.e. v Severo-Zapadnom Prichernomorye (chetyre contseptsii krizisa)'. *Vestnik drevney istorii 1999* , 3: 76–91.

Bruyako, V. 2005. *Rannie kochevniki v Evrope: X–V vv. do R. Kh.* Kishinev: Vysshaya antropologicheskaya shkola.

Bylkova, V. P. 2007. *Nizhnee Podneprov'e v antichnuyu epokhu (po materialam raskopok poseleniy)*. Kherson: Kherson University Press.

Chernenko, E. V., S. S. Bessonova, and J. V. Boltrik. 1986. *Skifskie pogrebal'nye pamjatniki stepey Severnogo Prichernomor'ya*. Kiev: Naukova Dumka.

Chochorowski, J. 1993. *Ekspansja kimmeryjska na tereny Europy środkowej (Die kimmerische Expansion in das mitteleuropäische Gebiet)*. Kraków: Uniwersytet Jagielloński.

Chochorowski, J., and S. Skoryj. 2000. 'Die Zentralbestattung des Gross-Grabhügels von Ryžanovka im rechtsseitigen Teil des ukrainischen Waldsteppengebietes', in *Pratiques funéraires dans l'Europe des 13e–4e s. av. J.-C. Actes du 3e Colloque International d'Archéologie Funéraire, organisé à Tulcea, 15–20 septembre 1997*: 105–122. Tulcea: Institut de Recherches Éco-Muséologiques de Tulcea.

Curtis, J. 1984. *Nush-i-Jan III: The Small Finds*. London: The British Institute of Persian Studies.

Dan, A. C., and H.-J. Gehrke. forthcoming. 'Zur Topographie der Taman-Halbinsel im Altertum', in U. Schlotzhauer and D. Zhuravlev (eds) *Die Geographie der Taman-(Halb) insel in der Antike: Untersuchungen zur Paläogeographie, historischen Topographie und Archäologie des asiatischen Teils des Kimmerischen Bosporus seit der griechischen Kolonisation*. Archäologie in Eurasien. Bonn: Habelt.

Daragan, M. 2009. *Geoinformazionnyj analiz transformatsii poselencheskikh struktur v nachale rannego zheleznogo veka v Srednem Podneprov'e: sostoyanie problemy i ,perspektivy issledovaniya*. Archeologiya i Geoinformatika 6. Moscow: Electronic publication.

Daragan, M. 2011. *Nachalo rannego zheleznogo veka v Dneprovskoy pravoberezhnoy lesostepi*. Kiev: KNT.

Dashevskaya, O. D. 1991. *Pozdnie skify v Krymu: Svod arkheologicheskikh istochnikov D1–07*. Moscow: Nauka.

Dubovskaya, O. R. 1997. 'Zur ethnischen und kulturellen Einordnung der "Novocherkassk-Gruppe"'. *Eurasia Antiqua* 3: 277–328.

Dudarev, S. L. 1991. *Iz istorii svyazey naseleniya Kavkaza s kimmeriysko-skifskim mirom*. Groznyi: Checheno-Ingushskiy gosudarstvennyi universitet.

Dvornichenko, V. V., and G. A. Fedorov-Davydov. 1993. 'Sarmatskoe pogrebenie skeptukha I v.n.e. u s. Kosika Astrakhanskoy oblasti'. *Vestnik drevney istorii* 1993, 3: 141–179.

Erlikh, V. R. 2007. *Severo-Zapadnyi Kavkaz v nachale zheleznogo veka: protomeotskaya gruppa pamyatnikov*. Moscow: Nauka.

Frolova, N. 1964. 'Monety skifskogo tsarya Skilura'. *Sovetskaya arkheologiya* 1: 44–55.

Galanina, L. K. 1997. *Die Kurgane von Kelermes: 'Königsgräber' der frühskythischen Zeit*. Berlin/ Moscow: Deutsches Archäologisches Institut, Eurasien-Abteilung.

Grakov, B. N. 1947. 'Γυναικοκρατουμενοι: perezhitki matriarkhata u sarmatov'. *Vestnik drevney istorii* 1947, 3: 100–121.

Gudkova, A. V., and M. M. Fokeev. 1984. *Zemledel'tsy i kochevniki v nizov'yakh Dunaya I–IV vv.n.e.* Kiev: Naukova dumka.

Gushchina, I. I., and I. P. Zasetskaya. 1994. *'Zolotoe kladbishche' rimskoy epokhi v Prikuban'e*. St Petersburg: Farn.

Iessen, A. A. 1953. 'K vorposu o pamyatnikakh 8.–7. vv. do n.e. na yuge Evropeyskoy chasti SSSR (Novocherkasskiy klad 1939 g.)'. *Sovyetskaya Arkheologiya* 18: 49–110.

Ivantchik, A. I. 2001. *Kimmerier und Skythen: kulturhistorische und chronologische Probleme der Archäologie der osteuropäischen Steppen und Kaukasiens in vor- und frühskythischer Zeit*. Berlin/Moscow: Deutsches Archäologisches Institut, Eurasien-Abteilung.

Ivantchik, A. I. 2005. *Am Vorabend der Kolonisation: Das nördliche Schwarzmeergebiet und die Steppennomaden des 8.–7. Jhs. v. Chr. in der klassischen Literaturtradition: Mündliche Überlieferung, Literatur und Geschichte*. Berlin/Moscow: Deutsches Archäologisches Institut, Eurasien-Abteilung.

Ivantchik, A. I. 2007. 'Zum Totenritual skythischer "Könige": Herodot und der archäologische Befund', in W. Menghin, H. Parzinger, A. Nagler, and M. Nawroth (eds) *Im Zeichen des goldenen Greifen: Königsgräber der Skythen*: 238–241. Berlin: Staatliche Museen zu Berlin, Preußischer Kulturbesitz.

Kamenetskiy, I. S. 1989. 'Meoty i drugie plemena Severo-Zapadnogo Kavkaza v VII v.do n.e.–III v.n.e.', in A. I. Melyukova (ed.) *Stepi Evropeyskoy chasti SSSR v skifo-sarmatskoe vremya*: 224–251. Moscow: Nauka.

Kamenetskiy, I. S. 2000. *Arkheologicheskie pamyatniki meotov Kubani*. Krasnodar: Kuban University Press.

Kashuba, M. T. 2000. 'Rannee zhelezo v lesostepi mezhdu Dnestrom i Siretom (kul'tura Cozia-Sacharna)'. *Stratum Plus* 2000, 3: 241–488.

Kashuba, M. T. 2008. 'Materiale ale culturii Şoldăneşti în bazinul Nistrului Mijlociu—observaţii preliminare'. *Tyragetia, Serie Nouă* 2, 1: 37–50.

Kashuba, M. T., M. Daragan, and O. Levitskiy. 2010. 'Technologicheskie novshestva rannego zheleznogo veka: perspektivy izucheniya ranney goncharnoy seroglinyanoy keramiki vostochnogo prikarpat'ya'. *Revista Arheologică, Serie Nouă* 5, 2: 28–61.

Kelterbaum, D., H. Brückner, A. Porotov, U. Schlotzhauer, and D. Zhuravlev. 2011. 'Geoarchaeology of Taman Peninsula (Kertch Strait, south-west Russia)—the example of the ancient Greek settlement of Golubitskaya 2'. *Die Erde* 142, 3: 235–258.

Kerschner, M., and U. Schlotzhauer. 2007. 'Ein neues Klassifikationssystem der ostgriechischen Keramik', in J. Cobet, V. von Graeve, W.-D. Niemeier, and K. Zimmermann (eds.) *Frühes Ionien: eine Bestandsaufnahme: Panionion-Symposion Güzelçamlı*: 295–317. Mainz: Philipp von Zabern.

Khakhutaishvili, D. A. 2009. *The Manufacture of Iron in Ancient Colchis*. British Archaeological Reports International Series 1905. Oxford: Archaeopress.

Khrapunov, I. N. 1991. 'Bulganakskoe pozdneskifskoe gorodishche'. *Materialy po arkheologii, istorii i etnografii Tavriki* 2: 3–34.

Khrapunov, I. N. 2007. 'Pogrebenie voina 2 v.n.e. iz mogil'nika Opushki', in Y. P. Zaytsev and V. I. Mordvintseva (eds) *Drevnyaya Tavrika*: 115–124. Simferopol: Universum.

Klejn, L. S. 1982. *Archaeological Typology*. British Archaeological Reports International Series 153. Oxford: Archaeopress.

Klepikov, V. M. 2002. *Sarmaty Nizhnego Povolzh'ya v IV–III vv.do n.e.* Volgograd: Volgograd University Press.

Kolotuchin, V. A. 1996. *Gornyy Krym v ėpochu pozdney bronzy, nachale zheleznogo veka: ėtnokulturnye processy*. Kiev: Juzhnogorodskie vedomosti.

Koltukhov, S. G. 1999. *Ukrepleniya Krymskoy Skifii*. Simferopol: Sonat.

Koltukhov, S. G. 2007. 'Osnovnoe pogrebenie kurgana Besh-Oba 4/2', in Y. P. Zaytsev and V. I. Mordvintseva (eds) *Drevnyaya Tavrika*: 193–206. Simferopol: Universum.

Koltukhov, S. G., and V. Y. Yurochkin. 2004. *Ot Skifii k Gotii: Ocherki istorii izucheniya varvarskogo neseleniya Stepnogo i Predgornogo Kryma (VII v. do n.e.–VII v.n.e.)*. Simferopol: Sonat.

Korobov, D. S., and A. V. Borisov. 2013. 'The origins of terraced field agriculture in the Caucasus. New discoveries in the Kislovodsk Basin'. *Antiquity* 87: 1086–1103.

Kossack, G. 1987. 'Von den Anfängen des skytho-iranischen Tierstils', in L. K. Galanina (ed.) *Skythika: Vorträge zur Entstehung des skytho-iranischen Tierstils und zu Denkmälern des Bosporanischen Reichs anläßlich einer Ausstellung der Leningrader Ermitage in München 1984*: 24–86. Munich: Verlag der Bayerischen Akademie der Wissenschaften.

Kostenko, V. I. 1993. *Sarmaty v Nizhnem Podneprov'e*. Dnepropetrovsk: Dnepropetrovsk University Press.

Kosyanenko, V. M. 2008. *Nekropol' Kobyakova gorodishcha (po materialam raskopok 1956–1962)*. Donskie Drevnosti 9. Azov: Azovskiy arkheologicheskiy musey.

Kovpanenko, G. T. 1986. *Sarmatskoe pogrebenie I v.n.e. na Yuzhnom Buge*. Kiev: Naukova dumka.

Kozenkova, V. I. 1992. *Seržen'-Jurt: Ein Friedhof der späten Bronze- und frühen Eisenzeit*. Materialien zur Allgemeinen und Vergleichenden Archäologie 48. Mainz: Phillip von Zabern.

Kozenkova, V. I. 2002. *U istokov gorskogo mentaliteta: mogil'nik ėpochi pozdney bronzy—rannego zheleza u aula Serzhen'-Jurt, Chechnya*. Materialy po izucheniyu istoriko-kul'turnogo naslediya Severnogo Kavkaza 3. Moscow: Pamjatniki Istoričeskoj Mysli.

Kris, Kh. I. 1981. *Kizil-kobinskaya kul'tura i tavry*. Moscow: Nauka.

Kryžytskiy, S. D. 1993. *Arkhitektura antichnykh gosudarstv Severnogo Prichernomor'ya*. Kiev: Naukova dumka.

Kutaisov, V. A., and V. B. Uzhentsev. 1997. 'Kalos-Limen (raskopki 1988–1995 gg.)'. *Arkheologiya Kryma* 1: 43–57.

Lantsov, S. 2003. *Antichnoe svyatilishche na zapadnom beregu Kryma*. Kiev: Stilos.

Leskov, A. M. (ed.) 1985. *Sokrovishcha kurganov Adygei*. Moscow: Katalog vystavki.

Leskov, A. M., and V. R. Erlikh. 1999. *Mogil'nik Fars-Klady: pamyatnik perekhoda ot epokhi pozdney bronzy k rannemu zheleznomu veku na Severo-Zapadnom Kavkaze*. Moscow: Gosudarstvennyi Muzei Vostoka.

Loboda, I. I., A. E. Puzdrovskiy, and J. P. Zajcev. 2002. 'Prunkbestattungen des 1. Jh. n. Chr. in der Nekropole Ust'-Al'ma auf der Krim. Die Ausgrabungen des Jahres 1996'. *Eurasia Antiqua* 8: 295–346.

Lysenko, A. 2009. 'Svyatilishcha rimskogo vremeni yuzhnoy chasti Gornogo Kryma (opyt sistematizatsii)'. *Stratum plus* 4: 374–400.

Magomedov, B. 2001. *Chernyakhovskaya kul'tura: Problema etnosa*. Lublin: Lublin University Press.

Maisuradze, B., and G. Gobedishvili. 2001. 'Alter Bergbau in Rača', in I. Gambashidze, A. Hauptmann, R. Slotta, and Ü. Yalcin (eds) *Georgien: Schätze aus dem Land des Goldenen Vlies*: 130–135. Bochum: Bergbaumuseum.

Makhortych, S. V. 1994. *Kimmeriytsy na Severnom Kavkaze*. Kiev: AN Ukrainy, Institut Archeologii.

Makhortych, S. V. 2005. *Kimmeriytsy Severnogo Prichernomor'ya*. Kiev: Shlyakh.

Makhortych, S. V., and M. M. Ievlev. 1992. 'Über die Anfangsperiode der Geschichte der Kimmerier'. *Acta Archaeologica Carpathica* 31: 107–122.

Maksimenko, V. E. 1983. *Savromaty i sarmaty na Nizhnem Donu*. Rostov-on-Don: Rostov University Press.

Mamontov, V. I. 2000. *Drevnee naselenie Levoberezh'ya Dona (po materialam kurgannogo mogil'nika Pervomayskiy VII)*. Volgograd: Volgograd University Press.

Marchenko, I. 1996. *Siraki Kubani*. Krasnodar: Kuban University Press.

Marchenko, I. I., and N. Limberis. 2008. 'Römische Importe in sarmatischen und maiotischen Denkmälern des Kubangebietes', in H. Parzinger (ed.) *Römische Importe in sarmatischen und maiotischen Gräbern zwischen Unterer Donau und Kuban*. Archäologie in Eurasien 25: 265–626. Mainz: Philipp von Zabern.

Marchenko, K. K. 1999. 'Osnovnye aspekty i rezul'taty varvaskich kontaktov i vzaimodejstvij v Severnom Pričernomor'e skifskoj ėpochi'. *Stratum Plus* 1999, 3: 333–353.

Medvedskaja, M. I. 1992. 'Periodizacija skifskoj archaiki i Drevnij Vostok'. *Rossijskaja Archeologija* 1992, 3: 86–107.

Menghin, W., H. Parzinger, A. Nagler, and M. Nawroth (eds). 2007. *Im Zeichen des goldenen Greifen: Königsgräber der Skythen*. Berlin: Staatliche Museen zu Berlin, Preußischer Kulturbesitz.

Metzner-Nebelsick, C. 2000. 'Kimmerier', in *Reallexikon der Germanischen Altertumskunde 16*: 504–523. Berlin/New York: Walter de Gruyter.

Metzner-Nebelsick, C. 2002. *Der 'Thrako-Kimmerische' Formenkreis aus der Sicht der Urnenfelder- und Hallstattzeit im südöstlichen Pannonien*. Vorgeschichtliche Forschungen 23. Rahden: Marie Leidorf.

Mordvintseva, V. I. 2008. 'Phalerae of horse harness in votive depositions of the 2nd–1st century BC in the North Pontic region and the Sarmatian paradigm', in P. Guldager Bilde and J. Petersen (eds) *Meetings of Cultures in the Black Sea Region: Between Conflict and Coexistence*. Black Sea Studies 8: 47–66. Aarhus: Aarhus University Press.

Mordvintseva, V. I. 2011. 'Kulturnye izmeneniya v Nizhnem Povolzh'e po materialam kompleksov s predmetami iz dragotsennykh metallov (III v. do n.e.–ser. III v.n.e.)', in S. Monakhov (ed.) *Antichnyi mir i arkheologiya*. Saratov: Saratov University Press.

Mordvintseva, V. I. 2013. 'The Sarmatians: the creation of archaeological evidence'. *Oxford Journal of Archaeology* 32: 203–219.

Mordvintseva, V. I., and N. V. Khabarova. 2006. *The Ancient Gold of the Volga Region*. Simferopol: Tarpan.

Mordvintseva, V. I., E. Khachaturova, and T. Yurchenko. 2010. *Treasures of Ancient Kuban*. Simferopol/Krasnodar: Universum.

Motzenbäcker, I. 1996. *Sammlung Kossnierska: Der digorische Formenkreis der kaukasischen Bronzezeit*. Museum für Vor- und Frühgeschichte Bestandskataloge, Band 3. Berlin: Staatliche Museen zu Berlin, Preußischer Kulturbesitz.

Mozolevskiy, B. N. 1979. *Tovsta mogila*. Kiev: Naukova Dumka.

Mozolevskiy, B. N., and S. V. Polin. 2005. *Kurgany skifskogo Gerrosa IV v. do n. ė.: Babina, Vodyana i Soboleva mogily*. Kiev: Stilos.

Murzin, V. Yu. 1984. *Skifskaya arkhaika Severnogo Prichernomor'ya*. Kiev: Naukova Dumka.

Myts, V., and A. Lysenko. 2001. 'Pozdneantichnoe svyatilishche Taraktash v Krymu', in M. Vakhtina, V. Zuev, E. Rogov, and V. Khrashanovskiy (eds) *Bosporskiy fenomen: kolonizatsiya regiona, formirovanie polisov, obrazovanie gosudarstva*: 96–100. St Petersburg: The State Hermitage Press.

Nicic, A. 2008. *Interferențe cultural-cronologie în nord-vestul Pontului Euxin la finele mil. II–începutul mil. I a. Chr.* Chișinău: Muzeul Național de Arheologie și Istorie a Moldovei.

Novichenkova, N. 2002. *Ustroystvo i obryadnost' svyatilishcha u perevala Gurzufskoe Sedlo*. Yalta: Crimean University of Humanities Press.

Ochotnikov, S. B. 1990. *Niznee Podnestrov'e: v VI–V vv.do n.e.* Kiev: Naukova Dumka.

Ochotnikov, S. B. 2006. 'The Chorai of the ancient cities in the lower Dniester area (6th century BC–3rd century AD)', in P. G. Bilde and V. F. Stolba (eds) *Surveying the Greek Chora: The Black Sea Region in a Comparative Perspective*: 81–98. Aarhus: Aarhus University Press.

Ol'chovskij, V. S. 1991. *Pogrebal'no-pominal'naya obrjadnost' naseleniya stepnoy Skifii (7–3 vv. do n. ė.)*. Moscow: Nauka.

Parzinger, H. 2004. *Die Skythen*. Munich: Beck.

Petrenko, V. G. 2006. *Krasnoeznamenskii burial-ground: Early Scythian elite burial-mounds in the Northern Caucasus*. Berlin/Bordeaux/Moscow: Paleograph Press.

Pieniążek, M. 2012. *Architektur in der Steppe: Spätbronzezeitliche Siedlungen im nordpontischen Raum*. Bonn: Habelt.

Pogrebova, N. N. 1956. 'Pogrebenie na zemlyanom valu akropolya Kamenskogo gorodishcha'. *Kratkie soobshcheniya Instituta istorii material'noy kul'tury* 1956: 94–97.

Pogrebova, N. N. 1961. 'Pogrebeniya v mavzolee Neapolya Skifskogo'. *Materialy i issledovaniya po arkheologii SSSR* 96: 103–213.

Polin, S. V. 1992. *Ot Skifii k Sarmatii*. Kiev: Arkheolog.

Polin, S. V. 2007. 'Fürstenkurgane in der ukrainischen Steppenzone', in W. Menghin, H. Parzinger, A. Nagler, and M. Nawroth (eds) *Im Zeichen des goldenen Greifen: Königsgräber der Skythen*: 256–267. Berlin: Staatliche Museen zu Berlin, Preußischer Kulturbesitz.

Polin, S. V., and M. Daragan. 2010. 'Raboty na Aleksandropol'skom kurgane v 2008 g', in A. A. Maslennikov, N. A. Gavriljuk, and A. A. Zavojkin (eds) *Symbola: antichnyi mir Severnogo Prichernomor'ya, Noveyshie nachodki i otkrytiya 1*: 187–205. Moscow: Triumf print.

Popa, A. 2012. 'Mythos "Spätskythen": Einige kritische Bemerkungen zu den "Spätskythen" und zur "spätskythischen" Kultur im nordwestlichen Schwarzmeergebiet und am unteren Dnjestr', in *Abstracts of the International Colloquium 'The Romans at the Black Sea During the Time of Augustus', Tulcea, 5–9 June 2012*. Tulcea: Institutul de Cercetări Eco-Muzeale Tulcea.

Popova, E. A. 2011. 'Pozdneskifskaya kul'tura: istoriya izucheniya, problemy, gipotezy'. *Vestnik Moskovskogo Universiteta* 1: 136–147.

Povalahev, N. 2008. *Die Griechen am Nordpontos: die nordpontische Kolonisation im Kontext der grossen griechischen Kolonisationsbewegung vom 8. bis 6. Jahrhundert v. Chr.* Munich: Utz.

Prokhorova, T. A., and V. K. Guguev. 1992. 'Bogatoe sarmatskoe pogrebenie v kurgane 10 Kobyakovskogo mogil'nika'. *Sovetskaya archaeologiya* 1992, 1: 142–161.

Puzdrovskiy, A. E. 2007. *Krymskaya Skifiya II v. do n.e.–III v.n.e. Pogrebal'nye pamyatniki*. Simferopol: Biznes-Inform.

Puzdrovskiy, A. E. 2013. 'Ust'-Al'ma: Die Siedlung und Nekropole', in S. Müller and M. Schmauder (eds) *Die Krim: Goldene Insel im Schwarzen Meer: Griechen–Skythen–Goten. Begleitbuch zur Ausstellung im LVR-LandesMuseum Bonn: 4. Juli 2013–19. Januar 2014*: 290–323. Frankfurt am Main: Primus Verlag.

Puzdrovskiy, A. E., and J. P. Zajcev. 2004. 'Prunkbestattungen des 1. Jh. n. Chr. in der Nekropole Ust'-Al'ma, Krim. Die Grabungen des Jahres 1999'. *Eurasia Antiqua* 10: 229–267.

Reinhold, S. 2007. *Die Spätbronze- und frühe Eisenzeit im Kaukasus: materielle Kultur, Chronologie und überregionale Beziehungen*. Bonn: Habelt.

Reinhold, S., A. B. Belinskiy, and D. S. Korobov. 2007. 'Landschaftsarchäologie im Nordkaukasus. Erste Ergebnisse der Untersuchung der Vorgebirgslandschaft bei Kislovodsk während der Spätebronze- und frühen Eisenzeit'. *Eurasia Antiqua* 13: 139–180.

Reinhold, S., D. S. Korobov, and A. B. Belinskiy. 2017. *Zwischen Mobilität und Sesshaftigkeit: Studien zu einer neu entdeckten bronzezeitlichen Kulturlandschaft im Hochgebirge des Nordkaukasus*. Archäologie in Eurasien 38. Bonn: Habelt.

Rolle, R., and V. J. Murzin. 1998. *Königskurgan Chertomlyk: Ein skythischer Grabhügel des 4. vorchristlichen Jahrhunderts*. Mainz: Philipp von Zabern.

Rostovtzeff, M. 1911. 'Svyatilishche frakiyskikh bogov i nadpisi benefetsiariev v Ay-Todore'. *Izvestiya Arkheologicheskoy Komissii* 40: 1–42.

Rostovtzeff, M. 1922. *Iranians and Greeks in South Russia*. Oxford: Oxford University Press.

Rostovtzeff, M. 1929. *The Animal Style in South Russia and China*. Princeton: Princeton University Press.

Ruban, V. V. 1985. 'Problemy istoricheskogo razvitiya Olviyskoy khory v IV–II vv.do n.e.'. *Vestnik drevney istorii* 1985, 1: 26–45.

Sergatskov, I. V. 2002. *Sarmatskie kurgany na Ilovle*. Volgograd: Volgograd University Press.

Sergatskov, I. V. 2009. 'Klad II v. do n.e. iz okrestnostej stanitsy Kachalinskoy'. *Rossiyskaya arkheologiya* 4: 149–159.

Shcheglov, A. N. 1998. 'Eshche raz o pozdneskifskoy culture Kryma (K probleme proiskhozhdeniya)'. *Problemy arkheologii* 4: 141–153.

Shilov, V. P. 1955. 'Novye dannye ob Elizavetovskom gorodishche po raskopkam 1952 g.'. *Sovetskaya arkheologiya* 23: 228–249.

Shilov, V. P. 1959. 'Kalinovskiy kurgannyi mogil'nik'. *Materialy i issledovaniya po arkheologii SSSR* 60: 323–523.

Shilov, V. P. 1975. *Ocherki po istorii drevnikh plemen Nizhnego Povolzh'ya*. Leningrad: Nauka.

Shults, P. N. 1957. 'Issledovaniya Neapolya skifskogo 1945–1950', in P. N. Shults (ed.) *Istoriya i arkheologiya drevnego Krima*: 62–93. Kiev: Naukova dumka.

Simonenko, A. V. 1993. *Sarmaty Tavrii*. Kiev: Naukova dumka.

Simonenko, A. V., I. I. Marchenko, and N. J. Limberis. 2008. *Römische Importe in sarmatischen Denkmälern des nördlichen Schwarzmeergebietes: Römische Importe in sarmatischen und maiotischen Gräbern zwischen Unterer Donau und Kuban*. Archäologie in Eurasien 25. Mainz: Philipp von Zabern.

Simpson, St J., and Pankova, S. V. (eds). 2017. *The BP Exhibition Scythians: Warriors of Ancient Siberia*. London: Thames and Hudson.

Skakov, A. J. 2009. 'Nekotorye problemy istorii Severo-Zapadnogo Zakavkaz'ya v ėpokhu pozdney bronzy—rannego zheleza'. *Kratkie Soobshcheniya Instituta Archeologii* 223: 143–172.

Skoryj, S. A. 1999. *Kimmeriytsy v ukrainskoy lesostepi*. Kiev: Poltava 'Arkheologiya'.

Skripkin, A. S. 1990. *Aziatskaya Sarmatiya: Problemy khronologii i ee istoricheskiy aspect*. Saratov: Saratov University Press.

Skripkin, A. S. 1997. *Etyudy po istorii i culture sarmatov*. Volgograd: Volgograd University Press.

Smirnov, K. F. 1960. 'Bykovskie kurgany'. *Materialy po istorii i arkheologii SSSR* 78: 167–268.

Smirnov, K. F. 1984. *Sarmaty i utverzhdenie ikh politicheskogo gospodstva v Skifii*. Moscow: Nauka.

Solov'ev, S. L. 1999. *Ancient Berezan: The Architecture, History and Culture of the First Greek Colony in the Northern Black Sea*. Leiden/Boston/Cologne: Brill.

Spitsyn, A. A. 1909. 'Falary yuzhnoy Rossii'. *Izvestiya arkheologicheskoy komissii* 29: 18–53.

Stoyanova, A. A. 2012. *Detskie pogrebeniya iz mogil'nika Opushki (po rezul'tatam raskopok 2003–2009 gg.)*. Simferopol: Dolya.

Symonovich, S. R. E. A. 1983. *Naselenie stolitsy pozdneskifskogo tsarstva*. Kiev: Naukova dumka.

Terenozhkin, A. I. 1976. *Kimmerijcy*. Kiev: Naukova Dumka.

Tokhtasyev, S. R. 2005. 'Sauromatae—Sarmatae—Syrmatae'. *Khersonesskiy sbornik* 14: 291–306.

Treister, M. 2005. 'On a vessel with figured friezes from a private collection, on burials in Kosika and once more on the "Ampsalakos School"'. *Ancient Civilizations from Scythia to Siberia* 11: 199–255.

Trofimova, A. A. 2007. *The Art of the Ancient Cities of the Northern Black Sea Region*. Los Angeles: J. Paul Getty Museum.

Vanchugov, V. P. 1990. *Belozerskie pamyatniki v Severo-Zapadnom Prichernomor'e*. Kiev: Naukova Dumka.

Vinogradov, Y. G. 1997. 'Khersonesskiy dekret o "nesenii Dionisa" IOSPE I 2 343 i vtorzhenie sarmatov v Skifiyu'. *Vestnik drevney istorii* 1997, 3: 104–124.

Vyaz'mitina, M. I. 1972. *Zolotobalkovskiy mogil'nik*. Kiev: Naukova dumka.

Vysotskaya, T. N. 1972. *Pozdnie skify v Yugo-Zapadnom Krymu*. Kiev: Naukova Dumka.

Vysotskaya, T. N. 1979. *Neapol—stolitsa gosudarstva pozdnikh skifov*. Kiev: Naukova Dumka.

Vysotskaya, T. N. 1994. *Ust'-Al'minskoe gorodishche i nekropol'*. Kiev: Naukova dumka.

Zaytsev, Y. P. 2004. *The Scythian Neapolis 2nd century BC to 3rd century AD: Investigation into the Graeco-Barbarian City on the Northern Black Sea Coast*. British Archaeological Reports International Series 1219. Oxford: Archaeopress.

Zaytsev, Y. P. (ed.) 2005. *Drevnie sokrovishcha Yugo-Zapadnogo Kryma: Katalog vystavki*. Simferopol: Tarpan.

Zaytsev, Y. P., and S. G. Koltukhov. 2004. 'Pogrebenie voina ellinisticheskogo vremeni u s. Chisten'koe v predgornom Krymu'. *Bosporskie issledovaniya* 7: 242–259.

Zaytsev, Y. P., V. I. Mordvintseva, and I. I. Nenevolya. 2007. 'Svyatilishche Beshik-Tau pervykh vekov n.e. v yugo-zapadnom Krymu', in N. O. Gavrilyuk (ed.) *Arkheologichny doslidzhennya v Ukraini 2005–2006*: 33–34. Kiev: Naukova dumka.

CHAPTER 16

EUROPE TO ASIA

LUDMILA KORYAKOVA

Introduction

THE area labelled 'Europe to Asia' embraces the European part of the Russian Federation. Geographically it coincides almost completely with the Russian plain. The dividing line between Europe and Asia is drawn along the watershed of the Ural mountains and the Ural river. In late prehistory, this vast area was occupied by societies of different social and economic character (nomadic, semi-nomadic, settled pastoralists, specialist metallurgists, hunters, and fishers), and different cultural identities. This chapter outlines the major cultural worlds of the eastern part of eastern Europe in the early Iron Age, chronologically spanning the period from the ninth/eight centuries BC to the third/fourth centuries AD, starting at the transition to the Iron Age and ending on the eve of the 'Great Folk Movement'.[1]

With regard to the introduction of iron into the area under consideration, we can define two basic subdivisions of the Iron Age: the early Iron Age (900/800 cal BC to AD 400) and the late Iron Age (AD 400 to 600), which in the Russian tradition is defined as the early medieval period. This framework is appropriate for the southern part of the region (steppe and forest steppe), but part of the northern (boreal) zone is characterized by different periods conditioned by a delayed technological evolution. In these northern areas, the Bronze Age effectively continued up to the fourth century BC, and development there was more gradual. The decline of the Bronze Age societies partly resulted from climate destabilization in the shape of the colder and wetter period that developed in Northern Eurasia in the climatic interval 3500–2500 cal BP (Budja 2015). Strictly speaking, over most of the first millennium BC, almost all forest cultures, with some exceptions, practised an economy based on bone and stone technology. In substantial parts of the forest zone, the widespread use of iron products, and so the start of the Iron Age proper, occurred in the late first millennium BC (Egoreichenko 2006; Koryakova and Kuzminykh 2021). Thus in this northern zone, the concept of the Iron Age is an archaeological construct that only partially reflects the realities of societal development there.

The east European (Russian) plain is one of the largest in the world. Its major characteristics are: (1) a mostly mild and arid continental climate, formed largely under the influence of the Atlantic and Arctic oceans, and (2) clearly expressed natural zones, the structure of which is greatly influenced by the flat relief and the neighbouring regions—central Europe, and north and central Asia. The Russian Plain has pronounced latitudinal zoning of soils and vegetation. There is a complex spectrum, from the Arctic tundra to the deserts of the temperate zone. The greater part is dominated by dark coniferous forest (*taiga*), merging into a zone of mixed forest consisting of various combinations of large- and small-leafed trees and spruces. In the south, the forests turn into the forest steppe, which gives way to steppe and semi-desert. In the recent past, the natural resources of the Russian plain were very rich and diverse (Milkov and Gvozdetskei 1975).

The people of eastern Europe became familiar with iron in the mid-second millennium BC, but it was some time before its benefits were realized. Among the regions where this metal was definitely produced earlier, one can mention south-eastern Europe and the Urals (Koryakova and Epimakhov 2007). Currently available data show that the earliest iron artefacts in the Volga-Kama area relate to the final Bronze Age, between 1200/1100 BC and the earlier ninth century BC (Kuzminykh and Chizhevsky 2009). The decline of Bronze Age societies partly resulted from climate destabilization into colder and wetter conditions. This change disrupted the basis of the settled pastoral economy; there followed an economic reorientation to nomadic pastoralism in the steppe area and cultural reorganization in the forest steppe. Some traditional raw material sources may have been exhausted and tin supplies became more difficult to acquire.

The transition to widespread use of iron tools and weapons in the temperate zone occurred between the eighth and third centuries BC. By the end of the ninth century BC, the population of eastern Europe had mastered the process of iron production, and in the eighth century BC they manufactured bimetallic swords and learned to make steel (Trans-Caucasus, northern Black Sea region, middle Volga). During a short period between the eighth and seventh centuries BC in these areas, all the major operations of the iron-making process were developed, namely the production of various types of steel, hot forging, welding, and surface and edge carburization. Once established, the technology spread from south-east Europe northwards and eastwards between the eighth and fifth centuries BC. One of the first recipients of the new technology was the Ananyino metallurgical centre in the Cis-Urals, whence it was passed on further north and west to Scandinavia (Chizhevsky 2011). From the outset, the Ananyino metallurgists were in close contact with the Caucasus and Black Sea centres, from where the so-called Cimmerian bronzes were imported (Terekhova et al. 1997). The development of metallurgy and the need to transport ore, metals, and products stimulated the development of a network of global and local trade and exchange communications of various lengths, up to thousands of kilometres. The invention of stiff horse harnesses and riding skills contributed to the creation of the cavalry.

During the last centuries BC and beginning of the first millennium AD, almost all zones entered the true Iron Age. Variations in degrees of technological and social advance are apparent between different regions and localities, some of which demonstrated internal unity and shared common cultural models, forming specific cultural worlds. Later, I will focus on those worlds that relate to the particular area of our interest. The first concerns the part of the nomadic world occupying the steppe zone between the Urals and the river Don. The cultural formations of the forest zone will also be examined. If the nomadic peoples and their material expressions are relatively well represented in Western publications, the same cannot be said of the people inhabiting the vast forests of north-east Europe. Figures 16.1 and 16.2 show the main cultural configurations of these zones during the earlier and later Iron Age respectively, while Table 16.1 sets out the cultural sequences and their dating in the different parts of the area under review.

The Nomadic World

The nomads of the early Iron Age were the first peoples to occupy the vast expanses of the steppes, including watersheds and arid areas, and came into close contact with state societies.[2] The early Eurasian nomads did not know writing. Some contradictory and fragmentary information relating to their history is preserved in ancient literary sources. Archaeological sites provide us with abundant data illuminating various aspects of nomadic culture. Pastoral nomadism as an economic, social, and cultural phenomenon emerged in the first millennium BC, though its preconditions matured during the Bronze Age.[3] In addition to the specific environmental conditions, in which large numbers of animals can be grazed year-round, it requires technological expertise and a suitable social context. An interregional division of labour and a corresponding level of overall economic and political structuring were both important requirements for Eurasian nomadism, since its narrowly specific economy is dependent on access to the production of sedentary societies. The degree of mobility, herd composition, and range and distance of migrations obviously depended on local environmental, social, and economic conditions, and the traditions of any given society (Khazanov 1984; Koryakova and Epimakhov 2007).

The nomadic world, stretching from Mongolia to the Great Hungarian plain (*puszta*), was composed of various cultures, which changed their configurations over space and time, but were united by a number of shared cultural attributes: a mobile mode of life, an animal herding economy, horse riding, burial under barrows, special types of material culture, religion and symbolic system. It should be stressed that the inhabitants of Eurasian steppes were not 'pure' nomads. This is especially true of the nomads of eastern Europe. They bred sheep, goats, horses, and cattle. Herd composition strongly depended on particular environments. The pastoral nomadic economy was of cyclical character; summer transmigrations were longer, and winter grazing involved shorter distances—mostly around the winter camps, where the nomads had some stable

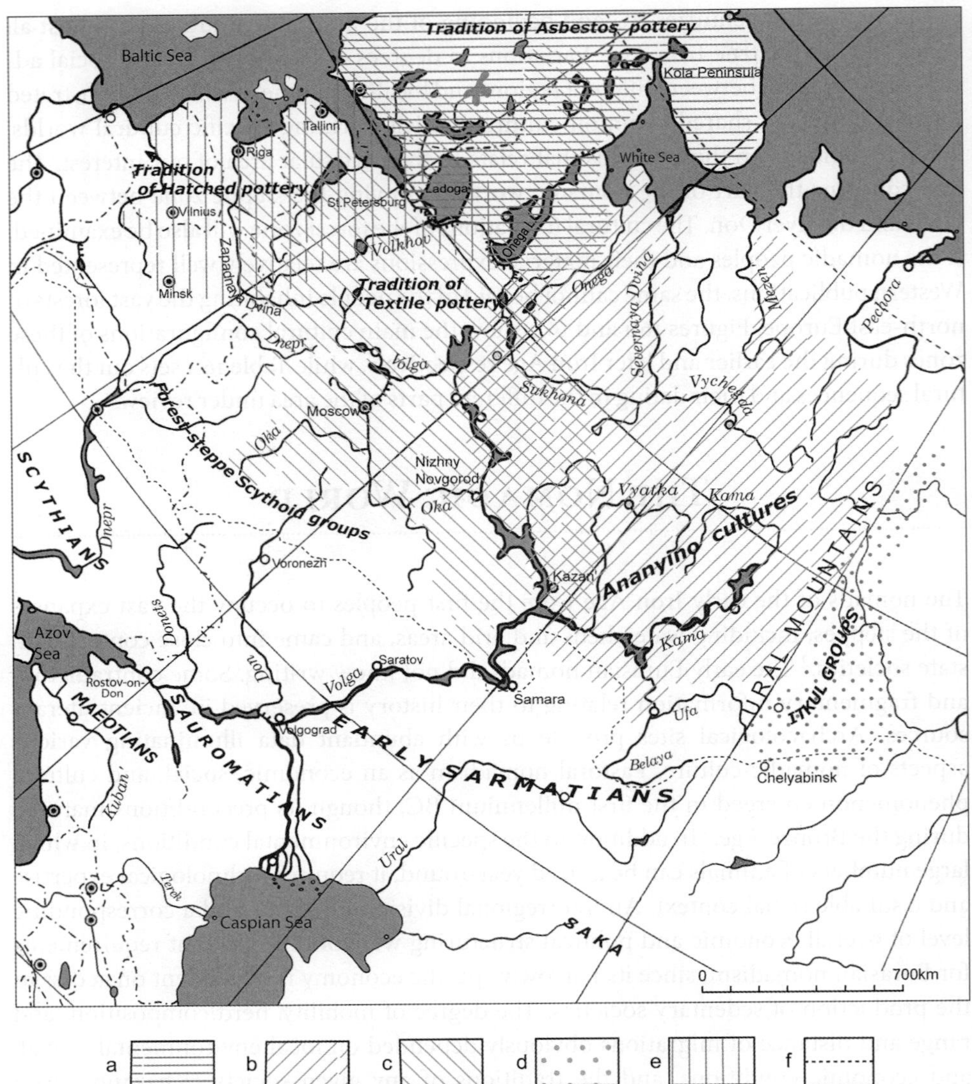

FIGURE 16.1 Cultural map of easternmost Europe, seventh to third centuries BC. Key: **a** area of the Asbestos pottery tradition; **b** area of the Ananyino culture and its influence; **c** area of the Textile pottery tradition; **d** area of the Itkul tradition; **e** area of the Hatched pottery tradition; **f** limits of the steppe.

settlements. Wooden houses are reproduced in the rich funerary chambers that have been excavated in many barrows. Usually, the ancestral cemeteries were located not far from the winter bases.

Animals were the private property of the families, and pasturing was regulated by lineages and clans; the tribe regulated the political sphere. The nomads appreciated their

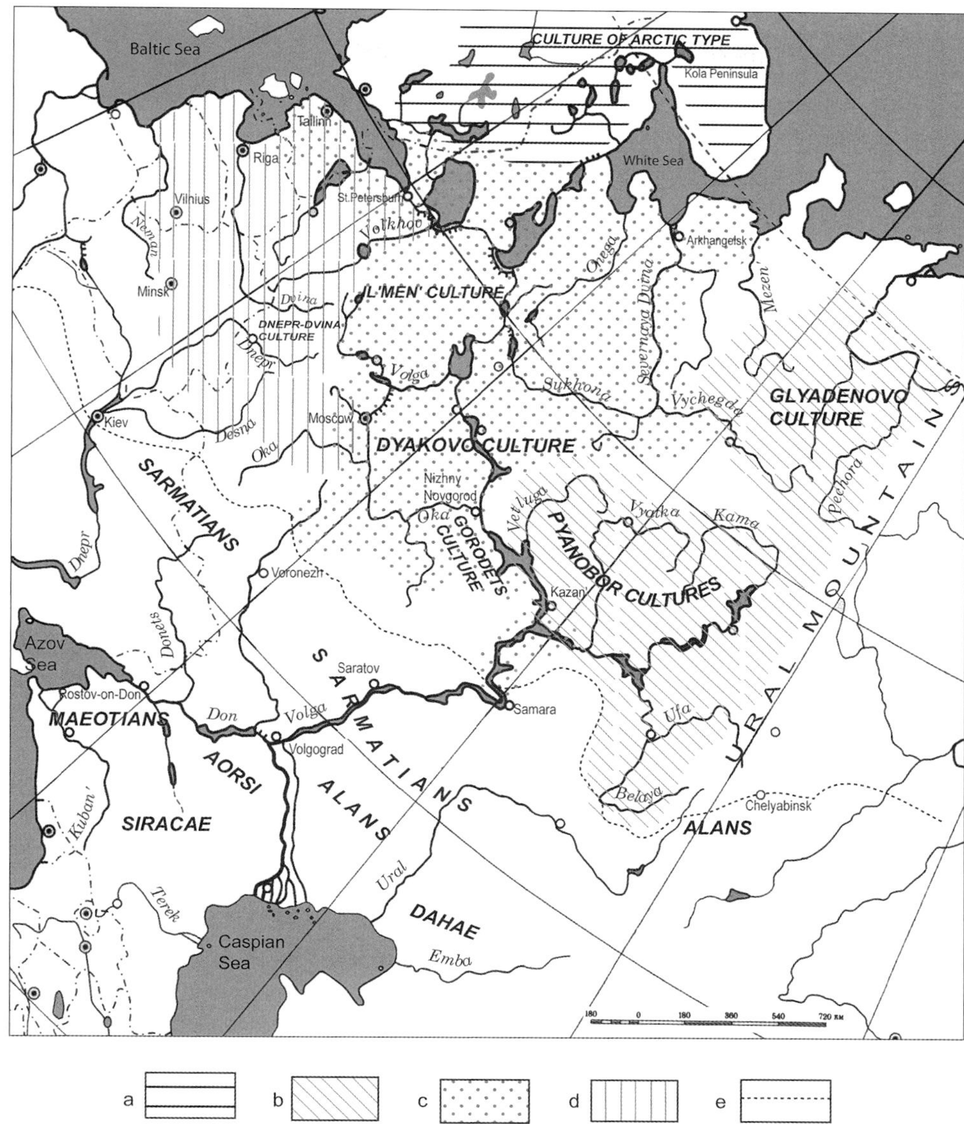

FIGURE 16.2 Cultural map of easternmost Europe, third century BC to third century AD. Key: **a** culture of Arctic type; **b** area of the Finno-Ugric cultures (proto-Finno-Permian); **c** area of Finno-Ugric cultures (proto-Finno-Volgaic); **d** area of the proto-Baltic cultures; **e** limits of the steppe.

status very much, but, if unable to maintain their usual way of life, they would settle. This often occurred near or among settled peoples, in the forest steppe or foothills, mixing with other populations. For example, in the early centuries AD, some Sarmatian settlements appeared in the Don delta area (Kobyakovo) as the result of such a process. Many rich Sarmatian kurgans were also concentrated in the lower Don region.

Table 16.1 Chronological chart for the steppe and forest zones in easternmost Europe

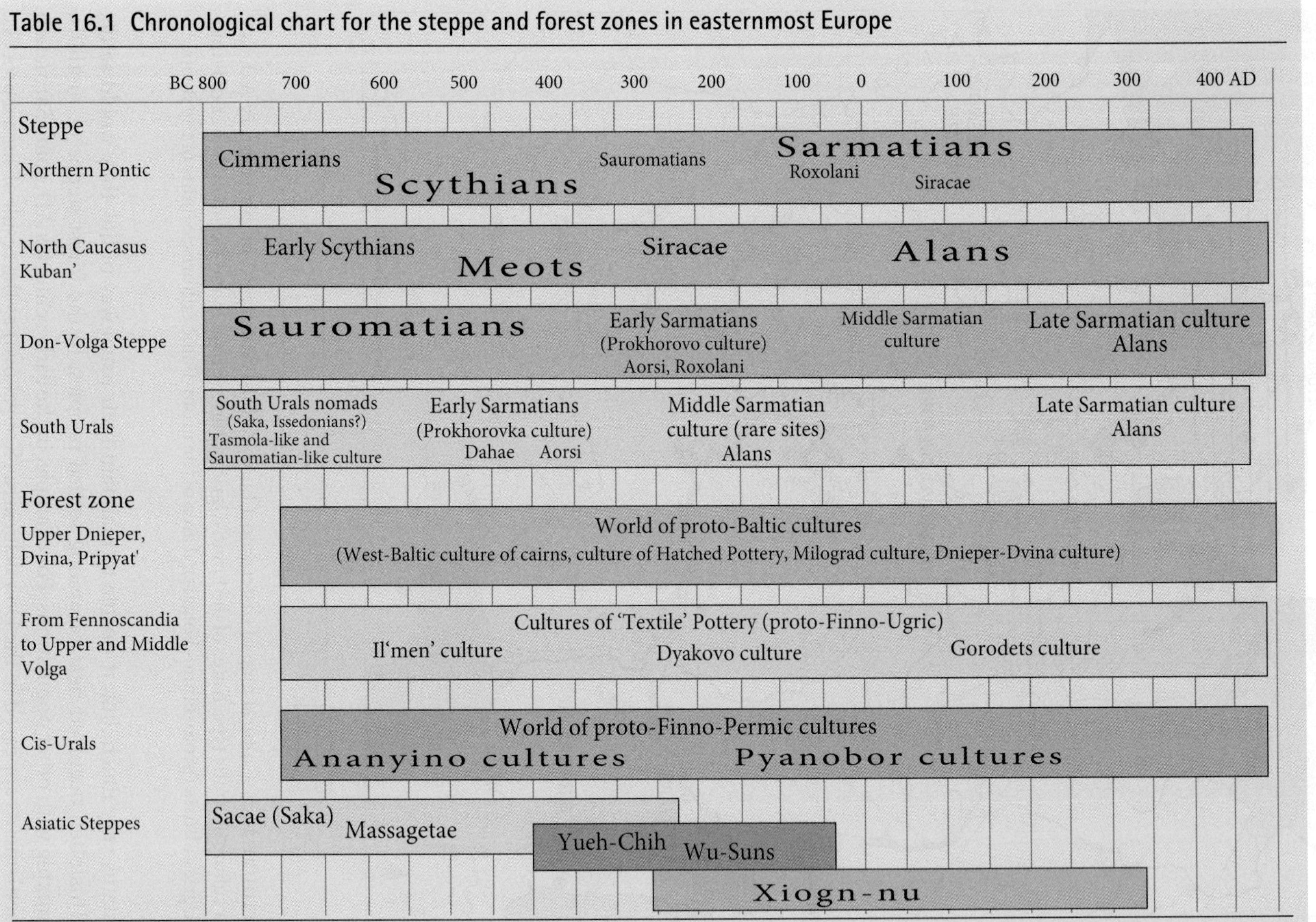

Literary sources give some information about nomadic tribes of the first millennium BC, most famously the Scythians and Sarmatians, but including many others.[4] They relocated repeatedly, and many of them migrated west into other parts of Europe, where their names eventually disappear from our sources. Despite local and chronological differences, the nomadic culture was united by common elements, such as general forms of weaponry (swords and arrows), horse harnesses (horse bits), and zoomorphic imagery (cross-legged deer, stylized animals on utilitarian and cult objects), and funerary practice (barrows of different size and detail, but constructed on similar principles). Sometimes this set is supplemented by bronze cauldrons and mirrors found everywhere in the Eurasian steppe and forest steppe.

The social consequences of transition to pastoral nomadism were very significant. The appearance of horseback riding entailed the whole range of technological innovation and change of social organization (see Chapter 32). A new social order, based on strong leadership, combined with a clan system, which became distinctly hierarchical when the nomads were drawn into more complex political units, or when they had long and active contacts with urban societies, endured for many centuries. War, trade, and diplomacy became integral parts of the new social and economic order created with the participation of nomads. In the later first millennium BC, the spheres of influence affecting this nomadic world were divided between the most powerful states. Interregional contacts, including long-distance relations, became an important factor in the historical development of Eurasia in the Iron Age. In this sense, Europe cannot be considered in isolation from Asia.

Nomadic studies have a long history in Russia.[5] The archaeology of the nomadic world is almost completely based on funerary sites, predominantly barrows. There are some settlements, located either in the forest steppe, or in the areas of politically organized nomadic states, which included some settled populations. The history of Eurasian nomadic culture is divided into two main periods, determined by the culture of the leading tribe. The first, Scythian, period, is conventionally dated to the seventh to third centuries BC; the second, the Sarmatian (or Hunnish-Sarmatian) period, spans the second century BC to fourth century AD. The transition from the Bronze Age to Iron Age in the eastern European steppe and forest steppe between the ninth and seventh centuries BC is known as the pre-Scythian or Cimmerian period; this relates to the origin of the Scythians and their culture, as well as other cultures of the nomadic world (see also Chapter 15). The archaeological record for this period is relatively modest compared with previous and succeeding times, with few burials and hoards.

The Scythians are well known from written sources; while giving their name to the whole era, they only continuously occupied the steppe and forest steppe of the northern Black Sea region and briefly the north Caucasus, creating an amazingly rich culture. The problem of the origin and appearance of the nomads in eastern Europe has long been debated. Without going into the details of this complex issue, I note that most current researchers emphasize the role of climatic factors as a stimulus, along with the influx of eastern nomadic groups at the start of the first millennium BC. Hereafter, I will focus mainly on the Sarmatians. They belonged to the north-east branch of Iranian-speaking

Indo-European peoples, and gave their name to many groups who occupied the steppes from the Urals to the Danube.

Cultural Trajectories between the River Don and the Urals

The ancient writers tell us about various barbarian tribes, among whom were the Sauromatians, the eastern neighbours of the Scythians. According to the legend reported by Herodotus (*Histories* 4.110–117), the Sauromatians originated from the marriage of young Scythian boys to Amazons, who did not speak the Scythian language properly. Their lands lay beyond the Tanais (river Don). The southern neighbours of the Sauromatians were collectively called the Maeotians, who inhabited the area along the east coast of the Sea of Azov, the Taman peninsula, and part of the Kuban river area (see Figure 16.1).

Before the early fourth century BC, the Sauromatians and Scythians did not bother one another, but gradually some Sauromatian groups moved west into Scythian lands, upsetting the pastoral and the demographic balance of the region. At the same time, in connection with the decline of Scythia, the ancient writers began to use the term Sarmatians (or Sirmatians), which eventually replaced the name Sauromatians or became its synonym. By the third century BC, the Sarmatians had crossed the river Don and invaded the north Pontic area. The expansionist politics of Alexander the Great are seen as one of the factors that stimulated the rise in dominance of these nomadic tribes and caused the displacement of others (Melukova 1989: 156–157). The Sarmatians became the most significant political agent in the western part of the nomadic world. They were not socially and politically consolidated, but consisted of many different groups, organized into rival nomadic chiefdoms. Textual sources of around the first century BC, notably Strabo's *Geography* (11.1–6), contain such terms as 'European' and 'Asiatic' Sarmatia, separated by the river Tanais. According to Skripkin (2014: 10), retrospective examination of the information about Sarmatia, from Ptolemy to Herodotus, allows us to assert that the territory between the Volga-Don interfluve and—probably—the Trans-Volga area equated to the early Sarmatia of the ancient sources.

As a kind of intermediary between the western and eastern nomads, and the forest peoples and states of Asia, the Sauromatians and Sarmatians became active participants in complex processes that occurred across the area from the river Danube to the Great Wall of China, and from the foothills of the Urals in the north to the Iranian plateau in the south (Berlizov 2011). Their culture evolved according to their own traditions, but in close interaction (voluntarily or not) with the civilizations of the ancient world. Nomads transmitted their achievements to the north, and, in turn, the ancient empires borrowed some nomadic achievements, for example in warfare. In Russian archaeology, the name Sauromatians used to be applied to nomadic tribes occupying the territory between the Don, Volga, and Ural rivers, to the east of Scythia. Currently archaeologists connect the historical Sauromatians with the lower Volga and Don areas, and place their political and military centre near the river Don (Ochir-Goryaeva 1992, 2012; Skripkin 2009). Nevertheless, all archaeological material from the kurgans of the seventh to fourth centuries BC between the Don-Volga region and the southern Urals is still placed under the Sauromatian umbrella. This presumes an ethnographic difference between the western sites (of the historical Sauromatians) and the eastern ones (of Uralian nomads—Dahae, Massagetae, or Issedonians).

Grakov (1947) divided the material from the kurgans between the Volga and the Urals into four cultural phases, which he identified with historical periods: (1) Sauromatian, sixth to fourth centuries BC; (2) early Sarmatian or Prokhorovo culture, fourth to second centuries BC; (3) middle Sarmatian, second century BC to second century AD; and (4) late Sarmatian, second to fourth centuries AD. All four stages were part of one overarching Sarmatian culture. This periodization is still widely used, but with the Prokhorovo or early Sarmatian phase now more tightly defined and also lengthened to include the fifth and first centuries BC (Skripkin 1990; Tairov 2000). This extended chronology spans its formation in the southern Urals, its spread over the Volga, and its latest development in the north Pontic area. The middle Sarmatian phase is consequently ascribed to a shorter period between the first century BC and first half of the second century AD (Moshkova 2002).

Since, for obvious reasons, pastoral nomads are often forced to change their habitats, it is hard to pin them down either geographically or chronologically in terms of distinct archaeological cultures, and the relationship between different variants of Sarmatian culture continues to be a matter of debate. However, we definitely can understand the meaning of fluid changes in nomadic culture coming out of the prescribed territorial limits of archaeological cultures, using them only as markers of their cultural deployment in time and space (Koryakova and Epimakhov 2007: 233).

Sauromatian and Early Sarmatian Presence in the Volga-Ural Area

Sites of the transitional period (tenth to eighth centuries BC) are rare, but some exist in marginal regions of the Urals and the Volga-Don steppe (Melukova 1989). There are a number of burials, in which the deceased were placed in pits of various kinds in a flexed or extended position, accompanied by a limited set of grave goods. Sites of the seventh to sixth centuries BC are also relatively uncommon in the east European steppe, but the late sixth century BC saw a notable demographic rise, to judge from the greater number of kurgans in the southern Urals (Figure 16.3), and along the Volga and Don rivers and their tributaries. Berlizov (2011) combines sites of the interval between the end of the seventh and third quarter of the sixth centuries BC into a separate chronological horizon and synchronizes them with the Greek and Scythian Archaic period.

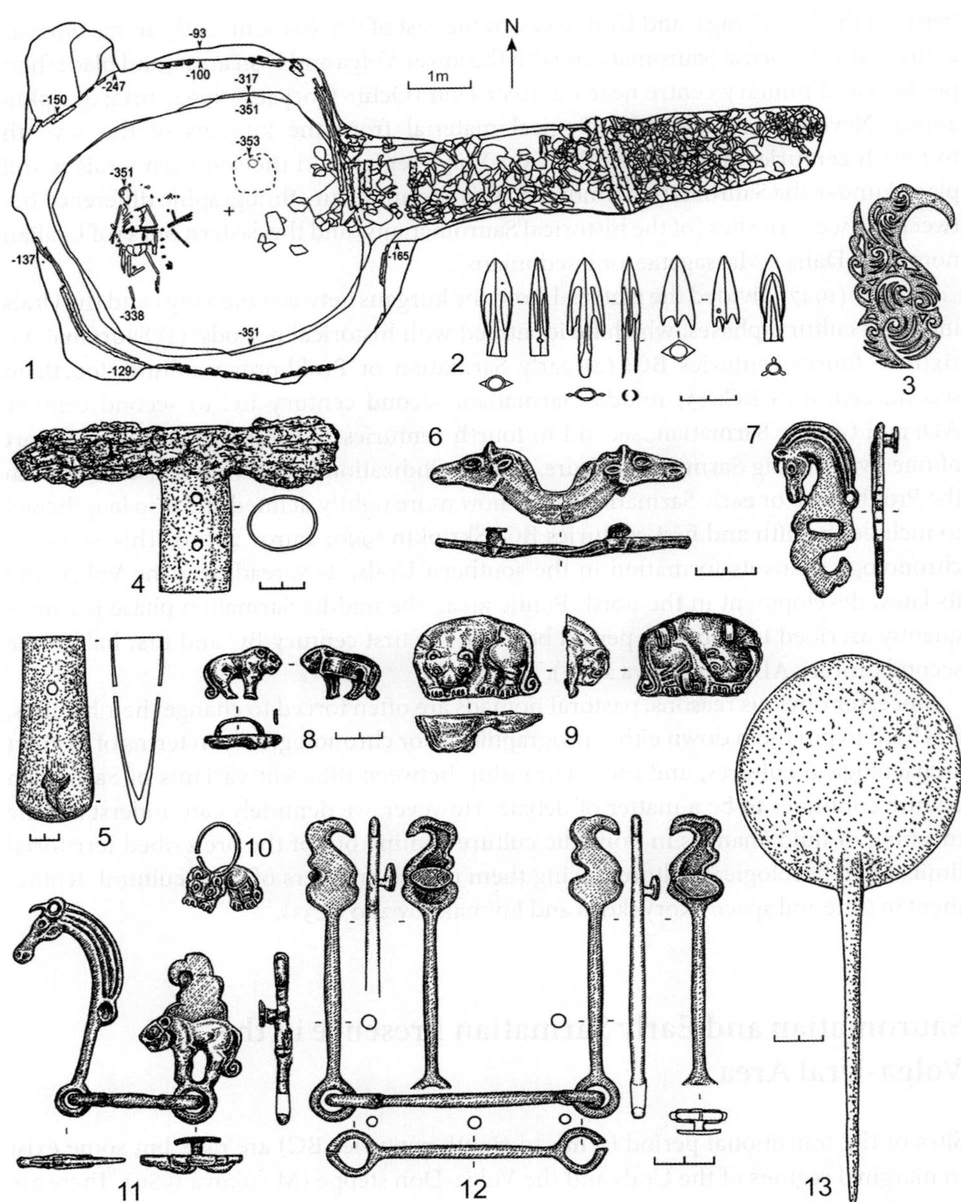

FIGURE 16.3 Kichigino cemetery, barrow 1, burial 1. (1) The large tomb, covered by a multilayered roof, was in the centre of the mound, approached by a long corridor (*dromos*). The tomb contained a man accompanied by rich grave goods. On his right there was a bimetallic battle hammer (4) with wooden handle ending in a bronze ferrule (5). The deceased had a leather belt, decorated with bronze attachments (6, 8), fastened by a buckle and hook (11). On the right, an iron dagger was attached to the belt with the help of a bronze three-part chain (12). The bronze mirror (13), which was fixed to the belt by a bronze hook (7), was underneath. On the left, there was a leather quiver with sixteen bronze arrows (2). The quiver was decorated by golden plaques (9, 10). A similar plaque was found on the breast, and a golden openwork plaque (3) decorated the headdress. On the left side of the cranium there was a massive gold ear-ring identical to plaque 9. Artefacts various scales.

Compiled after Tairov 2015: figs 2, 3

The majority of sites, however, date to the fifth to fourth centuries BC, pointing to an increase in the pastoral population in favourable environmental conditions.

The early Iron Age nomads constructed their burial mounds from earth; in the Urals, they also used stone. The burials were arranged in rectangular pit graves, some furnished with stepped walls or special side niches (*podboi*) constructed in the long wall. In the Volga area there were many narrow pits; these are typical for multiple secondary burials in the mound. The deceased were supine, in an extended position with their heads oriented to the west or north-west. Signs of organic bedding or a sprinkling of ash were found under the deceased, who were accompanied by grave goods, including daggers, bronze socketed (bilobate or trilobate) arrowheads, horse harnesses, composite belts, mirrors, stone altars, knives, and amulets. Sauromatian weaponry is of the same type as Scythian weaponry. Food for the afterlife is represented by sides of horses, decapitated sheep carcasses, or whole skeletons of horses, sheep, and sometimes dogs (Klepikov 2002). The burials vary in the number, type, and quality of grave goods. Male graves contained mainly weapons, while female graves contained mostly ornaments and cult objects, and sometimes (in about 15–20% of cases) items of weaponry. Pots containing beverages were placed in all graves, but their number varies. Burials can also be differentiated in terms of wealth, which varies from one or two pieces of meat, or several arrows or pots, to a large number of luxury objects. Horse burials, as well as various elements of horse harnesses, constituted an integral part of mortuary practice among Eurasian nomads (Ochir-Goryaeva 2012).

The Sauromatian period was a time of intensive exploration of new pastures, inevitably giving rise to conflicts over their possession. That is why male graves in the Ural-Volga steppes are full of weaponry (Myshkin 2010). A special kind of Animal style is associated with Sauromatian cultures. Although in general terms it belongs to the Scythian type, it has some differences (Smirnov 1976). The favourite images used to decorate weapons, harnesses, and stone altars were the elk, wolf, bear, and feline predators, sometimes with fantastical attributes or expressions. Animals are depicted as dynamic and aggressive: predators with fierce muzzles and eagles with overly large beaks. Sometimes they are polymorphic, combining parts of different creatures. The camel image is often used, unlike in Scythia.

Nomads of the southern Urals had winter camps near the Aral Sea, where they came into contact with nomadic groups from middle Asia and southern Kazakhstan, but their summer pastures were situated in the Uralian steppe. They were culturally connected with central Kazakhstan. On the other hand, indisputably Scythian (western) elements are also present in this area (Gutsalov 1998). These finds are interpreted as evidence of stable links with European Scythians and proof of the trade route mentioned by Herodotus (*Histories* 4.24), which is believed to have started in the late sixth century BC. Moreover, local mineral resources, especially gold and copper, could perhaps have attracted the western nomads. Bartseva (1981) states that around one-third of the metal objects from Scythian graves of the sixth to fourth centuries BC on the left bank of the Dnieper were manufactured from metal of Uralian origin. This demand could have stimulated the formation of the new metallurgical centres in the Urals, one of which

(Ananyino) was oriented to the Scythians from the very beginning, but gradually came under the control of Uralian nomadic clans.

In the period from the late sixth to the fifth century BC, changes occurred among the Uralian nomads, although the basic characteristics of their mortuary practice remained stable. Details such as occasional cremations, the burnt wooden roofs of funerary structures, wooden constructions at ground level, pit graves with steps, side niches (*podboi*), or corridors (*dromoi*), point to central Asia as the source of their emergence (Botalov and Tairov 2011; Tairov 2015). Additionally, new types of grave goods (beaked pots, flat-bottomed pear-shaped pots with small handles, bronze mirrors, stone altars with legs, spiral torcs) testify to the absorption of new ethnic groups from the south-east, followed by cultural and social consolidation. This is exemplified by the recently excavated Kichigino barrows (Figure 16.4).

The drift of the southern nomads to the Urals is thought to have been stimulated by the politics of the Achaemenid rulers of central Asia in the sixth century BC (Tairov 2000). The campaign of Cyrus II against the Massagetae in 530 BC ended in their victory, but the raid of Darius I on the Sacae in 519 BC was more successful for the Persians and undoubtedly affected the southern nomads. Any destabilization of the traditional pasture system entails regrouping in the nomadic environment. Some newcomers moved north-west to the sparsely populated Cis-Ural steppe and beyond, where ecological conditions from the later sixth century BC were favourable to nomadic pastoralism. The period was relatively humid, and the landscape consisted of multi-grass steppes, alternating with some forest (Tairov 2003).

Archaeological data demonstrate the rising prominence of military activities; the number of warrior graves, and the quantity and assortment of weapons of both eastern and western types increased dramatically. The concentration of large elite kurgans in the Cis-Ural steppe reflects the efforts of the nomadic aristocracy to control copper and iron deposits, and consequently, the flow of metal to Europe.

After the late sixth century BC, the nomads stepped up the pressure on their neighbours in the forested zone to the north. In the fifth century BC, the majority of arrowheads were produced in local Uralian workshops, whereas previously graves contained metal objects made of ores from central Kazakhstan. A process of cultural and social transformation among the Uralian nomads, provoked by the external factors already mentioned and promoted by climatic improvement, resulted in their involvement in western (Sauromatian) politics rather than in the eastern network, although traditional connections with their Saka relatives were maintained. This is reflected in the material culture, which gained a Sauromatian appearance, characteristic of the vast Volga-Ural steppe. It is possible that the Issedonians (Herodotus *Histories* 4.16–30) played a leading role in this process.

The majority of kurgans contained a single primary burial, placed in a pit grave within a wooden structure. However, some mounds were used for the deposition of several people, most probably relatives. The dead were generally in a supine, extended position with the head to the west. Some funerary sites, which have huge superstructures of 7–10 m in height, were presumably for the elite. These large kurgans are mainly

FIGURE 16.4 Kichigino burial ground, barrow 3, tomb no. 5. 1 general view of the remains during excavation; 2 anthropological reconstruction of the buried woman, by A. Nechvoloda; 3 grave goods.

Source: after Botalov and Tairov 2011

concentrated in the valleys o\f the Or and Ilek rivers (Smirnov 1975; Yablonsky 1996). Some of them (e.g. Filippovka) produced extremely rich gold objects manufactured in the Saka Animal style, and valuable foreign goods (Figure 16.5). The Filippovka funerary constructions are especially notable for the number of large burial chambers with corridors, hearths, collective burials, and tunnels leading from the foot of the mound to the central underground chamber. As Yablonsky (2008) has shown, these tunnels served for supplying the ancestors with ritual offerings. Such big kurgans with sophisticated

FIGURE 16.5 Objects from the Filippovka burial ground, excavations of L. N. Yablonsky. 1 strap buckle in the shape of a lying tiger, gold, length 83 mm; 2 cast bracelet with terminals in the shape of mountain goats, gold, width 80–90 mm; 3 strap buckle, silver and gold, height 63 mm; 4 quiver hook, silver, gold, length 50 mm; 5 amphora with a zoomorphic beaked handle, silver, height 255 mm.

Source: Yablonsky 2008

internal structures were primarily the funerary monuments of military leaders, but sometimes women were interred in them. Various kinds of weapons (sometimes newly made), items of horse harnesses, bronze cauldrons, flat-bottomed ceramic vessels, ornaments, handled mirrors, and cult objects were abundant in these burials. Some scholars explain the presence of rich foreign objects in Sauromatian burials as evidence of trade connections with the southern states, but others interpret these as payment for military service or subsidies extorted by some of the clans from the Achaemenid rulers.

Alternatively, these valuables might have been diplomatic gifts. Whatever the reason for their presence, their frequency and concentration in specific burials, together with the complexity of the funeral monuments and their abundant military attributes, leave no doubt about the existence of a strong social power, which above all wanted to emphasize its significance. The Filippovka necropolis fits well into the category of royal mortuary sites (*tsarski*) reflecting the transition from the Sauromatian to the early Sarmatian cultural phase.

Early Sarmatian Developments (the Prokhorovo Culture)

Research has shown that the material attributes that we principally associate with the early Sarmatians originated in the southern Urals, where the Prokhorovo culture formed during the fifth century BC. New cultural components, particularly round-based pots with talc temper, were introduced by the Trans-Ural forest steppe population, who maintained relationships with the nomads. Another view is that leading groups appeared (supposedly the Dahae and Aorsi) bringing elements of their culture, which they introduced to the indigenous milieu (Smirnov 1964). The site which gave its name to the archaeological culture of the early Sarmatians is a barrow cemetery near the village of Prokhorovka in the Cis-Urals. It was first excavated in 1916, and again in 2003–2005. Rich collections of weapons, female ornaments and cosmetic accessories, as well as imported wares, were found in the kurgans, characterizing the culture of the nomads dominating the Uralian steppe and forest steppe in the fourth century BC (Yablonsky 2010a).

Early Prokhorovo culture kurgans were made of earth or earth and stone. Stones were used as either a mound covering (cairn) or for forming circles around it. Wooden timber structures, as well as clay platforms, are frequently discovered under the mounds. Secondary burials are much more frequent in these barrows than in the preceding period, placed concentrically around the central grave (Figure 16.6). Such multi-grave barrows are interpreted as belonging to related persons. Soil analysis indicates that most early Sarmatian burials took place during warm periods. Thus, peripheral burials must have been postponed, so people who died in winter were buried in spring.

The funerary chambers take various forms: simple, with steps, with niches, subterranean catacombs, and corridors. They were often furnished with wooden structures, such as wooden frames, ceilings, a funeral bier or coffin, and a wooden or stone roof. Sprinkled powdered ochre or chalk, ash, and charcoal pieces frequently occur. The dead were placed supine, in an extended position, along the long wall, although diagonal positions are sometimes found. The orientation of the deceased was initially with the head to the west, but in the fourth to third centuries BC this was replaced by a southern orientation. Food offerings included sheep or horse shoulders with the foreleg attached. Compared with the preceding period, the cremation rite had practically died out. During the Prokhorovo phase, new kinds of weaponry appeared. Among them were heavy weapons, including the long sword and dagger, quivers with arrows,

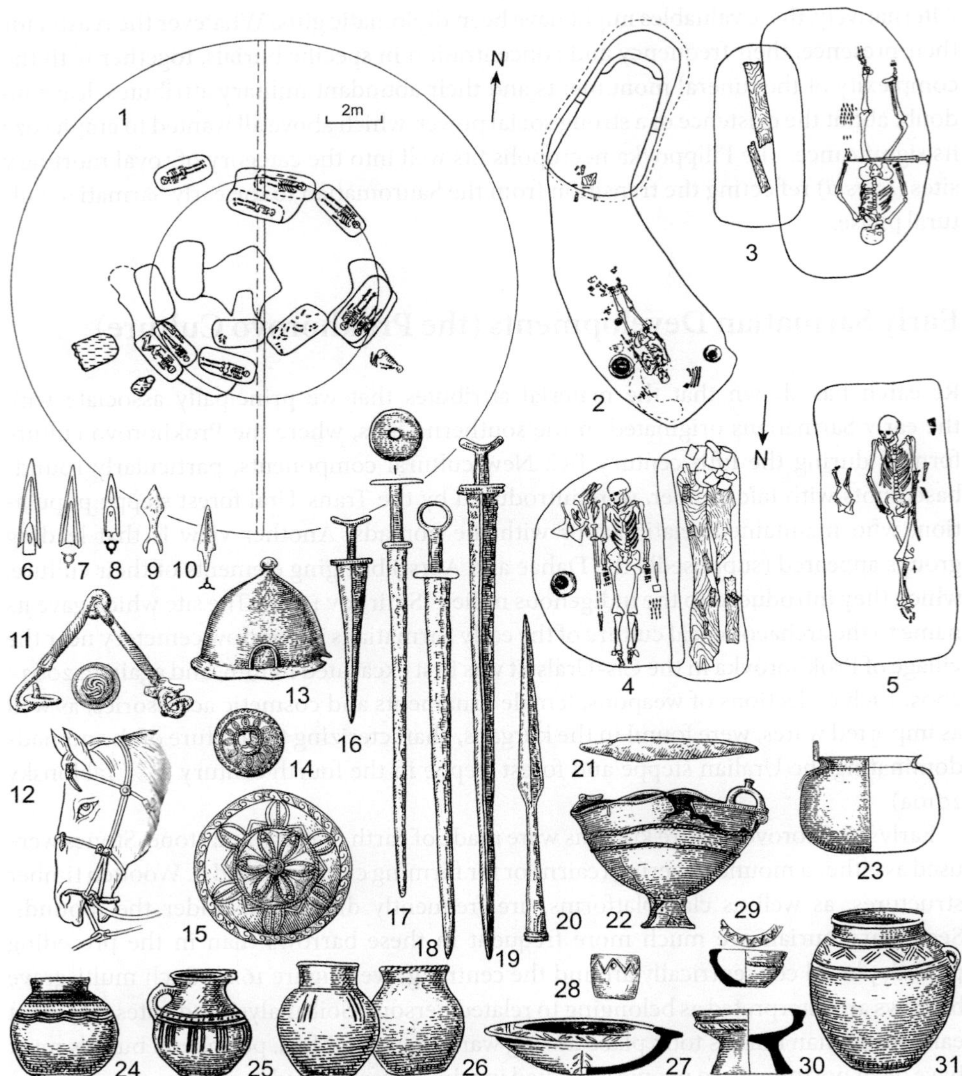

FIGURE 16.6 Early Sarmatian (Prokhorovo) culture. 1 Bykovo kurgan 3; 2–5 plans of burials from the Volga area (not to scale); 6–8 bronze arrowheads; 9–10 iron arrowheads; 11–12 iron horse bits; 13 helmet; 14–15 silver *phalerae*; 16–19 iron dagger and swords; 20 iron spearhead; 21 iron knife; 22–23 bronze cauldrons; 24–26, 31 handmade pots; 27–30 clay incense burners. Artefacts various scales.

Sources: Moshkova 1963; Melukova 1989

spears, helmets, cuirasses, and body armour. Iron trilobate tanged arrowheads came into common use. This evidence speaks of a change of military tactics towards the use of heavy cavalry and weapons for outfighting. The technology of making iron swords had also changed completely from that used in Scythian times (Terekhova 2011).

The number of fourth- to third-century BC sites in the Urals significantly exceeds that of other periods. Such a large concentration of nomadic population is explained partly by the more favourable ecological conditions here than in other areas. This was the original centre of the Sarmatian confederation. The region served as a sort of melting pot through which various groups of nomads travelled and spread out in various directions. In the fourth century BC, the Uralian nomads migrated, first to the south-west, and then—around the end of the same century—moved into the forest steppe of the foothills of the Urals and the Volga basin, introducing the Prokhorovo cultural complex, which gradually replaced the Sauromatian one.

The Sarmatians introduced multi-grave barrows, funerary chambers with niches (*podboi*), a southern orientation for the deceased, round-bottomed pots with some talc mixed into the fabric, and specific food offerings, which invariably included a sheep's foreleg. Female graves sometimes contained cult objects, such as stone portable altars or clay censers. The Animal style, so typical of the Scythian period, virtually disappeared, although some Sauramatian features did survive, especially in the Volga area.

The Prokhorovo culture between the Urals and the Don displays a substantial homogeneity of cultural attributes (funerary rite and artefacts), a unity indicative of the more consolidated character of early Sarmatian society. The finds unambiguously attest to pronounced social stratification and strong political power, barrows and burials varying in terms both of labour costs and the funerary gifts.

During the third to first centuries BC, the Sarmatians extended their territory up to the northern shore of the Black Sea. The ancient writers inform us about new tribal unions under the leadership of the Aorsi, Siracae, and Roxolani, who migrated westward. These events broke up former peaceful relations with the Scythians, who could no longer resist such a massive migration. Archaeologically, the rise of Sarmatian influence is reflected in the 'Sarmatization' of many Eurasian regions, in which local pottery was the only mark of an indigenous presence. However, some processes that would later affect much of Europe once again started in the east. At the turn of the third to second century BC, events with far-reaching consequences occurred in Mongolia, where the ambitious Modu Chanyu united the Xiung-nu tribes and began long wars with China and neighbouring tribes, causing a domino effect among the nomads first on a regional, then on a Eurasian scale.

In 128 BC, a frontal assault of nomadic tribes on the Graeco-Bactrian kingdom ended with its downfall. This provoked new movements among the eastern nomads, an increase in military activity, the incorporation of new ethnic groups, and a change of the general political situation in all parts of the nomadic world, including Asian Sarmatia.

The Rise of the Sarmatians

During the second and first centuries BC, a gradual increase in innovation took place in early Sarmatian culture. It was caused by internal factors, the incorporation of new ethnic groups, and interactions with the Greek Black Sea colonies, as well as with the inhabitants of the north Caucasus. This time, the source of the innovations was the Volga-Don area, where the middle Sarmatian culture emerged. This cultural development encompasses the period between the first century BC and the first to second centuries AD.

About a hundred mortuary sites dating to this time are known in the southern Trans-Urals and western Kazakhstan; most belong to the start of this period, with only single complexes at its end (Botalov 2009). Slightly more than a hundred complexes are recorded in the Cis-Urals, concentrated on the right bank of the Ural river. In the lower Volga-Don steppes, on the other hand, a larger number of barrows are recorded. The southern Urals, which previously looked almost depopulated, now became a periphery of the powerful tribal confederation of Asian Sarmatia, which centred on the lower Volga area. Such a situation is explained by dramatic climatic deterioration in the south Uralian steppe and the relocation of the strongest clans to the west (Tairov 2003). This relocation was not sudden and rapid; it took some time for newcomers and local nomads to build up relationships, establish new grazing systems, and develop new cultural norms. Processes of gradual transformation are generally not easy to see in the material record, but, in this case, archaeologists have succeeded in tracing the changes.

The new cultural complex in the Volga-Don area included new types of artefacts: cast bronze cauldrons of hemispherical form, and smaller kettles, often with zoomorphic designs on the handles; *tamga*-like signs;[6] rod-shaped cheek-pieces with decorated ends, often inlaid or clad with gold or silver; small alabaster vessels; swords with ring-shaped pommels; ceremonial short swords; scabbards with four lateral lobes; *phalerae*; and other items. Among the characteristics of middle and late Sarmatian culture were a new Animal style—ceremonial objects in the 'gold and turquoise' technique being the finest examples—and the relatively frequent finds of Italian and provincial Roman imports in the graves of the nobility (Khokhlach, Dachi, Zhutovo, Sadovyi, Kalinovka). The Sarmatian Animal style is characterized by the frequent use of inserts of carnelian, almandine, garnet, turquoise, coral, and coloured glass for the representation of the animals' thigh muscles, shoulder blades, eyes, ears, hooves, and claws (Figure 16.7).

As well as cast cauldrons, the Sarmatians used bronze and silver vessels, which come to them as tribute or as a gift for their service. These include bowls, cups, plates, *skyphoi*, jugs, and other vessels. As Shchukin (1994: 146) commented,

> the spread of Graeco-Bactrian-style objects from India to Mongolia, the Pontic steppes, and Thrace is the specific nomadic reflection of the complex epoch from the fall of the Graeco-Bactrian kingdom and the accession of Mithridates Eupator of Pontus, to the time of Pompey, Caesar, and the Dacian king Burebista. Nomadic aristocracy could perceive the complex world of symbols and images of the East Hellenistic ideology.

In the funerary sphere, individual barrows erected for one or more individuals, placed in a central rectangular or square grave, came to dominate. Graves with side niches became more common. Burial chambers containing caches of distinctive offerings (cauldrons, horse harness accessories, weapons) constitute a special group. These

FIGURE 16.7 Decorative objects of the middle and late Sarmatian culture in the lower Don area. 1 Torc from Khokhlach, gold, turquoise, coral, glass, diameter 164–178 mm; 2 Vessel for incense from Khokhlach, gold, coral, height 70 mm; 3 Cup with zoomorphic handle, gold, turquoise, coral, glass, height 75 mm; 4 Belt buckle from Khapry, gold, coral, glass, almandine, length 140–150 mm; 5 Dagger with decorated pommel and scabbard from the Dachi, iron, gold, cornelian, turquoise, overall length 450 mm; 6 Pectoral *phalera* of horse harness from Dachi, gold, coral, almandine, turquoise, diameter 145 mm.

Source: after Piotrovsky and Zasetskaya 2008: nos 10, 13, 21, 27, 29, 30

graves belonged to rich Sarmatians, who inhabited the left bank of the Don. In addition to the traditional extended position along the grave, a diagonal arrangement of the deceased also appeared. The dead were invariably buried with their head to the south (Skripkin 1990; Sergatskov 2009). Men and women are found with equally diverse grave goods, in accordance with their gender and age status. Sarmatian women were accompanied to the other world by toilet implements (mirrors, bone spoons, small alabaster or glass vessels, and cosmetic sets); they were dressed in the finest clothes, with rich ornaments (bronze, silver, and gold bracelets and ear-rings, various imported beads, and pendants). Men did not shy away from some decorations too. Three main social groups can be reconstructed from analysis of the burials: nomadic nobility, ordinary nomads, and people of the lowest status. There are also graves of so-called priestesses, which contained objects of cult meaning, such as portable altars and censers.

The weapons in the male graves demonstrate the development of fighting techniques. At the turn of era, the Sarmatian army was based mainly on troops of lightly armed cavalry (archers), but also included groups of heavily armed cavalry anticipating the famous Sarmatian cataphract (horse and rider both completely protected by scale armour). The men mostly possessed short iron swords with ring-shaped pommels and straight guards that they attached to a belt, on the right side. These short swords were short-range weapons, and replaced the long swords of the early Sarmatian period; the major weapon in combat on horseback was now the long spear. A bow with a set of arrows was also a necessary part of the weapon set. After the turn of era, the Sarmatians came to use a bigger and stronger composite bow, which was brought to the Volga-Don area by eastern nomads, who used it earlier. Ethnic and cultural relations between the nomads of central Asia, south Siberia, and eastern Europe, on the one hand, and state societies, on the other, are particularly evident in the military sphere. Each innovation in weapons and methods of warfare rapidly spread to a large area.

By the mid-second century AD, further changes occurred in the cultural facies of the nomads of eastern Europe, and the Uralian steppe came to life anew. A distinctive feature of late Sarmatian mortuary practice is the total dominance of a northern orientation for the deceased, a second marker being the custom of artificial cranial deformation. Both traits were known at an earlier date in and beyond the Urals and Trans-Volga area. New types of artefacts that became widespread in the second and third centuries AD included mirror-pendants, heavily shaped fibulae of the Bosporan series, iron swords and daggers without a metal pommel and guard, composite bows with bone linings of Hunnish type, and some special forms of pots. The large iron trilobate arrowheads correspond to the new bow type. In the southern Urals the majority of burials yielded rather modest goods, including handmade and wheelmade pottery, long swords with nephrite or sardonyx attachments, mirror-pendants, and numerous fibulae.

In the late Sarmatian cultural complex, *podboi*-type graves were more numerous than in the preceding period (Figure 16.8). Most barrows were not large—around 8–15 m in diameter. They contained mainly single burials (in the east), sometimes with secondary burials placed in the mound (in the west). Alongside these typical features, the culture of the southern Urals at this period shows very clear and specific differences from the area

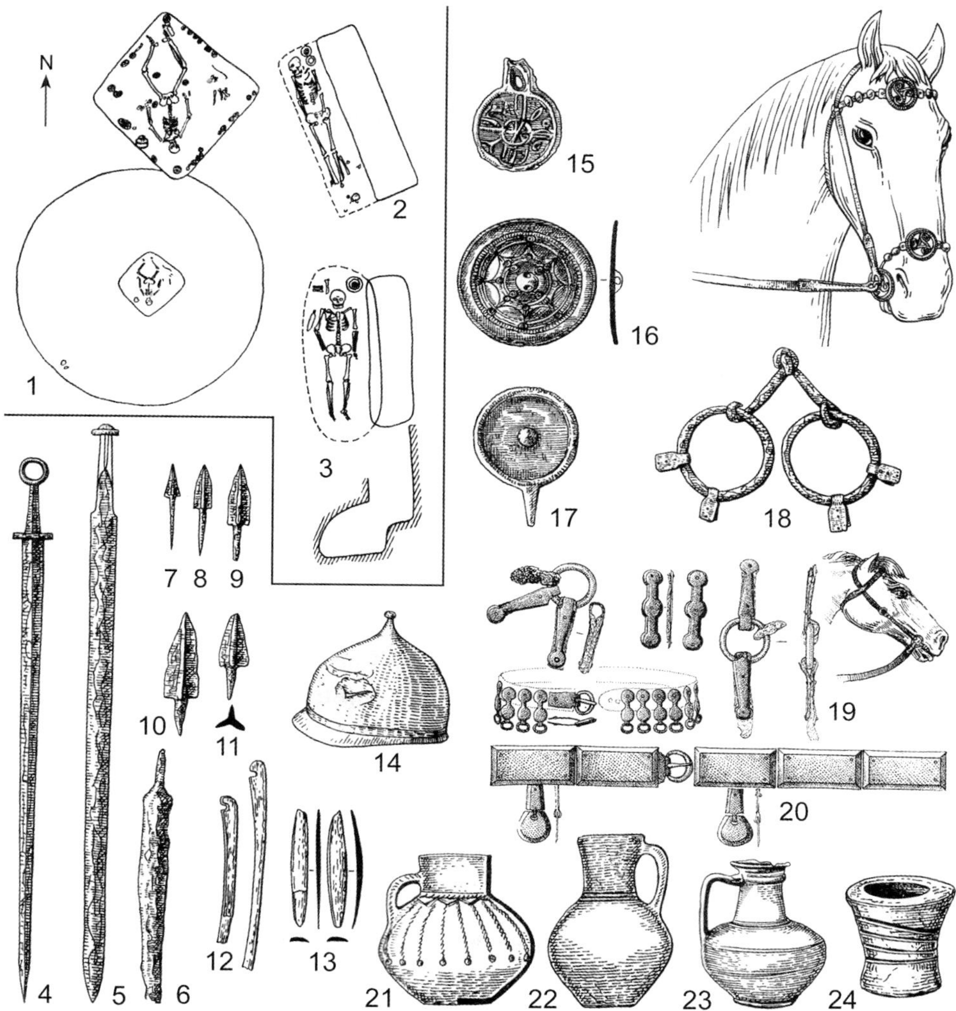

FIGURE 16.8 Middle and late Sarmatian culture. 1 Sorochinskyi I; 2–3 Lebedevka V and Kalinovka burials; 4–6 iron swords and dagger; 7–11 iron arrowheads; 12–13 bone plaques for Hunnish-type bow; 14 helmet; 15 bronze mirror-pendant; 16 Chinese mirror; 17 bronze handled mirror; 18 iron horse bits with cheek-pieces; 19–20 bronze plaques from horse harness and belt; 21–24 pottery. Various scales.

Sources: Melukova 1989; Botalov 2000

to the west. Cemeteries took the form of long chains of kurgans running north to south and comprising anything from two to a hundred mounds. Together with the standard funerary structures, there are some earthen sub-rectangular tombs, and elongated or dumb-bell-shaped kurgans (two kurgans linked by an earth bank). The number of narrow rectangular graves is greater than in the Volga region. Chinese mirrors are also more abundant. Aside from these items, the composite bow and cauldrons of Hunnish type, heavy tanged iron arrowheads, and new types of horse trappings of an eastern style came into widespread use (Bokovenko and Zasetskaya 1994; Botalov 2009).

Most scholars believe that these changes resulted from the new groups of nomads moving west. The question: 'Who was behind these groups?' has led to heated debate, but few would deny an eastern origin for these constant new arrivals. Skripkin (1990) identifies the early Sarmatian culture with the Aorsi and the Yantsai state of the Chinese sources. In his opinion, the main creators of middle Sarmatian culture were the Alani, who were initially either within the Kang-Ku state or under its political influence. They bypassed the Urals and went directly to Europe.

From the first century BC, a number of objects of eastern origin appeared in the Eurasian steppe and forest steppe: gold and turquoise zoomorphic objects, Chinese mirrors, raw opium, nephrite scabbard slides, lacquer objects, silk and other materials. Several extremely rich burials date to the first centuries AD. This rich material is concentrated in some regions, particularly Bactria, Mongolia, western Siberia, and the lower Don area. The last seems to be the centre of a powerful nomadic confederation, supposedly headed by the Alani. Some of these eastern objects may reflect trade along the northern branch of the Silk Road, which was in existence by this time, but it is unlikely that the massive sacred gold decorations of the rich barrows in the lower Don basin and the Dnieper region would have been mercantile trade items. Some items have parallels in Siberian and Hunnish assemblages. The international (not necessarily ethnic) military aristocracy was the most likely group to disperse polychrome style artefacts. The appearance in Europe of long Chinese swords with nephrite scabbard slides coincides with the equestrian horizon of the late Sarmatian culture (second to third centuries AD; Li Dgi Yn 2010). In Siberia, such swords were known earlier, in the last centuries of the first millennium BC.

Scholars believe in a successive development within the Sarmatian population, among whom new leading tribes arose from time to time, and these perpetual migrations from east to west were evidently at full pitch around the turn of era. The new nomadic groups also penetrated into the upper Don forest steppe area (Medvedev 1999; Berestnev 2016). Botalov (2009) groups all the sites of the second to fifth centuries AD in the Urals and Kazakhstan steppe into one Hunnish-Sarmatian culture, ascribing its creation to the Huns. Archaeological and anthropological data testify to a new drift of eastern nomads, who stopped first in the Urals, newly vacated by groups who had already moved westward. Taking into account the dramatic events that took place in central Asia, we should admit that the Huns might have been among the dislocated tribal groups seeking their fortunes in the west.

The late Sarmatian sites concluded the history of these tribes in Eurasia. In the west, the Goths defeated them at the turn of the second to third century AD. After the Hunnish invasion in the fourth century AD, some of the Sarmatians were killed; others joined the Huns and moved yet further west. However, some elements of their culture were inherited by later nomads and peoples of the northern Caucasus. The numerous migrations of the last centuries BC ultimately began the Great Folk Movement, which changed the ethnic and cultural make-up of Eurasia, precipitated the downfall of powerful states, and opened the way to the west for new peoples speaking Turkic languages.

The Forest Zone in North-East Europe

The worlds of the forest zone are composed of various cultures rooted in the traditions of the local Bronze Age (see Figures 16.1–16.2; Table 16.1). Compared to the southern part of eastern Europe, where the transition to the Iron Age was marked by widespread crises, significantly influenced by dramatic ecological changes (Medvedev 1999), the populations of the deep forests did not experience such severe disruption. Nevertheless, ecological conditions there also changed towards higher humidity while maintaining cool summers. The life of the forest dwellers was changed, but then evolved slowly for nearly a thousand years.

In the early Iron Age, the mixed forests between the western Bug and the upper Oka and Volga rivers were inhabited by people who left archaeological sites that many scholars believe to be associated with a proto-Baltic linguistic group. The correspondence of this region with that of Baltic river names lends support to this hypothesis. There are many ancient names in the north-west and central part of the Russian plain: the names of localities and villages go back to medieval times, but the river names are rooted in a more distant past. They are neither Russian nor Slavonic, being understood in Finno-Ugric and Baltic languages (Tretyakov 1966; Shchukin 1994).

According to archaeological typology, this territory is associated with the following cultures: West Baltic kurgan (Kaliningrad county, western Latvia, and Lithuania), Hatched pottery (eastern Lithuania and most of Byelorussia), Milograd (Pripyat'-Dniepr Polessye), and Dnieper-Dvina (partly Byelorussia and partly Russia). These cultural groups each have specific traits, but at the same time have much in common. Mark Shchukin (1994: 21–22) described them vividly:

> In all these cultures one cannot find brightly burnished pottery, nor jars, cups or bowls. The pottery is represented exclusively by poorly shaped and crudely fashioned vessels. Except for the western Baltic kurgans, sites are poor in non-ferrous metals, although they yield more numerous iron objects. The people built their settlements in places that were difficult to access and strengthened them with walls and moats.

Such hillforts became one of the integral attributes of the early Iron Age in the forest zone. They preserve the remains of wooden houses, which can be dispersed or regularly arranged; sometimes a long line of houses located around the edge of the hillfort formed a so-called 'inhabited wall'. The appearance of fortified settlements clearly reflects changes in the social sphere. Interestingly, such hillforts occur predominantly in the deep forest, but not so much in the southern area, which was closer to the steppe inhabitants—nomads—who might have been a danger. Thus, the hillforts were a response to internal processes within the forest zone. Except for the Milograd and West Baltic cultures, visible burials are unknown and mortuary practices uncertain.

The Dyakovo and Gorodets Cultures

To the east and north-east, in the forests which spread from the Finnish gulf to the upper and middle Volga, is another group of cultures. They are represented by both fortified and open settlements, and their pottery characteristically has surfaces covered by textile or network (reticulate) imprints. The cultures of the northernmost part, such as the late Kargopol tradition (Sukhona river) and the Asbestos pottery culture in Karelia, have a rather archaic appearance and limited material culture. These northern populations used mainly stone and bone for making tools and weapons for hunting and fishing, regardless of the large copper deposits available there. A more advanced economy and way of life is observable in the southern part of this world, represented by formations such as the Dyakovo (Krasnov 1974; Krenke 2011) and Gorodets (Smirnov and Trubnikova 1965) cultures.[7] These have much in common: hillforts with various combinations of buildings and fortifications, simple and crudely fashioned pottery, and artefacts such as the so-called *gruziki* of Dyakovo type (Figure 16.9, 5). The last are conical or bell-shaped clay objects, with a vertical perforation showing traces of wear, and decorated with dots, lines, swastikas, and other ornaments; it is uncertain whether they were used for cult or utilitarian purposes. They occur outside Dyakovo territory.

The hillforts were constructed on the elevated mesas within the river valleys, or on high and narrow promontories between a river and its tributary or a ravine. Researchers have repeatedly drawn attention to the fact that the settlements are located in groups or 'nests' (Syrovatko 2009: 30–32). Fortifications consisted of one to three lines of ditches and ramparts,[8] with wooden fences on top, or simple wooden stockades. The economy was based on territorial and chronologically expedient combinations of animal husbandry, hunting, fishing, metalworking, and slash-and-burn agriculture.[9] The last had been practised since the mid-first millennium BC, and was more typical of the Dyakovo culture than of the Gorodets culture. Of the two, the former is much better studied.

The Dyakovo culture spanned a thousand years: from the seventh century BC to the fifth or sixth century AD. More than 500 open and fortified settlements are recorded in the Volga-Oka interfluve and the upper Volga area. The hillforts, measuring from 0.1–0.3 ha, could accommodate from 50 to 200 people. The catchment zone of a hillfort was about 2–3 km in radius, and included hunting grounds, pasture, farming fields, open villages, and seasonal camps. Presumably such residential-economic complexes were at the top of the settlement hierarchy (Krenke 2011). Initially, people lived in round sunken houses, of 5–7 m in diameter, with a central hearth made of stone or clay. Later they built longhouses, divided into sections, and, in the last phase, a square wooden dwelling of 20 m^2 was dominant (Figure 16.9). The abundant assemblages of the Dyakovo culture sites

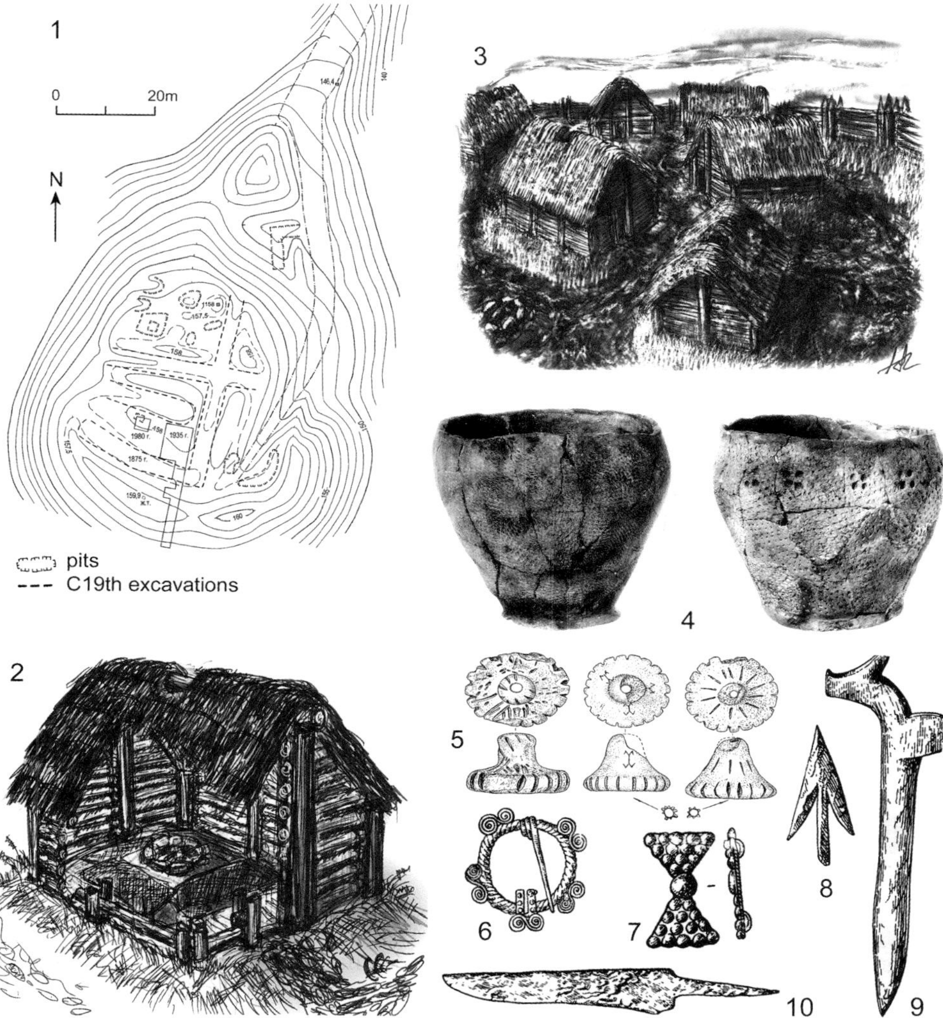

FIGURE 16.9 The Dyakovo culture. 1 Dyakovo hillfort, plan; 2–3 artist's reconstructions of the house and the hillfort interior; 4 'Textile' pots; 5 gruziki; 6–10 objects from Shcherbinskoye hillfort (6–7 bronze; 8–9 bone; 10 iron). Various scales.

Sources: after Dubynin 1974; Krenke 2011

comprised objects of everyday life, ornaments and clothing elements, weapons, objects connected with metal production, clay plaques, figurines, and other 'cult' objects. Most of the artefacts are made from bone and horn. To make pots, the people used a fabric which left net-like impressions on the pot surface combined with combing. Hoards of valuable metal objects are often found in hillforts. The sites also yield clay zoomorphic figurines, as well as bone objects with animal images, clay female statuettes, and other objects of small plastic art.

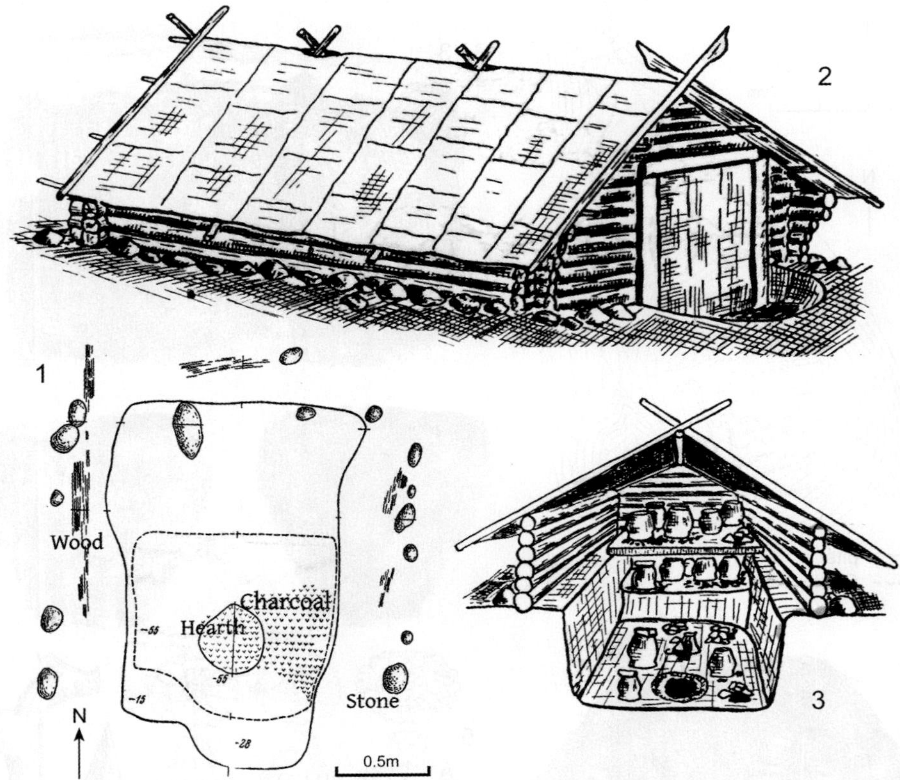

FIGURE 16.10 Dyakovo culture mortuary house. 1 plan; 2–3 artist's reconstructions.

Source: after Krasnov and Krasnov 1978: figs 1, 3

The Dyakovo economy was of diverse character. Animal breeding played an important part. At Dyakovo hillfort, the overall percentage ratio of bones of domestic to wild animals was about 80:20. The earlier sites demonstrate a predominance of pig bones, followed by horse, cattle, and sheep. Over time, the proportion of pig bones decreased, and horse became dominant. The role of meat declined in favour of plant foods. Millet, barley, wheat, cannabis (for textile making), and flax were cultivated. Specialists observe a significant reduction of the forests. Periods of balance between natural plant communities and cultivated fields were followed by hydrological changes and an increase in swampy areas. Palynologists have identified several such cycles during the life of Dyakovo hillfort (Krenke 2011).

Funerary sites of the Dyakovo culture are known at some late hillforts in the form of so-called mortuary houses (Figure 16.10), containing cremated bone intermixed with fragments of pottery, Dyakovo-type *gruziki*, and female ornaments. Dyakovo funerary rites are thought to have consisted of several phases: the exposing of the deceased at a place in or near the inhabited area, the cremating of the bones, and finally the placing of the remains in a mortuary house (Krenke 2011: 213).

Around the turn of era, the lifeways of the Dyakovo population underwent dramatic changes. Iron almost completely ousted bone in tool manufacture, and smithing developed significantly. The Dyakovo forgers used local bog-ores, which were widely accessible. Iron rings, which resulted from the smithing process, suitable for forging into finished artefacts, are frequently found in hillforts. In AD 100–500, textile-decorated pottery gave way to pottery with a smooth glossy surface. This change is explained by influence from the west, including the direct impact of populations from the Baltic region. It was a time of prosperity and consolidation for Dyakovo society. At the same time, some local traits became clearly visible, particularly in female decoration.

The Dyakovo people display contacts with various neighbouring regions. Initially, Scythian influence is particularly apparent, but by the end of the first millennium BC there was growing contact with the Sarmatians, whose northern border reached the forest zone (Medvedev 2008). At sites of the early first millennium AD, imports included some items from more distant sources—for example, Roman glass beads and beads produced in eastern Mediterranean lands (Galibin 2001). A Roman Aucissa brooch comes from Troitsk hillfort (Smirnov 1974). Such items penetrated to the upper Volga area through the agency of nomads, and some Dyakovo bone artefacts in pseudo-Animal style were manufactured under their influence. Despite changing styles, there was a basic continuity in material culture.

Related populations inhabited the Volga-Oka-Don watershed, where hillforts and open villages of the Gorodets culture are recorded. This culture spanned the period from the eighth or seventh centuries BC to the third or fourth centuries AD. In fact, the only real difference between Gorodets and Dyakovo material culture is the mat-like impressions on Gorodets ceramics. In the border area, settlements of both cultures occur alongside one another, while in the eastern part of the region Gorodets sites alternate with Ananyino and Pyanobor sites. The overall impression given by the Gorodets culture is rather modest and is primarily represented by pottery fragments. No hoards are found in its hillforts, and early sites yield very few metal objects. The pots have a net-like, mat-like or pseudo-mat-like, hatched, or smooth surface, marked with incisions or combing (Martyanov 2009). The people bred cattle, sheep, pigs, and horses, and hunted wild mammals and birds, which were abundant in the forest and forest steppe. There was little metallurgy in the early period, but smithing became more frequent in the early centuries AD.

The Dyakovo and Gorodets traditions are often interpreted as belonging to the Finno-Ugric ethno-linguistic group, with possible mixing with the Baltic language group in western Dyakovo territory (Tretyakov 1966). The cultures are seen as ancestral to groups of Volgaic Finno-Ugrians—Meria, Muroma, Ves', and Mordovians—known from the written sources. According to the data of pre-Slavic toponymy, the Meria spoke a language close to Mari, Vepsian, and Mordovian (Leontyev 1996; Matveyev 1997).[10]

Cultures of the Cis-Urals Forest Zone

The cultural world that scholars associate with Finno-Ugric development lies east of the Textile pottery zone. It includes several variants of the Ananyino and succeeding Pyanobor cultures, whose influence extended far beyond their core area in the Kama-Volga interfluve. Closeness to the mineral resources of the Urals, the legacy of Seima-Turbino metallurgy, and proximity to the nomadic world contributed to the more advanced technological level of these societies, although their way of life was of traditional forest character. These cultural entities give a special appeal to the early Iron Age of the east European forest zone (Koryakova and Epimakhov 2007). The two most significant formations lent their names to the earlier (eighth to third centuries BC), and later (second century BC to second century AD) phases of the local Iron Age. They are the Ananyino[11] and Pyanobor cultures, whose sites are concentrated mainly along the Kama valley, and on the adjacent lands of the middle Volga and north-east Europe. Continuous processes of economic, social, and cultural development culminated in the formation in the western Urals of ethnic groups such as the Komi-Permians, the Udmurts (Votyaks), and the Cheremis (Goldina 1999). Northern Fennoscandia, linked with the Ananyino metallurgical centres, is considered the westernmost component of this world. I share the widely accepted idea about the succession of the Ananyino and Pyanobor cultural traditions. Their territorial and chronological variability is mirrored in several local groups (or cultures). In the south, in the Volga-Ural forest-steppe, there was a buffer zone, a kind of "wild field" between the Ananyino territory and the area of nomads—representatives of the Sauromatian and Sarmatian archaeological cultures.

The Ananyino Cultural Groups

The Ananyino sites comprise numerous burial grounds, and both open and fortified settlements, located along the middle reaches of the Volga, and on the banks of the Kama river and its tributaries (the Vyatka, the Chusovaya, and the Belaya). Sites are also recorded in the basins of the Pechora, the Vychegda, and the Mesen' rivers in the extreme north-east of eastern Europe. To the south, there was a buffer zone between Ananyino territory and that of the south Uralian and Volga nomads. The mountain forest area to the east was inhabited by people who left sites of the archaic Gamayun tradition and the Itkul metal-producing culture (Koryakova and Epimakhov 2007). The extent of the Ananyino world is defined primarily by the spread of specific pottery types, funerary rites, and objects such as socketed axes and specific ornaments. Modern researchers distinguish three composite cultures of slightly different origins within the Ananyino world—Ananyino itself with corded and comb-corded ceramics, Akkozinskaya, and post-Maklasheyevskaya (Kuzminykh and Chizhevsky 2009).

The Ananyino tradition covers a period between the ninth and third centuries BC. Its early phase pre-dates the seventh century BC; the second covers the late eighth to fifth centuries BC; the third belongs to the fourth to third centuries BC (Kuzminykh and Chizhevsky 2014b). It should be stressed that start and end dates vary in different regions. For example, at the turn of the sixth to fifth century BC, the population abandoned the area of the low Kama, but in the Volga area this culture continued until the third century BC (Kuzminykh and Chizhevsky 2009).

The Ananyino settlement system includes several levels: (1) large fortified settlements up to 3 ha, serving as administrative and ceremonial centres; (2) small fortified settlements up to 0.4 ha, which functioned as subordinate centres; (3) open settlements; and (4) temporary hunting camps. Settlements accommodated numerous rectangular houses. Communal and tribal ritual centres functioned at some settlements and special places.

Much of the archaeological information is provided by cemeteries, which are located on high riverbanks and terraces, and are connected to specific villages. They comprise dozens or even hundreds of graves, laid out in rows parallel to the river, grouped according to kinship. The deceased were placed in oval or rectangular pits in an extended position, with their legs oriented to the river. Some cemeteries have small wooden mortuary houses with the remains of cremations. Ananyino mortuary practice was quite sophisticated, as evidenced by the variability of its archaeological expressions: individual, collective, secondary, and partial burials, with clear gender and status differences in the accompanying material (Figure 16.11).

Classic Ananyino pottery is characterized by shell temper in the clay. Pots are usually round bottomed, with a clearly profiled neck; the surface is quite smooth, sometimes polished. Corded and combed decoration, combined with holes, covers the upper part of the pot. Despite regional diversity, Ananyino societies shared a common economic basis: developed metalworking, stalled animal husbandry, and hunting and gathering. Cultivation can be inferred from implements such as hoes and grinding stones, but its extent is a matter of some debate. The bones of domestic animals (pigs, hornless cows, horses, sheep, and dogs resembling modern Siberian huskies) predominate in faunal assemblages. Bear, beaver, squirrel, hare, and deer were hunted for fur and skins, which were used for commercial exchange with neighbours. Ananyino bronze metallurgy was an advanced branch of the local economy, its products consumed both locally and more distantly. Iron production, which appeared here in the early first millennium BC under direct Caucasian influence, gradually replaced bronze in the economy, although the Ananyino culture is most famous for its bronzes.

The Ananyino groups effectively used natural resources that contributed to the local economy which, to judge from the number of sites, resulted in demographic growth in around the fifth to fourth centuries BC. Peripheral regions of the Ananyino world (the dark coniferous *taiga* forest of northern latitudes from Karelia to the polar Urals), however, experienced a 'prolonged' Bronze Age, in which hunting and fishing remained the basis of the economy (Kuzminykh and Chizhevsky 2009). The Ananyino culture was within the area where Animal style decoration was popular, but its repertoire of animal

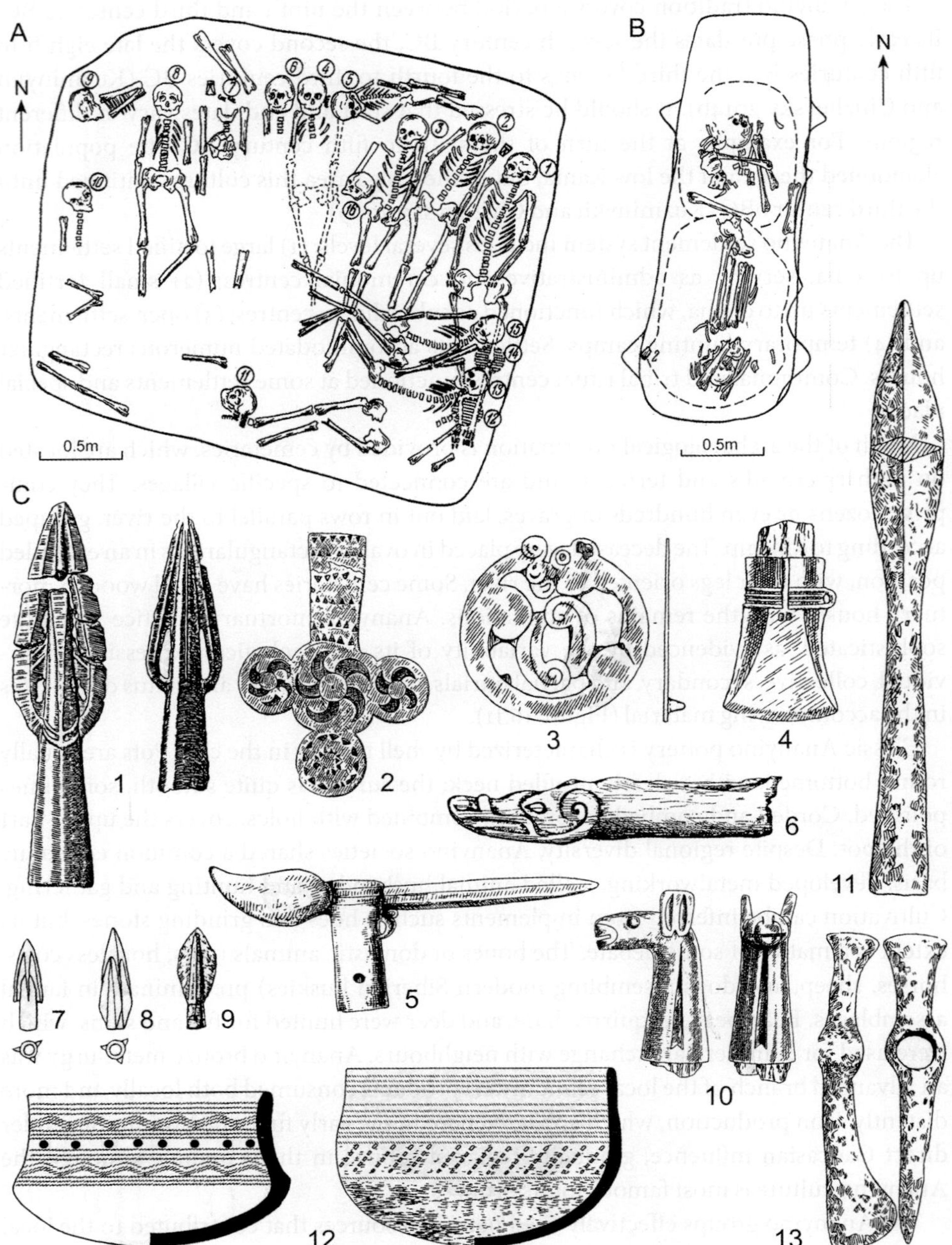

FIGURE 16.11 Akkozinsky burial ground: (A) Collective burial 46; (B) Plan of burial 32. (C) Artefacts from Ananyino cemeteries: 1, 11 spearheads; 2–3 plaques; 4 socketed axe; 5, 13 battle hammers; 6 zoomorphic object; 7–9 arrowheads; 10 pommel; 12 pots. (6 bone; 11, 13 iron; remainder bronze). Various scales.

Sources: after Koryakova and Epimakhov 2007; Kuzminykh and Chizhevsky 2009

images—which privileged elk, bear, and birds—was distinct from the Scythian Animal style, although heavily influenced by it in the beginning.

Ananyino society was organized into small tribal groups or simple chiefdoms; however, it preserved many egalitarian traditions and a tribal system with ill-defined boundaries between separate units. At the same time, Ananyino society displayed a greater degree of militarization than other societies of the Eurasian temperate forest zone. Analysis of the grave goods allows different social strata to be distinguished, which are more apparent among males. Imported objects (from Siberia, Kazakhstan, and central Asia) are numerous on early Ananyino sites and were concentrated in the possession of local chiefs.

The Pyanobor and Glyadenovo Cultural Groups

During the fourth to third and second centuries BC, the more or less homogenous Ananyino complex split into new archaeological entities represented by material culture inherited from the basic Ananyino traditions, but developed in a new social and economic climate. This separation occurred because groups experienced both local internal tensions and pressure from southern nomadic societies. Technologically, the new cultures depended almost entirely on iron production, and socially they were at a more advanced level. They span the period between the third century BC and the fifth century AD. The Pyanobor grouping is focused on the area of the middle and lower Kama, lower Belaya, and Vyatka rivers. Another formation derived from the Ananyino was the Glyadenovo grouping, which occupied the upper Kama area, the middle and upper Vychegda, and the upper Pechora rivers. These correspond to two subdivisions of Permic languages: proto-Udmurt and proto-Komi (Goldina 2004a).

The Pyanobor area consists of several variant local cultures. The Kara-Abyz culture occupied the broad-leafed forest and forest steppe along the middle Belaya river. It is characterized by vast open and fortified settlements and flat burial grounds, composed of thousands of shallow graves. In the cemeteries, the dead were placed on or wrapped in cloth, laid on their backs in an extended position, oriented with their legs toward a river, and accompanied by dress ornaments, particularly for belts. Male and female grave goods differed according to social status: male graves yielded a number of weapons—iron swords, daggers, spears, and horse harnesses. Female graves contained mainly ornaments (various kinds of ear-rings, ornaments that hung at the temple, necklaces, breast plaques, and pendants), utensils, and pottery. Ethnographic insight into women's costume is provided by leather belts crossed on the breast and decorated with numerous metal clips and round plaques, ending in lyre-shaped openwork plaques. The deceased were given a joint of meat: a leg of mutton or pork. This culture continued along Ananyino lines but with some Sarmatian (Prokhorovo) influence and the inclusion of population groups from beyond the Urals. Some scholars interpret this phenomenon as a result of sedentarization, when some nomads moved to a more stable economic and life regime (Koryakova and Epimakhov 2007: 262).

The best studied is the Cheganda sub-culture, also known as the Pyanobor culture. It was located along the river Kama near its confluence with the Belaya in a zone of coniferous and broad-leaf forest. Fortified settlements were of different sizes, and occur in clusters covering territories of 90–100 km^2, separated by 20–30 km of free space. The smallest sites appear to be refuges or outposts, but the biggest fortifications were surrounded by large residential areas. Burial sites were located on riverbanks, not far from the settlements. More than forty burial grounds with around 5,000 burials have been excavated; a cemetery could contain anything from 50 to 1,900 graves.

The fully excavated Tarasovo cemetery (1,900 burials) provides valuable information about Cheganda burial ritual, and the social and demographic structure of the population (Figure 16.12). Scholars believe that two lineages, each of which oriented their dead differently, founded this cemetery. The overwhelming majority of burials are inhumations, although there are traces of partial or complete cremation (Goldina 2004a, 2004b). The deceased were placed in a supine position, dressed in their best clothing, and decorated with many bronze ornaments. Epaulette-like belt buckles, temple pendants shaped like a question mark, round breast badges, and torcs are all characteristic of the Cheganda/Pyanobor material complex. The total weight of bronzes sometimes reached several kilograms, but included very few everyday objects. The cemeteries along the river Vyatka (a tributary of the Kama) are notable for combining inhumation and partial or full cremation, in bi-ritual mortuary practices, in which fire played a significant role. Vyatka graves can have up to 400 items in a single burial (Goldina 1999).

Cheganda society was evidently stratified and consisted of several units, ruled by local chiefs and united into a politically organized polity. This is evidenced by the systematic and hierarchical territorial distribution of fortresses, the high density of population, and the standardization of material culture, which is striking for its richness and sophistication. Statistical analysis of grave goods in the late cemeteries allowed Ostanina (1997: 134–136) to distinguish several different categories of female and male graves. From this she concluded that wealth and power were concentrated in lineages, which determined property and the social status of individuals.

The finds described earlier attest to the prosperity and economic rise of the corresponding societies, which occupied practically the whole Kama region, including the small river valleys in the forest zone. As well as the clustering of settlement around the large fortified sites, there were also dispersed small villages in cleared land. Social stratification, already visible in the Ananyino groups, became stronger in Pyanobor society, especially at the start of the first millennium AD. The social structure evolved from dominance of the extended family in the early period to that of the nuclear family in the late period. Metal production—primarily iron—became a specialized and autonomous branch of the economy. Complex technical operations, such as soldering and casting, which were used in the manufacture of ornaments, and relative standardization of artefacts, point to the existence of specialized craftworkers producing for intertribal exchange. Pyanobor decorations—specifically female ornaments, clearly symbols

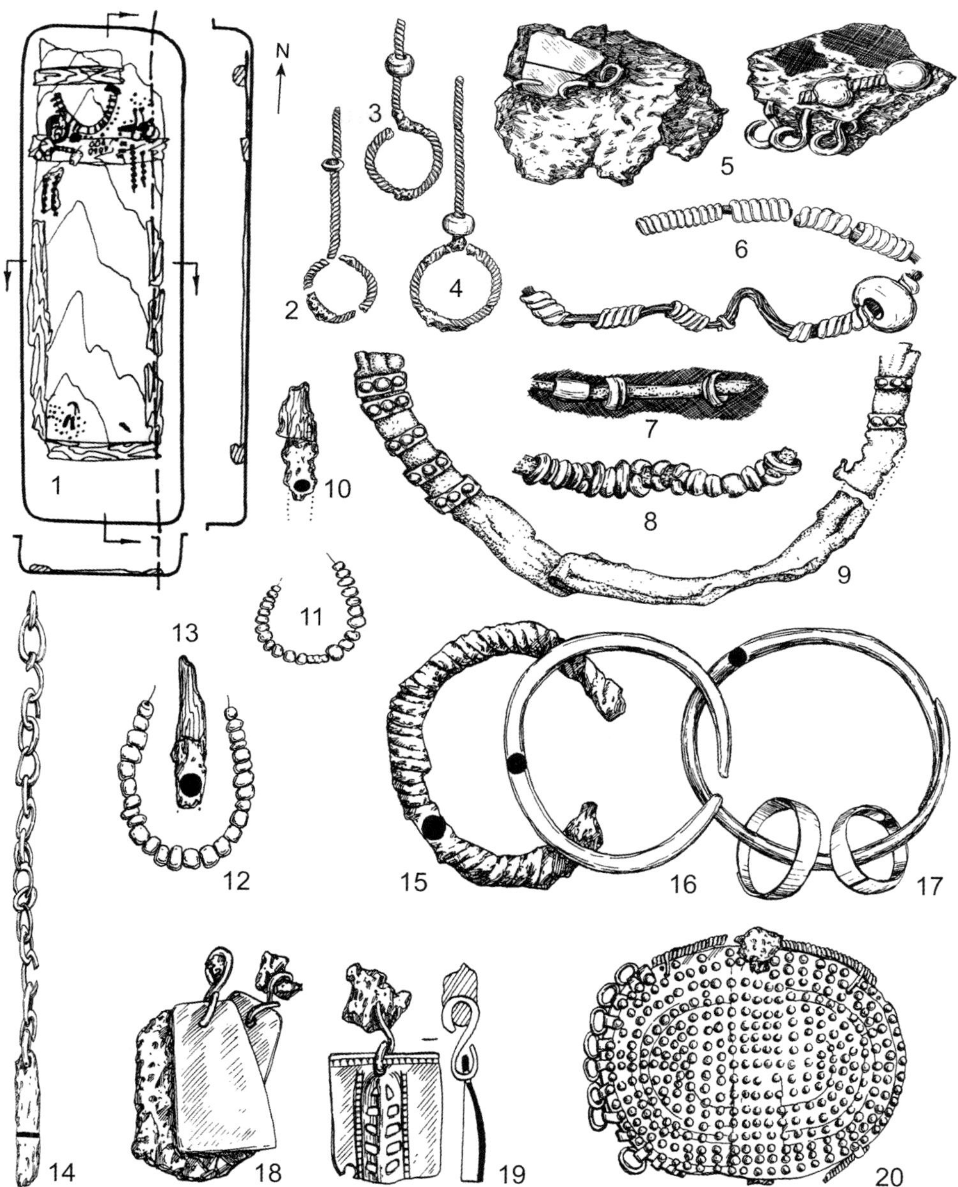

FIGURE 16.12 Tarasovo burial ground, Grave 185. 1 plan and sections; 2–4 ear-rings; 5 fragments of chain, beads, and tubules; 6 spiral and beads with leather strap; 7, 8 sleeve ornaments; 9 part of headdress; 10, 13 awl fragments; 11–12 beads; 14 chain; 15–16 bracelets; 17 bracelet with two finger-rings; 18–19 pendants; 20 fibula. (2–4 iron, bronze, glass; 5 iron, bronze, glass, fabric; 10, 13 iron, wood; 11–12 glass; 6–9 bronze, leather, fabric, glass; 14 bronze, iron; 18–20 iron, bronze). Various scales.

Source: after Goldina 2004b: figs 74–75

FIGURE 16.13 Female ornaments of the Pyanobor style.

Source: after Goldina 1999; 2004a

of local identity (Figure 16.13)—encountered outside their territory of origin, indicate intercultural contacts, perhaps through inter-group marriage.

Slash-and-burn arable farming was undoubtedly more important in the life of late Pyanobor communities. Grains of emmer wheat (*Triticum dicoccum*), barley, and oats have been found in the fortified settlements (Goldina 1999). Both metallurgy and farming required considerable investment of labour. At the same time, fishing and hunting supplemented the subsistence economy. Fur hunting remained of great importance: fur-bearing animals predominate among the bones of wild animals found on settlements. Animal husbandry was oriented to meat and milk, based on the rich grasslands of the Kama-Belaya valley. Horse, cattle, and pig were the preferred animals for breeding.

Pyanobor sites have produced a number of imported objects, which become more numerous in the second to third centuries AD. Silver items arrived from the Mediterranean lands and from central Asia, while beads imported from the Caucasus, Egypt, and Syria were also of wide popularity. Apart from this, the population of the forest and forest steppe zones of the Trans-Volga and Cis-Urals was closely connected with the late Sarmatian world, contacts which can be traced in both directions.

Glyadenovo groups occupied the southern and northern *taiga*, where hunting was of prime importance. This culture is represented by settlements, cemeteries, and communal ritual centres archaeologically characterized by large concentrations of bones and votive objects, known as *kostishche*. The richest Glyadenovo bone-producing site was discovered in the late nineteenth century. *Kostishche* are usually situated on the sites of earlier fortresses and are represented by several alternating stratigraphic layers. The components of the Glyadenovo *kostishche* are as follows: (1) a layer of burnt bones and ash, concentrated in the central area; (2) a layer of unburnt bones, deposited in a continuous mass around the first concentration; and (3) a great many artefacts—including ceramic vessels, bone, iron and copper tools, weapons (mostly arrowheads), knives, glass beads, small buckles, miniature copies of tools, and cult figurines of humans, mammals, and birds (Koryakova and Epimakhov 2007: 273–274). Zoological analysis has been limited, but the faunal remains were dominated by wild animals: bear, elk, reindeer, lynx, and boar.

The Glayedenovo *kostishche* yielded 12,900 glass beads with internal gilding, along with around 1,000 anthropomorphic cult figurines made from copper sheet. The figurines are simple schematic depictions of riders, archers, humans with serpents, and on dragons (Figure 16.14). Zoomorphic images include 460 dogs, as well as hares, squirrels, boars, bears, and some horses and cows. Birds are represented with outspread wings. There are also insects (bees) and snakes. These copper figurines are considered to be offerings to the local hunting gods. Also notable are a few Kushan and Chinese coins dating to the first and early second century AD (Koryakova and Epimakhov 2007: 274).

Several clusters of settlements, burial grounds, and sanctuaries, separated by 15–50 km, are distinguished within the Glyadenovo territory, which was isolated from the nomad invasions by the Kara-Abyz and Cheganda chiefdoms. Each cluster contains from two to seven sites, including one fortified settlement and some open villages, and corresponds to certain small tribal groups (Polyakov 2001).

The world of the Ananyino and Pyanobor groups displays a certain unity and progression of economic and cultural evolution. A steady development is noticeable in settlement pattern, pottery design, and belief system. These cultures produced distinctive objects of decorative art, elements of which are preserved in the folk art of the Permic peoples (the so-called Permic Animal style), which became their 'visiting card' in medieval times. There is no doubt that this world was more advanced than other forest formations. The diversified economy enabled local populations to generate stable food reserves, allowing the population growth reflected in the remarkable quantitative increase of first Ananyino, and then Pyanobor, settlements. In particular, some

FIGURE 16.14 Copper cult figurines from the Glyadenovo bone-producing site.

Source: after Gening 1988

5,000–7,000 people appear to have inhabited the Cheganda area, a density of around one person per km^2 (Gening 1988).

This type of economy ensured a substantial surplus production in the form of cattle, furs, metal, weapons, valuable ornaments, and other prestige goods, which could be plundered, exchanged, or stored in a fortress. Fortresses appear not only on the border with nomads but throughout the Ananyino, Pyanobor, and Glyadenovo areas, testifying to a rise in tension between different groups. The settlement hierarchy that emerged in the Ananyino cultural zone, developed further in the Pyanobor groups, accompanied by an increase in the size of fortresses. The Glyadenovo culture was more archaic, but preserved a rather unusual and unique type of communal sanctuary. These progressive developments tended to deepen social stratification, raising the role of local chiefs, and forming territorial units sharing common origins, language, and ideology. We can assume that the economic and political stability that existed in the forested Cis-Urals until the mid-first millennium AD promoted further ethnic consolidation and maintenance of cultural identities.

Until the second century AD, the Kama populations did not experience any great invasions. However, in the second century, the impact of Sarmatian groups on the Kara-Abyz territory can be seen in the archaeological record. The local population moved northward and mixed with the Cheganda groups. This movement is evidenced by mixed archaeological sites and led to a chain reaction of internal migrations within the Pyanobor world. At the end of the fourth century AD, new groups invaded the area of the Cis-Urals, both from the south-west (the Chernyakhov and Wielbark cultures) and from east of the Urals, as part of the wider Great Folk Movement. A very active process of interaction between the indigenous population and the newcomers changed the cultural make-up of the forest zone, and new cultures appeared there. Despite these invasions, traditions of the early Iron Age were preserved here for a long time.

Conclusions

During the early Iron Age the cultural and social landscape of eastern Europe, like the whole of Eurasia, underwent a major structural transformation. The broad decline of the Bronze Age cultures entailed an economic reorientation to pastoral nomadism in the steppe zone. On the one hand, this made possible the assimilation of a vast space and provided a partial solution to demographic problems. On the other hand, nomadic pastoralism had no great potential resources for social growth. Yet because the nomadic economy cannot exist without links to settled societies, even if these were not always peaceful, such contacts helped them to spread their achievements and to participate in the wider historical process. In becoming a pan-Eurasian phenomenon, nomadism opened the way to continuous invasions from east to west, but at the same time led to the growth of social contacts that transcended the boundaries of individual geographic zones.

I would like to stress that in the Iron Age, the temperate zone of eastern Europe was involved in a large interregional network, accompanied by growing militarization and social complexity. The start of the first millennium BC is represented by a clear rise of influence emanating from the regions occupied by established states. New world empires formed their own close peripheries, the sizes of which were determined by the level of social maturity of their populations. First the steppe (nomadic) population, then the forest steppe, and finally the forest groups were involved in the system of core/periphery relationships. However, for a long time the forest groups kept a slow pace of life and looser social structures, and their links with the centre were mediated by other polities.

The later first millennium BC demonstrates the evident complexity of economic, social, and political relations between societies within the major ecological zones and beyond them. Sites were more numerous throughout eastern Europe. The material points to demographic growth and a general increase in wealth, except, perhaps, in the northernmost areas. Almost all cultures were based on developed iron technology, while bronze became the metal used for manufacturing prestigious or cult objects. Gold was a metal of high value and a symbol of high status and power. Intensive local and interregional interactions also had negative effects, because not all of them were peaceful. Wars and conflicts became common, testifying to a gradual rise of tension within all cultural worlds. Ultimately, this tension resulted in the series of barbarian migrations that swept across the whole of Eurasia, and destroyed the old social and political order in Europe.

Acknowledgements

I would like to express my sincere gratitude to leading Russian archaeologists for permission to use illustrations from their publications. They are: L. T. Yablonsky, A. D. Tairov, S. G. Botalov, M. G. Moshkova, I. P. Zasetskaya, R. D. Goldina, N. N. Krenke, A. A. Chizhevsky, and S. V. Kuzminykh. Sadly, the great Russian archaeologist, and my friend, Leonid Yablonsky, passed away in 2016.

Notes

1. The 'Great Folk Movement' is the term used to characterize the large series of ethnic displacements and migrations in Eurasia *c.* 300–700 AD, which led to the settlement of numerous peoples such as the Goths, Huns, and Vandals within the territory of the Roman Empire; it is synonymous with the Migration period in western Europe.
2. For a recent overview of the archaeology and history of Eurasia, see Cunliffe (2015). Other useful surveys are Aruz et al. (2000); Basilov (1989); Brzezinski et al. 2002; Chernykh (2009); Davis-Kimball et al. 1995; Galanina et al. (1997); Lebedynsky (2002, 2009); Leciejewicz (1996); Parzinger (2006); Wegener (2010); Yablonsky (2010a, 2010b, 2013, 2015); Yablonsky et al. (2011).
3. Bronze Age pastoralism was not nomadic. It was practised mainly within the river valleys, as shown by the results of a recent Russian-German multidisciplinary project on Bronze Age settlement (Krause and Koryakova 2013).
4. Other groups attested in the ancient sources include the Maeotians, Saka (or Sacae), Issedonians, Arimaspians, Massagetae, Dahae (Dakhi), Roxolani, Siracae, Yazygs (Iasyges), Aorsi, Alani, amongst others.
5. There is no opportunity to cover the subject in detail here. The most prominent Russian nomadologists include M. Rostovtsev, P. Rau, B. Grakov, M. Grayznov, K. Smirnov, M. Moshkova, V. Skripkin, and L. Yablonsky, to name but a few. Their hard work and data collection form the foundation of all current research.

6. Abstract symbols, which were the emblem of a clan or family.
7. The former is named after the fortified settlement (gorodishche) of Dyakovo, located on a promontory on the right bank of the river Moskva, in the Kolomenskoye 'museum-reserve' in Moscow, the latter after Gorodets hillfort, discovered by V. A. Gorodtsov in 1899 in Ryazan' county (Smirnov and Trubnikova 1965; Levenok and Mironov 1976).
8. Soil studies of the ramparts in some Dyakovo hillforts demonstrate high levels of organic materials, including dung, within them. In other words, the ramparts were partly a refuse dump (Gol'eva et al. 2014). The Dyakovo fortifications provide fundamentally important insights into the development of this culture: as well as furnishing information on military affairs, the embankments and deposits in the ditches are sources of other data such as spore-pollen spectra (Syrovatko 2009: 41).
9. People changed their place of residence depending on the state of resources.
10. The Mari and Mordovians are often combined into one group according to their language. Mordva and Mari form a separate subgroup of the Finno-Ugric and Uralic languages; the name of the Volga Finno-Ugric peoples is therefore a geographical rather than an ethno-linguistic term (Belykh 2006: 23).
11. Named after the cemetery excavated by Alabin in 1858 near Ananyino on the river Vyatka. This discovery caused much interest among scholars and was an important event for Russian archaeology, opening new pages on the ancient history of the local population. For a review of the important contribution to the discovery and study of Cis-Urals antiquities made by the Finnish scientist A. M. Tallgren (1885–1945), see Kuzminykh and Chizhevsky (2014a).

References

Aruz, J., A. Farkas, A. Alekseev, and E. Korolkova (eds). 2000. *The Golden Deer of Eurasia: Scythian and Sarmatian Treasures from the Russian Steppes*. New York: Metropolitan Museum of Art.

Bartseva, T. I. 1981. *Tsvetnaya metalloobrabotka skifskogo vremeni*. Moscow: Nauka.

Basilov, V. N. 1989. *Nomads of Eurasia*. Los Angeles: Natural History Museum of Los Angeles County, Denver Museum of Natural History, and US National Museum of Natural History.

Belykh, S. K. 2006. *Istoriya narodov Volgo-Uralskogo regiona*. Izhevsk: UDGU.

Berestnev, R. S. 2016. 'Sarmaty v lesostepnom mezhdurechy'e Dona I Volgi (Itogi issledovaniya)'. *Vestnik Voronezhskogo Gosudarstvennogo Universiteta. Seriya Istoriya, politologiya, sociologiya* 4: 19–26.

Berlizov, N. E. 2011. *Ritmy Sarmatiyi: Savromato-Sarmatskiye plemena Yuzhnoi Rossiyi v VII–V vv. do n.e.* Krasnodar: Parabellum.

Bokovenko, N., and I. P. Zasetskaya. 1994. 'The Origin of Hunnish cauldrons in East-Europe', in B. Genito (ed.) *The Archaeology of the Steppes: Methods and Strategies*: 701–724. Naples: Instituto Universale Orientale.

Botalov, S. G. 2009. *Huns and Turks (The Historical and Archaeological Reconstructions)*. Chelyabinsk: Riphei.

Botalov, S. G., and A. D. Tairov. 2011. 'Excavations at the Kichigino burial site (South Urals) in 2007: Preliminary results'. *Ancient West and East* 10: 349–358.

Botalov, S. V. 2000. 'Pozdnyaya drevnost', in N. O. Ivanova (ed.) *Drevnyaya istoriya Yuzhnogo Zaural'ya*: 208–288. Chelyabinsk: Izadel'stvo YurGU.

Brzezinski, R., M. Mielczarek, and G. A. Embleton. 2002. *The Sarmatians, 600 BC–AD 450*. Oxford: Osprey.

Budja M. 2015. 'Archaeology and rapid climate changes: From the collapse concept to a panarchy interpretative model'. *Documenta Praehistorica* 42: 171–184.

Chernykh, E. N. 2009. *Stepnoi poyas Evraziyi: phenomen kochevykh kultur*. Moscow: Rukopisnaye pamytniki Drevnei Rusi.

Chizhevsky, A. A. 2011. 'Nachalo rannego zheleznogo veka v Volgo-Kamye', in V. A. Alekshin and V. S. Bochkarev (eds) *Perekhod on epokhi bronzy k epokhe zheleza v Severnoi Evraziyi*: 41–45. Saint Petersburg: Hermitage.

Cunliffe, B. W. 2015. *By Steppe, Desert and Ocean: The Birth of Eurasia*. Oxford: Oxford University Press.

Davis-Kimball, J., V. A. Bashilov, and L. T. Yablonsky (eds). 1995. *Nomads of the Eurasian Steppes in the Early Iron Age*. Berkeley: Zinat Press.

Dubynin, A. F. 1974. 'Sherbinskoye gorodishche', in Y. A. Krasnov (ed.) *Dyakovskaya kultura*: 198–280. Moscow: Nauka.

Koryakova, L. N., and S. V. Kuzminykh. 2021. 'Origin and introduction of Iron in northern Eurasia', in E. Kaiser and W. Schier (eds) *Time and Materiality: Periodization and Regional Chronologies at the Transition from Bronze to Iron Age in Eurasia (1200-600 BCE)*: 299–332. Rahden: Marie Leidorf.

Egoreichenko, A. A. 2006. *Kultury shtrikhovannoi keramiki*. Minsk: BGU.

Galanina, L. K., A. I. Ivanchik, and H. Parzinger. 1997. *Die Kurgane von Kelermes: 'Königsgräber' der frühskythischen Zeit*. Moscow: Institut für allgemeine Geschichte der Russischen Akademie der Wissenschaften.

Galibin, V. A. 2001. *Sostav stekla kak istorichesky istochnik*. St Petersburg: Peterburgskoye vostokovedeniye.

Gening, V. F. 1988. *Etnicheskaya istoria Zapadnovo Priuralia na rubrzhe nachei ery*. Moscow: Nauka.

Goldina, R. D. 1999. *Drevnyaya i srednevekovaya istoriya udmurtskogo naroda*. Izhevsk: Udmurt University.

Goldina, R. D. 2004a. *Tarasovskyi mogilnik I-V vv. n.e. na Srednei Kame, Vol. 1*. Izhevsk: Udmurtia.

Goldina, R. D. 2004b. *Tarasovskyi mogilnik I-V vv. n.e. na Srednei Kame, Vol. 2*. Izhevsk: Udmurtia.

Gol'eva, A. A., A. S. Syirovatko, and A. A. Troshina. 2014. 'Some construction features of the shafts at the Dyakovo hillforts: first results of scientific research' in S. V. Kuzminykh and A. A. Chizhevsky (eds) *Ananyinsky mir: istoki, razvitiye, svyazi, istoricheskiye sud'by*: 420–426. Kazan': Otechestvo.

Grakov, B. N. 1947. 'Naikokrato menoi (perezhitki matriarkhata u sarmatov)'. *Vestnik drevney istorii* 1947, 3: 100–121.

Gutsalov, S. Y. 1998. 'Kurgan ranneskifskogo vremeni na Ileke', in N. L. Morgunova (ed.) *Arkheologicheskiye pamyatniki Orenburzh'ya*: 136–142. Orenburg: Demer.

Khazanov, A. M. 1984. *The Nomads and the Outside World*. Cambridge: Cambridge University Press.

Klepikov, V. M. 2002. *Sarmaty Nizhnego Povilzhya v IV–III vv. do n.e.* Volgograd: Volgograd State University Press.

Koryakova, L. N., and A. V. Epimakhov. 2007. *The Urals and Western Siberia in the Bronze and Iron Ages*. Cambridge: Cambridge University Press.

Koryakova, L. N., and S. V. Kuzminykh. 2021. 'Origin and introduction of Iron in northern Eurasia', in E. Kaiser and W. Schier (eds) *Time and Materiality: Periodization and Regional Chronologies at the Transition from Bronze to Iron Age in Eurasia (1200–600 BCE)*: 299–332. Rahden: Marie Leidorf.

Krasnov, Y. A. (ed.) 1974. *Dyakovskaya kultura*. Moscow: Nauka.

Krasnov, Y. A., and N. A. Krasnov. 1978. 'Pogrebalnoye sooruzheniye na gorodishche dyakova tipa', in V. I. Kozenkova and Y. A. Krasnov (eds) *Voprosy drevnei i srednevekovovoi arkheologiyi Vostochnoi Evropy*: 140–152. Moscow: Nauka.

Krause, R., and L. Koryakova (eds). 2013. *Multidisciplinary investigations of the Bronze Age settlements in the Southern Trans-Urals (Russia)*. Bonn: Habelt.

Krenke, N. A. 2011. *Dyakovo gorodishche: Kultura naselenya basseina Moskvy-reki v I tys. do n.e.—I tys. n.e.* Moscow: Institute of Archaeology RAS.

Kuzminykh, S. V., and A. A. Chizhevsky. 2009. 'Ananyinsky mir: vzglyad na sostoyanie problemy', in A. A. Chizhevsky and S. V. Kuzminykh (eds) *U istokov arkheologiyi Volgo-Kamya (k 150-letiyu otkrytiya Ananyinskogo mogilnika)*: 29–55. Elabuga: Institut istoriyi AN RT.

Kuzminykh, S. V., and A. A. Chizhevsky (eds). 2014a. *Ananyinsky mir: istoki, razvitiye, svyazi, istoricheskiye sud'by*. Kazan': Otechestvo.

Kuzminykh, S. V., and A. A. Chizhevsky (eds). 2014b. 'Chronology of the early period of the Ananyino cultural and historical unity'. *Povolzhskaya archeologiya* 3, 9: 101–137.

Kuzminykh, S. V., and A. A. Chizhevsky. 2017. 'Introduction to the Archeology of the Ananyino Cultural-Historical Region: Northeast Europe in the Final Bronze and Early Iron Ages'. *Archaeology of the Eurasian Steppes* 3: 22–36.

Lebedynsky, I. 2002. *Les Sarmates: Amazones et lanciers cuirassés entre Oural et Danube, VIIe siècle av. J.-C.–VIe siècle apr. J.-C.* Paris: Errance.

Lebedynsky, I. 2009. *Scythes, Sarmates et Slaves: l'influence des anciens nomades iranophones sur les Slaves*. Paris: Harmattan.

Leciejewicz, L. 1996. 'The Baltic region: Scandinavians, Balts, Finno-Ugrians', in J. Herrmann and E. Zurcher (eds) *History of Humanity: From the Seventh Century BC to Seventh Century AD*: 276–280. London: Routledge.

Leontyev, A. E. 1996. *Arkheologiya meri: K predistoriyi Severo-Vostochnoi Rusi*. Moscow: MGU publisher.

Levenok, V. P., and V. G. Mironov. 1976. 'K voprosu o novom rayone gorodetskoi kultury na Donu'. *Sovetskaya arkheologiya* 2: 15–25.

Li Dgi Yn. 2010. 'Kitaiskyi import v pamyatnikakh yuga Rossiyi (100 BC–300 AD)'. PhD dissertation, Rostov University.

Martyanov, V. N. 2009. *Volgo-Kamye v epokhu zheleza*. Arzamas: AGPI.

Matveyev, A. K. 1997. 'K probleme rasseleniya letopisnoi Meri'. *Izvestiya Uralskogo gosudarstvennogo universiteta* 7: 5–17.

Medvedev, A. P. 1999. *Ranni zheleznyi vek lesostepnogo Podonya*. Moscow: Nauka.

Medvedev, A. P. (ed.) 2008. *Sarmaty v verkhovyakh Tanaisa*. Moscow: Taus.

Melukova, A. I. (ed.) 1989. *Stepi evropeiskoi chasti SSSR v skofo-sarmatskoye vremya*. Moscow: Nauka.

Milkov, F. N., and N. A. Gvozdetskei. 1975. *Phizicheskaya geographia SSSR*. Moscow: Mysl'.

Moshkova, M. G. 1963. *Pamyatniki peokhorovskoi kultury: Svod arkheologicheskikh istochnikov*. Moscow: Nauka.

Moshkova, M. G. (ed.) 2002. *Statisticheskaya obrabotka porebalnykh pamyatnikov Aziatskoi Sarmatiyi: Srednesarmatskaya kultura*. Moscow: Institute of Archaeology RAS.

Myshkin, V. N. 2010. 'O subkulture elity kochevnikov samaro-uralskogo regiona v VI–V vv. do n.e.', in A. S. Skripkin (ed.) *Nizhnevolzhskyi arkheologicheski sbornik*: 120–190. Volgograd: Volgograd State University Press.

Ochir-Goryaeva, M. A. 1992. 'Savromatskaya problema v skifo-sarmatskoi arkheologiyi'. *Rossiakaya arkheologiya* 2: 32–40.

Ochir-Goryaeva, M. A. 2012. *Drevniye vsadniki stepei Evraziyi*. Moscow: Taus.

Ostanina, T. I. 1997. *Naseleniye Srednego Prikamy'a v III–V vv. n. e.* Izhevsk: Udmurt Institute of History, Language and Literature.

Parzinger, H. 2006. *Die frühen Völker Eurasiens: Vom Neolithikum bis zum Mittelalter*. Munich: Beck.

Piotrovsky, B. B., and I. P. Zasetskaya. 2008. *Sokrovishcha sarmatov: katalog vystavki*. St Petersburg/Azov: Izd-vo Azovskogo muzeya-zapovednika.

Polyakov, Y. A. 2001. 'Glyadenovskaya kultura', in A. F. Melnichuk (ed.) *Arkheologiya i etnografiya Srednego Priuraly'a*: 10–19. Berezniki: Perm State University.

Sergatskov, I. V. 2009. 'Pogrebalyi obryad srednesarmatskoi kultury Nizhnego Povolzhya', in A. G. Furasyev (ed.) *Gunny, gotyy i sarmaty mezhdu Volgoi i Dunayem*: 41–64. St Petersburg: St Petersburg University.

Shchukin, M. B. 1994. *Na rubezhe er*. St Petersburg: Farn Ltd.

Skripkin, A. S. 1990. *Asiatskaya Sarmatiya: Problemy khronologii i ee istoricheskii aspekt*. Saratov: Saratov University.

Skripkin, A. S. 2009. 'Savromaty Gerodota', in A. G. Furasyev (ed.) *Gunny, goty i sarmaty mezhdu Volgoi i Dunayem*: 29–39. St Petersburg: St Petersburg University.

Skripkin, A. S. 2014. 'Sarmaty (problemy proiskhozhdeniya, rasseleniya I politicheskoi organizatsiyi)'. *Nizhnevolzhsky arkheologicheskyi vestnik* 14: 7–20.

Smirnov, A. P., and N. V. Trubnikova. 1965. *Gorodetskaya kultura*. Moscow: Nauka.

Smirnov, K. A. 1974. 'Dyakovskaya kultura', in Y. A. Krasnov (ed.) *Dyakovskaya kultura*: 7–96. Moscow: Nauka.

Smirnov, K. F. 1964. *Savromaty: rannaya istoria i kul'tura Sarmatov*. Moscow: Nauka.

Smirnov, K. F. 1975. *Sarmaty na Ileke*. Moscow: Nauka.

Smirnov, K. F. 1976. 'Savromato-sarmatskyi zverinyi stil', in A. I. Melukova and M. G. Moshkova (eds) *Skifo-sibirskyi zverinyi stil' v iskusstve narodov Evraziyi*: 74–89. Moscow: Nauka.

Syrovatko, A. S. 2009. *South-East Moscow Region during the Iron Age: Local Variants of Dyakovo Culture*. Moscow: ChuBuk.

Tairov, A. D. 2000. 'Rannij zheleznyi vek', in N. O. Ivanova (ed.) *Drevnyaya istoriya Yuzhnogo Zaural'ya*: 4–205. Chelyabinsk: Izadel'stvo YurGU.

Tairov, A. D. 2003. *Izmemeniya klimata stepei i lesostepei Tsentralnoi Evraziyi vo II-I tys. do n.e.: meterialy k istoricheskim rekonstruktsiyam*. Chelyabinsk: Rifei.

Tairov, A. D. 2015. 'The early Saka complex in the kurgan 5 Kichigino I cemetery (South Trans-Urals)', in A. Z. Baseynov (ed.) *Sak Culture of Saryarka in the Context of the Study of Ethnic and Sociocultural Processes of Steppe Eurasia: The Collection of Scientific Articles Dedicated to the Memory of Archaeologist Kemal Akishev*: 300–394. Almaty: HARC 'Begazy-Tasmola'.

Terekhova, N. N. 2011. 'Tekhnologiya proizvodstva mechei I kinzhalov Yuzhnogo Priuralya skifssko I sarmatskogo vremeni', in D. A. Machinskyi (ed.) *Evropeiskaya Sarmatia*: 68–84. St Petersburg: Nestor.

Terekhova, N. N., L. S. Rozanova, V. I. Zav'yalov, and V. V. Tolmacheva. 1997. *Ocherki po istoriyi drevnei zhelezoobrabotki v Vostochnoi Evrope*. Moscow: Metallurgiya.

Tretyakov, P. N. 1966. *Finno-Ugry, balty i slavyane na Dnepre i Volge*. Moscow: Nauka.

Wegener, R. 2010. *Sauromatisches und sarmatisches Fundgut nordöstlich und östlich des Kaspischen Meeres: Eine Bestandsaufnahme bisheriger Forschungen unter besonderer Berücksichtigung der Waffengräber*. British Archaeological Reports International Series 2072. Oxford: Archaeopress.

Yablonsky, L. T. (ed.) 1996. *Kurgany levoberezhnogo Ileka*. Moscow: Institute of Archaeology RAS.

Yablonsky, L. T. 2008. *Sokrovishcha sarmatskikh vpzhdei*. Orenburg: Dimur.

Yablonsky, L. T. 2010a. *Prokhorovka: u istokov sarmatskoi arkheologiyi*. Moscow: Taus.

Yablonsky, L. T. 2010b. 'New excavations of the early nomadic burial ground at Filippovka (Southern Ural Region, Russia)'. *American Journal of Archaeology* 114, 1: 129–143.

Yablonsky, L. T. 2013. *Zoloto sarmatskikh vozhdei: Elitnyi nekropol' Filippovka 1 (po materialam raskopok 2004–2009 gg.)*. Katalog kollektsiyi. Kn.1. Moscow: Institute of Archaeology RAS.

Yablonsky, L. T. 2015. 'New unusual findings at Filippovka-1 burial mound 1, southern Urals'. *Archaeology, Ethnography, and Anthropology of Eurasia* 43, 2: 97–108.

Yablonsky, L. T., I. V. Rukavishnikova, and M. S. Shemakhanskaya. 2011. 'L'epée dorée de Filippovka'. *Archeologia* 494, December 2011: 5–57.

CHAPTER 17

EDGES AND INTERACTIONS BEYOND EUROPE

NAOÍSE MAC SWEENEY AND PETER S. WELLS

Introduction

The boundaries of Europe are again under discussion as this book goes to press, and European identity is hotly debated in political discourse. We are reminded once more that continental boundaries are social constructs and do not necessarily reflect meaningful cultural and social borders. This is true of Iron Age Europe no less than its contemporary counterpart. When considering the Iron Age, it is not always possible to identify a clear boundary marking a division between Europe and its neighbouring regions. Indeed, there is increasing evidence for cultural, economic, social, and political interactions across the lines of modern continental borders. The Iron Age was a period of high mobility which saw objects, ideas, techniques, customs, practices, and people moving between the different regions.

Iron Age communities in what we now call Europe were in contact with and interacted, directly or indirectly, with communities in lands beyond the continent's edges, in Asia, Africa, and even—at the end of the first millennium AD—North America. Until recently, the study of the European Iron Age has paid very little attention to connections with other continents, except in a few exceptional cases. More attention has been focused on interactions within Europe—either between temperate and Mediterranean Europe, or between different regions within temperate Europe (e.g. Lang and Salač 2002). This trend has changed in recent decades, with more research being undertaken on long-distance and intercontinental interactions.

The reasons behind this shift are due to changes in archaeological theory and practice. Archaeology is becoming a truly global discipline, no longer dominated by European and North American schools of thought. More research than ever is being directed at questions of connectivity, networks, and intercultural exchange. This work is helping us to gain a better understanding of connectivity in prehistory. Indeed, recent research has demonstrated that 'globalization' is not a strictly modern phenomenon (Hodos 2017).

We have come to realize that the Iron Age offers considerable evidence for interaction between Europe and the other continents, and we are beginning to understand the effects of those interactions on European communities (Pitts 2017). These interactions are critical for understanding the changes that were taking place in Europe at this time.

In this chapter, we shall not attempt to theorize the nature of cultural interaction in the abstract, nor to discuss the methods and approaches available for investigating prehistoric connectivity. Such topics are amply covered in the existing literature (e.g. Cusick 1998; van Dommelen and Knapp 2010; Knappett 2011). Nor is it our aim to explain the reasons for transcontinental interactions in the European Iron Age, or to explore the diverse and far-reaching effects of such interaction (for which see Chapter 27). Instead, we present a brief overview of the archaeological evidence for transcontinental interaction in Iron Age Europe. Even within this remit, the chapter makes no claim to be comprehensive. We do not suppose to list every artefact, site, or class of evidence which stands testament to intercontinental links. However, we hope to provide an accessible introduction to the topic, and, crucially, to offer directions for further reading and investigation.

We focus on interactions at the southern and northern edges of Europe, as interactions with continental Asia to the east are discussed elsewhere in this volume (Chapter 16). For our purposes, the southern edge of Europe consists of the Near East and north Africa, while the northern comprises the North Atlantic and Greenland. We first outline the main developments and introduce the main groups active in these regions during the Iron Age. We then discuss the evidence for interaction between Mediterranean Europe and its southern neighbours, before turning to focus on the intercontinental interactions of temperate Europe. In particular, we examine three categories of evidence for interaction. One is the movement of objects, in particular the import of objects into Europe. The second is the movement of ideas, in particular the adoption of certain styles, social practices, and technologies by people in Europe. The third is the movement of people—a phenomenon that is particularly difficult to investigate and has provoked much archaeological debate. Finally, we close the chapter by reflecting briefly on the idea of Europe in the Iron Age as a coherent entity.

The Edges of Europe

This section introduces the people and societies ranged around the southern and northern edges of Iron Age Europe, starting in Anatolia and working clockwise round to Greenland. The Iron Age in the southern zone starts around 1150 BC, and is usually thought to end with the establishment of imperial Roman rule. We have therefore taken for our chronological endpoint the creation of Roman provinces in north Africa in

149 BC. In the north Atlantic, including Greenland, the chronological span of what is considered the Iron Age starts and ends considerably later.

Anatolia

During the Iron Age, the Anatolian peninsula (modern Turkey) was home to many different groups of people (Sagona and Zimansky 2009: ch. 10). Western Anatolia was occupied by a diverse patchwork of city states and principalities, and modern scholarship has applied a range of ethnic labels to these groups. Mysians (Malay 1999), Carians (Adiego Lajara 2007; Rumscheid 2009), and Lycians (Bryce 1986; Keen 1998) are thought to have been the indigenous populations of the region, occupying the northern, central, and southern areas respectively. They are said to have lived in communities interspersed with Greek city states (Cobet et al. 2007; Crielaard 2009; Greaves 2010, 2011; Mac Sweeney 2013). While it is clear from textual sources that these ethnic terms were indeed used in antiquity, in practice it seems that distinctions between ethnic groups were rarely clear. The archaeological evidence suggests hybridization in terms of material culture, ritual and cult, and domestic practices. This can be studied alongside a rich corpus of literary and epigraphic evidence, from the epic poetry of Homer to the funerary epigrams found on Lycian tombs. It should be noted, however, that the textual evidence from western Anatolia is dominated by sources in Greek. This is partly because of the Greek 'epigraphic habit' of inscribing texts in stone, and partly because of the classical manuscript tradition which has preserved the works of many western Anatolian authors such as Homer and Herodotus.

To the east, the kingdom of Phrygia dominated much of the central Anatolian plateau, with its capital at Gordion (Kealhofer 2005; Roller 2011; Voigt 2011). This city consisted of an extensive lower city and a citadel mound, where impressive monumental architecture stood testament to the wealth and power of the state. From the ninth century BC until the Hellenistic period, the Phrygian elite buried their dead in tumuli around Gordion (Figure 17.1), some mounds still standing as high as 53 m tall (Young 1981). Both settlement and tumuli have yielded rich archaeological finds, allowing for the use of scientific methods to establish a firm basis for Phrygian chronology (Rose and Darbyshire 2011). There is a small but steadily increasing corpus of inscriptions in the Phrygian language, written in its own alphabetic script similar to Greek. In addition to these Phrygian texts, classical and Neo-Assyrian sources can sometimes add nuance to our understanding of Phrygia. Classical mythology, for example, records several stories of the Phrygian King Midas, who was said to have donkey's ears (e.g. Ovid *Metamorphoses* 11.85–145); potentially the same royal name is preserved in Neo-Assyrian sources as King Mita of the Muški (Wittke 2004).

The power of the Phrygians in Anatolia was eclipsed by that of the Lydians in the seventh century BC (Hanfmann and Mierse 1983; Cahill 2008; Roosevelt 2009, 2012; Greenewalt 2011). With their capital at Sardis, the Lydians also appear frequently in classical myth and were actively involved in the Greek world. The last king of Lydia, Croesus, was known for his legendary wealth, which he is said to have displayed through conspicuous benefactions to Greek temples (Herodotus *Histories* 1.51). The wealth of Lydia

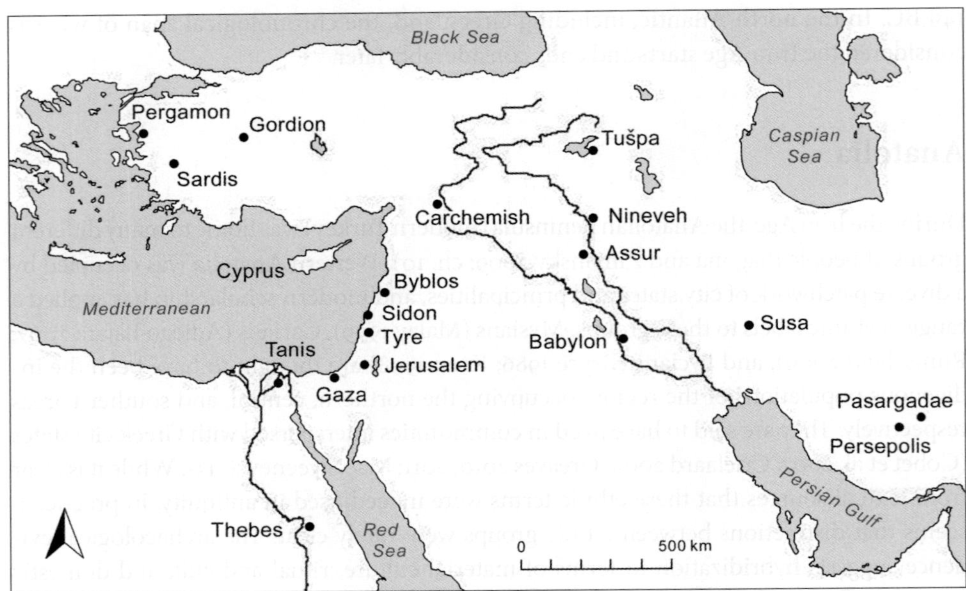

FIGURE 17.1 The Near East in the Iron Age, with principal sites mentioned in the text.

seems to have been more than hearsay, however, as it is the first place known to have minted coinage, and a substantial goldworking installation has been excavated at Sardis (Ramage and Craddock 2000). Like their Phrygian neighbours, the Lydian elite were buried in massive tumuli, the most impressive concentration of which is north of Sardis at the royal cemetery of Bin Tepe (Luke and Roosevelt 2016).

East of Phrygia and Lydia, the kingdom of Urartu prospered between the ninth and the sixth centuries BC (Zimansky 1998, 2011; Köroğlou and Konyar 2011; Ayvazian 2012). The capital at Tušpa, close to Lake Van, was a strong mountain fortress. From here the Urartians were able to dominate the highlands of eastern Anatolia, frequently coming to blows with their southerly neighbours, the Neo-Assyrians. Although we usually use the name 'Urartu'—the word itself is a Neo-Assyrian term—and the people of Tušpa themselves called their kingdom *Biainele*. The Urartian language belongs neither to the Indo-European family like its western neighbour Phrygian, nor to the Semitic language family like its southern neighbour Assyrian. Instead, it seems only to be related to the earlier language Hurrian, and is known from inscriptions in a modified version of cuneiform, the syllabic script developed in Mesopotamia and used widely across the Near East during the Bronze and Iron Ages.

Cyprus

During the Iron Age, the island of Cyprus acted as a node of interaction between Anatolia, the northern Levant, and the Aegean. The island seems to have been divided into a number of separate kingdoms, as attested by both epichoric inscriptions and

Neo-Assyrian documents (Counts and Iacovou 2013). Several of these kingdoms were focused on proto-urban centres that eventually developed into Greek polis-type city states (e.g. Paphos, Amathous, Kition). Epigraphic evidence suggests that a range of languages were used on the island—not only Greek (written in a syllabic script unique to Cyprus), but also Aramaic, and a local language that has been dubbed 'Eteocypriot' (also written in the Cypriot syllabary; Steele 2013). Linguistic variations do not seem to have mapped onto significant cultural distinctions, and the material culture across the island incorporated hybridized forms derived from the Aegean, Levant, and Anatolia, as well as peculiarly Cypriot features (Knapp 2008: 281–347).

A wide variety of types of site are known on the island, from urban centres to small villages, sanctuaries, and specialized locations for the production of copper, iron, and pottery (Todd and Warren 2012). Cyprus is believed to have the earliest evidence for the regular production of iron in Europe, from the twelfth century BC onward (Muhly 2006; Muhly and Kassianidou 2012). Ironworking spread rapidly, and from the eleventh century BC a variety of implements occur on settlements, attesting to the early use of the metal for everyday purposes. Production of bronze continued for the manufacture of some categories of objects, and intensified during the final centuries BC. The archaeological evidence reflects active commerce with other societies in coastal regions of the Mediterranean. Phoenician merchants are attested on Cyprus by the ninth century BC, and by the late sixth century BC some urban centres there were minting their own coins (Broodbank 2013).

The Levant

Along the long coastline of the Levant, independent city states and small principalities were the most common form of political organization, as in the Bronze Age. In the area of current-day Syria and south-east Turkey, a group of city states known as Neo-Hittite, or Hittite Successor States, flourished (Sagona and Zimansky 2009: ch. 8; Bryce 2012). These states came into being following the demise of the Hittite empire at the end of the Bronze Age, but unlike their Anatolian neighbours chose to preserve the tradition of Hittite monumental architecture and sculpture, as well as the use of the Luwian hieroglyphic script. Important Neo-Hittite sites include Carchemish (ancient Kargamiš), Zincirli Höyük (ancient Sam'al), Tell Tayinat (perhaps ancient Kinalua), Til Barsip, and the temple at Ain Dara. South of the Neo-Hittite states, in the area of modern Syria and Lebanon, and in the north of the ancient region known as Canaan, lay the city states of Phoenicia (Markoe 2006).

'Phoenicia' is a Greek rather than an indigenous term, and derives from the Greek word *phoinikes*, for the valuable purple dye produced from *murex* shells in this area. It is unclear whether these various independent states shared any type of collective identity in the Iron Age. The name is significant, however, in that it highlights a crucial activity for which the Phoenicians are especially famous—maritime trade. The purple dye was only one of many commodities traded by Phoenician merchants. Bulk goods, such as timber and metals, seem to have been transported, as well as elite and semi-luxury items which are more easily traced in the archaeological record, such as intricately worked ivories, glassware, and metal objects. Phoenician cities in the Levant such as Sidon, Tyre, Byblos, and Sarepta were nodes within extensive networks of trade and exchange, which stretched from the Near East across the Mediterranean (Aubet 2001; Sommer 2007). Phoenician colonization in north Africa and the central and western Mediterranean has stimulated a rich scholarly literature, often in parallel with the roughly contemporary phenomenon of Greek colonization (e.g. Osborne 1998; Aubet 2001; Tsetskhladze 2006, 2008; Arodaky 2007). The Phoenicians are also known for the development of the alphabet, which was adopted and adapted by Greek and other later alphabetic scripts.

South of the Phoenicians, in the area of modern Israel, Palestine, Jordan, and inland Syria, lay a group of larger territorial states—the kingdoms of Aram-Damascus, Israel, Judah, Ammon, Moab, and Edom. The political structures of these kingdoms are primarily known from historical sources, including a small number of local Aramaic inscriptions, Neo-Assyrian documents, and biblical texts. Among these states, archaeological attention has focused primarily on Israel and Judah, due to the popularity of biblical archaeology as a discipline and modern political pressures on the region (Mazar 2001; Lipiński 2006; Fantalkin and Yasur-Landau 2008; Cline 2009). Interpretation is often heavily dependent on textual sources, despite archaeological identification of political entities remaining problematic.

Distinct from these territorial states were several independent city states on the southern Levantine coast, occupied by a group known to us as the Philistines. According to biblical texts, their five main cities were Gaza, Ashkelon, Ashdod, Ekron, and Gath. There is an ongoing debate concerning the identity of this group. Following the biblical tradition, one school considers the Philistines to be an intrusive migrant group from the Aegean who arrived in Canaan at the start of the Iron Age (Dothan 1982; Yasur-Landau 2010); another argues that a Philistine identity may have emerged out of the complex social and economic conditions of the late Bronze to early Iron Age transition (Bauer 1998; Maeir et al. 2013). In either case, it appears that the Philistine cities shared many cultural similarities with their neighbours in the southern Levant, whether through acculturation or common tradition.

Egypt

Egypt during the Iron Age was in the middle of the Third Intermediate Period (Kitchen 1986; Van De Mieroop 2011: ch. 11). During this time, Egypt was divided. In the eleventh and tenth centuries BC, this took the form of political instability, with the pharaohs of the 21st Dynasty based at Tanis sharing power with the high priests based at Thebes. The tenth to eighth centuries BC saw increased fragmentation, with different dynasties and kings establishing themselves in different areas. Stability only returned in the eighth century, when the Nubian kings incorporated the entire Nile valley into the wider kingdom of Kush (Török 1997; Edwards 2004). This stability was short-lived, however, as in 671 BC the Neo-Assyrian King Esarhaddon invaded Egypt, reducing it to vassal status within the Neo-Assyrian empire. This state of affairs proved equally transitory, however, and in 664 BC Psamtek I established the 26th Dynasty, which was to rule until the Persian invasion of 525 BC. The archaeology of this period in Egypt has traditionally received less attention than that of earlier periods. Nonetheless, the rich royal cemeteries at Tanis have attracted much scholarly and popular interest (Stierlin et al. 1987), while research has also been done at the royal city of Sais (Wilson 2006) and at the Greek colony at Naukratis (Leonard 1997, 2001).

Mesopotamia

The Neo-Assyrians successfully conquered not only Egypt, but also all of the Levantine states, from the Neo-Hittites in the far north to the Philistines in the far south, over a long period between the ninth and seventh centuries BC. The Assyrian heartland lay in northern Mesopotamia, and over the course of the Iron Age the Neo-Assyrian kings expanded their territories to include Babylonia in southern Mesopotamia, Elam in modern Iran, south-eastern Anatolia, the entire Levantine coastline, and Egypt (Parpola and Whiting 1997; Postgate 2007; Altaweel 2008; Pedde 2012). Several Assyrian capital cities and their royal palaces have been excavated, mostly in the nineteenth and early twentieth centuries, yielding the spectacular architectural sculpture which today adorns the walls of many European and North American museums. The remains at Nimrud (Oates and Oates 2001; Curtis et al. 2008), Khorsabad (Loud 1936; Loud and Altman 1938), Nineveh (Russel 1991), and Assur (Renger 2003) have furnished us not only with impressive archaeological and architectural finds, but also with a vast corpus of imperial archives.

Discerning the imprint of the Neo-Assyrians elsewhere in the empire is somewhat more complex (Parker 2003, 2012). In the seventh century BC, internal strife in Assyria allowed their Babylonian neighbours to seize control of the empire, establishing the somewhat short-lived Neo-Babylonian empire in its stead. From their capital at Babylon, the Neo-Babylonian kings ruled over a slightly reduced empire from that of their Neo-Assyrian predecessors. In the main, there is little material change to mark the transition from Assyrian to Babylonian rule, although impressive remains have been uncovered at the cities of Babylonia (Kuhrt 2001; Baker 2012).

The Persian Empire

In the mid-sixth century BC, the Achaemenid king of Persia, Cyrus the Great, swept across vast swathes of the Near East and established the Persian empire in all the regions so far discussed. The Achaemenid dynasty itself originally came from Fars, in modern Iran. However, at its height, their empire stretched from Afghanistan in the east to Greece in the west, from Nubia in the south to Scythia in the north, incorporating most of the Near East, including Mesopotamia and Egypt (Briant 2002; Allen 2005; Kuhrt 2007). For nearly 200 years between *c.*500 and 330 BC, the Persians maintained this empire through a combination of centralized strength and local flexibility. The strengths of the empire lay not only in its military force, but also in a rapid and efficient system of communications and a meticulous system of administration and bureaucracy. The language of this administration was Aramaic, and important imperial archives have been found in Egypt, Persepolis in Iran, and Bactria in modern Afghanistan.

On a local level, imperial structures were often very flexible. Frequently, local dynastic rulers and elites were maintained in their roles, local laws and customs were upheld, and local cults and religions were maintained. This is evident from the archaeology of the Achaemenid provinces, where there is often considerable continuity as well as innovative hybridization (e.g. Dusinberre 2003; Briant and Boucharlat 2005; Ivantchik and Licheli 2007; Khatchadourian 2012).

Achaemenid archaeology remains under-studied, as the relevant levels of many sites in the provinces have been destroyed by later Hellenistic and Roman building. In addition to the provincial sites, several of the imperial centres in Persia itself have been excavated (Henkelman 2012), including Pasargadae (Stronach 1978), Persepolis (Schmidt 1953, 1957, 1970), and Susa (Boucharlat 1990). The Achaemenid empire was conquered by Alexander of Macedon in 330 BC, and dismembered by Alexander's competing successors after his death in 323 BC. The eastern Mediterranean region and the Near East moved into the Hellenistic period, beyond the chronological remit of this chapter.

North Africa

North Africa west of Egypt followed a different trajectory from that of the regions previously discussed. In the Iron Age, the area covered by the modern countries of Libya, Tunisia, Algeria, and Morocco was occupied by several distinct Berber groups, as well as by migrants from elsewhere in the Mediterranean region. The Iron Age archaeological record is scanty and heavily weighted in favour of the coast. This is partly due to the uneven history of excavation, although recent research is beginning to address this issue, as we shall see. However, the imbalance may also be partly due to the nature of the remains. It seems that many inland groups were pastoralists or semi-pastoralists, leaving a relatively lighter imprint on the archaeological record than the well-preserved settlements on the coast. In addition, historical information about the coastal cities is more plentiful.

Historical records are also relatively abundant for the eastern edge of this region, where local Berber groups frequently clashed with the Egyptian state. Indeed, for some time, conquering Libyan groups ruled parts of Egypt under the 22nd and 23rd Dynasties, and assumed prominent roles in Egyptian society (Kemp 2006: 42–46). Indigenous Berber groups also interacted with Greek colonists in Cyrenaica, where a cosmopolitan mercantile society seems to have developed from the seventh century BC onwards (Barker et al. 1985; Luni 2010). Five cities known as the 'Pentapolis' were established—Cyrene, Taucheira, Euesperides, Balagrae, and Barca (Figure 17.2). Save for Cyrene itself, all these sites now lie under modern cities,[1] and archaeological work has necessarily been intermittent (e.g. Marzano 2006). More is known about Cyrene and its hinterland, where there is strong archaeological evidence for the mixing of Greek, Egyptian, and local Berber customs, styles, and social practices (Hodos 2006: ch. 4).

West of Cyrenaica, the Mediterranean coast of north Africa was, in the Iron Age, dominated by Phoenician and later Punic settlements. Many of these sites were initially founded by Phoenicians as trading colonies between the tenth and sixth centuries BC. These included Leptis Magna, Oea (Tripoli), and Sabrata in Libya; Hadrumetum, Utica, and Carthage in Tunisia; and Lixus in Morocco. While these settlements may originally have had close ties with their mother-cities in the Levant, by the mid-sixth century BC Carthage had become the major power in the region. Carthage dominated the western and central Mediterranean with its strong naval power and control of trade routes from southern Spain to the Balearic Islands, Sardinia, and Sicily, as well as much of coastal north Africa (Lipiński 1987; Hoyos 2010). The rise of Carthage in the sixth century BC marks the beginning of the Punic period, as distinct from the Phoenician period that preceded it, and archaeology has uncovered a diversity of cultural styles and practices across the area of Carthaginian control. The mixing of Punic and local cultural forms is frequent, both in the Carthaginian territories overseas and also in the north African cities themselves (van Dommelen 2002; Arruda et al. 2007; Crawley Quinn 2011).

Further inland, the kingdom of the Garamantes prospered throughout the Iron Age, reaching the peak of its power in the Roman period (Ruprechtsberger 1997; Mattingly 2004; Mattingly et al. 2003, 2007, 2010). The name Garamantes was used first by Greek, and later by Roman, commentators, but remains in general use given the lack of any emic alternative. Contrary to the reports of classical authors, the Garamantes were a complex sedentary society, using sophisticated irrigation technologies to support agriculture and engaging in trans-Saharan trade. Their capital in the Iron Age seems to have been Zinchecra, moving in the Roman period to the nearby site of Garama.

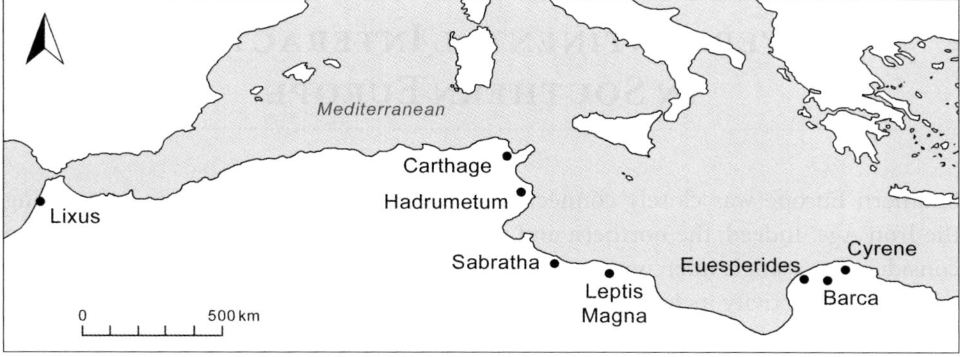

FIGURE 17.2 North Africa in the Iron Age, with principal sites mentioned in the text.

In the area of modern Algeria, other Berber states were established relatively late in the Iron Age. In the third century BC, several disparate groups came together and formed the kingdom of Numidia (Horn and Rüger 1979; Storm 2001; Kunze 2011). The term 'Numidian' is sometimes also applied to the local Berber population who lived in the Punic-dominated areas, but this usage must be recognized as distinct from Numidia as a later political entity. The capital of Numidia was the city of Cirta, although the coastal town of Hippo Regius may also have been an important royal seat. Numidia allied itself variously with both Rome and Carthage over the course of the second century BC. This political intriguing came to an end with the gradual extension of Roman control over north Africa. After the defeat of Carthage by Rome in the Third Punic War (149–146 BC), the Romans became involved in a Numidian succession dispute, and the dynasty was reduced to vassal kings.

The North Atlantic

The north-western and northern edges of Europe are geographically separated from the regions just discussed, and in these areas the Iron Age occupies a later chronological period. At the end of this 'long Iron Age' in northern Europe, at the end of the first millennium AD, peoples from what is now Scandinavia ventured west to Iceland, Greenland, and, briefly, North America. No clear indications of human settlement have been found on Iceland before Scandinavians settled there late in the ninth century AD (Vésteinsson and McGovern 2012). Parts of Greenland had been occupied by groups from North America, today referred to as Dorset peoples, before the arrival there of the Norse late in the tenth century, when they established what are known as the Eastern Settlement and the Western Settlement. According to present evidence, the European settlements of Greenland did not encounter any other peoples until a couple of centuries later (Odess et al. 2000). Only on Newfoundland, at L'Anse aux Meadows, is there evidence for interaction between Europeans and other peoples, sometime around AD 1000 (Wallace 2009).

Intercontinental Interactions in Southern Europe

Southern Europe was closely connected to north Africa and the Near East during the Iron Age. Indeed, the northern and southern shores of the Mediterranean can be considered as a single interconnected region during this time (Sherratt 2017). This zone of dense connectivity includes the 'European' lands of eastern Spain, southern France, Italy, Albania, Greece, and Turkish Thrace; as well as the 'Asian' territories of Anatolia, Mesopotamia and the Levant; and the 'African' countries of modern Egypt, Libya,

Tunisia, Algeria, and Morocco. Interactions around this zone have received much scholarly attention in recent decades (e.g. Foxhall 1998; Horden and Purcell 2000; Sherratt 2010; Hodos 2006; Broodbank 2008, 2013; Malkin et al. 2009; van Dommelen and Knapp 2010). We do not, therefore, intend to repeat this work here. Instead, we seek to offer a brief overview of some of the evidence from southern Europe specifically for intense and frequent interactions southwards.

The Movement of Objects and Commodities

The volume of objects traded around this extended area was high, and the range broad. They include not only high-value, low-bulk items for elite consumption, but also bulk goods, such as raw materials and staple foods, as well as semi-luxuries such as fine ceramics and desirable foodstuffs. The range of objects and commodities which moved around this entire Mediterranean–Near Eastern zone is testament to the frequency and regularity of contacts, and the density of the social and economic networks that held the region together.

Small, portable items imported to southern Europe from the Near East and Egypt were often used as a means to mark elite status and signify wealth (Helms 1988). Such items included jewellery, weapons, and other exotic objects, and have often been found deposited in mortuary contexts as grave offerings. One celebrated example of this is the cemetery at Toumba, in Lefkandi on the Greek island of Euboea (Nightingale 2007). From the very start of the early Iron Age in the tenth century BC, rich burials in this cemetery contained precious objects from the Near East such as Phoenician scarabs, vessels made from Egyptian faience, and Syrian cylinder seals. These kinds of valuable items were also often deposited as votives in sanctuaries, with small metal figurines of eastern gods often appearing as votive offerings in early Greek temple deposits (Treister 1995). The market for elite items such as these grew over the course of the Iron Age, and by the Roman period items can be found imported into southern Europe from places as far south as Meroë in Sudan (Allason-Jones 2004), and as far east as India (Tomber 2008) and even China (Thorley 1971).

Bulk goods were also widely traded, especially by maritime routes. Archaeological evidence for such trade is relatively poor, as bulk trade was often in commodities which leave little trace in the archaeolgical record—for example grain, raw metals, timber, and slaves. Instead, written texts and iconographic sources provide our fullest sources for bulk trade. Perhaps the most important bulk commodity entering southern Europe in the Iron Age was grain—in the Roman period in particular, grain from north Africa was crucial in maintaining the food supplies of the urban Italian population. According to the historian Josephus, one third of Rome's grain was supplied by Egypt and the remaining two-thirds from the rest of north Africa (Josephus *Jewish Wars* 2.383, 386). But our sources suggest that Europe exported more in the way of bulk produce than it imported. In particular, the Black Sea region was a vital source of timber, animal hides, and slaves for the empires of the Near East, while the Iberian Peninsula was mined for raw metals by Phoenician traders (Aubet 2001).

The Iron Age also saw the movement of many 'semi-luxury' products around this extended area. These items may perhaps be thought of as 'aspirational'—of high enough value to put them out of the reach of those on the breadline, but of low enough value to be potentially accessible beyond the narrow elite groups. They would include desirables such as high-quality wine, perfumed oils, well-crafted textiles, and decorated pottery.

Trade around the maritime networks of the Iron Age Mediterranean was complex and regular. Excellent evidence for this comes from a number of Iron Age shipwrecks, found at various locations around the Mediterranean. One particularly well-known example is the Bajo de la Campana shipwreck, found off the coast of Cartagena in Spain (Polzer and Reyes 2011). The cargo of this Phoenician trading vessel included bulk goods in the form of ingots of copper, lead, and tin; semi-luxuries in the form of ceramics; and luxury goods such as elephant ivory, Baltic amber, and items for personal grooming. These objects came from across the Near East, north Africa, and Europe—for example, the ivory came from Egypt; the amber from northern Europe; the metals from the Iberian peninsula.

The Movement of Ideas

The same networks that allowed for the movement of objects in and around Europe's southern edges also allowed for the movement of ideas, technologies, and social practices. For example, motifs and ideas from the Near East were incorporated into the local artistic styles of southern Europe in the late eighth and seventh centuries BC. This is known as the Orientalizing phenomenon, and resulted in the creation of new styles in ceramics, decorative arts—including the bronze *situlae* of northern Italy, Slovenia, and Austria (Frey 2011)—and monumental art among the Greeks and early Italic groups (Gunter 2012). Traditions of life-size sculpture; the incorporation of visual elements such as griffins, lotus flowers, and other motifs; and techniques of craftworking from the Levant, in particular, were all adopted and adapted. The processes by which this artistic interaction happened remain debated, but it is evident that the transmission of knowledge and ideas did not necessarily mean that they were slavishly imitated in a new context, nor that social meanings remained the same (Burkert 1992; Riva and Vella 2006).

Another important trend is the adoption, adaptation, and spread of alphabetic systems of writing in the Iron Age (Chapter 36). This happened first in lands along the Mediterranean coasts, and later, and to a very limited extent, further inland in temperate Europe (Robinson 2007). Although an alphabetic writing system is known from the late Bronze Age at Ugarit (Sivan 1997), the scripts of the Iron Age were developed from the alphabetic system used by the Phoenicians in the Levant from the eleventh century BC onwards. The Greek alphabet was developed using Phoenician letters from the ninth century BC, initially appearing in several local variants (Bakker 2010; Horrocks

2010: xviii). In the century or so that followed, the Etruscan alphabet was developed using one of these variants, as were several other Old Italic alphabets used by different groups within the Italian peninsula. The Etruscan alphabet was the ancestor of the Latin alphabet which is so widely used today, while some of these other Old Italic scripts were adopted and adapted in continental Europe, eventually becoming the various runic alphabets (Bonfante and Bonfante 2002). Independently from these developments in the central Mediterranean and continental Europe, the Phoenician alphabet also served as a starting point for the Palaeohispanic scripts of the Iberian peninsula, which integrated alphabetic and syllabic signs (de Hoz 1993).

The interaction necessary for the movement of ideas such as these involves regular and ongoing cultural exchange, and the building of social as well as economic and trading relationships. People communicated and engaged with one another, and adapted and innovated on each other's ideas. Indeed, from what we know of the movement of people around this area, we should not be surprised at the extent and closeness of this interaction.

The Movement of People

It is already evident that there were ongoing and regular movements of people around the Mediterranean and Near East. They included the movements of traders and craftspeople, mercenaries, and diplomats. This kind of continuous mobility can be compared to Brownian motion in particles, and produced an extremely febrile environment of ongoing cultural exchange. In addition to this background mobility, however, we can also identify some more discrete horizons where particular groups of people moved in more identifiable ways, and with a clearer sense of direction.

One of the best known of these were the 'colonization' movements of the Greeks and Phoenicians. New Greek communities emerged outside the Aegean during the course of the eighth to fifth centuries BC—some in Mediterranean Europe and the Black Sea region, others in north Africa in Egypt and Cyrenaica (Osborne 1996: 119–129; Hodos 2009; Dietler 2010). Phoenicians from the Levant began to create new communities around the same time, locating their new settlements in north Africa, but also in the Iberian peninsula, Sicily, and Sardinia (Aubet 2001; Arodaky 2007; Hoyos 2010). Some of the new settlements in southern Europe seem to have been settled from the north African Punic communities, rather than directly from the Phoenician homeland. In both the Greek and Phoenician cases, the establishment of new settlements seems to correlate with trade routes. The use of the word 'colony' in this context should not be taken to imply parallels with later European imperialism or colonization, but rather should be understood as a phenomenon in its own right (van Dommelen 1998, 2002; Hurst and Owen 2005; Cipolla and Hayes 2015). At both the Phoenician/Punic settlements in Europe, and the Greek settlements in north Africa, indigenous and new cultural elements can be found alongside one another. Relations between locals and newcomers were complex and variable, and cannot be assumed to conform to the later models of historical colonialism that we are more familiar with today (Vlassopoulos 2013: 78–128).

Another well-documented instance of people moving are the migrations of 'Celts', or 'Gauls', from Europe to Anatolia, and to a lesser extent, to northern Africa (Szabó 1991; Mitchell 1993: 13–23; Müller-Karpe 2006; Rustoiu 2006). Classical texts in Greek and Latin bear testament to these movements, although of course these texts cannot be taken at face value (Tomaschit 2002; Hauschild 2010). The Anatolian case is usually presented in the context of Gaulish military campaigns in the third century BC (Mitchell 1993: 14). The texts tend to emphasize their violence and hostility to the local populations (Darbyshire et al. 2000: 78), while the epigraphic record (referring to the Gauls as 'Galatians') suggest more complex forms of interaction (Mitchell 1993: 18). The quantity and quality of the archaeological evidence for Europeans in Anatolia is nowhere near as rich as the textual sources. Müller-Karpe (1988, 2006) summarizes the evidence, consisting of a number of European-style bronze fibulae, some ring jewellery, and fine painted pottery. Another source of material evidence for the 'Celtic' presence in Anatolia consists of the sculptures from Pergamon, which depict with great precision weapons of characteristic middle La Tène form (Darbyshire et al. 2000: 83; Müller-Karpe 2006: 120). In seeking archaeological evidence for 'Celtic' emigration, scholars disagree on whether or not there is evidence for the abandonment of landscapes in temperate Europe (Villes 1995; Arnold 2005: 17; Schönfelder 2007). On this point, the evidence remains inconclusive.

Evidence for the transcontinental movement of people at Europe's southern edges is complex and variable. Nonetheless, it is evident that people did move across what we now think of as a continental boundary in a range of different ways, and for a range of different reasons. This included the regular and ongoing Brownian motion of small groups and individuals that facilitated the sharing of ideas and transport of objects, but also on occasion larger-scale movements by larger groups seeking new homelands in which to settle.

The Movement of Objects into Temperate Europe

In temperate Europe, the evidence of imports is markedly different from that of southern Europe, and studies have focused on objects coming from the Mediterranean region, and the Greek, Etruscan, and Roman worlds in particular (e.g. Adam 2007; Hansen and Böhr 2011). However, objects have been recovered archaeologically in the non-Mediterranean regions of Europe that originated from much further afield as well. Some representative examples are discussed here, with no attempt at a comprehensive catalogue.

It has been argued that fundamental changes were taking place across Eurasia during the Iron Age in the ways commerce was organized, which spurred great increases in the production and widespread dissemination of goods (Ehret 2002; Harris 2007: 53; Fletcher 2012). The essence of these changes in the Mediterranean basin and the Near East was a shift in the control of commerce from political elites into the hands of independent merchants. The changes were a powerful economic stimulus across the whole of this zone and help to explain the increased evidence for external contact that we observe in temperate Europe.

Relative to the enormous quantity of archaeological material that has been excavated, studied, and published from Iron Age Europe, these imported objects are few. But the small number is no reason to doubt their powerful cultural significance to indigenous communities, nor the importance of the contacts to which they attest. Issues of preservation and identification are also relevant, and we are undoubtedly only seeing the tip of a much larger iceberg.

Metals

Metal objects arrived in Europe in a variety of forms. One particularly common import was the Near Eastern metal vessel. For example, in a burial at the early Iron Age centre of Stična in Slovenia (Figure 17.3) that contained a complete set of weapons, a bronze bowl decorated with floral patterns in relief was recovered (Gabrovec 1966: 11, fig. 5, 4). The bowl has its strongest stylistic parallels among vessels made during the fifth century BC in the Achaemenid world of the Near East (Curtis and Tallis 2005). The dating of the Stična grave to the mid-fifth century BC on the basis of the local objects in it, is consistent with the bowl's probable date of manufacture. Similarly, at the early La Tène settlement at Straubing on the Danube in Bavaria, a small bronze *situla* was recovered in a pit (Tappert and Mielke 1997; Tappert 2002). This object (Figure 17.4) is also believed to come from the Near East, most probably from the Levant area (C. Tappert pers. comm.). In some rich burials in eastern Europe, such as that at Filippovka, just east of the southern part of the Ural mountains, vessels of gold and silver manufactured in the Achaemenid Near East have been recovered. They represent components of feasting sets and include amphorae, jars, and *rhytons* (Pshenichniuk 2000a, 2000b, 2000c).

Glass

Items made from glass were imported from the Near East (Chapter 24). A well-outfitted burial at Ihringen near the early Iron Age centre of Breisach on the upper Rhine contained an intact bowl of greenish-blue glass (Dehn 1997). This bowl finds it closest parallels in the Achaemenid Near East, where such vessels were often placed in richly outfitted burials, and is believed to have been made there (Curtis and Tallis 2005: 174–180; Kistler 2010). Among the grave goods in another richly equipped burial in the mound known as Römerhügel, part of the tumulus group around the early Iron Age centre of the Hohenasperg just north of Stuttgart, was a small reddish-brown glass

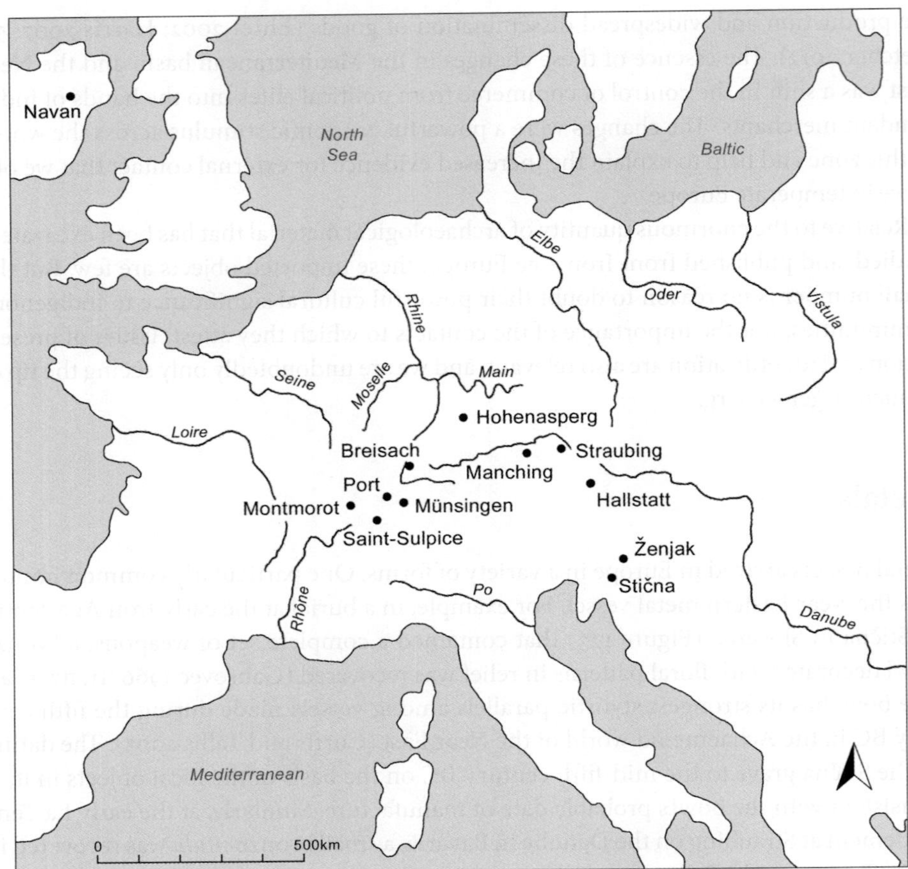

FIGURE 17.3 Principal sites in temperate Europe mentioned in the text.

bottle of squarish cross-section with white wavy lines around the outside (Paret 1921: 69, fig. 13, 5; Dehn 1951: 32–34, fig. 3, 2; Kimmig 1988: 26). Although Dehn suggests that the bottle is later and cannot belong to the burial assemblage, Paret reports it as part of the burial assemblage, and Kimmig reasserts that it was clearly mentioned in the original report. Again, parallels are to be found to the east, with similar vessels noted in Anatolia and Iran (Barag 1985:78–79).

Imported glass also often occurs as beads. For example, two beads in the form of masks of coloured opaque glass were recovered in the grave of a young woman dated to the fourth century BC in the cemetery of Saint-Sulpice on Lake Geneva, Switzerland (Haevernick 1981; Kaenel 1990: 295–296, pl. 22; Müller 2009: 95). Scholarly opinion is that they were made in the Carthage area, where large numbers of similar beads have been recovered (Jaffé 1978: 21–22). The same grave contained a polychrome eye-bead of a type with a very wide distribution, occurring as far away as China (Haevernick 1981: 402, fig. 5, 403, fig. 6).

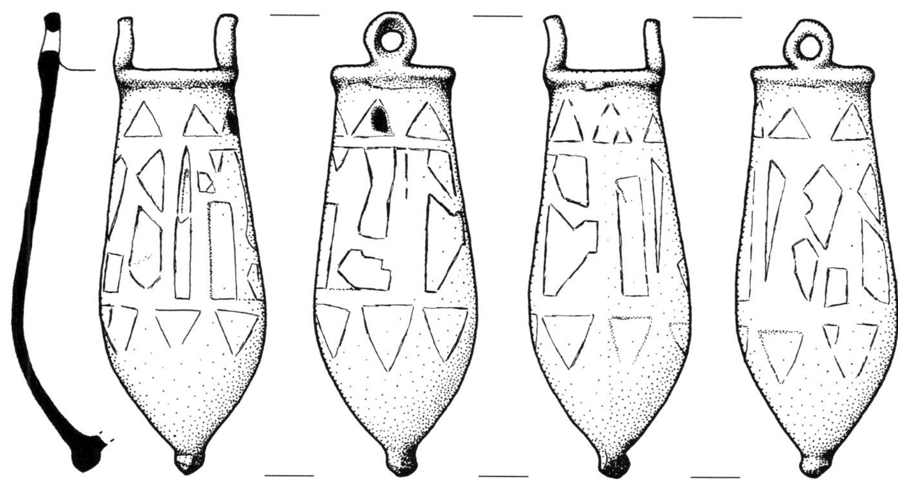

FIGURE 17.4 Bronze *situla* from Straubing, Bavaria, Germany, four views. Height 104 mm.
Drawing courtesy of Claudia Tappert

Ivory

A considerable quantity of ornaments made of material identified as ivory has been reported from early Iron Age contexts in temperate Europe. To judge by the extraordinary wealth and character of ivory finds in the looted Grafenbühl tumulus, as well as by the smaller quantities of pieces in other burials, and by the relatively widely distributed early Iron Age sword pommels and handle ornaments carved from ivory, much more ivory was probably in use than is preserved today.

The Grafenbühl tumulus, like the Römerhügel, is part of the group around the Hohenasperg. Among a large quantity of unusual objects recovered from this grave—which was looted in antiquity—were carved and polished ivory ornaments that adorned a piece of furniture. Zürn (1970), Herrmann (1970: 29–30), and Fischer (1990) all suggest that it was a couch, but Jung (2007) argues that it was a throne. The Grafenbühl grave also contained a small ornamented ivory disc, perhaps part of a mirror (Herrmann 1970: 30–31) or a fan (Spindler 1980), thought to have been made in the Near East. Other fragmentary ivory objects in the grave include a carved lion's foot and a small sphinx (Herrmann 1970: 25–28).

Early Iron Age sword pommels and/or hilt ornaments carved from ivory are an especially informative category of import. Since at least eight examples are known, we can learn from the distribution across Europe of the specific types of implements. Three are from graves at Hallstatt in Upper Austria (Kromer 1959), one each from burials at Emmerting-Bruck (Kossack 1959: pl. 118, 12), Kinding/Ilbling (Meixner et al. 1997), and Deisslingen in Germany (Oeftiger 1984: 56, fig. 16), and from Chaffois (Millotte 1971: 380, fig. 9) and Marainville-sur-Madon (Olivier 1988: 278, fig. 8) in France.

Among these eight well-documented examples,[2] two distinct types can be identified, each with three specimens, and two outliers. The pommels from Hallstatt grave 573 (Figure 17.5), Chaffois, and Marainville-sur-Madon are very similar to one another. The bottom part of the pommel is cylindrical, the sides slope upward in a concave curve that narrows toward the top, then widens just before the termination at the top. The pommel from Hallstatt grave 573 is the most complete. There are five horizontal zones, each separated from its neighbours by a band. In each zone is a delicate carved pattern of zigzag lines. In the lowest, cylindrical, zone, the zigzag lines form diamond shapes. In the other four zones, they are simply zigzag lines. The spaces between the lines (and inside the diamonds) are filled with carved amber.[3]

Very different are the pommels from Hallstatt graves 697 and 910 and from Deisslingen. All three have the same basic shape as the three just discussed, but without the carving or amber inlay. One might think that they were intended to be 'finished' like the three already discussed, but were never completed, although, as all three had been attached to swords and placed in burials, in this sense they were finished.

Since both varieties of ivory pommel occur over overlapping regions of the continent, the differences cannot be ascribed simply to different styles used by local craft workers. Ivory was a rare and exotic material, commonly associated with high status (as is particularly clear at Grafenbühl), so it is highly likely that every sword with a pommel carved of ivory was used by an individual of special status. Perhaps the more elaborate versions, carved with linear ornament and with inset amber, thus including another material from another distant source area, were signs of even higher status than the plainer

FIGURE 17.5 Ivory and amber pommel on an iron sword from Hallstatt Grave 573 (Austria). This combination of ivory and amber is especially important, because it connects two rare substances from distant, and different, source areas in a single object intended for display.

Photo: Alice Schumacher, © Natural History Museum Vienna

ivory pommels. Andreas Lippert (2011) has recently suggested similar status distinctions based on the number of repoussé circular decorations on Pass Lueg-type helmets.

In addition to ivory from Grafenbühl and on the early Iron Age swords, smaller ivory objects have also been identified in Iron Age contexts in temperate Europe. An example is the assemblage of three little rings and a small cylindrical ornament recovered in the late Hallstatt burial at Apremont in Haute-Saône (Mohen et al. 1988: 76, 93, fig. 117).

The carved ivory ornaments and sword hilts represent two different phenomena. Whereas the ornaments in the Grafenbühl grave are most likely to have been brought to the site as finished products, the hilt pieces were probably carved locally. They were shaped to fit the sword handles and do not match any known forms in the Near East or elsewhere. The presence of no fewer than three examples in graves at Hallstatt led Stöllner (2004: n. 58) to suggest that there may have been a workshop producing these hilts at Hallstatt itself, although there is no direct evidence for this (there is very little settlement evidence at Hallstatt), and the wide distribution of ivory hilts makes it unlikely that Hallstatt was a production centre.

The principal sources of ivory among societies of the Mediterranean region were elephant tusks from Africa and Asia, and hippomotamus canines and incisors from Africa and the Levant (Krzyszkowska 1990: 12–20). Elephant and hippopotamus ivory are distinctive (see e.g. Pulak 2008a: 328, fig. 197; 2008b: 329, fig. 198 a, b), but identifying the exact geographical origin of a piece of ivory is not easy (Caubet 2008). Investigators ordinarily use information about the distribution of these species, together with knowledge of trade routes, to suggest where specific pieces may have come from.

Textiles

Some imported materials leave relatively little trace in the archaeological record, yet the evidence suggests trade in textiles and other organic goods between Europe and neighbouring regions. There has been much discussion about the identification of silk textile in burials of late Hallstatt and early La Tène contexts, but these identifications are still matters of dispute (Good 1995; Banck-Burgess 1999; Stöllner 2004: 148; Chapter 26). Only scientific analyses will be able to reveal whether amino acids in the fabric are of plant or animal origin. Stöllner mentions the recent identification of silk from the salt mines at the Dürrnberg in Austria. In the Scythian burials at Semibratniy in Ukraine, Gleba (2008: 26) notes the presence of what has been identified as Chinese silk. For the antiquity of the 'Silk Roads', which may well have been active during Iron Age times, see Werning (2008) and von Falkenhausen (2010).

The Barbary Ape from Navan

A different perspective on contacts between Europe and Africa is given by a find from Navan fort in Ireland. During excavations at this important Iron Age centre, skeletal remains of a young adult male Barbary ape (*Macaca sylvanus*) were recovered and radiocarbon dated to the later Iron Age (Waterman 1997: 120–125). It seems likely that this animal arrived via seaborne contacts along the Atlantic coast, ultimately stretching all the way to north Africa, where the species originates. Whether it was an exotic gift, or was brought for some other reason, we can only speculate.

The Movement of Ideas into Temperate Europe: Styles, Practices, and Knowledge

It was not merely objects that moved between the continents during the Iron Age; various ideas were shared and transmitted across intercontinental boundaries. The movement of these less tangible phenomena can be difficult to identify in the archaeological record, but good evidence does nonetheless exist. This implies interaction and engagement on more than purely an economic or commercial level. Exchanging raw materials and artefacts with people from another place does indeed demonstrate contact with that place. However, learning about technologies, ritual practices, social activities, or visual styles from another place necessarily involves a qualitatively different kind of contact. Crucially, the transfer of knowledge through personal contacts, resulting perhaps from mechanisms such as the hiring of specialists from other regions, interactions between craft specialists working in different traditions, and diplomatic relationships, as opposed to objects, indicates a close and personal level of engagement. Again, we cannot attempt a complete catalogue of the different styles, ideas, and practices that were exchanged between Iron Age Europe and its neighbours here, but instead offer a representative discussion of some of the key and most common instances of intercontinental knowledge transfer.

Styles

The movement of visual or artistic styles usually involves a style originating in one area being adopted, imitated, and often locally adapted in another (Chapter 43).

Other examples of the movement of visual styles into Europe are the shared ornamental motifs and decorative elements recognizable in archaeological contexts, from Britain and Ireland in the west, to China in the east. These connections are especially apparent from the fifth century BC onward, with the development of the La Tène style. S-curves and spirals are important elements in early La Tène design (Megaw and Megaw 2001), just as they are in the design patterns of the Caucasus, Georgia, and Siberia (e.g. Reeder 1999: 109, 7; Parzinger et al. 2007: 78–79; Kacharava and Kvirkvelia 2008: 133–140). Cast bronze figurines from China between the eighth and third centuries BC (von Falkenhausen 2006: 251, fig. 49 top left; Michaelson 2007: 96, fig. 93), and from Anatolia during the sixth and fifth centuries BC (Farkas 2000: 9, fig. 8), often bear striking resemblances to figurines cast in temperate Europe during the fifth and fourth centuries BC. This is not the place to argue in detail for the nature of the connections that resulted in such similar motifs and figurines being produced in these widely separated regions. The important point is that in the mid-first millennium BC, much of the expressive material culture of Europe shared fundamental similarities with material culture throughout Eurasia (see also Teržan 2009), indicating the development and cultivation of intensive connections, the precise nature of which remains to be examined in detail.

Social Practices

Social practices and activities were also communicated across continental borders. Shared social practices can include ways of engaging in cult or ritual activity, ways of burying the dead, and ways of organizing social, urban, and domestic space. A key area which has generated much archaeological discussion is the way in which social identities were constructed and communicated. In particular, certain social practices became closely linked to the articulation of social status and power in Iron Age Europe, and these practices seem to have developed as a result of contacts with peoples on other continents.

As in many societies throughout human history, feasts—ritual banquets commonly involving both large quantities and special kinds of food and drink—played a major role in the social and political dynamics of Iron Age Europe (Chapter 39; Dietler 1996; Krausse 2004). Material representations of feasts are frequently present in richly outfitted Iron Age burials, particularly in the form of vessels used on these occasions. Krausse (1993) argues that at least two of the feasting practices evident in rich burials in west-central Europe derived from Near Eastern practices, not from Greece or Etruria (although they are likely to have reached temperate Europe via one of those regions). A particularly cogent part of his argument is that the earliest drinking horns, such as the great iron horn in the Hochdorf burial (Biel 1985), and couches like the one from Hochdorf (Biel 1985), are not copies of Greek or any other known originals. He suggests that they were crafted by local manufacturers on the basis of *ideas* of drinking horns and couches based on Near Eastern models, but the craft workers were not attempting to copy directly any specific prototypes. In contrast, a generation or two later, the elites of this region were importing actual Attic pottery and Greek and Etruscan bronze vessels, and sometimes making altered versions of the imported originals.

Technical Knowledge

The transmission of technologies and of knowledge is evidence for the movement of ideas on yet another distinct level. Once again, the movement of technologies and knowledge does not indicate passivity on the part of the people receiving these ideas—rather, the active acquisition of knowledge and the innovative adaptation of existing ideas is characteristic of the Iron Age. The spread of iron metallurgy, specific metalworking techniques, and other craft technologies, such as the potter's wheel, are examples of this phenomenon.

From the sixth century BC, there is evidence that writing technologies were being transmitted from the Mediterranean coasts of Europe into the central regions of the continent. Sherds recovered at Montmorot in eastern France have letters incised into them (Verger 2001). The Vix krater has Greek letters incised on the neck and on the attachments (Rolley 2003). Barth (1984) reports incised lines that are believed to be letters on wooden support beams in the mines at Hallstatt in Austria dating to the fifth century BC. A glass bead in a grave dating to around 300 BC, at Münsingen in Switzerland, has letters incised into the surface (Gambari and Kaenel 2001). An iron sword of late La Tène date from Port in Switzerland has the name *Korisios* in Greek letters stamped into the upper part of the blade (Wyss 1956). Two sherds of pottery recovered at Manching in Bavaria, Germany, have Greek letters incised into them, one spelling *Boios*, the other fragmentary (Krämer 1982). Finally, bronze helmets recovered at Ženjak, near Negova (German Negau) in Slovenia, bear inscriptions thought to date to around 100 BC in what is described as a north Italic alphabet (Nedoma 2002). These are just a few examples that show that some individuals and communities in temperate Europe were familiar with alphabetic scripts at the same time that writing was becoming increasingly common among peoples of the Mediterranean coastal lands.

Movements of People between Temperate Europe and Other Continents

In recent years, there has been a growing recognition that all cultural exchange and contact relies, to some extent, on mobility. It should be recognized that the mobility of individuals and small groups does not necessarily imply large-scale migration. Whereas once, archaeologists often employed models of migrations as discrete, unidirectional population movements, now the tendency is to use the concept of 'mobility', which can refer to many different modes of movement. From itinerant traders to bands of settlers or refugees, from individuals setting out to seek their fortunes to exogamous marriages, there is good evidence that the people of the Iron Age were much more mobile than once thought, in the pre-Roman period as much as later (e.g. Oelze et al. 2012).

In the Iron Age, there is ample evidence for people moving into and out of what we would now call Europe on a regular and frequent basis. Evidence for this mobility can be found not only in the archaeological record, but also from textual sources (Chapter 37). Combining the two must be done carefully and with considerable attention to the relative strengths and limits of both source types, but can produce fruitful results. In this section, we could have discussed many examples of intercontinental mobility at length: Greek traders and settlers in the Near East, at sites such as Naukratis in Egypt and Cyrene in modern Libya, or around the Black Sea; migrants from central Europe settling in Anatolia; the legendary migrations of Lydians and Trojans to the Italian peninsula; or the movement of steppe peoples from central Asia into central and southern Europe (Chapter 16). Instead however, we have chosen to focus on three well-attested examples: the Phoenician and Punic colonization movements, the Gallic and Celtic settlement in Anatolia, and the North Atlantic colonization.

Colonization of the North Atlantic

At the end of the 'long Iron Age' of northern Europe, Europeans from Scandinavia migrated westward, first to Iceland, then to Greenland, and finally, for a period thought not to have exceeded a decade or two around the year AD 1000, to Newfoundland, where the site of L'Anse aux Meadows has been identified as the only confirmed Norse settlement in North America (Wallace 2009). House architecture, smelting remains, textile-working tools, and a bronze pin are among the material remains left by the Norse settlers and recovered through archaeological excavation.

From the time of the establishment of the Norse settlements on Greenland toward the end of the tenth century AD, those communities produced a variety of goods for export to Europe. It is not clear at present just when the different categories of materials began to be shipped to Europe, but by the middle of the twelfth century they included walrus tusks, sealskins, and cattle hides (Arneborg 2000).

The Edges of Europe Revisited

All this exchange, movement, and migration highlights the fact that Europe in the Iron Age was part of a much wider, interconnected world. New research at the edges of Europe shows that there were no clear continental boundaries—instead, there was a continuum of interaction between different societies and communities, whereby objects, ideas, and people moved around regularly. Especially from the middle of the final millennium BC, Europe was part of a world of intensifying interregional interaction, with widespread changes in the character of commerce in Eurasia stimulating growing networks between peoples, both regionally and interregionally (Wells 2006, 2012: chs 11–12; Fletcher 2012; Stark 2012). The quantities of archaeological evidence attesting to these connections are still relatively small, but are steadily increasing. They make it clear that some European communities, at least, were open not only to products from distant lands, but also to motifs, styles, practices, and ideas from outside as well. Future studies will be able to document more thoroughly the roles that these interactions and the ideas that circulated through them played in the changes that are readily apparent in Iron Age Europe.

All along the edge of Europe during the Iron Age, objects, ideas, and people were constantly moving across what we would now consider to be continental boundaries. All four edges of the Mediterranean were connected by complex networks of interaction, mobility, and exchange—not just the northern and western edges of the sea, which are now classed as Europe, but also its southern edge which is now classed as Africa and its eastern edge which belongs to the Middle East. The southern and south-eastern edges, then, were far from clearly defined; nor was there a distinct boundary with Asia to the east. On the northern and north-western edges of Europe, the later periods of the Iron Age saw mobility and settlement into the north Atlantic as well.

Given the permeability of its boundaries, developments in regions we would now consider to lie beyond the edges of the continent had a major impact on the European Iron Age. Indeed, the concept of 'Europe' was not universally recognized in the Iron Age. The term 'Europe' was in use among the Greeks from the eighth century BC, but its meaning was unclear and remained contested for many centuries. Herodotus, the famous Greek historian of the fifth century BC, complained that he couldn't understand why people tried to divide the earth up into continents, when it was clearly all part of the same interconnected world (*Histories* 4.45). It is important that we, as archaeologists, adopt a similar approach and recognize both the permeability and artificiality of continental boundaries. The lines of modern borders do not necessarily correspond to meaningful distinctions in the past. While there are clear benefits for considering the 'European Iron Age' as a whole within this handbook, it is also important to highlight the lack of clear boundaries.

Acknowledgments

For helpful information and for publications used in preparation of this chapter, NMS would like to thank Eleftheria Pappa and David Mattingly; PSW thanks Bettina Arnold, Jörg Biel, Matthew Canepa, Heather Flowers, J. D. Hill, Daniel Potts, Aurel Rustoiu, John Soderberg, Simon Stoddart, and Claudia Tappert.

Notes

1. Taucheria lies under Tocra, Euesperides under Benghazi, Balagrae under Bayda, and Barca under El Merj.
2. A fragment of ivory from a grave that contained an iron sword at Ohnenheim in Alsace may also come from a pommel or handle (Egg 1987: 79, figs 2, 3), but this is uncertain.
3. Neither the Chaffois nor the Marainville-sur-Madon examples is as complete as the Hallstatt piece, but it seems that they were very similar. The bottom cylindrical part of the Chaffois pommel contains diamond shapes similar to those on the Hallstatt object, and the next zone also seems very similar. On the Marainville pommel, the bottom zone is not preserved, but the upper zones with their zigzag lines are very like those on the Hallstatt piece. On both pommels, the spaces are also filled with carved amber.

References

Adam, A.-M. 2007. 'Les importations méditerranéennes en Gaule interne aux IVe et IIIe siècles avant notre ère', in C. Mennessier-Jouannet, A.-M. Adam, and P.-Y. Milcent (eds) *La Gaule dans son contexte européen aux IVe et IIIe siècles avant notre ère*: 255–263. Lattes: Association pour le Développement de l'Archéologie en Languedoc-Roussillon.

Adiego Lajara, I. J. 2007. *The Carian Language*. Leiden: Brill.

Allason-Jones, L. 2004. 'Porringer' and 'Skillet handle', in D. A. Welsby and J. R. Anderson (eds) *Sudan: Ancient Treasures: 173*. London: British Museum Press.

Allen, L. 2005. *The Persian Empire*. Chicago: University of Chicago Press.

Altaweel, M. 2008. *The Imperial Landscape of Ashur: Settlement and Land Use in the Assyrian Heartland*. Heidelberg: Heidelberger Orientverlag.

Arneborg, J. 2000. 'Greenland and Europe', in W. W. Fitzhugh and E. I. Ward (eds) *Vikings: The North Atlantic Saga*: 304–317. Washington: Smithsonian Institution Press.

Arnold, B. 2005. 'Mobile men, sedentary women? Material culture as a marker of regional and supra-regional interaction in early Iron Age southwest Germany', in H. Dobrzánska, J. V. S. Megaw, and P. Poleska (eds) *Celts on the Margin: Studies in European Cultural Interaction (7th century BC–1st century AD) Dedicated to Zenon Wozniak*: 17–26. Krakow: Institute of Archaeology and Ethnology of the Polish Academy of the Sciences.

Arodaky, B.-E. 2007. *La Méditerranée des Phéniciens: De Tyr à Carthage*. Paris: Somogy éditions d'art.

Arruda, A. M., C. Gómez Bellard, and P. van Dommelen (eds). 2007. *Sítios e paisagens rurais do Mediterrâneo púnico: Actas do VI Congresso Internacional de Estudos Fenícios e Púnicos*. Lisbon: Colibri/Centro de Arqueologia da Universidade de Lisboa.

Aubet, M. E. 2001. *The Phoenicians and the West: Politics, Economy and Trade*, 2nd edition. Cambridge: Cambridge University Press.

Ayvazian, A. 2012. 'The Urartian Empire', in D. T. Potts (ed.) *A Companion to the Archaeology of the Ancient Near East*: 877–895. Oxford: Wiley-Blackwell.

Baker, H. D. 2012. 'The Neo-Babylonian Empire', in D. T. Potts (ed.) *A Companion to the Archaeology of the Ancient Near East*: 914–930. Oxford: Wiley-Blackwell.

Bakker, E. J. (ed.) 2010. *A Companion to the Ancient Greek Language*. Oxford: Wiley-Blackwell.

Banck-Burgess, J. 1999. *Hochdorf IV: Die Textilfunde aus dem späthallstattzeitlichen Fürstengrab von Eberdingen-Hochdorf (Kreis Ludwigsburg) und weitere Grabtextilien aus hallstatt- und latènezeitlichen Kulturgruppen*. Forschungen und Berichte zur Vor- und Frühgeschichte in Baden-Württemberg 70. Stuttgart: Theiss.

Barag, D. 1985. *Catalogue of Western Asiatic Glass in the British Museum, Vol. 1*. London: British Museum Publications.

Barker, G., J. A. Lloyd, and J. M. Reynolds (eds). 1985. *Cyrenaica in Antiquity*. British Archaeological Reports International Series 236. Oxford: British Archaeological Reports.

Barth, F. E. 1984. 'Eine prähistorische Stempelzimmerung aus dem Salzbergwerk Hallstatt'. *Archaeologia Austriaca* 68: 63–71.

Bauer, A. A. 1998. 'Cities of the sea: Maritime trade and the origin of Philistine settlement in the early Iron Age'. *Oxford Journal of Archaeology* 17: 149–168.

Biel, J. 1985. *Der Keltenfürst von Hochdorf*. Stuttgart: Theiss.

Bonfante, G., and L. Bonfante. 2002. *The Etruscan Language: An Introduction*, revised edition. Manchester: Manchester University Press.

Boucharlat, R. 1990. 'Suse et la Susiane à l'époque achémenide. Données archéologiques', in H. Sancisi-Weerdenburg and A. Kuhrt (eds) *Centre and Periphery*. Achaemenid History 4: 149–175. Leiden: Netherlands Institute for the Near East.

Briant, P. 2002. *From Cyrus to Alexander: A History of the Persian Empire* (trans. P. D. Daniels). Winona Lake, IN: Eisenbrauns.

Briant, P., and R. Boucharlat. 2005. *L'archéologie de l'empire achéménide: nouvelles recherches. Actes du colloque organisé au Collège de France par le 'Réseau international d'études et de recherches achéménides' (GDR 2538 CNRS), 21–22 novembre 2003*. Paris: de Boccard.

Broodbank, C. 2008. 'The Mediterranean and its hinterland', in B. W. Cunliffe, C. Gosden, and R. Joyce (eds) *The Oxford Handbook of Archaeology*: 677–722. Oxford: Oxford University Press.

Broodbank, C. 2013. *The Making of the Middle Sea: A History of the Mediterranean from the Beginning to the Emergence of the Classical World*. London: Thames and Hudson.

Bryce, T. R. 1986. *The Lycians in Literary and Epigraphic Sources*. Copenhagen: Museum Tusculanum Press.

Bryce, T. R. 2012. *The World of Neo-Hittite Kingdoms: A Political and Military History*. Oxford: Oxford University Press.

Burkert, W. 1992. *The Orientalizing Revolution*. Cambridge, MA: Harvard University Press.

Cahill, N. (ed.) 2008. *Love for Lydia: A Sardis Anniversary Volume Presented to Crawford H. Greenewalt, Jr*. Cambridge, MA: Harvard University Press.

Caubet, A. 2008. 'Ivory, shell, and bone', in J. Aruz, K. Benzel, and J. M. Evans (eds) *Beyond Babylon: Art, Trade, and Diplomacy in the Second Millennium BC*: 406–407. New York: Metropolitan Museum of Art.

Cipolla, C. N., and K. H. Hayes (eds). 2015. *Rethinking Colonialism: Comparative Archaeological Approaches*. Gainesville: University Press of Florida.

Cline, E. H. 2009. *Biblical Archaeology: A Very Short Introduction*. Oxford: Oxford University Press.

Cobet, J., V. von Graeve, W.-D. Niemeier, and K. Zimmerman (eds). 2007. *Frühes Ionien: Eine Bestandsaufnahme. Akten des Symposions 100 Jahre Milet, 1999*. Mainz: Philipp von Zabern.

Counts, D. B., and M. Iacovou. 2013. 'New Approaches to the Elusive Iron Age Polities of Ancient Cyprus'. *Bulletin of the American Schools of Oriental Research* 370: 1–13.

Crawley Quinn, J. 2011. 'The cultures of the Tophet: Identification and identity in the Phoenician diaspora', in E. Gruen (ed.) *Cultural Identity in the Ancient Mediterranean*: 338–413. Los Angeles: Getty Research Institute.

Crielaard, J. P. 2009. 'The Ionians in the Archaic period: Shifting identities in the changing world', in T. Derks and N. Roymans (eds) *Ethnic Constructs in Antiquity: The Role of Power and Tradition*. Amsterdam Archaeological Studies 13: 37–84. Amsterdam: Amsterdam University Press.

Curtis, J., H. McCall, D. Collon, and L. al-Gailani Werr (eds). 2008. *New Light on Nimrud. Proceedings of the Nimrud Conference 11th–13th March 2002*. London: British Institute for the Study of Iraq.

Curtis, J., and N. Tallis (eds). 2005. *Forgotten Empire: The World of Ancient Persia*. London: The British Museum Press.

Cusick, J. G. (ed.) 1998. *Studies in Culture Contact: Interaction, Culture Change, and Archaeology*. Carbondale, IL: Center for Archaeological Investigations, Illinois University.

Darbyshire, G., S. Mitchell, and L. Vardar. 2000. 'The Galatian settlement in Asia Minor'. *Anatolian Studies* 50: 75–97.

de Hoz, J. 1993. 'La lengua y la escritura ibéricas, y las lenguas de los iberos', in *Actas del V Colloquio sobre lenguas y culturas prerromanas de la Peninsula Ibérica*: 635–666. Salamanca: University of Salamanca.

Dehn, R. 1997. 'Riche découverte funéraire dans la nécropole tumulaire d'Ihringen-Gündlingen, lieu-dit "Nachtwaid-Ried"', in P. Brun and B. Chaume (eds) *Vix et les éphémères principautés celtiques: les VIe–Ve siècle avant J.-C. en Europe centre-occidentale*: 53–55. Paris: Errance.

Dehn, W. 1951. 'Einige Bemerkungen zu süddeutschem Hallstattglas'. *Germania* 29: 25–34.

Dietler, M. 1996. 'Feasts and commensal politics in the political economy: food, power and status in Prehistoric Europe', in P. Wiessner and W. Schiefenhovel (eds) *Food and the Status Quest*: 87–126. Oxford: Berghahn Books.

Dietler, M. 2010. *Archaeologies of Colonialism: Consumption, Entanglement and Violence in Ancient Mediterranean France*. Berkeley/Los Angeles: University of California Press.

Dothan, T. 1982. *The Philistines and their Material Culture*. New Haven, CT: Yale University Press.

Dusinberre, E. R. M. 2003. *Aspects of Empire in Achaemenid Sardis*. Cambridge: Cambridge University Press.

Edwards, D. E. 2004. *The Nubian Past: An Archaeology of Sudan*. London: Routledge.

Egg, M. 1987. 'Das Wagengrab von Ohnenheim im Elsass', in F. E. Barth (ed.) *Vierrädrige Wagen der Hallstattzeit: Untersuchungen zu Geschichte und Technik*. RGZM Monographien 12: 77–102. Mainz: Römisch-Germanisches Zentralmuseum.

Ehret, C. 2002. *The Civilizations of Africa: A History to 1800*. Charlottesville (VA): University of Virginia Press.

Fantalkin, A., and A. Yasur-Landau. 2008. *Bene Israel: Studies in the archaeology of Israel and the Levant during the Bronze and Iron Ages in honour of Israel Finkelstein*. Leiden: Brill.

Farkas, A. 2000. 'Filippovka and the art of the Steppes', in J. Aruz, A. Farkas, A. Alekseev, and E. Korolkova (eds) *The Golden Deer of Eurasia: Scythian and Sarmatian Treasures from the Russian Steppes*: 3–17. New York: Metropolitan Museum of Art.

Fischer, J. 1990. 'Zu einer griechischen Kline und weiteren Südimporten aus dem Fürstengrabhügel Grafenbühl, Asperg, Kr. Ludwigsburg'. *Germania* 68: 115–127.

Fletcher, R. N. 2012. 'Opening the Mediterranean: Assyria, the Levant and the transformation of early Iron Age trade'. *Antiquity* 86: 211–220.

Foxhall, L. 1998. 'Cargoes of the heart's desire: The character of trade in the archaic Mediterranean world', in N. Fisher and H. van Wees (eds) *Archaic Greece*: 295–309. London/Swansea: Duckworth/The Classical Press of Wales.

Frey, O.-H. 2011. 'The world of Situla art', in L. Bonfante (ed.) *The Barbarians of Ancient Europe: Realities and Interactions*: 282–312. Cambridge: Cambridge University Press.

Gabrovec, S. 1966. 'Zur Hallstattzeit in Slowenien'. *Germania* 44: 1–48.

Gambari, F. M., and G. Kaenel. 2001. 'L'iscrizione celtica sulla perla da Münsingen: una nuova lettura'. *Archäologie der Schweiz* 24, 4: 34–37.

Gleba, M. 2008. 'You are what you wear: Scythian costume as identity', in M. Gleba, C. Munkholt, and M.-L. Nosch (eds) *Dressing the Past*: 13–28. Oxford: Oxbow.

Good, I. 1995. 'On the question of silk in pre-Han Eurasia'. *Antiquity* 69: 959–968.

Greaves, A. M. 2010. *The Land of Ionia: Society and Economy in the Archaic Period*. Oxford: Wiley-Blackwell.

Greaves, A. M. 2011. 'The Greeks in western Anatolia', in S. R. Steadman and G. McMahon (eds) *The Oxford Handbook of Ancient Anatolia (c. 10,000–323 BCE)*: 500–516. Oxford: Oxford University Press.

Greenewalt, C. H. Jr. 2011. 'Sardis. A first millennium B.C.E. capital in western Anatolia', in S. R. Steadman and G. McMahon (eds) *The Oxford Handbook of Ancient Anatolia (c. 10,000–323 BCE)*: 1112–1129. Oxford: Oxford University Press.

Gunter, A. C. 2012. *Greek Art and the Orient*. Cambridge: Cambridge University Press.

Haevernick, T. E. 1981. 'Funde aus fernen Ländern', in *Beiträge zur Glasforschung: Die wichtigsten Aufsätze von 1938 bis 1981 von Thea Elisabeth Haevernick*: 399–403. Mainz: Philipp von Zabern.

Hanfmann, G. M. A., and W. E. Mierse. 1983. *Sardis from Prehistoric to Roman Times: Results of the Archaeological Exploration of Sardis, 1958–1975*. Cambridge, MA: Harvard University Press.

Hansen, L., and E. Böhr. 2011. 'Ein seltener Fund aus Westhofen (Lkr. Alzey-Worms): Fragment einer attischen Trinkschale'. *Archäologisches Korrespondenzblatt* 41: 213–230.

Harris, W. V. 2007. 'The Late Republic', in W. Scheidel, I. Morris, and R. Saller (eds) *The Cambridge Economic History of the Greco-Roman World*: 511–539. Cambridge: Cambridge University Press.

Hauschild, M. 2010. '"Celticised" or "assimilated"? In search of foreign and indigenous people at the time of the Celtic migrations', in S. Berecki (ed.) *Iron Age Communities in the Carpathian Basin. Proceedings of the International Colloquium from Târgu Mureş, 9–11 October* 2009: 171–180. Cluj-Napoca: Editura Mega.

Helms, M. W. 1988. *Ulysses' Sail: An Ethnographic Odyssey of Power, Knowledge, and Geographical Distance*. Princeton: Princeton University Press.

Henkelman, W. F. M. 2012. 'The Achaemenid heartland: An archaeological-historical perspective', in D. T. Potts (ed.) *A Companion to the Archaeology of the Ancient Near East*: 931–983. Oxford: Wiley-Blackwell.

Herrmann, H.-V. 1970. 'Die südländischen Importstücke', in H. Zürn (ed.) *Hallstattforschungen in Nordwürttemberg: Die Grabhügel von Asperg (Kr. Ludwigsburg), Hirschlanden (Kr. Leonberg) und Mühlacker (Kr. Vaihingen)*: 25–34. Stuttgart: Müller & Gräff.

Hodos, T. 2006. *Local Responses to Colonization in the Iron Age Mediterranean*. London: Routledge.

Hodos, T. 2009. 'Colonial engagements in the global Mediterranean Iron Age'. *Cambridge Archaeological Journal* 19, 2: 221–241.

Hodos, T. (ed.) 2017. *The Routledge Handbook of Globalization and Archaeology*. London: Routledge.

Horden, P., and N. Purcell. 2000. *The Corrupting Sea: A Study of Mediterranean History*. London: Blackwell.

Horn, H. G., and C. B. Rüger. 1979. *Die Numider: Reiter und Könige nördlich der Sahara*. Cologne: Rheinland-Verlag.

Horrocks, G. C. 2010. *Greek: A History of the Language and its Speakers*. Oxford: Wiley-Blackwell.

Hoyos, B. D. 2010. *The Carthaginians*. London: Routledge.

Hurst, H., and S. Owen. 2005. *Ancient Colonization: Analogy, Similarity and Difference*. London: Duckworth.

Ivantchik, A., and V. Licheli. 2007. *Achaemenid Culture and Local Traditions in Anatolia, Southern Caucasus and Iran: New Discoveries*. Leiden: Brill.

Jaffé, M. 1978. *Glass at the Fitzwilliam Museum*. Cambridge: Cambridge University Press.

Jung, M. 2007. 'Kline oder Thron? Zu den Fragmenten eines griechischen Möbelpfostens aus dem späthallstattzeitlichen "Fürstengrab" Grafenbühl in Asperg (Kr. Ludwigsburg)'. *Germania* 85: 95–107.

Kacharava, D., and G. Kvirkvelia. 2008. 'The Golden Graves of ancient Vani', in D. Kacharava and G. Kvirkvelia (eds) *Wine, Worship, and Sacrifice: The Golden Graves of Ancient Vani*: 126–205. Princeton: Princeton University Press.

Kaenel, G. 1990. *Recherches sur la période de La Tène en Suisse occidentale: Analyse des sépultures*. Lausanne: Bibliothèque historique vaudoise.

Kealhofer, L. 2005. *The Archaeology of Midas and the Phrygians: Recent Work at Gordion*. Philadelphia: University of Pennsylvania Museum of Archaeology.

Keen, A. G. 1998. *Dynastic Lycia*. Leiden: Brill.

Kemp, B. J. 2006. *Ancient Egypt: Anatomy of a Civilisation*. London: Routledge.

Khatchadourian, L. 2012. 'The Achaemenid provinces in archaeological perspective', in D. T. Potts (ed.) *A Companion to the Archaeology of the Ancient Near East*: 963–983. Oxford: Wiley-Blackwell.

Kimmig, W. 1988. *Das Kleinaspergle: Studien zu einem Fürstengrabhügel der frühen Latènezeit bei Stuttgart*. Forschungen und Berichte zur Vor- und Frühgeschichte in Baden-Württemberg 30. Stuttgart: Theiss.

Kistler, E. 2010. 'Großkönigliches *symbolon* im Osten—exotisches Luxusgut im Westen: Zur Objektbiographie der archämenidischen Glasschale aus Ihringen', in R. Rollinger, B. Gufler, M. Lang, and I. Madreiter (eds) *Interkulturalität in der Alten Welt: Vorderasien, Hellas, Ägypten und die vielfältigen Ebenen des Kontakts*: 63–95. Wiesbaden: Harrassowitz Verlag.

Kitchen, K. A. 1986. *The Third Intermediate Period in Egypt (1100–650 BC)*. Warminster: Aris and Phillips.

Knapp, A. B. 2008. *Prehistory and Protohistoric Cyprus: Identity, Insularity, and Connectivity*. Oxford: Oxford University Press.

Knappett, C. 2011. *An Archaeology of Interaction: Network Perspectives on Material Culture and Society*. Oxford: Oxford University Press.

Köroğlou, K., and E. Konyar (eds). 2011. *Urartu: Transformation in the East*. Istanbul: Yapı Kredi Yayınları.

Kossack, G. 1959. *Südbayern während der Hallstattzeit*. Römisch-Germanische Forschungen 25. Berlin: De Gruyter.

Krämer, W. 1982. 'Graffiti auf Spätlatènekeramik aus Manching'. *Germania* 60: 489–499.

Krausse, D. 1993. 'Trinkhorn und Kline. Zur griechischen Vermittlung orientalischer Trinksitten an die frühen Kelten'. *Germania* 71: 188–197.

Krausse, D. 2004. 'Komos und Kottabos am Hohenasperg? Überlegungen zur Funktion mediterraner Importgefässe des 6. und 5. Jahrhunderts aus Südwestdeutschland', in M. A. Guggisberg (ed.) *Die Hydria von Grächwil: Zur Funktion und Rezeption mediterraner Importe in Mitteleuropa im 6. und 5. Jahrhundert v. Chr.*: 193–201. Bern: Bernisches Historisches Museum.

Kromer, K. 1959. *Das Gräberfeld von Hallstatt*. Florenz: Sansoni.

Krzyszkowska, O. 1990. *Ivory and Related Materials*. London: Institute of Classical Studies.

Kuhrt, A. 2001. 'The palaces of Babylon', in I. Nielsen (ed.) *The Royal Palace Institution in the First Millennium BC*: 77–94. Athens: Danish Institute at Athens.

Kuhrt, A. 2007. *The Persian Empire: A Corpus of Sources from the Achaemenid Period*. London: Routledge.

Kunze, C. 2011. 'Carthage and Numidia, 201–149 BC', in D. Hoyos (ed.) *A Companion to the Punic Wars*: 393–411. Oxford: Wiley-Blackwell.

Lang, A., and V. Salač (eds). 2002. *Fernkontakte in der Eisenzeit*. Prag: Archäologisches Institut der Akademie der Wissenschaften der Tschechischen Republik.

Leonard, A. Jr. 1997. *Ancient Naukratis: Excavations at Greek Emporium, Vol. 1: The Excavations at Kom Hadid*. Atlanta: Scholars Press.

Leonard, A. Jr. 2001. *Ancient Naukratis: Excavations at Greek Emporium, Vol. 2: The Excavations at Kom Ge'if*. Atlanta: Scholars Press.

Lipiński, E. (ed.) 1987. *Carthago*. Leuven: Peeters.

Lipiński, E. 2006. *On the Skirts of Canaan in the Iron Age: Historical and Topographical Researches*. Leuven: Peeters.

Lippert, A. 2011. *Die zweischaligen ostalpinen Kammhelme und verwandte Helmformen der späten Bronze- und frühen Eisenzeit*. Archäologie in Salzburg 6. Salzburg: Salzburg Museum.

Loud, G. 1936. *Khorsabad, Vol. 1: Excavations in the Palaces and at a City Gate*. Chicago: University of Chicago Press.

Loud, G., and C. B. Altman. 1938. *Khorsabad, Vol. 2: The Citadel and the Town*. Chicago: University of Chicago Press.

Luke, C., and C. H. Roosevelt. 2016. 'Memory and meaning in the cemetery in Bin Tepe, the Lydian cemetery of the "Thousand Mounds"', in O. Henry and U. Kelp (eds) *Tumulus as Sema: Space, Politics, Culture and Religion in the First Millennium BC*. Topoi Excellence Cluster volume 27: 407–428. Berlin: De Gruyter.

Luni, M. 2010. *Cirene e le Cirenaica nell'antichità*. Roma: Bretschneider.

Mac Sweeney, N. 2013. *Founding Myths: The Politics of Settlement in Ancient Ionia*. Cambridge: Cambridge University Press.

Maeir, A. M., L. A. Hitchcock, and L. K. Horowitz. 2013. 'On the constitution and transformation of Philistine identity'. *Oxford Journal of Archaeology* 32: 1–38.

Malay, H. 1999. *Researches in Lydia, Mysia and Aeolis*. Vienna: Verlag der Österreichischen Akademie der Wissenschaften.

Malkin, I., C. Constantakopoulou, and K. Panagopoulou. 2009. *Greek and Roman Networks in the Mediterranean*. London: Routledge.

Markoe, G. 2006. *The Phoenicians*. London: Folio Society.

Marzano, A. 2006. 'Preserving cultural heritage and developing a modern city: The difficult case of Euesperides'. *Libyan Studies* 37: 89–94.

Mattingly, D. J. 2004. 'Surveying the desert: From the Libyan valleys to the Saharan oases', in M. Iacovou (ed.) *Archaeological Field Survey in Cyprus: Past History, Future Potentials*. British School at Athens Studies 11. London: British School at Athens.

Mattingly, D. J., C. M. Daniels, J. N. Dore, D. Edwards, and J. Hawthorne. 2003. *The Archaeology of Fazzān, Vol. 1: Synthesis*. London: Society for Libyan Studies/Department of Antiquities.

Mattingly, D. J., C. M. Daniels, J. N. Dore, D. Edwards, and J. Hawthorne. 2007. *The Archaeology of Fazzān, Vol. 2: Gazetteer, Pottery and Other Finds*. London: Society for Libyan Studies/Department of Antiquities.

Mattingly, D. J., C. M. Daniels, J. N. Dore, D. Edwards, and J. Hawthorne. 2010. *The Archaeology of Fazzān, Vol. 3: Excavations of C. M. Daniels*. London: Society for Libyan Studies/Department of Antiquities.

Mazar, A. 2001. *Studies in the Archaeology of the Iron Age in Israel and Jordan*. Sheffield: Sheffield Academic Press.

Megaw, R., and J. V. S. Megaw. 2001. *Celtic Art: From its Beginnings to the Book of Kells*, revised edition. London: Thames and Hudson.

Meixner, G., K. H. Rieder, and M. Schaich. 1997. 'Das hallstattzeitliche Grabhügelfeld von Kinding/Ilbling'. *Das archäologische Jahr in Bayern* 1996: 90–93.

Michaelson, C. 2007. 'Qin gold and jade', in J. Portal (ed.) *The First Emperor: China's Terracotta Army*: 94–103. London: British Museum Press.

Millotte, J.-P. 1971. 'Circonscription de Franche-Comté'. *Gallia Préhistoire* 14, 2: 377–392.

Mitchell, S. 1993. *Anatolia: Land, Men, and Gods in Asia Minor, Vol. 1: The Celts in Anatolia and the Impact of Roman Rule*. Oxford: Clarendon Press.

Mohen, J.-P., A. Duval, and C. Eluère. 1988. 'Apremont', in J.-P. Mohen, A. Duval, and C. Eluère (eds) *Trésors des princes celtes*: 75–94. Paris: Editions de la Réunion des musées nationaux.

Muhly, J. D. 2006. 'Texts and technology: The beginnings of iron metallurgy in the eastern Mediterranean', in T. P. Tassios and C. Polyvou (eds) *Ancient Greek Technology*: 19–31. Athens: Technical Chamber of Commerce.

Muhly, J. D., and V. Kassianidou. 2012. 'Parallels and diversities in the production, trade and use of copper and iron in Crete and Cyprus from the Bronze Age to the Iron Age'. *British School at Athens Studies* 20: 119–140.

Müller, F. (ed.) 2009. *Art of the Celts 700 BC to AD 700*. Bern: Bernisches Historisches Museum.

Müller-Karpe, A. 1988. 'Neue galatische Funde aus Anatolien'. *Istanbuler Mitteilungen* 38: 189–199.

Müller-Karpe, A. 2006. 'Zur historischen Deutung von Funden keltischer Trachtelemente in Anatolien', in M. Szabó (ed.) *Celtes et Gaulois: l'archéologie face à l'histoire: Les Civilisés et les Barbares du Ve au IIe siècle avant J.-C.* Collection Bibracte 12/3: 119–123. Glux-en-Glenne: Centre archéologique européen du Mont Beuvray.

Nedoma, R. 2002. 'Negauer Helm: Inschriften', in *Reallexikon der germanischen Altertumskunde 21*: 56–61. Berlin: Walter de Gruyter.

Nightingale, G. 2007. 'Lefkandi. An important note in the international exchange network of jewellery and personal adornment', in I. Galanaki, H. Tomas, Y. Galanakis, and R. Laffineur (eds) *Between the Aegean and Baltic Seas: Prehistory Across Borders*. Aegaeum 27. Liège/Austin: Université de Liège, University of Texas at Austin.

Oates, J., and D. Oates. 2001. *Nimrud: An Imperial City Revealed*. London: British Institute for the Study of Iraq.

Odess, D., S. Loring, and W. W. Fitzhugh. 2000. 'Skraeling: First peoples of Helluland, Markland, and Vinland', in W. W. Fitzhugh and E. I. Ward (eds) *Vikings: The North Atlantic Saga*: 193–205. Washington: Smithsonian Institution Press.

Oeftiger, C. 1984. 'Hallstattzeitliche Grabhügel bei Deisslingen, Kreis Rottweil'. *Fundberichte aus Baden-Württemberg* 9: 41–79.

Oelze, V. M., J. K. Koch, K. Kupke, O. Nehlich, S. Zäuner, J. Wald, et al. 2012. 'Multi-isotopic analysis reveals individual mobility and diet at the early Iron Age monumental tumulus of Magdalenenberg, Germany'. *American Journal of Physical Anthropology* 148, 3: 406–421.

Olivier, L. 1988. 'Le tumulus à tombe à char de Marainville-sur-Madon (Vosges): Premiers résults', in J.-P. Mohen, A. Duval, and C. Eluère (eds) *Les princes celtes et la Méditerranée*: 271–301. Paris: La Documentation Française.

Osborne, R. 1996. *Greece in the Making*. London: Routledge.

Osborne, R. 1998. 'Early Greek colonization? The nature of Greek settlements in the west', in N. Fisher and H. van Wees (eds) *Archaic Greece: New Approaches and New Evidence*: 251–269. London: Routledge.

Paret, O. 1921. *Urgeschichte Württembergs mit besonderer Berücksichtigung des mittleren Neckarlands*. Stuttgart: Strecker und Schröd.

Parker, B. J. 2003. 'Archaeological manifestations of Empire: Assyria's imprint on southeastern Anatolia'. *American Journal of Archaeology* 107: 525–557.

Parker, B. J. 2012. 'The Assyrians abroad', in D. T. Potts (ed.) *A Companion to the Archaeology of the Ancient Near East*: 867–876. Oxford: Wiley-Blackwell.

Parpola, S., and R. M. Whiting. 1997. *Assyria 1995*. Helsinki: The Neo-Assyrian Text Corpus Project.

Parzinger, H., W. Menghin, and M. Nawroth. 2007. *Im Zeichen des goldenen Greifen: Königsgräber der Skythen*. Munich: Prestel.

Pedde, F. 2012. 'The Assyrian heartland', in D. T. Potts (ed.) *A Companion to the Archaeology of the Ancient Near East*: 851–866. Oxford: Wiley-Blackwell.

Pitts, M. 2017. 'Deep histories of globalization and Europe: beyond Eurocentrism', in T. Hodos (ed.) *The Routledge Companion to Globalization and Archaeology*: 505–508. London: Routledge.

Polzer, M., and J. Reyes. 2011. 'The final season of the Claude and Barbara Duthuit expedition to the Bajo de la Campana, Spain. Excavation of a late seventh-century B.C.E. Phoenician shipwreck'. *The INA Annual* 4: 6–17.

Postgate, J. N. P. 2007. *The Land of Assur and the Yoke of Assur: Studies on Assyria, 1971–2005*. Oxford: Oxbow.

Pshenichniuk, A. 2000a. 'Amphora with mouflon-shaped handles terminating in a lion's paw', in J. Aruz, A. Farkas, A. Alekseev, and E. Korolkova (eds) *The Golden Deer of Eurasia: Scythian and Sarmatian Treasures from the Russian Steppes*: 152–153. New York: Metropolitan Museum of Art.

Pshenichniuk, A. 2000b. 'Rhyton with calf protome', in J. Aruz, A. Farkas, A. Alekseev, and E. Korolkova (eds) *The Golden Deer of Eurasia: Scythian and Sarmatian Treasures from the Russian Steppes: 154*. New York: Metropolitan Museum of Art.

Pshenichniuk, A. 2000c. 'Vessel with flaring neck', in J. Aruz, A. Farkas, A. Alekseev, and E. Korolkova (eds) *The Golden Deer of Eurasia: Scythian and Sarmatian Treasures from the Russian Steppes*: 88–89. New York: Metropolitan Museum of Art.

Pulak, C. 2008a. 'Elephant tusk', in J. Aruz, K. Benzel, and J. M. Evans (eds) *Beyond Babylon: Art, Trade, and Diplomacy in the Second Millennium BC*: 328–329. New York: Metropolitan Museum of Art.

Pulak, C. 2008b. 'Hippopotamus teeth', in J. Aruz, K. Benzel, and J. M. Evans (eds) *Beyond Babylon: Art, Trade, and Diplomacy in the Second Millennium BC*: 329–330. New York: Metropolitan Museum of Art.

Ramage, A., and P. Craddock. 2000. *King Croesus' Gold: Excavations at Sardis and the History of Gold Refining*. Archaeological Exploration of Sardis 11. Cambridge, MA: Harvard University Art Museums.

Reeder, E. (ed.) 1999. *Scythian Gold: Treasures from Ancient Ukraine*. New York: Harry Abrams.

Renger, J. 2003. 'Assur 1903–2003. 100 Jahre Ausgrabung der DOG in Assur und ein Bericht über das Assur-Projekt'. *Mitteilungen der Deutschen Orient-Gesellschaft* 135: 121–129.

Riva, C., and N. C. Vella (eds). 2006. *Debating Orientalization: Multidisciplinary Approaches to Processes of Change in the Ancient Mediterranean*. London: Equinox.

Robinson, A. 2007. *The Story of Writing*. London: Thames and Hudson.

Roller, L. E. 2011. 'Phrygia and the Phrygians', in S. R. Steadman and G. McMahon (eds) *The Oxford Handbook of Ancient Anatolia (c. 10,000–323 BCE)*: 560–578. Oxford: Oxford University Press.

Rolley, C. (ed.) 2003. *La tombe princière de Vix*. Paris/Châtillon-sur-Seine: Picard.

Roosevelt, C. 2009. *The Archaeology of Lydia, from Gyges to Alexander*. Cambridge: Cambridge University Press.

Roosevelt, C. 2012. 'Iron Age western Anatolia: The Lydian empire and dynastic Lycia', in D. T. Potts (ed.) *A Companion to the Archaeology of the Ancient Near East*: 896–913. Oxford: Wiley-Blackwell.

Rose, C. B., and G. Darbyshire (eds). 2011. *The New Chronology of Iron Age Gordion*. Gordion Special Studies 6. Philadelphia: University of Pennsylvania Museum of Archaeology and Anthropology.

Rumscheid, F. 2009. *Die Karer und die Anderen: Internationales Kolloquium an der Freien Universität Berlin 13. bis 15. Oktober 2005*. Bonn: Habelt.

Ruprechtsberger, E. M. 1997. *Die Garamanten: Geschichte und Kultur eines Libyschen Volkes in der Sahara*. Mainz: Philipp von Zabern.

Russel, J. M. 1991. *Sennacherib's Palace without Rival at Nineveh*. Chicago: University of Chicago Press.

Rustoiu, A. 2006. 'A journey to Mediterranean: Peregrinations of a Celtic warrior from Transylvania'. *Studia Universitatis 'Babeş-Bolyai', Historia* 51, 1: 42–85.

Sagona, A., and P. E. Zimansky. 2009. *Ancient Turkey*. London and New York: Routledge.

Schmidt, E. F. 1953. *Persepolis I: Structures, Reliefs, Inscriptions*. Chicago: University of Chicago Press.

Schmidt, E. F. 1957. *Persepolis II: Contents of the Treasury and Other Discoveries*. Chicago: University of Chicago Press.

Schmidt, E. F. 1970. *Persepolis II: The Royal Tombs and Other Monuments*. Chicago: University of Chicago Press.

Schönfelder, M. 2007. 'Zurück aus Griechenland—Spuren keltischer Söldner in Mitteleuropa'. *Germania* 85: 307–328.

Sherratt, S. 2010. 'Greeks and Phoenicians: perceptions of trade and traders in the early 1st millennium BC', in A. Agbe-Davies and A. Bauer (eds) *Trade as Social Interaction: New Archaeological Approaches*: 119–142. Walnut Creek: Left Coast Press.

Sherratt, S. 2017. 'A globalizing Bronze and Iron Age Mediterranean', in T. Hodos (ed.) *The Routledge Handbook of Globalization in Archaeology*: 602–617. London: Routldege.

Sivan, D. 1997. *A Grammar of the Ugaritic Language*. Leiden: Brill.

Sommer, M. 2007. 'Networks of commerce and knowledge in the Iron Age: The case of the Phoenicians'. *Mediterranean Historical Review* 22, 1: 97–111.

Spindler, K. 1980. 'Zur Elfenbeinscheibe aus dem hallstattzeitlichen Fürstengrab vom Grafenbühl'. *Archäologisches Korrespondenzblatt* 10: 239–248.

Stark, S. 2012. 'Nomads and networks: Elites and their connections to the outside world', in S. Stark, K. S. Rubinson, Z. S. Samashev, and J. Y. Chi (eds) *Nomads and Networks: The Ancient Art and Culture of Kazakhstan*: 106–138. New York: Institute for the Study of the Ancient World at New York University.

Steele, P. M. 2013. *A Linguistic History of Ancient Cyprus: The Non-Greek Languages and their relations with Greek, c. 1600–300 BC*. Cambridge: Cambridge University Press.

Stierlin, H., C. Ziegler, and J. Leclant. 1987. *Tanis: Trésors des pharaons*. Paris: Éditions du Seuil.

Stöllner, T. 2004. '"Verborgene Güter"—Rohstoffe und Spezereien als Fernhandelsgut in der Späthallstatt- und Frühlatènezeit', in M. A. Guggisberg (ed.) *Die Hydria von Grächwil: Zur Funktion und Rezeption mediterraner Importe in Mitteleuropa im 6. und 5. Jahrhundert v. Chr.*: 137–158. Bern: Bernisches Historisches Museum.

Storm, E. 2001. *Massinissa: Numidien in Aufbruch*. Stuttgart: Franz Steiner.
Stronach, D. 1978. *Pasargadae: A Report on the Excavations Conducted by the British Institute of Persian Studies from 1961–63*. Oxford: Oxford University Press.
Szabó, M. 1991. 'Mercenary activity', in S. Moscati, O.-H. Frey, V. Kruta, B. Raftery, and M. Szabó (eds) *The Celts*: 333–336. New York: Rizzoli.
Tappert, C. 2002. 'Straubing—ein Verkehrsknotenpunkt der Späthallstatt-/Frühlatènezeit', in A. Lang and V. Salač (eds) *Fernkontakte in der Eisenzeit*. Prague: Archäologisches Institut der Akademie der Wissenschaften der Tschechischen Republik.
Tappert, C., and D. P. Mielke. 1997. 'Eine kleine syrische Bronzesitula aus frühkeltischer Zeit'. *Jahresbericht des Historischen Vereins für Straubing und Umgebung* 99: 15–31.
Teržan, B. 2009. 'Kaukasisches Symbolgut in Südosteuropa. Bemerkungen zu Goldfibeln von Michalków—Fokoru—Dalj', in J. Apakidze, B. Govedarica, B. Hänsel, and E. Sava (eds) *Der Schwarzmeerraum vom Äneolithikum bis in die Früheisenzeit (5000–500 v. Chr.)*: 190–216. Rahden: Marie Leidorf.
Thorley, J. 1971. 'The silk trade between China and the Roman Empire at its height, circa A.D. 90–130'. *Greece & Rome (second series)* 18, 1: 71–80.
Todd, I. A., and P. Warren. 2012. 'Islandscapes and the built environments: the placing of settlements from village to city state (third to first millennia BC) in Cyprus and Crete'. *British School at Athens Studies* 20: 47–59.
Tomaschit, K. 2002. *Die Wanderungen der Kelten in der antiken literarischen Überlieferung*. Vienna: Österreichische Akademie der Wissenschaften.
Tomber, R. 2008. *Indo-Roman Trade: From Pots to Pepper*. London: Duckworth.
Török, L. 1997. *The Kingdom of Kush: Handbook of the Napatan-Meriotic Civilization*. Leiden: Brill.
Treister, M. Y. 1995. *The Role of Metals in Ancient Greek History*. Leiden: Brill.
Tsetskhladze, G. R. 2006. *Greek Colonisation: An Account of Greek Colonies and Other Settlements Overseas, Vol. 1*. Leiden: Brill.
Tsetskhladze, G. R. 2008. *Greek Colonisation: An Account of Greek Colonies and Other Settlements Overseas, Vol. 2*. Leiden: Brill.
Van de Mieroop, M. 2011. *A History of Ancient Egypt*. Oxford: Wiley-Blackwell.
van Dommelen, P. 1998. *On Colonial Grounds: A Comparative Study of Colonialism and Rural Settlement in First Millennium BC West Central Sardinia*. Archaeology Studies. Leiden: Leiden University.
van Dommelen, P. 2002. 'Ambiguous matters: Colonialism and local identities in Punic Sardinia', in C. Lyons and J. Papadopoulos (eds) *The Archaeology of Colonialism*: 121–147. Los Angeles: Getty Research Institute.
van Dommelen, P., and A. B. Knapp (eds). 2010. *Material Connections in the Ancient Mediterranean: Mobility, Materiality and Identity*. London: Routledge.
Verger, S. 2001. 'Un graffite archaique dans l'habitat hallstattien de Montmorot (Jura, France)'. *Studi Etruschi* 64: 265–316.
Vésteinsson, O., and T. H. McGovern. 2012. 'The peopling of Ireland'. *Norwegian Archaeological Review* 45: 206–218.
Villes, A. 1995. 'A propos des mouvements celtiques aux IVe–IIIe siècles: confrontation habitats et necropoles en Champagne', in J.-J. Charpy (ed.) *L'Europe celtique du Ve au IIIe siècle avant J.-C.: contacts, échanges et mouvements de populations: Actes du IIe symposium international d'Hautvillers, 8–10 octobre 1992*: 125–160. Sceaux: Kronos B.Y. Editions.
Vlassopoulos, K. 2013. *Greeks and Barbarians*. Cambridge: Cambridge University Press.

Voigt, M. M. 2011. 'Gordion: The changing political and economic roles of a first millennium B.C.E. city', in S. R. Steadman and G. McMahon (eds) *The Oxford Handbook of Ancient Anatolia (c. 10,000–323 BCE)*: 1069–1094. Oxford: Oxford University Press.

von Falkenhausen, L. 2006. *Chinese Society in the Age of Confucius (1000–250 BC): The Archaeological Evidence*. Los Angeles: Cotsen Institute of Archaeology.

von Falkenhausen, L. 2010. 'Notes on the history of the "silk routes" from the rise of the Xiongnu to the Mongol conquest (250 BC–AD 1283)', in V. Mair (ed.) *Secrets of the Silk Road*: 58–68. Santa Ana, CA: Bowers Museum.

Wallace, B. 2009. 'L'Anse Aux Meadows, Leif Eriksson's home in Vinland'. *Journal of the North Atlantic* 2, 2: 114–125.

Waterman, D. M. 1997. *Excavations at Navan Fort 1961–71*. Northern Ireland Archaeological Monographs 3. Belfast: The Stationery Office.

Wells, P. S. 2006. 'Mobility, art, and identity in early Iron Age Europe and Asia', in J. Aruz, A. Farkas, and E. V. Fino (eds) *The Golden Deer of Eurasia: Perspectives on the Steppe Nomads of the Ancient World*: 18–23. New York: Metropolitan Museum of Art.

Wells, P. S. 2012. *How Ancient Europeans Saw the World: Vision, Patterns, and the Shaping of the Mind in Prehistoric Times*. Princeton: Princeton University Press.

Werning, J. 2008. 'Ursprünge der Seidenstrasse'. *Archäologie in Deutschland 2008*, 1: 66–69.

Wilson, P. 2006. *The Survey of Sais (Sa el-Hagar), 1997–2002*. London: Egypt Exploration Society.

Wittke, A.-M. 2004. *Mušker und Phryger: Ein Beitrag zur Geschichte Anatoliens vom 12. bis zum 7. Jh. v. Chr.* Wiesbaden: Reichert.

Wyss, R. 1956. 'The sword of Korisios'. *Antiquity* 30: 27–28.

Yasur-Landau, A. 2010. *The Philistines and Aegean Migration at the End of the Late Bronze Age*. Cambridge: Cambridge University Press.

Young, R. S. 1981. *The Gordion Excavations (1950–1973) Final Reports, Vol. 1: Three Great Early Tumuli*. Philadelphia: University of Pennsylvania Museum of Archaeology.

Zimansky, P. E. 1998. *Ancient Ararat: A Handbook of Urartian Studies*. Delmar (NY): Caravan Books.

Zimansky, P. E. 2011. 'Urartian and the Urartians', in S. R. Steadman and G. McMahon (eds) *The Oxford Handbook of Ancient Anatolia (c.10,000–323 BCE)*: 548–559. Oxford: Oxford University Press.

Zürn, H. 1970. 'Der "Grafenbühl" bei Asperg, Kr. Ludwigsburg', in H. Zürn (ed.) *Hallstattforschungen in Nordwürttemberg: Die Grabhügel von Asperg (Kr. Ludwigsburg), Hirschlanden (Kr. Leonberg) und Mühlacker (Kr. Vaihingen)*: 7–51. Stuttgart: Müller und Gräff.

PART III

THEMES IN IRON AGE ARCHAEOLOGY

LIFEWAYS

CHAPTER 18

FOOD, FOODWAYS, AND SUBSISTENCE

HANSJÖRG KÜSTER

Introduction

In the Iron Age nearly all components of daily nutrition were locally produced, as in most traditional rural economies until the present day. The vast majority of Iron Age people were involved in food production all day long, most of them as peasants. This is often overlooked when the material culture of this period is considered, which—for archaeologists—is normally dominated by artefacts such as ceramics and iron tools. The local environment of settlements was first and foremost used for food production. The everyday lives of people, the character of their environment, and their food were interconnected within one of several different systems of life and land-use, which were not compatible with one another. During the Iron Age, different subsistence systems existed in parallel on the European continent.

Three 'Belts' of Subsistence in Europe

In the first millennium BC, the first part of the Iron Age, three subsistence 'belts' can be distinguished in Europe: a southern belt around the Mediterranean Sea, a central belt in the centre of the continent, and a northern belt in the Arctic and Subarctic regions. In later times—i.e. the early centuries AD up to the beginning of Middle Ages—the borders between these belts shifted somewhat to the north, partly influenced by the progress of iron technology (for more detail on different land-use systems and their landscapes, see Küster 2012).

In the south of Europe, an established system of states and infrastructures existed, primarily in the context of the Greek and Roman civilizations. In these societies permanent settlements existed, and crop fields could be located in the same place for long periods of time. The long-term settlement strategy allowed the establishment of orchards, where grafted olive and fruit trees were cultivated. Grafting techniques and long-term cultivation were also preconditions for viticulture. Vineyards existed only in the vicinity of permanent settlements as part of their land-use system (Zohary and Hopf 1988). Established networks allowed the transport of food from sites of surplus to sites of shortage, mainly on the Mediterranean and the waterways that connected with it. This was important for food distribution in antiquity. In principle, each crop could grow in any part of the Mediterranean region as climatic conditions were comparable on all coasts and islands. Almost exactly the same crops were cultivated in each part of the Mediterranean region, and in some cases it is not easy to detect where some rarely cultivated spices and other plants originated. Trade did not serve as a precondition for every region to receive each of the Mediterranean cultivated plants; it was important for another reason. Crop fields or sensitive fruit tree cultures could be destroyed by locally unfavourable weather conditions, such as storms, drought, or frost. These hazards did not normally affect the entire Mediterranean world in the same way and to the same extent, so that the harvest would only be destroyed in some places. Where the failures occurred, they could be mitigated as long as there was a surplus of food elsewhere, from where supplies could be transported by water to the site of shortage. Around the Mediterranean, enough sea salt was available to preserve food against pests during long sea voyages.

In central Europe, farming was also well developed during the Iron Age. Crop growing and livestock keeping had a long tradition going back to the Neolithic, but was practiced within a quite different land-use system from the one in the Mediterranean world. Trade was nowhere near as well developed as in the more complex societies of the Mediterranean area. If there was a shortage of bulk goods such as crops or timber, it was not possible to deliver the required goods because appropriate routes either did not exist or were not reliable enough. Problems linked to crop shortages and—perhaps more often—shortages of timber for the construction of houses could not be resolved in the same way as in Mediterranean societies (that is, by transport and trade). Instead, people were forced to shift their settlements and cultivated land after living in one place for some decades. They had to leave that place and move to another site inside the woodlands, where timber was still available for constructing new houses. This may have been one of the most important reasons for the fact that most Iron Age settlements—like all other earlier prehistoric settlements—were not permanent (Hvass 1982). In the vicinity of settlements which only existed for a few decades or centuries at most it was not possible to establish orchards, to plant and to graft fruit trees, and to cultivate wine. Especially for fruit orchards and vineyards, long-term settlements were needed. These could only flourish in a complex civilization, but not in the vicinity of a typical Iron Age or other prehistoric settlement (Zohary and Hopf 1988). Settlements and their fields would generally have been abandoned before cultivated trees and shrubs delivered optimal yields. Cultivated fruits, wine, spices, and other crops were sometimes imported from ancient Greece or Rome to Iron Age settlements in temperate Europe. Furthermore, in the pre-Roman Iron Age it was generally impossible to support people living at sites where crops could not be harvested successfully every year. This was a problem in coastal areas, in some high mountainous areas, and in the far north of the continent. People could only live permanently in such locations if an infrastructure was available which allowed trading contacts. By means of trade, surpluses could reach people living in areas which suffered from poor weather conditions. Some of these areas were settled in the Roman Iron Age, others not until medieval times, but in each case only when the regions were integrated to a political, social, and economic infrastructure.

In the far north of Europe, iron technology was also well developed (see Chapter 23), but was only used to manufacture tools for hunting and fishing. Farming was not yet introduced to these areas, possibly not for climatic reasons but rather because the soils were too stony. It was not therefore possible to cultivate them with the tools available at the time. Settlements of hunters and fishers were not stable either—like settlements of prehistoric farmers. They shifted from one place to another one, as a consequence of the quality of the conditions for hunting and fishing. But there were reasons why such settlements might have had a certain degree of stability. It was complicated to ensure that nutrition was available every day. Hunting for permanent nutrition was only possible in an open environment such as steppe and tundra. Few animals lived inside the dense woodlands and it was hard to hunt them. Needless to say, fishing was possible only in the vicinity of open water such as lakes, creeks, rivers, and seas. There were only a few places in Europe where permanent fishing communities were possible, such as northern Sweden and Finland, and also along some other Baltic Sea coasts. There, the prehistoric lifestyle of hunting and fishing survived for a very long time, in places nearly up to the present day. There were contacts between people living in all three subsistence 'belts', but their sociocultural, political, and economic systems were incompatible with one another. Therefore a 'mixture' between these systems did not exist. People relied either on hunting and gathering, farming without infrastructure, or farming inside a state infrastructure.

Crop Farming

The nuclear area of the European Iron Age was the centre of the continent. From there, many contacts existed with the Graeco-Roman world. Farming was practised much as in the Neolithic, but no longer just on fertile loess soils which are largely stone-free. The technological advances of the Iron Age permitted crops to be grown on other less amenable soils with a higher stone content, which would have destroyed Neolithic or Bronze Age ploughs or other tools used for tilling. Fens and damp grasslands along rivers were also cultivated for the first time during the late Bronze Age or Iron Age.

Farmers relied on the cultivation of at least two different cereal species. This brought several advantages, as different species had to be sown and harvested at different times. If one crop ripened at an inconvenient weather period with poor harvesting conditions, farmers could hope for better conditions during the harvest of the other crop. Cultivation of two crops also had economic and social advantages. Work on the fields did not all have to be done during one short period but was spread over a longer period, so that fewer people were involved in ploughing, sowing, harvesting, and threshing.

Another part of the population was free to pursue other activities such as caring for livestock and—very important during the Iron Age—mining and processing iron and salt.

Typical crops in the classical world—and also beyond, e.g. in the Iberian peninsula (Buxó i Capdevila et al. 1997)—were barley (*Hordeum vulgare*) and naked wheat. It is very difficult to determine, from the morphology of carbonized cereal grains found during excavations, whether tetraploid macaroni wheat (*Triticum durum*) or hexaploid bread or club wheat (*Triticum aestivum*) was grown. Generally it is only possible to determine naked wheat grains from the Mediterranean area as belonging to *Triticum aestivum* or *durum*. The Romans evidently induced farmers to grow naked or macaroni wheat, which are excellent bread crops, but these wheat species have an important disadvantage: their grains are 'naked' or 'free-threshing', which means they are not tightly hulled and protected by glumes. It is therefore hard to preserve them for a long time. Especially under damp climatic conditions, solid granaries were needed to store naked wheat. When such granaries were available, the growing and storing of free-threshing crops was possible—then it was advantageous to grow naked or free-threshing crops because they are easier to process than hulled crops. It was no longer necessary to dehusk crops before grinding the grains, which was a complicated procedure.

Wheat normally was grown as a winter crop, which means that the fields were prepared and the grains sown in autumn. The plants started to grow in late autumn and early winter, survived the cold season on the field, and started to grow again in mild phases of the winter and in spring. Winter crops could be harvested earlier than summer crops. Barley was probably a summer crop, sown in spring and harvested in summer a little later than the winter crops.

North of the Alps, spelt (*Triticum spelta*) was often grown instead of naked wheat, in combination with barley (Kreuz and Schäfer 2008; Küster 1995: 105–136; Rösch 1998). Spelt is also an excellent bread crop, but a hulled wheat species. The glumes are tightly attached to the grains so that it is not possible to separate grains and glumes by threshing alone. Special dehusking techniques had to be applied: it was necessary to dry crops carefully before dehusking. Afterwards, dehusking was achieved using a rotary quern to burst the glumes. This could be done by soft grinding or by lifting the moving quernstone, so that the grains were not damaged, but the dry glumes burst from the grains. After this, the glumes can be separated from the grains, for example by winnowing, because they have different weights (Körber-Grohne 1987: 71). Cultivation of hulled cereals allowed storage for longer periods, even under less favourable conditions and without a dry granary. It is possible to preserve hulled (but not naked) grain (spelt, hulled barley) for an entire winter season in a simple earth-cut pit (Lüning and Meurers-Balke 1980).

In north central Europe, spelt was normally replaced by emmer (*Triticum dicoccon*), another hulled crop (e.g. Buurman 1993; Matterne-Zech 1996). Like barley, emmer could be cultivated as a summer crop and is consequently known in German as *Sommerdinkel* ('summer spelt'). Both sowing and harvesting periods for emmer and barley were slightly different as well. Yields of emmer were certainly not comparable to those of naked wheat or spelt, but people received high-quality flour suitable for baking bread.

Grains and flour of all *Triticum* species are richer in protein than barley flour and have a better baking quality. Bread wheat, macaroni wheat, spelt, and also emmer could be used for baking bread. Barley flour could only be used for bread-making if it was mixed with other flour, perhaps prepared from legumes such as lentils or peas. Otherwise barley flour could be used for preparing a kind of porridge, or for brewing beer, which sometimes becomes apparent when sprouted grains are found in prehistoric grain assemblages (Stika 1996). Barley is also very suitable as fodder for livestock.

On the fields, crop rotation may have been practiced. This means that summer crops were regularly grown after winter crops, and a fallow phase was perhaps included in the third year (Küster 1995: 130–132). Crop rotation protects cultivated plants against pests such as insects or fungi which need single plant species for their development. With rotation and different crops on the fields each year, these insects and fungi could not propagate so well. With a fallow phase, additional minerals could be extracted from the soil by spontaneously growing plants. If these plants were left on the field after the growing season, organic materials were decomposed, but the minerals were left as ash on the field. These minerals would support crop cultivation the following year. In later times, such as the Middle Ages, it is well known that livestock grazed on fallow land (Ellenberg 1978: 57). Through this a lot of manure was spread on the land, so that additional nutrients such as nitrates and phosphates were dispersed on the fields. Possibly this was already practiced in the Iron Age.

Sometimes millet (*Panicum miliaceum*) was cultivated as a third cereal, mainly in the early Iron Age. Millet—like barley—is poor in proteins, so it too could only be used for porridge, or millet flour was mixed with legume flour. Perhaps it was not cultivated for human consumption, but for feeding horses (Küster 2010: 122–124). These animals had frequently been kept since the Bronze Age. Horses needed special treatment and nutrition: they are normally fed not only with grass or hay, but also with crops like millet. Other common domestic animals such as cattle, sheep, and goats are ruminants. Ruminants live in symbiosis with micro-organisms which propagate in the first stomachs of the animals and break down cellulose, allowing the animals to feed on grass and herbs. Horses are not ruminants, but also have symbiotic micro-organisms in their digestive systems, especially in their intestines, which can decay cellulose, but not as efficiently as ruminants. This means that horses need more fodder which is poor in cellulose, mainly grains such as millet and oats.

During the Iron Age, oats (*Avena sativa*) were also sometimes grown. This plant may have evolved from the wild oat (*Avena fatua*) inside crop fields where other cereals were grown and oats originally existed only as a weed. This weed was harvested together with cereal plants. The growing and harvesting together with the crops allowed a selection of weed individuals with similar attributes as cultivated plants. All grains must stick to the plants until harvest, whereas weeds should lose their grains as soon as possible so that they can germinate and grow. In, for example, barley fields, some oat plants developed which became suitable as cultivated plants as their grains were tightly attached to the plants. Such a development is not singular and is typical for a so-called secondary cultivated plant. The development of cultivated oats possibly took place in north-west Europe during the Bronze and Iron Age (Körber-Grohne 1987: 57–62). One of the oldest occurrences of oat cultivation is known from Iron Age Rullstorf near Lüneburg in north-west Germany (second to first century BC; Kroll 1980). There are further records of oats, mainly from sites near the North Sea coast, in the following centuries (Körber-Grohne 1987: 61–62). Possibly the spread of this additional cereal crop was indirectly influenced by the Romans. This will be discussed later.

Oats, too, are poor in proteins and, like barley and millet flour, their flour is not well suited to baking bread. Instead, oat grains are typically used for preparing porridge or horse feed. With the beginning of oat cultivation a replacement of millet cultivation probably started, resulting in its eventual disappearance in Europe (albeit not until the last few centuries), whereas oat cultivation is still practiced and oats are still well known as a special diet for horses. Another oat species which has sometimes been cultivated since the Iron Age, especially in sandy and infertile but also damp regions of north-west Europe, was the bristle oat (*Avena strigosa*; Körber-Grohne 1987: 62).

There were further crops at some sites such as einkorn (*Triticum monococcum*), a species frequently cultivated in the Neolithic, but only rarely at later periods. Rye (*Secale cereale*) was grown in south-east Europe, for instance in the region of present-day Ukraine. It can only develop in areas with hard frosts in winter because its sprouting is triggered by low winter temperatures. Rye was therefore never grown in the areas directly alongside the Mediterranean, and it was not introduced to central Europe at this time. Foxtail millet (*Setaria italica*) was sometimes cultivated in regions where exchange with Mediterranean cultures was possible, such as the northern fringes of the Alps and on the Iberian Peninsula (e.g. Alonso 2008).

Charred cereal grains are frequently found during archaeological excavations, possibly because crops had been dried in the vicinity of open fire, where they sometimes became carbonized by accident. This means that carbohydrates, such as starch, were transformed into pure carbon. This happens easily and quickly during contact with a fire or heat, as can be demonstrated today when preparing toasted bread! The drying of grain was a precondition for successful dehusking after harvesting, threshing, and storing, but before grinding and baking, as already mentioned. Apart from the fact that cereal grains are frequently found during excavation, it is highly likely that they were the most important basis of human nutrition. Starch has been a very important element of nutrition for humans since farming started in the Neolithic.

Legumes, Oil-Plants, and Other Cultivated Plants

For a well-balanced diet, it was important to cultivate not only plants rich in starch, but also legumes, with their high protein content, and oil plants, which contain herbal fat. Lentils (*Lens culinaris*) and peas (*Pisum sativum*) were grown in central Europe from the Neolithic. From the Bronze Age onwards, horse bean (*Vicia faba*) was also cultivated. In some regions, especially in the south and the centre of the continent, bitter vetch (*Vicia ervilia*) is also often identified in archaeological contexts. This crop is interesting as it can possibly be regarded as an import from the Mediterranean region where it was widely grown in antiquity. But it has also been identified among plant remains from Iron Age settlements from southern Germany and other regions in contact with Mediterranean cultures (Buxó 2008; Küster 1995: 127; Stika 1999).

Linseed or flax (*Linum usitatissimum*) was the predominant oil plant from the Neolithic onward and was also used to obtain fibres for producing textiles. Gold of pleasure (*Camelina sativa*) was probably cultivated as another oil plant, perhaps mainly in north-western central Europe—e.g. in the lower Rhine area (Knörzer 1978; Körber-Grohne 1987: 392–394). Sometimes opium poppy (*Papaver somniferum*) is recorded; this is mostly regarded as an oil plant, rather than as a spice or a source of opium. This last reason for poppy cultivation, however, cannot be totally excluded, as it is known that the Scythians also used hemp (*Cannabis sativa*) as a drug (Körber-Grohne 1987: 388). Possibly the Scythians introduced hemp to Europe from central Asia. Like flax, hemp was used for textile fabrication (Körber-Grohne 1985: 102–107). Hemp seeds have also been found in late Iron Age settlement layers at Budapest (Dálnoki and Jacomet 2002).

Some rare finds of walnut (*Juglans regia*), chestnut (*Castanea sativa*), fig (*Ficus carica*) (Stika 1999), and vine (*Vitis vinifera*), including grape pips (Küster 1992; Ulbert 1959), must be imports from southern Europe. The same is possibly the case for spices and condiments such as dill (*Anethum graveolens*) and celery (*Apium graveolens*; Bakels 1999; Lodwick 2014), which are rarely recorded in Iron Age contexts (e.g. Wiethold 1996). It is not obvious that these trees were regularly cultivated in orchard plots during the Iron Age; indeed as noted at the start of the chapter it is more than questionable whether orchards existed at all at this era; they were not elements of the land-use system of prehistoric communities. Sometimes wild fruits were collected, including wild strawberries (*Fragaria vesca*), wild apples (*Malus sylvestris*), cherries (*Prunus avium*), wild vine berries (*Vitis sylvestris*), and hazelnuts (*Corylus avellana*). There is no evidence for the cultivation of these fruits in gardens or orchards, as they are only detected as rare single occurrences.

Livestock

During the Iron Age, cattle, sheep, goats, and pigs were all kept under conditions that had changed little from Neolithic (see also Chapter 19). Animals browsed on woodlands so that woods became gradually more open through time. It was characteristic of woodlands, in many cases even up to the nineteenth century, that sites for producing timber and firewood were not clearly separated from sites of grazing. Some woodland may already have developed the character of grazed woodland or even open heath during the Iron Age. Both are caused by extensive grazing over long periods. Treeless grazing areas were generally not available except on some fresh-water and especially salt-water marshes. But such areas were often sparsely settled in the Iron Age owing to the lack of timber, which was such an important prerequisite for the establishment of prehistoric settlement.

Meadows for the preparation of winter fodder did not exist. Mowed grassland can only be managed if some kind of manure is available, as otherwise yields of grasses and herbs are not sufficient. During the Iron Age, manure for meadows was not available as it was probably used up in manuring crop fields. It was also not possible to harvest grasses and herbs for hay with stone tools. Producing iron sickles or—better—iron scythes, which became possible in the Iron Age, was an important precondition for the management of mowed grasslands in later times such as the Roman period. The only possible method of making winter fodder was by pollarding and pruning trees. Pollarding was typically practiced in late spring or early summer, soon after fresh leaves were fully developed. Twigs were dried during summer, perhaps by hanging them on the pollarded trees. After drying, twigs were brought to barns or stables as winter fodder. Some tree species can stand pollarding better than others, such as lime (*Tilia cordata, Tilia platyphyllos*), hornbeam (*Carpinus betulus*), and ash (*Fraxinus excelsior*). Elm species (*Ulmus glabra, Ulmus laevis, Ulmus campestris*) were often harmed by pests after pollarding, so they became rarer in woodlands as early as the Neolithic. This is the most likely reason for the well-known 'elm-decline' evident on so many pollen diagrams (for more discussion, see Küster 1988: 84–87).

In the Iron Age, horses were also kept as livestock. They were possibly used—like cattle—for working in the fields, and also as a source of meat. But first and foremost horses were undoubtedly used for riding and fighting, as can be deduced from the many parts of harnesses from excavations on Iron Age sites (Chapter 32). Horses require better fodder than ruminants like cattle, sheep, and goats. They should graze mainly on damp, fertile grasslands, possibly with a high content of young sprouting plants with a lower cellulose content, or they should eat crops such as millet, oats, and legumes (see earlier).

Shifting Colonization and Permanent Utilization of Woodlands

Much as in the Neolithic, many Iron Age people did not live in permanent dwelling places. Settlements shifted from time to time, perhaps as a result of reducing yields and more likely as a consequence of a gradual shortage of timber. After some decades of living at one place, suitable timber was no longer available in the vicinity of a settlement for renovating or rebuilding dilapidated houses. In such a situation, especially after a fire during which one or more houses burnt down, it might have been more convenient to rebuild a settlement and its houses in or near a patch of woodland where enough timber was available than to rebuild it on the same site (Küster 2008: 86–92).

After a settlement was abandoned, a secondary succession of woodland could start. At first herbs, shrubs, and pioneer trees expanded, such as birch (*Betula pendula*), poplar (*Populus nigra*), willow (*Salix* sp.) and pine (*Pinus sylvestris*). Under the canopy of these pioneer trees, slower-growing trees could follow, among them oak (*Quercus* sp.) and beech (*Fagus sylvatica*). Oak was already common across much of Europe before the first settlements were founded and woodlands cleared in the Neolithic, but beech was then still confined to some mountainous areas of southern Europe; its subsequent spread across the rest of Europe was dependent on human activity. Beech was not propagated intentionally but spread spontaneously in secondary successions of woodland, which developed after settlement sites had been abandoned. Although now regarded as a major component of the climax vegetation, beech is not a typical natural element of central European vegetation, its distribution being indirectly influenced by prehistoric settlement. It essentially reached its maximum distribution at the end of the pre-Roman Iron Age, as a result of the reduction in settlement mobility; however, in some northern European regions outside the Roman Empire beech was able to continue spreading until the Migration period (Küster 1997).

In many pollen diagrams from central Europe, characteristic maxima of beech percentages can be observed. It was recognized at an early stage of pollen analysis that these maxima might have been synchronous (Firbas 1949; Paul and Ruoff 1927, 1932) and assumed that they were a product of climate change, which triggered synchronous woodland development over large areas (indeed, beech maxima increases and decreases were used to date pollen diagrams before radiocarbon dates were widely available). More recently, it has been argued that there was a marked climatic decline in the Iron Age, but it is more likely that the increase of beech and its maximum were not predominantly influenced by climate, as for several millennia beech spread under both warmer and colder conditions. However, the preconditions for the spread of beech and the maximum of its distribution really can be dated to the same range of time in different regions, because the 'prehistoric' strategy of shifting settlement was the same in many different regions, and ended at these places at very much the same point of time. The end of the beech spread was marked by the time when dwelling places did not shift any more, so that secondary succession of woodland did not take place and beech consequently became rarer thereafter.

In the vicinity of permanent settlements different parts of the surrounding landscape were utilized permanently as field systems, areas for grazing livestock, and woodland. Long-term exploitation of woodlands resulted in a spread of coppices and woodlands which looked similar to developed coppices with standards. In coppices, trees and shrubs are frequently cut back and regenerate afterwards by the growth of young shoots. Some tree species are able to regenerate in this way; others are not. As a consequence, hornbeam (*Carpinus betulus*), hazel (*Corylus avellana*), and oak (*Quercus* sp.) became more frequent in woodland. Beech cannot withstand permanent coppicing and is not able to regenerate repeatedly by forming young shoots after several cuts. Therefore the representation of beech decreases in pollen diagrams at the same time as permanent settlement and utilization of the environment spread. As a result, the percentages of beech increase in pollen diagrams under the influence of shifting colonization, and decrease in a period when permanent colonization took place.

In other regions, beech expansion ended earlier, notably in iron and salt mining areas. There, wood charcoal was used as fuel to produce the high temperatures needed in furnaces to smelt ores. This was necessary to obtain pure iron. Much wood was also needed to heat salt pans at salt springs and mines. In mining areas such as the Siegerland in western Germany, the spread of coppices is clear from Iron Age pollen spectra (Pott 1985). Beech also became rarer in an area north of the Alps where atmospheric deposits of trace minerals indicate that ore smelting took place (Küster and Rehfuess 1997).

After the Roman period, shifting colonization prevailed again in the Migration period. This was connected with less coppice management. Again, secondary woodland successions resulted in an additional and last phase of beech expansion, taking the species to the outer limits which still exist today: southern Scandinavia, north-east Poland, and south-east England.

Iron Age Agriculture in Contact with the Infrastructure-Based Economy of the Roman Empire

During the centuries around the birth of Christ, the Roman Empire and land-use system, including its characteristic attributes, expanded into areas where an Iron Age economy prevailed before. In some places, Roman and Iron Age land-use systems came into direct contact. This was not just the case along the *limes* and Hadrian's Wall but over a wider area, especially in the North Sea region, where Roman imports are frequently found at settlements of Roman Iron Age date (Ulbert 1977; Erdrich 2001). As a consequence of the Roman influence on this area, infrastructure expanded, an important contributory factor in the settlement and cultivation of the North Sea marshes from the beginning of the Roman Iron Age onwards.

The North Sea marshes are unique in several respects. As they are sometimes flooded by salt water, central European trees cannot grow on this terrain. Only some halophytes—plants which are adapted to withstand salt water floods—can grow in such marshes. On the other hand, the North Sea marshes are the only region with large natural grasslands in central Europe where profitable livestock breeding could be established. Because of the lack of timber, livestock breeders could only settle in the marshes if a regular supply of timber could be secured, which became possible inside an infrastructure influenced by the Roman Empire. On the other hand, the farmers had to breed livestock and produce livestock goods—principally milk products and wool—to be able to buy timber on the markets in order to construct timber houses. Their settlements had a higher stability than earlier or contemporary 'normal' farming settlements in the hinterland, such as Feddersen Wierde near Bremerhaven, a coastal settlement occupied from the first to the fifth century AD (Kossack et al. 1984).

During phases with more numerous and higher floods, dwelling mounds were erected to protect people and livestock against flooding. Some cultivated plants were also grown on the highest places in the marshes, namely ones which can develop in a short period during summer when floods normally happen only rarely (Körber-Grohne 1967). Among them, barley, oats, horse bean, and gold of pleasure were important. Barley, in particular, can withstand a small amount of salt in the soil—as in dry regions in the Near East. Iron Age dwellers along the North Sea coast also cultivated dyer's woad (*Isatis tinctoria*), a plant containing the same dye products as indigo; it is therefore also known as 'German indigo'. This plant was certainly cultivated to dye textiles, especially wool, and so could be sold both as a raw material and as a processed good in the form of textiles. Remains of cultivated dyer's woad have been found in Roman Iron Age settlement layers on the North Sea coast, and Caesar reported that people in Britain were coloured in blue, which could only be possible by using dyer's woad as this is the only European dye plant that can be used to produce blue colours (Körber-Grohne 1987: 412–413; see Chapter 26).

Romans or sailors working inside their infrastructure also traded crops along the North Sea coast. This was important to support coastal farmers who probably were not able to have a good harvest every year. Sometimes summer floods might destroy their fields, or the salt content of the soils might be too high to allow optimal growth of cultivated plants demanding fresh water conditions. Perhaps occurrences of crops with naked grains on coastal sites in the Roman Iron Age can be interpreted as imports. It is more likely that indigenous farmers cultivated hulled crops which could be preserved more easily as already mentioned.

On the island of Amrum, a large amount of grains of both hulled (*Hordeum vulgare*) and naked (*Hordeum vulgare nudum*) barley were found. They were totally clean of weed seeds, suggesting they were part of a stored crop (Feindt 1987). Stocks of naked crops were also detected in an Iron Age granary in northern Jutland, dated to the period around the birth of Christ. In Overbygård, not only were many grains of naked barley found but also naked wheat, which was very uncommon in coastal areas at that time (Henriksen and Robinson 1996). But naked wheat was cultivated and traded by the Romans (Küster 1993); it could be stored in solid granaries. Such a building existed in Overbygård, and the stocks were stored in vessels and leather sacks which were affixed to the roof of the granary. The authors who presented the evidence thought that these naked crops were locally grown, but they could also be interpreted as Roman imports, transported as trading goods from places inside the Roman Empire (e.g. from the mouth of the River Rhine) to sites along the coast to the north.

In spite of the fact that Roman infrastructure was possibly the main reason for the development of settlements along the coast, the Romans themselves did not settle in areas which were not used for farming in the Iron Age. Local traditions of cereal production were also continued. In southern Germany and other areas of the northern fringe of the Alps, they used spelt, just like the Iron Age inhabitants who lived there before Roman rule. Both the crop and the techniques of crop processing were taken over (Guyan 1954). The Romans were not familiar with processing techniques for hulled crops, as naked crops prevailed in the warm and dry Mediterranean region. The tradition of spelt cultivation from the Iron Age to the Roman period suggests that the crop was possibly cultivated by local farmers and delivered to Roman settlements. Existing Iron Age farming communities continued to cultivate their land under the influence of the Roman Empire and introduced their crops into the trading network of the Roman economy (Küster 1995: 231).

Possibly under Roman influence, additional crops were now propagated, perhaps to allow permanent crop cultivation and settlement. This is evident from the distribution of rye. This crop, which was previously cultivated only in eastern Europe, was now cultivated in Roman contexts, as is evident from archaeobotanical analyses from, for example, Lampoldshausen in south-west Germany (Piening 1982) and Künzing in Bavaria (Küster 1995: 219). Rye was only rarely cultivated in central Europe before. But now it was also grown in Iron Age settlements outside the Roman Empire, presumably in areas along the North Sea coast which became integrated into the Roman economic infrastructure. This must be one reason why rye was the predominant crop in the Roman Iron Age settlement of Flögeln-Eekhöltjen near Bremerhaven in north-west Germany (Behre 1992). This site is not situated on the North Sea coastal marshes, but lies only a few kilometres away from potential waterways on which grain could be transported also into areas outside the Roman Empire. The same is true with Rullstorf, the site with the oat record mentioned earlier. In following centuries, both rye and oats became important crops in north-central Europe. Rye, in particular, could be grown every year on the same field if it was manured in a special way, by using so-called *plaggen*, pieces of turf which were cut in the heathlands, then used as bedding in stables over the winter where they became mixed with dung, before being transported to the fields in the spring. Field surfaces became elevated as a consequence of this practice.

Preconditions for Medieval Farming: Iron Technology and Stability

The tradition of agriculture and the introduction of new crops provide evidence that Iron Age technology and the infrastructure-based political and economic system of the Romans allowed the development of medieval culture in Europe north of the Alps. Without iron technology it would have been impossible to cultivate stony soils permanently. If the same areas were to be ploughed every year, iron ploughs were needed: with such implements it was possible to work the long narrow strip-fields, which became typical of the medieval agrarian landscape. One of the oldest records of such a field may have been found under the east gate of the Iron Age *oppidum* of Manching in Bavaria (Gensen 1965). It is slightly older than the gate, which was erected at the end of the second century BC. These strip-fields were possibly as long as they were because it was difficult to turn the plough team and animals. Iron was also in demand for special knifes which were used to castrate bulls. Oxen were best suited to draw ploughs on stony soils as they were patient enough to rest when the plough was stopped by heavy stones, so that the plough did not break; horses and bulls were less inclined to stop during ploughing, so frequently the implements were damaged or even destroyed.

Iron was also used to make sickles and scythes. The availability of scythes was a precondition for cultivating meadows. The oldest evidence for meadows comes from the Roman Iron Age (Körber-Grohne and Piening 1983). Meadows became very important in the medieval economy, providing hay as winter fodder for the livestock. The livestock had to be kept in stables to collect dung which could be used to manure permanently cropped fields. Another important precondition for the development of economic infrastructure and permanent settlement was availability of salt. Salt was used in antiquity to preserve food like meat, meat products, fruits, milk, and milk products such as cheese during long-distance transport by sea—for instance, on the Mediterranean. Salt could be processed from salt water, which was heated by the sun on sea shores, but was not commonly available until the Iron Age in many inland regions. Large-scale Iron Age mining, as at Hallstatt in Austria or in Romania, allowed wider distribution of salt. Iron pans were necessary to heat salt water from salt springs and mines to extract clean salt. When salt was generally available, trade networks could expand to the innermost parts of the European continent.

Conclusions

Iron Age agriculture was the most highly developed prehistoric land-use system outside complex Mediterranean societies. There were contacts between the two zones, but their land-use systems were not compatible. Iron technology was an important precondition for Roman economic expansion into southern, central, and western Europe, and subsequently for infrastructural expansion during the Middle Ages. On the one hand, the establishment of the medieval economy depended on a system of stable settlements and infrastructure inherited from the Roman world. On the other, medieval expansion of stable settlements, states, infrastructures, and culture to nearly all parts of Europe, with their different soils and climates, would have been impossible without Iron Age technology—in other words, the general availability of iron tools and implements and of salt to conserve food for storage and transport.

References

Alonso, N. 2008. 'Crops and agriculture during the Iron Age and Late Antiquity in Cerdanyola del Vallès (Catalonia, Spain)'. *Vegetation History and Archaeobotany* 17, 1: 75–84.

Bakels, C. 1999. 'Archaeobotanical investigations in the Aisne valley, northern France, from the Neolithic up to the early middle ages'. *Vegetation History and Archaeobotany* 8, 1–2: 71–77.

Behre, K.-E. 1992. 'The history of rye cultivation in Europe'. *Vegetation History and Archaeobotany* 1, 3: 141–156.

Buurman, J. 1993. 'Carbonized plant remains from a pre-Roman Iron Age house site at Opperdoes, West Friesland, The Netherlands'. *Vegetation History and Archaeobotany* 2, 2: 69–78.

Buxó, R. 2008. 'The agricultural consequences of colonial contacts on the Iberian Peninsula in the first millennium B.C.'. *Vegetation History and Archaeobotany* 17, 1: 145–154.

Buxó i Capdevila, R., N. Alonso, D. Canal, C. Echave, and I. Gonzalez. 1997. 'Archeobotanical remains of hulled and naked cereals in the Iberian Peninsula'. *Vegetation History and Archaeobotany* 6, 1: 15–23.

Dálnoki, O., and S. Jacomet. 2002. 'Some aspects of Late Iron Age agriculture based on the first results of an archaeobotanical investigation at Corvin tér, Budapest, Hungary'. *Vegetation History and Archaeobotany* 11, 1–2: 9–15.

Ellenberg, H. 1978. *Vegetation Mitteleuropas mit den Alpen in ökologischer Sicht*, 2nd edition. Stuttgart: Ulmer.

Erdrich, M. 2001. *Rom und die Barbaren. Das Verhältnis zwischen dem Imperium Romanum und den germanischen Stämmen vor seiner Nordwestgrenze von der späten römischen Republik bis zum Gallischen Sonderreich*. Römisch-Germanische Forschungen 58. Mainz: Philipp von Zabern.

Feindt, F. 1987. 'Zum Getreidefund von Amrum, Kreis Nordfriesland'. *Offa* 44: 101–106.

Firbas, F. 1949. *Spät- und nacheiszeitliche Waldgeschichte Mitteleuropas nördlich der Alpen I. Allgemeine Waldegeschichte*. Jena: G. Fischer.

Firbas, F. 1952. *Spät- und nacheiszeitliche Waldgeschichte Mitteleuropas nördlich der Alpen II. Waldgeschichte der einzelnen Landschaften*. Jena: G. Fischer.

Gensen, R. 1965. 'Manching III. Die Ausgrabung des Osttores in den Jahren 1962 bis 1963'. *Germania* 43: 49–62.

Guyan, W. U. 1954. *Mensch und Urlandschaft der Schweiz*. Zürich: Büchergilde Gutenberg.

Henriksen, P. S., and D. Robinson. 1996. 'Early Iron Age agriculture: Archaeobotanical evidence from an underground granary at Overbygård in Northern Jutland, Denmark'. *Vegetation History and Archaeobotany* 5, 1–2: 1–11.

Hvass, S. 1982. 'Ländliche Siedlungen der Kaiser- und Völkerwanderungszeit in Dänemark'. *Offa* 39: 189–195.

Knörzer, K.-H. 1978. 'Entwicklung und Ausbreitung des Leindotters (*Camelina sativa* L.)'. *Berichte der Deutschen Botanischen Gesellschaft* 91: 187–195.

Körber-Grohne, U. 1967. *Geobotanische Untersuchungen auf der Feddersen Wierde*. Wiesbaden: Steiner.

Körber-Grohne, U. 1985. 'Die biologischen Reste aus dem hallstattzeitlichen Fürstengrab von Hochdorf, Gemeinde Eberdingen (Kreis Ludwigsburg)', in H. Küster and U. Körber-Grohne (eds) *Hochdorf I*. Forschungen und Berichte zur Vor- und Frühgeschichte in Baden-Württemberg 19: 85–265. Stuttgart: Theiss.

Körber-Grohne, U. 1987. *Nutzpflanzen in Deutschland: Kulturgeschichte und Biologie*. Stuttgart: Theiss.

Körber-Grohne, U., and U. Piening. 1983. 'Die Pflanzenreste aus dem Ostkastell von Welzheim mit besonderer Berücksichtigung der Graslandpflanzen', in U. Körber-Grohne and et al.

(eds) *Flora und Fauna im Ostkastell von Welzheim*. Forschungen und Berichte zur Vor- und Frühgeschichte in Baden-Württemberg 14: 17–88. Stuttgart: Theiss.

Kossack, G., K.-E. Behre, and P. Schmid (eds). 1984. *Archäologische und naturwissenschaftliche Untersuchungen an ländlichen und frühstädtischen Siedlungen im deutschen Küstengebiet vom 5. Jahrhundert v. Chr. bis zum 11. Jahrhundert n. Chr. Band 1: Ländliche Siedlungen*. Acta Humaniora. Weinheim: VCH.

Kreuz, A., and E. Schäfer. 2008. 'Archaeobotanical consideration of the development of pre-Roman Iron Age crop growing in the region of Hesse, Germany, and the question of agricultural production and consumption at hillfort sites and open settlements'. *Vegetation History and Archaeobotany* 17, Supplement 1: 159–179.

Kroll, H. 1980. 'Einige Vorgeschichtliche Vorratsfunde von Kulturpflanzen aus Norddeutschland'. *Offa* 37: 372–383.

Küster, H. 1988. *Vom Werden einer Kulturlandschaft. Vegetationsgeschichtliche Studien am Auerberg (Südbayern)*. Acta Humaniora. Weinheim: VCH.

Küster, H. 1992. 'Vegetationsgeschichtliche Untersuchungen', in F. Maier, U. Geilenbrügge, E. Hahn, H.-J. Köhler, and S. Sievers (eds) *Ergebnisse der Ausgrabungen 1984–1987 in Manching*: 433–476. Die Ausgrabungen in Manching 15. Stuttgart: Steiner.

Küster, H. 1993. 'Getreidevorräte in römischen Siedlungen an Rhein, Neckar und Donau', in K.-H. Knörzer, A. J. Kalis, and J. Meurers-Balke (eds) *7000 Jahre bäuerliche Landschaft: Entstehung, Erforschung, Erhaltung*. Archaeo-Physika 13: 133–137. Cologne: Rheinland-Verlag.

Küster, H. 1995. *Postglaziale Vegetationsgeschichte Südbayerns. Geobotanische Studien zur Prähistorischen Landschaftskunde*. Berlin: Akademie Verlag.

Küster, H. 1997. 'The role of farming in the Postglacial expansion of beech and hornbeam in the oak woodlands of Central Europe'. *The Holocene* 7, 2: 239–242.

Küster, H. 2008. *Geschichte des Waldes: Von der Urzeit bis zur Gegenwart*, 3rd edition. Munich: Beck.

Küster, H. 2010. *Geschichte der Landschaft in Mitteleuropa: Von der Eiszeit bis zur Gegenwart*, 4th edition. Munich: Beck.

Küster, H. 2012. *Die Entdeckung der Landschaft: Einführung in einer neue Wissenschaft*. Munich: Beck.

Küster, H., and K.-E. Rehfuess. 1997. 'Pb and Cd concentrations in a Southern Bavarian bog profile and the history of vegetation as recorded by pollen analysis'. *Water, Air, and Soil Pollution* 100: 379–386.

Lodwick, L. 2014. 'Condiments before Claudius: new plant foods at the late Iron Age oppidum at Silchester, UK'. *Vegetation History and Archaeobotany* 23: 543–549.

Lüning, J., and J. Meurers-Balke. 1980. 'Experimenteller Getreideanbau im Hambacher Forst, Gemeinde Elsdorf, Kr. Bergheim/Rheinland'. *Bonner Jahrbücher* 180: 305–344.

Matterne-Zech, V. 1996. 'A study of the carbonized seeds from a La Tène D1 rural settlement, "Le Camp du Roi" excavation at Jaux (Oise), France'. *Vegetation History and Archaeobotany* 5, 1–2: 99–104.

Paul, H., and S. Ruoff. 1927. 'Pollenstatistische und stratigraphische Mooruntersuchungen im Südlichen Bayern I'. *Berichte der Bayerischen Botanischen Gesellschaft* 29: 1–84.

Paul, H., and S. Ruoff. 1932. 'Pollenstatistische und stratigraphische Mooruntersuchungen im Südlichen Bayern II'. *Berichte der Bayerischen Botanischen Gesellschaft* 30: 1–264.

Piening, U. 1982. 'Botanische Untersuchungen an verkohlten Pflanzenresten aus Nordwürttemberg. Neolithikum bis Römische Zeit'. *Fundberichte aus Baden-Württemberg* 7: 239–271.

Pott, R. 1985. *Vegetationsgeschichtliche und pflanzensoziologische Untersuchungen zur Niederwaldwirtschaft in Westfalen.* Abhandlungen aus dem Westfälischen Museum für Naturkunde 47.4. Münster: Westfälisches Museum für Naturkunde, Landschaftsverband Westfalen-Lippe.

Rösch, M. 1998. 'The history of crops and crop weeds in South-Western Germany from the Neolithic period to modern times, as shown by archaeobotanical evidence'. *Vegetation History and Archaeobotany* 7, 2: 109–125.

Stika, H.-P. 1996. 'Traces of a possible Celtic brewery in Eberdingen-Hochdorf, Kreis Ludwigsburg, Southwest Germany'. *Vegetation History and Archaeobotany* 5, 1–2: 81–88.

Stika, H.-P. 1999. 'Approaches to reconstruction of early Celtic land-use in the central Neckar region in Southwestern Germany'. *Vegetation History and Archaeobotany* 8, 1–2: 95–103.

Ulbert, G. 1959. 'Römische Holzfässer aus Regensburg'. *Bayerische Vorgeschichtsblätter* 24: 6–29.

Ulbert, G. 1977. 'Die römischen Funde von Bentumersiel'. *Probleme der Küstenforschung im südlichen Nordseegebiet* 12: 33–65.

Wiethold, J. 1996. 'Late Celtic and early Roman plant remains from the oppidum of Bibracte, Mont Beuvray (Burgundy, France)'. *Vegetation History and Archaeobotany* 5, 1–2: 105–116.

Zohary, D., and M. Hopf. 1988. *Domestication of Plants in the Old World: The Origin and Spread of Cultivated Plants in West Asia, Europe, and the Nile Valley*. Oxford: Oxford University Press.

CHAPTER 19

ANIMALS AND ANIMAL HUSBANDRY

MAAIKE GROOT

Broad Trends

Attempting to write a chapter on animal husbandry in Iron Age Europe is quite a challenge. Not only is there a large variation in climate and topography within Europe (see Chapter 3), but culture and society in different parts of Europe vary just as much. As a result, there is no one 'Iron Age animal husbandry', but rather a whole range of different animal husbandries, dependent on local conditions, the nature and complexity of society, and cultural preferences. As well as food, animals provided wool, hides, horn, and bone. Furthermore, animals not only played a role in the agrarian economy and diet, but also in sanctuaries and funerary ritual, and in trade, whether as transport animals or as traded items. All that is possible in this short chapter is to make some general remarks on species proportions, husbandry strategies, and animal size, and then to focus on selected regions in greater detail. Four regions have been chosen for their differences in society and animal husbandry strategies. The broader discussion is based on zooarchaeological data from over 400 sites or phases within sites.

Most people in Iron Age Europe were farmers and practised mixed farming (Chapter 18). In this system, growing crops and raising animals are complementary and mutually dependent. For example, cattle provide manure and draw ploughs, supporting the growing of crops, and they benefit from arable farming by grazing on stubble fields or being fed fodder crops. Growing crops and raising animals for meat and milk provides a complete diet and spreads risk, which means that people could be mostly self-sufficient. Risk was further avoided by growing a range of crops and keeping several different species of livestock. In case of food shortages, fishing and hunting wild animals provided an additional source of food.

Animal husbandry basically relied on four species: cattle, sheep, goats, and pigs. Horses, dogs, chickens, and in some regions donkeys, cats, and domestic geese were also kept, but the number of bones of these other species is usually relatively small compared to the principal livestock. Even when chronology within the Iron Age, type of site, or local environmental conditions are not taken into account, broad trends in species proportions between different parts of Europe are visible. Of course, such an approach ignores variability within and between smaller regions and changes over time. Broadly speaking, some regions in north-western Europe and the Mediterranean show high proportions of one species—cattle in what is now the Netherlands and northern Germany, sheep and goats in what is now Spain and Greece (Figure 19.1). In other parts of Europe, proportions between the main livestock species are more balanced. In northern France, pig is generally the most common species. In central Europe and Italy, proportions of pig can also be quite high, but in the rest of Europe, it is usually the least important of the main livestock species. Goats were rarer than sheep in central and northern Europe, but occurred much more frequently in the Mediterranean. The ratio of goat to sheep increases from south to north, from 1:0.9 in Greece to 1:18 for northern Germany.

Slaughter ages of livestock indicate what products animals were exploited for, since, for example, cattle exploited for milk will be killed at older ages than cattle exploited for meat. For cattle, different husbandry strategies are found. An emphasis on older cattle (for milk and traction) is found most often, but Iron Age sites with a focus on younger cattle (for meat) and those with a mixed exploitation are also common. Sheep were generally slaughtered young or as young adults for their meat. Although wool was certainly used, it seems that it was not necessary to maintain the flock especially for this product. In Greece and the Balkans, the emphasis is on adult sheep and goats, which suggests that the use of milk and wool was more important here than in other regions. Pigs were only kept for their meat, and therefore it is not surprising to find little difference in exploitation. Most were killed in their second or third year, when they would have reached their maximum size.

In many parts of Europe, meat from horses and dogs was consumed, although the generally low proportions of fragments found for these species suggest that this was not an everyday occurrence. An exception is northern France, where butchery marks on horse and dog bones are common, and where many of these animals are young, which suggests that they were kept for their meat (Méniel 1987a, 1987b). In some cases, consumption of dogs is associated with sacrifice, such as in Lipari, Italy and the northern French sanctuaries at Gournay-sur-Aronde and Ribemont-sur-Ancre (Villari 1991; Méniel 1987b). With the exception of northern France, horses usually lived to an old age, which fits with their main use as transport animals (Chapter 32).

Chickens, domesticated in south-east Asia, first reached southern and eastern Europe in the Bronze Age (Benecke 1994: 116). During the Iron Age, chickens spread through most of Europe, although they did not reach some areas until the Roman period. For example, chickens are found on sites in Greece, Italy, and Spain from 700/600 BC, present on some Hallstatt sites in central Europe but uncommon until the La Tène period, and rare on sites in the Netherlands and northern Germany. It has been suggested that chickens were initially kept for their colourful feathers (von den Driesch and Boessneck

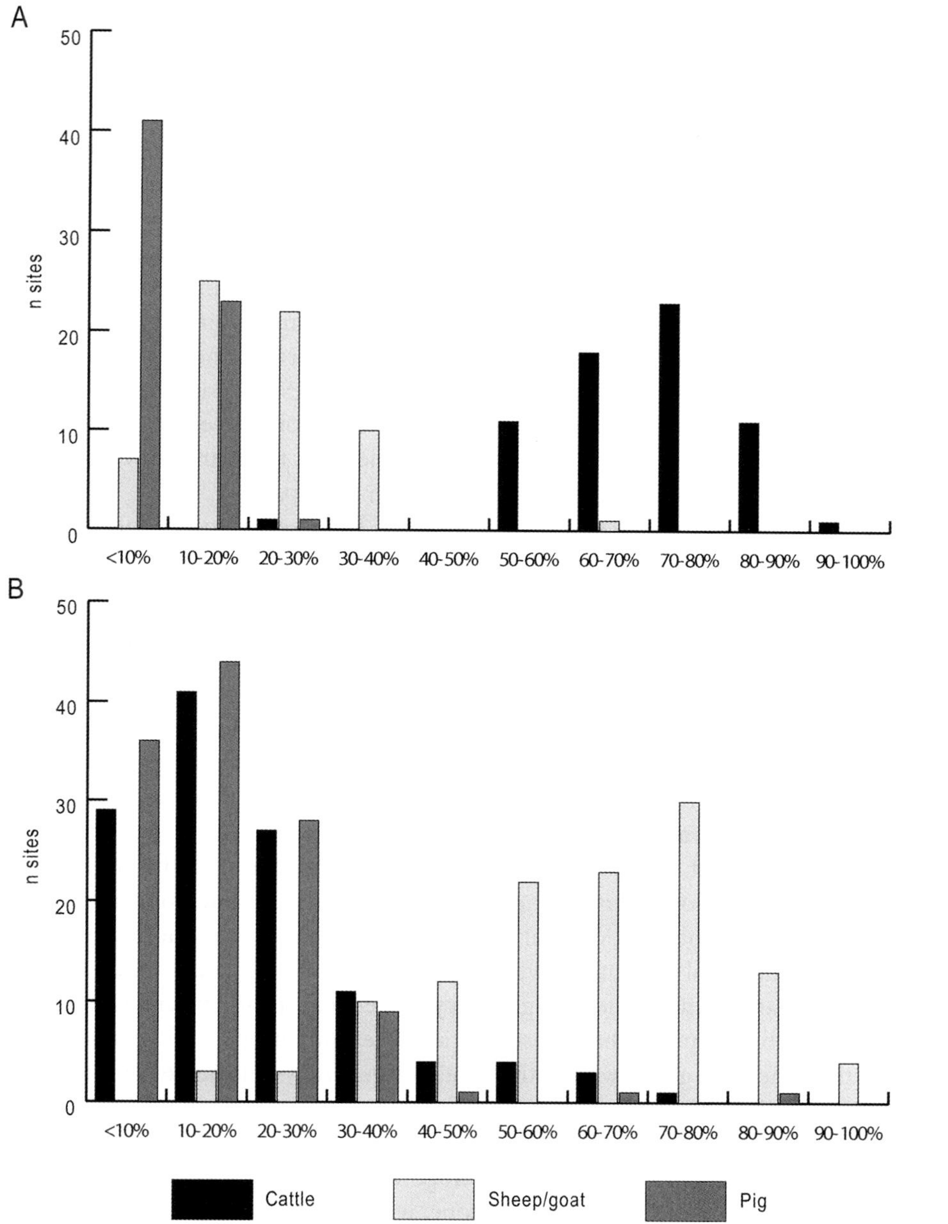

FIGURE 19.1 Species proportions for the main domestic livestock on Iron Age sites in: (A) what is now the Netherlands and northern Germany (n = 65 sites), and (B) Greece and the Iberian Peninsula (n = 118 sites).

Author

1989: 151), but at Roseldorf-Sandberg in Austria, chickens were killed young, implying they were kept for meat (Bruckner-Höbling and Pucher 2008: 76). In Iron Age Hungary, chicken was a preferred species in cemeteries (Bartosiewicz and Gál 2010: 123); this is similar to the Roman Netherlands, where chicken—a newcomer in this context as well—seems to have been selected for funerary ritual (Groot 2008). Their symbolic importance is also clear from the deposit of three chickens in a pit, as well as occurrences in graves, in Switzerland (Schibler et al. 1999: 131).

Domestic geese were introduced in the Iron Age. Literary sources indicate the presence of domestic geese in eighth-century BC Greece. Differentiating between wild and domestic geese is difficult, and as a result it is hard to pin down exactly when and where domestic goose occurs. Some of the oldest certain finds of domestic goose are skeletons from late Hallstatt/early La Tène graves in Slovakia (Benecke 1994: 117). Benecke believes it is no coincidence that the domestication of geese occurs at the same time as the introduction of chickens. Once people were familiar with the concept of keeping birds, local domestication of geese was a small step.

Iron Age cattle were small and slender in build. There seems to have been little variation in cattle size in Europe, but not all regions could be included due to a lack of information for some. Most cattle had withers heights between 100 and 125 cm, with considerable differences between cows, bulls, and oxen. At the end of the Iron Age a larger, Mediterranean type of cattle spread north and west of the Alps, together with other traded goods such as amphorae (Moser 1986: 2; Abd el Karem 2011). Cattle skins from the Dürrnberg (Austria) provide a rare insight into the coat colour, which varied from blond and light brown to red and brown/black, with the lighter colours more common. Variation in colour within the same skin suggests that pied cattle already existed (Groenman-van Waateringe 2002).

The withers height of sheep varies between 48 and 70 cm, with the largest animals found in central Europe. Female sheep were often hornless, and woollen textiles and skins from the Dürrnberg show that sheep with brown wool were more common than those with white wool (Groenman-van Waateringe 2002; Stöllner 2003: 154). Goats have a larger size range, with withers heights varying between 48 and 79 cm. Goats in Spain seem to have been smaller than those in France, central Europe, and Bosnia. Pigs were larger than sheep or goats, with withers heights generally between 65 and 80 cm, and little variation between regions.

A study on horse size identified two main types of horse: a western (average withers height 126 cm) and an eastern type (average withers height 136 cm; Bökönyi 1964). The first is found in western central Europe, while the second occurs in eastern central Europe, eastern Europe, and south-eastern Europe. Two possible explanations for the size difference are given: first, that environmental conditions in the east were better suited to horses, and second, that horses were selectively bred in the east. The size of horses in Austria, Switzerland, France, and the Netherlands fits with the smaller, western type. In Germany, some larger horses are also found, so perhaps the division is not as clear-cut as Bökönyi´s study suggests. Dogs were generally medium-sized (Benecke 1994: 142), but there were also some very large dogs, for example in the coastal region of the Netherlands (e.g. Prummel 2008: 140). Small dogs, similar in size to fox terriers and miniature schnauzers, were found at Manching (Boessneck et al. 1971: 92).

Hunting was generally of little importance as a contribution to the diet, accounting for less than 5% at most sites, although its symbolic role as a marker of elite status may have been more significant. There are exceptions of sites with higher proportions, or regions where more than 10% wild mammals are common, such as the Iberian Peninsula. Since the presence of fish and bird remains is largely dependent on whether sieving is used to collect animal bones, it is impossible for many areas to say much about the importance of fishing and bird hunting. Finds of fish traps prove that fishing occurred (Uerpmann and Uerpmann 2006; Kooistra 2015; Dütting and van Rijn 2017), but the contribution of fish to the diet cannot be established. Based on the current state of knowledge, wild animal resources were not exploited to any great extent, and in Britain it is suggested that fish were deliberately avoided for cultural reasons (Dobney and Ervynck 2007).

Animal Husbandry and Sacrifice in Ancient Greece

It has been claimed that the majority of the meat consumed by the ancient Greeks came from sacrificial animals (Jameson 1988: 87; Detienne 1989: 3, 11; Ekroth 2007: 251, 2008a: 259). The fact that animal bones—representing food refuse—are also found in settlement contexts clearly proves that this statement cannot be completely correct. Animals were slaughtered and their meat consumed outside sanctuaries as well. Nevertheless, sacrificial meat was an important part of rituals and festivities, and must have provided a large amount of the meat that was consumed. Ideally, animal husbandry should be investigated through animal remains from agrarian settlements, where the animals were raised. However, if a large proportion of livestock was slaughtered in sanctuaries rather than in settlements, data from both types of site should be analysed together. For Iron Age Greece, in fact, we do not have much choice, since most of the data on animal bones for this period comes from sanctuaries (Figure 19.2). Although selection of sacrificial animals may have taken place, based on species, age, and sex, local animal husbandry must have been able to sustain these choices. Therefore, the animal remains from sanctuaries provide indirect information on animal husbandry regimes. The carcasses of sacrificial animals were treated in a different way from animals butchered in a settlement context. After the animal was killed, the thigh bones and tail of the sacrificial animal were burnt on the altar as a gift to the gods, which means that these elements are usually completely burnt and missing among the food remains. This practice is known from literary and iconographic sources and supported by zooarchaeological studies (e.g. Groot 2014). Most of the meat was prepared for communal meals, chopped into small pieces and stewed so that differences in the quality of the meat would be obscured (Ekroth 2008a, 2008b).

FIGURE 19.2 Attic red-figure bell *krater* showing a sacrificial animal being led to the altar, produced at Athens *c.*450–425 BC. Although the vessel belongs to the classical period, the elements of the sacrifice had not changed.

Photo: © Collection Allard Pierson Museum Amsterdam

A different kind of ritual, which did not include meat consumption, is seen on Cyprus in the eighth to seventh centuries BC, where pairs of horses were sacrificed and buried together with chariots in chamber tombs. In less wealthy graves, donkeys instead of horses are found (Kosmetatou 1993).

Although there were cultural differences as well as differences in environment and climate between different parts of Greece, the available data set for the Iron Age is too small to be divided into regions. The Greek Iron Age covers two main periods: the early Iron Age (*c.*1100–700 BC) and the Archaic period (*c.*700–480 BC). Sheep or goats dominate in the majority of cases; at most sites they represent more than two-thirds of the main domestic livestock. Cattle are the dominant species in the settlement of Nichoria and the sanctuary of Hera on Samos (Sloan and Duncan 1978; Boessneck and von den Driesch 1988). While pig is the most common animal in the sanctuary at Messene, it is closely followed by cattle (Nobis 1997).

In most assemblages, either sheep or goat is dominant (this occurs in roughly equal numbers), but at a minority of sites, the proportions are more or less equal. Overall, this suggests that while there may be a preference for one species in certain sanctuaries, their importance to the agrarian economy was similar. There seems to have been a shift over time from an emphasis on goat in the Geometric period (early Iron Age) to one on sheep in the Archaic period. Sheep and goats were slaughtered both young and as adults. Many sites seem to show a preference for one of these broad age categories. In the Geometric period, there are more sites with a preference for younger animals, whereas in the Archaic period more sites preferred to slaughter adult sheep. Only the Heraion shows a dominance of females; in the other sites both sexes are represented. The adult sheep would have provided wool and milk before slaughter, while the younger animals would have been raised just for meat.

Cattle were mostly killed as young adults or adults. As with sheep and goats, a shift to older animals is noticeable in the Archaic period. In the Heraion, there was a clear preference for cows, while both sexes were present at Kalapodi (Stanzel 1991). Most pigs were killed at ages below two years. Just as for the other species, female pigs were selected for the Heraion. Horses and donkeys are present in settlements and some sanctuaries, but only in very small proportions. Dogs are present at most sites, but always in small numbers. Evidence for the consumption of dog meat was found in the Archaic sanctuary at Eretria (Studer and Chenal-Velarde 2003). Animal bones sometimes show evidence for long-distance connections, such as the hippopotamus teeth and crocodile skull found in the Heraion on Samos (Boessneck and von den Driesch 1988). In the two sites in modern Turkey, camel and dromedary were present (Peters and von den Driesch 1992; Bammer 1998: 38–39; Forstenpointner 2003).

Animal bone data clearly show the importance of sheep and goats in the pastoral economy. While cultural preference may have played a role, the undemanding nature of sheep and goats and their adaptation to upland and dry areas were certainly important factors. The roughly equal proportions of sheep and goats and the slaughter of adult animals suggest that wool and milk were important products. Dairy products, especially cheese, may have provided more calories in the diet than meat (Payne 1985: table 5; Jameson 1988: 103). While the climate and geography make it likely that transhumance was practised, there is little evidence for this. However, transhumance could have taken place over short distances, with herds being grazed on communal pastures (Skydsgaard 1988). While in northern Europe, autumn is the time for slaughter, since winter is a time when grazing is scarce, in the Mediterranean animals were culled in late spring, since here the heat and drought of summer limited the availability of pasture (Jameson 1988: 100). Pigs require woodland or fodder, which can be waste from arable farming and horticulture. They were probably kept in small numbers. Horses, donkeys, and mules were used as pack or riding animals and to thresh crops. Cattle were prestigious as animal sacrifices, but their main role was as plough animals. In fact, the number of plough animals was one of the factors that determined how much arable land could be cultivated (Foxhall 2003). Cattle thrive best in lowland areas with good grazing, which were limited in Greece.

A Complex Society at the Heart of Iron Age Europe

Modern Austria lies at the heart of the Hallstatt and La Tène area. Society here was more complex than in some other regions of Europe, with a variety of sites: agrarian settlements, cemeteries, industrial salt-mining centres, and large proto-urban centres. People working and living in the last two types of site were partly or wholly dependent on others for their food, and there is indeed evidence for both long-distance trade and local food supply. Salt mining in the Alps started in the late Bronze Age. Salt was important in preserving perishable foods. Since a considerable investment of time was needed before the salt was reached, salt mining required a developed and stable political system, and the ability to provide food for the miners (Stöllner 2003: 128).

In recent years, several large animal bone assemblages dating to the Hallstatt and La Tène periods have been analysed and published in detail. Cattle are the dominant species in most assemblages, sheep and goats in a handful, and pigs in just one. However, only in two cases does the dominant species (cattle in this case) represent more than two-thirds of the bones of the four main domesticates. Sheep are much more common than goats, with a ratio of goat to sheep of 1:7. Horses, dogs, and wild mammals are generally unimportant with regard to numbers (less than 5%), but there are a few exceptions, including the large sanctuary at Roseldorf where the proportion of horse bones is as high as 11% (Abd el Karem 2011). There is an explanation for this: cattle and horses were selected for ritual treatment in this sanctuary. Meat from horses and dogs was consumed, but since these two species were not very common, their meat was not eaten as regularly as that of the other animals.

The Dürrnberg has provided much information on Iron Age salt mining. The total number of people working in and around the Dürrnberg mine has been estimated at around 200. To feed these people, one cow a day had to be slaughtered (Stöllner 2003: 136–138). Nowhere else in the region is such a high proportion of cattle found (80%). The cattle reached the Dürrnberg on the hoof, where they were slaughtered. It is possible that some of the meat was preserved with salt from the mine, to be traded regionally and long-distance (Stöllner 2003: 164, 179). The absence of young cattle confirms that livestock was not raised locally; most of the cattle were young adult cows. The dominance of cows fits with the traditional alpine focus on milk production, but the increase in oxen over time attests to a growing demand for beef (Stöllner 2003: 166).

Another important site is Roseldorf-Sandberg, an extensive open site in lowland Austria, where parts of the settlement and the sanctuaries have been excavated. The cattle supplied to the inhabitants were mostly oxen, and younger than in farming sites (Bruckner-Höbling and Pucher 2008). Pigs, sheep, and goats were still kept in the settlement, but cattle were not raised by the people living in Roseldorf. This reflects the urban character of the site. In the agrarian sites, cattle were mainly slaughtered as adults, and cows outnumbered oxen. Bulls were only ever kept in small numbers, since not many are needed to safeguard the next generation. Sheep and goats were slaughtered young or as (young) adults. The sex ratio for sheep and goats seems to have been balanced, which, together with the slaughter ages, suggests a combined exploitation for meat, milk, and wool. Pigs were mostly slaughtered as young adults. The cemeteries do not show a clear selection of species that deviates from that found in the other sites (Schmitzberger 2006; Abd el Karem 2012).

Contacts with the Mediterranean world are visible from an early time, and not just in material culture (e.g. Attic pottery, Etruscan flagons, and a coin from Massalia, all found on the Dürrnberg; Stöllner 2003: 183), but also in herbs (aniseed on the Dürrnberg; Stöllner 2003: 149, and dill in Roseldorf; Abd el Karem 2011: 78) and animals. Chickens are already present at some Hallstatt-period sites, while a large, foreign type of cattle, presumably imported from Italy, is found in the large sanctuary of Roseldorf (Abd el Karem 2011: 26). Amber, found on the Dürrnberg, shows that contacts did not just reach south, but also north, to the Baltic (Stöllner 2003: 178).

THE EASTERN IBERIAN PENINSULA: SPECIALIZATION, TRADE, AND RITUAL DEPOSITS

In the Iron Age, the region of Valencia in the eastern Iberian Peninsula was characterized by a highly urbanized and socially stratified society (Iborra Eres and Pérez Jordà 2013). The Iberian culture spans the period from the sixth to the first century BC (Chapter 10). There were contacts with Phoenician and Greek colonists, and a certain degree of integration into Mediterranean trade routes. Sites include *oppida*, small towns, hillforts, hamlets, and farmsteads. Trading sites were mostly located on the coast. Generally, mixed farming was practised, with some specialization in wine and olive oil. The large wine and olive presses that have been found in coastal sites indicate the scale of production, and the local manufacture of amphorae indicate that wine and olive oil were produced for export. Inland, a different situation is found. The *oppidum* of La Bastida de les Alcusses had a population of *c*.450 to 840 people, and was occupied in the fifth and fourth centuries BC. Agriculture here was aimed at self-sufficiency. Cereals dominated among the crops, which can partly be related to the rich soils in the vicinity. Livestock was mainly exploited for secondary products, i.e. products that are provided by the living animal, such as milk and wool. Grapes and olives were cultivated, but processed at a much smaller scale than on the coast. The territory of Edeta has a hierarchy of sites, which were largely self-sufficient, but show some division in specialization, with oil, wine, and cured pork as trade products. Sites produced either wine or olive oil and presumably traded among one another. The animal bone data set for Valencia is quite rich, and includes assemblages from various types of site dated from the eighth to first centuries BC (von den Driesch 1973; Iborra Eres 2004; Pérez Jordà et al. 2007).

The strength of recent research in this area is the integration with the archaeobotanical information.

The island of Mallorca was characterized in the Iron Age by the Talaiot society. Social differentiation did not play a role until the end of the Iron Age (Valenzuela et al. 2013). Trade started in the seventh century BC, when a Carthaginian colony was founded nearby, but only really took off from the fourth century BC. Subsistence farming, with pastoralism of sheep and goats, is believed to have been the main farming strategy on Iron Age Mallorca, although mixed farming may also have occurred.

Sheep and goats are the dominant species in nearly all sites in Valencia and Mallorca. On Mallorca, they account for more than two-thirds of fragments in most cases; for Valencia numbers are slightly lower in general. The high proportion of sheep and goats on Mallorca may be related more to the limits of the environment than to any conscious choice (Valenzuela et al. 2013: 214). Overall, sheep is about twice as common as goat in Valencia. However, there is considerable variation between individual sites. There does not seem to be any relationship between the proportions of goat and sheep and the date of the assemblage. High proportions of goat from a site in Toscanos, Andalucia, have been interpreted as an indication of the presence of a non-agrarian class, keeping goats on the side (Uerpmann and Uerpmann 1973).

The differences in proportions of sheep and goat alone suggest variability in the exploitation of small ruminants. Slaughter ages provide more information for Valencia. Although there are a few sites with mainly slaughter of either young or adult sheep and goats, most show a mixture of young and older animals. The adults reached ages of up to ten years in some cases, which indicates that secondary products were important. Since sheep is the commoner species, wool is the most likely secondary product, but goats are likely to have been milked. On Mallorca, a mixed exploitation of sheep and goats for meat, wool, and milk has been suggested, with an increased emphasis on dairy and wool in the late Iron Age (Valenzuela et al. 2013: 216–217). There is little information on slaughter ages of cattle and pigs, but it is likely that cattle were used for traction, while pigs were kept for their meat.

Hunting was more important in Valencia than in other parts of Europe, with about a third of sites in Valencia showing proportions of wild mammals over 15%. Red deer, hares, and rabbits form the main prey. Hunting is likely to have been carried out for food, but may also have been done to protect crops from damage. Finds of mature male red deer at some sites are suggestive of trophy hunting (Iborra Eres and Pérez Jordà 2013).

The Iberian culture is also found in present-day Catalonia. This region has yielded evidence for the ritual use of animals (Carme Belarte and Valenzuela-Lamas 2013). Deposits of animal remains were found in domestic contexts in towns, villages, and *oppida*. The remains were buried below the house floor and close to a wall, usually in a small pit. In most cases, deposits consist of sheep remains, but goats, dogs, pigs, and chickens are also found. The sheep are mostly young, younger than in domestic food waste from the same sites. The deposits show clear patterning of anatomical elements, with three types occurring: head and feet (Figure 19.3), complete skeletons, and

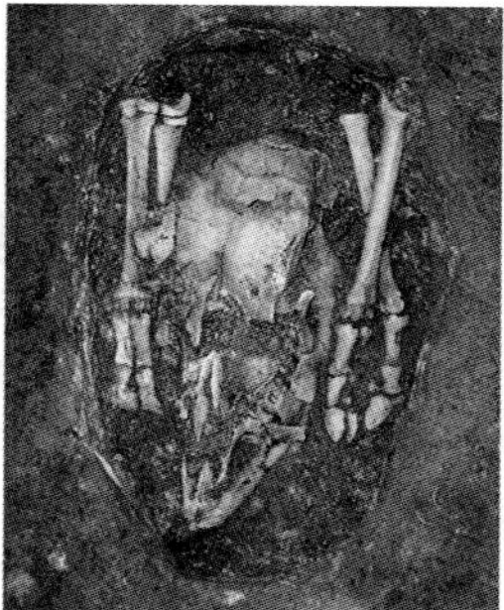

FIGURE 19.3 Three ritual deposits of a sheep's head and feet, Alorda Park, Catalonia, fifth to fourth centuries BC.

Source: Carme Belarte and Valenzuela-Lamas 2013

skeletons without the head and feet. The deposits have been interpreted as a reflection of propitiatory ritual or working feasts.

Subsistence in the Lowlands

Iron Age society in the river area of the Netherlands was very different from that in the regions discussed so far: it was mostly egalitarian, with perhaps a local elite, but no clear settlement hierarchy and no distinction between farmers and consumers. There was some exchange of goods, but this was limited and focused on luxury items rather than food. Farming was aimed at subsistence, and while arable farming and animal husbandry were combined, there seems to have been an emphasis on raising livestock. This is easy to understand when the local environmental conditions are taken into account: before dykes were built to control the rivers, they regularly flooded and changed their course. The area of land suitable for growing crops was limited, but the flood basins—which could be flooded in winter but were dry in summer—offered large areas of rich grassland (Groot and Kooistra 2009).

Cattle is the dominant species in all animal bone assemblages from the river area, and accounts for over two-thirds of fragments in half the cases. Sheep or goat is the second most common species, and played a significant role on some sites. Liver fluke, a parasite which occurs in damp (freshwater) pasture and affects the health of sheep, is sometimes given as an explanation for low proportions of sheep or goats. In the Dutch river area, however, the parasite clearly did not stop people from keeping sheep. Pigs were kept in small numbers. This could be related to a lack of woodland, as oak and beech provide mast in the autumn on which pigs can be fattened. When such woodland is not available, pigs can be fed on crops or waste from crop processing. In the first case, enough crops have to be grown to feed both pigs and people. The limits on arable farming may not have allowed this. Alternatively, the relative lack of pigs could be due to cultural preferences.

The typical house found in the region is the byre-house, divided into a stable and a section for people (Figure 19.4). Cattle and perhaps other livestock as well were stabled. One reason to stable animals is to collect the manure (Zimmermann 1999). Living under one roof with one's cattle also suggests a strong symbolic connection between human and animal. Cattle were not just of economic importance, but also played an important role in social transactions (Roymans 1999). The cattle bones are mostly from adult cows, with some younger animals. This would suggest that milk was an important product. However, while interpretations of age and sex are usually concerned with rational, economic decisions, other factors should also be considered. If cattle were used as exchange items in social transactions, then their value would be as living animals rather than meat or producers of milk (van Dijk and Groot 2013). It is likely that cattle had an intrinsic value, and sustaining the herd would be the first aim. At the same time, cows were milked and manure was collected. Young males as well as adult cows were occasionally killed for their meat. Another factor that would have influenced decisions

FIGURE 19.4 A byre-house excavated at Ezinge, northern Netherlands, showing the stable section with cattle stalls.

Photo: © Rijksuniversiteit Groningen, Groninger Instituut voor Archeologie on whether to slaughter a cow is the small size of the communities in this region. Cattle may have been slaughtered only at gatherings of people, where the large amount of meat would not go to waste. Preserving meat is possible, but would require large quantities of salt.

Goats were rare in this region, and sheep were killed at all ages, which indicates a mixed exploitation for meat, milk, and wool. Sheep would provide a more manageable supply of meat for a small community. Horses are found in larger numbers than in other parts of Europe (but never make up more than 20% of fragments) and several sites have yielded evidence for the consumption of horsemeat. Hunting is negligible in the river area, with wild mammals accounting for less than 1% of animal bones in general.

We have no information on funerary ritual for the river area, but a number of late Iron Age cemeteries have been excavated not far to the south in modern Noord-Brabant and Noord-Limburg. Since the sandy soils here do not preserve animal bones well, the only information comes from cremated bones found in graves. Only part of the population ended up in graves. Pottery (probably filled with food or drink) and portions of meat were placed on the funeral pyre and burnt together with the body. After the cremation some of the cremated human and animal remains and often also burnt pottery sherds and charcoal were buried in a pit (Hiddink 2003). Complete pottery vessels that had not been on the pyre were often placed in the burial pit. It is possible that unburnt portions of meat were also buried; no trace of them has been preserved in the sandy soils, but this practice is known from Roman funerary ritual in the river area (Groot 2008). In the late Iron Age, pig is the species most commonly found in cremation burials, followed by sheep. Cattle are rarely found, and only one case of cremated horse bones is known (Groot and Hiddink 2008). The preference for pigs and sheep in funerary ritual continues into the Roman period, and is then also found in the river area (Groot 2008). The body part that was placed on the pyre is most often the hind leg, probably because it carried a lot of meat. There was no preference for either the left or right side.

Conclusion

Iron Age society in Europe was overwhelmingly agrarian: there were towns in some regions, but the majority of people were farmers. Mixed farming was practised, with crops and livestock complementing and supporting each other. Animal husbandry is characterized by a high degree of variety, which can be related to differences in climate, geography, and the complexity of society. The main animal species were cattle, pigs, sheep, and goats, with the proportions varying between regions. Cattle were the most common species in northern Europe, while sheep and goats dominated in many Mediterranean regions. Pigs and sheep or goats were mainly kept for their meat and therefore generally slaughtered young, while the older slaughter ages of cattle indicate their importance for traction, milk, and as exchange items. Meat from dogs and horses was consumed in parts of Europe, but only supplied a small proportion of the total meat consumed. Hunting was of little importance for food supply, but probably carried important symbolic associations. There is some evidence for the movement of animals or animal parts, such as livestock that is larger than the local animals and the presence of exotic animals. Animals also played a role in ritual, from domestic rituals involving burial of sheep body parts under house floors to animal sacrifice and ritual meals in sanctuaries. The use of animals in funerary ritual is diverse, and includes the burial of whole animals in tombs and the burning of meaty parts on the funeral pyre. A link between chickens and funerary ritual is seen in several regions. Animals played a large role in the daily life of Iron Age people, as their agrarian economy and diet depended on them, but their meaning went beyond that, as animals were also used for sacrifice.

References

Abd el Karem, M. 2011. 'Analyse der Tierreste aus dem Objekt 1 ('Großes Heiligtum') der mittellatènezeitlichen Siedlung Roseldorf-Sandberg (NÖ) und Überlegungen zum frühen Erscheinen italischer Rinder nördlich der Alpen'. Diplomarbeit, Universität Wien.

Abd el Karem, M. 2012. 'Die Tierknochenfunde', in G. Tiefengraber and K. Wiltschke-Schrotta (eds) *Der Dürrnberg bei Hallein: Die Gräbergruppe Moserfeld-Osthang*. Dürrnberg-Forschungen 6: 331–339. Rahden: Marie Leidorf.

Bammer, A. 1998. 'Sanctuaries in the Artemision of Ephesus', in R. Hägg (ed.) *Ancient Greek Cult Practice from the Archaeological Evidence. Proceedings of the Fourth International Seminar on Ancient Greek Cult, organized by the Swedish Institute at Athens, 22–24 October 1993. Skrifter Utgivna av Svenska Institutet i Athen 8–15*: 38–39. Stockholm: Svenska Institutet i Athen.

Bartosiewicz, L., and E. Gál. 2010. 'Living on the frontier: "Scythian" and "Celtic" animal exploitation in Iron Age northeastern Hungary', in D. V. Campana, P. Crabtree, S. D. deFrance, J. Lev-Tov, and A. M. Choyke (eds) *Anthropological Approaches to Zooarchaeology: Colonialism, Complexity and Animal Transformations*: 115–127. Oxford: Oxbow.

Benecke, N. 1994. *Archäozoologische Studien zur Entwicklung der Haustierhaltung in Mitteleuropa und Südskandinavien von den Anfängen bis zum ausgehenden Mittelalter*. Schriften zur Ur- und Frühgeschichte 46. Berlin: De Gruyter.

Boessneck, J., and A. von den Driesch. 1988. *Knochenabfall von Opfermahlen und Weihgaben aus dem Heraion von Samos (7. Jh. V. Chr.)*. Munich: Institut für Palaeoanatomie, Domestikationsforschung und Geschichte der Tiermedizin der Universität München.

Boessneck, J., A. von den Driesch, U. Meyer-Lemppenau, and E. Wechsler-von Ohlen. 1971. *Die Tierknochenfunde aus dem Oppidum von Manching*. Die Ausgrabungen in Manching 6. Wiesbaden: Steiner.

Bökönyi, S. 1964. 'Angaben zur Kenntnis der Eisenzeitlichen Pferde in Mittel- und Osteuropa'. *Acta Archaeologica Academiae Scientiarum Hungaricae* 16: 227–239.

Bruckner-Höbling, T., and E. Pucher. 2008. 'Vom Knochenmüll zum Leben in der Keltenstadt von Roseldorf (Niederösterreich)', in E. Lauermann and P. Trebsche (eds) *Heiligtümer der Druiden: Opfer und Rituale bei den Kelten*. Katalog des Niederösterreichischen Landesmuseums Neue Folge 474: 71–83. Asparn/Zaya: Niederösterreichisches Landesmuseum.

Carme Belarte, M., and S. Valenzuela-Lamas. 2013. 'Zooarchaeological evidence for domestic rituals in the Iron Age communities of north-eastern Iberia (present-day Catalonia) (sixth–second century BC)'. *Oxford Journal of Archaeology* 32, 2: 163–186.

Detienne, M. 1989. 'Culinary practices and the spirit of sacrifice', in M. Detienne and J. P. Vernant (eds) *The Cuisine of Sacrifice among the Greeks*: 1–20. Chicago/London: University of Chicago Press.

Dobney, K., and A. Ervynck. 2007. 'To fish or not to fish? Evidence for the possible avoidance of fish consumption during the Iron Age around the North Sea', in C. Haselgrove and T. Moore (eds) *The Later Iron Age in Britain and Beyond*: 403–418. Oxford: Oxbow Books.

Dütting, M. K., and P. van Rijn. 2017. 'Wickerwork fish traps from the Roman period in the Netherlands', in T. Kaszab-Olschewski and I. Tamerl (eds) *Wald- und Holznutzung in der römischen Antike*. Archäologische Berichte 27: 37–59. Kerpen-Loogh: Deutschen Gesellschaft für Ur- und Frühgeschichte e.V.

Ekroth, G. 2007. 'Meat in ancient Greece: sacrificial, sacred or secular?' *Food and History* 5, 1: 249–272.

Ekroth, G. 2008a. 'Burnt, cooked or raw? Divine and human culinary desires at Greek animal sacrifice', in E. Stavrianopoulou, A. Michaels, and C. Ambos (eds) *Transformations in Sacrificial Practices from Antiquity to Modern Times*: 87–111. Berlin: LIT Verlag.

Ekroth, G. 2008b. 'Meat, man and god. On the division of the animal victim at Greek sacrifices', in A. P. Matthaiou and I. Polinskaya (eds) *Mikros hieromnemon: Meletes eis mnemen Michael H. Jameson*: 259–290. Athens: Greek Epigraphical Society.

Forstenpointner, G. 2003. 'Promethean legacy: investigations into the ritual procedure of "Olympian" sacrifice', in E. Kotjabopoulou, Y. Hamilakis, P. Halstead, C. Gamble, and P. Elefanti (eds) *Zooarchaeology in Greece: Recent Advances*. British School at Athens Studies 9: 203–213. Athens: British School at Athens.

Foxhall, L. 2003. 'Cultures, landscapes, and identities in the Mediterranean world'. *Mediterranean Historical Review* 18, 2: 75–92.

Groenman-van Waateringe, W. 2002. 'Haut- und Fellreste vom Dürrnberg', in C. Dobiat, S. Sievers, and T. Stöllner (eds) *Dürrnberg und Manching: Wirtschaftsarchäologie im ostkeltischen Raum. Akten des internationalen Kolloquiums in Hallein/Bad Dürrnberg vom 7. bis 11. Oktober 1998*. Kolloquien zur Vor- und Frühgeschichte 7: 117–122. Bonn: Habelt.

Groot, M. 2008. *Animals in Ritual and Economy in a Roman Frontier Community. Excavations in Tiel-Passewaaij*. Amsterdam Archaeological Studies 12. Amsterdam: Amsterdam University Press.

Groot, M. 2014. 'Burned offerings and sacrificial meals in Geometric and Archaic Karystos. Faunal remains from Plakari (2011–2012)'. *Pharos* 20, 2: 25–52.

Groot, M., and H. Hiddink. 2008. 'Dierlijk bot', in H. Hiddink (ed.) *Bewoningssporen uit de Vroege IJzertijd en een grafveld uit de Late IJzertijd te Panningen-Stokx, gemeente Helden*. Zuidnederlandse Archeologische Rapporten 32: 43–50. Amsterdam: Archeologisch Instituut Vrije Universiteit.

Groot, M., and L. I. Kooistra. 2009. 'Land use and the agrarian economy in the Roman Dutch River Area'. *Internet Archaeology* 27. Available at http://intarch.ac.uk/journal/issue27/5/1.html [accessed 16 May 2018].

Hiddink, H. A. 2003. *Het grafritueel in de Late IJzertijd en Romeinse tijd in het Maas-Demer-Scheldegebied, in het bijzonder van twee grafvelden bij Weert*. Amsterdam: Archeologisch Instituut Vrije Universiteit.

Iborra Eres, M. P. 2004. *La ganadería y la caza desde el Bronce Final hasta el Ibérico Final en el territorio Valenciano*. Valencia: Servicio de investigación prehistórica, Diputación provincial de Valencia.

Iborra Eres, M. P., and G. Pérez Jordà. 2013. 'Three systems of agrarian exploitation in the Valencian region of Spain (400–300 BC)', in M. Groot, D. Lentjes, and J. Zeiler (eds) *Barely Surviving or More than Enough?: The Environmental Archaeology of Subsistence, Specialisation and Surplus Food Production*: 131–150. Leiden: Sidestone Press.

Jameson, M. H. 1988. 'Sacrifice and animal husbandry in Classical Greece', in C. R. Whittaker (ed.) *Pastoral Economies in Classical Antiquity*: 87–119. Cambridge: Cambridge Philological Society.

Kooistra, L. I. 2015. *Botanische resten uit de IJzertijd en Romeinse tijd van Houten Castellum*. BIAXiaal 855. Zaandam: BIAX Consult.

Kosmetatou, E. 1993. 'Horse sacrifices in Greece and Cyprus'. *Journal of Prehistoric Religion* 7: 31–41.

Méniel, P. 1987a. *Chasse et élevage chez les Gaulois*. Paris: Errance.

Méniel, P. 1987b. 'L'élevage en Gaule: les structures de l'élevage en France septentrionale à la fin de l'âge du Fer'. *Archaeozoologia* 1, 2: 149–166.

Moser, B. 1986. 'Die Tierknochenfunde aus dem latènezeitlichen Oppidum von Altenburg-Rheinau. I. Charakterisierung des Fundgutes. Pferd, Hund, Hausgeflügel und Wildtiere'. PhD dissertation, Ludwig-Maximilians-Universität München.

Nobis, G. 1997. 'Tieropfer aus einem Heroen- und Demeterheiligtum des antiken Messene (SW-Peloponnes, Griechenland)—Grabungen 1992 bis 1996'. *Tier und Museum* 5, 4: 97–111.

Payne, S. 1985. 'Zooarchaeology in Greece: a reader's guide', in N. C. Wilkie and W. D. E. Coulson (eds) *Contributions to Aegean Archaeology: Studies in Honor of William A. McDonald*: 211–244. Dubuque: Kendall/Hunt.

Pérez Jordà, G., N. Alonso Martínez, and M. P. Iborra Eres. 2007. 'Agricultura y ganadería protohistóricas en la península Ibérica: modelos de gestión', in A. Rodríguez Díaz and I. Pavón Soldevilla (eds) *Arqueología de la tierra: Paisajes rurales de la protohistoria peninsular*: 327–373. Cáceres: Universidad de Extremadura.

Peters, J., and A. von den Driesch. 1992. 'Siedlungsabfall versus Opferreste: Essgewohnheiten im archaischen Milet'. *Istanbuler Mitteilungen* 42: 117–125.

Prummel, W. 2008. 'Dieren op de wierde Englum', in A. Nieuwhof (ed.) *De Leege Wier van Englum: Archeologisch onderzoek in het Reitdiepgebied*. Jaarverslagen van de Vereniging voor Terpenonderzoek 91: 116–159. Groningen: Vereniging voor Terpenonderzoek.

Roymans, N. 1999. 'Man, cattle and the supernatural in the Northwest European plain', in C. Fabech and J. Ringtved (eds) *Settlement and Landscape: Proceedings of a Conference in Århus, Denmark, May 4–7 1998*: 291–300. Højberg: Jutland Archaeological Society.

Schibler, J., B. Stopp, and J. Studer. 1999. 'Haustierhaltung und Jagd—Élevage et chasse', in F. Müller, G. Kaenel, and G. Lüscher (eds) *Die Schweiz vom Paläolithikum bis zum frühen Mittelalter IV: Eisenzeit*: 116–136. Basel: Schweizerische Gesellschaft für Ur- und Frühgeschichte.

Schmitzberger, M. 2006. 'Tierknochen aus dem hallstattzeitlichen Gräberfeld von Statzendorf, NÖ', in K. C. Rebay (ed.) *Das hallstattzeitliche Gräberfeld von Statzendorf, Niederösterreich*. Universitätsforschungen zur Prähistorischen Archäologie 135: 342–355. Bonn: Rudolf Habelt.

Skydsgaard, J. E. 1988. 'Transhumance in ancient Greece', in C. R. Whittaker (ed.) *Pastoral Economies in Classical Antiquity*: 75–86. Cambridge: Cambridge Philological Society.

Sloan, R. E., and M. A. Duncan. 1978. 'Zooarchaeology of Nichoria', in G. Rapp and S. E. Aschenbrenner (eds) *Excavations at Nichoria in Southwest Greece, Vol. 1: Site, Environs, and Techniques*: 60–77. Minneapolis: University of Minnesota Press.

Stanzel, M. 1991. 'Die Tierreste aus dem Artemis-Apollon-Heiligtum bei Kalapodi in Böotien/ Griechenland'. PhD dissertation, Ludwig-Maximilians-Universität München.

Stöllner, T. 2003. 'The economy of Dürrnberg-bei-Hallein: An Iron Age salt mining centre in the Austrian Alps'. *The Antiquaries Journal* 183: 123–194.

Studer, J., and I. Chenal-Velarde. 2003. 'La part des dieux et celle des hommes: offrandes d'animaux et restes culinaires dans l'aire sacrificielle nord', in S. Huber (ed.) *L'aire sacrificielle au nord du sanctuaire d'Apollon Daphnéphoros*. Eretria 14: 175–184. Gollion: Infolio.

Uerpmann, H.-P., and M. Uerpmann. 1973. 'Tierknochenfunde aus der phönizischen Faktorei von Toscanos und anderen phönizisch beeinflussten Fundorten der Provinz Málaga in Südspanien'. *Studien über frühe Tierknochenfunde von der Iberischen Halbinsel* 4: 35–100.

Uerpmann, M., and H.-P. Uerpmann. 2006. 'Hallstattzeitliche Berufsfischer am Federsee?', in H.-P. Wotzka (ed.) *Grundlegungen:Beiträge zur europäischen und afrikanischen Archäologie für Manfred K. H. Eggert*: 541–549. Tübingen: Francke.

Valenzuela, A., J. A. Alcover, and M. A. Cau. 2013. 'Tracing changes in animal husbandry in Mallorca (Balearic Islands, Western Mediterranean) from the Iron Age to the Roman period', in M. Groot, D. Lentjes, and J. Zeiler (eds) *Barely Surviving or More than Enough?: The Environmental Archaeology of Subsistence, Specialisation and Surplus Food Production*: 201–223. Leiden: Sidestone Press.

Van Dijk, J., and M. Groot. 2013. 'The late Iron Age–Roman transformation from subsistence to surplus production in animal husbandry in the central and western parts of the Netherlands', in M. Groot, D. Lentjes, and J. Zeiler (eds) *Barely Surviving or More than Enough?: The Environmental Archaeology of Subsistence, Specialisation and Surplus Food Production*: 175–200. Leiden: Sidestone Press.

Villari, P. 1991. 'The faunal remains in the bothros at Eolo (Lipari)'. *Archaeozoologia* 4, 2: 109–126.

Von den Driesch, A. 1973. 'Nahrungsreste tierischer Herkunft aus einer tartessischen und einer spätbronzezeitlichen bis iberischen Siedlung in Südspanien'. *Studien über frühe Tierknochenfunde von der Iberischen Halbinsel* 4: 9–31.

Von den Driesch, A., and J. Boessneck. 1989. 'Abschlußbericht über die zooarchäologischen Untersuchungen an Tierknochenfunden von der Heuneburg', in E. Gersbach (ed.) *Ausgrabungsmethodik und Stratigraphie der Heuneburg: Heuneburgstudien VI*. Römisch-Germanische Forschungen 45: 131–157. Mainz: Philipp von Zabern.

Zimmermann, W. H. 1999. 'Stallhaltung und Auswinterung der Haustiere in ur- und frühgeschichtlicher Zeit'. *Beiträge zur Mittelalterarchäologie in Österreich* 15: 27–33.

CHAPTER 20

HOUSEHOLDS AND COMMUNITIES

LEO WEBLEY

Introduction

The household and the local community were fundamental building blocks of Iron Age societies. They provided the context for much of daily life, and were arguably the social arenas with the greatest day-to-day significance for Iron Age people. Recent years have seen increasing interest in exploring the social dynamics of the household and the local community, providing a challenge to traditional narratives of social change during the Iron Age, in which these spheres are often portrayed as peripheral or irrelevant. This chapter will examine how the household and the community were constituted in different Iron Age societies, and attempt to grasp their internal social relations. Evidence will be drawn mainly from the ways that people ordered and inhabited their houses and settlements. The picture that emerges is one of great regional diversity and change through time.

Domestic Architecture

Iron Age settlement evidence is abundant across much of Europe, although superstructural remains of houses are largely confined to areas where stone was used as a building material. As a result, our perspective on domestic architecture is inevitably a little two-dimensional. Contemporary artistic representations of houses are available in only a few regions, such as Italy and Greece (e.g. Bartoloni et al. 1987; Schattner 1990), and even here it is questionable whether the form of real domestic buildings was faithfully reproduced. Parallels from historical vernacular architecture have been used to interpret Iron Age house construction in some regions, on the assumption that continuity in building techniques is likely (e.g. Črešnar 2007), though there is clearly a danger here of creating an anachronistically timeless image of rural life. Experimental reconstruction has also been used to elucidate the technical challenges involved in building an Iron Age house (e.g. Draiby 1991).

Although many Iron Age houses were simple single-roomed structures, more elaborate or even monumental buildings were also constructed in some places. While there is enormous regional and chronological variation across Europe in house forms, building materials, and constructional techniques, a few broad trends can be highlighted here.

In the Mediterranean region, houses at the beginning of the Iron Age were often small, single-roomed, and subcircular or apsidal in plan, with wattle-and-daub or mud walls and thatched roofs (Figure 20.1, 1–2). Over time, there was a shift to rectilinear plans, and larger multi-roomed houses appeared, in some cases arranged around an open courtyard (Figure 20.1, 3). Such developments can be seen from the late eighth century BC in Greece (Lang 2007; Mazarakis Ainian 2001), from the seventh/sixth century BC in parts of Italy (e.g. Izzet 2001), and from the sixth/fifth century BC onwards in southern France and eastern Iberia (Belarte 2009, 2010). These changes were associated with increased use of mud brick and stone as building materials, with tiled roofs also appearing in some areas.

Across much of temperate continental Europe, the typical Iron Age house was a rectangular structure with timber or wattle-and-daub walls and a thatched roof. Often the roof was supported by one or more rows of internal posts, creating an aisled layout of internal space (Figure 20.2, 1), while in other cases the wall posts were the load-bearing element. Some other houses had load-bearing walls incorporating a sill beam (Figure 20.2, 2), or formed of jointed horizontal timbers (the *Blockbau* technique). The latter method is spectacularly illustrated by the waterlogged buildings at the pile settlement of Donja Dolina in Bosnia-Herzegovina (Truhelka 1904) and at the Biskupin lake village in Poland, where houses had a raised loft (Rajewski 1959). *Blockbau* houses are particularly common in the Alpine regions, where the timbers were often placed on a drystone wall foundation. Examples include the 'Raetian' houses of the eastern Alps, which often had two storeys: a sunken stone-walled cellar accessed by a covered passageway, and an upper living area (Migliavacca 1993). Sunken-featured buildings (SFBs; *Grubenhäuser*) are also found at many settlements in central and eastern Europe, especially in the La Tène period, and spread further across northern Europe during the first millennium AD. These fairly small, rectangular buildings were partially sunken into the ground. They have often been seen as ancillary buildings used for crafts such as weaving. However, in some parts of central and eastern Europe evidence for buildings other than SFBs is scarce (e.g. Michałowski 2010). It is uncertain whether SFBs were the normal form of dwelling in these areas, or the remains of surface-level buildings have simply not survived.

Further north, the region stretching from the Rhine delta through north-west Germany to southern and central Scandinavia was dominated by aisled longhouses (Figure 20.2, 3; Brabandt 1993; Meyer 2010). These were built of timber or wattle and daub, sometimes with an outer wall layer of turf or stone. During the pre-Roman Iron

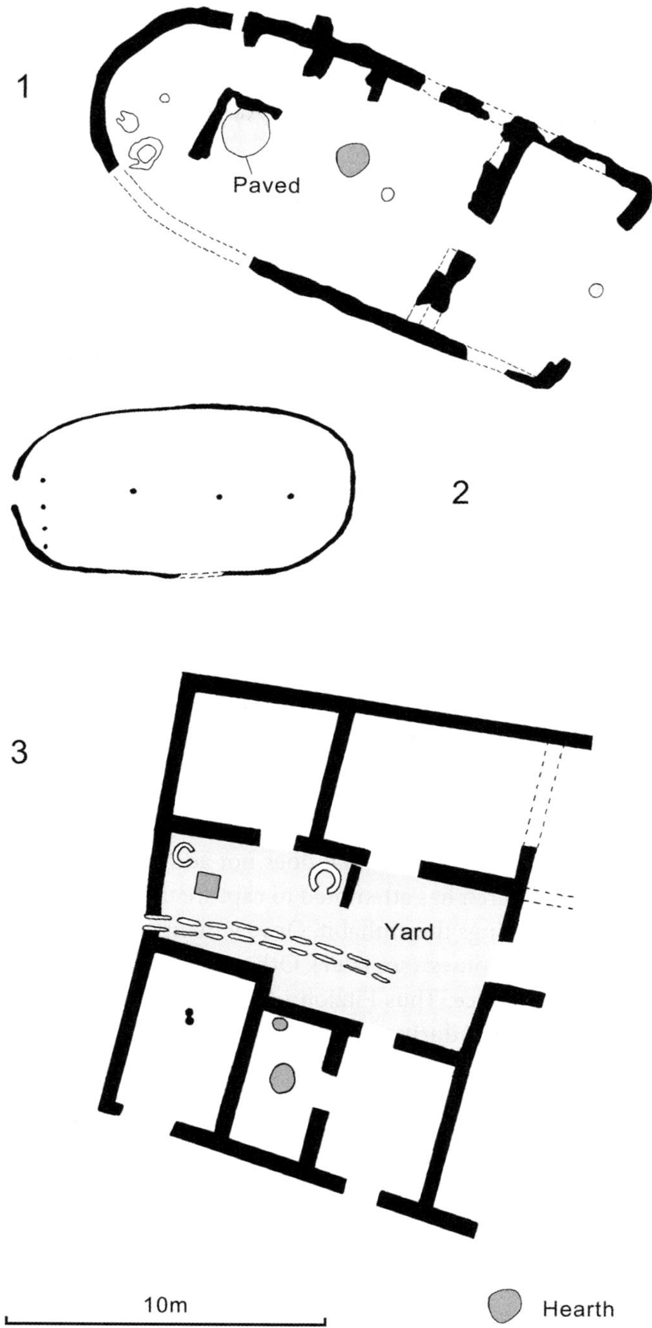

FIGURE 20.1 Iron Age houses from Mediterranean Europe. 1 Nichoria, Greece, ninth century BC. 2 San Giovenale, Italy, eighth to seventh century BC. 3 Lattes, southern France, courtyard house, early second century BC.

Author, after Nevett 2012 (1); Izzet 2001 (2); Py 1996 (3)

Age, most longhouses had a simple two-room plan with a dwelling at one end and an animal shed at the other. Larger longhouses with more complex multi-room layouts became increasingly common during the first millennium AD. The longhouse tradition did not extend to Finland, where regular patterns in house form are difficult to discern (Asplund 2002).

Roundhouses with conical roofs were the dominant form of domestic architecture in Britain, Ireland, and north-west Iberia, and also occur at some sites in northern France (Figure 20.2, 4; Ayán Vila 2008; Harding 2009). Again, a variety of building materials were used, including timber, wattle, stone, and turf. In many cases, no internal room divisions are apparent. Exceptions include the complex stone roundhouses of northern and western Scotland, such as the monumental multi-storey tower houses known as brochs, built during the later first millennium BC and early centuries AD.

Other structures associated with individual houses in temperate Europe could include smaller ancillary buildings, granaries, storage pits, wells, or paved yards. In some cases the boundary of the domestic unit was demarcated by a ditch, fence, or wall.

The question of why Iron Age domestic architecture took the forms that it did has been approached in varying ways. Traditionally, house form has been seen either as a response to functional imperatives, such as the availability of building materials, or as a matter of 'tradition' or ethnic identity. Since the 1980s, there has been increased interest in the symbolic aspects of domestic architecture, influenced by ethnographic parallels and structuralist theory. Thus the circularity of British roundhouses and the fact that they often had doorways oriented towards the rising sun has been claimed to embody a cosmology emphasizing diurnal and life cycles (e.g. Parker Pearson 1999). Such work has provided important insights, but can be criticized for its neglect of agency, implying that all members of society blindly followed a universal conceptual scheme. It also tends to produce an essentially static picture that does not address change through time. In response, some recent research has attempted to capture the dynamic relationships between people and the buildings they inhabit. One element of this has been the growing interest in household 'biographies' (see later). Other recent work has focused on the experiential aspects of built space. Thus Fitzjohn (2011) describes how changes in house architecture at Lentini, Sicily, during the eighth century BC produced new sensory experiences for the inhabitants of these buildings. In both these approaches, the key point is that houses cannot be understood in isolation from the households that they contained.

Characterizing the Household

The household has been portrayed as the basic building block of many Iron Age societies, and is often viewed as a 'natural' and unproblematic unit. This contrasts with anthropological work on the household, which has emphasized the slipperiness of the concept. Anthropologists generally define the household by co-residence,

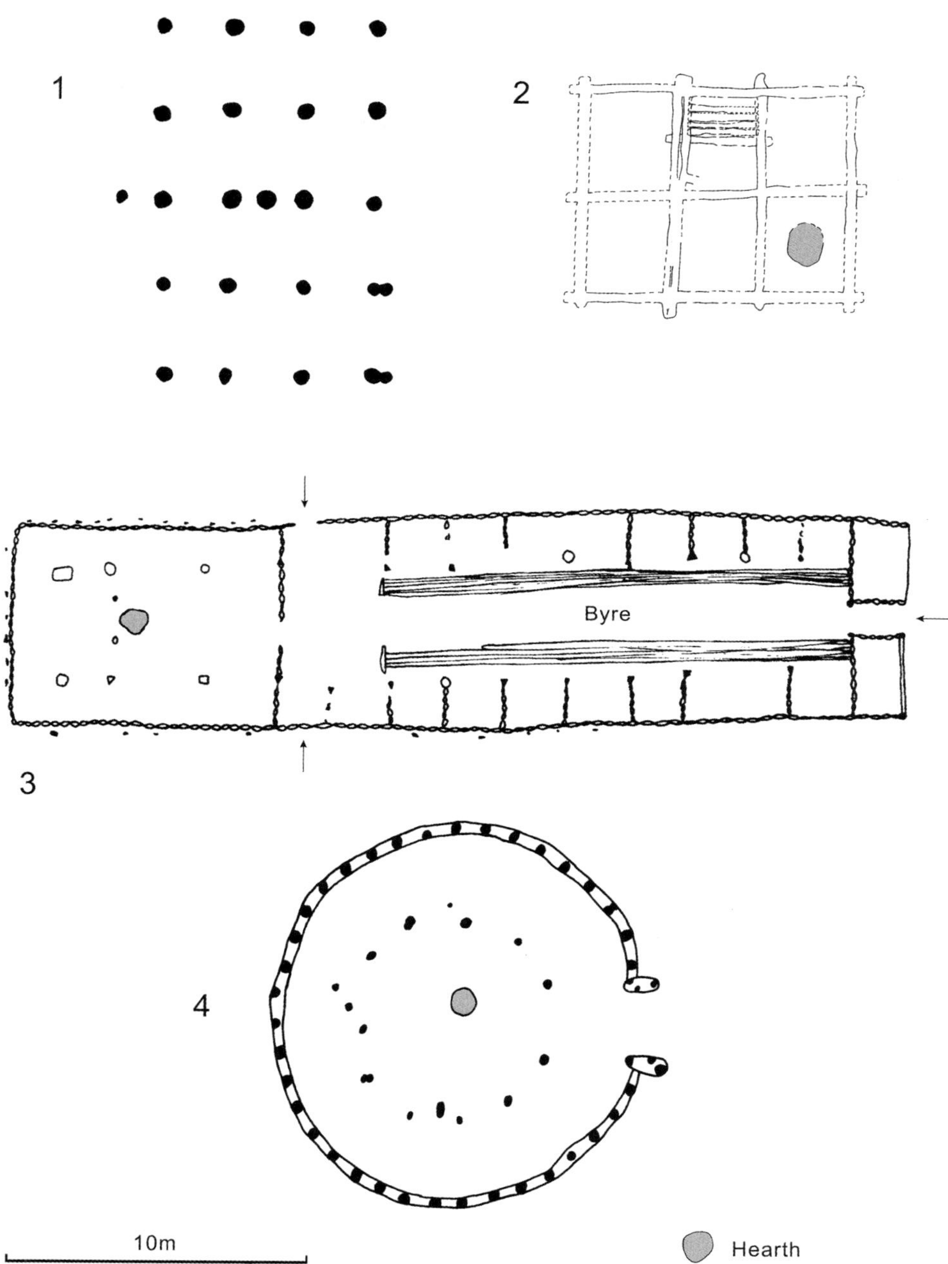

FIGURE 20.2 Iron Age houses from temperate Europe. 1 Grisy-sur-Seine, northern France, sixth to fifth century BC. 2 Heuneburg, south-west Germany, house with sill beam construction, sixth century BC. 3 Feddersen Wierde, north Germany, longhouse, first to second century AD. 4 West Plean, Scotland, roundhouse, pre-Roman Iron Age.

Author, after Haselgrove 2007 (1); Gersbach 1995 (2); Kossack et al. 1984 (3); Cunliffe 2005 (4)

distinguishing it from the family, the members of which need not reside together. This is not always straightforward, however, as some households may share members, or go through seasonal cycles of dispersal and reassembly. Also problematic is the common assumption that households formed the basic unit of production and consumption, and were the main focus for 'domestic' activities such as child-rearing and food preparation. In reality, the groups that undertake different domestic tasks may cross-cut residential units and one another (Yanagisako 2001). Such issues are obviously difficult to resolve in prehistoric archaeology. For the European Iron Age, it has often simply been assumed that one house (along with any associated ancillary buildings) represents a discrete household unit. This may be a reasonable hypothesis in cases where individual houses were dispersed across the landscape. Where settlements contain many neighbouring houses it may be less clear whether one house or several formed a household, or whether in fact households are an appropriate unit of analysis at all. This should not cause despair, however, as delineating the boundaries of the household unit is not a prerequisite for exploring social relations in the domestic sphere (Tringham 2001; see also Meadows 1999 for an Iron Age example).

Various estimates have been provided for the average size of Iron Age households in different regions, often based on floor area. For example, Nielsen (1999) suggests that three to five people (excluding infants) formed a typical household in pre-Roman Iron Age Denmark, by allowing for one person per 10 m^2 of living space. Such calculations should be treated with caution as ethnographic evidence shows that house occupant densities can vary widely between and within societies. Nevertheless, the disparities in the floor area of domestic units across Iron Age Europe are so great that they must surely in part reflect different patterns of residence. While the typical Iron Age household was probably fairly small, the occurrence of very large houses or domestic compounds covering hundreds of square metres suggests that extended residential groups existed in some places (Table 20.1).

While there has been much discussion of social distinctions between households within Iron Age communities (see later), there has been much less work on the composition of the household in terms of age, gender, and other categories, and the social relations within this group (Therkorn 1987; Webley 2008). One factor that would have influenced household structure in all Iron Age societies is a relatively low life expectancy (see Chapter 33). As a result, most household members would have been young by today's standards, and fosterage of orphaned children would have been common. To gain further insights into household structure, some archaeologists have turned to written sources. Thus Karl (2006) provides a detailed discussion of an idealized 'Celtic' household based largely on Caesar's *Gallic War* and early medieval Irish and Welsh law codes, while Woolf (1997) more loosely outlines the 'barbarian' household of the 'long Iron Age', referring to sources including Tacitus, Anglo-Saxon law, and the Icelandic sagas. In both cases the picture presented is one of hierarchic households, led by a male head with one or more wives, and in some cases incorporating non-kin such as fosterlings, servants, or slaves. Caution is needed here, however, as the sources are difficult to interpret and were, in many cases, written long after the Iron Age. Idealized

Table 20.1 Typical roofed area of domestic units in selected areas of Iron Age Europe. No account is taken of upper storeys.

Region	Period	Typical area	Reference
North-eastern Iberia	525–200 BC	Mostly 20–50m^2; exceptionally 500m^2+	Belarte 2008
Languedoc, southern France	550–0 BC	Mean 24–41m^2; exceptionally 500m^2+	Belarte 2009; Dedet 1999
Eastern Alps ('Rhaetian' houses)	7th–1st century BC	Mostly 20–40m^2; maximum 144m^{2} *	Migliavacca 1993
Wessex, southern Britain	400/300–100/50 BC	c. 20–175m^2; median c. 38m^{2} *	Sharples 2010
Biskupin, Poland	8th century BC	72–86m^2	Rajewski 1959
Jutland, Denmark	500–250 BC	50–120m^{2} †	Webley 2008
Jutland, Denmark	0–200 AD	60–310m^{2} †	Webley 2008

* = average area of individual houses, not necessarily equivalent to domestic units.

† = includes byres.

descriptions of 'Celtic' or 'barbarian' households also sit uneasily with the diversity in the organization of domestic space apparent in the archaeological record.

The premise that the social organization of the household will find expression in its spatial organization provides the starting point for other approaches. Architectural divisions and fixtures place material constraints on movement and visibility, and provide cues to 'correct' practice. Where domestic space is partitioned—either between different buildings or between multiple rooms within a single building—this may embody a concern to keep particular activities separate and different social groups distinct. Applications of these ideas include Foster's (1989) access analysis of broch settlements in Scotland, where a complex, nested arrangement of built space is equated with a complex and hierarchical social organization.

A limitation of analyses that focus exclusively on building plans is that while architecture may express spatial ideals it does not directly evince how domestic space was actually used in everyday practice. This can be investigated through chemical and micromorphological analyses of floor deposits, as at the early Iron Age settlement at Waldmatte in Switzerland (Jospin and Favrie 2008). More usually, however, the issue has been approached through analysis of artefact and ecofact distributions. A classic example is Clarke's (1972) controversial study of the later pre-Roman Iron Age settlement at Glastonbury in southern England, where a recurring household module was claimed, subdivided into female and male activity areas. More recent examples include work on La Tène enclosed farmsteads in northern France (e.g. Gransar et al. 1997). Density plots of artefacts, animal bone, and plant remains from ditches, pits, and postholes have been used to identify areas used for craft, storage, and living. A problem with much of this kind of work is that insufficient attention is paid to site formation processes, and the possibility of 'structured' or ritualized deposition of material culture is ignored. Even where artefacts are found lying directly on intact house floors or yard surfaces their distributions will often reflect activities during and after the abandonment of the settlement, rather than during its use-life (LaMotta and Schiffer 1999). Valuable therefore are cases where the occupation of a building was interrupted by a sudden, unforeseen catastrophe such as a fire, although care must be taken to distinguish this from deliberate burning as a planned abandonment practice (see later).

The evidence of architecture and the residues of daily practice together suggest wide variations in the organization of the domestic group between different Iron Age societies, but a few general points can be made. Firstly, it seems that common architectural forms could be interpreted through practice in differing ways in neighbouring regions, and also between households within individual communities. For example, roundhouses from different sites across southern and central Britain have been variously argued to show centre/periphery (Hingley 1990), left/right (e.g. Webley 2007: fig. 9; Sharples 2010) or front/back (Pope 2007) patterns in the use of space, based on evidence including artefact distributions and phosphate analysis. This suggests that there was no universal template for the organization of daily life in the British Iron Age, even though the same basic house form was shared.

Secondly, as a broad generalization, domestic units in most Iron Age societies in temperate Europe were not characterized by complex or rigid spatial divisions. Household members would have typically spent much of their time sharing the same (small) spaces and experiencing frequent face-to-face interaction, despite any differences of social position that may have existed between them. That said, more complex forms of domestic organization are discernible in some areas. In Jutland (Denmark), for example, the domestic unit during the pre-Roman Iron Age was typically represented by a single longhouse divided between a fairly small dwelling room and an animal shed. Artefact distributions from burnt-down houses show a simple arrangement of space within the dwelling, with food preparation usually confined to the rear (Figure 20.3). Larger farmsteads developed in the early centuries AD, which after AD 200 contained multi-roomed longhouses with indications of functional differences between rooms. This suggests a shift to larger and more internally differentiated households, at a time of wider social change usually characterized in terms of increasing hierarchy (Webley 2008).

In Mediterranean Europe, there is clearer evidence for complex domestic arrangements already in the pre-Roman Iron Age. As we have seen, many regions around the Mediterranean show a shift from single-roomed to multi-roomed houses over time, a process that has been particularly well studied in the nucleated settlements of southern France (Py 1996; Dedet 1999; Belarte 2009; Belarte et al. 2010). Here, houses of the fifth to fourth centuries BC typically had one or a few rooms. These show a recurring pattern in the use of space, illustrated for example by burnt fourth-century BC houses from Martigues (Figure 20.3; Damotte 2003). Storage and craftwork was normally confined to the rear, with food preparation and consumption occurring towards

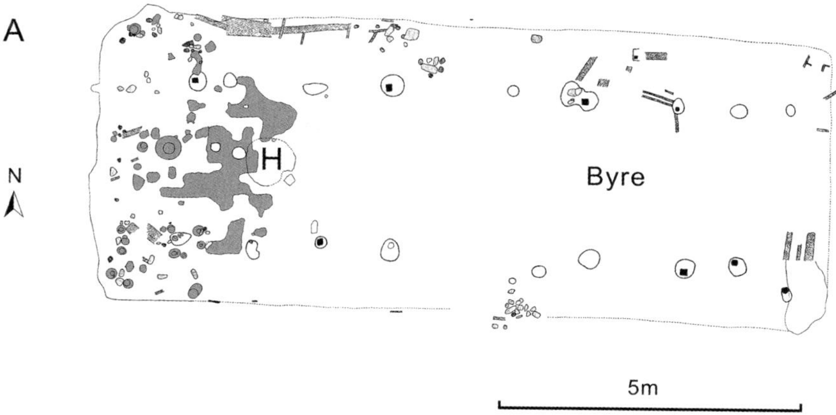

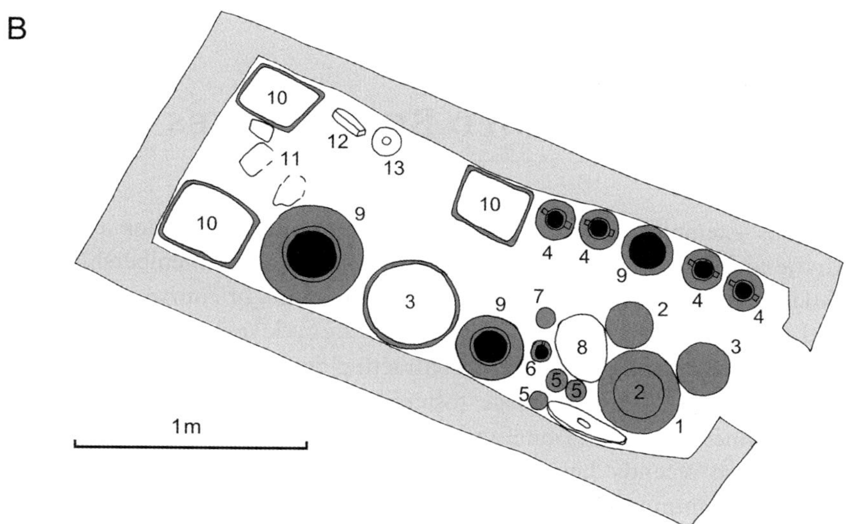

FIGURE 20.3 Burnt houses showing floor artefact distributions. (A) Gørding Hede, Denmark. House 3, dated *c.*500–250 BC. Pottery shown in grey. (B) L'Île, Martigues, southern France. Reconstructed plan of 'house' (or room) IIcA6, dated fourth century BC (1 clay oven; 2 ceramic bowl; 3 clay bowl; 4 amphora; 5 ceramic urn; 6 ceramic jug; 7 ceramic bowl; 8 hearth; 9 *dolium*; 10 rectangular clay silo; 11 quern base; 12 basalt rubber; 13 clay ring).

Author, sources Webley 2008, after C.-J. Becker (A); Damotte 2003 (B)

the front, by the entrance. In some cases, hearths were in fact placed outside the entrance, in the street. The high visibility of food preparation in the presentation of the household to outsiders contrasts with the Jutland example, hinting at different forms of gender relations. During the third to second centuries BC, larger multi-roomed houses appeared, often arranged around an open courtyard (Figure 20.1, 3). Hearths were now brought within the domestic area, and houses generally became more inward looking. Individual rooms within these houses often have similar fixtures and artefact assemblages. It has thus been suggested that courtyard houses represent a shift towards larger domestic groups, subdivided into smaller 'nuclear family' units of roughly equal status (Dietler et al. 2008; Belarte 2009). This contrasts with interpretations of contemporary courtyard houses in north-eastern Iberia, which are seen as elite residences with marked functional differences between rooms (Belarte 2008).

In both the Jutland and Mediterranean France examples, shifts in domestic relations occurred in the context of broader social change, in the latter case bound up with indigenous engagement with Greek colonists. It is however important that changes in domestic organization are not seen as merely a reflection of, or response to, higher-level social processes. For Iron Age people, interaction in the domestic sphere would have been central to the generation of *habitus*—that is, an understanding of one's place in the world. As such, action in the domestic sphere would have played an active role in maintaining or renegotiating wider social or political relations (Hendon 1996: 47; Webley 2008).

Household Biographies

The previous examples show how norms of domestic organization could change through the course of the Iron Age. At a more detailed level, the membership, activities, and spatial organization of any individual household are, of course, unlikely to have remained static. A household can be said to have a life cycle tied to those of its members, changing in fortunes and growing and contracting as individuals enter and leave the group (through birth, death, marriage, fosterage, and so on). Group membership and tasks can also fluctuate over seasonal and daily cycles.

Attempts have recently been made to investigate the biographies of Iron Age households by examining the sequences of development of the buildings they inhabited (Gerritsen 2003; Webley 2008). The initial construction of a house would often have made labour demands beyond a single domestic group, requiring the cooperation of a wider kin group or community. Such collective labour may have helped to maintain a shared understanding of architectural norms, reflected in the house 'traditions' we see in the archaeological record. The initial form of a building was not immutable, however, and many Iron Age houses show complex sequences of later alteration or extension, reflecting the unique history of each household group. Architectural changes may often have corresponded with shifts in household membership or status. For example, in some societies the construction of the hearth is an important act that marks the point at which a household becomes fully independent of the parental house. It is thus notable that some Iron Age houses began life with a simple burnt patch on the floor that was only later replaced by a properly made hearth (Webley 2008: 69). The construction or alteration of a house could have been an occasion for festivities and rituals. In many Iron Age societies this is evinced by 'offering' deposits of artefacts or animal bone placed in postholes or beneath floors, hearths, walls, or thresholds (e.g. Carlie 2004; Trebsche 2008). Human burials were also interred within houses and other settlement features in many parts of Europe (e.g. Zanoni 2011), emphasizing the link between the biographies of a house and its inhabitants. The abandonment of a house could also be ritualized, involving placed deposits or the deliberate burning of the building (e.g. van den Broeke 2002; Webley 2007).

The biographical approach is most powerful when we examine why the life cycles of households in different Iron Age societies followed differing trajectories. In some areas, houses were typically abandoned after a relatively short period, perhaps corresponding with a single human generation (Gerritsen 2003: 39). Elsewhere, houses could be occupied for centuries, being repeatedly repaired or rebuilt on the same plot. Broad trends towards increased house longevity can be seen at varying stages of the Iron Age in several different parts of Europe. Such developments occur, for example, around 800 BC in parts of Iberia (Blanco-González 2011) and during the late pre-Roman Iron Age across a swathe of north-west Europe, from northern France to southern Scandinavia (Gerritsen 2003; Mathiot 2011; Nouvel et al. 2009; Webley 2008). This greater emphasis on continuity has implications for the nature of the household and its relationship to systems of land tenure and inheritance. It suggests that the domestic group was now perpetuated for several generations, maintaining ties to a particular place and perhaps also passing down use-rights to land and resources.

This recalls Lévi-Strauss' concept of the House society, in which the House is defined as 'a corporate body holding an estate made up of both material and immaterial wealth, which perpetuates itself through the transmission of its name, its goods and its titles down a real or imaginary line' (Lévi-Strauss 1983: 174). It may incorporate one household or several related households. A feature of many historical and ethnographic House societies is that there is a close identification between the House and the building(s) that it occupies. These buildings are thus often elaborated and ornamented over time, providing a visible expression of the history and status of the House. This observation may be relevant to some Iron Age groups. For example, Blanco-González (2011) and González-Ruibal (2005) argue for the existence of House societies in central and north-western Iberia respectively. Houses in these regions—which could be repeatedly rebuilt on the spot over periods of centuries—show impressive investment in decoration, in the form of painted wall plaster, stone sculpture, or ornamented hearths.

Characterizing the Community

'Community' is a concept widely applied to the European Iron Age, but rarely defined in detail. Broadly, however, communities have been taken to be locally based groups, forming a middle level of social organization between individual households and larger entities such as 'tribes', chiefdoms, or ethnic groups. More or less implicitly, it has traditionally been assumed that members of a local community would to some degree have shared similar cultural practices and beliefs, and feelings of solidarity and belonging (Gerritsen 2004). In this section, I will explore some of the ways that local communities may have been constituted within different Iron Age societies. As issues of power and the political organization of Iron Age societies are discussed by Collis and Karl (Chapter 29), more of a bottom-up perspective will be taken here, focusing particularly on the relationship between the household and the community. I will also primarily be concerned with the rural communities that formed most Iron Age societies (for urban sites see Chapter 21).

Iron Age communities have generally been defined with reference to the settlement record, being equated with a 'village' or with a group of more dispersed settlements within a local area (generally no more than a few kilometres across). This would seem to reflect a premise that pre-industrial communities were essentially sustained through face-to-face interaction. In a few other cases, the community has been defined through funerary evidence, as the people who buried their dead within a particular cemetery (e.g. Bietti Sestieri 1992), though often this is based on the assumption that these people would also have resided in the same local area. Communities defined by locality would not necessarily have corresponded with kin groups, and would probably in fact have been cross-cut by kinship ties. In other words, an individual may have had kinship links with many, but not all, other people within their community, while also having links to some people in other communities (Hill 2011). The focus on locality rather than kinship in defining the community is, of course, partly a matter of analytical convenience, given the difficulties in approaching kinship though the archaeological record. The main criticism that can be levelled at work linking community to locality is that it has sometimes seemed to imply rather simplistically that community is a direct outcome of shared residence in a particular place. Recent approaches to the Iron Age have instead been characterized by increasing interest in elucidating the varying, culturally specific forms of social interaction that created and maintained different local communities. In tandem with this, there has been a shift away from a view of communities as neatly bounded, homogeneous units, and a greater appreciation of the fluid and overlapping nature of group identities (Cohen 1985; Gerritsen 2004; Giles 2008).

The spatial organization of local communities was highly varied across Iron Age Europe, but a broad contrast can be drawn between the trajectories followed in southern and temperate Europe. In many Mediterranean regions, large nucleated settlements—including proto-urban or urban centres—developed as early as the eighth to sixth centuries BC (Osborne and Cunliffe 2005). Nucleated sites were often enclosed within defensive circuits, and were densely built-up, with houses arranged along a network of streets (Figure 20.4, 1–2). Population estimates are difficult, though the largest sites must have had thousands of occupants. For example, the two neighbouring (400 m apart) later Iron Age settlement nuclei at Ullastret in north-east Iberia (Figure 20.4, 2) had a combined area of *c.*15 ha, and a suggested population of around 6,000 (Belarte 2010). Such major centres are often assumed to represent the peak of a settlement hierarchy that included smaller villages and farmsteads in their hinterland. Beyond the Mediterranean

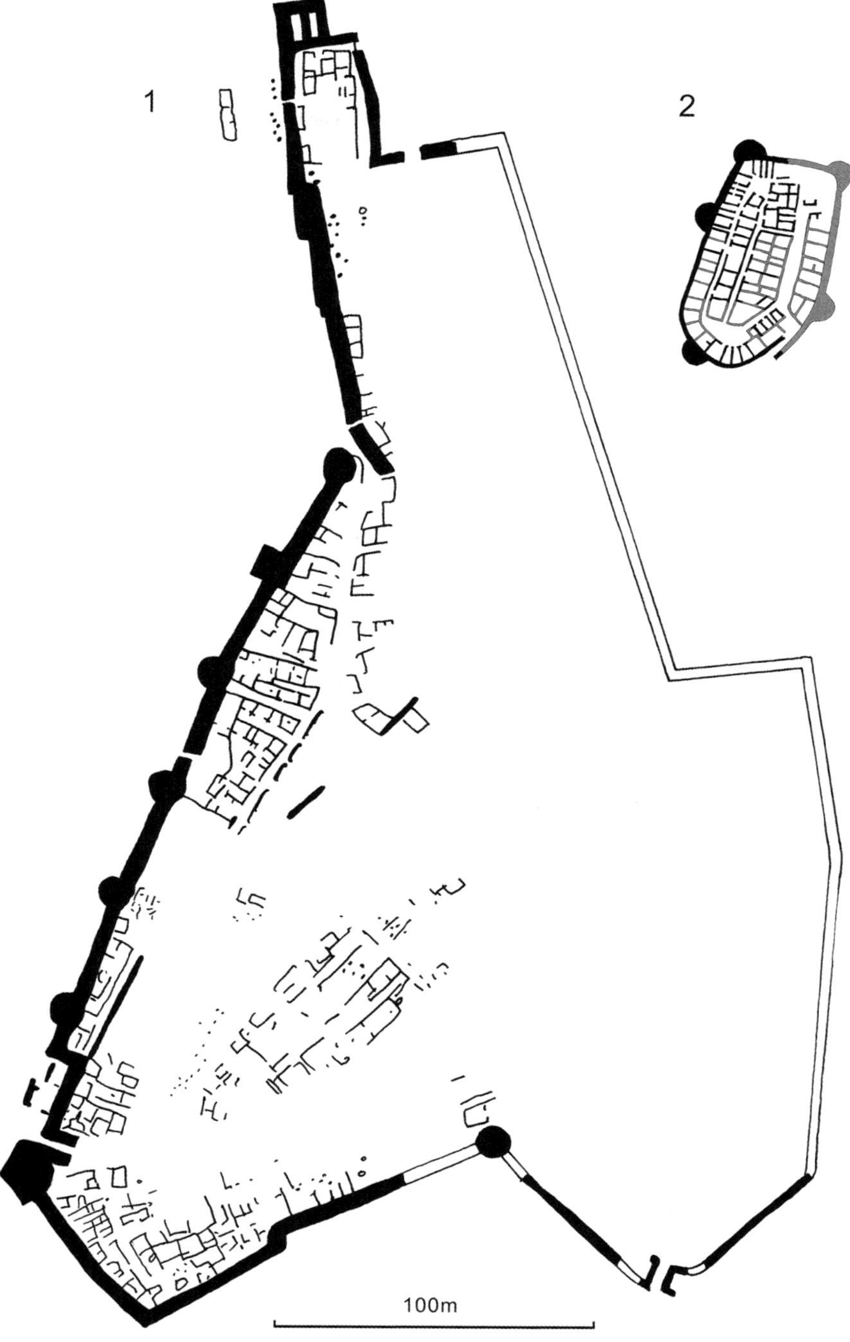

FIGURE 20.4 Multi-household settlements from Mediterranean Europe. 1 L'Île, Martigues, southern France, fifth century BC. 2 Puig de Sant Andreu, Ullastret, Catalonia, sixth to third century BC.

Author, after Belarte 2009 (1); Belarte 2008 (2)

region, in north-west Iberia, densely occupied hillforts (*castros*) of around 1 ha to tens of hectares in size are the only known form of settlement throughout the Iron Age in many areas (Ayán Vila 2008).

In contrast, in central and northern Europe settlement patterns were often looser, with more limited nucleation. In parts of Scandinavia, for example, dispersed farmsteads dominate the picture throughout the Iron Age. In other regions, hamlet- or village-sized sites did occur, but rarely comprised more than a dozen or so contemporary households (Figure 20.5, 1–3). This aversion to nucleation does not necessarily imply low population densities. For example, in some parts of lowland Britain farmstead- or hamlet-sized later pre-Roman Iron Age settlements are spaced as little as 0.5–1 km apart, suggesting that a local community a few kilometres across could have had a population in the low hundreds (Hill 2011: 250). Despite this general pattern of fairly small settlements across temperate Europe, in some regions large nucleated sites did appear at certain stages of the Iron Age. These include the defended settlements of early Iron Age Poland, such as the famous 'lake village' at Biskupin (Figure 20.5, 4). Here the enclosed area of 1.3 ha contained over 100 near-identical houses arranged in rigid rows (Rajewski 1959). In south-west Germany, densely occupied hillforts with putative 'proto-urban' characteristics arose during the sixth to fifth centuries BC. The best known of these is the Heuneburg, where the defended area of 3.2 ha is claimed to have housed a population of around 700–800 (van den Boom 2006), and was fringed by extensive extramural settlement. The middle and late La Tène period saw the development of (proto-)urban centres across a wider area of central Europe, initially in the form of open agglomerations, later followed by enclosed *oppida*.

Such variations in settlement form suggest differences in conceptions of community. People may have lived together in nucleated settlements through choice or compulsion, but either way it would have involved more frequent contact and interaction with one's neighbours. This may have fostered a greater sense of community (though it could also have led to rivalries and disputes). The construction of enclosures around nucleated settlements could also have made a visible statement of collective identity and distinctness from other groups. Equally, enclosure could also be used to emphasize the distinctness or autonomy of particular households or social groups from the rest of the community, as could, for example, be the case with the sub-compounds seen within some enclosed *oppida* (Chapter 21).

Studies that explore how settlement structure embodied conceptions of community include Hingley's (1984) discussion of the Upper Thames valley in southern Britain. Here, a contrast is drawn between the valley floor, with its unenclosed agglomerations of closely spaced settlement units, and the neighbouring uplands, dominated by small, dispersed enclosures. Hingley argues that the upland settlements embody an ideological emphasis on the independence of the individual 'local social group' (in many cases probably equivalent to a household), while in the valleys these units were bound into larger-scale cooperative groups. A slightly different approach is taken by Trebsche (2010), who compares the early Iron Age settlements at Biskupin and Milejowice in Poland, using

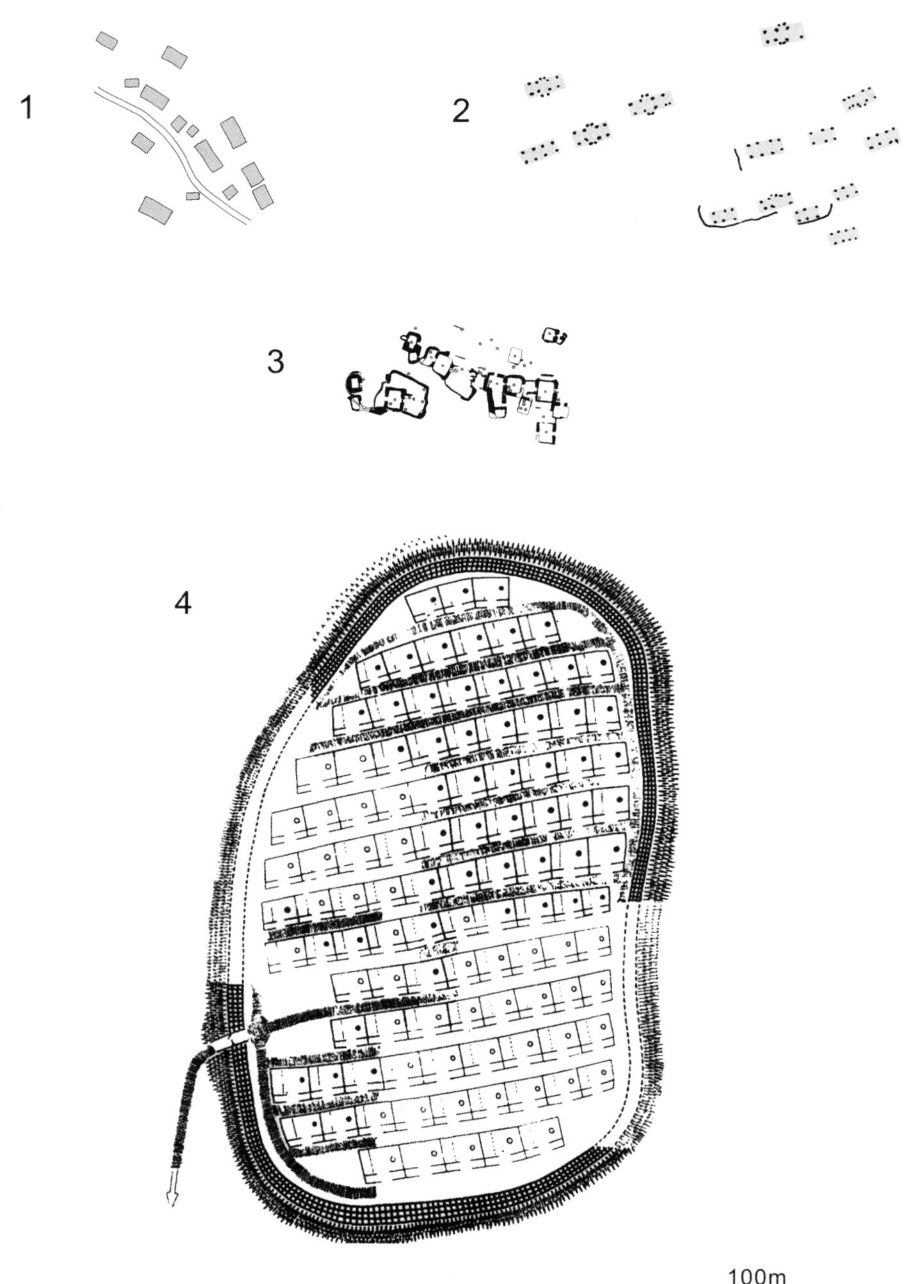

FIGURE 20.5 Multi-household settlements from temperate Europe. 1 Brig-Glis/Waldmatte, Switzerland, late seventh to early sixth century BC. 2 Priorsløkke, Denmark, first to second century AD. 3 Goulvars, western France, second to first century BC. 4 Biskupin, Poland, eighth century BC.

Author, after Jospin and Favrie 2008 (1); Kaul 1986 (2); Hyvert and Le Bihan 1990 (3); Rajewski 1959 (4)

concepts developed by the American archaeologist Gary Feinman. Biskupin, with its common defensive circuit and lack of differentiation between houses (Figure 20.5, 4), is argued to embody the 'corporate mode' of organization in which there is an ideological emphasis on community and power is embedded in group affiliation. Milejowice, with its lack of communal constructions, more dispersed layout, and evidence for differentiation between domestic units, is seen as an example of the 'network mode' in which personal networks were of greater social importance.

This does not of course imply that the nature of the community can simply be 'read off' from settlement structure. In particular, it should not be assumed that living closer together necessarily implies greater social or economic ties between households. In historical European societies there was often little relationship between the degree of settlement nucleation and the extent to which households were economically integrated and cooperated in agricultural labour (Riddersporre 1999), and this may also have been the case in the Iron Age. In some regions, dispersed settlements were integrated into large-scale systems of field boundaries and trackways, examples including the 'Celtic field' systems of northern Europe and the varying forms of land division attested in Britain. This demonstrates that dispersed households could be linked by shared frameworks of land tenure. In most Iron Age societies it is likely that use rights to farmland and resources, such as pasture and woodland, were controlled or mediated by the community—though as we have seen, in some regions there may have been an increasing emphasis through the course of the period on the inheritable rights of individual households.

No Iron Age households could have been truly self-sufficient, and some degree of economic interdependence between domestic groups will have been a feature of any community. That said, there are few universal patterns in the specific activities conducted, and resources controlled, at household and community levels respectively. In some cases, foodstuffs such as grain may have been stored collectively at communal sites, as has been suggested for some hillforts in Britain (Cunliffe 2005). Elsewhere, food storage was associated with individual domestic units, as in the nucleated settlements of Mediterranean France where houses frequently contain abundant grain silos and *dolia*. Evidence for the penning of livestock within these densely occupied settlements is, however, notably absent (Dedet 1999). This contrasts with communities in northern Europe, where the longhouse with its integral animal shed embodies a clear concern with the control of livestock by individual households. Craft activities often carried out at household level include textile working, as suggested by the near ubiquity of spindle whorls and loom weights from Iron Age settlements across much of Europe. Some other crafts may have only been carried out in a few households within each community. Within the *castros* of north-west Iberia, for example, metalworking was often restricted to a single domestic unit which—in contrast to other households—lacked food storage facilities. This suggests that the households of these communities were linked by exchange networks involving metal and food (Sastre 2008). Within most Iron Age communities, economic specialization of households or individuals was, however, fairly limited, with crafts probably pursued on a part-time basis. In Durkheimian terms, these were communities characterized by mechanical rather than organic solidarity. Clear spatial (and hence social) separation of different occupation groups was essentially restricted to the urban centres of the Mediterranean region and some of the major nucleated sites of middle to late La Tène central Europe.

Beyond fulfilling 'economic' requirements, shared participation by members of different households in exchange networks, or in tasks such as agricultural labour, could have played a significant role in reaffirming (or renegotiating) social and emotional bonds within the community. Giles (2007) has, for example, argued that the shared experience of collective labour in digging and maintaining boundary ditches contributed to the creation of communities in Iron Age East Yorkshire. Elsewhere, the construction and use of monuments or ritual sites could have played a similar role. Thus in southern Britain it has been argued that hillforts acted as centres for collective gatherings and rituals, providing a measure of social 'glue' between dispersed households that otherwise had an ideological emphasis on independence (Hill 1995). In the early Iron Age of the southern Netherlands—where households were also dispersed—shared use of large ancestral cemeteries is argued to have been key to the creation of community (Gerritsen 2003). Warfare is another activity that could have fostered community identity in some Iron Age societies (e.g. Sastre 2008). These varying examples illustrate the point that the forms of social interactions that sustained community would have been culturally specific. The extent to which it was felt necessary to explicitly display and reaffirm community identity would also have varied, and may often have been heightened at times of change or perceived external threat.

Social Differentiation within the Community

Relationships between households need not of course have been a matter of cooperation among equals. A recurring theme in many studies of Iron Age settlements has been a concern with identifying status or 'wealth' differences between households, often combined with an argument that such differentiation increased through the course of the Iron Age. What these status differences imply for the nature of the relationships and interactions between households is often not clearly specified, however.

'High-status' households have typically been identified through features such as greater house size or monumentality, the use of special building materials, or finds of 'prestige' artefacts. Examples of this approach include Malrain et al.'s (2002) model for the emergence of a four-tier hierarchy of farmsteads in middle to late La Tène northern France. These farmsteads are ranked based on the labour expenditure shown by their construction (absence/presence and elaborateness of enclosure), the 'wealth' of their artefact assemblages (including imported goods), and their faunal assemblages (best meat cuts). Malrain et al. argue that the basis for hierarchy was control of agrarian production, evinced by the abundant grain storage capacity of some farmsteads. They are cautious over how exactly this control was articulated, but others have specifically argued for clientship relationships between high- and low-status households in later La Tène central and western continental Europe (Wendling 2010). Karl (2007) has similarly claimed that contemporary multiple-ditched enclosed farmsteads in Britain were the homes of an elite, and that the labour for constructing the enclosure ditches was provided as part of the clientship obligations of their dependants.

In northern Europe, attention has instead focused on comparing the length of the animal sheds within longhouses. This is assumed to reflect the size of the herd controlled by each household, and hence its 'wealth' and prestige. The classic model for a hierarchically organized community comes from the late pre-Roman Iron Age 'village' at Hodde in Denmark, where the largest farmstead is associated with a concentration of fine pottery (Hvass 1985). Again, it has been argued that differentiation between households increased through the course of the Iron Age, and in Denmark the largest households of the early centuries AD have been characterized as 'chieftain's farms' dominating their local communities (Ethelberg 1995).

Such arguments have attracted increasing criticism in recent years. For the pre-Roman Iron Age longhouse societies of northern Europe, Brandt (2010) has critiqued the assumption that larger houses were necessarily higher status. He argues against the existence of relations of dominance and dependency between households, suggesting that the heads of successful households were at most 'big men' with the power to influence. In Britain, heterarchical models for community organization have been in vogue over the past two decades, often based on versions of Marx's Germanic mode of production. Unstable competitive relations between households, rather than permanent elites, are envisaged, with some groups achieving more prestige than others, but unable to maintain this success in the long term (Hill 1995, 2011). Heterarchical models have also been applied to north-west Iberia, influenced by Clastres' concept of 'societies against the state' (e.g. Sastre 2008).

Clearly, we cannot assume that relationships between households within Iron Age communities were necessarily based on institutionalized differences of wealth and power. That said, it is important that we do not retreat into a 'cosy' view of Iron Age communities which glosses over competition and conflict (see Chapter 30). Even in communities lacking formal hierarchy, rivalries and disputes between households and individuals are likely to have been common. The challenge now facing Iron Age archaeology is to move beyond the hierarchy/heterarchy debate to develop more nuanced approaches to the social dynamics of local communities.

References

Asplund, H. 2002. 'Houses or huts? Early Iron Age building remains in SW Finland', in H. Ranta (ed.) *Huts and Houses: Stone Age and Early Metal Age Buildings in Finland*: 227–233. Helsinki: National Board of Antiquities.

Ayán Vila, X. M. 2008. 'A round Iron Age: The circular house in the hillforts of the northwestern Iberian Peninsula'. *e-Keltoi* 6: 903–1003.

Bartoloni, G., F. Buranelli, V. D'Atri, and A. De Santis. 1987. *Le urne a capanna rinvenute in Italia*. Rome: Bretschneider.

Belarte, M. C. 2008. 'Domestic architecture and social differences in north-eastern Iberia during the Iron Age (*c*.525–200 BC)'. *Oxford Journal of Archaeology* 27: 175–199.

Belarte, M. C. 2009. 'Courtyard houses and other complex buildings in the protohistory of southern Gaul: From architectural to social changes'. *Journal of Mediterranean Archaeology* 22: 235–259.

Belarte, M. C. 2010. 'Los individuos en el espacio doméstico en la protohistoria de Cataluña'. *Arqueología Espacial* 28: 109–134.

Belarte, M. C., E. Gailledrat, and J. Principal. 2010. 'The functional and symbolic uses of space in western Mediterranean protohistory: The Pech Maho example (Sigean, western Languedoc, France)'. *Oxford Journal of Archaeology* 30: 57–83.

Bietti Sestieri, A. M. 1992. *The Iron Age Community of Osteria dell'Osa*. Cambridge: Cambridge University Press.

Blanco-González, A. 2011. 'From huts to "the house": The shift in perceiving home between the Bronze Age and the early Iron Age in central Iberia (Spain)'. *Oxford Journal of Archaeology* 30: 393–410.

Brabandt, J. 1993. *Hausbefunde der römischen Kaiserzeit im freien Germanien*. Halle: Landesmuseum für Vorgeschichte.

Brandt, J. 2010. 'Haus, Gehöft, Weiler, Dorf—Siedlungsstrukturen der vorrömischen Eisenzeit aus sozialanthropologischer Sicht', in M. Meyer (ed.) *Haus—Gehöft—Weiler—Dorf: Siedlungen der Vorrömischen Eisenzeit im nördlichen Mitteleuropa*. Berliner Archäologische Forschungen 8: 17–30. Rahden: Marie Leidorf.

Carlie, A. 2004. *Forntida byggnadskult*. Stockholm: Riksantikvarieambetet.

Clarke, D. L. 1972. 'A provisional model of an Iron Age society and its settlement system', in D. L. Clarke (ed.) *Models in Archaeology*: 801–869. London: Methuen.

Cohen, A. P. 1985. *The Symbolic Construction of Community*. London: Tavistock.

Črešnar, M. 2007. 'Wooden house construction types in Bronze Age and early Iron Age Slovenia', in M. Blečić, M. Črešnar, B. Hänsel, A. Hellmuth, E. Kaiser, and C. Metzner-Nebelsick (eds) *Scripta praehistorica in honorem Biba Teržan*. *Situla* 44: 321–339.

Cunliffe, B. W. 2005. *Iron Age Communities in Britain: An Account of England, Scotland and Wales from the Seventh Century BC until the Roman Conquest*, 4th edition. London: Routledge.

Damotte, L. 2003. 'Mobilier céramique et faciès culturel de l'habitat gaulois de l'Île de Martigues'. *Documents d'archéologie Méridionale* 26: 171–234.

Dedet, B. 1999. 'La maison de l'oppidum languedocien durant la protohistoire'. *Gallia* 56: 313–355.

Dietler, M., A. Kohn, A. Moya i Garra, and A. Rivalan. 2008. 'Les maisons à cour des IIIe–IIe s. av. J.-C. à Lattes'. *Gallia* 65: 111–122.

Draiby, B. 1991. 'Studier i jernalderens husbygning', in B. Madsen (ed.) *Eksperimentel arkæologi*: 103–133. Lejre: Historisk-Arkæologisk Forsøgscenter.

Ethelberg, P. 1995. 'The chieftain's farms of the Over Jerstal group'. *Journal of Danish Archaeology* 11: 111–135.

Fitzjohn, M. 2011. 'Constructing identity in Iron Age Sicily', in M. Gleba and H. W. Horsnaes (eds) *Communicating Identity in Italic Iron Age Communities*: 155–166. Oxford: Oxbow.

Foster, S. 1989. 'Analysis of spatial patterns in buildings (access analysis) as an insight into social structure: Examples from the Scottish Atlantic Iron Age'. *Antiquity* 63: 40–50.

Gerritsen, F. 2003. *Local Identities: Landscape and Community in the Late Prehistoric Meuse-Demer-Scheldt region*. Amsterdam Archaeological Studies 9. Amsterdam: Amsterdam University Press.

Gerritsen, F. 2004. 'Archaeological perspectives on local communities', in J. Bintliff (ed.) *A Companion to Archaeology*: 141–154. Oxford: Blackwell.

Gersbach, E. 1995. *Baubefunde der Perioden IVc–IVa der Heuneburg*. Römisch-Germanische Forschungen 53. Mainz: Philipp von Zabern.

Giles, M. 2007. 'Refiguring rights in the early Iron Age landscapes of East Yorkshire', in C. Haselgrove and R. Pope (eds) *The Earlier Iron Age in Britain and the Near Continent*: 103–118. Oxford: Oxbow.

Giles, M. 2008. 'Identity, community and the person in later prehistory', in J. Pollard (ed.) *Prehistoric Britain*: 330–350. Oxford: Blackwell.

González-Ruibal, A. 2005. 'House societies vs. kinship-based societies: An archaeological case from Iron Age Europe'. *Journal of Anthropological Archaeology* 25: 144–173.

Gransar, F., F. Malrain, and V. Matterne. 1997. 'Analyse spatiale d'un établissement rural à enclos fossoyés du début de La Tène finale: Jaux "Le Camp du Roi" (Oise)', in A. Bocquet (ed.) *Espaces physiques espaces sociaux dans l'analyse interne des sites du Néolithique à l'âge du Fer*: 159–181. Paris: Éditions du CTHS.

Harding, D. 2009. *The Iron Age Round-house: Later Prehistoric Building in Britain and Beyond*. Oxford: Oxford University Press.

Haselgrove, C. 2007. 'Rethinking earlier Iron Age settlement in the eastern Paris Basin', in C. Haselgrove and R. Pope (eds) *The Earlier Iron Age in Britain and Beyond*: 400–428. Oxford: Oxbow.

Hendon, J. 1996. 'Archeological approaches to domestic labor: Household practice and domestic relations'. *Annual Review of Anthropology* 25: 45–61.

Hill, J. D. 1995. 'How should we understand Iron Age societies and hillforts? A contextual study from southern Britain', in J. D. Hill and C. Cumberpatch (eds) *Different Iron Ages: Studies on the Iron Age in Temperate Europe*. British Archaeological Reports International Series 602: 45–66. Oxford: Archaeopress.

Hill, J. D. 2011. 'How did British middle and late pre-Roman Iron Age societies work (if they did)?', in T. Moore and X.-L. Armada (eds) *Atlantic Europe in the First Millennium BC: Crossing the Divide*: 242–263. Oxford: Oxford University Press.

Hingley, R. 1984. 'Towards social analysis in archaeology: Celtic society in the Iron Age of the Upper Thames valley', in B. W. Cunliffe and D. Miles (eds) *Aspects of the Iron Age in Central Southern Britain*. OUCA Monograph 2: 72–88. Oxford: Oxford University Committee for Archaeology.

Hingley, R. 1990. 'Domestic organisation and gender relations in Iron Age and Romano-British households', in R. Samson (ed.) *The Social Archaeology of Houses*: 125–149. Edinburgh: Edinburgh University Press.

Hvass, S. 1985. *Hodde: Et Vestjysk landsbysamfund fra Ældre Jernalder*. Copenhagen: Akademisk Forlag.

Hyvert, J., and J.-P. Le Bihan. 1990. 'Les habitats cotiers Armoricains à l'âge du Fer', in A. Duval, J.-P. Le Bihan, and Y. Menez (eds) *Les Gaulois d'Armorique*. Revue Archéologique de l'Ouest supplément 3: 71–84.

Izzet, V. E. 2001. 'Putting the house in order: the development of Etruscan domestic architecture', in J. R. Brandt and L. Karlsson (eds) *From Huts to Houses: Transformations of Ancient Societies*: 41–49. Stockholm: Svenska Institutet i Rom.

Jospin, J. P., and T. Favrie. 2008. *Premier bergers des Alpes*. Gollion: Infolio.

Karl, R. 2006. *Altkeltische Sozialstrukturen*. Archaeolingua Main Series 18. Budapest: Archaeolingua.

Karl, R. 2007. 'Der Haushalt des "Landesherrn" – Zum Verhältnis von *tegesākos und *mrogirīgs im eisenzeitlichen Wales', in P. Trebsche, I. Balzer, C. Eggl, J. K. Koch, H. Nortmann, and J. Wiethold (eds) *Die unteren Zehntausend—auf der Suche nach den Unterschichten der Eisenzeit. Beiträge zur Tagung der AG Eisenzeit in Xanten 2006*: 57–70. Langenweißbach: Beier und Beran.

Kaul, F. 1986. 'Priorsløkke—en befæstet jernalderlandsby fra ældre romersk jernalder ved Horsens'. *Nationalmuseets Arbejdsmark* 1986: 172–183.

Kossack, G., K.-E. Behre, and P. Schmid. 1984. *Archäologische und naturwissenschaftliche Untersuchungen an ländlichen und frühstädtischen Siedlungen im deutschen Küstengebiet vom 5. Jahrhundert v. Chr. bis zum 11. Jahrhundert n. Chr. Band 1: Ländliche Siedlungen*. Weinheim: Acta Humaniora.

LaMotta, V., and M. Schiffer. 1999. 'Formation processes of house floor assemblages', in P. Allison (ed.) *The Archaeology of Household Activities*: 19–29. London: Routledge.

Lang, F. 2007. 'House—community—settlement: the new concept of living in Archaic Greece', in R. Westgate, N. Fisher, and J. Whitley (eds) *Building Communities: House, Settlement and Society in the Aegean and Beyond*: 183–193. London: British School at Athens.

Lévi-Strauss, C. 1983. *The Way of the Masks*. London: Cape.

Malrain, F., V. Matterne, and P. Méniel. 2002. *Les paysans Gaulois (IIIe siècle–52 av. J.-C.)*. Paris: Errance.

Mathiot, D. 2011. 'Person, family and community. The social structures of the Iron Age societies seen through the organisation of their housing', in T. Moore and L. Armada (eds) *Atlantic Europe in the First Millennium BC: Crossing the Divide*: 358–374. Oxford: Oxford University Press.

Mazarakis Ainian, A. 2001. 'From huts to houses in early Iron Age Greece', in J. R. Brandt and L. Karlsson (eds) *From Huts to Houses: Transformations of Ancient Societies*: 139–161. Stockholm: Svenska Institutet i Rom.

Meadows, K. 1999. 'The appetites of households in early Roman Britain', in P. Allison (ed.) *The Archaeology of Household Activities*: 101–120. London: Routledge.

Meyer, M. (ed.) 2010. *Haus—Gehöft—Weiler—Dorf. Siedlungen der vorrömischen Eisenzeit im nördlichen Mitteleuropa*. Rahden: Marie Leidorf.

Michałowski, A. 2010. 'Die Siedlungen der Jastorf-Kultur in Großpolen', in M. Meyer (ed.) *Haus—Gehöft—Weiler—Dorf: Siedlungen der vorrömischen Eisenzeit im nördlichen Mitteleuropa*: 169–198. Rahden: Marie Leidorf.

Migliavacca, M. 1993. 'Lo spazio domestico nell'Età del Ferro. Tecnologia edilizia e aree di attività tra VII e I secolo a. C. in una porzione dell'arco alpino orientale'. *Preistoria Alpina* 29: 5–161.

Nevett, L. 2012. 'Housing and households in Ancient Greece', in S. E. Alcock and R. Osborne (eds) *Classical Archaeology*, 2nd edition: 209–227. Oxford: Blackwell.

Nielsen, S. 1999. *The Domestic Mode of Production and Beyond*. Copenhagen: Det Kongelige Nordiske Oldskriftselskab.

Nouvel, P., P. Barral, S. Deffressigne, V. Riquier, J.-M. Séguier, N. Tikonoff, et al. 2009. 'Rythmes de création, fonctionnement et abandon des établissements ruraux de la fin de l'âge du Fer dans l'est de la France', in I. Bertrand, A. Duval, J. Gomez de Soto, and P. Maguer (eds) *Habitats et paysages ruraux en Gaule et regards sur d'autres régions du monde celtique. Actes du XXXIe Colloque de l'AFEAF, 17–20 mai 2007, Chauvigny*: 109–151. Chauvigny: Association des Publications Chauvinoises.

Osborne, R., and B. W. Cunliffe (eds). 2005. *Mediterranean Urbanization 800–600 BC*. Proceedings of the British Academy 126. Oxford: Oxford University Press.

Parker Pearson, M. 1999. 'Food, sex and death: Cosmologies in the British Iron Age with particular reference to East Yorkshire'. *Cambridge Archaeological Journal* 9: 43–69.

Pope, R. 2007. 'Ritual and the roundhouse: a critique of recent ideas on domestic space in later British prehistory', in C. Haselgrove and R. Pope (eds) *The Earlier Iron Age in Britain and the Near Continent*: 204–228. Oxford: Oxbow.

Py, M. 1996. 'Les maisons protohistoriques de Lattara (IVe–Ier s. av. n. è.)'. *Lattara* 9: 141–258.

Rajewski, Z. 1959. *Biskupin: Polish Excavations*. Warsaw: Polonia Publishing House.

Riddersporre, M. 1999. 'Village and single farm. Settlement structure or landscape organisation', in C. Fabech and J. Ringtved (eds) *Settlement and Landscape*: 167–175. Højbjerg: Jysk Arkæologisk Selskab.

Sastre, I. 2008. 'Community, identity, and conflict: Iron Age warfare in the Iberian northwest'. *Current Anthropology* 49, 6: 1021–1051.

Schattner, T. G. 1990. *Griechische Hausmodelle*. Berlin: Gebrüder Mann.

Sharples, N. 2010. *Social Relations in Later Prehistory: Wessex in the First Millennium BC*. Oxford: Oxford University Press.

Therkorn, L. 1987. 'The inter-relationships of materials and meanings: Some suggestions on housing concerns within Iron Age Noord-Holland', in I. Hodder (ed.) *The Archaeology of Contextual Meanings*: 102–110. Cambridge: Cambridge University Press.

Trebsche, P. 2008. 'Rituale beim Hausbau während der Spätbronze- und Eisenzeit', in C. Eggl, P. Trebsche, I. Balzer, J. Fries-Knoblach, J. K. Koch, H. Nortmann, and J. Wiethold (eds) *Ritus und Religion in der Eisenzeit*: 67–78. Langenweißbach: Beier und Beran.

Trebsche, P. 2010. 'Architektursoziologie und prähistorische Archäologie: Methodische Überlegungen und Aussagepotenzial', in P. Trebsche, N. Müller-Scheeßel, and S. Reinhold (eds) *Der gebaute Raum: Bausteine einer Architektursoziologie vormoderner Gesellschaften*: 143–170. Münster: Waxmann.

Tringham, R. 2001. 'Household archaeology', in N. J. Smelser and P. B. Baltes (eds) *International Encyclopedia of the Social and Behavioral Sciences*: 6925–6929. Oxford: Elsevier.

Truhelka, Ć. 1904. 'Der vorgeschichtliche Pfahlbau im Savebette bei Donja Dolina (Bezirk Bosnisch-Gradiška)'. *Wissenschaftliche Mitteilungen aus Bosnien und der Herzegowina* 9: 3–156.

Van den Boom, H. 2006. 'Häuser und Haushalte der Heuneburg', in W.-R. Teegen, R. Cordie, O. Dörrer, S. Rieckhoff, and H. Steuer (eds) *Studien zur Lebenswelt der Eisenzeit*. Reallexikon der Germanischen Altertumskunde Ergänzungsbände 5: 353–368. Berlin: Walter de Gruyter.

Van den Broeke, P. 2002. 'Een vurig afscheid? Aanwijzingen voor verlatingsrituelen in ijzertijdnederzettingen', in H. Fokkens and R. Jansen (eds) *2000 Jaar Bewoningsdynamiek: Brons- en ijzertijdbewoning in het Maas-Demer-Scheldegebied*: 45–61. Leiden: Leiden University.

Webley, L. 2007. 'Using and abandoning roundhouses: A reinterpretation of the evidence from late Bronze Age–early Iron Age southern England'. *Oxford Journal of Archaeology* 26: 127–144.

Webley, L. 2008. *Iron Age Households*. Højbjerg: Jysk Arkæologisk Selskab.

Wendling, H. 2010. 'Landbesitz und Erbfolge—Ein ethnographisches Modell zur Sozialstruktur und Raumgliederung der mitteleuropäischen Latènezeit', in P. Trebsche, N. Müller-Scheeßel, and S. Reinhold (eds) *Der gebaute Raum: Bausteine einer Architektursoziologie vormoderner Gesellschaften*: 325–354. Münster: Waxmann.

Woolf, A. 1997. 'At home in the long Iron Age: a dialogue between households and individuals in cultural reproduction', in J. Moore and E. Scott (eds) *Invisible People and Processes: Writing Gender and Childhood into European Prehistory*: 68–74. London: Leicester University Press.

Yanagisako, S. J. 2001. 'Household in anthropology', in N. J. Smelser and P. B. Baltes (eds) *International Encyclopedia of the Social and Behavioral Sciences*: 6930–6934. Oxford: Elsevier.

Zanoni, V. 2011. *Out of Place: Human Skeletal Remains in Non-Funerary Contexts: Northern Italy in the 1st Millennium BC*. British Archaeological Reports International Series 2306. Oxford: Archaeopress.

CHAPTER 21

URBANIZATION AND *OPPIDA*

STEPHAN FICHTL

First Steps Towards Town Building in the Early Iron Age

Even if we agree that the late Iron Age *oppida* constitute the first form of urbanization north of the Alps (Collis 1975; Cunliffe and Rowley 1976; Werner 1979; Collis 1984; Audouze and Buchsenschutz 1989; Guichard et al. 2000; Fichtl 2000, 2005; Poux 2011; Rieckhoff and Fichtl 2011), we must still ask whether there are other, more ancient phenomena which can be interpreted as attempts at urbanization (Sievers and Schönfelder 2012). Recent excavations at a number of early Iron Age complexes in both Germany and France have opened up new perspectives. The most interesting site in this regard is undoubtedly the Heuneburg in Baden-Württemberg (Kurz 2009, 2010; Krausse et al. 2016). During the first half of the sixth century BC this fortified 'princely site' of about 3 ha, resembling a fortified acropolis, acquired a veritable suburb covering almost 100 ha. This extension consists of a small fortified section, the *Vorburg*, right against the foot of the hill, but then, notably, a series of enclosures aligned along the major north–south axis. This pattern reflects an incipient form of urbanism.

At Bourges in central France, the situation is slightly different, but similar characteristics can be observed. Beyond the fortified spur itself (Augier et al. 2007), recent excavations have revealed artisanal districts situated either immediately outside the wall, as at Saint-Martin-des-Champs (Milcent 2007, 2012), or further away from it as at Port-Sec. These suburbs seem likewise to have been laid out in a regular fashion. Again, this site suggests a readiness to introduce urban organization.

These two cases, although chronologically relatively close, are probably not part of the same phenomenon. At the Heuneburg, the suburb had only a relatively short lifespan of less than a century; it appears that after two or three generations the structures erected, along with the mud-brick wall, had run their course. This could have been for straightforward economic reasons: at the end of the sixth century, over-exploitation of the land around the site may have created social tensions, with the inhabitants drifting back to their places of origin. Conversely, at Bourges, all of the areas of activity located around the fortified site appear to have functioned throughout this first phase of occupation.

The Emergence of Artisan Settlements

The first examples of urbanism in Iron Age Europe were not as successful as might be supposed. Very soon the predominant, if not the only kind of, settlement was once again the isolated rural settlement. But one or even two centuries before the appearance of *oppida*, a second major step towards urbanization can be traced in sites known generally in the literature as 'open settlements', as distinct from *oppida*, which are fortified with a rampart. However, this term is now being dropped in favour of 'artisan settlements'.

At these sites, which appear at the end of the third century BC and the beginning of the second, it is economic activity which predominates—mainly artisanal, but also commercial. A large number of them grew up along the main lines of communication and became important places of trade. These villages or townlets are found throughout Celtic Europe. We know of more than eighty to date, but the number is undoubtedly much higher. Examples include Roseldorf in Austria, Němčice in Moravia (Čižmář et al. 2008), Lovosice in northern Bohemia, Manching and Berching-Pollanten in Bavaria (Fischer et al. 1984; Schäfer 2010), Kirchzarten, Breisach-Hochstetten, and Basel-Gasfabrik on the Rhine knee, Verdun-sur-le-Doubs in Burgundy, Nanterre and Bobigny in Île-de-France, Orléans and Levroux in Centre (Buchsenschutz et al. 2000), Aulnat and Varennes-sur-Allier in Auvergne, Saint-Gence in Limousin, Quimper in Brittany, and finally Lacoste and Villeneuve-sur-Lot in Aquitaine (Fichtl 2013).

This blanket term covers a number of differences in both status and function. Acy-Romance in Champagne has all the hallmarks of a village of arable and livestock farmers (Lambot and Méniel 1992, 2000; Méniel 1998). Here, artisanship is rudimentary, just as on any farmstead of the period. So the site is not comparable with contemporaneous major artisan settlements defined by the quantity and variety of objects they produce. These show such artisanal activities as bronze and iron metalworking, manufacture of glass jewellery and fancy objects. In some cases exploitation of a raw material is the predominant function, as at Lovosice with its extensive trade in quernstones made of gneiss. The economic importance of such sites is most apparent in glass jewellery production. The greatest quantity of glass bracelets come from three open settlements: Manching, with more than 600 bracelet fragments, Němčice with over 400 fragments, and Berching-Pollanten also with about 400 fragments. These figures are much higher than those for the *oppida*. Other sites, such as Lacoste, appear to have specialized in iron-work: thousands of objects connected with artisanal activity have been gathered from excavations and field surveys: offcuts, finished items, semi-products, and objects in the course of manufacture, as well as associated tools. The output here was mainly jewellery and iron weapons.

Where the extent of these sites is known, their area is very variable. They can be quite small, though often exceeding 10 ha (18 ha for Acy-Romance, 24 ha for Levroux), or they can be very much larger, as at Roseldorf or Němčice, with field survey estimates of 32 ha and 35 ha respectively, or Lovosice, reckoned to be between 40 and 60 ha.

These settlements appear in the third century BC in central Europe, but seem to be somewhat more recent in Gaul, where most arose during the second century. A new phase of site building is identifiable in the first century BC. A great many sites continued to be occupied into the Roman period, and met with varying fortunes. Some seem to have been abandoned in favour of a nearby *oppidum*, as at Levroux, where the open settlement of Village des Arènes was abandoned in favour of the *oppidum* of La Colline des Tours. In other cases an open settlement acquired a rampart, as at Manching, where a perimeter wall was built in the second half of the second century BC. Presumably the construction of this rampart changed the nature of the site from a simple settlement to a town. Elsewhere again, settlements continued as open sites and became secondary Roman settlements. Two sites in the territory of the Segusiavi, Feurs and Roanne (Loire), are good examples of this. Feurs even became the administrative centre of its province under the Romans.

Can we talk about urbanization for these sites? In fact their internal layout is rarely known. If we take the best-known plan, that of Acy-Romance—just a farming village, however—it appears that a perfectly structured internal layout was in place right from the start. This is seen even more clearly at Manching. The division of the centre of the site into large rectangular lots was also carried out at the beginning of the second century BC—i.e. more than half a century before the establishment of the *oppidum*. Its public facilities are poorly known, but in at least three cases we may note the presence of shrines: Acy-Romance, Roseldorf, and Manching. These elements, tenuous as they are, indicate a preliminary form of urbanization in the middle and late La Tène period, foreshadowing the *oppida*.

Defensive Walls: Architecture and Function

The last and most important urban phase was incontestably that of the *oppida*. These fortified sites appeared more or less simultaneously in Europe, from the Atlantic to central Europe. By the last third of the second century BC, this wide area was covered with large-scale fortified sites that can be regarded as the first towns north of the Alps.

The Large Scale of the *Oppida*

The area covered by an *oppidum* can easily be calculated from the plan of the surrounding wall, but the area actually occupied was not necessarily in direct proportion to the size of the interior. There could be many reasons for this. Sometimes it is simply a matter of the terrain. An *oppidum*, such as Mont Beuvray, contains within its walls many steep areas that are not suitable for building on, at least not without extensive earthmoving (Goudineau and Peyre 1993). But this argument cannot apply to an *oppidum* such as Manching, situated on the Danube plain. Here we might ask whether the extent of the wall was influenced by a political desire to attract a large population to the city, a project which never quite came off. Elsewhere, as at the Bavarian *oppidum* of Kelheim, an additional wall was erected to protect an ore-mining zone. This phenomenon recurs in certain Roman cities in Gaul which, although walled, contained large areas within the circuit that were not built on, as can be seen at Avenches, capital of the Helvetii, or Vienne in the territory of the Allobroges.

The *oppida* of northern Gaul, and of Celtic Europe in general, are known for the large amount of ground they cover. The minimum qualifying size has been the subject of much debate. In 1962, W. Dehn drew up a definition which advocated a minimum of 30 ha (Dehn 1962), which remains influential in German archaeology. At the Bavay and Mons conference of 1982, several alternatives were proposed. J.-P. Guillaumet recommended a size of 50 ha, whereas A. Duval suggested applying the term to sites as low as 10 ha (Cahen-Delhaye et al. 1984). The difficulty in agreeing on a minimum size can be explained by significant regional differences. The largest *oppida* are concentrated in southern Germany: Rheinau (233 ha), Manching (380 ha), Kelheim (600 ha), and Heidengraben bei Grabenstetten (over 1,600 ha). In Bohemia, although the *oppidum* of Závist reached a maximum extent of 118 ha and Stradonice attained 90 ha (Píč 1906; Rybová and Drda 1994), most of the sites identified as *oppida* are between 20 and 40 ha. Further east, in Hungary, the range is from 12 to 25 ha. Similarly, in Gaul, notwithstanding large sites such as Villejoubert in Limousin at 300 ha, the Donnersberg in the Palatinate (240 ha; Zeeb Lanz 2008), Bibracte in Burgundy (200 ha), the Fossé de Pandours in Alsace (170 ha) and Saint-Désir in Normandy (170 ha), most sites do not exceed 100 ha, and many of these are a mere 10 ha or so. The latter are probably secondary *oppida* for the most part, lying within the territories of well-organized Gaulish polities. So, when applying the term *oppidum*, there is an accepted critical threshold of 10–15 ha. This is still substantial compared with the size of sites in southern Gaul at the time, or the forts of the Bronze Age and early Iron Age.

The Place of *Oppida* in the Landscape

The defining feature of an *oppidum* is a wall enclosing the site. As with the great majority of protohistoric defences, the rampart is closely bound up with topography. Thus some sites depend on a rocky spur which can be easily defended by building a simple barrier. These promontory forts were very numerous among the smaller sites of Bronze Age and Hallstatt date, but they also occur during the late Iron Age, for example at Finsterlohr (Baden-Württemberg), Saint-Samson-de-la-Roque (Eure), and Langres (Haute-Marne) (Pierrevelcin 2012a). Similar in principle is the interfluvial fort, where

FIGURE 21.1 Aerial view of the *oppidum* of Besançon (Vesontio), capital of the Sequani, in a bend of the River Doubs in eastern France.

Photo: R. Goguey, D. Lebrun

the *oppidum* is situated in the triangle formed by the confluence of two rivers. One of the best examples is Kelheim in Bavaria, with others of this type at Sandouville (Seine-Maritime), Moulay (Mayenne), and Gondole (Puy-de-Dôme). A variation on this theme uses the curve of a river meander as a boundary, for instance at Vesontio-Besançon (Doubs; Figure 21.1), Jœuvres (Loire), Villeneuve-Saint-Germain (Aisne), Altenburg-Rheinau (Baden-Württemberg/Switzerland), and Bern (Switzerland). Finally, the sea also can act as a natural defence, as at Bracquemont (Seine-Maritime), where the *oppidum* backs on to the chalk cliff overlooking the English Channel (Figure 21.2). In other cases, entire coastal promontories are defended, as with the Pointe de Meinga (Ille-et-Vilaine), Cité d'Alet (Ille-et-Vilaine), and Hengistbury Head, Dorset (Cunliffe 1987).

Where there are no easily exploited natural defences, *oppida* may take the form of contour forts, typically hilltops completely encircled by a rampart, such as the *oppidum* of Bibracte on Mont Beuvray, where a double line of ramparts encloses three peaks over an area of around 200 ha. In less mountainous terrain, for instance at the *oppida* of Manching in Bavaria, Camp d'Attila at La Cheppe (Marne), Reims-Durocortorum (Marne), and Chartres-Autricum, the ramparts form an almost perfect circle.

If the defensive enclosures of the late Iron Age display strong continuity with earlier periods, there are nonetheless several new features to be noted. Regarding size, with the *oppida* of the second and first centuries BC we are talking of fortified sites of exceptional

FIGURE 21.2 The *oppidum* of Bracquemont on the chalk cliffs of Seine-Maritime, northern France.

Photo: R. Agache, Ministère de la Culture

size covering tens or even hundreds of hectares. The defences have also made striking advances. Ramparts may, as indicated, be tied to the topography, but now they very often take an independent course. Thus the *oppidum* is no longer simply reliant on a natural defensive feature, but has the added protection of a constructed perimeter. This is well illustrated by the *oppida* of Fossé des Pandours at Col de Saverne (Alsace) and the Titelberg (Luxembourg). The *oppidum* has broken free from the topography: its walls plunge down slopes, span streams and small valleys. This is clearly seen at Mont Beuvray, at Heidetränk near Frankfurt (Hesse), and at the *oppidum* of Závist in Bohemia.

Architecture of Late Iron Age Ramparts and Gateways

The architecture of ramparts in the late Iron Age can be divided into three broad categories, the first two using wood as a framework for the rampart, coupled with a drystone cladding and with an earthwork *talus* providing the bulk of the fortification (Buchsenschutz and Ralston 1981; Fichtl 2010, 2012a: 25–38). The third category, the massive dump rampart, simply relies on the sheer volume of earth (Wheeler and Richardson 1957).

In the eastern part of the Celtic world, the predominant construction method goes by the German name of *Pfostenschlitzmauer* (post-slot wall). This consists of a series of solid wooden uprights deeply embedded in a drystone facing which runs between them. The posts were probably anchored at the top by a bank of earth or rubble (*talus*) piled against the inner face of the wall. Recent excavations have uncovered structural variations in the timber frameworks which allow a more detailed classification. Kelheim-style ramparts consist only of posts and the outer stone facing (Figure 21.3). Excavations at *oppida* such as Metz, La Heidenstadt, and Fossé des Pandours have shown that the posts sometimes had horizontal beams attached to them by means of mortice-and-tenon joints. Finally, a third subtype has been discovered at Mont Vully (Kaenel et al. 2004), again with horizontal beams inserted in the stone facing but connected to a second row of uprights located inside the *talus* (Fichtl 2012a: 32). Given the poor state of preservation of these protohistoric ramparts, it is often difficult to decide between the three subtypes. It is also uncertain whether the first category ever actually existed as it was derived from examples that lacked proper elevation. Excavations at Yverdon on Lake Neuchâtel, moreover, clearly indicate from partly preserved timbers that some of these posts were not horizontal but could have exhibited a sharp incline of nearly 14 degrees (Brunetti 2007).

FIGURE 21.3 Reconstruction of rampart with vertical post construction at the *oppidum* of the Donnersberg, Rheinland-Pfalz, Germany.

Photo: G. Pierrevelcin

In Gaul, the preference was for a horizontal beam structure: the *murus gallicus*, described by Caesar in his *Gallic War*. This featured a grid of horizontal wooden beams held together by large iron spikes. Here too the outer face of the wall was protected by a drystone cladding. Again, the wooden frame was buried within the bulk of the rampart. Recent field data suggest that this category also has three subtypes, based on the method used to attach the beams to the cladding. The first type occurs at the *oppidum* of Bibracte (Buchsenschutz et al. 1999). Here the ends of beams perpendicular to the cladding protrude through it visibly, while the beams running parallel to the cladding are placed behind it (Figure 21.4). In the second type, found at the *oppidum* of Fossé des Pandours in Alsace and at Manching in Bavaria, the beams are inserted in the cladding, but are not visible on the outside. The third type, which seems to be of slightly later date, since it is found on two ramparts of the Augustan period at Alésia and Vertault in Burgundy, features heavy beams around 10 cm thick laid horizontally across the whole width of the cladding (Fichtl 2012a: 32).

Study of these different construction techniques confirms that these protohistoric ramparts are the product of timber architecture rather than drystone architecture. The stone in the walls had a primarily aesthetic function, providing a vertical facing but in no case capable of withstanding the thrust of the earth piled against it. It fell to timber technology to fulfil this design function. The 'massive dump' ramparts, built for the most part over old wood and stone walls, follow a different architectural logic. It is sheer

FIGURE 21.4 Reconstruction of the *murus gallicus* at the Porte du Rebout entrance to the *oppidum* of Bibracte on Mont Beuvray, Burgundy.

Photo: S. Fichtl

size which makes these structures what they are. They have a much more purely defensive role therefore.

The most monumental part of the enclosure is undoubtedly the gateway. The ground plans of *oppida* gateways are all quite similar (Fichtl 2012a: 38–40). They usually take the form of two segments of the curtain wall turning in at right angles to form a corridor. They are known by the German term *Zangentor*, or pincer-gate (Dehn 1961; van Endert 1987). At the end of the corridor is a large monumental gatehouse barring access. Most of these gateways measure 7–8 metres wide by 20 metres long. The structure at the end of the corridor is generally raised on a set of six, nine, or even twelve posts stout enough to support an upper storey. A row of central posts along the corridor suggests dual lanes. These entrances have a real defensive function, the gateway being a weak point in any fortification. Attackers are forced to approach through a corridor where they are exposed to missiles from three sides. But most of all they have a symbolic function: it is the compulsory pathway between the rural world outside and the urban world within. Nor should the element of sheer ostentation be lost sight of. This is the only way into town and so here, clearly, the most effort has been lavished to impress the visitor.

But alongside these monumental gateways we must imagine each site possessing several other much smaller gates, or posterns. The length of the wall necessitated numerous openings for quick and easy access to the entire circuit, if only to maintain the stone facings. These openings, of more perfunctory construction, are no longer easy to detect.

The Function of *Oppida* Walls in the Late Iron Age

There are three functions which can always be ascribed to ramparts at any stage in history: a military and defensive function, a function concerned with prestige and ostentation, and a symbolic function (Fichtl 2005). The walls of *oppida* are no exception. The defensive function is particularly apparent in the ground plans of gateways designed for siege warfare. Caesar himself praised the quality of Gallic architecture. Of the *murus gallicus* at Avaricum, the present-day town of Bourges, he says: 'It is also very practical and perfectly suited to the defence of cities, for the stone protects it from fire, and the wood from the battering ram, since the wood, being joined internally to forty-foot long beams, can be neither smashed through nor torn apart' (*de Bello Gallico* 7.23). The massive dump ramparts he encountered in Belgic Gaul caused him similar problems, 'on account of the width of the ditch and the height of the walls, he was unable to take it by storm' (*de Bello Gallico* 2.12).

The ostentatious aspect of these structures is also much in evidence. Caesar, still speaking of Avaricum, acknowledges the structure's aesthetic quality: 'This work, with its alternate rows of beams and stones, is not unsightly …' (*de Bello Gallico* 7.23). In a world where dressed stone is not the rule, there are many ramparts which do feature it. The best examples are the *muri gallici* at Hérisson in Allier (Lallemand 2010; Figure 21.5) and at Fossé des Pandours, Saverne. In the latter, we see that particular care has been focused on the aesthetics of the facing of the earthwork barrier, this being the main access to the site and a traveller's first view of the *oppidum*. On contour forts, conversely, where access is more difficult, the dressing of the stone blocks is much cruder. Clearly this reflects choices based on aesthetics and ostentation, not on architectural necessity. Ostentation is also much in evidence on the rampart of the *oppidum* of Třísov in Bohemia. The architecture here has a facing consisting of rows of edge-laid stone slabs, which from a distance give the impression of massive cyclopean blocks.

It would certainly have been the symbolic function that was uppermost in the *oppida* of the late La Tène period. Just as with the Etrusco-Roman *pomerium*,[1] the perimeter defined a boundary between the rural and the urban world. The rampart was the physical embodiment of this boundary. We have no clear idea of the legal and religious rules that were associated with it, but as with the city of Rome several taboos must have existed. The examples of Bibracte and the Titelberg (Metzler-Zens et al. 1999) provide evidence for the location of cemeteries: as in Roman cities these were consigned to sites outside the walls and placed where they could be clearly seen from the *oppidum*'s approach roads. Other constraints must have existed, especially with regard to people. We know from Caesar's account that the chief magistrate of the Aedui, the *vergobret*, was forbidden during his year of office from travelling beyond the borders of his *civitas*. This prohibition is not unlike that of the first magistrate of the city of Rome, the urban

FIGURE 21.5 Stone facing of the *murus gallicus* at the *oppidum* of Hérisson, Allier, France.
Photo: D. Lallemand

praetor, who also could not cross the boundaries of the city. If we add that during the imperial period the *vergobrets* bore the title *praetor*, we may reasonably assume that in the matter of these legal rules there were strong similarities between the Gaulish and the Roman worlds.

Was There Town Planning?

The number of *oppida* which have been extensively excavated remains small, and it would no doubt be risky to attempt to extrapolate from a few better-known examples to all *oppida*. Yet the more extensively excavated sites all indicate that their internal organization owes nothing to chance, but instead follows a predefined plan. Three features recur regularly in the examples studied: the presence of a (probably hierarchical) road system, a division into lots or blocks, unaltered throughout the life of the site, and finally a spatial organization into districts.

Streets and Plots in the *Oppida*

We know only little about the street system inside the *oppida*, but a frequently observed feature is a large main thoroughfare linking the gateways. This is seen both on hilly sites such as the *oppidum* of Bibracte, and on more level sites such as the Titelberg (Metzler 1995), Moulay, and Manching.

Internally the *oppida* seem to be divided up according to precise rules suggestive of urban cadastration. Excavations have shown that the land within *oppida* was divided into lots which appear to correspond to dwelling units. We find this right across the region: in Gaul, for example, at Villeneuve-Saint-Germain and Variscourt/Condé-sur-Suippe (Picardy), in southern Germany at Manching (Bavaria), and in the Czech Republic at Hrazany (Bohemia) and Staré Hradisko (Moravia). The layout consists of fenced enclosures containing one or two larger houses, interpretable as residential buildings, along with ancillary structures such as granaries, silos, and wells. The area of the enclosures, where it is known, is often large: thus at Variscourt/Condé-sur-Suippe sizes range between 1,500 and 2,000 m^2, while at Villeneuve-Saint-Germain they exceed 1,000 m^2. At Manching the large enclosures at the centre of the *oppidum* even approach 6,500 m^2 (Figure 21.6). In all cases these are large open spaces in which roofed elements account for only a small part of the total area. In contrast to sites from earlier periods, such as Biskupin in Poland or those of Mediterranean Gaul, where lack of space seems to have been the main influence on internal layouts, such constraints seem not to have existed in the *oppida* of the late Iron Age.

The most representative example is probably the *oppidum* of Variscourt/Condé-sur-Suippe (Picardy; Pion et al. 1997). Here, aerial survey and excavations have revealed an urban grid over large parts of the site. The principal excavated area

FIGURE 21.6 Model of the plots or *îlots* in the centre of Manching, Bavaria.
Photo: S. Fichtl, courtesy of Kelten Römer Museum Manching

revealed two parallel roadways some 10 metres wide with, grouped around them, rectangular enclosures with an average area of 2,000 m^2. These had boundary fences and in most cases contained one large building with associated granaries, silos, and wells. They would therefore seem to be housing units. The parcelling up of the site appears to have been planned at the time it was constructed. The two roads and the square which linked them remained clear of buildings during the first phase of occupation. In a second phase, the units encroached slightly on the open spaces without altering the original divisions. The roads run parallel to the south-west rampart and perpendicular to the south-east rampart; they were laid out at the same time as the ramparts, which for their part were aligned with the River Suippe. The Variscourt *oppidum* therefore implies a predetermined plan, as might occur with a new town.

Another interesting example is the central section of Manching, which features what amount to residential blocks (Schubert 1994, Beilage 21; Sievers 2003: 43). The areas about which most is known, complexes A, B, and C, are bounded by open porticos on parallel streets intersecting at right angles, reflecting a regular grid-based system. It is interesting to note that this dates from the early second century BC, the period of the middle La Tène open settlements.

If these arrangements give the impression of farms grouped behind the walls of the *oppidum*, the objects found on these sites tell a very different story, predominantly of artisanal activities, as evidenced by significant remains of amber working at Staré Hradisko or metal production at Variscourt. The routine presence of grain storage facilities should not be interpreted as proof of agricultural activity, but is related to the inhabitants' food supply.

In other cases there are no traces of fences in the soil to mark exact boundaries, but the core property is clearly discernible. A good illustration of this is the districts of Côme Chaudron and Champlain at the *oppidum* of Bibracte (Guillaumet and Dhennequin 2008: 70–74). Several buildings clustered along the main roadway have been carefully excavated in recent years. Several stages have been identified in each of these buildings, from earlier phases in timber to later ones using stone. Yet despite this technical change, the line of the walls is maintained throughout the life of the buildings, the stone walls rising precisely over the postholes of the previous phase. This cannot be attributable to technical constraints—quite the opposite in fact—but rather to the need to respect urban boundaries. It is not just the side boundaries of the properties which remain fixed, but also the front. Only when the main roadway was widened did these buildings have to shift their front wall, whereupon all the buildings were realigned along the new route. Here we have a case of a public redevelopment (the road) impinging directly on private properties—the workshops of Côme Chaudron and Champlain. The same continuity can be observed at the *domus* or upper-class residence known as PC1 (Paunier and Luginbühl 2004: 170–176). The first phase identified here consisted of a fenced enclosure whose orientation and shape would be maintained throughout its entire existence. The third phase, still of timber, adopted the same broad lines as the previous development, and prefigured the ground plan of the stone *domus* to come. Thus in two locales differing sharply in terms of both architecture and importance, we note the persistence of boundaries which appear to have been imposed over large parts of the site.

Specialized Districts

The existence of specialized districts at the *oppidum* of Bibracte was first raised by Joseph Déchelette in his handbook of Celtic archaeology (Déchelette 1914: 948–957), in which he identifies an artisan quarter, Côme Chaudron, an aristocratic quarter, the Parc aux Chevaux, and a religious quarter located around the *fanum* (temple). While recent excavations have somewhat modified this picture, particularly with regard to the religious aspects, the division into zones of specialized activity has been confirmed.

Entering at the Porte du Rebout and following the main road, one does indeed traverse an area which groups together a number of metalworking workshops, as evidenced by manufacturing waste: iron, bronze, and enamel. The waste metal suggests highly specialized products, as at workshop 1977 at Côme Chaudron, which mainly produced objects made from sheet iron. Another workshop, room 1014 at Champlain, can be interpreted as an enamelling workshop, to which bronze craftsmen probably brought their products for the application of a decorative layer of enamel. In front of the Rebout gate was a workshop specializing in the manufacture of brooches. A particular feature is that it went through two major phases: during the first it made iron brooches, then it switched to bronze. It is interesting that despite the use of quite different metals, and hence techniques, this workshop retained its specialization in a particular product, brooches. Other crafts—ceramics, bone, and glass working—have not so far been observed, but there could be other artisanal districts, within or immediately outside the walls, where they were located.

The aristocratic residential quarter is also clearly identifiable, with its series of houses of the Roman *domus* type, in the Parc aux Chevaux. The best known *domus* is PC1, one of the largest of the Republican period, though with PC2 and PC33 close by it was not secluded. The presumed strict division into districts needs to be somewhat qualified, because substantial houses have also been identified in other parts of the *oppidum* (Meylan 2008: 22–30). The existence of specialized districts elsewhere is demonstrated by the recent excavation of the *oppidum* at Moulay in Mayenne (Le Goff and Moreau 2012: 157). A residential area has been identified at the southern end, comprising some fifteen buildings of very similar architecture and proportions, most combined with a grain store. Here we encounter a repeated modular design that is characteristic of this sector of the *oppidum*. In the central area, by contrast, a large artisanal and commercial quarter was excavated, around a ditched enclosure in which ritually mutilated weapons have been unearthed. This was undoubtedly a place of worship.

Public Monuments: Squares and Temples

The major development of the last fifteen years has been the uncovering of public squares, for the most part related to temples (Fichtl et al. 2000; Fichtl 2012b). Two examples have been the subject of recent excavations and give a good idea of what public squares were like in an *oppidum*.

The 1990s excavations at the Titelberg, capital of the Treveri, revealed extremely interesting public amenities (Metzler et al. 2000, 2016; Metzler and Gaeng 2005). On this site of just under 50 ha, an area of 10 ha is marked off at one end by a broad ditch 4 m wide and 2 m deep, with a mud-brick wall behind. This would seem to have been an assembly area for political and religious events. Within this open space a public structure has been uncovered on the highest part of the Titelberg plateau which underwent several changes in the decades around the Roman conquest. In its first incarnation, around the end of the second century or the beginning of the first century BC, the area contained a series of parallel fences forming corridors more than 60 m long and nearly 4 m wide, running perpendicular to the main road through the *oppidum*. The excavating team's preferred interpretation is that this was a voting facility, comparable to the Roman *saepta*. In the second quarter of the first century BC this location underwent major changes. There now appeared in the same place a rectangular building of monumental scale, 14 by 15 m, incorporating four rows of posts. This would have been a hall with three aisles and was entirely open. It fronted onto an esplanade some 40 m long, in the middle of which was a square-shaped foundation aligned with the great hall, interpreted as the remains of an altar. The location of this monumental building, which would have been of significant height, is not accidental: it is situated on the highest point of the plateau precisely on a line between the two gates of the *oppidum*. In the first half of the first century AD the timber hall gave way to a building 12 metres square, also open, and in the middle of the second century AD to a small temple (*fanum*). So in the same location at this *oppidum* we have a succession of political and religious activities which confirms the close relationship between these two functions. The organization of space also calls to mind the forum in the Roman world.

More recently, the *oppidum* of Corent, capital of the Arverni, has provided another good example (Poux 2011). Excavations since the early 2000s in the centre of the *oppidum* have yielded evidence of a monumental temple, founded in the second half of the second century BC (Poux and Demierre 2016). It takes the form of a fenced enclosure 43 m square, more or less aligned with the cardinal points. At the start of the first century BC it underwent significant changes: while retaining its original form, the fence was replaced by four open porticos which increased the width per side to 50 m. The temple fronted onto a large square devoid of buildings which must have covered at least 2,500 m^2. Excavations in 2011 to the south-west of this spot uncovered a semicircular structure including a *cavea*[2] and a *podium*, which can be compared to a *comitium* or *curia*—i.e. a meeting place for the town's chief magistrates (Figure 21.7).

These two examples, to which may be added the *oppida* of Manching, Gournay-sur-Aronde (Oise), and more recently Moulay (Mayenne), clearly show that public spaces with political and religious functions have existed since the second century BC. The basilica complex discovered at Bibracte, dating from the 40s BC, is no more than a transcription into Roman architecture of monumental complexes which probably already existed in most *oppida*. The main interest of this discovery lies in its exceptionally early adoption of Roman architecture.

The Function of *Oppida*

The *oppida*, like all towns, were political and religious centres—clearly illustrated by the monumental public areas at Titelberg and Corent—and at the same time important commercial centres. As we have seen, the existence of true artisanal districts is apparent at Bibracte and Moulay. But even where division of the land for different artisanal activities is less easily demonstrated, these activities were still omnipresent, as can be seen at Manching, Variscourt, and Villeneuve-Saint-Germain.

FIGURE 21.7 Part of the public centre at the *oppidum* of Corent in the Auvergne, based on excavations by M. Poux.

Model CoursJus Production

We should also probably add coin production to our picture of the *oppida*. Although no actual mint has yet been definitely identified, it is on these sites that we find the greatest quantities of coins outside temple coffers. Perhaps the only certain example is the small Hungarian *oppidum* of Szalacska, where a mint was discovered in 1906. Six coin dies were found, three obverse and three reverse, along with several coins struck with these dies. Coin dies have been found at other *oppida*. Two from Bibracte correspond to different varieties of Aeduan silver units bearing helmeted heads (*tête casquée*; Gruel and Popovitch 2007: 25). From Manching comes a bronze stamp for making coin dies for silver units with a cross symbol, a coin type frequently found at the *oppidum*. Two more examples may be cited from the Swiss Plateau. A fourth die for striking silver units, in this case belonging to the Kaletedou series, was discovered at the *oppidum* of Mont Vully (Kaenel and Auberson 1996), while a die for striking gold coins, now at Avenches, could have come from the nearby Bois de Châtel *oppidum*. Another frequent indicator of coin production are spoiled potins (cast-metal coins), of which still-connected strings have been found on some sites: spoiled castings of potins with a boar symbol were found in a well at the *oppidum* of the Mediomatrici at Fossé des Pandours, and also at the *oppidum* of the Leuci at Boviolles.

The quantity of coinage in circulation at the *oppida*, and the mixed provenance of the coins, reflect intensive trading activities, both with the Mediterranean world and between the different regions of Celtic Europe (Pierrevelcin 2012b). Which goods were traded is harder to determine. Only the thousands or even tens of thousands of amphorae and associated containers, whether of metal, such as strainers, or pottery, such as Campanian ware, give any reflection of this commerce.

The *Oppidum* as Capital of the Gaulish *Civitas*

In the first century BC, Gaul was divided into around sixty civitates. These autonomous city-states were mostly organized around one or more *oppida* (Fichtl 2004). In some cases, it seems that one of these can be regarded effectively as a capital. This is apparent not only from archaeological data, but also from textual records.

If the ancient texts never explicitly refer to a capital of a Gaulish *civitas*, several passages nonetheless stress the predominance of one or another *oppidum*. Three references from Caesar's *Gallic War* are fairly clear on this matter: they concern Bourges-Avaricum, Besançon-Vesontio, and Mont Beuvray-Bibracte:

- Bourges, the former Avaricum, an *oppidum* of the Bituriges, is called 'the most beautiful [*oppidum*] of all Gaul, which is the strength and ornament of their civitas' (quae praesidio et ornamento sit civitati; *de Bello Gallico* 7.15.4), also 'the most important and best defended' (maximum munitissimumque; *de Bello Gallico* 7.13.3).
- Vesontio (Besançon), for its part, is described as 'the largest *oppidum* of the Sequani' (maximum oppidum Sequanorum; *de Bello Gallico* 1.38.1).
- Bibracte (Mont-Beuvray) is considered 'by far the largest and richest *oppidum* of the Aedui' (oppido Haeduorum longe maximo et copiosissimo; *de Bello Gallico*, 1.23).

The concept of a capital is more difficult to perceive archaeologically. One criterion is generally not enough; several yardsticks must be used. For instance, size is often considered to be the characteristic which defines the chief *oppidum* of a civitas. It is also the most readily accessible. The underlying idea is that the area of a site is closely related to its importance. This is undoubtedly true in absolute terms, but needs qualification. There is no standard size for principal *oppida*. In the case of the Aedui the main *oppidum* was Bibracte, which at its greatest extent covered an area of 200 ha. But go further west, to the home of a smaller group such as the Turones, and its biggest site, the *oppidum* of Amboise, occupies only 52 ha. Even so it is much larger than their other fortified sites, none of which exceed 12 ha. Similarly, the *oppidum* of the Mediomatrici at Fossé des Pandours is, at 170 ha, far and away the largest in the *civitas*, the other sites hovering around 12–20 ha.

Another problem to consider is the contemporaneity of sites. Gaulish polities did not stay the same size throughout their existence, which could affect where the capital might be. To continue with the example of the Mediomatrici, the *oppidum* at Fossé des Pandours was clearly the capital until the middle of the first century BC. However, after the Gallic Wars the *civitas* was stripped of its eastern sector, and Fossé des Pandours, located in just that part of the territory, declined rapidly, if it was not completely abandoned. Another *oppidum*, this time Metz, assumed its functions, and went on to become the capital of the Roman *civitas*.

Other criteria may also be considered, although they are often difficult to apply. The importance of monumental embellishments should be mentioned, in terms of both size and architectural quality. The existence of a public meeting space reflects the political and civic role of the town. Finally, the presence of a mint also confirms its political importance. But none of these criteria, taken individually, is enough to determine the capital of a *civitas*.

The *Oppidum* as a Structuring Element of Territory

Oppida undoubtedly shaped the territory of Gaulish civitates. The sixty *civitates* were, in many cases, subdivided into smaller territorial units called *pagi* by Caesar. These subdivisions can sometimes be detected through archaeology, particularly by studying the distribution of *oppida* within the *civitates*.

One *civitas* illustrates this perfectly: the territory of the Bellovaci in the west of Belgic Gaul, encompassing the present-day département of Oise. We know of four *oppida* in this territory—Gouvieux, Bailleul-sur-Thérain, Vendeuil-Caply, and Gournay-sur-Aronde. These four sites appear to correspond with the four *pagi* of the Merovingian period: *pagus belvacensis, pagus vindoliensis, pagus rossontentis*, and *pagus camliacensis*. The four-way division of Bellovaci territory must therefore not only go back to the pre-Roman period, but was very probably established relatively early on, because three of the *oppida* in question are associated with shrines which date back at least to the beginning of the third century BC.

Similarly in the case of the Treveri, who inhabited the lower valley of the Moselle, we find six *oppida* evenly distributed around the *civitas*: Donnersberg, Martberg, Otzenhausen, Kastel, Wallendorf, and Titelberg. If we project the theoretical territory of these *oppida* by means of Thiessen polygons onto a map of the Treveran region, we find that five of them have territories of similar size, and only the *oppidum* on the Donnersberg, opening onto the Rhine plain, has a larger territory. Moreover, these boundaries coincide quite closely with the boundaries of the medieval dioceses, themselves derived from the Gaulish divisions. We can therefore infer that the Treveri were subdivided from the outset into six *pagi*, each organized around an *oppidum*.

However, not all *civitates* can so easily be divided into areas dominated by an *oppidum*. Some contained only one *oppidum*, properly speaking, perhaps allied with lesser fortified sites, but not such as to allow division of the land into *pagi*. This is particularly true of the Turones, whose only real *oppidum* was the site at Amboise, which, with an area of 50 ha, can be considered their capital. It was associated with three small fortified sites of a mere dozen hectares, Rochecorbon, Fondette, and Sainte-Maure-de-Touraine, but their location does not represent an even division of the territory. Perhaps the *civitas* of the Turones, corresponding more or less to the present-day département of Indre-et-Loire, and thus among the smaller polities, was never subdivided into *pagi*.

The situation is different with the Senones. This group inhabited a large territory in east central Gaul, neighbouring the Aedui. However, it is difficult to postulate a division of their territory based on *oppida*. Indeed, only one fortified site can be regarded as a true *oppidum*: Villeneuve-sur-Yonne, which at 140 ha is among Gaul's larger *oppida*. Other fortified sites are found in this territory, but modest in scale, such as the promontory fort at Triguères, 'le Donjon', which is around 9 ha, or Mont-Avrollot at Avrolles, no bigger than 1.5 ha. Caesar does mention several hillforts in the western part of the territory, including Vellaunodunum, but the position of this site remains hypothetical. In the north-west of the territory lay Metlosedum, identified as present-day Melun. Iron Age settlement here is well documented for the first century BC, but the absence of any trace of a rampart at the ancient city presents problems in identifying it as an *oppidum*. The *civitas* seems to have been organized along the valley of the Yonne, with its succession of open settlements such as Bonnard, Senan, Sens-Quartier St Paul, Saint-Martin du Tertre, Varennes-sur-Seine, and Melun-Metlosedum. There is therefore a different model of organization for the Senones, not centred on *oppida*.

Conclusion

The *oppida* clearly represent the first real urban forms north of the Alps. These sites emerged over the last third of the second century BC, only to disappear in the middle or at the end of the first century BC. They are thus characterized by a very short lifespan, some not lasting more than half a century. In Gaul, many of them were abandoned in favour of a new Roman town, built a few kilometres away, on more favourable terrain. Yet a significant number of *oppida*, among them Besançon, Langres, Reims, Angers, and Poitiers, gave rise to Roman cities on the same site, on which in turn stand most of the leading French cities of today.

Notes

1. In Etruria and Rome, the *pomerium* designated a sacred area around a town, which was traced out at the time of its foundation. No building was permitted there, and armed soldiers were not allowed to cross it. It formed a symbolic limit to the town.
2. *Cavea* is the architectural term for the raked seating in Roman theatres and amphitheatres.

References

Audouze, F., and O. Buchsenschutz. 1989. *Villes, villages et campagnes de l'Europe celtique.* Paris: Hachette.

Augier, L., O. Buchsenschutz, and I. Ralston. 2007. *Un complexe princier de l'âge du Fer. L'habitat du promontoire de Bourges (Cher) (VIe-IVe s. av. J.-C.). Bituriga Monographie 3. Revue archéologique du Centre de la France supplément 32.* Bourges/Tours: FERACF.

Brunetti, C. 2007. *Yverdon-les-Bains et Sermuz à la fin de l'âge du Fer.* Cahiers d'archéologie romande 107. Lausanne: Bibliothèque historique vaudoise.

Buchsenschutz, O., A. Colin, G. Firmin, B. Fischer, J.-P. Guillaumet, S. Krausz, et al. 2000. *Le village celtique des Arènes à Levroux: Synthèses. Levroux 5.* Revue archéologique du Centre de la France supplément 19. Levroux: FERACF/ADEL.

Buchsenschutz, O., J.-P. Guillaumet, and I. Ralston. 1999. *Les remparts de Bibracte. Recherches récentes sur la Porte du Rebout et le tracé des fortifications.* Collection Bibracte 3. Glux-en-Glenne: Centre archéologique européen du Mont Beuvray.

Buchsenschutz, O., and I. Ralston. 1981. 'Les fortifications des âges des Métaux'. *Archéologia* 154: 26–35.

Cahen-Delhaye, A., A. Duval, G. Leman-Delerive, and P. Leman. 1984. *Les Celtes en Belgique et dans le nord de la France: Les fortifications à l'âge du Fer. Actes du sixième colloque tenu à Bavay et Mons.* Villeneuve d'Ascq: Revue du Nord.

Čižmář, M., E. Kolníková, and H.-C. Noeske. 2008. 'Němčice-Víceměřice—ein neues Handels- und Industriezentrum der Latènezeit in Mähren'. *Germania* 86, 2: 655–700.

Collis, J. R. 1975. *Defended Sites of the Late La Tène in Central and Western Europe.* British Archaeological Reports International Series 2. Oxford: British Archaeological Reports.

Collis, J. R. 1984. *Oppida, Earliest Towns North of the Alps.* Sheffield: University of Sheffield.

Cunliffe, B. W. 1987. *Hengistbury Head, Dorset: The Prehistoric and Roman Settlement, 3500 BC–AD 500.* OUCA Monograph 13. Oxford: Oxford University Committee for Archaeology.

Cunliffe, B. W., and T. Rowley. 1976. *Oppida: The Beginnings of Urbanisation in Barbarian Europe.* British Archaeological Reports International Series 11. Oxford: British Archaeological Reports.

Déchelette, J. 1914. *Manuel d'archéologie préhistorique, celtique et gallo-romaine. II-3: Second âge du Fer ou époque de La Tène.* Paris: Picard.

Dehn, W. 1961. 'Zangentore an spätkeltischen Oppida'. *Památky Archeologické* 52: 390–396.

Dehn, W. 1962. 'Aperçu sur les oppida d'Allemagne à la fin de l'époque celtique'. *Celticum* 4: 329–386.

Fichtl, S. 2000. *La ville celtique: Les oppida de 150 av. J.-C. à 15 apr. J.-C.* Paris: Errance.

Fichtl, S. 2004. *Les peuples gaulois: IIIe-Ier siècles av. J.-C.* Paris: Errance.

Fichtl, S. 2005. 'Murus et pomerium? Réflexions sur la fonction des remparts protohistoriques'. *Revue Archéologique du Centre de la France* 44: 55–72.

Fichtl, S. 2010. *Murus celticus: Architecture et fonctions des remparts de l'âge du Fer.* Collection Bibracte 19. Glux-en-Glenne: Centre archéologique européen du Mont Beuvray.

Fichtl, S. 2012a. *Les premières villes de Gaule: Le temps des oppida.* Lacapelle-Marival: Éditions Archéologie Nouvelle.

Fichtl, S. 2012b. 'Places publiques et lieux de rassemblement? À la fin de l'âge du Fer dans le monde celtique', in A. Bouet (ed.) *Le forum romain en Gaule et dans les régions voisines.* Collection 'Mémoires': 41–53. Bordeaux: Ausonius.

Fichtl, S. 2013. 'Les agglomérations gauloises de la fin de l'âge du Fer en Europe celtique (IIIe–Ier s. av. J.-C.)', in D. Garcia (ed.) *L'habitat en Europe celtique et en Méditerranée préclassique—Domaines urbaines*: 19–43. Paris: Errance.

Fichtl, S., J. Metzler, and S. Sievers. 2000. 'Le rôle des sanctuaires dans le processus d'urbanisation', in V. Guichard, S. Sievers, and O.-H. Urban (eds) *Le processus d'urbanisation à l'âge du Fer—Eisenzeitliche Urbanisationsprozesse*. Collection Bibracte 4: 143–150. Glux-en-Glenne: Centre archéologique européen du Mont Beuvray.

Fischer, T., S. Rieckhoff-Pauli, and K. Spindler. 1984. 'Grabungen in der spätlkeltischen Siedlung im Sulztal bei Berching-Pollanten, Lkr. Neumarkt, Oberpfalz'. *Germania* 2: 311–372.

Goudineau, C., and C. Peyre. 1993. *Bibracte et les Éduens: À la découverte d'un peuple gaulois*. Paris: Errance.

Gruel, K., and L. Popovitch. 2007. *Les monnaies gauloises et romaines de l'oppidum de Bibracte*. Collection Bibracte 13. Glux-en-Glenne: Centre archéologique européen du Mont Beuvray.

Guichard, V., S. Sievers, and O.-H. Urban (eds). 2000. *Le processus d'urbanisation à l'âge du Fer—Eisenzeitliche Urbanisationsprozesse*. Collection Bibracte 4. Glux-en-Glenne: Centre archéologique européen du Mont Beuvray.

Guillaumet, J.-P., and L. Dhennequin. 2008. 'Les ateliers du métal et leur production', in L. Dhennequin, J.-P. Guillaumet, and M. Szabó (eds) *L'oppidum de Bibracte (Mont Beuvray, France): Bilan de 10 années de recherches (1996–2005)*. Acta Archaeologica Academiae Scientiarum Hungaricae 59: 68–77. Budapest: Akadémiai Kiadó.

Kaenel, G., and A.-F. Auberson. 1996. 'Un coin monétaire celtique au Mont Vully (canton de Fribourg)'. *Archéologie suisse* 19: 106–111.

Kaenel, G., P. Curdy, and F. Carrard. 2004. *L'oppidum du Mont-Vully: Un bilan des recherches 1978–2003*. Archéologie fribourgeoise 20. Freiburg: Academic Press.

Krausse, D., M. Fernández-Götz, L. Hansen, and I. Kretschmer. 2016. *The Heuneburg and the Early Iron Age Princely Seats: First Towns North of the Alps*. Budapest: Archaeolingua.

Kurz, S. 2009. 'Neue Herren auf der Burg? Ein Beitrag zur historischen Interpretation der Heuneburg am Ende der Periode IV', in J. Biel, J. Heiligmann, and D. Krausse (eds) *Landesarchäologie. Festschrift für Dieter Planck zum 65. Geburtstag*: 143–161. Stuttgart: Theiss.

Kurz, S. 2010. 'Zur Genese und Entwicklung der Heuneburg in der späten Hallstattzeit', in D. Krausse (ed.) *'Fürstensitze' und Zentralorte der frühen Kelten. Abschlusskolloquium des DFG-Schwerpunktprogramms 1171 in Stuttgart, 12.–15. Oktober 2009*: 239–256. Stuttgart: Theiss.

Lallemand, D. 2010. 'L'oppidum de Cordes-Chateloi à Hérisson (Allier): premiers résultats des fouilles archéologiques conduites sur la porte de Babylone', in S. Fichtl (ed.) *Murus celticus: Architecture et fonctions des remparts de l'âge du Fer*. Collection Bibracte 19: 257–279. Glux-en-Glenne: Centre archéologique européen du Mont Beuvray.

Lambot, B., and P. Méniel. 1992. *Le site protohistorique d'Acy-Romance (Ardennes) I: l'habitat gaulois 1988–1990*. Mémoires de la Société Archéologique Champenoise 7, supplément 2. Dossiers de Protohistoire 4. Reims: Société Archéologique Champenoise.

Lambot, B., and P. Méniel. 2000. 'Le centre communautaire et cultuel du village gaulois d'Acy-Romance dans son contexte régional', in S. Verger (ed.) *Rites et espaces en pays celte et méditerranéen: étude comparée à partir du sanctuaire d'Acy-Romance (Ardennes, France)*. Collection de l'École française de Rome 276: 7–139. Rome: École française de Rome.

Le Goff, E., and C. Moreau. 2012. 'Moulay, un oppidum de l'ouest de la Gaule revisité'. *Nouveaux champs de la recherche Archéologique*. Archéopages, Hors-série 3: 153–159.

Méniel, P. 1998. *Les animaux et l'histoire d'un village gaulois: Le site protohistorique d'Acy-Romance (Ardennes) 3*. Mémoires de la Société Archéologique Champenoise H.S. 14. Reims: Société Archéologique Champenoise.

Metzler, J. 1995. *Das treverische Oppidum auf dem Titelberg (G.-H. Luxemburg)*. Dossier d'Archéologie du Musée National d'Histoire et d'Art 3. Luxembourg: Musée National d'Histoire et d'Art.

Metzler, J., R. Bis, C. Gaeng, and P. Méniel. 2000. 'Vorbericht zu den Ausgrabungen im keltisch-römischen Heiligtum auf dem Titelberg', in A. Haffner and S. von Schnurbein (eds) *Kelten, Germanen, Römer im Mittelgebirgsraum zwischen Luxemburg und Thüringen*. Kolloquien zur Vor- und Frühgeschichte 5: 431–445. Bonn: Habelt.

Metzler, J., and C. Gaeng. 2005. 'Le fossé d'enclos du centre public de l'oppidum du Titelberg', in F. Le Brun-Ricalens, L. Brou, F. Valotteau, J. Metzler, and C. Gaeng (eds) *Les collections du musée national d'histoire et d'art 1: Préhistoire et Protohistoire au Luxembourg*: 212–215. Luxembourg: Musée national d'histoire et d'art.

Metzler, J., C. Gaeng, and P. Méniel. 2016. *L'espace public du Titelberg*. Dossiers d'archéologie 17. Luxembourg: Centre National de la Recherche Archéologique.

Metzler-Zens, N., J. Metzler-Zens, and P. Méniel. 1999. *Lamadelaine, une nécropole de l'oppidum du Titelberg*. Dossier d'Archéologie du Musée National d'Histoire et d'Art 6. Luxembourg: Musée National d'Histoire et d'Art.

Meylan, F. 2008. 'Les influences romaines dans l'architecture et l'urbanisme: apport des fouilles anciennes', in L. Dhennequin, J.-P. Guillaumet, and M. Szabó (eds) *L'oppidum de Bibracte (Mont Beuvray, France): Bilan de 10 années de recherches (1996–2005)*. Acta Archaeologica Academiae Scientiarum Hungaricae 59: 22–30. Budapest: Akadémiai Kiadó.

Milcent, P.-Y. 2007. *Bourges-Avaricum, un centre proto-urbain celtique du Ve siècle av. J.-C. Les fouilles de Saint-Martin-des-Champs et les découvertes des établissements militaires*. Bituriga Monographie 1. Bourges: Éditions de la Ville de Bourges.

Milcent, P.-Y. 2012. 'Résidences aristocratiques et expérience urbaine hallstattiennes en France (VIe–Ve s. av. J.-C.)', in S. Sievers and M. Schönfelder (eds) *Die Frage der Protourbanisation in der Eisenzeit: La question de la proto-urbanisation à l'âge du Fer*. Kolloquien zur Vor- und Frühgeschichte 16: 91–113. Bonn: Habelt.

Paunier, D., and T. Luginbühl. 2004. *Le site de la maison 1 du Parc aux Chevaux (PC 1)*. Collection Bibracte 8. Glux-en-Glenne: Centre archéologique européen du Mont Beuvray.

Píč, J.-L. 1906. *Le Hradischt de Stradonitz en Bohême* (transl. J. Déchelette). Leipzig: Hiersemann.

Pierrevelcin, G. 2012a. *Les grands sites gaulois: Atlas des oppida*. Lacapelle-Marival: Éditions Archéologie Nouvelle.

Pierrevelcin, G. 2012b. 'L'oppidum, un centre économique: place de marché et lieu de production', in S. Fichtl (ed.) *Les premières villes de Gaule: Le temps des oppida*: 61–68. Lacapelle-Marival: Éditions Archéologie Nouvelle.

Pion, P., C. Pommepuy, G. Auxiette, B. Hénon, and F. Gransar. 1997. 'L'oppidum de Condé-sur-Suippe/Variscourt (Aisne) (fin IIe–début Ier s. av. J.-C.): approche préliminaire de l'organisation fonctionnelle d'un quartier artisanal', in G. Auxiette, L. Hachem, and B. Robert (eds) *Espaces physiques, espaces sociaux dans l'analyse interne des sites du Néolithique à l'Âge du Fer. Actes du 119e Congrès national des sociétés historiques et scientifiques*: 275–310. Paris: Éditions du CTHS.

Poux, M. 2011. *Corent: Voyage au cœur d'une ville gauloise*. Paris: Errance.

Poux, M., and M. Demierre. 2016. *Le sanctuaire de Corent (Puy-de-Dôme, Auvergne): Vestiges et rituels*. Gallia supplément 62. Paris: CNRS.

Rieckhoff, S., and S. Fichtl. 2011. *Keltenstädte aus der Luft*. Archäologie in Deutschland, Sonderheft 2011 PLUS. Stuttgart: Theiss.

Rybová, A., and P. Drda. 1994. *Hradiště by Stradonice: Rebirth of a Celtic Oppidum*. Prague: Institute of Archaeology of the Czech Academy of Sciences.

Schäfer, A. 2010. *Die Kleinfunde der jüngerlatènezeitlichen Siedlung von Berching-Pollanten, Lkr. Neumarkt i. d. Oberpfalz*. Marburger Studien zur Vor- und Frühgeschichte 24. Rahden: Marie Leidorf.

Schubert, F. 1994. 'Zur Maß- und Entwurfslehre keltischer Holzbauten im Oppidum von Manching'. *Germania* 72, 1: 133–192.

Sievers, S. 2003. *Manching: Die Keltenstadt. Führer zu archäologischen Denkmälern in Bayern. Oberbayern* 3. Stuttgart: Theiss.

Sievers, S., and M. Schönfelder (eds). 2012. *Die Frage der Protourbanisation in der Eisenzeit: La question de la proto-urbanisation à l'âge du Fer. Akten des 34. internationalen Kolloquiums der AFEAF vom 13.–16. Mai 2010 in Aschaffenburg*. Kolloquien zur Vor- und Frühgeschichte 16. Bonn: Habelt.

Van Endert, D. 1987. *Das Osttor des Oppidums von Manching*. Die Ausgrabungen in Manching 10. Stuttgart: Steiner.

Werner, J. 1979. 'Die Bedeutung des Stadtwesens für die Kulturentwicklung des frühen Keltentums', in L. Pauli (ed.) *Spätes Keltentum zwischen Rom und Germanien* (first published as *Die Welt als Geschichte* 5, 1939): 1–20. Munich: Beck.

Wheeler, M., and M. Richardson. 1957. *Hill Forts of Northern France*. Reports of the Research Committee of the Society of Antiquaries of London 19. London: Society of Antiquaries of London.

Zeeb-Lanz, A. 2008. *Der Donnersberg, eine bedeutende spätkeltische Stadtanlage*. Archäologische Denkmäler in der Pfalz 2. Speyer: Generaldirektion Kulturelles Erbe Rheinland-Pfalz.

CHAPTER 22

MONUMENTS

HOLGER WENDLING AND MANFRED K. H. EGGERT

Introduction: Envisaging Iron Age Landscapes

In general, ancient descriptions of landscapes and the spatial arrangement of Iron Age communities in temperate and northern Europe are limited and severely biased. Thus, Caesar's and Tacitus' accounts of Celtic and Germanic tribes and their habitat convey the image of a largely uncultivated wilderness with some dispersed single farms, hamlets, and villages, as well as a few *oppida* or towns. The description of woodlands dominating the landscape, and impenetrable forest impeding the spread of more complex Roman civilization, is certainly part of the larger endeavour of contrasting one's own world with that of supposedly barbarian savages (see last section, 'Forest exploitation and fortifications'). However, a closer look at the narratives reveals indirect evidence of a quite different character. For instance, Caesar mentions the rapidity of oral transmission of important news over considerable distances, which indirectly suggests that large parts of the landscape were cleared (*de Bello Gallico* 7.3.2). Moreover, huge amounts of grain were required to feed the Roman army, and this, in turn, presupposed extended areas under cultivation. Consequently, classical sources implicitly suggest Iron Age clearance of woodland, a fact also supported by archaeobotanical analysis. Pollen studies reveal a constant decline of tree pollen in favour of an increase in grass and plants indicating agricultural activity (Rösch et al. 2008: 341–343). Also, the landscape was deliberately opened up by infrastructural devices like bridges and roads. Even difficult terrain like swamps and peat bogs were made accessible by log causeways, according to classical sources (Caesar *de Bello Gallico* 7.19.2; Tacitus *Annals* 1.63.3; see Schetter and von Uslar 1971). Thus, the written record attests to a considerable human impact on the Iron Age landscape.

Traditionally, Iron Age archaeology focused on cemeteries and, to a much lesser degree, on settlements. With the intensification of settlement research after World War

II, attention was directed towards human interaction with the landscape and its impact on it. This led, for example, since the early 1960s, to an ecological approach in the American new archaeology (see Eggert 1978). In general, the development towards an ecological perspective was fundamentally influenced by the growing significance of natural sciences, such as palaeoethnobotany and zooarchaeology, in the context of archaeological research on settlements. More recently, structuralist, hermeneutical, and phenomenological approaches try to trace the position of communities in a natural and social environment considered as being both adaptable and resistant to internal and external pressure. In post-processual 'landscape archaeology', research is based on the social dimensions of the appropriation and use of space. Theoretical considerations related to this have had a positive impact on environmental studies, enabling indirect inferences from the residues of human spatial behaviour to the social foundations and—to a lesser degree—the intentions of prehistoric societies. Furthermore, the extraordinary development of IT tools and programs using geographical data effectively to analyse large-scale environmental information has profoundly altered present interpretations of archaeological landscapes (Limp 2008; Posluschny et al. 2011). Nowadays, landscape is perceived both as a setting for monuments and an encompassing monument in itself, which is composed of a multitude of anthropogenic and ecological traits and features.

Appropriating Ancient Monuments

Iron Age communities across Europe did not take possession of an unaltered pristine environment, but rather flourished in a landscape marked by a variety of structures erected during the Neolithic and Bronze Ages. A repeated appropriation of ancient cultural objects in creating new monuments which structured the landscape of an early Iron Age community is found at Rottenburg in south-west Germany (Reim 2006). Several burial mounds of a Hallstatt C–D cemetery contained complete or fragmentary anthropomorphic stone sculptures. These stelae were either part of the stone chamber in the centre of the earth mounds containing cremations, or displayed on top of the mounds. Contrary to earlier assumptions, a re-evaluation of the sculptures confirmed a late Neolithic or early Bronze Age date and a secondary usage in a seventh-century BC context. Probably the burial ground was arranged around a Neolithic grave structure, which might still have been visible at that time.

Only about eight kilometres from this site, the stone circle encompassing the base of a Hallstatt tumulus at Kilchberg contained three similar stelae also attesting to some kind of local cultural heritage. This might have served to integrate local traditions in a new temporal and spatial framework. The ostentatious acquisition and reuse of a time-honoured sacred environment referencing actual or fictitious ancestors might have legitimized land ownership and ideologically enhanced status and power.

Similar intentions might have guided late Iron Age communities when making use of the capacity of ancient burial mounds as prominent markers and structural elements of the landscape. Thus, in northern Germany, Iron Age cremations frequently occur in megalithic and other Neolithic and Bronze Age tombs (Schuldt 1972: 82; Sopp 1999; Bradley 2002: 124–130). During the Danish early Iron Age (500–150 BC) about a third of all cremation burials are related to, or placed within, existing Bronze Age mounds of the second millennium BC (Parker Pearson 1999: 126). More than a simple reuse of a funerary monument, this implies an intentional act of taking over the tradition of local beliefs and power. This was also intended in placing late Iron Age burials in Bronze Age and early Iron Age tumuli in the upper Rhine area (Wendling 2012: 239). People established themselves within an existing pattern of monumental structures, which they integrated into their own emerging landscape of monuments (Bradley and Williams 1998; Bradley 2002).

A direct connection with land property and the evocation of traditional rights regarding the landscape might be identified in a late Iron Age phenomenon called *Viereckschanzen*. These monumental earthen structures are often spatially related to ancient, mostly Bronze or early Iron Age, burial mounds (Wieland 1999: 76–78; Bradley 2002: 132, 139; Wendling 2016). The very act of building a farmstead next to ancestral monuments, and sometimes even incorporating a mound into the whole settlement, seems to reveal an urgent desire to assure ancestral land rights by reverting to local sacral forces. At Pulversheim in Alsace (France), a direct connection between a rectangular enclosure and an ancient mound, which was surely perceived as an ancestral monument, is apparent (Wendling 2012: no. 196). Adjacent to a *Viereckschanze* at Heiligkreuztal (south-west Germany) several groups of Hallstatt burial mounds indicate their integration into the late La Tène sacred landscape (Bittel et al. 1981: 94–95). The Hohmichele tumulus, with its original height of about 13.5 m, one of the most outstanding early Iron Age funerary monuments in Europe, is only about 75 m away. This spatial arrangement denotes an ideological appropriation of ancient monuments (Figure 22.1).

Integration of certain aspects of the past through referencing older monuments influenced the setting and orientation of early Iron Age hillforts in south-east England. In this context, the presence of Bronze Age barrows and the visibility of ancient places of resource procurement at a distance seem to have held significant symbolic importance (Hamilton and Manley 2001: 13). All this seems to indicate that the actual occupation of the landscape was often linked to the symbolic appropriation of remnants of the past.

It might be assumed, however, that the collective mental map which structured the environment transcended the sphere of ancient anthropogenic structures. In fact, it seems reasonable to imagine that natural features like trees, ridges, bogs, springs, or forests were also part of that map. They probably played an important role in establishing a structured environment that could be accessed physically and mentally (Bradley 2000). Ethnographic examples show how deeply such elements of vegetation and topography influence the way traditional societies perceive and experience the space they live in. The Kassena in Burkina Faso (Africa), like many other traditional societies, respect zones of restricted access or limited use according to the assumed presence of ancestral spirits (Hahn 2000a: 144–145). Trees mark single burials, but also visually localize narratives and events in times past. The localities which make up such a mental map are

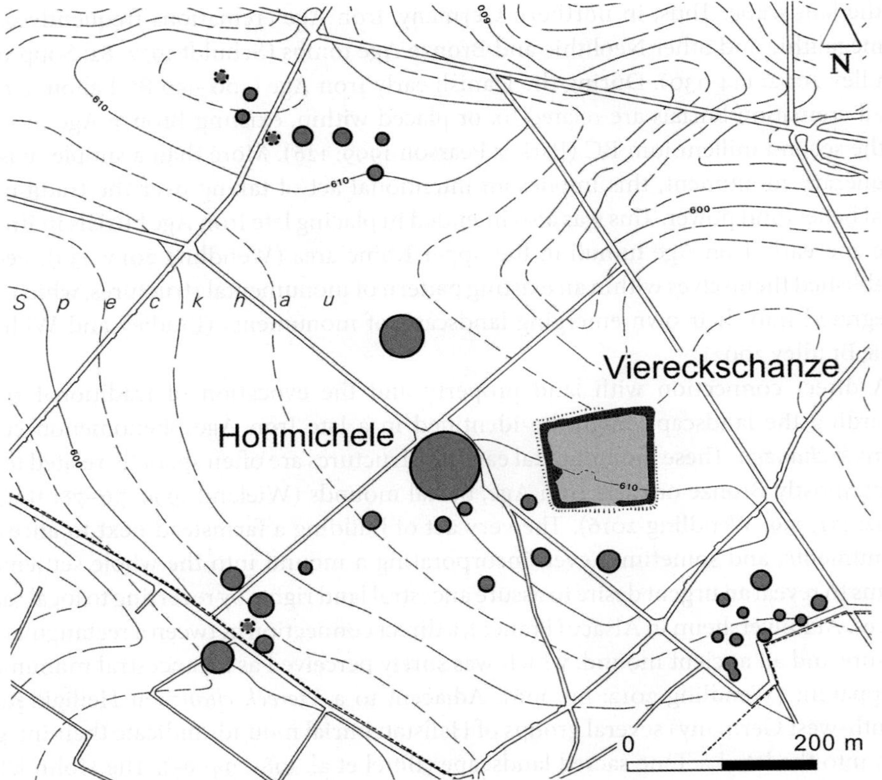

FIGURE 22.1 The proximity of a late La Tène fortified farmstead (*Viereckschanze*) to older Hallstatt barrows around the giant Hohmichele tumulus near the Heuneburg (south-west Germany) denotes an intentional spatial arrangement and ideological appropriation of ancient monuments.

Source: Bittel et al. (1981): fig. 31

not necessarily tangible, but are subject to continuous re-evaluation, being an integral part of religious practice. Natural features—which may often be of monumental size themselves—link the spatial concept with a temporal prospect and thus create a cosmological belief system (Hahn 2000b: 241–242, 251).

It seems reasonable to assume that similar beliefs and concepts determined mental constructs of landscape in European Iron Age societies. In most cases those natural phenomena have long vanished. Only rarely do we have indications of their former presence. For instance, some breaks and minor swerves in the course of British earthworks have been interpreted as showing the position of trees that might have been protected from felling by taboos, or were deliberately integrated into the new structures that were to form the landscape (Giles 2007: 113). Other sites were chosen as special places due to their monumental and singular morphology. For example, the Heidentor, a naturally formed rock gateway near Egesheim in south-west Germany, was used as a place of deposition in Hallstatt D and La Tène A (Bauer and Kuhnen 1995; Rieckhoff and Biel 2001: 195–196; Dehn 1992). The material found there suggests activity complementary to contemporaneous funerary practices in that certain finds categories are mutually exclusive at the Heidentor and in late Hallstatt/early La Tène graves (Dehn 1992: 105). Thus, this natural monument was considered as part of a wider landscape with burials and settlements. In sum, it constituted a complementary system of natural and cultural devices for the creation of a communal universe.

Another important factor in the building and acquisition of land and property was access to, and control over, water. Rivers and lakes not only structured and divided the landscape, but represented monumental features in themselves. Being especially important in economic terms, they differed markedly from small, but vitally critical springs and wells. In spite of their small size, the latter undoubtedly played a major role in the mental and factual construction of the landscape. Sometimes their significance had a strong impact on the structure and large-scale organization and monumentalization of the landscape. For instance, several monumental earthworks converge at the spring site of Tancred Pit Hole in East Yorkshire, forming a huge radiating pattern which focuses on the source (Giles 2007: 111). Water as a vital resource fundamentally influenced the cultural conditioning of the landscape.

The positioning of settlements was crucially dependent on water, and therefore springs were frequently protected and integrated using monumental architecture. At several La Tène hillforts in eastern France, southern Germany, and Bohemia, springs were enclosed in order to safeguard the settlement's water supply (Hansen and Pare 2008: 73–80; Klopsch 1994). This was most effectively realized at the hillforts of Ipf bei Bopfingen, Altkönig, and the Glauberg, near Frankfurt am Main, where water sources were protected by earthwork annexes (Figure 22.2). Similarly, at the hillfort of Vladař near Prague, an area of natural springs was incorporated into an older fortification during La Tène A (Chytráček et al. 2010). Timber and stone basins were built for spring water collection. Their monumental size and technical complexity indicate the importance of water storage and distribution. Generally, these provisions are interpreted as a reaction to social and political stress and threat (Hansen and Pare 2008: 79). Moreover, they probably represented an ideological indicator of political control over water resources.

Integrating Monuments and Landscapes

As indicated, Iron Age communities constantly interacted with their natural and cultural environment. An important part of this consisted of adding new monuments to those which already existed. In large parts of Europe, these were mainly burial mounds, as one of the standard features of early Iron Age funerary practice. This meant a distinctive

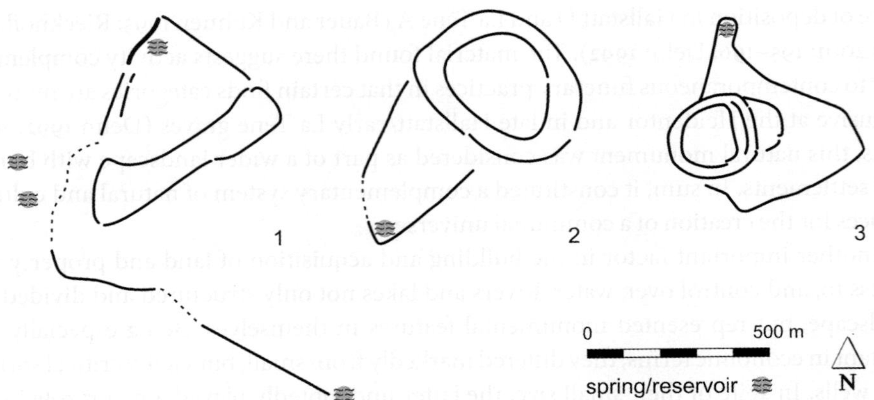

FIGURE 22.2 At the early Iron Age hillforts of Glauberg (1), Altkönig (2), and Ipf (3) in Germany, natural springs and reservoirs were subsequently incorporated into the fortified area by annexe walls.

Author, after Hansen and Pare (2008): fig. 9

rupture with earlier traditions of cremation and large urnfield cemeteries as the standard form of burial in late Bronze Age societies. In spite of persistent cremation burials between mounds, as at Untereggersberg in Bavaria (Germany), inhumations covered by tumuli became the preferred form of burial again (Rieckhoff and Biel 2001: 67, 178–179). From Hallstatt C times into the later Iron Age, tumuli were the commonest mode of burying the dead, creating a visual connection with the ancestors and at the same time perpetuating the presence of the community in the landscape.

At the cemetery of Schirndorf in south-east Germany, about a hundred burial mounds with inhumations or cremations in stone chambers were erected during Hallstatt C and Hallstatt D (Müller-Scheeßel 2009). They formed a honeycomb-like complex of stone revetments and barrows. Secondary interments within and between the mounds suggest a certain social differentiation. The barrows are all of modest size, but indicate an intention of displaying individual as well as communal status and wealth. Probably a limited internal competition for power and prestige of different families coincided with a collective external endeavour to exhibit status and create a common identity by monumental work—at Schirndorf, the cemetery as a whole represents a single monument (Figure 22.3).

Iron Age funerary practice in northern Europe was also dominated by burial mounds, albeit of rather small size. Related to the practice of interring cremations in Bronze Age tumuli, these miniature mounds might be interpreted as copies of the ancient tradition of placing the dead under an earth monument. The cemeteries were situated at some distance from the settlements and thus were not physically integrated in, or related to, the sphere of the living community. The restricted wealth of both funerary and settlement finds, the relative uniformity of burial offerings, and the limited and consistent size of the actual barrows, all imply limited social hierarchy (Parker Pearson 1999: 126).

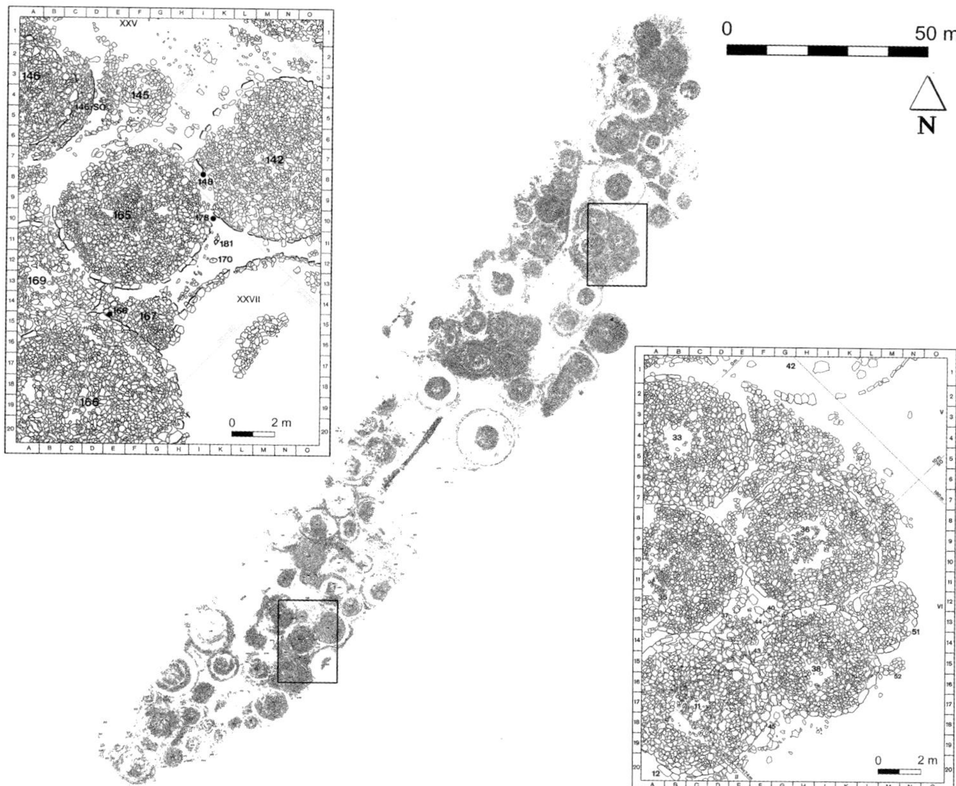

FIGURE 22.3 At Schirndorf, south-east Germany, Hallstatt C and D burial monuments form a honeycomb-like complex of barrows, stone chambers, and revetments. As an encompassing monument, the cemetery might have portrayed communal status and identity.

Sources Müller-Scheeßel (2009): fig. 1; Stroh (1979): table 12, (2000): table 65

In this case, therefore, the intention seems to have been simply to indicate the place of the dead by means of minimal monumentality of the burial mounds, instead of marking status internally and externally.

The distribution of the barrows sometimes indicates a correlation with a possible routeway, as at Grundsheim in south-west Germany (Bittel et al. 1981: 131–132; Figure 22.4). This linear sequence gives a clear notion of how cemeteries may have played a role in the transmission of information along major lines of communication. In a sense, they connected the world of the living with the realm of death and the ancestors—an idea based on the close linkage of the sacred and profane which are not considered as different spheres in traditional societies.

During the early phases of the Heuneburg hillfort in south-west Germany, a multitude of small settlements, each supplemented by a cemetery consisting of several smaller or single giant tumuli, existed in the surrounding area (Kurz 2012). Such a largely uniform distribution of burial mounds as markers of territories and local rights to land indicates

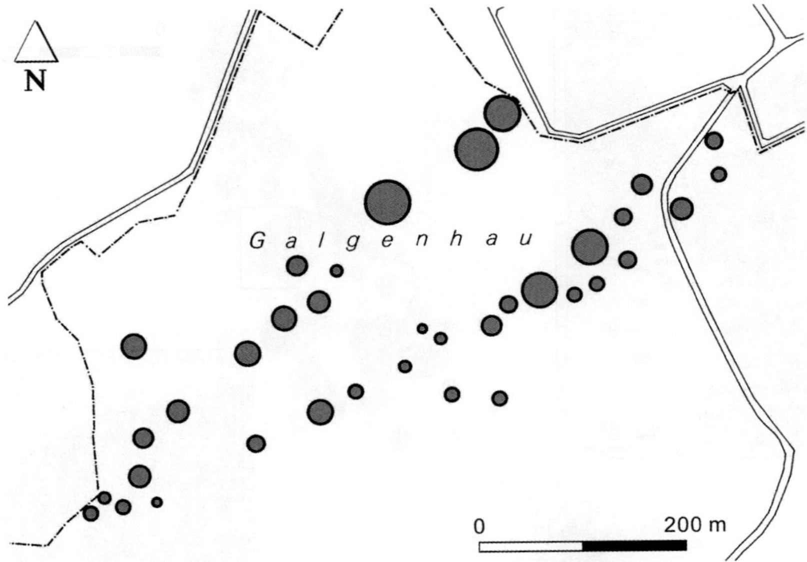

FIGURE 22.4 The line of barrows at Grundsheim, south-west Germany, retraces the course of a contemporary routeway. Situated along lines of communication, the burial monuments both transmitted information to external communities and connected the spheres of the living and the dead.

Authors, after Bittel et al. (1981): fig. 60

a comparatively moderate hierarchy of settlements and communities. A similar interpretation is proposed for the late Hallstatt communities of the Berry in central France. The number and distribution of elite burials in giant mounds suggest an even distribution of political power and territories. Their hinterland is supposed to have been of limited extent—it differs quite obviously from the territory of some very few major settlements, like those at Vix, Bourges, and Troyes. These major settlements with large mounds containing a rich and varied inventory of often precious finds in their environs have been termed 'princely sites' (Milcent 2012: 107–109; for a general discussion of the concept, see Schweizer 2006). The associated burial mounds are of impressive size and were surely pre-eminent landmarks which acted as stimuli in the creation of identities. Several characteristics contributed to their outstanding appearance, their size being the most prominent feature. The Magdalenenberg near Villingen in south-west Germany is the largest late Hallstatt tumulus in central Europe. Apart from the huge oak-and-stone chamber of its central grave, the earthen barrow, with an original diameter of about 105 m and a height of 10–12 m, contained 136 Hallstatt D1 burials (Spindler 1999).

Apart from the aforementioned Hohmichele, there is a concentration of giant mounds in the direct vicinity of the Heuneburg. A combination of four huge tumuli dated to Hallstatt D2/3, each of which is around 50 m in diameter and 5–7 m high, is located just north of the hillfort in the Giessübel-Talhau area. Other mounds, with even larger dimensions and rising up to about 6 m above ground, to this day define the landscape around the Heuneburg (Kurz 1997; Kurz and Schiek 2002). Similarly, several large mounds are to be found around the Hallstatt period hillfort on the Hohenasperg near Stuttgart (Germany). Like the Römerhügel, Grafenbühl, and Kleinaspergle, the tumulus at Hochdorf is of exorbitant dimensions, with a diameter of about 60 m and an original height of 6 m (Biel 1985; Kimmig 1988; Balzer 2008).

Apart from the size of these burial monuments, architectural features contributed to their outward appearance in order to impress and convey prestige and status. Stone walls and wooden stelae were arranged around the feet of several mounds—for instance, at Hochdorf and at mound 2 of the Giessübel-Talhau necropolis at the Heuneburg. Often a shallow ditch surrounded the foot of the mound, probably dividing the innermost sacral funerary sphere from the world of the living. Some tumuli were supposedly crowned by wooden or stone stelae on their top, thus enhancing their height by another two or three metres. The near life-size stone statues found at Hirschlanden, Holzgerlingen, and Glauberg contributed to the monumental character of the barrows, being themselves earliest examples of monumental depiction of men in temperate Europe (Kurz 1997: 57–63; Frey 2002).

Complexity of architectural layout is further proof of a deliberately created monumental setting. Some 'princely mounds' reveal an intricate internal structure. A geophysical survey of a 50 m-wide barrow in the vicinity of the Ipf hillfort revealed a segmented structure with radiating anomalies (Krause et al. 2008: 262–263, fig. 21). Equivalent features have been excavated at mounds of the Giessübel-Talhau necropolis near the Heuneburg, the Hochdorf barrow, and at the Magdalenenberg, with wooden divisions structuring the mound into different compartments (Biel 1985; Kurz 1997; Spindler 1999). Whether these are purely technical devices to facilitate the building up of the mound, or segments indicating the 'compartments' of different working groups, is not clear. The latter might correspond to different kinship-related or other social groups which, through a common effort, created different parts of a collective monument (Kurz 1997: 55–57).

The communal work involved investment of time and labour, and is a major factor in the establishment of monuments. The mobilization of the workforce and the supply of food and accommodation meant a fundamental effort for the community. Initial estimates of the time and labour needed to construct a mound like the Magdalenenberg have been questioned on the basis of ethnographic analogies. These suggest a rather moderate effort both in time and labour which can easily be achieved by quite small communities (Eggert 2011: 353–358). However, the community had to make a certain number of people available for the task, who were then unavailable for food procurement or other crucial activities during the building of the mound. The provision of building materials necessary for the creation of the monument was another major factor. Stones for covering the wooden chamber sometimes had to be transported from quite distant sources; trees for the construction of the chambers had to be felled and brought to the funerary site. However, all this has been duly accounted for in the model calculation for the Magdalenenberg. Nevertheless, like the ostentatious display of wealth through funerary offerings, labour, resources, and monumentality were used as prestigious media of social competition. With respect to 'labour as potlatch', Niall Sharples' (2007: 179–180) interpretation of enclosure boundaries as 'conspicuous consumption of resources' can also be transferred to burial mounds and other monuments.

Monuments and Territoriality

It is quite difficult to assess the spatial domain of Iron Age sites. Attempts have been made to estimate the territory surrounding the Hochdorf grave through the analysis of pollen and macrobotanical residues from the tumulus. The original interpretation supposed a wide-ranging zone of influence, but reconsideration of the data suggests a considerably smaller territory extending for some 20 or 30 km in radius. The same applies to the area around the Glauberg hillfort (Eggert 2007: 288–291). In the late Iron Age, the limestone used for the revetment of the *murus gallicus* erected around the *oppidum* of Manching in Bavaria was extracted from sources up to 20 km away, and probably transported by ship on the Danube (Streit 1987; see also later in the chapter). This might give a certain indication of this site's minimal territorial control.

Another aspect of territoriality is closely connected with the monumentality and visibility of burial mounds in the landscape. It has been suggested that barrows, together with other monuments or natural landmarks, may indicate territorial boundaries. For example, GIS-viewshed analysis of the area around the Glauberg demonstrated that, within a radius of 5 km, several mounds correlate with the maximum extent of visibility from inside the hillfort. Furthermore, this distribution along the boundaries of the perceivable landscape roughly corresponds to a presumed hinterland based on cost surface analyses (Posluschny 2008: 171–172). According to the positioning of burial mounds in the environment, the landscape itself becomes a monument which is strictly delimited in terms of monumentality. Consequently, patterns in the environment help to build the landscape and enable its cultural—and thus mental—perception.

In order to provide access to the surroundings of a settlement, roads and paths organized the landscape in the form of linear monuments. For example, marshlands and bogs of northern Europe were made accessible by linear log causeways which involved a substantial effort both in labour investment and supply of timber. The work involved in their construction and procurement was certainly not inferior to other monuments and represented an ambitious common undertaking. A singular example of a late Hallstatt/early La Tène road system with a surface of pebbles and stones has been found at Großhöbing in Bavaria (Schussmann 2008: 317). Its construction might have been initiated by a local elite, and similarly reveals significant investment of labour in a monumental project.

Early Iron Age linear ditches and earthworks in south-east England may equally have perpetuated the influence and control of central sites, settlements, or cemeteries in the landscape. Even if primarily interpreted as boundaries, they might also have served as devices for the flow of communication and movements. Whereas earlier, Bronze Age land divisions (often erroneously known as 'Celtic fields', from which they differ considerably), were relatively small-scale, Iron Age linear ditches and pit alignments enclosed quite extensive plots of land (Bradley and Yates 2007: 98–99). Together with an increase of enclosed settlements and hillforts towards the insular middle Iron Age, the decline of land division may be interpreted as a tendency towards communal access to the landscape and the management of agricultural production and surplus. Therefore, the hillforts might no longer have served as power centres of a ruling elite, but rather as ritual, storage, and distribution centres for an entire community (Hill 1995; Bradley and Yates 2007: 100; Thomas 1997).

On the continent, land division by 'Celtic fields' as one of the main methods of structuring the landscape was different from the earlier insular setting. Both along the continental coast and in central France, a complex system of small ditches and plots structured the hinterland of settlements and indicates a specific concept of land ownership and management of agricultural land. In spite of chronological difficulties, the reconfiguration of the field systems through time gives ample proof of manifold social and economic changes. In the valley of the River Oise in northern France, several shifts in orientation and structure of the enclosure system took place from middle La Tène to Roman times, with a significant increase in allotments and parcelling out (Malrain and Pinard 2006: 59–63). It seems that the landscape was constantly being rebuilt and realigned. The reasons and factors which caused these reconfigurations are a topic of ongoing archaeological debate. One model, based on ethnographic evidence, suggests a fractioning and discursive rearrangement of land property and social status which is evoked by traditional laws of succession (Wendling 2010a, 2012: 245–250). Inheritance leads to social differentiation, which in turn initiates a rearrangement of economic wealth, being highly dependent on control over agricultural land. Irrespective of the exact legal regulations, this generates increasing subdivision or consolidation of land, which might leave traces in the archaeological record in the form of plots and 'Celtic fields'. The landscape is subject to social inequality and transformation and is constantly rearranged and rebuilt.

The Monument as Landscape—the Landscape as Monument

The appropriation of the landscape and the monumentalization of the built environment were guided by sacral—i.e. ideological—and economic intentions. Both used funerary architecture to display wealth and power and to achieve visual and mental connections with the ancestors. Apart from burial mounds as prime features in the creation of monuments, house architecture was regarded as another appropriate means of visualizing the ability to create large-scale monuments. Generally, differentiation of the built environment within a settlement tends to reflect social variability. Form, function, and size do distinguish a building and its inhabitants. The apsidal building dominating the plateau at the late Hallstatt hillfort of Mont Lassois in Burgundy (France) evidently conveyed both prestige and power (Chaume 2011; Milcent 2012: 96–101). With more than 700 square metres of roofed space, and an assumed height of 15 m, it must have been an impressive building, which would necessarily have created intrasocietal awareness of rank and distinction. Architectural monumentality was a key signifier of social distinction throughout the Iron Age. In its later phases, the agricultural aristocracy resided in rectangular and possibly multistorey 'halls' within fortified farmsteads throughout La Tène Europe (Fichtl 2013; Wieland 1999: 35–37). Buildings of similar type at late Iron Age *oppida* such as Manching suggest that members of the elite were dwelling (at least temporarily) in these settlements (Figure 22.5). The dimensions of houses in these urban centres reflect marked differences of social status in the community (Wendling 2013: 473–476).

The European Iron Age yields numerous instances of creating and incorporating space by enclosures and fortifications. Even small settlements interpreted as fortified farmsteads were fitted with quite substantial enclosures. In early Iron Age Bavaria, '*Herrenhöfe*' or 'chiefs' estates' reveal complex palisaded enclosures and multiple ditch systems (Berg-Hobohm 2005). Their size and lateral dimensions attest functions which go far beyond simple protective needs. Rather, they seem to indicate a desire to exhibit economic strength gained from agricultural surplus. This display of power may result from an economic and social shift away from older habits. While during the late Bronze Age wealth was displayed by exchange, deposition, and conspicuous consumption of goods, early Iron Age communities tended towards monumentality in settlements and burials (Sharples 2007). Similar developments occurred towards the end of the continental Iron Age in different parts of Europe. In southern Germany, during La Tène C2 and La Tène D1, small rectangular enclosures, some of which had been in existence since La Tène B, were massively enlarged. They were monumentalized to become *Viereckschanzen*, fortified farmsteads enclosed by an earth bank and a V-shaped ditch of up to 4 m deep. The defences not only assured protection from external enemies but were also a means of competition between members of the agricultural elite. Equivalent developments took place between the sixth and first centuries BC in Brittany and other regions of Gaul, where aristocratic residences were massively fortified, gradually enlarged, and became regional political and economic centres (Menez 2012). In a highly competitive social system of clans and families striving for power and influence, the expression of military force by building monuments was of vital importance.

Similar needs might have led to the establishment of hillforts and *oppida*, which might have been initiated either by members of a ruling elite, or by communal engagement in an urban society. A unique example of the visualization of foreign contacts and military power is represented by the late Hallstatt mud-brick wall at the Heuneburg. Built in a technique that was completely unknown north of the Alps, both the 'exotic' architecture and the ability to engage a supposedly Greek architect must have aroused envy and admiration among rival chiefs. The outward appearance, which included a

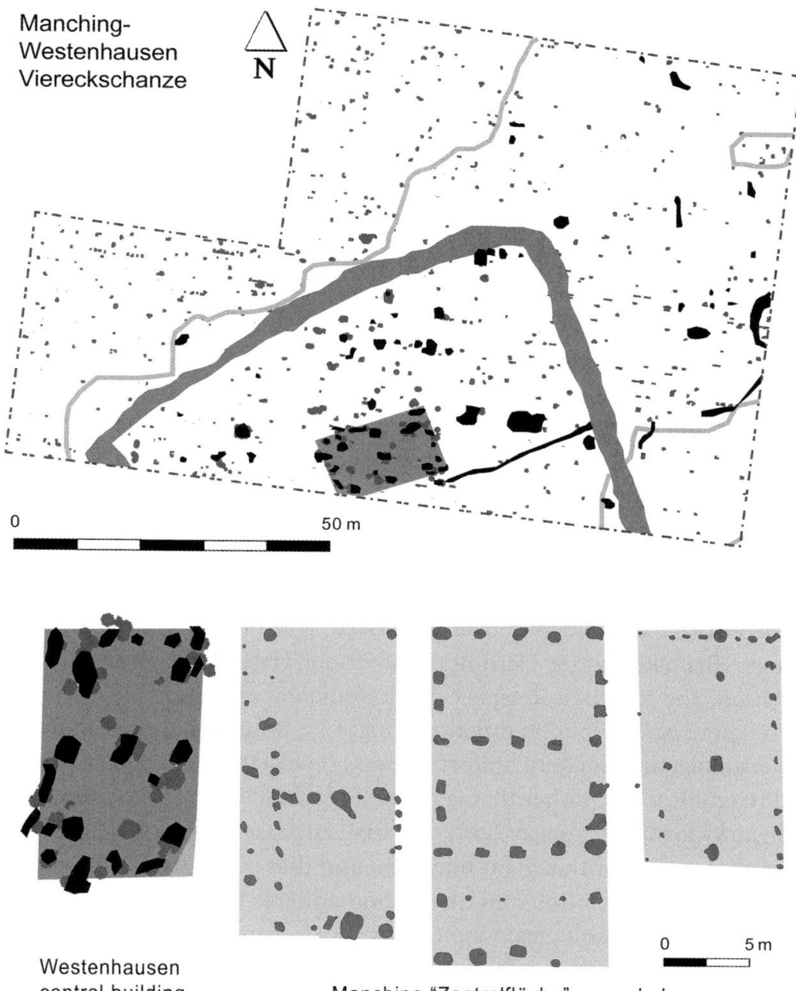

FIGURE 22.5 A combined digital interpretation of geomagnetic and aerial survey at a *Viereckschanze* farmstead near Manching, Bavaria, shows a large building in the centre of the enclosure. Buildings of equal scale and layout also figure in the adjacent urban centre. As aristocratic residences, they illustrate the ostentatious display of wealth and power through monumental architecture.

Drawing H. Wendling, © Römisch-Germanische Kommission

monumental gateway based on a massive stone foundation, made the hillfort a landmark which transferred its importance into the landscape (Kurz 2008). The Heuneburg is not the only site where use of a specific building material contributed a distinctive quality to the fortification and the enclosed settlement. At the early and middle Iron Age hillfort of Segsbury Camp on the Berkshire Downs in England, non-local chalk was incorporated into the wall without being visible. This suggests that the act of incorporation—rather than mere knowledge of its existence—was significant for the community. Incorporating chalk in the wall might have reflected the integration of a territory into a central place and the creation of links between places in the landscape (Gosden and Lock 2007: 289, 291). Again, the process of building a monumental defensive system seems to have played a significant role in creating a communal identity and in social competition.

Large-scale fortifications of European *oppida* transmitted a notion of togetherness among the inhabitants of the urban centre. The monumental perimeter ostentatiously demonstrated the unity of the *oppidani* (Caesar *de Bello Gallico* 2.7.1); Caesar's very term may suggest a self-assured distinction from the peasantry. At any rate, in addition to its military function, the enclosure symbolized the separation of the 'town' from the rural environs. The construction of the enclosure, while promoting a nexus within the community on the one hand, might have been a means of prestigious rivalry among different members of the community or its ruling class on the other. The *murus gallicus* at Manching reveals differences in building techniques that might be traced back to competitive action in terms of building the biggest, the most complex, or the most impressive part of the rampart (Sievers 2010; Wendling 2010b: 77, 2013: 479).

The creation of a common identity by adhering to notions of being 'inside' or 'outside' an enclosure has frequently been discussed, and plays a major role in Iron Age archaeology (Brunaux 2000; Harding et al. 2006; Haselgrove 2007). In prestigious representation, the ideological aspect of monumental enclosures becomes apparent, whereas religious and symbolic functions might be transmitted on a more enigmatic level. For example, the Glauberg hillfort in Hesse (Germany) seems to have been a symbolic and religious focus, rather than a purely economic centre. Massive linear ditches and earthworks form an extensive complex that surpasses a merely defensive function (Figure 22.6). Together with a giant burial mound that is integrated into the system of banks and ditches, its position and orientation adheres to astronomical patterns and thus creates a giant cosmological map (Deiss 2008). Pursuing a notion of 'inside/outside', a linear 'processional road' which leads to the monumental barrow seems to connect both spheres. The outward 'sphere of the dead' is apparently linked to the inside 'world of the living' at this focal point in the landscape (Posluschny 2008: 172). By transferring these ideas of life, death, and birth into a landscape monument, the landscape itself might have been furnished with meaning as a cosmological prospect.

The building of an enclosure or settlement in correspondence with religious beliefs and cosmological thoughts is frequently attested in ethnographic reports on traditional societies (Rapoport 1969: 49–58). Similar to medieval Celtic peoples, among Iron Age societies, the geographical 'north' might have had pejorative connotations. Accordingly, it was usually neglected in the orientation of the main axis of houses and enclosures. Another cosmological principle is manifested at Manching, where the circular rampart and eastern and southern gates are mathematically positioned according to an older, middle La Tène temple at the very centre of the settlement (Eller et al. 2012: 310; Sievers 2012; Wendling 2013: 479). As a religious centre it existed long before the construction of the wall and served as an *omphalos* or navel for the existing world. The landscape

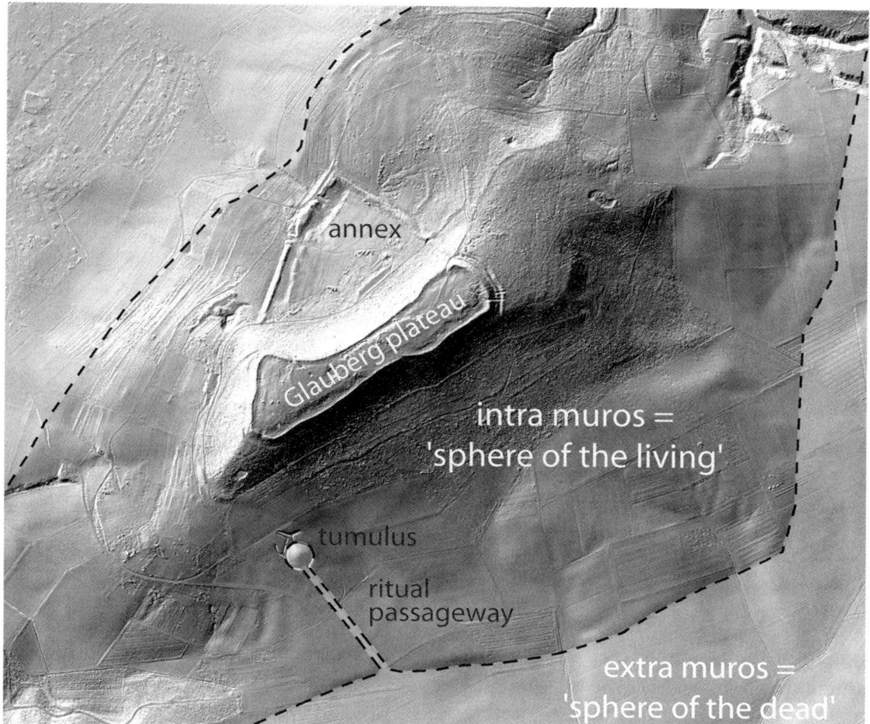

FIGURE 22.6 Massive linear ditches and earthworks, together with a large tumulus, form a landscape complex around the Glauberg hillfort. Following an underlying concept of inside/outside and an architectural fusion of the realms of the living and the dead, the landscape was transformed into a giant cosmological map.

Source: Posluschny (2008): fig. 4, LiDAR image © Römisch-Germanische Kommission

as a monument is built and created in a reflection of the cosmological *imago mundi*. During the process of fortification, the Manching environment was severely altered and decisively incorporated into, or excluded from, the materialized circular world view. Small rivers were redirected to form natural obstacles. Large parts of the landscape were integrated into the settlement and used as pasture, fields, or habitation areas (Eller et al. 2012: 310).

The integration of large parts of the landscape into a settlement area building an all-embracing monumental enclosure is a common phenomenon of late La Tène territorial *oppida*. The cultivated area was extended into the 'natural' environment either gradually, like at the *oppidum* of Závist in Bohemia, or in a monumental venture, as at the Heidengraben in south-west Germany (Knopf 2006; Motyková et al. 1990; Rieckhoff and Fichtl 2011: 61–72). Natural topographical features like clefts, gorges, and cliffs became part of the monumental defensive system. With a total area of 1,770 ha secured by lengths of wall or escarpments, the Heidengraben integrates all aspects of monumentality: natural monuments, ancient burial mounds, and monumental fortifications

FIGURE 22.7 Natural features like gorges and cliffs were effectively incorporated into the defensive system of the Heidengraben *oppidum*, south-west Germany. The landscape thus became a monument in its own right at the large territorial *oppida* of the late Iron Age.

Photo: O. Braasch, L7522-012-03_906-23, 14.11.1989, © Landesamt für Denkmalpflege im Regierungspräsidium Stuttgart

built a large-scale complementary unit—the landscape became a monument itself (Figure 22.7).

Spheres of the Iron Age Forest

Generally, the natural landscape, irrespective of whether or not and to what degree it has been influenced by human agency, is a vital factor for any community. This was certainly true for the Iron Age. Specific features of the physical environment may play an important role in the cultural perception and integration of the landscape, including among others, forests and swamps. The following sections highlight some points of general interest with respect to forests.

In 1992, Robert Pogue Harrison published an inspiring book with the provocative title *Forests: The Shadow of Civilization*. It was meant as an historically saturated treatise on the ongoing entanglement of humans and nature in the Old World which is attested even in very early written sources. As has been observed in another context, the title of Harrison's book evokes both a kind of arc between two poles—forest and civilization—and the mutual interdependence of these poles. In juxtaposing the forest with civilization, it represents the shadow of the latter in a twofold manner. On the one hand the forest may be considered as the origin and refuge of all that is contrary to civilization, and thus is constantly repressed and fought against in civilized settings. It is, in short, the dark side—the shadow—of the radiant 'brightness' of civilization. But then, at the same time, the shadow of the forest is constantly threatening what seems to belong to the safe haven of civilized life (Eggert 2011: 175–176).

The forest as representation of a dark, menacing, and impenetrable wilderness is deeply ingrained in the collective subconscious of the west. Some evidence of this is documented in ancient written sources, where it links up with the *topos* of barbarian peoples and countries. There is, as will be shown later, another sphere of the forest which is important in our context. This is much more mundane in that it concerns two aspects of the extremely wide range of utilization to which wood, as the main resource of the forest, was put.

The Forested Landscape

As far as Greek and Roman authors commented on what we are used to calling the 'Iron Age landscape' they concurred as to the density of forest cover. In *de Bello Gallico*, Caesar often mentions large forests and swamps (e.g. 6.5.4, 7; 6.29.4). Sometimes, villages, hamlets, and even single homesteads and residences were located deep in the forest. For instance, Ambiorix and his companions were lucky enough to retreat to a residence in the middle of a forest which was hard for Caesar's horsemen to attack (*de Bello Gallico* 6.30.3–4). Forests and marshes also play an important role in Tacitus' *Germania*. Although this work mainly concerns the territory of the Germanic tribes, some of what its author relates may also apply to the Celts and their homeland. It is, however, difficult to differentiate between the two.

According to a famous dictum of Tacitus, the country of the Germanic tribes consisted mostly of horrible forests and hideous swamps (Tacitus *Germania* 5.1). While the landscape appears generally inimical to humans, there is nevertheless some variation in it, as Tacitus admits. Unfortunately, he does not specify this (Tacitus *Germania* 5.1). In fact, there can be little doubt that primaeval forests and swamps are part of the *cliché* of 'barbarous' landscapes (Perl 1990: 142–143; for an analysis of the natural setting as presented by Tacitus, see Timpe 1992). In this case, however, it is probable—as Gerhard Perl (1990: 143) noted—that Tacitus' opinion was based on information derived from Roman military campaigns in north-western Germany.

Fifty years ago, Herbert Jankuhn (1966) published an article on the credibility of Tacitus' *Germania* as a historical source. Regarding Tacitus' remarks on the natural setting, Jankuhn (1966: 413) relied on the results of settlement archaeology he had himself undertaken in northern Germany. He argued that in the first centuries AD *Germania magna* was predominantly woodland. Ulrich Willerding (1992), an archaeobotanist, who in a critical article confronted the information of Tacitus on climate and vegetation with the palaeoethnobotanical evidence, provided a much more detailed account. In summary, however, he concluded that the forests of *Germania magna* must have made a rather dreadful impression on the Roman soldiers (Willerding 1992: 349). Willerding left no doubt that, in spite of much progress in the last decades, many questions concerning the environment and land use in *Germania* in general, and Tacitus' account of it in particular, were still unanswered. An in-depth study by Manfred Rösch et al. (2008) on Iron Age land use in southern central Europe is a very important update of Willerding's contribution. It gives a detailed, data-rich account of the current state of research without brushing aside the many problems with regard to the availability and quality of on-site and off-site indicators (see also Chapter 18).

The Forest as Sanctuary

The term 'sanctuary' carries a double meaning. On the one hand it is used to indicate a place of safety and protection for people in danger, as is exemplified by the retreat of Ambiorix and his men into the middle of a forest. On the other, however, 'sanctuary' refers to a location or building where cult activities are carried out; it is thus considered as holy by a people or group. Caesar himself relates very little about Gaulish religious places—he just mentions that spoil seized in battle was accumulated in heaps at sacred places by the Gauls (*de Bello Gallico* 6.17.3–4). Unfortunately, he does not specify these places. In contrast, he conveys some important information about the druids who, as priests, were held in the greatest esteem by the Gaulish tribes (*de Bello Gallico* 6.13–14, 6.16).

Another to refer to the druids was the Roman poet Lucan (AD 39–65). According to him, their ceremonies consisted of barbarous rites and weird religious customs, and they dwelt in deep forests with sequestered groves (Lucan *de Bello Civili* 1, 450–454). In Book Three of his work, the poet provides interesting details of a sacred grove in the vicinity of Massalia, which had not been touched by men's hands since ancient times (Figure 22.8). Within it, the gods were worshipped with savage rites, the altars supplied with hideous offerings, and every tree was splattered with human blood. During his siege of Massalia, Caesar ordered this grove to be felled since it was too near to his siege installations. When he realized that his soldiers showed great reluctance to comply with his order for fear of the place, he himself grabbed an axe and cut down a tree to reassure his men (Lucan *de Bello Civili* 3, 439–449). Lucan mentions priests, though not specifically druids, but Christian-J. Guyonvarc'h and Françoise Le Roux (1986: 230) think that druids served as priests in this kind of sanctuary.

Caesar relates that at a certain time in the year the druids assembled for an important convention at a consecrated place in the territory of the Carnutes (*de Bello Gallico* 6.13.10). Sometimes it is assumed that this place was situated in a forest, but as Gilbert-Charles Picard (1977: 229–230) has argued, there is nothing to support this view. He instead links such locations with the largely uninhabited borderland between tribal territories where religious ceremonies were carried out within simple enclosures. Several more recent books on Iron Age religion and the druids (Maier 2004, 2009; Brunaux 2009; Aldhouse-Green 2010; Chapter 42) provide a critical treatment of the role of

FIGURE 22.8 Middle La Tène gold foil-covered representation of an ivy-leaved branch or small tree from Manching. This ritual object provides archaeological support for Greek and Roman sources that indicate Celtic veneration of trees and sacred groves.

Photo: J. Bahlo, © Römisch-Germanische Kommission

druids in Celtic society and the question of cult sites, as well as a succinct summary of the current state of archaeological research on the latter.

Forest Exploitation and Fortifications

Iron Age settlements were often secured by fortifications. The various rampart types then in use showed a range in details of construction. While earth was always an important element, stone was often used too, sometimes as drystone walling. At any rate, once defences became more elaborate, the need for wood in the form of timber and planks implied an important effort for the community. The most elaborate timber-framed and timber-laced rampart was the *murus gallicus*, which Caesar mentions on various occasions, providing a very detailed account of its construction in relation to the defence of Avaricum in central France (*de Bello Gallico* 7.23).

Thanks to more than six decades of archaeological investigation at Manching, we are extremely well informed about its *murus gallicus* and two subsequent ramparts of *Pfostenschlitzmauer* type (Köhler and Maier 1992; Sievers 2010; Wendling 2010b, 2013: 476–479). The Manching fortifications enclosed about 380 ha and had a length of approximately 7 km (Figure 22.9). Heinz-Jürgen Köhler and Ferdinand Maier (1992: 350–351) estimated that for the timber used in construction of the *murus gallicus* alone, a very large amount of 25–30 year-old oaks, with a diameter of around 20 cm, would have been needed. As to the extent of the oak forest necessary to supply the community with the oak trees for the timber framework of their fortifications, they arrived at a minimum of about 370 ha (see also Lorenz 1986: 25–28). This, evidently, implies not only a considerable effort of tree-felling and timber-cutting activity, but also deliberate forest management. Since we have no clear idea of the timespan in which the impressive *murus gallicus* of Manching was erected, all estimates and calculations of the kind effected by Köhler and Maier necessarily remain hypothetical. But even if speculative, they provide a rough idea of the input of labour and material in such a defence structure (Figure 22.9). That this structure will then constitute an important element for both 'outsiders' and 'insiders' in a thus altered landscape need not be stressed after what has been outlined here.

Köhler and Maier (1992: 350) argued that oak trees for the timber framework of the *murus gallicus* were to be found in the floodplain forests in the immediate surroundings of the *oppidum*. However, this seems altogether less convincing when we consider the amount of wood required and the surface area of the forest needed for it. The palaeobotanist, Hansjörg Küster (1992: 455), limits his remarks on the provenance of the Manching oaks to the statement that they must have been provided from outside the settlement. The gravelly soil on which the *oppidum* was situated supported only very light woodland, which would in addition have been diminished by human and animal activity linked to agriculture and herding.

Although only partly related to forest exploitation, another aspect of the Manching defensive wall should at least be mentioned. It concerns its visual might which resided in its stone front. This front was erected in dry-wall technique, interrupted by the heads of the rectangular timbers of its oak framework (Figure 22.9). As already noted, we possess some rough estimates for the stone and soil needed for the *murus gallicus* (Lorenz 1986: 30–32). According to Reinhard Streit (1987: 115, 117–118), the limestone came from the southern Franconian Alb situated about 20 km from Manching, north of the Danube. They might have been mainly collected on the surface and transported by boat. Herbert Lorenz (1986: 30) estimated that around 120,000 m^3 of stone and soil was needed to infill the timber framework of the wall; this does not include the material for the earth ramp erected to stabilize the wall proper. According to Lorenz, it might have required the same amount of earth (Lorenz 1986).

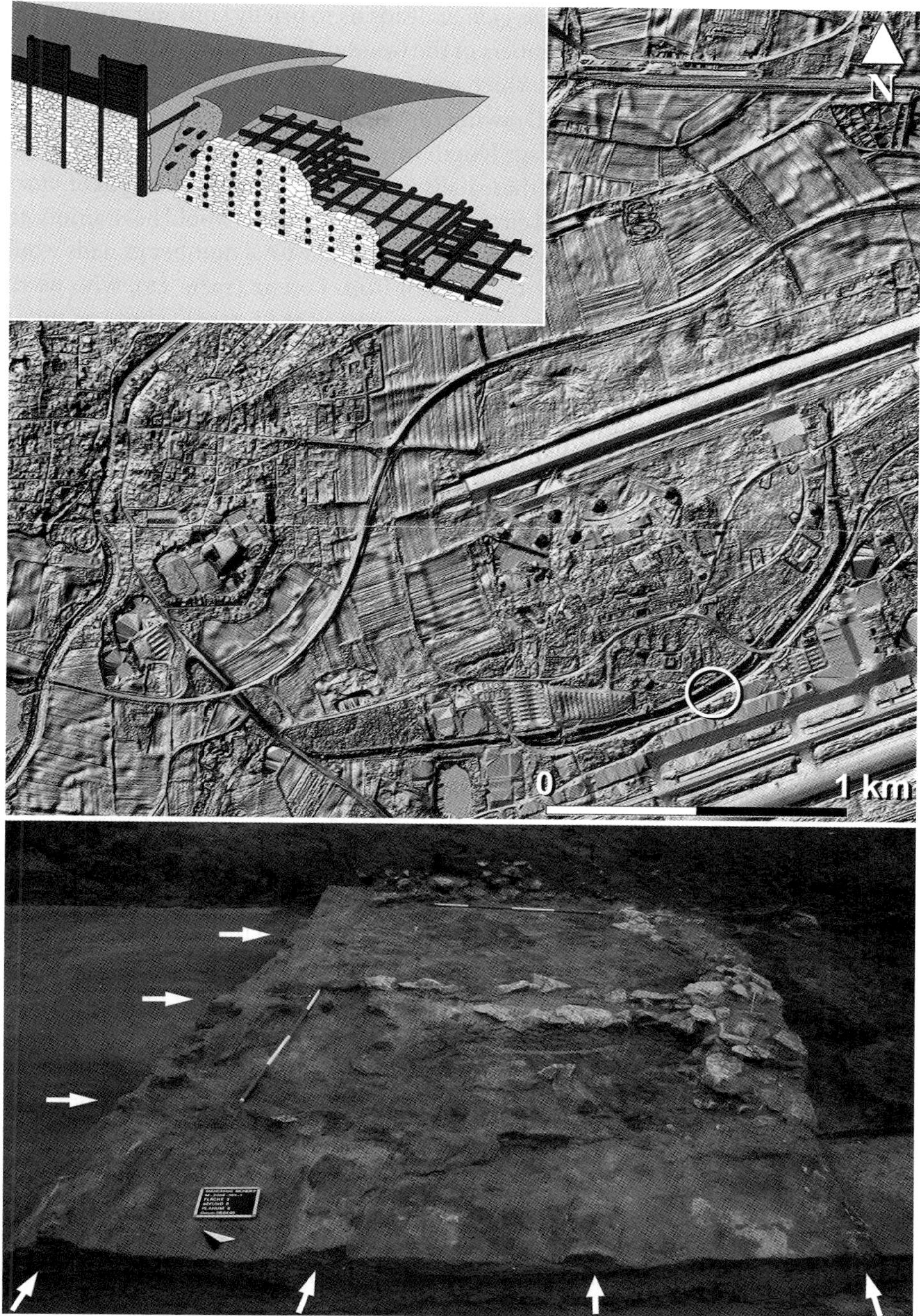

FIGURE 22.9 The monumental three-phase fortification at Manching figures prominently in a LiDAR topographical model; it required an immense investment of labour and building materials. The reconstruction of the sequence of building techniques (top left), and a preserved segment of the framework of vertical beams of the *murus gallicus* phase (bottom), illustrate the extent of human impact on the landscape caused by ancient wood clearance.

Photo: H. Wendling, © Römisch-Germanische Kommission

The example of the Manching *murus gallicus* leads us to briefly consider another feature of its construction. The lowest timbers of the wooden framework were fixed at their crossing points by means of iron nails which were more or less square in section and had a maximum length of about 23 cm. Drawing on the evidence of the 1938 and 1985–87 excavations, and working on an average length of 20 cm, Köhler and Maier (1992: 351) calculated that about twenty-three of these nails were needed for a 10 m length of *murus gallicus*. Extrapolated around the total circumference of 7 km, this would have amounted to 16,100 nails. Taking a weight of 126 g for a 20 cm nail, the total number of nails would have corresponded to approximately two tons of iron. Lorenz (1986: 28), who used a nail length of 25–30 cm and a weight of 300–400 g, arrived at a figure of about 7.5 tons of iron, including smaller nails for the parapet on top of the stone facing. Whatever the real figure, it is clear that the demand for iron was very high, and certainly not only for iron that was destined to be transformed into nails. It is here where the forest comes in again.

Charcoal and Iron Production

Traditional iron production using the bloomery process placed a very high demand on charcoal. Figures for the ratio of iron to charcoal vary widely in the literature. The same is true for that of fresh wood to charcoal. Seven experiments in charcoal production using different techniques—earth-covered pit, earth-covered piles, as well as open-fire and quenching—showed that, on average, 5.5 kg of wood yields 1 kg of charcoal (Holsten et al. 1991: 382–388). With respect to charcoal consumption, Radomír Pleiner (2000: 126) advances an educated guess based on experimental work that the weight of the charcoal must have been ten to fifteen times greater than that of the iron produced. This means that at least 10 kg of charcoal was needed for the reduction of 1 kg of iron. Pleiner's estimate accords with experimental results reported by Kazimierz Bielenin (1992: 265). On the other hand, R. F. Tylecote et al. (1973: 34, table 10) published the results of fifteen iron ore smelting experiments, where the average ratio of charcoal to iron was 18.5 to 1.

To return to the Manching *murus gallicus*, the figures on which Lorenz (1986: 28) based his estimates are within the range outlined here. If we operate with his guess of 7.5 tons of iron for the nails to fix the lowest level of the timber framework as well as the parapet, about 375 tons of charcoal must have been produced. Even if this is only a rough approximation, there was certainly an enormous demand for charcoal. It led Lorenz (Lorenz 1986) to the statement that whole forests must have been transformed into fuel for the reduction of iron ore.

Generally, archaeological evidence for Hallstatt and La Tène iron production is still scarce, although there has been important research in the Neuenbürg area in the northern Black Forest of south-west Germany (Gassmann et al. 2006; see also Brauns et al. 2013). From the pollen evidence, it seems that late Hallstatt and early La Tène iron ore reduction activities in the northern Black Forest had a considerable impact on the vegetation, in that common beech and white fir forests gave way to hazel, birch, and oak coppice (Gassmann et al. 2006: 298). If we take as an example the pollen counts from cores from the Stadtsee of Bad Waldsee in Upper Swabia, there is a clear trend towards a higher human impact and deforestation during the Hallstatt, La Tène, and Roman periods compared to the Bronze Age and the final Neolithic (Rösch et al. 2008: 339, table 6).

Apart from rare instances like these, archaeobotanical research on the correlation of early iron production and its consequences for the forest cover is very much wanting. Pleiner (2000: 126–129), whose book includes a section on wood consumption and deforestation, has little doubt that centres of iron production must have had a devastating effect on the vegetation, but until the status quo detailed by Rösch et al. (2008; see earlier) is radically altered, we are still a far cry from adequately assessing the impact of the bloomery technique on the natural environment.

A prolonged intensification of archaebotanical research is also important for achieving a realistic understanding of the reliability of the ancient sources which deal with the parts of Europe we have focused on here. Although this is no easy task, we are optimistic that research on the natural environment will continue at its current pace. In Germany, this research has profited very much from large projects on the Iron Age funded by the *Deutsche Forschungsgemeinschaft* in recent years (see e.g. Krausse 2010; Rösch et al. 2008), and we are witnessing some promising new research directions with respect to the Iron Age natural landscape to which the last sections of this chapter were devoted.

References

Aldhouse-Green, M. J. 2010. *Caesar's Druids: Story of an Ancient Priesthood*. London/ Newhaven: Yale University Press.

Balzer, I. 2008. 'Die Erforschung der Siedlungsdynamik im Umfeld des frühkeltischen Fürstensitzes Hohenasperg, Kr. Ludwigsburg, auf archäologischen und naturwissenschaftlichen Grundlagen. Mit einem Nachtrag "zu den Anfängen des Projektes" von Jörg Biel', in D. Krausse (ed.) *Frühe Zentralisierungs- und Urbanisierungsprozesse: Zur Genese und Entwicklung frühkeltischer Fürstensitze und ihres territorialen Umlandes. Kolloquium des DFG-Schwerpunktprogramms 1171 in Blaubeuren, 9.–11. Oktober 2006*. Forschungen und Berichte zur Vor- und Frühgeschichte in Baden-Württemberg 101: 143–161. Stuttgart: Theiss.

Bauer, S., and H.-P. Kuhnen. 1995. 'Ein "starker Ort": Der frühkeltische Opferplatz bei Egesheim, Lkr. Tuttlingen', in A. Hafner (ed.) *Heiligtümer und Opferkulte der Kelten*. Archäologie in Deutschland, Sonderheft 1995: 51–54. Stuttgart: Theiss.

Berg-Hobohm, S. 2005. 'Umfriedete Höfe der Hallstattzeit in Bayern. Aktueller Forschungsstand zu den Herrenhöfen und den zeitgleichen rechteckigen Grabenwerken'. *Berichte zur Bayerischen Bodendenkmalpflege* 43/44 (2002/2003): 161–189.

Biel, J. 1985. *Der Keltenfürst von Hochdorf*. Stuttgart: Theiss.

Bielenin, K. 1992. *Starożytne górnictwo i hutnictwo żelaza w Górach Świętokrzyskic* [*Ancient Mining and Iron Smelting in the Holy Cross Mountains*]. Kielce: Kieleckie Towarzystwo Naukowe.

Bittel, K., W. Kimmig, and S. Schieck. 1981. *Die Kelten in Baden-Württemberg*. Stuttgart: Theiss.

Bradley, R. 2000. *An Archaeology of Natural Places*. London: Routledge.

Bradley, R. 2002. *The Past in Prehistoric Societies*. London: Routledge.

Bradley, R., and H. Williams (eds). 1998. *The Past in the Past: The Reuse of Ancient Monuments*. World Archaeology 30, 1. Abingdon: Routledge.

Bradley, R., and D. Yates. 2007. 'After "Celtic" fields: the social organisation of Iron Age agriculture', in C. Haselgrove and R. Pope (eds) *The Earlier Iron Age in Britain and the Near Continent*: 94–102. Oxford: Oxbow.

Brauns, M., R. Schwab, G. Gassmann, G. Wieland, and E. Pernicka. 2013. 'Provenance of Iron Age iron in southern Germany: A new approach'. *Journal of Archaeological Science* 40, 2: 841–849.

Brunaux, J.-L. (ed.) 2000. *Les enclos celtiques: Actes de la 4e table ronde de Ribemont-sur-Ancre (Somme, 5 et 6 septembre 1999)*. Revue Archéologique de Picardie 2000, 1–2. Amiens: RAP.

Brunaux, J.-L. 2009. *Druiden: Die Weisheit der Kelten*. Stuttgart: J. G. Cotta.

Chaume, B. 2011. *Le complexe aristocratique de Vix: Nouvelles recherches sur l'habitat, le système de fortification et l'environnement du mont Lassois*. Dijon: Éditions Universitaires de Dijon.

Chytráček, M., L. Šmejda, A. Danielisová, P. Pokorný, R. Křivánek, P. Kočár, et al. 2010. 'Blockbalkenkonstruktionen des 5. Jahrhunderts v. Chr. im Feuchtbodenmilieu der Vorburg des Burgwalls Vladař in Westböhmen', in M. Chytráček, H. Gruber, J. Michálek, R. Sandner, and K. Schmotz (eds) *Archäologische Arbeitsgemeinschaft Ostbayern/West- und Südböhmen/ Oberösterreich: Archeologická pracovní skupina východní Bavorsko/západní a jižní Čechy/ Horní Rakousko. 19. Treffen/setkání 17.–20. Juni 2009 in Prachatice*: 183–192. Rahden: Marie Leidorf.

Dehn, R. 1992. 'Das "Heidentor" bei Egesheim, Kreis Tuttlingen. Ein bedeutendes archäologisches Denkmal der Hallstatt- und Frühlatènezeit durch Raubgrabungen zerstört'. *Archäologische Ausgrabungen in Baden-Württemberg* 1991: 102–105.

Deiss, B. 2008. 'Zur Struktur und Orientierung der Grabensysteme um die Fürstengrabhügel am Glauberg', in G. M. Schwitalla (ed.) *Der Glauberg in keltischer Zeit: Zum neuesten Stand der Forschung. Öffentliches Symposium, 14.–16. September 2006 in Darmstadt*. Fundberichte aus Hessen Beiheft 6: 279–294. Wiesbaden: Landesamt für Denkmalpflege Hessen.

Eggert, M. K. H. 1978. 'Prähistorische Archäologie und Ethnologie: Studien zur amerikanischen New Archaeology'. *Praehistorische Zeitschrift* 53: 6–164.

Eggert, M. K. H. 2007. 'Wirtschaft und Gesellschaft im früheisenzeitlichen Mitteleuropa: Überlegungen zum "Fürstenphänomen"'. *Fundberichte aus Baden-Württemberg* 29: 255–310.

Eggert, M. K. H. 2011. 'Der "Urwald" als Lebens- und Projektionsraum: Das innere Zentralafrika'. *Saeculum* 61: 161–187.

Eller, M., S. Sievers, H. Wendling, and K. Winger. 2012. 'Zentralisierung und Urbanisierung—Manchings Entwicklung zur spätkeltischen Stadt', in S. Sievers and M. Schönfelder (eds) *Die Frage der Protourbanisation in der Eisenzeit: La question de la proto-urbanisation à l'âge du Fer. Akten des 34. internationalen Kolloquiums der AFEAF vom 13.–16. Mai 2010 in Aschaffenburg*. Kolloquien zur Vor- und Frühgeschichte 16: 303–318. Bonn: Habelt.

Fichtl, S. 2013. 'À propos des résidences aristocratiques de la fin de l'âge du Fer: l'exemple de quelques sites du Loiret', in S. Krausz, A. Colin, K. Gruel, I. Ralston, and T. Dechezleprêtre (eds) *L'âge du Fer en Europe: Mélanges offerts à Olivier Buchsenschutz*: 329–343. Bordeaux: Ausonius.

Frey, O.-H. 2002. 'Menschen oder Heroen? Die Statuen vom Glauberg und die frühe Keltische Großplastik', in H. Baitinger and B. Pinsker (eds) *Glaube—Mythos—Wirklichkeit: Das Rätsel der Kelten vom Glauberg*: 208–218. Stuttgart: Theiss.

Gassmann, G., M. Rösch, and G. Wieland. 2006. 'Das Neuenbürger Erzrevier im Nordschwarzwald als Wirtschaftsraum während der Späthallstatt- und Frühlatènezeit'. *Germania* 84, 2: 273–306.

Giles, M. 2007. 'Refiguring rights in the early Iron Age landscapes of East Yorkshire', in C. Haselgrove and R. Pope (eds) *The Earlier Iron Age in Britain and the Near Continent*: 103–118. Oxford: Oxbow.

Gosden, C., and G. Lock. 2007. 'The aesthetics of landscape on the Berkshire Downs', in C. Haselgrove and R. Pope (eds) *The Earlier Iron Age in Britain and the Near Continent*: 279–292. Oxford: Oxbow.

Guyonvarc'h, C.-J., and F. Le Roux. 1986. *Les druides: De Mémoire d'Homme: L'Histoire*. Rennes: Éditions Ouest-France.

Hahn, H. P. 2000a. 'Raumkonzepte bei den Kassena (Burkina Faso)'. *Anthropos* 95: 129–148.

Hahn, H. P. 2000b. 'Siedlungsgeschichte bei den Kassena: orale Traditionen und Lokalität'. *Zeitschrift für Ethnologie* 125: 241–263.

Hamilton, S., and J. Manley. 2001. 'Hillforts, monumentality and place: A chronological and topographic review of first millennium BC hillforts of south-east England'. *European Journal of Archaeology* 4, 1: 7–42.

Hansen, L., and C. Pare. 2008. 'Der Glauberg in seinem mikro- und makroregionalen Kontext', in D. Krausse (ed) *Frühe Zentralisierungs- und Urbanisierungsprozesse: Zur Genese und Entwicklung frühkeltischer Fürstensitze und ihres territorialen Umlandes. Kolloquium des DFG-Schwerpunktprogramms 1171 in Blaubeuren, 9.–11. Oktober 2006*. Forschungen und Berichte zur Vor- und Frühgeschichte in Baden-Württemberg 101: 57–96. Stuttgart: Theiss.

Harding, A., S. Sievers, and N. Venclová (eds). 2006. *Enclosing the Past: Inside and Outside in Prehistory*. Sheffield Archaeological Monographs 15. Sheffield: J. R. Collis Publications.

Harrison, R. P. 1992. *Forests: The Shadow of Civilization*. Chicago/London: University of Chicago Press.

Haselgrove, C. 2007. 'The age of enclosure: Later Iron Age settlement and society in northern France', in C. Haselgrove and T. Moore (eds) *The Later Iron Age in Britain and Beyond*: 492–522. Oxford: Oxbow.

Hill, J. D. 1995. 'How should we understand Iron Age societies and hillforts? A contextual study from southern Britain', in J. D. Hill and C. Cumberpatch (eds) *Different Iron Ages: Studies on the Iron Age in Temperate Europe*. British Archaeological Reports International Series 602: 45–66. Oxford: Archaeopress.

Holsten, H., M. Lund, A. Moser, and F. Nikulka. 1991. 'Holzkohlegewinnung im Experiment', in Staatliches Museum für Naturkunde und Vorgeschichte Oldenburg (ed.) *Experimentelle Archäologie: Bilanz 1991*. Archäologische Mitteilungen aus Nordwestdeutschland, Beiheft 6: 365–391. Oldenburg: Isensee.

Jankuhn, H. 1966. *Archäologische Bemerkungen zur Glaubwürdigkeit des Tacitus in der Germania: Nachrichten der Akademie der Wissenschaften in Göttingen. I.* Philologisch-Historische Klasse 10. Göttingen: Vandenhoeck & Ruprecht.

Kimmig, W. 1988. *Das Kleinaspergle: Studien zu einem Fürstengrabhügel der frühen Latènezeit bei Stuttgart*. Forschungen und Berichte zur Vor- und Frühgeschichte in Baden-Württemberg 30. Stuttgart: Theiss.

Klopsch, E. 1994. 'Zur Frage der Wasserversorgung hessischer Ringwälle im 1. Jahrtausend v. Chr.', in C. Dobiat (ed.) *Festschrift für Otto-Herman Frey zum 65: Geburtstag*. Marburger Studien zur Vor- und Frühgeschichte 16: 305–315. Marburg: Hitzeroth.

Knopf, T. 2006. *Der Heidengraben bei Grabenstetten: Archäologische Untersuchungen zur Besiedlungsgeschichte*. Universitätsforschungen zur prähistorischen Archäologie 141. Bonn: Habelt.

Köhler, H.-J., and F. Maier. 1992. 'Der nördliche Wall', in F. Maier, U. Geilenbrügge, E. Hahn, H.-J. Köhler, and S. Sievers (eds) *Ergebnisse der Ausgrabungen 1984–1987*. Die Ausgrabungen in Manching 15: 340–356. Stuttgart: Steiner.

Krause, R., K. Euler, and K. Fuhrmann. 2008. 'Der frühkeltische Fürstensitz auf dem Ipf bei Bopfingen im Nördlinger Ries (Ostalbkreis, Baden-Württemberg). Neue Forschungen zur Burg und deren Siedlungsumfeld', in D. Krausse (ed.) *Frühe Zentralisierungs- und Urbanisierungsprozesse: Zur Genese und Entwicklung frühkeltischer Fürstensitze und ihres territorialen Umlandes. Kolloquium des DFG-Schwerpunktprogramms 1171 in Blaubeuren, 9.–11. Oktober 2006*. Forschungen und Berichte zur Vor- und Frühgeschichte in Baden-Württemberg 101: 249–279. Stuttgart: Theiss.

Krausse, D. (ed.) 2010. *'Fürstensitze' und Zentralorte der frühen Kelten. Abschlusskolloquium des DFG-Schwerpunktprogramms 1171 in Stuttgart, 12.–15. Oktober 2009*. Forschungen und Berichte zur Vor- und Frühgeschichte in Baden-Württemberg 120. Stuttgart: Theiss.

Kurz, G. 2008. 'Ein Stadttor und Siedlungen bei der Heuneburg (Gemeinde Herbertingen-Hundersingen, Kreis Sigmaringen). Zu den Grabungen in der Vorburg von 2000 bis 2006', in D. Krausse (ed.) *Frühe Zentralisierungs- und Urbanisierungsprozesse: Zur Genese und Entwicklung frühkeltischer Fürstensitze und ihres territorialen Umlandes. Kolloquium des DFG-Schwerpunktprogramms 1171 in Blaubeuren, 9.–11. Oktober 2006*. Forschungen und Berichte zur Vor- und Frühgeschichte in Baden-Württemberg 101: 185–208. Stuttgart: Theiss.

Kurz, S. 1997. *Bestattungsbrauch in der westlichen Hallstattkultur*. Tübinger Schriften zur Ur- und Frühgeschichtlichen Archäologie 2. Münster: Waxmann.

Kurz, S. 2012. 'La Heuneburg. État des dernières recherches', in S. Sievers and M. Schönfelder (eds) *Die Frage der Protourbanisation in der Eisenzeit: La question de la proto-urbanisation à l'âge du Fer. Akten des 34. internationalen Kolloquiums der AFEAF vom 13.–16. Mai 2010 in Aschaffenburg*. Kolloquien zur Vor- und Frühgeschichte 16: 15–27. Bonn: Habelt.

Kurz, S., and S. Schiek. 2002. *Bestattungsplätze im Umfeld der Heuneburg*. Forschungen und Berichte zur Vor- und Frühgeschichte in Baden-Württemberg 87. Stuttgart: Theiss.

Küster, H. 1992. 'Vegetationsgeschichtliche Untersuchungen', in F. Maier, U. Geilenbrügge, E. Hahn, H.-J. Köhler, and S. Sievers (eds) *Ergebnisse der Ausgrabungen 1984–1987*. Die Ausgrabungen in Manching 15: 433–476. Stuttgart: Steiner.

Limp, W. F. 2008. 'Combining Maps and Data: Geographical Information Systems', in H. Eiteljorg, II, *Archaeological Computing*, 2nd edition: 105–146. Bryn Mawr, PA: Center for the Study of Architecture. Available at http://archcomp.csanet.org/ftp/outgoing/ArchCompSEdup.pdf [accessed 30 April 2018].

Lorenz, H. 1986. *Rundgang durch eine keltische 'Stadt'*, 2nd edition. Pfaffenhofen: W. Ludwig.

Maier, B. 2004. *Die Religion der Kelten: Götter—Mythen—Weltbild*, 2nd edition. Munich: Beck.

Maier, B. 2009. *Die Druiden*. Munich: Beck.

Malrain, F., and E. Pinard. 2006. *Les sites laténiens de la moyenne vallée de l'Oise du Ve au Ier s. avant notre ère: Contribution à l'histoire de la société gauloise*. Revue Archéologique de Picardie Numéro spécial 23. Amiens: RAP.

Menez, Y. 2012. 'Die Entstehung städtischer Siedlungen bei befestigten Adelssitzen der jüngeren Eisenzeit in Gallien: Das Beispiel von Paule (Côtes d'Armor)', in S. Sievers and M. Schönfelder (eds) *Die Frage der Protourbanisation in der Eisenzeit: La question de la proto-urbanisation à l'âge du Fer. Akten des 34. internationalen Kolloquiums der AFEAF vom 13.–16. Mai 2010 in Aschaffenburg*. Kolloquien zur Vor- und Frühgeschichte 16: 289–301. Bonn: Habelt.

Milcent, P.-Y. 2012. 'Résidences aristocratiques et expérience urbaine hallstattiennes en France (VIe-Ve siècle av. J.-C.)', in S. Sievers and M. Schönfelder (eds) *Die Frage der Protourbanisation in der Eisenzeit: La question de la proto-urbanisation à l'âge du Fer. Akten des 34. internationalen Kolloquiums der AFEAF vom 13.–16. Mai 2010 in Aschaffenburg*. Kolloquien zur Vor- und Frühgeschichte 16: 91–113. Bonn: Habelt.

Motyková, K., P. Drda, and A. Rybová. 1990. 'Die Siedlungsstruktur des Oppidums Závist zum heutigen Forschungsstand'. *Archäologisches Korrespondenzblatt* 20: 415–426.

Müller-Scheeßel, N. 2009. 'Zum Gräberfeld von Schirndorf: ein Beitrag zur Chronologie der Hallstattzeit Nordostbayerns'. *Praehistorische Zeitschrift* 84, 2: 191–201.

Parker Pearson, M. 1999. *The Archaeology of Death and Burial*. Stroud: Sutton.

Perl, G. 1990. *Tacitus—Germania: Lateinisch und deutsch von G. Perl. Schriften und Quellen der Alten Welt: Griechische und lateinische Quellen zur Frühgeschichte Mitteleuropas bis zur Mitte des 1. Jahrtausends u. Z. 37*, 2. Berlin: Akademie-Verlag.

Picard, G.-C. 1977. 'César et les druides', in *Hommage à la mémoire de Jérôme Carcopini. Collection d'Études Anciennes*: 227–233. Paris: Les Belles Lettres/Société Archéologique de l'Aube.

Pleiner, R. 2000. *Iron in Archaeology: The European Bloomery Smelters*. Prague: Archeologický ústav AV ČR.

Posluschny, A. 2008. 'GIS as a Means to Investigate "Princely Sites", Space and Environ. New Ways to Answer Old Questions', in C. Gandini, F. Favory, and L. Nuninger (eds) *ARCHÆDYN: 7 Millennia of Territorial Dynamics: Settlement Pattern, Production and Trades from Neolithic to Middle Ages. Final Conference—University of Burgundy, Dijon, 23–25 June 2008*: 167–174. Dijon: ArchæDyn.

Posluschny, A., P. Verhagen, and A. Danielisová (eds). 2011. *Go Your Own Least Cost Path: Spatial Technology and Archaeological Interpretation. Proceedings of the GIS Session at EAA 2009, Riva del Garda*. British Archaeological Reports International Series 2284. Oxford: Archaeopress.

Rapoport, A. 1969. *House Form and Culture*. Foundations of Cultural Geography Series. Englewood Cliffs: Prentice Hall.

Reim, H. 2006. 'Der Menhir von Weilheim—Zu neolithischen und frühbronzezeitlichen Steinbildwerken im Neckartal zwischen Rottenburg und Tübingen', in H.-P. Wotzka (ed.) *Grundlegungen: Beiträge zur europäischen und afrikanischen Archäologie für Manfred K. H. Eggert*: 445–460. Tübingen: Francke.

Rieckhoff, S., and J. Biel. 2001. *Die Kelten in Deutschland*. Stuttgart: Theiss.

Rieckhoff, S., and S. Fichtl. 2011. *Keltenstädte aus der Luft*. Archäologie in Deutschland, Sonderheft 2011 PLUS. Stuttgart: Theiss.

Rösch, M., E. Fischer, H. Müller, M. Sillmann, and H.-P. Stika. 2008. 'Botanische Untersuchungen zur eisenzeitlichen Landnutzung im südlichen Mitteleuropa', in D. Krausse (ed.) *Frühe Zentralisierungs- und Urbanisierungsprozesse: Zur Genese und Entwicklung frühkeltischer Fürstensitze und ihres territorialen Umlandes. Kolloquium des DFG-Schwerpunktprogramms 1171 in Blaubeuren, 9.–11. Oktober 2006*. Forschungen und Berichte zur Vor- und Frühgeschichte in Baden-Württemberg 101: 319–347. Stuttgart: Theiss

Schetter, W., and R. von Uslar. 1971. 'Zu den pontes longi (Tac. ann. 1, 63, 3)'. *Gymnasium* 78, 3: 201–224.

Schuldt, E. 1972. *Die mecklenburgischen Megalithgräber: Untersuchungen zu ihrer Architektur und Funktion*. Beiträge zur Ur- und Frühgeschichte der Bezirke Rostock, Schwerin und Neubrandenburg 6. Berlin: VEB Deutscher Verlag der Wissenschaften.

Schussmann, M. 2008. 'Die östlichen Nachbarn der Hallstattfürsten—Siedlungshierarchien und Zentralisierungsprozesse in der Südlichen Frankenalb zwischen dem 9. und 4. Jh. v. Chr.', in D. Krausse (ed.) *Frühe Zentralisierungs- und Urbanisierungsprozesse: Zur Genese und Entwicklung frühkeltischer Fürstensitze und ihres territorialen Umlandes. Kolloquium des DFG-Schwerpunktprogramms 1171 in Blaubeuren, 9.–11. Oktober 2006*. Forschungen und Berichte zur Vor- und Frühgeschichte in Baden-Württemberg 101: 299–318. Stuttgart: Theiss

Schweizer, B. 2006. 'Fürstengrab und Fürstensitz: Zur Frühgeschichte zweier Begriffe in der Westhallstatt-Archäologie', in H.-P. Wotzka (ed.) *Grundlegungen: Beiträge zur europäischen und afrikanischen Archäologie für Manfred K. H. Eggert*: 81–100. Tübingen: Francke.

Sharples, N. 2007. 'Building communities and creating identities in the first millennium BC', in C. Haselgrove and R. Pope (eds) *The Earlier Iron Age in Britain and the Near Continent*: 174–184. Oxford: Oxbow.

Sievers, S. 2010. 'Die Wallgrabungen von Manching im Vergleich', in S. Fichtl (ed.) *Murus celticus: Architecture et fonctions des remparts de l'âge du Fer*. Collection Bibracte 19: 175–186. Glux-en-Glenne: Centre archéologique européen du Mont Beuvray.

Sievers, S. 2012. 'Manching—ein Oppidum nach Plan?', in W. Raeck and D. Steuernagel (eds) *Das Gebaute und das Gedachte: Siedlungsform, Architektur und Gesellschaft in prähistorischen und antiken Kulturen*. Frankfurter Archäologische Schriften 21: 115–123. Bonn: Habelt.

Sopp, M. 1999. *Die Wiederaufnahme älterer Bestattungsplätze in den nachfolgenden vor- und frühgeschichtlichen Perioden in Norddeutschland*. Antiquitas 3, 39. Bonn: Habelt.

Spindler, K. 1999. *Der Magdalenenberg bei Villingen: Ein Fürstengrabhügel des 7. vorchristlichen Jahrhunderts*, 2nd edition. Führer zu archäologischen Denkmälern in Baden-Württemberg 5. Stuttgart: Theiss.

Streit, R. 1987. 'Zur Herkunft der Bausteine für die Mauer', in D. van Endert (ed.) *Das Osttor des Oppidums von Manching*. Die Ausgrabungen in Manching 10: 115–118. Stuttgart: Steiner.

Stroh, A. 1979. *Das hallstattzeitliche Gräberfeld von Schirndorf, Ldkr. Regensburg I*. Materialhefte zur Bayerischen Vorgeschichte A 35. Kallmünz: Lassleben.

Stroh, A. 2000. *Das hallstattzeitliche Gräberfeld von Schirndorf, Ldkr. Regensburg, III*. Materialhefte zur Bayerischen Vorgeschichte A 37. Kallmünz: Lassleben.

Thomas, R. 1997. 'Land, kinship relations and the rise of enclosed settlement in first millennium BC Britain'. *Oxford Journal of Archaeology* 16, 2: 211–218.

Timpe, D. 1992. 'Die Landesnatur der Germania nach Tacitus', in G. Neumann and H. Seemann (eds) *Beiträge zum Verständnis der Germania des Tacitus, II, Bericht über die Kolloquien der Kommission für die Altertumskunde Nord- und Mitteleuropas im Jahre 1986 und 1987*. Abhandlungen der Akademie der Wissenschaften in Göttingen, Philologisch-Historische Klasse, Dritte Folge 195: 258–277. Göttingen: Vandenhoeck & Ruprecht.

Tylecote, R. F., J. N. Austin, and A. E. Wraith. 1973. 'Iron smelting experiments with a shaft furnace of the Roman period', in W. U. Guyan, R. Pleiner, and R. Fabešová (eds) *Die Versuchsschmelzen und ihre Bedeutung für die Metallurgie des Eisens und dessen Geschichte. Comité de la Sidérurgie ancienne UISPP affiliée à l'UNESCO*: 25–49. Schaffhausen: Internal print.

Wendling, H. 2010a. 'Landbesitz und Erbfolge—Ein ethnographisches Modell zur Sozialstruktur und Raumgliederung der mitteleuropäischen Latènezeit', in P. Trebsche,

N. Müller-Scheeßel, and S. Reinhold (eds) *Der gebaute Raum: Bausteine einer Architektursoziologie vormoderner Gesellschaften*: 325–354. Münster: Waxmann.

Wendling, H. 2010b. 'Opus deforme non est … Neue Erkenntnisse zur Konstruktion des Manchinger murus, Landkreis Pfaffenhofen a. d. Ilm, Oberbayern'. *Das archäologische Jahr in Bayern* 2009: 75–78.

Wendling, H. 2012. *Der Münsterberg von Breisach in der Spätlatènezeit: Siedlungsarchäologische Untersuchungen am Oberrhein*. Materialhefte zur Archäologie in Baden-Württemberg 94. Stuttgart: Theiss.

Wendling, H. 2013. 'Manching reconsidered: New perspectives on settlement dynamics and urbanization in Iron Age central Europe'. *European Journal of Archaeology* 16, 3: 459–490.

Wendling, H. 2016. 'Fingierte Tradition und kulturelles Gedächtnis—Die Aneignung der Vergangenheit im Siedlungswesen der mitteleuropäischen Latènezeit'. *Ethnographisch-Archäologische Zeitschrift* 55, 1–2: 91–118.

Wieland, G. 1999. *Keltische Viereckschanzen: Einem Rätsel auf der Spur*. Stuttgart: Theiss.

Willerding, U. 1992. 'Klima und Vegetation der Germania nach vegetationsgeschichtlichen und paläo-ethnobotanischen Quellen', in G. Neumann and H. Seemann (eds) *Beiträge zum Verständnis der Germania des Tacitus, II: Bericht über die Kolloquien der Kommission für die Altertumskunde Nord- und Mitteleuropas im Jahre 1986 und 1987*. Abhandlungen der Akademie der Wissenschaften in Göttingen. Philologisch-Historische Klasse. Dritte Folge 195: 332–373. Göttingen: Vandenhoeck & Ruprecht.

ECONOMY

CHAPTER 23

IRON AND IRON TECHNOLOGY

TIMOTHY CHAMPION

Introduction

The working and use of iron is, of course, the defining characteristic of the Iron Age in the Three Age System as codified by Thomsen in the early nineteenth century. Since then, archaeology has successfully demonstrated that iron was not, as once thought, a technology introduced into the rest of Europe by the Romans, but that there was an indigenous iron technology for a millennium or more before the Roman conquest of parts of Europe, and indeed that the skills developed in the non-Mediterranean regions were sometimes superior to those of the classical world.

Much of the discussion of the archaeology of Europe in the first millennium BC is still influenced very heavily by the ideas of the Three Age System: directly, in the chronological division of the subject and its specialisms into a Bronze Age and an Iron Age (as seen in the scope of this volume), which tends to generate questions about the transition from one age to another, and more indirectly through the technological basis of the System, with its underlying assumption of progress, which tends to generate similar questions about the transition from a bronze technology to an iron one; the rise of iron is therefore intimately linked to the decline of bronze. In addition to the linking of iron and bronze in a causal relationship (often but not always rooted in a notion of the superiority of iron), discussion of the rise and use of iron has often been based on the diffusionist assumption of an outward spread from a single point of origin, from Anatolia through the south-east of Europe in a generally north-westwards direction. Recent research makes these assumptions less clear and the picture more complicated: evidence for early ironworking in central and western Europe is making the diffusionist argument more problematic, and it is becoming clear that the regional adoption of iron was highly variable, and the pattern of technological development very patchy.

This chapter will give an account of the development of the basic technologies of making iron and the subsequent working of iron into finished products, the growth in scale of the iron industry and the emergence of major centres of production, and the impact that iron objects had in other spheres of Iron Age economy and society. Our knowledge of ironworking in Iron Age Europe is somewhat variable: chronologically, we know much more about the later stages than the earlier, and geographically there has been more research in central, western, and northern Europe than in parts of the west Mediterranean region and eastern Europe. Our knowledge has also been shaped by the nature of the archaeological record: Iron Age societies made decisions about what to select for deposition, what to recycle and what to discard; survival of iron is poor in many environments; and there is likely to be a bias against the recognition, identification and recovery of prehistoric iron in fieldwalking and even metal-detecting. The patterns of archaeological research have varied from region to region: concentration on cemeteries rather than settlements in some areas has shaped the range of objects available for study, which is dominated by items from graves, hoards, and ritual deposits. Recent research has led to a rapid increase in the quantity, quality, and range of evidence available through new discoveries, especially in advance of major development projects, and new analytical programmes; there has been a particular concentration of recent research in France (e.g. Mangin 1994; Feugère and Serneels 1998; Milcent 2007; Dubreucq 2013; Berranger 2014).

Iron Production

Iron ores are widely distributed throughout Europe, unlike those of the metals previously exploited—gold, copper, tin, and lead. Early technologies (Pleiner 2000) were much less efficient than those of later periods (some prehistoric slag tips were later reworked for the residual iron), so only the richer ores may have been of interest to Iron Age smelters; on the other hand, even quite small ore sources would have been economically viable. The commonest sources were oxide ores such as haematite and limonite; in northern Europe, iron ores were formed in bogs and other watery places, and these bog ores were widely exploited. These ores varied considerably in their trace element composition, especially in manganese, phosphorus, nickel, and cobalt, which have a significant effect on the quality of the iron; the special properties of particular ores would have been widely recognized. Sulphide ores such as iron pyrites ('fool's gold') may have been technically usable with thorough roasting, but there was a high risk of an admixture of sulphur with the iron, resulting in a very brittle metal; nevertheless, these ores may have been widely used.

Unlike copper, iron ores are generally located near the surface; limonites, in particular, are widely found as weathered exposures of other mineral ores. The primary collection or extraction of the ores has therefore left little archaeological trace, though in some locations clusters of pits have been interpreted as ore quarries. Caesar (*de Bello*

Gallico 7.22) and Strabo (*Geography* 4.2.2) refer to underground iron mines in central France, but these were clearly exceptional at this period.

Iron production in prehistoric Europe was by the 'direct' or 'bloomery' process, in which iron is produced in the form of a spongy lump or 'bloom'. The temperatures achievable in prehistoric furnaces were not high enough to produce liquid iron in a regular or controllable way, though small quantities might occur under certain conditions (Crew et al. 2011). This dictated all later stages of ironworking: unlike copper and its alloys, iron was not cast in a mould, but had to be shaped in a solid state, predominantly by heating and hammering; the technology to produce cast iron was developed in China before about 500 BC, but was not known in Europe until the fifteenth century AD. As well as the ore, the smelting process also required large quantities of clay for the construction of hearths and furnaces, and of charcoal for fuel. The acquisition of these materials, as well as the actual smelting process, would have been very labour-intensive, and the demand for charcoal would have had an impact on the local environment (e.g. Mighall and Chambers 1997); the comparatively small scale of the earliest iron production may have meant that impacts were localized and perhaps not permanent, though their severity increased greatly with the larger-scale workings of the late Iron Age and Roman period (Mighall et al. 2017; see also Chapter 22).

The first stage in smelting was the preparation or dressing of the ore. This involved crushing the ore and selecting the most useful parts, discarding the waste. The ore might then be roasted on a simple clay hearth: sulphide ores, if used, would certainly have needed roasting to remove much of the sulphur, and other ores would have benefited from the removal of water content. These processes would leave little archaeological trace.

The actual smelting required a hearth or furnace with an air supply. The simplest form was a bowl furnace, formed in a hollow in the ground lined with clay or stone; air would have been supplied by a bellows. Such simple hearths are found throughout prehistoric Europe, and were in use throughout the Iron Age alongside more complex versions that developed later. One such development was the domed hearth, certainly in use in the late Iron Age and possibly earlier. With a flat base and a clay dome, it was more akin to a pottery kiln or a domestic oven, and may not have been a particularly successful experiment.

More successful was the shaft furnace. The addition of a wall of clay around the bowl, perhaps originally just to retain the charge of ore and fuel in place, was the basis for this new form of furnace. As the clay wall was heightened to form a shaft, the smelting operation took place higher up and the bowl no longer operated as a hearth; instead, it acted as a sump into which the molten slag drained, until it was full, ending the operation. Such shaft furnaces with slag pits were common in much of central and western Europe in the late Iron Age and possibly earlier, though frequently the pit or a block of slag is all that survives. Later forms of shaft furnace were developed which did not have a slag pit; instead the slag was either raked out from the base of the shaft, or tapped and allowed to run off. These were difficult processes and risked serious loss of heat in the furnace, but allowed longer periods of operation. Such shaft furnaces became common in the Roman Iron Age in much of Europe, but it is unclear when they began to be used.

When the smelting was complete, the metallic iron had to be removed. In the case of a bowl furnace the bloom could be lifted out and separated manually from the slag and fuel ash; shaft furnaces had to be broken open to retrieve the bloom, though they were frequently rebuilt and reused. The bloom was a conglomerate of iron, slag, and ash, and needed further treatment to remove as much as possible of the slag and to consolidate the metallic iron. This was best achieved by reheating the bloom and hammering it, a process often repeated several times. The hearths used for such reheating and bloom-smithing were typically open and shallow, and produced characteristic plano-convex cakes of slag. The final result was a bloom of usable iron; examples that have been found are seldom more than 1 kg in weight, though larger ones are known.

The iron produced by this bloomery process could vary considerably in its finished state, depending on many factors such as the quality of the ore, the nature of pre-treatment, the ratio of ore and fuel in the furnace, the rate of charging the furnace with ore and fuel, the nature of the air supply, the method of slag removal, and the duration of the smelting; modern experimental work has demonstrated the complexities of this apparently simple technology (Crew 2013). These complexities would have made it a rather unpredictable process for early smelters, though increased practical experience would have brought better control of the outcome. Much of the finished metal was a low-carbon iron, though small quantities of phosphorous would have given a harder product; such iron could be comparatively easily worked into a variety of rods, bars, sheets, tools, and implements. A small percentage of the output was a higher-carbon steel, for which manganese-rich ores were especially suitable; this metal was particularly valuable for making hard, sharp edges for blades.

Archaeological evidence for these processes is found widely throughout Europe, though it is much more common in the later periods. In theory, the various stages of the smelting process could have been located in different places, and the iron transported in various forms from the untreated ore to the finished bloom, though it seems most likely that the commonest form of long-distance distribution was as finished iron ready for smithing. Individual elements of production in the form of hearths, furnaces, and various types of slag are well known, but much rarer is the recovery of a whole smelting complex including all stages of production and any associated settlement features. Rare examples such as that at Waschenberg in Austria (Pleiner 2000: 58 and fig. 14.2), dating to the early La Tène period, or from Bryn y Castell, north Wales (Figure 23.1; Crew 1986, 1988; Mighall and Chambers 1997), dating to the late Iron Age, are particularly important for the evidence they show of the organization of smaller-scale industrial sites. Elsewhere, modern large-scale excavations have revealed some details of the spatial and industrial organization of the developed industry: at Les Clérimois, France, for instance, a fourth-century episode of smelting was followed at the end of the Iron Age by much more extensive and technologically more complex operations (Dunikowski and Cabboi 1995). At Levroux 'Les Arènes', France, ironworking was part of a large industrial agglomeration: excavations have shown the spatial organization of activity spanning the

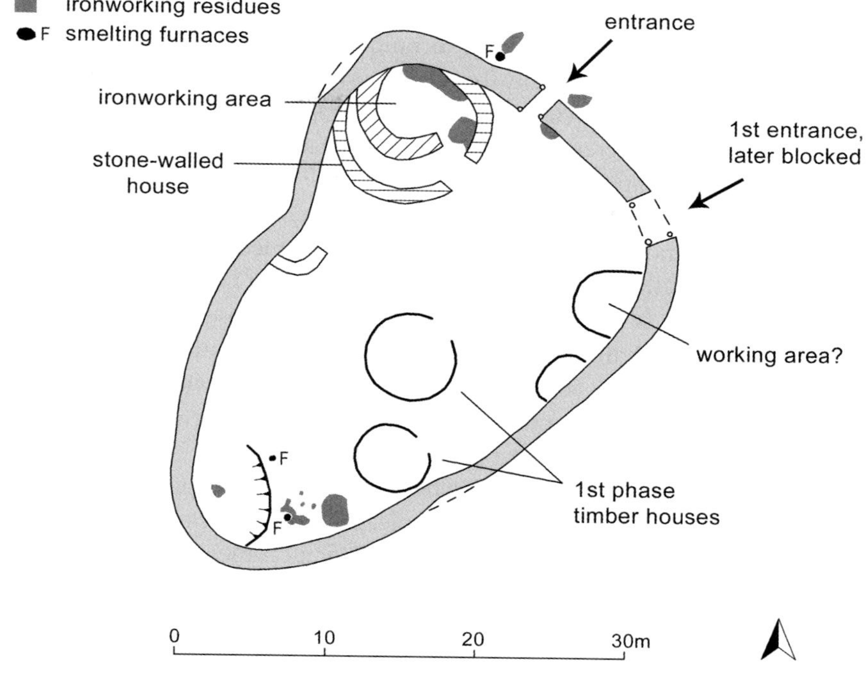

FIGURE 23.1 The small stone-walled hilltop enclosure at Bryn y Castell, north Wales, was later the location of ironworking in the late Iron Age and early Roman periods, especially the smelting of local ores, as shown by well-preserved smelting furnaces and extensive deposits of ironworking residues.

Author, adapted from Crew 1986, 1988

second century BC, which did not include primary smelting, but specialized in bloom-smithing and object fabrication, including brooches, scabbards, and blades (Berranger and Fluzin 2014).

In view of the high level of expertise involved, it is highly likely that the craft of smelting was practised by only a limited subset of the population, but we have little evidence to suggest how the craft was organized or how the skills were transmitted or developed. It is only in the late Iron Age that we can begin to see some evidence of the organization of production, by that time on an increasingly centralized scale, as discussed later.

Iron Smithing

The second stage in ironworking was the fabrication of individual artefacts from the stock of iron, an entirely separate process that could be, and often was, practised well away from the location of smelting (Pleiner 2006). It required a hearth or furnace to heat the iron to a point where it was malleable, as well as appropriate tools and skill derived from practical experience. Some of the techniques could be adapted from previous practice of bronzeworking, especially the use of hammer and anvil for cold working, but the need for constant heating of the metal required new expertise. Different types of iron needed to be worked at different temperatures; for instance, the higher the proportion of carbon, the lower the temperature.

An appropriate quantity of iron for the intended object had to be cut from the stock of metal with hammer and chisel; the iron could then be formed by a set of basic processes such as thinning, lengthening or widening ('drawing down'), thickening ('upsetting'), bending and rolling, twisting, splitting and piercing. These needed robust tools, including a solid anvil, hammers, chisels, punches, and tongs to hold the hot metal, tools which were themselves all made of iron. Where uniform widths or sections were required, for instance for nails, rods and wires, these could be formed in grooves in the anvils or by using special tools for shaping iron (swages).

Larger and more complex objects could be formed by welding pieces of iron together by hammering. This was a comparatively simple, if laborious, task where the two pieces were of the same type of metal, but much more difficult if they were of different composition requiring different temperatures. This was an important technique for the production of objects requiring a harder and sharper edge, such as swords; the body of the implement could be made of low-carbon wrought iron, while a higher-carbon steel was more suitable for the edge. More complex still were objects made from metal comprising layers of different types of metal ('piling') to increase its efficiency while maximizing the value of higher-quality material.

A further technique for improving the quality of blade edges was carburization, or the deliberate addition of carbon to a selected portion of the object. This could be achieved by prolonged exposure of the iron to a carbon source, typically charcoal; thus the blade edge could be enclosed in a bed of charcoal while the rest of the object was masked, to procure a harder steel.

Another technique acquired in the Iron Age, but used more rarely, was quenching. This involved heating the object and then rapid cooling in a medium such as oil or water. High-carbon steel quenched in this way was very hard, but also brittle; the brittleness could be reduced by tempering, which meant heating again and allowing to cool. Quenching and tempering could in theory allow fine control over the hardness of the finished metal.

These techniques were all known and practised by the end of the Iron Age, and there was clearly a very general pattern of increasing technical competence through the course of the period; Pleiner (1986: 82; see also Pleiner 1980: tables 11.1 and 11.3) has shown that the proportion of iron objects made from simple wrought iron as distinct from hardened metal (whether from the selection of high-carbon steel for the object, or from the welding of wrought iron and steel, or from carburization) fell from 61% in early La Tène, to 37% in middle La Tène, and 27% in late La Tène. At a more detailed level, however, it is difficult to see a consistent picture. Much of our evidence comes from a limited area of central and northern Europe, and there is a need for more technical analyses of iron artefacts from some of the less studied regions, but the picture is one of regional and chronological variability. Though the techniques of carburization and quench hardening were known at least as early as the fifth century BC in some places, as documented by chisels from Danebury in southern England (Ehrenreich 1985: 63), they were used only intermittently thereafter; the effects of quenching may have been little understood, since examples are known of the quenching of low-carbon wrought iron, on which it would have had no effect.

The artefacts that have received the most intensive study are swords, which were frequently placed in graves and ritual deposits of the La Tène period (Lang 1986, 2006; Pleiner 1993; Senn Bischofberger 2005; Mihok and Kotigoroschko 2011). These studies have shown that advanced techniques, though already known, may not have been generally applied to sword manufacture: for example, some swords continued to be made from single pieces of iron after the invention of piling techniques. One form of piling, edge to edge, comprised the welding of strips which each ran the length of the blade, typically sandwiching a harder iron between two strips of softer iron to provide the blade edges, a technique known at least by early La Tène times. Another form, strip piling, meant using strips that ran from surface to surface of the blade, not edge to edge; this was known at least by middle La Tène times. Though these methods would have produced stronger and more effective swords, they were not always adopted.

While the properties of high-carbon steel were well appreciated, especially for piled blades, it was not always used. A detailed study of iron technology in the north Alpine region (Senn Bischofberger 2005) shows that in the early La Tène swords were typically made of three layers, with a central core of hardened steel between two strips of low-carbon wrought iron; in middle La Tène the technology switched to the use of a single piece of high-phosphorus iron, while in the late Iron Age swords were made from multiple metals worked into a single blade. In general, swords here show little sign of quenching and tempering. A well-known passage by Polybius (*Histories* 2.33), describing the battle of Telamon in 225 BC between the Romans and the Gauls, recounts how the Gauls' iron swords bent on impact and required straightening. It is difficult to match this account with the modern analyses; some of the swords may well have been of poor quality, suggesting a demand for a long sword rather than an effective sword, but the historical sources may well be exaggerating the problems. A study of Dacian smithing skills from the late Iron Age showed careful selection of metals for different purposes and a variety of techniques in use for fabricating swords, including carburization, quenching, and tempering; some of the weapons were judged excellent, others merely serviceable (Mihok and Kotigoroschko 2011).

It is clear that smiths could distinguish basic low-carbon wrought iron from high-phosphorus iron, and from non-hardenable and hardenable steels. What is less clear is why they chose to use particular types of metal and particular fabrication methods at different times; fluctuating availability of different metals, regional differences in craft skills, variability in the personal expertise or knowledge of individual smiths may all have been significant. These detailed studies show the high degree of variability in the quality of the iron artefacts at any one time, and the lack of a clear pattern of what, with hindsight, we might see as technological progress through the period. It is difficult to disagree with Pleiner (1986: 82) that investigations

> regularly reveal examples of high-class work which lead to the skills of the ancient master-craftsmen being exaggerated. A closer study of the difference in their work and of the various categories of quality and fabrication methods often reveals the existence of unsuccessful artefacts, ... which demonstrate how difficult it must have been for early smiths to become familiar with different types of material, which was often poor in quality.

Evidence for smithing is found on many settlement sites of the Iron Age, but it is often difficult to gauge the scale of the activity. Small-scale working, including fabrication of simple objects or minor repairs, may have been practised by many people, but it seems likely that the manufacture of larger or more complex objects was a more restricted skill.

The Adoption of Iron: From Bronze to Iron?

The traditional model for the adoption of ironworking in prehistoric Europe has been a diffusionist one, based on the assumption of a spread of the knowledge of the relevant skills from Greece north-westwards through the continent (e.g. Pleiner 1980); in Iberia the role of the Phoenicians or the Greeks as agents of diffusion has been debated (Rovira 1998; Rovira Hortalà 2007), while in eastern Europe a hypothetical migration of Cimmerians following an alternative route north of the Black Sea has also been invoked (Berciu 1964; Piggott 1964). These processes have sometimes been linked with a three-stage model of adoption in which the new metal was first used for a small number of small objects or as an inlay, followed by a stage with more general use, and finally by large-scale production and use in the later periods (Pleiner 1980). The adoption of iron has also been linked to the decline of the bronze industry; though the precise nature of the relationship has seldom been expounded in detail, there are two main accounts: either iron was adopted because it was a superior metal, following the assumptions of technological progress implicit in the Three Age System, leading to the decline of bronze (e.g. Burgess 1979: 275; Kristiansen 1998: 211–213), or it was adopted as an alternative to bronze, despite the newness of the technology, as bronze supplies failed to meet the demand for metal (e.g. Bradley 1988) or the late Bronze Age economies collapsed totally (Bouzek 1985).

The picture is now more complex. Recent discoveries have begun to document an increasing number of iron objects throughout Europe from well before the decline of the bronze industry (Sørensen and Thomas 1989). They have been reported from Romania (Stoia 1989) and south-eastern Europe more generally (Taylor 1989); from central

Europe (Bouzek 1989) and Switzerland (Speck 1981); from France (Gomez de Soto and Mohen 1981; Gomez de Soto and Kerouanton 2009), Britain (Collard et al. 2006: 409–414) and the Netherlands (van der Broeke 2005), as well as Denmark (Nørbach 1998) and Sweden (Hjärthner-Holdar 1993). While the evidence for early iron in Iberia is less definite (Rovira Hortalà 2007), it is clear that iron objects were in use from about 1100 BC throughout much of Europe, and possibly earlier; although numbers were small, they became more common in the final phases of the Bronze Age. Good archaeological evidence for primary smelting does not appear that early. The earliest securely dated smelting furnace may be that from Messingham, England, operating in the period 800–700 BC (Pitts 2016); others, such as that at Choisy-au-Bac, France (Blanchet 1984: 413–419), may be only a little later. Slag deposits may also be good evidence of smelting and smithing: indeed in Denmark, smelting slags are the only evidence for iron production, rather than use, before the eventual appearance of furnaces in the late Iron Age (Nørbach 1998; Jouttijärvi and Voss 2011). Early slag deposits have been claimed in southern England (Collard et al. 2006) dating to the period 1000–900 BC, and in Sweden, similarly dated to Montelius IV (Hjärthner-Holdar 1993). In Germany, however, the first evidence of smelting does not appear until the sixth century BC (Gassman and Schäfer 2014).

Given the widespread evidence of iron production and usage in the late Bronze Age, it is impossible to maintain the link between the initial interest in iron and the decline of the bronze supply. It is also hard to support an argument for the replacement of bronze by a superior metal, in the light of the very limited quantity of iron in the early Iron Age and its highly variable quality, as discussed later. Though the eventual decline in the bronze industry may have been a stimulus to the development of the skills of iron production and fabrication, the initial working of iron in the late Bronze Age is best regarded as a separate phenomenon. It would have been quite possible for an original awareness of the potential of iron to be acquired independently in different locations in Europe in the late Bronze Age, where there was a high level of metallurgical skill in working copper, tin, gold, and lead, where there were efficient networks of metallurgical information, and where there were plentifully available iron ores. Nevertheless, the balance between the relative contributions of indigenous metallurgical skill and experimentation and the diffusion of the knowledge of iron from external sources can still be debated. Technological factors may have been less relevant than broader socio-economic ones (Thomas 1989), and it may not be reasonable to look for a single explanation for all the various regions of Europe.

The Development of the Industry

The development of the technologies of smelting and smithing has already been discussed, but it is also necessary to consider the growth of the iron industry and its role in society, as well as the nature of its products. At first, iron was used to make a range of small tools or ornaments; it was sometimes used for decorative rather than functional purposes, as an inlay in bronze objects such as pins or razors. As it became more common, it was used to replicate forms previously made in bronze, especially certain types of tool and weapon. Small personal ornaments such as pins and brooches continued to be made in bronze, but iron forms became more frequent. Iron was not well suited to use in sheet form, and most vessels such as cauldrons, bowls, and jugs were still made in bronze. Iron did, however, lend itself to the manufacture of tools and other implements, and the range of objects made in this metal widened enormously.

It is difficult to assess the scale of iron use in the earliest phases of the Iron Age. The metal certainly became more common from the second half of the eighth century BC. Our evidence is mostly derived from graves, with limited excavation of settlement sites, which have mostly produced little iron; recycling may have been important. In central Europe, iron was used almost exclusively for the production of elite items such as weaponry, wagon fittings, and occasional ornaments (Dubreucq 2013: 299–300). The large iron swords were impressive products of these early technologies, but must have consumed a considerable proportion of the available metal (Milcent 2004: 73–134; Brun et al. 2009).

The frequency of iron objects continues to increase in the sixth century BC, but the nature of the evidence, which is dominated by aristocratic burial and settlement sites, makes it difficult to judge its real availability. In a diachronic study of the use of iron in France, Berranger and Fluzin (2012) have suggested that production and circulation of the metal in the late Hallstatt and earliest La Tène periods was still very restricted, though a few sites were capable of larger-scale production, as at Bragny-sur-Saône (Flouest 2007). Iron was certainly in use in increasing volumes at the aristocratic sites, for a wide variety of utilitarian functions (Dubreucq 2013), and it is possible that the amount of iron in use more generally, and the uses to which it was put, have been underestimated (Dubreucq 2007).

The period from the fifth to the second century BC saw a significant rise in the use of iron. This can be seen in graves, although the widespread adoption of the rite of furnished inhumation and the fashion for the excavation of such cemeteries may be distorting the picture through preferential selection for deposition and recovery. It can also be seen in the increasing number of semi-products, or metal in the form of half-finished objects, indicating the growth of specialized production and the distribution of manufactured iron (Berranger and Fluzin 2012; Berranger 2014: 64–79), discussed in more detail later.

The final period of the Iron Age, starting perhaps in the third or second century BC, witnessed a massive rise in the production and use of iron in many parts of Europe. This can be seen in the rise of major production centres in various regions. The area of Noricum, in modern Austria, was an important production zone for high-quality iron and steel, exploiting the local ores with a high manganese content; *ferrum noricum* was well known and highly valued in the Roman world. The site of Magdalensberg was a major centre, with much evidence for both smelting and smithing (Dolenz 1998; Straube 1996). Another important area was in the Danube valley of southern

Germany: the *oppidum* at Kelheim was a centre for the extraction and smelting of iron ore; both smelting and smithing were important parts of the economy of the *oppidum* at Manching, while the nearby site at Pollanten specialized in smithing (Schäfer 2002). Another production zone with archaeological evidence was in central Poland (Czarnecka 2000); the sites in the Holy Cross Mountains, at their peak in the early centuries AD, have produced some of the most extensive evidence for iron smelting anywhere in Europe (Bielenin 1964).

Such evidence for large-scale production is matched by increased evidence for trade (Berranger and Fluzin 2012). It can also be matched by increased numbers of finds of iron objects in hoards (Bataille and Guillaumet 2006); these include many large hoards of ironwork, but the rise in the number of such hoards in the late Iron Age may be distorting the picture. More convincing is the greatly increased number of finds from settlement sites, in particular from many *oppida* such as Manching (Jacobi 1974), but also from elsewhere—for example, the hillfort of Danebury in southern England (Salter and Ehrenreich 1984: fig. 10.6).

Production, Distribution, and Trade

Iron ores occur widely in Europe, but vary greatly in quality and accessibility, and, though local production was always important, certain areas came to dominate the production and working of iron. The development of specialized production centres meant the growth of distribution systems, and iron became an item of exchange, often in ingot or semi-fabricated form, as discussed earlier. The discovery of these semi-products has provided important evidence for the nature and scale of the production of iron, as well as for studies of provenance (e.g. Berranger 2014: 64–79, 88–107).

Goods in transit can rarely be seen archaeologically, except for the occasional disasters, such as shipwrecks, that interrupt their safe passage. A group of such shipwrecks with cargoes of iron has been investigated at Saintes-Maries-de-la-Mer at the mouth of the Rhône (Pagès et al. 2011); they date to the first century AD, but iron seems curiously absent from earlier cargoes so far found in the western Mediterranean (Dietler 1997: 294–296).

Most of the evidence for the distribution of iron stock is in the form of more or less standardized ingots or semi-fabricated objects (Berranger 2007; 2014: 64–79; Berranger and Fluzin 2012). These are known from at least late Hallstatt times in central Europe; chronology is often difficult since many are found in hoards which cannot be easily dated with precision. A very common form is the double-pyramidal ingot found widely distributed in central Europe through much of the Iron Age. Other forms were used elsewhere. In Britain, a variety of types known generically as 'currency bars' were produced, in the form of swords, ploughshares and spits: different forms may have indicated different production sources (Allen 1967; Hedges and Salter 1979; Hingley 1990; Crew 1994). The standardized shapes and roughly standardized weights of the objects would have acted as indicators of the source, quality, and quantity of metal in exchange transactions. Though many such objects are known in complete form from hoard deposits, most were presumably broken up to be used as the raw material for smithing, as seen for instance at Danebury (Crew 1995).

Another approach is to study the supply of iron to a site, especially ones with large assemblages. At Danebury, for instance, where there was little evidence for smelting, the iron reached the site as semi-products from at least four different sources (Crew 1995). In addition to metallurgical studies designed to examine the production technology of the finished objects, modern scientific methods have been increasingly applied to the analysis of the composition of the iron in order to determine its provenance. These methods include chemical analysis of the iron and comparison with potential ore sources, analysis of isotope ratios in the iron and similar comparison with sources, and analysis of residual slag inclusions in the finished object and comparison with smelting slags or potential ores (for a summary of such research, see Schwab et al. 2006; Brauns et al. 2013; Charlton 2015). Analysis of included slag has been a particularly profitable approach; early work such as that of Hedges and Salter (1979) showed the potential, and more recent work, coupled with appropriate statistical methods for the comparison of the analytical results, has produced useful results (e.g. Blakelock et al. 2009; Charlton et al. 2012, with further references). It has, for instance, been possible to demonstrate that the source of the iron used at Manching in the late Iron Age was the local bog iron of the Danube valley (Schwab et al. 2006), while bog iron was also used in northern Germany, but with a variety of different smelting techniques to exploit its properties (Heimann et al. 2001).

The Impact of Iron

Although the development of iron technologies may have been slow, with well-made artefacts becoming widely available only comparatively late in the Iron Age, the impact of the new material was significant and cumulatively dramatic, not least in its ability to supply better-quality tools for other industries, thus compounding the economic benefit. In his early writings, Childe emphasized the ready availability of cheap iron tools and their role in the clearing and settlement of new areas, and hence in population growth (Childe 1936), and even spoke of an Iron Age revolution (Childe 1935: 8); most famously, he wrote that 'Cheap iron democratised agriculture and industry and warfare too' (Childe 1942: 183). Though he later emphasized more strongly his Neolithic and Urban revolutions, he continued to stress the significance of the plentiful availability of iron, in contrast to the rarer copper and tin, though he drew differing conclusions about its social significance: it could provide the opportunity for ordinary people to gain access to metal 'independent of kings or chieftains', thus helping to undermine aristocratic or monarchical power (Childe 1946: 30–31), but it could also lead to new forms of dominance through the control of forces armed with effective iron weapons (Childe 1950: 222).

In the longer run, there can be little doubt about the significance of the Eurasian mastery of iron, and some writers have clearly identified it as a key factor in later European global dominance (e.g. Diamond 1998). Here, however, the emphasis is on its more immediate economic and technological impact during the Iron Age itself, though these were undoubtedly integral to other social developments in the period.

The ready availability of iron ore could, as Childe suggested, have made it potentially available to many and therefore a difficult commodity to exploit for power. Ore, however, was not the only requisite, and the control of fuel, labour, skills, and the distribution and use of finished objects of iron may have been more important. The use of iron may have been limited in the earliest phases; its restricted use for elite items in Hallstatt C in central Europe was noted earlier, and there are conflicting arguments about its role in the support of later social elites. Berranger and Fluzin (2012) have suggested a connection with the elites of the late Hallstatt *Fürstensitze*, but for the early La Tène period Driehaus' (1965) suggestion of the exploitation of iron ores as a source of the power and prestige of the Rhineland chiefs has been questioned (Diepeveen-Jansen 2001: 11, 65). Certainly, by the end of the Iron Age the large-scale production of iron associated with the *oppida* would have been a major source of their economic power. In general, however, the collapse of the late Bronze Age societies based on long-distance trading networks would have led to the formation of societies with very different sets of social relations, in which iron would have been intricately involved, not just in the practice of warfare and craft skills but in the creation of metaphorical meanings (Giles 2007).

By the end of the Iron Age, iron was being used to manufacture a wide range of tools for use in various technologies, including those of metal, leather, and wood, as well as in agriculture. Standard tool types had been developed which continued with little change into the Roman period (Gaitzsch 1980) and would have remained familiar to medieval and early modern workers (Audouze and Buchsenschutz 1991: 47–48). Though many of the products of these technologies were organic, and hence the direct evidence has rarely survived, the effect of better, sharper, and longer-lasting tools was of huge importance for many areas of craft production. The range of products can be best appreciated in large assemblages such as those from Manching (Jacobi 1974) or Numantia (Manrique Mayor 1980), but similar tools were widespread throughout Europe.

The forging of iron artefacts required suitably robust tools, and anvils, hammers, tongs, and hearth shovels were all manufactured for this purpose. Tools for agriculture were perhaps the most common products, and sickles, billhooks, knives, axes, points for ploughshares, and blades for spades were all produced in iron. Specialist tools for working leather had already been made in bronze at the end of the late Bronze Age, and the semicircular knife blades were continued in iron; a variety of awls and punches may also have been used on leather.

Improved tools for woodworking had a major impact on the range and size of objects produced. Saws, axes, adzes, chisels, gouges, augers, files, and hammers were critical for carpentry, as were smaller items such as tacks, nails, and clamps for joining and finishing. Complex objects such as iron-bound buckets and barrels were produced, some of great size. Some of the most complex objects showed the importance of iron for both working and fixing wooden structures. Iron tools allowed the construction of complex spoked wheels for wagons and chariots; early examples from Hallstatt C were held fast by an iron tyre nailed on and held with clamps (Kossack 1971), but by the La Tène period a single-piece iron tyre was shrunk into place, a skill perfected in the Iron Age but later lost and only rediscovered by early-modern wheelwrights (Piggott 1983: 167, 216–217); the earliest dated example is from Scotland in the fifth century BC (Carter et al. 2010). By the late Iron Age, fortification techniques included the use of massive timbers, a method known as *murus gallicus* from its description by Caesar (*de Bello Gallico* 7.23); these were sometimes fixed by large iron spikes, often in extravagant quantities, as documented at sites such as Manching (van Endert 1987; see also Chapters 21 and 22).

One technology that combined developments in woodworking and ironworking skill was shipbuilding. Little is known about the boats and ships of the earlier Iron Age after the sewn-plank boats of the later Bronze Age (Ellmers 1969; van der Noort 2011: 160–169); the Hjortspring craft is a solitary exception (Randsborg 1995: 21–25). In the first century BC, however, Caesar gives a detailed description of the boats of the Veneti in Brittany (*de Bello Gallico* 3.13); they included timbers up to a foot thick, fastened by iron spikes 'the size of a man's thumb'. This is the first evidence for the use of iron nails in ship construction: though no physical evidence for such ships has survived, the description is similar to the Romano-Celtic ships well-documented in western Europe from the first century AD onwards, in which timbers were fixed to frames with large iron nails (McGrail 1995; van der Noort 2011: 166–169). Caesar also records that the anchors of the Veneti were attached by iron chains; a large iron anchor with six metres of iron chain attached was found in a late Iron Age hoard in the hillfort of Bulbury, southern England, possibly an example of such an object (Cunliffe 1972).

Another area in which iron played a significant role was that of arms and armour (Rapin 1999; Zeller 1980). Established forms of swords and spears were immediately copied in iron: some of the most impressive pieces of early ironwork are the long Hallstatt C swords, mentioned earlier, seen in cemeteries such as Hallstatt itself. These were followed by a long series of daggers and swords in use throughout the Iron Age (de Navarro 1972; Sievers 1982; Pleiner 1993; Stead 2006); the technology of sword-making has already been discussed. Iron played a smaller role in the production of defensive armour. It was used occasionally for the edge-binding of shields of organic material, and more often to strengthen the boss and protect the handgrip. In central Europe and Italy it was used to make an important group of helmets (Schaaff 1974). One striking development was the production of mail corselets, an innovation attributed by the Roman author Varro to the Celts (*de lingua latina*, V, 24, 116); these are known from the late fourth century BC, in widespread contexts such as the warrior graves at Ciumești, Romania (Rusu 1969) and Kirkburn, England (Stead 1991: 54–56), and the bog deposit at Hjortspring, Denmark (Randsborg 1995: 26–30).

Iron was also used to manufacture prestige items for use in feasting. By the end of the Bronze Age items such as buckets, cauldrons, spits, and flesh-hooks were made in bronze, and some of these were later made in iron. Iron was, however, less well suited to use in sheet-metal vessels and, despite a few iron examples, most were made in bronze.

By the end of the Iron Age, iron chains for suspending cauldrons, as well as firedogs (or andirons; Piggott 1971) and gridirons were in use, mostly appearing in aristocratic graves or as deposits in lakes or bogs. An elaborately decorated firedog from Capel Garmon, north Wales, shows that iron could also on occasion be used for decorative as well as purely functional purposes (Jope 2000: 109, 268, and pl. 174; Figure 23.2).

Most attention has been paid to tools and weapons, and in particular to the types of object selected for burial in graves or hoards, compounding the problems caused by poor survival and difficulties of recovery and interpretation; occasionally, however, these contexts provide a glimpse of a wider range of iron products, such as surgical instruments (de Navarro 1955) or slave chains (Fox 1946: 37–39). Domestic contexts are more problematic: many sites produce small items of iron whose original function is uncertain—possibly small tools or fixtures and fittings for complex objects. It is quite possible that the role of iron in domestic life in the Iron Age, or at least its later phases, has been seriously underestimated; its use permeated many areas of daily activity and its material presence was an everyday feature of Iron Age life (Dubreucq 2007, 2013; Serneels 2009).

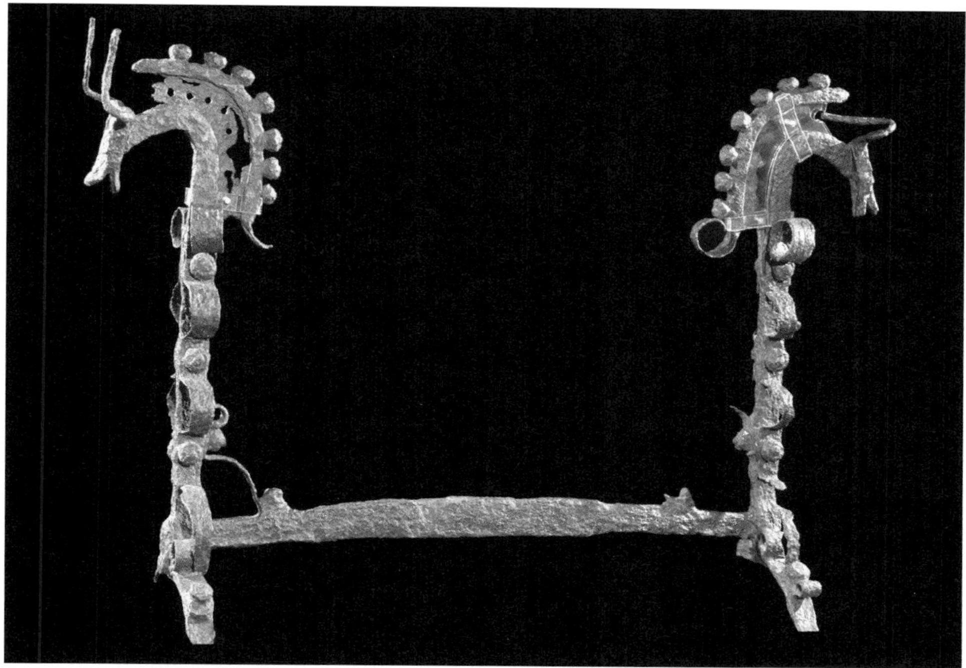

FIGURE 23.2 Iron firedog from Capel Garmon, north Wales. Found in a peat bog in 1852, it would originally have been one of a pair. On most firedogs the terminals of the uprights are decorated with simple ox heads, but here the animal heads are more elaborate with prominent horns and crests. Height 75 cm.

The Ideology of Iron

Historical and ethnographic studies of ironworking in other cultures (Rowlands 1971; Herbert 1993; Hinton 2003, 2011; Blakely 2006; Hedeager 2011) suggest that the industry is often surrounded with ideological beliefs and practices, reflected in later mythologies. This is hardly surprising, in view of the transformative processes of smelting and smithing, the hard labour on the part of the smith, and the impressive sights and sounds of the smithy. It is impossible to reconstruct the ideology of prehistoric iron and ironworking in detail, and it is uncertain how far later traditions should be pushed back into prehistory (Gillies 1981). It is, however, possible to use recurring patterns in the archaeological evidence to show something of the practices associated with the craft and the treatment of iron objects; Hingley (1997) has outlined some possible areas for study, and has emphasized the need to pay more detailed attention to the location and contextual associations of evidence for ironworking, as well as the treatment and deposition of iron artefacts. We may not be able to recover prehistoric ideas about smelting, or to test suggestions that the process was thought of as something akin to the agricultural cycle or human childbearing, though research on the association of iron and ironworking waste with materials such as burnt grain may shed light on this.

We can say more about the process of smithing and the history of iron artefacts. The nearest we can get to the smith in person is through a small number of graves in which sets of ironworking tools were buried with the dead person, such as Au am Leithagebirge Grave 13 in Austria (Nebehay 1973) or Rudston Grave 154, Yorkshire, England (Stead 1991: 205). These are burials of the La Tène period; artefacts deposited in graves of this tradition frequently represent variations in social identity on the basis of age, gender, status, and place of origin, but indications of an occupational or skill-based identity, such as that of a smith, are very rare. This suggests that the role of the smith, or at least of some smiths, presumably the most skilled, was invested with a special significance. The characteristic sets of smith's tools were also regarded as suitable items for ritual deposition in other contexts, such as disused pits (e.g. Halkon 2011: 157 and illus. 19), rivers (e.g. Manning 1985: 8–12), or caves, as at Býcí skála, Moravia, where, it seems, the remains of a smithy were deposited (Parzinger et al. 1995).

Little research has yet been done on the biography or symbolic meaning of iron objects. Aldhouse-Green (2002) has discussed classical references to Iron Age prohibitions on the use of iron in certain rituals, emphasizing the dual nature of iron as both beneficial and threatening. Some of the largest, and most socially significant, iron objects were undoubtedly the swords, though much more is known about their role in the post-Roman world. A number of these weapons are marked with small stamps, some inlaid with gold (Zeller 1980: Abb. 4); these marks may indicate a maker, but possibly also had a magical significance. One sword from Port in Switzerland (Wyss 1954) was stamped with the name Korisios in Greek letters, most likely the name of the smith who made it.

As well as smithing tools, iron objects were regarded as appropriate items for deposition in a wide variety of contexts (Manning 1972; Kurz 1995; Bataille and Guillaumet 2006), though it is not clear whether they were deposited because they were made of iron, or because of the functional or symbolic meaning of their form. Many of these deposits were in wet or watery places, such as at the site of La Tène itself (de Navarro 1972). Much less attention has been paid to the deposition of iron objects in settlement sites, though they were clearly selected for special deposition in the same way as animals, human remains, quernstones, and other items. Hingley (1990, 2006) has argued that there was a preference for the edge of a settlement or its surrounding ditch as a location for deposition.

Conclusions

As the evidence reviewed suggests, research on iron in Iron Age Europe has been dominated by questions of the technology of smelting and smithing, and, although there are still many questions about the chronology and social context of technical developments, the broad outline is clear (Pleiner 2000, 2006). Recent archaeological activity has brought to light much new evidence for the manufacture and deposition of iron, and new methods of scientific analysis are being applied more frequently. There are also new approaches to the understanding of the significance of iron in Iron Age society: new theoretical approaches, especially those using the concept of the *chaîne opératoire* (Serneels 1998; Fluzin et al. 2000), are transforming our understanding of the organization of the industry; regional studies of the industry (Ehrenreich 1985; Feugère and Serneels 1998; Schäfer 2002; Senn Bischofberger 2005) are helping to elucidate the patterns of technical development, while landscape studies (Halkon 2011) are placing ironworking in a broader social perspective.

References

Aldhouse-Green, M. J. 2002. 'Any old iron! Symbolism and ironworking in Iron Age Europe', in M. J. Aldhouse-Green and P. Webster (eds) *Artefacts and Archaeology: Aspects of the Celtic and Roman World*: 8–19. Cardiff: University of Wales Press.

Allen, D. F. 1967. 'Iron currency bars in Britain'. *Proceedings of the Prehistoric Society* 33: 307–335.

Audouze, F., and O. Buchsenschutz. 1991. *Towns, Villages and Countryside of Celtic Europe*. London: Batsford.

Bataille, G., and J.-P. Guillaumet (eds). 2006. *Les dépôts métalliques au second âge du Fer en Europe tempérée. Actes de la table ronde organisée par l'UMR 5594 CNRS-Culture, Université de Bourgogne, Archéologie, cultures et société en Bourgogne et en France orientale, Equipe 3, la société gauloise, Glux-en-Glenne, 13–14 octobre 2004*. Collection Bibracte 11. Glux-en-Glenne: Centre archéologique européen du Mont Beuvray.

Berciu, D. 1964. 'Pour une voie Cimmérienne de diffusion de la métallurgie du fer'. *Archeologické Rozhledy* 16: 264–279.

Berranger, M. 2007. 'Les demi-produits de fer au Ier millénaire a. C. en Europe continentale: potentialités d'études', in P.-Y. Milcent (ed.) *L'économie du fer protohistorique: de la production à la consommation du métal. Actes du XXVIIIe colloque de l'AFEAF, Toulouse 20–23 mai 2004*. Aquitania supplément 14/2: 133–143. Bordeaux: Fédération Aquitania.

Berranger, M. 2014. *Le Fer, entre matière première et moyen d'échange, en France, du VIIe au Ier siècle avant J.-C. Approches interdisciplinaires*. Dijon: Editions Universitaires de Dijon.

Berranger, M., and P. Fluzin. 2012. 'From raw iron to semi-product: quality and circulation of materials during the Iron Age in France'. *Archaeometry* 54, 4: 664–684.

Berranger, M., and P. Fluzin. 2014. 'Levroux "Les Arènes" (Indre, France): Organisation and specialisation of post-reduction activities in an open agglomeration of the Celtic Iron Age (2nd century–beginning of 1st century BC)', in B. Cech and T. Rehren (eds) *Early Iron in Europe*: 117–132. Montagnac: Monique Mergoil.

Bielenin, K. 1964. *Starożytne hutnictwo świętokrzyskie. II wydanie poszerzone i uzupełnione*. Warsaw.

Blakelock, E., M. Martinón-Torres, H. A. Veldhuijzen, and T. Young. 2009. 'Slag inclusions in iron objects and the quest for provenance: an experiment and a case study'. *Journal of Archaeological Science* 36, 8: 1745–1757.

Blakely, S. 2006. *Myth, Ritual, and Metallurgy in Ancient Greece and Recent Africa*. Cambridge: Cambridge University Press.

Blanchet, J.-C. 1984. *Les premiers metallurgistes en Picardie et dans le nord de la France: Chalcolithique, âge du Bronze et début du premier âge du Fer*. Mémoires de la Société préhistorique française 17. Paris: Société préhistorique française.

Bouzek, J. 1985. 'Kotázkám počátku doby železné ve střední Evropě'. *Archeologické Rozhledy* 37: 83–92.

Bouzek, J. 1989. 'The eastern Mediterranean and central Europe: The beginning of the Iron Age', in M. L. Sørensen and R. Thomas (eds) *The Bronze Age–Iron Age Transition in Europe*. British Archaeological Reports International Series 483: 36–42. Oxford: British Archaeological Reports.

Bradley, R. J. 1988. 'Hoarding, recycling, and the consumption of prehistoric metalwork: Technological change in western Europe'. *World Archaeology* 20: 249–260.

Brauns, M., R. Schwab, G. Gassmann, G. Wieland, and E. Pernicka, 2013. 'Provenance of Iron Age iron in southern Germany: A new approach'. *Journal of Archaeological Science* 40, 2: 841–849.

Brun, P., B. Chaume, L. Dhennequin, and B. Quilliec. 2009. 'Le passage du l'âge du bronze à l'âge du fer … au fil de l'épée', in M.-J. Roulière-Lambert, A. Daubigney, P.-Y. Milcent, M. Talon, and J. Vital (eds) *De l'âge du Bronze à l'âge du Fer en France et en Europe occidentale: Xe–VIIe siècle av. J-C. La moyenne vallée du Rhône aux âges du Fer, actualité de la recherche. Actes du XXXe Colloque International de l'AFEAF, Saint-Romain-en-Gal, 26–28 mai 2006*. Revue archéologique de l'Est supplément 27: 477–485. Dijon: SAE, APRAB, AFEAF.

Burgess, C. B. 1979. 'A find from Boyton, Suffolk, and the end of the Bronze Age in Britain and Ireland', in C. B. Burgess and D. Coombs (eds) *Bronze Age Hoards: Some Finds Old and New*. British Archaeological Reports British Series 67: 269–283. Oxford: British Archaeological Reports.

Carter, S., F. Hunter, and A. Smith. 2010. 'A 5th century BC Iron Age chariot burial from Newbridge, Edinburgh'. *Proceedings of the Prehistoric Society* 76: 31–74.

Charlton, M. F. 2015. 'The last frontier in "sourcing": The hopes, constraints and future for iron provenance research'. *Journal of Archaeological Science* 56: 210–220.

Charlton, M. F., E. Blakelock, M. Martinón-Torres, and T. Young. 2012. 'Investigating the production provenance of iron artifacts with multivariate methods'. *Journal of Archaeological Science* 39, 7: 2280–2293.

Childe, V. G. 1935. 'Changing methods and aims in prehistory (Presidential address for 1935)'. *Proceedings of the Prehistoric Society* 1: 1–15.

Childe, V. G. 1936. *Man Makes Himself*. London: Watts.

Childe, V. G. 1942. *What Happened in History*. Harmondsworth: Penguin.

Childe, V. G. 1946. 'The social implications of the Three "Ages" in archaeological classification'. *The Modern Quarterly* n.s. 1: 18–33.

Childe, V. G. 1950. *Prehistoric Migrations in Europe*. Oslo: Aschehoug.

Collard, M., T. Darvill, and M. Watts. 2006. 'Ironworking in the Bronze Age: Evidence from a 10th century BC settlement at Hartshill Copse, Upper Bucklebury, West Berkshire'. *Proceedings of the Prehistoric Society* 72: 367–421.

Crew, P. 1986. 'Bryn y Castell hillfort: A late prehistoric iron working settlement in north-west Wales', in B. G. Scott and H. Cleere (eds) *The Crafts of the Blacksmith*: 91–100. Belfast: UISPP Comité pour la Sidérurgie Ancienne and the Ulster Museum.

Crew, P. 1988. 'Bryn y Castell hillfort, Gwynedd, North Wales: A preliminary analysis of ironworking debris', in J. E. Jones (ed.) *Aspects of Ancient Mining and Metallurgy. Acts of a British School at Athens Centenary Conference at Bangor, 1986*: 129–135. Bangor: Department of Classics, University College of North Wales.

Crew, P. 1994. 'Currency bars in Great Britain: Typology and function', in M. Mangin (ed.) *La sidérurgie ancienne de l'Est de la France dans son contexte européen: archéologie et archéométrie. Actes du colloque de Besançon, 10–13 novembre 1993*. Annales littéraires de l'Université de Besançon 536: 345–350. Paris: Belles Lettres.

Crew, P. 1995. 'Aspects of the iron supply', in B. W. Cunliffe (ed.) *Danebury: An Iron Age Hillfort in Hampshire, Vol. 6: A Hillfort Community in Perspective*: 276–284. London: Council for British Archaeology.

Crew, P. 2013. 'Twenty-five years of bloomery experiments: Perspectives and prospects', in D. Dungworth and R. C. P. Doonan (eds) *Accidental and Experimental Archaeometallurgy*: 25–50. London: The Historical Metallurgy Society.

Crew, P., M. F. Charlton, P. Dillmann, P. Fluzin, C. Salter, and E. Truffaut. 2011. 'Cast iron from a bloomery furnace', in J. Hošek, H. Cleere, and Ľ. Mihok (eds) *The Archaeometallurgy of Iron: Recent Developments in Archaeological and Scientific Research*: 239–262. Prague: Institute of Archaeology of the ASCR.

Cunliffe, B. 1972. 'The Late Iron Age metalwork from Bulbury, Dorset'. *Antiquaries Journal* 52: 293–308.

Czarnecka, K. 2000. 'Iron smelting in the pre-Roman and Roman period in central Poland', in M. Feugère and M. Guštin (eds) *Iron, Blacksmiths and Tools: Ancient European Crafts. Acts of the Instrumentum Conference at Podsreda (Slovenia) in April 1999*: 89–91. Montagnac: Monique Mergoil.

de Navarro, J. M. 1955. 'A doctor's grave of the Middle La Tène period from Bavaria'. *Proceedings of the Prehistoric Society* 21: 231–248.

de Navarro, J. M. 1972. *The Finds from the Site of La Tène, Vol. 1: Scabbards and the Swords Found in Them*. London: Oxford University Press for the British Academy.

Diamond, J. M. 1998. *Guns, Germs and Steel: A Short History of Everybody for the Last 13,000 years*. London: Vintage.

Diepeveen-Jansen, M. 2001. *People, Ideas and Goods: New Perspectives on 'Celtic Barbarians' in Western and Central Europe (500–250 BC)*. Amsterdam Archaeological Studies 7. Amsterdam: Amsterdam University Press.

Dietler, M. 1997. 'The Iron Age in Mediterranean France: Colonial encounters, entanglements, and transformations'. *Journal of World Prehistory* 11, 3: 269–358.

Dolenz, H. 1998. *Eisenfunde aus der Stadt auf dem Magdalensberg*. Klagenfurt: Verlag des Landesmuseums für Kärnten.

Driehaus, J. 1965. 'Fürstengräber und Eisenerze zwischen Mittelrhein, Mosel und Saar'. *Germania* 43: 32–49.

Dubreucq, E. 2007. 'Le petit mobilier en fer des habitats du Hallstatt D—La Tène A: un mobilier sous-exploité', in P.-Y. Milcent (ed.) *L'économie du fer protohistorique: de la production à la consommation du métal. Actes du XXVIIIe colloque de l'AFEAF, Toulouse, 20–23 mai 2004*. Aquitania supplément 14/2: 329–354. Bordeaux: Fédération Aquitania.

Dubreucq, E. 2013. *Métal des premiers Celtes: productions métalliques sur les habitats des provinces du Hallstatt centre-occidental*. Dijon: Éditions universitaires de Dijon.

Dunikowski, C., and S. Cabboi. 1995. *La sidérurgie chez les Sénons: les ateliers celtiques et gallo-romains des Clérimois, Yonne*. Documents d'archéologie française 51. Paris: Éditions de la Maison des sciences de l'homme.

Ehrenreich, R. M. 1985. *Trade, Technology and the Ironworking Community in the Iron Age of Southern Britain*. British Archaeological Reports British Series 144. Oxford: British Archaeological Reports.

Ellmers, D. 1969. 'Keltischer Schiffbau'. *Jahrbuch des Römisch-Germanischen Zentralmuseums Mainz* 16: 73–122.

Feugère, M., and V. Serneels (eds). 1998. *Recherches sur l'économie du fer en Méditerranée nord-occidentale*. Montagnac: Monique Mergoil.

Flouest, J. L. 2007. 'Approches quantitatives de la production de fer sur le site hallstattien de Bragny-sur-Saône (Saône-et-Loire)', in P.-Y. Milcent (ed.) *L'économie du fer protohistorique: de la production à la consommation du métal. Actes du XXVIIIe colloque de l'AFEAF, Toulouse 20–23 mai 2004*. Aquitania supplément 14/2: 265–270. Bordeaux: Fédération Aquitania.

Fluzin, P., A. Ploquin, and V. Serneels. 2000. 'Archéométrie des déchets de production sidérurgique. Moyens et méthodes d'identification des différents éléments de la chaîne opératoire directe'. *Gallia* 57: 101–121.

Fox, C. 1946. *A Find of the Early Iron Age from Llyn Cerrig Bach, Anglesey*. Cardiff: National Museum of Wales.

Gaitzsch, W. 1980. *Eiserne römische Werkzeuge*. British Archaeological Reports International Series 78. Oxford: British Archaeological Reports.

Gassman, G., and A. Schäfer. 2014. 'Early iron production in Germany: A short review', in B. Cech and T. Rehren (eds) *Early Iron in Europe*: 21–32. Montagnac: Monique Mergoil.

Giles, M. 2007. 'Making Metals and Forging Relations: Iron Working in the British Iron Age'. *Oxford Journal of Archaeology* 26, 4: 395–413.

Gillies, W. 1981. 'The craftsman in early Celtic literature'. *Scottish Archaeological Forum* 11: 70–85.

Gomez de Soto, J., and I. Kerouanton. 2009. 'Les premiers objets en fer en France à l'âge du bronze', in M.-J. Roulière-Lambert, A. Daubigney, P.-Y. Milcent, M. Talon, and J. Vital (eds) *De l'âge du Bronze à l'âge du Fer en France et en Europe occidentale: Xe–VIIe siècle av. J-C. La moyenne vallée du Rhône aux âges du Fer, actualité de la recherche. Actes du XXXe Colloque International de l'AFEAF, Saint-Romain-en-Gal, 26–28 mai 2006*. Revue archéologique de l'Est supplément 27: 501–506. Dijon: SAE, APRAB, AFEAF.

Gomez de Soto, J., and J. P. Mohen. 1981. 'Les plus vieux objets en fer de France', in H. Haefner (ed.) *Frühes Eisen in Europa. Festschrift Walter Ulrich Guyan zu seinem 70. Geburtstag*: 53–56. Schaffhausen: Peter Meili.

Halkon, P. 2011. 'Iron, landscape and power in Iron Age East Yorkshire'. *Archaeological Journal* 168: 133–165.

Hedeager, L. 2011. *Iron Age Myth and Materiality: An Archaeology of Scandinavia, AD 400–1000*. London: Routledge.

Hedges, R. E. M., and C. J. Salter. 1979. 'Source determination of iron currency bars through analysis of the slag inclusions'. *Archaeometry* 21: 161–175.

Heimann, R. B., U. Kreher, I. Spazier, and G. Wetzel. 2001. 'Mineralogical and chemical investigations of bloomery slags from prehistoric (8th century BC to 4th century AD) iron production sites in Upper and Lower Lusatia, Germany'. *Archaeometry* 43, 2: 227–252.

Herbert, E. W. 1993. *Iron, Gender, and Power: Rituals of Transformation in African Societies*. Bloomington: Indiana University Press.

Hingley, R. 1990. 'Iron Age "currency bars": The archaeological and social context'. *Archaeological Journal* 147: 91–117.

Hingley, R. 1997. 'Iron, ironworking and regeneration: A study of the symbolic meaning of metalworking in Iron Age Britain', in A. Gwilt and C. Haselgrove (eds) *Reconstructing Iron Age Societies*: 9–18. Oxford: Oxbow.

Hingley, R. 2006. 'The deposition of iron objects in Britain in the later prehistoric and Roman periods: Contextual analysis and the significance of iron'. *Britannia* 37: 213–257.

Hinton, D. A. 2003. 'Anglo-Saxon smiths and myths', in D. G. Scragg (ed.) *Textual and Material Culture in Anglo-Saxon England: Thomas Northcote Toller and the Toller Memorial Lectures*: 261–282. Cambridge: D. S. Brewer.

Hinton, D. A. 2011. 'Weland's work: Metal and metalsmiths', in M. C. Hyer and G. R. Owen-Crocker (eds) *The Material Culture of Daily Living in the Anglo-Saxon World*: 185–200. Exeter: University of Exeter Press.

Hjärthner-Holdar, E. 1993. *Järnets och järnmetallurgins introduktion i Sverige*. AUN 16. Uppsala: Societas Archaeologica Upsaliensis.

Jacobi, G. 1974. *Werkzeug und Gerät aus dem Oppidum von Manching*. Die Ausgrabungen in Manching 5. Wiesbaden: Steiner.

Jope, E. M. 2000. *Early Celtic Art in the British Isles*. Oxford: Oxford University Press.

Jouttijärvi, A., and O. Voss. 2011. 'The oldest iron smelting furnaces in Denmark', in J. Hošek, H. Cleere, and Ľ. Mihok (eds) *The Archaeometallurgy of Iron: Recent Developments in Archaeological and Scientific Research*: 55–64. Prague: Institute of Archaeology of the ASCR.

Kossack, G. 1971. 'The construction of the felloe in Iron Age spoked wheels', in J. Boardman, M. A. Brown, and T. G. E. Powell (eds) *The European Community in Prehistory: Studies in Honour of C. F. C. Hawkes*: 141–163. London: Routledge and Kegan Paul.

Kristiansen, K. 1998. *Europe before History*. Cambridge: Cambridge University Press.

Kurz, G. 1995. *Keltische Hort- und Gewässerfunde in Mitteleuropa: Deponierungen der Latènezeit*. Materialhefte zur Archäologie in Baden-Württemberg 33. Stuttgart: Theiss.

Lang, J. 1986. 'The technology of Celtic iron swords', in B. G. Scott and H. Cleere (eds) *The Crafts of the Blacksmith*: 61–72. Belfast: UISPP Comité pour la Sidérurgie Ancienne and Ulster Museum.

Lang, J. 2006. 'The technology of some of the swords', in I. M. Stead (ed.) *British Iron Age Swords and Scabbards*: 85–114. London: British Museum Press.

McGrail, S. 1995. 'Romano-Celtic boats and ships: Characteristic features'. *International Journal of Nautical Archaeology* 24, 2: 139–145.

Mangin, M. (ed.) 1994. *La sidérurgie ancienne de l'Est de la France dans son contexte européen: archéologie et archéométrie. Actes du Colloque de Besançon, 10–13 novembre 1993*. Annales littéraires de l'Université de Besançon 536. Paris: Belles Lettres.

Manning, W. H. 1972. 'Ironwork hoards in Iron Age and Roman Britain'. *Britannia* 3: 224–250.

Manning, W. H. 1985. *Catalogue of the Romano-British Iron Tools, Fittings and Weapons in the British Museum*. London: British Museum Publications.

Manrique Mayor, M. 1980. *Instrumentos de hierro de Numancia: conservados en el Museo Numantino (Soria)*. Madrid: Ministerio de Cultura, Dirección General del Patrimonio Artistico, Archivos y Museos, Patronato Nacional de Museos.

Mighall, T. and F. Chambers 1997. 'Early ironworking and its impact on the environment: Palaeoecological evidence from Bryn y Castell hillfort, Snowdonia, North Wales'. *Proceedings of the Prehistoric Society* 63: 199–219.

Mighall, T., S. Timberlake, A. Martínez-Cortizas, N. Silva-Sánchez, and I. D. L. Foster. 2017. 'Did prehistoric and Roman mining and metallurgy have a significant impact on vegetation?' *Journal of Archaeological Science: Reports* 11: 613–625.

Mihok, Ľ. and Kotigoroschko, G. 2011. 'The craft of the Dacian blacksmith', in J. Hošek, H. Cleere and Ľ. Mihok (eds) *The Archaeometallurgy of Iron: Recent Developments in Archaeological and Scientific Research*: 107–122. Prague: Institute of Archaeology of the ASCR.

Milcent, P.-Y. 2004. *Le premier âge du fer en France centrale*. Mémoires de la Société préhistorique française 34. Paris: Société préhistorique française.

Milcent, P.-Y. (ed.) 2007. *L'économie du fer protohistorique: de la production à la consommation du metal. Actes du XXVIIIe colloque de l'AFEAF, Toulouse 20–23 mai 2004*. Aquitania supplément 14/2. Pessac: Fédération Aquitania.

Nebehay, S. 1973. *Das latènezeitliche Gräberfeld von der Kleinen Hutweide bei Au am Leithagebirge: p.B. Bruck a.d. Leitha, NÖ*. Archaeologia Austriaca Beiheft 11. Vienna: Deuticke.

Nørbach, L. C. 1998. 'Ironworking in Denmark from the late Bronze Age to the early Roman Iron Age'. *Acta Archaeologica* 69: 53–75.

Pagès, G., P. Dillmann, P. Fluzin, and L. Long. 2011. 'A study of the Roman iron bars of Saintes-Maries-de-la-Mer (Bouches-du-Rhône, France): A proposal for a comprehensive metallographic approach'. *Journal of Archaeological Science* 38, 6: 1234–1252.

Parzinger, H., J. Nekvasil, and F. E. Barth. 1995. *Die Býčí skála-Höhle: ein hallstattzeitlicher Höhlenopferplatz in Mähren*. Römisch-Germanische Forschungen 54. Mainz: Philipp von Zabern.

Piggott, S. 1964. 'Iron, Cimmerians and Aeschylus'. *Antiquity* 38: 300–303.

Piggott, S. 1971. 'Firedogs in Iron Age Britain and beyond', in J. Boardman, M. A. Brown, and T. G. E. Powell (eds) *The European Community in Prehistory: Studies in Honour of C. F. C. Hawkes*: 243–270. London: Routledge and Kegan Paul.

Piggott, S. 1983. *The Earliest Wheeled Transport: From the Atlantic Coast to the Caspian Sea*. London: Thames and Hudson.

Pitts, M. 2016. 'Oldest iron smelting site found by Tata plant'. *British Archaeology* 146: 6–7.

Pleiner, R. 1980. 'Early iron metallurgy in Europe', in T. A. Wertime and J. D. Muhly (eds) *The Coming of the Age of Iron*: 375–415. New Haven and London: Yale University Press.

Pleiner, R. 1986. 'Examination of some early La Tène period knives from Bohemia', in B. G. Scott and H. Cleere (eds) *The Crafts of the Blacksmith*: 73–82. Belfast: UISPP Comité pour la Sidérurgie Ancienne and the Ulster Museum.

Pleiner, R. 1993. *The Celtic Sword*. Oxford: Oxford University Press.

Pleiner, R. 2000. *Iron in Archaeology: The European Bloomery Smelters*. Prague: Archeologický ústav AV ČR.

Pleiner, R. 2006. *Iron in Archaeology: Early European Blacksmiths*. Prague: Archeologický ústav AV ČR.

Randsborg, K. 1995. *Hjortspring: Warfare and Sacrifice in Early Europe*. Aarhus: Aarhus University Press.

Rapin, A. 1999. 'L'armement celtique en Europe: chronologie de son évolution technologique du Ve au Ier s. av. J.-C.'. *Gladius* 19: 33–67.

Rovira, C. 1998. 'Les premiers objets en fer de Catalogne (VIIe–VIe s. av. n. è.)', in M. Feugère and V. Serneels (eds) *Recherches sur l'économie du fer en Méditerranée nord-occidentale*. Monographies instrumentum 4: 45–55. Montagnac: Monique Mergoil.

Rovira Hortalà, C. 2007. 'Producíon e intercambio de los primos objectos de hierro del nordeste de la Península Ibérica (s. VII–VI a.C.)', in P.-Y. Milcent (ed.) *L'économie du fer protohistorique: de la production à la consommation du métal. Actes du XXVIIIe colloque de l'AFEAF, Toulouse 20–23 mai 2004*. Aquitania supplément 14/2: 167–175. Bordeaux: Fédération Aquitania.

Rowlands, M. 1971. 'The archaeological interpretation of prehistoric metalworking'. *World Archaeology* 3, 2: 210–224.

Rusu, M. 1969. 'Das keltische Fürstengrab von Ciumeşti'. *Bericht der Römisch-Germanischen Kommission* 50: 267–300.

Salter, C., and R. M. Ehrenreich. 1984. 'Iron Age iron metallurgy in central southern Britain', in B. W. Cunliffe and D. Miles (eds) *Aspects of the Iron Age in Central Southern Britain*: 146–161. Oxford: University of Oxford Committee for Archaeology.

Schaaff, U. 1974. 'Keltische Eisenhelme aus vorrömischer Zeit'. *Jahrbuch des Römisch-Germanischen Zentralmuseums Mainz* 21: 149–204.

Schäfer, A. 2002. 'Manching—Kelheim—Berding-Pollanten', in C. Dobiat, S. Sievers, and T. Stöllner (eds) *Dürrnberg und Manching: Wirtschaftsarchäologie im ostkeltischen Raum. Akten des internationalen Kolloquiums in Hallein/Bad Dürrnberg vom 7. bis 11. Oktober 1998*. Kolloquien zur Vor- und Frühgeschichte 7: 219–241. Bonn: Habelt.

Schwab, R., D. Heger, B. Höppner, and E. Pernicka. 2006. 'The provenance of iron artefacts from Manching: A multi-technique approach'. *Archaeometry* 48, 3: 433–452.

Senn Bischofberger, M. 2005. *Das Schmiedehandwerk im nordalpinen Raum von der Eisenzeit bis ins frühe Mittelalter: Internationale Archäologie*. Naturwissenschaft und Technologie 5. Rahden: Marie Leidorf.

Serneels, V. 1998. 'La chaîne opératoire de la sidérurgie ancienne', in M. Feugère and V. Serneels (eds) *Recherches sur l'économie du fer en Méditerranée nord-occidentale*: 7–44. Montagnac: Monique Mergoil.

Serneels, V. 2009. 'Qu'est-ce qui change dans la vie quotidienne lorsque l'on remplace le bronze par le fer?', in M.-J. Roulière-Lambert, A. Daubigney, P.-Y. Milcent, M. Talon, and J. Vital (eds) *De l'âge du Bronze à l'âge du Fer en France et en Europe occidentale: Xe–VIIe siècle av. J-C. La moyenne vallée du Rhône aux âges du Fer, actualité de la recherche. Actes du XXXe Colloque International de l'AFEAF, Saint-Romain-en-Gal, 26–28 mai 2006*. Revue archéologique de l'Est supplément 27: 433–439. Dijon: SAE, APRAB, AFEAF.

Sievers, S. 1982. *Die mitteleuropäischen Hallstattdolche.* Prähistorische Bronzefunde VI, 6. Munich: Beck.

Sørensen, M. L., and R. Thomas (eds). 1989. *The Bronze Age–Iron Age Transition in Europe.* British Archaeological Reports International Series 483. Oxford: British Archaeological Reports.

Speck, J. 1981. 'Frühes Eisen in den Ufersiedlungen der Spätbronzezeit'. *Helvetia Archaeologica* 45–48: 265–271.

Stead, I. M. 1991. *Iron Age Cemeteries in East Yorkshire.* English Heritage Archaeological Report 22. London: English Heritage/British Museum Press.

Stead, I. M. 2006. *British Iron Age Swords and Scabbards.* London: British Museum Press.

Stoia, A. 1989. 'The beginning of iron metallurgy in Romania (1200–700 BC)', in M. L. Sørensen and R. Thomas (eds) *The Bronze Age–Iron Age Transition in Europe.* British Archaeological Reports International Series 483: 43–67. Oxford: British Archaeological Reports.

Straube, H. 1996. *Ferrum Noricum und die Stadt auf dem Magdalensberg.* Vienna/New York: Springer.

Taylor, T. 1989. 'Iron and Iron Age in the Carpatho-Balkan region: Aspects of social and technological change 1700–1400 BC', in M. L. Sørensen and R. Thomas (eds) *The Bronze Age–Iron Age Transition in Europe.* British Archaeological Reports International Series 483: 68–92. Oxford: British Archaeological Reports.

Thomas, R. 1989. 'The bronze–iron transition in southern England', in M. L. Sørensen and R. Thomas (eds) *The Bronze Age–Iron Age Transition in Europe.* British Archaeological Reports International Series 483: 263–286. Oxford: British Archaeological Reports.

Van der Broeke, P. W. 2005. 'Blacksmiths and potters: Material culture and technology', in L. P. Louwe Kooijmans, P. W. van der Broeke, H. Fokkens, and A. L. van Gijn (eds) *The Prehistory of the Netherlands*: 603–625. Amsterdam: Amsterdam University Press.

Van der Noort, R. 2011. *North Sea Archaeologies: A Maritime Biography, 10,000 BC to AD 1500.* Oxford: Oxford University Press.

Van Endert, D. 1987. *Das Osttor des Oppidums von Manching.* Die Ausgrabungen in Manching 10. Stuttgart: Steiner.

Wyss, R. 1954. 'Das Schwert des Korisios: zur Entdeckung einer griechischen Inschrift'. *Jahrbuch des Bernischen Historischen Museums in Bern* 34: 201–222.

Zeller, K. W. 1980. 'Kriegswesen und Bewaffnung der Kelten', in L. Pauli (ed.) *Die Kelten in Mitteleuropa: Kultur, Kunst, Wirtschaft*: 111–132. Salzburg: Salzburger Landesausstellung.

CHAPTER 24

RAW MATERIALS, TECHNOLOGY, AND INNOVATION

RUPERT GEBHARD

INTRODUCTION

In Iron Age Europe, technological progress proceeds in a regionally divergent manner and depends on access to raw materials and supra-regional exchange links. Development in the earlier Iron Age is frequently determined by external cultural influences, especially from Mediterranean cultures. The encounter with the Etruscan and Greek civilizations acts as a stimulus, not only through direct contact with the Greek colonies of southern France and along the Iberian coast, and through transalpine trade in the area of the Adriatic and northern Italy, but also through contact with the Balkans in the eastern Hallstatt zone.

In the later Iron Age, the high level of interrelatedness between leading settlements (the so-called '*oppida* culture') gave rise both to regional innovations and a rapid transfer of technology. Late Iron Age products hardly differ in quality from the products of the Graeco-Roman world. In this chapter I shall attempt to give an outline of the development of Iron Age technology by describing its capabilities in the fields of mechanics and technologies that use the power of fire. The presentation and choice of the raw materials treated here will also try to take account of the various challenges research in these domains poses.

Metal raw Materials: Iron, Copper, Tin, and Precious Metals

During the course of the first millennium BC, iron became established as the leading metal raw material. Unlike copper, it is widely found in many parts of Europe and is also easily obtainable from the different types of ores. As a result, the use of metal increases compared to the Bronze Age, and in the process causes a change in the economic value, and thus also the social worth, of raw materials. The accumulation of wealth based on the value of copper (bronze), which in the Bronze Age had been used for prestige and social dominance, no longer applied in the same measure to iron.

The material properties of iron are better suited for use in many domains, such as making weapons, implements, or tools (Figure 24.1), than those of bronze, which increasingly loses importance as a raw material in the course of the Iron Age. The value placed on iron is mainly based on its workability and hardness, or ability to be transformed into steel (Schwab 2002). A type of steel—*ferrum noricum*—is legendary in this respect: its technology was developed in the late Iron Age in Noricum, and the Romans preferred it to their own steel, even in Imperial times.

Bronze is an alloy of copper and tin, well known for its material properties. The technology for processing the alloy did not develop much further: forging, casting, and lost-wax casting were widely known. The use of steel tools and turning lathes made it possible to achieve a finer and more precise finish. Bronze was most commonly used for the manufacture of ornaments or jewellery, and composite objects made with different materials were also produced on a larger scale to achieve a multicoloured effect. Amber, coral, glass, and enamel were typical materials worked together with bronze. Towards the end of the Iron Age, copper alloys were increasingly brought into play for making coinage; of note are certain alloys, such as 'billon', a mixture of copper, silver, and tin, used to imitate silver coinage.

Precious metals were used in the early Iron Age, mainly for prestige jewellery, and in the late Iron Age they provided the basis for coinage. As the possession of gold was restricted to the elite in the Hallstatt period, its distribution broadly coincides with the erstwhile centres of power. Particular beating techniques provide evidence for local craftworkers, engaged for example in the production of the neck- and arm-rings of the western Hallstatt sphere. Because Hallstatt period gold is analytically not very different from Bronze Age gold, it must be assumed that the previously known sources of gold continued to be exploited. In the majority of cases these are river gold from the European continent and islands—for example, from the Rhine, the Danube, and their tributaries (Cauuet 1999). Indirect evidence for gold mining exists in the form of gold objects containing more than 25% silver. The 'golden quadrangle' of Transylvania, to which numerous gold artefacts are attributed in the Bronze Age, must be mentioned as a source of raw material. The introduction of coinage in the third century BC created an increased demand for gold and silver in Celtic Europe. The underlying principle is that

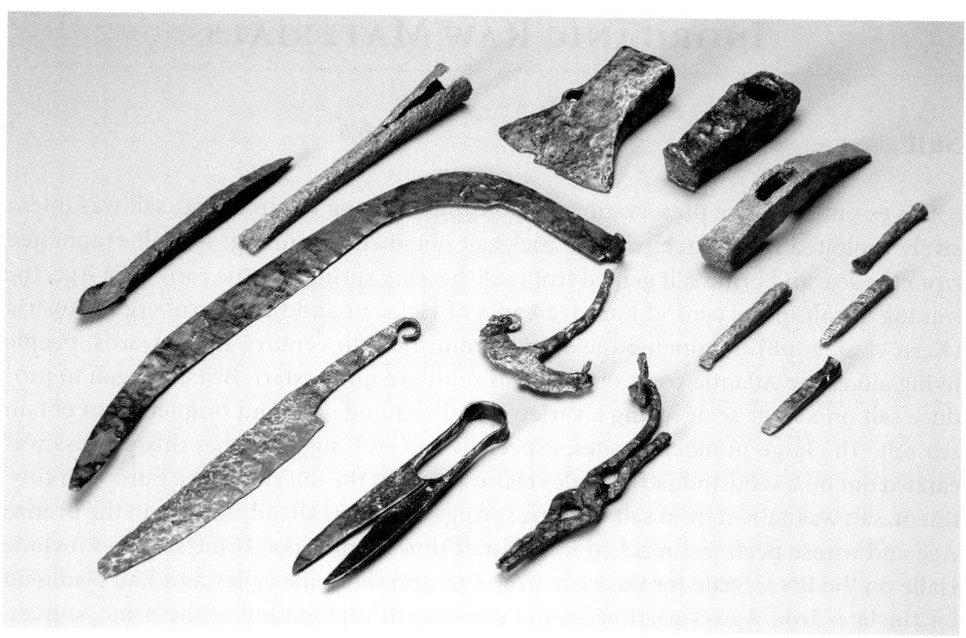

FIGURE 24.1 Tools and equipment of the third to first centuries BC from the *oppidum* of Manching, Bavaria.

Photo: Manfred Eberlein, GD 2002-6, © Archäologische Staatssammlung Munich

the weight and material are linked to the value of the coins, as will be explained later in this chapter. The gold used for coinage may largely have consisted of Mediterranean gold that reached Celtic Europe as payment to mercenaries, or as loot. Analyses showing the inclusion of significant amounts of platinum group metals have been interpreted as documenting this phenomenon (Steffgen et al. 1998), although recent research casts doubt on the extent of mercenary involvement in the introduction of gold coinage to Celtic Europe (e.g. Pion 2012; Nieto-Pelletier and Olivier 2016; see also Chapter 28). In western Europe, gold was produced mainly by mining. In France, Béatrice Cauuet (1999, 2004) has been able to demonstrate the existence of hundreds of mines, with the Limousin one of the key areas. It thus seems that Gaul was able to meet its needs mostly from its own gold deposits.

The sources of silver are still largely unknown. From a metallurgical viewpoint, the manufacture of silver is complex and laborious. As evidence for the primary exploitation of silver is completely lacking to date, it must be assumed that silver was imported. Indeed a few clues point in this direction: quantities of old and foreign coins destined for recycling were found in the large *oppidum* of Altenburg, mainly Republican *denarii* and their imitations (Burkhardt 2012). There are currently no indications that raw silver was used directly from the major production centres of Spain and Greece. It is much more likely that silver was obtained from secondary sources, by melting down artefacts like coins and jewellery.

Inorganic Raw Materials

Salt

Salt is essential for the preservation of foodstuffs. During the Iron Age, salt was intensively exploited from three sources: rock salt obtained by mining, sea salt evaporated from the sea, and brine salt gained from salt-bearing springs. In the early Iron Age, the mining of salt in the central European area of Hallstatt and the Dürrnberg in Austria (Kern et al. 2008) dominated the scene. From the fifth century BC onwards, people living along the Atlantic coast of Gaul and southern and eastern Britain began to produce salt on a large scale, using a variety of salt-boiling pans and briquetage to obtain sea salt. The large number of sites, especially in Gaul, suggests that this process was carried out on a semi-industrial scale (Daire 2003). In the interior of the European continent, salt was gained from salt-bearing springs, a process already known in the Bronze Age and whose peak was reached in Hallstatt times. Important brine salt sites include Halle on the River Saale for the early Iron Age, and the Seille valley and Bad Nauheim for the later Iron Age. Variations in the intensity of exploitation of the brine sources, and salt mines of the Alpine zone, make it evident that the production of salt in Europe developed into a supra-regional network governed by supply, demand, and competition for a product so vital for the preservation of food. This is illustrated in Lorraine, where the evidence points to a significant increase in production—which began in the Bronze Age—during Hallstatt times, and a considerable reduction in capacity in the late Iron Age. The salt produced in the mines of Hallstatt and the Dürrnberg also followed this principle. Given that sea salt production on the Atlantic coast grew at the same time into a large-scale industry, it is tempting to make a causal link between these observations. Support for this hypothesis comes from the differentiated, largely coinage-based, system of trade that developed in the European interior during the later Iron Age.

Glass

Glass is an amorphous, artificially made material. Raw glass is obtained by melting a mixture of quartz sand and fluxing agents. Adding metal ions—for example iron, copper, cobalt, lead, manganese, or antimony—produces differently coloured glass. By the late Iron Age, glass based on sodium carbonate and soda-lime had become the dominant type. But in the early Iron Age there were also other kinds of glass, which is attributable to the preponderance of beads originating from a variety of local raw glass production centres. The dominance of soda-lime glass in the late Iron Age suggests long distance trade. The sodium carbonate contained in the glass exists in such high concentrations that it can only have been added in mineral form. Ultimately only Egypt (Wadi Natrum) could have supplied such raw material. As recent isotope analysis by Julian Henderson et al. (2005) has demonstrated, the raw glass found at Manching and in southern England was made from sands obtained in Lebanon. This result makes it highly likely that all the late Iron Age raw glass of soda-lime type was imported from the Levant. A homogeneous source of raw material also seems likely for red enamel, which invariably occurs in the form of copper-lead glass.

Compared to the few centres that apparently produced raw glass, there is a multitude of local redistribution centres, which were active particularly in the late Iron Age, supplying the supra-regional trade in glass ornaments. Information on centres of glass production in the early Iron Age is, at present, inadequate. Glass beads of various colours and shapes were manufactured following a late Bronze Age tradition (the so-called 'Frattesina beads'), and traded over long distances. Apart from blue beads, compound eye beads were particular favourites for their apparently magical properties. The large quantities of glass beads found in the cemeteries of Slovenia suggest extensive production there, although no workshop has yet been discovered. Glass vessels are extremely rare in the Hallstatt period. A group of small, thin-walled beakers with ribbed bodies is found in the eastern Hallstatt zone, where they occur as a prestige item in rich graves. The glass bowl from Ihringen is a unique piece, imported from the eastern Mediterranean into the area of the princely centres in the sixth century BC. From the fifth century BC onwards, there is evidence for the import of small bottles made around a sand core (*Sandkernfläschen*), imported for the scents they contained. Phoenician beads also occur sporadically, well beyond the Mediterranean area.

The most common glass artefact produced in the third to first centuries BC in La Tène Europe is the seamless glass bracelet. The area of origin of this novel piece of adornment is still obscure. The first larger collections of such bracelets are found between Bohemia and the Swiss plateau. The earliest examples north of the Alps, such as those from the princely grave of Reinheim, dated to around 400 BC, appear to be imports, possibly from the area of Celtic incursions into Italy between the plain of the Po and Ancona. Several monographs and extensive analyses ensure that, today, this category of objects is well researched (Haevernick 1960; Gebhard 1989; Karwowski 2004; Wagner 2006; Gebhard 2010). The *c.*250-year-long period of production of glass bracelets can be subdivided into several phases of typological evolution and use of different kinds of raw glass and colours. The oldest phase is characterized by lightly coloured glass made of raw glass using sands with a high zirconium and low strontium content. In the second phase, glass coloured with cobalt appears for the first time, and other innovations include applying yellow glass sheets to the inside of translucent glass bracelets to mimic the appearance of gold bracelets. The third phase is characterized by further typological developments leading to hybrid forms. A stylistic break occurs in the late La Tène period, ending with the exclusive manufacture of smooth, narrow bracelets produced in only two colours—blue and purple.

Red Glass/Enamel

Red glass/enamel is mentioned here separately because it became a popular material for decorating bronze artefacts, especially in the late Iron Age (Challet 1992). Red glass can be subdivided analytically into two groups: glass containing copper, and glass with copper and lead content. Lead isotope analyses of glass from the Hill of Tara (Ireland) revealed a probable eastern Mediterranean origin for the lead. Given that the basic metal technology (copper, lead) is closely linked to the production of bronze, it is not impossible that local production centres existed. Red glass is a typical replacement for another material, in this case coral. Coral was dominant for the red ornamentation of bronze artefacts (fibulae, helmets, swords) up to the end of the fifth century BC or beginning of the fourth, but was almost completely replaced by red glass in the late Iron Age.

Stone

Stone was an important material for erecting buildings, particularly in southern Europe, but its use in constructing defences is more widespread. For logistical reasons, these employ mainly local materials. For large constructions, for example the 7 km-long defences of Manching, limestone was transported over a distance of more than 30 km (Streit 1987). The location of Manching on the banks of the Danube was ideal for fluvial transport as the *oppidum* had its own harbour inside the defensive circuit. Apart from building materials, certain types of stone were suited to special purposes, such as making grinding stones and whetstones, or door weights and, especially in the late Iron Age, rotary querns (Jacobi 1974). Workshops for the latter were established near quarry sites. Stefanie Wefers' study of protohistoric rotary querns in the region between Mayen in Germany and Lovosice in Bohemia (2012) showed that the quernstones produced in their quarries were much prized for their quality in the La Tène period. Their distribution to distant settlements makes an excellent case study for examining the extent of economic influence of centres of production in the late Iron Age. Wefers' approach was to combine a systematic petrographic analysis with a culture-historical interpretation. Further remarks on the introduction of rotary querns will be found in the section 'Technology and innovation'.

The suitability of a particular stone for making specific artefacts is especially well demonstrated in Iron Age sculpture. Indigenous (non-Greek and non-Etruscan) large sculptures are found among Italic, Iberian, Celtiberian, and Celtic populations, with well-known examples at Capestrano, Sanfins, Glauberg, Vix, and Roquepertuse. The types of stone chosen are almost always local, e.g. sandstone (Glauberg) or limestone, which could also be painted (Capestrano, Roquepertuse), and even granite (in Lusitania), which is difficult to work but extremely resistant.

Clay

Clay was the main material for ceramics in the Iron Age, as in other periods. It was particularly well washed and levigated for wares destined to be wheel-turned. Wheel-turned wares were introduced at different times in different regions; in central Europe,

FIGURE 24.2 Pottery of the second to first centuries BC, from Manching.
Photo: Manfred Eberlein, GD 2002-2, © Archäologische Staatssammlung Munich

they first appear in the princely centres of the late Hallstatt period. When archaeometric analyses are available, they show that for pottery production local clay sources were used in the majority of cases. The vessels were shaped in the fashion of the day, transmitted through technique and style (Figure 24.2). The analysis of over 1,000 vessel fragments from Manching and its surroundings provides an excellent example. Here, ceramic forms of similar appearance—for example, smooth wheel-turned pottery or graphite wares—were primarily made from locally available clay (Gebhard and Wagner 2002; Gebhard et al. 2004a). The graphite needed for the production of graphite-clay ceramics was imported (Kappel 1969). Use of graphite as a material for slips and decoration began in the Hallstatt period in central Europe. In the late Iron Age, graphite was added directly to the clay as a temper, or as the main component of the mixture, to improve its material properties. The most significant effect is likely to have been an increase in porosity, given that better heat conductivity cannot be proven (Bott et al. 1994). Pottery turned on a fast wheel reached mass production levels over much of Celtic Europe in the late Iron Age, but in the Germanic area, in the Celtic contact zone north of the Mittelgebirge (Thuringia and Saxony), wheel-turned wares take over for only a short time. Only in the late La Tène period did Germanic wheel-turned pottery also develop sporadically in the so-called Oder-Warthe group. Painted pottery (Céramique peinte 1991) constitutes a specific sub-group of smooth wheel-turned pottery, whose painted decoration was always applied as a coloured slip before firing in oxidizing conditions. Painted pottery, which also featured figurative representations or mythological motifs, was highly valued by the Celts and the Iberians. In this manner, a tradition which was already visible in the pottery and relief metalwork of the Hallstatt period endures. For the sake of completeness, mention must also be made of Greek painted pottery, which may have served as a model in certain cases.

Pigments

How colourful the material culture of protohistoric peoples was can only be partly reconstructed, as it depends so much on conditions of preservation. It is often possible to prove the presence of mineral pigments but, because they adhere poorly to their background, they decay on the surface, especially when buried. Natural pigments have been used for painting and ornamentation since the Stone Age (Rapp 2009). Earths coloured by iron oxides could be used to obtain red and yellow tones; wood or bone charcoal would have been used for black, and mixtures containing lime for white. This palette was widely used in the Iron Age: walls, pottery, stone sculptures, carved furniture, and other carved objects could all be painted. The latter are only very seldom preserved, a rare example being the couch (*kline*) and associated chest carved with meander motifs painted red and black from Grave 352 at the Dürrnberg in Austria (Egg and Zeller 2005). Pigments could be obtained locally, but there were also centres (e.g. in the Veneto) where pigments were exploited and therefore traded in greater quantities. The frescoes on the walls of the burial chambers at Vergina in northern Greece (*c.*340 BC) provide a magnificent illustration of the use of the entire range of the known palette.

Besides the wide spectrum provided by natural pigments (Kakoulli 2002), the artificially obtained pigment Egyptian blue ($CaCuSi_4O_{10}$) deserves a mention (Filippakis et al. 1979). Egyptian blue was known in Greece from the third millennium BC as a rare and expensive pigment, used in frescoes as well as for the colouring of sculptures. The wall paintings at the Iberian settlement of Tos Pelat near Moncada (Valencia, Spain) show that this pigment was already used in the west in the fourth millennium BC: analysis demonstrated the presence of Egyptian blue, as well as vermillion (Roldán García et al. 2005). At this point, it is opportune to note that the colouring of stone sculptures, which research into classical sculpture has pursued systematically in the last few years, also applies in principle to Celtic statuary, as shown by the Roquepertuse figures from southern France (Barbet 1991).

Organic Raw Materials

Within the vast range of organic materials used in pre- and protohistory, we shall focus only on those most important for the Iron Age. Archaeological evidence for these materials depends on the prevailing conditions of preservation, thus introducing an element of randomness. Some materials, for example wax, can nearly always only be detected in scientific analysis, although they must have played an important part in technical processes such as bronze casting. There are large gaps in the record, particularly for the raw materials for clothing, and the animal and vegetal materials used in textile and leather manufacture. The largest pieces of textile and leather come from bog finds, especially in Denmark (for example, Huldremose: Frei et al. 2009), and from the excavations of the salt mines at Hallstatt and the Dürrnberg in Austria (Bichler et al. 2005; Kern et al. 2008).

Wool was the most frequently used fibre; the yarns are finer in the Hallstatt period than they had been in the Bronze Age, and a thread thickness of 0.2–0.3 mm allows a density of fifty threads per centimetre. Plant dyes and interweaving ensured that the wool was coloured in different shades. There is also evidence for dyes being made using insects, particularly scale insects (the Coccoidea family). Different kinds of scale insects have different habitats, such as the Mediterranean for the kermes insect, and north-eastern Europe for the Polish cochineal. Insects used for dyes must therefore count among the non-proven traded goods that had to be imported in many regions of Iron Age Europe. The import of silk in Hallstatt princely burials is treated variously in the older literature but, to date, no proof has come from scientific analysis. In other regions too, as recently shown by the analysis of textiles from Kerameikos in classical Greece, potential evidence for the presence of silk has not been confirmed (Maragariti et al. 2011); in this instance, cotton seems to have been present. In most cases where silk had previously been claimed, the fabrics appear to have been made from particularly fine wool.

Wood and Charcoal

Wood is among the most essential universal materials of the past, providing energy in countless domestic uses, from cooking, heating, and lighting (tapers) to craft activities. The choice of hardwood or softwood depended on requirements. In metallurgy especially, wood was used in the form of charcoal to achieve the highest possible temperatures. Large-scale charcoal production must be assumed, even though there is no unequivocal evidence from excavation. The charcoal burners of the past were presumably independent. The most comprehensive 'sociological study' of this occupation has survived in Aristophanes' comedy *The Acharnians*, which contains all sorts of common preconceptions about these 'oak-ash-hardwood veterans'.

Apart from its use as a source of energy, wood was one of the most important building materials. Increasing settlement density in the Iron Age, for example in the zone of the Hallstatt princely seats or later with the birth of *oppida*, may have caused local timber supplies to dwindle and necessitated transport of timber over long distances. A study of the vegetation history of the Manching environs has shown that the surroundings of the *oppidum* were deforested (Küster 1992). With a population in the second century BC estimated at between 5,000 and 10,000 inhabitants, the 380 ha *oppidum* needed enormous amounts of wood. Completing the framework of the 7 km-long *murus gallicus* alone required 11,800 m^3 of timber (Maier et al. 1992; see also Chapter 22).

Just as for building, different types of wood were selected for their material properties when making tools and equipment. The adoption of the lathe meant that it was particularly important to grow timber free of knots and easy to split. The early Iron Age deposit of over a hundred wooden utensils found at the moor site of Schöllberg-Göge in the Weißenbach valley in southern Tyrol provides a good example (Steiner et al. 2009). It contained shovels, palettes, ladles, and scoops. The objects have a certain resemblance to the artefacts from the late Iron Age settlement of Cologne-Porz Lind (Joachim 2002). Similar moor or bog deposits are also known from northern Germany (Thorsberg Moor in Schleswig-Holstein), Poland, and Denmark (Rappendam in Zealand) (Jankuhn 1970). The utensils from the Schöllberg-Göge deposit are made of Swiss pine (*Pinus cembra*) native to the central Alps, indicating that indigenous types of wood were generally used. The import of foreign or unusual wood species cannot be quantified for lack of wood identifications, but, at the very least, mention must be made of cedar in Greek lands.

Fossil Materials

Amber was one of the most sought-after raw materials for making jewellery, amulets, and decorative elements from the Bronze Age; besides deposits of unworked material, it constituted a coveted prestige item in the Iron Age. Although there are a few locally used sources—for example, in the Simeto valley near Agrigento in Sicily—most of the amber found in the Mediterranean area between the Bronze Age and Roman times comes from the Baltic or peri-Baltic zone (Nava 2011). While relatively little amber reached southern Europe during the Bronze Age, trade in amber increased markedly in the Iron Age. The north–south trade network or 'amber route' is divided into an eastern and a western corridor. The routes of this ancient trade network are not known in detail, but can be mapped approximately from the distribution of finds of amber, with Alpine passes acting as fixed points. In eighth-century BC Italy, the Etruscans were the most important importers of amber, with a production centre based in Verucchio. In the seventh and sixth centuries BC, workshops spread over the whole of Italy, and Greek craftsmen in *Magna Graecia* (see Chapter 12) began to produce amber objects. It appears that trade in amber became the monopoly of the Piceni along the Adriatic coast. A further increase in the import of amber took place during the sixth century BC. Amber was mainly used in conjunction with ivory in the production of carved furniture. In the south, Ionian craftworkers gave a new impetus to work with amber. Sculptures carved in amber were particularly numerous in the sixth to fourth centuries BC in the area between *Magna Graecia* and the Etrusco-Padanian zone, but by the fourth century BC most amber workshops in Italy ceased to function, and the flow of imports from the north was interrupted. The incursions of the Celts from the north, and the attendant collapse of Padanian Etruria, are seen as the main cause. Only under the Roman Empire did the creation of new markets lead to a renewal of imports of amber.

Two other fossil materials were also worked into ornaments. Both are most easily turned on a lathe in moist conditions, and were popular for making light arm-rings. Jet (also known as black amber or gagate) is a bitumen-rich fossil product from the wood of coniferous trees. There are various sources of jet in Europe, which were also used in antiquity, including the north-east coast of England near Whitby, and in the Asturias, southern France, Austria, and Württemberg. Jet beads and broad armlets were made during the Hallstatt period, the most impressive being large barrel-shaped armlets (*Tonnenarmbänder*).

Sapropelite is a fossil shale formed from decayed mud. The most important sources exploited in the Iron Age are located in Bohemia and Moravia. There, mass production of simple smooth arm-rings, worn on the upper arm or the wrist, developed in the fourth and third centuries BC.

Ivory and Bone

Ivory was a luxury item in Iron Age Europe. The majority of imports stem from Phoenician or Syrian workshops, but in Italy there are also artefacts made from African or Indian ivory, such as hilts of prestige weapons or implements, but most frequently furniture ornaments. Such objects are often found in sanctuaries and graves of the eighth to seventh centuries BC in Greece and Asia Minor (e.g. at the sanctuary of Artemis Orthia in Sparta, or on the island of Samos). Tomb 79 from the cemetery of Salamis (Famagusta, Cyprus) provides the most complete impression of a bed and throne decorated in ivory. The many early ivory artefacts of the eighth to seventh centuries BC found in Italy include small cylindrical boxes or *pyxides* (Marsiliana d'Albegna in Tuscany: Circolo degli Avori), drinking-horn fittings (Populonia: Tumulo dei Carri), combs (Populonia: Tomba dei Flabelli), and sword or dagger hilts (Matelica near Ancona: Tomb 182). The Matelica dagger is paralleled at Kinding in Bavaria by an item probably made in the same workshop, a typical illustration of the tight network that existed between central Italy and the region north of the Alps. The sword pommels from Hallstatt, on the other hand, show local working of ivory. The best known furniture fittings from central Europe are those from Grafenbühl (Baden-Württemberg), including two sphinxes with amber knobs from the region of Taranto dated to around 600 BC. The same burial also contained an older, eastern Phoenician ivory plaque dated to the eighth or seventh century BC.

Animal bone, of course, was available everywhere, and was used for making ornaments and a variety of equipment (Jacobi 1974), including, for example, fittings for boxes, hinges, knobs, needles, tool handles, gaming pieces, and dice.

Pitch

Pitch from birch was used as an adhesive and for waterproofing. It is often found on pottery vessels (Stöckli et al. 1979) but can also serve to seal wood, as shown by the hub of a wheel from Bad Nauheim covered in pitch (Schönfelder 2003). Since birch pitch can only come from regions where birch trees grow, it follows that many European regions, especially in the south, would have had to import it.

Technology and Innovation

Technology and innovation play an important part in the cultural evolution of the Iron Age. A precondition of the diffusion of new ideas and techniques over the whole of Europe is a tight-knit network of communication based on high mobility. The generalized spread of the horse and cart was instrumental in this process. In contrast to the Neolithic and Bronze Age, the Iron Age experiences processes of innovation at 'high speed', for which archaeological methods are often inadequately equipped to recognize the modalities of flux and spread. Thus these developments can only be outlined in general terms.

We shall not dwell on iron technology here, since it is treated by Champion in Chapter 23. Technically iron technology occupies a key position because it is linked with the ability to master extremely high temperatures, necessary not only for metallurgy but also for glass manufacture and high-quality ceramics. It was possible to reach temperatures of over 1,000°C solely by using charcoal as fuel and bellows for improving oxygenation.

The transmission of expertise gained from dealing with high temperatures in iron metallurgy to other crafts stimulated innovation (Gebhard 1995). The advantage of working with high temperatures is that it leads directly to a detailed knowledge of other temperature-resistant materials—for example, heat-resistant ceramics. A general connection between the various production sites (ovens or furnaces), temperatures, and atmospheres required, and the metal or mineral materials used can thus be posited. In general, there is extensive expertise in the field of pyrotechnology in the Iron Age, inherited from Bronze Age traditions. Furnaces were operated selectively under reducing or oxidizing conditions. This influences, for example, the colours in glass production, and the reduction in oxygen prevents oxidization of the surface in the process of melting metal alloys. In ceramic production, double chamber kilns appear from the middle of the fifth century BC onwards, offering multiple possibilities to control firing (Gebhard et al. 2002, 2004b). Many of the metallurgical techniques developed in the Iron Age can be reconstructed through archaeometric analysis. In a few rare cases the entire contents of workshops have survived (Figure 24.3). The hoard from the Illyrian

FIGURE 24.3 Ceramic vessels with hammer-scale and iron remnants from a forge at Manching suggest that metal recycling was widespread in the second to first centuries BC.

Photo: Stefanie Friedrich, D 2011-263, © Archäologische Staatssammlung Munich

city of Daorson (Ošanići near Stolac, Bosnia and Herzegovina; Gebhard 1991) provides an insight into the workplace of a jeweller: apart from hammers, punches, and anvils—tools that have been part of a metalworker's toolkit since the Bronze Age—there are numerous tools and implements which appear to be Iron Age innovations, including tongs, compasses, draw-plates for iron wire, forming dies, and soldering pipes. The introduction of soldering technology made it possible to join together different metal parts, especially in jewellery. Reaction soldering predominates, but soft soldering is also known. A special variant consists of using liquid bronze as a conjoining or decorative element—for example, in sheet-metal statuary such as the 'iron horse of Manching' (Krämer 1989). The advantages of soldering are that raw material can be saved by making hollow rings and work can be carried out by a team. The famous torcs and bracelets from Erstfeld (Uri, Switzerland) were assembled from separate pieces, which had been made by several goldsmiths. Compensating weights were inserted inside the hollow artefacts (Guggisberg 2000). Experience in soldering precious metals could have had a general impact on knowledge of precious metal alloys. Gold and silver metallurgy is characterized by great diversity, and was deployed on a large scale in the production of coinage.

Research into coins combines three aspects: metallurgy, metrology, and economic history. The production of blanks followed a process which started with pellet moulds with rows of depressions in which coin blanks were cast (Gebhard et al. 1995, 1998, 1999). The analysis of coin hoards reveals that this process could achieve great consistency of gold alloys (Moesta and Franke 1995). Today, Iron Age coinage is given almost as much consideration in ancient numismatics as Greek and Roman coinage, and enormous numbers were struck (Figure 24.4). In the last few decades hundreds of new types have emerged, indicating that a fully functioning coinage circulated throughout Celtic Europe by the second and first centuries BC. This coin-using zone extended from Britain, through Gaul to northern Italy, Noricum, and regions influenced by Celtic culture on the middle and lower Danube (Chapter 28).

The diversity of coins found in central places like the *oppidum* of Manching shows that, beside regional exchange, coins circulated over hundreds of kilometres within a trade network, implying that coinage had a universal validity. Value was determined not by the design of the coins but by their material (gold, silver, bronze) and their weight. Coins made of the same material and of the same weight had an equivalent value. A gold coin (stater, *c.*7.2–8 g) served as the basic unit, which could be subdivided up to 1/72. This gold coinage was supplemented by silver and bronze coins. The weighing of subdivisions of these coins on simple small scales could achieve a precision ± 0.01 g.

FIGURE 24.4 Coin dies made of iron with corresponding coins from Kleinsorheim, Bavaria, first century BC.

Photo: Manfred Eberlein, GD 1999-491, © Archäologische Staatssammlung Munich

The various regions of Europe show different usage of gold and silver coins, depending on access to sources of precious metal, but also for historically contingent reasons. Thus silver coinage is dominant in Noricum and northern Italy, starting relatively late, in the middle of the second century BC, and soon coming under strong influence from trade with Rome. Gold coinage dominates in central Europe. The gold hoards found predominantly in southern Germany and Bohemia are particularly spectacular. Opinion is divided as to their interpretation, ranging from diplomatic gifts, payment of bribes, payment to soldiers, concealment of wealth, to exceptional votive deposits. The southernmost of these hoards was discovered at Campiglia Marittima in the province of Livorno, with its older issues of coins of the Boii suggesting a direct connection with the hoard of Großbissendorf in Bavaria and the great hoards of Bohemia.

In much of western and central Europe, coinage emerges as early as the fourth century BC. A direct link with Greek coinage, which replaced barter in the fifth century BC, is given by the choice of two Greek coins as the dominant models: the stater of Philip II and the stater of Alexander the Great. The Celts came into contact with Greek coinage through their expansion eastwards and their activity as mercenaries. While the first Iron Age coins imitate Greek exemplars, they evolve rapidly into variants that diverge markedly from the model. The autonomy of Celtic coinage accounts for its countless new creations, including designs with mythical creatures, human heads, animals, and ornaments.

Iron Age people possessed not only precise and widespread weighing systems, but also ways of measuring capacity and distances, along with complex geometric ornamental designs that give us a glimpse of the mathematics and geometry involved. This domain is generally approached through research into buildings; these frequently show that universal designs and underlying systems of measurement existed in the late Iron Age. The application of the Hippodamian grid plan in urban construction, reflected in the structures of some *oppida*, suggests influence from the Hellenistic world. Although a critical analysis is needed in individual cases, it appears that units of measurement (the 'Celtic foot') can be discerned in the construction of certain buildings. According to Schubert (1992, 1994), this unit was 309 mm at Manching, confirmed by the discovery of an iron scale measuring 154.5 mm, or half a foot. Other late Celtic settlements have produced very similar units of measurement. The construction of the monumental granite basin at Bibracte followed an elaborate design based on Pythagoras' theorem, using a basic unit of measurement of 304.2 mm (Almagro Gorbea and Gran Aymerich 1991). Albeit just another single instance, but remarkable for its similarity, the principle underlying the construction of a post-built house in the Etruscan settlement of the Forcello at Bagnolo San Vito near Mantua uses a unit of length of 308 mm (de Marinis 1986).

Schubert's studies show that we must assume a high and complex level of knowledge in 'barbarian' Europe. As can also be gleaned from Caesar's comments, access to this knowledge—which includes writing—was restricted to certain social groups. A grandiose monument like the Gallo-Roman Coligny calendar, which would be unimaginable without a long-term calendrical record spanning the entire Iron Age, gives us an inkling of the extent of this knowledge (Le Contel 1997; Bernecker 1998).

Apart from pyrotechnology and systems of measurements, examining how mechanics were mastered provides a further way of expressing how technical know-how was used. At this point it is necessary to briefly outline the position of mechanics in Greece (Schürmann 1991). The foundation of the Mouseion in Alexandria around 300 BC, the greatest and most important research centre in the entire Graeco-Roman world, marks a decisive break for the whole of society in antiquity. The foundation was linked to individuals like Ktesibios, Philon, and Heron, and covered all available attainments in the fields of μηχανικη τεχνη (the mechanical arts), the aim being to take these achievements further. The knowledge enshrined in the Mouseion built on a long history of innovation, which can be traced back through the first half of the first millennium BC, and to some extent it represents the entire European and Near Eastern cultural system. In nearly all domains of mechanics in antiquity—warfare technology, agriculture, logistics, the private sphere (*symposium*), the religious realm, official time measurement, and precision instruments—the Iron Age emerges as the great age of invention. Transmission benefited from two factors: on the one hand, the Greeks were able to interact with barbarian Europe through their colonies, especially in the western Mediterranean; and on the other, the role of neighbouring cultures, like for example the Etruscan culture (Sassatelli 2011), had a catalysing effect. As there are hardly any systematic studies of this phenomenon for Iron Age central Europe, we shall confine ourselves to a few examples. It should be noted at this juncture that the severe absence of wooden artefacts deprives us of a substantial section of the material culture presented here.

Levers were well known and intuitively used from the Stone Age. They were deliberately employed in construction and for tools in the Iron Age. Sleeve mounts on gouges or turning tools make it possible to attach longer handles and apply greater force through leverage. Pliers are a typical example of the use of levers, which, depending on how much force is required, have different length ratios between the jaw and the handles. There are also many 'hidden' areas where levers play a role, for example horse curb bits, or keys and locks, the latter exhibiting a spectacular diversity of forms and types in the second half of the first millennium BC.

Rotation is the second mechanical principle mentioned here. In its practical application, it is mainly in turning, or lathe-turning, that it played an important role in the Iron Age. All sorts of materials can be worked on a lathe: wood, ivory, bone, amber, coral, and also metals. The bases of sheet-metal containers of the Hallstatt period were partly finished by pressing the sheet metal into a turned wooden form.

Apart from lathes, the fast potter's wheel is among the significant innovations of Iron Age Europe. It had been known in Mesopotamia and Egypt from the fourth millennium BC onwards, and spread to the eastern Mediterranean during the third to second millennia. In Italy, it was the Etruscans who took on the role of transmitters, after it was introduced to the western Mediterranean by Greek colonists. Whether this linear 'diffusion model' reflects the reality of this process of innovation is debatable. Since general knowledge of wheels and lathes—which were also used for making wooden vessels—was already present, an independent, indigenous development cannot be excluded. The earliest wares produced on a fast wheel north of the Alps come from the late Hallstatt princely centres, the best-known assemblage being that of the Heuneburg (Lang 1974). In the late Iron Age, fast wheel-turned pottery was produced in large quantities, so it is apposite to speak of 'semi-industrial' production.

Rotary querns are first documented north of the Alps around the fourth century BC (Wefers 2012), and are found in Britain not much later. Their size implies that they were all operated by hand. Large mills operated by animals, as known from the Roman Empire, are so far unknown. The use of water power and waterwheels to drive mills is likely to have existed in the eastern Mediterranean from the third century BC at the earliest, based on the interpretation of written sources (Vitruvius, Philon, Archimedes: Schürmann 1991: 94). It is unlikely that the technique stalled until the late first century BC/early first century AD, as waterwheels and watermills were already present in Iron Age Europe (Landels 1980; Wikander 2000).

Mechanical aids to water management must have been known. The gold mine at La Fagassière in the Limousin had an elaborate underground drainage system in late La Tène times, whose exit channel could only be reached by overcoming a difference in height. Since water flowed continuously through a feeder channel, the excavator of the mine, Béatrice Cauuet (1999, 2004), suggested that an Archimedean screw was installed at this point.

This cursory look at the most important innovations and technical achievements of the first millennium BC must nevertheless include two peripheral areas firmly established in social life, but which are difficult to capture archaeologically. Medicine appears to have received clear influences from the south in Hellenistic times. The earliest example of the use of surgical instruments comes from Burial 7 at München-Obermenzing, dated to the third century BC (Krämer 1985). The grave contained a retractor, a scalpel, and a bone saw. Trepanation with such saws is documented at contemporary Manching (Lange 1983). Numerous single finds of medical probes and other implements from the *oppida* of the second and first centuries BC indicate that knowledge of medical treatment was spreading throughout Europe. Anthropological analyses undertaken on Iron Age skeletons, which often show evidence for the surgical treatment of fractures and wounds from striking blows, constitute a rich source of material.

Music belongs to an area of life, which, like language, generally eludes archaeologists; but reconstruction of musical instruments at least restores some soundscapes and harmonics. Music was an integral part of religious and social practice and was included in funerals and feasts (*symposia*). There is Iron Age evidence in both these areas. Instruments may originate in local traditions, such as the rattles of the Hallstatt period, or be imported. The fragment of a *crotale*, an Etruscan metal castanet, from the princely burial of Grafenbühl, provides an impressive example.

Apart from percussion instruments (frame drums, rattles), the two main musical instrument groups are wind instruments and string instruments. A spectacular discovery of seven metal trumpets (*carnyces*) was made in 2004 in the sanctuary of Tintignac (Maniquet 2008). Previously, some had been found fragmented (Deskford in Scotland, Mandeure in France), but they were mainly known from representations on coins and on the famous Gundestrup cauldron (Hunter 2001, 2009). *Carnyces* belong to a group of trumpets or horns on which a natural scale can be played. In the Nordic area, such bronze instruments, known as *luren* (lurs), appear in the fourteenth to seventh centuries BC. They are also known from burial assemblages and iconographic sources in the musical repertoire of the early Iron Age and Etruscan period (e.g. Populonia, Tumulo dei Carri). Outside the Mediterranean, stringed instruments are documented only in the form of rare images. The best-known representation of a lyre exists on a stone figure from Paule (Saint-Symphorien, Côtes-d'Armor, France) dated to the second century BC. With its soundbox and bridge between the arms, it bears such a close resemblance to the Greek *kithara* that an origin in the Mediterranean world must be supposed.

Conclusion

It has not been possible to cover in detail the regional distinctiveness sketched at the beginning of this brief overview of Iron Age raw materials, innovations, and techniques. The term 'Iron Age' has been used here in the way that Joseph Déchelette defined it in his groundbreaking manual (Déchelette 1913, 1914), as the period of time between the end of the Bronze Age and the beginning of the Roman Empire. Strictly speaking, this only applies to non-Greek and—after the end of the first century BC—non-Roman regions of Europe, which had not reached the level of 'higher civilization' at that time.

This also overlooks the fact that northern and eastern Europe—i.e. the zone occupied by 'Germanic tribes'—continued to exist in an Iron Age environment during the Roman period and eschewed the technological innovations of the Roman Empire. In Scandinavia especially, the notion of the Iron Age continues to be valid. After the fall of the Roman Empire and the migrations connected to it, many former Roman provinces returned to a 'prehistoric or Iron Age cultural level', where a renaissance of Roman achievements takes place in only a few areas—for example, watermills. The contemporary, gradual adoption of writing and large-scale restructuring of the political landscape by an aristocratic class announces the beginning of a new era, rightly described by the term 'early Middle Ages'.

References

Almagro Gorbea, M., and J. Gran Aymerich (eds). 1991. *El Estanque Monumental de Bibracte (Borgoña, Francia): Memoria de las Excavaciones del Equipo Franco Español en el Mont Beuvray 1987–1988*. Complutum, Extra 1. Madrid: Universidad Complutense.

Barbet, A. 1991. 'Roquepertuse et la polychromie en Gaule méridionale à l'époque préromain'. *Documents d'Archéologie Méridionale* 14: 53–81.

Bernecker, A. 1998. *Der gallorömische Tempelkalender von Coligny*. Bonn: Habelt.

Bichler, P., K. Grömer, R. Hofmann-de Keijzer, A. Kern, and H. Reschreiter (eds). 2005. *Hallstatt Textiles: Technical Analysis, Scientific Investigation and Experiment on Iron Age Textiles*. British Archaeological Reports International Series 1351. Oxford: Archaeopress.

Bott, R. D., R. Gebhard, F. E. Wagner, and U. Wagner. 1994. 'Mössbauer Study of Graphite Ware from the Celtic Oppidum of Manching'. *Hyperfine Interactions* 91: 639–644.

Burkhardt, A. 2012. 'Die Analysen der keltischen Münzen und Metalle der spätlatènezeitlichen Großsiedlungen in der Rheinschleife bei Altenburg ("Schwaben")'. *Fundberichte aus Baden Württemberg* 31, 1: 673–716.

Cauuet, B. (ed.) 1999. *L'Or dans l'Antiquité: de la Mine à l'Objet*. Aquitania supplément 9. Bordeaux: Fédération Aquitania.

Cauuet, B. 2004. *L'or des Celtes du Limousin*. Limoges: Culture et Patrimoine en Limousin.

Céramique peinte. 1991. *La céramique peinte celtique dans son contexte Européen: Actes du Symposium International d'Hautvillers, 9–11 octobre 1987*. Mémoires de la Société archéologique champenoise 5. Reims: Société archéologique champenoise.

Challet, V. 1992. *Les Celtes et l'émail*. Documents préhistoriques 3. Paris: Comité des travaux historiques et scientifique, Section de préhistoire et de protohistoire.

Daire, M.-Y. 2003. *Le sel des Gaulois*. Paris: Errance.

De Marinis, R. C. 1986. 'L'abitato etrusco del Forcello de Bagnolo S. Vito', in R. C. de Marinis (ed.) *Gli Etruschi al nord del Po*: 140–168. Mantua: Campanotto.

Déchelette, J. 1913. *Manuel d'archéologie préhistorique, Celtique, et Gallo-Romaine. II-2: Premier âge du fer ou époque de Hallstatt*. Paris: Picard.

Déchelette, J. 1914. *Manuel d'archéologie préhistorique, Celtique, et Gallo-Romaine. II-3: Second âge du fer ou époque de La Tène*. Paris: Picard.

Egg, M., and K. W. Zeller. 2005. 'Zwei hallstattzeitliche Grabkammern vom Dürrnberg bei Hallein—Befunde und Funde'. *Archäologisches Korrespondenzblatt* 35: 345–362.

Filippakis, S. E., B. Perdikatsis, and K. Assimenos. 1979. 'X-Ray analysis of pigments from Vergina, Greece'. *Studies in Conservation* 24, 2: 54–58.

Frei, K. M., I. Skals, M. Gleba, and H. Lyngstrøm. 2009. 'The Huldremose Iron Age textiles, Denmark: An attempt to define their provenance applying the strontium isotope system'. *Journal of Archaeological Science* 36, 9: 1965–1971.

Gebhard, R. 1989. *Der Glasschmuck aus dem Oppidum von Manching*. Die Ausgrabungen in Manching 11. Stuttgart: Steiner.

Gebhard, R. 1991. 'Aus der Werkstatt eines antiken Feinschmiedes. Zum Depotfund von Osaníci bei Stolac in Jugoslawien'. *Zeitschrift für Schweizerische Archäologie und Kunstgeschichte* 48: 2–11.

Gebhard, R. 1995. 'Industry in Celtic oppida. Aspects of high temperature processes', in G. Morteani and P. Northover (eds) *Prehistoric Gold in Europe: Mines, Metallurgy and Manufacture: Proceedings of the NATO Advanced Research Workshop on Prehistoric Gold in Europe, Seeon, Germany, September 27–October 1, 1993*. NATO ASI Series, Series E: Applied Science 280: 261–272. Dordrecht: Kluwer Academic.

Gebhard, R. 2010. 'Celtic glass', in B. Zorn and A. Hilgner (eds) *Glass along the Silk Road from 200 BC to AD 1000*: 3–13. Mainz: Verlag des Römisch-Germanischen Zentralmuseums.

Gebhard, R., R. Bott, N. Distler, J. Michálek, J. Riederer, F. E. Wagner, et al. 2004a. 'Ceramics from the Celtic oppidum of Manching and its influence in central Europe', in U. Wagner (ed.) *Mössbauer Spectroscopy in Archaeology: Hyperfine Interactions* 154, 1–4: 199–214.

Gebhard, R., E. Guggenbichler, W. Häusler, J. Riederer, K. Schmotz, F. E. Wagner, et al. 2002. 'Mössbauer study of a Celtic pottery-making kiln in Lower Bavaria', in E. Jerem and K. Biró (eds) *Archaeometry 98: Proceedings of the 31st Symposium, Budapest, April 26–May 3, 1998*. British Archaeological Reports International Series 1043: 555–563. Oxford: Archaeopress.

Gebhard, R., E. Guggenbicher, W. Häusler, J. Riederer, K. Schmotz, F. E. Wagner, et al. 2004b. 'A Celtic pottery-making kiln in Lower Bavaria', in U. Wagner (ed.) *Mössbauer Spectroscopy in Archaeology: Hyperfine Interactions* 154, 1–4: 215–230.

Gebhard, R., G. Lehrberger, G. Morteani, C. Raub, U. Steffgen, and U. Wagner. 1999. 'Production techniques of Celtic gold coins in Central Europe', in B. Cauuet (ed.) *L'Or dans l'Antiquité: de la mine à l'objet*. Aquitania supplément 9: 217–233. Bordeaux: Fédération Aquitania.

Gebhard, R., G. Lehrberger, G. Morteani, C. Raub, F. E. Wagner, and U. Wagner. 1995. 'Coin moulds and other ceramic material: A key to Celtic precious metal working', in G. Morteani and P. Northover (eds) *Prehistoric Gold in Europe: Mines, Metallurgy and Manufacture: Proceedings of the NATO Advanced Research Workshop on Prehistoric Gold in Europe, Seeon, Germany, September 27–October 1, 1993*. NATO ASI Series, Series E: Applied Science 280: 272–301. Dordrecht: Kluwer Academic.

Gebhard, R., G. Lehrberger, G. Morteani, C. Raub, F. E. Wagner, and U. Wagner. 1998. 'Melting and alloying techniques of Celtic gold coins in central Europe', in A. Oddy and M. Cowell (eds) *Metallurgy in Numismatics*, Vol. 4: 518–525. London: Royal Numismatic Society.

Gebhard, R., and U. Wagner. 2002. 'Das wirtschaftliche Umfeld von Manching: Möglichkeiten von Keramik Untersuchungen', in C. Dobiat, S. Sievers, and T. Söllner (eds) *Dürrnberg und Manching: Wirtschaftsarchäologie im ostkeltischen Raum: Akten des Internationalen Kolloquiums in Hallein-Bad Dürrnberg vom 7. bis 11. Oktober 1998*. Kolloquien zur Vor- und Frühgeschichte 7: 243–252. Bonn: Habelt.

Guggisberg, M. 2000. *Der Goldschatz von Erstfeld: Ein keltischer Bildzyklus zwischen Mitteleuropa und der Mittelmeerwelt*. Antiqua 32. Basel: Schweizerische Gesellschaft für Geschichte.

Haevernick, T. E. 1960. *Die Glasarmringe und Ringperlen der Mittel- und Spätlatènezeit auf dem europäischen Festland*. Bonn: Habelt.

Henderson, J., J. A. Evans, H. J. Sloane, M. J. Leng, and C. Doherty. 2005. 'The use of oxygen, strontium and lead isotopes to provenance ancient glasses in the Middle East'. *Journal of Archaeological Science* 32: 665–673.

Hunter, F. 2001. 'The carnyx in Iron Age Europe'. *Antiquaries Journal* 81: 77–108.

Hunter, F. 2009. 'The carnyx and other trumpets on Celtic coins', in J. van Heesch and I. Heeren (eds) *Coinage in the Iron Age: Essays in Honour of Simone Scheers*: 231–248. London: Spink.

Jacobi, G. 1974. *Werkzeug und Gerät aus dem Oppidum von Manching*. Die Ausgrabungen in Manching 5. Wiesbaden: Steiner.

Jankuhn, H. (ed.) 1970. *Vorgeschichtliche Heiligtümer und Opferplätze in Mittel- und Nordeuropa*. Abhandlungen der Akademie der Wissenschaften in Göttingen, Folge 3, 74. Göttingen: Vandenhoeck & Ruprecht.

Joachim, H.-E. 2002. *Porz-Lind: Ein Mittel- bis spätlatènezeitlicher Siedlungsplatz im "Linder Bruch" (Stadt Köln)*. Rheinische Ausgrabungen 47. Mainz: Philipp von Zabern.

Kakoulli, I. 2002. 'Late Classical and Hellenistic painting techniques and material: A review to the technical literature'. *Reviews in Conservation* 3: 56–67.

Kappel, I. 1969. *Die Graphittonkeramik von Manching*. Die Ausgrabungen in Manching 2. Wiesbaden: Steiner.

Karwowski, M. 2004. *Latènezeitlicher Glasringschmuck aus Ostösterreich*. Mitteilungen der Prähistorischen Kommission 55. Vienna: Verlag der Österreichischen Akademie der Wissenschaften.

Kern, A., K. Kowarik, A. W. Rausch, and H. Reschreiter (eds). 2008. *Salz—Reich. 7000 Jahre Hallstatt*. Veröffentlichungen der Prähistorischen Abteilung 2. Vienna: Naturhistorisches Museum Wien.

Krämer, W. 1985. *Die Grabfunde von Manching und die latènezeitlichen Gräberfelder in Südbayern*. Die Ausgrabungen in Manching 9. Stuttgart: Steiner.

Krämer, W. 1989. 'Das eiserne Roß von Manching. Fragmente einer mittellatènezeitlichen Pferdeplastik'. *Germania* 67, 2: 519–539.

Küster, H. 1992. 'Vegetationsgeschichtliche Untersuchungen', in F. Maier, U. Geilenbrügge, E. Hahn, H.-J. Köhler, and S. Sievers (eds) *Ergebnisse der Ausgrabungen 1984–1987*. Die Ausgrabungen in Manching 15: 433–476. Stuttgart: Steiner.

Landels, J. G. 1980. *Die Technik in der antiken Welt*. Munich: Beck.

Lang, A. 1974. *Die geriefte Drehscheibenkeramik der Heuneburg (1950–1970) und verwandte Gruppen: Heuneburgstudien III*. Römisch-Germanische Forschungen 34. Berlin: Walter de Gruyter.

Lange, G. 1983. *Die menschlichen Skelettreste aus dem Oppidum von Manching*. Die Ausgrabungen in Manching 7. Wiesbaden: Steiner.

Le Contel, J.-M. 1997. *Un calendrier celtique: Le calendrier gaulois de Coligny*. Paris: Errance.

Maier, F., U. Geilenbrügge, E. Hahn, H.-J. Köhler, and S. Sievers. 1992. *Ergebnisse der Ausgrabungen 1984–1987*. Die Ausgrabungen in Manching 15. Stuttgart: Steiner.

Maniquet, C. 2008. 'Le dépôt cultuel du sanctuaire gaulois de Tintignac à Naves (Corrèze)'. *Gallia* 65: 273–326.

Margariti, C., S. Protopapas, and V. Orphanou. 2011. 'Recent analyses of the excavated textile find from Grave 35 HTR73, Kerameikos cemetery, Athens, Greece'. *Journal of Archaeological Science* 38, 3: 522–527.

Moesta, H., and P. R. Franke. 1995. *Antike Metallurgie und Münzprägung: Ein Beitrag zur Technikgeschichte*. Basel/Boston/Berlin: Birkhäuser.

Nava, M. L. 2011. 'La Tradizione Millenaria dell'mbra', in F. Marzatico, R. Gebhard, and P. Gleirscher (eds) *Le grandi vie delle civiltà: Relazioni e scambi fra Mediterraneo e il centro Europa dalla Preistoria alla Romanitá*: 158–167. Trento: Castello del Buonconsiglio.

Nieto-Pelletier, S., and J. Olivier. 2016. 'Les statères aux types de Phillipe II de Macédoine: de l'Égée à la Gaule, des originaux aux imitations'. *Revue Numismatique* 173: 171–229.

Pion, P. 2012. 'La monnaie mercenaire: une approche anthropologique des premiers monnayages celtiques au nord-ouest du complexe nord-alpin (IIIe siècle av. J.-C.)', in P. Pion, B. Formoso, and R. Etienne (eds) *Monnaie antique, monnaie moderne, monnaies d'ailleurs: Métissages et hybridations*. Colloques de la Maison René-Ginouvès 8: 151–164. Paris: de Boccard.

Rapp, G. 2009. 'Pigments and colorants', in G. Rapp (ed.) *Archaeomineralogy, Natural Science in Archaeology*: 201–221. Berlin/Heidelberg: Springer.

Roldán García, C., J. L. Ferrero Calabuig, V. Primo Martín, C. Mata Parreñom, and J. Burriel Alberich. 2005. 'Analysis of Iberian wall paintings from "Tos Pelat" (4th century B.C.)', in C. Parisi, G. Buzzanca, and A. Paradisi (eds) *Proceedings of Art '05—8th International Conference on Non Destructive Investigations and Microanalysis for the Diagnostics and Conservation of the Cultural and Environmental Heritage*: 1–14. Lecce: University of Lecce.

Sassatelli, G. 2011. 'I rapporti tra Mediterraneo ed Europa e il ruolo degli Etruschi', in F. Marzatico, R. Gebhard, and P. Gleirscher (eds) *Le grandi vie delle civiltà: Relazioni e scambi fra Mediterraneo e il centro Europa dalla Preistoria alla Romanitá*: 254–267. Trento: Castello del Buonconsiglio.

Schönfelder, M. 2003. 'Räder, die nicht mehr rollen ... Hölzerne Naben keltischer Wagen aus dem Salinenbereich', in B. Kull (ed.) *Sole und Salz schreiben Geschichte: 50 Jahre Landesarchäologie: 150 Jahre archäologische Forschung in Bad Nauheim*: 271–274. Mainz: Philipp von Zabern.

Schubert, F. 1992. 'Metrologische Untersuchungen zu einem keltischen Längenmaß'. *Germania* 70: 293–305.

Schubert, F. 1994. 'Zur Maß- und Entwurfslehre keltischer Holzbauten im Oppidum von Manching'. *Germania* 72, 1: 133–192.

Schürmann, A. 1991. *Griechische Mechanik und Antike Gesellschaft: Studien zur staatlichen Förderung einer Technischen Wissenschaft*. Stuttgart: Steiner.

Schwab, R. 2002. 'Evidence for carburized steel and quench-hardening in the "Celtic" oppidum of Manching'. *Historical Metallurgy* 36, 1: 6–16.

Steffgen, U., R. Gebhard, G. Lehrberger, and G. Morteani. 1998. 'Platinum group metal inclusions in Celtic gold coins', in A. Oddy and M. Cowell (eds) *Metallurgy in Numismatics*, Vol. 4: 202–207. London: Royal Numismatic Society.

Steiner, H., A. Putzer, H. Oberrauch, A. Turner, and K. Nicolussi. 2009. 'Vorgeschichtliche Moorfunde aus der Schöllberg-Göge in Weissenbach (Gde. Ahrntal/Südtirol)'. *Archäologisches Korrespondenzblatt* 39: 489–508.

Stöckli, W. E., M. Hopf, and J. Riederer. 1979. *Die Grob- und Importkeramik von Manching*. Die Ausgrabungen in Manching 8. Wiesbaden: Steiner.

Streit, R. 1987. 'Zur Herkunft der Bausteine für die Mauer', in D. van Endert (ed.) *Das Osttor des Oppidums von Manching*. Die Ausgrabungen in Manching 10: 115–118. Stuttgart: Steiner.

Wagner, H. 2006. *Glasschmuck der Mittel- und Spätlatènezeit am Oberrhein und den angrenzenden Gebieten*. Remshalden: Bernhard Albert Greiner.

Wefers, S. 2012. *Latènezeitliche Mühlen aus dem Gebiet zwischen den Steinbruchrevieren Mayen und Lovosice*. Vulkanpark-Forschungen 9. RGZM Monographien 95. Mainz: Verlag des Römisch-Germanischen Zentralmuseums.

Wikander, Ö. 2000. 'The water-mill', in Ö. Wikander (ed.) *Handbook of Ancient Water Technology, Technology and Change in History*, 2: 371–400. Leiden: Brill.

CHAPTER 25

MATERIAL WORLDS

FRASER HUNTER

Introduction

The material worlds of the European Iron Age are best known as a series of treasures displayed in special exhibitions across the continent which focus on ancient 'peoples'—the Celts, the Iberians, the Ligurians, the Piceni, and so forth (e.g. Moscati et al. 1991; Govignon 1997; de Marinis and Biaggio Simona 2000; Colonna et al. 2001; de Marinis and Spadea 2004; Jimeno Martínez 2005). These exhibitions showcase the great and the good, the splendid and the shiny. Such items, generally displayed as art objects, are of course critical in understanding the European Iron Age, but they also give a very partial view. As any excavator knows, the everyday reality is potsherds and rusting iron fragments, broken bone tools, and the odd brooch. Rich assemblages are the exceptional ones, from places where something unusual was happening. It is between these two worlds, the rich and the mundane, that we must move if we are to explore the material worlds of the European Iron Age, for the latter is the basis of the former.

The period offers an unparalleled diversity of material compared to earlier prehistory. During the first millennium BC, new or previously rare raw materials such as iron, glass, and terracotta became markedly more widespread. Formats such as stone sculpture were experimented with more extensively; coinage became commonplace over the southern half of the continent; innovations such as the rotary quern spread widely; iron ploughshares opened up more land to cultivation. If you pick up an Iron Age excavation report from virtually any European country, the artefact categories will be familiar even if the types are regionally distinctive: agricultural tools such as sickles and plough components, often deposited in unusual and intriguing ways; tools for the processing and consumption of cereals, especially quernstones; a diversity of pottery, from storage through cooking to serving; a range of iron tools, increasing in diversity towards the end of the period as this metal became commonplace; decorative material, whether in ornate stone, glass, or copper alloy; and increasing interest in personal grooming, marked by combs, tweezers, and related material. The key themes—agriculture, food consumption, craft, ornament—are common in earlier and later periods, but the wider range of materials, the diversity of find types (especially in iron), and the advent of new or previously rare objects (the glass bead, the rotary quern) stand distinct from earlier times.

Innovations and Contacts: A Diachronic Picture

Yet underlying such similarities is a diversity across the continent. The range of materials and technologies used was notable, but their uptake was partial. Glass jewellery saw very variable adoption north of the Mediterranean region (see Chapter 24). Beads and bangles became relatively common in La Tène cultural areas during the later Iron Age, but with marked regional 'hotspots' (e.g. Venclová 1990: 142–156). In contrast, glass jewellery remained rare across most of northern Europe until the Roman Iron Age but became dominant there in the mid-first millennium AD (e.g. Tempelmann-Mączyńska 1985: 93–98).

Over much of temperate Europe iron use was sporadic until the late Iron Age, with the last couple of centuries BC and early centuries AD seeing an explosion in its production (see Chapter 23). This is well illustrated by the example of nails, which only became common towards the end of the Iron Age as iron became more abundant (e.g. Hunter 1998: 366–367; Gaudefroy, Malrain, and Pommepuy 2006: 164). The rotary quern may have greatly speeded up crop processing, but its development and adoption was very partial and staccato (Wefers 2011). There are good arguments for its origins lying in the western Mediterranean region in the Phoenician world by the sixth century BC; north-east Spain was a major centre of innovation by the fifth century, with current evidence suggesting a western/Atlantic spread at least as far as Britain in the fifth century (Figure 25.1). Yet the heart of temperate continental Europe seemingly did not adopt the device extensively for another two or three centuries (Wefers 2011; Jaccottey et al. 2013), while Greece retained a less effective local variant until the Roman conquest (Peacock 2013: 55).

Some areas consciously rejected such new technology: in Jutland, the rotary quern was not adopted until around AD 200, although these societies were open to other innovations and foreign goods (Webley 2008: 127). It is likely this was not just conservatism but a concern over the changes new technologies would bring to existing social relations built on a particular division of labour (Webley 2008). These diverse responses are a useful reminder that the Greek and Roman worlds did not have a monopoly on innovation, nor were they necessarily the sole drivers of cultural choice and change. Such influences could operate in more than one direction; Mediterranean connections were one narrative, but not the only one.[1]

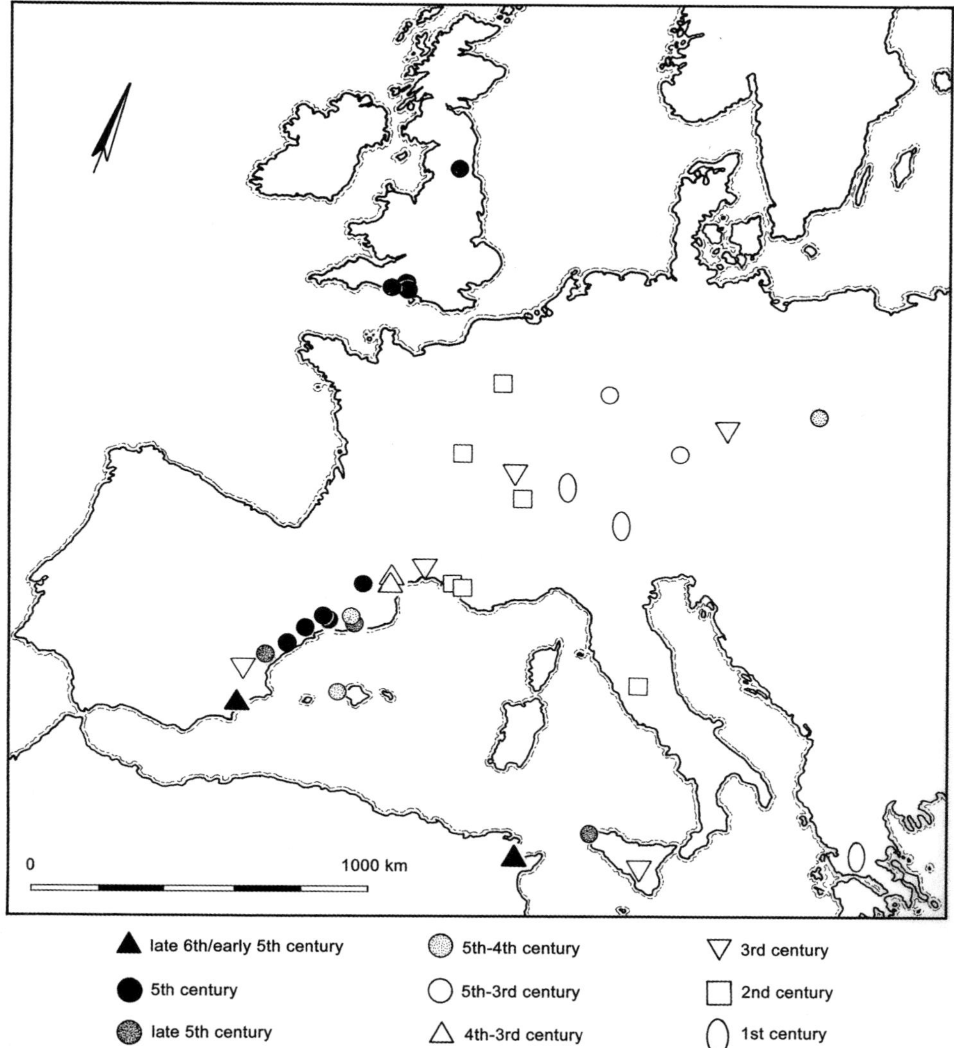

FIGURE 25.1 Datable finds of rotary querns from the European Iron Age.

Redrawn by Alan Braby, after Wefers 2011: fig. 2

The wheel offers a similar example—not in its Bronze Age advent but its subsequent development. Rather clunky spoked wheels are found widely in the earlier Iron Age around the Mediterranean (Crouwel 2011) and in the Hallstatt world (Pare 1992), but light spoked wheels in Europe were a feature of the La Tène cultural zone, attested in burials from fifth- to third-century BC Britain, northern France, western Germany, and Bohemia (Guštin and Pauli 1984). Some featured the high-technology solution of an iron tyre heat-shrunk onto the wheel without any fixings such as nails. The earliest evidence for this from north of the Alps comes from Britain, where the technique became standard (Figure 25.2; Carter et al. 2010: 54): the rarity of such evidence in the Mediterranean (Crouwel 2011: 33) suggests this was a northern innovation. Linguistic

FIGURE 25.2 Reconstruction of the chariot from Newbridge, Edinburgh. The wheel has a one-piece rim with the iron tyre shrunk onto it; no nails were used to fix the tyre to the wheel.

Photo: Neil McLean, © National Museums Scotland

evidence confirms that developments in vehicle manufacture reached the Latin language from Celtic-speaking areas (Piggott 1983: 230–234).

This rotary theme offers further examples of diversity. Wheel-made pottery was another stop–start technology, not a continuous development. The earliest examples north of the Alps come from late Hallstatt contexts in central Europe, and it became widespread in the continental La Tène area (see Chapter 24, Chapter 8). The technique's history in the Germanic world was rather different: distribution and dating suggest eastern/Black Sea origins, with some stimulus from the Roman world (Hegewisch 2007), while the technique was largely abandoned after introduction in much of central Europe (Bochnak 2013). This disinterest in certain new technologies is also seen in Britain: while the south adopted wheel-turned pottery in the late Iron Age, the north did not, with local handmade wares persisting although people here were exposed to (and used) wheel-turned pottery during the Roman period. In Ireland pottery use was abandoned entirely after the late Bronze Age for over a thousand years, until the later first millennium AD (Raftery 1995; Armit 2008).

Other technological innovations of Mediterranean origin show interesting and complicated adoption processes across temperate Europe. The goldworking techniques of granulation, filigree, and wire chains were widely used in Greek and Etruscan jewellery, and adopted extensively in Roman and Iberian areas (Armbruster 2013). Their use north of the Alps in western Europe was more sporadic. Rare examples from late Hallstatt and early La Tène contexts are likely to be special commissions (Müller 2009: 72; Schorer 2012), while the emulation of the techniques in repoussé and 'false filigree' castings shows they were desirable yet technically difficult to copy (e.g. Szabó 1975; Hautenauve 2005: 166–168). Even by the late La Tène period they are found only sporadically on indigenous gold jewellery (Figure 25.3) and often mark imported special commissions (e.g. the chain-like torcs in a hoard from Winchester, United Kingdom; Hill et al. 2004). But in some areas the technology was transferred and further developed. It was adopted into local cultures from Greek colonies north of the Black Sea; from there, the techniques spread around the change of era to southern Scandinavia, where they flourished (e.g. Andersson 1995: 222–224).

A similar distant flourishing of an originally Mediterranean habit is seen with enamels and glass inlays.[2] The habit originated in the Greek world in the later second millennium BC (Künzl 2012: 9), and glass inlays are found on a small scale in La Tène areas from *c.*400 BC (Megaw and Megaw 1990: 40–41; Challet 1992; Defente 2012), but its use exploded in Britain in the period from *c.*50 BC through the early Roman period. Such technical habits may have been inspired ultimately from Mediterranean cultures, but their differential uptake and subsequent history stress the diversity of material uses across the continent. Rather than simple pictures of linear and derivative influences, they show innovation and development. Links to the Mediterranean should not be ignored, but they are only part of the story. For instance, the significance of the amber trade to the Mediterranean is well attested from the Bronze Age onwards, but its movement elsewhere within Europe is also worth noting, especially for beads and

FIGURE 25.3 Hybrid torc from Blair Drummond (Stirling, Scotland). The form is a typical Iron Age ring-terminal torc, but the terminals use Mediterranean technologies of filigree, granulation, and chain-making.

Photo: Neil McLean, © National Museums Scotland

amulets (Nava 2011, esp. Abb. 1; for a long-term overview see Pauli 1975, esp. 131–133; for a Czech case study see Čižmářová 1996).[3]

The Materials

The increasing availability of iron and the wealth of other raw materials have rather overshadowed study of more traditional substances, notably stone and bone. Stone is rarely considered as a material at this period except for quernstones, and yet in some areas it retained a key role as a ubiquitous local resource, especially before the widespread adoption of iron. Early prehistorians scrutinize hammerstones, polishers, and flints, but later prehistorians rarely consider them. Review of excavation reports across the La Tène cultural zone produces only a thin scatter of polishers, whetstones, and pounders, which receive little substantive comment (e.g. Jacobi 1974: 129–130, 243–244, Taf. 83–85, 96; Gallet de Santerre 1980: 146–147), though some do appear as specialist tools on craftworking sites (e.g. Daire et al. 2001: 87–89, cobble tools connected to salt working; Colin et al. 2011: 69, polishers used in pottery manufacture; Tomo 2012, tools for ore-preparation in iron smelting). In contrast, stone tools are reported in quantity from northern Europe (see Lang 2007: 109 and Webley 2008: 75, 130 for summaries of Estonian and Jutland finds; they are also abundant in Scotland, e.g. over 800 from the Howe, Orkney; Ballin Smith 1994: 185–212). Do recognition and recovery bias play a role here, or are these real regional differences? And are they related primarily to the availability of iron (after which whetstones are the main stone tool type), or did other factors shape preferences?

One stone type which has received recent attention on a continental scale is black jewellery (primarily bangles) of shale, lignite, jet, and similar materials (Venclová 1998; Baron 2012; Hunter 2015: 230–233; see Chapter 24). Its geologically limited occurrence gives it an interest for distribution studies, while well-preserved working debris provides insights into workshop practices. Bone and antler is another category that receives lavish attention in early prehistory but is largely overlooked in the Iron Age, partly due to its variable survival—large areas of Europe have little or no bone preservation. It was also a less critical raw material than in earlier periods since metal had replaced many earlier bone tool types. Worked bone finds are rare across the La Tène world on the continent—or at least rarely reported (Krausz 2000: 131–132).[4] For instance, excavations of workshop areas of the sixth to fifth centuries BC at Port Sec, Bourges, France, produced over 110,000 animal bone fragments (Durand et al. 2012) but under 200 pieces of working debris and only some twenty finished artefacts (Augier et al. 2009: 45–50; Pescher 2012: fig. 123). Yet clusters of finds did indicate particular working areas; the debris showed that pins, perhaps needles, and discs for beads or counters were being produced, and there was also some evidence for horn working. A survey of later Iron Age finds in the Oise valley, France, showed that bone and antler objects were common in the early La Tène period but declined thereafter (Gaudefroy, Malrain, and Pommepuy 2006: 148, fig. 109). Occasional publications testify to a wide range of uses, from tools to ornaments and more decorative material (e.g. Krausz 2000; Jacobi 1974: 241–243, Taf. 81–82). Bone and antler have seen more substantive study in areas where preservation conditions are more favourable, for instance in Britain and the Netherlands (e.g. Roes 1963; Hallén 1994). Here an impressive diversity of tool types, fittings, and ornaments is recorded (Figure 25.4). There was clearly an overlap conceptually between items made in wood and bone/antler, especially in areas where the former was scarce; note, for example, spades and ploughshares of whalebone from the Western Isles of Scotland (Clarke 1971). Major lacunae remain in understanding the function of stone and bone artefacts. For both, a combination of experimental work, microwear studies (more typical of earlier prehistory), and scientific analysis of residues would be of great value (e.g. Adams 2002; Poissonnier 2002; Olsen 2003; Struckmeyer 2011; Peacock 2013: 189–191).

Pottery is viewed as ubiquitous for scholars whose focus is the Mediterranean and across much of temperate Europe. However, there are areas (such as Ireland and parts of western Britain) where it saw little or no use, even though other ceramic technologies such as moulds and crucibles were expertly adopted (e.g. Raftery 1995). Here, the need for vessels must have been met by organic materials, but these rarely survive. As with all periods of the past, the gaps in our picture of Iron Age material worlds are greater than the surviving parts because of the near total loss of organic finds—wood, hides, fibres,

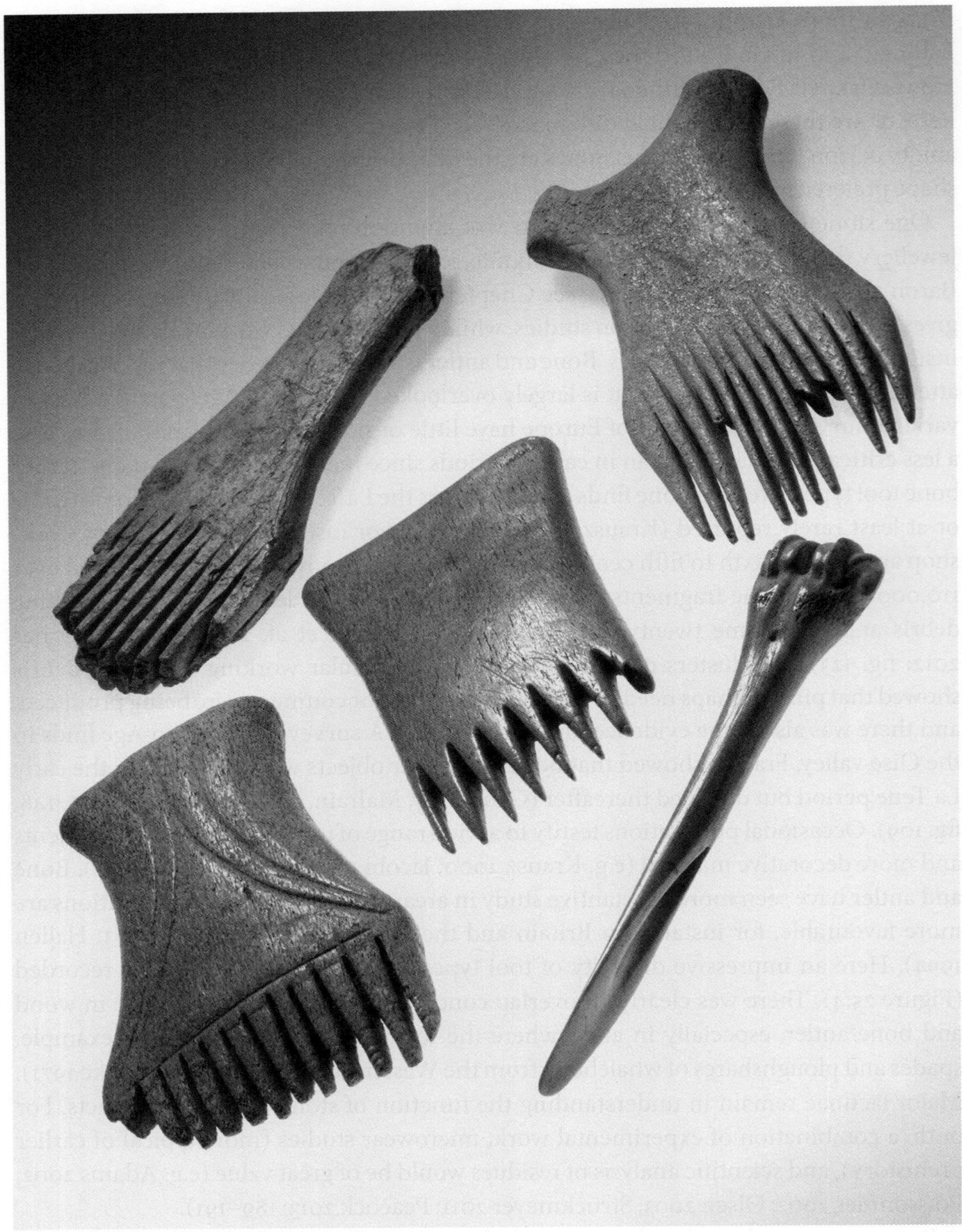

FIGURE 25.4 Bone and antler combs for textile processing and a bone hide-rubber from Midhowe and Gurness (Orkney, Scotland).

Photo: Neil McLean, © National Museums Scotland

and textiles (Hurcombe 2014)—though surviving inorganic objects can provide useful proxies for lost material. For instance, Gaudefroy, Malrain, and Pommepuy (2006: 160–161) noted a decline in spindle whorls in the Oise valley over the course of the La Tène period, suggesting increasingly centralized rather than domestic textile production, casting light on an otherwise all-but-invisible craft.

Rare survivals such as the wooden finds from the Hjortspring, Denmark, or Oberdorla, Germany, bog deposits, or the permafrozen Pazyryk (Siberia, Russia) burials provide tantalizing glimpses of what has been lost (Rosenberg 1937; Rudenko 1970; Gossel-Raeck et al. 1991: 182–215; Behm-Blancke 2003). But these also provide hints of regional and chronological variety. Chris Evans (1989) noted the rarity of decorated organic material in Iron Age waterlogged contexts in Britain and Ireland, in marked contrast to the Hjortspring or Pazyryk finds. Dutch bogs have produced a wealth of organic material, but wooden vessels are notably rare, and it seems ceramics were preferred here (van den Broeke 2005: 620).

The Everyday and the Exceptional

So far we have concentrated on the fragments which survive of everyday lives. The evidence from settlements is a painfully partial one, not a picture of life—materially rich, messy sites were by no means the rule. Many sites produce small and/or essentially prosaic assemblages, strongly biased to material that was disposable or hard to recycle once smashed—notably pottery. The quantitative mismatch between pottery and other items is striking. Of course the fragmentation of a pot creates an impressive sherd count, but even allowing for this, pottery dominates the record because of its survivability and its virtual uselessness once broken. For instance, Raimund Karl's survey of 332 settlement assemblages from Lower Austria showed that 90% of finds were ceramic (Karl 1996: 22); metal was very rare indeed. Of 206 Iron Age sites examined on the island of Fyn in Denmark, all produced pottery but only 28% had stone items, 9% produced ironworking evidence (but only 5% had iron finds), and only 1% produced glass or copper alloy (Webley 2008: 130, table 7.1). The late La Tène settlement site of Porz-Lind (Nordrhein-Westfalen, Germany) produced *c.*9,700 sherds from some 120–150 vessels, but only around thirty other inorganic finds, half of which were slingshots; however, it did produce a vital assemblage of almost 1,200 wooden items, a further reminder of how partial the picture normally is because of preservation conditions (Joachim 2002).

This settlement picture stands in marked contrast to the one from burials and hoards—which provide the raw material for exhibition catalogues and illustrate general books. Traditions of lavishly accompanied burial or rich hoards are, of course, diachronically varied. For instance, Pion and Guichard (1993) plotted the great regional variability in the occurrence of mid- to late La Tène cemeteries in France, while Schönfelder (2012: 100–105) has noted large-scale variations in hoarding at this time across continental Europe: weaponry is common in rivers from the Sâone to the upper Danube but rare beyond this; in western and northern France, it is found instead in sanctuaries, while in central and eastern Europe hoards are more often linked to big settlements and rarely involve weapons. It seems that later prehistoric societies in any particular area did not generally choose to deposit the same kinds of valued items in both burials and hoards (e.g. Bradley 1990: 99–114).

The issue of why accompanied burials or hoards were prevalent at particular times and places lies beyond the scope of this contribution; what is of interest here are the limits this places on our knowledge owing to the selectivity of what was deposited in different settings. This is not just true of hoards and burials. It is increasingly clear that much material on settlements was not simply left behind as rubbish. Often it formed carefully chosen groups, ritually deposited in special contexts such as entranceways—even broken sherds could be carefully and deliberately selected (e.g. Hill 1995; Malrain 2006; Webley 2008: 129–148; Wells 2016). The assemblages from burials, settlements, and hoards are notably distinct: there were clear and widespread perceptions of appropriateness in terms of what should be used in which context. There are obvious examples—rich jewellery and weaponry come overwhelmingly from hoards and burials—but also other, less obvious ones. For instance, quernstones are exceedingly rare in burials, though they appear in both settlements and (less commonly) hoards; bone tools are common on settlements but exceedingly rare in burials and were not often hoarded. There was selectivity within material categories as well. An obvious example is pottery in burials, which was often more elaborate than settlement material and may comprise a different functional spectrum; the same is true of jewellery (e.g. Gaudefroy, Malrain, and Pommepuy 2006: 167–168, figs 125–127; Gaudefroy, Pinard, and Malrain 2006: 110). Figure 25.5 illustrates this in two widely separated case study areas where contemporary settlements and burials have been examined: the early La Tène settlement of Inzersdorf-Walpersdorf (Ramsl 1998) and nearby cemetery of Inzersdorf ob der Traisen (Neugebauer 1996) in the Traisen valley in Lower Austria; and East Yorkshire, where a project was specifically targeted at recovering settlement assemblages (Rigby 2004) to compare with those from large-scale cemetery excavations (Stead 1991). This emphasizes the dominance of metal and glass finds from cemeteries and pot and bone from settlements (stone items were generally uncommon in both areas).

This is not a simple matter of one category of context providing a 'corrective' to another. Burials do not just flesh out the mundane picture from settlements: both assemblages are selective. A study of Iron Age material culture must consider all the available evidence, but too often the burial and hoard finds dominate at the expense of the everyday. A rare exception, synthesizing material from both cemetery and settlement excavations in the Oise valley, France, shows the value of a comparative approach for a more rounded picture (Gaudefroy, Malrain, and Pommepuy 2006; Gaudefroy, Pinard, and Malrain 2006). One corollary of this is that we must be very cautious not to assume areas are poor or peripheral when this reflects societies or periods which shunned accompanied burial or hoards (as in the early Iron Age of most of Britain and Ireland). In these circumstances, the surviving assemblages are a particularly weak reflection of reality.

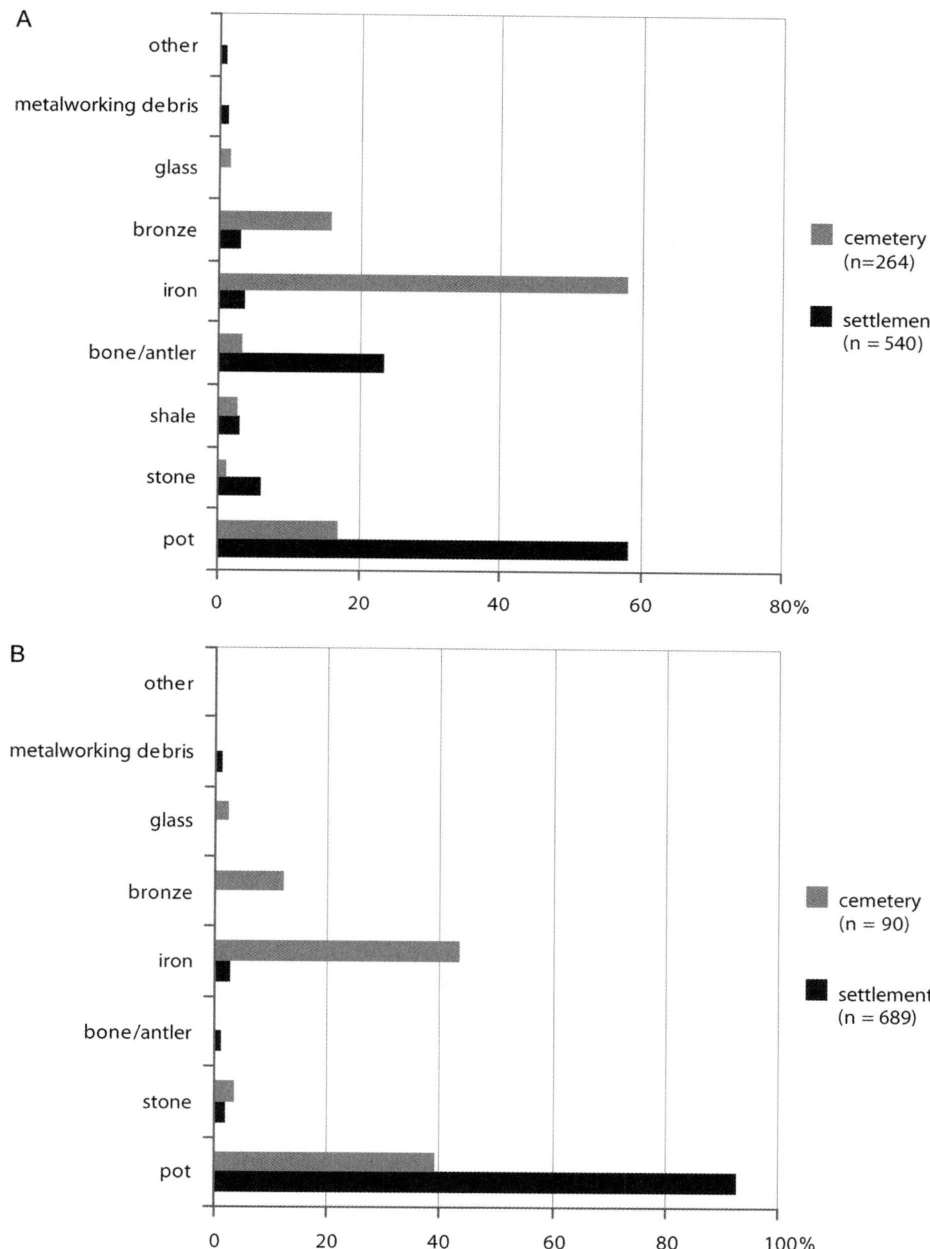

FIGURE 25.5 Comparison of the proportions of different material types found in settlement and cemetery contexts: A from East Yorkshire, England; B from the Traisen valley, Austria. With the Yorkshire material, note that the settlement finds have a longer time span (from the late Bronze Age to the late Iron Age) than the cemetery finds (which are mostly third to second century BC).

Sources: Rigby 2004; Stead 1991 (A); Ramsl 1998; Neugebauer 1996 (B)

Social Arenas and Identities

Material from burials and hoards consistently falls into a restricted number of social arenas: warfare, feasting, adornment, and transport dominate the material, with finds often using exotic raw materials and/or rare craft skills. These are recurring features of human display behaviour over millennia, but comparative studies of how these social arenas were expressed are rare. A notable exception is Diepeveen-Jansen's (2001) study of early La Tène burials in the Aisne-Marne area of France and the Hunsrück-Eifel area of Germany. She considered the categories of vehicles, feasting, and weaponry in terms of how concepts of hospitality and martial behaviour were expressed through burial practices, and how these changed over time. Similarly, Desenne et al.'s (2009) long-term view of the material from 700 burial assemblages in Picardy, France, spanning the whole La Tène period, allowed significant chronological variation to be explored: for instance, the role of brooches varied from rare and distinctive individual items to a more commonplace element of costume, to fasteners for a bag holding the deceased's ashes. The authors could also track changes in male versus female fashion over this period.

To explore one arena in a little more detail, personal ornaments are a recurring feature across Iron Age societies (as in many others), but larger-scale patterns tend to get obscured in more detailed studies. Torcs are often seen as typical of 'Celtic Europe', following the classical authors' preconceptions about Celts wearing them, but some types are characteristic of northern Europe (such as the late Bronze Age/early Iron Age *Wendelringe* and the Iron Age crown torcs; Heynowski 2000; Jensen 2013: 643–644), while others show a mixture of styles (such as the Danish ball torcs with Celtic art motifs; Kaul 1991). Their social roles also varied: Hautenauve (2005: 23–45) has noted the shift in La Tène gold torcs from female ornaments in the fifth to early third centuries BC to male warrior ornaments in middle La Tène period, and increasingly as attributes of gods towards the end of the Iron Age.

In many areas of northern Europe pins were preferred to brooches for most of the Iron Age, and it was only with the adoption of La Tène styles of fibulae from the third century BC that brooches became common (von Freeden and von Schnurbein 2006: 198; Müller and Steuer 2011: 58, 61). Belts were another area of changing fashion, with decorated belt plates commonly used in the Hallstatt and La Tène cultural zones in the sixth to fifth century BC, belt chains being widely used in the third century BC, but with belts generally falling from significance thereafter. Peter Wells (2008: 64–80) has discussed examples of ornaments over the long Iron Age in terms of patterns of visibility when worn on the body; such approaches allow broad views of the changing nature of display.

Broad-scale patterns can also be seen in preferences for prestige metals. Derek Allen (1980: 6–9) usefully classified early coinages north of the Alps into a southern 'silver belt' forming a broad swathe from the Bay of Biscay to the mouth of the Danube, and a 'gold belt' to its north, west of the middle Danube (see Chapter 28). Only in northern Iberia and south-west France was there a significant early bronze coinage. Metal use was of course affected by geological availability and access to trade goods, with the spread of Roman Republican silver coinage having a wide impact from the second century BC. Nonetheless, as Allen noted, '[t]his banding was only to some degree consequential on the location of mines and minerals; ... it was fundamentally a matter of choice' (1980: 9). This merits comparison to other uses of precious metal. In eastern Europe, silver was indeed the dominant metal (Venedikov 1976; Fol et al. 1989; Jevtović 1990; Vasić et al. 2004), though among the Thracians in particular gold was also popular (e.g. Marazov 1998). In contrast, gold was the prestige metal for torcs and other jewellery across western Europe, and silver was rare (Hautenauve 2005: 9, map 1). This was true both in areas which also used gold coinage, and in south-west France and northern Italy where coinage was predominantly silver. In Iberia, both silver and gold were used widely for jewellery (with some regional variety), but not for coin (Almagro-Gorbea 1991: 398; García Vuelta 2002: fig. 1; Barril Vicente 2002: fig. 7). It suggests rather different concepts of metal values and symbolism in different areas. These prestige ornaments yield interesting patterns at a large scale, but it is also necessary to embed 'treasure' within its local context. An excellent example is Spânu's (2012) study of Dacian silver, which started with typology and patterns of association, but then moved on to consider issues such as iconography, social meaning, and the reasons behind changes through time.

Such 'treasures' are typically seen as elite material, but there is a developing and valuable critique on the nature of Iron Age societies, particularly those which show little or no sign of centralized places with urban functions (such as most of Britain, or the early La Tène core areas, in contrast to the late Hallstatt *Fürstensitze*). This suggests that these groups were essentially small-scale in nature, including those lavishing rich grave goods (e.g. Diepeveen-Jansen 2001: 209). What was an elite in such a society, if indeed they existed at all (e.g. Hill 2006)? One strand of debate argues that prestige material was embedded in extended networks of connections, with the objects reliant on these links for both their creation and social meaning, carrying something of this story in the minds of the people who used the finds. People may not have had ownership of such prestige objects but temporary curation in their role as war leader, seer, or intermediary with the gods (e.g. Garrow and Gosden 2012). But these should still be seen as restricted items: such finds are uncommon, high craft skills were involved, and (especially in the case of objects with complex decoration such as Celtic art) knowledge was required both to make and decode such material, which implies a more exclusive status. We should note, though, that many of these finds are not absolutely rare; while there are exceptional burials such as Hochdorf, Vix, or Glauberg, well-furnished burials are not uncommon in early La Tène core areas such as the Marne or the Hunsrück-Eifel. In looking at catalogues of burials (e.g. Haffner 1976), one sees the same basic combinations of goods emerging again and again. These are almost stereotypes being played out—not so much competing for status, perhaps, but carrying out a necessary social role.

Decoration

Decoration in the European Iron Age is often considered specifically in terms of art, especially definable traditions like the stylized Celtic art or semi-naturalistic Thracian art, but it is important to look beyond this when considering ornament and aesthetics (e.g. Sharples 2008: 203; Joy 2011). Simple geometric recurring motifs, many familiar from the Bronze Age, continued to play a key role, especially on more everyday objects. A key missing element is colour: rare instances like painted pottery, the permanent colours of glass jewellery, and the fugitive traces from scant surviving textiles offer hints of what has been lost. This makes our understanding of the aesthetics of any region sparse indeed. The choice of material itself would have significant aesthetic and symbolic properties, as noted earlier in discussion of prestige metalwork. For example, the silver-rich jewellery of Illyria has very simple decoration by the standards of Celtic metalwork: the impact of massive pieces of silver is the visually dominant element (Jevtović 1990). It is clear also that decoration was unevenly applied in both material and character: not all items were decorated, and not always with the same styles. A sample of artefacts from the 'long Iron Age' in Pomerania (north-east Germany/north-west Poland) demonstrates this (Table 25.1; Eggers and Stary 2001). Here, only brooches were typically decorated; with all other categories of object decoration was less common or rare, varying from 30–40% of pots and belt hooks to 15% or less for spindle whorls, swords, and spears. Even this seems generous in comparison to other areas: for instance, at the long-lived hillfort settlement of Broxmouth (East Lothian, United Kingdom), only 15 of 190 bone/antler artefacts (8%) were decorated (Figure 25.6; Hunter et al. 2013: 260–261).

Table 25.1 Ratio of decorated to undecorated material culture in Pomerania (Germany/Poland)

Category	Decorated: undecorated	% decorated (of total)	Notes
Brooches	130:28	82%	Various forms of decoration (three-dimensional [occasionally zoomorphic], incised, openwork)
Belt hooks	23:36	39%	
Pots	198:450	31%	
Spindle whorls	5:28	15%	
Swords	3:20	13%	All decorated ones seem to be imports
Spears	3:58	5%	

Calculated from illustrations in Eggers and Stary 2001.

FIGURE 25.6 Bone and antler objects with varying styles of decoration from Broxmouth (East Lothian, Scotland). Left: pin, length 43.6 mm; top right: fastener, height 24 mm; bottom right: offcut from a decorated object, perhaps a handle, height 24.5 mm.

Photos: Neil McLean, © National Museums Scotland

In the later Iron Age across the La Tène cultural zone, prestige metalwork came to carry the complex styles of 'Celtic art' which took up and transformed earlier Iron Age habits, eastern styles, and the naturalistic traditions of Greek art (see Chapter 43). Peter Wells (2012: 201–207) has advocated the need to see this on a broad canvas, placing Celtic art within the much more extensive development of complex art across Eurasia around this time. Most striking is the emergence and development of stylized animal art in the Scythian world in the seventh to fourth centuries BC, influenced both by the Greek world and by wider contacts across the Eurasian steppe, and leading in turn to distinctive Thracian art styles from the fifth century BC onwards (e.g. Sandars 1985: 389–392; Taylor 1987; Gossel-Raeck et al. 1991: 42–151; Aruz et al. 2000).[5] It is likely that these complex art styles were linked to expressions of belief (Megaw and Megaw

2001: 21). They were also restricted, being uncommon finds which often used unusual or exotic materials (such as gold or coral) or special craft skills. It has been tempting to see such art as evidence of elites in the Iron Age, an oversimple view capable of critique (see earlier), but the complex and connected decoration does imply spheres of socially restricted but geographically widespread knowledge. This was not a common habit: only certain groups of people could understand these shared visual languages, but they served to mark their links over large areas.

Early Celtic art was an innovation of particular core areas (north-east France, south-west Germany, Bohemia, and the upper Danube) which was widely adopted and adapted, reaching from the Irish Sea to the Black Sea, and the Mediterranean fringe to Scandinavia. Older scholarship linked this to the idea of large-scale Celtic migrations, but the realities were much more complex. The spread of La Tène-style swords, for instance, which became the dominant form in temperate Europe, is better seen as deliberate adoption of a fashionable type of very effective weapon—the AK47 of the period (Schönfelder 2010: 47). Likewise, La Tène brooch styles were widely emulated. Such visible affiliations marked fashion and contacts, not simply migrations—as seen clearly in the history of La Tène swords in Romania. Here they were adopted as a deliberate signal of wider affiliations in the third century BC, but were abandoned in favour of a local style of curved sword in the later first century BC as powerful groups began to assert their local identity instead (Rustoiu 2007). This serves as a useful reminder of how much it was the idea embodied in an object, whether international or regional, which was key to its use—it was not just a simple marker of the spread of an ethnic group.

Research on Celtic art focuses on a lateral swathe from central France to Hungary, with Britain and Ireland treated as unusual offshoots (though see Farley and Hunter 2015 for a more integrated view). Yet the style influences of Celtic art can be traced widely (e.g. Dobrzańska et al. 2005), and Flemming Kaul (2007) has stressed the need to look beyond any simple idea of Celtic versus Germanic art, emphasizing the importance of considering not just movement of imports but the creation of versions and new forms in the areas north of the 'Celtic' world. Equally, large parts of the continent did not participate extensively in Celtic art (notably much of northern Europe) or developed different styles (such as the Iberian Peninsula; Almagro-Gorbea 1991, 2013). A good example is the late Iron Age painted pottery from Numantia in north-central Spain, with stylized but recognizable humans and animals set in narrative scenes; Marco Simón (2008) took a rather pan-Celtic view of their interpretation, but they make more sense when viewed as versions of more local, specific tales.

With all such decoration, original meaning is hard to approach. Much more profitable is contextual study (e.g. Garrow and Gosden 2012): rather than divorcing art as a separate category, considering objects it appears on, the contexts they occur in, and the relationships embodied.

Conclusions

A topic as broad as this chapter inevitably misses far more than it hits. My aim has been to pick some themes which have relevance beyond any one region or country, to look at recurring problems and possibilities across large areas of the European Iron Age. Often this will be in the sense of analogies rather than direct linkages (for instance, considering the effects of taphonomic bias), but there are large-scale linked themes that touch on big issues in European prehistory, such the development, selective adoption, and adaptation of new technologies, linkages to the Mediterranean world, or the role of art. There are also major areas of research in the archaeology of the everyday: the prosaic tools and other items which are too often ignored beyond the narrow confines of a specialist report, but merit attention in understanding the changing lives of people in the European Iron Age. Here, best practice in other areas and periods allied to comparative work could serve a valuable role in casting fresh light on these fascinating material worlds.

Acknowledgements

I am grateful to the editors for their patience during the extended gestation of this piece and for helpful guidance on content, to Martin Goldberg and Tanja Romankiewicz for comments on an earlier version, and to the Römisch-Germanisches Zentralmuseum Mainz for hospitality which allowed the core of the research to be conducted.

Notes

1. As can be seen in military equipment, which was widely adopted by the Roman army from the 'barbarians' they met. For example, chain mail was an Iron Age innovation, while Roman cavalry harness was adopted from the Gauls (Bishop 1988: 112–116; Stead 1991: 56).
2. Much Iron Age inlay work is glass rather than enamel. The glass was heated to soften it, pushed into place, and held mechanically, for example by the form of the cell or a rivet; enamel was fused to the substrate.
3. One could also consider the creation of local coinages from Mediterranean models, and the episodic development of naturalistic stone sculpture in Mediterranean-influenced areas such as southern Germany, southern France, and southern Spain. These influences were not just taken on wholesale, but were transformed for local needs.
4. There are notable exceptions, such as the *oppida* of Stradonice, Czech Republic, and Velem St Vid, Hungary, while the site museum at Ensérune, France, contains a remarkable wealth of worked bone, little of it published (Píč 1906: pls XLII–XLVIII; von Miske 1908: Taf. 4–8; Gallet de Santerre 1980: 143–144, pls 39–40).
5. At the time of writing this is the focus of a major Leverhulme-funded project, *European Celtic Art in Context*, led by Professor Chris Gosden at Oxford University, which is expected to cast significant new light on the topic.

References

Adams, J. L. 2002. *Ground Stone Analysis: A Technological Approach*. Salt Lake City: University of Utah Press.

Allen, D. F. 1980. *The Coins of the Ancient Celts*. Edinburgh: Edinburgh University Press.

Almagro-Gorbea, M. 1991. 'The Celts of the Iberian peninsula', in S. Moscati, O.-H. Frey, V. Kruta, B. Raftery, and M. Szabó (eds) *The Celts*: 388–405. Milan: Bompiani.

Almagro-Gorbea, M. 2013. 'L'art des oppida celtiques de la péninsule Ibérique', in S. Krausz, A. Colin, K. Gruel, I. Ralston, and T. Dechezleprêtre (eds) *L'Âge du Fer en Europe. Mélanges offerts à Olivier Buchsenschutz*: 595–607. Bordeaux: Ausonius.

Andersson, K. 1995. *Romartida guldsmide i norden III. AUN 21*. Uppsala: Uppsala University.

Armbruster, B. 2013. 'Les techniques de l'orfèvrerie orientalisante: un case de transfert technologique au début de l'Âge du Fer', in L. Callegarin and A. Gorgues (eds) *Les transferts de technologie au premier millénaire av. J.-C. dans le Sud-Ouest de l'Europe*. Mélanges de la Casa de Velázquez nouvelle série 43-1: 65–83. Madrid: Casa de Velázquez.

Armit, I. 2008. 'Irish-Scottish connections in the first millennium AD: An evaluation of the links between souterrain ware and Hebridean ceramics'. *Proceedings of the Royal Irish Academy* 108C: 1–18.

Aruz, J., A. Farkas, A. Alekseev, and E. Korolkova (eds). 2000. *The Golden Deer of Eurasia: Scythian and Sarmatian Treasures from the Russian Steppes*. New York: Metropolitan Museum of Art.

Augier, L., A. Baron, A. Filippini, P.-Y. Milcent, B. Pescher, and M. Salin. 2009. 'Les activités artisanales de la fin du VIe et du Ve s. av. J-C attestées sur le site de Bourges (Cher)', in O. Buchsenschutz, M.-B. Chardenoux, S. Krausz, and M. Vaginay (eds) *L'âge du Fer dans la boucle de la Loire: Les Gaulois sont dans la ville*. Revue Archéologique du Centre de la France supplément 35: 39–66. Paris/Tours: FERACF.

Ballin Smith, B. 1994. *Howe: Four Millennia of Orkney Prehistory*. Edinburgh: Society of Antiquaries of Scotland.

Baron, A. 2012. *Provenance et circulation des objets en roches noires ('lignite') à l'âge du Fer en Europe celtique (VIIIème–Ier s av J-C)*. British Archaeological Reports International Series 2453. Oxford: Archaeopress.

Barril Vicente, M. 2002. 'Los torques de plata más representativos an el Museo Arqueológico Nacional', in M. Barril Vicente and A. Romero Riaza (eds) *Torques, belleza y poder*: 111–128. Madrid: Museo Arqueológico Nacional.

Behm-Blancke, G. 2003. *Heiligtümer der Germanen und ihrer Vorgänger in Thüringen. Die Kultstätte Oberdorla. Forschungen zum alteuropäischen Religions- und Kultwesen*. Stuttgart: Theiss.

Bishop, M. C. 1988. 'Cavalry equipment of the Roman army in the first century AD', in J. C. Coulston (ed.) *Military Equipment and the Identity of Roman Soldiers*. British Archaeological Reports International Series 394: 67–195. Oxford: Archaeopress.

Bochnak, T. 2013. 'Przyczyny zaniku ceramiki toczonej na ziemiach polskich w początkach i wieku po chr.—zapomniany sekret, uwarunkowania społeczno-psychologiczne czy czynniki ekonomiczne? (The decline of wheel-turned pottery in the territory of Poland in early 1st century AD—a forgotten secret, social-psychological circumstances or economic factors?)'. *Wiadomści Archeologiczne* 64: 85–95.

Bradley, R. 1990. *The Passage of Arms: An Archaeological Analysis of Prehistoric Hoards and Votive Deposits*. Cambridge: Cambridge University Press.

Carter, S., F. Hunter, and A. Smith. 2010. 'A 5th century BC Iron Age chariot burial from Newbridge, Edinburgh'. *Proceedings of the Prehistoric Society* 76: 31–74.

Challet, V. 1992. *Les Celtes et l'émail*. Section de préhistoire et de protohistoire 3. Paris: Comité des travaux historiques et scientifique.

Čižmářová, J. 1996. 'Bernstein auf dem keltischen Oppidum Staré Hradisko in Mähren'. *Arheološki vestnik* 47: 173–182.

Clarke, D. V. 1971. 'Small finds in the Atlantic province: problems of approach'. *Scottish Archaeological Forum* 3: 22–54.

Colin, A., C. Sireix, and F. Verdin. 2011. *Gaulois d'Aquitaine*. Bordeaux: Ausonius.

Colonna, G., L. Franchi Dell'Orlo, and P. Marchegiani. 2001. *Piceni: popolo d'Europa*. Rome: De Luca Editore.

Crouwel, J. H. 2011. *Chariots and Other Wheeled Vehicles in Italy before the Roman Empire*. Oxford: Oxbow.

Daire, M.-Y., H. Hautenauve, E. Le Bozec, K. Le Nagard, and F. Nedelec. 2001. 'Un complexe artisanale de l'âge du Fer à Enez Vihan en Pleumeur-Bodou, Côtes d'Armor'. *Revue archéologique de l'Ouest* 18: 57–93.

de Marinis, R. C., and S. Biaggio Simona. 2000. *I Leponti: tra mito e realità*. Locarno: Gruppo Archeologia Ticino.

de Marinis, R. C., and G. Spadea (eds). 2004. *I Liguri: Un antico popolo europeo tra Alpi e Mediterraneo*. Geneva/Milan: Skira.

Defente, V. 2012. 'Red glass in Iron Age continental Europe: Technical innovation and technological transfer', in A. Kern, J. K. Koch, I. Balzer, J. Fries-Knoblach, K. Kowarik, C. Later, P. C. Ramsl, P. Trebsche, and J. Wiethold (eds) *Technologieentwicklung und -transfer in der Eisenzeit: Bericht der Internationalen Tagung der AG Eisenzeit und des Naturhistorischen Museums, Prähistorische Abteilung—Hallstatt 2009*. Beiträge zur Ur- und Frühgeschichte Mitteleuropas 65: 219–225. Langenweissbach: Beier und Beran.

Desenne, S., G. Auxiette, J.-P. Demoule, S. Gaudefroy, B. Henon, S. Thouvenot, and T. Lejars. 2009. 'Dépôts, panoplies et accessoires dans les sépultures du Second Âge du Fer en Picardie'. *Revue Archéologique de Picardie* 2009, 3–4: 173–186.

Diepeveen-Jansen, M. 2001. *People, Ideas and Goods: New Perspectives on 'Celtic Barbarians' in Western and Central Europe (500–250 BC)*. Amsterdam Archaeological Studies 7. Amsterdam: Amsterdam University Press.

Dobrzańska, H., V. Megaw, and P. Poleska (eds). 2005. *Celts on the Margin: Studies in European Cultural Interaction, 7th century BC–1st century AD, Dedicated to Zenon Woźniak*. Krakow: Institute of Archaeology and Ethnology of the Polish Academy of Sciences.

Durand, R., D. Germinet, P. Maçon, and M. Salin. 2012. 'Les vestiges osseux', in L. Augier, O. Buchsenschutz, R. Durand et al. (eds) *Bourges—un complexe princier de l'âge du Fer: le quartier artisanal de Port Sec Sud à Bourges (Cher)*. Revue Archéologique du Centre de la France supplément 41: 71–118. Bourges/Tours: Bourges Plus, FERACF.

Eggers, H. J., and P. Stary. 2001. *Funde der vorrömischen Eisenzeit, der römischen Kaiserzeit und der Völkerwanderungszeit in Pommern*. Lübsow: Archäologisches Landesmuseum für Mecklenburg-Vorpommern.

Evans, C. 1989. 'Perishables and worldly goods—artefact decoration and classification in the light of wetlands research'. *Oxford Journal of Archaeology* 8: 179–201.

Farley, J., and F. Hunter (eds). 2015. *Celts: Art and identity*. London: British Museum/National Museums Scotland.

Fol, A. N., B. N. Tsvetkov, G. I. Mihailov, I. Y. Venedikov, and I. R. Marazov. 1989. *The Rogozen Treasure*. Sofia: Bulgarian Academy of Sciences.

Gallet de Santerre, H. 1980. *Ensérune: les silos de la terrasse est*. Gallia supplément 39. Paris: Éditions du CNRS.

García Vuelta, O. 2002. 'Los torques áureos más representativos del Museo Arqueológico Nacional', in M. Barril Vicente and A. Romero Riaza (eds) *Torques, belleza y poder*: 97–111. Madrid: Museo Arqueológico Nacional.

Garrow, D., and C. Gosden. 2012. *Technologies of Enchantment? Exploring Celtic Art in Britain 400 BC to AD 100*. Oxford: Oxford University Press.

Gaudefroy, S., F. Malrain, and C. Pommepuy. 2006. 'L'outillage et la parure'. *Revue Archéologique de Picardie Numéro spécial* 23: 147–178.

Gaudefroy, S., E. Pinard, and F. Malrain. 2006. 'Le vaisselier de La Tène ancienne à La Tène finale'. *Revue Archéologique de Picardie Numéro spécial 23* : 101–146.

Gossel-Raeck, B., B. Kaeser, B. Vierneisel-Schlörb, and K. Vierneisel (eds). 1991. *L'or des Scythes: Trésors de l'Ermitage, Leningrad*. Brussels: Musées Royaux d'Art et d'Histoire.

Govignon, B. 1997. *Les Ibères*. Barcelona: Lunwerg.

Guštin, M., and L. Pauli (eds). 1984. *Keltski Voz*. Brežice: Posavski Muzej Brežice.

Haffner, A. 1976. *Die westliche Hunsrück-Eifel-Kultur*. Römisch-Germanische Forschungen 36. Berlin: De Gruyter.

Hallén, Y. 1994. 'The use of bone and antler at Foshigarry and Bac Mhic Connain, two Iron Age sites on North Uist, Western Isles'. *Proceedings of the Society of Antiquaries of Scotland* 124: 189–231.

Hautenauve, H. 2005. *Les torques d'or du second Âge du Fer en Europe: techniques, typologies et symbolique*. Rennes: Association des Travaux du Laboratoire d'Anthropologie de l'Université de Rennes 1.

Hegewisch, M. 2007. 'Ceramica modelată la roată din vestul Germanei Magna şi paralele ei în cadrul culturii Sântana de Mureş-Černeahov (Germanische Drehscheibenkeramik im western der Germania Magna und die Sântana de Mureş-Černjachov Kulture)'. *Ephemeris Napocensis* 16–17: 177–225.

Heynowski, R. 2000. *Die Wendelringe der späten Bronze- und der frühen Eisenzeit*. Bonn: Habelt.

Hill, J. D. 1995. *Ritual and Rubbish in the Iron Age of Wessex*. British Archaeological Reports British Series 242. Oxford: Archaeopress.

Hill, J. D. 2006. 'Are we any closer to understanding how later Iron Age societies worked (or did not work)?', in C. Haselgrove (ed.) *Celtes et Gaulois: l'Archéologie face à l'Histoire. Les mutations de la fin de l'âge du Fer. Actes de la table ronde de Cambridge, 7–8 juillet 2005*. Collection Bibracte 12/4: 169–179. Glux-en-Glenne: Centre archéologique européen du Mont Beuvray.

Hill, J. D., A. Spence, S. La Niece, and S. Worrell. 2004. 'The Winchester hoard: a find of unique Iron Age gold jewellery from southern England'. *The Antiquaries Journal* 84: 1–22.

Hunter, F. 1998. 'Iron', in L. Main, 'Excavation of a timber round-house and broch at the Fairy Knowe, Buchlyvie, Stirlingshire, 1975–78'. *Proceedings of the Society of Antiquaries of Scotland* 128: 356–367 [293–417].

Hunter, F. 2015. 'Craft in context: Artifact production in later prehistoric Scotland', in F. Hunter and I. Ralston (eds) *Scotland in Later Prehistoric Europe*: 225–246. Edinburgh: Society of Antiquaries of Scotland.

Hunter, F., A.-M. Gibson, and J. Gerken. 2013. 'Worked bone and antler', in I. Armit and J. McKenzie (eds) *An Inherited Place: Broxmouth Hillfort and the South-East Scottish Iron Age*: 251–309. Edinburgh: Society of Antiquaries of Scotland.

Hurcombe, L. M. 2014. *Perishable Material Culture in Prehistory: Investigating the Missing Majority*. London: Routledge.

Jaccottey, L., N. Alonso, S. Defressigne, C. Hamon, S. Lepareux-Coutourier, V. Brisotto, et al. 2013. 'Le passage des meules va-et-vient aux meules rotatives en France', in S. Krausz, A. Colin, K. Gruel, I. Ralston, and T. Dechezleprêtre (eds) *L'Âge du Fer en Europe. Mélanges offerts à Olivier Buchsenschutz*: 405–419. Bordeaux: Ausonius.

Jacobi, G. 1974. *Werkzeug und Gerät aus dem Oppidum von Manching*. Die Ausgrabungen in Manching 5. Wiesbaden: Steiner.

Jensen, J. 2013. *The Prehistory of Denmark: From the Stone Age to the Vikings*. Copenhagen: Gyldendal.

Jevtović, J. (ed.) 1990. *Masters of Silver: The Iron Age of Serbia*. Belgrade: National Museum.

Jimeno Martínez, A. (ed.) 2005. *Celtíberos: Tras la estela de Numancia*. Soria: Museo Numantio de Sorio.

Joachim, H.-E. 2002. *Porz-Lind. Ein Mittel- bis spätlatènezeitlicher Siedlungsplatz im 'Linder Bruch' (Stadt Köln)*. Rheinische Ausgrabungen 47. Mainz: Philipp von Zabern.

Joy, J. 2011. '"Fancy objects" in the British Iron Age: why decorate?'. *Proceedings of the Prehistoric Society* 77: 205–229.

Karl, R. 1996. *Latènezeitliche Siedlungen in Niederösterreich: Untersuchungen zu Fundtypen, Keramikchronologie, Bautypen, Siedlungstypen und Besiedlungstrukturen*. Historica Austria 2. Vienna: Österreichischer Archäologie Bund.

Kaul, F. 1991. 'The ball torques. Celtic art outside the Celtic world', in S. Moscati, O.-H. Frey, V. Kruta, B. Raftery, and M. Szabó (eds) *The Celts*: 540. Milan: Bompiani.

Kaul, F. 2007. 'Celtic influences during pre-Roman Iron Age in Denmark', in S. Möllers, W. Schlüter, and S. Sievers (eds) *Keltische Einflüsse im nördlichen Mitteleuropa während der mittleren und jüngeren vorrömischen Eisenzeit. Akten des Internationalen Kolloquiums in Osnabrück vom 29. März bis 1. April 2006*. Kolloquien zur Vor- und Frühgeschichte 9: 327–345. Bonn: Habelt.

Krausz, S. 2000. 'L'exploitation des matières animaux: objets et déchets artisanaux', in O. Buchsenschutz, A. Colin, G. Firmin, B. Fischer, J.-P. Guillaumet, S. Krausz, et al. (eds) *Le village celtique des Arènes à Levroux: Synthèses. Levroux 5*. Revue archéologique du Centre de la France supplément 19: 131–140. Levroux: FERACF/Association pour la défense et l'étude du canton de Levroux.

Künzl, E. 2012. 'Enamelled vessels of Roman Britain', in D. J. Breeze (ed.) *The First Souvenirs: Enamelled Vessels from Hadrian's Wall*: 9–22. Kendal: Cumberland and Westmorland Antiquarian and Archaeological Society.

Lang, V. 2007. *The Bronze and Early Iron Ages in Estonia*. Estonian Archaeology 3. Tartu: Tartu University Press.

Malrain, F. 2006. 'Les "dépots" d'objets dans l'habitat'. *Revue Archéologique de Picardie Numéro spécial 23* : 238.

Marazov, I. (ed.) 1998. *Ancient Gold: The Wealth of the Thracians: Treasures from the Republic of Bulgaria*. New York: Harry N. Abrams.

Marco Simón, F. 2008. 'Images of transition: The ways of death in Celtic Hispania'. *Proceedings of the Prehistoric Society* 74: 53–68.

Megaw, J. V. S., and R. Megaw. 1990. *The Basse-Yutz Find: Masterpieces of Celtic Art*. London: Society of Antiquaries of London.

Megaw, R., and J. V. S. Megaw. 2001. *Celtic Art: From its Beginnings to the Book of Kells*, 2nd edition. London: Thames and Hudson.

Moscati, S., O.-H. Frey, V. Kruta, B. Raftery, and M. Szabó (eds) 1991. *The Celts*. Milan: Bompiani.

Müller, F. (ed.) 2009. *Art of the Celts 700 BC to AD 700*. Bern: Bernisches Historisches Museum.

Müller, R., and H. Steuer (eds). 2011. 'Fibel und Fibeltracht', in *Reallexikon der Germanischen Altertumskunde 8*: 411–607. Berlin: De Gruyter.

Nava, M. L. 2011. 'Die jahrtausendealte Tradition des Bernsteins', in R. Gebhard, F. Martzatico, and P. Gleirscher (eds) *Im Licht des Südens: Begegnungen antiker Kulturen zwischen Mittelmeer und Zentraleuropa*: 40–49. Munich: Archäologische Staatssammlung.

Neugebauer, J.-W. 1996. 'Eine frühlatènezeitliche Gräbergruppe in Inzersdorf ob der Traisen, NÖ', in E. Jerem, A. Krenn-Leeb, J.-W. Neugebauer, and O. H. Urban (eds) *Die Kelten in den Alpen und an der Donau: Akten des internationalen Symposions, St Pölten, 14.–18. Oktober 1992. Studien zur Eisenzeit im Ostalpenraum*: 111–178. Budapest: Archaeolingua.

Olsen, S. L. 2003. 'The bone and antler artefacts: Their manufacture and use', in N. Field and M. Parker Pearson (eds) *Fiskerton: An Iron Age Timber Causeway with Iron Age and Roman Votive Offerings, the 1981 Excavations*: 92–111. Oxford: Oxbow.

Pare, C. F. E. 1992. *Wagons and Wagon-Graves of the Early Iron Age in Central Europe*. OUCA Monograph 35. Oxford: Oxford University Committee for Archaeology.

Pauli, L. 1975. *Keltischer Volksglaube: Amulette und Sonderbestattungen am Dürrnberg bei Hallein und im eisenzeitlichen Mitteleuropa*. Münchner Beiträge zur Vor- und Frühgeschichte 28. Munich: Beck.

Peacock, D. 2013. *The Stone of Life: Querns, Mills and Flour Production in Europe up to c. AD 500*. Southampton: Highfield Press.

Pescher, B. 2012. 'L'instrumentum', in L. Augier, O. Buchsenschutz, R. Durand, et al. (eds) *Bourges—un complexe princier de l'âge du Fer: le quartier artisanal de Port Sec Sud à Bourges (Cher)*. Revue Archéologique du Centre de la France supplément 41: 119–155. Bourges/Tours: Bourges Plus, FERACF.

Píč, J.-L. 1906. *Le Hradischt de Stradonitz en Bohême* (trans. J. Déchelette). Leipzig: Hiersemann.

Piggott, S. 1983. *The Earliest Wheeled Transport: From the Atlantic Coast to the Caspian Sea*. London: Thames and Hudson.

Pion, P., and V. Guichard. 1993. 'Tombes et nécropoles en France et au Luxembourg entre le IIIème et le Ier siècles avant J.-C. Essai d'inventaire', in D. Cliquet, M. Remy-Watt, V. Guichard, and M. Vaginay (eds) *Les Celtes en Normandie: Les Rites Funéraires en Gaule (IIIème–Ier siècle avant J.-C.)*. Revue Archéologique de l'Ouest supplément 6: 175–200. Rennes: Association RAO.

Poissonnier, B. 2002. 'Pilons, broyeurs, bouchardes, marteaux et autres percuteurs: les interprétations fonctionnelles au risque de l'expérimentation', in H. Procopiou and R. Treuil (eds) *Moudre et broyer: L'interprétation fonctionnelle de l'outillage de mouture et de broyage dans la Préhistoire et l'Antiquité. I: Méthodes*: 141–152. Paris: CTHS.

Raftery, B. 1995. 'The conundrum of Irish Iron Age pottery', in B. Raftery, V. Megaw, and V. Rigby (eds) *Sites and Sights of the Iron Age: Essays on Fieldwork and Museum Research Presented to Ian Mathieson Stead*: 149–156. Oxford: Oxbow.

Ramsl, P. C. 1998. *Inzersdorf—Walpersdorf. Studien zur späthallstatt-latènezeitlichen Besiedlung im Traisental, Niederösterreich*. Fundberichte aus Österreich Materialheft A6. Vienna: Bundesdenkmalamt.

Rigby, V. 2004. *Pots in Pits: The British Museum Yorkshire Settlements Project 1988–92*. East Riding Archaeologist 11. Hull: East Riding Archaeological Society.

Roes, A. 1963. *Bone and Antler Objects from the Frisian Terp-mounds*. Haarlem: H. D. Tjeenk Willink & Son.

Rosenberg. 1937. *Hjortspringfudnet. Nordiske Fortidsminder III, Bind 1*. Copenhagen: Nordisk Forlag.

Rudenko, S. I. 1970. *Frozen Tombs of Siberia: The Pazyryk Burials of Iron Age Horsemen*. London: J. M. Dent and Sons.

Rustoiu, A. 2007. 'Thracian sica and Dacian falx. The history of a "national" weapon', in S. Nemeti, F. Fodorean, E. Nemeth, S. Cociş, I. Nemeti, and M. Pîslaru (eds) *Dacia Felix: studia Michaeli Bărbulescu oblate*: 67–82. Cluj-Napoca: Editura Tribuna.

Sandars, N. K. 1985. *Prehistoric Art in Europe*, 2nd edition. New Haven/London: Yale University Press.

Schönfelder, M. 2010. 'Keltische Wanderungen—welche Modelle bleiben bestehen?', in M. Schönfelder (ed.) *Kelten! Kelten? Keltische Spuren in Italien: Mosaiksteine. Forschungen am Römisch-Germanischen Zentralmuseum*: 46–48. Mainz: Römisch-Germanisches Zentralmuseum.

Schönfelder, M. 2012. 'L'Âge du fer: vue d'ensemble', in A. Testart (ed.) *Les armes dans les eaux: questions d'interprétation en archéologie*: 97–105. Paris: Errance.

Schorer, B. 2012. 'Filigran und Granulation. Mediterrane Techniken', in R. Röber et al. (eds) *Die Welt der Kelten: Zentren der Macht—Kostbarkeiten der Kunst. Ausstellungskatalog Stuttgart 2012*: 229. Sigmaringen: Thorbecke.

Sharples, N. 2008. 'Comment I. Contextualising Iron Age art', in D. Garrow, C. Gosden, and J. D. Hill (eds) *Rethinking Celtic Art*: 203–213. Oxford: Oxbow.

Spânu, D. 2012. *Tezaurele dacice. Creaţia în metale preţioase din Dacia preromană*. Bucharest: Editura Simetria.

Stead, I. M. 1991. *Iron Age Cemeteries in East Yorkshire*. English Heritage Archaeological Report 22. London: English Heritage.

Struckmeyer, K. 2011. *Die Knochen- und Geweihgeräte der Feddersen Wierde*. Rahden: Marie Leidorf.

Szabo, M. 1975. 'Sur la question du filigrane dans l'art des Celtes orientaux', in J. Fitz (ed.) *The Celts in Central Europe*: 147–165. Székesfehérvár: Szent Istvan Kiraly Museum.

Taylor, T. 1987. 'Flying stags: Icons and power in Thracian art', in I. Hodder (ed.) *The Archaeology of Contextual Meaning*: 117–132. Cambridge: Cambridge University Press.

Tempelmann-Mączyńska, M. 1985. *Die Perlen der römischen Kaiserzeit und der frühen Phase der Völkerwanderungszeit im mitteleuropäischen Barbaricum*. Mainz: Philipp von Zabern/ Römisch-Germanische Kommission.

Tomo, N. 2012. 'Steingeräte eisenzeitlicher Verhüttungsplätze in Neuenbürg-Waldrennach (Enzkreis, Deutschland)', in A. Kern, J. K. Koch, I. Balzer, et al. (eds) *Technologieentwicklung und -transfer in der Eisenzeit. Bericht der Internationalen Tagung der AG Eisenzeit und des Naturhistorischen Museums, Prähistorische Abteilung—Hallstatt*: 171–172. Langenweissbach: Beier und Beran.

Van den Broeke, P. 2005. 'Blacksmiths and potters. Material culture and technology', in L. L. P. Kooijmans, P. W. van Den Broeke, H. Fokkens, and A. L. van Gijn (eds) *The Prehistory of the Netherlands*: 603–625. Amsterdam: Amsterdam University Press.

Vasić, R., V. Krstić, M. Tapavički-Ilić, P. Popović, and T. Bader. 2004. *Silber der Illyrer und Kelten im Zentralbalken*. Eberdingen: Keltenmuseum Hochdorf.

Venclová, N. 1990. *Prehistoric Glass in Bohemia*. Prague: Institute of Archaeology of the Czech Academy of Sciences.

Venclová, N. 1998. 'Black materials in the Iron Age of central Europe', in F. Müller (ed.) *Münsingen-Rain, ein Markstein der keltischen Archäologie*. Schriften des Bernischen Historischen Museums 2: 287–298. Bern: Bernisches Historisches Museum.

Venedikov, I. 1976. *Thracian Treasures from Bulgaria*. London: British Museum.

Von Freeden, U., and S. von Schnurbein (eds). 2006. *Germanica: unsere Vorfahren von der Steinzeit bis zum Mittelalter*. Augsburg: Weltbild.

Von Miske, K. 1908. *Die prähistorische Ansiedlung Velem St. Vid. I. Band: Beschreibung der Raubbaufunde*. Vienna: Carl Konegen.

Webley, L. 2008. *Iron Age Households*. Højbjerg: Jysk Arkæologisk Selskab.

Wefers, S. 2011. 'Still using your saddle quern? A compilation of the oldest known rotary querns in western Europe', in D. Williams and D. Peacock (eds) *Bread for the People: The Archaeology of Mills and Milling*: 67–76. Oxford: Archaeopress.

Wells, P. S. 2008. *Image and Response in Early Europe*. Duckworth Debates in Archaeology. London: Duckworth.

Wells, P. S. 2012. *How Ancient Europeans Saw the World: Vision, Patterns, and the Shaping of the Mind in Prehistoric Times*. Princeton: Princeton University Press.

Wells, P. S. 2016. 'Special pit deposits on late La Tène settlements. A case study at the oppidum of Kelheim'. *Archäologisches Korrespondenzblatt* 46: 89–100.

CHAPTER 26

TEXTILES AND PERISHABLE MATERIALS

JOHANNA BANCK-BURGESS

Introduction: History of Research

The distribution of textile finds of the pre-Roman Iron Age is uneven, being geographically and chronologically extremely dependent on the prevailing conditions for the preservation of textiles, when the textiles were excavated and studied, and which research approach was followed. A comprehensive discussion of the textile craft in the European Iron Age cannot be attempted in the current state of knowledge. Furthermore, a handful of unique assemblages such as the textiles from the Danish bogs, the precious fabrics from the late Hallstatt burial of Hochdorf in south-western Germany, the finds from the Austrian salt mines, or those of the Villanovan burials of Verucchio or Sasso di Furbara in Italy, would dominate the discussion. Given that most textiles are preserved on the corroded surfaces of metal grave goods, it follows that cultural areas, which are characterized by cremations or by burials with few or modest grave goods, for example the Jastorf culture of northern Germany, are underrepresented.

The intensity of research investment, directly linked to spectacular finds, is also relevant in terms of finds density and level of analysis. An excellent example is provided by the long tradition of research in Denmark, recently consolidated by an interdisciplinary research project established at the University of Copenhagen (Research Programme of the Danish National Research Foundation's Centre for Textile Research, CTR). The textiles from the Danish bog sites and from the weapon deposits of the pre-Roman and Roman Iron Age form its core since 2006. Of special note for central Europe is the work of Hans-Jürgen Hundt at the Römisch-Germanisches Zentralmuseum in Mainz, which laid the foundations for research on Iron Age textiles. His preliminary reports and the exceptional finds from the Hochdorf burial marked a turning point in establishing the discipline of textile archaeology in the State Office for the Conservation of Monuments (*Landesamt für Denkmalpflege*) of Baden-Württemberg at Esslingen. Similarly, there is a focus on textile archaeology at the Natural History Museum in Vienna, built around the Bronze and Iron Age textiles from the salt mines of Hallstatt and the Dürrnberg (Bichler et al. 2005; Grömer 2005, 2012; Kern et al. 2008). Countries from which there have been few publications of Iron Age finds documenting the textile craft and its products are underrepresented in research and can therefore hardly be assessed for Iron Age textile manufacture as a whole.

It is not without reason that the most recent comprehensive study of prehistoric—predominantly Iron Age—textiles in Europe (Gleba and Mannering 2012), organized by country, contains entries for Austria, Denmark, Greece, Italy, Latvia, Norway, Poland, the Slovak and Czech Republics, Spain, Sweden, Switzerland, Ukraine, the United Kingdom, and Ireland, but none for the Netherlands, Belgium, France, or Hungary. Even in countries where textile manufacture has been studied intensively—for example, Poland—the Iron Age evidence can only be outlined with difficulty (Maik 2012). A single complex, like the princely burial of Hochdorf, can form the basis for far-reaching conclusions about the culturally specific meaning of textiles and textile manufacture, which countless single finds can hardly provide. Blank areas in the distribution of finds or gaps in research history must therefore be treated with caution when discussing the history of textiles. Quite often they hide precious information, whose value is only now being realized, researched, and published, for example the textiles from the Villanovan graves of Verucchio in Italy. The enormous expansion of textile archaeology over the past fifteen years, which has catapulted textile research from a niche discipline into the realm of fundamental, culturally relevant research objectives in archaeology, as well as raised completely new questions, was determined to a large degree by a close interdisciplinary collaboration with the natural sciences.

Apart from aspects of distribution, it is mainly the approach and research focus of individual specialists that set the agenda when presenting material. Lise Bender Jørgensen, in her presentation of the Iron Age textile finds from Scandinavia (1986) and the whole of Europe (1992, 2005), emphasizes the way textiles were made (materials, types of weave, and thread twist), an approach that can be criticized from a methodological viewpoint (Hägg 1985; Bender Jørgensen 1987). Comparable presentations of finds, which barely touch on their context, exist as appendices by Hans-Jürgen Hundt in numerous site reports, cited by Bender Jørgensen (1992). Based on the technical characteristics that she defined, Bender Jørgensen identified a series of textile types from which chronologically and regionally different distribution areas can be outlined. In their re-examination of older Danish bog finds dated to the Iron Age, Margarita Gleba and Ulla Mannering put the acquisition of information through scientific analyses, including data on the provenance of the wool and the processes involved in dyeing, as well as questions of context interpretation and research into clothing, at the centre of their investigations.

In her research on the Hochdorf princely burial and its Iron Age textiles, Johanna Banck-Burgess (1999) gave prominence to the context of the assemblage, concentrating on the practical function and meaning that connected the burial with its fabrics. Iconographic sources were at the core of the publication by Katharina von Kurzynski (1996) on Celtic textile craft and clothing, while Antoinette Rast-Eicher (2008) highlighted the importance of analysing fibres, in this case wool fibres, in her study of

Iron Age textiles from Switzerland. A comprehensive compilation of the investigations of a number of disciplines exists in Karina Grömer's book on the textile art of central Europe (2010, 2016): her evaluation of the Iron Age textile craft gives equal weight to the textiles and the equipment needed to make them, to the various results of scientific analyses and culture-historical enquiries, and to the insights offered by experimental archaeology. For textiles and clothing of the Roman Iron Age, not considered here, the recent publication, which is mainly based on the international research project 'DressID—Clothing and Identities: New Perspectives on Textiles in the Roman Empire', offers the newest results (Tellenbach et al. 2013). This European project, carried out by the Reiss-Engelhorn Museum in Mannheim between 2007 and 2012, put a special accent on interdisciplinary research.

Of course one would not do justice to the craft of making textiles if treatment of the subject was restricted to weaving and production; this will however largely be the case here, given the sources available. Indeed it leaves out not only the countless processes involved in making textiles known from the Neolithic onwards, but also the representations of their use in daily life as containers, strainers, nets, or backing materials (Banck-Burgess 2005; Grömer 2016; Gleba and Mannering 2012). Because of the light weight, flexibility, durability and enormous adaptability of products made from textile raw materials—i.e. tree bark, wool, and linen in our context—there was probably no other group of material employed as frequently as textiles (Banck-Burgess 2005, 375–376). The amount of information available on European Iron Age textiles which are not counted among woven fabrics, such as sprang, a kind of warp-twining (Hald 1980, 240–277), found preserved among the Danish bog finds, is slight and will only marginally be considered here. The fact that some production techniques are missing from the record may be due to gaps in research, a fact well illustrated by an example from Spain. Finds published from that country include the very fine wicker lining of a helmet and fishing containers (creels and baskets) from the Greek shipwreck of Cala San Vicenc (Pollensa, Majorca) dated to *c.*520 BC (Alfaro Giner 2011; 2012: 341), as well as the remains of fishing nets like the fine fourth-century BC hemp net from La Albufereta (Alicante; Alfaro Giner 2010, 2012: 342, fig. 16.11.). Finally, while proof for everyday textiles is largely missing, the textiles from high-status contexts, such as the precious fabrics and prestige textiles from the late Hallstatt cultural sphere, or contemporary examples from Eurasia, indicate how much influence textiles exerted in the Iron Age.

Textile Craft

Equipment and Looms

Among the instruments and looms used for producing textiles, the largest group of objects is formed by the spindle whorls and finds associated with warp-weighted looms. While spindle whorls occur in burials as well as in settlements, significant evidence for looms is found exclusively in settlements. Weaving equipment was often showcased in early textile research (von Kimakowicz-Winnicki 1910; von Stokar 1938), as little attention was paid to the remains of textiles preserved on the corroded surfaces of metal grave goods. Equipment used in textile manufacture occurs mainly in female burials of the early Iron Age east and north of the Alps, in equal proportions in cremations and inhumations. Investigations at the cemetery of Satzendorf in Lower Austria, dated to between 800 and 600 BC, show that spindle whorls and sewing needles are present in graves of all social classes (Rebay 2006). Margarita Gleba has demonstrated the importance of the presence of implements to prove the existence of textile production, especially in the Italian area (Gleba 2008: 159), where they start to appear in the Orientalizing and Archaic periods (Gleba 2008: 183–187, 2012: 237). She suggests that in Italy the large number of standardized tools used in textile manufacture during the Orientalizing (750 to 600 BC) and Archaic (650 to 450 BC) periods points to increasing specialization, in stark contrast to the Bronze Age, when weaving was confined to the domestic sphere (Gleba 2003, 2012: 237). Poggio Civitate di Murlo can be cited as an example of increasing specialization (Gleba 2008: 197). Detailed evidence for the production of textiles in the third to second century BC was gathered by Francesco Meo (2011), based on loom weights found in individual houses in the city of Heraclea in southern Italy.

Evidence for equipment used in textile manufacture begins to decrease markedly in some parts of central Europe from the fourth century BC onwards, a situation that is however primarily linked to the decrease in the number of graves, and therefore grave goods. So, for example, the number of inhumations dating to the fourth to second centuries BC found in southern Germany is generally very small compared with the corresponding number of settlements. Unusual inhumations, such as those from the *oppidum* of Manching (Dobiat et al. 2003; Sievers 2003), suggest that only a small proportion of the population received a form of burial that is recognizable today.

While the products of the weaving shed are to be found predominantly as grave goods, production can also be traced in settlements. Loom weights and examples of starting edges on fabrics bear witness to the presence of warp-weighted looms. Other types of loom, or simpler weaving equipment, which must surely have been used for making narrow weaves, have not been documented on settlements. Specific types of loops found in textiles from Denmark and northern Germany suggest that circular looms were used (Hald 1980; Gleba and Mannering 2012; Möller-Wiering 2012). Loom weights, which are taken to prove the presence of warp-weighted looms, are absent from the settlements of this region (Bender Jørgensen 1992: 120–122). Instances from more southerly regions where the fallen loom weights are found *in situ* still in rows allow us to gain a better impression of the width of warp-weighted looms. Examples from Austria and Slovakia indicate widths of between 60 and 90 cm, and 120 and 160 cm (Belanová-Stolcová and Grömer 2010: 15–17).

An assemblage from the Hallstatt settlement of Nové Košariská in Slovakia suggests that production was on a domestic scale, with loom weights from one house indicating that there were two looms of different widths standing at right angles to each other (Grömer 2010: 119). Instances of looms over 3 m wide also seem to concentrate in the eastern Hallstatt area. Thus the find from the hilltop 'princely seat' of Kleinklein in Austria (Dobiat 1990), which had long been considered a unique instance of the production of prestige textiles, is no longer an isolated case. The Hallstatt period lowland settlement of Hafnerbach in Lower Austria has also produced loom weights laid out in a 4 m-long double row (Preinfalk 2004: 17, fig. 12). To date, little is known about the use of such wide fabrics. Given that their manufacture required enormous bodily strength, the insights of experimental archaeology have proved helpful. Weaving on the reconstructed warp-weighted loom of Kleinklein required moving 60 kg of material when raising two braiding bars simultaneously to make a twill. The weight of the 107 loom weights was 118 kg. The considerable amount of strength required for weaving, and the 3.70 m width of the loom, suggest that at least two persons were needed (Grömer 2010: 256). Currently it is hardly possible to judge whether finds indicating that conspicuously wide fabrics were woven point to the presence of centres of production. Gleba (2012: 237) proposes such centres in Italy, though they only appear prominently in the Hellenistic period (300 to first century BC).

Loom weights are pyramid-shaped in the majority of cases known from central Europe, but other types are documented in the Iron Age. Loom weights decrease in size from the time of the Urnfield culture and in the Hallstatt period, becoming narrower and disc- or pyramid-shaped. According to Grömer (2010: 117–121) this trend is largely due to the relationship between the shape of the loom weights and the density of the warp, and therefore the fineness of the fabric. Indeed, compared to Bronze Age examples, the majority of textiles from the early Iron Age onwards have finer threads and higher densities.

Centres of Production

The existence of textile production centres has so far been difficult to document from the evidence of settlement assemblages. In Italy, the concentration in many sanctuary areas of equipment used in textile manufacture, as well as its deposition as votive objects during the Orientalizing and Archaic periods, suggest that textile production had a special significance (Gleba 2008: 183–187, 2012: 237). In the La Tène settlement areas of the Dürrnberg, where this question was actively pursued, equipment used for making textiles, such as spindle whorls, loom weights, needles with eyes, and scissors, was found dispersed among several households (Brand 1995: fig. 84). The contexts and assemblages from the Hallstatt hillfort of Smolenice-Molpír in Slovakia, where over 700 spindle whorls and numerous instances of looms are documented, suggest that it was a textile production centre (Belanová 2007; Belanová-Stolcová and Grömer 2010: 9–20). The presence of iron shears in male graves from the Middle La Tène period onwards is linked by Antoinette Rast-Eicher with changes in pastoralism and the selective production of wool. Whereas in earlier times wool was plucked from sheep—i.e. in the spring, the coarser outer wool was shed or lightly teased off—there were now sheep whose fleece grew throughout the year. These mixed-wool sheep no longer moulted naturally. Keeping sheep in flocks and the quantity and quality of their wool contributed, according to Rast-Eicher, to an economic and social transformation, and the shears found in the male burials of Switzerland are interpreted as symbolizing ownership of flocks (Rast-Eicher 2008: 156).

Currently it is mainly the fabrics themselves that provide information on centres of production and the processes involved in textile manufacture. Thus the quality and composition of the textiles from the Hochdorf burial lead to the conclusion that they are the products of a specialist craft, an economic factor that contributed significantly to the regional power structures (Banck-Burgess 1999: 127–132, 2012b). The textiles from the cemetery and salt mines of Hallstatt belong to an affluent group of the population; given the local environment, they were probably not manufactured locally but obtained through exchange for salt (Grömer 2010: 230–231, 244–245). Such a model implies textile production elsewhere, at a scale beyond domestic production.

Fabrics

Finds of woven material are traditionally described on the basis of a few production attributes which include the type of weave, the use of yarn or twine for the two threading systems (warp and weft), the twisting of the thread, its strength and size, and the materials used. Although remains of fabrics are a category of find frequent among metal grave goods, wide-ranging groupings based on these technical characteristics can only hint at trends, and their distribution cannot form the basis for reliable conclusions about manufacturing traditions. Circumstances such as differences in the intensity of research, variations in preservation conditions for animal and vegetal products, or lack of detail about the use of the fabrics are too random and, consequently, too unrepresentative. There is hardly another category of artefact that is as elusive as textiles, in terms of their form, dimensions, appearance, or function. The circumstance that research has so far given much space to attributes relating to production must not detract from the fact that their interpretation is biased by this selfsame emphasis.

In this respect, results obtained by experimental archaeology have shown that manufacturing attributes are insufficient to capture the essence of specific textiles (Hammarlund and Vestergaard Petersen 2007). Despite the difficulties mentioned, the textile types that Bender-Jörgensen has presented (1992: 120–122)—including the Huldremose type (weave: tabby or twill with s/s twist direction), the Haraldskær type (weave: tabby or twill with z/z twist direction), the Viring type (weave: 2/2 twill, lozenge or diamond twill; z/s twist direction; wool), and the Dürrnberg type (weave: 2/2 twill)—continue to provide useful guidance when trying to categorize fabric assemblages in textile archaeology. How limited our understanding of textiles from the pre-Roman Iron Age, based on the production attributes of single finds, really is, is illustrated by Möller Wiering's (2012) compilation of finds from Germany. While in the north the Jastorf culture was part of the Scandinavian sphere of influence, the Hunsrück-Eifel culture of central and western Germany was predominantly marked by the late Hallstatt and La Tène cultural groupings of southern Germany. Differences in burial rituals and strong variations in the numbers of surviving grave goods contribute to the differential quantities of preserved textiles (Möller Wiering 2012: 124). If one tries to describe the archaeological findscape according to criteria of textile production (Möller Wiering 2012: 130–133), the exception becomes the rule—i.e. the grouping of combinations of attributes is of limited use.

A similar situation exists among finds from Greece, where, although plain-weave fabrics are dominant, other production attributes vary (Spantidaki and Moulherat 2012: 198–199). In many countries, such as Latvia (Zeiere 2012: 271–272), Sweden (Franzén et al. 2012), Norway (Halvorsen 2012), Scotland, and Ireland (Wincott Heckett 2012), it is barely possible to assess the Iron Age craft of textile making owing to the paucity of published finds. In countries which have seen intensive research into textiles over the last few years, such as the Slovak and Czech Republics (Belanová 2005; Belanová-Stolcová 2012) or Switzerland (Rast-Eicher 2008; 2012), or where finds are made more frequently, such as Denmark (Hald 1980; Mannering et al. 2012: 104), a marked change is observable between Bronze Age and Iron Age textiles. Whereas in the Bronze Age plain weaves with a low density of threads predominate, in the early Iron Age the 2/2 twill (*Gleichgratköper* K2/2) becomes dominant in many European countries. Textile fibres are mainly wool and linen, but the presence of nettles, hemp, and hairs of goat, horse, badger, and other animals shows that the range of fibres available was far greater.

The lack of fabrics made from vegetal fibres in certain regions is often the consequence of unfavourable conditions of preservation. This is the case in Denmark, where the nettle fibre found with Huldremose Woman (Mannering et al. 2012: 104) constitutes an exception among the bog finds. The dominance of woollen fabrics in the early Iron Age of central Europe has meant that research has concentrated on this type of fibre (Ryder 1983, 2001; Rast-Eicher 2008: 121–162). Publications dealing with linen or the production of linen fabrics are relatively rare (Gleba 2004).

The high standard of textile manufacture in the European Iron Age is mostly documented by unique sites, in which substantial assemblages have survived thanks to unusual conditions of preservation. This high standard is also attested by a large quantity of fine fabrics, distinguished by the structure of their weave (mainly twills), patterning, colour, and feel. Twills (mostly 2/2 twill), but also chevron, herringbone or lozenge twills, chequered patterns, spin-patterning, and tablet weaving are equally represented among the Villanovan burial finds of Sasso di Furbara (Masurel and Mamez 1992) and Verucchio (eighth century BC), as well as in the late Hallstatt burial assemblages of the Hohmichele or Hochdorf (Riek and Hundt 1962; Hundt 1985; Ræder Knudsen 1999; Banck-Burgess 1999, 2012a) or the recycled fabrics from the Austrian salt mines. The latter were found at Hallstatt (Eastern Group, *c.* 900 to 300 BC) and at the slightly later Dürrnberg (late sixth to third–second centuries BC). They had originally been used above ground, but were later reused in mining activities (von Kurzynski 1996; Grömer 2007, 2010). Remarkable single finds, such as the twill from the first half of the sixth century BC recovered from Oakbank Crannog on Loch Tay in Scotland (Wincott

Heckett 2012: 437), and a diamond twill with tablet-woven starting borders from the La Tène-period burials of Burton Fleming and Rudston in East Yorkshire (Crowfoot 1991: 124–125; DeRoche 2012: 447), and a twill with a pattern made of yarns spun in different directions from Orton Meadow near Peterborough in England (DeRoche 2012: 446) show that such high-quality weaves were also present at this time in north-western Europe.

Tablet Weaves

Tablet-woven borders can be singled out from the mass of textile finds for the richness of their patterns (Figures 26.1 and 26.2). The finds from Hochdorf, Apremont (France), Sasso di Furbara, and Verucchio highlight the magnificence of such borders. The tablet weaves of Hochdorf in particular, which at times employed more than 120 tablets (Ræder Knudsen 1999), show the complex and time-consuming process involved in making these borders. Their pattern zones, divided into longitudinal stripes, are ornamented with chevron, diamond, and swastika motifs in repeat patterns. While the tablet-weave borders of Hochdorf were sown or woven onto the fabric, those of Verucchio were exclusively woven as borders and followed both straight and curved edges as well as contours within the fabric, like neck openings (Ræder Knudsen 2012: 261). Neither site has produced starting borders in tablet weaves, but these are known from the La Tène-period burials of Burton Fleming and Rudston in East Yorkshire (Crowfoot 1991: 124–125; DeRoche 2012: 447).

That this technique continued to be used is documented by the well-known hooded woollen cape from Orkney in Scotland, which is dated to the later Iron Age (AD 250–615). Its striking appearance is due to a sewn-on tablet-woven border from which hangs an extremely long fringe comparable to the warp threads of starting edges (Henshall 1950; Gabra Sanders 2001: 89–89; Wincott Heckett 2012: 438–439). Grave 200 at El Cigarralejo, Mula, Murica, in Spain, dating to the fourth century BC, provides a rare combination of tablet weaves and the equipment necessary for such weaving. Tablet weaves and other plain weaves of remarkably fine quality were found together with square boxwood tablets with sides 3 cm long (Hundt 1968; Alfaro Giner 1984:119–121, 138–141; Cardito Rollán 1996; Alfaro Giner 2012: 341–342).

Colours and Dyes

Intensive research, mainly in the last decade, into the colouring agents used in the Iron Age has led to a far better understanding of the dyes and dyeing processes employed, for example at Hochdorf (Walton Rogers 1999) and Hallstatt (Hofmann-de Keijzer et al. 2005). An examination of the dyes from early Iron Age textile finds from Denmark has been undertaken by Vanden Berghe and colleagues (Vanden Berghe et al. 2009, 2010). Among the dyes used for Hallstatt- and La Tène-period textiles, woad (*Isatis tinctoria* L)

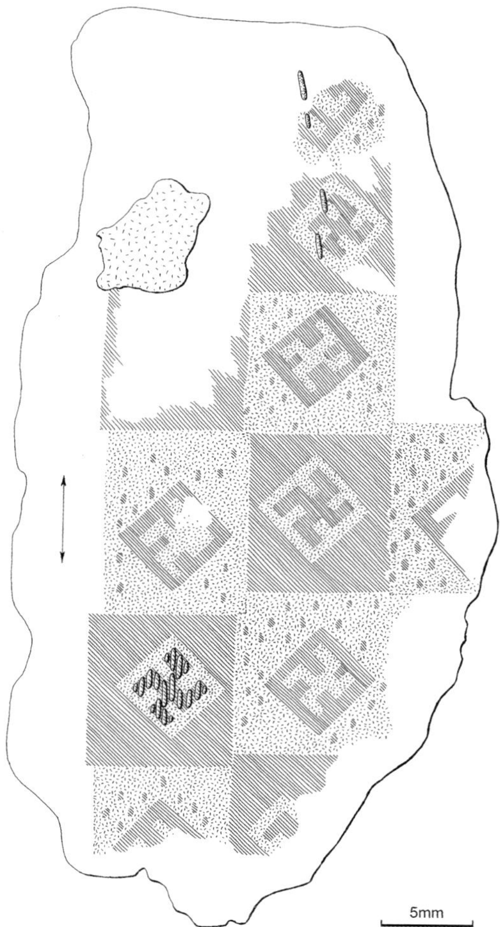

FIGURE 26.1 Tablet-woven fabric from the late Hallstatt burial at Hochdorf, south-west Germany. The swastika was one of the most common motifs at Hochdorf.

for blue colours, and madder (Rubiceae) or more rarely crimson (from *Kermes vermilio*) for red, are frequently documented. Other colours were obtained by mixing colouring agents and adding tanning agents (Hofmann-de Keijzer 2010: 143–162, fig. 74). Documentary evidence indicates that workshops for dyeing existed on the Italian coast of Taranto (Mar Piccolo); it refers in particular to purple dy (Forbes 1956: 136, 162; De Juliis 2000: 81; Gleba 2012: 237).

If one compares the results obtained for Iron Age fabrics with those gained for the Bronze Age, it is evident that many aspects of textile manufacture changed during the Iron Age, ultimately leading to higher quality products (Grömer 2016; Gleba and Mannering 2012: 55–60, 133, 114–115). But we must bear in mind that the differences recognized are mostly based on assemblages from rich Iron Age burials, therefore

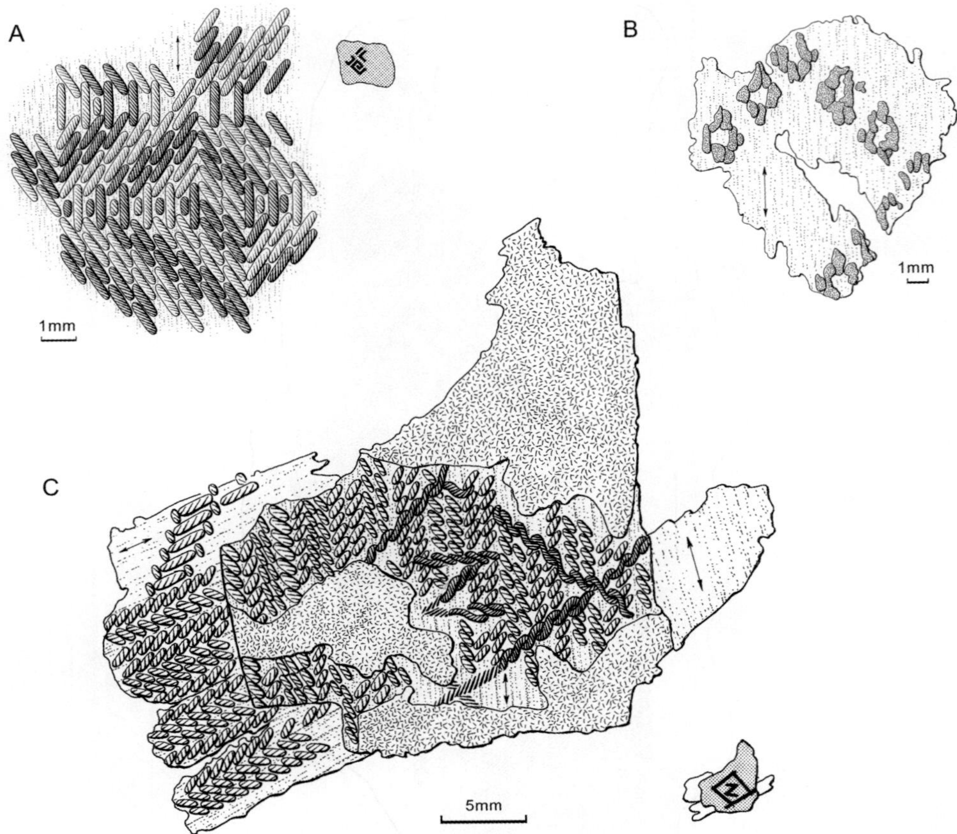

FIGURE 26.2 Tablet-woven textiles from Hochdorf. (A) Part of a meander pattern, with red and blue threads. (B) Fragment found on the wagon. (C) Textile with additional pattern in soumak technique.

making them less suitable for comparison with preceding periods; instead, they must be seen as representing the 'state of the art' for early Iron Age prestige textiles. The richly patterned fabric from the Bronze Age wetland settlement of Molina di Ledro in northern Italy (Bazzanella et al. 2003: 161–163, 2005: 151–160; Bazzanella and Mayr 2009: 212–215) alone highlights that high-value textiles were already being made in the Bronze Age; it is likely that the lack of finds emphasizes differences, making them more apparent than real.

The known remains of textiles are predominantly burial finds, and even then they document only a part of what was actually available. Everyday textiles—i.e. functional fabrics—are hardly known. And even in burial contexts the function of individual fabrics—surely an essential aspect of the processes and attributes of their production—remains for the most part elusive. If a fragment is found near a body—for example, in connexion with elements of a belt—it may represent uses other than clothing, such as a shroud, wrappings, special offerings, elements of dressing a collapsed burial chamber, or fragments of upholstery. Distributions of attributes of production therefore hardly allow us to reach far-ranging conclusions, since such characteristics may in fact reflect burial rites—for example, the introduction of the use of shrouds.

Changes in Production in the Middle La Tène Period

While twill weaves are dominant during the late Hallstatt and early La Tène period, textile finds show a different configuration from the middle La Tène period at the latest. Plain weaves using a simple yarn in both warp and weft predominate, and the richly patterned weaves of the late Hallstatt period, such as diamond twills or weaves with patterns made of yarns spun in different directions, are largely absent from the assemblages. The reasons for such a change are multiple. Extensive analyses of the burial assemblages, from which one may deduce changes in burial rites, are yet to be undertaken. It is conceivable that simple shrouds to wrap the bodies, or the offering of specific cloths, which would have acted at the same time as shrouds, were introduced. From the standardization of woollen cloths recognizable in Switzerland, Antoinette Rast-Eicher suggests this was largely linked to changes in pastoralism. The newly available wool from sheep producing mixed wool had longer fibres than the undercoat of the hairy sheep of the Hallstatt period, and its pigmentation made it less easy to dye. A twisted warp was no longer necessary (Rast-Eicher 2008: 189–190). Other factors leading to the production of simpler textiles are to be sought in the technical sphere, such as the introduction of new types of looms like the Nordic round loom, or frame looms more suited to the production of plain weaves (Rast-Eicher 2008: 189; Grömer 2010: 225).

Prestige Textiles

The large fabrics from the princely grave of Hochdorf mark them out as prestige textiles not only because of the fine quality of the weave. Their precious dyes, including crimson (*Kermes vermilio*) imported from the Mediterranean, and the magnificent tablet-woven borders, put these items at the heart of any social occasion. It is mainly the exclusive nature of the materials that brings textiles with gold or silk (but see later in the chapter) thread within the realm of power and wealth. Apart from single finds of textiles with gold threads, such as the finds of gold wire from the late Hallstatt burial of Grafenbühl (Banck-Burgess 1999: 204), or from the well-known fourth-century BC royal grave in Vergina (Macedonia), the written sources indicate that a centre for the production of gold thread existed in Taranto in southern Italy during the Hellenistic period (De Juliis 1984: 331). The tapestry fabric from Vergina, deposited in a golden shrine and consisting of the finest gold threads and red woollen yarns (dyed purple), shows various vegetal motifs and curvilinear meander patterns (Andronikos 1979: 366, pl. XL a; Andronikos 1984: 191–192, figs 156–157; Flury-Lemberg 1988: 234–235, cat. 51; Spantidaki and Moulherat 2012: 196, fig.7.17). The fabric does not seem to have been a unique product of Greek textile making, since it can also be found in the Greek colonies along the Black Sea coast of Eurasia (Gleba and Krupa 2012: 409–413).

Clear proof of the existence of silk is more difficult to establish in the current state of research. The problematic finds from the Hochdorf and Hohmichele burials, which Hundt had considered as possibly containing silk (Riek and Hundt 1962; Hundt 1969, 1985), can now be discounted categorically on the basis of amino-acid compositional analysis (Banck-Burgess 1999: 235). As for the find from Altrier, no scientific analyses are available to date. The most recent investigations indicate that the find from Kerameikos in Athens is not silk either (Margariti et al. 2011). Contrary to the view of Good (2011), who continued to consider these finds as silk, there is to date no published scientific evidence that the finds in question are fibres of silk made of the *Bombyx mori* L. variety. Less impressive, but nevertheless important, is the evidence for prestige textiles found in connection with countless tiny metal objects, mainly in late Hallstatt contexts. Hundreds of small bronze wire rings were worked into the fabric of textiles at Brno-Židenice in Moravia (Berg 1962, pl. 5/2 Grave 26, pl. 21/1 Grave 72, and pl. 27/1 Grave 86). In a La Tène-period princely burial at Waldalgesheim, numerous wire rings and ringlets of bronze were worked in various ways, and using different production techniques, into a fabric which is interpreted as part of a breastplate (Hundt 1995: 141–147, figs 104–106). The support for metal objects was provided not only by textiles, but also by leather. The most impressive example comes from the prestige wagon burial of Mitterkirchen on the eastern periphery of the west Hallstatt cultural sphere: there, thousands of small bronze buttons, found over the entire body of the female inhumation, are interpreted as the remains of a leather cloak (Kern et al. 2008).

Textiles from Eurasia

The Iron Age textile finds from Eurasia, particularly those from Pazyryk, which became famous the world over as the fabrics of Scythian nomads, must not be overlooked. Pieces of clothing (Polos'mak 2001; Parzinger et al. 2007) and other organic finds from the permafrost burials of the Pazyryk Group (fifth to third century BC) of the Altai highlands, which include artfully finished rugs, saddlecloths, and other ornaments made of felt (Parzinger 2006: 590–596, fig. 194) bear witness to the richness of this central Asian art form. Finds from the early Iron Age document a long tradition of making such elaborate and costly textiles. Remains of such prestige clothing are present in the assemblages of the barrow burials of Tuva in southern Siberia (Aržan I; Parzinger 2006: 609). These early finds, which mark the beginning of the Scythian form vocabulary in Siberia in the ninth to eighth century BC, are echoed by later finds from the large *kurgan* of Aržan 2/Grave 5 (seventh to sixth century BC), which also contains prestigious garments. These include a man's cloak onto which thousands of small figures of panthers were sown, arranged in curvilinear patterns resembling a plumage. The inside of the four walls of a timber burial chamber were draped in red felt (Parzinger 2006: 613). A glance at the Iron Age textile remains from the European continent reveals, on the basis of very few finds, a comparable force of expression. The gold fabrics found in the Greek and Roman colonies of the Ukraine in western and eastern Crimea (Gleba and Krupa 2012: 409–411) also count among the most precious textiles of Eurasia.

Textiles as Means of Communication

Archaeological textiles only rarely allow us to ascertain a function in which the processes involved in their manufacture and the features indicative of their later use can be assumed to match. The appearance of textiles must have been a powerful means of non-verbal communication. This is easily recognizable in striped and chequered fabrics, which are well represented in the European early Iron Age. Patterns with stripes, block checks, or hound's-tooth check were made in countless variants, in combinations of different threads, wefts, sizes, and composition of groups of threads. Striped and chequered fabrics were not limited to central Europe. They were present in the pre-Roman Iron Age of northern Europe, as well as south of the Alps, as early as in the Villanova culture on sites such as Sasso di Furbara and Verucchio (Masurel and Mamez 1992; Banck-Burgess 1999; Stauffer 2002, 2012; Gleba and Mannering 2012: 104). It may be that the appearance of these fabrics, which presumably acted as code rendered in textile, was used to distinguish between different communities or groups of people, allowing outsiders to be easily recognized or pointing to the origin of travellers.

The pattern combinations used may not necessarily have corresponded to our contemporary understanding of symmetry. At both Hallstatt and Hochdorf there were fabrics in which the basic patterns, such as a chequered pattern or the lozenges of a diamond twill, were covered by additional longitudinal stripes which did not take account of the basic patterning (Banck-Burgess 1999: 115–118; Grömer 2010: 169). At Hochdorf and at Hallstatt, patterns made by yarns spun in different directions were quite frequent: in these, the chequered or tabby patterning was created by reflecting the light differentially. Groups of differently spun threads formed the basis of such patterns, which could then also be overlain by additional colour patterns.

Besides the surface patterns created while the basic structure of the fabric was being made, there are also some instances where additional patterns were worked into the weave as the fabric was being woven. This 'flying thread' technique, also known as the Soumak technique, is mainly known in the late Hallstatt burials of Hochdorf and the Hohmichele. Such elaborate craftsmanship was apparently preferred to embroidery—which would have been much easier—suggesting that textiles were not just used purely as supports for ornament. These elaborate techniques of manufacture would indicate a translation of content specific to textiles—in other words, a meaning intrinsic to textiles (Banck-Burgess 1998, 1999: 130–132). Thus the swastika symbol, which dominates the fabrics at Hochdorf, is not found on other artefacts such as the Hallstatt pottery found between the Rhône valley and the Carpathian Basin (Brosseder 2004: 333–334).

Case Study: Hochdorf

Since the excavations concluded at the end of the 1970s, the late Hallstatt barrow burial of Hochdorf has been hugely influential in Iron Age archaeology (Krausse 2010). Hochdorf is unique, not so much for the quantity, quality, or individuality of its assemblage (Biel 1985; Krausse 1996; Bieg 2002; Koch 2006; Hansen 2010), but for the insights provided by the combination, or rather interrelationships, between site and assemblage. The undisturbed burial, whose configuration, construction, and inner arrangements could largely be reconstructed, shows the extent to which burial practice was used as a means of communication by late Hallstatt communities (Verger 2006; Biel 2009). Jörg Biel, its excavator, interprets this burial as a way of demonstrating power, whose staging also ensured its preservation (Biel 2009).

The textiles found at Hochdorf illustrate impressively that their significance can only be understood when approached in the context of the entire burial complex (Banck-Burgess 1999, 2012a, 2012b). The high value and composition of the textile assemblage represented not only the social status of the deceased, but also stood for a craft, which undoubtedly contributed to the establishment and consolidation of power structures in the central Neckar area. The textiles' patterns and colours indicate that they played an important role as a non-verbal way of communicating within indigenous ethnic and cultural boundaries, as well as in exchanges with other culture areas. Autochthonous traditions of manufacture had an important role to play in the realization of the fabric patterns. This suggests that the optical effect determined the value of textiles as much as the material itself.

To date there are no direct parallels for the pattern combinations displayed by the richly patterned tablet-woven borders of Hochdorf in the European Iron Age, but the basic pattern configurations—lozenges, checks, and hound's-tooth motifs—can be found all over Europe. However, there are some differences in aspects of the manufacturing process, such as the density of the weave, the use of yarns or threads or the direction of twist of the threads. The combination of patterns, which is based on the foundation created by warp and weft, and uses variations in colour, or materials, or the differential light-reflecting properties of s- and z-spun threads, reveals a multiplicity of expressions of patterns at a single site, making the textiles a focal point of the Hochdorf community. The swastika was the dominant motif among textiles (Figure 26.1), but it is absent from other late Hallstatt artefacts. While the textiles found in the burial, as manufactured products or as means of non-verbal expression or communication, provide information about the world of the living, other textile finds give direct insight into the burial rites and beliefs connected to the afterworld. How extensively wrapping of the dead and of the grave goods appropriate to their status, which would have negated the

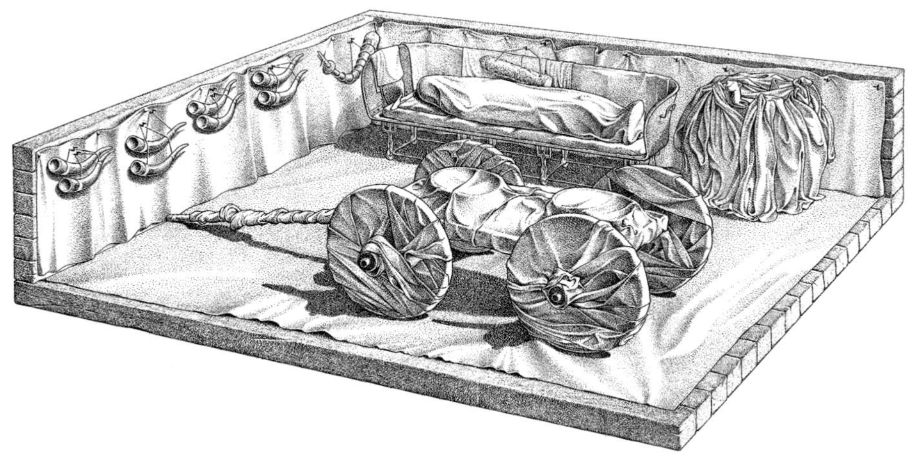

FIGURE 26.3 All the grave goods in the burial chamber at Hochdorf were wrapped with simple fabrics.

© J. Banck-Burgess/Landesamt für Denkmalpflege, Esslingen

optical effect of these objects, either during or after the funeral, was carried out, remains unknown. This burial rite, which is documented for the entire Iron Age (Bartel 1998; Banck-Burgess 1999: 18–28; Banck-Burgess 2012c), suggests that demonstrating earthly values on the way to the afterworld or the world of the dead followed a different set of values (Figure 26.3).

How far cremation rites encompassed similar beliefs is, at present, unknown. The wrapping of ashes and of grave goods is common in Greece from the beginning of the Iron Age in the Geometric period, or the end of the eleventh century BC (Spantidaki and Moulherat 2012: 197). Further clues about the conduct of funerals are given by the damaged textiles of Hochdorf: the fine tablet-woven borders, the wall hangings pierced by crude iron hooks, and twisted remains of fabrics which once covered the floor of the chamber let us suppose that the deposition of the grave goods was undertaken in haste. The reasons why this should be so remain open to question for the time being, but the indications are that different phases of the funeral are represented.

Research Into Clothing

The pre-Roman Iron Age finds from the bogs of northern Germany and Denmark (Hald 1980; Gleba and Mannering 2012) provide clear illustrations of specific garments. Secure evidence of individual pieces of clothing that are preserved nearly intact are rare in Europe, but include the leggings and pair of socks from Vedretta di Ries (Ries Glacier in the Italian southern Tyrol; Bazzanella et al. 2003: 180–182, 2005: 151–160) and two mantles from the Villanova-period site of Verucchio (Stauffer 2002, 2012). Deducing particular items of clothing from the position of clothing elements or accessories in graves is a difficult exercise. Iconographic evidence is only appropriate for the derivation of garments if the sources have been suitably assessed.

The documented garments of the pre-Roman Iron Age—here mainly restricted to 'Germanic finds'—are largely confined to trousers, sheet-like cloaks and shirt-like 'smocks' for men, and blouse, skirt, and '*peplos*-like' garments for women (Hald 1980; Gleba and Mannering 2012). These, and other generic elements such as tunics, are usually cited when describing Iron Age clothing, in an attempt to better define the appearance of such clothing on the basis of fibulae or iconographic indications (Birkhan 1999; Rast-Eicher 2008: 180–185; Grömer 2010: 392, fig. 196). This implies a large degree of uniformity in the clothes worn during the European Iron Age, which is highly unlikely, if only for the functional and status-bound importance of clothing. The contemporary clothing of the Scythians alone gives an impression of how diverse garments can be.

Clothing Accessories

In many parts of Europe, knowledge of Iron Age garments is based on the position of clothing accessories, especially pins, fibulae, and belts. These clothing accessories are grouped together with items of personal ornament or jewellery under the umbrella term of costume. Textile components, which in the original ethnographic study of costume were naturally considered part and parcel of the costume, are missing from archaeological research into dress. The analysis of textile remains which have survived together with dress accessories have so far yielded little information on clothing (Banck-Burgess 2000; Rast-Eicher 2008: 177, 187).

In traditional archaeological research into costume, the formal and stylistic attributes of fibulae occupy the centre ground (Mansfeld 1994; Maute 1994; Müller 2001), but it is the archaeological or textile-archaeological context that produces results for the reconstruction of garments. The late Hallstatt custom of dressing—i.e. wearing one fibula each on the left and right side (Mansfeld 1994: 439–443, fig. 81)—is often taken as an indication of the existence of a garment comparable to the classical *peplos* (Grömer 2010: 392, fig. 196). In La Tène assemblages from Switzerland (La Tène A to C1), it is assumed that this is an outer garment, pulled up to the chest and fastened in the area of the shoulders by a small pair of fibulae (Maute 1994: 464–466, fig. 92). The practical function of fibulae is rarely discussed—for example, the tendency to use smaller fibulae during the late Hallstatt period, which is seen to be associated with the use of finer textiles (Mansfeld 1994: 441–442). The significance of fibulae as items of personal ornament, which can change appearance quite rapidly according to the rules of fashion, takes centre stage in Iron Age brooch research and counts as a foundation for the delimitation of distribution areas and thus for the definition of cultural, or even ethnic, groups (Mansfeld 1994: esp. 442; Pabst-Dörrer 2000).

If one considers the possibility that fibulae and fabrics as components of clothing had regionally and chronologically varied functions, then the distribution patterns of textile and fibula types could, where applicable, be interpreted differently, or might not permit comparison. Protection against the weather, work-related purposes, embellishment of the body, expressions of gender or of the individual's age or status, functions linked to social obligations, representation in social contexts, meanings within and without cultural groupings, not to forget expressions of power (Banck-Burgess 2000; Brather 2009: 5, fig. 3; Grömer 2016; Banck-Burgess 2012b), are all among the diverse roles of clothing and clothing accessories, but do not have to encompass them. The narrow model of the 'local costume' (*Volkstracht*) is no longer applicable, as Brather (most recently 2009: 4) has pointed out.

Numerous textile remains are preserved on the corroded surfaces of dress accessories and jewellery made of metal. To identify these as fabric from clothes is only possible if an analysis of the relevant context is available and no other function is likely; such functions include shrouds or body wrappings, special offerings of textiles deposited close to the person, fabrics that once hung on a collapsed burial chamber, or textile fragments of upholstery used in bedding for the dead. Detailed observations made during excavation are often missing from publications, so that at present clothing fabrics cannot be described separately.

Garments

Unequivocal evidence for Iron Age clothing is limited to a very few sites. From the area of the Riesenferner glacier in the southern Tyrol come pairs of leggings and a pair of sewn foot-coverings (dated 795 to 499 BC), which may have acted, as the case may be, as inner linings for shoes (Bazzanella et al. 2005; Gleba 2012: 224). Among the most impressive items of Iron Age clothing from south of the Alps are two semicircular garments from the Villanovan site of Verucchio. They are described as mantles and come from graves dated to the eighth century BC (Stauffer 2002: 196–212, figs 64–65, figs 72–73, figs 77–78, 2012). According to Greek sources, they were known to the Etruscans as '*tebenna*' (Bonfante 2003: 48–55; Stauffer 2012: 251). With a length of 86 and 88 cm respectively, and a width of 240 and 264 cm, they are indeed impressive garments.

In the Germanic north, the bog finds of northern Germany (Schlabow 1976) and Denmark (Hald 1980) represent the most comprehensive source of Iron Age clothing. The older bog finds have often been the subject of corrections or changes of position concerning their dating, understanding of the circumstances of discovery, and analysis of the garments (Mannering et al. 2010; Gleba and Mannering 2012). Male garments include leg wraps and skin caps, while long skirts and sprang caps are ascribed to women (Gleba and Mannering 2012). Tubular garments are interpreted as skirts or *peploi*, depending on their lengths. They consist either of a piece of woven cloth sown together with a seam, or a tubular fabric woven on a round loom. By analogy with the Greek *peplos*, it is assumed that the tubular fabrics were pulled up to chest or shoulder height and fastened on both shoulders by fibulae. Hald (1980: 359) notes that no *peplos*-like garment has been found in Danish graves dating to between the late Bronze Age and the beginning of the Roman Iron Age. The representations of Germanic people on the columns of Trajan and Marcus Aurelius in Rome, dated to the second century AD, are often seen as proof of the existence of the Germanic *peplos* in the Iron Age (Hald 1980: 362, fig. 445 and 363, fig. 446). There the *peplos* belongs to female attire, while the mantle is worn by men, in the form of large sheets. Both types of garment are remarkably richly draped. The *peplos* and the large sheets of the male clothing are taken to indicate a change in north and central European dress that occurred at the beginning of the Iron Age at the latest. This change includes a departure from tailored and close-fitting garments, as are known from the northern Bronze Age (Gleba and Mannering 2012).

The ability to make finer, and therefore lighter, fabrics, which made it possible to wear richly draped clothing, is seen as another reason for this change. The fabrics were largely used as they came off the loom. Such characteristics contrast with the much simpler, coarser, and therefore heavier, fabrics of the Bronze Age (Ehlers 1999). Hems and seams, preserved in the case of the fabrics from the salt mines (Mautendorfer 2005), are largely absent from Iron Age textiles. Stuart Piggott shifts the change in costume back into the late Bronze Age on the basis that pairs of pins found in the area of the shoulders indicate *peplos*-like garments (Piggott 1965; Hägg 1996), but Rast-Eicher (2008: 187) on the strength of her detailed examination of textile remains and elements of costume from Switzerland, has shown that there is no evidence for *peploi* in the Hallstatt and early La Tène periods. Only in the middle and late La Tène periods could arrangements for closing garments in the area of the shoulders be indicative of the existence of *peploi*.

In Danish textile archaeology, the focus is on the tubular textiles from bog finds, which are documented in a variety of dimensions, such as 100 × 50 cm, 150 × 100 cm or 260 × 140 cm. The interpretation of some cloths as *peploi* has been questioned recently (Gleba and Mannering 2012: 15), as in the case of a fabric from Thorup II in northern Jutland, where the context does not allow an unequivocal interpretation—i.e. it is not certain that the fabric came from a garment. Sheet fabrics, which are attributed to male as well as female bog bodies, may also have been used as covers, or to wrap the body. Fastenings included strings, pins, or fibulae. Deposition of a cloth under the body is also recorded (Gleba and Mannering 2012: 105–106). In the case of the well-known bog body of Windeby I in northern Germany, which the most recent research suggests is the body of a boy dated to the first century AD (AD 41 to 118), and not, as previously assumed, of a girl, his clothes were laid under his body (Gebühr 2002: 47). Sheet-like fabrics are also documented at the late Hallstatt princely grave of Hochdorf. Although they enveloped the body, it is not possible to ascertain whether they were covering sheets or garments made of sheet fabric.

Trousers, which are attributed to both Germanic and Celtic people (von Kurzynski 1996, 2000), are known among the bog finds of Schleswig-Holstein and Lower Saxony only from the period of the Roman Empire onwards. Besides the finds of Damendorf and Dätgen, the pair of woollen trousers with attached foot coverings from Thorsberg Moor in Schleswig-Holstein is often cited. Textiles from weapon deposits, to which the well-known items of clothing from Thorsberg Moor belong, have been presented in a recent publication by Susan Möller-Wiering (2011).

Visual Representations of the Textile Craft and Clothing

To describe the craft of making textiles and clothing in Iron Age Europe, iconographic representations are often pressed into service. The early Hallstatt vessel with a conical neck, featuring scenes of spinning and weaving on its exterior surface, from the grave of a young woman (Tumulus 27) in the cemetery of Sopron-Burgstall (Várhely in Hungary; Dobiat 1982) is frequently cited in an early Iron Age context. Equally often cited is the *tintinabulum* (rattle or wind chime) from the Tomba degli Ori at the Arsenale Militare cemetery at Bologna (Morigi Govi 1971), dated to *c.*630 BC, both sides of which are decorated with scenes of textile making, including spinning, setting up a warp, and working at a loom. The people depicted are thought to be female, and the literature concerned with making textiles tends to attribute the craft to women (Gleba 2008; Grömer 2016: 270).

The situla art that flourished in the fifth and fourth centuries BC in the south-eastern Alpine and pre-Alpine region (Frey 2005) is another frequently used source. This mainly illustrates scenes which had little to do with daily life, like wrestling, acrobatics and dancing, and journeys or processions by cart. Although there is a broad consensus in the literature concerning these sources that the representations have a communicative character, the current perception of the level of realism of the figurative representations has to be set against the perspective of the people of that time. The direct translation from the outlines of representations of people into dress patterns and, by extension, garments, is methodologically questionable (Lenneis 1972). Stylistic attributes tend to be transferred largely uncritically when describing details relevant to clothing (Mautendorfer 2007; Grömer 2010: 216–217, 363–372). Culturally specific formal principles, such as the triangular shape of the human body on vessels of the eastern Hallstatt sphere, though understood to be symbolic, are interpreted just like other traits that include aspects of textile manufacture as 'real' elements (Eibner 2001).

The possibility that in certain cases what was represented was comprehensible only to a given community of onlookers who understood the symbolic character of such representations is overlooked. Considering the different interpretations of situla art from the perspectives of today's archaeologists alone makes it clear how difficult it is to understand its content. While Otto-Herman Frey (2005) interprets the scenes as the exclusive activities of an early Iron Age nobility, Kossack (1970: 166) sees the situla art images as a 'call to association'. Christoph Huth (2005) posits that they served to glorify the dead and were far from any form of reality, and Kull (1997: 403) understands the sculpture from the Glauberg in Hessen in the context of a 'deification of conspicuously buried individuals'. From this perspective, the representations acquire another dimension and may have transmitted values as a metaphorical language—values which would have been understood regionally and probably also beyond, but which certainly had no reliable value as realistic representations.

It should be stressed that a critical assessment of the iconographic evidence from a limited area can, however, lead to meaningful conclusions about clothing. Thus Yasmine Freigang (1997) examined the Gallo-Roman burials of the first to third centuries AD in the Moselle area of Gallia Belgica from the viewpoint of the self-representation of a community. In this context, significant insights into the meaning of clothing could be gained, and the wearing of specific items of clothing appropriate to the occasion could be ascertained. Interestingly, such informed studies never set out to visualize individual items of clothing, but aim to understand the meaning of clothing as means of social expression on the basis of characteristic attributes. Regardless of what intention is hidden in the cited iconographic sources, archaeological finds are more likely to yield reliable information on the craft of making textiles and clothing. In contrast to regions north of the Alps, the written and iconographic evidence that refers to textile manufacture or clothing in Italy (Gleba 2012: 237) can be interpreted more authentically. A close link with chronological and geographical context is available more frequently there.

References

Alfaro Giner, C. 1984. *Tejido y cestería en la Península Ibérica: Historia de su técnica e industrias desde la Prehistoria hasta la romanización*. Bibliotheca Prehistorica Hispana 21. Madrid: Consejo Superior de Investigaciones Cientificas, Instituto Espanol de Prehistoria.

Alfaro Giner, C. 2010. 'Fishing nets in the ancient world: The historical and archaeological evidence', in T. Bekker-Nielsen and D. Bernal Casasola (eds) *Ancient Nets and Fishing Gear. Proceedings of the International Workshop on Nets and Fishing Gear in Classical Antiquity: A First Approach. Cádiz, November 15–17, 2007*: 55–82. Cádiz/Aarhus: Servicio de Publicaciones de la Universidad de Cádiz, Aarhus University Press.

Alfaro Giner, C. 2011. 'Approches méthodologiques et perspectives sur la corderie et la vannerie grecque archaique: les trouvailles de cala Sant Vicenc (Pollensa, Mallorca)', in F. Blondé (ed.) *L'artisanat grec: Approches méthodologiques et perspectives*: 68–98. Lille: Presses Universitaires du Septentrion.

Alfaro Giner, C. 2012. 'Spain', in M. Gleba and U. Mannering (eds) *Textiles and Textile Production in Europe: From Prehistory to AD 400*. Ancient Textiles Series 11: 332–346. Oxford: Oxbow.

Andronikos, M. 1979. *The Finds from Royal Tombs at Vergina*. Proceedings of the British Academy 65. London: British Academy.

Andronikos, M. 1984. *Vergina: The Royal Tombs and the Ancient City*. Athens: Ekdotike Athenon.

Banck-Burgess, J. 1998. 'Prähistorische Textiltraditionen', in B. Fritsch, M. Maute, I. Matuschik, J. Müller, and C. Wolf (eds) *Traditionen und Innovation: Prähistorische Archäologie als Historische Wissenschaft. Festschrift für Christian Strahm*. Internationale Archäologie, Studia honoraria 3: 469–478. Rahden: Marie Leidorf.

Banck-Burgess, J. 1999. *Hochdorf IV. Die Textilfunde aus dem späthallstattzeitlichen Fürstengrab von Eberdingen-Hochdorf (Kreis Ludwigsburg) und weitere Grabtextilien aus hallstatt- und latènezeitlichen Kulturgruppen*. Forschungen und Berichte zur Vor- und Frühgeschichte in Baden-Württemberg 70. Stuttgart: Theiss.

Banck-Burgess, J. 2000. 'Kleidung', in *Reallexikon der Germanischen Altertumskunde 16*: 603–614. Berlin: Walter de Gruyter.

Banck-Burgess, J. 2005. 'Textilien', in *Reallexikon der Germanischen Altertumskunde 30*: 372–392. Berlin: Walter de Gruyter.

Banck-Burgess, J. 2012a. 'Case study: The textiles from the princely burial at Eberdingen-Hochdorf, Germany', in M. Gleba and U. Mannering (eds) *Textiles and Textile Production in Europe: From Prehistory to AD 400*. Ancient Textiles Series 11: 139–150. Oxford: Oxbow.

Banck-Burgess, J. 2012b. *Mittel der Macht: Textilien bei den Kelten [Instruments of Power: Celtic Textiles]*. Hemsbach: Theiss.

Banck-Burgess, J. 2012c. 'Wrapping as an element of early Celtic burial customs: The princely grave from Hochdorf and the cultural context', in S. Harris and L. Douny (eds) *Wrapping and Unwrapping Material Culture: Archaeologial and Anthropological Perspectives*: 147–156. London: Left Coast Press and Institute of Archaeology.

Bartel, A. 1998. 'Die organischen Reste an der bronzenen Schnabelkanne des Keltenfürsten von Glauberg-Glauberg, Wetteraukreis', in O.-H. Frey and F.-R. Herrmann (eds) *Ein frühkeltischer Fürstengrabhügel am Glauberg im Wetteraukreis, Hessen. Bericht über die Forschungen 1994–1996*: 68–87. Wiesbaden: Archäologische Gesellschaft in Hessen.

Bazzanella, M., L. Dal Rì, A. Maspero, and I. Tomedi. 2005. 'Iron Age textile artefacts from Riesenferner/Vedretta di Ries (Bolzano/Bozen-Italy)', in P. Bichler, K. Grömer, R. Hofmann-de Keijzer, A. Kern, and H. Reschreiter (eds) *Hallstatt Textiles: Technical Analysis, Scientific Investigation and Experiment on Iron Age Textiles*. British Archaeological Reports International Series 1351: 151–160. Oxford: Archaeopress.

Bazzanella, M., and A. Mayr. 2009. *I reperti tessili, le fusaiole e i pesi da telaio dalla palafitta di Molina di Ledro2*. Trento: Provincia autonoma di Trento.

Bazzanella, M., A. Mayr, L. Moser, and A. Rast-Eicher. 2003. *Textiles: intrecci e tessuti dalla preistoria europea. Catalogo della mostra tenutasi a Riva del Garda dal 24 maggio al 19 ottobre 2003*. Trento: Esperia.

Belanová, T. 2005. 'The state of research of La Tène Textiles from Slovakia and Moravia', in P. Bichler, K. Grömer, R. Hofmann-de Keijzer, A. Kern, and H. Reschreiter (eds) *Hallstatt Textiles: Technical Analysis, Scientific Investigation and Experiment on Iron Age Textiles*. British Archaeological Reports International Series 1351: 175–189. Oxford: Archaeopress.

Belanová, T. 2007. 'Archaeological textile finds from Slovakia and Moravia revisited', in A. Rast-Eicher and R. Windler (eds) *Archäologische Textilfunde—Archaeological Textiles: Report from the 9th NESAT Symposium, 18–21 May 2005 in Braunwald*: 41–48. Ennenda: ArcheoTex.

Belanová-Stolcová, T. 2012. 'Slovak and Czech Republics', in M. Gleba and U. Mannering (eds) *Textiles and Textile Production in Europe: From Prehistory to AD 400*. Ancient Textiles Series 11: 304–331. Oxford: Oxbow.

Belanová-Stolcová, T., and K. Grömer. 2010. 'Weights, spindles and textiles—textile production in central Europe from Bronze Age to Iron Age', in E. Andersson Strand, M. Gleba, U. Mannering, C. Munkholt, and M. Ringgard (eds) *North European Symposium for Archaeological Textiles X*: 9–20. Oxford: Oxbow.

Bender Jørgensen, L. 1986. *Forhistoriske textiler i Skandinavien [Prehistoric Scandinavian Textiles]*. Copenhagen: Det Kongelige Nordiske Oldskriftselskab.

Bender Jørgensen, L. 1987. 'Metoder og kildekritik i Textilforskningen. Et svar på et debatoplæg'. *Tor* 21: 263–281.

Bender Jørgensen, L. 1992. *North European Textiles until AD 1000*. Aarhus: Aarhus University Press.

Bender Jørgensen, L. 2005. 'Hallstatt and La Tène textiles from the archives of central Europe', in P. Bichler, K. Grömer, R. Hofmann-de Keijzer, A. Kern, and H. Reschreiter (eds) *Hallstatt Textiles: Technical Analysis, Scientific Investigation and Experiment on Iron Age Textiles*. British Archaeological Reports International Series 1351: 133–150. Oxford: Archaeopress.

Berg, F. 1962. *Das Flachgräberfeld der Hallstattkultur von Maiersch*. Veröffentlichungen der Österreichischen Arbeitsgemeinschaft für Ur- und Frühgeschichte 4. Vienna: Institut für Ur- und Frühgeschichte der Universität Wien.

Bichler, P., K. Grömer, R. Hofmann-de Keijzer, A. Kern, and H. Reschreiter (eds). 2005. *Hallstatt Textiles: Technical Analysis, Scientific Investigation and Experiment on Iron Age Textiles*. British Archaeological Reports International Series 1351. Oxford: Archaeopress.

Bieg, G. 2002. *Hochdorf V. Der Bronzekessel aus dem späthallstattzeitlichen Fürstengrab von Eberdingen-Hochdorf (Kr. Ludwigsburg)*. Forschungen und Berichte zur Vor- und Frühgeschichte in Baden-Württemberg 83. Stuttgart: Theiss.

Biel, J. 1985. *Der Keltenfürst von Hochdorf*. Stuttgart: Theiss.

Biel, J. 2009. 'Das frühkeltische Fürstengrab von Eberdingen-Hochdorf. Eine Inszenierung', in J. Biel, J. Heiligmann, and D. Krausse (eds) *Landesarchäologie. Festschrift für Dieter Planck zum 65. Geburtstag*. Forschungen und Berichte zur Vor- und Frühgeschichte in Baden-Württemberg 100: 163–174. Stuttgart: Theiss.

Birkhan, H. 1999. *Celts: Images of their Culture*. Vienna: Österreichische Akademie der Wissenschaften.

Bonfante, L. 2003 [1975]. *Etruscan Dress*, 2nd edition. Baltimore: Johns Hopkins University Press.

Brand, C. 1995. *Zur eisenzeitlichen Besiedlung des Dürrnberges bei Hallein*. Internationale Archäologie 19. Espelkamp: Leidorf.

Brather, S. 2009. 'Ethnische Identitäten aus archäologischer Perspektive', in Landesmuseum Bonn und Verein von Altertumsfreunden im Rheinlande (eds) *Kelten am Rhein, Akten des dreizehnten Internationalen Keltologiekongresses [Proceedings of the Thirteenth International Congress of Celtic Studies]. Erster Teil: Archäologie, Ethnizität und Romanisierung*. Beihefte der Bonner Jahrbücher 58: 1–12. Mainz: Philipp von Zabern.

Brosseder, U. 2004. *Studien zur Ornamentik hallstattzeitlicher Keramik zwischen Rhonetal und Karpatenbecken*. Universitätsforschungen zur Prähistorischen Archäologie 106. Bonn: Habelt.

Cardito Rollán, L. M. 1996. 'Les manufacturas textiles en la prehistoria: Las Placas de telar en el Calcolítico peninsular [Textile manufacture in Prehistory: Tablet-weaving in the Copper-Age in the Iberian Peninsula]'. *Zephyrus* 49: 124–145.

Crowfoot, E. 1991. 'The textiles', in I. M. Stead (ed.) *Iron Age Cemeteries in East Yorkshire*. English Heritage Archaeological Report 22: 119–125. London: English Heritage.

De Juliis, E. 1984. *Gli ori di Taranto in Etá Ellenistica*. Milan: Mondadori.

De Juliis, E. 2000. *Taranto*. Bari: Edipuglia.

DeRoche, D. 2012. 'England: Bronze and Iron Ages', in M. Gleba and U. Mannering (eds) *Textiles and Textile Production in Europe: From Prehistory to AD 400*. Ancient Textiles Series 11: 443–450. Oxford: Oxbow.

Dobiat, C. 1982. 'Menschendarstellungen auf ostalpiner Hallstattkeramik. Eine Bestandsaufnahme'. *Acta Archaeologica Academiae Scientiarum Hungaricae* 34: 279–322.

Dobiat, C. 1990. *Der Burgstallkogel bei Kleinklein I: Die Ausgrabungen der Jahre 1982 und 1984*. Marburger Studien zur Vor- und Frühgeschichte 13. Marburg: Hitzeroth.

Dobiat, C., S. Sievers, and T. Stöllner (eds). 2003. *Dürrnberg und Manching: Wirtschaftsarchäologie im ostkeltischen Raum. Akten des internationalen Kolloquiums in Hallein 1998*. Kolloquien zur Vor- und Frühgeschichte 7. Bonn: Habelt.

Ehlers, S. K. 1999. 'Die bronzezeitlichen Textilien aus Schleswig-Holstein. Eine technische Analyse und Funktionsbestimmung'. PhD thesis, Universität Kiel.

Eibner, A. 2001. 'Die Stellung der Frau in der Hallstattkultur anhand der bildlichen Zeugnisse'. *Mitteilungen der Anthropologischen Gesellschaft in Wien* 130/131: 107–136.

Flury-Lemberg, M. 1988. *Textilkonservierung im Dienste der Forschung*. Schriften der Abegg-Stiftung Bern 7. Bern: Abegg-Stiftung Bern.

Forbes, R. J. 1956. *Studies in Ancient Technology, Vol. 4*. Leiden: Brill.

Franzén, M.-L., E. Lundwall, A. Sundström, and E. Andersson Strand. 2012. 'Sweden', in M. Gleba and U. Mannering (eds) *Textiles and Textile Production in Europe: From Prehistory to AD 400*. Ancient Textiles Series 11: 347–364. Oxford: Oxbow.

Freigang, Y. 1997. 'Die Grabmäler der gallo-römischen Kultur im Moselland. Studien zur Selbstdarstellung einer Gesellschaft'. *Jahrbuch des Römisch-Germanischen Zentralmuseums* 44, 1: 277–440.

Frey, O.-H. 2005. 'Situlenkunst', in *Reallexikon der Germanischen Altertumskunde 28*: 527–535. Berlin: Walter de Gruyter.

Gabra Sanders, T. 2001. 'The Orkney hood, re-dated and reconsidered', in P. Walton Rogers, L. Bender Jørgensen, and A. Rast-Eicher (eds) *The Roman Textile Industry and its Influence: A BirthdayTribute to John Peter Wild*: 98–104. Oxford: Oxbow.

Gebühr, M. 2002. *Moorleichen in Schleswig-Holstein*. Neumünster: Wachholtz.

Gleba, M. 2003. 'Textile production in proto-historic Italy: from specialists to workshops', in C. Gillis and M. L. Nosch (eds) *Ancient Textiles: Production, Craft and Society. International Conference on Ancient Textiles held at Lund, Sweden and Copenhagen, Denmark*. Ancient Textiles Series 1: 71–76. Oxford: Oxbow.

Gleba, M. 2004. 'Linen production in pre-Roman and Roman Italy', in C. Alfaro, J. P. Wild, and B. Costa (eds) *Purpureae vestes: Actas del I Symposium International sobre Textiles y Tintes del Mediterráneo en época romana (Ibiza, 8 al 10 de noviembre, 2002)*: 29–38. València: Universitat de València.

Gleba, M. 2008. *Textile Production in Pre-Roman Italy*. Ancient Textiles Series 4. Oxford: Oxbow.

Gleba, M. 2012. 'Italy: Iron Age', in M. Gleba and U. Mannering (eds) *Textiles and Textile Production in Europe: From Prehistory to AD 400*. Ancient Textiles Series 11: 214–241. Oxford: Oxbow.

Gleba, M., and T. Krupa. 2012. 'Ukraine', in M. Gleba and U. Mannering (eds) *Textiles and Textile Production in Europe: From Prehistory to AD 400*. Ancient Textiles Series 11: 397–425. Oxford: Oxbow.

Gleba, M., and U. Mannering (eds). 2012. *Textiles and Textile Production in Europe: From Prehistory to AD 400*. Ancient Textiles Series 11. Oxford: Oxbow.

Good, I. 2011. 'Stands of connectivity: Assessing the evidence for long distance exchange of silk in later prehistoric Eurasia', in T. C. Wilkinson, S. Sherratt, and J. Bennet (eds) *Interweaving Worlds: Systemic Interactions in Eurasia, 7th to 1st Millennia BC*: 218–230. Oxford: Oxbow.

Grömer, K. 2005. 'The textiles from the prehistoric salt-mines at Hallstatt', in P. Bichler, K. Grömer, R. Hofmann-de Keijzer, A. Kern, and H. Reschreiter (eds) *Hallstatt Textiles: Technical Analysis, Scientific Investigation and Experiment on Iron Age Textiles*. British Archaeological Reports International Series 1351: 17–40. Oxford: Archaeopress.

Grömer, K. 2007. 'Bronzezeitliche Gewebefunde aus Hallstatt: Ihr Kontext in der Textilkunde Mitteleuropas und die Entwicklung der Textiltechnologie zur Eisenzeit'. PhD thesis, Universität Wien.

Grömer, K. 2010. *Prähistorische Textilkunst in Mitteleuropa: Geschichte des Handwerkes und der Kleidung vor den Römern*. Vienna: Verlag des Naturhistorischen Museums.

Grömer, K. 2012. 'Austria: Bronze and Iron Age', in M. Gleba and U. Mannering (eds) *Textiles and Textile Production in Europe: From Prehistory to AD 400*. Ancient Textiles Series 11: 25–64. Oxford: Oxbow.

Grömer, K. 2016. *The Art of Prehistoric Textile Making. The development of craft traditions and clothing in Central Europe*. Vienna: Natural History Museum.

Hägg, I. 1985. 'Textilhitoria, statistik och källkritik 1'. *Tor* 20: 259–278.

Hägg, I. 1996. 'Textil und Tracht als Zeugnis von Bevölkerungsverschiebungen'. *Archäologische Informationen* 19, 1/2: 135–147.

Hald, M. 1980. *Ancient Danish Textiles from Bogs and Burials*. Copenhagen: The National Museum of Denmark.

Halvorsen, S. 2012. 'Norway', in M. Gleba and U. Mannering (eds) *Textiles and Textile Production in Europe: From Prehistory to AD 400*. Ancient Textiles Series 11: 273–290. Oxford: Oxbow.

Hammarlund, L., and K. Vestergaard Petersen. 2007. 'Textile appearance and visual impression: Craftknowledge applied to archaeological textiles', in A. Rast-Eicher and R. Windler (eds) *Archäologische Textilfunde-Archaeological Textiles. Nordeuropäisches Symposium für archäologische Textilien IX in Braunwald 18.–20. Mai 2005*: 213–219. Ennenda: ArcheoTex.

Hansen, L. 2010. *Hochdorf VIII. Die Goldfunde und Trachtbeigaben des späthallstattzeitlichen Fürstengrabes von Eberdingen-Hochdorf (Kr. Ludwigsburg)*. Forschungen und Berichte zur Vor- und Frühgeschichte in Baden-Württemberg 118. Stuttgart: Theiss.

Henshall, A. S. 1950. 'Textiles and weaving appliances in prehistoric Britain'. *Proceedings of the Prehistoric Society* 16: 130–162.

Hofmann-deKeijzer, R. 2010. 'Färben', in K. Grömer (ed.) *Prähistorische Textilkunst in Mitteleuropa: Geschichte des Handwerkes und der Kleidung vor den Römern*: 143–162. Vienna: Verlag des Naturhistorischen Museums.

Hofmann-de Keijzer, R., M. R. van Bommel, and I. Joosten. 2005. 'Dyestuff and element analysis on textiles from the prehistoric salt-mines of Hallstatt', in P. Bichler, K. Grömer, R. Hofmann-de Keijzer, A. Kern, and H. Reschreiter (eds) *Hallstatt Textiles: Technical Analysis, Scientific Investigation and Experiment on Iron Age Textiles*. British Archaeological Reports International Series 1351: 17–40. Oxford: Archaeopress.

Hundt, H.-J. 1968. 'Die verkohlten Reste von Geweben, Geflechten, Seilen und Schnüren aus Grab 200 von El Cigarralejo'. *Madrider Mitteilungen* 9: 187–205.

Hundt, H.-J. 1969. 'Über vorgeschichtliche Seidenfunde'. *Jahrbuch des Römisch-Germanischen Zentralmuseums Mainz* 16: 59–71.

Hundt, H.-J. 1985. 'Die Textilien im Grab von Hochdorf', in D. Planck (ed.) *Der Keltenfürst von Hochdorf: Methoden und Ergebnisse der Landesarchäologie. Katalog zur Ausstellung, Stuttgart, Kunstgebäude vom 14. August–13. Oktober 1985*: 106–115. Stuttgart: Theiss.

Hundt, H.-J. 1995. 'Reste eines Zierrates', in H.-E. Joachim (ed.) *Waldalgesheim: Das Grab einer keltischen Fürstin*. Kataloge des Rheinischen Landesmuseums Bonn 3: 141–147. Cologne: Rheinland-Verlag.

Huth, C. 2005. 'Situlenfest', in *Reallexikon der Germanischen Altertumskunde 28*: 522–527. Berlin: De Gruyter.

Kern, A., K. Kowarik, A. W. Rausch, and H. Reschreiter (eds). 2008. *Salz—Reich. 7000 Jahre Hallstatt*. Veröffentlichungen der Prähistorischen Abteilung 2. Vienna: Naturhistorisches Museum Wien.

Koch, J. 2006. *Hochdorf VI. Der Wagen und das Pferdegeschirr aus dem späthallstattzeitlichen Fürstengrab von Eberdingen-Hochdorf (Kr. Ludwigsburg)*. Forschungen und Berichte zur Vor- und Frühgeschichte in Baden-Württemberg 89. Stuttgart: Theiss.

Kossack, G. 1970. *Gräberfelder der Hallstattzeit an Main und Fränkischer Saale*. Materialhefte zur bayerischen Vorgeschichte 24. Kallmünz: Lassleben.

Krausse, D. 1996. *Hochdorf III. Das Trink- und Speiseservice aus dem späthallstattzeitlichen Fürstengrab von Eberdingen-Hochdorf (Kr. Ludwigsburg)*. Forschungen und Berichte zur Vor- und Frühgeschichte in Baden-Württemberg 64. Stuttgart: Theiss.

Krausse, D. (ed.) 2010. *'Fürstensitze' und Zentralorte der frühen Kelten. Abschlusskolloquium des DFG-Schwerpunktprogramms 1171 in Stuttgart, 12.–15. Oktober 2009*. Forschungen und Berichte zur Vor- und Frühgeschichte in Baden-Württemberg 120. Stuttgart: Theiss.

Kull, B. 1997. 'Tod und Apotheose: zur Ikonographie in Grab und Kunst der jüngeren Eisenzeit an der unteren Donau und ihrer Bedeutung für die Interpretation von "Prunkgräbern"'. *Berichte der Römisch-Germanischen Kommission* 78: 197–466.

Lenneis, E. 1972. 'Die Frauentracht des Situlenstils. Ein Rekonstruktionsversuch'. *Archaeologia Austriaca* 51: 16–57.

Maik, J. 2012. 'Poland', in M. Gleba and U. Mannering (eds) *Textiles and Textile Production in Europe: From Prehistory to AD 400*. Ancient Textiles Series 11: 291–303. Oxford: Oxbow.

Mannering, U., M. Gleba, and H. M. Bloch. 2012. 'Denmark', in M. Gleba and U. Mannering (eds) *Textiles and Textile Production in Europe: From Prehistory to AD 400*. Ancient Textiles Series 11: 89–118. Oxford: Oxbow.

Mannering, U., G. Possnert, J. Heinemeier, and M. Gleba. 2010. 'Dating Danish textiles and skins from bog finds by means of ^{14}C AMS'. *Journal of Archaeological Science* 37: 261–268.

Mansfeld, R. 1994. 'Fibel und Fibeltracht: Ältere Eisenzeit in südlichen Mitteleuropa', in *Reallexikon der Germanischen Altertumskunde 18*: 438–444. Berlin: Walter de Gruyter.

Margariti, C., S. Protopapas, and V. Orphanou. 2011. 'Recent analyses of the excavated textile find from Grave 35 HTR73, Kerameikos cemetery, Athens, Greece'. *Journal of Archaeological Science* 38: 522–527.

Masurel, H., and L. Mamez. 1992. 'Étude complémentaire des vestiges textiles trouvés dans l'embarcation de la nécropole du Caolino à Sasso di Furbara'. *Origini* 16: 295–310.

Maute, M. 1994. 'Fibel und Fibeltracht: La Tènezeit: Fibeltypen und Verbreitung', in *Reallexikon der Germanischen Altertumskunde 18*: 458–467. Berlin: Walter de Gruyter.

Mautendorfer, H. 2005. 'Genähtes aus dem prähistorischen Hallstatt', in P. Bichler, K. Grömer, R. Hofmann-de Keijzer, A. Kern, and H. Reschreiter (eds) *Hallstatt Textiles: Technical Analysis, Scientific Investigation and Experiment on Iron Age Textiles*. British Archaeological Reports International Series 1351: 41–54. Oxford: Archaeopress.

Mautendorfer, H. 2007. 'Schnitttechnische Interpretationen anhand hallstattzeitlicher Darstellungen', in R. Karl and J. Leskovar (eds) *Interpretierte Eisenzeiten: Fallstudien,*

Methoden, Theorien. Tagungsbeiträge der 2. Linzer Gespräche zur interpretativen Eisenzeitarchäologie: 263–276. Linz: Oberösterreichisches Landesmuseum.

Meo, F. 2011. 'Rediscovering ancient activities: Textile tools in a 3rd–2nd century BC context from Herakleia, southern Basilicata, Italy'. *Archaeological Textiles Newsletter* 53: 2–11.

Möller-Wiering, S. 2011. *War and Worship: Textiles from 3rd to 4th-century AD Weapon Deposits in Denmark and Northern Germany*. Ancient Textiles Series 9. Oxford: Oxbow.

Möller-Wiering, S. 2012. 'Germany: Bronze and pre-Roman Iron Ages', in M. Gleba and U. Mannering (eds) *Textiles and Textile Production in Europe: From Prehistory to AD 400*. Ancient Textiles Series 11: 122–138. Oxford: Oxbow.

Morigi Govi, C. 1971. 'Il tintinnabulo della "tomba degli ori" dell'arsenale militare di Bologna'. *Archeologia Classica* 23: 211–235.

Müller, R. 2001. 'Nadelformen der Eisenzeit', in *Reallexikon der Germanischen Altertumskunde* 20: 496. Berlin: Walter de Gruyter.

Pabst-Dörrer, S. 2000. *Untersuchungen zu hallstattzeiltichen Frauentrachten mit Spiralbrillenfibeln zwischen Alpen, Karpaten und Ostsee*. Internationale Archäologie 51. Rahden: Marie Leidorf.

Parzinger, H. 2006. *Die frühen Völker Eurasiens: Vom Neolithikum bis zum Mittelalter*. Munich: Beck.

Parzinger, H., W. Menghin, and M. Nawroth. 2007. *Im Zeichen des goldenen Greifen: Königsgräber der Skythen*. Munich: Prestel.

Piggott, S. 1965. *Ancient Europe: From the Beginnings of Agriculture to Classical Antiquity*. Chicago: Aldine.

Polos'mak, N. V. 2001. 'Zur Kleidung der Pazyryk-Bevölkerung aus Ukok, Südaltaj', in R. Eichmann and H. Parzinger (eds) *Migration und Kulturtransfer: Der Wandel vorder- und zentralasiatischer Kulturen im Umbruch vom 2. und 1. vorchristlichen Jahrtausend*. Kolloquien zur Vor- und Frühgeschichte 6: 101–126. Bonn.

Preinfalk, F. 2004. 'KG Hafnerbach', in C. Farka (ed.) *Fundberichte aus Österreich 42, 2003*: 15–17. Vienna: Die Abteilungen für Bodendenkmalpflege des Bundesdenkmalamtes.

Ræder Knudsen, L. 1999. 'Exkurs: Technical description of the fragments of the broad tablet woven band found on the big cauldron from Eberdingen-Hochdorf', in J. Banck-Burgess (ed.) *Hochdorf IV. Die Textilfunde aus dem späthallstattzeitlichen Fürstengrab von Eberdingen-Hochdorf (Kreis Ludwigsburg) und weitere Grabtextilien aus hallstatt- und latènezeitlichen Kulturgruppen*. Forschungen und Berichte zur Vor- und Frühgeschichte 70: 80–82. Stuttgart: Theiss.

Ræder Knudsen, L. 2012. 'Case study: The tablet-woven borders of Verucchio', in M. Gleba and U. Mannering (eds) *Textiles and Textile Production in Europe: From Prehistory to AD 400*. Ancient Textiles Series 11: 254–263. Oxford: Oxbow.

Rast-Eicher, A. 2008. *Textilien, Wolle, Schafe der Eisenzeit in der Schweiz*. Antiqua 44. Basel: Archäologie der Schweiz.

Rast-Eicher, A. 2012. 'Switzerland: Bronze and Iron Age', in M. Gleba and U. Mannering (eds) *Textiles and Textile Production in Europe: From Prehistory to AD 400*. Ancient Textiles Series 11: 378–396. Oxford: Oxbow.

Rebay, K. C. 2006. *Das hallstattzeitliche Gräberfeld von Statzendorf, Niederösterreich*. Universitätsforschungen zur Prähistorischen Archäologie 135. Bonn: Habelt.

Riek, G. 1962. *Der Hohmichele: Ein Fürstengrabhügel der späten Hallstattzeit bei der Heuneburg*. Heuneburgstudien I. Römisch-Germanische Forschungen 25. Berlin: De Gruyter.

Ryder, M. L. 1983. *Sheep and Man*. London: Duckworth.

Ryder, M. L. 2001. 'Fibres in Iron Age Textiles from the Dürrnberg (Austria)'. *Archaeological Textiles Newsletter* 33: 2–5.

Schlabow, K. 1976. *Textilfunde der Eisenzeit in Norddeutschland.* Göppinger Schriften zur Vor- und Frühgeschichte 15. Neumünster: Wachholtz.

Sievers, S. 2003. *Manching: Die Keltenstadt.* Führer zu archäologischen Denkmälern in Bayern. Oberbayern 3. Stuttgart: Theiss.

Spantidaki, Y., and C. Moulherat. 2012. 'Greece', in M. Gleba and U. Mannering (eds) *Textiles and Textile Production in Europe: From Prehistory to AD 400.* Ancient Textiles Series 11: 82–200. Oxford: Oxbow.

Stauffer, A. 2002. 'Tessuti', in P. von Eles (ed.) *Guerriero e Sacerdote: Autorità e comunità nell'Età del Ferro a Verucchio: La Tomba del Trono.* Quaderni di Archeologia dell'Emilia Romagna 6: 192–214. Florence: All'insegna del Giglio.

Stauffer, A. 2012. 'Case study: The textiles from Verucchio, Italy', in M. Gleba and U. Mannering (eds) *Textiles and Textile Production in Europe: From Prehistory to AD 400.* Ancient Textiles Series 11: 242–253. Oxford: Oxbow.

Tellenbach, M., S. Schulz, and A. Wieczorek. 2013. *Die Macht der Toga: DressCode im Römischen Weltreich.* Publikation der Reiss-Engelhorn-Museen in Kooperation mit dem Roemer- und Pelizaeus-Museum, Band 56. Mannheim: Schnell & Steiner.

Vanden Berghe, I., M. Gleba, and U. Mannering. 2009. 'Towards the identification of dyestuffs in Early Iron Age Scandinavian peat bog textiles'. *Journal of Archaeological Science* 36, 9: 1910–1921.

Vanden Berghe, I., M. Gleba, and U. Mannering. 2010. 'Dyes: to be or not to be? Investigation of dyeing in Early Iron Age Danish bog textiles', in E. Andersson Strand, M. Gleba, U. Mannering, C. Munkholt, and M. Ringgaard (eds) *North European Symposium for Archaeological Textiles X.* Ancient Textiles Series 5: 247–251. Oxford: Oxbow.

Verger, S. 2006. 'La grande tombe de Hochdorf, mise en scène funéraire d'un cursus honorum tribal hors pair'. *Siris* 7: 5–44.

Von Kimakowicz-Winnicki, M. 1910. *Spinn- und Webewerkzeuge: Entwicklung und Anwendung in vorgeschichtlicher Zeit Europas. Darststellungen über früh- und vorgeschichtliche Kultur-, Kunst- und Völkerentwicklung.* Mannus Bibliothek 2. Würzburg: Kabitzsch.

Von Kurzynski, K. 1996. '*... und ihre Hosen nennen sie bracas*': *Textilfunde und Textiltechnologie der Hallstatt-und Latènezeit und ihr Kontext.* Internationale Archäologie 22. Eselkamp: Leidorf.

Von Kurzynski, K. 2000. 'Hose', in *Reallexikon der Germanischen Altertumskunde* 15: 131–139. Berlin: De Gruyter.

Von Stokar, W. 1938. *Spinnen und Weben bei den Germanen—eine vorgeschichtlich-naturwissenschaftliche Untersuchung.* Mannus-Bücherei 59. Leipzig: Curt Kabitzsch.

Walton Rogers, P. 1999. 'Farbstoffanalysen an Probenaus Eberdingen-Hochdorf und dem Hohmichele', in J. Banck-Burgess (ed.) *Hochdorf IV. Die Textilfunde aus dem späthallstattzeitlichen Fürstengrab von Eberdingen-Hochdorf (Kreis Ludwigsburg) und weitere Grabtextilien aus hallstatt- und latènezeitlichen Kulturgruppen.* Forschungen und Berichte zur Vor- und Frühgeschichte in Baden-Württemberg 70: 240–246. Stuttgart: Theiss.

Wincott Heckett, E. 2012. 'Scotland and Ireland', in M. Gleba and U. Mannering (eds) *Textiles and Textile Production in Europe: From Prehistory to AD 400.* Ancient Textiles Series 11: 426–442. Oxford: Oxbow.

Zeiere, I. 2012. 'Latvia', in M. Gleba and U. Mannering (eds) *Textiles and Textile Production in Europe: From Prehistory to AD 400.* Ancient Textiles Series 11: 264–272. Oxford: Oxbow.

CHAPTER 27

TRADE AND EXCHANGE

CHRIS GOSDEN

Introduction

Not that long ago, the topic of trade and exchange was one of the most important in Iron Age studies. There were a number of reasons for this. Much discussion of the Iron Age took place within a broadly social evolutionary idiom, which saw the earlier Iron Age as dominated by tribes and chiefdoms, while the later period witnessed the emergence of states. The change from chiefdom to state was paralleled, and partly caused, by the transition from gift to commodity, it was argued. Chiefdoms operate through the idiom of kinship, with chiefly power limited by social obligations of reciprocity. Movements of agricultural and craft products from the producing commoners to a non-producing elite were countered to some degree by the movement of high-value craft products down the social pyramid. Exchanges took place through the idiom of the gift, with its triple obligations to give, to receive, and to repay, following Mauss (1969 [1924]; see also Gregory 1982). States, it was thought, broke free from the bonds of kinship, seeing the emergence of classes to some extent at least. Relations of class are economic and political, influenced by access to the means of production, the most basic of which was land. The lowest class, most likely slaves in the ancient world, owned nothing, not even their own bodies or labour, and certainly not land, which was owned or controlled by an elite, aristocratic class. A small, but important, class of specialist producers and traders sold and bought for profit in a nascent price-fixing market. Control of land and trade freed the elite from some social obligations, fettering their power less than previously. The role of coinage was debated. Was it money in a modern sense or a new aesthetically structured mode of exchange, as important for relations with the gods as with other people?

New methods were developed which could help on the modes of exchange in operation. The work of Renfrew (1975, 1977) concentrated on fall-off curves of materials moving away from a known source, following his own chemical characterizations of obsidian. More relevant to the Iron Age was the characterization of pottery, where

Peacock (1968, 1981) and others took a lead, followed by research into pottery industries in Germany and France (Magetti and Galetti 1980). Attempts to look at the circulation of metal were always less successful, either through the analysis of metals themselves or the styles of vessels produced (Frey and Schwappach 1973; Northover 1982, 1984). Salt and amber moved (Morris 1994) providing minor but informative trails of evidence of connection. Renfrew's fall-off curves aimed to spot and understand the operation of central people and places. Other things being equal (and of course they never were) one would expect a regular decline in the amounts of a material with increasing distance from its source, and the relationship between amount and distance could be graphed. An unexpectedly large amount of an item given the distance of a site from its source, might indicate the existence of a chief with the power to attract sought-after items. But it might also indicate a market, where the larger amounts of material transacted through a site would lead to loss and deposition there. Renfrew's methods were effective in distinguishing egalitarian from more centralized exchange, but less good at resolving, what was then a central question for the Iron Age, the existence of chiefs and markets.

To make such a distinction, recourse to a broader scope of archaeological evidence was needed. Here the question of central places becomes important. Two periods and sets of sites were pertinent here: the earlier was the so-called *Fürstensitze* of Hallstatt D in eastern France, Switzerland, and southern Germany; secondly were the much more widespread *oppida* of La Tène D, which at their most generous interpretation were found from Britain to central Europe in a band across the middle latitudes of Europe.

For the Hallstatt D and La Tène D instances a further relationship was important—that between the Mediterranean and Europe north of the Alps. For Hallstatt D, a prestige goods economy was seen to be key, predicated in turn on an unequal, core–periphery relation between the Mediterranean world and continental Europe (Frankenstein and Rowlands 1978) drawing on the work of Wallerstein (1974)—see also the subsequent world systems literature, for instance (Frank and Gills 1993; Denemark et al. 2000). Frankenstein and Rowlands (1978) identified four levels of chiefdom, ranging from a paramount chief with access to Mediterranean imports and the best locally produced objects, down to minor chiefs with rich locally produced items only. For the Heuneburg in Baden-Württemberg, they saw a paramount chief living in the central settlement, mobilizing local resources to obtain Greek pottery. Local resources came partly in the form of craft production in evidence through metalworking and pottery production inside the Heuneburg. Local, and especially Mediterranean, items were distributed from the paramount to vassal chiefs to maintain their allegiance, being also used to cement marriage alliances and in prestige-maintaining feasts. Levels of chiefdomship were most obviously manifest archaeologically through burials under barrows with different amounts of local and long-distance items placed as grave goods. Against long-distance items may have been traded archaeologically invisible products, such as metals, food, and slaves. The meeting of the Mediterranean and continental European systems of exchange was the encounter of two different systems of value in which items that were locally cheap to produce could be distantly traded to great advantage (Frankenstein and Rowlands 1978:79–80). There was an instability of local centres of power across the

Hallstatt D and La Tène periods, as new centres of exchange concentrated developers, such as at the salt mining site of the Dürrnberg in Austria (Moosleitner et al. 1974; Pauli 1978).

The rise of the late Iron Age sites, the *oppida*, was due only in part, it was thought, to the influence of the Mediterranean societies and, more specifically, Rome. Some of the biggest agglomerations of people towards the eastern end of the distribution of *oppida*, such as Manching and Staré Hradisko (Čižmář 2005), were never the result of Roman influence. Here, urban development derived more obviously from trade internal to continental Europe, fuelled by a considerable scale of production within the *oppida* (see Chapter 21). To the west, the situation was always different, in present-day France, Belgium, the Netherlands, and Britain. Mediterranean imports were generally lacking in continental Europe in La Tène B and C, but the sites such as Aulnat, near Clermont Ferrand, produced small amounts of Italian Campanian wares, as well as artefacts from across Europe, such as a bronze jug from Slovakia, in La Tène C (Collis 1984: 149). After the Roman occupation of southern France between 125–121 BC, trade between Mediterranean towns such as Massalia and the interior increased markedly (Dietler 2010). Particularly after Caesar's annexation of Gaul in the 50s BC, the impact of Roman materials north and west increased.

In an early attempt to model this systematically for Britain, Haselgrove (1982) reprised the prestige goods model, examining the effects of cross-channel trade on a core set of tribes in an area from north Kent, up the Thames, and then across to southern East Anglia. These groups interacted with a periphery of the Iceni, Coritani, Dobunni, Durotriges, and Atrebates who supplied metals, salt, and agricultural products, complemented by an outer supply zone in highland Britain. This was a world of multiple cores and peripheries, so that the core in south-east England was linked to northern France, which in turn had a series of links back to the Mediterranean. Haselgrove's article, mobilized around a pair of most effective maps (Haselgrove 1982: figs 10.4, 10.6) has been much discussed (see Hill 2007: 16–17) and subject to criticisms which themselves have helped structure the debate. Current opinion would acknowledge the influence of people and materials from across the Channel on south-east England, but tending to put more emphasis on local insular developments. As I will discuss below, most British *oppida*—apart perhaps from Silchester—do not now look like centres of concentrated and large-scale populations (see Chapter 4).

I have tried to give a sense of the varied influences that led to the centrality of discussions of trade and exchange: the impact of provenancing studies and attendant statistical analyses of artefact distributions, the role of the literatures on gifts and commodities, core and periphery, as well as gift exchange in general. At the heart of all this effort was an attempt to characterize and understand social boundaries and forms of organization in the Iron Age, impulses found throughout the social sciences. Going back to Marx's modes of production, or Durkheim's distinction between mechanical (for tribal societies) and organic (for industrial, class-based forms) solidarity, discussions of the movement from tribes to states found new impetus mid-twentieth century in the work of Polanyi (Polanyi et al. 1957), reinforced by later anthropology (for instance, Sahlins 1974; Meillassoux 1981). Social structure or organization is much easier to model in extant societies, where relationships can be observed, but rather harder with prehistoric archaeological evidence. The analysis of the movement of raw materials and finished artefacts was seen as a most useful proxy for an understanding of social relations more broadly.

Quite why interest moved away from trade and exchange is an interesting question. In the English-speaking world, post-processualism shifted the agenda from any explanation deemed economic (such as those based on production and exchange), and indeed social structure, towards an emphasis on the individual and identity. The deconstruction of broader narratives led to a return to more local and particularistic studies, within the rise of a basically relational framework of discussion. Relational thought holds these things to be self-evident: that no entity is self-sustaining and separate, but exists through a network of relations with other entities, be they people, plants, animals, or objects. Identities, genders, group adherence, or sexuality are not characteristics that inhere in an individual, but derive rather from a complex web of links to significant others.

Such approaches slightly complicated a stress on trade and exchange, but it was the move away from any economic form of explanation that was more effective in making the topic more marginal; of course, empirical considerations were also important. The most cogent critique of the prestige goods model, as applied to the Hallstatt chiefdoms, came from Arafat and Morgan (1994). In a broad survey of the uses of Greek pottery outside Greece, they point out the relative paucity of finds. Some forty sherds of black-figure ware had then been found at the Heuneburg spanning a period of ninety years from around 540 BC, whereas from Mont Lassois some 300 sherds were found (representing *c.*24 reconstructable vessels) against a background of millions of locally produced sherds (Arafat and Morgan 1994: 123–124). They go on to point out the necessity of understanding imports against a background of local practices, so it might be that the preference for black-figure ware at the Heuneburg was due to its resonance with local, amber-coloured graphite burnished pots (Arafat and Morgan 1994). The emphasis on the generation and negotiation of local values in contact with material from outside, and mediated through material things, brought a welcome new dimension to the debate.

What Should Our Approach to Trade and Exchange Be Today?

Any human society sees two sets of circulation systems: that of people and that of things. Objects can move through relatively static populations from one group to another; people can move taking objects with them, so that the objects move but stay in the same human hands. Most commonly both objects and people are on the move, with people setting objects in motion, but also the object world (in the form of raw materials or finished goods) attracting people to them. The older prestige goods models had links between objects and people built into them through notions of kinship links and bride price. Part of the reason people desired particular artefacts was to conduct marriage alliances, maintaining or increasing the numbers in their group. The most successful traders enjoyed the greatest demographic growth (here, African ethnography was a considerable influence: Meillassoux 1981; Ekholm 1972; Terray 1972). The Heuneburg grew as a centre of population due to its success as a centre of trade, following the argument.

However, if we follow the Arafat and Morgan (1994) critique, emphasizing the relative lack of imported wares, then such a model is harder to sustain. Maybe instead we should reverse the causal relationship between population and imports, seeing imports coming in to areas with centres of population? In the following section I shall compare two early Iron Age centres—the Heuneburg and Massalia—founded in similar times, and which have both been central to debates about trade and exchange.

A Tale of Two Centres: The Heuneburg and Massalia

At the time when Frankenstein and Rowlands and others were writing in the 1970s, only limited evidence was available from the Heuneburg from excavations of the plateau top and a rather patchy understanding of grave finds. Excavations this century by Kurz (2001, 2002) and Reim (2001, 2002) have transformed our knowledge (for an overview, see Krausse et al. 2016). From the new excavations and survey it has become apparent that the main settlement was not on the plateau top, surrounded by the mud-brick wall, but rather in the so-called lower town and outer settlements. From the seventh century BC, a set of scattered farms and hamlets were found in the Heuneburg area, which coalesced into a larger settlement around 650 BC. The mud-brick wall enclosed 3 ha of plateau around 600 BC, and the enclosed outer settlement and lower town also developed suddenly into a conglomeration of some 5,000 people within a 100 ha enclosed area. The outer town was made up of buildings within their own enclosures, perhaps representing kinship groups. One large timber hall located in the later area of the Gießübel-Talhau burial mounds has been compared in size to the contemporary Etruscan palaces (Krausse et al. 2016). The plateau occupation, with buildings ordered in rows, seems to represent craft producers, with the main settlement outside. Around 550 BC a major fire destroyed the mud-brick wall and plateau occupation; whether due to an attack or an accident is not known. The mud-brick wall was replaced by an earth and timber rampart, the outer town was abandoned, and the tumuli of Gießübel-Talhau partially placed over the top of it. The lower town saw an intensification of use, now with much evidence of craft production, and the plateau saw a more haphazard settlement compared to the previous rows of artisans' buildings. It is to this period that the main Mediterranean imports were dated. The settlement as a whole was abandoned around

450 BC, at the same time as Mont Lassois and broadly contemporary with the start of La Tène A.

Much could be said about the new evidence, which I have not even covered in outline here. I will, however, concentrate on two issues, one briefly, the other slightly more fully. Slightly surprisingly, given that my main subject is trade and exchange, I shall give little attention to the Mediterranean imports, but rather more to the accumulation of people. As we have seen, Mediterranean imports at the Heuneburg were always small in number, and now that we know how many people lived there this number is further diminished in comparison to the people. These imports come late in the complex history of the settlement, making it very hard to see that links with the Mediterranean world were crucial to the wealth and size of the Heuneburg settlement.

A key aspect of the continental Iron Age, from early to late, is the rapid and often temporary accumulations of population. It is estimated that, at its height, the Heuneburg was inhabited by 5,000 people. This represented the gathering together of a large number of previously discrete communities, presumably from smaller settlements in the surrounding countryside. These people and their descendants stayed together for some 200 years—eight generations—before, presumably, dispersing around 450 BC. The process of temporarily coming together and dispersing has never been problematized, although it was a key part of Iron Age life, influencing many patterns of production and exchange. Derrida, not a name generally associated with Iron Age studies, developed a notion of hospitality to look at how groups were brought together, or boundaries of exclusion were set up. A host is hospitable and welcoming, but also in a position of power, so able to bring people together and with the resources to act as a host (Derrida 2000; Derrida and Dufourmantelle 2000). Behind the apparent open-handedness and generosity of the host lie issues of power, an important contradiction for Derrida, who also sees the relationship between host and guest can be upturned when the cosmopolitanism of guest may throw the homeliness of the host into relief. Derrida was partly thinking here of issues of multiculturalism, nationalism, and prejudice in the context of a modern nation state, but such ideas may also resonate in earlier periods.

It is thought that the enclosures of the later town at the Heuneburg represent various kinship groups, although this is hard to demonstrate. If so, the mechanisms behind such a coming together are interesting, whether this was through the invitation of one group or individual, or a more spontaneous coalescence. The existence of the large 'palace' structure may indicate the former. The building of the mud-brick wall around the plateau once the settlement had coalesced is a striking indication of outside influence of some kind, quite possibly a local individual who had been in the Mediterranean region and brought back knowledge and/or skilled workers with them. As the relatively small number of imported sherds arrived well into the history of the settlement, Mediterranean links had nothing to do with its origin. Nevertheless, far-flung links may have been locally important, adding an extra, exotic lustre to local power (Helms 1988, 1993).

Whatever the mechanisms by which such a large number of people came together, their joint effects on production and exchange would have been marked in the local region and far beyond. The picture of the Heuneburg is still so novel that the implications in human and material terms will take some time to work through, and the nature of production on the site and the regional effects will be key. A site which starts contemporaneously with the Heuneburg, has a very different history, and a considerable influence on trade and exchange is Massalia (modern-day Marseille), which we will consider next.

At the end of the second millennium BC contacts are seen throughout the Mediterranean zone, as evidenced by the movement of Mycenaean pots to sites in Italy, Sicily, Sardinia, and Spain, or the production locally of Mycenaean style wares (Sherratt 1998). Cyprus has links with Sardinia, which is at the western end of the distribution of ox-hide ingots found in Babylon in the east around 1200 BC (Osborne 1996: 113). The standard sizes of these ingots indicate some standardization of value in exchange. Trade continued throughout the Mediterranean region despite the collapse of the palace economies around 1200 BC. By 800 BC, the Phoenicians were starting to move along the southern Mediterranean coastline, and shortly afterwards settlements were set up at Pithekoussai and on Sicily. Whether these were Greek colonies or not has been debated (Osborne 1998; Gosden 2004). So, for instance, Pithekoussai was founded just before 750 BC on the island of Ischia in the Bay of Naples, and grew to 5,000–10,000 inhabitants within a generation. It seems unlikely that all these people came from a single Greek place to found a colony: their pottery came from a variety of Greek sources, alongside locally made copies; the ironworkers may well have used ores from sources in mainland Etruria (Osborne 1996: 114–118). The possibilities of production and trade may have drawn people to these new cities from many areas, making them less colonies and more accumulations of groups from across the Mediterranean. People accumulated wealth, but wealth also accumulates people.

Massalia sits within one of the best natural harbours in Mediterranean France, not far from the mouth of the Rhône, the major conduit to inland areas. From 650 BC, Etruscan traders worked these waters mainly selling wine in distinctive Etruscan amphorae and drinking vessels made in Etruria, such as black *bucchero* wares. From 600 BC, a dramatic new phase commenced with the founding of Massalia. The conventional view is that this was a Phocaean colony settled by a group from the mother city of Phocaea on the coast of Asia Minor, reinforced by new migrants when that city fell to Cyrus the Great in 545 BC (Dietler 2010: 104–106). Others (Osborne 1998: 269), including myself (Gosden 2004: 65–72), disagree. In the one view, the northern shore of the Mediterranean was dominated by Greek colonists and colonies, with the southern shore and parts of Iberia being trading areas of Phoenicians/Carthaginians. In the other view, the Mediterranean region was a melting pot of people, ideas, and materials, with slightly different circulation systems, later claiming links to Greece or Carthage (Malkin 2011). In reality the two views are not so far apart, with Dietler (2010: 105–106) noting that neither Greek nor Phocaean was a stable and fixed identity; people claimed (or denied) such identities for strategic reasons, and those reasons always included trade and exchange.

For the discussion here I am less interested in colonies and cultural links and more concerned with the contrasting histories of Massalia and the Heuneburg. Both were established around 600 BC. Population estimates are difficult, but it is possible that the very earliest populations of both were of similar size—around 5,000 people. Massalian occupation covered some 12 ha initially, with evidence around Fort Saint-Jean and Butte Saint-Laurent, both on a promontory sticking out into the sea, with the ancient shoreline closer in than now (Dietler 2010: 308). The earliest dated rampart, *c.*510 BC, probably enclosed a much larger area, including the Butte des Moulins and the Butte des Carmes (although there is some debate about this). Within a century of the founding, Massalia expanded from 12 to 40 ha, not far from its maximum known Roman extent when it had 15,000–20,000 inhabitants. Such massive growth is unlikely to have come from Aegean colonists alone, and must have included locals as well. The different grid layouts (possibly five?) in the earliest periods may have been due to variations in topography or the existence of a variety of kin or political groups (as is also surmised for the Heuneburg lower town). No monumental buildings have yet been found for the earliest phases.

The very earliest pottery assemblages at Massalia have a predominance of Etruscan wares, but often *c.*550 BC locally produced colonial creamwares, and grey-monochrome pots take over, and it is from this period that wine is locally produced. In the area west of the Rhône, in Languedoc, Etruscan wares form 10–15% of assemblages between 625–540 BC, with Massalian-produced wares peaking at 50% of assemblages around 400 BC, with Roman Dressel 1 amphorae becoming most common for a century from 125 BC. Similar patterns are found in Provence as well (Dietler 2010: 206–207). At Emporion in present-day Spain, Massalian sherds are never more than 15% of totals, with Ibero-Punic amphorae (and presumably locally produced wine) dominant.

We can discern a series of different regions of wine production and consumption arising after 540–530 BC when Etruscan influence declines, perhaps due to internal problems in Etruria. These remain more or less stable and centred around large sites such as Emporion or Massalia until the Roman trade takes off around 125 BC. This trade is massively different. From 600 BC onwards, trade is local and certainly coastal with very little material moving inland, as we have seen with the Heuneburg. Roman amphorae of Dressel 1 type are suddenly found all over Gaul (e.g. Olmer 2003; Loughton 2014), with good numbers turning up in Britain (Fitzpatrick 1985) and elsewhere. The Roman trade is commercial, large-scale, and in many areas a prelude to empire; in earlier periods we can chart mainly local networks linked by small amounts of exotic goods moving longer distances.

When we compare the Mediterranean and inland areas for the two centres from 600 BC, similarities and differences can be seen. We would now accept sites like the Heuneburg, and probably others, such as Bourges (Buchsenschutz and Frénée 2009; Buchsenschutz et al. 2009), as having considerable concentrations of population, having previously restricted this to late Iron Age *oppida*. Substantial numbers of people came together, engaging mainly in local production and exchange, with some exotics. These represent unprecedented numbers and new forms of organization, possibly through different kin groups confederating. In the case of the Heuneburg, this lasted for several generations before dispersal in early La Tène. The case of Bourges is still less well known, with domestic structures being difficult to recognize.

The Mediterranean centres have widespread links initially, such as those between Provence and Etruria down to *c*.540 BC, but then develop their own local areas of trade and exchange, best defined by pottery concerned with wine. These centres are part of a first wave of urbanization across the Mediterranean from east to west between 800 and 600 BC. The Mediterranean centres are founded at much the same time as those in the north, but have more continuous histories, with Massalia morphing over 2,600 years into modern Marseille. No town exists on the ancient Heuneburg, which flourished briefly, if spectacularly, only in the early Iron Age.

The fluctuating history of urbanism, which underpins a great deal of the movement of materials, takes on a new phase in the second century BC in temperate Europe when new towns emerge. By this time, many in the Mediterranean world had long and continuous histories. It is to the late Iron Age that we now turn.

Late Iron Age Trade and Exchange

La Tène B and C saw few Mediterranean imports into temperate Europe, and in some of the Mediterranean centres, such as Massalia, levels of longer distance trade declined. Such a decline in obvious links with the Mediterranean world is found generally across Europe at this time, and might be connected to drops in population levels in temperate Europe between *c*.400 and 200 BC. This is indicated by a smaller number of find-spots, but also by the pollen evidence (Krausse 2006; Fernández-Götz 2012: 346). Quite why this happened is debatable and might be some sort of response to more centralized forms of power between 600–400 BC, or due to the historically documented movement of Celtic peoples south and east, which in itself might be part of such a response.

After *c*.200 BC (La Tène C2), a second phase of centralization begins in a band from France across to Hungary and beyond. Some sites are more or less new foundations, such as Manching, Bavaria, but others develop on the sites of earlier hillforts, such as those in the Hunsrück-Eifel area (Fernández-Götz 2012). As is well known, there has been a long debate over whether the *oppida* were towns, seeing too the rise of cultural forms with a more obvious economic base with price-fixing markets and the sale of commodities for profit. Certainly conditions in Europe had changed compared with those found around the centres of the early Iron Age. This is due in considerable part to startling new levels of production and exchange emanating from Roman Italy. The contrast in the number and distribution of Mediterranean imports between the early and later Iron Age is stark. Just looking at amphorae, very few Greek, Etruscan, and Massalian amphorae are found inland from Mediterranean shores, but huge amounts of Dressel 1 and subsequent forms are seen after 125 BC, from the mouth of the Rhône Valley up into north-west Europe (Dietler 2010: ch. 7). There are similar increases in drinking vessels from Campania and later *terra sigillata*, with the latter produced within France. There can be little doubt about the scale and ubiquitous nature of this trade, with even small sites receiving Mediterranean items. Elsewhere (Gosden 2005) I have tried to sketch out the influence the new demands that novel material culture, food and drink might have made on people.

As well as long-distant trade, local production, especially within the *oppida*, sees a marked upturn. The vast row of monographs on Manching demonstrates the importance of pottery production, including graphite-tempered and painted wares, ironmaking and recycling, bronze smelting and casting, and so on. In the Altenfeld area was a series of pits, possible storage structures, evidence for the working of bronze and the recycling of iron, and also indications of a harbour on an old arm of the Danube (Sievers 2003; Sievers et al. 2013). A hoard of 483 gold coins indicates connections with Bohemia, a link reinforced through the results of isotopic analyses of human bone. The excavations at Altenfeld make it more likely that there were specialist craftworking areas inside Manching (despite extensive excavations, only around 8% of the interior has been investigated) (Maier 1992). The long-distance connections indicated there are reinforced by finds of Baltic amber and considerable amounts of Roman amphorae (Stöckli et al. 1979).

Similar patterns are found elsewhere, with the large-scale excavations at Mont Beuvray in central France showing specialist metal production around the Porte du Rebout with a building with equipment for smelting, casting, forging, and finishing metalwork. The multiple internal structures also evidence metalworking and other crafts, together with large amounts of Roman amphorae (Guichard et al. 2000; Olmer 2003). Such examples could be multiplied through sites such as Staré Hradisko in Moravia to the east (Čižmář 2005). For both Mont Beuvray and Manching, population estimates range between 5,000–10,000 people, overlapping with the Heuneburg at the lower end, but rather less than the 15,000–20,000 people estimated for Massalia at the time of the Roman invasion in 125 BC. Such numbers are modest by modern standards, but unprecedented for ancient Europe, causing considerable internal demand for food and goods, new modes of social regulation, and a probable need for incomers to replace those dying from disease in newly crowded conditions.

In Britain, *oppida* are lacking in large populations—with the arguable exception of Silchester (Fulford and Timby 2000)—although there is considerable evidence of production on various sites. Centres such as Camulodunum (Colchester; Hawkes and Crummy 1995), Verulamium (St Albans; Niblett 1999, 2001), and Bagendon (Moore 2006) have complex ditches enclosing large areas within which are centres of productive activity and burials, but small living populations. Most sites were not in previously settled areas, demonstrating a certain novelty of power relations at the end of the Iron Age (Hill 2007). Coins had become common in the last century BC, and were minted in gold, silver, and bronze in some areas, presumably with differing values. Coins were minted in sites such as Silchester, as well as St Michael's enclosure in Verulamium (Haselgrove and Millett 1997: 284). There has been considerable debate as to whether a widespread coinage was due to a market economy, or whether it complemented and nuanced more socially based exchanges (Collis 1971). The *oppida* and contemporary burials, such as those at Welwyn Garden City (Stead 1967), Lexden (Foster 1986), and Folly Lane (Niblett 1999) contained considerable numbers of Roman imports, including amphorae, pottery, and metalwork. Britain, as elsewhere, was connected to the long-distance trade deriving from the Mediterranean world in a manner never seen previously, although this was most obvious in the south and east of the country.

In writing about Celtic art in Britain, Duncan Garrow and I felt that throughout the Iron Age and into the Roman period people's efforts to produce, exchange, use, and deposit items, both local and exotic, were enmeshed in a broader sets of values linking to the material world and the cosmological powers seen to animate it (Garrow and Gosden 2012: chs 1, 9). Human, material, and cosmological values were all mixed, so that the search for individual or group advantage could not be seen in solely economic terms as we would understand these today. Looking across late Iron Age Europe, we can see novel political forms and modes of identity, with something like the tribal groups, noted by Caesar and others, coming into being in the last 150 years BC. People become more themselves by trading with outsiders, particularly with material culture designated as Roman (although important items of trade, such as *terra sigillata*, were produced at La Graufenesque and other sites in Gaul with distributions to northern Britain, north Africa, across the *limes* into eastern Europe and even Italy). Extensive excavations in recent decades of a number of *oppida* and smaller settlements have yet to lead to proper syntheses of individual sites, and without this sustained comparison and contrasts between sites is not possible. The internal structure, local effects, and long-distance connections of *oppida* are still poorly understood, although potentially knowable from the information we have. Unprecedented levels of local production and of population dynamics, as well as regional exchange, are in evidence, but need more thought.

On that note I shall turn to some final reflections, which contain indications of further directions, but within a further consideration of the history of work done on trade and exchange.

Final Thoughts

Thirty years ago I finished a PhD thesis on the production and exchange of early wheel-turned pottery in central Europe (Gosden 1983), and this anniversary might account for the historical nature of this chapter. Back then, as I mentioned in the opening, trade and exchange were central topics in Iron Age studies, being seen as cause rather than effect, and operating in a *sui generis* manner as a link between the productive base and the social infrastructure (Marx was in fashion back then too). The evidence for the Iron Age has changed out of all recognition since the 1980s, mainly as a result of developer-funded archaeology. We are nowhere near assimilating this mass of new data. Key sites, such as the Heuneburg, can now be seen as centres of population, with much more extensive occupation than just that required for artisan's workshops and specialist traders. The same may be true of Bourges and other early centres. Population concentration in the early Iron Age invites comparison with the much longer recognized concentrations of people in *oppida*, along with the now obvious contrast between the lack of Mediterranean trade in the early period and its high levels in the late Iron Age.

Linked to such empirical realizations, we now view trade and exchange less as processes on their own, and as more embedded within other aspects of culture, which helped to define the values attached to artefacts, where the term value is broadly conceived. Consequently, trade and exchange become effects as much as causes. The relatively large numbers of people in the Heuneburg might have drawn in Mediterranean and other imports in modest numbers, rather than the imports being the reason for the centralization of power, people, and productivity. More generally, we might be inclined to link things up, so that changing distributions of people concentrating, dispersing, and concentrating again between Hallstatt D and La Tène D, were linked to changing distributions of productive powers and of exchanged objects. I have drawn out the different histories of population concentration (urbanism) in the Mediterranean world and in temperate Europe. A marked change happens in many places around 600 BC with new centres of population. Massalia starts around this date with roughly 5,000 people, grows rapidly and continually to perhaps twice its original size within a century, and grows more slowly through to the Roman period and down to today as Marseille. Quite a number of the Mediterranean towns show the same history, and it is the defended hilltops, such as Entremont, which are abandoned before the coming of the Romans (Armit et al. 2012). In temperate Europe, the Hallstatt D centres are generally found in previously unoccupied places, then last for several generations to disappear without being reoccupied in many cases. On some occasions, such as in the Hunsrück-Eifel, some of the earlier sites are reoccupied from La Tène C onwards to become *oppida* (Fernández-Götz 2012: 347). However, even more *oppida* are on 'green field' sites, although there are intriguing indications that a number might have been picked out as centres of cult and burial in the earlier La Tène, as is the case with Manching. Most *oppida* are abandoned before the coming of the Romans (Manching) or soon after (the move from Mont Beuvray to Autun). The sequence in southern Britain is different again, with unprecedented population in some hillforts, such as Danebury from 600 BC, which continues until the start of the late Iron Age (Cunliffe 2009). Populations are probably hundreds and not thousands, but leave considerable evidence of agricultural and craft activity, with some evidence of local (pottery, salt) and long-distance exchange (coral, amber, and possibly metals). The few early Iron Age Greek pots that have been found in Britain come from rivers, and not population centres (Bradley and Smith 2007: fig. 3.3). Hillforts do not become *oppida* in Britain, but then none of the British late Iron Age centres are towns in any sense that we would understand, although many have cult and industrial activities in evidence. As far as we can tell, no more people lived in them than lived in the hillforts. Towns only start in Britain with the Romans. The *oppida* do show evidence of items moving in long-distance exchange, so were part of broader European links and the changes in power and identity to which these were in turn connected.

As the older model of trade and exchange has declined, so too has the connected change from early Iron Age chiefdoms to late Iron Age states. We are increasingly aware that generalizations drawn from ethnography, such as chiefdom and state, are not helpful in understanding late prehistoric cultural forms and their practices. The prestige goods model of a few decades ago no longer seems to work, nor do we have a full and coherent alternative. Present archaeologists are faced with a newly massive empirical base, and in some ways are working up from this, with generalized theories of practice, culture, and ontology. If the present is somewhat uncertain, future prospects for novel understandings are bright.

References

Arafat, K., and C. Morgan. 1994. 'Athens, Etruria and the Heuneburg: Mutual misconceptions in the study of Greek–barbarian relations', in I. Morris (ed.) *Classical Greece: Ancient Histories and Modern Archaeologies*: 108–134. Cambridge: Cambridge University Press.

Armit, I., C. Gaffney, and A. Hayes. 2012. 'Space and movement in an Iron Age oppidum: Integrating geophysical and topographical survey at Entremont, Provence'. *Antiquity* 86: 191–206.

Bradley, R., and A. Smith. 2007. 'Questions of context: A Greek cup from the River Thames', in C. Gosden, H. Hamerow, P. De Jersey, and G. Lock (eds) *Communities and Connections: Essays in honour of Barry Cunliffe*: 30–42. Oxford: Oxford University Press.

Buchsenschutz, O., C. Cribellier, A. Luberne, B. Pescher, and J. Troadec. 2009. 'Réflexions sur 40 ans de fouilles à Bourges (Cher) et à Levroux (Indre)', in O. Buchsenschutz, M.-B. Chardenoux, S. Krausz, and M. Vaginay (eds) *L'âge du Fer dans la boucle de la Loire: Les Gaulois sont dans la ville. Actes du XXXIIe Colloque de l'AFEAF, Bourges, 1–4 mai 2008*. Revue Archéologique du Centre de la France supplément 35: 237–250. Paris/Tours: FERACF.

Buchsenschutz, O., and E. Frénée. 2009. 'Structures d'habitat de l'âge du Fer dans la boucle de la Loire', in O. Buchsenschutz, M.-B. Chardenoux, S. Krausz, and M. Vaginay (eds) *L'âge du Fer dans la boucle de la Loire: Les Gaulois sont dans la ville. Actes du XXXIIe Colloque de l'AFEAF, Bourges, 1–4 mai 2008*. Revue Archéologique du Centre de la France supplément 35: 103–120. Paris/Tours: FERACF.

Čižmář, M. 2005. *Keltské oppidum Staré Hradisko*, 2nd edition. Archeologické Památky Střední Moravy 4. Olomouc: Olomouc Museum.

Collis, J. R. 1971. 'Functional and theoretical interpretations of British coinage'. *World Archaeology* 3: 71–84.

Collis, J. R. 1984. *The European Iron Age*. London: Batsford.

Cunliffe, B. W. 2009. 'Continuity and change in a Wessex landscape', in R. Johnston (ed.) *2008 Lectures, Proceedings of the British Academy 162*. Oxford/London: Oxford University Press/ British Academy.

Denemark, R. A., J. Friedman, B. Gills, and G. Modelski. 2000. *World System History: The Social Science of Long-Term Change*. London: Routledge.

Derrida, J. 2000. 'Hospitality'. *Angelaki: Journal of the Theoretical Humanities* 5: 3–18.

Derrida, J., and A. Dufourmantelle. 2000. *Of Hospitality*. Stanford: Stanford University Press.

Dietler, M. 2010. *Archaeologies of Colonialism: Consumption, Entanglement and Violence in Ancient Mediterranean France*. Berkeley/Los Angeles: University of California Press.

Ekholm, K. 1972. *Power and Prestige: The Rise and Fall of the Kongo Kingdom*. Gothenburg: Etnologiska Museet.

Fernández-Götz, M. 2012. 'Identität und Macht: das Mittelrhein- und Moselgebiet von der frühen Eisenzeit bis zur Romanisierung (600 v. Chr.—70 n. Chr.)'. *Archäologische Informationen* 35: 343–350.

Fitzpatrick, A. P. 1985. 'The distribution of Dressel 1 amphorae in north-west Europe'. *Oxford Journal of Archaeology* 4: 305–340.

Foster, J. 1986. *The Lexden Tumulus: A Reappraisal of an Iron Age Burial from Colchester, Essex*. British Archaeological Reports British Series 156. Oxford: British Archaeological Reports.

Frank, G., and B. Gills. 1993. *The World System: Five Hundred Years or Five Thousand?* London: Routledge.

Frankenstein, S., and M. Rowlands. 1978. 'Early Iron Age society in southwest Germany'. *Bulletin of the Institute of Archaeology* 15: 73–112.

Frey, O.-H., and F. Schwappach. 1973. 'Studies in early Celtic design'. *World Archaeology* 4: 341–356.

Fulford, M., and J. Timby. 2000. *Late Iron Age and Roman Silchester: Excavations on the Site of the Forum-Basilica, 1977, 1980–6*. Britannia Monograph Series 15. London: Society for the Promotion of Roman Studies.

Garrow, D., and C. Gosden. 2012. *Technologies of Enchantment?: Exploring Celtic Art in Britain 400 BC to AD 100*. Oxford: Oxford University Press.

Gosden, C. 1983. 'Iron Age Pottery Trade in Central Europe'. PhD thesis, University of Sheffield.

Gosden, C. 2004. *Archaeology and Colonialism: Cultural Contact from 5000 BC to the Present*. Cambridge: Cambridge University Press.

Gosden, C. 2005. 'What do objects want?' *Journal of Archaeological Method and Theory* 12, 3: 193–211.

Gregory, C. 1982. *Gifts and Commodities*. New York: Academic Press.

Guichard, V., S. Sievers, and O. H. Urban (eds). 2000. *Les processus d'urbanisation à l'âge du Fer: Eisenzeitliche Urbanisationsprozesse*. Collection Bibracte 4. Glux-en-Glenne: Centre archéologique européen du Mont Beuvray.

Haselgrove, C. 1982. 'Wealth, prestige and power: the dynamics of late Iron Age political centralisation in south-east England', in C. Renfrew and S. Shennan (eds) *Ranking, Resource and Exchange*: 79–88. Cambridge: Cambridge University Press.

Haselgrove, C., and M. Millett. 1997. 'Verlamion reconsidered', in A. Gwilt and C. Haselgrove (eds) *Reconstructing Iron Age Societies*. Oxbow Monograph 71: 282–296. Oxford: Oxbow.

Hawkes, C. F. C., and P. Crummy. 1995. *Camulodunum 2*. Colchester Archaeological Report 11. Colchester: Colchester Archaeological Trust.

Helms, M. W. 1988. *Ulysses' Sail: An Ethnographic Odyssey of Power, Knowledge and Geographical Distance*. Princeton: Princeton University Press.

Helms, M. W. 1993. *Craft and the Kingly Ideal: Art, Trade, Power*. Austin: University of Texas Press.

Hill, J. D. 2007. 'The dynamics of social change in Later Iron Age eastern and south-eastern England *c.*300 BC–AD 43', in C. Haselgrove and T. Moore (eds) *The Later Iron Age in Britain and Beyond*: 16–40. Oxford: Oxbow.

Krausse, D. 2006. *Eisenzeitlicher Kulturwandel und Romanisierung im Mosel-Eifel-Raum: Die keltisch-römische Siedlung von Wallendorf und ihr archäologisches Umfeld*. Römisch-Germanische Forschungen 63. Mainz: Philipp von Zabern.

Krausse, D., M. Fernández-Götz, L. Hansen, and I. Kretschmer. 2016. *The Heuneburg and the Early Iron Age Princely Seats: First Towns North of the Alps*. Budapest: Archaeolingua.

Kurz, S. 2001. 'Siedlungsforschungen bei der Heuneburg, Gde. Herbertingen-Hundersingen, Kreis Sigmaringen—Zum Stand des DFG-Projektes'. *Archäologische Ausgrabungen in Baden-Württemberg 2001*: 61–63.

Kurz, S. 2002. 'Siedlungsforschungen im Umfeld der Heuneburg bei Hundersingen, Gde. Herbertingen, Kreis Sigmaringen'. *Archäologische Ausgrabungen in Baden-Württemberg 2002*: 77–79.

Loughton, M. 2014. *The Arverni and Roman Wine: Roman Amphorae from Late Iron Age Sites in the Auvergne (Central France): Chronology, Fabrics and Stamps*. Archaeopress Roman Archaeology 2. Oxford: Archaeopress.

Magetti, M., and G. Galetti. 1980. 'Composition of fine ceramics from Châtillon-sur-Glâne (kt. Fribourg, Switzerland) and the Heuneburg (Kr. Sigmaringen, West Germany)'. *Journal of Archaeological Science* 7: 87–91.

Maier, F. 1992. 'Nachwort', in F. Maier, U. Geilenbrügge, E. Hahn, H.-J. Köhler, and S. Sievers (eds) *Ergebnisse der Ausgrabungen 1984–1987*. Die Ausgrabungen in Manching 15. Stuttgart: Steiner.

Malkin, I. 2011. *A Small Greek World: Networks in the Ancient Mediterranean*. Oxford: Oxford University Press.

Mauss, M. 1969. *The Gift*. London: Routledge and Kegan Paul.

Meillassoux, C. 1981. *Maidens, Meal and Money: Capitalism and the Domestic Economy*. Cambridge: Cambridge University Press.

Moore, T. 2006. *Iron Age Societies in the Severn-Cotswolds: Developing Narratives of Social and Landscape Change*. British Archaeological Reports British Series 421. Oxford: Archaeopress.

Moosleitner, F., L. Pauli, and E. Penninger. 1974. *Der Dürrnberg bei Hallein II: Katalog der Grabfunde aus der Hallstatt- und Latènezeit*. Münchner Beiträge zur Vor- und Frühgeschichte 17. Munich: Beck.

Morris, E. 1994. 'Production and distribution of pottery and salt in Iron Age Britain: A review'. *Proceedings of the Prehistoric Society* 60: 371–393.

Niblett, R. 1999. *The Excavation of a Ceremonial Site at Folly Lane, Verulamium*. Britannia Monograph Series 14. London: Society for the Promotion of Roman Studies.

Niblett, R. 2001. *Verulamium: The Roman City of St Albans*. Stroud: Tempus.

Northover, P. 1982. 'The exploration and long distance movement of bronze in Bronze Age and early Iron Age Europe'. *Bulletin of the Institute of Archaeology* 19: 45–72.

Northover, P. 1984. 'Iron Age bronze metallurgy in central southern England', in B. W. Cunliffe and D. Miles (eds) *Aspects of the Iron Age in Central Southern England*. OUCA Monograph 2: 126–145. Oxford: Oxford University Committee for Archaeology.

Olmer, F. 2003. *Les amphores de Bibracte, 2. Le commerce du vin chez les Eduens d'après les timbres d'amphores*. Collection Bibracte 7. Glux-en-Glenne: Centre archéologique européen du Mont Beuvray.

Osborne, R. 1996. *Greece in the Making, 1200–479 BC*. London: Routledge.

Osborne, R. 1998. 'Early Greek colonization? The nature of Greek settlement in the West', in N. Fisher and H. van Wees (eds) *Archaic Greece: New Approaches and New Evidence*: 251–269. London: Duckworth.

Pauli, L. 1978. *Der Dürrnberg bei Hallein III: Auswertung der Grabfunde*. Münchner Beiträge zur Vor- und Frühgeschichte 18. Munich: Beck.

Peacock, D. 1968. 'Petrological study of certain Iron Age pots from western England'. *Proceedings of the Prehistoric Society* 34: 414–427.

Peacock, D. 1981. 'Archaeology, ethnography and ceramic production', in H. Howard and E. Morris (eds) *Production and Distribution: A Ceramic Viewpoint*. British Archaeological Reports International Series 120: 187–194. Oxford: British Archaeological Reports.

Polanyi, K., C. M. Arensberg, and H. W. Pearson. 1957. *Trade and Market in Early Empires: Economies in History and Theory*. Glencoe: The Free Press.

Reim, H. 2001. 'Siedlungsarchäologische Forschungen im Umland der frühkeltischen Heuneburg bei Hundersingen, Gemeinde Herbertingen, Kreis Sigmaringen'. *Jahrbuch Heimat- und Altertumsverein Heidenheim* 9: 12–33.

Reim, H. 2002. 'Die Außenbefestigungen der Heuneburg bei Hundersingen, Gde. Herbertingen, Kreis Sigmaringen'. *Archäologische Ausgrabungen in Baden-Württemberg* 2002: 72–76.

Renfrew, C. 1975. 'Trade as action at a distance. Questions of integration and communication', in J. A. Sabloff and C. C. Lamberg-Karlovsky (eds) *Ancient Civilization and Trade*: 3–59. Albuquerque: New Mexico Press.

Renfrew, C. 1977. 'Alternative models for exchange and spatial distribution', in T. Earle and J. Ericson (eds) *Exchange Systems in Prehistory*: 71–90. New York: Academic Press.

Sahlins, M. 1974. *Stone Age Economics*. London: Tavistock.

Sherratt, S. 1998. ' "Sea peoples" and the economic structure of the late second millennium in the eastern Mediterranean', in S. Gitin, A. Mazar, and E. Stern (eds) *Mediterranean Peoples in Transition: Thirteenth to Early Tenth Centuries BC*: 292–313. Jerusalem: Israel Exploration Society.

Sievers, S. 2003. *Manching, Die Keltenstadt: Führer zu archäologischen Denkmälern in Bayern: Oberbayern 3*. Stuttgart: Theiss.

Sievers, S., M. Leicht, and M. Ziegaus. 2013. *Ergebnisse der Ausgrabungen in Manching-Altenfeld 1996–1999*. Die Ausgrabungen in Manching 18. Wiesbaden: Reichert Verlag.

Stead, I. 1967. 'A La Tène III burial at Welwyn Garden City'. *Archaeologia* 101: 1–62.

Stöckli, W. E., M. Hopf, and J. Riederer. 1979. *Die Grob- und Importkeramik von Manching*. Die Ausgrabungen in Manching 8. Wiesbaden: Steiner.

Terray, E. 1972. *Marxism and Primitive Societies*. New York: Monthly Review Press.

Wallerstein, I. 1974. *The Modern World-System*. New York: Academic Press.

CHAPTER 28

COINAGE AND COIN USE

COLIN HASELGROVE

Introduction

An invention of the Greek peoples of Asia Minor in the seventh century BC, coinage spread rapidly through the Mediterranean world, and around 300 BC began to penetrate north into temperate Europe. By the second century BC, indigenous coinages were in use over a zone stretching from the Black Sea and Danube basin via Bohemia and southern Germany to the Atlantic coasts of France and Spain. Most groups who issued coins were Celtic speakers, but they also included Germans, Iberians, Illyrians, Ligurians, and Thracians. The inhabitants of Britain were among the last to adopt the idea, continuing to mint coins in the first century AD after most coin-using peoples had been absorbed into the Roman Empire. During the Roman Iron Age, large quantities of imperial coinage found its way to groups beyond the frontiers, but in much of northern Europe coinage remained alien until the early Medieval period.

In recent decades, Iron Age coin studies have advanced rapidly, driven by new finds from excavations and metal detecting, detailed die studies, and scientific analysis. At major centres and religious sites, finds often run into hundreds, if not thousands, although they are rarer on rural settlements. Types once known from only a few examples are now common, permitting secure geographical and typological attribution—although many gaps remain, especially for early series. There has also been a shift in theoretical orientation, with scholars abandoning older paradigms that viewed Iron Age coinage through the lens of modern Western economies in favour of anthropologically informed approaches that emphasize its social and religious dimensions (e.g. Roymans 1990; Aarts 2005; Haselgrove and Wigg-Wolf 2005; Roymans and Aarts 2009; García-Bellido et al. 2011; Farley 2012; Howgego 2013).

The chapter begins with a short overview of Iron Age coinage in non-Mediterranean Europe and evidence for minting and manufacturing.[1] It then examines debate about why the idea of coinage—by then well established in the classical world—was rapidly adopted around 300 BC by many Iron Age peoples, but seemingly resisted by those in Scandinavia and the North European Plain until centuries later. The evolving role and function of Iron Age coins are then explored in greater depth, drawing on contextual studies of coin loss and deposition on archaeological sites across the continent. A significant issue in seeking to understand Iron Age coinage is the absence of internal references to its use and meaning, while a handful of references by classical authors to the use of gold or money in Iron Age Europe (see Allen 1976) may not be wholly dependable or even relate to coins. This renders material evidence the most viable route to progress (Howgego 2013: 13–16).

The Spread of Coinage in Non-Mediterranean Europe

At the outset, Iron Age coins were made of gold or silver and derived from Greek models. Coins of the powerful Macedonian rulers, Philip II (died 336 BC) and Alexander the Great (died 323 BC), were the most influential prototypes, but issues of later Hellenistic rulers and Greek colonies such as Massalia (Marseille), Rhode (Rosas), and Emporion (Ampurias) were also copied. Near the Mediterranean, the Greek models adopted were nearly all of silver, whereas north of the Alps communities generally opted for gold (Figure 28.1). Over time, distinctive regional traditions emerged as indigenous issuers added features and designs of their own. None of the early coins were meaningfully inscribed, but from the second century BC, moneyers began to put names—and occasionally other details such as a title or mint—on coins. Most legends were in Greek or Latin letters, or a mixture of the two, and Iberian, Illyrian, and Italiote scripts were all used in certain areas (Allen 1980; Chapter 36). As Rome became the dominant Mediterranean power after defeating Carthage in the Second Punic War (218–201 BC), its coinage was increasingly widely imitated. Many Iron Age peoples began to mint in more than one metal, although bronze was essentially confined to western Europe, and tri-metallic coinages are exceptional, and mostly post-date Caesar's conquest of Gaul.

Throughout southern Europe, from the Balkans and Danube basin, via the Po plain in Italy, to the Garonne basin in France, silver was the preferred metal for Iron Age coinage (Table 28.1). In the east, the earliest types were faithful imitations of posthumous *tetradrachms* of Philip II of Macedon, with a bearded head on one side and a horseman on the other. These were not so much a local coinage as substitutes for the real thing (Nash 1987). The first unmistakeably native coinages emerged in the early third century BC and were all based on this model, except close to the Black Sea, where *tetradrachms* of Alexander the Great or his successor Philip III were the preferred model; these portray a seated figure instead of the horseman. A few Greek gold types were also copied in this area, but not for long. Over the next century, silver coinage spread across eastern Europe, sometimes employing other Greek models, and its volume increased

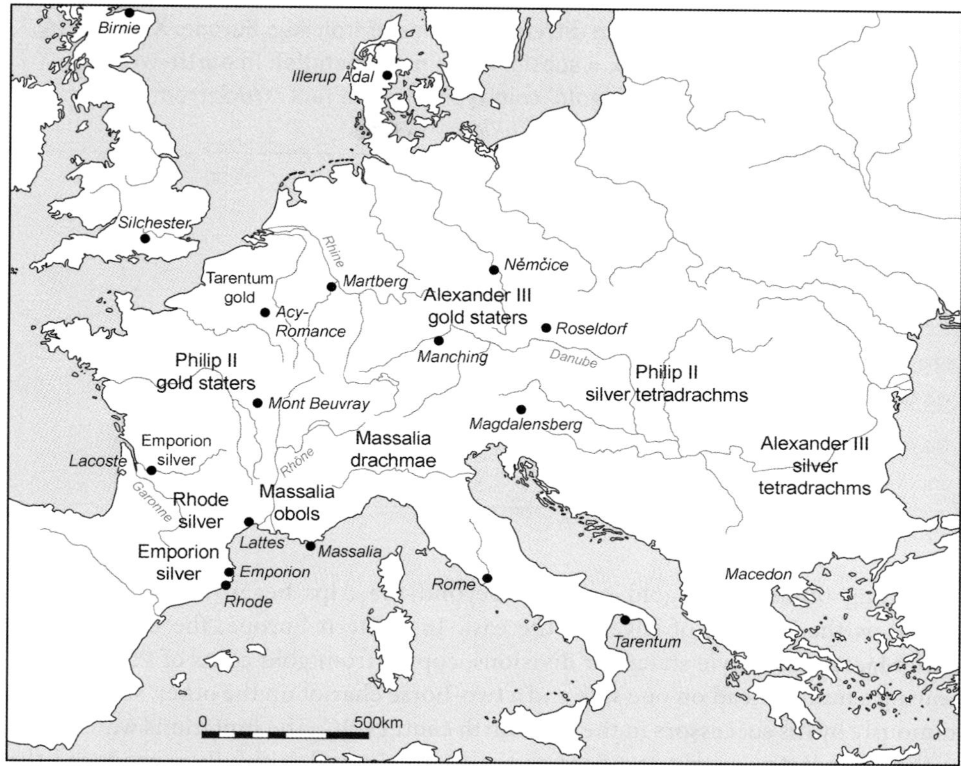

FIGURE 28.1 Greek prototypes copied by the earliest Iron Age coinages in Celtic Europe, and location of key sites mentioned in the text.

Drawing: author

markedly; distinctive regional traditions developed, stylistically further removed from the prototypes. Eventually, in the first century BC, many groups abandoned Hellenistic models for Roman types, added legends, but then stopped striking coinage altogether. Silver fractions also occur, but bronze coins are restricted to Pannonia.

Elsewhere in the silver zone, initial models were mostly provided by coinages of the Greek colonies (Hiriart et al. 2020). As early as the fourth century BC, some communities in the Po basin struck silver coins copying heavy *drachms* of Massalia (Arslan 2017), to which legends in Italiote characters were later added. The designs of the first silver coins of the Rhône valley were derived from early *obols* of Massalia, although their date is still rather uncertain. In south-west France, several peoples issued coinages with a distinctive cross-shaped emblem on one side, copied from the Greek colony of Rhode in north-east Spain. This series started in the third century BC and lasted to the early first century BC. The peoples of west-central France opted instead to copy coins issued by the neighbouring city of Emporion; these later provided the model for the first, small-scale silver coinages in northern France and Britain.

Table 28.1 Principal coinages in different regions of Iron Age Europe. X = primary coinage metal(s); x = subsidiary coinage metal(s). In north-west France, many later 'gold' coin types were in fact struck from a silver and copper alloy known as *billon*.

	Gold	Silver	Potin	Bronze
Balkans-Danube basin		X		(x)
Alps-North Italy	x	X		
Southern France		X		x
Spain		x		X
Southern Germany-Czechia	X	x		
Northern France-Belgium-Luxembourg	X	x	X	X
South-east Britain	X	X	x	x

Minting of Iron Age gold coinages beyond the Alps began around the same period as the copying of silver in the east. In western Europe, the earliest coins were Macedonian-style staters or divisions, copied from gold coins of Philip II and bearing a human head on one side and a two-horse chariot on the other, struck posthumously by his successors in the late fourth century BC. The imitations were struck to the same 'Attic' weight standard as the originals, and faithfully reproduced the symbols used by individual Greek mints, allowing different groups of primary copies to be identified, dispersed over an area extending from south-west Germany via Switzerland to Atlantic France (e.g. Scheers 2004; Nieto-Pelletier and Olivier 2016). Over time, distinct regional series developed. In Picardy, some types copied coins minted by the Greek city of Tarentum (Taranto) in southern Italy, while Brittany was home to a series of ornate coinages often depicting a human-headed horse, which, in their later stages, were struck from debased silver-bronze alloys known as billon rather than gold.

In central Europe, developments were more complex (Militký 2013). The earliest gold coins in Bohemia and Moravia imitated staters of Alexander the Great with a standing Victory on the reverse, and were in turn copied in other areas like the upper Danube. In the mid- to late third century BC, the Alexander copies were supplanted by superficially similar types, this time influenced by Roman and Greek silver coinage.[2] This 'Alkis' series is notable for its many fractions (1/3, 1/8, 1/24 staters). It, too, had various derivatives, including virtually formless coins shaped rather like mussels. Around the same time, silver coins and fractions appeared in lower Austria, Moravia, and Bohemia alongside the Alkis and mussels types.[3] Minting in both metals then continued down to the first century BC. The late mussels types inscribed 'Biatec' are linked by this legend to a series of large, inscribed silver coins from south Slovakia, some of which closely copied Roman *denarii* and were amongst the last Iron Age coinages of central Europe (Nash 1987).

Much earlier Roman influence is often claimed for some tiny gold coins (1/24 staters) of late third century BC date from southern Germany, depicting a janiform (double) head, although their imagery may actually be derived from Danubian *tetradrachms* (Sills 2003: 113). The janiform coins and another early series of 1/24 staters with a human-headed horse from the same area (Hiriart et al. 2020: 193–194) were soon supplanted in southern Germany by an extensive series of concave coins of full weight known as rainbow cups, with affinities to the mussels tradition; these bear a range of designs, starting with coins depicting a coiled serpent on one side and a torc enclosing six pellets on the other. The rainbow cup coinage in due course spread into the middle Rhineland, and finally—in very debased form and bearing a triskeles design—to the lower Rhine region (Roymans 2001).

Early in the second century BC, many peoples in non-Mediterranean France and south-east Britain began to make cast bronze coins known as potins after their high tin (and often lead) content, which gave them a distinctive silvery appearance (Haselgrove 1999). These started as close copies of bronze coins of Massalia with a butting bull on the reverse, but various regional traditions, often with purely native designs, soon emerged. Many potin series occur over enormous areas, cross-cutting regional boundaries marked by coinages in other metals. Around the mid-second century BC, and reflecting the expanding political and military reach of Rome, groups in eastern France and the Rhône valley began striking inscribed silver units at a weight standard close to half a *denarius*, many of them directly inspired by Roman types; the Kaletedou series copying features from a *denarius* of 151 BC is one of most extensive and probably the earliest (Martin 2015).

These silver '*quinarius*' coinages soon spread into other areas such as the Rhineland, or, as in central and western France, stimulated silver issues on a slightly different weight standard. Around the same time—perhaps earlier in areas such as the south-eastern Alps (Kos 2007)—Roman coins started to occur alongside local types, and copying of *denarii* became widespread in parts of eastern Europe. Dacia (modern Romania) has a concentration of hoards mixing late Republican *denarii* and local copies of such high quality that differentiating them has given rise to almost as much debate as the reasons for this influx of *denarii* to the area (Crawford 1985; Lockyear 2004; Chapter 14). The bronze and (more occasionally) silver coins struck by local groups in Iberia and the Narbonne region in the second and early first centuries BC were essentially modelled on Roman coinage, although their types and legends are distinct (Crawford 1985; García-Bellido 2004; Ripollès 2017; Chapter 10).

By the mid-first century BC, gold coinage was in retreat in many regions, with the principal exceptions of northern Gaul and Britain, while, over a zone extending from the middle Rhineland to Bohemia, cultural changes linked to Germanic population movements ended coin use altogether. Caesar's conquests accelerated the changes. Gold coins largely vanished from circulation in Gaul, many doubtless taken as booty by the Romans, while silver *quinarius* types proliferated and for a while even expanded in volume in places. Potin coins were superseded by struck bronze, which until the first century BC had been uncommon in most of Gaul,[4] but were now minted almost everywhere. In contrast to the supra-regional distributions of early potin types, the late bronze issues were often quite localized and some reveal strong Roman influence. None of these developments were sustained for long, however; within half a century of Caesar, most Iron Age peoples had ceased issuing coins, or turned to producing versions of official Roman bronze types.

The exception was Britain. Here, silver came into widespread use alongside gold in the later first century BC, legends were added, and struck bronze replaced potin around the Thames estuary. Several leaders minted coinage with overt Roman imagery and legends that sometimes included the title *rex* (king) or a mint name (Creighton 2000). Much of their silver output was coined out of recycled *denarii*, presumably gifts or subsidies to friendly rulers. In an echo of the Augustan monetary reforms, some rulers introduced rare copper and brass denominations as well as bronze units at a different weight standard. The Roman invasion in AD 43 effectively brought insular minting to an end; within not much more than a generation, Iron Age coins had disappeared from circulation, with large amounts hoarded on sacred sites.

Minting and Manufacture

Although the overall evolution of Iron Age coinage is well understood and secure sequences have been established for most regions, close dating remains a problem, owing to the many uninscribed issues and slender historical sources, even when legends became common. In the past, numismatists often sought to date their material by linking specific coinages and hoard horizons with events recorded in the texts, but this approach is full of pitfalls, even for well-documented episodes such as the Gallic War (Haselgrove 2019), leading scholars to turn to archaeology as a more neutral means of dating.

A pioneering study of coins from La Tène graves (Polenz 1982) and subsequent research on stratified coin finds from settlement sites (e.g. Haselgrove 1988, 1995; Pion 2008) have established that many Iron Age silver and base metal types were significantly earlier than the received numismatic dating allowed. For many coin series, however, the actual period of issue remains elusive, since, by its very nature, archaeological evidence is often only able to furnish an approximation of when coins circulated. Between the dates of the Greek models and the growing number of second-generation derivatives found in La Tène C1 contexts, it is now clear that the minting of gold beyond the Alps began around the turn of the fourth and third centuries BC (Nieto-Pelletier and Olivier 2016; Hiriart et al. 2020), but the chronologies of many later gold types remain open to debate due to the lack of independent dating (Sillon 2014; Sills 2017; Haselgrove 2019).

Knowledge of the technical aspects of minting, especially in precious metal, has benefited from extensive programmes of metal analysis (e.g. Cowell 1992; Northover 1992; Barrandon et al. 1994; Burkhardt et al 1994; Roymans et al. 2012; Sillon 2014; Nieto-Pelletier 2016). In northern Gaul, for example, gold coinage was gradually debased by adding silver and copper in the ratio 2:1, which enabled its yellow colour to be maintained for a long time. When a point of no return was eventually reached, there was an abrupt switch to copper-rich alloys. Similar patterns of debasement are found in other regions, but did not happen simultaneously (Nieto and Barrandon 2002; Nieto-Pelletier 2016). A major change in metal stock in northern Gaul around the start of the first century BC was apparently the result of mixing the existing stock with gold from east of the Rhine (Sillon 2014).

Coupled to metal analyses, die studies (Figure 28.2) allow us to estimate the sizes of different coinages and how much metal they required.[5] Some later gold coinages were vast, running into the high hundreds of thousands, if not millions (de Jersey 2009). Even the early series could have required between 1 to 2 tonnes of gold, as well as substantial amounts of silver and copper (Nieto-Pelletier 2016: 238–239). This not only has implications for the scale of metal extraction in Iron Age Europe (Cauuet 1999), but also underlines how little of the coinage once in circulation survives in the archaeological record. Much of it was presumably withdrawn and reminted, or converted into other objects; indeed, outlines of melted coins can be observed in silver ingots from Britain and elsewhere (Bland et al. 2020: 246). A number of authors have noted the coincidence in timing between the emergence of Iron Age coinage and intensified mining of gold- and silver-bearing ores in south-west Gaul and elsewhere in the late fourth and third centuries BC (Meunier and Luaces 2021).

Many Iron Age coinages were probably minted when need arose, rather than continuously (Sills 2003; Talbot 2017). Over sixty dies and punches are known, including a workshop hoard from Kleinsorheim (Germany) (Ziegaus 2011; Gruel et al. 2017; Chapter 24). In the west, dies were generally made of bronze, whereas east of the Rhine they were iron. Many finds of coin-making equipment, including hoards from Szalacska, Hungary, and Tilişca, Romania, come from fortified sites (*oppida*) and other major centres of La Tène C–D date. However, dies also occur at rural and cult sites, which, if this was their place of use, implies that not all minting was centralized or controlled. Minting could even have been itinerant (Lauwers 2015); dies are readily portable and much of the other necessary equipment such as hammers or scales was used by all metalworkers. Some supra-regional series like the Kaletedou *quinarii* were certainly minted at multiple locations, and even at places named on late coins there is little evidence for permanent mints. Pits containing debris from workshops which may have been engaged in manufacturing coins have been found at Corent (an *oppidum*) and Les Rochereaux (a rural site) in France (Toledo I Mur and Pernot 2008; Gruel et al. 2017).

Potin coins were cast in bivalve moulds made out of bronze—like the unique example from Romilly in the Saône valley (Delestrée and Pilon 2014)—or clay. If metal moulds were in common use, they must have been recycled when exhausted. A die for a potin mould has been found in Britain, albeit for a Gaulish type (SUR-08FD05).

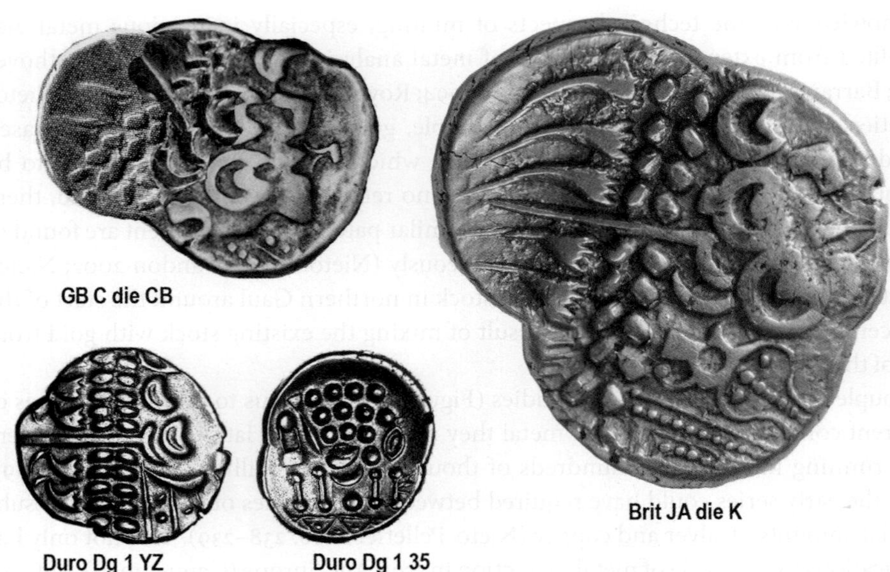

FIGURE 28.2 Composite images of Iron Age coins struck from a single die: (A) Gallo-Belgic C gold; (B) British J gold; (C) South-Western silver stater. Dies typically had larger surface areas than the coins minted from them, but by overlapping images of different coins, the full designs can be reconstructed (see Talbot 2017: 4–5). Not to scale.

Photos: John Talbot

Sometimes actual coins were used to impress designs, another possible sign of uncontrolled minting. Reject strip castings of potins occur at several French *oppida*, including Villeneuve-Saint-Germain and Fossé-des-Pandours. Flans for struck coins were sometimes made in bivalve moulds and the *cire perdue* technique may have been used for making plated coins (Gruel et al. 2017).

Whether the baked-clay pellet trays found on many Iron Age sites were used in minting—as opposed to other forms of non-ferrous metalworking—continues to be debated (Tournaire et al. 1982; Landon 2016; Gruel et al. 2017), but the shape of some examples, e.g. from Mont Beuvray, France, implies that not all were used in making coin flans (Gruel and Popovitch 2007). Examples are known from over 100 sites, many but by no means all of them major centres. Perhaps tellingly, they include finds from sites beyond the normal areas of Iron Age coin production, at Janków in Poland and Scotch Corner in Britain, the latter site associated with a workshop used over several decades (Fell 2020). A study of pellet trays from Britain suggests that they were made in the autumn (Landon 2016), which might imply that the activities for which they were destined were also seasonal.

New discoveries underline the difficulty of linking coinages with groups named in classical sources. Many gold, silver, and potin types have extensive distributions that do not correspond to any polity. Major changes in group territories and sociopolitical organization occurred from the fourth to first centuries BC (Fichtl 2004) and, as noted, the extent to which minting was centralized is open to question. Gruel (2002) has postulated four different models for minting and circulation in Gaul, and other possibilities exist (Collis 1981). Even where coinages form coherent sets linked by legends or designs, the constituent types often display complementary distributions, suggesting they circulated via separate networks (Leins 2012). This might reflect the different roles of e.g. gold and silver, but is less easy to explain for gold staters and divisions. This reminds us of the complex and undoubtedly shifting sociopolitical realities that underlay the fossilized coin distributions that survive today. And while later Iron Age coinages were much more regionalized (Wigg-Wolf 2011), not all of them can be easily equated with the administrative groupings adopted by the Romans.

Why Was Coinage Adopted and Minted in Iron Age Europe?

The impulse behind the near-synchronous expansion of Greek-style coinages over a large area of the continent centuries after they appeared in the Mediterranean littoral of southern Europe has long exercised scholars. Contacts and trade that had existed for millennia must have led to some familiarization with coins in regions nearer the Mediterranean, but seemingly not yet beyond the Alps. For some decades, the prevailing explanation for the inception of coinage in these more distant parts has been that Celts serving as mercenaries for Hellenistic rulers in the recurrent wars following the death of Alexander the Great became accustomed to being paid off in precious metal coins. On returning, these warriors introduced the concept to their homelands, whence the idea spread (e.g. Nash 1987; Sills 2003; Scheers 2004; Pion 2012; Krmnicek 2019).

There are, however, problems with the 'mercenary hypothesis'. Very few Greek originals are known from the areas where they were copied, and metal analysis provides no evidence for recycling of refined gold on the scale anticipated if many Greek coins had been brought back.[6] The indications from Gaul are that the prototypes arrived in a short-lived episode around the end of the fourth century BC,[7] whereas most mentions of Celts serving as mercenaries in Mediterranean wars date to well after the adoption of coinage (Nieto-Pelletier 2016). In addition, while it is easy to see why motifs such as severed heads and chariots might have appealed to Iron Age peoples, this does not explain why the specific Greek types were selected from the much wider spectrum circulating in the Mediterranean, or why only either gold or silver coins were replicated, given that mercenaries would have been exposed to both as well as to base metal issues. Italic and Punic coins dating to the fourth or third century BC also occasionally found their way to sites north of the Alps, and could have been brought back by mercenaries (Wigg-Wolf 2017: 136–137), but were not imitated.

There is also the question of why, if peoples across a large part of Europe suddenly became receptive to the idea of coinage, their neighbours to the north displayed no such enthusiasm. This was not due to ignorance, as coins occur at Iron Age sites beyond their normal spheres of circulation (e.g. Dulęba and Wysocki 2017).[8] Rudnicki (2014) has even suggested that Nowa Cerekwia in Poland and other aggregations along the Amber Route to the Danube (Chapter 7) were assembly points for warriors setting off to the Mediterranean, whose return from the Second Punic war would explain why so many bronze coins of this period from the classical world occur at these sites, notably Němčice (Czechia; Čižmář et al. 2008). If north European war bands were engaged in Mediterranean warfare, mercenary service on its own is insufficient to explain the adoption of coinage; other factors must have been involved.

Given the issues, many scholars now reject the 'mercenary hypothesis' as an overarching explanation for the spread of coinage, while acknowledging that it could have had a role in certain parts of Europe such as the Balkans (Baray 2014; Nieto-Pelletier 2016; Nieto-Pelletier and Olivier 2016). Long-distance trade also seems an unlikely mechanism given the high value of the Greek coins, but what other factors might have led to such rapid and widespread adoption of the idea of minting coins is less clear. One could be the appeal of the imagery and renown of the Macedonian warrior kings among Iron Age societies whose martial preoccupations can be inferred from the weapon deposits found at many religious sanctuaries in this period (Fichtl 2004). It may also be more than coincidence that Celtic migrations into southern and eastern Europe—not always readily distinguishable from mercenary service in the sources—ended around the time coinage was adopted (Chapter 37). This may have increased competition over land and other resources beyond the Alps, creating a social and political arena in which coinage would flourish.

Other scholars who still subscribe to the 'mercenary hypothesis' have shifted their focus to the context in which local minting started, albeit diverging over the role of coinage in this process and its monetary status. Pion (2012) sees coinage as the preserve of returning warrior bands formed from the cadet branches of society and habituated to being paid in coin, whose rise to dominance destabilized the old order. Martin (2015) prefers to emphasize the social and territorial transformation implied by the emergence of regional sanctuaries during La Tène B2, which rendered this new social order receptive to the innovation. For Wigg-Wolf (2011, 2017), coins provided elites across Europe with a versatile new medium for fulfilling the obligations (alliance, dowries, tribute, etc.) that helped to distance them from the rest of society, consolidating their power within the existing hierarchy. Precious metal coins were also a convenient new store of wealth.

Like many scholars, Martin sees Iron Age coins from the outset as a form of money in the conventional sense, citing the rapid emergence not only of fractional units—down to the 1/24 coins of central Europe—but also of plated forgeries (cf. Gruel 1989). A problem with this view is that even small gold and silver coins would surely have been unsuited to minor everyday transactions. Pion and Wigg-Wolf take a more anthropological perspective, arguing that those who adopted coinage perceived the earliest coins merely as a new form of valuable that could be assimilated into existing transactional spheres alongside traditional prestige objects such as torcs, with which they had a degree of equivalence (cf. Haselgrove 1987; Nash 1987). This tallies with the evidence from the lower Danube, where prestige objects were generally made of silver, and this was the metal adopted for coins (Lockyear 2004; Howgego 2013). Conversely, the failure of the peoples of northern Europe to adopt coinage might simply be because it conflicted with their existing value system and ideology. Whether or not these were based on cattle (Roymans 1999), both settlements and burials suggest these societies were organized on quite different principles to their neighbours in temperate Europe.

Despite this diversity of views over their adoption, a consensus exists that Iron Age coinages were generally struck by powerful individuals or leaders of specific groups, not on behalf of entire communities. As in the classical world, they were not minted to facilitate exchange, but to meet the issuers' needs to make specific payments, such as distributions to secure the loyalty of followers after a change of ruler (Wigg-Wolf 2017). Some scholars take a much narrower view, arguing that precious metal coins were primarily minted to secure or reward military service in times of crisis (Nash 1987; Sills 2003; Pion 2012), but while this may have been true of the Roman Republic (Crawford 1985) and certainly also happened in Iron Age Europe, notably during the Gallic War, the recovery of coin-making equipment from a wide range of sites (see earlier) suggests a plurality of needs. The view that minting was solely to finance warfare has also led to essentially circular arguments whereby coinages are equated with known (or failing that, inferred) episodes of warfare, from which an absolute chronology is constructed (Haselgrove 2019: 244).

Growing acceptance and availability of the medium in the late third and second centuries BC is indicated by the greater number of coins entering the archaeological record (Haselgrove 2005; Wigg-Wolf 2011). Coin hoards, too, which were initially rare, became more common in the second century BC. Many contain groups of die-linked coins and there are die links between widely separated hoards (Nick 2005; Figure 28.3). While attesting the extent of long-distance elite networks, this also implies that the coins spent much of their life immobile, and were exchanged infrequently and in batches rather than circulating individually (Wigg-Wolf 2011: 17). Many of the hoards also contain torcs, and seem to have been deposited in a votive or ritual context, which may extend to many single coin finds (see later).

The early minting of silver coinages alongside gold in central Europe, and of potin in the west, points to an expansion of coin use, but for both metals this was still largely limited to elite-centred transactions. The first of these developments occurred at the interface of the original gold and silver belts and may well reflect more a local blending of these traditions than the creation of bimetallic coinage sets—as those who see Iron Age coins as all-purpose money tend to have it (e.g. Hiriart et al. 2020: 196–201). Similarly, it would be wrong to assume that potins were necessarily intended to meet a need for low-value coins for everyday exchange. Their original silvery appearance implies that they too were primarily meant for discharging social or religious obligations, whatever functions they subsequently acquired. And in much of western Europe—if less so east of the Rhine—the slightly later spread of Roman-style *quinarius* coinages essentially

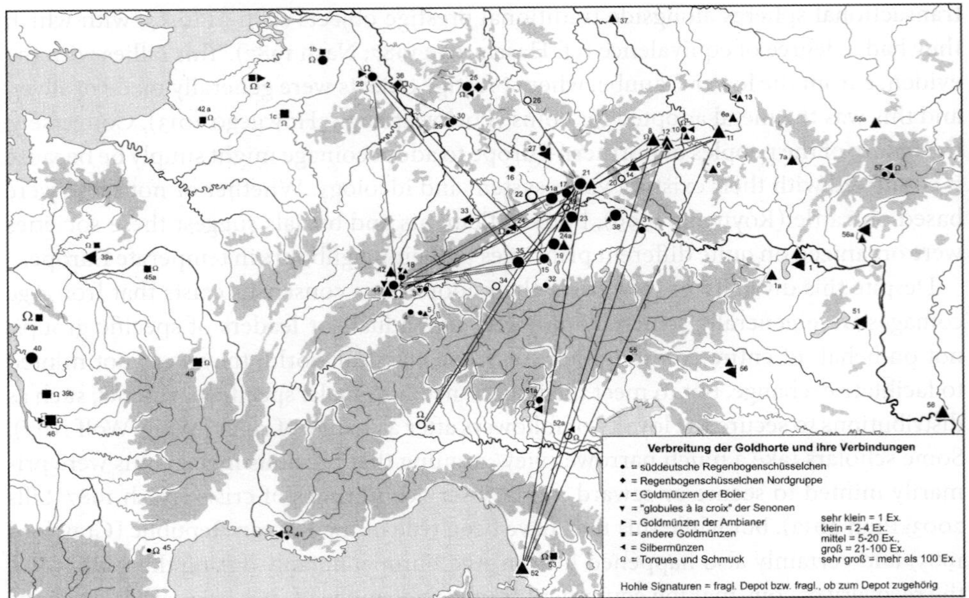

FIGURE 28.3 Distribution of Iron Age gold coin hoards containing rainbow cup or mussels staters, showing the extent of die-linking between hoards.

Source: after Nick 2005: Abb. 1

supplanted gold as the principal coinage metal rather than complementing it, bringing this zone into line with the Mediterranean world, where gold issues were always in the minority (Crawford 1985; Martin 2015; Nieto-Pelletier 2016).

The causes of the explosion of struck bronze coinages after the Roman conquest of Gaul should similarly be sought primarily in the preoccupations of a leading stratum of society—now deprived of control of precious metal resources—with maintaining their authority and status in a new political and cultural arena. Unlike potins with their wide distributions, most struck bronzes occur close to their place of origin and they are strongly associated with large centres and religious sites (Haselgrove 2005). This is equally true of the bronze coins struck in Britain after Caesar by rulers allied to Rome. The implication is that use of bronze coins was essentially restricted to places where their 'value'—which may have been substantial—was guaranteed by the issuers (or their gods), although now possibly in a wider range of transactions and by more people.

Iconography

The peri-conquest period saw a parallel evolution in Iron Age coin iconography, which was also to some extent a culmination of developments under way since the second century BC (Wigg-Wolf 2017). The earliest types drew on a limited range of inherited Greek designs, whereas after 200 BC issuers increasingly exploited coin types to distinguish themselves from others, using an expanded vocabulary of imagery and symbolism—although this still pertained largely to the political-military-religious milieu that was the preserve of the elite and their adherents—allowing regional types to have currency outside their place of origin. The addition of legends from the later second century BC allowed individuals competing for power to project their identity via coins that increasingly adhered to recognizable regional norms; some series also began to reference the growing power of Rome.

Following the conquest, we see explicit incorporation of Roman iconography by leaders who owed their continuing position to Roman support, a message now aimed more at their subordinates than their peers (Wigg-Wolf 2017). This practice found its fullest expression in the reign of Augustus, where across the Channel in Britain client rulers invoked Latin titles and copied a wide range of Roman coin types and motifs, albeit with the iconography subtly adjusted for local consumption and tastes (Creighton 2000; Williams 2005).

Archaeological Perspectives on Iron Age Coin Circulation and Deposition

It is also from the second century BC that we start to encounter significant numbers of coins on Iron Age sites. This enables us to interrogate coin use from the perspective of the types of sites at which different series occur, the archaeological contexts in which they were lost or deposited, and associated material. Stratified coins offer the best insights, along with crucial dating evidence, but judicious comparison of site assemblages (even unstratified) can yield valuable data, for example as to external contacts, coin loss in different sectors of a site, or whether an individual site conforms to wider regional and chronological trends (Haselgrove 1987; Delestrée 1996).

Here I will focus on coin finds from rural settlements, proto-urban centres, and religious contexts (although there is not always a clear divide between these categories), privileging extensively excavated sites. As many authors have noted, the final resting place of a coin is only the endpoint of a potentially long and complex biography; many details of circulation and use may be difficult or impossible to reconstruct (e.g. Wigg-Wolf 2011: 303–304).

Coinage and Rural Settlements

The Iron Age societies that adopted coinage during La Tène B2–C1 were essentially rural. Large permanent centres of population were rare at this period. Across Europe, cemeteries, religious sanctuaries, and natural foci such as caves provided periodic meeting places for these dispersed rural communities, but, with a few exceptions, the earliest coins show little or no attachment to archaeological sites of any kind.

Coins start to occur on farms and other small rural settlements from La Tène C2–D1, but in low numbers and at a minority of sites (Haselgrove 2005: 143–144). A mere 15% of excavated rural sites in France north of the Loire have Iron Age coins, although this hides regional variations linked to the types in circulation and the nature of the settlement pattern (Martin et al. 2016). Values tend to be highest in regions that adopted potin or replaced gold with silver after 150 BC, but below the mean in areas such as Brittany that remained faithful to the gold stater, even heavily debased. An exception is the lower Rhine region, where the population remained focused on rural sites until the Roman period, leading to more finds from small farmsteads (Roymans 2001).

On the basis that transactions with coins mostly took place elsewhere, we would expect few accidental losses to occur on rural sites (Roymans 2004: 96). Where coins are found, they often seem to have been carefully placed in features such as postholes, pits, and enclosure boundaries, perhaps as foundation or closure deposits, like three gold coins deposited at intervals in a ditch containing other unusual objects surrounding the coastal site at Urville-Nacqueville (Haselgrove and Webley 2016). Votive practices were far from uniform, however, and could differ even within a region. In Picardy, potins occur regularly at farms along the Aisne valley, but not in the neighbouring Oise valley, where they are instead concentrated at religious sanctuaries (Martin et al. 2016). Since the two valleys have similar histories of archaeological investigation as well as similar coinage, this contrast is hard to explain other than in terms of discrepant cultural traditions.

The strongest evidence of deliberate deposition apparently without any intention of retrieval comes from a handful of coin hoards mostly of precious metal from rural sites (Haselgrove and Webley 2016). The Behringen (Belgium) and Niederzier (Germany) hoards of gold coins and torcs were both buried in what may have been sacred spaces within the settlement. Other hoards were placed in building postholes (Saint-Denis-lès-Sens; Val-de-Reuil, France) and enclosure ditches (Ifs; La-Chaize-le-Vicomte), just like the single coins. Further hoards are known from outside rural sites in Brittany and elsewhere (Gruel and Pion 2009), although some of these might have been for safekeeping.

The presence of sizeable gold and silver coin hoards at farmsteads concurs with other signs of a continued association between coinage and a rurally based social elite, even when larger population centres developed. In northern Gaul, gold is more common in the countryside than at larger sites (Wigg-Wolf 2011: 309–310) and the majority of Roman-period rural sites with Iron Age coin finds can be classified as 'villas', with implications for the status of their previous occupants, always assuming continuity of ownership (Haselgrove 2005: 143–144).

Coinage and Urban Aggregations

In contrast to rural sites, Iron Age coins are plentiful at large centres. Their abundance at fortified *oppida* all the way from Mont Beuvray in France to Stradonice in Czechia was long ago adopted by Déchelette as one of the defining attributes of the late La Tène period and as support for his model—still widely followed (Chapter 21)—of *oppida* being not only centres of production and long-distance trade, but also markets for the local people (Déchelette 1914: 931–932, 947–948). More recently, it has become apparent that coins were already common at the unfortified lowland settlements that preceded the rise of the *oppida*. While some of these earlier aggregations had an agricultural character, most were engaged in specialist manufacturing of commodities such as pottery, iron, glass, and salt.

In central Europe, the earliest lowland aggregations developed at around much the same time as coinage itself was introduced, whereas west of the Rhine, few sites pre-date the start of La Tène C2. As with the *oppida* later, the coins from these aggregations point to extensive contacts with counterparts north of the Alps and in the Mediterranean world. Němčice has coins from Gaul, the Balkans, many Italian cities, and even Egypt and Cyrenaica (Kolníková 2012). It is also the site of the earliest known glass workshop in temperate Europe, making it unlikely that all these imports are to be explained by mercenaries returning from the Second Punic War (see earlier). The *oppidum* of Manching, which began as an unfortified aggregation, displays strong numismatic links with eastern Gaul (Gruel 2009) and Bohemia (a hoard of mussels staters), as well as south of the Alps. Massaliote coins are common at major centres in the Garonne basin of France (Hiriart 2019), while coins from the south-west and other parts of Gaul travelled in the opposite direction to sites in Mediterranean France such as Lattes (Py 2006). Similar long-distance links are evident at many *oppida*, although blurred by the movement of non-local coinages with troops during and after the Gallic War—illustrated by the Gaulish coin finds from the Roman siege camps around the stronghold of Alesia (Martin 2015: 402). Across the Channel, the *oppidum* at Silchester has coins from every coin-using region of Britain as well as from several parts of Gaul. Here, we know that the rulers had political ties with some of these other regions, a reminder that Iron Age coins could have been transported for many reasons apart from trade.

At many Iron Age centres, the assemblages consist predominantly of metal-detected surface finds and/or poorly recorded older discoveries (e.g. Němčice, Kolníková 2012; Stradonice, Militký 2015), limiting what we might otherwise be able to deduce about the context and duration of these links or about coin use within the settlements. Investigating these questions depends on a smaller, if growing, corpus of sites that have been sufficiently extensively excavated to compare finds from different zones, and where there is enough archaeological information to establish the context of coin loss or deposition.

A valuable case study is provided by the Celtic-speaking port at Lattes. A thriving hub from the sixth century BC, Lattes never minted coins of its own (Py 2006). Instead, the majority of coins used there came from Massalia, first appearing in the later fourth century BC, 200 years after the Greek colony itself began minting. Over the next two centuries, coin losses at Lattes remained modest, rising only slightly after Massaliote bronzes were introduced, although the burial of four silver hoards on the settlement periphery shows that some people had access to substantial amounts of coinage. Only after Roman intervention in the later second century BC do numbers rise, accompanied by a fall in the proportion of silver types. From this time on, too, coins occur in specialist workshops and industrial premises, whereas previously most finds were from domestic contexts (Luley 2008). From this evidence, the excavator suggests that in the pre-Roman period only a minority of individuals—those controlling commodities sought by foreign merchants—were involved in monetary transactions, and then only occasionally (Py 2006: 1160–1162). While the introduction of bronze coins may gradually have enabled more of society to participate in a wider range of transactions, developments associated with Roman occupation were the main driver for the monetization of the local population. A similar expansion of coin use after the Roman conquest in 106 BC has been noted at Toulouse Sainte-Roche (Verrier and Dieulafait 2019: 241).

Allowing for the different cultural and chronological contexts, many elements of this picture are repeated north of the Alps, notably the growth in stratified coins after the mid-second century BC and differences between zones of the same site. Exogenous coins often exhibit discrete patterns of deposition. At the extensively excavated site of Manching, there are less than 150 stratified coins and very few from the pre-*oppidum* phase,[9] although, as at Lattes, this is balanced by the hoard of mussels staters and three silver coin hoards (Ziegaus 2013). All the coins of Mediterranean origin come from the central area and imported potins cluster in specific sectors of the site, whereas local silver is widely distributed, dominating in the peripheral zones. At the much later *oppidum* of Silchester in Britain, Gaulish imports and local silver types are prominent in the central part of the site, whereas Insula IX towards the periphery of the settlement has more bronze coins and types from other parts of Britain; there are few Iron Age coins from pre-Roman contexts in either area (Haselgrove 2018). At Mont Beuvray, occupied throughout the first century BC, stratified coins are numerous from the outset. Potins dominate throughout, supplemented from the mid-first century BC by Gaulish bronzes and in the Augustan period by Roman bronze. There are concentrations of potins in the workshop quarter, and, to a lesser extent, in the residential and sanctuary areas (Gruel and Popovitch 2007). Silver is scarcer in the workshop area and best represented in the residential zone, where Roman *denarii* were already present before the conquest. The only recorded hoard (mostly of *denarii* and post-conquest coins) is also from here, although there are hints of dispersed hoards among the site finds. Coinage is also strongly associated with a workshop quarter at the open settlement at Berching-Pollanten, near Manching, although here too local silver dominates.

Manching was abandoned in the early first century BC, whereas at *oppida* like Mont Beuvray, that were occupied into the Roman period, coin loss typically increased sharply after the conquest, accompanied by a rise in struck bronze at the expense of other metals. Pion's (2005) study of coin densities from successive sites in Picardy reveals the magnitude of the increase: the rate of loss at Pommiers (La Tène D2b) is 20 times higher than at Condé-sur-Suippe (La Tène D1b) abandoned only 30 years earlier. This implies a rapid acceleration of monetization associated with Roman intervention, much as we saw at Lattes, albeit initially confined largely to the sections of society most involved in dealings with Roman troops, officials, and traders quartered in *oppida*.

Otherwise we would expect greater penetration of struck bronze beyond the environs of the main centres. Only after the Augustan reorganization of Gaul and through exposure to Roman commerce, taxation, and practices like money-lending (Howgego 2013: 26–27) did a wider spectrum of society come to participate in monetary transactions, often now conducted with Roman rather than Iron Age coinage. This would seem to be borne out at Mont Beuvray, where Roman (and indeed Gaulish) bronzes have more extensive distributions across the site than Iron Age potin and silver (Gruel and Popovitch 2007).

If monetization largely took hold only after the Gallic War, what of the argument that *oppida* and other proto-urban settlements were market centres at an earlier date? Hiriart (2019: 433) suggests that large empty spaces with multiple coin finds at Lacoste (France) and Roseldorf (Austria) were market places, but it seems inherently unlikely that so many precious metal coins, even fractions, would have been lost in everyday exchanges. The coins could be from scattered hoards like those found intact at Lattes or Manching; disturbed remnants of closure deposits akin to those at Acy-Romance (Haselgrove and Webley 2016); or ploughed-out offerings from sacred areas. Not all coin-rich sanctuaries possessed built shrines; in Britain, the Snettisham hoards came from a low hill seemingly devoid of contemporary features.[10] While the surface coin finds from Roseldorf are largely mutually exclusive of the seven temple and shrine structures so far identified at the aggregation (Holzer 2014), this is not in itself a decisive argument in favour of a secular context for their loss.

Acy-Romance is far from the only large settlement where many coin finds were intentionally deposited rather than accidentally lost. At the centre of Manching, there is a cluster of coins, including a small gold hoard in a bronze purse, around a palaeochannel or wet area. This sector was also a focus for unusual deposits, many of them horse-related, and is plausibly interpreted as a ritual zone. Many of the coins depict horses, which may be why they were selected for deposition (Haselgrove and Webley 2016; Wigg-Wolf 2018). Elsewhere at the *oppidum*, the mussels hoard was found near a possible high-status burial, which included another gold coin of this type, while three silver coins with cut marks resembling those from many Iron Age temples (see later) were recovered not far from putative shrine buildings. Several more coins were in features containing human bone or in pits with structured deposits, patterns repeated at Basel-Gasfabrik (Switzerland), where many of the >600 coins (including another purse hoard) were from artefact-rich pits within the settlement. If, as the excavators suggest, these pit deposits originated in ritual practices, it seems plausible that coins featured in these activities (Haselgrove and Webley 2016; Nick 2018).[11]

Ritualized deposits incorporating Iron Age coins have been recognized at proto-urban centres all the way from Lattes in southern France (Luley 2008) to the Dacian fortress of Costești-Cetățuie in Romania (Găzdac 2018). At the Roman trading settlement on the Magdalensberg in Austria, occupied *c*.40 BC–AD 50, over half of the stratified coins are thought to have been deposited intentionally, whether singly or in groups (Krmnicek 2012).[12] They range from finds in pits, postholes, or wet contexts to coins incorporated in walls or hearths, or placed beneath the foundations or floors of domestic structures and workshops. Almost all the Iron Age coins are local silver types, whereas the majority of Roman coins are bronzes that reached Noricum after the kingdom was annexed in 16 BC. Interestingly, the people enacting these deposits seem to have been slower to adopt Roman coins into their ritual practices than for economic transactions; intentional deposits were still made almost exclusively with local silver issues until the final phase of occupation, even though Roman issues already account for over half the losses in the Augustan period. A higher proportion of deliberately deposited Roman coins are precious metal (including two *aurei*) than among the accidental losses, although this is perhaps to be expected.

With its resident Italian traders, the Magdalensberg was not a typical Iron Age centre, and the high rate of intentional deposits there cannot automatically be translated to other proto-urban sites. On the other hand, the hilltop topography has resulted in the preservation of walls and other features containing coins that rarely survive on Iron Age sites, where most coins left behind in the fabric when a structure was demolished or collapsed would have ended up in other deposits, where archaeologists find them. When we also factor in the evidence from Manching and elsewhere, this strongly suggests that we have underestimated the extent of intentional coin deposition at Iron Age centres. In turn, this reinforces the view rehearsed earlier that, prior to Roman expansion, coinage was largely reserved for transactions in the sphere of elite competition, or linked to long-term reproduction of the social and religious order (Wigg-Wolf 2011). In short, Iron Age coins rarely entered the record by chance.

Coinage and Religion

One form of intentional deposition—with potential to provide insights into Iron Age beliefs and the role of coinage—is the sporadic inclusion of coins in graves, a practice that began within a generation of the adoption of coinage itself. At Dobian (Germany), two Alexander-Victory staters were found with a burial dating to the second quarter of the third century BC in a tumulus; other early finds include two 1/24 Janus staters and a Massaliote obol from La Tène C1 graves in Switzerland (Polenz 1982). Over time, the incidence of Iron Age coins in graves increased, a trend that carried on after the Roman conquest, but while geographically widespread, the practice was always restricted. Across northern Gaul, coins are recorded from over 100 Iron Age and early Roman cemeteries (Haselgrove 2005), but rarely in more than one grave in the same burial ground, and some coins are from ditched enclosures around the graves and were probably deposited as part of the rites accompanying burial. Coins are slightly more common at some cemeteries belonging to larger agglomerations,[13] as at Bern-Reichenbachstrasse (Switzerland), the Lamadeleine cemetery at the Titelberg (Luxembourg), and Acy-Romance, but still occur only in a few graves (six to eight), representing a small proportion of the deceased. Another burial at the Titelberg, this time in the eastern cemetery, contained a punch for the reverse of a bronze type of Arda, whose coins were almost certainly issued at this *oppidum* (Metzler et al. 2016: 409).

Overall, coins are much rarer in graves than goods such as brooches or bracelets.[14] From other grave goods and a minority of inhumations excavated under modern conditions, it seems that most individuals accompanied by coins were adult females, including all six at Bern. Beyond this, there is no clear pattern as to why a select minority were interred with coins. Most graves contain only a single coin, but sometimes a small group was included in a pouch of perishable material (Acy-Romance, Basel-Gasfabrik, all potins). At Bern, a metal vessel containing six silver coins was laid on the chest of the dead woman; another at Sion had 30 silver coins in a purse on her belt (Jud and Ulrich-Bochsler 2014). In other Swiss La Tène C2 graves, including several at Bern, coins were placed in the mouth of the dead, echoing the Graeco-Roman custom of Charon's *obol*. If borrowing was involved, Massalia is a more likely source than Rome, since Massaliote *obols* also occur in contemporary Swiss burials. The increased representation of coins in Gaulish graves after the conquest may similarly reflect the influence of Roman burial customs.

After the earliest period, silver and potin coins predominate in graves, eventually giving way to bronze. Interestingly, given the elite associations of coinage, few graves with coins seem to be of the highest rank, and these burials are post-conquest and so belong to a different milieu, and the coins are Roman bronzes (e.g. Fléré-la-Rivière, France). At Esvres-sur-Indre, also in central France, another Augustan grave containing a sword included a curated potin, placed in a pouch with some amulets (Riquier 2004).[15] A burial from Chassenard contained two pairs of iron dies for gold or silver coins of Tiberius, presumably symbolizing real or imagined ties to the Emperor (Wigg-Wolf 2017), but, as with the swords, also harking back to traditional elite prerogatives and privileges.

Prior to the first century BC, very few Iron Age coins were deposited at formal religious sites. Only eleven were found in excavations of the Roseldorf temples (Holzer 2019). The small third-century BC gold hoard from Ribemont-sur-Ancre (France) was not a dedicated offering, but belonged to one of the dead warriors whose remains were displayed there as trophies with their weapons (Wigg-Wolf 2018). There are good grounds, however, for thinking that many precious metal coins found not on sites but 'in the landscape', whether singly or in hoards, were in fact deposits at significant natural foci or open-air ritual sites. While coin hoards might sometimes have been concealed near a prominent feature such as a rock outcrop as an aid to later recovery (Bland et al. 2020), this is inherently unlikely for most wet deposits (e.g. the famous finds at La Tène and the mass of potins from Lake Zurich; Nick 2018).

The recurrent choice of certain categories of natural location and often the presence of other distinctive finds both argue in the same direction. Across Europe, individual coins and hoards occur at river sources and springs (e.g. Tayac, France), in marshy areas or caves, and on hilltops and mountains (cf. Haselgrove 2008; Sîrbu and Bodo 2011). High in the Alps at Piller Sattel (Austria), Iron Age silver coins[16] were just one late element of a wide spectrum of deposits extending back over 1,500 years, starting with burnt offerings. A single rainbow cup coin found near the rock arch known as Heidentor (Germany) is surely linked to the tradition, stretching back to the sixth century BC, of scattering offerings of food and drink and personal items from this rock (Nick 2018). Some discoveries come from older prehistoric monuments such as tombs, implying these retained or acquired a significance for the later inhabitants of the landscape. Small-scale coin offerings at open-air sites continued in the final phases of the Iron Age, even increasing in some areas, although in others, foci of this kind were replaced by formal temples, or themselves acquired built shrines (Haselgrove 2008).

After 100 BC, and above all during La Tène D2b and the Augustan period, coin deposition at temples and sanctuaries rose dramatically—including at religious complexes within *oppida*, as at Corent[17] or Martburg (Germany)—supplanting the earlier tradition of depositing weapons and human remains at older foci like Ribemont-sur-Ancre. Allowing for regional variations, these developments essentially mirrored wider changes in coin use and circulation in western Europe during this period (Wigg-Wolf 2018). Precious metal coins and especially potins tend to be prevalent in earlier horizons, but give way almost entirely to bronze issues after the Gallic War (except in outlying regions of Britain). The new emphasis on coinage was only one of many changes in votive behaviour at this time. Among other categories now regularly deposited at cult sites, albeit with some pronounced regional variations, were brooches, pots, and miniature objects, notably wheels (*rouelles*) made in different metals and sizes. Around 30,000 of these wheels were found at Villeneuve-au-Châtelet (France), where they could well have been used in similar ways to Iron Age coins, of which there were 1,900 at the site (Nick 2018). Many cult sites also have evidence of animal sacrifice and feasting.

Although our interpretation of the role of coins in religious practices is hindered by the mixing of layers and deposits at many sanctuaries and temples, compounded by our ignorance of the dedicants' beliefs and the meaning of the rituals they enacted, certain points can nevertheless be made. Coin offerings were not a feature of all Iron Age religious sites—though this could be because they were first displayed (for which there is some evidence) and later removed—and variations can occur between temples within a single sanctuary. At Martberg, some structures within the precinct have no coins, and when they were deposited the same practices were not always followed (Wigg-Wolf 2018).[18] Different types of coins were clearly also sometimes treated differently at the same site—at the admittedly unusual cult site at Mormont (Switzerland), potins come primarily from pits, whereas silver *quinarii* are mostly from layers corresponding to the old ground surface (Nick 2018). On occasions, it may be possible to draw a convincing link between coin offerings and a specific cult or deity from the identity of the Roman god or goddess worshipped at a temple, as at Empel (Netherlands; Roymans and Aarts 2005), but given the uncertainties over the nature of religious syncretism, this is yet another approach full of pitfalls.

A specific practice found at some but not all Iron Age religious sites is chopping or cutting of coins. This was presumably a form of ritual killing, analogous to the bending or breaking of many weapons deposited at earlier sanctuaries. At the Martberg, many gold and silver coins exhibit cut marks, invariably on the horse on the reverse (Figure 28.4). This resonates with the horse-related deposits at Manching (see earlier) and with the important role of horses in the rituals and symbolism of elite power and leadership

FIGURE 28.4 Cut-marked 'sitting person' silver coins from the Martberg (type Scheers 55). Not to scale.

Photo: David Wigg-Wolf

in Iron Age societies (Creighton 2005; Chapter 32). Conceivably, at Martberg and elsewhere, these cut-marked coins acted as substitutes for sacrificial animals, with the horse being killed symbolically rather than the coin being sacrificed in its own right as an object of value (Wigg-Wolf 2018). Cut-marking could also have served to prevent coins re-entering normal circulation after they had entered the ritual sphere in a transaction with the deities, particularly if this involved a phase of public display. A point on which classical authors agree is that vast quantities of precious metal were put on view at Iron Age sanctuaries—where they would have served to demonstrate the value of the material sacrificed and the resources at the command of the donors.

The rich and often fantastic imagery of the designs on Iron Age coins suggests intimate links with the religious beliefs and rituals that underpinned power and status in Iron Age societies, which would have extended to all aspects of their life cycle from the metals out of which they were created, to their makers, and the persons with whom they were associated (Haselgrove and Wigg-Wolf 2005). This applies to potin and bronze as much as precious metal. When gold and silver disappeared from circulation after the Gallic War, bronze coins were clearly deemed appropriate for use in a religious setting. The employment of low-value coins to fulfil religious obligations hitherto met with precious metals was undoubtedly a factor in the near exponential rise in temple finds during the mid- to late first century BC. As in other spheres, bronze coins may also have opened up rituals and sacrifices once reserved for the elite to new participants, and led to the use of coins for more transactions (Wigg-Wolf 2018). The greater number of personal objects deposited at temples and sanctuaries alongside coins is consistent with the participation of a wider section of society in religious rituals at this period.

Across the Channel in Britain, coin-rich temples on the continental model are the exception, with coin deposition focusing on other types of sacred site. The temple on Hayling Island is essentially an insular outlier of a distinctive group of Gaulish sanctuaries, leaving Harlow as the only built shrine with hundreds of mostly bronze coin finds. In Britain, the peri-conquest period is marked by a distinctive horizon of mixed Iron Age and Roman coin hoards in client kingdoms that had initially welcomed the Roman invaders (Talbot 2017). Where excavated, as at Hallaton and Wanborough, the find-spots proved to be open-air sanctuaries (e.g. Score 2011), suggesting that these hoards had been placed on sacred sites under the safekeeping of the gods in a rapidly changing political climate.

Postscript: Coinage in Roman Iron Age Europe

From the reign of Augustus onwards, Roman coins began to penetrate the regions beyond the Rhine and Danube in substantial numbers (Bursche et al. 2008). Despite far greater exposure to this medium than before, its recipients remained resolutely resistant to minting coins of their own, beyond some copying of *denarii* (e.g. Dymowski 2019)—though not on the scale of first-century BC Dacia—and, later, of Roman gold coins (e.g. Bursche 2014). Although Roman bronze coins are not uncommon, silver was the metal of choice, especially in hoards (Horsnaes 2008; Wigg-Wolf 2008, 2020); gold is rare until the late period. Although the circumstances in which individual societies encountered Roman coins (and other imports) varied according to their external contacts and proximity to the Roman Empire, the numismatic pattern is surprisingly uniform from Britain and Ireland to the Russian plain. A notable cluster of brass *sestertii* in the southern Baltic coastal region—perhaps, but not certainly, an instance of targeted export to meet a local cultural preference—merely emphasizes the homogeneity of Roman coin finds elsewhere, especially compared to La Tène Europe (Howgego 2013).[19] Otherwise, only slight regional differences are apparent (e.g. between south and north Scandinavia; Chapter 5).

The most important mechanism behind the bulk export of Roman *denarii* to northern Europe was the Antonine return to the practice of giving bribes, gifts, and payoffs to friends and enemies beyond the frontier as an instrument of imperial policy. Other factors contributing to the northward flow of Roman coins in the early centuries AD included warfare—as with the finds from Kalkriese (Germany), the site of the catastrophic Augustan defeat in AD 9; cross-border trade in the frontier zone;[20] and, less certainly, Germanic auxiliaries returning to their homelands after military service.[21] *Denarius* hoards are particularly numerous in parts of Scotland, Denmark, Poland, Ukraine, and on some Baltic islands, all but the first a long distance from the nearest frontiers. In these areas, hoarding peaked in the later second and early third century AD—typified by two hoards excavated at the rural site at Birnie (Scotland; Figures 28.5). These close in AD 193 and 196, just before the campaigns launched by the Emperor Severus north of Hadrian's Wall (Hunter 2007; Blackwell et al. 2017). Minor differences between regions suggest that these *denarius* hoards were not the product of a blanket policy, but rather responses to particular frontier troubles.[22] After Severus, the number of *denarius* hoards fell away rapidly, probably due to a combination of shifts in policy and the sharp debasement of Roman silver.

The ways in which different societies beyond the frontiers integrated Roman silver coins into their specific practices and beliefs varied. Gaps in the distribution of *denarius* hoards might be because some groups rejected Roman coins altogether, or generally melted them down to make other objects, of which there is ample evidence (e.g. Bursche 2008). In Scotland, many *denarius* hoards come from wet places and other ritual foci (Hunter 2007), implying that here coins were incorporated into traditional votive practices involving the sacrifice of prestige objects, comparable to many Iron Age coin-using areas. The Birnie hoards were buried in a part of the settlement which has other unusual deposits, and may have been a sacred space. In Scotland, *denarii* do not seem to have circulated extensively after their arrival—many were buried when still fresh. As with Iron Age coins, this need not preclude their use in bulk transactions in the elite sphere, but if so, there was no attempt to replace them once the supply dried up.

This contrasts with the continent, where *denarii* often remained in circulation throughout the third and fourth centuries AD, long after they disappeared within the Empire. In Denmark, some *denarii* were worn smooth before they were finally buried (Blackwell et al. 2017). Here, Roman coins were evidently used in the military sphere. Many of the dead warriors placed in a lake in the third century AD at Illerup Ådal (Denmark) along with their weapons and equipment had pouches or purses containing *denarii* attached to their belts. Like the purse of Iron Age gold coins found among the collapsed military trophies at Ribemont-sur-Ancre (see earlier), the Illerup purses are clearly incidental to the primary martial offerings (Wigg-Wolf 2018). This is quite different from the Scottish wetland hoards, where the coins themselves formed the offerings, if only for the prestige value of the metal. Other notable Danish finds include *denarius* hoards from excavated settlements at Ginderup and Dankirke in Jutland, and over 1,200 Roman coins from the extended complex of Gudme-Lundeberg on Funen (Bjerg 2011; Horsnaes 2008, 2010). With its ceremonial core and workshop trading area, Gudme-Lundeberg recalls many middle La Tène aggregations (see earlier). The vast majority of the coins are silver or gold, but here many of them are certainly from hoards, some still *in situ*. Roman coins have also been found in at least twenty-five graves in Denmark.

FIGURE 28.5A The second of two *denarius* hoards discovered at the Roman Iron Age settlement at Birnie. Both hoards were placed in locally made pots, each containing two batches of coins, originally contained in leather pouches.

Photo: © National Museums Scotland; Fraser Hunter

FIGURE 28.5B The hoards were buried less than 10 m apart in the heart of the settlement, close to this circular building.

Photo: © National Museums Scotland; Fraser Hunter

The late Roman army relied on recruitment beyond the frontiers. This was undoubtedly a key factor in the flow of gold coins—with which soldiers were now normally paid—into northern Europe from the late third century AD onwards, as warrior bands returned home from Roman military service. The resumption of pay-offs to external enemies was another factor, along with mounting Germanic incursions and raiding into the Empire.[23] Along with gold, Roman hacksilver was increasingly used for military pay and diplomatic subsidies;[24] it too occurs in many hoards outside the Empire, with clusters in Scotland and Denmark. While gold was now the favoured payment medium on the continent, in Scotland (and Ireland) local groups evidently preferred the silver, to which they were accustomed. Scottish hacksilver hoards include a few Roman silver coins, but no gold, whereas many continental hoards contain both metals (Blackwell et al. 2017: 51–58). As with the *denarius* hoards, many Scottish hacksilver finds come from ritual foci and many Danish hoards from settlements, where they perhaps acted as stores of wealth for individual families.

In sum, coin finds show that many peoples beyond the frontiers of the Empire were familiar with Roman coinage, which they adapted to their own practices and world view. Rising above differences of detail, coins were clearly employed in a more restricted manner than within the Roman world. Both silver and gold were too valuable for everyday transactions (Wigg-Wolf 2008). Not only is this reminiscent of the first phase of coin use in La Tène Europe, but developments in the Roman Iron Age also unfolded in a broadly similar manner. Over much of northern Europe, leading sections of society—some of whom had hitherto resisted the idea—now began to use coins (and other prestige imports) to discharge social, political, or religious obligations traditionally performed with other media—albeit with one key difference to the La Tène world: *denarius* hoards rarely contain items other than coins (Wigg-Wolf 2020), perhaps indicating that they were not perceived as equivalent to other valuables. The transactions into which coins were drawn (e.g. tribute, ransom, blood money, dowry, reward) would have varied from society to society, but must have included interregional exchanges, as die-linked *denarius* copies made outside the Empire occur far apart from each other (Wigg-Wolf 2008). Many of these copies originated in Ukraine in territory occupied from *c.*AD 200 by the Chernyakhov culture—identifiable, at least in part, with the historical Goths (Dymowski 2019; Chapter 7). Over time, aided by their universality, Roman coins may well have come to serve as a standard of value for exchanges between discrete spheres (Hedeager 1992: 234–236), or with traders and outsiders. Coins would have been a convenient store of wealth for actors in such transactions, as we see at pre-Roman sites like Lattes.

Throughout the Roman Iron Age, coinage formed a reservoir of precious metal for societies beyond the frontier, demonstrated by similar compositions of coins, ornaments, and militaria (Bursche 2008). What proportion of imported silver and gold was recycled is not easy to establish, but melted *denarii* have been found in workshops and some votive deposits of *denarii* include scrap metal, while in the late Empire, large numbers of gold coins were clearly converted into traditional valuables like spiral rings, or made into status symbols such as medallions and bracteates. Nor is there a simple way to compare the overall amounts of coinage available to pre-Roman and Roman Iron Age societies, but if single and site finds are any guide, the quantities circulating among some late La Tène peoples could well have been an order of magnitude higher—although we should remember that population densities were probably somewhat lower in much of northern Europe.

The question remains of why Roman Iron Age societies did not initiate their own coinages, given their appetite for the medium. One possible answer is that the amount of imported coinage was already more than adequate to satisfy local requirements. Cultural, demographic, and organizational differences between these groups and the peoples of La Tène Europe may also be relevant. While many northern European societies show signs of having become more centralized during the Roman Iron Age (Hedeager 1992), it does not follow that their leaders need have shared the avid interest of La Tène elites in using coin production and iconography to promote their own standing, nor indeed that this avenue was even feasible for them. In the world beyond the frontier, Roman coins may essentially have owed their prestige value to their foreign origin and even the link with the Emperor himself—properties that locally minted coins would have lacked. In this scenario, the power of local leaders rested on the implied direct relationship with the individual at the apex of Roman society, of which payments in coin were proof.[25]

Certainly, the iconography of Roman coins—and the imperial image in particular—came to play an increasingly important role in the symbolic language of Roman Iron Age societies in Scandinavia and the North European Plain. Roman coins were widely reused as amulets and ornaments—pierced coins often formed part of necklaces alongside glass and amber beads[26]—and gold plaques cast from coins appear as fittings on weapons and caskets. In the late period, representations of the Emperor in the form of coins or medallions, particularly in gold, were routinely worn by high-ranking individuals as symbols of their own power and prestige (Bursche 2008).[27] These tendencies continued into the early Migration period. Some imitation medallions and bracteates show imperial images and insignia next to local power symbols and Roman titles written in runes and, rather than adopting distinctive coinages of their own, the Germanic kingdoms that emerged within the old western Empire generally imitated Roman or Byzantine pieces and even sometimes struck coins in the names of particular emperors (Wigg-Wolf 2008).

Conclusion

Whatever the initial impulse(s) to the adoption of coinage in Iron Age Europe, a range of factors clearly contributed to its rapid spread and acceptance. One was the cultural interconnectedness of the La Tène world, expressed not only in shared decorative metalwork traditions and symbolism, but also in similar mortuary and ritual practices and perhaps underlying belief systems. Celtic migrations of the fifth and fourth centuries

BC helped spread these traits across Europe and may have been instrumental in social changes that helped create conditions conducive to acceptance of the new medium. The decisive rejection of coinage across northern Europe at this stage is also instructive and speaks of different value systems and ideologies between the two zones. Once in place, this boundary between coin-users and their neighbours to the north hardly altered for over three centuries. The late expansion of coin use into the lower Rhine region and Britain was little more than a prelude to the large-scale penetration of Roman coinage into other areas beyond the frontier in the early centuries AD.

In emphasizing broader La Tène cultural unity, the degree of regional diversity in other regards should not be overlooked. Beyond the initial blanket preference for silver by groups already to some extent familiar with Greek colonial coinage nearer the Mediterranean, and for gold beyond the Alps where this was the metal of choice for elite symbols of power, this underlying heterogeneity is evident in the emergence of divergent regional coin traditions, as issuers opted for specific units and divisions, and added their own features and designs. Until the widespread adoption of Roman-style silver coinages in the face of the growing power of Rome restored a degree of unity, Iron Age coinages continued to evolve along largely distinct pathways in different parts of Europe, despite a striking degree of convergence in some other regards, not least the precocious development of coin-rich aggregations engaged in specialist manufacturing at the interface of the gold and silver belts in the Garonne basin in the west, and where the Amber Route and the Danube intersect in central Europe (Hiriart et al. 2020).

It is likely that, not just at the outset but throughout their period of use, Iron Age coinages were employed predominantly in transactions linked to elite needs and obligations, or undertaken by them to underpin the traditional social and cosmic order. This was also the case in the early centuries AD for Roman coins exported beyond the frontiers of the Empire. In pre-Roman and Roman Iron Age societies alike, coins functioned alongside a range of other prestige goods and valuables (including imports) in the elite sphere, and probably also in tandem with other forms of special purpose currencies appropriate to different spheres of conveyance—concerned, for example, with subsistence or the procurement of raw materials.

Monetary objects used in other transactional spheres will have varied from region to region, but candidates in Iron Age Europe range from cattle, salt, and textiles to stone or glass beads and bracelets, which were often deliberately halved or quartered,[28] and standardized iron ingots and semi-products (Chapter 23). Small precious (and base) metal bars and rings of various types occur widely in Europe from the pre- to the post-Roman period (e.g. García-Bellido et al. 2011; Hedeager 1992). They were sometimes hoarded with coins and, as with hacksilver, they could have been used in their own right in payments.[29] By the time of Roman expansion, Iron Age coins might have supplanted these other media in certain transactions, but it is unlikely that they put an end to all of them. Only with the upsurge in bronze issues after the conquest did a wider spectrum of Iron Age society come to participate in monetary transactions and, even then, the extent to which coins were routinely used as general-purpose money in exchange for many goods or services remains an open question.

As the contextual study of Iron Age site finds shows, depositional practices incorporating coins were far from uniform. This hints at variations in the social and conceptual significance of coins among peoples using what seem to us to be similar types ultimately derived from the same models. While it has always been accepted that there is a selective aspect to site finds, this has clearly been underestimated for Iron Age settlements (Haselgrove and Webley 2016). Structured deposition in the broadest sense is apparent on urban and rural settlements, as well as religious sites. In many cases, an element of intentional deposition is likely. This, in turn, may often have had a ritual significance, although this need not be the only explanation.

Coin specialists therefore need to move beyond the assumption that every Iron Age coin find that is not demonstrably a votive deposit or part of a 'wealth concealment' hoard must be a chance loss. As with other forms of material culture, the depositional practices behind coin assemblages from settlements were complex. In certain respects, site finds do adhere to modern preconceptions—base metal issues generally predominate where present, while gold coins are rare and often show signs of special treatment—but they are not just a straightforward reflection of economic activity. Depositional patterns and context, and the extent to which these reflect intentional behaviours on the part of coin owners and users, must be carefully assessed. At the same time, despite considerable diversity across Europe, we can discern commonalities in the ways that Iron Age coins ended their lives. Even if simple economic interpretations are rejected, coins were used in broadly similar ways by different Iron Age societies. The challenge is to make full use of the accumulating archaeological data to establish more precisely the roles and functions of Iron Age coins and how these evolved over time.

Notes

1. For general surveys of Iron Age coinage, see Allen 1980; Nash 1987; Gruel 1989; Ziegaus 2010.
2. The helmeted head on the 'Alkis' coins is derived in a roundabout way from Roman *didrachms* of *c.*265–242 BC; the reverse figure of Athena Alkis is copied from *tetradrachms* of Antigonus II Gonatas (*c.*277–239 BC) or Philip V of Macedon (*c.*221–210 BC), or, much less likely, from earlier *tetradrachms* of Ptolemy I of Egypt (*c.*310–305 BC). See Venclová and Militký (2014: 396).
3. Stratified finds from radiocarbon-dated deposits in the cult areas at Roseldorf (Austria) indicate that silver coinage developed in this region during La Tène C (Holzer 2019), much earlier than once thought, but until the Roseldorf evidence is published in full, exactly when silver was first introduced remains somewhat uncertain.
4. An exception is the middle Loire region, where struck bronze coins occur alongside potins from the second century BC onwards (Martin 2015).
5. Exact estimates are rendered hazardous by the many unknowns and variables, ranging from the numbers of coins typically struck from a single die to the extent of metal recycling from earlier to later issues. See Talbot (2017: 64–84) for further discussion of the issues in relation to the gold and silver coinages of the Iceni.
6. These points would similarly seem to rule out the arrival of Greek coinage through long-distance trade as responsible for its widespread adoption beyond the Alps (Wigg-Wolf 2011).

7. Between the late 320s and the 270s BC (Nieto-Pelletier 2016; Hiriart et al. 2020: 183).
8. As well as Iron Age coins, some Republican *denarii* from Przeworsk culture settlements in Poland could be pre-Roman Iron Age imports, although most were later arrivals (Dymowski and Romanowski 2017).
9. The ratio of small to large silver coins has also increased in recent decades, suggesting a bias against the recovery of small coins in the early excavations.
10. A polygonal ditched enclosure around the hilltop was originally thought to mark the limits of the Iron Age sanctuary, but in fact probably dates to the Roman period, when a small stone temple was also constructed on the hill (information Dr J. Farley). The earliest hoards from Snettisham were mostly of torcs with few coins, but from the mid-first century BC onwards, coins dominated. Deposition culminated in the first century AD with the so-called 'bowl hoard', comprising a silver bowl containing over 6,000 silver coins, with a separate deposit of 500 gold coins and ingots beneath (Talbot 2017: 109–110, 223–225).
11. The artefact-rich pits at Basel-Gasfabrik are reminiscent of south-east European 'pit field' sanctuaries such as Bucharest-Snagov (Romania) or Bagachina (Bulgaria), where there were also many coins among the finds (Sîrbu and Bodo 2011). There is some debate about whether the material from these pit field sites is domestic in origin, but many of them show a longevity of ritual practice that sets them apart from settlements.
12. Most of the coins in question were found singly or in small groups, along with a minority of larger deposits which qualify as hoards (Krmnicek 2012).
13. The earliest grave find from a major centre is a gold rainbow cup quarter-stater in a female cremation burial at the salt mining complex at Dürrnberg-bei-Hallein (Austria). The grave, which also contained four brooches and burnt fragments of a glass arm ring, dates to the start of La Tène C2 (Schachinger and Wendling 2019).
14. It is not uncommon for coins to be associated in settlements with the same dress accessories as in graves. At Acy-Romance, Iron Age coins are often found in disused storage pits with animal and human bone, brooches, beads, and bracelets identical to those in burials surrounding the site. Conceivably, the pit deposits were generated by mortuary rituals enacted elsewhere and brought back to the settlement, perhaps as a closure rite. At this period, formal burials are far too few to account for more than a minority of the population and many of the dead must have been disposed of in ways that leave little if any archaeological trace. A family link between storage pits and the individuals whose possessions were buried in them is also possible.
15. The human bones did not survive. The other five graves from Esvres with Iron Age coins all have goods normally seen as female.
16. All the Iron Age coin are non-local types with origins in the upper Rhine area; seven Republican *denarii* from the site may be contemporary deposits (Nick 2018: 41–42).
17. At Corent, the site of the sanctuary was first identified from the concentration of coin finds on the surface (Poux and Demierre 2015).
18. There are also differences between the overall spectrum of coins from the temple precinct at Martberg and from the adjacent settlement, where gold is rarer (Wigg-Wolf 2017, 2018).
19. Many of these *sestertii* were deposited in graves (Bursche 2008; Chapter 6), a timely reminder that distributions of coin finds are shaped by depositional behaviour. Similar coins may have reached other areas beyond the frontier without this being apparent from the record, as Wheeler (1954: 40–41) long ago cautioned.
20. Stray finds from different parts of Germany show that Roman base metal coins are somewhat more common close to the frontier. While this supports the idea of some

cross-border commerce, the proportion of base-metal issues is tiny compared even to rural areas of the Empire, indicating that small denominations were not used intensively beyond the frontier (Wigg-Wolf 2008, 2020).

21. This has been questioned by James (2005), who argues that there is little evidence in the early Empire for auxiliary veterans returning to homelands deep in Germany; at this period, recruitment of Germanic troops from outside the Empire appears to have been limited to the border regions.
22. For example, in Scotland *denarius* hoards rose in number after the Antonine Wall was abandoned; initially, the focus was on the central region; it then shifted first to the north-east, and then—after Severus—back to the hinterland of Hadrian's Wall. The difference in date between the two Birnie hoards implies that they left the Empire a few years apart and might therefore be separate payments (Blackwell et al. 2017: 23–24. 29).
23. From his study of gold finds beyond the frontier, particularly from modern Ukraine, Bursche has argued that after defeating the Roman army at Abritus (in modern Bulgaria) in AD 251, the Goths returned home with a large amount of Roman gold, mostly coins but probably also ingots, seized when they captured part of the treasury carried by the emperor on campaign (Bursche and Myzgin 2020).
24. Silver tableware and personal objects chopped up into pieces and often carefully apportioned into Roman weight units. Unlike the third-century silver coinage, such items were made of high-purity metal. Hacksilver hoards from outside the Empire were for a long time interpreted as booty from Germanic raids and incursions across the frontier, but while this may be true in some cases, it seems unlikely of the majority.
25. Interestingly, making ornaments from recycled Roman silver in Scotland seems to start after hacksilver had supplanted *denarii* in diplomatic payments. This might just be due to the greater purity or amounts of hacksilver, but could be because at an earlier period coin payments were valued for their personal link to the emperor.
26. Pre-Roman coins, especially potins, were treated in the same way by Germanic settlers within the Empire. Late Roman and early medieval graves often contain curated Iron Age coins in necklaces or with suspension loops, or occasionally reused as balance weights (Haselgrove 2008). In at least one case, troop movements or resettlement led to Iron Age coins being transported wholesale to territories outside their area of origin.
27. Unlike gold, silver coins were rarely pierced or mounted for use as personal adornments in the Roman Iron Age. This could well stem from different perceptions of the two metals (chiming with Tacitus' claim that the Germans preferred silver to gold), resulting in their assimilation into separate spheres, one concerned with elite exchanges, the other with status display (Wigg-Wolf 2020: 29–30).
28. Roymans and Vernier (2010: 212) reject the idea of glass bracelets as primitive money, on the grounds both of their fragility and the lack of hoards, arguing that they were ornaments worn exclusively by females.
29. As with coins, gold-plated metal bars sometimes occur, e.g. at Roseldorf.

References

Aarts, J. G. 2005. 'Coins, money and exchange in the Roman world. A cultural-economic perspective'. *Archaeological Dialogues* 12, 1: 1–27.

Allen, D. F. 1976. 'Wealth, money and coinage in a Celtic society', in J. V. S. Megaw (ed.) *To Illustrate the Monuments: Essays on Archaeology Presented to Stuart Piggott*: 200–208. London: Thames and Hudson.

Allen, D. F. 1980. *The Coins of the Ancient Celts*. Edinburgh: Edinburgh University Press.

Arslan, E. A. 2017. 'La moneta celtica in Italia Settentrionale', in P. Piana Agostinetti (ed.) *Celti d'Italia: I Celti dell'eta di La Tène a sud delle Alpi, Atti del Convegno internazionale sui Celti dell'eta di La Tène a sud delle Alpi, Roma 2010*: 429–489. Biblioteca di Studi Etruschi 59. Rome: Giorgio Bretschneider.

Baray, L. 2014. *Les mercenaires celtes et la culture de La Tène: critères archéologiques et positions sociologiques*. Dijon: University of Dijon.

Barrandon, J.-N., G. Aubin, J. Benusiglio, J. Hiernard, D. Nony, and S. Scheers. 1994. *L'or gaulois: Le trésor de Chevanceax et les monnayages de la façade atlantique*. Cahiers d'Ernest-Babelon 6. Paris: CNRS.

Bjerg, L. M. H. 2011. 'Die Denare aus Siedlungen der römischen und germanischen Eisenzeit in Jütland'. *Germania* 89, 1–2: 231–275.

Bland, R., A. Chadwick, E. Ghey, C. Haselgrove, D. Mattingly, A. Rogers, et al. 2020. *Iron Age and Roman Coin Hoards in Britain*. Oxford: Oxbow Books.

Blackwell, A., M. Goldberg, and F. Hunter. 2017. *Scotland's Early Silver: Transforming Roman Pay-Off to Pictish Treasures*. Edinburgh: National Museums Scotland.

Burkhardt, A., G. Helmig, and W. B. Stern. 1994. *Keltische Münzen aus Basel: Numismatische Untersuchungen und Metallanalysen*. Basel: Antiqua 25.

Bursche, A. 2008. 'Function of Roman coins in Barbaricum of Later Antiquity. An anthropological essay', in A. Bursche, R. Ciołek, and R. Wolters (eds) *Roman Coins Outside the Empire: Ways and Phases, Contexts and Functions*: 395–416. Collection Moneta 82. Wetteren: Moneta.

Bursche, A. 2014. 'Gold barbarian imitations of Roman coins: the Ulów type,' in R. Madyda-Legutko and J. Rodzińska-Nowak (eds) *Honoratissimum assensus genus est armis laudare: Studia dedykowane Profesorowi Piotrowi Kaczanowskiemu z okazji siedemdziesiątej rocznicy urodzin*: 317–327. Krakow: Jagiellonian University, Institute of Archaeology.

Bursche, A., and K. Myzgin. 2020. 'The Gothic invasions of the mid-3rd century AD and the battle of Abritus: Coins and archaeology in east-central Barbaricum'. *Journal of Roman Archaeology* 33: 195–229.

Bursche, A., R. Ciołek, and R. Wolters. (eds) 2008. *Roman Coins Outside the Empire: Ways and Phases, Contexts and Functions*. Collection Moneta 82. Wetteren: Moneta.

Cauuet, B. 1999. 'L'exploitation de l'or en Gaule à l'Age du Fer', in B. Cauuet (ed.) *L'or dans l'Antiquité: De la mine à l'objet*: 31–86. Aquitania supplement 9. Toulouse: Fédération Aquitania.

Čižmář, M., E. Kolníková, and H. C. Noeske. 2008. 'Němčice-Víceměřice—ein neues Handels- und Industriezentrum der Latenezeit in Mähren'. *Germania* 86, 2: 655–700.

Collis, J. R. 1981. 'A typology of coin distributions'. *World Archaeology* 13, 1: 122–128.

Cowell, M. R. 1992. 'An analytical survey of the British Celtic gold coinage', in M. Mays (ed.) *Celtic Coinage: Britain and Beyond*: 207–233. British Archaeological Reports British Series 222. Oxford: Tempus Reparatum.

Crawford, M. H. 1985. *Coinage and Money Under the Roman Republic*. London: Methuen.

Creighton, J. 2000. *Coins and Power in late Iron Age Britain*. Cambridge: Cambridge University Press.

Creighton, J. 2005. 'Gold, ritual and kingship', in C. Haselgrove and D. Wigg-Wolf (eds) *Iron Age Coinage and Ritual Practices*: 69–83. Studien zu Fundmünzen der Antike 20. Mainz am Rhein: Philipp von Zabern.

Déchelette, J. 1914. *Manuel d'Archéologie préhistorique, celtique et gallo-romaine, II-3: Second âge du fer ou époque de La Tène*. Paris: Picard.

Delestrée, L.-P. 1996. *Monnayages et peuples Gaulois du Nord-Ouest*. Paris: Errance.

Delestrée, L.-P., and F. Pilon. 2014. 'Le moule à potins en bronze de Romenay (Saône-et-Loire, France)'. *Numismatic Chronicle* 174: 61–74.

Dulęba, P., and P. Wysocki. 2017. 'A new discovery of a Celtic coin hoard from western Lesser Poland'. *Archäologisches Korrespondenzblatt* 47, 1: 51–66.

Dymowski, A. 2019. 'The CERES group of Barbarian imitations of Roman denarii'. *Numismatic Chronicle* 179: 179–204.

Dymowski, A., and A. Romanowski. 2017. 'Finds of Roman Republican coins from the Przeworsk culture settlement concentration in the middle Prosna drainage'. *Numismatický sborník* 31: 176–184.

Farley, J. 2012. 'At the edge of empire: Iron Age and early Roman metalwork in the East Midlands'. PhD thesis, University of Leicester.

Fell, D. 2020. *Contact, Concord and Conquest: Britons and Romans at Scotch Corner*. Northern Archaeological Associates Monograph Series 5. Barnard Castle: Northern Archaeological Associates.

Fichtl, S. 2004. *Les peuples gaulois. IIIe–Ier s. av. J.-C.* Paris: Errance.

García-Bellido, M. P. 2004. 'The Roman impact and the Hispano-Celtic coinage', in K. Strobel (ed.) *Forschungen zur Monetarisierung und ökonomischen Funktionaliserung von Geld in den nordwestlichen Provinzen des Imperium Romanum: Die Entstehung eines europäische Wirtschaftraumes. Akten des 2. Trierer Symposiums zur antiken Wirtschaftsgeschichte*: 61–89. Trierer Historische Forschungen 49. Trier: Kliomedia.

García-Bellido, M. P., L. Callegarin, and A. Jiménez Díez. (eds) 2011. *Barter, Money and Coinage in the Ancient Mediterranean 10th–1st centuries BC: Actas del IV Encuentro peninsular de Numismática antigua EPNA, Madrid 2010*. Madrid: CSIC.

Găzdac, C. 2018. 'The coin assembly as a votive deposit in the Iron Age. The case of coins in the ritual complex at the Dacian fortress of Costești-Cetățuie Hunedoara county, Romania'. *Journal of Ancient History and Archaeology* 5, 3: 55–65.

Gruel, K. 1989. *La monnaie chez les Gaulois*. Paris: Errance.

Gruel, K. 2002. 'Monnaies et territoires', in D. Garcia and F. Verdin (eds) *Territoires celtiques: espaces ethniques et territoires des agglomérations protohistoriques d'Europe occidentale. Actes du 24e colloque international de l'AFEAF, Martigues, 1–4 juin 2000*: 205–212. Paris: Errance.

Gruel, K. 2009. 'Comparaison des faciès monétaires des oppida de Bibracte et de Manching', in S. Grunwald, J. K. Koch, and D. Mölders (eds) *Artefact: Festschrift für Sabine Rieckhoff*: 467–476. Universitätsforschungen zur prähistorischen Archäologie 172. Bonn: Habelt.

Gruel, K., and P. Pion. 2009. Les « trésors monétaires » en Gaule chevelue: faciès régionaux et contextes sociaux des dépôts, in S. Bonnardin, C. Hamon, M. Lauwers, and B. Quilliec (eds) *Du matériel au spirituel: Réalités archéologiques et historiques des « dépôts » de la Préhistoire à nos jours*: 381–395. XXIXe Rencontres Internationales d'Archéologie et d'Histoire d'Antibes. Antibes: Éditions APDCA.

Gruel, K., and L. Popovitch. 2007. *Les Monnaies gauloises et romaines de l'oppidum de Bibracte*. Collection Bibracte 13. Glux-en-Glenne: Centre Archéologique Européen du Mont Beuvray.

Gruel, K., S. Nieto-Pelletier, M. Demierre, and E. Hiriart. 2017. 'Evaluation des indices de métallurgie monétaire au second âge du Fer', in S. Marion, S. Defressigne, J. Kaurin, and G. Bataille (eds) *Production et proto-industrialisation aux âges du Fer: Actes du 39e colloque international de l'AFEAF, Nancy 2015*: 497–518. Bordeaux: Ausonius.

Haselgrove, C. 1987. *Iron Age Coinage in South-East England: The Archaeological Context*. British Archaeological Reports British Series 174. Oxford: British Archaeological Reports.

Haselgrove, C. 1988. 'The archaeology of British potin coinage'. *Archaeological Journal* 145, 1: 73–88.

Haselgrove, C. 1995. 'Le potin au personnage courant en contexte archéologique. Les potins gaulois: typologie, diffusion, chronologie, état de la question'. *Gallia* 52: 51–59.

Haselgrove, C. 1999. 'The development of Iron Age coinage in Belgic Gaul'. *Numismatic Chronicle* 159: 111–168.

Haselgrove, C. 2005. 'A new approach to analysing the circulation of Iron Age coinage'. *Numismatic Chronicle* 165: 129–174.

Haselgrove, C. 2008. 'Iron Age coin finds from religious sites and contexts in northern Gaul', in R. Haussler and A. King (eds) *Continuity and Innovation in Religion in the Roman West. Vol. II. Numismatic, Linguistic and Epigraphic Studies*: 7–23. Journal of Roman Archaeology Supplementary Series 67.2. Portsmouth, RI: Journal of Roman Archaeology.

Haselgrove, C. 2018. 'The Iron Age coins', in M. Fulford, A. Clarke, E. Durham, and N. Pankhurst, *Late Iron Age Calleva: The Pre-Conquest Occupation at Silchester Insula IX*. Britannia Monograph 32: 77–91. London: Society for the Promotion of Roman Studies.

Haselgrove, C. 2019. 'The Gallic War in the chronology of Iron Age coinage', in A. P. Fitzpatrick and C. Haselgrove (eds) *Julius Caesar's Battle for Gaul: New Archaeological Perspectives*: 241–266. Oxford: Oxbow Books.

Haselgrove, C., and L. Webley. 2016. 'Lost purses and loose change? Coin deposition on settlements in Iron Age Europe', in C. Haselgrove and S. Krmnicek, *The Archaeology of Money*: 85–113. Leicester Archaeology Monograph 24. Leicester: School of Archaeology and Ancient History.

Haselgrove, C., and D. Wigg-Wolf. 2005. 'Introduction: Iron Age coinage and ritual practices', in C. Haselgrove and D. Wigg-Wolf (eds) *Iron Age Coinage and Ritual Practices*: 183–206. Studien zu Fundmünzen der Antike 20. Mainz: Philipp von Zabern.

Hedeager, L. 1992. *Iron Age Societies: From Tribe to State in Northern Europe 500 BC to AD 700*. Oxford: Blackwell.

Hiriart, E. 2019. 'Les agglomérations artisanales et l'apparition de l'usage monétaire dans le monde celtique IIIe s. et début du IIe s.av. J.-C', in S. Fichtl, P. Barral, G. Pierrevelcin, and M. Schönfelder (eds) *Les agglomérations ouvertes de l'Europe celtique IIIe–Ier s. av. J.-C. Table ronde internationale Glux-en-Glenne, 28–30 October 2015*: 419–436. Mémoires d'Archéologie du Grand Est 4. Strasbourg: AVAGE.

Hiriart, E., T. Smělý, J. Genechesi, K. Gruel, S. Nieto-Pelletier, and D. Wigg-Wolf. 2020. 'Coinages and economic practices between the 3rd century and the beginning of the 2nd century BC in temperate Europe', in G. Pierrevelcin, J. Kysela, and S. Fichtl (eds) *Unité et diversité du monde celtique: Actes du 42e colloque international de l'AFEAF, Prague 2018*: 181–212. Collection AFEAF 2. Paris: AFEAF.

Holzer, V. 2014. 'Roseldorf—an enclosed settlement of the early and middle La Tène period in lower Austria Roseldorf/Němčice centre', in M. Fernández-Götz, H. Wendling, and K.

Winger (eds) *Paths to Complexity: Centralisation and Urbanisation in Iron Age Europe*: 122–131. Oxford: Oxbow Books.

Holzer, V. 2019. 'Die Großsiedlung Roseldorf/Niederösteereich und ihrer Heiligtümer—Varanten, Opfer and Rituale', in S. Fichtl, P. Barral, G. Pierrevelcin, and M. Schönfelder (eds) *Les agglomerations ouvertes de l'Europe celtique IIIe–Ier s. av. J.-C. Table ronde internationale Glux-en-Glenne, 28–30 October 2015*: 389–410. Mémoires d'Archéologie du Grand Est 4. Strasbourg: AVAGE.

Horsnaes, H. 2008. 'Roman coins and their contexts in Denmark', in A. Bursche, R. Ciołek, and R. Wolters (eds) *Roman Coins Outside the Empire: Ways and Phases, Contexts and Functions*: 135–146. Collection Moneta 82. Wetteren: Moneta.

Horsnaes, H. 2010. *Crossing Boundaries: An Analysis of Roman Coins in Danish Contexts, Vol. 1: Finds from Sealand, Funen and Jutland*. Studies in Archaeology and History 18. Copenhagen: National Museum.

Howgego, C. 2013. 'The monetization of temperate Europe'. *Journal of Roman Studies* 103: 16–45.

Hunter, F. 2007. 'Silver for the barbarians: interpreting *denarii* hoards in North Britain and beyond', in R. Hingley and S. Willis (eds) *Roman Finds: Context and Theory*: 214–224. Oxford: Oxbow Books.

James, S. 2005. 'Large-scale recruitment of auxiliaries from Free Germany?', in Z. Visy (ed.) *Limes XIX: Proceedings of the XIXth International Congress of Roman Frontier Studies, Pécs, Hungary, 2003*: 273–279. Pécs: University of Pécs.

Jersey, P. de 2009. 'Some experiments in Iron Age coin production and some implications for the production of Gallo-Belgic E', in J. van Heesch and I. Heeren (eds) *Coinage in the Iron Age: Essays in Honour of Simone Scheers*: 257–269. London: Spink.

Jud, P., and S. Ulrich-Bochsler. 2014. *Bern, Reichenbachstrasse: Neue Gräber aus dem latènezeitlichen Oppidum auf der Engehalbinsel*. Bern: Archäologischer Dienst des Kantons Bern.

Kolníková, E. 2012. *Němčice: Ein Macht-, Industrie- und Handelszentrum der Latenezeit in Mahren und Siedlungen am ihren Rande*. Spisy Archeologického Ústavu Brno 43. Brno: Czech Academy of Sciences.

Kos, P. 2007. 'The beginning of coinage of Celtic tribes in the southeastern Alps'. *Slovenská Numizatika* 18: 59–68.

Krmnicek, S. 2012. 'Coins in walls, floors and foundations: a contextual approach. The case of the Magdalensberg, Austria', in G. Pardini (ed.) *Preatti del I Workshop Internazionale di Numismatica: Numismatica e archeologia: Monete, stratigrafie e contesti*: 519–530. Rome: Dipartimento di Scienze dell'Antichità.

Krmnicek, S. 2019. 'Introduction. Money made the ancient world go round', in S. Krmnicek (ed.) *A Cultural History of Money in Antiquity*: 1–19. London: Bloomsbury Press.

Landon, M. 2016. *Making a Mint: Comparative Studies in Late Iron Age Coin Mould*. Oxford: Archaeopress.

Lauwers, C. 2015. 'Coins et ateliers monétaires celtes: de l'oppidum aux artisans itinerants'. *Revue Belge de Numismatique* 161: 55–72.

Leins, I. 2012. 'Numismatic data reconsidered: Coin distributions and interpretation in studies of late Iron Age Britain'. PhD thesis, University of Newcastle.

Lockyear, K. 2004. 'The late Iron Age background to Roman dacia', in W. S. Hanson and I. P. Haynes (eds) *Roman Dacia: The Making of a Provincial Society*: 33–73. Journal of Roman Archaeology Supplementary Series 56. Portsmouth, RI: Journal of Roman Archaeology.

Luley, B. 2008. 'Coinage at Lattara. Using archaeological context to understand ancient coins'. *Archaeological Dialogues* 15, 2: 174–195.

Martin, S. 2015. *Du statere au sesterce: Monnaie et romanisation dans la Gaule du Nord et de l'Est IIIe s. a.C. / Ier s. p.C.* Scripta Antiqua 78. Bordeaux: Ausonius.

Martin, S., F. Malrain, and T. Lorho. 2016. 'La circulation monétaire dans les campagnes gauloises de l'âge du Fer. Éléments de synthèse à partir des découvertes répertoriées dans la base de données des établissements ruraux du second âge du Fer', in S. Martin (ed.) *Monnaies et monétisation dans les campagnes de la Gaule du Nord et de l'Est, de l'âge du Fer à l'Antiquité tardive*: 133–159. Scripta Antiqua 9. Bordeaux: Ausonius.

Metzler, J., C. Gaeng, and P. Méniel. 2016. *L'espace public du Titelberg*. Dossiers d'Archéologie 17. Luxembourg: Centre National de Recherche Archéologique.

Meunier, E., and M. Luaces. 2021. 'Mining in south-west Gaul at the crossroads of the Celtic and Mediterranean worlds. The case of the mining area of the Arize mountains (central Pyrenees) during the fourth and third centuries BC'. *Oxford Journal of Archaeology* 40, 2: 191–210.

Militký, J. 2013. 'Coinage in the La Tène period', in N. Venclová (ed.) *The Late Iron Age—The La Tène Period*. The Prehistory of Bohemia 6: 127–134. Prague: Czech Academy of Sciences.

Militký, J. 2015. *Oppidum Hradiště u Stradonic: Komentovaný katalog mincovních nálezů a dokladů mincovní výroby/Das Oppidum Hradiště bei Stradonice. Kommentierter Katalog der Münzfunde und Belege der Münzproduktion*. Prague: Czech Academy of Sciences.

Nash, D. 1987. *Coinage in the Celtic World*. London: Seaby.

Nick, M. 2005. 'Am Ende des Regenbogens . . . Ein Interpretationsversuch von Hortfunden mit keltischen Goldmünzen', in C. Haselgrove and D. Wigg-Wolf (eds) *Iron Age Coinage and Ritual Practices*: 115–155. Studien zu Fundmünzen der Antike 20. Mainz: Philipp von Zabern.

Nick, M. 2018. 'The impact of coinage on ritual offering during the late Iron Age *c*.250–25/15 BC', in N. Myrberg Burstrom and G. Tarnow Ingvardson (eds) *Divina Moneta: Coins in Ritual and Religion*: 30–48. Abingdon: Routledge.

Nieto, S., and J.-N. Barrandon. 2002. 'Le monnayage en or arverne: essai de chronologie relative á partir des données typologiques et analytiques'. *Revue Numismatique* 159: 37–91.

Nieto-Pelletier, S. 2016. *De l'imitation à l'individualisation: genèse des monnayages d'or en Gaule: Regards croisés*. Mémoire de HDR. Paris: EPHE.

Nieto-Pelletier, S., and J. Olivier. 2016. 'Les statères aux types de Philippe II de Macédoine: de l'Égée à la Gaule, des origines aux imitations'. *Revue Numismatique* 173: 171–229.

Northover, J. P. 1992. 'Materials issues in the Celtic coinage', in M. Mays (ed.) *Celtic Coinage: Britain and Beyond—The Eleventh Oxford Symposium on Coinage and Monetary History*: 235–299. British Archaeological Report 222. Oxford: Tempus Reparatum.

Pion, P. 2005. 'Les caractères généraux et l'évolution de la circulation monétaire en Gaule nord-orientale aux IIe et Ier siècles avant J.C.', in J. Metzler and D. Wigg-Wolf (eds) *Die Kelten und Rom: neue numismatische Forschungen*: 39–57. Studien zu Fundmünzen der Antike 19. Mainz: Philipp von Zabern.

Pion, P. 2008. '"La monnaie de l'absolu": un siècle de numismatique gauloise dans les chronologies du second âge du Fer', in A. Lehoërff (ed.) *Construire le temps: Histoire et méthodes des chronologies et calendriers des derniers millénaires avant notre ère en Europe occidentale Actes du 30e colloque international de Halma-Ipel, Lille 2006*: 349–358. Collection Bibracte 16. Glux-en-Glenne: Centre Archéologique Européen du Mont Beuvray.

Pion, P. 2012. 'La monnaie mercenaire: une approche anthropologique des premiers monnayages celtiques au nord-ouest du complexe nord-alpin IIIe siècle av. J.-C.', in P. Pion and B. Formoso (eds) *Monnaie antique, Monnaie moderne, Monnaie d'ailleurs . . . Métissages et hybridations*: 151–164. Paris: De Boccard.

Polenz, H. 1982. 'Münzen in latènezeitlichen Gräbern Mitteleuropas aus der Zeit zwischen 300 und 50 vor Christi Geburt'. *Bayerische Vorgeschichtsblätter* 47: 28–222.

Poux, M., and M. Demierre. 2015. *Le sanctuaire de Corent Puy-de-Dôme, Auvergne*. Gallia supplément 62. Paris: CNRS.

Py, M. (ed.) 2006. *Les monnaies préaugustéennes de Lattes et la circulation monétaire protohistorique en Gaule méridionale*. Lattara 19. Lattes: Association pour le développement de l'Archéologie en Languedoc-Roussillon.

Riquier, S. 2004. 'La nécropole gauloise de "Vaugrignon" à Esvres-sur-Indre (Indre-et-Loire)'. *Revue Archéologique du Centre de la France* 43, 1: 21–113.

Ripollès, P. P. 2017. 'The Iberian Coinages, 6th–1st century BC'. *Numismatic Chronicle* 177: 1–8.

Roymans, N. 1990. *Tribal Societies in Northern Gaul: An Anthropological Perspective*. Cingula 12. Amsterdam: University of Amsterdam.

Roymans, N. 1999. 'Man, cattle and the supernatural in the Northwest European Plain', in C. Fabech and J. Ringtved (eds) *Settlement and Landscape: Proceedings of a Conference in Åarhus, Denmark 4–7 May 1998*: 291–300. Mooesgård: Åarhus University Press.

Roymans, N. 2001. 'The Lower Rhine triquetrum coinages and the ethnogenesis of the Batavi', in T. Grünewald and H.-J. Schalles (eds) *Germania Inferior: Besiedlung, Wirtschaft und Gesellschaft an der Grenze der römisch-germanischen Welt*: 93–145. Berlin: Walther de Gruyter.

Roymans, N. 2004. *Ethnic Identity and Imperial Power: The Batavians in the Early Roman Empire*. Amsterdam Archaeological Studies 10. Amsterdam: Amsterdam University Press.

Roymans, N., and J. Aarts. 2005. 'Coins, soldiers and the Batavian Hercules cult. Coin deposition at the sanctuary of Empel in the Lower Rhine region', in C. Haselgrove and D. Wigg-Wolf (eds) *Iron Age Coinage and Ritual Practices*: 337–359. Studien zu Fundmünzen der Antike 20. Mainz: Philipp von Zabern.

Roymans, N., and J. Aarts. 2009. 'Coin use in a dynamic frontier region. Late Iron Age coinages in the Lower Rhine area'. *Journal of the Archaeology of the Low Countries* 1: 5–26.

Roymans, N., G. Creemers, and S. Scheers. 2012. *Late Iron Age Gold Hoards from the Low Countries and the Caesarian Conquest of Northern Gaul*. Amsterdam Archaeological Studies 18. Amsterdam: Amsterdam University Press.

Roymans, N., and L. Vernier. 2010. 'Glass La Tène Bracelets in the Lower Rhine Region. Typology, chronology and social interpretation'. *Germania* 88, 1/2: 195–219.

Rudnicki, M. 2014. 'Nowa Cerekwia. *A celtic centre for craft and commerce of interregional importance north of the Carpathians*', in S. Berecki (ed.) *Iron Age Crafts and Craftsmen in the Carpathian Basin*: 33–70. Targu Mureş: Editura MEGA.

Schachinger, U., and H. Wendling. 2019. 'Numismatik einer Salzmetropole, Fundmünzen und Edelmetallguss der Latène- und Römerzeit auf den Dürrnberg und in Hallein (Salzberg)'. *Bayerische Vorgeschichtsblätter* 84: 171–210.

Scheers, S. 2004. 'La naissance du monnayage d'or en Gaule d'après les influences étrangères', in K. Strobel (ed.) *Forschungen zur Monetarisierung und ökonomischen Funktionaliserung von Geld in den nordwestlichen Provinzen des Imperium Romanum. Die Entstehung eines europäische Wirtschaftraumes Akten des 2. Trierer Symposiums zur antiken Wirtschaftsgeschichte*: 7–26. Trierer Historische Forschungen 49. Trier: Kliomedia.

Score, V. 2011. *Hoards, Hounds and Helmets: A Conquest-Period Ritual Site at Hallaton, Leicestershire*. Leicester Archaeology Monograph 21. Leicester: School of Archaeology and Ancient History.

Sillon, C. 2014. 'L'or monnayé dans le Nord de la Gaule: Recherches sur les monnaies d'or frappées dans le Nord de la Gaule entre le IIIe et le Ier siècle avant notre ère'. PhD thesis, University of Orléans.

Sills, J. 2003. *Gaulish and Early British Gold Coinage*. London: Spink.

Sills, J. 2017. *Divided Kingdoms: The Iron Age Gold Coinage of Southern England*. Aylsham: Chris Rudd.

Sîrbu, V., and C. Bodo. 2011. 'Coins from Geto-Dacian sacred sites', in M. Guštin and M. Jetvić (eds) *The Eastern Celts: The Communities between the Alps and the Black Sea*: 207–218. Belgrade: Koper.

Talbot, J. 2017. *Made for Trade: A New View of Icenian Coinage*. Oxford: Oxbow Books.

Toledo I Mur, A., and M. Pernot. 2008. 'Un atelier monétaire gaulois près de Poitiers. Les Rochereaux à Migné-Auxances (Vienne)'. *Gallia* 65: 231–272.

Tournaire, J., O. Buchsenschutz, J. Henderson, and J. R. Collis. 1982. 'Iron Age coin moulds from France'. *Proceedings of the Prehistoric Society* 48, 1: 417–435.

Venclová, N., and J. Militký. 2014. 'Glass-making, coinage and local identities in the Middle Danube region in the third and second centuries BC', in S. Hornung (ed.) *Produktion—Distribution—Ökonomie: Siedlungs und Wirtschaftsmuster der Latenezeit*: 387–406. Bonn: Rudolf Habelt.

Verrier, G., and F. Dieulafait. 2019. 'Monnaies et agglomération au IIe S. av. n.è.: le cas de la ZAC Niel à Toulouse Saint-Roch', in E. Hiriart, S. Martin, S. Nieto-Pelletier, and F. Olmer (eds) *Monnaies et archéologie en Europe celtique: Mélanges en l'honneur de Katherine Gruel*: 237–242. Collection Bibracte 29. Glux-en-Glenne: Centre Archéologique Européen du Mont Beuvray.

Wheeler, R. E. M. 1954. *Rome Beyond the Imperial Frontiers*. London: Penguin.

Wigg-Wolf, D. 2008. 'Coinage on the periphery', in A. Bursche, R. Ciołek, and R. Wolters (eds) *Roman Coins Outside the Empire: Ways and Phases, Contexts and Functions*: 35–48. Collection Moneta 82. Wetteren: Moneta.

Wigg-Wolf, D. 2011. 'The function of Celtic coinages in Northern Gaul', in M. P. García-Bellido, L. Callegarin, and A. Jiménez Díez (eds) *Barter, Money and Coinage in the Ancient Mediterranean 10th–1st centuries BC: Actas del IV Encuentro peninsular de Numismática antigua EPNA, Madrid 2010*: 301–314. Madrid: CSIC.

Wigg-Wolf, D. 2017. 'Of warriors, chiefs and gold. Coinage and exchange in the late pre-Roman Iron Age', in D. Brandherm, E. Heymans, and D. Hofmann (eds) *Gifts, Goods and Money: Comparing Currency and Circulation Systems in Past Societies*: 133–154. Oxford: Archaeopress.

Wigg-Wolf, D. 2018. 'Death by deposition? Coins and ritual offering in the late Iron Age and early Roman transition in northern Gaul', in N. Myrberg Burstrom and G. Tarnow Ingvardson (eds) *Divina Moneta: Coins in Ritual and Religion*: 13–29. Abingdon: Routledge.

Wigg-Wolf, D. 2020. 'The adoption of coinage by non-state societies. Two case studies from Iron Age northern Europe', in E. D. Heymans and M. K. Termeer (eds) *Politics of Value: New Approaches to Early Money and the* State: 25–38. Archaeology and Economy in the Ancient World 23. Heidelberg: Propylaeum. DOI: https://doi.org/10.11588/propylaeum.574

Williams, J. H. C. 2005. '"The newer rite is here": vinous symbolism on British Iron Age coins', in C. Haselgrove and D. Wigg-Wolf (eds) *Iron Age Coinage and Ritual Practices*. Studien zu Fundmünzen der Antike 20: 25–42. Mainz: Philipp von Zabern.

Ziegaus, B. 2010. *Kelten Geld: Münzen der Kelten und angrenzender nichtgriechischer Völkerschaften: Sammlung Christian Flesche*. Munich: Staatliche Münzsammlung.

Ziegaus, B. 2011. 'Celtic workmanship and die production in the West and the East', in M. P. García-Bellido, L. Callegarin, and A. Jiménez Díez (eds) *Barter, Money and Coinage in the Ancient Mediterranean 10th–1st centuries BC: Actas del IV Encuentro peninsular de Numismática Antigua EPNA, Madrid 2010*: 289–299. Madrid: CSIC.

Ziegaus, B. 2013. 'Münzen und Münzwerkzeuge', in S. Sievers, M. Leicht, and B. Ziegaus (eds) *Ergebnisse der Ausgrabungen in Manching-Altenfeld 1996–1999*: 425–619. Ausgrabungen in Manching 18. Wiesbaden: Reichert.

COMPLEXITY

CHAPTER 29

POLITICS AND POWER

JOHN COLLIS AND RAIMUND KARL

INTRODUCTION

THROUGHOUT the first millennium BC we can see two conflicting forces at work, both in the Latin and Greek written sources and in various aspects of the archaeological record. On the one hand we can see ever increasing social differentiation, which reaches its apogee in the last decades of the millennium when substantial areas of Mediterranean and temperate Europe were under the rule of just one man, the Roman emperor Augustus. On the other hand there was an ideology of egalitarianism, most famously in the Athenian concept of democracy, and even Augustus in his rise to power had to use sleight of hand to disguise the reality of what was happening, and he assiduously avoided the use of the term 'king', claiming he was only the leading citizen, the *primus inter pares*.

The complexity of the societies with which we are dealing are, as a broad generalization, grouped around two major axes. The first is geographical: the further societies are to the north and west of the Mediterranean the less complex they are politically, socially, economically, and technologically. The second axis is time: societies everywhere tend to become more complex from the beginning to the end of the millennium. However we must beware of thinking of this as a simple, unilinear development. In all areas—Mediterranean, temperate, and northern European—there is great variety with, for instance, urbanized and non-urban societies existing side by side. And in some places there are very clear reversions, with hierarchical or urban societies being replaced with simpler decentralized societies—in Greece at the beginning of the first millennium BC, in much of central and western temperate Europe in the fourth century BC, or in southern Germany and the Czech Republic in the first century BC.

The Nature of the Evidence

Contemporary Written Sources

Written sources from the Greek and Roman world are the best informants we have for social and political structure and evolution, but in addition to the usual scepticism we need to use—political and social biases of the authors, a tendency to use stereotypes or to plagiarize earlier sources—even for the Greek world, for instance, we may have considerable information for Athens or Sparta, but for the majority of *poleis* and colonies we have no information, perhaps not even the precise location of the site.

Discussion of social and political structures at this time revolves around three poles. At one extreme is monarchy, which in the Roman world starts with semi-mythical hereditary kings; though they were credited with the foundation of the city, the organization of religious rituals, and the setting up of a legal system, in the end the last king, Tarquinius Superbus, abused his power and was ousted. Under the subsequent Republic, in military or political crises a supreme leader, the *dictator*, might be appointed for a limited time only. The ideal was the semi-mythical Cincinnatus who was summoned to take control while ploughing his fields, and laid aside power as soon as he had completed the tasks required of him. The abhorrence of kingship in the first century BC was symbolized by Julius Caesar's rejection of the crown, and Augustus disguising his steps to supreme power. In the Greek world it was the *tyrannos*, usually someone who seized power during a period of internal political and social conflict (*stasis*). We have evidence of similar pressures outside the Mediterranean world, such as the successful attempt by Luernios to establish a ruling dynasty among the Arverni of central Gaul in the second century BC, and the stories related by Caesar of the joint but abortive attempts by Orgetorix of the Helvetii, Casticus of the Sequani, and Dumnorix of the Aedui to seize autocratic power.

The second pole was oligarchy. In most societies in the first millennium BC, certain people were able to exploit economic and social conditions to make others indebted to them unless there were counter-pressures. Quite how these individuals gained this influence is unclear as the rise of an aristocracy had already happened before we have written texts, and status was something largely inherited; it may have been power obtained through leading a powerful lineage, but also through characteristics such as greater energy or intelligence or charisma. In both the Greek and Roman worlds, and probably beyond, the major problem was access to land to cultivate, leading to the appearance of an urban poor who had no land to inherit, and also a rural poor of subsistence farmers who produced too little surplus to survive bad harvests, the effects of warfare, or the normal demographic upsets such as illness. This problem was the catalyst for the constitutional reforms in Athens of Solon and Cleisthenes. In Rome, by the late second century BC aristocrats had built up large holdings of land by making loans to poorer individuals who could not repay their debts. In the 130s BC, Tiberius Gracchus, and later his brother Gaius, attempted to reform land ownership, which was the main basis of power in the city-states, and gave access to magisterial posts and other sources of power. In Rome it was the estate-owning group which held most legislative power through membership of the senate, and we hear of similar bodies elsewhere—for instance, Caesar refers to the 'senate' of the Aedui, but who these people were, how they achieved their membership, and how much it may, or may not, have resembled the Roman senate is unclear. In many of the *polis* societies there was a second class of elite, the knights who could, like Maecenas, the patron of the poet Horace, be wealthier than many of the land-owning aristocracy. Their wealth could be accumulated through activities such as industrial production and trade, which were closed to the senatorial class, though senators might invest in the form of loans.

The third pole was democracy, which gave varying degrees of power to the male citizens of a state, and also privileges as in Athens, where citizens had the right to serve as jurors in court cases and were paid for it. Normally, citizen status was inherited through birth, but could be acquired, for instance though military service, or by becoming a *libertus*, a freed slave—indeed this could be a way of social advancement, with poor people handing over children as slaves to rich sponsors with the agreement that they would be educated and later freed. In Athens and Rome there was the right to attend assemblies to elect certain magistrates (e.g. the tribunes of the plebs) and to pass laws. We hear of such assemblies elsewhere; Caesar talks about an assembly called by the Treveri to decide whether to declare war. But given the potential for such events to foment unrest, mass assemblies are only likely to have taken place in more democratic states.

The pressure towards democracy was usually defence. Though major empires in the Near East often relied on impressed troops supplied by their subject peoples, and though tyrants such as Dionysus of Syracuse employed mercenaries and Athens had its police force of Scythian archers, the main defence was the citizen army. Social status could be measured in terms of how a warrior was armed: the horses of the aristocracy and the knights, the bronze armour of the heavy hoplites, and lighter arms for skirmishing forces. In Athens, where the fleet was the power base of the state, the citizen rowers formed the backbone and they demanded payment. This was a problem which hit the Roman army during the protracted siege of Veii in 396 BC, but it was not until the reforms of Marius in the war against the Cimbri and Teutones in 105–101 BC that the army became fully professional.

The political power of women in most of these societies was very limited, though we hear of cases such as Boudicca and Cartimandua in Britain who were referred to as 'queens' in the Roman texts. They certainly had political power, perhaps in her own right in the case of Cartimandua, and for Boudicca inherited from her husband and perhaps more in the form of personal influence rather than any formal rights; both certainly had a major political influence on their subjects.

The lower classes may have been free, but did not necessarily have citizen rights; in the case of the Greek cities foreign craftsmen, the metics or *metaoikoi*, formed an important class. Below them were the slaves, with limited or no freedom and no citizen rights. Though the ancient world is often portrayed as a slave-based economy, this was probably relatively undeveloped in the early first millennium BC. It was the pressure for cheap labour for the increasing production from mining and quarrying and the appearance of large agricultural estates, the *latifundia*, in the last two or three centuries BC that led to the full development of the slave economy, helped by a ready supply of slaves from the wars of conquest. But not all slaves were of a lowly exploited status; educated Greek slaves, for instance, could hold influential positions—such as Marcus Tullius Tiro, the secretary to Cicero.

Burial Evidence

From the 1970s onwards there have been many attempts by archaeologists to escape from earlier simplistic interpretations of burials, for instance that 'rich' burials are those of 'kings', 'princesses', 'warriors', etc., often based on medieval feudal models, and to use more anthropologically based criteria and nomenclature. Before that time interest was mainly based on the objects in the graves, and studies of the human remains themselves were rare, except to identify 'racial' characteristics through craniology. Even distinctions between genders were usually based on the grave goods and there was little interest in burials with few or no associated finds. An early attempt to look at age and gender was Ludwig Pauli's study (1973) of the late Hallstatt and early La Tène burials from southern Germany and Austria, identifying, for instance, certain classes of objects ('amulets') found especially in graves of young/unmarried (?) females, or triple brooches with more mature women (married?, mothers?). The more recent use of methods such as stable isotope analysis, DNA, etc. on skeletal remains has shown a potential to identify individual or communal migration and familial relationships, which has yet to be fully realized (see Chapter 37). Rich female burials have been interpreted in various ways, for instance that gold jewellery worn by a woman reflected her husband's standing, but in cases where female burials were the primary interments under barrows, as in Pauli's study, this could indicate a matrilineal form of inheritance or in exceptional circumstances a possibility of female inheritance. However, this does not indicate that these women held a higher political status than the men, and the concept of 'matriarchy' (rule by women) as postulated in some nineteenth-century evolutionary schemes is not something that can be demonstrated. In cases such as the woman in the late sixth-century BC burial at Vix in central France on the upper Seine with her wagon, gold torc, and the huge Greek *krater* (supposedly used for mixing wine and water), the probability that her status was her own and not dependent on any males appears to be rather high.

However we face a number of major limitations; over much of the Atlantic area—Britain, Ireland, western and central France, and Iberia—burials are usually very rare, and even in societies such as classical Athens only a minority of the population is recognizable in the burial rites, and the lower classes have virtually disappeared (Morris 1987). In other periods cremation is predominant and information from burnt bones is more limited. In key areas such as the Hunsrück-Eifel on either side of the river Moselle the soil is too acidic for bones to survive.

Though we agree that grave goods symbolize something, there are many things which may indicate relative wealth. A burial with many grave goods may be of someone with many family members, each of whom brought a pot; the presence of weapons may indicate social status rather than someone who was a warrior; wealthy goods with a child may indicate inherited rather than acquired status, though other interpretations are possible (e.g. a child with rich parents, or of a 'messenger to the gods' for the community); rich grave goods may indicate socially unstable times and an attempt by the heirs to bolster their position in an ostentatious destruction of wealth; or there could be taboos on inheriting certain classes of object, which thus need to be destroyed; and finally there is the question of how much 'wealth' was necessarily accompanied by direct political power (cf. Maecenas, who had the ear of Augustus but could not take up any major political offices because of his legal status as an *eques*). In some societies status at death may be deliberately suppressed in the burial rite—in Athens Solon is credited with instigating a law limiting expenditure on funerals; in others it may be deliberately inflated. Thus different societies choose different features to signify—wealth or poverty, gender, age, occupation, social position—but usually burial representation is even more complex, with several statuses being signified simultaneously. In the male cemetery of Großromstedt (Hachmann 1960) in late Iron Age northern Germany, one interpretation sees two different hierarchies: one social, symbolized by imported bronze vessels, and a military one with complete, fragmentary, or miniaturized weapons, with a full panoply of sword, shield, and spear at the top. But burials are also likely to include personal idiosyncrasies specific to the deceased.

Settlement Hierarchies and Layout

The foundation of new settlements, which happened frequently in the first millennium BC, gave a society the opportunity to express its social ideology in physical and spatial terms. In this we can often see the expression of egalitarian principles with similar sized houses which may be sited singly, in clusters, or linked together with shared partition walls: in Greek colonies; the forts in Poland such as Biskupin dating to the seventh century BC (Harding and Raczkowski 2010); the roundhouses on British hillforts such as Danebury and Moel-y-Gaer (Cunliffe 2005); the hilltop towns of southern France such as Nages or Entremont starting from the third century BC (Py 2012); the small hillforts in northern Spain laid out in radial form around a communal space in the centre and backing onto the ramparts; or Roman colonies for retired soldiers, where land was laid out in equal shares by centuriation. But on some of these sites, such as Greek and Roman colonies or hilltop towns like Ensérune in southern France, we can also see this egalitarianism breaking down as plots of land and buildings were joined together under one owner, perhaps around a private courtyard, or were embellished with painted wall plaster, mosaic pavements, and columns.

Some new foundations, however, show a pre-existing hierarchy as on the late Iron Age *oppida* of central Gaul. Mont Beuvray in Burgundy from its foundation in the late second century was divided into specialist quarters with the small wooden buildings on the Côme Chaudron occupied especially by metalworkers and other craftsmen, in contrast with the Parc aux Chevaux (PC), which was an aristocratic habitation area. The house PC1 started as a large complex of timber buildings which, by the time the site was abandoned at the start of the first century AD, had evolved into a multi-courtyard palatial building with mosaics, heated rooms, and an ornamental garden with water features (Paunier and Luginbühl 2004). Urban settlements began to take on something of the concentric layout of Sjoberg's (1960) 'pre-industrial city' with a core consisting of religious and administrative buildings and the houses of the aristocracy; a middle zone occupied by specialist middle-class groups and concentrated on streets or in defined areas perhaps forming guilds (e.g. merchants, butchers, metal and leather workers); and on the periphery the urban poor of labourers, food producers, etc.

Models such as Sjoberg's can give us an indicator that the size and opulence of a domestic house is linked with political power by its siting in an urban or village setting, and the presence of public buildings nearby indicate the concentration of political power, as in Rome. This is less obvious when settlement is dispersed; the size and layout of a building may be an indicator of wealth, but unless there is evidence of exceptional resources being brought together, the construction of the house may only be an indicator of wealth or the size of the group inhabiting it. One example of this is the large roundhouses of 15–20 m diameter in the late Bronze Age/earliest Iron Age of southern Britain, a contrast with the subsequent early and middle Iron Age at hillforts such as Danebury, where the norm is a diameter of about 8–10 m and large houses are lacking. This is also true of the late Bronze Age to Roman Iron Age in north-western Europe (e.g. Netherlands and Denmark), where the farmhouses had accommodation for the family at one end and a byre for the cattle at the other, and the size of the byre is assumed to indicate the size of the herd and so the wealth of the inhabitants (see Chapter 20). But in neither of these cases does there seem to be separate sleeping quarters for the head of the household. On the other hand, settlement landscapes with contemporary unenclosed, enclosed, and monumentalized homesteads, as in much of Wales during the early, middle, and later Iron Age, may indicate the existence of a decentralized, rural social hierarchy. Monumentalization can take various forms, from the provision of multiple ramparts to a homestead not obviously for reasons for defence, as occurs in highland areas of Britain such as the Cheviots, to the construction of luxury dwelling houses which, for instance, started in the middle of the first millennium BC in areas such as central Italy, and were to become very much a feature of the Roman landscape over much of central and western Europe as well, in the form of villas. Such investment in rural properties over the long term is also an indicator of the importance of land as a measure of status, and probably also of political power.

Other Archaeological Indicators of Wealth and Power

In most, perhaps all, societies social status is indicated by material culture, but objects do not possess this power within themselves; the status has to be assigned, and for identical objects this may vary from one society to another. One example is Attic red-figure ware of the fifth century BC. This had a certain status in Athens as a fineware service (much like the mass-produced painted or transfer-ware china such as 'Willow Pattern' in nineteenth-century Britain), but it was widely diffused throughout society and only the very poor were unable to purchase it. However, when such pottery was traded considerable distances, its role as a status indicator changed. In central Italy and southern France, Attic pottery was fairly well distributed, but not universally, and it turns up, for instance, in rich burials. Further north at Bourges in central France (Milcent 2007; Augier et al. 2012), at this time perhaps a royal site, it is virtually confined to the one settlement, showing its special status, but within the site it is scattered all over the occupied area, suggesting that it was not an indicator of special status among the inhabitants. In southern Germany, in contrast, Attic pottery is rare, and may be a clear indicator of high status; it only turns up in the richest burials and settlements, and in one case, Klein Aspergle, two broken cups had been mended, and decorated gold leaf was used to mask the breaks (Megaw 1970: fig. 41; Hoppe 2012).

Perhaps the most important indicator of wealth is dress, but textiles such as clothing, carpets, and wall hangings only rarely survive, e.g. at Pazyryk in the Altai Mountains (Rudenko 1970), as threads in burials such as Hochdorf, or small pieces in the salt mines at Hallstatt (see Chapter 26). Other goods associated with textiles were traded, like the purple dye produced in the Levant and used by elite males in Rome to indicate their senatorial status. But normally we are limited to metal objects such as ornaments and dress adjuncts like fibulae. Where in rich burials we find silver and gold brooches, in more normal burials they are of bronze or iron, and we can infer higher status, especially of wealth for the precious metals.

Grave goods in burials tend to be interpreted as indicators of the status of the individual, as items for personal use in a future life after death, or as items which were taboo and so could not be passed on by the dead to the living. However, in burials such as Hochdorf we see something transcending this, with a deliberate and ostentatious destruction of wealth. At Hochdorf the dagger and its sheath were covered with gold foil and the dead man's shoes were adorned with gold strips. These items showed no sign of wear, and several other gold objects shared common features with them—for example the punches used to decorate them—indicating that they were made at the time of the burial (Biel 1985). Highly visible burial markers such as large tumuli or the statues marking graves on sixth-century BC burials in southern Germany or the cemeteries of the Archaic period in Greece fall into a similar category. In these cases the main aim may have been political, demonstrating the ability of the heirs to take over the powers and status of the dead person.

Such deliberate destruction of wealth is not confined to funerary contexts; it also occurs in the context of gift-giving and feasting, most famously in the potlatch of native tribes such as the Kwakiutl on the Pacific coast around Vancouver (Mauss 1954). It can also appear in ritual contexts such as the gold treasure dredged from a lake by the Roman army when they captured Toulouse in 125–123 BC. Deposition of rich objects in watery contexts such as lakes, marshes, and rivers is very much a feature of the Atlantic coast from Portugal to Scandinavia in the middle and especially the late Bronze Age, but it continues into the Iron Age, mainly in rivers such as the Rhine, the Seine (Bonnamour 2000a), the Saône (Bonnamour 2000b), the Thames (Cunliffe 2005), and the Witham (Field and Parker Pearson 2003)—for example the Amfreville helmet or the Battersea, Wandsworth, and Witham shields—but also in lakes such as Llyn Fawr and Llyn Cerrig Bach in Wales (Cunliffe 2005), and most notably at La Tène on Lake Neuchâtel (Lejars 2013). Deposition of this kind can also occur on dry land, and in western Europe in the second to first centuries BC there are hoards of gold coins and torcs at sites such as Snettisham (Norfolk; Fitzpatrick 2005). It has been claimed that such activities are characteristic of periods of political instability and change (Luernios in the second century BC achieved the kingship of the Arverni through largesse), but it also occurs in times of relative stability such as in the burials of Hallstatt C (eighth to seventh century BC) in central Europe. Also, while we may largely be dealing with the activities of individuals or small groups, wealth destruction can also be a communal act, as has been claimed for the deposition of gold torcs in north-western Iberia in the hillfort (*castro*) communities which in other respects look relatively egalitarian (e.g. Sastre 2011).

Later Sources for Interpreting Iron Age Archaeology

In addition to the written sources previously discussed, sources produced by or about considerably later societies can also be used to help interpret how power could be exerted, and what political means and mechanisms may have been available in first millennium BC societies in Europe. These later sources include both ethnographic records collected in more modern times, which can be used as anthropological analogies, and 'indigenous' sources produced by literate societies in temperate and northern Europe, mainly during the early and high middle ages, which can also be useful as analogies.

Using these later sources is riddled with various difficulties, also requiring the usual scepticism. Earlier scholarship did not always fully recognize these difficulties and applied ideas gathered in such sources directly to first millennium BC societies, as if the societies described in the later sources were identical to the much earlier ones. Thus, interpretations of, for instance, early Irish literature as a 'Window on the Iron Age' (Jackson 1964) were both overly optimistic and simplistic in their assumptions of what later written sources could tell us about pre-Roman Iron Age societies. Similarly, the application of 'loaded' medieval 'feudal' terms like *Fürstengrab, Adelssitz*, or 'aristocratic seat' by early scholars (e.g. Kimmig 1969; see Jung 2005) for the rich burials and hillforts of the late Hallstatt and early La Tène periods simply back-projected a distinctly medieval model of social organization onto Iron Age societies without the necessary reflection on its general applicability. And the same, it has been argued, also applies to the simplistic application of (often cherry-picked) modern ethnographic analogies to the Iron Age (Eggert 1988, 1999; Krausse 1999).

The usefulness of modern ethnography, if used with the appropriate reflectiveness, is largely accepted in archaeology today. The use of early and high medieval written sources is much more disputed, both by those who happily use modern analogies but largely reject medieval ones (e.g. Collis 1994, 2011), and those who are happy to use classical sources but reject later ones more or less generally, and medieval ones specifically (e.g. Rieckhoff and Biel 2001). Despite this, there is a long tradition of developing anthropological models from medieval sources; not least, Engels' model of the 'military democracy' (mentioned again later in this chapter) is mainly based on his reading of extant early medieval 'Celtic' and 'Germanic' laws (Engels 1892). Equally, there is a long tradition of using comparisons of classical and medieval sources to interpret political and social developments in the first millennium BC (e.g. Wenskus 1977).

The available medieval European sources come from a variety of literary genres, ranging from quasi-historical texts, through myths and epic poetry and prose, to law texts. Obviously, these were put into writing in medieval contexts and first and foremost reflect their contemporary medieval societies. Despite this (nowadays) undisputed fact, it cannot be ruled out that some social practices and institutions described in these texts changed very little between the Iron Age and the medieval period. For instance, taking J. D. Hill's descriptions of how (some) British Iron Age societies (may have) worked (e.g. Hill 2011)[1] as reasonably correct, and comparing his main points to the description of medieval Irish societies found in their extant laws, there are a surprising number of similarities (e.g. Karl 2008).

Models of mechanisms of social interaction gathered by a thorough analysis of such medieval sources can similarly help us understand how certain historically attested political features of Iron Age societies may have come about: in societies with partible patrilineal inheritance rules, (inherited) land ownership determined social status and political power, and with marriage alliances and fosterage as important mechanisms for (political) alliance-building, political disputes between brothers (or other close relatives) are highly likely to occur (Karl 2006). This may help to explain the conflict between the brothers Diviciacus and Dumnorix, both drawing external allies into an apparently primarily internal conflict within the Aeduans; or more generally why Caesar states that 'In Gaul, not only in every state and every canton, but almost in each single household, there are competing parties' (*de Bello Gallico* 6.11); and possibly even why north-western European Iron Age societies seem to have been inherently politically unstable.

Both authors of this chapter agree (at least in theory, though perhaps less in practice) that these medieval sources can be helpful if used like any other ethnographic analogy (i.e. explicitly: Karl 2007; Collis 2011). Our main disagreement is about which sources for analogies should be preferred as a first port of call when looking for possible explanations for features found in the archaeological record of Iron Age societies. One of us (Collis 1994, 2011) would argue that the ethnographic analogies are more suitable as a first port of call because they provide a much wider range of, and often (but not always) much more reliably recorded, sources for analogies. The other (Karl 2007) would argue the same for the medieval sources, because much more frequently than with (often randomly picked) ethnographic analogies, there is a proven rather than just an assumed similarity (for example, but by no means exclusively, ecological, technological conditions, and linguistic environment) between them as the source and the Iron Age targets of the application of the analogy, improving the methodological rigour of its application (Bernbeck 1997). Importantly, where we both agree again is that neither kind of analogy should be forced on archaeological evidence as an explanatory straitjacket, but rather any analogy (whatever its source) must be dismissed if it does not fit the evidence (Karl 2007; Collis 1994, 2011).

The Basis of Power

Studies of power structures in the ancient world too often start with basic and erroneous assumptions about what the key element may have been. Thus, in the nomenclatures used of the rich burials and wealthy centres of the sixth to fifth centuries BC (Hallstatt D and La Tène A) terms such as *Fürsten-* and *Adelssitz*, or 'princely tombs' are used, taken from the medieval nomenclature of feudal society, carrying with it the danger of assuming that the control and ownership of land was the basis of power for a traditional elite which did not engage in demeaning activities such as trade and industry—see the attitudes as late as the early nineteenth century in English society in the books of Jane Austen. An alternative model for such societies is that of the 'military democracy' in theories of social evolution in authors such as Friedrich Engels, perpetuated in the communist doctrines of eastern Europe into the late twentieth century, or in the 'warrior societies' of Daphne Nash (1984, 1987) and Barry Cunliffe (1988). The reality is likely to be much more complicated, with a number of factors interacting, and not necessarily what we would expect. Thus Dumnorix, in his attempts to seize control of the Aeduan state, chose the auctions for the rights to collect customs dues and other taxes as a key source of wealth to finance his ambitions. As a particularly powerful and popular member of an aristocratic family, everyone else allegedly felt so threatened by him that no one dared bid against him.

Through archaeology we can often recognize 'wealth' in certain societies (see Chapter 31), but we cannot always be sure that this equated to political power. This is especially true for women. In his narrative of the Gallic War, Caesar hardly ever mentions women; he states that Dumnorix had built up interstate alliances by himself marrying a Helvetian lady, arranging for his mother to marry a Biturigan, and other members of the family also married outside the *civitas* (*de Bello Gallico* 1.18). At the battle of Gergovia the only part played by the women to defend themselves when Roman soldiers mounted the rampart was to bare their breasts and 'offer themselves up to' the enemy troops. These limited mentions by Caesar may reflect the lack of political power of women both in Roman and Gallic society, where all political posts were closed to them. But this was not true of all Iron Age societies, as in Britain a century later both the 'queens' Boudicca and Cartimandua seem to have held real political influence. We do not know what marriage entailed for the women; did they lose all rights to their wealth and property (as in nineteenth-century Britain), or did they (as in medieval Icelandic society) still maintain their property rights if the marriage failed? Whatever the case may be, it seems that in most Iron Age societies, the best a woman could hope for was to 'influence' the male members of her family, and influence was perhaps also the only political power of the 'knights' and other classes in Roman and Athenian society. We do, however, find rich female burials, indicating non-political status.

Ownership of land, especially agricultural land, was certainly often a key element in power and status in most city-states. Ownership of estates was often a prerequisite of senatorial status, as in Rome, and thus loss of one's land could also mean loss of citizen rights, for instance in the land crisis of the 130s and 120s BC which the Gracchi tried to resolve. In the cases of successful city-states such as Rome and Athens, increasing population could lead to a shortage of land to support the population as a whole, but also often led to the concentration of land into fewer and fewer hands. Solutions could include the redistribution of land, or expansion onto less fertile terrain, or simply the removal of part of the population through colonization elsewhere. But in temperate and northern Europe the situation may have been very different. Livy, when discussing the Gallic invasions of Italy and central Europe by the Gauls, talks of central Gaul being overpopulated, and in this case, as in the Mediterranean, only part of the population migrated. But in other cases such as the Cimbri and Teutones, and especially the Helvetii, the home territory was largely, if not entirely, abandoned, so perhaps ownership of a specific piece of land was not particularly important. Certainly in temperate Europe both rural and urban settlement patterns seem to have been much more fluid than in the Mediterranean countries.

We also do not usually know whether ownership was individual or communal, or something in between. The latter could vary in character; in medieval England under the 'open field system' land would be reallocated each year by common agreement among the farmers, as still happens in the village of Laxton in Nottinghamshire. In the Scottish Highlands it was the clans who corporately farmed the land under their clan chief. Both systems collapsed when the leaders decided it was in their personal interest to take over ownership of the land—a doubtfully legal procedure—in England through the 'Enclosure Acts' passed over 200–300 years in Parliament, and in Scotland through the 'Clearances' of the eighteenth and nineteenth centuries in which the peasant communities were simply dispersed. Whether such political sleights of hand occurred in the ancient world is unknown, but by the time we have documentary evidence, ownership of land by individuals seems to have been fairly universal.

Ultimately, all societies or groups within societies rely on force to protect their rights and persons, either directly by bearing arms themselves, or by relying on a proxy organization such as the state to act on their behalf. The first millennium BC probably saw a gradual transition from small groups within a society performing this role: households, family groups, lineages, or the clients of a powerful individual. At the same time societies needed to defend themselves from external threat, a threat that produces a sort of arms race, as enemies grow larger and stronger, with conflict between states, or empire against empire, and alliances against common enemies: the Delian League of the fifth century BC under the leadership of Athens against the expanding Persian Empire; or the attempt by the tribal states of Gaul to unite under Vercingetorix against Julius

Caesar and the might of Rome. We also see the gradual professionalization of military forces, firstly by the payment of citizen soldiers, as in Rome after the siege of Veii, or by Athens for the rowers of its fleet; the increasing use of paid mercenaries by rulers like Dionysus of Syracuse, often recruited from the less politically advanced societies of the 'periphery'—Scythians, Celts, Iberians, Numidians; and finally the full professionalization of the army, for instance under the reforms of the Roman army under Marius in the late second century BC. Archaeologically this process can be documented in the increasing size and elaboration of defended sites, which can also give an idea of the scale of the societies that constructed them: the generally small hillforts of the sixth and fifth centuries BC in temperate Europe compared to the much larger *oppida* of the second and first centuries BC; or by the large size of the deposits of arms and human remains in religious, funerary, and ritual contexts like those from La Tène, Gournay-sur-Aronde, or Ribemont-sur-Ancre (see Chapter 41).

But we must avoid simplistic correlations such as thinking an increase in weapons or defended sites indicates a period of unrest, or the presence of weapons in graves signifies warriors. The clustering together of villages in the late Bronze Age and early Iron Age at places such as Athens and Rome was probably for mutual defence, but it was not until the sixth to fifth century BC that they were physically linked together by the construction of shared defensive walls, as at Rome and Veii. The fourth and third centuries are notable for the general lack of defended sites in temperate Europe, but were a period of military expansion by the Celts. In areas such as Bohemia, Moravia, and the Hungarian Plain, burials with weapons are common, but at the same time in central Gaul they are virtually unknown in the most powerful tribal states such as the Arverni in the Auvergne, and defended *oppida* only appear after their defeat by the Romans in 123 BC. The nature of warfare is one variable, e.g. the 'smash and grab' nature of raiding in contrast with the longer-term nature of conquest of territory and of siege warfare (see Chapter 30). The construction of defended sites may be a successful deterrent against attack, but may only be a symbol of the prestige of the community or of individual leaders, and not meant for warfare; the *oppidum* of Ulaca near Ávila has impressive stone ramparts when viewed from the plain, but only a nominal wall facing the mountains (Álvarez Sanchís 1999, 2003; Collis 2004). Symbolism is even more obvious in the case of burial rites; weapons may mean someone of warrior status, but may also indicate only social not military status. At Münsingen (Hodson 1968), burials with weapons gradually disappear during the three hundred years the cemetery was in use, but this was replaced by deposition of weapons in nearby lakes and rivers, notably at La Tène, so shifting from an individual to a communal context.

From the anthropological record, in contrast to traditional assumptions that ownership of land and military force are the bases of power, we find that high status and political power can be achieved through industrial production and especially from trade and exchange. This was barred to land-owning elites like the Roman senators for whom such activity was unbecoming if not illegal, although financing lower-class merchants and industrialists and sharing the profits was usually permitted. As an example, the traditional interpretation of the cemetery at Hallstatt was that the rich graves were those of people who controlled the mining, using lower classes, if not slaves, to do the hard work. Recent studies of the skeletal remains, however, suggest the people with the richest grave goods were themselves miners and used to hard physical labour (Pany et al. 2003). The distribution of rich graves in the fifth century BC in temperate Europe was oriented in many cases not towards the best agricultural land or trade routes, but towards the occurrence of raw materials, especially salt, gold, and haematite iron ores in Austria (Hallstatt and the Dürrnberg), southern Bohemia (Písek), and in western Germany on the upper reaches of the river Nahe in the Hunsrück (Driehaus 1965). In contrast, the sixth-century rich graves and *Fürstensitze* lay on major trade routes, such as points where land routes linking river systems met navigable rivers: Vix/Mont Lassois on the upper Seine, and the Heuneburg on the upper Danube (Collis 1984a). Control of trade (for instance, 'administered trade', where the goods and the quantities are exchanged at fixed prices agreed between states rather than by market forces) has also been suggested as a reason for the rapid rise of kingdoms in south-east England (e.g. of Cunobelin at Colchester) in the first centuries BC/AD (Collis 1984b). Trade, however, does not necessarily lead to social differentiation, as for instance around the port site of Hengistbury Head in Dorset in the first century BC (Fitzpatrick 2001).

Access to special knowledge can also be a vital source of power. It falls into two main categories: legal and religious. The knowledge of law changes fundamentally in the first millennium BC with the adoption of writing. Before that legal knowledge would have been oral, and Caesar notes that the Druids spent twenty years learning their lore and nothing of it was written down, even though some members of Gallic society had been literate from the fifth century BC. However, in some Mediterranean societies such as Athens and Rome law was recorded in writing, restricting access to it to a small, largely senatorial class, and even a newcomer like Cicero could reach the pinnacle of political power, the consulship, through his legal expertise and success as a prosecutor in the law courts. The training of the Druids was also religious, and we hear that they possessed the power to impose sanctions on offenders to exclude them from religious ceremonies and from making sacrificial offerings, and also to condemn criminals to death, for instance the burning of people imprisoned in wicker figures. But religion in this period in Europe (see Chapter 42) was not so closely linked with political power as in Near Eastern empires such as Egypt, where kings and pharaohs were considered to be gods. Such concepts where generally abhorrent in European societies, but were gradually adopted as the Romans conquered Near Eastern towns where the emperor would be given divine honours; in Rome it was only under Augustus that humans were deified, first, posthumously, Julius Caesar, and finally Augustus himself. Before that, even though to become chief priest (*pontifex maximus*) brought great prestige and honour, it was not a primarily political post like the consulship.

Personal charisma was also a major element in gaining political power, in terms of building up both alliances and support, but rhetoric was also a vital skill. There may be no close equivalents of Adolf Hitler, who rose from a lowly social status to supreme power, but there were fifth-century demagogues in Athens who were criticized for their lowly origins; the most successful Athenian orator and politician, Pericles, was however of high status. The rise of Octavian to become the emperor Augustus owed much to his political skill; his only assets as a young man were his wealth and the fact that he was the adopted heir of Julius Caesar, and at the beginning of his career he was an unlikely candidate for supreme power. We must assume similar qualities in Gallic leaders such as Luernios, who used largesse and feasting as a mechanism to become king of the Arverni, and it was another Arvernian, Vercingetorix, who was chosen as supreme commander of the Gallic army to oppose Caesar. Personal character as well as military expertise would have been essential to hold together mobile armies such as those of the Cimbri and Teutones, or of the Helvetii, although most of the names of leaders we are given may well be mythical: Segovesus and Belovesus who led the Gallic invasions of northern Italy and central Europe, or the two leaders called Brennus who led the attacks on Rome and on Delphi. In Italy both Hannibal and Spartacus successfully kept armies in the field for several years with spectacular successes.

Basic Trends in the First Millennium BC

As mentioned in the introduction to this chapter, the general trend in the first millennium BC is towards greater social differentiation, starting in the south-east (e.g. Greece) and spreading north and west. For burial rites, where burials are archaeologically recognizable, there is an almost pan-European ethos of egalitarianism at the beginning of the millennium with little differentiation in the number of grave goods, mainly pottery vessels, with very few metal objects. This is especially true for the 'Urnfield' burials found from Romania to southern France and central Spain, and to southern Italy. Where inhumation dominated, as in Greece and eastern Italy, the same ethos appears, with just a few personal ornaments such as brooches—a stark contrast with the previous Mycenaean burial rites. Along the Atlantic seaboard burials largely disappear for much of the millennium (e.g. Ireland, Britain, and northern Spain) and while burial under barrows continued in the later Nordic Bronze Age, by the early Iron Age this area too had succumbed to egalitarian cremation cemeteries.

But this apparent egalitarianism masks a rather different reality. In hoard finds we encounter prestige bronze items such as body armour (helmets, cuirasses, greaves) or shields, the latter at least for display rather than warfare, alongside swords and spears. Status ornaments in gold, be they communal or individual symbols, are not uncommon, especially twisted torcs or the 'gorgets' found in Ireland. There is also a wealth of objects associated with feasting: gold cups, bronze spits, cauldrons, and *situlae*. In Greece, there are also a handful of richer burials with iron swords and body armour, as at Tiryns and Argos, or the male and female burials found in the remains of a large apsidal timber building at Lefkandi, the cremated bones of the man placed in an imported bronze vessel (Bintliff 2012: 211; see also Chapter 12).

The Lefkandi burials are a forerunner of a trend which hit much of central and southern Europe from the eighth century BC onwards, the appearance of ostentatious destruction of material goods in a funeral context. These are usually associated with individuals buried under tumuli, but occasionally in a family context like the chamber tombs of the Etruscan world or the multiple burials in tumuli in Slovenia and southern Germany during Hallstatt D, e.g. the Hohmichele. At first these richer burials were simply found among the ordinary burials, e.g. burial AA1 in the cemetery of Quattro Fontanili at Veii with its decorated bronze urn, shield, and iron sword. But individuals were quickly differentiated not merely by the wealth of their grave goods but also by the burial rite, with a shift away from cremation to inhumation in the richer burials in Italy and central Europe, burial in wooden chambers under mounds and, in some cases, physical distancing from the ordinary burials, as in the rich burials from Salamis on Cyprus, likely to be those of the 'kings' mentioned in Assyrian sources. But the 'ordinary' burials themselves are unlikely to include the lower echelons of society, something most clearly demonstrated in Greece (Morris 1987).

The grave goods in these richer burials are mainly local—personal ornaments, weapons, vehicles, pottery vessels—but from the start included exotic imported items, from the faience scarabs and figurines at Lefkandi imported from the Levant and Egypt, to the huge wine-mixing *krater* at Vix in central France. There is clearly a causal relationship that increasing trade produced increasing wealth and probably also social differentiation, but this does not mean that the wealth of these individuals was necessarily based on controlling the trade. We can contrast trading in the Icelandic world of the later first millennium AD, where a leader would both provide the boat and himself take part in the voyage, with sixteenth-century Europe where a monarch like Elizabeth I of England would help finance a voyage and share in the profits, but never participate personally. Though in the early first millennium BC there is an emphasis on weaponry in the deposition of hoard and ritual finds, by the time we have documentary evidence in Greece and central Italy it is control of land—rather than military force or trading—that seems to provide the wealth which formed the basis of power for the elite classes. Archaeologically this trend of rich burials and imported luxury items continued expanding to the north and west, reaching northern Germany and south-east Britain in the first century BC, and then beyond the Roman frontier throughout the Roman and early medieval periods until it encompassed southern Scandinavia as well. The spread of formal temple sites where objects, especially but by no means exclusively military, were deposited runs parallel with the burials, starting in Greece in the early first millennium, reaching central Italy in the middle of the millennium, Gaul in the third to second century BC, and south-eastern Britain in the first century BC.

The antithesis of this process, in the form of evidence for an egalitarian ethos, shows no obvious patterns in time or space. It is most clearly visible in the foundation of nucleated, usually defended, settlements, whether established due to social processes internal to the societies or by settlement of outsiders. Thus we see it in Poland in the marsh fort at Biskupin dating to the second half of the eighth century BC with its rows of identical houses. It is a feature of southern France, for instance the defended *oppida* of

Nages, dating to the third and second centuries BC, and Entremont in the second century BC (Py 2012), or in central and northern Spain, for instance at Cortes de Navarra. It is also a feature of some Greek colonies and new foundations as the result of synoecism, e.g. Olynthus (discussed in Bintliff 2012: 297–299). This last case warns us that such outward signs of egalitarianism may mask a different reality, as we know that Greek society was hierarchical at this time, and we need additional evidence in support. The relative egalitarianism that we see on British hillforts such as Danebury is somewhat backed by the relative lack of other items indicative of a hierarchical society, for instance the absence of gold objects and imported goods, while the most prestigious items in these societies, two-wheeled carts or chariots with decorative metalwork, seem widely spread among members of the society. But in the case of Britain, the range of social differentiation may differ between adjacent societies; the Arras burials in East Yorkshire include male and female individuals buried with a chariot, one of them with a coat of mail and an elaborately decorated sword, suggestive of a more hierarchical setup in this particular group. These burials do not, however, show the extremes of wealth seen in those of the sixth and fifth centuries BC in southern Germany and eastern France, where markedly hierarchical societies seem to have been replaced in the fourth to third centuries by a less differentiated society, though still with distinctions between men buried with weapons and women with bronze ornaments and those with minimal grave goods.

Conclusion

This rapid survey of Europe in the pre-Roman Iron Age demonstrates that the evidence for political power is very ambiguous, with different types of evidence often being contradictory, and that very different societies could exist alongside one another. As has been argued by Hill (e.g. 2011) and others, as well as by ourselves, we cannot presume a hierarchical society—as for instance has often been assumed for 'Celtic society'—and each area needs to be investigated in its own right. Though general trends are visible, there is no simple evolution.

Note

1. Hill (2011) argues that British Iron Age societies were not necessarily hierarchical with clearly established, hereditary elites, but were potentially more heterarchical and 'non-triangular', characterized more by semi-independent households linked by kinship ties and the need to cooperate mainly on a very local level, rarely exceeding more than 15–20 km in extent, thereby creating rather loose networks of social connections and only occasionally coalescing rather fluidly into what, in historical sources, would perhaps be described as larger 'tribes'.

References

Álvarez-Sanchís, J. R. 1999. *Los Vettones*. Biblioteca Archaeologica Hispana 1. Madrid: Real Academia de la Historia.

Álvarez Sanchís, J. R. 2003. *Los Señores del Ganado: Arqeología de los Pueblos prerromanos en le Occidente de Iberia*. Madrid: Edicione.

Augier, L., O. Buchsenschutz, R. Durand, A. Filippini, D. Germinet, P. Macon, et al. 2012. *Bourges—un complexe princier de l'Âge du Fer: le quartier artisanal de Port Sec sud à Bourges (Cher)*. Revue Archéologique du Centre de la France supplément 41. Bourges/Tours: Bourges Plus, FERACF.

Bernbeck, R. 1997. *Theorien in der Archäologie*. Tübingen: Francke.

Biel, J. 1985. *Der Keltenfürst von Hochdorf*. Stuttgart: Theiss.

Bintliff, J. L. 2012. *The Complete Archaeology of Greece, from Hunter-Gatherers to the 20th Century AD*. Chichester: Wiley-Blackwell.

Bonnamour, L. (ed.) 2000a. *Archéologie des fleuves et des rivières*. Paris: Errance.

Bonnamour, L. 2000b. *Archéologie de la Saône: le fleuve gardien de la mémoire*. Paris: Errance.

Collis, J. R. 1984a. *The European Iron Age*. London: Batsford.

Collis, J. R. 1984b. *Oppida: Earliest Towns North of the Alps*. Sheffield: Department of Prehistory and Archaeology.

Collis, J. R. 1994. 'Reconstructing Iron Age society', in K. Kristiansen and J. Jensen (eds) *Europe in the First Millennium BC*: 31–39. Sheffield: J. R. Collis.

Collis, J. R. 2004. 'Hill-Fort Study Group, visit to Ávila, Spain, April 20th–23rd 2004: Guide'. Unpublished guidebook.

Collis, J. R. 2011. '"Reconstructing Iron Age Society" revisited', in T. Moore and X. L. Armada (eds) *Western Europe in the First Millennium BC: Crossing the Divide*: 223–241. Oxford: Oxford University Press.

Cunliffe, B. W. 1988. *Greeks, Romans and Barbarians: Spheres of Interaction*. London: Batsford.

Cunliffe, B. W. 2005. *Iron Age Communities in Britain: An Account of England, Scotland and Wales from the Seventh Century BC until the Roman Conquest*, 4th edition. London: Routledge.

Driehaus, J. 1965. 'Fürstengräber und Eisenerze zwischen Mittelrhein, Mosel und Saar'. *Germania* 43: 42–49.

Eggert, M. K. H. 1988. 'Riesentumuli und Sozialorganisation. Vergleichende Betrachtungen zu den sogenannten "Fürstenhügeln" der späten Hallstattzeit'. *Archäologisches Korrespondenzblatt* 18: 263–274.

Eggert, M. K. H. 1999. 'Der Tote von Hochdorf: Bemerkungen zum Modus archäologischer Interpretation'. *Archäologisches Korrespondenzblatt* 29: 211–222.

Engels, F. 1892. *Der Ursprung der Familie, des Privateigenthums und des Staats: Im Anschluss an Lewis H. Morgan's Forschungen*, 4th edition. Stuttgart: Dietz.

Field, N., and M. Parker Pearson. 2003. *Fiskerton: An Iron Age Timber Causeway with Iron Age and Roman Votive Offerings*. Oxford: Oxbow Books.

Fitzpatrick, A. P. 2001. 'Cross-Channel exchange, Hengistbury Head, and the end of the hillforts', in J. R. Collis (ed.) *Society and Settlement in Iron Age Europe: L'habitat et l'occupation du sol en Europe. Actes du XVIIIe Colloque de l'AFEAF, Winchester, avril 1994*: 82–97. Sheffield: J. R. Collis Publications.

Fitzpatrick, A. P. 2005. 'Gifts for the golden gods: torques and coins', in C. Haselgrove and D. Wigg-Wolf (eds) *Iron Age Coinage and Ritual Practices*. Studien zu Fundmünzen der Antike 20: 157–182. Mainz: Philipp von Zabern.

Hachmann, R. 1960. 'Die Chronologie der jüngeren vorrömischen Eisenzeit. Stand der Forschung in nördlichen Mitteleuropa und in Skandinavien'. *Bericht der Römisch-Germanische Kommission* 41: 1–275.

Harding, A., and W. Raczkowski. 2010. 'Living on the lake in the Iron Age: New results from aerial photographs, geophysical survey and dendrochronology on sites of Biskupin type'. *Antiquity* 84: 386–404.

Hill, J. D. 2011. 'How did British middle and late pre-Roman Iron Age societies work (if they did)?', in T. Moore and X.-L. Armada (eds) *Atlantic Europe in the First Millennium BC: Crossing the Divide*: 242–263. Oxford: Oxford University Press.

Hodson, F. R. 1968. *The La Tène Cemetery of Münsingen-Rain*. Acta Bernensia 5. Bern: Stämpfli.

Hoppe, T. 2012. 'Südliche Vorbilder und keltische Interpretation—das Ensemble aus dem Kleinaspergle', in R. Röber, M. Jansen, S. Rau, C. von Nikolai, and I. Frech (eds) *Die Welt der Kelten: Zentren der Macht, Kostbarkeiten der Kunst*: 246–247. Ostfildern: Jan Thorbecke.

Jackson, K. 1964. *The Oldest Irish Tradition: A Window on the Iron Age*. Cambridge: Cambridge University Press.

Jung, M. 2005. 'Nochmals zum Problem späthallstattzeitlicher Adelssitze. Eine kritische Wiederlektüre des Textes von Wolfgang Kimmig', in R. Karl and J. Leskovar (eds) *Interpretierte Eisenzeiten. Fallstudien, Methoden, Theorie. Tagungsbeiträge der 1. Linzer Gespräche zur interpretativen Eisenzeitarchäologie*. Studien zur Kulturgeschichte von Oberösterreich, Folge 18: 181–190. Linz: Oberösterreichisches Landesmuseum.

Karl, R. 2006. *Altkeltische Sozialstrukturen*. Archaeolingua Main Series 18. Budapest: Archaeolingua.

Karl, R. 2007. 'Grundlagen der Analyse sozialer Komplexität in der eisenzeitlichen Keltiké', in H. Birkhan (ed.) *Kelten-Einfälle an der Donau*: 325–346. Vienna: Verlag der Österreichischen Akademie der Wissenschaften.

Karl, R. 2008. 'Random coincidences? Or: the return of the Celtic to Iron Age Britain'. *Proceedings of the Prehistoric Society* 74: 69–78.

Kimmig, W. 1969. 'Zum Problem späthallstättischer Adelssitze', in K.-H. Otto and J. Herrmann (eds) *Siedlung, Burg, Stadt: Studien zu ihren Anfängen. Festschrift Paul Grimm*. Schriften der Sektion für Vor- und Frühgeschichte 25: 95–113. Berlin: Akademie-Verlag.

Krausse, D. 1999. '"Der Keltenfürst" von Hochdorf: Dorfälterster oder Sakralkönig? Anspruch und Wirklichkeit der sog. kulturanthropologischen Hallstatt-Archäologie'. *Archäologisches Korrespondenzblatt* 29: 339–358.

Lejars, T. 2013. *La Tène: la collection Schwab (Bienne, Suisse). La Tène, un site, un mythe 3. Vols 1–2*. Cahiers d'Archéologie Romande 140–141. Lausanne: Cahiers d'Archéologie Romande.

Mauss, M. 1954. *The Gift: Forms and Functions of Exchange in Archaic Societies*. London: Cohen and West.

Megaw, J. V. S. 1970. *Art of the European Iron Age: A Study of the Elusive Image*. Bath: Adams and Dart.

Milcent, P.-Y. 2007. *Bourges-Avaricum: un centre proto-urbain celtique du Ve siècle av. J.-C. Les fouilles de Saint-Martin-des-Champs et les découvertes des établissements militaires*. Bituriga Monographie 1. Bourges: Éditions de la Ville de Bourges.

Morris, I. 1987. *Burial and Ancient Society: The Rise of the Greek City State*. Cambridge: Cambridge University Press.

Nash, D. 1984. 'The basis of contact between Britain and Gaul in the late pre-Roman Iron Age', in S. Macready and F. H. Thompson (eds) *Cross-Channel Trade between Gaul and Britain in the Pre-Roman Iron Age*: 92–107. London: Society of Antiquaries.

Nash, D. 1987. *Coinage in the Celtic World*. London: Seaby.

Pany, D., M. Teschler-Nicola, and H. Wilfing. 2003. 'Miners or mine owners—Do the Hallstatt skeletons reflect occupation and social structure?' *American Journal of Physical Anthropology* Supplement 36: 164.

Pauli, L. 1973. *Untersuchungen zur Späthallstattkultur in Nordwürttemberg: Analyse eines Kleinraumes im Grenzbereich zweier Kulturen*. Hamburger Beiträge zur Archäologie 2. Hamburg: Buske.

Paunier, D., and T. Luginbühl. 2004. *Bibracte. Le site de la maison du Parc aux Chevaux (PC1) des origines de l'oppidum au regne de Tibère*. Collection Bibracte 8. Glux-en-Glenne: Centre archéologique européen du Mont Beuvray.

Py, M. 2012. *Les Gaulois du Midi de la fin de l'âge du Bronze à la conquête romaine*. Paris: Errance.

Rieckhoff, S., and J. Biel. 2001. *Die Kelten in Deutschland*. Stuttgart: Theiss.

Rudenko, S. I. 1970. *Frozen Tombs of Siberia: The Pazyryk Burials of Iron Age Horsemen*. London: J. M. Dent and Sons.

Sastre, I. 2011. 'Social inequality during the Iron Age: Interpretation models', in T. Moore and X.-L. Armada (eds) *Atlantic Europe in the First Millennium BC: Crossing the Divide*: 264–284. Oxford: Oxford University Press.

Sjoberg, G. 1960. *The Pre-Industrial City, Past and Present*. New York: Free Press.

Wenskus, R. 1977. *Stammesbildung und Verfassung: Das Werden der frühmittelalterlichen gentes*, 2nd edition. Cologne/Vienna: Böhlau.

CHAPTER 30

WARRIORS, WAR, AND WEAPONS; OR ARMS, THE ARMED, AND ARMED VIOLENCE

SIMON JAMES

Introduction

Iron Age Europe is widely seen as suffused by war, its societies dominated by warriors, often ruled by 'warrior elites'. This perception originates in Graeco-Roman accounts of bellicose northern 'barbarians': Scythians and Sarmatians, Thracians and Dacians, Gauls and Germans, Celtiberians and Caledonians. It was then apparently confirmed by nineteenth-century finds of splendid weaponry ascribed to these groups—the type site of La Tène produced many swords—and by the dating of many hillforts to the era.

However, recent research on many, especially earlier, Iron Age societies, notably in Britain, has identified little evidence of carnage, weaponry or fortifications, let alone of 'warrior classes', leading to questioning of received ideas, particularly of warlike Celts with warrior elites. Arguably swinging to the opposite extreme, many British archaeologists have even interpreted structures long labelled hillforts as communal monuments for purposes other than conflict (Armit 2007; Lock 2011). Emphasis on agrarian life, symbolism, and social power resulted in largely tacit 'pacification of the Iron Age' (James 2007; on wider 'pacification of the past' see Keeley 1997 and Vandkilde 2006).

Is absence of evidence of weapons and mayhem in some Iron Age cultural contexts consequently being fallaciously taken as evidence of absence? Have awkward data from others (hillforts do look like fortifications) been ignored or explained away? Or could the received image of a war-torn Iron Age actually be substantially a myth, rooted in Graeco-Roman propaganda, uncritically accepted by early modern scholars who venerated classical texts? Might emphasis on 'combat culture' at least in many societies of the later pre-Roman and Roman Iron Age really mark responses to increasing threats from Greek, and particularly Roman, aggression—a 'violent edge of empire effect' (Ferguson and Whitehead 1992)? Or would framing indigenous Europeans as peaceable until externally destabilized be a simplistic postcolonial inversion of received ideas of a 'warlike Iron Age'?

Paradoxically, apparently mutually exclusive traditional and revisionist readings of the same evidence tend to share a critical implicit assumption: that combat weapons and their use simply equate to warfare. Hence any armed Iron Age individual is often automatically labelled a 'warrior', any burial accompanied by weapons a 'warrior grave', an equation long challenged by Collis (1994: 36–37).

There are serious dangers in shoving weaponry, its wielders, and their practices into a box labelled 'war'. As we shall see, much armed violence in European societies was not warfare, and there may often have been no 'warriors' on any definition of the term. Even more dangerous is the further implication, often tacitly drawn: that everything outside the box-called-war constituted 'peace', which equalled 'normal' life. The war-box illusion, and its implicit reciprocal of peaceful normality in the European Iron Age, arise from a combination of factors. Firstly, the simple equation 'weapons = warriors + warfare' is the superficial impression given by our historiographical starting point: classical texts recount wars against, more than internal dynamics of, Iron Age societies. I believe this has been overlain by cultural assumptions of post-World War II generations of Europeans whose shared default experience has involved little or no exposure to weapons and combat, in our societies the preserve of specialist minorities (professional soldiers, armed police). For us, wars generally happen far away. More local incidents of armed violence constitute rare aberrations mostly known only indirectly through news media. When thinking about 'normal life' in our own world, Europeans do not usually have to consider weapons and bloodshed. This mindset seems often to be simply back-projected onto the Iron Age: weapons were about warfare, and wars dysfunctional aberrations occurring at political boundaries. Literally and figuratively peripheral to social life, armed violence may then simply be ignored as a factor in modelling Iron Age societies. However, recent years have seen increasing willingness, notably in Scandinavia and among UK-based investigators, to consider the grim realities of armed aggression, based on new finds, reanalysing old data, and rethinking assumptions. (For an approach to wider questions of violence in Iron Age and Roman Britain, see also Redfern 2020).

Terminology: 'War' and 'Warriors'?

In discourse on the European Iron Age, the terms 'war' and 'warrior' are rarely examined or defined. 'War' (except 'civil war') is commonly understood to connote organized collective armed violence between polities. Yet in many historically attested societies, possessing, displaying, and using lethal weaponry are/were not about war primarily, and sometimes hardly at all. Rather, weapons may articulate social dynamics, mutual fear, and conflict within a polity—as exemplified by the contemporary United States.

In 2007, the USA averaged eighty-eight civilian firearms per hundred people: around 270 million guns, by far the world's highest absolute and relative numbers (Small Arms Survey 2007: ch. 2, annexe 4). Many are for hunting, but millions are ostensibly for protection against fellow citizens. In 2011 alone, 8,583 Americans were murdered by firearms (Federal Bureau of Investigation 2011). This figure, rather low by historical standards, dwarfs US combat fatalities by an order of magnitude: 5,324 over more than a decade of wars in Iraq and Afghanistan (as of 15 August 2014: Department of Defense 2014). In terms of personal weapon 'culture' and body count, in the USA internal armed violence far outweighs external war in importance.

I suggest similar patterns prevailed in other cultural contexts across time, including many societies of Iron Age Europe. It is, then, unjustifiable, and potentially profoundly misleading, automatically to discuss archaeological evidence of weapons and their use solely in terms of warfare. Conversely, much violence in war is committed not with dedicated weapons but with fist, foot, and phallus; war is not even simply a subset of armed violence. Rather, there exists a broad field of interpersonal violence, in which war and weapon use only partially overlap.

Similar lack of critical analysis of the term 'warrior', in archaeology in general, has been addressed by Vandkilde (2006: 393–403). Her work, undertaken in the context of a study of Copper Age Europe, identified in anthropological literature several different forms of 'warriordom'. This is a valuable contribution, yet still limited in that she focuses on war and the specialized war-fighter, without really considering armed violence in contexts other than war between polities. Nor does she much examine the question of who possessed and used weapons. While it seems that in later prehistory, as in historical times, females did not normally directly participate in armed violence, there were some striking Iron Age exceptions, notably on the Eurasian steppe.

Ukrainian sites have produced graves of over a hundred females, mostly younger adults, buried with arms between the seventh and third centuries BC, some also bearing injuries from arrows and handheld weapons (Guliaev 2003: 114–115). Some Scythian women evidently possessed combat skills, although systematic differences in weaponry between male and female interments probably reflect gender distinctions in fighting styles. Such armed women are plausibly the inspiration for Herodotus' Amazons (*Histories* 4.110–117). Away from the steppes, in Iron Age Europe inflicting armed violence appears to have been near universally a male practice, often closely tied to masculine ideology. One weapon burial from Rudston (R163; Stead 1991: 205, fig. 113) suggests that biological females were not entirely excluded from using arms in Iron Age East Yorkshire, although it is unclear how this individual's gender was constructed culturally (Giles 2012: 166), and s/he may well have been regarded as entirely masculine (see also Redfern 2008 on females and violence in Iron Age Dorset.) Nevertheless, in general, wielding weapons was, as it still is, especially associated with young adult males at the height of their strength and aggressiveness.

Given the foregoing, rather than the more traditional 'weapons, warriors, and warfare', this chapter is framed in terms of 'arms, the armed, and armed violence' which, where involving confrontation between armed opponents rather than using weapons on the unarmed, comprised 'combat'.

To investigate these matters, we should turn first to the direct testimony left by Iron Age peoples themselves: archaeological remains. We have material evidence for fortified places, specialized weapons, and graphic instances of their impact on human bodies. However, while such evidence confirms—unsurprisingly—that at least some Iron Age Europeans valued arms and used them, what does it tell us about contexts and purposes of such use, or about the raising of armies among Iron Age European societies? What actually is the evidence for arms, the armed, and armed violence in Iron Age Europe, and what does it mean? What surviving traces might we expect to find of cultural phenomena which, in physical terms, were episodic, explosive, and transient?

Bones of the Dead: Direct Evidence of Armed Violence—or Its Absence?

Human remains potentially offer us the most direct surviving evidence of armed violence. However, while it does attest specific incidents, some extremely graphic, taken as a whole this source of testimony can be highly problematic. A profound general limitation is that, with the rare exceptions of bog bodies, we are dealing at best with the bones of the dead; no soft-tissue evidence survives (see later in this section). Worse, for much of the era, we have only cremated remains, or none at all, due to soil conditions or disposal of the dead by means other than burial.

Where they survive, Iron Age skeletons may be examined for evidence of Sharp-Force Trauma (SFT)—injuries from the points or edges of metal weapons. However, we cannot always assume that any single injury on a body is evidence of deliberate armed assault. A proportion of injuries inevitably resulted from misadventure with blades or projectiles in working, hunting, training, or play, rather than calculated aggression. Even injuries unequivocally inflicted with combat weapons need not reflect deliberate violent killing. For example, a skull from Danebury hillfort, in southern England, had been transfixed by a spear through the forehead (Cunliffe 2003: 41; Figure 30.1). This injury looks calculated, was perimortem (inflicted around the time of death), and would almost certainly have been lethal; yet even so, it was not necessarily the actual cause of death. This could, for example, represent spearing of a body already dead (the fragment also bears serious blunt-force injuries), as part of funerary rites like those attested in East Yorkshire where spears were thrust into corpses already laid in their graves (Giles 2012: 1–2). However, the pattern of evidence on this bone strongly suggests armed violence.

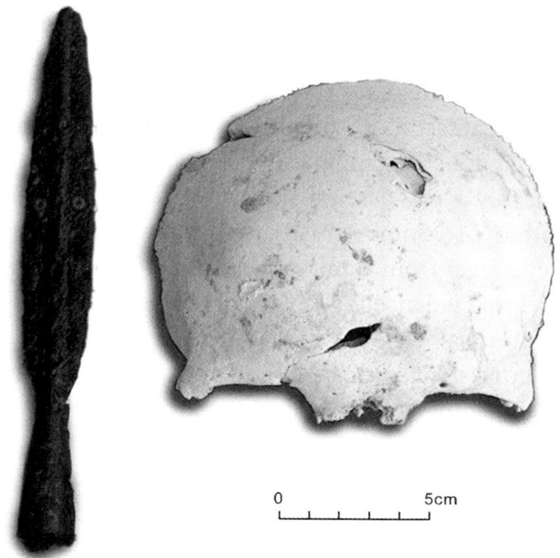

FIGURE 30.1 Skull fragment from Danebury hillfort, southern England, exhibiting blunt-force trauma and a graphic perimortem injury from a spear, closely similar to this example also found at the site.

Photos: Simon James

Reciprocally, lack of skeletal trauma does not constitute evidence of absence of armed violence in a particular cultural context. The absence may be more apparent than real, especially with small bone assemblages, where some kinds of injuries suffered in a population may not be encountered due to simple statistical chance. On poorly preserved remains, traces of violence may survive but go unrecognized. Even in substantial bone assemblages, smaller skeletal injuries and, equally, healed ante-mortem damage which have been called the 'subtle stigmata' of armed violence, may be missed simply because they are not looked for carefully enough (Knüsel 2005).

Slight bone wounds can attest devastating soft tissue damage. Further, modern trauma medicine and forensic pathology show that many lethal injuries—including those inflicted through preferred modes of attack—need leave no skeletal trace at all (Shepherd et al. 1990; Redfern 2011: 131). Throat wounds, and puncture wounds between the ribs or piercing the abdomen, can kill within minutes or hours through respiratory failure, blood loss, and shock. Even superficial flesh wounds may kill through infection (James 2010: 49). Without surviving soft tissues, these are wholly vanishing stigmata of violence. There are also taphonomic considerations: even mass casualties of huge battles, in which the defeated dead were despoiled and left to rot, need leave no detectable traces. The site of a previously unknown battle *c.*AD 230 between Romans and Germans at Harzhorn, Germany, was identified through scatters of Roman metal items which had escaped scavengers and corrosion; no bones survived (Geschwinde et al. 2009). Similar scatters at Kalkriese near Osnabrück, Germany, led to the discovery of some pits of collected human remains, deriving from the historically attested massacre of Varus' three legions by Arminius in AD 9; but only a handful of more than 10,000 dead are known archaeologically (Schlüter and Wiegels 1999; Derks and Burmeister 2009).

Direct bioarchaeological testimony of armed violence, then, can be elusive and, even where identified, ambiguous or enigmatic. However, larger patterns of trauma, on individuals and especially across assemblages, provide our best evidence for deliberate violence, armed or otherwise. Some British case studies illustrate this.

In comparing assemblages from Hampshire and East Yorkshire, King (2010) detected extensive skeletal trauma evidence for violent practices (healed as well as perimortem injuries) in both regions, albeit exhibiting different patterns. Notably, SFT on East Yorkshire bodies is consistent with ritualized intragroup duelling (see later in the chapter), while in Hampshire such injuries more probably attest slaughter and special disposal of foreign enemies in war (King 2010: 235–243).

Redfern's reanalysis of the bones from Maiden Castle hillfort, Dorset, identified perimortem and healed trauma indicating that armed violence was indeed not confined to the Roman conquest of southern Britain during the AD 40s; that was apparently just the last of a series of violent episodes resulting in death or injury of adult males, females, and children (Redfern 2011: 133–134). She attributed this evidence to 'intra- or intertribal warfare' (Redfern 2011: 111), and in other work has argued that groups in Iron Age Dorset were far from being internally harmonious either. Her study of Iron Age remains from multiple sites revealed extensive blunt-force trauma suggestive of 'domestic violence' inflicted on, and likely often by, females as well as males (Redfern 2008).

The Iron Age peoples of southern Italy—especially the Samnites—offer further good case studies as they interred their dead in cemeteries, often on geologies favouring bone survival. A number of skeletal assemblages have been studied for violent trauma. For example, Paine's study of cranial injuries among males buried during the sixth and fifth centuries BC at Alfedena concluded that they faced a high risk of meeting a violent end (Paine et al. 2007). Sparacello's work on the same assemblage makes a compelling, if not conclusive, case that unusually high levels of asymmetric development of the upper limbs among the males in this population resulted from habitual training with the weaponry interred with them (Sparacello et al. 2011).

Another important skeletal assemblage with dramatic evidence of SFT, found with weaponry, comes from Ribemont-sur-Ancre (Somme, France), one of a number of northern Gaulish sanctuary sites of the middle La Tène, long before the coming of Roman influence (Brunaux 1999, 2001; Craig et al. 2005: 172–174). Disarticulated skeletons of several hundred young adult males were found, with whole and fragmentary weapons, and remains of horses. Many bones bear sharp-force trauma consistent with combat wounds, while gnaw marks and corrosion on the weapons suggest the bodies were exposed before burial, even if Brunaux's original idea that one group of around seventy-five individuals were suspended on a wooden rack (Brunaux 2001) now looks unlikely. Strikingly, heads are almost entirely absent. The Ribemont deposits probably represent multiple battles in the third century BC, following which collected headless corpses of defeated enemies and their weapons were ritually displayed for collective triumphing before eventual burial (Armit 2012: 198–201). Individuals perhaps took the heads as personal trophies, consistent with classical accounts of later Iron Age Gaulish combat practices (see also Chapter 41, on the complexities behind 'Celtic headhunting').

Similarly dramatic skeletal evidence indicating battle comes from recent finds at Alken Enge, Jutland, in Denmark. Remains apparently of hundreds of adult males were deposited around the turn of the first millennia BC/AD in Lake Mossø (Skanderborg Museum 2012). The bones, some of which exhibit SFT, had been exposed for some time and been dismembered before deposition, accompanied by evidence of feasting. This evidence is yet to be fully studied, but the bones are thought to represent the dead of a defeated army ritually processed and deposited (Maribo 2014). They echo a number of earlier wetland finds from Denmark and North Germany, of mass offerings of weapons rather than bodies. At a spot just 5 km up the Illerup Ådal (river valley) from Alken Enge, *c.*200 years after the bones were deposited, the equipment of what seems to be another entire defeated army was sacrificed to the waters (Ilkjær 2000). The Illerup Ådal finds bring us on to the testimony of the artefacts of armed violence.

Portable Material Culture of Armed Violence

Just as evidence for armed violence on Iron Age bodies often proves elusive or ambiguous, similarly few signs have yet been identified of damage on Iron Age weapons certainly resulting from actual combat. As with bone injuries, combat damage can be hard to distinguish from other phenomena—e.g. 'ritual killing' of weaponry prior to deposition by hacking cutting edges, bending blades, or denting shield bosses (as at Illerup), or as a result of post-depositional damage. However, we can say much more by turning our attention from the elusive results of acts of armed violence to the more plentiful evidence for intent and preparation implied by the weapons themselves.

In contrast to much modern armament, which inflicts multiple deaths at great distances, Iron Age weaponry was about one individual directly inflicting violent trauma on another, at short range, and especially within arm's reach. Even battles against invading Roman armies were largely aggregations of 1:1 encounters, more or less mediated by team training and organization into battle lines.

Co-evolution of material culture, practices, and ideologies of armed violence during the era exhibited a widespread cultural preference for toe-to-toe (or horse-to-horse) combat on open ground. Nevertheless, like so much else in Iron Age European archaeology, there is great spatio-temporal variation and diversity in the material culture of armed violence—much of which, most unambiguously helmets, shields, and body armour, is specifically designed for combat. We can identify two distinct large-scale traditions: the primarily equestrian 'combat culture' of the steppe grasslands, from the Great Hungarian Plain to the Urals (and beyond: this is a Eurasian tradition), and the mainly foot-fighting culture of the rest of Europe, shared with much of the Mediterranean: Greek and Italian fighting styles belonged to this tradition, more suited to farmed and hilly landscapes. We will examine this latter tradition first.

Archaeological finds show that, while in some areas of the broad western zone slings inflicting blunt-force injury at a distance were employed in fighting, and bows and javelins were also known, design of offensive weaponry focused on infliction of direct sharp-force trauma using handheld weapons at close quarters, mostly on foot, but sometimes (and increasingly commonly towards the end of the late pre-Roman Iron Age) from horseback. The principal offensive weapons were iron-tipped thrusting spears (Figure 30.1) and iron swords (Figure 30.2). Material countermeasures to these primarily comprised wooden shields, sometimes with metal fittings and occasionally full metal facings. Shields were generally wielded by a single, central, horizontal handle, protected by a projecting boss, allowing the shield to be used to strike the opponent. In some contexts, shields were supplemented by helmets. In such defensive kit, copper alloy was also increasingly (but not entirely) displaced by stronger iron. From the fourth century BC, body armour also rapidly became known across a swathe of the continent, in the form of iron mail ('chain mail' of interlocking rings). Sophisticated late pre-Roman Iron Age iron helmets and swords, at least partly made of steel, attest growing mastery of ironworking in several regions of Europe. Archaeological evidence is consistent with classical texts recording that the Romans copied innovations in weapons technology developed by 'barbarians', from the Gauls mail and, later, iron helmet designs, and from Iberia sword technology which provided later Republican legionaries with the famous *gladius Hispaniensis* (Figure 30.2: 1–3).

Great regional variations in repertoires of combat equipment reflect differential access to materials and technical know-how, cultural differences, or ideological choices. For example, the late pre-Roman Iron Age peoples of the western Baltic and Scandinavia appear rarely to have possessed anything like the sophisticated swords and armour seen in contemporary Gaul, perhaps an expression of relative material poverty. Conversely, from the late pre-Roman Iron Age, like Gaul much of Britain produced elaborate weaponry, including mail shirts, but notably few helmets; this might perhaps represent a cultural disinclination among the islanders to fight helmeted. As explored later in the chapter, functional practicality and protection could be trumped by ideological considerations, like notions of masculine prowess and display.

The predominantly foot-combat culture of most of Europe contrasted strongly with modes of armed violence among the primarily pastoralist steppe peoples. In the mid-first millennium BC these lands were home to groups the Greeks called Scythians, and during the late pre-Roman Iron Age and Roman Iron Age to Sarmatian groups, whose styles of fighting were closely integrated with those of the Asiatic steppe lands as far as China. Here ecology, economy, and sheer distances resulted in mounted combat becoming the norm, with corresponding technological differences from further west. Lances and swords indicate the importance of close-quarter fighting, but the compound or composite bow, today more often associated with later peoples such as the Huns and Mongols, was also already important in the late pre-Roman Iron Age (Figure

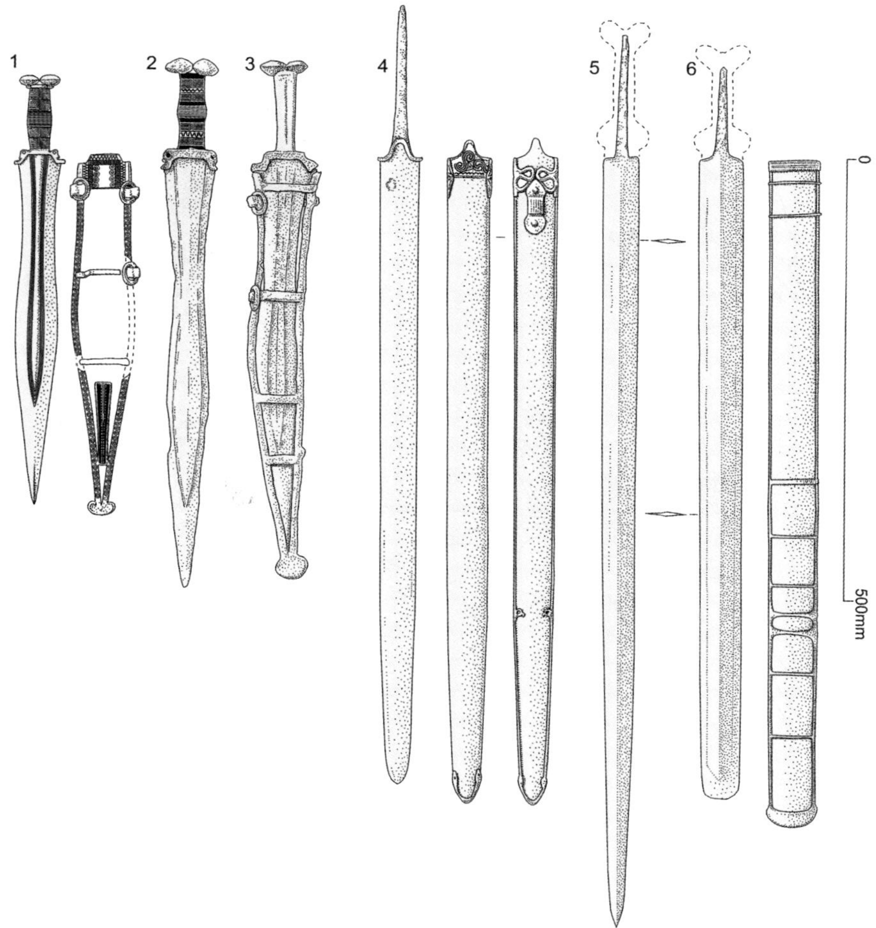

FIGURE 30.2 Iron Age swords. Left: pre-Roman Iron Age weapons from Spain: 1 Altillo del Cerropozo, Guadalajara; 2 Monreal de Ariza, Zaragoza; 3 Osma, Soria. Centre: 4 a sword and both sides of its scabbard, from La Tène, Switzerland, third century BC. Right: restorations of late pre-Roman Iron Age weapons from Port Nidau, Switzerland, respectively optimized for thrusting (5) and slashing (6).

Drawings: Simon James

30.3). Primacy of lance and bow, both two-handed weapons, explains the apparent lack of use of shields on the steppe; however, by the Roman Iron Age iron helmets and mail body armour were introduced (Goroncharovski 2006), probably supplementing earlier defences made of organic materials.

Conflicts among the steppe peoples, between them and the sophisticated armies of the Hellenistic world, and then with their similarly equipped southern neighbours the Arsacids (Parthians) of Mesopotamia and Iran, were likely responsible for key refinements of equestrian steppe combat and collective warfare in the last centuries

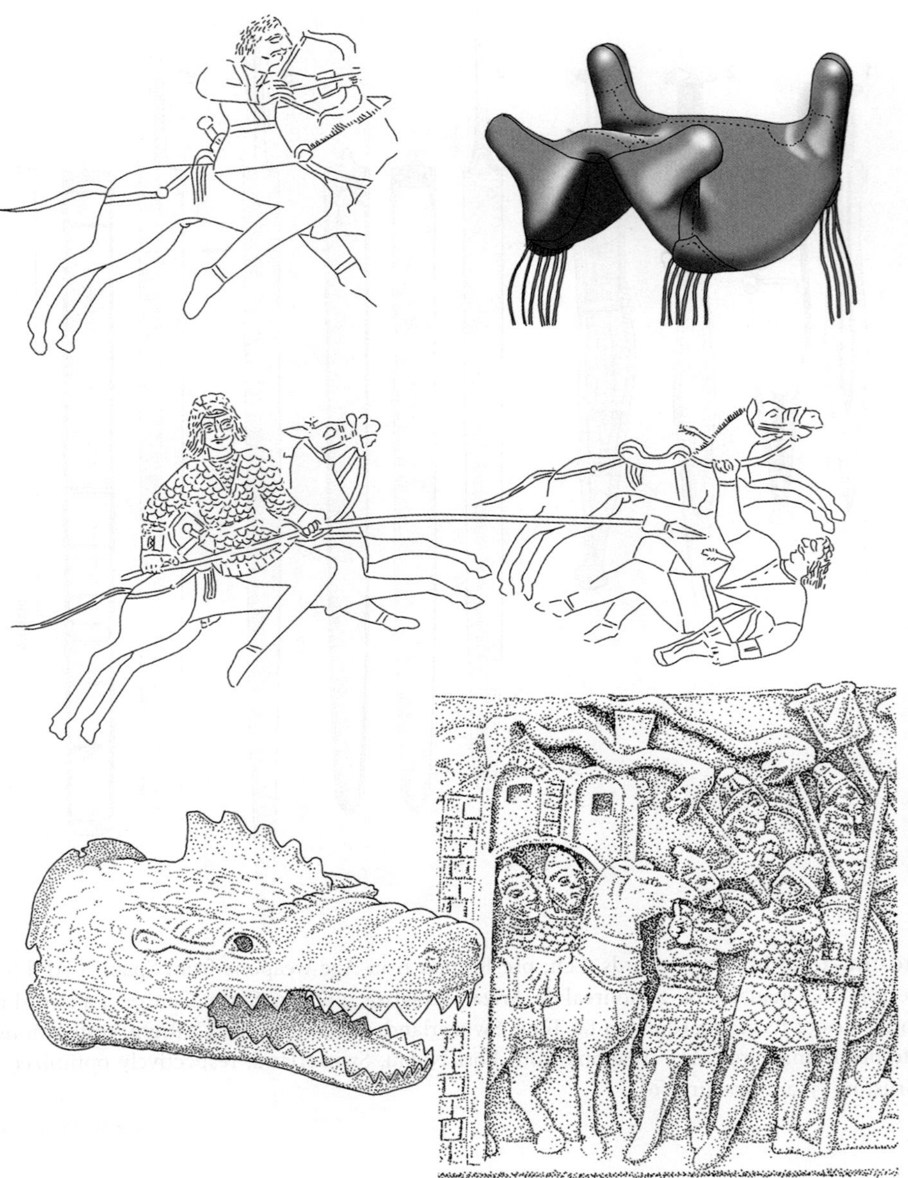

FIGURE 30.3 Top left and centre: steppe equestrian combat with bow and lance: engraved figures from the Kosika cup, *c.*50 BC to AD 50 (scale unknown; after Treister 1998). Top right: reconstruction of Roman saddle design, probably of steppe origin. Bottom left: head of a Roman draco from Niederbieber, Germany, and bottom right: perhaps some of the Sarmatian troops who introduced such windsock standards to Roman service, on the Arch of Galerius, Thessaloniki, Greece.

Drawings: Simon James

BC. These involved combinations of horse archers and lance-wielding cavalry with both man and horse encased in armour. This mounted combat tradition, which Roman legions found very hard to cope with, depended not just on weapons but also on equestrian equipment; and it evolved long before the introduction of stirrups. Only in the 1980s did we begin to understand Roman Iron Age horse harnesses, especially saddles. Archaeological finds of Roman saddle fragments were reconstructed to reveal a four-pommel design which, modern experimentation with replicas shows, provides a secure seat for wielding weapons (Connolly and Van Driel-Murray 1991; Figure 30.3). This very effective riding technology probably originated on the Eurasian steppe during the last millennium BC.

In many areas of western Europe, too, the horse played roles in combat during the Iron Age, initially pulling chariots (Chapter 32). By the late pre-Roman Iron Age mounted fighting was an established and developing tradition, notably in Iberia, Gaul, and parts of Germany, probably independent developments enhanced by adoption of the four-pommel saddle from the steppe via regions like Thrace. Here equestrian skills were especially highly developed, under strong influence from nearby 'Scythian' and then Sarmatian groups. A Chinese-made jade belt slide from a sword scabbard deposited in early Roman times in a Thracian tomb at Chatalka in Bulgaria (Werner 1994) attests the immense reach of these (probably down-the-line) connections. The four-pommel saddle probably entered Roman use via Thracian, Gaulish, or Parthian auxiliaries. Steppe mounted-combat culture literally based on this saddle was also so effective that imperial Rome subsequently adopted horse archers and armoured lancers on a substantial scale.

Despite regional differences and change over time, Iron Age European weapon technologies shared certain fundamentals. In contrast to modern pyrotechnic weaponry, which injures through blast waves and heat as much as direct impact of metal, most Iron Age arms worked by concentrating kinetic energy derived from human (sometimes supplemented by horse) muscle power into sharpened metal points or edges shot, thrown, thrust, or swung directly against human bodies (James 2010). This was intended to inflict sharp-force trauma to incapacitate or kill the victim, through direct disruption of muscle, nerve, and bone, or blood loss and shock. If such weapon blows could not be escaped by flight or evaded by dodging (and the Greeks inculcated agility in combat through dance), then effects of impacts could be mitigated through parrying or deflecting with a shield. For some people, in some places at some times, helmets and armour offered additional protection to the body, but this was a trade-off: armour required major investment of resources to make and maintain, and was heavy and potentially debilitating to wear, especially in hot weather. Nevertheless, it offered the prospect of absorbing some of the energy of otherwise deadly blows, and a chance of converting potentially lethal sharp-force impacts into perhaps more survivable blunt-force injuries by dispersing their energy over a larger area. However, design and especially embellishment of much Iron Age weaponry indicates that it also had other, perhaps equally effective, modes of operation involving no physical contact with the foe at all, working on the mind as much as the body.

A striking example of this is furnished by a sword from a third- or second-century BC grave (K3) in the cemetery at Kirkburn, East Yorkshire (Stead 1991: 66–70, 224–225). The sword is fused into its scabbard, but the general size and form of the weapon, and details from X-rays, reveal a two-edged blade with a long point, potentially capable of slashing but probably optimized for close-quarters thrusting. This functional interpretation looks to be confirmed by the gorgeous decoration of hilt and scabbard, specifically the red glass detail inlaid into the polished iron and copper alloy. This appears to simulate, symbolize, and celebrate the tip of the sword covered in gore, and the bloodied hand of its (by implication) victorious wielder. Here was a weapon designed to impress and intimidate while sheathed, as well as—as much as? instead of?—when drawn in anger.

Similarly, Gallic helmets were sometimes gorgeously embellished, and frequently sported crest holders. Crests—e.g. of feathers or metal—had little practical function, although characteristic forms could identify leaders or contingents. Their more general purpose was to exaggerate the apparent size of the wearer to intimidate antagonists, like the arched back and raised fur of an aggressively posturing cat. Such material observations, suggesting conscious attempts to undermine the opponent or intended victim psychologically—and also to boost the wearer's own sense of size and power—are consistent with classical descriptions of Gallic champions strutting, boasting, and seeking to belittle and demoralize their foes before actual fighting started (Diodorus Siculus *Library of History* 5.29.3).

The Gauls also used fearsome-looking animal-headed war-trumpets, or *carnyces*, to whip their own side into a battle frenzy and to intimidate the enemy (Figure 30.4). Similarly, Sarmatian 'dragon'-headed windsock standards, doubtless valuable for marshalling contingents, also had a powerful impact on the enemy, as the Sarmatian riders charged in with hissing, writhing monsters flying above their heads. The Romans adopted such *dracones* for their own cavalry (Figure 30.3). Trumpets and standards were psychological weapons.

Emphasis on armed display and posturing, intended to challenge but also to intimidate in advance (perhaps often instead) of actually inflicting blows with weapons, brings us to the role of fear. Threat of the use of weapons may often have been at least as important in influencing people's behaviour as the consequences of actual explosions of armed violence. Such equipment exemplifies 'technologies of enchantment' (Gell 1992). Gell proposed that artefacts were less about aesthetics and meanings than about mediating social action, through the effects they had on those who encountered them, a perspective applied to the study of 'Celtic art', much of which appears on arms (Gosden and Hill 2008; Garrow and Gosden 2012). 'Enchantment', a term connoting seductive fascination, but equally encompassing loss of willpower and terror, seems especially appropriate to portable artefacts intended for the theatre of combat and killing—including fortifications.

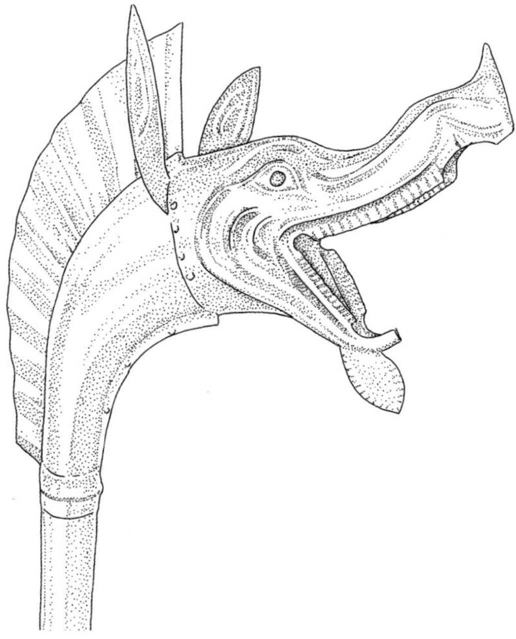

FIGURE 30.4 Reconstruction of a Gallic war-trumpet (*carnyx*), one of several found at Tintignac, France.

Drawing: Simon James

Fortified Places and Their Functions

As with Iron Age weaponry, fortified sites varied greatly in numbers and kind across Europe, with substantial areas and eras apparently lacking them; and where they existed, they undoubtedly operated in psychological and ideological as well as practical ways.

The term 'fortification' applied to many Iron Age sites presupposes a military function, but there is good reason to conclude that, across much of Britain for example, substantial bank-and-ditch earthworks around smaller later Iron Age settlements were about protecting livestock from predators, animal or human, and so were 'secured' rather than fortified. That even huge earthwork enclosures need not be military is epitomized by Tara and other Iron Age 'royal' sites of Ireland where the enclosures have the ditch inside the bank, and so were not practically defensible. Here other potential functions of massive enclosures come to the fore: of separation and privileging of internal space, and of impressing with power other than military. As mentioned earlier, in Britain especially, much recent discourse on those Iron Age sites with one or more ditches to the outside of one or more massive embankments, which we conventionally call 'hillforts', has emphasized their likely symbolic, social, cosmological, and other roles while, more controversially, playing down their potentially violent implications.

The shift of focus onto internal social dynamics—the community who built the site, and lived in or around it—as being critical in motivating construction of defensible enceintes of hillforts, or indeed *oppida*, is a key advance. However, I think questionable conclusions have been drawn, largely due to a continued tendency to 'pacify the past'. Social competition, conflict, coercion, and domination may well have been factors as significant as bonding, cohesion, and willing collaboration in 'building communities', even among relatively egalitarian Iron Age societies such as those envisaged by J. D. Hill (2006). The internal political purpose of constructing and maintaining ramparts and gates could then have been more about imposing social control than developing and expressing community. In practical terms, most of the time, enceintes likely served to hinder small-scale infiltration (e.g. raiding/theft by outsiders or outcasts), but equally deterred unsanctioned movement out of such places. Topographical location of hillforts also facilitated surveillance of surrounding lands—and not just for signs of foreign incursion. Many enceintes, then, may well have been more about social regulation of the home community than communal defence. However, the overtly defensible form of such sites indicates at least ideological framing of their rationale in terms of external threat.

Take, for example, the late Hallstatt defences at the Heuneburg, overlooking the Danube in southern Germany (Krausse et al. 2016). Here a hilltop enceinte exceptionally boasted projecting towers; these, and the plastered mud brick from which they were built, imitate Mediterranean (or Middle Eastern?) urban defences, whose towers exposed attackers to projectiles from three directions. Yet the Heuneburg towers are unnecessarily closely spaced and—crucially—were built only on the sides facing a substantial lower town and sprawling 'suburbs'. This suggests the towers' purpose was more visual impact on—and domination of?—the home community than practical defence. However, the lower town was itself walled and possessed a massive gate, expressing exclusion of outsiders, if not fear and perhaps real danger, of attack—matters strongly implicit in Sharples' (2010) picture of a mosaic of xenophobic Wessex polities.

It would today be simplistic and naive to seek to explain the vastness and complexity of the gates and ramparts of Maiden Castle hillfort primarily in tactical terms of fields of 'fire' for defending slingers, even if such observations fit the facts (Wheeler 1943: 49–51). It is equally doubtless that such massive undertakings were meant to work on human minds, through enchantment akin to the impact of splendid helmets with towering crests: impressing the resident population within and around, whether with their own collective effort or the authority of the dominant. At the same time, the earthworks sought also to overawe would-be attackers. Similar intertwining of ideological—symbolic and practical—tactical motivations may be seen at British hillfort gates. The preferential eastern orientation of main entrances of many British hillforts plausibly has a cosmological explanation, yet gate design was still necessarily largely driven by practical considerations, of surveillance and regulation of movement of people and livestock, of communal security, and—at least at some times in some places—a need for military vigilance. The elaboration of Danebury's eastern gate makes sense in tactical defensive terms, and it seems ultimately to have been attacked (Cunliffe 2003: 66–68).

However, 'poliorcetics'—sophisticated siegecraft using complex engineering (machines, ramps, mining)—was apparently unknown in Iron Age Europe. Originating in the Middle East, it was developed by Greeks (who invented torsion artillery) and perfected by the Romans, who introduced it to the transalpine world. Only wealthy states possessed the means to acquire and sustain such military capabilities, which demanded vast resources and technical expertise. Most Iron Age enceintes were created in a world in which the plausible dangers were mass assault with simple ladders (escalade), surprise attack on open gates, or treachery (which brings us back to internal dynamics).

In such circumstances, even simple circuits could have been militarily effective, deterring large-scale attack by making it difficult and potentially very costly. Equally significantly, what we know historically, or can infer from archaeology of masculine ideologies across Iron Age Europe, suggests that both aggressors and defenders preferred to avoid fighting across fortifications—or in many regions refrain from creating them at all. On the steppe especially, the cultural centrality of the horse generally rendered fortifications superfluous. For both single combat and collective warfare, Iron Age societies widely exhibited a strong cultural preference, and material equipment, for face-to-face fighting rather than defending walls.

The Samnite peoples of southern Italy offer a good protohistorical example. They had hillforts but, it seems, did not expect them to withstand large-scale attack. In 293 BC, before they had developed sophisticated siege capabilities, the Romans faced fierce resistance when they advanced to assault Saepinum. The Samnites, who according to Livy habitually defended their settlements with their right arms in preference to walls, attacked the approaching legions in the open field and, even once forced back inside Saepinum's defences, sought to keep the invaders at bay by aggressive sorties rather than passively from the ramparts (Livy *History of Rome* 10.45; Salmon 1967: 30, fn. 3).

Defenders, then, often opted to fight far from their own walls, even if they possessed them, while attackers preferred not to have to throw themselves against fortifications. Even after becoming expert military engineers, Romans exhibited a bloodthirsty preference for sword combat, lauding open battle over costly and potentially less glorious sieges.

Where they existed, Iron Age fortifications may have been built because in most circumstances they proved effective enough, in creating areas of sanctuary from endemic risk and episodic reality of serious 'brigandage' or war in the local landscape. Yet no fortification is invulnerable, and it may be that Iron Age defended sites actually suffered successful attack more often than we have hitherto realized, because archaeological evidence for carnage can be surprisingly ephemeral.

Fin Cop: A Case of War and Massacre?

Excavations at Fin Cop hillfort in the Derbyshire Peak District of England (Waddington 2012) provide a recent case study in the identification of Iron Age conflict through archaeological evidence, which suggests that the material 'stigmata' of ancient violence may be very subtle indeed. They may not even reside on the bones of the dead, but be detectable only in patterns in other data—in this case in interment of multiple bodies, demography of the group, and the way they had been buried. These enigmatic traces, taken together, suggest a long-forgotten Iron Age atrocity.

Stratigraphy and radiocarbon dating indicate that the earthwork perimeter of Fin Cop was a new foundation of the middle Iron Age. Stone from a rock-cut ditch was used to build a rampart 3–4 m high, around the end of the fifth century BC. A second outer rampart was subsequently started, but still far from complete when the circuit was deliberately slighted and the site abandoned, probably in the second half of the fourth century BC (Waddington 2012: 223–224). Widely spaced trenches across the rampart ditch have so far produced fifteen bodies buried in its fill (Waddington 2012: 214–217, 231). The known distribution and density of bodies (roughly a corpse per metre of ditch) implies several hundred along its length. Those recovered so far have been identified as adult women, babies, and one adolescent, possibly male. No adult males have been encountered, a curious fact unlikely to be statistical fluke, although males might perhaps lie concentrated in the unexcavated stretches of ditch. Equally curiously, the corpses lay not in graves dug into the ditch fill, but were interleaved within layers of a deliberate single-phase demolition of the hillfort rampart. The bodies were apparently placed—or thrust—into the ditch from the outside while the rampart material was being thrown back in from the inside: i.e. their burials were apparently simultaneous, and contemporaneous with—indeed integral to—destruction of the hillfort (Waddington 2012: 226).

What happened here? If the Fin Cop community was destroyed and its settlement ritually abandoned as a result of some epidemic, where are the adult males? Their apparent absence forms part of a chain of argument leading to an even grimmer alternative: that we are dealing here with violent extirpation of an entire community and its central and symbolic place. The skeletons recovered so far have revealed no gross violent trauma that could have been the cause of death (Waddington 2012: 226). However, as we saw, many lethal wounds leave no skeletal trace. The Fin Cop dead could have been strangled or had their throats cut. The argument for a massacre as an act of war, with simultaneous slighting of the fort indicating the intention was obliteration not conquest (Waddington 2012: 224–226, 228–229), is largely circumstantial, but is cumulative and compelling.

Perhaps what happened was something like this: the community centred on Fin Cop was one of many in the region, each of the scale of some hundreds to a thousand or more individuals. For unknown reasons, during the fifth century BC violent conflict, up to the scale of war between communities, become a threat prompting construction of a number of defensible sites in the area, including Fin Cop. A generation or two later the decision to strengthen the defences further may indicate increasing risk or occurrence of conflict, and perhaps itself precipitated pre-emptive attack from a neighbouring group before work could be completed. Bodies of adult males are absent from the site because they went to confront the attackers in open battle, to keep them away from the unfinished and perhaps vulnerable hillfort, and/or because, as among Romans and Gauls, prevailing combat culture decreed open-field confrontation. However, they were defeated, all slain in fighting and ensuing rout, captured and killed or made fugitives. Following this, the victors rounded up all the women and children at Fin Cop itself. The community was then practically and symbolically obliterated, by annihilating the rest of the population and their central place in a combined act of slaughter and physical destruction, as Waddington has argued.

We may then have, at Fin Cop, testimony of a calculated act not just of war, but of small-scale genocide. This is, of course, a lurid and horrifying scenario, yet there are parallels—e.g. the Native American mass grave at Crow Creek, South Dakota, *c.*AD 1325 (Zimmerman 1997). The people of Crow Creek were, like the similar-scale Fin Cop community seventeen centuries earlier, in the process of enhancing their settlement defences when they were attacked. The remains recovered attest massacre, accompanied by widespread mutilation, of apparently the entire five-hundred-strong population—except for young female adults who are underrepresented in the mass grave (Zimmerman 1997: 84).

Perhaps at Fin Cop too, along with loot and livestock, the conquerors also spared the young females, making this rather a case of 'ethnocide'—i.e. destruction of a self-identifying group, distinct from genocide in that there were biological survivors forcibly absorbed into another group. An even larger-scale example of just such an atrocity as that envisaged at Fin Cop is described in the Bible (*Book of Numbers* 31: 7–18, King James Version): the obliteration of the Midianites by the Israelites:

> And they warred against the Midianites, as the LORD commanded Moses; and they slew all the males. And they slew the kings of Midian ... And the children of Israel took all the women of Midian captives, and their little ones, and took the spoil of all their cattle, and all their flocks, and all their goods. And they burnt all their cities wherein they dwelt, and all their goodly castles, with fire... And Moses said unto them, 'Have ye saved all the women alive? ... Now ... kill every male among the little ones, and kill every woman that hath known man by lying with him. But all the women children, that have not known a man by lying with him, keep alive for yourselves.'

The historicity of this appalling account may be questioned, yet it was already current among the Jews, taken to be true, and regarded as a just, divinely sanctioned act by the time the archaeologically attested events at Fin Cop unfolded.

Armed Violence in Iron Age Europe

How can we make sense of the fragmentary, often enigmatic, yet sometimes lurid evidence for carnage and combat culture in Iron Age Europe? Can development of large armies, at least, be attributed to a 'violent edge of empire effect', responses to the encroachment of Roman imperialism? This certainly looks to be a major factor during the Roman Iron Age. For example, the defeated army, apparently comprising men from Norway and Sweden, whose equipment was buried at Illerup around AD 200 (see earlier), included many Roman-made sword blades, likely attesting Roman political interference in the north. Generations of fighting against, and indeed for, Rome appears to have led some Germanic groups to develop quite sophisticated armies with distinct tactical components. When a Frankish army faced a Roman force at Strasbourg in AD 357, its right wing attempted flanking tactics (Ammianus Marcellinus *History* 16.12). This wing was commanded by a king with the Graeco-Roman name Serapio, his father having spent years in Roman Gaul where he learnt the mysteries of Greek religion (Ammianus Marcellinus *History* 16.12.26)—and perhaps also Roman tactics?

Yet, as we have seen, there is extensive evidence that northern Iron Age Europeans were fighting and sometimes massacring each other long before Rome impinged on their world. The likely dynamics of armed violence within and between societies through the Iron Age might be understood through cross-cultural comparison with better attested analogous contexts, from wider anthropology, and not least from one corner of the Iron Age world itself: Italy, in transition to history.

The anthropology of recent 'honour cultures', classically based on studies of Mediterranean pastoral and rural societies (Péristiany 1966), provides analogies for Iron Age Europeans. Those living in small-scale societies without large-scale collective institutions live in conditions of chronic insecurity, and must depend on their own physical capacities, plus family and personal allies, for security of their lives and livelihoods. This often requires a capacity for violence: at least a credible deterrent threat based on skill with weapons. Personal reputation for fighting prowess can become vital to social standing; conflict may arise from competition within groups (duelling, feuding) as much as between them (which may or may not deserve the label 'war'). From the later Bronze Age, dedicated combat weapons, not least swords, became more common in Europe. Through the ensuing millennium, sword designs remained generally double-edged, also providing a pertinent metaphor: armed violence could protect or give advantage, while also threatening self-inflicted injuries to a community through internecine strife. Increasing elaboration of material culture of armed violence as means of deterrence or active aggression ran in tandem with the development of social codes to seek to limit mayhem; development of 'honour cultures' codified the prestige of masculine courage and aggression, while at same time providing rules of engagement and means of negotiating conflict.

Danger of internal conflict was one of several major driving forces (including demographic expansion) in the creation of larger, more complex polities—e.g. during Italy's Iron Age, generating fora for non-violent competition and conflict resolution—in the case of archaic Rome, the literal, original forum. Many of the diverse peoples of Iron Age Italy seem to have become dominated by armed and violent aristocrat-led 'clans', prone to fighting each other as much as outsiders (Terrenato 2001, 2007; Motta and Terrenato 2006). A major function of the Italian city states and ethnic leagues developing from the eighth century BC was collective regulation of internal conflict, facilitating competition for prestige through non-violent means (i.e. religious, political, and economic activities). These institutions also sought to control armed violence, in part by religious and legal sanctions, but largely through channelling masculine aggression into less internally disruptive ends: war against outsiders. Capacity for armed violence thus remained central to Italian masculinity, values shared by Greeks and Samnites as well as Latins and Etruscans. Personal honour and social standing increasingly derived from performance in war on behalf of the community (McDonnell 2006). The peoples of Iron Age Italy thus evolved in parallel from baseline chronic insecurity towards a different, binary system of 'peace' and 'war', both collective enterprises requiring organization and maintenance. Nevertheless, Italian polities were often unstable; civil strife could still be as dangerous as foreign wars.

As it turned out, one city state, Rome, developed a unique talent for alliance building in tandem with its military capacities (Eckstein 2006), facilitating peaceful integration of Italy's multi-ethnic societies through diverting and harnessing their armed aggression in the now traditional way: directing it outwards. The vast imperial power which then proceeded to conquer much of Europe was a product as much of earlier Italian Iron Age traditions of armed violence as of the special qualities of the Roman Republic (James 2011: 53–63).

Much of the rest of Iron Age Europe probably followed similar trajectories, albeit of varying speed and degree. The large polities of late pre-Roman Iron Age Transalpine Gaul, as depicted in the pages of Caesar's *Gallic War*, exhibited characteristics strikingly similar to those of archaic Italy: armed masculinity, aristocratic regimes prone to internal instability, and propensity for external war. The preceding centuries had seen a number of large-scale Gaulish plunder-raids into Italy and, less spectacular but perhaps more important, many Gauls, alongside Celtiberians, Thracians and others, serving Mediterranean powers as mercenaries (Szabó 1991). Thus Gaulish societies usefully neutralized armed and dangerous young males by exporting them, either to die abroad or return rich—as it turns out, bringing new ideas like coinage (Wells 1999: 46–47, 54) and perhaps political ideas facilitating larger polities. During the Roman Iron Age, Germans and Sarmatians would also become mercenaries or recruits in Roman service. Late Roman hiring of entire 'barbarian' armies simply marked the culmination of a long tradition of mercenary service.

However, until the Roman era, many more distant European societies remained small-scale in organization, still with patterns of violence likely reflecting tensions within society as much as external raiding and war, as Giles envisages for society in later

Iron Age East Yorkshire. Here the gorgeous weapons in graves, and the injuries they inflicted on the bodies, probably reflect intragroup duelling more than warfare (Giles 2012: 107, 235–238).

Later Iron Age Europeans, then, were by no means simply victims reacting as best they could to imperialist aggression. Many were willing and active participants in martial interactions with the classical Mediterranean world, contacts which reshaped, redirected, and perhaps intensified pre-existing violent practices. Development of large-scale armies and warfare were the reverse of the coin of development of civil society emergent in various parts of Europe during the Iron Age.

Acknowledgements

I am grateful to Colin Haselgrove, Peter Wells, and Katharina Rebay-Salisbury for their patience during the overlong gestation of this piece. Many thanks also to John Collis, Mel Giles, Heinrich Härke, Sarah King, Rebecca Redfern, and Clive Waddington for references and valuable discussions, though none of them necessarily agree with the views expressed here.

References

Armit, I. 2007. 'Hillforts at war: From Maiden Castle to Taniwaha pa'. *Proceedings of the Prehistoric Society* 73: 25–40.

Armit, I. 2012. *Headhunting and the Body in Iron Age Europe*. Cambridge: Cambridge University Press.

Brunaux, J.-L. 1999. 'Ribemont-sur-Ancre: Bilan préliminaire et nouvelles hypothèses'. *Gallia* 56: 177–283.

Brunaux, J.-L. 2001. 'Gallic blood rites'. *Archaeology* 54, 2: 54–57.

Collis, J. R. 1994. 'Reconstructing Iron Age society', in K. Kristiansen and J. Jensen (eds) *Europe in the First Millennium BC*: 31–39. Sheffield: J. R. Collis.

Connolly, P., and C. Van Driel-Murray. 1991. 'The Roman cavalry saddle'. *Britannia* 22: 33–50.

Craig, R., C. J. Knüsel, and G. Carr. 2005. 'Fragmentation, mutilation and dismemberment: An interpretation of human remains on Iron Age sites', in M. Parker Pearson and N. Thorpe (eds) *Warfare, Violence and Slavery in Prehistory*. British Archaeological Reports International Series 1374: 165–180. Oxford: Archaeopress.

Cunliffe, B. W. 2003. *Danebury Hillfort*. Stroud: Tempus.

Department of Defense. 2014. [untitled current casualty statistics page]. Available at https://www.defense.gov/casualty.pdf [accessed 15 August 2014].

Derks, H., and S. Burmeister (eds). 2009. *Varusschlacht in Osnabrücker Land*. Mainz: Philipp von Zabern.

Eckstein, A. M. 2006. *Mediterranean Anarchy, Interstate War, and the Rise of Rome*. Berkeley/Los Angeles/London: University of California Press.

Federal Bureau of Investigation. 2011. Crime in the United States 2011: Table 20, Murder. Available at http://www.fbi.gov/about-us/cjis/ucr/crime-in-the-u.s/2011/crime-in-the-u.s.-2011/tables/table-20 [accessed 20 August 2014].

Ferguson, R. B., and N. L. Whitehead. 1992. 'The violent edge of empire', in R. B. Ferguson and N. L. Whitehead (eds) *War in the Tribal Zone: Expanding States and Indigenous Warfare*: 1–30. Santa Fe, NM: School of American Research Press.

Garrow, D., and C. Gosden. 2012. *Technologies of Enchantment? Exploring Celtic Art in Britain 400 BC to AD 100*. Oxford: Oxford University Press.

Gell, A. 1992. 'The technology of enchantment and the enchantment of technology', in J. Coote and A. Shelton (eds) *Anthropology, Art and Aesthetics*: 40–66. Oxford: Clarendon.

Geschwinde, M., H. Hassmann, P. Lönne, M. Meyer, and G. Moosbauer. 2009. 'Roms vergessener Feldzug: Das neu entdeckte Schlachtfeld am Harzhorn in Niedersachsen', in S. Berke, S. Burmeister, and H. Kenzler (eds) *2000 Jahre Varusschlacht: Imperium—Konflikt—Mythos*: 228–232. Stuttgart: Theiss.

Giles, M. 2012. *A Forged Glamour: Landscape, Identity and Material Culture in the Iron Age*. Oxford: Windgather Press.

Goroncharovski, V. A. 2006. 'Some notes on defensive armament of the Bosporan cavalry', in M. Mode and J. Tubach (eds) *Arms and Armour as Indicators of Cultural Transfer: The Steppes and the Ancient World from Hellenistic Times to the Early Middle Ages*: 445–452. Wiesbaden: Reichert.

Gosden, C., and J. D. Hill. 2008. 'Introduction: Reintegrating "Celtic" Art', in D. Garrow, C. Gosden, and J. D. Hill (eds) *Rethinking Celtic Art*: 1–14. Oxford: Oxbow.

Guliaev, V. 2003. 'Amazons in the Scythia: New finds at the Middle Don, Southern Russia'. *World Archaeology* 35, 1: 112–125.

Hill, J. D. 2006. 'Are we any closer to understanding how later Iron Age societies worked (or did not work)?', in C. Haselgrove (ed.) *Celtes et Gaulois: l'archéologie face à l'histoire: Les mutations de la fin de l'âge du Fer. Actes de la table ronde de Cambridge, 7–8 Juillet 2005*. Collection Bibracte 12/4: 169–179. Glux-en-Glenne: Centre archéologique européen du Mont Beuvray.

Ilkjær, J. 2000. *Illerup Ådal: Archaeology as a Magic Mirror*. Moesgård: Moesgård Museum.

James, S. T. 2007. 'A bloodless past: the pacification of Early Iron Age Britain', in C. Haselgrove and R. Pope (eds) *The Earlier Iron Age in Britain and the Near Continent*: 160–173. Oxford: Oxbow.

James, S. T. 2010. 'The point of the sword: What Roman-era weapons could do to bodies—and why they often didn't', in A. W. Busch and H.-J. Schalles (eds) *Waffen in Aktion: Akten der 16. Internationalen Roman Military Equipment Conference (ROMEC)*. Xantener Berichte 16: 41–54. Mainz am Rhein: Von Zabern.

James, S. T. 2011. *Rome and the Sword: How Warriors & Weapons Shaped Roman History*. London/New York: Thames & Hudson.

Keeley, L. H. 1997. *War Before Civilization*. Oxford: Oxford University Press.

King, S. S. 2010. 'What Makes War? Assessing Iron Age Warfare Through Mortuary Behaviour and Osteological Patterns of Violence'. PhD thesis, University of Bradford.

Knüsel, C. 2005. 'The physical evidence of warfare—subtle stigmata?', in M. Parker-Pearson and N. Thorpe (eds) *Warfare, Violence and Slavery in Prehistory*. British Archaeological Reports International Series 1374: 49–66. Oxford: Archaeopress.

Krausse, D., M. Fernández-Götz, L. Hansen, and I. Kretschmer. 2016. *The Heuneburg and the Early Iron Age Princely Seats: First Towns North of the Alps*. Budapest: Archaeolingua.

Lock, G. 2011. 'Hillforts, emotional metaphors, and the Good Life: A response to Armit'. *Proceedings of the Prehistoric Society* 77: 355–362.

McDonnell, M. 2006. *Roman Manliness: Virtus and the Roman Republic*. Cambridge: Cambridge University Press.

Maribo, S. H. 2014. 'Violent aftermath for the warriors at Alken Enge'. Available at http://cas.au.dk/en/currently/news/singlenews/artikel/translate-to-english-in-alken-enge/ [accessed 23 August 2014].

Motta, L., and N. Terrenato. 2006. 'The origins of the state par excellence: Power and society in Iron Age Rome', in C. Haselgrove (ed.) *Celtes et Gaulois: l'Archéologie face à l'Histoire: Les mutations de la fin de l'âge du Fer. Actes de la table ronde de Cambridge, 7–8 Juillet 2005*. Collection Bibracte 12/4: 225–234. Glux-en-Glenne: Centre archéologique européen du Mont Beuvray.

Paine, R. R., D. Mancinelli, M. Ruggieri, and A. Coppa. 2007. 'Cranial trauma in iron age Samnite agriculturists, Alfedena, Italy: Implications for biocultural and economic stress'. *American Journal of Physical Anthropology* 132, 1: 48–58.

Péristiany, J. G. 1966. *Honour and Shame: The Values of Mediterranean Society*. Chicago: University of Chicago Press.

Redfern, R. C. 2008. 'A bioarchaeological analysis of violence in Iron Age females: A perspective from Dorset, England (mid to late C7th BC to the C1st AD)', in O. Davis, N. Sharples, and K. Waddington (eds) *Changing Perspectives on the First Millennium BC: Proceedings of the Iron Age Research Student Seminar 2006*: 139–160. Oxford: Oxbow.

Redfern, R. C. 2011. 'A re-appraisal of the evidence for violence in the late Iron Age human remains from Maiden Castle hillfort, Dorset, England'. *Proceedings of the Prehistoric Society* 77: 111–138.

Redfern, R. C. 2020. 'Gendered violence in Iron Age and Roman Britain', in G.G. Fagan, L. Fibiger, M. Hudson, and M. Trundle (eds) *The Cambridge World History of Violence, Vol. 1: The Prehistoric and Ancient Worlds*: 320–341. Cambridge: Cambridge University Press.

Salmon, E. T. 1967. *Samnium and the Samnites*. Cambridge: Cambridge University Press.

Schlüter, W., and R. Wiegels (eds). 1999. *Rom, Germanien und die Ausgrabungen von Kalkriese*. Osnabrück: Universitätsverlag Rasch.

Sharples, N. 2010. *Social Relations in Later Prehistory: Wessex in the First Millennium BC*. Oxford: Oxford University Press.

Shepherd, J. P., M. Shapland, N. X. Pearce, and C. Scully. 1990. 'Pattern, severity and aetiology of injuries in victims of assault'. *Journal of the Royal Society of Medicine* 83, 2: 75–78.

Skanderborg Museum. 2012. 'Alken Enge—the mass grave at Lake Mossø'. Available at http://www.skanderborgmuseum.dk/Alken_Enge-English_version-1070.aspx [accessed 23 August 2014].

Small Arms Survey. 2007. *Small Arms Survey 2007: Guns and the City*. Available at http://www.smallarmssurvey.org/publications/by-type/yearbook/small-arms-survey-2007.html [accessed 20 August 2014].

Sparacello, V. S., O. M. Pearson, A. Coppa, and D. Marchi. 2011. 'Changes in skeletal robusticity in an iron age agropastoral group: The samnites from the Alfedena necropolis (Abruzzo, central Italy)'. *American Journal of Physical Anthropology* 144, 1: 119–130.

Stead, I. M. 1991. *Iron Age Cemeteries in East Yorkshire*. English Heritage Archaeological Report 22. London: English Heritage.

Szabó, M. 1991. 'Mercenary activity', in S. Moscati, O.-H. Frey, V. Kruta, B. Raftery, and M. Szabó (eds) *The Celts*: 333–336. New York: Rizzoli.

Terrenato, N. 2001. 'A tale of three cities: The Romanization of northern coastal Etruria', in S. J. Keay and N. Terrenato (eds) *Italy and the West: Comparative Issues in Romanization*: 54–67. Oxford: Oxbow.

Terrenato, N. 2007. 'The clans and the peasants: Reflections on social structure and change in Hellenistic Italy', in P. van Dommelen and N. Terrenato (eds) *Articulating Local Cultures: Power and Identity Under the Expanding Roman Republic*. Journal of Roman Archaeology Supplement 63: 13–22.

Treister, M. 1998. 'New discoveries of Sarmatian complexes of the first century AD: A survey of publications in VDI'. *Ancient Civilizations from Scythia to Siberia* 4, 1: 35–100.

Vandkilde, H. 2006. 'Warriors and warrior institutions in Copper Age Europe', in T. Otto, H. Thrane, and H. Vandkilde (eds) *Warfare and Society: Archaeological and Social Anthropological Perspectives*: 393–421. Aarhus: Aarhus University Press.

Waddington, C. 2012. 'Excavations at Fin Cop, Derbyshire: An Iron Age hillfort in conflict?' *Archaeological Journal* 169: 159–236.

Wells, P. S. 1999. *The Barbarians Speak: How the Conquered Peoples Shaped Roman Europe*. Princeton: Princeton University Press.

Werner, J. 1994. 'Chinesischer Schwerttragbügel der Han-Zeit aus einem thrakischen Häuptlingsgrab von Catalka (Bulgarien)'. *Germania* 72: 269–282.

Wheeler, R. E. M. 1943. *Maiden Castle, Dorset*. Reports of the Research Committee of the Society of Antiquaries of London 12. Oxford: Society of Antiquaries.

Zimmerman, L. 1997. 'The Crow Creek massacre, archaeology and prehistoric plains warfare in contemporary perspective', in J. Carman (ed.) *Material Harm: Archaeological Studies of War and Violence*: 75–94. Glasgow: Cruithne Press.

CHAPTER 31

WEALTH, STATUS, AND OCCUPATION GROUPS

TOM MOORE

Introduction

The pre-Roman Iron Age is often regarded as a period when larger, more complex social entities formed in Europe. In order to understand how such social systems operated we need to examine how groups and individuals expressed wealth and status. Did they mark themselves out through consumption of resources, martial prowess, or controlling exchange? Or were disparities in status relatively rare or deliberately constrained? Such questions are at the heart of how we envisage Iron Age societies, underpinning explanations of how, and why, things changed in the first millennium BC. If we envisage, for example, that wealth was expressed through ownership of exotic imports, the availability of such items will have had a dramatic impact on the nature of Iron Age communities, their structure, survival, and development. The nature of wealth and status also has implications for determining whether stratified societies existed with clearly defined specialist groups. This chapter will explore the varied ways in which wealth and status were expressed across Iron Age Europe and the evidence for occupation groups, classes, and specialist roles within the variety of European societies. Finally, it will assess whether broader trends can be discerned from this evidence.

Defining Wealth and Status in Iron Age Europe

Before we can examine concepts of wealth and status in Iron Age societies we must first consider what we mean by such terms. In the past, simplistic associations have often been drawn between the richness of material culture and the rank and status of individuals, communities, and regions. The origins of studying the period were dominated by a drive to investigate the perceived elites in society, focusing attention on the more visible burial tumuli of central Europe, or a search for the richest metalwork, as in southern Scandinavia (Weill 2003). Anachronistic concepts of wealth have inevitably led to value judgements in our terminology; descriptions for individuals such as the Vix 'princess' to refer to the late Hallstatt burial in central France (Brun 1987), or more general terms such as *Fürstengräber* (princely graves), are defined largely on the perceived wealth of their grave goods and derive from the antiquarian context in which they emerged (Fischer 1995: 34).

This focus on certain areas and periods has led to a distorted view, often overlooking more nuanced concepts of wealth that may have existed in many Iron Age societies. This approach has led to the application of a universal 'Celtic' model of society, which includes implicit understanding of the nature of wealth and status. This is based largely on Julius Caesar's description of the Aedui in central France in the first century BC, in which he describes distinct social classes: commoners, a religious class (druids), and a warrior class (*equites*), largely dedicated to warfare (*de Bello Gallico* 6.13–15). This has been allied with other textual sources (such as early medieval Irish texts) and the archaeological evidence to argue that all Iron Age communities were highly stratified societies, where status was maintained via warrior prowess and the control and redistribution of wealth (Figure 31.1; see Chapter 29). However, the varied evidence from across the European Iron Age increasingly suggests that such a universal model is highly problematic (Hill 2011). Not least, it is notable that proponents of this generalized model of society tend to ignore the evidence elsewhere in classical sources which indicate that many societies had very different social structures and value systems. Both Caesar (*de Bello Gallico* 6.22) and Tacitus (*Germania* 7; 11) describe, for example, how German societies were organized in more egalitarian and consensual terms. Concepts of wealth, therefore, are at the forefront of this debate: defining whether Iron Age societies can be reconstructed as hierarchical or more egalitarian, and what we mean by terms such as 'elite' or 'chief' (Hill 2011: 247).

Changing modes of obtaining and distributing wealth have also been linked to discussions of social complexity, with Kristian Kristiansen (1998: 394) seeing a correlation between the presence of wealth in burials and hoards and the rise of more hierarchical and elite-dominated societies. The challenge is to determine whether there is a correlation between elaborate objects or large monuments and the position of people within, and the nature of, society. As we shall see, Iron Age studies are far from developing a common approach to these issues (Collis 1994: 31). Some continue to regard concepts of wealth and status as easily definable, using the 'Celtic' model just outlined, or assuming that these communities can be placed within a certain stage of social evolution, such as a 'chiefdom', where status is always expressed in similar ways. Others meanwhile, often utilizing ethnographic comparisons, emphasize the varied ways in which status can be obtained and expressed in human societies, arguing that not all Iron Age societies were dominated by wealthy elites.

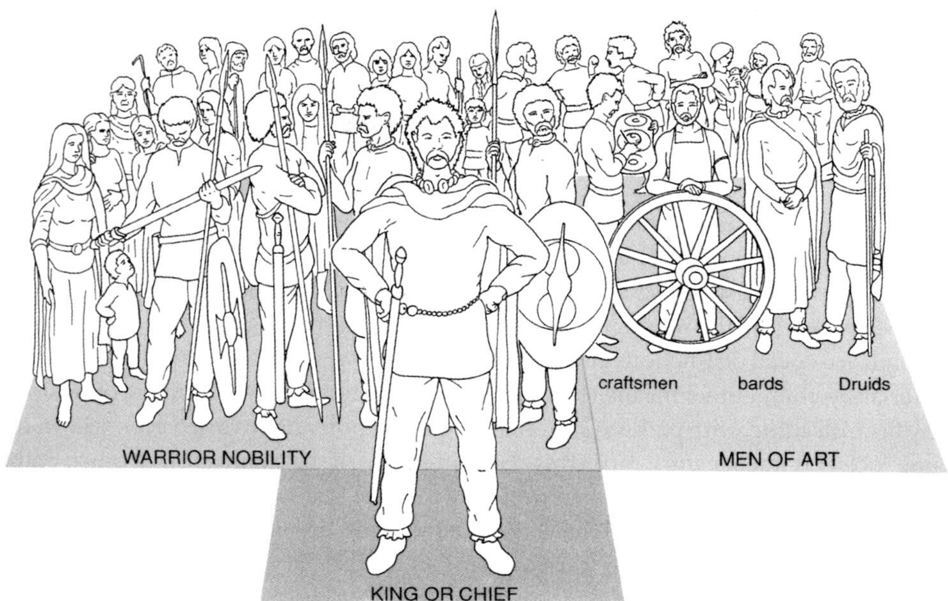

FIGURE 31.1 The traditional model of Celtic society.

Drawing © Simon James (1993), with permission

Anthropological studies certainly provide us with a complex picture of what can represent wealth and status, and how it can be articulated. We may take a Marxist approach that wealth was based on the control of production, perhaps indicated by the placement of late La Tène *oppida* (such as Kelheim and Manching, Germany) close to iron ore sources or evidence of wealthy burials close to early Iron Age salt mines at the Dürrnberg and Hallstatt, Austria (Stöllner et al. 2003: 184; Kern et al. 2008). But for most Iron Age societies there is little evidence that status rested purely on the control of natural resources, land, or craft production. Ethnographic accounts demonstrate that in many societies wealth is demonstrated more in the social obligations and relationships it engenders and contains, than in objects or monuments (Graeber 2001: 94). Such studies indicate that many societies have 'levelling mechanisms' which control the amount of wealth any individual or group can amass. This could take the form of socially undermining the more successful in society (Boehm 1993) or mechanisms such as competitive feasting (e.g. potlatches: described in 'Status through conspicuous consumption'). It seems unlikely that the concept of private wealth truly existed in Iron Age Europe. Even those individuals who may have amassed 'wealth' in the form of exotic objects, metalwork, or land are marked out by their need to demonstrate that wealth. In this sense, wealth only had value through its display, destruction (conspicuous consumption), or exchange (gift giving) to other members of the community (Graeber 2001).

Evidence from classical sources also reminds us of the different and varied value systems which existed across Iron Age Europe. For example, Diodorus Siculus' claim (*Library of History* 5.26.1) that the Gauls would exchange one slave for one amphora of wine has struck some as indicating the Celts' thirst for alcohol, but in reality this probably reflected its value in Iron Age ritual practices and maintaining social status (Poux 2004: 214). We need to be careful, therefore, of our own prejudices in determining symbols of wealth and status: why should torcs be symbols of power, and brooches merely ornamentation (Pope and Ralston 2011: 376)? Does this reflect our own gender-laden and materialistic obsessions rather than how wealth and status were expressed in the Iron Age? While we might seek to contrast those Iron Age societies who largely downplayed social distinctions and those where status was expressed through amassing material by competitive means (Price and Feinman 2010: 4), such binary opposition may be misleading, with pathways to obtaining status potentially varied even within the same society (Graeber 2001: 100). This also reminds us of the challenge that much of the material we see may not mark differences in 'wealth' or 'status' but represent markers of gender or age (Collis 1994: 33). Objects and monuments are likely to have had multiple roles and meanings, expressing varied identities and social relationships in different contexts.

Variations in Wealth

The existence of somewhat simplistic approaches to what constituted wealth in the past has inevitably distorted our picture of its presence across Iron Age Europe. This has often led to broader value judgements: the 'poverty' of a northern European Iron Age compared to that of central and southern Europe (Moore and Armada 2011: 5). It is clear, however, that deposition patterns varied enormously across Europe, ensuring that what occurs in burials or on settlement sites does not necessarily reflect the 'wealth' of material available to living groups, let alone mark an objective reflection of how 'wealthy' an individual was. For example, the so-called chariot burials of East Yorkshire present a range of items, including elaborately decorated martial equipment (Giles 2012: 120–174; Chapter 30), but this does not mean that such objects were not present elsewhere in Britain. In other regions, where elaborate burials were largely absent, such as the south and east, swords were more commonly deposited in wet places (Stead 2006: 80). Similarly, the paucity of material culture on Iron Age sites in certain parts of north-western Europe is likely to reflect not the poverty of those communities but decisions over what was deposited in pits and ditches as part of larger processes of structured deposition (Hill 1995a; Becker 2009: 359). For some societies, displays of status and wealth may have been through other means, which are harder to see archaeologically, such as the ownership of livestock (as indicated by some classical sources, such as Tacitus *Germania* 34).

The varied deposition patterns and distributions of certain types of objects are, however, likely to reflect different modes of displaying wealth. The distribution of metalwork in Britain indicates a greater preponderance of such items in East Anglia compared to northern and western Britain (Figure 31.2; Garrow and Gosden 2012: 137). It is possible that this reflects the 'wealth' of such communities, but it is more likely that it marks how those communities chose to display and consume that 'wealth', as votive offerings in wet places or sanctuaries. This potentially reflects a broader division in how status and power were expressed by different societies: depositing elaborate metalwork in some areas contrasting with the exploitation of labour elsewhere. While such simple divisions are likely to obscure the complexities of social systems, they emphasize how communities in relatively close proximity might have measured wealth and displayed status in quite different ways.

Depositing Wealth

For the preceding Bronze Age, wealth in societies across much of north-western Europe appears to have been marked by the consumption and deposition of bronze metalwork. This represented the ritualized destruction of wealth, allowing elites to maintain, but also regulate, their place in society (Bradley 1998; Kristiansen 1998: 73). This was often through deposition in wet places, such as rivers and bogs. In the eighth to seventh centuries BC, there was a dramatic cessation in the deposition of bronze metalwork across north-west Europe, denoting the end of the Bronze Age. This marked major changes in the ways in which wealth and status were demonstrated in the earliest Iron Age; in central France (Milcent 2004: 66) and the Low Countries (De Mulder and Bourgeois 2011: 307), for example, the decline in depositing metalwork in wet places can be contrasted with an increased deposition of weaponry in burials (Figure 31.3). Meanwhile, in Britain resources seemed to be switched to the construction of structures, such as large roundhouses (Needham 2007: 57). The reasons for these changes are undoubtedly complex, but they may indicate that wealth and status in the Iron Age were expressed more through ownership of land and the control of food production than through control of metal resources and objects (Kristiansen 1998: 218; Needham 2007: 58).

The practice of depositing elaborate objects in wet places did not, however, die out entirely. Finds of decorated martial equipment in major rivers in Britain (such as the Battersea and Witham shields) and elsewhere in Europe, notably at sites like La Tène in Switzerland, indicate that in some areas deposition continued to be significant (Bradley 1998). In southern Scandinavia deposition in bogs continued, sometimes with the deposition of exceptional objects such as the second- or first-century BC silver cauldron from Gundestrup, Denmark (Nielsen et al. 2005), indicating that the removal from circulation of valuable items continued as a way of maintaining social prestige into the first millennium AD (Hedeager 1992).

FIGURE 31.2 The varied expression of wealth and status through metalwork: the distribution of gold torcs in Europe.

Redrawn by author, after Hautenauve (2005): map 1

Such destruction of wealth may also be seen in deposits such as that from a bog at Hjortspring, Denmark, an apparent votive offering of the equipment and boat of a defeated fourth-century BC warrior band (Randsborg 1995). This deliberate destruction of weaponry and wealth echoes classical authors' accounts of late La Tène Gaul (e.g. Julius Caesar's *de Bello Gallico* 6.17) and is reflected by the evidence from excavated temples such as Gournay-sur-Aronde and Ribemont-sur-Ancre in northern France,

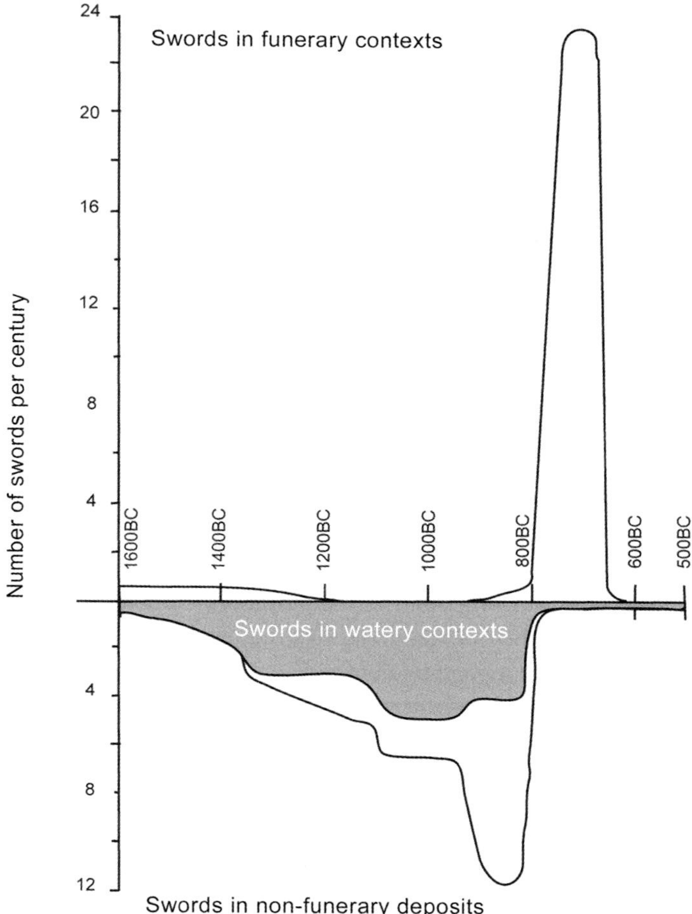

FIGURE 31.3 Graph showing change in deposition of metalwork in the latest Bronze Age/earliest Iron Age of central France.

Redrawn after Milcent (2004): fig. 31

which have produced large quantities of weaponry, much of it deliberately broken and damaged (Brunaux 2000; Chapter 30). While often explained as votive deposition, the act of disposing of metalwork in wet places or at sanctuaries is also likely to have related to how status and social order were maintained through the conspicuous consumption of high-status material by elites or the wider community (Fitzpatrick 1984: 187). Such items were potentially deliberately taken out of circulation, perhaps to ensure that control of resources continued to reside with those who had access to the production and exchange of material wealth.

Burial, Status, and Exchange

One of the clearest ways in which status and wealth are often thought to have been expressed is through burial. Perhaps one of the best examples of the ways archaeologists have understood the nature of wealth in the Iron Age and how status was obtained, is that of the late Hallstatt societies of central Europe. These burials are discussed elsewhere in the book, but it is worth noting here that many of them were characterized by very rich grave goods, including objects imported from Greek and Etruscan societies. In some instances, such items were elaborate and exotic, like the Greek wine mixing *krater* from Vix, France, and the couch from Hochdorf, Germany. The presence of such grave goods has been the focus of understanding these societies and the role of Mediterranean imports in displaying status. Susan Frankenstein and Mike Rowlands (1978: 84–85) argued this could be regarded as part of a prestige goods economy; the wealth and status of individuals could be discerned from the range and types of items included in their burials. They suggested the status of chiefs relied on obtaining prestige items and controlling circulation of them to their vassals. Their status was maintained by continued connections to Greek and Etruscan traders to obtain such items and, in return, to supply them with the raw resources they required (Frankenstein and Rowlands 1978: 77). As status was maintained by obtaining and circulating prestige goods, such a society was inherently unstable as others could acquire status by obtaining similar items (Kristiansen 1998: 267).

Defining status on the basis of quantity and quality of grave goods has been attempted for other periods and regions, such as the burial tumuli of the Sarmatians and Scythians in southern central Asia (Hanks 2000; Davis-Kimball 2002). Here too it has been argued that status was related to the elites' relationship with the Mediterranean world (Kristiansen 1998: 288). Late La Tène cremation burials found in north-eastern France and south-eastern England also provide a range of grave goods, including imports from the Roman world. This too has been seen as the conspicuous consumption by aristocratic elites controlling new exchange routes between Rome and its peripheries (Haselgrove 1982; Cunliffe 1988: 141).

In these examples, the status of putative elites has been suggested by many authors to be based on control over exchange and trade. However, we need to be wary of envisioning such status as representing control over proto-market economies. Exchange potentially had complex roles within Iron Age societies (see Chapter 27); as the idea of prestige goods suggests, the value of objects may not necessarily have been related merely to their inherent value. Drawing on the work of anthropologist Mary Helms (1988), it has been suggested that such items could have been imbued with power relating to their complex artefact biographies from being passed through many hands (Diepeveen-Jansen 2001: 26). Such concepts need not only relate to tangible objects; the unusual Greek-style mud-brick ramparts of the late Hallstatt *Fürstensitz* at the Heuneburg, Germany (Krausse et al. 2016: 52) or the outlying broch of Edin's

Hall, south-east Scotland (Harding 2004: 187), both far from the main focus of such structures, may have conveyed status by associating their builders with exotic knowledge of worlds far removed from most inhabitants.

Status Through Conspicuous Consumption

There are a number of problems in interpreting status from burials in the ways suggested in the previous section. Most significantly, we must remind ourselves that material wealth in burials need not necessarily reflect the status of the deceased, but instead those of the living (Parker Pearson 1999: 84), potentially creating status through interments representing 'ancestors' (Diepeveen-Jansen 2001: 29). The models described also rely on imported material from the Mediterranean acting as the source of wealth for elites who controlled exchange. In contrast, Michael Dietler (1990) has argued that the way in which status was obtained may not have been through controlling the supply of prestige items from the Mediterranean, but that these were only a part of a broader way of expressing wealth and maintaining social status. The lack of exotic or imported objects beyond a small number of graves and locations suggests that they were not significantly redistributed, and thus unlikely to have been part of a prestige goods network (Dietler 1990: 386). Dietler instead emphasizes that much of the material from late Hallstatt and early La Tène graves (the drinking horns from Schwarzenbach, cauldron from Hochdorf, and wine mixing vessel or *krater* from Vix) places an emphasis on communal eating and drinking. Using the concept of 'potlatch', derived from ethnographic studies of North America, Dietler (1990: 382) argues that this emphasis on feasting was part of maintaining status through hospitality, a mechanism which already existed in these communities. In ethnographic examples of potlatch, individuals competed with each other to hold festivals where large amounts of material, in the form of gifts from social debtors, were consumed (destroyed) and provided through feasting, to outshine rivals. This process was often reciprocal, the indebted communities providing comparable potlatches, maintaining status levels, rather than allowing one group or individual to become wealthier (Rosman and Rubel 1971). In such cases, objects were a by-product of obtaining and displaying wealth and status through competitive consumption or 'potlatch'. In the late Hallstatt, therefore, consumption of Mediterranean items potentially differentiated an 'elite' or marked status differences between groups, but within an existing feasting process. Potlatches to maintain status need not have just relied on consuming material objects; Niall Sharples (2007) has suggested that in middle Iron Age Wessex, labour may have been consumed in a similar way, through the accruing of social debts to construct massive monuments, in the form of hillforts.

The late Hallstatt is not the only period when status may have been maintained by large-scale feasting and conspicuous consumption. The presence of large cauldrons from France and Britain dating to the middle and late La Tène indicates that communal eating, frequently aimed at displaying the status of the provider(s), was relatively common (see Chapter 39). The large middens found in southern Britain, dating to the latest Bronze Age and earliest Iron Age (for example at Potterne and East Chisenbury), have also been argued as sites of intensive feasting (and the destruction of wealth), perhaps representing neutral locations for surrounding communities (Waddington 2008: 164). The destruction of wealth through such 'potlatches', as a means of displaying status and maintaining the amount of material in circulation, may have been relatively common in Iron Age societies and has been used to explain much of the other evidence we have for the deliberate destruction of valuable objects, such as the metalwork found in wet places and in other burials across Europe (Brun 1987: 162; Sharples 2010: 97).

Adornment and Display

Modes of eating and feasting may have been used to maintain status and also to express it, differentiating sectors of the community. The late La Tène of north-western Europe sees the appearance of new forms of dining equipment alongside new forms of drink, especially wine, and changing consumption patterns. The presence of fire-dogs (andirons) in late La Tène burials from southern England and northern Gaul (such as Baldock and La Mailleraye-sur-Seine) or the range of wine drinking equipment from Welwyn, England, and Goeblingen-Nospelt, Luxembourg, implies that these too may have denoted the ability to provide feasting opportunities for vassals (Poux 2004: 222–224; Hill 2007: 27). However, both the claimed imitation of the Mediterranean *symposium* by late Hallstatt elites (Krausse 1999: 205) and the late La Tène adoption of imported dining equipment marked more complex ways of differentiating sections of society than just adopting markers of status from elsewhere. Only those inculcated into such practices would have understood (and been able to participate in) these dining events, marking them out from the rest of the community. These changing modes of dining were reflected by changing patterns of adornment, with increasing quantities of brooches and new forms of dress and appearance (Hill 1997) marking new ways in which status was expressed. By contrast, the lack of evidence for differences in diet in the apparently stratified society of middle Iron Age East Yorkshire (Jay and Richards 2006) may mean that foodways were not always related to status. Anthropological studies (e.g. Lévi-Strauss 1969) caution us, however, that variation in the cooking and quality of food may have been more significant than the types of food consumed.

Adornment seems to have frequently been part of displaying social differentiation. Torcs (neck-rings) are perhaps one of the most widely recognized items from the Iron Age which potentially signified status. Some of these were in precious metals, such as the gold examples from Vix (France) in the early fifth century BC and Waldalgesheim (Germany) in the fourth century BC or those of very different style from north-western Iberia, such as the examples from Burela (Spain) and Vilas-Boas (Portugal), dating to the fourth to first centuries BC (Figure 31.4). The fact that torcs are also displayed on various statues, such as the fifth-century BC example from the Glauberg, Germany (depicting the same torc found at the site), and the late Hallstatt figure from Hirschlanden, Germany, suggests they conveyed the status of the wearer (Frey 2002; Armit and Grant 2008: 413). Elsewhere, the decorated headdress from the second-century BC 'warrior burial' from Deal, England (Parfitt 1995), the elaborate gold headdress and clothes of the individual from the fourth- to third-century BC Scythian burial at Issyk, Kazakstan (Davis-Kimball 2002: 346), and the massive decorated arm-rings of the first and second centuries AD from north-east Scotland (Harding 2004: 193) have all been argued as evidence that elaborate costume was used to mark status.

Although the richness of burials changes over the Iron Age, status need not have been represented just by elaborate objects. The flat inhumation cemeteries found across many areas of central Europe in the middle La Tène, although lacking imports, still appear to have used items to mark social status. Glass bangles, brooches, torcs, finger-rings, weaponry, and occasional gold objects (e.g. at Wallendorf and Mannersdorf) were clearly used to differentiate status, alongside expressing other forms of identity, such as gender and age (Kaenel 1990; Bühler et al. 2008; Ramsl 2011). Whether objects such as gold torcs were also imbued with ritual significance is difficult to determine, but the mistletoe-style headdress found at the Glauberg (Baitinger and Pinsker 2002),

FIGURE 31.4 Gold torc and bracelets from Waldalgesheim, Rheinland-Pfalz, Germany.
Photo: Jürgen Vogel, © LVR-Landesmuseum Bonn

alongside the possible ritual roles of individuals like the woman from Vix (Knüsel 2002), may imply that secular and spiritual status were often combined (Hedeager 1992: 27–31; Fitzpatrick 2005).

The 'wealth' of such objects may not necessarily have been in their material value, but as results of deliberate acts of conspicuous consumption. The late La Tène bronze mirrors from Britain, for example, may have conveyed the complexity of skills and artistic ranges of the artisans, as well as the natural resources 'consumed' by such an object (Joy 2011: 208). The first-century BC gold brooches found at Corent, France (Poux 2012: 236), and Winchester, England (Hill et al. 2004), alongside the two chain torcs from Winchester and from Broighter, Ireland—all potentially made by jewellers from the Mediterranean (Hill et al. 2004: 16)—might also have conveyed exotic contacts and expert craftsmanship. We should be wary of necessarily regarding such metalwork as the preserve of elites (Giles 2008); some of these objects, such as the Snettisham torcs or items from late Hallstatt burials, may have been symbols of communal, rather than individual, status (Eggert 1999; Hill 2007: 21). While we can say how complex and prestigious an item may have been, we cannot be certain such items were worn by a chief whose status was achieved through warrior prowess or someone whose status was conferred by the community. The latter might have been similar to the 'big man' societies anthropologists have recognized in the Pacific (Brun and Ruby 2008: 84), or like the elected *vergobrets* of late La Tène Gaul (Caesar *de Bello Gallico* 1.16; Hill 2011: 247). Even by the late Iron Age, when individuals whom we can label 'kings' appear—their names recorded on the newly emerging inscribed coinage with labels such as *rex* (Creighton 2000)—they seem to have held their status in trust rather than as a right. Within the larger social entities of the late La Tène, power and status appear to have remained fluid (Moore 2011). Coinage, for example, while marking a new form of portable wealth, appears to have been used primarily to create and maintain social obligations (clientage; Creighton 2000: 14). Strabo's (*Geography* 4.2.3) account of Luernios, king of the Arverni in Gaul, scattering gold and silver coins to his people potentially represents one way rulers used largesse to maintain their status. New forms of material culture could also challenge existing ways of establishing status; coinage not only signalled wealth and patronage, but much of its imagery, echoing that of early Imperial Roman coinage, also signified connections to a new external source of status: Rome (Creighton 2000).

Monuments and Status: Hierarchies or Heterarchies?

For much of the preceding discussion the emphasis has been on objects: the transfer, ownership, and deposition of material culture. Yet in many parts of Europe, wealth and status are likely to have consisted largely of other things, in particular the control of land, agricultural resources, and the ability to mobilize labour. Much of Iron Age Europe is characterized by the presence of enclosed monuments, such as the elaborate multivallate hillforts of the middle Iron Age in Britain (Cunliffe 2005: 388–396), the *castros* of northwestern Iberia (Sastre 2011), and timber fortifications, like the early Iron Age lakeside settlements in Poland (Harding and Rączkowski 2010). The extent to which the presence of such monuments reflects the existence of highly stratified societies has been a focus of debate over the last thirty years. For many, the existence of fortified sites has been regarded as further evidence for warrior elites whose status was manifested through elaborate ramparts. Barry Cunliffe (1995: 93–95) suggests that hillforts like Danebury, Hampshire, represented central places, commanding the control and redistribution of agricultural resources by a resident elite whose status and position were maintained through raiding on competing groups. This vision relies heavily on the Celtic model described earlier, combining archaeological and textual evidence to emphasize a highly stratified society dominated by a warrior elite (see Chapter 29).

The relationship between such monuments and status is potentially complex, however. In Britain, J. D. Hill's (1996) detailed analysis of evidence from the Danebury environs suggested that many hillforts were unlikely to represent displays of consumption by an individual chief or warrior elite. Hill demonstrated that there was little evidence that Danebury had greater storage capacity than other settlements and there was little supporting evidence (for example the presence of more metalwork) to signify the presence of an elite. Evidence for the existence of elites within these societies might be sought elsewhere, for example in differentiation in house sizes: larger structures marking chiefly residences. Yet evidence for status expressed through household architecture is largely lacking; Clarke's (1972) assertion that variance in house size at Glastonbury, Britain, reflected social status no longer corresponds with the archaeological evidence (Coles and Minnit 1995). The role of large houses in the British late Bronze Age and early Iron Age, marking significant consumption of resources perhaps to denote status (Sharples 2010: 206), is starkly contrasted with the flimsier house structures and lack of house-size differentiation at major hillforts in the middle Iron Age, including Danebury (Hill 1995b: 49; Sharples 2010: 237). Elsewhere, it could be argued that the large apsidal building from the late Hallstatt *Fürstensitz* at Mont Lassois, Burgundy (Brun and Ruby 2008: 64), or much larger roundhouses surrounded by clusters of smaller ones, as at the early Iron Age hillfort of Crickley Hill, England (Dixon 1976), or the brochs situated within larger 'villages', as at Howe, Orkney (Armit 2003: 98), represent chiefly residences. However, in all cases other roles, as communal meeting places or sanctuaries, are just as plausible.

Hill (1996, 2011) and others (e.g. Crumley 1995; Moore 2007) suggest that for many areas of Europe, particularly Britain and northern Iberia, it seems more likely that forms of segmentary or heterarchical social organization existed. In some models the household owned land and resources largely for its own consumption (Hingley 1984; Hill 1995b) and there were limits to the extent to which status disparities could exist. Hillforts in such societies could represent communal 'wealth' and networks of social obligations from other communities (Hill 2011; Sastre 2011). In some instances the construction of monumental ramparts, in the form of hillforts (Figure 31.5), may have

FIGURE 31.5 The elaborate earthworks of Maiden Castle hillfort, southern England, potentially reflecting potlatch labour exchange.

Photo: © Historic England, with permission

marked differences in the size and social obligations of each community, but they need not have been the residences of elites (cf. Sharples 2010). A similar debate has taken place concerning the monumental stone-built brochs of western and northern Scotland. Some have argued that the monumentality of brochs must mean they represented the elite status of their owners (Sharples and Parker Pearson 1997). Others argue there is little evidence to suggest brochs represented the top of a settlement hierarchy; instead they seem to represent autonomous communities in which most people lived (Armit 2003: 84). Such relatively 'acephalous' societies did not only exist in north-western Iberia and Britain, but can also be argued for in areas traditionally perceived as hierarchical, such as middle La Tène northern Gaul (Haselgrove 2012: 51) and the very different societies of the southern French coast. In this last area, settlement form and widespread consumption of imported foodstuffs implies an emphasis on levelling status disparities (Dietler 2010). Even the massive stone-faced ramparts of late La Tène *oppida* such as Bibracte in France, or the earthworks of polyfocal complexes such as Bagendon in Britain (Moore 2012), normally seen as evidence of an elite, could be regarded as expressions of community status and negotiated forms of power (Moore 2017).

Envisioning many Iron Age societies as heterarchical does not mean that status differentiations did not exist. Within and between communities there were almost certainly some individuals and households who held more social capital than others (Hill 2011: 257), but such claims to status were fluid and temporary. Such differences might be seen in the varied treatment of the dead in Britain (Chapter 4), which might have signified varying status or social role. The construction of enclosures around smaller settlements may also have marked status differentiation. The elaborate nature of small enclosures in areas such as the Welsh Marches and Cheviot hills of Britain and the small *castros* (hillforts) of some parts of north-western Iberia suggests a potentially excessive use of labour beyond the requirements and capabilities of the community enclosed. In some areas, this may have marked competition (Frodsham et al. 2007; González-García et al. 2011), but such enclosures might also signify cooperation between communities (Wigley 2007). Acting as a 'levelling mechanism', the mutual exchange of labour to construct these enclosures could maintain social relationships and might even deliberately downplay status differences between communities. Processes of exchange, akin to the reciprocal gift-giving noted by anthropologists such as Mauss (1954) and Godelier (1999), could act in similar way: the exchange of objects such as quernstones or ceramics maintaining sets of social obligations between communities, while also ensuring status disparities did not become excessive (Moore 2007).

Occupation Groups and Status

As the discussion in the previous section illustrates, how we use the varied evidence to reconstruct Iron Age societies, as highly stratified or more egalitarian, dictates to what extent we can envision specific social groups. Hierarchical models, like that created for Danebury, have frequently used the evidence from classical sources to argue for the existence of defined social roles in Iron Age societies. However, as discussed, it is clear that Iron Age communities across Europe varied in time and space and it is unlikely they all mirrored Caesar's image of the Aedui. There is, however, evidence from many regions and periods of social groups with particular roles in society.

Warriors, Slaves, and Druids

Many visions of Iron Age society regard status as having been obtained through warrior prowess; indeed, some have seen warfare as the 'cultural means of defining status and recruiting dependants' in the Iron Age (Rowlands 1994: 4). Implicit in these accounts and identified in the 'Celtic' model of society is the existence of specialist warriors. The inclusion of martial grave goods in various burial traditions from Britain (Hunter 2005), Scythia (Davis-Kimball 2002), and Iberia (Graells Fabregat 2011) among others, has led to their identification as 'warrior burials'. The presence of weapons might signify status, but need not mark the existence of a specialized warrior elite (Collis 1994: 33). For north-western Iberia it has been suggested that skill in warfare need not have automatically led to political power (Sastre 2008) but was a status granted by the community, rather than imposed (González García et al. 2011: 288). Others have argued that the limited number of warrior burials in many areas, such as the British Isles, suggests warfare was relatively rare, or at least not the main way in which status was acquired. Instead, warfare may have been a periodic activity by people who were, for the majority of the time, farmers of relatively equal standing (Hill 1996; Sastre 2011: 280; cf Chapter 30).

Many classical sources highlight the presence of slaves in Iron Age society, while models of exchange between the Mediterranean and Iron Age worlds often stress their importance as a commodity (Arnold 1988). Evidence for slaves also comes from archaeological examples of slave chains, such as that from Llyn Cerrig Bach, Wales (Taylor 2001), and from *oppida* such as Manching (Arnold 1988: 180). However, some sources (e.g. Tacitus *Germania* 25) indicate that the place of slaves in society could be very different from that of those in the classical world, sometimes holding social roles similar to other members of the community. We need to be cautious, therefore, in using texts to define social classes in Iron Age societies, remembering that they refer to specific times and locations. Most importantly, we are seeing these communities through the subjective accounts of Mediterranean observers (Dunham 1995).

The existence of Iron Age ritual specialists has also been drawn largely from classical sources. Evidence for priests or druids is explored by Aldhouse-Green (Chapter 42), but some have suggested that particular items, such as bronze spoons from Britain, represent evidence for such ritual specialists (Fitzpatrick 2007). The inclusion of Roman medical instruments in the late Iron Age burial at Stanway, Essex (Crummy et al. 2007), and that from Pottenbrunn, Austria (Ramsl 2002), are unlikely to represent 'doctors' but more likely ritual specialists. The nature of such burials demonstrates the close relationship between ritual, medical knowledge, status, and other specialized skills, such as smithing (Budd and Taylor 1995: 139), reflected in the multiple roles druids appear to have had (Caesar *de Bello Gallico* 6.13). This reminds us that, for most of the European Iron Age, there is limited evidence for the presence of a dedicated priestly caste; instead, ritual behaviour was most likely conducted largely within the domestic sphere by people engaged for the majority of time in other activities (see Chapter 41).

Craftworkers, Miners, and Traders

Since V. G. Childe's claim that knowledge of bronze was brought to temperate Europe by itinerant smiths, the existence of craft specialists has been central to many visions of later prehistoric Europe (Gibson 1996; Wells 1996: 85). Evidence from Hallstatt and the Dürrnberg, Austria, indicates that salt mining was being undertaken by skilled workers, with evidence from their diets that mining was a year-round occupation by specialized communities (Kristiansen 1998: 230; Stöllner et al. 2003). The appearance of fortified sites and focus of production at central locations, as at the Heuneburg in the late Hallstatt, indicates an increasing specialization of manufacture. Some of the material from related burials, such as Hochdorf, may even represent production at specialist workshops (Wells 1996: 90), while the quality of some 'Celtic' metalwork has been regarded as the product of specialized 'artists' (Jope 2000: 208). The striking similarity of certain objects, such as the curved weapons from southern Iberia, might also suggest that specialized, itinerant craftspeople existed (Quesada et al. 2000).

By the late La Tène, the *oppida* of Gaul and central Europe, such as Bibracte, were producing particular objects in specific workshops (Guillaumet 2006: 88), marking the emergence of specialized craft groups as part of increased control over manufacture (Henderson 1991; Wells 1996: 92). Specialists at such *oppida* also probably included die engravers and coin minters who produced the intricately designed coinage in circulation across much of Europe at this period (Cunliffe 1997: 131). Such specialization in the middle and late La Tène was also seen in other material culture, such as glass beads and bangles. Specialized centres for the production of glass objects, such as Meare, Somerset, and Culbin Sands, near Inverness, and the appearance of craft-focused open settlements in central Europe may mark the emergence of specializing communities (Henderson 1991).

The pattern is not a simple one, however. Many *oppida* in central Europe and in Gaul appear to have been divided into smaller family or kin units, each potentially relatively economically independent (Wells 1996: 91). This suggests that, as with the more dispersed patterns of manufacturing seen in many middle La Tène communities, the individuals involved may not always have been specialists. Indeed, most of north-west Europe may have consisted of communities who were unable to support full-time specialists. This does not mean that activities such as salt producing and pottery manufacture were not dedicated crafts, but that the individuals involved were more likely to have undertaken such activities seasonally, alongside acting as farmers (Gibson 1996: 113; Giles 2007: 398; Moore 2007). The same appears likely of those involved in facilitating trade. For most of the Iron Age systems of down-the-line exchange seem the most likely explanation for the spread of objects. Distributions of artefacts along coastlines, such as salt briquetage along the western British coast and material from Brittany in central southern Britain, implies seaborne trade (Matthews 1999; Fitzpatrick 2001), but the relatively small-scale nature of these exchanges suggests dedicated traders are unlikely for most of the Iron Age.

There is relatively little evidence of the status of groups such as craftworkers. Metalworking tools in some graves, such as those from Rudston, England (Figure 31.6; Giles 2012: 160), St Geogen, Austria (Wells 1996: 92), and Bibracte (Guillaumet 2006: 89), and tools alongside rich grave goods (as at Hochdorf) might suggest some individuals were being marked out for their specialist role, but whether this reflected their different status is unclear. It has been suggested that the inherently magical processes involved in skills such as metalworking may have been linked to social status (Giles 2007). Others suggest that blacksmiths were itinerant, fringe members of society, explaining the location of metalworking on the edges of settlements as a reflection of the liminal role of these activities and the individuals involved (Hingley 1997). It has been suggested too that the miners from the Dürrnberg were controlled by an elite and their role held no particular status (Stöllner et al. 2003).

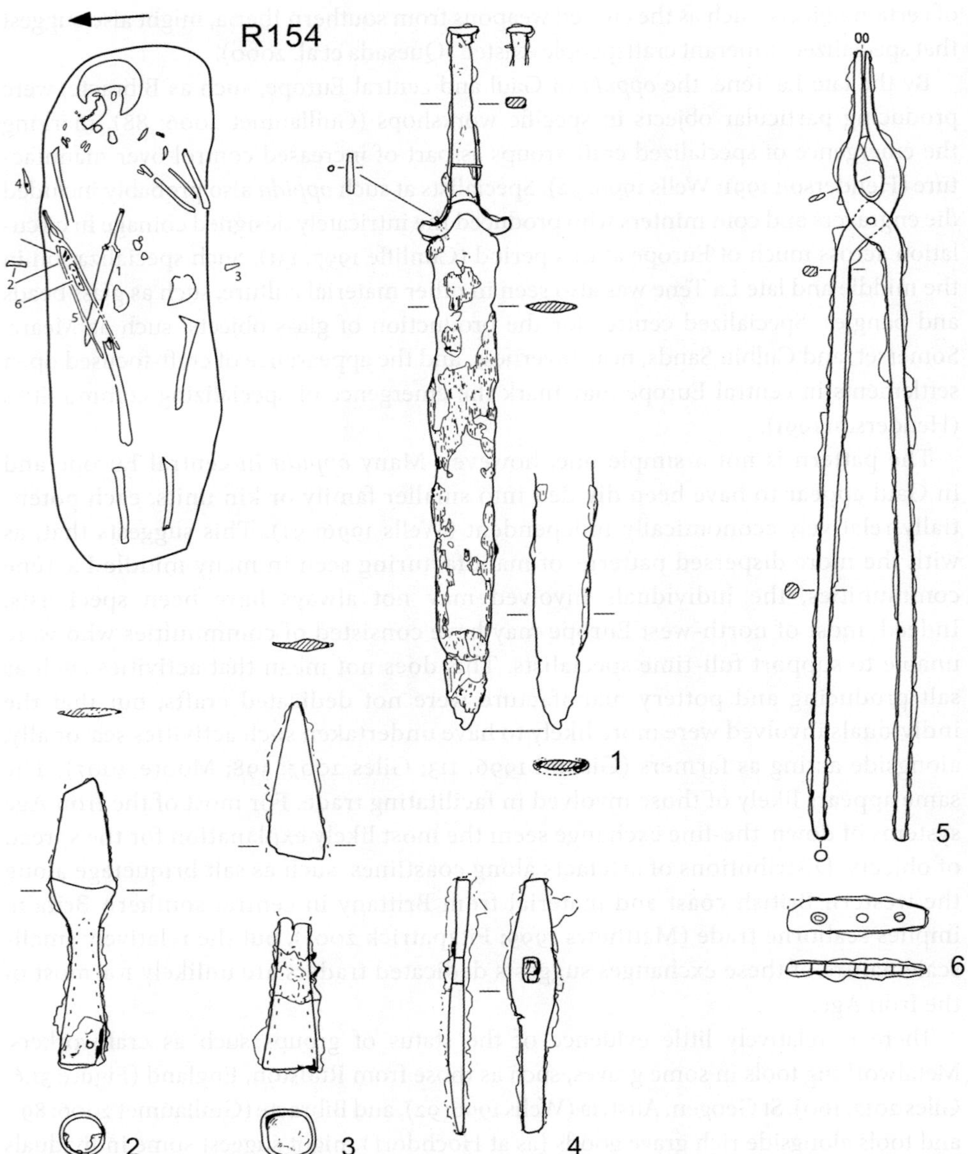

FIGURE 31.6 Grave of possible ironworker from Rudston, East Yorkshire, England. Various scales.

Drawing © Melanie Giles (2012): fig. 5.19, with permission

Gender, Age, and Status

I have sketched out the varied ways in which status and wealth were obtained and expressed and what specialist occupation groups may have existed, but who was able to obtain status or perform such roles, and to what extent was this constrained by age or gender? It has frequently been implied in the past that evidence of martial equipment, in burials or as votive offerings, signifies that status was a particularly male preserve (see Pope and Ralston 2011). The presence of rich material in female burials has often been explained away in the past; the elaborate burial at Vix, for example, has been interpreted as the daughter of a Greek trader or nobleman rather than a woman of status in her own right (Kristiansen 1998: 273; see also Chapter 34). Yet a striking element of many areas of the European Iron Age is that rich grave goods were frequently not restricted to one particular sex: for example in early La Tène central Europe (Arnold 1995: 155; Diepeveen-Jansen 2001), Britain (Pope and Ralston 2011), and Scythia (Davis-Kimball 2002). Similarly, classical writers' identification of Boudicca and Cartimandua as powerful queens in the late Iron Age indicates that women could obtain high status in Iron Age societies (Cunliffe 1997: 109). Such evidence may indicate that status was achieved through means, such as warrior prowess or social networks, irrespective of gender (Arnold 1995: 164). Age too does not appear to have been a barrier to social roles. Analysis of the shoes from the mine-working at the Dürrnberg, Austria, suggests that children were frequently employed as miners from an early age (Stöllner et al. 2003: 138). Meanwhile, treatment of the dead does not indicate that status was restricted only to elders in the population (Pope and Ralston 2011).

Conclusion and Long-Term Perspectives

Through examining some of the varied ways in which European Iron Age societies expressed wealth and status, it becomes increasingly apparent that overarching models of how status was obtained and wealth expressed are highly problematic. Status was likely to have been obtained by a number of intertwined means: ritual, charisma, control of prestige goods, warrior prowess, clientage, and maintaining social obligations. Even within the same societies the emphasis on such aspects is likely to have changed over time.

From this varied evidence, some key themes emerge which are fundamental to how we approach the European Iron Age. The first is that definitions of wealth and status underpin reconstructions of these societies and the broader debate between regarding them as predominantly hierarchical or as some form of heterarchy. For many parts of Europe, there is little evidence for the stratified, warrior elite-dominated societies which many past models envisaged. Instead, status and wealth were expressed through very different mechanisms or downplayed. Even where rich burials and elaborately decorated objects exist, what we often perceive as evidence of status (rich grave goods, precious metal objects, monuments) may be markers of communal feasting, conspicuous consumption, or power held in trust. These were part of levelling mechanisms (potlatch, gift exchange) that minimized status disparities and limited the development of fixed hierarchies. Even in seemingly more complex societies, such as those in late Iron Age Gaul and southern Britain, status roles such as 'king' could be acquired and demonstrated in more nuanced ways than simple hierarchical models imply (Crumley 1995; Hill 2011).

Despite the diversity of modes of expressing wealth and status, it is apparent that there are longer-term regional and chronological trends in the Iron Age record. In areas such as the Low Countries wealth was persistently based on the construction of houses and ownership of land and/or livestock (see e.g. Gerritsen 2003; Webley 2008). Elsewhere, in Ireland and eastern England, wealth (or symbols of status) seems largely portable for much of the Iron Age. By contrast, in central southern Britain status (by individuals or communities) appears persistently demonstrated through the consumption of labour in earthworks and settlement boundaries. Such trends have sometimes been explained as related to underlying economics: pastoralists tending to be more egalitarian, for example. However, such simple equations between economy and expressions of wealth have been challenged by anthropology (e.g. Boehm 1993) and should be viewed with caution. It largely remains to be seen whether forms of levelling mechanism as discussed here perpetuated modes of displaying status over time; there certainly needs to be caution in seeing deposition of metalwork in burials or wet places as marking the same social mechanisms across time and space. Such broader patterns may also mask a greater diversity, as appears to be the case in Britain. On the continent, local variations such as potentially more heterarchical societies in parts of northern and western France may have been obscured by the focus on certain areas where rich burials have been found, and such processes were undoubtedly dynamic rather than static (Gerritsen 2003: 254).

Past concepts of increasingly stratified and hierarchical societies over the Iron Age as part of social evolution are also hard to match against the evidence. Even in the late La Tène, where more defined social groups such as crafts specialists and druids existed, it seems likely that many roles, such as warrior, and any status they conveyed, were temporary; most of Europe consisted largely of farming communities where variations in social rank were limited or largely downplayed. The appearance of highly stratified societies may have been the exception rather than the rule. However, whether the appearance of rich burials and clearer social distinctions at certain times and places represents a traditional 'Celtic' vision of elites or not, its emergence (and disappearance) requires explanation. In the past such processes have been aligned with the ebbing and flowing of the impact of the Mediterranean world: more stratified societies dependent on exchange with the Greeks and Etruscans, declining once Mediterranean influence disappears, only to re-emerge in the late Iron Age with opportunities for wealth and status provided by the expansion of Rome (e.g. Cunliffe 1988; Kristiansen 1998). Such patterns, however, underplay the very different ways in which status was expressed between such societies; with some exceptions (noted in this chapter), the elites of the late Iron Age often seem to have expressed power more communally through monuments (*oppida*) than via elaborate burials.

Changes in levels of stratification and modes of status display may also have had more to do with internal developments and social pressures. For example, new expressions of wealth and status in the late Iron Age, through new burial rites and material culture, may have been a corollary of managing the larger social entities emerging as a result of increased production and population rise, rather than depending on wealth generated from trade with the Mediterranean (e.g. Sharples 2010: 170 on Wessex; Webley 2008: 153 on Jutland). We must be cautious, too, of transferring relatively discrete and sometimes short-lived examples of wealth and status expression to the rest of the Iron Age. We need to ask ourselves to what extent the focus of study of Iron Age societies has 'created' the significance of these regions and periods, rather than reflecting the reality of social processes in the first millennium BC (Moore and Armada 2011). These expressions might be seen as exceptions, resulting from particular combinations of social and economic pressures, but not necessarily part of an underlying trend in how Iron Age societies expressed wealth and status.

Acknowledgements

I am very grateful to Jody Joy, Niall Sharples, Katharina Rebay-Salisbury, and Colin Haselgrove for their insightful comments on an earlier draft of this chapter. My thanks to Simon James for permission to reproduce his reconstruction drawing of 'Celtic' society, Mel Giles for permission to reproduce the image of the Rudston burial, and the Landesmuseum Bonn for permission to reproduce the photograph of the Waldalgesheim torc.

References

Armit, I. 2003. *Towers in the North: The Brochs of Scotland*. Stroud: Tempus.

Armit, I., and P. Grant. 2008. 'Gesture politics and the art of ambiguity: The Iron Age statue from Hirschlanden'. *Antiquity* 82, 316: 409–422.

Arnold, B. 1988. 'Slavery in late prehistoric Europe: Recovering evidence for social structure in Iron Age society', in D. B. Gibson and M. N. Geselowitz (eds) *Tribe and Polity in Late Prehistoric Europe: Demography, Production, and Exchange in the Evolution of Complex Social Systems*: 179–192. New York: Plenum.

Arnold, B. 1995. '"Honorary males" or women of substance? Gender, status and power in Iron Age Europe'. *Journal of European Archaeology* 3, 2: 153–168.

Baitinger, H., and B. Pinsker. 2002. *Das Rätsel der Kelten vom Glauberg: Glaube—Mythos—Wirklichkeit*. Stuttgart: Theiss.

Becker, K. 2009. 'Iron Age Ireland—finding an invisible people', in G. Cooney, K. Becker, J. Coles, M. Ryan, and S. Sievers (eds) *Relics of Old Decency: Archaeological Studies in Later Prehistory. Festschrift for Barry Raftery*: 353–361. Dublin: Wordwell.

Boehm, C. 1993. 'Egalitarian behaviour and reverse dominance hierarchy'. *Current Anthropology* 34, 3: 227–254.

Bradley, R. 1998. *The Passage of Arms: An Archaeological Analysis of Prehistoric Hoards and Votive Deposits*, 2nd edition. Oxford: Oxbow.

Brun, P. 1987. *Princes et princesses de la Celtique: Le premier âge du Fer (850–450 av. J.C.)*. Paris: Errance.

Brun, P., and P. Ruby. 2008. *L'âge du Fer en France. Premières villes, premiers états celtiques.* Paris: La Découverte.

Brunaux, J.-L. 2000. *Les religions Gauloises (Ve–Ier siècles av. J.C.): Nouvelles approches sur les rituels Celtiques de la Gaule indépendante.* Paris: Errance.

Budd, P., and T. Taylor. 1995. 'The Faerie Smith meets the bronze industry: Magic versus science in the interpretation of prehistoric metal making'. *World Archaeology* 27: 133–143.

Bühler, B., J. V. S. Megaw, M. R. Megaw, and P. C. Ramsl. 2008. 'Grab 115 des latènezeitlichen Gräberfeldes von Mannersdorf am Leithagebirge (Niederösterreich): Typologische, technologische und stilistiche Studien zu den beiden Goldarmreifen'. *Germania* 86: 103–134.

Clarke, D. L. 1972. 'A provisional model of an Iron Age society and its settlement system', in D. L. Clarke (ed.) *Models in Archaeology*: 801–869. London: Methuen.

Coles, J., and J. Minnit. 1995. *Industrious and Fairly Civilised: The Glastonbury Lake Village.* Taunton: Somerset Levels Project and Somerset County Council Museums Service.

Collis, J. R. 1994. 'Reconstructing Iron Age society', in K. Kristiansen and J. Jensen (eds) *Europe in the First Millennium BC*: 31–39. Sheffield: J. R. Collis.

Creighton, J. 2000. *Coins and Power in Late Iron Age Britain*. Cambridge: Cambridge University Press.

Crumley, C. 1995. 'Heterarchy and the analysis of complex societies', in C. Crumley, R. Ehrenreich, and J. Levy (eds) *Heterarchy and the Analysis of Complex Societies.* Archaeological Papers of the American Anthropological Association 6: 1–5. Ann Arbor: American Anthropological Association.

Crummy, P., S. Benfield, N. Crummy, V. Rigby, and D. Shimmin. 2007. *Stanway: An Elite Burial Site at Camulodunum*. Britannia Monograph Series 24. London: Society for the Promotion of Roman Studies.

Cunliffe, B. W. 1988. *Greeks, Romans and Barbarians: Spheres of Interaction*. London: Batsford.

Cunliffe, B. W. 1995. *Danebury: An Iron Age Hillfort in Hampshire, Vol. 6: A Hillfort Community in Perspective*. CBA Research Report 102. London: Council for British Archaeology.

Cunliffe, B. W. 1997. *The Ancient Celts*. Oxford: Oxford University Press.

Cunliffe, B. W. 2005. *Iron Age Communities in Britain: An Account of England, Scotland and Wales from the Seventh Century BC until the Roman Conquest*, 4th edition. London: Routledge.

Davis-Kimball, J. 2002. 'Statuses of eastern early Iron Age nomads'. *Ancient West and East* 1, 2: 332–356.

De Mulder, G., and J. Bourgeois. 2011. 'Shifting centres of power and changing elite symbolism in the Scheldt fluvial basin during the late Bronze Age and the Iron Age', in T. Moore and X.-L. Armada (eds) *Atlantic Europe in the First Millennium BC: Crossing the Divide*: 302–318. Oxford: Oxford University Press.

Diepeveen-Jansen, M. 2001. *People, Ideas and Goods: New Perspectives on 'Celtic Barbarians' in Western and Central Europe (500–250 BC)*. Amsterdam Archaeological Studies 7. Amsterdam: Amsterdam University Press.

Dietler, M. 1990. 'Driven by drink: The role of drinking in the political economy and the case of early Iron Age France'. *Journal of Anthropological Archaeology* 9: 352–406.

Dietler, M. 2010. *Archaeologies of Colonialism: Consumption, Entanglement and Violence in Ancient Mediterranean France*. Berkeley and Los Angeles: University of California Press.

Dixon, P. 1976. 'Crickley Hill, 1969–1972', in D. W. Harding (ed.) *Hillforts: Later Prehistoric Earthworks in Britain and Ireland*: 162–175. London: Academic Press.

Dunham, S. B. 1995. 'Caesar's perception of Gallic social structures', in B. Arnold and D. Blair-Gibson (eds) *Celtic Chiefdom, Celtic State: The Evolution of Complex Social Systems in Prehistoric Europe*: 110–115. Cambridge: Cambridge University Press.

Eggert, M. K. H. 1999. 'Der Tote von Hochdorf: Bemerkungen zum Modus archäologischer Interpretation'. *Archäologisches Korrespondenzblatt* 29: 211–222.

Fischer, D. 1995. 'The early Celts of west central Europe: The semantics of social structure', in B. Arnold and D. Blair Gibson (eds) *Celtic Chiefdom, Celtic State: The Evolution of Complex Social Systems in Prehistoric Europe*: 34–40. Cambridge: Cambridge University Press.

Fitzpatrick, A. P. 1984. 'The deposition of La Tène Iron Age metalwork in watery contexts in southern England', in B. W. Cunliffe and D. Miles (eds) *Aspects of the Iron Age in Central Southern Britain*. OUCA Monograph 2: 178–190. Oxford: University of Oxford Committee for Archaeology.

Fitzpatrick, A. P. 2001. 'Cross-Channel exchange, Hengistbury Head, and the end of the hillforts', in J. R. Collis (ed.) *Society and Settlement in Iron Age Europe; L'Habitat et l'Occupation du Sol en Europe. Actes du XVIIIe Colloque de l'AFEAF, Winchester - Avril 1994*: 82–97. Sheffield: J. R. Collis publications.

Fitzpatrick, A. P. 2005. 'Gifts for the Golden Gods: Iron Age hoards of torques and coins', in C. Haselgrove and D. Wigg-Wolf (eds) *Iron Age Coinage and Ritual Practices*. Studien zu Fundmünzen der Antike 20: 157–182. Mainz: Phillip von Zabern.

Fitzpatrick, A. P. 2007. 'Druids: Towards an archaeology', in C. Gosden, H. Hamerow, P. de Jersey, and G. Lock (eds) *Communities and Connections: Essays in Honour of Barry Cunliffe*: 287–318. Oxford: Oxford University Press.

Frankenstein, S., and M. J. Rowlands. 1978. 'The internal structure and regional context of early Iron Age society in south-western Germany'. *Bulletin of the Institute of Archaeology of the University of London* 15: 73–112.

Frey, O.-H. 2002. 'Menschen oder Heroen? Die Statuen vom Glauberg und die frühe Keltische Großplastik', in H. Baitinger and B. Pinsker (eds) *Glaube—Mythos—Wirklichkeit: Das Rätsel der Kelten vom Glauberg*: 208–218. Stuttgart: Theiss.

Frodsham, P., I. Hedley, and R. Young. 2007. 'Putting the neighbours in their place? Displays of position and possession in northern Cheviot "hillfort" design', in C. Haselgrove and T. Moore (eds) *The Later Iron Age in Britain and Beyond*: 250–265. Oxford: Oxbow.

Garrow, D., and C. Gosden. 2012. *Technologies of Enchantment? Exploring Celtic Art in Britain 400 BC to AD 100*. Oxford: Oxford University Press.

Gerritsen, F. 2003. *Local Identities: Landscape and Community in the Late Prehistoric Meuse-Demer-Scheldt Region*. Amsterdam Archaeological Studies 9. Amsterdam: Amsterdam University Press.

Gibson, D. B. 1996. 'Death of salesman: Childe's itinerant craftsman in the light of present knowledge of late European craft production', in B. Wailes (ed.) *Craft Specialization and Social Evolution: In Memory of V. Gordon Childe*. University Museum Monograph 93: 107–122. Philadelphia: University of Pennsylvania Museum of Archaeology and Anthropology.

Giles, M. 2007. 'Making metals and forging relations: Iron working in the British Iron Age'. *Oxford Journal of Archaeology* 26, 4: 395–413.

Giles, M. 2008. '"Seeing red": The aesthetics of martial objects in the Iron Age of East Yorkshire', in D. Garrow, C. Gosden, and J. D. Hill (eds) *Rethinking Celtic Art*: 59–77. Oxford: Oxbow.

Giles, M. 2012. *A Forged Glamour: Landscape, Identity and Material Culture in the Iron Age*. Oxford: Windgather Press.

Godelier, M. 1999. *The Enigma of the Gift*. Chicago: University of Chicago Press.

González García, F. J., C. Parcero-Oubiña, and X. Ayán Vila. 2011. 'Iron Age societies against the state: An account of the emergence of the Iron Age in north-western Iberia', in T. Moore and X.-L. Armada (eds) *Atlantic Europe in the First Millennium BC: Crossing the Divide*: 285–301. Oxford: Oxford University Press.

Graeber, D. 2001. *Toward an Anthropological Theory of Value: The False Coin of Our Own Dreams*. New York: Palgrave.

Graells Fabregat, R. 2011. 'Warriors and heroes from the north-east of Iberia: A view from the funerary contexts', in T. Moore and X.-L. Armada (eds) *Atlantic Europe in the First Millennium BC: Crossing the Divide*: 575–589. Oxford: Oxford University Press.

Guillaumet, J.-P. 2006. 'Les productions manufacturées à la fin de l'âge du fer', in C. Haselgrove (ed.) *Celtes et gaulois: l'archéologie face à l'histoire: Les mutations de la fin de l'âge du fer. Actes de la table ronde de Cambridge, 7–8 juillet 2005*. Collection Bibracte 12/4: 83–92. Glux-en-Glenne: Centre archéologique européen du Mont Beuvray.

Hanks, B. 2000. 'Iron Age nomadic burials of the Eurasian steppe: A discussion exploring burial ritual complex', in J. Davis-Kimball, E. Murphy, L. Koryakov, and L. Yablonksy (eds) *Kurgans, Ritual Sites, and Settlements: Eurasian Bronze and Iron Age*. British Archaeological Reports International Series 890: 19–30. Oxford: Archaeopress.

Hautenauve, H. 2005. *Les torques d'or du second Âge du Fer en Europe: techniques, typologies et symbolique*. Rennes: Association des Travaux du Laboratoire d'Anthropologie de l'Université de Rennes 1.

Harding, A., and W. Rączkowski. 2010. 'Living on the lake in the Iron Age: New results from aerial photographs, geophysical survey and dendrochronology on sites of Biskupin type'. *Antiquity* 84: 386–404.

Harding, D. 2004. *Northern Britain: Celts, Romans, Natives and Invaders*. London: Routledge.

Haselgrove, C. 1982. 'Wealth, prestige and power: The dynamics of late Iron Age political centralisation in south-east England', in C. Renfrew and S. Shennan (eds) *Ranking, Resource and Exchange*: 79–88. Cambridge: Cambridge University Press.

Haselgrove, C. 2012. 'Reflections on the Iron Age background to the emergence of villa landscapes in northern France', in N. Roymans and T. Derks (eds) *Villa Landscapes in the Roman North: Economy, Culture and Lifestyles*. Amsterdam Archaeological Studies 17: 45–60. Amsterdam: Amsterdam University Press.

Hedeager, L. 1992. *Iron Age Societies: From Tribe to State in Northern Europe 500 BC to AD 700*. Oxford: Blackwell.

Helms, M. W. 1988. *Ulysses' Sail: An Ethnographic Odyssey of Power, Knowledge and Geographical Distance*. Princeton: Princeton University Press.

Henderson, J. 1991. 'Industrial specialisation in late Iron Age Britain and Europe'. *The Archaeological Journal* 148: 104–148.

Hill, J. D. 1995a. 'How should we understand Iron Age societies and hillforts? A contextual study from southern Britain', in J. D. Hill and C. Cumberpatch (eds) *Different Iron Ages: Studies on the Iron Age in Temperate Europe*. British Archaeological Reports International Series 602: 45–66. Oxford: Tempus Reparatum.

Hill, J. D. 1995b. *Ritual and Rubbish in the Iron Age of Wessex*. British Archaeological Reports British Series 242. Oxford: Tempus Reparatum.

Hill, J. D. 1996. 'Hillforts and the Iron Age of Wessex', in T. Champion and J. Collis (eds) *The Iron Age in Britain and Ireland: Recent Trends*: 95–116. Sheffield: J. R. Collis Publications.

Hill, J. D. 1997. 'The end of one kind of body and the beginning of another kind of body? Toilet instruments and Romanization', in A. Gwilt and C. Haselgrove (eds) *Reconstructing Iron Age Societies*: 96–107. Oxford: Oxbow Books.

Hill, J. D. 2007. 'The dynamics of social change in later Iron Age eastern and south-eastern England *c.*300 BC–AD 43', in C. Haselgrove and T. Moore (eds) *The Later Iron Age in Britain and Beyond*: 16–40. Oxford: Oxbow.

Hill, J. D. 2011. 'How did British middle and late pre-Roman Iron Age societies work (if they did)?', in T. Moore and X.-L. Armada (eds) *Atlantic Europe in the First Millennium BC: Crossing the Divide*: 242–263. Oxford: Oxford University Press.

Hill, J. D., A. Spence, S. La Niece, and S. Worrell. 2004. 'The Winchester hoard: A find of unique Iron Age gold jewellery from southern England'. *The Antiquaries Journal* 84: 1–22.

Hingley, R. 1984. 'Towards social analysis in archaeology: Celtic society in the Iron Age of the Upper Thames valley', in B. W. Cunliffe and D. Miles (eds) *Aspects of the Iron Age in Central Southern Britain*. OUCA Monograph 2: 72–88. Oxford: Oxford University Committee for Archaeology.

Hingley, R. 1997. 'Iron, iron working and regeneration: A study of the symbolic meaning of metalwork in Iron Age Britain', in A. Gwilt and C. Haselgrove (eds) *Reconstructing Iron Age Societies*: 9–18. Oxford: Oxbow.

Hunter, F. 2005. 'The image of the warrior in the British Iron Age—coin iconography in context', in C. Haselgrove and D. Wigg-Wolf (eds) *Iron Age Coinage and Ritual Practices*. Studien zu Fundmünzen der Antike 20: 43–68. Mainz: Phillip von Zabern.

James, S. 1993. *Exploring the World of the Celts*. London: Thames and Hudson.

Jay, M., and M. Richards. 2006. 'Diet in the Iron Age cemetery population at Wetwang Slack, East Yorkshire, UK: Carbon and nitrogen stable isotope evidence'. *Journal of Archaeological Science* 33, 5: 653–662.

Jope, M. 2000. *Early Celtic Art in the British Isles*. Oxford: Clarendon Press.

Joy, J. 2011. '"Fancy objects" in the British Iron Age: Why decorate?'. *Proceedings of the Prehistoric Society* 77: 205–229.

Kaenel, G. 1990. *Recherches sur la période de La Tène en Suisse occidentale: Analyse des sépultures*. Lausanne: Bibliothèque historique vaudoise.

Kern, A., K. Kowarik, A. W. Rausch, and H. Reschreiter (eds). 2008. *Salz—Reich: 7000 Jahre Hallstatt*. Veröffentlichungen der Prähistorischen Abteilung 2. Vienna: Naturhistorisches Museum Wien.

Knüsel, C. 2002. 'More Circe than Cassandra: The princess of Vix in ritualised social context'. *European Journal of Archaeology* 5, 3: 275–308.

Krausse, D. 1999. 'Der "Keltenfürst" von Hochdorf: Dorfälterster oder Sakralkönig? Anspruch und Wirklichkeit der sog. kulturanthropologischen Hallstatt-Archäologie'. *Archäologisches Korrespondenzblatt* 29: 339–358.

Krausse, D., M. Fernández-Götz, L. Hansen, and I. Kretschmer. 2016. *The Heuneburg and the Early Iron Age Princely Seats: First Towns North of the Alps*. Budapest: Archaeolingua.

Kristiansen, K. 1998. *Europe Before History*. Cambridge: Cambridge University Press.

Lévi-Strauss, C. 1969. *The Raw and the Cooked: Introduction to a Science of Mythology*. London: Pimlico.

Matthews, K. 1999. 'The Iron Age of north-west England and Irish sea trade', in B. Bevan (ed.) *Northern Exposure: Interpretative Devolution and the Iron Age in Britain*. Leicester Archaeology Monograph 4: 173–196. Leicester: School of Archaeology and Ancient History.

Mauss, M. 1954. *The Gift: Forms and Functions of Exchange in Archaic Societies*. London: Cohen and West.

Milcent, P.-Y. 2004. *Le premier âge du Fer en France centrale*. Mémoire 34 de la Société Préhistorique Française. Paris: Société Préhistorique Française.

Moore, T. 2007. 'Perceiving communities: Exchange, landscapes and social networks in the later Iron Age of western Britain'. *Oxford Journal of Archaeology* 26, 1: 79–102.

Moore, T. 2011. 'Detribalizing the later prehistoric past: Concepts of tribes in Iron Age and Roman studies'. *Journal of Social Archaeology* 11: 334–360.

Moore, T. 2012. 'Beyond the Oppida: Polyfocal Complexes and Late Iron Age Societies in Southern Britain'. *Oxford Journal of Archaeology* 31, 4: 391–417.

Moore, T. 2017. 'Alternatives to urbanism? Reconsidering oppida and the urban question in Late Iron Age Europe'. *Journal of World Prehistory* 30, 3: 281–300.

Moore, T., and X.-L. Armada. 2011. 'Crossing the divide: Opening a dialogue on approaches to western European first millennium BC studies', in T. Moore and X.-L. Armada (eds) *Atlantic Europe in the First Millennium BC: Crossing the Divide*: 3–77. Oxford: Oxford University Press.

Needham, S. 2007. '800 BC, the great divide', in C. Haselgrove and R. Pope (eds) *The Earlier Iron Age in Britain and the Near Continent*: 39–63. Oxford: Oxbow.

Nielsen, S., J. H. Andersen, J. A. Baker, et al. 2005. 'The Gundestrup cauldron: New scientific and technical investigations'. *Acta Archaeologica* 76, 2: 1–58.

Parfitt, K. 1995. *Iron Age Burials from Mill Hill, Deal*. London: British Museum Press.

Parker Pearson, M. 1999. *The Archaeology of Death and Burial*. Stroud: Sutton.

Pope, R., and I. Ralston. 2011. 'Approaching sex and status in Iron Age Britain with reference to the nearer Continent', in T. Moore and X.-L. Armada (eds) *Atlantic Europe in the First Millennium BC: Crossing the Divide*: 375–416. Oxford: Oxford University Press.

Poux, M. 2004. *L'âge du vin: Rites de boisson, festins et libations en Gaule indépendante*. Protohistoire Européenne 8. Montagnac: Monique Mergoil.

Poux, M. 2012. *Corent: Voyage au cœur d'une ville gauloise*, 2nd edition. Paris: Errance.

Price, T. D., and G. M. Feinman. 2010. *Pathways to Power: New Perspectives on the Emergence of Social Inequality*. New York: Springer.

Quesada, F., M. Zamora, and F. Requena. 2000. 'Itinerant smiths in the Iberian Iron Age (6th–2nd centuries BC)', in M. Feugère and M. Guštin (eds) *Iron, Blacksmiths and Tools: Ancient European Crafts. Acts of the Instrumentum Conference at Podsreda (Slovenia), April 1999*: 15–20. Montagnac: Monique Mergoil.

Ramsl, P. C. 2002. *Das eisenzeitliche Gräberfeld von Pottenbrunn*. Fundberichte aus Österreich, Materialhefte A 11. Horn: Berger.

Ramsl, P. C. 2011. *Das latènezeitliche Gräberfeld von Mannersdorf im Leithagebirge, Flur Reinthal Süd, Niederösterreich*. Mitteilungen der Prähistorischen Kommission 74. Vienna: Österreichische Akadamie der Wissenschaften.

Randsborg, K. 1995. *Hjortspring: Warfare and Sacrifice in Early Europe*. Aarhus: Aarhus University Press.

Rosman, A., and P. Rubel. 1971. *Feasting with Mine Enemy: Rank and Exchange among Northwest Coast Societies*. New York: Columbia University Press.

Rowlands, M. 1994. 'From "The Gift" to market economies: The ideology and politics of European Iron Age studies', in K. Kristiansen and J. Jensen (eds) *Europe in the First Millennium BC*. Sheffield Archaeological Monographs 6: 1–6. Sheffield: J. R. Collis Publications.

Sastre, I. 2008. 'Community, identity, and conflict: Iron Age warfare in the Iberian northwest'. *Current Anthropology* 49, 6: 1021–1051.

Sastre, I. 2011. 'Social inequality during the Iron Age: Interpretation models', in T. Moore and X.-L. Armada (eds) *Atlantic Europe in the First Millennium BC: Crossing the Divide*: 264–284. Oxford: Oxford University Press.

Sharples, N. 2007. 'Building communities and creating identities in the first millennium BC', in C. Haselgrove and R. Pope (eds) *The Earlier Iron Age in Britain and the Near Continent*: 174–184. Oxford: Oxbow.

Sharples, N. 2010. *Social Relations in Later Prehistory: Wessex in the First Millennium BC*. Oxford: Oxford University Press.

Sharples, N., and M. Parker Pearson. 1997. 'Why were brochs built? Recent studies in the Iron Age of Atlantic Scotland', in A. Gwilt and C. Haselgrove (eds) *Reconstructing Iron Age Societies*: 254–265. Oxford: Oxbow.

Stead, I. M. 2006. *British Iron Age Swords and Scabbards*. London: British Museum Press.

Stöllner, T., H. Aspöck, N. Boenke, C. Dobiat, H.-J. Gawlick, W. Groenman-van Waateringe, et al. 2003. 'The economy of Dürrnberg-bei-Hallein: An Iron Age salt mining centre in the Austrian Alps'. *The Antiquaries Journal* 183: 123–194.

Taylor, T. 2001. 'Believing the ancients: Quantitative and qualitative dimensions of slavery and the slave trade in later prehistoric Eurasia'. *World Archaeology* 33, 1: 27–43.

Waddington, K. 2008. 'Topographies of accumulation at late Bronze Age Potterne', in O. P. Davis, N. M. Sharples, and K. E. Waddington (eds) *Changing Perspectives on the First Millennium BC*: 161–184. Oxford: Oxbow.

Webley, L. 2008. *Iron Age Households: Structure and Practice in Western Denmark, 500 BC–AD 200*. Aarhus: Jutland Archaeological Society.

Weill, S. 2003. 'Denmark's bog find pioneer. The archaeologist Conrad Engelhardt and his work', in L. Jørgensen, B. Storgaard, and L. Gebauer (eds) *The Spoils of Victory: The North in the Shadow of the Roman Empire*: 66–83. Copenhagen: Nationalmuseet.

Wells, P. S. 1996. 'Location, organization and specialization of craft production in late prehistoric central Europe', in B. Wailes (ed.) *Craft Specialization and Social Evolution: In Memory of V. Gordon Childe*: 85–98. Philadelphia: University of Pennsylvania Museum of Archaeology and Anthropology.

Wigley, A. 2007. 'Rooted to the spot: The "smaller enclosures" of the later first millennium BC in the central Welsh Marches', in C. Haselgrove and T. Moore (eds) *The Later Iron Age in Britain and Beyond*: 173–189. Oxford: Oxbow.

CHAPTER 32

HORSES, WAGONS, AND CHARIOTS

KATHARINA REBAY-SALISBURY

Introduction

Horses played an important role in the lives of Iron Age people, particularly the elite. They are versatile animals; trained correctly, they serve as riding, pack, and draught animals in peace and war, they are useful companions for hunting and partners in sport, perform as status symbols in funerary and ritual contexts, aid in agriculture, give milk and, in the end, provide meat and hides. In comparison to bovines, horses exhibit greater endurance and speed, which enabled long-distance transport and trade; their ability to react quickly and reliably to human command revolutionized warfare. Horses can carry about one-fifth of their own weight (*c.*70 kg) and pull about double their weight (*c.*700 kg; Schwindt 1995). Iron Age horses were smaller than modern breeds and their performance was weaker, but they still reached a speed of 3.2 to 4.3 km/h and travelled 50–60 km a day as pack animals (Bökönyi 1993: 26). Over shorter distances a horse may reach up to 45–52 km/h at a full gallop (Junkelmann 1990: 46). War chariots, pulled by two horses, may have reached a speed of 38 km/h over a distance of 1,000 m (Spruytte 1977: 39). Training and keeping horses, however, required considerable expense and seems to have been primarily the domain of the elites. Evidence of horses, wagons, and chariots comes from many sources in the Iron Age, from depictions in art and animal bones to the horse gear and paraphernalia found in various archaeological contexts. This chapter provides an overview of the use of horses in the Iron Age, through which their significance for the time period will become apparent.

Breeding, Training, and Grooming Horses

The percentage of horse bones in Iron Age faunal assemblages varies widely: in central Europe, between 4% and 10% is common, depending on the cultural context (see Chapter 19). There is little doubt that horses were eaten, but attitudes to horsemeat were culturally contingent and fluctuated through time. Animal bone evidence from settlements such as the Heuneburg, Manching, and Basel-Gasfabrik show that horse bones were subject to the same cutting and butchering patterns as other domestic animals. The age of the slaughtered animals suggests they were butchered and eaten after their use as riding, draught, or pack animals (Müller et al. 1999: 121). It is noticeable that in Hungary, sites associated with Scythian populations have higher proportions of horses in their faunal assemblages and horsemeat was regularly consumed (Bartosiewicz and Gál 2010). Romans considered horsemeat disgusting and did not generally eat it. In northern Europe, horses were eaten in the early Iron Age, but this decreased during the late Iron Age and was given up in the Viking Age (Nilsson 2003). Germanic peoples consumed horse until the pope forbade it as a pagan practice in the eighth century AD (Reichstein 2003: 32–33). Today, horsemeat is avoided in countries with Germanic history, while those of Roman heritage consider horsemeat a delicacy.

Iron Age horses were probably comparable to modern Icelandic horses in weight, height, and speed. The height at the withers of an average horse at the transition from the Bronze to the Iron Age was under 130 cm (Benecke 1994: 113–114), though larger animals were found in centres such as the Heuneburg or Manching, where they were most likely specially selected and bred. Horses of central and eastern Europe can be divided into two groups that can be demarcated by imagining a line from Venice to Vienna and continuing northwards. According to animal bone evidence (Bökönyi 1968, 1993: 46), eastern horses interbred with horses of the nomadic cultures of the steppes had stronger legs and were larger, with an average of 136 cm height, while in the west horses tended to be of smaller build, 126 cm on average. Both types of horses are shown in a battle scene on the belt plate from Vače, Slovenia (Figure 32.1; Lucke and Frey 1962: pl. 55; Powell 1971). The horse on the left is noticeably taller and has a shorter skull, typical of the eastern horse type; the short or braided mane may be more practical for archers. The rider wears his hair long and carries lances. The horse on the right, in contrast, has a long skull and flowing mane; the horseman is armed with helmet, axe, and lances typical of the Slovenian Iron Age. An image on the *situla* from Este-Benvenuti, Italy (Lucke and Frey 1962: pl. 65), shows a seated man holding the reins of a horse, while another man inspects its hind leg. This may show the quality control of a purchase; the Venetian and Slovenian areas were equine centres in the early Iron

FIGURE 32.1 Two breeds of horses on the belt plate from Vače, Slovenia, fifth century BC.
Photo: Lessing Archive, © Natural History Museum Vienna, Austria

Age. Although there is little evidence for horse bridle bits in the region, burials and votive figurines of horses are widespread in the Veneto (Azzaroli 1980: 296). Horses used by the Veneti and the Etruscans (Azzaroli 1980) seem to be closely related to Mediterranean breeds.

Slovenian *situlae*, such as the one from Dolenjske Toplice (Egg and Eibner 2005: fig. 4) show the whole range of horse training and use: in the first register, a rider sitting on a horse being led by a man suggests breaking the horse; next is a horse and chariot, followed by a horse led on the lunge line from behind, again followed by a horse led on short reins, another chariot and a rider. The Scythian princely tomb from Čertomlyk, Ukraine, contained an electrum vessel with a depiction of several men trying to get a horse to kneel, which is particularly tricky (Rolle 1979: 111).

The oldest surviving horse training manual, *The Art of Horsemanship*, was written by the Athenian historian and soldier Xenophon (*c*.430–354 BC) and contains information on selecting a young and an older horse, caring and grooming, riding and training the horse for parade and battle. The advice seems modern in that Xenophon suggests having respect for the horses' nature in training; rather than beating them into submission, he advocates handling them gently and making them obedient through reward. Xenophon stresses the importance of caring for the horses' hooves, being gentle with the bit, and using the volte (riding in small circles) as an exercise to bend the horse—time-tested advice that any modern rider will recognize.

Horseshoes were generally unknown in the ancient world. The only evidence that they might have existed comes from a fourth-century BC Etruscan tomb at Tarquinia, Italy (Bates 1902), where a set of four bronze half-shoes with three holes each were found together with part of the jaw of a 12 year-old horse. Romans used iron hipposandals to protect the hoof from heavy wear. Evidence of nailed iron shoes from the tomb of the Frankish King Childeric I at Tournai, Belgium (Périn and Kazanski 1996: 176), is uncertain, but they were introduced in Europe by eastern nomads and were widespread by the late medieval period.

Riding Horses

Riding on horseback enhances the speed of human transport, and lends an entirely different quality to hunting and warfare. Artefactual evidence for riding comes from associated material culture such as bits, bridles and other horse gear, saddles, and riding aids such as crops and whips. Additional insights are provided by contemporary depictions.

The main tool for controlling a horse is the bridle, which is placed on the horse's head and guides its movements. Although it is possible to ride without bits or with organic bits (known from late Bronze Age lake site contexts, cf. Hüttel 1981: no. 165, no. 169), metal bits, first made of bronze, were in use from the third millennium BC onwards in the Carpathian basin and further east (Uckelmann 2013: 401). Bridles used in the Iron Age normally consisted of the bit, halters, and reins. Bits comprise a mouthpiece and elements that connect the bit to the reins. Halters comprise various leather straps, including the crownpiece over the head behind the ears, and cheek-pieces attached to either side of the crownpiece; browband, noseband, and throat lash usually accompany the set and prevent slipping. All leather straps and crossings may be decorated with metal elements such as rivets, knobs, *tutuli*, or *phalerae*.

New types of bridles appeared in the ninth and eighth centuries BC, which are frequently associated with Cimmerian and Scythian contacts (Kromer 1986; Metzner-Nebelsick 1998) and influenced the development of horse gear in the early Iron Age. The complex of three horse bridles—one with D-ringed ends, two with ringed toggles and a number of zoomorphic cheek-pieces—found with a battle axe and fragment of a cup in Stillfried/March, Austria (Kaus 1989), for example, is best paralleled in the central Dnieper basin and demonstrates far-reaching contacts. The landscape of the Carpathian basin and the steppes further east is ideally suited for keeping and using horses; undoubtedly the cultures of eastern nomads contributed substantially to the development of horse culture in the rest of Europe.

As a material for bits, bronze was very quickly replaced by iron, which was much better suited for the purpose, as contact with the horse's saliva causes chemical reactions. Several different types were in use in the Iron Age, including plain straight bar bits with ring ends (from Bronze Age D), twisted straight bar bits with ring ends (from Hallstatt B3), bar or jointed bits with permanently fastened cheek-pieces (Hallstatt B3–C1), and jointed bits alone (Hallstatt B2–C1; Balkwill 1973). Bits were connected to the reins by D-rings, loose rings, or cheek-pieces, which were made of bone, horn, bronze, or iron and usually encompass three holes or rings, allowing for different positions of the reins. Their use depended on fashion as well as function: jointed bits act by applying direct pressure on the horse's mouth, whereas leverage bits extend pressure beyond the mouth on the poll and chin groove. Western European types include bar bits (Balkwill 1973), whereas central and eastern European bits are exclusively jointed (Metzner-Nebelsick 1994: 398). The bit does not normally have contact with the horse's teeth, as it lies in the edentulous (tooth-free) part of the mouth, although a horse that tries to move the bit out of its mouth may push it towards the premolars with its tongue; in such cases, traces on the premolars may be identified under the microscope. This is useful for distinguishing riding from pack animals, as the latter were not normally bridled with bits (Anthony 1994: 187). It is impossible to ascertain from the bits whether they were used for riding or driving; it is often assumed, however, that single bits indicate riding and pairs of bits indicate two bridles, and hence driving. Three bits might account for one horse for riding plus a pair for driving (Egg 1996b).

Grave 11 from Mindelheim, Germany, served as the basis for a reconstruction of a Hallstatt C bridle (Kossack 1954): it included two iron bits, four bronze cheek-pieces, thirteen closed bronze rings, ten bronze *tutuli* (discs with cross-shaped eyelets at the back), and two further rings, most likely attached to the yoke (Egg 1996a: 183). The burial mound at Hochdorf, Germany, contained bridles, which were deposited on the wagon in this exceptionally well-preserved and documented grave. They provide the best insights into how a Hallstatt D bridle was constructed (Koch 2006). The jointed bits were held in place by two wooden cheek-pieces, wrapped in sheet bronze; the cheek-pieces were fixed to the nose and cheek bands. The crownpiece was wrapped with thick bronze wire. A front band connected the browband and noseband. Sixteen large and eight small sheet metal discs decorated the bridle. It was closed by a small clasp on the side of the throat strap. This clasp usually faces the outside, which permits the differentiation of the right and left bridle; interestingly, they were placed on the 'wrong side' on the wagon in the grave. In the La Tène period, cheek-pieces became less common and the rings of the bit were directly connected to cheek-straps and reins. From the fourth century BC, Thracian and Italic types of curb bits gain importance throughout Europe (Koch 2003: 40–41).

Evidence for saddles in Iron Age Europe is scarce, except for the Scythian area. Skilled riders do not need saddles for balance, but blanket-like support structures held by a girth and/or via breast straps distribute weight more evenly and relieve the strain on the horse's back. Particularly when horses are used as pack animals, pack saddles are required. Scythian saddles consist of a wooden saddle tree, padded cushions, and felted covers; they are held in the right place via girths, breastplates, and cruppers. Examples with rich and imaginative decoration dating to the fifth century BC have been unearthed from the frozen tombs of Pazyryk in Siberia (Rudenko 1970). Saddles do not seem to have been widely used as they were not commonly depicted in early Iron Age art; images of saddles and saddle-like pads become more common in the late Iron Age and are shown, for instance, on the Gundestrup cauldron (Olmsted 1979; Nielsen et al. 2005; Figure 32.2). Stirrups did not spread to Europe before the migration period.

There is solid evidence for the use of crops and whips as riding aids. In its simplest form, the crop is a straight and flexible wooden rod, which does not leave archaeological traces. Forked whips are shown in early Iron Age situla art, for instance on the belt plate from Magdalenska gora (Lucke and Frey 1962: pl. 41b). Spurs appear in Slovenian and southern Italian graves in the fifth century BC (Baitinger 2004: 372), and slightly later in Greece. They became popular with Celtic and Germanic riders in the middle and late La

FIGURE 32.2 Riders with saddles and spurs depicted on the Gundestrup cauldron, Denmark, second to first century BC.

Photo: © National Museum of Denmark

Tène period (Van Endert 1991: 41). Graves with spurs dating to La Tène C and D cluster in the central Rhine/Moselle area (Schönfelder 2002: 324); the riders depicted on the Gundestrup cauldron (Olmsted 1979; Nielsen et al. 2005) wore spurs.

Riding is a popular motif in Iron Age art, which depicts many different contexts in which riding took place: sports, travelling, hunting, military marches, parades, and warfare. Figurines of riders such as the ceramic ones from Speikern, Germany (Vollrath 1964), and Großmugl, Austria (Kromer 1958), or lead figurines from Frög, Austria (Tomedi 2002), all depict male riders naked, most likely to underline their virility.

Horse racing as a sport, a competitive physical activity following formal rules (Rebay-Salisbury 2012), is shown on the *situla* from Kuffern, Austria (Lucke and Frey 1962: pl. 75). It shows two bareback riders, naked except for long, pointed caps; their bodies appear tilted backwards, and the fists are held upright, gripping the reins. The second rider's arm is stretched towards the back, probably spurring on the horse with a whip. Ancient Greek, Etruscan, and Roman sports are relatively well documented (e.g. Crowther 2010; Futrell 2006), but Iron Age sports have to be reconstructed on the basis of depictions, artefacts, and their contexts. Images of Iron Age sports are most often found in graves and sanctuaries, suggesting that, as in the Greek world, competitions were often held in the context of funerary games and to honour the gods (Herrmann and Kondoleon 2004: 43).

Travellers are depicted differently from sportsmen (e.g. Vače, Slovenia, Lucke and Frey 1962: pl. 73, or Bologna-Certosa, Italy, Lucke and Frey 1962: pl. 64); they are always dressed and sit on their horse calmly. Riders are frequently part of a military march or parade, in which case they wear a helmet and carry spears and a shield, which often covers the whole body (e.g. Bologna-Arnoaldi, Lucke and Frey 1962: pl.

14). Hunting is much more frequently done on foot than on horseback in situla art, but a few images show riders in context with dogs as accompanying animals (e.g. Este-Nazari, Italy, Lessing 1980: fig. 56) or using a lance to strike a deer (e.g. Zagorje, Slovenia, Lucke and Frey 1962: pl. 54b). Hunting on horseback is a popular motif further north, in the north-eastern Hallstatt and Lausitz areas, as on finds from, for instance, Sopron-Várhely, Hungary (Eibner-Persy 1980: pl.28) or Łazy, Poland (Schlette 1984: 100). People standing on horseback are depicted on a vessel from Beilngries-Im Ried West, Germany (Torbrügge 1968: no. 246), perhaps indicating horse acrobatics.

Horses as Draught Animals

It is presently unclear whether horses were used as draught animals for ploughing. Wear and tear on such horses' skeletons would look identical to those on horses employed in pulling carts. From images on *situlae* which depict ploughing (e.g. Sanzeno, Italy, Lucke and Frey 1962: pl. 67; Nesactium, Croatia, Mihovilić 1992: app. 2), it cannot be determined which animal species was used. Ploughing frequently co-occurs with sex images and seems to have had significance for the assertion and passing of power between generations.

Wagons reached Europe from the Near East, where they had been in use since the third millennium BC; simple vehicles with wooden disc wheels for transport and farming had been in use ever since (Pare 1987a: 25). Horse-drawn wagons with spokes, however, constitute a different tradition. From around 800 BC ceremonial wagons became part of the elite funerary ritual and image canon in Italy and central Europe, whereas they remained an exception in eastern Europe, where a rich riding culture flourished. Two basic vehicle types serving different functions can be distinguished: the four-wheeled ceremonial wagon and the two-wheeled chariot.

Both types are drawn by a pair of horses with a similar harness; the bridle does not differ significantly from that of a riding horse. In prehistory, horses were harnessed with yokes, wooden beams that were fitted on the horses' necks in front of or just behind the withers. Today, yokes are only used on bovines, as they went out of use for horses with the invention of head collars in the medieval period. Horses' harnesses include various straps and belts, buckles and fasteners, as well as rings to guide the reins. The double yoke is symmetrical, with two lateral arches and straight centre section, which connects to the pole between the horses, which in turn connects to the vehicle. The connection between yoke and pole may be fastened with leather straps or via a nail. The yoke is fastened to the horse with breastplates, and harnesses with straps around the neck and chest of the animal. A double yoke made of maple wood was discovered in the Hochdorf burial mound. At 1.2 m long, it was anatomically formed and decorated with a pair of cast bronze horses (Koch 2006). Further yokes are known, for example from La Tène and Ezinge, but it is unclear if they were for horses (Piggott 1983: 218). The reins connect the bits in the horses' mouths to the hands of the driver; frequently they are led through rings and cross-linked so both horses may be steered together.

Four-Wheeled Ceremonial Wagons

Early Iron Age innovations in building wagons[1] included a new way of constructing wheels: felloes were generally made of two layers of wood—an inner layer of bent wood, and an outer layer composed of several bent pieces; they were held together by felloe clamps. The wheels were strengthened by iron tyres nailed to the wooden felloes. The intersection of the spokes and the axle was secured by a nave (Pare 1987b: 192). The wheels of the wagons usually comprise eight to ten spokes, although sixteen have been counted on the wheels from Großeibstadt, Germany, and their diameter ranges from 0.7 to 0.95 m. The pairs of front and rear wheels are each connected by an axle of 1.1 to 1.3 m length; the axles are set 1.4 to 1.8 m apart (Pare 1987b: 209). Tracks of early Iron Age wagons have been found at the Heuneburg, Germany, and Ütliberg, Switzerland (Biel 1985: 185).

A number of further fittings might have been fastened to the spokes, the nave, the axle, the wagon box, the pole, and the yoke; Hallstatt D wagons were especially richly adorned. The wagon boxes were generally rectangular and measured 0.6–0.84 m in width and 1.48–1.85 m in length. The side walls were kept low, although some wagons had more elaborate wooden constructions at the back. A T-shaped or forked perch connected the yoke to the wagon. The front axle, at least, must be attached to the wagon box in a movable way to permit steering (Piggott 1983: 156–158); this is usually ensured by a kingpin, which can be of wood. Nevertheless, a turning circle of at least 8.5 m was probably necessary to turn an Iron Age wagon around (Pare 1987b: 211).

Drivers commonly control horses by voice and reins; in addition, goads with sharp points were used in the Iron Age to spur horses on to higher performances. The Hochdorf burial mound contained a complete goad, 1.66 m long, made of snowball wood (*Viburnum opulus*) and wrapped in a spiral of thin sheet bronze and armed with an iron prickle (Koch 2006: 87, 275). Archaeological evidence in the form of goad tips has been found in Voltera, Tarquinia, Veii, and Bologna, Italy, as well as north of the Alps at the Heuneburg (Krausse 1992). Goads are depicted on the Hochdorf couch (Biel 1985: 95) and on several *situlae* (e.g. Bologna-Arnoaldi, Italy, Lucke and Frey 1962: pl. 12).

Four-wheeled wagons are a characteristic feature of the west Hallstatt elite burial rite, in which members of the elite were interred in rectangular wooden grave chambers under mounds (Figure 32.3). The main area of wagon distribution north of the Alps is southern Germany and surrounding areas; from Burgundy to Bohemia and Upper Austria about 260 wagon graves are known. Four-wheeled wagons are rare in the eastern Hallstatt area, where cremation was preferred, although a few have been found, as at Strettweg, Austria, and Somlóvásárhely, Hungary (Egg 1996a). The wagons in graves were frequently dismantled, with the wheels taken off and placed along the chamber walls. The body of the deceased person may be placed on the wagon box (e.g. Vix,

FIGURE 32.3 Four-wheeled ceremonial wagon used in the funerary display at Mitterkirchen, Austria, eighth to seventh century BC.

Drawing © Oberösterreichisches Landesmuseum Linz

France, Knüsel 2002), under it (e.g. Hohmichele VI, Germany, Riek 1962), or to the side (e.g. Hochdorf, Germany, Biel 1985). Both men and women were buried with wagons. Although male wagon burials occur more frequently, some very exceptional graves are in fact those of women, most famously at Vix in eastern France (Rolley 2003). A recent list of elite female burials lists twenty graves with four-wheeled wagons and fourteen graves with two-wheeled wagons from Hallstatt C to La Tène B in central Europe and Italy (Metzner-Nebelsick 2009: 250).

The wagons were probably used in funerary processions to transport the bodies to the graves, and some might even have been built for that very purpose. At Wehringen-Hexenbergle, Germany, one of the earliest Hallstatt wagons, wood samples of the burial chamber and the wagon nave have been dendrochronologically dated to 783–773 BC, early Hallstatt C1; claims that both the wagon and the chamber were made of the same oak tree (Friedrich and Hennig 1995) have only recently been contested (Eggert 2012: 281).

Only a handful of wagons are known from late Bronze Age cremation graves (e.g. Hart an der Alz and Poing, Germany, Winghart 1999), but small wagon models—frequently carrying vessels of different shapes and decorated with water birds—demonstrate that movement and transport were important parts of late Bronze Age ideology, linked to the cremation rite and ideas about the regeneration of life through the regular solar cycle. These traditions may be the roots of the use of four-wheeled ceremonial wagons in the early Iron Age (Pare 1992: 179). Although four-wheeled wagons are primarily found in the early Iron Age, the wagons from Boé, France (Schönfelder 2002), dating to La Tène D2 (*c.*80/70–30 BC) and the wagon from Dejbjerg, Denmark (Petersen 1888), dismantled and laid in a peat bog at the end of the first century BC, illustrate that the four-wheeled ceremonial wagon was used over the *longue durée*.

Interestingly, representations of four-wheeled wagons rarely occur where the vehicles themselves are found; the distribution of actual wagons and depictions is almost mutually exclusive (Pare 1987b: 212–223; Figure 32.4). Exceptions include the wagons on the back of the bronze couch from Hochdorf, and an image on a ceramic vessel from Schirndorf, Germany. Sketched or stamped on pottery, four-wheeled wagons are frequent motifs in the Lausatian and north-eastern Hallstatt areas (e.g. Sopron, Hungary, Eibner-Persy 1980: pl. 28; Gallus 1934: pl. 2). They are also depicted on *situlae* from Slovenia, again an area where no wagon graves have been found. The only representation of a four-wheeled wagon on a bronze vessel is from San Maurizio, Italy (Lucke and Frey 1962: 68), where four men are shown seated on the wagon box. A two-wheeled travel cart is shown on the Vače *situla* (Lucke and Frey 1962: pl. 73), where both driver and passenger are seated in the wagon box. In most other instances of travelling, chariots are depicted, which not only have a standing driver, but also a passenger standing on the step behind (e.g. Dolenjske Toplice, Slovenia, Egg and Eibner 2005: 195, fig. 4, or Rovereto, Italy, Lucke and Frey 1962: pl. 32, 12). These images show the same type of chariot as used in sporting events, and perhaps depict the journey to the funerary games. Chariots are further embedded in scenes of warriors and battles, such as on the *situla* from Este-Benvenuti, Italy (Lucke and Frey 1962: pl. 65), or on another with a ship battle scene from Nesactium (Mihovilić 1996: app. 3).

Two-Wheeled Chariots

Chariots emerged at the beginning of the second millennium BC in the Near East. Important innovations that define the chariot are the use of the spoked wheel, the exclusive use of horses, controlling horses by bits, using bow and arrow as primary weapons, and allowing a crew of two to stand abreast (Raulwing 2000: 42). Pictorial sources, for instance from Scandinavia and Spain, models of spoked wheels, and horse fittings all suggest that light, two-wheeled chariots were adopted during the early and middle Bronze Age in Europe (Pare 1989: 81), but they did not play a significant role in funerary ritual before the Iron Age.

Two-wheeled chariots in graves appeared in central Italy, in Etruria and Picenum, at about the same time as the central European four-wheeled wagons (*c.*800–600 BC). In fact, technological details reveal that some of the knowledge of building wheeled vehicles was shared over the Alps. In the early La Tène period, four-wheeled ceremonial wagons were replaced by two-wheeled chariots north of the Alps. They particularly cluster in Rheinland-Pfalz, Germany, and Champagne, France (Schönfelder 2000: 44). With the

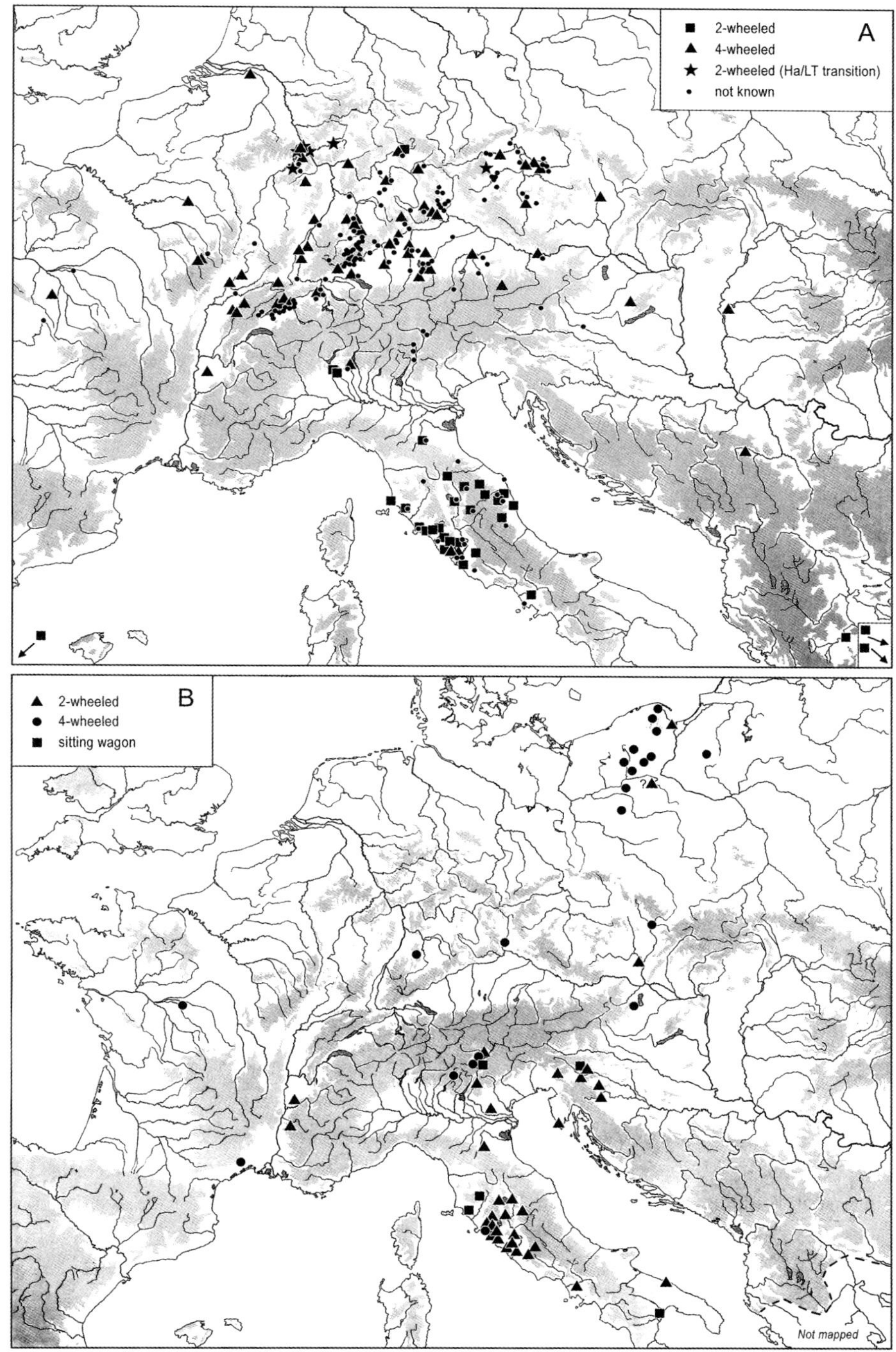

FIGURE 32.4 The distribution of wagon graves and depictions of wagons in the early Iron Age.

Source: after Pare 1987b: figs 13 and 14

transition to cremation, archaeological evidence becomes sparser during the middle and late La Tène period and the distribution of chariots shifted slightly to encompass fringe areas such as the lower Seine, the Paris basin, and eastern Celtic areas, particularly Bohemia. The custom of vehicle burials is also found in Britain. The earliest chariot burial, dating to the fifth century BC, was found at Newbridge, Edinburgh (Carter et al. 2010). For a short period of within a generation or so (Jay et al. 2012) in the third century BC, the local elite of the Arras culture in East Yorkshire was buried crouched in inhumation graves under square ditched burial mounds, each accompanied by a dismantled chariot (Stead 1979). By the second century BC, chariots went out of use in warfare in continental Europe and were replaced by cavalry, but remained in use in Britain and Ireland (e.g. mentioned in Caesar, *de Bello Gallico* 4.33.1, cf. James 1993: 78).

Iron Age chariots were smaller and lighter than wagons. Their construction includes a square or D-shaped platform for the driver (and passenger) to stand on, measuring approximately 1 m by 1 m, fixed to the single axle at the back in a flexible way. At least two types of superstructure are known: two low, bow-shaped railings made of bent wood on either side, or a D-shaped balustrade covering the front and sides of the box, often elaborately decorated with bronze fittings. Wheel diameters range from 0.7 to 1.2 m and were set 1.3 m apart in a standardized manner; this presumably permitted the vehicle to be manoeuvred along ruts (Pare 2006: 36).

Graves with chariots tend to be equipped with a full set of weapons, including a helmet, a sword, lances, and a shield, indicating a high-status warrior. The warrior in Grave 44/2 from Dürrnberg, Austria (Penninger 1972: 76), for example, was buried lying on top of the chariot with iron tyres and fittings. An 88 cm tall bronze *situla* and a small bronze bowl, a Greek vessel made between 480 and 450 BC, a bronze flask with compass ornaments, and a wooden jug, ornamented with a bronze mask in early Celtic style, were part of the grave furnishings. An iron sword, two lances, an elaborate belt, three razors, and a whetstone, together with several small ornaments, including amber and gold items, were personal possessions of the warrior. His helmet was placed at his feet.

The equipment of warriors with chariots does not differ significantly from that of warriors on foot; in combination with historical sources (Dobesch 1996), it has thus been suggested that the chariot served primarily as a 'taxi' to drive the warrior to and from battle, and for representation (Schönfelder 2002: 326). The chariot was not, however, purely an instrument of war; like the four-wheeled wagon, they could be elaborately ornamented and may have served to demonstrate the status of the elite in life and death. The existence of different types of two-wheeled chariots for travelling, war, and sport is likely, supported by the fact that two-wheeled vehicles are also found, to a limited extent, in elaborate women's graves, such as the one from Waldalgesheim, Germany (Joachim 1995).

The *situlae* from Kuffern, Austria, and Bologna-Arnoaldi, Italy (Lucke and Frey 1962: pl. 63), show chariot races. In both pictures, four pairs of horses with chariots and drivers in full motion race to the right. The chariot drivers hold on to long reins with both hands and carry a goad in their right hand to spur on the horses. The left arms of the charioteers are raised above their heads, while the right arms are held at waist height;

the reins, at least on the *situla* from Kuffern, are wrapped around the body, like Roman drivers (Greek drivers held the reins in their hands, cf. Futrell 2006: 191). Chariot drivers did not compete naked, but dressed in a short-sleeved garment with a belt. They wear long pointed caps unusual for *situla* images and perhaps particular to horse and chariot races.

Horse Burials

Horse burials, not to be confused with wagon burials and burials with horse gear (Ginoux et al. 2009), are definitely an eastern concept; in western Europe, horses are not generally buried, although exceptions are known. Among all the wagon burials of the western Hallstatt provinces, only one case is confirmed in which a pair of horses was buried too. The horses were found in a rectangular pit in a large burial mound at Unterfahlheim, Bavaria (Ambs 1998), but preservation was poor and no human remains were found. Horse burials are more frequent in the eastern Hallstatt provinces and beyond. The cemetery of Szentes-Vekerzug, Hungary, includes fourteen horse burials among the 151 graves (Kemenczei 2003; Párducz 1953: fig. 1). Many are located in a separate section at the southern fringe of the cemetery. Horses are rarely cremated, but the recently excavated burial mound (or kurgan) at Jalžabet, Croatia, dating to the first half of the sixth century BC contained not only a cremation and the remains of Scythian horse gear, arrowheads, and armour, but also the remains of cremated horses (Šimek 1998). The deposition of horses in the graves with elite individuals, who were normally cremated in the eastern Hallstatt provinces (Rebay-Salisbury 2017), apparently led to the merging of different practices and traditions. This is also apparent from Gemeinlebarn Tumulus 1, Austria, where a male cremation was buried with a classic Hallstatt C Mindelheim sword (Torbrügge 1992: 469). The body of the person was cremated directly outside the burial chamber with a wagon, and a horse was inhumed next to the burial chamber (Neugebauer 1997: 166). Wagon burials are not uncommon, in fact typical for west Hallstatt graves, but they are never cremated, and they do not include the horses.

Horse burials in Scythian kurgans of the sixth to fourth centuries BC are a feature of exceptional, high-status burials. One to sixteen horses are normally placed near the entrance to the main burial shaft (Rolle 1979: 96–112) in the Ukrainian steppes; further east, in the Kuban and Altai, the number of horses may be even higher (Chapter 15). Horses were killed and placed in rows, fully equipped with bridles, saddles, and breastplates. They are occasionally accompanied by a servant, most likely the groom. Wagons are also found dismantled in the corridors of the kurgans: they may have been used to drive the deceased around to relatives and friends for a final goodbye, before they were transported to the burial ground. Horse bones are also a frequent occurrence in the fill of the burial mounds, but have to be interpreted in a slightly different light. According to the Greek historian Herodotus (*Histories* 4.72), a memorial ceremony was held a year after a Scythian king's death, at which horses and attendants were strangled, disembowelled, filled with chaff, and arranged in full bridle as mounted horsemen on stakes and posts around the burial mound.

Villanovians did not bury horses, but Etruscans sometimes entombed racing horses with their chariots (Azzaroli 1980: 302). Late Iron Age sites in northern Italy such as Altino-Le Brustolade, Oppeano-Le Franchine, or Adria also include horse burials. At Adria, for example, a chariot with two horses plus one horse was buried behind the wagon. Ring cheek-pieces were used for the draught animals, whereas a bronze cheek bit and omega-shaped side pendants suggest the single horse was used for riding (Jerem 1998: 329). In the Carpathian basin, horses continued to be buried throughout the late Iron Age and into the Roman period (Steuer 2003: 61). At Sopron-Krautacker, Hungary, for example, a horse was included in a La Tène B2 burial, lying on its side with a riveted iron ring in the mouth (Jerem 1998: 328).

A remarkable discovery was recently made at the *oppidum* of Gondole, France (Cabezuelo et al. 2007), not far from the hilltop fortification unsuccessfully attacked by Julius Caesar at Gergovia. This comprised a grave pit of 3.6 m by 3.2 m, in which eight horses and eight men had been deposited in two rows of four. The dead lay on their right side, oriented south–north, looking east; the left arm of each person was arranged to embrace the man in front, expressing unity of the group. The horses were relatively small, with 1.2 m shoulder height, and stripped of all horse gear; the men did not carry any weapons or cloth fittings, but also showed no signs of battle injuries. Radiocarbon dates for the burial centre on the first century BC, which makes it likely that the grave can be seen in the context of the Gallic war (Deberge et al. 2014). In fact, Caesar recounts how the last unit of warriors arriving at the assembly point before a battle was sacrificed (*de Bello Gallico* 5.56.1–2). This seems the most likely explanation for this unusual find (Figure 32.5).

More often, whole horse cadavers and parts of horses are found in pits on later Iron Age settlements, which is also not uncommon for humans at this period. Examples range from southern England (e.g. Danebury, Cunliffe 1992) to France (e.g. Acy-Romance, Lambot and Méniel 1998) and Germany (e.g. Forchheim, Maise 1995). Such depositions are most unlikely to be purely disposal of refuse and may well have ritual connotations.

The Symbolic and Religious Dimensions of Horses

Images of horses and their riders, and of gods and goddesses in connection with horses go back to the early Iron Age. Horses were symbols of the elite and, as we have seen, their depiction often illustrates elite activities such as hunting, sports, and mounted

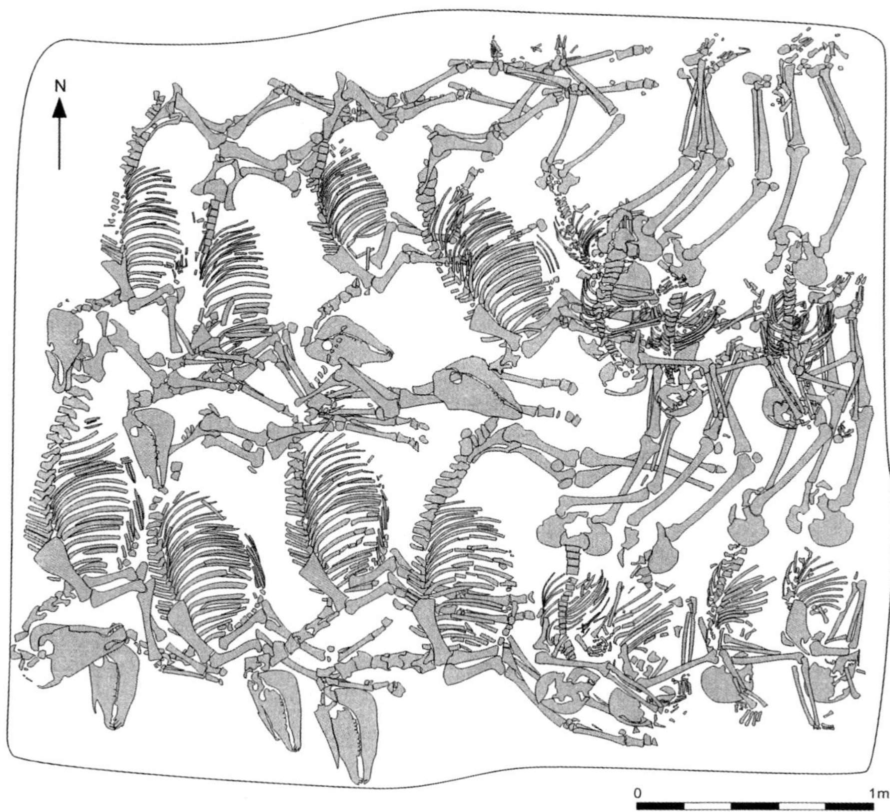

FIGURE 32.5 Burial of eight men and their horses at Gondole, France, first century BC.
After Cabezuelo et al. 2007: 370, fig. 6, © Inrap

warfare. The role of the horse as a symbol encompassed the notions of movement and transport, and may even have mediated between the heavens and the warrior sphere (Teržan 2011: 254). Images of horses—in particular Hallstatt and early La Tène horse-shaped fibulae in northern Italy and temperate Europe—are, however, most frequently associated with high-status female burials or found in sanctuaries. Women's ritual competence and their role as bestowers of sovereignty and legitimacy may be expressed by this equestrian symbolism (Metzner-Nebelsick 2007), which is also found in antique mythology.

Horse sculptures dating to the middle and late La Tène period are most often interpreted as devotional images for temples, or perhaps also as standards for the cavalry. The most famous is probably the iron horse from Manching, Germany (Krämer 1989), of which only the head and parts of the legs are preserved. It has a reconstructed length of 53 cm and was made in the second century BC. It exhibits clear traits of Celtic art, despite looking a little crude. Its eyes, for instance, are almond-shaped; the insert of bone or glass is missing. Mouth and nostrils are only rudimentarily formed and the legs are straight metal tubes rather than anatomically shaped: hoof and knee are only indicated by bulges. The horse was dismantled in antiquity, as apparent from the fact that its parts were found distributed over a large area. The closest parallels to the Manching horse are the bronze horses from Guerchy and Pogny, France. These are slightly smaller (22 and 21 cm), but were also fixed to a platform and may have served a similar function (Maier and Birkhan 2012: 1475).

Particularly tangible is Epona, a Gallo-Roman mother-goddess associated with fertility and abundance, who was worshipped all over Europe from Britain to Bulgaria, but especially in Gaul and the Rhineland (Chapter 42). Over 300 epigraphic and pictorial sources testify to her importance. Epona is frequently depicted as a female standing between two horses or riding a horse. As the protector of horses, donkeys, and mules, she was adopted by the Roman cavalry and worshipped all over the Roman Empire between the first and third centuries AD. She was further associated with the journey to the afterlife (Birkhan 1997: 526–527).

The Uffington White Horse in southern England connects the past to the present (Figure 32.6). This 110 m long stylized image of a horse is cut into the white chalk near an Iron Age hillfort and is seen best from the air (Darvill 1996: 222–226). Comparisons of the art style have long suggested that the horse dates to the Iron Age, but an excavation in 1990 recovered deposits that were scientifically dated to the late Bronze Age (Miles et al. 2003). It was also confirmed that the image was achieved by cutting trenches into the ground and filling them with layers of white chalk; simply removing the turf to reveal the white chalk below would not have sufficed to keep the monument visible in the long term. Nevertheless, the trenches have to be scoured and cleaned on a regular basis, a communal activity that, in the nineteenth century at least, was done as part of a fair held on the hill.

Conclusion

The long-term history of human relationships with horses began before the Iron Age and has lasted well into the modern era. What is striking about the evidence for horses, wagons, and chariots from the Iron Age is that they are strongly connected to elite identities, ideology, and religion. The archaeological sources include images in art, wagon and chariot burials, as well as horse burials, all of which were selectively and intentionally deposited in graves and sanctuaries. The patterns observed across the European continent therefore reflect specific depositional practices and highlight areas in which the horse played an important symbolic role in addition to its practical use. Animal bone evidence and stray finds from settlements prove, however, that horses were part of everyday Iron Age life.

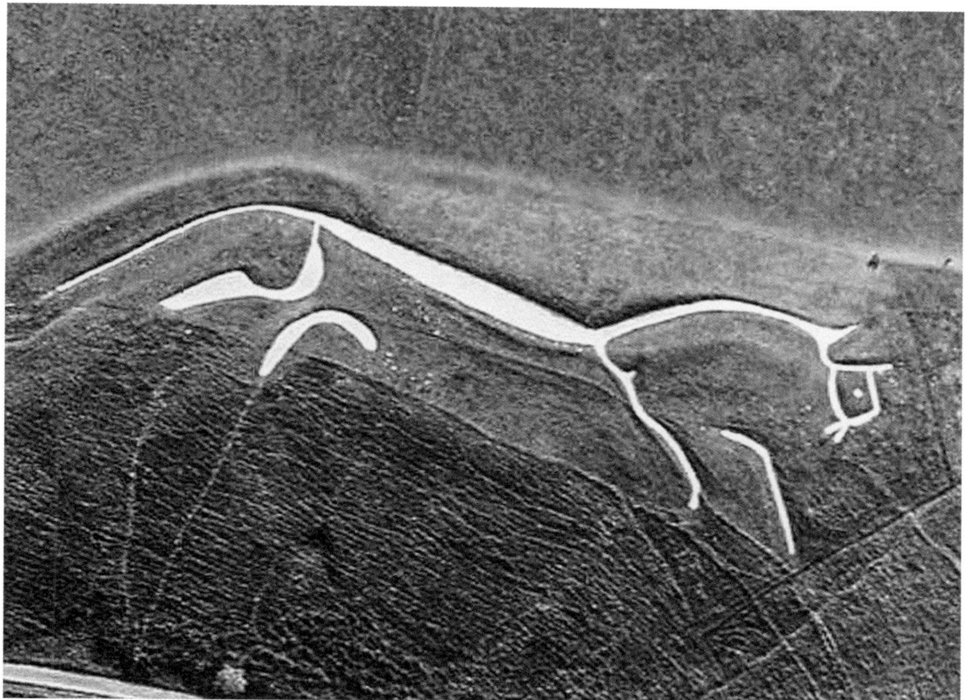

FIGURE 32.6 The Uffington Horse (Oxfordshire) from the air.

Image NASA, in the public domain

Postscript

The study of ancient horse DNA is rapidly advancing our understanding of horse domestication, which is now thought to have occurred in the western part of the Eurasian steppe around 3500 BC (Warmuth et al. 2012). Domesticated mares and stallions spread from this area, but genetic diversity is much greater in mares, which suggests that few stallions were domesticated, and wild mares continued to contribute to the gene pool of domesticated horses over a longer time (Wutke et al. 2018). Przewalski's horses, originally thought ancestral to the domesticated horse population, were found to be feral descendants of horses herded at Botai in Central Asia in the Bronze Age (Gaunitz et al. 2018). Analysis of 264 Eurasian horse genomes dating from c. 45,000 to 200 BC revealed that all modern horses' ancestry across Europe can be traced to the steppe grasslands of the Volga-Don region, replacing other domesticated linages from 2000 BC. Genetic evidence points to breeding for a physique suited to riding and pulling chariots, as well as a docile and stress-resistant temper (Librado et al. 2021). The small Celtic horses from today's Switzerland are thought to have been selected for monochrome bay, chestnut, and black colour (Elsner et al. 2016). A DNA study based on 873 equid samples from

Iron Age to modern France showed that only horses were present in the Iron Age, whilst mule breeding gained importance during Roman times (Lepetz et al. 2021). Future studies of Iron Age horse DNA will provide insights into strategies of selection, breeding practices, use, trade, and gift-giving of horses.

Note

1. For technical terms related to wagons, see Pare 1992: fig. 1.

References

Ambs, R. 1998. 'Eine hallstattzeitliche Bestattung zweier Pferde mit Schirrung und Wagen in einem Grabhügel bei Unterfahlheim, Gem. Nersingen/Schwaben'. *Bayerische Vorgeschichtsblätter* 63: 83–95.

Anthony, D. W. 1994. 'The earliest horseback riders and Indo-European origins: New evidence from the steppes', in B. Hänsel and S. Zimmer (eds) *Die Indogermanen und das Pferd. Festschrift für Bernfried Schlerath*. Archaeolingua Main Series 4: 185–195. Budapest: Archaeolingua.

Azzaroli, A. 1980. 'Venetic horses from Iron Age burials at Padova, northern Italy'. *Rivista di Scienze Preistoriche* 35: 281–308.

Baitinger, H. 2004. 'Hellenistisch-frühkaiserzeitliche Reitersporen aus dem Zeusheiligtum von Olympia'. *Germania* 82: 351–380.

Balkwill, C. J. 1973. 'The earliest horse-bits of western Europe'. *Proceedings of the Prehistoric Society* 39: 425–452.

Bartosiewicz, L., and E. Gál. 2010. 'Living on the frontier: "Scythian" and "Celtic" animal exploitation in Iron Age northeastern Hungary', in D. V. Campana, P. Crabtree, S. D. de France, J. Lev-Tov, and A. M. Choyke (eds) *Anthropological Approaches to Zooarchaeology: Colonialism, Complexity and Animal Transformations*: 115–127. Oxford: Oxbow.

Bates, W. N. 1902. 'Etruscan horseshoes from Corneto'. *American Journal of Archaeology* 6, 4: 398–403.

Benecke, N. 1994. *Archäozoologische Studien zur Entwicklung der Haustierhaltung in Mitteleuropa und Südskandinavien von den Anfängen bis zum ausgehenden Mittelalter*. Schriften zur Ur- und Frühgeschichte 46. Berlin: De Gruyter.

Biel, J. 1985. *Der Keltenfürst von Hochdorf*. Stuttgart: Theiss.

Birkhan, H. 1997. *Kelten: Versuch einer Gesamtdarstellung ihrer Kultur*. Vienna: Österreichische Akademie der Wissenschaften.

Bökönyi, S. 1968. 'Mecklenburg Collection, Part I: Data on Iron Age horses of central and eastern Europe'. *Bulletin of the American Schools of Prehistoric Research* 25: 3–71.

Bökönyi, S. 1993. *Pferdedomestikation, Haustierhaltung und Ernährung*. Archaeolingua Minor Series 3. Budapest: Archaeolingua.

Cabezuelo, U., P. Caillat, and P. Meniel. 2007. 'La sépulture multiple de Gondole', in C. Mennessier-Jouannet and Y. Deberge (eds) *L'archéologie de l'âge du fer en Auvergne. Actes du XXVIIe Colloque international de l'AFEAF, Clermont-Ferrand 2003*. Monographies d'Archéologie Méditerranéenne Hors-Série 2: 365–384. Lattes: Association pour le développement de l'archéologie en Languedoc-Roussillon.

Carter, S., F. Hunter, and A. Smith. 2010. 'A 5th century BC Iron Age chariot burial from Newbridge, Edinburgh'. *Proceedings of the Prehistoric Society* 76: 31–74.

Crowther, N. B. 2010. *Sport in Ancient Times*. Praeger Series on the Ancient World. Norman: University of Oklahoma Press.

Cunliffe, B. W. 1992. 'Pits, preconceptions and propitiation in the British Iron Age'. *Oxford Journal of Archaeology* 11: 69–83.

Darvill, T. 1996. *Prehistoric Britain from the Air: A Study of Space, Time and Society*. Cambridge: Cambridge University Press.

Deberge, Y., F. Baucheron, U. Cabezuelo, P. Caillat, E. Gatto, C. Landry, et al. 2014. 'Témoignages de la Guerre des Gaules dans le bassin clermontois, nouveaux apports'. *Revue archéologique du Centre de la France* 53. Available at http://racf.revues.org/2071 [accessed 18 May 2016].

Dobesch, G. 1996. 'Überlegungen zum Heerwesen und zur Sozialstruktur der Kelten', in E. Jerem, A. Krenn-Leeb, J.-W. Neugebauer, and O. H. Urban (eds) *Die Kelten in den Alpen und an der Donau. Akten des internationalen Symposions, St. Pölten, 14.–18. Oktober 1992*. Studien zur Eisenzeit im Ostalpenraum: 13–71. Budapest: Archaeolingua.

Egg, M. 1996a. *Das Hallstattzeitliche Fürstengrab von Strettweg bei Judenburg in der Obersteiermark*. RGZM Monographien 37. Mainz: Römisch-Germanisches Zentralmuseum.

Egg, M. 1996b. 'Zu den Fürstengräbern im Osthallstattkreis', in E. Jerem and A. Lippert (eds) *Die Osthallstattkultur. Akten des Internationalen Symposiums, Sopron, 10.–14. Mai 1994*. Archaeolingua Main Series 7: 53–86. Budapest: Archaeolingua.

Egg, M., and A. Eibner. 2005. 'Einige Anmerkungen zur figural verzierten Bronzesitula aus Dolenjske Toplice in Slowenien'. *Archäologisches Korrespondenzblatt* 35: 191–204.

Eggert, M. K. H. 2012. *Prähistorische Archäologie: Konzepte und Methoden*, 4th edition. Tübingen: Francke.

Eibner-Persy, A. 1980. *Hallstattzeitliche Grabhügel von Sopron (Ödenburg). Die Funde der Grabungen 1890–92 in der Prähistorischen Abteilung des Naturhistorischen Museums in Wien und im Burgenländischen Landesmuseum in Eisenstadt*. Wissenschaftliche Arbeiten aus dem Burgenland 62. Eisenstadt: Amt der Burgenländischen Landesregierung.

Elsner, J., S. Deschler-Erb, B. Stopp, M. Hofreiter, J. Schibler, and A. Schlumbaum. 2016. 'Mitochondrial d-loop variation, coat colour and sex identification of Late Iron Age horses in Switzerland'. *Journal of Archaeological Science: Reports* 6: 386–396.

Friedrich, M., and H. Hennig. 1995. 'Dendrochronologische Untersuchung der Hölzer des hallstattzeitlichen Wagengrabes 8 aus Wehringen, Lkr. Augsburg und andere Absolutdaten zur Hallstattzeit'. *Bayerische Vorgeschichtsblätter* 60: 289–300.

Futrell, A. 2006. *The Roman Games: A Sourcebook*. Oxford: Wiley-Blackwell.

Gallus, S. 1934. *A soproni Burgstall alakos urnái. Die figuralverzierten Urnen vom Soproner Burgstall*. Archaeologica Hungarica 13. Budapest: Magyar Történeti Múzeum.

Gaunitz, C., A. Fages, K. Hanghøj, A. Albrechtsen, N. Khan, M. Schubert, et al. 2018. 'Ancient genomes revisit the ancestry of domestic and Przewalski's horses'. *Science* 360, 6384: 111–114.

Ginoux, N., G. Leman-Delerive, and C. Severin. 2009. 'Le dépôt de pièces de char dans les tombes de Gaule Belgique entre le IIIe et le Ier s. avant J.-C.'. *Revue Archéologique de Picardie 2009*, 3–4: 211–222.

Herrmann, J. J., and C. Kondoleon. 2004. *Games for the Gods: The Greek Athlete and the Olympic Spirit*. Boston, MA: Museum of Fine Arts.

Hüttel, H.-G. 1981. *Bronzezeitliche Trensen in Mittel- und Osteuropa: Grundzüge ihrer Entwicklung*. Prähistorische Bronzefunde XVI, 2. Munich: Beck.

James, S. 1993. *Exploring the World of the Celts*. London: Thames and Hudson.

Jay, M., C. Haselgrove, D. Hamilton, J. D. Hill, and J. Dent. 2012. 'Chariots and context: New radiocarbon dates from Wetwang and the chronology of Iron Age burials and brooches in East Yorkshire'. *Oxford Journal of Archaeology* 31, 2: 161–189.

Jerem, E. 1998. 'Iron Age horse burial at Sopron-Krautacker (NW Hungary): Aspects of trade and religion', in P. Anreiter, L. Bartosiewicz, E. Jerem, and W. Meid (eds) *Man and the Animal World*. Archaeolingua Main Series 8: 319–334. Budapest: Archaeolingua.

Joachim, H.-E. 1995. *Waldalgesheim: Das Grab einer keltischen Fürstin*. Cologne: Rheinland-Verlag.

Junkelmann, M. 1990. *Die Reiter Roms I: Reise, Jagd, Triumph und Circusrennen*. Kulturgeschichte der Antiken Welt 45. Mainz: Philipp von Zabern.

Kaus, M. 1989. 'Kimmerischer Pferdeschmuck im Karpatenbecken. Das Stillfrieder Depot aus neuer Sicht'. *Mitteilungen der Anthropologischen Gesellschaft in Wien* 118/119: 247–257.

Kemenczei, T. 2003. 'The middle Iron Age: Scythians in the Tisza region (7th–5th centuries B.C.)', in Z. Visy (ed.) *Hungarian Archaeology at the Turn of the Millennium*: 179–183. Budapest: Ministry of National Cultural Heritage.

Knüsel, C. 2002. 'More Circe than Cassandra: The princess of Vix in ritualised social context'. *European Journal of Archaeology* 5, 3: 275–308.

Koch, J. K. 2003. 'Pferdegeschirr', in *Reallexikon der Germanischen Altertumskunde 23*: 35–50. Berlin/New York: Walter de Gruyter.

Koch, J. K. 2006. *Hochdorf VI. Der Wagen und das Pferdegeschirr aus dem späthallstattzeitlichen Fürstengrab von Eberdingen-Hochdorf (Kr. Ludwigsburg)*. Forschungen und Berichte zur Vor- und Frühgeschichte in Baden-Württemberg 89. Stuttgart: Theiss.

Kossack, G. 1954. 'Pferdegeschirr aus Gräbern der älteren Hallstattzeit Bayerns'. *Jahrbuch des Römisch-Germanischen Zentralmuseums Mainz* 1: 111–178.

Krämer, W. 1989. 'Das eiserne Roß von Manching—Fragmente einer mittellatenezeitlichen Pferdeplastik'. *Germania* 67, 2: 520–539.

Krausse, D. 1992. 'Treibstachel und Peitsche. Bemerkungen zur Funktion hallstattzeitlicher Stockbewehrungen'. *Archäologisches Korrespondenzblatt* 22: 515–523.

Kromer, K. 1958. *Gemeinlebarn, Hügel 1. Inventaria Archaeologica. Österreich Heft 2, A 11, Metallzeit*. Bonn: Habelt.

Kromer, K. 1986. 'Das östliche Mitteleuropa in der frühen Eisenzeit (7.–5. Jh. v. Chr.). Seine Beziehungen zu Steppenvölkern und antiken Hochkulturen'. *Jahrbuch des Römisch-Germanischen Zentralmuseums Mainz* 33, 1: 1–97.

Lambot, B., and P. Méniel. 1998. 'La question du sacrifice animal dans les rites funéraires en Gaule Belgique'. *Revue Archéologique de Picardie 1998* , 1–2: 245–251.

Lepetz, S., B. Clavel, D. Alioğlu, L. Chauvey, S. Schiavinato, L. Tonasso-Calvière, et al. 2021. 'Historical management of equine resources in France from the Iron Age to the Modern Period'. *Journal of Archaeological Science: Reports* 40: 103250.

Lessing, E. 1980. *Hallstatt: Bilder aus der Frühzeit Europas*. Vienna: Jugend und Volk.

Librado, P., N. Khan, A. Fages, M. A. Kusliy, T. Suchan, L. Tonasso-Calvière, et al. 2021. 'The origins and spread of domestic horses from the Western Eurasian steppes'. *Nature* 598: 634–640.

Lucke, W., and O.-H. Frey. 1962. *Die Situla in Providence (Rhode Island). Ein Beitrag zur Situlenkunst des Osthallstattkreises*. Römisch-Germanische Forschungen 26. Berlin: De Gruyter.

Maier, F., and H. Birkhan. 2012. 'Pferd', in S. Sievers, O. H. Urban, and P. Ramsl (eds) *Lexikon zur keltischen Archäologie*. Mitteilungen der Prähistorischen Kommission 73: 1474–1476. Vienna: Österreichische Akadamie der Wissenschaften.

Maise, C. 1995. 'Eine Pferdebestattung der Frühlatènezeit und hallstattzeitliche Siedlungsreste in Forchheim, Kr. Emmendingen'. *Archäologische Ausgrabungen in Baden-Württemberg* 1995: 110–112.

Metzner-Nebelsick, C. 1994. 'Die früheisenzeitliche Trensenentwicklung zwischen Kaukasus und Mitteleuropa', in P. Schauer (ed.) *Archäologische Untersuchungen zum Übergang von der Bronze- zur Eisenzeit zwischen Nordsee und Kaukasus*. Regensburger Beiträge zur prähistorischen Archäologie 1: 383–448. Regensburg: Universitätsverlag Regensburg.

Metzner-Nebelsick, C. 1998. 'Abschied von den "Thrako-Kimmeriern"?—Neue Aspekte der Interaktion zwischen karpatenländischen Kulturgruppe der späten Bronze- und frühen Eisenzeit mit der osteuropäischen Steppenkoine', in B. Hänsel and J. Machnik (eds) *Das Karpatenbecken und die osteuropäische Steppe*. Prähistorische Archäologie in Südosteuropa 12: 361–422. Rahden: Marie Leidorf.

Metzner-Nebelsick, C. 2007. 'Pferdchenfibeln. Zur Deutung einer frauenspezifischen Schmuckform der Hallstatt- und Frühlatènezeit', in M. Blečić, M. Črešnar, B. Hänsel, A. Hellmuth, E. Kaiser, and C. Metzner-Nebelsick (eds) *Scripta Praehistorica in honorem Biba Teržan*. Situla 44: 707–735. Ljubljana: Narodni muzej Slovenije.

Metzner-Nebelsick, C. 2009. 'Wagen- und Prunkbestattungen von Frauen der Hallstatt- und frühen Latènezeit in Europa. Ein Beitrag zur Diskussion der sozialen Stellung der Frau in der älteren Eisenzeit', in J. M. Bagley, C. Eggl, D. Neumann, and M. Schefzik (eds) *Alpen, Kult und Eisenzeit. Festschrift für Amei Lang zum 65. Geburtstag*. Internationale Archäologie, Studia honoraria 30: 237–270. Rahden: Marie Leidorf.

Mihovilić, K. 1992. 'Die Situla mit Schiffskampfszene aus Nesactium'. *Arheološki vestnik* 43: 67–78.

Mihovilić, K. 1996. *Nezakcij. Nalaz grobnice 1981. godine (Nesactium. The Discovery of a Grave Vault in 1981)*. Monografije i katalozi 6. Pula: Arheološki muzej Istre.

Miles, D., S. Palmer, G. Lock, C. Gosden, and A. M. Cromarty. 2003. *Uffington White Horse and its Landscape: Investigations at White Horse Hill, Uffington, 1989–95 and Tower Hill Ashbury, 1993–4*. Thames Valley Landscapes Monograph 18. Oxford: Oxford Archaeology.

Müller, F., G. Kaenel, and G. Lüscher (eds). 1999. *Die Schweiz vom Paläolithikum bis zum frühen Mittelalter. IV: Eisenzeit*. Basel: Schweizerische Gesellschaft für Ur- und Frühgeschichte.

Neugebauer, J.-W. 1997. 'Beiträge zur Erschließung der Hallstattkultur im Zentralraum Niederösterreichs', in L. D. Nebelsick, A. Eibner, E. Lauermann, and J.-W. Neugebauer (eds) *Hallstattkultur im Osten Österreichs*: 165–190. St Pölten/Vienna: Niederösterreichisches Pressehaus.

Nielsen, S., J. H. Andersen, J. A. Baker, C. Christensen, J. Glastrup, P. M. Grootes, et al. 2005. 'The Gundestrup cauldron: New scientific and technical investigations'. *Acta Archaeologica* 76, 2: 1–58.

Nilsson, L. 2003. 'Animal husbandry in Iron Age Uppåkra', in B. Hårdh (ed.) *Centrality—Regionality: The Social Structure of Southern Sweden during the Iron Age*: 89–103. Stockholm: Almqvist and Wiksell.

Olmsted, G. S. 1979. *The Gundestrup Cauldron: Its Archaeological Context, the Style and Iconography of its Portrayed Motifs, and their Narration of a Gaulish Version of Táin Bó Cúailnge*. Collection Latomus 162. Brussels: Éditions Latomus.

Párducz, M. 1953. 'Le cimetière hallstattien de Szentes-Vekerzug III'. *Acta Archaeologica Academiae Scientiarum Hungaricae* 6: 1–22.

Pare, C. F. E. 1987a. 'Der Zeremonialwagen der Urnenfelderzeit—seine Entstehung, Form und Verbreitung', in F. E. Barth (ed.) *Vierrädrige Wagen der Hallstattzeit. Untersuchungen zu Geschichte und Technik*. RGZM Monographien 12: 25–68. Mainz: Römisch-Germanisches Zentralmuseum.

Pare, C. F. E. 1987b. 'Der Zeremonialwagen der Hallstattzeit—Untersuchungen zu Konstruktion, Typologie und Kulturbeziehungen', in F. E. Barth (ed.) *Vierrädrige Wagen der Hallstattzeit. Untersuchungen zu Geschichte und Technik*. RGZM Monographien 12: 189–248. Mainz: Römisch-Germanisches Zentralmuseum.

Pare, C. F. E. 1989. 'From Dupljaja to Delphi: The ceremonial use of the wagon in later prehistory'. *Antiquity* 63: 80–100.

Pare, C. F. E. 1992. *Wagons and Wagon-Graves of the Early Iron Age in Central Europe*. OUCA Monograph 35. Oxford: Oxford University Committee for Archaeology.

Pare, C. F. E. 2006. 'Wagen und Wagenbau, Wagengrab', in *Reallexikon der Germanischen Altertumskunde* 33: 51–68. Berlin: Walter de Gruyter.

Penninger, E. 1972. *Der Dürrnberg bei Hallein I: Katalog der Grabfunde aus der Hallstatt- und Latènezeit*. Münchner Beiträge zur Vor- und Frühgeschichte 16. Munich: Beck.

Périn, P., and M. Kazanski. 1996. 'Das Grab Childerichs I', in A. Wieczorek, P. Périn, K. von Welck, and W. Menghin (eds) *Die Franken: Wegbereiter Europas*: 173–182. Mainz: Philipp von Zabern.

Petersen, H. 1888. *Vognfundene i Dejbjerg Præstegaardsmose ved Ringkjøbing 1881 og 1883*. Copenhagen: Reitzel.

Piggott, S. 1983. *The Earliest Wheeled Transport: From the Atlantic Coast to the Caspian Sea*. London: Thames and Hudson.

Powell, T. G. E. 1971. 'The introduction of horse-riding to temperate Europe: A contributory note'. *Proceedings of the Prehistoric Society* 37, 2: 1–14.

Raulwing, P. 2000. *Horses, Chariots and Indo-Europeans*. Archaeolingua Minor Series 13. Budapest: Archaeolingua.

Rebay-Salisbury, K. 2012. 'It's all fun and games until somebody gets hurt: Images of sport in early Iron Age art of central Europe'. *World Archaeology* 44, 2: 189–201.

Rebay-Salisbury, K. 2017. 'Rediscovering the body: Cremation and inhumation in early Iron Age central Europe', in J. I. Cerezo-Román, A. Wessman, and H. Williams (eds) *Cremation and the Archaeology of Death*: 52–71. Oxford: Oxford University Press.

Reichstein, H. 2003. 'Pferd. Zoologisch-Archäologisches', in *Reallexikon der Germanischen Altertumskunde* 23: 29–35. Berlin/New York: Walter de Gruyter.

Riek, G. 1962. *Der Hohmichele: Ein Fürstengrabhügel der späten Hallstattzeit bei der Heuneburg. Heuneburgstudien I*. Römisch-Germanische Forschungen 25. Berlin: De Gruyter.

Rolle, R. 1979. *Totenkult der Skythen, Teil 1: Das Steppengebiet*. Vorgeschichtliche Forschungen 18. Berlin: De Gruyter.

Rolley, C. (ed.) 2003. *La tombe princière de Vix*. Paris: Picard/Société des amis du Musée du Châtillonnais.

Rudenko, S. I. 1970. *Frozen Tombs of Siberia: The Pazyryk burials of Iron Age Horsemen*. London: J. M. Dent and Sons.

Schlette, F. 1984. *Die Kunst der Hallstattzeit*. Leipzig: Seemann.

Schönfelder, M. 2000. 'Der spätkeltische Wagen von Boé', in F. Cecchi, M. Egg, A. Emiliozzi, R. Lehnert, A. Romualdi, et al. (eds) *Zeremonialwagen—Statussymbole eisenzeitlicher Eliten*.

Sonderdruck aus dem Jahrbuch des Römisch-Germanisches Zentralzuseums 46: 44–58. Mainz: Römisch-Germanisches Zentralmuseum.

Schönfelder, M. 2002. *Das spätkeltische Wagengrab von Boé (Dép. Lot-et-Garonne). Studien zu Wagen und Wagengräbern der jüngeren Latènezeit.* RGZM Monographien 54. Mainz: Römisch-Germanisches Zentralmuseum.

Schwindt, G. 1995. *Fahren mit Pferden*. Stuttgart: Franckh-Kosmos.

Šimek, M. 1998. 'Ein Grabhügel mit Pferdebestattung von Jalžabet, Kroatien', in B. Hänsel and J. Machnik (eds) *Das Karpatenbecken und die osteuropäische Steppe*. Prähistorische Archäologie in Südosteuropa 12: 493–510. Rahden: Marie Leidorf.

Spruytte, J. 1977. *Études expérimentales sur l'attelage: Contribution à l'histoire du cheval.* Paris: Crépin-Leblond.

Stead, I. M. 1979. *The Arras Culture*. York: Yorkshire Philosophical Society.

Steuer, H. 2003. 'Pferdegräber', in *Reallexikon der Germanischen Altertumskunde* 23: 50–96. Berlin/New York: Walter de Gruyter.

Teržan, B. 2011. 'Hallstatt Europe: Some aspects of religion and social structure', in G. R. Tsetskhladze (ed.) *The Black Sea, Greece, Anatolia and Europe in the First Millennium BC*: 233–264. Leuven: Peeters.

Tomedi, G. 2002. *Das hallstattzeitliche Gräberfeld von Frög. Die Altgrabungen von 1883 bis 1892.* Archaeolingua Main Series 7. Budapest: Archaeolingua.

Torbrügge, W. 1968. *Bilder zur Vorgeschichte Bayerns*. Konstanz: Thorbecke.

Torbrügge, W. 1992. 'Die frühe Hallstattzeit (HA C) in chronologischen Ansätzen und notwendige Randbemerkungen II. Der sogenannte östliche Hallstattkreis'. *Jahrbuch des Römisch-Germanischen Zentralmuseums Mainz* 39, 2: 425–615.

Uckelmann, M. 2013. 'Land transport in the Bronze Age', in H. Fokkens and A. Harding (eds) *The Oxford Handbook of the European Bronze Age*: 398–413. Oxford: Oxford University Press.

Van Endert, D. 1991. *Die Bronzefunde aus dem Oppidum von Manching*. Die Ausgrabungen in Manching 13. Stuttgart: Steiner.

Vollrath, F. 1964. 'Das Reiterlein von Speikern'. *Vorzeit* 1/2: 15–20.

Warmuth, V., A. Eriksson, M. A. Bower, and A. Manica. 2012. 'Reconstructing the origin and spread of horse domestication in the Eurasian steppe'. *Proceedings of the National Academy of Sciences* 109, 21: 8202–8206.

Winghart, S. 1999. 'Die Wagengräber von Poing und Hart a.d. Alz. Evidenz und Ursachen spätbronzezeitlicher Elitenbildung in der Zone nordwärts der Alpen', in *Eliten in der Bronzezeit. Ergebnisse zweier Kolloquien in Mainz und Athen*. RGZM Monographien 43.1: 515–532. Mainz: Römisch-Germanisches Zentralmuseum.

Wutke, S., E. Sandoval-Castellanos, N. Benecke, H.-J. Döhle, S. Friederich, J. Gonzalez, et al. 2018. 'Decline of genetic diversity in ancient domestic stallions in Europe'. *Science Advances* 4, 4: eaap9691.

IDENTITY

CHAPTER 33

DEMOGRAPHIC ASPECTS OF IRON AGE SOCIETIES

STEFAN BURMEISTER AND MICHAEL GEBÜHR[†]

Introduction

The study of demography offers a key to understanding the development of not only recent, but also historic and prehistoric populations. People are born, they have children, they may migrate, and they die. The sum of these individual life trajectories results in the demographic composition of a population. The ratio of different age groups, birth rate, rate of survival beyond childhood, and age at death constitute the fundamental building blocks of an age pyramid. It provides a first insight into the living conditions of a society. Numerous historical examples show that demographic trends can also play socially and historically determinant roles, and this is the case in the Iron Age too (e.g. Wierschowski 1994). Hence palaeodemography is a central element of the investigation of Iron Age societies.

The European Iron Age comprises diverse societies, in part living under completely different conditions, and which do not form a homogeneous cultural sphere. Thus it is to be expected that the demographic circumstances prevailing in the Faroe Islands were quite different from those of the *oppida* civilization of central Europe, or the populations of the Eurasian steppes. An overview like this can only deal with the subject in outline, with the aim of giving a general impression of the demography of Iron Age societies. We shall therefore content ourselves with sketching out general trends. And because our research interests lie in central, northern, and north-western Europe, we shall concentrate on the societies of those regions in the Iron Age.

In the first part of the chapter, the methods of palaeoanthropology, their possibilities and limitations, will be briefly presented using some Iron Age examples. We shall confine bibliographic references and explanations of anthropological procedures to what is necessary for archaeological and historical interpretation. The second part will enter into more detail and draw on our research on Iron Age cemeteries in order to outline the demographic development of Germanic societies and point to further possibilities that palaeodemographic studies offer.

Palaeodemography

Palaeodemography is a scientific subdiscipline at the intersection of physical anthropology and archaeology. Introductions to the subject exist in a series of standard works (e.g. Acsádi and Nemeskéri 1970; Hoppa and Vaupel 2002; Chamberlain 2006), but the Iron Age, though it has yielded many thousands of well-studied burials, is largely ignored in these overviews. In our opinion, the established approaches leave an enormous potential for palaeodemographic analyses unexploited. Historical demography especially lets us glimpse the further possibilities that demographic research can offer (e.g. Imhof 1977).

Skeletal data acquired through examination by physical anthropologists constitute the main source of information for palaeodemographic studies. Age at death and sex are crucial, as they form the basis of all further considerations. The quality of such evidence depends on how precisely physical anthropologists can identify their specimens. The rite of cremation that was practised among many Iron Age communities, which often reduces the bones to unidentifiable fragments, makes the analysis of skeletal data much harder. In cases where the same cremation assemblages were examined independently by different specialists, there have been serious discrepancies in the results (e.g. Articus 2004: 191, table 2, 230, table 10). Further progress in diagnostic methods should help to reduce such problems.

The fundamental parameters for constituting the demographic profile of a society are the ratio of sex and age groups. Here the emphasis is on sex; this must not be taken as an indication that the gender debate is being ignored by biologists, but rather that the focus is on biological sex and the inherent capacity to reproduce. Essentially, three demographic factors determine the status and development of a population: fertility, mortality, and migration. The relationship between the number of births and the mortality rate, as well as shifts in population due to migration, determines whether a population remains stable, grows, or shrinks.

Palaeodemography has been severely criticized within its own ranks, because the methods of age determination as a prerequisite for estimating age distributions created 'artefacts' (e.g. Bocquet-Appel and Masset 1982) and the model building rested on false premises (e.g. Petersen 1975). These difficulties have so far not been resolved satisfactorily (for discussions see Buikstra and Konigsberg 1985; Meindl and Russell 1998; Hoppa 2002). Two fundamental problems should be briefly touched on: on the one hand, the assumed stability of prehistoric populations, and, on the other, the disputed question of how representative the skeletal data are.

The rough temporal resolution of archaeological dating leads to a situation in which the data from broader periods is treated as though they were quasi-contemporaneous.

It is indeed impossible to circumscribe single generations or year cohorts. In addition, entire cemeteries are taken as a reference unit on the basis of a very few cases that are capable of being analysed. Thus an average population is defined, smoothing out and in consequence obscuring the original demographic dynamics. If this course is followed, then inevitably many populations under consideration will appear stable. But the culture-historical conclusions drawn from this exercise will remain factually groundless. The procedures currently employed to model dynamic populations (e.g. Gage 1985; Wood et al. 2002) unfortunately fail when it comes to the level of data recorded archaeologically. Beyond the chronological resolution of individual burial data, it is of course possible to identify different temporal horizons, which can be analysed on their own. The sequence of these stages can at its best allow an identification of demographic trends.

The second problem—the lack of representativeness of the skeletal data—is possibly more serious. The figures for fertility and mortality in a population are given by the ratio of the different age groups and illustrated in mortality tables. It is thus obvious that if a specific age group is under-represented in the archaeological data, this relationship, and therefore the demographic picture, shifts. The ethnological evidence clearly shows that, for a variety of reasons, burial practices were selective and that certain groups of people were given burials outside the ordinary cemeteries (Huntington and Metcalf 1991). We cannot therefore assume that all the dead of a given group were interred in their burial grounds. In particular, the often observed lack of children and old people suggests that we are faced with a lack of representativeness. Serious distortions can thus arise in demographic calculations. A deficit among adults aged over 45 years increases the crude birth rate by 10–20%, while a deficit of children lowers the fertility rate as well as the crude birth rate by 20–25% (Paine and Harpending 1998). The reasons behind such deficits may be found in the methods of identification used, in the specific conditions of preservation of children's skeletal remains, or again in the cultural practices of the time.

A series of procedures has been devised to test to what extent a cemetery population represents the living population of the time. These are based on model tables of death rates, derived from historic populations, i.e. recent populations in different social contexts collected by the United Nations (Weiss 1973). A neonate and child mortality of 40–50% is inferred from this, and the supposed deficit in subadults is adjusted mathematically. Such a formulation is legitimate as an approximation, but presents methodological difficulties because the transfer from model populations to Iron Age conditions cannot be verified. Populations in modern developing countries, which have been taken as a reference, live in marginalized conditions today, largely deprived of their traditional cultural practices of reacting to specific situations. European historic populations, which have also been used as a reference, were generally subjected to compulsory residence, an aspect of society that has its roots in the medieval and early modern social system. In both cases it must be assumed that the living conditions of the reference populations influenced the demographic factors in a way that cannot be expected a priori for prehistoric populations.

Based on model populations, a sample of the population is taken as broadly demographically representative if the ratio of children aged 5–9 years to those aged 10–14 years is greater than or equal to 2:1, and the ratio of children aged 5–15 years to adults does not fall below 0.1:1 (Bocquet-Appel and Masset 1977). The resulting indices allow for deficits within individual age groups to be corrected. For the Hallstatt period in southern Germany a deficit of neonates and infants of 34 % on average can thus be postulated. Based on the available burial data, this would indicate a mortality of neonates and infants of 43.4 % ± 4.1 % (Burmeister 2000a: 83).

Such methods of testing can only provide approximations for calculating a population size, because, independently of the validity of the basic assumptions, the error margin in calculations remains wide, particularly when determining the number of adults (cf. Dollhopf 2002). But, despite all the methodological problems encountered, there are as yet no alternatives to the procedures employed by palaeodemography. The data derived from physical anthropology are the only way that provides at least some insights into the demographic composition of prehistoric societies.

In many cases demographic trends follow an inherent logic: children not born today cannot have offspring tomorrow. Changes in demographic parameters, due for instance to the selective emigration of young adults or to losses of men in wars, lead to a decrease in the birth rate, which in turn has further demographic effects (e.g. Stangl 2008: 116–171).

For us it is ultimately not the demographic arithmetic that is of interest, but the social causes and effects of demographic processes. The data provided by physical anthropology are not to be read as protocols of the past; at best they reflect social processes that can be interrogated in terms of their history of effects. Historical demography teaches us that the structure of a local population, conditioned as it is by a number of fundamental factors, can be completely different from one place to another. We would abandon the ability to recognize such local conditions if we worked out the mortality curves of individual populations based on the averaged-out standard values of the UN mortality curves. In historical demography we recognize powerful demographic differences from region to region—partly dictated by law, religion, and social and economic circumstances. Cultural practices influence demographic trends; for example infant mortality increases when mothers with newborns are involved in the economic work process (Imhof 1977: 69–70), or certain religious constraints lead to specific attitudes towards children and hence to differences in child mortality (Heller-Karneth 2000). Only an examination of the social framework can help us to understand the demographic processes at work and the historical developments associated with them.

Population Densities

Many social factors have an effect on demography. Social complexity and the population size related to it are prominent among them, and here we can argue with concrete figures. Socio-economic evolution and the increase in social complexity are closely linked to population growth in Iron Age societies (for Britain, see Cunliffe 1978). Roman textual evidence gives us some indications about the size of certain peoples that came to the attention of Roman authors. So, for example, 160,000 Cimbri are reported to have stood against the Romans at the battle of Vercellae, over 260,000 Helvetii are said to have left their homeland, and 80,000 Vandals are recorded as having entered North Africa under Genseric. Such figures are fundamentally unreliable, as the Romans largely exaggerated the numbers of their opponents for propaganda reasons (Gerlinger 2008). Though the enemies of Rome were generally subsumed under an ethnonym, as a rule this designated polyethnic alliances (Wolfram 1979; Jarnut 1993), hence the size of the constituents of any of these alliances remains obscure too.

In this respect it is only through studying the size of cemeteries and settlements that we can advance our subject, although once again we face the problem of representativeness. Nils Müller-Scheeßel (2007) calculates that barely 9% of the Hallstatt period cemeteries of southern Germany are known. Adjusting for this deficit, this would imply that there were around 80,000 people alive at any one time in the Hallstatt C period in southern Germany, and around 200,000 in Hallstatt D. This corresponds to population densities of 0.77 and 1.82 inhabitants per km^2 respectively. Müller-Scheeßel concludes that at least for the earlier Hallstatt period these values are too low, and that we have to expect that not all the deceased were buried in the cemeteries.

The difficulties thrown up by such calculations are also illustrated by population estimations for La Tène period in north-western France. Demoule (1999) calculated a population density of 3.3 persons per km^2 for La Tène A, and 0.6 for La Tène B1, whereas Chossenot (1997), starting from different initial assumptions about the representativeness of the recorded burials, estimated a density of 1–5 persons per km^2 for La Tène A and 8–14 persons per km^2 for La Tène D (cf. Eggl 2009: 327).

In their cross-period analysis, Zimmermann et al. (2009) estimated a figure of 4 persons per km^2 for western Germany in the Iron Age. This value was based on several factors and fits well into the demographic development from the Neolithic to modern times. Yet such indications can only be understood as rough estimations or approximations and cannot be taken as standard values for Iron Age societies in general. Even if we can assume a population density of below 10 persons per km^2 in a given area, there were local exceptions, such as, for example, the north German coast, where in a small region a density of *c.*37 inhabitants per km^2 can be assumed for the Roman Iron Age (see Rau 2010: 498).

A different approach consists of attempting to define the recruitment area of Germanic warrior bands. Based on the catchment area of Germanic princely graves as well as the archaeological distribution of war booty sites in southern Scandinavia, it is possible to postulate that the size of warrior bands ranged from several hundred to 2,000–3,000 men (Steuer 2007). Again, certain assumptions underpin these calculations, such as the number of occupants of individual farmsteads or the ratio of recruits drawn from a given population (see Rau 2010: 499 for an overview). According to the settlement density of north-western Germany and Denmark during the Roman

Iron Age, regions of 1000 km^2 such as Anglia (Schleswig-Holstein/southern Jutland) could raise warrior bands of several hundred men. When combined with the war booty sites, it becomes possible to obtain a figure for the size of supra-regional political units.

Age at Death

Age at death is the starting point for reconstructing the demographic composition of prehistoric societies. It is only at death that individuals manifest themselves with their biographical data in the archaeological record and that they as members of a cemetery population can be incorporated into palaeodemographic analysis. The age-at-death distribution of the population being examined is obtained by allocating the individuals within a burial group proportionally to their age ranges—taking account of the degree of precision of their respective age determinations. This is illustrated by a histogram or 'mortality curve' which shows how many people died in which age category. If one looks at a mortality curve, reading from the base upwards (i.e. from young to old), the following picture normally emerges (e.g. Gebühr 2007: 29, fig. 1.2): a comparatively large number of young children up to seven years old is followed by a smaller number of older children up to 13 years old, and the next stage (i.e. juveniles) with even fewer individuals. The curve then grows markedly with young adults or middle adults (around 20 years and older), and it is often here that the maximum number of individuals is represented. Older age categories are represented by far fewer numbers and the curve generally fades out with the transition from mature to senile (Figure 33.1). In general, the accuracy of age determination—within the framework of morphological examination, the method most commonly applied—is greatest for children and young adults and decreases with older age.

Such a mortality curve or one very similar to it can be found almost everywhere in Iron Age Europe, among the Celts, Germanic peoples, Slavs, Vikings, and also—slightly modified—on the gravestones of the Roman Empire. The shape of the curve is presumably due to common factors that go beyond cultural traits: the physical strain and hazards to which people were exposed, be it disease, hunger, or accidents, in different age groups (Gebühr 2007). It starts with the vulnerability of newborns to disease, and continues, via accidents in childhood, with increasing exposure in adult life to risk in civilian and military life, and in pregnancy and childbirth, and ends with fragility and the specific afflictions of old age. The juvenile phase, on the other hand, when the body is already developed and before the individual is burdened with the higher risks of work, weapon bearing, and reproduction, appears to result in the lowest death toll. The average age at death is generally above 25 and under 35 years old. This figure must not be confused with the average age of the *living population*; the latter is as a rule about a quarter lower than the average age at death, since the living have not yet reached their maximum age.

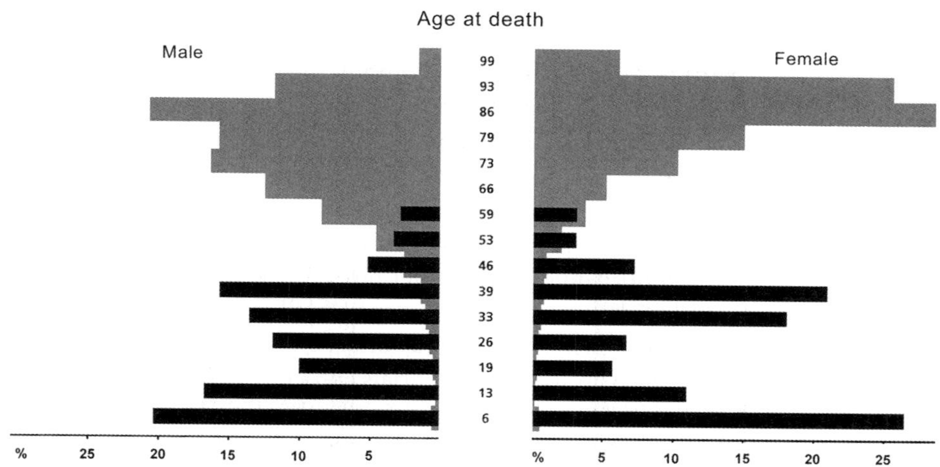

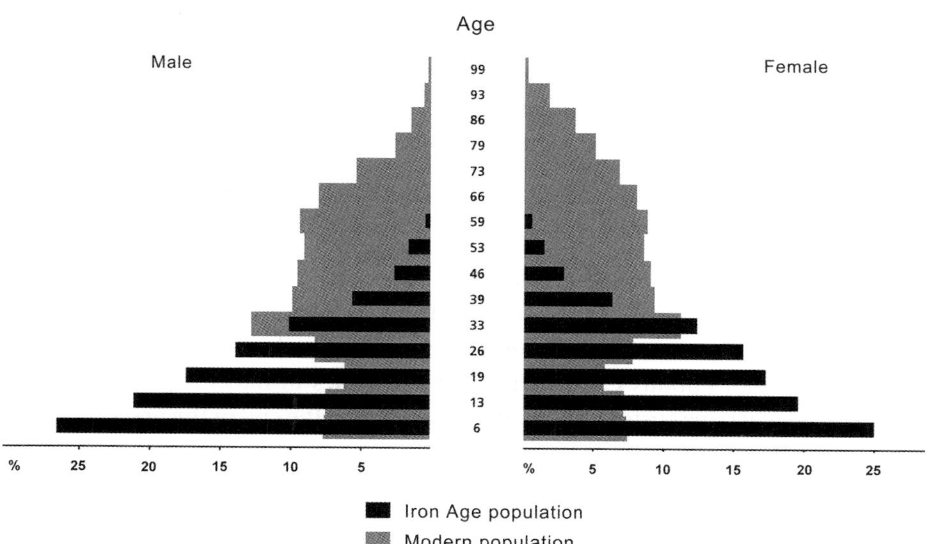

FIGURE 33.1 Mortality curve and life pyramid of the Iron Age population in Schleswig-Holstein, north Germany. The diagrams are based on anthropological data from the cemeteries of Schwissel and Hamfelde. For comparison, the modern population of Schleswig-Holstein.

Authors

Divergences from this standard mortality curve require explanations that must be found in specific causes. If they are not due to the vagaries of data acquisition, they may reflect culture-historical determinants. The low numbers of infants is a commonly observed departure from the standard pattern—when compared, for example, with mortality rates derived from parish registers or mortality curves of traditional societies and developing countries. The reason for child deficit in the archaeological record is mainly explained by the poor state of preservation of children's bones. But there are also cultural causes behind the scarcity of infants in cemeteries. The Iron Age cremation cemeteries of Schleswig-Holstein in northern Germany show evidence of a marked break around 100 BC: while in the earlier phase there are clearly demarcated age-group-specific grave goods, urns, and burial shape as well as a 30 % ratio of children, this changes in the ensuing centuries. Age-related burial equipments disappear progressively and children only make up 16 % of the burials (Brock 2007). The lower ratio of children's burials in the later phase could be explained either by a lowered child mortality rate or by an increased deficit in the representation of children. Since the change in the relative ratio of children's burials to the total number of people buried appears to be accompanied by a transformation in age-related burial practices, it seems more likely that we are seeing a different attitude to age and infant mortality which largely excludes children from the burial population. This is especially apparent in the cremation cemetery of Schwissel in Holstein (Krambeck 1992), which was in use from the fourth century BC to the first century AD. In the early phases all the infants were tightly clustered in a separate group, surrounded by loosely distributed adult burials; in the following centuries the great majority of infants are found on the outer edges of the cemetery; and in the final phase they disappear altogether—and single infant burials turn up on settlement sites.

If natality is largely subject to biological parameters, then the demography and number of children represented are different from the pattern shown when additional cultural, social, or economic conditions determine reproduction. The Roman politician and historian Publius Cornelius Tacitus describes in his ethnographic account *Germania* the marriage customs of Germanic peoples at the end of the first century AD. He reports that the man provided a dowry in the form of cattle, a horse and bridle, and a set of weapons (*Germania* 18). This has been variously interpreted as a form of bride price, but, strictly speaking, this is not the case. The groom does not buy the bride but brings goods in advance of marriage, gifts that will return to his household afterwards. It is thus rather a proof of the groom's economic potential, since the marriage can only be concluded if the family of the bride is satisfied. Such an arrangement is rather reminiscent of customs observed in early modern times in various parts of Europe. In France it was a common custom among rural communities that a marriage could only take place if a farmstead was in possession. Since the number of farmsteads could not just be increased, this meant in practice that a new couple could only be formed if another had ceased to exist (Imhof 1977: n. 80). Similar customs are known from various parts of the North Sea coast (Kersten and La Baume 1958: 78).

A marriage presupposes a certain minimum level of prosperity; only then, in general, can 'reproduction' begin. If marriage is delayed for economic reasons, conjugal fertility is delayed too. Although the frequency of births generally increases when reproduction starts later, this does not compensate for 'lost years' in terms of childbirths; entering a marriage five years earlier results on average in 15 % more children (Imhof 1977: 74–76). This can lead to economically induced fluctuations in population numbers. In times of economic hardship fewer people marry, fewer children are born, and the population shrinks, without migration playing a significant role. In contrast, in times of prosperity the average age of marriage decreases, the number of children increases, and the population grows without immigration playing a significant part. Demographic simulation runs produce similar results based on an economically supported marriage and hence reflect a (positive as well as negative) population growth in line with material prosperity (Gebühr 1994: 82). Such a pattern is to be expected in large parts of Iron Age Europe—at least in northern central Europe but presumably also far beyond.

Increased child mortality, or more precisely a larger number of dead children, is generally interpreted as a sign of adversity, poor hygiene, or cultural attitudes to breastfeeding. In the model presented here it signals rather the opposite, since in times of adversity marriages are started later and fewer children are born; if there are fewer children (who may be looked after by proportionally more adults), fewer will die and therefore the child mortality represented in cemeteries will be less prominent. By contrast, if many children are buried in a cemetery, this may reflect a prosperity-induced reproductive exuberance. It remains to be shown how far such considerations apply to the Iron Age and whether the archaeological evidence confirms such a scenario. It is, however, already apparent that a high child mortality rate in Iron Age burial grounds is in no way self-evident in all cases. The demographic side effects of migrations may also have an influence on the ratio of children buried (see later in the chapter).

Linking demography with cultural aspects of burial has its attractions. Was it—according to the type of burial and value attached to the grave goods—young or old who were elaborately buried? Men or women? In general there is a tendency, independent of variations in social status, to provide older men and younger women with particularly well-furnished burials (Figure 33.2). But sometimes we see the opposite, for example in the Viking period in Denmark, where the most valuable female grave goods (rich assemblages of fibulae) accompany older women, 50 years old on average. Similar trends can be observed in northern Europe as early as the beginning of the first century AD: occasionally there are highly elaborate burials of older women such as that of Juellinge II on Lolland (Müller 1911; Gebühr 1997a). It is unclear why it is in northern Europe that older women are relatively often richly furnished. It may be related to a somewhat different attitude towards women in general—as repeatedly reflected in Roman historical sources. Perhaps it stems from the legal position of women, which grants property ownership to them, and, as recorded in the later Sagas they were repeatedly widowed as a consequence of feuds, this wealth frequently increased through inheritance (see also Chapter 29).

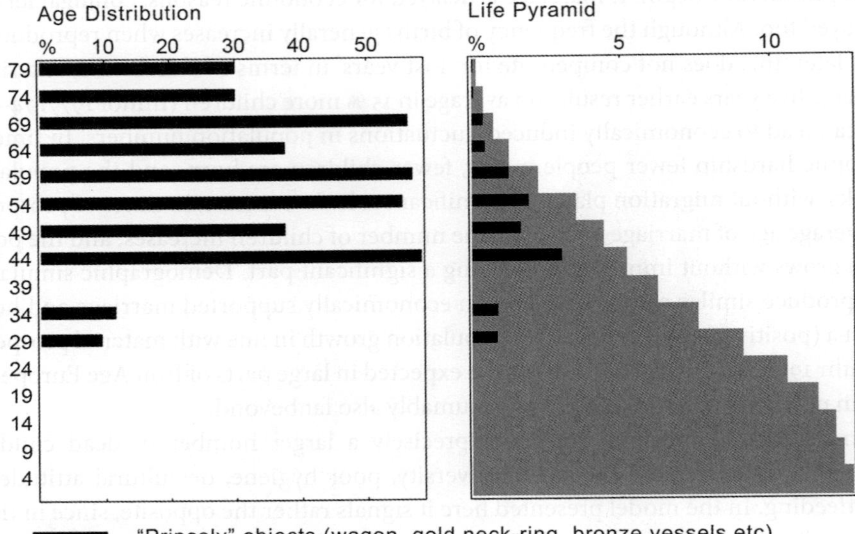

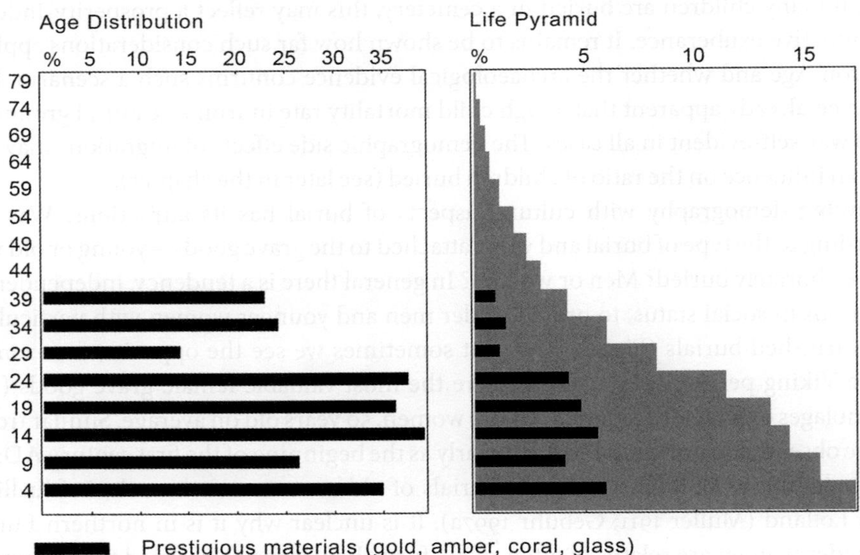

FIGURE 33.2 Gender- and age-specific high-status burials in late Hallstatt south-west Germany.

Authors

The analysis of age at death recorded in the burials of northern Europe appears to indicate a general change in pattern. In the final centuries BC, the trend was to furnish the graves of older people more elaborately, but this seems to change in the early centuries AD, when the status of women, compared to that of men, was enhanced in the burial customs of many regions (Gebühr 1994: 78–79; Derks 2012). This may indicate influence from the neighbouring Roman Empire. There, while respect for the dignity of old age (*senatus*) marked the Republican period, a new regard for youth ensued when young emperors began to rule, and leading women gradually discarded their virtuous reserve to take greater part in active political life (e.g. Balsdon 1962; Kunst 2013). This is likely to have had an effect in neighbouring barbarian regions, which were affected, even in the remotest corners, by the arrival of Roman goods and impulses.

The correlation between the various types of grave goods and age at death provides insights into certain 'stages of initiation' at a given age: when does a boy become a 'man'—or at least receive the equipment of a man—and when is a growing girl considered a woman? It seems that in large parts of northern and central Europe young men acceded to a new status and a new social role—signalled in particular by weapons—around the age of 20, marking the passage to adulthood. By contrast, girls appear to have been kitted out 'like a woman' in terms of personal ornaments from childhood onwards; their gender status was evidently recognized earlier than that of boys. Such a pattern can be observed for example in southern Germany during Hallstatt times (Burmeister 2000a: 89–94) as well as during the Roman Iron Age in Germany (Derks 2012: 175–187). In the Iron Age graves at the Dürrnberg in Austria, elaborate female ornaments were reserved to girls in the majority of cases. A supra-regional study comparing such customs is yet to be undertaken.

Roman gravestones (Acsádi and Nemeskéri 1970: 224, table 78) illustrate how different social groups can have quite distinct mortality curves. The spread of the average life expectancy ran from 17.5 years of age for slaves in the city of Rome to 58.6 years for members of the priestly classes. It is striking that life expectancy was lower on average in the city of Rome compared to a life spent in the countryside. The life expectancy of women could, depending on their occupation, also fall several years below that of men; only slaves and priests had a similar life expectancy among men and women—ideally both groups were expected to be celibate, which removed the greatest risk of death for women, i.e. death in childbirth (Figure 33.3). Though enjoying better living conditions, even the Roman upper classes had trouble with progeny: on the one hand, despite presumably better hygiene and material conditions, they did not manage to stem the tide of child mortality among their ranks; on the other, too many male offspring were not desired, because the apportioning of inheritance could result in their lacking the minimum fortune required for senatorial rank, with wide-ranging political and social consequences for the family (see Wierschowski 1994: 362, 360 fn. 21). Such nuanced demographic research is unfortunately not possible for Iron Age societies on the basis of the archaeological record alone.

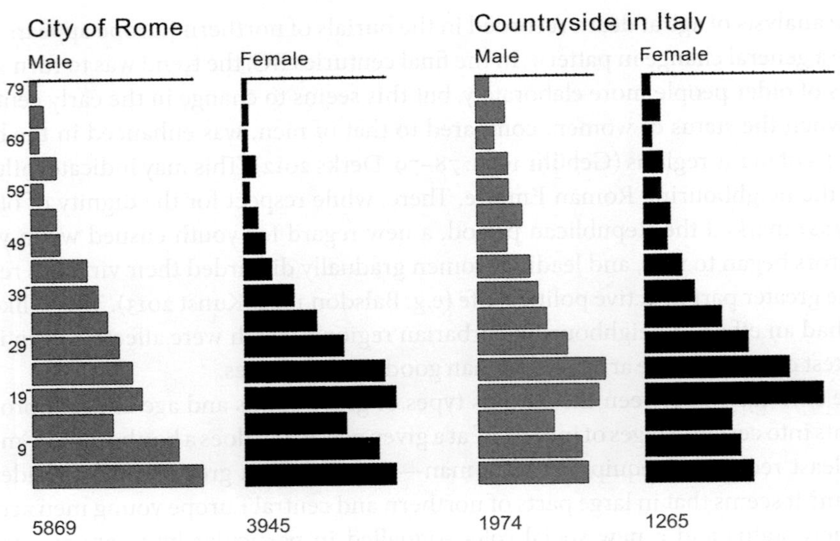

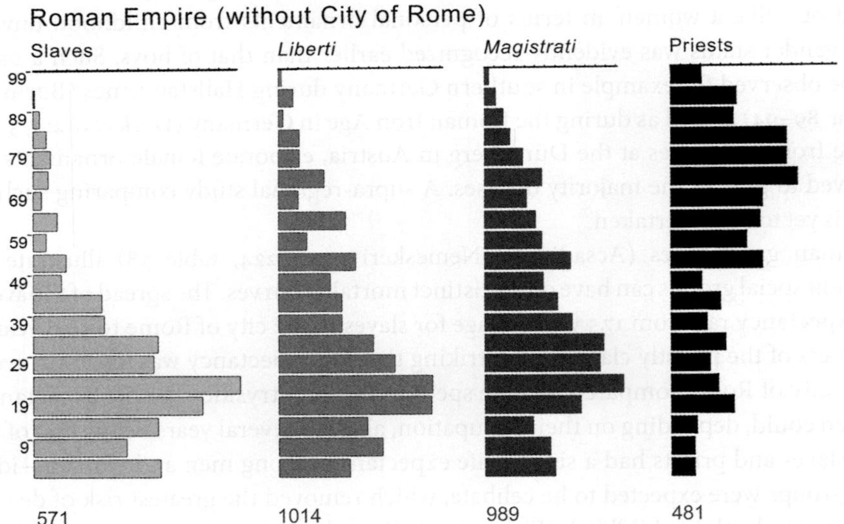

FIGURE 33.3 Mortality in the Roman Empire according to epitaphs on gravestones, first to sixth centuries AD.

Authors, data after Szilágyi 1961, 1962, 1963

AGE

If an acceptably reliable mortality curve is established, the average age composition of a living community can be reconstructed in a 'life pyramid'. The method rests on the principle used to calculate the headcount of a living population and employs the following formula: (number of dead) × (average age at death) ÷ (occupation span of cemetery); the procedure is simple (for further details see Gebühr and Kunow 1976: 193). Given the lack of precision of age determinations we can only generate approximate average values. The fact that people may have emigrated or immigrated while a cemetery was in use does not matter, as it is not the size of a settled community that is being considered, but literally the deceased population, wherever its members spent their lives.

The life pyramid is mostly a relatively flat pyramid with somewhat irregular edges. Even when over the course of time the actual population composition sometimes adopts another form, on the whole and considering all graves, it is always a pyramid that represents the average situation. As expected, the average age of the living lies clearly below the average age at death (see above; Figure 33.1).

If the mortality curve is similar to the expected life pyramid, then there are grounds to suspect a catastrophe, a massacre, or an epidemic, which claimed victims among the different age groups regardless of their average probability of dying; were the entire living population to die at the same time, then the mortality curve would match one to one the age composition of the 'life pyramid' of the previously living population.

Such may have been the case in the Viking period town of Hedeby (Haithabu) in Schleswig-Holstein in the ninth and tenth centuries AD (Gebühr 1994: 80). The mortality curve of the burials is as expected. It can be reconstructed into a correspondingly 'normal' life pyramid. In the settlement itself further skeletal elements have been recovered—partly dispersed and partly in small groups; the mortality curve derived from these individuals is less like the cemetery mortality curve and much more like the life pyramid derived from the cemetery data (Figure 33.4). Historic textual sources report that Hedeby was attacked several times and even captured, and occasional epidemics cannot be excluded either. It may be that such events could explain the resulting 'catastrophe curve'.

A low average age has all sorts of cultural and social consequences. For example, the question arises of the provision for children and their welfare, were their parents to die early—a problem that presumably had to be addressed in earlier prehistoric times, too. In the Iron Age, however, there is contemporary textual evidence that may provide some answers. Writing of Germanic people in the first century AD, Tacitus records that sons were held in as much esteem by their mother's brother as by their father, implying that some children grew up in their uncle's household (*Germania* 20). Thus a growing child received security and later support from its wider family circle, as well as the care of its natural parents. Such foster fathers are also occasionally recorded in early medieval literature, and foster parents are known from ancient Celtic sources too (Karl

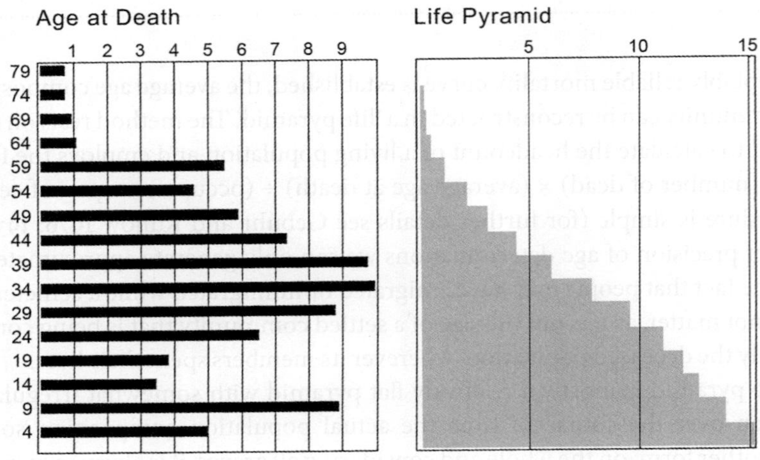

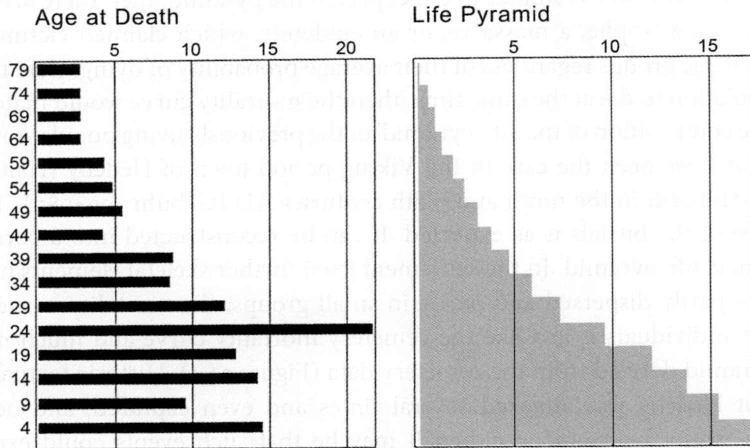

FIGURE 33.4 Opposing mortality curves and life pyramids of the Viking Age population from the cemeteries and settlement of Haithabu, Denmark. The mortality curve of the population interred in the settlement rather than in the formal cemeteries corresponds more closely with the life pyramid; this might be caused by catastrophic incidents.

Authors

2006: 437–440). Müller-Scheeßel et al. (2015) could demonstrate by strontium isotope analysis for Hallstatt and La Tène period populations that juveniles were often living outside the households of their biological parents. From the age of 6 onwards they left their home and moved to a new family—in some cases it was probably the family of the mother.

The comparison between life span and age at death has considerable repercussions on what grave goods may reveal in terms of cultural meaning—if we assume that the provision of these articles is characteristic of the deceased shortly before death. The burial assemblage reflects the equipment of a given individual at the end of his or her life, but not the material that this person previously had in his or her lifetime, which quantitatively is of far greater importance to the living. Were we today to follow the custom of putting into the grave attributes that reflected our lives shortly before death, there would be numerous pacemakers, walking aids, wheelchairs, and hearing aids—but hardly ever the skateboard of a young victim of an accident. Yet in a living Iron Age society, the young are on average several times more frequently represented than the old at any similar range of age; a comparison of the mortality curve with the reconstructed life pyramid of a given population makes this clear (Figure 33.1). Thus the burial assemblage of the old is always over-represented—with regard to the living population—compared to that of the young. Yet it is the representation of a living community that historical research mainly strives for. The 'dead society' we encounter in cemeteries merely serves as a starting point. The reconstructed life pyramid allows us to make inferences from the one to the other, in terms of the quantitative significance of specific grave goods. An example illustrates this point: the early Roman Iron Age female cemetery of Neubrandenburg in Mecklenburg contained only four graves with bronze belt elements, but twenty-five with iron exemplars. Since the latter are only found with older women, it follows that more—young—women with bronze belt ornaments would be encountered in the living population (Gebühr et al. 1989: fig. 8). At the Merovingian cemetery of Marktoberdorf in Bavaria (Christlein 1966) the percentage of (rather older) warriors bearing swords is halved when the figure is converted to the living; by contrast the archers increase. In general, long-range weapons (bows, spears) are found more frequently in the graves of younger men, suggesting that such weapons had a quantitatively greater importance for the living troops than would be suspected from the grave goods.

Women and Men

Other questions concern the ratio of the sexes—is there a clear surplus of males or females? What could cause such an imbalance? Selective infanticide? One-sided exogamy? Were men missing because they were killed in wars, or taken prisoner, or lost at sea, or because they emigrated? For many areas of Iron Age central and northern Europe asking such questions is admittedly of limited use. The vast majority of the dead recorded to date were cremated; in most cases the sexing of the skeletal material is insufficiently accurate, and results remain vague. Moreover it was the custom at least in large parts of northern Europe—a few exceptions aside—to bury men and women in separate cemeteries; to date not one 'matching pair of cemeteries' has been found.

Occasionally there are references to the marital age of men and women in ancient textual records. For example, Germanic people are said to marry somewhat later than their Roman counterparts (Tacitus *Germania* 20). According to Book 6 of Caesar's *de Bello Gallico*, a marriage contracted before the age of 20 was considered a 'very great disgrace'. Such claims must not be taken at face value, yet they appear to find corroboration in the anthropological material—assuming that the added risk of complications connected with pregnancy and childbirth is clearly expressed in the mortality curves of women. Such an expression could be attested by an abrupt rise in mortality or in a maximum mortality, providing an indication of the start of the age of reproduction and hence of marital age in general. A comparison of the mortality curve of women in the Roman Empire—based on their gravestones—with that derived from Roman Iron Age female cemeteries of northern central Europe—based on the identification of skeletal elements from inhumations or cremations—shows clear differences. Female mortality registers later in the north than in the Roman Empire. The maximum values can be as much as ten years apart (Gebühr et al. 1989: figs 19–20). We should therefore expect a later average age of marriage in the north, as the written sources suggest.

A consequence of the low life expectancy and late age of marriage is reflected in the question of the women left behind when men are killed in wars. It would be natural to think of mothers, widows, and orphans, but the demographic results and the written sources paint a rather different picture. Following Tacitus (e.g. *Germania* 15), it seems likely that founding a family was done towards the end of the time a man spent in arms, a period used to a very considerable extent to meet the economic conditions set for acquiring a bride (Burmeister 2009). The correlation of weapons with age at death shows that hardly anyone under the age of 20 was a warrior. Women, married after the age of 20 and fertile for 25 years on average, were thus unlikely to see their sons become warriors before they themselves were 45 years old. Since the average age of mothers hardly ever overstepped the 35–40 years mark, there cannot have been many who mourned their fallen sons. A similar situation applies to widows and orphans. If families were founded only after the end of the time spent as a warrior, a man killed in action was unlikely to leave behind a widow and orphans. The bereaved women were therefore probably mainly the sisters and girlfriends of the deceased (Gebühr 2000: 26–27).

Migrations

Migrations are a decisive demographic parameter. That emigration or immigration of population groups has an effect on demography is stating the obvious. But the migration of an entire population is highly unusual, although there seem to be exceptions, as with the Helvetii. As a rule migration is selective, i.e. a certain portion of a population emigrates, and it is mostly those of 20–30 years of age, especially men, who do so (Burmeister 2000b: 543; Chapter 37). Since this is the age group that produces the next generation, its departure (or arrival) has a particularly long-lasting effect on the wider demographic pattern. Yet the historical example of the Anglo-Saxon migrations shows that very specific and diverse processes are at work when large population movements are involved (Burmeister 2000b: 548–552; Härke 2011). Two separate processes are at play: the immigration of individual warrior groups and the family-based incoming of settler groups. It is easily understandable that each of these ideal types of population movement has demographic repercussions both in the area left behind and in the region of arrival.

The written sources frequently cite 'land-hunger' as the cause of the Germanic migrations. This suggests that soil exhaustion—and also a growing population—was involved. In addition, displacement at the hands of neighbouring tribes played a role, in which case an explanation should be sought in the land-hunger of the neighbouring groups. The heterogeneous nature of the various Germanic population movements alone shows that no single cause can be evoked for migrations.

Most Iron Age migrations recorded in written sources are, from an archaeological point of view, of little use in demographic research. Single finds of luxury goods accompany the Migration period, and individual cemeteries, generally small or of medium size at best, tend to be considered from an antiquarian rather than an anthropological angle. The Anglo-Saxon migration into Britain offers a relatively large number of burials, and hence a more or less reliable basis for demographic analysis. The Danish island of Fyn, and the cremation cemeteries of Issendorf in Lower Saxony and Spong Hill in East Anglia provide relevant case studies.

Only very limited anthropological data are available for Fyn, although with 3,600 Iron Age burials from 215 sites the island is archaeologically exceptionally well recorded. Moreover, the population pattern—insofar as the burials indicate—shows strong similarities in its sequence with the pattern exhibited by its neighbours, the Angles (Gebühr 1998), whose fate the island appears to share: first a slow growth up to AD 200, then an exponential increase in the number of burials, followed by an abrupt break around AD 400.

The quality and quantity of the grave goods show a clear increase in the second and third centuries AD; very few graves lack grave goods, and non-ferrous and precious metals become noticeably more frequent. Unless this gradual growth is a function of the source data or can be explained by an escalation in ritual behaviour, it is likely to indicate a general increase in prosperity, boosted by the favourable climatic conditions of the first centuries AD. If we retain the notion of a population growth induced by prosperity, as described earlier, a gradual lowering of the age of marriage and consequently an increased growth in population numbers are to be expected. Fyn does not provide sufficient anthropological data to be statistically significant; but in neighbouring regions with similar conditions, a decrease (albeit based on a small number of instances) in age for the maximum female mortality is observable (e.g. Gebühr et al. 1989: 100). At any rate the marked growth in the number of graves in the subsequent period is obvious.

It is not difficult to appreciate that such population growth would lead to a food crisis, given unchanging productivity—or even declining capacity resulting from over-exploitation—within a space that remained constant; furthermore the climate appears to have deteriorated after AD 300, with cold and wet conditions reducing the yield of harvests. Other factors must be considered and they point in the same direction. In the face of worsening conditions, overpopulation increasingly results in military conflict or migrations. Both are attested by different sources in the south-western Baltic region. Simulation models which test this hypothesis from the available data (Gebühr 1990) suggest that, besides other factors (climate change, the collapse of Roman long-distance trade, military unrest), demographically induced overpopulation appears to trigger migration. This result is based on the quantity and spatial distribution of the settlement evidence, and the archaeological patterns support such a conclusion remarkably accurately over more than 600 years.

Incidentally, when the simulation run was proceeded, the living environment was shown to have initially recovered more quickly than the descendant population managed to fill it, and that after some time—without outside interference—renewed population growth led to a new crisis, resulting in migration in the late Viking period. It is not necessary to dwell on this case, but the overarching question remains: is a population that remains largely unchanged and stable the norm, or should we not also consider the possibility—triggered by changes from 'outside' (climate change, plagues, wars)—of a 'pulsating' population pattern, as occasionally observed in predator–prey relationships as well as in the field of microbiology (Schäfer 1971)?

How a strong population movement alters the population pattern over the longer term, both in the area left behind and in the target region, is shown by the fifth- to sixth-century AD cemeteries of Issendorf and Spong Hill. Issendorf, located near Stade in Lower Saxony, contained over 3,000 urned cremations (Weber 1998), and Spong Hill in East Anglia more than 2,000 cremations (Hills and Lucy 2013). Some 700 km separate the two sites, yet they are more alike than any other two cemeteries of this period. They contained roughly equal numbers of both sexes, whereas the Angles of Schleswig Holstein (the presumed area of origin of Anglian migration) have separate cemeteries for men and women; they had a small proportion of east–west oriented inhumations, whereas in the region of the Angles the rite is exclusively cremation; and specific urn features are almost identical, as is the combination of grave goods and the correlation of certain grave goods with age at death. The two burial grounds resemble each other more than either of them resemble their respective neighbouring cemeteries in Lower Saxony and East Anglia. It could almost be argued that part of the Anglo-Saxon migration took place directly between the two sites (Gebühr 1998: 68–71; see also Hills and Lucy 2013: 318–319).

It was possible to determine, with the aid of the simulation program, how the demographic profile of the two cemeteries changed, from one region—out of which a proportion of young men (and to a lesser extent young families) moved over the decades—to the other (Gebühr 1997b), as predicted by the preferred migration model. The results are surprising. In the simulation run, the 'exit cemetery' contains a greater number of children and is rather biased towards the young; the situation in the 'target cemetery' is exactly the opposite. The young people who left the original area can no longer be buried in old age in the original cemetery; instead the cemetery in the new area is filled with older people. Given that at least in the initial stages of migration there are more men than women on the move, the rate of reproduction in the target area drops. The

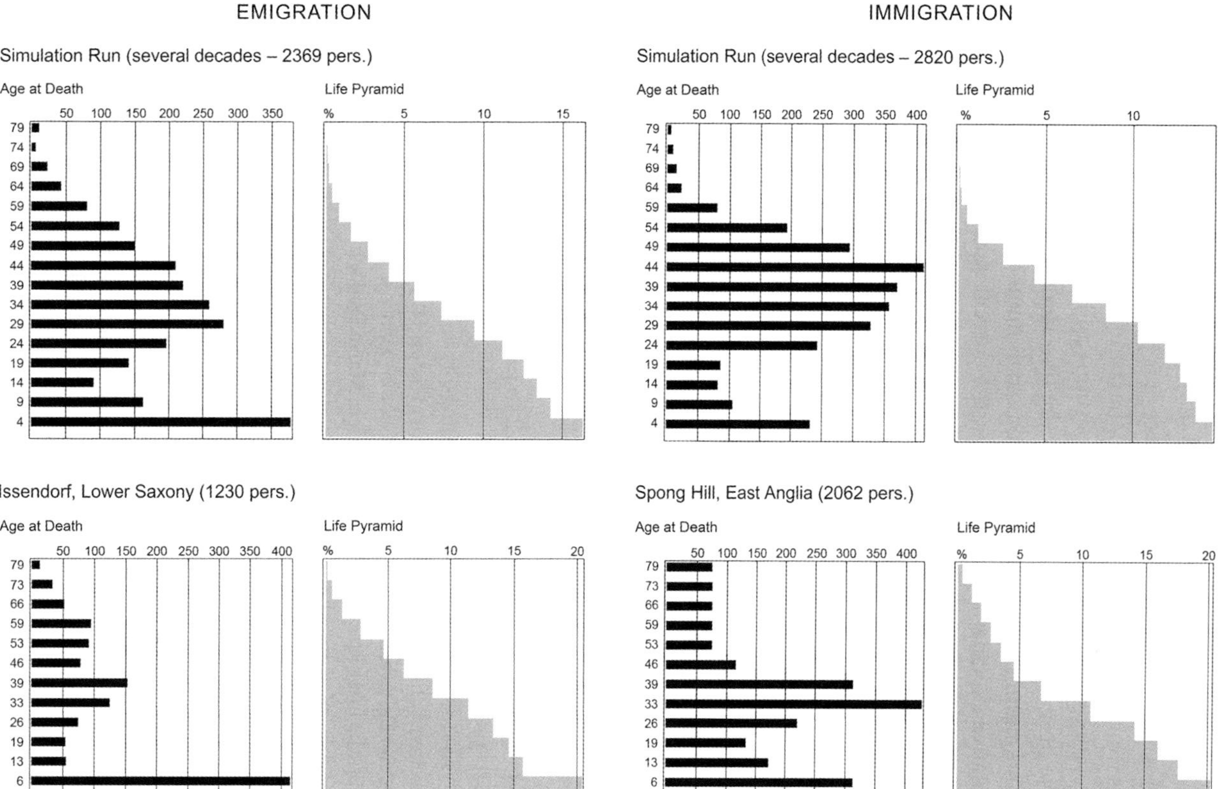

FIGURE 33.5 Simulated mortality curve and life pyramid of a population experiencing a long-lasting emigration vs a population experiencing immigration; in comparison the mortality curves and life pyramids of Migration period/early Anglo-Saxon populations from Issendorf, Lower Saxony, Germany, and Spong Hill, East Anglia, England.

Authors

model provided by the simulation run seems to be confirmed by the actual cemeteries in Lower Saxony and East Anglia. Issendorf, in the presumed emigration area, contains a surprising number of children's graves, and Spong Hill is biased towards older people (Figure 33.5). Only the sex ratio contradicts the model: the ratio of women at Spong Hill is no lower than at Issendorf (Gebühr 1998: 78–80). A supplementary hypothesis may help explain this situation: as observed elsewhere, it is possible that in the immigration area indigenous women were incorporated into the community (Härke 2011).

Such interpretations are beset with many questions and doubts from case to case—starting with the limitations brought about by the uncertainties of dating and skeletal identification and ending with the often still too small number of graves and the possibility of alternative explanations. But to us, in the current state of knowledge of the material and methodology, they appear to provide a better account of the evidence than competing explanations.

References

Acsádi, G., and J. Nemeskéri. 1970. *History of Human Life Span and Mortality*. Budapest: Akadémiai Kiadó.

Articus, R. 2004. *Das Urnengräberfeld von Kasseedorf, Lkr. Ostholstein. Die Entwicklung des südöstlichen Schleswig-Holsteins während der jüngeren römischen Kaiserzeit*. Internationale Archäologie 74. Rahden: Marie Leidorf.

Balsdon, J. P. V. D. 1962. *Roman Women: Their History and Habits*. London: Bodley Head.

Bocquet-Appel, J.-P., and C. Masset. 1977. 'Estimateurs en paléodémographie'. *L'Homme* 17: 65–90.

Bocquet-Appel, J.-P., and C. Masset. 1982. 'Farewell to paleodemography'. *Journal of Human Evolution* 11: 321–333.

Brock, T. 2007. 'Wo sind die Kinder? Zum Bestattungsort von Säuglingen und Kleinkindern im prähistorischen Schleswig-Holstein', in S. Burmeister, H. Derks, and J. von Richthofen (eds) *Zweiundvierzig—Festschrift für Michael Gebühr zum 65. Geburtstag*. Internationale Archäologie, Studia honoraria 25: 283–294. Rahden: Marie Leidorf.

Buikstra, J. E., and L. W. Konigsberg. 1985. 'Paleodemography: Critiques and controversies'. *American Anthropologist New Series* 87, 2: 316–333.

Burmeister, S. 2000a. 'Archaeology and migration: Approaches to an archaeological proof of migration'. *Current Anthropology* 41: 539–567.

Burmeister, S. 2000b. *Geschlecht, Alter und Herrschaft in der Späthallstattzeit Württembergs*. Tübinger Schriften zur Ur- und Frühgeschichtlichen Archäologie 4. Münster: Waxmann.

Burmeister, S. 2009. 'Fighting wars, gaining status: On the rise of Germanic elites', in D. Sayer and H. Williams (eds) *Mortuary Practices and Social Identities in the Middle Ages: Essays in Burial Archaeology in Honour of Heinrich Härke*: 46–63. Exeter: University of Exeter Press.

Chamberlain, A. 2006. *Demography in Archaeology*. Cambridge Manuals in Archaeology. Cambridge: Cambridge University Press.

Chossenot, M. 1997. *Recherches sur La Tène moyenne et finale en Champagne. Étude des processus de changement*. Mémoires de la Société archéologique champenoise 12. Reims: Société archéologique champenoise.

Christlein, R. 1966. *Das alamannische Reihengräberfeld von Marktoberdorf im Allgäu.* Materialhefte zur bayerischen Vorgeschichte 21. Kallmünz: Lassleben.

Cunliffe, B. W. 1978. 'Settlement and population in the British Iron Age: Some facts, figures and fantasies', in B. W. Cunliffe and T. Rowley (eds) *Lowland Iron Age Communities in Europe.* British Archaeological Reports International Series 48: 3–24. Oxford: British Archaeological Reports.

Demoule, J.-P. 1999. *Chronologie et société dans les nécropoles celtiques de la culture Aisne-Marne du VIe au IIIe siècle avant notre ère.* Revue archéologique de Picardie Numéro spécial 15. Amiens: RAP.

Derks, H. 2012. *Gräber und 'Geschlechterfragen'—Studie zu den Bestattungssitten der älteren Römischen Kaiserzeit.* Archäologische Berichte 24. Bonn: Habelt.

Dollhopf, K.-D. 2002. 'Erwachsenenrepräsentanz oder Erosionsverlust? Gedanken zu einem Dogma der Paläodemographie des frühen Mittelalters'. *Germania* 80: 295–304.

Eggl, C. 2009. 'Überlegungen zur demographischen Repräsentanz und Aussagekraft latènezeitlicher Bestattungsplätze', in J. M. Bagley, C. Eggl, D. Neumann, and M. Schefzik (eds) *Alpen, Kult und Eisenzeit. Festschrift für Amei Lang zum 65. Geburtstag.* Internationale Archäologie, Studia honoraria 30: 323–334. Rahden: Marie Leidorf.

Gage, T. B. 1985. 'Demographic estimation from anthropological data: New methods'. *Current Anthropology* 26, 5: 644–647.

Gebühr, M. 1990. 'Experiment: Ursachen für die Räumung Fünens im 5. Jahrhundert n. Chr.', in M. Fansa (ed.) *Experimentelle Archäologie in Deutschland.* Archäologische Mitteilungen aus Nordwestdeutschland Beiheft 4: 45–54. Oldenburg: Isensee.

Gebühr, M. 1994. 'Alter und Geschlecht. Aussagemöglichkeiten anhand des archäologischen und anthropologischen Befundes', in B. Stjernquist (ed.) *Prehistoric Graves as a Source of Information.* Kungliga Vitterhets Historie och Antikvitets Akademien, Konferenser 29: 73–86. Stockholm: Kungliga Vitterhetsakademien.

Gebühr, M. 1997a. 'The Holsteinian housewife and the Danish diva: Early Germanic female images in Tacitus and cemetery evidence'. *Norwegian Archaeological Review* 30: 113–122.

Gebühr, M. 1997b. 'Überlegungen zum archäologischen Nachweis von Wanderungen am Beispiel der angelsächsischen Landnahme in Britannien'. *Archäologische Informationen* 20, 1: 11–24.

Gebühr, M. 1998. 'Angulus desertus?'. *Studien zur Sachsenforschung* 11: 43–85.

Gebühr, M. 2000. *Nydam und Thorsberg. Opferplätze der Eisenzeit. Begleitheft zur Ausstellung.* Schleswig: Archäologisches Landesmuseum.

Gebühr, M. 2007. 'Tod und Jenseits in der Eisenzeit', in M. Freudenberg (ed.) *Tod und Jenseits. Totenbrauchtum in Schleswig-Holstein von der Jungsteinzeit bis zur Eisenzeit*: 28–37. Schleswig: Archäologisches Landesmuseum.

Gebühr, M., U. Hartung, and H. Meier. 1989. 'Das Gräberfeld von Neubrandenburg. Beobachtungen zum anthropologischen und archäologischen Befund'. *Hammaburg* 9: 85–108.

Gebühr, M., and J. Kunow. 1976. 'Der Urnenfriedhof von Kemnitz, Kr. Potsdam-Land. Untersuchungen zur anthropologischen Bestimmung, Fibeltracht, sozialen Gliederung und "Depot"sitte'. *Zeitschrift für Archäologie* 10: 185–222.

Gerlinger, S. 2008. *Römische Schlachtenrhetorik. Unglaubwürdige Elemente in Schlachtendarstellungen, speziell bei Caesar, Sallust und Tacitus.* Heidelberg: Winter.

Härke, H. 2011. 'Anglo-Saxon immigration and ethnogenesis'. *Medieval Archaeology* 55: 1–28.

Heller-Karneth, E. 2000. 'Konfession und Demographie—Plädoyer für eine differenzierte Betrachtung', in M. Matheus and W. G. Rödel (eds) *Landesgeschichte und Historische Demographie*. Geschichtliche Landeskunde 50: 69–80. Stuttgart: Steiner.

Hills, C., and S. Lucy. 2013. *Spong Hill, Part IX: Chronology and Synthesis*. Cambridge: McDonald Institute for Archaeological Research.

Hoppa, R. D. 2002. 'Paleodemography: looking back and thinking ahead', in R. D. Hoppa and J. W. Vaupel (eds) *Paleodemography: Age Distributions from Skeletal Samples*: 9–28. Cambridge: Cambridge University Press.

Hoppa, R. D., and J. W. Vaupel (eds). 2002. *Paleodemography: Age Distributions from Skeletal Samples*. Cambridge: Cambridge University Press.

Huntington, R., and P. Metcalf. 1991. *Celebrations of Death: The Anthropology of Mortuary Ritual*, 2nd edition. Cambridge: Cambridge University Press.

Imhof, A. E. 1977. *Einführung in die Historische Demographie*. Munich: Beck.

Jarnut, J. 1993. 'Die Landnahme der Langobarden in Italien aus historischer Sicht', in M. Müller-Wille and R. Schneider (eds) *Ausgewählte Probleme europäischer Landnahmen des Früh- und Hochmittelalters. Methodische Grundlagendiskussion im Grenzbereich zwischen Archäologie und Geschichte, Teil I*: 173–194. Sigmaringen: Thorbecke.

Karl, R. 2006. *Altkeltische Sozialstrukturen*. Archaeolingua Main Series 18. Budapest: Archaeolingua.

Kersten, K., and P. La Baume. 1958. *Vorgeschichte der nordfriesischen Inseln. Die nordfriesischen Inseln Amrum, Föhr und Sylt (Kreis Südtondern)*. Neumünster: Wachholtz.

Krambeck, K. 1992. 'Das Brandgräberfeld von Schwissel, Kreis Segeberg. Studien zum archäologischen und anthropologischen Befund'. MA thesis, Universität Hamburg.

Kunst, C. 2013. *Matronage. Handlungsstrategien und soziale Netzwerke Herrscherfrauen*. Osnabrücker Forschungen zu Altertum und Antike-Rezeption 19. Rahden: Marie Leidorf.

Meindl, R. S., and K. F. Russell. 1998. 'Recent advances in method and theory in paleodemography'. *Annual Review of Anthropology* 27: 375–399.

Müller, S. 1911. *Juellinge-Fundet og den romerske Periode. Nordiske Fortidsminder II, Hefte 1*. Copenhagen.

Müller-Scheeßel, N. 2007. 'Bestattungsplätze nur für die oberen Zehntausend? Berechnungen der hallstattzeitlichen Bevölkerung Süddeutschlands', in P. Trebsche, I. Balzer, C. Eggl, J. Koch, H. Nortmann, and J. Wiethold (eds) *Die unteren Zehntausend—auf der Suche nach den Unterschichten der Eisenzeit. Beiträge zur Tagung der AG Eisenzeit in Xanten 2006*. Beiträge zur Ur- und Frühgeschichte Mitteleuropas 47: 1–10. Langenweißbach: Beier und Beran.

Müller-Scheeßel, N., G. Grupe, and T. Tütken. 2015. 'In der Obhut von Verwandten? Die Zirkulation von Kindern und Jugendlichen in der Eisenzeit Mitteleuropas', in R. Karl and J. Leskovar (eds) *Interpretierte Eisenzeiten. Fallstudien, Methoden, Theorie. Tagungsbeiträge der 6. Linzer Gespräche zur interpretativen Eisenzeitarchäologie*. Studien zur Kulturgeschichte von Oberösterreich 42: 9–42. Linz: Oberösterreichisches Landesmuseum.

Paine, R. R., and H. C. Harpending. 1998. 'Effect of sampling bias on paleodemographic fertility estimates'. *American Journal of Physical Anthropology* 105: 231–240.

Petersen, W. 1975. 'A demographer's view of prehistoric demography'. *Current Anthropology* 16, 2: 227–245.

Rau, A. 2010. *Nydam Mose 1. Die personengebundenen Gegenstände. Grabungen 1989–1999*. Jysk Arkæologisk Selskabs skrifter 72. Århus: Århus Universitetsforlag.

Schäfer, W. 1971. *Der kritische Raum. Über den Bevölkerungsdruck bei Tier und Mensch*. Kleine Senckenberg Reihe 4. Frankfurt: Kramer.

Stangl, G. 2008. *Antike Populationen in Zahlen. Überprüfungsmöglichkeiten von demographischen Zahlenangaben in antiken Texten*. Grazer Altertumskundliche Studien 11. Frankfurt: Lang.

Steuer, H. 2007. 'Besiedlungsdichte, Bevölkerungsgrößen und Heeresstärken während der älteren Römischen Kaiserzeit in der Germania magna', in G. A. Lehmann and R. Wiegels (eds) *Römische Präsenz und Herrschaft im Germanien der augusteischen Zeit. Der Fundplatz von Kalkriese im Kontext neuerer Forschungen und Ausgrabungsbefunde*: 337–362. Göttingen: Vandenhoeck & Ruprecht.

Szilágyi, J. 1961. 'Beiträge zur Statistik der Sterblichkeit in den westeuropäischen Provinzen des römischen Imperiums'. *Acta Archaeologica Academiae Scientiarum Hungaricae* 13: 125–155.

Szilágyi, J. 1962. 'Beiträge zur Statistik der Sterblichkeit in der illyrischen Provinzgruppe und in Norditalien (Gallia Padana)'. *Acta Archaeologica Academiae Scientiarum Hungaricae* 14: 297–396.

Szilágyi, J. 1963. 'Die Sterblichkeit in den Städten Mittel- und Süditaliens sowie in Hispanien'. *Acta Archaeologica Academiae Scientiarum Hungaricae* 15: 129–224.

Weber, M. 1998. 'Das Gräberfeld von Issendorf, Niedersachsen. Ausgangspunkt für Wanderungen nach Britannien?'. *Studien zur Sachsenforschung* 11: 199–212.

Weiss, K. M. 1973. *Demographic Models for Anthropology*. Memoirs of the Society for American Archaeology 27. Washington, DC: Society for American Archaeology.

Wierschowski, L. 1994. 'Die historische Demographie—ein Schlüssel zur Geschichte? Bevölkerungsrückgang und Krise des Römischen Reiches im 3. Jh. n. Chr.'. *Klio* 76: 355–380.

Wolfram, H. 1979. *Geschichte der Goten. Von den Anfängen bis zur Mitte des sechsten Jahrhunderts. Entwurf einer historischen Ethnographie*. Munich: Beck.

Wood, J. W., D. J. Holman, K. A. O'Connor, and R. J. Ferrell. 2002. 'Mortality models for paleodemography', in R. D. Hoppa and J. W. Vaupel (eds) *Paleodemography: Age Distributions from Skeletal Samples*: 129–168. Cambridge: Cambridge University Press.

Zimmermann, A., J. Hilpert, and K. P. Wendt. 2009. 'Estimations of population density for selected periods between the Neolithic and AD 1800'. *Human Biology* 81, 2–3: 357–380.

CHAPTER 34

GENDER AND SOCIETY

RACHEL POPE

Introduction: Understanding Iron Age Societies Through Analysis of Gender

Over the last twenty-five years, archaeologists have been battling to disentangle Iron Age studies from the twin problems of masculine classical comment, and a male-dominated archaeology of the later twentieth century—which together bequeathed to us a somewhat imbalanced view of European Iron Age society (Pope and Ralston 2011; Arnold 2012). For Arnold (1991), treatment of Iron Age women had ranged from 'benign neglect to active sabotage', with a similar trend recognized in studies of Celtic history (Berresford Ellis 1995: 78). Later twentieth-century archaeological methodologies continued to rely on historical and/or anthropological analogy to reconstruct social organization—essentially an unrelenting circular argument, endlessly reproducing a familiar, romantic, patriarchal Celtic society.

Out of the post-processual movement came the reaction against analogy (Wylie 1985) and a move against two fundamental assumptions concerning Iron Age society: social hierarchy (Hill 1989) and patriarchy (Ehrenberg 1989; Arnold 1991). Subsequently, the tendency has been to jettison top-down social modelling in favour of more contextual methodologies, with gender archaeology providing one clear route towards a new understanding of Iron Age societies built up from the archaeological evidence (Sørensen 2000; Pope 2007). There has been important work on Iron Age gender in several parts of Europe since the 1990s, pioneered by Frank Hodson at Hallstatt, Stefan Burmeister and Bettina Arnold for Baden-Württemberg, and Pierre-Yves Milcent and Stéphane Verger for France; yet the dominant thinking on Iron Age social systems in Britain remains largely notional, and notably androcentric (Hill 2011).

Where are we now with a gendered archaeology of Iron Age Europe? While still grappling with various issues—such as the meaning of grave goods and costume as social or individual identity, and the low volume of sexed data—mortuary evidence remains the securest route to understanding gender in society (Pope 2007, contra Arnold 2012). Cemetery corpora (e.g. Hodson 1968, 1990; Pare 1992; Burmeister 2000; Rebay 2007) and syntheses (e.g. Demoule 1999; Baray 2000; Diepeveen-Jansen 2001; Evans 2004; Pope and Ralston 2011; Verger and Pernet 2013) now provide trends based on thousands of burials. Research on gendered structuring principles from mortuary traditions—e.g. via analysis of grave costume, goods, body position, feasting traditions, and barrow size—has enormous potential for integration with wider study of Iron Age society and regional cultural traditions.

In parallel, osteoarchaeology has developed rapidly, revealing the gender of social structures and social activities such as mobility, kinship, diet, labour, and violence (e.g. Kiesslich et al. 2005; Pany and Teschler-Nicola 2007; Jay et al. 2008; Redfern 2008; Oelze et al. 2012; Scheeres et al. 2013). Neither Iron Age gender nor the gender of power is as straightforward as once assumed, requiring a more 'intersectional' approach (Diaz-Andreu et al. 2005; Arnold 2016). Data from the centuries prior to interaction with Rome can then be compared with the classical texts. Combining this new evidence for gender and Iron Age societies, we can now challenge post-colonial interpretations and offer a more nuanced understanding of pre-Roman Europe, which we can compare to contemporary Mediterranean societies. As Fernández-Götz (2014: 101) has observed, 'it seems indisputable that women of the so-called Celtic and Germanic societies enjoyed greater liberty and freedom of action than their Greek or Roman contemporaries'.

This chapter focuses primarily on the good evidence that we now have for gender and society in the Hallstatt west (Figure 34.1), before turning to the growing evidence from the La Tène phase down to 250 BC. It closes with a review of gender from the first-century BC texts.

Salt and a New Social Order

In western Europe, our evidence for the earliest Iron Age (800–600 BC) reveals typically masculine items dominating burial traditions. Gündlingen swords are found across Britain and Ireland, and in male burials further afield—for example at Haroué, Magny-Lambert, Diarville T2 primary (France), Wijchen (Netherlands), and Pilsting-Oberndorf (Bavaria). In France, swords are often accompanied by razors; in the Netherlands by wagons (Fontijn and Fokkens 2007). We accept a cultural continuity of late Bronze Age traditions, celebrating men, swords, horses, and travel (Milcent 2015). In Germany, the emphasis is very much on high-status men—both in Bavaria (e.g. Schirndorf, with primary male interments and women buried at mound peripheries) and in the west, where men had large burial feasts with twenty to thirty ceramic vessels (Rebay-Salisbury 2016). The new cremation rite occurs first with individuals bearing swords. A degree of early contact with Italy is seen in male burials in Germany—e.g. Grosseibstadt G1, with four bronze vessels, or Frankfurt-Stadtwald with four bronze

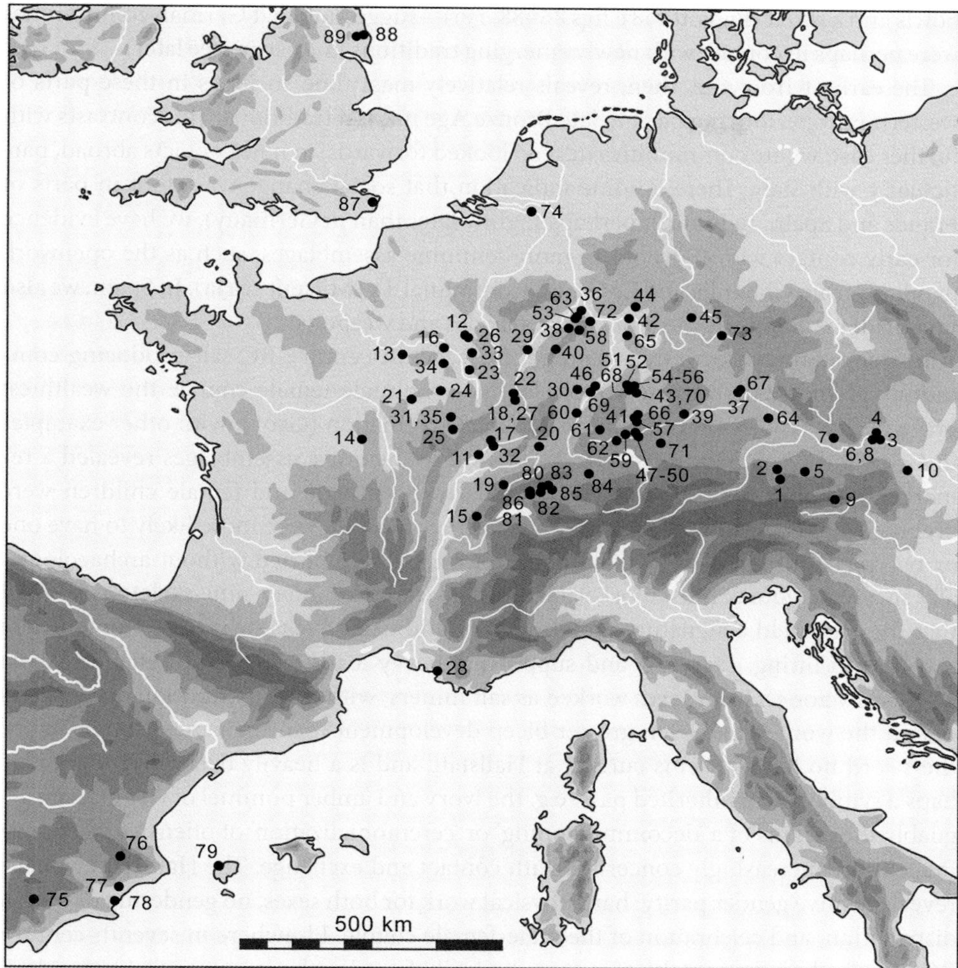

FIGURE 34.1 Map of sites mentioned in the text. *Austria*: 1 Bischofshofen-Pestfriedhof, 2 Dürrnberg, 3 Gemeinlebarn, 4 Grafenwörth, 5 Hallstatt, 6 Inzersdorf an der Traisen, 7 Mitterkirchen, 8 Statzendorf, 9 Strettweg, 10 Zagersdorf. *France*: 11 Apremont, 12 Aure, 13 Barbey, 14 Bourges, 15 Chemilla, 16 Chouilly Les Jogasses, 17 Courtesoult, 18 Diarville, 19 Le Grand Communal (La Rivière-Drugeon), 20 Grandvillars, 21 Gurgy, 22 Haroué, 23 Heiltz-l'Evêque, 24 Lavau, 25 Magny-Lambert, 26 Manre, 27 Marainville-sur-Madon, 28 Massalia, 29 Mondelange, 30 Nordhouse, 31 Sainte-Colombe-sur-Seine, 32 Savoyeux, 33 Somme-Bionne, 34 Vert-Toulon, 35 Vix. *Germany*: 36 Bell, 37 Beratzhausen, 38 Bescheid, 39 Dillingen-Kicklingen, 40 Elm-Sprengen, 41 Engstingen-Großengstingen, 42 Frankfurt-Stadtwald, 43 Gerlingen, 44 Glauberg, 45 Großeibstadt, 46 Heiligenbuck, 47–50 Heuneburg environs (Bettelbühl, Gießübel-Talhau, Hohmichele, Speckhau), 51 Hirschlanden, 52 Hochdorf, 53 Hochscheid, 54–56 Hohenasperg environs (Grafenbühl, Kleinaspergle, Ludwigsburg-Römerhügel), 57 Hohenstein-Oberstetten, 58 Hoppstädten, 59 Inzigkofen-Vilsingen, 60 Kappel-Grafenhausen, 61 Magdalenenberg, 62 Neuhausen ob Eck, 63 Niederweiler, 64 Pilsting-Oberndorf, 65 Reinheim, 66 Sankt Johann, 67 Schirndorf, 68 Schöckingen, 69 Söllingen, 70 Stuttgart-Bad Cannstatt, 71 Tannheim, 72 Waldalgesheim, 73 Weismain-Görau. *Netherlands*: 74 Wijchen. Spain: 75 Baza, 76 Cerro de los Santos, 77 Elche, 78 Guardamar, 79 Ibiza. *Switzerland*: 80 Allenlüften, 81 Châtonnaye, 82 Düdingen, 83 Grächwil, 84 Gunzwil-Adiswil, 85 Münsingen-Rain, 86 Payerne. *UK*: 87 Mill Hill, 88 Rudston, 89 Wetwang Slack.

bowls and a *situla* (Piggott 1983: figs 86–88, 139)—suggesting that German communities were perhaps in contact with newly emerging traditions in Austria (see later).

The earliest Iron Age, then, reveals relatively masculine societies in these parts of western Europe, looking back to late Bronze Age martial traditions. This contrasts with further east, where communities instead looked forwards, to new contacts abroad, particularly with Italy. There is some indication that social change was afoot in parts of France and Spain. In France (perhaps slightly later than in Germany), we have evidence for early contact with Italy, but in more feminine assemblages, such as the openwork pendants from Chemilla and Le Grand Communal T2 (Milcent 2013a). In Spain, we also find diadems alongside the more usual vehicles and weapons.

In stark contrast to western Europe, the seventh-century BC salt-producing community at Hallstatt seems to have celebrated the male-female couple: the wealthiest grave in the cemetery was a joint male/female cremation (G507), with other examples in G504 and G299. Hodson's (1990) seriation of the grave assemblages revealed a remarkable gender parity (Table 34.1); similarly, both male and female children were accorded status. Among the lowest status burials, women were more likely to have one or two pieces of jewellery, while one in four men were buried without archaeologically surviving goods. Musculoskeletal stress-markers in ninety-nine skeletons showed that the men held a signature of hammering and using picks, while the women were involved in lifting, carrying, and supporting heavy loads (Pany and Teschler-Nicola 2007; Pany 2009). Both sexes worked as salt miners, with task distribution on the basis of sex; the women had even greater bicep development than their men. Interestingly, the sword no longer seems current at Hallstatt, and is a heavily decorative item, perhaps a symbol of an inherited past (e.g. the ivory and amber pommel of G507), even arguably the origins of a 'decommissioning' or 'ceremonialization' of offensive weaponry in a culture increasingly concerned with contact and exchange. The Hallstatt evidence reveals relative gender parity: hard physical work for both sexes, no gendering of wealth distribution, and celebration of the male-female couple. Elsewhere in seventh-century BC Austria, however, wealth was more typically found with women, as at Statzendorf, Mitterkirchen, and Zagersdorf T1 (Pare 1992; Kiesslich et al. 2005; Rebay 2007).

As Hodson (1990) noted, connections displayed in Austria were often to the south and east: to Italy, Slovenia, and perhaps even to Scythia—communities where women shared high status—and in contrast to Germany, contact with Italy was considered appropriate for either sex. It was also women and children who received the first inhumations in Austria (e.g. Grafenwörth, Inzersdorf an der Traisen; Rebay-Salisbury 2016: 71). Communities in Germany and Austria had very different attitudes to gender at this time. By the sixth century BC, we see a peak in elite burials in the eastern Alps, alongside what appears to be a move towards female authority at the Dürrnberg (T59) and Hallstatt (G505), where the gold belt attachment might be read as a sword skeuomorph, utilizing the sun/wheel symbolism of the wealthiest Hallstatt C grave (G507) a generation earlier (Figure 34.2). The heavily decorated amber-inlaid ivory pommel of the Mindelheim sword of Hallstatt G573[1]—now dated to Hallstatt D1 after its parallel

Table 34.1 Gendered grave assemblages and status groups for the Ramsauer graves at Hallstatt, Austria

Status	Masculine		Feminine	
Group 1	No grave goods	26%	Bracelets, fibulae	45%
Group 2	Iron fragments, pins and/or axe/spear/knife/whetstone	51%	Bead necklaces and/or decorated belts + bracelets, fibulae	34%
Group 3 *household heads*	Sword (Ha C)/dagger (Ha D), *phalerae* (Ha C) and/or metal vessel + axe/spear/ knife/whetstone, iron fragments, pins	19%	Headdresses, hairpins/coil set, anklet, rod-link chain, wheel symbols/jangles, lunate fibulae + necklaces and/or decorated belts, bracelets, fibulae	16%
Group 4 *elites*	Specialist tools, axe sceptre, armour + sword/dagger, *phalerae*, metal vessel, axe/ spear/knife/ whetstone, iron fragments, pins	4%	Gold jewellery, heavy bronze ring, multiple chain, ox figurine, metal vessels + headdresses, wheels/jangles, necklaces and/or decorated belts, bracelets, fibulae	5%

After Hodson (1990): tables 13–14; 99

from Marainville-sur-Madon (Milcent 2013b)—exhibits a degree of decoration that is disproportionate: less socially current, more ritual than functional.

High-status motifs at Hallstatt were sacrifical animals, drinking, feasting, travel/contact, and cattle, water bird, and wheel—the last two together and of direct Italian inspiration (Kossack 1954; Merhart 1969). Following Hodson (1990) on cattle symbols at Hallstatt, the divinity figures of Strettweg, Gemeinlebarn (stag sacrifice), and Demlfeld may suggest that high-status women gained authority through practices of sacrifice and divination, certainly by the late seventh century BC. Although limited, the evidence suggests a fairly equitable seventh-century BC society, in line with communities to the south and east, giving way to greater female authority in the sixth century BC. Disproportionate female wealth seems to continue at the Dürrnberg, where we find two 'priestess' graves at Eislfeld T59 and T118 (Moosleitner 1997: 200; Moser 2009).

Mobility and Social Equity

At the end of Hallstatt C and in the first two generations of Hallstatt D1, a display of individual status is apparent, particularly in Baden-Württemberg, but also

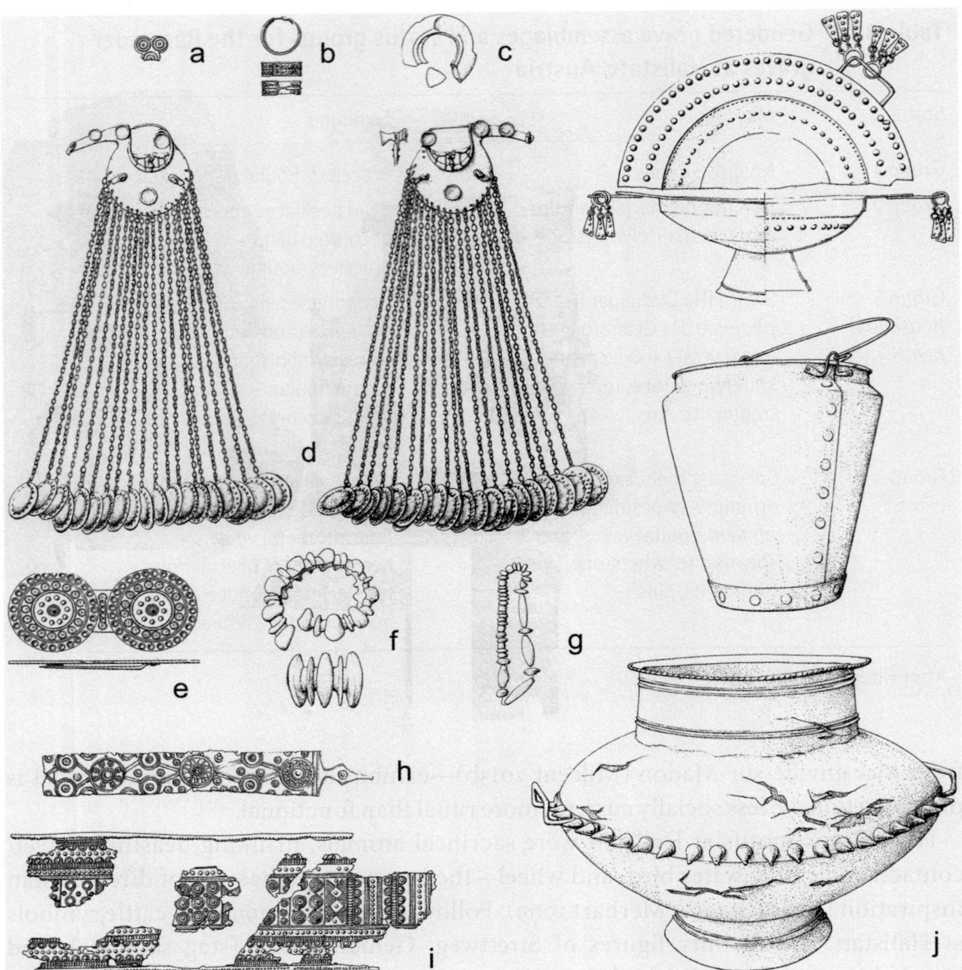

FIGURE 34.2 Hallstatt Grave 505. Gold: a, b, e, h; amber: c, g; bronze: d, f, i, j. Items not shown: second gold ear-ring, and coil; bronze belt hook and second ribbed arm-ring; and further amber beads. Not to scale.

Source: Hodson (1990), pls 35–36

further west (Stöllner 2014). This is evidenced by the huge tumuli raised for the men of Magdalenenberg (100 m in diameter) and Heiligenbuck (72 m), and the women of Hohmichele I (80 m) and Apremont (70 m), and perhaps also by the statue of Hirschlanden and the stelae of north-east Spain (Biel 1997). The social circumstances of the early sixth century BC meant that these individuals, and perhaps their achievements, were important—they represented something worth remembering in this new social system; they were well respected by their communities, who sought to monumentalize them on death and ensure that their stories continued.

Crucially, these individual 'founder burials' in Hallstatt D1 are both male and female—and the wealthiest burial assemblages (e.g. Hohmichele I and VI) occur with women (Ehrenberg 1989: 171; Pare 1992; Arnold 1995: 44; Frey 1997: 86). Contemporary with these individuals there is evidence for growing contact between Italy and Baden-Württemberg (bronze vessels at Hohmichele, Heiligenbuck, Sankt Johann, Kappel-Grafenhausen, and Engstingen-Großengstingen) and eastern France (Le Grand Communal T2, Chemilla, Nordhouse, Apremont, Marainville-sur-Madon, Diarville, and Gurgy). This development is roughly contemporary with the establishment of Massalia around 600 BC, with indications that this contact may have somewhat earlier origins in Germany. We also now have evidence for individuals who grew up in the Alps or northern Italy being interred at the Magdalenenberg in Hallstatt D1. The implication is a period of real mobility during the early sixth century BC, and one that seems not to have been gendered.

In sixth-century BC Austria, we find a greater proportion of female burials than male burials (e.g. Hallstatt, Bischofshofen-Pestfriedhof; Figure 34.3). For southern Germany, Arnold (2016) suggests that subadults were gendered female up to age 14. Alternatively, this may reveal a degree of gendered out-migration. In Bavaria, although clearly related to neighbouring Austria, the wagon burials reveal a more male-authored society, concerned with appearance (toilet sets, razors, pins). This more masculine society, with relaxed gender norms, displays a gender equity more akin to sixth-century BC Baden-Württemberg than Austria (Brun 1987; Pare 1992; Rebay-Salisbury 2016). Bavaria also appears more insular, with less Italian contact, almost as if stating its difference to Austria. One wonders if this community may have seen a degree of migration from Austria. Meanwhile, we see the Hallstatt community reducing Mediterranean contact, looking instead to the people of the Magdalenenberg and the Heuneburg/Hohmichele, themselves now clearly looking south. The sixth century BC represents a period of mobility and gender equity in Baden-Württemberg. Isotope analysis at the Magdalenenberg reveals a 'highly mobile' society between 616 and 575 BC. The 144 secondary burials comprised similar numbers of men and women, both with status items, and no gendered access to proteins—although a group of men with weapons did have higher protein levels (Oelze et al. 2012: 409, 413–415). This gender equity may in fact be linked to mobility—with individuals interred at the Magdalenenberg having grown up in relatively female-authored communities, such as the Heuneburg, Hallstatt, and northern Italy (Oelze et al. 2012: 416). Importantly, the isotope work revealed no relationship between sex and mobility.

At the Magdalenenberg, seriation data and osteological assessment (Zäuner and Wahl 2013) reveal a far greater number of items with secure female associations (bronze neck-ring, armband pair, bronze needles, amber, bronze belt adornments, spacers) than male (razors, as well as female items made in iron: belt plate, needle). Hallstatt D assemblages in Baden-Württemberg do not divide neatly into binary gender, with 10–15% of burials containing elements of both masculine and feminine attire (Burmeister 2000; Burmeister and Müller-Scheeßel 2005). This practice is most apparent with elders and children—the latter potentially receiving a token from each parent (contra Koch

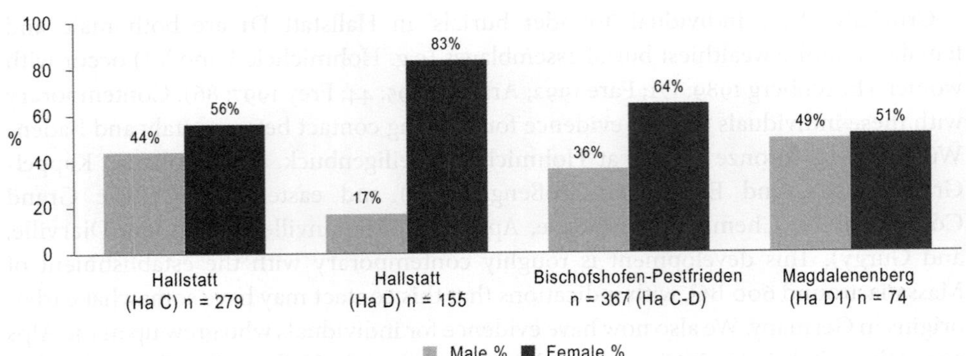

FIGURE 34.3 Gendered cemetery populations.

Sources Hodson (1990): table 12; Oelze et al. (2012); Rebay-Salisbury (2016)

2013). At the same time, a wide *range* of female items found at the Magdalenenberg with male bodies (arm/anklets, bronze belt plates, ear-rings, feminine brooches) suggests that grave goods were the by-product of very individual selection, with women perhaps more often placing tokens in male graves. Individual relationships were evidently well respected in mortuary behaviour, rather than the latter being governed by more formal social rules. Four of six sexed Magdalenenberg men with weapons were among those with more feminine items, with elders more likely to have daggers (Burmeister and Müller-Scheeßel 2005); they were perhaps also able to perform a more relaxed gender in their later years. As elsewhere, age seems the more significant structuring principle (Pope and Ralston 2011; Arnold 2016), with (elder) martial male identity also receiving greater access to proteins (Oelze et al. 2012).

Fluid Identities and Daggers

Beyond the Magdalenenberg, in the rest of Baden-Württemberg, gender seems yet more fluid for both men and women. A number of Hallstatt D1 graves, particularly in the south of the region, mix items categorized by seriation as either masculine or feminine, albeit mostly in the absence of osteological confirmation (Burmeister 2000; Burmeister and Müller-Scheeßel 2005; Figure 34.4). In addition to Burmeister's 'masculine' burials with typically feminine armlets/belt plates, there are also 'feminine' burials, with otherwise exclusively feminine neck-rings and hair ornaments, as well as typically masculine daggers/spears—notably Gerlingen 4/1 and Neuhausen ob Eck 1/1; other possible examples are Hohenstein-Oberstetten 2/2, Tannheim 5/1,[2] and two wagon burials at Kappel-Grafenhausen T3 and Sankt Johann. Of the other twelve high-status wagon burials where sex can be suggested (Pare 1992), four are women (Bettelbühl, Hohmichele I, Inzigkofen-Vilsingen, Engstingen-Großengstingen); the two wagon burials with the

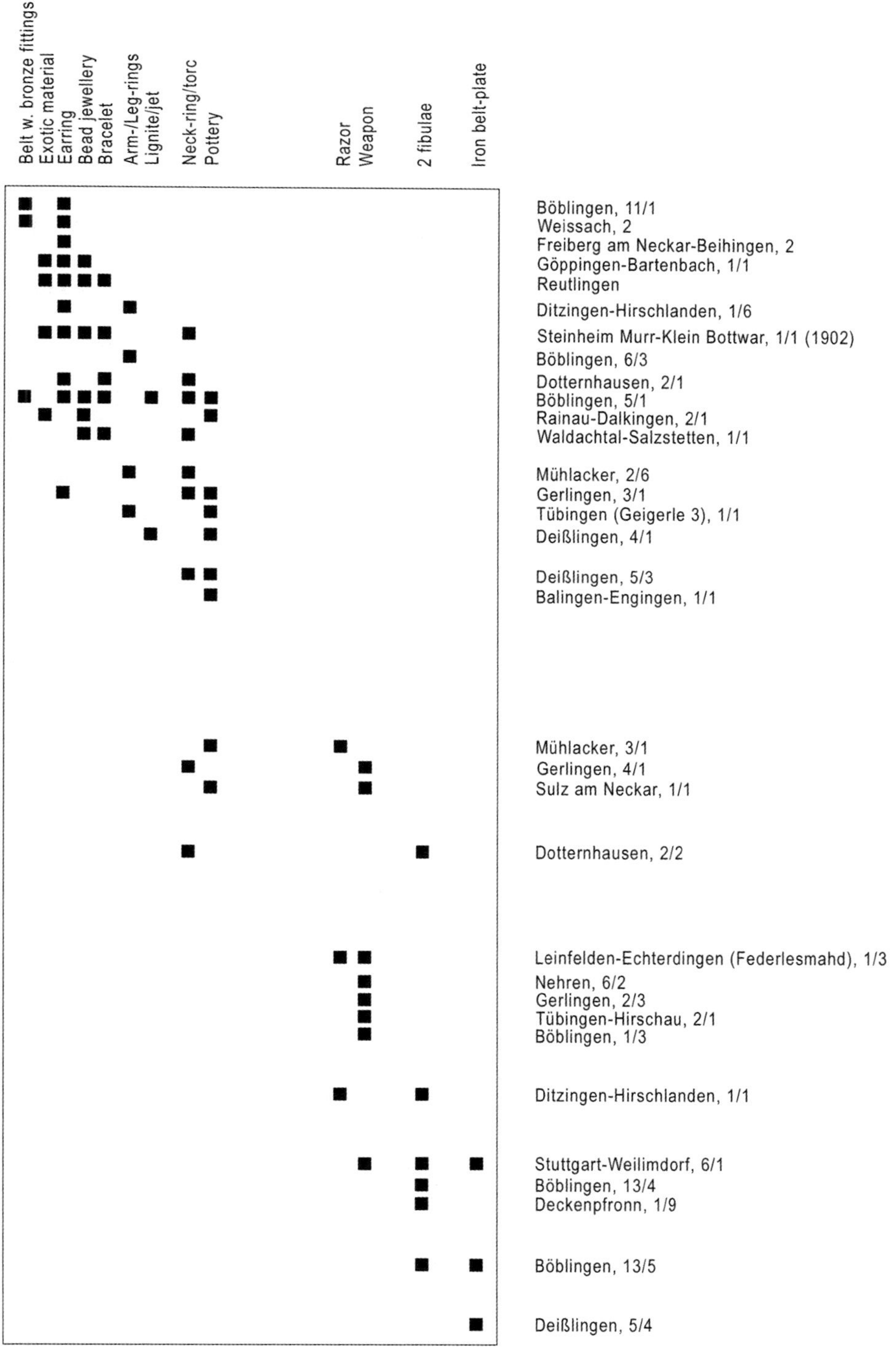

FIGURE 34.4 Burmeister's seriation methodology: North Württemberg, Germany, Hallstatt D1.

After Burmeister (2000): fig. 7

greatest evidence of Mediterranean contact were both female (Inzigkofen-Vilsingen, Kappel-Grafenhausen T3).

Other high-status women with wagons wear gold but, interestingly, do not have Mediterranean vessels (Bettelbühl, Hohmichele I). We can thus differentiate two distinct elite female identities in Baden-Württemberg: one with gold, but no Mediterranean contact (perhaps indigenous); the other with weapons and Mediterranean contact (perhaps linked to Greece). This pattern sits well perhaps with evidence for a more feminine male culture in Bavaria focused on appearance. As we move through Hallstatt D1, feminine burials do maintain elite status (e.g. Hohmichele I, Neuhausen ob Eck, Kappel-Grafenhausen T3). High-status men are present, but seem somehow under stress (e.g. Hirschlanden's 'mask' or Heiligenbuck's dagger hilt with no blade); alongside this, Burmeister's data point to growing gender fluidity (around 13% of the population). This might perhaps be related to an out-migration of men from Baden-Württemberg into the Rhineland after 550 BC (see later).

Following increasingly decorative swords among the well connected of Hallstatt, daggers appear by the start of Hallstatt D1 (620 BC), perhaps earlier in Switzerland (Sievers 1982; Hodson 1990). Swords decline more generally by 580 BC—primary Magdalenenberg man is without—but occur at 600 BC Gemeinlebarn (Austria), Hallstatt D1 Beratzhausen (Bavaria), and Diarville T2 (Meurthe-et-Moselle, France). The transition from sword to dagger seems very relevant to understanding gender in Hallstatt society. A defining moment exists at Apremont (Haute Saône), where the early sixth-century BC deceased had a ritually killed sword at her feet, perhaps representing the final 'death' of late Bronze Age culture. Between 580 and 425 BC, there was an interlude of five generations when high status was represented by daggers, particularly in

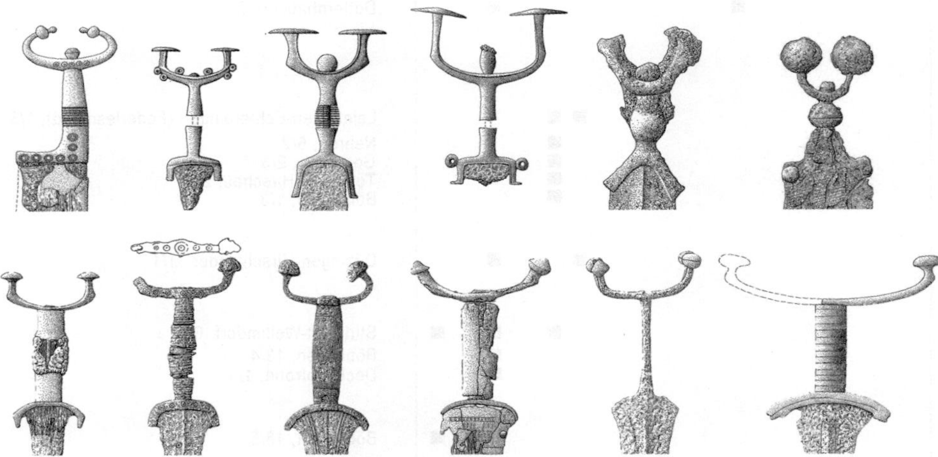

FIGURE 34.5 Selection of Hallstatt D dagger handles, revealing anthropomorphism focused on the belly and symmetrical ornament (especially Austria and France) and cattle symbolism (wider geographical spread).

After Sievers (1982)

Germany (Figure 34.5). Daggers occur first in high-status feminine assemblages (e.g. Neuhausen ob Eck, Kappel-Grafenhausen T3) contemporary with the Hohmichele VI man—who is notably without dagger.

The 'holding up' motif of Hallstatt D1 anthropomorphic daggers is also seen on the Strettweg wagon (600 BC), and later on the Hochdorf couch or *kline* (530 BC) and Reinheim mirror (450–400 BC)—these examples of the motif all gendered female. While Bronze Age studies accept swords and daggers as representing different fighting styles (Harding 2000: 277), Iron Age studies twenty years ago thought the dichotomy might reflect an inverse relationship with female authority (Frey 1997: 121). As contact abroad increased and Hallstatt traditions became more female-authored, daggers may have come to symbolize an ancestral, martial past. In Germany, swords are found only with men over the age of twenty, and daggers with elder men, suggesting that weapon type was related to age and social role, and that the dagger was a representation of former heroicism, linked more to elevated status than to active combat (Burmeister and Müller-Scheeßel 2005). While in seriation work, weapons are generally considered male, they do have feminine associations in elite assemblages; this is an area where we need increasingly contextual work with burial assemblages.

While Baden-Württemberg seems to mix male and female high status, and Bavaria seems more masculine, Hallstatt D1 eastern France seems to be under exclusively female authority, more like contemporary Austria, but (unlike Austria) with continuing strong links to Italy, and also clear links back to indigenous Bronze Age feminine tradition (Verger and Pernet 2013). Several female 'founder' barrows are known (Milcent 2003, 2004); they begin relatively modestly at 12–16 m in diameter, with indications that female lineage and authority were already important to communities, as perhaps seen most clearly at Courtesoult, almost a century before Vix (*c*.500 BC). Perhaps the most striking story comes from Apremont—arguably the first Hallstatt D leader in France—who had a particularly large barrow (70 m), akin to those of contemporary Heuneburg/Hohmichele, but otherwise echoed pre-existing feminine traditions in France (Verger and Pernet 2013). This woman—with our first gold neck-ring, four amber beads, five gold ornaments near the neck, a belt with ivory rings, and bronze cauldron with gold cup—had a masculine cremation (with razor at her feet), complete with ritually killed sword. Also relevant is Diarville, where the woman of T7 (40 m) had shoes, perhaps similar to Vix (Verger 1995: 445). Vix had a long lineage behind her that can be traced back to Germany/Austria, with links to Italy and central Europe remaining important. A similarly balanced social system seemingly existed in north-east Spain and in Britain, although gender information for both regions remains limited (Graells Fabregat 2011; Pope and Ralston 2011).

By the sixth century BC, out of a wealthy, gender-balanced salt trade in Austria, with strong Italian links, we see the growth of more feminine cultural traditions. Contemporary are the more equitable communities of the Magdalenenberg, the Heuneburg, and Bavaria (620–600 BC), while in France, we see the same feminine trend at Apremont and Courtesoult (600/580 BC), raising questions about the role of Greek contact through Massalia. The apparent westward shift at this period ties in chronologically with Livy's migrations south and east, to Italy and Bohemia, resulting from overpopulation, around 600 BC. After 550 BC, contact with Italy—which was again markedly feminine—developed further in both France and Germany, as with Nordhouse and Hirschlanden (Freidin 1982; Cunliffe 1997). In Baden-Württemberg, the largest Hallstatt D1 Mediterranean assemblages are from arguably feminine graves (Kappel-Grafenhausen T3 with fourteen bronze vessels; Inzigkofen-Vilsingen with eight). The last individual also has a Rhodian flagon—currently the earliest Greek item. The Greek contacts of these two burials anticipate Hallstatt D2/3 developments and may represent the origins of that tradition. As noted, isotope work at the Magdalenenberg has revealed a very mobile early Hallstatt D1, which material culture suggests continued throughout Hallstatt D. A pressing question is whether these Germanic/Celtic/Italic/Greek people were travelling, trading, allying, exchanging, settling, or—most likely—varying combinations of these social mechanisms, with some perhaps taking partners and settling abroad. The sixth century BC was a fluid period in identities, too, seen best in those of the women who came to dominate the Austrian salt trade, Bavarian men concerned with appearance, gender equity at the Magdalenenberg, Baden-Württemberg men with items of female dress, women with daggers, and the French lineage prior to Vix.

By Hallstatt D2/3, more women in Baden-Württemberg were buried with weaponry—best known is Stuttgart-Bad Cannstatt 1 (Arnold 1991)—with perhaps ten such women now identified in Germany, a few potentially appropriating masculine dress (e.g. with two fibulae, a typically masculine feature according to seriation; Burmeister 2000). Meanwhile some men in the north of Baden-Württemberg appropriated female items (bronze neck-rings, and several armlets or anklets), following the older southern tradition, where some men were buried with typically female belt plates and armlets. In sixth-century BC eastern France—where the evidence for high-status weaponry is more limited in this notably more feminine society—we also see an apparent 'mixing' of masculine and feminine items, such as the gold neck-rings at Apremont 2, Diarville T2, and Châtonnaye (Switzerland) with dagger, sword, and dagger chape respectively.

Daggers seem to be an artefact linked to more feminine social systems (Frey 1997). Arguably functioning as sword skeuomorphs—their high degree of symbolic imagery is fundamental—perhaps references to a heroic past. Daggers appear more appropriate for women as well as elder men (cf. Burmeister and Müller-Scheeßel 2005), and perhaps adolescents too (e.g. the small sword from Barbey; Marion 2004: 185). With origins in Germany at 620 BC, in Champagne we find British-Jogassian daggers dating to between 525–425 BC (Milcent 2015). In north-east Spain, burials of women and children, as well as men, contain notably short swords; daggers also appear on the warrior statues of northern Portugal. Swords, however, seem an artefact of more masculine and/or more actively martial societies (both earlier in Hallstatt C, and later during the La Tène period) and are more appropriate in the burials of younger men (20–40 years).

Gendered Lineages

In contrast to the evidence for elite women in France, gold neck-rings were a typically male item in Hallstatt D2/3 Germany (Hochdorf, Ludwigsburg-Römerhügel, Gießübel-Talhau), apart from one female example at Stuttgart-Bad Cannstatt and perhaps another at Kappel-Grafenhausen T1. Accepting the gold neck-ring as the symbol of authority, it seems that leadership was more often male in later sixth century BC Germany. Despite clear links with France, Italy, and Greece, Germany appears increasingly martial at this date (weaponry). Leadership seems even more masculine in the generation after 550 BC (Hochdorf, Ludwigsburg, Gießübel-Talhau, Söllingen), following greater contact with Greece, although the enhanced authority of these men in Germany, with their strong external links, was perhaps not welcomed by all.

The elder of Hochdorf (530 BC) stands out for the lavishness of the grave assemblage, his body resting on a *kline*, on badger fur and a pillow of herbs, his dagger gold-plated to match his shoes (Olivier 1999). During his lifetime, heavily martial societies formed in the Rhineland and Bavaria (Haffner 1997; Diepeveen-Jansen 2001)—perhaps masculine out-migration away from what Baden-Württemberg had become. Hochdorf's apparent heir, Grafenbühl (500 BC), with mirror and belt hook, may however have been a woman, a contemporary of Vix in France; the assemblage displays both extraordinary wealth and very strong Mediterranean connections akin to those of Hochdorf. Given the tendency to write powerful women out of the past (Arnold 1991, 2012), this burial should be reconsidered. Meanwhile in the eastern Alps, the older elite burials decline as they increase in the west (Rebay-Salisbury 2016). At Hallstatt, we have the antenna-hilted daggers (Sievers 1982), as at Dürrnberg Simonbauernfeld, with female authority perhaps until 470 BC (Moser 2009).

In eastern France, a more feminine social system continued, with a shift from collective to individual barrows at the start of Hallstatt D2/3 (Baray 2000: fig. 14)—the largest for the women of Sainte-Colombe-sur-Seine—suggesting that individual status remained important here during the later sixth century BC, just as it was developing even further in contemporary Germany, with the ostentatious displays of Hochdorf and Grafenbühl (albeit with smaller barrows). Vix was not the first woman with a gold neck-ring; as we have seen, they occur in feminine burials across the sixth century BC (Apremont, Diarville, Savoyeux, Mondelange, Grandvillars), placing the origins of female leadership in France in Hallstatt D1. In Switzerland, too, five women had gold neck-rings (Allenlüften, Düdingen, Gunzwil-Adiswil, Payerne, and perhaps Châtonnaye). In both countries, the majority of wagon burials were female (Milcent 2003; Baray 2000), perhaps suggesting a degree of gendered migration. Female high status is typical in the Hallstatt D2/3 cemeteries of eastern and central France (Diarville, Mondelange, Chouilly Les Jogasses, Aure, Manre, Heiltz-l'Evêque, Courtesoult, Bourges), with burial often in gendered groups (Diepeveen-Jansen 2001: 167; Fernández-Götz 2014: 95). Hallstatt D2/3 women in eastern France also display strong Mediterranean contact, with access to both Greek (Sainte-Colombe La Butte, Vix) and especially Etruscan drinking culture (Sainte-Colombe La Garenne; cf. Dietler 1990), the latter with parallels to Grafenbühl. In Switzerland, with its evidence for earlier Greek contact, we find the Grächwil *hydria* with female divinity figure (540 BC).

The huge barrows of Sainte-Colombe-sur-Seine (70–76 m in diameter) echo those of Hallstatt D1 Apremont and Hohmichele. Hallstatt D2/3 barrows for men are typically less than half the size at 20–40 m (Pare 1992). Vix—the richest grave in Celtic Europe—and her contemporary Grafenbühl are arguably heirs to a political system linking back to the Heuneburg, and ultimately to Hallstatt. Much ink has been spilled over Vix and her claim to authority (see Arnold 2016: 834); her torc was at first considered a 'diadem', despite its clear position around her neck. In Britain, one generation accorded her elite status—for Collis (1984) she was 'chiefly', for Cunliffe (1997) 'princely'—whereas James (2005) considered her a 'noblewoman' compared to Hochdorf as 'chieftain'. Nevertheless, Vix herself made clear political statements on gender and authority (Rolley 2003). The crowning warrior parade on her *krater*—an item of the masculine Greek symposium—had been removed and replaced by a central female figure from a south Italian workshop made a generation earlier (540–530 BC; Baray 2000; Rebay-Salisbury 2016), and the choice of Greek ceramics celebrated female warfare with Greece (Amazons fighting Hoplites).

The Vix burial actively subverted Greek masculinity and, through Greek material culture no less, made reference to distinctly female Celtic leadership, as testified by her 480 g torc—then the heftiest in Europe, surpassed only by the 580 g torc from the rich burial found in 2015 at Lavau in Champagne (Dubuis et al. 2015; Inrap 2015). Lavau (dated 500–475 BC) shows this social system surviving into early fifth-century BC France. Understanding the gender of this individual is critical: despite the amber beads, gold bracelet-pair, and lignite armlet, which might suggest a female gender (Dubuis et al. 2015; Inrap 2015; Arnold 2016), the poorly preserved skeleton is believed to be male. A male leader at the end of this strong female line is certainly interesting, perhaps drawing parallels with the richest early La Tène burials in Germany, which were female at the end of a strong male line (see later).

As we have seen, alongside growth in individual status, true social elites developed during Hallstatt D—first in Germany, arguably a generation later in France. Elite status involved several motifs: old drinking traditions, and long-lived contact with Italy (going back to Hallstatt C in Austria and surviving into La Tène B in Germany); daggers (popular between 580–425 BC, with Swiss/Austrian origins); neck-rings (female/gold across France; female/bronze in Hallstatt D1 Germany, subsequently becoming gold and appropriate for either sex); and latterly, contact with Greece, established first in Germany and in evidence down to 475 BC. Contact with Etruscan Italy became showier in Germany, and in Hallstatt D2/3, we find cauldrons/vessels with both sexes, but also now elite items, such as the Grafenbühl furniture and mirror, and later mirror at Reinheim. In Bavaria, a bronze bowl in three masculine burials and one cauldron with a woman suggests limited, and more typically masculine, contact.

In France, the old contact with Etruscan Italy was largely represented by cauldrons, and in Switzerland by single bronze vessels, in both cases with women. In Germany, elite burials were both male and female throughout Hallstatt D.[3] Milcent (2003) sees elite Hallstatt D1 France (Courtesoult, Apremont, Diarville, Gurgy) as a matriarchal society, and in Hallstatt D2/3, elite status remains feminine (Sainte-Colombe-sur-Seine, Savoyeux), peaking with Vix, followed by Lavau. In Germany, the growth of elites seems linked to masculine out-migrations to the Rhineland and Bavaria at the time of Hochdorf (530 BC), whereas in France, the out-migration to Champagne (450 BC) took place a generation after the final Hallstatt burial at Lavau. In both cases, the out-migrations ultimately gave rise to new, more egalitarian La Tène societies.

Twenty years ago, Frey (1997) suggested that the later sixth-century BC cultural system typified by Hochdorf influenced later developments in France, such as Vix. This general principle does work, but extends back to the start of Hallstatt D1. A generation before the construction of the Heuneburg, we have a male founder burial at Magdalenenberg under an enormous barrow, while the secondary interments reveal links back east to the Heuneburg, Hallstatt, and the Alps/northern Italy. Following this, we have evidence for links between Germany and France in the similarly sized barrows of Hohmichele I (80 m), Heiligenbuck (72 m)—broadly contemporary with the Heuneburg at 600 BC—and early sixth-century BC, and Apremont (70 m).

By the later sixth century BC, the links go back the other way: earlier Burgundian female burial traditions, such as gold neck-rings, are replicated at Stuttgart-Bad Cannstatt, Kappel-Grafenhausen T1, and by male leaders in Baden-Württemberg—perhaps the sons of this French sister-dynasty to the west. We find Courtesoult (600 BC) influencing male Hirschlanden (550 BC) and perhaps Speckhau T18 in concentric rings of burials (Arnold 2016); Apremont's gold cup akin to that of Hochdorf two generations later, and her 70 m barrow influencing Ludwigsburg. Piggott (1983) saw parallels between Apremont's wagon and that from Hallstatt D2–3 Stuttgart-Bad Cannstatt (female). Apremont (with ritually killed sword at her feet) seems particularly important. If the early sixth century BC burials in eastern France were the daughters of the Heuneburg, their sons seem to have returned to Baden-Württemberg by the later part of that century, as discord is apparent in the Rhineland and Bavaria. Later, parallels exist between Hallstatt D2/3 female leaders in the two regions, such as the comparably sized barrows of Sainte-Colombe-sur-Seine (70–76 m) and Kappel-Grafenhausen T1 (74 m); and the Etruscan tripods of Sainte-Colombe La Garenne and Grafenbühl. Iron Age societies in Germany and France were thoroughly linked, and very probably related, across the sixth century BC (Figure 34.6).

Greece and the Decline of Hallstatt

Our first gendered evidence for Greek contact comes from a female Hallstatt D1 wagon burial at Inzigkofen-Vilsingen (Germany), and the Grächwil *hydria* with its

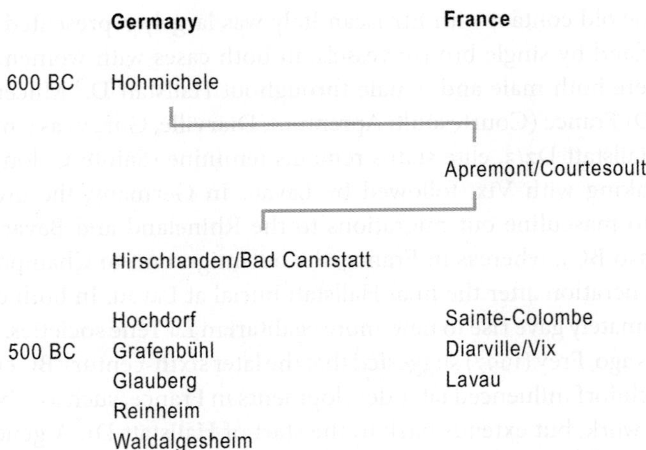

FIGURE 34.6 Links between German and French 'dynasties', potentially denoting kinship.

female goddess (540 BC). This new high-status contact was continued after 530 BC by Hochdorf, and a generation later Grafenbühl's intense contact with Greece and Italy produced a burial with an array of Mediterranean furniture and vessels. In eastern France, such extreme wealth is not found prior to 500 BC; developed contact with Greece seems the salient factor here. Two women reveal Greek contact between 530–475 BC: Sainte-Colombe La Butte with Greek ceramics and Massalian wine; Vix with krater and Attic cups; to whom we can now add Lavau with Greek cauldron and black-figure *œnochoe*. This developed elite contact with Greece seems current in Germany and France after 550 BC.

Greece made no inroads with the newer Hallstatt D2/3 cultures of Bavaria or the Rhineland, and was clearly more at home with the elites and relaxed gender norms of the older Hallstatt-derived communities in Germany and eastern France. We have two to three generations of elite contact with Greece (550–475 BC), first associated with women, and comprising a more ostentatious display of wealth and status. The mixing of Celtic and Greek traditions in these assemblages suggests political alliances, perhaps even kinship—Vix actively playing with, even subverting, the masculinity of Greek rule. Lavau sits well with Cunliffe's (1997) end date for an elite exchange system—arguably the cessation of direct contact with Greece. Contact was perhaps sustained, however, down to 400 BC further north and west, with Attic ceramics at Bourges (spanning the fifth century BC) and an Attic cup at Somme-Bionne (420 BC). It may have been this developed contact with Greece that sparked La Tène.

Alongside the well-known move out of the Hallstatt heartland (550–450/430 BC), first in Germany and then in France, and the new popularity of two-wheeled rather than four-wheeled vehicles, Greek contact—central to the last elite Hallstatt burials (Hochdorf, Grafenbühl, Vix, Lavau)—ended, alongside the rise of Athens and ensuing troubles with Sparta. This political move away from Greece, however, did not see the immediate decline of older Hallstatt traditions, which took place slowly across the subsequent century. In particular, the cessation of Greek contact at 450 BC did not impact on traditional connections with Italy, which were maintained for another two generations. Arnold's (1995) end date of 400 BC (transition to La Tène B), seems a good fit for the end of Etruscan contact (Reinheim, Kleinaspergle, Hoppstädten, Hochscheid, Bescheid, the Dürrnberg), although Waldalgesheim pushes this to 350 BC.

Etruscan vessels continue to be found predominantly with high-status women (Reinheim, Waldalgesheim), but also occur with children (Hoppstädten, Bescheid), while a man at Hochscheid was accompanied by two beaked flagons. At the Dürrnberg, Hallstatt traditions continued, with display of the old drinking culture down to 400 BC, and continued celebration of the male-female couple (Moosleitner 1997: 200). Female authority continued in several areas, particularly in Switzerland, Germany and—following male out-migration—Champagne (Champion 1995: 413; Verger 1995; Roualet 1997). We do, however, begin to see the ritual decline of these older social systems in La Tène A—notably the disproportionate deposition of inherited feminine wealth in Bavaria, Austria, and Switzerland; and often with the young—as the decline of Hallstatt traditions meant the women themselves jettisoned the status associated with these artefacts (Table 34.2; Moser 2009: 171). This seems to be the decline of female power, as wealth sits again with couples in Austria. After 400 BC, the old contact with Italy, as displayed through Etruscan vessels in funerary contexts, also ended—social networks and traditions that had lasted over two centuries.

The old Hallstatt lineage continued strongly in Germany, with masculine high status, but typically feminine authority—e.g. Reinheim and Kleinaspergle (with parallels to Vix)—arguably grander than Bescheid or Glauberg. That Kleinaspergle was considered female on excavation, but reinterpreted as male on finding alcoholic residues, is a sad indictment of twentieth-century reasoning (Arnold 1991, 2012). This final Hallstatt lineage became steeped in ritual at Reinheim, Glauberg, and ultimately Waldalgesheim (whose goldwork links back to Glauberg). These assemblages reference mistletoe headdresses and a dejected masculinity—the misery of Glauberg warrior, and Reinheim's stunted penises. Reinheim has eight human representations: women depicted in gold, men in bronze. This ritualized end to Hallstatt Germany comes nicely full circle, mirroring the ritual employed at its origins almost three centuries earlier in Austria (Hodson 1990).

Importantly, Hallstatt culture—and the feminine ritual traditions that retained its memory—did not finally end until the death of Waldalgesheim (350 BC). We do not see the same growth of active martial culture in this old heartland—with swords coral-decorated and no helmets—unlike contemporary Champagne and Austria. After 450 BC, we find rich female cremations in central France, near Bourges. Meanwhile, in southern Spain, elite female status at 450 to 350 BC is revealed in statuary (Las Damas de Baza, Elche, and Guardamar), linked perhaps to continued Greek contact. Running counter to the increase in swords elsewhere, north-east Spain sees an absence of weaponry after 450 BC, while further south, Baza (female, richest tomb in cemetery) has weapon deposition. In Britain, we have mirrors in East Yorkshire with female founder burials at Wetwang Slack after 300 BC. Akin to final Hallstatt Germany two generations earlier, by the third century BC, high female status also seems to have taken on a more

Table 34.2 Examples of disproportionate deposition in graves in late Hallstatt and early La Tène Europe

Cemetery	Grave	Sex/age	Disproportionate deposition
Hallstatt D Bavaria			
Weismain-Görau	T3	Female?	9 bronze neck-rings, 20 arm-rings
Bad Königshofen-Merkershausen	1897	Female?	13 bronze ankle-rings, 9 fibulae
Schesslitz-Demmelsdorf	-	Female?	5 bronze neck-rings, 10 arm-rings, 12 ear-/hair-rings
La Tène A Austria			
Dürrnberg	-	Female	Large number of fibulae
La Tène A Switzerland			
Münsingen-Rain	G12	Child, 7–14 yrs	Iron neck-ring, 140-bead amber necklace, bracelet and anklet pair, 5 finger-rings, 5 fibulae, glass bead, perforated antler coronet (off-cut from spindle whorl manufacture?)
	G23	Child	51-bead necklace (amber, blue glass), bronze neck-ring, bracelet and anklet pair, decorated clay ball, 3 fibulae
	G62	Child, with milk teeth	38-bead necklace (amber, blue glass), fine bronze chain, 2 bracelet pairs, ankle-ring pair, bronze finger-ring, 8 fibulae
	G149	Female, 14–20 yrs	118-bead necklace (blue glass, amber), iron and bronze chain, 3 bracelets, 2 anklet pairs, 4 finger-rings (2 silver, 2 bronze), 16 fibulae

ritual dimension in southern Spain with Las Damas de Ibiza and Cerro de los Santos (300–250 BC), alongside growth of new La Tène martial culture to the north.

New La Tène Traditions

The origins of a new La Tène social system are first seen in the Rhineland after 550 BC, where a more masculine community seems to have grown out of the old order, with wagons and neck-rings (and even a gold ear-ring at Elm-Sprengen); representing perhaps a degree of out-migration from Baden-Württemberg, during the leadership of Hochdorf—a newly opulent male authority, with links back to the sister-dynasty in France, and very heavy links to Greece. Unlike the situation in Baden-Württemberg, but perhaps more akin to Bavaria, the new Rhineland community had limited interest in the Mediterranean—although late Hallstatt wagon burials (i.e. Niederweiler with cauldron;

Bell with *situla*) do reveal earlier Rhineland links with Italy. Similarly, the Rhineland had no interest in ostentatious display; instead, the emphasis was on spears, and it is here that we see the first chariots—the new Rhineland identity was martial. This community was overtly masculine, with an apparent absence of women (Haffner 1997: 175), and leadership was strongly male. It was around this time that men begin to be found with daggers in Baden-Württemberg (Ludwigsburg, Gießübel-Talhau, Hochdorf) and spears became appropriate for elite women too (Stuttgart-Bad Cannstatt). Hochdorf's dagger, however, was gold covered, and the grave depicted ritualized scenes of martiality (especially the swords on the *kline*). It is the motif of combat that becomes important among Hallstatt leadership during this time of apparent out-migration to the north and east. Those in the Rhineland seem unimpressed by the new links to Greece (or perhaps back to France), or the ostentation of Hochdorf, choosing instead to build more equitable societies north of the old heartland. From the material culture, it seems that they may not have left without a fight. The same seems to have been true on Baden-Württemberg's eastern border.

Out of a more male-authored Hallstatt D1 Bavaria—which may itself have involved an earlier out-migration from Austria—we see a different social trajectory. In Hallstatt D2/3 Bavaria, wagon burials were predominantly male (85%), although not high status, and associated with weaponry (Pare 1992), perhaps suggesting that travel was associated with combat, rather than the more positive wagon association between contact and exchange. This swell of male chariot burials in Hallstatt D2/3 might again suggest movement out of Baden-Württemberg at the time of Hochdorf to this established, different society in Bavaria, with its Hallstatt D1 origins. Like the Rhineland, but unlike its neighbours in Baden-Württemberg, late Hallstatt Bavaria was less concerned with absorbing Mediterranean culture.

In Bavaria too, however, the wealthiest wagon burials were again female, revealing perhaps the roots of Hallstatt social traditions. Within this, we again see disproportionate deposition (e.g. the nine neck-rings and twenty arm-rings with the woman of Weismain-Görau 3); this seems to be an active deposition of old feminine Hallstatt wealth, in this reconfiguring society, very much like the slightly later episode among the women and children of Münsingen-Rain and the Dürrnberg (Table 34.2). This is wealth that had lost its social currency. Instead, society was increasingly martial, as in the Rhineland, to the extent that even the distinctly feminine high-status burial of Dillingen-Kicklingen was provided with a spear. In a more martial era, this high-status woman seems to have adopted the more masculine qualities of her time. A move towards greater equity in society was accompanied by a new austerity, with traditions less linked to the old Austrian values to the south—based on wealth accumulation via trade in salt—and different from the new display of Baden-Württemberg to the west—based on elite contact with Greece.

Beyond Germany, we see related social change in Austria, with higher-status male burials at the Dürrnberg after 470 BC (Moser 2009); proximity to the newer Bavarian social norms was perhaps taking effect. By 450 BC, a generation or two later than in Germany, this new, male-led cultural shift had also begun in eastern France, delayed perhaps by the more radically female Hallstatt social system there. In Champagne, the transitional (late Hallstatt to early La Tène) cemeteries of Chouilly Les Jogasses and Heiltz-l'Évêque remained divided by sex (Fernández-Götz 2014: 95). So too among the later burials at Courtesoult (530 to 370 BC), women were buried to the north-east and men to the south-east of the tumulus (Verger 2013; Milcent 2013c: 141)—old gender traditions persisted on death, as they declined in life.

Meanwhile, the first early La Tène chariot burials are again male, while in Champagne we find helmets (Piggott 1983). Evidence for north Italian contact continues, as at Bourges Route de Dun, and in Champagne at Somme-Bionne and Chouilly Les Jogasses. We find a strongly male gender for what seem to be a series of out-migrations from the more feminine Hallstatt heartland over three generations between 550/540 BC (Rhineland/Bavaria) and 470/450 BC (Austria/France). Despite the martial nature and initial male leadership of these societies, we do not see evidence for patriarchal lifeways, representing both a physical and an ideological move away from the old traditions, which celebrated elite wealth, gender division, and foreign contact—values now actively in decline. Although still active in Germany, Hallstatt traditions had become heavily ritualized, and we see disproportionate deposition of feminine wealth—first in Hallstatt D2/3 Bavaria, and by La Tène A at the Dürrnberg (Austria) and Münsingen-Rain (Switzerland). Alongside the slow decline of the old traditions, the new La Tène societies that first emerged in the Rhineland and Bavaria were beginning to have an impact on communities in Austria and northern France by 450 BC.

After 450 BC, we instead find evidence for female high status further west—e.g. in south-east Spain and central France—with rich female cremations near Bourges, where the long-lived Hallstatt contact with Italy continued down to 400 BC (Pope and Ralston 2011). Further north, by 430 BC, influenced perhaps by social changes in Champagne, we see a La Tène society forming in the upper Seine basin, characterized again by martial material culture—spears (Evans 2004). In this next generation, however, society was less actively gendered male. Burial was now by family group, implying a new social order, very different from the old gendered Hallstatt traditions (Demoule 1999; Diepeveen-Jansen 2001: 167). This move towards social equity and gender parity, perhaps because of its strong female heritage, was later echoed in Britain (Evans 2004; Pope and Ralston 2011). Conceivably the notion of gendered power structures was actively rejected in France, in favour of a clear social alternative, meaning that male authority did not translate into androcentrism (Roualet 1997).

The richest La Tène A burials in the Hunsrück-Eifel were male, reflecting perhaps the region's heritage of typically more masculine leadership. Around the La Tène A1–A2 transition (425 BC), we find a renewed popularity of swords (Aisne-Marne, upper Seine, middle Rhine, the Dürrnberg), again marking a departure from Hallstatt cultural traditions, and the growth of a new martial age. This readoption of swords was associated with the same generation that saw the final, cordial contact with communities in the Mediterranean. Some swords remained highly decorated, as at Vert-Toulon, Hochscheid G2, and Bescheid G6, although these last two, both with coral, are from the old Hallstatt heartland. From the end of La Tène A, swords became much less decorative in France (Diepeveen-Jansen 2001), in parallel with the increasing focus on martiality in these societies.

Marking both the cessation of traditional links with Italy, and the end of salt production at Hallstatt and the Dürrnberg, 400 BC is an important date. Champagne was becoming ever more martial (chariots, swords, spears), with La Tène B swords notably standardized to a fairly uniform Hatvan-Boldog type (Diepeveen-Jansen 2001: 159; Evans 2004), almost utilitarian after 400 BC, with society increasingly structured around martial identities. The low number of swords in Champagne after 400 BC apparently reflects a distinct lack of men—something also seen in the Rhineland and ostensibly in accord with textual accounts of migrations to Italy; although more locally we see population rise elsewhere in north-eastern France and in Britain (Collis 2003; Haselgrove and Pope 2007). The women of Champagne, however, seem to have remained, and true to their heritage began to perform greater wealth display (Roualet 1997: 170) and continued to attain very high status in a markedly 'egalitarian' society. This was followed by almost total population decline in Champagne and the Rhineland after 350 BC—in line with the end of Hallstatt traditions in Germany, and the appearance of a new egalitarian society, akin to Champagne, in Britain. Particularly interesting here are the female founder burials of Wetwang Slack, with blue glass bead-strings (Giles 2012).

Unlike La Tène France, Britain does not see a decline in sword decoration, and swords became longer over time (Stead 2006), perhaps linked to equestrianism; some were deposited outside burial contexts, reflecting older indigenous customs. Other Hallstatt echoes include gendered burial clusters, mirrors—which Piggott (1983) linked back to Reinheim at Arras T3—and after 300 BC, chariots (Pope and Ralston 2011: 398; Jay et al. 2012). In Britain, status goods are found equally between the sexes, with women more likely to receive meat in the grave (Pope and Ralston 2011: figs 17.5–17.6). Isotope analysis for Wetwang reveals a diet high in meat and dairy protein, with no sex-based differences, apart from a dietary trend for men over 35 (Jay and Richards 2006, 2007). Age, not sex, was the defining structuring principle.

Gender Roles and Identity

New work on fertility and childrearing is key to understanding gender roles. The number of neonate/infant burials in Britain, and the 13% infant burial figure for late Hallstatt France, are both considered low, with subadults in Austria and Bavaria at 19–24% (Roualet 1997: 169; Giles 2012: 95; Rebay-Salisbury 2016). Our assumption has been that pre-industrial societies would see unrestricted fertility across childbearing years, with an estimate of 43% infant burial (Burmeister 2000: 85). Giles (2012) suggests the disparity is an artefact of survival, whereas Rebay-Salisbury (2016) considers it a result of infant burial in settlements (e.g. Baden-Württemberg, Bavaria, Britain). Certainly, the youngest in the Yorkshire and Dürrnberg cemeteries were 2 to 3 years old, suggesting that infants were often kept close to the living, rather than buried in communal cemeteries (Lally 2008; Giles 2012: 95; Müller-Scheeßel et al. 2013). Alternatively, our high estimates may simply not be appropriate for pre-Roman Iron Age Europe, with evidence now for Iron Age women at Wetwang controlling their maternity by restricting breastfeeding via early introduction of supplementary foods (Jay et al. 2008). Regarding childcare as a gendered activity, it is notable that Rebay-Salisbury's (2016) analysis of over 3,000 early Iron Age human representations in central Europe revealed no association between women and domestic/childcare roles. As the archaeological evidence increasingly indicates, the roles of women in pre-Roman Iron Age societies were not restricted to domesticity, as earlier scholars might have assumed (Pope 2007). An association between spinning and women of some status is now accepted for some regions, although this seems not to transfer to elite grave assemblages, nor to Baden-Württemberg and Spain (Pope and Ralston 2011; Giles 2012; Arnold 2016; Rebay-Salisbury 2016).

Early Iron Age elite men and women both had access to a culture of drinking, wealth, travel, and Mediterranean contact. We also have growing evidence for women's involvement in ritual leadership—e.g. in late Hallstatt Austria (Strettweg, Hallstatt, Gemeinlebarn, the Dürrnberg), early La Tène Germany (Reinheim, Waldalgesheim), and La Tène B–C Britain (Wetwang Slack, Mill Hill). Several scholars now conclude that—beyond late Hallstatt eastern France, where the female gender seems primary—age, rather than sex, was the more important social factor in Iron Age Europe. Burmeister's (2000) analysis of Hallstatt D Baden-Württemberg showed that adult women (aged between 20 and 40) had both the largest burial chambers and the most grave goods; in Britain, gender identities were relatively fluid for women (Pope and Ralston 2011: 409).

In La Tène Yorkshire, younger men received special, martial rites, with a more fixed martial masculine identity; in Baden-Württemberg, young men were more likely to have swords (Burmeister and Müller-Scheeßel 2005; Pope and Ralston 2011; Giles 2012). Gender seemingly became more fluid for elder men in Hallstatt D Württemberg, as some 50% reached high status; elders seem also to have been accorded martial status—something removed from the more active martial identities of younger men (Burmeister and Müller-Scheeßel 2005; Pope and Ralston 2011: 393). Some high-status and elder women also seem involved in martial identities in both these regions. At the Magdalenenberg, (elder) martial men had higher protein levels (Oelze et al. 2012); at Wetwang, diet was similarly different for men over 35; while elder Rudston women were accorded an equivalent status, involving burial with pig/pork (Jay and Richards 2006, 2007; Pope and Ralston 2011). Were the elders gifted more meat, elder men during their life, elder women on their death? By the La Tène period, we can see age as the more defining social category.

Gender from the Texts

Having explored aspects of gender in Iron Age societies prior to Roman influence, we can turn briefly to observations on gender from first-century BC texts. Most of our information comes from Gaul—from the Greek writers Diodorus Siculus and Strabo, and the Roman Julius Caesar (Chapter 36). This focus on Gaul was perhaps the result of its old gender traditions as outlined here, making it sufficiently worthy of comment. While Caesar describes Gallic women as weak and treacherous (*de Bello Gallico* 7.26, 7.47–48), the Greeks consider them a match for their men, both in stature and in courage (Diodorus Siculus *Library of History* 5.32; Strabo *Geography* 3.4.17; 4.4.6). This difference between Greek and Roman comment regarding the female sex is of interest.

Caesar records noble-born leadership as a uniquely male concern, regional in scope, and second only to Druidic rule, which is also male in Gaul (*de Bello Gallico* 6.13–14, 7.4). Nevertheless, we hear from Strabo of a terrifying female ritual community near the mouth of the Loire, who would sail to the mainland purely to have sex with the men (*Geography* 4.4.6). In Gaul, the texts present a fairly liberal society, as women gave dowries to their husbands on marriage, and could inherit subsequent joint wealth, while men delighted in homosexuality over marital sex—although a woman could be killed if a noble man died suspiciously (*de Bello Gallico* 6.19; *Library of History* 5.32). Regarding parenting, boys were not permitted to approach their parents openly until grown, to harden them for war, and food was served by the youngest children, both male and female (*de Bello Gallico* 6.18; *Library of History* 5.28). In essence, the textual evidence on Gaul accords well with our understanding of gender from the archaeological evidence from the region for the La Tène period.

Beyond Gaul, Caesar had German women surrounding the battle weeping, or hidden in the woods (*de Bello Gallico* 1.51, 4.19, 2.16, 2.28), whereas Strabo tells us of elder Cimbri priestesses active in battle, beating the stretched wagon hides to produce an 'unearthly noise' (*Geography* 7.2.3). Unlike Gaul (no gods, Druids, nor sacrifices), Germans worshiped the sun, moon, and fire, and elder women used divination, with the authority to stay any battle (*de Bello Gallico* 1.50, 6.21). This apparent link between the fourth-century BC archaeology (e.g. Reinheim, Waldalgesheim) and first-century BC texts, regarding female ritual leadership, is intriguing. We also hear of male German chastity, with sex before 20 considered disgraceful (*de Bello Gallico* 6.21). In northern Spain, women received dowries, gave away their brothers in marriage, and were noted for their courage—pregnant women apparently digging ditches or working in the fields, and looking after their men, even on the day of childbirth (Strabo *Geography* 3.3.7, 3.4.17–18). In Britain, we hear that marriage took place while a virgin, becoming polygamous, with children of uncertain paternity readily accepted by the initial husband; and in Ireland of ritual incest (*de Bello Gallico* 5.14; *Library of History* 5.32; *Geography* 4.5.4). The further west one travels, the more different these peoples are made to seem by our commentators. To finish, we have a tantalizing statement from Strabo on gender roles among the Belgae:

> But as for their custom relating to the men and the women (I mean the fact that their tasks have been exchanged, in a manner opposite to what obtains among us), it is one which they share in common with many other barbarian peoples.
>
> (*Geography* 4.4.3)

Conclusions

The available evidence suggests a complex picture of Iron Age society, with gender identities and roles neither constant across time, nor between regions, nor even across a lifetime. In the earliest Iron Age west, a male-authored society looked back to late Bronze Age traditions; further east, a gender-equal salt trade came to be led by women, perhaps linked to their role in ritual, and connections to Etruscan Italy. What may be a series of non-gendered migrations (620 to 580 BC) saw equitable communities in Germany becoming more male-authored after 550 BC, and female-authored in eastern France. Both regions maintained traditional contact with Italy, and notably with each other. Contemporary with elite contact with Greece (550 to 475 BC) was a male-authored move away from old Hallstatt traditions (550 to 450 BC)—first in the Rhineland and Bavaria, then in Austria, then in France—with development of distinctly martial, more 'egalitarian' La Tène-type communities. The years around 400 BC saw the departure of traditional links with Italy, the Austrian salt trade, and men in central Champagne and the Rhineland, alongside population increase in the Paris basin and Britain, with the women remaining in Champagne regaining very high status. Population decline took place in Champagne and the Rhineland after 350 BC, in line with the end of Hallstatt traditions in Germany and Switzerland (markedly female and ritual), as old Hallstatt echoes began to be found in western France, Spain, and finally Britain.

The archaeological evidence shows gender as critical to transitions from late Bronze Age to Hallstatt to La Tène societies; without understanding gender, we cannot understand society. In addition, the texts reveal differences between Celtic and classical gender norms. Regarding kinship, there are hints of lineages at Hallstatt, and between Hallstatt D Germany and France, and in our less masculine societies children were accorded status (Hallstatt, Münsingen-Rain), with parental tokens perhaps in children's graves at the Magdalenenberg. Sex was an important structuring principle in some Iron Age societies—Hallstatt C western Europe (masculine), Hallstatt D Austria and France (feminine), Hallstatt D Bavaria (masculine), and La Tène Switzerland (feminine). However, gender equity has also been noted for Hallstatt C Austria, Hallstatt D Bavaria, and for La Tène communities in France and Britain. Regarding gender identities, we find complementary, rather than separate, social roles for Iron Age men and women, often with a degree of overlap, and relatively fluid gender identities, with elders of both sexes accorded higher status (e.g. greater access to proteins). More work that breaks down gender by age and sex is needed—advancing our attempts at contextual archaeological method by dissecting the evidence to give greater chronological precision, refined regional narratives, and more detailed gender patterning.

Notes

1. Illustrated in Chapter 17, Figure 17.5.
2. Magdalenenberg G19 also falls into this category.
3. Hallstatt D1: Hohmichele VI (couple); Hohmichele I, Neuhausen ob Eck, Kappel-Grafenhausen T3 (feminine); Heiligenbuck (masculine). Hallstatt D2/3: Hirschlanden, Hochdorf, Ludwigsburg, Gießübel-Talhau (masculine); Schöckingen (with gold headdress), Grafenbühl, Kappel-Grafenhausen T1, Stuttgart Bad-Cannstatt 1 (feminine).

References

Arnold, B. 1991. 'The deposed princess of Vix. The need for an engendered European prehistory', in D. Walde and N. D. Willows (eds) *The Archaeology of Gender: Proceedings of the 22nd Annual Chacmool Conference*: 361–374. Calgary: University of Calgary.

Arnold, B. 1995. '"Honorary males" or women of substance? Gender, status and power in Iron Age Europe'. *Journal of European Archaeology* 3, 2: 151–168.

Arnold, B. 2012. 'The Vix Princess Redux: A retrospective on European Iron Age gender and mortuary studies', in L. Prados Torreira (ed.) *La Arqueología funeraria desde una perspectiva de género*: 211–232. Madrid: UA Ediciones.

Arnold, B. 2016. 'Belts vs. blades: The binary bind in Iron Age mortuary contexts in southwest Germany'. *Journal of Archaeological Method and Theory* 23, 3: 831–853.

Baray, L. 2000. 'Évolution socio-économique et adaptations architecturales. Tumulus et concentration de pouvoir en Bourgogne de la seconde moitié du IXe au milieu du Ve s. av. J.-C.', in B. Dedet, P. Gruat, G. Marchand, M. Py, and M. Schwaller (eds) *Archéologie de la mort, archéologie de la tombe au Premier Âge du Fer. Actes du XXIe Colloque de l'AFEAF, Conques-Montrozier 1997*. Monographies d'Archéologie Méditerranéenne 5: 191–211. Lattes: UMR 154 du CNRS.

Berresford Ellis, P. 1995. *Celtic Women: Women in Celtic Society and Literature*. London: Constable.

Biel, J. 1997. 'The Celtic princes of Hohenasperg (Baden-Württemberg)', in S. Moscati, O.-H. Frey, V. Kruta, B. Raftery, and M. Szabó (eds) *The Celts*: 121–131. New York: Rizzoli.

Brun, P. 1987. *Princes et princesses de la Celtique: le premier âge du Fer (850–450 av. J.C.)*. Paris: Errance.

Burmeister, S. 2000. *Geschlecht, Alter und Herrschaft in der Späthallstattzeit Württembergs*. Tübinger Schriften zur Ur- und Frühgeschichtlichen Archäologie 4. Münster: Waxmann.

Burmeister, S., and N. Müller-Scheeßel. 2005. 'Der Methusalemkomplex. Methodologische Überlegungen zu Geschlecht, Alter und Sozialstatus am Beispiel der Hallstattzeit Süddeutschlands', in J. Müller (ed.) *Alter und Geschlecht in ur- und frühgeschichtlichen Gesellschaften. Tagung Bamberg 20.–21. Februar 2004*. Universitätsforschungen zur Prähistorischen Archäologie 126: 91–125. Bonn: Habelt.

Champion, S. 1995. 'Jewellery and adornment', in M. Green (ed.) *The Celtic World*: 411–419. London: Routledge.

Collis, J. R. 1984. *The European Iron Age*. London: Batsford.

Collis, J. R. 2003. *The Celts: Origins, Myths and Inventions*. Stroud: Tempus.

Cunliffe, B. W. 1997. *The Ancient Celts*. Oxford: Oxford University Press.

Demoule, J.-P. 1999. *Chronologie et société dans les nécropoles celtiques de la culture Aisne-Marne du VIe au IIIe siècle avant notre ère*. Revue archéologique de Picardie Numéro spécial 15. Amiens: RAP.

Diaz-Andreu, M., S. Lucy, S. Babić, and D. N. Edwards. 2005. *The Archaeology of Identity: Approaches to Gender, Age, Status, Ethnicity, and Religion*. Oxford: Routledge.

Diepeveen-Jansen, M. 2001. *People, Ideas and Goods: New Perspectives on 'Celtic Barbarians' in Western and Central Europe (500–250 BC)*. Amsterdam Archaeological Studies 7. Amsterdam: Amsterdam University Press.

Dietler, M. 1990. 'Driven by drink: The role of drinking in the political economy and the case of early Iron Age France'. *Journal of Anthropological Archaeology* 9: 351–406.

Dubuis, B., D. Josset, E. Millet, and C. Villenave. 2015. 'La tombe princière du Ve siècle avant notre ère de Lavau "ZAC du Moutot" (Aube)'. *Bulletin de la société préhistorique française* 112, 2: 371–374.

Ehrenberg, M. 1989. *Women in Prehistory*. London: British Museum Press.

Evans, T. L. 2004. *Quantitative Identities: A Statistical Summary and Analysis of Iron Age Cemeteries in North-Eastern France 601–130 BC*. British Archaeological Reports International Series 1226. Oxford: Archaeopress.

Fernández-Götz, M. 2014. *Identity and Power: The Transformation of Iron Age Societies in Northeast Gaul*. Amsterdam Archaeological Studies 21. Amsterdam: Amsterdam University Press.

Fontijn, D., and H. Fokkens. 2007. 'The emergence of early Iron Age "chieftain's graves" in the southern Netherlands: Reconsidering transformations in burial and depositional practices', in C. C. Haselgrove and R. E. Pope (eds) *The Earlier Iron Age in Britain and the Near Continent*: 351–373. Oxford: Oxbow.

Freidin, N. 1982. *The Early Iron Age in the Paris Basin: Hallstatt C and D*. British Archaeological Reports International Series 131. Oxford: British Archaeological Reports.

Frey, O.-H. 1997. ' "Celtic Princes" in the sixth century BC', in S. Moscati, O.-H. Frey, V. Kruta, B. Raftery, and M. Szabó (eds) *The Celts*: 81–102. New York: Rizzoli.

Giles, M. 2012. *A Forged Glamour: Landscape, Identity and Material Culture in the Iron Age*. Oxford: Windgather Press.

Graells Fabregat, R. 2011. 'Warriors and heroes from the north-east of Iberia: A view from the funerary contexts', in T. Moore and X.-L. Armada (eds) *Atlantic Europe in the First Millennium BC: Crossing the Divide*: 571–589. Oxford: Oxford University Press.

Haffner, A. 1997. 'The princely tombs of the Celts in the middle Rhineland', in S. Moscati, O.-H. Frey, V. Kruta, B. Raftery, and M. Szabó (eds) *The Celts*: 173–190. New York: Rizzoli.

Harding, A. F. 2000. *European Societies in the Bronze Age*. Cambridge: Cambridge University Press.

Haselgrove, C., and R. Pope. 2007. 'Characterising the earlier Iron Age', in C. Haselgrove and R. Pope (eds) *The Earlier Iron Age in Britain and the Near Continent*: 1–23. Oxford: Oxbow.

Hill, J. D. 1989. 'Rethinking the Iron Age'. *Scottish Archaeological Review* 6: 11–24.

Hill, J. D. 2011. 'How did British middle and late pre-Roman Iron Age societies work (if they did)?', in T. Moore and X.-L. Armada (eds) *Atlantic Europe in the First Millennium BC: Crossing the Divide*: 241–263. Oxford: Oxford University Press.

Hodson, F. R. 1968. *The La Tène Cemetery at Münsingen-Rain: Catalogue and Relative Chronology*. Acta Bernensia 5. Bern: Stämpfli.

Hodson, F. R. 1990. *Hallstatt. The Ramsauer Graves: Quantification and Analysis*. RGZM Monographien 16. Mainz: Römisch-Germanisches Zentralmuseum.

Institut de recherches archéologiques préventives (Inrap). 2015. *Une tombe princière celte du Ve siècle avant notre ère découverte à Lavau*. Available at http://www.inrap.fr/une-tombe-princi ere-celte-du-ve-siecle-avant-notre-ere-decouverte-lavau-1369 [accessed 15 May 2015].

James, S. 2005. *Exploring the World of the Celts*, 2nd edition. London: Thames and Hudson.

Jay, M., B. T. Fuller, M. P. Richards, C. J. Knusel, and S. S. King. 2008. 'Iron Age breastfeeding practices in Britain: Isotopic evidence from Wetwang Slack, East Yorkshire'. *American Journal of Physical Anthropology* 136, 3: 321–337.

Jay, M., C. Haselgrove, D. Hamilton, J. D. Hill, and J. Dent. 2012. 'Chariots and context: New radiocarbon dates from Wetwang and the chronology of Iron Age burials and brooches in East Yorkshire'. *Oxford Journal of Archaeology* 31, 2: 161–189.

Jay, M., and M. P. Richards. 2006. 'Diet in the Iron Age cemetery population at Wetwang Slack, East Yorkshire, UK: Carbon and nitrogen stable isotope evidence'. *Journal of Archaeological Science* 33, 5: 651–662.

Jay, M., and M. P. Richards. 2007. 'British Iron Age diet: Stable isotopes and other evidence'. *Proceedings of the Prehistoric Society* 73: 161–190.

Kiesslich, J., F. Neuhuber, H. J. Meyer, M. P. Baur, and J. Leskovar. 2005. 'DNA analysis on biological remains from archaeological findings—sex identification and kinship analysis on skeletons from Mitterkirchen, Upper Austria', in R. Karl and J. Leskovar (eds) *Interpretierte Eisenzeiten* 1: 141–154. Linz: Oberösterreichisches Landesmuseum.

Koch, J. K. 2013. 'Cross-gender in Bronze and Iron Age in Central Europe? A question of interpretation'. Unpublished paper given at EAA Pilsen (2013).

Kossack, G. 1954. *Studien zum Symbolgut der Urnenfeld- und Hallstattzeit Mitteleuropas*. Römisch-Germanische Forschungen 20. Berlin: De Gruyter.

Lally, M. 2008. 'Death and difference in the Iron Age of southern England', in M. Lally (ed.) *(Re) thinking the Little Ancestor: New Perspectives on the Archaeology of Infancy and Childhood*. British Archaeological Reports International Series 2271. Oxford: Archaeopress.

Marion, S. 2004. *Recherches sur l'Âge du Fer en Ile-de-France*. British Archaeological Reports International Series 1231. Oxford: Archaeopress.

Merhart, G. von 1969. *Hallstatt und Italien: Gesammelte Aufsätze zur frühen Eisenzeit in Italien und Mitteleuropa* (ed. G. Kossack). Mainz: Römisch-Germanisches Zentralmuseum.

Milcent, P.-Y. 2003. 'Statut et fonctions d'un personnage féminin hors norme', in C. Rolley (ed.) *La tombe princière de Vix*: 311–327. Paris: Picard/Société des amis du Musée du Châtillonnais.

Milcent, P.-Y. 2004. *Le premier âge du Fer en France centrale*. Mémoire XXXIV de la Société Préhistorique Française. Paris: Société Préhistorique Française.

Milcent, P.-Y. 2013a. 'Une "dynastie" féminine? La Rivière Drugeon, le Grand Communal, tumulus 2 (Doubs)', in S. Verger and L. Pernet (eds) *Une odyssée gauloise: Parures de femmes à l'origine des premiers échanges entre la Grèce et la Gaule*. Collection Archéologie de Montpellier Agglomération 4: 141–145. Arles: Errance.

Milcent, P.-Y. 2013b. 'Le pommeau d'épée en ivoire et ambre de Chaffois (Doubs)', in S. Verger and L. Pernet (eds) *Une odyssée gauloise: Parures de femmes à l'origine des premiers échanges entre la Grèce et la Gaule*. Collection Archéologie de Montpellier Agglomération 4: 181–189. Arles: Errance.

Milcent, P.-Y. 2013c. 'La nouvelle place des femmes dans l'espace funéraire en Gaule: Des tombes à épée Hallstattienne aux tombes à riche parure feminine', in S. Verger and L. Pernet (eds) *Une odyssée gauloise: Parures de femmes à l'origine des premiers échanges entre la Grèce et la Gaule*. Collection Archéologie de Montpellier Agglomération 4: 131–141. Arles: Errance.

Milcent, P.-Y. 2015. 'Bronze objects for Atlantic elites in France and beyond (13th–8th century BC)', in F. Hunter and I. B. M. Ralston (eds) *Scotland in Later Prehistoric Europe*: 11–46. Edinburgh: Society of Antiquaries of Scotland.

Moosleitner, F. 1997. 'The Dürrnberg near Hallein: A centre of Celtic art and culture', in S. Moscati, O.-H. Frey, V. Kruta, B. Raftery, and M. Szabó (eds) *The Celts*: 191–203. New York: Rizzoli.

Moser, S. 2009. 'Life and death at Dürrnberg', in A. Kern, K. Kowarik, H. Reschreiter, and A. W. Rausch (eds) *Kingdom of Salt: 7000 Years of Hallstatt*. Veröffentlichungen der Prähistorischen Abteilung 3: 171–173. Vienna: Natural History Museum.

Müller-Scheeßel, N., C. Berszin, G. Grupe, A. Schwentke, A. Staskiewicz, and J. Wahl. 2013. 'Ältereisenzeitliche Siedlungsbestattungen in Baden-Württemberg und Bayern', in N. Müller-Scheeßel (ed.) *'Irreguläre' Bestattungen in der Urgeschichte: Norm, Ritual, Strafe . . .? Akten der Internationalen Tagung in Frankfurt a. M. vom 3. bis 5. Februar 2012*. Kolloquien zur Vor- und Frühgeschichte 19: 409–424. Bonn: Habelt.

Oelze, V. M., J. K. Koch, K. Kupke, O. Nehlich, S. Zäuner, J. Wahl, et al. 2012. 'Multi-isotopic analysis reveals individual mobility and diet at the early Iron Age monumental tumulus of Magdalenenberg, Germany'. *American Journal of Physical Anthropology* 148, 3: 401–421.

Olivier, L. 1999. 'The Hochdorf "princely" grave and the question of the nature of archaeological funerary assemblages', in T. Murray (ed.) *Time and Archaeology*. One World Archaeology 37: 101–138. London: Routledge.

Pany, D. 2009. 'The Early Iron Age occupation of the High Valley', in A. Kern, K. Kowarik, A. W. Rausch, and H. Reschreiter (eds) *Kingdom of Salt: 7000 Years of Hallstatt*. Veröffentlichungen der Prähistorischen Abteilung 3: 131–141. Vienna: Natural History Museum.

Pany, D., and M. Teschler-Nicola. 2007. 'Working in a salt mine—everyday life for the Hallstatt females?' *Lunula* 15: 81–97.

Pare, C. F. E. 1992. *Wagons and Wagon-Graves of the Early Iron Age in Central Europe*. OUCA Monograph 35. Oxford: Oxford University Committee for Archaeology.

Piggott, S. 1983. *The Earliest Wheeled Transport: From the Atlantic Coast to the Caspian Sea*. London: Thames and Hudson.

Pope, R. 2007. 'Ritual and the roundhouse: A critique of recent ideas on domestic space in later British prehistory', in C. Haselgrove and R. Pope (eds) *The Earlier Iron Age in Britain and the Near Continent*: 204–228. Oxford: Oxbow.

Pope, R., and I. Ralston. 2011. 'Approaching sex and status in Iron Age Britain with reference to the nearer continent', in T. Moore and X.-L. Armada (eds) *Atlantic Europe in the First Millennium BC: Crossing the Divide*: 371–414. Oxford: Oxford University Press.

Rebay, K. 2007. 'Plotting social change: The cemetery of Statzendorf Austria as an example of changing burial rites at the beginning of the Early Iron Age in central Europe', in R. Salisbury and D. Keeler (eds) *Space—Archaeology's Final Frontier? An Intercontinental Approach*: 131–156. Newcastle: Cambridge Scholars Publishing.

Rebay-Salisbury, K. 2016. *The Human Body in Early Iron Age Central Europe: Burial Practices and Images of the Hallstatt World*. London: Routledge.

Redfern, R. 2008. 'A bioarchaeological analysis of violence in Iron Age females: A perspective from Dorset, England (4th century BC to the 1st century AD)', in O. Davis, N. Sharples, and K. Waddington (eds) *Changing Perspectives on the First Millennium BC: Proceedings of the Iron Age Research Student Seminar 2006*: 131–160. Oxford: Oxbow.

Rolley, C. (ed.) 2003. *La tombe princière de Vix*. Paris: Picard/Société des amis du Musée du Châtillonnais.

Roualet, P. 1997. 'The Marnian culture of Champagne', in S. Moscati, O.-H. Frey, V. Kruta, B. Raftery, and M. Szabó (eds) *The Celts*: 165–172. New York: Rizzoli.

Scheeres, M., C. Knipper, M. Hauschild, M. Schönfelder, W. Siebel, D. Vitali, et al. 2013. 'Evidence for "Celtic migrations"? Strontium isotope analysis at the early La Tène (La Tène B) cemeteries of Nebringen (Germany) and Monte Bibele (Italy)'. *Journal of Archaeological Science* 40: 3611–3625.

Sievers, S. 1982. *Die mitteleuropäischen Hallstattdolche*. Prähistorische Bronzefunde VI, 6. Munich: Beck.

Sørensen, M. L. S. 2000. *Gender Archaeology*. Cambridge: Polity Press.

Stead, I. M. 2006. *British Iron Age Swords and Scabbards*. London: British Museum Press.

Stöllner, T. 2014. 'Between ruling ideology and ancestor worship: The *mos maiorum* of the early Celtic "Hero Graves"', in C. Gosden, S. Crawford, and K. Ulmschneider (eds) *Celtic Art in Europe: Making Connections*: 111–136. Oxford: Oxbow.

Verger, S. 1995. 'De Vix à Weiskirchen: la transformation des rites funéraires aristocratiques en Gaule du nord et de l'est au Ve siècle avant J.-C.'. *Mélanges de l'École française de Rome (Antiquité)* 107: 331–458.

Verger, S. 2013. 'La tombe du Mia à Saint-Georges-les-Baillargeaux (Vienne) et trésors de femmes en France central et méridionale (Xe–VIe siècles avant J.-C.)', in S. Verger and L. Pernet (eds) *Une odyssée gauloise: Parures de femmes à l'origine des premiers échanges entre la Grèce et la Gaule*. Collection Archéologie de Montpellier Agglomération 4: 151–156. Arles: Errance.

Verger, S., and L. Pernet (eds). 2013. *Une odyssée gauloise: Parures de femmes à l'origine des premiers échanges entre la Grèce et la Gaule*. Collection Archéologie de Montpellier Agglomération 4. Arles: Errance.

Wylie, A. 1985. 'The reaction against analogy', in M. B. Schiffer (ed.) *Advances in Archaeological Method and Theory*: 61–111. New York: Academic Press.

Zäuner, S., and J. Wahl. 2013. 'Zur demographischen Struktur der Bestattungen im späthallstattzeitlichen Grabhügel vom Magdalenenberg'. *Fundberichte aus Baden Württemberg* 33: 131–146.

CHAPTER 35

REGIONS, GROUPS, AND IDENTITY

An Intellectual History

T. L. THURSTON

Introduction

Regional identity in the European Iron Age has long been an important, yet ever-changing topic in archaeological research. Our knowledge of what identity is, and how it figures in human societies, has changed so much in the last few decades that the contrast between the early and current usage of the identity concept is astounding. The meaning of what we understand as 'regional' has also shifted a great deal over time.

For the purpose of understanding our current perspective, we need only go back to the earlier nineteenth century, when archaeologists understood identity through the lens of colonialism's collision with non-Western cultures, which was growing towards its peak. Additionally, the Napoleonic wars, which threatened discrete national identities, had recently been won. Identity thus became a key issue in European and American quests for national 'character' and ethnic genealogies in the later nineteenth and early twentieth centuries, and by the early to mid-twentieth century new archaeological concepts, largely reductionist in nature, cast identity as a device for explaining an orderly and understandable past. Since the mid-twentieth century, informed by both social science and humanist research, identity has been seen as a much less tidy quality, which operates simultaneously in unique but also somewhat predictable ways. Because of this, it is viewed as important for reconstructing a period about which we know much less than we once thought.

When discussing identity on levels broader than the individual or smallest family unit, what do we mean? Identity is an amorphous concept with which it can be difficult to grapple. Definitions typically refer to an array of characteristics through which someone can be recognized or defined, or a set of behavioural qualities through which an individual is acknowledged as a member of a group. Despite this emphasis on *people*, much that has been written on the Iron Age concerns the archaeologist's best understanding of geographic territories, and the difference and similarity of the objects, structures, and settlements found there—regions such as Iberia, Ireland, and Mediterranean France. Some of these 'regions' were understood to represent peoples recorded in the historic texts of antiquity; some were identified solely by types of material culture.

Reference to the *identity of a region* therefore implies a geographic, bounded area. In recent times, for reasons outlined later in the chapter, the regional focus has been replaced by the study of *groups*. When one says 'group identity' this implies not a random group, but a group with some rationale for cohesion—an ethnic group or a cultural group, which are not the same thing. Often these words, 'region' and 'group', are used interchangeably at all scales, as in the Germanic region, or the region of the Votadini, yet if one unpacks the concepts, they are not equivalent things, or even similar units of analysis. This conflation also implies that all inhabitants of a region or members of a group will hold the same identity cards, a condition now understood to be nearly inconceivable. It also suggests that regions are so central to identity that it would be lost in other settings: also untrue. All these concepts have different implications and an important place in the history of Iron Age archaeology.

Early Concepts of Regional Identity

The earliest modern attempts at theorizing ancient identity are attached to the German Romanticists of the eighteenth and nineteenth centuries, whose inspiration combined theology, philosophy, and literature. Primary among them was Johann Herder, who equated language with the 'nation'—not the modern nation state, but those peoples whose ancient unity of origin and long-term development gave them a special character. This idea gave birth to a variety of later concepts, such as Boas' cultural relativism, but also the *Kulturkreis* or 'culture circle' concept (Rebay-Salisbury 2011), which, rather than stressing similarities across groups, stressed difference and isolation. A popular nineteenth-century notion was the metaphor of cultural *hearths* or homelands, core territories, places of origin, which spread broadly throughout the archaeological discipline.

Despite the fact that they characterized identity as 'tribal' or peopled by 'folk' groups and 'barbarians', Iron Age scholars of that era had little notion of what tribalism was, or what ancient ways of life entailed. Their concepts surrounding past people—primitives—were partly simple ignorance found in the early days of all disciplines, and partly self-deception constructed by their own beliefs, couched in a period of intense nationalism throughout nineteenth-century Europe, where each society, as well as the academics in their universities, was most concerned with *national identities*, those attached to the nation state (Kohl 1998; Meskell 2002). As the major players jockeyed for power and position at home and through their colonial empires, ensuing periods of warfare and rapacious economic competition inspired political leaders to make nationalistic appeals toward support for local and global enterprises. The anthropological literature of the times is replete with compendia of a hundred 'nations', illustrating their 'national costumes', typical implements, houses, and other materials, often illustrated in highly detailed, full-colour lithographs (e.g. Bodmer 1839–1843).

Thus, when we say 'regional identity' in archaeology, we are really making reference to a set of very specific ideas from the nineteenth and early twentieth centuries. As has been elaborated in many other publications (Hodder 1982; Jones 1996, 1997; Lyman et al. 1997; Wells 2001), the nineteenth-century European archaeological paradigm known as *culture history* grew from these roots and also found ready acceptance elsewhere in the Anglophone world. Culture history was the crystallization of these concepts projected into the past for archaeological and historical purposes.

Despite describing the Iron Age peoples as primal and autochthonous, scholarly minds went immediately to the people of a bounded, geographic nation state; they linked borders and supposed long-time 'boundedness' with the belief that they were occupied by homogeneous and essentialized populations, all exhibiting some fundamental, wholly shared quality of identity, all imbued with an antique version of nationalistic ideologies (Watson 1995; Lyman et al. 1997). In archaeological terms, following assumptions that all people native to a region would display indistinguishable self-projections, identity was thought to be observable in the burial customs and grave goods, symbolism interpreted from weapons or jewellery, house shapes, and the nature of public monuments, representing the equivalent of their prehistoric national costume, customs, and traditions, which could also distinguish one 'tribe' from another. For the terminal Iron Age, the names of peoples reported by the Greeks and Romans were added into the mix.

Many recent publications touch on Iron Age 'peoples' described as barbarian tribes following Greek and Roman frames (Wells 1999; Green 2004; Hedeager 2011). These represent the most current interpretations in the discipline on who and especially *what* they were. Yet these contemporary works are not necessarily what generates the general academic and public perception of Iron Age identities.

It is common now to attribute to Kossinna (1911, 1926) the mapping of tribal entities, based on Roman and other sources, in what Sommer (2008) calls the age of patriotic antiquarianism. Kossinna was actually a latecomer to this tradition, drawn not from prehistoric archaeology but from popular cartography, classical history, geography, and philology. Kossinna initially studied classical philology before turning to German prehistory and linguistics, absorbed the work of eighteenth- and nineteenth-century classicists, and applied a pseudo-ethnographic approach to create his prehistoric settlement archaeology.

As European archaeology formed its disciplinary basis, the impact of earlier scholars was enormous. Historical atlases (e.g. Spruner and Menke 1865) were fashionable, as were the works of ancient historians like Mommsen (1854–1856, 1885), who is still cited by classicists today. The first three parts of his multi-volume *History of Rome* were published in German in the 1850s, around the time Kossinna was born. Mommsen was awarded a Nobel Prize—still the only non-fiction, historical work ever to receive it—for his vivid characterization of Romans and barbarians, which captured the public's imagination, including that of future archaeologists. In Volume 5, *Die Provinzen von Caesar bis Diokletian* (1885), the chapter 'Roman Germany and the Free Germans' enumerated the plethora of tribes and traced their complex political histories and movements within and without the Imperial Limes. The Celts were 'men whose courage despised death ... their mode of fighting ... as novel as it was terrible; sword in hand the Celts precipitated themselves with furious onset on the Roman phalanx, and shattered it at the first shock' (Mommsen 1886: 428).

Several far more obscure authors may have been among the most influential. E. H. Bunbury, an otherwise little-known English classics professor, in 1879 produced *A History of Ancient Geography Among the Greeks and Romans From the Earliest Ages Till The Fall Of The Roman Empire with 20 illustrative maps.* He noted that most major works detailing ancient peoples, places, and countries were in German, and thus offered an English source which appeared in several editions, the maps especially popular as they simplified works such as Mannert (1788–1825), Ukert (1821), and Forbiger (1848), each in their time presenting complex maps, based on Julius Caesar, Ptolemy, and others, illustrating the 'territories' of the barbarian tribes.

Kossinna entered university in 1876, beginning in classical philology and only dedicating himself to German prehistory in 1894. He was thus familiar with the cartographic and textual tradition in Classics, yet in his later, more strident work on German prehistory (Kossinna 1919, 1926, 1931) often failed to cite a single contemporary classicist, despite extensive discussion of the sources. Sometimes petty and vindictive, he may have felt animus at typical assertions that Germans were inferior to Romans.

With many decades of source criticism and deconstruction, the ethnic attributions in ancient texts are today understood differently. In addition to the idea that Caesar 'invented' the Germans, his ethnogeographical descriptions of Gaul and Britain display great detail on peoples and terrain, causing 'the Roman reader to recognize that the Roman general has ... this space intellectually mastered' (Krebs 2006: 117), while Germania is 'an infinite extension without any interior patterns except for infinite forest ... he saves his and his soldiers' lives by leaving in timely fashion' (Krebs 2006: 112). The emphasis on wild, trackless desolation and wilderness may have conveniently explained why he had failed to conquer Germania—since his knowledge of all three territories was equivalent (Krebs 2006: 120). It is possible that his politicized presentation of 'peoples and tribes' created generations of archaeological analyses based on ancient dissembling.

It was standard practice to label a set of artefacts that were restricted in time and space as a culture. Kossinna (1911) equated sets of material objects and patterns of settlement with culture groups, and Childe (1925, 1929), despite his different views, also defined a 'culture' as a set of diagnostic artefacts. In the United States, Kidder (1924) used similar concepts, and McKern (1939) specifically excluded any aspect of the actual culture of a human group from his definition of the archaeological culture, which was based purely on the form of objects.

Such misconstructions fuelled many excesses of the late nineteenth and twentieth centuries: Western European colonialism, Russian expansionism, German imperialism—all of which suffered from severe critique after World War II. The unfortunate use of this notion by the German National Socialists to support the 'reoccupation' of their presumed primordial homelands has been detailed in many recent works (e.g. Arnold 1992; Härke 2000; Fazioli 2012).

Ironically, the nation states of the nineteenth century itself were not populated by such primordially descended peoples, displaying homogeneous identities: in the era's regions, some material items were bounded, others were not, languages and religions were scrambled together, and the long-term history that supposedly lay behind the nation states was shallow and only disguised many diversities even within the borders as they were then drawn. This understanding of how nineteenth-century scholars constructed their views is acknowledged, and is a common trope among historians, including historians of archaeology. Yet in some ways these views have continued into recent times. In many parts of the world, culture history was never rejected, only modified; even after the dismissal of culture history in North America, the set of artefacts from a bounded region as representational of 'a people' remained an important concept—an array of behaviours, indicated by artefacts and other material remains, and limited to a particular place and time period (Binford 1962, 1965). Attempts were made to stress that such a collection was not a de facto culture, but that the culture itself could never be studied—only its material correlates. Despite efforts to keep these cognitive categories separate, they were usually conflated.

Today, archaeologists stress the difference between what is called an *archaeological culture*, which relates only to a set of material objects that co-occur, and an actual *culture*, a group of people linked together in a variety of ways. This distinction is critical, as different cultural groups may use similar sets of objects, and members of one group may frequently use or wear items manufactured by, or in imitation of, those associated with other groups. This may signify an important relationship, or it may signify a fashion, or mere availability—in any case, it is clear that objects may not simply stand in for people.

From Region to Group

This intellectual history has led us to a current framework where it is *not* very typical for contemporary archaeologists to discuss *regional* identities—though some undoubtedly do. A large amount of research shows that identity rarely, if ever, works in such a fashion, and the quest for grasping its true inner workings and outer expression, the one that we can most easily hope to study, has propelled many archaeologists through an ever-changing landscape of ideas.

We can postulate that reasonably cohesive Iron Age groups existed, at least over short periods of time; the difficulty comes in using archaeological data to identify them. If we cannot identify them with any certainty, or understand how identity (or rather multiple internal identities) was constructed, and what this signified for society, then it is subsequently risky to discuss their differences or similarities to other groups, as well as their interactions. This realization was, in fact, the main justification for the culture historians' insistence that they should *describe* what they found but never *interpret* what it meant (Lyman et al. 1997), one of the reasons culture history was rejected by many scholars.

We also have not usually known, using the older models of identity, whether people in past times believed themselves to be members of the same or related groups, or significantly alien from one another. Occasionally, textual reports—based on 'outsider' observations, sometimes containing presumable self-descriptions of group affiliation, interaction, and membership—are available for the Greek colonial era and the Roman conquest. These, however, have been filtered through the authors' lens (Buchsenschutz and Ralston 1988; Wilkes 2007), may represent new conditions related more to violent conflict, conquest, and colonialism than earlier organization, and only relate to groups in contact with Greece and Rome—not those beyond the colonial landscape or *limes*. Thus they are useful, but only in a limited way (Wells 1999, 2001).

Despite these inescapable drawbacks, much has changed in the methods and theories of the social sciences and humanities since the mid-twentieth century, and it is no longer the case that material remains are mute, impenetrable barriers to understanding (Wells 1999). Newer ways of both imagining the past, and seeking the data with which to investigate it, have brought us considerably closer to answers. During the twentieth century, as the drawbacks of the 'regional identity' study grew apparent, a quest for *group* identities began: the term 'group' can refer to many rationales for cohesion, as groups are not tied to geography and can transcend and evade borders. The notion of collective identities also emerged, meaning that in addition to subconscious shared ideas of 'togetherness' there are also publicly acknowledged group identities that are sometimes congruent with implicit identity and sometimes not. Such identities include ethnic groups, political groups, political factions within groups, and groups based on religion, ideology, gender, sex, economic status, social status, age, occupation, and—if we use contemporary ethnographic data as a guide—even dietary preference, community residence, and mutual interests (warrior societies, fraternal/sororal organizations, clubs, parties), all of which have certain material indications in at least some archaeologically studied societies, worldwide.

Group identity can be addressed by a wide variety of disciplines, among them the visual studies, history, and literature—yet to understand some very useful issues around such identity, we must often turn to the social sciences. In this realm, the ways in which the identities of groups are built, shared, passed on, and changed have been intensively studied, as well as how they are expressed to the outside world. Such scholarship addresses both intellectual aspects of such expression and also its materiality, through the solid and observable 'things' or patterns of everyday life. It must be stressed, though, that many caveats remain. Contemporary scholars are often careful to note how much we do *not* know about identity, and what assumptions we should *not* make, perhaps with more frequency than they make positive statements about the subject.

Studying Group Identity: Ethnic Identity

While much could be written about the wide variety of identity groups in the past, a chapter must have limits. One of the main avenues of research on group identity in the Iron Age has been ethnicity, a 'social identification based on the presumption of shared history and a common cultural inheritance' (Brumfiel 1994). Thus, the remainder of this discussion will concern ethnic identity,[1] although many of its points and conclusions are valid for any type of identity group, as *all* of them, including ethnicity, are culturally constructed categories. The term 'cultural construction' is sometimes misapprehended outside ethnography and sociology. It does not mean invented or not real; it refers to the notion that the behaviours and activities of group members come with a set of expectations created by the larger society. What is acceptable for and expected of 'youth' in one society might be outlawed in another.

As with much research in the social sciences, a series of ideas was put forth by scholars during the mid- to late twentieth century, evaluated by peers, and rejected or amended in light of accumulating data (Emberling 1997). The social sciences are inherently comparative, thus some examples, used later, of how such ideas have been used are drawn from global archaeological contexts with applications in the European Iron Age. We can understand this history of such intellectual experiment by examining the history of theories. Three major approaches to ethnic identity can be traced in the social sciences: the isolationist/primordialist approach, the instrumentalist/constructivist/integrationist approach, and the power/domination approach.

Identity Primordialism and Isolationist Concepts

The first approach, which is associated with the culture historic perspective, sees groups as discrete social units whose traditions and material culture are ancient, unchanging, distinctive, and unique to each group, due mainly to geographical differences and isolation, creating a culture that is easily distinguishable from other groups. Archaeologically speaking, there are certain implications that come with this theory. If group identity, and by extension some presumed territorial identity, is formed in isolation or separation of strongly bounded groups, one would predict that each discrete ethnic entity would use highly differing, non-overlapping sets of material culture and also perform certain types of unique behaviours. In addition to the realization that few groups are really isolated, the isolationist hypothesis was discredited largely by observation, not only by anthropologists and sociologists, but by archaeological research as well.

Interaction, Cultural Construction, and Identity Instrumentalism

One of the most important seminal works on this subject, which critiqued the first approach and defined the second, is Barth's (1969) *Ethnic Groups and Boundaries: The Social Organization of Culture Difference*. Barth's observations led social scientists toward the development of the instrumentalist or social constructivist view of group identity, in which ethnic affiliation is seen as a tool, or instrument, for obtaining a desired outcome; by creating a group of social allies, constructed from symbols of group affiliation, individuals in a group can better position themselves vis-à-vis other groups for various types of advantages (Barth 1969). While later scholarship added to Barth's thesis (Eller and Coughlan 1993; Nagel 1994; Cerulo 1997; Verkuyten 2005), it stands as a turning point in our understanding of group identity, especially in terms of how archaeologists understand the Iron Age.

Barth (1969) emphasized that rather than focusing on identities formed in isolation, we should concentrate on those formed in dynamic interaction spheres, where people often need to distinguish themselves from others, by *affiliating*, or choosing to form shared loyalties based on the *presumption* or *construction* of shared history and common cultural inheritance—often, but not always real. Barth (1969: 14) identified two ways in which groups distinguished themselves: first, 'overt signals or signs—the diacritical features that people look for and exhibit to show identity, often such features as dress, language, house-form, or general style of life', and second, 'basic value orientations: the standards of morality and excellence by which performance is judged'.

Socially relevant factors alone become diagnostic for membership, not the overt, 'objective' differences which are generated by other factors. It makes no difference how dissimilar members may be in their overt behaviour—if they say they are A, in contrast to another cognate category B, they are willing to be treated and let their own behaviour be interpreted and judged as A's and not as B's; in other words, they declare their allegiance to the shared culture of A. The effects of this, as compared to other factors influencing actual behaviour, can then be made the object of investigation (Barth 1969: 14). The idea most detrimental to the culture historic view is summed up thus: 'The critical focus of investigation from this point of view becomes the ethnic boundary that defines the group, not the cultural stuff that it encloses' (Barth 1969: 15).

In his important ethnoarchaeological work in Kenya and the Sudan, inspired by the findings of Barth and other ethnographers, Hodder (1977, 1978, 1979, 1982, 1985) studied the interactions of different, self-identified ethnic groups, to test the assumption that material culture uniformly reflects differences that mark a group out as distinct, and whether objects could even be classified as to their use or meaning. What he found was that the assumptions of archaeologists were completely at odds with reality, both in theory and in practice. The age-old notion that a group can be identified by the distribution of objects or styles, or that such styles can be assumed to correspond with a language or even a religion, proved false. People of different language groups shared styles; those speaking different languages used similar material culture, while practising different *or* the same religions. In addition, the groups observed by Hodder lived in communities close together—making it impossible to tell groups apart 'archaeologically' by any sort of material distributions. Several types of artefacts with overtly utilitarian uses were in fact symbolic of different age- and gender-related roles. There were virtually no simple correspondences between ethnicity and the very traits that archaeologists were sure could label an ethnic group. Despite these conditions, groups in close proximity for centuries lost none of their ethnic distinctiveness.

For many archaeologists, Hodder's work cast grave doubts on the linkages, and thus inferences, between bounded geographic regions, material culture, and ethnic identities in archaeology. In actuality group identities are even more complex than such studies indicate. Many diacritica used by groups to distinguish themselves are based on superficial and recently adopted symbols of membership that only serve to construct an identity different from other groups (Barth 1969; Hobsbawm and Ranger 1983). Individuals frequently changed their ethnicity, by simply declaring themselves as such, and choosing to live in differently ascribed ways (Waters 1990). More recent ethnoarchaeological work (Saetersdal 1999) notes that two groups of Maconde, one in Tanzania and one Mozambique, closely identify as one group, although their material culture became starkly different as they adjusted to different social environments. Other groups, such as the Hutu and Tutsi, are in fact the identical ethnic group, who only since the colonial era, due to German and Belgian ascription of different statuses, insist on difference to the point of genocide (Bowen 1996).

Brumfiel (1994), citing Barth (1969) on ethnicity and Apter (1965) on politics and ethnic traditions, discussed the possible archaeological correlates for such conditions in her discussion of Imperial Aztec ethnic identity in Mexico, a study that has had broad impacts on the archaeological study of identity globally. If a group with self-perceived ethnic identity was using it as an instrument to obtain specific goals or create a place for themselves, as ethnohistories of the early immigrant Mexica group (later Aztec) indicate, it might be expected that while they would share a number of material similarities with neighbouring groups, early Mexica households, gathering areas, or public spaces should yield an identifiable set of artefacts, styles, and behaviours (burial traditions, spatial preferences) that are symbolically unique to the group (Brumfiel 1994: 96). In other words, these would have been symbols that purposefully delineated differences between the Mexica and others as they strove to rise above their peers; Brumfiel proceeded to provide a strong case study documenting such a set of conditions.

Situations do arise in which multiple ethnic groups are suddenly brought together rather than having coexisted for long periods of time, for example during episodes of magnet immigration, when multiple groups are drawn to a single location or area. With magnet immigration, it is understood that the group's cultural and material repertoire is not distinct due to isolation in the homeland (as in primordialist theory), but due to a sudden juxtaposition. What happens under such circumstances? Is there evidence that they would maintain difference? Or that once-distinct cultural inventories would blur and lose their differences with time? The latter is sometimes called the 'melting pot' expectation, and might be observed in modern nations where immigration has brought unfamiliar groups into contact—East Asian and African, European and South American: classically Canada, Australia, the United States, but now many contexts across the globe. This might characterize England during the long Iron Age's early Anglo-Saxon period (Härke 2011), Gaul in the early fifth century AD when various Germanic groups migrated into the former Roman province (Halsall 2000; Goffart 2009), and other periods when specific areas were rapidly colonized by people from a variety of groups. For England, some studies have indicated that early migrants' origins can be traced to Sweden, Norway, Denmark, the Netherlands, and elsewhere based on differing material culture, materially observable customs, and biology (Crawford 1997; Russell 2007; Härke 2011). After some time, the process of structuration modified or fused many such differences, and inspired novel styles, producing new forms. But did it erase people's view of their own ethnicities? Did immigrants ever distinguish themselves based on ancestry or origins? If they did, how long was it before they no longer did so?

Studies show that for over a century, in modern times, despite differing conditions in Canada and the United States, for example, while the experience of individual groups has been varied, in most cases cultural pluralism has been the result of in-migration by highly differentiated groups. Sometimes called multiculturalism, some attributes of immigrant cultures persist, while others have melted together (Palmer 1976). So far, this appears to be determined by the level of desire (or necessity) to assimilate, the rejection of immigrant assimilation due to discrimination by other groups, and changes in political conditions and government policies over time. Sociological surveys indicate varied levels of internal, psychological, or ideological integration, that are not always equal with materiality (Barlow et al. 2000), ranging from long-term citizens who remain psychologically 'foreigners', to others who feel assimilated yet perceive rejection by the dominant culture, and those who deny any historical ethnic differences (Perks 1984; Cheryan and Monin 2005; Devos and Banaji 2005; Manning and Roy 2007). If we seek to find similar conditions in fully or largely prehistoric times, we might discover similar patterns, but also fail to know if more than superficial, material markers were involved, or know that other more subtle processes of identity were at work. The possibilities and difficulties of recognizing such conditions archaeologically, informed by contemporary social theory, have been successfully explored in several contexts (e.g. Pauketat 2003; Knapp 2008). Manning and Roy (2007) have discussed the statistical probability that those who emigrate from poorer places with social problems 'feel' a new or hybrid ethnicity much more quickly than those who were better off, and that many who are dissatisfied return-migrate, even with a high level of inconvenience or cost. Identifying the livelihood conditions of early first-generation immigrants could play to the strengths of research using material culture.

For the Iron Age, we remain unsure, even if such initial material differences diminish, whether this penetrates beyond the purely material and into social memory—witness the ongoing debate as to whether an apartheid-like system separated Germanic immigrants from Britons—or whether over time, integration occurred (Pattison 2007, 2011; Thomas et al. 2008); populations, if not identities, are being studied using demographic statistics, biology, and genetics, in addition to archaeology and textual records.

Ethnic Power and Social Dominance Hierarchies

The idea of identity as a tool of power and domination was introduced by Comaroff (1987, 1998). This idea deals with more than instrumental competition and advantage-seeking between groups; it concerns the hierarchical order of various groups seen in many societies, where ethnic and/or other group identity is used to justify the privileges of one group over another, and even suppression of the rights of others. Comaroff (1987) defined dominance, in this paradigm, as the use of ethnic identity to legitimate its own privileges by claiming to have superior cultural or biological traits.

In such cases, some specific concepts are useful: *affiliation* is a positive force in which people decide on or are drawn to self-identification with their group, while *attribution* is a more negative quality that indicates the 'labelling' of a group by others (Comaroff 1987). Brumfiel's Aztec case study, along with ample European Iron Age imperial and colonial examples, illustrates how ethnic awareness in a context of several groups gives rise not only to differentiation, but also to a pecking order. Brumfiel (1994: 96), in her discussion of Aztec imperialism, indicated that when studying a context in which the power/domination conditions might be operating, the process of identifying ethnic attribution is essential. Dominant groups have good reasons to maintain ethnic loyalties, as they contain a part of the group's leverage for remaining at the top of the social, political, and economic hierarchy. Yet conversely, in many cases, those who belong to other, less advantaged or even downtrodden ethnic groups are just as insistent on maintaining and displaying markers of their own identities (Barth 1969), unifying no matter what indignities they suffer, accepting scorn as a badge of their mutual dilemma, developing shared strategies for coping with their position, and perhaps using their agency to improve it.

Archaeologists seeking evidence of such a context might expect to find unflattering external attributions associated with certain groups in the archaeological record, but would also find other internal markers of their shared identity. Brumfiel (1994: 96) asserted that evidence of both attribution and affiliation processes can be seen in a fairly straightforward way through representational art, murals, and sculptures depicting clearly indexed items of dress, adornment, body presentation—which we find as artefacts, contexts, and sometimes biological phenomena such as intentional or unintentional body deformations.

Archaeologically, ethnic attribution would be expected to yield some demeaning images of other ethnic groups, a visual (or textual) indication of subservience, related to known insults or slurs. Essentialized markers of dress, style, occupation, and other ethnic 'traits' can be seen for example on Trajan's Column (Lepper and Frere 1988;

Kampen 1995; Davies 1997; Stevenson 2001; Dillon 2006), showing the conquest and subjugation of the Dacians. This is just one clear example of attribution—among many other Roman monuments reflecting the labelling, essentializing, or humiliation of a group, such as the column of Marcus Aurelius and the Severan Arch (Dillon 2006; Lusnia 2006). Accompanying visual signs of such attribution, there might also be signs of more social and physical alienation, and more economic distance between such groups and a conquering or dominating culture over time.

Such relationships themselves must not be stereotyped, or the direction of power assumed. For the Iron Age, with its many and complex intercultural and intergroup interactions, it might be useful for archaeologists to consider the term *transculturation* (Ortiz 1947), a multilateral process in which groups 'select, appropriate, and invent from materials transmitted to them by other groups in the contact zone' (MacDonald and Butz 1998: 336). A number of archaeologists have discussed the evidence for this process in the Roman provinces after conquest (Webster 1997; Häussler 2001), especially in terms of how religion was syncretized, at once forced by the Romans yet creatively enacted by Britons, Gauls, and others. Among the most successful and influential works has been that of Jones (1997), which dove into the controversy and complexity with newer ideas and methods, many drawn from the social sciences, to examine ethnicity as a dynamic phenomenon of overlapping identities using the Roman conquest of the Britons as a case study. Jones teased apart many intersecting identities by focusing on specific types of places, with the expectation that they characterized different social, religious, political, and economic groups, as well as public and private spheres of activity. The test implication most clearly supported was that Roman culture was differentially adopted and that people expressed British or Roman identity differently in different contexts.

This agrees with Ortiz (1947: 102), who noted that unlike the acculturation notion, which indicated acquiring a new culture while being forced to lose the other, transculturation refers to the creation of new cultural phenomena, through complex and ongoing processes. This begins early in colonial contact when 'those above and those below, living together in the same atmosphere of terror and oppression, the oppressed in terror of punishment, the oppressor in terror of reprisals', and while groups on the subordinate end of the continuum are initially coerced or otherwise induced to adopt the dominant society's constructions, as time goes on, in most cases of imperial domination such groups may have a great deal of self-determination about 'what they adopt and how they make use of these foreign constructions' (MacDonald and Butz 1998: 336).

Finally, it must be noted that such biases grow from dominant groups' desire to legitimize inequality (Comaroff 1987, 1998). In the beginning, a conquering group—say the Romans—might create conditions of inequality, in this case between themselves and Germanic or Celtic peoples, elite and non-elite. This early relationship might result in suffering: economic, social, and physical, which are aspects of *material domination*. Yet as structuration proceeds into the future, and inequality has been internalized, subordinate groups may attain similar levels of wealth, education, even power in society. At this point, it is no longer inequality that forms the social framework, but prejudice, and as such, prejudice will still induce *status domination*, or 'practices which deny standing or dignity to subordinates—humiliation, insults, assaults on self-respect—and emphasize their subordination' (MacDonald and Butz 1998: 337).

In the beginning status domination strengthens and supports material domination, yet even after inequality is effectively levelled, and material domination diminishes, status domination may remain strongly in place. Thus, archaeologically speaking, it is not enough to imagine a single snapshot of time along the colonial continuum. It is necessary to consider multiple time slices, and it is to the attributive markers that archaeologists must return in mature colonial or interaction spheres. For example, in late Roman Gaul and Iberia, uprisings among the indigenes occurred, in which they themselves created and used the name *bacaudae*, which was soon also used by those against whom they were rising up (Thompson 1952; Lee 2007). This group and their phenomenon have been called mysterious, 'described by some as peasant rebels and by others as local notables showing too strong an inclination toward independence from the state' (Lee 2007: 9). The *bacaudae* would provide an excellent archaeological context for understanding whether after several centuries there was still some stigma attached to their ethnic origins, whereas it is usually presumed that indigenous people came to 'feel Roman'. Such a study would have to establish markers of ethnicity, but also of class, economic status, and other possible determinants of conflict.

Importantly, 'traits' used for ethnic attribution are often unimportant to, or not particularly noted by, members of the subordinate group (Barth 1969; Brumfiel 1994). For example, men of such a group might not consider that a particular style of facial hair essentializes them, even if they largely embrace such a style. Dominant groups pick what is visibly or behaviourally most recognizable to use as a labelling, 'othering' device. These may include not only objects but behaviours claimed to be 'typical'—for example, in the nineteenth century, and to some degree more recently, many people in the United States, a society with multiple subordinate ethnic groups, used racial and ethnic slurs that characterized Asians as 'scheming and inscrutable', Mexicans as 'lazy', Jews as 'money-hungry', Italians as 'criminal', and Irish as 'brawling'.

Thus it can be seen that when we characterize, for example, Germanic groups as 'warlike' we are simply buying into the attributions of the Iron Age! While no one doubts that the Romans could wage an effective war, because of the textual emphasis on their sciences, arts, and intellectual achievements, we rarely call them equally 'warlike' in the same breath with which we label Germanic or Celtic people. It has been only recently that Viking scholars have gained broad acceptance for the notion that the Scandinavians were neither more nor less aggressive than their neighbours, and just as likely as their neighbours to engage in trade and other non-violent interactions. This represents the improved understanding of such behaviours as situational and instrumental—a paradigm shift that has not yet caught on to such a degree for the earlier Iron Age.

Conflict as a 'habitual strategy' between groups in this light is not as clear-cut as once thought: it is indicated, for example, by Julius Caesar that various peoples could be allies when expedient, and fall into conflict when it was necessary or desirable from some internal perspective. While is it common now to recognize as normal the fluid fragmenting, consolidating, and reorganizing among the Germanic people or the Celts, it is also the case across these groups that were once characterized as vastly differing. If it is to be taken as relatively accurate, in Caesar's description of Ariovistus, a Germanic leader who allied with and then fell out with Gaulish counterparts among the Sequani, it is implicit that there is no special way to characterize a group's (or region's) way of interacting with other entities. All were capable of peaceful interaction, diplomacy, or warfare; all could instrumentally and rapidly shift strategies.

A group's identity does not necessarily change with their economy—groups the world over shift frequently from foraging to herding to farming to urban life, and back. Similarly, in the strategies with which they engage others, warfare and trade are only decisions made on expedient grounds, as can be seen between any modern or former entities who waged brutal wars only a few decades ago but now engage in warm trading and manufacturing relationships with their former antagonists.

If it is a fallacy to believe that the identity of a group lies in a piece of land or territory, or in its strategies of conflict or cooperation, it is also a fallacy that it resides in an economic system or even a religion or social structure. This is an artefact of older essentialist views. In the 1970s and 1980s, for example, it was popular to discuss the extinction of the Ju/'hoansi of southern Africa, once called Bushmen, and their 'degradation', as they had been impacted so deeply by colonialism and modernization that their cultural identity no longer existed. Then how, in current times, can ethnographers be studying the impact of HIV/AIDS on their lives, as they conduct a circular migration between the savannah, rural towns, and the urban centres of South Africa (Susser 2007; Klaits 2010), with many of their traditions altered and hybridized, but their identities still intact? How can the transgendered Mapuche shamans of Chile turn from evoking ancestors to scold misbehaving families in their isolated villages, to trancing in the city, announcing their displeasure with the government for eroding indigenous rights (Bacigalupo 2007)? It is recognized that so-called identity markers shift with each generation, even each significant set of interactions, and an acquired non-regional tradition quickly becomes integrated into a group's cultural repertoire—one generation's norms could be distant from or even alien to the experience of their temporally close descendants, still while maintaining identity.

Contemporary ethnographers often say that there are no 'real' claims of cultural authenticity, because everyone's identity is authentic. Groups worldwide both enjoy their cultural identity in relatively private group activities, and in public use it as an instrument for making appeals, lobbying governments, seeking rights, and improving or leveraging their positions. There is nothing wrong with this, it is an apparently long-standing element of human organization, yet those studying groups and cultures should not reify authenticity claims, creating a reality out of a cultural construct that is sometimes only situational—today as well as in the past.

In this light, it is each individual archaeologist's task to understand the place and time that they are studying, emplace it within a longer timescale with which to understand change, and interpret their finds in light of the current understanding of how culture works among both past and present groups.

Current and Future Directions for the Study of Iron Age Identities

More and more layers are added to our research problems when underlying group identities relate to wider social, political, religious, and economic concerns. In eras like the Iron Age, with ample communication across great distances, distinct regional traditions were stacked together with overarching continuities, some holdovers from earlier times, some apparently newly conceptualized. We can hypothesize all these processes of identity for Iron Age societies, with their cosmopolitan interactions, their clashes between expanding empire and local populations, and constant jostling for advantage in a field of many similar small social units. We understand that group identity stems from complex sets of culturally constructed internal and external determinants. Regions are inhabited by groups made up of individuals and smaller social agglomerations: families, lineages, clans, or socially and politically connected co-residential groups, each with multiple shifting identities involving kinship, social status, gender, age, occupation, shared experience, and personal biography. No 'group' experiences its own society in the same way as other groups.

What does this mean for the future archaeological study of regional and group identities? Even among groups or between regions with competitive interests, cooperation or detente between neighbours is as likely as conflict according to ethnographic parallels; trade, travel, and familiarity can result in a co-mingling of material culture, actions, and ideas, while still preserving self-recognized differences. There are several ways in which archaeologists, some discussed in this chapter, have begun to grapple with these acknowledged difficulties.

Because of the interactions on so many levels and so many scales, not to mention spheres—political, economic, social, and sacred—which may differ from one another, we should also remember the term *intersectionality*, a shorthand in social science for describing how group (and individual) identities exist on many multidimensional levels and scales at one time (Crenshaw 1989; Jordan-Zachery 2007). This is of course one of the most difficult aspects confronting archaeologists. Brumfiel noted that gender, class, political faction, and many other nuclei of identity operate simultaneously or sequentially in individuals and groups (Brumfiel 1992; also 1989, 1994).

Intersectionality, informed by social science research, has been investigated for the Iron Age with the intent of both presenting case studies of nested identities and underscoring the complexity once overlooked by earlier scholars (James 1999; Sjöberg 2011; Fahlander 2012; Thedéen 2012; Fernández-Götz 2013). With skill, and the right kind of data, we can at least pluck out one or two of these intersectional identities and follow their courses through time.

A major direction in identity studies has been to use ethnographic analogies to produce understanding of the various affordances available to past people, and then seek understanding of which ones they chose to make use of, and in what way. There has been a long-standing debate in archaeology about such analogies, but in this case they are usually used only to suggest a starting place for research and inform a variety of interpretations of archaeological data.

One may ask, how can studies of current social processes be used to study very different past societies? The answer is twofold. First, if the processes studied are *cognitive*, that is, related to the limbic system or based on the structure of the brain, they are usually deemed by psychologists to be generally cross-cultural and relatively cross-temporal, and studied as such by other researchers. Examples might be comparative study of responses to war-induced forced migration in west Africa and central America, or comparative study of the experience of homelessness between the Great Depression beginning in 1929 and the Great Recession beginning in 2009. Predictable and comparable responses to unchosen homelessness, and forced migration in general, are both understood to be cognitive responses in the literature, and we understand that between the Iron Age and today the human brain and limbic system have not evolved biologically. Such cognitive responses might be expected at 15, 150, or 1,500 years in the past.

Psychologists have documented the specific *psychosocial* reasons why these phenomena are experienced in such similar ways through time and across space (Summerfield 1996; Baron 2002; Eisenbruch et al. 2004)—for example, that overt or hidden conflicts between groups can frequently be linked with a strengthening of group identity, 'us versus them'. Thus, archaeologists wondering if conflict was a possible condition of life in the place and time period they study, might look for traces of a similar strengthening of identities in their prehistoric or protohistoric contexts. Such flaring of identity awareness might be apparent through an increase in symbols, monumental commemorations, texts, or other media, and if so, the possibility of conflict might be highlighted.

Human responses can also sometimes be examined in light of the findings of neurologists who understand responses that are cognitive, or related to the structure and anatomy of the human brain, as differentiated from the 'mind' studied by social scientists. While there is never a fully certain parallel between studies of current or recent people's and past people's behaviours, such data are often helpful in imagining the full range of human choices in various circumstances, and perhaps in interpreting what decisions they made.

Second, when responses are not explicitly cognitive, we assume that they are part of a constellation of possible responses; since the social sciences work within a deductive framework, one does not expect to 'prove' any response, only to identify evidence as to whether it occurred, and if not, move on to test other possible sets of conditions and responses, in this case against the archaeological record. Thus, any 'test implication' or evidence that might be expected under a set of conditions is simply a starting point for research that may end up with quite different conclusions.

There is growing scholarly consensus (Jones 1996, 1997) that certain materially observable classes of behaviour are more likely to reflect acquired styles while others indicate indigenous traditions. Typically, a comparison of material culture that is more private, perhaps within the household, retains long-standing traditions, the group's internal affiliative identity, while outward shows of style and form may more accurately reflect public group identity—the attributive identity, constructed by the dominant culture and presented to the group itself and its neighbours, local and distant.

Another recent tool adding to our ability to unlock the black box of identity is the notion of *technological choice*. This body of theory stems from the archaeologically well-used theories of practice, structure, and agency in which ethnic (and other) identities are seen as specifically linked to material productions through the subconscious patterns of everyday activities (Bourdieu 1977, 1990)—*practice*—which in turn reflect a set of acquired patterns of thought, behaviour, and taste—the *habitus* (Bentley 1987). Habitus in turn is strongly influenced by the material and spatial conditions in which people live (Dietler and Herbich 1998). Because practice is ongoing and constant, and habitus all-pervasive, identity is maintained and reinforced continually through these processes. Over time, conditions of stasis or change in practice, habitus, and identity are determined by the structuration process (Giddens 1979, 1984), in which people simultaneously influence and are influenced by the cultural rules of the world around them.

Research on technological choice specifically demonstrates that while people may change the way in which they decorate, style, or organize material culture, they usually continue to construct it in older, more traditional ways. This work, rooted in the French school of *techniques* (Mauss 1934; Leroi-Gourhan 1964) has been pioneered by a small number of scholars (Lemonnier 1986, 1993; Dobres and Hoffman 1994; Cumberpatch and Blinkhorn 1997; Costin and Wright 1998; Stark 1998; Gosselain 2000; Sillar 2000; Sillar and Tite 2000; Stark et al. 2000; Fazioli 2011, 2012). Study of the underlying technology is a way that archaeologists can determine what sort of change is apparent and at what level or scale it has occurred (Lemonnier 1986, 1993; Cumberpatch and Blinkhorn 1997).

In other words, a pot may be painted with the new or hybridized designs of a dominant or influential—or merely neighbouring—culture, yet the vessel itself is made in clear and distinctive technological fashion, showing continuity with the ceramic technology of earlier generations. Earlier styles may simply be out of fashion or no longer instrumental in communicating cultural knowledge. This would indicate that the group's identity is intact, and that only the style has changed. Understanding that identity persists behind a stylistic change could alter the entire interpretation of a cultural trajectory.

Conclusions

Because of the past misuse of concepts like ethnicity, and the fact that identity is not easy to study, many once asserted that identity research was either impossible or unnecessary. For archaeologists, the many realizations about the slippery nature of identity were at first daunting. It made impossible what had once been a straightforward task of describing a piece of jewellery in a burial and linking it to 'identity' with much wider implications. Now that many have readjusted the expectation of how we study these issues, in recent times recognition of its importance has inspired many new approaches to the archaeological study of identity. One cannot really separate or ignore such cross-cutting connections without the risk of misinterpreting the evidence: a key factor in archaeological studies is to identify the appropriate scale at which to study different types and levels of identity. Untangling the ways in which a group's identity is best made visible, how one group interacts with others, and its relation to so many other factors, is difficult at best.

In the end, archaeologists must work with 'things'—material culture—and physical traces of their organization, and link them to the ways of life, practices, and actions that produced them. They must also try to understand what it all meant on different levels—what the makers were trying to express, and what that tells us about the overall story of their society through time. There is no complete agreement about the precise ways that past identity worked at either the personal or social level, or on how identity was formed, maintained, dissolved, and recreated. Yet a combination of new methods and a vastly enhanced array of theoretical approaches have made the difficult study of identity into a rewarding avenue for understanding the European Iron Age.

Note

1. For an exhaustive review of ethnicity and archaeology, see Emberling 1997.

References

Apter, D. E. 1965. *The Politics of Modernization*. Chicago: University of Chicago Press.

Arnold, B. 1992. 'The past as propaganda: How Hitler's archaeologists distorted European prehistory to justify racist and territorial goals'. *Archaeology* July/Aug: 30–37.

Bacigalupo, A. M. 2007. *Shamans of the Foye Tree: Gender, Power, and Healing among the Chilean Mapuche*. Austin: University of Texas Press.

Barlow, K. M., D. M. Taylor, and W. E. Lambert. 2000. 'Ethnicity in America and feeling "American"'. *Journal of Psychology* 134, 6: 581–601.

Baron, N. 2002. 'Community based psychosocial and mental health services for Southern Sudanese refugees in long term exile in Uganda', in J. De Jong (ed.) *Trauma, War, and Violence: Public Mental Health in Socio-Cultural Context*: 157–203. New York: Springer.

Barth, F. 1969. *Ethnic Groups and Boundaries: The Social Organization of Culture Difference*. Boston: Little, Brown.

Bentley, G. C. 1987. 'Ethnicity and Practice'. *Comparative Studies in Society and History* 29, 1: 24–55.

Binford, L. 1962. 'Archaeology as Anthropology'. *American Antiquity* 28, 2: 217–225.

Binford, L. R. 1965. 'Archaeological systematics and the study of culture process'. *American Antiquity* 31, 2: 203–210.

Bodmer, K. 1839–1843. *Travels in the Interior of North America in the Years 1832 to 1834*. London: Ackermann and Company.

Bowen, J. R. 1996. 'The myth of global ethnic conflict'. *Journal of Democracy* 7, 4: 3–14.
Bourdieu, P. 1977. *Outline of a Theory of Practice*. Cambridge: Cambridge University Press.
Bourdieu, P. 1990. *The Logic of Practice*. Cambridge: Polity Press.
Brumfiel, E. M. 1989. 'Factional competition in complex society', in D. Miller, M. Rowlands, and C. Tilley (eds) *Domination and Resistance*: 127–139. London: Unwin Hyman.
Brumfiel, E. M. 1992. 'Distinguished lecture in archeology: Breaking and entering the ecosystem. Gender, class, and faction steal the show'. *American Anthropologist* 94, 3: 551–567.
Brumfiel, E. M. 1994. 'Factional competition and political development in the New World: An introduction', in E. M. Brumfiel and J. W. Fox (eds) *Factional Competition and Political Development in the New World*: 3–14. Cambridge: Cambridge University Press.
Buchsenschutz, O., and I. Ralston. 1988. 'En réalisant la guerre des Gaules'. *Aquitania* supplément 1: 383–387.
Bunbury, E. H. 1879. *A History of Ancient Geography among the Greeks and Romans: From the Earliest Ages till the Fall of the Roman Empire, Vol. 2*. London: J. Murray.
Cerulo, K. A. 1997. 'Identity construction: New issues, new directions'. *Annual Review of Sociology* 23: 385–409.
Cheryan, S., and B. Monin. 2005. '"Where are you really from?": Asian Americans and identity denial'. *Journal of Personality and Social Psychology* 89, 5: 717–730.
Childe, V. G. 1925. *The Dawn of European Civilization*. London: Kegan Paul.
Childe, V. G. 1929. *The Danube in Prehistory*. Oxford: Clarendon Press.
Comaroff, J. 1987. 'Of totemism and ethnicity: Consciousness, practice and the signs of inequality'. *Ethnos: Journal of Anthropology* 52, 3–4: 301–323.
Comaroff, J. 1998. 'Reflections on the colonial state, in South Africa and elsewhere: Factions, fragments, facts and fictions'. *Social Identities* 4, 3: 321–362.
Costin, C. L., and R. Wright (eds). 1998. *Craft and Social Identity*. Arlington, VA: American Anthropological Association.
Crawford, S. 1997. 'Britons, Anglo-Saxons and the Germanic burial ritual', in J. Chapman and H. Hamerow (eds) *Migrations and Invasions in Archaeological Explanation*. British Archaeological Reports International Series 664: 45–72. Oxford: Archaeopress.
Crenshaw, K. 1989. 'Demarginalizing the intersection of race and sex: A Black feminist critique of antidiscrimination doctrine, feminist theory and antiracist politics'. *The University of Chicago Legal Forum* 165: 139–167.
Cumberpatch, C. G., and P. W. Blinkhorn (eds). 1997. *Not so Much a Pot, More a Way of Life: Current Approaches to Artefact Analysis in Archaeology*. Oxbow Monograph 83. Oxford: Oxbow.
Davies, P. J. E. 1997. 'The politics of perpetuation: Trajan's Column and the art of commemoration'. *American Journal of Archaeology* 101, 1: 41–65.
Devos, T., and M. R. Banaji. 2005. 'American = White?'. *Journal of Personality and Social Psychology* 88, 3: 447–466.
Dietler, M., and I. Herbich. 1998. 'Habitus, techniques, style: An integrated approach to the social understanding of material cultures and boundaries', in M. T. Stark (ed.) *The Archaeology of Social Boundaries*: 232–263. Washington, DC: Smithsonian Institute Press.
Dillon, S. 2006. 'Women on the columns of Trajan and Marcus', in S. Dillon and K. E. Welch (eds) *Representations of War in Ancient Rome*: 244–271. Cambridge: Cambridge University Press.
Dobres, M. A., and C. R. Hoffman. 1994. 'Social agency and the dynamics of prehistoric technology'. *Journal of Archaeological Method and Theory* 1, 3: 211–258.

Eisenbruch, M., J. T. V. M. de Jong, and W. van de Put. 2004. 'Bringing order out of chaos: A culturally competent approach to managing the problems of refugees and victims of organized violence'. *Journal of Traumatic Stress* 17, 2: 123–131.

Eller, J. D., and R. M. Coughlan. 1993. 'The poverty of primordialism: The demystification of ethnic attachments'. *Ethnic and Racial Studies* 16, 2: 183–202.

Emberling, G. 1997. 'Ethnicity in complex societies: Archaeological perspectives'. *Journal of Archaeological Research* 5, 4: 295–344.

Fahlander, F. 2012. 'Facing gender. Corporeality, materiality, intersectionality and resurrection', in I. M. Back Danielsson and S. Thedéen (eds) *To Tender Gender: The Pasts and Futures of Gender Research in Archaeology*. Stockholm Studies in Archaeology 58: 137–152. Stockholm: Stockholm University.

Fazioli, K. P. 2011. 'Technology, Identity, and Time: Studies in the Archaeology and Historical Anthropology of the Eastern Alpine Region from Late Antiquity to the Early Middle Ages'. PhD dissertation, State University of New York, University at Buffalo.

Fazioli, K. P. 2012. 'Ceramic technology in the southeastern Alpine region in Late Antiquity and the Early Middle Ages: Results of macroscopic and microscopic analyses'. *Arheološki vestnik* 63: 199–234.

Fernández-Götz, M. 2013. 'Revisiting Iron Age ethnicity'. *European Journal of Archaeology* 16, 1: 116–136.

Forbiger, A. 1848. *Handbuch der alten Geographie, aus den Quellen bearbeitet*. Leipzig: Gustav Mayer.

Giddens, A. 1979. *Central Problems in Social Theory*. London: Macmillan.

Giddens, A. 1984. *The Constitution of Society. Outline of a Theory of Structuration*. Cambridge: Polity Press.

Goffart, W. 2009. *Barbarian Tides: The Migration Age and the Later Roman Empire*. Philadelphia: University of Pennsylvania Press.

Gosselain, O. P. 2000. 'Materializing identities: An African perspective'. *Journal of Archaeological Method and Theory* 7, 3: 187–217.

Green, M. A. 2004. *An Archaeology of Images: Iconology and Cosmology in Iron Age and Roman Europe*. London: Routledge.

Halsall, G. 2000. 'Archaeology and the late Roman frontier in northern Gaul: The so-called Föderatengräber reconsidered', in W. Pohl and H. Reimitz (eds) *Grenze und Differenz im früheren Mittelalter*: 167–180. Vienna: Österreichische Akademie der Wissenschaften.

Härke, H. 2000. *Archaeology, Ideology and Society: The German Experience. Gesellschaften und Staaten im Epochenwandel 7*. Frankfurt: Europäischer Verlag der Wissenschaften.

Härke, H. 2011. 'Anglo-Saxon immigration and ethnogenesis'. *Medieval Archaeology* 55: 1–28.

Häussler, R. 2001. 'Fusion and resistance in native religion in Gallia Narbonensis and Britain'. *Veleia* 18–19: 79–116.

Hedeager, L. 2011. *Iron Age Myth and Materiality: An Archaeology of Scandinavia, AD 400–1000*. London: Routledge.

Hobsbawm, E., and T. Ranger (eds) 1983. *The Invention of Tradition*. Cambridge: Cambridge University Press.

Hodder, I. 1977. 'The distribution of material culture items in the Baringo district, western Kenya'. *Man* 12: 239–269.

Hodder, I. 1978. 'The spatial structure of material "cultures": A review of some of the evidence', in I. Hodder (ed.) *The Spatial Organisation of Culture*: 93–111. London: Duckworth.

Hodder, I. 1979. 'Economic and social stress and material culture patterning'. *American Antiquity* 44, 3: 446–454.

Hodder, I. 1982. *Symbols in Action: Ethnoarchaeological Studies of Material Culture.* Cambridge: Cambridge University Press.

Hodder, I. 1985. 'Boundaries as strategies: An ethnoarchaeological study', in S. W. Green and S. M. Perlman (eds) *The Archaeology of Frontiers and Boundaries*: 141–159. Orlando, FL: Academic Press.

James, S. 1999. *The Atlantic Celts: Ancient People or Modern Invention?* London: British Museum Press.

Jones, S. 1996. 'Discourses of identity in the interpretation of the past', in P. Graves-Brown, S. Jones, and C. Gamble (eds) *Cultural Identity and Archaeology: The Construction of European Communities*: 62–80. London: Burns & Oates.

Jones, S. 1997. *The Archaeology of Ethnicity: Constructing Identities in the Past and Present.* New York: Routledge.

Jordan-Zachery, J. S. 2007. 'Am I a black woman or a woman who is black? A few thoughts on the meaning of intersectionality'. *Politics and Gender* 3, 2: 254–263.

Kampen, N. B. 1995. 'Looking at gender: The column of Trajan and Roman historical relief', in D. C. Stanton and A. J. Stewart (eds) *Feminisms in the Academy*: 46–73. Ann Arbor: University of Michigan Press.

Kidder, A. V. 1924. *An Introduction to the Study of Southwestern Archaeology.* New Haven, CT: Yale University Press.

Klaits, F. 2010. *Death in a Church of Life: Moral Passion during Botswana's Time of AIDS.* Berkeley: University of California Press.

Knapp, A. B. 2008. *Prehistoric and Protohistoric Cyprus: Identity, Insularity, and Connectivity.* Oxford: Oxford University Press.

Kohl, P. L. 1998. 'Nationalism and archaeology: On the constructions of nations and the reconstructions of the remote past'. *Annual Review of Anthropology* 27: 223–246.

Kossinna, G. 1911. *Die Herkunft der Germanen: Zur Methode der Siedlungsarchäologie.* Leipzig: Kabitzsch.

Kossinna, G. 1919. *Altgermanische Kulturhöhe: ein Kriegsvortrag.* Jena: Nornen Verlag.

Kossinna, G. 1926. *Ursprung und Verbreitung der Germanen in vor- und frühgeschichtlicher Zeit.* Berlin: Germanen Verlag.

Kossinna, G. 1931. *Germanische Kultur im 1. Jahrtausend.* Leipzig: Kabitzsch.

Krebs, C. B. 2006. '"Imaginary geography" in Caesar's *Bellum Gallicum*'. *American Journal of Philology* 127, 1: 111–136.

Lee, A. D. 2007. *War in Late Antiquity: A Social History.* Oxford: Blackwell.

Lemonnier, P. 1986. 'The study of material culture today: Toward an anthropology of technical systems'. *Journal of Anthropological Archaeology* 5: 147–186.

Lemonnier, P. (ed.) 1993. *Technological Choices: Transformations in Material Cultures Since the Neolithic.* London: Routledge.

Lepper, F., and S. S. Frere. 1988. *Trajan's Column.* Gloucester: Alan Sutton.

Leroi-Gourhan, A. 1964. *Le geste et la parole 1: technique et langage.* Paris: Albin Michel.

Lusnia, S. 2006. 'Battle imagery and politics on the Severan Arch in the Roman Forum', in S. Dillon and K. E. Welch (eds) *Representations of War in Ancient Rome*: 272–299. Cambridge: Cambridge University Press.

Lyman, R. L., M. J. O'Brien, and R. C. Dunnell. 1997. 'Culture history, cultural anthropology, and cultural evolution', in *The Rise and Fall of Culture History*: 207–226. New York: Plenum Press.

MacDonald, K. I., and D. Butz. 1998. 'Investigating portering relations as a locus for transcultural interaction in the Karakorum region of northern Pakistan'. *Mountain Research and Development* 18, 4: 333–334.
McKern, W. 1939. 'The Midwestern taxonomic method as an aid to archaeological culture study'. *American Antiquity* 4: 301–313.
Mannert, K. 1788–1825. *Geographie der Griechen und Römer*. Nürnberg.
Manning, A., and S. Roy (ed.) 2007. *Culture Clash or Culture Club? The Identity and Attitudes of Immigrants in Britain*. CEP Discussion Paper 790. London: Centre for Economic Performance/London School of Economics and Political Science.
Mauss, M. 1934. 'Les techniques du corps'. *Journal de Psychologie* 32: 271–293.
Meskell, L. 2002. 'The intersections of identity and politics in archaeology'. *Annual Review of Anthropology* 31: 279–301.
Mommsen, T. 1854–1856. *Römische Geschichte, I–III*. Leipzig: Reimer & Hirsel.
Mommsen, T. 1885. *Römische Geschichte, V: Die Provinzen von Caesar bis Diokletian*. Berlin: Weidmann.
Mommsen, T. 1886. *The Provinces of the Roman Empire from Caesar to Diocletian* (trans. W. P. Dickson). London: R. Bentley & Son.
Nagel, J. 1994. 'Constructing ethnicity: Creating and recreating ethnic identity and culture'. *Social Problems* 41, 1: 152–176.
Ortiz, F. 1947. *Cuban Counterpoint: Tobacco and Sugar*. New York: Knopf.
Palmer, H. 1976. 'Mosaic versus melting pot? Immigration and ethnicity in Canada and the United States'. *International Journal* 31, 3: 488–528.
Pattison, J. E. 2007. 'Estimating inbreeding in large semi-isolated populations: Effects of varying generation length and of migration'. *American Journal of Human Biology* 19: 495–510.
Pattison, J. E. 2011. 'Integration versus Apartheid in post-Roman Britain: A response to Thomas et al. (2008)'. *Human Biology* 83, 6: 715–733.
Pauketat, T. R. 2003. 'Resettled farmers and the making of a Mississippian polity'. *American Antiquity* 68, 1: 39–66.
Perks, R. B. 1984. '"A feeling of not belonging": Interviewing European immigrants in Bradford'. *Oral History* 12, 2: 64–67.
Rebay-Salisbury, K. 2011. 'Thoughts in circles: Kulturkreislehre as a hidden paradigm in past and present archaeological interpretations', in B. Roberts and M. Vander Linden (eds) *Investigating Archaeological Cultures*: 41–59. New York: Springer.
Russell, C. K. 2007. 'Whence Came the English? Exploring Relationships Between the Iron Age, Romano-British and Anglo-Saxon Periods in Britain and Denmark: A Craniometric Biodistance Analysis'. PhD thesis, Durham University.
Saetersdal, T. 1999. 'Symbols of cultural identity: A case study from Tanzania'. *The African Archaeological Review* 16, 2: 121–135.
Sillar, B. 2000. *Shaping Culture: Making Pots and Constructing Households. An Ethnoarchaeological Study of Pottery Production, Trade and Use in the Andes*. British Archaeological Reports International Series 883. Oxford: Archaeopress.
Sillar, B., and M. S. Tite. 2000. 'The challenge of "technological choices" for materials science approaches in archaeology'. *Archaeometry* 42: 2–20.
Sjöberg, B. L. 2011. 'More than just gender: The classical Oikos as a site of intersectionality', in R. Laurence and A. Strömberg (eds) *Family in the Greco-Roman World I*: 48–59. London: Continuum.

Sommer, U. 2008. 'Choosing ancestors. The mechanisms of ethnic ascription in the age of patriotic antiquarianism (1815–1859)', in N. Schlanger and J. Nordbladh (eds) *Archives, Ancestors, Practices: Archaeology in the Light of its History*: 233–245. New York: Berghahn Books.

Spruner, K. V., and T. Menke. 1865. *Spruner-Menke Atlas Antiquus: Historisch-Geographischer Hand-Atlas*. Gotha: Perthes.

Stark, M. T. (ed.) 1998. *The Archaeology of Social Boundaries*. Washington, DC: Smithsonian Institution Press.

Stark, M. T., R. L. Bishop, and E. Miksa. 2000. 'Ceramic technology and social boundaries: Cultural practices in Kalinga clay selection and use'. *Journal of Archaeological Method and Theory* 7: 295–331.

Stevenson, T. 2001. 'On Trajan's Column: Readings, functions and symbolism'. *Ancient History* 31, 1: 28–68.

Summerfield, D. 1996. *The Impact of War and Atrocity on Civilian Populations: Basic Principles for NGO Interventions and a Critique of Psychosocial Trauma Projects*. Network Paper 14. London: Overseas Development Institute.

Susser, I. 2007. 'Confounding conventional wisdom: The Ju/'hoansi and HIV/AIDS', in R. Hitchcock, K. Ikeya, M. Biesele, and R. B. Lee (eds) *Updating the San: Image and Reality of an African People in the 21st Century. Senri Ethnological Studies 70*: 45–61. Osaka: National Museum of Ethnology.

Thedéen, S. 2012. 'Box brooches beyond the border. Female Viking Age identities of intersectionality', in I. M. Back Danielsson and S. Thedéen (eds) *To Tender Gender: The Pasts and Futures of Gender Research in Archaeology*. Stockholm Studies in Archaeology 58: 61–82. Stockholm: Stockholm University.

Thomas, M. G., M. P. Stumpf, and H. Härke. 2008. 'Integration versus apartheid in post-Roman Britain: A response to Pattison'. *Proceedings of the Royal Society B* 275: 2419–2421.

Thompson, E. A. 1952. 'Peasant revolts in late Roman Gaul and Spain'. *Past and Present* 2: 11–23.

Ukert, F. A. 1821. *Geographie der Griechen und Römer von den frühesten Zeiten bis auf Ptolemäus*. Weimar: Geographisches Institut.

Verkuyten, M. 2005. *The Social Psychology of Ethnic Identity*. New York: Psychology Press.

Waters, M. C. 1990. *Ethnic Options: Choosing Identities in America*. Berkeley: University of California Press.

Watson, P. J. 1995. 'Archaeology, Anthropology, and the Culture Concept'. *American Anthropologist* 97: 683–694.

Webster, J. 1997. 'Necessary comparisons: A post-colonial approach to religious syncretism in the Roman provinces'. *World Archaeology* 25: 324–338.

Wells, P. S. 1999. *The Barbarians Speak: How the Conquered Peoples Shaped Roman Europe*. Princeton: Princeton University Press.

Wells, P. S. 2001. *Beyond Celts, Germans and Scythians*. London: Duckworth.

Wilkes, J. 2007. 'Sailing to the Britannic Isles: Some Mediterranean perspectives on the remote northwest from the sixth century BC to the seventh century AD', in C. Gosden, H. Hamerow, P. de Jersey, and G. Lock (eds) *Communities and Connections: Essays in Honour of Barry Cunliffe*: 3–14. Oxford: Oxford University Press.

CHAPTER 36

WRITING, WRITERS, AND IRON AGE EUROPE

DAPHNE NASH BRIGGS

Introduction

READING and writing are different skills. Reading is more accessible than writing but can still seem almost magical to a non-reader (Polybius *Histories* 10.47.5–10). Writing is far more specialized, and attested early uses are commonly in the realm of religion, divination, and magic, sending messages through space and time to the living, the dead, and the gods. Since writing is what leaves a material trace, this chapter is about early European writing.

Typical Steps in the Acquisition of Writing

Writing can make any surface bear a message, and many of the earliest intelligible texts are inscribed on personal valuables, grave markers, dedications, or boundary stones, making the item speak: 'I am Nestor's cup, good to drink with ...' (Euboian Greek, Pithekoussai, *c*.720 BC); 'Manios made me for Numasios' (Latin, gold fibula, Praeneste, late seventh century BC). These are short, functional messages: a brooch, cup, or stone announce themselves, like honoured guests. Writing at this point is the preserve of rare and spooky specialists attached to senior social elites, perhaps initially often foreign visitors: metalworkers and other travellers with privileged rights to cross political and territorial boundaries (Hedeager 2011: 139–145).

Next come longer texts, still formulaic and functional, used to regulate contractual relations among members of social elites and their dealings with foreigners: accounts, contracts (sometimes helpfully bilingual), letters of introduction, diplomatic correspondence, oaths, prayers, and curses addressed to the gods. Eventually, there also appear public calendars and laws, the prerogative of rulers, arbitrators, and religious specialists: Athens' first written law code, *c*.621/620 BC; the Twelve Tables of Roman law, first inscribed in 451/450 BC; or Frankish Salic law written down at a similar point in their own post-Roman process, *c*.AD 507–511. At the point of transition to more generalized use of writing, this step may extend to recording oracular utterances and other matters of religious importance (Greek oracles, Etruscan prophecies and religious books, the Gaulish Coligny Calendar, *c*. late second century AD). This category includes some of the longest known samples of otherwise unrecorded, and sometimes now unintelligible, languages: the Celtiberian Botorrita plaque (early first century BC; Meid 1994a; Russell 1995: 202–203; Koch 2013a: 3); the Chamalières and Larzac inscriptions in Gaulish (both in the realm of magic, first century AD; Lambert 1994: 150–159, 160–172; Meid 1994b; Russell 1995: 4–5); or the official record of the first Roman treaty with Carthage (509–508 BC), viewed by the Greek historian Polybius in the early second century BC: 'I have given as accurate a translation as I can of this, but the language of the ancient Romans differs so much from the modern that even the most intelligent, with effort, can only decipher some of it. The treaty is more or less as follows ...' (*Histories* 3.22.3–4). This was the language of the 'Duenos' inscription (seventh to fifth century BC) on a ceramic vessel from a votive context in Rome, that seems to record an oath, perhaps connected with a solemn marriage contract, but scholars today, like Polybius, can barely understand it (Figure 36.1; Forsythe 2005: 88–89). The Visigoth Ulfila's translation of the Bible into Gothic in the fourth century AD, by far the longest continuous text in an early Germanic language, also belongs to this class of early document.

As a final step, writing can extend to recording canonical versions of high-order oral tradition—the Homeric poems, *Beowulf*, the *Táin Bo Cuailgne*, the *Poetic Edda*—then to composing new songs, poems, and prose literature, and to writing 'anything the human mind can conceive' (Ammianus Marcellinus *History* 17.4.10). In an advanced urban culture, literacy had myriad extensions in general use and entertainment, as illustrated in all the provinces of the Roman Empire. This step becomes apparent when writing utensils, practice alphabets, and graffiti start appearing in everyday household rubbish. Literacy had by then become an essential skill in public life, practised from childhood, and gave rise in the educated classes to specialized literacies that produced the historians, geographers, and other ancient writers on whom we now depend for verbal accounts of their non-literate contemporaries. Where inland Europe is concerned, book-based education, with a marked emphasis on rhetoric, took off with especially impressive speed among the Gauls: Massalia had a 'school for Gauls' before the first century BC (Strabo *Geography* 4.1.5). By AD 21 the 'noblest youth of Gaul' were receiving a 'liberal education' at Augustodunum (Tacitus *Annals* 3.43), and in AD 48 Claudius could recommend leading Gauls for admission to the Senate in Rome (Tacitus *Annals* 11.23; Smallwood 1967: no. 369). Later, Burdigala (Bordeaux) had a fine university, celebrated by the fourth-century

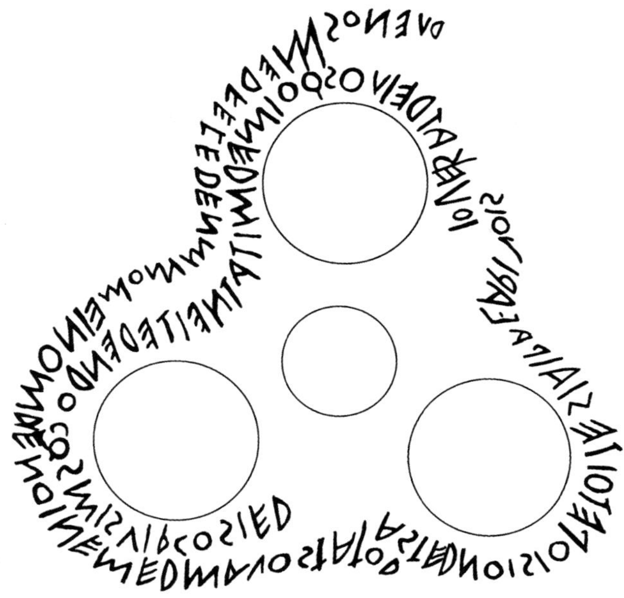

FIGURE 36.1 'Duenos' inscription on the shoulders of three conjoint vases, Rome, *c.* sixth century BC. In oldest archaic Latin: 'iovesat deivos qoi med mitat, nei ted endo cosmis virco sied. As ted noisi opetoitesiaipacarivois / Duenos med feced en mano meinom duenoi. Ne med malos tatod' = (?) 'he swears by the gods [or 'the god swears'] who sends/gives me . . . ? . . . that the fair maiden not be against thee. / A good man [or personal name Duenos] made me as a fine gift for a good man. Let not a bad man touch (?) me.' (Forsythe 2005: 88–89).

Author

AD poet Ausonius, who taught rhetoric there, and in post-Roman Britain a high standard of Latin went on being taught into the seventh century and beyond (Dark 1994: 181; Henig 2010: 124, 131).

Archaeologically Attested European Writing Systems

The writing systems with which this chapter is concerned all employ short, ordered sets of symbols to represent the sounds of particular languages. As a result, inscriptions can provide unique evidence for spoken language, changes through time, and synchronous regional dialects. Two writing systems are found in early Europe: (1) the semi-syllabic systems of Iberia in the first millennium BC that combined alphabetic symbols for single vowels and consonants with syllabic symbols for a fixed set of stop-consonant–vowel pairs (Figure 36.2; Koch 2010, 2016: 445–469, with lucid explanations); and

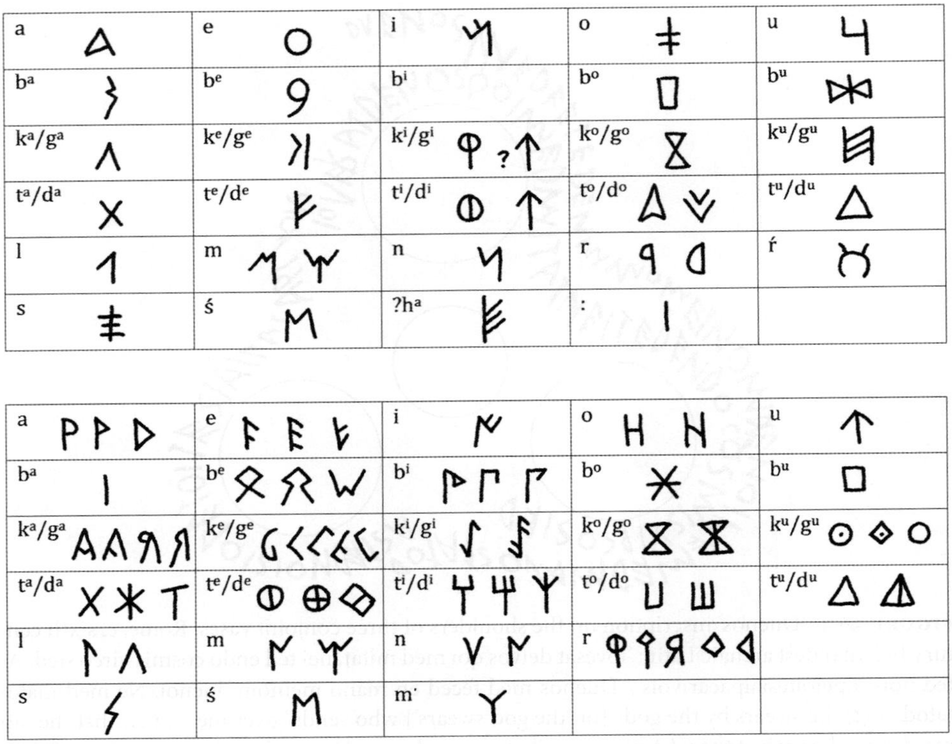

a	e	i	o	u
b^a	b^e	b^i	b^o	b^u
k^a/g^a	k^e/g^e	k^i/g^i ?	k^o/g^o	k^u/g^u
t^a/d^a	t^e/d^e	t^i/d^i	t^o/d^o	t^u/d^u
l	m	n	r	ŕ
s	ś	?h^a	:	

a	e	i	o	u
b^a	b^e	b^i	b^o	b^u
k^a/g^a	k^e/g^e	k^i/g^i	k^o/g^o	k^u/g^u
t^a/d^a	t^e/d^e	t^i/d^i	t^o/d^o	t^u/d^u
l	m	n	r	
s	ś	m˙		

FIGURE 36.2 Tartessian symbols (above) and Celtiberian symbols (below).

Author, sources: Koch 2010: 206 (1); various (2)

(2) alphabetic systems that used one symbol per phoneme—these include ogam and the runic futhark, and are generally named for the sounds that their first few symbols represent, e.g. Greek alphabet, carried over into Latin; Tartessian abekatu; runic futhark; Anglo-Frisian futhorc. It is unknown what the symbols on Pictish inscriptions represent.

No one system could be used unchanged to write all the sounds even of regional dialects, much less those of a completely foreign language (the modern International Phonetic Alphabet illustrates the complexity required to adapt one alphabet to the sounds of any language). Thus, the Greek and Tartessian scripts teed off independently from the Phoenician alphabet and made importantly different choices to represent vowel sounds, which were absent in the parent code. Likewise, regional Etruscan alphabets were variously adapted to write Latin, Oscan, Lepontic, Venetic, and other languages in the Italian peninsula and Alps (Figure 36.3).

All ancient scripts were designed by people already literate in another language; all contained innovations; all underwent subsequent modifications; and all were passed on in the same effective and time-consuming way by guided copying out of memorized symbol sequences and rote recitation of sound–symbol combinations. Learning to

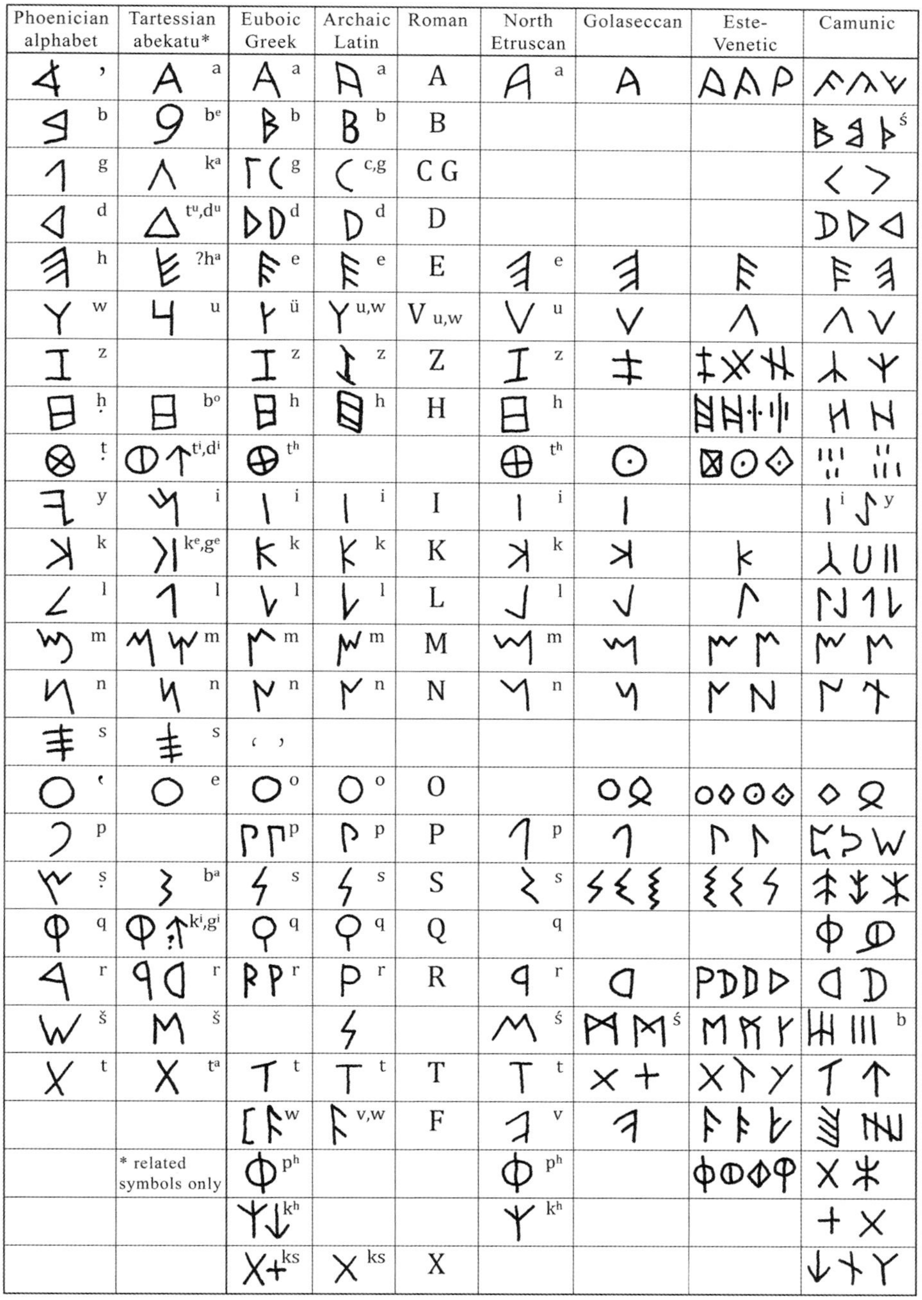

Phoenician alphabet	Tartessian abekatu*	Euboic Greek	Archaic Latin	Roman	North Etruscan	Golaseccan	Este-Venetic	Camunic
ʾ	a	a	a	A	a			
b	b^e	b	b	B				ś
g	k^a	g	c,g	C G				
d	t^u,d^u	d	d	D				
h	$?h^a$	e	e	E	e			
w	u	ü	u,w	V u,w	u			
z		z	z	Z	z			
ḥ	b^o	h	h	H	h			
ṭ	t^i,d^i	t^h			t^h			
y	i	i	i	I	i			i y
k	k^e,g^e	k	k	K	k			
l	l	l	l	L	l			
m	m	m	m	M	m			
n	n	n	n	N	n			
s	s							
ʿ	e	o	o	O				
p		p	p	P	p			
ṣ	b^a	s	s	S	s			
q	k^i,g^i	q	q	Q	q			
r	r	r	r	R	r			
š	š				ś	ś		b
t	t^a	t	t	T	t			
		w	v,w	F	v			
	* related symbols only	p^h			p^h			
		k^h			k^h			
		ks	ks	X				

FIGURE 36.3 Alphabets mentioned in the text, arranged to show morphological connections.

Author, sources: Tartessian after Koch 2010: 206; North Etruscan after Haynes 2000: 66; Golaseccan, Este-Venetic, Camunic after Markey 2001

write was not a trivial accomplishment. Archaeologically attested writing codes and the spread of specific scripts reflect chains of personal teacher–pupil contact because of how they had to be taught: the 'influence' of one attested script on another reflects an actual process of individual instruction, however mediated. As such, early writing belongs to the otherwise unwritten social histories of their societies, reflecting and celebrating aspects of selected group identity as these began to form in contrast with significant outsiders.

The geographical routes through which writing spread in early Europe (Figure 36.4) coincide rather strikingly with archaeologically attested medium- to long-range networks of exchange through which high-value goods from inland, especially rare metals and amber, horses and slaves, are all known to have passed towards the Mediterranean (see e.g. Kristiansen 1998; Cunliffe 2001, 2008; Koch 2007, 2016: *passim*). This phenomenon must reflect entrenched patterns of personal contact at elite level between literate guests and their hosts, perhaps primarily diplomatic envoys and specialist traders who would be foreign guests for most of their journeys and would need safe passage, introductions, hospitality, and records of agreements and transactions—all contexts in which early uses of writing are attested. The sole passing reference in Homer to 'signs' on a folded tablet that appear to be writing—an object, in that context, of justified suspicion—was a letter of introduction ordering the bearer's execution (*Iliad* 6.166–170). Learning to read was at the very least a safeguard against treachery. Spread of styles of script is highly visible in the material record in those places where writing was applied to metal, ceramic, and stone.

In historical order of the first appearance of writing, these geographical systems were:

1. [Phoenician]–Iberia–Atlantic
2. [Phoenician–Greek]–Etruscan–north Italian–Alpine–Scandinavian
3. [Greek]–Rhône valley–eastern Gaul; limited spread in the hinterland of Greek colonies in Iberia and the Black Sea
4. [Greek–Etruscan]–Latin–western Roman provinces.

1: [Phoenician]–Iberia–Atlantic

Phoenicians were in Spain from at least the ninth/eighth century BC (Aubet 2001; Koch 2007, 2016: *passim*; Cunliffe 2013: 244–249). Homer gives an anecdotal sketch of eighth-century Phoenician sea-trading: a ship arrives on an island, its captain is received at the big house and does some initial business; he leaves to do more business elsewhere on the island; then, when the crew are ready to depart, he returns, sells some amber jewellery to the ladies of the big house; and in this particular tale the Phoenician slave woman in charge of the toddler son of the house kidnaps him and steals some gold and silver tableware in exchange, she thought, for her own passage home (*Odyssey* 15.403–484; Nash Briggs 2006).

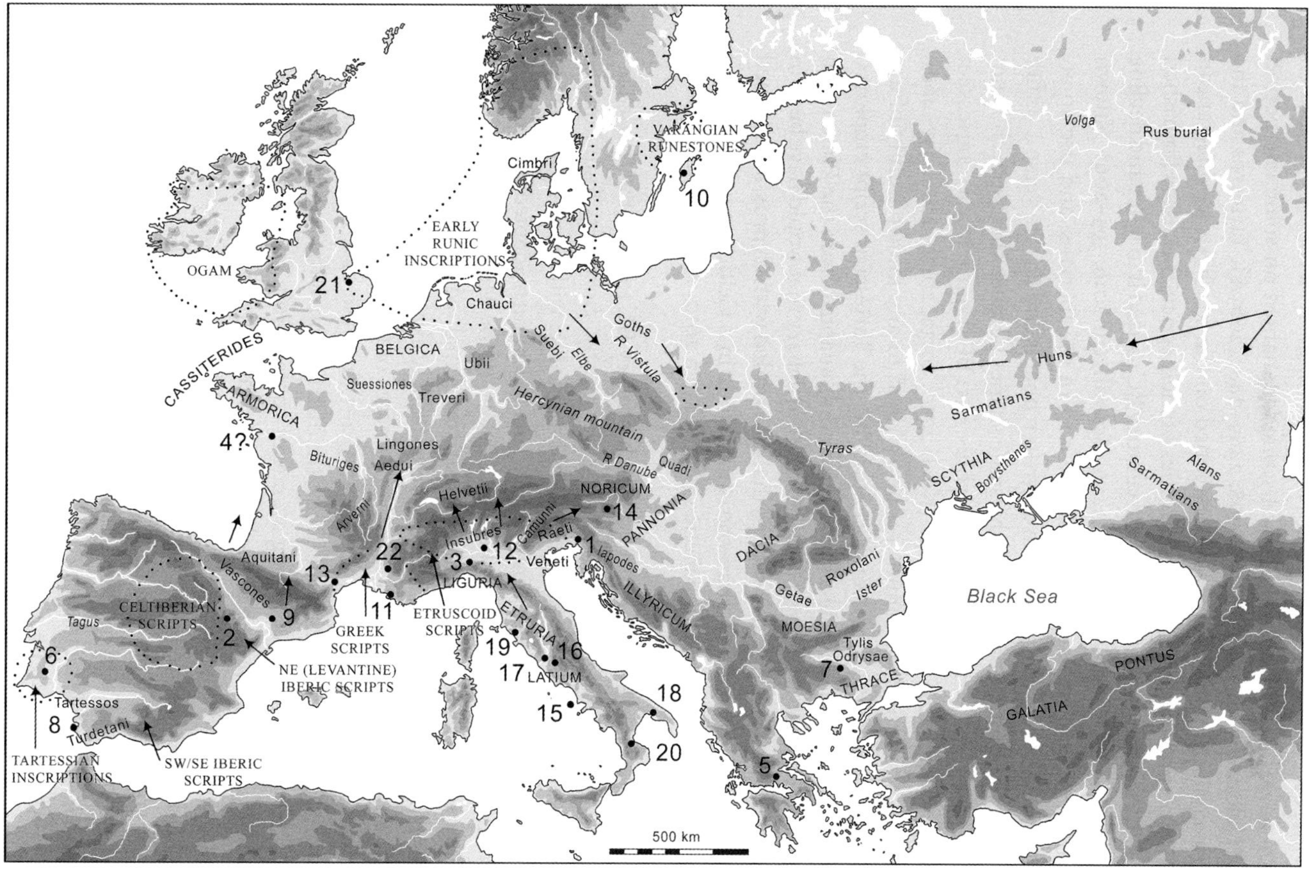

FIGURE 36.4 Schematic map showing spread of early writing systems based on Iberian, Etruscan, Greek, and Latin scripts. Key to numbered places: 1 Aquileia, 2 Botorrita, 3 Briona, Novara, 4 Corbilo (uncertain location), 5 Delphi, 6 Espanca, Castro Verde, 7 Ezerovo, 8 Cadiz (Gadir/Gades), 9 Ilerda, 10 Kylver, 11 Marseille (Massalia/Massilia), 12 Milan (Mediolanum), 13 Montlaurès, near Narbonne (Narbo), 14 Negova (Negau), 15 Pithekoussai, 16 Praeneste, 17 Rome, 18 Tarentum, 19 Telamon, 20 Thurii, 21 Undley, 22 Vaison-la-Romaine.

Author

The mutually very profitable silver-trading arrangements between Phoenicians at Gadir and the local elites supported the early emergence of a literate archaic civilization in Tartessos, with rulers entitled Arganthonios or 'silver-master' (Herodotus 1.163; Koch 2010, 2016: 459–462), like a Gaulish official, *Argantodan*, named on some late-period coins in Gaul (Delestrée and Tache 2002–2008: 2485–2487, 2663A). Tartessos and the unrelated Iberic civilization that soon also developed on the southern Mediterranean coast were entirely comparable with Etruscan cities of their epoch. Tartessos flourished until changes in Phoenician activity in the sixth century BC caused it to falter and decline without wholly losing its identity (Koch 2013a: 6; Brandherm 2016: 195–206). Known as Turdetani to the Romans, they were 'ranked wisest of the Iberians, and use an alphabet, and have ancient records in the form of written poems and laws in verse ... other Iberians also use an alphabet but not with the same shapes because their speech is not the same' (Strabo *Geography* 3.1.6, reporting Polybius, *c.*151 BC; Figure 36.5, 1). Tartessian has proved to be an archaic Celtic language (Koch 2010, 2013a, 2013b, 2016: 457–468), while Iberic was not, and indeed cannot yet be ascribed to any known family of ancient languages. From perhaps the seventh century BC the Tartessian script employed a unique system that combines single-phoneme symbols adapted from the Phoenician alphabet with syllabic symbols inspired by the Cypriot syllabary that would have been in concurrent use by scribes on Phoenician ships that also traded with Cyprus, a combined system beautifully adapted to some characteristic sounds in a Celtic language that are difficult to represent with a simple alphabetic system (Koch 2010, with details, 2013a: 6; 2016: 445–449).

Tartessian script was adapted in the fifth to fourth century BC to write the Iberic language, represented by thousands of barely intelligible, mostly short texts found on the Mediterranean side of the Iberian peninsula and in Languedoc: with some local variants it remained in use until the early first century AD. This was in turn adapted, probably in the second century BC, to write the Celtiberian language of the Meseta, at a time when the Roman conquest of Hispania was under way; it, too, remained in use until the early first century AD. Iberic and Celtiberian scripts were strongly expressive of regional identity, and both were used on the silver and bronze coinages of their respective areas, generally naming settlements and peoples (Figure 36.5, 2–3), not the individuals that were customary on coins in contemporary Gaul. There, the distribution of Iberic script on coins (e.g. Figure 36.5, 4) reflects a long-standing avenue of contact from gulf to gulf between Languedoc and the Atlantic, reported in the late fourth century by Pytheas from Massalia (see later). Third-century BC gold coins found between Nantes and Angers bearing the syllabic symbol KO (DT 2022–2025) may perhaps name Korbilo, an unidentified port of trade in that area still active in the 150s BC (Strabo *Geography* 4.2.1); some third-century Armorican gold coins used design elements from the Iberian coinage of Ilerda (Sills 2003: 65, 112, 120, cf. 110), while far to the north, around Namur, one series of third-century gold coins bears what seems to be a careful inscription in characters either of Iberic or conceivably proto-runic type (Scheers 1977: 237, type 6 class 2, fig. 43). In the first century BC the horseman and Celtiberian inscription of a coinage of the Vascones (Figure 36.5, 2) served as model for a Belgic bronze issue in the Somme valley (Scheers 1977: no. 104).

FIGURE 36.5 1 Espanca stone (Castro Verde, Portugal), *c.* seventh to fifth century BC: two sets of Tartessian abekatu or similar palaeo-Hispanic signary. 2 Silver *denarius, c.*150–100 BC, Vascones (Navarre, Spain), with Iberic inscription: BeNCoDa / BaSCuNES. 3 Silver *denarius, c.*120–30 BC, Segobriges (Spain), with Celtiberian inscription: SECoBiRICeS. 4 Bronze *as, c.* first century BC, people of Narbo (Montlaurès, Hérault, France), with Iberic inscription: NERONCeN.

(1) Author, after Koch 2010: 207; (2–4) Coin images © Chris Rudd.

2: [Phoenician–Greek]–Etruscan–North Italian–Alpine–Scandinavian

A long non-literate interval followed the loss of Mycenean writing in the twelfth century BC, until ninth- to eighth-century Greeks in Ionia adopted the Phoenician alphabet to write their own language 'but changing the sound and shape of a few [letters] ... I myself saw Cadmean characters engraved upon some tripods in the temple of Apollo Ismenias in Boeotian Thebes ... One of the tripods is inscribed, "Amphitryon dedicated me, on return from the Teleboans"' (Herodotus *History* 5.58–59: this inscription was in verse).

Greeks from Euboea brought their version of the alphabet to their early trading outpost on Pithekoussai (Ischia) in the Bay of Naples. The inscription on a cup placed in a young boy's grave *c.*720 BC, mentioned earlier, contains the oldest known reference to Homer and is one of the earliest examples of Greek writing in the west (Lane

Fox 2009: 157–158, 357). The Villanovan elites of central Italy were non-literate. As in Tartessos, organized trading relations in metals and slaves with Phoenicians in Sardinia and with Greeks at Pithekoussai promoted social change in coastal centres in central Italy, transforming Villanovans into Etruscans, as local elites formed a regional network of independent cities with a shared non-Indo-European language and a rich archaic culture. They called themselves *Rasna* or *Rasenna* (*Tyrrhenoi* or *Tyrsenoi* to the Greeks, *Tusci* or *Etrusci* in Latin), with a shared ceremonial life structured around a revealed religion that was from an early point dependent on written texts allegedly dictated by the divine child Tages who sprang from ploughed earth in Tarquinia (Haynes 2000: 29). Etruscan civilization was becoming fully literate by the seventh century BC, as attested by everyday finds of practice alphabets, inscribed weaving equipment (women might even have been first to write), and sundry graffiti.

The Etruscans in turn taught regional versions of their alphabet to other peoples of the Italian peninsula with whom they engaged under treaty or as rulers, each of whom adapted it to the sounds of their own different languages: early examples include the Praeneste fibula in primitive Latin (*c.*600 BC or later); similarly, early Faliscan inscriptions in Tolfa and Cività Castellana; and in *c.*600–580 BC the earliest Lepontic (Celtic) inscriptions of the Golaseccan culture in north-western Italy at Castelletto Ticino (see Figure 36.6, 1–2 for later examples). Etruscans in northern Italy had a well-documented formative influence on non-Etruscan elite cultures on both sides of the Alps in the sixth to fifth centuries BC, notably Hallstatt C and D (proto-Transalpine Gauls), Este (proto-Veneti), and Golasecca (proto-Insubrian Gauls)—for all of which see Haynes (2000) and Camporeale (2001). Copious Baltic amber reached Picenum and Etruria from the head of the Adriatic (Nava and Salerno 2007; cf. Pliny *Natural History* 37.11.42–45); salt and slaves may have been prime imports from Hallstatt centres (Nash Briggs 2003), and the Veneti were known for their horses.

A number of small but powerful Alpine populations, through whose territory long-range travellers were obliged to pass and with whom they had to negotiate, adapted north Etruscan alphabets to their various languages (Markey 2001); the historical Raetii, who held the northern passes to the headwaters of the Rhine and Danube, spoke an Etruscan dialect and wrote a modified Etruscan script; another, the Camunni (Val Camonica), with an as yet unintelligible language, seem to have integrated writing into their community cult, and their script was the likeliest model for the earliest known sample of writing in a Germanic language, from an important votive deposit of twenty-six Etruscoid bronze helmets at Negau in Slovenia (Markey 2001; Zimmer 2020). These may well originally have been fifth- or fourth-century BC trophies from one of the countless conflicts among Etruscans and their north Italian neighbours for which there is ample historical evidence that Transalpine reinforcements had long been conscripted, but with rising intensity in the period to which the helmets belong (Livy *History of Rome* 5.32–33; Polybius *Histories* 2.17). Several of these heirlooms were given short dedicatory inscriptions, the latest probably in the mid-first century BC, before they were ceremonially buried: this was a time when the local population was under pressure first from the Geto-Dacian king Burebista (Strabo *Geography* 7.3.11) and then from Rome.

FIGURE 36.6 1 Briona stone (Novara, Italy), *c.* third century BC. Cisalpine Gaulish, Etruscoid script: 'the sons of Dannotalos, Quintos legatos, Andocombogios, Setubogios, and [the sons of] Essandecot[t]os, Anarevisseos, Dannotalos, raised [this]'. 2 Silver drachm, *c.* second to first century BC, Insubres (above Milan, Italy), with Lepontic inscription: TOVTIOPOVOS. 3 Celtic inscription on Negau Helmet A: SIRAKV: TVRPI, *c.*60–50 BC or earlier. 4 Germanic inscription on Negau Helmet B: HARIGASTI TEIVA ///?, *c.*60–50 BC. 5 Inscription ARATIEPOS, Celtic language in modified Venetic script, from silver tetradrachms in the Ribnjačka hoard, third/early second century BC. 6 Earliest complete sequence of old runic futhark: [f] u þ a r k g [w] h n i j p î z s t b e m l ng d o. Kylver stone (Gotland, Sweden), *c.*AD 400.

(1) Author, after Lambert 1994: 72; (2) Image © Chris Rudd; (3–4) Author, after Markey 2001: 112; (5) Author, after Kos and Mirnik 1999: pls 28–31; (6) Author

Of the two intelligibly inscribed Negau helmets, A, was dedicated in a Celtic language in a Rhetic script (Figure 36.6, 3), and the legible part of helmet B's inscription, in an adapted Camunic script, is unmistakably Germanic: *harigasti teiva*, naming a man, or an epithet, and a god (Figure 36.6, 4; Markey 2001: 105–112, 122; Zimmer 2020: 64–70 for details). Similarly, silver tetradrachms in a third- to early second-century BC hoard from Ribnjačka in Croatia bear the name Aratiepos (Celtic) in a modified Venetic script (Figure 36.6, 5; T. Markey, pers. comm.; Kos and Mirnik 1999).

These inscriptions bring together several observations relevant to the current discussion. In the first place they reflect the mixed ethnic origin of unattached young men in many of the warbands and armed retinues of distinguished military leaders throughout Iron Age Europe, whose unit name while on the move may convey almost nothing about where its members originated (*Tectosages*, for instance, simply means 'Travellers')—a source of unending confusion for anyone attempting to place and classify Celts and Germans in antiquity or today (Strabo *Geography* 4.1.13; Wells 2001; Looijenga 2003: 69–70; Koch 2007: 23–29). It also illustrates the long-term persistence of personal links between northern Europe, the upper Danube, and the northern Adriatic. Ariovistus, for instance, a contemporary with the Negau inscriptions and the first German leader to whom Julius Caesar introduced his readers, was in Franche-Comté in the 60s–59 BC with mercenary soldiers on behalf of the Sequani and with numerous would-be settlers from across the Rhine. His reported name is Gaulish (Delamarre 2003: 54–55); he had two wives, one a categorically Germanic Sueban 'from his home', the other a sister of king Voccio of Noricum, presumably Celtic-speaking, who had been sent to him in Gaul (Caesar *de Bello Gallico* 1.53.4).

Whether Camunic script was taken to the far north in the first century BC we cannot know for sure. Tacitus mentioned Germans using 'special marks' for divination (*Germania* 10.1), and while it cannot be proved that these were proto-runic letters, neither can it be disproved. The third-century coins from near Namur may or may not bear an Alpine type of script. What is clear is that the likeliest linear ancestor of the older runic *futhark* is Camunic (Figure 36.6, 6; Markey 2001). On linguistic grounds, the *futhark* was probably created early in the Roman period, probably among the Ubii (Looijenga 2003: 82–88, 101), though the earliest surviving examples date from the late second or early third century AD. It was designed specifically to write a Germanic language at a time of vigorous cultural development amongst north European elites (Elliott 1963; Todd 1975: 186; Green 1998: *passim*; Looijenga 2003: *passim*; Hedeager 2011: 21). Early examples, with the short, formulaic texts and religious associations common in early writing, are scattered around eastern Britain, *Germania Magna*, and southern Scandinavia. Runic scripts were already diversifying by the fifth century AD, when suitably modified symbols were employed to write the earliest known sample of archaic Old English, on a fifth-century gold bracteate found at Undley in Suffolk (Hines and Odenstedt 1987; Nash Briggs 2020).

3: [Greek]–Rhône Valley–Eastern Gaul; Other Greek Colonial Hinterlands

The only other Greek alphabets that had a remotely comparable uptake were those of Phocaean Massalia and its outposts and colonies in Gaul and north-eastern Iberia. In Alicante and Murcia the Greek alphabet was adapted to write Iberic, but it was most extensively naturalized in Provence, where there are many Gallo-Greek inscriptions

(Figure 36.7, 1), and inland along the Rhône valley corridor (Duval 1985–2002, Vol. I: *passim*), largely overlapping with the geographical distribution of Massaliote wine amphorae. The Phocaeans at Massalia are said to have taught letters to the Gauls, who wrote contracts in Greek (Strabo *Geography* 4.1.5).

Inland, the Greek alphabet was also used for indigenous inscriptions on late second- to early first-century BC silver coins of the Lingones (Figure 36.7, 2) and Aedui—some giving versions in Greek and in Latin letters. A gold coinage of similar date inscribed in Greek appears in Touraine (Delestrée and Tache 2002–2008: 2536, S2536 A–B), and outlying examples are found in northern Gaul on first-century BC coins of the Suessiones (Delestrée and Tache 2002–2008: 64, 207, 208, 232) and Treveri (Delestrée and Tache 2002–2008: 601). Greek letters were also used for the inscription *Korisios* (a Gaulish name), together with a pictorial stamp, on a fine iron sword from near Bern, Switzerland (context *c.*100–60 BC: Duval 1985–2002, Vol. I: G-280; see Hedeager 2011: 140 for the possible significance of placing a name on a sword). It is relevant in this connection that in 59 BC Julius Caesar said that Orgetorix, preparing to lead an enormous mixed contingent of Helvetii and other migrants from Switzerland to Saintonge, kept his records in Greek script (*de Bello Gallico* 1.29.1). Caesar's general statement that the Druids used Greek script for public and private record-keeping (*de Bello Gallico* 6.14.3) must primarily apply to these areas: he did not mention that the Latin alphabet and language were also by then in widespread use, though we see it everywhere on coinage, and when in winter 54 BC he needed to get an urgent message through the Nervian blockade of Q. Cicero's camp in northern Belgica, he wrote it in Greek to make sure that it would not be understood if intercepted (*de Bello Gallico* 5.48.4).

By contrast, inland from the Greek trading posts and colonies on the Black Sea, the Thracians, Scythians, and a long succession of other nomadic and semi-nomadic peoples scarcely used writing at all and never devised their own scripts; the vanishingly few pre-Roman inscriptions are either in Greek—for example, on coins of King Kotys I of the Odrysae and precious utensils in his name with his artisan Egbeo (383–359 BC), and on third-century BC coinage in Tylis (Figure 36.7, 3) —or, rarely, employ the Greek alphabet to write a native language (Figure 36.7, 4; Fol and Marazov 1977: 46, 54, 82). Greek letters coexisted with the Roman alphabet in the Roman Danubian provinces of Moesia, Dacia, and Pannonia (Figure 36.7, 5).[1]

4: [Greek–Etruscan]–Latin–Western Roman Provinces

The Latin alphabet spread beyond Italy with Italian trade and Roman conquests, and becomes evident outside directly administered areas from the second century BC onwards, especially on indigenous coinage. Coin inscriptions were clearly subject to the same scrupulous compositional attention as the rest of the design (Creighton 2000: 37–54; Nash Briggs 2011, 2017), and the Latin alphabet had to be adapted both in the spelling of several phonemes and in the shape of one of its letters to represent sounds that were absent from the Latin language (Figure 36.7, 6; see Allen 1978, 1987 for the pronunciation

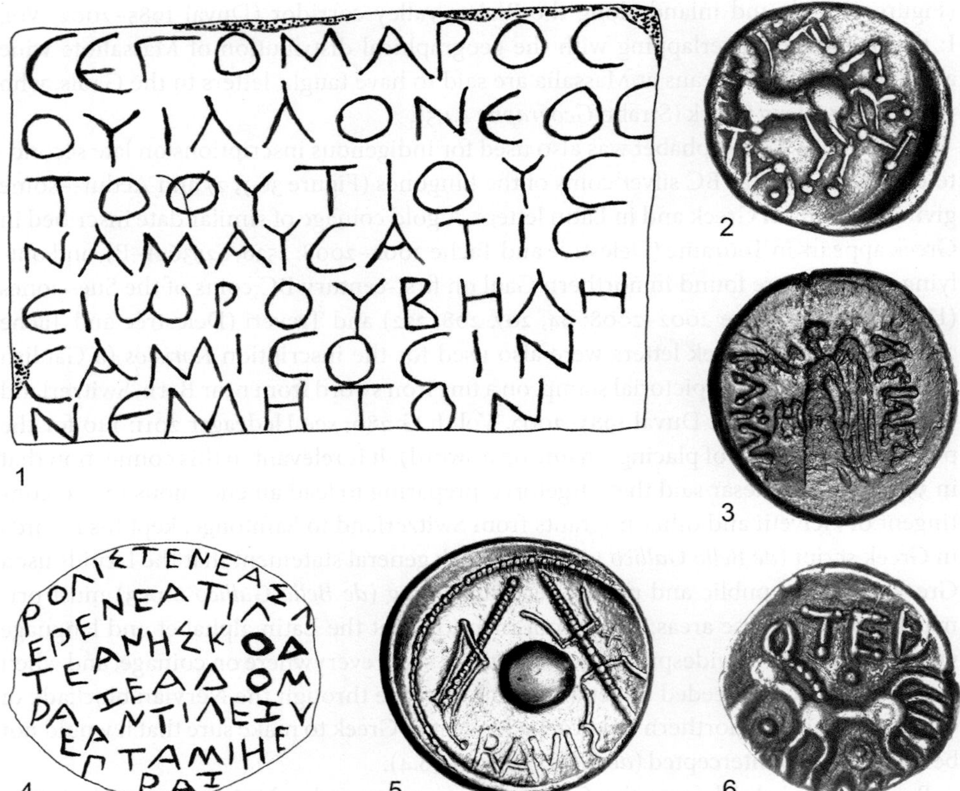

FIGURE 36.7 1 Stone from Vaison-la-Romaine (Vaucluse, France), *c.* third century BC. Gaulish language in Greek script: 'Segomaros son of Villonos, citizen of Nemausus, dedicated this sacred enclosure to Belisama'. 2 Silver unit inscribed KALETEDOU, Lingones (Gaul), *c.*120–50 BC. Gaulish language, Greek script. 3 Bronze coin of Kavaros (a Gaulish king); Greek language, Tylis (Thrace), *c.*225–218 BC. 4 Gold ring from Erezovo (Bulgaria), fifth century BC. Thracian language in Greek script: 'I am Rolisteneas, descended from Nereneas. Tilezipta, an Arazian woman, delivered me to the ground'. 5 Silver *denarius* inscribed RAVIS (Roman script), Eravisci (Pannonia), *c.* first century BC. 6 Silver unit inscribed [AN]TEÐ (= *tau Gallicum*; Cottam et al. 2010, *ABC* 2072), *c.*AD 20–43.

(1) Author, after Lambert 1994: 84; (4) Author, after Fol and Marazov 1977: 81; (2–3, 5–6) Coin images © Chris Rudd

of classical Latin and Greek, and Russell 1995: 202, 207 for use of the Greek *theta* or a barred D designed in Britain or Belgic Gaul to represent Gaulish/Brittonic *tau gallicum*). Some 'friendly kings' (Braund 1984, 1986) close to the provincial frontiers in Noricum, Gaul, central Europe, and Britain, many of whom will have received a Roman education as hostages in their teens, issued coinages with Roman-style imagery which depart from previous norms of iconographic representation and even have legends in the Latin language or with Latin spellings of their names, suggesting a shift in relationship between these rulers and their learned elite: this development is most apparent in the last generations before Caesar's conquest of eastern and central Gaul and Claudius' conquest of Britain. The Latin alphabet was normally employed on the relatively rare occasions when vernacular languages were written in Roman imperial provinces, often in Roman cursive hands. In the post-Roman period, Latin manuscript hands were adapted to create the Gothic, Irish, and Old English literary scripts.

Other Writing Codes

Two other inscriptional writing codes are known from the late imperial period in the British Isles. Ogam (Figure 36.8), in use from the late fourth to the sixth century AD, was a unique alphabetic code mainly preserved on numerous standing stones with short inscriptions of Type 1 or 2 in Ireland and parts of Britain. Ogam transposed the Roman alphabet almost letter for letter to write archaic Old Irish (Russell 1995: 208–211), probably as a deliberate act of ethnic self-definition. At much the same time, Pictish glyphs were carved on stones in Scotland and are presumed to be another linguistic code, but their system is undeciphered. Whatever their content, they, like ogam, identified their makers as indigenous people with a high-order, specialized artisanal culture.

Coinage

Coinage occupies a privileged position in the space between archaeology, inscriptions, and history. It connects with written history more than any other class of portable artefact, partly because it was issued by warlords and community leaders during conflicts that are sometimes historically documented. If writing (which coinage often also carries) spread primarily through civilian, religious, and commercial relationships, coinage also spread through military and administrative channels, together with a high order of associated organizational and technical skills. Painstaking study of pre-Roman coinages from the Danube basin to Britain in the period from around 270 BC to the mid-first century AD allows otherwise undocumented histories to be pieced together with remarkable precision (e.g. Scheers 1977; Nash 1978a; de Jersey 1994; Sills 2003, 2017; Cottam et al. 2010, all with bibliographies). Here a few general points can be made (see also Chapter 28).

Designing a coinage and setting up a mint demanded organizational competence normally associated with high-ranking authorities in a stratified political hierarchy: commanders-in-chief, kings, and the officials of regional consortia. Striking coinage was an expensive and potentially risky thing to do with accumulated treasure, as many Mediterranean states that paid mercenaries discovered to their cost. It has been argued that Iron Age coinage in precious metals was only ever issued episodically, to finance a current crisis or, as in the case of Britain in 54–51 BC, to pay tribute

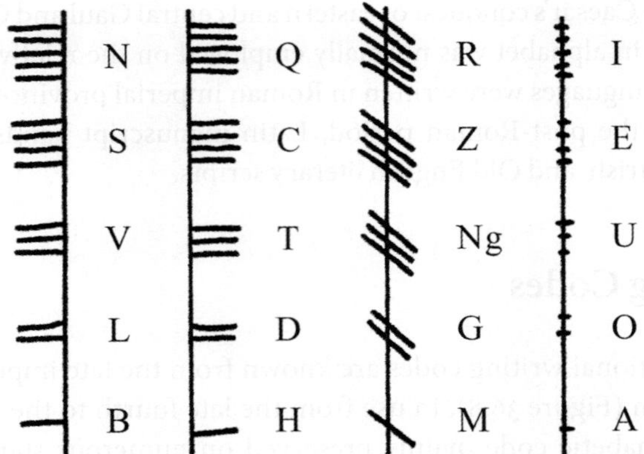

FIGURE 36.8 Ogam script, basic system.

Author, after Russell 1995: 209

or a war indemnity (Sills 2003: 350–351, 2017: 2–8, 721–732). The initial technology belonged to the highest order of metalworking skills and was almost always imported or acquired abroad, employing already proficient, sometimes literate, even actually Mediterranean, die-cutters. Transmission of their skills to indigenous craftworkers can only have been through lengthy personal apprenticeship, and it is often possible to identify the exact source from which the first die-cutters of a new coinage learned their skills. Countless case histories have been written, sometimes shedding unexpected light on long-range relationships, like soldiers from the Somme who must have been among the mercenaries fighting for Tarentum in the third century BC (Scheers 1977; Sills 2003: 120–121).

Coin design was generally conservative, with its iconographic content probably always subject to detailed religious supervision (Creighton 2000: 37–54); when inscriptions appear, they lend precious insight into language, literacy at the mint, and structures of authority. Once established, highly distinctive regional styles of die-cutting and design repeatedly emerged, often with rather well-defined geographical boundaries, together with regionally distinctive choices of metal, alloy, and denomination shared by several separate coin-issuing authorities (e.g. Allen 1980; Nash 1987). This must reflect preferential networks through which technical skills were exercised and learned, and in most cases also some otherwise undocumented aspects of regional political history and identity: the formation, for instance, of relatively cohesive multi-member leagues akin to Etruscans, Latins, Achaeans, and other well-known consortia in the Mediterranean world. We find these in northern Italy, Celtiberia, Languedoc, the Rhône valley, Armorica, Belgica, Bohemia, the Rhineland, Britain, the Danube basin, and elsewhere. The later history of Iron Age coinage is a valuable guide to ongoing change in political organization and patterns of dominance among the relevant ruling elites. In the most developed coinages, smaller denominations and specialized types of coin may well have been used to finance domestic projects in the larger kingdoms and proto-urban states that formed in parts of Gaul and Britain towards the end of their independence from Rome.

The Written Historical Record

On the threshold of fully fledged literacy a dynamic tension can sometimes be observed between two modes of advanced elite learning: memorized oral transmission and reliance on written texts. We are, for instance, told that in the mid-first century BC, Druids in Gaul might spend twenty years acquiring their skills by memory, that Britain had specialist centres for advanced learning attended also by sons of the Gaulish nobility, and that the Druids opposed transcribing their knowledge, Caesar thought partly in order not to disseminate their knowledge and partly for fear of losing their memory skills (Caesar *de Bello Gallico* 6.14.4). This was at a time when many of the Gauls personally known to Caesar and his contemporaries, including a pro-Roman Aeduan Druid, Diviciacus, were in fact already at least minimally literate and had even visited Rome, so knew what this change to their system of learning might entail. A book-based classical education started in childhood, likewise took decades to acquire, and while large amounts of poetry and law were in fact learned by heart, readers could indeed allow their memories to lapse. Both systems were based on one-to-one master–pupil relationships, both took a lifetime to master, and both encompassed a variety of intellectually contrasting schools of advanced learning: diversity in the classical tradition needs no special reference (for evidence of divergent Druidic doctrines see e.g. Green 1997: 50–51).

We sometimes glimpse the contrast between traditional styles of learning and literate expectations at an early point of contact with the Roman Empire, for instance when children of free German and British elites who had been taken to Italy and the provinces as guarantees to secure treaty arrangements and given a Roman education were later sent back to their communities to assume positions of authority. While some, including, probably, Prasutagus of the British Iceni (Nash Briggs 2011), were successfully reintegrated, others, including German Maroboduus, were eventually rejected because of their threat to established norms (e.g. Strabo *Geography* 7.1.3, Tacitus *Annals* 2. 44; Thompson 1965: 17–28).

Most conspicuously, none of early Europe's long and varied succession of pastoral nomads, with their continuously mobile, highly specialized ways of life and inherently conservative social values, seems ever to have integrated writing. They remained 'ignorant of writing and unpractised in it up to the present day; they neither have any writing-master nor do their children grow up toiling over their letters' (Procopius *History of the Wars* 8.19.8–9, describing the Utigur Huns in the AD 550s).

Even the powerful kings of the relatively settled agro-pastoral tribes of Thrace, with their immense wealth invested in personal display, their cultural emphasis on high-order oral poetry and song, and uninterrupted involvement with the Greek world since the Homeric epoch (Fol and Marazov 1977; Kristiansen 1998: 193–195), never committed their traditions to writing. Until this region became a Roman province in the mid-first century AD, its rulers scarcely used writing at all (see earlier), and their craftworkers developed instead an elaborate mythological idiom that had many points in common with the artistic expression of non-literate La Tène elites in central Europe and beyond: an effective means of arcane narrative representation for those who could 'read' it, variously seen on elite metalwork, textiles, and in coinage design (Fischer 2009; Hedeager 2011: 71).

Written Traditions

In the Greek world, transition to full literacy occurred with the transcription of high-end oral tradition. Here, the Homeric poems occupy a class of their own as distinguished, preliterate, bardic compositions of around the mid-eighth century BC (West 2007; Lane Fox 2009) passed on from memory until transcribed from dictation in their current form a century or so later. Homer was a poet, not an ethnographer or historian. Nonetheless the Homeric and other early Greek poems afford helpful insights into aspects of the pre-classical Aegean world and its neighbours. The older background includes Greek, Trojan, Thracian, and Near Eastern kings, aristocrats, and warriors; gift exchange; slave-taking; war chariots; and Patroclus' funeral. Thrace has numerous tribal groupings, and one king, Rhesus, equalled the Trojans in wealth (cf. Fol and Marazov 1977: 140). From the recent past and eighth-century present come anecdotal glimpses of Phoenician sea-traders and life on an aristocratic estate (Nash Briggs 2007). Iron exists but is scarce and valuable; writing might as well not exist.

Then history began. The Athenian historian Thucydides (*c*.460/455–*c*.400 BC) described, with examples, how difficult it was to reconstruct the preliterate past. Together with Hecataeus and Herodotus (see later), he set standards for history writing backed by evidence that earned lasting respect. In particular, he mistrusted poets, who dramatized their themes, and prose writers whose authorities could not be checked and whose older subject matter drifted into fable (*Peloponnesian War* 1.20–21).

The historical framework that the classical Greeks worked out was assimilated by the Romans and passed in due course, cross-referenced with Biblical chronologies, into the Middle Ages. The events of the *Iliad* and *Odyssey* were located in the last 150 years of the Mycenean period, preceded by a legendary seafaring Age of Minos, and the Trojan War was dated to *c*.1190 BC on our own reckoning. Later non-Greek societies often worked revered figures from the Trojan War and Greek mythological cycles into their legendary pasts when they came to compile their own ancient histories: Aeneas by the Romans, Priam by the Franks, and a Trojan Brutus in Geoffrey of Monmouth's (*c*.AD 1100–1155) learned but fantastical tales of the earliest kings of Britain (Cunliffe 2013: 8–13).

A number of indirectly preserved indigenous origin stories are embedded in some of the classical histories, and we are occasionally reminded that certain population groups, for instance some fifth-century Rugi amongst the Goths, might go to great lengths to preserve their ethnic identity and traditions (Procopius *History of the Wars* 7.2.1–3; Hedeager 2011: 49–50). Tacitus says the Germani had songs that served as history, and reports in detail an origin myth for their three component groupings (*Germania* 2).

Many others apparently lost track of their origins: Strabo was perplexed (*Geography* 4.1.13), as were many other ancient researchers, that, for instance, Brennos who led the Delphi expedition was said to be a Prausan, but Strabo could not say where on earth the Prausans had formerly lived (on which see Sills 2003: 88, 320), nor could he locate places where two out of three of the Galatian tribes in Asia Minor might have originated. Poetic imagination could then step in. Thus we find a mixture of history and myth for the origins of Tartessos (Freeman 2010). Several Celtic origin myths feature Heracles and may also come from Iberia, ably summarized by Timagenes, a scholarly Greek in Augustan Rome, who wrote a lost *History of the Gauls* (cited by Ammianus Marcellinus *History* 15.9). The Augustan historian Livy (*History of Rome* 5.34) gives an Insubrian origin legend for the Gauls of northern Italy in which Ambigatus, a long-lived and successful sixth-century BC king of the Bituriges, arranged for his sister's sons to lead emigrations—Segovesus into central Europe and Bellovesus into Italy (Koch 2007: 12). This was indeed a time when the Golaseccan ancestors of the historical Insubres were in cultural contact with Transalpine elites and were already writing a Celtic language in an adapted Etruscan alphabet, so the Insubres may have had records that Livy's informants could refer to—but their archaeology suggests their ancestors had in fact been resident in their lands since the Bronze Age. Livy, who actually came from Milan, retold this legend, and the rest of his history of Gaulish settlement in northern Italy, in the hindsight of Caesar's recent conquest of Gaul. All the peoples he mentions in Bellovesus' exodus, except the Insubres themselves, had Gaulish namesakes that played roles in Caesar's war commentaries: Bituriges, Arverni, Senones, Aedui, Ambarri, Carnutes, and Aulerci: not the Laevi, Lebecii, Insubres, and Cenomani listed by Polybius (see later), who wrote before Rome was involved in any way with Transalpine Gaul. Livy or his sources have, perhaps, selectively reworked some old traditions to suit the Augustan age. This may also account for the appearance of Alesia in a Gaulish origin myth otherwise featuring Heracles, retold by Diodorus Siculus within living memory of the decisive Roman victory at Alesia in 52 BC (*Library of History* 5.24).

Chroniclers could 'find' mythical ancestors to align an indigenous tradition with an admired foreign narrative, and selectively recast it, but not completely overwrite it while people still knew how the story should go and could correct it. If, however, an oral tradition lapsed without being written down it might be impossible to resurrect an authentic story if history produced a new elite in need of an ancient lineage. This must often have happened in Roman provinces, when indigenous peoples' unwritten history dropped into a folkloric background and was no longer celebrated at community festivals, as the guardians of the old elite's traditions were variously suppressed, relegated to peripheral niches, or were re-educated in the Roman imperial story: see Tacitus (*Agricola* 21, AD 79) for cultural policy in Britain, and Strabo (*Geography* 4.4.5) on suppression of unacceptable religion (cf. Green 1997: 52–53). With the help of archaeology and coinage, we actually know more today about the royal houses of southern Britain in the late pre-Roman Iron Age than Gildas, Bede, or Nennius were able to discover in the seventh to ninth centuries AD (see Cottam et al. 2010: *passim*; Sills 2017: 699–786).

In contrast, fragments of potentially authentic origin stories do seem to have been preserved by many successful elites outside the reach of the Roman Empire, to inform late Antique and early medieval histories of the Goths, Lombards, Danes, and other northern peoples (Hedeager 2011: 41–58).

Classical Writers as Foreign Observers: Geographers, Ethnographers, Historians

This is not the place for an exhaustive list or detailed critique of the countless ancient writings relevant to Iron Age Europe. Instead, what follows is a condensed handlist, in historical sequence, of those ancient authors whose known work contains the most detailed treatments of matters of potential interest to an archaeologist and is also in every case based either on the author's personal experience of the peoples and places described, or on reported information from reliable eyewitnesses within living memory. This series allows changes in Greek and Roman knowledge of inland Europe to be followed in reasonable detail.

For the sake of economy, I will simply give authors' name, dates, origin, professional role as writer/observer, known works relevant to Iron Age Europe, what these contain that is new in their own generation, and any general remarks.

Hecataeus, *c.*550–*c.*476 BC

Well-connected Ionian Greek from Miletus writing *c.*510–490 BC; private citizen, adviser to his city authorities; extensive personal foreign travel. Original writings lost but more than 370 excerpts and citations survive in later authors from Herodotus onwards, especially the sixth-century AD grammarian Stephanus of Byzantium (*Geographical Dictionary*) and, in Latin verse that collated information from Hecataeus and nine other early sources, the fourth-century AD Roman scholar Avienus (*Descriptio Orbis* and *Ora Maritima*). Book 2 of Hecataeus' *Gês Periodos* or *Travel around the Earth* described Europe, correcting an earlier map by Anaximander, and listed places and people on the coasts of the Black Sea, the Mediterranean and its islands, and the southernmost tip of Atlantic Iberia. Hecataeus gave well-researched accounts of the lower Danube, Scythia, Iberia, and Tartessos; he mentioned Celti inland from the coast in Gaul and Iberia. For other sixth- to fifth-century BC Greek and Punic voyagers reporting the same Atlantic route from Gadir and Tartessos to Ierne

(Ireland) and Albion (Britain), see Avienus (*Ora Maritima* 42–50), Cunliffe (2002: 25–72), and Freeman (2010).

Herodotus, *c.*484–420 BC

Ionian Greek from Halicarnassus, later living in Thurii (southern Italy). Well-connected private citizen; visited the Black Sea, but had no first-hand knowledge west of Italy, for which he depended on others, including Hecataeus. Herodotus' vastly influential *History* (of the Persian wars and their background) survives largely intact; Book 4 is important for the Black Sea hinterland including Thrace and Thracians.

New material: on the rivers of Scythia including the lower Danube (4.47–54) and detailed observation of pastoral nomads, on which see also Lebedynsky (2010), Kristiansen (1998: 185–209, 277–288), and Cunliffe (2015: 222–236). Herodotus' account of royal Scythian burials is corroborated by kurgan excavations. Herodotus had a strong personal interest in religious matters and often also mentions language; like Hecataeus, he was mistrustful of oral tradition and hearsay (5.9–10): he said nothing was reliably known north of the Ister apart from the Sigynnae, and nothing at all for the far north (4.16, 45). Had no reason to investigate temperate western Europe but does report Celts as people furthest west, next to the Kynetes (2.33, 4.49; Koch 2007: 12; 2013b: 126–127; Cunliffe 2013: 244). In a much-debated and derivative passage (4.19) he has the Ister [Danube] rise amongst the Celts, apparently in the far west of Europe.

Pytheas, *c.*350–*c.*289 BC

Greek from Massalia, private citizen, voyager, and geographer. Wrote *On the Ocean*, which is lost, but frequently cited by Polybius, Diodorus, Strabo, Pliny the Elder, and others.

New descriptions: of places, peoples, agriculture, and customs in Britain (*Pretannikê Nêsos* or *British Island*, cf. Welsh *Ynys Prydein*); he named its promontories Kantion (Kent), Belerion (Cornwall), and Orkas (Orkney); described Ireland; also the south-western British source of tin, emporia at Ictis/Mictis off Britain, Corbilo on the Loire estuary, and overland transport thence to Narbo and Massalia; the North Atlantic; the Baltic as far as the Vistula with an abundant source of amber; details of ocean tides, pancake ice, the midnight sun, and other peri-arctic phenomena; and a northernmost Atlantic island Thule, possibly Iceland (Cunliffe 2002: 116–133). Pytheas' latitude of 65 degrees N would be correct for this (Strabo *Geography* 2.5.8), although Thule was generally understood by the Ancients to mean arctic Scandinavia. Influential detractors from Polybius and Strabo onwards discounted Pytheas' evidence, together with the remarkably exact cartography derived from it by the mathematical geographer Eratosthenes (*c.*275–194 BC) and the astronomer Hipparchus (Strabo *Geography* 1.1.18), who made accurate measurements of his own for Europe north of the Borysthenes (Dnieper) and agreed with Pytheas. Many centuries of needless ignorance and distorted maps resulted from the rejection of Pytheas' work: see Cunliffe (2002: *passim*) for cogent discussion.

Polybius, *c.*200–*c.*118 BC

A Greek from Arcadia of distinguished political family, deported as hostage to Rome after the battle of Pydna 168 BC amongst 1,000 leading Achaeans; became close friend and mentor of the Roman general and politician Scipio Aemilianus, witnessing the destruction of Carthage in 146 BC. Wrote *Histories* in forty books to explain to the Greeks the fifty-three years between the war with Hannibal and the victory at Pydna (220–168 BC) during which the Romans mastered the whole Mediterranean. Books 1–5 survive, excerpts only from the rest.

New for Europe: a formidable Illyrian queen Teuta (*Histories* 2.4–12); European mercenary soldiers everywhere in Hellenistic and Carthaginian armies; Gauls on the move with families and wagons in the east; their attack on Byzantium; Gallic disaster at Delphi; Comontorius' kingdom of Tylis (4.45–46).

Limits of knowledge: 3.37: the Celts occupy lands near the Narbo river and beyond as far as the Pyrenees; the parts that lie along the Outer or Great Sea have no general name but are densely populated, and northern Europe between the Don and the Narbo is unknown to us (i.e. the whole of Transalpine Gaul).

Polybius had recent information from the Roman historian and senator Fabius Pictor who fought the Gauls at Telamon in 225 BC and reported details of the Gauls' military organization, dress, and chariots; also the *Gaesatai* (literally 'spearsmen' in Gaulish) 'so called because they serve for hire' (2.22.1), La Tène warriors of mixed origin recruited in 231 BC from the Alps and beyond by the Insubres and Boii to confront the Romans and raid in Italy (2.23); for their likely role in the adoption of gold coinage see Nash (1987: 43) and Sills (2003: 90–92). Polybius reports the first Roman contacts with second-century Thrace (30.17), with Transalpine Gaul, aiding Massalia against Ligurians besieging Nicaea (Nice) and Antipolis (Antibes: 33.8, 155–154 BC), and with Noricum (Book 34 quoted by Strabo *Geography* 4.6.12), describing Aquileia and a Tauriscan gold mine exploited by Italians until they were ejected for greed. Polybius also personally visited Iberia and coastal Gaul (with Scipio) and travelled the outer sea beyond Gades, no further than Brittany 'mostly to correct errors and make them known to the Greeks' (3.59). See Cunliffe (2002: 160) for likely reasons for his excessive objections to Pytheas.

Polybius and his sources are especially important because they are uncontaminated by subsequent Roman knowledge of Transalpine Gaul. He describes the Po valley from his own observation and reports history drawn from older sources about the Gauls in Italy from the fifth century BC: their close involvement with Etruscans and the 'epidemic of war' in northern Italy during the entire third century BC (2.14–17). He often calls the Italian Gauls *Keltoi*, especially when allied with Carthage or Etruscans (e.g. 1.6, 3.68, cf. earlier remarks on Herodotus), and differentiates them from the Veneti, who had different customs, dress, and language (2.17.7); when referring generically to Gaul and northern Italy he also uses *Galatia* (e.g. 3.59).

Poseidonios (Posidonius in Latin) *c.*135–*c.*51/50 BC

Greek, originally from Apamea in Syria, educated in Athens, then active in public life in Rhodes. Rhodian ambassador to Rome 87/86 BC, where he also taught; lasting personal connections with leading Romans in the 70s and 60s BC. Foremost scholar of his age: philosopher, historian, ethnographer, astronomer, geographer; conducted his own research for several years in the 80s BC in western Mediterranean provinces: in Hispania, where he stayed for thirty days at Gades (Strabo *Geography* 3.1.5), Gaul, Liguria, Italy, and Dalmatia. Extensive writings, all lost, included fifty-two books of *Histories* that continued where Polybius left off.

New: much on Iberia (in Strabo *Geography* Book 3) including recent information about the British Cassiterides obtained during P. Crassus' proconsular term in Further Spain (96–93 BC); an important study of Gaul, in connection with the Roman wars first with the Arverni and Allobroges in 125 BC, then in 113–101 BC with mobile mixed forces of raiders and migrants led by Cimbri, Teutones, and Ambrones: best fragments survive in Diodorus Siculus, Athenaeus, and Strabo. These contain much information about Provence, Languedoc, the Arverni, and Allobroges; also introduce Cimbri and the tradition that they left homes on the northern Ocean shortly before 113 BC because of a sudden inundation or even a tsunami (Strabo *Geography* 7.2.1–2). Poseidonios gave vivid descriptions of the customs and beliefs of various Gauls, including the earliest account of a learned class of bards, seers, and Druids. He classified as Celts peoples along the Alps, above Massilia, and on the Mediterranean side of the Pyrenees, Galatae as peoples inland from Celtica as far as the Ocean, the Hercynian mountain [wooded heights of Bohemia and Thuringia], and all the people beyond them as far as Scythia, but said Romans used 'Gauls' for both (Diodorus *Library of History* 5.32). Poseidonios considered the present condition of less civilized peoples as representing early states of culture in the Graeco-Roman world, and draws attention to resemblances between Gauls and Homeric heroes. Of especial interest because writing before Caesar's invasion of Transalpine Gaul. For assembled texts with translation and commentaries see Tierney (1960); those from Julius Caesar and Strabo include updated information that Poseidonios cannot have had, and Diodorus blends sources from different periods without always drawing attention to this.

C. Julius Caesar, 100–44 BC

Leading Roman politician, consul in 59 BC; proconsular governor and military commander-in-chief in provinces of Cisalpine Gaul, Illyricum, and, by special legislation, Transalpine Gaul from 59–48 BC; invaded Gaul beyond the provincial boundary in

59 BC; by 51 had driven the Roman frontier to the Rhine, Atlantic, and Channel. Wrote seven annual commentaries *de Bello Gallico* on his activities, all containing fresh information; an eighth book (51 BC) was ghostwritten by Aulus Hirtius after Caesar had left Gaul. All survive. Of similar outlook to Poseidonios, whom Caesar must have known and tacitly updates in his own excursus into Gallic ethnography (6.13–28).

New: contributions are too numerous to list but include geographical data for Britain, the Channel, northern Gaul, and the Rhineland, and political and cultural differences among inland peoples and regional groupings. In 59/58 BC he classified Aquitania, Celtica, and Belgica as different in 'language, customs, and laws' (1.1); he later gave the first detailed descriptions of Germans and Britons; as events unfolded, Armorica emerged as a distinct region (5.53.6, 7.75.4), and it became apparent that neither Belgae nor Germani were all the same. Everywhere there are passing allusions to social and political organization: obvious state-level institutions in central Gaul with laws, magistrates, military levies, and elections, which correlate well with evidence from coins (e.g. Nash 1978a, 1978b). Introduces Belgae (a regional confederacy), previously unreported, their recent history during movements of the Cimbri and Teutones, and their ongoing relations with Britain and Germany, also corroborated by coinage (Sills 2003: *passim*); he had less to say about Aquitania, which was left to his legates and was quiescent until the general uprising in 52/51 BC and Hirtius' account of the siege of Uxellodunum in Book 8.

Allowance must be made for observations made during a foreign invasion, influencing the way the Gauls, Germans, and Britons behaved and also Caesar's need to justify his position. He could forget to mention embarrassing mistakes (it is more than likely that he originally planned a two-pronged invasion of Britain, ruined by the Veneti, accounting for the exceptional brutality of his reprisals against them), but he could not invent episodes or tell outright lies: he had many critics on his military staff and in Gaul on other business who were in touch with contacts in Rome, as he makes Ariovistus remind himself in 59 BC (1.44.12). A man of wide-ranging intellect and accomplishments, Caesar made his own enquiries and observations, and knew many of the leading Gauls in person; even found time in Gaul to write a (lost) philosophical treatise *De Analogia* on the origins of human language. When he said Celts, Belgae, and Aquitani spoke different languages, he knew what he meant (and when he had to change interpreter), even if we don't.

Strabo, 64/63 BC–*c*.AD 24

Greek of eminent birth from Amaseia in Pontus; scholar, philosopher, and geographer, widely travelled but not in Europe outside the Mediterranean. Knew Poseidonios. All seventeen books of his *Geography* survive. A key secondary source of information about every part of the known world in the reign of Tiberius. See Book 2.5 for Scythia; Book 3 *passim* for Iberia and its peoples, with abundant older information otherwise lost and updates into his own time under Roman administration; Book 4 *passim* on Transalpine

Celtica and Britain; older information from Poseidonios and Caesar but important updates on Roman Gaul under Augustus and Tiberius, including river communications (4.1.14, 4.2.1, 4.3.4), and discussion of the differences between Gauls and Germans (4.4.2). See 5.1.3 for Cisalpine Celtica; 5.1.4 Liguria; 5.1.8 Aquileia at the head of the Adriatic, a Roman emporium for the tribes of Illyrians who live near the Ister [Danube]; 6.4.2 for the Bosphorus area; Book 7 for parts 'beyond the Rhine and Celtica and to the north of the Ister', territories of 'Galatai and Germani' (7.1.1) as far as the Borysthenes.

New since Caesar: flourishing trade and diplomatic relations with the dynasts of Britain (4.5.3, cf. 2.5.8); seeing British boys at Rome (4.5.2); the history of Maroboduus, the Suebi, and many more remote German peoples known to Rome through wars under Augustus and Tiberius (7.1.3–4); Cimbri still resident in their homeland, sending a gift of a sacred cauldron to Augustus in apology for the second-century raids (7.2.1); in the east: Iapodes, war-mad people with armour like the Celts and tattoos like Illyrians and Thracians (7.5.4); Getae, Scythians, Roxolani, and other nomads evidently in his own time (7.3.1–17); distinguishes Dacians, towards Germany and the sources of the Danube (now securely located) from Getae towards Pontus and the east.

Limits of Strabo's information: explicit statement (1.1.23) that he would only address the big picture, not fine details and component parts. With reference to anything that might lie north of Britain: 'for the purposes of government, there would be no advantage in knowing about such countries and their inhabitants, especially if they live in the sort of islands that can neither injure nor benefit us in any way because of their isolation' (2.5.8), reflecting Tiberius' conservative policy on imperial expansion. Hence: parts beyond the Albis [Elbe] near Ocean are wholly unknown to us (7.2. 4); Ierne [Ireland] is nowadays the remotest voyage north, about which he had no reliable information, but was said to be a wretched place on account of the cold and occupied by cannibalistic savages; and that anywhere further north must be uninhabitable (2.1.13, 2.5.8, 4.5.4); in the east, that Roxolani are the remotest of known Scythians, living beyond the Borysthenes; that the sources of the Tyras [Dniester], Borysthenes [Dnieper], and Hypanis [Bug] have never been explored, and that regions further north are even less known (2.4.6, 2.5.7).

C. Plinius (Pliny the Elder), AD 23/4–79

From Como; author and natural historian, personal friend of the emperor Vespasian; in public life, commanded infantry, then cavalry, in Lower Germany from AD 46–56, took part in the conquest of the Chauci in AD 47, and wrote a twenty-book *History of the German Wars*, sadly lost, on which Tacitus relied for the rich information in his *Annals* and *Germania*. The thirty-seven books of Pliny's *Natural History* are liberally scattered with items of relevance to inland Europe in his own time and in the past, many drawn from his long service in Lower Germany, and are often on subjects for which Pliny is the first or only surviving authority. These include the famous account of Druids culling mistletoe (16.249–251) and a section on amber (37.11.30–46), with a detailed critique of earlier speculation and with accurate information from AD 16 to his own time: says

Germans take it from the Baltic to Pannonia; Veneti take it into Italy; and that a Roman knight in the AD 60s was commissioned to travel from Carnuntum (Pannonia) to the Baltic to fetch fabulous quantities for a gladiator show in Nero's Rome.

P. Cornelius Tacitus, *c.*AD 56–117

Of Narbonensian or north Italian descent; Roman senator and historian; his *Agricola* and *Germania* survive in full, his *Histories* and *Annals* in part. These contain detailed secondary information obtained from living participants in Roman wars since the death of Augustus (AD 14), especially in the Germanies and Britain. Major known sources include Pliny the Elder's lost *History of the German Wars* and Tacitus' own father-in-law Cn. Julius Agricola (AD 40–93), who served in Britain under Suetonius Paullinus AD 58–62, governed Britain in AD 77–85, and led Roman armies into Wales (Ordovices), the Isle of Man, and Scottish highlands, had Britain circumnavigated, and may have considered invading Ireland, having an exiled Irish king under his protection. Valid information available to Roman historians now extends almost to the limits of Britain; the middle and upper reaches of the Danube to northern Germany, Scandinavia, and the Baltic; and Ireland reappears as a real place from a new perspective.

Claudius Ptolemy, *c.*AD 90–*c.*168, fl. 127–148

Roman Greek from Egypt; astronomer and mathematical geographer. His *Geography* provided a series of detailed maps (of which only medieval or later versions survive) of the entire known world, each with a list of place names and landscape features, their position in degrees of longitude and latitude, and general remarks about every region including its peoples. Important as evidence of awareness of the world outside the Roman Empire in the first half of the second century AD, due primarily to Roman military action and reconnaissance. It shows good knowledge now of the entire Irish coastline, listing sixteen peoples and six rivers; likewise Scotland; greater Germany including Scandinavia as far as the Finns; Upper and Lower Pannonia, Sarmatia, Dacia, Upper and Lower Moesia, and Thrace. Beyond the nomads of Sarmatia (*Geography* 5), 'unknown land' is largely blank, stretching far into the northern plains towards the tundra.

Ammianus Marcellinus, *c.*AD 330–395

Well-born Roman Greek from Syrian Antioch; on active military service in Gaul under the Caesar Julian, whom he admired. After 378 settled in Rome; as the last great classical historian writing in Latin, his *Res Gestae*, originally in thirty-one books, brought Tacitus' *Annals* down to AD 378. Only the years 353–378 survive. Constant passing references to barbarians inside and outside the Empire, not now in connection with Roman military initiatives in their homelands, but as foreign peoples with interests of their own in Roman territory and possessions.

New: events in Britain under Valentinian and Theodosius with information about Picts, Attacotti, Scots, and Saxons; close contemporary views of Alamanni (western empire), and Goths (eastern empire); of Quadi and Sarmatians (esp. Book 29); geography and peoples beyond the Tanaïs (Don) and Maeotic Gulf (Sea of Azov: 22.8.29–36); first detailed descriptions of origin, manners, and customs of the Huns (31.2.1–12), described as horsemen from beyond the Sea of Azov and towards the frozen sea, short, beardless, and dark, constantly on the move, 'almost glued to their horses' (31.2.6), 'burning with an infinite thirst for gold' (31.2.11); and of Alans, 'once known as Massagetae' (31.2.13–23), pastoral nomads on the measureless wastes of Scythia: tall, tending to blond, numerous subgroupings, living in wagons, driving herds of horses and cattle; valuable details of cultural and religious practices resembling information in Poseidonios (Gauls) and Tacitus (Germans).

Strabo, writing under Tiberius when imperial expansion had paused but was incomplete, expressed little interest in nomads beyond the Bosphorus who 'are of no use for anything because they do not mix with others, and only require watching' (*Geography* 6.4.2). For Ammianus, however, they were objects of urgent historical concern: in AD 376 peoples of the north were stirring up commotions (31.4.1): Huns were driving Alans west; Alans were harassing settled Goths; Goths were seeking refuge in the Empire; and accepting some Goths into Thrace in that year 'brought ruin into the Roman world' (31.4.6). On these movements see Cunliffe (2015: 281–284, 334–338).

Procopius, *c.*AD 500–after 562

Eminent Byzantine Greek from Caesarea in Palestine, trained in rhetoric and law; military experience as senior officer and personal adviser to Justinian's marshal Belisarius in Italy during the Gothic wars (AD 536–540); later wrote *History of the Wars* in eight books, mostly surviving. Constant incidental information and many ethnographic digressions about northern peoples involved in his narrative.

New: in Italy and the west, accounts of Franks, Gepids, and Lombards ('Franks' and 'Germans' are interchangeable terms, e.g. 6.25); Franks are said still to use human sacrifice to make prophecies and are differentiated from Goths; Cisalpine Gaul north of the Po is now called Liguria. In the north: Book 6 for the Danish peninsula and Thule (northern Scandinavia), including winter night and a ceremony to greet the returning sun, Procopius' own enquiries into how they counted days when there was constant day or night, and plausible descriptions that he himself barely credited about hunting peoples of the tundra and arctic (6.15); also (8.20) a vastly populous Scandinavian 'island of Brittia', close to the Ocean between Britain and Thule whose Angili, Frissones, and Brittones annually migrate south into the Franks (cf. earlier reports of this kind, e.g. Caesar *de Bello*

Gallico 2.4.1–2: did they often go to join elite households?). Procopius reports a Brittian funerary custom (burial at sea?) and his own unease with the 'dream-like' account he was given of it (8.20.42–58). Distant 'Brittia' may in fact be somewhere on the North Sea coast of post-Roman Britain (Koch 2013a: 11)—e.g. Lincolnshire or Norfolk (Behr and Pestell 2014; Nash Briggs 2020)—lands that were indeed then inhabited by 'Angili, Frissones, and Brittones'. In the east: events in Thrace include detailed accounts of the Hunnic Antae and Sclaveni north of the Danube (7.14.23); the hinterland of the Black Sea and river Don 'once held by Cimmerians, now called Utigurs (Huns)' (8. 4); Goths (some Christian) on the Don estuary; Tetraxitae Goths who said they used to be called Scythians because everyone there was Scythian: Procopius was understandably baffled by nomads, who were born in one place, raised in another, moved somewhere else later on, and could not tell you where they came from (Ammianus Marcellinus 31.2.10). Important excursus on the Caucasus area with more Hunnic tribes; eastern shores of the Black Sea still 'unknown' even to Byzantine Greeks. Careful account of the ongoing debate about the boundaries of Asia and Europe (8.6).

Ahmad Ibn Fadlan, Tenth Century AD

Sent as ambassador in AD 921 by the Caliph of Baghdad to a king of the Volga Bulgars, and wrote a meticulous travel memoir in Arabic (Frye 2005; Lunde and Stone 2012; Cunliffe 2015: 403–409) recounting 'what he saw in the land[s] of the Turks, the Khazars, the Rus, the Saqaliba, the Bashkirs and others, of the many types of their religion, of the histories of their kings, and [of] the way they act in many affairs of their life' (Frye 2005: 25).

New: earliest eyewitness report of (Scandinavian) Volga Rus (Cunliffe 2015: 373–378): their appearance, flat swords of Frankish type, wooden halls, trading customs; selling women and furs; getting drunk on mead; some details of religion; and a lengthy description of the ship cremation of a chief who had died there, which included sacrifice of a slave girl (Taylor 2002: 170–222; Frye 2005: 63–71; Hedeager 2011: 108–109; Lunde and Stone 2012: 50–54). This ritual featured an old woman, the Angel of Death, who stabbed the victim with a broad-bladed dagger, resembling a Cimbric sacrificial practice described by Poseidonios (Strabo *Geography* 7.2.3). The reported procedures for when a Rus king dies (Frye 2005: 71; Lunde and Stone 2012: 54–55) resemble what Caesar said happened in Gaul 'a little before living memory' (*de Bello Gallico* 6.19.5). These Rus were probably Varangians: cf. ninth- to eleventh-century runic inscriptions in Uppland and Gotland commemorating men who had died in the east.[2] For relevant observations of the tenth-century Rus by other Arab writers see Lunde and Stone (2012).

This series concludes in the latest post-Roman Iron Age with Bishop Adam of Bremen's account of geography, peoples, and customs in Scandinavia, and especially Sweden, in his *Descriptio Insularum Aquilonis* of AD 1075 (and see Hedeager 2011: 102–103).

Concluding Remarks

Procopius' *History*, in Greek, was the last great work of its kind in the classical tradition and bears favourable comparison with Herodotus and Thucydides. In most respects ancient historians all did exactly what we would expect from a historian today, attempting to leave a permanent and accurate record of current and past events, offering rational explanations, and drawing conclusions for the benefit of their readers, generally also expressing the hope that future generations might learn from the past.

It is sometimes said that the Ancients did not perceive change among barbarians. This is not quite true. Caesar and Strabo, for instance, often remark on differences between reported past conditions and what obtained in their own day. Caesar in particular gives invaluable insights into political change over several generations among the Belgae, Arverni, and Aedui that bear comparison with the earliest histories of Greece and Italy. It would be more accurate to say that the Ancients took change in foreign people for granted, but seldom felt inspired to dwell on it, either because they were preoccupied with a particular historic moment or because they were more generally impressed, especially since Poseidonios, with what seemed to be living illustrations of their own cultures' imagined simple lives and heroic values in the distant past. They were all aware of potential flaws in their information, which most discuss openly at some point.

We ourselves have to contend with the drastically fragmentary state of written evidence for the European Iron Age. Authors were selective in what they reported; much of what they did write has since been lost; and errors in manuscript transmission have taken a disproportionately heavy toll on unfamiliar and unpronounceable foreign places and names as fragile old papyrus rolls were serially copied from dictation and eventually transcribed onto parchment. Like foreigners everywhere, Greeks and Romans had difficulty representing some sounds in other language groups in their own alphabets: this is why every culture, then and now, is obliged to modify the characters and/or spelling of a parent script as it embarks on literacy.

One example of this extremely common problem can stand for many others. Only Tacitus (*Agricola* 16.1; *Annals* 14.31, 35, 37) and Cassius Dio (*Roman History* 62.2, 6, 7, 12), who retold Tacitus' story of the British uprising of AD 60–61 more than a century after Tacitus' death, name *Boudicca, Boodicia, uo adicca, Bouidicta, Voadicca, Voaduca* (Tacitus, in Latin), *Boudouika, Boundouika, Bodouika*, or *Boudouike* (Dio, in Greek) as its Icenian leader. Nowhere is the usual modern emendation of her name, **Boudica* (Brittonic for 'Victorious'), actually attested, though on purely philological grounds that or **Bodica* is probably correct. Inscriptions that write indigenous names in their own place and time sometimes help to correct mistakes in the manuscripts: in Britain, for example, the erstwhile Coritani should be Corieltavi and the Durotriges should be Durotrages (Breeze 2002a, 2002b). Strabo (*Geography* 4.5.3) said some British dynasts had sought Augustus' friendship; the extant fragments of inscriptions bearing Augustus' own public record of his reign are damaged in the place where he himself names these kings as 'Dumnobellaunus and Tin[…]' (*Res Gestae Divi Augusti* 32). It was long conjectured on perfectly reasonable grounds that Tin …'s full name was Tincommius, but it is now known from fully inscribed gold and silver coinage that he was in fact Tincomarus (Figure 36.9). Without such archaeological windfalls, we are in the dark.

Despite all this, the ancient writers have left testimony of incalculable value for what it adds to the solid base of archaeology. Their writings contain verbal descriptions of individual communities and of larger population groups *in situ*, of relations among foreign groups, of peoples on the move, of foreign soldiers employed in Mediterranean armies, and of war bands on destructive raids. They name places, rivers, landmarks, and peoples, and offer especially vivid ethnographical sketches when 'new' peoples entered the scene as history unfolded. And we get narrative pictures of living individuals, with values and beliefs, attitudes, aptitudes, and deficiencies, and details of their interactions with others. We even sometimes glimpse what foreigners made of their observers: some Vettones during Roman wars in the upper Tagus valley, who thought Roman officers strolling around their camp must have lost their minds, and led them back to their tents, thinking they should either be sitting quietly indoors or fighting (Strabo *Geography* 3.4.16); two Frisian kings, 'in so far as Frisii are under kings', who came to Rome on public business and were being shown the sights while waiting for Nero, asking their host embarrassing questions while bored by a show in Pompey's theatre and promoting themselves to better seats (Tacitus *Annals* 13.54); or one of the Rus collapsing in laughter after the interpreter had given a solemn and probably disingenuous answer to the rather pompous Ibn Fadlan when he asked what the two had been saying while they watched the Rus chief's pyre blaze (Frye 2005: 70; Lunde and Stone 2012: 54).

1 2

FIGURE 36.9 British kings named by Augustus. Note Latin spelling of both names. 1 Gold stater inscribed DVBNOVELLAVNV[S] (Cottam et al. 2010, *ABC* 2392), *c.*5 BC–AD 10. 2 Gold stater inscribed TINCOMARVS (*ABC* 1052), *c.*25 BC–AD 10.

Images © Chris Rudd

Notes

1. For the inherent social conservatism of the royal elites of Thrace, Dacia, Pannonia, and Scythia in the classical period see Fol and Marazov 1977: *passim*; Kristiansen 1998: 185–209; Lebedynsky 2010: *passim*.
2. For a detailed inventory see Project Samnordisk Runtextdatabas Svensk, http://www.nordiska.uu.se/forskn/samnord.htm [Rundata].

References

Allen, D. F. 1980. *The Coins of the Ancient Celts*. Edinburgh: Edinburgh University Press.

Allen, W. S. 1978. *Vox Latina: The Pronuciation of Classical Latin*. Cambridge: Cambridge University Press.

Allen, W. S. 1987. *Vox Graeca: The Pronunciation of Classical Greek*. Cambridge: Cambridge University Press.

Aubet, M. E. 2001. *The Phoenicians and the West: Politics, Economy and Trade*, 2nd edition. Cambridge: Cambridge University Press.

Behr, C., and T. Pestell. 2014. 'The bracteate hoard from Binham—an early Anglo-Saxon central place? With a note on the runic inscription on the B-bracteates by John Hines'. *Medieval Archaeology* 58: 47–82.

Brandherm, D. 2016. 'Stelae, funerary practice, and group identities in the Bronze and Iron Ages of SW Iberia: A *moyenne durée* perspective', in J. T. Koch and B. W. Cunliffe (eds) *Celtic from the West 3: Atlantic Europe in the Metal Ages. Questions of Shared Language*: 179–217. Oxford: Oxbow.

Braund, D. 1984. *Rome and the Friendly King: The Character of the Client Kingship*. London: Croom Helm.

Braund, D. 1986. *Ruling Roman Britain*. London: Routledge.

Breeze, A. 2002a. 'Does Corieltavi mean "warband of many rivers"?'. *Antiquaries Journal* 82: 307–309.

Breeze, A. 2002b. 'Not Durotriges but Durotrages'. *Notes and Queries for Somerset and Dorset* 35, 357 (2003): 213–215.

Camporeale, G. 2001. *Gli Etruschi fuori d'Etruria*. San Giovanni Lupatoto: Arsenale Editrice.

Cottam, E., P. de Jersey, C. Rudd, and J. Sills. 2010. *Ancient British Coins*. Aylsham: Chris Rudd.

Creighton, J. 2000. *Coins and Power in Late Iron Age Britain*. Cambridge: Cambridge University Press.

Cunliffe, B. W. 2001. *Facing the Ocean: The Atlantic and its Peoples 8000 BC–AD 1500*. Oxford: Oxford University Press.

Cunliffe, B. W. 2002. *The Extraordinary Voyage of Pytheas the Greek*. London: Penguin.

Cunliffe, B. W. 2008. *Europe Between the Oceans*. New Haven: Yale University Press.

Cunliffe, B. W. 2013. *Britain Begins*. Oxford: Oxford University Press.

Cunliffe, B. W. 2015. *By Steppe, Desert, and Ocean: The Birth of Eurasia*. Oxford: Oxford University Press.

Dark, K. R. 1994. *Civitas to Kingdom: British Political Continuity 300–800*. London: Leicester University Press.

De Jersey, P. 1994. *Coinage in Iron Age Armorica*. OUCA Monograph 39. Oxford: Oxford University Committee for Archaeology.

Delamarre, X. 2003. *Dictionnaire de la langue gauloise. Une approche linguistique du vieux-celtique continental*. Paris: Errance.

Delestrée, L.-P., and M. Tache. 2002–2008. *Nouvel Atlas des Monnaies Gauloises, Vols I–IV*. Saint-Germain-en-Laye: Éditions Commios.

Duval, P.-M. (ed.) 1985–2002. *Recueil des Inscriptions Gauloises, Vols I–IV*. Paris: CNRS.

Elliott, R. W. V. 1963. *Runes: An Introduction*. Manchester: Manchester University Press.

Fischer, B. 2009. 'L'iconographie des monnaies gauloises: Rapports et perspectives', in J. van Heesch and I. Heeren (eds) *Coinage in the Iron Age: Essays in Honour of Simone Scheers*: 99–106. London: Spink.

Fol, A., and I. Marazov. 1977. *Thrace and the Thracians*. London: Cassell.

Forsythe, G. 2005. *A Critical History of Early Rome: From Prehistory to the First Punic War*. Berkeley: University of California Press.

Freeman, P. M. 2010. 'Ancient references to Tartessos', in B. W. Cunliffe and J. T. Koch (eds) *Celtic from the West: Alternative Perspectives from Archaeology, Genetics, Language and Literature*: 303–334. Oxford: Oxbow.

Frye, R. 2005. *Ibn Fadlan's Journey to Russia: A Tenth-Century Traveller from Baghdad to the Volga River*. Princeton: Markus Wiener.

Green, D. H. 1998. *Language and History in the Early Germanic World*. Cambridge: Cambridge University Press.

Green, M. 1997. *Exploring the World of the Druids*. London: Thames and Hudson.

Haynes, S. 2000. *Etruscan Civilization: A Cultural History*. London: British Museum.

Hedeager, L. 2011. *Iron Age Myth and Materiality: An Archaeology of Scandinavia, AD 400–1000*. London: Routledge.

Henig, M. 2010. *The Heirs of King Verica: Culture and Politics in Roman Britain*, 2nd edition. Stroud: Amberley.

Hines, J., and B. Odenstedt. 1987. 'The Undley bracteate and its runic inscription'. *Studien zur Sachsenforschung* 6: 73–94.

Koch, J. T. 2007. *An Atlas for Celtic Studies: Archaeology and Names in Ancient Europe and Early Medieval Ireland, Britain and Brittany*. Oxford: Oxbow.

Koch, J. T. 2010. 'Paradigm shift? Interpreting Tartessian as Celtic', in B. W. Cunliffe and J. T. Koch (eds) *Celtic from the West: Alternative Perspectives from Archaeology, Genetics, Language and Literature*: 185–301. Oxford: Oxbow.

Koch, J. T. 2013a. 'Prologue: Ha C Ia ≠ PC ("the earliest Hallstatt Iron Age cannot equal Proto-Celtic")', in J. T. Koch and B. W. Cunliffe (eds) *Celtic from the West 2: Rethinking the Bronze Age and the Arrival of Indo-European in Atlantic Europe*: 1–16. Oxford: Oxbow.

Koch, J. T. 2013b. 'Out of the flow and ebb of the European Bronze Age: Heroes, Tartessos, and Celtic', in J. T. Koch and B. W. Cunliffe (eds) *Celtic from the West 2: Rethinking the Bronze Age and the Arrival of Indo-European in Atlantic Europe*: 101–146. Oxford: Oxbow.

Koch, J. T. 2016. 'Phoenicians in the West and the break-up of the Atlantic Bronze Age and Proto-Celtic', in J. T. Koch and B. W. Cunliffe (eds) *Celtic from the West 3: Atlantic Europe in the Metal Ages: Questions of Shared Language*: 431–476. Oxford: Oxbow.

Kos, P., and I. Mirnik. 1999. 'The Ribnjačka hoard (Bjelovar, Croatia)'. *Numismatic Chronicle* 159: 298–306.

Kristiansen, K. 1998. *Europe Before History*. Cambridge: Cambridge University Press.

Lambert, P.-Y. 1994. *La langue gauloise*. Paris: Errance.

Lane Fox, R. 2009. *Travelling Heroes: Greeks and their Myths in the Epic Age of Homer*. London: Penguin.

Lebedynsky, I. 2010. *Les Scythes*. Paris: Errance.

Looijenga, T. 2003. *Texts and Contexts of the Oldest Runic Inscriptions*. Leiden: Brill.

Lunde, P., and C. Stone. 2012. *Ibn Fadlán and the Land of Darkness: Arab Travellers in the Far North*. London: Penguin.

Markey, T. 2001. 'A tale of two helmets—the Negau A and B inscriptions'. *Journal of Indo-European Studies* 29: 69–172.

Meid, W. 1994a. *Celtiberian Inscriptions*. Budapest: Archaeolingua.

Meid, W. 1994b. *Gaulish Inscriptions*. Budapest: Archaeolingua.

Nash, D. 1978a. *Settlement and Coinage in Central Gaul c. 200–50 BC*. British Archaeological Reports International Series 39. Oxford: British Archaeological Reports.

Nash, D. 1978b. 'Territory and state formation in central Gaul', in D. Green, C. Haselgrove, and M. Spriggs (eds) *Social Organisation and Settlement: Contributions from Anthropology, Archaeology and Geography*. British Archaeological Reports International Series 47: 455–475. Oxford: British Archaeological Reports.

Nash, D. 1987. *Coinage in the Celtic World*. London: Seaby.

Nash Briggs, D. 2003. 'Metals, salt, and slaves: economic links between Gaul and Italy from the eighth to the late sixth centuries BC'. *Oxford Journal of Archaeology* 22, 3: 243–259.

Nash Briggs, D. 2006. 'Servants at a rich man's feast: early Etruscan household slaves and their procurement'. *Etruscan Studies* 9 (2002–2003): 153–176.

Nash Briggs, D. 2007. 'Home truths from travellers' tales on the transmission of culture in the European Iron Age', in C. Gosden, H. Hamerow, P. de Jersey, and G. Lock (eds) *Communities and Connections: Essays in Honour of Barry Cunliffe*: 15–29. Oxford: Oxford University Press.

Nash Briggs, D. 2011. 'The language of inscriptions on Icenian coinage', in J. A. Davies (ed.) *The Iron Age in Northern East Anglia: New Work in the Land of the Iceni*. British Archaeological Reports British Series 549: 83–102. Oxford: Archaeopress.

Nash Briggs, D. 2017. 'Multilingual coin inscriptions and their context in pre-Roman East Anglia'. *Philology* 3: 149–168.

Nash Briggs, D. 2020. 'An emphatic statement: the Undley-A gold bracteate and its message in fifth-century AD East Anglia', in N. Sekunda (ed.) *Wonders Lost and Found. A Celebration of the Work of Professor Michael Vickers*: 160–184. Oxford: Archaeopress.

Nava, M. L., and A. Salerno (eds). 2007. *Ambre: Trasparenze dall'Antico*. Milan: Mondadori Electa.

Russell, P. 1995. *An Introduction to the Celtic Languages*. London: Longman.

Scheers, S. 1977. *Traité de Numismatique celtique II: La Gaule belgique*. Paris: Belles Lettres.

Sills, J. 2003. *Gaulish and Early British Gold Coinage*. London: Spink.

Sills, J. 2017. *Divided Kingdoms: The Iron Age Gold Coinage of Southern England*. Aylsham: Chris Rudd.

Smallwood, E. M. 1967. *Documents Illustrating the Principates of Gaius, Claudius and Nero*. Cambridge: Cambridge University Press.

Taylor, T. 2002. *The Buried Soul: How Humans Invented Death*. London: Fourth Estate.

Tierney, J. J. 1960. 'The Celtic ethnography of Poseidonius'. *Proceedings of the Royal Irish Academy* 60: 189–275.

Thompson, E. A. 1965. *The Early Germans*. Oxford: Clarendon Press.

Todd, M. 1975. *The Northern Barbarians 100 BC–AD 300*. Oxford: Blackwell.

Wells, P. S. 2001. *Beyond Celts, Germans and Scythians*. London: Duckworth.

West, M. 2007. *Indo-European Poetry and Myth*. Oxford: Oxford University Press.

Zimmer, S. 2020. 'Celtic, Germanic and HARIGASTI TEIWA', in T. L. Markey and L. Repanšek (eds) *Revisiting Dispersions Celtic and Germanic ca. 400 BC–ca. 400 AD. Proceedings of the International Interdisciplinary Conference held at Dolenjske muzej, Novo mesto, Slovenia October 12–14, 2018*: 48–80. Washington, DC: Journal of Indo-European Studies Monograph 67.

CHAPTER 37

MIGRATION

ANDREW P. FITZPATRICK

Introduction

For over 150 years migration has been a defining theme of the European Iron Age. In the mid-nineteenth century, the idea of prehistory was still emerging but the works of classical writers such as Livy and Julius Caesar were well known. They recorded the wars of the Greeks and Romans, the invasions they made, and the colonies they founded. They also recorded migrations and invasions by peoples they called Celts, some of which were into the territories of Greece and Rome. Although these authors cited different reasons for the incursions, principally resettlement, raiding for booty, and mercenary service, they were often subsumed within a single interpretative category of migrations. Linguistic evidence for the dispersal of Celtic and Germanic languages helped ensure that migration—usually envisaged as the mass migration of whole tribes—became the most important and widely accepted way of explaining archaeological change.

Migration remained the pre-eminent explanatory framework until well into the twentieth century: changes in archaeologically defined cultural groups and in technologies, from the Neolithic to the Iron Age, were all explained by invasions. In the Anglophone world, the later twentieth century saw a series of reactions against migration, headed by Grahame Clark's 1966 'The invasion hypothesis in British archaeology'. The 'Celtoscepticism' debate may, in part, be traced to this rejection of invasion to explain change, although the focus here was on defining the Celts and their presumed origins. Even so, connections between the classical world and temperate Europe have remained a constant theme in Iron Age studies, including the role of the Mediterranean world as the source of luxury imports that inspired Celtic art, or as an arena for mercenary service.

Outside Celtic art studies, the potential importance of migration in these connections has been largely ignored in Anglophone scholarship. Elsewhere, particularly in central and eastern Europe, the importance of migration endured (Härke 1998); as a result, at a European level, its current study is uneven. Most effort has been expended on trying to identify what has been conceived of as the expansion of the Celts and, because of this, the archaeological evidence for the migrations of the Celtic peoples in the pre-Roman Iron Age is the principal focus of this chapter.

The great majority of evidence comprises objects placed in graves. There are few studies of stable isotopes and fewer still of ancient DNA. However, the migrations of other peoples, notably the Germans in the pre-Roman and Roman Iron Ages, and other types of movement had major consequences. One of the most notable was Greek colonization from the sixth century BC. The colonies in Italy drew the south and east of the peninsula into the Greek world, while the trade and exchange facilitated by Massalia is argued to have played a key role in creating social hierarchization among the late Hallstatt and early La Tène elites of central and north-western Europe. Colonies also enabled the transfer of influences from the Persian world that helped to create a distinctively Celtic art. The Phoenician and Greek colonies in Iberia, too, acted as a conduit for external influences that contributed to a distinctively Iberian culture.

Defining Migration

In the nineteenth century migration was typically envisaged as mass population movement (Champion 1990, 2013); this is reflected in the types of evidence that were anticipated for prehistoric migrations. In Britain, many of the criticisms of migration as an explanatory framework for the Iron Age compared the evidence interpreted as showing migration with that anticipated on the basis of Childe's concept of an archaeological culture. From this perspective, relevant evidence might be expected to include the contemporary appearance of new types of settlement architecture and morphology, burial rites, and material culture in a given area, and the presence of the same traits in another region at the same date or earlier (e.g. Hodson 1962, 1964). In practice, this burden of proof was rarely applied. Rather than rethinking migration and its possible archaeological correlates, the existence of several suggested migrations continued to be accepted, usually based on monothetic traits such as similarities between artefacts in different regions or the introduction of new funerary rites (e.g. Hodson 1964; Clark 1966). Instead, attention turned towards new interpretative frameworks, notably social and economic archaeology. Despite attempts to introduce greater rigour to the study of migration (e.g. Chapman and Hamerow 1997; Burmeister 2000), the topic has not returned to mainstream studies. It was, as Anthony (1990, 1997) described, a case of throwing out the baby with the bathwater.

In the regions where migration continued to be regarded as an important explanatory framework, studies were based largely on Iron Age funerary evidence, particularly grave goods, which were—and still are—seen as indices of ethnicity. Little attention was paid either to settlement evidence, which can provide indicators of settlement density, or to palaeoenvironmental data that might attest soil degradation and exhaustion, and provide proxies for climate change.

Although it was recognized that resettlement could take place for a variety of reasons and at a variety of scales (Dehn 1979), it was generally assumed that most migrations were mass events of the sort apparently described by classical writers. It was usually stated that the Celts were lured to migrate by the wealth of the classical world, but studies of modern migration point to a balance between 'push' factors that make leaving a place possible and 'pull' factors that make it viable (e.g. Anthony 1997). Most migration is local in geographical scale, and some is circular or 'tethered' in the sense that it is not permanent and there is a homecoming. Mass migration is rare, and usually thought to comprise a series of smaller migrations in which one group follows another into what would otherwise be unfamiliar territory, creating a 'chain migration'. Chain migrations often require a phase of exploration or contact to gain the assent of other parties to secure safe passage through their lands, or to establish the likely success of armed conquest. Warfare and raiding can lead to coerced migration as captives or slaves.

The scale of migration also varies. The individual, the group (defined on social, ethnic, religious, or many other grounds), the community, and the nation can all migrate, whether permanently or for shorter periods. 'Push' factors for resettlement can include:

- movement to a different type of settlement, for example to urban settlements
- to relieve pressure on land because of overpopulation
- climate change
- fosterage or marriage for personal or family reasons, or to secure political alliances
- religious beliefs
- to enter service, for example as a servant or a soldier
- to establish colonies, often for trading purposes
- to escape persecution
- banishment
- being held hostage or enslaved.

Some of these might not routinely be considered as migration, for example fosterage, or giving hostages, which is a type of coerced migration. Differentiating on archaeological grounds between such journeys and ones made for other reasons is not straightforward. For example, an individual might undertake circular migration:

- to prospect for metals
- to accrue status by visiting foreign lands and gain exotic knowledges and materials
- for religious beliefs, for example as a pilgrimage, or
- on military service, either for their community (for example as an auxiliary) or to join a cause, or as a mercenary.

Archaeological methods are strong in identifying the 'foreign', but interpreting this is complex. Short-term mobility and long-term settlement are difficult to distinguish; it is equally hard to determine whether archaeological evidence represents the migration of people who carried ideas and/or objects with them, or trade and exchange. External contacts can result in the transfer of immaterial things, such as new types of behaviour and ideologies, or new technologies and techniques (Venclová 2002; Sievers 2007; Defente 2012).

Creating 'the Celts'

The Celtic invasions of the classical world played a key role in determining how the European Iron Age was defined and why such different concepts (cultural = Celtic, geographical = Europe, and chronological = Iron Age) came to be regarded as synonymous (Fitzpatrick 1996). The resultant construct reflects the importance of historical sources and the dominance of history as a way of understanding the past. Key assumptions were that objects of La Tène Iron Age date and type are 'Celtic' because classical writers state that many of the areas in which they are found were inhabited by Celtic peoples. Two key inferences are (i) that these La Tène type objects were all used by people whose ethnicity was Celtic, and (ii) that these peoples spoke Celtic languages. Celtic art is often seen as an expression of a quintessentially 'Celtic spirit'.

Critiques of the 'traditional orthodoxy' and related models of Celtic Europe have been called 'Celtoscepticism' (e.g. Collis 2003, 2014). They emphasize the assumptions made in correlating archaeological data with much more recently recorded linguistic evidence, and point out that language is not synonymous with ethnicity. The classical writers used a variety of names to describe the peoples interpreted today as Celtic: groups were variously and inconsistently called Celtae/Κέλτοι and Galli or Galatai/Γαλάται, with no precise description of those to whom they were referring. Many finds have been called Celtic based on a single, monothetic trait rather than the polythetic groups envisaged by Frank Hodson or David Clarke (1968). Objects of La Tène type are also found in areas that the classical writers describe as being occupied by other ethnic groups, notably among the Germans. Even so, 'Celtic' remains a well-understood, if contentious, shorthand descriptor that helps distinguish between the major cultural groupings of Europe, which also include Germans, Iberians, Scythians, and Thracians, as well as Greeks and Romans, and is used here in that sense (see Chapter 1). A subject of ongoing debate is how ethnicity and other social identities were constituted and how they might be identified archaeologically (e.g. Fernández-Götz 2014; Chapter 35); this will be central to future studies of migration in the European Iron Age.

In the nineteenth century, the origins of Celticity were seen to lie in central Europe and its eventual distribution over the rest of Europe to result from migration and diffusion from this core: the so-called 'Celtic expansion' (Figure 37.1). The interpretation was also predicated on the assumption that societies were sedentary and typically farmers. As such, the Celts could be seen as the predecessors of modern western Europeans, whereas peoples characterized as nomadic, such as the Scythians, have little place in this interpretative model.

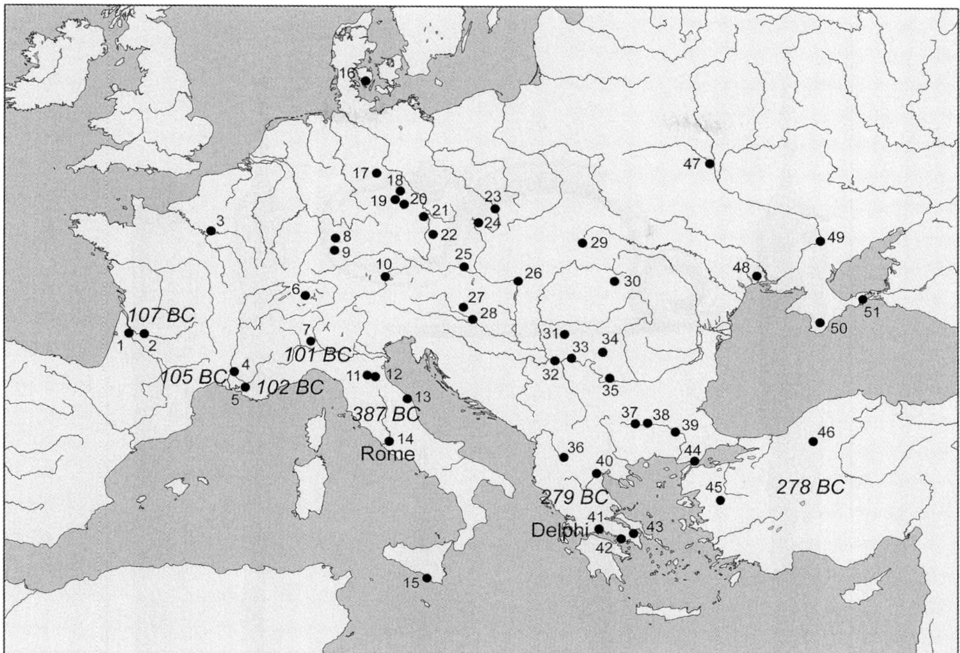

FIGURE 37.1 Map of selected sites mentioned in the text. 1 Bordeaux, 2 Tayac, 3 Le Plessis Gassot, 4 Orange, 5 Aix-en-Provence, 6 Münsingen-Rain, 7 Vercelli, 8 Dühren, 9 Nebringen, 10 Dornach, 11 Monte Bibele, 12 Monterenzio Vecchio, 13 Montefortino d'Arcevia, 14 Rome, 15 Camarina, 16 Gundestrup, 17 Westerhausen, 18 Dorna, 19 Groitsch, 20 Liebau, 21 Radovesice, 22 Kuntá Hora, 23 Němčice-Víceměřice, 24 Nowa Cerekwia, 25 Mannersdorf, 26 Szob, 27 Orehova, 28 Srednica, 29 Galish-Lovachka, 30 Ciumeşti, 31 Remetea Mare, 32 Belgrade, 33 Kostolac-Pećine, 34 Teleşti, 35 Gorni Tsibar, 36 Ohrid, 37 Pistiros, 38 Plovdiv, 39 Mal Tepe, 40 Vergina, 41 Delphi, 42 Corinth, 43 Athens, 44 Lyismachia, 45 Pergamon, 46 Karalar, 47 Zalissya, 48 Olbia, 49 Vyshhetarasivka, 50 Neapolis, 51 Nymphaion.

Drawing: Liz James

Equally important to nineteenth-century thinking was the formalization of the Three Age System. An integral part of its application was the recognition and naming of cultures and type sites. Shortly after what became the type site of the second Iron Age was discovered at La Tène, several slightly earlier cemeteries were found in western Switzerland. Many finds from these sites were decorated with Celtic art and, as it was now possible to compare objects from across Europe, the Alpine region came to be seen as the homeland of the La Tène culture. At almost the same time, similarities between objects found in France and Italy were being correlated with the Celtic invasions of Italy in the fourth century BC. In 1870 Gabriel de Mortillet drew attention to strikingly similar finds from northern Italy and north-eastern France, illustrating them side by side (Figure 37.2). Here, it seemed, was archaeological evidence for the historically attested Celtic invasion of Italy.

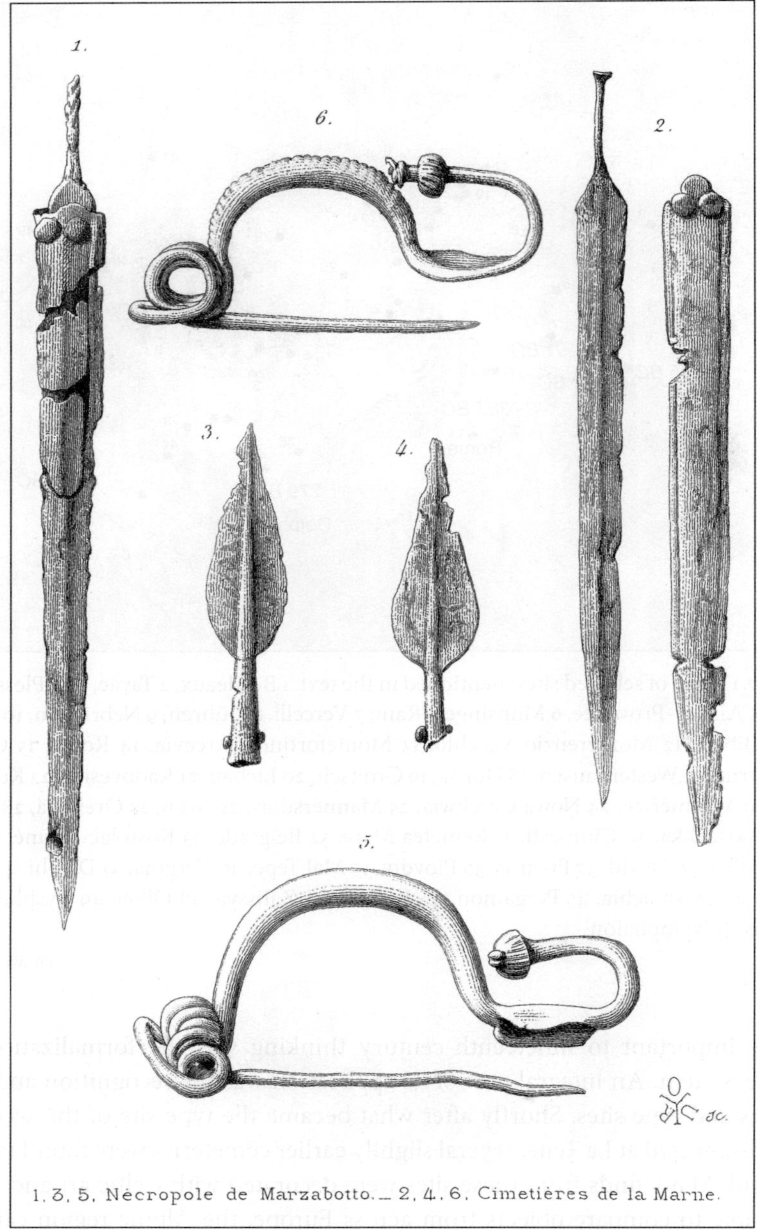

FIGURE 37.2 The discovery of the Celtic migration to Italy. In 1871 Gabriel de Mortillet used this engraving to illustrate the similarities between objects found in graves at Marzabotto in north-east Italy (1, 3, 5) and in the Marne region of north-eastern France (2, 4, 6).

Source: de Mortillet 1871: pl. XXII

Joseph Déchelette provided the first Europe-wide assessment of the later Iron Age—his '*second âge du fer ou époque de La Tène*'—and developed the concept of the 'Gaulois' as a Celtic ethnic and cultural group. One of the first illustrations in his *Manuel d'Archéologie* was of objects from the Marne and Bohemia placed side by side. Although he stressed the importance of commerce as well as '*bouleversements ethnographiques*' (1914: 915, figs 385–6), it was migration that became the popular explanation for these similarities (Kaenel 2007: 387–388). The identification of Celtic place names and elements that might be associated with historic migrations and invasions became an important parallel theme in linguistic studies in regions such as the Balkans, the Black Sea, and even beyond (e.g. Sims-Williams 2006).

The Celts in the Classical World: The View Outwards

The sacking of Rome by Gauls in 387/386 BC and the attack on Delphi in 279 BC were landmark events in Roman and Greek history. Although the written accounts are compelling, the difficulties in using them should not be forgotten: in many regards the classical sources about other peoples are statements of self-definition of the Greek and Hellenistic worlds relative to a barbarian 'other' (Tomaschitz 2002). Putting aside textual criticism of what are often only fragments of larger works, some of the principal difficulties include:

- the use of lost earlier works that cannot now be assessed critically
- a cultural geography very different from modern cartography, resulting in uncertainty about the geographical areas from which, and sometimes to which, people travelled
- differentiating between real events and origin myths (so-called aetiological accounts)
- the accuracy and credibility of the numbers of people said to have been involved in migrations and raids
- the dates when those journeys were made
- the motives for the journeys, and
- the authenticity of stories about individuals.

In some cases, it is unknown when—or even if—the claimed migrations occurred. Diodorus Siculus stated that the Celtiberians were descended from the Celts (*Library of History* 5.33), but there is no consensus that such an event or process can be identified archaeologically. Julius Caesar reported that the Helvetii abandoned and burnt their cities before they began their migration of 58 BC, but the archaeological evidence from western Switzerland does not support this claim (Kaenel 2012). Despite the caveats, the written sources do provide information about migrations that might not be deduced on archaeological grounds. They also contain insights into the motives of the migrants.

The Roman World

The best-known account of the Gaulish migration to Italy is by Livy (Peyre 2007). In *History of Rome* Book 5, Livy relates how around 600 BC Ambicatus of the Bituriges, described as the king of the Celts (said to make up one of the three divisions of Gaul), decided that part of his kingdom should colonize new territories. The stated reason was overpopulation. Ambicatus chose two nephews to lead the migration; they were to go to wherever the gods led them, as decided by augury. Segovesus travelled east into the Hercynian forest (southern Germany; the northern boundary of the known world to the Romans); Bellovesus travelled south to Italy and 'taking with him the surplus populations of his tribes, the Bituriges, Arveni, Senones, Haedeui, Ambarri, Carnutes, Aulerci, he marched with vast numbers of infantry and cavalry' (Peyre 2007: 5.34). Livy describes how the Gauls settled in the Po valley of northern Italy, which became known as *Gallia Cisalpina* or 'Gaul on this side of the Alps'. In Rome, the enduring fear of another invasion became known as the *metus gallicus*.

As Livy's account was written 400 years later, in the late first century BC, it must have drawn on earlier sources. It may also have been influenced by more recent contacts with Gaul, particularly Caesar's campaign, and the territories of the named tribes may have changed in the intervening period. It has also been asked whether parts of Livy's history were intended to provide an aetiological account rather than an 'accurate' historical one. The date of the migration is uncertain; Livy says around 600 BC but Polybius, who wrote a century before Livy and is generally regarded as reliable, placed it 200 years later (which is more consistent with the archaeological evidence). Some aspects of Livy's geography are also very general, notably the location of the Hercynian forest. Pompeius Trogus, who wrote at about the same time as Livy, gave additional information (preserved in Justin *Epitome* 24.4), stating that some of the 300,000 Gauls involved in this migration travelled past the head of the Adriatic and settled in Pannonia (broadly equivalent to modern Hungary).

Although it is important to treat these written sources cautiously, Livy made an important observation when he stated that the migration occurred in stages. Once the first migration was successful, the Cenomani, Libui, Saluvii, Boii, Lingones, and Senones all migrated successively. Livy implies that this was done as individual tribes. The lands to which they migrated were occupied variously by Etruscans, Umbrians, and Ligurians, who were all expelled after defeat in battle. Livy says that the last Celtic tribe to migrate were the Senones, who had to travel through the territories already settled; their territory in the Marches (central eastern Italy) became the southernmost Celtic settlement in Italy. This suggests a chain migration rather than a single event; the decision to migrate was in part based on information obtained from the first groups to settle, and the process was facilitated by them.

The classical writers give a variety of motives for Celtic migrations, but often emphasized greed and cupidity. Livy stated that overpopulation was the cause of the first migration from Gaul, but he also related how the Etruscan Arrunte used the lure of figs and wine to entice the Celts into his city of Chiusi to right a wrong done to him (*History of Rome* 33.3–4). Writing in the late first century AD, Pliny recounted how the Helvetian Helicus, who had worked in Rome as a blacksmith, took figs, oil, and wine back to his home (in modern Switzerland), and the desire for more such luxuries prompted the migration (*Natural History* 12.5). Livy also recorded that in 387/386 BC the Celts were persuaded to call off their seven-month siege of Rome on receipt of a large ransom.

The 'economic' lure of loot and luxuries became a classical literary trope that has often been accepted by modern scholars as the underlying motive for Celtic migration to Italy. But rather than taking the comments of Livy and Pliny as a balanced assessment of why the migrations started, they should be seen as attempts to explain them to a contemporary Roman audience. The same may be true for Livy's suggestion that the foundation of Massalia and the migration to Italy were contemporary. Both were famous events involving Gauls and, in the absence of a clear chronology, he sought to associate them. As described by Livy, the riches of Italy were not a factor in the migration to the east led by Segovesus.

The Greek and Hellenistic World

The Celts were also associated with dramatic events in the Greek and Hellenistic world. In 380 BC, shortly after the sacking of Rome, Celts are mentioned as fighting the Ardiacians, an Illyrian people whose territory was on the coast of Dalmatia in modern Montenegro and northern Albania (Theopompus *Fragments* 40). This is broadly consistent with Pompeius Trogus' account of a migration past the head of the Adriatic. In 335 BC, Celtic emissaries from the Adriatic famously met Alexander the Great during his campaign in the Balkans and lower Danube. On being asked what they feared, the Celtic warriors replied that they feared nothing on earth except that the sky might fall down. In the Greek world, this answer was seen as brave and naive in equal measure; the diplomatic answer would have been that they feared Alexander (Arrian *Anabasis* 1.4).

After Alexander's death in 323 BC, no single successor emerged, and a series of regional wars ensued among the rivals (the Diadochi), who fought to control the vast empire he had created, causing instability in the Balkan peninsula as elsewhere. Some conflicts were due to the unravelling of the arrangements with groups that Alexander had conquered, such as the Thracian Triballi of southern Serbia and western Bulgaria. Others were wars between competing Hellenistic leaders. Celts are mentioned frequently in the accounts of these wars, sometimes as aggressors and often as mercenaries employed by Hellenistic kings; on occasion, their involvement led to their resettlement.

In 310 BC, a Celtic force described as 31,000 strong was led by Molistomos into Illyria. This caused the Antariatae to flee, whereupon they ran into a Macedonian army. Cassander, one of Alexander's successors, resettled 20,000 of them on his own frontier. In 298 BC, incursions into the successor kingdom of Lysimachus in Thrace and Macedonia were halted by Cassander. The eventual collapse of Lysimachus' kingdom in 281 BC and the murder of Selucus I created a power vacuum that provided an opportunity for Celtic incursions through the Balkan peninsula.

The most famous of these Celtic raids were in 280–279 BC, when large numbers travelled through the Balkans to Greece and across the Bosphorus to Anatolia. In 280 BC three separate armies comprising 85,000 soldiers passed through Thrace into the Balkans. In 279 BC, the army led by Bolgios defeated the Illyrians, led by King Monunius, and then the Macedonians, led by King Ptolemy Keraunos, the son of Lysimachus. However, instead of pursuing this military advantage, the Celtic armies withdrew. On their return, Brennos, who had led the army that marched into Paeonia, called for a united assault on the south later that year, which various Balkan tribes joined. Greek colonies were plundered and, famously, the temple of Apollo at Delphi was attacked. Greek and Roman sources do not agree on whether the temple was sacked, the Greeks saying it was spared. The force led by Brennos is said to have comprised 152,000 infantry and 24,400 cavalry. Such large numbers are often thought to be incredible, but they may be accepted as providing an order of magnitude of a massive force. Even so, the force was defeated and retreated northwards before being defeated again by Antigonos Gonatos near Lysimacheia in 278 or early in 277 BC.

These events had an impact on the Greek world comparable to that caused by the sacking of Rome a century earlier, and an annual festival of commemoration, the *soteria*, was instituted. Here, it seemed, was confirmation that the Celts were fearless warriors whose ambition was to plunder the treasures of the civilized world. However, as with the invasions of Italy, different explanations are given for the raids, which undermine this literary trope. Pausanius (*Guide* 10.19) explained it as motivated by a greed for loot, Justin cited overpopulation (*Epitome* 24.4), while Memnon (*History of Heracleia* 12.4) explained it as due to famine.

Few of the invaders stayed, but one group settled in eastern Bulgaria in 277 BC and this kingdom of Tylis survived until 218 BC. Others settled further north where there was already a Celtic presence. In Croatia and Serbia one group became known as the Scordisci. They fought many wars with what became Roman Macedonia, until their eventual defeat in 88 BC. The Taurisici are also recorded as settling in northern Serbia. Famously, another group settled in Anatolia in 278 BC after being summoned by King Nicomedes I of Bithynia to him help defeat his brother (Zipoetes II) to secure the throne and defend it from attack by the Seleucid Empire led by Antiochus I Soter. Some 20,000 people, including women and children, are said to have crossed the Hellespont. Their territory became known as Galatia, and once established there, they are recorded as launching many raids and looting expeditions, forcing the payment of taxes or tribute, and serving as mercenaries.

The power of the Galatians was eventually challenged by King Attalus I, whose victories over them in 230 BC were celebrated by the building of a huge monument on the acropolis of Athena Nikephoros at Pergamon. Built by Attalus or a descendant, probably Antochius, the monument was adorned with sculptures depicting the defeat of the Galatians along with victories over other barbarians, both historical—the Persians—and mythical—giants and Amazons. One of the most iconic images of the Celts, the sculpture known as 'The Dying Gaul', is thought to be a Roman copy of part of a group from the Pergamon acropolis (Figure 37.3). In 166 BC, Eumenes II (an ally of Rome) won a decisive victory over the Galatians. This triumph, too, was marked at Pergamon, where friezes were added to the altar, and other monuments celebrating the victory were built in Athens and Ephesus. The statuary that adorned these Hellenistic monuments and comparable Roman monuments celebrating the victories over the Celts in northern

FIGURE 37.3 Celtic migration embodied: the 'Dying Gaul', an ancient and modern icon of the Celtic migrations. The Roman marble statue is a copy of a bronze sculpture that was part of a group on the acropolis of Athena Nikephoros at ancient Pergamon, western Turkey.

Photo: Antonio Idini, by permission of the Museo Capitolino, Rome

Italy, notably the terracotta figures from the sanctuary at Civitalba, provides some of the most defining images of the Celts in the classical world.

Iberia

If the invasions of Greece and Italy are well attested in the classical texts and, as discussed later, there is corresponding archaeological evidence, this is not the case for Iberia. A Celtic migration to Iberia was recorded by Diodorus Siculus, who said that the origin of the Celtiberians was in a migration (*Library of History* 5.33), although this suggestion was derided (along with the term Celtoscythians) by his near contemporary, Strabo (*Geography* 1.2).

Writing in the fifth century BC, Herodotus implied that Iberia was inhabited by Celts, and later writers were clear that a major part of east-central Spain was occupied by the Celtiberian people and that there were also other Celtic groups elsewhere in the peninsula, including the Celtici in the south. Iberia has a rich and varied epigraphic record which demonstrates that several languages were spoken in the Iron Age, and considerable efforts have been made to correlate the archaeological and linguistic evidence. The focus of much current linguistic research is on Indo-European and the emergence of proto-Celtic languages (e.g. Koch 2010, 2013), but earlier studies concentrated on the origins of Celtiberian, a language considered to be the most archaic Celtic language known.

The migration mentioned by Diodorus Siculus is usually assumed to relate to the Celtic element of the compound name—which indicates a mixture of Celts and Iberians—but there is little indisputable archaeological evidence for migrations to the peninsula in the Iron Age. Similarities between early La Tène brooches and weapons in Iberia and temperate Europe are sometimes taken to indicate a Celtic settlement contemporary with that of Italy (Lenerz de Wilde 1991, 2001), but archaeological correlates for the migration are more usually sought amongst late Bronze Age Urnfield groups (e.g. Ruiz Zapatero 1993), which is problematic both linguistically and archaeologically (e.g. Lorrio 2006).

Migrants or Mercenaries?

Figural representations of Celts are often interpreted as portraits of migrants but it is likely that many were mercenaries employed by Hellenistic kings. Celtic warriors were common subjects in the minor arts, appearing on painted pottery and as small terracotta figurines. There is extensive literary evidence for Celtic mercenaries across the eastern Mediterranean. According to Justin (*Epitome* 25.2), no king of the east 'carried on a war without a mercenary army of Gauls, nor if they were driven from their thrones, did they seek protection with any other people than the Gauls' (Griffith 1935).

Such mercenary service was widespread. As well as serving the Hellenistic kings, Celts were also employed by Carthaginians, Etruscans, and Romans, though in some instances they were auxiliaries rather than mercenaries—an important distinction. The first written reference to Celts on the Greek mainland is when Dionysius I, the tyrannical ruler of Syracuse in southern Italy, sent an expeditionary force of Celtic and Iberian mercenaries to the aid of the Spartans in 367 BC (Xenophon *Hellenica* 7.1). It has been suggested, however, that the use of mercenaries was already well established and even that the sack of Rome in 387/386 BC was ordered by Dionysius (Bridgman 2003). A few finds may hint at such earlier mercenary service: it has been suggested that the representation of a Celtic shield at Camarina, Sicily, may be associated with the 'Elesian and Ligurian' mercenaries recorded as fighting with the Greeks at the Battle of Himera on Sicily in 480 BC (Rapin 2001).

Celtic mercenaries are mentioned much more frequently after the invasion of Greece in 279/278 BC. The two main pretenders to the Macedonian throne after Ptolemy Keraunos was killed by the Celts in 279 BC, Antigonus Gonatus and Pyrrhus, both made extensive use of mercenaries. Antigonus offered to pay each one who had carried a shield but this was refused and payment demanded for the whole group (Polyaenus *Stratagems* 4.6). The presence of women and children foreshadows the composition of the groups who settled in Galatia in 278 BC.

Whether or not all the mercenaries thus described were 'Celts'—rather than other northern peoples such as Thracians or Illyrians (Diepeveen-Jansen 2001: 205–206; Džino 2008: 53)—these soldiers travelled far and wide. In 277–276 BC Ptolemy II Philadelphus, king of Egypt (the half-brother of Ptolemy Keraunos), employed 4,000 Celts in a civil war against his brother Maugus. When they mutinied he famously besieged them on an island in the Nile, where they died, through either hunger or suicide.

Summary

These historical accounts have been decisive in how migration in the European Iron Age has been interpreted, with little consideration given to their inherent difficulties. The written sources should arguably be used as a framework rather than a detailed guide; the ways in which barbarian peoples were characterized as 'other' in classical writing were part of a process of self-definition and the reasons given for the migrations are often literary tropes, which tend to emphasize 'pull' factors in the classical world. Where 'push' factors are given, they are often inconsistent, and may also be literary devices.

Nonetheless, when viewed in the round, the texts provide an important and broadly internally consistent narrative of migrations and raids into the Roman and Greek worlds between *c.*400 and 200 BC, although the evidence for Iberia is less cogent. The accounts of the migration to Italy indicate that hundreds of thousands of people from central and eastern France moved in a chain migration. Around a century later, large numbers, many probably from the middle Danube and the Carpathian basin, invaded the Balkan peninsula and travelled as far as the Aegean and Asia Minor. At least some permanent settlement in Anatolia and the Balkans ensued. This settlement was by tribal groups, who retained their social structure and their tribal names. Other groups returned north to settle among existing Celtic groups, which may also be seen as a chain migration.

Archaeological Evidence: The View Inwards

The written accounts of migrations are corroborated not only by classical sculpture and other figural art, but also by numerous objects with close parallels north of the Alps from the regions implicated (e.g. Kaenel 2007). Many of these items come from graves: in northern Italy, in the middle Danube region, and further east into the Carpathian basin (Hungary) and Transylvania (Romania), where they are reasonably interpreted as archaeological correlates for Livy's account of migrants following two separate routes. The finds in eastern Europe are distinctive variants of those from central Europe and are attributed to the so-called 'eastern Celts'. Some relevant objects have also been discovered in Greece and Turkey.

Italy

Celtic finds from Italy are usually studied in terms of the tribal territories recorded in accounts of the Roman conquest of northern Italy during the third and second centuries BC (e.g. Kruta 1981). This power was consolidated by a different type of migration: the establishment of urban colonies and the settlement of veteran soldiers.

Archaeological evidence makes it clear that transalpine contact existed long before the fourth century BC. The distribution of Golasecca culture material from the Alps to the Po valley is often considered to represent an earlier stage of migration, while finds of French objects of Hallstatt D date in Greek and Sicilian sanctuaries suggest that journeys to the Mediterranean were long established (Verger 2003). Enduring relations between the Alpine communities probably enabled Celtic groups to cross the mountains safely using passes that were always difficult and often hazardous. Clear links across the Alps are shown by distinctive types of La Tène A openwork belt hooks (Frey 1991; Stöllner 2010).

Most of the evidence for the migrations in Italy comes from graves, although a few graffiti from settlements give Celtic names (e.g. Vitali 1998; Vitali and Kaenel 2000). Contra Livy, some of the earliest graves are the most southerly, from the Marches (e.g. Lejars 2006). Many of the most famous finds are old discoveries about which information is limited. Although many well-furnished burials incorporated both Celtic and classical grave goods, emphasis has been placed on the 'Celtic' objects as indicators of ethnicity; these are usually weapons, typically swords, and sometimes spears and bronze or iron helmets. Grave groups containing 'Celtic' objects associated with females appear to be less frequent. Montefortino d'Arcevia is a good example of the older discoveries. In the late nineteenth century, approximately fifty graves spanning the late fourth and third centuries BC were excavated. Almost half contained Celtic swords and some of them helmets. The other male graves and almost all the female graves, however, lacked objects typical of burials north of the Alps, apart from a few women's graves with torcs and multiple arm-rings that are late in the life of the cemetery.

The best-examined cemeteries in northern Italy are at Monte Bibele, Monterenzio, and Monterenzio Vecchio, south-east of Bologna in the Apennines, in the area settled by the Boii and not far from Marzabotto. The Monte Bibele cemetery is close to the hilltop settlement of Pianella di Monte Savino, and provides a detailed insight into the processes of migration and acculturation (Vitali and Verger 2008). It contained at least 170 burials, mainly inhumations. The earliest graves were on the summit and burials then expanded downhill, providing an important horizontal stratigraphy. Graffiti on pots in the earlier graves (*c*.350–330 BC) show that the burials were of Etruscans who lived in the associated settlement. Burials regarded as Celtic are mainly of males and typically include swords in their scabbards, sword belts, and brooches. Over 40% of the graves contained weapons; initially these followed the horizontal stratigraphy, but later formed a discrete group. There are also age-related distinctions: younger males were buried with spears, old men without weapons. While the swords and scabbards may be identified as Celtic, there is less certainty about the spears, some of which are related to the Italian tradition of *pila*. The helmets, although derived from Celtic examples, are of a variety found mainly in Italy. Grave 14 contained weapons and a set of pottery vessels for two people, one of which has a graffito in Etruscan, 'Petnei'. This may be the name of the wife of the dead man, who is assumed to have been Celtic. At Monterenzio Vecchio, almost 60% of the graves of adolescents and adults contained weapons.

The types of objects and the Celtic art on some of them also reflect the assimilation of the Greek culture and customs that had been adopted in Etruria and south-east Italy. Greek and Etruscan objects found in graves at Monte Bibele include wine services of bronze or pottery, cauldrons and skewers for cooking meat, and strigils for cleaning oil from the body. These are seen as symbolizing the ideas of the *symposium*, banquet, and athlete (Verger 2006), although the first two were already well known north of the Alps. Tools for textile working, jewellery, mirrors, and *unguentaria* (perfume jars) were also found. On the other hand, some swords were bent and broken in a manner that is more familiar north of the Alps, whereas the metal armour and Greek-style helmets and swords of the Etruscans, Samnites, and other Italian peoples were not adopted.

This evidence has been interpreted as reflecting the garrisoning of an elite group of Celtic soldiers in an Etruscan settlement at Monte Bibele and the gradual cultural assimilation of these men and those buried at Monterenzio Vecchio into Umbrian-Etruscan society and its 'Hellenizing' or Greek influences. However, this assimilation was not universal. At the nearby cemeteries of Casalecchio (zone A) and Marzabotto, objects that symbolized the *symposium*, banquet, and athlete were absent.

Livy (*History of Rome* 6–7) and other writers referred to Celts in southern Italy in the fourth century BC, but evidence from this region is confined to isolated finds, such as the helmet from Canosa di Puglia in Apulia, which may just as well reflect booty or mercenary service.

While a trade in slaves to Italy is often suggested, and enslavement is envisaged as happening during warfare and raiding (e.g. Arnold 1988; Nash Briggs 2003), there is little evidence for such coerced migration before the late Iron Age when writers such as Poseidonios described the exchange of slaves for wine. By this time the Roman *Provincia* in southern France provided a conduit for the movement of people to the slave-based *latifundia* of Italy. Roman campaigns also provided a regular and sometimes prodigious supply of slaves. Finds of slave chains and fetters from across Europe provide some material evidence for the existence of slavery as a social institution (Peschel 1971; Schönfelder 2015).

'Traditional' archaeological interpretations of Celtic migration into Italy have relied primarily on the written sources and artefact typologies. There has been little consideration of the finds as assemblages or how they compare with those north of the Alps, while scientific analyses of human residence patterns are only just beginning. Strontium isotopes in teeth provide information about the geological environment in which a person grew up, and oxygen isotopes about geographical and climatic conditions, but the few studies undertaken on Iron Age populations have mostly been in Germany (e.g. Vohberger 2007), with some in Britain (e.g. Jay et al. 2013). Analyses of ancient DNA are rarer still (e.g. Scholz et al. 1999).

The most significant project to date has sought to examine residential change during the period of the Celtic migrations (Hauschild 2010a; Scheeres et al. 2013, 2014; Scheeres 2014). Cemeteries of La Tène B date (*c*.380–250 BC) were selected for isotope or aDNA analysis based on their geographical location, size, length of use, and the presence of typologically diagnostic grave goods. The cemeteries analysed include Nebringen (Germany), Münsingen-Rain (Switzerland), Kuntá Hora and Radovesice I and II (Czech Republic), and Monte Bibele and Monterenzio Vecchio (Italy).

The strontium analyses from Monte Bibele offer little support for the historical and artefact-based interpretation. The great majority of people buried there (81%) appear to have been local, although the homogeneous geology could obscure local movement. Males appear to have changed residency after childhood more often than females, but there was no clear correlation between this and the carrying of arms. The later graves contained both Celtic and Etruscan grave goods, and these were found with both local and non-local individuals. Occasionally graves contained objects that may not be local, but while the isotopes are consistent with this possibility, they are rarely conclusive. For example, the woman buried in Grave 20 had an ear-ring characteristic of the Great Hungarian Plain, but while the isotope ratios can be matched in that region, they are not exclusive to it. The implication is that migrants formed only a small, if arguably significant, proportion of the community who used the cemetery. The Celtic objects would appear to reflect processes of acculturation and the creation of new social identities as much as ethnic origins.

Western and Central Europe

La Tène-type finds earlier than Livy's date of *c*.400 BC for the migrations into Italy are widely distributed in France, Germany, and central Europe, and in many cases display a clear development from local Hallstatt types. These early La Tène objects share many similarities across great distances, usually explained by concepts such as emulation. However, similarities between objects dating after 400 BC are often explained as indicating migration, even though the differences between them and earlier objects are often less pronounced than those between Hallstatt finds and their La Tène successors.

Assessments of mobility have typically concentrated on a single trait, for example burial in flat inhumation graves, or types of object such as swords, brooches, or wheel-turned pottery. Similarities in styles and decoration apparent on metal objects across Europe are often cited as evidence for the networks maintained by migrating communities. Duchcov- and Münsingen-type brooches (Kruta 1979) are a classic example. These ornaments are found widely across central Europe and although many regional groups can be identified, the stylistic similarities they share is often used to argue for migration (e.g. Bujna 1998: fig. 2; Waldhauser 1998). Considerable emphasis has also been placed on objects decorated in the 'Plastic style' as evidence for links between northern France and central Europe (e.g. Charpy 1991; Čižmář 1995; Ginoux 2007a). Perhaps the most striking example is the distribution of La Tène C scabbards decorated with 'dragon pairs' (Figure 37.4). They belonged to a panoply of weapons so

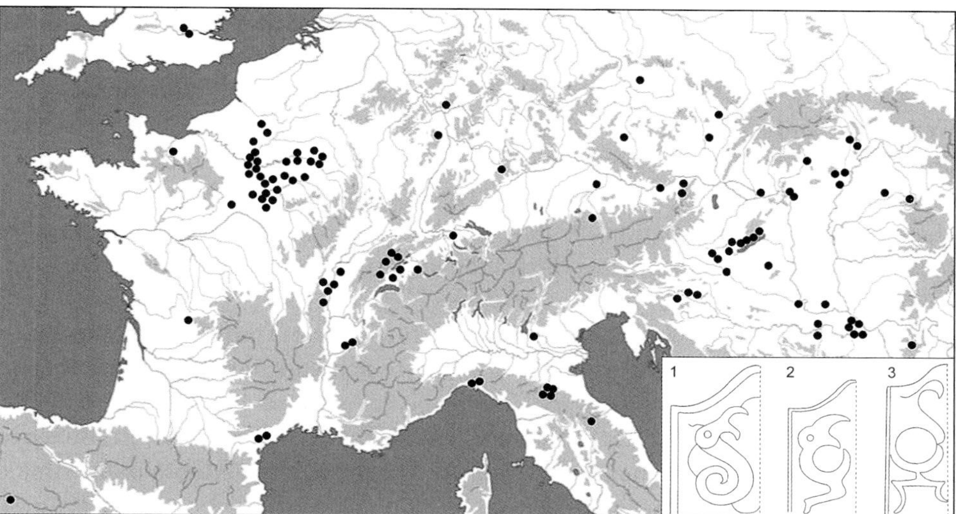

FIGURE 37.4 The leitmotif of the 'dragon pair' on sword scabbards. Most of the find-spots are graves and so the map reflects the distribution of funerary rites, but the widespread distribution of this probably apotropaic motif also illustrates a value shared across much of temperate Europe.

Source: Ginoux 2012: fig. 1

similar across much of temperate Europe that they have been described as a 'standard' that shared the same visual language (e.g. Ginoux 2007b, 2009, 2012).

Correlations between cemeteries and settlements, which are generally much less well studied, have rarely been attempted. Although the depopulation of areas from which people left to migrate to Italy is often suggested, it is rarely demonstrated. In Champagne, there is a marked decline in the number of cemeteries in use at the end of the fifth century BC. This has been widely interpreted as demonstrating a mass migration to Italy (e.g. Charpy 1991), but the settlement evidence is thought to demonstrate continuity (Villes 1995). A more sharply focused chronology of the funerary evidence in fact reveals considerable intra-regional variability (Charpy 2009). However, a little further north-east, the appearance of high-status female burials in the Rhineland in La Tène A—as at Reinheim—is suggested to reflect a period in which many males were absent from the region and there was a change in how social ranking was expressed (Arnold 1995).

The Arras burials of East Yorkshire in England are often still accepted as evidence for a migration from northern France, even after the rejection of the invasion hypothesis by British scholars and despite the lack of typological, chronological, or isotopic data to support the view (Stead 1979; Van Endert 1986; Anthoons 2007, 2010, 2013; Jay et al. 2012, 2013).

In areas such as Moravia that are close to the zone where La Tène styles emerged, the appearance of new styles may reflect acculturation rather than migration. Many of the objects that are found across central Europe are common types, particularly weapons, brooches, and bracelets, which must have been widely manufactured. They indicate connections over long distances, but not necessarily migration. As mentioned, while some artefacts such as swords and brooches have supra-regional distributions, certain types of jewellery could be grouped and worn differently. This is particularly true for female costume, in which different numbers of brooches were worn and superficially similar bangles could be worn as armlets, bracelets, or anklets in different numbers and in different combinations (Lorenz 1978, 1985). When assessed with regionally distinctive types of objects such as belt hooks and belt chains or pottery, combinations of grave goods have the potential to illuminate more localized patterns of movement which may indicate residence patterns such as exogamy (e.g. Dizdar 2009).

Even so, La Tène-type objects clearly appeared further east at progressively later dates. The evidence comes primarily from the appearance of inhumation graves that contain Celtic objects, and the chronology of these can be fine-grained. In the Czech Republic, finds appear in western and central Bohemia in La Tène B1a, and in eastern Bohemia in La Tène B1b. Similarly, finds from Lower Austria are later than those in the Alpine regions to the west (e.g. Neugebauer 1996; Sankot 2003; Ramsl 2007; Tappert 2012). While the absolute chronology continues to be refined (e.g. Guštin and Kavur 2016), these regional sequences support models of the steady introduction of new rites and material culture that might be due to chain migration or settlement expansion, rather than widespread and contemporary changes in religious beliefs or changes in settlement patterns within existing communities.

An even stronger case can be made further away from the 'Celtic core'. Based largely on a small number of brooches, Ramsl (2010) suggests that some of the people buried in the Mannersdorf cemetery in Lower Austria came from Switzerland, while other finds, particularly the weapons, display the wide-ranging contacts typical of La Tène metalwork (Ginoux and Ramsl 2014).

The northernmost Celtic finds in central Europe are from southern Poland, where they first appeared in La Tène B in the basins of the rivers Oder and Vistula. The initial contacts are often interpreted as representing 'Latèneization' or acculturation, but the underlying cause of change is usually assumed to be migration (Chapter 7). The distinctive objects are again mainly swords and brooches, most of which occur in Tyniec group cremation burials. The swords were often deliberately broken before being placed on the pyre. Most of the brooches, swords and scabbards, spearheads, spurs, and tools from Poland are very like examples from further south, though the similarities are with different regions. Thus, the finds from Lower Silesia around the rivers Oder, Bystrzyca, and Oława, and from Mount Ślęża have direct links to Bohemia and indirect ones to western Europe. Finds from settlements in Upper Silesia (Little Poland) around the Głubczyce upland show stronger links with 'eastern Celtic' finds and have analogies with Moravia, while objects from the San basin in south-east Poland are linked with the upper Tisza area in Hungary and Ukraine south of the Carpathians (Olędzki 2005). Although the groups on the Vistula around Krakow are regarded as a 'pure' Celtic group initially, in La Tène B2 and C1, the influence of the Przeworsk culture led to the formation of distinctive groups such as the Tyniec and Púchov groups in the Krakow region (Poleska 2005; Bochnak 2006, 2011).

Isotope analyses of six inhumation cemeteries in the 'Celtic core' are now available. The results from the small La Tène B2 cemetery at Dornach, southern Bavaria, suggest limited change in residencies, although some individuals were non-local, perhaps from Bohemia and particularly Moravia, further to the east (Eggl 2003: 528–530, fig. 10). The presence in the graves of bracelets of a type best known in Moravia appears to support this suggestion, while the possible non-local interred in Grave 534 was buried with a scabbard decorated with the dragon pair motif. Comparable results have been obtained from the broadly contemporary Germanic cemetery to the north at Westerhausen, Sachsen-Anhalt, where two of fourteen individuals analysed were not local (Nehlich et al. 2009). There are fewer analyses of early Iron Age burials, but individual mobility is also attested (e.g. Oelze et al. 2012).

Larger studies include the key Swiss cemetery of Münsingen-Rain. The cemetery's clear horizontal stratigraphy and long use (*c.*220 graves) have given it a prominent position in chronological and cultural studies (Müller 1998). Morphological kinship analysis based on epigenetic characteristics of the teeth and skulls revealed important results. The population displayed an above average homogeneity and a distinctive, deformed skull shape suggested that many of the deceased were biologically related.

Two 'founder families' were identified, whose descendants used the cemetery for at least ten generations over some 250 years (Alt et al. 2005; Müller et al. 2008).

Isotope analyses (Hauschild et al. 2013; Scheeres 2014) indicate that most of the individuals buried at Münsingen-Rain were local, and some evidence could indicate Alpine transhumance. A small proportion of people (14.7%), both females and males, came from relatively nearby communities. Such movements seem to have occurred regularly though not frequently, which might indicate reciprocal marriage arrangements. A few females may have come from further afield, including one buried in Grave 6, who may have grown up near the Mediterranean. This combination of morphological and isotope analyses provides important evidence for the scale of social networks of stable and long-lived communities.

A similar pattern of largely local residence is seen at Nebringen in south-west Germany. This small mixed-rite cemetery contained twenty-seven graves suggested as belonging to six family groups, based on the regular proximity of graves of females, males, and children. It was used for five or six generations or around 150 years (Krämer 1964). Assuming the cemetery was fully defined, *c*.80% of the inhumations were analysed for strontium isotopes (only). Although differences in the strontium isotopes of the first and last teeth to be formed were observed in half of the individuals, this might simply be due to regular changes in the location of cultivated land, as the local geology is very heterogeneous. However, one female appears to be non-local; she was buried with a type of brooch known from Hungary and Romania, although the isotope ratios are not exclusive to those regions. One of the Nebringen burials was accompanied by a distinctive type of neck-ring (or torc) decorated with discs; such *Scheibenhalsringe* are one of the few types of metal object that provide evidence for long-distance journeys.

In contrast, the cemeteries at Radovesice I and II, and Kuntá Hora in Bohemia, where both oxygen and strontium were analysed, display considerable evidence for the movement of women, men, and children (Scheeres et al. 2014). Approximately 75% of the population are thought to come from different geological regions within Bohemia, although again the heterogeneous regional geology makes it difficult to be precise. Most males who were buried with weapons had moved residencies, but it is also possible that entire families had moved. Some males clearly came from outside the region—particularly the man buried in Grave 19 at Kuntá Hora—and the objects as a group also display signs of contacts with Moravia and the Danubian region. This could indicate continuing connections with communities who had migrated to the east. Settlements in Bohemia typically appear to have been occupied continuously from the early Iron Age, and one such settlement close to the Radovesice I cemetery is thought to be associated with it (Waldhauser 1987).

Although there is greater evidence for mobility in the Bohemian cemeteries than further west or in Italy, the nature of the local geology is critical in determining whether it is possible to identify migration using strontium isotopes alone. Even so, a critical implication of the Bohemian analyses is that there may be different reasons for changes in residence of individuals buried in the same cemetery, and even considerable evidence for mobility need not equate to mass migration. Scheeres et al. (2014) suggest that female residency may be related to an exogamous marriage and patrilocal residence pattern, whereas male residency may be related to warrior status. Changes in the residency of children might tentatively be linked to fosterage.

Eastern Europe

The evidence for the migration of Celtic peoples further to the east also takes the form of the appearance of new material culture, often associated with new burial rites of which cremation was now the most common. There was an increasing emphasis on including parts of objects rather than the whole, as a form of *pars pro toto*. Many objects are distinctive 'eastern Celtic' varieties of widely distributed types (e.g. Szabó 1992, 2001, 2006). The dating of these graves is not straightforward. The regional chronology has traditionally been linked directly to the historical evidence and, as a result, La Tène B2 has been supposed to finish after the Balkan invasion in 279 BC, typically after *c.*260 BC (cf. Rapin 1995). However, most of the (admittedly relatively few) Celtic objects in Asia Minor are typologically La Tène C1. If the historically based chronology is correct and most of the objects reached Asia Minor with the new arrivals of 278 BC, this would suggest that material of La Tène C1 type was already current before then, perhaps as early as 300 BC (Blečić Kavur and Kavur 2012). There is insufficient evidence to determine whether this view of a single typological sequence is correct, but the resulting uncertainty has important consequences for its interpretation.

The funerary evidence indicates a steady eastward progression in the appearance of Celtic material, plausibly interpreted as representing the progress of Celtic groups. Graves of La Tène A date occur mainly in the middle Danube-Carpathian basin, although individual objects are also found in indigenous contexts in Serbia and Croatia. Burials dated to La Tène B1/B2 further to the east indicate continuing migrations and/or processes of acculturation that extended through the Great Hungarian Plain and the upper Tisza basin, before continuing into Romania along the Carpathian Apuseni mountains and then into Transylvania. The finds from the San valley in south-east Poland are contiguous and part of this distribution.

In Romania, most graves and cemeteries with Celtic objects in the west and centre of the country were established from late in La Tène B1, but comparable graves do not appear in the east and far south of the country until La Tène B2 (Figure 37.5; Rustoiu 2008, 2011, 2014). Grave goods span a range of Celtic types: swords, brooches (including Duchcov and Münsingen types), distinctive bronze hollow knobbed bracelets (*Hohlbuckelringe*) worn by females, and wheel-turned pottery (Zirra 1991, 1998; Szabó 2001; Rustoiu 2008). *Scheibenhalsringe* neck-rings occur mainly along the upper Rhine but there are several from Hungary and Romania, some being noticeably worn (Figure 37.6). As there are few finds in the intervening areas, it seems likely that

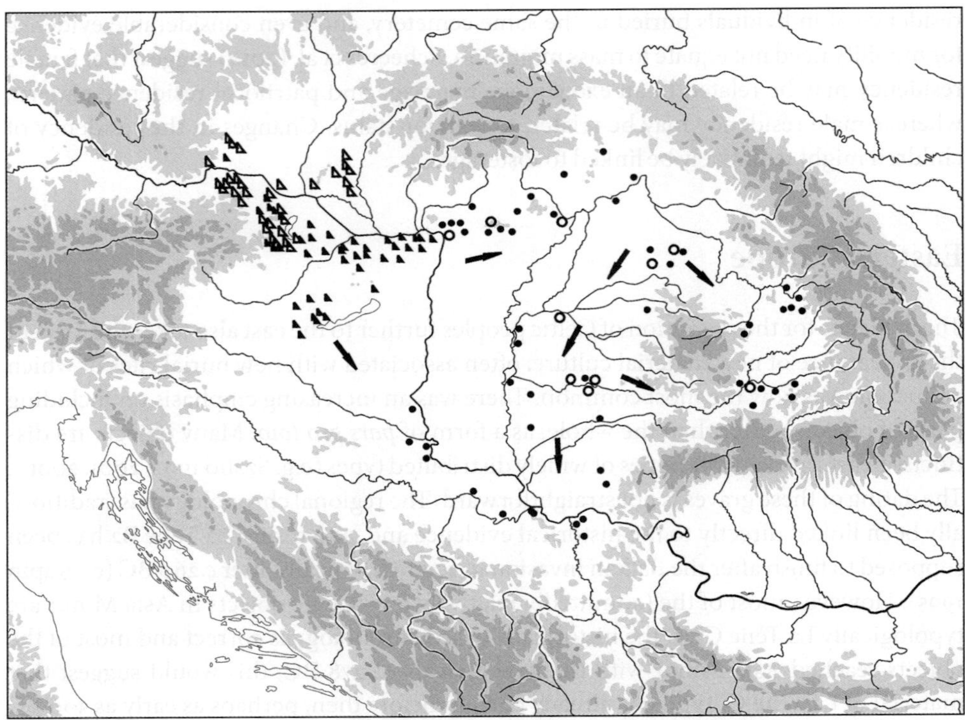

FIGURE 37.5 The distribution of early La Tène burials in the Carpathian basin and the possible directions of Celtic migration. Open triangles: cemeteries of La Tène A date; black triangles: cemeteries of La Tène B1 date; open dots: cemeteries beginning in La Tène B1/B2; black dots: cemeteries beginning in La Tène B2.

Source: Rustoiu 2011: fig. 1

their wearers had made long journeys from the west (Müller 1989). In contrast, some cemeteries, such as Fântânele-Dâmbul Popii, appear typically Celtic in their rites and rituals but many, if not all, of the objects are distinctive regional versions.

It is usually assumed that most, if not all, of those who invaded Greece in 279/278 BC came from the Carpathian basin (e.g. Szabó 1995, 2001; Horváth 2005)—a view supported by the occurrence of Thracian objects in graves north of the Danube in Transylvania and the Banat (Rustoiu 2011: 164)—but it is possible that groups from Slovenia were also involved (Lubšina-Tušek and Kavur 2011; Guštin 2011; Jovanović 2011). Recent discoveries in eastern Slovenia imply that some groups also migrated through Transdanubia (western Hungary) to the south-west. Some graves at Srednica-Zgornja Hajdina and Orehova date to La Tène B1 and several objects from Srednica have parallels with finds from southern Slovakia, and this small cemetery of just four graves is clearly an intrusive rite in the local context (Lubšina-Tušek and Kavur 2009, 2011).

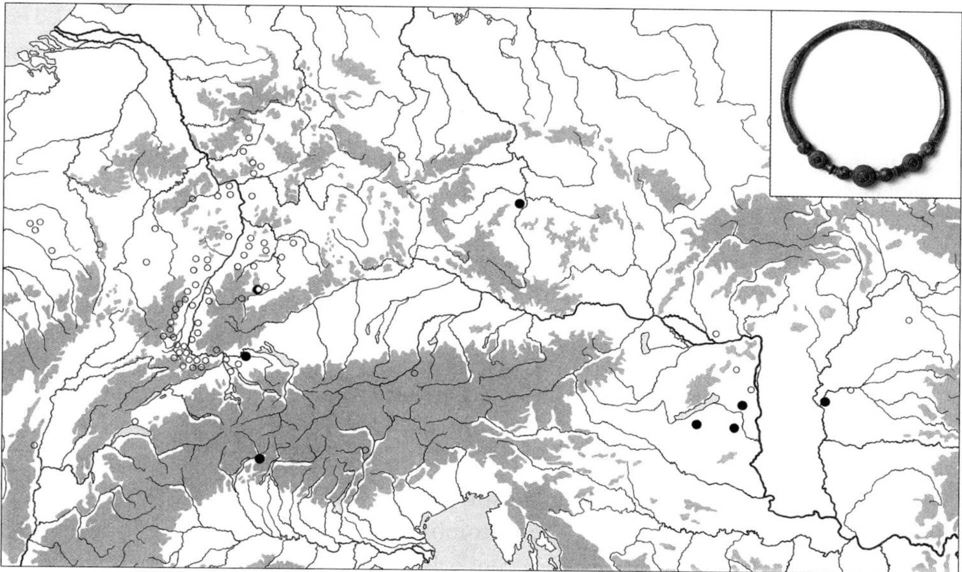

FIGURE 37.6 Heavily worn neck-rings (*Scheibenhalsringe*; black dots) in relation to all neck-rings (open circles). Most examples are from the upper Rhine region; the higher proportion of worn examples in the Carpathian basin may indicate that they were old when they were deposited, having been brought by migrants. Inset: neck-ring from Andelfingen, Switzerland.

Source: Müller 1989: Abb. 33

The Balkan Peninsula

Celtic objects found in the Balkan peninsula are traditionally interpreted as evidence of Celts involved in the invasion of 279 BC, but the situation is both subtler and more complicated. According to the historical sources, the Balkans were inhabited by several peoples including Thracians, Geto-Dacians, Scythians, and Greeks; perhaps because of this, assemblages composed solely of distinctive Celtic objects are rare. Most Celtic objects are single finds of brooches and bracelets from indigenous Thracian contexts. At this time, the Thracians were emulating many aspects of Hellenistic culture from the Aegean, Anatolia, and the eastern Mediterranean, including urbanism and coinage. These items are as likely to indicate trade and exchange between Thracians and Celts and/or acculturation as they are to indicate invaders; moreover, some objects may have arrived before the invasions and settlements. The gold torc with Waldalgesheim-related decoration from Gorni Tsibar, northern Bulgaria, is likely to date to the late fourth century BC (Megaw 2004, 2005); along with other high-status objects it could have arrived through exogamous marriage or in gift exchange (Emilov 2007; Rustoiu 2011).

In fact, only a comparatively small number of Celtic objects come from south of the Balkan mountains and even fewer from contexts plausibly associated with the invasions. Even so, these include settlements, burials, and hoards. The Hellenistic city or *emporion* of Pistiros in south-west Bulgaria was destroyed twice in the early third century BC. The first destruction is dated to *c.*300 BC, which has been linked to the attacks on Thrace that were stopped by Lysimachus in 298 BC, although there is no conclusive evidence. The city was soon rebuilt but did not survive the second assault. This time the finds from the destruction levels include several fragmentary La Tène swords and scabbards, spears, and a Duchcov brooch. A large hoard of Hellenistic coins beneath the floor of a building ends with issues of Lysimachus. The damage ended urban life in Pistiros and the attack is plausibly associated with Belgios in 279/278 BC (Bouzek 2005a). A contemporary destruction level at the nearby fortress of Krakra may also be associated with this attack (Emilov 2005). However, most of the major settlements in Thrace appear to have been unaffected.

A different strand of evidence comes from the Macedonian royal cemetery at Vergina/Aegae, in north-east Greece, best known for what is very probably the tomb of Philip of Macedon. Pyrrhus reportedly employed Celtic mercenaries in his struggle with Antigonus Gonatus for the Macedonian throne and Plutarch relates how they infamously desecrated and plundered the royal tombs at Vergina in 276 BC (*Life of Pyrrhus* 26.6). Several destroyed tombs have recently been excavated and fragments of once sumptuous gold grave goods recovered.

However, as we have seen, correlating individual objects with historical accounts is not straightforward. A pair of *Hohlbuckelringe* from the Spanos well near the temple of Isthmia at Corinth were long associated with the events of 279 BC (e.g. Krämer 1961; Maier 1973; Müller-Karpe 1988) but their find context dates to *c.*350–325 BC (Blečić Kavur and Kavur 2012). A brooch from the sanctuary of Apollo in Delos and a sword from Dodona are also likely to pre-date the raid (Szabó 1971; Megaw 2004). Such finds continue the practice of depositing Celtic objects in sanctuaries, as evidenced at the nearby sanctuary of Heraion of Perachora (Shefton 2004) and elsewhere (Verger 2003), and by later finds in Sicily and Italy (Baitinger 2012). Celtic weapons are also mentioned in an inventory dating to the first half of the fourth century BC from the temple of Athena on the acropolis in Athens (Freeman 1996). Rather than being spoil from the great Celtic expedition dedicated by the victors, these finds, like the gold torc from Gorni Tsibar, may reflect earlier contacts of a different kind.

The vaulted tomb or *tholos* at Mal Tepe, Mezek, in south-east Bulgaria, is a famous find of Celtic objects for which different interpretations have been advanced. The tomb had been disturbed, and because it contained secondary interments it is unclear with which burial(s) some objects were associated, although the Celtic finds are recorded as found in the corridor leading to the tomb. The tomb was probably built in the later fourth century BC, but if the Plastic style decoration of the chariot fittings dates to the third century BC (as seems likely on typological grounds), these were probably associated with the secondary burials. It has been suggested that the *tholos* was reused for a Celtic chariot burial, but it is not certain that all the chariot was present and, as the fittings are the only Celtic-type objects in the tomb, it has also been argued that they could be trophies collected from the battlefield at Lysimachia where the Celts were defeated in 277 BC, placed in the grave to symbolize the deeds of the deceased, who might have been a general to Antigonus Gonatas (Emilov and Megaw 2012). Although some distance from Lysimachia (*c.*100 km), Mal Tepe is still one of the most southerly finds of Celtic objects in Bulgaria.

Other graves have been proposed as those of invading Celts, among them three in the large cemeteries at Ohrid-Gorna-Porta, the Hellenistic city of Lychnidos, in south-west Macedonia. Cremation grave 138 contained a typical east Celtic helmet, a sword, scabbard and sword chain, three spears, and a shield boss. Based on the panoply of weapons, the deceased can plausibly be identified as a Celt, but the grave also contained a circular shield boss of Macedonian type and a curved knife commonly found in Illyria (Guštin et al. 2012). A similar mixture of grave goods and funerary rites occurs in Bulgaria, for example at Plovdiv (Bouzek 2005b: 67, figs 7–9; Emilov 2005: 107, 2010: 79–82, figs 4–7). There are also several Celtic swords in Bulgaria (e.g. Anastassov 2011; Anastassov et al. 2013), but as they are older discoveries about which little information is available, the mixture of objects in graves like Ohrid-Gorna-Porta and Plovdiv cautions against interpreting such single finds as denoting the grave of a Celt.

This mixture of Celtic and Thracian objects also occurs in settlement contexts. Most excavated Celtic finds in Bulgaria come from indigenous sites north of the Balkan mountains, particularly in the north-east where there are concentrations at fortified Thracian settlements that have strong Hellenistic influences. At Sboryanovo—identified as Helis, the capital of the Getae, and thought to have been destroyed by an earthquake around 250 BC—over 60% of the brooches from recent excavations are Celtic types, and many were probably made there. They are a mixture of Duchcov and Münsingen varieties, closely related to examples in the Carpathian basin in Hungary and Romania, and local forms. One or two *Hohlbuckelringe* found near the south gate and graphite-coated pottery of central European type suggest contact with the north (Emilov 2005). Conversely, Celtic objects from the graves of high-status females in some Thracian cemeteries in north-east Bulgaria have been interpreted as indicating marriage alliances between Celtic and Thracian elites. The production of Celtic types of brooches in Bulgaria could indicate the adoption of Celtic fashions by other ethnic groups.

When the Celts retreated from Delphi, they established the kingdom of Tylis amongst the Thracians. The kingdom is traditionally located in south-east Bulgaria (e.g. Emilov 2005; Falileyev 2010), but 73% of Celtic-type objects of all dates come from the north-east. The finds include the core distribution of coins issued by Kavaros, the last Celtic king of Tylis (Anastassov 2011).

Other Celtic settlement areas founded or reformed after the raids of 279 BC include those of the Scordisci and the Triballi in the southern Carpathian basin, but the impact of the returning groups may perhaps be identified more widely. Some cemeteries founded in La Tène B2 as far apart as Belgrade-Karaburma, Serbia, and Remetea Mare in the Romanian Banat have a high proportion of graves with weapons—up to 70%. These have been suggested as the graves of military groups returning from the Balkan venture rather than typical agrarian communities (Rustoiu 2006: 61–62). Lower numbers of weapons in the subsequent La Tène C1 cemeteries may reflect changing rites and a lesser emphasis on warrior status, but could also indicate an increase in mercenary service from which many never returned.

Two graves illustrate the complexity of the archaeological evidence. The woman buried in Grave 3 at Remetea Mare stands out as the only inhumation in a La Tène B2/C1 cremation cemetery, and might be from Thrace (Rustoiu 2006: 215–216, figs 6–8). Her belt plate is of a style well known in the north Balkans and typical of the Scordisic area, but a Thracian-style brooch, as well as pottery and iron tweezers, are interpreted as showing that she had travelled north to Remetea Mare from a contact zone between the Thracians and the Illyrian Scordisci, where inhumation was the dominant rite. Conversely, an isolated grave at Teleşti, Oltenia, in southern Romania, which contained typical La Tène C1 jewellery (brooches, a belt chain, and bracelets) and also a horse bit, may be that of a woman from a Celtic territory who moved to a Thracian community, perhaps after marrying a Get (Rustoiu 2005, 2011). This offers another example of how individuals might change residences, perhaps in marriage, probably at an elite level.

Graves with mixed grave goods at Mannersdorf in Lower Austria (e.g. Grave 76) have also been interpreted in the context of the Great Raid (Ramsl 2007: 327–328, figs 15–16, 2011). Other likely evidence for the aftermath of the raid comes from small white or translucent vase-shaped glass beads. These were made in Greece but their distribution encompasses Slovenia and the Carpathian basin, and extends into Austria, Slovakia, and the Czech Republic, where they are often found in female graves (Schönfelder 2007). It is not known if the beads were worn by women from Greece, or whether just the beads were brought back or exchanged.

The few other Greek and Macedonian objects found to the north are often interpreted as loot from the raid. A Greek bronze *kylix* from the Szob cemetery near Budapest is the only such find north of the Balkan peninsula (Szabó 1992: 156). But other interpretations are possible: the fourth-century BC Macedonian bronze *situla* and cup (*phiale*) from Grave 22 at Belgrade-Karaburma, and a ceramic *oinochoe* from Grave 316 at Kostolac-Pećine, Serbia (Blečić Kavur and Kavur 2012), both pre-date the raid and could indicate the adoption of Greek customs before 279 BC. Some La Tène A graves in Germany and northern France containing long iron spear ferrules whose construction imitates Greek examples may also reflect earlier contact. The ferrule (*sauroter*) fitted onto the long lance used by Hoplites; knowledge of their use is likely to have been gained on the battlefields of the Greek world (Schönfelder 2007, challenged by Baray 2014).

Delphi: 279 BC

Although the emphasis of the Greek writers is on the Great Raid of 279 BC, archaeological evidence paints a more wide-ranging and subtle picture. While discoveries like the destruction levels at Pistiros are compatible with this narrative, some Celtic finds in the Balkans are earlier and require a different explanation, as do the *sauroter*-derived ferrules in central and western Europe. While the 'early' finds could be associated with the previous invasions of 298 or even 310 BC, several come from pan-Hellenic sanctuaries, suggesting earlier and regular contacts. It should be remembered that after 335 BC the Celts of the Adriatic agreed a treaty with Alexander the Great and a delegation of Celts was among those who travelled to Babylon in 323 BC to pay their respects. The gold torc from Gorni Tsibar might represent one such diplomatic alliance, this time with a Thracian group, while a few Macedonian objects found in Serbia suggest that some Hellenistic customs were adopted by Celtic groups before 279 BC. The implications of an earlier dating of La Tène C have yet to be considered fully but imply that Celtic settlement extended south at an earlier date than traditionally thought. It seems likely that the Great Raid followed at least half a century of direct contact between Celts and the Hellenistic *koiné*. In many ways, the raids were dramatic events that illuminated longer and more slow-moving processes.

Most Celtic objects in the Balkan peninsula come from a mixed milieu. Most finds in Bulgaria come from Thracian cities, and while some seem likely to indicate the area of Celtic settlement after 279 BC, others were used and made by Thracians. Brooches may indicate that Thracians adopted aspects of Celtic dress at the same time as they were embracing Hellenistic culture. North of the Danube, graves of females buried with complete costumes that were foreign to the area (not just a single brooch) suggest that exogamy was one of the social institutions that facilitated this assimilation.

In this multicultural environment (Rustoiu 2014; Vranić 2014), soldiers from different groups used the weapons of other groups. They would have experienced the utility of the weaponry both as opponents and when serving alongside one another as allies or mercenaries and being paid with the same coinage. Men identified as Celtic were buried with their own weapons and those of Macedonians in the cemeteries of Hellenistic Lychnidos, which suggests that they had been integrated into a different culture. At the same time, the high proportion of weapons in some cemeteries in Serbia and Romania may indicate that these were the burial grounds of groups returning from the south.

The main consequences of the Celtic migration for Celtic groups were thus twofold. In the Balkan peninsula, there was an assimilation of Celtic peoples and the adoption of Celtic traits within an already multicultural environment. To the north, some migrant peoples created new settlements and communities (such as the Scordisci: Mihajlović 2014), but others returned to lands north of the Danube to join established communities in a form of chain migration.

Anatolia (Asia Minor)

In many regards the archaeological evidence for Asia Minor is comparable to that from the Balkan peninsula. As noted, some 20,000 people from three tribes are reported to have crossed the Hellespont in 278 BC. They settled in northern Anatolia, inland from the Black Sea, where they were known as the Galatae. But few distinctively Celtic objects and no clearly Celtic settlements are known, and (perhaps more noteworthy) there are no distinctively Celtic burials. The royal cemetery at Karalar is identified as Galatian rather than Hellenistic because of a Greek inscription. The most common Celtic finds in

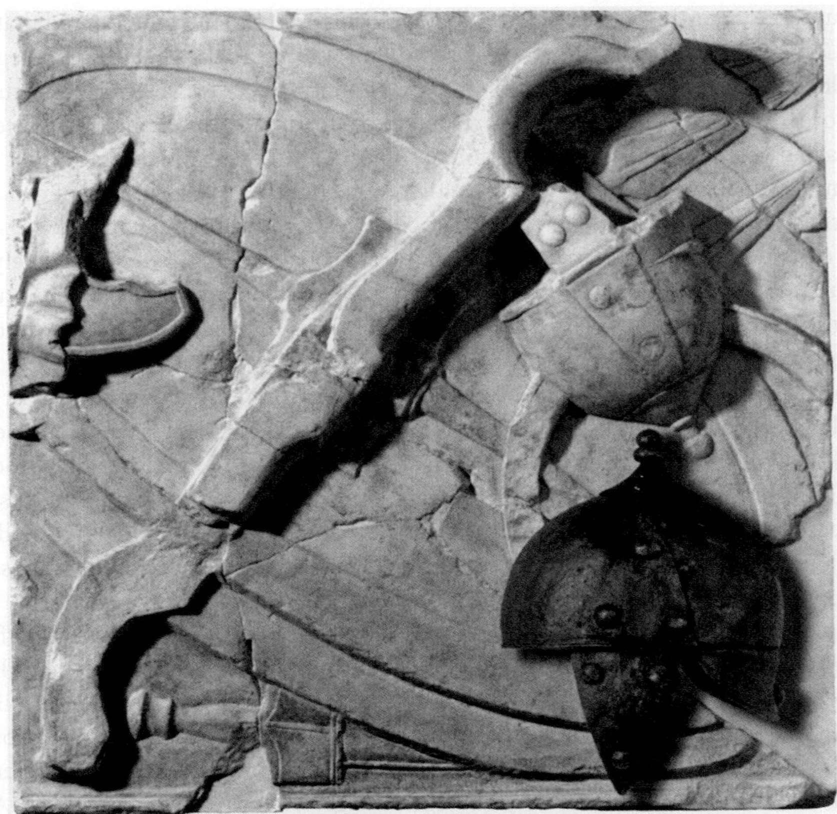

FIGURE 37.7 Detail from a relief from the acropolis of Athena Nikephoros at Pergamon with a photograph of an actual Celtic helmet from Batina, Croatia, superimposed. Although the original object does not have horns, the similarities between the two helmets are clear and the sculpture vividly depicts the presence of ancient Celts in modern Turkey.

Source: Hauschild 2010b: Abb. 3

Anatolia are La Tène C brooches, although jewellery—particularly bracelets—and occasional pots are also found (Polenz 1978: fig. 15; Müller-Karpe 1988, 2006). The Galatian Celts rapidly adopted a Hellenistic material culture, and the clearest evidence for their presence is arguably the great monuments at Pergamon built by the kings of Bithynia to commemorate their victories over them (Figure 37.7).

A few La Tène brooches are known from the east Mediterranean, in Syria and Lebanon, which are usually associated with either Galatian raids or mercenary service after 279/278 BC (Courbin 1999; Bouzek 2005a: 93). A well-preserved wooden shield from Kasr el-Harit, in the Fayum oasis, Egypt, is often associated with Celts because of its oval shape (e.g. Kimmig 1940; Cunliffe 1997), but the use of multiple layers of wood to make it, its convex profile, and its shape are just as consistent with it being a Roman *scutum* (but see Künzl 2003).

Ukraine and Belarus

Celtic objects occur sporadically in the north Pontic region and adjacent areas, notably in the Zakarpats'ka region of south-west Ukraine, continuing the distribution from south-east Poland and northern Hungary. Some come from inhumation burials, but most are settlement finds, associated with sunken-featured buildings, wheel-thrown pottery, ironworking, and some glassworking; they are usually dated to La Tène C. The appearance of these new features in the early third century BC in the north Thracian Kushtanovycya group is usually interpreted as indicating the arrival of outsiders. The largest assemblage, from the settlement at Galish-Lovachka, includes Celtic swords and linchpins from vehicles. A handful of cremation burials mix Thracian and Celtic grave goods (Olędzki 2005; Kazakevich 2012).

The situation is less clear-cut to the south and east. Celtic-type objects occur in several Greek colonies along the western Black Sea coast (Zirra 1979), but a scatter of finds from Moldova and Ukraine east of the Carpathians is often seen as evidence for migration (e.g. Machinskiy 1974; Cunliffe 1997). An inscription from Olbia on the north Black Sea coast commemorates Protogenes for funding the renewal of the defences when the Greek colony was threatened by Celts in the late third or earlier second century BC. However, the interpretation of individual finds, which are mostly from the Dniester and Dnieper basins, is not straightforward. Those from the Dniester valley are broadly contemporary with the Celtic finds in the Balkan peninsula and share the emphasis on female jewellery seen in Thrace, as well as technical traits (e.g. double springs); while the identification of some brooches as Celtic is debatable (Babeş 2005), features of others ('Zarubincy fibulae') find parallels in the middle Danube region.

Some brooches occur in graves of the Pomeranian and Zarubincy groups but most are stray finds. A mould for making bracelets is known from Olbia, so, as in Bulgaria, the Celtic-style brooches and other ornaments may be regional products, indicating the adoption of Celtic styles of clothing and fashion rather than migration. However, viewed as an assemblage, the composition of the finds from the Dniester basin is comparable to that from Anatolia (largely jewellery, with small quantities of pottery), there interpreted as indicating a migration because of the historical sources.

Further east in Scythia Magna, a scatter of finds along the Dnieper basin extends as far as Belarus. The northern Black Sea region was populated by a complex range of societies, not solely nomadic pastoralists like the Sarmatians or Scythians, although this characterization may be broadly correct for the Volga/Don and Ural steppes (Mordvintseva 2013; Chapter 15). Consequently, the interpretation of various objects, for example neck-rings, as of Celtic manufacture is uncertain (e.g. Almássy 2010). Some items—such as the bronze bracelets, glass beads, and a possible iron sword chain from the Milograd culture hillfort at Goroshkov—might indicate trade. However, a cremation burial found in 1900 at Zalissya in the Chernobyl district was accompanied by a bronze Duchcov brooch and a pot that can be compared to examples in eastern Europe.

Lower down the Dnieper valley at Vyshhetarasivka, a La Tène B2/C sword comparable to Bulgarian examples was found in an inhumation grave, although the integrity of the group is uncertain (Schukin 1995: 207, fig. 3; Kazakevich 2012: 183–184, fig. 7). Two swords and a brooch were also found in Crimea in a mausoleum in Neapolis, the capital of the Scythian kingdom. One, dating to La Tène C2, accompanied a burial interpreted as that of Skilurus, the king of Scythia Minor in the late second century BC; the other grave goods are Scythian (Reith 1965; Kazakevich 2012: 184–185, fig. 8).

The dates of the numerous Montefortino-type helmets found around the northern Black Sea littoral and Sea of Azov (Raev et al. 1995) have not yet been established satisfactorily. Often dated to the third century BC, many may actually be Roman, and associated with the Mithridatic wars of the first century BC. Other finds claimed to demonstrate the presence of Celts include representations of oval shields. A graffito on a third-century BC fresco from Nymphaion (Crimea) shows a Hellenistic ship called the Isis with four oval shields. Although the shape of shields is not a reliable guide to the ethnicity of their owners (Gunby 2000), these appear to have winged umbos typical of Celtic shields. They have been interpreted as indicating mercenaries, and the graffito to represent one of Ptolemy II of Egypt's ships present during the negotiations with the Bosporan King Persiades II in 280 and 254 BC.

An oval shield and a possibly Celtic anthropomorphic-handled sword are depicted on coins of the later third-century BC Bosporan ruler Leucon II (Treister 1993: 790, fig. 1). Similar shields are depicted on Bosporan gravestones of this date, while small terracotta figurines dating to the second century BC from the north Pontic Greek towns represent figures naked to the waist who might therefore be Celtic, along with others in Persian or Thracian dress (Gunby 2000). As no representations or finds are known in the adjoining regions, the contacts they represent were presumably by sea. The representations could be associated with the later La Tène-type brooches found in Anatolia and Crimea that some have interpreted as evidence of continuing mercenary activity by the Galatae, even though they had long been defeated as an independent power (Müller-Karpe 2006).

Mercenaries

The importance of mercenaries in Mediterranean armies, particularly those of the Hellenistic kings, is well attested, leading scholars to question whether some classical representations taken to show invading or migrating Celts might actually be of mercenaries. Archaeological studies of this institution in barbarian Europe have begun to appear only recently (Péré-Noquès 2007, 2013; Baray 2014), but certain burials have been identified as those of Celtic mercenaries and some innovations, notably the adoption of coinage, are often argued to be associated with it.

The grave goods from the La Tène C1 burial at Ciumeşti, Romania, included the famous iron helmet surmounted by a bird whose wings flap,[1] a suit of chain mail, and two bronze greaves that must have been made in the Hellenistic world. As greaves were made-to-measure, this suggests that the dead man portrayed himself as a Hellenistic officer. Other non-local objects from the Ciumeşti cemetery, such as a horse bit of a Thracian type well known in Bulgaria, could represent diplomatic gifts, probably of horses (Rustoiu 2006). The medical knowledge implicit in a small number of burials in central and eastern Europe that contain surgical instruments (Künzl 1991) may also have been accelerated by mercenary service.

Far away in France, the grave of a man buried in the fourth century BC in the small cemetery at Le Plessis Gassot near Paris has also been interpreted as the grave of a mercenary who had fought in Italy before returning to his homeland (Ginoux 2009). It contained weapons that have parallels in Italy and two Etruscan black-figure dishes (which are very rare in northern Europe). A small number of glass gaming pieces from France might also reflect return journeys from Italy, if they indicate the introduction of the game itself rather than trade (Diliberto and Lejars 2011). Some early third-century BC coins in Belgic Gaul are thought to be imitations of the coins of Syracuse used to pay mercenaries. In eastern Europe, coins of Philip II and Thasos provided the prototypes for the first coinages and it is often suggested that coinage was adopted by groups across Europe as a form of special purpose money to pay for military service, albeit not necessarily as a mercenary (e.g. Kruta 1982; Szabó 1983; Nash 1987; Fischer 1991)—although this has been challenged (Pion 2012; Baray 2014).

The networks connected with Mediterranean mercenary activity appear to have been far-reaching. The settlement at Nowa Cerekwia in Silesia (Poland) has yielded numerous Mediterranean coins, some of them Greek (Rudnicki 2012). The coins from the La Tène C1–2 trading settlement of Němčice-Víceměřice, Moravia, show a strong correlation with the Second Punic War between Rome and Carthage (218–201 BC) and, more surprisingly, the Sixth Syrian War between Ptolemaic Egypt and the Seleucid Empire (170–168 BC). Such distinctive patterns seem likely to indicate that these coins entered the coin pool circulating in central Europe with returning mercenaries.

Mercenary service may also have extended beyond Celtic areas. A few graves with a panoply of Celtic weapons are known in areas with no other obvious traces of Celtic settlement. In Saxony, there are La Tène A graves at Liebau and Dorna an der Mulde, and a La Tène B2/C1 grave at Groitzsch. The Liebau grave has been seen as that of the leader of a group of foreign metal prospectors from north-east Bavaria or west Bohemia exploring the rich copper resources of the Elbe valley near Dresden (Spehr 2002: 196, figs 13–17), but the grave at Dorna contains a ferrule from a Greek-style lance, suggesting an alternative interpretation.

Migrations of German Peoples

While the Celtic migrations have been the main focus of attention of the European pre-Roman Iron Age, they were only one of several cultural groupings, which included Celtiberians and Germans. The archaeological entity associated with the Germanic peoples for much of the later pre-Roman Iron Age in northern Germany, the Netherlands, and the coastal areas of western and central Scandinavia is the Jastorf culture.

Where Germanic migrations in the pre-Roman Iron Age are mentioned, it is again in relation to the Mediterranean world. The best known is the migration of the Cimbri and Teutones and their allies the Ambrones and Tignurni between 113 and 101 BC. While the historical sources outline where these peoples went during what was for Rome the Cimbrian War, they are silent on from where they came. Their homelands are inferred from later writers such as Ptolemy, who placed the Teutones in Jutland, leading to the assumption that they were Germanic.

The Cimbri and Teutones are first recorded in the Danube region, where they fought the Scordisci in *c.*113 BC. They then defeated Roman armies at Noreia (southern Austria or northern Slovenia) in 112 BC, in southern France in 109 BC, at Burdigala (Bordeaux) in 107 BC, and at Arausio (near Orange) in 105 BC. After fighting the Arverni, they set out towards the Pyrenees in 103 BC, but decided instead to attack north Italy. The tribes separated, with the Teutones and Ambrones taking a coastal route, and the Cimbri travelling north and east, entering Italy through the Tyrol. Both groups were then defeated by Marius—the Teutones at Aquae Sextiae (Aix-en-Provence) in 102 BC, and the Cimbri at Vercellae in 101.

The numbers reported are large, allegedly hundreds of thousands, but little archaeological evidence can be associated with these events. The case for linking coin hoards, such as that from Tayac, Gironde, to the raids is weak, but the site of the battle of Orange has plausibly been identified (Luginbühl 2014). The paucity of evidence may be compared with that relating to the Celtic attack on Delphi. In both cases the intent was to raid and plunder rather than settle. However, Julius Caesar's claim that the Aduatuci of northern Gaul were descended from a group of 6,000 whom the Cimbri and Teutones left behind (*de Bello Gallico* 2.29.4–5) is consistent with the slightly later material evidence that shows a fusion of Celtic and Germanic elements, although not all of Caesar's comments find archaeological support (e.g. the migration of the Helvetii).

Indirect evidence for the raids to the Danube and eastern Alps might conceivably come from the Gundestrup cauldron, found in a bog in Jutland. Its decorative style is a mixture of Celtic and Thracian. If such a fusion originated with the Scordisci, the migration of the Cimbri close to their territory could have provided the mechanism for the cauldron reaching Denmark (Bergquist and Taylor 1987). Other strands of Celtic influence have been identified in the north: cauldrons, display carts, and ball torcs; while numerically few, they are argued to have been very influential (Klindt-Jensen 1950; Kaul and Mertens 1995; Kaul 2007).

In contrast, archaeological evidence for the later migration of Germanic peoples is cogent. For much of the pre-Roman Iron Age, the dominant direction of cultural influence was from south to north (Müller 2007). Many locally made Celtic-style objects—primarily brooches, neck-rings, and bangles—have been found in graves and they copied types found to the south in Thuringia, Bohemia, and Moravia. It is suggested that these objects were used primarily in ritual contexts (Brandt 2001, 2010). It was only towards the end of the pre-Roman Iron Age that objects from the west were copied, at about the same time as strong Germanic influences became apparent in southern Germany, the Czech Republic, and Slovakia (Chropovský 1977; Nortmann 2007; Schäfer 2007; Salač and Bemmann 2009). These influences include distinctively Germanic belt hooks and Przeworsk-culture-style cremation urns. There was also considerable interchange of ideas, and many objects regarded as Celtic, particularly weaponry, have been found in Germanic areas and in southern Scandinavia, particularly Denmark. In the late pre-Roman Iron Age, it is not always possible to differentiate between what is German or Celtic (e.g. Brandt 2010; Łuciewicz 2010). A few finds, such as a brooch of central German origin from the well-furnished grave at Dühren, Baden-Württemberg, imply that long-distance and elite contacts played a part in these processes (Bockius 1990; Bockius and Łuczkiewicz 2004; Spohn 2009).

The changes in southern Germany east of the Rhine in the later second and first centuries BC include the abandonment of *oppida* and the end of coinage. It has been argued that these were associated with an overall decline in population that led to a vacuum across much of southern Germany (Rieckhoff-Pauli 1995). This steady 'Germanization' is widely accepted as indicating migration (e.g. Brandt 2001), and while it is this aspect of mobility that is usually emphasized, there is also evidence for mobility within some Germanic areas, albeit at an elite level (Schuster 2013).

These observations are consistent with the commentaries of Caesar, who describes a constant pressure from peoples east of the Rhine to resettle on the west side. This was largely due to the Suebi, some of whom had already settled among the Sequani, and others were preparing to cross the river. The Germanic Usipetes and Tencteri are said to have settled in the lower Rhine region to seek refuge from the Suebi. Although Caesar is widely considered to have overemphasized the role of the Rhine as a cultural boundary between Germans and Celts, and the lower Rhine appears to have been an area of cultural fusion, his broader narrative is consistent with archaeological evidence.

The lower Rhine was clearly not a major boundary and the aftermath of Caesar's campaign saw the resettlement of several tribes from the east bank. The Batavi are said by Tacitus to have originated as a group within the Chatti on the east bank of the middle Rhine, the Cugerni (originally part of the Sugambri) were forced to move by the Romans and the Ubii may have been too. Late Iron Age finds support Tacitus' account: the *triquetrum* coinage has links to the middle Rhine, while other objects are paralleled at the Dünsberg *oppidum* east of the Rhine, including brooches and distinctive types of pendants. These new tribes appeared and developed their own distinctive material culture in the territory formerly occupied by the Eburones, who were virtually destroyed by Caesar after they rebelled in 54 BC. It is possible that their territory was deliberately resettled (Roymans 2004).

These lower Rhine settlements are the first traces of the Germanic migrations of the Roman Iron Age. A massive Roman military presence on what became a permanent frontier along the Rhine and Danube, the establishment of cities and veteran colonies, trade beyond the frontier, and service as Roman auxiliaries all contributed to transforming Germanic society. The invasion of the Alemannic coalition in AD 231 and their subsequent settlement in the *Agri Decumates* marked the beginning of a series of invasions that lasted over 200 years—mostly to the south, or south-west to Gaul, although the Angles and Saxons migrated west to Britain. The Franks settled in Gaul with Roman permission, but according to Roman writers other settlements were born of violent conflicts. This aggression was to become an important theme in later Roman history.

Overview

The study of migration in Iron Age Europe has been driven by an interpretative model that reflects the dominance of the historical texts. Studies of migrations have thus focused geographically on the regions adjoining the Graeco-Roman world and chronologically on the later pre-Roman and Roman Iron Ages. The migrations of the Celts have been pre-eminent and were one of the key factors in the construction of a Celtic Iron Age, but movements of Germanic peoples were arguably no less significant.

Thanks to this model, except for the Phoenician and Greek colonies, migration was assumed to be mass migration that occurred rapidly and caused population displacement, and population and language replacement. This is partly because classical authors mostly wrote about 'barbarian' peoples when they appeared on the margins of their own lands as dangerous war bands thought to have been attracted by Mediterranean wealth. Nothing is known of the Cimbri and Teutones before they reached the territory of a Roman ally in the Tyrolean Alps, or of the eastern Celts until they were drawn into the internal conflicts of the Diadochi. In some cases, the claimed origins of peoples find little archaeological support (the Celtiberians), and they could be aetiological or origin myths as much as statements of historical fact.

A consequence of the historical emphasis is that the study of migration in the European Iron Age has been weakly theorized. Explanations have generally focused on the motives cited by classical writers, rather than on internal factors such as changes in social organization or population growth, or environmental causes such as soil exhaustion or climate change. Reasons given by classical writers often contradict one another, suggesting that they were stock phrases. Even if we accept Livy's explanation of overpopulation for the migration to Italy, his is an outside view of processes that may also have included regular fission of small groups from societies to provide opportunities for younger males or others to advance themselves socially. Such 'push' factors need to be included in a balanced interpretation of migration. The lure or 'pull' of Mediterranean riches and the cupidity or 'push' of the Celts do not in themselves provide a satisfactory explanation. While Livy mentions the migrations to the east, the focus on Rome has led to their receiving less attention, despite the more cogent archaeological evidence. The dominance of historical interpretation has resulted in the writing of 'tribal histories' that accept mass migration as the basis of settlement and as constituting an accurate historical framework for events. This has led to a corresponding emphasis on the correlation of archaeological remains with named peoples, such as the Anarti in the upper Tisza basin or the Scordisci around the confluence of the Sava, Drava, and Danube, and small numbers of distinctive grave goods have consequently been taken as reliable indicators of ethnicity.

While the ancient writers imply that most migrations were mass events, it is not clear how common this was. The planned migration of whole communities would have required familiarization with the lands to be passed through, the securing of safe passage, and knowledge of where they might be allowed or able to settle, whether peacefully or by force. Travel would have been along established routes (tracks, not roads), on foot, assisted by beasts of burden. Sea crossings would have been rare and limited by the number of seagoing vessels. The migration of a community is a process that, once started, might take many years, and it seems clear that the migrations to Italy and eastern Europe consisted of many small migrations that cumulatively comprised a chain migration.

There is little evidence for the wholesale population replacement anticipated by the mass migration model, largely because studies have concentrated on the lands that migrants travelled to, rather than those they left, and most of the archaeological evidence considered is funerary. Abrupt decreases in burial numbers can occasionally be identified, but without any corresponding change in the settlement evidence, as in Champagne in the third century BC. Where burials can be interpreted as those of migrants, they typically occur in small groups. Large cemeteries are rare, and isotope analyses indicate only a small proportion of migrants. Different mortuary rites and material cultures were shared rapidly between indigenous and migrant communities, creating a further layer of difficulty. Thus, Monte Bibele in Italy is interpreted as a Celtic cemetery on the basis of some La Tène objects, although there are more Etruscan and Greek ones. Other cemeteries, such as Pişcolt in Romania, have a few finds of central or western European origin, but most grave groups mix local varieties of Celtic types and indigenous objects. Little, if anything, is distinctively Celtic in the burial rites of the groups who settled in Bulgaria and Anatolia.

In the case of eastern Europe, this might indicate that migration was a slow process that lasted for generations, and the establishment of new Celtic cemeteries in Romania progressively further to the east and south is consistent with this. This also raises the question of whether the process might be better interpreted as acculturation rather than migration. The adoption of new objects and styles across large distances was well established in the Iron Age, exemplified by the occurrence of early La Tène belt hooks from northern Italy to northern France, or Duchcov-Münsingen brooches from Switzerland to Romania. Similarly, many Celtic objects in the Balkan peninsula are found with Thracian ones, those in south-west Ukraine with Zarubincy objects. Such an adoption of selected traits is often referred to by central European scholars as 'Latènization' or 'Germanization', albeit usually predicated on an implicit assumption that migration would be indicated by a normative or 'complete' archaeological culture.

Isotope analyses combined with high-precision radiocarbon dating have the potential to discriminate between such possibilities, but the few studies to date have not identified significant numbers of migrants, even among the earliest burials. This may be a factor of small sample size, and there are insufficient data to assess any differences between migrant cemeteries and parent communities. It may be anticipated that 'typical' patterns of movement will include changes in residency due to marriage, and in certain regions seasonal changes reflecting pastoral practices and transhumance, or the exploitation of marine resources. Such mobility is the product of regular social processes, rather than migration, and exogamous marriage may well provide a more accurate interpretation of several female burials accompanied by foreign or exotic grave goods in eastern Europe.

In contrast, some historically attested 'migrations' are perhaps better seen as short events. The Great Raid of 279/278 BC left few traces in the Balkan peninsula and apparently saw little booty returned. These events did, however, lead to the settlement of Celtic peoples as the kingdom of Tylis in Bulgaria, as the Scordisci in Croatia, and as the Galatae in Anatolia. There is archaeological evidence for all three settlements, although its precise interpretation, particularly in Bulgaria, is not without dispute.

Service in the armies of Hellenistic and other leaders around the Mediterranean world was responsible for the development of mercenary service as a distinctive social institution of the pre-Roman Iron Age in several regions. Mercenary service (as opposed to auxiliary service in the Roman army) was a form of circular migration that involved large numbers of men. The distances they travelled provides one explanation for the wide-ranging similarities in weaponry and the use of specific decorative motifs as a shared visual code that helped define warrior identities, that were more precisely defined than those presented by the distributions of late Bronze Age weapons. The use of Celtic weaponry may have been encouraged to sustain the identity—and perhaps the courage—of the soldiers (Lejars 2006), and in this sense the identity was situational. Many finds previously interpreted as indicating migration should probably instead be associated with mercenary service. The interregional and reciprocal scale of this institution again presents a challenge of how to move between different scales of analysis. Most Iron Age studies are at a local or regional scale; how they might contribute to analyses of ethnically defined peoples such as the Celtiberians or Germans is weakly theorized, despite the Anglophone 'Celtosceptic' debate.

Since the nineteenth century migration has been a defining theme of the European Iron Age, and the archaeological evidence across much of Europe is broadly consistent with the accounts of the classical writers. A wealth of new evidence from across Europe and new scientific techniques now provide the opportunity to recast the grand narratives into well-dated regional ones. Funerary evidence has the potential to allow detailed stories to be developed around individuals, but this needs to be integrated with palaeoenvironmental and settlement data. Other challenges include how to move between the classical accounts describing migration at a tribal or larger scale and the small scale of most archaeological studies, which reveal complex connections between material cultures, while the definition of identity and ethnicity is yet to be addressed fully. Another obstacle is the need to bridge different specialisms, for example between Thracian and Celtic archaeology, or between proto-historic archaeology and classical studies. Renewed interest in migration has great potential but will only be fulfilled by rethinking how the European Iron Age is studied.

Postscript

The preliminary results of the first large-scale studies of Iron Age DNA in western Europe are now becoming available (e.g. Armit 2023; Fischer et al. 2022 and literature cited therein). While these studies have not identified large-scale genetic changes of the sorts that transformed understandings of earlier periods, they confirm that, when combined with stable isotope analyses, fine-grained detail about the relationships between the people buried in Iron Age cemeteries will be available shortly.

Note

1. Illustrated in Chapter 14, Figure 7.

References

Almássy, K. 2010. 'Some new data on the Scythian-Celtic relationship', in E. Jerem, M. Schönfelder, and G. Wieland (eds) *Nord-Süd, Ost-West. Kontakte während der Eisenzeit in Europa. Akten der Internationalen Tagungen der AG Eisenzeit in Hamburg und Sopron 2002*. Archaeolingua Main Series 17: 9–25. Budapest: Archaeolingua.

Alt, K. W., P. Jud, F. Müller, N. Nicklisch, A. Uerpmann, and W. Vach. 2005. 'Biologische Verwandtschaft und soziale Struktur im latènezeitlichen Gräberfeld von Münsingen-Rain'. *Jahrbuch des Römisch-Germanischen Zentralmuseums* 52, 1: 157–210.

Anastassov, J. 2011. 'The Celtic presence in Thrace during the 3rd century BC in light of new archaeological data', in M. Guštin and M. Jevtić (eds) *The Eastern Celts: The Communities between the Alps and the Black Sea*: 7–15. Koper/Belgrade: University of Primorska/University of Belgrade.

Anastassov, J., R. Megaw, V. Megaw, and E. Mircheva. 2013. 'Walt Disney comes to Bulgaria. A bronze mount in the Museum of Archaeology, Varna', in S. Krausz, A. Colin, K. Gruel, I. Ralston, and T. Dechezleprêtre (eds) *L'âge du Fer en Europe: Mélanges offerts à Olivier Buchsenschutz*: 551–565. Bordeaux: Ausonius.

Anthony, D. W. 1990. 'Migration in archaeology: The baby and the bathwater'. *American Anthropologist* 92: 23–42.

Anthony, D. W. 1997. 'Prehistoric migration as social process', in J. Chapman and H. Hamerow (eds) *Migrations and Invasions in Archaeological Explanation*. British Archaeological Reports International Series 664: 21–32. Oxford: Archaeopress.

Anthoons, G. 2007. 'The origins of the Arras culture: Migration or elite networks?', in R. Karl and J. Leskovar (eds) *Interpretierte Eisenzeiten. Fallstudien, Methoden, Theorien. Tagungsbeiträge der* 2. Linzer Gespräche zur interpretativen Eisenzeitarchäologie: 141–151. Linz: Oberösterreichisches Landesmuseum.

Anthoons, G. 2010. 'Les gestes funéraires et l'échange culturel entre la Gaule et la culture d'Arras du Yorkshire de l'Est', in P. Barral, B. Dedet, F. Delrieu, P. Giraud, I. Le Goff, S. Marion, and A. V.-L. Tiec (eds) *L'âge du Fer en Basse-Normandie. Gestes funéraires en Gaule au Second Âge du Fer. Actes du XXXIIIe colloque international de l'AFEAF, Caen, 20–24 mai 2009*.

Annales littéraires de l'université de Franche-Comté 883/Série Environnement, sociétés et archéologie 14: 31–35. Besançon: Presses universitaires de Franche-Comté.

Anthoons, G. 2013. 'La mobilité des druides et la diffusion de gestes funéraires', in A. Colin and F. Verdin (eds) *L'âge du Fer en Aquitaine et sur ses marges. Mobilité des hommes, diffusions des idées, circulation des biens dans l'espace européen à l'âge du Fer. Actes du XXXVe colloque de l'AFEAF, Bordeaux, juin 2011*. Aquitania supplément 30: 417–428. Bordeaux: Fédération Aquitania.

Armit, I. 2023. 'The COMMIOS project', in M. Fernández-Götz, C. Nimura, P. Stockhammer, and R. Cartwright (eds) *Rethinking Mobility in Late Prehistoric Eurasia. Proceedings of the British Academy* 254: 280–291. London: The British Academy.

Arnold, B. 1988. 'Slavery in late prehistoric Europe: recovering evidence for social structure in Iron Age society', in D. B. Gibson and M. N. Geselowitz (eds) *Tribe and Polity in Late Prehistoric Europe: Demography, Production, and Exchange in the Evolution of Complex Social Systems*: 179–192. New York: Plenum.

Arnold, B. 1995. '"Honorary males" or women of substance? Gender, status and power in Iron Age Europe'. *Journal of European Archaeology* 3, 2: 153–168.

Arnold, B. 2005. 'Mobile men, sedentary women? Material culture as a marker of regional and supra-regional interaction in Iron Age Europe', in H. Dobrzańska, V. Megaw, and P. Poleska (eds) *Celts on the Margin: Studies in European Cultural Interaction, 7th century BC–1st century AD Dedicated to Zenon Woźniak*: 17–26. Krakow: Institute of Archaeology and Ethnology of the Polish Academy of Sciences.

Babeş, M. 2005. 'The brooch from Horodnica: Dacian, Celtic or Germanic?', in H. Dobrzańska, V. Megaw, and P. Poleska (eds) *Celts on the Margin: Studies in European Cultural Interaction, 7th century BC–1st century AD Dedicated to Zenon Woźniak*: 121–129. Krakow: Institute of Archaeology and Ethnology of the Polish Academy of Sciences.

Baitinger, H. 2012. 'Fibeln vom Mittelatèneschema auf Sizilien und Kalabrien'. *Archäologisches Korrespondenzblatt* 59: 365–389.

Baray, L. 2014. *Les mercenaires celtes et la culture de La Tène. Critères archéologiques et positions sociologiques*. Dijon: Éditions universitaires de Dijon.

Bergquist, A., and T. Taylor. 1987. 'The origin of the Gundestrup cauldron'. *Antiquity* 61: 10–24.

Blečić Kavur, M., and B. Kavur. 2012. 'Grob 22 iz beogradske nekropole Karaburma: retrospektiva i perspektiva'. *Starinar* 60: 57–84.

Bochnak, T. 2006. 'Les Celtes et leurs voisins septentrionaux', in M. Szabó (ed.) *Celtes et Gaulois: l'archéologie face à l'histoire. Les Civilisés et les Barbares du Ve au IIe siècle avant J.-C. Actes de la table ronde de Budapest, 17–18 juin 2005*. Collection Bibracte 12/3: 159–183. Glux-en-Glenne: Centre archéologique européen du Mont Beuvray.

Bochnak, T. 2011. 'The eastern Celts in the north', in M. Guštin and M. Jevtić (eds) *The Eastern Celts: The Communities between the Alps and the Black Sea*: 13–17. Koper/Belgrade: University of Primorska/University of Belgrade.

Bockius, R. 1990. 'Das reiche Grab von Dühren—ein Zeugnis politischer Verflechtungen Europas im 2. Jahrhundert v. Chr.'. *Jahrbuch des Römisch-Germanischen Zentralmuseums Mainz* 37: 675–677.

Bockius, R., and P. Łuczkiewicz. 2004. *Kelten und Germanen im 2.–1. Jahrhundert vor Christus. Archäologische Bausteine zu einer historischen Frage*. Mainz: Römisch-Germanisches Zentralmuseum.

Bouzek, J. 2005a. The Duchcov fibula in Bulgaria and the destructions of Pistiros in 279/8 BC, in H. Dobrzańska, V. Megaw, and P. Poleska (eds) *Celts on the Margin: Studies in European*

Cultural Interaction, 7th century BC–1st century AD Dedicated to Zenon Woźniak: 93–101. Krakow: Institute of Archaeology and Ethnology of the Polish Academy of Sciences.

Bouzek, J. 2005b. *Thracians and their Neighbours*. Studia Hercyna 9. Prague: Institute of Classical Archaeology, Charles University.

Brandt, J. 2001. *Jastorf and Latène. Kultureller Austausch und seine Auswirkungen auf soziopolitische Entwicklungen in der vorrömische Eisenzeit*. Internationale Archäologie 66. Rahden: Marie Leidorf.

Brandt, J. 2010. 'Die Latènisierung der Jastorfkultur. Kulturkontakt als Folge germanischer Raum-Zeit-Konzeptionen', in E. Jerem, M. Schönfelder, and G. Wieland (eds) *Nord-Süd, Ost-West. Kontakte während der Eisenzeit in Europa. Akten der Internationalen Tagungen der AG Eisenzeit in Hamburg und Sopron 2002*. Archaeolingua Main Series 17: 51–59. Budapest: Archaeolingua.

Bridgman, T. P. 2003. 'The "Gallic disaster". Did Dionysus I of Syracuse order it?'. *Proceedings of the Harvard Celtic Colloquium* 23: 40–51.

Brown, K. 2014. 'Women on the move. The DNA evidence for female mobility and exogamy in prehistory', in J. Leary (ed.) *Past Mobilities*: 155–173. Farnham: Ashgate.

Bujna, J. 1998. 'Münsingen-Rain und die keltischen Gräberfelder im mittleren Donaugebiet. Kontakte im Spiegel des frühlatènezeitlichen Fundmaterials', in F. Müller (ed.) *Münsingen-Rain. Ein Markstein der keltischen Archäologie. Funde, Befunde und Methoden im Vergleich*. Schriften des Bernischen Historischen Museums 2: 171–203. Bern: Bernisches Historisches Museum.

Burmeister, S. 2000. 'Archaeology and migration: Approaches to an archaeological proof of migration'. *Current Anthropology* 41: 539–567.

Champion, T. C. 1980. 'Mass migration in later prehistoric Europe', in P. Sörbom (ed.) *Transport, Technology and Social Change*: 31–42. Stockholm: Tekniska Museet.

Champion, T. C. 1990. 'Migrations reviewed'. *Danish Journal of Archaeology* 9: 214–218.

Champion, T. C. 2013. 'Protohistoric European migrations', in *The Encyclopedia of Global Human Migration*. Chichester: Wiley. onlinelibrary.wiley.com/doi/10.1002/9781444351071.wbeghm425/references

Chapman, J., and H. Hamerow (eds). 1997. *Migration and Invasions in Archaeological Explanation*. British Archaeological Reports International Series 664. Oxford: Archaeopress.

Charpy, J.-J. 1991. 'Esquisse d'une ethnographie en Champagne aux IVe et IIIe siècles avant J.-C.'. *Études celtiques* 28: 75–125.

Charpy, J.-J. 2009. 'La question de la continuité ou de la discontinuité dans les nécropoles celtiques de la Champagne'. *Revue Archéologique de Picardie* 2009, 3–4: 71–83.

Chropovský, B. (ed.) 1977. *Symposium Ausklang der Latène-Zivilisation und Anfänge der germanischen Besiedlung im mittleren Donaugebiet*. Bratislava: VEDA, Vydavateľstvo Slovenskej akadémie vied.

Čižmář, M. 1995. 'Beitrag zur Erkenntnis der fremden Einflüsse auf dem mährischen Gebiet in der Stufe La Tène B1', in J.-J. Charpy (ed.) *L'Europe celtique du Ve au IIIe siècle avant J.-C.: contacts, échanges et mouvements de populations. Actes du IIe symposium international d'Hautvillers, 8–10 octobre 1992*: 69–75. Sceaux: Kronos B.Y. Editions.

Čižmář, M. 2005. 'Contacts between Moravia and the territory of the Scordisci', in H. Dobrzańska, V. Megaw, and P. Poleska (eds) *Celts on the Margin: Studies in European Cultural Interaction, 7th century BC–1st century AD Dedicated to Zenon Woźniak*: 131–134. Krakow: Institute of Archaeology and Ethnology of the Polish Academy of Sciences.

Čižmář, M., E. Kolníková, and H.-C. Noeske. 2008. 'Němčice-Víceměřice—ein neues Handels- und Industriezentrum der Latènezeit in Mähren'. *Germania* 86, 2: 655–700.

Clark, G. 1966. 'The invasion hypothesis in British archaeology'. *Antiquity* 40: 172–189.

Clarke, D. L. 1968. *Analytical Archaeology*. London: Methuen.

Collis, J. R. 2003. *The Celts: Origins, myths, inventions*. Stroud: Tempus.

Collis, J. R. 2014. 'The Celts. More myths and inventions', in C. N. Popa and S. Stoddart (eds) *Fingerprinting the Iron Age: Approaches to Identity in the European Iron Age. Integrating South-Eastern Europe into the Debate*: 290–305. Oxford: Oxbow.

Courbin, P. 1999. 'Une fibule de La Tène à Bassit (Syrie)', in B. Chaume, J.-P. Mohen, and P. Périn (eds) *Archéologie des Celtes. Mélanges à la mémoire de René Joffroy*. Protohistoire europèene 3: 93–97. Montagnac: Monique Mergoil.

Cunliffe, B. W. 1997. *The Ancient Celts*. Oxford: Oxford University Press.

de Mortillet, G. 1871. 'Les Gaulois de Marzabotto dans l'Apennin'. *Revue Archéologique* 22: 288–290.

Déchelette, J. 1914. *Manuel d'archéologie préhistorique, celtique et gallo-romaine, II-3: Second âge du Fer ou époque de La Tène*. Paris: Picard.

Defente, V. 2012. 'Red glass in Iron Age continental Europe: technical innovation and technological transfer', in A. Kern, J. K. Koch, I. Balzer, J. Fries-Knoblach, K. Kowarik, C. Later, P. C. Ramsl, P. Trebsche, and J. Wiethold (eds) *Technologieentwicklung und -transfer in der Eisenzeit. Bericht der Internationalen Tagung der AG Eisenzeit und des Naturhistorischen Museums, Prähistorische Abteilung, Hallstatt 2009*. Beiträge zur Ur- und Frühgeschichte Mitteleuropas 65: 219–225. Langenweißbach: Beier und Beran.

Dehn, W. 1979. 'Einige Überlegungen zum Charakter keltischer Wanderungen', in P.-M. Duval and V. Kruta (eds) *Les mouvements celtiques du Ve au Ier siècle avant notre ère. Actes du XXVIIIe colloque organisé à l'occasion du IXe Congrès International des Sciences Préhistoriques et Protohistoriques, Nice, le 19 septembre 1976*: 15–20. Paris: Centre National de la Recherche Scientifique.

Diepeveen-Jansen, M. 2001. *People, Ideas and Goods: New Perspectives on 'Celtic Barbarians' in Western and Central Europe (500–250 BC)*. Amsterdam Archaeological Studies 7. Amsterdam: Amsterdam University Press.

Dietler, M. 1994. 'Our ancestors the Gauls: archaeology, ethnic nationalism, and the manipulation of Celtic identity in modern Europe'. *American Anthropologist* 96: 584–605.

Diliberto, M., and T. Lejars. 2011. 'Mobilità celtica. A proposito di una pedina da gioco centro-italica trovata in Gallia', in S. Casini (ed.) *'Il Filo del Tempo'. Studi di preistoria e protostoria in onore di Raffaele Carlo de Marinis*. Notizie Archeologiche Bergomensi 19: 411–425. Bergamo: Comune di Bergamo.

Dizdar, M. 2009. 'Željezni pojasi tipa zvonimirovo LT 6 kao dio Ženske srednjolatenske nošnje u zapadnoj panoniji i na jugoistočnoalpskom prostoru'. *Vjesnik Arheološkog muzeja u Zagrebu, 3 serija* 42: 271–304.

Džino, D. 2008. 'The people who are Illyrians and Celts: Strabo and the identities of the barbarians from Illyricum'. *Arheološki vestnik* 59: 371–380.

Eggl, C. 2003. 'Ost-West Beziehungen im Flachgräberlatène Bayerns'. *Germania* 81: 513–538.

Emilov, J. 2005. 'Changing paradigms: Modern interpretations of Celtic raids in Thrace reconsidered', in H. Dobrzańska, V. Megaw, and P. Poleska (eds) *Celts on the Margin: Studies in European Cultural Interaction 7th century BC–1st century AD Dedicated to Zenon Woźniak*: 103–108. Kraków: Institute of Archaeology and Ethnology of the Polish Academy of Sciences.

Emilov, J. 2007. 'La Tène finds and the indigenous communities in Thrace. Interrelations during the Hellenistic period', Actes du colloque images et techniques: l'art des anciens Celtes et leurs contemporains, Prague, 23–26 juin 2005. *Studia Hercynia* 11: 57–75. Prague: Institute of Classical Archaeology, Charles University.

Emilov, J. 2010. 'Ancient texts on the Galatian royal residence of Tylis and the context of La Tène finds in southern Thrace. A reappraisal', in L. F. Vagalinski (ed.) *In Search of Celtic Tylis in Thrace (III BC). Proceedings of the Interdisciplinary Colloquium arranged by the National Archaeological Institute and Museum at Sofia and the Welsh Department, Aberystwyth University, held at the National Archaeological Institute and Museum, Sofia*, 8 May 2010: 67–87. Sofia: Bulgarian Academy of Sciences, National Archaeological Institute and Museum.

Emilov, J., and V. Megaw. 2012. 'Celts in Thrace? A re-examination of the tomb of Mal Tepe, Mezek with particular reference to the La Tène chariot fittings'. *Archaeologia Bulgarica* 16, 1: 1–32.

Falileyev, A. 2010. 'Ancient place-names of the eastern Balkans: Defining Celtic areas', in L. F. Vagalinski (ed.) *In Search of Celtic Tylis in Thrace (III BC). Proceedings of the Interdisciplinary Colloquium arranged by the National Archaeological Institute and Museum at Sofia and the Welsh Department, Aberystwyth University, held at the National Archaeological Institute and Museum, Sofia, 8 May 2010*: 121–129. Sofia: Bulgarian Academy of Sciences, National Archaeological Institute and Museum.

Fernández-Götz, M. 2014. *Identity and Power: The Transformation of Iron Age Societies in Northern Gaul*. Amsterdam Archaeological Studies 21. Amsterdam: Amsterdam University Press.

Fischer, C.-E., M.-H. Pemonge, I. Ducossau, A. Arzellier, M. Rivollat, F. Santos, et al. 2022. 'Origin and mobility of Iron Age Gaulish groups in present-day France revealed through archaeogenomics'. *iScience* 25: 104094. https://doi.org/10.1016/

Fischer, B. 1991. 'Les différentes monétaires des premières imitations du statère de Philippe II du Macédonie'. *Études celtiques* 28: 137–155.

Fitzpatrick, A. P. 1996. ' "Celtic" Iron Age Europe: The theoretical basis', in P. Graves-Brown, S. Jones, and C. Gamble (eds) *Cultural Identity and Archaeology: The Construction of European Communities*: 238–255. London: Routledge.

Freeman, P. M. 1996. 'The earliest Greek sources on the Celts'. *Études celtiques* 32: 11–48.

Frey, O.-H. 1991. 'Einige Bemerkungen zu den durchbrochenen Frühlatènegürtelhaken', in A. Haffner and A. Miron (eds) *Studien zur Eisenzeit im Hunsrück-Nahe-Raum. Symposium Birkenfeld 1987*. Trierer Zeitschrift Beiheft 13: 101–111. Trier: Rheinisches Landesmuseum Trier.

Ginoux, N. 2007a. 'L'iconographie celtique en Ile-de-France et ses connexions avec l'Europe central au IIIe s. av. J.-C.: inventaire et bilain des données', Actes du colloque Images et techniques: l'art des anciens Celtes et leur contemporains, Prague, 23–26 juin, 2005. *Studia Hercynia* 11: 11–26. Prague: Institute of Classical Archaeology, Charles University.

Ginoux, N. 2007b. *Le thème symbolique de 'la paire de dragons' sur les fourreaux celtiques (IVe–IIe siècles avant. J.-C.). Étude iconographique et typologie*. British Archaeological Reports International Series 1702. Oxford: Archaeopress.

Ginoux, N. 2009. *Élites guerrières au nord de la Seine au début du IIIe siècle av. J.-C. La nécropole celtique du Plessis-Gassot (Val-d'Oise)*. Revue du Nord, Hors-série Art et Archéologie 15. Lille: Université Charles-de-Gaulle.

Ginoux, N. 2012. 'Images and visual codes of early Celtic warriors (5th–4th centuries BC)', in C. Pare (ed.) *Kunst und Kommunikation. Zentralisierungsprozesse in Gesellschaften des europäischen Barbarikums im 1. Jahrtausend v. Chr*. RGZM Tagungen 15: 179–190. Mainz: Römisch-Germanisches Zentralmuseum.

Ginoux, N., and P. Ramsl. 2014. 'Art and craftsmanship in elite-warrior graves: from Boii to Parisii and back again', in S. Crawford, S. Ulmschneider, and C. Gosden (eds) *Celtic Art in Europe—Making Connections: Festschrift in honour of Vincent Megaw on his 80th Birthday*: 274–285. Oxford: Oxbow.

Griffith, G. T. 1935. *The Mercenaries of the Hellenistic World*. Cambridge: Cambridge University Press.

Gunby, J. 2000. 'Oval shield representation on the Black Sea littoral'. *Oxford Journal of Archaeology* 19: 359–365.

Guštin, M. 2011. 'On the Celtic tribe of Taurisci. Local identity and regional contacts in the ancient world', in M. Guštin and M. Jevtić (eds) *The Eastern Celts: The Communities Between the Alps and the Black Sea*: 119–128. Koper: Univerza na Primorskem.

Guštin, M., and B. Kavur. 2016. 'Early La Tène warrior graves from Unterpremstätten-Zettling and Dobl-Zwaring (Styria/Austria)', in S. Berecki (ed.) *Iron Age Chronology in the Carpathian Basin. Proceedings of the International Colloquium from Târgu Mureş, 8–10 October 2015*: 65–74. Cluj-Napoca: Editura Mega.

Guštin, M., P. Kuzman, and V. Mlenko. 2012. 'Ein keltischer Krieger in Lychnidos Ohrid, Macedonia'. *Folis Archaeologica Balkanica* 2: 181–196.

Härke, H. 1998. 'Archaeologists and migrations: A problem of attitude?'. *Current Anthropology* 39: 19–45.

Hauschild, M. 2010a. '"Celticised" or "assimilated"? In search of foreign and indigenous people at the time of the Celtic migrations', in S. Berecki (ed.) *Iron Age Communities in the Carpathian Basin. Proceedings of the International Colloquium from Târgu Mureş, 9–11 October 2009*: 171–180. Cluj-Napoca: Editura Mega.

Hauschild, M. 2010b. 'Keltische Söldner im Süden' in M. Schönfelder (ed.) *Kelten! Kelten? Keltische Spuren in Italien. Mosaiksteine*. Forschungen am Römisch-Germanischen Zentralmuseum 7: 28–29. Mainz: Römisch-Germanisches Zentralmuseum.

Hauschild, M., M. Schönfelder, M. Scheeres, C. Knipper, K. W. Alt, and C. Pare. 2013. 'Nebringen, Münsingen und Monte Bibele—zum archäologischen und bioarchäometrischen Nachweis von Mobilität im 4./3. Jahrhundert v. Chr.'. *Archäologisches Korrespondenzblatt* 43: 345–364.

Hodson, F. R. 1962. 'Some pottery from Eastbourne, the Marnians and the pre-Roman Iron Age in southern England'. *Proceedings of the Prehistoric Society* 28: 140–155.

Hodson, F. R. 1964. 'Cultural groupings within the British pre-Roman Iron Age'. *Proceedings of the Prehistoric Society* 30: 99–110.

Horváth, L. 2005. 'Grave of a Celtic warrior from Magyarszerdahely (Zala County)'. *Zalai Múzeum* 14: 61–73.

Janković, M. A. 2014. 'Negotiating identities at the edge of the Roman empire', in C. N. Popa and S. Stoddart (eds) *Fingerprinting the Iron Age: Approaches to Identity in the European Iron Age. Integrating South-Eastern Europe into the Debate*: 89–107. Oxford: Oxbow.

Jay, M., C. Haselgrove, D. Hamilton, J. D. Hill, and J. Dent. 2012. 'Chariots and context: New radiocarbon dates from Wetwang and the chronology of Iron Age burials and brooches in East Yorkshire'. *Oxford Journal of Archaeology* 31, 2: 161–189.

Jay, M., J. Montgomery, O. Nehlich, J. Towers, and J. Evans. 2013. 'British Iron Age chariot burials of the Arras culture: A multi-isotope approach to investigating mobility levels and subsistence practices'. *World Archaeology* 45: 473–491.

Jovanović, A. 2011. 'Middle La Tène female grave 56 from Brežice, Slovenia', in M. Guštin and M. Jevtić (eds) *The Eastern Celts: The Communities between the Alps and the Black Sea*: 31–50. Koper: Univerza na Primorskem.

Kaenel, G. 2007. 'Les mouvements de populations celtiques: aspects historiques et confrontations archéologiques', in C. Mennessier-Jouannet, A.-M. Adam, and P.-Y. Milcent (eds) *La Gaule dans son contexte européen aux IVe et IIIe siècles avant notre ère. Actes du XXVIIe colloque international de l'AFEAF, Clermont-Ferrand, 29 mai-1er juin 2003*. Monographies d'Archéologie Méditerranéenne Hors-Série 2: 385–398. Lattes: Association Française pour l'Étude de l'Âge du Fer.

Kaenel, G. 2012. *L'an –58. Les Helvètes: Archéologie d'un peuple celte*. Collection Le savoir Suisse 82. Lausanne: Presses polytechniques et universitaires romandes.

Kaul, F. 2007. 'Celtic influences during Pre-Roman Iron Age in Denmark', in S. Möllers, W. Schlüter, and S. Sievers (eds) *Keltische Einflüsse im nördlichen Mitteleuropa während der mittleren und jüngeren vorrömischen Eisenzeit. Akten des Internationalen Kolloquiums in Osnabrück vom 29. März bis 1. April 2006*. Kolloquien zur Vor- und Frühgeschichte 9: 327–345. Bonn: Habelt.

Kaul, F., and J. Mertens. 1995. 'Southeast European influences in the Iron Age of southern Scandinavia. Gundestrup and the Cimbri'. *Acta Archaeologica Academiae Scientiarum Hungaricae* 66: 111–161.

Kazakevich, G. 2012. 'Celtic military equipment from the territory of Ukraine: Towards a new warrior identity in the pre-Roman eastern Europe', in M. Fomin, V. Blažek, and P. Stalmaszczyk (eds) *Transforming Traditions: Studies in Archaeology, Comparative Linguistics and Narrative. Proceedings of the Fifth International Colloquium of Societas Celto-Slavica held at Příbram*. Studia Celto-Slavica 6: 177–212. Łódź: Wydawnictwo Uniwersytetu Łódzkiego.

Kimmig, W. 1940. 'Ein Keltenschild aus Aegypten'. *Germania* 24: 106–111.

Klindt-Jensen, O. 1950. *Foreign Influences in Denmark's Early Iron Age*. Copenhagen: Munksgaard.

Koch, J. T. 2010. 'Paradigm shift? Interpreting Tartessian as Celtic', in B. W. Cunliffe and J. T. Koch (eds) *Celtic from the West: Alternative Perspectives from Archaeology, Genetics, Language and Literature*: 185–301. Oxford: Oxbow.

Koch, J. T. 2013. 'Prologue: Ha C1a ≠ PC. ("The earliest Hallstatt Iron Age cannot equal Proto-Celtic")', in J. T. Koch and B. W. Cunliffe (eds) *Celtic from the West 2: Rethinking the Bronze Age and the Arrival of Indo-European in Atlantic Europe*: 1–16. Oxford: Oxbow.

Krämer, W. 1961. 'Keltische Hohlbuckelringe vom Isthmus von Korinth'. *Germania* 39: 32–42.

Krämer, W. 1964. *Das keltische Gräberfeld von Nebringen (Kreis Böblingen)*. Veröffentlichungen des staatlichen Amtes für Denkmalpflege Stuttgart, Reihe A 8. Stuttgart: Silberburg.

Kruta, V. 1979. 'Duchcov-Münsingen: nature et diffusion d`une phase Laténienne', in P.-M. Duval and V. Kruta (eds) *Les mouvements celtiques du Ve au Ier siècle avant notre ère. Actes du XXVIIIe colloque organisé à l'occasion du IXe Congrès International des Sciences Préhistoriques et Protohistoriques, Nice, le 19 septembre 1976*: 81–117. Paris: Centre National de la Recherche Scientifique.

Kruta, V. 1981. 'Les Sénons de l'Adriatique d'après l'archéologie (prolégomènes)'. *Études celtiques* 18: 7–38.

Kruta, V. 1982. 'Archéologie et numismatique. La phase initiale du monnayage celtique'. *Études celtiques* 19: 35–50.

Kruta, V. 2008. 'Les Sénons dans les Marches au IVe et IIe siècles avant J.-C. État de la question'. *Études celtiques* 36: 7–20.

Künzl, E. 1991. 'The tomb of the warrior and surgeon of München-Obermenzing and other archaeological evidence of Celtic medicine', in S. Moscate, O.-H. Frey, V. Kruta, B. Raftery, and M. Szabó (eds) *The Celts*: 372–373. London: Thames and Hudson.

Künzl, E. 2003. 'Waffendekor und Zoologie in Alexandrien: Der hellenistiche Prunkschild im Württembergischen Landesmuseum, Stuttgart'. *Jahrbuch des Römisch-Germanisches Zentralmuseum Mainz* 50: 279–306.

Lejars, T. 2006. 'Les celtes d'Italie', in M. Szabó (ed.) *Celtes et Gaulois: l'archéologie face à l'histoire. Les Civilisés et les Barbares du Ve au IIe siècle avant J.-C. Actes de la table ronde de Budapest, 17–18 juin 2005*. Collection Bibracte 12/3: 77–96. Glux-en-Glenne: Centre archéologique européen du Mont Beuvray.

Lenerz de Wilde, M. 1991. *Iberica Céltica: Archäologishe Zeugnisse keltischer Kultur auf der Pyrenäenhalbinsel*. Stuttgart: Steiner.

Lenerz de Wilde, M. 2001. 'Los Celtas en Celtiberia'. *Zephyrus* 53–54: 323–351.

Lorenz, H. 1978. 'Totenbrauchtum und Tracht. Untersuchungen zu regionalen Gliederungen der frühen Latènezeit'. *Bericht der Römisch-Germanischen Kommission* 59: 1–380.

Lorenz, H. 1985. 'Regional organization in the western Early La Tène province: The Marne-Mosel and Rhine-Danube groups', in T. C. Champion and J. V. S. Megaw (eds) *Settlement and Society: Aspects of West European Prehistory in the 1st Millennium BC*: 109–122. Leicester: Leicester University Press.

Lorrio, A. J. 2006. 'Les Celtibères', in M. Szabó (ed.) *Celtes et Gaulois: l'archéologie face à l'histoire. Les Civilisés et les Barbares du Ve au IIe siècle avant J.-C. Actes de la table ronde de Budapest, 17–18 juin 2005*. Collection Bibracte 12/3: 43–61. Glux-en-Glenne: Centre archéologique européen du Mont Beuvray.

Lubšina-Tušek, M., and B. Kavur. 2009. 'A sword between. The Celtic warriors grave from Srednica in north-eastern Slovenia', in G. Tiefengraber, B. Kavur, and A. Gaspari (eds) *Keltske študije II. Studies in Celtic Archaeology. Papers in Honour of Mitja Guštin*. Protohistoire Européenne 11: 125–142. Montagnac: Monique Mergoil.

Lubšina-Tušek, M., and B. Kavur. 2011. 'Srednica near Ptuj. A contribution to the beginning of the La Tène period in eastern Slovenia', in M. Guštin and M. Jevtić (eds) *The Eastern Celts: The Communities between the Alps and the Black Sea*: 31–50. Koper: Univerza na Primorskem.

Łuciewicz, P. 2010. 'Die spätlatènezeitlichen Trinkhornbeschläge. Zeugnisse germanischer Einflüsse im keltischen Gebiet?', in E. Jerem, M. Schönfelder, and G. Wieland (eds) *Nord-Süd, Ost-West. Kontakte während der Eisenzeit in Europa. Akten der Internationalen Tagungen der AG Eisenzeit in Hamburg und Sopron 2002*. Archaeolingua Main Series 17: 165–181. Budapest: Archaeolingua.

Luginbühl, T. 2014. 'La migration des Cimbres et des Teutons: une histoire sans archéologie?', in C. Gaeng (ed.) *Hommage à Jeannot Metzler*. Archaeologia Mosellana 9: 343–360. Luxembourg: Centre National de la Recherche Archéologique, Musée National d'Histoire et d'Art.

Machinskiy, D. 1974. 'Kelty na zemliah k vostoku ot Karpat' (Celts in the lands to the east of the Carpathians)', in V. N. Yartseva (ed.) *Kelty i keltskie jazyki (Celts and the Celtic Languages)*: 31–41. Moscow: Nauka.

Maier, F. 1973. 'Keltische Altertümer in Griechenland'. *Germania* 51: 459–477.

Megaw, J. V. S. 2004. 'In the footsteps of Brennos? Further archaeological evidence for the Celts in the Balkans', in B. Hänsel and E. Studenikova (eds) *Zwischen Karpaten und Ägäis. Neolithikum und ältere Bronzezeit. Gedenkschrift für Viera Nemejcová Pavúková*: 93–107. Rahden: Marie Leidorf.

Megaw, J. V. S. 2005. 'Celts in Thrace? A reappraisal', in J. Bouzek and L. Domaradzka (eds) *The Culture of Thracians and their Neighbours*. British Archaeological Reports International Series 1350: 209–214. Oxford: Archaeopress.

Megaw, R., and V. Megaw. 1989. *Celtic Art: From its Beginnings to the Book of Kells*. London: Thames and Hudson.

Mihajlović, V. D. 2014. 'Tracing Ethnicity Backwards: the Case of the 'Central Balkan Tribes'', in C. N. Popa and S. Stoddart (eds) *Fingerprinting the Iron Age: Approaches to Identity in the European Iron Age. Integrating South-Eastern Europe into the Debate*: 97–107. Oxford: Oxbow.

Mordvintseva, V. 2013. 'The Sarmatians: The creation of archaeological evidence'. *Oxford Journal of Archaeology* 32: 203–219.

Müller, F. 1989. *Die frühlatènezeitlichen Scheibenhalsringe*. Römisch-Germanische Forschungen 46. Mainz: Philipp von Zabern.

Müller, F. (ed.) 1998. *Münsingen-Rain, ein Markstein der keltischen Archäologie*. Schriften des Bernischen Historischen Museums 2. Bern: Bernisches Historisches Museum.

Müller, F., P. Jud, and K. W. Alt. 2008. 'Artefacts, skulls and written sources: The social ranking of a Celtic family buried at Münsingen-Rain'. *Antiquity* 82: 462–469.

Müller, R. 2007. 'Die östliche Kontaktzone zwischen dem keltischen Kulturraum und dem Norden', in S. Möllers, W. Schlüter, and S. Sievers (eds) *Keltische Einflüsse im nördlichen Mitteleuropa während der mittleren und jüngeren vorrömischen Eisenzeit. Akten des Internationalen Kolloquiums in Osnabrück vom 29. März bis 1. April 2006*. Kolloquien zur Vor- und Frühgeschichte 9: 265–282. Bonn: Habelt.

Müller-Karpe, A. 1988. 'Neue galatische Funde aus Anatolien'. *Istanbuler Mitteilungen* 38: 189–199.

Müller-Karpe, A. 2006. 'Zur historischen Deutung von Funden keltischer Trachtelemente in Anatolien', in M. Szabó (ed.) *Celtes et Gaulois: l'archéologie face à l'histoire. Les Civilisés et les Barbares du Ve au IIe siècle avant J.-C.* Collection Bibracte 12/3: 119–123. Glux-en-Glenne: Centre archéologique européen du Mont Beuvray.

Nash, D. 1987. 'Syracusan influence upon the earliest gold coinage of western Gaul', in C. Bémont, C. Delpace, B. Fischer, K. Gruel, C. Peyre, and J.-C. Richard (eds) *Mélanges offerts au Docteur J.-B. Colbert de Beaulieu*: 647–653. Paris: Le Léopard d'Or.

Nash Briggs, D. 2003. 'Metals, salt, and slaves: Economic links between Gaul and Italy from the eighth to the late sixth centuries BC'. *Oxford Journal of Archaeology* 22, 3: 243–259.

Nehlich, O., J. Montgomery, J. Evans, M. P. Richards, V. Dresely, and K. W. Alt. 2009. 'Biochemische Analyse stabiler Isotope an prähistorischen Skelettfunden aus Westerhausen, Lkr. Harz'. *Jahresschrift für Mitteldeutsche Geschichte* 91: 329–350.

Neugebauer, J.-W. 1996. 'Eine frühlatènezeitliche Gräbergruppe in Inzersdorf ob der Traisen, NÖ', in E. Jerem, A. Krenn-Leeb, J.-W. Neugebauer, and O. H. Urban (eds) *Die Kelten in den Alpen und an der Donau. Akten des internationalen Symposions, St. Pölten, 14.-18. Oktober 1992*. Studien zur Eisenzeit im Ostalpenraum: 111–178. Budapest: Archaeolingua.

Nortmann, H. 2007. 'Zur westlichen Kontaktzone zwischen dem keltischen Kulturraum und dem Norden', in S. Möllers, W. Schlüter, and S. Sievers (eds) *Keltische Einflüsse im nördlichen Mitteleuropa während der mittleren und jüngeren vorrömischen Eisenzeit. Akten des Internationalen Kolloquiums in Osnabrück vom 29. März bis 1. April 2006*. Kolloquien zur Vor- und Frühgeschichte 9: 283–292. Bonn: Habelt.

Oelze, V. M., J. K. Koch, K. Kupke, O. Nehlich, S. Zäuner, J. Wahl, et al. 2012. 'Multi-isotopic analysis reveals individual mobility and diet at the Early Iron Age monumental tumulus of Magdalenenberg, Germany'. *American Journal of Physical Anthropology* 148, 3: 406–421.

Olędzki, M. 2005. 'Anarti and Anartophracti: Transcarpathian cultural and settlement relations of the Celts', in H. Dobrzańska, V. Megaw, and P. Poleska (eds) *Celts on the Margin: Studies in European Cultural Interaction 7th century BC–1st century AD Dedicated to Zenon Woźniak*: 145–152. Krakow: Institute of Archaeology and Ethnology of the Polish Academy of Sciences.

Péré-Noquès, S. 2007. 'Les Celtes et le mercenariat en Occident (IVe et IIIe siècle av. n.è.)', in C. Mennessier-Jouannet, A.-M. Adam, and P.-Y. Milcent (eds) *La Gaule dans son contexte européen aux IVe et IIIe siècles avant notre ère. Actes du XXVIIe colloque international de l'AFEAF, Clermont-Ferrand, 29 mai–1er juin 2003*. Monographies d'Archéologie Méditerranéenne Hors-Série 2: 353–361. Lattes: Association pour le développement de l'archéologie en Languedoc-Roussillon.

Péré-Noquès, S. 2013. 'Aux limites de l'interprétation: mercenariat et mobilité au Second âge du Fer', in A. Colin and F. Verdin (eds) *L'âge du Fer en Aquitaine et sur ses marges. Mobilité des hommes, diffusions des idées, circulation des biens dans l'espace européen a l'âge du Fer. Actes du XXXVe colloque de l'AFEAF, Bordeaux, juin 2011*. Aquitania supplément 30: 429–437. Bordeaux: Fédération Aquitania.

Peschel, K. 1971. 'Zur Frage der Sklaverei bei den Kelten während der vorrömischen Eisenzeit'. *Ethnographisch-Archäologische Zeitschrift* 12: 527–539.

Peyre, C. 2007. 'Les migrations gauloises vers l'Italie d'après le témoinage de Tite-Livre', in C. Mennessier-Jouannet, A.-M. Adam, and P.-Y. Milcent (eds) *La Gaule dans son contexte européen aux IVe et IIIe siècles avant notre ère. Actes du XXVIIe colloque international de l'AFEAF, Clermont-Ferrand, 29 mai–1er juin 2003*. Monographies d'Archéologie Méditerranéenne Hors-Série 2: 363–375. Lattes: Association pour le développement de l'archéologie en Languedoc-Roussillon.

Pion, P. 2012. 'La monnaie mercenaire: une approche anthropologique des premiers monnayages celtiques au nord-ouest du complexe nord-alpin (IIIe siècle av. J.-C.)', in P. Pion, B. Formoso, and R. Etienne (eds) *Monnaie antique, monnaie moderne, monnaies d'ailleurs. Métissages et hybridations*. Colloques de la Maison René-Ginouvès 8: 151–164. Paris: de Boccard.

Polenz, H. 1978. 'Gedanken zu einer Fibel vom Mittellatèneschema aus Káyseri in Anatolien'. *Bonner Jahrbücher* 178: 181–216.

Poleska, P. 2005. 'The Celtic settlement microregion in the area near Kraków', in H. Dobrzańska, V. Megaw, and P. Poleska (eds) *Celts on the Margin: Studies in European Cultural Interaction, 7th century BC–1st century AD Dedicated to Zenon Woźniak*: 187–194. Krakow: Institute of Archaeology and Ethnology of the Polish Academy of Sciences.

Popović, P. 1996. 'Early La Tène between Pannonia and the Balkans'. *Starinar* 47: 105–125.

Prammer, J., R. Sandner, and C. Tappert (eds). 2007. *Siedlungsdynamik und Gesellschaft. Beiträge des internationalen Kollquiums zur keltischen Besiedlungsgeschichte im bayerischen Donauraum, Österreich und der Tschechischen Republik, 2–4 März im Gäubodenmusuem Straubing*. Jahresbericht des Historischen Vereins für Straubing und Umgebung, Sonderband 3. Straubing: Historischer Verein.

Raev, B. A., A. V. Simonenko, and M. Treister. 1995. 'Etrusco-Italic and Celtic helmets in eastern Europe'. *Jahrbuch des Römisch-Germanischen Zentralmuseums Mainz* 38: 465–496.

Ramsl, P. C. 2007. 'L'Autriche aux IVe et IIIe s. av. n. e.: état de la recherche, structures et nouveaux aspects', in C. Mennessier-Jouannet, A.-M. Adam, and P.-Y. Milcent (eds) *La Gaule dans son contexte européen aux IVe et IIIe siècles avant notre ère. Actes du XXVIIe colloque international de l'AFEAF, Clermont-Ferrand, 29 mai–1er juin 2003*. Monographies d'Archéologie Méditerranéenne Hors-Série 2: 319–332. Lattes: Association pour le développement de l'archéologie en Languedoc-Roussillon.

Ramsl, P. C. 2009. 'Eine Omeganadel im latènezeitlichen Gräberfeld von Mannersdorf am Leithagebirge, Niederösterreich', in G. Tiefengraber, B. Kavur, and A. Gaspari (eds) *Keltske*

Študije II. Studies in Celtic Archaeology. Papers in honour of Mitja Guštin. Protohistoire Européenne 11: 117–124. Montagnac: Monique Mergoil.

Ramsl, P. C. 2010. 'Verbindende Randzonen des Karpatenbeckungs in der Frühlatènezeit', in E. Jerem, M. Schönfelder, and G. Wieland (eds) *Nord-Süd, Ost-West. Kontakte während der Eisenzeit in Europa. Akten der Internationalen Tagungen der AG Eisenzeit in Hamburg und Sopron 2002*. Archaeolingua Main Series 17: 241–255. Budapest: Archaeolingua.

Ramsl, P. C. 2011. *Das latènezeitliche Gräberfeld von Mannersdorf im Leithagebirge, Flur Reinthal Süd, Niederösterreich*. Mitteilungen der Prähistorischen Kommission 74. Vienna: Österreichische Akadamie der Wissenschaften.

Rapin, A. 1995. 'Propositions pour un classement des équipements militaires celtiques en amont et en aval d'un repère historique: Delphes 278 avant J.-C.', in J.-J. Charpy (ed.) *L'Europe celtique du Ve au IIIe siècle avant J.-C.: contacts, échanges et mouvements de populations. Actes du IIe symposium international d'Hautvillers, 8–10 octobre 1992*: 275–290. Sceaux: Kronos B.Y. Editions.

Rapin, A. 2001. 'Un bouclier celtique dans la colonie grecque de Camarina (Sicilie)'. *Germania* 79: 274–296.

Reith, A. 1965. 'Bemerkungen zu einem keltischen Langschwert von Neapolis auf der Krim'. *Germania* 43: 159–163.

Rieckhoff-Pauli, S. 1995. *Süddeutschland im Spannungsfeld von Kelten, Germanen und Römern. Studien zur Chronologie der Spätlatenezeit im südlichen Mitteleuropa*. Trierer Zeitschrift Beiheft 19. Trier: Rheinisches Landesmuseum.

Roymans, N. 2004. *Ethnic Identity and Imperial Power: The Batavians in the Early Roman Empire*. Amsterdam Archaeological Studies 10. Amsterdam: Amsterdam University Press.

Rudnicki, M. 2012. 'Pieniądz celtycki na Śląsku', in W. Garbaczewski and R. Macyra (eds) *Pieniądz i banki na Śląsku. Studia nad Dziejami Pieniądza i Bankowości w Polsce*: 33–68. Poznań: Muzeum Narodowe w Poznaniu.

Ruiz Zapatero, G. 1993. 'El concepto de Celtas en la prehistoria europea y española', in M. Almagro-Gorbea and G. Ruiz-Zapatero (eds) *Los Celtas: Hispania y Europa*. Actas de El Escorial 4: 23–62. Madrid: Universidad Complutense.

Rustoiu, A. 2005. 'Archäologische und historische Hinweise betreffend den Anfang der keltischen Kolonisation des innerkarpatischen Raumes'. *Apulum* 42: 55–76.

Rustoiu, A. 2006. 'A journey to the Mediterranean. Peregrinations of a Celtic warrior from Translyvania'. *Studia Universitatis 'Babes-Bolyai'. Series Historia* 51, 1: 42–85.

Rustoiu, A. 2008. 'Celţic din Transilvania şi comunităţile indigene nord-balcanice. Schimburi culturale şi mobilitate individuală (The Celts from Transylvania and the indigenous communities from northern Balkans. Cultural exchanges and individual mobility)'. *Ephemeris Napocensis* 18: 25–44.

Rustoiu, A. 2011. 'The Celts from Transylvania and the eastern Banat and their southern neighbours. Cultural exchanges and individual mobility', in M. Guštin and M. Jevtić (eds) *The Eastern Celts: The Communities between the Alps and the Black Sea*: 163–170. Koper/Belgrade: University of Primorska/University of Belgrade.

Rustoiu, A. 2014. 'Indigenous and colonist communities in the eastern Carpathian basin at the beginning of the Late Iron Age. The genesis of the eastern Celtic world', in C. N. Popa and S. Stoddart (eds) *Fingerprinting the Iron Age: Approaches to Identity in the European Iron Age: Integrating South-Eastern Europe into the Debate*: 142–156. Oxford: Oxbow.

Salač, V., and J. Bemmann (eds). 2009. *Mitteleuropa zur Zeit Marbods. Tagung Roztoky u Křivoklátu 4.-8. 12. 2006 anlässlich des 2000jährigen Jubiläums des römischen Feldzuges gegen Marbod. 19. Internationales Symposium Grundprobleme der frühgeschichtlichen Entwicklung im mittleren Donauraum*. Prague/Bonn: Archeologický ústav AV ČR/Vor- und Frühgeschichtliche Archäologie der Rheinischen Friedrich-Wilhelms-Universität Bonn.

Sankot, P. 2003. *Les épées du début de La Tène en Bohême*. Fontes archaeolgici Pragenses 28. Prague: Museum Nationale Pragae.

Schäfer, A. 2007. 'Nördiche Einflüsse auf die Latènekultur', in S. Möllers, W. Schlüter, and S. Sievers (eds) *Keltische Einflüsse im nördlichen Mitteleuropa während der mittleren und jüngeren vorrömischen Eisenzeit. Akten des Internationalen Kolloquiums in Osnabrück vom 29. März bis 1. April 2006*. Kolloquien zur Vor- und Frühgeschichte 9: 347–360. Bonn: Habelt.

Scheeres, M. 2014. 'High Mobility Rates during the Period of the "Celtic Migrations"? 87Sr/86Sr and δ^{18}O Evidence from Early La Tène Europe'. PhD thesis, Johannes-Gutenberg-Universität Mainz.

Scheeres, M., C. Knipper, M. Hauschild, M. Schönfelder, W. Siebel, C. Pare, et al. 2014. '"Celtic migrations": Fact or fiction? Strontium and oxygen isotope analysis of the Czech cemeteries of Radovesice and Kutná Hora in Bohemia'. *American Journal of Physical Anthropology* 155: 496–512.

Scheeres, M., C. Knipper, M. Hauschild, M. Schönfelder, W. Siebel, D. Vitali, et al. 2013. 'Evidence for "Celtic migrations"? Strontium isotope analysis at the early La Tène (LT B) cemeteries of Nebringen (Germany) and Monte Bibele (Italy)'. *Journal of Archaeological Science* 40: 3614–3625.

Scholz, M., J. Hald, P. Dicke, S. Hengst, and C. M. Pusch. 1999. 'Das frühlatènezeitliche Gräberfeld von Gäufelden-Nebringen. Neue Erkenntnisse zur inneren Gliederung unter Anwendung archäobiologischer Analyseverfahren'. *Archäologisches Korrespondenzblatt* 29, 2: 223–235.

Schönfelder, M. 2007. 'Zurück aus Griechenland—Spuren keltischer Söldner in Mitteleuropa'. *Germania* 85: 307–328.

Schönfelder, M. (ed.) 2010. *Kelten! Kelten? Keltische Spuren in Italien. Mosaiksteine*. Forschungen am Römisch-Germanischen Zentralmuseum 7. Mainz: Römisch-Germanisches Zentralmuseum.

Schönfelder, M. 2015. 'Sklaven und Sklavenketten in der jüngeren Latènezeit: zu neuen Nachweismöglichkeiten', in S. Wefers, M. Karwowski, J. Fries-Knoblach, P. Trebsche, and P. C. Ramsl (eds) *Waffen—Gewalt—Krieg. Beiträge zur Internationalen Tagung der AG Eisenzeit und des Instytut Archeologii Uniwersytetu Rzeszowskiego—Rzeszów 19.–22. September 2012*. Beiträge zur Ur- und Frühgeschichte Mitteleuropas 79: 83–91. Langenweißbach: Beier and Beran.

Schukin, M. 1995. 'The Celts in eastern Europe'. *Oxford Journal of Archaeology* 14: 201–227.

Schuster, J. 2013. 'Frühe Gräber weiblicher Eliten bei den Germanen und ihre Vernetzung im Barbaricum', in D. Quast (ed.) *Weibliche Eliten in Frühgeschichte. Female Elites in Protohistoric Europe. Internationale Tagung vom 13. bis zum 14. Juni im RGZM im Rahmen des Forschungsschwerpunktes Eliten*: 307–320. Mainz: Römisch-Germanisches Zentralmuseum.

Shefton, B. 2004. 'The Grächwil hydria: The object and its milieu beyond Grächwil', in M. Guggisberg (ed.) *Die Hydria von Grächwil: zur Funktion und Rezeption mediterraner Importe in Mitteleuropa im 6. und 5. Jahrhundert v.Chr. Akten Internationales Kolloquium anlässlich des 150. Jahrestages der Entdeckung der Hydria von Grächwil*. Schriften des Bernischen Historischen Museums 5: 29–45. Bern: Bernisches Historisches Museum.

Sievers, S. 2007. 'Formen des Kulturtransfers', in S. Möllers, W. Schlüter, and S. Sievers (eds) *Keltische Einflüsse im nördlichen Mitteleuropa während der mittleren und jüngeren vorrömischen Eisenzeit. Akten des Internationalen Kolloquiums in Osnabrück vom 29. März bis 1. April 2006*. Kolloquien zur Vor- und Frühgeschichte 9: 245–253. Bonn: Habelt.

Sims-Williams, P. 2006. *Ancient Celtic Place-Names in Europe and Asia Minor*. Oxford: Blackwell.

Spehr, R. 2002. 'Kulturelle und personelle Fernbeziehungen im sächsischen Latène', in A. Lang and V. Salač (eds) *Fernkontakte in der Eisenzeit, Konferenz Liblice 2000*: 194–229. Prague: Archeologický ústav AV ČR.

Spohn, J. 2009. 'Das spätkeltische Prunkgrab von Sinsheim-Dühren—ein Zeugnis sozialer "Eliten" am Unterlauf des Neckars?', in R. Karl and J. Leskovar (eds) *Interpretierte Eisenzeiten 3. Fallstudien, Methoden, Theorie. Tagungsbeiträge der 3*. Linzer Gespräche zur interpretativen Eisenzeitarchäologie: 65–80. Linz: Oberösterreiches Landesmuseum.

Stead, I. M. 1979. *The Arras Culture*. York: Yorkshire Philosophical Society.

Stöllner, T. 2010. 'Kontakt, Mobilität und Kulturwandel im Frühlatènekreis—das Beispiel Frühlatènegürtelhaken', in E. Jerem, M. Schönfelder, and G. Wieland (eds) *Nord-Süd, Ost-West. Kontakte während der Eisenzeit in Europa. Akten der Internationalen Tagungen der AG Eisenzeit in Hamburg und Sopron 2002*. Archaeolingua Main Series 17: 277–319. Budapest: Archaeolingua.

Szabó, M. 1968. 'Zur Frage des keltischen Fundes von Isthmia'. *Acta Antiqua Academiae Scientiarum Hungaricae* 16: 173–177.

Szabó, M. 1971. *The Celtic Heritage in Hungary*. Budapest: Corvina.

Szabó, M. 1983. 'Audoleon und die Anfänge der ostkeltischen Münzprägung'. *Alba Regia* 20: 43–56.

Szabó, M. 1992. *Les Celtes de l'Est. Le second âge du Fer dans la cuvette des Karpathes*. Paris: Errance.

Szabó, M. 1995. 'Guerriers celtiques avant et après Delphes. Contribution à une periode critique du monde celtique', in J.-J. Charpy (ed.) *L'Europe celtique du Ve au IIIe siècle avant J.-C.: contacts, échanges et mouvements de populations. Actes du IIe symposium international d'Hautvillers, 8–10 octobre 1992*: 49–67. Sceaux: Kronos B.Y. Editions.

Szabó, M. 2001. 'La formation de la communauté culturelle des Celtes orientaux aux IIIe s. av. J.-C.'. *Comptes-rendus de l'Académie des Inscriptions et Belle-Lettres* 145: 1705–1724.

Szabó, M. 2006. 'Les celts de l'est', in M. Szabó (ed.) *Celtes et Gaulois: l'archéologie face à l'histoire. Les Civilisés et les Barbares du Ve au IIe siècle avant J.-C. Actes de la table ronde de Budapest, 17–18 juin 2005*. Collection Bibracte 12/3: 97–117. Glux-en-Glenne: Centre archéologique européen du Mont Beuvray.

Tappert, C. 2012. 'Der Beginn der Drehscheibenkeramik im östlichen Frühlatènekreis und ihre Entwicklung bis zum Ende der Stufe Lt A', in A. Kern, J. K. Koch, I. Balzer, J. Fries-Knoblach, K. Kowarik, C. Later, P. C. Ramsl, P. Trebsche, and J. Wiethold (eds) *Technologieentwicklung und -transfer in der Eisenzeit. Bericht der Internationalen Tagung der AG Eisenzeit und des Naturhistorischen Museums, Prähistorische Abteilung—Hallstatt 2009*. Beiträge zur Ur- und Frühgeschichte Mitteleuropas 65: 121–138. Langenweißbach: Beier und Beran.

Tomaschitz, M. 2002. *Die Wanderungen der Kelten in der antiken literarischen Überlieferung*. Mitteilungen der Prähistorischen Kommission 47. Vienna: Österreichische Akademie der Wissenschaften.

Treister, M. J. 1993. 'The Celts in the north Pontic area: A reassessment'. *Antiquity* 67: 789–804.

Van Endert, D. 1986. 'Zur Stellung der Wagengräber der Arras-Kultur'. *Berichte der Römisch-Germanischen Kommission* 67: 203–288.

Venclová, N. 2002. 'External contacts: Visible and invisible', in A. Lang and V. Salač (eds) *Fernkontakte in der Eisenzeit. Konferenz Liblice 2000*: 77–82. Prague: Archeologický ústav AV ČR.

Verger, S. 2003. 'Des objets gaulois dans les sanctuaires archaïques de Grèce, de Sicile et d'Italie'. *Comptes-rendus de l'Académie des Inscriptions et Belle-Lettres* 147: 525–573.

Verger, S. 2006. 'La grande tombe de Hochdorf, mise en scène funéraire d'un cursus honorum tribal hors pair'. *Siris* 7: 5–44.

Villes, A. 1995. 'A propos des mouvements celtiques aux IVe-IIIe siècles: confrontation habitats et necropoles en Champagne', in J.-J. Charpy (ed.) *L'Europe celtique du Ve au IIIe siècle avant J.-C.: contacts, échanges et mouvements de populations. Actes du IIe symposium international d'Hautvillers, 8–10 octobre 1992*: 125–160. Sceaux: Kronos B.Y. Editions.

Vitali, D. 1998. 'I Celti e Spina', in F. Rebecchi (ed.) *Spina e il delto padano: Riflessioni sul catalogo sulla mostra ferrarese*: 253–273. Rome: Bretschneider.

Vitali, D., and G. Kaenel. 2000. 'Un Helvète chez les Étrusques vers 300 av. J.-C.'. *Archéologie Suisse* 23: 115–122.

Vitali, D., and S. Verger (eds). 2008. *Tra mondo celtico e mondo italico: La necropoli di Monte Bibele. Atti della Tavola Rotonda*. Bologna: Università di Bologna Dipartimento di Archeologia.

Vohberger, M. 2007. 'Herkunftsbestimmung anhand stabiler Sauerstoff- und Strontiumisotopie—die naturwissenschaftliche Lösung einer archäologischen Fragestellung', in J. Prammer, R. Sandner, and C. Tappert (eds) *Siedlungsdynamik und Gesellschaft: Beiträge des internationalen Kolloquiums zur keltischen Besiedlungsgeschichte im bayerischen Donauraum, Österreich und der Tschechischen Republik 2.-4. März 2006 im Gäubodenmuseum Straubing*. Jahresbericht des Historischen Vereins für Straubing und Umgebung, Sonderband 3: 251–259. Straubing: Historischer Verein.

Vranić, J. 2014. '"Hellenisation" and ethnicity in the continental Balkan Iron Age', in C. N. Popa and S. Stoddart (eds) *Fingerprinting the Iron Age: Approaches to Identity in the European Iron Age. Integrating South-Eastern Europe into the Debate*: 161–172. Oxford: Oxbow.

Waldhauser, J. 1987. 'Keltische Gräberfelder in Böhmen'. *Bericht der Römisch-Germanischen Kommission* 68: 25–179.

Waldhauser, J. 1998. 'Die Goldfingerringe von Münsingen-Rain und ihre Vergleichsstücke aus Flachgräberfeldern im Gebiet zwischen dem schweizerischen Mittelland und dem Karpatenbecken', in F. Müller (ed.) *Münsingen-Rain. Ein Markstein der keltischen Archäologie. Funde, Befunde und Methoden im Vergleich*. Schriften des Bernischen Historischen Museums 2: 85–121. Bern: Bernisches Historisches Museum.

Zirra, V. 1979. 'À propos de la présence des éléments laténiens sur la rive occidentale de la Mer Noire', in P.-M. Duval and V. Kruta (eds) *Les mouvements celtiques du Ve au Ier siècle avant notre ère. Actes du XXVIIIe colloque organisé à l'occasion du IXe Congrès International des Sciences Préhistoriques et Protohistoriques, Nice, le 19. septembre 1976*: 189–193. Paris: Centre National de la Recherche Scientifique.

Zirra, V. 1991. 'Les plus anciennes fibules en Roumanie'. *Dacia* 35: 177–184.

Zirra, V. 1998. 'Die relative Chronologie des Gräberfeldes von Pişcolt (Kr. Satu Mare, Rumänien)', in F. Müller (ed.) *Münsingen-Rain, Ein Markstein der keltischen Archäologie: Funde, Befunde und Methoden im Vergleich*. Schriften des Bernischen Historischen Museums 2: 145–160. Bern: Bernisches Historisches Museum.

CHAPTER 38

INDIGENOUS COMMUNITIES UNDER ROME

ADAM ROGERS

Introduction

The Roman Empire in Europe stretched from Greece in the east to Britain in the west, expanding out of Italy over a long time period from the third century BC to the second century AD, incorporating the existing communities in these lands, but also causing a range of social changes before conquest. The nature of the lifeways and other expressions and indications of identity, and processes of continuity and change, across this huge area and timescale can best be approached thematically. These themes include geography and landscape, settlement, buildings and space, religion and ritual, death and burial, and production and material culture. As the Empire expanded, new styles of settlement such as cities and villas, material culture, and new forms of political and administrative organization appeared in many areas, creating an apparent uniformity on the surface. Continuity from the Iron Age, however, also forms an important part of understanding indigenous communities under Rome, and the complexities of these continuities, resulting in local differences and varying influences from Rome, are being increasingly recognized and documented. This chapter examines the way in which archaeological material can be used to examine these complexities during the Roman period and into post-Roman times. There was also considerable impact beyond the official bounds of the Empire but this chapter concentrates on the peoples within its boundaries.

The nature of the theoretical framework in interpreting the archaeological material is also important in analysing the nuances of continuity and change. European Iron Age studies, as part of the tradition of prehistoric archaeology, have acknowledged and positively utilized the theoretical nature of archaeological interpretation to develop some stimulating approaches to explore the complexities of the material evidence. The investigation of Roman archaeology has traditionally relied on historical frameworks and theoretical discussions have been slower in development but are now becoming more important, especially to explore themes such as identity within the Empire. Studies of late antiquity, however, have tended to be more conventional in the nature of archaeological interpretation, but by bridging the gap between the different specialisms it is possible to recognize the complexity in the relationship between continuity, change, and identity which will be explored through the themes of this chapter.

Historical Background to the Era and the Study of Identity Within the Empire

The areas of Europe that were incorporated into the Empire had rich histories and unique circumstances which produced provinces with many differing characteristics. A vast array of local differences existed within each province. The incorporation of the Iberian peninsula into the Empire began at the end of the third century BC, but it took nearly 200 years before it was complete and the provinces of Baetica, Lusitania, and Tarraconensis were created (Keay 2003). Expansion into Gaul from the second century BC onwards was equally drawn out, leading to the eventual creation of four provinces: Gallia Narbonensis, Gallia Aquitania, Gallia Lugdunensis, and Gallia Belgica (Woolf 1998). Conquest in Britain took many years after the initial invasion of AD 43 (Mattingly 2006), and influences from Rome and the Continent had already begun to cause social changes before this (cf. Creighton 2006). The provinces of Dalmatia, Noricum, Raetia, Pannonia, and Moesia in central Europe and the Balkans were created at the end of the first millennium BC, although there had also already been considerable contact between them and Rome before then (Lengyel and Radan 1980; Fischer 2002; Gassner et al. 2002; Davison et al. 2006; Mirković 2007). Germania Inferior and Germania Superior were established in AD 85 (Carroll 2001; Bechert 2007), and Dacia after the wars of AD 101–102 and AD 105–106 (Haynes and Hanson 2004; Oltean 2007). While the province of Macedonia was established in the second century BC, in southern Greece Achaea was not created until the end of the first century BC (Alcock 1993: 8–9). The nature of the conquest, including the level of force used, in a particular area might provide some reflection of local attitudes to Rome and the continued importance attached to local identities and traditions. Uprisings also occurred as for example in Britain, Dacia, and Pannonia/Dalmatia in an attempt to reassert local power (see Dyson 1971 for a list of documented uprisings).

The ancient Greek and Roman writers created general labels for other peoples such as Celt, German, Illyrian, and Dacian, which are just as inadequate for understanding community identities under Rome as in the Iron Age (cf. Jones 1997; James 1999). By the time of the Roman conquest, some peoples, such as the Dacians, were apparently under the rule of a single leader (Oltean 2007), but this does not mean that all groups in the kingdom necessarily considered themselves Dacian, with individual tribal identities instead remaining important. Sources indicate a vast complexity of different tribes across Europe but it is increasingly recognized that Roman influence may have played an important role in the consolidation of these entities through conquest and the creation of the *civitas* system; before this groups were in fact probably less homogeneous and more fluid (cf. Moore 2011) and local forms of identity expression probably continued to exist within the *civitates*. Tribes may have existed as much through individuals' fluctuating capabilities of commanding power and allegiance rather than reflecting local group identities (cf. James 1999; Hill 2006). Ethnic identity is situational and fluid in nature, rooted in daily practice and historical experience (Barth 1969; Cohen 1978; Jones 1997). Jones (1997: 13) has questioned the importance of pursuing ethnicity for understanding 'the basic, underlying essence or character of a group of people'. Identity can be expressed at a number of different levels; individual settlements or dwellings may well have contributed more of importance to the understanding of the self than anything of larger scale. This creates great potential for studying the way in which indigenous communities continued to express their identities in, and reacted to, the Roman Empire.

The dominant model for understanding indigenous communities under Rome has been that of 'Romanization', whereby local lifestyles and practices represented by settlements, goods, and land organization were gradually replaced by ones reflecting Roman influences. Where Roman styles were not adopted, this was seen as representing a failure, mainly through a lack of economic means. There have been a number of hugely influential figures in Roman studies and their pioneering work has contributed much to our understanding of the organization of the Empire and Roman provincial archaeology. The focus of their work, particularly the emphasis on Romanization, set the research agenda in Roman archaeology for much of the twentieth century. These scholars include Theodor Mommsen in Germany (1817–1903), whose most important works were the three-volume *History of Rome* (*Römische Geschichte*) covering the Republic (Mommsen 1854–1856), followed by a fourth volume on *The Provinces of the Roman Empire from Caesar to Diocletian* (*Die Provinzen von Caesar bis Diocletian*; Mommsen 1885). Mommsen was immensely influential on the next generation of scholars including Camille Jullian (1859–1933), who wrote a monumental eight-volume *Histoire de la Gaule* (Jullian 1908–1926), and Francis Haverfield (1860–1919), whose *Romanization of Roman Britain* (Haverfield 1912) was really one of the first works to take a modern scholarly approach to Roman archaeology in Britain. As the title indicates, however, his perspective was very much focused on the way in which the Empire transformed and benefited Britain.

The historiography of Roman studies has emphasized the importance of the social and political context in which the theory of 'Romanization' developed (e.g. Mattingly 1997; Hingley 2000; Freeman 2007), but it continues to remain a highly influential interpretative framework in Roman archaeology across Europe (cf. Hingley 2001). Moving beyond 'Romanization' and the context in which it developed, opens up a range of alternative ways of examining the complexity of reactions to Rome by indigenous communities. One such concept is 'cultural resistance', as opposed to active rebellion and violence, which argues that in the face of powerful external cultural influences there was a deliberate maintenance and reproduction of traditions (Wells 1999: 170). Though useful, the emphasis is on deliberate action against Rome when in many cases there may simply have been a lack of engagement with the Roman world. Resistance, moreover, does not help to explain the complex interaction of local and Roman traditions which is often recognized where there was a continuation of local attributes alongside newly introduced elements. The linguistic term 'creolization', recognizing the merging of two languages into a dialect that blends the two, has been adopted by some as a replacement for Romanization to explain this interaction of Roman and non-Roman, because it places less emphasis on the cultural superiority of Rome (Webster 2001).

Another concept is that of 'discrepant experience', which puts an emphasis on the fact that identities could be expressed in a variety of ways within the Roman imperial context (Mattingly 2004, 2006, 2011). There was no standard process or recipe for being Roman or being part of the Roman Empire—instead, we find a huge number of responses ranging from close integration to active resistance. Discrepant experience gives a voice to the individual and suggests that they had more power over their lives than has often been envisaged: some people may have wished to use their situation within the Empire to change their lives and others may not have done so. There was a coexistence of options where identities would have been continually reconstituted and redefined (Alcock 2002: 88). Perhaps no framework will ever adequately explain the vast range of experiences and lifeways possible within the Empire but this chapter will explore these further through a number of themes relating to the archaeological material.

Geography and Landscape

Maps of the Empire were produced for a Roman audience depicting the conquered lands and demonstrating dominance and control, but it is unlikely that most of the inhabitants of this vast area would have been aware of this new way of defining the land in which they lived. The maps were also highly selective in what they displayed and were designed for specific purposes: the *Tabula Peutingeriana* (Peutinger Map), for instance, depicts principally the *cursus publicus*, the main road network and the forts and cities along it, although it does show some mountains, rivers, and forests (Talbert 2010). Modern maps of the Roman Empire and its provinces are equally selective and tend to focus on features of governance, dominance, and elite society (cf. Alcock et al. 2001; Mattingly 2002). This reflects not only the dominant archaeological research traditions with their emphasis on Roman influences, but also the early modern European context of map-making and its relationship with imperialism (cf. Hingley 2006). Through detailed regional surveys of all known archaeological material of Roman date, however, it is possible to demonstrate the huge range of rural settlements relating to indigenous communities that existed within the Empire (e.g. Taylor 2007). Such work can dramatically redefine our understanding of local landscapes and settlement patterns.

Landscape archaeology, especially large-scale fieldwalking surveys, have been an important means of examining rural settlement patterns through time in a number of parts of Europe, for example in Spain (Castro López and Gutiérrez Soler 2001) and Greece (Alcock 1993, 1997; Cavanagh et al. 2002), as well as in Italy beyond Rome (e.g. Percossi et al. 2006; Witcher 2006; Bradley et al. 2008). Knowledge of settlement in Dacia has increased considerably through a detailed programme of aerial surveys (Hanson and Oltean 2003). It is clear that changes occurred in the Roman period, but rather than being uniform economic and social responses to Rome, these surveys have emphasized important differences across regions and micro-regions. In Republican Italy, for example, the level of urbanization, the extent to which settlements changed from indigenous types, and the change from using indigenous locally produced pottery to imports (Terrenato 1998; Sterry 2008) varied across and within regions, especially between coastal and inland locations. Surveys have shown a general numerical decline in rural sites in the Greek Peloponnese, but also regional differences and differences within regions relating to levels of site continuity and landholding patterns (e.g. Cavanagh et al. 2002). What is important to recognize is that at the individual settlement level there would also have been continuities in perceptions and organizations of space, and in the way in which the landscape was experienced, drawing on the long-term meanings attached to these landscapes.

Focusing on settlements of Roman date provides only a partial view of landscapes as they were inhabited in the Roman period. The time-depth of these landscapes will have been an important factor in the way in which they were experienced; prehistoric monuments and other sites, and also other features such as lakes, rivers, marshes, hills, and woodlands, will have continued to form elements of the cultural geography just as they did before the conquest (cf. Rogers 2012). Roman roads provided a new form of connectivity and way of moving through the landscape, as has been studied for Roman-period Greece (Malkin et al. 2009), but pre-existing routeways—and ways of experiencing the landscape—will have remained important (Alcock 2002). Prehistoric monuments continued to provide foci of activity, such as Silbury Hill in Britain (Leary and Field 2010), as did many Iron Age hillforts and *oppida* where, for example, Roman-period shrines and temples were constructed, as at Bibracte in France (Rebourg 1998). Such features were important landmarks and components of ritualized landscapes. Prehistoric burial monuments, in particular, may have been foci for the continuation of local ancestor cults with Roman-period inhabitants actively continuing or reworking pre-Roman values (Vermeulen and Bourgeois 2000). At Sint-Gillis-Waas in East Flanders (Belgium), for example, a number of early Roman cremation graves were located close to a Bronze Age barrow and a Roman-period settlement was found nearby (Vermeulen and Bourgeois 2000). The continuation of local traditions in perceiving and experiencing the land and environment has not received as much attention as it could, but it seems likely that landscapes will always have been contested between local peoples and incomers with different backgrounds and intentions.

Settlements, Buildings, and Space

New forms of settlement relating to the political and administrative functions of the Empire appeared across many parts of Europe, including colonies, *municipia*, and what are often termed *civitas* capitals. While they were usually new foundations, these sites could be located on or near pre-existing settlements, but had distinctive characteristics with their grid networks of paved streets, public buildings, and courtyard houses. They have traditionally formed an important focus of investigation in Roman archaeology, encouraged by descriptions of their importance in classical texts (e.g. Aristides *Orationes*), and often form the subject of major publications (e.g. Bedon et al. 1988; Wacher 1995; Šašel Kos and Scherrer 2002). The city of Augusta Raurica (Noricum) near Augst/Kaiseraugst in Switzerland, for example, has been the subject of an over forty-volume series *Forschungen in Augst* relating to the excavations and artefact studies. There were other forms of town-like settlements, however, often grouped under the heading of 'small town' or 'secondary agglomeration', which remain poorly understood and problematic to categorize. Often founded along Roman roads, they appear to have played important roles in the *civitates* but exhibit styles of organization that equate much more to local traditions than Roman influences. It is possible that they represent some kind of local interpretation of Roman urbanism (cf. Hingley 1997), or other trajectories in urban development that do not fit the classical city model, as perhaps Iron Age *oppida* also were. Regionally these settlements are now receiving more attention, as in Dacia (Oltean 2007), Gaul (Massy 1997), and Britain (Burnham and Wacher 1990), but also require detailed investigation to elucidate their biographies and the experiences associated with each individual settlement.

Roman cities, of course, were more than buildings and streets—they were stages of movement, interaction, and experience, and much of this will have related to indigenous attitudes to space. The Gallic city of Augustodunum (Autun), for example, was founded near the *oppidum* of Bibracte and although it was planned as a characteristic Roman city, its unusual shape appears to echo that of the earlier *oppidum* along with its size and the width and shape of its gates, which may reflect continued expression of local identities as the settlement developed (cf. Woolf 1998; Meylan 2000; Hurst 2005). Woolf (2006), moreover, has argued that it might be possible to view the monumental ramparts of Autun in terms of a further elaboration of those at Bibracte, continuing the pattern and importance of repeated and ritualized monumentalization of sites that occurred in prehistory. It might also be possible to recognize a similar form of organization within the city, with the industrial activities moving from Bibracte, which already had some elaborate Roman-style buildings at the time of its abandonment (Meylan 2000). In Britain, it is becoming increasingly clear that some of the earthworks traditionally associated with late Iron Age *oppida* were only constructed around or after the AD 43 invasion, and they continued to be important as towns developed around or near them, as at Silchester, the Bagendon/Ditches complex near Cirencester, and Colchester.

This, too, suggests a continuation of pre-Roman ideas of landscape monumentalization and the use of space. On the other side of the Empire in Greece, cities existed before the Roman period and although the infrastructures were often altered in Roman times, the surviving geography of the cities, and the histories and meanings associated with them will have continued to form important elements of the city identities, maintaining links with the pre-Roman past (cf. Alcock 2002).

It is important that the archaeological evidence is studied independently of any assumed historical frameworks. The relationship between existing settlements and Roman urbanism was not simply one of disuse and replacement by new forms. Major forms of Iron Age settlement such as hillforts and *oppida* did not necessarily go out of use after the appearance of Roman towns. A good example is provided by the *castros* and other upland settlement forms of the Iberian peninsula. *Castros*, with their stone-built roundhouses and open spaces surrounded by drystone walls in hilly settings of north-west Iberia, have traditionally been assumed to go out of use after the Roman conquest. There is now, however, increasing evidence for continued use and alteration of these places in the Roman period. In the upland areas of Baetica, the southernmost Roman province in Spain, there has been a lot of work documenting the extent of settlement continuity (e.g. Fortea Pérez and Bernier Lugue 1970). Torreparadones, for example, enclosing over 100,000 m^2, was a focus of occupation from the sixth century BC into the medieval period, including the use of a pre-existing shrine in the Roman period (Cunliffe and Fernández Castro 1999). There was a much more complex mix of sites in Spain than has generally been recognized, with native sites and new Roman towns being occupied at the same time.

Indigenous-style domestic architecture is often known in at least the early phases of cities, as at Atuatuca Tungrorum (Tongeren) in Belgium (Figure 38.1; Vanderhoeven 1996) and London in Britain (Perring and Roskams 1991; Hill and Rowsome 2011; Perring 2011). Increasingly, attention is being given to recognizing and studying indigenous-style buildings continuing in the Roman period. The form of domestic architecture and the materials used in construction related to more than just practicality and cost: they embody local choices, daily life, and ways of expressing and understanding identity and being in the world. The internal organization of the spaces, moreover, would have been deeply embedded in indigenous cosmologies. Investigation of individual structures, then, can reveal much about indigenous lifeways and continuities in the Roman period. The process of construction itself may well have formed an important part of the building and its meaning, and would have been a significant social activity perhaps rooted in local traditions (cf. McFadyen 2006; Sharples 2010).

In Britain the pre-Roman tradition of roundhouses, as opposed to Roman-period rectangular structures, continued and has been recognized even in the south of the province. Excavations at Snettisham, Norfolk, for example, uncovered part of what appears to have been a fairly extensive rural settlement with a mixed economy of farming and craft activity. The buildings were timber roundhouses, all built after the Roman conquest and dated from the mid-first to late second century AD (Flitcroft 2001). A decision was made to build in this style despite there being a number of Roman villas in

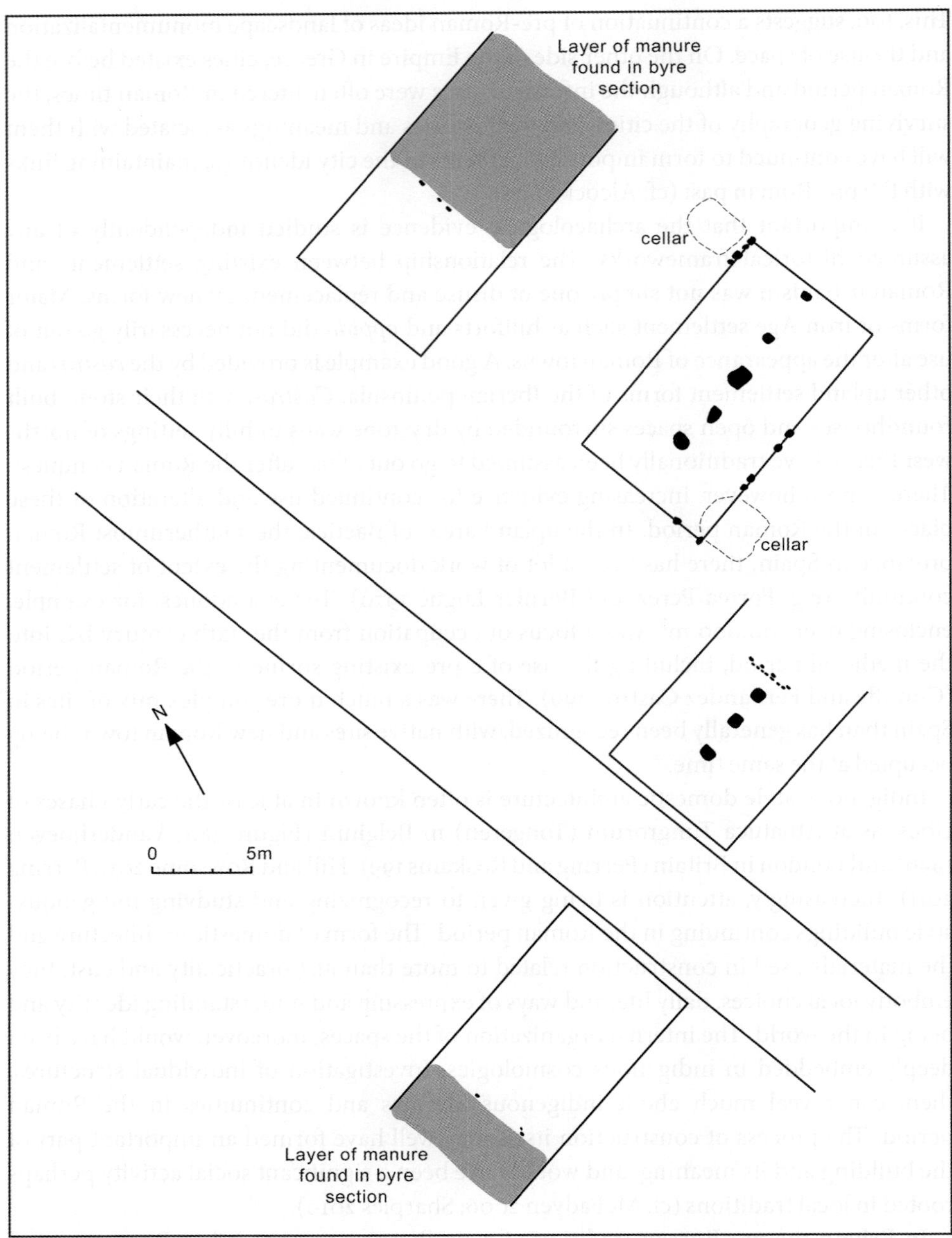

FIGURE 38.1 Period 2 Alphen-Ekeren-type timber buildings at Kielenstraat, Tongeren, Belgium, probably dating to the beginning of the first century AD. The remains of the walls consist of shallow inserted posts and some structures have evidence of internal partitions.

Author, adapted from Vanderhoeven (1996): fig. 4

the area. There was a large amount of local handmade pottery on the site. Analysis of the distribution of material from another Roman-period roundhouse at Birdlip Quarry, Gloucestershire, suggests that there had been a left/right and front/back organization of the activities that took place in the structure (Figure 38.2; Mudd 1999: 247). The internal space was ordered and will have formed an important way in which lives were reconstituted on a daily basis. A traditional focus in the expression of identity may have been more important than wider notions of belonging; identities were constructed through daily practices and could be fluid, flexible, and multidimensional.

It is also important to recognize, however, that replacing roundhouses with rectangular buildings need not necessarily represent a significant alteration in the way in which internal spaces were inhabited and organized (cf. Hingley 1999). Often the same form of internal divisions between central and peripheral space can be recognized, whether consisting of two rows or a circle of posts. Moreover, rectangular structures

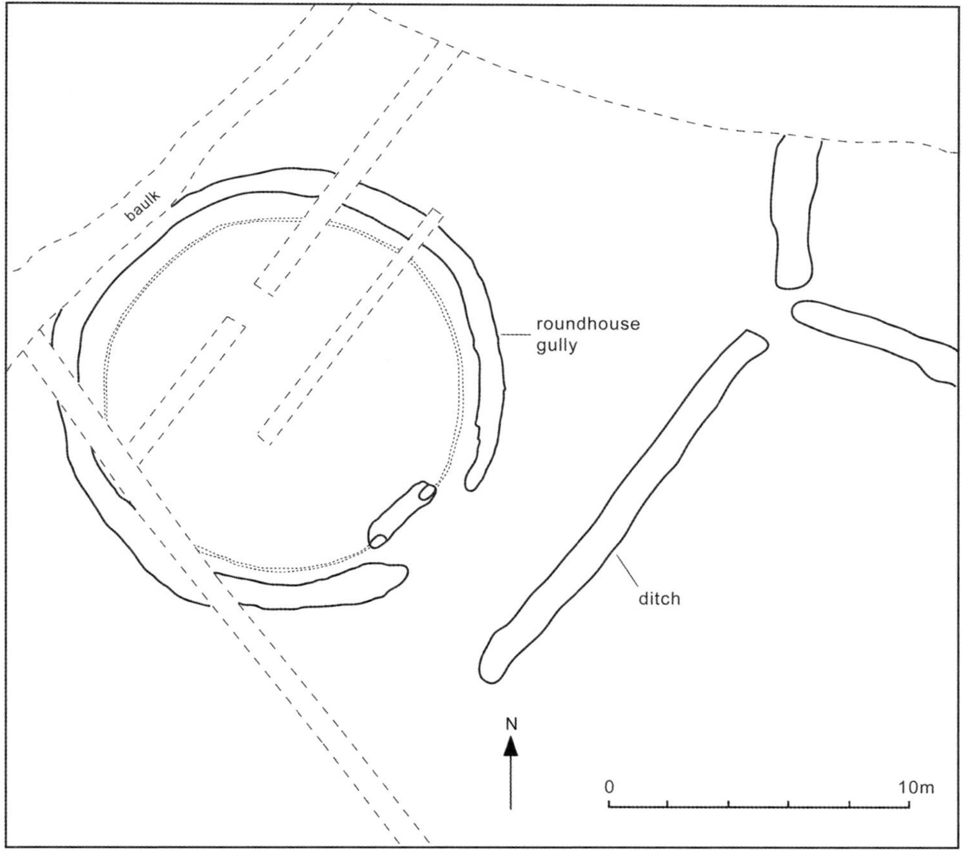

FIGURE 38.2 Birdlip Quarry, Gloucestershire, England: plan of roundhouse structure 1464 and nearby features.

Author, adapted from Mudd (1999): fig. 4.48

were often built in timber, which could relate as much to the importance of existing building traditions as the lack of means for a masonry building. More investigation is needed on the way in which regional and local pre-Roman traditions of architecture and spatial organization influenced settlement patterns and building styles in the Roman period. Smith's (1997) Empire-wide analysis of Roman villa plans, for example, has indicated that many of the villas of Dacia, Pannonia, and Moesia show sufficient differences from Italy or the western provinces to suggest that they may have been influenced by local traditions of spatial organization and family relationships, but this is as yet poorly understood and needs further work.

Across much of Europe, local forms of timber rectangular structures continued to be built in the Roman period. For example, the site of Rijswijk in the western Netherlands has been comprehensively excavated, providing evidence of continuous occupation from the early first century AD until the second half of the third century (Bloemers 1978). The earliest phase was a farmstead consisting of a house and ancillary buildings. The farmhouse was a three-aisled timber building with human occupation confined to one end and cattle kept at the other. This building was replaced by a slightly larger structure divided into two rooms, with the larger one being used to keep animals. The structure was then enlarged again, still using traditional architectural techniques; by the second century AD there were three farmsteads on the site. Locally made pottery remained important from the early first into the third century AD. Like roundhouses, these structures and their organization represented local value systems, social structures, and ideologies (Roymans 1995; Gerritsen 2003). Cosmological principles underlay the construction, spatial organization, and decorative schemes of buildings which may well have been difficult to lose or replace in the Roman period.

Ritual and Religion

The expansion of the Roman Empire saw the spread of new official forms of religion and architecture such as the Imperial cult, classical-style temples, statuary, and altars. While Roman religion has been the subject of considerable study (e.g. Beard et al. 1998), the nature of religious beliefs and ritual practices means that they can often survive beyond other forms of social change and the introduction of new religious forms. In each Roman province, a vast range of religious activities took place, forming important elements of daily life and the expression of local identities. The process often referred to as *interpretatio Romana*, after Tacitus' description of Roman and German gods (*Germania* 43), is usually evoked to demonstrate that attempts were made to control indigenous gods by associating them with Roman deities and naming them in ways that they had not been previously. The way in which this influenced religious practices, however, is unclear and numerous dedicatory remains indicate that local gods continued to be worshipped in their own right (cf. Mattingly 2006: 215). There would also have been countless other forms of local religious beliefs and practices that were much more difficult for the authorities to pin down and manage. Many indigenous gods were represented in new ways, including in anthropomorphic form by manufacturing statues and statuettes which drew on the classical tradition. The forms, however, often exhibited local attributes, and it could be argued that the importance of the local gods was strengthened through this new method of representation rather than being weakened by assimilation. From eastern and central Gaul, for example, statuettes of indigenous gods include the horse goddess Epona and the hammer god Sucellus, who wears a distinctive Gallic cloak or *sagum* (Webster 2003). There was a complex negotiation of ideas relating to new representations and the continuation of pre-existing religion and belief.

In studying the expression of indigenous identities through religion and ritual it is important to look beyond temples, altars, and statues. Most excavations of Roman rural settlements, for example, do not produce religious inscriptions, altars, or shrines in the same way that towns or military sites do, suggesting that, as in the Iron Age, religious activities took other forms. One form of religious expression that is recognizable in the archaeological record, continuing from prehistory, is structured deposition; this has been identified not only on rural settlements but also in cities. Documenting such activity requires detailed contextualization and analysis of archaeological finds from excavations as well as the recognition of the religious significance of the material and its context.

Where the standards of excavation and recording are high enough, it is possible to reconstruct such activity retrospectively, as with the Victorian and Edwardian excavations at the Roman town of Calleva Atrebatum (Silchester, southern Britain). Fulford (2001) has been able to document a rich collection of objects found in wells and pits across the Roman town, including complete pottery and bronze vessels, animal remains, and other finds. Rather than simply representing rubbish thrown away, Fulford argues that this material indicates the persistence of existing religious traditions. Placed deposits of objects in pits, wells, and other contexts are common in the Roman period, as in prehistory, and the significance of such material for studying religious practice needs to be recognized. These contexts may have been regarded as entry points into the godly world (cf. Ross 1967; Cunliffe 1992), and offerings may have been made to negotiate the difficulties of everyday life.

There has been considerable work done on documenting religious activity and ritual actions inferred from cultural material in prehistoric central and eastern Europe, including the analysis of pit deposits and the development of the fragmentation premise for interpreting human action from object distribution in the archaeological record (Chapman 2000; Chapman and Gaydarska 2007). Detailed analysis of the contexts in which objects were found suggests a rich tradition of social behaviour whereby objects were deliberately broken and meaningfully used after breakage. The study of Roman-period material culture has tended to focus on object function, and materials and method of construction. Analysis of use-life and deposition is still in its infancy but it seems likely that rich traditions of cultural activity such as are known from prehistory will have influenced behaviour in Roman times. Archaeological literature discusses rubbish pits and other forms of disposal but there remains considerable potential for scrutinizing the way in which archaeological deposits are interpreted.

Some classical sources, as well as archaeological evidence, hint at the wide range of locations that attracted religious activity in the Iron Age, including rivers, lakes, wetlands, and hilltops (Webster 1995) as with Poseidonios' description of sacred lakes near Toulouse in southern France recorded by Strabo (*Geography* 4.1.13). Their religious importance often survived into the Roman period, which impacts on our understanding of the experience of settlement and place (cf. Rogers 2008). At the source of the River Seine in east-central France, for example, wooden sculptures of humans and human body parts, along with metal objects, were deposited at the spring in the late Iron Age. In the Roman period, statuary dedicated to the pre-Roman river deity was placed in or around the spring (Derks 1998). In north-west Iberia, the upland sanctuary of Panóias consists of three rock outcrops into which steps were cut and rectangular hollows were cut into the tops of the large rocks (Richert 2005: 15). The sanctuary remained in use in the Roman period. The Roman military clearly recognized and were keen to appease local deities in the landscapes that they occupied, as the large number of objects deposited in the River Tees at the base at Piercebridge in north-east England demonstrates (Cool and Mason 2008). Local gods needed to be placated if possible.

Death and Burial

The Roman period saw a considerable standardization of burial practices across Europe in the form of cremations, and large cemeteries were established outside towns. Amidst this uniformity, local practices influenced Roman-style funerary rites, and pre-Roman traditions continued. In reality there was a huge range of variation across and within cemeteries in the precise way in which individuals were buried—a combination of human action and expression of identity. The burial evidence represents processes, rituals, and ceremonies relating to the funerary event and beliefs concerning death and the afterlife (Sharples 2010: 247). It seems likely, then, that pre-existing traditions and beliefs could survive even if the style of burial itself changed.

In provincial settings, burial evidence can be very varied, exhibiting differing degrees of external influence and the continuation of individual expressions and traditions within the community. At the cemetery of Wadern-Oberlöstern in north-west Saarland (Germany), excavations indicate continuation of the local tradition of tumuli enclosed by a boundary, but fused with Roman influences including the use of funerary monuments (Figure 38.3; Abegg-Wigg 2000). Local decisions and choices were also being made regarding the type of grave goods placed in graves, reflecting local traditions and individual identities. This can be seen even in urban settings such as the eastern cemetery outside the town of Bavay in northern Gaul (Loridant and Deru 2009). In the Low Countries and parts of Germany a strong martial culture continued in the Roman period and many male graves contained weapons, continuing pre-existing traditions

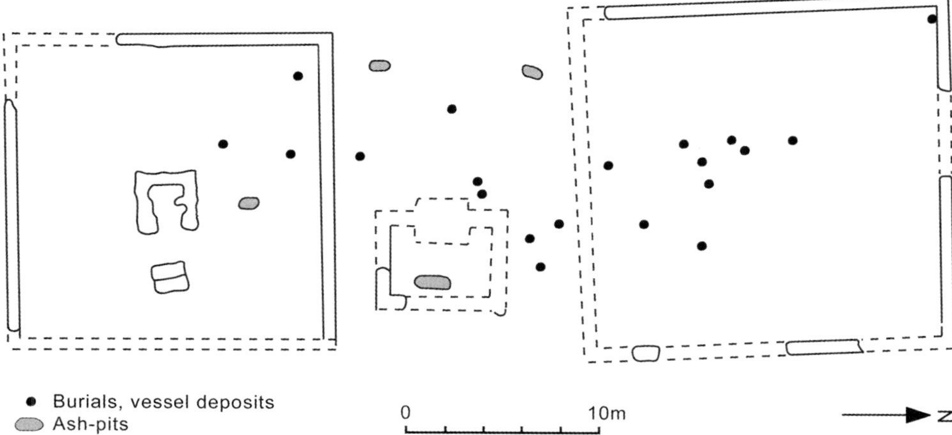

FIGURE 38.3 The cemetery of Wadern-Oberlöstern, Saarland, Germany, in the east of the *Civitas Treverorum*.

Author, adapted from Abegg-Wigg (2000): fig. 12.2

of expressing identity, as at the Goeblingen-Nospelt cemetery in Luxembourg (Metzler 1984; Nicolay 2007). Local styles of burial can indicate persistence of pre-Roman traditions, while also using Roman-style ceramic tableware and other objects as grave goods. In the Berry area of central France, for example, there were tombs consisting of square chambers, which were probably covered with mounds, containing the human remains together with weapons, ceramic and metal vessels, amphorae, and food remains (Ferdière and Villard 1993). The Roman-style objects, then, were probably incorporated into local rites and beliefs about death and the afterlife. There are also more distinctive cases of local traditions: in West Yorkshire, Roman-period crouched burials have been found, drawing on pre-Roman traditions (Chadwick 2009).

As in prehistory, burials—whether cremations or inhumations—were not the only methods used to dispose of bodies in the Roman period. The discovery of human bone in contexts other than formal burials is suggestive of other ways of disposing of the dead. It is a well-known statistic that in Europe there is a general shortage of prehistoric burials compared with the number of people who must have lived at that time, indicating that there were other ways of disposing of the dead. There is evidence that body parts formed elements of special deposits and were also placed in rivers and other watery contexts (Wait 1985; Brück 1995; Sharples 2010: 251–253). Some at least of these traditions continued in the Roman period, with body parts being found in various contexts both on land and in water. In London the site of Moor House lay just outside the north boundary of the Roman town, in a wet and low-lying area in the Walbrook valley (Figure 38.4). Within the numerous small river channels and marshy ground were a large number of disarticulated human body parts, with a noticeable concentration of specific bone types, suggesting that the bones did not simply represent disturbed burials (Butler 2006: 38–41). The evidence may indicate that people from a wide area

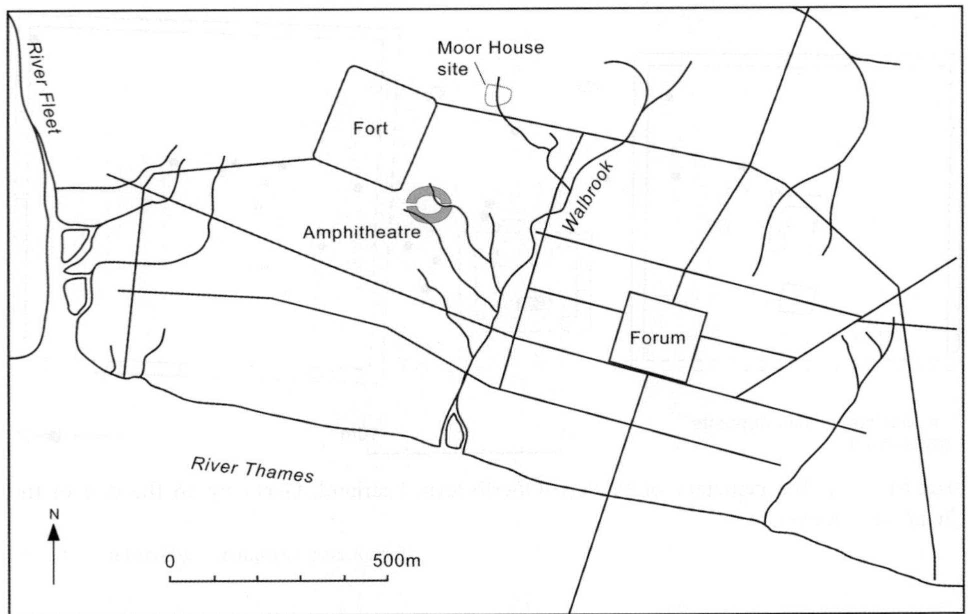

FIGURE 38.4 The location of the Moor House excavations in relation to Roman London and the upper Walbrook valley.

Author, adapted from Butler (2006): fig. 7

were converging at this location to dispose of their dead through ritual ceremonies and traditional means. Significantly, the Walbrook was used in prehistory for the deposition of large numbers of human skulls (Merrifield 1995), reinforcing the idea of a continued tradition (cf. Schulting and Bradley 2014). Much work is still needed on documenting the variety of traditions of burial and body disposal that undoubtedly existed in the Roman period amongst indigenous communities. The Walbrook valley certainly seems to have attracted veneration through ritual deposition throughout the Roman period (cf. Merrifield and Hall 2008; Leary and Butler 2012).

Production, Material Culture, and Art

Objects play a central role in archaeological and anthropological studies and important themes of research include object biography, the relationship between object and identity, and the symbolism and meaning in object production (Gosden and Marshall 1999). In the Roman period mass-produced objects spread across the Empire, but opportunities remained to express local identities through the choices made to use particular objects, especially dress accessories, and the way in which objects were treated. In post-medieval colonial archaeology there has been considerable work documenting the way in which objects were used to express identity and resistance through the way they were used, treated, and altered (e.g. Deetz 1977). Detailed studies of the distribution of object types is one important way of assessing local choices in object use and the way in which this might reflect expressions of identity. Eckardt's (2002) comprehensive study of the distribution of lighting equipment found across Roman Britain is a good example, demonstrating many local variations in the types of equipment that were chosen. There were also areas where no Roman-style lighting equipment was used, suggesting that indigenous traditions remained important; lighting can also be hugely symbolic and relates to the experience and organization of social space. The presence and quantity of Roman-style material culture on a settlement site has conventionally been used as an indicator of the status and wealth of the inhabitants, but many factors were involved in the formation (and deposition) of artefact assemblages, including the accessibility of goods, the desirability of using Roman-style material, and local traditions of object use and wealth disposal. Indeed, wealth may have been expressed in many different ways, some not easily represented in the archaeological record, including the ownership of animals (cf. Matthews 1997; Fincham 2002). It is also important to recognize that the way in which objects were perceived and experienced in terms of factors such as shape, colour, and feel will have differed depending on local traditions and circumstances (Wells 2008b).

As well as new forms of material culture introduced into conquered provinces, continuity is often seen in the use of existing forms of objects and methods of manufacture. Pottery is a good indicator of the persistence of traditions because it survives well and it is possible to recognize local styles and techniques. Studies of pottery from Roman Dacia, for example, have demonstrated considerable continuity in the production of local handmade pottery, including a number of distinctive types (Negru 2003). In Germany, as well as local handmade wares, pottery was produced in imported styles, but using local dark-coloured reduced fabrics rather than the colourful oxidized wares of the originals (Carroll 2001: 85). Seemingly, new styles of pottery were being interpreted through local ideas of how pottery should be made and what it should look like.

Traditions of production are an important aspect of understanding material culture and local identity expression. The act of manufacture was a cultural activity deeply embedded in local traditions and beliefs and imbued with ritual symbolism, thereby influencing the way in which objects were used and treated. Craft processes were learnt through traditions, and rituals passed on through the generations (cf. Budd and Taylor 1995). The processes of metal production and metalworking, for example, were charged with religious symbolism, and this cultural significance may have survived even if the type of objects manufactured had changed. At Southwark in Roman London, excavations along the main road leading to London Bridge uncovered an iron smithing workshop (Drummond-Murray and Thompson 2002: 97). As well as smithing debris, the site yielded a so-called 'smith urn' from a well, which depicted a representation of a smith god complete with hammer, pincers, and anvil. From the same well and two adjacent pits came the remains of twenty dog skeletons, which appear to have been ritual deposits (cf. Smith 2006). This suggests that indigenous traditions relating to ironworking survived and were still taking place in Roman London where indigenous people came into the new settlement to carry out ironworking activities.

Artwork is another important form of expression. Provincial artwork has traditionally been viewed in negative terms in comparison to art from Greece and Rome—being considered as inferior attempts at imitation (e.g. Haverfield 1912). Postcolonial perspectives, however, help us to regard local artwork according to indigenous expressions and ways of perceiving the world. The artists were not incompetent but rather were being actively creative according to the demands of existing traditions (cf. Webster 2003).

The End of Roman Rule and Beyond

The historical events of the later Roman Empire are complex; in observing developments and changes, studies have tended to focus on Rome itself and the lives of the elite across the Empire. Archaeology permits a more detailed investigation of the impact of the end of the Empire at a local level, where there might be no written records of events. The concept of 'decline' has been hugely influential in interpreting late Roman archaeological material; it is also linked with Romanization, which puts an emphasis on classical buildings and material culture, which begin to change in late Roman times. More recently, however, there has been much useful work redressing the concept of decline in late Roman and early post-Roman archaeology (e.g. Cameron 2003; Christie 2006a; Wells 2008a; Rogers 2011). A central aspect of this chapter has been to emphasize the huge variety of lifeways, building types, and styles of material culture throughout the Roman period, in many cases continuing pre-existing traditions. Similarly, adoption of Roman styles need not necessarily indicate significant change in local behaviours or world views. Many late Roman buildings were constructed in timber in various parts of Europe, but rather than decline this implies continued vitality and sophistication. Timber structures, moreover, could be monumental in their own right, as they were in prehistory—there was also a continuity in the importance of these materials and the significance of the processes of construction and creation.

The concept of the 'Celtic Revival' has long been a popular interpretative framework for understanding a perceived resurgence of indigenous expressions through building styles and material culture in the later Roman west, as Roman influences weakened (e.g. Seebohm 1883; Vinogradoff 1905; Rice Holmes 1907; Haverfield 1912; Collingwood and Myres 1936). After many centuries as part of the Empire, there will have been a complex relationship between indigenous and external influences; the concept of 'being Roman' will have constantly evolved (cf. Gardner 2007), so it seems unlikely that we can think in terms of a revival of things pre-Roman. The later Roman period saw considerable instability through incursions of peoples from outside the Empire, and established supply routes were jeopardized. This may be another reason for the apparent resurgence in locally produced pottery and other goods, as has been argued for fourth- and fifth-century Pannonia (Christie 2006b). Political troubles in Rome centred on the elite and it is unlikely that the lives of most people in rural communities in the provinces will have been greatly affected as the Roman period passed into post-Roman times. There are examples of indigenous settlements that show little if any sign of change between the Iron Age and the later Roman period or beyond. Many settlements in Cornwall in south-west England, for example, appear to show relatively little engagement with the Roman world, for instance in the distinctive stone-built circular structures known as Rounds which remained in use into post-Roman times (e.g. Quinnell 2004).

It is also possible to consider long-term continuities and importance in the symbolism attached to landscapes from prehistory into post-Roman times. There appears to have been considerable continuity in behaviour and experience of the land into post-Roman times. Prehistoric monuments still provided a special focus for religious and burial places in early medieval Europe (e.g. Williams 2006). At Kelheim in southern Bavaria, a number of graves dating from the sixth to seventh century AD appear to have deliberately focused on the long-abandoned *oppidum* as a suitable place for burial, indicating that it remained an important and symbolic element of the landscape (Suppe 1993: 156). In Lincolnshire, the prehistoric causeways across the wetland of the Witham valley formed a focus of ritual deposition into the water from pre-Roman into post-Roman times, indicating a continuing significance of this landscape (Stocker and Everson 2003). In early medieval times, many of these causeways became foci for the establishment of churches, indicating continued recognition of the religious dimensions of this environment. Building styles and material culture may have altered, but longer-term local continuities are apparent in the habitation and use of the landscape. Such considerations form an important part of understanding the lives of communities under Rome.

References

Abegg-Wigg, A. 2000. 'A Roman cemetery in the eastern Civitas Treverorum. Preliminary report on the excavations in Wadern-Oberlöstern in northwestern Saarland (Germany)', in J. Pearce, M. Millett, and M. Struck (eds) *Burial, Society and Context in the Roman World*: 112–117. Oxford: Oxbow Books.

Alcock, S., H. Dey, and G. Parker. 2001. 'Sitting down with the Barrington Atlas'. *Journal of Roman Archaeology Supplement* 14: 454–461.

Alcock, S. E. 1993. *Graecia Capta: The Landscapes in Roman Greece*. Cambridge: Cambridge University Press.

Alcock, S. E. 1997. 'Greece: A landscape of resistance?', in D. J. Mattingly (ed.) *Dialogues in Roman Imperialism: Power, Discourse and Discrepant Experiences in the Roman Empire*. Journal of Roman Archaeology Supplementary Series 23: 103–115. Portsmouth (RI): Journal of Roman Archaeology.

Alcock, S. E. 2002. *Archaeologies of the Greek Past: Landscape, Monuments and Memories*. Cambridge: Cambridge University Press.

Barth, F. 1969. 'Introduction', in F. Barth (ed.) *Ethnic Groups and Boundaries: The Social Organisation of Culture Difference*: 9–38. London: George Allen and Unwin.

Beard, M., J. North, and S. Price. 1998. *The Religions of Rome*. Cambridge: Cambridge University Press.

Bechert, T. 2007. *Germania Inferior: eine Provinz an der Nordgrenze des Römischen Reiches*. Mainz: Philipp von Zabern.

Bedon, R., R. Chevallier, and R. Pinon. 1988. *Architecture et urbanisme en Gaule romaine, Tome 2: L'urbanisme en Gaule romaine*. Paris: Errance.

Bloemers, J. H. F. 1978. *Rijswijk (Z.H.) 'De Bult': Eine Siedlung der Canenefaten*. Den Haag: Staatsuitgeverij.

Bradley, G., D. Fossataro, and O. Menozzi. 2008. 'The Iuvanum Survey Project, Abruzzo, Chieti, Italy', in G. Lock and A. Faustoferri (eds) *Archaeology and Landscape in Central Italy: Papers in Memory of John A. Lloyd*: 137–150. Oxford: Oxford University School of Archaeology.

Brück, J. 1995. 'A place for the dead: The role of human remains in late Bronze Age Britain'. *Proceedings of the Prehistoric Society* 61: 245–277.

Budd, P., and T. Taylor. 1995. 'The Faerie Smith meets the bronze industry: Magic versus science in the interpretation of prehistoric metal making'. *World Archaeology* 27: 133–143.

Burnham, B. C., and J. Wacher. 1990. *The Small Towns of Roman Britain*. London: Batsford.

Butler, J. 2006. *Reclaiming the Marsh: Archaeological Excavations at Moor House, City of London*. PCA Monograph 6. London: Pre-Construct Archaeology.

Cameron, A. 2003. 'Ideologies and agendas in Late Antique studies', in L. Lavan and W. Bowden (eds) *Theory and Practice in Late Antique Archaeology*: 3–21. Leiden: Brill.

Carroll, M. 2001. *Romans, Celts and Germans: The German Provinces of Rome*. Stroud: Tempus.

Castro López, M., and L. Gutiérrez Soler. 2001. 'Conquest and Romanization of the upper Guadalquivir valley', in S. Keay and N. Terrenato (eds) *Italy and the West: Comparative Issues in Romanization*: 145–160. Oxford: Oxbow Books.

Cavanagh, W., J. Crouwel, R. W. V. Catling, and G. Shipley. 2002. *Continuity and Change in a Greek Rural Landscape: The Laconia Survey*. London: The British School at Athens.

Chadwick, A. M. 2009. *An Archaeological Research Agenda for West Yorkshire: The Iron Age and Romano-British Periods in West Yorkshire*. Wakefield: The West Yorkshire Archaeology Advisory Service.

Chapman, J. 2000. *Fragmentation in Archaeology: People, Places and Broken Objects in the Prehistory of South Eastern Europe*. London: Routledge.

Chapman, J., and B. Gaydarska. 2007. *Parts and Wholes: Fragmentation in Prehistoric Context*. Oxford: Oxbow Books.

Christie, N. 2006a. *From Constantine to Charlemagne: An Archaeology of Italy AD 300–800*. Aldershot: Ashgate.

Christie, N. 2006b. 'From the Danube to the Po: The defence of Pannonia and Italy in the fourth and fifth centuries AD', in A. Poulter (ed.) *The Transition to Late Antiquity on the Danube and Beyond*: 547–578. Oxford: Oxford University Press.

Cohen, R. 1978. 'Ethnicity: Problems and focus in anthropology'. *Annual Review of Anthropology* 7: 379–403.

Collingwood, R. G., and J. N. L. Myres. 1936. *Roman Britain and the English Settlements*. Oxford: Clarendon Press.

Cool, H. E. M., and D. W. Mason (eds). 2008. *Roman Piercebridge: Excavations by D. W. Harding and Peter Scott 1969–1981*. AASDN Research Report 7. Durham: Architectural and Archaeological Society of Durham and Northumberland.

Creighton, J. 2006. *Britannia: The Creation of a Roman Province*. London: Routledge.
Cunliffe, B. W. 1992. 'Pits, preconceptions and propitiation in the British Iron Age'. *Oxford Journal of Archaeology* 11: 69–83.
Cunliffe, B. W., and M. C. Fernández Castro. 1999. *The Guadajoz Project: Andalucía in the First Millennium BC, Vol 1: Torreparedones and its Hinterland*. Oxford: Institute of Archaeology, University of Oxford.
Davison, D., V. Gaffney, and E. Marin (eds). 2006. *Dalmatia: Research in the Roman Province 1970–2001: Papers in Honour of J. J. Wilkes*. British Archaeological Reports International Series 1576. Oxford: Archaeopress.
Deetz, J. 1977. *In Small Things Forgotten: An Archaeology of Early American Life*. New York: Bantam Doubleday Dell.
Derks, T. 1998. *Gods, Temples and Ritual Practices: The Transformation of Religious Ideas and Values in Roman Gaul*. Amsterdam Archaeological Studies 2. Amsterdam: Amsterdam University Press.
Drummond-Murray, J., P. Thompson, and C. Cowan. 2002. *Settlement in Roman Southwark: Archaeological Excavations (1991–8) for the London Underground Limited Jubilee Line Extension Project*. MoLAS Monograph 12. London: Museum of London Archaeology Service.
Dyson, S. 1971. 'Native revolts in the Roman Empire'. *Historia. Zeitschrift für Alte Geschichte* 20: 239–274.
Eckardt, H. 2002. *Illuminating Roman Britain*. Monographies Instrumentum 16. Montagnac: Éditions Monique Mergoil.
Ferdière, A., and A. Villard. 1993. *La tombe augustéene de Fléré-la-Rivière (Indre) et les sépultures aristocratiques de la cité des Bituriges*. Revue Archéologique du Centre de la France supplément 7. Saint Marcel: Musée d'Argentomagus.
Fincham, G. 2002. *Landscapes of Imperialism: Roman and Native Interaction in the East Anglian Fenland*. British Archaeological Reports British Series 338. Oxford: Archaeopress.
Fischer, T. 2002. *Noricum*. Mainz: Philipp von Zabern.
Flitcroft, M. 2001. *Excavations of a Romano-British Settlement on the A149 Snettisham Bypass, 1989*. East Anglian Archaeology Report 93. Dereham: Norfolk Museums and Archaeology Service.
Fortea Pérez, J., and J. Bernier Lugue. 1970. *Recintos y fortificaciones ibéricos en la Bética*. Salamanca: Universidad de Salamanca.
Freeman, P. W. M. 2007. *The Best Training-Ground for Archaeologists: Francis Haverfield and the Invention of Romano-British Archaeology*. Oxford: Oxbow Books.
Fulford, M. 2001. 'Links with the past: Pervasive "ritual" behaviour in Roman Britain'. *Britannia* 32: 199–218.
Gardner, A. 2007. *Archaeology of Identity: Soldiers and Society in Later Roman Britain*. Walnut Creek: Left Coast Press.
Gassner, V., S. Jilek, and S. Ladstätter. 2002. *Am Rande des Reiches: die Römer in Österreich*. Vienna: Ueberreuter.
Gerritsen, F. 2003. *Local Identities: Landscape and Community in the Late Prehistoric Meuse-Demer-Scheldt Region*. Amsterdam Archaeological Studies 9. Amsterdam: Amsterdam University Press.
Gosden, C., and Y. Marshall. 1999. 'The cultural biography of objects'. *World Archaeology* 31, 2: 169–178.
Hanson, W. S., and I. A. Oltean. 2003. 'The identification of Roman buildings from the air: Recent discoveries in Western Transylvania'. *Archaeological Prospection* 10: 101–117.

Haverfield, F. 1912. *The Romanization of Roman Britain*. Oxford: Clarendon Press.

Haynes, I. P., and W. S. Hanson. 2004. 'An introduction to Roman Dacia', in W. S. Hanson and I. P. Haynes (eds) *Roman Dacia: The Making of a Provincial Society*. Journal of Roman Archaeology Supplementary Series 56: 11–31. Portsmouth (RI): Journal of Roman Archaeology.

Hill, J., and P. Rowsome. 2011. *Roman London and the Walbrook Stream Crossing: Excavations at 1 Poultry and Vicinity, City of London*. MoLA Monograph 37. London: Museum of London Archaeology.

Hill, J. D. 2006. 'Are we any closer to understanding how later Iron Age societies worked (or did not work)?', in C. Haselgrove (ed.) *Celtes et Gaulois: l'archéologie face à l'histoire: Les mutations de la fin de l'âge du Fer*. Collection Bibracte 12/4: 169–179. Glux-en-Glenne: Centre archéologique européen du Mont Beuvray.

Hingley, R. 1997. 'Resistance and domination: Social change in Roman Britain', in D. J. Mattingly (ed.) *Dialogues in Roman Imperialism: Power, Discourse and Discrepant Experiences in the Roman Empire*. Journal of Roman Archaeology Supplementary Series 23: 145–166. Portsmouth (RI): Journal of Roman Archaeology.

Hingley, R. 1999. 'The imperial context of Romano-British studies and proposals for a new understanding of social change', in P. P. A. Funari, M. Hall, and S. Jones (eds) *Historical Archaeology: Back from the Edge*: 137–150. London: Routledge.

Hingley, R. 2000. *Roman Officers and English Gentlemen*. London and New York: Routledge.

Hingley, R. (ed.) 2001. *Images of Rome: Perceptions of Ancient Rome in Europe and the United States in the Modern Age*. Journal of Roman Archaeology Supplementary Series 44. Portsmouth (RI): Journal of Roman Archaeology.

Hingley, R. 2006. 'Projecting Empire: The mapping of Roman Britain'. *Journal of Social Archaeology* 6: 328–353.

Hurst, H. 2005. 'Roman Cirencester and Gloucester compared'. *Oxford Journal of Archaeology* 24: 293–305.

James, S. 1999. *The Atlantic Celts: Ancient People or Modern Invention?* London: British Museum Press.

Jones, S. 1997. *The Archaeology of Ethnicity: Constructing Identities in the Past and Present*. London/New York: Routledge.

Jullian, C. 1908–1926. *Histoire de la Gaule, Vols I–VIII*. Paris: Librairie Hachette.

Keay, S. 2003. 'Recent archaeological work in Roman Iberia (1990–2002)'. *Journal of Roman Studies* 93: 146–211.

Leary, J., and J. Butler. 2012. *Roman Archaeology in the Upper Reaches of the Walbrook Valley: Excavations at 6–8 Tokenhouse Yard, London EC2*. PCA Monograph 14. London: Pre-Construct Archaeology.

Leary, J., and D. Field. 2010. *The Story of Silbury Hill*. Swindon: English Heritage.

Lengyel, A., and G. T. B. Radan. 1980. *The Archaeology of Roman Pannonia*. Lexington: University Press of Kentucky.

Loridant, F., and X. Deru. 2009. *Bavay: la nécropole gallo-romaine de 'La Fache des Près Aulnoys'*. Revue du Nord hors série Collection Art et Archéologie 13. Lille: Revue du Nord.

McFadyen, L. 2006. 'Building technologies, quick architecture and early Neolithic long barrow sites in southern Britain'. *Archaeological Review from Cambridge* 21, 1: 117–134.

Malkin, I., C. Constantakopoulou, and K. Panagopoulou. 2009. *Greek and Roman Networks in the Mediterranean*. London: Routledge.

Massy, J.-L. (ed.) 1997. *Les agglomérations secondaires de la Lorraine Romaine*. Annales Littéraires de l'Université de Franche-Comté 647. Besançon: Université de Franche-Comté.

Matthews, K. J. 1997. 'Immaterial culture: Invisible peasants and consumer subcultures in northwest Britannia', in K. Meadows, C. Lemke, and J. Heron (eds) *TRAC96: Proceedings of the Sixth Annual Theoretical Roman Archaeology Conference*: 120–132. Oxford: Oxbow Books.

Mattingly, D. 1997. *Dialogues in Roman Imperialism: Power, Discourse and Discrepant Experiences in the Roman Empire*. Journal of Roman Archaeology Supplementary Series 23. Portsmouth (RI): Journal of Roman Archaeology.

Mattingly, D. 2002. 'Review of "Historical Map and Guide of Roman Britain"'. *Britannia* 33: 383–384.

Mattingly, D. 2004. 'Being Roman: Expressing identity in a provincial setting'. *Journal of Roman Archaeology* 17: 5–25.

Mattingly, D. 2006. *An Imperial Possession: Britain in the Roman Empire*. London: Penguin.

Mattingly, D. 2011. *Imperialism, Power and Identity: Experiencing the Roman Empire*. Princeton: Princeton University Press.

Merrifield, R. 1995. 'Roman metalwork from the Walbrook—rubbish, ritual or redundancy?' *Transactions of the London and Middlesex Archaeological Society* 46: 27–44.

Merrifield, R., and J. Hall. 2008. 'In its depths what treasures—the nature of the Walbrook stream valley and the Roman metalwork found therein', in J. Clark, J. Cotton, J. Hall, R. Sherris, and H. Swain (eds) *Londinium and Beyond: Essays on Roman London and its Hinterland for Harvey Sheldon*. CBA Research Report 156: 121–127. York: Council for British Archaeology.

Metzler, J. 1984. 'Treverische Reitergräber von Goeblinger-Nospelt', in H. Cüppers (ed.) *Trier: Augustusstadt der Treverer*: 87–99. Mainz: Philipp von Zabern.

Meylan, F. 2000. 'Éléments d'urbanisme à Bibracte: les maisons du Parc aux Chevaux', in V. Guichard, S. Sievers, and O.-H. Urban (eds) *Les processus d'urbanisation à l'âge du Fer*. Collection Bibracte 4: 197–201. Glux-en-Glenne: Centre archéologique européen du Mont Beuvray.

Mirković, M. 2007. *Moesia Superior: eine Provinz an der mittleren Donau*. Mainz: Philipp von Zabern.

Mommsen, T. 1854–1856. *Römische Geschichte, Vols I–III*. Leipzig: Reimer and Hirsel.

Mommsen, T. 1885. *Römische Geschichte: Die Provinzen von Caesar bis Diocletian*. Leipzig: Reimer and Hirsel.

Moore, T. 2011. 'Detribalizing the later prehistoric past: Concepts of tribes in Iron Age and Roman studies'. *Journal of Social Archaeology* 11: 334–360.

Mudd, A. 1999. *Excavations alongside Roman Ermin Street, Gloucestershire and Wiltshire, 1: Prehistoric and Roman Activity*. Oxford: Oxford Archaeological Unit.

Negru, M. 2003. *The Native Pottery of Roman Dacia*. British Archaeological Reports International Series 1097. Oxford: Archaeopress.

Nicolay, J. 2007. *Armed Batavians: Use and Significance of Weaponry and Horse Gear from Non-Military Contexts in the Rhine Delta (50 BC to AD 450)*. Amsterdam Archaeological Studies 11. Amsterdam: Amsterdam University Press.

Oltean, I. A. 2007. *Dacia: Landscape, Colonisation, Romanisation*. London: Routledge.

Percossi, E., G. Pignocchi, and F. Vermeulen. 2006. *I siti archeologici della Vallata del Potenza: Conoscenza e tutela*. Ancona: Il lavoro editoriale.

Perring, D. 2011. 'Two studies on Roman London'. *Journal of Roman Archaeology* 24, 1: 249–282.

Perring, D., S. Roskams, and C. Allen. 1991. *Early Development of Roman London West of the Walbrook: The Archaeology of Roman London 2*. CBA Research Report 70. London: Museum of London/Council for British Archaeology.

Quinnell, H. 2004. *Trethurgy: Excavations at Trethurgy Round, St Austell: Community and Status in Roman and Post-Roman Cornwall*. Truro: Cornwall County Council.

Rebourg, A. 1998. 'L'urbanisme d'Augustodunum (Autun, Saône-et-Loire)'. *Gallia* 55: 141–236.

Rice Holmes, T. 1907. *Ancient Britain and the Invasions of Julius Caesar*. Oxford: Clarendon Press.

Richert, E. 2005. *Native Religion under Roman Domination: Deities, Springs and Mountains in the Northwest of the Iberian Peninsula*. British Archaeological Reports International Series 1382. Oxford: Archaeopress.

Rogers, A. 2008. 'Religious place and its interaction with urbanization in the Roman era'. *Journal of Social Archaeology* 8: 37–62.

Rogers, A. 2011. *Late Roman Towns in Britain: Rethinking Change and Decline*. Cambridge: Cambridge University Press.

Rogers, A. 2012. 'Water and the urban fabric: A study of towns and waterscapes in the Roman period'. *International Journal of Nautical Archaeology* 41, 2: 327–339.

Ross, A. 1967. *Pagan Celtic Britain: Studies in Iconography and Tradition*. London: Routledge and Kegan Paul.

Roymans, N. 1995. 'Romanisation, cultural identity and the ethnic discussion: The integration of lower Rhine populations in the Roman Empire', in J. Metzler, M. Millett, N. Roymans, and J. Slofstra (eds) *Integration in the Early Roman West: The Role of Culture and Ideology*. Dossiers d'Archéologie du Musée National d'Histoire et d'Art 4: 47–64. Luxembourg: Musée national d'histoire et d'art.

Šašel Kos, M., and P. Scherrer. 2002. *The Autonomous Towns of Noricum and Pannonia (Die autonomen Städte in Noricum und Pannonien)*. Ljubljana: Narodni muzej Slovenije.

Schulting, R., and R. Bradley. 2014. 'Of human remains and weapons in the neighbourhood of London: New AMS 14C dates on Thames "river skulls" exhibiting injuries'. *Archaeological Journal* 170: 31–77.

Seebohm, F. 1883. *The English Village Community Examined in its Relations to the Manorial and Tribal Systems and to the Common or Open Field System of Husbandry: An Essay in Economic History*. London: Longmans, Green and Co.

Sharples, N. 2010. *Social Relations in Later Prehistory: Wessex in the First Millennium BC*. Oxford: Oxford University Press.

Smith, J. T. 1997. *Roman Villas: A Study in Social Structure*. London: Routledge.

Smith, K. 2006. *Guides, Guards and Gifts to the Gods: Domesticated Dogs in the Art and Archaeology of Iron Age and Roman Britain*. British Archaeological Reports British Series 422. Oxford: Archaeopress.

Sterry, M. 2008. 'Searching for identity in Italian landscapes', in C. Fenwick, M. Wiggins, and D. Wythe (eds) *TRAC 2007: Proceedings of the Seventeenth Annual Theoretical Roman Archaeology Conference, London 2007*: 31–43. Oxford: Oxbow Books.

Stocker, D., and P. Everson. 2003. 'The straight and narrow way: Fenland causeways and the conversion of the landscapes in the Witham valley, Lincolnshire', in M. Carver (ed.) *The Cross Goes North: Processes of Conversion in Northern Europe AD 300–1300*: 271–288. York: York Medieval Press.

Suppe, F. 1993. 'Continuity of religious tradition at Kelheim and the foundation of Weltenburg Abbey', in P. S. Wells (ed.) *Settlement, Economy and Cultural Change at the*

End of the European Iron Age: Excavations at Kelheim in Bavaria, 1987–1991: 156–161. Ann Arbor: International Monographs in Prehistory.

Talbert, R. J. A. 2010. *Rome's World: The Peutinger Map Reconsidered*. Cambridge: Cambridge University Press.

Taylor, J. 2007. *An Atlas of Roman Rural Settlement in England*. CBA Research Report 151. York: Council for British Archaeology.

Terrenato, N. 1998. 'Tam Firmum Municipium. The Romanization of Volterrae and its cultural implications'. *Journal of Roman Studies* 88: 94–114.

Vanderhoeven, A. 1996. 'The earliest urbanisation in northern Gaul. Some implications of recent research in Tongres', in N. Roymans (ed.) *From the Sword to the Plough: Three Studies on the Earliest Romanisation of Northern Gaul*. Amsterdam Archaeological Studies 1: 189–245. Amsterdam: Amsterdam University Press.

Vermeulen, F., and J. Bourgeois. 2000. 'Continuity of prehistoric burial sites in the Roman landscape of Sandy Flanders', in J. Pearce, M. Millett, and M. Struck (eds) *Burial, Society and Context in the Roman World*: 143–161. Oxford: Oxbow Books.

Vinogradoff, P. 1905. *The Growth of the Manor*. London: Allen and Unwin.

Wacher, J. 1995. *The Towns of Roman Britian*. London: Batsford.

Wait, G. 1985. *Ritual and Religion in Iron Age Britain*. British Archaeological Reports British Series 149. Oxford: British Archaeological Reports.

Webster, J. 1995. 'Sanctuaries and sacred places', in M. Green (ed.) *The Celtic World*: 441–464. London and New York: Routledge.

Webster, J. 2001. 'Creolizing the Roman provinces'. *American Journal of Archaeology* 105: 209–222.

Webster, J. 2003. 'Art as resistance and negotiation', in S. Scott and J. Webster (eds) *Roman Imperialism and Provincial Art*: 24–51. Cambridge: Cambridge University Press.

Wells, P. S. 1999. *The Barbarians Speak: How the Conquered Peoples Shaped Roman Europe*. Princeton: Princeton University Press.

Wells, P. S. 2008a. *Barbarians to Angels: The Dark Ages Reconsidered*. New York: W. W. Norton.

Wells, P. S. 2008b. *Image and Response in Early Europe*. Duckworth Debates in Archaeology. London: Duckworth.

Williams, H. M. R. 2006. *Death and Memory in Early Medieval Britain*. Cambridge: Cambridge University Press.

Witcher, R. 2006. 'Settlement and society in early imperial Etruria'. *Journal of Roman Studies* 96: 88–123.

Woolf, G. 1998. *Becoming Roman: The Origins of Provincial Civilization in Gaul*. Cambridge: Cambridge University Press.

Woolf, G. 2006. 'The end of "the end of the Iron Age"?', in C. Haselgrove (ed.) *Celtes et Gaulois: l'archéologie face à l'histoire: Les mutations de la fin de l'âge du Fer*. Collection Bibracte 12/4: 267–276. Glux-en-Glenne: Centre archéologique européen du Mont Beuvray.

RITUAL AND EXPRESSION

CHAPTER 39

FEASTING AND COMMENSAL RITUALS

JODY JOY

Introduction

THE communal consumption of food and drink is a critical mechanism for the generation of society (Lévi-Strauss 1968; Goody 1982), and the importance of its ritual consumption, particularly feasting, to Iron Age society is increasingly being recognized (e.g. Arnold 1999; Dietler 1996, 2001). However, discussions of feasting tend to focus on extraordinary finds, or elite activities as evidenced by elaborate tableware from rich graves, or Greek and Etruscan imports of feasting vessels, and exotic foods and drink, especially wine. Rich grave finds from the late Hallstatt and early La Tène periods in south-west Germany, eastern France, and parts of Switzerland containing feasting equipment and Greek and Etruscan imports are frequently discussed, as are specific regions such as the Auvergne (Loughton 2009), where large concentrations of wine amphorae have been discovered. Outside these contexts, feasting is something that is assumed to have regularly taken place but it is often discussed only in passing. This is changing as scholars begin to realize the value of the evidence associated with feasting, with its potential to shift interpretations towards social relationships and the active role of material culture (Ralph 2007: 2).

Feasts, defined as the ritualized, communal consumption of food and/or drink (Dietler and Hayden 2001: 3), take place in public, domestic, religious, and funerary contexts (Hamilakis and Sherratt 2012: 187) and provide an opportunity for larger social gatherings to celebrate and arrange important events such as marriages, to mark religious festivals, to bring together animal stock, organize labour for large-scale activities such as house building, and to reaffirm social and family obligations. They can be a stage-setting for social, economic, and political transactions (Dietler 2001: 65), and are frequently accompanied by singing, dancing, and storytelling (Dietler and Hayden 2001: 4).

Table 39.1 Sources of evidence for feasting

Literary sources

- Contemporary Greek and Roman writers recorded Iron Age feasting practices.
- Early medieval Irish and Welsh mythic literature, written in the vernacular, includes descriptions of feasts and feasting that have been drawn on as evidence for earlier practices.

Archaeological evidence

- Comparative evidence from the late Bronze Age and the classical world.
- Special eating and drinking equipment (ceramic, metal, and perishable materials such as wood). Includes: imported food and drinking equipment, and transport vessels, such as amphorae. Distinguished from everyday tableware by rarity, special forms, and/or elaborate decoration.
- Large collections of animal bones and other archaeobotanical material.
- Organic residues of special foods or drink associated with feasting equipment.
- Large-scale storage equipment and facilities, indicating the collection of food and drink for feasts.
- Special architecture.
- 'Special locations': hillforts, *oppida*, temples, shrines, regional centres, ports-of-trade, and particular locations in the landscape could all be locations for feasts.

Source Hayden (2001): table 2.1

Potential sources of evidence for feasting activity are outlined in Table 39.1. There are two main sources: literary and archaeological. Comparative evidence taken from the late Bronze Age and contemporary Mediterranean societies has also been influential to some studies.

Literary Evidence

Feasts are documented by contemporary Graeco-Roman authors, such as Poseidonios. Texts describing Iron Age peoples date to as early as the sixth century BC, but the majority were written after 120 BC when the Romans came into direct contact with Iron Age peoples in southern France (Webster 1995: 445). Medieval Irish and Welsh mythic literature, written in the vernacular, is also used as a source of evidence. The myths were written down from the late sixth century AD by Christian monks, but arguably have earlier origins. Sometimes both sources of evidence are combined. In these texts and myths, feasts are described as arenas for social competition, particularly among young men aspiring to positions of status (Cunliffe 1997: 105–107; Green 1998; Arnold 1999: 72–76). According to these accounts, feasts were highly structured with social status marked by seating position and other factors such as who is served food or drink first, or who is entitled to eat particular cuts of meat. They are also seen to be the domain of men, particularly young warriors, and were often drunken and violent affairs. A social convention of hospitality by which food and drink should be offered to strangers is also highlighted in some accounts.

This textual evidence can be heavily influential, especially to general accounts of feasting practice. For example, in *The Ancient Celts*, Barry Cunliffe states:

> The feast was evidently a highly structured affair organized rigorously according to status. The arrangement of the participants and the serving of the meat provided the occasions for the definition of the social hierarchy and its public affirmation. If anyone felt demeaned by the ordering, he would contest it, and the ensuing conflict could lead to single combat and death.
>
> (Cunliffe 1997: 105)

This example is taken from a general book covering a vast geographical area and a broad time span, and Cunliffe (1997: 105) himself states that feasts were clearly more varied. Nevertheless, a reliance on the literary evidence as a primary source restricts the parameters of interpretation and excludes smaller-scale and non-elite activities from consideration. Too heavy a reliance on literary sources can also promote a 'universal' and 'generalist' interpretation of feasting, masking regional and temporal variation (see Fitzpatrick 1991: 127). For example, the majority of classical texts drawn on as evidence for feasting practices describe events in southern and central France during the late La Tène period. Yet these accounts have been used to interpret evidence from Britain, Germany, France, and Switzerland dating from the early to the late Iron Age (see Loughton 2009: 77–78). As Loughton states, 'it is questionable how relevant many of these classical accounts are towards understanding drinking and feasting behaviours in non-Mediterranean France during the late Iron Age, let alone during the preceding Hallstatt and early La Tène periods' (Loughton 2009: 78), or indeed activities which occurred hundreds of miles from southern France.

Another danger of being too heavily reliant on the literary evidence is that both classical and early medieval texts were written by individuals from a different culture with diverse social and political motivations (see Hutton 1991: 144–150). For example, eating and drinking was one of the means by which Greeks and Romans defined themselves as different from continental Europeans. Certain practices such as drinking to excess, drinking beer, and the consumption of undiluted wine were all seen as uncivilized or barbaric (Cool 2006: 81), and consequently evidence for these customs may have been fabricated or exaggerated for narrative effect.

Comparative Evidence

Interpretations of Iron Age feasting have also been influenced by evidence originating in the late Bronze Age and the classical world.

Late Bronze Age to Early Iron Age

During the late Bronze Age specialist feasting equipment such as bronze buckets, cauldrons, flesh-hooks, and spits were used. These feasting objects are especially prevalent in central and northern Europe, Italy, and the Atlantic seaboard, including Britain, Ireland, western France, and Iberia (Gomez de Soto 1993; Needham and Bowman 2005; Gerloff 2010; Armada 2011). The presence of these objects has been linked to the conspicuous consumption of meat and drink in commensal and feasting rituals (Armada 2011: 168). For example, cauldrons (many of which have capacities of up to 70 litres) were used to boil meat, providing substantial quantities of food for large social gatherings. Whether these were communally organized gatherings, or events laid on by social elites to display their wealth and power of redistribution, is more difficult to establish. Evidence for the use and significance of late Bronze Age cauldrons is drawn on to interpret later Iron Age cauldrons, as the available contextual data for these objects are often poor (Baldwin and Joy 2017).

In southern England, especially the Vale of Pewsey, a number of exceptionally large mounds, known as middens, have been discovered dating to the late Bronze Age and early Iron Age. Examples include Potterne, East Chisenbury, and Runnymede Bridge (McOmish 1996; Needham and Spence 1997; Lawson 2000). These mounds are often located close to routeways and contain huge amounts of animal dung, as well as animal bone and ceramics. Consequently, they have been interpreted as locations where large numbers of people congregated at particular times of the year, bringing their livestock with them. Judging by the animal remains and ceramics, feasting appears to be one of the major activities that took place at these sites (Sharples 2010: 52–53). Middens have been influential in terms of highlighting the possibility for large social gatherings.

The Classical World

Commensality, the act of eating together, was very significant to the Greeks, Etruscans, and Romans and there is plenty of evidence for specialist rooms and architecture designed for communal eating (Dunbabin 2003). Lying down to eat and drink while being served by others was a particular indicator of civilization and prestige. This practice derives from the *symposium*, a Greek custom which appeared by the seventh century BC at the latest (Dunbabin 2003: 11). The practice of dining while reclining continued into the Roman period, where dining was accompanied by other rituals such as hand-washing using specially made jugs and pans (Cool 2006: 81; Fitzpatrick 2009: 395). Mixing wine with hot or cold water was also important, with the exact ratios of mixing tailored to the tastes of individual diners (Dunbabin 2003: 22). Many of the rich Iron Age graves containing feasting equipment and Etruscan and Greek imports have been interpreted from the perspective of classical practices of eating and drinking, especially the *symposium* (Fitzpatrick 2009: 392).

Archaeological Evidence for Feasting

Feasting and Funerary Rituals

The ceremonial consumption of food and drink often accompanies funerary rituals and many rich graves containing feasting equipment have been discovered. For example, a grave found under the mound at Kleinaspergle, Baden-Württemberg, southwest Germany, dating to the mid-fifth century BC, was found to contain, amongst other items such as a belt and gold ornaments, a drinking service for two participants, which includes two Greek cups, an Etruscan bronze *stamnos*, a bronze flagon, two drinking horns and a ribbed bucket (Frey 1991: 127). This grave is one of many dating to the late Hallstatt and early La Tène periods in parts of Switzerland, western Germany, and eastern France that contain feasting equipment. They sometimes include imported Greek and Etruscan objects and have been interpreted as graves of an elite whose status was based on the redistribution of food and drink and control of access to exotic comestibles and beverages, such as olives and wine.

Pottery vessels used for drinking and eating are found in many graves, but very often these were everyday items selected as grave goods. The term 'feasting equipment' is used here to describe specialist vessels and other related paraphernalia made for and used on special occasions. It should be stressed that feasting equipment is not found in every rich grave. Therefore its inclusion in graves is more significant than a simple display of wealth or power through control of trade (Arnold 1999: 88). As will be discussed in the context of the grave from Hochdorf (see 'Hunting and sacrifice'), detailed examination of individual graves (e.g. Krausse 1996, 1999) is revealing their complexity; however, the inclusion in graves of drinking and dining sets for multiple participants is an indicator of the importance of the consumption of food and drink to social relations at this time.

In addition to feasting equipment, many graves also contain animal remains (see Chapter 19). These meat cuts can be interpreted as grave goods intended for consumption by the deceased in the afterlife. Special selection of particular cuts of meat from certain animals also hints at the ritual consumption and redistribution of meat during funerary rituals. Preferences for different cuts or types of meat vary. For example, graves from East Yorkshire, dating from the fourth to first centuries BC, often contain specific joints, represented by bones of the forequarters of pig or the left humeri of sheep, with the rear parts of the animals presumably consumed by the living. Cattle are almost completely absent from graves in this region even though their remains are frequently found at settlement sites (Parker Pearson 1999: 53). Excavations of cemeteries in the Champagne region of France have revealed multiple late La Tène cremation graves containing burnt and unburnt animal bones (Stead et al. 2006). Of the cremated animal bones extracted from the burials, 54% were pig bone, 22% chicken or other bird bones, and only 4% sheep (Stead et al. 2006: 114–117). Many of these showed signs of butchering. Some of the late La Tène burials also contained unburnt animal bones. Again pig was the most popular, represented especially by legs, skulls cut in half, and vertebrae. There was a preference for the left side of skulls and of hind legs rather than forelegs. A number of graves also contained headless but otherwise complete chickens. One exceptional grave (J2) from Juniville contained the burnt remains of a pig, dog, goose, and chicken and unburnt remains of a dog(s), pig(s), goose, and chicken (Stead et al. 2006: 246–249, fig. 100).

This evidence implies that in East Yorkshire mutton, and more rarely pork, was consumed at funerals. Singeing and burning on some bones could indicate that meat was consumed communally, prepared over an open fire; alternatively, cuts of meat could have been divided between the mourners for later consumption (Giles 2012: 181). In contrast, in Champagne, pork and poultry were the meats of choice. In East Yorkshire the forequarters of animals were reserved for the dead, while in Champagne it was the hindquarters. In the context of East Yorkshire, Melanie Giles (2012: 181–182) has questioned what kind of feasting this evidence represents. She suggests that a funeral was a context in which the family of the dead could demonstrate prestige through 'lavish generosity':

> The communal eating of meat, particularly at events such as the funeral served to bind the community together—defining internal roles and relations, and allowing some of its members to jostle for power—whilst enhancing the general prestige of the family concerned.
>
> (Giles 2012: 182)

Evidence for feasting has also been discovered on the fringes of burials and cemeteries (Ralph 2005: 58) with, for example, signs of feasting activity including discrete pottery deposits found within enclosures related to late Iron Age cremations and burials at Brisley Farm, Kent (Stevenson 2013).

Deposition

Large assemblages of feasting equipment are not restricted to grave contexts. As with other types of Iron Age material culture, feasting equipment is also deposited in the landscape or as 'special deposits' at settlements.

For example, a large assemblage of vessels, including two metal cauldrons, a wooden bucket, and beautifully made wheel-thrown vessels, was recovered during rescue excavations in 2009 at the late La Tène (150–80 BC) Basel-Gasfabrik settlement in Switzerland (Hüglin and Spichtig 2012). In an exemplary excavation, the entire deposit was lifted as a 9-ton block and excavated under laboratory conditions. The vast majority of the objects were confined to an area 1 m in diameter and were possibly originally buried in a large organic cylindrical container such as a barrel. No skeletal or cremated remains were recovered so the deposit is not thought to be a burial. The vessels were deposited at a time when the settlement was still occupied and they include many items

FIGURE 39.1 Layout of the cauldrons in the pit at Chiseldon, Wiltshire, England.
Drawing: Stephen Crummy © The Trustees of the British Museum

necessary to host a feast of some size. Were these items deposited for storage or were they an offering of some kind (Hüglin and Spichtig 2012: 13)?

A second example was discovered in southern England in 2004 by a metal detector user, who recovered fragments of copper-alloy sheet from a field near Chiseldon, Wiltshire. Excavation of the find-spot in 2005 by Wessex Archaeology and conservators from the British Museum revealed the remains of a large hoard containing seventeen complete cauldrons, dating to the late fourth or early third centuries BC, and two cow skulls (Baldwin and Joy 2017). Many of the cauldrons show signs of usage and repair, thus indicating that they were not manufactured especially for deposition. The hoard was placed in a pit which was lined with an organic material, possibly straw, and the cauldrons were carefully positioned within it (Figure 39.1). Some of the cauldrons are fancily decorated: two iron plaques in the form of cows' heads are mounted underneath the handles of one vessel (Figure 39.2); two more cauldrons are ornamented with decoration in the Vegetal style, and others are finished with scalloped edges and carefully shaped patches. Organic residues adhering to some of the cauldrons have been shown to contain animal fats, indicating that they were used to prepare meat dishes, perhaps some form of meat stew. The find-spot itself was probably the location of a small settlement. It is located close to the Ridgeway, a trackway of possible ancient origin spanning the Berkshire and Marlborough Downs, and is overlooked by Barbury Castle and Liddington Castle hillforts (see Payne et al. 2006: 103 and 118).

Interpretation of this site is difficult because it is unprecedented and represents the greatest concentration of complete cauldrons ever discovered. Cauldrons are large

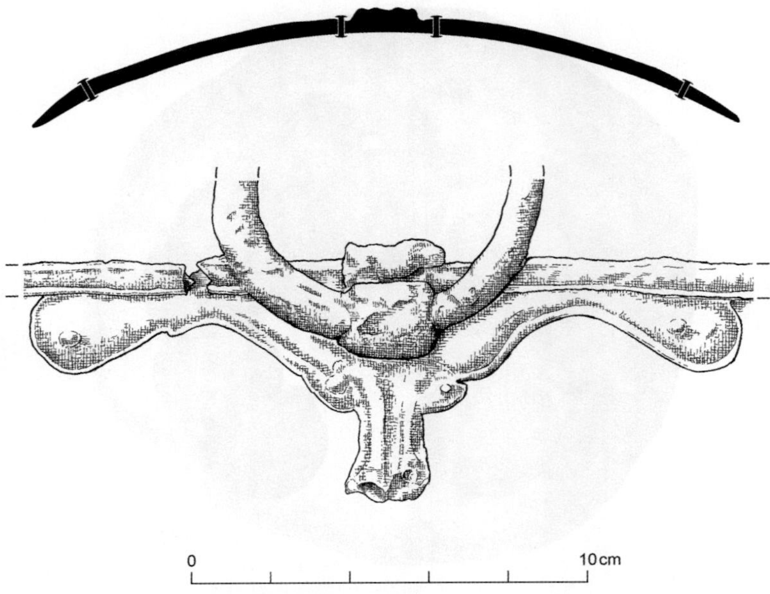

FIGURE 39.2 Decorated cauldron from Chiseldon, detail.
Drawing: Craig Williams, © The Trustees of the British Museum

vessels capable of containing generous quantities of food and drink. They are rarely found and were therefore probably not used for everyday purposes. It is probable that they were used to prepare and serve food, and possibly drink, during feasts. The location of the Chiseldon site on the Ridgeway seems to be ideal for a large gathering of people. The careful placement of the cauldrons in a lined pit and the selection of decorated objects also indicate the special nature of the deposit. The cow skulls may have been intended to represent the meat consumed in the cauldrons. The hoard therefore probably represents the actual or symbolic remains of a large feast. On this occasion the feast was marked by the ritual deposition of the serving vessels, perhaps symbolically bringing a significant event or tradition of gathering at that site to a close. The large number of vessels in the hoard exemplifies the capacity at the time to host large feasts attended by hundreds if not thousands of participants.

Specialized Architecture

Feasting does not require a specialized architecture and can occur in landscape locations, with the very act of feasting creating meaning, significance, and social memories (Ralph 2005: 57), but occasionally evidence for specialist architecture associated with feasting events is uncovered in the form of structures and/or earthworks. For example, thousands of animal bones and a series of circular structures comprised of upright wooden posts have been discovered dating to the Iron Age phase of the site (dated fifth century

BC to third century AD) at Dún Ailinne, just south-west of Dublin (Crabtree 2003). The vast majority of the bones were of cattle, pig, sheep/goat, and horse, particularly cattle and pigs. Most of the cattle bones were from young animals, especially suckling calves, and the faunal data overall indicate that people returned to the site periodically during the pre-Christian Iron Age to consume large quantities of veal, beef, pork, and sometimes mutton and horse (Crabtree 2003: 65). As the site is very different from contemporary settlements, it is interpreted as a long-standing location of ritual feasting. The exact role of the posts is not known, but they may have acted to demarcate or divide up space for particular activities or participants. Evidence for feasting activity in the form of large numbers of animal remains has also been uncovered from Navan Fort and Tara (McCormick 2009).

Finds made at Hallaton, Leicestershire, draw our attention to a particular type of communal site that may be more widespread in Britain, which facilitated gatherings of distinct social groups and where activities such as feasting and the ceremonial deposition of artefacts took place (Score 2011). A polygonal ditch with an entrance was located on a hilltop. At least sixteen hoards of Iron Age gold and silver coins and Roman *denarii* have been discovered, as well as a huge scatter of young pig bones found outside the entrance. The ditch and entrance may have structured and divided access to activities at the site. The finds date from the later first century BC into the Roman period, but the main focus of activity was shortly before or after the Roman conquest. Pigs are ideal for a feasting food as they have large litters and are fast-growing animals: one adult pig will feed up to sixty people (Ralph 2007: 44, 58). Parker Pearson (1999: 46) suggests that in Britain pigs had a kind of 'totemic significance' as a special feasting food, and they were specifically favoured in the late Iron Age in southern England and in France where their remains are preferentially found at sites categorized as 'high status' or 'ritual'.

Feasting events can also mark the destruction or transformation of sites. At Mas Castellar de Pontós, north-east Spain, a large pit was dug on the ruins of a fortified village, shortly after its destruction (between 375 and 325 BC; Garcia and Pons 2011). The pit was filled in a number of layers but appears to contain the remains of a feast, including vessels and utensils related to eating and drinking and animal remains totalling around 300 kg of meat—sufficient for a meal for several hundred participants. The excavators interpret the remains as representing a feast or banquet celebrating a social, economic, or political alliance (Garcia and Pons 2011: 244), perhaps related to the abandonment of the site.

Feasting Equipment

The physical characteristics of feasting equipment can provide clues as to the types of social activities for which it was made and used. Feasting equipment is often complex, providing multiple means by which it can be interpreted through its usage at feasts. There is a two-way relationship, as the type of feast influences the material culture that is used and the material culture also influences the types of feast people have. Three case studies are presented here to illustrate the possible influence of material culture on feasts of various scales; many other examples could have been selected including bowls, buckets, cups, platters, and roasting spits.

The pair of flagons from a probable grave at Basse Yutz (Figure 39.3), north-east France (Megaw and Megaw 1990), are lined with layers of clay and beeswax to waterproof the vessels and perhaps avoid tainting the liquid they were made to serve and pour—probably wine, based on the presence of the two Etruscan *stamnoi* (wine storage vessels) with which they were deposited. The flagons are decorated in a mixture of styles and inlaid with red glass and coral from the Mediterranean coast. The handles, in the form of a dog or a wolf, are reminiscent of Greek or Etruscan-style art. The use of palmette forms under each spout, though popular in Celtic art, ultimately derives from Egypt, via Greece (Megaw and Megaw 1990: ch. 4). The ducks at the end of the spout are a purely native element of the decoration. The act of serving and pouring is of great importance as it demonstrates hospitality in a very dramatic fashion (see Hamilakis and Sherratt 2012: 191). In this instance, flagons decorated in a style drawing on diverse influences are used to serve imported wine. Indeed, the decoration acts to bring this performance to life, as the ducks appear to be swimming on a river of wine as it is poured (Figure 39.4). These vessels ooze exclusivity, made for and used by the elite for the conspicuous serving and consumption of imported wine.

Wooden tankards with metal handles and sometimes with metal stave bands or coverings (Figure 39.5) are a feature of the later Iron Age and early Roman period in Britain and are found in a range of contexts including hoards and graves (Horn 2015). It is thought they were used to serve and consume alcoholic beverages, most probably beer (Sealey 2007: 12). A feature of these tankards is that the handle opening is only wide enough to accommodate up to three adult-sized fingers. Surviving wooden remains and metal coverings indicate that tankards are of a consistent size, with an average capacity of around 4.2 pints or 2.3 litres (Horn 2015: 311). As Corcoran (1952: 87–88) suggested, it would be impractical to lift a full tankard using the handle alone. Far more likely, the tankard was lifted using two hands, one hand with fingers placed through the handle to prevent slippage (Corcoran 1952: 88; Jackson 1990: 45). The relatively large capacity of these tankards is nearly double that of a 'yard of ale', which has a capacity of 2.5 pints or 1.4 litres. This means that, although possible, tankards are unlikely to have been used like a yard of ale which is 'downed in one' by an individual. Tankards may therefore have been passed between a small group of drinkers who each took gulps of beer before they passed the tankard on to the next drinker. Tankards were therefore designed for more intimate social gatherings, for the sharing of drink between close associates.

Cauldrons dating to the late Iron Age are found in small numbers across much of Britain, Ireland, and continental Europe (Joy 2014). They are all watertight and have large ring handles, implying that they were designed for suspension and to contain liquid. Sooting on the exterior of cauldron bowls indicates they were suspended over an open fire. Analysis of residues shows they were used to prepare and serve meat (Baldwin and Joy 2017), but like the example from Hochdorf (see 'Hunting and sacrifice'), they

FIGURE 39.3 One of a pair of copper-alloy flagons, Basse-Yutz, Lorraine, France.

FIGURE 39.4 Basse-Yutz flagon: close-up of the duck swimming on a 'river' of wine.

FIGURE 39.5 Copper-alloy stave bindings and handle of a tankard found near Brackley, Northamptonshire, England.

may also have been used to serve alcoholic beverages. Many cauldrons have capacities of 50 litres or more. All of this evidence combined suggests that they were used in collective ceremonies involving large gatherings of people. In this instance cauldrons would have taken centre stage, suspended above the hearth, with people serving themselves or brought individual servings. If some individuals were served and others not, social differences would have been emphasized. Alternatively, if everyone served themselves, communal identity would have been reinforced.

Food Storage

There is widespread evidence from across Europe for the underground storage of grain in pits (Wood 2000: 99). These pits vary in size and form but they all work in the same way: grain is poured in from the top, which is then plugged; when the grain at the edges of the pit germinates all of the oxygen is used up, hermetically sealing the pit and ensuring good storage conditions.

The dominant interpretation has viewed such pits as a means of preserving seed corn for spring sowing (e.g. Jones 1984; Cunliffe 1992). However, the pits from southern England, many of which have been discovered at hillforts, have recently been reinterpreted by Marijke van der Veen and Glynis Jones. One of the crops most often found in pits—spelt wheat—is best suited to autumn sowing, meaning that long-term storage is not necessary (Van der Veen and Jones 2006: 224; Van der Veen 2007: 119). This fact, combined with the occurrence of pits at hillforts, has led to the suggestion that grain was stored in pits not simply as part of the agricultural cycle, but rather to be consumed as food and beer at feasts. This interpretation has been developed in two ways. Van der Veen and Jones (2006) take a long-term view following changes in the morphology and usage of hillforts. In the early Iron Age, hillforts acted as foci for social interaction and rituals, and surpluses of grain were stored for occasional large communal gatherings. By the middle Iron Age, when the majority of hillforts went out of use and the earthworks of a small number were modified and extended, pits were linked to the organization of labour, with particular groups or individuals able to raise the person power required to modify hillforts by giving 'work party' feasts, a transaction of labour exchanged for food and drink with the end results 'owned' by the hosts of the feast. The absence of storage pits in the late Iron Age is explained as agricultural surpluses being diverted to exchange or to acquire new consumer goods such as Roman pottery and metal vessels, glass, and exotic foods such as wine and figs (Van der Veen and Jones 2006: 226).

Martin Jones, on the other hand, examines in detail potential feasting activity at the site of Danebury, Hampshire. Based on an estimate of a total number of 3,600 grain storage pits at the site, which was occupied for approximately 450 years, he suggests there could have been an average of eight feasts per year (Jones 2007: 148). Established by the size of the pits and estimates of the average daily food and beer consumption of one individual, he identifies three types of feast. The majority of the pits contained enough sustenance to provide for a week-long feast for 170 people; 5% of the pits were roughly double this size and could therefore supply sustenance for twice as many people. The frequency of such feasts would perhaps be something like once every three years. A final, much rarer, 'super-pit' could supply enough food for 500 people for one week and may have occurred no more than once every 25 years (Jones 2007). These are clearly rough estimates and do not include consumption of other foods, particularly meat. However, even if only some of the pits contained food for feasts, this interpretation demonstrates the potentially central role of feasting to society in southern England as a means of pooling labour to construct hillforts and to facilitate large social gatherings.

What Was Consumed at Feasts?

For the most part, Iron Age Europe was a world of farmers, with most people living in small farmsteads (Wood 2000), and they are likely to have consumed relatively simple meals. For example, evidence from the preserved stomach contents of European bog bodies indicates they ate relatively simple last meals, such as gruel of mixed cereals, or bread (Joy 2009: 30). Based on the variety and size of the ceramics utilized in East Anglia during the middle Iron Age, Hill (2002: 148) argues that people primarily ate carbohydrate-rich stews and porridges. It would not take much variation in the quantity and availability of food and drink at a feasting event for it to stand out against this culinary backdrop.

Meat

The high cost and symbolic value of meat makes it a desirable food for feasts. Meat is unlikely to have been consumed in large quantities by the vast majority of Iron Age peoples (Wood 2000). Animals are valuable. Their consumption at feasts represents a destruction of wealth but can also act to highlight the prestige of the host(s) and the significance of the feast as a special occasion. The act of taking an animal's life is also likely to have been negotiated through ritual, giving meat a special symbolism (Wright 2004: 52). Animals may have had to be killed in a particular way, such as by sacrifice. This has to be undertaken by someone with specialist knowledge. Different cuts of meat may also have been deemed appropriate for consumption by different people of varying social status or gender. The consumption of large quantities of meat also provides an arena for special forms of consumption: boiled in vessels or roasted on a spit or firedog.

Hunting and Sacrifice

The symbolic value of meat is clearly highlighted by the contents of the grave from Hochdorf in south-west Germany (Biel et al. 1985; Krausse 1996) which is frequently drawn on as evidence for feasting practices (e.g. Koch 2003: 130–132; Fitzpatrick 2009: 390–393). The large, wood-lined grave of a middle-aged man dates from between 540 and 520 BC (Verger 2006: 6) and contains all the accoutrements necessary to host a large feast, including a cauldron containing residues of mead and nine drinking horns, eight of which are made from aurochs horns. The grave also contains iron fish-hooks, a quiver of arrows (presumably originally with a now decayed bow), and animal skins. Many of these items could be 'hunting trophies' (Krausse 1999; Fitzpatrick 2009: 393), symbolizing the role of the host as 'provider'. Loaded on a large four-wheeled wagon were copper-alloy dishes and basins, as well as an iron axe, knife, and other implements.

Krausse (1999) suggests these objects could have been used in the ritual sacrifice of animals (see also Fitzpatrick 2009).

Animal sacrifice is well known from Mycenaean, Greek, Etruscan, and Roman culture (Krausse 1999; Wright 2004: 51) and evidence for animal sacrifice has been found from Iron Age contexts. For example, the bronze model wagon found in a late Hallstatt burial at Strettweg, near Graz in Austria, presents a scene which is thought to represent a stag hunt and/or sacrifice and contains various figures including stags, human figures standing and mounted on horses, and a woman with outstretched arms (Egg 1996). At Gournay-sur-Aronde, northern France, pits dug during the fourth and third centuries BC were found to contain huge quantities of animal bone (Brunaux 1988). The age and sex of many of the animals from these pits differ from animal remains from settlement sites, as does the manner of death. For example, older, male cattle were preferentially selected at Gournay and these were killed by expert axe blows delivered to the nape of the neck (Fitzpatrick 2009: 393–394).

Alcohol

Alcohol is a special class of foodstuff with psychoactive properties, making it a potent social artefact (Dietler 2006: 229). Evidence for alcohol consumption includes special drinking and storage receptacles, chemical residues, descriptions in historical texts, and even possible evidence for brewing (Dietler 2006: 233). Alcohol can be made from a wide variety of sugary foods but the primary types of alcohol made in continental Europe during the first millennium BC were mead, beer, and wine.

Mead is a fermented drink made by mixing honey with water (Koch 2003: 125). Evidence for the consumption of mead in Europe dates back to the Bronze Age and honey residues have been discovered in pots and bark buckets from rich graves. The earliest evidence from the Iron Age is the pollen residues found at the bottom of the huge cauldron of Greek manufacture, with a capacity of 500 litres, from the Hochdorf grave (see 'Hunting and sacrifice'). It is calculated that the pollen derives from approximately 100 litres of honey. The cauldron was around three-quarters full when deposited, meaning that it probably contained around 350 litres of mead (Koch 2003: 132).

On a smaller scale, the two La Tène A (450–400 BC) burials excavated from a mound close to the hilltop settlement known as the Glauberg, Hesse, Germany, both included jugs containing honey residues (Bartel et al. 1998). The jug from Grave 1 was wrapped in cloth and residues indicate it contained around 1.4 litres of mead. Lower concentrations of pollen were found in the jug from Grave 2, suggesting a different kind of drink containing only a small quantity of honey (Koch 2003: 133–135).

Greek and Roman written sources indicate that beer was the main form of alcohol consumed by European peoples living outside the Mediterranean world (see Laubenheimer et al. 2003: 52–53). For example, Iberian beer is praised for its good taste and long life (Stika 1996: 81). In the main, however, the consumption of beer rather than wine is viewed by classical authors pejoratively as a characteristic of barbarians.

Archaeological evidence directly related to beer production is rare. Large quantities of germinated barley grains were discovered in two U-shaped ditches at the late Hallstatt/early La Tène (600–400 BC) settlement at Hochdorf (Stika 1996). The ditches have been interpreted as kilns for malting, which is part of the brewing process, with the barley grains heated on a structure made of mud bricks and a wooden frame with a textile cover (Stika 1996: 87). Evidence for beer making has also been discovered from a fifth-century house at Roquepertuse in southern France (Bouby et al. 2011). However, in this instance brewing seems to have occurred as an ordinary domestic activity, as the building the barley was recovered from is a typical dwelling for the region (Bouby et al. 2011: 356). All that is required to brew beer is grain, containers to soak the grain, a flat area to spread out the grain during germination, an oven to dry it, grindstones to grind malted grain, and water and containers for fermentation, storage, and serving (see Laubenheimer et al. 2003). Evidence for all of these processes was uncovered from the Roquepertuse house. The oven was particularly suited to drying malt (Bouby et al. 2011: 356–357).

Interestingly, wine was available in southern France at the same time that beer was being brewed, both in the form of wine made in the Greek colony of Massalia and wine produced by 'locals'. It could be that wealthier people drank wine and poorer people drank beer made in domestic dwellings. However, this is probably overly simplistic. Ethnographic evidence demonstrates a complex picture of alcoholic consumption, with beverages such as beer taking on many different political, cultural, and symbolic values (Dietler 1990; Arthur 2003; Bouby et al. 2011: 358). For example, in many African societies beer is a substantial contributor to yearly calorie intake but it is also regarded as a luxury food and is consumed at feasts and other religious ceremonies (Arthur 2003). The production of beer in domestic dwellings and its possible everyday consumption are not contradictory therefore to its role as a special kind of food (Dietler 2006).

A critical property of wine is that it is less perishable than other types of alcohol and actually improves with age, making it more suitable than beer or mead for storage and trade (Arnold 1999: 74). Wine was already being produced in Greece by the third millennium BC (Sherratt 1995: 18) and was consumed by the Minoan and Mycenaean elites (Hamilakis 1998). It spread to Italy and Spain through Greek and Phoenician colonization by the seventh and eighth centuries (Dietler 2006: 233–234) and Etruscan wine was traded in France by the late seventh century (Dietler 1990: 353). A limited number of finds of domesticated grapes dating to the late Bronze Age and early Iron Age have been made north of the Alps, suggesting the cultivation of vines, probably for wine production, for example at Stillfried in Austria (Rebay 2003). Wine consumption, particularly during the early Iron Age in central Europe, also adopted some aspects of Mediterranean practices, including mixing wine with water and spices (Rebay 2003). Evidence for the wine trade has also been found along the Mediterranean coast and the lower Rhône basin in the form of Etruscan wine amphorae and other pottery forms associated with mixing and serving wine, as well as metal vessels and small numbers of wine-drinking cups from Greece.

As already stated, the first wine produced in France was at the Greek colony of Massalia (Marseille), founded around 600 BC (Dietler 1996: 109). Evidence of trading wine in the immediate region can be seen in the form of the distinctive Massaliote amphorae. Between the last half of the sixth century BC and the beginning of the fifth, small numbers of objects of Mediterranean origin, especially those related to the consumption of wine, are found hundreds of kilometres up the Rhône in southern Germany and Switzerland (Dietler 1996: 355). Due to the restricted type of contexts in which these objects have been discovered—specifically rich graves and fortified settlements—and the impressive nature of some of these objects, the control of the trade of 'prestige' items and the consumption of wine have most often been discussed in relation to social and political changes in the region and early Iron Age elite practices (e.g. Brun 1987). As Dietler (1990: 358) argues, less attention has been paid to the fact that the majority of these Mediterranean imports are associated with drinking, many objects appear to be heavily used, and they are often deposited alongside 'native' objects. Trade therefore appears to be limited in terms of the quantity and range of artefacts, suggesting the adaption of classical material culture to existing institutions rather than the adoption and emulation of classical drinking customs. A different pattern can be seen in southern France, where numerous amphorae and wine-drinking ceramics are found at a wide variety of different types of site. Again this appears to be adaption and selection rather than emulation, as when compared to regions such as North Africa with similar access and opportunity to trade, the range of imports in southern France is far more selective (Dietler 1990: 357).

Evidence for importation and consumption of Italian wine is prevalent in Gaul and southern England during the later Iron Age (*c.*200–20 BC; e.g. Fitzpatrick 1985; Poux 2004; Sealey 2009). Interpretations of this evidence have tended to be influenced by the evidence from the Hallstatt and early La Tène periods (Loughton 2009: 77).

Social Models of Feasting

Primarily through the work of Michael Dietler (1996, 2001), Iron Age case studies have been at the centre of debate concerning the social role of feasting in archaeology. Dietler identifies three different patterns of feast, which he calls 'entrepreneurial' or 'empowering', 'patron-role', and 'diacritical'. Each is seen to serve a different social function. 'Entrepreneurial' or 'empowering' feasts provide a mechanism by which to acquire influence or prestige in societies without institutionalized political roles or fixed hereditary hierarchies. Hosting a feast, the giving of food and drink, creates debts and obligations on participants, but this is not always recognized by the protagonists as the overt intention of the host. This pattern of feasting includes feasts conceived of as celebrations of community identity, which can also be arenas for negotiations of social influence (Dietler 2001: 76–77). In pre-capitalist societies one method of mobilizing labour for large-scale tasks is the 'work feast' where food and particularly alcohol are provided in exchange for a day's labour (Dietler 2001: 79–80). In the 'patron-role' feast there is no expectation for equal reciprocation; rather, unequal social hierarchies are in part supported or generated by an obligation on the part of the social elite to host feasts. The final pattern of feast, 'diacritical', uses different styles of food and drink and ways of consuming them to reinforce social differences. This type of feasting creates what Appadurai (1986: 21) terms 'tournaments of value', defining the membership and parameters of competition of a social elite. Diacritical feasts are prone to emulation as special foods, ways of consumption, and feasting paraphernalia can be copied by lower social classes (Dietler 2001: 86).

Dietler (e.g. 1996: 107–115) has used these feasting patterns to examine the relationships between food, power, and society in the early Iron Age of western Europe. Fitzpatrick (2009) links archaeological remains, particularly grave assemblages, with Dietler's feast patterns. For example, he suggests that burials containing special feasting paraphernalia, including objects for storing and serving wine, are the graves of the givers of patron-role feasts, in Dietler's terminology. Similarly, Ralph (2007: 85) suggests the remains from Fison Way, Thetford, Norfolk, are a possible location of a work-party feast. Another study influenced by Dietler is Matthieu Poux's (2004) *L'âge du vin*. Poux examines the remains of feasts in the geographical area which later became the Roman province of Gaul and, based on the contents of their graves, identifies the organizers of feasts and guests (*convives*) of varying levels of importance (Poux 2004: figs 124–125).

Conclusions and Future Directions

While the role of the conspicuous consumption of food and drink in negotiations of power is clearly very important, so too are smaller-scale events and feasts. These have often been neglected, partly because it can be difficult to distinguish evidence for smaller-scale commensal rituals from the everyday consumption of food and drink (see Ralph 2007: 36). The potential sensual and emotional experiences that are generated during the performance of social eating and drinking, as well as the role of feasting in the creation of social memory (see Hamilakis 1998: 117), are also themes which are yet to be fully explored in Iron Age contexts. For example, the role of memory is often neglected in interpretations of rich Hallstatt and La Tène graves. The burial of individuals with feasting equipment could be interpreted to be as much about forgetting as remembrance, because by placing these artefacts in burials, their 'social lives' are ended. Through the performance of burial, 'what is "killed" therefore is not the memory of the person itself, but the memory of the social person as player and participant in the construction of social experience' (Hamilakis 1998: 117). This creates new 'social' space for living people to occupy.

Viewing feasting as a social mechanism has many implications for how we can interpret/reinterpret the Iron Age. For example, in pre-money economies work-party feasts represent one of the few mechanisms of pooling labour (see Dietler 1990: 365). Other benefits include prestige gained from giving the best food or drink, which in turn may attract more workers to the next work-party feast. Work-party feasts were very likely involved in major construction projects such as building hillforts, houses, and field boundaries (see Sharples 2010: 123). They may also have been a significant part of metal-working activities, as a method of rewarding the people who gathered ores or fuel, or even the metalworkers themselves (see Loughton 2009: 92).

References

Appadurai, A. 1986. 'Introduction. Commodities and the politics of value', in A. Appadurai (ed.) *The Social Life of Things: Commodities in Cultural Perspective*: 3–63. Cambridge: Cambridge University Press.

Armada, X.-L. 2011. 'Feasting metals and the ideology of power in the Late Bronze Age of Atlantic Iberia', in G. Aranda, S. Montón-Subías, and M. Sánchez (eds) *Guess Who's Coming to Dinner? Feasting Rituals in the Prehistoric Societies of Europe and the Near East*: 158–183. Oxford: Oxbow.

Arnold, B. 1999. '"Drinking the feast": Alcohol and the legitimation of power in Celtic Europe'. *Cambridge Archaeological Journal* 9, 1: 71–93.

Arthur, J. W. 2003. 'Brewing beer: Status, wealth and ceramic use alteration among the Gamo of south-western Ethiopia'. *World Archaeology* 34, 3: 516–528.

Baldwin, A., and J. Joy. 2017. *A Celtic Feast: The Iron Age Cauldrons from Chiseldon, Wiltshire*. London: British Museum Press.

Bartel, A., O.-H. Frey, F.-R. Herrmann, A. Kreuz, and M. Rösch. 1998. 'Ein frühkeltischer Fürstengrabhügel am Glauberg im Wetteraukreis, Hessen: Bericht über die Forschungen 1994–1996'. *Germania* 75: 459–550.

Biel, J., H.-J. Hundt, U. Körber-Grohne, W. Gauer, and A. Hartmann. 1985. 'Das Grab des Keltenfürsten', in J. Biel (ed.) *Der Keltenfürst von Hochdorf: Katalog zur Ausstellung Stuttgart, Kunstgebäude vom 14. August bis 13.Oktober 1985*: 78–163. Stuttgart: Theiss.

Bouby, L., P. Boissinot, and P. Marinval. 2011. 'Never mind the bottle. Archaeobotanical evidence of beer-brewing in Mediterranean France and the consumption of alcoholic beverages during the 5th century BC'. *Human Ecology* 39: 351–360.

Brun, P. 1987. *Princes et princesses de la Celtique: Le premier âge du Fer (850–450 av. J.C.)*. Paris: Errance.

Brunaux, J.-L. 1988. *The Celtic Gauls: Gods, Rites and Sanctuaries*. London: Seaby.

Cool, H. E. M. 2006. 'Sustenance in a strange land', in P. Ottaway (ed.) *A Victory Celebration: Papers on the Archaeology of Colchester and Late Iron Age Roman Britain Presented to Philip Crummy*: 75–82. Colchester: Friends of Colchester Archaeological Trust.

Corcoran, J. X. W. P. 1952. 'Tankards and tankard handles of the British Early Iron Age'. *Proceedings of the Prehistoric Society* 23: 85–102.

Crabtree, P. J. 2003. 'Ritual feasting in the Irish Iron Age: Re-examining the fauna from Dún Ailinne in light of contemporary archaeological theory', in A. Ervynck, S. J. O'Day, and W. van Neer (eds) *Behaviour Behind Bones: The Zooarchaeology of Ritual, Religion, Status and Identity. Proceedings of the 9th ICAZ Conference, Durham*: 62–65. Oxford: Oxbow.

Cunliffe, B. W. 1992. 'Pits, preconceptions and propitiation in the British Iron Age'. *Oxford Journal of Archaeology* 11: 69–83.

Cunliffe, B. W. 1997. *The Ancient Celts*. Oxford: Oxford University Press.

Dietler, M. 1990. 'Driven by drink: The role of drinking in the political economy and the case of Early Iron Age France'. *Journal of Anthropological Archaeology* 9: 352–406.

Dietler, M. 1996. 'Feasts and commensal politics in the political economy: Food, power and status in prehistoric Europe', in P. Wiessner and W. Schiefenhovel (eds) *Food and the Status Quest*: 87–126. Oxford: Berghahn Books.

Dietler, M. 2001. 'Theorizing the feast: Rituals of consumption, commensal politics, and power in African contexts', in M. Dietler and B. Hayden (eds) *Feasts: Archaeological and Ethnographic Perspectives on Food, Politics and Power*: 65–114. Tuscaloosa: University of Alabama Press.

Dietler, M. 2006. 'Alcohol: Anthropological/archaeological perspectives'. *Annual Review of Anthropology* 35, 1: 229–249.

Dietler, M., and B. Hayden. 2001. 'Digesting the feast: Good to eat, good to drink, good to think', in M. Dietler and B. Hayden (eds) *Feasts: Archaeological and Ethnographic Perspectives on Food, Politics and Power*: 1–22. Tuscaloosa: University of Alabama Press.

Dunbabin, K. M. D. 2003. *The Roman Banquet: Images of Conviviality*. Cambridge: Cambridge University Press.

Egg, M. 1996. *Das Hallstattzeitliche Fürstengrab von Strettweg bei Judenburg in der Obersteiermark*. RGZM Monographien 37. Mainz: Römisch-Germanisches Zentralmuseum.

Fitzpatrick, A. P. 1985. 'The distribution of Dressel 1 amphorae in north-west Europe'. *Oxford Journal of Archaeology* 4: 305–340.

Fitzpatrick, A. P. 1991. 'Celtic (Iron Age) religion: Traditional and timeless?' *Scottish Archaeological Review* 8: 123–128.

Fitzpatrick, A. P. 2009. 'The champion's portion: Feasting in the Celtic pre-Roman Iron Age', in G. Cooney, K. Becker, J. Coles, M. Ryan, and S. Sievers (eds) *Relics of Old Decency: Archaeological Studies in Later Prehistory. Festschrift for Barry Raftery*: 389–404. Dublin: Wordwell.

Frey, O.-H. 1991. 'The formation of the La Tène culture in the fifth century B.C.', in S. Moscati, O.-H. Frey, V. Kruta, B. Raftery, and M. Szabó (eds) *The Celts*: 127–145. New York: Rizzoli.

Garcia, L., and E. Pons. 2011. 'The archaeological identification of feasts and banquets: Theoretical notes and the case of Mas Castellar', in G. A. Jiménez, S. Montón-Subías, and M. Sánchez Romero (eds) *Guess Who's Coming to Dinner?: Feasting Rituals in the Prehistoric Societies of Europe and the Near East*: 224–245. Oxford: Oxbow.

Gerloff, S. 2010. *Atlantic Cauldrons and Buckets of the Late Bronze and Early Iron Ages in Western Europe: With a Review of Comparable Vessels from Central Europe and Italy*. Prähistorische Bronzefunde II, 18. Stuttgart: Steiner.

Giles, M. 2012. *A Forged Glamour: Landscape, Identity and Material Culture in the Iron Age*. Oxford: Windgather Press.

Gomez de Soto, J. 1993. 'Cooking for the elite: Feasting equipment in the Late Bronze Age', in C. Scarre and F. Healy (eds) *Trade and Exchange in Prehistoric Europe*. Oxbow Monograph 33: 191–197. Oxford: Oxbow.

Goody, J. 1982. *Cooking, Cuisine and Class: A Study in Comparative Sociology*. Cambridge: Cambridge University Press.

Green, M. J. 1998. 'Vessels of death: Sacred cauldrons in archaeology and myth'. *Antiquaries Journal* 78: 63–84.

Hamilakis, Y. 1998. 'Eating the dead: Mortuary and the politics of memory in the Aegean Bronze Age societies', in K. Branigan (ed.) *Cemetery and Society in the Aegean Bronze Age*. Sheffield Studies in Aegean Archaeology 1: 115–132. Sheffield: Sheffield Academic Press.

Hamilakis, Y., and S. Sherratt. 2012. 'Feasting and the consuming body in Bronze Age Crete and Early Iron Age Cyprus', in G. Cadogan, M. Iakavou, K. Kopaka, and J. Whitley (eds) *Parallel*

Lives: Ancient Island Societies in Crete and Cyprus. BSA Studies 20: 187–205. London: British School at Athens.

Hayden, B. 2001. 'Fabulous feasts: A prolegomenon to the importance of feasting', in M. Dietler and B. Hayden (eds) *Feasts: Archaeological and Ethnographic Perspectives on Food, Politics and Power*: 23–64. Tuscaloosa: University of Alabama Press.

Hill, J. D. 2002. 'Just about the potter's wheel? Using, making and depositing Middle and Later Iron Age pots in East Anglia', in A. Woodward and J. D. Hill (eds) *Prehistoric Britain: The Ceramic Basis*: 143–160. Oxford: Oxbow.

Horn, J. A. 2015. 'Tankards of the British Iron Age'. *Proceedings of the Prehistoric Society* 81: 311–341.

Hüglin, S., and N. Spichtig. 2012. 'Turned upside down. An exceptional deposit from the Late La Tène settlement from Basel-Gasfabrik'. *The European Archaeologist* 37: 4–13.

Hutton, R. 1991. *The Pagan Religions of the Ancient British Isles: Their Nature and Legacy*. Oxford: Blackwell.

Jackson, R. 1990. *Camerton: The Late Iron Age and Early Roman Metalwork*. London: British Museum Press.

Jones, M. 1984. 'The plant remains', in B. W. Cunliffe (ed.) *Danebury: An Iron Age Hillfort in Hampshire, Vol. 2*. CBA Research Report 52: 483–495. London: Council for British Archaeology.

Jones, M. 2007. 'A feast of Beltain? Reflections on the rich Danebury harvests', in C. Gosden, H. Hamerow, P. de Jersey, and G. Lock (eds) *Communities and Connections: Essays in Honour of Barry Cunliffe*: 142–153. Oxford: Oxford University Press.

Joy, J. 2009. *Lindow Man*. London: British Museum Press.

Joy, J. 2014. 'Fire burn and cauldron bubble: Iron Age and early Roman cauldrons of Britain and Ireland'. *Proceedings of the Prehistoric Society* 80: 327–362.

Koch, E. 2003. 'Mead, chiefs and feasts in later prehistoric Europe', in M. Parker Pearson (ed.) *Food, Culture and Identity in the Neolithic and Early Bronze Age*. British Archaeological Reports International Series 1117: 125–143. Oxford: Archaeopress.

Krausse, D. 1996. *Hochdorf III. Das Trink- und Speiseservice aus dem späthallstattzeitlichen Fürstengrab von Eberdingen-Hochdorf (Kr. Ludwigsburg)*. Forschungen und Berichte zur Vor- und Frühgeschichte in Baden-Württemberg 64. Stuttgart: Theiss.

Krausse, D. 1999. 'Der "Keltenfürst" von Hochdorf: Dorfälterster oder Sakralkönig? Anspruch und Wirklichkeit der sog. kulturanthropologischen Hallstatt-Archäologie'. *Archäologisches Korrespondenzblatt* 29: 339–358.

Laubenheimer, F., P. Ouzoulias, and P. Van Ossel. 2003. 'La bière en Gaule. Sa fabrication, les mots pour le dire, les vestiges archéologiques: première approche'. *Revue Archéologique de Picardie* 2003, 1–2: 47–63.

Lawson, A. J. 2000. *Potterne 1982–1985: Animal Husbandry in Later Prehistoric Wiltshire*. Salisbury: Wessex Archaeology.

Lévi-Strauss, C. 1968. *L'Origine des Manières de Table*. Paris: Plon.

Loughton, M. E. 2009. 'Getting smashed: The deposition of amphorae and the drinking of wine in Gaul during the Late Iron Age'. *Oxford Journal of Archaeology* 28, 1: 77–110.

McCormick, F. 2009. 'Ritual feasting in Iron Age Ireland', in G. Cooney, K. Becker, J. Coles, M. Ryan, and S. Sievers (eds) *Relics of Old Decency: Archaeological Studies in Later Prehistory. Festschrift for Barry Raftery*: 405–412. Dublin: Wordwell.

McOmish, D. 1996. 'East Chisenbury: Ritual and rubbish at the British Bronze Age–Iron Age transition'. *Antiquity* 70: 68–76.

Megaw, J. V. S., and R. Megaw. 1990. *The Basse-Yutz Find: Masterpieces of Celtic Art—The 1927 Find in the British Museum*. London: Society of Antiquaries of London.

Needham, S., and S. Bowman. 2005. 'Flesh-hooks, technological complexity and the Atlantic Bronze Age feasting complex'. *European Journal of Archaeology* 8, 2: 93–136.

Needham, S., and T. Spence. 1997. 'Refuse and the formation of middens'. *Antiquity* 71: 77–90.

Parker Pearson, M. 1999. 'Food, sex and death: Cosmologies in the British Iron Age with particular reference to East Yorkshire'. *Cambridge Archaeological Journal* 9: 43–69.

Payne, A., M. Corney, and B. W. Cunliffe. 2006. *The Wessex Hillforts Project: Extensive Survey of Hillfort Interiors in Central Southern England*. London: English Heritage.

Poux, M. 2004. *L'âge du vin: Rites de boisson, festins et libations en Gaule indépendante*. Protohistoire Européenne 8. Montagnac: Éditions Monique Mergoil.

Ralph, S. 2005. 'Constructive consumption: Feasting in Iron Age Britain and Europe'. *Archaeological Review from Cambridge* 20, 1: 55–69.

Ralph, S. 2007. *Feasting and Social Complexity in Later Iron Age East Anglia*. British Archaeological Reports British Series 451. Oxford: Archaeopress.

Rebay, K. 2003. 'Wein in der Eisenzeit', in J. Leskovar, G. Schwanzar, and G. Winkler (eds) *Worauf wir stehen: Archäologie in Oberösterreich*: 289–297. Linz: Oberösterreichisches Landesmuseum.

Score, V. 2011. *Hoards, Hounds and Helmets: A Conquest-Period Ritual Site at Hallaton, Leicestershire*. Leicester Archaeology Monograph 21. Leicester: University of Leicester Archaeological Services.

Sealey, P. R. 2007. *A Late Iron Age Warrior Burial from Kelvedon, Essex*. East Anglian Archaeology Report 118. Colchester: Colchester Museums/Colchester Borough Council.

Sealey, P. R. 2009. 'New light on the wine trade in Julio-Claudian Britain'. *Britannia* 40: 1–40.

Sharples, N. 2010. *Social Relations in Later Prehistory: Wessex in the First Millennium BC*. Oxford: Oxford University Press.

Sherratt, A. 1995. 'Alcohol and its alternatives: Symbol and substance in pre-industrial cultures', in J. Goodman, P. E. Lovejoy, and A. Sherratt (eds) *Consuming Habits: Global and Historical Perspectives on How Cultures Define Drugs*: 11–45. London: Routledge.

Stead, I. M., J.-L. Flouest, and V. Rigby. 2006. *Iron Age and Roman Burials in Champagne*. Oxford: Oxbow.

Stevenson, J. 2013. *Living by the Sword: The Archaeology of Brisley Farm, Ashford, Kent*. Spoilheap Monograph 6. Portslade: Archaeology South-East/Surrey County Archaeological Unit.

Stika, H.-P. 1996. 'Traces of a possible Celtic brewery in Eberdingen-Hochdorf, Kreis Ludwigsburg, southwest Germany'. *Vegetation History and Archaeobotany* 5, 1–2: 81–88.

Van der Veen, M. 2007. 'Food as an instrument of social change: Feasting in Iron Age and early Roman southern Britain', in K. Twiss (ed.) *The Archaeology of Food and Identity*: 112–129. Carbondale: Southern Illinois University.

Van der Veen, M., and G. Jones. 2006. 'A re-analysis of agricultural production and consumption: Implications for understanding the British Iron Age'. *Vegetation History and Archaeobotany* 15: 217–228.

Verger, S. 2006. 'La grande tombe de Hochdorf, mise en scène funéraire d'un cursus honorum tribal hors pair'. *Siris* 7: 5–44.

Webster, J. 1995. 'Sanctuaries and sacred places', in M. Green (ed.) *The Celtic World*: 441–464. London and New York: Routledge.

Wood, J. W. 2000. 'Food and drink in European prehistory'. *European Journal of Archaeology* 3, 1: 89–111.

Wright, J. C. 2004. 'A survey of evidence for feasting in Mycenaean society', in J. C. Wright (ed.) *The Mycenaean Feast*. (Also published as *Hesperia* 73, 2): 13–58. Princeton: American School of Classical Studies at Athens.

CHAPTER 40

FUNERARY PRACTICES

PATRICE BRUN

Introduction

The archaeological study of funerary practices has advanced greatly in recent years. Protocols for on-site recording and observation techniques capturing fine detail in the laboratory have lifted the veil on practices whose variability was often unforeseen. This might be seen to lend support to the idea that the mortuary practices lacked any overriding rationale, or at least were independent of social organization. However, an homogeneous thread can in fact be perceived behind this diversity, comprising a recurrent pattern of symbols and an underlying logic suggesting that a funerary ceremony represented a codified form of expression, an ideological 'discourse' linked to real historical circumstances. Like other rites of passage, this diversity 'spoke' in some way about the society to which those close to the deceased belonged, and of their world view. Funerary practices are not therefore a faithful and passive reflection of the way societies were organized, but nor are they a purely ideological product disconnected from economic and political contingencies. This is clearly apparent during the Iron Age, a period that spans, for most parts of Europe, the last eight centuries BC, continuing into the early centuries AD beyond the frontiers of the Roman Empire. We shall follow the chronological and spatial development of these practices in pre-Roman Europe, examining the most significant archaeological evidence available.

Methodological and Theoretical Framework

Humans did not always bury their dead. In Iron Age Europe, the majority of communities did not bury all their dead, and some seem to have buried none at all.

This means that unburied bodies, though no doubt treated with respect as in all human societies, escape archaeological detection. Among the filters that come between the actual funerary practices of a distant era and our current understanding of them, the decision to bury or not to bury appears increasingly to be one of the most significant. It is combined with other similarly cultural choices, such as the level of restraint inherent in the funerary deposits, the number of graves located in a single place, and the degree of permanence or monumentality of the burials. All these elements obviously have a significant bearing on the chances of discovering graves and understanding their distinctive features. Such social filters come on top of other constraints, which are often easier to quantify; these include natural erosion, later human intervention, or the level of effort invested in field research. Burials thus represent merely the tip of an enormous iceberg which encompasses the totality of all funerary practices. The concept of the grave or tomb, which defines a place where a person was buried, comes from the Greek *tumbos*, meaning burial mound, and from the Latin *tumere*, meaning swelling, in the sense of a mound marking a burial pit, where—however slight the relief—the living can remember the dead. The role of a grave was also to materialize symbolically the relationship between a social group and the land it inhabited, exploited, and from which it drew its sustenance, as well as to perpetuate the memory of the deceased in the consciousness of the survivors.

Among the people who were not formally buried, by far the majority during the Iron Age, some have nevertheless left archaeological traces: these include individuals accidentally or deliberately placed in natural hollows or scoops dug for reasons that had nothing to do with commemorating the dead; we shall later see that a high proportion of these individuals are very likely to have been the victims of human sacrifice.

As stated, only a fraction of the population received formal burial during the Iron Age, but in proportions that varied according to the region or period. This fraction is often equated with the political, economic, and religious elites. There is little doubt that this was the case when the grave goods are significantly richer, or some burials more monumental than others, but it is less obvious when the burials of a given community show little differentiation. Indeed, among societies of broadly equivalent political complexity, some were remarkably restrained in their burial practices, while others exhibited very significant differences between graves. This suggests that funerary practices did not always reflect economic and political organization. Rather, they conveyed an ideological message (Figure 40.1). They showed not what these communities were, but how they wanted to appear, depending on their ethical values and the circumstances of the time (Morris 1987). Such a discourse is not explicit, but close observation of differences between graves and cemeteries yields much information on the communities' conception of social relations, especially between rank, gender, and age groups, even when differences in rank were removed for religious reasons or to promote cohesion when solidarity was vital. Significant differences between graves, as well as between groups of graves and cemeteries, can thus be perceived from elements such as the number of burials, the relative distribution of men, women, and children, the period of use, the grave goods, the treatment

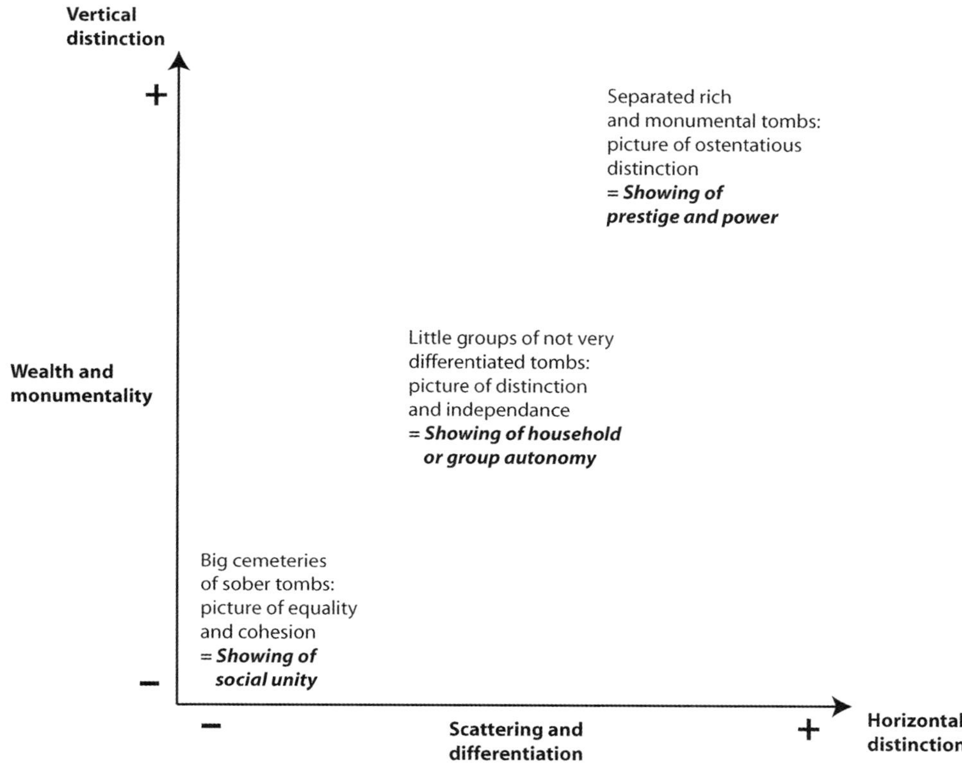

FIGURE 40.1 Model of the ideological messages conveyed by funerary practices, in particular through the wealth of funerary deposits, monumentality, location, and relative differentiation of graves.

Author

of the body, or the durability of markers on the ground to avoid recutting. Overall, the development of these funerary traits over several centuries and on a Europe-wide scale reveals trends which, when compared with patterns in other spheres of activity (domestic, artisan, cult-related, agro-pastoral, commercial, or diplomatic), provide precious insights.

The use of iron is attested over most of Europe from the eighth century BC, at the time city-states were emerging in Greece and then Italy (see Chapter 23, also Chapters 12–14). Based on current knowledge, urbanization is detectable mainly through funerary and religious remains. Vast cemeteries developed on the outskirts of towns because of the high density of inhabitants, the permanence of the settlements, and probably also because more people were now being buried than disposed of in ways that left no archaeologically detectable traces; the exposure of bodies on platforms, and the cremation and scattering of remains on the ground or on water in selected locations, all require space to be available nearby, which becomes more limited or more difficult to access in an urban environment. As its name implies, a necropolis *sensu stricto* tends to accompany a *polis*, i.e. an urban agglomeration. Outside urban settings—which applies to the greater part of the Iron Age—large cemeteries indicate, if not the existence of villages, then at least the presence of long-lived territorial communities, whose shared burial ground becomes a symbolic centre. Conversely, the permanence of a territorial community did not necessarily give rise to the growth of large cemeteries; societies evidently made choices about their funerary practices, and, although these were undoubtedly carried out with respect, they did not result in interment for the majority of the deceased. We shall survey Europe from south to north and in chronological sequence to follow the non-linear and seemingly random development of funerary practices, using key sites which are statistically representative of the period. In this way we shall examine the variability of these practices and how they have been read in terms of their ideological and social significance.

The Development of Networks

This first section will examine mortuary practices from the eighth to fifth centuries BC, with a particular focus on the phenomenon of so-called 'princely' burials. In much of Europe, the overall picture is one of broad continuity with late Bronze Age burial traditions, but with increasing investment in funerary rites; some areas, however, seem to lack formal burials altogether in the earlier Iron Age. In various regions, from Iberia to the Ukraine, very ostentatious tombs appear. These contain exotic luxury goods which attest to one of the hallmarks of this period—the intensification of long-distance supra-cultural exchange networks. These networks allowed certain players to establish powerful dynasties which held sway for three or four generations. We will begin with the rich mortuary evidence from the Circum-Alpine zone.

The Circum-Alpine Zone

At the beginning of the Iron Age, the new metal was mainly used for weapons, especially the long iron swords often placed as status symbols in the graves of the male social elite. These graves, which are isolated or grouped in small clusters, were often covered by a small round barrow. Within the usable corpus of 179 burials in the Circum-Alpine zone dated to between 800 and 625 BC and containing at least one iron object, iron swords are frequently the only metal artefact present. No standard panoply stands out. The burial rite (inhumation or cremation) varies too. There are, however, some preferred associations: first with iron knives (nearly always found near faunal remains), then with wagons, then with objects of personal adornment or toiletry sets made of iron or bronze, and finally with iron axes, especially in the eastern Alps (Dhennequin 2005). Such patterns show that the adoption of iron metallurgy proceeded very slowly in Europe.

While a significant threshold in its spread was passed around 730 BC, iron nevertheless remained the prerogative of social elites, who used it for military equipment and for prestige, especially in ceremonial funerals.

At the turn of the eighth to seventh century BC, the emerging city-states of Greece and Italy gave new impetus to exchanges with the north of the European continent, particularly across the eastern Alps. The *situlae* with narrative representations, which were often deposited in graves, are evidence of this network. They illustrate court scenes inspired from the figurative manner typical of the Orientalizing style (Frey 1962). The societies that used these *situlae* were organized in territorial groups and possessed fortified centres with ostentatious burials under barrows close by, and had relations with groups further north as far as the Austrian Danube and, more diffusely, beyond. The impressive funerary deposits in some burials show this without any ambiguity. The burial of Stična (Božič 2009) in Slovenia, and the Strettweg grave with cult wagon (Egg 1996), the Kröllkogel barrow at Kleinklein with bronze burial mask and hands (Egg and Kramer 2005), the grave with an elephant-ivory sword pommel at Hallstatt (Kromer 1959), and wagon burials of richly attired women such as Mitterkirchen (Pertlwieser 1982)—all in Austria—are particularly telling. To a lesser extent, the numerous wagon burials from across this zone, including a high concentration in the Prague region (Chytráček et al. 2010), are surely affirmation of a stratified social organization closely following wide-ranging exchange networks along several alternative routes between the Adriatic and the Baltic seas. A variety of goods travelled along this multi-branched axis, of which Baltic amber is the easiest to identify archaeologically. The barrow cemetery of Stična—with six burials in one barrow producing over 20,000 glass beads (a material and technique originating in the Near East) and a large quantity of Baltic amber beads assembled into elaborate pendants (Wells 1981)—is a perfect example of such a structure resting on networks that were previously disconnected.

At the cemetery of Hallstatt in Austria, excavated repeatedly since 1846, over 2,000 graves have been recovered, several containing very rich assemblages. That is why the burial ground was quickly adopted as representative of the early Iron Age and gave its name to the period. The wealth displayed in this cemetery, located 340 m above an Alpine lake at the end of the high valley of the Salzberg and very close to the Hallstatt salt mines, is probably related to the exploitation of this exportable commodity and to the control that the local community was able to exert over the one of the most frequently used exchange routes in the seventh century BC linking the Adriatic to the Baltic via the eastern Alps. The Hallstatt cemetery was used between *c.*730 and 430 BC by an average population of some 330 people. The deceased were either inhumed or buried after cremation on a pyre, most often singly, but sometimes accompanied by one to three other individuals. A gradual shift from cremation to inhumation took place. Men and women, in equal numbers, seem to have occupied distinct areas of the cemetery, but both groups exhibit an identical socio-economic profile, with 20% of rich graves, among which 4% represent an even more lavishly furnished subsection. Over its three centuries of use, the cemetery's social structure remained the same, although signs of far-flung connections became fewer after the end of the seventh century BC (Hodson 1990).

It is notable that the graves of women are often among the most prestigious burials in this era. This echoes practices known in Italy at the end of the Villanovan and early Etruscan periods. Two extremely rich female graves of the first half of the seventh century BC, consequently dubbed 'princely graves' by our Italian colleagues, spring to mind: the Regolini-Galassi tomb at Cerveteri with gold jewellery by the dozen, and the Barberini tomb at Preneste with its spectacular Orientalizing objects (Winther 1997). However, in contrast to what took place later, artefacts made in the emerging Mediterranean city-states reached central Europe in small numbers only (Chapter 27). Exchange was from one to another, at a sporadic rate, and probably took place in an indirect manner.

Exchange increased in the course of the sixth century BC, with the most prestigious funerary displays including tablewares made in Greek or Etruscan city-states. This is the case both north-west of the Alps, and in various parts of the European hinterland in contact with Greek colonies on the Black Sea and the Mediterranean coast. Mediterranean objects, many of which were destined from the outset for distant clients—for example, the oversized Vix *krater* (Joffroy 1962), Illyrian amber figurines (Palavestra 1994), and Graeco-Thracian and Graeco-Scythian gold and silverwork (Moscalu 1989; Schiltz 1994)—became the markers of social dominance. They featured especially in the largest and richest burials furnished with grave goods of diverse provenance.

The archaeological complex of Vix-Mont Lassois (Chaume and Mordant 2011), interpreted as a princely centre of the sixth and early fifth centuries BC, consists of a defended hilltop site and three wagon burials, among them the particularly richly furnished Vix burial (Figure 40.2). Originally covered by a large barrow, 38 m in diameter, the underground burial chamber contained a huge Greek bronze *krater* 1.60 m high, decorated with masks of Gorgons and a parade of warriors, two Attic cups, a Greek silver bowl, as well as two Etruscan bronze basins and an *oenochoe*. The woman lay in the body of a wagon whose four wheels had been dismantled and stacked along the walls of the chamber. She died aged 30–35, and was bedecked with jewellery of local manufacture, sometimes adorned with beads of exotic provenance (Baltic amber and Mediterranean coral), as well as a heavy gold torc with terminals in the form of a lion's paw supporting a tiny winged horse and ending in a sphere. The other two wagon burials were located in the neighbouring commune of Sainte-Colombe. As well as the remains of a wagon, one of them contained an Etruscan basin with three griffins' heads, and an iron and bronze tripod; the other produced two bracelets and two ear pendants made of gold, and an iron axe.

Another burial has recently been discovered near the River Seine at Lavau (Aube), 70 km north of Vix. Here too a tumulus was erected over a large burial chamber. The body of the deceased, originally laid out in the body of a wagon, was adorned with a gold torc and bracelets, and accompanied by a dozen metal vessels imported from the Mediterranean, including a large cauldron, two wine jugs, a sieve, and a goblet. This tomb lay close to three more previously known rich graves of the same period, around 450 BC. The group is thus a perfect transitional ensemble, marking the end of the earlier Iron Age and the north Alpine princely phenomenon, as well as its north-western limit.

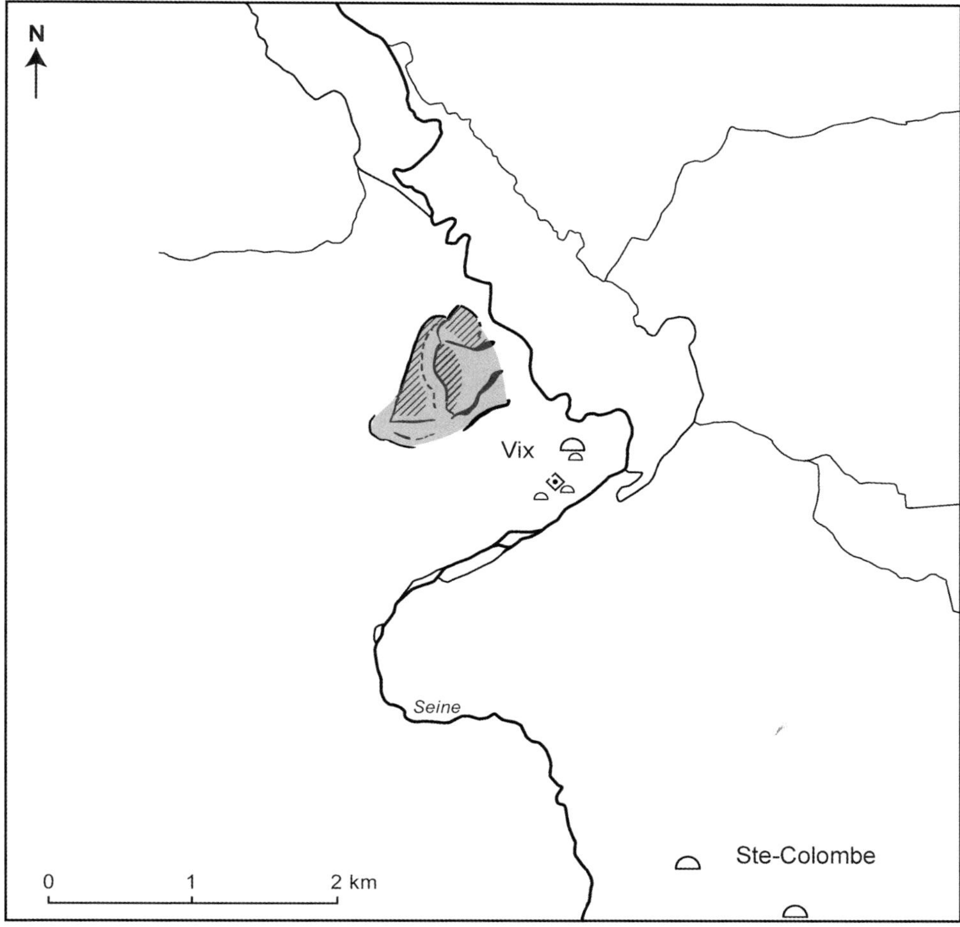

FIGURE 40.2 The Vix-Mont Lassois complex, Burgundy, comprising the large fortified hilltop settlement on Mont Lassois, the Vix and Sainte-Colombe barrow burials, and the contemporary sanctuary at Vix, all found within a radius of 4 km.

Author

Some twenty princely centres of this type are known in a zone between western Bavaria and eastern Berry in central France (Krausse et al. 2016). Their distribution, at a distance of some 100 km from one another, suggests the development of centralized princely territories of roughly similar size. Never before had territories of this scale been unified under a single power. Yet these polities were fragile and their rulers unable to stay in power for long, most probably because they were dependent on exchange relations binding them to Mediterranean powers, and they collapsed after the middle of the fifth century BC. The princely graves played a major part within these societies as territorial and dynastic markers. The best-excavated of these graves, at Hochdorf (Baden-Württemberg), shows that they were not always erected at the capital of these autonomous political units. It is also worth noting that many burials were robbed after only a short interval (Kimmig 1983), as with the Grafenbühl and Hohmichele in south-west Germany, and Ütliberg in Switzerland. The pillaging of the Magdalenenberg (also in south-west Germany), less than half a century after the funerary chamber was built, demonstrates that any ideological taboos protecting these burials were not universally observed, even before the full floruit of the princely phenomenon.

South-Western and South-Eastern Europe

The Circum-Alpine zone was not the only region to exhibit signs of ostentatious burial. In the south of the Iberian peninsula, in the kingdom of Tartessos, the richest tombs known are those of Almuñecar, La Joya, Niebla, Carmona, and Setefilla. Imported items, as well as prestigious goldwork, have also been recovered from the remains of palaces or temples such as at Cancho Roano. In the Spanish Levante too, burials were organized along hierarchical lines, with 'royal' or monarchic tombs, and 'princely' or aristocratic burials dominating all the others (Almagro-Gorbea 1983). The most prestigious tombs were capped by funerary monuments made of cut and sculpted stone. The tombs contained Attic wares, and objects of personal adornment are also found more frequently there than elsewhere in the Iberian peninsula (Nicolini 1990). This political organization lasted a century and a half at most, and collapsed as Phoenician trade was disrupted and the communities of the Iberian interior became increasingly threatening (Almagro-Gorbea and Ruiz Zapatero 1992). The practice of ostentatious burial ceased at the end of the sixth century BC, but towns such as Carmo, Hasta Regia, or Castulo, which occupied an area up to 50 ha in extent, continued to rule over small independent territories as long as the late third century BC. Such manifestations of power are related to the privileged links that the indigenous elites forged with Phoenician and Greek colonies. Archaic states emerged in the Levante towards the middle of the fifth century BC, around the cities of Hemeroskopaion (near Alicante) and Sagonte, which adopted an Ionian alphabet (Ruiz and Molinos 1993).

Turning to the ancient region of Illyria in the Balkans, the five graves of Pilatovíci, Atenica, Novi Pazar, Pécka Banja, and Trebenište (Tomb VII) are richer and more monumental than the others, with prestigious burial accorded equally to individuals of either gender or sex (Babić 2002). More ordinary graves, but still containing imported goods, are also known, suggesting at least three, if not four, levels of status. The imported bronze vessels from Novi Pazar and Trebenište seem to have been made by the same southern Italian Greek workshops as those of Hochdorf, Grächwil, and Vix north of the Alps. Amber is also abundant in some Balkan graves, having passed through workshops established in Picenum or southern Italy (Parović-Pešikan 1964; Palavestra 1994). These prestige goods crossed the Adriatic and were then transported overland, or continued by sea to the area of the modern port of Dubrovnik. Significantly, these wealthy graves were located on communication networks that were still important in the Middle Ages for caravan traffic between the Adriatic and the Balkan hinterland. The region's mineral wealth, especially the silver ores, hints at what was being exchanged for the fine tableware and precious jewellery. To this we must probably add other goods, still being transported by caravan in the Middle Ages: leather, wool, furs, livestock, wax, honey, resin, timber, rare plants, and slaves. The medieval caravans could consist of several hundred pack animals and an armed escort (Palavestra 1994). Those of the sixth and fifth centuries BC were probably not so very different.

In Thrace, the majority of princely burials date to the beginning of the fourth century BC, but are conveniently considered here as part of this tradition. The tombs at Strelca, Brezovo, Rozovec, Dalboki, Daskal Atanasovo, and Kalajanovo run from east to west over a distance of some 200 km between the Gate of Trajan and Yambol. Others are spread along the Danube basin: Vraca (Vratsa), Sofronievo, Peretu, Chirnogi, Gavani, and Agighiol; two more are located in Transylvania: Dobolii de Jos and Sfântu Gheorghe (Fol and Marazov 1977; Moscalu 1989; Bouzek 1990; see Chapter 14). These probably reflect attempts at legitimating the power of aristocratic families who controlled exchanges with Greek city-states, as some accompanying settlements resemble those we know north of the Alps: Zimnicea in the Danube valley, some 300 km from the Black Sea, for example, has produced—in addition to Thracian, Getan, and Scythian products—fragments of hundreds of Greek amphorae which reached the site from around 430 BC onwards. These wine containers also travelled to Piscu Crasani further north and as far as the slopes of the Carpathians at Cetatenii din Vale (Danov 1990). Among the Scythians, ostentatious burials also illustrate attempts at legitimating increased power. Their elites were buried with the traditional bow, trilobite arrows, *akinakes* or short sword, massive spears, and body armour, as well as with people put to death to accompany them in the grave (Moscalu 1989).

In all these zones with rich burials, a distinct hierarchy of at least three levels is apparent within the graves. Furthermore, the very richest burials or groups of burials were not randomly distributed but lay at quite regular intervals from one another. Where the settlement pattern is known sufficiently, the richest sites show a distribution that mirrors the burials. It suggests a very centralized model whose major sites can be used to define influence over a hypothetical territory—i.e. the degree of integration. The most ostentatious burials included grave goods from Greek and Etruscan city-states, suggesting a causal link between the wealth of the family of the deceased, the importance of its role in long-distance exchange networks, the extent of its political power, and the probably tyrannical nature of that power. The message sent by the burials is thus not just an indication of a high level of organizational complexity, but also of the form of political regime. Elsewhere, funerary practices were more restrained (even if with differences demonstrating some social inequality), which appears to reflect the probably less authoritarian, more respectful character of lineage-based or village-based power structures in these regions.

North-Western Europe

Even further north, the south–north exchange axis is marked by fewer and less ostentatious burials in the eighth and seventh centuries BC, like the large barrow at Voldtofte on the island of Fyn (Denmark), or that of Seddin in Mecklemburg (Wüstemann 1974). Greek and Etruscan artefacts are extremely rare, but cordoned buckets and bronze *situlae*—made in the southern Alpine foothills (or even copied on the middle Rhine) and consequently of lower local social value—were given to the northern political leaders. These ceremonial vessels are known from graves located along the Meuse up to the Rhine delta and the lower Weser in the Bremen area. Others were present in the region of Seddin and along the Oder and Neisse. Further afield, in Scandinavia and the British Isles, finds of such objects are extremely rare (Kimmig 1983; Stary 1993, 1995).

Formal graves are practically absent from the British Isles for much of the Iron Age, apart from in one or two areas such as East Yorkshire (discussed later), as other funerary practices were in existence. The absence of durable traces suggests that it may have been less important for those communities to keep a distinctly reified place commemorating the social elites.

Turmoil and Reconfiguration

The start of the second half of the first millennium BC saw significant changes in the funerary record. The overall number and size of cemeteries increased markedly, with particularly striking concentrations in some areas such as Champagne and the middle Rhine-Moselle region (e.g. Diepeveen-Jansen 2001). Distinctions in wealth and monumentality were also reduced in many areas. This reflects the collapse of the old despotic dynasties and probably a reduction in politically autonomous territories. These upheavals were magnified in the fourth and third centuries BC by the onset of migration by sections of these north Alpine societies, which brought about the demise of the supra-cultural exchange networks. Cremation burial remained the dominant rite in the north German plain, and became increasingly prevalent in the final centuries BC in many other parts of north-west Europe, when we again begin to see a return to more ostentatious funerary practices around the fringes of the expanding Roman Empire. These changes correspond to a reconfiguration of the supra-cultural networks, which now extended much further north. This section follows the same geographical framework as before, again adopting a necessarily selective approach.

The Circum-Alpine Zone

Since the nineteenth century, tens of thousands of inhumation graves have been discovered in the Champagne region, where some 400 cemeteries are known, on average only about 3.5 km apart from one another. The calcareous subsoil has contributed to good preservation, but unfortunately the majority of these were dug in the past without adequate care or recording. Some graves contained vehicles, and at least three have produced an Etruscan *oenochoe*. The tradition can be traced back to the end of the sixth century BC. At that time, as illustrated by the large cemetery of Chouilly-Les Jogasses, women were buried in one half of the funerary area, and men in the other, on either side of a four-wheeled wagon burial. Thereafter, when the cemetery grew outwards from this nucleus, the graves were arranged, no longer according to the sex of the occupants, but probably in family groups that included men, women, and children.

All told, remains of vehicles—mostly two-wheeled chariots—have been found in more than 250 graves, most often in male burials, but associated with women in some twenty cases. In seven instances, two individuals were found superimposed in the same grave, and in six of these the woman was uppermost. Only one grave contained two men. On two occasions three individuals were recorded in the same grave. The study of well-recorded graves belonging to the Aisne-Marne culture has made it possible to take social analysis much further (Demoule 1999). Weapons belonged to men, and torcs signalled women. Among the graves without neck-rings, but containing other items of personal adornment like fibulae or belt hooks, three-quarters were female. A similar proportion of the graves that produced only pottery, or had no grave goods at all, were male. Each cemetery contained equal proportions of men and women. It is possible to distinguish four levels of wealth overall, both among men and women (Demoule 1999). At the top, obviously, come the chariot burials, followed by the warrior graves (10–20% of the total). Wealthy women are represented in similar numbers, and their graves were located in the same parts of the cemeteries as those of the warriors and of children with rich grave goods. The cemeteries were thus organized in family groups of different status, who used the same space for several generations. More than half the burials were those of men without weapons and of women with little jewellery. The last group consisted of men and women without any grave goods at all.

In this region the cemeteries are densely and evenly distributed, but overall differences in wealth are perceptible. Thus chariot burials are generally present only in cemeteries of more than a hundred graves. Local communities appear to coexist independently. Some exhibit greater opulence than others, but the rich chiefs do not appear to have extended their power over a larger territory. These small political units, clearly hierarchical, characterize the Celtic world during the period of the great migrations, a period when the number of cemeteries decreases regularly after experiencing a strong and rapid growth in the middle of the fifth century BC. Burials with Greek and Italic vessels, such as Châlons-sur-Marne, Somme-Bionne, Somme-Tourbe (Figure 40.3), or Pernant count among the richest. Among the most prestigious, male burials remain in the majority, but the proportion of female burials turns out to be higher than expected. At Bucy-le-Long (Aisne), for example, four out of the five cart burials uncovered were those of women. Moreover, it was a woman who was laid to rest in the richest burial of the fourth century BC, at Waldalgesheim (Rheinland-Pfalz, Germany).

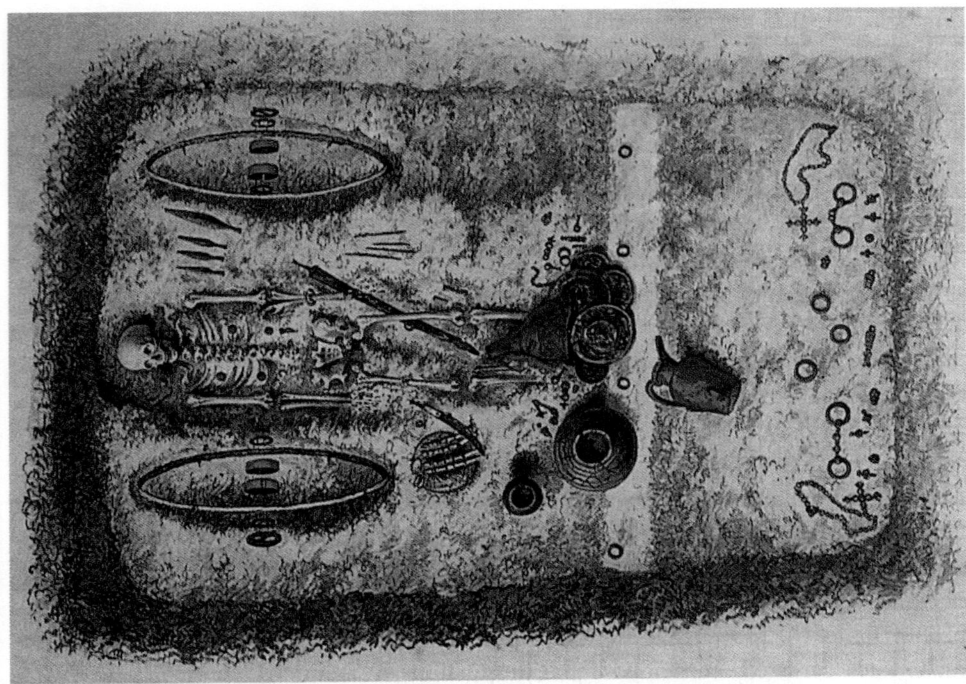

FIGURE 40.3 Plan and section of the burial with cart and Mediterranean imports at La Gorge-Meillet in Somme-Tourbe, Marne, France.

Drawing: E. Gastebois, in Fourdrignier 1877

As an example of a late Iron Age cemetery where the cremation rite predominates, we may examine Lamadeleine, Luxembourg (Metzler-Zens et al. 1999). In use during the first century BC, this lay outside the western gate of the monumental Titelberg *oppidum*. The cemetery was organized in three groups of graves, containing seventy-nine cremations and six inhumations (all perinatal deaths). An unknown number of graves had undoubtedly been destroyed prior to excavation (Metzler-Zens et al. 1999: 18), but the age and sex profile of the surviving remains consisted of at least fifty-two adults, two young adults, one immature, one adolescent, three older children, eighteen young children or infants (including the six perinatals), and five too fragmentary to identify (Metzler-Zens et al. 1999: 249). As always, the proportion of subadults is much lower than would be expected in a normal population (see Chapter 33). The cemetery expanded into a new area about every twenty years, with use of the pre-existing clusters diminishing before ceasing altogether (Figure 40.4).[1]

Lamadelaine is one of the very rare well-analysed and published examples of a cemetery associated with a large fortified town-like settlement belonging to the end of Gaulish independence. Even allowing for lost burials, the number of individuals interred here was clearly low compared to the likely number of inhabitants. The number of datable graves in any single twenty-year span was eight, sixteen, thirteen, thirteen, and finally five. A permanent grave in this burial ground would appear to have been a privilege reserved to a minority. However, more recently, hundreds of new graves have been discovered outside the eastern gate of the Titelberg (Metzler et al. 2016: 411). This second cemetery was clearly far larger than Lamadelaine and would appear finally to bring this agglomeration closer to an urban model.

South-Western and South-Eastern Europe

In the fourth century BC in southern Spain, the sculpted funerary monuments of the Iberian sovereigns, like that of Pozo Moro, were replaced by monuments with heroic iconography, such as the *heroon* of Porcuna (Chapa Brunet 1985). This new mode of expression probably sanctioned the rise to power of a warrior aristocracy in a more fragmented political landscape, as though a compression and concomitant tightening of the level and scale of integration were at play. It seems to be a phenomenon similar to contemporary developments in Celtic areas north of the Alps.

The Celtic migrations, however, set many more people in motion (Chapter 37). Some descended on northern Italy, others penetrated Lower Austria, south-western Slovakia, and northern Transdanubia. They settled there and consolidated their hold, as attested by many cemeteries, like those of Sopron-Bécsidomb or Ménfőcsanak (Szabó 1992). At the beginning of the third century BC a series of chieftain's tombs were built, including that at Ciumeşti, famous for its helmet topped by a bird of prey with wings that move, but also containing among the other artefacts greaves of Greek manufacture. Several of these burials yielded Hellenistic bronze vessels. It is unlikely that these luxury goods all

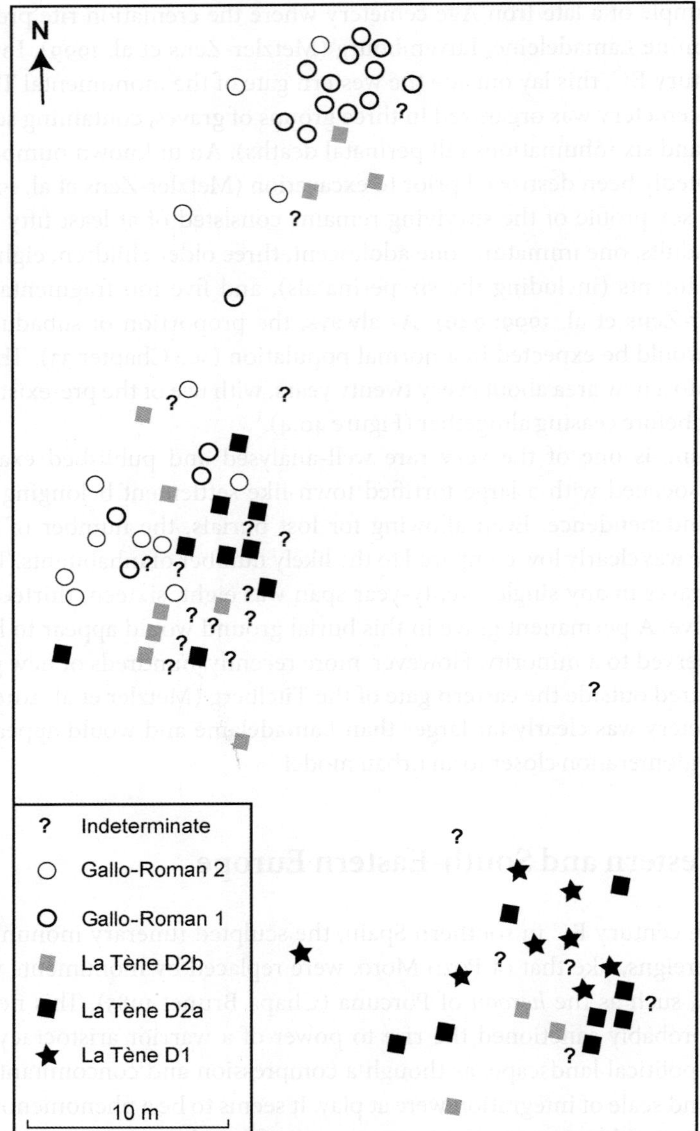

FIGURE 40.4 Plan of the sequence of graves at the cemetery of Lamadeleine near the *oppidum* of the Titelberg, Luxembourg.

Author, after Metzler-Zens et al. 1999

represent loot brought back by valiant warriors. The majority were probably acquired through commercial exchanges and/or as diplomatic gifts (Szabó 1992).

An important example of funerary practices *not* faithfully reflecting social organization is provided by the Dacians. Between 130 and 31 BC, vast quantities of

Roman coins reached the Carpathians (over 25,000 Roman *denarii* and local copies have been discovered in some one hundred coin hoards), but other Roman products are much rarer than in other parts of central Europe. This choice is most likely to stem from Dacian religious prohibitions. These affected most social activities, but only screened certain objects among the goods exchanged with the Mediterranean civilizations. Such ritual particularities call to mind a monotheistic belief system, which could conceivably have been inspired by religions practised in more complex societies: Buddhism introduced via the steppe regions, Judaism recently adopted in the Crimean kingdom, or Egyptian cults in the Hellenistic cities of southern Thrace. The binding rules of this Dacian state-run religion not only obscured the underlying social organization, but also seem to have encoded funerary practices, ensuring that no individual was associated with grave goods or equipment indicative of his or her status. Further archaeological evidence shows the high level of complexity of such a social organization. The vast settlement of Sarmizegetusa, spread over 3 km and centred on an imposing timber and stone sanctuary of Hellenistic inspiration, is interpreted as the capital of a state that disintegrated at the death of its leader, Burebista (Glodariu 1976).

North-Western Europe

In Scandinavia, little evidence of social distinction is discernible in burials between the sixth and early second centuries BC. Cemeteries consist of cremation graves that resembled one another in their generalized sobriety. The adoption of iron metallurgy, which thereafter rested on local resources, was accompanied by a tendency for communities to turn inwards. Furthermore, regional style differences appear to confirm that community identities were being strengthened (Kristiansen 1998). However, some caution is required in the face of this apparent return to more egalitarian social relations; indeed, field boundaries suggest that differential access to land was institutionalized, even if the extent of such power largely escapes us.

Clear social differences become apparent again in the second century BC. Richer graves in many parts of north-west Europe also signal, through the exotic goods found in them, that long-distance links had been re-established via the social elites. Relations with the Roman world in particular grew rapidly, and 'principalities' or 'kingdoms' become perceptible (Hedeager 1978, 1992).

In Britain, the middle Iron Age Arras culture is named after the nineteenth-century discovery of a large cemetery in East Yorkshire (Stead 1979; Giles 2012). Dating to between 400 and 150 BC, its funerary practices mark it out as distinct, bar a few exceptions, from the rest of Britain (Figure 40.5). The Arras tradition is characterized by individual inhumation burials surrounded by a quadrangular ditch, sometimes containing a two-wheeled vehicle, as was the case at the same time on the Continent. There are, however, specifically local traits: the dead were laid to rest on their side in a flexed position, the vehicle was dismantled, and the funerary assemblage was indigenous in character. These attributes suggest not immigration, but partial borrowing by local elites of practices from the other side of the Channel to manifest their prestige. It is, however, worth noting that a recent excavation of a chariot burial at Ferry Fryston revealed the presence of a possible outsider within this elite: strontium isotope analysis

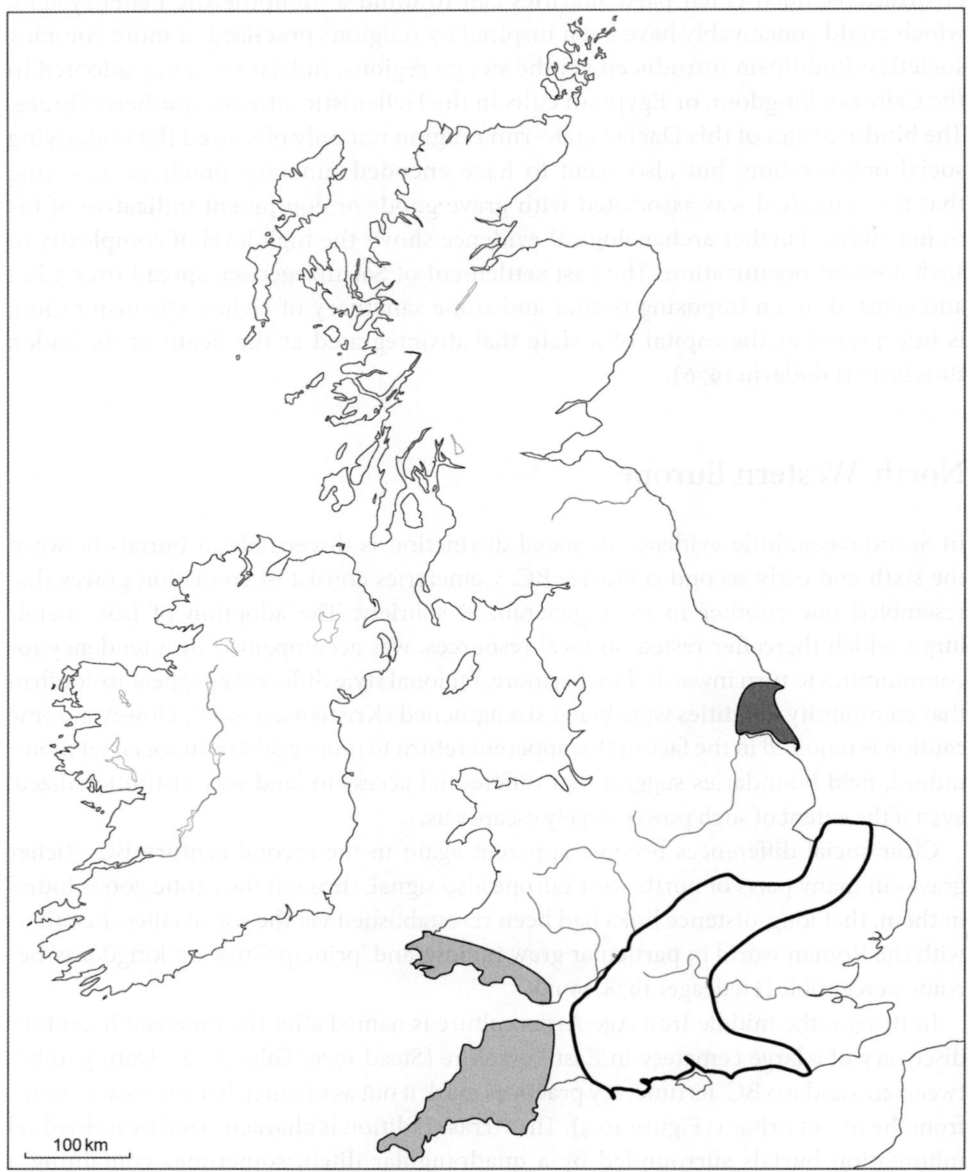

FIGURE 40.5 Mortuary practices in Britain. Dark grey: Arras burials; light grey: Atlantic cist burials; black outline: central-southern pit burials.

Author, after Cunliffe 1993

shows that the man might have grown up much further north, in the Highlands of Scotland or even in Scandinavia (Brown et al. 2007: 154). Only a minority of the Arras burials contained goods, and these were mostly fairly modest—a bracelet of bronze, jet, or shale, or a brooch. Just a few individuals buried with chariots exhibited signs of greater opulence: two men with swords, and a woman with an iron mirror and bronze container at Wetwang Slack; a man with a mail coat at Kirkburn; and a woman with another iron mirror and a string of tiny blue glass beads, wrapped around a coral-decorated brooch at Wetwang village (Giles 2012).

South-east England was marked by a stronger current of influence during the first century BC, as shown by the widespread adoption of cremation burial, coinage, and the potter's wheel. Cremation cemeteries—not unlike those across the Channel, but again displaying distinctive insular characteristics—became more frequent: they were generally small, with only two known that contained over a hundred cremations. They show very uneven degrees of wealth, with a few particularly ostentatious burials containing imported wine amphorae and Roman pottery—for example, the Welwyn-type burials found in the region north of the Thames. As we have seen, this reappearance of individual rich burials is part of a wider phenomenon evident around the fringes of the expanding Roman Empire, which continued into the Roman Iron Age in northern Europe (Hedeager 1992).

More than a thousand individuals dated to the Iron Age have been recovered from the bogs of north-west Europe, where the acid and anaerobic environment ensured exceptional preservation, including soft tissue and hair. Many of the individuals appear to have been executed: strangled, or with their throat slit or skull broken, they were thrown into the bogs and pushed into the mud with the help of poles and sticks (Chapter 41). It is of course difficult to establish whether the executions were carried out as punishment for wrong-doing, or represent human sacrifices. Some bodies, like Tollund Man (Denmark) or Lindow Man (England), were recovered still with the rope that was used to strangle them. Lindow Man, found near Manchester and dated to the first century AD, had been fatally struck three times on the head, his throat was slit, and he had been bled, as well as garrotted (asphyxiated) until his neck was finally broken (Joy 2009). This triple execution is likely to be ritual. The individuals found in this type of context appear for the most to belong to a relatively high level of society. They were well-nourished and do not show physical signs of heavy labour, and in some cases they even had manicured nails (Glob 1966; Aldhouse-Green 2001).

Similar suggestions have been made for bodies found in disused cereal storage pits. These are not formal graves, but rather attest to sacrificial practices involving both humans and animals (Cunliffe 1993). A marked increase in this practice, which was probably destined to ensure good harvests in the gift of supernatural powers, is noticeable from the fifth to the third century BC in Lower Austria, the south of Germany, the Paris basin, and central southern England.

The Social Significance of Funerary Practices

The death of someone close deeply affects the survivors, leaving them moved and distressed. In traditional societies, their whole world view is shaken to the core. After the death of one of its members, the community needed to restore its view of the world order. Not only did people have to dispose of the body rapidly for reasons of hygiene, but they also had to make sense of the separation from that inert body and its rapid physical decay. They had lost an individual who had previously contributed in all sorts of ways to the community, which, above all, was suffering the loss of a link in its own social and reproductive chain. Consequently the family and the whole community needed to mourn in a ritualized manner, a practice that involved interaction with supernatural powers.

Archaeological data are only partly representative of actual funerary practices, especially those reflecting their more ostentatious elements. When graves are monumental in character, they reveal unambiguously the will to mark, both in the soil and in memory, the social role of the deceased. But the contents do not necessarily or unambiguously reflect his or her status, as objects could have been previously destroyed ceremonially without leaving any traces. This constitutes a serious challenge for archaeology. Indeed, there is no guarantee that the artefacts deposited in a grave are representative of what was destroyed or expended during the funeral—i.e. everything that constituted the funeral ceremony. The frequent use of the same categories of objects in the most richly furnished mortuary deposits all over Iron Age Europe, however, implies that a largely shared model—symbolizing identity and status differences (accoutrements, toilet instruments), generosity (vessels used in banquets), mobility (horse gear, vehicles), and, for males, armed force (weapons)—was in operation. The main variations observable across the continent relate to the proportion of people who were buried. Not all the dead of a community were interred, and those who were buried may not have been accorded any signs of distinction. In this respect, major differences can be seen between Iron Age societies of similar complexity. The grave should be conceived, not as a faithful reflection of the life and status of an individual, but as the expression of an 'ideal' or symbolic status that the community or group bestowed on the dead. Funerary practices fit into a sequence that conforms to other rites of passage: rites of separation are followed by rites of integration into the community of ancestors (Van Gennep 1909). For the Iron Age, such practices appear to take different forms articulated between two poles:

- integration into a large community of equals, rendering social differences practically imperceptible
- assimilation within the mythical genealogy of a dominant or emerging group, be it a family, a lineage, an aristocratic or economic group; in this instance, the markers of group membership are clearly displayed.

Rites of passage are fundamentally aimed at the submission of those they are celebrating. It is conceivable that funerary rites fulfilled the function of integrating the dead into a 'useful' category, whether useful to the community as a whole, or to an already dominant or emerging social group, for instance a new dynasty (Kristiansen 1998).

Here too we must neither confine ourselves to social analysis at a local scale, nor undertake a narrowly defined thematic enquiry such as solely archaeological or solely palaeopathological studies. Mortuary practices are full of meanings that are obscure but also intimately connected to other social dimensions. This contradicts the idea of a myriad of meanings that escape our understanding, a myriad that is entirely unpredictable and can only be described, without any hope of higher-level explanation. It is possible to draw out structural meaning related to the more or less ostentatious nature of power and the more or less intensive character of social, political, and economic exchanges.

Feasting was a tradition common to north-Alpine social elites from at least the fourteenth century BC onwards (Chapter 39). The abundance and/or luxury of the tableware found in their graves signals the importance of the banquet to members of the social elites buried with great ceremony; it symbolizes the funeral feast, of course, but more generally the banquet was a crucial element in their power strategies. These high-ranking individuals offered lavish hospitality, in a range of contexts, in order to pose as models of conviviality, solidarity, sociability, and generosity, and to parade their wealth, power, good fortune, and divine protection—i.e. their legitimacy. Literary and ethnographic sources show how universal such practices were in hierarchical societies and how frequent the occasions for organizing a spectacular feast were: births, rites of passage to adulthood, marriages, military victories, changes of status, collective enterprises, funerals, etc (Dietler and Hayden 2001; Poux 2004). At funerals, those close to the deceased also demonstrated that they had the capacity and the will to assume the roles of political and religious leaders and guarantee continuity. They thus conveyed a message, transforming the ceremony into a huge communications event aimed at the local population, but conceivably also foreign potentates invited for the occasion. Indeed, expenditure was not limited to attracting the favour of those invited or merely to impressing them at the time: by marking the landscape, the intent was to make a lasting impression on the collective memory. It is likely that the more unstable the position of the dominant group—for instance, in times of political or economic strife—the greater their outlay, especially those whose territories controlled communication networks, or major routes for the exchange of goods, people, and ideas. Such situations promote material and intellectual improvement, but are potentially unsettling for the organization of traditional societies (Brun et al. 2010). Material improvement seems almost invariably to lead to changes in social balance, and new ideas inevitably shake up traditional conceptual frameworks.

This approach conforms to the 'dual-processual' theory (Blanton et al. 1996), which holds that leaders use different kinds of politico-economic strategies on a continuum from exclusive and highly centralized 'networks', to inclusive and more decentralized 'corporate' strategies. The 'network' mode emphasizes personal prestige, wealth exchange, individual power of accumulation, elite progression, lineage-based models of inheritance and descent, particularizing ideologies, personal networks, and specialized craft workshops. Archaeological evidence of this mode takes the form of individualization, exchange systems for prestige goods, and ostentatious burials. The 'corporate' mode stresses basic food production, communal ritual, public construction, power-sharing, cooperative large-scale projects, with the segments of society linked together by rituals of integration and by ideological means. Hierarchy is present but not individualized; economic distinctions are limited or even completely absent from mortuary practices.

The available evidence, the most significant of which we have reviewed in this chapter, shows that distinctive trends were at work during the seven or eight centuries under consideration. From south to north the size, durability, and materiality of funerary assemblages increases. This tendency unfolded in two main phases, separated by a temporary reversal from the fourth to second centuries BC; however, this was not so much a general outward diffusion as a dendritic spread along the main river networks. In its first phase, this translates into burials that were monumental, richly, or very richly furnished, and either isolated or in small groups; in the second, cemeteries are larger and the burials more clearly materialized, but with less evident distinctions in terms of wealth and monumentality.

These observations suggest that funerary practices too were sensitive to the intensification of contacts among the different societies occupying the European continent. Such relationships bring in their wake changes in all domains of activity: economic, of course, political because they tend to change the social equilibrium (in other words, traditional power structures), but also ideological because they foster the introduction of new ideas. The latter were sometimes a result of simple borrowings, but more often a product of difficulties created by the opening up of the community to other societies, exacerbating the causes of conflict and requiring the reinforcement of internal solidarities in compensation. Such a scenario could explain why many Iron Age communities in Europe chose to express their internal solidarity symbolically by having a greater number of people buried in communal cemeteries, and by adopting more uniform forms of burial. Where funerary deposits are very restrained, the intention may have been to show that equal value was accorded to all individuals in the face of death, a death risked to safeguard the community. Less extreme cases of restraint in mortuary rite seem instead to reflect a type of political regime where power was exercised in a more consensual manner, or at least less despotically, than in the so-called 'princely' societies.

Note

1. For a more recent analysis of the cemetery, see Deweirdt et al. 2012, although this does not fundamentally change the picture.

References

Aldhouse-Green, M. J. 2001. *Dying for the Gods: Human Sacrifice in Iron Age and Roman Europe*. Stroud: Tempus.

Almagro Gorbea, M. 1983. 'Pozo Moro. El Monumento orientalizante, su contexto socio-cultural y sus paralelos en la arquitectura funeraria ibérica'. *Madrider Mitteilungen* 24: 191–287.

Almagro Gorbea, M., and G. Ruiz Zapatero. 1992. 'Paleoetnologia de la Peninsula Ibérica. Reflexiones y perspectivas de futuro', in M. Almagro Gorbea and G. Ruiz Zapatero (eds) *Paleoetnologia de la Peninsula Ibérica, Complutum 2–3*: 469–499. Madrid: Editorial Complutense.

Babić, S. 2002. '"Princely graves" of the central Balkans: A critical history of research'. *European Journal of Archaeology* 5, 1: 70–88.

Blanton, R., G. Feinman, S. Kowalewski, and P. Peregrine. 1996. 'A dual-processual theory for the evolution of Mesoamerican civilization'. *Current Anthropology* 37: 1–14: 65–68.

Bouzek, J. 1990. *Studies of Greek Pottery in the Black Sea Area*. Prague: Charles University.

Božič, D. 2009. 'A Hallstatt grave containing a cuirass, excavated near Stična by the Duchess of Mecklenburg in 1913. The reliability of grave groups from the Mecklenburg Collection'. *Arheološki vestnik* 60: 63–95.

Brown, F., C. Howard-Davis, M. Brennand, A. Boyle, T. Evans, S. O'Connor, et al. 2007. *The Archaeology of the A1 (M) Darrington to Dishforth DBFO Road Scheme*. Lancaster Imprints 12. Lancaster: Oxford Archaeology North.

Brun, P., I. Aubry, C. Galinand, F. Pennors, V. Quenol, and P. Ruby. 2010. 'Elite and prestige goods during the early and middle Bronze Age in France', in H. Meller and F. Bertemes (eds) *Der Griff nach den Sternen: Wie Europas Eliten zu Macht und Reichtum Kamen, International Symposium (16–21 02 2005)*: 199–206. Halle: Landesamt für Denkmalpflege und Archäologie Sachsen-Anhalt, Landesmuseum für Vorgeschichte.

Chapa Brunet, T. 1985. *La Escultura ibérica zoomorfa*. Madrid: Ministerio de Cultura.

Chaume, B., and C. Mordant (eds). 2011. *Le complexe aristocratique de Vix: Nouvelles recherches sur l'habitat, le système de fortification et l'environnement du Mont Lassois*. Dijon: Éditions Universitaires de Dijon.

Chytráček, M., A. Danielisová, M. Trefný, and M. Slabina. 2010. 'Zentralisierungsprozesse und Siedlungsdynamik in Böhmen (8.–4. Jh. v. Chr.)', in D. Krausse (ed.) *'Fürstensitze' und Zentralorte der frühen Kelten: Abschlusskolloquium des DFG-Schwerpunkprogramms 1171 in Stuttgart, 12.–15. Oktober 2009*. Forschungen und Berichte zur Vor- und Frühgeschichte in Baden-Württemberg 20.2: 155–173. Stuttgart: Theiss.

Cunliffe, B. W. 1993. *Fertility, Propitiation and the Gods in the British Iron Age*. Amsterdam: Museum voor Anthropologie en Praehistorie.

Danov, C. 1990. 'Characteristics of Greek colonization in Thrace', in J.-P. Descœudres (ed.) *Greek Colonists and Native Populations*: 151–155. Oxford: Clarendon Press.

Demoule, J.-P. 1999. *Chronologie et société dans les nécropoles celtiques de la Culture Aisne-Marne du VIe au IIIe siècle avant notre ère*. Revue Archéologique de Picardie Numero spécial 15. Amiens: RAP.

Deweirdt, E., P. De Maeyer, P. Méniel, J. Metzler, C. Petit, and J. Bourgeois. 2012. 'L'analyse spatiale des nécropoles revisitée: L'exemple de la nécropole de l'âge du Fer final et du début de l'époque gallo-romaine de Lamadeleine (Grand-Duché du Luxembourg)'. *Archäologisches Korrespondenzblatt* 42, 2: 185–204.

Dhennequin, L. 2005. 'L'armement au premier âge du Fer en Europe tempérée'. PhD thesis, Université de Paris 1.

Diepeveen-Jansen, M. 2001. *People, Ideas and Goods: New Perspectives on 'Celtic Barbarians' in Western and Central Europe (500–250 BC)*. Amsterdam Archaeological Studies 7. Amsterdam: Amsterdam University Press.

Dietler, M., and B. Hayden (eds). 2001. *Feasts: Archaeological and Ethnographic Perspectives on Food, Politics, and Power*. Washington, DC: Smithsonian.

Egg, M. 1996. *Das Hallstattzeitliche Fürstengrab von Strettweg bei Judenburg in der Obersteiermark*. RGZM Monographien 37. Mainz: Römisch-Germanisches Zentralmuseum.

Egg, M., and D. Kramer. 2005. *Krieger—Feste—Totenopfer. Der letzte Hallstattfürst von Kleinklein in der Steiermark. Mosaiksteine*. Forschungen am Römisch-Germanischen Zentralmuseum 1. Mainz: Römisch-Germanisches Zentralmuseum.

Fol, A., and I. Marazov. 1977. *Thrace and the Thracians*. London: Cassell.

Fourdrignier, E. 1877. 'Double sépulture gauloise de la Gorge Meillet'. *Mémoire de la Société d'Agriculture, Commerce, Sciences et Arts du Département de la Marne* 1875–1876: 125–157.

Frey, O.-H. 1962. 'Der Beginn der Situlenkunst im Ostalpenraum'. *Germania* 40: 56–73.

Giles, M. 2012. *A Forged Glamour: Landscape, Identity and Material Culture in the Iron Age*. Oxford: Windgather Press.

Glob, P. V. 1966. *Les hommes des tourbières*. Paris: Fayard.

Glodariu, I. 1976. *Dacian Trade with the Hellenistic and Roman World*. British Archaeological Reports International Series 8. Oxford: British Archaeological Reports.

Hedeager, L. 1978. 'A quantitative analysis of Roman imports in Europe north of the Limes (0–400 A.D.), and the question of Roman-Germanic exchange', in K. Kristiansen and C. Paludan-Müller (eds) *New Directions in Scandinavian Archaeology*: 191–217. Odense: National Museum of Denmark.

Hedeager, L. 1992. *Iron Age Societies: From Tribe to State in Northern Europe 500 BC to AD 700*. Oxford: Blackwell.

Hodson, F. R. 1990. *Hallstatt: The Ramsauer Graves: Quantification and Analysis*. RGZM Monographien 16. Mainz: Römisch-Germanisches Zentralmuseum.

Joffroy, R. 1962. *Le Trésor de Vix: Histoire et portée d'une grande découverte*. Paris: Fayard.

Joy, J. 2009. *Lindow Man*. London: British Museum Press.

Kimmig, W. 1983. 'Die griechische Kolonisation im westlichen Mittelmeergebiet und ihre Wirkung auf die Landschaften des westlichen Mitteleuropa'. *Jahrbuch des Römisch-Germanischen Zentralmuseums Mainz* 30: 5–78.

Krausse, D., M. Fernández-Götz, L. Hansen, and I. Kretschmer. 2016. *The Heuneburg and the Early Iron Age Princely Seats: First Towns North of the Alps*. Budapest: Archaeolingua.

Kristiansen, K. 1998. *Europe Before History*. Cambridge: Cambridge University Press.

Kromer, K. 1959. *Das Gräberfeld von Hallstatt*. Florence: Sansoni.

Metzler, J., C. Gaeng, and P. Méniel. 2016. *L'espace public du Titelberg*. Dossiers d'Archéologie 17. Luxembourg: Centre National de la Recherche Archéologique.

Metzler-Zens, N., J. Metzler-Zens, and P. Méniel. 1999. *Lamadelaine, une nécropole de l'oppidum du Titelberg*. Dossiers d'Archéologie 6. Luxembourg: Musée National d'Histoire et d'Art.

Morris, I. 1987. *Burial and Ancient Society: The Rise of the Greek City State*. Cambridge: Cambridge University Press.

Moscalu, E. 1989. 'Das thrako-getische Fürstengrab von Peretu in Rumänien'. *Bericht der Römisch-Germanischen Kommission* 70: 129–190.

Nicolini, G. 1990. *Techniques des ors antiques: La bijouterie ibérique du VIIe au IVe siècle.* Paris: Picard.

Palavestra, A. 1994. 'Prehistoric trade and a cultural model for princely tombs in the central Balkans', in K. Kristiansen and J. Jensen (eds) *Europe in the First Millennium B.C.* Sheffield Archaeological Monographs 6: 45–56. Sheffield: J. R. Collis Publications.

Parović-Pešikan, M. 1964. 'Les Illyriens au contact des Grecs'. *Archaeologia Iugoslavia* 5: 61–82.

Pertlwieser, M. 1982. 'Hallstattzeitliche Grabhügel bei Mitterkirchen, Pol. Bez. Perg, OÖ (Vorbericht)'. *Jahrbuch des Oberösterreichischen Musealvereins* 127, 1: 9–24.

Poux, M. 2004. *L'âge du vin: Rites de boisson, festins et libations en Gaule indépendante.* Protohistoire Européenne 8. Montagnac: Monique Mergoil.

Ruiz, A., and M. Molinos. 1993. *Los Iberos: Analisis arqueologico de un proceso historico.* Barcelona: Critica.

Schiltz, V. 1994. *Les Scythes et les Nomades des steppes VIIIe siècle avant J.-C.–Ier siècle après J.-C. L'Univers des Formes.* Paris: Gallimard.

Stary, P. F. 1993. 'Der Mittelgebirgsraum als Transit- und Vermittlungszone hallstatt- und latènezeitlicher Kulturelemente aus Mitteleuropa ins westliche Ostseegebiet'. *Bericht der Römisch-Germanischen Kommission* 74: 537–564.

Stary, P. F. 1995. 'Italic and Etruscan imports in the Baltic Sea area and in the British Isles during the pre-Roman Iron Age: Analogies, differences and backgrounds', in J. Swaddling, S. Walker, and P. Roberts (eds) *Italy in Europe: Economic Relations 700 BC–AD 50.* BM Occasional Paper 97: 93–106. London: British Museum Press.

Stead, I. M. 1979. *The Arras Culture.* York: Yorkshire Philosophical Society.

Szabó, M. 1992. *Les Celtes de l'Est: Le second âge du Fer dans la cuvette des Karpathes.* Paris: Errance.

Van Gennep, A. 1909. *Les rites de passage.* Paris: E. Nourry.

Wells, P. S. 1981. *The Emergence of an Iron Age Economy: The Mecklenburg Grave Groups from Hallstatt and Stična.* Meklenburg Collection, Part III. American School of Prehistoric Research Bulletin 33. Cambridge, MA: Harvard University Press.

Winther, H. C. 1997. 'Princely tombs of the Orientalizing period in Etruria and Latium Vetus'. *Acta Hyperborea* 7: 423–446.

Wüstemann, H. 1974. 'Zur Sozialstruktur im Seddiner Kulturgebiet'. *Zeitschrift für Archäologie* 8: 67–107.

CHAPTER 41

RITUAL SITES, OFFERINGS, AND SACRIFICE

IAN ARMIT

Ritual and Ritualization in Iron Age Europe

As is the case throughout prehistory, ritual permeated all aspects of Iron Age life. Although we can see the emergence in many parts of Europe of formalized places of religious significance, ritual acts of various kinds, and at various scales, were also performed in less formal settings: in houses, on hilltops, in peat bogs, at lakesides, and elsewhere. Before embarking on a survey of 'ritual sites' across Iron Age Europe, therefore, it is worth considering what is meant by the term. For the purposes of this review, 'ritual sites' are defined simply as places within which ritualized behaviour took place, following Bradley's definition of ritualization as a 'way of acting which reveals some of the dominant concerns of society, and a process by which certain parts of life are selected and provided with an added emphasis' (2005: 34). This definition is useful as it emphasizes that ritual is not simply a synonym for religion, but encompasses a variety of *formalized* and *elaborated* behaviours or performances that can relate to a range of social concerns. It is worth remembering, too, that ritual acts were not empty gestures, but were intended to have directly practical outcomes—whether to ensure the fertility of the community, to provide success in war, to bring wealth, or to heal the sick. As in many more recent societies, ritual acts were central to social life.

Some of the most obvious and dramatic rituals would have involved large gatherings of people at special locations set aside for the purpose, and were probably intended to mediate between the worlds of the living and the supernatural. Some would have occurred at predetermined times based around calendrical observances, such as the autumn festival of Samhain. Others might have been conducted more expediently—for example, when kings were inaugurated. But ritualized acts, in the sense used here, need not be so large in scale. Small-scale ritual performance, familial, private, and perhaps even individual, can also be widely observed within the domestic sphere across much of Iron Age Europe.

Just as the scale of ritual performance varied, so too did the role of ritualists. For the larger-scale public ritual monuments we might legitimately infer the presence of dedicated priests, such as the Druids described by Poseidonius and Caesar. Elsewhere, small-scale ritualized activities associated with individual households or village-sized communities may have been officiated by part-time ritualists belonging to looser collectives, or individuals more akin to shamans, with a consequently more fluid and expedient approach to the choreography of ritual performance. Some ritualized actions might have been repeated many times, and adherence to prescribed ways of doing things may have been perceived as critical to their efficacy. Other rituals might express creative variations on a set of commonly understood themes, based on individual judgements about what is appropriate in a given set of circumstances. Across an area as large as Iron Age Europe, we might expect a good deal of innovation and variety in such matters.

Although ritual frequently embodies interactions between the participants and the supernatural, it need not be exclusively religious in character: indeed, some rituals may be primarily secular, centred on establishing and maintaining relationships between the participants themselves, and between the participants and their audience—as, for example, with a modern military parade. I have suggested elsewhere (Armit 2012) that ritualized action can be understood heuristically as pertaining to three interwoven themes: cosmology, religion, and ideology. Cosmology relates to deep-rooted communal understandings of the nature of the world, its origins, and the place of humans within it, and to the mental geographies by which the local landscape and its relationship to the wider world was understood. Religion, while related to cosmology, is defined here as a body of commonly held beliefs relating to the nature and workings of the supernatural. In essentially small-scale societies like those that characterized much of Iron Age Europe, such beliefs would have been uncodified and probably quite fluid across both time and space. Ideology, as understood here, is essentially a set of ideas concerning social relationships and power relations both within and between communities. Although frequently underpinned by cosmological or religious ideas, ideology can nonetheless be understood as a potentially distinct arena of ritual practice.

These themes frequently come together, as can be seen in the processional displays depicted on situla art (Chapter 43) from the sixth to fourth centuries BC in northern Italy, Slovenia, and the east Alpine region. The Vače *situla*, for example, found with an inhumation burial under a small tumulus in a Slovenian cemetery, is a small vessel made from thin copper-alloy sheet, and covered with delicate repoussé motifs depicting a complex range of figural scenes organized into three superimposed registers (Frey 2011). The uppermost depicts a procession of horsemen and chariots moving to the left (Figure 41.1), while the lowermost depicts a procession of animals heading the opposite way; the central register shows scenes of feasting, music, and boxing. Such processional displays, common on *situlae*, are intrinsically ritualized, with the participants being

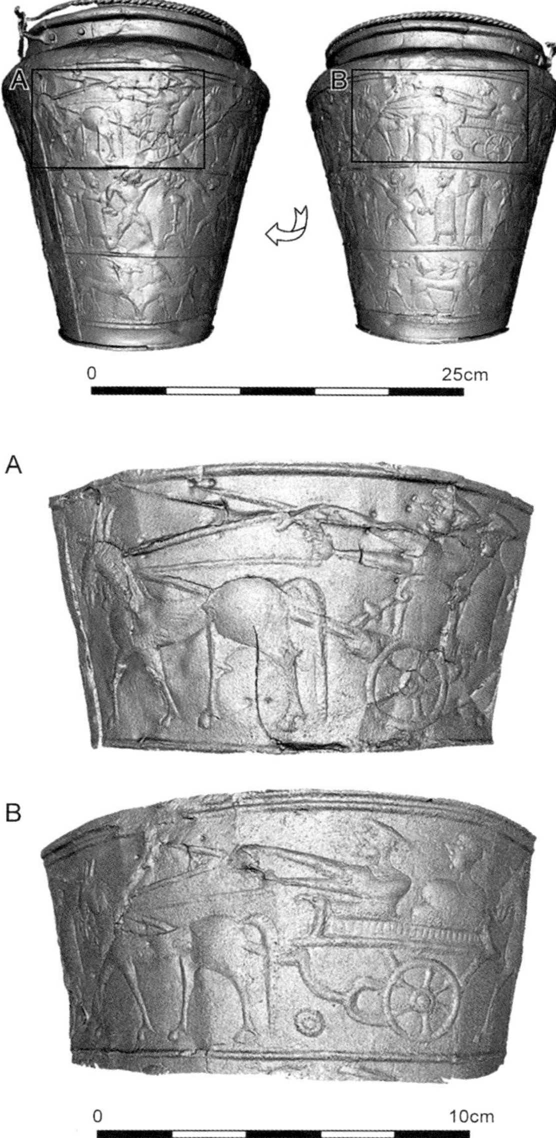

FIGURE 41.1 Details of wagon and chariot from the upper frieze of the *situla* from Vače, Slovenia, from digital 3D model.

Images Adrian Evans and Rachael Kershaw, courtesy of Fragmented Heritage/Bradford Visualisation and the National Museum of Slovenia

consciously sorted and arranged in linear order according to conventions of relative status and role. In this sense they are ideological rituals, serving to create and maintain a social order. This essentially arbitrary set of social relations is, however, given legitimacy by its incorporation within a wider ordering of the natural (and sometimes supernatural) worlds, with the processional display extended to animals, similarly ordered and ranked. In this sense it embodies a cosmological vision. Overtly religious ideas, while less obvious to the modern observer, may be embodied by the enthroned figure on the central panel being offered drink by a high-status woman (perhaps a priestess), and perhaps by the birds that hover over certain characters in the processions. Most importantly perhaps, the ritualized displays represented on east Alpine situla art remind us that ritual need not leave any material residue. A long procession of richly attired riders and warriors, with accompanying clatter and music, would have been a powerful and memorable sight. Yet it is only by chance that their echoes survive through the medium of situla art. Much Iron Age ritual would have involved events and performances like these, which left no material trace.

In the following discussion I avoid sites with a primarily funerary focus, as these are covered elsewhere in the volume (Chapter 40). Nonetheless, many of the sites discussed contain human remains, treated and processed in various ways. I also avoid discussion of formal religion, codified beliefs, or the named gods that can sometimes be identified in the later part of the Iron Age: these form the focus of Chapter 42.

Ritualization in the Domestic Sphere

Iron Age Europe is characterized by a remarkable ritualization of domestic life. In many regions, certain objects, often including human body parts, were deposited in or around people's homes, in pits, walls, and floors. Some of the best evidence comes from northern Scotland where the remarkable survival of dry-stone Atlantic roundhouses and wheelhouses has enabled the superstructures of domestic buildings to be carefully dissected. At the wheelhouse of Cnip in Lewis, for example, articulated animal bones, complete pottery vessels, and the fleshed head of a seabird were among the offerings placed within the wall fabric during construction, in the first centuries BC/AD (Armit 2006). Further deposits of animal and human remains were placed in pits below thresholds, under floors, and (in the case of a perforated human cranial fragment) perhaps hung from the rafters. The most striking domestic deposit of this kind comes from another wheelhouse-like structure, at Hornish Point in South Uist, dating from the first or second centuries BC (Armit 2012: 204–207). Here the remains of a young boy had been placed within four pits underneath the floor of the building, before occupation began. The boy had a suffered two fatal stab wounds to his back, recalling the statement by Strabo, writing in the first century AD, that the Gauls would sacrifice live human victims by stabbing them in the back, and make prophecies based on their death spasms (*Geography* 4.1.13). The partially articulated state of the body suggests that it had been preserved for a significant period (perhaps by being dried or smoked) before being buried along with the remains of young animals that had been butchered and cooked, perhaps as part of a feast to inaugurate the building.

Similar deposits, although less well preserved, can be traced in other parts of Britain. At Broxmouth hillfort in southern Scotland, for example, the walls of roundhouses dating to the first centuries BC/AD contained human cranial fragments, animal skulls, and objects of stone and bone (Armit and McKenzie 2013). Two blackened and polished antler domes from behind a late wall of House 4 seem to belong to the same set as another buried in a pit a couple of generations earlier (Büster and Armit 2021). This suggests that at least some of these deposits were intended to form links between the occupants of the house and their ancestors. Across southern Britain, domestic buildings are seldom so well preserved, but similar deposits are nonetheless frequently found (Wilson 1981; Hill 1995).

Similar types of small-scale domestic deposit are found elsewhere in Europe, including a significant concentration in southern France, where domestic buildings are again well preserved (Nin 1999). Houses from the neighbouring Provençal *oppida* of L'Île de Martigues and Saint-Pierre de Martigues have produced numerous small pits containing animal burials (mostly sheep, goats, and pigs) dating from the fifth to the first centuries BC (Chausserie-Laprée 2005). Elsewhere, there is a particular preference for wild animals, such as the fox cub pierced with bronze needles found buried under the threshold of a house at the *oppidum* of Saint-Blaise, Provence, or the wild birds and snakes found within Languedocien *oppida*, at Les Castels de Nages, Ambrussum, and Ensérune. The avoidance of large domesticates, like cattle or horses, and the location of these deposits in private dwellings, suggests that these are the residues of small-scale rituals associated with individual families. The frequent finding of neonatal human remains under house floors across many parts of Europe, as at Dürrnberg, Austria (Wiltschke-Schrotta 2012), and in many domestic sites in the Languedoc (e.g. Dedet and Schwaller 1990), may be a related practice.

In southern England and northern France, structured deposits are often found in the fills of large grain storage pits located close to domestic dwellings. The best known come from Danebury hillfort in Hampshire, where human remains ranged from fully articulated skeletons to severed heads and other isolated body parts (Cunliffe 1995). The Danebury finds are complex and probably derive from a range of sources; some may be fragments of excarnated bodies from the hillfort community itself, while others appear to derive from outsiders who had met violent deaths (Craig et al. 2005). Occasional examples, particularly some individuals who appear to have been bound, may represent executions or sacrifices carried out as part of the rituals associated with the closure of the pits. The same deposits frequently contain animal remains, including dogs, ravens, and horses, as well as the more common domesticates, and a range of other objects. Similar deposits from sites in northern and central France include several where successive deposits of human remains had been made, usually over a relatively short time period, as at Lazenay, Bourges, and La Grande Paroisse, Seine-et-Marne (Delattre 2000). In most cases the bodies appear to have been thrown into the pits. Again, some individuals seem to have been bound, as at Les Jardins du Luxembourg, Paris, and La Normée, Marne (Delattre 2000). These grain pit deposits appear to have been offerings to the gods, and were presumably intended to ensure the ongoing fertility of the crops. Such deposits are a good example of the practical intent of ritual deposition.

While these rituals used pre-existing pits that had been used to store grain, at other sites human bodies occur in specially created pits. In one part of the settlement complex at Acy-Romance, in the Ardennes, at least nineteen young men were found buried in a constricted seated position, suggesting that their bodies were either bound or constricted within some form of timber box (Verger 2000). They were conceivably alive when buried, and the formal and consistent manner of their deposition suggests that they were victims of ritual sacrifice. Elsewhere, disarticulated human bones, including cranial remains showing signs of decapitation, are a frequent find on major settlements, including the *oppidum* of Manching, in Bavaria (Sievers 2002), the sprawling unenclosed Basel-Gasfabrik settlement in Switzerland (Hüglin and Spichtig 2010), and numerous other late Iron Age settlements.

Ritualizing the Natural World

The idea that the ancient Celts practised their religion in the open air, eschewing the formal temples characteristic of Mediterranean civilizations, is a long-standing trope. The poet Martial, writing in the first century AD, for example, mentions a sacred oak grove, as well as mountains and springs of religious importance in his native Iberia. His contemporary Lucan, writing about the events of the previous century, provides a vivid and much-quoted description of a sacred forest glade near Massalia (modern Marseille), housing rough and rotting wooden images of gods, and trees festooned with human gore (*Pharsalia* 3). Restoring the passage to its original context, however, reveals that Lucan's epic poem abounds with overblown descriptions of murder and mayhem, and cannot be relied upon as an accurate description of any real place: formal built sanctuaries had in any case existed within this very region just a few generations earlier—for example, at Entremont, Glanon, and Roquepertuse (see below). Nonetheless, it is clear from archaeological evidence that much Iron Age ritual was indeed practised at natural places.

Often these were places on the margins of the day-to-day farming landscape, separate from areas of settlement, and perhaps in unoccupied boundary zones or 'no man's lands'. Such liminal places may have been judged especially suited to communication between different worlds. Dramatic landscape features, such as caves, lakes, or hilltops may have been regarded as the dwelling places of ancestors, gods, or spirits. They would have formed important elements within the mental geographies by which landscapes were tamed, humanized, and understood, visited and venerated over many generations.

Watery places, and especially still bodies of water such as lakes and stagnant pools within peat bogs, were frequent foci of ritual practice throughout the Iron Age, as they had been in earlier periods. Although the ritual use of these places persisted, however, the nature of deposition changed: whereas earlier generations had deposited large quantities of bronze metalwork, their Iron Age descendants carried out more varied rites, with human bodies playing an increasingly significant role.

Human bodies deposited in peat bogs have been found recurrently over the past two centuries across northern Europe, notably north Germany, southern Scandinavia, the Netherlands, Britain, and Ireland (Van der Sanden 1996). Since the application of scientific dating methods it has become increasingly apparent that the great majority of these individuals died between the beginning of the Iron Age and the first couple of centuries AD, suggesting that this was a distinctively Iron Age rite, shared across a wide geographical area. The bodies themselves display several recurrent features: many died violent and unusually complex deaths, some were apparently of high status, many were buried either naked or with minimal and/or unusual clothing, and several were staked down firmly into the bog.

One of the most dramatic recent finds is Old Croghan Man, discovered in a peat bog in Co. Offaly in Ireland and dated to the fourth or third centuries BC (Kelly 2006). Although his remains comprise only the upper torso and arms, they conform to all three characteristics previously outlined. The man was exceptionally tall (some 1.98 m), in his early to mid-twenties, and had manicured nails suggestive of high status. Cut marks on his arms suggest that he died trying to defend himself, perhaps from the deep stab wound visible in his chest. Once felled, and perhaps shortly after death, he was decapitated and his entire upper torso was separated from the rest of his body (the division of the body echoing the treatment of the Hornish boy). The remaining portion of the body preserved signs of earlier torture, including deep cuts to each nipple and a hazel withy strung through his arm muscles. The extreme nature of this individual's death and his likely status are both reflected in the best-known British bog body, from Lindow Moss in Cheshire, which probably dates to the first century AD (Joy 2009). This young man, again in his twenties, also had manicured nails and a neatly trimmed beard. After being led into the bog, he was garrotted, had his throat cut, and received crushing blows to his skull; each injury was individually sufficient to kill him. While Old Croghan Man was apparently naked save for a plaited leather armband, Lindow Man wore nothing but a fox fur bracelet.

Many of the best-known bog bodies come from Denmark, including a particularly important group from Jutland. One of these, Grauballe Man, broadly contemporary with Old Croghan Man, was also found naked and with his throat slashed (Asingh and Lynnerup 2007). Although his smooth hands may suggest a privileged status, studies of his teeth suggest that he had undergone periods of nutritional deprivation earlier in life. Another Jutland find of similar date, known as Tollund Man, was also found naked except for a sheepskin cap, a hide belt, and a noose around his neck: he had apparently been hanged (Van der Sanden 1996). Tollund Man's hair, preserved under his cap, had been closely cropped—a trait shared with other bog bodies, including the Yde Girl from the Netherlands, who was deposited with one half of her head shaved and the other half bearing long hair. Close by the Tollund find were discovered the remains of the Elling Woman, also hanged, with her naked body wrapped in a sheepskin and a leather cape. The north European bog finds also include severed heads like that of Roum Man, from Jutland, found wrapped in sheepskin, Osterby Man from Schleswig Holstein, and Worsley Man from Lancashire (north-west England), who had been garrotted and received a blow to the head before being decapitated: these finds link the rite of bog burial to the act of headhunting discussed later.

Individuals buried in peat bogs frequently appear to have been the victims of ritualized killing, either as religious sacrifices, executions, or a mixture of both. Reference is often made to Tacitus' late first-century AD account of the Germanic tribes, which states that cowards, shirkers, and those guilty of unnatural acts were cast into bogs and pinned down with wooden hurdles (*Germania* 12), a description that immediately recalls the circumstances of numerous north European bog bodies, including the Haraldskær Woman, from Jutland, found naked and pinned down below a wooden hurdle. Tacitus also mentions that traitors and deserters were hanged, recalling the pre-depositional treatment of Tollund Man and the Elling Woman. Judicial punishment may well be one major reason behind the elaborate killings that led to the preservation of these bog bodies.

As well as the manicured nails and smooth hands of individuals like Grauballe Man, Lindow Man, and Old Croghan Man, elaborate hairstyles such as the Suebian knot worn atop the decapitated heads of Osterby Man and Dätgen Man, both in northern Germany, and the knotted braid worn by the Elling Woman from Jutland, hint that important figures within the community were unusually frequent victims (e.g. Aldhouse-Green 2015). Conceivably they may have been high-ranking outsiders, captured during episodes of conflict, but others may have been killed by members of their own communities.

Even if social wrong-doing was the proximate cause of victim selection, the heavily ritualized qualities of the killings suggest that more was at stake than the disposal of undesirables. Strabo's reference to divination based on the death spasms of sacrificed human victims may have resonance with the complex treatment of brutally murdered bog bodies, as it did with bodies in domestic locations (see earlier). Bog bodies habitually show signs of dehumanizing treatments that would have robbed them of their individuality in the lead-up to their death. As we have seen, many were naked, or else wearing only unusual items of skin, leather, or hide—perhaps symbols of the wild, in contrast to the woven textiles common in everyday life. Some had their heads wholly or partially shaved. They were thus transformed into something less than human, perhaps closer to the gods, or perhaps simply more acceptable to kill. Much has also been made of the mistletoe pollen found in the stomach of Lindow Man—supposedly the most sacred plant of the Druids, and perhaps ingested as part of some transformative rite. The ritualized performance of the killing itself often involved several stages and multiple lethal injuries, perhaps inflicted by more than one individual, none of whom need have regarded themselves as wholly responsible for the death (Armit 2011).

Although bog bodies have understandably received a great deal of attention, these same bogs were also the scene of many other ritual activities. The numerous animal deposits placed in waterlogged peat cuttings in Jutland, for example, contain a preponderance of dog and horse remains. At Hedelisker, the remains of thirteen dogs had been deposited with human bones, broken pottery, and a carved wooden phallus (Van der Sanden 1996). Some finds, such as the anthropomorphic wooden idol from Ballachulish in western Scotland, dating from the seventh or sixth centuries BC, and found under a wooden hurdle, closely echo the rituals associated with bog bodies. The deposition of anthropomorphic wooden idols, such as those from Wittemoor in Lower Saxony (Germany), and Corlea, Co. Longford (Ireland), also resonate with the sacrificial rituals associated with bog bodies. A series of ard deposits from Danish bogs suggest the practice of rituals associated with fertility. Best known of all the Scandinavian bog finds is the Gundestrup silver cauldron, which probably dates to the later second or first century BC, and was most likely imported from south-east Europe. This precious object, elaborately decorated with figural scenes of religious and/or cosmological character, was deliberately dismantled and deposited in a Jutland peat bog.

Several Scandinavian finds in bogs and lakes point to deposition on an even grander scale, involving large numbers of people. At Hjortspring, Nydam, and Ejsbøl, in Denmark, for example, large wooden boats had been carried overland to be deposited in peatlands, along with large quantities of weaponry. The three sites are within 50 km of one another, but they span many centuries, from Hjortspring in the fourth century BC, to the last of the Nydam boats in the fourth century AD, and they clearly represent a long-lasting regional tradition. Further large-scale depositions were made at the lake of Illerup Ådal, in Jutland, where some 15,000 deliberately broken weapons and associated objects had been deposited, some of them burnt and many of them wrapped in bundles, in a series of discrete episodes between around AD 200–500 (Ilkjær 2000). Within a few kilometres of Illerup Ådal, the remains of several hundred adult male warriors appear to have been exposed, during the first century AD, along a channel between two lake basins (Mollerup et al. 2010). Further north, at the broadly contemporary site of Skedemosse, Öland, Sweden, we see once again the deposition of large quantities of iron weaponry, several gold arm-rings, animal bones, and human remains representing around fifty men, women, and children. At Skedemosse, as at several of the other sites, the presence of many non-indigenous objects suggests that these were the spoils of war, offered to the gods. The treatment of war booty at Scandinavian sites may find some reflection in the writings of Paulus Orosius, in the early fifth century AD, who describes the destruction of enemy weaponry, and the slaughter of prisoners and captured horses by Cimbric warriors (who may very well have originated in Jutland) in the wake of military victories during their late second-century BC incursions into southern Europe (*Historia Adversus Paganos* 5, 16). Deposits containing objects of a similar martial character, if on a much smaller scale, can be seen elsewhere in northern Europe, as at Llyn Cerrig Bach in Wales, Lisnacrogher, in Co. Armagh, and Deskford, in north-east Scotland.

Away from the peatlands of northern Europe, deposits of a similar character are found in lakes. The classic example is, of course, at the Swiss lake site of La Tène, where large quantities of weaponry have also been recovered alongside human and animal remains. As is often the case, crania considerably outweigh other bones among the human remains, and decapitated skeletons are also present (Jud 2007). The remains of substantial timber structures projecting into the lake suggest that offerings were cast into the waters from a bridge or platform. Similar features can be seen in England, as at Fiskerton, Lincolnshire, where a long timber causeway is associated with deposition around the fifth and fourth centuries BC, and in Wales, at Llyn Cerrig Bach, where fine La Tène metalwork was deposited between around 300 BC to AD 100. While the still waters encountered in peatlands and lakes seem to have been favoured, much elaborate metalwork has also been recovered from rivers, especially in northern Europe, with notable concentrations in the Thames and its tributaries, the Bann, and the Meuse.

Another set of landscape features frequently associated with Iron Age ritual activity were caves and rock shelters. Among the best known is the extensive limestone cave system of the Trou de Han, in the Belgian Ardennes, where concentrations of late Bronze Age and Iron Age metalwork have been recovered, particularly from the bed of the River Lesse where it runs underground through the caves (Warmenbol 1996). Many human remains, including isolated crania, have been found, again dating to the late Bronze and Iron Age. In one case, a group of seven human mandibles showing signs of decapitation, and with radiocarbon dates ranging from around 200 BC to AD 100, had been collected and placed beneath a late Iron Age hearth. Eugène Warmenbol's description of the Trou de Han as 'the mouth of hell' (*la bouche des enfers*) nicely captures both the liminal qualities of such caves, providing points of access to the underworld, and the visceral nature of the rites enacted there.

Evidence of decapitation and cranial modification can be found at numerous other European cave sites, including the especially spectacular seventh-century BC deposits from the Býčí skála Cave, in the Moravian karst, where a human skull fashioned into a drinking cup was found along with other deposits including the remains of around forty individuals, mutilated horses, exotic bronzes, and vehicle parts. At the Sculptor's Cave, in north-east Scotland, the remains of numerous decapitated individuals dating to the Roman Iron Age were found on a site venerated from at least the late Bronze Age to the early medieval period (Armit et al. 2011).

While conspicuous natural formations, such as caves, hilltops, and watery places, are consistent foci for deposition across many parts of Europe, ritual offerings were also made in locations that have an apparently less dramatic character. In the Alps, for example, numerous open-air sites display evidence for the deliberate burning of metalwork, including weaponry and personal ornaments of various kinds, and animal bones. The gold torcs from Snettisham in Norfolk, eastern England, are some of the finest examples of Iron Age metalworking in Europe, yet there is nothing immediately striking about their dryland find-spot, a low hill overlooking the Wash. The same can be said for many other dryland depositions of coins and jewellery seen across northern and western Europe during the late Iron Age.

THE CREATION OF RITUAL PLACES

Whatever the enduring significance of certain natural places, Iron Age communities in Europe also built formal places of ritual and worship. As might be expected, it is in those regions closest to the Mediterranean that we see the creation of buildings most obviously analogous to those of the classical and Hellenistic worlds, and those are considered first, before examining ritual places further north.

Sanctuaries in Mediterranean Europe

Along the southern coasts of France and north-eastern Iberia, Iron Age ritual sites seem to have developed initially in prominent natural places. From the beginning of the Iron Age, hilltops and rock shelters became foci for the deposition of modest offerings of metalwork, such as pins, brooches, and polished bronze discs. The site that was later to emerge as the regional capital of Entremont, for example, began as just one of many sacred hilltops set apart from the day-to-day settlement landscape. The Hellenized centre at Glanon, in the Alpilles, also developed from an original focus on a sacred spring overlooked by a series of natural rock shelters.

The closest we can come to a coherent biography of one of these sites is at Roquepertuse, Provence, where the original sanctuary was established in the early Iron Age at the base of a sheer-sided limestone peak overlooking the valley of the River Arc. It seems initially to have comprised an informal collection of oval, timber-framed buildings scattered around the base of the outcrop, invisible from the valley below (Boissinot and Gantès 2000). A series of small stelae hint at activity in the earliest part of the Iron Age, but firmer dates come from the series of near life-size warrior statues, carved from soft local limestone, found redeposited in later contexts. Stylistic analysis of these serene, almost buddhic, cross-legged warriors places their origins in the fifth century BC (Rapin 2003). This is primarily based on their distinctive costume, which includes cuirasses with stiffened back-plates, geometric painted designs, and square neck-guards. The early dating is strengthened by their remarkable similarities to the tiny warrior figure perched on the rim of the mid-fifth-century bronze flagon from one of the tombs at Glauberg, Hesse (Baitinger and Pinsker 2002). Around ten stone figures are represented by fragments found at Roquepertuse, and similar statues come from sites from across the region, including a remarkable series from Glanon. The close similarities in size, pose, clothing, and personal ornament show adherence to widely shared conventions of representation.

Although little is understood of the layout of the early sanctuary, recent excavations at Roquepertuse have clarified much about its later development, as a monumental, terraced complex set into a natural amphitheatre against the base of the limestone outcrop. This transformation, which occurred around 300 BC, included the construction of a building supported by lintels and pillars that contained carefully shaped niches carved to accommodate and display severed human heads in various states of preservation. At least two clay-coated crania remained fixed within one of the pillars when it was excavated in the 1920s. The brightly painted decoration on these blocks also included images of horses, serpents, and carrion birds. Ravens and crows are a frequent symbol for the journey from life to death, as witnessed, for example, by images on Iberian pottery from Numantia, Soria, dating to the first century BC, showing dead warriors being consumed by carrion birds. Silius Italicus (*Punica* 3, 342–348) and Aelian (*De Natura Animalium* 10, 22), writing in the first two centuries AD, both describe the deliberate exposure of the bodies of high-ranking Celtiberians to carrion birds, enabling their souls to escape their earthly bodies. Ravens are common also in other ritual contexts, such as the Danebury grain pits, as well as being frequently depicted in situla art. Scattered fragments of three-dimensional sculpture from Roquepertuse include further horse and bird imagery, and two complete horse skeletons, perhaps the remains of sacrifices, were also found buried close to the monumental terrace. Horses have frequently been interpreted as spirit guides, or psychopomps, charged with conducting the dead to the Otherworld.

Whatever the specificity of the symbolism, it is a reasonable assumption that the rituals conducted at Roquepertuse were concerned with the treatment of the dead and the passage of souls. Yet its monumental form and increasing elaboration suggest that Roquepertuse was also an important place in the secular world, and it may be for this reason that the sanctuary was destroyed, and much of its statuary deliberately shattered and ground down in a flurry of iconoclastic activity, sometime around 250 BC. Although it was soon reoccupied, there seems to have been no further production or display of overtly religious imagery, and the site may have continued primarily as a small *oppidum* rather than an important religious centre.

Head niches similar to those at Roquepertuse, as well as carved depictions of severed or disembodied heads, occur at several other sites in the region and appear to represent a widespread tradition of head curation and display. Although some niches may have held ancestral relics, the evidence more usually suggests that they relate to the display of trophy heads. An important series of potentially early Iron Age carvings were found redeposited in second-century BC deposits at Entremont. The well-known 'head pillar', reused as a threshold slab in the mid-second-century BC 'hypostyle' building (the principal communal building on the site, its roof supported by columns), but probably originating in an earlier sanctuary on the hill, bears images of twelve carefully arranged, stylized, mouthless heads (Arcelin and Rapin 2003; Armit 2011: 89–95). The more recently discovered *bloc aux épis*, built into the early second-century BC rampart, has similar columns of heads depicted on two faces, paired with carved ears of wheat on the other: the association between severed heads and crop fertility can be paralleled widely among headhunting societies, from the nineteenth-century Nagas of north India to the Classic Maya (Armit 2012). These ordered groups of stylized and anonymous heads, seen also at Provençal sites like Badasset and Saint-Michel-de-Valbonne, seem to represent a distinct regional tradition in the early part of the Iron Age, during which we also see frequent deposits of human crania in domestic contexts.

The imagery of headhunting emerges even more forcefully at Entremont with the appearance of the remarkable group of third-century BC warrior statues, whose heavily fragmented remains were found in the make-up of a late roadway close to the 'hypostyle' (Arcelin 2006). The remains of at least nine warriors are represented, although they had been so thoroughly destroyed that no single example can be confidently reconstructed (Figure 41.2). These warriors share much with the earlier figures of Roquepertuse type, in their near life-size representation, their calm, cross-legged posture, the detailed representation of body armour (including chain-mail) and jewellery, and their final violent destruction. Unlike the earlier statues, however, the Entremont warriors are represented explicitly as headhunters; each clasps one or more trophy heads. Unlike earlier examples, these severed heads are no longer stylized and anonymous but, like the warrior heads themselves, they are carefully individualized. In a non-literate society it would appear that quite specific messages of domination, subjugation, and incorporation were being communicated through the medium of sculpture (Armit 2012).

The Entremont warriors were created at the time when the Saluvian confederacy was emerging as the dominant regional power, and they were most probably housed in the original hilltop sanctuary. With the foundation of the *oppidum*, the statues were redisplayed at the centre of the settlement, where the main arterial routeway passes in front of the 'hypostyle' (Armit et al. 2012). Their long and complex biography ended with their deliberate destruction and dispersal—an act which must surely be connected to a shift in power among the Saluvian hierarchy. The symbol of the severed head remained central, however, as the 'hypostyle' was latterly used to display at least fifteen of them, pinned to its walls with massive iron nails—heads that bore numerous violent injuries.

Around the head of the Adriatic the focus on human remains disappears, and activity at sanctuaries appears dominated by the deposition of votives. At Este, in the Po valley, a sanctuary dedicated to the local goddess, Reitia, was a focus for the deposition of a range of objects including small bronze *laminae* bearing scenes reminiscent of those of situla art. These appear to have been generally personal dedications perhaps associated with the goddess' perceived role as a healer. The objects vary quite markedly between the many known sanctuaries in the Veneto, suggesting the evolution of quite localized traditions (de Nardi 2007).

Votive depositions also dominate certain Illyrian sanctuaries across the Adriatic, as at Turska Kosa, near Topusko in central Croatia (Čučković 2004). Depositions in 'cultic place 1' at Turska Kosa from the sixth to third centuries BC include numerous human and animal figurines, crudely made of local ceramics. Although the human figures lack any facial detail, breasts and genitals identify their sex, and elements of personal jewellery, particularly necklaces, are elaborately modelled. Although the large collection from Turska Kosa is associated with earlier cremation pyres, and may reflect a local ancestor cult, it has also been suggested (Čučković 2004) that the general distribution of these figurines relates to their role in the ritual surrounding iron production.

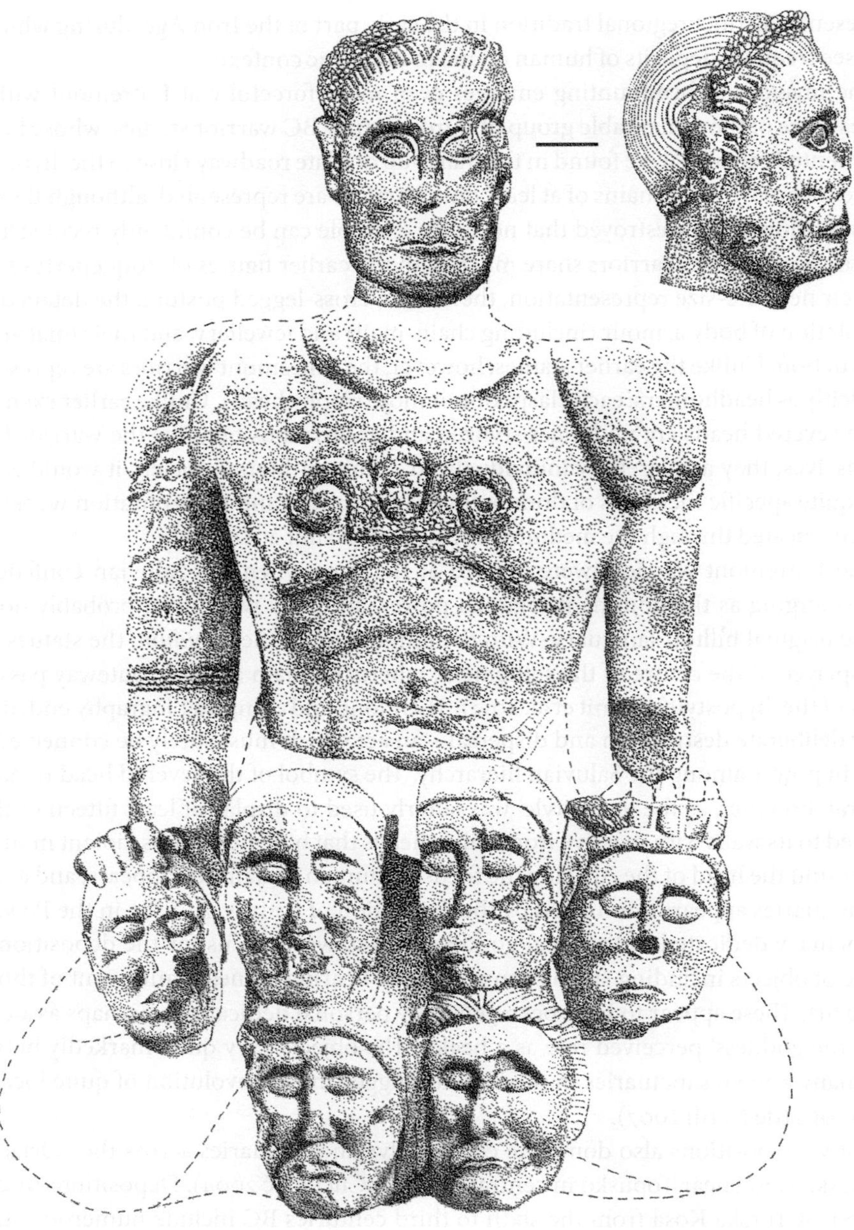

FIGURE 41.2 One of the warrior statues from Entremont, southern France, reconstructed from fragments. Given the level of fragmentation it is impossible to be sure that they all originally belonged to the same statue rather than another in the series.

Drawing: Libby Mulqueeny, after Salviat 1993: nos 3, 8, 22 and 23

Sanctuaries in Temperate Europe

One of the major transformations in our understanding of Iron Age ritual life over the last few decades has been the intensive work on the middle La Tène sanctuaries of northern France, of which the best-known examples remain Gournay-sur-Aronde and Ribemont-sur-Ancre, both in Picardy. The sanctuary at Gournay, which had its *floruit* in the third to second centuries BC, contained a complex sequence of buildings contained within a quadrangular enclosure with sides some 40 m long, defined by a deep ditch and external palisade with an east-facing entrance.

Over several centuries, Gournay seems to have been the focus for elaborate, large-scale rituals (Brunaux 2003a). Large quantities of bent and broken weaponry, including thousands of swords, spearheads, and shield fittings, appear to have been displayed in the open air before finally becoming incorporated into the ditch and pit fills, in varying states of decay. The quantity and condition of the weapons suggest that they were battle trophies, recalling Caesar's description, from the first century BC, of *loci consecrati* where the Gauls dedicated captured weaponry to the gods (*de Bello Gallico* 6.17). The sanctuary seems also to have been the focus for animal sacrifice, and there is clear evidence for the differential treatment of certain species. Young sheep and pigs, for example, are mostly represented by meat-bearing bones suggestive of butchery outside the sacred area and feasting within. Unbutchered horses, however, were deposited whole, and with some ceremony (perhaps after a period of exposure) in the ditches, while the main pits in the central area contained the remains of similarly unbutchered elderly cattle (probably valued traction animals). Brunaux has suggested that these animals were effectively being 'fed' to chthonic deities as their bodies rotted in the sacrificial pits. As time progressed the architecture of the central area appears to have become increasingly formalized with the construction of successive buildings (plausibly temples) over the pits.

The thematic connections that sites like Gournay share with contemporary sanctuaries of the Mediterranean (especially Greek) world have not gone unnoticed; the presence of elaborate and structured animal sacrifice alongside the dedication of battle trophies in sacred spaces characterized by formal religious architecture, suggests that certain forms of communal religious expression in temperate Europe may have been closer to those of the Mediterranean world than classical writers were inclined to admit.

Alongside the metalwork and animal bones, there were also human remains at Gournay, including notable concentrations of cranial fragments near the entrance, suggestive of the display of decapitated human heads. However, it is the evidence from the broadly contemporary sanctuary of Ribemont-sur-Ancre, 50 km to the north, which is most significant in this regard (Fercoq du Leslay 1996, 2000; Brunaux 2003b). Ribemont comprises a group of ditched enclosures, each producing substantial quantities of human remains showing complex postmortem treatments. The northern, square enclosure is superficially similar to Gournay, although its empty interior has suggested to some that it may have contained a sacred grove of trees, analogous to those described by

Lucan, Martial, and others. In the corners of this enclosure, however, were constructed at least three ossuaries, with sides some 1.6 m long, built entirely of human long bones, with occasional fragments of iron weaponry and horse bones; around 300 men and 50 horses were represented in the best-preserved example, which contained at its centre a pit full of cremated human and animal bone.

In the adjoining trapezoidal enclosure excavations have revealed dense concentrations of human remains representing several hundreds of individuals, associated with weapons dating to the beginning of La Tène C1 (*c.*260 BC), and gold coins from north-west France that might suggest the origin of some of the dead. These were virtually all men of fighting age, many with perimortem weapon trauma. Heads were virtually absent, and many cervical vertebrae showed signs of decapitation. The bodies, found in discrete heaps, appear to have decayed *in situ*, perhaps exposed upright on timber scaffolds. Like the metalwork at Gournay, the remains of these decapitated warriors seem to represent battle trophies offered up to the gods. Another circular enclosure seems to have been used for the (perhaps more respectful) deposition of around sixty warriors and their weapons. This last enclosure had subsequently been commemorated by the emplacement of fifty squat sandstone stelae around its infilled ditch.

Elsewhere in France, similar rectilinear enclosures housed other forms of ritual deposit. At Tintignac, in Limousin, for example, underneath the Gallo-Roman temple, was an earlier enclosure with a central timber building and a pit in one corner densely packed with deliberately broken weaponry, including ten or more helmets and at least five *carnyces*—long, animal-headed war-trumpets fashioned from sheet bronze (Maniquet et al. 2011). As at Gournay, the objects seem to have been displayed above ground before burial.

Morphologically, sites like Gournay and Ribemont parallel the widespread quadrangular enclosures, known as *Viereckschanzen*, that are found widely across central Europe (Murray 1995), several of which have also yielded evidence for unusual depositional practices. One of the wells in the eastern *Viereckschanze* at Holzhausen in Bavaria, for example, contained a sharpened vertical stake, and may have acted to receive sacrificial offerings. Wooden animal figures, around 1 m high, from the base of a well in the *Viereckschanze* of Fellbach-Schmiden, Baden-Württemberg (Wieland 1999), may originally have formed part of an elaborately carved structure: they have been dated by dendrochronology to 123 BC. At the Bohemian *Viereckschanze* of Mšecké Žehrovice, a ritualistic dimension is suggested by the well-known stone head found adjacent to the enclosure (Venclová 1998). Excavations of *Viereckschanzen* have also sometimes yielded evidence of important buildings in corner locations, similar to the ossuaries at Ribemont. At Bopfingen, Baden Württemberg, for example, such buildings were located in the north-east and south-east corners, while a third, larger building occupied the western side of the enclosure. In general, however, the evidence for ritual deposition in *Viereckschanzen* is less dramatic than in the northern French sanctuaries, and there is more evidence for settlement and industrial activity: excavations at Mšecké Žehrovice, for example, suggest that it was a centre for ironworking, and the ritual activity on the site may be concerned with the efficacy of this industrial production. Other *Viereckschanzen* are sited close to burial mounds and areas of settlement, and one apparently lies at the heart of the *oppidum* of Manching, suggesting that the practices carried out at these sites might be quite varied in character. A role as elite settlements appears to be the emerging consensus (e.g. von Nicolai 2009), but a ritual dimension would not of course be out of keeping with such an interpretation.

While rectilinear architecture was commonly used for domestic as well as sacred architecture across most of Europe, domestic buildings in Britain and Ireland were almost exclusively circular, and square or rectangular architecture seems usually to have signalled some specifically ritualistic intent. Thus the series of square structures at the centre of Danebury hillfort have been interpreted as shrines, in contrast to the roundhouses around the periphery of the interior, even in the absence of obviously votive deposits (Cunliffe 1995).

Ancestral Landscapes

In several parts of Iron Age Europe it is possible to identify ritual landscapes that extend far beyond any single identifiable archaeological site. Some of the clearest examples are found in Ireland, where the well-known 'royal sites' (Tara, Rathcroghan, Navan, and Knockaulin) survived long enough in communal memory to be recorded as important pagan places in the written records of the early Christian period. As a landscape, the best understood is probably the 'royal site' on the Hill of Tara, Co. Meath. Although the complex covers a large area (the sixth- to fourth-century BC Lismullin enclosure, some 2 km to the north-east being the most recently discovered element) and encompasses the remains of numerous Bronze Age burial monuments, its focus appears to have been the Neolithic chambered tomb known as the Mound of the Hostages which occupies the highest point of the hill. This was surrounded during the Iron Age by a large hengiform enclosure, in and around which several large earthwork enclosures were created (Newman 1997). One of the principal roles of the Hill of Tara, certainly in later periods, and probably during the Iron Age, was the inauguration of kings. Much of the complex seems to have been laid out to choreograph the movement of participants in these and other rituals, the various elements of the landscape acting as mnemonic aids in the recounting of ancient Irish cosmology. By the Iron Age, the already incomprehensibly ancient Mound of the Hostages seems to have been venerated as some kind of *axis mundi* or portal to the Otherworld.

The northern 'royal site' of Navan, Co. Armagh, which appears in early documentary accounts as Emain Macha, shares much in common with Tara. Here the middle Iron Age activity focuses on a sequence of large figure-of-eight timber buildings on the summit of a small hill, in an area with a deep history of activity, including a large multivallate hillfort a short distance to the west, and a series of linear earthworks and barrows (Waterman 1997). The timber buildings at Navan do not appear to have been domestic in character and seem related instead to the long-lived ritual use of the hilltop. Among the finds from the wall trenches was the skull of a Barbary ape of likely north African origin, demonstrating the long-distance links of the community or its leaders. The figure-of-eight buildings are closely paralleled, though on a larger scale, by structures excavated at Knockaulin, Co. Kildare, suggesting that conventions of ritual architecture were widely shared between members of the politico-religious elite.

At the beginning of the first century BC, however, a remarkable transformation took place at Navan, with the emplacement of a large hengiform enclosure (mirroring the one at Tara) around the hilltop, and the construction of a massive timber structure at its centre, directly over the remains of the figure-of-eight buildings. This central circular structure measured some 40 m in diameter and was supported by densely packed concentric circles of oak posts. The central post has been dated by dendrochronology to around 95 BC. This massive construction, however, was never intended to have been occupied; before any deposits had accumulated on its floor it was set on fire and, while the charred posts remained standing, the building was infilled with earth to create a circular mound, capped with limestone rubble. It might be conjectured that the purpose of this enormous undertaking, so costly in labour and resources, was to create a mound replicating the 'Mound of the Hostages' at Tara, and may give some insight into what sort of structure the Iron Age communities of Ireland understood that great monument to be.

While the excavated remains are less clear it can be suggested that *oppida* in late Iron Age Britain, such as those at Verlamion in the south, and Stanwick in the centre, may have been organized around similar principles, incorporating funerary monuments, areas of settlement, and industrial zones spread across extensive areas of landscape, between which movement would have been controlled and structured. A similar focus on movement and procession can be seen in around the Glauberg, in Hesse, with its lengthy linear earthworks channelling movement around the hillfort and its associated tumuli, with their prominent post settings (Baitinger and Pinsker 2002). Phil Mason (2008) has highlighted the emphasis on movement around Slovenian Iron Age landscapes, where well-built roadways, like that close to Vinji Vrh, appear to lead the traveller through various zones of industrial, funerary, and settlement activity on their approach to the major hillfort centres.

Offerings and Sacrifice

As the elaborate but ephemeral processions represented on situla art remind us, much Iron Age ritual will have left no physical trace. Archaeology, however, can only ever reveal the material residues of ritual actions. Our evidence is thus skewed towards the identification of those rituals that involved the placing of material into the ground, into water, or into the structural fabric of buildings or enclosures. It is no surprise then that much of our evidence suggests a concern with sacrifice: the offering of people, animals, produce, or other items to the gods, ancestors, or spirits. The motivations behind these deposits were undoubtedly diverse. In domestic buildings, some offerings would have been made to imbue the house with luck, protect it from evil spirits, and ensure the well-being of its inhabitants. Others may have had more individual intent—for example, to heal some specific malady (much like *muti* in present-day southern Africa), or to bring personal wealth or status. Those offerings placed in grain silos at the end of their use-lives were perhaps intended as a thanksgiving for the safe storage of the crop, and a plea for future fertility of the fields.

Although other objects are often present, there is a recurrent visceral theme to Iron Age ritual deposition. Iron Age ritual could be bloody, dramatic, and violent. While animal remains are most common, often featuring a ritual menagerie of horses, dogs, and birds, a great many sites display an emphasis on the curation and processing of human remains. These range from small-scale domestic deposits in Scottish roundhouses, to the huge and macabre displays at sites like Ribemont-sur-Ancre. Throughout the period, the human body seems to have been a potent symbol that could be manipulated to embody a range of ideas. Although whole bodies are not uncommon, there is a widespread emphasis on the human head. In some areas, particularly southern France and Iberia, this clearly relates to a long-established practice of headhunting, and this is probably also the case in many other parts of Europe. Although the accrual of trophy heads had close links to the maintenance of fertility (for crops, animals, and humans), it seems also to have become a metaphor for chiefly power, imbuing secular leaders with cosmological and religious authority.

Perhaps the most spectacular of all Iron Age ritual sites were associated with the sacrifice of war booty, at places like Gournay-sur-Aronde, Ribemont-sur-Ancre, Hjortspring, and Illerup Ådal. Such sites display the sacrifice of weaponry, humans, and animals on a huge scale, reflecting the coordinated actions of large communities under the direction of ritualists adhering to widely shared conventions of ritual practice. These were places where large numbers of people came together, in regions largely without major population centres, to express group cohesion and identity—places where the close association of warfare and sacrifice illustrates the interplay of secular power, religion, and cosmology.

References

Aldhouse-Green, M. 2015. *Bog Bodies Uncovered*. London: Thames and Hudson.

Arcelin, P. 2006. 'Avant Aquae Sextiae: l'oppidum d'Entremont', in F. Mocci and N. Nin (eds) *Aix-en-Provence, Pays d'Aix, Val de Durance*. Carte Archéologique de la Gaule 13.4: 125–168. Paris: Fondation Maison des Sciences de l'Homme.

Arcelin, P., and A. Rapin. 2003. 'L'iconographie anthropomorphe de l'âge du Fer en Gaule Méditeranéenne', in O. Buchsenschutz, A. Bulard, M.-B. Chardenoux, and N. Ginoux (eds) *Décors, images et signes de l'âge du Fer européen. Actes du XXVIe Colloque de l'AFEAF, Paris et Saint-Denis, 9–12 mai 2002*. Revue Archéologique du Centre de la France supplément 24: 183–220. Tours: FERACF.

Armit, I. 2006. *Anatomy of an Iron Age Roundhouse: The Cnip Wheelhouse Excavations, Lewis*. Society of Antiquaries of Scotland Monograph Series. Edinburgh: Society of Antiquaries of Scotland.

Armit, I. 2011. 'Violence and society in the deep human past', *British Journal of Criminology* 51, 3: 499–517.

Armit, I. 2012. *Headhunting and the Body in Iron Age Europe*. Cambridge: Cambridge University Press.

Armit, I., C. Gaffney, and A. Hayes. 2012. 'Space and movement in an Iron Age oppidum: Integrating geophysical and topographic survey at Entremont, Provence'. *Antiquity* 86: 191–206.

Armit, I., and J. McKenzie. 2013. *An Inherited Place: Broxmouth and the Southern Scottish Iron Age*. Society of Antiquaries of Scotland Monograph Series. Edinburgh: Society of Antiquaries of Scotland.

Armit, I., R. J. Schulting, C. J. Knüsel, and I. A. G. Shepherd. 2011. 'Death, decapitation and display: The Bronze and Iron Age human remains from the Sculptor's Cave, Covesea, NE Scotland'. *Proceedings of the Prehistoric Society* 77: 251–278.

Asingh, P., and N. Lynnerup (eds). 2007. *Grauballe Man: An Iron Age Bog Body Revisited*. Moesgård: Moesgård Museum.

Baitinger, H., and B. Pinsker. 2002. *Das Rätsel der Kelten vom Glauberg: Glaube—Mythos—Wirklichkeit*. Stuttgart: Theiss.

Boissinot, P., and L.-F. Gantès. 2000. 'La chronologie de Roquepertuse. Propositions préliminaires à l'issue des campagnes 1994–1999'. *Documents d'Archéologie Méridionale* 27: 249–271.

Bradley, R. 2005. *Ritual and Domestic Life in Prehistoric Europe*. London: Routledge.

Brunaux, J.-L. 2003a. 'Notice 9: Gournay-sur-Aronde (Oise)', in P. Arcelin and J.-L. Brunaux (eds), *Gallia 60: Cultes et sanctuaires en France à l'âge du Fer*: 58–59. Paris: CNRS Éditions.

Brunaux, J.-L. 2003b. 'Notice 14: Ribemont-sur-Ancre (Somme)', in P. Arcelin and J.-L. Brunaux (eds) *Gallia 60: Cultes et sanctuaires en France à l'âge du Fer*: 64–68. Paris: CNRS Éditions.

Büster, L., and I. Armit. 2021. 'Materialising memories: Inheritance, performance and practice at Broxmouth hillfort, south-east Scotland', in S. Stoddart, E. D. Aines, and C. Malone (eds) *Gardening Time: Reflections on Memory, Monuments and History in Scotland and Sardinia*: 27–36. Cambridge: McDonald Institute for Archaeological Research.

Chausserie-Laprée, C. 2005. *Martigues, Terre Gauloise Entre Celtique et Méditerranée*. Paris: Errance.

Craig, R., C. J. Knüsel, and G. Carr. 2005. 'Fragmentation, mutilation and dismemberment: An interpretation of human remains on Iron Age sites', in M. Parker Pearson and N. Thorpe (eds) *Warfare, Violence and Slavery in Prehistory*. British Archaeological Reports International Series 1374: 165–180. Oxford: Archaeopress.

Čučković, L. 2004. 'The Colapiani', in D. Balen-Letunič (ed.) *Ratnici na razmeđu istoka i zapada starije željezno doba u kontinentalnoj Hrvatskoj*: 173–210. Zagreb: Arheološki muzej.

Cunliffe, B. W. 1995. *Danebury: An Iron Age Hillfort in Hampshire, Vol. 6: A Hillfort Community in Perspective*. CBA Research Report 102. London: Council for British Archaeology.

De Nardi, S. 2007. 'Landscapes of the prehistoric Veneto, Italy. A plurality of local identities reflected in cult and landscape perception'. *Papers from the Institute of Archaeology* 18: 39–56.

Dedet, B. and M. Schwaller. 1990. 'Pratiques cultuelles et funéraires en milieu domestique sur les oppidums languedociens'. *Documents d'Archéologie Méridionale* 13: 137–162.

Delattre, V. 2000. 'Les inhumations en silos dans les habitats de l'âge du fer du Bassin parisien', in S. Marion and G. Blancquaert (eds) *Les Installations Agricoles de l'Âge du Fer en France Septentrionale*. British Archaeological Reports International Series 1374: 299–311. Oxford: Archaeopress.

Fercoq du Leslay, G. 1996. 'Chronologie et analyse spatiale à Ribemont-sur-Ancre'. *Revue Archéologique de Picardie* 1996, 3–4: 189–208.

Fercoq du Leslay, G. 2000. 'L'apport des fossés de Ribemont-sur-Ancre (Somme) à la chronologie et à l'interprétation du site'. *Revue Archéologique de Picardie* 2000, 1–2: 113–146.

Frey, O.-H. 2011. 'The world of situla art', in L. A. Bonfante (ed.) *The Barbarians of Ancient Europe: Realities and Interactions*: 282–312. Cambridge: Cambridge University Press.

Hill, J. D. 1995. *Ritual and Rubbish in the Iron Age of Wessex*. British Archaeological Reports British Series 242. Oxford: Tempus Reparatum.

Hüglin, S, and N. Spichtig. 2010. 'War crime or élite burial: Interpretations of human skeletons within the Late La Tène settlement Basel-Gasfabrik, Basel, Switzerland'. *European Journal of Archaeology* 13, 3: 313–335.

Ilkjær, J. 2000. *Illerup Ådal: Archaeology as a Magic Mirror*. Moesgård: Moesgård Museum.

Joy, J. 2009. *Lindow Man*. London: British Museum Press.

Jud, P. 2007. 'Les ossements humains dans les sanctuaires laténiens de la région des Trois-Lacs', in P. Barral, A. Daubigny, C. Dunning, G. Kaenel, and M.-J. Roulière-Lambert (eds) *L'âge du Fer dans l'arc jurassien et ses marges: Dépôts, lieux sacrés et territorialité à l'âge du Fer. Actes du XXIXe colloque international de l'AFEAF, Bienne, 5–8 mai 2005*: 391–398. Besançon: Presses Universitaires de Franche-Comté.

Kelly, E. P. 2006. *Kingship and Sacrifice: Iron Age Bog Bodies and Boundaries*. Archaeology Ireland Heritage Guide 35. Wicklow: Wordwell.

Maniquet, C., T. Lejars, B. Armbruster, M. Pernot, M. Drieux-Daguerre, P. Mora, and L. Espinasse. 2011. 'Le carnyx et le casque-oiseau celtiques de Tintignac (Naves-Corrèze). Description et étude technologique'. *Aquitania* 27: 63–150.

Mason, P. 2008. 'Places for the living, places for the dead and places in between: Hillforts and the semiotics of the Iron Age landscape in central Slovenia', in G. Children and G. Nash (eds) *Semiotics in the Landscape II: The Archaeology of Semiotics and the Social Order of Things*. British Archaeological Reports International Series 1833. Oxford: Archaeopress.

Mollerup, L., A. K. Ejgreen Tjellden, E. Hertz, and M. K. Holst. 2010. 'The postmortem exposure interval of an Iron Age human bone assemblage from Alken Enge, Denmark'. *Journal of Archaeological Science Reports* 10: 819–827.

Murray, M. 1995. 'Viereckschanzen and feasting: Socio-political ritual in Iron Age central Europe'. *Journal of European Archaeology* 3, 2: 125–151.

Newman, C. 1997. *Tara: An Archaeological Survey*. Discovery Programme Monograph 2. Dublin: Discovery Programme and The Royal Irish Academy.

Nin, N. 1999. 'Les espaces domestiques en Provence durant la Protohistoire. Aménagements et pratiques rituelles du VIe s. av. n. è. à l'époque augustéene'. *Documents d'Archéologie Méridionale* 22: 221–278.

Rapin, A. 2003. 'De Roquepertuse à Entremont, la grande sculpture du Midi de la Gaule'. *Madrider Mitteilungen* 44: 223–246.

Salviat, F. 1993. 'La sculpture d'Entremont', in D. Coutagne (ed.) *Archéologie d'Entremont au Musée Granet*: 165–239. Aix-en-Provence: Association des Amis du Musée Granet.

Sievers, S. 2002. 'Manching revisited'. *Antiquity* 76: 943–944.

Van der Sanden, W. 1996. *Through Nature to Eternity: The Bog Bodies of North West Europe*. Amsterdam: Batavian Lion International.

Venclová, N. 1998. *Mšecké Žehrovice in Bohemia: Archaeological Background to a Celtic Hero*. Sceaux: Kronos.

Verger, S. (ed.) 2000. *Rites et Espaces en Pays Celte et Méditerranéen: Étude comparée à partir du sanctuaire d'Acy-Romance (Ardennes, France)*. Rome: École Française de Rome.

Von Nicolai, C. 2009. 'La question des "Viereckschanzen" d'Allemagne du Sud revisitée', in I. Bertrand, A. Duval, J. Gomez De Soto and P. Maguer (eds) *Habitats et paysages ruraux en Gaule et regards sur d'autres régions du monde celtique. Actes du XXXIe colloque international de l'AFEAF, 17–20 mai 2007, Chauvigny*: 245–280. Chauvigny: Association des publications chauvinoises.

Warmenbol, E. 1996. 'L'or, la mort et les hyperboréens. La bouche des enfers ou le Trou de Han à Han-sur-Lesse', in M. Almagro Gorbea (ed.) *Archäologische Forschungen zum Kultgeschehen in der jüngeren Bronzezeit und frühen Eisenzeit Alteuropas. Ergebnisse eines Kolloquiums in Regensburg 4.-7. Oktober 1993*: 203–234. Regensburg: Universitätsverlag.

Waterman, D. M. 1997. *Excavations at Navan Fort 1961–71*. Northern Ireland Archaeological Monographs 3. Belfast: The Stationery Office.

Wieland, G. 1999. *Keltische Viereckschanzen: Einem Rätsel auf der Spur*. Stuttgart: Theiss.

Wilson, C. E. 1981. 'Burials within settlements in southern Britain during the pre-Roman Iron Age'. *Bulletin of the Institute of Archaeology London* 18: 127–169.

Wiltschke-Schrotta, K. 2012. 'Anthropologische Auswertung des Gräberfeldes Dürrnberg-Kammelhöhe/Sonneben', in S. Moser, G. Tiefengraber, and K. Wiltschke-Schrotta (eds) *Der Dürrnberg bei Hallein: Die Gräbergruppen Kammelhöhe und Sonneben*. Dürrnberg-Forschungen 5, Abteilung Gräberkunde: 211–236. Rahden: Marie Leidorf.

CHAPTER 42

FORMAL RELIGION

MIRANDA ALDHOUSE-GREEN

Introduction: A 'Formal' Religion?

This chapter's focus is the late La Tène period through to the beginnings of Christianity in western Europe; this emphasis is in large part due to the comparatively rich assemblage of evidence available for this tranche of time. Is it possible to impose a formal religious structure or belief system on the European Iron Age? Even if such systems were to have been in place, how would they be recognized in the archaeological record? Formal religion implies a formulaic set of rituals and repetitive or persistent ways of expressing the sacred, and perhaps also belief in divine beings, as recipients of offerings and sacrifices (see Chapter 41). It *is* possible to recognize such 'formality', to some degree, during the Roman provincial period. This was perhaps due largely to the presence of more formalized political systems and the development of common governance and urbanization. More importantly, the introduction of religious inscriptions and identifiable cult iconography enabled the recognition of deities, complete with mythologies, responsibilities, and constellations of emblems.

By contrast, the material culture of the pre-Roman Iron Age seldom allows for the recognition of unequivocal belief systems and cosmologies, and it is necessary to exercise extreme caution in making assumptions based on the more evidence-rich Roman period, and running the risk of thus imposing its structures on the relatively blank canvas of the Iron Age. For most of this period of later European prehistory, it is possible only to suggest a religious system that was pivoted upon natural phenomena. The deeply rooted and widespread custom of depositing valuable artefacts in water, for instance, strongly implies an acknowledgement by its perpetrators of a perceived numinosity associated with rivers, bogs, and pools (Bradley 1990; Field and Parker Pearson 2003; Macdonald 2007). One of the most evocative such deposits was the set of four late Iron Age ceremonial trumpets placed in a small lake at Loughnashade, at the foot of the great ceremonial circular building erected at Navan in Co. Armagh (Ireland) in the early first century BC. The presence of human skulls in the lake reinforces its identity as a holy place, and it is tempting to see Druids presiding over its rituals (Lynn 1992; Raftery 1994). The persistence of focus on water and its spirit-force into the provincial Roman horizon is exemplified by the great temple to the British divinity Sulis (twinned with Minerva), built in recognition of the powerful and continuous gushing of hot springs close to the River Avon at Bath (Cunliffe 1988; Cunliffe and Davenport 1985), and the Burgundian shrine at *Fontes Sequanae* (the springs of Sequana) dedicated to the female personification of the spring source of the River Seine on the limestone plateau near Dijon (Deyts 1983, 1994; Aldhouse-Green 1999).

A multipronged approach may be made to the problem of identifying a 'formal' religion for the European Iron Age, while always acknowledging regional diversity and the bias in the evidence base towards Britain and the near Continent. First, there is sufficient data on the Druids, based largely, though no longer wholly, on the statements of Greek and Roman authors concerning the very latest Iron Age of Gaul and Britain, tentatively to suggest the role of the Druids in coordinating and formalizing ritual and belief across a large part of western Europe. A second prong is exhibited by classical literary references to deities with Gallo-British names, arguably worshipped before full Roman occupation, albeit not until late in the Iron Age, whose veneration is supported by Roman-period epigraphic evidence. Thirdly, it is both useful and necessary—as long as it is done judiciously—to consider to what extent Roman-period evidence is at all relevant to the later Iron Age. For instance, it is unlikely that such indigenous Gallic divinities as Epona, as represented in Roman-period inscriptions and iconography, sprang fully fledged into the Gallo-Roman religious repertoire. Instead, she may well have possessed a pre-Roman ancestry, albeit altered. However, certain deities—such as mother-goddesses—who were venerated only on a local scale in the late pre-Roman Iron Age may well have morphed in the Roman period into tribal or even supra-tribal divinities. Others—if indeed they existed in any formalized sense prior to provincial annexation—remained as personifications of specific features in the landscape: Sequana is a good example.

Taranis, Esus, and Teutates: Lucan's Contribution

> And those Gauls who propitiate with human sacrifices the merciless gods Teutas, Esus and Taranis—at whose altars the visitant shudders because they are as awe-inspiring as those of Scythian Diana
>
> (Lucan *Pharsalia* 1, lines 444–446)

The *Pharsalia* is an epic poem written in the mid-first century AD about the civil war between Pompey and Caesar that culminated in the former's defeat at Pharsalus in Greece in 48 BC. Who are these deities? Should any credence be placed on an author who is not known to have visited Gaul and who, in any case, died in his mid-twenties.

Robert Graves (1956) describes Lucan as 'the father of yellow journalism' and 'the father of the costume-film'. Further, he comments on the poem, 'It consists of carefully chosen, cunningly varied, brutally sensational scenes, linked by a tenuous thread of historical probability.' Even if Lucan's remarks about these three deities are taken at face value, a fundamental problem with this reference is that he does not make clear to which polities these three named gods belonged, although the context of his discourse is southern Gaul. Just before his comment about the divine triad, he mentions Gallic tribes whose territories included regions between the Rhône and the Saône, the Cevennes and Liguria, but he seems here simply to be alluding to the withdrawal of Caesar's garrisons from Gaul in preparation for his march on Rome. However, despite the epic (and romantic) genre of his poem, Lucan's three deities with Gaulish names cannot be dismissed as invention, for all three names occur in the epigraphy of the western Roman provinces, albeit sparsely and (in the case of Taranis) mostly outside Gaul. Lucan's text provides no information on the responsibilities and remit of these gods, apart from the apparent need to propitiate them with human sacrificial victims. However, the etymology affords some clues, particularly in the case of Taranis, whose name is derived from the Gaulish (and Welsh) *Taran*, meaning thunder.

Only a handful of Roman-date inscribed altars mentioning Taranis are recorded (Green 1984: 359, cat. D1–7), but three of these link his name with that of the Roman sky/father god Jupiter: from Scardona, Croatia (*C.I.L.* III, 2804), from Chester in Britain (Collingwood and Wright 1965: no. 452; Green 1982); and from Thauron, Creuse, France (Perrier 1960: 195–197). This is an apt pairing because, of course, Jupiter was lord of the firmament and his weapons included thunder and lightning. The key question has to be whether Taranis, in whatever form, was identified and invoked prior to the Roman period in the lands within which inscriptions are recorded. Perhaps the only clue consists of miniature copper-alloy wheel-amulets (*rouelles*), many of which are of Iron Age date and come from sanctuaries (like those from Champlieu and Bolards in France; Green 1984: 311, A72, 319, A173) or cemeteries (for example at Tregnes, Belgium; Green 1984: 317, A155). The link is tenuous but credible, in so far as several Gallo-Roman and Romano-British altars or imagery dedicated to Jupiter include solar wheel imagery, as from Aigues-Mortes and Nîmes in southern France (Espérandieu 1910: no. 2650; 1925: no. 6849), or Birdoswald, Cumbria, Britain (Wright and Phillips 1975: 69, no. 179), which does not belong to the symbolic repertoire of the god in Roman tradition.

Esus is even more elusive, in so far as his presence is only attested on one or two monuments. Most notable is the inscribed image on one of the panels of the stone pillar monument dedicated to Jupiter in Paris by the *Nautes Parisiacae* (guild of Seine river boatmen) in AD 26 (Espérandieu 1911: no. 3134; Green 1989: 103, fig. 44). In this scene, Esus is depicted as a woodcutter, engaged in felling, or perhaps pollarding, a willow tree (Figure 42.1).[1] The etymology of Esus' name suggests a title rather than a name per se, for it appears to mean simply 'lord' (Ross 1967: 279). In this context, the link between Esus and the willow tree may represent his control over the natural world, a theme that chimes both with Iron Age evidence for environmental numinosity and with classical literary references to Gallo-British sacred groves.

FIGURE 42.1 Stone carving of a woodman, bearing the inscription 'Esus'. Part of the *Nautes Parisiacae* monument set up by a guild of Seine boatmen and dedicated to Jupiter in Paris AD 26.

Drawing © Paul Jenkins, for author

Teutates likewise possesses a generic title rather than a specific name, for the roots of the word lie in the Gaulish term for tribe or polity (as in old Irish *tuath*). A scattering of inscriptions reflect his worship and, if he was a tribal deity, his responsibility probably relates to protection of his people, because his name is linked with that of Mars. Teutates may well have been venerated as a divine hero, as argued forcefully in a recent study of Iberian material (Almagro-Gorbea and Lorrio Alvaredo 2011), and such an identification sits easily with a warrior/guardian role associated with the very being of tribe, polity, or clan. Mars Teutates was invoked by a devotee who dedicated an inscribed silver 'feather' plaque to him at Barkway (Hertfordshire; Toynbee 1978: no. 26). Here several similar plaques were offered to Mars and Vulcan. Britain seems to have been a focus for the cult of Teutates, for other inscriptions that mention him occur in the province, notably at Kelvedon in Essex, where the word 'Toutatis' was roughly scratched on a sherd of local black pottery. Furthermore, another fragment in virtually identical ceramic depicts what can only be interpreted as a Trinovantian warrior god, a horseman with stiff, spiky hair (that tallies with Diodorus Siculus' description of Gallic warriors, their hair stiffened with washed-in lime to make them look taller and more formidable to their enemies (*Library of History* 5.28)). He carries a late La Tène-style hexagonal shield and a curious long-shafted, crook-ended object that might have been a ritual stave, or even a British version of a Roman augurer's *lituus*, a tool used in divining rituals (Aldhouse-Green 2010: 164). Could this image be that of the Gallo-British guardian god Teutates? Or is it more likely to have represented the Trinovantian warrior knight, buried with full military honours in the mid-first century BC here at Kelvedon?[2] Teutates also occurs further afield, for instance at Seckau in Styria (Austria), and was even exported to Rome (de Vries 1963: 54), but *never occurs in Lucan's area of Gaul.*

Sena and Pomponius Mela

Sena means 'The Old'. The name *Senae* (to Sena 'the Old One') is inscribed on a small altar from Saint-Bertrand-de-Comminges in Pyrenean southern France, found reused in the cathedral. This female deity is referred to in the plural at Tiffen in Noricum (cf. singular and plural versions of Lugoves; see Marco Simón 2010). Sena also appears on a silver leaf from Britain and a cognate deity Senuna, also British, has several dedications (de Bernardo Stempel 2008). In one and the same hoard from Baldock (Hertfordshire), which yielded nineteen votive plaques, Sena and Senuna were both invoked, but here they were equated with Minerva (Mattingly 2006: 484). Sena also appears at Bibracte in Burgundy. The first-century AD Roman writer Pomponius Mela mentions Sena ('Sena in Britannico mare Ossismicis adversa litoribus, Gallici numinis oraculo insignis est'; *Chorographia* 3.47–3.48). His text is usually taken to refer to a sacred island called Sena inhabited by virgin oracular priestesses (Chadwick 1997: 79), but it could also be an obscure allusion to a wise old goddess (de Bernardo Stempel 2008) and, if so, Mela may be describing a British divinity already well established by the time of the Claudian invasion.

Tacitus and Nerthus

Tacitus wrote his *Germania* in AD 98. In the introduction to his translation, Harold Mattingly (1948) discusses the reliability or otherwise of the text, expressing confidence in it as a work of genuine reportage, citing the manner in which the author's descriptions of German material culture tally with archaeological evidence. Perhaps, then, it is possible to regard Tacitus' comments on German gods and goddesses with a greater sense of security than—say—those of Lucan on his three *dei horribili*. Tacitus says most about an earth goddess called Nerthus.[3] Is Nerthus credible? Perhaps she is. There is plenty of Rhenish evidence for 'mother goddesses', in both epigraphy (where they are often referred to as *Matronae*) and iconography. In common with their worship in other western Roman provinces, they were frequently represented in triplicate (von Petrikovits 1987; Green 1989: 194–198). Tacitus' account is full of detail and, if we accept his testimony, the ritual is so exact as to argue for its establishment for a considerable length of time prior to his reporting at the end of the first century AD.

The name Nerthus is interesting for, in common with Venus, it is a neuter rather than a feminine word. Tacitus makes it clear that her cult was widespread among the German polities, yet her sanctuary was located at a specific *locus consecratus* and this suggests that it was a place of annual pilgrimage, perhaps involving arduous journeys over long distances. Nerthus' rituals were hedged about with prohibitions concerning the eschewance of warfare and presumably the taboo on iron reflects such avoidance of weapons. It is tempting (though perhaps rash) to make broad connections between iron objects and the depositions containing ironwork that occur, for instance, in late Iron Age British watery contexts such as Carlingwark in Scotland, where in the first century AD local people sank a cauldron in a sacred marshy pool containing large quantities of broken ironwork (Manning 1972; Green 1998; Aldhouse-Green 2002: 10). The negative association between a German fertility goddess and iron contains an apparent counterpoint to the perception of metalworking in many present-day traditional societies (notably in parts of Africa), where the winning and working of iron is perceived as closely analogous to the production of bread and, indeed, to human and animal fertility and reproduction (Herbert 1993; Hingley 1997: 9–10).

The intense, and multi-layered sacrality in Nerthus' cult needs to be addressed, particularly as its complexity lends weight to its authenticity, while still acknowledging that Tacitus may have embroidered his evidence or have been partially ignorant in his interpretation of his material. The sanctity of the wagon, which only the priest could touch, suggests something akin to the 'electrical' charge of numinosity with which the Old Testament Ark of the Covenant was suffused (2 *Samuel* 6: 6–7), a charge so powerful that a profane touch resulted in instant death for the offender. Tacitus' testimony presents a highly complex association between Nerthus and water, which is perceived as both an agent of purification and a context for the enactment of human sacrifice. The archaeological links between water and iron have been discussed earlier in the chapter. In terms of sacrifice, it is significant that persons of lowly status were employed to cleanse the goddess' wagon, and that they were then ritually executed. Perhaps such an act accords with some of the north European bog bodies, who were denied grave goods and were sometimes subjected to abuse and restraint prior to their deaths (van der Sanden 1996; Aldhouse-Green 2001b). It is tempting to relate the cult of Nerthus to a Burgundian goddess of the third century AD, Berecynthia, recorded in the sixth century AD by

Gregory, Bishop of Tours (in his *The Glory of the Confessors*; de Nie 1987). Her agricultural festival included her procession in a wagon around the fields.

Celtiberia

The singular material culture from north-east Spain, centred on the Iron Age fortified stronghold of Numantia, provides unique insights into complex Iron Age cosmologies. Metalwork, including copper-alloy brooches and sceptre terminals, suggests the presence of a warrior horseman cult associated with the depiction of disembodied human heads (Figure 42.2; Lorrio 1997: pls. 3, 4; Martínez 1999: 7; Aldhouse-Green 2001b: 100, fig. 39). The military theme is similarly occurrent on pre-conquest Numantine polychrome pottery, but here the religious emphasis is on solar imagery, together with a funerary ritual associated with sky deities represented by vultures, which consume the exposed bodies of warriors who are slain honourably in battle (Aldhouse-Green 2001b: col. pl. 3). Written testimony on these excarnatory ceremonies is provided by Roman authors (Aelian *de Natura Animalium* 10, 22; Silius Italicus *Punica* 3, 242–348).

While most of the decorated ceramic material belongs to the post-conquest horizon, some of it has been dated to the pre-Roman period. A recently discovered pre-conquest polychrome vessel from Segeda dates to a period prior to the start of the Celtiberian wars in 153 BC (Marco Simón 2007: 104–105, fn. 12). Its imagery has been interpreted in terms of display of 'an indigenous cosmological vision founded on three stages or layers: the celestial world, dominated by the sun, an earth-world imagined by water and the fertility of animals, and a final infernal layer'. Francisco Marco Simón (2010: 15–16) cites both the iconography on this early pot and other coeval imagery, such as a funerary plaque from a cemetery at Alpanseque, Soria, as evidence of an ancestral Celtiberian cosmology on whose foundations were built the elaborate cults played out on post-conquest painted pottery. It is apparent that the origins of both celestial and warrior cults pre-date the Roman annexation of Celtiberia. Life-size stone armed, torc-wearing soldiers, known as *guerreros Gallaicos*, guarded the perimeters of Iron Age strongholds such as Ávila, providing further evidence for cults associated with war or protection of territory. Most of these images date to the middle to later Iron Age, although a few bear Latin inscriptions (Tranoy 1988; Aldhouse-Green 2004a: 41, fig. 2.6).

Back-Projection and *Romanitas*

Scholars such as Jane Webster (1995) rightly protest against the all-too-common explanation of Iron Age European religion as viewed through the evidence-rich lens of *romanitas*. It is indeed tempting to travel down this pathway, simply because it

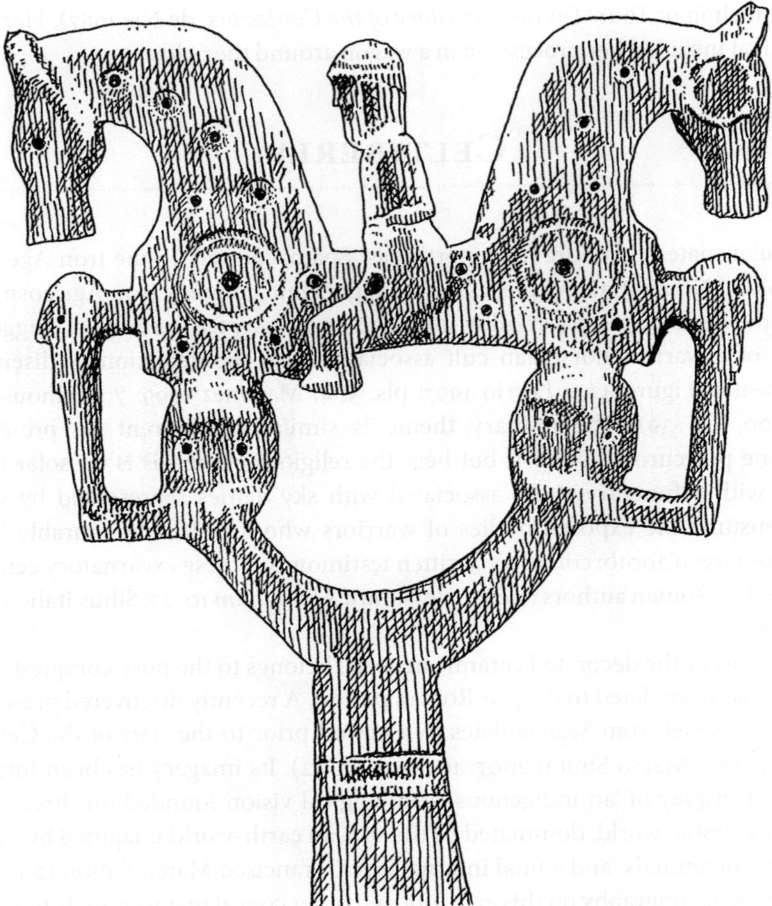

FIGURE 42.2 Copper-alloy sceptre head depicting a pair of back-to-back horses, a horseman, and disembodied human heads beneath the horses' front hooves and bodies. From a high-status cremation grave in a cemetery at Numantia, Spain, second century BC.

Drawing © Paul Jenkins, for author

promises to provide a context for the myriad of new (and apparently indigenous) gods' names and images that appear in the Roman provinces, borne on the new wave of religious epigraphic and iconographical expression that, according to the evidence base, had little Iron Age background or previous tradition. But that is insufficient cause to claim silent prehistoric roots for these Gallo-Roman, Romano-British, or other provincial constellations of deities. On the contrary, there is reason to believe that new local religious movements were actually constructed in the Roman period and that 'Romano-Celtic' panthea were largely new-minted under Imperial rule (Woolf 1998: 215–220). However, there may be exceptions. A good candidate for the possession of an Iron Age pedigree is Epona, a horse goddess whose cult was widespread in the

Roman west, where she is amply represented both in images and in epigraphy (Magnen and Thévenot 1953).

A search for a direct Iron Age antecedent for Epona leads to a dead end. However, it might be possible to find an ancestor for her in late Iron Age coinage, particularly in Breton issues. A particular iconographic theme on the reverse of some gold coinage minted by the Redones and neighbouring Armorican polities is the image of a naked horsewoman, who gallops along brandishing weapons, shields, torcs, or branches of trees (Figure 42.3). A cognate image is that of an armed female charioteer (Duval 1987: 31, 43, 45). Is it possible that she represents an Iron Age war goddess, whose cavalry imagery persisted into the Roman period when she was transformed into a peaceful horse goddess, bringer of fertility and prosperity? It is possible that the foliage borne by some of the pre-Roman coin images (together with the obvious and heavy-breasted nudity on some issues; Duval 1987: frontispiece) hints at this dimension already. It is also feasible to argue that Epona's clear responsibility for the shepherding of the dead, exhibited in some of her Gallic iconography, where she appears with the keys to the Otherworld (Espérandieu 1908: no. 1618; 1915: no. 4894; Green 1989: 18, 22), reflects her inheritance from an ancestral war deity. Given a Roman Imperial provincial milieu in which aggressive, militarized indigenous cult expression is likely to have been discouraged, it is highly possible to imagine the retention of Iron Age spirit entities under different guises. Numerous broad analogies to such reconfiguration

FIGURE 42.3 Armorican Iron Age gold coin depicting a naked horsewoman with shield and sword, accompanied by wheel and lyre symbols, first century BC.

on the part of subjugated communities, belonging to more modern contexts, may be cited. One instance is that of seventeenth-century New Mexico, where local pagan religious expression, in the form of imagery on painted ceramics, went underground and hid its potency beneath a blanket of seemingly innocent blandness (Spielmann et al. 2006).

Trouble with Images

One of the most important late Iron Age European religious objects is the Gundestrup cauldron, a great silver-gilt repoussé vessel, found dismantled into its thirteen component plates, where it had been deliberately deposited on a dry island within a peat bog in Jutland in about 100 BC (Kaul 1991). The cauldron is unique, not only in its metal but in the elaborate scenes and portraits decorating its inner and outer surfaces. It is highly likely that a precious object such as this was at the centre of ritual practices in the locality where it was used, and no doubt the iconography represents both mythic narratives and expressions of the gods. Perhaps the most powerful image on the vessel is that of a human figure wearing red deer antlers and a torc, and seated cross-legged, holding a second neck-ring in one hand and a snake with rams' horns in the other (Figure 42.4). The Gundestrup cauldron is uninscribed, but the antlered image accords with a range of iconography dating to the late Iron Age and Roman periods from Britain, Gaul, and the Rhineland. On the same *Nautes Parisiacae* monument that displays the name and image of Esus, erected in Paris in AD 26, is the depiction of a bearded human antlered head (Espérandieu 1911: no. 3133), a torc hanging from each antler; above it is the inscribed word '[C]ERNUNNO' ('to the horned one'). Thus, this singular image has a name or title, given to it early in the Gallo-Roman period. Unlike the imagery associated with many provincial deities with local names, similar iconography occurs in several Iron Age contexts: for instance, it is present severally on the rock art of Val Camonica in northern Italy (Priuli 1988: nos. 134, 136–137; 1996: 29, fig. 51; Aldhouse-Green 2001a: 82), on a copper-alloy late Iron Age statuette from Bouray in eastern France (Joffroy 1979: no. 78; Aldhouse-Green 2004a: 190, fig. 7.8), and on a British silver coin dating to about AD 10 (Boon 1982). Perhaps because the imagery of the antlered deity (if, indeed, it does represent a divine being rather than a 'shaman' wearing an antler headdress) contained no intrinsic message of resistance or aggression, it carried on, unchanged, into the Roman period, resulting in such stone carvings as the serpent-grasping image from Corinium (modern Cirencester in south-west England; Henig 1993: no. 93) and the much grander and more formal-looking enthroned figure, flanked by the Roman gods Apollo and Mercury, from Reims, France (Espérandieu 1913: no. 3653). On this last image, the message given out by the iconography is one of syncretized harmony and prosperity, the latter symbolized by the cascade of coins or grain falling from an open sack on the antlered image's lap. The 'marriage' between *romanitas* and *gallitas*, indicated by the presence of Roman and Gallic deities on the

FIGURE 42.4 Inner plate from a gilded silver cauldron, depicting an antlered human figure accompanied by a stag, a ram-horned snake, and other creatures, second to first century BC. From a bog at Gundestrup, Denmark.

Drawing © Paul Jenkins, for author

same stone, is perhaps enhanced further by the imagery of a stag and a bull that stand facing one another at the god's feet: the depiction of wilderness and domestication together may be a deliberate evocation of cultural unification.

The trouble with images, particularly in the form of stone statuary or copper-alloy figurines, is that they are extremely rare in Iron Age Europe. Where they do occur, unless they chime with Roman-period iconography that is tied into identities provided, for instance, by epigraphy (as is the case—perhaps—with Cernunnos and antlered imagery), it is impossible to discern their identity or meaning. It is even difficult to be sure whether they have any kind of religious significance. A case in point is a small granite carving from Lanneunoc in Brittany (Clément 1986: 143; Aldhouse-Green 2004a: 84–85, fig. 3.16). Its head is missing, it is utterly featureless, except for crudely fashioned arms that meet at its stomach in a pair of hands with raised and over-large thumbs. It might be a god, a ruler, or indeed any human figure. It cannot advance understanding of Iron Age religion. The only glimmer of enlightenment is in the treatment of the Lanneunoc figure's thumbs, for similar exaggeration occurs on Iron Age Gallic coin images on issues struck by the Turones in the middle Loire region and by the Redones of Armorica, where figures of female charioteers exhibit these *pouces levées* (Duval 1987: 43, 46).

The blankness of the Lanneunoc image exemplifies the problem of Iron Age iconography at its most challenging. Equally problematical, for other reasons, is the fragmentary ragstone carving from far away to the east at Mšecké Žehrovice in the Czech Republic (Megaw and Megaw 1989: fig. 178; Aldhouse-Green 2004b: 307, fig. 4). This at least has a context: a pit within a ritual enclosure in which it had been deposited in the third or second century BC. The nearly life-size head is that of a mature man with a luxuriant curling moustache and matching eyebrows; round the truncated neck is a large buffer torc. Before its deposition, the head had been severed from its body (the latter never found) and broken into several pieces, of which at least one was removed prior to the head's interment. What is more, the treatment of the hair is curious: a thick *en brosse* fringe running horizontally from ear to ear but with the cranium behind it completely bare, as if shaven. In an innovative paper, Natalie Venclová (2002) makes the tentative suggestion that such a style might indicate some form of tonsure, as if of a religious official, perhaps even a Druid, citing other broadly coeval sculptures from Germany (at Freinsheim-Dackenheim; Kimmig 1987: fig. 32) and Brittany (at Yvignac: Daire and Langouet 1992: fig. 8). But it is not easy to interpret the head from Mšecké Žehrovice: did it represent a deity, a leader, a war hero, or some other individual? Why was it decapitated and the head deliberately fragmented so that it was interred incomplete? Was this an act of enchainment,[4] insult, or reverence? Could it, following Venclová, have been a Druid? The issue of Druids is addressed in the following section.

The Druids: Fact and Fiction

In seeking to ascribe formal or formalized religious systems to the communities of Iron Age Europe, it is necessary to venture into the problematic arena of the Druids and their portrayal in classical literature (Chadwick 1997; Aldhouse-Green 2010: 20–38). Caesar, the most useful and contemporary source, starkly informs us that:

> The Druids are in charge of religion. They have control over public and private sacrifices, and give rulings on all religious questions.
>
> (*de Bello Gallico* 6.13)

Over thirty Greek and Roman authors mention the Druids (Chadwick 1997: xxi–xxx), most of whom stress their roles as diviners or prophets. However, many—like Lucan (*Pharsalia* 1, lines 422–465) and Pliny (*Natural History* 30.4) in the first century AD—barbarize the Druids, presenting them as synonymous with all that was perceived as worst about unconquered, uncivilized territories beyond the *nomos* (a Greek word meaning law and order) of the Mediterranean world. It is tempting to dismiss the Druids as nothing more than the figment of the over-fertile imaginings of spin doctors and romantic poets, but Caesar falls into neither category and, what is more, he was a first-hand witness of Gaulish society and customs in the mid-first century BC.

One of the problems with Druids is that the literature stands proud of material culture. While there is considerable archaeological evidence for ritual equipment (sceptres, sacrificial knives, headdresses, and 'divination' spoons; see for example Aldhouse-Green 2010: 146–168) and cult practices (see Chapters 39–41), up until recently, no concrete links between archaeology and ancient Druidic literature have been possible. However, a discovery from France made in 2005 may at last provide such a connection, albeit rather a curious one. The find was made at Chartres, whose ancient ancestor Autricum was the tribal capital of the Carnutes. It was in their territory that Caesar places the annual pan-Gallic Druidic Assembly:

> On a fixed date each year they assemble in a consecrated place in the territory of the Carnutes; that area is supposed to be the centre of the whole country of Gaul. People who have disputes to settle assemble there from all over the country and accept the rulings and judgements of the Druids.
>
> (*de Bello Gallico* 6.13)

The discovery was made during excavations for an underground car park in the centre of Chartres (Gordon et al. 2010; Joly et al. 2010). The collapsed remains of a burnt-out Gallo-Roman house had sealed its cellar intact, and an assemblage of ritual objects indicates that this 'crypt' had been used as a shrine during the late first/early second century AD. The liturgical equipment included a range of pottery vessels and lamps, a broad-bladed knife (or *culter*) similar to those habitually used in animal sacrifice, and, most significantly of all, the remains of three large *turibula* (incense burners) of which one was virtually intact. All of the material had been safely tucked away beneath the stairs, for safekeeping or secrecy. The presence of the censers is remarkable enough in itself, but the surface of the complete vessel was covered with cursive inscriptions, scratched on with a stylus when the pot was leather-hard but before firing. Fragments of two other identical vessels have been recovered from the site, and there may well have originally been four (see below).

The inscriptions on the complete *turibulum* (Figure 42.5) are divided into four panels, each one occupying a block running from the top collar of the vessel to its base. Each panel begins with a directional word: *oriens, meridie, occidens*, and *septemtrio* (east, south, west, and north), but beneath these compass words the wording of each panel is virtually identical. Each consists of a prayer: in it Gaius Verius Sedatus summons up the *numina omnipotentia* (all-powerful spirits) and demands benefits and blessings from them because he is *vester custos* ('your guardian'). There then follows a list of 'magical' names, of which all are obscure (and arguably invented) except for a significant one: '*Dru*'. While it could be argued that this incomplete term simply refers to the Gaulish root-word *dru* (wisdom), it could be that the Druids are being invoked and, if so, they have been transformed from priests into spirits. Sedatus was clearly a relatively well-educated and respected citizen of Chartres, but there is evidence that he was dabbling in esoteric magic (some of the pottery, including snake-handled vases, and some of the wording used on the inscribed censers suggest a familiarity with Graeco-Egyptian magical traditions and texts). The shrine is of Roman date and Sedatus was almost certainly (because of his possession of a *cognomen*) a Roman citizen. What Sedatus seems to have been doing is to 'reinvent' an eclectic magical cult that included the 'revivification' of an ancient Gaulish tradition by the inclusion of '*Dru*' in his list of magical words. We can imagine the experience of attendance at the shrine: the four smoking

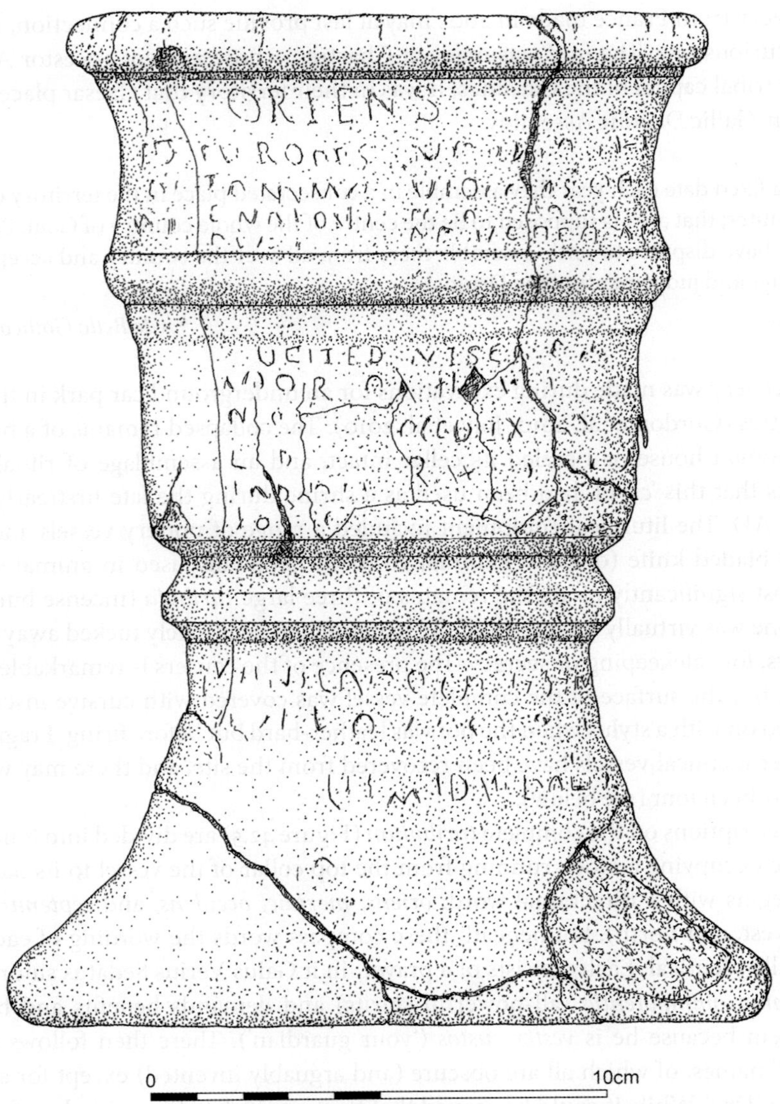

FIGURE 42.5 One of four ceramic *turibula* (incense-burners) from an underground sanctuary at Chartres (Autricum), France. The censer is inscribed with 'magical' words including 'Dru'. First to second century AD.

Drawing © Ian Dennis, for author

censers (the directional words suggest that one vessel may once have been positioned at each of the four corners of a demarcated sacred space), perhaps burning psychotropic, trance-inducing substances, the shadowy figure of Sedatus amid the swirling smoke, the flickering lamps and the darkness, his resonant voice reciting arcane words as he conjured up the spirits, the heightened sensations of the devotees, and the cathartic climax of the ceremony as the sacrifice was enacted in the secrecy of the underground cavern. What is important about the Chartres site, in the context of genuinely ancient Iron Age Druids, is their continued resonance in a Gallo-Roman situation, and it is surely no coincidence that Sedatus chose to invoke the Druids at the very place where, long ago, their annual assembly had taken place.

According to Caesar and others, the Druids were by no means the only religious functionaries operating in Iron Age Europe. Although it is possible, perhaps, to push the named existence of the Druids as far back as the third century BC, it is clear that other groups of holy men (and women) took responsibility for religious affairs, with varying degrees of influence over different territories. For most of his commentaries, Caesar speaks of *sacerdotes*, the normal Latin term for priests: it is only in Book 6 of *de Bello Gallico* that he introduces the Druids. But in Book 8 (8.38) we also encounter another ritual specialist, a *gutuater* (a Gallic word meaning 'Master of Voice' or 'Father of Inspiration'; Chadwick 1997: 38–39; Le Bohec 2005), a highly charged title, suggesting the power invested in someone who had the ear of the spirits and the means of communicating effectively with both them and the people. The reference to this individual in the final (posthumous) book of Caesar's war diaries, written by Hirtius, does not refer to other than a political arena for the *gutuater* (Goudineau 2003)—indeed it appears to be the personal name of a Bellovacan rebel. However, Roman-period Gallic epigraphy appears to reflect the clerical role of someone bearing this title. The most striking example is a small altar from Autun, capital of the Burgundian Aedui (Caesar's closest Gallic allies), dedicated to the spirit of the emperor and to a local deity Anvallus by one Norbaneius Thallus, who calls himself a *gutuater*, in the first century AD (Coulon 2000: 52; Aldhouse-Green 2010: 53, fig. 16).

The power with which words could be invested is demonstrated by the Chartres *turibula* and by the title *gutuater*. It is also emphasized in Tacitus' description of the first-century AD Batavian prophetess Veleda, whose gift of divination was so great that her people considered her to be virtually a goddess (Tacitus *Histories* 4.65). Like the Cumaean Sybil of Virgil's *Aeneid* (Book 6), Veleda spoke in tongues and her utterances had to be interpreted by a male relative. No archaeological evidence for Veleda has been recorded, but Tacitus' reference serves as a reminder that many different kinds of religious authority must have existed in late Iron Age and early Roman Europe, including female as well as male clergy.

Interpreters of Dreams: From Lydney to Thetford

A study of Roman Britannia reveals that *britannitas* was by no means submerged by *romanitas*, in terms of religious expression. On the contrary, new local religious movements appear to have sprung up in the late third and fourth centuries AD, all the more significant because that was the time when Christianity was beginning to emerge as an important new cult that, to a degree, challenged pagan polytheism. The late Roman sanctuary at Lydney Park (Gloucestershire) exemplifies this new wave of paganism: here a classically styled stone-built temple, set within the bounds of an Iron Age hillfort and ironworking site, was positioned to give magnificent views of the River Severn and its spectacular tidal bore (Wheeler and Wheeler 1932; see Smith 2006: 68–69 for an illustrated description of the bore in action). Inscriptions demonstrate that the presiding deity was a British healer/hunter god called Nodons, and devotees who visited the shrine left ex-votos in the form of dog statuettes, including a superbly naturalistic copper-alloy figurine of a young deerhound (Wheeler and Wheeler 1932: pl. 25) and a sheet metal plaque depicting a dog with a human face (Wheeler and Wheeler 1932: pl. 26, no. 119; Green 1997: fig. 7; Aldhouse-Green 2010: 248, fig. 77). There is some evidence for the presence of formal religious officials here: an inscribed mosaic laid on the floor of the inner sanctum reveals that one of them, Victorinus, was an 'Interpreter of Dreams' (Henig 1995: 120), a prophetic role that aligns with one of the principal responsibilities of the early Druids.

The sanctuary at Lydney was built within the confines of a much earlier site, perhaps because the place was already numinous. The same notion of sacred 'landscapes of memory'—the title of a Holocaust autobiographical narrative by Ruth Kluger (2004) —might also be present in the territory of the Iceni, at Thetford in Norfolk. Before the Boudican uprising in AD 60, a great wooden structure was erected at Fison Way, almost certainly intended as a place of assembly and, perhaps, religious ceremony (Gregory 1992). The great timber edifice resonates with the huge circular construction erected at Navan in Northern Ireland in 94 BC, almost certainly a ceremonial structure that was 'sacrificed' by being burnt down immediately after its erection (Lynn 1992). At the time of the rebellion, the Roman army systematically dismantled the Fison Way monument, probably to prevent its further use as a rallying point for freedom fighters or as a martyrs' memorial. But 300 years later, a hoard of precious metalwork was deliberately deposited immediately adjacent to the site of the early building. Among the objects interred here was a set of thirty-three silver spoons, many of them inscribed with the names of hitherto unrecorded local divinities, some twinned with the obscure Italian woodland deity Faunus (Johns and Potter 1983; Painter 1997). These spoons were intended for liturgical use, and would have been used formally to measure out libations or other offerings (Painter 1997; Aldhouse-Green 2004c: 216). The hoard also contained wine strainers, and one of the spoons was dedicated to Medugenus (Johns and Potter 1983: no. 54, fig. 27), whose name means 'mead-begotten': implicit in this title might be the trance state achieved by the imbibing of mind-altering substances and the ability to attain an out-of-body visionary state, perhaps analogous to the interpreter of dreams at Lydney.

From Polytheism to Monotheism: Christianity

In a sense Christianity could be perceived as irrelevant to a study of the European Iron Age. However, as a finale to this chapter, one or two issues are worthy of brief attention because the interface between polytheistic paganism and the monotheistic new faith was by no means clear-cut. When Christianity first took its place in the religious arena of the late western provinces of the Roman Empire, it was added to the melting pot of already well-established cults, and it was possible for individuals to espouse Christianity as well as to adhere to their old faiths and rituals. Material culture demonstrates this blurring of the edges. In 1975, a rich hoard of Constantinian Christian religious silver was discovered at Water Newton in Cambridgeshire (Painter 1977). The treasure almost certainly came from an early *ecclesia*, a formal church, and among the hidden church plate was a series of feather-shaped plaques adorned with gilded chi-rho symbols. The form of these Christian-inscribed sheets is important, for 'feather' or 'leaf' plaques were commonly offered as votive gifts by devotees worshipping in pagan temples (Toynbee 1978). It is likely that the very form of the Water Newton feather plaques was deliberately chosen to express Christian values (Painter 1977), in order to provide a bridge of understanding between old and new religions.

Conclusion: Keeping the Faith?

A single object, the disembodied stone head from Caerwent in south Wales, exemplifies the complex relationship between indigenous religion, Roman paganism, and Christianity in the later Roman Empire (Aldhouse-Green 2012). Furthermore, this particular piece also represents the tenacity of pre-Roman Iron Age religious expression. The human head (see Chapter 41) is an iconic motif in Iron Age European ritual and cosmology. Yet the Caerwent head comes from a shrine at the bottom of the garden belonging to a fourth-century Briton who may himself have been a Christian (Boon 1976; Brewer 1986: no. 53, pl. 20).[5] It has generally been interpreted as a pagan image, perhaps dedicated by a member of the house owner's staff. However, study of the stone statue of Mercury from Uley (Gloucestershire; Croxford 2003) opens up alternative interpretations for the Caerwent image. Early in the post-Roman period, the Uley statue was broken up and the head alone reverentially deposited in a pit on an early Christian site. Could it be that the Mercury head was 'recycled' as an image of Christ? Should the Caerwent head be seen as an expression of a 'retro' cult that harked back to the Iron Age or was it, like the Uley head, magnificently appropriated as a symbol of the new Christian religious movement? Looking to Ireland, barely touched by *romanitas*, it is perhaps significant that the great Christian traditions of imagery in metalwork, monumental crosses, and illuminated manuscripts included an emphasis on the human head (Green 1996: 156–157, 163, 166) that surely referenced a pagan Irish tradition that produced such objects as the disembodied stone heads from Corleck in Co. Cavan (Raftery 1994: 73–74).

It is hard to pin down 'formal' religion in the European Iron Age. Perhaps the best hope lies with the Druids, even with all the pitfalls associated with their interpretation. However, classical writers occasionally provide clues to the worship of divinities that can also be identified in material culture. Images are an important but ambiguous source: generally, the iconographic record is poor, but coins and—for Celtiberia—ceramics provide abundant material. The temptation to back-project from the Roman period into the more silent Iron Age needs to be resisted or, at least, used with restraint. One of the most interesting areas—as far as Britain is concerned—is the manner in which locally grown cults survived, and indeed flourished anew, more than three centuries after Roman annexation. It is even possible that early Christian symbolism became enmeshed in pagan traditions of expression. In any event, neither *romanitas* nor Christianity appear to have prevented the pulse of Iron Age religious traditions from continuing to power local belief systems until long after the European Iron Age had ceased to be.

Notes

1. Almost identical iconography appears at Trier in the Moselle valley (Schindler 1977: 32, fig. 91), although on the latter monument, Esus' name is absent.
2. Paul Sealey, pers. comm. Toutatis is represented also in northern Britain, for instance in Cumbria (possibly Old Carlisle: Collingwood and Wright 1965: no. 1017; Aldhouse-Green and Raybould 1999). The Kelvedon sherds are in the Castle Museum, Colchester. I am grateful to Dr Paul Sealey for giving me access and information.
3. 'They [the Germans] are distinguished by a common worship of Nerthus, or Mother Earth. They believe that she interests herself in human affairs and rides through their peoples. In an island of Ocean stands a sacred grove, and in the grove stands a car draped with a cloth which none but the priest may touch. The priest can feel the presence of the goddess in this holy of holies, and attends her, in deepest reverence, as her car is drawn by kine. Then follow days of rejoicing and merrymaking in every place that she honours with her advent and stay. No one goes to war, no one takes up arms; every object of iron is locked away; then, and then only, are peace and quiet known and prized, until the goddess is again restored to her temple … After that, the car, the cloth and, believe it if you will, the goddess herself are washed clean in a secluded lake. This service is performed by slaves who are immediately afterwards drowned in the lake' (Tacitus *Germania* 40; Mattingly 2006: 133–134).
4. Enchainment is a process in which objects are deliberately fragmented and distributed widely in order to maintain and reinforce bonding within and between groups of people (Chapman 2000).
5. The Christian affiliations of the houseowner have been suggested on the grounds of the 'Orphic' mosaic in the house.

References

Aldhouse-Green, M. J. 1999. *Pilgrims in Stone: Stone Images from the Gallo-Roman Healing Sanctuary of Fontes Sequanae*. British Archaeological Reports International Series 754. Oxford: Archaeopress.

Aldhouse-Green, M. J. 2001a. 'Animal iconographies: Metaphor, meaning and identity', in G. Davies, A. Gardner, and K. Lockyear (eds) *TRAC 2000: Proceedings of the Tenth Theoretical Roman Archaeology Conference, London, 2000*: 81–93. Oxford: Oxbow.

Aldhouse-Green, M. J. 2001b. *Dying for the Gods: Human Sacrifice in Iron Age and Roman Europe*. Stroud: Tempus.

Aldhouse-Green, M. J. 2002. 'Any old iron! Symbolism and ironworking in Iron Age Europe', in M. J. Aldhouse-Green and P. Webster (eds) *Artefacts and Archaeology: Aspects of the Celtic and Roman World*: 1–19. Cardiff: University of Wales Press.

Aldhouse-Green, M. J. 2004a. *An Archaeology of Images: Iconology and Cosmology in Iron Age and Roman Europe*. London: Routledge.

Aldhouse-Green, M. J. 2004b. 'Crowning glories: Languages of hair in later prehistoric Europe'. *Proceedings of the Prehistoric Society* 70: 291–325.

Aldhouse-Green, M. J. 2004c. 'Gallo-British deities and their shrines', in M. Todd (ed.) *A Companion to Roman Britain*: 191–219. Oxford: Blackwell.

Aldhouse-Green, M. J. 2010. *Caesar's Druids: Story of an Ancient Priesthood*. London/Newhaven: Yale University Press.

Aldhouse-Green, M. J. 2012. 'Singing stones: Contexting body-language in Romano-British iconography'. *Britannia* 43: 115–134.

Aldhouse-Green, M. J., and M. E. Raybould. 1999. 'Deities with Gallo-British names recorded in inscriptions from Roman Britain'. *Studia Celtica* 33: 91–135.

Almagro-Gorbea, M., and A. Lorrio Alvaredo. 2011. *Teutates: El Héroe Fundador*. Madrid: Real Academia de la Historia.

Boon, G. C. 1976. 'The shrine of the head, Caerwent', in G. C. Boon and J. M. Lewis (eds) *Welsh Antiquity*: 161–175. Cardiff: University of Wales Press.

Boon, G. C. 1982. 'A coin with the head of the Cernunnos'. *Seaby Coin and Medal Bulletin* 769: 271–282.

Bradley, R. 1990. *The Passage of Arms*. Cambridge: Cambridge University Press.

Brewer, R. 1986. *Corpus Signorum Imperii Romani, 1.5: Wales*. Oxford: Oxford University Press.

Chadwick, N. 1997. *The Druids*. Cardiff: University of Wales Press.

Chapman, J. 2000. *Fragmentation in Archaeology*. London: Routledge.

C.I.L. 1873. *Corpus Inscriptionum Latinarum, Vol. III*, ed. T. Mommsen. Berlin: Berlin-Brandenburgische Akademie der Wissenschaften.

Clément, M. 1986. 'Les dieux gaulois', in *Au Temps des Celtes Ve–Ier siècle avant J.-C.*: 131–143. Quimper: Musée Départemental Breton/Association Abbaye de Daoulas.

Collingwood, R. G., and R. P. Wright. 1965. *The Roman Inscriptions of Britain 1: Inscriptions on Stone*. Oxford: Clarendon Press.

Coulon, G. 2000. 'La survivance du druidisme à l'époque gallo-romaine', in V. Guichard and F. Perrin (eds) *Les Druides. L'Archéologue, Hors Série* 2: 51–55. Paris: Errance.

Croxford, B. 2003. 'Iconoclasm in Roman Britain?' *Britannia* 34: 81–95.

Cunliffe, B. W. 1988. *The Temple of Sulis Minerva at Bath. Vol. 2: The Finds from the Sacred Spring*. OUCA Monograph 16. Oxford: Oxford University Committee for Archaeology.

Cunliffe, B. W., and P. Davenport. 1985. *The Temple of Sulis Minerva at Bath. Vol. 1: The Site.* OUCA Monograph 7. Oxford: Oxford University Committee for Archaeology.

Daire, M.-Y., and L. Langouet. 1992. 'Une sculpture anthropomorphe gauloise dans un enclos à Yvignac (Côte d'Armor)'. *Les Dossiers du Ce.R.A.A.* 20: 1–16.

De Bernardo Stempel, P. 2008. 'The "old" Celtic goddess Sena: A new testimony from Aquitania'. *Veleia* 21–25: 1201–1206.

De Nie, G. 1987. *Views from a Many-Windowed Tower: Studies of Imagination in the Works of Gregory of Tours*. Amsterdam: Rodopi.

De Vries, J. 1963. *La Religion des Celtes*. Paris: Payot.

Deyts, S. 1983. *Les Bois Sculptés des Sources de la Seine*. Gallia supplément 13. Paris: Centre national de la recherche scientifique.

Deyts, S. 1994. *Un peuple de pèlerins: Offrandes de pierre et de bronze des sources de la Seine*. Revue Archéologique de l'Est et du Centre-Est supplément 13. Dijon: Revue archéologique de l'Est.

Duval, P.-M. 1987. *Monnaies gauloises et mythes celtiques*. Paris: Hermann.

Espérandieu, E. 1908. *Recueil général des bas-reliefs, statues et bustes de la Gaule romaine, Vol. 2*. Paris: Imprimerie Nationale/Ernest Leroux.

Espérandieu, E. 1910. *Recueil général des bas-reliefs, statues et bustes de la Gaule romaine, Vol. 3*. Paris: Imprimerie Nationale/Ernest Leroux.

Espérandieu, E. 1911. *Recueil général des bas-reliefs, statues et bustes de la Gaule romaine, Vol. 4*. Paris: Imprimerie Nationale/Ernest Leroux.

Espérandieu, E. 1913. *Recueil général des bas-reliefs, statues et bustes de la Gaule romaine, Vol. 5*. Paris: Imprimerie Nationale/Ernest Leroux.

Espérandieu, E. 1915. *Recueil général des bas-reliefs, statues et bustes de la Gaule romaine, Vol. 6*. Paris: Imprimerie Nationale/Ernest Leroux.

Espérandieu, E. 1925. *Recueil général des bas-reliefs, statues et bustes de la Gaule romaine, Vol. 9*. Paris: Imprimerie Nationale/Ernest Leroux.

Field, N., and M. Parker Pearson. 2003. *Fiskerton: An Iron Age Timber Causeway with Iron Age and Roman Votive Offerings*. Oxford: Oxbow.

Gordon, R., D. Joly, and W. van Andringa. 2010. 'A prayer for blessings on three ritual objects discovered at Chartres Autricum (France/Eure et Loir)', in R. Gordon and F. Marco Simón (eds) *Magical Practice in the Latin West: Papers from the International Conference held at the University of Zaragoza 2005*: 481–518. Leiden: Brill.

Goudineau, C. 2003. 'Le gutuater gaulois. Idéologie et histoire'. *Gallia* 60: 381–387.

Graves, R. 1956. *Lucan. Pharsalia: Dramatic Episodes of the Civil Wars*. Harmondsworth: Penguin.

Green, M. J. 1982. 'Tanaris, Taranis and the Chester altar'. *Journal of the Chester Archaeological Society* 65: 31–44.

Green, M. J. 1984. *The Wheel as a Cult-Symbol in the Romano-Celtic World*. Collection Latomus 83. Brussels: Éditions Latomus.

Green, M. J. 1989. *Symbol and Image in Celtic Religious Art*. London: Routledge.

Green, M. J. 1996. *Celtic Art: Reading the Messages*. London: Weidenfeld and Nicolson.

Green, M. J. 1997. 'Images in opposition: Polarity, ambivalence and liminality in cult-representation'. *Antiquity* 71: 891–911.

Green, M. J. 1998. 'Vessels of death: Sacred cauldrons in archaeology and myth'. *Antiquaries Journal* 78: 61–84.

Gregory, T. 1992. *Excavations at Thetford, 1980–1982: Fison Way*. East Anglian Archaeological Report 53. Norwich: Norfolk Field Archaeology Division.

Henig, M. 1993. *Corpus Signorum Imperii Romani. Great Britain 1.7: Roman Sculptures from the Cotswold Region*. London/Oxford: British Academy/Oxford University Press.

Henig, M. 1995. *The Art of Roman Britain*. London: Batsford.

Herbert, E. W. 1993. *Iron, Gender and Power: Rituals of Transformation in African Societies*. Bloomington, IN: Indiana University Press.

Hingley, R. 1997. 'Iron, ironworking and regeneration: A study of the symbolic meaning of metalworking in Iron Age Britain', in A. Gwilt and C. Haselgrove (eds) *Reconstructing Iron Age Societies*: 1–18. Oxford: Oxbow.

Joffroy, R. 1979. *Musée des Antiquités Nationales, Saint-Germain-en-Laye*. Paris: Éditions de la Réunion des Musées Nationaux.

Johns, C., and T. Potter. 1983. *The Thetford Treasure*. London: British Museum Press.

Joly, D., W. van Andringa, and S. Willerval. 2010. 'L'attirail d'un magicien rangé dans un cave de Chartres (Autricum)'. *Gallia* 67, 2: 121–208.

Kaul, F. 1991. *Gundstrup Kedelen*. Copenhagen: Nationalmuseet.

Kimmig, W. 1987. 'Eisenzeitliche Grabstelen in Mitteleuropa'. *Fundberichte aus Baden-Württemberg* 12: 251–297.

Kluger, R. 2004. *Landscapes of Memory: A Holocaust Girlhood Remembered*. London: Bloomsbury Press.

Le Bohec, Y. 2005. 'Le clergé celtique et la guerre des Gaules historiographique et politique'. *Latomus: Revue d'études Latines* 64, 4: 871–881.

Lorrio, A. J. 1997. *Los Celtibéros*. Madrid/Alicante: Universidad de Alicante/Universidad Complutense de Madrid.

Lynn, C. 1992. 'The Iron Age mound in Navan Fort: A physical realization of Celtic religious beliefs?' *Emania* 10: 31–57.

Macdonald, P. 2007. *Llyn Cerrig Bach: A Study of the Copper Alloy Artefacts from the Insular La Tène Assemblage*. Cardiff: University of Wales Press.

Magnen, R., and É. Thévenot. 1953. *Epona*. Bordeaux: Delmas.

Manning, W. H. 1972. 'Iron work hoards in Iron Age and Roman Britain'. *Britannia* 3: 221–250.

Marco Simón, F. 2007. 'A lost identity: Celtiberian iconography after the Roman conquest', in R. Haeussler and A. C. King (eds) *Continuity and Innovation in Religion in the Roman West*. Journal of Roman Archaeology Supplementary Series 67: 101–115. Portsmouth, RI: Journal of Roman Archaeology.

Marco Simón, F. 2010. 'Dioses espacios sacros y sacerdotes', in F. Burillo Mozota (ed.) *VI Simposio sobre Celtiberos: Ritos y Mitos*: 11–25. Segeda: Fundación Segeda Centro Celtibérico.

Martínez, A. J. 1999. 'Religión y Ritual Funerario Celtibéricos'. *Revista de Soria* 25: 1–18.

Mattingly, D. 2006. *An Imperial Possession: Britain in the Roman Empire*. London: Allen Lane.

Mattingly, H. 1948. *Tacitus: On Britain and Germany*. Harmondsworth: Penguin.

Megaw, R., and V. Megaw. 1989. *Celtic Art: From its Beginnings to the Book of Kells*. London: Thames and Hudson.

Painter, K. S. 1977. *The Water Newton Early Christian Silver*. London: British Museum.

Painter, K. S. 1997. 'Silver hoards from Britain in their late Roman context'. *L'Antiquité Tardive* 5: 91–110.

Perrier, J. 1960. 'L'autel de Thauron (Creuse)'. *Gallia* 18: 191–197.

Priuli, A. 1988. *Incisioni rupestri della Val Camonica: Quaderni di Cultura Alpina*. Turin: Collana.

Priuli, A. 1996. *Le più antiche manifestazioni spirituali: arte rupestre: paleoiconografia camuna e delle genti alpine*. Ivrea: Priuli & Verlucca.

Raftery, B. 1994. *Pagan Celtic Ireland*. London: Thames and Hudson.

Ross, A. 1967. *Pagan Celtic Britain*. London: Routledge and Kegan Paul.

Schindler, R. 1977. *Führer durch des Landesmuseum Trier*. Trier: Rheinisches Landesmuseum.

Smith, K. T. 2006. *Guides, Guards and Gifts to the Gods: Domesticated Dogs in the Art and Archaeology of Iron Age and Roman Britain*. British Archaeological Reports British Series 422. Oxford: Archaeopress.

Spielmann, K., J. L. Mobley-Tanaka, and J. M. Potter. 2006. 'Style and resistance in the seventeenth-century Salinas province'. *American Antiquity* 71, 4: 621–647.

Toynbee, J. M. C. 1978. 'A Londinium votive leaf or feather and its fellows', in J. Bird, H. Chapman, and J. Clark (eds) *Collectanea Londinensia: Studies in London Archaeology and History presented to Ralph Merrifield*: 121–148. London: London and Middlesex Archaeological Society.

Tranoy, A. 1988. 'Du héros au chef: l'image du guerrier dans les societés indigènes du nord-ouest de la péninsule ibérique (IIe siècle avant J.-C.–Ier siècle après J.-C.)', in *Le Monde des Images en Gaule et dans les Provinces Voisines: Actes du Colloque 11–17 mai 1987, Université de Tours*. Caesarodunum 23: 211–228. Paris: Errance.

Van der Sanden, W. 1996. *Through Nature to Eternity: The Bog Bodies of Northwest Europe*. Amsterdam: Batavian Lion International.

Venclová, N. 2002. 'The Venerable Bede, druidic tonsure and archaeology'. *Antiquity* 76: 451–471.

Von Petrikovits, H. 1987. 'Matronen und verwandte Gottheiten. Zusammenfassende Bemerkungen', in G. Neumann and G. Bauchhenss (eds) *Matronen und verwandte Gottheiten: Ergebnisse eines Kolloquiums veranstaltet von der Göttinger Akademiekommission für die Altertumskunde Mittel- und Nordeuropas*. Beihefte der Bonner Jahrbücher 44: 241–254. Cologne: Rheinland-Verlag.

Webster, J. 1995. 'Interpretatio: Roman word power and the Celtic Gods'. *Britannia* 26: 151–161.

Wheeler, R. E. M., and T. V. Wheeler. 1932. *Report on the Excavation of the Prehistoric, Roman and Post-Roman Site in Lydney Park, Gloucestershire*. Reports of the Research Committee of the Society of Antiquaries of London 9. Oxford: Society of Antiquaries.

Woolf, G. 1998. *Becoming Roman: The Origins of Provincial Civilization in Gaul*. Cambridge: Cambridge University Press.

Wright, R. P., and E. J. Phillips. 1975. *Roman Inscribed and Sculptured Stones in Carlisle Museum*. Carlisle: Tullie House Museum.

CHAPTER 43

ART ON THE NORTHERN EDGE OF THE MEDITERRANEAN WORLD

MARTIN GUGGISBERG

INTRODUCTION

THE need to express wealth and power grew as hierarchically structured societies led by the aristocracy developed in Iron Age Europe. Artfully ornamented and skilfully made artefacts of high value of all sorts—primarily those of the male warrior world, but also the dress ornaments of women—became essential signals of social status and identity. Prestigious luxury goods from far afield reached the indigenous world in increasing quantities over an ever more complex network of foreign contacts. They acted as a stimulus for the emulation of technologies and confrontation of different forms of artistic expression. The result was artistic creative processes in different regions of Europe, in which local traditions were combined with foreign impulses into new, independent forms of style, which from today's perspective are often assigned eponymous labels, such as the art of the Celts, the Thracians, the Scythians, and the Iberians. However, more often than not, we lose sight of the fact that the creators of this art in no way belonged to an ethnically homogeneous group and that the styles themselves are internally more heterogeneous and diverse than they appear at first sight.

Consequently, the term 'art of the European Iron Age' is deliberately defined here in broad terms. In this chapter, we shall try to characterize the nature of this art and explore both the differences and common traits of the various Iron Age styles against the background of their confrontation with the Mediterranean and Eurasian–Near Eastern world. The main focus is on Celtic art, in which indigenous traditions quintessentially meld with influences from Greek–Etruscan and Near Eastern art. The intention is not so much to recount by phase and style a 'history of Celtic art', but rather to launch a debate into overarching questions about the specific character of Celtic artistic creation as well as that of other European Iron Age cultures.

What is art anyway? What specific stylistic features determined the appearance of Celtic art and parallel phenomena in Iron Age Europe? What social and religious content is at the root of the representations? It goes without saying that there are no definitive answers to these questions. Nevertheless, they open important perspectives on the conceptual foundations of the processes of artistic creation that have so significantly marked the Iron Age cultures of Europe.

Approaching Art, Artists, and Artisans

Anyone who engages with European Iron Age art has immediately to grapple with the question of defining the concept and its applicability to the evidence of past material culture that has survived (Müller 2009: 24–29; 2012a: 14–20; Guggisberg and Hoppe 2012). Art, as an intellectual and creative force, is a universal form of human expression. Accordingly it is firmly embedded in the social and ideological parameters of the community that generates it. In Europe, the idea that artistic creation should be set free from its social and religious straitjacket to become an independent force was first put forward in the Enlightenment. In antiquity, and especially during the European Iron Age, art did not subscribe to this form of free artistic expression. As a rule art was related to purpose: it served to imbue artefacts and monuments with a higher ideological meaning, which was used in daily life or on particular social, political, and religious occasions. Thus the passage from art to craft is fluid.

What Iron Age art meant in the eyes of the population is difficult to fathom in the absence of written sources. Greek and Roman societies had the concept of τεχνη and *ars*, which encompassed a wide range of creative activities from mundane crafts, via iconographic and poetic rendering, to genial inventions (Philipp 1968, 1990; Burford 1985). The artist and artisan (τεχνίτης, *artifex*) of antiquity was characterized in the first place by perfect mastery of his or her craft. This could be measured either by the skilful handling of materials and techniques, or by the accuracy and naturalism of the images represented. Works of art that fulfilled those conditions were admired and marvelled at, and their creators praised. It seems not unreasonable to assume that similar ideas prevailed in Europe beyond the Mediterranean. In any case, here too art is defined time and again by the highest level of technical and formal refinement. However, naturalism—the canon of Graeco-Roman art—is not sought, at least not in the sense of a lifelike organic design. Instead, abstraction and stylization occupy the centre ground, a means of expression that to all intents and purposes can encompass a comparable intrinsic content: so, for example, it seems appropriate to see in the distinctive dynamism of Celtic and also Scythian art the artistic expression of the power and richness of nature, just as it exists behind the naturalistic representations of Greek and Roman art.

Little is known about the social status of indigenous artists and their relationship with those who commissioned the work. But a look at the relationships that existed in the Mediterranean world can offer some clues. There it is generally assumed that artists worked to order in the majority of cases, though no written contracts survive. The famous story of Archimedes, who had to test the weight in gold of a royal commission for a crown, can however serve as an example of contract work. Hieron, the ruler of Syracuse, had given the goldsmith not only the contract to make the crown, but had also provided the necessary quantity of raw material, i.e. gold (Vitruvius *de Architectura* IX.9; Plutarch *Moralia* 1094C). In another well-known case, King Minos of Crete imprisoned his 'star artist' Daedalus in his palace to prevent him from working for other patrons (Ovid *Metamorphoses* 8). In the archaeological record, such contract activity is evidenced by the products of Greek goldsmiths and other artists who worked for the Scythian aristocracy in the Black Sea region (Schiltz 1994: 131–179, esp. 133; Dally 2007).

The artisans and artists' status as βάναυσοι (*banausoi*) in the Greek and Roman world was on the lower rung of the social scale (Himmelmann 1983). Although they liked to sign their work, and in the fifth century BC proudly represented themselves in vase painting and other artistic monuments, few managed to rise permanently on the social ladder. The god of smiths, Hephaistos—the only one of the twelve Olympian gods to be disabled and defined as an outsider in the community of gods—stands as an example of the status of artists and artisans.

The conditions of the Graeco-Roman world obviously cannot be transferred wholesale to the indigenous populations of Europe. Nevertheless it seems very likely that the great demand for high-value artistic and artisan products, as can be assumed and is partly documented in the vicinity of the aristocratic power centres of central Europe and Eurasia, was similarly met by subordinate specialists under contract.

Art of the Hallstatt and La Tène Periods

Paul Jacobsthal sets the beginning of Celtic art at the onset of the La Tène period in the early fifth century BC in his seminal work on *Early Celtic Art* published in 1944. He simply ascribes the status of 'source' to the previous Hallstatt culture, from which early Celtic art drew part of its artistic character. Research is only gradually beginning to free itself from this view and take notice of the art of the Hallstatt period in its own original and creative right (Reichenberger 1995; Müller 2009: 67–73, 2012a: 24–31; Hoppe and Schorer 2012).

The Geometric Style of the Hallstatt Culture

The Hallstatt culture almost exclusively uses geometric motifs in the shape of zigzag bands, lozenges, triangles, crosses, circles, and more, which are combined in a sort of *horror vacui* on surfaces carpeted in motifs. The geometric ornamental style—which, with a certain time lag, is associated with comparable early Iron Age elements in Greece and Italy—reached a first heyday in the so-called Alb-Hegau pottery of the eighth and seventh centuries BC, attested primarily in southern Germany and the neighbouring regions of Switzerland and Alsace (Figure 43.1). It consists of handmade pottery made specifically for funerary purposes, which stands out not only for the richness of its decoration but also for its polychromy and eccentric vessel shapes, among which figure the so-called stepped plates (*Stufenteller*). There are hardly any links with the south, but the stamping technique used for part of the ornamentation, as well as the polychromy, suggest at least indirect exchange with the Iron Age pottery of northern Italy. The same canon of geometric patterns appears on metalwork, particularly on belt plates and barrel-shaped armlets (*Tonnenarmbänder*), as well as textiles.

In the sixth century BC, the repertoire is defined by quadrangular patterns which are combined to cover entire surfaces. Felix Müller has recently suggested that the division of the surface into quadrangular fields can be traced back to textile art (Müller 2012a: 27–28). The preference for such decoration on bronze belt plates and arm-rings thus finds a plausible explanation in the rendering in metal of wristbands and belts made of cloth, a hypothesis supported by the few surviving remains of textiles, such as those from the Hochdorf burial in south-west Germany (Banck-Burgess 1999; Chapter 26). However, attributing the preference for geometric ornament solely to technological parameters

FIGURE 43.1 Stepped plate (*Stufenteller*) of Alb-Hegau ware from Gomadingen-Sternberg, south-west Germany, seventh century BC. Diameter 550 mm.

Photo: P. Frankenstein, H. Zwietasch, courtesy of Landesmuseum Württemberg, Stuttgart is surely too simplistic. More probably the geometric, abstract art of the Hallstatt period reveals an overarching cultural world view, which endures in altered form into the La Tène period. Patterns and surface-covering decoration continued to be much appreciated in the art of the fifth and fourth centuries BC.

The art of the Hallstatt period is characterized by an almost total lack of human and animal representation. Only in late Hallstatt times do the first figurative representations appear, under the growing influence of the south. Horses, deer, and simple human stick figures, whose gender is more often than not unidentifiable, are preferred. The repertoire is a little more extensive in the eastern Hallstatt sphere, which had been exposed to earlier and stronger southern influences than the west (Nebelsick 1992; Reichenberger 1995). The famous model of a wagon from Strettweg (Egg 1996) can be taken as representative of other works; it features a naked female figure, probably a goddess, holding a cauldron aloft. She is accompanied by a procession of male and female figures on horseback and on foot leading a deer to be sacrificed, the whole arranged in mirror-image fashion. Without going into the meaning of the representation here, this wagon model of the late seventh century BC makes two points clear: on the one hand, there was a close link with the anthropomorphic art of northern Italy, and on the other there was a concern to create an iconographic composition of narrative character. Both elements appear elsewhere in the eastern Hallstatt world, whereas in the western part figurative representation appears only later; images with multiple figures are almost entirely absent.

Lack of contact with the Mediterranean world can only be held responsible to a limited extent for this persistence in representing a geometric cosmos, since imports bearing figurative representations from Etruria and other regions of Italy, and perhaps even Greece, appear as early as the seventh century BC in central Europe. An example is the *pyxis* (a cylindrical vessel) from Appenwihr in Alsace, decorated with lion or sphinx figures in relief, for which recent research suggests an origin in Vetulonia (Jehl and Bonnet 1968; Camporeale 2009). It is more likely that a conscious aversion to the narrative, figurative art of the south, or—to put it more positively—a particular predilection for traditional forms of artistic expression, was a factor in this preference.

Responses to southern stimuli increased in the late Hallstatt period. Besides the two Mediterranean lions on its rim, the large bronze cauldron from Hochdorf features a third similar animal figure, which was probably created north of the Alps (Figure 43.2; Bieg 2002). The stylistic confidence with which the artist reproduced an animal that he or she could not have known in real life is striking. Although the stylization does not yet presage the dynamism of the later art of the early La Tène period, creations like lion no. 3 from Hochdorf suggest that the artistic conditions for the subsequent development of La Tène art were already taking shape in the second half of the sixth century BC (Fischer 1984; Kimmig 1988: 277–278). The new early La Tène style makes its entrance about half a century later, in works that are still firmly anchored in the Hallstatt culture. In this context, mention must be made of the famous gold torc from Vix in Burgundy, whose smooth back swells to a spherical shape (Rolley 2003: 170–188, pl. 13), and the two silver-plated bronze bracelets from Unterlunkhofen in Switzerland whose gold-plated catches

FIGURE 43.2 The lion figures from the Hochdorf cauldron. Lengths 337–344 mm.
Photo: courtesy of Landesmuseum Württemberg, Stuttgart

are ornamented with a highly stylized ribbon of lotus flowers over a pattern of simple St Andrew's crosses (Berger 1999: 232, fig. 106.1; Müller 2012a: 38–39). The petals end in dots which bear a close relationship to the circular motifs of slightly later creations of La Tène art. Remarkably, the find-spots of both these creations lie outside the region where early La Tène art flourished only slightly later, in the area of the middle Rhine and Marne.

How exactly the geographical origin of La Tène art is to be envisaged, and how the traditional centres of Hallstatt culture in south-west Germany were transposed to the middle Rhine region, is still the subject of much debate (Steffen 2012). Ultimately, what profound cultural and possibly also religious changes were responsible for the emergence of La Tène art and its rapid spread over large parts of Europe is just as uncertain.

Art of the La Tène Period

A radical change in the artistic forms of expression of the Celts took place in the early fifth century BC with the passage from the Hallstatt to the La Tène culture. In place of the persistent geometric configurations, dynamically structured images began to emerge, with a much-modified basis in vegetal, human, and animal motifs.

The Early Style

Since Paul Jacobstahl's seminal study (1944: 155), the triple origin of the Early style has gained acceptance: a fertile combination of the traditional Hallstatt formal repertoire and stimuli from the Mediterranean world and the Near East. The crucial aspect is that the process of reception was not limited merely to adopting foreign iconographic motifs, but gave rise to artistic fusion and a creative development of different traditions. The resultant style is defined by transformation and abstraction, rhythm and movement, but also symmetry and paratactic repetition. This creative process is best illustrated by comparing the handle attachment of the bronze beaked flagon (*Schnabelkanne*) from Kleinaspergle (Baden-Württemberg) with the attachments of an Etruscan *stamnos* (bucket) found in the same grave (Figure 43.3; see Kimmig 1988: 87–103, fig. 22, pls 1–9 for the *Schnabelkanne* and 104–106, fig. 30, pls 10–17 for the *stamnos*; Röber et al. 2012: 97–98). The Celtic artist reproduced the bearded Silenus heads of the Etruscan vessel in the smallest detail, but not as a whole, dissecting them instead into individual parts. So the ears become horns, the moustaches are transformed into mutton chops, and the lower lip turns into a bulbous chin. But the most ingenious transformation is the way the artist has treated the ivy leaf framing of the attachment. It is a palmette-shaped creation under the chin of the demon creature, made out of overlapping leaves which are stacked in multiple layers, to evoke sometimes a beard and at other times a vegetal motif. The companion of the classical god of wine Dionysos has been turned into a fantastical composite being of Celtic countenance, such as populate the art of the early La Tène period in ever-changing variations.

Celtic artists constantly subvert the mental map of people trained in classical Greek art. Human and animal figures are broken into their individual components and then reassembled. The complexity of the artistic message in ornament, which in many instances covers the entire surface of vessels and implements like a carpet, is particularly marked. The openwork gold foil from Schwarzenbach (Germany), which probably once decorated the mouth of a drinking horn, serves as an example (Figure 43.4). Depending on how one looks at it, the negative (i.e. the cut-out zones) or the filled-in components combine into vegetal ornaments. Individual palmette or flower elements borrowed from Mediterranean art are immediately recognizable. The ornament, however, eschews a clear reading *à la grecque*.

Despite its vegetal composition, the careful construction of the Schwarzenbach ornamental band can be recognized at first sight (Frey 2007: fig. 20). It is based on a compass-drawn circle, which significantly shaped the appearance of the Early style and later developed into an artistic climax, especially in the British Isles.

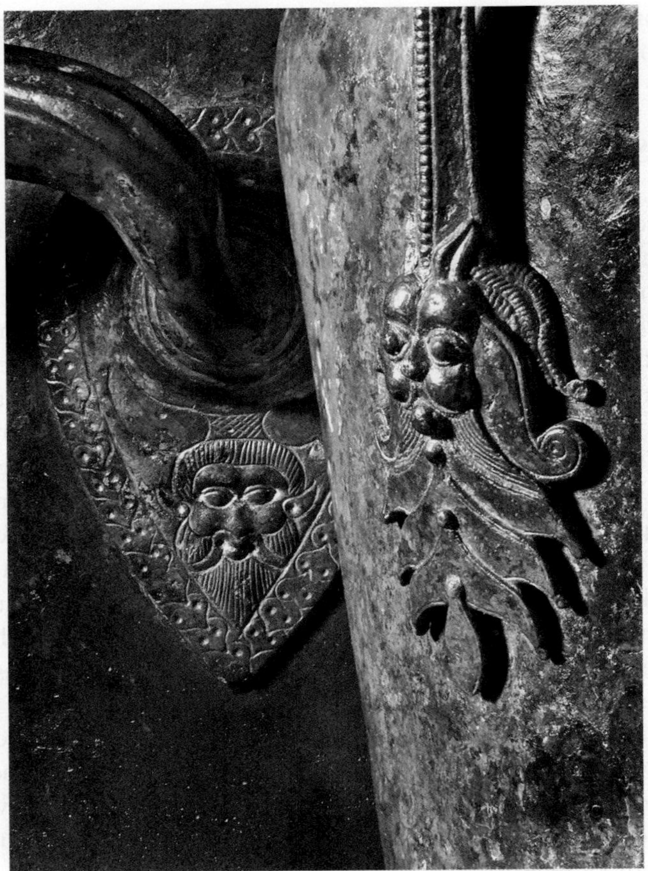

FIGURE 43.3 Handle attachment of the beaked flagon (*Schnabelkanne*) and *stamnos* from Kleinaspergle, south-west Germany.

Photo: P. Frankenstein, H. Zwietasch, courtesy of Landesmuseum Württemberg, Stuttgart

The Waldalgesheim Style

La Tène art opens up to new currents in the age of the historically documented Celtic migrations of the fourth century BC. It is characterized by a predominantly vegetal style, named after the princely burial in Rheinland-Pfalz shaping the research agenda of Celtic art (Joachim 1995; Müller 2012a: 52–62, 2012b). The focus of the so-called Waldalgesheim style is formed by the wavy scroll, a pattern based on the Mediterranean vine scroll, which once again distinguishes itself markedly from its Mediterranean counterparts through the prism of abstraction. While in principle the Mediterranean scroll grows continuously in one direction, its Celtic counterpart is characterized by the fact that each advancing wavy curve gives rise to a tendril in a contrary direction,

FIGURE 43.4 Gold openwork mount from Schwarzenbach, Saarland, Germany, probably from a drinking horn. Diameter 126 mm.

Photo: bpk/Johannes Laurentius, courtesy of Antikensammlung, Staatliche Museen zu Berlin

which interrupts the flow. The result is a turbulent, but at the same time very dynamic, configuration, which reveals itself as a consecutive scroll only on closer inspection. The goldsmiths who created the annular jewellery of the Waldalgesheim burial heightened the artistic appeal of their creations further by coiling the irregular wavy scroll in three dimensions around the body of the rings (Figure 43.5). Only by turning and moving the objects can the observer fully appreciate the intricate design of the ornamentation.

The questions of the origin of the new style and what led to its genesis cannot yet be answered with certainty. However it is clear that the old La Tène A centres on the middle Rhine and in the Marne region played only a marginal role in the development of the new style. The Waldalgesheim burial stands alone as a last representative of the early La Tène custom of prestige burials in a cultural landscape which was only peripherally involved in the process of Celtic expansion to the south and east (Frey 1976, 1995: 203–206), where the new centres of power were located. The idea that the lively Waldalgesheim style, if anything, owes its origin to Celtic migrants to Italy does not seem too fanciful, given that some of the most significant creations of the new style belong to the area of settlement of the Senones and Boii in northern Italy: the torc and weapon decorations of Filottrano near Ancona, or the metal appliqués of Comacchio near Spina.

FIGURE 43.5 The torc from Waldalgesheim, Rheinland-Pfalz, Germany: detail of terminal decorated with a palmette and tendrils. Diameter of neck-ring 211 mm.

Photo: J. Vogel, courtesy of Rheinisches Landesmuseum, Bonn

The Plastic Style

Increased contacts with the city-based cultures of the Mediterranean world brought about by the southward and eastward expansion of the Celts had a significant influence on the appearance of Celtic art. It does not seem unreasonable to assume that the third style defined by Paul Jacobsthal, the so-called Plastic style, also owes its expansive, three-dimensional character to contact with the Mediterranean world, especially the Hellenistic sphere. The Plastic style is characterized by the translation of the traditional repertoire of patterns into three dimensions (Müller 2009: 108–110, 220 cat. no. 20, 2012b: 62–66; Megaw 2012a, 2012b). Scrolls and spirals are turned into baroque shapes, which are transformed into grotesque human faces, depending on the angle and field of view. The five bronze terrets or rein guides from the chariot burial of Mezek in Bulgaria serve as an example: their plastic circular eyes suddenly become a human face with a pointy nose. Of note too is a bronze knob with exuberant scroll decoration (Figure 43.6), thought to have originated in Hungary and which was only recognized by accident as a Celtic artefact, published recently by Felix Müller (2011). These artefacts show that Celtic art—in contrast to that of the Mediterranean world—was still primarily an applied art in the third century BC, exhibiting a preference for ornamenting artefacts in daily use. Linchpins and other vehicle components played a privileged role as carriers of artistic expression from the Hallstatt period onwards, suggesting that, apart from prestige, such artistic ornamentation also carried apotropaic meaning.

Finds of artefacts executed in the Plastic style are concentrated in eastern Europe, leading to the assumption that the carriers of this style were the eastern Celts, who came into close contact with the Hellenistic world in the third century BC during their raids and in mercenary service (Chapter 37). But let us remember that masterpieces of the Plastic style survive in the west too, in the Paris basin as well as in Languedoc and Ireland. As in the previous phases, Celtic art of the third century BC is linked with an elite, which was highly mobile and widely connected.

FIGURE 43.6 Bronze knob in Plastic style. Diameter 35 mm. Private collection.

Photo: Yvonne Hurni, courtesy of Bern Historical Museum

The 'Sword Styles'

The same applies to the so-called 'Sword styles', which developed in parallel with the Plastic style in various areas of the Celtic *koine* (Lejars 2012; Müller 2012b: 66–68, 2009: 111–113). Fantastical scrollwork, which evolves primarily on surfaces in linear fashion, is characteristic of the 'Sword styles'. Sword scabbards and spearheads are especially well represented as carriers of this style, the iron scabbard from Cernon-sur-Coole in Champagne being a remarkable example (Megaw 1973; Duval and Kruta 1986; Müller 2009: 216 cat. no. 18): the back is decorated with a fantastical mythical creature, whose narrow head with long, tightly curled beak, upright comb, and beard immediately strike the observer (Figure 43.7). Its body is transformed into an S-shape ending in a network of small spirals. The Cernon-sur-Coole creature is closely paralleled on a scabbard from Drňa in Slovakia. For this reason, but also because stylistically related artefacts of the so-called 'Hungarian sword style' are concentrated in the Transdanubian area, it was long assumed that the Cernon-sur-Coole sword was an eastern import.

Recently it has become apparent that the number of weapons decorated in the 'Hungarian sword style' is considerably larger in the west than previously thought, the uneven distribution being primarily due to differences in research emphasis and in the source material. The highly mobile Celtic warrior groups could just as easily be responsible for the pan-European distribution of the new style and its regional variants at the turn of the fourth to third centuries BC as close contacts and supra-regional links between Celtic elites. The 'Hungarian sword style' is characterized by the asymmetry that nearly always underpins the patterns. This distinguishes it from other groups which feature greater symmetry in their decoration, such as the scabbards ornamented with pairs of birds or griffins arranged in mirror-image fashion. They resemble closely the composition of early La Tène belt hooks, and are often interpreted as a symbol of salvation or protection among Celtic warriors (for example Stöllner 2010: 302). Further regional Sword style groups are also present in Switzerland, Britain, and Ireland.

Later La Tène Art

The creative energy and innovative spirit of La Tène art gradually loses ground with the advance of the Romans into the Po plain and southern France during the course of the second century BC, particularly with regard to metalwork. Precious weapons and dress accessories continued to be made and were sometimes ornamented with exclusive designs, but overarching formal criteria, which would make it possible to define a 'style', are only peripherally discernible. Accordingly, the notion of style is hardly ever used for the late period. An increase in human and animal representations is noticeable and can only be interpreted as a response to Mediterranean art. The wooden sculptures of Fellbach-Schmiden (Baden-Württemberg), with a dendrochronological date of *c.*127

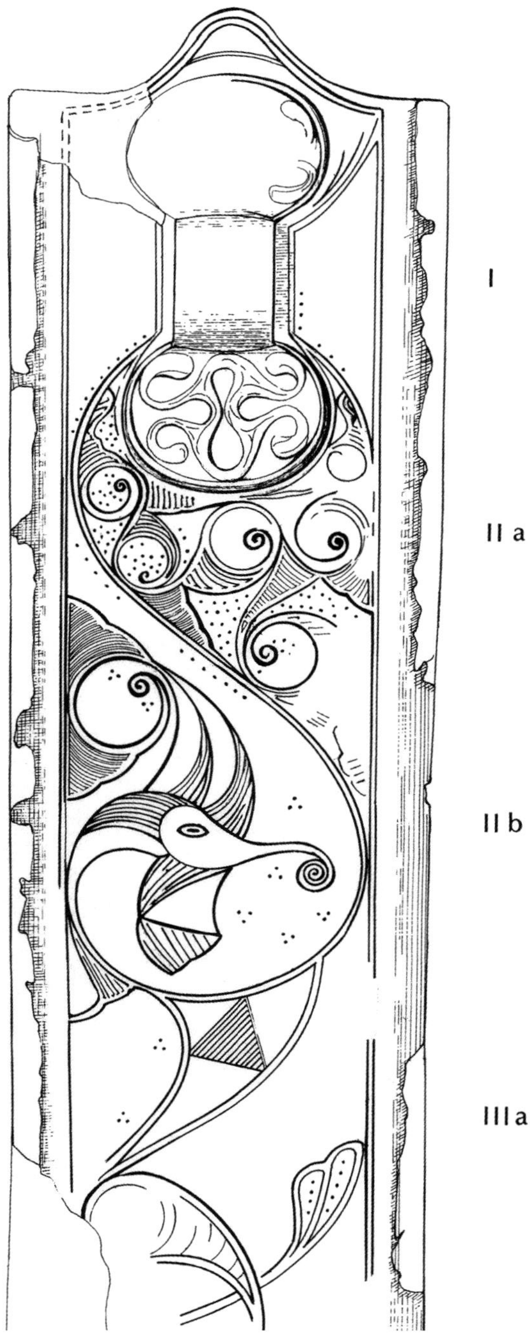

FIGURE 43.7 Scabbard from Cernon-sur-Coole, Marne, France. Length 620 mm

After Duval and Kruta 1986: fig. 20

BC (Planck 1985; Müller 2009: 238–240, cat. no. 28), represent a high point (Figure 43.8). Two billy goats flank a now missing human figure, reprising the old motif of the Master or Mistress of Animals. The third animal, a stag standing upright, may have belonged—together with a lost counterpart—to a similar group. The original function of the wooden sculptures is unknown. The long, narrow proportions and the huge eyes, ears, and horns define the appearance of these animals, their abstraction calling to mind works of the early La Tène period such as the rams on the Rodenbach bracelet.

The animal representations on late La Tène ceramics in central France (Müller 2009: 234–237, cat. no. 27) also bear witness to the continued vitality of Celtic stylization and capacity for abstraction. A quadruped with a beaked head and enormous ears or outspread antlers, executed in stylistically confident curving lines painted on a white background, takes centre stage in most representations (Figure 43.9). The background is hatched, and the antlers are sometimes stylized into a self-contained ornament of typically La Tène character. Here too there are references back to the ornamentation of earlier times, such as the fan-shaped antlers of the impressive quadruped from one of the vessels from Rue Elisée-Reclus, Clermont-Ferrand, which is reminiscent of a human face.

FIGURE 43.8 Wooden figure from Fellbach-Schmiden, south-west Germany, detail. Height 770 mm.

Photo: P. Frankenstein, H. Zwietasch, courtesy of Landesmuseum Württemberg, Stuttgart

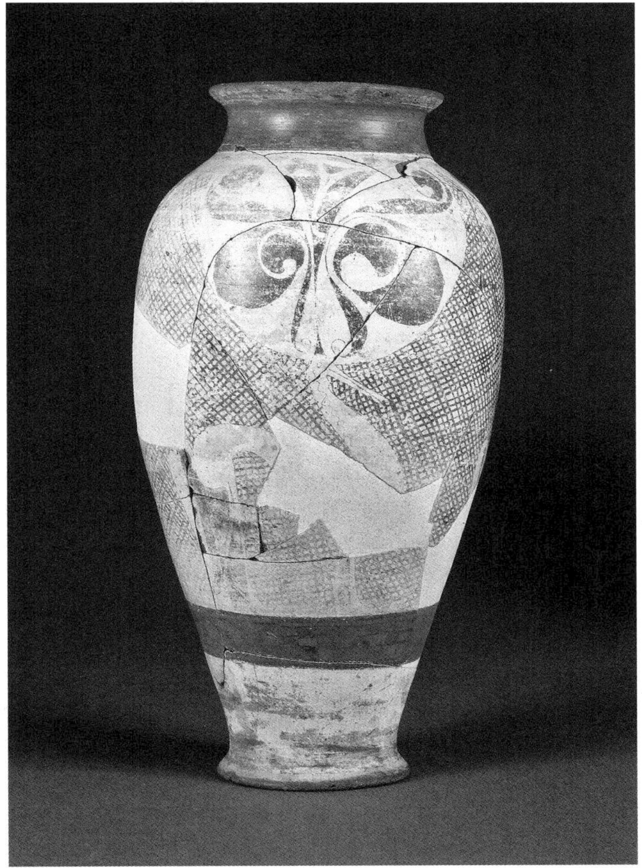

FIGURE 43.9 Vessel with deer figure from Puy de la Poix, Clermont-Ferrand, Auvergne, France. Height 278 mm.

Photo: V. Guichard

As powerful and self-assured as the creations of late La Tène art may still be in isolated cases, the integration of Gaul into the Roman Empire in the mid-first century BC signals the abrupt death of Celtic artistic endeavour. Only the British Isles, which fell under Roman control at a later date, see a late flourishing of La Tène art around the turn of the millennium, reflected most impressively in works such as the Desborough mirror (Müller 2009: 250 cat. no. 32). Once again intricate sinuous design, symmetry, and alternating patterned and smooth surfaces are artfully combined in a puzzle which reveals a Celtic mask—the 'mirror-image' of the person looking into the mirror, who thus becomes part and parcel of the artistic message. Celtic art remained established in Ireland and Scotland until well into the sixth or seventh centuries AD, not least in manuscript illumination, which begins to rise as a new means of communication.

Orientalizing Influences

From the outset, Celtic artistic creation was influenced by borrowings from Near Eastern art. Vegetal ornamentation as well as figurative compositions belong to the repertoire that the Celts took up and freely transformed—just as they did with Greek and Etruscan models. Lion no. 3 on the Hochdorf cauldron, most probably produced north of the Alps, must be among the earliest examples: although he formally emulates the other two 'Greek' lions on the rim, he belongs to an exotic species of animal inhabiting the Near East. One could argue that such a representation was created out of necessity and should be interpreted merely as a repair. But the very fact that the paws of a lion are represented on the only slightly later gold torc from Vix indicates that the Celts were particularly interested in this exotic feline (Rolley 2003: 170–188, pls 13–17). The lion image was quickly absorbed into the iconography of indigenous predators in La Tène art, but mythical traits also start to become more visible. The handle of the beaked flagon (*Schnabelkanne*) from the Borscher Aue in Thuringia (Jacobsthal 1944: 33, pl. 223; Storch 1986) features a lion that has become a wolf, and on the flagon from the Dürrnberg (Austria), it is turned into a mythical creature with a human-like head.

It is apparent from this briefly sketched evolution that Celtic art was open from the outset to the phenomenon of the Orientalizing style, which spread over large parts of the Mediterranean world and its contact zones from the early first millennium BC onwards. The causes of this wide-ranging spread of the Orientalizing style are multiple and can hardly be grouped under a single denominator. The common feature uniting the regional manifestations of the phenomenon is, however, their link to a specific aristocratic set of values and the luxurious lifestyle connected to it, a way of life that also becomes manifest, after a certain time lag, in the sixth and fifth centuries BC in the *Keltike* (compare for example Aubet 1982; Prayon and Röllig 2000; Serra Ridgway 2002; Riva and Vella 2006; van Dommelen 2006; Rathje 2008; Brisart 2011; Gunter 2012).

Naturally, the process of Orientalization comprises far more than the mere emulation of oriental iconographic models. Particular motifs are taken from the rich imagery of the oriental world, and translated into an individual stylistic and pictorial language. Sphinxes and griffins, but also the 'Master or Mistress of Animals' motif that dominates early La Tène imagery, form the focus of the Orientalizing artistic endeavours of the fifth and early fourth century BC (Guggisberg 2010). With the advent of the Waldalgesheim style, the figurative components fade into the background in favour of vegetal ornamentation and the Orientalizing haze is clearing over Celtic art. Reverberations can however still be felt in the late La Tène period, perhaps most distinctly in the Fellbach-Schmiden sculptures, which are devoted anew to the theme of the 'Master or Mistress of the Animals'.

With the exception of the Ihringen glass bowl (Dehn 1996, 1997; Kistler 2010), there is up to now no evidence of original Near Eastern imports into central Europe. Consequently the consensus is that the Orientalizing stimuli were transmitted to central

Europe in the first instance via the Etruscans and their neighbours in northern Italy and the southern fringes of the Alps. It is worthwhile noting, however, that the Orientalizing phenomenon becomes manifest in La Tène art only after a time lag of over a century. Celtic art thereby follows the situla art established in the southern foothills of the Alps, where a strongly Orientalizing iconographic and stylistic language on its eponymous bronze containers lingers on into the fifth and fourth centuries BC (Lucke and Frey 1962; Frey 1969). Contacts between situla art and figurative early La Tène art are documented primarily in the eastern Celtic world, for example in the frieze depicting young hares on a ceramic bowl from Libkovice in northern Bohemia (Schwappach 1974: 123–127, fig. 13). Imported works of situla art may have served as sources of inspiration, as evidenced by isolated finds from Austria and Thuringia. Contacts with the western centres of early La Tène art in the middle Rhine and Marne regions on the other hand appear to have been rather indirect. As yet, there is nothing to demonstrate the presence of figurative works of the situla art there, and the influence of situla art is equally difficult to detect in western early La Tène art. It therefore seems more likely that the basis for the interest in the Orientalizing style—which incidentally conforms to a common preference for archaic forms of expression—lies in a comparable set of social values among the various populations rather than in a direct cultural exchange across the Alps.

The Orientalizing phenomenon is by no means limited to the Celtic world. It also left traces in Iberia (Aubet 1982, 2006; Le Meaux 2010) and among the Scythians (Schiltz 1994). In Spain, the Orientalizing style appears through Phoenician transmission from the start of the seventh century BC onwards, where it is especially manifest in early ivory carvings (Aubet 1979–1980). The well-known motif of the duel between human and animal or human and griffin is encountered repeatedly on the ivories and also on goldwork such as the belt from the La Aliseda treasure (Blech et al. 2001: 575, pl. 138); this motif returns as late as the fifth century BC among the stone sculptures of Cerillo Blanco near Porcuna, illustrating the longevity of the Orientalizing iconographic language in the Iberian Peninsula (Koch 1998: 255–256, cat. no. 19; Blech et al. 2001: pl. 223).

Griffins play a central role in Scythian art, too, where they are often shown in combat against other animals. The majority of the representations date to the fifth century BC and later. However, the integration of Orientalizing imagery and style forms into Scythian creation goes back much further. Two gold-decorated short swords from the *kurgan* of Litoj and *kurgan* 1 of the cemetery of Kelermes bear witness already in the seventh century BC to an iconography unmistakably rooted in Near Eastern artistic tradition (Kossack 1987: 30–35; Schiltz 1994: 89–102). Griffins, horned lions, winged bulls, and mythical creatures adorn both scabbards (Figure 43.10). They owe their form to direct stimuli from Assyrian or Urartian art, as do the winged genies pollinating the tree of life at the mouth of the scabbard and on the hilt of the sword. While the latter are still relatively close to their original models, the mythical animal creatures on the scabbard mix foreign Near Eastern imagery with an indigenous, Scythian creative urge: the wings of the animals are formed out of carnivorous fish with open mouths which grow out of the bodies of the mythical creatures in the way so typical of the Scythian Animal style. As in other Orientalizing cultural areas, it can be assumed that the reception of

FIGURE 43.10 Scabbard from Kelermes, north Caucasus, Russia, with procession of griffins: detail of lion griffin. Length of scabbard *c.*500 mm. St Petersburg, State Hermitage Museum.

Source: Piotrovsky et al. 1986: fig. 35

(Near) Eastern imagery in Scythian art was accompanied by the adoption of the social and religious world views of the monarchic cultures of the Near East (see also Reeder 1999: 48–49).

Two aspects distinguish the Scythians' access to oriental art from the Orientalizing cultures of the Mediterranean world: on the one hand their geographical proximity, which allowed them to confront the art of the oriental world directly, and on the other the circumstance that Orientalization followed two different paths—directly in the sense described above and indirectly though transmission by Greeks who worked on contract for the Scythians in the coastal establishments of the Black Sea.

The Animal Style

The figurative imagery of Iron Age Europe centres on animals. Humans—under influence from the Mediterranean and the Near East—are introduced only hesitantly into the indigenous figurative repertoire. There is particular emphasis on animals in Scythian art, where it is not the natural, physical appearance of creatures, but a symbolic, emblematic rendering in abstract form that is accentuated (for a summary of the Scythian Animal style, see Jettmar 1964; Kossack 1987; Schiltz 1994; Jacobson-Tepfer 1995; Langner 2008; Becker 2015). The longevity of the types of images and their unchanged inner coherence is remarkable, suggesting that the animal images retained their symbolic meaning as signs of a bond between humans and the world of the animals that surrounded them for centuries.[1]

The artists of the steppes developed a rich repertoire of iconographic formulae, capable of expressing the speed, agility, danger, and also the sheer grace of the animals. 'Rolling animals', which can be traced back to the eighth century BC, embody the concentrated power of a predator ready to pounce (Schiltz 1994: 87). Turning the rear of the body through 180°, i.e. using so-called 'inversion' (Schefold 1938: 38–39; Schiltz 1994: 39; Guggisberg 1998: 569), but also reproducing the flexed or fully outstretched legs, allowed the Scythian artists to give their animal images dynamism and vitality (Figure 43.11). A further characteristic of this art consists of the cumulative association of whole animals or individual parts of animals (so-called 'zoomorphic conjunction') whereby—it is assumed—the power of the animals is multiplied (Schefold 1938: 38; Guggisberg 1998: 554–555). Devices of abstract art were also employed, such as the duplication of specific elements of the body, for example the two halves of a face in frontal view, or the symmetrical rendering of horns and antlers (Schiltz 1994: 41). Particularly important body parts—claws, paws, horns, antlers, and heads of birds of prey—were often emphasized by exaggerating their size or stylizing them.

FIGURE 43.11 Wooden bridle attachment in the shape of a mouflon from *Kurgan* 3, Pazyryk, Siberia, Russia. Height 104 mm. St Petersburg, State Hermitage Museum.

Source: Vierneisel 1984: no. 123

The fascination with animals defines Celtic art too, if to a lesser extent. Although they have to compete with vegetal ornament to attract the attention of the observer, animals occupy at all times a decisive position in Celtic creativity. Just as in Scythian art, it is the essence of the animal that is accentuated through transformation and abstraction. Significant body parts such as beaks, claws, and talons are often represented in exaggerated form here too. It is not rare to find animals of different species combined into a new figure: for example, the tail of the animal on the handle of the Borscher Aue beaked flagon ends in a bird's head and the rear legs of the predator are turned into wings. Worth noting too are the apparently peaceful rams on the gold bracelet from Rodenbach, whose front legs are stretched out in front, like a predator. In a manner similar to the rendering of the griffins with fish-shaped wings, horned lions, and winged bulls on the Litoj and Kelermes short swords described earlier, it seems that the artist intended to emphasize the supernatural power of the animals by using different animal components.

The representation of several deer figures on late La Tène painted wares from the French Massif Central (Guichard 1987, 2003: 98–99, figs 11–15; Müller 2009: 234–236, figs 310, 312) is worth dwelling on (Figure 43.9). The animals standing at rest are characterized by bold, sinuous body contours and long legs, by the dynamism of their upwardly stretched necks, and by their small heads adorned with magnificent sets of antlers. The latter are represented in frontal view—unlike the rest of the body, which is shown in profile—and hence can develop into an independent abstract ornament; in at least one case the frontal aspect of the antlers has been turned wholesale into a typical, fan-shaped design. A similar way of turning antlers into an ornament is also seen among Scythian animal representations, for example the standing stag depicted on a silver-plated relief from *kurgan* 2 of the Seven Brothers barrow cemetery (Figure 43.12; Minns 1913: fig. 115; Jacobsthal 1944: pls 221–222; Artamonov 1970: fig. 113), or the recumbent stag on a bridle plaque from barrow 4 of the same cemetery (Schiltz 1994: 43, fig. 26).

The possibility of points of contact between the Eurasian and Celtic animal styles has been debated for many years (Guggisberg 1998: 549, n. 2). Recently Vincent Megaw (2005) has vehemently argued anew against the existence of such contacts. Since no secure finds of Scythian–Eurasian provenance have turned up to date in western central Europe, caution is certainly advisable when assessing the question. Many of the stylistic attributes of eastern Celtic art could have reached central Europe indirectly via Greece and Italy, if indeed they were not newly invented independently by local artists. Yet the possibility of sporadic contacts cannot be excluded a priori, given the mounting evidence for contact between the Scythian-inspired Vekerzug culture and the early La Tène culture in precisely the middle Danube region and Transdanubia (see Teržan 1998: esp. 534, n. 176; Stöllner 2010: 301–302). The representation of a griffin with head curled backwards on an early La Tène belt buckle from Ossarn in the Traisen valley has not so long ago been convincingly argued by Otto-Herman Frey (2001) as linked to Scythian prototypes.

In this context it is worth noting the decoration of the bird appliqué executed in early La Tène style on the fibula from Panenský Týnec in Bohemia (Jacobsthal 1944: no. 318,

FIGURE 43.12 Breastplate with stags, bird of prey, and undetermined prey animal from the Seven Brothers *kurgan*, Taman peninsula, Russia. Height 343 mm. St Petersburg, State Hermitage Museum.

Photo: Classical Archaeology, University of Basel

pl. 161; Binding 1993: 228, no. 459, pl. 7.2; a good photograph of the punched motif on the bird's back exists in Megaw 1972: pl. 21.3). The bird is seen from above with wings spread out wide. Its plumage is rendered in geometric patterns: hatched squares organized in a chequerboard pattern are visible on the wings, and a lattice of tiny punched squares covers the body of the bird. While the former pattern belongs to the standard Celtic repertoire, the latter has no parallels in La Tène art. Similar patterns are, however, quite often present in Thracian art, where they decorate the bodies of various mythical animals, especially birds and bird-like animal components.[2]

The New York silver beaker decorated with an animal frieze is of particular interest. The antlers, ending in numerous bird protomes, of the eight-legged stag as well as the body of a large bird of prey are covered by a dense pattern of small punched squares

(Jacobsthal 1944: pl. 226 a–d). The same applies to another stag with antlers also ending in bird protomes, this time on the silver beaker of Agighiol (Figure 43.13; Berciu 1969; Roth 1994: 164, no. 49.5). Although the motif of punched squares is not limited to bird or bird-like representations, the possibility exists that the artist who made the Panenský Týnec fibula was inspired by examples from the lower Danube region, given that punched squares, as already mentioned, are otherwise unknown in Celtic art. Though a single instance should not be made to carry too much weight, the Panenský Týnec fibula—together with the Ossarn belt hook—is of significance for the question of the existence of an inner European axis of communication for the Animal style in so far as the stag on the New York beaker carries a set of antlers ending in bird protomes, which unmistakably references Scythian models. Last but not least, the symmetrical stylization of the frontally viewed antlers, reminiscent of the above-mentioned images of deer in late La Tène and Scythian art, is worthy of attention.

In sum, the contacts between the animal styles of the various regions of central and eastern Europe in the Iron Age appear rather slight. Concordances in the abstract rendering and transformation of animal images and in the choice of animals represented, which—with the exception of horses—belong mainly to the wild, could instead be the result of ways of handling the natural and animal world common to groups connected by their social and cultural ways of life.

Monumentality

It is one of the peculiarities of European Iron Age art that its creations—outside the Mediterranean area—are only very rarely monumental in nature. Moreover, stone, which is so well suited to monumental representation, is used conservatively. Yet there are stone representations in many Iron Age cultures. In the majority of cases, these are merely roughly worked stone blocks or stelae (for the Scythian sphere, see Reeder 1999: 268–271, nos 132, 133). Thus evidence for a more sophisticated confrontation with the plastic arts is all the more significant. It is for the most part influenced directly or indirectly by Greek and Etruscan art, which embraced large-scale sculpture particularly early and comprehensively. The Hirschlanden and Glauberg warrior statues can be taken here as examples of Celtic art, as can the figures of sitting warriors from southern France, which new research suggests may have begun to be made as early as the sixth or fifth century BC (Arcelin and Rapin 2003; Py 2011; Girard 2013). At around the same time, the first large stone sculptures of the Iberian cultural sphere begin to emerge (Blech in Blech et al. 2001: 451–455). One may recall the enigmatic set of stone sculptures of Cerillo Blanco near Porcuna (Figure 43.14). Large sculptures are also known from Sardinia (Thimme 1980: 368–369, nos 42, 43; Tronchetti 1988: 73–79, pls 30–33; Tronchetti and van Dommelen 2005; Tronchetti 2012) and from Nesactium in Croatia (Mihovilić 2001: 117–130). The peoples of the Balkan interior appear to have discovered monumental sculpture for themselves

FIGURE 43.13 Silver beaker from Agighiol, Romania. Height 187 mm. New York, Metropolitan Museum of Art.

Photo: http://www.metmuseum.org/art/collection/search/324029 [accessed 30 January 2017]

only in Hellenistic times, and large figurative statuary remains largely unknown in the Eurasian cultural sphere.

The use of wooden sculpture has been invoked to help explain the rarity of monumental stone sculpture in Iron Age Europe. The 55 cm high sculpture of a naked man from Seurre (Côte d'Or), dating to the late Hallstatt period (Bonenfant et al. 1998: 22–23, figs 5–6), may be cited as an example. Several, sometimes larger than life, wooden statues of the late second and first century BC are known from western Switzerland (Geneva, Villeneuve, and Yverdon; Müller 2009: 244–246, no. 30). The well-known wooden sculptures from Fellbach-Schmiden (see earlier) are of similar date. These examples leave no doubt that wooden statuary was present in the Celtic world, just as other Iron Age cultural groups mastered woodcarving to the highest degree, as illustrated by the

FIGURE 43.14 Griffin sculpture from Cerrillo Blanco de Porcuna, Andalusia, Spain. Height 700 mm. Jaén Museum.

Source: Blech et al. 2001: pl. 222b

impressive carving of a griffin devouring the head of a deer from the Pazyryk cemetery in the Altai mountains of Siberia (Schiltz 1994: 271, fig. 202).

A fundamental difference exists, however, between stone and wooden sculpture. While stone sculptures were intended to last for a long time, wooden statuary is by definition less durable. There are many reasons for the origin of Greek marble statuary, but one of them may have been the wish of aristocratic patrons to commemorate their own person in a permanent form for posterity (Kyrieleis 1996). The wooden sculptures of the Iron Age were hardly capable of fulfilling such a purpose. It seems therefore more than mere coincidence that monumental statuary appears among the Celts precisely when ideological links with the Mediterranean world were at their strongest. The artistic and above all technical quality of the sculpture suggests a direct transfer of technology controlled by the elites who commissioned the works. In any case, working stone in the round presupposes a confrontation with the three-dimensional physicality of representing the human body, a process for which there are few preliminary stages documented in Iron Age Europe.

Image and Narrative

A central concern of Greek and Etruscan art was the telling of stories. As early as the Geometric period, besides *prothesis* and *ekphora* (funerary scenes showing the laying out of the corpse and its ceremonial transport to the grave), battles, nautical scenes, and hunting adventures are represented in great detail. Later the wide iconographic palette embraces mythology in all its facets. Although heraldic compositions and animal friezes still play a significant part in Archaic times in the art of the eastern Aegean and in Corinthian art—both strongly influenced by Near Eastern models—narrativity takes on a decisive role in latter artistic landscapes at an early stage too.

Despite their knowledge of Greek and Etruscan products, indigenous cultures on the periphery of the Mediterranean and Black Seas showed limited interest in the narrative elements of Mediterranean art for a long time. The focus was on animal and human representations, which appear either on their own, in frieze-like rows, or in heraldic compositions. Interaction between the individual figures, beyond the fighting animals motif or comparable imagery, occurs only very rarely. The figures of the Strettweg cult wagon (see earlier) are an example of a narrative composition, as is the famous early La Tène scabbard from Hallstatt (Jacobsthal 1944: no. 96, pl. 60). In Scythian art interest in figurative, often narrative, representation grows with increasing Greek influence from the fifth century BC onwards. However the well-known scenes depicting the life of Scythian warriors, as they appear on vessels and precious metal jewellery, are largely works of Greek artists imprisoned in their own artistic traditions.

The reticence shown by Iron Age art towards narrative images undoubtedly has many causes. One could be related to the function of the supports for the art, which—*contra* the Greek and Etruscan world—belong mainly to personal equipment (dress, weapons, horses, vehicles). The fine tablewares needed for the banquet, which in the Mediterranean world are among the essential supports of narrative imagery, are only rarely decorated with figures among the indigenous cultures of Europe.[3] Evidence for other genres, such as architectural sculpture or reliefs, is found only in isolated cases. Might we conclude that figurative imagery in the art of the north and east was valued primarily for its personal, emblematic content? The fact that the images are often reproduced on supports made of precious materials, or themselves consist of these materials, is testimony to their prestigious status and suggests that they were preferentially used by their owners in religious and other forms of social and ideological self-expression (for the Scythian area, see Dally 2007: 294). Further afield, however, the late Bronze Age and early Iron Age rock art of the Altai region, with its comprehensive hunting scenes, is also worth noting (e.g. Jacobson 1999, figs 3–10; Jacobson-Tepfer 2015).

Conclusion: A Cultural Sphere on the Periphery of the Mediterranean World

The art of the Iron Age cultures located on the northern edge of the Mediterranean Sea and in the neighbouring Eurasian steppes is so multifaceted that it is difficult to reach general conclusions. A common trait is that the art that has come down to us is rooted in highly hierarchical elite societies, which had the power and economic resources to give expression to their need for social representation through artistically prominent prestige goods frequently chosen to accompany their owners in death.

External stimuli, especially from the expansive Near Eastern and Graeco-Roman worlds, were a welcome source of inspiration for the consistently independent indigenous art, and led to a fruitful dialogue between the respective spheres. The result was a process of artistic creation, which led to regionally and culturally very different forms of expression, but also to a remarkably homogeneous European Iron Age art when taken at a general level of comparison. An interest in depicting animals, a predilection for abstraction and stylization, and a preference for reproducing images on objects of personal equipment characterize and connect the different artistic regions, which developed a related stylistic and formal language partly in parallel and partly in sequence. Human representations play only an ephemeral role in most stylistic regions of Iron Age art, a circumstance that emphasizes the profound differences between the anthropocentric cultures of the Mediterranean city states and their neighbours in northern and eastern Europe, who were more committed to the natural world.

These characteristics clearly distinguish the art of Iron Age Europe from the contemporary art of the Greeks, Etruscans, and Romans, which focuses on the organic appearance of people, plants, and animals. Reasons for this distinction may be sought in different perceptions of the relationship between humans and their environment within the sociocultural and religious fabric of the respective cultures.

Notes

1. For example the existential link between humans and animals is illustrated by the zoomorphic tattoos on human bodies, as found preserved in the Pazyryk burials in Siberia.
2. The Thracian artefacts with punched chequered patterns are usually dated to the later fourth century BC. The Panenský Týnec fibula belongs to a late type of Certosa fibula, which was used well into the fourth century BC (Teržan 1976: especially Variant X, and appendix 1.2 for dating).
3. In this context, it is worth noting that the iconography of Graeco-Scythian art, namely the narrative scenes from Scythian (warrior) daily life, appears preferentially on drinking and pouring vessels. It is not unthinkable that it denotes the greater influence of the Greek culture of drinking and debating in banquets and *symposia*.

References

Arcelin, P., and A. Rapin. 2003. 'Considérations nouvelles sur l'iconographie anthropomorphe de l'âge du Fer en Gaule méditerranéenne', in O. Buchsenschutz and A. Bulard (eds) *Décors, images et signes de l'âge du Fer européen. Actes du XVIe colloque de l'AFEAF, Paris et Saint-Denis, 9–1 mai 2002*. Revue Archéologique du Centre de la France supplément 24: 183–219. Tours/Paris: FERACF.

Artamonov, M. I. 1970. *Goldschatz der Skythen in der Eremitage*. Hanau am Main: W. Dausien.

Aubet, M. E. 1979–1980. *Marfiles fenicios del Bajo Guadalquivir*. Studia Archaeologica 1 and 2. Valladolid: Universidad de Valladolid.

Aubet, M. E. 1982. 'Zur Problematik des orientalisierenden Horizontes auf der Iberischen Halbinsel', in H. G. Niemeyer (ed.) *Phönizier im Westen: Die Beiträge des Internationalen Symposiums über 'Die phönizische Expansion im westlichen Mittelmeerraum' in Köln vom 24. bis 27. April 1979*: 309–332. Mainz: Philipp von Zabern.

Aubet, M. E. 2006. 'On the organization of the Phoenician colonial system in Iberia', in C. Riva and N. C. Vella (eds) *Debating Orientalization: Multidisciplinary Approaches to Change in the Ancient Mediterranean*: 94–109. London: Equinox.

Banck-Burgess, J. 1999. *Hochdorf IV: Die Textilfunde aus dem späthallstattzeitlichen Fürstengrab von Eberdingen-Hochdorf (Kreis Ludwigburg) und weitere Grabtextilien aus hallstatt- und latènezeitlichen Kulturgruppen*. Forschungen und Berichte zur Vor- und Frühgeschichte in Baden-Württemberg 70. Stuttgart: Theiss.

Becker, V. 2015. 'Zur Entstehung und Ausbreitung der "zoomorphen Junktur" in der skythischen Kunst', in R. Gleser and F. Stein (eds) *Äusserer Anstoss und innerer Wandel: Festschrift für Rudolf Echt zum 65. Geburtstag*. Studia Honoraria 37: 59–74. Rahden: Marie Leidorf.

Berciu, D. 1969. 'Das thrako-getische Fürstengrab von Agighiol in Rumänien'. *Berichte der Römisch-Germanischen Kommission* 50: 209–265.

Berger, L. 1999. 'Kunst und Kunstgewerbe in Mittelland und Jura', in F. Müller, G. Kaenel, and G. Lüscher (eds) *Die Schweiz vom Paläolithikum bis zum frühen Mittelalter, IV: Eisenzeit*: 229–242. Basel: Schweizerische Gesellschaft für Ur- und Frühgeschichte.

Bieg, G. 2002. *Hochdorf V: Der Bronzekessel aus dem späthallstattzeitlichen Fürstengrab von Eberdingen-Hochdorf (Kr. Ludwigsburg)*. Forschungen und Berichte zur Vor- und Frühgeschichte in Baden-Württemberg 83. Stuttgart: Theiss.

Binding, U. 1993. *Studien zu den figürlichen Fibeln der Frühlatènezeit*. Universitätsforschungen zur prähistorischen Archäologie 16. Bonn: Habelt.

Blech, M., M. Koch, and M. Kunst. 2001. *Hispania Antiqua: Denkmäler der Frühzeit*. Mainz: Philipp von Zabern.

Bonenfant, P.-P., J.-P. Guillaumet, and F. Boyer. 1998. *La statuaire anthropomorphe du premier âge du Fer*. Annales littéraires de l'Université de Franche-Comté 667. Série archéologie et préhistoire 43. Besançon: Presses universitaires franc-comtoises.

Brisart, T. 2011. *Un art citoyen: Recherches sur l'orientalisation des artisanats en Grèce proto-archaïque*. Brussels: Académie royale de Belgique, Classe des lettres.

Burford, A. 1985. *Künstler und Handwerker in Griechenland und Rom*. Mainz: Philipp von Zabern.

Camporeale, G. 2009. 'Da Vetulonia verso la Renania e la costa d'oro nel VII secolo a.C.'. *Studi Etruschi* 73: 3–15.

Dally, O. 2007. 'Skythische und graeco-skythische Bildelemente im nördlichen Schwarzmeerraum', in W. Menghin, H. Parzinger, A. Nagler, and M. Nawroth (eds) *Im*

Zeichen des goldenen Greifen: Königsgräber der Skythen: 291–298. Berlin: Staatliche Museen zu Berlin, Preußischer Kulturbesitz.

Dehn, W. 1996. 'Ein Fürstengrab der späten Hallstattzeit von Ihringen', in S. Plouin, P. Jud, and C. Dunning (eds) *Trésors Celtes et Gaulois: Le Rhin supérieur entre 800 et 50 avant J.-C.*: 112–118. Colmar: Musée d'Unterlinden.

Dehn, R. 1997. 'Riche découverte funéraire dans la nécropole tumulaire d'Ihringen-Gündlingen, lieu-dit "Nachtwaid-Ried"', in P. Brun and B. Chaume (eds) *Vix et les éphémères principautés celtiques: Les VIe–Ve siècle avant J.-C. en Europe centre-occidentale*: 53–55. Paris: Errance.

Duval, P.-M., and V. Kruta. 1986. 'Le fourreau celtique de Cernon-sur-Cool (Marne)'. *Gallia* 44: 1–27.

Egg, M. 1996. *Das Hallstattzeitliche Fürstengrab von Strettweg bei Judenburg in der Obersteiermark*. RGZM Monographien 37. Mainz: Römisch-Germanisches Zentralmuseum.

Fischer, F. 1984. 'Württemberg und der Dürrnberg bei Hallein'. *Fundberichte aus Baden-Württemberg* 9: 223–248.

Frey, O.-H. 1969. *Die Entstehung der Situlenkunst: Studien zur figürlich verzierten Toreutik von Este*. Römisch-Germanische Forschungen 31. Berlin: De Gruyter.

Frey, O.-H. 1976. 'Du premier style au style de Waldalgesheim, remarques sur l'évolution de l'art celtique ancien', in P.-M. Duval and C. F. C. Hawkes (eds) *Celtic Art in Ancient Europe: Five Protohistoric Centuries. Proceedings of the Colloquy held in 1972 at the Oxford Maison Française*: 141–163. London: Seminar Press.

Frey, O.-H. 1995. 'Das Grab von Waldalgesheim. Eine Stilphase des keltischen Kunsthandwerkes', in H.-E. Joachim (ed.) *Waldalgesheim: Das Grab einer keltischen Fürstin*: 159–206. Cologne: Rheinland-Verlag.

Frey, O.-H. 2001. 'Ein frühlatènezeitlicher Gürtelhaken aus Ossarn, Nieder-Österreich', in D. Büchner (ed.) *Studien in memoriam Wilhelm Schüle*. Studia honoraria 11: 157–163. Rahden: Marie Leidorf.

Frey, O.-H. 2007. *Keltische Kunst in vorrömischer Zeit*. Kleine Schriften aus dem Vorgeschichtlichen Seminar Marburg 57. Marburg: Philipps-Universität Marburg.

Girard, B. 2013. *Au fil de l'épée: Armes et guerriers en pays celte méditerranéen. Catalogue d'exposition du 4 mai au 31 décembre 2013 au Musée archéologique de Nîmes*. Nîmes: Musée archéologique.

Guggisberg, M. 1998. 'Zoomorphe Junktur und Inversion. Zum Einfluss des skythischen Tierstils auf die frühe keltische Kunst'. *Germania* 76: 549–571.

Guggisberg, M. 2010. 'The Mistress of Animals, the Master of Animals: Two complementary or oppositional religious concepts in early Celtic art?', in D. B. Counts and B. Arnold (eds) *The Master of Animals*. Archaeolingua Main Series 24: 223–236. Budapest: Archaeolingua.

Guggisberg, M., and T. Hoppe. 2012. 'Von Zirkeln, Ranken und anderen Dingen. Kunst und Künstler der Kelten', in R. Röber, M. Jansen, S. Rau, C. von Nicolai, and I. Frech (eds) *Die Welt der Kelten: Zentren der Macht—Kostbarkeiten der Kunst. Ausstellungskatalog Stuttgart 2012*: 42–51. Sigmaringen: Thorbecke.

Guichard, V. 1987. 'La céramique peinte à décor zoomorphe des IIe et Ier s. avant J.-C. en territoire ségusiave'. *Études Celtiques* 24: 103–143.

Guichard, V. 2003. 'Un dernier moment de folie: le repertoire ornemental de la céramique peinte dans le nord-est du Massif central au IIe siècle avant J.-C.', in O. Buchsenschutz, A. Bulard, M.-B. Chardenoux, and N. Ginoux (eds) *Décors, images et signes de l'âge du Fer européen. Actes du XXVIe Colloque de l'AFEAF, Paris et Saint-Denis 9–12 mai 2002*. Revue Archéologique du Centre de la France supplément 24: 91–112. Tours: FERACF.

Gunter, A. C. 2012. *Greek Art and the Orient*. Cambridge: Cambridge University Press.

Himmelmann, N. 1983. *Alexandria und der Realismus in der griechischen Kunst*. Tübingen: E. Wasmuth.

Hoppe, T., and B. Schorer. 2012. 'Geometrisches Ornament', in R. Röber, M. Jansen, S. Rau, C. von Nicolai, and I. Frech (eds) *Die Welt der Kelten: Zentren der Macht—Kostbarkeiten der Kunst. Ausstellungskatalog Stuttgart 2012*: 209–225. Sigmaringen: Thorbecke.

Jacobson, E. 1999. 'Early nomadic sources for Scythian art', in E. Reeder (ed.) *Scythian Gold: Treasures from Ancient Ukraine*: 59–69. New York: Harry Abrams.

Jacobson-Tepfer, E. 1995. *The Art of the Scythians: The Interpenetration of Cultures at the Edge of the Hellenic World*. Handbuch der Orientalistik 8. Leiden: Brill.

Jacobson-Tepfer, E., 2015. *The Hunter, the Stag, and the Mother of Animals: Image, Monument, and Landscape in Ancient North Asia*. Oxford: Oxford University Press.

Jacobsthal, P. 1944. *Early Celtic Art*. Oxford: Clarendon Press.

Jehl, M., and C. Bonnet. 1968. 'La pyxide d'Appenwihr (Haut-Rhin)'. *Gallia* 26: 295–300.

Jettmar, K. 1964. *Die frühen Steppenvölker: Der eurasiatische Tierstil, Entstehung und sozialer Hintergrund*. Baden-Baden: Holle.

Joachim, H.-E. 1995. *Waldalgesheim. Das Grab einer keltischen Fürstin*. Cologne: Rheinland-Verlag.

Kimmig, W. 1988. *Das Kleinaspergle: Studien zu einem Fürstengrabhügel der frühen Latènezeit bei Stuttgart*. Forschungen und Berichte zur Vor- und Frühgeschichte in Baden-Württemberg 30. Stuttgart: Theiss.

Kistler, E. 2010. 'Grosskönigliches Symbolon im Osten—exotisches Luxusgut im Westen: Zur Objektbiographie der achämenidischen Glasschale aus Ihringen', in R. Rollinger, B. Gufler, M. Lang, and I. Madreiter (eds) *Interkulturalität in der Alten Welt: Vorderasien, Hellas, Ägypten und die vielfältigen Ebenen des Kontakts*. Philippika 34: 63–95. Wiesbaden: Harrassowitz.

Koch, M. (ed.) 1998. *Die Iberer: Ausstellungskatalog der Kunst- und Ausstellungshalle der Bundesrepublik Deutschland Bonn, 15. Mai–23. Aug. 1998*. Munich: Hirmer Verlag.

Kossack, G. 1987. 'Von den Anfängen des skytho-iranischen Tierstils', in L. K. Galanina (ed.) *Skythika: Vorträge zur Entstehung des skytho-iranischen Tierstils und zu Denkmälern des Bosporanischen Reichs anläßlich einer Ausstellung der Leningrader Ermitage in München 1984*: 24–86. Munich: Verlag der Bayerischen Akademie der Wissenschaften.

Kyrieleis, H. 1996. *Der grosse Kuros von Samos*. Samos 10. Bonn: Habelt.

Langner, M. 2008. 'Skythischer Tierstil und graeco-skythische Tierbilder', in A. Alexandridis, M. Wild, and L. Winkler-Horacek (eds) *Mensch und Tier in der Antike: Grenzziehung und Grenzüberschreitung Symposion vom 7. bis 9. April 2005 in Rostock*: 397–416. Wiesbaden: Reichert.

Le Meaux, H. 2010. *L'iconographie orientalisante de la péninsule Ibérique: questions de styles et d'échanges (VIIIe–VIe siècles av. J.-C.)*. Madrid: Casa de Velázquez.

Lejars, T. 2012. 'Der Schwertstil', in R. Röber, M. Jansen, S. Rau, C. von Nicolai, and I. Frech (eds) *Die Welt der Kelten: Zentren der Macht—Kostbarkeiten der Kunst. Ausstellungskatalog Stuttgart 2012*: 318–325. Sigmaringen: Thorbecke.

Lucke, W., and O.-H. Frey. 1962. *Die Situla in Providence (Rhode Island): Ein Beitrag zur Situlenkunst des Osthallstattkreises*. Römisch-Germanische Forschungen 26. Berlin: De Gruyter.

Megaw, J. V. S. 1972. 'Style and style groupings in continental early La Tène art'. *World Archaeology* 3, 3: 276–292.

Megaw, J. V. S. 1973. 'The decorated sword-scabbard of iron from Cernon-sur-Cool (Marne) and Drňa, Rimavská Sobota (Slovakia)'. *Hamburger Beiträge zur Archäologie* 3, 2: 119–137.

Megaw, J. V. S. 2005. 'Early Celtic art without Scythians?', in H. Dobrzańska, J. V. S. Megaw, and P. Poleska (eds) *Celts on the Margin: Studies in European Cultural Interaction (7th Century BC–1st Century AD) Dedicated to Zenon Woźniak*: 33–47. Krakow: Institute of Archaeology and Ethnology of the Polish Academy of Sciences.

Megaw, J. V. S. 2012a. 'Der plastische Stil', in R. Röber, M. Jansen, S. Rau, C. von Nicolai, and I. Frech (eds) *Die Welt der Kelten: Zentren der Macht—Kostbarkeiten der Kunst. Ausstellungskatalog Stuttgart 2012*: 304–307. Sigmaringen: Thorbecke.

Megaw, J. V. S. 2012b. 'Micky Mouse im Grab. Mezek und der Disney Stil', in R. Röber, M. Jansen, S. Rau, C. von Nicolai, and I. Frech (eds) *Die Welt der Kelten: Zentren der Macht—Kostbarkeiten der Kunst. Ausstellungskatalog Stuttgart 2012*: 316–317. Sigmaringen: Thorbecke.

Mihovilić, K. 2001. *Nezakcij: Prapovijesni nalazi 1900–1953 [Nesactium. Prehistoric finds 1900–1953]*. Monografije i katalozi 11. Pula: Arheološki muzej Istre.

Minns, E. H. 1913. *Scythians and Greeks: A Survey of Ancient History and Archaeology on the North Coast of the Euxine from the Danube to the Caucasus*. Cambridge: Cambridge University Press.

Müller, F. (ed.) 2009. *Kunst der Kelten: 700 v. Chr.–700 n. Chr. Katalog zur Ausstellung*. Stuttgart: Belser.

Müller, F. 2011. 'Ein latènezeitlicher Zierknopf im plastischen Stil'. *Archäologisches Korrespondenzblatt* 41: 521–529.

Müller, F. 2012a. *Die Kunst der Kelten*. Munich: Beck.

Müller, F. 2012b. 'Keltische Ornamentik par excellence', in R. Röber, M. Jansen, S. Rau, C. von Nicolai, and I. Frech (eds) *Die Welt der Kelten: Zentren der Macht—Kostbarkeiten der Kunst. Ausstellungskatalog Stuttgart 2012*: 295–299. Sigmaringen: Thorbecke.

Nebelsick, L. D. 1992. 'Figürliche Kunst der Hallstattzeit am Nordostalpenrand im Spannungsfeld zwischen alteuropäischer Tradition und italischem Lebensstil', in A. Lippert and K. Spindler (eds) *Festschrift zum 50jährigen Bestehen des Institutes für Ur- und Frühgeschichte der Leopold-Franzens-Universität Innsbruck*. Universitätsforschungen zur prähistorischen Archäologie 8: 401–432. Bonn: Habelt.

Philipp, H. 1968. *Tektonon Daidala: der bildende Künstler und sein Werk im vorplatonischen Schrifttum*. Berlin: Hessling.

Philipp, H. 1990. 'Handwerker und bildende Künstler in der griechischen Gesellschaft', in H. Beck, P. C. Bol, and M. Bückling (eds) *Polyklet: Der Bildhauer der griechischen Klassik. Ausstellungskatalog Frankfurt*: 79–110. Mainz: Philipp von Zabern.

Piotrovsky, B., L. Galanina, and N. Grach. 1986. *Scythian Art: The Legacy of the Scythian World: Mid-7th to 3rd Century B.C.* Leningrad: Aurora Art Publishers.

Planck, D. 1985. 'Die Viereckschanze von Fellbach-Schmiden', in D. Planck (ed.) *Der Keltenfürst von Hochdorf. Ausstellungskatalog Stuttgart*: 340–353. Stuttgart: Theiss.

Prayon, F., and W. Röllig (eds). 2000. *Akten des Kolloquiums zum Thema 'Der Orient und Etrurien': Zum Phänomen des 'Orientalisierens' im westlichen Mittelmeerraum (10.–6. Jh. v. Chr.), Tübingen, 12.–13. Juni 1997*. Biblioteca di Studi Etruschi 35. Pisa/Rome: Istituti editoriali e poligrafici internationali.

Py, M. 2011. *La sculpture gauloise méridionale*. Paris: Errance.

Rathje, A. 2008. 'Tracking down the Orientalizing'. *Bollettino di Archeologia On Line*. Available at http://www.bollettinodiarcheologiaonline.beniculturali.it/documenti/generale/2_RATHJE.pdf [accessed 20 May 2018].

Reeder, E. (ed.) 1999. *Scythian Gold: Treasures from Ancient Ukraine*. New York: Harry Abrams.

Reichenberger, A. 1995. 'Figürliche Kunst: Hallstattzeit', *Reallexikon der Germanischen Altertumskunde* 9: 13–20. Berlin/New York: Walter de Gruyter.

Riva, C., and N. C. Vella (eds). 2006. *Debating Orientalization: Multidisciplinary Approaches to Change in the Ancient Mediterranean*. London: Equinox.

Röber, R., M. Jansen, S. Rau, C. von Nicolai, and I. Frech (eds). 2012. *Die Welt der Kelten: Zentren der Macht—Kostbarkeiten der Kunst. Ausstellungskatalog Stuttgart 2012*. Sigmaringen: Thorbecke.

Rolley, C. (ed.) 2003. *La tombe princière de Vix*. Paris: Picard/Société des amis du Musée du Châtillonnais.

Roth, J. (ed.) 1994. *Goldhelm, Schwert und Silberschätze: Reichtümer aus 6000 Jahren rumänischer Vergangenheit. Sonderausstellung*. Frankfurt am Main: Museum für Vor- und Frühgeschichte/Schirn-Kunsthalle.

Schefold, K. 1938. 'Der skythische Tierstil in Südrussland'. *Eurasia Septentrionalis Antiqua* 12: 1–78.

Schiltz, V. 1994. *Die Skythen und andere Steppenvölker. 8. Jahrhundert v. Chr. bis 1. Jahrhundert n. Chr*. Universum der Kunst 39. Munich: Beck.

Schwappach, F. 1974. 'Zu einigen Tierdarstellungen der Frühlatènekunst'. *Hamburger Beiträge zur Archäologie* 4: 103–140.

Serra Ridgway, F. R. 2002. 'Orientalizing motifs in Etruscan art'. *Opuscula Romana* 27: 109–122.

Steffen, M. 2012. 'Komplexe Zentren nördlich der Alpen. Die Entstehung der Fürstensitze', in R. Röber, M. Jansen, S. Rau, C. von Nicolai, and I. Frech (eds) *Die Welt der Kelten: Zentren der Macht—Kostbarkeiten der Kunst. Ausstellungskatalog Stuttgart 2012*: 94–97. Sigmaringen: Thorbecke.

Stöllner, T. 2010. 'Kontakt, Mobilität und Kulturwandel im Frühlatènekreis—das Beispiel Frühlatènegürtelhaken', in E. Jerem, M. Schönfelder, and G. Wieland (eds) *Nord-Süd, Ost-West: Kontakte während der Eisenzeit in Europa. Akten der Internationalen Tagungen der AG Eisenzeit in Hamburg und Sopron 2002*. Archaeolingua Main Series 17: 277–319. Budapest: Archaeolingua.

Storch, H. 1986. 'Die Rekonstruktion der keltischen Schnabelkanne von Borsch, Kr. Bad Salzung, in der Sammlung des Bereichs Ur- und Frühgeschichte der Friedrich-Schiller-Universität Jena'. *Wissenschaftliche Zeitschrift der Friedrich-Schiller-Universität Jena* 35: 411–421.

Teržan, B. 1976. 'Certoška fibula'. *Arheološki vestnik* 27: 317–536.

Teržan, B. 1998. 'Auswirkungen des skythisch geprägten Kulturkreises auf die hallstattzeitlichen Kulturgruppen Pannoniens und des Ostalpenraumes', in B. Hänsel and J. Machnik (eds) *Das Karpatenbecken und die osteuropäische Steppe*. Prähistorische Archäologie in Südosteuropa 12: 511–560. Rahden: Marie Leidorf.

Thimme, J. (ed.) 1980. *Kunst und Kultur Sardiniens: Vom Neolithikum bis zum Ende der Nuraghenzeit. Ausstellung Badisches Landesmuseum Karlsruhe im Karlsruher Schloss vom 18. April–13. Juli 1980*. Karlsruhe: Müller.

Tronchetti, C. 1988. *I Sardi: traffici, relazioni, ideologie nella Sardegna arcaica*. Milan: Longanesi.

Tronchetti, C. 2012. 'La statuaria di Monte Prama nel contesto delle relazioni tra Fenici e Sardi', in P. Bernardini and M. Perra (eds) *I Nuragici, i Fenici e gli altri: Sardegna e Mediterraneo tra bronzo finale e prima età del ferro: atti del I Congresso internazionale in occasione del venticinquennale del Museo Genna Maria di Villanovaforru, 14–15 dicembre 2007*: 181–192. Sassari: Comune di Villanovaforru/Museo archeologico di Villanovaforru/Università di Sassari.

Tronchetti, C., and P. van Dommelen. 2005. 'Entangled objects and hybrid practices. Colonial contacts and elite connections at Monte Prama, Sardinia'. *Journal of Mediterranean Archaeology* 18, 2: 183–209.

Van Dommelen, P. 2006. 'The Orientalizing phenomenon: Hybridity and material culture in the western Mediterranean', in C. Riva and N. C. Vella (eds) *Debating Orientalization: Multidisciplinary Approaches to Change in the Ancient Mediterranean*: 135–152. London: Equinox.

Vierneisel, K. (ed.) 1984. *Gold der Skythen aus der Leningrader Eremitage. Ausstellung der Staatlichen Antikensammlungen am Königsplatz in München, 19. September bis 9. Dezember 1984*. Munich: Staatliche Antikensammlungen und Glyptothek.

Index

Abano Terme, Vicenza (Italy) 369
Abchazia valley 535
Abingdon (England) 112
Abritus (Bulgaria) 916
absolute dating 46–52
Abul (Portugal) 316
acculturation 1090
Achaeans 1118, 1124, 1188
Achaemenid dynasty 625–6
  glass artefacts 633
  metal artefacts 502, 633
  politics 586
  valuable grave goods associated with 588
Acharnians, The (Aristophanes) 805
Acy-Romance (France) 68
  artisanship 718–19
  coins 903, 904, 905, 915
  horse-related finds 1012
  ritual practices 90, 96, 112, 1266
Adam of Bremen, Bishop 1130
Adelssitz 934, 936
Adige basin 360, 361, 366
Adige, River 367, 369
adornment 980–2
Adriatic 22–3, 40, 200, 345–90
  amber 1112
  Celtic links 1114, 1145, 1163
  horse-related finds 1012
  map of sites 371
  migration through 1144
  trade 797, 806, 1241, 1244–5
  votive depositions 1273
Aduatuci 121, 1168
Aedui 1121
  capital (Autun) 1297
  capital (Bibracte) 93, 238, 733
  chief magistrate (*vergobret*) 726
  coins 732, 1115
  Diviciacus of 935, 1119
  Dumnorix of 928, 935, 936
  political change 1131
  senate 929
  and Senones 735
  social classes 972, 985
Aegae *see* Vergina/Aegae
Aegean 23, 40, 407–17, 479
  art 1329
  artefacts 463–4
  connection with northern Greece and the central Balkans 449–51
  contact with Chalkidike 453
  contact with Cyprus 622–3
  contact with Sardinia 437, 438
  contact with Thapsos 430
  contact with Thracians 1159
  development 470
  dualist view 469
  imports 454
  iron artefacts 480
  map of sites 408
  migration through 455, 631, 1149
  Philistines from 624
  population movements 28, 878
  pottery 453, 490
  rivers and mountains 462, 463
  written traditions 1120
Aelian, *De Natura Animalium* 1272, 1289
Aeneas 1120
Aeneid (Virgil) 1297
Aeolian Islands 434, 436
Aestii (*Aestiorum gentes*) 174, 208–9
Aetolia, cult activity 416
affiliation 1086, 1089

Afghanistan, Persian empire 625–6
Africa 40, 626–8, 1092
  Barbary ape/macaque remains 108, 637–8, 1277–8
  beer consumption 1228
  contact with Europe 22, 108, 619, 628–9, 637–8
  ironworking 1288
  ivory 637, 807
  migration through 1094
  Phoenicians in 624, 631
  population movements 631–2
  Roman provinces 620–1
  trade with Europe 629–30, 881, 1229
  Vandals in 1029
Agde (France) 277, 301
  Agathé colony 295
  cemeteries 280–1, 282
  settlements 284
age 1026
  at death 1030–6
  life pyramids 1037–9
  representation in cemeteries 1039
  and social status 989
Age of Minos 1120
agglomerations
  Britain 112
  central Europe 245–6
  France 286, 291
  Iberia 326
  north-west Europe 90–4, 105
  see also nucleated settlements
Agighiol (Romania) 500, 501, 1245
  silver beaker 1326, 1327
Agios Dimitrios (Greece), cemeteries 457
Agios Panteleimonas (Greece) 450
  inhumations 457
Agout (France) 281
Agricola (Tacitus) 122, 123, 1121, 1128, 1131
agriculture 660–1
  Britain 84
  climate suitable for 26
  crops 661–4
  cultivated plants 664–5
  eastern Baltic 188
  France 289–90
  Iberian peninsula 683–5
  and iron technology 670–1
  livestock 665–6, 685–7
  on marshes 668–70
  Netherlands 685–7
  in north-west Europe 69–71
  Pyanobor culture 608
  and the Roman Empire 668–70
  single-generation farms 83
  use of horses 1005–11
Agri Decumates 1169
agro-silvo-pastoral system 351
Aigues-Mortes (France) 1285
Ain Dara 623
Aineia (Greece) 470
Aisne-Marne region 77–8, 81, 88
  burial practices 121, 123, 830, 1247
  swords 1068
  see also Champagne
Aisne, River 90, 91
Aisne valley (France) 44, 93, 95
  potins 900
Ai-Todor (Crimea) 556
Aix-en-Provence/Aquae Sextiae (France) 1141, 1168
akinakes (short sword or dagger) 499
Ak-Kaya (Crimea) 550, 551
Akkozinskaya culture 602, 604
Akornion of Dionysopolis 507
Alamanni 1129
Alani/Alans 529–30, 559, 596, 1129
Albacete (Spain) 320
Albanese Procelli, R. M. 436, 442
Albania 450, 458–62, 628, 1145
Albenga (Italy) 346, 351
Alb-Hegau pottery 1308
Alchedar (Moldova) 540
Aldhouse-Green, M. J. 788, 986
ale consumption 1222
Alemannic coalition 1169
Alentejo 316
Alesia 724, 1121
  artefacts 47
  battlefield 43, 121
  brooches 45
  coins 901
Alessandri, J. 439

Alexander the Great 513, 582, 626, 811, 888, 1145–6
  image on coins 890
  treaty with the Celts 1163
Alexandria (Romania) 499
Alexandropol' (Ukraine) 544–5
Alfedena (Italy) 952
Alföld group/Vekerzug culture 491, 492, 1324
Algarve 316
Algeria 626, 628–9
Aliakmon, River 451, 456
Alicante 1114
Aligor (Crimea) 555
Alken Enge (Denmark) 159, 166, 953
Alkis coins 890, 914
Allen, D. 830–1
Allenlüften (Switzerland) 1051, 1061
Allobroges 1125
alluvium 25
Almagro-Gorbea, M. 330
Alma-Kermen (Crimea) 551
Almuñecar (Spain) 1244
Almwirtschaft 535
Alorda Park (Spain) 324, 685
Alpanseque (Spain) 1289
Alpenrheintal 360
alphabetic systems 630–1, 1107, 1109
  archaeologically attested 1105–17
  Camunic script 1113, 1114
  Celtiberian 1106, 1110
  Greek 1114–15
  Iberic script 1110
  Latin 1115–17
  Ogam script 119, 1117, 1118
  Phoenician 1106, 1108–14
  Pictish inscriptions 1106
  spelling 1131
  Tartessians 1106, 1110–11
Alphen-Ekeren type houses 98, 1194
Alpilles 282, 291, 292, 297
Alpine regions 22, 345, 354, 1141, 1246
  alphabetic systems 1106, 1108, 1112, 1114
  amber 806
  architecture 752
  art 234, 861, 1264, 1321
  Augustus' campaign 239
  biogeography 29
  cattle 678
  cemeteries 221, 225, 233, 282, 1154
  central 360–5
  ceremonial wagons 1006
  chariots 1008
  Circum-Alpine zone 1240–4, 1246–9
  climate 27, 28
  clothing 859, 861–2
  coins 830, 890–2, 895, 901–2
  contact 1150
  crops 662, 664, 669
  dendrochronology 50
  elite burials 1052, 1061, 1255
  fortified sites 719
  glass artefacts 801
  goldworking 823, 888
  Hallstatt culture 193, 220
  houses 694, 699
  iron technology 670, 779, 822
  ivory 807
  migration through 13
  military 1124
  movement through 250
  pottery 487, 812–13, 823
  princely seats 73
  religious sectors 251
  ritual practices 1270
  salt mines 49, 220, 230, 682, 800
  settlements 387
  south-eastern 379
  textile works 846, 855, 861–2
  urbanization 717
  woodland 668, 806
Alsace 221, 229, 1308, 1309
Altai mountains 525, 854, 933
  art 1328, 1329
  horse-related finds 1011
Alta Rocca Caleca-Lévie (Corsica) 439
Altenburg-Rheinau oppidum (Germany/Switzerland) 720, 721
  coins 799
Altenfeld (Germany) 880
Altillo del Cerropozo, sword from 955
Altino (Italy) 346, 369, 1012
Altkönig (Germany) 745–6
Alt-Laari (Estonia) 186
Altmühl valley 220, 223
Altno 369

Altrier (Luxembourg) 854
Alu (Estonia) 179
Amazons 582, 949, 1062, 1147
Ambarri 1121, 1144
amber 636, 683, 806–7, 1244–5
  Lugiorum nomen 204–6
  trade in eastern central Europe 194, 203–6
Amber Route 806, 896, 913
Ambigatus/Ambicatus of the
    Bituriges 1121, 1144
Ambiorix 757, 758
Ambisonti 373
Amboise (France) 733, 735
Ambracia *see* Arta
Ambrones 1125, 1168
Ambrussum (France) 277, 294, 1265
Ameglia (Italy) 346, 351, 352
America 619, 628, 641, 1083
Amfreville helmet 934
Ammianus Marcellinus 1128–9, 1130
  History 964, 1104, 1121
Ammon 624
Ampass-Demlfeld (Austria) 218, 252
Ampurias/Emporion (Spain) 277, 323, 878
Amrum island 669
Amrum Wyk (Germany) 146, 158
Anabasis (Arrian) 513, 1145
Ananyino 578, 586, 601–5, 606, 609–11
  metallurgical centre 576
Anarti 1170–1
Anatolia 13, 40, 490, 621–2, 625, 628
  art 638
  brooches 1166
  Celtic links 1159, 1171
  droughts 28
  glass artefacts 634
  ironworking 38, 56, 773
  migration through 632, 1146, 1163–4
Anaximander 1122
ancestral landscapes 1277–8
ancient DNA (aDNA)
  analysis 7, 32, 95, 229, 1152
  horses 1015–16
  studies of 1138
Ancona (Italy) 801
Andalusia 316, 318, 320–1, 327
Andelfingen (Switzerland) 1159
Andros island 416
Anethum graveolens (dill) 665
Anfimov, N. V. 529
'Angel of Death' 1130
Ångermanland 147, 152
Angers (France) 735, 1110
Angili 1129–30
Angles 1041–2, 1170
Anglo-Frisian 1106
Anglo-Saxons 149, 1088
  halls 167
  migrations 1040–3
  time period 56
animal bones *see* bones: animal bones
animal farming/husbandry 155, 675–9
  Dolenjska group 383
  Iberian peninsula 683–5
  Netherlands 685–7
  and sacrifice 679–81
  Scandinavia and northern Germany 150
animals 682–3
  belonging to nomads 578–9
  brought to middens 1216
  as decoration 369
  domestic
    Dyakovo culture 600
    eastern Baltic 188
    in north-west Europe 70
  fur as textiles 849
  in Glyadenovo culture 609
  as livestock 665–6
  meat in burials 585
  in north-west Europe 70
  as offerings 251, 1275
  from outside Europe 681
  water deposits 1268–9
  wild 608, 1265
animal sacrifices 109, 330–1, 511, 679–81, 682,
    688, 1227, 1265
Animal style art 562–3, 585, 591, 1322–6
  Ananyino 603–5
  golden figurines 540
  Permic 609
  pseudo 601
  Saka 587
  Sarmatian 529, 592
  Scythian 539, 833

Annals (Tacitus) 122–3, 741, 1104, 1119, 1127–8, 1131, 1132
Antariatae 1146
Antes 211
Anthony, D. W. 1138
anthropological models 935
Antigonus II Gonatas 914, 1146, 1149, 1160–1
antimony 535
Antioch (Syria) 1128
Antiochus I Soter 1146–7
antler 162, 250–1, 825–6, 834, 1265
Antonine Wall (Scotland) 916
Anvallus 1297
Aorsi 530, 556, 589, 591, 596, 612
Apamea (Syria) 1125
Apennines 234, 345, 348, 349
Apium graveolens (celery) 665
Apollo
  carvings 1292
  sanctuary in Delos 1160
  temple in Delphi 1146
Apollonia (Albania) 498
Appadurai, A. 1230
Appenwihr (Alsace) 1309
Appian, *Illyrian Wars* 507
apples (*Malus sylvestris*) 665
Apremont (France) 637, 850, 1051, 1054–5
  barrows 1062, 1063
  burial practices 1058, 1059–60, 1061
Apter, D. E. 1087
Apuani 351
Apulian pottery 379, 383
Aquae Sextiae *see* Aix-en-Provence
Aquileia 366, 1109, 1124, 1127
Aquitaine 280, 288, 300
Aquitania 71, 120, 1126
Arabic language 1130
Arafat, K. 874–5
Aragón 322, 323
Aral Sea 585
Aramaic language 623, 624, 626
Aram-Damascus 624
Aratiepos 1113
Arausio *see* Orange
Arbedo (Italy) 346, 354, 358
Arbury Camp (England) 102
Arcadia 1124
archaeological culture 1083
archaeomagnetic dating 52
Archimedes 813, 1307
architecture
  for feasting 1220–1
  France 286–8
  housing 693–6
  ramparts 722–5
  Scandinavia and northern Germany 163
Arch of Galerius 956
Arc, River 1271
Arctic 576, 579, 659
Arda 904
Ardèche 297
Ardennes 69, 78, 1266, 1270
  houses 98
Ardiacians 1145
Areopagus 413, 414
Arganthonios 1110
Argos (Greece) 416, 940
Århus (Denmark) 147
Ariapeites 544
Arimaspians 612
Ariovistus 1092, 1114, 1126
Aristides, *Orationes* 1192
'aristocratic seat' 934
aristocratic settlements 73–7, 729–30
  see also elites
Aristophanes, *The Acharnians* 805
Aristotle 416
Arles (France) 277, 285, 288, 291, 292, 297
Arminius 122, 952
Armorica 76, 1110, 1118, 1126
  coins 1291
  Redones of 1293
armour, iron used in 786
Arnac-La-Poste (France) 96
Arnold, B. 1049, 1055, 1065
Arras burials 942, 1010, 1069, 1154, 1251–3
Arrian, *Anabasis* 513, 1145
Arruda, A. M. 316
Arrunte 1145
Arsacids 955–7
Arse/Saguntum (Spain) 336, 337
Arta/Ambracia (Greece) 450, 462
Artand (Hungary) 491

artefacts
  made from iron 777–80
  Scandinavia and northern Germany 162–5
Artemis Orthia sanctuary (Greece) 807
artisan settlements 718–19
  see also craftworking
artists 1305–7
Art of Horsemanship, The (Xenophon) 1001
artworks 1305–30
  Animal style 562–3, 585, 591, 1322–6
    Ananyino 603–5
    golden figurines 540
    Permic 609
    pseudo 601
    Saka 587
    Sarmatian 529, 592
    Scythian 539, 838
  central Europe 249
  Early style 1311–12
  and ethnic identity 1089
  Geometric style 1307–10
  iconography 1329
  La Tène period 1307, 1309–21
  Orientalizing style 1241, 1320–2
  Plastic style 1314–15
  representations of textile craft 861–2
  Roman Empire 1202
  'Sword styles' 1316
  Waldalgesheim style 1312–14
Arverni 928, 934, 938, 940, 982, 1121, 1125, 1131, 1168
  capital Corent 731
Aržan (Siberia) 854
Asarhaddon 528
Asbestos pottery 578, 598
Ascona complex 347
Ashdod 624
Ashkelon 624
Ashurbanipal II 541
Asia
  art 854
  burial practices 978
  chickens from 676
  coastline 39
  connection with Europe 24, 1130
  Europe to Asia area 575–612
  hemp from 665
  horses 1015
  ivory 637
  nomads 28
  racial stereotypes 1091
  steppes 525–6, 530, 563, 641
  see also Eurasia
Asiago plateau 366
Asia Minor 480, 490, 543, 807, 1163–4
  Celtic objects 1157
  coins 887
  Galatian tribes 1121
Aspromonte massif 422
Assas (France) 277, 278
Assendelver Polders (Netherlands) 68, 78
Assiros (Greece) 452
Assur 625
Assyria 527–8, 537, 625
  art 1321
  kings 941
  Neo-Assyrian sources 621–5
Asturias 315, 328, 807
Asva (Estonia) 174
Atenica 1244
Athena 428
  temple of 1160
Athena Alkis 914
Athenaeus 1125
Athena Nikephoros acropolis, Pergamon 1147, 1164
Athens (Greece) 408, 680, 928–9, 937–40, 1141
  Acropolis 19
  Attic pottery in 933
  burial practices 930–1
  burials 38, 413–14
  contact with the Near East 410
  temple of Athena 1160
  written law 1104
Atlantic roundhouses 103, 116, 1264
Atlantic zone 69, 620–1
  Britain 86, 103–4, 113, 115–16
  burial practices 940, 1252
  climate 26, 576
  coastline 22, 24, 155, 638, 933
  colonization 641
  communities 309
  North Atlantic 628, 641

rivers 305, 319–20
salt production 800
settlements 316
Atrebates 873
Attacotti 1129
Attalus I 1147
Attica 413–14, 428
Attic pottery 75, 78, 325, 361, 368, 420, 1244
black-figure 47, 359, 874
cups 81, 1064, 1242
imports 639
Protogeometric 415
red-figure 237, 359, 680, 932–3
and status 933
Attila 210, 211
attribution 1089–90
Atuatuca Tungrorum *see* Tongeren
Aucissa brooch from Troitsk 601
Aude-Garonne axis 300
Aude valley 282, 284, 288
Augst/Kaiseraugst/Augusta Raurica (Switzerland) 1192
Augustan period 99, 299, 350, 550, 724
burial practices 905
coins 906, 908
Roman bronze 902–3, 904
Augusta Raurica *see* Augst/Kaiseraugst
Augustodunum *see* Autun
Augustus 927–8, 931, 939–40, 1127
British kings named by 1132
campaigns 48, 239
coins 337, 892
death 1128
defeat 909
Aukštadvaris (Lithuania) 185, 187
Aulerci 1121, 1144
Aulnat (France) 294, 718, 873
Aulnat-Gandaillat 68, 90, 95, 121
Le Pâtural 95
Aulus Hirtius 1126, 1297
Aumes (France) 290, 295
Aure (France) 1051, 1061
Ausetani 325
Ausonian II 409, 434, 436
Ausonius 1105
Austen, Jane 936
Austria 682, 1052, 1055, 1059
bronze *situlae* 630
burial practices 230–1
coins 890
dendrochronology 50
gender 1065, 1067–8
horses 678
jet 807
salt mines 849
salt trade 1059–60
settlements 827
textile works 844
transition to La Tène period 244, 387
wagons 1006, 1241
weaving looms 846
Autka (Crimea) 555
Autricum *see* Chartres
Autun/Augustodunum (France) 1104, 1192, 1297
Auvergne 72, 90, 92, 95, 1213
Avaldsnes (Norway) 167
Avaricum *see* Bourges
Avena fatua (wild oats) 663
Avena sativa (oats) 663
Avena strigosa (bristle oats) 664
Avenches (Switzerland) 720, 732
Bois de Châtel *oppidum* 732
Avienus 1122, 1123
Avignon (France) 277, 292
Ávila (Spain) 1289
Avon, River 1284
awls 174
Axios/Vardar valley 451, 453–4, 456, 470
Aylesbury (England) 109
Aylesford (England) 109, 111, 112
Azov Sea 23, 526–7, 542, 543, 1129
cemeteries near 546, 550
helmets 1166
settlements 582
Aztec groups 1087, 1089

Babadag culture 464, 483, 489–90, 538
Babylon 877, 1163
Babylonia 625
bacaudae 1091
Bactria (Afghanistan) 596, 626
Badajoz 318
Badasset (France) 1272

Bad Buchau (Germany) 50
Baden-Württemberg 50, 225, 237, 246, 843
  burial practices 1066–7
  gender 1055, 1056, 1058–63, 1069–70
  status 1053
Bad Königshofen-Merkershausen (Germany) 1066
Bad Nauheim (Germany) 218, 245, 248
  pitch 808
  salt mines 800
Baetica 1188, 1193
baetyli (sacred stones) 331
Bagachina (Bulgaria) 915
Bagendon (England) 69, 105, 122, 880, 984, 1192
Bagienni 351
Bagnolo San Vito (Italy) 811
Bailleul-sur-Thérain (France) 734
Băiţa (Romania) 492
Baix Priorat 323
Bajkaj (Albania) 459
Bajo de la Campana shipwreck 630
Bajo Guadalquivir 317
Bakšiai (Lithuania) 187
Balagrae 627, 642
Bălăneşti (Romania) 499
Balaton, Lake 345, 384
Baldock (Herts) 111, 112, 980, 1287
Balearic Islands 306, 308, 325, 627
Balkan-Danube basin 890
Balkan-Danubian Hallstatt groups 539
Balkans 24, 40, 449–70, 479
  Alexander the Great's campaign 1145
  amber 1244
  animals 676
  Balkan peninsula 1159–62, 1163, 1171–2
  burial practices 505–6
  daggers 504
  maps of sites 371, 494
  migration through 1146
  northern 499–503, 505–6
  soil 25
Balksbury (England) 82–3
Ballachulish (Scotland) 1269
Ballinderry (Ireland) 87
Balline (Ireland) 118
Ballinrees (Ireland) 118
Baltic languages 601
Baltic region 21, 24, 40, 597
  amber 194, 630, 806, 880, 1112, 1123, 1241
  coastline 206–8
  coins 908
  eastern Baltic 21, 173–89
    sub-regions 187
  marine mammal oil 155
  Romans in 203
  solidi 158
  urns 195
  weaponry 954
  wetlands 25
Balto-Slavic languages 32
Balts 208–9, 212–13
Balzer, I. 247
Balzers (Liechtenstein) 361
Bambolo-type axes 360
Banat region 232, 480, 484, 486–7, 501, 508, 1158
Banck-Burgess, J. 844
banjo enclosures 105
Bann, River 1270
banquets *see* feasting
Baranja region 384, 387
Baranovka (Ukraine) 533
Baratella (Italy) 369
barbarians 582
Barbaricum 193, 204, 208
Barbary ape/macaque remains 108, 637–8, 1277–8
Barbey (France) 1051, 1060
Barbury Castle (England) 1219
Barca (Libya) 627, 642
Barkway (England) 1287
barley (*Hordeum vulgare*) 662–3, 669, 1228
barrages 160
Barrees (Ireland) 69, 119
barrow burials 72, 87
  central Europe 220
  eastern Baltic 178, 183, 184–5
Barry (France) 294
Bârseşti group 492, 498
Barth, F. E. 640, 1086
Bartseva, T. I. 585
Basarabia 479, 489, 498

Basarabi culture 232, 464, 483, 487, 490, 498, 539
Basel (Switzerland) 90
Basel-Gasfabrik 31, 121, 218, 244, 718
  animal bones 1000
  coins 903, 905
  deposition 1218
  pits 915
Bashkirs 1130
basileus 234
Basilicata 421, 422, 423–6
Baška (Croatia) 371, 378, 379
Basque language 306
Basse Yutz (France) 218, 249, 1222, 1223
Bastarnae 199–200, 503, 565
Batavi 1169
Bâtca Doamnei (Moldavia) 509
Batilly-en-Gâtinais (France) 68, 94
Batina (Croatia) 371, 384, 1164
Battersea shield 934, 975
Battle of Himera 1149
Baubliai (Lithuania) 187
Baudouvin-la-Bigoye (France) 277, 285
Bauska (Latvia) 178
Bavaria 50, 52, 219
  barrows 220
  burial practices 224–5, 239, 242, 244, 1055, 1066–7
  farmsteads 246
  gender 1058–63, 1069
  imports 237
  pottery 247
  semi-nomadic lifestyles in 222
  settlements 235–6
Bavay (France) 1198
Bayesian approach 50–4, 71
Bay of Biscay 830
Bay of Bothnia 155
Bay of Naples 877, 1111
Baysrath (Ireland) 69, 119
Baza (Spain) 1051
Bâzdâna (Romania) 500
beads, imported glass 634
beaked flagons (*Schnabelkannen*) 358–9
Beaumont Leys (England) 105
Beckford (England) 102, 105
Bede 1122
beech trees (*Fagus sylvatica*) 667–8
Beeglen, cemetery (Netherlands) 79
beer consumption 1227–8
Befort (Germany) 50
Behringen (Belgium) 900
Beilngries-Im Ried West (Germany) 1005
Beira 316
Bela cerkev (Slovenia) 383
Bela krajina region 379
Belarus 21, 1165–6
Belasica/Kerkini mountains 453, 462
Belaya, River 602, 605–6
Belerion (Cornwall) 1123
Belgae 1126, 1131
Belgica 71, 1115, 1118, 1126
Belgic Gaul 91, 109, 111–12, 120, 725, 1116, 1167
Belgios 1160
Belgium 72, 78, 844, 873
  cult enclosures 99
  loess belt 94, 98
Belgrade (Serbia) 388, 1141
  Belgrade-Karaburma 1161, 1162
Beliaus (Crimea) 551
Beli Most-Petrovo (North Macedonia) 454
Belisarius (Italy) 1129
Beljak/Villach (Austria) 371, 384
Bell Beaker pottery 330
Bell (Germany) 1051, 1067
Bellini collection 389
Bellovaci territory 734
Bellovesus 940, 1121, 1144
belly amphora 414
Belogrudovskaya 531, 532
Belozërka culture 531, 534
Belsk (Ukraine) 534
belts 203, 830
Benacci cemetery, Bologna (Italy) 348
Bender Jørgensen, L. 844, 848
Benecke, N. 678
Benvenuti, Este (Italy) 389
  situla 369
  tomb 122, 368
Beowulf 166, 168, 1104
Beram (Croatia) 371, 374
Beratzhausen (Germany) 1051, 1058
Berber groups 626–8

Berching-Pollanten (Germany) 218, 245, 246, 248, 718, 902
Berecynthia, deity 1288–9
Berezan island 525, 543
Berëzovka culture 532
Beringen (Belgium) 68, 99
Berkshire Downs 753, 1219
Berkshire Ridgeway 85
Berlizov, N. E. 583
Bernisse (Netherlands) 68, 98
Bern (Switzerland) 721, 905, 1115
  Bern-Reichenbachstrasse cemetery 904
Berranger, M. 782, 785
Berrocal-Rangel, L. 312
Berru helmets 240
Berry (France) 72, 95, 748, 1199, 1243
Besançon/Vesontio (France) 90, 91, 721, 733
Bescheid (Germany) 1051, 1065, 1068
Bessan (France) 277, 284, 286, 295
Bethlehem 167
Bettelbühl (Germany) 218, 1051, 1056, 1058
  dendrochronology 49
  grave 226
Betula pendula (birch) 666
Béziers (France) 277, 286, 291, 295
Biainele kingdom 622
'Biatec' 890
Bible
  Book of Numbers 963
  translations 1104
Bibracte (France) 5, 93, 238, 720, 721, 724, 726, 727, 729, 731–3, 811, 984, 987, 1191, 1192, 1287
  Côme Chaudron and Champlain 729–30, 931–2
  Parc aux Chevaux 932
  see also Mont Beuvray
Bielenin, K. 762
Biel, J. 856
Biel Water (Scotland) 53
'Big Men' 278, 283
Bila Cerkva (Ukraine) 496
Billendorf group 221
Binisafuller shipwreck 325
Bin Tepe cemetery (Turkey) 622
biogeography 29–32
birch (*Betula pendula*) 666
  pitch from 808
bird helmets 97
Birdlip Quarry (England) 1195
Birdoswald (England) 1285
birds
  hunting 679
  symbolism 1272
Birnie (Scotland) 69, 117, 909–10, 916
Bischofshofen-Pestfriedhof (Austria) 218, 231, 1051, 1055
Bisenzio (Italy) 348, 419
Biskupin (Poland) 194, 694, 699, 706–8, 727, 931, 941
  dendrochronology 49
Bitak necropolis (Crimea) 553
Bithynia 1146, 1164
bitter vetch (*Vicia ervilia*) 664
Bituriges 93, 733, 936, 1121, 1144
Björnhovda (Sweden) 160
black-figure ware 47, 359, 874
Black Forest 30, 248, 762
Black Loch crannog (Scotland) 49, 55, 86
Black Sea region 23, 24, 26
  barbarians 199
  early Iron Age 531–4
  Greek colonies 48, 464, 490, 494, 497–8, 508, 543, 854, 1165
  helmets 1166
  indigenous cultures 1329
  invasion of Huns 210
  northern 525–34
  Ostrogoths 211
  records 1122, 1123
  Sarmatians 591
  Scythian migration 492–3, 542–3, 581, 1307, 1322
  trade 629–30
  transport route 480, 780
blacksmithing 987
Blackwater estuary 112
Blagoevgrad basin 463
Blair Drummond (Scotland) 69, 109, 110, 824
Blanco-González, A. 703
Blandiana (Romania) 504
Blockbau technique 245, 694
blockhouses 86
blood sacrifice 251–2
bloomery process 776

blue pigment 804
Boas, F. 1080
Bobda (Romania) 480
Bobigny (France) 68, 88, 90, 93, 718
Bodensee 50
Bodrishtë (Albania) 459
Boé (France) 95, 1008
bog bodies 26, 108, 950, 1199, 1226, 1266–8, 1267–9, 1288
  animals as 1268–9
  clothing 860
  Netherlands 114, 123
  preservation of organic materials 26
bog deposits 806, 827, 976, 1008, 1168, 1292–3
bog environments 5, 787, 805
  Denmark 843, 844, 845, 849
  Germany 859
bog iron 784
bog ores 154, 601, 774
Bohemia 24, 219, 221, 231–2, 236, 237, 242, 244, 720, 1155, 1156–7
  coins 890, 901
Boh, River 208
Boii 242, 507, 811, 1124, 1144, 1151, 1313
Boito (Italy) 389
Bökönyi, S. 678
Bolgios 1146
Bollène (France) 294
Bologna (Italy) 42, 346, 348, 350, 355–8, 369, 1004, 1151
  Arsenale Militare cemetery 861
  Bologna-Arnoaldi *situla* 1006, 1010
Bombyx mori 854
Bondarikha culture 526, 531
bones 7, 825–6, 1199
  animal bones 9, 82, 188, 223, 233–4, 424, 433
    cattle 685–6
    craftworking with 807
    Crimea 555–6
    domestic animals 603, 682, 685
    evidence of long distance contact 681
    evidence of meat eating 676, 679, 1218, 1221, 1275
    fish and birds 679
    horse bones 233, 687, 1000, 1012
    limbs 511, 560, 563
    ratios 600, 676, 1217–18
    ritual practices 679, 702–3
    sheep and goats 681
    wild animals 608
  children's 1032
  craftworking with 75, 539
  cremated 116, 178, 184, 201, 222, 232, 360–1, 930
  decorative features 834
  decorative objects 834
  difficulties with analysing 1026
  economic value 575
  effect of soil 26–7, 69, 687, 930
  evidence of armed violence 950–3, 962
  evidence of decapitation 1266, 1270
  evidence of lifestyle 242
  isotope studies 30, 32, 880
  kostishche 609
  medical treatment of 813
  objects made from 412, 532, 559, 594–5, 599, 604, 807, 825–6
    replaced by iron 601
  working with 347, 509, 812
Bopfingen (Germany) 218, 246, 1276
Bordeaux (France) 1141
Borg (Norway) 146, 147, 153, 160, 163
Bornholm (Denmark) 203
Borremose fort (Denmark) 146, 159
Borscher Aue (Germany) 1320, 1324
Borysthenes 1123, 1127
Bosnia 22, 222, 678
Bosphorus 1129, 1146
Bosporan kingdom 543, 550, 554, 565, 594, 1166
Botai (Central Asia) 1015
Botalov, S. G. 596
Boudicca 929, 936, 989, 1131
Bouray (France) 1292
Bourges/Avaricum (France) 68, 73, 75–6, 91, 93, 717–18, 725, 733, 760, 878
  attic pottery 1064
  gender 1068
  status 933
Boviolles (France) 96, 732
Boyne, River 118
Bozkova, A. 463
Bozna (Romania) 484
bracelet roughouts 94

bracelets, glass 718, 801
Brachnówko (Poland) 196
Bracquemont (France) 721, 722
Bradano, River 424
Bradley, R. 1261
Bragny-sur-Saône (France) 68, 782
  elite settlement 76
Brandopferplätze 9, 360
Brandt, J. 710
Brather, S. 859
Braughing-Puckeridge (England) 112
breastfeeding 1069
breastplates 1325
Breiddin (Wales) 69
Bredon Hill (England) 69, 101–2
Breg/Frög 371, 379, 384, 1004
Breglnica, River 451, 456
Brennos 1121
Breno-Dos dell'Arca culture 362
Brežec (Slovenia) 371, 372
Brežice Gate 379
bridge building 53, 67
brine salt 800
Briona stone 1113
Brisley Farm (England) 1218
bristle oats (*Avena strigosa*) 664
Britain
  coins 892, 908
  earlier Iron Age 81–7
  fishing 71
  funerary practices 1252–3
  genetic studies of 'Celts' 31–2
  iron production 783–4
  later Iron Age 100–11
  maritime connection to Europe 21
  technical development 823
  texts on gender 1071
  trade 880–1
Brittany, elite settlements 76
Britzgyberg (France) 218, 237
Brnijca culture 454–5
Brno-Židenice (Czech Republic) 854
brochs 103–4, 115–16, 699
Broglio di Trebisacce (Italy) 408, 421, 422, 427
Broighter (Ireland) 69, 118, 982
Bromfield (England) 87
bronze 798
  coins 891–2, 898
  hoards 81, 482
  musical instruments 814
  objects in sanctuaries 369–70
  transition to iron 780–1
Bronze Age
  eastern Baltic 174–5
  feasting 1216
  Italy 346–9
bronze ornaments 187
  horse-related finds 363
bronzeworking 778
brooches 830
  radiocarbon dating 51
  Roman Iron Age 117–18
  status displays 982
  use in dating systems 44, 45
  see also fibulae
Broxmouth (Scotland) 69, 86, 103, 108
  chronology 51
  decorative features 832, 833
  ritual practices 1265
Brumfiel, E. M. 1087, 1089
Brunaux, J. L. 88–9, 952, 1275
Brun, J.-P. 423
Bryher (England) 69, 109, 118
Brylevka kurgan (Ukraine) 548
Bryn y Castell (Wales) 776, 777
bucchero 352, 356, 877
Bucy-le-Long (France) 88, 1247
Buffe-Arnaud (France) 48, 277, 297
buffer torcs 118
Bug, River 597
bulk trade 629–30
Bunbury, E. H. 1082
Bu (Orkney) 86
Burdigala 1104–5
Burebista, King 504, 507–8, 510
Burela (Spain) 980
Burgstallkogel (Austria) 383, 384
Burgundian culture 203
burial chambers 541
burial mounds 5, 222, 487, 506, 585, 746–50, 1238
  appropriation of 742–3
  barrows 178

chariots 1010
Crimea 550
disappearance in later Iron Age 14
Dolenjska group 380
elite burials 528, 560
giant 754
Gießübel-Talhau 875
Heuneburg plateau 236
Hochdorf 1003, 1005, 1006
horse burials 1011–12
Kelermes 540
Kraznoe Znamya 541
Kuban region 556
kurgans 8, 560–3
Magdalenenberg 30, 49, 225, 235
Norrie's Law 117
number and type of tombs 459–62
Rehovë 460
Romania 485
Sboryanovo 501
Scythian 542, 544
Styrian-Pannonian group 385
tarand graves 180–3
Velika Gruda 461
Vergina/Aegae 457
see also cemeteries; kurgans

burial practices
barrow burials 72, 87
central Europe 220
eastern Baltic 178, 183, 184–5
Bobigny 88
Britain 108–11, 112–13
celebrating male/female couples 1052
central Italy 419–20
changing over time 14
chariot burials 77
child burials
Crimea 553–4
Dacian kingdom 511
coins in 904–8
Dacian kingdom 511
Danube basin 503
Dyakovo culture 600–1
eastern Baltic 175–9
egalitarianism 940, 941–2
elite burials 978–9, 1062
Britain 113–14
end of the Iron Age 95–6
Scandinavia and northern Germany 163
end of the Iron Age 95–7
and gender 1050–2
Greece 412–13
of horses 1011–12, 1013
within houses 703
Iberian peninsula 310
Istrian peninsula 374
later Iron Age 108–11
lower Dnieper region 546–50
lower Volga region 562
Maeotians 563
Morgantina Cittadella (Sicily) 433
Netherlands 687
north Caucasus 537
northern Adriatic 368
North European Plain 97–8
and political structure 930–1
Prokhorovo culture 589–91
representativeness 1027
Roman Empire 1198–200
Scandinavia 149
status displays 978–9, 981
Thrace 466
Transylvania 487
types 6
unurned cremations 108
with wagons 1006–8, 1009
water deposits *see* bog bodies
see also funerary practices; grave goods

Burmeister, S. 1049, 1057–8, 1070
burnt offerings 168, 252, 361, 369
Burriac-Ilturo (Spain) 324, 326
Burrough Hill (England) 69, 102, 105
Burton Fleming (England) 850
Bury Hill (England) 105
Byblos 624
Býčí skála cave (Czech Republic) 788, 1270
Bykovo kurgan (Russia) 590
Bylany group 231
byre-houses 98, 114, 686
byres 151
Bystrzyca, River 1155

Cabrera II shipwreck 325
Caerwent (Wales) 1299

cairn graves, eastern Baltic 176
Calabria 421
Calleva Atrebatum *see* Silchester
Camarina (Sicily) 1141
cambisols 25
Camelina sativa (gold of pleasure) 665
Camonica valley 362–5
Ca' Morta (Italy)
  'Helmet tomb' 359
  wagon burial 355
Campania 417, 421
Campanian wares 873
Campolungo (Italy) 363
Camunian rock art 364–5
Camunic script 1113, 1114
Canaan 624
Cancho Roano (Spain) 309, 317, 331
Canegrate culture 347, 349
Cannabis sativa (hemp) 665
Cantabrian strip 308, 310–12
Canterbury (England) 112
Capel Garmon (Wales) 787
Capo di Ponte (Italy) 363
carburization 778–9
Carcassone (France) 277, 300
Carchemish 623
Carians 621
Carinthia 222
Carlingwark (Scotland) 1288
Cârlomănești (Romania) 508
Carmona/Carmo (Spain) 320, 1244
Carn Euny (England) 104, 113
Carnutes 1121
carnyces (trumpets) 97, 813–14, 958, 959
Carpathian and Danubian region 23, 477–513
Carpathian basin 206, 477–9
  Celtic horizon 493–7
  earlier Iron Age 482–8
  early iron use 480–2
  La Tène burials 1158
  seventh to third centuries BC 491–7
Carpathian mountains 198
Carrickmines Great (Ireland) 69, 106
Carthage (Tunisia) 627
Cartimandua 929, 936
caryatids 501
Casa di Ricovero cemetery (Italy) 367–9
  Tomb 23 368–9
  Tomb 236 368
Casalmoro settlements 366
casa retica 361
Căscioarele (Romania) 500
casemate technique 452
cashels 119
Cassius Dio 1131
  Roman History 508–9
Castanea sativa (chestnut) 665
Castellace (Italy) 422
Castellazzo della Garolda (Italy) 346, 366
Castellet de Banyoles (Spain) 324, 335
Castelletto Ticino (Italy) 346, 356, 358
Castell Henllys (Wales) 69, 103
Castellieri culture 374
Castelnau-le-Lez (France) 278
Casticus of the Sequani 928
Castle O'er (Scotland) 116
Castro Lezenho (Portugal) 333, 334
Castro Marim (Portugal) 316
castros (fortified sites) 308–10, 314, 318, 983, 1193
catacombs 559
Catalonia 307
Caterthuns (Scotland) 69
cattle 676, 678, 681, 682–3
  Netherlands 685–7
cauldrons 10, 109, 1216, 1219–20, 1222–3
  iron fixings for 787
Causse necropolis, Labruguière (France) 281
Cauuet, B. 799, 813
caves 1270
  as cult sites 89
celery (*Apium graveolens*) 665
Celestino, S. 317
Celtiberia 307, 314, 335, 336, 1106, 1110, 1143, 1148, 1289
Celtic art 5, 832–3, 881, 958, 1137–8, 1140–1, 1324
  animals in 1324
  in Bohemia 221
  continuing tradition 1319
  early 1307, 1311–15
  Early style 1311–12
  and Greek culture 1151, 1305–6
  iron horse sculpture 1013–14

Orientalizing style 1320–1
palmette forms 1222
warrior statues 1326
Celtic Baeturia 316, 318
'Celtic fields' 150, 708, 751
Celtic horizon 493–7
Celtic period *see* La Tène period
Celtic Revival 1202
Celtoscepticism 1140
Celts 14
in the classical world 1143–50
coins 811
genetic studies 31–2
mercenaries 14, 1148–9, 1166–7
migration 1140–50
to Anatolia 1163–4
to Balkan peninsula 1159–62
to eastern Europe 1157–9
to Italy 1150–2
to Ukraine and Belarus 1165–6
to western and central Europe 1153–7
myths 1121
script 1113
social structure 973
cemeteries 6–7, 108–9, 221–2, 331
Aylesford-type 112
Baltic region 181
barrows 116, 220, 226, 229
chariot burials 78, 108
cremation 311, 314, 322
dating 56
in defensive settlements 319
elite burials 240
flat grave 6, 14, 232, 242–4
Jastorf culture 199
Oksywie culture 201
Scythian Age 491
France 72
gendered 1056
genetic studies 31
Germany 225–6
Hallstatt site (Austria) 4, 12, 30, 43, 219, 230
Iapodic 377
inhumation 51, 87, 112, 208, 210
isotope studies 31
Istrian peninsula 374
La Tène 197–8
narratives 166–7
Oksywie culture 206
pit graves 179, 184, 279–82
representativeness 1027
in rural settlements 94, 98
Scandinavia 146
Scandinavia and northern Germany 166–7
sizes 79
stone constructions 183–4
with stone constructions 183–4
tumulus 233, 234–5, 253
Urnfield 78, 80, 194–5
weapons 201
Wielbark culture 208
Zarubincy culture 200
see also burial mounds
Cenabum *see* Orléans
central Alpine region 360–5
central Europe 22, 217–54
Celtic migration to 1153–7
chronological frameworks 42–3
earlier Iron Age 219–22, 235–7
later Iron Age 238–9, 247–52
La Tène mortuary evidence 239–44
material culture 247–9
religion and ritual 249–52
settlements 235–9
central Mediterranean and the Aegean 23, 407–42
Central Meseta 305
ceramic dating 51
cereal-drying kilns 119
cereal grains 664
Čergoviče/Tscherberg (Austria) 371
Cernon-sur-Coole (France) 1316–17
Cerrillo Blanco de Porcuna (Spain) 329, 334, 1328
Cerro de los Santos (Spain) 1051, 1066
Čertomlyk (Ukraine) 1001
Cerveteri (Italy) 348
Regolini-Galassi tomb 1242
Cessetania 324
Chaffois (France) 635–6
chaîne opératoire 789
chain migrations 1139
chains, Roman Iron Age 117
Chalcolithic period 278–9

Chalkidike 451, 453
Chalkis (Greece) 411
chamber graves 166, 231–2
  Crete 415
Champagne region 1008, 1060, 1068–9, 1154
  meat in burials 1218
  see also Aisne-Marne region
Chao Samartín (Spain) 309
charcoal production 762, 805–6
chariot burials 77, 80–1, 87, 108
  timespan 53
  two-wheeled 1008–11, 1247
Chartres-Autricum (France) 721, 1295–7
Chassenard (France) 905
Chatalka (Bulgaria) 957
Châteaumeillant (France) 68
  oppidum 90
  ramparts 91, 92
Châtillon-sur-Glâne (Switzerland) 218, 237
Châtonnaye (Switzerland) 1051
Chatyr-Dag mountain 555
Chavéria (France) 68, 218, 229
  barrow burials 72
Chechenia 537
Cheganda sub-culture 606
Chemilla (France) 1051
Chenopodium album (fat hen) 152
Cheremis 602
Chernogorovka culture 526, 527, 532
Chernoles-Zhabotin cultures 526, 532, 534
chernozems 25
Chernyakhov culture 207, 211, 546, 911
cherries (*Prunus avium*) 665
Chertomlyk (Ukraine) 544, 545
Chester (England) 1285
chestnut (*Castanea sativa*) 665
Chiavari (Italy) 346, 351, 352–3
chickens 676–8, 683
chiefdoms 871, 872
childbirth 1033, 1040, 1069–70
child burials 1069
  Crimea 553–4
  Dacian kingdom 511
  mortality rates 1027–8, 1032–3
childcare roles 1070
Childe, V. G. 784–5, 986, 1082
China, imported glass 634
Chiscani (Romania) 500
Chiseldon (England) 109, 1219–20
Chisten'koe (Crimea) 555
Chiusi (Italy) 419
Choisy-au-Bac (France) 781
Chorygi (Greece) 450, 454
Chossenot, M. 1029
Chouilly Les Jogasses (France) 1051, 1060, 1068, 1247
Chřín (Czech Republic) 218, 237
Christianity 1299–300
chronological frameworks 41–6
  inconsistencies 43
chronology
  central Mediterranean and the Aegean 408–10
  in north-west Europe 71–2
  Scandinavia and northern Germany 147–9
  scientific methods 48–55
Ciceu-Corabia (Romania) 484
Cimbri 940, 1029, 1071, 1168
Cimmerian route 480, 486
Cimmerians 527–8, 780
circular architecture 67–8
Circum-Alpine zone
  funerary practices 1240–4, 1246–9
  timber road and bridge building 53
cist graves 366–7, 457
cists 357
Cis-Urals 576, 586
  forest zone 602–11
Cité d'Alet (France) 721
cities
  Roman Empire 1192–3
  see also urbanization
Ciumeşti (Romania) 495, 786, 1141, 1166–7, 1249
civitas 733–5, 1189
Civitas Camunnorum 364–5
civitates 93, 1189, 1192
Clachtoll (Scotland) 69, 116
Clarke, D. L. 699, 983, 1140
Clark, G. 1137
class 871
  and democracy 929–30
classical civilizations, as a marker of the end of the Iron Age 39

classical writers 1120–30
Claudius, invasion of Britain 71
clay 802–3
  see also wheel-thrown pottery
Clearances (Scottish) 937
Cliffs End Farm (England) 31
Clifton Quarry (England) 83
climate 26–9
  catastrophe of AD 536–550 152, 153, 189
  eastern Baltic 173–4
cloche-graves 196
Clonycavan (Ireland) 69
  Clonycavan Man 108
Cloongownagh (Ireland) 69
clothing 859–61
  accessories 858–9
  see also textiles
club wheat (*Triticum aestivum*) 662
Cnip (Scotland) 69, 104, 1264
coarsewares 433
coastal settlements, North European Plain 78–9
coastland 152
coastlines 24
Cochan-Satovcha (Bulgaria) 450, 463
cognitive processes 1094
coins 887–916
  adoption in Iron Age Europe 895–9
  Britain 892, 908
  bronze 891–2, 898
  circulation 899–908
  colours 893
  cut-marked 906–7
  Dacian kingdom 510
  depositions 899, 903–4, 905–8, 914
  designs 891
  eastern Baltic 187
  gold 798–9, 811, 890, 891–2
  horse imagery 1291
  Iberian peninsula 337
  iconography 898–9, 912
  inscriptions 888, 1117–19, 1132
  later Iron Age
    Britain 109–10
    north-west Europe 89–90
  minting 890–1, 892–5
  North European Plain 99
  preference for 'prestige' metals 830–1
  production 810, 894
    in *oppida* 732–3
  and religion 904–8
  Roman Iron Age 117–18, 908–12
  in rural settlements 899–900
  Scandinavia 156–7
  silver 798–9, 811, 888–9, 891
  status displays 982
  urbanization 900–4
  use in dating systems 48
Colchester (England) 69
Colchis culture 535–6
Collis, J. 52–3, 246, 948, 1062
colonization 152
Comacchio (Italy) 1313
Comaroff, J. 1089
Combo de la Semal (France) 295
combs 826
communities 703–9
  eastern Baltic 188
  social stratification 709–10
Como (Italy) 346, 355
Condé-sur-Suippe (France) 68, 91, 727, 902
  see also Variscourt/Condé-sur-Suippe
conflict 1091–2
connectivity 619–20
conspicuous consumption 979–80
Conțești (Romania) 511
Conwy Mountain (Wales) 103
cooking vessels, Dacian kingdom 508
copper 482, 798
  cult figurines 610
  mines 535
coral 802
Corbières 299
Corcoran, J. X. W. P. 1222
Cordillera Cantábrica 305
Corent (France) 68, 92, 96, 732, 906
Corinth (Greece) 431, 1141
Corlăteni-Chișinău culture 483, 489
Corlea (Ireland) 69, 106, 1269
Cornwall (England) 1203
Corsica 438–40
Corylus avellana (hazelnuts) 665
Costești-Cetățuie (Romania) 903
Cotnari (Romania) 499

Coțofenii din Dos (Romania) 500
Cotswold Community site (England) 83, 104
couches 228
Courland (Latvia) 177
Courtesoult (France) 1051, 1059, 1063, 1068
Covesea Caves (Scotland) 116
Cozia group 483, 489
Cozia-Sacharna culture 526, 539–40
Cozza Torte (Corsica) 439
Cozzo Presepe (Italy) 408, 424, 425
craftworking 75, 155, 708
  Britain, later Iron Age 100
  central Europe 247–8
  France 295–6
  settlements 718–19
  and social status 986–8
  textiles 861–2
cremation
  difficulties with analysing 1026
  in north-west Europe 72
creolization 1190
Crete 410, 415–16
Crévéchamps (France) 68, 72–3, 218, 221, 235
Crick (England) 69, 105
Crickley Hill (England) 69, 85, 983
Crimea 526–7, 534–5, 550–5
  sanctuaries 555–6
'crisis of 400' 318
Croatia 222, 1146
Croesus, King 621
crops 660, 661–4
  cultivated plants 664–5
  on marshes 669–70
cross-dating 46–7
crouched inhumations 118, 1199
Crow Creek (USA) 963
crown neck-rings 199
crypts 551, 553–5
Cuciurpula (Corsica) 408, 438–40
Cucorăni (Romania) 489
Cugir (Romania) 506
Culbin Sands (Scotland) 987
cult sites 88–9, 99
Cults Loch (Scotland) 69, 86
  dendrochronology 49, 55
cultural construction 1085
culture history 1081–3
cult wagon 9, 388
Cumae (Italy), foundation dates 48
Cunliffe, B. 307, 936, 983, 1062, 1215
currency bars 783–4
cut-marked coins 906–7
Cvinger (Slovenia) 379
Cyprus 413, 622–3
  early iron use 38
  sacrifice of horses 680
Cyrenaica 626
Cyrene 627
Cyrus the Great 877
cystic fibrosis 32

Dacian kingdom 503–12, 1188–9
  Roman conquest 512–13
daggers 1058–9, 1060
  heart-shaped handles (*akinakai*) 537
  sica type 511
Dalj (Croatia) 371
Dalmatia 1188
Damendorf (Germany) 860
Danebury hillfort (England) 69, 85–6, 100–1, 931, 983
  animal deposits 1012, 1065
  egalitarianism 942
  feasting 1224–5
  human remains 950, 951, 1265
  iron production 779, 783–4
  roundhouses 931, 932
  settlement in environs 52, 84, 105
  shrines 1277
Dankirke (Denmark) 909
Danube basin 194
  lower 488–90, 497–503, 538–9
Danube, River 24, 203, 217
Daorson (Bosnia-Herzegovina) 808–9
Dätgen (Germany) 860
  Dätgen Man 1268
dating schemes 41–6
  scientific methods 48–55
Daugava basin 179
Deal (England) 69, 981
de Architectura (Vitruvius) 1307
death rates 1027–8
de Bello Civili (Lucan) 758

de Bello Gallico (Caesar) 120, 757–8, 774–5, 1071, 1115, 1126
- Book 1 733, 936, 982
- Book 2 725, 754, 1168
- Book 3 786
- Book 4 1010
- Book 5 1012
- Book 6 507, 935, 972, 976, 986, 1040, 1119, 1130, 1275, 1294–5, 1297
- Book 7 91, 92, 725, 733, 741, 760, 786

decapitations 952–3, 1265–6
- in caves 1270
- and religion 1299–300

Decebalus, King 504, 510
Deceneus, King 510
Déchelette, J. 44, 238–9, 729, 901, 1143
decorative features 832–4
- animals 369
- Danube basin 502
- Geometric style 1307–10
- on helmets 958
- horses 1290–1
- Italian pottery 358
- movement into temperate Europe 638–9
- pigments 804
- red glass/enamel 801–2
- Sarmatian culture 593
- Scandinavia and northern Germany 162
- and status display 980–2
- styles 13
- textile craftwork 861–2

deer motifs 1319
deforestation 29, 152, 154
Dehn, W. 634, 720
de Hoz, J. 335
Deisslingen (Germany) 635, 636
Dejbjerg (Denmark) 146, 160
- wagon 156, 1008

de Lanfranchi, F. 439
Delev, P. 468
Delphi (Greece) 1141, 1162–3
Demir Kapija gorge 451
Demlfeld (Austria) 252, 1053
democracy 929–30
demographics 1025, 1026–8
- grave goods 1033–4
- migration 1040–4, 1042–4

de Mortillet, G. 1141–2
Demoule, J.-P. 1029
denarius hoards 117, 118, 510, 891, 902, 909
dendrochronology 49–50, 54–5
Den Haag (Netherlands) 68
Denmark
- bog bodies 1267, 1269
- German peoples 1169
- textiles research 843–4, 850–1, 860

dependency 155
depopulation 210
deposits 9, 81, 96–7, 915, 1269–70
- agricultural tools 819
- alcohol 1227
- in Britain 108–11, 113
- coins 899, 903–4, 905–8, 914
- domestic 1264–6
- feasting equipment 1218–20
- horses 1011–12
- human bodies 1267–8, 1294
- iron 788–9
- ritual 484, 487, 511, 678, 897, 903, 908, 933, 1200, 1264–6
  - burnt offerings 361, 369
  - central Europe 250–2
  - France 1276
  - Iberian peninsula 684–5
  - Lincolnshire (England) 1203
  - pottery 81
  - Scotland 1279
- vessels 485, 487, 511
- votive 363, 369, 556, 629, 847, 1273
- warriors 953
- water 9, 250, 355, 933–4, 1198
  - of dead bodies 1199
- and wealth 974–7, 1065–8
- weapons 941
- *see also* grave goods

Derrida, J. 876
Desenne, S. 830
Deskford (Scotland) 1269
destruction of wealth 933, 1201
diadem belts 332
Diarville (France) 1051, 1058
Díaz-Andreu, M. 330
Diepeveen-Jansen, M. 830
dies (coin minting) 893–4

diet 30
Dietler, M. 877, 979, 1229–30
Difesa di San Biagio (Italy) 423–4
dill (*Anethum graveolens*) 665
Dillingen-Kicklingen (Germany) 1051, 1067
Diodorus Siculus 430, 529, 974, 1071, 1121, 1143, 1148
Dionysius of Halicarnassus, *Roman Antiquities* 389
discrepant experience 1190
Diviciacus of the Aedui 935, 1119
DNA
  ancient DNA (aDNA)
    analysis 7, 32, 95, 229, 1152
    horses 1015–16
    studies of 1138
  mitochondrial DNA (mtDNA) 31–2
Dnieper region, lower 545–50
Dnieper, River 526, 528
Dniester region 199
Dniester, River 479, 539
Dobian (Germany) 904
Dobolii de Jos (Romania) 1245
Dobova group 380
Dobrina (Bulgaria) 499
Dobrogea/Dobrudzha 479, 480, 489, 490, 499, 508, 528
Dobroselie (Ukraine) 491
Dobrzankowo (Poland) 201, 202
Dobunni 873
Dodona (Greece) 1160
dogs 678–9, 681
  as meat 676
  water deposits 1269
Doiran basin 451, 453
Dolenjska group 379–83, 385, 387
Dolenjske Toplice (Slovenia) 1001
dolmens 466–7
domestic animals
  Dyakovo culture 600
  eastern Baltic 188
  in north-west Europe 70
domestic architecture 693–6
Domitian 509, 511, 512
domus 729
Donec hills 526
Donja Brnjica (Kosovo) 450, 454–6
Donja Dolina (Bosnia-Herzegovina) 694
Donnersberg (Germany) 720, 723, 734
Don, River 23, 193, 208, 526–7, 579, 582–3, 594, 596, 1130
  region 560–3
Doppelspitzenbarren 248
Dorians 462
Dorna an der Mulde (Germany) 1141, 1167
Dornach (Switzerland) 1141, 1155
Dorset peoples 628
Dorsey earthwork (Ireland) 107
Dos Gustinaci facies 360
Doubs, River 76, 91, 721
Douix (France) 9, 250
dracones 958
Dragonby (England) 105
dragon pair 1153
Dragoyna (Bulgaria) 450, 465
Drava, River 345
dream interpretation 1297–8
dress accessories 209
Driehaus, J. 785
drinking vessels 118
  Danube basin 502
  Germany 227–8
  Italy 352
  La Tène style 239, 241
Drňa (Slovakia) 1316
dromos (passages) 233, 385, 586
druids 986
Druids 1262, 1284, 1294–7
Drumanagh (Ireland) 69, 118
Dryburn Bridge (Scotland) 108
drying kilns 119
drystone structures 103, 759
dual-processual theory 1255–6
Dublin (Ireland) 118
Dubovskaya, O. R. 532, 533, 537, 542
Duchcov/Dux (Czech Republic) 9, 43, 218, 242, 250, 1153, 1160, 1161
Düdingen (Switzerland) 1051, 1061
'Duenos' inscription 1104, 1105
Duero valley 311, 312–13
Dühren (Germany) 1141, 1169
Dumnorix of the Aedui 928, 935, 936
Dún Ailinne (Ireland) 54, 1221

Dún Aonghasa (Ireland) 69, 87
Dun Glashan (Scotland) 103
Dunnicaer (Scotland) 69, 116
Dünsberg (Germany) 218, 250, 1169
Durkheim, E. 873
Durocortorum *see* Reims
Durotriges 873, 1131
Dürrnberg (Austria) 8, 50, 218, 230–1, 1051, 1065–6
  amber 683
  animal skins 678
  burial chambers 240
  burial practices 221
  child burials 1069, 1265
  children working in mines 989
  decorative objects 1320
  dendrochronology 49
  elite female burials 1035, 1052–3
  grave goods 48
  male burials 1067
  pigments 804
  salt mines 25, 248, 682, 800, 986
  silk from 637
  textiles 844, 847, 848
  warrior grave 1010
Dutch Rivers area 79, 685
Duval, A. 720
dwelling mounds 669
Dyakovo culture 598–601
Dyakovo hillfort (Russia) 599–600
dyes 669, 805, 850–3
Dying Gaul sculpture 1147
dyke complexes 111–12, 159

Early style art 1311–12
ear-rings 414
East Chisenbury (England) 1216
eastern Baltic 21, 173–89
  sub-regions 187
eastern central Europe 21–2, 193–213
  early Iron Age 193–8
  Germanic tribes 198–203
  Great Migration Period 210–13
  La Tène influence 197–8
  Roman Iron Age 203–13
eastern Europe
  Celtic migration to 1157–9
  chronological frameworks 41
  climate 28–9
  silver coins 831
East Yorkshire 829
  chariot burials 974
  evidence of violence 952
  female burials 1065
  funerary practices 1251
  meat in burials 1217–18
  Tancred Pit Hole spring 745
  weapons in burials 949
Ebro, River 305
Ebro valley 311–13
Eckardt, H. 1201
economies
  eastern Baltic 188–9
  and group identity 1092
  Scandinavia and northern Germany 150–8
Eddic myth 162
Edeta (Spain) 683
Edin's Hall (Scotland) 978–9
Edom 624
education 1119
Egbeo 1115
Egesheim (Germany) 9, 218, 250
Egg, M. 234
Egypt 624–5, 800
Egyptian blue 804
Ehrenbürg (Germany) 218, 245
einkorn (*Triticum monococcum*) 664
Eislfeld (Germany) 231
Eketorp (Sweden) 146, 147, 153, 160, 165
Eklizi-Burun sanctuary (Crimea) 555
Ekron 624
Elam (Iran) 625
Elbe, River 199, 201
Elbląg (Poland) 207
Elche/Ilici (Spain) 332–3, 1051
elite burials 978–9, 1062
  Britain 113–14
  end of the Iron Age 95–6
  Scandinavia and northern Germany 163
elites 971–91
  aristocratic settlements 73–7, 729–30
  destruction of wealth 933
  differences in skeletons 30
  exchange of prestige goods 873

elites (*cont.*)
prestige materials 831
Scandinavia and northern Germany 156–7
see also social stratification
Elizavetinskaya 556
Ellekilde cemetery (Denmark) 167
Elling Woman 1267–8
El Molí d'Espígol (Spain) 325
Elm-Sprengen (Germany) 1051
El Palomar (Spain) 317
El Sec shipwreck 325
Els Estinclells (Spain) 325
El Soto de Medinilla (Spain) 311
Els Vilars d'Arbeca (Spain) 309, 325
El Turó de Ca n'Oliver (Spain) 324
El Turuñelo (Spain) 317
Elymii 430
Emmerting-Bruck 635
emmer wheat (*Triticum dicoccum*) 608, 662
Empel (Netherlands) 68, 99, 906
emplecton technique 500, 509
Emporion *see* Ampurias
enamel/red glass 801–2
enceintes 960–1
enchantment 958
Enclosure Acts 937
enclosures 9, 53, 75, 119, 122
Alpine regions 237
around nucleated settlements 706
banjo enclosures 105
for burials 98, 176, 354, 367
cult 99, 246
ditched 76, 83, 88–9, 106, 251, 710, 730, 904, 915
farmsteads 94, 752–3
fenced 729, 731
figure-of-eight (Navan) 54, 87
France 1275–6
gateways 725
hengiform 1277–8
hilltop sites 51, 82, 84, 86, 777
Ireland 959
kinship groups 876
monumental 754–5
multiple 103, 113, 180
in *oppida* 727
palisaded 83, 86, 96, 752
for ritual practices 1293
tower-enclosures 318
urban communities 288
Wales 985
walled (*enceinte*) 283, 329, 464
Engadine 360
Engels, F. 936
Engstingen-Großengstingen (Germany) 1051
Enns, River 221
Ensérune (France) 277, 284, 295, 299, 931
Entremont (France) 48, 277, 298, 931, 942
warriors 1273–4
Epirus 449, 458–9
Epitome (Justin) 301
Epona 1014, 1197, 1290–1
Epulon 375
Ercavica (Spain) 337
Eretria (Greece) 411
Erezovo (Bulgaria) 1116
Erkenbrechtsweiler (Germany) 356–7
Erstfeld (Switzerland) 218, 250
Esarhaddon, King 625
Espanca stone 1111
Espeyran (France) 277, 285, 294
Este culture 366
Este (Italy) 9, 346, 366, 367–8
Estonia
barrow burials 185
climate 173–4
coastal 187, 188
hillforts 185–6
social structure 188
stone cist graves 175–6
tarand graves 178
Esus 1285–6
Esvres-sur-Indre (France) 905
Étang de Berre (France) 285
ethnē 416, 470
ethnic labels 217
group identities 1085–92
Iberian peninsula 330
and power 1089–92
stereotypes 1091
ethnoarchaeology 1087
ethnographic records 934–5
Etruria 419, 877, 878

Etruscans 193–4, 348–9, 418, 420–1, 1112
alphabetic systems 631
horses 1012
Etruscoid script 1113
Euboea 410, 411, 420, 1111
Euesperides 627
Eurasia, textiles from 854–5
Europe
boundaries 619, 620–8, 641–2
climate 26–9
division into zones 19–24
soils 24–5
topography 24
European Union (EU) 19
Europe to Asia 23, 575–612
Evans, C. 827
events, use in dating systems 48
excavations
of burial mounds 5
scale of 4
exchange 871–83
late Iron Age 879–81
executions 96, 1253, 1268
Extremadura 308, 317–18
Ezinge (Netherlands) 68, 79, 99, 686

fabrics 805, 848–56
see also textiles
face-urns 195, 196
Fadlan, Ahmad Ibn 1130
Fagus sylvatica (beech trees) 667–8
falx type swords 511
family living 1037–8, 1040
childcare roles 1070
households 696–703
Scandinavia and northern Germany 150
Fântânele-Dâmbul Popii (Romania) 1158
farming *see* agriculture
farmsteads 7, 8, 706, 1196
coin hoards 900
elite 236
fortified (*Viereckschanze*) 8, 246, 743–4, 752, 753, 1276–7
hierarchical 709–10
and land ownership 154, 743
large 237, 246, 700
and rules on marriage 1032
single 179, 185, 235, 246
surrounded by ditches 94–5, 104, 236
fashions 830
fat hen (*Chenopodium album*) 152
feasting 109, 234, 330–1, 1213–31
archaeological evidence 1217–25
classical world 1216
comparative evidence 1215–16
equipment 980, 1217–20, 1221–3
food eaten in 1226–9
in funerals 1255
Iberian peninsula 330–1
iron artefacts 786–7
literary evidence 1214–15
movement of social practices 639
social models 1229–30
specialized architecture 1220–1
as status display 979–80
storage for 1224–5
Fécamp type fortifications 91
Feddersen Wierde (Germany) 114–15, 146, 147, 668, 697
Feinman, G. 708
Fellbach-Schmiden (Germany) 218, 1276, 1316–18, 1320
felloes 1006
Fennoscania 29
Ferigile group 492, 498
Fernández-Götz, M. 236, 1050
ferrum noricum 782, 798
Ferry Fryston (England) 1252–3
fertility 1033, 1069–70
Fesques (France) 88
Feurs (France) 294, 719
fibulae 242, 252, 858–9
see also brooches
Ficus carica (fig) 665
fields 152
eastern Baltic 188
field systems 83
fig (*Ficus carica*) 665
figurines, Glyadenovo culture 610
Filippovka burial ground (Russia) 587–9, 633
Filottrano (Italy) 1313
Fin Cop (England) 69, 100, 962–3
finger-rings 244
Finland 21, 156, 177, 180, 183, 187–8, 661, 696

Finnic languages 173
Finno-Ugric cultures 579, 601
Finsterlohr (Germany) 720
fire
  'crisis of 400' 318
  destruction in 151, 236
firedogs 787, 980
Firth of Forth 116
Fischer, J. 635
fishing 679
Fiskerton (England) 69, 109
Fison Way (England) 69, 108, 113, 1230, 1298
Fitzjohn, M. 435, 696
Fitzpatrick, A. P. 1230
flagons 1223–4
flans (coin minting) 894
flat grave cemeteries 6, 14, 232, 242–4
  Crimea 551
  Jastorf culture 199
  Oksywie culture 201
  Scythian Age 491
flax (*Linum usitatissimum*) 665
Fléré-la-Rivière (France) 68, 95–6
Flögeln-Eekhöltjen (Germany) 114, 146, 147, 670
flooding 668–9
Florensac (France) 277
fluted pottery 489
Fluzin, P. 782, 785
Fochteloo (Netherlands) 114
Fokkens, H. 79
Folly Lane, St Albans (England) 111, 880
Fontes Hispaniae Antiquae 306
Fontes Sequanae 1284
food 1226
  cultivated 660–5
  dairy products 681
  storage 1224–5
  see also feasting
'fool's gold' 774
Foppe di Nadro (Italy) 364
Forbiger, A. 1082
forest zone 666–8, 756–9
  Cis-Urals 602–11
  exploitation 759–63
  north-east Europe 597–601
  ritual practices 1266
  as sanctuary 758–9
fortifications 103, 959–61
  Crimea 551
  Dacian kingdom 506–7, 509
  Fécamp type 91
  in north-west Europe 73–6
  status displays 983
  see also hillforts; hilltop sites
Fossé de Pandours (France) 720, 722, 723
  as *civitas* capital 733–4
  coin production 732, 894
  muri gallici 725–6
fossil materials 806–7
foster parents 1037–8
Foster, S. 699
founder burials 1055
foxtail millet (*Setaria italica*) 664
Fragaria vesca (strawberries) 665
Francavilla-Marittima (Italy) 408, 422, 426, 427
  Macchiabate cemetery 426
France 275–301
  burial practices 229–30
  economies 283
  gender 1061, 1063
  pre-urban societies 276–83
  settlements 284–8, 296–300
  urbanization 284–96
Franche-Comté 1114
Franconia 220, 232
Frankenstein, S. 872, 875, 978
Frankfurt-Stadtwald (Germany) 218, 220, 1051
Franzhausen (Austria) 32
Frattesina (Italy) 346, 347
Freigang, Y. 862
Frey, O.-H. 861, 1063
Fritzens-Sanzeno culture 234, 361
  bowls 252
Frög/Breg (Austria) 371, 379, 384, 1004
frontiers, Roman Iron Age 114–19
fruits 665
Führholz (Austria) 371
Fulford, M. 1197
funerary practices 1237–56
  Circum-Alpine zone 1240–4, 1246–9
  north-west Europe 1246, 1251–3

Przeworsk culture 201
Scandinavia and northern Germany 166
social significance 1254–6
southern Europe 1244–5, 1249–51
see also burial practices
fur hunting 608
furnaces 186–7, 310
Fürstensitze (princely sites) 7, 236, 717, 748, 785, 872, 939
funerary practices 1242–4
in north-west Europe 73–7
Fyn (Denmark) 1041

Galanina, L. K. 540
Galatia 1147
Galicia 307
Galician-Lusitanian warriors 329
Galindai 209
Galish-Lovachka (Ukraine) 1141
Gallicos, River 451
Gallic War 54, 111, 903, 906
Gallipoli peninsula 467
Gallo-Roman imports 112
Gánovce (Slovakia) 480
Garamantes 627
Garn Boduan (Wales) 103
Garrow, D. 881
Garton-Wetwang (England) 69
Gascony 72
gateways 725
Gath 624
Gauls 10, 1144
civitas 733–5
invasions 71, 937
texts on gender 1071
Gáva culture 482–3, 486, 489
Gaza 624
geese 678
Geldermalsen (Netherlands) 69, 99
Gell, A. 958
gelysols 25
Gemeinlebarn (Austria) 1051, 1053, 1058
gender 1049–73
fluidity 1056–60
roles and identity 1069–70
and social status 989
in texts 1070–1
genetic studies 31–2
Genna Maria (Sardinia) 437
Genoa (Italy) 346
Genoa-Portofranco 351
Geoffrey of Monmouth 1120
Geography (Ptolemy) 207
Geography (Strabo) 388, 508, 582, 775
Geometric period 681
Geometric pottery 453, 464
Geometric art style 1307–10
geopolitical units 19–21
Gergovia, battle of 936
Gerlingen (Germany) 1051
Germania (Tacitus) 10, 174, 204, 207, 208, 757, 1032
Germanic tribes, in eastern central Europe 198–203
Germans
ancient writings about 10
migration 1167–70
Germany
burial practices 222–9
texts on gender 1071
Getica (Jordanes) 211
Gevgelija (North Macedonia) 450
Ghidici (Romania) 488
Giessübel-Talhau area 748–9, 875
Giles, M. 709, 965–6, 1069, 1218
'Gimirrāia' 527–8
Gimpera, P. B. 306
Ginderup (Denmark) 909
Giubiasco (Italy) 346
gladius Hispaniensis 954
Glanon (France) 277, 278, 281, 297, 1271
glass artefacts 801
drinking vessels 118
flask (*aryballos*) 245
imports 633–4
inlays 823
red glass/enamel 801–2
glass beads 162–3, 801
glass production 800–1
colours 808
Glastonbury (England) 5, 54, 69, 105, 699, 983
Glastonbury Lake Village 51, 105

Glauberg (Germany) 9, 218, 241–3, 251, 746, 750, 754–5, 1051
torcs 981
warrior 1065
Gleba, M. 844, 846, 847
Glenfield (England) 105, 109
Gluhite Kamani (Bulgaria) 450, 468, 469
Glyadenovo groups 609–11
goats 251, 676, 681, 682–3
decorative features 1318
Iberian peninsula 684
Netherlands 687
Godelier, M. 985
gods 167–8
Goeblange-Nospelt (Luxembourg) 68, 980, 1199
Goincet (France) 299
Golasecca (Italy) 76, 346, 350, 353–9, 361, 389, 1112, 1150
gold 798–9
Carpathian basin 482
coins 798–9, 811, 890, 891–2
in decorative features 162
jewellery 118, 240, 333
later Iron Age, Britain 109–10
as prestige metal 831
soldering 809
thread 853
weighing system 158
Goldberg (Germany) 218, 235
Golden cemetery 559
gold of pleasure (*Camelina sativa*) 665
goldworking 482, 823
Golubić (Croatia) 371, 375
Gomadingen-Sternberg (Germany) 1308
Gondole (France) 92, 121, 721, 1012–13
Gondreville (France) 218, 235
González Ruibal, A. 310, 703
Good, I. 854
Gørding Hede (Denmark) 701
Gordion 621
Gorjanci hills 379
Gornea-Kalakača group 483–4, 486–7, 532
Gorni Tsibar (Bulgaria) 1141, 1159, 1160, 1163
Gornja Stražava (Montenegro) 450, 455
Gorodets culture 598, 601, 613
Gorodtsov, V. A. 613
Goroshkov (Belarus) 1165
Gosden, C. 835, 881, 882
Gospič-Lipe (Croatia) 371, 375
Goths 206–9, 551, 556, 596, 916, 1129–30
Gotland 149, 152–3, 158, 168, 176, 180, 203, 1113
Goulvars (France) 707
Gournay-sur-Aronde (France) 9, 68, 88–9, 93, 122, 676, 731, 734, 976, 1227, 1275–6
Gouvieux (France) 734
Gracchi 937
Grächwil (Switzerland) 1051, 1062, 1063–4
Grădiştea de Munte (Romania) 508
Graeco-Bactrian kingdom 591
Grafenbühl tumulus (Germany) 635, 813, 1061, 1062
Grafenwörth (Austria) 1051
graffiti 508, 1151, 1166
grain storage 1224–5
deposits 1266
Grakov, B. N. 583
granaries 414
Grandate (Italy) 369
Grand Bassin I cemeteries 280–2
Grandvillars (France) 1051
grapes 423
graphite clay pottery 247, 803
Grauballe Man 1267
grave goods 6–7
and age at death 1035
Crimea 557
demographics 1033–4
elites 157, 831
evidence of feasting 1217–18
Fyn (Denmark) 1041
Italy 356
Kichigino cemetery 584
northern Adriatic 372
prestige materials 831
Sarmatian culture 594
Scandinavia and northern Germany 163
and social status 933, 941, 978–9, 981
Styrian-Pannonian group 385
in *tarand* graves 178
use in dating systems 47–8
see also burial practices
Gravelly Guy (England) 83
graves *see* grave goods; inhumations

Graves, R. 1285
Great Caucasus mountains 527
Great Folk Movement 575, 596–7
Great Hungarian Plain 477–9, 482, 485–6, 1157
Great Migration Period, eastern central Europe 210–13
Great Raid (279 BC) 1162–3, 1172
Greece 410–17
- animal husbandry 676, 680
- cross-dating 47
- early iron use 38
- gender 1063–6
- mechanical principles 812
- textiles 849

Greeks 1060, 1145–8
- alphabetic systems 1114–15
- coins 895
- feasting 1216
- in the north Black Sea area 543
- written sources 10

Greenland, ice cores 27
grid plan construction 419, 811
griffins 1320, 1321
- sculptures 1328

Grisy-sur-Seine (France) 697
Groitsch (Germany) 1141
Grömer, K. 845, 847
Gromovka (Crimea) 548
Grøntoft (Denmark) 146, 147, 159
Großbissendorf (Germany) 811
Großeibstadt (Germany) 218, 223, 1006, 1051
Großhöbing (Germany) 750
Großmugl (Austria) 1004
Großromstedt (Germany) 931
Grotte des Perrats (France) 68, 89
group identities 1083–5
- dominant groups 1089–92
- ethnic labels 1085–92

Grubenhäuser (sunken-featured buildings; SFBs) 246, 694
Gruel, K. 895
Grunas (Albania) 450, 459
Grundsheim (Germany) 747–8
gruziki 598
Guadalquivir, River 319–20
Guadiana, River 317
Guadiana valley 319
Guardamar (Spain) 1051
Guardamonte (Italy) 346
Gubin group 199
Gudme-Lundeberg (Denmark) 123, 146, 147, 160, 909
Guerchy (France) 1014
guerreros Gallaicos 1289
Guichard, V. 827
Guillaumet, J.-P. 720
Guisando (Spain) 313
Gundestrup (Denmark) 10, 146, 156, 813, 975, 1003–4, 1141, 1168, 1269, 1292–3
Gündlingen swords 224, 1050
Gunzwil-Adiswil (Switzerland) 1051
Gurgy (France) 1051
Gurness (Scotland) 69, 104, 115, 826
gutuater 1297
Guyonvarc'h, C.-J. 758

habitus 1095
Hacilar (Turkey) 467
hacksilver 118, 911
Hadrian's Wall 116
Hadrumetum (Tunisia) 627
haemorrhagic fever 32
Haggis, D. 415
Haithabu *see* Hedeby
Hald, M. 860
Hallaton (England) 69, 113, 908, 1221
halls, Scandinavia and northern Germany 167
Hallstatt culture
- Geometric style 1307–10
- Italic influence 234

Hallstatt–La Tène framework 41–2
Hallstatt period
- burial practices 222–35
- decline of 1063–6
- division into stages 219
- Hallstatt C, wagons 224
- Hallstatt D 73–8
  - economy 872–3
  - swords in Britain 81
  - swords in Germany 224
  - wagons 225
- population data 1029

Hallstatt plateau (dating) 71

Hallstatt site (Austria) 3, 218, 1051
cemetery 4, 219
dendrochronology 49, 55
evidence of early iron use 39
male/female cremation 1052
pommels 636
salt mines 25, 26
sword scabbard 9
Hallstatt zone 219
eastern central Europe 194
Hamfelde (Germany) 1031
Ham Hill (England) 69, 101
Hannibal 940
Hannut (Netherlands) 69
Haps (Netherlands) 69
Haps type houses 98
Haraldskær type textile 848
Haraldskær Woman 1268
Harii 204
Harlyn Bay cemetery (England) 108
Haroué (France) 1051
Harrison, R. P. 756
harvesting 152
Hasdingi 206
Haselgrove, C. 873
Hasta Regia (Spain) 320
Hatched pottery 578, 597
Hatvan-Boldog type swords 493, 495
Haughey's Fort (Ireland) 86
Hautenauve, H. 830
Haverfield, F. 1189
Hayling Island temple (England) 113, 908
hazelnuts (*Corylus avellana*) 665
headhunting 1273
hearths 701–2
Hecataeus of Miletus 1120, 1122–3
Hedeby/Haithabu (Germany) 146, 158, 1037–8
Hedges, R. E. M. 784
Heidengraben (Germany) 218, 246, 249, 720, 755–6
Heidentor (Germany) 744–5, 905–6
Heidetränk (Germany) 722
Heiligenbuck (Germany) 1051, 1054, 1058
Heiligkreuztal (Germany) 743
Heiltz-l'Evêque (France) 1051, 1068
Helicus 1145
Hellenistic world 1145–8
helmets 495
decorative features 958
at Grotte des Perrats 89
in Italy 1151
Pass Lueg-type 637
Roman Iron Age 113
Styrian-Pannonian group 382
Helms, M. 978
Helvetii 1040
hemp (*Cannabis sativa*) 665
Henderson, J. 800–1
Hengistbury Head (England) 69, 111, 118, 721
Henkeldellenbecher 362
Hephaistos 1307
Heracles 1121
Heraion of Perachora sanctuary (Greece) 1160
Hercynian forest 1144
Herder, J. 1080
Hérisson (France) 91, 725, 726
heritage management 145–7
Herodotus 10, 31, 217, 527, 582, 585, 642, 1011–12, 1120, 1123
Heroon 412–13, 414
Herrenhöfe 752
Herrmann, H.-V. 635
Hesse 220, 239
Heuneburg (Germany) 7, 8, 50, 218, 236, 706, 717–18, 875–9, 1051
black-figure ware 874
defences 960
dendrochronology 49
dwellings and workshops 75
elite female burials 226, 1063
fortification 73
genetic studies 32
imports 882
mud-brick wall 752, 978
necropolis 749
pottery 247, 813, 872
wagons 1006
Heunen (Netherlands) 69
Heybridge (England) 112
hides 155
Hieron of Syracuse 1307
Hildebrand, H. 238
hillforts 947, 959, 960, 983–5, 1224

Britain
earlier Iron Age 84–6
later Iron Age 100–2, 751, 882
central Europe 221–2, 233, 235, 236, 245, 253, 745–6
Dyakovo culture 598–601
eastern Baltic 179–80, 185–6, 197
Ireland 86–7
northern Adriatic 351, 372, 374, 378
north-east Europe forest zone 597–8
north Pontic region 534, 539
time period for construction 53
see also fortifications; hilltop sites
Hill, J. D. 935, 942, 960, 983, 1226
hilltop sites 5, 8, 245, 299, 361, 431, 453, 931, 1243
barrow culture 197
Britain 82–3, 84, 86, 101
burial practices 241, 1227
cemeteries 383
Chorygi (Greece) 454
coins 904
elites 244, 847, 1242
fortification 379–80, 384, 465
France 90, 286, 292
Germany 227, 235
huts 419
Lipari 435
'Lucanian' communities 423
in north-west Europe 78
oppida 246, 292, 721, 1273
Pianella di Monte Savino 1151
radiocarbon dating 51, 180–1
and the slave trade 121
time period 55, 82
unfortified 458
use 236
Wales 777
see also fortifications; hillforts
Hingley, R. 706, 788, 789
Hinova hoard (Romania) 482, 488
Hippo Regius (Algeria) 628
Hiriart, E. 903
Hirschlanden (Germany) 9, 218, 981, 1051, 1058, 1063
Hisar/Leskovac (Serbia) 450, 454
Histories (Polybius) 326, 388, 779, 1104
History (Ammianus Marcellinus) 964, 1104, 1121
History of Rome (Livy) 388, 1144–5
Histria/Istros (Romania) 498
Hittite Successor States 623
Hjortspring (Denmark) 146, 149, 159, 786, 827, 976, 1269, 1279
Hoby (Denmark) 146, 158, 167
Hochdorf burial (Germany) 218, 844, 860, 1051
alcohol 1227–8
cauldron 1227, 1309–10, 1320
couch 978, 1006, 1008, 1059
dagger 1067
drinking horns 639
feasting practices 1226
gender 1061, 1063
grave goods 47, 226–7, 229, 857, 933
Hochdorf man 228–9
politics 1243–4
tablet weaves 850–2
textiles 843, 848, 853–4, 855, 856–7, 1308
tumulus 749, 750, 1003, 1005
wooden chambers 6
Hochdorf-Reps settlement (Germany) 237
Hochscheid (Germany) 1051, 1068
Hodde (Denmark) 146, 159, 710
Hodder, I. 1086–7
Hodson, F. R. 44, 1049, 1052, 1053, 1140
Hohenasperg (Germany) 218, 237, 633, 1051
Hohenstein-Oberstetten (Germany) 1051
Hohlbuckelringe 1160, 1161
Hohmichele tumulus (Germany) 743–4, 849
Holy Cross Mountains 783
Holzer, V. 250–1
Holzgerlingen (Germany) 218, 251
Holzhausen (Germany) 218, 1276
Homer 1104, 1108, 1120
honeycomb-like complexes 746–7
honour cultures 964
Hoppstädten (Germany) 1051
Hordeum vulgare (barley) 662–3, 669, 1228
horizontal stratigraphy 44
horn-blower's grave 167
horse beans (*Vicia faba*) 664

horse-gear 357, 1323
  for agriculture 1005–11
  equipment for wagons 222–3
  Kachalinskaya hoard 549
  for riding 1002–5
  Stična 381
  Thracian type 504–5
horses 678, 999–1016
  breeding 1000
  burials 1011–12, 1013, 1275
  in combat 956–7
  consumption 1000
  decorative features 1290–1
  DNA analysis 1015–16
  as draught animals 1005–11
  as livestock 666, 676
  racing 1004
  riding 1001, 1002–5
  sacrifice 680
  sculptures of 1013–14
  Scythian Age 491, 545
  symbols of elite status 501, 1012–14
horseshoes 1001
households 696–702
  biographies 702–3
housing
  architecture 693–6
  Corsica 439
  Crete 415–16
  Greece 411–12
  on marshes 669
  residential blocks 728
  Scandinavia and northern Germany 150, 164–5
  southern Italy 424, 428
  status displays 983
Howe (Scotland) 69, 86, 104, 983
Hownam sequence 46
Hradenín (Czech Republic) 6
Hrazany (Czech Republic) 727
Huelva (Spain) 320, 420
Huldremose type 848, 849
Hundt, H.-J. 843, 844
Hungarian sword style 1316
Hunnish-Sarmatian culture 596
Huns 211
Hunsbury (England) 69
  hillfort 102
Hunsrück-Eifel region 78, 221, 240, 830, 848–9, 879, 882
  burial practices 930, 1068
hunting 146, 152, 661, 679, 1226–7
  fur 608
  on horseback 1005
  Iberian peninsula 684
  in north-west Europe 70
Huşi-Suruceni group 492, 498
Huth, C. 861
Hutu group 1087
hydriai 491

Iapodes 375–7
  jewellery 376
Iberian peninsula 22, 305–38
  animals 683–5
  Celtic migration to 1148
  chronological frameworks 41
  north-east 322–6
  north-west 307–10
  provinces 1188
  social life and traditions 329–36
  south-east 320–2
  southern 319–20
  urbanization 326–9
Iberian range 308, 314–15
Iberic script 1110
Ibiza (Spain) 1051, 1066
Iceni 1298
iconography 1292–4, 1329
  of coins 898–9, 912
identities 830–1
  ethnic groups 1085–92
  future studies 1093–5
  gender roles 1069–70
  regional 1079–85
  Roman Empire (Romanization) 1188–90
Idrija group 373
Iessen, A. A. 527
Ifs (France) 68, 94
Ihringen glass bowl (Germany) 1320
Ilek, River 587
Ilercavonia (Spain) 324
Ilici *see* Elche
Ilipla (Spain) 320
Illeberis (France) 277, 295

Illerup Ådal (Denmark) 158, 166, 909, 953, 964, 1269
Illyria 1161, 1244–5
Illyrians 449, 458–9
  Octavian's campaign 508
Illyrian Wars (Appian) 507
imago mundi 755
imports
  and absolute dating 47, 48
  to central Italy 420
  into eastern Baltic 174
  glass 633–4
  ivory 635–7
  from Mediterranean to Heuneburg 876
  metals 633
  Roman Iron Age 116–17
  from Rome to Scandinavia and northern Germany 156
  into temperate Europe 632–8
  textiles 637
  transcontinental 629–30
incastellamento 15, 93
incense-burners (*turibula*) 1296
Incoronata (Italy) 408, 424–5
Indigecia 324
indigenous communities under Roman Empire 1187–203
inequality, group identities 1090–1
Ingermanland (Russia) 177
inhumations 118
  crouched 118, 1199
  Scandinavia and northern Germany 166
  textiles used in 846
  women and children 1052
injuries 950–1
Inn valley 221
inorganic raw materials 800–4
insects, for dyes 805
Ins (Switzerland) 218, 356–7
Insula Banului group 483, 489
interfluvial forts 720–1
intersectionality 1093–4
Inzersdorf ob der Traisen (Austria) 828, 1051
Inzersdorf-Walpersdorf (Austria) 828
Inzigkofen-Vilsingen (Germany) 1051, 1060, 1063
Ionic alphabet 336
Ipf (Germany) 218, 237, 746, 749
Iran 541
Ireland
  burial sites 87
  climate 28
  earlier Iron Age 81–7
  early iron use 39
  genetic studies of 'Celts' 31–2
  later Iron Age 105–8
  radiocarbon dating 55
  Roman Iron Age 117–19
  textiles 849
Irish Sea 67
Iron Age
  absolute dating 46–52
  beginning 37–9
  chronological frameworks 41–6
  chronology 37–41
  division into Hallstatt and La Tène periods 3
  end 39–40
  time period 3–4, 5
Iron Age Cold Epoch 28
iron production 155, 205–6, 774–7
  around the start of the Iron Age 38–9, 40, 174–5
  in eastern Europe 576
  need for wood charcoal 668, 762–3
  specialized settlements 8
  and trade 783–4
iron technology 198, 201, 248, 773–4
  in Britain 70–1, 100
  development 781–3
  effect on industry 784–7
  high temperatures 808
  importance in farming 670–1
  in northern Europe 661
  properties of iron 798
  shift in economy 253
ironworking 249, 382, 559, 590, 595, 607
  bracelets 178
  in Britain 81–2, 1202
  decorative objects 199
  early appearance 410, 413, 422, 480–2, 780–1
  ideology 788–9
  iron bars 109
  iron-clad wagons 224

ironworking (*cont.*)
  nails 820
  ritual practices 1288
  smelting furnaces 186–7
  smithing 777–80, 788
  swords 72, 81, 359, 594, 636, 640
  tools 197, 785–6
  tyres 822
  weapons 954–5, 1240
Iru (Estonia) 174
Isatis tinctoria (woad) 669, 850–1
Ischia (Italy) 877
Isle-Saint-Georges (France) 68, 72
Isola Farnese, Veii (Italy) 418
Isola Rizza (Italy) 369
isolationist hypothesis 1085–6
isotope studies 7, 31, 800–1, 930, 1055, 1060, 1069, 1155, 1172
  lead 323, 802
  oxygen 27, 30, 1152
  of skeletons 30
  strontium 30, 494, 1038, 1152, 1156, 1252–3
Israel 624
Issedonians 586
Issendorf (Germany) 1041, 1042–4
Issyk (Kazakstan) 981
Istrian peninsula 374–5
Istros, River 217
  see also Danube, River
Italy
  Bronze Age 346–9
  Celtic migration to 1150–2
  central 417–21
  southern 421–9
  textile production 847
ithyphallic horsemen 375
Ivanovka (Azerbaijan) 533
ivory 347, 635–7, 807, 1321

Jacobstahl, P. 1311, 1314
Jägala (Estonia) 179
Jagodnja Gornja (Croatia) 371
Jakuszowice (Poland) 205, 210
Jalžabet (Croatia) 371, 383, 1011
James, S. 1062
janiform coins 891
Jankuhn, H. 757
Jastorf culture 195, 198–9, 848
  migration and influence 199–201
Jenišův Újezd (Czech Republic) 6
Jesus Christ 167
jet 807
jewellery 718
  black-coloured 825
  Danube basin 502
  eastern central Europe 205
  glass bracelets 718, 801
  gold 482
  Iapodic 377
  Iberian peninsula 333
  La Tène style 240
  Liburni 379
  Oksywie culture 206
  status displays 980–2
  tools for production 809
Jezerine (Croatia) 371
Joeuvres (France) 721
Jones, G. 1225
Jones, M. 1225
Jones, S. 1090, 1189
Jordanes 207–8
  Getica 211
Judah 624
Juglans regia (walnuts) 665
Julius Caesar 10, 940, 1091–2, 1125–6, 1262
  de Bello Gallico see *de Bello Gallico* (Caesar)
  democracy 929
  invasion of Gaul 71
  muri gallici 91
Jullian, C. 1189
Jung, M. 635
Jupiter 1285
Justin 1146, 1148
  Epitome 301
Jutland (Denmark) 700, 702, 820

Kachalinskaya votive hoard (Russia) 549
Kaiseraugst *see* Augst
Kakavia (Albania) 459
Kalajanovo tomb (North Macedonia) 1245
Kalapodi (Greece) 408, 416, 431, 681
Kalenderberg group 221, 232–3, 390
Kaletedou series 732, 891, 893
Kaliningrad (Russia) 597

Kalinovka (Russia) 592, 595
Kalkriese (Germany) 908, 951
Kama, River 606
Kama valley 602, 603, 605, 608, 611
Kamenicë (Albania) 450, 459–60
Kamenka (Ukraine) 546
Kamenska Čuka (Bulgaria) 450, 463
Kamyshevakha (Ukraine) 542
Kang-Ku state 596
kantharos cups 497
Kapan-Shahumyan (Armenia) 32
Kapf hillfort (Germany) 30
Kappel (Germany) 218, 227–9
  Kappel-Grafenhausen 1051, 1055, 1056–61, 1063
Kaptol (Croatia) 371, 383
Kara-Abyz culture 605, 609, 611
Karabournaki (Greece) 450, 456
Karagač (Kosovo) 450, 455
Karalar (Turkey) 1141, 1163
Kara-Tobe (Crimea) 551
Kardla (Estonia) 187
Karelia 603
  pottery 598
Kargopol tradition 598
Karl, R. 698, 710, 827
Karmazinai (Lithuania) 184, 185
Karphi (Crete) 408, 410, 415
Kashuba, M. T. 539
Kasr el-Harit (Egypt) 1164
Kassena of Burkina Faso 743
Kastanas (Greece) 450, 452
Kastel (Germany) 734
Kastro (Greece) 450, 457
Katharinenkogel (Austria) 371, 384
Kaul, F. 833
Kaushany (Moldova) 533
Kavaros, King 1116, 1161
Kavkazskaya (Russia) 556
Kavousi area (Crete) 415
Kazakhstan 585, 586, 592, 596
Kelermes (Russia) 528, 539–40, 1321–2, 1324
Kelheim-Alkimoennis (Germany) 8, 218
  iron quarries 246
  oppidum 720–1, 723, 783, 1203
Kelvedon (England) 1287, 1300
Kemmelberg (Belgium) 68, 78
Kenya 1086
Kerameikos cemetery, Athens (Greece) 413, 454, 455, 805, 854
Kerch peninsula 543
Kergoven (France) 90
Kerkini/Belasica mountains 453, 462
Kerkūzi (Latvia) 185
Kermenchik/Neapolis Scythica (Crimea) 550–1, 552, 554, 555, 1141
Kermes vermilio 227, 851, 853
Kersebleptes 502
Kessel-Lith (Netherlands) 99–100
Khapry, belt buckle 593
Kharax (Crimea) 556
Khokhlach (Russia) 592–3
Khorsabad (Iraq) 625
Kichigino cemetery (Russia) 584, 586, 587
Kidder, A. V. 1082
Kietrz (Poland) 194
Kiev culture 207, 211
Kilchberg (Switzerland) 742
Killalane (Ireland) 69, 119
Killibury (England) 103
Killoran (Ireland) 69, 119
Kimmeridge shale 94
Kimmig, W. 634
Kinding (Bavaria) 807
King David's hall (Bethlehem) 167
King, S. S. 952
kinships 1037
Kirchzarten (Germany) 718
Kirkburn (England) 786, 958, 1253
Kirnsulzbach (Germany) 50
Kirpili valley 556, 557, 566
Kislovodsk basin 537
Kition (Greece) 623
Kivti (Latvia) 185
Ķivutkalns (Latvia) 179
Kizil Koba culture 526, 531, 535–6
Klasro (Sweden) 147
Kleinaspergle (Germany) 218, 239, 241, 749, 933, 1051, 1065, 1217, 1311–12
Kleinklein (Austria) 218, 229, 233–5, 254, 371, 383, 386–7, 847, 1241
Kleinsorheim (Bavaria) 810, 893
Klin Yar burial ground (Russia) 537
Kluçka/Skopje (North Macedonia) 450, 455

Kluger, R. 1298
Knapp, A. B. 28
knobbed ware 490
Knockaulin (Ireland) 69, 106, 107–8, 122, 1277–8
Knockcommane (Ireland) 69, 106
Knossos (Crete) 408, 410, 415
Knowes (Scotland) 53
knowledge, as source of power 939
Knowth (Ireland) 118
Koban-Colchis culture 526, 531, 535–7
Kobarid (Slovenia) 370–1
Kobyakovo culture 526, 535, 563, 564, 579
Kogaionon 508
Köhler, H.-J. 760, 761–2
Kohtla (Estonia) 187
Kokmuiža (Latvia) 187
Kolomenskoye (Russia) 613
Kolotuchin, V. A. 535
Kolpa, River 375
Komi-Permians 602
Kompolje (Slovenia) 371, 375, 376, 377
Kõmsi (Estonia) 178
Komstromskaya (Russia) 541
Koningsbosch (Netherlands) 69, 98
Konterbia Karbika (Spain) 337
Kontich-Alfberg (Belgium) 68
Koprivlen (Bulgaria) 450, 463
Koralpe mountains 383, 384
Korçë basin (Albania) 458, 460
Korčula 378
Korenovsk (Russia) 560
Korisios 1115
Kosika burials (Russia) 562
  cups 956
Kosovo 23, 450, 454, 457
Kossack, G. 219–20, 223, 540, 861
Kossinna, G. 1081–2
kostishche 609
Kostolac-Pećine (Serbia) 1141, 1162
Kostychi (Ukraine) 533
Kotor bay (Montenegro) 461
Kotys 502
Kotys I, King 1115
Koukos (Greece) 455
Kovrovo (Russia) 209
Krakow (Poland) 1155
Krakra (Bulgaria) 1160
Krasnaya Polyana (Russia) 533
Krasnokutinskiy (Ukraine) 545
Kras-Notranjska group 370, 372, 379
Krasnozorenskoe 551
Krausse, D. 229, 236, 639, 1227
Kraznoe Znamya (Russia) 539, 541
Kremastos hill, Asar-tepe (Greece) 465
krepis 541, 544
Krepostnoe 563
Kresna gorge 463
Kristiansen, K. 24, 338, 972, 1123
Križna gora (Slovenia) 371, 372
Krka, River 377
Kröllkogel grave, Kleinklein (Austria) 229, 233, 385–6, 1241
Kronwinkl-type burials 244
Krško plain 383
Ktesibios 812
Kuban region 528–9, 535–7, 543, 556–60, 563, 565, 1011
Kuban, River 527, 582
Kuffern (Austria) 1004, 1010–11
Kujawy region 198, 201, 203
Kulchuk (Crimea) 551
Kull, B. 861–2
Kul' Oba mound (Crimea) 544
Kulturkreis concept 1080
Kuma-Manych basin 23, 526
Kuma, River 527
Kuntá Hora (Czech Republic) 1141, 1152, 1156
Künzing (Bavaria) 670
Kurd-type *situla* 227, 356
Kurevere (Estonia) 178
kurgans 8, 529, 533, 546, 557–63, 595
  composition 589
  Crimea 550, 555
  cultural phases 583
  elite burials 586–8
  finds 548
  horse burials 1011
  as sanctuaries 560
  types 554–5
  see also burial mounds
Kurmaičiai (Lithuania) 178, 184
Kurz, S. 875
Kush Kaya (Bulgaria) 450, 465

Kush kingdom 624
Kushtanovycya group 1165
Küster, H. 760
Kutná Hora (Czech Republic) 30, 31
Kvarner coast 375, 377
Kvitki (Ukraine) 532
Kwakiutl (Canada) 933
Kylver stone, Gotland 1109, 1113
Kynetes 1123

Laba, River 557
Lacoste (France) 68, 718
Lady of Baza 333, 334, 1065
Lady of Elche 333
La Génibrette necropolis, Lautrec (France) 281
La Gorge-Meillet (France) 1248
La Gourjade (France) 281
La Joya (Spain) 1244
lake margin settlements 72
lakes
  depositions 934
  sacred 1198
  submersion of people 168
  votive 166
lake settlements 706
  preservation of organic materials 26
La Lagaste (France) 299
Lalapaşa (Turkey) 450, 466–7
La Liquière (France) 277
Lamadeleine cemetery, Titelberg (Luxembourg) 904, 1249
L'Amastuola (Italy) 408, 422, 428
La Mata de Campanario (Spain) 318
Lambay Island 118
La Moulinasse (France) 277, 284
Lampoldshausen (Germany) 670
Lamprechtskogel-Waisenberg (Austria) 371
land division, earlier Iron Age, Britain 83–4
land-hunger 1041
landscape 756–9
  as monuments 751–6
  ritual practices 1266
  Roman Empire 1190–1
Langadas basin 451
Langres (France) 720
languages
  acquisition of 1104
  Anatolian 622
  Arabic 1130
  Aramaic 623, 624, 626
  Baltic 601
  Balto-Slavic 32
  Finnic 173
  movement of writing systems 630–1
  see also writing systems
Lanneunoc (France) 1293
La Normée (France) 1266
L'Anse aux Meadows (Newfoundland) 628, 641
La Platrière de Lazer, Gap (France) 297
Lăpuş (Romania) 480, 485
La Ramasse (France) 277, 278, 279, 295
Lascuta (Spain) 320
La Serreta d'Alcoi (Spain) 337
later Iron Age
  Britain and Ireland 100–11
  north-west Europe 87–100
La Tène culture 31, 493, 833, 913
  burial practices 239–44, 830, 1217
  connection with Celts 1140–1
  cultural traditions 1066–9
  in eastern central Europe 197–8
  eastern Europe 1157–9
  gender roles 1070
  influences 197–8, 352, 362, 368, 373, 377, 387
  jewellery 820, 823
  pottery 199, 803
  swords 955
  wheels 821
La Tène period 6, 30, 76, 221
  art 1307, 1309–21
  cemeteries 494, 503
  chronology 42–4, 49–50, 56, 219, 238–9
    Italy 350
  Dacian kingdom 504–6
  elite burials 95
  farmsteads 699, 709, 744, 752
  graves 47, 48
  hillforts 745
  iron production 762, 778
  La Tène A 73–8
  material culture 247–9

La Tène period (*cont.*)
  north-west Europe 78
  oppida 122, 719, 726, 755, 872, 901
  ritual practices 249–52, 759
  road system 750
  rural communities 94–5
  settlements 237, 244–6
  structures 121
  swords 122
  textiles 853, 858
  urban communities 90, 706
  weapons 383
  see also Celtic period
La Tène site (Switzerland) 3, 9, 218, 238, 789
  deposition of wealth 975
  early finds 4–5
  weapons 955, 1269–70
La Tène style 13–14, 51–2, 99, 638, 1153–5, 1324
  in Britain 100
  brooches 45, 81, 199, 201, 203, 830, 833
  glass bracelets 801
  metalwork 106
  swords 511, 640, 779, 833
lathe-turning 812
Latin alphabet 1115–17
Latobici 383
La Traytié (France) 281
Lattes (France) 277, 278, 280, 285, 286, 294–5, 299, 420, 695
  coins 901–2
Latvia
  barrow burials 185
  textiles 849
Lavariškės (Lithuania) 186
Lavau (France) 68, 1051, 1062, 1063, 1242
Laxton (England) 937
Layetania 324
lead sculptures 384
leaf-blade swords 455
Lebanon 801
Le Baou-Roux (France) 277, 285, 292
Lebedevka V burial (Ukraine) 595
Le Calla de Durban (France) 295
Le Cayla (France) 284
Le Cluzel (France) 300
Le Cros (France) 277, 284
Leekfrith (England) 109
Lefkandi (Greece) 408, 411–13, 414, 940–1
Łęg Piekarski (Poland) 204
Le Grand Communal (France) 1051
legumes 664–5
Leicester (England) 69, 112
Leighton, R. 430
Lejre/Old Lejre (Denmark) 146, 152, 160, 168
Le Marduel (France) 276, 277, 290
Le Mont-Garou (France) 292
Le Moulin, Peyriac-de-Mer (France) 277, 285
Lenerz-de Wilde, M. 249
Lens culinaris (lentils) 664
lentils (*Lens culinaris*) 664
Lentini (Sicily) 408, 421, 435–6, 696
Léon 328
Le Pègue (France) 278, 292
Le Peyra (France) 277, 281
Le Plan des Ribiers (France) 297
Le Plessis-Gassot (France) 68, 1141, 1167
Lepontic script 1113
Leptis Magna 627
Le Puy d'Issolud (France) 68
Le Roux, F. 758
Les Baou de Saint-Marcel (France) 277, 292
Les Caisses de Saint-Jean (France) 276
Les Clérimois (France) 776
Les Jardins du Luxembourg, Paris (France) 1266
Leskovac/Hisar (Serbia) 450, 454
Lessini mountains 366
Les Touriès (France) 276, 277, 278
Leuci *oppidum* 732
Leucon II 1166
Levant 28, 623–4
  early iron use 38
  main cities 624
levelling mechanisms 973, 985
levers 812
Lévi-Strauss, C. 703
lev-names 160–1
lev-villages 160–1
Levroux (France) 68, 90, 718, 776–7
  La Colline des Tours 719
  Village des Arènes 719
Lexden tumulus, Colchester (England) 111, 880
Liatovouni (Greece) 450, 460

Libkovice (Czech Republic) 1321
Libna (Slovenia) 371
Liburni 377–8
  jewellery 378
Liebau (Poland) 1141
life pyramids 1037–9
Liguria 349–53
Lika region 375
L'Ile de Martigues (France) 277, 292, 293–4, 1265
  houses 700–1, 705
lilia 159
Limagne plain 95
limonites 774
Limska gradina (Croatia) 371
Lindow Man 108, 1253, 1267
linear dykes *see* dyke complexes
linen 849
Linum usitatissimum (flax) 665
Linz-St Peter (Austria) 218, 221
lion figures 1310, 1320
Lipari (Italy) 408, 434–5
Lippert, A. 637
Lisičić, Predgrađe-Asseria (Croatia) 378
Lismullin (Ireland) 106
Lisnacrogher (Ireland) 1269
literacy 112, 1103–5
  Scandinavia 149, 165–6
literature 934–5, 1104, 1120–30
  evidence for feasting 1214–15
lithosols 25
Lithuania
  barrow burials 184–5
  climate 173–4
  hillforts 186
  iron production 174–5
Little Woodbury (England) 69, 83, 87
Livy 1121, 1152
  History of Rome 388, 1144–5
Lixus (Morocco) 627
Ljubljana (Slovenia) 371, 387
Llanmaes (Wales) 69, 82
Llíria (Spain) 329
Llyn Cerrig Bach (Wales) 69, 109, 113, 934, 986, 1269–70
Llyn Fawr (Wales) 934
  votive hoard 81
Lodève (France) 277
Lodévois valley 284
loess 25
Lofkënd (Albania) 450
Loire, River 91
long barrows 185
Longbridge Deverill Cow Down (England) 83
longhouses 79, 98, 694–7
  animal sheds 710
looms 155, 426, 845–7
loom weights 846–7
Lorenz, H. 760, 762
Loretto (Austria) 218, 232
Lorraine 221
  salt production 800
Lough Gara (Ireland) 69, 87, 106
Loughton, M. E. 1215
Lovosice (Czech Republic) 8, 218, 248, 718–19, 802
lowland Britain, later Iron Age 104–5
Luant (France) 68, 91
Luaras (Albania) 450, 459
Łubiana (Poland) 210
Lübsow burials 115
Lucan 1266, 1288
  de Bello Civili 758
  Pharsalia 1284–5
Luco culture 360–1
Ludwigsburg (Germany) 1063
Lugiorum nomen 204–6
luminescence dating 52
Lunan Bay cemetery (Scotland) 116
Lusatian culture 194, 221
Lusitania 1188
luvisols 25
Luwian script 623
Lycians 621
Lydians 621–2
Lydney Park (England) 1298
Lyismachia, battle of 1141
Lyon-Vaise (France) 68
  elite settlement 76
lyres 814
Lysimachus 1160–1
Lyubimovka (Ukraine) 547

macaroni wheat (*Triticum durum*) 662
Macedonia 449, 450–1, 1161, 1188
  east 462–3
  west 456–8
Maconde groups 1087
madder (Rubiceae) 851
Maeotians 529, 563
Magdalenenberg (Germany) 6, 49, 218, 225, 748–9, 1051, 1054–6, 1058
  differences between elite and non-elite skeletons 30
  gender 1070, 1072
  isotope studies 1060
  male burials 1063, 1070
Magdalensberg (Austria) 903–4
Magdalenska gora (Slovenia) 6, 371, 380, 1003
magical practices 512
Magna Graecia 806
magnet immigration 1087–8
Magny-Lambert (France) 1051
Maiden Castle (England) 69
  hillfort 85–6, 101, 952, 960, 984
Maier, F. 760
Maiersch (Austria) 218, 232
mail corselets 786
Mailhac (France) 277, 280, 281, 284, 295
  Grand Bassin and Le Moulin cemeteries 281
Main, River 201
Makhortych, S. V. 532–3
Maliq, lake 458
Mallorca 325, 684
Malrain, F. 94, 709–10
Mal Tepe (Bulgaria) 1141, 1160–1
Malus sylvestris (apples) 665
mammal oil 155
Manching *oppidum* (Germany) 8, 218
  agriculture 670–1
  burial practices 846
  coins 732, 810, 901, 902–3
  craftworking 880
  dogs 679
  elites 752
  farmsteads 1277
  finds 799, 803
  glass bracelets 718
  horizontal stratigraphy 44
  horse-related finds 906
  human skeletons 244
  'iron horse of Manching' 809, 1014–15
  pottery 640, 803, 809
  ritual practices 754–5, 759
  smithing 783
  source of iron 784
  structures 724, 727–8
  units of measurement 811
  urbanization 90
  vegetation 805
  walls 719–20, 750, 754, 760–1, 762, 802
  wine consumption 249
Manětín-Hrádek (Czech Republic) 218, 242
Mannering, U. 844
Mannersdorf (Austria) 218, 244, 1141
Mannert, K. 1082
Manning, S. W. 28
manors 154
Manre (France) 1051
mantles 859–60
manuring 152
maps of Roman Empire 1190
Marainville-sur-Madon (France) 635–6, 1051, 1053
Maramureş region 496
Marchenko, I. 557–9
Marcomanni 204, 206
Marco Simón, F. 1289
Marcus Aurelius 1090
Marignane (France) 277
Maritsa valley 464
Marktoberdorf (Bavaria) 1039
Marly (France) 218, 235
Maroboduus 1119
marriage 1032–3, 1039–40
Marsal (France) 68, 218
Marseille/Massalia (France) 275, 277, 292, 297, 877–9, 882, 1051
  coins 889
  foundation dates 48
marshes 668–70
Marsiliana d'Albegna (Italy) 356
'Mars von Gutenberg' 361
Martburg (Germany) 906–7
Martial 1266
Martijanec (Croatia) 371, 383
Martinet (France) 281

Martin, S. 896
Marvinci (North Macedonia) 450
Marzabotto (Italy) 1142
Mas Castellar de Pontos (Spain) 1221
Mason, P. 1278
mass production 14
'Master or Mistress of the Animals' 251, 1320
Masurian lakes 197, 213
Matelica dagger 807
material culture 819–35, 1094–5
  armed violence 953–9
  central Europe 247–9
  eastern Baltic 187–8
  Roman Empire 1200–2
  Scandinavia and northern Germany 162–5
  social practices 830–1
material domination 1090–1
Mattingly, H. 1287–8
matt-painted pottery 462
Mauss, M. 871, 985
Mayen (Germany) 218, 802
McKern, W. 1082
mead 1227
Meare (England) 5, 105, 987
measurement systems 157–8, 811
meat 1226
  in burials 585, 1217–18
  from horses 1000
  as an offering 223, 243, 1227
mechanical principles 812
medicine 813
Mediterranean region 5, 22–3, 660, 823
  African coastline 627
  art 1305–30
  cattle 678
  central 40, 407–42
  climate 26
  coastline 1242
  coins 895, 902
  commerce 283, 289–90
  contact with Atlantic communities 309–10, 315, 317
  contact with Britain 119
  contact with Celts 251, 253, 1148
  crops 664
  decorative styles 501
  eastern 497, 812–13
  and gender 1058
  horses 1001
  imports 75, 76, 81, 99, 237, 245, 853, 872–3, 875–6, 978, 1248
  maps of sites 277, 408
  mercenaries 1166–7, 1170
  politics 927
  ritual practices 1271–4
  trade 321, 327, 347, 351–2, 683, 877, 879–82
  warfare 895–6, 1132
  western 774, 783, 812, 820
  wine consumption 1228–9
  written sources 10, 13
Medugenus 1298
Medvedskaja, M.I. 540
megalithic tombs 466–8
Megara Hyblaea (Sicily) 429
Megaw, V. 1324
Meillonydd (Wales) 69, 86
Melegunìs Lipára, Lipari (Italy) 436
'melting pot' theory 1088
Melton (England) 87
Memnon 1146
Mende (Greece) 450, 453, 456
Ménföcsanak (Hungary) 1249
menhirs (standing stones) 467–8
Meo, F. 846
mercenaries
  'Celtic' 14, 1148–9, 1166–7
  Roman Iron Age 965
  and use of coins 896
mercenary hypothesis 896
Mercury statue 1299
Meseta 307, 308
  northern 312–14
  southern 318–19
Mesopotamia 625
Messingham (England) 781
metal artefacts 25
  deposits 9
  imports 633
metalwork
  coin production 1118
  hoarding 109
  Ireland 106
    Roman Iron Age 118
  raw materials 798–9

Metapiccola (Sicily) 435
Metaponto settlement (Italy) 425–6
Metohija region 457–8
Metz, dendrochronology 54
Meuse-Demer-Scheldt region 99
Mexico, ethnic identity 1087
Mezek (Bulgaria) 1315
Mez-Notariou (France) 68, 82
Mezőcsát group 483, 486
Midas, King 621
midden sites 1216
  Britain 82–3, 980
Middle East 642
'Midgard' 168
Midhowe (Scotland) 826
Midianites 963
Mierlo-Hout (Netherlands) 69, 79, 80
migration 1137–73
  Anglo-Saxons 1040–3
  Celts 1140–50
    to Anatolia 1163–4
    to Balkan peninsula 1159–62
    to eastern Europe 1157–9
    to Italy 1150–2
    to Ukraine and Belarus 1165–6
    to western and central Europe 1153–7
  definition 1138–40
  German peoples 1167–70
  Jastorf culture 199–201
  magnet immigration 1087–8
  push factors 1139
  Scythians 492–3, 542–3, 581, 1307, 1322
  through Alpine regions 13
  through Anatolia 632, 1146, 1163–4
  through Slovenia 1158
  through the Adriatic 1144
  through the Aegean 455, 631, 1149
  through the Balkans 1146
  through west Africa 1094
  transcontinental 631–2, 640–1
Migration period 4, 174, 210–13
  coins 912
  'Great Folk Movement' 612
  luxury goods 1041
  mortality curves 1043
  sites 180, 183–4, 186–9
Milan (Italy) 346
Milcent, P.-Y. 1049
Milejowice (Poland) 706–8
Miletus (Turkey) 543
military activity 158, 938
  defence of democracy 929
  Dolenjska group 380–1
  Roman Iron Age 114–19
  Volga-Ural steppe 586
military belts 160
military democracy 201
Milla Skerra (Scotland) 69, 86
millet (*Panicum miliaceum*) 663
Mill Hill, Deal (England) 108, 1051
millstones 430
Milogrady culture 195, 197
Mincio, River 366
Mindelheim (Germany) 1003, 1052–3
minerals 25
  Danube basin 479
Mineral Waters area 535, 536–7
miners 987
  both sexes 1052
Minos of Crete, King 1307
Miraveche-Monte Bernorio culture 311
Mirebeau-sur-Bèze (France) 89
mirrors 982, 1065
mitochondrial DNA (mtDNA) 31–2
Mittelgebirge 803
Mitterkirchen (Austria) 31, 218, 221, 854, 1007, 1051, 1052, 1241
Moab 624
mobility 30–1
  and gender 1053–6
model boats 118
Mödling (Austria) 218
Modu Chanyu 591
modular farms 154
Moel-y-Gaer (Wales) 931
Moesia 1188
Mokronog group 383, 387
Moldavia 479, 489
Molinos, M. 327
Möller Wiering, S. 848, 861
Mommsen, T. 1081–2, 1189
monarchy 928
Moncucco, Como (Italy) 355
Mondelange (France) 1051

Moñes (Spain) 332
Monreal de Ariza, sword from 955
Mont Beuvray (France) 55, 68, 91, 92, 218
  burial practices 95
  coins 900, 903
  oppidum 720, 722, 724
  trade 880
  see also Bibracte
Montebelluna (Italy) 346
Monte Bernorio (Spain) 311
Monte Bibele (Italy) 31, 1141, 1151, 1152
Montefortino d'Arcevia (Italy) 1141, 1151
Montelius, O. 41
Monte Molião (Portugal) 309
Monterenzio Vecchio (Italy) 1141, 1151
Montfau (France) 277, 284, 295
Monti della Tolfa mountain range 418
Montjean (France) 277, 292
Mont Lassois (France) 7, 75, 237, 752, 874, 983
  see also Vix
Montlaurès (France) 277, 299–300
Mont Vully (Switzerland) 723
monuments 741–63, 1326–9
  appropriation of 742–5
  construction 745–50
  France 276–9
  as landscape 751–6
  public 730–1
  Roman Iron Age 117
  status displays 982–5
  and territoriality 750–1
Moor House, London (England) 1199–200
moraine landscapes 173
Moravia 222, 1154, 1155
Morgan, C. 874–5
Morgantina Cittadella (Sicily) 408, 421, 431–4
Mormont (Switzerland) 906
Morris, I. 38
mortality rates 1030–6
  children 1027–8, 1032–3
  and life pyramids 1037
  in women 1040
mortuary houses 600
mortuary practices *see* burial practices
Moselle-Hunsrück region 244
Mossø, Lake 953
Most na Soči (Slovenia) 372
Moulay (France) 68, 721
Mount El'brus volcano 527
mourning 1254
Mouseion of Alexandria 812
movement of ideas 630–1
  into temperate Europe 638–40
movement of objects 629–30
  into temperate Europe 632–8
movement of people *see* migration
Mozsolics, A. 482
Mšec (Czech Republic) 8
Mšecké Žehrovice (Czech Republic) 218, 251, 1276, 1293–4
Mucking (England) 69, 83, 104
  burial practices 112
Mühlacker (Germany) 218, 226
Müller, F. 1308, 1315
Müller-Scheeßel, N. 1029, 1038
multiculturalism 1088
München-Obermenzing burial (Germany) 813
Münsingen-Rain (Switzerland) 6, 31, 43–4, 218, 243, 640, 1051, 1066, 1141, 1155
  brooches/fibulae 242, 1153, 1161, 1171
  burials with weapons 938
  dress accessories 244
  glass artefacts 640
  isotope studies 1156
Münsterberg (Germany) 218, 237, 247
Muntenia region 488
Mureş valley 509
muri gallici 91, 724, 725–7, 760–2
  iron fixings for 786
musical instruments 813–14
mussels staters 890, 898, 902
Must Farm (England) 26, 69, 82
Mycenae (Greece) 410
  pottery 421–2
Mysians 621
myths 1121
  Scandinavia and northern Germany 166, 167–8

Nages (France) 277, 294, 931
Nagyberki-Szalacska (Hungary) 371, 384
Nahanarvali 204

Nahe, River 939
Nanterre (France) 718
Napoleonic Wars 1079
Naquane (Italy) 364–5
Narbonne (France) 277
Nash, D. 936
national identities 1080–1
nations, boundaries 19
Natural History (Pliny) 388
Naukratis (Egypt) 625
Nautes Parisiacae 1285–6, 1292
Navan (Ireland) 69, 106–8, 1277–8, 1283–4
  enclosure 87
Nea Michaniona (Greece) 450
Neapolis Scythica *see* Kermenchik
Near East 20, 622, 626
  glass imports 633–4
  metal imports 633
Nebringen (Germany) 31, 1141, 1152, 1156
Nechvoloda, A. 587
necklaces 118
neck-rings 110, 118, 830
  deposition 976
  gender 1061
  Germany 227
  Roman Iron Age 117
  Scheibenhalsringe 1156, 1157–9
  status displays 980–1
  Waldalgesheim (Germany) 1314
needles 846
Negau Helmet 1113
Němčice Nad Hanou (Czech Republic) 90, 198, 218, 245–6, 718
  coins 896, 901
Němčice-Víceměřice (Czech Republic) 1141
Nemetios 349
Neo-Assyrian sources 621–5
Neo-Hittite sites 623, 625
Nerka Trostaia, tomb of 368
Nero 204
Nerthus 1288–9
Nesactium/Nezakcij (Croatia) 371, 374, 375
Nestos valley 463
Netherlands
  animal husbandry 685–7
  climate 28
  communities 709
Nettlebank Copse (England) 105
nettle fibre 849
networks 1255–6
Neubrandenburg (Germany) 1039
Neuchâtel, Lake 238, 934
Neuenbürg (Germany) 218
Neuhausen ob Eck (Germany) 1051
Newbridge (Scotland) 87, 822
Newcastle Great Park (England) 69, 83
Newfoundland 628
Newgrange (Ireland) 69, 118
New York silver beaker 1325
niche graves 553–4
niches 468, 469, 585, 1272
  podboi (side niches) 586, 591, 594
Nichoria (Greece) 408, 410–11, 412, 695
Nicomedes I, King 1146
Niebla (Spain) 1244
Niederbieber (Germany) 956
Niedererlbach (Germany) 218, 226
Niederkaina (Germany) 218, 221
Niederweiler (Germany) 1051
Niederzier (Germany) 900
Nielsen, S. 698
Nijmegen area, chariot burials 80–1
Nile valley 624–5
Nîmes (France) 277, 291, 294
Nimrud 625
Nin (Croatia) 371, 379
Nineveh 625
nomads 577–82
Noordbarge (Netherlands) 98
Norbaneius Thallus 1297
Nordhouse (France) 1051
Nordic area, chronological frameworks 41
Noricum 782, 1188
Nørre Tranders (Denmark) 146, 151
north Africa 20, 40, 626–8
  Barbary ape/macaque remains 108, 637–8, 1277–8
  contact with Europe 22, 108, 619, 628–9, 637–8
  Phoenicians in 624, 631
  population movements 631–2
  Roman provinces 620–1
  trade with Europe 629–30, 881, 1229
  Vandals in 1029

North America 619, 628, 641, 1083
North Atlantic 628
  Gulf Stream 26
North Bersted (England) 109
north Caucasus 535–8
  early Iron Age 530–1
  Scythians in 539–41
north-east Europe, forest zone 597–601
northern Adriatic 22–3, 40, 200, 345–90
  amber 1112
  Celtic links 1114, 1145, 1163
  horse-related finds 1012
  map of sites 371
  migration through 1144
  trade 797, 806, 1241, 1244–5
  votive depositions 1273
northern Black Sea and north Caucasus 23, 525–66
northern Europe, chronological frameworks 41
northern Greece and the central Balkans 23
North European Plain 24, 78–81
  later Iron Age 97–100
north Pontic Greeks 525
North Sea marshes 668–70
north-west Europe 21, 67–120
  chronological frameworks 41
  earlier Iron Age 72–81
  funerary practices 1246, 1251–3
  later Iron Age 87–100
  map of sites 68
  rural settlements 94–5
Notranjska group 370–2
Nové Košariská (Slovakia) 846
Noves (France) 277
Novoalexandrovka (Ukraine) 542
Novocherkassk (Russia) 527–8, 532
Novo mesto (Slovenia) 371
Nowa Cerekwia (Poland) 206, 896, 1141
Nuciaresa (Corsica) 438, 439
nucleated settlements 88, 99, 114, 441–2, 704, 706, 708–9, 941–2
  in central Mediterranean and Aegean 411, 415, 428
  in Iberia 326–9
  in northern Greece and central Balkans 458–9
  in southern France 292–6, 700
  see also agglomerations
Numana (Italy) 369
Numancia/Numantia (Spain) 309, 329, 332, 785, 834, 1272, 1289, 1290
Numidia 628
nuraghi (stone towers) 437–8
Nydam (Denmark) 5, 159, 1269
Nymphaion (Crimea) 1141, 1166
Nynice (Czech Republic) 218, 232
Nysa, River 199

Oakbank Crannog (Scotland) 849
oak trees (*Quercus* sp.) 667, 760
oats (*Avena sativa*) 663
Ocna Mureş hoard (Romania) 482
Ocniţa (Moldova) 508, 510
Octavian 940
Oder basin 196, 198, 210
Oder, River 199, 1155
Oder-Warthe group 803
Odiel, River 320
Odin 167–8
Oea/Tripoli 627
oenochoe 284, 542, 1064, 1247
Ogam/ogham script 119, 1117, 1118
Oguz (Ukraine) 544
Ohrid-Gorna-Porta (North Macedonia) 1141, 1161
oil
  mammal 155
  plants 665
Oinotrians 426
Oise, River 751
Oise valley 828, 900
Oka, River 597
Oksywie culture 200, 201–3, 206–7
Öland, island of
  ring forts 158, 164
  wall construction 163–4
Oława, River 1155
Olbia (Ukraine) 545, 1141, 1165
  foundation dates 48
Old Croghan (Ireland) 69
  Old Croghan Man 108, 1267
Old Scatness (Scotland) 69, 104
Old Sleaford (England) 112
Old Uppsala (Sweden) 146, 152, 160, 168

oligarchy 928–9
olive oil 683
olives 423
Olmo di Nogara (Italy) 347
Olsztyn group 212–13
Oltenia 489, 506
Olynthus (Greece) 942
omphalos cups 361
Onuba (Spain) 320
open field system 937
open settlements
  Ananyino 603
  artisan type 718, 728, 735, 902, 987
  Britain and Ireland 83, 86, 102, 113, 119
  Carpathian and Danube area 484
  central Europe 195, 221, 235
  Dyakovo culture 598
  eastern Baltic 179, 186, 188–9
  northern Greece and Balkans 458, 465
  see also agglomerations; nucleated settlements
opium poppy (*Papaver somniferum*) 665
Oppeano (Italy) 368, 1012
oppida 8, 90–4, 246, 319, 717–35
  Britain 880–2
  coins 893–4, 900–3
  craftworking in 496
  debate over 879
  decline of 292
  division into smaller communities 987
  early appearance 328
  elite settlement precursors 76–7
  fortification 318, 754
  functions 731–3
  grid plan construction 811
  increasing numbers 14–15
  iron production 785
  medical knowledge 813
  network 300
  '*oppida* culture' 797
  reasons for building 14, 313, 316–17
  rulers of 322
  size 720
  town planning 727–30
  walls (*muri gallici*) 91, 724, 725–7
  warfare 938
optical stimulated luminescence dating 52
Oram's Arbour (England) 101
Orange/Arausio (France) 1141
Orationes (Aristides) 1192
orators 939–40
Orehova (Slovenia) 1141
organic materials 804–8
  preservation 26–7
Orgetorix of the Helvetii 928, 1115
Orientalizing style 1241, 1320–2
Orkney islands 117, 850
Orléans/Cenabum (France) 68, 91, 92, 718
Orlovec (Bulgaria) 540
ornaments, Pyanobor culture 608
Ornavasso (Italy) 359
  chronologies 47
Or, River 587
Orsi, P. 429
Ortiz, F. 1090
Orton Meadow (England) 850
Orvieto (Italy) 356, 419
Osanna, M. 424
Osma, sword from 955
Ossarn belt hook 1326
Oss (Netherlands) 69, 79, 80
  Oss-Almstein 98
  Oss-Schalkskamp 98
osteoarchaeology 1050
Osterby Man 1268
ostrich eggs 347
Ostrogoths 211
Otherworld 1272, 1277, 1291
Otomani culture 480
Ottoman Empire 156
Otzenhausen (Germany) 734
Ourique (Portugal) 316
outhouses 151
Ouvèze valley 292
overgrazing 154
Over Rig (Scotland) 69, 116
Owslebury 'warrior' (England) 108

Pada (Estonia) 182
Padanian Etruria 358
Padea-Panagjurski Kolonii group 506, 507, 508, 511
Padua (Italy) 346, 368
painted pottery 803

Palace of Nestor, Pylos (Greece) 410
palaeodemography 1025, 1026–8
Palazzo (Italy) 422
Palio Gynaekokastro (Greece) 450
palisades 83, 86, 96, 484, 752
Panenský Týnec (Bohemia) 1324, 1326
Pangaion (Greece) 468
Panicum miliaceum (millet) 663
Pannonia 383–8, 1188, 1203
Panóias (Portugal) 1198
Pantalica (Sicily) 408, 429
Papadopoulos, J. 470
Papaver somniferum (opium poppy) 665
Paret, O. 634
Pasargadae 626
Pashkovskaya (Russia) 556
passages (*dromos*) 233, 385, 586
Pass Lueg-type helmets 637
Paule-Saint-Symphorien (France) 68, 88
  elite settlements 76–7
Paulus Orosius 1269
Pausanius 1146
Payerne (Switzerland) 1051
Pazhok (Albania) 450, 460
Pazyryk (Siberia) 827, 854, 1003, 1323
Pčinja, River 451, 453
Peacock, D. 872
Pearson, P. 1221
peas (*Pisum sativum*) 664
peat bogs 1268
Pech-Maho (France) 277, 284, 290
Pećka-Banja (Kosovo) 1244
Pecs-Jakabhegy (Hungary) 371, 384
Peelo (Netherlands) 98
Pelagonia 456–7
pellet moulds 810
Peloponnese 410–11, 1191
Pentalofos (Greece) 450, 452
Pentapolis (the five cities) 626–7
peploi 859–60
Peretu (Romania) 501
Pergamon (Turkey) 632, 1141
  see also Athena Nikephoros acropolis
Pericles 939–40
Perl, G. 757
Persian empire 625–6, 937
Persepolis 626
petroglyphs 363, 468
Peutinger Map (*Tabula Peutingeriana*) 1190
Pézenas (France) 277
Pfalzfeld (Germany) 218, 251
Pfostenschlitzmauer (post-slot walls) 722–3, 760
Phantassie (Scotland) 116
Pharos (Croatia) 371
Pharsalia (Lucan) 1284–5
Philip II of Macedon 811, 888, 1160
Philistines 624
Phoenicians 623–4
  alphabetic systems 1106, 1108–14
  early iron use 38
  glass beads 801
  ivory 807
  in Portugal 315–16
  pottery 420
Phoenician-Tartessian area 333
Phrygia 621
Pianella di Monte Savino (Italy) 1151
Piatra Craivii (Romania) 507, 510
Piazza d'Armi, Veii (Italy) 419
Picard, G.-C. 758
Picardy 890, 900, 902
Piceni 806
Píč, J. 238
Pictish inscriptions 1106
Picugi (Croatia) 371
Piercebridge (England) 1198
Pieria region 456–7
Piggott, S. 860, 1063
pigments 804
pigs 676, 681, 683
  for feasting 1221
  found at midden sites 82
  Netherlands 685–6
piling techniques 779
Piller Sattel (Austria) 218, 252, 905
Pilsting-Oberndorf (Germany) 1051
Pimperne (England) 69, 84
pincer-gates (*Zangentor*) 725
Pion, P. 827, 896, 902
Piórkowo (Poland) 196
Pirin Macedonia 462–3
Pistiros (Bulgaria) 1141, 1160
Pisum sativum (peas) 664

pitch 808
pit graves
  eastern Baltic 184
  France 280
  northern Adriatic 367
Pithekoussai (Italy) 408, 417, 423, 877, 1111–12
  foundation dates 48
pithoi 290, 432–3
pit houses 154, 165
pits 484, 1221, 1224–5
  deposits 1266
plaggen system 152, 670
plague, genetic studies 32
plaques 240, 360, 584
Plastic style art 1153, 1314–15
platinum 799
Pleiner, R. 762, 778, 780
Plessis-Gassot (France) 88
Pliny the Elder 203–4, 1127–8
  Natural History 388
ploughing 1005
Plovdiv (Bulgaria) 1141, 1161
pluvisols 25
Poanse (Estonia) 178
Pöcking (Germany) 218, 223
Pocklington (England) 69, 108
podboi (side niches) 586, 591, 594
Podmokly-Kobily group 199
Podzemelj (Slovenia) 371
podzols 25
Poetic Edda 1104
Poggio Civitate di Murlo (Italy) 846
Pogny (France) 1014
Poieneşti-Lukaševka culture 199, 200, 503
Pointe de Meinga (France) 721
Poland, Celtic migration to 1155
Polanyi, K. 873–4
poleis 416, 470
Polichni (Greece) 450, 456
Polin, S. V. 542
poliorcetics 961
political structure 927–42
  Britain and Ireland 87
  burial evidence 930–1
  eastern central Europe 198
  first millennium BC 940–2
  France 290–1
  later Iron Age 93
  power structures 936–40
  settlement hierarchies 931–2
  and social status 932–4
  written sources 928–30
pollarding 666
pollen data 28, 741
Polog region 456–7
Polybius 1121, 1124–5
  Histories 326, 388, 779, 1104
Polychrono (Greece) 456
Pomeranian culture 194–6, 832, 1165
pommels 636–7, 807, 1052–3
Pompeius Trogus 1145
Pomponius Mela 1287
Pontic region 477
Pont-Valperga group 349
population change, in Scandinavia 149
population
  density 153, 1028–30
  expansion 14, 1041–2
Populonia (Italy) 356
Po, River 345, 801
Pörnullbacken (Finland) 146, 152, 153
portcullis gates 160
Portonaccio, Veii (Italy) 419
Port-Sec (France) 717
Port (Switzerland), swords from 640, 788, 955
Portugal 307–8, 315–17, 1060
Poseidonios 1125, 1198, 1214, 1262
Posočje region 370
Poštela (Slovenia) 371, 384, 387
post-slot walls (*Pfostenschlitzmauer*) 722–3, 760
Post-Zarubincy culture 205
poterie grise 247
potin coins 892, 893–4, 900
potlatches 979–80, 984
Pottenbrunn (Austria) 218, 244, 249, 986
Potterne (England) 26, 1216
potter's wheel 110
pottery
  Ananyino 603
  Attic pottery *see* Attic pottery
  Cozia-Sacharna culture 540
  finds 827
  fluted 489

France 296
Geometric 464
Germany 223–4
graphite clay pottery 247
Greek influenced 543
Hatched 578, 597
imported into Italy 347
Italy 358, 420–2, 424
matt-painted 462
Mycenaen 421–2
northern Adriatic 367
oenochoe 284, 542
Pomeranian culture 196
Portugal 316
poterie grise 247
Roman Empire 1201
use in dating systems 44–6, 52
in Wessex 82
West Balt barrow culture 197
wheel-thrown 198, 199, 247, 498–9, 802–3
technical development 823
Willow Pattern 933
Pöttsching (Austria) 32
Poux, M. 1230
Po valley 346, 351, 417, 889, 1273
power structures 936–40
ethnic identity 1089–92
natural leaders 939–40
Pozo Moro (Spain) 332–3, 1249
Pradines (France) 277, 280, 281
Præstestien (Denmark) 146, 154, 159, 165
Prasutagus of the Iceni 1119
precious metals 798–9
coins 798–9, 811
soldering 809
see also gold; platinum; silver
Preneste (Italy)
Barberini tomb 1242
Preuteşti (Romania) 489
Priam, King 1120
priests 986
Primorskiy (Russia) 542
princely sites (*Fürstensitze*) 7, 236, 717, 748, 785, 872, 939
funerary practices 1242–4
in north-west Europe 73–7
Priorsløkke (Denmark) 707
Procopius 1129–30, 1131
Prokhorovo culture 589–91
propylaion 89
Prosdocimi, A. 366
Proto-Maeotian culture 526, 536
Proto-Villanovan groups 347
Prozor (Bosnia-Herzegovina) 371
Prunus avium (cherries) 665
Prut, River 539
Przewalski's horses 1015
Przeworsk culture 200, 201, 202, 204, 205, 207, 1155
cemeteries 210
Pšeničevo culture 483, 489
Ptolemy 209, 1128
Geography 207
Ptolemy Keraunos, King 1146
Púchov group 1155
Puente Tablas 309, 327
Puglia 421
Pula (Croatia) 371
Pulversheim (France) 743
punched square motif 1325–6
Punic War
Second 301, 326, 336, 896
Third 628
Punta Chiarito (Italy) 408, 423
Puy de la Poix (France) 1319
Pyanobor culture 602, 605–9
Pyrene 236
Pyrenees 282
Pyrrhus 1160
Pytheas 1123–4
pyxis 1309

Quattro Fontanili cemetery, Veii (Italy) 941
quenching 778–9
Quercus sp. (oak trees) 667, 760
querns/quernstones 8, 102, 157, 662, 718, 789, 802, 819, 828
base 701
rotary 67, 106, 120, 248, 662, 802, 813, 819, 820–1
'Quiet Corner' 212
Quimper (France) 718
quinarius coins 891–2, 893

Raab group 384
Racha valley 535
racial stereotypes 1091
Raddatz, K. 238
Rădeni hoard (Romania) 490
radiocarbon dating 49–52, 53, 55
  in north-west Europe 71
Radovesice (Czech Republic) 31, 1141, 1152, 1156
Radovin (Croatia) 371, 379
Raetia 1188
Raeti communities 360, 361, 1112
rainbow cup coins 891, 898, 905–6
Ralph, S. 1230
ramparts 722–5
  Britain
    earlier Iron Age 86
    later Iron Age 91–2
Ramsauer graves, Hallstatt 1053
Ramsl, P. C. 1155
Rast-Eicher, A. 844–5, 847, 853, 860
Rathcrogan (Ireland) 69, 106
Rathgall (Ireland) 69, 86–7
Rathoy (Scotland) 103
raths 119
Ravna (Bulgaria) 499
raw materials 823–7
  inorganic 800–4
  metals 798–9
  organic 804–8
Rebay-Salisbury, K. 1069–70
rectangular houses 67–8, 1196
Redfern, R. C. 952
red glass/enamel 801–2
regional framework 20, 21–4
regional identity 1079–85
regosols 25
Rehovë (Albania) 450, 459–60
Reim, H. 875
Reims/Durocortorum (France) 68, 721
reindeer herding 152
Reinecke, P. 44, 219, 238
  Reinecke periodization 43, 71
Reinheim (Germany) 218, 240–1, 249, 1051, 1059, 1065
Reiss-Engelhorn Museum 845
Reitia 1273
religion 96–7, 1283–300
  beliefs 167
  central Europe 249–52
  and coins 904–8
  Dacian kingdom 511–12
  France 290–1
  funerary practices 1251
  and horses 1012–14, 1291
  iconography 1292–4
  and monuments 754
  Roman Empire 1196–8
  see also ritual practices
religious sanctuaries 88–9
Remetea Mare (Romania) 495, 1141, 1162
Renfrew, C. 871–2
representations of humans and animals 9–10
rescue archaeology 147
research
  division of Europe into zones 19–24
  on the Iberian peninsula 306
  traditions 15
residential blocks 728
Rheinland-Pfalz 1008
Rhesus, King 1120
Rhineland 1154
Rhine-Moselle region 227, 239
Rhine, River 24
Rhodope mountains 463–8
Rhône valley 879, 889
Rhynie (Scotland) 116
Ribe area 154, 158
Ribemont-sur-Ancre (France) 9, 68, 88–9, 97, 676, 905–6, 952–3, 976, 1275–6, 1279
Ribnjačka (Croatia) 1113
Riccu (Corsica) 438
Ricovero *see* Casa di Ricovero
Ridgeway, the 1219–20
Riedenburg-Untereggersberg (Germany) 218, 223
Riesenferner glacier 859
Rijnieki (Latvia) 187
Rijswijk (Netherlands) 1196
Rila mountain 462
Rimini (Italy) 349
ring forts 119
  eastern Baltic 180
Riotinto, River 320

ritual practices 8, 9, 1261–79
abandonment of houses 83, 703
ancestral landscapes 1277–8
Angel of Death 1130
animal sacrifices 109, 330–1, 511, 679–81, 682, 688, 1227, 1265
blood sacrifice 251–2
buildings for 709
burial practices 374, 377, 606
coins in 903–4
depositions 484, 487, 511, 678, 897, 903, 908, 933, 1200
burnt offerings 168, 361, 369
central Europe 250–2
France 1276
Iberian peninsula 684–5
Lincolnshire 1203
pottery 81
Scotland 1279
destruction of objects 383, 730, 906–7, 953, 1058
domestic sphere 1264–6
elite female burials 233, 1065, 1068
feasting 109, 234, 330–1, 1213–31
female leadership 1071
funerals 545, 687
human killings 544, 1253
iron taboos and prohibitions 788, 1288
later Iron Age 95–7, 99, 249–52
natural world 1266–70
objects of 759
offerings on land 168
perspectives 12
of power and wealth 229, 975
Roman Empire 1196–8, 1200
sacrifices 1278–9
animals *see* ritual practices: animal sacrifices
sanctuaries 1271–7
Scandinavia and northern Germany 166–9
social inequality 321, 359
social practices 639
specialists 986, 1035, 1262
submersion in water 168
Thracian Highlands 464–5
violent practices 952
see also burial practices; religion
Riva, C. 418
rivers in Europe 24
deposition in 250, 975
Rizza, G. 436
road building 53, 1191
Roanne (France) 294, 299, 719
Robernier-Monfort (France) 277, 278
Rocavecchia (Italy) 421
Roccagloriosa (Italy) 421
roches moutonnées 363
rock art 363–5
rock-cut tombs 433, 467
rock salt 800
Rocky mountains 26
Rodenbach (Germany) 218, 240, 241
Rogaland 147, 149, 150, 152
Rogozen hoard (Bulgaria) 502
Rogozinovo (Bulgaria) 465
Röhrenkanne (bronze jug) 240
Roma-Colli Albani group 348
Roman Antiquities (Dionysius of Halicarnassus) 389
Roman conquests 3–4, 13, 40–1, 239
Balkans 508
Carpathian and Danubian area 512–13
defence from 91
Iberian peninsula 312, 326, 336
iconography 899
northern Adriatic 349, 350, 359, 374–5
Transylvania 479
Roman Empire 155–8, 1144–5
and agriculture 668–70
aristocrats in 96
burial practices 1198–200
chronology 42, 71–2
climate during 29
coins 47, 510
economy 154
end of Roman rule 1202–3
equestrian mask 168
geography and landscape 1190–1
identities (Romanization) 1188–90
imports 48, 95
indigenous communities under 1187–203
material culture 1200–2
mortality rates 1036
population data 1029

Roman Empire (*cont.*)
  pottery 509
  ritual practices 1196–8, 1200
  sanctuaries 96
  settlements 1192–6
  structures 1193–6
  temples 99
  traders 92
  written sources 10, 13, 15
Roman forts, use in dating systems 48
Roman Forum 19
Roman Gaul 1091
Roman History (Cassius Dio) 508–9
Romania 477, 483, 485, 1157
Roman Iron Age 21, 55, 122–3, 149, 152
  agriculture 155
  Britain 111–19
  burial practices 155, 163
  chronology 174
  coins 908–12
  decorative objects 162
  eastern Baltic 180–7, 188
  eastern central Europe 203–13
  hillforts 103
  hut circles 103
  mercenaries 965
  Scandinavia and northern Germany 165, 167
  structures 164
  warfare 159–62
romanitas 1289–92
Roman mythology 1285
Roman Warm Period 29
Rome (Italy) 301, 315, 328, 1141
  alliance building 965
  society 417
  wars 351, 353
Römerhügel (Germany) 633
Romerike (Norway) 147
Roncone (Italy) 346, 362
roofing 164
Roquepertuse (France) 277, 278, 1228, 1271–2
Rösch, M. 763
Roseldorf (Austria) 9, 198, 218, 245, 245–6, 250, 682–3, 905
Rosepark (Ireland) 69, 119
Roşia Montană (Romania) 479
Rostovtzeff, M. I. 529–30
rotary querns 67, 106, 120, 248, 662, 802, 813, 819, 820–1
  see also querns/quernstones
rotation 812
Roum Man 1268
roundhouses 102, 103, 696, 700, 931, 1193–6
  Pimperne 84
  Scotland 86
Roussillon 280, 282, 284, 290, 295, 300
Rowbury Farm (England) 84
Rowlands, M. 872, 875, 978
Roxolani 591
Roymans, N. 98, 99
Rozavlea (Romania) 480
Rubiceae (madder) 851
Rudnicki, M. 896
Rudston (England) 788, 850, 987–8, 1051
  gender roles 1070
Rue Elisée-Reclus, Clermont-Ferrand (France) 1318
Ruibal, G. 310
Ruiz Rodríguez, A. 327
Runnymede Bridge (England) 1216
rural settlements
  coins 899–900
  north-west Europe 94–5
Ruscino (France) 277, 284, 295
Russia
  barrow burials 185
  European part (Europe to Asia) 23, 575–612
Russian Plain 576
rye (*Secale cereale*) 152, 664, 670
Ryzhanovka tumulus (Ukraine) 544
Rzadkowo (Poland) 196

Sabrata (Libya) 627
Sa Caleta 325
Sacharna (Moldova) 539
sacred stones (*baetyli*) 331
Saghegy (Hungary) 371, 384
Saharna-Solonceni group 483, 489
Saint-Bertrand-de-Comminges (France) 1287
Saint-Blaise (France) 277, 285, 292, 293, 297
Sainte-Colombe (France) 218, 229, 1051, 1061–2, 1063
Saintes-Maries-de-la-Mer (France) 783

Saint-Etienne-de-Dions (France) 292
Saint-Gence (France) 718
Saint-Just-d'Ardèche (France) 297
Saint-Laurent, Vaison-la-Romaine (France) 292
Saint-Martin-des-Champs, Bourges (France) 717
Saint-Michel-de-Valbonne (France) 1272
Saint-Pierre-de-Martigues (France) 277, 1265
Saint-Samson-de-la-Roque (France) 720
Saint-Thibéry (France) 277, 295
Saint Walburg-Ulten (Austria) 252
Sais (Egypt) 625
Sajópetri (Hungary) 31, 503
  Sajópetri-Hosszú-dűlő 496
Sakar mountain 464, 467
Salač, V. 246
Salamis cemetery, Famagusta (Cyprus) 807, 941
Salter, C. 784
salt mines 8, 25, 230, 682, 986
  economic value 231
  silk from 637
  women and children working in 30, 1052
  wood samples from 49, 55, 668
salt production 70, 94, 100, 248, 800
salt springs 478–9, 489, 671
salt trade 1059–60, 1067, 1072
Saluvians 1273
Sambian peninsula 197
Samhain festival 1261
samian ware 118
Samnites 952, 961
Sanary (France) 277
Sanchorreja (Spain) 313
sanctuaries 369–70, 1271–7
  Crimea 555–6
  Dacian kingdom 511
  forests as 758–9
sand barrows, eastern Baltic 178, 183, 184–5
Sandouville (France) 721
San Giovenale (Italy) 418, 695
Sanislău-Nir group 491–2
Sankt Johann (Germany) 1051
San Maurizio (Italy) 1008
San Mauro hills 435
San Pietro-Montagnon (Italy) 346
Santa Barbara, Muggia (Italy) 371
Santa Lucia group 369, 370–3
Santa Olaia (Portugal) 316
Sant'Imbenia (Sardinia) 408, 438
Santu Antine (Sardinia) 408, 437
Sanzeno (Italy) 346, 361, 363
sapropelite 807
Sarakini (Greece) 450
Sardinia 437–8
Sarepta 624
Sargon II 528
Sarmatian period 562–3
Sarmatians 14, 41, 528–9, 583–9
  Prokhorovo culture 589–91
  rise of 591–7
Sarmizegetusa Regia (Romania) 504, 509–10
Šašel, J. 373
Sasso di Furbara, Cerveteri (Italy) 849, 850
Satzendorf (Austria) 846
Sauromatians *see* Sarmatians
Sava, River 345
Savoyeux (France) 1051
Saxo Grammaticus 166
Sboryanovo (Bulgaria) 500, 501, 502, 1161
scabbards 1322
  dragon pair 1153
Scandinavia 628
  bog bodies 1269
  communities 706
  funerary practices 1251
Scandinavia and northern Germany 21
  contact with the Roman world 155–8
Scardona (Croatia) 1285
'scarecrow' burials 563
Schandorf (Austria) 218
Scheibenhalsringe 1156, 1157–9
Schirndorf (Germany) 746–7, 1008, 1051
Schleswig-Holstein (Germany) 860, 1031, 1037
Schnabelkannen (beaked flagons) 358–9
Schöckingen (Germany) 1051
Schöllberg-Göge (Austria) 806
Schönfelder, M. 827
Schubert, F. 811
Schulten, A. 306
Schwab, H. 238
Schwarzenbach (Germany) 218, 240, 1311, 1313

Schwissel (Germany) 1031, 1032
scientific methods, use in dating systems 48–55
Scirii 199
Scordisci 387, 1146, 1161, 1162
Scotland
 clans 937
 climate 28
 denarius hoards 909
 hacksilver 911
 textiles 849
 writing systems 1117
scrolls 1312–13, 1316
Sculptor's Cave (Scotland) 1270
Scuol (Switzerland) 369
Scythia Magna 1165
Scythians 8, 525, 528–9, 531, 534, 537, 581
 Animal style 539, 833
 art 1306, 1321–4, 1326, 1329
 burial practices 539–44, 1245
 contact with Sauromatians 582, 585
 finds 538
 gender 949
 hemp 665
 horses 1000, 1001, 1003, 1011–12
 late settlements 546–7, 550
 migration to Black Sea region 492–3, 542–3, 581, 1307, 1322
 population movements 29
 raids 194, 513
 Scythian Age 491–3
 silk 637
 textiles 854, 858
seal blubber 155
Sea of Azov 23, 526–7, 542, 543, 1129
 cemeteries near 546, 550
 helmets 1166
 settlements 582
Sea Peoples 28, 455
sea salt 800
sea transport, in north-west Europe 67
Secale cereale (rye) 664, 670
Seckau (Austria) 1287
Sedatus, Gaius Verius 1295–7
Segobriges 1111
Segovesus 1144
Segsbury Camp (England) 753–4
Segusiavi 719
Seille valley 800
Seleucid Empire 1146
Sena 1287
Senones 1121
Serapio 964
Serbia 1146
Sereni, E. 351
Serzhen'-Yurt cemetery (Russia) 537, 538
Sesto Calende (Italy) 346, 356, 369
Setaria italica (foxtail millet) 664
Setefilla (Spain) 1244
settlements 7–9
 agricultural 70
 artisan 718–19
 Britain
  earlier Iron Age 86
  Roman Iron Age 113
 central Europe
  earlier Iron Age 235–7
  later Iron Age 238–9
 changing understanding of 8
 and community 706
 Dacian kingdom 509–10
 desertion 152
 domestic architecture 693–6
 eastern Baltic 179–80, 185–6
 eastern central Europe 194
 enclosed *see* enclosures
 France 284–8, 296–300
 increasing populations 14
 Italy
  central 418–19
  southern 426
 lake margins 72
 northern Adriatic 367–8
 North European Plain 78–81, 98–9
 in north-west Europe 72–3
 open *see* open settlements
 political structure 931–2
 replaced by woodland 666–8
 Roman Empire 1192–6
 specialized 729–30
 status displays 984
 tell settlements 452
 see also nucleated settlements; *oppida*
Seurre 1327

Seven Brothers barrow cemetery (Russia) 1324–5
Severan Arch, Rome 1090
Severn, River 1298
sewing needles 846
sex, biological 1026, 1039–40
shaft furnaces 775–6
Shala valley 459
shared history in group identity 1086
Sharp-Force Trauma (SFT) 950, 952–3
Sharples, N. M. 101, 960, 979
Shcherbinskoye hillfort (Russia) 599
Shchukin, M. 592, 597
sheep 155, 676, 678, 681, 682–3
  Iberian peninsula 684
  Netherlands 687
  Scandinavia and northern Germany 150
  wool 155, 805, 847–8, 853
shields 954
shipbuilding 786
shrines 331
shrouds 853
Siberia 596
  climate 29
sica type daggers 511
Sicily 421, 429–37
side niches (*podboi*) 586, 591, 594
Sidon 624
Sierentz (France) 218, 235
Sierra Morena 305
Sigbert, King 168
Sikans 430
Sikels 430
Silbury Hill (England) 1191
Silchester/Calleva Atrebatum (England) 69, 111–12, 901, 1197
Silesia 194, 197
Silesian-Platěnice group 221
Silius Italicus 1272
silk 637, 805, 854
Silk Road 596, 637
silver 156, 799
  beakers 1325–6, 1327
  coins 798–9, 811, 888–9, 891
  Dacian kingdom 512
  as prestige metal 831
  Roman Iron Age 117
  soldering 809
  tableware 335
  trading 1110
  used in alloys 798
Simferopol *see* Kermenchik/Neapolis Scythica
Simón, M. 834
Sindos (Greece) 450, 453
single-generation farms 83
Sint-Gillis-Waas (Belgium) 1191
Siracae 591
Siret valley 508, 509–10
Sistema Ibérico 305
Situla art 10, 234
situlae 227, 1241, 1262–3
  basket-shaped 358–9
  from Germany 635
Sjoberg, G. 932
Skedemosse (Sweden) 1269
skirts 859
Skopje/Kluçka (North Macedonia) 450, 455
Skoryj, S. A. 533
Skripkin, A. 530, 582, 596
skulls 1269–70
slag deposits 781
slave trade 1152
Slavonia/Slavonija region 384, 387
Slavs 211–12, 213, 545, 1030
Ślęża, Mount 1155
Slovakia 23, 221–2, 384, 477, 484, 491, 493, 846
  bronze jug 873
  silver coins 890
Slovenia 22, 217, 219, 369, 630
  migration through 1158
  situlae 1001, 1008
  Slovenian Iron Age 1000, 1278
  spurs 1003
  tumuli 941, 1262
Slovenian Dolenjsko 225, 230, 235, 248, 372
Šmarjeta (Slovenia) 371
smelting furnaces 775–7, 781
Šmihel (Slovenia) 371
smithing 777–80, 788, 1201–2
Smith, J. T. 1196
Smolenice-Molpír (Slovakia) 371, 384, 847
Snettisham (England) 9, 69, 110, 903, 915, 934, 982, 1270
  roundhouses 1193

Snodgrass, A. M. 38
Snorre Sturluson 166
Soboleva mogila (Ukraine) 544
social gatherings 1216, 1221
  see also feasting
social groups 985–8
social practices 830–1
  movement into temperate Europe 639
social sciences 1085
social stratification 154, 155, 971–91
  within communities 709–10
  eastern Baltic 189
  in Iapodic culture 377
  Iberian peninsula 332
  and political structure 932–4
  Styrian-Pannonian group 386
  see also elites
social structure
  Britain and Ireland 87
  eastern Baltic 188–9
  eastern central Europe 198
Sofievka (Ukraine) 533
soft tissue damage 951
soil
  effect on preservation of organic materials 26–7
  types 24–5
Soldanesti (Moldova) 540
soldering 809
solidi 158, 160
Söllingen (Germany) 1051
Solokha (Ukraine) 544
Solontsy (Russia) 548
Solotvino (Ukraine) 496
Someren (Netherlands) 69, 79
Somlóhegy (Hungary) 371, 384
Somlóvásarhely (Hungary) 218, 1006
Somme-Bionne (France) 1051
Somme-Tourbe (France) 1248
Sommer, U. 1081
Şona (Romania) 484
Sonneben barrow group, Dürrnberg (Austria) 240
Sopron-Bécsidomb (Hungary) 1249
Sopron-Burgstall (Hungary) 218, 233, 861
Sopron-Krautacker (Hungary) 387, 1012
Sopron-Varhely (Hungary) 371, 384, 387
Sorochinskyi I 595
Soto de Medinilla group 312
soumak technique 852, 855
souterrain construction 113
south-eastern Europe, funerary practices 1244–5, 1249–51
southern Africa 1092
southern Europe, transcontinental interaction 628–32
southern France 22
Southwark (England) 1201–2
south-western Europe, funerary practices 1244–5, 1249–51
Soyons (France) 292
Spain 1060
Spanos well, Corinth (Greece) 1160
Spânu, D. 831
Spartacus 940
Spasskoe (Russia) 533
specialized settlements 729–30
Speckhau (Germany) 1063
Speikern (Germany) 1004
spelt crops (*Triticum spelta*) 662, 1225
sphinxes 1320
Spina (Italy) 346
spindle whorls 845–6
Spong Hill (England) 1041, 1042–3
sports, horse racing 1004
Springhead (England) 113
squares, public 730–1
Srednica (Slovenia) 1141, 1158
Staffelberg (Germany) 218, 245
St Albans/Verlamion/Verulamium (England) 69, 1278
  King Harry Lane cemetery 111
  see also Folly Lane
Stânceşti (Romania) 499
standing stones (menhirs) 467–8
Stanway (England) 986
Stanwick (England) 69, 112, 1278
Staré Hradisko (Czech Republic) 727, 873, 880
Starnberg, Lake 223
Starokorsunskaya (Russia) 558
statues 1326–7
status displays 155, 971–91
status domination 1091
Statzendorf (Austria) 218, 232, 1051, 1052

steel 779, 798
stelae, France 276–9
Stelnica cemetery (Romania) 500
Stephanus of Byzantium 1122
stepped plates 1308
steppes 24
  Great Hungarian Plain 477–9
St Geogen (Austria) 987
Stična (Slovenia) 6, 369, 371, 382, 1241
  metal artefacts 633
  stone walls 379
  swords in graves 47
  tumulus 380, 381
Stillfried (Austria) 218, 233, 1228
Stöllner, T. 231
stone circles
  eastern Baltic 183
  Roman Iron Age 117
stone cist graves, eastern Baltic 175–6
stone production 802, 824–5
stone sculptures 242–3, 313, 1328
  Iberian peninsula 332–4
  Nesactium/Nezakcij 375
storage pits 1224–5
  increase in later Iron Age 88
Strabo 287, 366, 1071, 1121, 1126–7, 1268
  Geography 388, 508, 582, 775
Stradonice (Bohemia) 5, 218, 238–9, 720, 835
  coins 900
Strait of Kerch 527
Strandzha mountain 464
Straubing (Germany) 635
strawberries (*Fragaria vesca*) 665
street systems 727–9
Streit, R. 760
Strettweg (Austria) 218, 233, 234, 371, 387, 1051, 1053
  cult wagon 388, 1059, 1227
  Styrian-Pannonian group 383
  swords 47
  wagons 9, 1006
strip-fields 670–1
strip piling 779
structures
  Lipari 434–5
  North European Plain 98
  Roman Empire 1193–6
  Scandinavia and northern Germany 163–4
Struma valley 463
Stuttgart-Bad Cannstatt (Germany) 1051, 1061, 1063
St Walburg-Ulten (Italy) 218
Styria 222
Styrian-Pannonian group 383–8
subsistence, belts 659–61
subsistence crisis 152–3
Suceava 489
Sucellus 1197
Suddern Farm (England) 108
Sudeten mountains 194
Sudinoi 209
Suebi 1169
Sulcis (Sardinia) 437
Sulm/Solba valley 383
sulphur 774
sunken-featured buildings (SFBs; *Grubenhäuser*) 246, 694
supine inhumations 118
Susa 626
Süttő (Hungary) 371, 384
Sutton Common (England) 69, 102
Svantia valley 535
Svilengrad (Bulgaria) 450, 464
Swabian Alb 225
swastika motif 851, 855–6
Switzerland
  burial practices 230
  gender 1061–2
swords 955
  deposited in Britain 81
  falx type 511
  Hatvan-Boldog type 493, 495
  leaf-blade 455
  manufacture 779
  use in dating systems 47
sword scabbards 9
'Sword style' art 1316
Sybaris (Italy) 422, 426
symbolism 938
Syracuse (Sicily) 421
Százhalombatta (Hungary) 371, 384
Szentes-Vekerzug (Hungary)
  culture 387
  cemetery 1011

Szob (Hungary) 1141
Szymborze (Poland) 196

tablet weaves 850, 851–2
Tabula Peutingeriana (Peutinger Map) 1190
Tacitus 114, 1121, 1128, 1287–8
  Agricola 122, 123, 1121, 1128, 1131
  Annals 122–3, 741, 1104, 1119, 1127–8, 1131, 1132
  Germania 10, 174, 204, 207, 208, 757, 1032
Taganrog (Russia) 543
Táin Bo Cuailgne 1104
Tajo, River 315–16
Tajo valley 318, 319
Talaiot society 684
talus (earthwork bank) 723
Taman peninsula 1325
Tamaris (France) 277, 286
Tancred Pit Hole (England) 745
tankards 1222, 1224
Tannheim (Germany) 1051
Tápiószele (Hungary) 504
Tap O'Noth (Scotland) 69, 103, 116
Tappert, C. 247
Taradeau (France) 277, 296
Tara (Ireland) 69, 106, 107–8, 1278
  Hill of Tara 802, 1277
  Mound of the Hostages chambered tomb 1277
tarand graves, eastern Baltic 176–8, 180–3
Taranis 1285
Taranto/Taras/Tarentum (Italy) 428, 851, 890
Tarascon (France) 277, 297
Tarasovo cemetery, Russia 606–7
Tarquinia (Italy) 408, 418–19
Tarraconensis 1188
Tarracon-Kese (Spain) 324
Tartessians 315, 1106, 1110–11
Taucheira 627
Taurapilis (Lithuania) 189
Taurini-Salassi 349, 388
Taurisici 387, 1146
taxation 154
Tayac (France) 1141, 1168
tebenna (mantles) 859
technical knowledge, movement into temperate Europe 639–40
technological choice 1095
technologies
  and innovation 808–14
  mechanical principles 812
  raw materials
    inorganic 800–4
    metals 798–9
    organic 804–8
Teleac (Romania) 481, 484–5
Teleşti (Romania) 1141, 1162
tell settlements 452
Tell Tayinat 623
Temir gora (Crimea) 539, 542–3
tempering 779
temples 730–1
  Crimea 556
  Dacian kingdom 510
Tencteri 1169
Tenginskaya (Russia) 560
Terenozhkin, A. I. 527–8
Termito (Italy) 421, 422
Terramare culture 347
territoriality 750–1
territorial models 327
Testimonia Hispaniae Antiqua 306
tetradrachms 891
Teutates 1286–7
Teutones 940, 1168
Teutonic Knights 209
textiles 843–62
  dyes for 669, 805, 850–3
  from Eurasia 854–5
  imports 637
  materials 805, 848–56
  as means of communication 855–6
  prestige materials 853–4
  production
    centres 847–8
    changes in middle La Tène period 853
    equipment 845–7
  research 843–5, 848, 857–61
  and social status 933
  weave structure 849–50
texts, earliest in Europe 4
Thames, River 9, 82
  Attic cup 81
  metal finds 892

settlements 104
water deposits 934
Thames valley 87, 102, 706
Thapsos (Sicily) 408, 430–1
Thapsos cups 430–1
Thasos (Greece) 450, 467
Thauron (France) 1285
Thermaic Gulf 451
Thermon (Greece) 408, 416–17
Thessaly 462
Thetford (Norfolk) 1298
Thézy-Glimont (France) 68, 92
tholos tombs 411
Thomsen, C. J. 41, 773
see also Three Age System
Thorsberg Moor (Germany) 860–1
Thrace 464–6, 1119–20, 1159–60
funerary practices 1245
Thracians 449, 1162
language 1116
Three Age System 3, 41, 56, 305, 773, 780, 1141
three-aisled buildings 79, 98, 114
Thucydides 430, 453, 1120
Thuringia 220
Tiberius Gracchus 928–9
Tiel-Passewaaij (Netherlands) 69, 98
Til Barsip 623
Timpone della Motta *see* Francavilla Marittima
tin 798
Tincomarus 1132
Tinner, W. 28
Tintignac (France) 68, 97, 1276
tintinabulum 861
Tirol 480
Tiryns (Greece) 408, 410, 940
Tischler, O. 43, 44, 238
Tiszafüred-Maratvapart (Hungary) 504
Tisza region 491
Titelberg (Luxembourg) 68, 78, 96, 722, 1250
burial practices 95
Lamadeleine cemetery 904, 1249
public monuments 730
Tollund Man 1253, 1267
Tolmin (Slovenia) 371
Tolstaya/Tovsta mogila (Ukraine) 544
Tomblaine (France) 218, 245
Tongeren/Atuatuca Tungrorum (Belgium) 1193, 1194
topography, France 287–8
torcs 110, 118, 830
deposition 976
gender 1061
Germany 227
Roman Iron Age 117
Scheibenhalsringe 1156, 1157–9
status displays 980–1
Waldalgesheim (Germany) 1314
Torone (Greece) 450, 456
Torre di Mordillo (Italy) 422
Torre d'Inferrata (Italy) 422
Torre di Satriano (Italy) 408, 422, 424, 425
Torre Galli (Italy) 422
Torreparadones (Spain) 1193
Tos Pelat (Spain) 804
Toulouse Sainte-Roche (France) 902
Toumba cemetery, Lefkandi (Greece) 412, 413, 450
toumbas 451–2
Toumba Thessaloniki (Greece) 452, 456
Touraine 1115
town planning 727–30
Trachsel, M. 43, 56, 239
trade 871–83
control of 939
late Iron Age 879–81
status displays 978
transcontinental 629–30
Traisen valley 829
Trajan 509, 511, 512, 860
Trajan's Column 1089–90
Transalpine Europe 47, 53
Transalpine Gaul 965, 1112, 1124–5
Trans-Caucasus 576
transcontinental interaction 619–20
southern Europe 628–32
transculturation 1090
Transdanubia (Hungary) 379, 384, 387, 493
transhumance 681
Trans-Ural steppe 589, 592
Trans-Volga area 582, 594, 609
Transylvania 222, 477–89, 492–8, 501, 504–8, 510, 798, 1158

Traprain Law (Scotland) 53, 69, 115, 116, 117
'treasure' 831
Trebenishte (North Macedonia) 470
Trebsche, P. 706–7, 706–8
tree-ring dating *see* dendrochronology
trees 666–8
Trégueux (France) 68, 91–2
Trémuson (France) 121
Trentino 360–2
Trent, River 105
trepanation 813
Tre'r Ceiri (Wales) 103
Trethellan Farm (England) 108
Trevelgue Head (England) 69, 86, 103
Treveri 734, 929, 1115
Triballi 506, 513, 1161
Triguères (France) 735
Třísov (Czech Republic) 726
Triticum aestivum (club wheat) 662
Triticum dicoccum (emmer wheat) 608, 662
Triticum durum (macaroni wheat) 662
Triticum monococcum (einkorn) 664
Triticum spelta (spelt) 662, 1225
Troitsk hillfort (Russia) 601
Trojans 641, 1120
Trojan War 1120
Tropaeum Augusti 389
Trou de Han (Belgium) 1270
trousers 860–1
Troy 490
Troyes (France) 748
trumpets (*carnyces*) 813–14, 958, 959
Trumpington (England) 83
Trumplini 389
Tscherberg/Čergoviče (Austria) 371
Tsouka (Greece) 465
tumuli *see* burial mounds
Turdetania 316
turibula (incense-burners) 1296
Turska Kosa (Croatia) 1273
Tuscany 417
Tušpa (Turkey) 622
Tutsi group 1087
twill 849–50, 853
two-aisled houses 98
two-wheeled chariots 1008–11, 1247
Tylecote, R. F. 762
Tylis (Bulgaria) 1115, 1116, 1146, 1161
Tyniec group 1155
tyrannos 928
Tyre 624

Ubii 1114
Udmurts 602
Uffington White Horse (England) 1014–15
Ugarit 630
Uioara de Sus (Romania) 492
Ukert, F. A. 1082
Ukraine 949, 1165–6
Uley (England) 1299–300
Ul' kurgan mound (Russia) 560
Ullastret (Spain) 324, 326, 704, 705
Ulyap kurgan mound (Russia) 560
Una River 375
Untereggersberg (Germany) 746
Unterfahlheim (Germany) 1011
Unterlunkhofen-Bärhau
(Switzerland) 218, 230
unurned cremations 108
Uppåkra (Sweden) 146, 160, 168
Urals 582–97
Urartu 622
urbanization 717–35
  enclosure and districts 288
  France 284–96
  Iberian peninsula 326–9
  Italy 421
  Macedonia 470
  north-west Europe 90–4
  and political structure 932
  and use of coins 900–4
Urnfield
  burial tradition 79, 940
  cemeteries 78, 80, 194, 195, 222
urn graves 378
urns
  Brnijca culture 455
  Jastorf culture 199
  Pomeranian culture 195–6
Urtenen (Switzerland) 218
Urville-Nacqueville (France) 68, 94–5, 111, 900
Usipetes 1169
Ust'-Al'ma (Crimea) 554, 555

Utica (Tunisia) 627
Ütliberg (Switzerland) 218, 237, 1006
Uusküla (Estonia) 178

Vače (Slovenia) 371, 1001, 1008
  situla 1262–3
Vadena (Italy) 346, 360
Vaison-la-Romaine (France) 1116
Val Camonica (Italy) 1292
Valencia region 683–4
Vale of Pewsey *see* middens
Vallhagar (Sweden) 146, 147, 155
Valtellina valley 362
Vandals 206
Vanden Berghe, I. 850
van der Veen, M. 1225
Vandkilde, H. 949
Van, Lake 622
Vardar/Axios valley 451, 453–4, 456, 470
Vardar–Morava corridor 480
Vardar, River 453
Varennes-sur-Allier (France) 718
Variscourt/Condé-sur-Suippe (France) 727–9
  see also Condé-sur-Suippe
Varro 786
Vascones 306
Vasil'evka (Ukraine) 533, 548
Vedretta di Ries (Italy) 857
vegetation, biogeography 29
Veii (Italy) 408, 418, 419, 938
Veii-Gevelinghausen amphora type 356
Vekerzug culture/Alföld group 491, 492, 1324
Veleda 1297
Velem Szentvid (Hungary) 371, 384
Velika Gruda (Montenegro) 450, 461
Velika Košariská (Slovakia) 371, 384
Venantius Fortunatus 168
Venclová, N. 1294
Veneti 365–70
Venetic script 1113
Vercelli (Italy) 1141
Vercingetorix 48, 937–8, 940
Verdun-sur-le-Doubs (France) 718
Verger, S. 1049
Vergina/Aegae (Greece) 450, 1141, 1160
  early iron use 38
  frescoes 804
  tombs 501
  tumuli 457
Verkhnee Pogromnoe (Russia) 561
Verlamion/Verulamium *see* St Albans
Verona (Italy) 346
verracos (stone sculptures) 313
vertical stratigraphy 44–5
Vert-Toulon (France) 1051, 1068
Verucchio (Italy) 806, 844, 849, 850, 857
Vesontio *see* Besançon
Vettonian communities 313–14, 318
Vetulonia (Italy) 356, 357, 419, 1309
Vicenza (Italy) 346, 368
Vicia ervilia (bitter vetch) 664
Vicia faba (horse beans) 664
Vidivarii 211
Vienne (France) 292, 297–9
Viereckschanze (fortified farmsteads) 8, 246, 743–4, 752, 753, 1276–7
Vigna di Mezzo burial, Como (Italy) 355
Viking age 4, 174
  buildings 164
  farms 154
  horsemeat 1000
  mortality curves 1038
  silver 156
Vilas-Boas (Portugal) 980
Villa Benvenuti, Este (Italy) 366
Villach/Beljak (Austria) 371, 384
villages 115
Villanovan culture 388, 420–1, 1012, 1112
Villejoubert (France) 68
Villeneuve-Saint-Germain (France) 68, 91, 721, 727
  coin production 894
Villeneuve-sur-Lot (France) 718
Villeneuve (Switzerland) 218
Vimose (Denmark) 5
vine berries (*Vitis sylvestris*) 665
vine (*Vitis vinifera*) 665
vineyards 660
Vinji Vrh (Slovenia) 1278
violence 964–6
  evidence of 947–8, 950–3
  executions 96, 1253, 1268
  at Fin Cop 962–3
  material culture 953–9

Virgil, *Aeneid* 1297
Viring type textile 848
Viştea (Romania) 480
Vistula basin 196, 198, 199, 201, 210, 1155
visual styles, movement into temperate Europe 638–9
viticulture 660
Vitis sylvestris (vine berries) 665
Vitis vinifera (vine) 665
Vitruvius, *de Architectura* 1307
Vix (France) 6, 68, 218, 1051, 1062–4
  brooches 43
  'Dame de Vix'/'Princess of Vix' 30, 73–4, 237, 972
  elite women 230, 930, 982, 989, 1007, 1059
  gold 980, 1309, 1320
  krater 237, 640, 930, 941, 978, 979, 1242
  map of complex 1243
  princely seats 73
  river systems 939
  stone statues 9
  see also Mont Lassois
Vladař (Czech Republic) 218, 237, 745
Voldtofte (Denmark) 1246
Volga region 560–3
Volga, River 597
Volga-Ural steppe 529–30, 583–9
Volovăţ (Romania) 489
Volterra (Italy) 419
von Kurzynski, K. 844
votive depositions 363, 369, 556, 629, 847, 1273
  Crimea 560
votive lakes 166
votive practices 116
Vouga, E. and P. 238
Vouga, River 315
Vraca group 492, 498, 501
Vukovar (Croatia) 371
Vulchitran hoard (Bulgaria) 490
Vulci (Italy) 418
Vyatka, River 606
Vyshhetarasivka (Ukraine) 1141, 1166
Vysochino (Russia) 542
Vysokaya mogila (Russia) 533

Wadern-Oberlöstern (Germany) 1198–9
wagons 9, 1005
  four-wheeled ceremonial 1006–8, 1009
  Germany 224, 225
  horse equipment for 222–3, 232
  Hungary 232
Walachia 480
Walbrook valley, London (England) 1199–200
Waldalgesheim (Germany) 218, 240–1, 249, 854, 980, 981, 1051, 1065, 1247
  artistic style 1312–14
Waldmatte (Switzerland) 699, 707
Wallendorf (Germany) 78
walls, Scandinavia and northern Germany 163–4
walnuts (*Juglans regia*) 665
Wanborough (England) 908
war chariots 999
warfare
  eastern central Europe 198
  at Fin Cop 962–3
  Scandinavia and northern Germany 158–62
  social status 985–6
  terminology around 948–50
Warmenbol, E. 1270
war offerings 166
warrior elites 493
warriors 162, 223, 225–6, 947–66, 1273
  personal honour 965
  in rock art 364–5
  social status 985–6
  terminology around 948–50
Warta basin 196, 198, 199
Waschenberg (Austria) 776
water deposits 9, 250, 355, 933, 1198
  of dead bodies *see* bog bodies
water management 813
Water Newton (England) 1299
wax 804
wealth 971–91
  and deposition 974–7, 1065–8
  destruction of 933, 1201
  ritual practices 229, 975
weapon graves 159
weapons 827–8, 964–6
  central Europe 249
  in cremation burials 233
  culture 949
  as evidence of violence 953–9
  as evidence of war 948
  iron used in 786

in religious sanctuaries 89
technologies 957–8
weather events, AD 536–550 152, 153, 189
weaving looms 845–7
Webster, J. 1289
Wederath-Belginum (Germany) 218
Weert (Netherlands) 69
Weert-Laarderweg 98
Wefer, S. 802
Wehringen-Hexenbergle (Germany) 218, 224, 1007
dendrochronology 49
weight systems 157–8
Weiskirchen (Germany) 218, 240
Weismain-Görau (Germany) 1051
Wells, P. 830
Welwyn Garden City (England) 880
Wessex earlier Iron Age 82–3
west Africa, migration through 1094
West Balt barrow culture 195, 196, 197, 200, 205, 207
Westerhausen (Germany) 1141
western Europe
Celtic migration to 1153–7
chronological frameworks 42–3
Westhampnett 69, 109
West Plean (Scotland) 697
wetlands 5, 25
burials 118
dendrochronology 49
deposition 187
fortification 194
Humber 102
Lincolnshire 1203
preservation 79
preservation of organic materials 26
Scotland 909
settlements 478, 852
weapons 953
Wetwang Slack (England) 1051, 1065, 1069, 1253
whale blubber 155
wheat 608, 662–4, 1225
wheelhouses 104, 115–16
wheels
development 821–3
mechanical use of 812
wheel-thrown pottery 198, 199, 247, 498–9, 802–3
technical development 823
Wicina (Poland) 194
'Widsith' (poem) 160, 166
Wielbark culture 205, 206–8, 206–9, 210, 611
Wietenberg culture 480
'wiggle-matching' 55
Wigg-Wolf, D. 896
Wijchen (Netherlands) 1050, 1051
Wijster (Netherlands) 114
wild oats (*Avena fatua*) 663
Willerding, U. 757–8
Willow Pattern 933
Winchester (England) 69, 108, 113, 118, 823, 982
Windeby boy 860
wine consumption 96, 878, 1228
vessels 1222
wine production 683, 878, 1228
Winklebury (England) 83
Winsum (Netherlands) 123
Winterbourne Kingston (England) 69, 105
Witham, River 9, 55, 87, 934, 975, 1203
Witham valley 1203
Wittemoor (Germany) 1269
Wittenham Clumps (England) 69, 82, 102
woad (*Isatis tinctoria*) 669, 850–1
Wolfgantzen (France) 218, 235
women
bereaved 1040
buried with weapons 949
costumes in the northern Adriatic 372, 378
decorated graves 414
divinities (*heroon*) 374
elite burials 88, 226–7, 1241–2
Dürrnberg 1035, 1052–3
Heuneburg 226, 1063
ritual practices 233, 1065, 1068
first inhumations 1052
mortality rates 1040
political power 929, 936–7
sculptures of 375
social status 233, 989
wooden artefacts 162
wooden sculptures 1327–8
wooden structures 492
woodland 666–8
see also forest zone

wood tar production 155
woodworking 805–6
  iron tools for 785–6
wool 155, 805, 847–8, 853
Woolf, A. 698, 1192
World War II 19, 1083
Worsley Man 108, 1268
Wožniak, Z. 506
writing systems 1107, 1109
  acquisition of 1103–5
  archaeologically attested 1105–17
  Camunic script 1113, 1114
  Celtiberian 1106, 1110
  Greek 1114–15
  Iberic script 1110
  Latin 1115–17
  movement of 630–1
  Ogam script 119, 1117, 1118
  Phoenician 1106, 1108–14
  Pictish inscriptions 1106
  spelling 1131
  Tartessian 1106, 1110–11
written sources 4, 1119–20
  on coins 888, 1117–19
  on gender 1070–1
  literature 934–5
  Mediterranean region 10
  on political structure 928–30
written traditions 1120–30
Wrocław-Zakrzów (Poland) 206
Württemberg 232, 1057
Wyss, R. 238

Xenophon, *The Art of Horsemanship* 1001
Xeropolis *see* Lefkandi
Xiungnu people 565, 591

Yablonsky, L. T. 587–8
Yankovo (Bulgaria) 502
Yantsai state 596
Yarnton (England) 69, 83, 108
Yde girl 123, 1267
Yersinia pestis 32
Yonne, River 92, 735
Yorkshire
  cemeteries 1069
  La Tène period 1070
  settlements 113
  see also East Yorkshire
Ÿue-chi 529
Yverdon (Switzerland) 723, 1327
Yvignac (France) 1294

Zadar (Croatia) 371, 379
Zagersdorf (Austria) 218, 233, 1051, 1052
Zagora (Greece) 416
Zakarpats'ka region 1165
Zalissya (Ukraine) 1141, 1165
Zangentor (pincer-gates) 725
Zapatero, R. 312
Zarubincy culture 200–1, 211, 1165
Závist (Czech Republic) 218, 237, 245, 720, 722, 755
Zeijen (Netherlands) 69, 98
Zeist (Netherlands) 69
  Zeist-Kroostweg Noord 98
Ženjak (Slovenia) 640
Zevio (Italy) 369
Zhabotin culture 532, 534
Zimmermann, A. 1029
Zimnicea (Romania) 500, 501
Zincirli Höyük (Turkey) 623
Zürn, H. 219, 635
Žuto Brdo-Gârla Mare culture 488